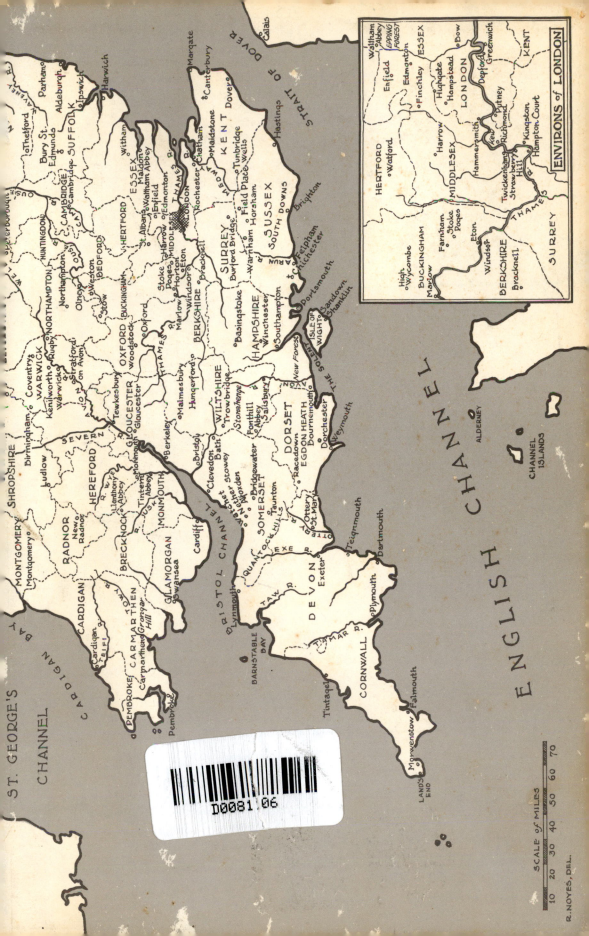

ENGLISH ROMANTIC

POETRY AND PROSE

ENGLISH ROMANTIC

POETRY and PROSE

SELECTED AND EDITED WITH ESSAYS AND NOTES BY

RUSSELL NOYES, *Professor of English, Indiana University*

New York · OXFORD UNIVERSITY PRESS · 1956

Copyright © Oxford University Press, Inc., 1956
Library of Congress Catalogue Card Number: 56–5118
Ninth Printing, with corrections and
expanded Bibliographies, 1967

Sixteenth printing 1980

PREFACE

THIS WORK is designed to provide representative readings and an adequate critical apparatus for the student undertaking his first long excursion in the literature of the English Romantic movement. Without departing radically from the canon of settled acceptance, the editor has sought to produce a fresh and stimulating anthology. He has included, besides numerous 'new' short pieces, several long works—a notable example is Shelley's *Cenci* —which have never before appeared uncut in a survey text in English romanticism. Another special feature is the generous representation from the letters of the time. The Romantic writers have left us many superb letters, which not only are delightful reading in themselves but which also often provide insight into the personalities of their authors and illuminate the intentions of their more formal work.

Prose fiction, except for several selections from Gothic romance and Peacock's burlesque of that type of writing, is outside the scope of this work. It has seemed hardly feasible to represent by excerpts the many-faceted power of Scott in the novel. The serious student should read at least one of his novels of Scottish life in the eighteenth century, and if possible one of the medieval romances, and one of the great drawings of English history of the sixteenth or seventeenth century. Single volumes of Scott's novels are available in several inexpensive editions. The short story, 'Wandering Willie's Tale,' from *Redgauntlet,* complete in itself, is included in this text as a masterly example of Scott at his story-telling best.

With the exception of prose fiction, however, all the forms of literature are fully displayed. The minor writers are represented by some new faces and much new material, which includes besides the indispensable poetical selections, passages from diaries, journals, biography, political tracts, and literary criticism. A plentiful gathering of humorous material, chosen largely from among the minor Romantic voices should provide a welcome light touch to balance the high seriousness of the major poets.

The text is fully annotated, with headnotes and footnotes printed on the page with the selections. This arrangement is intended to save the student who is after the facts the often troublesome maneuvering for information in the 'back of the book.' To give added authenticity to the annotations, wherever feasible the editor has drawn upon original prefaces and notes and other contemporary materials.

Writers are presented generally in chronological order but with some attention paid to their associations with one another. The selections for each author are arranged in strict chronological order according to the dates of composition in so far as known. Where two dates are given the first is the date of composition and the second is the date of publication. The line numberings giving the location of passages from Shakespeare refer to Kittredge's *Complete Works of Shakespeare.*

In an Introductory Survey the editor has sought to provide an orientation to English romanticism. The predominant features of Romantic literature are described in an historical framework and the backgrounds of social, economic, and political events are sketched in. Additional details of literary history are woven into some of the introductory essays on the Pre-romantic writers. All of the authors represented are provided with descriptive biographical outlines. For the major figures these outlines are given in considerable fullness and an attempt has been made through the selection of significant detail to bring the subjects to life. The critical essays enlarge upon the personality traits of these writers and trace their intellectual and artistic progress from its beginnings to its fulfillment. Critical bibliographies useful to the student of English romanticism are provided. Included in the bibliographies are general works covering political, economic, and social history and literary criticism as well as selected references on each author.

The text of the present work is based (with a few exceptions noted elsewhere) upon the last editions known to have been approved or edited by the authors. Contemporary English spelling, capitalization, and punctuation have been retained in all the selections.

Abbreviations used in the bibliographies and notes are as follows: *ELH*, Journal of English Literary History; *JEGP*, Journal of English and Germanic Philology; *JHI*, Journal of the History of Ideas; *MLN*, Modern Language Notes; *MLQ*, Modern Language Quarterly; *MLR*, Modern Language Review; *MP*, Modern Philology; *N&Q*, Notes and Queries; *PMLA*, Publications of the Modern Language Association of America; *PQ*, Philological Quarterly; *RES*, Review of English Studies; *SP*, Studies in Philology; *TLS*, Times Literary Supplement (London); *UTQ*, University of Toronto Quarterly.

It is a pleasure to acknowledge the many obligations which the editor has incurred in the long labor of preparing this volume. He has drawn heavily upon innumerable printed sources for his factual and critical materials. The general indebtedness to books may be understood to be covered by the titles listed in the bibliographies, but more specific mention must be made of studies by Grierson, Phelps, Herford, Symons, Elton, Legouis and Cazamian, Bernbaum, Fairchild, Beach, Lovejoy, Bush, and McKillop. For biographical and critical materials on individual authors in addition to those already named, the editor has found studies or critical editions by the following writers to have been especially helpful: for BLAKE, Damon, Mona Wilson, Bronowski, Schorer, Kazin, and Frye; for BURNS, Snyder, Ferguson, and Daiches; for COLERIDGE, Lowes, Chambers, Griggs, and Hanson; for LANDOR, Colvin and Elwin; for SCOTT, Lang, Buchan, and Grierson; for WORDSWORTH, Harper, Beatty, Herford, Stallknecht, and Havens; for BYRON, Ethel Mayne, Chew, Drinkwater, Bredvold, and Rice; for DE QUINCEY, Eaton, Sackville-West, and Stern; for HAZLITT, Zeitlin, Howe, and Maclean; for KEATS, Colvin, Murry, Thorpe, and de Selincourt; for LAMB, Lucas, Blunden, and French; for SHELLEY, Solve, Grabo, White, Kurtz, Barnard, Baker, and Cameron.

The editor desires to express his thanks for the courtesies extended him at many libraries: the Widener Library at Harvard University, the Library of Congress, the Newberry Library at Chicago, the libraries at the Universities of Illinois and Michigan,—above all, the library at Indiana University where most of the work of textual transcription and annotation was done. Thanks are due also to the President and the Board of Trustees at Indiana University for a Sabbatical leave and other release from teaching, and for financial grants-in-aid. To the many persons who through the various stages of the preparation of this work have assisted with their criticisms and suggestions the editor owes a heavy debt of gratitude: to Wallace Douglas for a critical reading of the sketch on Wordsworth; to Thomas C. Edwards for help on Landor; to John R. Moore for stimulating criticism on Scott and the Preromantics; to his Indiana colleagues, Newton P. Stallknecht, George Barnett, Philip Daghlian, Donald Smalley, and Edson Richmond, for numerous helpful suggestions; to Edward Seeber and Norman Pratt for assisting with the translations from foreign languages. He wishes further to acknowledge the many helpful suggestions of Carlos H. Baker of Princeton University, Marcel Kessel of the University of Connecticut, James V. Logan of Ohio State University, Leslie A. Marchand of Rutgers University, R. L. Purdy of Yale University, and the late Charles F. Harrold of Ohio State University who examined portions of the manuscript at the request of the publisher.

He expresses his sincere thanks to Howard Lowry for his early encouragement of this undertaking when he was general editor of Oxford University Press, and to William M.

Oman and Charles E. Pettee and others on the staff of the Oxford University Press for constant helpfulness extending over a period of several years. It is his further pleasure to express his gratitude to a succession of research assistants—Georgia Anderson, William Carroll, William Seat, Mrs. Suzanne Miller, and Mrs. Joan Nist—who spent long hours preparing manuscripts and checking texts, bibliographies, and annotations. Thanks are due also to Agnes Elpers for expertly typing most of the biographical and critical portions of the manuscript.

Finally, and not the least, the editor is indebted to his wife for her unfailing encouragement and for help in all stages of the work and in ways too numerous to specify.

R.N.

Bloomington, Indiana
November 1955

ACKNOWLEDGMENTS

FOR KIND PERMISSION to reproduce copyrighted materials the editor is indebted to Constable and Co., Ltd., and Harvard University Press for selections from *Coleridge's Shakespearean Criticism*, ed. T. M. Raysor; to J. M. Dent and Sons, Ltd., and Yale University Press for the letters of Lamb (in the text nos. 1, 2, 4, 7, 8, 9, 11, 13), ed. E. V. Lucas; to J. M. Dent and Sons, Ltd., and E. P. Dutton and Co., Inc., for *Crows in Spring* and *Silent Love* by John Clare; to the Lutcher Stark Library, University of Texas, for the letter of Lamb to Wordsworth; to the Huntington Library for Lamb's letters to Manning, nos. 5 and 12; to Sir Isaac Pitman and Sons, Ltd., for the selections from *Shelley's Letters and Prose*, ed. Ingpen and Peck; to John Murray for Byron's two letters to Lady Caroline Lamb, his letters to Miss Milbanke, Augusta Leigh, and Lady Byron taken from *Letters and Journals of Lord Byron*, ed. R. E. Prothero, and his letter to Kinnaird from *Lord Byron's Correspondence*, ed. Sir John Murray; to Oxford University Press for selections from *The Letters of John Keats*, ed. M. B. Forman, and for selections from *Henry Crabb Robinson on Books and Their Writers*, ed. Edith Morley.

CONTENTS

Contents

HOW TO USE THIS BOOK

THIS TEXTBOOK will be useful primarily for the selected readings it contains of fifty-four representative English Romantic writers. It is axiomatic that the study of any literature should begin and end in what the men of letters themselves created. But the meaning and worth of romantic literature (as of any literature) can be fully arrived at only by specific knowledge of persons, places, and events that appear in the writings; by secondary and supporting writings; by full and accurate biographical information; by the interpretations of later scholars; by critical orientations which embrace the total writings of the individual authors; by historical orientations, including the literary origins of romanticism and the sociological, political, and economic milieu which conditioned the origin, growth, and ultimate attainments of English romanticism. All these helps will be found in this textbook. Naturally they cannot be used all at once.

The order and choice of the authors read will vary with each instructor using the book. Some will wish to begin with the romantic period proper and to open with such major figures as Blake, Wordsworth, and Coleridge. If this approach is used, the student may profitably first read over with care the biographical outline and the first two or three paragraphs of the critical sketch on the author chosen. The instructor can elaborate in class, if he chooses, with further biographical details, anecdotes, and contemporary appraisals. Abundant cross reference materials are to be found throughout the textbook. If Blake is selected, for example, the student could profitably read Crabb Robinson's first-hand account of Blake (text, p. 465).

After a biographical and general orientation to the chosen author has been achieved, the student may then read and interpret with his instructor's guidance the writings as they appear. Here the headnotes and footnotes on the pages with the text will give the dates and, wherever they are significant, the circumstances of composition. For the more important writings, critical interpretations are given in the introductory author essays; hence, as the student proceeds, he should turn back to these for further help. Again using Blake for an example, there are separate paragraphs on *Poetical Sketches, Songs of Innocence, Songs of Experience, The Marriage of Heaven and Hell,* and other important works. This same pattern is followed throughout for all the major authors. When the study of an author is concluded, the student may wish to reread the entire introductory author essay for review and to check it against his own evaluations.

Perhaps the study of English romanticism is best begun with the major figures; but whatever the order of study, it will never be complete and satisfactory until the student comes to some understanding of what the origins and patterns of development of the Romantic Movement were, what gave it its drive and direction, what the temper of romanticism was, what values it created, how these values challenged neo-classicism and are now challenged by our contemporary world. These larger considerations are the concern of the Introductory Survey which opens this volume.

For the instructor who prefers to 'begin at the beginning,' the early portion of the Introductory Survey should serve as a useful accompaniment to the reading of the Pre-romantics. As Thomson, Dyer, Shenstone, Gray, Collins, and Cowper are read, the student may be helpfully oriented by reading the introductory paragraphs on 'The Return to Nature'; as Walpole, Radcliffe, Chatterton are read he may turn for guidance to the section on 'The Medieval Revival'; and so on. Also, it should be noted, the introductory author essays to the Pre-romantics often usefully supplement the historical account of pre-romanticism—e.g. the story of the ballad revival is told under Bishop Percy, and orientalism is described under William Beckford.

In whatever order the Romantics are read, it would not much benefit the beginning student to read through the Introductory Survey before he was fortified with direct knowledge of the literature itself. However, as he proceeds from time to time he may profitably check back for reinforcing information and orientation. When the student is near the end of his course, if he then rereads the Introductory Survey in its entirety, it should be with something like a true understanding of what the English Romantic Movement was and of how the various authors of the time made their individual contributions to the building up of that complex and wonderful creation of the human spirit which we call *romanticism*.

INTRODUCTORY SURVEY

Major Aspects of English Romanticism

THE ROMANTIC MOVEMENT DESIGNATED

THE European Romantic Movement covered a span of approximately a hundred years from the mid-eighteenth century to the mid-nineteenth century. During these years there occurred a vast upheaval in the philosophical, social, economic, and political systems of Europe. Traditional beliefs and institutions were abolished and empires overthrown; and upon the ruins of the old order, new creeds and institutions and new frames of government were built. A multitude of revolutionary, often complex and contradictory, currents of thought and feeling swept over Europe which men of creative genius caught up and gave lasting expression in literature, philosophy, music, and art. Indeed by their writings and their example, the philosophers and men of letters in particular as often directed, as they were directed by, the revolutionary forces which surrounded them and of which they were a part. The individual roles they played in the progress of that momentous epoch cannot easily be exaggerated.

Of the nations England, Germany, and France were chiefly involved in the Romantic Movement and, to a lesser degree, Italy and Spain; but no European country was left untouched, even the Scandinavian countries and Russia, and America across the ocean. In England the literary movement was well under way by the 1760's, sprang to full maturity with Blake, Wordsworth, and Scott, and was continued in subsequent romantic literature of the nineteenth century. In Germany the *Romantische Schule* with a definite program and a definite type of literature flourished from 1795 to 1820. In France romanticism was momentarily delayed by the Revolution and the Napoleonic wars, but under the militant leadership of Victor Hugo emerged triumphant from 1820 to 1840. In contrast to the romantic movements in Germany and France, which were provided with clearly defined programs, there was in England no consciously directed 'movement.' The same forces were at work, but in England romanticism developed instinctively and informally.

MEDIEVAL AND RENAISSANCE ROMANTICISM

Romanticism must not be thought of as being exclusively a modern affair. It is as old in European literature as Greek mythology and the *Odyssey,* even older. However, romanticism as we think of it is largely a development of medieval and modern philosophy and literature. Its first great era coincides with the blossoming of secular romance in the twelfth and thirteenth centuries in such characteristic works as *Launcelot and Guinevere, Tristan and Iseult,* and *Aucassin and Nicolette.* These works embodied the spirit of chivalry in revolt against the undue preoccupation of men with an ascetic ideal. They reflected men's growing enthusiasm for human adventure, passion, and delight. In the fourteenth century the extravagances of medieval romanticism were lightly satirized by Chaucer, yet even he paid his debt of honor to the traditions of romance.

During the Renaissance, romanticism had a second flowering. The writers of that age, for all their magnificent intellectual achievements, were characteristically romantic in their individualism, their youthful enthusiasm, and their love of splendor. They went to the past for a glamorous interpretation of life and gloried in the extravagant, the supernatural, and the mystic. Spenser with his great pageantry of chivalry, moral idealism, and sensuous beauty of style was their most celebrated romancer. But he was not at all an isolated figure. Shakespeare and his fellow dramatists, as well as a host of prose romancers and lesser poets, likewise worked predominantly in the spirit of a romantic tradition.

The third great wave of European romanticism reached its height, as we have seen, in the late eighteenth and early nineteenth century. Elements of medieval and renaissance romance were embodied in modern romanticism, but many new elements were added also.

CLASSICISM

The traditional opposite to romanticism is classicism. Classicism in European literature is associated with those periods in the histories of nations when men felt that their age was more serene, universal, and wise than the one which preceded them. Classicism suggests a balancing of forces, a sense of social solidarity and wholeness. The first, and supreme, classical age flourished in Athens during the rule of Pericles (460 B.C.–429 B.C.); the second great classical age rose to its climax in Rome during the reign of the Emperor Augustus (27 B.C.–A.D. 14): the third great classical age had its start in France in the early years of the reign of Louis XIV (1643–1715) and lagged behind in England, but reached its height in that country in the reign of Queen Anne (1702–14). English classicism, or neo-classicism, with which we are concerned here, developed in an atmosphere of new scientific and critical rationalism ushered in by such leaders as Hobbes and Newton. The spirit of rationalism encouraged an objective, verifiable appraisal of men and manners, and emphasized the universal significance of common, human experience. Men of letters of the time, in sympathy with the new dry-eyed approach to life, came to distrust the faith in intuition, in enthusiasm, and in unchecked imagination which had characterized the late renaissance. They stood opposed to anything wildly improbable; they wearied of the extravagances of the metaphysical style. The neo-classicists, in short, in their belief inclined toward a comfortable deism, and in their poetry aimed at being respectable, humane, and social. They showed a special partiality for satire and, indeed, did much of their best work in this genre. In language and style they strove for precision, polish, and control.

A key-word in neo-classical doctrine was 'nature,' but to Pope and his colleagues nature was the general, traditional norm in all departments of human activity. In poetic practice, since the poet imitates nature, and since the ancients were the supreme imitators, to follow nature meant, as Pope said, to copy them. For good poets the principle of imitation of authors encouraged an active awareness of enduring standards of form and style, of good sense and good taste. During the high tide of neo-classicism, sturdy English individualism and common sense kept application of 'the rules' within a healthy flexibility. Among lesser men, however, a too strict adherence to the authority of tradition tended to reduce human behavior to codes of etiquette and respectability and to debase literature to stereotyped formalism and didacticism. It was the imitative practices of neo-classicism which ultimately quenched its spirit. The eighteenth century achieved a rich and solid culture by means of a nicely sustained equilibrium, but it did so at a price. When the comparative stability broke down, their art disintegrated and a wave of fresh thought and emotion poured over the nation.

ROMANTICISM

The word 'romantic' is of English origin, its use dating from the period of the popularity of medieval and French heroical romances in the middle of the seventeenth century. It originally meant 'like the old romances,' but since these works had to do with improbable adventures remote from ordinary life, 'romantic' came to mean something unreal or far-fetched as opposed to fact. During the eighteenth century the word 'romantic' gained increasing currency in some such sense as fictitious, or extravagant. In time it came to be used as a descriptive term for pleasing scenes and situations described in the romances, but more often it was applied specifically to the literature of earlier times which described these scenes. The term 'romanticism,' a later semantic development, has come to refer generally to the resurgence of progressive thought and emotion which eighteenth-century rationalism never wholly repressed.

Wordsworth and his contemporaries did not think of themselves as belonging to a 'romantic' age, nor did they use the term 'romantic' except to apply it in a general sense. But the men of Wordsworth's generation were 'caught in the chronological net.' Because they lived at a particular time and place and responded to the conditions of their age in the way they did, posterity has chosen to call them 'Romanticists.' It has become a matter of convenience to label them with this tag, and to consider nearly all those English authors as 'Romanticists' the bulk of whose mature work falls within the limits of the years from 1789 to 1832, and 'historic English romanticism' as the sum total of the characteristics of those years as represented by the productions of the artists, philosophers, and poets then living. But whereas the artistic and philosophical tenets of neo-classicism can be neatly summed up, as indeed they were by Pope, the features of romanticism are so numerous, varied, and complex as to challenge any easy packaging in a prescriptive formula. Nevertheless, some generalizations about romanticism may be ventured.

Romanticism began and prevailed in a spirit of revolt against the dogma of reason, or against the actual or supposed neo-classicist conception of it, which comprehended the reflection of a mechanized universe and a mechanized philosophy as well as the rejection of seventeenth- and eighteenth-century literary forms and themes which to the Romantics seemed effete. The world of the neo-classicists had been proclaimed by the philosophers to be the best of all possible worlds, made for man's delight. Man need no longer, they felt, foster gloomy convictions of sin nor harbor any enthusiastic yearning for salvation; neither should he concern himself about changing social conditions: for all was divinely ordered. The consequence of this kind of 'optimism' was a gospel of hopelessness, a belief that society was unimprovable. Dynamic men of the eighteenth century rejected such a degraded acceptance of the *status quo*. Rousseau and Diderot in France and Wesley in England challenged the implications of a static creation and a fixed society. By degrees the concept of a mechanistic universe was discarded for an evolutionary one. Men turned to the abolition of avoidable evils and looked to an indefinite progress toward perfection. By the end of the century in a climate of resurgent emotionalism an 'optimism of progress' superseded an 'optimism of acceptance.' Thus, whereas neo-classicism had shown an essential preference for static, rational discipline and the balancing of forces, romanticism rejected this for expansive emotion and freedom of action.

The anti-rationalist revolt was carried forward on all levels of society and manifested itself in a great variety of ways: *in a turning from a satisfaction with sober reason to an indulgence in passion and sensibility; from a confidence in the unversality of reason to an emphasis upon the diversity of truth; from a compact, stable society to an unstable, revolutionary society; from a concentration on the general to a search for the minute and the singular; from an adherence to the agreed standards of the age to an eccentric, anti-social disregard of convention; from scientific mechanism to philosophical idealism; from the Newtonian world of science to the supernatural world of myth and mysticism; from a religion of* *comfortable deism to a religion of optimistic theism; from the uniformity of behavior to the differentness of men and their opinions; from the civilized and the modern to the simple, the rustic, and the primitive; from a preference for urban life to a love of country life, natural scenery, and solitudes; from preoccupation with human nature to a preoccupation with aesthetic and spiritual values of external nature; from a concern with the species to a concern with the individual; from traditional creeds to individual speculations and revelations; from the ideal of order to the ideal of expansiveness; from a distrust in originality to a faith in the validity of novelty; from an interest in the usual, the 'natural' to an absorption with the abnormal, the eccentric, and the peculiar; from imitation of classic authors to glorification of native tradition, especially the medieval; from a love of the simple and the direct to a preference for the complex and the fanciful; from the conception that poetry is an acquired art to the conception that poetry is the gift of nature; from a poetry of prose statement to a poetry of image and symbol; from satire to lyric; from the Augustan couplet to earlier verse patterns and variations upon them; from poetic diction to common language; from indifference toward social problems to a broad humanitarianism; from the ascendancy of the reason to the ascendancy of the imagination.*

These are the sub-headings of our topic which, needless to say, are capable of qualifications in both directions. In subsequent sections of this essay the characteristics of romanticism will be so qualified and expanded. Many levels and diverse values will appear in the appraisal of romanticism: some good, creative, or enduringly desirable; others false, destructive, fleeting, or wasteful.

PRE-ROMANTICISM

The term Pre-romanticism is used in this essay to designate English literary tendencies of the eighteenth century up to 1789 which resemble, or which influenced, the romanticism of the age which followed. It is a generally useful term, although not strictly definable and although applied to different authors for different reasons. The contributions of any one of the Pre-romantics to romanticism was partial, superficial, or with respect to one or two restricted subjects or features. Some authors, e.g., Gray and Goldsmith, are placed with the Pre-romantics because of their less important work. With others, e.g., Macpherson, Bowles, Chatterton, their pre-romanticism is about the only reason for still reading them. Burns, whose publication dates fall each side of a somewhat arbitrary dividing line, has been classed as both a Pre-romantic and a Romantic. A strict interpretation of pre-romanticism, then, is neither possible nor important, but an approach to romanticism historically through pre-romanticism can be helpful to the student in discerning the growth and the main characteristics of the Romantic Movement.

This approach is the one that will be used in this essay. In such topics as 'Return to Nature,' 'Romantic Melancholy,' 'Primitivism,' 'Medievalism,' and others, eighteenth-century feelings, thoughts, and tastes will be carried through from their origins to their chief points of development by the greater nineteenth-century Romantics. More extensive discussions of these and related topics, as they were handled by nineteenth-century Romantic authors, will be found in the essays preceding each section of the selections.

In approaching romanticism first through pre-romanticism the student must be warned against thinking that all the art and vital concern of the Romantic poets had eighteenth-century sources. The chief concerns of the Romantics, while they bear some relation to earlier tendencies, are the product of the individual poets and the temper of the time in which they lived. The Romantics were far more original than they were derivative. This obvious fact has caused some writers on our subject to make a plea for interpreting the Romantic Age as if it were dis-continuous, i.e. as if it were a literary age self-established and self-contained. New revolutionary forces were, admittedly, at work within the Romantic Age and a new cluster of geniuses was living to respond to them in their own original way. But it would appear to this writer to be a partial and hampering view of the Romantic Movement to minimize the role of eighteenth-century romantic philosophers and writers. The major Romantics were deeply influenced by what they learned from their predecessors. The new romanticism is—and can profitably be studied as—the *total* impulse of tradition plus contemporaneous events, thoughts, and feelings as assimilated and reshaped by the then living men of genius. If the tradition had been different, the contemporary age would have been different and romanticism as we now know it might never have been.

THE RETURN TO NATURE

In literature the principle of equilibrium and interruption of equilibrium, of convention and revolt, holds. Yet we must guard against the assumption that the advance of English poetry in the eighteenth century was an open conflict between pre-romantic tendencies or schools and the reigning mode. The century was predominantly classical. The transition to romanticism, though fundamental and pervasive, was leisurely and largely unselfconscious, proceeding in successive advances by no means regular.

The first romantic element which comes into prominence is a new awareness of external nature. In the fifty years or more before Pope there had been an almost complete indifference toward nature, but by the second quarter of the eighteenth century there occurred a vigorous reviviscence of enjoyment in nature manifested in an enthusiasm for wildness, grandeur, and solitude. The beginnings came in the verse of Thomson and Dyer. These men pioneered by stressing in their poetry the pictorial wonders of nature. Their emphasis derived from an admiration widely shared at the time of the Italian landscape paintings of Claude Lorrain, Salvator Rosa, and Nicolas Poussin. The 'fair visionary world' of these painters was transferred to their poetry with no loss of the delightful picturesqueness of extended prospects done on canvas—of landscapes with cliffs, cascades, darkening woods, still lakes, and feudal castles lit up with the glow of the setting sun. After Thomson (who was often called 'the Claude of poets') the poetry of nature was inseparably linked with the rise of landscape painting. Nature was looked at as if it were an infinite series of more or less well-composed subjects for painting.

By mid-century—influenced chiefly by Rosa who was remarkable beyond other painters for the irregular, the wild, and the sublime—the 'cult of the picturesque' came into fashion. Horace Walpole on a continental excursion must view the Savoy 'as picturesquely as possible.' Gray found exaltation in the terrors of mountainous regions; and on a walking tour of the English lakes—'prospect' glass in hand—made a record of aesthetic adventures. The fad for the picturesque was carried to excess, but it got men to looking at the landscape with an artist's gusto. Moreover, the better nature poets followed their own bent and showed from the start more exactitude and restraint than the Italian idealizations.

Closely tied in with the rise of the picturesque is the development of informal landscape gardening in England. The new English gardens were made to imitate nature. 'Artificial-natural' grounds were laid out with winding paths, solitary grottoes, picturesque vistas, even with 'ruins' constructed to give an antique and romantic setting. William Shenstone's *Leasowes* was one of the most famous of these artificial reconstructions of nature; another in the mode was Horace Walpole's *Strawberry Hill*. In gardening, as in descriptive verse, the aim was to achieve lonely scenes among 'ruins' and frowning rocks, which by the light of the sunrise or sunset would cast their shimmering reflections on the gleaming lakes. A close correspondence, it should be noted, existed between the new gardening and the new freedom of form in verse. Near the close of the century the fashion of descriptive landscape even spread to prose fiction where Mrs. Ann Radcliffe brought 'the landscape with pictures' to life and made landscape as background a convention in novels. Cowper and possibly some others felt at least a medicinal if not a spiritual influence from nature. Wordsworth afterward went on to formulate and refine such concepts.

The nineteenth-century Romantics profited from the abundant accumulation of enthusiastic, appreciative renderings of external nature which preceded them. The revival of interest in nature quickened their powers of observation, gave them a feeling for the beauty and exquisiteness of the animate world, and brought a new awareness of its kinship to man and of its value to the artist and the poet. It fostered in them a renewed sensibility, sharpened their vision, and led them to discover profound and new meanings in common things. Some of the major Romanticists were most fascinated by nature's silence and solitude, as were Wordsworth and Keats; others by its panorama and magnitude as was Byron; still others by nature's contrasting moods and combinations of moods. Wordsworth stands supreme among the romantic generation for the precision, diversity, and profundity of his interpretation of nature, but hardly less wonderful are the living delineations of Shelley, the exquisitely fresh and vivid passages of natural beauty of Keats, the spectacular renderings of Byron, and the mysteriously supernatural-natural verses of Coleridge. A rendering of external nature in poetry was not only the starting point of the new romanticism; but the Romantic poets' extraordinary, various, intimate, and subtle interpretations of the natural world became one of the age's most prominent features and chief glories. (For detailed discussions of 'Nature' as handled by the major Romantics see especially the introductions to Wordsworth, Shelley, and Keats.)

ROMANTIC MELANCHOLY

In pre-romantic literature the pleasures of nature were often fused with those of melancholy. When Thomson and other early eighteenth-century poets drew their landscapes in subdued, twilight tones they appropriated for their verses the melancholy sentiments then fashionable in Augustan literature of philosophical retirement. As the century advanced, the meditative melancholy of Milton's *Il Penseroso*, the pietistic solemnity of Puritan funeral elegies, and the deliberately pathetic gloom of the new evangelicalism all gave impetus to a varied and ever-increasingly popular literature of melancholy. With the appearance of Young's *Night Thoughts* (1742) and Blair's *The Grave* (1743) the literature of melancholy became an established vogue. The 'grave-yard school,' as it has come to be called, flourished in the middle decades of the century. Besides Young and Blair, who may be thought of as the founders, the school included in its membership the Warton brothers, Collins, and Gray. Some writers of the group stressed a harsh, gloomy melancholy and found solace in visitations to places of skulls and in midnight philosophizing upon man, death, and immortality. Others preferred a sadly-pleasing, meditative melancholy and emphasized a love of quiet, solitary musing. But soon all shades and degrees of melancholy were exhibited by the host of imitators who swelled this 'grave-yard' literature to flood tide in the succeeding decades of the century. Words such as 'sequestered,' 'mouldered,' 'mouldering,' 'contemplative,' 'pensive,' and 'votary,' became universal favorites. The preferred theme was the contemplation of ruins, dilapidated statues, tombs, and grave-yards (all symbols of man's futility) viewed by moonlight near a hermit's cell and accompanied by the plaintive cry of night-birds. To the literature of melancholy were drawn closely related themes, such as, the sentimentalized idealization of retirement, the unhappiness of love, the sufferings of humanity, the horrific, and the superstitious. In fiction Mrs. Radcliffe achieved new atmospherical shades of melancholy with her somber castles in ruins viewed by moonlight or threatening storm.

The mood of melancholy did not abate in the early nineteenth century, but as the century opened many things contributed to touch eighteenth century pseudo-melancholy with its resounding generalizations and capitalized abstractions and deepen it into a true romantic *Weltschmerz.* Wordsworth, looking both outward and inward, heard more deeply interfused 'the still, sad music of humanity.' Coleridge projected into the poetry of melancholy an acute introspective awareness of suffering and frustration. Byron added an accent of pessimistic despair. Finally, Shelley and Keats with their poignant lyrics of dejection and their poetical sublimations of death brought the literature of melancholy to its creative climax. (For a further discussion of 'Romantic Melancholy' and related topics see below under 'Individualism and Exoticism'; also the introductions to Coleridge, Shelley, and Keats.)

PRIMITIVISM

The 'return to nature' for the romantic generation not only meant a new delight in external nature but also involved the belief that the natural, or earliest, conditions of man and human society are the best conditions. This belief, which is known as primitivism, found a highly favorable climate in the eighteenth century and rapidly reached a growth of amazing proportions. Primitivism was nourished by the philosophers, who encouraged the doctrine of natural goodness and extended the principle of benevolence to include the benevolence of primitive men. Voyaging and discovery, which was marked by rapid development following the accession of George III, also quickened the general interest to see and study man in his primitive state. Support for the philosophers' doctrine of natural goodness poured in from the multitude of accounts of voyages both real and imaginary. According to these accounts, the golden age yet lingered in the South Seas where the natives lived without toil or labor upon the bounty of nature. Good savages, sage Chinese, noble Indians, honest Negroes, wise and tolerant heathen of every color were described and extolled. The most extraordinary emotional outbursts were inspired by Captain Cook's reports on the life of primitive South Sea islanders and amazing enthusiasm was awakened for the island chieftain, Omai, exhibited in London as representative of his noble race.

In literary circles as early as the second quarter of the century Thomson in the *Seasons* toyed with the 'noble savage' idea. Joseph Warton in *The Enthusiast,* 1740, extolled a life of idyllic innocence among naked Indians. Collins in *An Ode on the Popular Superstitions of the Highlands of Scotland* (written in 1749) by precept and example supported the poetic use of popular superstitions found among primitive peoples. Shortly after the mid-century Gray with his *Bard* gave high sanction to the figure of the primitive singer. With the Ossianic poems of Macpherson in the 'sixties, primitivism reached a climax. After Macpherson the cult of primitivism spread throughout Europe. In England, hardly a romantic writer was untouched by some aspect or another of its creed. There were appeals to the patriarchal state and laments for the passing of ancient grandeur. The savage and the peasant, it was believed, had become virtuous by living close to nature. Urban sophistication, on the contrary, had brought a train of evils which were greatly to be lamented. Goldsmith denounced even the decay of rural goodness; while Cowper pleaded to his countrymen for a less intricate design for living and a return to the virtues of their forefathers.

In general, sentimental primitivism is represented in the earlier, cruder, and more extravagant aspects of the romantic movement. Wordsworth, Coleridge, and Southey in the days of their romantic sensibility were vaguely favorable to primitivism, but rather early in their careers they abandoned the grosser implications of its creed. Still there persists in Wordsworth's major poetry significant parallels between his noble dalesmen and the 'noble savage' of tradition. His rustic heroes live in innocence, exempt from urban temptations. By nature's molding power they are given physical health, moral strength, and uncorrupted speech. Wordsworth's Michael is 'nature's venerable patriarch.'

Tied in with the glorification of the primitive and the natural was the idealization of the child and childhood. The child, like the peasant, absorbed benign influences from natural scenery. He derived physical beauty from nature; his communion with natural objects fostered an exquisite sensitiveness and moral instinct independent of, often hostile to, analytical reason. Wordsworth and Coleridge placed supreme confidence in the intuitive wisdom of the child; Blake enshrined the child in a mystical aura. Byron in certain moods revealed a close adherence to the formula of sentimental primitivism. For example, his ideal of love between the sexes called for a primitive setting and the removal of all the barriers of civilized society—a re-enacting, as in the episode of Haidee in *Don Juan,* of the paradisiacal story of Adam and Eve. On higher levels most of the romantic poets, following Wordsworth's lead, took up and developed with insight the true harmony between man and nature which Rousseau had been the first vividly to perceive. Wordsworth's discovery of the infinite significance of common things and Shelley's passionate humanitarianism were both founded ultimately upon the belief in a primal universal sympathy existing between organic nature and man.

SENTIMENTALISM

Primitivism and romantic melancholy are partial manifestations of the larger emotional advance which all along the line was breaking down neo-classical rationalism. Early in the eighteenth century the philosopher Shaftesbury had given sanction to a sentimental morality founded upon feelings of sympathy and benevolence. There was opposition to the presumptions of Shaftesbury's sentimental doctrine by such tough-minded realists as Mandeville and Swift, but by mid-century the satirists were losing ground. The new sentimentalism was not revealed immediately, or regularly, in thought or style. Until the eighth decade the majority of authors were writing from impulses which were for the most part rational; but sentimentalism which was meager in the Age of Pope is clearly prevalent in the Age of Johnson.

The advance of the program was greatly aided by a vast social upheaval which had created in its wake a host of bourgeois readers and writers. These new literates insisted upon the validity of man's emotions, instincts, and passions as opposed to a narrowly intellectual view of his nature. The emotional religious awakening led by Wesley was, likewise, widely influential in spreading the cult of feeling. The new religion softened and civilized the spirit of the masses and reasserted through the emphasis on 'conversion' the importance of an emotionally realized faith. As early as the 1740's, the theologian Edward Young (*Night Thoughts,* 1742) self-consciously displayed middle class religious sentiment in a vein antithetical to almost all that neo-classical rationalism stood for. In the area of belles-lettres the Warton brothers (*The Enthusiast,* 1740, *The Pleasures of Melancholy,* 1744) similarly were in conscious revolt from neo-classical standards and were calling for something much more emotional. In the field of the novel, Richardson, (*Pamela,* 1740, *Clarissa,* 1747–48) employed the feelings to support a moral code, and by a tender-minded manipulation of characters and situations set the feminine world a-weeping. As the century advanced there was not only an increase in the growth of sensibility, but also a more pronounced indulgence in emotional thrills for their own sake. Macpherson with his vague nostalgic sorrowings over Fingal and other Ossianic heroes and heroines (*Fingal,* 1762) established the fashion for a steady increase in the volume of sighs and tears, sorrowful deaths, and general unhappiness. By the time of the American Revolution sentimentalism in English literature was all-pervasive, and by the time Wordsworth and Coleridge began their careers a tradition of sentimental thinking and writing had become solidly established.

The effects of sentimentalism in romantic literature were both beneficial and deleterious. Just as the Augustans had carried the pretentions of rationalism to a sterile extreme, so the Romanticists in their revolt went too far in an opposite direction. With the Romanticists sentimentalism often degenerated into an abnormal stress upon the subjective or a display of idiosyncracies. At the same time, sentimentalism had built a body of ideas and feelings, of themes and patterns, on which creative originality could operate. Perhaps most importantly it was discovered that tradesmen, seamen, and country folk could share in the great human drama after all. Wesley saved their souls. Dr. Johnson was their defender. Oglethorpe, Howard, and other enlightened reformers won them better schools and prisons. Wilberforce, the great evangelical, led the way to the abolition of the slave trade. The poor, the oppressed, the underprivileged, even dumb animals were included in an ever enlarging sympathy for all living creatures. It is possible to trace these expansive benevolent impulses gaining upon characteristic eighteenth-century authors. With the coming of the nineteenth century, intellectual earnestness was added to eighteenth-century sentimental-humanitarianism, thereby immeasurably enlarging the sense of human brotherhood and the conception of love in its universal application. The development of these themes will be explored in a later section; meanwhile some of the less constructive consequences of sentimentalism in Romantic literature must be examined.

INDIVIDUALISM AND EXOTICISM

Some eighteenth-century authors, chiefly the novelists, warned against the folly of excessive sensibility; yet among certain nineteenth-century romantic writers there was if anything an increase in the display of new and strange sensibilities. Taking a cue from Rousseau ('If I'm not better than other people, at least I'm different.') there were Romanticists who became unduly preoccupied with themselves and the pursuit of their idiosyncracies. Extremes of imaginative sensibility were indulged in without moral or social restraint. The whole gamut of emotional changes was run from joyous ecstasy to despondency and disillusionment. In the life within these Romantics saw themselves beautifully displayed; their desires, aspirations, joys, and griefs were made sublime. They wore their hearts on their sleeves. They unblushingly confessed their most secret habits, sins, and passions in a burst of public confidences.

Rousseau with his *Confessions* (1782) set the fashion for a great spawning of confessional literature. In English romanticism, to name notable examples, we have De Quincey's *Confessions of an Opium Eater,* Lamb's *Confessions of a Drunkard,* Hazlitt's *Liber Amoris,* and Byron's *Childe Harold.* With some Romantics self-revelation went hand in hand with an inordinate self-esteem. Byron is the extreme example of unremitting egotism, exhibiting his ego in all its varied forms of self-pity, self-culture, and self-esteem. He is against government, conventions, and the church. He is the Satan of the romantic crew, the arch-rebel. But almost any one of the Romantics was more often than not on the side of the individual as against society. Not finding the world about them attractive, some Romantics built for themselves a picture of life within for the sustenance and fulfillment of impulses cramped by society or reality. Their introspection was not necessarily morbid nor did all romantic writers live in a make-believe region of dreams. There were, however, notable dreamers among them, the most famous being Coleridge and De Quincey; Lamb, too, had 'his sublime moments of nostalgic reverie.'

Certain of the Romantics not only tended to escape into self-indulging sensibilities and the world of their own dreams, they also sought emotional experience in the world external to themselves in the pursuit of the remote in time and space. They enthusiastically explored the monuments of the past and the hopes for the future, and the dim vistas and picturesque customs of far-off lands. They delighted to place their tales of adventure among strange people and exotic scenes. They felt the 'magic of distance'; they lost themselves in 'the thing desired rather than the thing known.' Their emotions were quickened by the appeal of suggestion and mystery. They had a craving for the 'unfamiliar, the marvelous, the supernatural'; a fondness for ivy-mantled towers and moonlit waters, for the unnatural and the horrible. Their passionate desire

was for 'strangeness added to beauty.' (For further details on 'Exoticism' see especially the introductions to Coleridge, De Quincey, and Byron; for a discussion of 'Orientalism' see the introduction to Beckford.)

THE MEDIEVAL REVIVAL

In their search for the magic of the remote and the wonderful, romantic writers found a spiritual home in the life and thought of the Middle Ages. Medievalism richly satisfied the longing for all that was distant, unfamiliar, and mysterious. Also, because the Middle Ages appeared so strikingly different, it was conceived as a better place and therefore a place the Romantic thought he would like to be. As early as the second quarter of the eighteenth century, pre-romantic writers had developed a sentimental tendency to dwell upon the castle in ruins and the moss-grown priory. By mid-century a deeper curiosity about life in earlier times was sending antiquarians to searching out and interpreting old manuscripts, legends, and popular traditions. Sometimes the interest of an author extended to no more than the romances of Spenser. At other times it included English history, early English literature, Chaucer, balladry, even the study of Milton and Shakespeare; for in the enthusiasm for antiquities no line was drawn between the Elizabethan period and the Middle Ages.

In these varied interests associated with the revival of the past, the work of the Wartons is representative. Thomas Warton in his *History of English Poetry* (1774–81) pioneered in opening up the treasures of early literature, and in his critical studies and his poetry made positive contributions to the advance of the Gothic. Joseph Warton, similarly in his poetry, but more especially by his critical manifesto in the *Essay on Pope* (1757–82), bolstered the revolt against didactic poetry and the return to earlier native tradition. During the latter half of the century, following the lead of the Wartons, medieval poetry was vaguely antique and picturesque with a strong sentimental coloring. In this vein was the work of Thomas Chatterton, the wonder boy of Bristol, who attempted to foist upon the learned world his pseudo-archaic fabrications known as the Rowley poems (first published, 1777).

Throughout the earlier stages of the medieval revival, enthusiasm for feudal architecture went hand in hand with a love for the older literature.

Horace Walpole, wealthy collector of antiquities, reconstructed his villa at *Strawberry Hill* into a Gothic castle and made the castle the scene for a sentimental novel of adventure. The medievalism of Walpole's novel, *The Castle of Otranto* (printed 1764, published 1765) is wholly superficial; nevertheless, it quickly became a landmark in taste and engendered an enormous progeny in Gothic fiction. Among the most famous of this multitudinous family were William Beckford's *Vathek* (1786), Ann Radcliffe's *Mysteries of Udolpho* (1794), Matthew G. Lewis's *The Monk* (1796), and Mary Shelley's *Frankenstein* (1818). In reaction to Gothic absurdities, Jane Austen (*Northanger Abbey,* 1818) and Thomas Love Peacock (*Nightmare Abbey,* 1818) gave delight with their satires of the genre; while Sir Walter Scott with vigor and imagination worked out Walpole's formula in terms of genius (*Ivanhoe,* 1819; *Quentin Durward,* 1823).

But it was not in fiction alone that Scott turned romantic medievalism to good account. In his poetry as well as in his great historical novels Scott erected a monument of patriotic literature built with deep affection upon the rich lore of Scottish customs and national heroic legends. The fervid nationalism of Scott ('This is my own, my native land') was shared, too, by Burns in his dedicated revitalization of the songs of his people and by Wordsworth in his memorable series of patriotic sonnets. Among major Romantic poets, Wordsworth and Coleridge were profoundly influenced by the ballad revival: Wordsworth by the vigor of the narratives and the directness and simplicity of the diction; Coleridge by these qualities and, in addition, the dramatic appeal of the supernatural. The unprecedented vogue of the medieval produced in romantic literature a vast quantity of lesser Gothic poetry, specter balladry, macabre verse, and sentimental claptrap. The whole millennium from 500 to 1500 was seen through the rose-colored spectacles of poetic glamor. The customs of chivalry, the medieval baron's castle, the mystical, the medieval church suffused in the unreal colors of the imagination, the wildest caprices of the supernatural, and many another pseudo-medieval extravagance were spread across the land. Yet on levels above the shoddy and the transient, there were enduring achievements in romantic medieval poetry; Gray's *The Bard;* Scott's *The Lay of the Last Minstrel;* Coleridge's *The Rime of the Ancient Mariner* and *Christabel;* Keats' *The Eve of St. Agnes* and, choicest flowering of all, *La Belle Dame Sans Merci.* (For a detailed account of the popular ballad in romantic literature turn to 'Thomas Percy and the Ballad Revival.')

REVOLUTION AND ROMANTICISM

We have followed romantic tendencies gathering head throughout the eighteenth century on English soil and we have seen how in various ways the love of external nature, the cult of melancholy, primitivism, sentimentalism, exoticism, and the return to the medieval developed into prominent aspects of romantic literature of the nineteenth century. But romanticism was much more than the result of a literary evolution working strictly within the boundaries of a well-defined literary tradition. The years spanned by the lives of Blake, Wordsworth, and Shelley witnessed a succession of earth-shaking revolutions—social, intellectual, economic, and political—such as the western world had not known since the dawn of the Christian era. During the period roughly from 1760 to 1840, the combined shock and challenge of intellectual advances in science and political economy, of far-reaching geographic voyage and discovery, of the no less than revolutionary social and political reforms in England, of the Industrial Revolution, of the American Revolution, and of the French Revolution and the Napoleonic Wars —all these released new forces which immeasurably enlarged and enriched the content of English romantic literature.

Political revolution dramatically broke loose in America with 'the shot heard round the world' at Lexington (1775) and in France with the Storming of the Bastille (1789). Far in advance of these events, however, vast, powerful currents of revolutionary thought and feeling had been rising in England, France, and America during the seventeenth and eighteenth centuries. In England the empirical philosophers Locke, Hume, Hartley, and Priestley had provided the needed body of intellectual revolutionary doctrine. The sentimentalists, too, were in the revolutionary camp; though probably such writers as Shaftesbury, Richardson, Macpherson, and Cowper were quite unconscious of any design of fostering revolutionary intentions. Nevertheless, their popularizations of the belief in the essential goodness of man and their enthusiastic sanction for a 'return to Nature' were profoundly instrumental in spreading revolutionary tendencies. The Methodist revival appears to have diverted the English nation from violent political revolution in favor of the established order. Religious sentiment coupled with British common sense saved England from violence such as shattered France. Revolution was none-the-less, as Leslie Stephen has pointed out, as much of a reality in England as in France, without mass bloodshed, yet not without protracted suffering and struggle.

In France, Rousseau was the most eloquent voice of the spirit of change. In 1761 he electrified all Europe with two epoch-making books, the *Contrat social* and *Émile.* 'Man is born free, and everywhere is in chains,' is the first sentence of the *Contrat social.* The first sentence of *Émile* is, 'God made all things good; man meddles with them and they become evil.' In the *Contrat social* Rousseau proclaims the worth and dignity of natural man. He repudiates the doctrine of original sin, explaining that man is born naturally good but is held in check by the errors and vicious principles of the past. A return to natural law, he insists, would return sovereignty to the people, who by the exercise of the 'general will' would establish civil liberty and make a reality of the dream of the modern, liberal bourgeois state. In *Émile,* Rousseau presents a persuasive picture of the child of nature, living alertly with his first-hand sensory impressions in surroundings of simple, country life, unchecked by the errors of artificial restraint and arriving by himself to the full, untrammeled strength of manhood. In these two revolutionary masterpieces—and to a lesser degree in *La Nouvelle Héloïse*—Rousseau with fervent eloquence drove home his fundamental doctrine of the 'return to Nature.' Many of Rousseau's countrymen similarly proclaimed the doctrine of natural man. Holbach and the French Encyclopedists taught that nature is a defiant Titaness who would dethrone the established gods and overturn all earthly altars and thrones. Man, they explained, is a part of nature; all our misfortunes come from neglecting and departing from nature. With Rousseau and his followers, the 'return to Nature' meant a return to a simple social order. It meant getting rid of kings, nobles, and priests by clearing away the accumulated debris of obsolete institutions.

While a multitude of writers on both sides of the channel were lamenting the loss of natural primitive simplicity, another multitude were concentrating on the idea of *progress* from the simple to the complex. From the English empirical philosophers stemmed a new faith in reason as an agency in the progress of human society. They argued that man is solely the product of his environment and that, therefore, if he would but use his reason to control his environment, each individual, and society at large, would move toward unlimited perfection. A wave of philosophical optimism rapidly gained momentum and moved through the eighteenth century with something of the force of a new religion. The French revolutionary theorists, Helvetius, Holbach, and Condorcet, extolled the virtues of the new materialistic philosophy and in the name of reason called for an end of the tyranny founded upon superstition and supernatural religion. They were convinced that once the stupid veneration for ancient laws and customs was destroyed by reason an unhindered advance to perfection would come of necessity. Through Godwin, Paine, and other popularizers, above all through the hostile and passionate opposition of Burke, the idea of progress and perfectibility became known and fiercely debated throughout Europe and America. By either course that the philosophers laid out—the leveling of the old order or the advance to the new—Reason was the revolutionary watchword. But if Reason laid the foundations upon which the pyre of revolution was built, Emotion was the flame which ignited it. The faith in Reason continued, of course, long after the cult of sensibility achieved the ascendancy and the revolutionary struggle was carried on in the name of both; yet after the 1760's the political emotional temperature ran increasingly higher until, at the last, revolution came in a fiery outburst of human passion. With the Fall of the Bastille the dreams of the philosophers and the sentimentalists had become an actuality; the old regime was blown to pieces.

In England, the French Revolution was received with feverish admiration by its partisans and with disapproval mingled with despair by the defenders of tradition. A favorable sermon by Price called forth the denunciations of Burke (*Reflections on the French Revolution*, 1790). Burke felt that the Revolution constituted a menace by destroying the whole complex organization of human society necessary to ordered living, and called for an orderly growth in social change. Burke's plea for order and tradition was answered in Parliament by Fox and Sheridan and was attacked by scores of others in books and pamphlets. Of the numerous replies none was so effective as that of Tom Paine (*The Rights of Man,* 1791), who made a vigorous popular appeal by championing the cause of liberty. But to Godwin it was left to enunciate in *Political Justice,* 1793, the extreme conclusions that revolutionary philosophy reached in England. Godwin saw the French Revolution as nothing less than the inevitable, long hoped-for liberation of mankind. Sharing Godwin's ardent progressivism was Mary

Wollstonecraft, who in her *Vindication for the Rights of Woman,* 1792, made a forthright plea for the enfranchisement of modern womanhood. The active vision of revolutionary idealism was fading at the very moment when many ardent patriots of humanity were rallying to sustain it, but the spiritual energies released lasted long enough to make a great poetic age.

The years 1789 to 1832 mark a triumph of the creative spirit in English literature. The outbreak of the French Revolution was the shock that broke down the last barriers of tradition. The French Revolution and Napoleon made a clean sweep; after them it was no longer possible to think, act, or write as if the old forms still had life. In the year that witnessed the Storming of the Bastille and Blake's *The Songs of Innocence* the forces for human redemption were joined. We rightly date English romanticism from Blake and Burns; Wordsworth and Coleridge in 1798 but intensify the break begun in 1789. The Revolution inspired Burns to surmount the limitations of nationalism and sing of the day when 'Man to man the world o'er / Shall brithers be for a' that.' Blake in his younger days associated with such revolutionary sympathizers as Godwin, Priestley, and Paine, and he wrote fiery verses in liberty's defense. Wordsworth was a resident in France during the early years of the Revolution and gave his whole being to the cause. He wrote *Descriptive Sketches* and *Guilt and Sorrow* in the full tide of revolutionary enthusiasm and even in the years of sober conservatism never yielded in his first loyalty to the liberties of men. Coleridge wrote ardent revolutionary pieces and planned with Southey and others to establish an ideal community on the banks of the Susquehanna. Southey in his years of liberalism wrote a rash drama in praise of regicide. But republicanism with Wordsworth, Coleridge, and Southey was short-lived. At the turn of the century a tide of conservative reaction set in, and these men moved with it. It was left to the second generation of romantic writers, after the defeat of Napoleon, to carry to ultimate fulfillment the consequences of the revolutionary dream.

INDUSTRIAL REVOLUTION AND REFORM

The Industrial Revolution had an even more profound and lasting effect upon the English nation than the French Revolution and the Napoleonic Wars. In its social consequences the Industrial Revolution was at first largely destructive, but ultimately it built up forces which brought about important economic, social, and political transformations. The movement dates from the early years of the reign of George III. At the time of the king's accession in 1760 there had been no canals; few hard roads; practically no cotton industry; few capitalist manufactures; little smelting of iron; and, as yet, but slight disruption of rural community life through the enclosure of farm land. In these and in many other respects, however, changes due to new mechanical inventions and applications were in full progress soon after 1760.

By the closing decade of the century the pace of industrial advance had become terrific. Then, too, it became disastrously involved in the cross currents of politics and the economic consequences of the war with France. To Dr. Johnson and his contemporaries the world was good enough as it was and their aim was to preserve it as they found it. But resistless change ignored them; the world moved on. To eliminate antiquated, wasteful methods of farming, Parliament abolished the open fields and most of the commons and had them enclosed by fences and merged into large, privately owned farms. The enclosures of land changed the face of rural England 'with the rapidity of an earthquake.' Open-field farmers and cottagers who had worked the hand-looms in their homes were forced to remove from the country to urban industrial centers. There, with their old freedoms undermined, they crowded together in close quarters in unwholesome surroundings. Grave social evils had already existed under the old economic system and when, after the Industrial Revolution had changed everything else, the old fabric of government was preserved unaltered in its smallest detail, the laborers of the nation suffered prolonged moral and physical catastrophe.

England had achieved a parliamentary form of government in the settlement of 1688–89. With the coming of the Hanoverian dynasty the king had been shorn of his executive powers, which were transferred to the Prime Minister. In the latter half of the eighteenth century the country had become a haven of liberals, yet as late as 1800 England was far from becoming a true democracy. Less than 5 per cent of the adult males were permitted to vote. Anglicans as the favored religious group controlled education and were alone eligible to sit in the House of Lords. Statesmen, including Burke, Pitt the elder, and Earl of Chatham, as well as political free-lancers, such as Tom Paine and 'Jack' Wilkes, had worked for the alleviation of social evils and reform in government. But it was not until the Industrial Revolution had made the lives of large classes of society in field and factory intolerable, and had collected great masses of them together in industrial districts, that democracy began slowly to commend itself to the victims as a means of liberation.

In the early years of the French Revolution the idea of reform, though suppressed and persecuted, first took root. Fox, Priestley, Paine, and other liberals hailed the revolution as the dawn of world-wide political enfranchisement and of religious and social equality. But the extreme radicalism of the supporters of the French Revolution and the approaching threat of war combined to put control of affairs completely into the hands of the anti-Jacobin Tories. Priestley's house and scientific instruments were destroyed by the 'Church and State' mob of Birmingham. Tom Paine, convicted of seditious writings and hunted by the government, fled for his life to France. *The Rights of Man* and other similar publications were suppressed; radical publishers were seized and sentenced to prison; free speech and free press ceased to be the rights of Englishmen.

During the long years of war, reformers continued to be savagely prosecuted, societies and public meetings were banned, the *Habeas Corpus Act* was suspended, and Trade Unions were declared illegal. These panicky and gravely injurious actions were in large part the result of the shock given to the English mind by the spectacle of increasing disorder and violence in French society. The Storming of the Bastille, the September massacres, the French conquest of Belgium and the Rhineland, the threatened invasion of Holland, the execution of Louis XVI, and the distracting struggle for national preservation and military victory combined to overwhelm the Reform movement as a serious issue for years to come. The sufferings of the working class during the years of exhausting war were increased by the uncertainties of employment and inflationary prices. The bulk of the population craved peace, but British patriotism doggedly endured privation and hardship in anticipation of the day of victory. The genius of Nelson gave England the supremacy of the seas, and the leadership of Wellington the brilliant series of land victories culminating in the battle of Waterloo that brought Napoleon to final defeat.

By the time the war had come to a close, the evil effects of land enclosures and industrialization had reached a climax. The decadence of cottage industry, higher prices, an increasing population, unemployment, and the enactment of Poor Laws which forced day laborers upon parish rates had led to the pauperization of one-quarter of the

laborers in all England. Factory working conditions were appalling. Women and children toiled from twelve to fifteen hours each day under the most unhygienic conditions. Life in the mines was oppressive, and for the shopkeepers and small businessman, not much better. The economic doctrine of *laissez faire,* given authority by Adam Smith in *The Wealth of Nations* (1777), was always invoked against the less fortunate, never in their behalf.

In the course of the almost unbroken war of twenty years, social progress had stood still, so that when peace came there was a violent revulsion. Demands by the workingmen for the alleviation of their miseries through popular suffrage were renewed. Brougham, Bentham, Owen, and Cobbett were among those who led the social and political revolt against the Tory aristocracy. Jeremy Bentham (1748–1832), the 'utilitarian' philosopher, impressed upon his countrymen the notion that existing institutions should be judged by results and perpetually readjusted so as to produce 'the greatest good to the greatest number.' Robert Owen (1771–1858), manufacturer and social planner, made his factories a model of humane and intelligent provisions for his workers. William Cobbett (1763–1835), most reckless of the reformers, by the very extravagance of his economics aroused the entire country to an awareness of the wrongs and sufferings of the poor. By demonstrating to the working class that the remedy for their ills was to be found in legislation, he prepared the way for Parliamentary Reform.

Cobbett was the leader of the masses in the industrial districts among whom fierce agitation had at length broken out. Peace had brought stern competition of foreign markets, bankruptcy, widespread unemployment; and then when a series of bad harvests had sent the price of bread to prohibitive heights, the working men grew desperate and took to rioting. There was much destruction of machinery, burning of hayricks, plundering of shops, and other disorderly proceedings. So tense were the times in 1817 that the government suspended the *Habeas Corpus Act* and declared all combinations of workers illegal. Two years later when the laws against public meetings were relaxed, a monster meeting of workingmen to demand universal suffrage was held at St. Peter's Field, Manchester. An attempt to suppress the meeting by the local magistrates and government troopers was bungled with the result that eleven persons were killed and over a hundred were wounded. Agitation was temporarily quelled and for three more years the government passed further measures to suppress sedition. But Peterloo gave the death-blow to the old Toryism.

Home reforms followed in rapid succession in the 1820's, although it was not until 1832 that the 'sovereignty of the people,' proclaimed by the reformers nearly half a century before, was at last recognized. The great Reform Act of that year provided for the popular election of members of Parliament and the redistribution of seats in the House among the large centers of population. The Reform Act of 1832 was only a beginning, but it provided the opening wedge for more and broader reforms to follow.

HUMANITARIANISM AND IDEALISM

Throughout the period of the Industrial Revolution there was a growing awareness of the evils that industrialism had brought to English society and a determination on the part of the men of creative genius, as well as the professional reformers, to do something to mitigate these evils. Humanitarianism had broadened and deepened toward the close of the eighteenth century. With the Fall of the Bastille philanthropy entered upon its revolutionary apotheosis. One need only contrast the work of Goldsmith and Blake, who wrote only twenty years after, to observe the chasm between them. Blake's human sentiment was deeper, subtler, and more impassioned. The anvil blows of revolution and war rang in his mind; the specters of hunger and raggedness haunted his spirit. Blake abhorred the nation's indifference to social ills. In trenchant language he called upon men to shake off the mind-forged manacles that bound them and to rebuild Jerusalem 'in England's green and pleasant land.' Wordsworth expressed profound compassion for those people in low station overtaken by misfortune—for beggars, idiots, social derelicts (both men and women) whose homes were broken by economic disaster and forced by society's indifference into a dreary vagrant life. Coleridge dedicated himself in the name of Heavenly Love to the establishment of a true social Christian brotherhood.

When Byron and Shelley began to write, the Napoleonic War was nearing its close and the 'dear years' of the postwar period were soon to bring the misery of the populace to its greatest depths. These two, and other young authors, like the poets of the older generation, were also quick to throw their support to the common man. Byron delivered two Parliamentary speeches in behalf of the laborers of Nottingham. In his poetry

he fearlessly exposed the corruption and hypocrisy of the ruling classes. Shelley inveighed against the abuses of privilege and wealth and passionately preached the doctrine of universal sharing. Hazlitt also was a vociferous champion of the underdog. Leigh Hunt led the liberal press and went to prison for his defiance of arbitrary authority. Tom Hood sang the 'Song of the Shirt' and aroused the public to the miseries of the sweat shop. These men, and others, spoke out in bitter social protest over the spectacle they beheld of widespread misery, poverty, and abuse.

After Waterloo the revolutionary dream of social amelioration was also revived on its more theoretical, idealistic level especially by Shelley. Shelley believed in the inherent greatness of men's souls and aspired to discover a new way of freedom for the human spirit. He believed that not only man's mode of life but man himself is capable of endless improvement, that man's will can completely master reality and transform it. Shelley's major poetry glows with Utopian visions of man's earthly perfection. But Shelley is not alone among the Romantic generation in expressing profoundly ethical-religious idealism. His moral earnestness was shared by Blake, Wordsworth, Coleridge, and Keats. These five major poets all opposed in their most characteristic work the traditions of eighteenth-century materialism. Blake fed his mystical imagination upon the theosophical writings of Swedenborg and Boehme. The work of Wordsworth, Coleridge, Shelley, and Keats is impermeated with the idealistic philosophy of Plato and the neo-Platonists.

The most enduring intellectual influence of the age, however, came not from the Greeks but from the idealistic philosophers of Germany—Fichte, Schelling, Schlegel, and most of all Kant. The German philosophers showed how the real and the ideal may be made one through goodness and beauty; how art by carrying out the ideal that men imagine may bring them deliverance. Kant demonstrated how men may attain freedom through transferring the seat of authority for knowledge from the world without to the world within. His great doctrine was that individual man through the integrity and activity of the mind has power to weave together impressions and so give to thought unity and validity. For Kant experience was a totality, united by self-consciousness, and formally determined by the thinking subject. His belief in the supremacy of the individual in intellectual and moral spheres was more effective than any other in establishing the reign of philosophical idealism in nineteenth-century Europe. By Kant's doctrine the mind of man becomes the creative interpreter of nature and society; the will of man may master destiny and achieve true freedom even for the most degraded and enslaved of men. The transcendental philosophy of Kant and his school was disseminated widely in England through Coleridge. Its law of higher reason found expression in Wordsworth's best poetry of the middle years, in the essays of De Quincey, in the many philosophical-religious works of Coleridge—and from him the 'transcendental' spirit was fully appropriated and spread abroad by Carlyle and by the young apostles of the Oxford movement.

ROMANTIC STYLE

The new freedoms of thought and emotion of the Romantic Age were united to new freedoms in expression. On all sides the new spirit was finding the traditional forms inadequate. A new romantic style in poetry can be distinguished. Its language is rich and musical, its rhythms varied and subtle, its imagery full of sensuous appeal and overtones of emotional shadings. It is shot through with strange beauties of thought and vision, of phrase and pattern. The romantic style was fully developed by Wordsworth, Coleridge, Shelley, and Keats, and after his manner by Byron, and in varying degrees by a host of lesser poets.

The neo-classical couplet, which had been brought to its highest perfection by Pope, had deteriorated in the hands of Pope's imitators and died in the hands of Moore and Rogers. The lofty and heroic style of the older English writers early attracted the favor of eighteenth-century poets with romantic leanings. Once the impulses were given, the poets of the Romantic Revival progressively revitalized the verse forms of the old masters, adapting them to their own use and—using them as points of departure—creating new forms and rhythms.

As early as 1726, when Pope still had eighteen years to live, Milton inspired two poems (Thomson's *Seasons* in blank verse and Dyer's *Grongar Hill* in octosyllabic couplets) that served as enjoyment and example to many. Among Preromantic writers, the Wartons, Collins, and Gray owed in great part their poetic inspiration to Milton's minor poems, especially *Il Penseroso*. Still the minor poems were less influential than *Paradise Lost*. After *The Seasons*, Miltonic blank verse was used in over four hundred eighteenth-century poems and the tradition continued un-

diminished in *The Prelude, Prometheus Unbound,* and *Hyperion.*

Spenser, too, was 'discovered' early. There were scores of imitations of Spenserian verse even in the Augustan age, at first in the spirit of parody or burlesque (such was essentially Thomson's *Castle of Indolence*), but as time went on writers fell in love with the real beauties of Spenser and tried to reproduce in their own verses his exquisite rhythms, pictorial charm, and rich imaginative beauty. Against the pallid vigor and hard perfection of neo-classical diction Spenser's language contended with a new glamor of enchantment. Throughout the eighteenth century Spenser's example encouraged a constantly increasing use of new verse forms and antique diction and, like Milton, his example set the pattern for some of the most notable poems of the major Romantics —*Childe Harold, Adonais,* and *The Eve of Saint Agnes.*

The enthusiasm for Milton and Spenser was extended to the eager study and exploitation of the Elizabethans, Drayton, Sidney, Chapman, and others, and to a deeper reading and comprehension of Shakespeare. The great tradition of the medieval was first opened up by the Warton brothers and exploited to the full by the entire generation of Romantic writers. The older ballad gave extraordinary impetus to the new freedom in style. Jacobean literature and Elizabethan drama yielded up rich stores from the quarryings of Hunt and Charles Lamb. Coleridge, Lamb, and De Quincey discovered a varied storehouse in seventeenth-century prose.

Two new creditors of the Romantic generation appear in the form of literary debts to Germany and Italy. The German impact was felt by the early Scott and the later Wordsworth, by De Quincey, Byron, and Crabb Robinson. The literature of Italy wrought its spell most fully upon the younger generation of poets, Byron, Shelley, and Keats. Some of the best writing of this famous triumvirate was inspired by the Italian masters. Leigh Hunt, Hazlitt, and Landor also were strongly attracted to Italian themes.

Finally, the revival of Hellenism is of major importance in romantic literature. Shelley and Keats work profoundly in the spirit of Greek literature and art. The mature poetry of Shelley is indisputably united with Aeschylus and Plato. Keats through his close study of Greek sculpture deeply perceived the meaning of Greek life and surmounted the barrier of language. Landor, too, who was steeped in the classical tradition, vitally transfers the spirit of Hellenism into the life stream of English literature.

The widespread use of earlier English literature and of modern foreign and Classical literatures served the Romantics, Elton reminds us, 'as a staff, a standard of control, and a storehouse of new inspiration.' By the study of Aeschylus, *Paradise Lost*, and the *Faerie Queene* poetic perceptions were sharpened and new energies were released. But each artist fashioned his instrument in his own way with the result that the dead old forms of the classicists had to go and their place to be taken by a new poetic vocabulary and a bewilderingly rich and varied romantic style.

ROMANTIC IMAGINATION

The literature of the Romantic Age is predominantly a literature produced by young writers or by writers during their earlier years. Consequently it shares the characteristics and sometimes the faults of youth. Writing was done at a time of life when emotions were volatile and when it was easy to avoid the discipline of strict, prolonged thought. Such youthful topics as the vanity of human wishes, the instability of beauty, and the inevitability of death occur only too often. There is also among Romantic writers—though not always confined to young writers—a tendency to withdraw from what might have been rewarding contacts with society and in isolation to indulge in sentimental explorations of themselves or in yearnings for the unusual and the unattainable. Sentimentalism, a fault of youth, was the crying fault of the age. But in fairness it must be said that though no author escaped from the contamination of sentimentalism, every major author very nearly, if not entirely, ultimately worked himself free from it. And if romantic literature did possess the shortcomings of youth, it also possessed the gifts and energies of youth. The poets in particular were endowed in an extraordinary degree with the supreme gift of creative imagination.

Imagination operated for the entire generation as a great lever of liberation. It reawakened in them a sense of beauty and opened the way to explore, to enjoy, and to express every kind of human experience. The Romantic poets came to believe that through imagination they could create life and add to the totality of experience. They dedicated themselves to the task of discovering a transcendental order in which the defects of the temporal world without losing their individuality are dissolved in the vast, spiritual perfection of the eternal. In this creative operation of the imagination visible things came to have a special new significance, for visible things were the tangible means through which the imagination moved to this higher reality. Even the commonplace and the trivial in the external world of nature awakened in the Romantics a constant sense of new beauty and wonder. Some of the lesser Romantic writers and some less inspired pieces of the greater writers may be thought of as escapist. On the whole, however, the English Romantics were more constructive than escapist; the hunger for illusion was balanced by respect for actuality and the love of the concrete. They rediscovered the full, rich variety of the real world—the total world in which we live. For are not even dreams in the final analysis a part of reality? De Quincey's great ambition was to recapture the experience of the dream as the most fleeting, but in some ways the most real, form of human experience. The supernatural, too, in history and in the folk mind as imaginatively re-created by the Romantics becomes a portion of reality.

Most of all, however, the Romantics sought through imaginative reconstruction a more satisfactory world in which to live their daily lives. Those portions of reality which they did not like, they proposed to change. They believed in the worth of the individual. They had a special sense of a humanitarian mission for mankind. Out of the great material and mental occasions of the age, such as the French Revolution, the Napoleonic Wars, and the idealistic philosophy of Kant, they opened up new vistas towards the truths that should make men free. (For the best statements by the Romantics on the Imagination see Wordsworth's *Prelude*, Book XIV, and Preface to the *Lyrical Ballads;* Coleridge's *Biographia Literaria;* Shelley's *A Defence of Poetry;* Keats's *Letters.* See also the commentary on Wordsworth's *Prelude.*)

ROMANTICISM IN THE VICTORIAN PERIOD

In foregoing sections of this essay we have followed the rise of modern English romanticism in the eighteenth century and have marked its many sea changes during the years of triumph. To round out our account, it remains to tell briefly what further transmutations of romanticism took place in the nineteenth and twentieth centuries, what

the generations coming after have thought of romanticism, and finally how romanticism stands
today.

The great Romantic Age virtually ended with
the death of Scott in 1832, but romanticism lived
on in Victorian literature without serious challenge until the mid-century. Tennyson in his
earlier collections (1830, 1832, 1843) proclaimed
himself Keats's follower by his ornate manner
and deliberate richness of melody. Like his predecessors Tennyson excelled in pictorial descriptions of nature. Browning also carried on from
the Romantics. In his youth he was the avowed
disciple of Shelley. In his maturity he developed
an all-embracing faith in human and divine love
which has affinities to Shelleyan optimism. Browning also shared with Tennyson the Romantics'
belief in progress. Arnold was a victim of modern skepticism, yet he welcomed the 'healing
power' of Wordsworth and in his poetry revealed
at times a quiet Wordsworthian sensitiveness to
natural beauty.

Whereas Tennyson, Browning, and Arnold
each in his different way richly used the romantic heritage to interpret man as a social being,
the Pre-Raphaelite poets—Rossetti, Morris, and
Swinburne—sought less to interpret the world
than to escape from it. Rossetti, who was the
leader of this younger group of Victorian poets,
turned away from the new challenges of science
and philosophy to a region of dreams and decorations. Taking his lead from Keats, he proclaimed the worship of beauty for beauty's sake.
He became absorbed in detached symbols, strange
rich colors, and sensuousness. Morris went even
deeper than Rossetti did into the past to become,
among other things, a connoisseur of Gothic art
and architecture. His poetry, which has marked
similarities to that of Coleridge and Keats, as well
as to that of Rossetti, kept alive the spirit of the
mysterious and the mystical in medieval romanticism. Swinburne, too, looked to Rossetti; but in
his over-intensity, exoticism, lyric fervor, radicalism, and unchastened imagination he proclaimed
himself the romantic heir of Shelley. Swinburne's
lavishness of style and excessive impressibility of
all forms of sensuous beauty carried the neo-
romantic manner of making verse decorative and
melodious about as far as it would go. Stevenson,
Kipling, and Hardy rejected the lead which the
Pre-Raphaelites had given; but in spite of scattered opposition, toward the end of the century
an aesthetic romanticism which employed color
effects, unique symbols, and escape from reality

had become the dominant mode in English poetry.

The Romantics had resisted the materialistic
implications of seventeenth- and eighteenth-century scientific thought by proclaiming the purposiveness of the universe and assigning moral
and spiritual values to nature. But with the appearance of Darwin's *Origin of Species* (1859),
the doubts, which had been increasing, about
those faiths held by the romantic generation were
now confirmed. For many Victorians supposed
that Darwin's theory of evolution proved con-
clusively that the processes of nature were lacking in purposiveness, that natural selection happened wholly by chance. According to their
understanding of the new theory, humanity was
merely the product of heredity and environment
and was capable of being explained altogether
in terms of these. Purely mechanistic ideas were,
therefore, brought back into fashion. Man lost
the dignified and heroic stature to which the Romantics had lifted him; in the minds of the late
Victorians man became a helpless animal in a
meaningless universe and at the mercy of the
forces around him. Independently of evolution,
moreover, a tendency toward what we call realism had already set in. Browning's addiction to
precise historical reconstructions in his poetry
and Tennyson's exactitude of description pointed
toward the realistic treatments of the Victorian
novelists who were themselves moving in the direction of naturalism without being aware of the
fact.

With the ascendancy of realism and naturalism
in Victorian fiction and the retirement of Victorian poetry to the confines of aestheticism, by
the end of the nineteenth century romanticism
had lost its potency.

ROMANTICISM IN THE TWENTIETH CENTURY

Two world wars and the specter of a third
one, the decline of religious faith and of moral
values, the widespread acceptance of the naturalistic view of life, the mechanization of both
external existence and of individual personality,
the disintegrating force of an industrialized society—these are some of the factors which in the
twentieth century brought about a crucial break
in the romantic tradition. It was in the 'twenties,
soon after the close of World War I (1914–18),
that the changed conditions of our environment
were markedly reflected in anti-romantic attitudes in English fiction, poetry, and criticism.

In twentieth-century fiction previous to the First World War, romanticism retained a lingering vitality in the work of such writers as Conrad, Galsworthy, Bennett, and H. G. Wells. But in the work of Henry James (1843–1916) new attitudes and methods in fiction were developed. A prominent disciple of James was the Irish novelist, James Joyce (*Ulysses,* 1922). Joyce plumbed the depths of the subconscious, glorified the life-urge, and drew ironic, desolate pictures of contemporary society. He performed astonishing feats with language, symbols, and technical devices to create a still further modification in fictional form. Allied in spirit to Joyce in the disrupted years between the two World Wars were D. H. Lawrence (1885–1930) and Aldous Huxley (1894–   ). Joyce, Huxley, and Lawrence—the most distinguished of British writers in the bleak 'twenties and 'thirties—typified the prevailing mood during the years when the old faiths and dignities had been discarded. Since World War II (1939–45) there are signs that both the fiction writers and the public have become tired of cynicism. But as yet no novelist of stature has cast the formula of hope into impressive artistic form.

The development of twentieth-century poetry roughly parallels that of modern fiction. In poetry there was no abrupt break in the tradition of aesthetic romanticism up to or during World War I. A group of Georgian poets, among whom were De la Mare, G. K. Chesterton, and D. H. Lawrence, mildly protested the Pre-Raphaelite decadence. But it was a group of young writers calling themselves Imagists who first hurled a direct challenge at 'exuberance, sentiment, and cloudily romantic lushness in poetry.' The Imagists were under the leadership of T. E. Hulme (1883–1917) and included in their group, Amy Lowell, Ezra Pound, and Richard Aldington. Not all Romantics were anathema to them, but with the Imagists the points of sympathy with the Romantics were overshadowed by the points of antipathy. The Imagists' principal objective was a verse of hard and dry clarity, a goal chiefly inspired by the example of French symbolism. The Symbolists, like the English Pre-Raphaelites with whom they were associated and from whom they derived, shunned a society that displeased them and became preoccupied with a solitary life of introspection and vision. The poetry produced by symbolism appealed to a limited audience, but before it went out of fashion it left its mark not only upon the Imagists but upon two writers— William Butler Yeats and T. S. Eliot—who were

to become pre-eminent in modern poetry. Imagism, symbolism, and other anti-romantic elements operating through these two poets and their disciples brought twentieth-century poetry into a position of sharp opposition to romanticism.

During the 'twenties and the 'thirties, through Eliot's example, mechanism, disbelief, and isolation became fashionable. Poetry between the two World Wars lost touch with the problems of society and did its best to ignore and keep free from them altogether. The poet came to feel that he was living in a world of chaos and desolation, a world hostile to the artist. Poetry came to be practiced by a small coterie indifferent to social values, haunted by the decay of religious faith, convinced of the validity of the naturalistic view of life, of the mechanization of existence, and of the triumph of blind chance. In the last dozen years or so, possibly encouraged by Eliot's overt shift to religious themes (*Ash Wednesday* and *Four Quartets*) and by the critical leadership of Herbert Read and others, there has been a turning away from philosophical defeatism to private experience and simple, natural things. There are also signs of a retreat from sophisticated exclusiveness in style and a return to an idiom, such as was recommended by Wordsworth, in the common tradition and intelligible to a wide audience. It would be misleading to suggest, however, that the new poetical stirrings have as yet seriously challenged the dominance of modernist techniques derived from the seventeenth-century Metaphysicals, the French Symbolists, and elsewhere, and given the wide sanction of authority by Yeats and Eliot. In the use of poetical idiom the Modernists stand opposed to both the neoclassic and the Romantic poets. As of this mid-twentieth century it is the Modernists who are very much in the ascendant.

There is close relationship between modernist poetical practice and twentieth-century anti-romantic criticism. Since the 1920's, the Romantic poets have run into increasingly rough critical opposition from T. E. Hulme, T. S. Eliot (*The Sacred Wood,* 1920), I. A. Richards (*Principles of Literary Criticism,* 1924), and their rapidly growing band of disciples on both sides of the Atlantic. Eliot from his high station as England's most influential critic has called down thunder on the romantic generation. Following Eliot's lead, a host of modern critics has moved forward to assault the standings of the Romantics and to extol the virtues of such unromantic poets as Donne and Pope. Yet Eliot has spoken of 'the surprising, varied, and abundant contribution of the Romantic period'; of Wordsworth's greatness about which there is 'something integral'; of the attractiveness of Blake and Landor; of Keats's notable letters and his 'philosophic' mind; and of the deep insight of Coleridge's critical writings (*The Use of Poetry,* 1933). Thus even with Eliot critical judgment on the Romantics is not wholly one of condemnation. Nor have the literary historians and scholars at large by any means forsaken the camp of the Romantics. Year by year undiminished numbers of fresh critical appraisals, textual studies, biographies, monographs, and essays bespeak the unceasing attraction the great Romantics still hold for innumerable readers. Eliot and his followers, it should be noted, admit a profound debt to the critical methods and philosophy of Coleridge. It should also be placed on record that Blake has had a twentieth-century revival paralleling, perhaps exceeding, that of Donne.

The most hostile anti-romantic criticism has come from those who have assumed that modern science has made it rationally impossible to maintain romantic beliefs about man and nature. They have concluded that science has proved nature to be wasteful, cruelly savage, and brutal. They have seen man as the mere product of matter, a prisoner of blind chance without choice and without will in a horrible prison house. In such a world the Romantics appear to be childish dreamers; their pictures of natural beauty, mere illusions; their moral values, utter emptiness. But it may be properly asked whether these pessimistic conclusions of the anti-romantics are well-founded. During the 1920's and even earlier there appeared among some scientists a radical revision in the interpretation of scientific data. Biologists discovered abundant evidence of the role of mutual helpfulness (symbiosis) in the emergence of new life forms; struggle and cruelty play their roles, but not necessarily, as formerly implied, the chief one. Moreover, in the process of analyzing the character of nature itself, science finds that the emergence of organisms depends on a selective process that is akin to purpose.

In the realm of the physical sciences the anti-romantics have pessimistically assumed the quantum theory to be the final report of despair. According to this theory, the universe is discontinuous and is made up of quanta or particles; there is no causality or determinism; everything is based wholly on chance. But in 1953 an American professor of mathematics reported the solution of a set of equations that establishes harmony between the quantum theory and the unified field theory of electromagnetism. Now the intricacies of higher mathematics are far beyond the grasp of most of us and even if they were not the testing of the new hypothesis can only be done by experimental methods. Nonetheless the harmonizing of these theories renews the picture of the universe as continuous and well ordered. Albert Einstein favored such a concept. He once said, 'I cannot believe that God plays dice with the cosmos!' A century and a half ago Wordsworth wrote,

> Thou dost preserve the stars from wrong;
> And the most ancient heavens, through
>   Thee, are fresh and strong.

Could it be that the Romantics were right after all about the orderliness of the physical universe?

Whether it is the Modernists or the Romanticists who are right about the nature of the universe, or about who or what keeps it going, or about whether there are or are not eternal truths, or about other unsolved mysteries of existence, we have seen in tracing the history of romanticism in modern times that the most formidable opposition to romanticism has come from philosophic and scientific mechanism. The Romantic Revolt, through the agencies of human faith and human imagination, challenged the pessimistic implications of eighteenth-century deism and political conservatism; then in a counter-revolt, seemingly sanctioned by the negations of science, twentieth-century modernism (at least in its most anti-romantic revulsions in the 'twenties and 'thirties) confirmed the darkest implications of mechanism.

We are now living in a time of uncertainties. If there could be a working-out of world tensions and the establishment of an era of good will among nations, it is possible that in some future day the faiths of the Romantics will come back into fashion again. Over the years it is likely that romanticism will be powerfully helped by the perennial optimism of human nature. Nearly all Romantics, as indeed most Classicists, have been on the side of optimism. They believe that the universe is rich in potentials for the happiness, not the despair of man. Historically, the very heart of romantic doctrine was a democratic idealism proclaiming the dignity and hope of man. The implications and aspirations of romanticism, therefore, far from being dead, are very much alive. To know twentieth-century values and directions—no less, to orient and test our own beliefs—we greatly need to know the romantic wellsprings from which in so large measure they derive.

R.N.

ENGLISH ROMANTIC

POETRY AND PROSE

1700 · JAMES THOMSON · 1748

1700 Born at Ednam on the Scottish border, the son of a minister. Studied for the ministry at Edinburgh University but did not take a degree.

1725 Went to London and there under the stress of poverty wrote *Winter*. Became tutor to the son of Lord Binning.

1726 Published *Winter*, followed by *Summer* (1727) and *Spring* (1728).

1730 Published *The Seasons* including the first appearance of *Autumn* and *A Hymn on the Seasons*. *Sophonisba*, a tragedy, produced at Drury Lane. Traveled in France and Italy as tutor to Charles Talbot, son of the solicitor-general.

1733–7 Served as Secretary of Briefs in the Court of Chancery. Published a long poem entitled *Liberty* (1734–6).

1738 *Agamemnon* produced at Drury Lane, with Quin in the leading role. Awarded an annual pension from the Prince of Wales.

1739 Published *Edward and Eleonora*.

1740 Collaborated with David Mallet to write a masque, *Alfred*, containing the famous song *Rule, Britannia*, attributed to Thomson.

1744–6 Published revised editions of *The Seasons*. Served as Surveyor-General of the Leeward Islands.

1745 *Tancred and Sigismunda*, the most successful of his plays, produced at Drury Lane with Garrick.

1748 Published *The Castle of Indolence*. Died. *Coriolanus* produced posthumously the next year.

JAMES THOMSON, whose literary works bear points of resemblance to those of his contemporaries, Pope and Addison, earned a large measure of his fame from plays written after classical models; but in his most significant contribution to English poetry, *The Seasons*, he dissociated himself from neo-classical tradition. Always good-humored and sociable by nature (he fitted easily into the courtly world of Queen Caroline), Thomson nevertheless had a deep and private delight in nature. He knew the 'poet's rapture' and possessed the poet's gift for accurate firsthand observation. He excelled in reporting odors, sounds, and colors and in capturing the ever-varying light and shade of the 'face of nature.' In *The Seasons* by means of a rich fullness of detail he aroused in his readers a new awareness of the myriad goings-on of the natural world. Thomson delighted also in the panoramic view, in large expansiveness, and 'atmospheric' effects. Like his friend and rival John Dyer, he was a landscape painter and gives us, particularly in *Summer*, a gallery of paintings—Claudian sunrises and sunsets, extended views, and Arcadian scenes of pastoral charm. He also glories in motion and change, not merely in set composition. He loved the titanic exuberance of nature—the river flood, the windstorm, and the deluge. Taking his excellences all together, Thomson is hard to beat as a poet of pictorial landscape.

The Seasons, however, is not solely a series of pictures. It contains narrative and didactic passages as well as descriptive. The author reveals an interest in natural religion, in the new findings of science, and in the ideals of philanthropy. He takes his stand for a more humane treatment of animals and for prison reform. He tells us what man and nature are doing; what man as affected by nature is experiencing. He rejoices in the infinite diversity and beauty of Nature; he finds the very contemplation of Nature's magnificence awe-inspiring. He believes, as did Shaftesbury, that the universal harmony and grandeur of nature are a glorification of God. But Nature is God's handiwork, not God: 'God is not all, but Lord of All.' Unlike Wordsworth and the Romantics, Thomson made no attempt to interpret the inner life of the Nature he delineates. In *A Hymn on the Seasons,* he foreshadows the deeper intuition of Nature's oneness found in Wordsworth's *Tintern Abbey,* but with a difference. With Thomson, observation and moralizing are in separate compartments; with Wordsworth, observation and philosophy are joined. Thomson's conception of Nature was substantially that of his age.

Thomson's manner of expression like his philosophy is not free from the academic biases of the neo-classicists. He modeled his verse after Milton, but distorted it with the antithetical points and balances of Pope. 'The blank verse of *The Seasons,*' H. A. Beers aptly observes, 'is a blank verse which has been passed through the strainer of the heroic couplet.' Thomson yielded to the allure of the swelling, sounding phrase and the verbose diction which were fashionable in his day. His style is not lacking in crudities of language, diffuseness, and cumbersome cadences. But when he shakes himself free from the artificialities of style and forgets his moralizing we get the blooming fullness of the natural world for the first time in many years. With Thomson, 'something old and precious returned to English verse, and a step was taken towards the rediscovery of an almost forgotten world.' Thomson is the first of modern writers to emphasize the 'living activities and operant magic of the earth.' Nature was to him always a fresh and abiding source of wonder, of attractiveness, and of solace.

The Seasons enjoyed an immense popularity and was widely imitated both in England and on the Continent. By its example Thomson successfully challenged the ideal of artificiality in English poetry and inaugurated a new era in the sentiment for Nature. There was hardly a single English writer of verse between 1725 and 1750 who was not in some manner guided or biased by the author of *The Seasons.* And until 1850 Thomson remained one of the most celebrated British poets of the first half of the eighteenth century. Wordsworth and his associates paid him the tribute of imitation. Hazlitt called him 'incomparably the best of our descriptive poets.'

The Castle of Indolence, though a slighter poem than *The Seasons* and built upon a trivial subject, helped to spread Thomson's fame. It is written in the Spenserian stanza with the Spenserian archaisms then in fashion. By a rare felicity of phrase, metrical spontaneity, and rich portraiture Thomson created in *Indolence* one of the best imitations of Spenserian melody and descriptive techniques in the language. Later poets regarded this as the most exquisite and charming of Thomson's works. Its Oriental elements and dreamy Spenserian rhythms widely reappear in poetry of the school of Coleridge and Keats. As late as the Victorian era a famous descendant of *Indolence* may be identified in Tennyson's languorous *Lotos-Eaters.*

From THE SEASONS

WINTER

PREFACE TO THE SECOND EDITION

Let poetry once more be restored to her ancient truth and purity; let her be inspired from heaven, and in return her incense ascend thither; let her exchange her low, venal, trifling, subjects for such as are fair, useful, and magnificent; and let her execute these so as at once to please, instruct, surprise, and astonish: and then of necessity the most inveterate ignorance, and prejudice, shall be struck dumb; and poets yet become the delight and wonder of mankind.

But this happy period is not to be expected, till some long-wished, illustrious man of equal power and beneficence rise on the wintry world of letters: one of a genuine and unbounded greatness and generosity of mind; who, far above all the pomp and pride of fortune, scorns the little addressful flatterer; pierces through the disguised designing villain; discountenances all the reigning fopperies of a tasteless age: and who, stretching his views into late futurity, has the true interest of virtue, learning, and mankind entirely at heart—a character so nobly desirable that to an honest heart it is almost incredible so few should have the ambition to deserve it.

Nothing can have a better influence towards the revival of poetry than the choosing of great and serious subjects, such as at once amuse the fancy, enlighten the head, and warm the heart. These give a weight and dignity to the poem; nor is the pleasure—I should say rapture—both the writer and the reader feels unwarranted by reason or followed by repentant disgust. To be able to write on a dry, barren theme is looked upon by some as the sign of a happy, fruitful genius:—fruitful indeed! like one of the pendant gardens in Cheapside, watered every morning by the hand of the Alderman himself. And what are we commonly entertained with on these occasions save forced unaffecting fancies, little glittering prettinesses, mixed turns of wit and expression, which are as widely different from native poetry as buffoonery is from the perfection of human thinking? A genius fired with the charms of truth and nature is tuned to a sublimer pitch, and scorns to associate with such subjects. . . .

I know no subject more elevating, more amusing; more ready to awake the poetical enthusiasm, the philosophical reflection, and the moral sentiment, than the works of Nature. Where can we meet with such variety, such beauty, such magnificence? All that enlarges and transports the soul! What more inspiring than a calm, wide survey of them? In every dress nature is greatly charming—whether she puts on the crimson robes of the morning, the strong effulgence of noon, the sober suit of the evening, or the deep sables of blackness and tempest! How gay looks the Spring! how glorious the Summer! how pleasing the Autumn! and how venerable the Winter!—But there is no thinking of these things without breaking out into poetry; which is, by-the-by, a plain and undeniable argument of their superior excellence.

For this reason the best, both ancient, and modern, Poets have been passionately fond of retirement, and solitude. The wild romantic country was their delight. And they seem never to have been more happy, than when, lost in unfrequented fields, far from the little busy world, they were at leisure, to meditate, and sing the Works of Nature.

Lines 224–389

THE keener Tempests come: and fuming dun
From all the livid East, or piercing North,
Thick Clouds ascend; in whose capacious Womb
A vapoury Deluge lies, to Snow congeal'd.
Heavy they roll their fleecy World along;
And the Sky saddens with the gather'd Storm.
Thro' the hush'd Air the whitening Shower descends,   230
At first thin-wavering; till at last the Flakes
Fall broad, and wide, and fast, dimming the Day,
With a continual Flow. The cherish'd Fields

Put on their Winter-Robe, of purest White.
'Tis Brightness all; save where the new Snow melts,
Along the mazy Current. Low, the Woods
Bow their hoar Head; and, ere the languid Sun
Faint from the West emits his Evening-Ray,
Earth's universal Face, deep-hid, and chill,
Is one wild dazzling Waste, that buries wide   240
The Works of Man. Drooping, the Labourer-Ox
Stands cover'd o'er with Snow, and then demands
The Fruit of all his Toil. The Fowls of Heaven,
Tam'd by the cruel Season, croud around
The winnowing Store,[1] and claim the little Boon
Which PROVIDENCE assigns them. One alone,
The Red-Breast, sacred to the household Gods,
Wisely regardful of th' embroiling Sky,
In joyless Fields, and thorny Thickets, leaves
His shivering Mates, and pays to trusty Man   250
His annual Visit. Half-afraid, he first
Against the Window beats; then, brisk, alights
On the warm Hearth; then, hopping o'er the Floor,
Eyes all the smiling Family askance,
And pecks, and starts, and wonders where he is;
Till more familiar grown, the Table Crumbs
Attract his slender Feet. The foodless Wilds
Pour forth their brown Inhabitants. The Hare,
Tho' timorous of Heart, and hard beset
By Death in various Forms, dark Snares, and
          Dogs,   260
And more unpitying Men, the Garden seeks,
Urg'd on by fearless Want. The Bleating Kind
Eye the bleak Heaven, and next the glistening
          Earth,
With Looks of dumb Despair; then, sad dispers'd,
Dig for the wither'd Herb thro' Heaps of Snow.
     Now, Shepherds, to your helpless Charge be
          kind,
Baffle the raging Year, and fill their Pens
With Food at Will; lodge them below the Storm,
And watch them strict: for from the bellowing
          East,
In this dire Season, oft the Whirlwind's Wing   270
Sweeps up the Burthen of whole wintry Plains
In one wide Waft, and o'er the hapless Flocks,
Hid in the Hollow of two neighbouring Hills,
The billowy Tempest whelms; till, upward urg'd,
The Valley to a shining Mountain swells,
Tipt with a Wreath, high-curling in the Sky.
     As thus the Snows arise; and foul, and fierce,
All Winter drives along the darken'd Air;
In his own loose-revolving Fields, the Swain
Disaster'd stands; sees other Hills ascend,   280
Of unknown joyless Brow; and other Scenes,
Of horrid Prospect, shag the trackless Plain:
Nor finds the River, nor the Forest, hid

---

1 of grain.

Beneath the formless Wild; but wanders on
From Hill to Dale, still more and more astray;
Impatient flouncing thro' the drifted Heaps,
Stung with the Thoughts of Home; the Thoughts
    of Home
Rush on his Nerves, and call their Vigour forth
In many a vain Attempt. How sinks his Soul!
What black Despair, what Horror fills his
    Heart!   290
When from the dusky Spot, which Fancy feign'd
His tufted Cottage rising thro' the Snow,
He meets the Roughness of the middle Waste,
Far from the Track, and blest Abode of Man:
While round him Night resistless closes fast,
And every Tempest, howling o'er his Head,
Renders the savage Wilderness more wild.
Then throng the busy Shapes into his Mind,
Of cover'd Pits unfathomably deep,
A dire Descent! beyond the Power of Frost,   300
Of faithless Bogs; of Precipices huge,
Smooth'd up with Snow; and, what is Land un-
    known,
What Water, of the still unfrozen Spring,
In the loose Marsh or solitary Lake,
When the fresh Fountain from the Bottom boils.
These check his fearful Steps; and down he sinks
Beneath the Shelter of the shapeless Drift,
Thinking o'er all the Bitterness of Death,
Mix'd with the tender Anguish Nature shoots
Thro' the wrung Bosom of the dying Man,   310
His Wife, his Children, and his Friends unseen.
In vain for him th' officious Wife prepares
The Fire fair-blazing, and the Vestment warm;
In vain his little Children, peeping out
Into the mingling Storm, demand their Sire,
With Tears of artless Innocence. Alas!
Nor Wife, nor Children, more shall he behold,
Nor Friends, nor sacred Home. On every Nerve
The deadly Winter seizes; shuts up Sense;
And o'er his inmost Vitals creeping cold,   320
Lays him along the Snow, a stiffen'd Corse,
Stretch'd out, and bleaching in the northern Blast.
   Ah little think the gay licentious Proud,
Whom Pleasure, Power, and Affluence surround;
They, who their thoughtless Hours in giddy Mirth,
And wanton, often cruel, Riot waste;
Ah little think they while they dance along,
How many feel, this very Moment, Death
And all the sad Variety of Pain!
How many sink in the devouring Flood,   330
Or more devouring Flame. How many bleed,
By shameful Variance betwixt Man and Man.
How many pine in Want, and Dungeon Glooms;
Shut from the common Air, and common Use
Of their own Limbs. How many drink the Cup

Of baleful Grief, or eat the bitter Bread
Of Misery. Sore pierc'd by wintry Winds,
How many shrink into the sordid Hut
Of chearless Poverty. How many shake
With all their fiercer Tortures of the Mind,   340
Unbounded Passion, Madness, Guilt, Remorse;
Whence tumbled headlong from the Height of
    Life,
They furnish Matter for the Tragic Muse.
Even in the Vale, where Wisdom loves to dwell,
With Friendship, Peace, and Contemplation
    join'd,
How many, rack'd with honest Passions droop
In deep retir'd Distress. How many stand
Around the Death-Bed of their dearest Friends,
And point the parting Anguish. Thought fond
    Man
Of these, and all the thousand nameless Ills,   350
That one incessant Struggle render Life,
One Scene of Toil, of Suffering, and of Fate,
Vice in his high Career would stand appall'd
And heedless rambling Impulse learn to think;
The conscious Heart of Charity would warm,
And her wide Wish Benevolence dilate;
The social Tear would rise, the social Sigh;
And into clear Perfection, gradual Bliss,
Refining still the social Passions work.
   And here can I forget the generous Band,   360
Who, touch'd with human Woe, redressive
    search'd
Into the Horrors of the gloomy Jail?[2]
Unpity'd, and unheard, where Misery moans;
Where Sickness pines; where Thirst and Hunger
    burn,
And poor Misfortune feels the Lash of Vice.
While in the Land of Liberty, the Land
Whose every Street and public Meeting glow
With open Freedom, little Tyrants rag'd:
Snatch'd the lean Morsel from the starving
    Mouth;
Tore from cold wintry Limbs the tatter'd
    Weed;   370
Even robb'd them of the last of Comforts, Sleep;
The free-born BRITON to the Dungeon chain'd,
Or, as the Lust of Cruelty prevail'd,
At pleasure mark'd him with inglorious Stripes;
And crush'd out Lives, by secret barbarous Ways,
That for their Country would have toil'd, or bled.
O great Design! if executed well,
With patient Care, and Wisdom-temper'd Zeal.
Ye Sons of Mercy! yet resume the Search;
Drag forth the legal Monsters into Light,   380
Wrench from their Hands Oppression's iron Rod,

---

2 In 1729 a parliamentary committee investigated and brought to
light the shocking conditions of the debtors' prisons.

And bid the Cruel feel the Pains they give.
Much still untouch'd remains; in this rank Age,
Much is the Patriot's weeding Hand requir'd.
The Toils of Law, (what dark insidious Men
Have cumbrous added to perplex the Truth,
And lengthen simple Justice into Trade)
How glorious were the Day! that saw These broke,
And every Man within the Reach of Right.

1725   1726

SUMMER

Lines 516–37, 585–628, 1371–1400

STILL let me pierce into the midnight depth
Of yonder Grove, of wildest largest growth,
That, forming high in air a woodland Quire,
Nods o'er the Mount beneath. At every step,
Solemn and slow the Shadows blacker fall,   520
And all is awful list'ning Gloom around.
  These are the haunts of Meditation, these
The Scenes where ancient Bards th' inspiring
      Breath
Ecstatic felt, and, from this World retir'd,
Convers'd with Angels and immortal Forms,
On gracious Errands bent—to save the fall
Of Virtue struggling on the Brink of Vice;
In waking Whispers and repeated Dreams
To hint pure Thought, and warn the favour'd Soul,
For future Trials fated, to prepare;   530
To prompt the Poet, who devoted gives
His Muse to better Themes; to soothe the Pangs
Of dying Worth, and from the Patriot's Breast
(Backward to mingle in detested War,
But foremost when engag'd) to turn the Death;
And numberless such Offices of Love,
Daily and nightly, zealous to perform.

          .   .   .

  Thus up the Mount, in airy Vision rapt,
I stray, regardless whither; till the sound
Of a near fall of Water every sense
Wakes from the charm of Thought: swift-shrink-
      ing back,
I check my Steps and view the broken Scene.
  Smooth to the shelving Brink a copious
      Flood   590
Rolls fair and placid; where, collected all
In one impetuous Torrent, down the steep
It thundering Shoots, and shakes the Country
      round.
At first, an azure sheet, it rushes broad;
Then, whit'ning by degrees as prone it falls,
And from the loud-resounding Rocks below
Dash'd in a Cloud of Foam, it sends aloft
A hoary Mist and forms a ceaseless Shower.

Nor can the tortured Wave here find repose;
But, raging still amid the shaggy Rocks,   600
Now flashes o'er the scatter'd Fragments, now
Aslant the hollow Channel rapid darts;
And, falling fast from gradual Slope to Slope,
With wild infracted Course and lessened Roar
It gains a safer Bed, and steals at last
Along the Mazes of the quiet Vale.
  Invited from the Cliff, to whose dark brow
He clings, the steep-ascending Eagle soars
With upward Pinions thro' the Flood of Day,
And, giving full his Bosom to the Blaze,   610
Gains on the Sun; while all the tuneful Race,
Smit by afflictive Noon, disorder'd droop
Deep in the Thicket, or, from Bower to Bower
Responsive, force an interrupted Strain.
The Stock-dove only thro' the Forest coos,
Mournfully hoarse; oft ceasing from his Plaint,
Short interval of weary Woe! again
The sad Idea of his murder'd Mate,
Struck from his Side by savage Fowler's Guile,
Across his Fancy comes; and then resounds   620
A louder Song of Sorrow thro' the Grove.
  Beside the dewy Border let me sit,
All in the freshness of the humid Air,
There on that hollow'd Rock, grotesque and wild,
An ample Chair moss-lin'd, and over head
By flowering Umbrage shaded; where the Bee
Strays diligent, and with th' extracted balm
Of fragrant Woodbine loads his little Thigh.

          .   .   .

  The Sun has lost his rage: his downward Orb
Shoots nothing now but animating Warmth
And vital Lustre; that with various Ray,
Lights up the Clouds, those beauteous robes of
      Heaven,
Incessant roll'd into romantic Shapes,
The Dream of waking Fancy! Broad below,
Cover'd with ripening Fruits, and swelling fast
Into the perfect Year, the pregnant Earth
And all her Tribes rejoice. Now the soft Hour
Of walking comes for him who lonely loves   1380
To seek the distant Hills, and there converse
With Nature, there to harmonize his Heart,
And in pathetic Song to breathe around
The harmony to Others. Social Friends,
Attun'd to happy Unison of Soul—
To whose exulting Eye a fairer World,
Of which the Vulgar never had a glimpse,
Displays its Charms; whose Minds are richly
      fraught
With philosophic Stores, superior Light;
And in whose Breast enthusiastic Burns   1390
Virtue, the Sons of Interest deem Romance—

Now call'd abroad, enjoy the falling Day:
Now to the verdant PORTICO of Woods,
To Nature's vast LYCEUM, forth they walk;
By that kind SCHOOL where no proud Master reigns,
The full free converse of the friendly Heart,
Improving and improv'd. Now from the World,
Sacred to sweet Retirement, Lovers steal,
And pour their Souls in Transport, which the SIRE
Of Love approving hears, and *calls it good.*   1400

AUTUMN
Lines 960–1047, 1363–84

BUT see the fading many-colour'd Woods,   960
Shade deepening over Shade, the Country round
Imbrown; a crouded Umbrage, dusk, and dun,
Of every Hue, from wan declining Green
To sooty Dark. These now the lonesome Muse,
Low-whispering, lead into their leaf-strown Walks,
And give the Season in its latest View.

Mean-time, light-shadowing all, a sober Calm
Fleeces[3] unbounded Ether; whose least Wave
Stands tremulous, uncertain where to turn
The gentle Current: while illumin'd wide,   970
The dewy-skirted Clouds imbibe the Sun,
And thro' their lucid Veil his soften'd Force
Shed o'er the peaceful World. Then is the Time,
For those whom Wisdom and whom Nature charm,
To steal themselves from the degenerate Croud,
And soar above this little Scene of Things;
To tread low-thoughted Vice beneath their Feet;
To sooth the throbbing Passions into Peace;
And woo lone Quiet in her silent Walks.

Thus solitary, and in pensive Guise,   980
Oft let me wander o'er the russet Mead,
And thro' the sadden'd Grove, where scarce is heard
One dying Strain, to chear the Woodman's Toil.
Haply some widow'd Songster pours his Plaint,
Far, in faint Warblings, thro' the tawny Copse.
While congregated Thrushes, Linnets, Larks,
And each wild Throat, whose artless Strains so late
Swell'd all the Music of the swarming Shades,
Robb'd of their tuneful Souls, now shivering sit
On the dead Tree, a dull despondent Flock!   990
With not a Brightness waving o'er their Plumes,
And nought save the chattering Discord in their Note.
O let not, aim'd from some inhuman Eye,
The Gun the Music of the coming Year
Destroy; and harmless, unsuspecting Harm,

Lay the weak Tribes, a miserable Prey,
In mingled Murder, fluttering on the Ground!

The pale descending Year, yet pleasing still,
A gentler Mood inspires; for now the Leaf
Incessant rustles from the mournful Grove,   1000
Oft startling such as, studious, walk below,
And slowly circles thro' the waving Air,
But should a quicker Breeze amid the Boughs
Sob, o'er the Sky the leafy Deluge streams;
Till choak'd, and matted with the dreary Shower,
The Forest-Walks, at every rising Gale,
Roll wide the wither'd Waste, and whistle bleak.
Fled is the blasted Verdure of the Fields;
And, shrunk into their Beds, the flowery Race
Their sunny Robes resign. Even what remain'd   1010
Of bolder Fruits falls from the naked Tree;
And Woods, Fields, Gardens, Orchards, all around
The desolated Prospect thrills the Soul.

He comes! he comes! in every Breeze the POWER
Of PHILOSOPHIC MELANCHOLY comes!
His near Approach the sudden-starting Tear,
The glowing Cheek, the mild dejected Air,
The soften'd Feature, and the beating Heart,
Pierc'd deep with many a virtuous Pang, declare.
O'er all the Soul his sacred Influence breathes;   1020
Inflames Imagination; thro' the Breast
Infuses every Tenderness; and far
Beyond dim Earth exalts the swelling Thought.
Ten thousand thousand fleet Ideas, such
As never mingled with the vulgar Dream,
Croud fast into the Mind's creative Eye.
As fast the correspondent Passions rise,
As varied, and as high: Devotion rais'd
To Rapture, and divine Astonishment;
The Love of Nature unconfin'd and, chief,   1030
Of Human Race; the large ambitious Wish,
To make them blest; the Sigh for suffering Worth,
Lost in Obscurity; the noble Scorn,
Of Tyrant Pride; the fearless great Resolve;
The Wonder which the dying Patriot draws,
Inspiring Glory thro' remotest Time;
Th' awaken'd Throb for Virtue, and for Fame;
The Sympathies of Love, and Friendship dear;
With all the *social Offspring of the Heart.*   1040

Oh bear me then to vast embowering Shades!
To twilight Groves, and visionary Vales!
To weeping Grottoes, and prophetic Glooms!
Where Angel-Forms athwart the solemn Dusk,
Tremendous sweep, or seem to sweep along;
And Voices more than human, thro' the Void
Deep-sounding, seize th' enthusiastic Ear.

---

3 spreads over.

Oh, Nature! all-sufficient! over all!
Inrich me with the Knowledge of thy Works!
Snatch me to Heaven; thy rolling Wonders there,
World beyond World, in infinite Extent,
Profusely scatter'd o'er the void Immense,
Shew me; their Motions, Periods, and their Laws,
Give me to scan; thro' the disclosing Deep
Light my blind Way: the mineral *Strata*
    there;   1370
Thrust, blooming, thence the vegetable World;
O'er that the rising System, more complex,
Of Animals; and higher still, the Mind,
The vary'd Scene of quick-compounded Thought,
And where the mixing Passions endless shift;
These ever open to my ravish'd Eye:
A Search, the Flight of Time can ne'er exhaust!
But if to that unequal; if the Blood,
In sluggish Streams about my Heart, forbid
That *best* Ambition; under closing Shades,   1380
Inglorious, lay me by the lowly Brook,
And whisper to my Dreams. From THEE begin,
Dwell all on THEE, with THEE conclude my Song:
And let me never never stray from THEE!

1730

A HYMN ON THE SEASONS

THESE, as they change, ALMIGHTY FATHER, these,
Are but the *varied* GOD. The rolling Year
Is full of Thee. Forth in the pleasing Spring
THY Beauty walks, THY Tenderness and Love.
Wide-flush the Fields; the softening Air is Balm;
Echo the Mountains round; the Forest smiles;
And every Sense, and every Heart, is Joy.
Then comes THY Glory in the Summer-Months,
With Light and Heat refulgent.[1] Then THY Sun
Shoots full Perfection thro' the swelling Year. 10
And oft THY Voice in dreadful Thunder speaks;
And oft at Dawn, deep Noon, or falling Eve,
By Brooks and Groves, in hollow-whispering
    Gales.
THY Bounty shines in Autumn unconfin'd,
And spreads a common Feast for all that lives.
In Winter awful THOU! with Clouds and Storms
Around THEE thrown, Tempest o'er Tempest
    roll'd,
Majestic Darkness! on the Whirlwind's Wing,
Riding sublime, THOU bidst the World adore,
And humblest Nature with THY northern Blast. 20
   Mysterious Round! what Skill, what Force
    divine,
Deep-felt, in These appear! a simple Train,
Yet so delightful mix'd, with such kind Art,

Such Beauty and Beneficence combin'd;
Shade, unperceiv'd, so softening into Shade;
And all so forming an harmonious Whole;
That, as they still succeed, they ravish still.
But wandering oft, with brute unconscious Gaze,
Man marks not THEE, marks not the mighty
    Hand,
That, ever-busy, wheels the silent Spheres;   30
Works in the secret Deep; shoots, streaming,
    Thence
The fair Profusion that o'erspreads the Spring:
Flings from the Sun direct the flaming Day;
Feeds every Creature; hurls the Tempest forth;
And, as on Earth this grateful Change revolves,
With Transport touches all the Springs of Life.
   Nature, attend! join every living Soul,
Beneath the spacious Temple of the Sky,
In Adoration join; and, ardent, raise
One general Song! To HIM, ye vocal Gales,   40
Breathe soft, whose SPIRIT in your Freshness
    breathes:
Oh talk of HIM in solitary Glooms!
Where, o'er the Rock, the scarcely-waving Pine
Fills the brown Shade with a religious Awe.
And ye, Whose bolder Note is heard afar,
Who shake th' astonish'd World, lift high to
    Heaven
Th' impetuous Song, and say from whom you
    rage.
HIS Praise, ye Brooks, attune, ye trembling Rills;
And let me catch it as I muse along.
Ye headlong Torrents, rapid, and profound;   50
Ye softer Floods, that lead the humid Maze
Along the Vale; and thou, majestic Main,
A secret World of Wonders in thyself,
Sound HIS stupendous Praise; whose greater Voice
Or bids you roar, or bids your Roarings fall.
Soft-roll your Incense, Herbs, and Fruits, and
    Flowers,
In mingled Clouds to HIM; whose Sun exalts,
Whose Breath perfumes you, and whose Pencil
    paints,
Ye Forests bend, ye Harvests wave, to HIM;
Breathe your still Song into the Reaper's
    Heart,   60
As home he goes beneath the joyous Moon.
Ye that keep watch in Heaven, as Earth asleep
Unconscious lies, effuse[2] your mildest Beams,
Ye Constellations, while your Angels strike,
Amid the spangled Sky, the Silver Lyre.
Great Source of Day! best Image here below
Of thy Creator, ever pouring wide,
From World to World, the vital Ocean round,
On Nature write with every Beam HIS Praise.

---

1 radiant; resplendent.

2 send forth.

The Thunder rolls: be hush'd the prostrate
    World;   70
While Cloud to Cloud returns the solemn Hymn.
Bleat out afresh, ye Hills; ye mossy Rocks,
Retain the Sound: the broad responsive Low,
Ye Valleys, raise; for the GREAT SHEPHERD reigns;
And his *unsuffering* Kingdom yet will come.
Ye Woodlands all, awake: a boundless Song
Burst from the Groves; and when the restless
    Day,
Expiring, lays the warbling World asleep,
Sweetest of Birds! sweet Philomela, charm
The listening Shades, and teach the Night HIS
    Praise.   80
Ye chief, for whom the whole Creation smiles;
At once the Head, the Heart, and Tongue of all,
Crown the great Hymn! in swarming Cities
    vast,
Assembled Men, to the deep Organ join
The long-resounding Voice, oft-breaking clear,
At solemn Pauses, thro' the swelling Base;
And, as each mingling Flame increases each,
In one united Ardor rise to Heaven.
Or if you rather chuse the rural Shade,
And find a Fane in every sacred Grove;   90
There let the Shepherd's Flute, the Virgin's Lay,
The prompting Seraph, and the Poet's Lyre,
Still sing the GOD OF SEASONS, as they roll.
For me, when I forget the darling Theme,
Whether the Blossom blows, the Summer-Ray
Russets the Plain, *inspiring* Autumn gleams;
Or Winter rises in the blackening East;
Be my Tongue mute, may Fancy paint no more,
And, dead to Joy, forget my Heart to beat!
    Should Fate command me to the farthest
      Verge   100
Of the green Earth, to distant barbarous Climes,
Rivers unknown to Song; where first the Sun
Gilds *Indian* Mountains, or his setting Beam
Flames on th' *Atlantic* Isles; 'tis nought to me;
Since GOD is ever present, ever felt,
In the void Waste as in the City full;
And where HE vital spreads there must be Joy.
When even at last the solemn Hour shall come,
And wing my mystic Flight to future Worlds,
I chearful will obey. There, with new Powers,   110
Will rising Wonders sing: I cannot go
Where UNIVERSAL LOVE not smiles around,
Sustaining all yon Orbs and all their Suns,
From *seeming Evil* still educing *Good,*
And *Better* thence again, and *Better* still,
In infinite Progression.————But I lose
Myself in HIM, in LIGHT INEFFABLE!
Come then, expressive Silence, muse HIS Praise.
    1730

THE CASTLE OF INDOLENCE

ADVERTISEMENT

    This poem being writ in the manner of Spenser, the obsolete words, and a simplicity of diction in some of the lines which borders on the ludicrous, were necessary to make the imitation more perfect. And the style of that admirable poet, as well as the measure in which he wrote, are as it were appropriated by custom to all allegorical poems writ in our language—just as in French the style of Marot, who lived under Francis I, has been used in tales and familiar epistles by the politest writers of the age of Louis XIV.

From CANTO I
Lines 10–108, 172–98, 289–396

IN lowly dale, fast by a river's side,   10
With woody hill o'er hill encompass'd round,
A most enchanting wizard did abide,
Than whom a fiend more fell is no where found.
It was, I ween, a lovely spot of ground;
And there a season atween June and May,
Half prank't with spring, with summer half im-
    brown'd,
A listless climate made, where, sooth to say,
No living wight could work, ne cared even for
    play.

Was nought around but images of rest:
Sleep-soothing groves, and quiet lawns
    between;   20
And flowery beds that slumbrous influence kest,[1]
From poppies breath'd; and beds of pleasant
    green,
Where never yet was creeping creature seen.
Mean time unnumber'd glittering streamlets
    play'd,
And hurled every-where their waters sheen;
That, as they bicker'd through the sunny glade,
Though restless still themselves, a lulling murmur
    made.

Join'd to the prattle of the purling rills,
Were heard the lowing herds along the vale,
And flocks loud-bleating from the distant hills,   30
And vacant[2] shepherds piping in the dale;
And now and then sweet Philomel would wail,
Or stock-doves plain amid the forest deep,
That drowsy rustled to the sighing gale;
And still a coil the grashopper did keep:
Yet all these sounds yblent[3] inclined all to sleep.

Full in the passage of the vale, above,

---

1 cast.
2 carefree.
3 blended.

A sable, silent, solemn forest stood;
Where nought but shadowy forms were seen to
   move,
As *Idless* fancy'd in her dreaming mood.   40
And up the hills, on either side, a wood
Of blackening pines, ay waving to and fro,
Sent forth a sleepy horror through the blood;
And where this valley winded out, below,
The murmuring main was heard, and scarcely
   heard, to flow.

A pleasing land of drowsy-hed it was:
Of dreams that wave before the half-shut eye;
And of gay castles in the clouds that pass,
For ever flushing round a summer-sky:
There eke the soft delights, that witchingly   50
Instil a wanton sweetness through the breast,
And the calm pleasures always hover'd nigh;
But whate'er smack'd of noyance, or unrest,
Was far far off expell'd from this delicious
   nest.

The landskip such, inspiring perfect ease,
Where INDOLENCE (for so the wizard hight)
Close-hid his castle mid embowering trees,
That half shut out the beams of Phœbus bright,
And made a kind of checker'd day and night.
Mean while, unceasing at the massy gate,   60
Beneath a spacious palm, the wick'd wight
Was plac'd; and to his lute, of cruel fate,
And labour harsh, complain'd, lamenting man's
   estate.

Thither continual pilgrims crouded still,
From all the roads of earth that pass there by:
For, as they chaunc'd to breathe[4] on neighbour-
   ing hill,
The freshness of this valley smote their eye,
And drew them ever and anon more nigh,
'Till clustering round th' enchanter false they
   hung,
Ymolten[5] with his syren melody;   70
While o'er th' enfeebling lute his hand he flung,
And to the trembling chords these tempting verses
   sung:

'Behold! ye pilgrims of this earth, behold!
See all but man with unearn'd pleasure gay.
See her bright robes the butterfly unfold,
Broke from her wintry tomb in prime of May.
What youthful bride can equal her array?
Who can with her for easy pleasure vie?
From mead to mead with gentle wing to stray,

From flower to flower on balmy gales to fly,   80
Is all she has to do beneath the radiant sky.

'Behold the merry minstrels of the morn,
The swarming songsters of the careless grove,
Ten thousand throats! that, from the flowering
   thorn
Hymn their good GOD, and carol sweet of love,
Such grateful kindly raptures them emove:[6]
They neither plough, nor sow; ne, fit for flail,
E'er to the barn the nodding sheaves they drove;
Yet theirs each harvest dancing in the gale,
Whatever crowns the hill, or smiles along the
   vale.   90

Outcast of nature, man! the wretched thrall
Of bitter-dropping sweat, or sweltry pain,
Of cares that eat away thy heart with gall,
And of the vices, an inhuman train,
That all proceed from savage thirst of gain:
For when hard-hearted *Interest* first began
To poison earth, *Astræa*[7] left the plain;
Guile, violence, and murder seiz'd on man;
And, for soft milky streams, with blood the rivers
   ran.

'Come, ye, who still the cumbrous load of life   100
Push hard up hill; but as the farthest steep
You trust to gain, and put an end to strife,
Down thunders back the stone with mighty sweep,
And hurls your labours to the valley deep,
For-ever vain: come, and, withouten fee,
I in oblivion will your sorrows steep,
Your cares, your toils, will steep you in a sea
Of full delight: O come, ye weary wights, to
   me!'

He ceas'd. But still their trembling ears retain'd
The deep vibrations of his witching song;
That, by a kind of magic power, constrain'd
To enter in, pell-mell, the listening throng.
Heaps pour'd on heaps, and yet they slip'd along
In silent ease: as when beneath the beam
Of summer-moons, the distant woods among,
Or by some flood all silver'd with the gleam,
The soft-embodied fays through airy portal
   stream.   180

By the smooth demon so it order'd was,
And here his baneful bounty first began:

---

4 rest.
5 melted.

6 move.
7 the 'star' maid, who dwelt among men in the golden age, but
when that age had passed away she withdrew and was placed
among the stars.

Though some there were who would not further
    pass,
And his alluring baits suspected han.[8]
The wise distrust the too fair-spoken man.
Yet through the gate they cast a wishful eye:
Not to move on, perdie,[9] is all they can;
For do their very best they cannot fly,
But often each way look, and often sorely sigh.

When this the watchful wicked wizard saw,   190
With sudden spring he leap'd upon them strait;
And soon as touch'd by his unhallow'd paw,
They found themselves within the cursed gate;
Full hard to be repass'd, like that of fate.
Not stronger were of old the giant-crew,[10]
Who sought to pull high *Jove* from regal state;
Though feeble wretch he seem'd, of sallow hue:
Certes, who bides his grasp, will that encounter
    rue.

                  .   .   .

The doors, that knew no shrill alarming bell,
Ne cursed knocker ply'd by villain's hand,   290
Self-open'd into halls, where, who can tell
What elegance and grandeur wide expand
The pride of *Turkey* and of *Persia* land?
Soft quilts on quilts, on carpets carpets spread,
And couches stretch around in seemly band;
And endless pillows rise to prop the head;
So that each spacious room was one full-swelling
    bed.

And every where huge cover'd tables stood,
With wines high-flavour'd and rich viands
    crown'd;
Whatever sprightly juice or tasteful food   300
On the green bosom of this earth are found,
And all old ocean genders in his round:
Some hand unseen these silently display'd,
Even undemanded, by a sign or sound;
You need but wish, and, instantly obey'd,
Fair-rang'd the dishes rose, and thick the glasses
    play'd.

Here freedom reign'd, without the least alloy;
Nor gossip's tale, nor ancient maiden's gall,
Nor saintly spleen durst murmur at our joy,
And with envenom'd tongue our pleasures
    pall.   310
For why? there was but one great rule for all;
To wit, that each should work his own desire,
And eat, drink, study, sleep, as it may fall,

Or melt the time in love, or wake the lyre,
And carol what, unbid, the muses might inspire.

The rooms with costly tapestry were hung,
Where was inwoven many a gentle tale;
Such as of old the rural poets sung,
Or of *Arcadian* or *Sicilian* vale:
Reclining lovers, in the lonely dale,   320
Pour'd forth at large the sweetly-tortur'd
    heart;
Or, looking tender passion, swell'd the gale,
And taught charm'd echo to resound their smart,
While flocks, woods, streams, around repose and
    peace impart.

Those pleas'd the most, where, by a cunning hand,
Depainted[11] was the patriarchal age;
What time Dan *Abraham* left the *Chaldee* land,[12]
And pastur'd on from verdant stage to stage,
Where fields and fountains fresh could best
    engage.
Toil was not then. Of nothing took they heed,   330
But with wild beasts the silvan war to wage,
And o'er vast plains their herds and flocks to feed:
Blest sons of nature they! true golden age indeed!

Sometimes the pencil, in cool airy halls,
Bade the gay bloom of vernal landskips rise,
Or autumn's varied shades imbrown the walls:
Now the black tempest strikes the astonish'd eyes;
Now down the steep the flashing torrent flies;
The trembling sun now plays o'er ocean blue,
And now rude mountains frown amid the
    skies;   340
Whate'er *Lorrain* light-touch'd with softening
    hue,
Or savage *Rosa* dash'd, or learned *Poussin* drew.[13]

Each sound too here to languishment inclin'd,
Lull'd the weak bosom, and induced ease.
Aerial music in the warbling wind,
At distance rising oft, by small degrees,
Nearer and nearer came, till o'er the trees
It hung, and breath'd such soul-dissolving airs,
As did, alas! with soft perdition please:
Entangled deep in its enchanting snares,   350
The listening heart forgot all duties and all cares.

A certain music, never known before,
Here lull'd the pensive melancholy mind;

8 have.
9 a mild oath from the French, *par Dieu,* by God.
10 the Titans.

11 depicted.
12 Genesis, xi, 31.
13 Claude Lorrain, Salvator Rosa, and Nicolas Poussin, the three
great seventeenth-century landscape painters, were well known
in England and extremely influential on the work of landscape
poets such as Thomson.

Full easily obtain'd. Behoves no more,
But sidelong, to the gently-waving wind,
To lay the well-tun'd instrument reclin'd;
From which, with airy flying fingers light,
Beyond each mortal touch the most refin'd,
The God of winds drew sounds of deep delight:
Whence, with just cause, *The harp of Æolus* it
    hight. 360

Ah me! what hand can touch the strings so fine?
Who up the lofty diapasan[14] roll
Such sweet, such sad, such solemn airs divine,
Then let them down again into the soul?
Now rising love they fan'd; now pleasing dole
They breath'd, in tender musings, through the
    heart;
And now a graver sacred strain they stole,
As when seraphic hands an hymn impart:
Wild warbling nature all, above the reach of
    art!

Such the gay splendor, the luxurious state, 370
Of *Caliphs* old, who on the *Tygris'* shore,
In mighty *Bagdat,* populous and great,
Held their bright court, where was of ladies store;
And verse, love, music still the garland wore:

When sleep was coy, the bard, in waiting there,
Chear'd the lone midnight with the muse's lore;
Composing music bade his dreams be fair,
And music lent new gladness to the morning air.

Near the pavilions where we slept, still ran
Soft-tinkling streams, and dashing waters fell, 380
And sobbing breezes sigh'd, and oft began
(So work'd the wizard) wintry storms to swell,
As heaven and earth they would together mell:[15]
At doors and windows, threatening, seem'd to call
The demons of the tempest, growling fell,
Yet the least entrance found they none at all;
Whence sweeter grew our sleep, secure in massy
    hall.

And hither *Morpheus* sent his kindest dreams,
Raising a world of gayer tinct and grace;
O'er which were shadowy cast Elysian gleams, 390
That play'd, in waving lights, from place to place,
And shed a roseate smile on nature's face.
Not *Titian*'s pencil e'er could so array,
So fleece with clouds the pure etherial space;
Ne could it e'er such melting forms display,
As loose on flowery beds all languishing lay.

1736–48 1748

---

14 entire compass of tones.

15 mingle.

1699 · JOHN DYER · 1757

1699   Born in Carmarthenshire, in southern Wales. Educated at Westminster School. Studied painting under Jonathan Richardson. Was a member of a London literary coterie that included James Thomson and Richard Savage.

1724–5   Studied painting in Italy.

1726   *Grongar Hill* and *The Country Walk,* a companion piece, printed in Poetical Miscellanies for the year.

1734–7   Engaged in gentleman-farming.

1740   Published *The Ruins of Rome,* a tourist poem.

1741–57   Took holy orders and held various curacies in England.

1757   Published *The Fleece,* a descriptive-didactic blank-verse poem on sheep-raising and the woolen industry.

1757   Died.

JOHN DYER is best remembered for *Grongar Hill,* a delightful 'prospect piece' of his native vale of Towy describing rivers, woods, and hills as they open in a wide expanse to the eye of a climber. In the midst of the natural scene, the poet moralizes amiably (as a true son of his age) and with winning simplicity bids us share his musing on the hillside and his joy in the song of the thrush. In a day of city poets, Dyer found inspiration in the beauty and simple pleasures of nature. He therefore takes his place in literary history (a modest one, to be sure) alongside Thomson and other early eighteenth-century writers who were inaugurating a revival of interest in external nature. *Grongar Hill* (which made its appearance in the same year as Thomson's *Winter*) won an immediate and brilliant success. In after times it found favor with such diverse judges as Dr. Johnson, Wordsworth, and Byron.

GRONGAR HILL

SILENT Nymph,[1] with curious eye!
Who, the purple ev'ning, lie
On the mountain's lonely van,[2]
Beyond the noise of busy man,
Painting fair the form of things,
While the yellow linet sings;
Or the tuneful nightingale
Charms the forest with her tale;
Come with all thy various hues,
Come, and aid thy sister Muse;   10
Now while Phœbus riding high
Gives lustre to the land and sky!
Grongar Hill[3] invites my song,
Draw the landskip bright and strong;
Grongar, in whose mossy cells
Sweetly-musing Quiet dwells;
Grongar, in whose silent shade,
For the modest Muses made,
So oft I have, the evening still,
At the fountain of a rill,   20
Sate upon a flow'ry bed,

---

[1] the Muse of painting.
[2] summit.

[3] in southwestern Wales, near Aberglasney, where Dyer was born.

With my hand beneath my head;
While stray'd my eyes o'er Towy's[4] flood,
Over mead, and over wood,
From house to house, from hill to hill,
'Till Contemplation had her fill.
   About his chequer'd sides I wind,
And leave his brooks and meads behind,
And groves, and grottoes where I lay,
And vistoes shooting beams of day: 30
Wide and wider spreads the vale;
As circles on a smooth canal:
The mountains round, unhappy fate!
Sooner or later, of all height,
Withdraw their summits from the skies,
And lessen as the others rise:
Still the prospect wider spreads,
Adds a thousand woods and meads,
Still it widens, widens still,
And sinks the newly-risen hill.   40
   Now, I gain the mountain's brow,
What a landskip lies below!
No clouds, no vapours intervene,
But the gay, the open scene
Does the face of nature show,
In all the hues of heaven's bow!
And, swelling to embrace the light,
Spreads around beneath the sight.
   Old castles on the cliffs arise,
Proudly tow'ring in the skies!   50
Rushing from the woods, the spires
Seem from hence ascending fires!
Half his beams Apollo sheds
On the yellow mountain-heads!
Gilds the fleeces of the flocks:
And glitters on the broken rocks!
   Below me trees unnumber'd rise,
Beautiful in various dyes:
The gloomy pine, the poplar blue,
The yellow beech, the sable yew,   60
The slender fir, that taper grows,
The sturdy oak with broad-spread boughs.
And beyond the purple grove,
Haunt of Phillis, queen of love!
Gaudy as the op'ning dawn,
Lies a long and level lawn[5]
On which a dark hill, steep and high,
Holds and charms the wand'ring eye!
Deep are his feet in Towy's flood,
His sides are cloath'd with waving wood,   70
And ancient towers crown his brow,
That cast an aweful look below;
Whose ragged walls the ivy creeps,
And with her arms from falling keeps;

So both a safety from the wind
On mutual dependence find.
   'Tis now the raven's bleak abode;
'Tis now th' apartment of the toad;
And there the fox securely feeds;
And there the pois'nous adder breeds   80
Conceal'd in ruins, moss and weeds;
While, ever and anon, there falls
Huge heaps of hoary moulder'd walls.
Yet time has seen, that lifts the low,
And level lays the lofty brow,
Has seen this broken pile compleat,
Big with the vanity of state;
But transient is the smile of fate!
A little rule, a little sway,
A sun beam in a winter's day,   90
Is all the proud and mighty have
Between the cradle and the grave.
   And see the rivers how they run,
Thro' woods and meads, in shade and sun,
Sometimes swift, sometimes slow,
Wave succeeding wave, they go
A various journey to the deep,
Like human life to endless sleep!
Thus is nature's vesture wrought,
To instruct our wand'ring thought;   100
Thus she dresses green and gay,
To disperse our cares away.
   Ever charming, ever new,
When will the landskip tire the view!
The fountain's fall, the river's flow,
The woody vallies, warm and low;
The windy summit, wild and high,
Roughly rushing on the sky!
The pleasant seat, the ruin'd tow'r,
The naked rock, the shady bow'r;   110
The town and village, dome and farm,
Each give each a double charm,
As pearls upon an Æthiop's arm.
   See on the mountain's southern side,
Where the prospect opens wide,
Where the evening gilds the tide;
How close and small the hedges lie!
What streaks of meadows cross the eye!
A step methinks may pass the stream,
So little distant dangers seem;   120
So we mistake the future's face,
Ey'd thro' hope's deluding glass;
As yon summits soft and fair
Clad in colours of the air,
Which to those who journey near,
Barren, brown, and rough appear;
Still we tread the same coarse way,
The present's still a cloudy day.
   O may I with myself agree,

---

4 Towy is a river flowing into Carmarthen Bay.
5 grassy field.

And never covet what I see:
Content me with an humble shade,
My passions tam'd, my wishes laid;
For while our wishes wildly roll,
We banish quiet from the soul:
'Tis thus the busy beat the air;
And misers gather wealth and care.
   Now, ev'n now, my joys run high,
As on the mountain-turf I lie;
While the wanton Zephyr sings,
And in the vale perfumes his wings;
While the waters murmur deep;
While the shepherd charms his sheep;
While the birds unbounded fly,
And with musick fill the sky,

130

140

Now, ev'n now, my joys run high.
   Be full, ye courts, be great who will;
Search for Peace with all your skill:
Open wide the lofty door,
Seek her on the marble floor,
In vain you search, she is not there;
In vain ye search the domes of care!
Grass and flowers Quiet treads,
On the meads, and mountain-heads,
Along with Pleasure, close ally'd,
Ever by each other's side:
And often, by the murm'ring rill,
Hears the thrush, while all is still,
Within the groves of Grongar Hill.

150

1726

1683 · EDWARD YOUNG · 1765

1683   Born at Upham, son of the rector who was later chaplain to William and Mary, and Queen Anne. Educated at Winchester and at New College and Corpus Christi College, Oxford. Took the bachelor's and doctor's degrees in law at All Souls College.

1719   *Busiris* produced at Drury Lane, followed two years later by *The Revenge*.

1725–8   Wrote and published a series of Horatian satires, *The Love of Fame*.

1726   Granted a pension of £200 a year.

1728   Appointed one of the royal chaplains; published *Two Epistles to Mr. Pope*.

1730   Given the rectory of Welwyn in Hertfordshire.

1731   Married the widowed Lady Elizabeth Lee, granddaughter of Charles II; she died ten years later.

1742–6   Published *The Complaint; or Night Thoughts on Life, Death, and Immortality.* Immediately popular.

1753   *The Brothers* (written about 1724) produced at Drury Lane.

1754   Published *The Centaur not Fabulous*, a *Night Thoughts* in prose.

1759   Published *Conjectures on Original Composition*, written to his friend, the novelist Richardson.

1765   Died.

EDWARD YOUNG—dramatist, poet, and divine—by virtue of his wide influence was the central figure of a mid-eighteenth-century group of writers preoccupied with themes of night, death, and immortality.[1] Young's most famous work is *Night Thoughts*, a long religious poem in nine books of ejaculatory blank verse in which the author gives emotional support to the new moral and evangelical fervor which was at that time winning thousands of converts to Methodism. His avowed purpose is to establish a defense of the teachings of Christian orthodoxy in direct protest against the optimistic philosophy of the deists. To set the right 'tone' Young drew upon the 'contemplative' melancholy of the landscape school and, more especially, upon the heavily pietistic melancholy of the Puritan funeral elegies. However, a very real sorrow (the nearly simultaneous loss of three close relatives) gave him the original impetus to write. In *Night Thoughts* the poet invites the reader to share his personal grief and to join him in midnight musings on man and death and immortality. His theme is the mixed nature of man and his redemption through Christ. He sets up the infidel Lorenzo and denounces him; then he proceeds to reclaim him by making him sensible of his littleness and overwhelming his imagination with the endless variety and beauty of the starry universe. Nature is a volume that declares to all men the evil of skepticism, the might of the Creator, and the eternity to come. The human soul is a midway link in the great chain of

---

1 The so-called 'graveyard' poets were: Robert Blair, *The Grave* (written, 1738, published, 1743); Joseph Warton, *The Enthusiast* (written, 1740, published, 1744); Edward Young, *Night Thoughts* (1742); William Collins, *Odes* (1746); Thomas Warton, *The Pleasures of Melancholy* (1747); Thomas Gray, *Elegy Written in a Country Churchyard* (1751).

being; set free, man outweighs the planets and the stars together. Love and desire carry him impetuously to the great stretches beyond. Yet man is never allowed to forget that he is abject, pitiable, and a sinner. Life is an empty dream; the world is a lunatic asylum. Paradox and startling contrasts are constantly used by the author to shock his readers into emotional awareness. The poet is at once blackly pessimistic and exuberantly optimistic. He preaches the nothingness of man; then elevates him to the stars. Man is

> An heir of glory! a frail child of dust!
> Helpless immortal! insect infinite!
> A worm! a god!

The abasement of man and life prepares for the mysteries of Christian theology and the argument for immortality. The emphasis in *Night Thoughts* is on the theme of death. Young dramatizes the paradoxical 'death is life' theme later to be made famous by Shelley in *Adonais*. We exist here on earth in embryo, Young declares, waiting to be born into life. Death is the 'great pay-day'; death is the 'deliverer'; death is the 'crown of life'!

Though Young supports the conception of divine creativeness and allows, it would seem, ample room for an individual's potential for freedom and goodness, the preponderant tone of *Night Thoughts* is elaborately and deliberately pathetic. It is full of gloomy religious excitement which emphasizes an atrabilious view of the pleasures as well as the duties of life. The thought is commonplace; the style labored, sententious, and diffuse. Yet there are some attractions in the energetic, staccato blank verse. Young had an extraordinary knack for epigram. He seized his moments (especially in the first four books where the impetus of the original passion is best sustained), and he knew how to make rather common ideas strike his readers as important novelties. Young's remarkable vogue lay in his melodramatic concentration on the theme of death. He absorbed and powerfully crystallized the romantic sentiment of death, grief, and mystery. The intensity of passion and the absence of restraint made him more popular on the Continent than in England. Nocturnal meditations on death by the vague light of the moon spread their fascination over all Europe. By means of the *Conjectures on Original Composition,* in which he pleads for a going back to the original of things and the avoidance of 'copies' made by others, the author of *Night Thoughts* similarly gave powerful impetus, particularly in Germany, to the cult of original genius.

From THE COMPLAINT: OR NIGHT
THOUGHTS ON LIFE, DEATH,
AND IMMORTALITY

NIGHT THE FIRST

Lines 1–34, 54–89, 110–33, 204–33, 437–59

TIR'D Nature's sweet Restorer, balmy *Sleep!*
He, like the World, his ready Visit pays
Where Fortune smiles; the Wretched he forsakes:
Swift on his downy Pinion flies from Woe,
And lights on Lids unsully'd with a Tear.

  From short (as usual) and disturb'd Repose,
I wake: How happy they, who wake no more!
Yet that were vain, if Dreams infest the Grave.
I wake, emerging from a Sea of Dreams
Tumultuous; where my wreck'd, desponding
    Thought   10
From Wave to Wave of *fansy'd* Misery,
At random drove, her Helm of Reason lost.
Tho' now restor'd, 'tis only Change of Pain,
(A bitter Change!) severer for severe.

The *Day* too short for my Distress! and *Night,*
Even in the *Zenith* of her dark Domain,
Is Sunshine, to the Colour of my Fate.[1]
  Night, sable Goddess! from her *Ebon* Throne,
In rayless Majesty, now stretches forth
Her leaden Sceptre o'er a slumb'ring World.   20
Silence, how dead! and Darkness, how profound!
Nor Eye, nor list'ning Ear an Object finds;
Creation sleeps. 'Tis, as the gen'ral Pulse
Of Life stood still, and Nature made a Pause;
An awful Pause! prophetic of her End.
And let her Prophecy be soon fulfill'd;
Fate! drop the Curtain; I can lose no more.
  Silence, and *Darkness!* solemn Sisters! Twins
From antient *Night,* who nurse the tender Thought
To *Reason,* and on *Reason* build *Resolve,*   30
(That Column of true Majesty in Man)
Assist me: I will thank you in the Grave;

---

1 The death of Young's wife in 1741 and the deaths of two other close members of his family within a few months account in part for the undertone of despair in the early portions of this poem.

The Grave, your Kingdom: *There* this Frame shall
    fall
A Victim sacred to your dreary Shrine.

.   .   .

  The Bell strikes *One.* We take no Note of Time,
But from its Loss. To give it then a Tongue,
Is wise in Man. As if an Angel spoke,
I feel the solemn Sound. If heard aright,
It is the *Knell* of my departed Hours:
Where are they? With the Years beyond the
    Flood.
It is the *Signal* that demands Dispatch;   60
How much is to be done? my Hopes and Fears
Start up alarm'd, and o'er Life's narrow Verge
Look down—on what? A fathomless Abyss;
A dread Eternity! how surely *mine!*
And can Eternity belong to me,
Poor Pensioner on the Bounties of an Hour?
  How poor, how rich, how abject, how august,
How complicate, how wonderful, is Man?
How passing wonder HE, who made him such?
Who centred in our Make such strange
    Extremes?   70
From diff'rent Natures marvelously mixt,
Connection exquisite of distant Worlds!
Distinguish'd *Link* in Being's endless Chain!
Midway from *Nothing* to the *Deity!*
A Beam etherial sully'd, and absorbt!
Tho' sully'd, and dishonour'd, still Divine!
Dim Miniature of Greatness absolute!
An Heir of Glory! a frail Child of Dust!
Helpless Immortal! Insect *infinite!*
A Worm! a God!—I tremble at myself,   80
And in myself am lost! At home a Stranger,
Thought wanders up and down, surpris'd, aghast,
And wond'ring at her *own:* How Reason reels!
O what a Miracle to Man is Man,
Triumphantly distress'd! what Joy, what Dread!
Alternately transported, and alarm'd!
What can preserve my Life? or what destroy?
An Angel's Arm can't snatch me from the Grave;
Legions of Angels can't confine me There.

.   .   .

They live! they greatly live a Life on Earth   110
Unkindled, unconceiv'd; and from an Eye
Of Tenderness, let heav'nly Pity fall
On me, more justly number'd with the Dead.
This is the Desart, *this* the Solitude:
How populous! how vital, is the Grave!
This is Creation's melancholy Vault,
The Vale funereal, the sad *Cypress* Gloom;
The Land of Apparitions, empty Shades!
All, all on Earth is *Shadow,* all beyond

Is *Substance;* the Reverse is Folly's *Creed:*   120
How solid all, where Change shall be no more?
  This is the Bud of Being, the dim Dawn,
The Twilight of our Day, the Vestibule.
Life's Theatre as yet is shut, and Death,
Strong Death, alone can heave the massy Bar,
This gross Impediment of Clay remove,
And make us Embryos of Existence free.
From *real* Life, but little more remote
Is *He,* not yet a Candidate for Light,
The *future* Embryo, slumb'ring in his Sire.   130
Embryos we must be, till we burst the Shell,
Yon ambient, azure Shell, and spring to Life,
The Life of Gods: O Transport! and of Man.

.   .   .

  Death! Great Proprietor of All! 'tis thine
To tread out Empire, and to quench the Stars.
The Sun himself by thy Permission shines;
And, one Day, thou shalt pluck him from his
    Sphere.
Amid such mighty Plunder, why exhaust
Thy *partial* Quiver on a Mark so *mean?*
Why thy *peculiar* Rancour wreck'd on *me?*   210
Insatiate Archer! could not *One* suffice?
Thy Shaft flew *thrice;* and *thrice* my Peace was
    slain;
And thrice, ere thrice yon Moon had fill'd her
    Horn.
O *Cynthia!* why so pale? Dost thou lament
Thy wretched Neighbour? Grieve to see thy Wheel
Of ceaseless Change outwhirl'd in human Life?
How wanes my *borrow'd* Bliss! from Fortune's
    Smile,
Precarious Courtesy! not *Virtue's* sure,
Self-given, *solar,* Ray of sound Delight.
  In ev'ry vary'd Posture, Place, and Hour,   220
How widow'd ev'ry Thought of ev'ry Joy!
Thought, busy Thought! too busy for my Peace!
Thro' the dark Postern of Time long laps'd,
Led softly, by the Stilness of the Night,
Led, like a Murderer, (and such it proves!)
Strays, wretched Rover! o'er the pleasing *Past;*
In quest of Wretchedness perversely strays;
And finds all desart *now;* and meets the Ghosts
Of my departed Joys; a num'rous Train!
I rue the Riches of my former Fate;   230
Sweet Comfort's blasted Clusters I lament;
I tremble at the Blessings once so dear;
And ev'ry Pleasure pains me to the Heart.

.   .   .

  The spritely *Lark's* shrill Matin wakes the Morn;
Grief's sharpest Thorn hard-pressing on my Breast,
I strive, with wakeful Melody to chear

The sullen Gloom, sweet *Philomel!* like Thee, 440
And call the Stars to listen: Ev'ry Star
If deaf to mine, enamour'd of thy Lay.
Yet be not vain; there are, who thine excell,
And charm thro' distant Ages: Wrapt in Shade,
Pris'ner of Darkness! to the silent *Hours,*
How often I repeat their Rage divine,
To lull my Griefs, and steal my Heart from Woe!
I roll their Raptures, but not catch their Flames.
Dark, tho' not blind, like thee *Mæonides!*[2]
Or *Milton!* thee; ah could I reach your Strain! 450
Or *His,* who made *Mæonides* our *Own.*[3]
Man too He sung: *Immortal* Man, I sing;
Oft bursts my Song beyond the Bounds of Life;
What, *now,* but Immortality can please?
O had *He* press'd his Theme, pursu'd the Track,
Which opens out of Darkness into Day!
O had he mounted on his Wing of Fire,
Soar'd, where I sink, and sung *Immortal* Man!
How had it blest Mankind, and rescu'd me?

NIGHT THE THIRD

Lines 328–50, 486–536

LIVE ever here, LORENZO?[4]—shocking thought!
So shocking, they who wish, disown it too;
Disown from shame, what they from folly
    crave.   330
Live ever in the womb, nor see the light?
For what live ever here?—with lab'ring step
To tread out former footsteps? Pace the round
Eternal? to climb life's worn, heavy wheel,
Which draws up nothing new? to beat and beat,
The beaten track? to bid each wretched day
The former mock? to surfeit on the *same,*
And yawn our joys? or thank a misery
For change, tho' sad? To see what we have
    seen?   340
Hear, till unheard, the same old slabber'd tale?
To taste the tasted, and at each return
Less tasteful? O'er our palates to decant
Another vintage? Strain a flatter year,
Thro' loaded vessels, and a laxer tone?
Crazy machines to grind earth's wasted fruits!
Ill-ground, and worse concocted! Load, not Life!
The *rational* foul kennels of excess!
Still-streaming thoroughfares of dull debauch
Trembling each gulp, lest death should snatch
    the bowl.   350

Then welcome, death! thy dread harbingers,
Age and *disease*; disease, tho' long my guest;
That plucks my nerves, those tender strings of life;
Which, pluckt a little more, will toll the bell,   490
That calls my few friends to my funeral;
Where feeble nature drops, perhaps, a tear,
While reason and religion, better taught,
Congratulate the dead, and crown his tomb
With wreath triumphant. Death is victory;
It binds in chains the raging ills of life:
Lust and *ambition, wrath* and *avarice,*
Dragg'd at his chariot-wheel, applaud his power.
That ills corrosive, cares importunate,
Are not *immortal* too, O death! is thine.   500
Our day of dissolution!—name it right;
'Tis our great pay-day; 'tis our harvest, rich
And ripe: What tho' the sickle, sometimes keen,
Just scars us as we reap the golden grain?
More than thy balm, *O Gilead!*[5] heals the wound.
Birth's feeble cry, and *death's* deep dismal groan,
Are slender tributes low-taxt nature pays
For mighty gain: the gain of each, a life!
But O! the last the former so transcends,
Life dies, compar'd: *Life* lives beyond the
    grave.   510
And feel I, *death!* no joy from thought of thee,
Death, the great counsellor, who man inspires
With ev'ry nobler thought and fairer deed!
Death, the deliverer, who rescues man!
Death, the rewarder, who the rescu'd crowns!
Death, that absolves my birth; a curse without
    it!
Rich *death,* that realizes all my cares,
Toils, virtues, hopes; without it a chimera!
Death, of all pain the period, not of joy;
Joy's *source,* and *subject,* still subsist unhurt; 520
One, in my soul; and one, in her great Sire;
Tho' the four winds were warring for my dust.
Yes, and from winds, and waves, and central
    night,
Tho' prison'd there, my dust too I reclaim,
(To dust when drop proud nature's proudest
    spheres,)
And live *entire.* Death is the crown of life:
Were death deny'd, poor man would live in vain;
Were death deny'd, to live would not be life;
Were death deny'd, ev'n fools would wish to
    die.
Death wounds to cure: we fall; we rise; we
    reign!   530
Spring from our fetters; fasten in the skies;
Where blooming *Eden* withers in our sight:
Death gives us more than was in *Eden* lost.
This king of terrors is the prince of peace.

---

2 Homer.
3 Pope.
4 an infidel, probably an imaginary figure, to whom are addressed
the poet's arguments for orthodoxy.

5 Genesis xxxvii, 25

When shall I die to vanity, pain, death?
When shall I *die*?—When shall I live for ever?

1742

From CONJECTURES ON ORIGINAL COMPOSITION

BUT there are who write with vigour and success, to the world's delight and their own renown. These are the glorious fruits where genius prevails. The mind of a man of genius is a fertile and pleasant field, pleasant as *Elysium,* and fertile as *Tempe*; it enjoys a perpetual spring. Of that spring, *Originals* are the fairest flowers; *Imitations* are of quicker growth but fainter bloom. *Imitations* are of two kinds: one of nature, one of authors. The first we call *Originals,* and confine the term imitation to the second. I shall not enter into the curious enquiry of what is or is not, strictly speaking, *Original,* content with what all must allow, that some compositions are more so than others; and the more they are so, I say, the better. *Originals* are and ought to be great favourites, for they are great benefactors; they extend the republic of letters, and add a new province to its dominion. *Imitators* only give us a sort of duplicates of what we had, possibly much better, before, increasing the mere drug of books, while all that makes them valuable, *knowledge* and *genius,* are at a stand. The pen of an *original* writer, like *Armida's*[1] wand, out of a barren waste calls a blooming spring. Out of that blooming spring, an *Imitator* is a transplanter of laurels, which sometimes die on removal, always languish in a foreign soil. . . .

We read *Imitation* with somewhat of his languor who listens to a twice-told tale. Our spirits rouze at an *Original* that is a perfect stranger, and all throng to learn what news from a foreign land. And though it comes like an *Indian* prince, adorned with feathers only, having little of weight, yet of our attention it will rob the more solid, if not equally new. Thus every telescope is lifted at a new-discovered star; it makes a hundred astronomers in a moment, and denies equal notice to the sun. But if an *Original,* by being as excellent as new, adds admiration to surprize, then are we at the writer's mercy; on the strong wind of his imagination, we are snatched from *Britain* to *Italy,* from climate to climate, from pleasure to pleasure; we have no home, no thought, of our own till the magician drops his pen. And then falling down into ourselves, we

---

1 Armida was the enchantress who opposed the Crusaders in Tasso's *Jerusalem Delivered.*

awake to flat realities, lamenting the change, like the beggar who dreamt himself a prince. . . .

But why are *Originals* so few? Not because the writer's harvest is over, the great reapers of antiquity having left nothing to be gleaned after them; nor because the human mind's teeming time is past, or because it is incapable of putting forth unprecedented births; but because illustrious examples *engross, prejudice,* and *intimidate.* They *engross* our attention, and so prevent a due inspection of ourselves; they *prejudice* our judgement in favour of their abilities, and so lessen the sense of our own; and they *intimidate* us with the splendour of their renown, and thus under diffidence bury our strength. Nature's impossibilities and those of diffidence lie wide asunder.

Let it not be suspected, that I would weakly insinuate anything in favour of the moderns, as compared with antient authors; no, I am lamenting their great inferiority. But I think it is no *necessary* inferiority; that it is not from divine destination, but from some cause far beneath the moon. I think that human souls, through all periods, are equal; that due care, and exertion, would set us nearer our immortal predecessors than we are at present. And he who questions and confutes this, will show abilities not a little tending toward a proof of that equality, which he denies.

After all, the first antients had no merit in being *Originals.* They could *not* be *Imitators.* Modern writers have a *choice* to make; and therefore have a merit in their power. They may soar in the regions of *liberty,* or move in the soft fetters of easy *imitation;* and imitation has as many plausible reasons to urge, as *Pleasure* had to offer to *Hercules.* Hercules made the choice of an hero, and *so* became immortal.

Yet let not assertors of classic excellence imagine, that I deny the tribute it so well deserves. He that admires not antient authors, betrays a secret he would conceal, and tells the world, that he does not understand them. Let us be as far from neglecting, as from copying, their admirable compositions. Sacred be their rights, and inviolable their fame. Let our understanding feed on theirs: they afford the noblest nourishment. But let them nourish, not annihilate, our own. When we read, let our imagination kindle at their charms; when we write, let our judgement shut them out of our thoughts; treat even *Homer* himself as his royal admirer was treated by the cynic; bid him stand aside, nor shade our Composition from the beams of our own genius. For nothing *Original* can rise, nothing immortal, can ripen, in any other sun. . . .

Let us build our Compositions with the spirit,

and in the taste, of the antients; but not with their materials. Thus will they resemble the structures of *Pericles* at *Athens,* which *Plutarch* commends for having had an air of antiquity as soon as they were built. All eminence, and distinction, lies out of the beaten road; excursion, and deviation, are necessary to find it; and the more remote your path from the highway, the more reputable. . . .

Had *Milton* never wrote, *Pope* had been less to blame. But when in *Milton's* genius, *Homer,* as it were, personally rose to forbid *Britons* doing him that ignoble wrong, it is less pardonable, by that *effeminate* decoration, to put *Achilles* in petticoats a second time. How much nobler had it been, if his numbers had rolled on in full flow, through the various modulations of *masculine* melody, into those grandeurs of solemn sound which are indispensably demanded by the native dignity of heroick song! How much nobler, if he had resisted the temptation of that *Gothic* dæmon,[2] which modern poesy tasting, became mortal! O how unlike the deathless, divine harmony of three great names (how justly joined!) of *Milton, Greece,* and *Rome*! His verse, but for this little speck of mortality in its extreme parts, as his hero had in his heel, like him, had been invulnerable and immortal.[3] But unfortunately, *that* was undipt in *Helicon,* as *this* in *Styx.* Harmony as well as eloquence is essential to poesy; and a murder of his musick

is putting half *Homer* to death. *Blank* is a term of diminution; what we mean by blank verse is verse unfallen, uncurst; verse reclaimed, reënthroned in the true *language of the gods,* who never thundered, nor suffered their *Homer* to thunder, in rhyme. . . .

When such an ample area for renowned adventure in *original* attempts lies before us, shall we be as mere leaden pipes, conveying to the present age small streams of excellence from its grand reservoir of antiquity, and those too, perhaps, mudded in the pass? *Originals* shine like comets; have no peer in their path; are rivalled by none, and the gaze of all. All other compositions (if they shine at all) shine in clusters, like the stars in the galaxy, where, like bad neighbours, all suffer from all, each particular being diminished and almost lost in the throng.

If thoughts of this nature prevailed, if antients and moderns were no longer considered as masters and pupils, but as hard-matched rivals for renown, then moderns, by the longevity of their labours, might one day become antients themselves. And old time, that best weigher of merits, to keep his balance even, might have the golden weight of an *Augustan* age[4] in both his scales; or rather our scale might descend, and that of antiquity (as a modern match for it strongly speaks) might *kick the beam.*

1759

---

2 rime.
3 According to Greek legend, Achilles was dipped by his mother in the river Styx, and his body made invulnerable, except his heel by which he was held.

4 in any national literature the supreme age: so-called after Augustus Caesar in whose reign, 31 B.C.–A.D. 14, was the golden age of Roman literature.

1699 · ROBERT BLAIR · 1746

1699   Born in Edinburgh, eldest son of the Reverend Robert Blair, who was one of the king's chaplains. Educated at Edinburgh University and in Holland. Inherited a private fortune.

1731   Appointed to the living of Athelstaneford in East Lothian. His favorite leisure pursuits were gardening and the study of English poets.

1738   Composed *The Grave,* which he had sketched out ten years earlier.

1743   Published *The Grave.*

1746   Died at Athelstaneford.

ROBERT BLAIR'S only considerable work is *The Grave,* a didactic-blank-verse poem of some eight hundred lines celebrating the 'gloomy horrors of the tomb.' Though independently conceived, *The Grave* is almost contemporaneous with Young's *Night Thoughts* and serves as a kind of corollary to it. Both Blair and Young share the same didactic purpose, both adhere to the same commonplace philosophical-theological pretensions. Blair's poem, however, is mercifully shorter than Young's and much less ornate. *The Grave* is, in fact, superior throughout to *Night Thoughts* as poetry. It contains a wealth of picturesque, appropriately macabre detail; and it is written in sinewy language, which now and then breaks into ringing dramatic speech. Blair's models were Milton and the Elizabethan and Stuart tragedy. His greatest debt was to Shakespeare, particularly to the grave-digging scene in *Hamlet.* Upon its publication *The Grave* won an instant success and for well over half a century was enormously popular and influential on literature in Europe and America. William Blake designed a famous series of illustrations for *The Grave* and nineteen-year-old William Cullen Bryant composed his *Thanatopsis* soon after reading Blair's poem.

From THE GRAVE

Lines 1–71, 183–236, 447–90, 712–67

WHILE some affect the sun, and some the shade,
Some flee the city, some the hermitage;
Their aims as various, as the roads they take
In journeying thro' life;—the task be mine,
To paint the gloomy horrors of the TOMB;
Th' appointed place of rendezvous, where all
These travellers meet.—Thy succours I implore,
Eternal King! whose potent arm sustains
The keys of hell and death.—The GRAVE, dread
   thing!
Men shiver when thou'rt named: Nature
      appall'd,   10
Shakes off her wonted firmness.—Ah! how dark
Thy long extended realms, and rueful wastes!
Where nought but Silence reigns, and Night, dark
      Night,
Dark as was CHAOS, ere the infant sun
Was roll'd together, or had try'd his beams
Athwart the gloom profound.—The sickly taper,
By glimm'ring thro' thy low-brow'd misty vaults,
(Furr'd round with mouldy damps, and ropy
      slime,)
Lets fall a supernumerary horror,

And only serves to make thy night more irk-
    some.   20
Well do I know thee by thy trusty YEW,
Cheerless, unsocial plant! that loves to dwell
'Midst sculls and coffins, epitaphs and worms:
Where light-heel'd ghosts, and visionary shades,
Beneath the wan, cold moon (as fame reports)
Embody'd thick, perform their mystic rounds.
No other merriment, dull tree! is thine.

    See yonder hallow'd Fane;—the pious work
Of names once fam'd, now dubious or forgot,
And bury'd 'midst the wreck of things which
    were;   30
There lie interr'd the more illustrious dead.
The wind is up:—hark! how it howls!—Methinks,
'Till now, I never heard a sound so dreary:
Doors creak, and windows clap, and night's foul
    bird,
Rook'd in the spire, screams loud; the gloomy
    aisles
Black-plaster'd, and hung round with shreds of
    'scutcheons,
And tatter'd coats of arms, send back the sound,
Laden with heavier airs, from the low vaults,
The mansions of the dead.—Rous'd from their
    slumbers,
In grim array the grisly spectres rise,   40
Grin horrible, and, obstinately sullen,
Pass and repass, hush'd as the foot of Night.
Again the screech-owl shrieks—ungracious
    sound!
I'll hear no more—it makes one's blood run chill.

    Quite round the pile, a row of reverend elms
(Coeval near with that), all ragged shew,
Long lash'd by the rude winds. Some rift half
    down
Their branchless trunks; others so thin at top,
That scarce two crows can lodge in the same tree.
Strange things, the neighbours say, have
    happen'd here;   50
Wild shrieks have issued from the hollow tombs;
Dead men have come again, and walk'd about;
And the great bell has toll'd unrung, untouch'd.
(Such tales their cheer at wake or gossipping,
When it draws near to witching time of night.)

    Oft in the lone Church-yard at night I've seen,
By glimpse of moonshine chequering thro' the
    trees,
The school-boy, with his satchel in his hand,
Whistling aloud to bear his courage up,
And lightly tripping o'er the long flat stones, 60
(With nettles skirted, and with moss o'ergrown,)
That tell in homely phrase who lie below.
Sudden he starts, and hears, or *thinks* he hears,
The sound of something purring at his heels;

Full fast he flies, and dares not look behind him,
'Till, out of breath, he overtakes his fellows,
Who gather round, and wonder at the tale
Of horrid APPARITION tall and ghastly,
That walks at dead of night, or takes his stand
O'er some new-open'd grave; and (strange to
    tell!)   70
Evanishes at crowing of the cock.

.   .   .

    Absurd! to think to overreach the GRAVE,
And from the wreck of names to rescue ours!
The best-concerted schemes men lay for fame
Die fast away; only themselves die faster.
The far-fam'd SCULPTOR and the laurell'd BARD,
Those bold insurancers of deathless fame,
Supply their little feeble aids in vain—
The tapering PYRAMID, th' Egyptian's pride, 190
And wonder of the world, whose spiky top
Has wounded the thick cloud, and long out-liv'd
The angry shaking of the winter's storm;
Yet, spent at last by th' injuries of heaven,
Shatter'd with age and furrow'd o'er with years,
The mystic cone, with hieroglyphics crusted,
Gives way. Oh, lamentable sight! At once
The labour of whole ages lumbers down,
A hideous and misshapen length of ruins!
Sepulchral columns wrestle but in vain   200
With all-subduing Time; her cank'ring hand
With calm deliberate malice wasteth them.
Worn on the edge of days, the brass consumes,
The busto[1] moulders, and the deep-cut marble,
Unsteady to the steel, gives up its charge!
AMBITION, half convicted of her folly,
Hangs down the head, and reddens at the tale.

    Here all the mighty TROUBLERS OF THE EARTH,
Who swam to sov'reign rule thro' seas of blood;
Th' oppressive, sturdy, man-destroying
    villains,   210
Who ravag'd kingdoms, and laid empires waste,
And, in a cruel wantonness of power,
Thinn'd states of half their people, and gave up
To want the rest; now, like a storm that's spent,
Lie hush'd, and meanly sneak behind the covert.
Vain thought! to hide thee from the general scorn,
That haunts and doggs them like an injured ghost
Implacable.—Here, too, the PETTY TYRANT,
Whose scant domains GEOGRAPHER ne'er notic'd,
And, well for neighbouring grounds, of arms as
    short,   220
Who fix'd his iron talons on the poor,
And grip'd them like some lordly beast of prey;
Deaf to the forceful cries of gnawing Hunger,
And piteous plaintive voice of Misery;

---

[1] bust; statue.

(As if a SLAVE was not a shred of nature,
Of the same common nature with his LORD;)
Now tame and humble, like a child that's whipp'd,
Shakes hands with dust, and calls the worm his
        kinsman;
Nor pleads his rank and birthright. Under ground,
PRECEDENCY's a jest; Vassal and Lord,   230
Grossly familiar, side by side consume.

   When self-esteem, or other's adulation,
Would cunningly persuade us we are something
Above the common level of our kind;
The *Grave* gainsays the smooth-complection'd
        flatt'ry,
And with blunt truth acquaints us what we are.

                    .   .   .

   DEATH'S SHAFTS fly thick! Here falls the Village
        swain,
And there his pamper'd lord! The cup goes round,
And who so artful as to put it by?
'Tis long since DEATH had the majority,   450
Yet, strange, *the Living lay it not to heart.*
See yonder maker of the dead man's bed,
The SEXTON, hoary-headed chronicle,
Of hard unmeaning face, down which ne'er stole
A gentle Tear, with mattock in his hand
Digs through whole rows of Kindred and Ac-
        quaintance,
By far his juniors. Scarce a skull's cast up,
But well he knew its Owner and can tell
Some passage of his life. Thus hand in hand
The sot has walk'd with DEATH twice twenty
        years;   460
And yet ne'er Yonker on the green laughs louder,
Or clubs a smuttier tale; when Drunkards meet,
None sings a merrier catch or lends a hand
More willing to his cup. Poor wretch!, he minds
        not
That soon some trusty Brother of the trade
Shall do for him what he has done for thousands.
   On this side and on that, men see their friends
Drop off like leaves in autumn; yet launch out
Into fantastic schemes, which the long Livers
In the world's hale and undegenerate days   470
Could scarce have leisure for.—Fools that we are!
Never to think of DEATH and of OURSELVES
At the same time!—as if to learn to die
Were no concern of ours. Oh! more than sottish,
For creatures of a Day in gamesome mood
To frolic on Eternity's dread brink,
Unapprehensive; when, for aught we know,
The very first swoln Surge shall sweep us in!
Think we, or think we not, TIME hurries on
With a resistless unremitting stream,   480
Yet treads more soft than e'er did midnight thief,

That slides his hand under the Miser's pillow
And carries off his prize. What is *this World?*
What but a spacious *burial-field* unwall'd,
Strew'd with Death's spoils, the spoils of animals
Savage and tame, and full of dead men's bones!
The very turf on which we tread, once liv'd,
And we that live must lend our carcases
To cover our own offspring: In their turns
They too must cover theirs. 'Tis here all meet! 490

                Sure *the last end*
Of the good Man is PEACE.—How calm his EXIT!
Night-dews fall not more gently to the ground,
Nor weary worn-out winds expire so soft.
Behold him! in the evening tide of Life,
A life well spent, whose early care it was
His riper years should not upbraid his green
By unperceiv'd degrees he wears away;
Yet like the sun seems larger at his setting!   720
(High in his faith and hopes,) look how he reaches
After the prize in view! and, like a bird
That's hamper'd, struggles hard to get away!
Whilst the glad gates of sight are wide expanded
To let new glories in, the first fair fruits
Of the fast-coming harvest.——Then!——Oh
        then!
Each earth-born joy grows vile, or disappears,
Shrunk to a thing of nought.——Oh! how he
        longs
To have his passport sign'd, and be dismiss'd!
'Tis done, and now he's happy!——The glad
        SOUL   730
Has not a wish uncrown'd.——Ev'n the lag FLESH
RESTS too IN HOPE of meeting once again
Its better half, never to sunder more.
Nor shall it hope in vain:—The time draws on
When not a single spot of burial-earth,
Whether on Land, or in the spacious Sea,
But must give back its long-committed dust
Inviolate:—And faithfully shall these
Make up the full account;—not the least atom
Embezzl'd, or mislaid, of the whole tale.[2]   740
Each SOUL shall have a BODY ready-furnish'd;
And each shall have his own.——Hence, ye pro-
        fane:
Ask not how this can be.——Sure the same pow'r
That rear'd the piece at first, and took it down,
Can reassemble the loose scatter'd parts,
And put them as they were:——Almighty God
Has done much more: Nor is his arm impair'd
Thro' length of days; And what he can, he will:
His Faithfulness stands bound to see it done.
When the dread Trumpet sounds, the
        slumb'ring dust,   750

2 number.

(Not unattentive to the call,) shall wake;
And ev'ry joint possess its proper place,
With a new elegance of form, unknown
To its first state.—— Nor shall the conscious SOUL
Mistake its partner; but amidst the Crowd,
Singling its other half, into its arms
Shall rush, with all th' impatience of a Man
That's new come home, who, having long been
    absent,
With haste runs over ev'ry different room,

In pain to see the whole.——Thrice happy
    meeting! 760
Nor TIME, nor DEATH, shall ever part them more.
  'Tis but a Night, a long and moonless Night;
We make the GRAVE our bed, and then are gone.
  Thus, at the shut of ev'n, the weary Bird
Leaves the wide air, and in some lonely brake
Cow'rs down, and dozes till the dawn of day;
Then claps his well fledg'd wings and bears away.

1743

1721 · MARK AKENSIDE · 1770

1721   Born at Newcastle-upon-Tyne, son of a butcher. Studied theology but switched to medicine and rose to eminence in his profession. Besides *The Pleasures of Imagination* wrote numerous odes and minor poems of which the best is *Hymn to the Naiads* (written in 1746 and published in Dodsley's *Collection of Poems,* 1758).

1744   Published *The Pleasures of Imagination,* which met with great success.

1770   Died. The unfinished recast of *The Pleasures of Imagination* published posthumously in *Poems,* 1772.

MARK AKENSIDE is chiefly significant in the history of romanticism for *The Pleasures of Imagination,* though his odes, published at least two years before Gray had printed his, are of minor importance in the revival of supposedly Greek forms of lyric. *The Pleasures of Imagination* is a didactic-descriptive poem of two thousand lines in somewhat cramped Miltonic blank verse. Its title and some of its ideas come from Addison's essays (Spectator, 411–21), which, following the lead of the philosopher Locke, affirmed that man's aesthetic pleasures are derived from the senses. Unlike Addison, however, Akenside cannot fully account for man's intellectual pleasures merely on the basis of the empirical philosophy of Locke. Following Shaftesbury, he went back to Plato and Longinus, who stress a belief in man's innate powers. Like these ancient philosophers, Akenside perceived that the beauty and harmony of all nature is revealed directly to the purified intellect. Like them, he joins truth, beauty, and goodness in an attempt to enlarge man's sense of spiritual values. Despite the frigidity of Akenside's verse, there is a dignified exposition of a system of ideas that were considered important in his time and a certain idealistic fervor that animates his best passages. *The Pleasures of Imagination* was widely popular in the eighteenth century and was read and appreciated by the major romantic poets. In his psychological preoccupation of man's place in nature Akenside is the obvious forerunner of Wordsworth.

From THE PLEASURES OF IMAGINATION

BOOK I

Lines 1–138, 169–221, 472–89, 512–66

WITH what attractive charms this goodly frame
Of nature touches the consenting hearts
Of mortal men; and what the pleasing stores
Which beauteous imitation thence derives
To deck the poet's or the painter's toil,
My verse unfolds. Attend, ye gentle powers
Of Musical Delight! and while I sing
Your gifts, your honours, dance around my strain.

Thou, smiling queen of every tuneful breast,
Indulgent Fancy! from the fruitful banks   10
Of Avon, whence thy rosy fingers cull
Fresh flow'rs and dews to sprinkle on the turf
Where Shakespeare lies, be present; and with thee
Let Fiction come, upon her vagrant wings
Wafting ten thousand colours thro' the air,
Which by the glances of her magic eye
She blends and shifts at will thro' countless forms,
Her wild creation. Goddess of the lyre,
Which rules the accents of the moving sphere,
Wilt thou, eternal Harmony! descend   20

And join this festive train? for with thee comes
The guide, the guardian of their lovely sports,
Majestic Truth; and where Truth deigns to come,
Her sister Liberty will not be far.
Be present, all ye Genii who conduct
The wand'ring footsteps of the youthful bard,
New to your springs and shades; who touch his ear
With finer sounds; who heighten to his eye
The bloom of nature, and before him turn
The gayest, happiest attitude of things.   30

Oft have the laws of each poetic strain
The critic-verse employ'd; yet still unsung
Lay this prime subject, tho' importing most
A poet's name: for fruitless is th' attempt,
By dull obedience and by creeping toil
Obscure to conquer the severe ascent
Of high Parnassus. Nature's kindling breath
Must fire the chosen genius; Nature's hand
Must string his nerves, and imp his eagle-wings,
Impatient of the painful steep, to soar   40
High as the summit; there to breathe at large
Ethereal air, with bards and sages old,
Immortal sons of praise. These flatt'ring scenes,
To this neglected labour court my song;
Yet not unconscious what a doubtful task
To paint the features of the mind,
And to most subtile and mysterious things
Give colour, strength, and motion. But the love
Of Nature and the Muses bids explore,
Thro' secret paths erewhile untrod by man,   50
The fair poetic region, to detect
Untasted springs, to drink inspiring draughts,
And shade my temples with unfading flow'rs
Cull'd from the laureate vale's profound recess,
Where never poet gain'd a wreath before.

From Heav'n my strains begin; from Heav'n descends
The flame of genius to the human breast,
And love and beauty, and poetic joy
And inspiration. Ere the radiant sun
Sprang from the east, or 'mid the vault of night 60
The moon suspended her serener lamp;
Ere mountains, woods, or streams adorn'd the globe,
Or Wisdom taught the sons of men her lore;
Then liv'd the Almighty One: then, deep-retir'd
In his unfathom'd essence, view'd the forms,
The forms eternal of created things;
The radiant sun, the moon's nocturnal lamp,
The mountains, woods and streams, the rolling globe,
And Wisdom's mien celestial. From the first

Of days, on them his love divine he fix'd,   70
His admiration: till in time complete,
What he admir'd and lov'd, his vital smile
Unfolded into being. Hence the breath
Of life informing each organic frame,
Hence the green earth and wild resounding waves;
Hence light and shade alternate, warmth and cold,
And clear autumnal skies and vernal show'rs,
And all the fair variety of things.

But not alike to every mortal eye
Is this great scene unveil'd. For since the claims 80
Of social life to different labours urge
The active pow'rs of man, with wise intent
The hand of Nature on peculiar minds
Imprints a diff'rent bias, and to each
Decrees its province in the common toil.
To some she taught the fabric of the sphere,
The changeful moon, the circuit of the stars,
The golden zones of heav'n; to some she gave
To weigh the moment of eternal things,
Of time and space and fate's unbroken chain,   90
And will's quick impulse; others by the hand
She led o'er vales and mountains, to explore
What healing virtue swells the tender veins
Of herbs and flow'rs; or what the beams of morn
Draw forth, distilling from the clifted rind
In balmy tears. But some to higher hopes
Were destin'd; some within a finer mould
She wrought, and temper'd with a purer flame.
To these the Sire Omnipotent unfolds
The world's harmonious volume, there to read   100
The transcript of himself. On every part
They trace the bright impressions of his hand:
In earth or air, the meadow's purple stores,
The moon's mild radiance, or the virgin's form
Blooming with rosy smiles, they see portray'd
That uncreated beauty which delights
The Mind Supreme. *They* also feel her charms,
Enamour'd; *they* partake th' eternal joy.

For as old Memnon's image, long renown'd
By fabling Nilus, to the quiv'ring touch   110
Of Titan's ray, with each repulsive string
Consenting, sounded thro' the warbling air
Unbidden strains,[1] even so did Nature's hand
To certain species of external things,
Attune the finer organs of the mind:
So the glad impulse of congenial pow'rs,
Or of sweet sound, or fair proportion'd form,
The grace of motion, or the bloom of light,
Thrills thro' imagination's tender frame,

---

[1] According to tradition a colossal statue of the Egyptian Memnon near Thebes gave forth musical sounds when struck by the rays of the rising sun.

From nerve to nerve; all naked and alive   120
They catch the spreading rays; till now the soul
At length discloses every tuneful spring,
To that harmonious movement from without
Responsive. Then the inexpressive strain
Diffuses its enchantment: Fancy dreams
Of sacred fountains and Elysian groves,
And vales of bliss; the intellectual pow'r
Bends from his awful throne a wond'ring ear,
And smiles; the passions, gently sooth'd away,
Sink to divine repose, and love and joy   130
Alone are waking; love and joy, serene
As airs that fan the summer. Oh, attend,
Whoe'er thou art, whom these delights can touch,
Whose candid bosom the refining love
Of Nature warms, oh, listen to my song;
And I will guide thee to her fav'rite walks,
And teach thy solitude her voice to hear,
And point her loveliest features to thy view.

.   .   .

Wherefore darts the mind,
With such resistless ardour to embrace   170
Majestic forms; impatient to be free,
Spurning the gross control of wilful might;
Proud of the strong contention of her toils;
Proud to be daring? Who but rather turns
To heav'n's broad fire his unconstrainèd view,
Than to the glimmering of a waxen flame?
Who that, from Alpine heights, his lab'ring eye
Shoots round the wide horizon, to survey
Nilus or Ganges rolling his bright wave
Thro' mountains, plains, thro' empires black
     with shade   180
And continents of sand; will turn his gaze
To mark the windings of a scanty rill
That murmurs at his feet? The high-born soul
Disdains to rest her heav'n-aspiring wing
Beneath its native quarry. Tir'd of earth
And this diurnal scene, she springs aloft
Thro' fields of air; pursues the flying storm;
Rides on the volley'd lightning thro' the heav'ns;
Or, yok'd with whirlwinds and the northern blast,
Sweeps the long tract of day. Then high she
     soars   190
The blue profound, and hovering round the sun
Beholds him pouring the redundant stream
Of light; beholds his unrelenting sway
Bend the reluctant planets to absolve
The fated rounds of time. Thence far effus'd
She darts her swiftness up the long career
Of devious comets; thro' its burning signs
Exulting measures the perennial wheel
Of nature, and looks back on all the stars,
Whose blended light, as with a milky zone,   200

Invests the orient. Now amaz'd she views
Th' empyreal waste, where happy spirits hold,
Beyond this concave heav'n, their calm abode;
And fields of radiance, whose unfading light
Has travell'd the profound six thousand years,
Nor yet arrives in sight of mortal things.
     E'en on the barriers of the world untir'd
She meditates th' eternal depth below;
Till half recoiling, down the headlong steep
She plunges; soon o'erwhelm'd and swallow'd
     up   210
In that immense of being. There her hopes
Rest at the fated goal. For from the birth
Of mortal man, the Sovereign Maker said
That not in humble nor in brief delight,
Not in the fading echoes of renown,
Pow'r's purple robes, nor Pleasure's flow'ry lap,
The soul should find enjoyment: but from these
Turning disdainful to an equal good,
Thro' all the ascent of things enlarge her view,
Till every bound at length should disappear,   220
And infinite perfection close the scene.

.   .   .

Thus doth beauty dwell
There most conspicuous, even in outward shape,
Where dawns the high expression of a mind:
By steps conducting our enraptur'd search
To the eternal origin, whose pow'r,
Thro' all th' unbounded symmetry of things,
Like rays effulging from the parent sun,
This endless mixture of her charms diffus'd.   480
Mind, Mind alone, (bear witness, earth and
     heav'n!)
The living fountains in itself contains
Of beauteous and sublime: here hand in hand,
Sit paramount the Graces; here enthron'd,
Celestial Venus, with divinest airs,
Invites the soul to never-fading joy.
Look then abroad thro' nature, to the range
Of planets, suns, and adamantine spheres
Wheeling unshaken thro' the void immense;

.   .   .

Once more search, undismay'd, the dark profound
Where nature works in secret; view the beds
Of min'ral treasure, and th' eternal vault
That bounds the hoary ocean; trace the forms
Of atoms moving with incessant change
Their elemental round; behold the seeds
Of being, and the energy of life
Kindling the mass with ever-active flame:
Then to the secrets of the working mind   520
Attentive turn; from dim oblivion call
Her fleet, ideal band; and bid them, go!

Break thro' time's barrier, and o'ertake the hour
That saw the heav'ns created: then declare
If aught were found in those external scenes
To move thy wonder now. For what are all
The forms which brute, unconscious matter wears,
Greatness of bulk, or symmetry of parts?
Not reaching to the heart, soon feeble grows
The superficial impulse; dull their charms,   530
And satiate soon, and pall the languid eye.
Not so the moral species, nor the pow'rs
Of genius and design; th' ambitious mind
There sees herself; by these congenial forms
Touch'd and awaken'd, with intenser act
She bends her nerve, and meditates well-pleas'd
Her features in the mirror. For of all
Th' inhabitants of earth, to man alone
Creative Wisdom gave to lift his eye
To truth's eternal measures; thence to frame   540
The sacred laws of action and of will,
Discerning justice from unequal deeds,
And temperance from folly. But beyond
This energy of truth, whose dictates bind

Assenting reason, the benignant sire,
To deck the honour'd paths of just and good,
Has added bright imagination's rays:
Where Virtue, rising from the awful depth
Of Truth's mysterious bosom, doth forsake
The unadorn'd condition of her birth;   550
And dress'd by Fancy in ten thousand hues,
Assumes a various feature, to attract,
With charms responsive to each gazer's eye,
The hearts of men. Amid his rural walk,
Th' ingenuous youth, whom solitude inspires
With purest wishes, from the pensive shade
Beholds her moving, like a virgin muse
That wakes her lyre to some indulgent theme
Of harmony and wonder: while among
The herd of servile minds, her strenuous form   560
Indignant flashes on the patriot's eye,
And thro' the rolls of memory appeals
To ancient honour, or in act serene,
Yet watchful, raises the majestic sword
Of public pow'r, from dark ambition's reach
To guard the sacred volume of the laws.

1744

1722 · JOSEPH WARTON · 1800

1722 Born, son of Thomas Warton the elder, Oxford professor of poetry; brother of Thomas Warton the younger. Educated at Winchester (where he formed a friendship with William Collins) and Oriel College, Oxford. Took holy orders. Held various curacies and was headmaster of Winchester for many years.

1744 Published a volume of verse which included *The Enthusiast, or The Lover of Nature.*

1746 Published *Odes on Various Subjects.*

1757 *Essay on the Genius and Writings of Pope,* vol. I, and

1782 *Essay on the Genius and Writings of Pope,* vol. II.

1797 Edition of Pope's *Works* in nine volumes.

1800 Died.

J OSEPH WARTON was active in the revolt against the prevailing mode in eighteenth-century poetry. *The Enthusiast* (published in the year of Pope's death, though written four years earlier) is noteworthy because it is perhaps the earliest deliberate fusion of the cult of Rousseauistic primitivism, sentimental melancholy, and the love of the antique. It sings the pleasures of solitary communion with nature; the delights of the picturesque; the superiority of wild, even savage, and desolate scenes and naked Indians; and the wish to withdraw from the artificialities of European civilization to the idyllic innocence of America. These themes had made their appearance before in secondary roles or in isolation (notably in Thomson's *Seasons*), but in *The Enthusiast* the sentiment is joined and the melodrama heightened. Joseph Warton did his chief pioneering work, however, not in poetical composition but as leader of the revolution in eighteenth-century literary criticism. He took a firm stand against the prevailing taste for moral and ethical poetry. He was convinced that the fashion of moralizing in verse had gone too far and that what was needed was invention and imagination—the poet was to be 'bold without confine.' He scorned vagueness in description and called for more exactness in the naming of objects. His most definite opposition was to Pope. He put Pope in the second rank to Shakespeare, Spenser, and Milton on the ground that ethical poetry, however excellent, is an inferior species. As a literary critic Joseph Warton was a man of independent judgment and wide influence. He held his own even against Johnson in the Literary Club.

THE ENTHUSIAST: OR, THE LOVER OF NATURE[1]

YE green-rob'd *Dryads,* oft' at dusky Eve
By wondering Shepherds seen, to Forests brown,
To unfrequented Meads, and pathless Wilds,

Lead me from Gardens deckt with Art's vain Pomps.
Can gilt Alcoves, can Marble-mimic Gods,
Parterres embroider'd, Obelisks, and Urns
Of high Relief; can the long, spreading Lake,
Or Vista lessening to the Sight; can *Stow*
With all her *Attic* Fanes, such Raptures raise,

---

[1] Text is of the first edition.

As the Thrush-haunted Copse, where lightly
   leaps   10
The fearful Fawn the rustling Leaves along,
And the brisk Squirrel sports from Bough to
   Bough,
While from an hollow Oak the busy Bees
Hum drowsy Lullabies? The Bards of old,
Fair Nature's Friends, sought such Retreats, to
   charm
Sweet *Echo* with their Songs; oft' too they met,
In Summer Evenings, near sequester'd Bow'rs,
Or Mountain-Nymph, or Muse, and eager learnt
The moral Strains she taught to mend Mankind.
As to a secret Grot *Ægeria* stole   20
With Patriot *Numa,* and in silent Night
Whisper'd him sacred Laws, he list'ning sat
Rapt with her virtuous Voice, old *Tyber* leant
Attentive on his Urn, and husht his Waves.[2]
   Rich in her weeping Country's Spoils *Versailles*
May boast a thousand Fountains, that can cast
The tortur'd Waters to the distant Heav'ns;
Yet let me choose some Pine-topt Precipice
Abrupt and shaggy, whence a foamy Stream,
Like *Anio,*[3] tumbling roars; or some bleak
   Heath,   30
Where straggling stand the mournful Juniper,
Or Yew-tree scath'd; while in clear Prospect
   round,
From the Grove's Bosom Spires emerge, and
   Smoak
In bluish Wreaths ascends, ripe Harvests wave,
Herds low, and Straw-rooft Cotts appear, and
   Streams
Beneath the Sun-beams twinkle—The shrill Lark,
That wakes the Wood-man to his early Task,
Or love-sick *Philomel,* whose luscious Lays
Sooth lone Night-wanderers, the moaning Dove
Pitied by listening Milkmaid, far excell   40
The deep-mouth'd Viol, the Soul-lulling Lute,
And Battle-breathing Trumpet. Artful Sounds!
That please not like the Choristers of Air,
When first they hail th' Approach of laughing
   May.
   Creative *Titian,* can thy vivid Strokes,
Or thine, O graceful *Raphael,* dare to vie
With the rich Tints that paint the breathing Mead?
The thousand-colour'd Tulip, Violet's Bell
Snow-clad and meek, the Vermil-tinctur'd Rose,
And golden Crocus?—Yet with these the Maid, 50
Phillis or *Phœbe,* at a Feast or Wake.
Her jetty Locks enamels; fairer she,

In Innocence and home-spun Vestments drest,
Than if cœrulean Sapphires at her Ears
Shone pendant, or a precious Diamond-Cross
Heav'd gently on her panting Bosom white.
   Yon' Shepherd idly stretcht on the rude Rock,
Listening to dashing Waves, the Sea-Mews Clang
High-hovering o'er his Head, who views beneath
The Dolphin dancing o'er the level Brine,   60
Feels more true Bliss than the proud Ammiral,
Amid his Vessels bright with burnish'd Gold
And silken Streamers, tho' his lordly Nod
Ten thousand War-worn Mariners revere.
And great *Æneas* gaz'd with more Delight
On the rough Mountain shagg'd with horrid
   Shades,[4]
(Where Cloud-compelling *Jove,* as Fancy
   dream'd,
Descending shook his direful *Ægis* black)
Than if he enter'd the high Capitol
On golden Columns rear'd, a conquer'd World 70
Contributing to deck its stately Head:
More pleas'd he slept in poor *Evander's* Cott
On shaggy Skins, lull'd by sweet Nightingales,
Than if a *Nero,* in an Age refin'd,
Beneath a gorgeous Canopy had plac'd
His royal Guest, and bade his Minstrels sound
Soft slumb'rous *Lydian* Airs to sooth his Rest.
   Happy the first of Men, ere yet confin'd
To smoaky Cities; who in sheltering Groves,
Warm Caves, and deep-sunk Vallies liv'd and
   lov'd   80
By Cares unwounded; what the Sun and Showers,
And genial Earth untillag'd could produce,
They gather'd grateful, or the Acorn brown,
Or blushing Berry; by the liquid Lapse
Of murm'ring Waters call'd to slake their Thirst,
Or with fair Nymphs their Sun-brown Limbs to
   bathe;
With Nymphs who fondly clasp'd their fav'rite
   Youths,
Unaw'd by Shame, beneath the Beechen Shade,
Nor Wiles, nor artificial Coyness knew.
Then Doors and Walls were not; the melting
   Maid   90
Nor Frowns of Parents fear'd, nor Husband's
   Threats;
Nor had curs'd Gold their tender Hearts allur'd,
Then Beauty was not venal. Injur'd Love,
O whither, God of Raptures, art thou fled?
While Avarice waves his golden Wand around,
Abhorr'd Magician, and his costly Cup
Prepares with baneful Drugs, t'enchant the Souls
Of each low-thoughted Fair to wed for Gain.
   What tho' unknown to those primæval Sires,

---

2 Numa, second legendary king of Rome, derived his inspiration
from Ægeria, goddess of fountains, whom he met by night in her
sacred grove.
3 a river in Italy.

---

4 *Æneid,* Bk.v iii.

The well-arch'd Dome, peopled with breathing
    Forms   100
By fair *Italia*'s skilful Hand, unknown
The shapely Column, and the crumbling Busts
Of awful Ancestors in long Descent?
Yet why should Man mistaken deem it nobler
To dwell in Palaces, and high-rooft Halls,
Than in God's Forests, Architect supreme!
Say, is the *Persian* Carpet, than the Field's
Or Meadow's Mantle gay, more richly wov'n;
Or softer to the Votaries of Ease,
Than bladed Grass, perfum'd with dew-dropt
    Flow'rs?   110
O Taste corrupt! that Luxury and Pomp
In specious Names of *polish'd Manners* veil'd,
Should proudly banish Nature's simple Charms.
Tho' the fierce North oft smote with Iron Whip
Their shiv'ring Limbs, tho' oft the bristly Boar
Or hungry Lion 'woke them with their Howls,
And scar'd them from their Moss-grown Caves to
    rove,
Houseless and cold in dark, tempestuous Nights;
Yet were not Myriads in embattled Fields
Swept off at once, nor had the raving Seas   120
O'erwhelm'd the foundering Bark, and helpless
    Crew;
In vain the glassy Ocean smil'd to tempt
The jolly Sailor, unsuspecting Harm,
For Commerce was unknown. *Then* Want and
    Pine
Sunk to the Grave their fainting Limbs; but *Us*
Excess and endless Riot doom to die.
They cropt the poisonous Herb unweetingly,
But wiser we spontaneously provide
Rare powerful Roots, to quench Life's chearful
    Lamp.
    What are the Lays of artful *Addison*,   130
Coldly correct, to *Shakespear*'s Warblings wild?
Whom on the winding *Avon*'s willow'd Banks
Fair Fancy found, and bore the smiling Babe
To a close Cavern: (still the Shepherds shew
The sacred Place, whence with religious Awe
They hear, returning from the Field at Eve,
Strange Whisperings of sweet Music thro' the Air)
Here, as with Honey gather'd from the Rock,
She fed the little Prattler, and with Songs
Oft' sooth'd his wondering Ears, with deep
    Delight   140
On her soft Lap he sat, and caught the Sounds.
    Oft' near some crowded City would I walk,
Listening the far-off Noises, rattling Carrs,
Loud Shouts of Joy, sad Shrieks of Sorrow, Knells
Full slowly tolling, Instruments of Trade,
Striking mine Ears with one deep-swelling Hum.
Or wandering near the Sea, attend the Sounds

Of hollow Winds, and ever-beating Waves.
Ev'n when wild Tempests swallow up the Plains,
And *Boreas'* Blasts, big Hail, and Rains com-
    bine   150
To shake the Groves and Mountains, would I sit,
Pensively musing on th' outragious Crimes
That wake Heav'n's Vengeance: at such solemn
    Hours,
Dæmons and Goblins thro' the dark Air shriek,
While *Hecat* with her black-brow'd Sisters nine,
Rides o'er the Earth, and scatters Woes and
    Deaths.
Then too, they say, in drear *Ægyptian* Wilds
The Lion and the Tiger prowl for Prey
With Roarings loud! the list'ning Traveller
Starts Fear-struck, while the hollow-echoing
    Vaults   160
Of Pyramids encrease the deathful Sounds.
    But let me never fail in cloudless Nights,
When silent *Cynthia* in her silver Car
Thro' the blue Concave slides, when shine the
    Hills,
Twinkle the Streams, and Woods look tipt with
    Gold,
To seek some level Mead, and there invoke
Old Midnight's Sister Contemplation sage,
(Queen of the rugged Brow, and stern-fixt Eye)
To lift my Soul above this little Earth,
This Folly-fetter'd World; to purge my Ears,   170
That I may hear the rolling Planets Song,
And tuneful-turning Spheres: If this debarr'd,
The little *Fayes* that dance in neighbouring Dales,
Sipping the Night-dew, while they laugh and love,
Shall charm me with aërial Notes.—As thus
I wander musing, lo, what awful Forms
Yonder appear! sharp-ey'd *Philosophy*
Clad in dun Robes, an Eagle on his Wrist,
First meets my Eye; next, Virgin *Solitude*
Serene, who blushes at each Gazer's Sight;   180
Then *Wisdom*'s hoary Head, with Crutch in Hand,
Trembling, and bent with Age; last *Virtue*'s self
Smiling, in White array'd, who with her leads
Fair *Innocence,* that prattles by her Side,
A naked Boy!—Harass'd with Fear I stop,
I gaze, when *Virtue* thus—'Whoe'er thou art,
Mortal, by whom I deign to be beheld,
In these my Midnight-Walks; depart, and say
That henceforth I and my immortal Train
Forsake *Britannia*'s Isle; who fondly stoops   190
To Vice, her favourite Paramour.'—She spoke,
And as she turn'd, her round and rosy Neck,
Her flowing Train, and long, ambrosial Hair,
Breathing rich Odours, I enamour'd view.
    O who will bear me then to Western Climes,
(Since Virtue leaves our wretched Land) to Shades

Yet unpolluted with *Iberian* Swords;
With simple *Indian* Swains, that I may hunt
The Boar and Tiger thro' *Savannah*'s[5] wild?
There fed on Dates and Herbs, would I despise 200
The far-fetch'd Cates of Luxury, and Hoards
Of narrow-hearted Avarice; nor heed
The distant Din of the tumultuous World.
So when rude Whirlwinds rouze the roaring Main,
Beneath fair *Thetis* sits, in coral Caves,
Serenely gay, nor sinking Sailors Cries
Disturb her sportive Nymphs, who round her form
The light fantastic Dance, or for her Hair
Weave rosy Crowns, or with according Lutes
Grace the soft Warbles of her honied Voice. 210

From AN ESSAY ON THE GENIUS AND WRITINGS OF POPE

DEDICATION TO THE REVEREND DR. YOUNG

... I REVERE the memory of Pope, I respect and honour his abilities; but I do not think him at the head of his profession. In other words, in that species of poetry wherein Pope excelled, he is superior to all mankind, and I only say that this species of poetry is not the most excellent one of the art.

We do not, it should seem, sufficiently attend to the difference there is betwixt a *man of wit, a man of sense,* and a *true poet.* Donne and Swift were undoubtedly men of wit and men of sense, but what traces have they left of *pure poetry?* It is remarkable that Dryden says of Donne, 'He was the greatest wit though not the greatest poet of this nation.' Fontenelle[1] and La Motte[2] are entitled to the former character, but what can they urge to gain the latter? Which of these characters is the most valuable and useful is entirely out of the question; all I plead for is to have their several provinces kept distinct from each other and to impress on the reader that a clear head and acute understanding are not sufficient alone to make a *poet,* that the most solid observations on human life expressed with the utmost elegance and brevity are *morality,* and not *poetry,* that the *Epistles* of Boileau[3] in *rhyme* are no more poetical than the *Characters* of La Bruyère[4] in *prose,* and that it is a creative and glowing *Imagination,* 'acer spiritus

ac vis,'[5] and that alone that can stamp a writer with this exalted and very uncommon character which so few possess and of which so few can properly judge.

For one person who can adequately relish and enjoy a work of imagination, twenty are to be found who can taste and judge of observations on familiar life and the manners of the age. *The Satires* of Ariosto[6] are more read than the *Orlando Furioso* or even Dante. Are there so many cordial admirers of Spenser and Milton, as of Hudibras,[7] if we strike out of the number of these supposed admirers those who appear such out of fashion and not of feeling? Swift's *Rhapsody on Poetry* is far more popular than Akenside's noble *Ode to Lord Huntingdon.* The *Epistles* on the Characters of Men and Women and your sprightly Satires, my good friend, are more frequently perused and quoted than *L'Allegro* and *Il Penseroso* of Milton. Had you written only these Satires, you would indeed have gained the title of a man of wit and a man of sense, but, I am confident, would not insist on being denominated a *poet merely* on their account.

'Non satis est puris versum perscribere verbis.'[8]

It is amazing this matter should ever have been mistaken when Horace has taken particular and repeated pains to settle and adjust the opinion in question. He has more than once disclaimed all right and title to the name of *poet* on the score of his ethic and satiric pieces.

'—Neque enim concludere versum
    Dixeris esse satis——'[9]

are lines often repeated but whose meaning is not extended and weighed as it ought to be. Nothing can be more judicious than the method he prescribes, of trying whether any composition be essentially poetical or not; which is to drop entirely the measures and numbers and transpose and invert the order of the words, and in this unadorned manner to peruse the passage. If there be really in it a true poetical spirit all your inversions and transpositions will not disguise and extinguish it, but it will retain its lustre like a diamond unset and thrown back into the rubbish of the mine. Let us make a little experiment on the

---

5 treeless plains.

1 Bernard Fontenelle, 1657-1757, French author and wit, whose prose still lays some claim to remembrance.
2 Antoine Houdart de La Motte, 1672-1731, French dramatist, famous in his day for his wit and inquiring mind.
3 Nicolas Boileau, 1636-1711, most famous critic and poet of the French classical school.
4 Jean de la Bruyère, 1645-96, French ethical writer.

5 'vehement spirit and power'—Horace, *Satires,* I, iv, 46.
6 Ludovico Ariosto, 1474-1533, celebrated Italian writer whose *Orlando Furioso* is the greatest of Italian romantic epics.
7 Samuel 'Hudibras' Butler, 1612-80, author of the widely popular mock-heroic poem, *Hudibras,* which satirized Puritanism.
8 'It is not enough to write out a verse in plain language.'—Horace, *Satires,* I, iv, 54.
9 'You would not assert that it is enough merely to round out a verse.'—Horace, *Satires,* I, iv, 40-41.

following well-known lines, 'Yes, you despise the man that is confined to books, who rails at humankind from his study, though what he learns, he speaks, and may perhaps advance some general maxims or may be right by chance. The coxcomb bird, so grave and so talkative that cries, "whore, knave, and cuckold," from his cage, though he rightly call many a passenger, you hold him no philosopher. And yet, such is the fate of all extremes, men may be read too much, as well as books. We grow more partial for the sake of the observer to observations which we ourselves make, less so to written wisdom because another's. Maxims are drawn from notions, and those from guess'.[10] What shall we say of this passage? Why, that it is most excellent sense, but just as poetical as the 'qui fit Maecenas'[11] of the author who recommends this method of trial. Take ten lines of the *Iliad, Paradise Lost* or even of the *Georgics* of Virgil and see whether by any process of critical chemistry you can lower and reduce them to the tameness of prose. You will find that they will appear like Ulysses in his disguise of rags, still a hero, though lodged in the cottage of the herdsman Eumaeus.[12]

The sublime and the pathetic are the two chief nerves of all genuine poesy. What is there transcendently sublime or pathetic in Pope? In his works there is, indeed, 'nihil inane, nihil arcessitum; puro tamen fonti quam magno flumini proprior,'[13] as the excellent Quintilian remarks of Lysias.[14] And because I am, perhaps, unwilling to speak out in plain English, I will adopt the following passage of Voltaire, which, in my opinion, as exactly characterizes Pope as it does his model Boileau, for whom it was originally designed, 'Incapable peut-être du sublime qui élève l'ame, et du Sentiment qui l'attendrit, mais fait pour éclairer ceux à qui la nature accorda l'un et l'autre, laborieux, sévère, précis, pur, harmonieux, il devint, enfin, le poète de la Raison.'[15]

Our English poets may, I think, be disposed in four different classes and degrees. In the first class I would place our only three sublime and pathetic poets, Spenser, Shakespeare, Milton. In the second class should be ranked such as possessed the true poetical genius in a more moderate degree, but who had noble talents for moral, ethical and panegyrical poesy. At the head of these are Dryden, Prior, Addison, Cowley, Waller, Garth, Fenton, Gay, Denham, Parnell. In the third class may be placed men of wit, of elegant taste and lively fancy in describing familiar life, though not the higher scenes of poetry. Here may be numbered Butler, Swift, Rochester, Donne, Dorset, Oldham. In the fourth class the mere versifiers, however smooth and mellifluous some of them may be thought, should be disposed. Such as Pitt, Sandys, Fairfax, Broome, Buckingham, Landsdown. This enumeration is not intended as a complete catalogue of writers and in their proper order but only to mark out briefly the different species of our celebrated authors. In which of these classes Pope deserves to be placed the following work is intended to determine. . . .

1757

CONCLUSION TO VOLUME II

. . . Thus have I endeavoured to give a critical account, with freedom, but it is hoped with impartiality, of each of Pope's works; by which review it will appear, that the largest portion of them is of the didactic, moral, and satyric kind; and consequently, not of the most poetic species of poetry; whence it is manifest, that good sense and judgement were his characteristical excellencies, rather than fancy and invention: not that the author of *The Rape of the Lock* and *Eloisa* can be thought to want imagination; but because his imagination was not his predominant talent, because he indulged it not, and because he gave not so many proofs of this talent as of the other. This turn of mind led him to admire French models; he studied Boileau attentively; formed himself upon him, as Milton formed himself upon the Grecian and Italian sons of Fancy. He stuck to describing modern manners; but those manners, because they are familiar, uniform, artificial, and polished, are, in their very nature, unfit for any lofty effort of the Muse. He gradually became one of the most correct, even, and exact poets that ever wrote; polishing his pieces with a care and assiduity, that no business or avocation ever interrupted; so that if he does not frequently ravish and transport his reader, yet he does not disgust him with unexpected inequalities, and absurd improprieties. Whatever poetical enthusiasm he actually possessed, he withheld and stifled. The perusal of him affects not our minds with such

---

10 a paraphrase of the opening lines of Pope's *Moral Essays.*
11 'How does it happen, Maecenas'—opening phrase of the first satire of Horace. Gaius Maecenas, a celebrated Roman, was a benefactor to Virgil and Horace.
12 *The Odyssey,* Bk. XIV.
13 'nothing irrelevant, nothing artificial; but more characteristic of a clear spring than a great river'—Quintilian, *Institutio Oratoria,* X, i, 78.
14 a famous Greek orator, c.400 B.C.
15 'Incapable perhaps of that sublimity which elevates the soul and of the feelings which move it, but created for the enlightenment of those to whom nature had given those two gifts; laborious, severe, exact, pure, harmonious, he became, in short, the poet of Reason.'

strong emotions as we feel from Homer and Milton; so that no man of a true poetical spirit, is master of himself while he reads them. Hence, he is a writer fit for universal perusal; adapted to all ages and stations; for the old and for the young; the man of business and the scholar. He who would think the *Faerie Queene, Palamon and Arcite, The Tempest* or *Comus,* childish and romantic, might relish Pope. Surely, it is no narrow and niggardly encomium, to say he is the great Poet of Reason, the first of ethical authors in verse. And this species of writing is, after all, the surest road to an extensive reputation. It lies more level to the general capacities of men, than the higher flights of more genuine poetry. We all remember when even a Churchill[16] was more in vogue than a Gray. He that treats of fashionable follies and the topics of the day, that describes present persons and recent events, finds many readers, whose understandings and whose passions he gratifies. The name of Chesterfield on one hand, and of Walpole on the other, failed not to make a poem bought up and talked of. And it cannot be doubted that the *Odes* of Horace which celebrated, and the *Satires* which ridiculed, well-known and real characters at Rome, were more eagerly read, and more frequently cited, than the *Æneid* and the *Georgics* of Virgil.

Where then, according to the question proposed at the beginning of this Essay, shall we with justice be authorized to place our admired Pope? Not, assuredly, in the same rank with Spenser, Shakespeare, and Milton; however justly we may applaud the *Eloisa* and *Rape of the Lock;* but, considering the correctness, elegance, and utility of his works, the weight of sentiment, and the knowledge of man they contain, we may venture to assign him a place, next to Milton, and just above Dryden. Yet, to bring our minds steadily to make this decision, we must forget, for a moment, the divine *Music Ode* of Dryden; and may, perhaps, then be compelled to confess, that though Dryden be the greater genius, yet Pope is the better artist.

The preference here given to Pope above other modern English poets, it must be remembered, is founded on the excellencies of his works in general, and taken all together; for there are parts and passages in other modern authors, in Young and in Thomson, for instance, equal to any of Pope; and he has written nothing in a strain so truly sublime, as *The Bard* of Gray.

---

16 Charles Churchill, 1731-64, author of numerous political and social satires.

1782

1721 · WILLIAM COLLINS · 1759

1721 Born at Chichester, son of a hatter who was the town's mayor. Educated at Winchester, where he established a friendship with Joseph Warton, and Magdalen College, Oxford.

1742 Published *Persian Eclogues* while still an undergraduate.

1744 Entered upon a literary career in London. Formed a close friendship with James Thomson and became acquainted with Garrick, the actor, and with Dr. Johnson. *A Song from Shakespear's 'Cymbelyne'* appeared in the second edition of *Verses to Sir Thomas Hanmer* (first edition, 1743).

1746 Published *Odes Descriptive and Allegoric* (twelve in number and Collins' most significant work). Traveled on the Continent.

1749 Published *Ode Occasioned by the Death of Mr. Thomson;* wrote for John Home *Ode on the Popular Superstitions of the Highlands of Scotland* (published in 1788). Inherited £2000.

1751 Suffered a mental breakdown; recovered, but was ever afterward subject to melancholia. For a time was confined in a madhouse in Chelsea. After his release he lived until his death with a sister in Chichester,

1759 Died.

WITH THE PUBLICATION of his *Odes* in 1746 William Collins brought a new vitality and fresh inspiration to English poetry. Collins had been fully aware that the conditions of poetry in his day were not satisfactory and shared with his friend Joseph Warton a desire to unsettle the prevailing canons of Pope and his followers. To bring about a change he set up ancient classical literature and the poetry of Spenser, Shakespeare, and Milton as his models. Yet even with the substantial help of earlier traditions Collins was not altogether successful in outgrowing the strong influence of Pope. The younger poet's work shows clearly the struggle between his break for freedom and the hold established literary convention had on him. Collins was endowed with sincerity and a rare lyrical gift. He combined in his person, learning, idealism, imagination, sensitiveness to nature, awareness of public events, and tenderness. With these qualities he might ultimately have led the way to greater freedom in poetry, but his work was prematurely and tragically interrupted. His career lasted only a decade, ending before he was thirty years old. He produced only about a score of poems.

In the slender sheaf of poems which he has left us Collins opened up no new subjects, but he did bring to current themes an exquisite sensibility and lyric perfection. It is true that even the odes, which contain the best of his poetry, are marred at times by conventional diction and excessive personification; yet for pathos and delicacy, rare propriety of form, and lofty poetic suggestions the odes stand unrivaled in English verse. These high qualities of artistic finish and poetic myth-making are found especially in the *Ode to Evening* where twilight sounds, sights, and feelings are 'exquisitely harmonized in the subdued music of the unrhymed strophes and in the poet's own tender, meditative melancholy.' The diffused feeling for nature which permeates the *Ode to Evening* is present in nearly all of the odes. In his emphasis on nature Collins is following Thomson, though he did not see nature as realistically as the author of *The Seasons*. For the most part Collins' nature pictures are of a shadowy quality and accompanied by fanciful personifications. He was attracted to the landscape not for itself alone but for the ideas and emotions that the landscape evoked. He loved the secret solitary shade where in meditative reverie he could people nature with airy beings. His favorite delight was nature at twilight with beetle and bat, mossy hermitage, and 'darkening vale.' His themes and moods are in key with the new romantic melancholy of the mid-century but without the harsh or gloomy accents of the more somber poets of the 'graveyard school.' Collins shared with this school a taste for ruins and the past, and a curiosity for legends and popular traditions. In his *Ode on Popular Superstitions* he reveals a moral sympathy for the 'blameless manners' of the peasant and makes a plea for the full artistic use of the poetic materials so accessible in peasant folklore. It is in this particular ode that Collins falls in with the return to the past and the anti-intellectualism which in the very center of neo-classical traditions were setting up incipient romantic tendencies.

Although not fully appreciated in his own time and although his influence was delayed for more than a generation because of the loss of his most romantic poem (*Ode on Popular Superstitions,* not published until 1788), Collins, nevertheless, advanced the poetic position of romanticism. During the period from 1790 to 1825, he was a familiar figure whose works were imitated, quoted, and parodied. There was hardly a poet of these years who did not at one time in his career deem Collins worthy of imitation. Chatterton, Cowper, Burns, Blake, Bowles, Wordsworth, Coleridge, Scott, Byron, Shelley, Keats, Campbell, and Moore may be named among others who were influenced by the author of the *Ode to Evening*. Wordsworth and Burns addressed poems to Collins. Bowles shared his love of evening, his quiet melancholy, and his fondness for the enchantment of distance. Blake was attracted by his shadowy and visionary forms. Coleridge was drawn to Collins by his word magic and his use of superstition and classical lore. Among the younger romantics Keats is especially kin to Collins: *To Autumn* is in a direct line of descent from *Ode to Evening*. With the entire generation of the romantic poets, then, Collins' influence was steady and significant. They recognized in him the genuine imaginative quality of his verse.

A SONG FROM SHAKESPEAR'S 'CYMBELYNE'

SUNG BY GUIDERUS AND ARVIRAGUS OVER FIDELE, SUPPOS'D TO BE DEAD[1]

To fair FIDELE's grassy Tomb
  Soft Maids, and Village Hinds shall bring
Each op'ning Sweet, of earliest Bloom,
  And rifle all the breathing Spring.

No wailing Ghost shall dare appear
  To vex with Shrieks this quiet Grove:
But Shepherd Lads assemble here,
  And melting Virgins own their Love.

No wither'd Witch shall here be seen,
  No Goblins lead their nightly Crew: 10
The Female Fays shall haunt the Green,
  And dress thy Grave with pearly Dew!

---

1 Cf. *Cymbeline,* IV, ii.

The Redbreast oft at Ev'ning Hours
  Shall kindly lend his little Aid:
With hoary Moss, and gather'd Flow'rs,
  To deck the Ground where thou art laid.

When howling Winds, and beating Rain,
  In Tempests shake the sylvan Cell:
Or midst the Chace on ev'ry Plain,
  The tender Thought on thee shall dwell.   20

Each lonely Scene shall thee restore,
  For thee the Tear be duly shed:
Belov'd, till Life could charm no more;
  And mourn'd, till Pity's self be dead.

1744

ODE TO SIMPLICITY

O THOU by *Nature* taught,
  To breathe her genuine Thought,
In Numbers warmly pure, and sweetly strong:

Who first on Mountains wild,
In *Fancy* loveliest Child,
Thy Babe, or *Pleasure's*, nurs'd the Pow'rs of
    Song!

Thou, who with Hermit Heart
Disdain'st the Wealth of Art,
And Gauds,[1] and pageant Weeds, and trailing
    Pall[2]:
But com'st a decent[3] Maid   10
In *Attic* Robe array'd,
O chaste unboastful Nymph, to Thee I call!

By all the honey'd Store
On *Hybla's* Thymy Shore,[4]
By all her Blooms, and mingled Murmurs dear,
By Her,[5] whose Love-lorn Woe
In Ev'ning Musings slow
Sooth'd sweetly sad *Electra's* Poet's[6] Ear:

By old *Cephisus*[7] deep,
Who spread his wavy Sweep   20
In warbled Wand'rings round thy green
    Retreat,[8]
On whose enamel'd Side
When holy *Freedom* died
No equal Haunt allur'd thy future Feet.

O Sister meek of Truth,
To my admiring Youth,
Thy sober Aid and native Charms infuse!
    The Flow'rs that sweetest breathe,
    Tho' Beauty cull'd the Wreath,
Still ask thy Hand to range their order'd   30
    Hues.

While *Rome* could none esteem
But Virtue's Patriot Theme,[9]
You lov'd her Hills, and led her Laureate Band:
    But staid to sing alone
    To one distinguish'd Throne,[10]
And turn'd thy Face, and fled her alter'd Land.

No more, in Hall or Bow'r,
The Passions own thy Pow'r,
Love, only Love her forceless Numbers mean:

For Thou hast left her Shrine,   40
Nor Olive more, nor Vine,
Shall gain thy Feet to bless the servile Scene.

Tho' Taste, tho' Genius bless,
To some divine Excess,
Faints the cold Work till Thou inspire the
    whole;
What each, what all supply,
May court, may charm our Eye,
Thou, only Thou can'st raise the meeting Soul!

Of These let others ask,
To aid some mighty Task,   50
I only seek to find thy temp'rate Vale:
Where oft my Reed might sound
To Maids and Shepherds round,
And all thy Sons, O *Nature,* learn my Tale.

1746

ODE ON THE POETICAL CHARACTER

STROPHE

As once, if not with light Regard
I read aright that gifted Bard,[1]
(Him whose School above the rest
His Loveliest *Elfin* Queen[2] has blest.)
One, only One, unrival'd Fair,
Might hope the magic Girdle wear,[3]
At solemn Turney hung on high,
The Wish of each love-darting Eye;

Lo! to each other Nymph in turn applied,
    As if, in Air unseen, some hov'ring Hand,   10
Some chaste and Angel-Friend to Virgin-Fame,
    With whisper'd Spell had burst the starting
        Band,
It left unblest her loath'd dishonour'd Side;
    Happier hopeless Fair, if never
    Her baffled Hand with vain Endeavour
Had touch'd that fatal Zone to her denied!

Young *Fancy* thus, to me Divinest Name,
    To whom, prepar'd and bath'd in Heav'n,
    The Cest[4] of amplest Pow'r is giv'n:
    To few the God-like Gift assigns,   20
    To gird their blest prophetic Loins,
And gaze her Visions wild, and feel unmix'd her
    Flame!

---

1 ornaments.
2 a long cloak.
3 decorous.
4 Hybla was an ancient city on the east coast of Sicily, famous for honey.
5 The nightingale, for which Sophocles seems to have entertained a peculiar fondness.—(Collins.)
6 Sophocles, author of a Greek tragedy, *Electra.*
7 a river in *Attica.*
8 Athens.
9 that of physical courage.
10 of Augustus Caesar, patron of poets.

---

1 Spenser.
2 Elizabeth
3 Amoret was the one maiden who could wear the girdle of chastity. Cf. *The Faerie Queene,* IV, 5, 16–19.
4 girdle.

EPODE

The Band, as Fairy Legends say,
Was wove on that creating Day,
When He, who call'd with Thought to Birth
Yon tented Sky, this laughing Earth,
And drest with Springs, and Forests tall,
And pour'd the Main engirting all,
Long by the lov'd *Enthusiast* woo'd,
Himself in some Diviner Mood,   30
Retiring, sate with her alone,
And plac'd her on his Saphire Throne,
The whiles, the vaulted Shrine around,
Seraphic Wires were heard to sound,
Now sublimest Triumph swelling,
Now on Love and Mercy dwelling;
And she, from out the veiling Cloud,
Breath'd her magic Notes aloud:
And Thou, Thou rich-hair'd Youth of Morn,[5]
And all thy subject Life was born!   40
The dang'rous Passions kept aloof,
Far from the sainted growing Woof:
But near it sate Ecstatic *Wonder,*
List'ning the deep applauding Thunder:
And *Truth,* in sunny Vest array'd,
By whose[6] the Tarsel's[7] Eyes were made;
All the shad'wy Tribes of *Mind,*
In braided Dance their Murmurs join'd,
And all the bright uncounted *Pow'rs,*
Who feed on Heav'n's ambrosial Flow'rs.   50
Where is the Bard, whose Soul can now
Its high presuming Hopes avow?
Where He who thinks, with Rapture blind,
This hallow'd Work for Him design'd?

ANTISTROPHE

High on some Cliff, to Heav'n up-pil'd,
Of rude Access, of Prospect wild,
Where, tangled round the jealous[8] Steep,
Strange Shades o'erbrow the Valleys deep,
And holy *Genii* guard the Rock,
Its Gloomes embrown, its Springs unlock,   60
While on its rich ambitious Head,
An *Eden,* like his own, lies spread:

I view that Oak, the fancied Glades among,
  By which as *Milton* lay, His Ev'ning Ear,
From many a cloud that drop'd Ethereal Dew,
  Nigh spher'd[9] in Heav'n its native Strains
     could hear:

On which that ancient Trump he reach'd was
     hung;
  Thither oft his Glory greeting,
  From *Waller*'s Myrtle Shades retreating,[10]
With many a Vow from Hope's aspiring
     Tongue.   70

My trembling Feet his guiding Steps pursue;
  In vain—Such Bliss to One alone,[11]
  Of all the Sons of Soul was known,
  And Heav'n, and *Fancy,* kindred Pow'rs,
  Have now o'erturn'd th' inspiring Bow'rs,
Or curtain'd close such Scene from ev'ry future
     View.
                                        1746

ODE WRITTEN IN THE BEGINNING OF THE YEAR 1746[1]

How sleep the Brave, who sink to Rest,
By all their Country's Wishes blest!
When *Spring,* with dewy Fingers cold,
Returns to deck their hallow'd Mold,
She there shall dress a sweeter Sod,
Than *Fancy*'s Feet have ever trod.

By Fairy Hands their Knell is rung,
By Forms unseen their Dirge is sung;
There *Honour* comes, a Pilgrim grey,
To bless the Turf that wraps their Clay,   10
And *Freedom* shall a-while repair,
To dwell a weeping Hermit there!
                                        1746

ODE TO EVENING

If ought of Oaten Stop,[1] or Pastoral Song,
May hope, O pensive *Eve,* to sooth thine Ear,
  Like thy own brawling Springs,
  Thy Springs, and dying Gales,
O *Nymph* reserv'd, while now the bright-hair'd
     Sun
Sits in yon western Tent, whose cloudy Skirts,
  With Brede[2] ethereal wove,
  O'erhang his wavy Bed:

---

5 the sun.
6 i. e. by whose eyes.
7 the male falcon's.
8 difficult to climb.
9 placed in one of the spheres in which the heavenly bodies were
supposed to move.

---

10 An allusion to the trivial erotic poetry of Waller. The myrtle
was sacred to Venus.
11 Milton.

---

1 This ode commemorates the soldiers who fell at Fontenoy in
May 1745, at Prestonpans in September of the same year, and at
Falkirk in January 1746. In all these battles the English were de-
feated with great losses.

---

1 any music from a shepherd's flute.
2 embroidery.

Now Air is hush'd, save where the weak-ey'd
　　Bat,
With short shrill Shriek flits by on leathern　　10
　　Wing,
　　　　Or where the Beetle winds
　　　　His small but sullen Horn,
As oft he rises 'midst the twilight Path,
Against the Pilgrim born in heedless Hum:
　　　　Now teach me, *Maid* compos'd,
　　　　To breathe some soften'd Strain,
Whose Numbers stealing thro' thy darkning
　　Vale,
May not unseemly with its Stillness suit,
　　　　As musing slow, I hail
　　　　Thy genial lov'd Return!　　20

For when thy folding Star arising shews
His paly Circlet, at his warning Lamp
　　　　The fragrant *Hours,* and *Elves*
　　　　Who slept in Buds the Day,
And many a *Nymph* who wreaths her Brows with
　　Sedge,
And sheds the fresh'ning Dew, and lovelier
　　still,
　　　　The *Pensive Pleasures* sweet
　　　　Prepare thy shadowy Car.
Then let me rove some wild and heathy Scene,
Or find some Ruin 'midst its dreary Dells,　　30
　　　　Whose Walls more awful nod
　　　　By thy religious Gleams.
Or if chill blustring Winds, or driving Rain,
Prevent my willing Feet, be mine the Hut,
　　　　That from the Mountain's Side,
　　　　Views Wilds, and swelling Floods,
And Hamlets brown, and dim-discover'd Spires,
And hears their simple Bell, and marks o'er
　　all
　　　　Thy Dewy Fingers draw
　　　　The gradual dusky Veil.　　40

While *Spring* shall pour his Show'rs, as oft he
　　wont,
And bathe thy breathing Tresses, meekest *Eve!*
　　　　While *Summer* loves to sport,
　　　　Beneath thy ling'ring Light:
While sallow *Autumn* fills thy Lap with Leaves,
Or *Winter* yelling thro' the troublous Air,
　　　　Affrights thy shrinking Train,
　　　　And rudely rends thy Robes.
So long regardful of thy quiet Rule,
Shall *Fancy, Friendship, Science,* smiling
　　Peace,　　50
　　　　Thy gentlest Influence own,
　　　　And love thy fav'rite Name!

1746

AN ODE
ON THE POPULAR SUPERSTITIONS
OF THE HIGHLANDS OF SCOTLAND

CONSIDERED AS THE SUBJECT OF POETRY

[This poem is addressed to John Home, Scottish clergyman and dramatist, who visited London in 1749. The
manuscript, lacking a stanza and a half, was found
among Home's papers and first published in its fragmentary state in 1788.]

I

H[OME], thou return'st from Thames, whose
　　Naiads long
　　Have seen thee ling'ring, with a fond delay,
Mid those soft friends, whose hearts, some future
　　day,
　　Shall melt, perhaps, to hear thy tragic song.
Go, not unmindful of that cordial youth,[1]
　　Whom, long endear'd, thou leav'st by
　　　　Lavant's[2] side;
Together let us wish him lasting truth,
　　And joy untainted with his destin'd bride.
Go! nor regardless, while these numbers boast
　　My short-liv'd bliss, forget my social
　　　　name;　　10
But think far off how, on the southern coast,
　　I met thy friendship with an equal flame!
Fresh to that soil thou turn'st, whose ev'ry vale
　　Shall prompt the poet, and his song demand:
To thee thy copious subjects ne'er shall fail;
　　Thou need'st but take the pencil to thy hand,
And paint what all believe who own thy genial
　　land.

II

There must thou wake perforce thy Doric[3] quill,
　　'Tis Fancy's land to which thou sett'st thy
　　　　feet;
Where still, 'tis said, the fairy people meet　　20
　　Beneath each birken shade on mead or hill.
There each trim lass that skims the milky store
　　To the swart tribes[4] their creamy bowl allots;
By night they sip it round the cottage-door,
　　While airy minstrels warble jocund notes.
There every herd, by sad experience, knows
　　How, wing'd with fate, their elf-shot arrows
　　　　fly;
When the sick ewe her summer food foregoes,
　　Or, stretch'd on earth, the heart-smit heifers
　　　　lie.
Such airy beings awe th' untutor'd swain:　　30

1 John Barrow, a friend who had introduced Collins to Home.
2 The river Lavant flows through Chichester, Sussex.
3 simple; natural.
4 the brownies.

Nor thou, though learn'd, his homelier
    thoughts neglect;
Let thy sweet muse the rural faith sustain:
    These are the themes of simple, sure effect,
That add new conquests to her boundless reign,
And fill, with double force, her
    heart-commanding strain.

III

Ev'n yet preserv'd, how often may'st thou hear,
    Where to the pole the Boreal[5] mountains
    run,
Taught by the father to his list'ning son
    Strange lays, whose power had charm'd a
    SPENCER's ear.
At ev'ry pause, before thy mind possest,   40
    Old RUNIC bards[6] shall seem to rise around,
With uncouth[7] lyres, in many-coloured vest,[8]
    Their matted hair with boughs fantastic
    crown'd:
Whether thou bid'st the well-taught hind repeat
    The choral dirge that mourns some chieftain
    brave,
When ev'ry shrieking maid her bosom beat,
    And strew'd with choicest herbs his scented
    grave;
Or whether, sitting in the shepherd's shiel,[9]
    Thou hear'st some sounding tale of war's
    alarms;
When, at the bugle's call, with fire and steel, 50
    The sturdy clans pour'd forth their bony
    swarms,
And hostile brothers met to prove each other's
    arms.

IV

'Tis thine to sing, how framing hideous spells
    In SKY's lone isle[10] the gifted wizzard seer,
Lodged in the wintry cave [his wayward fits],
    Or in the depth of Uist's[11] dark forests dwells:
How they, whose sight such dreary dreams
    engross,
    With their own visions oft astonish'd droop,
When o'er the wat'ry strath[12] or quaggy moss
    They see the gliding ghosts unbodied
    troop.   60
Or if in sports, or on the festive green,
    Their [piercing] glance some fated youth
    descry,

---

5 northern.
6 poets who used the runic alphabet.
7 strange.
8 garb.
9 hut.
10 the Isle of Skye, largest of the Inner Hebrides.
11 an island of the Outer Hebrides.
12 river valley.

Who, now perhaps in lusty vigour seen
    And rosy health, shall soon lamented die.
For them the viewless forms of air obey,
    Their bidding heed, and at their beck repair.
They know what spirit brews the stormful day,
    And heartless,[13] oft like moody madness stare
To see the phantom train their secret work
    prepare.

[Stanza v lost.]

VI

[8 lines lost.]

What though far off, from some dark dell espied
    His glimm'ring mazes cheer th' excursive sight,
Yet turn, ye wand'rers, turn your steps aside,
    Nor trust the guidance of that faithless light;
For watchful, lurking 'mid th' unrustling reed,
    At those mirk hours the wily monster lies, 100
And listens oft to hear the passing steed,
    And frequent round him rolls his sullen eyes,
If chance his savage wrath may some weak
    wretch surprise.

VII

Ah, luckless swain, o'er all unblest indeed!
    Whom late bewilder'd in the dank, dark fen,
Far from his flocks and smoking hamlet then!
    To that sad spot [his wayward fate shall lead]:
On him enrag'd, the fiend, in angry mood,
    Shall never look with pity's kind concern,
But instant, furious, raise the whelming
    flood   110
    O'er its drown'd bank, forbidding all return.
Or, if he meditate his wish'd escape
    To some dim hill that seems uprising near,
To his faint eye the grim and grisly shape,
    In all its terrors clad, shall wild appear.
Meantime, the wat'ry surge shall around him
    rise,
    Pour'd sudden forth from ev'ry swelling
    source.
What now remains but tears and hopeless sighs?
    His fear-shook limbs have lost their youthly
    force,
And down the waves he floats, a pale and
    breathless corse.

VIII

For him, in vain, his anxious wife shall wait, 121
    Or wander forth to meet him on his way;
For him, in vain, at to-fall of the day,
    His babes shall linger at th' unclosing gate!
Ah, ne'er shall he return! Alone, if night

---

13 dismayed.

Her travell'd limbs in broken slumbers steep,
With dropping willows drest, his mournful sprite
Shall visit sad, perchance, her silent sleep:
Then he, perhaps, with moist and wat'ry hand,
  Shall fondly seem to press her shudd'ring
      cheek,   130
And with his blue swoln face before her stand,
  And, shiv'ring cold, these piteous accents
    speak:
Pursue, dear wife, thy daily toils pursue
  At dawn or dusk, industrious as before;
Nor e'er of me one hapless thought renew,
  While I lie welt'ring on the ozier'd[14] shore,
Drown'd by the KAELPIE's[15] wrath, nor e'er shall
  aid these more!

IX

Unbounded is thy range; with varied stile
  Thy muse may, like those feath'ry tribes[16]
    which spring
From their rude rocks, extend her skirting
    wing   140
  Round the moist marge of each cold Hebrid
    isle,
To that hoar pile[17] which still its ruin shows:
  In whose small vaults a pigmy-folk is found,
Whose bones the delver with his spade
    upthrows,
  And culls them, wond'ring, from the hallow'd
    ground!
Or thither where beneath the show'ry west
  The mighty kings of three fair realms are
    laid:[18]
Once foes, perhaps, together now they rest.
  No slaves revere them, and no wars invade:
Yet frequent now, at midnight's solemn
    hour,   150
  The rifted mounds their yawning cells unfold,
And forth the monarchs stalk with sov'reign
    pow'r
  In pageant robes, and wreath'd with sheeny
    gold,
And on their twilight tombs aerial council hold.

X

But O! o'er all, forget not KILDA's race,[19]
  On whose bleak rocks, which brave the
    wasting tides,
Fair Nature's daughter, Virtue, yet abides.

Go, just, as they, their blameless manners
  trace!
Then to my ear transmit some gentle song
  Of those whose lives are yet sincere and
    plain,   160
Their bounded walks the rugged cliffs along,
  And all their prospect but the wintry main.
With sparing temp'rance, at the needful time,
  They drain the sainted spring,[20] or, hunger-
    prest,
Along th' Atlantic rock undreading climb,
  And of its eggs despoil the Solan's[21] nest.
Thus blest in primal innocence they live,
  Suffic'd and happy with that frugal fare
Which tasteful[22] toil and hourly danger give.
. Hard is their shallow soil, and bleak and
    bare;   170
Nor ever vernal bee was heard to murmur there!

XI

Nor need'st thou blush, that such false themes
  engage
  Thy gentle[23] mind, of fairer stores possest;
For not alone they touch the village breast,
  But fill'd in elder time th' historic page.
There SHAKESPEARE's self, with ev'ry garland
  crown'd,
  In musing hour, his wayward sisters[24] found,
And with their terrors drest the magic scene.
From them he sung, when mid his bold design,
  Before the Scot afflicted and aghast,   180
The shadowy kings of BANQUO's fated line,
  Through the dark cave in gleamy pageant
    past.[25]
Proceed, nor quit the tales which, simply told,
  Could once so well my answ'ring bosom
    pierce;
Proceed, in forceful sounds and colours bold
  The native legends of thy land rehearse;
To such adapt thy lyre and suit thy powerful
  verse.

XII

In scenes like these, which, daring to depart
  From sober truth, are still to nature true,
And call forth fresh delight to fancy's view, 190
  Th' heroic muse employ'd her TASSO's art!
How have I trembled, when at TANCRED's
  stroke,
  Its gushing blood the gaping cypress pour'd;

---

14 overgrown with willows.
15 water-sprite's.
16 of gannets or solan geese.
17 a burial vault on the Island of Benbecula said to contain the bones of pigmies.
18 Kings of Norway, Scotland, and Ireland are said to be buried on the Island of Iona.
19 the inhabitants of St. Kilda, rocky island of the Outer Hebrides.

---

20 St. Kilda's Well.
21 the solan goose or gannet.
22 making food appetizing.
23 cultivated.
24 the Weird Sisters of *Macbeth.*
25 See *Macbeth,* IV, i.

When each live plant with mortal accents spoke,
  And the wild blast up-heav'd the vanish'd
    sword![26]
How have I sat, when pip'd the pensive wind,
  To hear his harp, by British FAIRFAX[27] strung.
Prevailing poet, whose undoubting mind
  Believ'd the magic wonders which he sung!
Hence at each sound imagination glows;   200
Hence his warm lay with softest sweetness
    flows;
  Melting it flows, pure, num'rous, strong and
    clear,
And fills th' impassion'd heart, and wins th'
    harmonious ear.

XIII

All hail, ye scenes that o'er my soul prevail,
  Ye [spacious] friths[28] and lakes which, far
    away,
Are by smooth ANNAN fill'd, or past'ral TAY,
  Or DON's romantic springs, at distance, hail!

The time shall come when I, perhaps, may tread
  Your lowly glens, o'erhung with spreading
    broom,
Or o'er your stretching heaths by fancy led: 210
Then will I dress once more the faded bow'r,
  Where JOHNSON sat in DRUMMOND's [social]
    shade;[29]
Or crop from Tiviot's[30] dale each [classic flower],
  And mourn on Yarrow's[30] banks [the widow'd
    maid.]
Meantime, ye Pow'rs, that on the plains which
    bore
  The cordial youth,[31] on LOTHIAN's[32] plains
    attend,
Where'er he dwell, on hill, or lowly muir,
  To him I lose, your kind protection lend,
And, touch'd with love like mine, preserve my
    absent friend.

1749   1788

---

26 Tasso, *Jerusalem Delivered*, xiii, 41–6.
27 Edward Fairfax translated the *Jerusalem Delivered* into English in 1600; this version had been reprinted in 1749.
28 arms of the sea.

29 alluding to the visit Ben Jonson paid in 1619 to the Scottish poet, William Drummond of Hawthornden.
30 The Teviot and Yarrow, rivers of the Scottish border, have long been associated with romance and balladry.
31 John Barrow (cf. l. 15).
32 the county of Lothian, in which Edinburgh is situated.

1716 · THOMAS GRAY · 1771

1716 Born in London, only survivor of twelve children. Educated at Eton, where his principal friends were Horace Walpole and Richard West, and at Peterhouse, Cambridge.

1739–41 Accompanied Walpole on a Continental tour but they quarreled and returned home separately. Their friendship was renewed in 1745.

1742 Resided at Cambridge where he studied law and began his work as an English poet. Composed *Ode on the Spring, Ode on a Distant Prospect of Eton College* (published in 1747), *Hymn to Adversity, Sonnet on the Death of Richard West.* Began *Elegy in a Country Church-yard* (published in 1751).

1748 *Ode on the Death of a Favorite Cat* (written in 1747 for Walpole) published in Dodsley's *Miscellanies.*

1757 *Odes by Mr. Gray* (including *The Progress of Poesy,* composed 1752–4, and *The Bard,* composed 1755–7) printed by Walpole as the first work of his Strawberry Hill Press. Declined an offer of the laureateship.

1767 Took a journey among the English Lakes, which is commemorated in the *Journal* (published 1775), Gray's most finished prose work.

1768 Became professor of modern history at Cambridge but never gave any lectures. Published collected poems including *The Fatal Sisters, The Descent of Odin, The Triumphs of Owen* (translations or imitations of old Norse poetry).

1771 Died and lies buried at Stoke Poges, the village associated with *Elegy in a Country Church-yard.*

THOMAS GRAY is among the most learned of all English poets. He was steeped in the classics; widely read in travel books, antiquities of all sorts, and modern literature; and was a close student of botany, music, painting, and architecture. By comparison with the long years that he devoted to study, the amount of time he gave to poetical composition was slight and the thin sheaf of poems he has left to the world but a small achievement. He had some sadness of spirit within him which paralyzed action and thwarted his poetical genius. Lack of incentive, ill-health, and an extreme fastidiousness also cut down his production. Gray was a scrupulous artist in verse with a passion for structure, economy, and finish. He labored for exact expressions of beauty, and studied and polished (sometimes for years on a single poem) until he was satisfied with every detail. In his high regard for the finished effect he falls in with Pope and his school, as he does also in his taste for moralizing and personification. Near the close of his career, however, Gray pointed the way toward a rejuvenation in literature by introducing new subject matter into his verse and by working with a freer poetic idiom. But he was not too much of a rebel against the accepted order. He loved tradition while courting novelty and anticipated the later poetry chiefly by 'working within the existing tradition in a fresh and original way' (Elton).

Though the bulk of his writing is small, Gray reveals a wide variety of verse forms, vigor and pace in execution, an exquisite sense of proportion, sincere inspiration, grace, and true sensibility. The early lyrics are written in a tenderly sensitive melancholy vein. The historical odes are more ambitious, being compact with learning and difficult for readers untrained in the classics, but they have 'wide horizons, ardor of feeling, and a splendid pomp of varying sound.' The famous *Elegy Written in a Country Churchyard* is Gray's greatest composition and one of the most perfect poems in the English language. It is unrivaled for its conciseness of expression, propriety and harmony of diction, and noble tone of tenderness. Its spring of emotion is a deep sympathy for common man and his common lot. It is a meditation on time, death, and human glory which speaks for and to everyone. The theme and treatment are firmly rooted in eighteenth-century tradition although in its attention to nature and humble life the Elegy anticipates the new romantic spirit. From the outset the poem was widely imitated, parodied, and translated and is today among the best-loved of English lyrics.

In his Celtic and Norse imitations and in his letters Gray mirrors something of the change of taste and the expansion of interests which were occurring all around him and to which he himself contributed. Fairly late in his career his archeological studies led him to the Middle Ages and Scandinavian antiquities. These enthusiasms were not long in finding expression in poetry: the medieval in *The Bard* and the Scandinavian in *The Decent of Odin* and *The Fatal Sisters*. These poetical antiques as well as their author's other antiquarian activities gave impetus to the steadily increasing interest in medieval subjects. *The Bard* in particular appears to have encouraged Macpherson in his Ossianic adventure and subsequently, through Macpherson's *Ossian* as well as directly, to have been responsible for the flood of primitivistic verse which spread over all Europe in the last decades of the century. The Norse fragments were admired for their vigorous language and metrics and had a salutary influence in a minor way in encouraging a less ornate diction. In his letters as well as in his poems Gray spread the gospel of the archaic and the Gothic. His letters also reveal another coming romantic enthusiasm—the love of scenery and nature. Gray delighted particularly in the wilder aspects of nature and could become eloquent in describing the sublimity of the Alps or the rugged mountains of the Scottish Highlands. In his *Journal in the Lakes* he shows himself to be a practical observer of color and detail and a sensitive recorder of nature's changing moods. Thus in prose Gray led the way to new facets in the appreciation of nature which Wordsworth was later to distill into poetry.

SONNET ON THE DEATH OF RICHARD WEST[1]

In vain to me the smileing Mornings shine,
    And redning Phœbus lifts his golden Fire:
The Birds in vain their amorous Descant joyn;
    Or chearful Fields resume their green Attire:
These Ears, alas! for other Notes repine,
    A different Object do these Eyes require.
My lonely Anguish melts no Heart, but mine;
    And in my Breast the imperfect Joys expire.
Yet Morning smiles the busy Race to chear,
    And new-born Pleasure brings to happier
        Men: 10
The Fields to all their wonted Tribute bear:
    To warm their little Loves the Birds complain:
I fruitless mourn to him, that cannot hear,
    And weep the more because I weep in vain.

        1742   1775

---

[1] Richard West was the closest of Gray's Eton friends and a poet of some promise.

HYMN TO ADVERSITY

[This poem was modeled on Horace's *Ode to Fortune,* and in turn influenced Wordsworth's *Ode to Duty.*]

Daughter of Jove, relentless Power,
Thou Tamer of the human breast,
Whose iron scourge and tort'ring hour,
The Bad affright, afflict the Best!
Bound in thy adamantine chain
The Proud are taught to taste of pain,
And purple Tyrants vainly groan
With pangs unfelt before, unpitied and alone.

When first thy Sire to send on earth
Virtue, his darling Child, design'd,   10
To thee he gave the heav'nly Birth,
And bad to form her infant mind.
Stern rugged Nurse! thy rigid lore
With patience many a year she bore:
What sorrow was, thou bad'st her know,
And from her own she learn'd to melt at others'
    woe.

Scared at thy frown terrific, fly
Self-pleasing Folly's idle brood,
Wild Laughter, Noise, and thoughtless Joy,
And leave us leisure to be good.   20
Light[1] they disperse, and with them go
The summer Friend, the flatt'ring Foe;
By vain Prosperity received,
To her they vow their truth, and are again
     believed.

Wisdom in sable garb array'd
Immers'd in rapt'rous thought profound,
And Melancholy, silent maid
With leaden eye, that loves the ground,
Still on thy solemn steps attend:
Warm Charity, the gen'ral Friend,   30
With Justice to herself severe,
And Pity, dropping soft the sadly-pleasing tear.

Oh, gently on thy Suppliant's head,
Dread Goddess, lay thy chast'ning hand!
Not in thy Gorgon terrors[2] clad,
Nor circled with the vengeful Band[3]
(As by the Impious thou art seen)
With thund'ring voice, and threat'ning mien,
With screaming Horror's funeral cry,
Despair, and fell Disease, and ghastly Poverty. 40

Thy form benign, oh Goddess, wear,
Thy milder influence impart,
Thy philosophic Train be there
To soften, not to wound my heart.
The gen'rous spark extinct revive,
Teach me to love and to forgive,
Exact my own defects to scan,
What others are, to feel, and know myself a Man.

1742   1748

ELEGY WRITTEN IN A COUNTRY CHURCH-YARD

[This celebrated poem was probably begun at Stoke Poges in 1742 but was not completed until June 1750 when it was circulated in manuscript. Gray persuaded Walpole to publish it anonymously in February 1751, in order to forestall the printing of an unauthorized version.]

THE Curfew tolls the knell of parting day,
The lowing herd wind slowly o'er the lea,
The plowman homeward plods his weary way,
And leaves the world to darkness and to me.

Now fades the glimmering landscape on the
     sight,
And all the air a solemn stillness holds,
Save where the beetle wheels his droning flight,
And drowsy tinklings lull the distant folds;

Save that from yonder ivy-mantled tow'r
The mopeing owl does to the moon complain 10
Of such, as wand'ring near her secret bow'r,
Molest her ancient solitary reign.

Beneath those rugged elms, that yew-tree's
     shade,
Where heaves the turf in many a mould'ring
     heap,
Each in his narrow cell for ever laid,
The rude[1] Forefathers of the hamlet sleep.

The breezy call of incense-breathing Morn,
The swallow twitt'ring from the straw-built shed,
The cock's shrill clarion, or the echoing horn,
No more shall rouse them from their lowly
     bed.   20

For them no more the blazing hearth shall burn,
Or busy housewife ply her evening care:
No children run to lisp their sire's return,
Or climb his knees the envied kiss to share.

Oft did the harvest to their sickle yield,
Their furrow oft the stubborn glebe has broke;
How jocund did they drive their team afield!
How bow'd the woods beneath their sturdy
     stroke!

Let not Ambition mock their useful toil,
Their homely joys, and destiny obscure;   30
Nor Grandeur hear with a disdainful smile,
The short and simple annals of the poor.

The boast of heraldry,[2] the pomp of pow'r,
And all that beauty, all that wealth e'er gave,
Awaits[3] alike th' inevitable hour.
The paths of glory lead but to the grave.

Nor you, ye Proud, impute to These the fault,
If Mem'ry o'er their Tomb no Trophies raise,
Where thro' the long-drawn isle and fretted vault
The pealing anthem swells the note of praise. 40

Can storied urn[4] or animated[5] bust
Back to its mansion call the fleeting breath?

---

1 swiftly.
2 The snaky head of Medusa (Gorgon) was so horrible that all who looked upon it were transformed to stone.
3 the Furies.

1 unlettered, simple-living.   2 noble lineage.
3 *hour* is the subject of *awaits*.   4 funeral urn with an inscription.
5 lifelike.

Can Honour's voice provoke[6] the silent dust,
Or Flatt'ry sooth the dull cold ear of Death?

Perhaps in this neglected spot is laid
Some heart once pregnant with celestial fire;
Hands, that the rod of empire might have
      sway'd,
Or wak'd to extasy the living lyre.

But Knowledge to their eyes her ample page
Rich with the spoils of time did ne'er unroll; 50
Chill Penury repress'd their noble rage,[7]
And froze the genial[8] current of the soul.

Full many a gem of purest ray serene,
The dark unfathom'd caves of ocean bear:
Full many a flower is born to blush unseen,
And waste its sweetness on the desert air.

Some village-Hampden,[9] that with dauntless
      breast
The little Tyrant of his fields withstood;
Some mute inglorious Milton here may rest,
Some Cromwell guiltless of his country's
      blood.   60

Th' applause of list'ning senates to command,
The threats of pain and ruin to despise,
To scatter plenty o'er a smiling land,
And read their hist'ry in a nation's eyes,

Their lot forbad: nor circumscrib'd alone
Their growing virtues, but their crimes confin'd;
Forbad to wade through slaughter to a throne,
And shut the gates of mercy on mankind,

The struggling pangs of conscious truth to hide,
To quench the blushes of ingenuous shame, 70
Or heap the shrine of Luxury and Pride
With incense kindled at the Muse's flame.

Far from the madding crowd's ignoble strife,
Their sober wishes never learn'd to stray;
Along the cool sequester'd vale of life
They kept the noiseless tenor of their way.

Yet ev'n these bones from insult to protect
Some frail memorial still[10] erected nigh,

With uncouth[11] rhimes and shapeless sculpture
      deck'd,
Implores the passing tribute of a sigh.   80

Their name, their years, spelt by th' unletter'd
      muse,
The place of fame and elegy supply:
And many a holy text around she strews,
That teach the rustic moralist to die.

For who to dumb Forgetfulness a prey,
This pleasing anxious being e'er resign'd,
Left the warm precincts of the chearful day,
Nor cast one longing ling'ring look behind?

On some fond breast the parting soul relies,
Some pious drops the closing eye requires; 90
Ev'n from the tomb the voice of Nature cries,
Ev'n in our Ashes live their wonted Fires.

For thee,[12] who mindful of th' unhonour'd Dead
Dost in these lines their artless tale relate;
If chance, by lonely contemplation led,
Some kindred Spirit shall inquire thy fate,

Haply some hoary-headed Swain may say,
'Oft have we seen him at the peep of dawn
Brushing with hasty steps the dews away
To meet the sun upon the upland lawn.   100

'There at the foot of yonder nodding beech
That wreathes its old fantastic roots so high,
His listless length at noontide would he stretch,
And pore upon the brook that babbles by.

'Hard by yon wood, now smiling as in scorn,
Mutt'ring his wayward fancies he would rove,
Now drooping, woeful wan, like one forlorn,
Or craz'd with care, or cross'd in hopeless
      love.

'One morn I miss'd him on the custom'd hill,
Along the heath and near his fav'rite tree; 110
Another came; nor yet beside the rill,
Nor up the lawn, nor at the wood was he;

'The next with dirges due in sad array
Slow thro' the church-way path we saw him
      born.

---

6 call forth.
7 enthusiasm.
8 endowed with genius.
9 John Hampden, 1595–1643, who lived in the county containing Gray's churchyard, refused in 1636 to pay taxes unlawfully imposed by Charles I.
10 always.

---

11 strange; odd.
12 'Thee' has been variously identified as (1) Gray himself; (2) Gray's college friend, Richard West, who died in young manhood; (3) a semiliterate stonecutter who marked the gravestones of the villagers. See F. H. Ellis, 'Gray's *Elegy:* The Biographical Problem in Literary Criticism.' *PMLA,* LXVI (1951), 971–1008.

Approach and read (for thou can'st read) the lay,
Grav'd on the stone beneath yon aged thorn.'[13]

THE EPITAPH

Here rests his head upon the lap of Earth
A Youth to Fortune and to Fame unknown.
Fair Science frown'd not on his humble birth,
And Melancholy mark'd him for her own.   120

Large was his bounty, and his soul sincere,
Heav'n did a recompence as largely send:
He gave to Mis'ry all he had, a tear,
He gain'd from Heav'n ('twas all he wish'd) a
*   friend.*

No farther seek his merits to disclose,
Or draw his frailties from their dread abode,
(There they alike in trembling hope repose,)
The bosom of his Father and his God.

1742–50   1751

THE PROGRESS OF POESY

A PINDARIC ODE

[In this and the next poem Gray undertook to follow
the exact construction of the Pindaric ode by laying out
three identical parts, each consisting of strophe, anti-
strophe, and epode—signifying the turn, the counter-
turn, and the stand of the choric dances in the Greek
theater. Gray's contemporaries found these odes difficult
to understand even with the help of his elaborate notes.
Later generations of readers have held widely diverse
opinions on their merits.]

I.   I.

Awake, Æolian lyre,[1] awake,
And give to rapture all thy trembling strings.
From Helicon's harmonious springs[2]
A thousand rills their mazy progress take;[3]
The laughing flowers, that round them blow,
Drink life and fragrance as they flow.
Now the rich stream of music winds along
Deep, majestic, smooth, and strong,
Thro' verdant vales, and Ceres' golden reign.[4]
Now rowling down the steep amain,   10
Headlong, impetuous, see it pour:

The rocks, and nodding groves rebellow to the
    roar.

I.   2.

Oh! Sovereign of the willing soul,[5]
Parent of sweet and solemn-breathing airs,
Enchanting shell![6] the sullen Cares,
And frantic Passions hear thy soft controul.
On Thracia's hills the Lord of War,[7]
Has curb'd the fury of his car,
And drop'd his thirsty lance at thy command.
Perching on the scept'red hand   20
Of Jove, thy magic lulls the feather'd king[8]
With ruffled plumes, and flagging wing:
Quench'd in dark clouds of slumber lie
The terror of his beak, and light'nings of his eye.

I.   3.

Thee the voice, the dance, obey,[9]
Temper'd to thy warbled lay.
O'er Idalia's[10] velvet-green
The rosy-crowned Loves are seen
On Cytherea's day
With antic Sports, an blue-eyed Pleasures,   30
Frisking light in frolic measures;
Now pursuing, now retreating,
Now in circling troops they meet:
To brisk notes in cadence beating
Glance their many-twinkling feet.
Slow melting strains their Queen's approach
    declare:
Where'er she turns the Graces homage pay.
With arms sublime,[11] that float upon the air,
In gliding state she wins her easy way:
O'er her warm cheek, and rising bosom,
    move   40
The bloom of young Desire, and purple light of
    Love.

II.   I.

Man's feeble race what Ills await,[12]
Labour, and Penury, the racks of Pain,
Disease, and Sorrow's weeping train,
And Death, sad refuge from the storms of Fate!

---

13 hawthorn tree.

1 an invocation to Pindar, master of the strict Greek ode, who
himself called his verse 'Æolian'—i.e. joyous and musical.
2 the fountain of the Muses on Mount Helicon in Boeotia.
3 The various sources of poetry, which gives life and lustre to all
it touches, are here described; its quiet majestic progress enriching every subject (otherwise dry and barren) with a pomp of diction and luxuriant harmony of numbers; and its more rapid and
irresistible course, when swoln and hurried away by the conflict
of tumultuous passions.—(Gray.)
4 fields of grain, presided over by Ceres, the divinity of crops.

5 Power of harmony to calm the turbulent sallies of the soul.—
(Gray.)
6 the lyre, said to have been made first by Hermes out of a tor-
toise shell.
7 Ares or Mars, who is particularly associated with Thrace.
8 Jove's eagle.
9 Power of harmony to produce all the graces of motion in the
body.—(Gray.)
10 a town in Cyprus containing a temple sacred to Venus (or
Cytherea, l. 29).
11 uplifted.
12 To compensate the real and imaginary ills of life, the Muse was
given to mankind by the same Providence that sends day by its
cheerful presence to dispel the gloom and terrors of the night.—
(Gray.)

The fond[13] complaint, my Song, disprove,
And justify the laws of Jove.
Say, has he giv'n in vain the heav'nly Muse?
Night, and all her sickly dews,
Her Spectres wan, and Birds of boding cry,   50
He gives to range the dreary sky:
Till down the eastern cliffs afar
Hyperion's[14] march they spy, and glitt'ring shafts
    of war.

II.   2.

In climes beyond the solar road,[15]
Where shaggy forms o'er ice-built mountains
    roam,
The Muse has broke the twilight-gloom
To chear the shiv'ring Native's dull abode.
And oft, beneath the od'rous shade
Of Chili's boundless forests laid,
She deigns to hear the savage Youth repeat   60
In loose numbers wildly sweet
Their feather-cinctured Chiefs, and dusky Loves.
Her track, where'er the Goddess roves,
Glory pursue, and generous Shame,
Th' unconquerable Mind, and Freedom's holy
    flame.

II.   3.[16]

Woods, that wave o'er Delphi's steep,[17]
Isles, that crown th' Egæan deep,
Fields, that cool Ilissus[18] laves,
Or where Mæander's[19] amber waves
In lingering Lab'rinths creep,   70
How do your tuneful Echoes languish,
Mute, but to the voice of Anguish?
Where each old poetic Mountain
Inspiration breath'd around:
Ev'ry shade and hallow'd Fountain
Murmur'd deep a solemn sound:
Till the sad Nine in Greece's evil hour
Left their Parnassus for the Latian plains.[20]
Alike they scorn the pomp of tyrant-Power,
And coward Vice, that revels in her chains. 80

---

13 foolish.
14 the sun-god's.
15 Extensive influence of poetic genius over the remotest and
most uncivilized nations: its connection with liberty, and the virtues that naturally attend on it. (See the Erse, Norwegian, and
Welsh Fragments, the Lapland and American songs.)—(Gray.)
16 Progress of poetry from Greece to Italy, and from Italy to England. Chaucer was not unacquainted with the writings of Dante
or of Petrarch. The Earl of Surrey and Sir Tho. Wyatt had traveled in Italy, and formed their taste there; Spenser imitated the
Italian writers; Milton improved on them; but this School expired
soon after the Restoration, and a new one arose on the French
model, which has subsisted ever since.—(Gray.)
17 Mount Parnassus, haunt of the Muses.
18 a river flowing past Athens.
19 a winding river in Asia Minor.
20 The Nine Muses, at the decline of Grecian civilization, took
up their abode in Italy.

When Latium had her lofty spirit lost,
They sought, oh Albion! next thy sea-encircled
    coast.

III.   1.

Far from the sun and summer-gale,
In thy green lap was Nature's Darling[21] laid,
What time, where lucid Avon stray'd,
To Him the mighty Mother did unveil
Her aweful face: The dauntless Child
Stretch'd forth his little arms, and smiled.
This pencil take (she said) whose colours clear
Richly paint the vernal year: 90
Thine too these golden keys, immortal Boy!
This can unlock the gates of Joy;
Of Horrour that, and thrilling Fears,
Or ope the sacred source of sympathetic Tears.

III.   2.

Nor second He,[22] that rode sublime
Upon the seraph-wings of Extasy,
The secrets of th' Abyss to spy.
He pass'd the flaming bounds of Place and Time:
The living Throne, the saphire-blaze,
Where Angels tremble, while they gaze,   100
He saw; but blasted with excess of light,
Closed his eyes in endless night.
Behold, where Dryden's less presumptuous car,
Wide o'er the fields of Glory bear
Two Coursers of ethereal race,
With necks in thunder cloath'd, and long-
    resounding pace.[23]

III.   3.

Hark, his hands the lyre explore!
Bright-eyed Fancy hovering o'er
Scatters from her pictur'd urn
Thoughts, that breath, and words, that burn. 110
But ah! 'tis heard no more——
Oh! Lyre divine, what daring Spirit[24]
Wakes thee now? Tho' he inherit
Nor the pride, nor ample pinion,
That the Theban Eagle[25] bear
Sailing with supreme dominion
Thro' the azure deep of air:
Yet oft before his infant eyes would run
Such forms, as glitter in the Muse's ray
With orient hues, unborrow'd of the Sun: 120
Yet shall he mount, and keep his distant way
Beyond the limits of a vulgar fate,

---

21 Shakespeare.
22 Milton.
23 Meant to express the stately march and sounding energy of
Dryden's rhymes.—(Gray.)
24 Gray himself.
25 Pindar.

Beneath the Good how far—but far above the Great.

1754   *1757*

THE BARD

The following ode is founded on a tradition current in Wales, that Edward the First, when he completed the conquest of the country, ordered all the bards that fell into his hands to be put to death.—(Gray's Prefatory Advertisement.)

The army of Edward I., as they march through a deep valley, and approach Mount Snowdon, are suddenly stopped by the appearance of a venerable figure seated on the summit of an inaccessible rock, who, with a voice more than human, reproaches the king with all the desolation and misery which he had brought on his country; foretells the misfortunes of the Norman race, and with prophetic spirit declares that all his cruelty shall never extinguish the noble ardour of poetic genius in this island; and that men shall never be wanting to celebrate true virtue and valour in immortal strains, to expose vice and infamous pleasure, and boldly censure tyranny and oppression. His song ended, he precipitates himself from the mountain, and is swallowed up in the river that rolls at its foot.—(Gray's outline of the poem in his Notebook.)

I. 1.

'RUIN seize thee, ruthless King!
Confusion[1] on thy banners wait,
Tho' fann'd by Conquest's crimson wing
They mock the air with idle state.
Helm, nor Hauberk's twisted mail,
Nor even thy virtues, Tyrant, shall avail
To save thy secret soul from nightly fears,
From Cambria's[2] curse, from Cambria's tears!'
Such were the sounds, that o'er the crested pride
Of the first Edward scatter'd wild dismay,   10
As down the steep of Snowdon's shaggy side
He wound with toilsome march his long array.
Stout Glo'ster[3] stood aghast in speechless trance:
To arms! cried Mortimer, and couch'd his quiv'ring lance.

I. 2.

On a rock, whose haughty brow
Frowns o'er old Conway's[4] foaming flood,
Robed in the sable garb of woe,
With haggard eyes the Poet stood;
(Loose his beard, and hoary hair
Stream'd, like a meteor, to the troubled air)[5]   20

And with a Master's hand, and Prophet's fire,
Struck the deep sorrows of his lyre.
'Hark, how each giant-oak, and desert cave,
Sighs to the torrent's aweful voice beneath!
O'er thee, oh King! their hundred arms they wave,
Revenge on thee in hoarser murmurs breath;
Vocal no more, since Cambria's fatal day,
To high-born Hoel's[6] harp, or soft Llewellyn's lay.[7]

I. 3.

Cold is Cadwallo's[8] tongue,
That hush'd the stormy main: 30
Brave Urien[8] sleeps upon his craggy bed:
Mountains, ye mourn in vain
Modred,[8] whose magic song
Made huge Plinlimmon[9] bow his cloud-top'd head.
On dreary Arvon's shore[10] they lie,
Smear'd with gore, and ghastly pale:
Far, far aloof th' affrighted ravens fail;
The famish'd Eagle screams, and passes by.
Dear lost companions of my tuneful art,
Dear, as the light that visits these sad eyes,   40
Dear, as the ruddy drops that warm my heart,
Ye died amidst your dying country's cries—
No more I weep. They do not sleep.
On yonder cliffs, a griesly band,
I see them sit, they linger yet,
Avengers of their native land:
With me in dreadful harmony they join,
And weave with bloody hands the tissue of thy line.

II. 1.

"Weave the warp, and weave the woof,[11]
The winding-sheet of Edward's race.   50
Give ample room, and verge enough
The characters of hell to trace.
Mark the year, and mark the night,
When Severn shall re-eccho with affright
The shrieks of death, thro' Berkley's roofs that ring,
Shrieks of an agonizing King![12]

---

1 destruction
2 Cambria is the old Latin name for Wales.
3 Earl of Gloucester, son-in-law of Edward I.
4 The Conway is a river in North Wales.
5 The image was taken from a well-known picture of Raphael, representing the Supreme Being in the vision of Ezekiel. There are two of these pictures (both believed original), one at Florence, the other at Paris.—(Gray.)
6 Howel ab Owain Gwynedd was a royal poet of the twelfth century.
7 the poem celebrating the generous-hearted Welsh king, Llewellyn.
8 Cadwallo, Urien, and Modred are introduced as ancient Welsh bards. No bard named Modred is known; perhaps Gray took the name from Arthurian legends.
9 a mountain in Wales.
10 opposite Anglesey, in Carnarvonshire county.
11 Lines 49–100 are chanted by a chorus of the spirits of the slain bards.
12 Edward II, who was cruelly murdered in Berkeley Castle.

She-Wolf of France,[13] with unrelenting fangs,
That tear'st the bowels of thy mangled Mate,
From thee be born, who o'er thy country hangs
The scourge of Heav'n.[14] What Terrors round
    him wait!   60
Amazement in his van, with Flight combined,
And sorrow's faded form, and solitude behind.

II.   2.

"Mighty Victor, mighty Lord,
Low on his funeral couch he lies!
No pitying heart, no eye, afford
A tear to grace his obsequies.
Is the sable Warriour[15] fled?
Thy son is gone.   He rests among the Dead.
The Swarm, that in thy noon-tide beam were
    born?
Gone to salute the rising Morn.   70
Fair laughs the Morn, and soft the Zephyr blows,
While proudly riding o'er the azure realm
In gallant trim the gilded Vessel goes;
Youth on the prow, and Pleasure at the helm;[16]
Regardless of the sweeping Whirlwind's sway,
That, hush'd in grim repose, expects his
    evening-prey.

II.   3.

'"Fill high the sparkling bowl,
The rich repast prepare,
Reft of a crown, he yet may share the feast:
Close by the regal chair   80
Fell Thirst and Famine scowl
A baleful smile upon their baffled Guest.[17]
Heard ye the din of battle bray,[18]
Lance to lance, and horse to horse?
Long Years of havock urge their destined course,
And thro' the kindred squadrons mow their way.
Ye Towers of Julius,[19] London's lasting shame,
With many a foul and midnight murther fed,
Revere his Consort's[20] faith, his Father's[21] fame,
And spare the meek Usurper's[22] holy head.   90
Above, below, the rose of snow,
Twined with her blushing foe, we spread;[23]

The bristled Boar[24] in infant-gore
Wallows beneath the thorny shade.
Now, Brothers, bending o'er th' accursed loom
Stamp we our vengeance deep, and ratify his
    doom.

III.   I.

'"Edward, lo! to sudden fate
(Weave we the woof.   The thread is spun)
Half of thy heart[25] we consecrate.
(The web is wove. The work is done.)"   100
Stay, oh stay! nor thus forlorn
Leave me unbless'd, unpitied, here to mourn:
In yon bright track, that fires the western skies,
They melt, they vanish from my eyes.
But oh! what solemn scenes on Snowdon's
    height
Descending slow their glitt'ring skirts unroll?
Visions of glory, spare my aching sight,
Ye unborn Ages, crowd not on my soul!
No more our long-lost Arthur we bewail.[26]
All-hail, ye genuine Kings, Britannia's[27]   110
    Issue, hail!

III.   2.

'Girt with many a Baron bold
Sublime their starry fronts they rear;
And gorgeous Dames, and Statesmen old
In bearded majesty, appear.
In the midst a Form divine![28]
Her eye proclaims her of the Briton-Line;
Her lyon-port, her awe-commanding face,
Attemper'd sweet to virgin-grace.
What strings symphonious tremble in the air,
What strains of vocal transport round her play! 120
Hear from the grave, great Taliessin,[29] hear;
They breathe a soul to animate thy clay.
Bright Rapture calls, and soaring, as she sings,
Waves in the eye of Heav'n her many-colour'd
    wings.

III.   3.

'The verse adorn again
Fierce War, and faithful Love,
And Truth severe, by fairy Fiction drest.[30]
In buskin'd measures[31] move

---

13 Isabel of France, Edward the Second's adulterous Queen.—
(Gray.)
14 Edward III.
15 Edward the Black Prince, who died before his father.
16 Lines 71-4, says Gray, are intended to suggest the 'magnificence of Richard the Second's reign.'
17 Gray cites in a note authority for the story that Richard II was
starved to death.
18 the Wars of the Roses.
19 the Tower of London.
20 Margaret of Anjou, wife of Henry VI.
21 Henry V.
22 Henry VI.
23 The white and red roses were emblems of the Houses of York
and Lancaster.

24 Richard III, whose emblem was a silver boar. He murdered
the two young sons of Edward IV.
25 Eleanor of Castile, queen of Edward I, at whose death the king
was overwhelmed with grief.
26 It was commonly believed in Wales that King Arthur would
return from fairyland to reign over Britain.
27 The House of Tudor, which was of Welsh origin.
28 Queen Elizabeth.
29 a Welsh bard of the sixth century.
30 in Spenser's *The Faerie Queene*.
31 in Shakespeare's tragedies.

Pale Grief, and pleasing Pain,
With Horrour, Tyrant of the throbbing breast. 130
A Voice,[32] as of the Cherub-Choir,
Gales from blooming Eden bear;
And distant warblings[33] lessen on my ear,
That lost in long futurity expire.
Fond impious Man, think'st thou, yon sanguine
    cloud,
Rais'd by thy breath, has quench'd the Orb of
    day?
To-morrow he repairs the golden flood,
And warms the nations with redoubled ray.
Enough for me: With joy I see
The different doom our Fates assign. 140
Be thine Despair, and scept'red Care,
To triumph, and to die, are mine.'
He spoke, and headlong from the mountain's
    height
Deep in the roaring tide he plung'd to endless
    night.

    1754–7   1757

THE FATAL SISTERS

[Gray's two Norse poems (*The Fatal Sisters* and *The Descent of Odin*) are free renderings from the Latin translations by Thomas Bartholin in his treatise on Scandinavian antiquities, *De Causis Contemptae Mortis*, 1689.]

In the Eleventh Century *Sigurd*, Earl of the Orkney-Islands, went with a fleet of ships and a considerable body of troops into Ireland, to the assistance of *Sictryg with the silken beard*, who was then making war on his father-in-law *Brian*, King of Dublin: the Earl and all his forces were cut to pieces, and *Sictryg* was in danger of a total defeat; but the enemy had a greater loss by the death of *Brian*, their King, who fell in the action. On Christmas-day, (the day of the battle,) a Native of *Caithness* in Scotland saw at a distance a number of persons on horseback riding full speed towards a hill, and seeming to enter into it. Curiosity led him to follow them, till looking through an opening in the rocks he saw twelve gigantic figures resembling women: they were all employed about a loom; and as they wove, they sung the following dreadful Song; which when they had finished, they tore the web into twelve pieces, and (each taking her portion) galloped Six to the North and as many to the South.—(From Gray's Preface.)

Now the storm begins to lower,
(Haste, the loom of Hell prepare,)
Iron-sleet of arrowy shower
Hurtles in the darken'd air.

Glitt'ring lances are the loom,
Where the dusky warp we strain,
Weaving many a Soldier's doom,
Orkney's woe, and *Randver*'s bane.

See the griesly texture grow,
('Tis of human entrails made,)   10
And the weights, that play below,
Each a gasping Warriour's head.

Shafts for shuttles, dipt in gore,
Shoot the trembling cords along.
Sword, that once a Monarch bore,
Keep the tissue close and strong.

Mista black, terrific Maid,
Sangrida, and *Hilda* see,
Join the wayward work to aid:
'Tis the woof of victory.   20

Ere the ruddy sun be set,
Pikes must shiver, javelins sing,
Blade with clattering buckler meet,
Hauberk crash, and helmet ring.

(Weave the crimson web of war)
Let us go, and let us fly,
Where our Friends the conflict share,
Where they triumph, where they die.

As the paths of fate we tread,
Wading thro' th' ensanguin'd field: 30
Gondula, and *Geira*, spread
O'er the youthful King[1] your shield.

We the reins to slaughter give,
Ours to kill, and ours to spare:
Spite of danger he shall live.
(Weave the crimson web of war.)

They,[2] whom once the desart-beach
Pent within its bleak domain,
Soon their ample sway shall stretch
O'er the plenty of the plain.   40

Low the dauntless Earl[3] is laid,
Gor'd with many a gaping wound:
Fate demands a nobler head;
Soon a King[4] shall bite the ground.

Long his loss shall Eirin weep,
Ne'er again his likeness see;
Long her strains in sorrow steep,
Strains of Immortality!

Horror covers all the heath,

---

1 Sictryg.
2 the Norse.
3 Sigurd.
4 Brian.

---

32 Milton.
33 the poets following Milton.

Clouds of carnage blot the sun.   50
Sisters, weave the web of death;
Sisters, cease, the work is done.

Hail the task, and hail the hands!
Songs of joy and triumph sing!
Joy to the victorious bands;
Triumph to the younger King.[1]

Mortal, thou that hear'st the tale,
Learn the tenour of our song.
Scotland, thro' each winding vale
Far and wide the notes prolong.   60

Sisters, hence with spurs of speed:
Each her thundering faulchion wield;
Each bestride her sable steed.
Hurry, hurry to the field.

1761   1768

In glitt'ring arms and glory drest,
High he rears his ruby crest.
There the thund'ring strokes begin,
There the press, and there the din;
Talymalfra's rocky shore[4]
Echoing to the battle's roar.
Where his glowing eye-balls turn,
Thousand Banners round him burn.
Where he points his purple spear,
Hasty, hasty Rout is there,   30
Marking with indignant eye
Fear to stop, and shame to fly.
There Confusion, Terror's child,
Conflict fierce, and Ruin wild,
Agony, that pants for breath,
Despair and honourable Death.

*   *   *

1764   1768

THE TRIUMPHS OF OWEN

A FRAGMENT

[This fragment is based on an English prose translation of a Welsh poem found in Evans' *Specimens of the
Ancient Welsh Bards*, 1764. It commemorates a battle in
which Owen, Prince of North Wales, repulses the combined attack of the Irish, Danish, and Norman fleets,
about 1160.]

Owen's praise demands my song,
Owen swift, and Owen strong;
Fairest flower of Roderic's stem,
Gwyneth's shield, and Britain's gem.
He nor heaps his brooded stores,
Nor on all profusely pours;
Lord of every regal art,
Liberal hand, and open heart.

Big with hosts of mighty name,
Squadrons three against him came;   10
This the force of Eirin[1] hiding,
Side by side as proudly riding,
On her shadow long and gay
Lochlin[2] plows the watry way;
There the Norman sails afar
Catch the winds, and join the war:
Black and huge along they sweep,
Burthens of the angry deep.

Dauntless on his native sands
The Dragon-Son of Mona[3] stands;   20

---
1 Sictryg.

---
1 Ireland.   2 Denmark.
3 As the descendant of Cadwallon, ancient British king, Owen
wore the device of a red dragon.

SELECTIONS FROM GRAY'S LETTERS

1   *To* His Mother

Lyons, 13 October, N.S. 1739

It is now almost five weeks since I left Dijon,
one of the gayest and most agreeable little cities
of France, for Lyons, its reverse in all these particulars. It is the second in the kingdom in big-
ness and rank, the streets excessively narrow and
nasty; the houses immensely high and large (that,
for instance where we are lodged, has twenty-five
rooms on a floor, and that for five stories); it
swarms with inhabitants like Paris itself, but
chiefly a mercantile people, too much given up
to commerce, to think of their own, much less of
a stranger's diversions. We have no acquaintance in the town, but such English as happen to
be passing through here, in their way to Italy and
the south, which at present happen to be near
thirty in number. It is a fortnight since we set out
from hence upon a little excursion to Geneva.
We took the longest road, which lies through Savoy, on purpose to see a famous monastery,
called the grand Chartreuse, and had no reason
to think our time lost. After having travelled [two]
days very slow (for we did not change horses, it
being impossible for a chaise to go post in these
roads) we arrived at a little village, among the
mountains of Savoy, called Échelles; from thence
we proceeded on horses, who are used to the way,
to the mountain of the Chartreuse. It is six miles
to the top; the road runs winding up it, com-

---
4 a bay on the northeast coast of Anglesea.

monly not six feet broad; on one hand is the rock, with woods of pine-trees hanging overhead; on the other, a monstrous precipice, almost perpendicular, at the bottom of which rolls a torrent, that sometimes tumbling among the fragments of stone that have fallen from on high, and sometimes precipitating itself down vast descents with a noise like thunder, which is still made greater by the echo from the mountains on each side, concurs to form one of the most solemn, the most romantic, and the most astonishing scenes I ever beheld. Add to this the strange views made by the crags and cliffs on the other hand; the cascades that in many places throw themselves from the very summit down into the vale, and the river below; and many other particulars impossible to describe; you will conclude we had no occasion to repent our pains. This place St. Bruno chose to retire to, and upon its very top founded the aforesaid Convent, which is the superior of the whole order. When we came there, the two fathers, who are commissioned to entertain strangers (for the rest must neither speak one to another, nor to any one else), received us very kindly; and set before us a repast of dried fish, eggs, butter, and fruits, all excellent in their kind, and extremely neat. They pressed us to spend the night there, and to stay some days with them; but this we could not do, so they led us about their house, which is, you must think, like a little city; for there are 100 fathers, besides 300 servants, that make their clothes, grind their corn, press their wine, and do everything among themselves. The whole is quite orderly, and simple; nothing of finery, but the wonderful decency, and the strange situation, more than supply the place of it. In the evening we descended by the same way, passing through many clouds that were then forming themselves on the mountain's side. Next day we continued our journey by Chamberry, which, though the chief city of the Duchy, and residence of the King of Sardinia, when he comes into this part of his dominions, makes but a very mean and insignificant appearance; we lay at Aix, once famous for its hot baths, and the next night at Annecy; the day after, by noon, we got to Geneva. I have not time to say anything about it, nor of our solitary journey back again. . . .

2 *To* Richard West

Turin, 16 November, N.S. 1739

After eight days' journey through Greenland, we arrived at Turin. You approach it by a hand-some avenue of nine miles long, and quite strait. The entrance is guarded by certain vigilant dragons, called Douâniers,[1] who mumbled us for some time. The city is not large, as being a place of strength, and consequently confined within its fortifications; it has many beauties and some faults; among the first are streets all laid out by the line, regular uniform buildings, fine walks that surround the whole, and in general a good lively clean appearance. But the houses are of brick plastered, which is apt to want repairing; the windows of oiled paper, which is apt to be torn; and everything very slight, which is apt to tumble down. There is an excellent opera, but it is only in the carnival; balls every night, but only in the carnival; masquerades too, but only in the carnival. This carnival lasts only from Christmas to Lent; one half of the remaining part of the year is passed in remembering the last, the other in expecting the future carnival. We cannot well subsist upon such slender diet, no more than upon an execrable Italian comedy, and a puppet-show, called *Rappresentazione d'un' anima dannata,*[2] which, I think are all the present diversions of the place; except the Marquise de Cavaillac's Conversazione, where one goes to see people play at ombre and taroc, a game with seventy-two cards all painted with suns and moons and devils and monks. Mr. Walpole has been at court; the family are at present at a country palace, called La Venerie. The palace here in town is the very quintessence of gilding and looking-glass; inlaid floors, carved panels, and painting, wherever they could stick a brush. I own I have not, as yet, anywhere met with those grand and simple works of art that are to amaze one, and whose sight one is to be the better for; but those of Nature have astonished me beyond expression. In our little journey up to the Grande Chartreuse, I do not remember to have gone ten paces without an exclamation, that there was no restraining: not a precipice, not a torrent, not a cliff, but is pregnant with religion and poetry. There are certain scenes that would awe an atheist into belief, without the help of other argument. One need not have a very fantastic imagination to see spirits there at noonday. You have Death perpetually before your eyes, only so far removed as to compose the mind without frighting it. I am well persuaded St. Bruno was a man of no common genius to choose such a situation for his retirement, and perhaps should have been a disciple of his, had I been born in his time. You may believe Abelard and Heloïse were

---

1 customs officers.
2 'Representation of a damned soul.'

not forgot upon this occasion. If I do not mistake, I saw you too every now and then at a distance among the trees; *il me semble, que j'ai vu ce chien de visage-là quelque part.*[3] You seemed to call to me from the other side of the precipice, but the noise of the river below was so great, that I really could not distinguish what you said; it seemed to have a cadence like verse. In your next you will be so good to let me know what it was. The week we have since passed among the Alps has not equalled the single day upon that mountain, because the winter was rather too far advanced, and the weather a little foggy. However, it did not want its beauties; the savage rudeness of the view is inconceivable without seeing it. I reckoned in one day thirteen cascades, the least of which was, I dare say, one hundred feet in height. . . . We set out for Genoa in two days' time.

3 *To* Horace Walpole

[*1760*]

I am so charmed with the two specimens of Erse poetry,[4] that I cannot help giving you the trouble to enquire a little farther about them, and should wish to see a few lines of the original, that I may form some slight idea of the language, the measures, and the rhythm.

Is there anything known of the author or authors, and of what antiquity are they supposed to be?

Is there any more to be had of equal beauty, or at all approaching to it?

I have been often told that the poem called *Hardicanute*[5] (which I always admired and still admire) was the work of somebody that lived a few years ago. This I do not at all believe, though it has evidently been retouched in places by some modern hand: but however, I am authorised by this report to ask whether the two poems in question are certainly antique and genuine. I make this enquiry in quality of an antiquary, and am not otherwise concerned about it: for, if I were sure that any one now living in Scotland had written them to divert himself, and laugh at the credulity of the world, I would undertake a journey into the Highlands only for the pleasure of seeing him.

---

3 'It seems to me that I have seen that abominable face everywhere.'
4 Ossianic poems, which Macpherson claimed he had collected in the Scottish Highlands and translated from the Gaelic or Erse.
5 An anonymous romance reprinted by Percy in the *Reliques*, 1765.

4 *To* the Reverend William Mason[6]

Pembroke Hall, 7 August 1760

. . . The Erse fragments have been published five weeks ago in Scotland, though I had them not (by a mistake) till last week. As you tell me new things do not soon reach you at Aston, I inclose what I can; the rest shall follow, when you tell me whether you have not got it already. I send the two which I had before, for Mr. Wood, because he has not *the affectation of not admiring*. I continue to think them genuine, though my reasons for believing the contrary are rather stronger than ever: but I will have them antique, for I never knew a Scotchman of my own time that could read, much less write, poetry; and such poetry too! I have one (from Mr. Macpherson) which he has not printed: it is mere description, but excellent, too, in its kind. If you are good and will learn to admire, I will transcribe it. . . .

[*c. 31 August 1760*]

Having made many enquiries about the authenticity of these fragments, I have got a letter from Mr. David Hume (the historian), which is more satisfactory than anything I have yet met with on that subject. He says—

'Certain it is that these poems are in everybody's mouth in the Highlands, have been handed down from father to son, and are of an age beyond all memory and tradition. Adam Smith, the celebrated professor in Glasgow, told me that the piper of the Argyleshire Militia repeated to him all those which Mr. Macpherson has translated, and many more of equal beauty. Major Mackay (Lord Rae's brother) told me that he remembers them perfectly well; as likewise did the Laird of Macfarlane (the greatest antiquarian we have in this country), and who insists strongly on the historical truth as well as the poetical beauty of these productions. I could add the Laird and Lady Macleod, with many more, that live in different parts of the Highlands, very remote from each other, and could only be acquainted with what had become (in a manner) national works. There is a country surgeon in Lochaber who has by heart the entire epic poem[7] mentioned by Mr. Macpherson in his preface; and, as he is old, is perhaps the only person living that knows it all, and has never committed it to writing, we are in the more haste to recover a monument which will certainly be regarded as a curiosity in the repub-

---

6 Gray's friend and biographer, 1724–97.
7 *Fingal.*

lic of letters: we have, therefore, set about a subscription of a guinea or two guineas apiece, in order to enable Mr. Macpherson to undertake a mission into the Highlands to recover this poem, and other fragments of antiquity.'

I forgot to mention to you that the names of Fingal, Ossian, Oscar, etc., are still given in the Highlands to large mastiffs, as we give to ours the names of Cæsar, Pompey, Hector, etc.

5 *To* Thomas Warton

[September 1765]

I deferred writing to you till I had seen a little more of this country[8] than you yourself had seen, and now being just returned from an excursion, which I and the major have been making into the Highlands, I sit down to tell you all about it....

We set out then the 11th of September, and continuing along the Strath[9] to the west passed through *Megill* (where is the tomb of *Queen Wanders, that was riven to dethe by staned-horses for nae gude that she did.* So the woman there told me, I am sure), through Cowper of Angus, over the river Ila, then over a wide and dismal heath fit for an assembly of witches, till we came to a string of four small lakes in a valley, whose deep blue waters, and green margin, with a gentleman's house or two seated on them in little groves, contrasted with the black desert in which they were inchased. The ground now grew unequal; the hills more rocky seemed to close in upon us, till the road came to the brow of a steep descent, and (the sun then setting) between two woods of oak we saw far below us the river Tay come sweeping along at the bottom of a precipice, at least 150 feet deep, clear as glass, full to the brim, and very rapid in its course. It seemed to issue out of woods thick and tall, that rose on either hand, and were overhung by broken rocky crags of vast height; above them to the west, the tops of higher mountains appeared, on which the evening clouds reposed. Down by the side of the river, under the thickest shades is seated the town of Dunkeld; in the midst of it stands a ruined cathedral, the towers and shell of the building still entire; a little beyond it a large house of the Duke of Athol with its offices and gardens extends a mile beyond the town; and as his grounds were interrupted by the streets and roads, he has flung arches of communication across them, that add to the scenery of the place, which of itself is built

of good white stone, and handsomely slated, so that no one would take it for a Scotch town till they came into it; here we passed the night. If I told you how, you would bless yourself. Next day we set forward to Taymouth twenty-seven miles farther west; the road winding through beautiful woods, with the Tay almost always in full view to the right, being here from three to four hundred feet over. The Strath-Tay, from a mile to three miles or more wide, covered with corn, and spotted with groups of people, then in the midst of their harvest; on either hand a vast chain of rocky mountains, that changed their face, and opened something new every hundred yards, as the way turned, or the clouds passed. In short, altogether it was one of the most pleasing days I have passed these many years, and at every step I wished for you. At the close of the day we came to *Balloch,* so the place was called, but now for decency *Taymouth;* improperly enough, for here it is that the river issues out of Loch Tay (a glorious lake fifteen miles long, and one and a half broad), surrounded with prodigious mountains. There on its northeastern brink impending over it, is the vast hill of Lawers; to the east is that monstrous creature of God, *She-khallian* (*i.e.* the Maiden's Pap), spiring above the clouds. Directly west (beyond the end of the lake) *Beni-more* (the great mountain) rises to a most awful height, and looks down on the tomb of Fingal.[10] ...

As evening came on, we approached the Pass of Gillikrankie, where in the year 1745 the Hessians with their prince at their head stopped short and refused to march a foot farther.

'Vestibulum ante ipsum primisque in faucibus Orci.'[11]

stands the solitary mansion of Mr. Robinson of Faseley. Close by it rises a hill covered with oak, with grotesque masses of rock staring from among their trunks, like the sullen countenances of Fingal and all his family frowning on the little mortals of modern days. From between this hill and the adjacent mountains, pent in a narrow channel, comes roaring out the river Tummell, and falls headlong down, enclosed in white foam, which rises into a mist all round it.—But my paper is deficient, and I must say nothing of the pass itself, the black river Garry, the Blair of Athol, Mount Beni-gloe, my return (by another road) to Dunkeld, the Hermitage, the *Stra-Brann,* and

---

8 Scotland.
9 valley.

10 epic hero of the Ossianic poems.
11 'Right before the entrance, in the very jaws of Oreus' —*Æneid,* VI, 273.

the rumbling Brigg. In short, since I saw the Alps I have seen nothing sublime till now.

From JOURNAL IN THE LAKES

3 October 1769. Wind at S.E.; a heavenly day. Rose at 7, and walked out under the conduct of my landlord to *Borrodale.* The grass was covered with a hoar frost, which soon melted, and exhaled in a thin blueish smoke. Crossed the meadows obliquely, catching a diversity of views among the hills over the lake and islands, and changing prospect at every ten paces; left Cockshut and Castlehill (which we formerly mounted) behind me, and drew near the foot of *Walla-crag,* whose bare and rocky brow, cut perpendicularly down above 400 feet, as I guess, awfully overlooks the way; our path here tends to the left, and the ground gently rising, and covered with a glade of scattering trees and bushes on the very margin of the water, opens both ways the most delicious view, that my eyes ever beheld. Behind you are the magnificent heights of *Walla-crag;* opposite lie the thick hanging woods of Lord Egremont, and *Newland* valley, with green and smiling fields embosomed in the dark cliffs; to the left the jaws of *Borrodale,* with that turbulent Chaos of mountain behind mountain, rolled in confusion; beneath you, and stretching far away to the right, the shining purity of the *Lake,* just ruffled by the breeze, enough to shew it is alive, reflecting rocks, woods, fields, and inverted tops of mountains, with the white buildings of *Keswick, Crosthwait* church, and *Skiddaw* for a background at a distance. . . . This scene continues to *Barrow-gate,* and a little farther, passing a brook called *Barrow-beck,* we entered *Borrodale.* The crags, named *Lodoor-banks,* now begin to impend terribly over your way; and more terribly, when you hear, that three years since an immense mass of rock tumbled at once from the brow, and barred all access to the dale (for this is the only road) till they could work their way through it. Luckily no one was passing at the time of this fall; but down the side of the mountain, and far into the lake lie dispersed the huge fragments of this ruin in all shapes and in all directions. Something farther we turned aside into a coppice, ascending a little in front of *Lodoor* waterfall, the height appears to be about 200 feet, the quantity of water not great, though (these three days excepted) it had rained daily in the hills for nearly two months before: but then the stream was nobly broken, leaping from rock to rock, and foaming with fury. On one side a towering crag, that spired up to equal, if not overtop, the neighbouring cliffs (this

lay all in shade and darkness) on the other hand a rounder broader projecting hill shagged with wood and illumined by the sun, which glanced sideways on the upper part of the cataract. The force of the water wearing a deep channel in the ground hurries away to join the lake. We descended again, and passed the stream over a rude bridge. Soon after we came under *Gowder crag,* a hill more formidable to the eye and to the apprehension than that of *Lodoor;* the rocks a-top, deep-cloven perpendicularly by the rains, hanging loose and nodding forwards, seem just starting from their base in shivers; the whole way down, and the road on both sides is strewed with piles of the fragments strangely thrown across each other, and of a dreadful bulk. The place reminds one of those passes in the Alps, where the Guides tell you to move on with speed, and say nothing, lest the agitation of the air should loosen the snows above, and bring down a mass, that would overwhelm a caravan. I took their counsel here and hastened on in silence. . . . Walked leisurely home the way we came, but saw a new landscape: the features indeed were the same in part, but many new ones were disclosed by the midday Sun, and the tints were entirely changed. Take notice this was the best or perhaps the only day for going up Skiddaw, but I thought it better employed: it was perfectly serene, and hot as midsummer.

In the evening walked alone down to the Lake by the side of *Crow-Park* after sunset and saw the solemn colouring of night draw on, the last gleam of sunshine fading away on the hill-tops, the deep serene of the waters, and the long shadows of the mountains thrown across them, till they nearly touched the hithermost shore. At distance heard the murmur of many waterfalls not audible in the daytime. Wished for the Moon, but she was *dark to me and silent, hid in her vacant interlunar cave.*[12]

8 October. Left Keswick and took the Ambleside road in a gloomy morning; wind east and afterwards northeast; about two miles from the Town mounted an eminence called *Castle Rigg,* and the sun breaking out discovered the most enchanting view I have yet seen of the whole valley behind me, the two lakes, the river, the mountain, all in their glory! had almost a mind to have gone back again. . . . Past by the little chapel of *Wiborn,* out of which the Sunday congregation were then issuing. Past a beck near *Dunmailraise* and entered Westmoreland a second time, now begin to see *Helm-crag* distinguished from its rugged neigh-

12 Cf. Milton, *Samson Agonistes,* 86–9.

bours not so much by its height, as by the strange broken outline of its top, like some gigantic building demolished, and the stones that composed it flung across each other in wild confusion. Just beyond it opens one of the sweetest landscapes that art ever attempted to imitate. The bosom of the mountains spreading here into a broad basin discovers in the midst Grasmere-water; its margin is hollowed into small bays with bold eminences: some of rock, some of soft turf that half conceal and vary the figure of the little lake they command. From the shore a low promontory pushes itself far into the water, and on it stands a white village with the parish-church rising in the midst of it, hanging enclosures, corn-fields, and meadows green as an emerald, with their trees and hedges, and cattle fill up the whole space from the edge of the water. Just opposite to you is a large farm-house at the bottom of a steep smooth lawn embosomed in old woods, which climb halfway up the mountain's side, and discover above them a broken line of crags, that crown the scene. Not a single red tile, no flaming Gentleman's house, or garden walls break in upon the repose of this little unsuspected paradise, but all is peace, rusticity, and happy poverty in its neatest, most becoming attire.

1775

1728 · THOMAS WARTON · 1790

1728   Born, son of Thomas Warton the elder, professor of poetry at Oxford; younger brother of Joseph Warton. Educated at his father's school at Basingstoke and at Trinity College, Oxford. Took holy orders.

1745   Wrote *The Pleasures of Melancholy* (published in 1747).

1754   Published *Observations on the Faerie Queene of Spenser.*

1757–67   Served as professor of poetry at Oxford. Wrote satirical and biographical works, and edited an anthology of university verse, *The Oxford Sausage.*

1774–81   Published *History of English Poetry* in three volumes.

1777   Published *Poems,* notable for their revival of the sonnet.

1785   Was appointed professor of ancient history at Oxford; became Poet Laureate; published an edition of Milton's shorter poems.

1790   Died.

IN HIS YOUTH Thomas Warton shared an enthusiasm for the poetry of pensive melancholy. His *Pleasures of Melancholy* abounds in the customary trappings of the 'Il Penseroso' school—solitude, delight in darkness, ruined abbeys, 'hollow charnels,' and favorite midnight haunts. As poetry, however, the *Pleasures* has little to recommend it. It is a patchwork of borrowed phrases, the chief indebtedness being, quite obviously, to Milton. In his scholarly writings Thomas Warton, like his brother Joseph, helped to prepare the way for the 'Gothic' revival. He genuinely felt the fascination of Gothic architecture and of medieval poetry. His *History* opened up to his contemporaries the rich stores of medieval and Elizabethan literature. His *Observations on the Faerie Queene* was revolutionary in its expression of admiration for Spenser. He insisted in that essay that the 'various and the marvellous' (the knights, dragons, and enchantresses) are legitimate sources of delight in serious and adult literature. He argued that the very subject matter of romance rouses and invigorates the imagination. With such critical points of view he helped to turn the tide against the rational standards of his age. In his later poetry Thomas Warton joins his love of the past with his love of nature. In his medieval poems he anticipates in a startling way the medieval lays of Walter Scott. (The opening of *The Grave of King Arthur* and the scenes, even the poetical cadences, of *The Lay of the Last Minstrel* are strikingly alike.) His sonnets with their pensive and commemorative style, are often near to Wordsworth. Thomas Warton is lacking in native richness of expression and in energy of imagination, yet he is no mere copyist. He made definite contributions to the advance of romanticism. A clear line of influence in the love of nature and personal reflection may be traced from Joseph Warton and Thomas Warton through Bowles (Joseph's student at Trinity) to Coleridge and Wordsworth, and in the revival of the spirit of the past directly to Walter Scott. Thomas Warton's work also parallels Scott's in its intimate connection between antiquarian studies and literary works.

From THE PLEASURES OF MELANCHOLY

Lines 1–69, 153–65, 196–210

MOTHER of musings, Contemplation sage,
Whose grotto stands upon the topmost rock
Of Teneriff;[1] 'mid the tempestuous night,
On which, in calmest meditation held,
Thou hear'st with howling winds the beating rain
And drifting hail descend; or if the skies
Unclouded shine, and thro' the blue serene
Pale Cynthia rolls her silver-axled car,
Whence gazing stedfast on the spangled vault
Raptur'd thou sitt'st, while murmurs indistinct 10
Of distant billows sooth thy pensive ear
With hoarse and hollow sounds; secure, self-blest,
There oft thou listen'st to the wild uproar
Of fleets encount'ring, that in whispers low
Ascends the rocky summit, where thou dwell'st
Remote from man, conversing with the spheres!
O lead me, queen sublime, to solemn glooms
Congenial with my soul; to cheerless shades,
To ruin'd seats, to twilight cells and bow'rs,
Where thoughtful Melancholy loves to muse, 20
Her fav'rite midnight haunts. The laughing scenes
Of purple Spring, where all the wanton train
Of Smiles and Graces seem to lead the dance
In sportive round, while from their hands they
    show'r
Ambrosial blooms and flow'rs, no longer charm;
Tempe, no more I court thy balmy breeze,
Adieu green vales! ye broider'd meads, adieu!
  Beneath yon ruin'd abbey's moss-grown piles
Oft let me sit, at twilight hour of eve,
Where thro' some western window the pale
    moon   30
Pours her long-levell'd rule of streaming light;
While sullen sacred silence reigns around,
Save the lone screech-owl's note, who builds his
    bow'r
Amid the mould'ring caverns dark and damp,
Or the calm breeze, that rustles in the leaves
Of flaunting ivy, that with mantle green
Invests some wasted tow'r. Or let me tread
Its neighb'ring walk of pines, where mus'd of old
The cloyster'd brothers: thro' the gloomy void
That far extends beneath their ample arch 40
As on I pace, religious horror wraps
My soul in dread repose. But when the world
Is clad in Midnight's raven-colour'd robe,
'Mid hollow charnel let me watch the flame
Of taper dim, shedding a livid glare
O'er the wan heaps; while airy voices talk
Along the glimm'ring walls; or ghostly shape
At distance seen, invites with beck'ning hand

My lonesome steps, thro' the far-winding vaults.
Nor undelightful is the solemn noon   50
Of night, when haply wakeful from my couch
I start: lo, all is motionless around!
Roars not the rushing wind; the sons of men
And every beast in mute oblivion lie;
All nature's hush'd in silence and in sleep.
O then how fearful is it to reflect,
That thro' the still globe's awful solitude,
No being wakes but me! till stealing sleep
My drooping temples bathes in opiate dews.
Nor then let dreams, of wanton folly born,   60
My senses lead thro' flow'ry paths of joy;
But let the sacred Genius of the night
Such mystic visions send, as Spenser saw,
When thro' bewild'ring Fancy's magic maze,
To the fell house of Busyrane, he led
Th' unshaken Britomart;[2] or Milton knew,
When in abstracted thought he first conceiv'd
All heav'n in tumult, and the Seraphim
Come tow'ring, arm'd in adamant and gold.[3]

Thro' POPE's soft song tho' all the Graces
    breathe,
And happiest art adorn his Attic[4] page;
Yet does my mind with sweeter transport glow,
As at the root of mossy trunk reclin'd,
In magic SPENSER's wildly warbled song[5]
I see deserted Una wander wide
Thro' wasteful solitudes, and lurid heaths,
Weary, forlorn; than when the fated fair[6]   160
Upon the bosom bright of silver Thames
Launches in all the lustre of brocade,
Amid the splendors of the laughing Sun.
The gay description palls upon the sense,
And coldly strikes the mind with feeble bliss.

The taper'd choir, at the late hour of pray'r,
Oft let me tread, while to th' according voice
The many-sounding organ peals on high,
The clear slow-dittied chaunt, or varied hymn,
Till all my soul is bath'd in ecstasies,   200
And lapp'd in Paradise. Or let me sit
Far in sequester'd iles of the deep dome,
There lonesome listen to the sacred sounds,
Which, as they lengthen thro' the Gothic vaults,
In hollow murmurs reach my ravish'd ear.
Nor when the lamps expiring yield to night,

---

1 largest of the Canary Islands.

2 *The Faerie Queene*, III, xi–xii.
3 *Paradise Lost*, VI, 110.
4 marked by classic qualities.
5 *The Faerie Queene*, I, iii and vi.
6 Pope's Belinda who was fated to lose her lock. See *The Rape of
the Lock*, ii.

And solitude returns, would I forsake
The solemn mansion, but attentive mark
The due clock swinging slow with sweepy sway,
Measuring Time's flight with momentary
    sound.   210

    1747

THE GRAVE OF KING ARTHUR

[King Henry II, on his way to suppress a rebellion in
Ireland raised by Roderick, King of Connaught, was entertained, in his passage through Wales, with the songs
of Welsh bards. The subject of their poetry was King
Arthur, whose history had been so long obscured by
legend that the place of his burial was scarcely remembered. But in one of the Welsh poems sung before Henry,
it was recited that King Arthur, after the battle of Camlan in Cornwall, was interred at Glastonbury Abbey
without external mark or memorial.]

STATELY the feast, and high the cheer:
Girt with many an armed peer,
And canopied with golden pall,
Amid CILGARRAN's castle hall,
Sublime in formidable state,
And warlike splendour, Henry sate;
Prepar'd to stain the briny flood
Of Shannon's lakes with rebel blood.
  Illumining the vaulted roof,
A thousand torches flam'd aloof: 10
From massy cups, with golden gleam
Sparkled the red metheglin's stream[1]:
To grace the gorgeous festival,
Along the lofty-window'd wall,
The storied tapestry was hung:
With minstrelsy the rafters rung
Of harps, that with reflected light
From the proud gallery glitter'd bright:
While gifted bards, a rival throng,
(From distant Mona,[2] nurse of song,   20
From Teivi,[3] fring'd with umbrage brown,
From Elvy's[4] vale, and Cader's[5] crown,
From many a shaggy precipice
That shades Ierne's[6] hoarse abyss,
And many a sunless solitude
Of Radnor's[7] inmost mountains rude,)
To crown the banquet's solemn close,
Themes of British glory chose;
And to the strings of various chime
Attemper'd thus the fabling rime.   30
  'O'er Cornwall's cliffs the tempest roar'd,
High the screaming sea-mew soar'd;

On Tintaggel's[8] topmost tower
Darksom fell the sleety shower;
Round the rough castle shrilly sung
The whirling blast, and wildly flung
On each tall rampart's thundering side
The surges of the tumbling tide:
When Arthur rang'd his red-cross ranks
On conscious Camlan's crimson'd banks: 40
By Mordred's[9] faithless guile decreed
Beneath a Saxon spear to bleed!
Yet in vain a paynim foe
Arm'd with fate the mighty blow;
For when he fell, an elfin queen,
All in secret, and unseen,
O'er the fainting hero threw
Her mantle of ambrosial blue;
And bade her spirits bear him far,
In Merlin's[10] agate-axled car,   50
To her green isle's enamel'd steep,
In the navel of the deep.
O'er his wounds she sprinkled dew
From flowers that in Arabia grew:
On a rich, inchanted bed,
She pillow'd his majestic head;
O'er his brow, with whispers bland,
Thrice she wav'd an opiate wand;
And, to soft music's airy sound,
Her magic curtains clos'd around.   60
There, renew'd the vital spring,
Again he reigns a mighty king;
And many a fair and fragrant clime,
Blooming in immortal prime,
By gales of Eden ever fann'd,
Owns the monarch's high command:
Thence to Britain shall return,
(If right prophetic rolls I learn)
Borne on Victory's spreading plume,
His antient sceptre to resume;   70
Once more, in old heroic pride,
His barbed courser to bestride;
His knightly table to restore,
And brave the tournaments of yore.'
  They ceas'd: when on the tuneful stage
Advanc'd a bard, of aspect sage;
His silver tresses, thin-besprent,
To age a graceful reverence lent;
His beard, all white as spangles frore
That cloath Plinlimmon's[11] forests hoar,   80
Down to his harp descending flow'd;
With Time's faint rose his features glow'd;
His eyes diffus'd a soften'd fire,

---

1 a fermented drink made of honey, water, and hot spices.
2 an island and county of Wales, northwest of the mainland.
3 a river in Pembrokeshire.
4 a river in Wales.
5 a mountain range in Wales.
6 Ireland's.
7 a county of South Wales.

8 a castle in Cornwall celebrated in Arthurian legend; the
reputed birthplace of Arthur.
9 the treacherous nephew of King Arthur.
10 the enchanter.
11 a mountain in Cardigan, Wales.

And thus he wak'd the warbling wire.
'Listen, Henry, to my read!
Not from fairy realms I lead
Bright-rob'd Tradition, to relate
In forged colours Arthur's fate;
Though much of old romantic lore
On the blest theme I keep in store: 90
But boastful Fiction should be dumb,
Where Truth the strain might best become.
If thine ear may still be won
With songs of Uther's glorious son,[12]
Henry, I a tale unfold,
Never yet in rime enroll'd,
Nor sung nor harp'd in hall or bower;
Which in my youth's full early flower,
A minstrel, sprung of Cornish line,
Who spoke of kings from old Locrine,[13]   100
Taught me to chant, one vernal dawn,
Deep in a cliff-encircled lawn,
What time the glistening vapours fled
From cloud-envelop'd Clyder's head;
And on its sides the torrents gray
Shone to the morning's orient ray.
   'When Arthur bow'd his haughty crest,
No princess, veil'd in azure vest,
Snatch'd him, by Merlin's potent spell,
In groves of golden bliss to dwell;   110
Where, crown'd with wreaths of misletoe,
Slaughter'd kings in glory go:
But when he fell, with winged speed,
His champions, on a milk-white steed,
From the battle's hurricane,
Bore him to Joseph's[14] towered fane,
In the fair vale of Avalon.[15]
There, with chanted orison,
And the long blaze of tapers clear,
The stoled fathers met the bier;   120
Through the dim iles, in order dread
Of martial woe, the chief they led,
And deep intomb'd in holy ground,
Before the altar's solemn bound.
Around no dusky banners wave,
No mouldering trophies mark the grave:
Away the ruthless Dane has torn
Each trace that Time's slow touch had worn;
And long, o'er the neglected stone,
Oblivion's veil its shade has thrown: 130
The faded tomb, with honour due,
'Tis thine, O Henry, to renew!
Thither, when Conquest has restor'd

Yon recreant isle, and sheath'd the sword,
When Peace with palm has crown'd thy brows,
Haste the, to pay thy pilgrim vows.
There, observant of my lore,
The pavement's hallow'd depth explore;
And thrice a fathom underneath
Dive into the vaults of death.   140
There shall thine eye, with wild amaze,
On his gigantic stature gaze;
There shalt thou find the monarch laid,
All in warrior-weeds array'd;
Wearing in death his helmet-crown,
And weapons huge of old renown.
Martial prince, 'tis thine to save
From dark oblivion Arthur's grave!
So may thy ships securely stem
The western frith,[16] thy diadem   150
Shine victorious in the van,
Nor heed the slings of Ulster's[17] clan:
Thy Norman pike-men win their way
Up the dun rocks of Harald's bay:
And from the steeps of rough Kildare
Thy prancing hoofs the falcon scare:
So may thy bow's unerring yew
Its shafts in Roderick's heart embrew.'
   Amid the pealing symphony
The spiced goblets mantled high,   160
With passions new the song impress'd
The listening king's impatient breast:
Flash the keen lightnings from his eyes;
He scorns awhile his bold emprise;
Ev'n now he seems, with eager pace,
The consecrated floor to trace;
And ope, from its tremendous gloom,
The treasure of the wonderous tomb:
Ev'n now, he burns in thought to rear,
From its dark bed, the ponderous spear,   170
Rough with the gore of Pictish kings:
Ev'n now fond hope his fancy wings,
To poise the monarch's massy blade,
Of magic-temper'd metal made;
And drag to day the dinted shield
That felt the storm of Camlan's field.
O'er the sepulchre profound
Ev'n now, with arching sculpture crown'd,
He plans the chantry's choral shrine,
The daily dirge, and rites divine.   180

1777

From OBSERVATIONS ON THE FAERIE QUEENE OF SPENSER

IT is absurd to think of judgeing either Ariosto
or Spenser by precepts which they did not attend

---

12 Arthur.
13 a mythical king of England.
14 Joseph of Arimathaea, who is supposed to have carried the
Holy Grail to Britain, where he built the abbey of Glastonbury.
15 in Celtic mythology, an earthly paradise in the western seas
where the great heroes were carried at death.

16 estuary.   17 Ireland's.

to. We who live in the days of writing by rule are apt to try every composition by those laws which we have been taught to think the sole criterion of excellence. Critical taste is universally diffused, and we require the same order and design which every modern performance is expected to have, in poems where they never were regarded or intended. Spenser, and the same may be said of Ariosto, did not live in an age of planning. His poetry is the careless exuberance of a warm imagination and a strong sensibility. It was his business to engage the fancy, and to interest the attention by bold and striking images, in the formation and the disposition of which, little labour or art was applied. The various and the marvellous were the chief sources of delight. Hence we find our author ransacking alike the regions of reality and romance, of truth and fiction, to find the proper decoration and furniture for his fairy structure. Born in such an age, Spenser wrote rapidly from his own feelings, which at the same time were naturally noble. Exactness in his poem would have been like the cornice which a painter introduced in the grotto of Calypso.[1] Spenser's beauties are like the flowers in Paradise,

> Which not nice Art
> In beds and curious knots, but Nature boon
> Pour'd forth profuse, on hill, and dale, and plain;
> Both where the morning sun first warmly smote
> The open field, or where the unpierc'd shade
> Imbrown'd the noon-tide bowers.
> —*Paradise Lost*, IV, 241.

If *The Faerie Queene* be destitute of that arrangement and economy which epic severity requires, yet we scarcely regret the loss of these while their place is so amply supplied by something which more powerfully attracts us; something which engages the affections, the feelings of the heart, rather than the cold approbation of the head. If there be any poem whose graces please because they are situated beyond the reach of art, and where the force and faculties of creative imagination delight because they are unassisted and unrestrained by those of deliberate judgement, it is this. In reading Spenser, if the critic is not satisfied, yet the reader is transported.

.　　.　　.

I cannot dismiss this section without a wish that this neglected author [Chaucer], whom Spenser proposed as the pattern of his style, and to whom he is indebted for many noble inventions,

1 a nymph living in the island of Ogygia, who detained Ulysses for seven years.

should be more universally studied. This is at least what one might expect in an age of research and curiosity. Chaucer is regarded rather as an old, than as a good, poet. We look upon his poems as venerable relics, not as beautiful compositions; as pieces better calculated to gratify the antiquarian than the critic. He abounds not only in strokes of humour, which is commonly supposed to be his sole talent, but of pathos and sublimity not unworthy a more refined age. His old manners, his romantic arguments, his wildness of painting, his simplicity and antiquity of expression, transport us into some fairy region, and are all highly pleasing to the imagination. It is true that his uncouth and unfamiliar language disgusts and deters many readers; but the principal reason of his being so little known and so seldom taken into hand, is the convenient opportunity of reading him with pleasure and facility in modern imitations. For when translation, and such, imitations from Chaucer may be justly called, at length becomes substituted as the means of attaining a knowledge of any difficult and ancient author, the original not only begins to be neglected and excluded as less easy, but also despised as less ornamental and elegant. Thus the public taste becomes imperceptibly vitiated, while the genuine model is superseded, and gradually gives way to the establishment of a more specious but false resemblance. Thus, too many readers, happy to find the readiest accommodation for their indolence and their illiteracy, think themselves sufficient masters of Homer from Pope's translation; and thus, by an indiscreet comparison, Pope's translation is commonly preferred to the Grecian text, in proportion as the former is furnished with more frequent and shining metaphors, more lively descriptions, and in general appears to be more full and florid, more elaborate and various.

.　　.　　.

In reading the works of a poet who lived in a remote age, it is necessary that we should look back upon the customs and manners which prevailed in that age. We should endeavour to place ourselves in the writer's situation and circumstances. Hence we shall become better enabled to discover how his turn of thinking, and manner of composing, were influenced by familiar appearances and established objects which are utterly different from those with which we are at present surrounded. For want of this caution, too many readers view the knights and damsels, the tournaments and enchantments, of Spenser with modern eyes; never considering that the encounters of chivalry subsisted in our author's age, that romances were then most eagerly and universally studied, and that consequently Spenser from the fashion of the times was induced to undertake a recital of chivalrous achievements, and to become, in short, a *romantic* poet.

Spenser, in this respect, copied real manners no less than Homer. A sensible historian observes that 'Homer copied true natural manners, which, however rough and uncultivated, will always form an agreeable and interesting picture; but the pencil of the English poet (Spenser) was employed in drawing the affectations and conceits and fopperies of chivalry.' This, however, was nothing more than an imitation of real life; as much, at least, as the plain descriptions in Homer, which corresponded to the simplicity of manners then subsisting in Greece.

Mechanical critics will perhaps be disgusted at the liberties I have taken in introducing so many anecdotes of ancient chivalry. But my subject required frequent proofs of this sort. Nor could I be persuaded that such enquiries were, in other respects, either useless or ridiculous; as they tended, at least, to illustrate an institution of no frivolous or indifferent nature. Chivalry is commonly looked upon as a barbarous sport or extravagant amusement of the dark ages. It had, however, no small influence on the manners, policies, and constitutions of ancient times, and served many public and important purposes. It was the school of fortitude, honour, and affability. Its exercises, like the Grecian games, habituated the youth to fatigue and enterprise, and inspired the noblest sentiments of heroism. It taught gallantry and civility to a savage and ignorant people, and humanized the native ferocity of the Northern nations. It conduced to refine the manners of the combatants by exciting an emulation in the devices and accoutrements, the splendour and parade, of their tilts and tournaments; while its magnificent festivals, thronged with noble dames and courteous knights, produced the first efforts of wit and fancy.

I am still further to hope that, together with other specimens of obsolete literature in general hinted at before, the many references I have made in particular to romances, the necessary appendage of ancient chivalry, will also plead their pardon. For however monstrous and unnatural these compositions may appear to this age of reason and refinement, they merit more attention than the world is willing to bestow. They preserve many curious historical facts, and throw considerable light on the nature of the feudal system. They are the pictures of ancient usages and customs; and represent the manners, genius, and character of our ancestors. Above all, such are their terrible Graces of magic and enchantment, so magnificently marvellous are their fictions and fablings, that they contribute, in a wonderful degree, to rouse and invigorate all the powers of imagination; to store the fancy with those sublime and alarming images which poetry best delights to display.

1754

1736 · JAMES MACPHERSON · 1796

1736 Born at Ruthven, Inverness, son of a poor farmer. Educated at King's College and Marischal College, Aberdeen, and at the University of Edinburgh; took no degree. Taught school in Ruthven, and later became a tutor.

1759 Met John Home, who encouraged him to do Gaelic translations.

1760 Published *Fragments of Ancient Poetry Collected in the Highlands of Scotland,* with an introduction by Dr. Hugh Blair declaring their authenticity. Journeyed to the Highlands to collect an 'epic.'

1761 Published *Fingal,* epic poem in six books.

1763 Published *Temora,* in eight books. Blair supported its authenticity in his *Critical Dissertation on the Poems of Ossian.*

1764 Appointed secretary to the governor at Pensacola, West Florida.

1765 Published *The Works of Ossian* (collected edition).

1766 Returned to England; became a political writer for the government.

1771 Published *An Introduction to the History of Great Britain and Ireland.*

1774 Authenticity of the Ossianic poems attacked by Johnson in his *Journey to the Western Islands of Scotland.*

1775 Published *The Secret History of Great Britain from the Restoration to the Accession of the House of Hanover.*

1780 Elected Member of Parliament,

1796 Died; buried in Westminster Abbey.

THE CULT of primitivism—the belief that the earliest conditions of man and human society are the best conditions—found a highly favorable climate in the eighteenth century and rapidly reached a growth of amazing proportions. Primitivism was nourished chiefly by the philosophers and men of letters, who encouraged the doctrine of natural goodness and extended the principle of benevolence to include the benevolence of primitive men. In literary circles, as early as the second quarter of the century, Thomson in the *Seasons* toys with the 'noble savage' idea. Joseph Warton in *The Enthusiast,* 1740, extols a life of idyllic innocence among naked Indians. Collins in *An Ode on the Popular Superstitions of the Highlands of Scotland* (written in 1749) by precept and example supports the poetic use of popular superstitions as found among primitive peoples. Shortly after the mid-century Gray with his *Bard* gives high sanction to the figure of the primitive singer. With the Ossianic poems of Macpherson in the 'sixties primitivism reaches a climax.

James Macpherson, a young Scottish clergyman and descendant of an obscure branch of a Highland clan, began collecting ancient Gaelic fragments for his own amusement. He published anonymously in 1760 a booklet of some seventy pages, and though he had a very imperfect knowledge of Gaelic, claimed his work to be a translation from the Gaelic language. The publication excited immediate interest, with the result that certain friends took up a subscription to make it possible for Macpherson to travel through the Highlands and the Hebrides in search of oral poetry. The no less than sensational result of this trip was *Fingal,* an epic in six books, 1761, to which Macpherson prefixed an essay attributing the work to Ossian, a bard of the third century. Another gathering, *Temora,* in eight books, appeared in 1763. Almost immediately a bitter controversy ensued over the genuineness of the Ossianic poems. To Gray, lover of antiquities, Ossian was a dream come true. Gray's enthusiasm for Macpherson's earliest efforts added considerably to the interest with which they were received by the host of Gray's literary friends. Eventually, however, Gray seems to have doubted the genuineness of the Ossianic poems, though he never failed to express admiration for the poetry. Dr. Johnson, on the other hand, was one of the most truculent skeptics; he both disputed their authenticity and denied them any poetic value. Macpherson finding himself discredited promised to produce his originals; but he never did. The controversy over Ossian blew hot and cold and was not satisfactorily settled until well over a century after the first angry outbursts. It appears there did exist both in Ireland and in the Scottish Highlands traditions, tales, and poems attributed to Oisin, the son of Finn Mac-Cumhail. But today experts agree that though Macpherson may have built his Ossianic poems upon a slender traditional foundation, they do not rest on traditional texts. Macpherson seems to have been carried away with Caledonian pride and the worship of the hour for national beginnings. In fabricating his manuscripts he probably got himself involved deeper than he had intended and once in he found it impossible to extricate himself without embarrassment or worse.

Leaving aside moral considerations, it must be admitted that Macpherson shrewdly gauged the public taste in ministering to the growing idealization of the primitive. His Ossianic poems aroused an immediate and astonishing popular response. To a generation weary of drawing-room conventions, Macpherson's world of heroic simplicity set in a region of mountains and mists was tremendously appealing. The wild, gigantesque landscape of Ossian fitted the newly awakened enthusiasm for what was called 'romantic' scenery. The ancient world of fictitious fancy excited in readers a vaguely caressing sense of noble feelings. Pathetically mournful tales of superstition, grief, and violence crowd close upon one another: ghosts move in the mists and dissolve in showers of blood; white-bosomed maids, forewarned of the deaths of their lovers, look with fear upon the impending battle; a father unknowingly slays his son and dies of grief; the aged Ossian pitifully lifts up his blind eyes to address the eternal sun. Today the falsetto quality of the Ossianic poems is easily apparent, but to their first audience they came like a strong voice out of a natural, primitive past. Also, the loosely rhythmical prose, which owes something to the Old Testament, came as a welcome change to the close regularity of Augustan versification.

The sentimental primitivism of Macpherson expressed the nostalgic mood of the hour. Ossianism swept like a tidal wave over all Europe. It influenced the youth of Goethe and Schiller and captured the imagination of Napoleon. In French literature its influence was very great; it arrived later but endured longer in France than in any other country. In England its direct influence was reflected in a host of imitations. Not only were Chatterton, Bowles, Southey, Moore, Campbell, and dozens of lesser writers beholden to Ossianic literature for melancholy inspiration or epithets, but Blake, Coleridge, Scott, and Byron show unmistakable evidence of having been taken in by the Ossianic fever. Though the impact upon the great English writers was slight and transient, epithets, sentiments, and rhythms of Macpherson echo and re-echo in English verse from the lowest to the highest. The only literary impulse of greater consequence in romantic literature was Percy's *Reliques.*

CARTHON: A POEM

ARGUMENT

This poem is complete, and the subject of it, as of most of Ossian's compositions, tragical. In the time of Comhal the son of Trathal, and father of the celebrated Fingal, Clessámmor the son of Thaddu and brother of Morna, Fingal's mother, was driven by a storm into the River Clyde, on the banks of which stood Balclutha, a town belonging to the Britons between the walls. He was hospitably received by Reuthámir, the principal man in the place, who gave him Moina his only daughter in marriage. Reuda, the son of Cormo, a Briton who was in love with Moina, came to Reuthámir's house, and behaved haughtily towards Clessámmor. A quarrel ensued, in which Reuda was killed; the Britons, who attended him, pressed so hard on Clessámmor, that he was obliged to throw himself into the Clyde, and swim to his ship. He hoisted sail, and the wind being favourable, bore him out to sea. He often endeavoured to return, and carry off his beloved Moina by night; but the wind continuing contrary, he was forced to desist.

Moina, who had been left with child by her husband, brought forth a son, and died soon after.—Reuthámir named the child Carthon, *i. e., the murmur of waves,* from the storm which carried off Clessámmor his father, who was supposed to have been cast away. When Carthon was three years old, Comhal the father of Fingal, in one of his expeditions against the Britons, took and burnt Balclutha. Reuthámir was killed in the attack; and Carthon was carried safe away by his nurse, who fled further into the country of the Britons. Carthon, coming to man's estate, was resolved to revenge the fall of Balclutha on Comhal's posterity. He set sail, from the Clyde, and falling on the coast of Morven, defeated two of Fingal's heroes, who came to oppose his progress. He was, at last, unwittingly killed by his father Clessámmor, in a single combat. This story is the foundation of the present poem, which opens on the night preceding the death of Carthon, so that what passed before is introduced by way of episode. The poem is addressed to Malvina the daughter of Toscar.

A TALE of the times of old! The deeds of days of other years!

The murmur of thy streams, O Lora! brings back the memory of the past. The sound of thy woods, Garmallar, is lovely in mine ear. Dost thou not behold, Malvina, a rock with its head of heath? Three aged pines bend from its face; green is the narrow plain at its feet; there the flower of the mountain grows, and shakes its white head in the breeze. The thistle is there alone, shedding its aged beard. Two stones, half sunk in the ground, shew their heads of moss. The deer of the mountain avoids the place, for he beholds a dim ghost standing there. The mighty lie, O Malvina! in the narrow plain of the rock.

A tale of the times of old! the deeds of days of other years!

Who comes from the land of strangers, with his thousands around him? the sunbeam pours its bright stream before him; his hair meets the wind of his hills. His face is settled from war. He is calm as the evening beam that looks from the cloud of the west, on Cona's silent vale. Who is it but Comhal's son, the king of mighty deeds! He beholds his hills with joy, he bids a thousand voices rise. 'Ye have fled over your fields, ye sons of the distant land! The king of the world sits in his hall, and hears of his people's flight. He lifts his red eye of pride; he takes his father's sword. Ye have fled over your fields, sons of the distant land!'

Such were the words of the bards, when they came to Selma's halls. A thousand lights from the stranger's land rose in the midst of the people. The feast is spread around; the night passed away in joy. 'Where is the noble Clessámmor?' said the fair-haired Fingal. 'Where is the brother of Morna, in the hour of my joy? Sullen and dark he passes his days in the vale of echoing Lora: but, behold, he comes from the hill, like a steed in his strength, who finds his companions in the breeze, and tosses his bright mane in the wind. Blest be the soul of Clessámmor, why so long from Selma?'

'Returns the chief,' said Clessámmor, 'in the midst of his fame? Such was the renown of Comhal in the battles of his youth. Often did we pass over Carun to the land of the strangers: our swords returned, not unstained with blood: nor did the kings of the world rejoice. Why do I remember the times of our war? My hair is mixed with grey. My hand forgets to bend the bow: I lift a lighter spear. O that my joy would return, as when I first beheld the maid; the white-bosomed daughter of the strangers, Moina, with the dark-blue eyes!'

'Tell,' said the mighty Fingal, 'the tale of thy youthful days. Sorrow, like a cloud on the sun, shades the soul of Clessámmor. Mournful are thy thoughts, alone, on the banks of the roaring Lora. Let us hear the sorrow of thy youth, and the darkness of thy days!'

'It was in the days of peace,' replied the great Clessámmor, 'I came in my bounding ship, to Balclutha's walls of towers. The winds had roared behind my sails, and Clutha's streams received my dark-bosomed ship. Three days I remained in Reuthámir's halls, and saw his daughter, that beam of light. The joy of the shell went round, and the aged hero gave the fair. Her breasts were like foam on the wave, and her eyes like stars of light: her hair was dark as the raven's wing: her soul was generous and mild. My love for Moina was great: my heart poured forth in joy.

'The son of a stranger came; a chief who loved the white-bosomed Moina. His words were mighty in the hall; he often half-unsheathed his sword. "Where," said he, "is the mighty Comhal, the restless wanderer of the heath? Comes he, with his host, to Balclutha, since Clessámmor is so bold?" "My soul," I replied, "O warrior! burns in a light of its own. I stand without fear in the midst of thousands, though the valiant are distant far. Stranger! thy words are mighty, for Clessámmor is alone. But my sword trembles by my side, and longs to glitter in my hand. Speak no more of Comhal, son of the winding Clutha!"

'The strength of his pride arose. We fought; he

fell beneath my sword. The banks of Clutha heard his fall; a thousand spears glittered around. I fought: the strangers prevailed: I plunged into the stream of Clutha. My white sails rose over the waves, and I bounded on the dark-blue sea. Moina came to the shore, and rolled the red eye of her tears: her loose hair flew on the wind; and I heard her mournful, distant cries. Often did I turn my ship; but the winds of the East prevailed. Nor Clutha ever since have I seen, nor Moina of the dark-brown hair. She fell in Balclutha, for I have seen her ghost. I knew her as she came through the dusky night, along the murmur of Lora: she was like the new moon, seen through the gathered mist: when the sky pours down its flaky snow, and the world is silent and dark.'

'Raise, ye bards,' said the mighty Fingal, 'the praise of unhappy Moina. Call her ghost, with your songs, to our hills, that she may rest with the fair of Morven, the sunbeams of other days, the delight of heroes of old. I have seen the walls of Balclutha, but they were desolate. The fire had resounded in the halls: and the voice of the people is heard no more. The stream of Clutha was removed from its place, by the fall of the walls. The thistle shook there its lonely head: the moss whistled to the wind. The fox looked out from the windows, the rank grass of the wall waved round its head. Desolate is the dwelling of Moina, silence is in the house of her fathers. Raise the song of mourning, O bards! over the land of strangers. They have but fallen before us: for one day we must fall. Why dost thou build the hall, son of the winged days? Thou lookest from thy towers today; yet a few years, and the blast of the desert comes; it howls in thy empty court, and whistles round thy half-worn shield. And let the blast of the desert come! we shall be renowned in our day! The mark of my arm shall be in battle; my name in the song of bards. Raise the song; send round the shell: let joy be heard in my hall. When thou, sun of heaven, shalt fail! if thou shalt fail, thou mighty light! if thy brightness is for a season, like Fingal, our fame shall survive thy beams!'

Such was the song of Fingal, in the day of his joy. His thousand bards leaned forward from their seats, to hear the voice of the king. It was like the music of harps on the gale of the spring. Lovely were thy thoughts, O Fingal! why had not Ossian the strength of thy soul? But thou standest alone, my father! who can equal the king of Selma?

The night passed away in song; morning returned in joy. The mountains shewed their grey heads; the blue face of ocean smiled. The white wave is seen tumbling round the distant rock; a mist rose, slowly, from the lake. It came in the figure of an aged man along the silent plain. Its large limbs did not move in steps; for a ghost supported it in mid-air. It came towards Selma's hall, and dissolved in a shower of blood.

The king alone beheld the sight; he foresaw the death of the people. He came in silence to his hall; and took his father's spear. The mail rattled on his breast. The heroes rose around. They looked in silence on each other, marking the eyes of Fingal. They saw battle in his face: the death of armies on his spear. A thousand shields at once are placed on their arms; they drew a thousand swords. The hall of Selma brightened around. The clang of arms ascends. The grey dogs howl in their place. No word is among the mighty chiefs. Each marked the eyes of the king; and half-assumed his spear.

'Sons of Morven,' begun the king, 'this is no time to fill the shell. The battle darkens near us; death hovers over the land. Some ghost, the friend of Fingal, has forewarned us of the foe. The sons of the stranger come from the darkly-rolling sea. For, from the water, came the sign of Morven's gloomy danger. Let each assume his heavy spear, each gird on his father's sword. Let the dark helmet rise on every head; the mail pour its lightning from every side. The battle gathers like a storm; soon shall ye hear the roar of death.'

The hero moved on before his host, like a cloud before a ridge of green fire, when it pours on the sky of night, and mariners foresee a storm. On Cona's rising heath they stood: the white-bosomed maids beheld them above like a grove; they foresaw the death of the youth, and looked towards the sea with fear. The white wave deceived them for distant sails; the tear is on their cheek! The sun rose on the sea, and we beheld a distant fleet. Like the mist of ocean they came, and poured their youth upon the coast. The chief was among them, like the stag in the midst of the herd. His shield is studded with gold; stately strode the king of spears. He moved towards Selma; his thousands moved behind.

'Go, with a song of peace,' said Fingal; 'go, Ullin, to the king of swords. Tell him that we are mighty in war; that the ghosts of our foes are many. But renowned are they who have feasted in my halls; they show the arms of my fathers in a foreign land: the sons of the strangers wonder, and bless the friends of Morven's race; for our names have been heard afar: the kings of the world shook in the midst of their host.'

Ullin went with his song. Fingal rested on his spear: he saw the mighty foe in his armour: he blest the stranger's son. 'How stately art thou, son of the sea!' said the king of woody Morven. 'Thy sword is a beam of fire by thy side: thy spear is a pine that defies the storm. The varied face of the moon is not broader than thy shield. Ruddy is thy face of youth! soft the ringlets of thy hair! But this tree may fall; and his memory be forgot! The daughter of the stranger will be sad, looking to the rolling sea: the children will say, "We see a ship; perhaps it is the king of Balclutha." The tear starts from their mother's eye. Her thoughts are of him who sleeps in Morven!'

Such were the words of the king, when Ullin came to the mighty Carthon; he threw down the spear before him; he raised the song of peace. 'Come to the feast of Fingal, Carthon, from the rolling sea! partake of the feast of the king, or lift the spear of war! The ghosts of our foes are many: but renowned are the friends of Morven! Behold that field, O Carthon! many a green hill rises there, with mossy stones and rustling grass: these are the tombs of Fingal's foes, the sons of the rolling sea!'

'Dost thou speak to the weak in arms!' said Carthon, 'bard of the woody Morven? Is my face pale for fear, son of the peaceful song? Why, then, dost thou think to darken my soul with the tales of those who fell? My arm has fought in battle; my renown is known afar. Go to the feeble in arms, bid them yield to Fingal. Have not I seen the fallen Balclutha? And shall I feast with Comhal's son? Comhal, who threw his fire in the midst of my father's hall? I was young, and knew not the cause, why the virgins wept. The columns of smoke pleased mine eye, when they rose above my walls! I often looked back with gladness when my friends fled along the hill. But when the years of my youth came on, I beheld the moss of my fallen walls. My sigh arose with the morning, and my tears descended with night. "Shall I not fight," I said to my soul, "against the children of my foes?" And I will fight, O bard! I feel the strength of my soul.'

His people gathered round the hero, and drew at once their shining swords. He stands in the midst, like a pillar of fire, the tear half-starting from his eye; for he thought of the fallen Balclutha. The crowded pride of his soul arose. Sidelong he looked up to the hill, where our heroes shone in arms; the spear trembled in his hand. Bending forward, he seemed to threaten the king.

'Shall I,' said Fingal to his soul, 'meet, at once, the youth? Shall I stop him, in the midst of his course, before his fame shall arise? But the bard, hereafter, may say, when he sees the tomb of Carthon, Fingal took his thousands to battle, before the noble Carthon fell. No: bard of the times to come! thou shalt not lessen Fingal's fame. My heroes will fight the youth, and Fingal behold the war. If he overcomes, I rush, in my strength, like the roaring stream of Cona. Who, of my chiefs, will meet the son of the rolling sea? Many are his warriors on the coast, and strong is his ashen spear!'

Cathul rose, in his strength, the son of the mighty Lormar: three hundred youths attend the chief, the race of his native streams. Feeble was his arm against Carthon: he fell, and his heroes fled. Connal resumed the battle, but he broke his heavy spear: he lay bound on the field: Carthon pursued his people.

'Clessámmor!' said the king of Morven, 'where is the spear of thy strength? Wilt thou behold Connal bound; thy friend, at the stream of Lora? Rise, in the light of thy steel, companion of valiant Comhal! Let the youth of Balclutha feel the strength of Morven's race.' He rose in the strength of his steel, shaking his grizzly locks. He fitted the shield to his side; he rushed, in the pride of valour.

Carthon stood on a rock; he saw the hero rushing on. He loved the dreadful joy of his face: his strength, in the locks of age! 'Shall I lift that spear,' he said, 'that never strikes, but once, a foe? Or shall I with the words of peace, preserve the warrior's life? Stately are his steps of age! lovely the remnant of his years! Perhaps it is the husband of Moina; the father of car-borne Carthon. Often have I heard that he dwelt at the echoing stream of Lora.'

Such were his words, when Clessámmor came, and lifted high his spear. The youth received it on his shield, and spoke the words of peace. 'Warrior of the aged locks! Is there no youth to lift the spear? Hast thou no son to raise the shield before his father to meet the arm of youth? Is the spouse of thy love no more? or weeps she over the tombs of thy sons? Art thou of the kings of men? What will be the fame of my sword should'st thou fall?'

'It will be great, thou son of pride!' begun the tall Clessámmor. 'I have been renowned in battle; but I never told my name to a foe. Yield to me, son of the wave, then shalt thou know, that the mark of my sword is in many a field.'

'I never yielded, king of spears!' replied the noble pride of Carthon: 'I have also fought in war; I behold my future fame. Despise me not, thou chief of men! my arm, my spear is strong.

Retire among thy friends; let younger heroes fight.'

'Why dost thou wound my soul?' replied Clessámmor, with a tear. 'Age does not tremble on my hand; I still can lift the sword. Shall I fly in Fingal's sight: in the sight of him I love? Son of the sea! I never fled: exalt thy pointed spear.'

They fought like two contending winds, that strive to roll the wave. Carthon bade his spear to err; he still thought that the foe was the spouse of Moina. He broke Clessámmor's beamy spear in twain: he seized his shining sword. But as Carthon was binding the chief, the chief drew the dagger of his fathers. He saw the foe's uncovered side, and opened there a wound.

Fingal saw Clessámmor low: he moved in the sound of his steel. The host stood silent in his presence; they turned their eyes to the king. He came like the sullen noise of a storm before the winds arise: the hunter hears it in the vale, and retires to the cave of the rock. Carthon stood in his place: the blood is rushing down his side: he saw the coming down of the king; his hopes of fame arose; but pale was his cheek: his hair flew loose, his helmet shook on high: the force of Carthon failed; but his soul was strong.

Fingal beheld the hero's blood; he stopt the uplifted spear. 'Yield, king of swords!' said Comhal's son; 'I behold thy blood. Thou hast been mighty in battle, and thy fame shall never fade.'

'Art thou the king so far renowned?' replied the car-borne Carthon. 'Art thou that light of death, that frightens the kings of the world? But why should Carthon ask? for he is like the stream of his hills, strong as a river in his course, swift as the eagle of heaven. O that I had fought with the king, that my fame might be great in song! that the hunter, beholding my tomb, might say he fought with the mighty Fingal. But Carthon dies unknown; he has poured out his force on the weak.'

'But thou shalt not die unknown,' replied the king of woody Morven: 'my bards are many, O Carthon! Their songs descend to future times. The children of years to come shall hear the fame of Carthon, when they sit round the burning oak, and the night is spent in songs of old. The hunter, sitting in the heath, shall hear the rustling blast, and, raising his eyes, behold the rock where Carthon fell. He shall turn to his son, and shew the place where the mighty fought; "There the king of Balclutha fought, like the strength of a thousand streams."'

Joy rose in Carthon's face: he lifted his heavy eyes. He gave his sword to Fingal, to lie within his hall, that the memory of Balclutha's king might remain in Morven. The battle ceased along the field, the bard had sung the song of peace. The chiefs gathered round the falling Carthon; they heard his words with sighs. Silent they leaned on their spears, while Balclutha's hero spoke. His hair sighed in the wind, and his voice was sad and low.

'King of Morven,' Carthon said, 'I fall in the midst of my course. A foreign tomb receives, in youth, the last of Reuthámir's race. Darkness dwells in Balclutha: the shadows of grief in Crathmo. But raise my remembrance on the banks of Lora, where my fathers dwelt. Perhaps the husband of Moina will mourn over his fallen Carthon.' His words reached the heart of Clessámmor: he fell in silence on his son. The host stood darkened around: no voice is on the plain. Night came: the moon, from the east, looked on the mournful field; but still they stood, like a silent grove that lifts its head on Gormal, when the loud winds are laid, and dark autumn is on the plain.

Three days they mourned above Carthon; on the fourth his father died. In the narrow plain of the rock they lie; a dim ghost defends their tomb. There lovely Moina is often seen, when the sunbeam darts on the rock, and all around is dark. There she is seen, Malvina! but not like the daughters of the hill. Her robes are from the stranger's land; and she is still alone!

Fingal was sad for Carthon; he commanded his bards to mark the day when shadowy autumn returned. And often did they mark the day, and sing the hero's praise. 'Who comes so dark from ocean's roar, like autumn's shadowy cloud? Death is trembling in his hand! his eyes are flames of fire! Who roars along dark Lora's heath? Who but Carthon, king of swords! The people fall! see how he strides, like the sullen ghost of Morven! But there he lies, a goodly oak which sudden blasts overturned! When shalt thou rise, Balclutha's joy? When, Carthon, shalt thou arise? Who comes so dark from ocean's roar, like autumn's shadowy cloud?' Such were the words of the bards, in the day of their mourning: Ossian often joined their voice, and added to their song. My soul has been mournful for Carthon; he fell in the days of his youth: and thou, O Clessámmor! where is thy dwelling in the wind? Has the youth forgot his wound? Flies he, on clouds, with thee? I feel the sun, O Malvina! leave me to my rest. Perhaps they may come to my dreams; I think I hear a feeble voice! The beam of heaven delights to shine on the grave of Carthon: I feel it warm around!

O thou that rollest above, round as the shield of my fathers! Whence are thy beams, O sun! thy everlasting light? Thou comest forth, in thy awful beauty; the stars hide themselves in the sky; the moon, cold and pale, sinks in the western wave; but thou thyself movest alone. Who can be a companion of thy course? The oaks of the mountains fall: the mountains themselves decay with years; the ocean shrinks and grows again: the moon herself is lost in heaven; but thou art for ever the same, rejoicing in the brightness of thy course. When the world is dark with tempests, when thunder rolls and lightning flies, thou lookest in thy beauty from the clouds, and laughest at the storm.

But to Ossian, thou lookest in vain; for he beholds thy beams no more; whether thy yellow hair flows on the eastern clouds, or thou tremblest at the gates of the west. But thou art, perhaps, like me, for a season; thy years will have an end. Thou shalt sleep in thy clouds, careless of the voice of the morning. Exult then, O sun, in the strength of thy youth! Age is dark and unlovely; it is like the glimmering light of the moon, when it shines through broken clouds, and the mist is on the hills; the blast of the north is on the plain; the traveller shrinks in the midst of his journey.

1760

1717 · HORACE WALPOLE · 1797

1717   Born in London, fourth son of Sir Robert Walpole, the great prime minister. Educated at Eton, where he formed a friendship with Thomas Gray, and at King's College, Cambridge. Obtained political sinecures through his father's influence which assured him of a comfortable income for life.

1739–41   Traveled in France and Italy with Gray, making long stays at Florence and Rome.

1747   Settled at Strawberry Hill, Twickenham, which he made into 'a little Gothic castle,' and where he collected various art-objects, relics, books, and manuscripts and gardened in the English manner on his fourteen acres.

1757   Set up a private printing press at Strawberry Hill, the first production being Gray's *Odes.*

1758   Published *Catalogue of Royal and Noble Authors,*

1762–80   *Anecdotes of Painting in England,* and

1764   *The Castle of Otranto.*

1765   To Paris, where he made the first of five visits with Madame du Deffand, celebrated and witty Frenchwoman.

1768   Privately printed *The Mysterious Mother,* a tragedy of incest.

1791   Succeeded to the family title as Earl of Orford.

1797   Died in London.

B Y THE MID-EIGHTEENTH CENTURY, fiction writers were abandoning analysis and ridicule, and were returning to magic, mystery, and chivalry. Smollett initiated the change in *Ferdinand Count Fathom* (1753) by effectively combining the use of superstition with violence and crime to awaken in his readers the emotions of pleasing horror and wonder. Critical encouragement for the school of terror was given by Burke's *Ideas of the Sublime and Beautiful* (1757) and for the revival of Gothic manners by Bishop Hurd's *Letters on Chivalry and Romance* (1762). It remained for Horace Walpole, man of fashion, politician, and amateur antiquary, to give to the narrative of violent emotions a Gothic habitation and a name. The new romance was in part an outgrowth of the architectural zeal of Englishmen, who, when the bonds of classicism began to break, were drawn to the study of ruins and monuments of the Middle Ages. Walpole, always a great collector and lover of the antique, pioneered in this activity. He transformed his villa at Strawberry Hill into a miniature Gothic castle. For a generation this architectural wonder excited great interest and attracted many visitors. By its example it served as a primary impulse in the revival of the Gothic mode in art, if indeed it did not give, via its creator's novel, the romantic movement in literature its greatest impetus. The actual creation of Walpole's *The Castle of Otranto* appears to have been an accidental sport. By Walpole's own account it originated in a dream. We may suppose that this lonely, fastidious bachelor, surrounded in his absurd Gothic castle by a heterogeneous collection of antique treasures, habitually escaped from the anxieties of ill health into a fantastical, medieval dream world. In any case, out of that strange world he created the romance that not inappropriately has been described as 'a dilettante's nightmare.' The setting, though assigned by Walpole to Italy of the twelfth and thirteenth centuries, has no definite historical background; the events are a sequence of sorrow, violence, and bewilderment; the characters are the wildest absurdities. Only the castle, which is none other than Strawberry Hill, has any substantial reality. But the castle and its trappings sufficed to carry the day. To Walpole's contemporaries the story was bold and amazing. Its thrills of emotion set in remote and mysterious times were a heady elixir for an age wearying of the chaste proportions of Palladian buildings and the narrow confines of neo-classical emotions. *The Castle of Otranto* quickly became a landmark in literary taste. After *Otranto* the medieval scene with its haunted castle—with cloister, black towers, long dark stairways, airy chambers, trap doors, and subterraneous passages—became the accepted locale for the sentimental novel of adventure. Walpole's romance thus became the acknowledged prototype of that class of novel afterward imitated by Clara Reeve (*The Old English Baron,* 1777), by Mrs. Ann Radcliffe (*The Mysteries of Udolpho,* 1794), and worked out in terms of genius by Sir Walter Scott.

From THE CASTLE OF OTRANTO
A GOTHIC STORY

PREFACE TO THE SECOND EDITION

The favourable manner in which this little piece has been received by the public, calls upon the author to explain the grounds on which he composed it. . . .

It was an attempt to blend the two kinds of romance —the ancient and the modern. In the former, all was imagination and improbability; in the latter, nature is always intended to be, and sometimes has been, copied with success. Invention has not been wanting; but the great resources of fancy have been dammed up, by a strict adherence to common life. But if, in the latter species, nature has cramped imagination, she did but take her revenge, having been totally excluded from old romances. The actions, sentiments, conversations, of the heroes and heroines of ancient days, were as unnatural as the machines employed to put them in motion.

The author of the following pages thought it possible to reconcile the two kinds. Desirous of leaving the powers of fancy at liberty to expatiate through the boundless realms of invention, and thence of creating more interesting situations, he wished to conduct the mortal agents in his drama according to the rules of probability; in short, to make them think, speak, and act as it might be supposed mere men and women would do in extraordinary positions. He had observed that, in all inspired writings, the personages under the dispensation of miracles, and witnesses to the most stupendous phenomena, never lose sight of their human character; whereas, in the production of romantic story, an improbable event never fails to be attended by an absurd dialogue. The actors seem to lose their senses, the moment the laws of nature have lost their tone. As the public have applauded the attempt, the author must not say he was entirely unequal to the task he had undertaken; yet if the new route he has struck out shall have paved a road for men of brighter talents, he shall own, with pleasure and modesty, that he was sensible the plan was capable of receiving greater embellishments than his imagination or conduct of the passions could bestow on it. . . .

CHAPTER I

MANFRED, Prince of Otranto, had one son and one daughter. The latter, a most beautiful virgin aged eighteen, was called Matilda. Conrad, the son, was three years younger, a homely youth, sickly, and of no promising disposition; yet he was the darling of his father, who never showed any symptoms of affection to Matilda. Manfred had contracted a marriage for his son with the Marquis of Vicenza's daugher, Isabella; and she had already been delivered by her guardians into the hands of Manfred that he might celebrate the wedding as soon as Conrad's infirm state of health would permit. Manfred's impatience for this ceremonial was remarked by his family and neighbours. The former indeed, apprehending the severity of their Prince's disposition, did not dare to utter their surmises on this precipitation. Hippolita, his wife, an amiable lady, did sometimes venture to represent the danger of marrying their only son so early, considering his great youth and greater infirmities; but she never received any other answer than reflections on her own sterility, who had given him but one heir. His tenants and subjects were less cautious in their discourses. They attributed this hasty wedding to the Prince's dread of seeing accomplished an ancient prophecy, which was said to have pronounced that *the Castle and Lordship of Otranto should pass from the present family whenever the real owner should be grown too large to inhabit it.* It was difficult to make any sense of this prophecy; and still less easy to conceive what it had to do with the marriage in question. Yet these mysteries or contradictions did not make the populace adhere the less to their opinion.

Young Conrad's birthday was fixed for his espousals. The company was assembled in the chapel of the castle, and everything ready for beginning the divine office, when Conrad himself was missing. Manfred, impatient of the least delay, and who had not observed his son retire, despatched one of his attendants to summon the young prince. The servant, who had not staid long enough to have crossed the court to Conrad's apartment, came running back breathless, in a frantic manner, his eyes staring, and foaming at the mouth. He said nothing, but pointed to the court. The company were struck with terror and amazement. The Princess Hippolita, without knowing what was the matter, but anxious for her son, swooned away. Manfred, less apprehensive than enraged at the procrastination of the nuptials, and at the folly of his domestic, asked imperiously what was the matter. The fellow made no answer, but continued pointing towards the court-yard; and at last, after repeated questions put to him, cried out,—

'Oh! the helmet! the helmet!'

In the meantime, some of the company had run into the court, from whence was heard a confused noise of shrieks, horror, and surprise. Manfred, who began to be alarmed at not seeing his son, went himself to get information of what occasioned this strange confusion. Matilda remained endeavouring to assist her mother, and Isabella staid for the same purpose and to avoid showing any impatience for the bridegroom, for whom, in truth, she had conceived little affection.

The first thing that struck Manfred's eyes was a group of his servants endeavouring to raise something that appeared to him a mountain of sable plumes. He gazed without believing his sight. 'What are ye doing?' cried Manfred, wrathfully. 'Where is my son?'

A volley of voices replied, 'Oh! my lord! the prince! the prince! the helmet, the helmet!'

Shocked with these lamentable sounds, and dreading he knew not what, he advanced hastily, but with a sight for a father's eyes! He beheld his child dashed to pieces and almost buried under an enormous helmet, an hundred times more large than any casque ever made for human being, and shaded with a proportionable quantity of black feathers.

The horror of the spectacle, the ignorance of all around how this misfortune had happened, and above all, the tremendous phenomenon before him, took away the Prince's speech. Yet his silence lasted longer than even grief could occasion. He fixed his eyes on what he wished in vain to believe a vision; and seemed less attentive to his loss than buried in meditation on the stupendous object that had occasioned it. He touched, he examined the fatal casque; nor could even the bleeding mangled remains of the young Prince divert the eyes of Manfred from the portent before him. All who had known his partial fondness for young Conrad were as much surprised at their Prince's insensibility, as thunder-struck themselves at the miracle of the helmet. They conveyed the disfigured corpse into the hall, without receiving the least direction from Manfred. As little was he attentive to the ladies who remained in the chapel. On the contrary, without mentioning the unhappy princesses, his wife and daughter, the first sounds that dropped from Manfred's lips were, 'Take care of the Lady Isabella.'

The domestics, without observing the singularity of this direction, were guided by their affection to their mistress to consider it as peculiarly addressed to her situation, and flew to her assistance. They conveyed her to her chamber more dead than alive, and indifferent to all the strange circumstances she heard except the death of her son. Matilda, who doted on her mother, smothered her own grief and amazement, and thought of nothing but assisting and comforting her afflicted parents. Isabella, who had been treated by Hippolita like a daughter, and who returned that tenderness with equal duty and affection, was scarce less assiduous about the Princess, at the same time endeavouring to partake and lessen the weight of sorrow which she saw Matilda strove to suppress, for whom she had conceived the warmest sympathy of friendship. Yet her own situation could not help finding its place in her thoughts. She felt no concern for the death of young Conrad, except commiseration; and she was not sorry to be delivered from a marriage which had promised her little felicity, either from her destined bridegroom or from the severe temper of Manfred, who, though he had distinguished her by great indulgence, had imprinted her mind with terror, from his causeless rigour to such amiable princesses as Hippolita and Matilda.

While the ladies were conveying the wretched mother to her bed, Manfred remained in the court, gazing on the ominous casque, and regardless of the crowd which the strangeness of the event had now assembled around him. The few words he articulated tended solely to enquiries whether any man knew from whence it could have come. Nobody could give him the least information. However, as it seemed to be the sole object of his curiosity, it soon became so to the rest of the spectators, whose conjectures were as absurd and improbable as the catastrophe itself was unprecedented. In the midst of their senseless guesses, a young peasant, whom rumour had drawn thither from a neighbouring village, observed that the miraculous helmet was exactly like that on the figure in black marble of Alfonso the Good, one of their former princes in the church of St. Nicholas.

'Villain! What sayest thou?' cried Manfred, starting from his trance in a tempest of rage, and seizing the young man by the collar. 'How darest thou utter such treason? Thy life shall pay for it.'

The spectators, who as little comprehended the cause of the Prince's fury as all the rest they had seen, were at a loss to unravel this new circumstance. The young peasant himself was still more astonished, not conceiving how he had offended the Prince; yet recollecting himself, with a mixture of grace and humility, he disengaged himself from Manfred's grip, and then with an obeisance which discovered more jealousy of innocence than dismay, he asked, with respect, of what he was guilty. Manfred, more enraged at the vigour, however decently exerted, with which the young man had shaken off his hold, than appeased by his submission, ordered his attendants to seize him, and if he had not been withheld by his friends, whom he had invited to the nuptials, would have poignarded the peasant in their arms.

During this altercation, some of the vulgar spectators had run to the great church, which stood near the castle, and came back open-mouthed, declaring that the helmet was missing from Alfonso's statue. Manfred, at this news, grew perfectly frantic; and, as if he sought a subject on which to vent the tempest within him, he rushed again on the young peasant crying, 'Villain! Monster! Sorcerer! 'Tis thou has done this! 'Tis thou hast slain my son!'

The mob, who wanted some object within the scope of their capacities on whom they might discharge their bewildered reasonings, caught the words from the mouth of their lord and reëchoed, 'Ay, ay; 'tis he; 'tis he; he has stolen the helmet from good Alfonso's tomb and dashed out the brains of our young Prince with it,' never reflecting how enormous the disproportion was between the marble helmet that had been in the church and that of steel before their eyes, nor how impossible it was for a youth, seemingly not twenty, to wield a piece of armour of so prodigious a weight.

The folly of these ejaculations brought Manfred to himself. Yet whether provoked at the peasant having observed the resemblance between the two helmets, and thereby led to the farther discovery of the absence of that in the church, or wishing to bury any fresh rumour under so impertinent a supposition, he gravely pronounced that the young man was certainly a necromancer, and that till the church could take cognisance of the affair, he would have the magician, whom they had thus detected, kept prisoner under the helmet itself, which he ordered his attendants to raise and place the young man under it, declaring he should be kept there without food, with which his own infernal art might furnish him.

It was in vain for the youth to represent against this preposterous sentence. In vain did Manfred's friends endeavour to divert him from this savage and ill-grounded resolution. The generality were charmed with their lord's decision, which, to their apprehensions, carried great appearance of justice, as the magician was to be punished by the very instrument with which he had offended. Nor were they struck with the least compunction at the probability of the youth being starved, for they firmly believed that by his diabolic skill he could easily supply himself with nutriment.

Manfred thus saw his commands even cheerfully obeyed; and appointing a guard with strict orders to prevent any food being conveyed to the prisoner, he dismissed his friends and attendants, and retired to his own chamber after locking the gates of the castle, in which he suffered none but his domestics to remain. . . .

As it was now evening, the servant who conducted Isabella bore a torch before her. When they came to Manfred, who was walking impatiently about the gallery, he started and said hastily: 'Take away that light, and begone!' Then shutting the door impetuously, he flung himself upon a bench against the wall, and bade Isabella sit by him. She obeyed trembling.

'I sent for you, lady,' said he, and then stopped under great appearance of confusion.

'My lord!'

'Yes, I sent for you on a matter of great moment,' resumed he. 'Dry your tears, young lady. You have lost your bridegroom. Yes, cruel fate! and I have lost the hopes of my race! But Conrad was not worthy of your beauty.'

'How! my lord,' said Isabella. 'Sure you do not suspect me of not feeling the concern I ought! My duty and affection would have always—'

'Think no more of him,' interrupted Manfred; 'he was a sickly puny child; and Heaven has perhaps taken him away that I might not trust the honours of my house on so frail a foundation.

The line of Manfred calls for numerous supports. My foolish fondness for that boy blinded the eyes of my prudence; but it is better as it is. I hope in a few years to have reason to rejoice at the death of Conrad.'

Words cannot paint the astonishment of Isabella. At first, she apprehended that grief had disordered Manfred's understanding. Her next thought suggested that this strange discourse was designed to ensnare her. She feared that Manfred had perceived her indifference for his son; and in consequence of that idea she replied,—

'Good my lord, do not doubt my tenderness. My heart would have accompanied my hand. Conrad would have engrossed all my care; and wherever fate shall dispose of me, I shall always cherish his memory, and regard your highness and the virtuous Hippolita as my parents.'

'Curse on Hippolita!' cried Manfred. 'Forget her from this moment, as I do. In short, lady, you have missed a husband undeserving of your charms. They shall now be better disposed of. Instead of a sickly boy, you shall have a husband in the prime of his age, who will know how to value your beauties, and who may expect a numerous offspring.'

'Alas! my lord,' said Isabella; 'my mind is too sadly engrossed by the recent catastrophe in your family to think of another marriage. If ever my father returns, and it shall be his pleasure, I shall obey, as I did when I consented to give my hand to your son. But until his return, permit me to remain under your hospitable roof, and employ the melancholy hours in assuaging yours, Hippolita's and the fair Matilda's affliction.'

'I desired you once before,' said Manfred, angrily, 'not to name that woman. From this hour she must be a stranger to you as she must be to me. In short, Isabella, since I cannot give you my son, I offer you myself.'

'Heavens!' cried Isabella, waking from her delusion; 'what do I hear? You! my lord! you! my father-in-law! the father of Conrad! the husband of the virtuous Hippolita!'

'I tell you,' said Manfred, imperiously, 'Hippolita is no longer my wife; I divorce her from this hour. Too long has she cursed me by her unfruitfulness. My fate depends on having sons; and this night I trust will give a new date to my hopes.'

At those words he seized the cold hand of Isabella, who was half dead with fright and horror. She shrieked and started from him. Manfred rose to pursue her, when the moon, which was now up and gleamed in at the opposite casement, presented to his sight the plumes of the fatal helmet, which rose to the height of the windows, waving backwards and forwards, in a tempestuous manner, and accompanied with a hollow and rustling sound. Isabella, who gathered courage from her situation, and who dreaded nothing so much as Manfred's pursuit of his declaration, cried,—

'Look! my lord. See! Heaven itself declares against your impious intentions.'

'Heaven nor hell shall impede my designs,' said Manfred, advancing again to seize the Princess. At that instant the portrait of his grandfather, which hung over the bench where they had been sitting, uttered a deep sigh and heaved its breast. Isabella, whose back was turned to the picture, saw not the motion, nor knew whence the sound came, but started, and said: 'Hark! my lord! What sound was that?' and at the same time made towards the door. Manfred, distracted between the flight of Isabella, who had now reached the stairs, and yet unable to keep his eyes from the picture, which began to move, had, however, advanced some steps after her, still looking backwards on the portrait, when he saw it quit its panel and descend on the floor with a grave and melancholy air.

'Do I dream?' cried Manfred, returning; 'or are the devils themselves in league against me? Speak, infernal spectre! Or, if thou art my grandsire, why dost thou too conspire against thy wretched descendant, who too dearly pays for—' Ere he could finish the sentence, the vision sighed again, and made a sign to Manfred to follow him.

'Lead on!' cried Manfred; 'I will follow thee to the gulf of perdition.' The spectre marched sedately, but dejected, to the end of the gallery and turned into a chamber on the right hand. Manfred accompanied him at a little distance, full of anxiety and horror, but resolved. As he would have entered the chamber, the door was clapped to with violence by an invisible hand. The Prince, collecting courage from this delay, would have forcibly burst open the door with his foot, but found that it resisted his utmost efforts.

'Since hell will not satisfy my curiosity,' said Manfred, 'I will use the human means in my power for preserving my race; Isabella shall not escape me.' . . .

Words cannot paint the horror of the Princess's situation. Alone in so dismal a place, her mind impressed with all the terrible events of the day, hopeless of escaping, expecting every moment the arrival of Manfred, and far from tranquil on knowing she was within reach of somebody, she knew not whom, who for some cause seemed concealed thereabouts,—all these thoughts crowded on her distracted mind, and she was ready to sink under her apprehensions. She addressed herself to every saint in heaven, and inwardly implored their assistance. For a considerable time she remained in an agony of despair. At last, as softly as was possible, she felt for the door, and having found it, entered trembling into the vault from whence she had heard the sigh and steps. It gave her a kind of momentary joy to perceive an imperfect ray of clouded moonshine gleam from the roof of the vault, which seemed to be fallen in, and from whence hung a fragment of earth or building, she could not distinguish which, that appeared to have been crushed inwards. She advanced eagerly towards this chasm, when she discerned a human form standing close against the wall.

She shrieked, believing it the ghost of her betrothed Conrad. The figure advancing said in a submissive voice: 'Be not alarmed, lady; I will not injure you.'

Isabella, a little encouraged by the words and tone of voice of the stranger, and recollecting that this must be the person who had opened the door, recovered her spirits enough to reply: 'Sir, whoever you are, take pity on a wretched princess standing on the brink of destruction. Assist me to escape from this fatal castle, or in a few moments I may be made miserable forever.'

'Alas!' said the stranger, 'what can I do to assist you? I will die in your defense; but I am unacquainted with the castle, and want—'

'Oh!' said Isabella, hastily interrupting him, 'help me but to find a trap-door that must be hereabout, and it is the greatest service you can do me, for I have not a minute to lose.' Saying these words, she felt about on the pavement, and directed the stranger to search likewise for a smooth piece of brass inclosed in one of the stones. 'That,' said she, 'is the lock, which opens with a spring, of which I know the secret. If we can find that, I may escape; if not, alas! courteous stranger, I fear I shall have involved you in my misfortunes. Manfred will suspect you for the accomplice of my flight, and you will fall a victim to his resentment.'

'I value not my life,' said the stranger; 'and it will be some comfort to lose it in trying to deliver you from his tyranny.'

'Generous youth,' said Isabella, 'how shall I ever requite—'

As she uttered those words, a ray of moonshine streaming through a cranny of the ruin above shone directly on the lock they sought.— 'Oh! transport!' said Isabella, 'here is the trap-door!' And taking out a key, she touched the spring, which starting aside discovered an iron ring. 'Lift up the door,' said the Princess. The stranger obeyed; and beneath appeared some stone steps descending into a vault totally dark. 'We must go down here,' said Isabella. 'Follow me. Dark and dismal as it is, we cannot miss our way; it leads directly to the church of St. Nicholas. But perhaps,' added the Princess, modestly, 'you have no reason to leave the castle; nor have I farther occasion for your service. In few minutes I shall be safe from Manfred's rage. Only let me know to whom I am so much obliged.'

'I will never quit you,' said the stranger eagerly, 'until I have placed you in safety. Nor think me, Princess, more generous than I am. Though you are my principal care—'

The stranger was interrupted by a sudden noise of voices that seemed approaching, and they soon distinguished these words: 'Talk not to me of necromancers. I tell you she must be in the castle. I will find her in spite of enchantment.'

'Oh, heavens!' cried Isabella, 'it is the voice of Manfred! Make haste or we are ruined! And shut the trap-door after you.' Saying this, she descended the steps precipitately, and as the stranger hastened to follow her he let the door slip out of his hands. It fell, and the spring closed over it. He tried in vain to open it, not having observed Isabella's method of touching the spring; nor had he many moments to make an essay. The noise of the falling door had been heard by Manfred, who directed by the sound, hastened thither, attended by his servants with torches.

1764

1729 · THOMAS PERCY · 1811
AND
THE BALLAD REVIVAL

THE EIGHTEENTH CENTURY saw a revival of interest in the popular ballad that proved to be of phenomenal importance in the development of romantic trends in literature. The ballad with its artlessness and passion appealed to feeling rather than to reason; it increased interest in the past, the remote, and the supernatural. Early in the century, as the circles of the learned developed an interest in medieval antiquities, ancient forms of poetry began to be revived and old-time texts to be published. Addison recovered the famous old ballad, *Chevy-Chase,* and sounded a note of praise for its heroic qualities (*Spectator,* Nos. 70 and 74). A successful *Collection of Old Ballads* (1723–5), doubtfully attributed to Ambrose Phillips, was issued with a large number of ballads 'corrected from the best and most ancient copies extant.' The Scottish interest in ballad material was significantly revealed in Allan Ramsay's *Tea-Table Miscellany* (1724–7). A favorite of the times was David Mallet's *William and Margaret* (1724), a remaking of a genuine popular ballad. By mid-century, as growing interest in authentic primitive poetry mounted to a high point with Gray's *Bard* (1757) and Macpherson's *Ossian* (1762), ballad publication was climaxed with the most famous collection of them all, Thomas Percy's *Reliques of Ancient English Poetry* (1765).

The editor of this notable work, Bishop Percy, was an intelligent clergyman 'of wide though desultory antiquarian and literary interests,' a member of the scholarly circle that included Goldsmith, Shenstone, and Dr. Johnson. He shared the generally dispersed enthusiasm for the antique and the primitive, and his publications give him a place in the Scandinavian revival. His greatest contribution, however, derives from his publication of selected materials from a manuscript which he rescued from neglect and mutilation in a Shropshire country house. This manuscript was a miscellaneous collection of old songs and verses copied by some unknown person in the seventeenth century. To Percy, ballads were rude survivals of the past, of value in that they might reveal ancient beliefs and customs, but of no great intrinsic value as poetry. This view determined his editorial handling of the materials for the *Reliques.* He altered his texts, smoothed out the crudeness, corrected careless copying, filled out gaps caused by the mutilation of the pages, and refined passages so as to make them in his judgment fit for the perusal of cultivated readers. He also included in his volume many Elizabethan and seventeenth-century pieces and 'modern' poems of his own composing to gain a wider public acceptance of his work.

The critical reception of the *Reliques* was at first cool. Dr. Johnson considered the ballads worthless as literature, though interesting as antiquarian curiosities. Joseph Ritson, a rival antiquary, openly and heatedly disapproved of Percy's textual methods, and even questioned the existence of a manuscript. But the liberties Percy took with his texts appear to have gained him readers. The popular success of the *Reliques* was immediate and very great. Within a short time numerous scholars were prompted to seek out and to publish similar traditional materials. The example of Percy's *Reliques* was of particular importance to the collectors of Scottish songs and ballads. It occasioned publications such as David Herd's *Scots Songs* (1769), Sir Walter Scott's *Minstrelsy of the Scottish Border* (1802–3), Robert Jamieson's *Popular Ballads and Songs* (1806), William Motherwell's *Minstrelsy Ancient and Modern* (1827), and many more. Meanwhile the *Reliques* had given a great impetus to Herder's theories of popular literature in Germany and, along with the Ossianic poems, it was responsible for inaugurating a new era in folk literature in that country. In England there developed an increasingly favorable criticism. Cowper praised the simplicity and ease of the ballad, and at the end of the century Wordsworth pointed directly to the great importance to literature of the influence of the *Reliques.* 'For our own country,' he declared, 'its poetry has been absolutely redeemed by it. I do not think that there is an able writer of verse today who would not be proud to acknowledge his obligation to *The Reliques.*' Scott was a boy of thirteen when he first fell under the spell of the ballads of Percy. He was entranced by them and for years afterward they largely shaped the direction of his literary interests and activities. His *Minstrelsy of the Scottish Border,* modeled after Percy's work, led him directly to the writing of the romantic lays which brought him his greatest fame as a poet. Besides the major influence of the *Reliques* on Wordsworth and Scott, an influence they freely acknowledged, there was scarcely a writer in the first third of the nineteenth century who in one way or another did not owe allegiance to the ballad revival. The ballads did more than all else to revive genuinely simple poetry. There was no great abundance of romantic poems which closely imitated the original form and spirit of the ballads. Coleridge's *Ancient Mariner,* though it may be said to owe its origin to the ballad and to be an imitation of the ballad, is overlaid with metaphysical and religious sophistication which make it 'something less and something infinitely more than a ballad' (Hustvedt). But aside from formal aspects, the ballad qualities and the ballad spirit permeated the thought and literature of the age in many and diverse ways. The ballad had its share in bringing about 'a renascence of wonder' and rejuvenated the sensibilities of a public grown tired of the falsely noble language and stilted sentiment of much of late eighteenth-century poetry. People discovered that their ancestors were genuine human beings capable of manly emotions. Sung 'to a well-known air,' ballads spread even to the illiterate, fostering a love of romance. The popularity of the ballad form among lesser versifiers did not lead altogether to the happiest results. But it may be confidently stated that taken as a whole the revival of the popular ballad was the most wholesome and most potent single liberating factor in the whole romantic movement.

From RELIQUES OF ANCIENT ENGLISH
POETRY

THOMAS PERCY, EDITOR

(Published, 1765)

THE ANCIENT BALLAD OF
CHEVY-CHASE

[This ballad, known also as *The Hunting of the Cheviot,* is based upon the historical battle of Otterburn, fought between the English and the Scots in August 1388. The battle originated in a rivalry between the neighboring families of Percy and Douglas over hunting rights in the Cheviot hills, which separated their domains. Popular imagination in recounting the events has distorted historical truth to the advantage of the English.]

THE FIRST FIT

THE Persè owt of Northombarlande,
  And a vowe to God mayd he,
That he wolde hunte in the mountayns
  Off Chyviat within dayes thre,
In the mauger of¹ doughtè Dogles,
  And all that ever with him be.

The fattiste hartes in all Cheviat
  He sayd he wold kill, and carry them away:
'Be my feth,' sayd the dougheti Doglas agayn,
  'I wyll let² that hontyng yf that I may.'   10

Then the Persè owt of Banborowe cam,
  With him a myghtye meany,³
With fifteen hondrith archares bold;
  The wear chosen out of shyars thre.

This begane on a Monday at morn
  In Cheviat the hillys so he;⁴
The chyld may rue that ys un-born,
  It was the mor pittè.

The dryvars thorowe the woodes went
  For to reas the dear;   20
Bomen bickarte⁵ uppone the bent⁶
  With ther browd aras⁷ cleare.

Then the wyld⁸ thorowe the woodes went
  On every syde shear;⁹

---

1 in spite of.

2 prevent.   3 band.   4 high.   5 swiftly coursed.
6 field.   7 arrows. 8 wild deer. 9 several.

Grea-hondes thorowe the greves[10] glent[11]
  For to kyll thear dear.

The begane in Chyviat the hyls above
  Yerly on a Monnym day;
Be that[12] it drewe to the oware off none[13]
  A hondrith fat hartes ded ther lay.   30

The blewe a mort[14] uppone the bent,
  The semblyd on sydis shear;
To the quyrry[15] then the Persè went
  To se the bryttlyng[16] off the deare.

He sayd, 'It was the Duglas promys
  This day to meet me hear;
But I wyste he wold faylle verament':[17]
  A gret oth the Persè swear.

At the laste a squyar of Northombelonde
  Lokyde at his hand full ny,   40
He was war ath[18] the doughetie Doglas comynge:
  With him a mightè meany,

Both with spear, byll, and brande:
  Yt was a myghti sight to se.
Hardyar men both off hart nar hande
  Wear not in Christiantè.

The wear twenty hondrith spear-men good
  Withouten any fayle;
The wear borne a-long be the watter a Twyde
  Yth[19] bowndes of Tividale.   50

'Leave off the brytlyng of the dear,' he sayde,
  'And to your bowys look ye tayk good heed,
For never sithe ye wear on your mothars borne
  Had ye never so mickle need.'

The dougheti Dogglas on a stede
  He rode att his men beforne;
His armor glytteryde as dyd a glede;[20]
  A bolder barne[21] was never born.

'Tell me what men ye ar,' he says,
  'Or whos men that ye be: 60
Who gave youe leave to hunte in this
  Chyviat chays in the spyt of me?'

The first mane that ever him an answear mayd,
  Yt was the good lord Persè:
'We wyll not tell the what men we ar,' he says,

'Nor whos men that we be;
But we wyll hount hear in this chays
  In the spyte of thyne, and of the.

The fattiste hartes in all Chyviat
  We have kyld, and cast[22] to carry them
    a-way.'   70
'Be my troth,' sayd the doughtè Dogglas agayn,
  'Ther-for the ton[23] of us shall de this day.'

Then sayd the doughtè Doglas
  Unto the lord Persè:
'To kyll all thes giltless men,
  A-las! it wear great pittè.

'But, Persè, thowe art a lord of lande,
  I am a yerle callyd within my contre;
Let all our men uppone a parti stande;
  And do the battell off the and of me.'   80

'Nowe Cristes corse[24] on his crowne,' sayd the
    lord Persè,
  'Who-soever ther-to says nay.
Be my troth, doughtè Doglas,' he says,
  'Thow shalt never se that day;

'Nethar in Ynglonde, Skottlonde, nar France,
  Nor for no man of a woman born,
But and fortune be my chance,
  I dar met him on man for on.'

Then bespayke a squyar off Northombarlonde,
  Ric[hard] Wytharynton was his nam;   90
'It shall never be told in Sothe-Ynglonde,' he says,
  'To kyng Herry the fourth for sham.

'I wat[25] youe byn great lordes twaw,
  I am a poor squyar of lande;
I wyll never se my captayne fight on a fylde,
  And stande my-selffe, and looke on,
But whyll I may my weppone welde,
  I wyll not fayl both harte and hande.'

That day, that day, that dredfull day:
  The first Fit here I fynde,   100
And you wyll here any mor athe hountyng athe
    Chyviat,
  Yet ys ther mor behynde.

THE SECOND FIT

The Yngglishe men hade ther bowys yebent,
  Ther hartes were good yenoughe;

---

10 groves.
13 hour of noon.
16 cutting up.
19 in the.

11 darted.
14 death note.
17 truly.
20 glowing coal.

12 when.
15 slaughtered game.
18 aware of.
21 man.

---

22 intend.
24 curse.

23 one.
25 know.

The first of arros that the shote off,
  Seven skore spear-men the sloughe.²⁶

Yet bydyes²⁷ the yerle Doglas uppon the bent,
  A captayne good yenoughe,
And that was sene verament,
  For he wrought hom²⁸ both woo and
    wouche.²⁹   110

The Dogglas pertyd his ost in thre,
  Lyk a cheffe cheften off pryde,
With suar³⁰ speares off myghttè tre
  The cum in on every syde.

Thrughe our Yngglishe archery
  Gave many a wounde full wyde;
Many a doughetè the garde³¹ to dy,
  Which ganyde them no pryde.

The Yngglyshe men let thear bowys be,
  And pulde owt brandes that wer bright;   120
It was a hevy syght to se
  Bryght swordes on basnites³² lyght.

Thorowe ryche male, and myneyeple,³³
  Many sterne³⁴ the stroke downe streght:
Many a freyke,³⁵ that was full free,
  Ther undar foot dyd lyght.

At last the Duglas and the Persè met,
  Lyk to captayns of myght and mayne;
The swapte³⁶ togethar tyll the both swat³⁷
  With swordes, that were of fyn myllàn.³⁸ 130

Thes worthè freckys for to fyght
  Ther-to the wear full fayne,
Tyll the bloode owte off thear basnetes sprente,³⁹
  As ever dyd heal or rayne.

'Hold the, Persè,' sayd the Doglas,
  'And i' feth I shall the brynge
Wher thowe shalte have a yerls wagis
  Of Jamy our Scottish kynge.

'Thoue shalte have thy ransom fre,
  I hight the hear⁴⁰ this thinge,   140
For the manfullyste man yet art thowe,
  That ever I conqueryd in filde fightyng.'

'Nay, then,' sayd the lord Persè,
  'I tolde it the beforne,

That I wolde never yeldyde be
  To no man of a woman born.'

With that ther cam an arrowe hastely
  Forthe off a mightie wane,⁴¹
Hit hathe strekene the yerle Duglas
  In at the brest bane.   150

Thoroue lyvar and longs bathe
  The sharp arrowe ys gane,
That never after in all his lyffe days,
  He spake mo wordes but ane,
That was, 'Fyghte ye, my merry men, whyllys ye
    may,
  For my lyff days ben gan.'

The Persè leanyde on his brande,
  And sawe the Duglas de;
He tooke the dede man be the hande,
  And sayd, 'Who ys me for the!   160

'To have savyde thy lyffe, I wold have pertyd with
  My landes for years thre,
For a better man of hart, nare of hande
  Was not in all the north countrè.'

Off all that se⁴² a Skottishe knyght,
  Was callyd Sir Hewe the Mongon-byrry,
He sawe the Duglas to the deth was dyght;⁴³
  He spendyd⁴⁴ a spear, a trusti tre:

He rod uppon a corsiare
  Throughe a hondrith archery;   170
He never styntyde, nar never blane,⁴⁵
  Tyll he cam to the good lord Persè.

He set uppone the lord Persè
  A dynte, that was full soare;
With a suar spear of a myghtè tre
  Clean thorow the body he the Persè bore,

Athe tothar syde, that a man myght se,
  A large cloth yard and mare:
Towe bettar captayns wear nat in Christiantè,
  Then that day slain wear thare.   180

An archer off Northomberlonde
  Say⁴⁶ slean was the lord Persè,
He bar a bende-bow in his hande,
  Was made off trusti tre:

An arow, that a cloth yarde was lang,
  To th' hard stele halyde⁴⁷ he;

---

26 they slew.   27 abides.   28 them.
29 harm.   30 sure; trusty.   31 they made.
32 helmets.   33 gauntlet.   34 bold ones.
35 man.   36 smote.   37 sweat.
38 Milan steel.   39 spurted.   40 promise thee here.

41 man.   42 saw.   43 doomed.   44 grasped.
45 ceased.   46 saw.   47 pulled.

A dynt, that was both sad and soar,
  He sat[48] on Sir Hewe the Mongon-byrry.

The dynt yt was both sad and sar,
  That he of Mongon-byrry sete;   190
The swane-fethars, that his arrowe bar,
  With his hart blood the wear wete.

Ther was never a freake wone foot wold fle,
  But still in stour[49] dyd stand,
Heawing on yche othar, whyll the myght
  dre,[50]
  With many a bal-ful brande.

This battell begane in Chyviat
  An owar befor the none,
And when even-song bell was rang
  The battell was nat half done.   200

The tooke 'on' on ethar hand
  Be the lyght off the mone;
Many hade no strength for to stande,
  In Chyviat the hyllys abone.

Of fifteen hondrith archars of Ynglonde
  Went away but fifti and thre;
Of twenty hondrith spear-men of Skotlonde,
  But even five and fifti:

But all wear slayne Cheviat within:
  The hade no strengthe to sand on hie; 210
The chylde may rue that ys un-borne,
  It was the mor pittè.

Thear was slayne with the lord Persè
  Sir John of Agerstone,
Sir Roge the hinde[51] Hartly,
  Sir Wyllyam the bolde Hearone.

Sir Jorg the worthè Lovele
  A knyght of great renowen,
Sir Raff the ryche Rugbè
  With dyntes wear beaten dowene.   220

For Wetharryngton my harte was wo,
  That ever he slayne shulde be;
For when both his leggis wear hewyne in to,
  He knyled and fought on hys kne.

Ther was slayne with the dougheti Douglas
  Sir Hewe the Mongon-byrry,
Sir Davye Lwdale, that worthè was,
  His sistars son was he:

Sir Charles a Murrè, in that place,
  That never a foot wolde fle;   230
Sir Hewe Maxwell, a lorde he was,
  With the Duglas dyd he dey.

So on the morrowe the mayde them byears[52]
  Off byrch, and hasell so gray;
Many wedous with wepyng tears
  Cam to fach ther makys[53] a-way.

Tivydale may carpe off[54] care,
  Northombarlond may mayk grat mone,
For towe such captayns, as slayne wear thear,
  On the March-perti[55] shall never be none.   240

Word ys common to Edden-burrowe,
  To Jamy the Skottishe kyng,
That dougheti Duglas, lyff-tenant of the Merches,
  He lay slean Chyviot with-in.

His handdes dyd he weal[56] and wryng,
  He sayd, 'Alas, and woe ys me!
Such another captayn Skotland within,'
  He sayd, 'y-feth[57] shuld never be.'

Worde ys commyn to lovly Londone
  Till the fourth Harry our kyng,   250
That lord Persè, leyff-tennante of the Merchis,
  He lay slayne Chyviat within.

'God have merci on his soll,' sayd kyng Harry,
  'Good lord, yf thy will it be!
I have a hondrith captayns in Ynglonde,' he sayd,
  'As good as ever was hee:
But Persè, and I brook[58] my lyffe,
  Thy deth well quyte[59] shall be.'

As our noble kyng made his a-vowe,
  Lyke a noble prince of renowen,   260
For the deth of the lord Persè,
  He dyd the battel of Hombyll-down:

Wher syx and thritte Skottish knyghtes
  On a day were beaten down:
Glendale glytteryde on ther armor bryght,
  Over castill, towar, and town.

This was the hontynge off the Cheviat;
  That tear[60] begane this spurn;[61]
Old men that knowen the grownde well yenoughe,
  Call it the Battell of Otterburn.   270

---

48 set.   49 combat.
50 endure.   51 courteous.

52 biers.   53 mates.   54 talk of.
55 border-side.   56 clench.   57 in faith.
58 enjoy.   59 avenged.   60 there.
61 conflict.

At Otterburn began this spurne
    Uppon a Monnyn day:
Ther was the dougghtè Doglas slean,
    The Persè never went away.

Ther was never a tym on the March-partes
    Sen the Doglas and the Persè met,
But yt was marvele, and the redde blude ronne not,
    As the reane doys in the stret.

Jhesue Christ our balys bete,[62]
    And to the[63] blys us brynge!   280
Thus was the hountynge of the Chevyat:
    God send us all good ending!

EDWARD, EDWARD

'WHY dois your brand sae drap wi bluid,
    Edward, Edward,
Why dois your brand sae drap wi bluid,
    And why sae sad gang yee O?'
'O I hae killed my hauke sae guid,
    Mither, mither,
O I hae killed my hauke sae guid,
    And I had nae mair bot hee O.'

'Your haukis bluid was nevir sae reid,
    Edward, Edward,   10
Your haukis bluid was nevir sae reid,
    My deir son I tell thee O.'
'O I hae killed my reid-roan steid,
    Mither, mither,
O I hae killed my reid-roan steid,
    That erst[1] was sae fair and frie O.'

'Your steid was auld, and ye hae got mair,
    Edward, Edward,
Your steid was auld, and ye hae got mair,
    Sum other dule[2] ye drie[3] O.'   20
'O I hae killed my fadir deir,
    Mither, mither,
O I hae killed my fadir deir,
    Alas, and wae is mee O!'

'And whatten penance wul ye drie for that,
    Edward, Edward?
And whatten penance will ye drie for that?
    My deir son, now tell me O.'
'Ile set my feit in yonder boat,
    Mither, mither,   30
Ile set my feit in yonder boat,
    And Ile fare ovir the sea O.'

'And what wul ye doe wi your towirs and your ha,
    Edward, Edward?
And what wul ye doe wi your towirs and your ha,
    That were sae fair to see O?'
'Ile let thame stand tul they doun fa,
    Mither, mither,
Ile let thame stand tul they doun fa,
    For here nevir mair maun[4] I bee O.'   40

'And what wul ye leive to your bairns and your wife,
    Edward, Edward?
And what wul ye leive to your bairns and your wife,
    Whan ye gang ovir the sea O?'
'The warldis room, late them beg thrae life,
    Mither, mither,
The warldis room, late them beg thrae life,
    For thame nevir mair wul I see O.'

'And what wul ye leive to your ain mither deir,
    Edward, Edward?   50
And what wul ye leive to your ain mither deir?
    My deir son, now tell me O.'
'The curse of hell frae me sall ye beir,
    Mither, mither,
The curse of hell frae me sall ye beir,
    Sic counseils ye gave to me O.'

SIR PATRICK SPENCE

THE king sits in Dumferling toune,
    Drinking the blude-reid wine:
'O quhar[1] will I get guid sailòr,
    To sail this schip of mine?'

Up and spak an eldern knicht,
    Sat at the kings richt kne:
'Sir Patrick Spence is the best sailòr,
    That sails upon the se.'

The king has written a braid letter,
    And signd it wi' his hand;   10
And sent it to Sir Patrick Spence,
    Was walking on the sand.

The first line that Sir Patrick red,
    A loud lauch[2] lauched he:
The next line that Sir Patrick red,
    The teir blinded his ee.

'O quha[3] is this has don this deid,
    This ill deid don to me;

---

62 troubles relieve.   63 thy.

1 once.   2 dole; sorrow.   3 suffer.

4 must.

1 where.   2 laugh.   3 who.

To send me out this time o' the zeir,[4]
  To sail upon the se?   20

'Mak hast, mak haste, my mirry men all,
  Our guid schip sails the morne';
'O say na sae, my master deir,
  For I feir a deadlie storme.

'Late, late yestreen I saw the new moone,
  Wi' the auld moone in hir arme;
And I feir, I feir, my deir mastèr,
  That we will com to harme.'

O our Scots nobles wer richt laith[5]
  To weet their cork-heild schoone;[6]   30
Bot lang owre[7] a' the play wer playd,
  Thair hats they swam aboone.[8]

O lang, lang, may thair ladies sit
  Wi' thair fans in their hand,
Or eir they se Sir Patrick Spence
  Cum sailing to the land.

O lang, lang, may the ladies stand
  Wi' thair gold kems[9] in their hair,
Waiting for thair ain deir lords,
  For they'll se thame na mair.   40

Have owre,[10] have owre to Aberdour,
  It's fiftie fadom deip:
And thair lies guid Sir Patrick Spence,
  Wi' the Scots lords at his feit.

From MINSTRELSY OF THE SCOTTISH
BORDER

SIR WALTER SCOTT, EDITOR

(Published 1802–3)

LORD RANDAL

'O WHERE hae ye been, Lord Randal, my son?
O where hae ye been, my handsome young man?'
'I hae been to the wild wood; mother, make my
  bed soon,
For I'm weary wi hunting, and fain wald lie down.'

'Where gat ye your dinner, Lord Randal, my son?
Where gat ye your dinner, my handsome young
  man?'
'I din'd wi my true-love; mother, make my bed
  soon,
For I'm weary wi hunting, and fain wald lie down.'

'What gat ye to your dinner, Lord Randal, my son?
What gat ye to your dinner, my handsome young
  man?'   10
'I gat eels boiled in broo; mother, make my bed
  soon,
For I'm weary wi hunting, and fain wald lie down.'

'What became of your bloodhounds, Lord Randal,
  my son?
What became of your bloodhounds, my handsome young man?'
'O they swelld and they died; mother, make my
  bed soon,
For I'm weary wi hunting, and fain wald lie down.'

'O I fear ye are poisond, Lord Randal, my son!
O I fear ye are poisond, my handsome young man!'
'O yes! I am poisond; mother, make my bed soon,
For I'm sick at the heart and I fain wald lie
  down.'   20

THE WIFE OF USHER'S WELL

THERE lived a wife at Usher's Well,
  And a wealthy wife was she;
She had three stout and stalwart sons,
  And sent them oer the sea.

They hadna been a week from her,
  A week but barely ane,
Whan word came to the carline wife
  That her three sons were gane.

They hadna been a week from her,
  A week but barely three,   10
Whan word came to the carlin wife
  That her sons she'd never see.

'I wish the wind may never cease,
  Nor fashes in the flood,
Till my three sons come hame to me,
  In earthly flesh and blood.'

It fell about the Martinmass,
  When nights are lang and mirk,[1]
The carlin wife's three sons came hame,
  And their hats were o the birk.[2]   20

It neither grew in syke[3] nor ditch,
  Nor yet in ony sheugh;[4]
But at the gates o Paradise,
  That birk grew fair eneugh.

4 year.   5 loth.   6 shoes.
7 ere.   8 above.   9 combs.
10 over.

1 dark.   2 birch.
3 trench.   4 furrow.

'Blow up the fire, my maidens,
  Bring water from the well;
For a' my house shall feast this night,
  Since my three sons are well.'

And she has made to them a bed,
  She's made it large and wide,   30
And she's taen her mantle her about,
  Sat down at the bed-side.

.   .   .

Up then crew the red, red cock,
  And up and crew the gray;
The eldest to the youngest said,
  ''T is time we were away.'

The cock he hadna crawd but once,
  And clapped his wings at a',
When the youngest to the eldest said,
  'Brother, we must awa.[5]   40

'The cock doth craw, the day doth daw,[6]
  The channerin[7] worm doth chide;
Gin we be mist out o our place,
  A sair[8] pain we maun bide.

'Faer ye weel, my mother dear!
  Fareweel to barn and byre![9]
And fare ye weel, the bonny lass
  That kindles my mother's fire!'

---

5 away.
7 fretting.
9 cow-house.

6 dawn.
8 sore.

From MINSTRELSY ANCIENT AND
MODERN

WILLIAM MOTHERWELL, EDITOR[1]

(Published, 1827)

BONNIE GEORGE CAMPBELL

HIE upon Hielands
  And low upon Tay,
Bonny George Campbell
  Rode out on a day.
Saddled and bridled
  And gallant rade he;
Hame came his gude horse,
  But never cam he!

Out cam his auld mither
  Greeting[2] fu' sair,   10
And out cam his bonnie bride
  Rivin' her hair.
Saddled and bridled
  And booted rade he;
Toom[3] hame cam the saddle,
  But never cam he!

'My meadow lies green,
  And my corn is unshorn;
My barn is to big,[4]
  And my babie's unborn.'   20
Saddled and bridled
  And booted rade he;
Toom hame cam the saddle,
  But never cam he!

---

1 William Motherwell, 1797–1835, was a judicious collector and editor of ballads and something of a poet in his own right. His *Minstrelsy* is highly regarded by ballad scholars for its careful recording of texts.

2 weeping.   3 empty.   4 build.

1730 · OLIVER GOLDSMITH · 1774

1730   Born in Ireland, the second son of a clergyman. Attended various village schools and Trinity College, Dublin, as a sizar, where he took the B.A. degree in 1749.

1749–52   Led an unsettled life; was rejected for ordination, acted as tutor, gambled away money for studying law, and toyed with the idea of going to America. Finally went to Edinburgh to study medicine.

1754   Sailed to Leyden, where he continued his medical studies. Wandered on foot about France, Switzerland, and Italy.

1756   Returned to London in destitution. After supporting himself with difficulty as physician, schoolteacher, and proofreader began his career as a literary hack, working for Griffiths' *Monthly Review.*

1759   Published *An Enquiry into the Present State of Polite Learning in Europe.*

1762   Published *The Citizen of the World,* a collection of 'Chinese Letters' written in 1760 for *The Public Ledger.*

1763   Became one of the charter members of Johnson's 'Club.'

1764   Published *A History of England in a Series of Letters* and *The Traveller,* a poem on the conditions of European society.

1766   Published *The Vicar of Wakefield.*

1768   *The Good Natured Man* produced at Covent Garden.

1769   Became first Professor of History of the Royal Academy. Wrote a history of Rome, followed later by histories of England and Greece, and *A History of Animated Nature* (1774).

1770   Published *The Deserted Village.*

1773   *She Stoops To Conquer* performed with great success at Covent Garden.

1774   Wrote *Retaliations, A Poem.* Died and was buried in Temple Church; at the expense of 'The Club' a monument to him was erected in Westminster Abbey.

OLIVER GOLDSMITH imagined that he had no sympathy with romantic tendencies in poetry; nevertheless, in two poems, *The Traveller* and *The Deserted Village,* his sentimentality, humanitarianism, and love of country life, bring him within the widening current of romanticism in the second half of the eighteenth century. In *The Traveller,* the author, in the character of a solitary, disillusioned observer of European society (not unlike the Byron of *Childe Harold* of a later day), tells of the countries he has visited in a vain search for happiness. He discovers that happiness is not dependent upon externals but is created deep in man's own nature. In *The Deserted Village,* a much better poem, Goldsmith elaborates upon the theme, already dealt with in *The Traveller,* of the sorrows of those driven by monopolizing wealth to seek relief in emigration. The poem is important as opposing rural innocence not merely to the conventional luxury and corruption of city life but to the swift and unforeseen economic changes of the period, the rise of the factory system, and the consequent breakup of the village community. Goldsmith achieves his humanitarian intention by contrasting the English village life of old with its present sad state of decay. He opens his poem with an idyllic description of

Sweet Auburn, loveliest village of the plain,

and recounts through a series of pictures the simple-hearted pleasures of the poor. (Auburn is, of course, no real locality but a composite of Irish and English villages transformed and exalted in the light of recollection.) As the poet proceeds he turns from a picture of the village in prosperity and shows it in decay. He imagines the hardships of life in distant, savage countries and pictures with moving pathos the departure of emigrants who are forced by poverty to leave their native England. Nine tenths of *The Deserted Village* has to do with human beings and the new humanitarianism. From Goldsmith's tragic exiles it is a short cry to Wordsworth's vagrants broken by industrialism or the backwash of war.

Goldsmith, like Gray, was a disciple of form and polish. *The Deserted Village* is typically classical in its compactness; there is not a superfluous line in it. The verse pattern is the traditional pseudo-classic couplet, though the antithetical sharpness favored by Pope and his followers is tempered in Goldsmith's lines by musical sensitiveness and romantic sentiment. The poet's drawings are wonderfully precise and true to the details of Nature. His portraits of the village preacher and the schoolmaster are done with Chaucer-like insight, and his pictures of the countryside and the innocent pleasures of the villagers with 'an exquisite simplicity and penetrative sweetness' hardly to be rivaled.

The Vicar of Wakefield may be numbered with *The Traveller* and *The Deserted Village* among Goldsmith's writings having romantic characteristics. It is an idyll in prose, full of romantic sentimentality, probably the best-loved drawing in our literature of English country life in all its sweetness and charm.

THE DESERTED VILLAGE

TO SIR JOSHUA REYNOLDS

Dear Sir,
    . . . Permit me to inscribe this Poem to you.

How far you may be pleased with the versification and mere mechanical parts of this attempt, I don't pretend to enquire; but I know you will object (and indeed several of our best and wisest friends concur in the opinion) that the depopulation it deplores is no where to be seen, and the disorders it laments are only to be found in the poet's own imagination. To this I can scarce make any other answer than that I sincerely believe what I have written; that I have taken all possible pains, in my country excursions, for these four or five years past, to be certain of what I alledge; and that all my views and enquiries have led me to believe those miseries real, which I here attempt to display.[1] But this is not the place to enter into an enquiry, whether the country be depopulating, or not; the discussion would take up much room, and I should prove myself, at best, an indifferent politician, to tire the reader with a long preface, when I want his unfatigued attention to a long poem.

In regretting the depopulation of the country, I inveigh against the encrease of our luxuries; and here also I expect the shout of modern politicians against me. For twenty or thirty years past, it has been the fashion to consider luxury as one of the greatest national advantages; and all the wisdom of antiquity in that particular, as erroneous. Still, however, I must remain a professed ancient on that head, and continue to think those luxuries prejudicial to states, by which so many vices are introduced, and so many kingdoms have been undone. Indeed so much has been poured out of late on the other side of the question, that, merely for the sake of novelty and variety, one would sometimes wish to be in the right.

I am,
Dear Sir,
Your sincere friend,
and ardent admirer,
Oliver Goldsmith.

SWEET AUBURN,[2] loveliest village of the plain,
Where health and plenty cheared the labouring
        swain,
Where smiling spring its earliest visit paid,
And parting summer's lingering blooms delayed,
Dear lovely bowers of innocence and ease,
Seats of my youth, when every sport could please,
How often have I loitered o'er thy green,
Where humble happiness endeared each scene;
How often have I paused on every charm,
The sheltered cot, the cultivated farm,   10
The never failing brook, the busy mill,
The decent church that topt the neighbouring hill,

---

[1] In the eighteenth century the enclosure of meadows and pasture lands previously held in common had, in fact, forced many thousands of yeomen and cottagers off the land. For the most part these displaced farming people found their way to the cities, where the new factories were calling for cheap labor.

[2] Auburn is an idealized English village.

The hawthorn bush, with seats beneath the shade,
For talking age and whispering lovers made;
How often have I blest the coming day,
When toil remitting lent its turn to play,
And all the village train, from labour free,
Led up their sports beneath the spreading tree;
While many a pastime circled in the shade,
The young contending as the old surveyed;   20
And many a gambol frolicked o'er the ground,
And slights of art and feats of strength went round;
And still as each repeated pleasure tired,
Succeeding sports the mirthful band inspired;
The dancing pair that simply sought renown
By holding out to tire each other down;
The swain mistrustless of his smutted face,
While secret laughter tittered round the place;
The bashful virgin's side-long looks of love,
The matron's glance that would those looks
    reprove: 30
These were thy charms, sweet village; sports like
    these,
With sweet succession, taught even toil to please;
These round thy bowers their chearful influence
    shed,
These were thy charms—But all these charms are
    fled.
    Sweet smiling village, loveliest of the lawn,
Thy sports are fled, and all thy charms withdrawn;
Amidst thy bowers the tyrant's hand is seen,
And desolation saddens all thy green:
One only master grasps the whole domain,
And half a tillage stints thy smiling plain;   40
No more thy glassy brook reflects the day,
But choaked with sedges, works its weedy way.
Along thy glades, a solitary guest,
The hollow sounding bittern guards its nest;
Amidst thy desert walks the lapwing flies,
And tires their ecchoes with unvaried cries.
Sunk are thy bowers, in shapeless ruin all,
And the long grass o'ertops the mouldering wall,
And trembling, shrinking from the spoiler's hand,
Far, far away thy children leave the land.   50
    Ill fares the land, to hastening ills a prey,
Where wealth accumulates, and men decay:
Princes and lords may flourish, or may fade:
A breath can make them, as a breath has made;
But a bold peasantry, their country's pride,
When once destroyed, can never be supplied.
    A time there was, ere England's griefs began,
When every rood of ground maintained its man;
For him light labour spread her wholesome store,
Just gave what life required, but gave no more: 60
His best companions, innocence and health;
And his best riches, ignorance of wealth.
    But times are altered; trade's unfeeling train

Usurp the land and dispossess the swain;
Along the lawn, where scattered hamlets rose,
Unwieldy wealth, and cumbrous pomp repose;
And every want to oppulence allied,
And every pang that folly pays to pride.
These gentle hours that plenty bade to bloom,
Those calm desires that asked but little room,   70
Those healthful sports that graced the peaceful
    scene,
Lived in each look, and brightened all the green;
These far departing seek a kinder shore,
And rural mirth and manners are no more,
    Sweet AUBURN! parent of the blissful hour,
Thy glades forlorn confess the tyrant's power.
Here as I take my solitary rounds,
Amidst thy tangling walks, and ruined grounds,
And, many a year elapsed, return to view
Where once the cottage stood, the hawthorn
    grew,   80
Remembrance wakes with all her busy train,
Swells at my breast, and turns the past to pain.
    In all my wanderings round this world of care,
In all my griefs—and GOD has given my share—
I still had hopes my latest hours to crown,
Amidst these humble bowers to lay me down;
To husband out life's taper at the close,
And keep the flame from wasting by repose.
I still had hopes, for pride attends us still,
Amidst the swains to shew my book-learned
    skill,   90
Around my fire an evening groupe to draw,
And tell of all I felt, and all I saw;
And, as an hare whom hounds and horns pursue,
Pants to the place from whence at first she flew,
I still had hopes, my long vexations past,
Here to return—and die at home at last.
    O blest retirement, friend to life's decline,
Retreats from care that never must be mine,
How happy he who crowns in shades like these,
A youth of labour with an age of ease;   100
Who quits a world where strong temptations try,
And, since 'tis hard to combat, learns to fly.
For him no wretches, born to work and weep,
Explore the mine, or tempt the dangerous deep;
No surly porter stands in guilty state
To spurn imploring famine from the gate,
But on he moves to meet his latter end,
Angels around befriending virtue's friend;
Bends to the grave with unperceived decay,
While resignation gently slopes the way;   110
And all his prospects brightening to the last,
His Heaven commences ere the world be past!
    Sweet was the sound when oft at evening's
    close,
Up yonder hill the village murmur rose;

There as I past with careless steps and slow,
The mingling notes came softened from below;
The swain responsive as the milk-maid sung,
The sober herd that lowed to meet their young,
The noisy geese that gabbled o'er the pool,
The playful children just let loose from school, 120
The watch-dog's voice that bayed the whispering
    wind,
And the loud laugh that spoke the vacant mind,
These all in sweet confusion sought the shade,
And filled each pause the nightingale had made.
But now the sounds of population fail,
No chearful murmurs fluctuate in the gale,
No busy steps the grass-grown foot-way tread,
For all the bloomy flush of life is fled.
All but yon widowed, solitary thing
That feebly bends beside the plashy spring;   130
She, wretched matron, forced, in age, for bread,
To strip the brook with mantling cresses spread,
To pick her wintry faggot from the thorn,
To seek her nightly shed, and weep till morn;
She only left of all the harmless train,
The sad historian of the pensive plain.

    Near yonder copse, where once the garden
        smil'd,
And still where many a garden flower grows wild;
There, where a few torn shrubs the place disclose,
The village preacher's modest mansion rose. 140
A man he was, to all the country dear,
And passing rich with forty pounds a year;
Remote from towns he ran his godly race,
Nor e'er had changed, nor wished to change his
    place;
Unpractised he to fawn, or seek for power,
By doctrines fashioned to the varying hour;
Far other aims his heart had learned to prize,
More skilled to raise the wretched than to rise.
His house was known to all the vagrant train,
He chid their wanderings, but relieved their
    pain;   150
The long remembered beggar was his guest,
Whose beard descending swept his aged breast;
The ruined spendthrift, now no longer proud,
Claimed kindred there, and had his claims allowed;
The broken soldier, kindly bade to stay,
Sate by his fire, and talked the night away;
Wept o'er his wounds, or tales of sorrow done,
Shouldered his crutch, and shewed how fields were
    won.
Pleased with his guests, the good man learned to
    glow,
And quite forgot their vices in their woe;   160
Careless their merits, or their faults to scan,
His pity gave ere charity began.
    Thus to relieve the wretched was his pride,

And even his failings leaned to Virtue's side;
But in his duty prompt at every call,
He watched and wept, he prayed and felt, for all.
And, as a bird each fond endearment tries,
To tempt its new fledged offspring to the skies;
He tried each art, reproved each dull delay,
Allured to brighter worlds, and led the way.   170
    Beside the bed where parting life was layed,
And sorrow, guilt, and pain, by turns dismayed,
The reverend champion stood. At his control,
Despair and anguish fled the struggling soul;
Comfort came down the trembling wretch to
    raise,
And his last faultering accents whispered praise.
    At church, with meek and unaffected grace,
His looks adorned the venerable place;
Truth from his lips prevailed with double sway,
And fools, who came to scoff, remained to
    pray.   180
The service past, around the pious man,
With steady zeal each honest rustic ran;
Even children followed with endearing wile,
And plucked his gown, to share the good man's
    smile.
His ready smile a parent's warmth exprest,
Their welfare pleased him, and their cares distrest;
To them his heart, his love, his griefs were given,
But all his serious thoughts had rest in Heaven.
As some tall cliff that lifts its awful form,
Swells from the vale, and midway leaves the
    storm,   190
Tho' round its breast the rolling clouds are spread,
Eternal sunshine settles on its head.
    Beside yon straggling fence that skirts the way,
With blossomed furze unprofitably gay,
There, in his noisy mansion, skill'd to rule,
The village master taught his little school;
A man severe he was, and stern to view,
I knew him well, and every truant knew;
Well had the boding tremblers learned to trace
The day's disasters in his morning face;   200
Full well they laugh'd with counterfeited glee,
At all his jokes, for many a joke had he;
Full well the busy whisper circling round,
Conveyed the dismal tidings when he frowned;
Yet he was kind, or if severe in aught,
The love he bore to learning was in fault;
The village all declared how much he knew;
'Twas certain he could write, and cypher too;
Lands he could measure, terms and tides presage,
And even the story ran that he could gauge.   210
In arguing too, the parson owned his skill,
For even tho' vanquished, he could argue still;
While words of learned length, and thundering
    sound,

Amazed the gazing rustics ranged around;
And still they gazed, and still the wonder grew,
That one small head could carry all he knew.
   But past is all his fame. The very spot
Where many a time he triumphed, is forgot.
Near yonder thorn, that lifts its head on high,
Where once the sign-post caught the passing
     eye,   220
Low lies that house where nut-brown draughts
     inspired,
Where grey-beard mirth and smiling toil retired,
Where village statesmen talked with looks pro-
     found,
And news much older than their ale went round.
Imagination fondly stoops to trace
The parlour splendours of that festive place;
The white-washed wall, the nicely sanded floor,
The varnished clock that clicked behind the door;
The chest contrived a double debt to pay,
A bed by night, a chest of drawers by day;   230
The pictures placed for ornament and use,
The twelve good rules,[3] the royal game of goose;[4]
The hearth, except when winter chill'd the day,
With aspen boughs, and flowers, and fennel gay,
While broken tea-cups, wisely kept for shew,
Ranged o'er the chimney, glistened in a row.
   Vain transitory splendours! Could not all
Reprieve the tottering mansion from its fall!
Obscure it sinks, nor shall it more impart
An hour's importance to the poor man's heart; 240
Thither no more the peasant shall repair
To sweet oblivion of his daily care;
No more the farmer's news, the barber's tale,
No more the wood-man's ballad shall prevail;
No more the smith his dusky brow shall clear,
Relax his ponderous strength, and lean to hear;
The host himself no longer shall be found
Careful to see the mantling bliss go round;
Nor the coy maid, half willing to be prest,
Shall kiss the cup to pass it to the rest.   250
   Yes! let the rich deride, the proud disdain,
These simple blessings of the lowly train;
To me more dear, congenial to my heart,
One native charm, than all the gloss of art;
Spontaneous joys, where Nature has its play,
The soul adopts, and owns their first born sway;
Lightly they frolic o'er the vacant mind,
Unenvied, unmolested, unconfined.
But the long pomp, the midnight masquerade,
With all the freaks of wanton wealth arrayed, 260
In these, ere triflers half their wish obtain,
The toiling pleasure sickens into pain;

3 rules of conduct ascribed to King Charles, which were printed
in broadside form and hung on the wall.
4 a game played with dice on a board.

And, even while fashion's brightest arts decoy,
The heart distrusting asks, if this be joy.
   Ye friends to truth, ye statesmen, who survey
The rich man's joys encrease, the poor's decay,
'Tis yours to judge, how wide the limits stand
Between a splendid and an happy land.
Proud swells the tide with loads of freighted ore,
And shouting Folly hails them from her shore; 270
Hoards, even beyond the miser's wish abound,
And rich men flock from all the world around.
Yet count our gains. This wealth is but a name
That leaves our useful products still the same.
Not so the loss. The man of wealth and pride,
Takes up a space that many poor supplied;
Space for his lake, his park's extended bounds,
Space for his horses, equipage, and hounds;
The robe that wraps his limbs in silken sloth,
Has robbed the neighbouring fields of half their
     growth;   280
His seat, where solitary sports are seen,
Indignant spurns the cottage from the green;
Around the world each needful product flies,
For all the luxuries the world supplies.
While thus the land adorned for pleasure, all
In barren splendour feebly waits the fall.
   As some fair female unadorned and plain,
Secure to please while youth confirms her reign,
Slights every borrowed charm that dress supplies,
Nor shares with art the triumph of her eyes. 290
But when those charms are past, for charms are
     frail,
When time advances, and when lovers fail,
She then shines forth, solicitous to bless,
In all the glaring impotence of dress.
Thus fares the land, by luxury betrayed;
In nature's simplest charms at first arrayed;
But verging to decline, its splendours rise,
Its vistas strike, its palaces surprize;
While scourged by famine from the smiling land,
The mournful peasant leads his humble band; 300
And while he sinks without one arm to save,
The country blooms—a garden, and a grave.
   Where then, ah where, shall poverty reside,
To scape the pressure of contiguous pride?
If to some common's fenceless limits strayed,
He drives his flock to pick the scanty blade,
Those fenceless fields the sons of wealth divide,
And even the bare-worn common is denied.
   If to the city sped—What waits him there?
To see profusion that he must not share;   310
To see ten thousand baneful arts combined
To pamper luxury, and thin mankind;
To see those joys the sons of pleasure know,
Extorted from his fellow-creature's woe.
Here, while the courtier glitters in brocade,

There the pale artist plies the sickly trade;
Here, while the proud their long-drawn pomps display,
There the black gibbet glooms beside the way.
The dome where Pleasure holds her midnight reign,
Here, richly deckt, admits the gorgeous train;   320
Tumultuous grandeur crowds the blazing square,
The rattling chariots clash, the torches glare.
Sure scenes like these no troubles e'er annoy!
Sure these denote one universal joy!
Are these thy serious thoughts?—Ah, turn thine eyes
Where the poor houseless shivering female lies.
She once, perhaps, in village plenty blest,
Has wept at tales of innocence distrest;
Her modest looks the cottage might adorn,
Sweet as the primrose peeps beneath the thorn;   330
Now lost to all; her friends, her virtue fled,
Near her betrayer's door she lays her head,
And pinch'd with cold, and shrinking from the shower,
With heavy heart deplores that luckless hour
When idly first, ambitious of the town,
She left her wheel and robes of country brown.

Do thine, sweet AUBURN, thine, the loveliest train,
Do thy fair tribes participate her pain?
Even now, perhaps, by cold and hunger led,
At proud men's doors they ask a little bread!   340
Ah, no! To distant climes, a dreary scene,
Where half the convex world intrudes between,
Through torrid tracts with fainting steps they go,
Where wild Altama[5] murmurs to their woe.
Far different there from all that charm'd before,
The various terrors of that horrid shore;
Those blazing suns that dart a downward ray,
And fiercely shed intolerable day;
Those matted woods where birds forget to sing,
But silent bats in drowsy clusters cling,   350
Those poisonous fields with rank luxuriance crowned,
Where the dark scorpion gathers death around;
Where at each step the stranger fears to wake
The rattling terrors of the vengeful snake;
Where crouching tigers wait their hapless prey,
And savage men, more murderous still than they;
While oft in whirls the mad tornado flies,
Mingling the ravaged landscape with the skies.
Far different these from every former scene,
The cooling brook, the grassy vested green,   260
The breezy covert of the warbling grove,
That only sheltered thefts of harmless love.

---

5 the river Altahama in Georgia.

Good Heaven! what sorrows gloom'd that parting day,
That called them from their native walks away;
When the poor exiles, every pleasure past,
Hung round their bowers, and fondly looked their last,
And took a long farewell, and wished in vain
For seats like these beyond the western main;
And shuddering still to face the distant deep,
Returned and wept, and still returned to weep.   370
The good old sire, the first prepared to go
To new found worlds, and wept for others woe.
But for himself, in conscious virtue brave,
He only wished for worlds beyond the grave.
His lovely daughter, lovelier in her tears,
The fond companion of his helpless years,
Silent went next, neglectful of her charms,
And left a lover's for a father's arms.
With louder plaints the mother spoke her woes,
And blest the cot where every pleasure rose;   380
And kist her thoughtless babes with many a tear,
And claspt them close in sorrow doubly dear;
Whilst her fond husband strove to lend relief
In all the silent manliness of grief.

O luxury! Thou curst by Heaven's decree,
How ill exchanged are things like these for thee!
How do thy potions, with insidious joy,
Diffuse their pleasures only to destroy!
Kingdoms, by thee, to sickly greatness grown,
Boast of a florid vigour not their own;   390
At every draught more large and large they grow,
A bloated mass of rank unwieldy woe;
Till sapped their strength, and every part unsound,
Down, down they sink, and spread a ruin round.

Even now the devastation is begun,
And half the business of destruction done;
Even now, methinks, as pondering here I stand,
I see the rural virtues leave the land:
Down where yon anchoring vessel spreads the sail,
That idly waiting flaps with every gale,   400
Downward they move, a melancholy band,
Pass from the shore, and darken all the strand.
Contented toil, and hospitable care,
And kind connubial tenderness, are there;
And piety, with wishes placed above,
And steady loyalty, and faithful love:
And thou, sweet Poetry, thou loveliest maid,
Still first to fly where sensual joys invade;
Unfit in these degenerate times of shame,
To catch the heart, or strike for honest fame;   410
Dear charming nymph, neglected and decried,
My shame in crowds, my solitary pride;
Thou source of all my bliss, and all my woe,
That found'st me poor at first, and keep'st me so;

Thou guide by which the nobler arts excell,
Thou nurse of every virtue, fare thee well.
Farewell, and O where'er thy voice be tried,
On Torno's[6] cliffs, or Pambamarca's[7] side,
Whether where equinoctial fervours glow,
Or winter wraps the polar world in snow,   420
Still let thy voice prevailing over time,
Redress the rigours of the inclement clime;

Aid slighted truth, with thy persuasive strain
Teach erring man to spurn the rage of gain;
Teach him that states of native strength possest,
Tho, very poor, may still be very blest;
That trade's proud empire hastes to swift decay,
As ocean sweeps the labour'd mole away;
While self-dependent power can time defy,
As rocks resist the billows and the sky.   430

---

6 Lake Tornea in northern Sweden.
7 a mountain in Ecuador.

1770

1752 · THOMAS CHATTERTON · 1770

1752   Born at Bristol, posthumous son of a poor schoolmaster, and nephew to the sexton of St. Mary Redcliffe Church. Attended Colston's Hospital (Bristol's charity school). A dreamy, solitary child he spent his leisure hours poring over medieval manuscripts of no particular value which his father had carried home from the muniment room of Redcliffe Church. Throughout his school days, he was fascinated by antiquities, especially heraldry and the surroundings of medieval life. When he was ten, wrote his first poem and began contributing to the local magazines.

1764   Wrote *Apostate Will,* a satiric poem, and other verses.

1767   Left school and became apprenticed to a Bristol attorney, John Lambert. About this time conceived the idea of an elaborate series of poems and prose pieces grouped about the figure of William Canynge, mayor of Bristol under Henry VI, purporting to be the work of one Rowley, a mythical fifteenth-century parish priest.

1768   Submitted to his townsmen a pseudo-archaic account of the opening of Bristol bridge in the thirteenth century. Began palming off Rowley poems and other fabricated documents upon George Catcott and Henry Burgum, two credulous Bristol pewterers, and William Barrett, a surgeon and antiquary who was writing a history of Bristol.

1769   Wrote to James Dodsley, the London publisher, offering to supply him with ancient poems that had fallen into his hands. Receiving no answer, wrote to Horace Walpole, who first showed interest and then, upon the advice of Mason and Gray, rejected Chatterton's work. *Elinoure and Juga,* the only Rowley poem published during the author's lifetime, appeared in *Town and Country Magazine.*

1770   Left Bristol for London and cast his fortune with the hazards of a literary career. Scribbled incessantly for the papers and magazines, receiving little or no pay. Wrote the last Rowley poem, *An Excelente Balade of Charitie.* At length oppressed by poverty and disease, and overcome with despair, he destroyed his remaining manuscripts, took poison, and died. The Rowley poems were first collected and published by Thomas Tyrwhitt in 1777.

Thomas Chatterton was gifted with a precocious talent, which from early childhood was turned eagerly, almost instinctively, to the study of medieval antiquities. By his sixteenth year the 'marvelous boy of Bristol' had constructed with great diligence and ingenuity the astounding fabrication known as the Rowley poems. In contrast to his own proudly arrogant nature or the sharp wit of his modern verse satires, the Middle Ages that his highly active imagination created was a world of simplicity and benevolence. His creation was partly an escape from reality, and it was partly the result of following Elizabethan rather than true medieval models. Chatterton's master was Spenser though he drew also with some frequency upon Shakespeare and Drayton. Besides those found in Spenser, he picked up quaint words (sometimes mistaking their sense), from Chaucer, Percy's *Reliques,* Anglo-Saxon dictionaries, Geoffrey of Monmouth, Camden, Holinshed, and others. His work abounds in unnatural spellings, misapplied diction, and anachronisms; but it also reveals extraordinary inventiveness and insight. Chatterton expertly adapted the Spenserian stanza and repeatedly shows skill in free and irregular meters. There is, however, no occasion (as some have done) to make extravagant claims for the Rowley poems. The best pieces have sincerity and cadenced beauty, but few critics would wish seriously to compare them with the finished work of Thomson, Collins, or Gray. As for their originality it must be kept in mind that the revival of a taste for Gothic literature and art predates Chatterton's writings. Moreover, as H. A. Beers has reminded us, his reconstruction of the antique, though more original than the imitative verse of the Wartons or the thin, diffused medievalism of Walpole, was still a 'poor, faint *simulacrum*' compared with Scott's.

It is hardly necessary to raise a moral issue over the Rowley poems. It was a day of literary forgeries. The Ossian controversy was raging and the tide of popular favor was running strong toward the antique. Chatterton hoped to gain the attention of the learned world with the announcement of the discovery of an unknown fifteenth-century poet. But Walpole quickly shied off and Tyrwhitt and other medieval scholars easily exposed the fabrication. Nevertheless, sensational interest attached to Chatterton's name for half a century after his death. To the succeeding generation of romantic poets he became the symbol of neglected genius and was commemorated in verse by a host of writers. Keats, who held a sort of psychical sympathy with Chatterton, dedicated *Endymion* to his memory and Shelley placed him in *Adonais* among 'the inheritors of unfulfilled renown.' The romantics tended to praise Chatterton's gifts rather than his poems, though his direct influence, working primarily through Coleridge, was of some slight consequence, too, in the writings of Coleridge himself and of Keats and Rossetti.

BRISTOWE TRAGEDIE: OR, THE DETHE OF SYR CHARLES BAWDIN[1]

THE featherd songster chaunticleer
  Han[2] wounde hys bugle horne,
And tolde the earlie villager
  The commynge of the morne:

Kynge EDWARDE sawe the ruddie streakes
  Of lyghte eclypse the greie;
And herde the raven's crokynge throte
  Proclayme the fated daie.

'Thou'rt ryght,' quod hee, 'for, by the Godde
  That syttes enthron'd on hyghe!   10
CHARLES BAWDIN, and hys fellowes twaine,
  To-daie shall surelie die.'

Thenne wythe a jugge of nappy ale
  Hys Knyghtes dydd onne hymm waite;
'Goe tell the traytour, thatt to-daie
  Hee leaves thys mortall state.'

Syr CANTERLONE thenne bendedd lowe,
  Wythe harte brymm-fulle of woe;

Hee journey'd to the castle-gate,
  And to Syr CHARLES dydd goe.   20

Butt whenne hee came, hys children twaine,
  And eke hys lovynge wyfe,
Wythe brinie tears dydd wett the floore,
  For goode Syr CHARLESES lyfe.

'O goode Syr CHARLES!' sayd CANTERLONE,
  'Badde tydyngs I doe brynge.'
'Speke boldlie, manne,' sayd brave Syr CHARLES,
  'Whatte says thie traytor kynge?'

'I greeve to telle, before yonne sonne
  Does fromme the welkinn flye,   30
Hee hath uponne hys honour sworn,
  Thatt thou shalt surelie die.'

'Wee all must die,' quod brave Syr CHARLES;
  'Of thatte I'm not affearde;
Whatte bootes to lyve a little space?
  Thanke JESU, I'm prepar'd:

'Butt telle thye kynge, for myne hee's not,
  I'de sooner die to-daie
Thanne lyve hys slave, as manie are,
  Tho' I shoulde lyve for aie.'   40

Thenne CANTERLONE hee dydd goe out,
  To telle the maior straite

---

1 Chatterton's poem is probably based upon the execution of Sir Baldwin Fulford at Bristol in 1461 after the accession of Edward IV. During the War of the Roses, Fulford had opposed Edward's claims to the throne.
2 has.

To gett all thynges ynne reddynesse
   For goode Syr CHARLESES fate.

Thenne Maisterr CANYNGE[3] saughte the kynge,
   And felle down onne hys knee;
'I'm come,' quod hee, 'unto your grace
   To move your clemencye.'

Thenne quod the kynge, 'Youre tale speke out,
   You have been much oure friende;   50
Whatever youre request may bee,
   Wee wylle to ytte attende.'

'My nobile liege! alle my request
   Ys for a nobile knyghte,
Who, tho' may hap hee has donne wronge,
   He thoghte ytt stylle was ryghte:

'Hee has a spouse and children twaine,
   Alle rewyn'd[4] are for aie;
Yff thatt you are resolv'd to lett
   CHARLES BAWDIN die to-daie.'   60

'Speke nott of such a traytour vile,'
   The kynge ynne furie sayde;
'Before the evening starre doth sheene,
   BAWDIN shall loose hys hedde:

'Justice does loudlie for hym calle,
   And hee shalle have hys meede:
Speke, Maister CANYNGE! Whatte thynge else
   Att present does you neede?'

'My nobile leige!' goode CANYNGE sayde,
   'Leave justice to our Godde,   70
And laye the yronne rule asyde;
   Be thyne the olyve rodde.

'Was Godde to serche our hertes and reines,[5]
   The best were synners grete;
CHRIST's vycarr only knowes ne synne,
   Ynne alle thys mortall state.

'Lett mercie rule thyne infante reigne,
   'Twylle faste thye crowne fulle sure;
From race to race thy familie
   Alle sov'reigns shall endure: 80

'But yff wythe bloode and slaughter thou
   Beginne thy infante reigne,

---

3 mayor of Bristol, patron of the imaginary poet Thomas
Rowley.
4 ruined.
5 loins.

Thy crowne uponne thy childrennes brows
   Wylle never long remayne.'

'CANYNGE, awaie! thys traytour vile
   Has scorn'd my power and mee;
Howe canst thou thenne for such a manne
   Intreate my clemencye?'

'My nobile leige! the trulie brave
   Wylle val'rous actions prize,   90
Respect a brave and nobile mynde,
   Altho' ynne enemies.'

'CANYNGE, awaie! By Godde ynne Heav'n
   That dydd mee beinge gyve,
I wylle nott taste a bitt of breade
   Whilst thys Syr CHARLES dothe lyve.

'By MARIE, and alle Seinctes ynne Heav'n,
   Thys sunne shall be hys laste.'
Thenne CANYNGE dropt a brinie teare,
   And from the presence paste.   100

Wyth herte brymm-fulle of gnawynge grief,
   Hee to Syr CHARLES dydd goe,
And satt hymm downe uponne a stoole,
   And teares beganne to flowe.

'Wee all must die,' quod brave Syr CHARLES;
   'Whatte bootes ytte howe or whenne;
Dethe ys the sure, the certaine fate
   Of all wee mortall menne.

'Saye why, my friend, thie honest soul
   Runns overr att thyne eye;   110
Is ytte for my most welcome doome
   Thatt thou dost child-lyke crye?'

Quod godlie CANYNGE, 'I doe weepe,
   Thatt thou so soone must dye,
And leave thy sonnes and helpless wyfe;
   'Tys thys thatt wettes myne eye.'

'Thenne drie the tears thatt out thyne eye
   From godlie fountaines sprynge;
Dethe I despise, and alle the power
   Of EDWARDE, traytor kynge.   120

'Whan throgh the tyrant's welcom means
   I shall resigne my lyfe,
The Godde I serve wylle soone provyde
   For bothe mye sonnes and wyfe.

'Before I sawe the lyghtsome sunne,
   Thys was appointed mee;

Shall mortal manne repyne or grudge
    Whatt Godde ordeynes to bee?

'Howe oft ynne battaile have I stoode,
    Whan thousands dy'd arounde;   130
Whan smokynge streemes of crimson bloode
    Imbrew'd the fatten'd grounde:

'How dydd I knowe thatt ev'ry darte,
    Thatt cutte the airie waie,
Myghte nott fynde passage toe my harte,
    And close myne eyes for aie?

And shall I nowe, forr feere of dethe,
    Looke wanne and bee dysmayde?
Ne! fromm my herte flie childyshe feere,
    Bee alle the manne display'd.   140

'Ah, goddelyke HENRIE![6] Godde forefende,[7]
    And guarde thee and thye sonne,
Yff 'tis hys wylle; but yff 'tis nott,
    Why thenne hys wylle bee donne.

'My honest friende, my faulte has beene
    To serve Godde and mye prynce;
And thatt I no tyme-server am,
    My dethe wylle soone convynce.

'Ynne Londonne citye was I borne,
    Of parents of grete note;   150
My fadre dydd a nobile armes
    Emblazon onne hys cote:

'I make ne doubte butt hee ys gone
    Where soone I hope to goe;
Where wee for ever shall bee blest,
    From oute the reech of woe:

'Hee taughte mee justice and the laws
    Wyth pitie to unite;
And eke hee taughte mee howe to knowe
    The wronge cause fromm the ryghte: 160

'Hee taughte mee wythe a prudent hande
    To feede the hungrie poore,
Ne lett mye sarvants dryve awaie
    The hungrie fromme my doore:

'And none can saye, butt alle mye lyfe
    I have hys wordyes kept;
And summ'd the actyonns of the daie
    Eche nyghte before I slept.

'I have a spouse, goe aske of her,
    Yff I defyl'd her bedde?   170
I have a kynge, and none can laie
    Blacke treason onne my hedde.

'Ynne Lent, and onne the holie eve,
    Fromm fleshe I dydd refrayne;
Whie should I thenne appeare dismay'd
    To leave thys worlde of payne?

'Ne! hapless HENRIE! I rejoyce,
    I shalle ne see thye dethe;
Moste willynglie ynne thye just cause
    Doe I resign my brethe.   180

'Oh, fickle people! rewyn'd londe!
    Thou wylt kenne peace ne moe;
Whyle RICHARD's sonnes[8] exalt themselves,
    Thye brookes wythe bloude wylle flowe.

'Saie, were ye tyr'd of godlie peace,
    And godlie HENRIE's reigne,
Thatt you dydd choppe[9] youre easie daies
    For those of bloude and peyne?

'Whatte tho' I onne a sledde bee drawne,
    And mangled by a hynde,[10]   190
I doe defye the traytor's pow'r,
    Hee can ne harm my mynde;

'Whatte tho', uphoisted onne a pole,
    Mye lymbes shall rotte ynne ayre,
And ne ryche monument of brasse
    CHARLES BAWDIN's name shall bear;

'Yett ynne the holie booke above,
    Whyche tyme can't eate awaie,
There wythe the sarvants of the Lorde
    Mye name shall lyve for aie.   200

'Thenne welcome dethe! for lyfe eterne
    I leave thys mortall lyfe:
Farewell, vayne worlde, and alle that's deare,
    Mye sonnes and lovynge wyfe!

'Nowe dethe as welcome to mee comes,
    As e'er the moneth of Maie;
Nor woulde I even wyshe to lyve,
    Wyth my dere wyfe to staie.'

Quod CANYNGE, ' 'Tys a goodlie thynge
    To bee prepar'd to die;   210

---

6 Henry VI, a pious but weak king, deposed by Edward IV and held by him in captivity.
7 defend: the true meaning is *forbid*.

8 Edward IV and Richard, Duke of Gloucester, later Richard III.
9 exchange.
10 peasant.

And from thys world of peyne and grefe
  To Godde ynne Heav'n to flie.'

And nowe the bell beganne to tolle,
  And claryonnes to sounde;
Syr CHARLES hee herde the horses feete
  A prauncyng onne the grounde:

And just before the officers,
  His lovynge wyfe came ynne,
Weepynge unfeigned teeres of woe,
  Wythe loude and dysmalle dynne.   220

'Sweet FLORENCE! nowe I praie forbere,
  Ynne quiet lett mee die;
Praie Godde, thatt ev'ry Christian soule
  Maye looke onne dethe as I.

'Sweet FLORENCE! why these brinie teeres?
  Theye washe my soule awaie,
And almost make mee wyshe for lyfe,
  Wyth thee, sweete dame, to staie.

' 'Tys butt a journie I shalle goe
  Untoe the lande of blysse;   230
Nowe, as a proofe of husbande's love,
  Receive thys holie kysse.'

Thenne FLORENCE, fault'ring ynne her saie,
  Tremblynge these wordyes spoke,
'Ah, cruele EDWARDE! bloudie kynge!
  My herte ys welle nyghe broke:

'Ah, sweete Syr CHARLES! why wylt thou goe,
  Wythoute thye lovynge wyfe?
The cruelle axe thatt cuttes thye necke,
  Ytte eke shall ende mye lyfe.'   240

And nowe the officers came ynne
  To brynge Syr CHARLES awaie,
Whoe turnedd toe his lovynge wyfe,
  And thus toe her dydd saie:

'I goe to lyfe, and nott to dethe;
  Truste thou ynne Godde above,
And teache thye sonnes to feare the Lorde,
  And ynne theyre hertes hym love:

'Teache them to runne the nobile race
  Thatt I theyre fader runne: 250
FLORENCE! shou'd dethe thee take—adieu!
  Yee officers, leade onne.'

Thenne FLORENCE rav'd as anie madde,
  And dydd her tresses tere;

'Oh! staie, mye husband! lorde! and lyfe!'—
  Syr CHARLES thenne dropt a teare.

'Tyll tyredd oute wythe ravynge loud,
  Shee fellen onne the flore;
Syr CHARLES exerted alle hys myghte,
  And march'd fromm oute the dore.   260

Uponne a sledde hee mounted thenne,
  Wythe lookes full brave and swete;
Lookes, thatt enshone[11] ne moe concern
  Thanne anie ynne the strete.

Before hym went the council-menne,
  Ynne scarlett robes and golde,
And tassils spanglynge ynne the sunne,
  Muche glorious to beholde:

The Freers of Seincte AUGUSTYNE next
  Appeared to the syghte,   270
Alle cladd ynne homelie russett weedes,[12]
  Of godlie monkysh plyghte:[13]

Ynne diffraunt partes a godlie psaume
  Moste sweetlie theye dydd chaunt;
Behynde theyre backes syx mynstrelles came,
  Who tun'd the strunge bataunt.[14]

Thenne fyve-and-twentye archers came;
  Echone the bowe dydd bende,
From rescue of kynge HENRIES friends
  Syr CHARLES forr to defend.   280

Bolde as a lyon came Syr CHARLES,
  Drawne onne a clothe-layde sledde,
Bye two blacke stedes ynne trappynges white,
  Wyth plumes uponne theyre hedde:

Behynde hym fyve-and-twentye moe
  Of archers stronge and stoute,
Wyth bended bowe echone ynn hande,
  Marched ynne goodlie route:

Seincte JAMESES Freers marched next,
  Echone hys parte dydd chaunt;   290
Behynde theyre backs syx mynstrelles came,
  Who tun'd the strunge bataunt:

Thenne came the maior and eldermenne,
  Ynne clothe of scarlett deck't;
And theyre attendyng menne echone,
  Lyke Easterne princes trickt:

---

11 showed.   12 homespun garments.   13 condition.
14 a stringed instrument, apparently the creation of Chatterton's imagination.

And after them, a multitude
  Of citizenns dydd thronge;
The wyndowes were alle fulle of heddes,
  As he dydd passe alonge.   300

And whenne hee came to the hyghe crosse,
  Syr CHARLES dydd turne and saie,
'O Thou, thatt savest manne fromme synne,
  Washe mye soule clean thys daie!'

Att the grete mynsterr wyndowe sat
  The kynge ynne myckle state,
To see CHARLES BAWDIN goe alonge
  To hys most welcom fate.

Soone as the sledde drewe nyghe enowe,
  Thatt EDWARDE hee myghte heare,   310
The brave Syr CHARLES hee dydd stande uppe,
  And thus hys wordes declare:

'Thou seest mee, EDWARDE! traytour vile!
  Exposed to infamie;
Butt bee assur'd, disloyall manne!
  I'm greaterr nowe thanne thee.

'Bye foule proceedyngs, murdre, bloude,
  Thou wearest nowe a crowne;
And hast appoynted mee to dye,
  By power nott thyne owne.   320

'Thou thynkest I shall dye to-daie;
  I have beene dede 'till nowe,
And soone shall lyve to weare a crowne
  For aie uponne my browe:

'Whylst thou, perhapps, for som few yeares,
  Shalt rule thys fickle lande,
To lett them knowe howe wyde the rule
  'Twixt kynge and tyrant hande:

'Thye pow'r unjust, thou traytour slave!
  Shall falle onne thye owne hedde'—   330
Fromm out of hearyng of the kynge
  Departed thenne the sledde.

Kynge EDWARDE's soule rush'd to hys face,
  Hee turn'd hys hedde awaie,
And to hys broder GLOUCESTER[15]
  Hee thus dydd speke and saie:

'To hym that soe-much-dreaded dethe
  Ne ghastlie terrors brynge,
Beholde the manne! hee spake the truthe,
  Hee's greater thanne a kynge!'

-----
15 afterward Richard III.

'Soe lett hym die!' Duke RICHARD sayde;
  And maye echone oure foes
Bende downe theyre neckes to bloudie axe,
  And feede the carryon crowes.'

And nowe the horses gentlie drewe
  Syr CHARLES uppe the hyghe hylle;
The axe dydd glysterr ynne the sunne,
  Hys pretious bloude to spylle.

Syrr CHARLES dydd uppe the scaffold goe,
  As uppe a gilded carre   350
Of victorye, bye val'rous chiefs
  Gayn'd ynne the bloudie warre:

And to the people hee dydd saie,
  'Beholde you see mee dye,
For servynge loyally mye kynge,
  Mye kynge most rightfullie.

'As longe as EDWARDE rules thys lande,
  Ne quiet you wylle knowe;
Youre sonnes and husbandes shalle bee slayne,
  And brookes wythe bloude shalle flowe.   360

'You leave youre goode and lawfulle kynge,
  Whenne ynne adversitye;
Lyke mee, untoe the true cause stycke,
  And for the true cause dye.'

Thenne hee, wyth preestes, uponne hys knees,
  A pray'r to Godde dydd make,
Beseechynge hym unto hymselfe
  Hys partynge soule to take.

Thenne, kneelynge downe, hee layd his hedde
  Most seemlie onne the blocke;   370
Whyche fromme hys bodie fayre at once
  The able heddes-manne stroke:

And oute the bloude beganne to flowe,
  And rounde the scaffolde twyne;
And teares, enow to washe't awaie,
  Dydd flowe fromme each mann's eyne.

The bloudie axe hys bodie fayre
  Ynnto foure parties cutte;
And ev'rye parte, and eke hys hedde,
  Uponne a pole was putte.   380

One parte dydd rotte onne Kynwulph-hylle,
  One onne the mynster-tower,
And one from off the castle-gate
  The crowen dydd devoure:

The other onne Seyncte Powle's goode gate,
  A dreery spectacle;
Hys hedde was plac'd onne the hyghe crosse,
  Ynne hyghe-streete most nobile.

Thus was the ende of BAWDIN's fate:
  Godde prosper longe oure kynge,   390
And grante hee maye, wyth BAWDIN's soule,
  Ynne heav'n Godd's mercie synge!
  1768   1772

From ÆLLA: A TRAGYCAL ENTERLUDE

I. MYNSTRELLES SONGE

Fyrste Mynstrelle

THE boddynge[1] flourettes bloshes atte the
  lyghte;
The mees[2] be sprenged[3] wyth the yellowe hue;
Ynn daiseyd mantels ys the mountayne dyghte;
The nesh[4] yonge coweslepe bendethe wyth the
  dewe;
The trees enlefèd, yntoe heavenne straughte,[5]
Whenn gentle wyndes doe blowe, to whestlyng
  dynne ys brought.

The evenynge commes, and brynges the dewe
  alonge;
The roddie welkynne sheeneth to the eyne;[6]
Arounde the alestake[7] mynstrelles synge the
  songe;
Yonge ivie rounde the doore poste do
  entwyne;   10
I laie mee onn the grasse; yette, to mie wylle,
Albeytte alle ys fayre, there lackethe somethynge
  stylle.

Seconde Mynstrelle

So Adam thoughtenne, whann, ynn Paradyse,
All heavenn and erthe dyd hommage to hys
  mynde;
Ynn womman alleyne mannès pleasaunce lyes;
As instrumentes of joie were made the kynde.[8]
Go, take a wyfe untoe thie armes, and see
Wynter and brownie hylles wyll have a charme
  for thee.

Thyrde Mynstrelle

Whanne Autumpne blake[9] and sonnebrente
  doe appere,

With hys goulde honde guylteynge the falleynge
  lefe,   20
Bryngeynge oppe Wynterr to folfylle the yere,
Beerynge uponne hys backe the ripèd shefe;
Whan al the hyls wythe woddie sede[10] ys whyte;
Whanne levynne fyres[11] and lemes[12] do mete from
  far the syghte:

Whann the fayre apple, rudde as even skie,
Do bende the tree unto the fructyle grounde;
When joicie peres, and berries of blacke die,
Doe daunce yn ayre, and call the eyne arounde;
Thann, bee the even foule or even fayre,
Meethynckes mie hartys joie ys steyncèd[13] wyth
  somme care.

Seconde Mynstrelle

Angelles be wroghte to bee of neidher kynde;[14]
Angelles alleyne fromme chafe[15] desyre bee
  free:
Dheere[16] ys a somwhatte evere yn the mynde,
Yatte,[17] wythout wommanne, cannot styllèd
  bee;
Ne seyncte yn celles, botte,[18] havynge blodde
  and tere,
Do fynde the spryte to joie on syghte of wom-
  manne fayre;

Wommen bee made, notte for hemselves, botte
  manne,
Bone of hys bone, and chyld of hys desire;
Fromme an ynutyle membere[19] fyrste beganne,
Ywroghte with moche of water, lyttele fyre;   40
Therefore theie seke the fyre of love, to hete
The milkyness of kynde, and make hemselves
  complete.

Albeytte wythout wommen menne were
  pheeres[20]
To salvage kynde,[21] and wulde botte lyve to
  slea,
Botte wommenne efte[22] the spryghte of peace
  so cheres,
Tochelod yn[23] Angel joie heie[24] Angeles bee:
Go, take thee swythyn[25] to thie bedde a wyfe;
Bee bante[26] or blessed hie[27] yn proovynge mar-
  ryage lyfe.

---

[1] budding.   [2] meadows.
[3] sprinkled.   [4] tender.
[5] stretched.   [6] The ruddy sky shines to the
                         eyes.
[7] alehouse sign.   [8] womankind.
[9] bare.

[10] willow seed.   [11] lightning.
[12] gleams.   [13] stained.
[14] sex.   [15] warm.
[16] there.   [17] that.
[18] but.   [19] a useless member, i. e.
                             Adam's rib.
[20] mates.   [21] savage creatures.
[22] often.   [23] dowered with.
[24] they.   [25] at once.
[26] accursed.   [27] highly.

II. MYNSTRELLES SONGE

O! synge untoe mie roundelaie,[28]
O! droppe the brynie teare wythe mee,
Daunce ne moe atte hallie daie,
Lycke a reynynge ryver bee;
 Mie love ys dedde,
 Gon to hys death-bedde,
 Al under the wyllowe tree.

Blacke hys cryne[29] as the wyntere nyghte,
Whyte hys rode[30] as the sommer snowe,
Rodde hys face as the mornynge lyghte,   10
Cale[31] he lyes ynne the grave belowe;
 Mie love ys dedde,
 Gon to hys deathe-bedde,
 Al under the wyllowe tree.

Swote hys tyngue as the throstles note,
Quycke ynn daunce as thoughte canne bee,
Defte hys taboure,[32] codgelle stote,[33]
O! hee lyes bie the wyllowe tree:
 Mie love ys dedde,
 Gone to hys deathe-bedde,   20
 Alle underre the wyllowe tree.

Harke! the ravenne flappes hys wynge,
In the briered delle belowe;
Harke! the dethe-owle loude dothe synge,
To the nyghte-mares as heie[34] goe;
 Mie love ys dedde,
 Gon to hys deathe-bedde,
 Al under the wyllowe tree.

See! the whyte moone sheenes onne hie;
Whyterre ys mie true loves shroude;   30
Whyterre yanne the mornynge skie,
Whyterre yanne the evenynge cloude;
 Mie love ys dedde,
 Gon to hys deathe-bedde,
 Al under the wyllowe tree.

Heere, uponne mie true loves grave,
Schalle the baren fleurs be layde,
Nee one hallie Seyncte to save
Al the celness[35] of a mayde.
 Mie love ys dedde,   40
 Gonne to hys deathe-bedde,
 Alle under the wyllowe tree.

Wythe mie hondes I'lle dente[36] the brieres
Rounde his hallie corse to gre,[37]

Ouphante[38] fairie, lyghte youre fyres,
Herre mie boddie stylle schalle bee.
 Mie love ys dedde,
 Gon to hys deathe-bedde,
 Al under the wyllowe tree.

Comme, wythe acorne-coppe & thorne,   50
Drayne mie hartys blodde awaie;
Lyfe and all yttes goode I scorne,
Daunce bie nete, or feaste by daie.
 Mie love ys dedde,
 Gone to hys death-bedde,
 Al under the wyllowe tree.

Waterre wytches, crownede wythe reytes,[39]
Bere mee to yer leathalle[40] tyde.
I die; I comme; mie true love waytes.
Thos the damselle spake, and dyed.   60

1768   1777

AN EXCELENTE BALADE OF CHARITIE:

AS WROTEN BIE THE GODE PRIESTE
THOMAS ROWLEY, 1464[1]

IN VIRGYNE[2] the sweltrie sun gan sheene,
And hotte upon the mees[3] did caste his raie;
The apple rodded[4] from its palie greene,
And the mole[5] pear did bende the leafy spraie;
The peede chelandri[6] sunge the livelong daie;
'Twas nowe the pride, the manhode of the
  yeare,
And eke the ground was dighte in its mose defte
  aumere.[7]

The sun was glemeing in the midde of daie,
Deadde still the aire, and eke the welken
  blue,
When from the sea arist in drear arraie   10
A hepe of cloudes of sable sullen hue,
The which full fast unto the woodlande drewe,
Hiltring attenes the sunnis fetive face,[8]
And the blacke tempeste swolne and gatherd up
  apace.

---

38 elfin.   39 reeds.   40 deadly.

1 Thomas Rowley, the author, was born at Norton Malreward,
in Somersetshire, educated at the Convent of St. Kenna, at Key-
nesham, and died at Westbury in Gloucestershire.—(Chatterton.)
2 the Virgin, the sign of the zodiac which the sun enters in
August.
3 meads.
4 reddened.
5 soft.
6 pied goldfinch.
7 mantle.
8 hiding at once the sun's beauteous face.

---

28 join in my song.   29 hair.
30 complexion.   31 cold.
32 a small drum.   33 stout cudgel.
34 they.   35 coldness.
36 plant.   37 grow.

Beneathe an holme,[9] faste by a pathwaie side,
Which dide unto Seyncte Godwine's covent[10]
    lede,
A hapless pilgrim moneynge[11] did abide.
Pore in his viewe,[12] ungentle in his weede,[13]
Longe bretful[14] of the miseries of neede,
Where from the hail-stone coulde the almer[15]
    flie?   20
He had no housen theere, ne anie covent nie.

Look in his glommed[16] face, his sprighte there
    scanne;
Howe woe-be-gone, how withered, forwynd,[17]
    deade!
Haste to thie church-glebe-house,[18] asshrewed
    manne!
Haste to thie kiste,[19] thie onlie dortoure[20] bedde.
Cale, as the claie whiche will gre on thie hedde,
Is Charitie and Love aminge highe elves;
Knightis and Barons live for pleasure and them-
    selves.

The gatherd storme is rype; the bigge drops
    falle;
The forswat[21] meadowes smethe,[22] and
    drenche[23] the raine;   30
The comyng ghastness[24] do the cattle pall,[25]
And the full flockes are drivynge ore the plaine;
Dashde from the cloudes the waters flott[26]
    againe;
The welkin opes; the yellow levynne[27] flies;
And the hot fierie smothe[28] in the wide lowings[29]
    dies.

Liste! now the thunder's rattling clymmynge[30]
    sound
Cheves[31] slowlie on, and then embollen[32] clangs,
Shakes the hie spyre, and losst, dispended,
    drown'd,
Still on the gallard[33] eare of terroure hanges;
The windes are up; the lofty elmen swanges; 40
Again the levynne and the thunder poures,

And the full cloudes are braste attenes in stonen
    showers.

Spurreynge his palfrie oere the watrie plaine,
The Abbote of Seyncte Godwynes convente
    came;
His chapournette[34] was drented with the reine,
And his pencte[35] gyrdle met with mickle shame;
He aynewarde tolde his bederoll[36] at the same;
The storme encreasen, and he drew aside,
With the mist[37] almes craver neere to the holme
    to bide.

His cope[38] was all of Lyncolne clothe so fyne, 50
With a gold button fasten'd neere his chynne;
His autremete[39] was edged with golden twynne,
And his shoone pyke a loverds mighte have
    binne;[40]
Full well it shewn he thoughten coste no sinne:
The trammels[41] of the palfrye pleasde his sighte,
For the horse-millanare[42] his head with roses
    dighte.

An almes, sir prieste! the droppynge pilgrim
    saide,
O! let me waite within your covente dore,
Till the sunne sheneth hie above our heade,
And the loude tempeste of the aire is oer;   60
Helpless and ould am I alas! and poor;
No house, ne friend, ne moneie in my pouche;
All yatte I call my owne is this my silver crouche.[43]

Varlet, replyd the Abbatte, cease your dinne;
This is no season almes and prayers to give;
Mie porter never lets a faitour[44] in;
None touch mie rynge[45] who not in honour live.
And now the sonne with the blacke cloudes did
    stryve,
And shettynge on the grounde his glairie raie,
The Abbatte spurrde his steede, and eftsoones
    roadde awaie.   70

Once moe the skie was blacke, the thunder
    rolde;
Faste reyneynge oer the plaine a prieste was
    seen;
Ne dighte full proude, ne buttoned up in golde;

---

9 oak.
10 It would have been *charitable* if the author had not pointed at
personal characters in this 'Ballad of Charity.' The abbot of St.
Godwin's at the time of the writing of this was Ralph de Bello-
mont, a great stickler for the Lancastrian family. Rowley was a
Yorkist.—(Chatterton.)

11 moaning.	12 appearance.
13 beggarly in his dress.	14 brimful.
15 beggar.	16 gloomy.
17 withered.	18 the grave.
19 coffin.	20 dormitory.
21 sunburned.	22 smoke.
23 drink.	24 terror.
25 frighten.	26 fly.
27 lightning.	28 vapor.
29 flashes.	30 noisy.
31 moves.	32 swollen, strengthened.
33 frightened.	

34 small round hat.
35 bright-colored.
36 He told his beads backwards; a figurative expression to signify
cursing.—(Chatterton.)
37 poor.
38 cloak.
39 loose white robe.
40 His pointed shoes might have been a lord's.
41 shackles, used to make a horse amble.
42 saddler.   43 crucifix.
44 vagabond.   45 door-knocker.

His cope and jape[46] were graie, and eke were
   clene;
A Limitoure he was of order seene;[47]
And from the pathwaie side then turned hee,
Where the pore almer laie binethe the holmen tree.

An almes, sir priest! the droppynge pilgrim
   sayde,
For sweete Seyncte Marie and your order sake.
The Limitoure then loosen'd his pouche
   threade,   80
And did thereoute a groate of silver take;
The mister[48] pilgrim dyd for halline[49] shake.

Here take this silver, it maie eathe[50] thie care;
We are Goddes stewards all, nete[51] of oure owne
   we bare.

But ah! unhailie[52] pilgrim, lerne of me,
Scathe[53] anie give a rentrolle to their Lorde.
Here take my semecope,[54] thou arte bare I see;
Tis thyne; the Seynctes will give me mie rewarde.
He left the pilgrim, and his waie aborde.[55]
Virgynne and hallie Seyncte, who sitte yn
   gloure,   90
Or give the mittee[56] will, or give the gode man
   power.

1770   1777

46 short surplice.
47 He was seen to be a limiter—i. e. a friar licensed to beg.
48 poor.
49 joy.

50 ease.   51 naught.
52 unhappy.   53 scarce.
54 under-cloak.   55 took up.
56 mighty.

1760 · WILLIAM BECKFORD · 1844

1760   Born at Fonthill-Giffard, Wiltshire, son of William Beckford, Lord Mayor of London; heir to enormous wealth. Educated by tutor; visited the Continent; toured England. Member of Parliament.

1780   Published anonymously *Biographical Memoirs of Extraordinary Painters.* Visited the Low Countries, Germany, and Italy.

1782   Wrote in French *The History of the Caliph Vathek.* Made a second journey to Italy.

1783   Printed travel sketches entitled *Dreams, Waking Thoughts and Incidents.*

1786   Anonymous and surreptitious English publication of *Vathek* by its translator, the Reverend Samuel Henley.

1787   The French original of *Vathek* published at Paris and Lausanne.

1787–96   Made trips to Portugal (wrote an account of Alcobaça and Batalha), Spain, Paris (saw the fall of the Bastille), and Switzerland (bought Gibbon's library).

1796–1822   Went into seclusion at Fonthill-Giffard; became a collector and connoisseur; gained notoriety for his architectural and artistic extravagance. Published *The Elegant Enthusiast* (1796) and *Amezia* (1797), burlesques on sentimental novels, and *Al Raoui* (1799).

1822   Forced to sell Fonthill and the greater part of its contents.

1834   Published *Italy, Spain, and Portugal,* the travel sketches of 1783, revised, with those on Spain and Portugal.

1835   Published *Recollections of an Excursion to the Monasteries of Alcobaça and Batalha.*

1844   Died.

D ATING FROM QUEEN ANNE'S time there had developed in eighteenth-century literature a persistent interest in Oriental culture. Fascination for the marvels of the East had been awakened by the English translation in 1708 of Galland's French version of *Arabian Nights.* An era of exploration to remote and strange lands confirmed the growing taste for exotic setting and violent emotions. By the mid-century Voltaire was making effective modern use of Eastern materials in his extravagant satiric fables. William Beckford in *The History of Caliph Vathek* (1782) carried on the humorous treatment of the Oriental tale, but went beyond Voltaire and others in reviving the imaginative dreaming and pleasure-loving luxury characteristic of the Eastern tradition.

William Beckford was a much-traveled, wealthy, and brilliant dilettante who amused himself by giving literary and architectural expression to his romantic visions. In much the same spirit as Horace Walpole, who transformed his home, Strawberry Hill, into a Gothic castle, Beckford built Fonthill Abbey, an immense mansion in Wiltshire, which cost a fortune and whose wild, exotic halls and towers embodied its builder's extravagant dreams of Oriental luxury. A more enduring expression of Beckford's Orientalism (the abbey fell to ruins before it was completed) is *Vathek,* the prose romance of his youth written according to the author at a single sitting of three days and two nights. In *Vathek* Beckford recklessly combines the bizarre and the terrible; with the Oriental-fantastic he intermixes liberal quantities of the Gothic-grotesque given currency by Walpole. The story takes place in an unreal and unmoral region of Oriental fantasy. Incidents of violence and horror follow each other in kaleidoscopic succession interrupted by wild comic interludes or brief passages of idyllic or voluptuous beauty, which exaggerate the grotesqueness or brutality of what went on before. The characters are whimsical compounds of violent and fanciful elements, scarcely credible except perhaps in the final tragic incident. The sensuous exoticism of the romance reaches a climax of grandeur in the closing scenes in the domain of Eblis with an impressive panoramic display of a florid kind of supernaturalism. Beckford's Hell has been named as one of the few worthy of the idea of Hell.

Vathek was enthusiastically admired by Byron, one side of whose nature was probably attracted by the romance's extravagant Orientalism, the other side by its portrayal of the struggle of a fierce and undisciplined nature against moral forces it could defy but could not control. The figure of Eblis ('Milton's Satan a little humanized') came to pervade fiction between Beckford and Scott. He is prominent as the 'anti-hero' in the works of Mrs. Radcliffe, Lewis, and Godwin. His outline is also familiar in Byron's men of mystery.

From THE HISTORY OF THE CALIPH VATHEK

VATHEK, ninth Caliph[1] of the race of the Abassides, was the son of Motassem, and the grandson of Haroun Al Raschid. From an early accession to the throne, and the talents he possessed to adorn it, his subjects were induced to expect that his reign would be long and happy. His figure was pleasing and majestic; but when he was angry one of his eyes became so terrible, that no person could bear to behold it, and the wretch upon whom it was fixed instantly fell backward, and sometimes expired. For fear, however, of depopulating his dominions and making his palace desolate, he but rarely gave way to his anger.

Being much addicted to women and the pleasures of the table, he sought by his affability to procure agreeable companions; and he succeeded the better as his generosity was unbounded, and his indulgences unrestrained, for he was by no means scrupulous, nor did he think with the Caliph Omar Ben Abdalaziz, that it was necessary to make a hell of this world to enjoy Paradise in the next.

He surpassed in magnificence all his predecessors. The palace of Alkoremi, which his father Motassem had erected on the hill of Pied Horses, and which commanded the whole city of Samarah, was in his idea far too scanty; he added, therefore, five wings, or rather other palaces, which he destined for the particular gratification of each of his senses.

In the first of these were tables continually covered with the most exquisite dainties, which were supplied both by night and by day according to their constant consumption, whilst the most delicious wines and the choicest cordials flowed forth from a hundred fountains that were never exhausted. This palace was called *The Eternal* or *Unsatiating Banquet.*

The second was styled *The Temple of Melody,* or *The Nectar of the Soul.* It was inhabited by the most skilful musicians and admired poets of the time, who not only displayed their talents within, but, dispersing in bands without, caused every surrounding scene to reverberate their songs, which were continually varied in the most delightful succession.

The palace named *The Delight of the Eyes,* or *The Support of Memory,* was one entire enchantment. Rarities collected from every corner of the earth were there found in such profusion as to dazzle and confound, but for the order in which they were arranged. One gallery exhibited the pictures of the celebrated Mani,[2] and statues that seemed to be alive. Here a well-managed perspective attracted the sight, there the magic of optics agreeably deceived it; whilst the naturalist on his part exhibited, in their several classes, the various gifts that Heaven had bestowed on our globe. In a word, Vathek omitted nothing in this palace that might gratify the curiosity of those who resorted to it, although he was not able to satisfy his own, for he was of all men the most curious.

The Palace of Perfumes, which was termed likewise *The Incentive to Pleasure,* consisted of various halls where the different perfumes which the

---

1 a title of the successors of Mohammed.

2 a Persian religious mystic of the third century, the founder of Manichaeism.

earth produces were kept perpetually burning in censers of gold. Flambeaux and aromatic lamps were here lighted in open day. But the too powerful effects of this agreeable delirium might be avoided by descending into an immense garden, where an assemblage of every fragrant flower diffused through the air the purest odours.

The fifth palace, denominated *The Retreat of Joy,* or *The Dangerous,* was frequented by troops of young females beautiful as the Houris[3] and not less seducing, who never failed to receive with caresses all whom the Caliph allowed to approach them; for he was by no means disposed to be jealous, as his own women were secluded within the palace he inhabited himself.

Notwithstanding the sensuality in which Vathek indulged, he experienced no abatement in the love of his people, who thought that a sovereign immersed in pleasure was not less tolerable to his subjects than one that employed himself in creating them foes. But the unquiet and impetuous disposition of the Caliph would not allow him to rest there; he had studied so much for his amusement in the lifetime of his father, as to acquire a great deal of knowledge, though not a sufficiency to satisfy himself; for he wished to know everything, even sciences that did not exist. He was fond of engaging in disputes with the learned, but liked them not to push their opposition with warmth; he stopped the mouths of those with presents whose mouths could be stopped, whilst others, whom his liberality was unable to subdue, he sent to prison to cool their blood, a remedy that often succeeded.

Vathek discovered also a predilection for theological controversy, but it was not with the orthodox that he usually held. By this means he induced the zealots to oppose him, and then persecuted them in return; for he resolved at any rate to have reason on his side.

The great prophet Mahomet, whose vicars the caliphs are, beheld with indignation from his abode in the seventh heaven the irreligious conduct of such a viceregent. 'Let us leave him to himself,' said he to the Genii,[4] who are always ready to receive his commands; 'let us see to what lengths his folly and impiety will carry him; if he runs into excess we shall know how to chastise him. Assist him, therefore, to complete the tower which, in imitation of Nimrod, he hath begun, not, like that great warrior, to escape being drowned, but from the insolent curiosity of pene-

trating the secrets of Heaven; he will not divine the fate that awaits him.'

The Genii obeyed, and when the workmen had raised their structure a cubit in the day time, two cubits more were added in the night. The expedition with which the fabric arose was not a little flattering to the vanity of Vathek. He fancied that even insensible matter showed a forwardness to subserve his designs, not considering that the successes of the foolish and wicked form the first rod of their chastisement.

His pride arrived at its height when, having ascended for the first time the eleven thousand stairs of his tower, he cast his eyes below and beheld men not larger than pismires, mountains than shells, and cities than beehives. The idea which such an elevation inspired of his own grandeur completely bewildered him; he was almost ready to adore himself, till, lifting his eyes upwards, he saw the stars as high above him as they appeared when he stood on the surface of the earth. He consoled himself, however, for this transient perception of his littleness, with the thought of being great in the eyes of others, and flattered himself that the light of his mind would extend beyond the reach of his sight, and transfer to the stars the decrees of his destiny.

With this view the inquisitive Prince passed most of his nights at the summit of his tower, till he became an adept in the mysteries of astrology, and imagined that the planets had disclosed to him the most marvellous adventures, which were to be accomplished by an extraordinary personage from a country altogether unknown. Prompted by motives of curiosity he had always been courteous to strangers, but from this instant he redoubled his attention, and ordered it to be announced by sound of trumpet, through all the streets of Samarah that no one of his subjects, on peril of displeasure, should either lodge or detain a traveller, but forthwith bring him to the palace.

Not long after this proclamation there arrived in his metropolis a man so hideous that the very guards who arrested him were forced to shut their eyes as they led him along. The Caliph himself appeared startled at so horrible a visage, but joy succeeded to this emotion of terror when the stranger displayed to his view such rarities as he had never before seen, and of which he had no conception.

In reality nothing was ever so extraordinary as the merchandize this stranger produced; most of his curiosities, which were not less admirable for their workmanship than splendour, had besides, their several virtues described on a parchment fastened to each. There were slippers which enabled the feet to walk; knives that cut without the motion of a hand; sabres which dealt the blow at the person they were wished to strike, and the whole enriched with gems that were hitherto unknown.

The sabres, the blades of which emitted a dazzling radiance, fixed more than all the Caliph's attention, who promised himself to decipher at his leisure the uncouth characters engraven on their sides. Without, therefore, demanding their price, he ordered all the coined gold to be brought from his treasury, and commanded the merchant to take what he pleased; the stranger complied with modesty and silence.

Vathek, imagining that the merchant's taciturnity was occasioned by the awe which his presence inspired, encouraged him to advance, and asked him, with an air of condescension, who he was, whence he came, and where he obtained such beautiful commodities. The man, or rather monster, instead of making a reply, thrice rubbed his forehead, which, as well as his body, was blacker than ebony, four times clapped his paunch, the projection of which was enormous, opened wide his huge eyes, which glowed like firebrands, began to laugh with a hideous noise, and discovered his long amber-coloured teeth bestreaked with green.

The Caliph, though a little startled, renewed his enquiries, but without being able to procure a reply; at which, beginning to be ruffled, he exclaimed: 'Knowest thou, varlet, who I am? and at whom thou art aiming thy gibes?' Then, addressing his guards, 'Have ye heard him speak? is he dumb?'

'He hath spoken,' they replied, 'though but little.'

'Let him speak again then,' said Vathek, 'and tell me who he is, from whence he came, and where he procured these singular curiosities, or I swear by the ass of Balaam[5] that I will make him rue his pertinacity.'

The menace was accompanied by the Caliph with one of his angry and perilous glances, which the stranger sustained without the slightest emotion, although his eyes were fixed on the terrible eye of the Prince.

No words can describe the amazement of the courtiers when they beheld this rude merchant withstand the encounter unshocked. They all fell prostrate with their faces on the ground to avoid the risk of their lives, and continued in the same abject posture till the Caliph exclaimed in a furi-

ous tone: 'Up, cowards! seize the miscreant! see that he be committed to prison and guarded by the best of my soldiers! Let him, however, retain the money I gave him; it is not my intent to take from him his property; I only want him to speak.'

No sooner had he uttered these words than the stranger was surrounded, pinioned with strong fetters, and hurried away to the prison of the great tower, which was encompassed by seven empalements of iron bars, and armed with spikes in every direction longer and sharper than spits.

The Caliph, nevertheless, remained in the most violent agitation; he sat down indeed to eat, but of the three hundred covers that were daily placed before him could taste of no more than thirty-two. A diet to which he had been so little accustomed was sufficient of itself to prevent him from sleeping; what then must be its effect when joined to the anxiety that preyed upon his spirits? At the first glimpse of dawn he hastened to the prison, again to importune this intractable stranger; but the rage of Vathek exceeded all bounds on finding the prison empty, the gates burst asunder, and his guards lying lifeless around him. In the paroxysm of his passion he fell furiously on the poor carcasses, and kicked them till evening without intermission. His courtiers and vizirs exerted their efforts to soothe his extravagance, but finding every expedient ineffectual they all united in one vociferation: 'The Caliph is gone mad! the Caliph is out of his senses!'

This outcry, which soon resounded through the streets of Samarah, at length reaching the ears of Carathis, his mother, she flew in the utmost consternation to try her ascendancy on the mind of her son. Her tears and caresses called off his attention, and he was prevailed upon by her entreaties to be brought back to the palace.

Carathis, apprehensive of leaving Vathek to himself, caused him to be put to bed, and seating herself by him, endeavoured by her conversation to heal and compose him. Nor could any one have attempted it with better success, for the Caliph not only loved her as a mother, but respected her as a person of superior genius; it was she who had induced him, being a Greek herself, to adopt all the sciences and systems of her country, which good Mussulmans hold in such thorough abhorrence. Judicial astrology was one of those systems in which Carathis was a perfect adept; she began, therefore, with reminding her son of the promise which the stars had made him, and intimated an intention of consulting them again.

'Alas!' sighed the Caliph, as soon as he could speak, 'what a fool have I been! not for the kicks

5 See Numbers, xxii.

bestowed on my guards who so tamely submitted to death, but for never considering that this extraordinary man was the same the planets had foretold, whom, instead of ill-treating, I should have conciliated by all the arts of persuasion.'

'The past,' said Carathis, 'cannot be recalled, but it behoves us to think of the future; perhaps you may again see the object you so much regret; it is possible the inscriptions on the sabres will afford information. Eat, therefore, and take thy repose, my dear son; we will consider, tomorrow, in what manner to act.' . . .

The Caliph submitted to the reasons of his mother, and sending for Morakanabad, his prime vizir, said: 'Let the common criers proclaim, not only in Samarah, but throughout every city in my empire, that whosoever will repair hither and decipher certain characters which appear to be inexplicable, shall experience the liberality for which I am renowned; but that all who fail upon trial shall have their beards burnt off to the last hair.[6] Let them add also that I will bestow fifty beautiful slaves, and as many jars of apricots from the isle of Kirmith, upon any man that shall bring me intelligence of the stranger.'

The subjects of the Caliph, like their sovereign, being great admirers of women and apricots from Kirmith, felt their mouths water at these promises, but were totally unable to gratify their hankering, for no one knew which way the stranger had gone.

As to the Caliph's other requisition, the result was different. The learned, the half-learned, and those who were neither, but fancied themselves equal to both, came boldly to hazard their beards, and all shamefully lost them.

The exaction of these forfeitures, which found sufficient employment for the eunuchs, gave them such a smell of singed hair as greatly to disgust the ladies of the seraglio, and make it necessary that this new occupation of their guardians should be transferred into other hands.

At length, however, an old man presented himself whose beard was a cubit and a half longer than any that had appeared before him. The officers of the palace whispered to each other, as they ushered him in, 'What a pity such a beard should be burnt!' Even the Caliph, when he saw it, concurred with them in opinion, but his concern was entirely needless. This venerable personage read the characters with facility, and explained them verbatim as follows: 'We were made where every thing good is made; we are the least of the won-

ders of a place where all is wonderful, and deserving the sight of the first potentate on earth.'

'You translate admirably!' cried Vathek; 'I know to what these marvellous characters allude. Let him receive as many robes of honour and thousands of sequins of gold, as he hath spoken words. I am in some measure relieved from the perplexity that embarrassed me!'

Vathek invited the old man to dine, and even to remain some days in the palace. Unluckily for him he accepted the offer; for the Caliph, having ordered him next morning to be called, said: 'Read again to me what you have read already; I cannot hear too often the promise that is made me, the completion of which I languish to obtain.'

The old man forthwith put on his green spectacles, but they instantly dropped from his nose on perceiving the characters he had read the day preceding had given place to others of different import.

'What ails you?' asked the Caliph; 'and why these symptoms of wonder?'

'Sovereign of the world,' replied the old man, 'these sabres hold another language today from that they yesterday held.'

'How say you?' returned Vathek—'but it matters not! tell me, if you can, what they mean.'

'It is this, my Lord,' rejoined the old man: 'Woe to the rash mortal who seeks to know that of which he should remain ignorant, and to undertake that which surpasseth his power!'

'And woe to thee!' cried the Caliph in a burst of indignation; 'today thou art void of understanding; begone from my presence, they shall burn but the half of thy beard, because thou wert yesterday fortunate in guessing;—my gifts I never resume.'

The old man, wise enough to perceive he had luckily escaped, considering the folly of disclosing so disgusting a truth, immediately withdrew and appeared not again.

But it was not long before Vathek discovered abundant reason to regret his precipitation; for though he could not decipher the characters himself, yet by constantly poring upon them he plainly perceived that they every day changed, and unfortunately no other candidate offered to explain them.

.   .   .

[The Caliph Vathek under the influence of his sorceress mother and of his own unbounded curiosity and megalomania becomes a servant of the Indian merchant, who is in reality Eblis (the Devil). The Caliph is promised a visit to the subterranean palace of fire if he will adjure Mahomet, but the journey can be begun only after he

---

6 Among the Mohammedans, the loss of the beard was regarded as a public disgrace.

has satisfied the Indian's thirst, with a blood sacrifice of fifty of his subjects' most beautiful children. After many adventures, he comes to the happy valley of the Emir Fakreddin where he falls in love with Nouronihar, the Emir's beautiful daughter. Contrary to her father's wishes, she accompanies Vathek on his way to the subterranean kingdom. As the company approaches the halls of Eblis, Mahomet permits various beneficent Genii to warn Vathek to abandon his evil purpose.]

Mahomet answered, with an air of indignation: 'He hath too well deserved to be resigned to himself; but I permit you to try if one effort more will be effectual to divert him from pursuing his ruin.'

One of these beneficent Genii, assuming without delay the exterior of a shepherd, more renowned for his piety than all the derviches[7] and santons[8] of the region, took his station near a flock of white sheep, on the slope of a hill; and began to pour forth from his flute such airs of pathetic melody as subdued the very soul; and, wakening remorse, drove far from it every frivolous fancy. At these energetic sounds, the sun hid himself beneath a gloomy cloud; and the waters of two little lakes, that were naturally clearer than crystal, became of a colour like blood. The whole of this superb assembly was involuntarily drawn towards the declivity of the hill. With downcast eyes, they all stood abashed; each upbraiding himself with the evil he had done. The heart of Dilara palpitated; and the chief of the eunuchs, with a sigh of contrition, implored pardon of the women whom for his own satisfaction he had so often tormented.

Vathek and Nouronihar turned pale in their litter; and regarding each other with haggard looks, reproached themselves—the one with a thousand of the blackest crimes; a thousand projects of impious ambition;—the other, with the desolation of her family; and the perdition of the amiable Gulchenrouz. Nouronihar persuaded herself that she heard, in the fatal music, the groans of her dying father; and Vathek, the sobs of the fifty children he had sacrificed to the Giaour.[9] Amidst these complicated pangs of anguish, they perceived themselves impelled towards the shepherd, whose countenance was so commanding that Vathek, for the first time, felt overawed; whilst Nouronihar concealed her face with her hands.

The music paused, and the Genius addressing

the Caliph said: 'Deluded prince! to whom Providence hath confided the care of innumerable subjects; is it thus that thou fulfillest thy mission? Thy crimes are already completed, and art thou now hastening towards thy punishment? Thou knowest that, beyond these mountains, Eblis and his accursed dives hold their infernal empire; and seduced by a malignant phantom, thou art proceeding to surrender thyself to them! This moment is the last of grace allowed thee: abandon thy atrocious purpose: return: give back Nouronihar to her father, who still retains a few sparks of life: destroy thy tower with all its abominations: drive Carathis from thy councils: be just to thy subjects: respect the ministers of the Prophet; compensate for thy impieties, by an exemplary life: and, instead of squandering thy days in voluptuous indulgence, lament thy crimes on the sepulchres of thy ancestors. Thou beholdest the clouds that obscure the sun: at the instant he recovers his splendour, if thy heart be not changed, the time of mercy assigned thee will be past forever.'

Vathek, depressed with fear, was on the point of prostrating himself at the feet of the shepherd; whom he perceived to be of a nature superior to man: but, his pride prevailing, he audaciously lifted his head, and, glancing at him one of his terrible looks, said: 'Whoever thou art, withhold thy useless admonitions: thou wouldst either delude me, or art thyself deceived. If what I have done be so criminal, as thou pretendest, there remains not for me a moment of grace. I have traversed a sea of blood, to acquire a power, which will make thy equals tremble: deem not that I shall retire when in view of the port; or, that I will relinquish her, who is dearer to me than either my life, or thy mercy. Let the sun appear! Let him illume my career! It matters not where it may end.'

On uttering these words, which made even the Genius shudder, Vathek threw himself into the arms of Nouronihar; and, commanded that his horses should be forced back to the road.

There was no difficulty in obeying these orders: for the attraction had ceased: the sun shone forth in all his glory, and the shepherd vanished with a lamentable scream.

The fatal impression of the music of the Genius remained notwithstanding in the heart of Vathek's attendants. They viewed each other with looks of consternation. At the approach of night, almost all of them escaped; and of this numerous assemblage there only remained the chief of the eunuchs, some idolatrous slaves, Dilara, and a

---

7 members of a Mohammedan religious order taking vows of poverty and austerity.
8 Turkish priests.
9 unbeliever; evil one.

few other women; who, like herself, were votaries of the religion of the Magi.

The Caliph, fired with the ambition of prescrib-
ing laws to the Intelligences of Darkness, was but
little embarrassed at this dereliction; the impetuosity of his blood prevented him from sleeping,
nor did he encamp any more as before. Nouronihar, whose impatience if possible exceeded his
own, importuned him to hasten his march, and
lavished on him a thousand caresses to beguile
all reflection; she fancied herself already more
potent than Balkis, and pictured to her imagination the Genii falling prostrate at the foot of her
throne. In this manner they advanced by moonlight, till they came within view of the two towering rocks that form a kind of portal to the valley,
at whose extremity rose the vast ruins of Istakhar.
Aloft on the mountain glimmered the fronts of
various royal mausoleums, the horror of which
was deepened by the shadows of night. They
passed through two villages almost deserted, the
only inhabitants remaining being a few feeble old
men, who, at the sight of horses and litters, fell
upon their knees and cried out:

'O Heaven! is it then by these phantoms that
we have been for six months tormented? Alas!
it was from the terror of these spectres and the
noise beneath the mountains, that our people
have fled, and left us at the mercy of maleficent
spirits!'

The Caliph, to whom these complaints were
but unpromising auguries, drove over the bodies
of these wretched old men, and at length arrived
at the foot of the terrace of black marble; there
he descended from his litter, handing down Nouronihar; both with beating hearts stared wildly
around them, and expected with an apprehensive shudder the approach of the Giaour; but
nothing as yet announced his appearance.

A deathlike stillness reigned over the mountain and through the air; the moon dilated on a
vast platform the shades of the lofty columns,
which reached from the terrace almost to the
clouds; the gloomy watchtowers, whose numbers
could not be counted, were veiled by no roof, and
their capitals, of an architecture unknown in the
records of the earth, served as an asylum for the
birds of darkness, which, alarmed at the approach
of such visitants, fled away croaking.

The chief of the eunuchs, trembling with fear,
besought Vathek that a fire might be kindled.

'No!' replied he, 'there is no time left to think
of such trifles; abide where thou art, and expect
my commands.'

Having thus spoken he presented his hand to
Nouronihar, and, ascending the steps of a vast
staircase, reached the terrace, which was flagged
with squares of marble, and resembled a smooth
expanse of water, upon whose surface not a leaf
ever dared to vegetate; on the right rose the watch-
towers, ranged before the ruins of an immense
palace, whose walls were embossed with various
figures; in front stood forth the colossal forms of
four creatures, composed of the leopard and the
griffin; and, though but of stone, inspired emotions of terror; near these were distinguished by
the splendour of the moon, which streamed full
on the place, characters like those on the sabres
of the Giaour, that possessed the same virtue
of changing every moment; these, after vacillating for some time, at last fixed in Arabic letters, and prescribed to the Caliph the following
words:

'Vathek! thou hast violated the conditions of
my parchment, and deservest to be sent back;
but, in favour to thy companion, and as the meed
for what thou hast done to obtain it, Eblis per-
mitteth that the portal of his palace shall be opened, and the subterranean fire will receive thee
into the number of its adorers.'

He scarcely had read these words before the
mountain against which the terrace was reared
trembled, and the watch-towers were ready to
topple headlong upon them; the rock yawned,
and disclosed within it a staircase of polished
marble that seemed to approach the abyss; upon
each stair were planted two large torches, like
those Nouronihar had seen in her vision, the cam-
phorated vapour ascending from which gathered
into a cloud under the hollow of the vault.

This appearance, instead of terrifying, gave new
courage to the daughter of Fakreddin. Scarcely
deigning to bid adieu to the moon and the firmament, she abandoned without hesitation the pure
atmosphere to plunge into these infernal exhalations. The gait of those impious personages was
haughty and determined; as they descended by
the effulgence of the torches they gazed on each
other with mutual admiration, and both appeared
so resplendent, that they already esteemed themselves spiritual Intelligences; the only circumstance that perplexed them was their not arriving at the bottom of the stairs; on hastening their
descent with an ardent impetuosity, they felt their
steps accelerated to such a degree, that they
seemed not walking, but falling from a precipice.
Their progress, however, was at length impeded
by a vast portal of ebony, which the Caliph without difficulty recognised; here the Giaour awaited
them with the key in his hand.

'Ye are welcome,' said he to them with a ghastly smile, 'in spite of Mahomet and all his dependants. I will now admit you into that palace where you have so highly merited a place.'

Whilst he was uttering these words he touched the enamelled lock with his key, and the doors at once expanded, with a noise still louder than the thunder of mountains, and as suddenly recoiled the moment they had entered.

The Caliph and Nouronihar beheld each other with amazement, at finding themselves in a place which, though roofed with a vaulted ceiling, was so spacious and lofty that at first they took it for an immeasurable plain. But their eyes at length growing familiar to the grandeur of the objects at hand, they extended their view to those at a distance, and discovered rows of columns and arcades, which gradually diminished till they terminated in a point, radiant as the sun when he darts his last beams athwart the ocean; the pavement, strewed over with gold dust and saffron, exhaled so subtle an odour as almost overpowered them; they, however, went on, and observed an infinity of censers, in which ambergris and the wood of aloes were continually burning; between the several columns were placed tables, each spread with a profusion of viands, and wines of every species sparkling in vases of crystal. A throng of Genii and other fantastic spirits of each sex danced lasciviously in troops, at the sound of music which issued from beneath.

In the midst of this immense hall a vast multitude was incessantly passing, who severally kept their right hands on their hearts, without once regarding anything around them; they had all the livid paleness of death; their eyes, deep sunk in their sockets, resembled those phosphoric meteors that glimmer by night in places of interment. Some stalked slowly on, absorbed in profound reveries; some, shrieking with agony, ran furiously about, like tigers wounded with poisoned arrows; whilst others, grinding their teeth in rage, foamed along, more frantic than the wildest maniac. They all avoided each other, and, though surrounded by a multitude that no one could number, each wandered at random, unheedful of the rest, as if alone on a desert which no foot had trodden.

Vathek and Nouronihar, frozen with terror at a sight so baleful, demanded of the Giaour what these appearances might mean, and why these ambulating spectres never withdrew their hands from their hearts.

'Perplex not yourselves,' replied he bluntly, 'with so much at once, you will soon be ac-

quainted with all; let us haste and present you to Eblis.'

They continued their way through the multitude, but, notwithstanding their confidence at first, they were not sufficiently composed to examine with attention the various perspectives of halls and of galleries that opened on the right hand and left, which were all illuminated by torches and braziers, whose flames rose in pyramids to the centre of the vault. At length they came to a place where long curtains, brocaded with crimson and gold, fell from all parts in striking confusion; here the choirs and dances were heard no longer, the light which glimmered came from afar.

After some time Vathek and Nouronihar perceived a gleam brightening through the drapery, and entered a vast tabernacle carpeted with the skins of leopards; an infinity of elders with streaming beards, and Afrits[10] in complete armour, had prostrated themselves before the ascent of a lofty eminence, on the top of which, upon a globe of fire, sat the formidable Eblis. His person was that of a young man, whose noble and regular features seemed to have been tarnished by malignant vapours; in his large eyes appeared both pride and despair; his flowing hair retained some resemblance to that of an angel of light; in his hand, which thunder had blasted, he swayed the iron sceptre that causes the monster Ouranabad, the Afrits, and all the powers of the abyss to tremble; at his presence the heart of the Caliph sunk within him, and for the first time, he fell prostrate on his face. Nouronihar, however, though greatly dismayed, could not help admiring the person of Eblis; for she expected to have seen some stupendous Giant. Eblis, with a voice more mild than might be imagined, but such as transfused through the soul the deepest melancholy, said:

'Creatures of clay, I receive you into mine empire; ye are numbered amongst my adorers; enjoy whatever this palace affords; the treasures of the pre-adamite Sultans, their bickering[11] sabres, and those talismans that compel the Dives to open the subterranean expanses of the mountain of Kaf, which communicate with these; there, insatiable as your curiosity may be, shall you find sufficient to gratify it; you shall possess the exclusive privilege of entering the fortress of Aherman, and the halls of Argenk, where are portrayed all creatures endowed with intelligence, and the various animals that inhabited that earth

---

10 powerful evil genii or demons in Arabian mythology.
11 clashing.

prior to the creation of that contemptible being, whom ye denominate the Father of Mankind.'

Vathek and Nouronihar, feeling themselves revived and encouraged by this harangue, eagerly said to the Giaour:

'Bring us instantly to the place which contains these precious talismans.'

'Come!' answered this wicked Dive, with his malignant grin, 'come! and possess all that my Sovereign hath promised, and more.'

He then conducted them into a long aisle adjoining the tabernacle, preceding them with hasty steps, and followed by his disciples with the utmost alacrity. They reached, at length, a hall of great extent, and covered with a lofty dome, around which appeared fifty portals of bronze, secured with as many fastenings of iron; a funereal gloom prevailed over the whole scene; here, upon two beds of incorruptible cedar, lay recumbent the fleshless forms of the Pre-adamite Kings, who had been monarchs of the whole earth; they still possessed enough of life to be conscious of their deplorable condition; their eyes retained a melancholy motion; they regarded each other with looks of the deepest dejection, each holding his right hand motionless on his heart; at their feet were inscribed the events of their several reigns, their power, their pride, and their crimes; Soliman Raad, Soliman Daki, and Soliman Di Gian Ben Gian, who, after having chained up the Dives in the dark caverns of Kaf, became so presumptuous as to doubt of the Supreme Power; all these maintained great state, though not to be compared with the eminence of Soliman Ben Daoud.

This king, so renowned for his wisdom, was on the loftiest elevation, and placed immediately under the dome; he appeared to possess more animation than the rest; though from time to time he laboured with profound sighs, and, like his companions, kept his right hand on his heart; yet his countenance was more composed, and he seemed to be listening to the sullen roar of a vast cataract, visible in part through the grated portals; this was the only sound that intruded on the silence of these doleful mansions. A range of brazen vases surrounded the elevation.

'Remove the covers from these cabalistic depositaries,' said the Giaour to Vathek, 'and avail thyself of the talismans, which will break asunder all these gates of bronze; and not only render thee master of the treasures contained within them, but also of the spirits by which they are guarded.'

The Caliph, whom this ominous preliminary had entirely disconcerted, approached the vases with faltering footsteps, and was ready to sink with terror when he heard the groans of Soliman. As he proceeded, a voice from the livid lips of the Prophet articulated these words:

'In my life-time I filled a magnificent throne, having on my right hand twelve thousand seats of gold, where the patriarchs and the prophets heard my doctrines; on my left the sages and doctors, upon as many thrones of silver, were present at all my decisions. Whilst I thus administered justice to innumerable multitude, the birds of the air librating over me served as a canopy from the rays of the sun; my people flourished, and my palace rose to the clouds; I erected a temple to the Most High, which was the wonder of the universe; but I basely suffered myself to be seduced by the love of women, and a curiosity that could not be restrained by sublunary things; I listened to the counsels of Aherman and the daughter of Pharaoh, and adored fire and the hosts of heaven; I forsook the holy city, and commanded the Genii to rear the stupendous palace of Istakhar, and the terrace of the watch-towers, each of which was consecrated to a star; there for a while I enjoyed myself in the zenith of glory and pleasure; not only men, but supernatural existences were subject also to my will. I began to think, as these unhappy monarchs around had already thought, that the vengeance of Heaven was asleep; when at once the thunder burst my structures asunder and precipitated me hither; where, however, I do not remain, like the other inhabitants, totally destitute of hope, for an angel of light hath revealed that, in consideration of the piety of my early youth, my woes shall come to an end when this cataract shall forever cease to flow; till then I am in torments, ineffable torments! an unrelenting fire preys on my heart.'

Having uttered this exclamation Soliman raised his hands towards Heaven, in token of supplication, and the Caliph discerned through his bosom, which was transparent as crystal, his heart enveloped in flames. At a sight so full of horror Nouronihar fell back, like one petrified, into the arms of Vathek, who cried out with a convulsive sob:

'O Giaour! whither hast thou brought us? Allow us to depart, and I will relinquish all thou hast promised. O Mahomet! remains there no more mercy?'

'None! none!' replied the malicious Dive. 'Know, miserable prince! thou art now in the abode of vengeance and despair; thy heart also will be kindled, like those of the other votaries of Eblis. A few days are allotted thee previous to this fatal period; employ them as thou wilt; re-cline on these heaps of gold; command the In-fernal Potentates; range at thy pleasure through these immense subterranean domains; no barrier shall be shut against thee; as for me, I have ful-filled my mission; I now leave thee to thyself.' At these words he vanished.

The Caliph and Nouronihar remained in the most abject affliction; their tears unable to flow, scarcely could they support themselves. At length, taking each other despondingly by the hand, they went faltering from this fatal hall, indifferent which way they turned their steps; every portal opened at their approach; the Dives fell pros-trate before them; every reservoir of riches was disclosed to their view; but they no longer felt the incentives of curiosity, pride, or avarice. With like apathy they heard the chorus of Genii, and saw the stately banquets prepared to regale them; they went wandering on from chamber to cham-ber, hall to hall, and gallery to gallery, all without bounds or limit, all distinguishable by the same lowering gloom, all adorned with the same awful grandeur, all traversed by persons in search of re-pose and consolation, but who sought them in vain; for, every one carried within him a heart tormented in flames: shunned by these various sufferings, who seemed by their looks to be up-braiding the partners of their guilt, they with-drew from them to wait in direful suspense the moment which should render them to each other the like objects of terror.

'What!' exclaimed Nouronihar; 'will the time come when I shall snatch my hand from thine?'

'Ah!' said Vathek; 'and shall my eyes ever cease to drink from thine long draughts of enjoyment! Shall the moments of our reciprocal ecstasies be reflected on with horror! It was not thou that broughtest me hither; the principles by which Carathis perverted my youth, have been the sole cause of my perdition!' Having given vent to these painful expressions, he called to an Afrit, who was stirring up one of the braziers, and bade him fetch the Princess Carathis from the palace of Samarah.

After issuing these orders, the Caliph and Nou-ronihar continued walking amidst the silent crowd, till they heard voices at the end of the gallery; presuming them to proceed from some unhappy beings, who like themselves were await-ing their final doom, they followed the sound, and found it to come from a small square cham-ber, where they discovered sitting on sofas five young men of goodly figure, and a lovely female, who were all holding a melancholy conversation by the glimmering of a lonely lamp; each had a gloomy and forlorn air, and two of them were embracing each other with great tenderness. On seeing the Caliph and the daughter of Fakreddin enter, they arose, saluted and gave them place; then he who appeared the most considerable of the group addressed himself thus to Vathek.

'Strangers! who doubtless are in the same state of suspense with ourselves, as you do not yet bear your hand on your heart, if you are come hither to pass the interval allotted previous to the inflic-tion of our common punishment, condescend to relate the adventures that have brought you to this fatal place, and we in return will acquaint you with ours, which deserve but too well to be heard; we will trace back our crimes to their source; though we are not permitted to repent, this is the only employment suited to wretches like us!'

The Caliph and Nouronihar assented to the proposal, and Vathek began, not without tears and lamentations, a sincere recital of every cir-cumstance that had passed. When the afflicting narrative was closed, the young man entered on his own. Each person proceeded in order, and when the fourth prince had reached the midst of his adventures, a sudden noise interrupted him, which caused the vault to tremble and to open. . .

Almost at the same instant the same voice an-nounced to the Caliph, Nouronihar, the five princes, and the princess, the awful and irrevo-cable decree. Their hearts immediately took fire, and they at once lost the most precious of the gifts of heaven—HOPE. These unhappy beings re-coiled with looks of the most furious distraction; Vathek beheld in the eyes of Nouronihar nothing but rage and vengeance, nor could she discern aught in his but aversion and despair. The two princes who were friends, and till that moment had preserved their attachment, shrunk back, gnashing their teeth with mutual and unchange-able hatred. Kalilah and his sister made recipro-cal gestures of imprecation, whilst the two other princes testified their horror for each other by the most ghastly convulsions, and screams that could not be smothered. All severally plunged themselves into the accursed multitude, there to wander in an eternity of unabating anguish.

Such was, and such should be, the punishment of unrestrained passions and atrocious actions! Such is, and such should be, the chastisement of blind ambition, that would transgress those bounds which the Creator hath prescribed to hu-man knowledge; and, by aiming at discoveries reserved for pure Intelligence, acquire that infatuated pride, which perceives not the condition appointed to man is to be ignorant and humble.

Thus the Caliph Vathek, who, for the sake of empty pomp and forbidden power, had sullied himself with a thousand crimes, became a prey to grief without end, and remorse without mitigation; whilst the humble and despised Gulchenrouz passed whole ages in undisturbed tranquility, and the pure happiness of childhood.

1783   1786

1764 · ANN RADCLIFFE · 1823

1764   Born in London, daughter of William and Ann Ward. A retiring individual who shunned public notice; next to writing romances, enjoyed reading Shakespeare and indulging her passions for music and wild scenery.

1787   Married William Radcliffe, proprietor and editor of the *English Chronicle.*

1789   Published anonymously *The Castles of Athlin and Dunbayne.*

1790   Published *A Sicilian Romance,*

1791   *The Romance of the Forest,*

1794   *The Mysteries of Udolpho,* and

1797   *The Italian,* a romance of the Inquisition.

1802   Wrote *Gaston de Blondeville* (published posthumously in 1826 with *St. Alban's Abbey).*

1816   Published *Poems.*

1823   Died.

ANN RADCLIFFE, arch-gothicizer, published five romances between 1789 and 1797 all of which were widely popular and widely circulated. Of the five *The Mysteries of Udolpho* is the best known, although *The Italian* is perhaps as good. For her formula Mrs. Radcliffe followed her English predecessors, Walpole and Clara Reeve, but she manipulated her materials with such resourcefulness and with such a power of emotional appeal that she did in effect create something new. She leans heavily upon dramatic suspense (used with only partial success by Walpole), which she sustains by means of wonder and terror awakened through supernatural agencies or (by the mere power of suggestion) through terrifying associations. She also frequently resorts to real and present dangers for terror and suspense.

Thus, though the horrors that Emily, the heroine of *Udolpho,* experiences are for the most part purely imaginary, there are times when her fears are well-grounded, as, for example, when she narrowly escapes abduction by a band of ruffians. It is this admixture of terrors, which Mrs. Radcliffe nicely distinguishes as 'real' and 'ideal,' that constitute the warp and woof of her long and ingeniously complicated romances. At the last all real dangers are by-passed and all mysteries are explained in terms of natural causes. Mrs. Radcliffe handles her plots well and displays great fertility of incident, yet most readers when they reach the end feel disappointed and cheated over her failure to fulfill expectations that were previously awakened.

Romantic love with an overload of sentiment is a staple of all Mrs. Radcliffe's stories. The hero is a gentleman of noble birth, likely as not in some sort of disgrace; the heroine, an orphan-heiress, high-strung and sensitive, and highly susceptible to music and poetry and to nature in its most romantic moods. A prominent role is given to the tyrant-villain. He is a man of fierce and morose passions obsessed by the love of power and riches. The villain can usually be counted on to confine the heroine in the haunted wing of a castle because she refuses to marry someone she hates. Whatever the details, Mrs. Radcliffe generally manages the plot and action so that the chief impression is a sense of the young heroine's incessant danger. On oft-repeated midnight prowls about the gloomy passageways of a rambling, ruined castle, the heroine in a quiver of excitement (largely self-induced) experiences a series of hair-raising adventures and narrow escapes. Her emotional tension is kept to the pitch by a succession of strange sights and sounds—'half-perceived and half-created' —and by an assorted array of sliding panels, trap doors, faded hangings, veiled portraits, bloodstained garments, and even dark and desperate characters.

Mrs. Radcliffe undeniably has a gift for creating atmosphere. Not only can she establish an interior mood of terror, but she is one of the first romancers to make extended use of natural description to give tone and setting to her stories. She knows how to make skillful use of atmospherical factors, such as sunset, storms, winds and thunders, and moonlight. Her favorite scene is the silhouetted castle in ruins, which she placed now in a sternly beautiful landscape, now in a sweetly poetical, idyllic one. She has an eye for large, romantic masses of architecture and a sure taste for the picturesque. Unfortunately she possessed no firsthand knowledge of the countries (France and Italy) where her scenes were laid. As a consequence, she was forced to draw largely upon her reading of the nature poets and her study of the landscape paintings of Salvator Rosa, though some details come from direct observation of the English landscape. Though Mrs. Radcliffe was praised in her day for her ability to describe scenes she had never visited, the total effect of her method is one of indefiniteness. Yet to this day Mrs. Radcliffe has few superiors in the art of creating poetical atmosphere. By the force of her example she made landscape in fiction a convention.

Mrs. Radcliffe's chief weakness is her failure to humanize her characters. Because of this weakness her romances are lacking in any logical relation of characters to action; in short, they fall to the level of melodrama. Yet in spite of this and other shortcomings, perhaps because of them, her 'terror' romanticism found huge public favor and exercised great influence on her contemporaries. The years following the publication of *The Mysteries of Udolpho* were the heyday for the Gothic romance, a time climaxed by the publication of *The Italian* and Lewis's *The Monk*. Mrs. Radcliffe herself never went far into the medieval. She was in this respect a transitional figure, developing tendencies and themes that had earlier been experimental and pointing out the way to Scott. But in mystery and the picturesque, either directly or by way of Scott, her influence is patent in nearly every variety of nineteenth-century fiction. The American tales of terror and wonder of Irving, Poe, and Hawthorne, the detective stories of Godwin and Brocton Browne, and the criminal romances of Dickens—all bear testimony to the fertile example of Mrs. Radcliffe's Gothic thrillers.

From THE MYSTERIES OF UDOLPHO

[The period of Mrs. Radcliffe's novel is the end of the sixteenth century. The principal scenes are laid in the gloomy Castle of Udolpho, isolated in the Italian Apennines. Emily St. Aubert, the beautiful daughter of a Gascon family, is the heroine; and the villain, who marries Emily's aunt for her money, is the sinister Signor Montoni. As the following scene opens, Montoni is conveying Emily and her unhappy aunt to the 'vast and dreary' confines of the castle.]

AT length the travellers began to ascend among the Apennines. The immense pine forests, which, at that period, overhung these mountains, and between which the road wound, excluded all view but of the cliffs aspiring above, except that, now and then, an opening through the dark woods allowed the eye a momentary glimpse of the country below. The gloom of these shades, their solitary silence, except when the breeze swept over their summits, the tremendous precipices of the mountains that came partially to the eye, each assisted to raise the solemnity of Emily's feelings into awe; she saw only images of gloomy grandeur, or of dreadful sublimity, around her; other images, equally gloomy and equally terrible, gleamed on her imagination. She was going she scarcely knew whither, under the dominion of a person from whose arbitrary disposition she had already suffered so much, to marry, perhaps, a man who possessed neither her affection nor esteem; or to endure, beyond the hope of succour, whatever punishment revenge, and that Italian revenge, might dictate. The more she considered what might be the motive of the journey, the more she became convinced that it was for the purpose of concluding her nuptials with Count Morano, with the secrecy which her resolute resistance had made necessary to the honour, if not to the safety, of Montoni. From the deep solitudes into which she was emerging, and from the gloomy castle, of which she had heard some mysterious hints, her sick heart recoiled in despair, and she experienced, that, though her mind was already occupied by peculiar distress, it was still alive to the influence of new and local circumstance; why else did she shudder at the image of this desolate castle?

As the travellers still ascended among the pine forests, steep rose over steep, the mountains seemed to multiply as they went, and what was the summit of one eminence proved to be only the base of another. At length they reached a little plain, where the drivers stopped to rest the mules, whence a scene of such extent and magnificence opened below, as drew even from Madame Montoni a note of admiration. Emily lost, for a moment, her sorrows in the immensity of nature. Beyond the amphitheatre of mountains that stretched below, whose tops appeared as numerous almost as the waves of the sea, and whose feet were concealed by the forests—extended the *campagna* of Italy, where cities and rivers and woods, and all the glow of cultivation, were mingled in gay confusion. The Adriatic bounded the horizon, into which the Po and the Brenta, after winding through the whole extent of the landscape, poured their fruitful waves. Emily gazed long on the splendours of the world she was quitting, of which the whole magnificence seemed thus given to her sight only to increase her regret on leaving it; for her, Valancourt alone was in that world; to him alone her heart turned, and for him alone fell her bitter tears.

From this sublime scene the travellers continued to ascend among the pines, till they entered a narrow pass of the mountains, which shut out every feature of the distant country, and in its stead exhibited only tremendous crags, impending over the road, where no vestige of humanity, or even of vegetation, appeared, except here and there the trunk and scathed branches of an oak, that hung nearly headlong from the rock, into which its strong roots had fastened. This pass, which led into the heart of the Apennine, at length opened to day, and a scene of mountains stretched in long perspective, as wild as any the travellers had yet passed. Still vast pine forests hung upon their base, and crowned the ridgy precipice that rose perpendicularly from the vale, while, above,

the rolling mists caught the sunbeams, and touched their cliffs with all the magical colouring of light and shade. The scene seemed perpetually changing, and its features to assume new forms, as the winding road brought them to the eye in different attitudes; while the shifting vapours, now partially concealing their minuter beauties, and now illuminating them with splendid tints, assisted the illusions of the sight.

Though the deep valleys between these mountains were, for the most part, clothed with pines, sometimes an abrupt opening presented a perspective of only barren rocks, with a cataract flashing from their summit among broken cliffs, till its waters, reaching the bottom, foamed along with louder fury; and sometimes pastoral scenes exhibited their 'green delights' in the narrow vales, smiling amid surrounding horror. There herds and flocks of goats and sheep, browsing under the shade of hanging woods, and the shepherd's little cabin, reared on the margin of a clear stream, presented a sweet picture of repose.

Wild and romantic as were these scenes, their character had far less of the sublime than had those of the Alps, which guard the entrance of Italy. Emily was often elevated, but seldom felt those emotions of indescribable awe, which she had so continually experienced in her passage over the Alps.

Towards the close of day, the road wound into a deep valley. Mountains, whose shaggy steeps appeared to be inaccessible, almost surrounded it. To the east, a vista opened, and exhibited the Apennines in their darkest horrors; and the long perspective of retiring summits rising over each other, their ridges clothed with pines, exhibited a stronger image of grandeur than any that Emily had yet seen. The sun had just sunk below the top of the mountains she was descending, whose long shadow stretched athwart the valley, but his sloping rays, shooting through an opening of the cliffs, touched with a yellow gleam the summits of the forest that hung upon the opposite steeps, and streamed in full splendour upon the towers and battlements of a castle that spread its extensive ramparts along the brow of a precipice above. The splendour of these illumined objects was heightened by the contrasted shade which involved the valley below.

'There,' said Montoni, speaking for the first time in several hours, 'is Udolpho.'

Emily gazed with melancholy awe upon the castle, which she understood to be Montoni's; for, though it was now lighted up by the setting sun, the Gothic greatness of its features, and its mouldering walls of dark grey stone, rendered it a gloomy and sublime object. As she gazed, the light died away on its walls, leaving a melancholy purple tint, which spread deeper and deeper, as the thin vapour crept up the mountain, while the battlements above were still tipped with splendour. From those, too, the rays soon faded, and the whole edifice was invested with the solemn duskiness of evening. Silent, lonely, and sublime, it seemed to stand the sovereign of the scene, and to frown defiance on all who dared to invade its solitary reign. As the twilight deepened, its features became more awful in obscurity, and Emily continued to gaze, till its clustering towers were alone seen rising over the tops of the woods, beneath whose thick shade the carriages soon after began to ascend.

The extent and darkness of these tall woods awakened terrific images in her mind, and she almost expected to see banditti start up from under the trees. At length the carriages emerged upon a heathy rock, and soon after reached the castle gates, where the deep tone of the portal bell, which was struck upon to give notice of their arrival, increased the fearful emotions that had assailed Emily. While they waited till the servant within should come to open the gates, she anxiously surveyed the edifice: but the gloom that overspread it, allowed her to distinguish little more than a part of its outline, with the massy walls of the ramparts, and to know that it was vast, ancient, and dreary. From the parts she saw, she judged of the heavy strength and extent of the whole. The gateway before her, leading into the courts, was of gigantic size, and was defended by two round towers, crowned by overhanging turrets, embattled, where, instead of banners, now waved long grass and wild plants, that had taken root among the mouldering stones, and which seemed to sigh, as the breeze rolled past, over the desolation around them. The towers were united by a curtain, pierced and embattled also, below which appeared the pointed arch of a huge portcullis, surmounting the gates: from these, the walls of the ramparts extended to other towers, overlooking the precipice, whose shattered outline, appearing on a gleam that lingered in the west, told of the ravages of war. Beyond these all was lost in the obscurity of evening.

While Emily gazed with awe upon the scene, footsteps were heard within the gates, and the undrawing of bolts; after which an ancient servant of the castle appeared, forcing back the huge folds of the portal to admit his lord. As the carriage-wheels rolled heavily under the portcullis,

Emily's heart sank, and she seemed as if she was going into her prison; the gloomy court, into which she passed, served to confirm the idea, and her imagination, ever awake to circumstance, suggested even more terrors than her reason could justify. . . .

[*Emily explores the mystery of the picture concealed behind the veil.*]

'Do you know which is my room?' said she to Annette, as they crossed the hall.

'Yes, I believe I do, ma'amselle; but this is such a strange rambling place! I have been lost in it already: they call it the double chamber, over the south rampart, and I went up this great staircase to it. My lady's room is at the other end of the castle.'

Emily ascended the marble staircase, and came to the corridor, as they passed through which Annette resumed her chat. 'What a wild lonely place this is, ma'am! I shall be quite frightened to live in it. How often, and often have I wished myself in France again! I little thought, when I came with my lady to see the world, that I should ever be shut up in such a place as this, or I would never have left my own country! This way, ma'amselle, down this turning. I can almost believe in giants again, and such like, for this is just like one of their castles; and, some night or other, I suppose, I shall see fairies too, hopping about in the great old hall, that looks more like a church, with its huge pillars, than anything else.'

'Yes,' said Emily, smiling, and glad to escape from more serious thought, 'if we come to the corridor, about midnight, and look down into the hall, we shall certainly see it illuminated with a thousand lamps, and the fairies tripping in gay circles to the sound of delicious music; for it is in such places as this, you know, that they come to hold their revels. But I am afraid, Annette, you will not be able to pay the necessary penance for such a sight; and, if once they hear your voice, the whole scene will vanish in an instant.'

'Oh! if you will bear me company, ma'amselle, I will come to the corridor, this very night, and I promise you I will hold my tongue; it shall not be my fault if the show vanishes.—But do you think they will come?'

'I cannot promise that with certainty, but I will venture to say, it will not be your fault if the enchantment should vanish.'

'Well, ma'amselle, that is saying more than I expected of you: but I am not so much afraid of fairies as of ghosts, and they say there are a plentiful many of them about the castle; now I should be frightened to death if I should chance to see any of them. But hush, ma'amselle, walk softly! I have thought, several times, something passed by me.'

'Ridiculous!' said Emily; 'you must not indulge such fancies.'

'Oh, ma'am! they are not fancies, for aught I know; Benedetto says these dismal galleries and halls are fit for nothing but ghosts to live in; and I verily believe, if I *live* long in them, I shall turn to one myself!'

'I hope,' said Emily, 'you will not suffer Signor Montoni to hear of these weak fears; they would highly displease him.'

'What, you know then, ma'amselle, all about it!' rejoined Annette. 'No, no, I do know better than to do so; though, if the signor can sleep sound, nobody else in the castle has any right to lie awake, I am sure.' Emily did not appear to notice this remark.

'Down this passage, ma'amselle; this leads to a back staircase. Oh! if I see anything, I shall be frightened out of my wits!'

'That will scarcely be possible,' said Emily, smiling, as she followed the winding of the passage, which opened into another gallery: and then Annette, perceiving that she had missed her way, while she had been so eloquently haranguing on ghosts and fairies, wandered about through other passages and galleries, till, at length, frightened by their intricacies and desolation, she called aloud for assistance: but they were beyond the hearing of the servants, who were on the other side of the castle, and Emily now opened the door of a chamber on the left.

'Oh, do not go in there, ma'amselle,' said Annette, 'you will only lose yourself further.'

'Bring the light forward,' said Emily, 'we may possibly find our way through these rooms.'

Annette stood at the door, in an attitude of hesitation, with the light held up to show the chamber, but the feeble rays spread through not half of it. 'Why do you hesitate?' said Emily; 'let me see whither this room leads.'

Annette advanced reluctantly. It opened into a suite of spacious and ancient apartments, some of which were hung with tapestry, and others wainscotted with cedar and black larch-wood. What furniture there was, seemed to be almost as old as the rooms, and retained an appearance of grandeur, though covered with dust, and dropping to pieces with damp, and with age.

'How cold these rooms are, ma'amselle!' said Annette: 'nobody has lived in them for many, many years, they say. Do let us go.'

'They may open upon the great staircase, perhaps,' said Emily, passing on till she came to a chamber hung with pictures, and took the light to examine that of a soldier on horseback in a field of battle.—He was darting his spear upon a man who lay under the feet of the horse, and who held up one hand in a supplicating attitude. The soldier, whose beaver was up, regarded him with a look of vengeance, and his countenance, with that expression, struck Emily as resembling Montoni. She shuddered, and turned from it. Passing the light hastily over several other pictures, she came to one concealed by a veil of black silk. The singularity of the circumstance struck her, and she stopped before it, wishing to remove the veil, and examine what could thus carefully be concealed, but somewhat wanting courage. 'Holy Virgin! what can this mean?' exclaimed Annette. 'This is surely the picture they told me of at Venice.'

'What picture?' said Emily. 'Why a picture—a picture,' replied Annette, hesitatingly—'but I never could make out exactly what it was about, either.'

'Remove the veil, Annette.'

'What! I ma'amselle!—I! not for the world!' Emily, turning round, saw Annette's countenance grow pale. 'And pray, what have you heard of this picture, to terrify you so, my good girl?' said she. 'Nothing, ma'amselle: I have heard nothing, only let us find our way out.'

'Certainly: but I wish first to examine the picture; take the light, Annette, while I lift the veil.' Annette took the light, and immediately walked away with it, disregarding Emily's call to stay, who not choosing to be left alone in the dark chamber, at length followed her. 'What is the reason of this, Annette?' said Emily, when she overtook her; 'what have you heard concerning that picture, which makes you so unwilling to stay when I bid you?'

'I don't know what is the reason, ma'amselle,' replied Annette, 'nor anything about the picture, only I have heard there is something very dreadful belonging to it—and that it has been covered up in black *ever since*—and that nobody has looked at it for a great many years—and it somehow has to do with the owner of this castle before Signor Montoni came to the possession of it—and——

'Well, Annette,' said Emily, smiling, 'I perceive it is as you say—that you know nothing about the picture.'

'No, nothing, indeed, ma'amselle, for they made me promise never to tell:——but——'

'Well,' said Emily, who perceived that she was struggling between her inclination to reveal a secret, and her apprehension for the consequence, 'I will inquire no further——'

'No pray, ma'am, do not.'

'Lest you should tell all,' interrupted Emily.

Annette blushed, and Emily smiled, and they passed on to the extremity of this suite of apartments, and found themselves, after some further perplexity, once more at the top of the marble staircase, where Annette left Emily, while she went to call one of the servants of the castle to show them to the chamber, for which they had been seeking.

While she was absent, Emily's thoughts returned to the picture; an unwillingness to tamper with the integrity of a servant, had checked her inquiries on this subject, as well as concerning some alarming hints, which Annette had dropped respecting Montoni; though her curiosity was entirely awakened and she had perceived that her questions might easily be answered. She was now, however, inclined to go back to the apartment and examine the picture; but the loneliness of the hour and of the place, with the melancholy silence that reigned around her, conspired with a certain degree of awe, excited by the mystery attending this picture, to prevent her. She determined, however, when daylight should have reanimated her spirits, to go thither and remove the veil. . . .

Montoni having refused Emily another chamber, she determined to bear with patience the evil she could not remove, and, in order to make the room as comfortable as possible, unpacked her books, her sweet delight in happier days, and her soothing resource in the hours of moderate sorrow: but there were hours when even these failed of their effect; when the genius, the taste, the enthusiasm of the sublimest writers, were felt no longer.

Her little library being arranged on a high chest, part of the furniture of the room, she took out her drawing utensils, and was tranquil enough to be pleased with the thought of sketching the sublime scenes beheld from her windows; but she suddenly checked this pleasure, remembering how often she had soothed herself by the intention of obtaining amusement of this kind, and had been prevented by some new circumstance of misfortune.

'How can I suffer myself to be deluded by hope,' said she, 'and, because Count Morano is not yet arrived, feel a momentary happiness? Alas! what is it to me, whether he is here to-day, or to-morrow, if he comes at all?—and that he will come —it were weakness to doubt.'

To withdraw her thoughts, however, from the subject of her misfortunes, she attempted to read, but her attention wandered from the page, and at length she threw aside the book, and determined to explore the adjoining chambers of the castle. Her imagination was pleased with the view of ancient grandeur, and an emotion of melancholy awe awakened all its powers, as she walked through rooms obscure and desolate, where no footsteps had passed probably for many years, and remembered the strange history of the former possessor of the edifice. This brought to her recollection the veiled picture, which had attracted her curiosity on the preceding night, and she resolved to examine it. As she passed through the chambers that led to this, she found herself somewhat agitated; its connexion with the late lady of the castle, and the conversation of Annette, together with the circumstance of the veil, throwing a mystery over the object that excited a faint degree of terror. But a terror of this nature, as it occupies and expands the mind, and elevates it to high expectation, is purely sublime, and leads us, by a kind of fascination, to seek even the object from which we appear to shrink.

Emily passed on with faltering steps, and having paused a moment at the door, before she attempted to open it, she then hastily entered the chamber, and went towards the picture, which appeared to be enclosed in a frame of uncommon size, that hung in a dark part of the room. She paused again, and then, with a timid hand, lifted the veil; but instantly let it fall—perceiving that what it had concealed was no picture, and, before she could leave the chamber, she dropped senseless on the floor.

1794

1762 · WILLIAM LISLE BOWLES · 1850

1762   Born at King's Sutton, Northamptonshire, son of the vicar.

1776–92   Studied at Winchester School, where Joseph Warton was headmaster, and at Trinity College, Oxford. Took holy orders.

1789   Published *Fourteen Sonnets*, which were followed soon after by more sonnets and in the next forty years by a quantity of other miscellaneous verse and prose.

1792–1850   Held vicarages, chiefly at Bremhill, Wiltshire, where he was greatly beloved by his parishioners. Was appointed chaplain to the prince regent and canon of Salisbury.

1806   Published an edition of Pope with a prefatory essay that involved Bowles in a heated controversy with Byron and Campbell over the merits of Pope's poetry.

1850   Died at Salisbury.

WILLIAM LISLE BOWLES began writing poetry as the result of a disappointment in love which sent him on a tour of England, Scotland, and the Continent in search of forgetfulness. On his travels he often wandered in the evening by 'sequestered' streams to listen to the plaintive notes of 'Philomel' or to muse upon 'romantic' ruins. At other times he would be roused from his apathy by contemplating the wild landscape of mountains or ocean. Under favoring circumstances, through imaginative transference accompanied by poetical composition, his own heartache would seem for the moment to be lightened. The handful of sonnets which are the record of his wandering are predominantly sentimental and almost wholly lacking in depth of thought or poetic force. Yet they were hailed with delight by Coleridge and his youthful contemporaries, who paid them the tribute of imitation. Their melodious versification, tenderness of feeling, and simplicity of language filled a need of the hour. By their break from conventional diction they were in fact a genuine, though slight, impulse toward a quiet and natural style in poetry. Moreover, in spite of their author's sentimental proclivities, the sonnets do reveal a sincere appreciation of the life and beauty of nature and Bowles's partial success, at least, in harmonizing the moods of nature with those of the mind.

AT DOVER CLIFFS

ON these white cliffs, that calm above the flood,
Uplift their shadowing heads, and, at their feet,
Scarce hear the surge that has for ages beat,
Sure many a lonely wand'rer has stood;
And, whilst the lifted murmur met his ear,
And o'er the distant billows the still Eve
Sail'd slow, has thought of all his heart must leave
Tomorrow; of the friends he lov'd most dear;
Of social scenes, from which he wept to part:
But if, like me, he knew how fruitless all   10
The thoughts that would full fain the past recall,
Soon would he quell the risings of his heart,
And brave the wild winds and unhearing tide—
The World his country, and his God his guide.

1789

121

THE BELLS OF OSTEND[1]

How sweet the tuneful bells' responsive peal!
As when, at opening morn, the fragrant breeze
Breathes on the trembling sense of pale disease,
So piercing to my heart their force I feel!
And hark! with lessening cadence now they fall!
And now, along the white and level tide,
They fling their melancholy music wide,
Bidding me many a tender thought recall
Of summer days, and those delightful years
When from an ancient tower, in life's fair prime, 10
The mournful magic of their mingling chime
First waked my wondering childhood into tears!
But seeming now, when all those days are o'er,
The sounds of joy once heard, and heard no more.

1787   1789

INFLUENCE OF TIME ON GRIEF

O TIME! who know'st a lenient hand to lay
Softest on sorrow's wounds, and slowly thence,
Lulling to sad repose the weary sense,
The faint pang stealest unperceiv'd away:
On Thee I rest my only hope at last,
And think, when thou hast dried the bitter tear
That flows in vain o'er all my soul held dear,
I may look back on every sorrow past,
And meet life's peaceful evening with a smile—
As some lone bird, at day's departing hour,   10
Sings in the sunbeam, of the transient show'r
Forgetful, though its wings are wet the while—
Yet ah! how much must that poor heart endure,
Which hopes from thee, and thee alone, a cure!

                                              1789

_____
1 a famous seashore resort in Belgium.

DISTANT VIEW OF ENGLAND FROM THE SEA

YES! from mine eyes the tears unbidden start,
As thee, my country, and the long-lost sight
Of thy own cliffs, that lift their summits white
Above the wave, once more my beating heart
With eager hope and filial transport hails!
Scenes of my youth, reviving gales ye bring,
As when erewhile the tuneful morn of spring
Joyous awoke amidst your hawthorn vales,
And fill'd with fragrance every village lane:
Fled are those hours, and all the joys they gave! 10
Yet still I gaze, and count each rising wave
That bears me nearer to my home again;
If haply, 'mid those woods and vales so fair,
Stranger to Peace, I yet may meet her there.

                                              1789

HOPE

As one who, long by wasting sickness worn,
Weary has watched the lingering night, and heard
Unmoved the carol of the matin bird
Salute his lonely porch; now first at morn
Goes forth, leaving his melancholy bed;
He the green slope and level meadow views,
Delightful bathed with slow-ascending dews;
Or marks the clouds, that o'er the mountain's
     head
In varying forms fantastic wander white;
Or turns his ear to every random song,   10
Heard the green river's winding marge along,
The whilst each sense is steeped in still delight.
So o'er my breast young Summer's breath I feel,
Sweet Hope! thy fragrance pure and healing in-
     cense steal!

                                              1789

1731 · WILLIAM COWPER · 1800

1731 Born, son of the rector of Great Berkhampstead. His mother claimed descent from Henry III and John Donne. Upon his mother's death, when he was six, was sent to a boarding school (where he was bullied) and afterward to Westminster School.

1749–64 Studied law and was called to the bar. Fell in love with his cousin Theodora, but her father refused to countenance the suit. Suffered periods of great depression which, agitated by nervousness over an impending examination for a clerkship in the House of Lords and the delusion that he was damned, developed into mania and caused him to attempt suicide. Was removed in 1763 to a private asylum at St. Albans.

1765–78 Recovered his health and became an inmate of the household of the Reverend Morley Unwin at Huntingdon. After the death of Unwin in 1767 moved with Mrs. Unwin and her two children to Olney. There he came under the influence of John Newton, the evangelical curate of that place. Became engaged to Mrs. Unwin but another attack of madness prevented their marriage.

1779 The influence of the strenuous Newton being withdrawn, Cowper entered upon the most peaceful period of his life. To occupy his mind began to write poetry. Publication of *Olney Hymns* (written in conjunction with Newton, 1771–3).

1780–82 Wrote eight moral satires: *The Progress of Error, Truth, Table Talk, Expostulation, Hope, Charity, Conversation,* and *Retirement* (published in 1782). Composed *On the Loss of the Royal George* and *John Gilpin.*

1783–4 Composed *The Task,* begun upon a suggestion by Lady Austen. Began a translation of Homer.

1785 Published *The Task,* together with *John Gilpin* and *Triocinium,* an attack upon the public schools.

1786–95 Moved to Weston, Norfolk, with Mrs. Unwin, where he wrote some of his finest short poems, including *On the Receipt of My Mother's Picture,* the sonnet *To Mrs. Unwin,* and the pathetically beautiful lines *To Mary.* Published the translation of Homer (1791).

1796 Death of Mrs. Unwin, which left the poet shattered in mind and body.

1799 Wrote his last poem, *The Castaway,* an allegory of his own condition.

1800 Died.

B Y THE MID-EIGHTEENTH CENTURY the effects of the Industrial Revolution were becoming acutely felt. Unrest among agricultural as well as factory workers was on the increase; the gap between wealth and poverty was rapidly widening. As the distress of the masses grew there developed a need for an emotional faith for them to hold to. Deism—a softened, sentimentalized religion teaching universal benevolence—had met certain wants for a time. But as the social order became increasingly unsettled and as sufferings among the lower classes mounted, the old deistical doctrines were no longer felt to be adequate. The crying need was for a religious outlet by which the untaught and the uncared for could find release from their discontent. This need was filled by Methodism. In its essentials Methodism was a revival of traditional Christianity based upon the fundamental doctrine of original sin. According to this belief man was utterly helpless and corrupt until redeemed through the incarnate God. John Wesley, the founder of Methodism, and his itinerant preachers spread their old-fashioned creed with great fervor throughout the length and breadth of England. A great wave of religious excitement stirred the people, chiefly among the middle and lower classes, though the evangelical spirit flourished for a while also within the more aristocratic membership of the English Church. The Methodist movement satisfied a real emotional hunger; it also resulted in positive good to the nation. The strong conviction of the evil side of human nature led to the condemnation of social evils. A crusading lower class quickened the social consciousness, strengthened civic solidarity, established moral precedents in politics, and made people more humane. Except for the hymns of Charles Wesley, however, there was practically no literary work of consequence as the direct product of Methodism. Yet more generally Methodism acted as a stimulating force upon the sensibilities of the people, helping to prepare the way for a poetry of more spontaneous seeing and feeling, of more appeal to the heart, and of aid in the regeneration of the mystical imagination.

Though William Cowper was not himself a Methodist, through his association with the English Church his creative thought and feeling were in no small way conditioned by the new evangelicanism. During various periods of his life his sensitive mind was nourished upon the gloomy doctrine of predestination fed to him by ill-chosen spiritual advisers. As a consequence, in times of mental depression he became possessed by a terrible and implacable conviction that he was a lost soul. In his hymns he persistently stresses the saving power of the atoning sacrifice, and throughout his religious verse he gives expression to the hard and revolting beliefs of inelastic Puritanism. He is convinced that things are going from bad to worse. He sees many signs that God's patience will not put up much longer with the avarice and luxury that are increasing on all sides. He mourns the selfishness of the nation's rulers who make war to satisfy their greed and ambition. He laments the lack of discipline in schools and colleges, where vice flourishes because the aims of the teachers are low and selfish. Slavery he condemns as a monstrous evil supported by the greed of the traders. Yet it would be a mistake to overemphasize the religious bias of Cowper's writing. He lamented England's vices not merely as a strait-laced theologian but as a fine humanitarian and patriot, and as a sensitive poet and lover of nature. He was persistent in his hopes for the brotherhood of man (he prophesied the fall of the Bastille), spoke out boldly against aggressive war, was dead in earnest in his pleas for the abolition of slavery, and was generous in his sentiment for all living things from man himself to the humblest forms of sentient life.

With Cowper religious worship and the love of Nature are closely linked. Nature becomes for him the symbol of the simple life which nourishes virtue and inner freedom. In Nature's presence consolation and peace are to be found, and joy in contemplating her. Nature is the teacher of the wise; meditation in quiet rural surroundings will better foster wisdom than will learning gleaned from books. Also, the country is the place of physical as well as mental health. Disease is caused by the worldling who is distracted by the false gaiety of the city. Rural sights and sounds, on the contrary, exhilarate and restore the human body and spirit. Cowper does not go so far as to say that civilized life is inimical to virtue, but he is suspicious of cities and the products of civilization. The beauty of the countryside is for him lovelier than the adulterated works of art. He knew the country, lived there all his adult life, and rejoiced in the simplicity and serenity he found there. His poetry is filled with a loving appraisal of Nature's gifts. He drew her portrait faithfully. His lines are filled with the ceaseless activity of the natural world recorded in minute realistic detail. Nothing is too small or obscure for his attention. Among eighteenth-century nature poets Cowper has partial rivals in Thomson, Collins, and Gray, but he is not surpassed in accuracy of detail or depth of sympathy for animate Nature.

In his early volumes Cowper followed the main lines of current thought and expression. It was in *The Task* that he emancipated himself. In this work, his masterpiece, he looked at the world and into his own mind and heart; expressed directly what he saw, thought, and felt; and in so doing recovered simplicity and truth in poetry. Large portions of *The Task* are admittedly dull reading and there are frequent lapses in the poem into eighteenth-century conventional diction. But despite a certain drag of conservatism, Cowper brought a new spirit into English verse and helped measurably to redeem it from artificiality and rhetoric. In *The Task* he reveals himself as essentially an original writer, singularly independent of theories, movements, and schools. In a well-known letter to his bookseller Cowper attacked Pope's smoothness and stated a preference for the 'manly rough line.' In utterances such as this we have a clear manifesto of the literary reformation in style afterward led by Wordsworth. Moreover, in the subject matter of poetry as well as in the manner Cowper was prophetic of much that was to characterize later writing. He anticipated the romantic generation in his political liberalism, in his humanitarianism, and most of all in his sympathetic and faithful rendering of external nature. Of historical importance also are the strong personal note in his poetry and the personal directness of treatment.

Cowper's poetry falls short of greatness by its lack of emotional intensity. Its charm is that of the leisureliness and intimacy of the personal essay. But if the poems approach the essay, the letters are in fact essays in miniature. With more liveliness than the poems, but with equal fidelity, they capture the details and oddities, the fireside enjoyments and home-born happiness of everyday life. As a man Cowper was shy, morbidly sensitive, and at times lost in the great darkness of insanity. Yet madness and unhappiness were only sporadic and did not essentially damage the fine integrity of his character. In the letters his playful humor and broad sympathies wonderfully shine forth to give us some of the most delightfully intimate and informal prose writing in the language.

From OLNEY HYMNS

[The *Olney Hymns* were written in partnership with the Reverend John Newton at Olney, chiefly in 1771 and 1772. Cowper contributed altogether 68 hymns to the collection.]

LIGHT SHINING OUT OF DARKNESS[1]

GOD moves in a mysterious way,
  His wonders to perform;
He plants his footsteps in the sea,
  And rides upon the storm.

Deep in unfathomable mines
  Of never failing skill;
He treasures up his bright designs,
  And works his sovereign will.

Ye fearful saints fresh courage take,
  The clouds ye so much dread   10
Are big with mercy, and shall break
  In blessings on your head.

Judge not the LORD by feeble sense,
  But trust him for his grace;
Behind a frowning providence,
  He hides a smiling face.

His purposes will ripen fast,
  Unfolding ev'ry hour;
The bud may have a bitter taste,
  But sweet will be the flow'r.   20

Blind unbelief is sure to err,
  And scan his work in vain;
GOD is his own interpreter,
  And he will make it plain.

1779

WALKING WITH GOD[1]

OH! for a closer walk with GOD,
  A calm and heav'nly frame;
A light to shine upon the road
  That leads me to the Lamb!

Where is the blessedness I knew
  When first I saw the LORD?
Where is the soul-refreshing view
  Of JESUS, and his word?

What peaceful hours I once enjoy'd!
  How sweet their mem'ry still!   10
But they have left an aching void,
  The world can never fill.

---

1 John, i, 5.

1 Genesis, v, 24.

Return, O holy Dove, return,
　　Sweet messenger of rest;
I hate the sins that made thee mourn,
　And drove thee from my breast.

The dearest idol I have known,
　　Whate'er that idol be;
Help me to tear it from thy throne,
　　And worship only thee.　　　　　　　　20

So shall my walk be close with GOD,
　　Calm and serene my frame;
So purer light shall mark the road
　　That leads me to the Lamb.

　　　　　　　　　　　　　　　1779

ADDRESSED TO A YOUNG LADY[1]

SWEET stream that winds thro' yonder glade,
Apt emblem of a virtuous maid—
Silent and chaste she steals along,
Far from the world's gay busy throng,
With gentle, yet prevailing, force
Intent upon her destin'd course;
Graceful and useful all she does,
Blessing and blest where'er she goes,
Pure-bosom'd as that wat'ry glass,
And heav'n reflected in her face.　　　　　　10

　1780　　　　　　　　　　　　　1782

From THE TASK

The history of the following production is briefly this:
A lady,[1] fond of blank verse, demanded a poem of that
kind from the author, and gave him the Sofa for a subject. He obeyed; and, having much leisure, connected
another subject with it; and, pursuing the train of thought
to which his situation and turn of mind led him, brought
forth at length, instead of the trifle which he at first intended, a serious affair—a Volume.—(From Cowper's
prefatory Advertisement.)

BOOK I

THE SOFA

Lines 109–80, 749–74

FOR I have lov'd the rural walk through lanes
Of grassy swarth, close cropt by nibbling sheep, 110
And skirted thick with intertexture firm
Of thorny boughs; have lov'd the rural walk
O'er hills, through valleys, and by rivers' brink,
E'er since a truant boy I pass'd my bounds

---

1 Miss Shuttleworth, sister-in-law of the Reverend William Unwin, Mrs. Mary Unwin's son.

---

1 Lady Austen, a friend of Cowper.

T' enjoy a ramble on the banks of Thames;
And still remember, nor without regret
Of hours that sorrow since has much endear'd,
How oft, my slice of pocket store consum'd,
Still hung'ring, pennyless and far from home,
I fed on scarlet hips[2] and stony haws,[3]　　　120
Or blushing crabs, or berries, that emboss
The bramble, black as jet, or sloes[4] austere.
Hard fare! but such as boyish appetite
Disdains not; nor the palate, undeprav'd
By culinary arts, unsav'ry deems.
No SOFA then awaited my return;
Nor SOFA then I needed. Youth repairs
His wasted spirits quickly, by long toil
Incurring short fatigue; and, though our years
As life declines speed rapidly away,　　　　130
And not a year but pilfers as he goes
Some youthful grace that age would gladly keep;
A tooth or auburn lock, and by degrees
Their length and colour from the locks they spare;
Th' elastic spring of an unwearied foot
That mounts the stile with ease, or leaps the fence,
That play of lungs, inhaling and again
Respiring freely the fresh air, that makes
Swift pace or steep ascent no toil to me,
Mine have not pilfer'd yet; nor yet impair'd　140
My relish of fair prospect; scenes that sooth'd
Or charm'd me young, no longer young, I find
Still soothing and of pow'r to charm me still.
And witness, dear companion of my walks,[5]
Whose arm this twentieth winter I perceive
Fast lock'd in mine, with pleasure such as love,
Confirm'd by long experience of thy worth
And well-tried virtues, could alone inspire—
Witness a joy that thou hast doubled long.
Thou know'st my praise of nature most sincere, 150
And that my raptures are not conjur'd up
To serve occasions of poetic pomp,
But genuine, and art partner of them all.
How oft upon yon eminence our pace
Has slacken'd to a pause, and we have born
The ruffling wind, scarce conscious that it blew,
While admiration, feeding at the eye,
And still unsated, dwelt upon the scene.
Thence with what pleasure have we just discern'd
The distant plough slow moving, and beside　160
His lab'ring team, that swerv'd not from the track,
The sturdy swain diminish'd to a boy!
Here Ouse, slow winding through a level plain
Of spacious meads with cattle sprinkled o'er,
Conducts the eye along its sinuous course

---

2 fruit of the dog-rose.
3 fruit of the hawthorn.
4 fruit of the black thorn.
5 Mrs. Mary Unwin.

Delighted. There, fast rooted in their bank,
Stand, never overlook'd, our fav'rite elms,
That screen the herdsman's solitary hut;
While far beyond, and overthwart the stream
That, as with molten glass, inlays the vale,   170
The sloping land recedes into the clouds;
Displaying on its varied side the grace
Of hedge-row beauties numberless, square tow'r,
Tall spire, from which the sound of cheerful bells
Just undulates upon the list'ning ear,
Groves, heaths, and smoking villages, remote.
Scenes must be beautiful, which, daily view'd,
Please daily, and whose novelty survives
Long knowledge and the scrutiny of years.
Praise justly due to those that I describe.   180

God made the country, and man made the town.
What wonder then that health and virtue, gifts 750
That can alone make sweet the bitter draught
That life holds out to all, should most abound
And least be threaten'd in the fields and groves?
Possess ye, therefore, ye, who, borne about
In chariots and sedans, know no fatigue
But that of idleness, and taste no scenes
But such as art contrives, possess ye still
Your element; there only can ye shine,
There only minds like your's can do no harm.
Our groves were planted to console at noon   760
The pensive wand'rer in their shades. At eve
The moon-beam, sliding softly in between
The sleeping leaves, is all the light they wish,
Birds warbling all the music. We can spare
The splendour of your lamps; they but eclipse
Our softer satellite. Your songs confound
Our more harmonious notes: the thrush departs
Scar'd, and th' offended nightingale is mute.
There is a public mischief in your mirth;
It plagues your country. Folly such as your's, 770
Grac'd with a sword, and worthier of a fan,
Has made, what enemies could ne'er have done,
Our arch of empire, stedfast but for you,
A mutilated structure, soon to fall.

BOOK II

THE TIME-PIECE

Lines 1–47

Oh for a lodge in some vast wilderness,
Some boundless contiguity of shade,
Where rumour of oppression and deceit,
Of unsuccessful or successful war,
Might never reach me more. My ear is pain'd,
My soul is sick, with ev'ry day's report
Of wrong and outrage with which earth is fill'd.

There is no flesh in man's obdurate heart,
It does not feel for man; the nat'ral bond
Of brotherhood is sever'd as the flax   10
That falls asunder at the touch of fire.
He finds his fellow guilty of a skin
Not colour'd like his own; and, having pow'r
T' enforce the wrong, for such a worthy cause
Dooms and devotes him as his lawful prey.
Lands intersected by a narrow frith
Abhor each other. Mountains interpos'd
Make enemies of nations, who had else,
Like kindred drops, been mingled into one.
Thus man devotes his brother, and destroys;   20
And, worse than all, and most to be deplor'd,
As human nature's broadest, foulest blot,
Chains him, and tasks him, and exacts his sweat
With stripes, that mercy, with a bleeding heart,
Weeps when she sees inflicted on a beast.
Then what is man? And what man, seeing this,
And having human feelings, does not blush,
And hang his head, to think himself a man?
I would not have a slave to till my ground,
To carry me, to fan me while I sleep,   30
And tremble when I wake, for all the wealth
That sinews bought and sold have ever earn'd.
No: dear as freedom is, and in my heart's
Just estimation priz'd above all price,
I had much rather be myself the slave,
And wear the bonds, that fasten them on him.
We have no slaves at home.—Then why abroad?
And they themselves, once ferried o'er the wave
That parts us, are emancipate and loos'd.
Slaves cannot breath in England,[6] if their lungs 40
Receive our air, that moment they are free;
They touch our country, and their shackles fall.
That's noble, and bespeaks a nation proud
And jealous of the blessing. Spread it then,
And let it circulate through ev'ry vein
Of all your empire; that where Britain's pow'r
Is felt, mankind may feel her mercy too.

BOOK III

THE GARDEN

Lines 108–38

I was a stricken deer, that left the herd
Long since; with many an arrow deep infixt
My panting side was charg'd, when I withdrew 110
To seek a tranquil death in distant shades.
There was I found by one who had himself
Been hurt by th' archers. In his side he bore,
And in his hands and feet, the cruel scars.

---

6 The court decision that 'Slaves cannot breathe in England' was
given by Lord Mansfield in 1772. The slave trade was abolished in
1811.

With gentle force soliciting the darts,
He drew them forth, and heal'd, and bade me live.
Since then, with few associates, in remote
And silent woods I wander, far from those
My former partners of the peopled scene;
With few associates, and not wishing more. 120
Here much I ruminate, as much I may,
With other views of men and manners now
Than once, and others of a life to come.
I see that all are wand'rers, gone astray
Each in his own delusions; they are lost
In chase of fancied happiness, still woo'd
And never won. Dream after dream ensues;
And still they dream that they shall still succeed.
And still are disappointed. Rings the world
With the vain stir. I sum up half mankind, 130
And add two thirds of the remaining half,
And find the total of their hopes and fears
Dreams, empty dreams. The million flit as gay
As if created only like the fly,
That spreads his motley wings in th' eye of noon,
To sport their season, and be seen no more.
The rest are sober dreamers, grave and wise,
And pregnant with discov'ries new and rare.

BOOK V

THE WINTER MORNING WALK

Lines 363–462

Whose freedom is by suff'rance, and at will
Of a superior, he is never free.
Who lives, and is not weary of a life
Expos'd to manacles, deserves them well.
The state that strives for liberty, though foil'd,
And forc'd t' abandon what she bravely sought,
Deserves at least applause for her attempt,
And pity for her loss. But that's a cause   370
Not often unsuccessful: pow'r usurp'd
Is weakness when oppos'd; conscious of wrong,
'Tis pusillanimous and prone to flight.
But slaves, that once conceive the glowing thought
Of freedom, in that hope itself possess
All that the contest calls for; spirit, strength,
The scorn of danger, and united hearts;
The surest presage of the good they seek.
Then shame to manhood, and opprobrious more
To France than all her losses and defeats,   380
Old or of later date, by sea or land,
Her house of bondage, worse than that of old
Which God aveng'd on Pharaoh—the Bastile![7]
Ye horrid tow'rs, th' abode of broken hearts;
Ye dungeons and ye cages of despair,

That monarchs have supplied from age to age
With music such as suits their sov'reign ears—
The sighs and groans of miserable men!
There's not an English heart that would not leap
To hear that ye were fall'n at last; to know   390
That ev'n our enemies, so oft employ'd
In forging chains for us, themselves were free.
For he who values liberty confines
His zeal for her predominance within
No narrow bounds; her cause engages him
Wherever pleaded. 'Tis the cause of man.
There dwell the most forlorn of human kind;
Immur'd though unaccus'd, condemn'd untried,
Cruelly spar'd, and hopeless of escape!
There, like the visionary emblem seen   400
By him of Babylon,[8] life stands a stump,
And, filletted about with hoops of brass,
Still lives, though all its pleasant boughs are gone.
To count the hour-bell and expect no change;
And ever, as the sullen sound is heard,
Still to reflect, that, though a joyless note
To him whose moments all have one dull pace,
Ten thousand rovers in the world at large
Account it music; that it summons some
To theatre, or jocund feast or ball: 410
The wearied hireling finds it a release
From labour; and the lover, who has chid
Its long delay, feels ev'ry welcome stroke
Upon his heart-strings, trembling with delight—
To fly for refuge from distracting thought
To such amusements as ingenious woe
Contrives, hard-shifting, and without her tools—
To read engraven on the mouldy walls,
In stagg'ring types, his predecessor's tale,
A sad memorial, and subjoin his own—   420
To turn purveyor to an overgorg'd
And bloated spider, till the pamper'd pest
Is made familiar, watches his approach,
Comes at his call, and serves him for a friend—
To wear out time in numb'ring to and fro
The studs that thick emboss his iron door;
Then downward and then upward, then aslant
And then alternate; with a sickly hope
By dint of change to give his tasteless task
Some relish; till the sum, exactly found   430
In all directions, he begins again—
Oh comfortless existence! hemm'd around
With woes, which who that suffers would not kneel
And beg for exile, or the pangs of death?
That man should thus encroach on fellow man,
Abridge him of his just and native rights,
Eradicate him, tear him from his hold
Upon th' endearments of domestic life
And social, nip his fruitfulness and use,

---

[7] the French royal prison, destroyed 14 July 1789 by the Revolutionists.

[8] See Daniel, iv, 10–18.

And doom him for perhaps an heedless word   440
To barrenness, and solitude, and tears,
Moves indignation; makes the name of king
(Of king whom such prerogative can please)
As dreadful as the Manichean god,[9]
Ador'd through fear, strong only to destroy.

'Tis liberty alone that gives the flow'r
Of fleeting life its lustre and perfume;
And we are weeds without it. All constraint,
Except what wisdom lays on evil men,
Is evil; hurts the faculties, impedes   450
Their progress in the road of science; blinds
The eyesight of discov'ry; and begets,
In those that suffer it, a sordid mind
Bestial, a meagre intellect, unfit
To be the tenant of man's noble form.
Thee therefore still, blame-worthy as thou art,
With all thy loss of empire, and though squeez'd
By public exigence till annual food
Fails for the craving hunger of the state,
Thee I account still happy, and the chief   460
Among the nations, seeing thou art free:
My native nook of earth!

BOOK VI

THE WINTER WALK AT NOON

Lines 57–117

The night was winter in his roughest mood;
The morning sharp and clear. But now at noon
Upon the southern side of the slant hills,
And where the woods fence off the northern
    blast,   60
The season smiles, resigning all its rage,
And has the warmth of May. The vault is blue
Without a cloud, and white without a speck
The dazzling splendour of the scene below.
Again the harmony comes o'er the vale;
And through the trees I view th' embattled tow'r
Whence all the music. I again perceive
The soothing influence of the wafted strains,
And settle in soft musings as I tread
The walk, still verdant, under oaks and elms,   70
Whose outspread branches overarch the glade.
The roof, though moveable through all its length
As the wind sways it, has yet well suffic'd,
And, intercepting in their silent fall
The frequent flakes, has kept a path for me.
No noise is here, or none that hinders thought.
The redbreast warbles still, but is content
With slender notes, and more than half suppress'd:
Pleas'd with his solitude, and flitting light

From spray to spray, where'er he rests he
    shakes   80
From many a twig the pendent drops of ice,
That tinkle in the wither'd leaves below.
Stillness, accompanied with sounds so soft,
Charms more than silence. Meditation here
May think down hours to moments. Here the heart
May give an useful lesson to the head,
And learning wiser grow without his books.
Knowledge and wisdom, far from being one,
Have oft-times no connexion. Knowledge dwells
In heads replete with thoughts of other men;   90
Wisdom in minds attentive to their own.
Knowledge, a rude unprofitable mass,
The mere materials with which wisdom builds,
Till smooth'd and squar'd and fitted to its place,
Does but encumber whom it seems t' enrich.
Knowledge is proud that he has learn'd so much;
Wisdom is humble that he knows no more.
Books are not seldom talismans and spells,
By which the magic art of shrewder wits
Holds an unthinking multitude enthrall'd.   100
Some to the fascination of a name
Surrender judgment, hood-wink'd. Some the style
Infatuates, and through labyrinths and wilds
Of error leads them by a tune entranc'd.
While sloth seduces more, too weak to bear
The insupportable fatigue of thought,
And swallowing, therefore, without pause or
    choice,
The total grist unsifted, husks and all.
But trees, and rivulets whose rapid course
Defies the check of winter, haunts of deer,   110
And sheep-walks populous with bleating lambs,
And lanes in which the primrose ere her time
Peeps through the moss that clothes the hawthorn
    root,
Deceive no student. Wisdom there, and truth,
Not shy, as in the world, and to be won
By slow solicitation, seize at once
The roving thought, and fix it on themselves.

1783–4   1785

ON THE RECEIPT OF MY MOTHER'S
PICTURE OUT OF NORFOLK[1]

THE GIFT OF MY COUSIN ANN BODHAM

OH that those lips had language! Life has pass'd
With me but roughly since I heard thee last.
Those lips are thine—thy own sweet smiles I see,
The same that oft in childhood solaced me;
Voice only fails, else, how distinct they say,
'Grieve not, my child, chase all thy fears away!'

---

9 the god worshipped by the followers of Manichaeism, a religion
founded by Mani in the third century, which prescribed a severely
rigid system of fasting, ritual, and prayer.

1 See Cowper's letter to Mrs. Bodham, text, p. 136.

The meek intelligence of those dear eyes
(Blest be the art that can immortalize,
The art that baffles time's tyrannic claim
To quench it) here shines on me still the same. 10
   Faithful remembrancer of one so dear,
Oh welcome guest, though unexpected, here!
Who bidd'st me honour with an artless song,
Affectionate, a mother lost so long,
I will obey, not willingly alone,
But gladly, as the precept were her own;
And, while that face renews my filial grief,
Fancy shall weave a charm for my relief—
Shall steep me in Elysian reverie,
A momentary dream, that thou art she.   20
   My mother! when I learn'd that thou wast dead,
Say, wast thou conscious of the tears I shed?
Hover'd thy spirit o'er thy sorrowing son,
Wretch even then, life's journey just begun?
Perhaps thou gav'st me, though unseen, a kiss;
Perhaps a tear, if souls can weep in bliss—
Ah that maternal smile! it answers—Yes.
I heard the bell toll'd on thy burial day,
I saw the hearse that bore thee slow away,
And, turning from my nurs'ry window, drew   30
A long, long sigh, and wept a last adieu!
But was it such?—It was.—Where thou art gone
Adieus and farewells are a sound unknown.
May I but meet thee on that peaceful shore,
The parting sound shall pass my lips no more!
Thy maidens griev'd themselves at my concern,
Oft gave me promise of a quick return.
What ardently I wish'd, I long believ'd,
And, disappointed still, was still deceiv'd;
By disappointment every day beguil'd,   40
Dupe of *to-morrow* even from a child.
Thus many a sad to-morrow came and went,
Till, all my stock of infant sorrow spent,
I learn'd at last submission to my lot;
But, though I less deplor'd thee, ne'er forgot.
   Where once we dwelt our name is heard no
      more,
Children not thine have trod my nurs'ry floor;
And where the gard'ner Robin, day by day,
Drew me to school along the public way,
Delighted with my bauble coach, and wrapt   50
In scarlet mantle warm, and velvet capt,
'Tis now become a history little known,
That once we call'd the past'ral house our own.
Short-liv'd possession! but the record fair
That mem'ry keeps of all thy kindness there,
Still outlives many a storm that has effac'd
A thousand other themes less deeply trac'd.
Thy nightly visits to my chamber made,
That thou might'st know me safe and warmly laid;
Thy morning bounties ere I left my home,   60

The biscuit, or confectionary plum;
The fragrant waters on my cheeks bestow'd
By thy own hand, till fresh they shone and glow'd;
All this, and more endearing still than all,
Thy constant flow of love, that knew no fall,
Ne'er roughen'd by those cataracts and brakes
That humour interpos'd too often makes;
All this still legible in mem'ry's page,
And still to be so, to my latest age,
Adds joy to duty, makes me glad to pay   70
Such honours to thee as my numbers may;
Perhaps a frail memorial, but sincere,
Not scorn'd in heav'n, though little notic'd here.
   Could time, his flight revers'd, restore the hours,
When, playing with thy vesture's tissued flow'rs,
The violet, the pink, and jessamine,
I prick'd them into paper with a pin,
(And thou wast happier than myself the while,
Would'st softly speak, and stroke my head and
      smile)
Could those few pleasant hours again appear, 80
Might one wish bring them, would I wish them
      here?
I would not trust my heart—the dear delight
Seems so to be desir'd, perhaps I might.—
But no—what here we call our life is such,
So little to be lov'd, and thou so much,
That I should ill requite thee to constrain
Thy unbound spirit into bonds again.
   Thou, as a gallant bark from Albion's coast
(The storms all weather'd and the ocean cross'd)
Shoots into port at some well-haven'd isle,   90
Where spices breathe and brighter seasons smile,
There sits quiescent on the floods that show
Her beauteous form reflected clear below,
While airs impregnated with incense play
Around her, fanning light her streamers gay;
So thou, with sails how swift! hast reach'd the
      shore
'Where tempests never beat nor billows roar,'[2]
And thy lov'd consort on the dang'rous tide
Of life, long since, has anchor'd at thy side.[3]
But me, scarce hoping to attain that rest,   100
Always from port withheld, always distress'd—
Me howling winds drive devious, tempest toss'd,
Sails ript, seams op'ning wide, and compass
      lost,
And day by day some current's thwarting force
Sets me more distant from a prosp'rous course.
But oh the thought, that thou art safe, and he!
That thought is joy, arrive what may to me.
My boast is not that I deduce my birth

---

2 inexactly quoted from *The Dispensary* by Sir Samuel Garth,
1661–1719.
3 Cowper's father died in 1756.

From loins enthron'd, and rulers of the earth;[4]
But higher far my proud pretensions rise—   110
The son of parents pass'd into the skies.
And now, farewell—time, unrevok'd, has run
His wonted course, yet what I wish'd is done.
By contemplation's help, not sought in vain,
I seem t'have liv'd my childhood o'er again;
To have renew'd the joys that once were mine,
Without the sin of violating thine:
And, while the wings of fancy still are free,
And I can view this mimic shew of thee,
Time has but half succeeded in his theft—   120
Thyself remov'd, thy power to sooth me left.

1790   1798

TO MARY

[This poem was addressed to Mrs. Mary Unwin, Cowper's closest friend and companion for more than half his lifetime.]

THE twentieth year is well-nigh past,
Since first our sky was overcast,[1]
Ah would that this might be the last!
          My Mary!
Thy spirits have a fainter flow,
I see thee daily weaker grow—
'Twas my distress that brought thee low,
          My Mary!
Thy needles, once a shining store,
For my sake restless heretofore,   10
Now rust disus'd, and shine no more,
          My Mary!
For though thou gladly wouldst fulfil
The same kind office for me still,
Thy sight now seconds not thy will,[2]
          My Mary!
But well thou play'dst the housewife's part,
And all thy threads with magic art
Have wound themselves about this heart,
          My Mary!   20
Thy indistinct expressions seem
Like language utter'd in a dream;
Yet me they charm, whate'er the theme,
          My Mary!
Thy silver locks, once auburn bright,
Are still more lovely in my sight
Than golden beams of orient light,
          My Mary!
For could I view nor them nor thee,
What sight worth seeing could I see?   30

The sun would rise in vain for me.
          My Mary!
Partakers of thy sad decline,
Thy hands their little force resign;
Yet, gently prest, press gently mine,
          My Mary!
And then I feel that still I hold
A richer store ten thousandfold
Than misers fancy in their gold,
          My Mary!   40
Such feebleness of limbs thou prov'st,
That now at every step thou mov'st
Upheld by two; yet still thou lov'st,
          My Mary!
And still to love, though prest with ill,
In wintry age to feel no chill,
With me is to be lovely still,
          My Mary!
But ah! by constant heed I know,
How oft the sadness that I show   50
Transforms thy smiles to looks of woe,
          My Mary!
And should my future lot be cast
With much resemblance of the past,
Thy worn-out heart will break at last,
          My Mary!

1793   1803

THE CASTAWAY

[This poem, the last that Cowper ever wrote, was suggested by an incident narrated in *Lord Anson's Voyage round the World*, 1748.]

OBSCUREST night involv'd the sky,
    Th' Atlantic billows roar'd,
When such a destin'd wretch as I,
    Wash'd headlong from on board,
Of friends, of hope, of all bereft,
His floating home for ever left.

No braver chief[1] could Albion boast
    Than he with whom he went,
Nor ever ship left Albion's coast,
    With warmer wishes sent,   10
He lov'd them both, but both in vain,
Nor him beheld, nor her again.

Not long beneath the whelming brine,
    Expert to swim, he lay;
Nor soon he felt his strength decline,
    Or courage die away;
But wag'd with death a lasting strife,
Supported by despair of life.

---

4 On his mother's side Cowper traced his ancestry to Henry III.

1 An attack of insanity in 1773 prevented Cowper's marriage to Mrs. Unwin.

2 In 1793, Mrs. Unwin, who was then seventy years of age, had suffered two paralytic strokes and was rapidly declining in health.

1 George, Lord Anson, 1697-1762, English admiral.

He shouted: nor his friends had fail'd
    To check the vessel's course,   20
But so the furious blast prevail'd,
    That, pitiless perforce,
They left their outcast mate behind,
And scudded still before the wind.

Some succour yet they could afford;
    And, such as storms allow,
The cask, the coop, the floated cord,
    Delay'd not to bestow.
But he (they knew) nor ship, nor shore,
Whate'er they gave, should visit more.   30

Nor, cruel as it seem'd, could he
    Their haste himself condemn,
Aware that flight, in such a sea,
    Alone could rescue them;
Yet bitter felt it still to die
Deserted, and his friends so nigh.

He long survives, who lives an hour
    In ocean, self-upheld;
And so long he, with unspent pow'r,
    His destiny repell'd;   40
And ever, as the minutes flew,
Entreated help, or cried—Adieu!

At length, his transient respite past,
    His comrades, who before
Had heard his voice in ev'ry blast,
    Could catch the sound no more.
For then, by toil subdued, he drank
The stifling wave, and then he sank.

No poet wept him: but the page
    Of narrative sincere,   50
That tells his name, his worth, his age,
    Is wet with Anson's tear.
And tears by bards or heroes shed
Alike immortalize the dead.

I therefore purpose not, or dream,
    Descanting on his fate,
To give the melancholy theme
    A more enduring date:
But misery still delights to trace
Its 'semblance in another's case.   60

No voice divine the storm allay'd,
    No light propitious shone;
When, snatch'd from all effectual aid,
    We perish'd, each alone:
But I beneath a rougher sea,
And whelm'd in deeper gulphs than he.

20 March, 1799   1803

SELECTIONS FROM COWPER'S LETTERS

1 *To* The Reverend William Unwin[1]

6 October, 1781

My dear Friend,
    What a world are you daily conversant with, which I have not seen these twenty years, and shall never seen again! The arts of dissipation (I suppose) are nowhere practised with more refinement or success than at the place of your present residence. By your account of it, it seems to be just what it was when I visited it, a scene of idleness and luxury, music, dancing, cards, walking, riding, bathing, eating, drinking, coffee, tea, scandal, dressing, yawning, sleeping; the rooms perhaps more magnificent, because the proprietors are grown richer, but the manners and occupations of the company just the same. Though my life has long been like that of a recluse, I have not the temper of one, nor am I in the least an enemy to cheerfulness and good humour; but I cannot envy you your situation; I even feel myself constrained to prefer the silence of this nook, and the snug fireside in our own diminutive parlour, to all the splendour and gaiety of Brighton.
    You ask me, how I feel on the occasion of my approaching publication.[2] Perfectly at my ease. If I had not been pretty well assured beforehand that my tranquillity would be but little endangered by such a measure, I would never have engaged in it; for I cannot bear disturbance. I have had in view two principal objects; first, to amuse myself,—and secondly, to compass that point in such a manner, that others might possibly be the better for my amusement. If I have succeeded, it will give me pleasure; but if I have failed, I shall not be mortified to the degree that might perhaps be expected. I remember an old adage (though not where it is to be found), *'bene vixit, qui bene latuit,'*[3] and if I had recollected it at the right time, it should have been the motto to my book. By the way, it will make an excellent one for *Retirement,* if you can but tell me whom to quote for it. The critics cannot deprive me of the pleasure I have in reflecting, that so far as my leisure has been employed in writing for the public, it has been conscientiously employed, and with a view to their advantage. There is nothing agreeable, to be sure, in being chronicled for a dunce; but I believe there lives not a man upon earth who would be less affected by it than myself. With all this

---

1 Mary Unwin's son.
2 *Poems,* published in 1782.
3 'He has lived well who has kept hidden.'—Ovid, *Tristia,* III, iv. 25.

indifference to fame, which you know me too well to suppose me capable of affecting, I have taken the utmost pains to deserve it. This may appear a mystery or a paradox in practice, but it is true. I considered that the taste of the day is refined, and delicate to excess, and that to disgust the delicacy of taste, by a slovenly inattention to it, would be to forfeit at once all hope of being useful; and for this reason, though I have written more verse this last year than perhaps any man in England, I have finished, and polished, and touched, and retouched, with the utmost care. If after all I should be converted into waste paper, it may be my misfortune, but it will not be my fault. I shall bear it with the most perfect serenity. . . .

W.C.

2   *To* The Reverend William Unwin

10 October, 1784

My dear William,

I send you four quires of verse,[4] which having sent, I shall dismiss from my thoughts, and think no more of, till I see them in print. I have not after all found time or industry enough to give the last hand to the points.[5] I believe, however, they are not very erroneous, though in so long a work, and in a work that requires nicety in their particular, some inaccuracies will escape. Where you find any, you will oblige me by correcting them.

In some passages, especially in the second book, you will observe me very satirical. Writing on such subjects I could not be otherwise. I can write nothing without aiming at least at usefulness: it were beneath my years to do it, and still more dishonourable to my religion. I know that a reformation of such abuses as I have censured is not to be expected from the efforts of a poet; but to contemplate the world, its follies, its vices, its indifference to duty, and its strenuous attachment to what is evil, and not to reprehend were to approve it. From this charge at least I shall be clear, for I have neither tacitly nor expressly flattered either its characters or its customs. I have paid one, and only one compliment, which was so justly due, that I did not know how to withhold it, especially having so fair an occasion;—I forget myself, there is another in the first book to Mr. Throckmorton,[6]—but the compliment I mean is to Mr. Smith.[7] It is however so managed, that nobody but himself can make the application, and you, to whom I disclose the secret; a delicacy on my part, which so much delicacy on his obliged me to the observance of.

What there is of a religious cast in the volume I have thrown towards the end of it, for two reasons; first, that I might not revolt the reader at his entrance,—and secondly, that my best impressions might be made last. Were I to write as many volumes as Lope de Vega, or Voltaire, not one of them would be without this tincture. If the world like it not, so much the worse for them. I make all the concessions I can, that I may please them, but I will not please them at the expense of conscience.

My descriptions are all from nature: not one of them second-handed. My delineations of the heart are from my own experience: not one of them borrowed from books, or in the least degree conjectural. In my numbers, which I have varied as much as I could (for blank verse without variety of numbers is no better than bladder and string,) I have imitated nobody, though sometimes perhaps there may be an apparent resemblance; because at the same time that I would not imitate, I have not affectedly differed.

If the work cannot boast a regular plan, (in which respect however I do not think it altogether indefensible,) it may yet boast, that the reflections are naturally suggested always by the preceding passage, and that except the fifth book, which is rather of a political aspect, the whole has one tendency: to discountenance the modern enthusiasm after a London life, and to recommend rural ease and leisure, as friendly to the cause of piety and virtue.

If it please you I shall be happy, and collect from your pleasure in it an omen of its general acceptance.

Yours, my dear friend,

W.C.

3   *To* The Reverend John Newton[8]

13 December, 1784

My dear Friend,

Having imitated no man, I may reasonably hope that I shall not incur the disadvantage of a comparison with my betters. Milton's manner was peculiar. So is Thomson's. He that should write like either of them, would, in my judgment,

---

4 The manuscript of *The Task,* which was published the following June.
5 the punctuation.
6 Squire of Weston,

7 an anonymous benefactor of the poor in Olney.
8 evangelical clergyman, formerly curate at Olney, who had recently criticized *The Task* adversely.

deserve the name of a copyist, but not of a poet. A judicious and sensible reader therefore, like yourself, will not say that my manner is not good, because it does not resemble theirs, but will rather consider what it is in itself. Blank verse is susceptible of a much greater diversification of manner, than verse in rhyme: and why the modern writers of it have all thought proper to cast their numbers alike, I know not. Certainly it was not necessity that compelled them to it. I flatter myself however that I have avoided that sameness with others, which would entitle me to nothing but a share in one common oblivion with them all. It is possible that, as the reviewer of my former volume found cause to say that he knew not to what class of writers to refer me, the reviewer of this, whosoever he shall be, may see occasion to remark the same singularity. At any rate, though as little apt to be sanguine as most men, and more prone to fear and despond, than to overrate my own productions, I am persuaded that I shall not forfeit any thing by this volume that I gained by the last.

As to the title, I take it to be the best that is to be had. It is not possible that a book, including such a variety of subjects, and in which no particular one is predominant, should find a title adapted to them all. In such a case, it seemed almost necessary to accommodate the name to the incident that gave birth to the poem; nor does it appear to me, that because I performed more than my task, therefore *The Task* is not a suitable title. A house would still be a house, though the builder of it should make it ten times as big as he first intended. I might indeed, following the example of the Sunday newsmonger, call it the *Olio*.[9] But I should do myself wrong; for though it have much variety, it has, I trust, no confusion.

For the same reason none of the interior titles apply themselves to the contents at large of that book to which they belong. They are, every one of them, taken either from the leading, (I should say the introductory,) passage of that particular book, or from that which makes the most conspicuous figure in it. Had I set off with a design to write upon a gridiron, and had I actually written near two hundred lines upon that utensil, as I have upon the Sofa, the Gridiron should have been my title. But the Sofa being, as I may say, the starting-post from which I addressed myself to the long race that I soon conceived a design to run, it acquired a just pre-eminence in my account, and was very worthily advanced to the titular honour it enjoys, its right being at least

so far a good one, that no word in the language could pretend a better.

The Time-piece[10] appears to me, (though by some accident the import of that title has escaped you,) to have a degree of propriety beyond the most of them. The book to which it belongs is intended to strike the hour that gives notice of approaching judgement, and, dealing pretty largely in the *signs* of the *times,* seems to be denominated, as it is, with a sufficient degree of accommodation to the subject. . . .

4   *To* Joseph Johnson, Bookseller[11]

[*December 1784?*]

I did not write the line that has been tampered with hastily, or without due attention to the construction of it; and what appeared to me its only merit is, in its present state, entirely annihilated.

I know that the ears of modern verse writers are delicate to an excess, and their readers are troubled with the same squeamishness as themselves. So that if a line do not run as smooth as quicksilver, they are offended. A critic of the present day serves a poem as a cook does a dead turkey, when she fastens the legs of it to a post and draws out all the sinews. For this we may thank Pope; but unless we could imitate him in the closeness and compactness of his expression, as well as in the smoothness of his numbers, we had better drop the imitation, which serves no other purpose than to emasculate and weaken all we write. Give me a manly rough line, with a deal of meaning in it, rather than a whole poem full of musical periods, that have nothing but their oily smoothness to recommend them!

I have said thus much, as I hinted in the beginning, because I have just finished a much longer poem[12] than the last, which our common friend will receive by the same messenger that has the charge of this letter. In that poem there are many lines which an ear so nice as the gentleman's who made the above-mentioned alteration would undoubtedly condemn; and yet (if I may be permitted to say it) they cannot be made smoother without being the worse for it. There is a roughness on a plum which nobody that understands fruit would rub off, though the plum would be much more polished without it. But, lest I tire you, I will only add that I wish you to guard me from all such meddling; assuring you that I always write as smoothly as I can; but that I never

---

10 title of the second book of *The Task.*
11 Cowper's publisher.
12 *The Task.*

did, never will, sacrifice the spirit or sense of a passage to the sound of it.

5 *To* Lady Hesketh[13]

12 October, 1785

My dear Cousin,

It is no new thing with you to give pleasure; but I will venture to say, that you do not often give more than you gave me this morning. When I came down to breakfast, and found upon the table a letter franked by my uncle, and when opening that frank I found that it contained a letter from you, I said within myself: 'This is just as it should be. We are all grown young again, and the days that I thought I should see no more are actually returned.' You perceive, therefore, that you judged well when you conjectured that a line from you would not be disagreeable to me. It could not be otherwise than, as in fact it proved, a most agreeable surprise, for I can truly boast of an affection for you, that neither years, nor interrupted intercourse, have at all abated. I need only recollect how much I valued you once, and with how much cause, immediately to feel a revival of the same value: if that can be said to revive, which at the most has only been dormant for want of employment, but I slander it when I say that it has slept. A thousand times have I recollected a thousand scenes, in which our two selves have formed the whole of the drama, with the greatest pleasure; at times, too, when I had no reason to suppose that I should ever hear from you again. I have laughed with you at the *Arabian Nights' Entertainments,* which afforded us, as you well know, a fund of merriment that deserves never to be forgot. I have walked with you to Netley Abbey, and have scrambled with you over hedges in every direction, and many other feats we have performed together, upon the field of my remembrance, and all within these few years. Should I say within this twelvemonth, I should not transgress the truth. The hours that I have spent with you were among the pleasantest of my former days, and are therefore chronicled in my mind so deeply, as to feel no erasure. Neither do I forget my poor friend, Sir Thomas.[14] I should remember him, indeed, at any rate, on account of his personal kindness to myself; but the last testimony that he gave of his regard for you endears him to me still more. With his uncommon understanding (for with many peculiarities he had more sense

than any of his acquaintance), and with his generous sensibilities, it was hardly possible that he should not distinguish you as he has done. As it was the last so it was the best proof that he could give, of a judgement that never deceived him, when he would allow himself leisure to consult it.

You say that you have often heard of me: that puzzles me. I cannot imagine from what quarter, but it is no matter. I must tell you, however, my Cousin, that your information has been a little defective. That I am happy in my situation is true; I live, and have lived these twenty years, with Mrs. Unwin, to whose affectionate care of me, during the far greater part of that time, it is, under Providence, owing that I live at all. But I do not account myself happy in having been for thirteen of those years in a state of mind that has made all that care and attention necessary; an attention, and a care, that have injured her health, and which, had she not been uncommonly supported, must have brought her to the grave. But I will pass to another subject; it would be cruel to particularize only to give pain, neither would I by any means give a sable hue to the first letter of a correspondence so unexpectedly renewed.

I am delighted with what you tell me of my uncles's good health. To enjoy any measure of cheerfulness at so late a day is much; but to have that late day enlivened with the vivacity of youth, is much more, and in these postdiluvian times a rarity indeed. Happy, for the most part, are parents who have daughters. Daughters are not apt to outlive their natural affections, which a son has generally survived, even before his boyish years are expired. I rejoice particularly in my uncle's felicity, who has three female descendants from his little person, who leave him nothing to wish for upon that head.

My dear Cousin, dejection of spirits, which, I suppose, may have prevented many a man from becoming an author, made me one. I find constant employment necessary, and therefore take care to be constantly employed. Manual occupations do not engage the mind sufficiently, as I know by experience, having tried many. But composition, especially of verse, absorbs it wholly. I write, therefore, generally, three hours in a morning, and in the evening I transcribe. I read also, but less than I write, for I must have bodily exercise, and therefore never pass a day without it.

You ask me where I have been this summer. I answer at Olney. Should you ask me where I spent the last seventeen summers, I should still answer, at Olney. Aye, and the winters also; I have seldom

---

13 the poet's cousin, a daughter of Ashley Cowper, with whom Cowper lived when he was studying law.
14 Lady Hesketh's husband, who had died in 1778.

left it, and except when I attended my brother in his last illness, never I believe a fortnight together.

Adieu, my beloved Cousin, I shall not always be thus nimble in reply, but shall always have great pleasure in answering you when I can.—Yours, my dear Friend and Cousin,

W.C.

6 *To* Mrs. Bodham[15]

Weston, 27 February, 1790

My dearest Rose,

Whom I thought withered and fallen from the stalk, but whom I find still alive: nothing could give me greater pleasure than to know it, and to learn it from yourself. I loved you dearly when you were a child, and love you not a jot the less for having ceased to be so. Every creature that bears any affinity to my mother is dear to me, and you, the daughter of her brother, are but one remove distant from her: I love you, therefore, and love you much, both for her sake and for your own. The world could not have furnished you with a present so acceptable to me as the picture which you have so kindly sent me. I received it the night before last, and viewed it with a trepidation of nerves and spirits somewhat akin to what I should have felt had the dear original presented herself to my embraces. I kissed it, and hung it where it is the last object that I see at night, and of course the first on which I open my eyes in the morning. She died when I had completed my sixth year; yet I remember her well, and am an ocular witness of the great fidelity of the copy. I remember, too, a multitude of the maternal tendernesses which I received from her, and which have endeared her memory to me beyond expression. There is in me, I believe, more of the Donne[16] than of the Cowper; and though I love all of both names, and have a thousand reasons to love those of my own name, yet I feel the bond of nature draw me vehemently to your side. I was thought in the days of my childhood much to resemble my mother, and in my natural temper, of which at the age of fifty-eight I must be supposed a competent judge, can trace both her, and my late uncle, your father. Somewhat of his irritability, and a little I would hope both of his and her——, I know not what to call it without seeming to praise myself, which is not my intention, but speaking to *you,* I will even speak out, and say *good nature.* Add to all this, I deal much in poetry, as did our venerable ancestor, the Dean of St. Paul's, and I think I shall have proved myself a Donne at all points. The truth is, that whatever I am, I love you all. . . .

W.C.

---

15 Cowper's cousin on his mother's side.

16 Cowper was related on his mother's side to the family of John Donne, the poet.

1759 · ROBERT BURNS · 1796

1759 Born at Alloway, the elder of two sons of an Ayrshire tenant farmer. His father was an austere man, ambitious to bring up his children both educated and God-fearing; his mother was without learning, but warm-hearted and imaginative. From his mother and an old relative, Betty Davidson, the boy came to know firsthand the ballads, legends, and songs of the Scottish peasantry. For two or three years attended the local school conducted by John Murdoch. Taught for the most part by his father during the long winter evenings. Was an apt pupil and devoured whatever books came within his reach. Eighteenth-century writers, Sterne, Mackenzie, and Macpherson were favorites. Heavy farm labor in his youth laid the foundation for rheumatic heart disease which eventually was to be the cause of his early death. Throughout his life was visited by periodic fits of depression, from which he sought refuge in company and conviviality.

1773 Boyish love for Nelly Kilpatrick, partner in the harvest field, inspired his first song.

1775 Briefly attended school in Kirkoswald, a near-by smuggling town, to study surveying; his studies overset by a transient flirtation with Peggy Thomson.

1777 Moved with his family to a farm near the villages of Tarbolton and Mauchline, which provided companionship, social atmosphere, and an appreciative audience.

1780 Was the prime mover in founding the Tarbolton Bachelors' Club, a debating society; attended dancing school, much against his father's wishes.

1781-2 Joined the Freemasons. Proposed marriage to Alison Begbie ('Mary Morison'), a neighboring farm girl, but was rejected. Went to Irvine, a flourishing seaport, to learn the trade of flax-dressing. Met Richard Brown, an educated sailor and man of the world, who encouraged him in authorship but who was a detrimental influence on his morals. Burning of the flax shop obliged him to give up his venture and to return dejected to the farm. Suffered his first serious illness.

1783 Began *First Commonplace Book,* which contains drafts of many early poems, and miscellaneous philosophical, religious, and critical observations.

1784 On the death of his father moved to Mossgiel, where he and his brother Gilbert farmed 118 acres in partnership until 1788. Bad seed and bad weather doomed their undertaking to eventual failure. Became involved with Elizabeth Paton, a former servant girl in the Burns's household. Suffered a second bout of serious illness, which brought him moods of depression and remorse.

1785 His friend and patron, Gavin Hamilton, urged him to write for publication. Fell in love with Jean Armour, daughter of a highly respectable Mauchline master mason.

1786 Early in the year, when his affair with Jean had become serious, Burns gave her a written document acknowledging her as his wife, but her father forced Jean to give up the paper and forbade the marriage. Burns felt that Jean had betrayed him. Began to talk of emigrating to Jamaica, where a post on a plantation had been offered him. Sought comfort in the love of Mary Campbell, a Highland servant girl. Seems to have promised her marriage, but

she died of a fever on her way to meet him.With Jean Armour was publicly reproved in
open church for their transgression. *Poems Chiefly in the Scottish Dialect* published at Kilmarnock in late July. In September Jean gave birth to twins, Jean and Robert. Highly favorable reception of his poems determined him to give up his plans for Jamaica, and instead to
visit Edinburgh to make arrangements for a second edition. Was feted at the capital by all
the literati and social bigwigs. Played his part well, though there were occasional moments
of bitterness and irritation. Friendship of Mrs. Dunlop, an aristocratic lady in her late fifties,
and of the Earl of Glencairn.

1787   Edinburgh edition of *Poems* appeared in April and brought him £500. Returned home
in June by way of the Border country. Toured the Highlands and other parts of Scotland.
Friendship with Peggy Chalmers, daughter of an Ayrshire gentleman farmer. During a second winter in Edinburgh eagerly assisted the engraver James Johnson with material for *The
Scots Musical Museum,* a collection of Scottish songs. Contributed some 200 songs, new or
adapted, to successive volumes of this publication (1787–1803). Began friendship and 'Cla-
rinda-Sylvander' correspondence with Mrs. James M'Lehose, an attractive and sentimental Edinburgh grass widow of his own age. The relationship with Mrs. M'Lehose was sustained through several years of voluminous correspondence and a handful of lyrics, but
terminated in 1791, when 'Clarinda' left Edinburgh to join her husband in the West Indies.

1788   Birth of a second set of twins by Jean; acknowledgment of her as his wife. Moved to
a farm at Ellisland. Friendship with Robert Riddell, which led to that with his sister-in-law,
Maria Riddell.

1789   Appointment as Excise officer in charge of the 'Dumfries First Itinerary.'

1791   *Tam O'Shanter* published in *Antiquities of Scotland* by Francis Grose, whom Burns
had met in 1789 through Riddell. Gave up farming and moved with his family to Dumfries
to live on his scanty salary as an exciseman.

1792   Began assisting George Thomson with material for *Select Scottish Airs.* Made new
friends in the Dumfries community.

1793   His liberal sympathies for the doctrines of the French Revolution inquired into
sharply by his superiors in the Excise and nearly cost him his post. Second Edinburgh edition of *Poems* published in two volumes.

1795   Active in Dumfries volunteers. By autumn his health failing.

1796   Died in July. Given a military funeral. A large subscription was raised for his family.

R OBERT BURNS was no illiterate peasant, as his early biographers represented him to be,
but a person of broad sympathies and extensive learning. His schooling, it is true, was
irregular and scanty; on the other hand, he had what was probably of much more importance, a quick wit, a receptive and expanding mind, and a burning ambition to learn. In his
father's cottage he sat at meals 'with a book in one hand and a spoon in the other.' By the
time he was fifteen he knew French and by young manhood had familiarized himself with
the standard eighteenth-century English and Scottish writers and with Shakespeare, Milton,
and the Bible. When he entered the drawing rooms of Edinburgh, he was able to hold his
own in high company with his resourceful, brilliant, and witty conversation. There were
times among the elite, to be sure, when his peasant tactlessness and sturdy independence
brought him into disrepute. Burns was always self-conscious about his rustic upbringing
and fiercely resented any reflections upon his social status. He hated all forms of hypocrisy,
hardness, and power in high places. He was openly rebellious against ecclesiastical authority, and blasted corruptions in the church with a complete disregard for consequence. His
spirited love of freedom led him to profound sympathy with the American colonies and
later with the French revolutionaries. He drank a health to George Washington; wore the
buff and blue (the badge of liberty); and once recklessly dispatched four carronades as a gift
to the French Convention. Not only in his patriotic zeal but also in his more personal behavior Burns was often wholly indiscreet and reckless. His personality was vibrant and

glowing, his nature passionate. Maria Riddell has described him as having 'an irresistible power of attraction.' As everybody knows he was involved in many affairs with women. Not that his kind of behavior was unusual among the Scottish peasantry of his day. And it can be said in Burns's behalf that he was sincerely tender and paternal toward his many children, whether born within or without wedlock, and was considerate of their care. It cannot be denied, however, that at times under the stress of passion or mortified vanity Burns allowed the ruder manners of the peasantry to overcome his better nature. His uncouthness cost him the friendship of at least two of the most admiring and finest of his women acquaintances, Mrs. Dunlop and Maria Riddell. With those above his station Burns 'never acquired finesse whether in toasting, flattering, or sinning' (Ferguson). Yet with those of his own kind he was perfectly at ease and among them enjoyed life-long sociability and friendship. He found grateful relief from recurrent 'blue devilism' in the conviviality of the tavern. But in an age when heavy drinking and rough-speaking were common, Burns seldom overstepped the bounds of propriety. His untimely death was not (as was once believed) the result of sheer dissipation, but of a heart condition of long standing, aggravated by overwork, disappointment, and exacerbated nerves. Burns was a canny, steady-going man of affairs, but the fires of genius roused in him passions, agonies, and desires that were not to be reconciled with the crude peasant surroundings to which fate had committed him. The raging conflict of natures within often brought him restlessness and misery; the miracle is that it also produced for posterity glorious satire, absorbing narrative, and immortal song.

Burns owed a great deal to a long line of gifted Scottish poets working in the vernacular who had preceded him. An unbroken tradition of native Scottish folk poetry reached from the Ayrshire poet as far back as the fifteenth and sixteenth centuries. Even in its early stages there is preserved in the fugitive and popular pieces of Dunbar, Douglas, and Lyndsay the later style and purposes of Burns. In the period beginning the seventeenth century, Scottish writers affected a more literary manner and wrote for the most part in standard English. By the opening of the eighteenth century, however, there was a vigorous reaction against literary artificialities and a revival of old themes and old ways which had been lying submerged but which had never been wholly forgotten. Allan Ramsay (1686–1758) pioneered in the revival with his immensely popular *Tea Table Miscellany,* 1724–32, a mixed collection in four volumes of old and new songs and ballads. Filled with themes dealing with humble life in country and town, the fun of taverns, domestic life in the rough, and the like, Ramsay's collection had a far-reaching influence in reawakening interest in native peasant poetry. Great seminal work was also done by James Watson as editor of *A Choice Collection of Scots Poems, Ancient and Modern,* 1706–11. Robert Fergusson (1750–74) carried forward the work of Ramsay and his associates and handed it on to Burns greatly enriched. Fergusson had a surprising, precocious talent which he employed in bringing vividly to life circumstantial or realistic Scottish objects, persons, and situations. Attracted by Fergusson's sure craftsmanship, his wit and irony, and sharing with him similar interests and attitudes, Burns often imitated (and as often surpassed) his youthful predecessor. Many of Burns's best subjects, such as *The Holy Fair, The Cotter's Saturday Night,* the epigrams and satires, bear obvious indications of having been suggested by Fergusson. In the use of the traditional Lowland Scots dialect, also, Burns followed Fergusson's lead and found it of inestimable help. The dialect intensified the humor, confirmed the realism, and gave spontaneity and fidelity to the emotion. Burns could handle standard English competently and wrote a few superb short lyrics and lyrical passages in English, but his tendency when using the literary idiom was to be consciously elegant and sentimental after the manner of eighteenth-century English writers. In Low Scots he found the perfect medium for the fullest expression of his genius. It is to be doubted whether in English Burns would have been anything more than a competent secondary poet.

After a very brief apprenticeship Burns struck out independently (late 1785 to early 1786) in a vigorous and brilliant series of religious satires. In the poet's day the old religion had degenerated in the country districts into an effete sham.The majority of the folk had long been restless under the extremes of doctrine and the ridiculous severities of church discipline meted out to them. As a consequence, Burns's attack upon ecclesiastical pretensions was gleefully welcomed. The satires were widely circulated in manuscript, and their author was universally hailed for his brilliant scoring of 'hits.' Burns's ire was first aroused at the senseless persecution by the elders of his good friend Gavin Hamilton. His indignation was all the fiercer because he realized that some members of the session were trafficking upon lingering superstitions to gratify their own lust or avarice. Chief among these was a certain William Fisher, whom Burns anatomizes with withering scorn in the satire, *Holy Willie's Prayer*. This solemn mockery, with its marvelous gleams of humor, is without doubt the most 'tremendous indictment of a kind of religion and of a kind of person' ever put in a poem. Burns takes a further fling at orthodoxy in *The Holy Fair*. Here he is working closely in the Scots literary tradition, following the pattern of Fergusson's *Leith Races* and *Hallow Fair*, but the development of the theme is Burns's own. *The Holy Fair* is no harsh satire, like *Holy Willie's Prayer*, but a poem of 'delighted acceptance of the bustling, variegated scene' and of amused tolerance for the kinds of hypocrisy, confusion, drinking, and love-making which are to be found there. By implication, however, the satire is vastly damaging to sham and bigotry. *Address to the Devil* is another light-hearted yet telling blow at the superstitious orthodoxy of that day. By using the devil of folklore rather than that of theology, and treating him in a mocking tone, the poet with amused tolerance led his readers to question a too literal-minded interpretation of fundamentalist doctrines. The period of the satires was short but during it Burns scored three or four of his greatest successes.

The vivid glimpses of Scottish social life given in the satires are multiplied and extended in several non-satirical poems of middle length. Of these *The Cotter's Saturday Night* is one of the best known and best loved. This poem has a fundamental veracity, which is doubtless responsible for its having a wide appeal. Artistically, however, *The Cotter's Saturday Night* is the least satisfactory of the major poems. It is marred by a tendency toward melodramatic sentiment and a confusing intermixture of the realistic language of Scots with that of eighteenth-century genteel convention. In a second piece, *The Jolly Beggars,* Burns worked more closely in the Scots tradition, though adapting tradition brilliantly to his own use, and achieved one of his finest imaginative triumphs. The original of the poem is a cantata in Ramsay's *Tea-Table Miscellany* entitled *Merry Beggars*. The unpromising scene is a den of corruption where a group of criminals and social outcasts are foregathered for carousal and drunken love-making. The chief point of the poem is the swaggering songs woven into a pattern by brief intermittent recitations. Burns has captured the feeling of conviviality and joyous abandon, the 'fierce and almost anarchistic acceptance of man at his lowest social level' (Daiches). The poetry is vivid, pungent, full of color and exuberance, and shows a magnificent command of rollicking rhythms. An overwhelming vitality fuses the whole composition into a single artistic unity. In a third major work, the narrative *Tam o'Shanter,* the poet again takes us into the world of conviviality and good fellowship. For the plot and the handling of the supernatural in this poem Burns drew from the fountain of genuine folklore. For the intimate, realistic details, he depended upon his own firsthand observation and experience. By every test *Tam o'Shanter* is a notable achievement. It has speed and verve, vivid realistic background, graphic characterization, comic exaggeration, drollery, power of selection, telling phrase, and suspense. The tone is at once 'shrewd yet irresponsible, mocking yet sympathetic'; there is a fine balance between the 'mere supernatural anecdote and the precisely etched realistic pictures' (Daiches). *Tam o'Shanter* is the only verse narrative that Burns ever wrote. Its surpassing perfection makes us wonder what rich legacy in the narrative kind the poet might have left us had he been more happily favored with leisure and encouragement.

Burns's creative energy was given an immense stimulus during the later years through his co-operation in compiling the two collections of national songs of Johnson and Thomson. After 1786 his chief enthusiasm went into these collections, for which altogether he rescued, improved, and re-created well over 300 songs. He was wholly unmindful of personal fame in this labor and steadfastly refused to accept any kind of a fee for his numerous contributions. He was driven by a deep patriotic fervor to give enduring life to the folk songs of his people. Many of the traditional songs that Burns recovered dealt frankly with the robust, physical side of love. Here was a quality in Scottish song which found a hearty responsiveness in its interpolator. Mirthfully and with a touch of swagger Burns sings in *Green Grow the Rashes* of the male's eternal allegiance to the fair sex. The note of the purely physical struck in this joyous song is fairly widespread in Burns and is likely to be found even in the most 'respectable' of the lyrics. In the finest love song of them all, *A Red, Red Rose,* for example, the lover's desire to possess and his pride of protectiveness give an unmatched sincerity to his passionate vows. The note of male protectiveness appears over and over again, but never more perfectly than in the tenderly gallant song, *O, Wert Thou in the Cauld Blast,* addressed to Jessie Lewars, who watched over Burns in his last illness. The range of Burns's love songs is extraordinary. He was not confined to his personal experience relating to love, but he could dramatize love from the woman's point of view and he could write beautifully of love in old age. In *John Anderson, My Jo* he skillfully avoids an overly sentimental treatment of the old couple by a concrete fusing of their long years of domesticity and companionship with their love for one another. Burns can also handle effectively personal experiences that do not deal with love. His superb drinking song, *Willie Brew'd a Peck o' Maut,* is a frank glorification of drunkenness, celebrating a memorable night over the tankards with his cronies. And a surprising number of Burns's songs do not relate to his personal experience at all. His patriotic songs belong to this class and include several of his unquestioned successes. Of these *Scots Wha Hae* (though less of a song perhaps than an exhortation) has a right ring to it. A much better, though less well-known, patriotic song is *It Was a' for our Rightfu' King.* The firm structure, the masterful handling of the cadence and verse form, and the skillful control of the emotion must place this among Burns's greatest lyric triumphs. The variety of Burns's songs is no less remarkable than their surpassing excellence. Hardly any two follow the same pattern. Several of his most successful lend themselves to declamatory recitation rather than to song. Such is the immensely popular *Is There for Honest Poverty,* a poem made up of revolutionary slogans of the day, sharpened by the use of the traditional refrain 'for a' that and a' that.' Some of Burns's songs are written in straight English. Included among them are the lovely pastoral *Sweet Afton,* the nostalgic *My Heart's in the Highlands,* and his impassioned elegy *To Highland Mary.* Many of the most appealing are in standard English 'just tipped with Scots.' These are not the songs of folk emotions, but the more formal songs of love or compliment. *Mary Morison* is one of the finest of this 'middle' class of song. Another is the heart-broken farewell to 'Clarinda,' *Ae Fond Kiss.* Of all the songs the best known, of course, and the most often sung is the universal favorite *Auld Lang Syne.* This is without question the world's greatest song of human fellowship and friendship. Who of us has ever sung it in company without a tugging at the heart? In working with traditional material Burns almost always wrote to an old tune for which he sought the appropriate words. After a first stanza was fairly well set up, he improved, pieced out, or supplied new stanzas. He had a sure sense of musical rhythm and a rare ability to harmonize his expressions with the thoughts of his people. The songs have directness and simplicity, intense feeling, swiftness, fine flowing quality, and 'heart-moving melody.' In the songs Burns's powers were at their highest. He gives us the many moods of love, humor, patriotic fervor, conviviality, and friendship—all these in a more abundant measure than any other poet of the eighteenth century.

Nature is seen by Burns not in a philosophical or religious light (as it is by the major Romantics), but simply as a fact of existence. Nevertheless, Burns was a keen and alert observer of the world about him and could sketch with rapid, sure strokes the appropriate natural setting to open or at any point to heighten a satire, descriptive piece, or narrative. The openings to *The Jolly Beggars* and *Tam O'Shanter* and the background scenes in *The Holy Fair* and the thunderstorm in *Tam O'Shanter* are hard to beat. In the love lyrics Burns uses imaginatively and with poignant effect the flowers, streams, trees, and songs of birds of his beloved Scottish countryside. In *To Highland Mary* memory broods over the 'banks and braes and streams' around the castle where the two lovers took their last farewell; in *Ye Flowery Banks* the song of a bird intensifies the heartache of the forsaken girl. Nearly everywhere in Burns, Nature sets the background and enhances the poetry. But essentially Burns is, of course, the poet not of Nature but of human nature. He lived close to the soil and shared intensely in the local circumstances and domestic emotions of the folk. He vividly depicts the customs, scenes, rustic beliefs, loves, and occasions of his fellow peasants. In particular, his own life of slavish toil begot in him a passionate kinship with the less fortunate. He brought within the circle of his sympathy the toil-worn cottager and the drunken prostitute, and extended the boundary of his fellowship to include friendly intercourse with animals and birds, even the flowers of the field. Burns kept intellectually abreast of the advanced reforms of the day and made fervent appeals in his poetry for the dignity and equality of all men. Thus, though he built his poetry from local characters and circumstances and is what we might call a 'regional' poet, he emphasizes those moods, images, and thoughts that are permanent and elemental in all humanity. Burns moves with the forces of revolutionary advance. Although he never set foot outside his native Scotland, he must be numbered among the citizens of the world. Also, in language and metrics, as well as in his humanity, Burns allied himself with progress. By using as a literary vehicle the real language of men ready at hand in the traditional folk literature of his country, he anticipated by nearly fifteen years in his Kilmarnock edition the return to precision and simplicity called for by Wordsworth in the *Lyrical Ballads.* Wordsworth expresses his admiration for Burns, vigorously defends him against the abuses of the critics, and acknowledges his poetical indebtedness to his neighbor over the border. It cannot be claimed that Burns's influence upon individual romantic poets was widespread, but through Wordsworth his example was salutary in bringing about a return both to homely subject matter and to sane diction. Burns's range was not wide and sometimes he fell into an excessively sentimental vein; yet his sense of humor saved him from too great extravagances. What Burns did do well, he did supremely well. And by the measure of that accomplishment this 'brilliant and troubled peasant poet of Scotland' has won the perpetual esteem and affection of his fellow men the world over.

MARY MORISON

O MARY, at thy window be,
  It is the wish'd, the trysted hour!
Those smiles and glances let me see,
  That make the miser's treasure poor:
How blythely wad I bide the stoure,[1]
  A weary slave frae sun to sun,
Could I the rich reward secure,
  The lovely Mary Morison.

Yestreen, when to the trembling string
  The dance gaed thro' the lighted ha',   10
To thee my fancy took its wing,
  I sat, but neither heard nor saw:
Tho' this was fair, and that was braw,[2]
  And yon the toast of a' the town,
I sigh'd, and said amang them a',
  'Ye are na Mary Morison.'

O Mary, canst thou wreck his peace,
  Wha for thy sake wad gladly die?
Or canst thou break that heart of his,
  Whase only faut is loving thee?   20
If love for love thou wilt na gie,
  At least be pity to me shown!

A thought ungentle canna be
The thought o' Mary Morison.

1781   1800

GREEN GROW THE RASHES,[1] O

CHORUS

GREEN grow the rashes, O;
  Green grow the rashes, O;
The sweetest hours that e'er I spend,
  Are spent amang the lasses, O!

There's nought but care on ev'ry han',
  In ev'ry hour that passes, O;
What signifies the life o' man,
  An' twere na for the lasses, O.

The warly[2] race may riches chase,
  An' riches still may fly them, O;   10
An' tho' at last they catch them fast,
  Their hearts can ne'er enjoy them, O.

But gie me a canny[3] hour at e'en,
  My arms about my dearie, O;

---

1 endure the strife.
2 fine; handsome.

---

1 rushes.
2 worldly.
3 happy.

An' warly cares, an' warly men,
  May a' gae tapsalteerie,[4] O!

For you sae douce,[5] ye sneer at this,
  Ye're nought but senseless asses, O:
The wisest man the warl' saw,
  He dearly lov'd the lasses, O.   20

Auld nature swears, the lovely dears
  Her noblest work she classes, O;
Her prentice han' she try'd on man,
  An' then she made the lasses, O.

    1784   1787

HOLY WILLIE'S PRAYER

And send the godly in a pet to pray—POPE.[1]

ARGUMENT

Holy Willie [William Fisher] was a rather oldish bachelor elder, in the parish of Mauchline, and much and justly famed for that polemical chattering which ends in tippling orthodoxy, and for that spiritualized bawdry which refines to liquorish devotion. In a sessional process with a gentleman in Mauchline—a Mr. Gavin Hamilton—Holy Willie and his priest, Father Auld, after full hearing in the Presbytery of Ayr, came off but second best, owing partly to the oratorical powers of Mr. Robert Aiken, Mr. Hamilton's counsel; but chiefly to Mr. Hamilton's being one of the most irreproachable and truly respectable characters in the country. On losing his process, the muse overheard him at his devotions as follows—

O Thou, wha in the Heavens dost dwell,
Wha, as it pleases best Thysel',
Sends ane to Heaven and ten to Hell,
    A' for Thy glory,
And no for ony guid or ill
    They've done afore Thee!

I bless and praise Thy matchless might,
Whan thousands Thou has left in night,
That I am here afore Thy sight,
    For gifts an' grace   10
A burnin' an' a shinin' light,
    To a' this place.

What was I, or my generation,
That I should get sic exaltation?
I, wha deserve most just damnation,
    For broken laws,
Sax thousand years 'fore my creation,
    Thro' Adam's cause.

4 topsy-turvy.
5 sedate; sober.

1 *The Rape of the Lock*, IV, 64.

When frae my mither's womb I fell,
Thou might hae plung'd me in Hell,   20
To gnash my gums, to weep and wail,
    In burnin' lakes,
Where damnèd devils roar and yell,
    Chain'd to their stakes;

Yet I am here a chosen sample,
To show Thy grace is great and ample;
I'm here a pillar in Thy temple,
    Strong as a rock,
A guide, a buckler, an example
    To a' Thy flock.   30

O Lord, Thou kens what zeal I bear,
When drinkers drink, and swearers swear,
And singin' there and dancin' here,
    Wi' great an' sma':
For I am keepit by thy fear
    Free frae them a'.

But yet, O Lord! confess I must
At times I'm fash'd[2] wi' fleshly lust;
An' sometimes too, in warldly trust,
    Vile self gets in;   40
But Thou remembers we are dust,
    Defil'd in sin.

O Lord! yestreen, Thou kens, wi' Meg—
Thy pardon I sincerely beg—
O! may 't ne'er be a livin' plague
    To my dishonour,
An' I'll ne'er lift a lawless leg
    Again upon her.

Besides I farther maun allow,
Wi' Lizzie's lass, three times I trow—   50
But, Lord, that Friday I was fou,[3]
    When I cam near her,
Or else Thou kens Thy servant true
    Wad never steer[4] her.

May be Thou lets this fleshly thorn
Beset Thy servant e'en and morn
Lest he owre high and proud should turn,
    That he's sae gifted;
If sae, Thy hand maun e'en be borne,
    Until Thou lift it.   60

Lord, bless Thy chosen in this place,
For here Thou hast a chosen race;
But God confound their stubborn face,
    An' blast their name,

2 plagued.   3 drunk.   4 molest.

Wha bring Thy elders to disgrace
        An' public shame.

Lord, mind Gawn Hamilton's deserts,
He drinks, an' swears, an' plays at cartes,[5]
Yet has sae mony takin' arts
        Wi' grit an' sma',   70
Frae God's ain priest the people's hearts
        He steals awa'.

An' when we chasten'd him therefor,
Thou kens how he bred sic a splore[6]
As set the warld in a roar
        O' laughin' at us;
Curse Thou his basket and his store,
        Kail and potatoes.

Lord, hear my earnest cry an' pray'r,
Against that Presbyt'ry o' Ayr;   80
Thy strong right hand, Lord, make it bare
        Upo' their heads;
Lord, weigh it down, an' dinna spare,
        For their misdeeds.

O Lord my God, that glib-tongu'd Aiken,
My very heart and soul are quakin',
To think how we stood sweatin', shakin',
        An' piss'd wi' dread,
While he, wi' hingin' lips and snakin',[7]
        Held up his head.   90

Lord, in the day o' vengeance try him;
Lord, visit them wha did employ him,
And pass not in Thy mercy by them,
        Nor hear their pray'r:
But, for Thy people's sake, destroy them,
        And dinna spare.

But, Lord, remember me and mine
Wi, mercies temp'ral and divine,
That I for gear an' grace may shine
        Excell'd by nane,   100
And a' the glory shall be Thine,
        Amen, Amen!

1785   1799

EPISTLE TO JOHN LAPRAIK

AN OLD SCOTTISH BARD, 1 APRIL 1785

WHILE briers an' woodbines budding green,
An' paitricks[1] scraichin'[2] loud at e'en,

---

5 cards.   6 disturbance.   7 sneering.

---

1 partridges.   2 screeching.

An' morning poussie whiddin'[3] seen,
        Inspire my Muse,
This freedom, in an unknown frien',
        I pray excuse.

On Fasten-een[4] we had a rockin',[5]
To ca' the crack[6] and weave our stockin';
And there was muckle fun and jokin',
        Ye need na doubt;   10
At length we had a hearty yokin'[7]
        At sang about.[8]

There was ae sang, amang the rest,
Aboon them a' it pleas'd me best,
That some kind husband had addrest
        To some sweet wife:
It thirl'd[9] the heart-strings thro' the breast,
        A' to the life.

I've scarce heard ought describ'd sae weel,
What gen'rous, manly bosoms feel;   20
Thought I 'Can this be Pope, or Steele,
        Or Beattie's wark!'
They tauld me 'twas an odd kind chiel[10]
        About Muirkirk.

It pat me fidgin' fain[11] to hear 't,
And sae about him there I spier'd;[12]
Then a' that kenn'd him round declar'd
        He had ingine,[13]
That nane excell'd it, few cam near 't,
        It was sae fine.   30

That, set him to a pint of ale,
An' either douce[14] or merry tale,
Or rhymes an' songs he'd made himsel,
        Or witty catches,
'Tween Inverness and Teviotdale,
        He had few matches.

Then up I gat, an' swoor an aith,
Tho' I should pawn my pleugh and graith,[15]
Or die a cadger pownie's[16] death,
        At some dyke-back,   40
A pint an' gill I'd gie them baith
        To hear your crack.[17]

But, first an' foremost, I should tell,
Amaist as soon as I could spell,

---

3 hare scurrying.   4 the evening before Lent.
5 spinning bee.   6 have a chat.
7 set-to.   8 a game in which each person
                      sings a song.
9 thrilled.   10 fellow.
11 made me tingling wild.   12 asked.
13 genius.   14 sober.
15 tools, gear.   16 peddlar's pony.
17 talk, chat.

I to the crambo-jingle[18] fell;
      Tho' rude an' rough,
Yet crooning to a body's sel,
      Does weel eneugh.

I am nae poet, in a sense,
But just a rhymer, like, by chance,   50
An' hae to learning nae pretence,
      Yet what the matter?
Whene'er my Muse does on me glance,
      I jingle at her.

Your critic-folk may cock their nose,
And say 'How can you e'er propose,
You wha ken hardly verse frae prose,
      To mak a sang?'
But, by your leaves, my learnèd foes,
      Ye're maybe wrang.   60

What's a' your jargon o' your schools,
Your Latin names for horns[19] an' stools;
If honest nature made you fools,
      What sairs[20] your grammars?
Ye'd better ta'en up spades and shools,[21]
      Or knappin'-hammers.[22]

A set o' dull conceited hashes[23]
Confuse their brains in college classes!
They gang in stirks,[24] and come out asses,
      Plain truth to speak;   70
An' syne[25] they think to climb Parnassus
      By dint o' Greek!

Gie me ae spark o' Nature's fire,
That's a' the learning I desire;
Then tho' I drudge thro' dub an' mire
      At pleugh or cart,
My Muse, though hamely in attire,
      May touch the heart.

O for a spunk[26] o' Allan's[27] glee,
Or Fergusson's,[28] the bauld an' slee,[29]   80
Or bright Lapraik's, my friend to be,
      If I can hit it!
That would be lear[30] eneugh for me,
      If I could get it.

Now, sir, if ye hae friends enow,
Tho' real friends, I b'lieve, are few,

Yet, if your catalogue be fou,[31]
      I'se no insist,
But gif ye want ae friend that's true,
      I'm on your list.   90

I winna blaw about mysel,
As ill I like my fauts to tell;
But friends, an' folks that wish me well,
      They sometimes roose[32] me;
Tho' I maun own, as mony still
      As far abuse me.

There's ae wee faut they whiles lay to me,
I like the lasses—Gude forgie me!
For mony a plack[33] they wheedle frae me,
      At dance or fair;   100
Maybe some ither thing they gie me
      They weel can spare.

But Mauchline race, or Mauchline fair,
I should be proud to meet you there;
We'se gie ae night's discharge to care,
      If we forgather,
An' hae a swap o' rhymin'-ware
      Wi' ane anither.

The four-gill chap,[34] we'se gar him clatter,[35]
An' kirsen[36] him wi' reekin[37] water;   110
Syne we'll sit down an' tak our whitter,[38]
      To cheer our heart;
An' faith, we'se be acquainted better
      Before we part.

Awa, ye selfish warly race,
Wha think that havins,[39] sense, an' grace,
Ev'n love an' friendship, should give place
      To catch-the-plack![40]
I dinna like to see your face,
      Nor hear your crack.   120

But ye whom social pleasure charms,
Whose hearts the tide of kindness warms,
Who hold your being on the terms,
      'Each aid the others,'
Come to my bowl, come to my arms,
      My friends, my brothers!

But to conclude my lang epistle,
As my auld pen 's worn to the gristle;

---

18 rhyming.
19 inkhorns.
20 serves.
21 shovels.
22 hammers for breaking stones.
23 blockheads.
24 young steers.
25 afterward.
26 spark.
27 Allan Ramsay (1686–1758), Scottish poet.
28 Robert Fergusson (1750–74), Scottish poet.
29 sly.
30 learning.

31 full.
32 praise.
33 four pence Scots.
34 drinking cup.
35 make him rattle.
36 christen.
37 steaming.
38 hearty draught.
39 good manners.
40 the hunt for coin.

Twa lines frae you wad gar me fissle,[41]
           Who am, most fervent,   130
While I can either sing, or whistle,
           Your friend and servant.

1785   1786

THE HOLY FAIR

A robe of seeming truth and trust
  Hid crafty observation;
And secret hung, with poison'd crust,
  The dirk of Defamation:
A mask that like the gorget show'd,
  Dye-varying, on the pigeon;
And for a mantle large and broad,
  He wrapt him in Religion.

HYPOCRISY A-LA-MODE

[In Burns's time and in his region of Scotland the
church observed the Sacrament of the Lord's Supper
only once in each twelvemonth on the second Sunday in
August, and usually several neighboring parishes united
to hold one joint service. Because of the crowds attending, the preaching was done in a tent pitched in the
churchyard, while the communion service was held inside the church. At Mauchline, a tavern stood almost
within the shadow of the preaching-tent, a circumstance
that contributed to the degeneration of 'The Occasion,'
as it was popularly called, and gave Burns the opportunity for the 'skillful juxtaposition of incongruities,' which
make his satire, though uniformly good-humored, so
devastating.]

Upon a simmer Sunday morn,
  When Nature's face is fair,
I walkèd forth to view the corn,
  An' snuff the caller[1] air.
The risin' sun, owre Galston muirs,
  Wi' glorious light was glintin';
The hares were hirplin'[2] down the furrs,[3]
  The lav'rocks[4] they were chantin'
           Fu' sweet that day.

As lightsomely I glowr'd[5] abroad,   10
  To see a scene sae gay,
Three hizzies,[6] early at the road,
  Cam skelpin'[7] up the way.
Twa had manteeles o' dolefu' black,
  But ane wi' lyart[8] lining;
The third, that gaed a wee a-back,
  Was in the fashion shining
           Fu' gay that day.

The twa appear'd like sisters twin,
  In feature, form, an' clae;[9]   20
Their visage wither'd, lang an' thin,
  An' sour as ony slaes:[10]
The third cam up, hap-stap-an'-lowp,
  As light as ony lambie,
An' wi' a curchie low did stoop,
  As soon as e'er she saw me,
           Fu' kind that day.

Wi' bonnet aff, quoth I, 'Sweet lass,
  I think ye seem to ken me;
I'm sure I've seen that bonnie face,   30
  But yet I canna name ye.'
Quo' she, an' laughin' as she spak,
  An' taks me by the hands,
'Ye, for my sake, hae gi'en the feck[11]
  Of a' the Ten Commands
           A screed[12] some day.

'My name is Fun—your crony dear,
  The nearest friend ye hae;
An' this is Superstition here,
  An' that's Hypocrisy.   40
I'm gaun to Mauchline Holy Fair,
  To spend an hour in daffin':[13]
Gin[14] ye'll go there, yon runkl'd[15] pair,
  We will get famous laughin'
           At them this day.'

Quoth I, 'Wi' a' my heart, I'll do't;
  I'll get my Sunday's sark[16] on,
An' meet you on the holy spot;
  Faith, we'se hae fine remarkin'!'
Then I gaed hame at crowdie-time,[17]   50
  An' soon I made me ready;
For roads were clad, frae side to side,
  Wi' mony a wearie bodie
           In droves that day.

Here farmers gash[18] in ridin' graith[19]
  Gaed hoddin' by their cotters;[20]
There swankies young in braw braid-claith
  Are springin' owre the gutters.
The lasses, skelpin' barefit,[21] thrang,[22]
  In silks an' scarlets glitter,   60
Wi' sweet-milk cheese, in mony a whang,[23]

---

41 thrill with pleasure.

1 cool.   2 limping.
3 furrows.   4 larks.
5 looked.   6 wenches.
7 hurrying.   8 gray.

9 clothes.   10 sloe berries.
11 greater part.   12 tear, rip.
13 fun.   14 if.
15 wrinkled.   16 shirt.
17 porridge-time, i.e. breakfast.   18 prosperous.
19 attire.   20 jogging by their cottagers.
21 hastening barefoot.   22 crowd.
23 slice.

An' farls²⁴ bak'd wi' butter,
    Fu' crump²⁵ that day.

When by the plate we set our nose,
    Weel heapèd up wi' ha'pence,
A greedy glow'r²⁶ Black Bonnet²⁷ throws,
    An' we maun draw our tippence.
Then in we go to see the show:
    On ev'ry side they're gath'rin';
Some carryin' deals,²⁸ some chairs an' stools, 70
    An' some are busy bleth'rin'²⁹
        Right loud that day.

Here stands a shed to fend the show'rs,
    An' screen our country gentry;
There racer Jess an' twa-three whores
    Are blinkin' at the entry.
Here sits a raw o' tittlin'³⁰ jades,
    Wi' heavin' breasts an' bare neck,
An' there a batch o' wabster³¹ lads,
    Blackguardin' frae Kilmarnock 80
        For fun this day.

Here some are thinkin' on their sins,
    An' some upo' their claes;
Ane curses feet that fyl'd³² his shins,
    Anither sighs an' prays:
On this hand sits a chosen swatch,³³
    Wi' screw'd up, grace-proud faces;
On that a set o' chaps, at watch,
    Thrang winkin' on the lasses
        To chairs that day. 90

O happy is that man an' blest!
    Nae wonder that it pride him!
Wha's ain dear lass, that he likes best,
    Comes clinkin' down beside him!
Wi' arm repos'd on the chair-back
    He sweetly does compose him;
Which, by degrees, slips round her neck,
    An' s loof³⁴ upon her bosom,
        Unkenn'd that day.

Now a' the congregation o'er 100
    Is silent expectation;
For Moodie³⁵ speels³⁶ the holy door,
    Wi' tidings o' damnation.

Should Hornie, as in ancient days,
    'Mang sons o' God present him,
The vera sight o' Moodie's face
    To 's ain het hame had sent him
        Wi' fright that day.

Hear how he clears the points o' faith
    Wi' rattlin' an' wi' thumpin'! 110
Now meekly calm, now wild in wrath,
    He 's stampin' an' he 's jumpin'!
His lengthen'd chin, his turn'd-up snout,
    His eldritch³⁷ squeal an' gestures,
O how they fire the heart devout,
    Like cantharidian plaisters,
        On sic a day!

But, hark! the tent has chang'd its voice;
    There's peace an' rest nae langer;
For a' the real judges rise, 120
    They canna sit for anger.
Smith opens out his cauld harangues,
    On practice and on morals;
An' aff the godly pour in thrangs
    To gie the jars an' barrels
        A lift that day.

What signifies his barren shine
    Of moral pow'rs an' reason?
His English style an' gesture fine
    Are a' clean out o' season. 130
Like Socrates or Antonine,³⁸
    Or some auld pagan Heathen,
The moral man he does define,
    But ne'er a word o' faith in
        That 's right that day.

In guid time comes an antidote
    Against sic poison'd nostrum;
For Peebles,³⁹ frae the water-fit,⁴⁰
    Ascends the holy rostrum:
See, up he's got the word o' God, 140
    An' meek an' mim⁴¹ has view'd it,
While Common Sense has ta'en the road,
    An' aff, an' up the Cowgate
        Fast, fast, that day.

Wee Miller,⁴² neist,⁴³ the Guard relieves,
    An' Orthodoxy raibles,⁴⁴

---

24 oat-cakes.   25 crisp.   26 stare.
27 the black-bonneted elder taking the collection.
28 planks.   29 talking nonsense.
30 whispering.   31 weaver.
32 dirtied.   33 sample.
34 the palm of his hand.
35 Alexander Moodie, a local minister noted for his great severity.
36 climbs, i.e. enters.

37 unearthly.
38 a celebrated Roman stoic philosopher.
39 William Peebles, a versifying divine from Newton-on-Ayr.
40 river's mouth.   41 primly.
42 Alexander Miller, a parish preacher in Ayr, whose career in the ministry was ruined by the present passage.
43 next.   44 gabbles.

Tho' in his heart he weel believes,
　An' thinks it auld wives' fables:
But, faith! the birkie[45] wants a Manse,
　So cannilie he hums them;[46]　　　　　　150
Altho' his carnal wit an' sense
　Like hafflins-wise[47] o'ercomes him
　　　　　At times that day.

Now, butt an' ben,[48] the Change-house[49] fills,
　Wi' yill-caup[50] Commentators;
Here's crying out for bakes an' gills,[51]
　An' there the pint-stowp clatters;
While thick an' thrang, an' loud an' lang,
　Wi' logic, an' wi' Scripture,
They raise a din, that in the end　　　　　160
　Is like to breed a rupture
　　　　　O' wrath that day.

Leeze me[52] on drink! it gi'es us mair
　Than either school or college:
It kindles wit, it waukens lair,[53]
　It pangs us fou o' knowledge.
Be't whisky gill, or penny wheep,[54]
　Or ony stronger potion,
It never fails, on drinkin' deep,
　To kittle[55] up our notion　　　　　170
　　　　　By night or day.

The lads an' lasses, blythely bent
　To mind baith saul an' body,
Sit round the table, weel content,
　An' steer about the toddy.
On this ane's dress, an' that ane's leuk,
　They're makin observations;
While some are cosy i' the neuk,
　An' formin' assignations
　　　　　To meet some day.　　　　　180

But now the Lord's ain trumpet touts,
　Till a' the hills are rairin',
An' echoes back return the shouts;
　Black Russel[56] is na sparin':
His piercing words, like Highlan' swords,
　Divide the joints an' marrow;
His talk o' Hell, where devils dwell,
　Our very 'sauls does harrow'
　　　　　Wi' fright that day!

A vast, unbottom'd, boundless pit,　　　　　190
　Fill'd fou o' lowin'[57] brunstane,
Wha's ragin' flame, an' scorchin' heat,
　Wad melt the hardest whun-stane![58]
The half-asleep start up wi' fear
　An' think they hear it roarin',
When presently it does appear
　'Twas but some neebor snorin'
　　　　　Asleep that day.

'Twad be owre lang a tale to tell
　How mony stories past,　　　　　200
An' how they crowded to the yill,[59]
　When they were a' dismist;
How drink gaed round, in cogs an' caups,[60]
　Amang the furms and benches;
An' cheese an' bread, frae women's laps,
　Was dealt about in lunches,
　　　　　An' dawds[61] that day.

In comes a gawsie,[62] gash[63] guidwife,
　An' sits down by the fire,
Syne draws her kebbuck[64] an' her knife;　　　210
　The lasses they are shyer.
The auld guidmen, about the grace,
　Frae side to side they bother,
Till some ane by his bonnet lays,
　An' gi'es them't like a tether,
　　　　　Fu' lang that day.

Waesucks![65] for him that gets nae lass,
　Or lasses that hae naething!
Sma' need has he to say a grace,
　Or melvie[66] his braw claithing!　　　　　220
O wives, be mindfu', ance yoursel
　How bonnie lads ye wanted,
An' dinna for a kebbuck-heel[67]
　Let lasses be affronted
　　　　　On sic a day!

Now Clinkumbell, wi' rattlin' tow,[68]
　Begins to jow an' croon;[69]
Some swagger hame the best they dow,[70]
　Some wait the afternoon.
At slaps[71] the billies halt a blink,　　　　230
　Till lasses strip their shoon:
Wi' faith an' hope, an' love an' drink,

---

45 fellow.　　　　　　　46 talks humbug.
47 nearly half.　　　　　48 kitchen and parlor.
49 tavern.　　　　　　　50 ale-cup.
51 biscuits and whiskey.　52 blessings.
53 learning.　　　　　　54 small ale.
55 tickle.
56 John Russell, a feared and hated schoolmaster and Calvinistic
minister of Kilmarnock.

57 flaming.　　　　　　58 mill-stone.
59 ale.　　　　　　　　60 wooden bowls and cups.
61 large portions.　　　62 buxom.
63 shrewd.　　　　　　64 cheese.
65 alas.　　　　　　　　66 soil with meal.
67 last piece of cheese.　68 bell-rope.
69 peal and toll.　　　　70 can.
71 fence-openings.

They're a' in famous tune
          For crack[72] that day.

How mony hearts this day converts
     O' sinners and o' lasses!
Their hearts o' stane, gin night, are gane
     As saft as ony flesh is.
There's some are fou o' love divine,
     There's some are fou o' brandy;
An' mony jobs that day begin,
     May end in houghmagandie[73]
               Some ither day.

          Autumn, 1785   1786

TO A MOUSE

ON TURNING HER UP IN HER NEST WITH THE
PLOUGH, NOVEMBER 1785

WEE, sleekit,[1] cow'rin', tim'rous beastie,
O what a panic's in thy breastie!
Thou need na start awa sae hasty,
          Wi' bickering brattle![2]
I wad be laith to rin an' chase thee
          Wi' murd'ring pattle![3]

I'm truly sorry man's dominion
Has broken Nature's social union,
An' justifies that ill opinion
          Which makes thee startle   10
At me, thy poor earth-born companion,
          An' fellow-mortal!

I doubt na, whiles,[4] but thou may thieve;
What then? poor beastie, thou maun live!
A daimen-icker in a thrave[5]
          'S a sma' request:
I'll get a blessin' wi' the lave,[6]
          And never miss 't!

Thy wee bit housie, too, in ruin!
Its silly wa's the win's are strewin'!
An' naething, now, to big[7] a new ane,   20
          O' foggage[8] green!
An' bleak December's winds ensuin',
          Baith snell[9] an' keen!

Thou saw the fields laid bare and waste,
An' weary winter comin' fast,

An' cozie here, beneath the blast,
          Thou thought to dwell,
Till crash! the cruel coulter past
          Out-thro' thy cell.   30

That wee bit heap o' leaves an' stibble
Has cost thee mony a weary nibble!
Now thou's turn'd out, for a' thy trouble,
          But house or hald,[10]
To thole[11] the winter's sleety dribble,
          An' cranreuch[12] cauld!

But, Mousie, thou art no thy lane,[13]
In proving foresight may be vain:
The best laid schemes o' mice an' men
          Gang aft a-gley,[14]   40
An' lea'e us nought but grief an' pain
          For promis'd joy.

Still thou art blest compar'd wi' me!
The present only toucheth thee:
But och! I backward cast my e'e
          On prospects drear!
An' forward tho' I canna see,
          I guess an' fear!

          1785   1786

THE JOLLY BEGGARS

A CANTATA

RECITATIVO

WHEN lyart[1] leaves bestrow the yird,
Or, wavering like the baukie bird,[2]
     Bedim cauld Boreas' blast;
When hailstanes drive wi' bitter skyte,[3]
And infant frosts begin to bite,
     In hoary cranreuch[4] drest;
Ae night at e'en a merry core[5]
     O' randie gangrel[6] bodies
In Poosie Nansie's held the splore,[7]
     To drink their orra duddies.[8]   10
          Wi' quaffing and laughing,
               They ranted an' they sang;
          Wi' jumping an' thumping
               The vera girdle[9] rang.

First, niest the fire, in auld red rags,
     Ane sat, weel brac'd wi' mealy bags,

---

72 talk.   73 fornication.

---

1 sleek.   2 scampering haste.
3 plough-staff.   4 at times.
5 an occasional ear in a shock of grain.
6 rest.   7 build
8 coarse grass.   9 biting.

10 without house or home.   11 endure.
12 hoarfrost.   13 not alone.   14 awry.

1 faded.   2 bat.
3 lash.   4 hoarfrost.
5 group.   6 disorderly, vagrant.
7 carousal.   8 to sell their spare rags for drink.
9 griddle.

And knapsack a' in order;
His doxy[10] lay within his arm;
Wi' usquebae[11] and blankets warm,
  She blinket on her sodger;   20
An' aye he gies the tosy[12] drab
The tither skelpin'[13] kiss,
While she held up her greedy gab,
Just like an aumous[14] dish:
  Ilk smack still did crack still
  Just like cadger's whip;[15]
  Then staggering, an' swaggering,
  He roar'd this ditty up—

AIR
TUNE—*Soldier's Joy*

I am a son of Mars, who have been in many wars,
  And show my cuts and scars wherever I come; 30
This here was for a wench, and that other in a
  trench,
  When welcoming the French at the sound of
  the drum.
                    Lal de daudle, &c.

My 'prenticeship I pass'd where my leader breath'd
  his last,
  When the bloody die was cast on the heights of
  Abrám;[16]
And I servèd out my trade when the gallant game
  was play'd,
  And the Moro low was laid[17] at the sound of
  the drum.

I lastly was with Curtis, among the floating
  batt'ries,[18]
  And there I left for witness an arm and a limb:
Yet let my country need me, with Elliot[19] to
  head me,   40
  I'd clatter on my stumps at the sound of a drum.

And now tho' I must beg, with a wooden arm and
  leg,
  And many a tatter'd rag hanging over my bum,
I'm as happy with my wallet, my bottle, and my
  callet,[20]
  As when I used in scarlet to follow a drum.

What tho' with hoary locks I must stand the winter shocks,
  Beneath the woods and rocks oftentimes for a
  home?

When the t'other bag I sell, and the t'other bottle
  tell,
  I could meet a troop of hell at the sound of the
  drum.
                    Lal de daudle, &c.

RECITATIVO

He ended; and the kebars sheuk[21]   50
  Aboon the chorus roar;
While frighted rattons[22] backward leuk,
  And seek the benmost bore.[23]
A fairy fiddler frae the neuk,
  He skirl'd[24] out *Encore!*
But up arose the martial chuck,[25]
  And laid the loud uproar.

AIR
TUNE—*Soldier Laddie*

I once was a maid, tho' I cannot tell when,
And still my delight is in proper young men;
Some one of a troop of dragoons was my daddie, 60
No wonder I'm fond of a sodger laddie.
                    Sing, Lal de dal, &c.

The first of my loves was a swaggering blade,
To rattle the thundering drum was his trade;
His leg was so tight, and his cheek was so ruddy,
Transported I was with my sodger laddie.

But the godly old chaplain left him in the lurch;
The sword I forsook for the sake of the church;
He ventur'd the soul, and I riskèd the body,—
'Twas then I prov'd false to my sodger laddie. 70

Full soon I grew sick of my sanctified sot,
The regiment at large for a husband I got;
From the gilded spontoon[26] to the fife I was
  ready,
I askèd no more but a sodger laddie.

But the peace it reduc'd me to beg in despair,
Till I met my old boy at a Cunningham fair;
His rags regimental they flutter'd so gaudy,
My heart it rejoic'd at a sodger laddie.

And now I have liv'd—I know not how long,
And still I can join in a cup or a song;   80
But whilst with both hands I can hold the glass
  steady,
Here's to thee, my hero, my sodger laddie!
                    Sing, Lal de dal, &c.

---

10 wench.   11 whiskey.
12 tipsy.   13 another smacking.
14 alms basin.   15 hawker's whip.
16 at Quebec, 1759.   17 at Santiago de Cuba, 1762.
18 at Gibraltar, 1782.   19 the defender of Gibraltar.
20 wench.

---

21 rafters shook.   22 rats.
23 farthest hole.   24 screamed.
25 darling.   26 halberd.

RECITATIVO

Poor Merry Andrew in the neuk
    Sat guzzling wi' a tinkler hizzie;[27]
They mind't na wha the chorus teuk,
    Between themselves they were sae busy.
At length, wi' drink an' courting dizzy,
He stoiter'd[28] up an' made a face;
    Then turn'd, an' laid a smack on Grizzy,
Syne tun'd his pipes wi' grave grimace.   90

AIR

TUNE—*Auld Sir Symon*

Sir Wisdom's a fool when he's fou,
    Sir Knave is a fool in a session;
He's there but a 'prentice I trow,
    But I am a fool by profession.

My grannie she bought me a beuk,
    And I held awa to the school;
I fear I my talent misteuk,
    But what will ye hae of a fool?

For drink I would venture my neck;
    A hizzie's the half o' my craft;   100
But what could ye other expect,
    Of ane that's avowedly daft?

I ance was tied up like a stirk,[29]
    For civilly swearing and quaffing;
I ance was abused i' the kirk,
    For touzling a lass i' my daffin.[30]

Poor Andrew that tumbles for sport,
    Let naebody name wi' a jeer;
There's even, I'm tauld, i' the Court,
    A tumbler ca'd the Premier.   110

Observ'd ye yon reverend lad
    Maks faces to tickle the mob?
He rails at our mountebank squad—
    It's rivalship just i' the job.

And now my conclusion I'll tell,
    For, faith! I'm confoundedly dry;
The chiel that's a fool for himsel',
    Gude Lord! he's far dafter than I.

RECITATIVO

Then niest outspak a raucle carlin,[31]
What kent fu' weel to cleek the sterling,[32] 120
For mony a pursie she had hookit,
And had in mony a well been dookit;

Her love had been a Highland laddie,
But weary fa' the waefu' woodie![33]
Wi' sighs an' sobs, she thus began
To wail her braw John Highlandman:—

AIR

TUNE—*O An' Ye Were Dead, Guidman*

A Highland lad my love was born,
The Lawlan[34] laws he held in scorn;
But he still was faithfu' to his clan,
My gallant braw John Highlandman.   130

CHORUS

Sing hey, my braw John Highlandman!
Sing ho, my braw John Highlandman!
There's no a lad in a' the lan'
Was match for my John Highlandman.

With his philibeg[35] an' tartan plaid,
And gude claymore[36] down by his side,
The ladies' hearts he did trepen,[37]
My gallant braw John Highlandman.

We rangèd a' from Tweed to Spey,[38]
And liv'd like lords an' ladies gay;   140
For a Lawlan' face he fearèd nane,
My gallant braw John Highlandman.

They banish'd him beyond the sea;
But ere the bud was on the tree,
Adown my cheeks the pearls ran,
Embracing my John Highlandman.

But oh! they catch'd him at the last,
And bound him in a dungeon fast;
My curse upon them every one!
They've hang'd my braw John Highlandman. 150

And now a widow I must mourn
The pleasures that will ne'er return;
No comfort but a hearty can,
When I think on John Highlandman.

RECITATIVO

A pigmy scraper wi' his fiddle,
Wha us'd at trysts[39] and fairs to driddle,[40]
Her strappin' limb and gaucy[41] middle
        (He reach'd nae higher)
Had hol'd[42] his heartie like a riddle,[43]
        And blawn't on fire.   160

27 tinker-wench.   28 staggered.
29 young steer.   30 play.
31 boisterous old woman.   32 pinch the ready cash.

33 bad luck to the gallows.   34 Lowland.
35 kilt.   36 two-handed Highland sword.
37 ensnare.
38 that is, from one end of the country to the other.
39 cattle-markets.
40 toddle.   41 plump.   42 pierced.   43 sieve.

Wi' hand on haunch, and upward ee,
He croon'd his gamut, one, two, three,
Then, in an *arioso*[44] key,
    The wee Apollo
Set aff, wi' *allegretto* glee,
    His *giga*[45] solo.

AIR

TUNE—*Whistle Owre the Lave*[46] *O't*

Let me ryke[47] up to dight[48] that tear,
And go wi' me and be my dear,
And then your every care an' fear
    May whistle owre the lave o't.   170

CHORUS

I am a fiddler to my trade,
And a' the tunes that e'er I play'd,
The sweetest still to wife or maid,
    Was *Whistle Owre the Lave O't.*

At kirns[49] and weddings we'se be there,
And oh! sae nicely 's we will fare;
We'll bouse about, till Daddie Care
    Sings *Whistle Owre the Lave O't.*

Sae merrily's the banes we'll pyke,
And sun oursels about the dyke,   180
And at our leisure, when ye like,
    We'll whistle owre the lave o't.

But bless me wi' your heav'n o' charms,
And while I kittle hair on thairms,[50]
Hunger and cauld, and a' sic harms,
    May whistle owre the lave o't.

RECITATIVO

Her charms had struck a sturdy caird,[51]
    As well as poor gut-scraper;
He taks the fiddler by the beard,
    An' draws a roosty rapier—   190
He swoor, by a' was swearing worth,
    To spit him like a pliver,[52]
Unless he would from that time forth
    Relinquish her for ever.

Wi' ghastly ee, poor Tweedle-Dee
    Upon his hunkers[53] bended,
And pray'd for grace wi' ruefu' face,
    And sae the quarrel ended.
But tho' his little heart did grieve

When round the tinkler prest her,   200
He feign'd to snirtle[54] in his sleeve,
When thus the caird address'd her:—

AIR

TUNE—*Clout*[55] *the Cauldron*

My bonnie lass, I work in brass,
    A tinkler is my station;
I've travell'd round all Christian ground
    In this my occupation;
I've ta'en the gold, I've been enroll'd
    In many a noble squadron;
But vain they search'd, when off I march'd
    To go and clout the cauldron.   210

Despise that shrimp, that wither'd imp,
    Wi' a' his noise and caperin';
And tak a share wi' those that bear
    The budget[56] and the apron;
And, by that stoup,[57] my faith an' houp!
    And by that dear Kilbaigie,[58]
If e'er ye want, or meet wi' scant,
    May I ne'er weet my craigie.[59]

RECITATIVO

The caird prevail'd—th' unblushing fair
    In his embraces sunk,   220
Partly wi' love o'ercome sae sair,
    An' partly she was drunk.
Sir Violino, with an air
    That show'd a man o' spunk,
Wish'd unison between the pair,
    An' made the bottle clunk
        To their health that night.

But urchin Cupid shot a shaft
    That play'd a dame a shavie;[60]
The fiddler rak'd her fore and aft,   230
    Behint the chicken cavie.[61]
Her lord, a wight of Homer's craft,[62]
    Tho' limpin' wi' the spavie,[63]
He hirpl'd[64] up, and lap like daft,[65]
    An' shor'd[66] them *Dainty Davie*
        O' boot[67] that night.

He was a care-defying blade
    As ever Bacchus listed;

---

44 melodious.
46 rest.
48 wipe.
50 tickle hair on catgut.
52 plover.

45 Italian for 'jig.'
47 reach.
49 harvest-homes.
51 tinker.
53 haunches.

54 snicker.
56 bag of tools.
58 a kind of whiskey.
60 trick.
62 ballad singing.
64 hobbled.
66 offered.

55 patch.
57 jug.
59 throat.
61 coop.
63 spavin.
65 leaped like mad.
67 free.

Tho' Fortune sair upon him laid,
 His heart she ever miss'd it.   240
He had nae wish—but to be glad,
 Nor want but—when he thirsted;
He hated nought but—to be sad,
 And thus the Muse suggested
   His sang that night.

AIR

TUNE—*For A' That, An' A' That*

I am a Bard of no regard
 Wi' gentlefolks, an' a' that;
But Homer-like, the glowrin' byke,[68]
 Frae town to town I draw that.

CHORUS

For a' that, and a' that,   250
 An' twice as meikle's a' that;
I've lost but ane, I've twa behin',
 I've wife eneugh for a' that.

I never drank the Muses' stank,[69]
 Castalia's burn,[70] an' a' that;
But there[71] it streams, and richly reams[72]—
 My Helicon I ca' that.

Great love I bear to a' the fair,
 Their humble slave, an' a' that;
But lordly will, I hold it still   260
 A mortal sin to thraw[73] that.

In raptures sweet this hour we meet
 Wi' mutual love, an' a' that;
But for how lang the flee may stang,
 Let inclination law[74] that.

Their tricks an' craft hae put me daft,
 They've ta'en me in, an' a' that;
But clear your decks, and *Here's the sex!*
 I like the jads for a' that.

For a' that, an' a' that,   270
 And twice as meikle's a' that,
My dearest bluid, to do them guid,
 They're welcome till't,[75] for a' that.

RECITATIVO

So sung the Bard—and Nansie's wa's
Shook with a thunder of applause,

Re-echo'd from each mouth;
They toom'd their pocks,[76] an' pawn'd their duds.
They scarcely left to co'er their fuds,[77]
 To quench their lowin'[78] drouth.
Then owre again the jovial thrang   280
 The Poet did request
To lowse his pack, an' wale[79] a sang,
 A ballad o' the best;
 He rising, rejoicing,
  Between his two Deborahs,
 Looks round him, an' found them
  Impatient for the chorus.

AIR

TUNE—*Jolly Mortals, Fill Your Glasses*

See the smoking bowl before us,
 Mark our jovial ragged ring;
Round and round take up the chorus,   290
 And in raptures let us sing—

CHORUS

A fig for those by law protected!
 Liberty's a glorious feast!
Courts for cowards were erected,
 Churches built to please the priest.

What is title? what is treasure?
 What is reputation's care?
If we lead a life of pleasure,
 'Tis no matter how or where!

With the ready trick and fable,   300
 Round we wander all the day;
And at night, in barn or stable,
 Hug our doxies on the hay.

Does the train-attended carriage
 Thro' the country lighter rove?
Does the sober bed of marriage
 Witness brighter scenes of love?

Life is all a variorum,
 We regard not how it goes;
Let them cant about decorum   310
 Who have characters to lose.

Here's to budgets, bags, and wallets!
 Here's to all the wandering train!
Here's our ragged brats and callets!
 One and all cry out *Amen!*

   1785   1799

---

68 staring crowd.   69 pool.
70 brook.   71 in his mug of ale.
72 foams.   73 thwart.
74 decide.   75 to it.

76 emptied their pockets.   77 cover their buttocks.
78 burning.   79 choose.

THE COTTER'S SATURDAY NIGHT

INSCRIBED TO ROBERT AIKEN, ESQ.[1]

Let not Ambition mock their useful toil,
Their homely joys, and destiny obscure;
Nor Grandeur hear, with a disdainful smile,
The short and simple annals of the poor.
—GRAY'S *Elegy*

[Although the general plan and title of this poem were taken from Fergusson's *The Farmer's Ingle*, the work is formed chiefly on English models and is the most imitative of all Burns's work. The influence of Gray's *Elegy* is conspicuous and there are echoes of other eighteenth-century writers and of Milton. The Spenserian stanza was imitated not from Spenser himself, whom Burns had not read, but from Shenstone and Beattie.]

My lov'd, my honour'd, much respected friend!
　No mercenary bard his homage pays:
With honest pride I scorn each selfish end,
　My dearest meed a friend's esteem and praise:
　To you I sing, in simple Scottish lays,
The lowly train in life's sequester'd scene;
　The native feelings strong, the guileless ways;
What Aiken in a cottage would have been—
Ah! tho' his worth unknown, far happier there, I
　　ween!

November chill blaws loud wi' angry sough;[2]　10
　The short'ning winter-day is near a close;
The miry beasts retreating frae the pleugh;
　The black'ning trains o' craws to their re-
　　pose:
　The toil-worn Cotter frae his labour goes,
This night his weekly moil is at an end,
　Collects his spades, his mattocks, and his hoes,
Hoping the morn in ease and rest to spend,
And weary, o'er the moor, his course does hame-
　　ward bend.

At length his lonely cot appears in view,
　Beneath the shelter of an agèd tree;　20
Th' expectant wee things, toddlin', stacher[3]
　　through
　To meet their Dad, wi' flichterin' noise an'
　　glee.
　His wee bit ingle,[4] blinkin bonnilie,
His clean hearth-stane, his thrifty wifie's smile,
　The lisping infant prattling on his knee,
Does a' his weary kiaugh[5] and care beguile,
An' makes him quite forget his labour an' his
　　toil.

Belyve,[6] the elder bairns come drapping in,
　At service out, amang the farmers roun';
Some ca'[7] the pleugh, some herd, some tentie[8]
　　rin　30
A cannie errand to a neibor town:
　Their eldest hope, their Jenny, woman-grown,
In youthfu' bloom, love sparkling in her e'e,
　Comes hame, perhaps to shew a braw new
　　gown,
Or deposite her sair-won penny-fee,
To help her parents dear, if they in hardship be.

With joy unfeign'd brothers and sisters meet,
　An' each for other's weelfare kindly spiers:[9]
The social hours, swift-wing'd, unnotic'd fleet;
　Each tells the uncos[10] that he sees or hears; 40
　The parents, partial, eye their hopeful years;
Anticipation forward points the view.
　The mother, wi' her needle an' her sheers,
Gars[11] auld claes look amaist as well's the new;
The father mixes a' wi' admonition due.

Their master's an' their mistress's command,
　The younkers a' are warnèd to obey;
An' mind their labours wi' an eydent[12] hand,
　An' ne'er, tho' out o' sight, to jauk[13] or play:
　'And O! be sure to fear the Lord alway, 50
An' mind your duty, duly, morn an' night!
　Lest in temptation's path ye gang astray,
Implore His counsel and assisting might:
They never sought in vain that sought the Lord
　　aright!'

But hark! a rap comes gently to the door;
　Jenny, wha kens the meaning o' the same,
Tells how a neibor lad cam o'er the moor,
　To do some errands, and convoy her hame.
　The wily mother sees the conscious flame
Sparkle in Jenny's e'e, and flush her cheek; 60
　Wi' heart-struck anxious care, inquires his
　　name,
While Jenny hafflins[14] is afraid to speak;
Weel pleas'd the mother hears it's nae wild worth-
　　less rake.

Wi' kindly welcome, Jenny brings him ben;[15]
　A strappin' youth; he takes the mother's eye;
Blythe Jenny sees the visit's no ill ta'en;
　The father cracks[16] of horses, pleughs, and kye.
　The youngster's artless heart o'erflows wi' joy,

---

1 Robert Aiken, 1739-1807, was Solicitor in Ayr, and one of Burns's earliest admirers.
2 sough, the sound of the wind.
4 fire.　　　　　　　3 stagger.
　　　　　　　　　　5 anxiety.

6 soon.　　　　　　　　　　　　7 drive.
8 heedful.
10 uncommon things.　　　　　　11 makes.
12 diligent.　　　　　　　　　　13 dally.
14 half.　　　　　　　　　　　　15 into the parlor.
16 talks.

But blate and laithfu',[17] scarce can weel behave;
  The mother, wi' a woman's wiles, can spy 70
What makes the youth sae bashfu' an' sae grave;
Weel-pleased to think her bairn's respected like the lave.[18]

O happy love! where love like this is found;
  O heart-felt raptures! bliss beyond compare!
I've pacèd much this weary mortal round,
  And sage experience bids me this declare—
    'If Heaven a draught of heavenly pleasure spare,
One cordial in this melancholy vale,
  'Tis when a youthful, loving, modest pair
In other's arms breathe out the tender tale, 80
Beneath the milk-white thorn that scents the evening gale.'

Is there, in human form, that bears a heart—
  A wretch, a villain, lost to love and truth—
That can, with studied, sly, ensnaring art,
  Betray sweet Jenny's unsuspecting youth?
    Curse on his perjur'd arts, dissembling smooth!
Are honour, virtue, conscience, all exil'd?
  Is there no pity, no relenting ruth,
Points to the parents fondling o'er their child?
Then paints the ruin'd maid, and their distraction wild? 90

But now the supper crowns their simple board,
  The halesome parritch,[19] chief of Scotia's food:
The sowpe their only hawkie[20] does afford,
  That 'yont the hallan[21] snugly chows her cood;
  The dame brings forth in complimental mood,
To grace the lad, her weel-hain'd kebbuck, fell:[22]
  And aft he's prest, and aft he ca's it good;
The frugal wifie, garrulous, will tell
How 'twas a towmond[23] auld sin' lint was i' the bell.[24]

The cheerfu' supper done, wi' serious face 100
  They round the ingle form a circle wide;
The sire turns o'er, wi' patriarchal grace,
  The big ha'-Bible,[25] ance his father's pride:
  His bonnet rev'rently is laid aside,
His lyart haffets[26] wearing thin an' bare;
  Those strains that once did sweet in Zion glide—
He wales[27] a portion with judicious care,

And 'Let us worship God!' he says with solemn air.

They chant their artless notes in simple guise;
  They tune their hearts, by far the noblest aim: 110
Perhaps Dundee's wild warbling measures rise,
  Or plaintive Martyrs, worthy of the name;
  Or noble Elgin beets[28] the heav'nward flame,
The sweetest far of Scotia's holy lays:
  Compar'd with these, Italian trills are tame;
The tickl'd ears no heartfelt raptures raise;
Nae unison hae they with our Creator's praise.

The priest-like father reads the sacred page,
  How Abram was the friend of God on high;
Or Moses bade eternal warfare wage 120
  With Amalek's ungracious progeny;
  Or how the royal bard[29] did groaning lie
Beneath the stroke of Heaven's avenging ire;
  Or Job's pathetic plaint, and wailing cry;
Or rapt Isaiah's wild seraphic fire;
Or other holy seers that tune the sacred lyre.

Perhaps the Christian volume is the theme,
  How guiltless blood for guilty man was shed;
How He who bore in Heaven the second name
  Had not on earth whereon to lay His head; 130
  How His first followers and servants sped;
The precepts sage they wrote to many a land:
  How he,[30] was lone in Patmos banishèd,
Saw in the sun a mighty angel stand,
And heard great Bab'lon's doom pronounc'd by Heaven's command.

Then kneeling down to Heaven's Eternal King
  The saint, the father, and the husband prays:
Hope 'springs exulting on triumphant wing'[31]
  That thus they all shall meet in future days:
  There ever bask in uncreated rays, 140
No more to sigh, or shed the bitter tear,
  Together hymning their Creator's praise,
In such society, yet still more dear;
While circling Time moves round in an eternal sphere.

Compar'd with this, how poor Religion's pride,
  In all the pomp of method and of art,
When men display to congregations wide
  Devotion's ev'ry grace, except the heart!
The Power, incens'd, the pageant will desert,
The pompous strain, the sacerdotal stole; 150
  But haply, in some cottage far apart,

---

17 shy and bashful.
19 oatmeal porridge.
21 partition.
23 twelvemonth.
25 hall-Bible.
27 chooses.

18 rest.
20 cow.
22 well-kept, tasty cheese.
24 since flax was in bloom.
26 gray locks.

---

28 kindles.
30 John.

29 David.
31 Pope, *Windsor Forest*, 112.

May hear, well pleas'd, the language of the soul;
And in His Book of Life the inmates poor enrol.

Then homeward all take off their sev'ral way;
    The youngling cottagers retire to rest:
The parent-pair their secret homage pay,
    And proffer up to Heav'n the warm request,
That He who stills the raven's clamorous nest,
    And decks the lily fair in flow'ry pride,
    Would, in the way His wisdom sees the best, 160
For them and for their little ones provide;
But chiefly in their hearts with Grace Divine pre-
side.

From scenes like these old Scotia's grandeur
    springs,
    That makes her lov'd at home, rever'd abroad:
Princes and lords are but the breath of kings,
    'An honest man's the noblest work of God';[32]
    And certes, in fair Virtue's heavenly road,
The cottage leaves the palace far behind;
    What is a lordling's pomp? a cumbrous load,
Disguising oft the wretch of human kind,   170
Studied in arts of Hell, in wickedness refin'd!

O Scotia! my dear, my native soil!
    For whom my warmest wish to Heaven is
    sent!
Long may thy hardy sons of rustic toil
    Be blest with health, and peace, and sweet
    content!
    And O! may Heaven their simple lives prevent
From Luxury's contagion, weak and vile;
    Then, howe'er crowns and coronets be rent,
A virtuous populace may rise the while,
And stand a wall of fire around their much-lov'd
isle.   180

O Thou! who pour'd the patriotic tide
    That stream'd thro' Wallace's undaunted
    heart,
Who dared to nobly stem tyrannic pride,
    Or nobly die—the second glorious part,
    (The patriot's God, peculiarly Thou art,
    His friend, inspirer, guardian, and reward!)
    O never, never, Scotia's realm desert;
But still the patriot, and the patriot-bard,
In bright succession raise, her ornament and guard!
    1785   1786

ADDRESS TO THE DEIL

O Prince! O Chief of many thronèd pow'rs!
That led th' embattl'd seraphim to war!
                                    —MILTON

32 Pope, *Essay on Man*, 248.

[Burns professed the strongest admiration for Milton's
Satan because of his 'desperate daring, and noble defiance of hardship.' It was chiefly, however, the excessively
illiberal set of beliefs held by the 'old church' party that
prompted his good-natured burlesque on the devil.]

O THOU! whatever title suit thee,
Auld Hornie, Satan, Nick, or Clootie,
Wha in yon cavern grim an' sootie,
            Clos'd under hatches,
Spairges[1] about the brunstane cootie,[2]
            To scaud poor wretches!

Hear me, auld Hangie,[3] for a wee,
An' let poor damnèd bodies be;
I'm sure sma' pleasure it can gie,
            Ev'n to a deil,   10
To skelp[4] an' scaud poor dogs like me,
            An' hear us squeal!

Great is thy pow'r, an' great thy fame;
Far kenn'd an' noted is thy name;
An', tho' yon lowin heugh's[5] thy hame,
            Thou travels far;
An' faith! thou's neither lag[6] nor lame,
            Nor blate nor scaur.[7]

Whyles[8] rangin' like a roarin' lion
For prey, a' holes an' corners tryin';   20
Whyles on the strong-wing'd tempest flyin',
            Tirlin' the kirks;[9]
Whyles, in the human bosom pryin',
            Unseen thou lurks.

I've heard my rev'rend grannie say,
In lanely glens ye like to stray;
Or, where auld ruin'd castles gray
            Nod to the moon,
Ye fright the nightly wand'rer's way,
            Wi' eldritch[10] croon.   30

When twilight did my grannie summon
To say her pray'rs, douce,[11] honest woman!
Aft yont the dyke[12] she's heard you bummin',[13]
            Wi' eerie drone;
Or, rustlin', thro' the boortrees[14] comin',
            Wi' heavy groan.

Ae dreary windy winter night
The stars shot down wi' sklentin'[15] light,

1 splashes.   2 brimstone tub.
3 hangman.   4 strike.
5 flaming pit is.   6 slow.
7 shy nor timid.   8 at times.
9 unroofing the churches.   10 unearthly.
11 sober.   12 beyond the wall.
13 humming.   14 elders.
15 slanting.

Wi' you mysel I gat a fright
      Ayont the lough;[16]   40
Ye like a rash-buss[17] stood in sight
      Wi' waving sough.[18]

The cudgel in my nieve[19] did shake,
Each bristl'd hair stood like a stake,
When wi' an eldritch stoor[20] 'quaick, quaick,'
      Amang the springs,
Awa ye squatter'd like a drake
      On whistlin' wings.

Let warlocks grim an' wither'd hags
Tell how wi' you on ragweed nags   50
They skim the muirs, an' dizzy crags
      Wi' wicked speed;
And in kirk-yards renew their leagues
      Owre howkit[21] dead.

Thence country wives, wi' toil an' pain,
May plunge an' plunge the kirn[22] in vain;
For oh! the yellow treasure's taen
      By witchin' skill;
An' dawtit[23] twal-pint Hawkie's[24] gane
      As yell's the bill.[25]   60

Thence mystic knots mak great abuse
On young guidmen, fond, keen, an' crouse;[26]
When the best wark-lume i' the house,
      By cantrip[27] wit,
Is instant made no worth a louse,
      Just at the bit.[28]

When thowes[29] dissolve the snawy hoord,
An' float the jinglin' icy-boord,
Then water-kelpies haunt the foord,
      By your direction,   70
An' 'nighted trav'llers are allur'd
      To their destruction.

An' aft your moss-traversing spunkies[30]
Decoy the wight that late an' drunk is:
The bleezin,[31] curst, mischievous monkies
      Delude his eyes,
Till in some miry slough he sunk is,
      Ne'er mair to rise.

When masons' mystic word an' grip
In storms an' tempests raise you up,   80

Some cock or cat your rage maun stop,
      Or, strange to tell!
The youngest brither ye wad whip
      Aff straught to hell.

Lang syne, in Eden's bonnie yard,
When youthfu' lovers first were pair'd,
And all the soul of love they shar'd,
      The raptur'd hour,
Sweet on the fragrant flow'ry swaird,
      In shady bow'r;   90

Then you, ye auld snick-drawing[32] dog!
Ye cam to Paradise incog.
An' play'd on man a cursed brogue,[33]
      (Black be you fa![34])
An' gied the infant warld a shog,[35]
      'Maist ruin'd a'.

D'ye mind that day, when in a bizz,
Wi' reekit[36] duds, an' reestit gizz,[37]
Ye did present your smoutie phiz
      'Mang better folk,   100
An' sklented[38] on the man of Uz[39]
      Your spitefu' joke?

An' how ye gat him i' your thrall,
An' brak him out o' house an' hal',
While scabs an' blotches did him gall
      Wi' bitter claw,
An' lows'd[40] his ill-tongu'd wicked scawl,[41]
      Was warst ava?[42]

But a' your doings to rehearse,
Your wily snares an' fechtin'[43] fierce,   110
Sin' that day Michael did you pierce,
      Down to this time,
Wad ding[44] a' Lallan[45] tongue, or Erse,
      In prose or rhyme.

An' now, aul Cloots, I ken ye're thinkin',
A certain Bardie's rantin', drinkin',
Some luckless hour will send him linkin',[46]
      To your black Pit;
But faith! he'll turn a corner jinkin',[47]
      An' cheat you yet.   120

But fare you weel, auld Nickie-Ben!
O wad ye tak a thought an' men'!

---

16 beyond the lake.
17 clump of rushes.
18 sough, the sound of wind.
19 fist.
20 harsh.
21 dug up.
22 churn.
23 petted.
24 twelve-pint cow.
25 as dry as the bull.
26 cocksure.
27 magic.
28 critical moment.
29 thaws.
30 will-o'-the-wisps.
31 blazing.
32 latch-lifting.
33 trick.
34 lot.
35 shake.
36 smoking.
37 singed face.
38 turned.
39 Job.
40 let loose.
41 scold—i.e. Job's wife.
42 worst of all.
43 fighting.
44 defy.
45 Lowland.
46 tripping.
47 dodging.

Ye aiblins[48] might—I dinna ken—
      Still hae a stake:[49]
I'm wae to think upo' yon den,
      Ev'n for your sake!

1785   *1786*

TO A LOUSE

ON SEEING ONE ON A LADY'S BONNET AT CHURCH

HA! wh'are ye gaun, ye crowlin' ferlie![1]
Your impudence protects you sairly:[2]
I canna say but ye strunt[3] rarely,
      Owre gauze and lace;
Tho' faith! I fear ye dine but sparely
      On sic a place.

Ye ugly, creepin', blastit wonner,
Detested, shunn'd by saunt an' sinner!
How dare yet set your fit[4] upon her,
      Sae fine a Lady?   10
Gae somewhere else, and seek your dinner
      On some poor body.

Swith,[5] in some beggar's haffet[6] squattle;
There ye may creep, and sprawl, and sprattle[7]
Wi' ither kindred jumping cattle,
      In shoals and nations;
Where horn nor bane[8] ne'er dare unsettle
      Your thick plantations.

Now haud[9] ye there, ye're out o' sight,
Below the fatt'rels,[10] snug an' tight;   20
Na, faith ye yet! ye'll no be right
      Till ye've got on it,
The very tapmost tow'ring height
      O' Miss's bonnet.

My sooth! right bauld ye set your nose out,
As plump an' gray as onie grozet;[11]
O for some rank mercurial rozet,[12]
      Or fell red smeddum![13]
I'd give you sic a hearty doze o't,
      Wad dress your
           droddum![14]   30

I wad na been surpris'd to spy
You on an auld wife's flannen toy;[15]

Or aiblins[16] some bit duddie[17] boy,
      On's wyliecoat;[18]
But Miss's fine Lunardi![19] fie,
      How daur ye do't?

O Jenny, dinna toss your head,
An' set your beauties a' abroad![20]
Ye little ken what cursèd speed
      The blastie's makin'!   40
Thae winks and finger-ends, I dread,
      Are notice takin'!

O wad some Pow'r the giftie gie us
To see oursels as others see us!
It wad frae mony a blunder free us,
      An' foolish notion:
What airs in dress an' gait wad lea'e us,
      And ev'n devotion!

1786   *1786*

ADDRESS TO THE UNCO GUILD,
OR
THE RIGIDLY RIGHTEOUS

My son, these maxims make a rule,
  And lump them ay thegither;
The Rigid Righteous *is a fool,*
  The Rigid Wise *anither:*
The cleanest corn that e'er was dight[1]
  May hae some pyles o' caff[2] in;
So ne'er a fellow-creature slight
  For random fits o' daffin.[3]

          SOLOMON—Eccles. vii, 16

A YE wha are sae guid yoursel,
      Sae pious and sae holy,
Ye've nought to do but mark and tell
      Your Neebours' fauts and folly!
Whase life is like a weel-gaun[4] mill,
      Supply'd wi' store o' water,
The heaped happer's[5] ebbing still,
      And still the clap[6] plays clatter.

Hear me, ye venerable Core,[7]
      As counsel for poor mortals,   10
That frequent pass douce[8] Wisdom's door
      For glaikit[9] Folly's portals;

---

48 perhaps.   49 chance.

1 crawling wonder.   2 greatly.
3 strut.   4 foot.
5 quick.   6 temples.
7 struggle.   8 horn nor bone, i.e. coarse nor fine comb.
9 hold.   10 ribbon-ends.
11 gooseberry.   12 rosin.
13 powder.   14 breech.
15 flannel cap.

16 perhaps.   17 small ragged.   18 flannel vest.
19 a balloon bonnet, named after the aeronaut Lunardi.
20 abroad.

1 winnowed.   2 chaff.   3 fun.
4 well-going.   5 hopper.   6 clapper.
7 company.   8 sober.   9 giddy.

I, for their thoughtless, careless sakes
  Would here propone[10] defences,
Their donsie[11] tricks, their black mistakes,
  Their failings and mischances.

Ye see your state wi' theirs compar'd,
  And shudder at the niffer,[12]
But cast a moment's fair regard
  What maks the mighty differ;[13]   20
Discount what scant occasion gave,
  That purity ye pride in,
And (what's aft[14] mair than a' the lave[15])
  Your better art o' hiding.

Think, when your castigated pulse
  Gies now and then a wallop,
What ragings must his veins convulse,
  That still eternal gallop:
Wi' wind and tide fair i' your tails,
  Right on ye scud your sea-way;   30
But, in the teeth o' baith[16] to sail,
  It makes an unco[17] leeway.

See Social-life and Glee sit down,
  All joyous and unthinking,
Till, quite transmugrify'd,[18] they're grown
  Debauchery and Drinking:
O would they stay to calculate
  Th' eternal consequences;
Or—your more dreaded hell to state—
  Damnation of expenses!   40

Ye high, exalted, virtuous Dames,
  Ty'd up in godly laces,
Before ye gie poor *Frailty* names,
  Suppose a change o' cases;
A dear-lov'd lad, convenience snug,
  A treacherous inclination——
But, let me whisper i' your lug,[19]
  Ye're aiblins nae temptation.

Then gently scan your brother Man,
  Still gentler sister Woman;   50
Tho' they may gang a kennin[20] wrang,
  To step aside is human:
One point must still be greatly dark,
  The moving *Why* they do it;
And just as lamely can ye mark,
  How far perhaps they rue it.

Who made the heart, 'tis *He* alone
  Decidedly can try us,

He knows each chord its various tone,
  Each spring its various bias: 60
Then at the balance let's be mute,
  We never can adjust it;
What's *done* we partly may compute,
  But know not what's *resisted.*
        1786   1787

TO A MOUNTAIN DAISY

ON TURNING ONE DOWN WITH THE PLOUGH IN
APRIL 1786

WEE modest crimson-tippèd flow'r,
Thou 's met me in an evil hour;
For I maun crush amang the stoure[1]
        Thy slender stem:
To spare thee now is past my pow'r,
        Thou bonnie gem.

Alas! it's no thy neibor sweet,
The bonnie lark, companion meet,
Bending thee 'mang the dewy weet
        Wi' spreckl'd breast,   10
When upward springing, blythe to greet
        The purpling east.

Cauld blew the bitter-biting north
Upon thy early humble birth;
Yet cheerfully thou glinted forth
        Amid the storm,
Scarce rear'd above the parent-earth
        Thy tender form.

The flaunting flow'rs our gardens yield
High shelt'ring woods and wa's maun shield,   20
But thou, beneath the random bield[2]
        O' clod or stane,
Adorns the histie[3] stibble-field,
        Unseen, alane.

There, in thy scanty mantle clad,
Thy snawy bosom sun-ward spread,
Thou lifts thy unassuming head
        In humble guise;
But now the share uptears thy bed,
        And low thou lies!   30

Such is the fate of artless maid,
Sweet flow'ret of the rural shade,
By love's simplicity betray'd,
        And guileless trust,

Til she like thee, all soil'd, is laid
        Low i' the dust.

Such is the fate of simple Bard,
On Life's rough ocean luckless starr'd:
Unskilful he to note the card[4]
        Of prudent lore,   40
Till billows rage, and gales blow hard,
        And whelm him o'er!

Such fate to suffering Worth is giv'n,
Who long with wants and woes has striv'n,
By human pride or cunning driv'n
        To mis'ry's brink,
Till wrench'd of ev'ry stay but Heav'n,
        He, ruin'd, sink!

Ev'n thou who mourn'st the Daisy's fate,
That fate is thine—no distant date;   50
Stern Ruin's ploughshare drives elate
        Full on thy bloom,
Till crush'd beneath the furrow's weight
        Shall be thy doom!

     1786   1786

OF A' THE AIRTS[1]

[This song was written as a compliment to Mrs. Burns shortly after the wedding. The poet was in Ellisland making ready their new home, while his wife was yet in Ayrshire.]

OF a' the airts the wind can blaw,
    I dearly like the west,
For there the bonnie Lassie lives,
    The Lassie I lo'e best.
There wild woods grow, and rivers row,[2]
    And monie a hill between;
But day and night my fancy's flight
    Is ever wi' my Jean.

I see her in the dewy flowers,
    I see her sweet and fair: 10
I hear her in the tunefu' birds,
    I hear her charm the air.
There's not a bonnie flower that springs
    By fountain, shaw,[3] or green,
There's not a bonie bird that sings,
    But minds me o' my Jean.

     1788   1790

GO FETCH TO ME A PINT O' WINE

Go fetch to me a pint o' wine,
    An' fill it in a silver tassie;

That I may drink, before I go,
    A service to my bonnie lassie.
The boat rocks at the pier o' Leith,
    Fu' loud the wind blaws frae the ferry,
The ship rides by the Berwick-Law,
    And I maun leave my bonnie Mary.

The trumpets sound, the banners fly,
    The glittering spears are rankèd ready;   10
The shouts o' war are heard afar,
    The battle closes thick and bloody;
But it's no the roar o' sea or shore
    Wad mak me langer wish to tarry;
Nor shout o' war that's heard afar,
    It's leaving thee, my bonnie Mary.

     1788   1790

AULD LANG SYNE[1]

CHORUS

FOR auld lang syne, my dear,
    For auld lang syne,
We'll tak a cup o' kindness yet
    For auld lang syne!

Should auld acquaintance be forgot,
    And never brought to mind?
Should auld acquaintance be forgot,
    And auld lang syne?

And surely ye'll be your pint-stowp,[2]
    And surely I'll be mine;   10
And we'll tak a cup o' kindness yet
    For auld lang syne!

We twa hae run about the braes,
    And pou'd the gowans[3] fine;
But we've wander'd monie a weary fit[4]
    Sin' auld lang syne.

We twa hae paidl'd in the burn,[5]
    Frae morning sun til dine;
But seas between us braid hae roar'd
    Sin' auld lang syne.   20

And there's a hand, my trusty fiere,[6]
    And gie's a hand o' thine;
And we'll tak a right guid-willie waught[7]
    For auld lang syne.

     1788   1796

---

4 compass-card.

---

1 directions.   2 roll.   3 woodland.

1 old long since, i.e. old times.
2 be good for your pint-cup.
3 pulled the daisies.
4 foot.
5 paddled in the brook.
6 comrade   7 hearty, good-will draught.

JOHN ANDERSON MY JO[1]

John Anderson my jo, John,
  When we were first acquent,
Your locks were like the raven,
  Your bonnie brow was brent;[2]
But now your brow is beld,[3] John,
  Your locks are like the snow;
But blessings on your frosty pow,[4]
  John Anderson, my jo.

John Anderson my jo, John,
  We clamb the hill thegither;   10
And mony a canty[5] day, John,
  We've had wi' ane anither:
Now we maun totter down, John,
  And hand in hand we'll go,
And sleep thegither at the foot,
  John Anderson, my jo.

1789   1790

SWEET AFTON

Flow gently, sweet Afton, among thy green
  braes,
Flow gently, I'll sing thee a song in thy praise;
My Mary's asleep by thy murmuring stream,
Flow gently, sweet Afton, disturb not her dream.

Thou stock-dove whose echo resounds thro' the
  glen,
Ye wild whistling blackbirds in yon thorny den,
Thou green-crested lapwing, thy screaming for-
  bear,
I charge you disturb not my slumbering fair.

How lofty, sweet Afton, thy neighbouring hills,
Far mark'd with the courses of clear winding
  rills;   10
There daily I wander as noon rises high,
My flocks and my Mary's sweet cot in my eye.

How pleasant thy banks and green valleys below,
Where wild in the woodlands the primroses blow;
There oft as mild Ev'ning weeps over the lea,
The sweet-scented birk[1] shades my Mary and me.

Thy crystal stream, Afton, how lovely it glides,
And winds by the cot where my Mary resides;
How wanton thy waters her snowy feet lave,
As gathering sweet flow'rets she stems thy   20
  clear wave.

Flow gently, sweet Afton, among thy green
  braes,
Flow gently, sweet river, the theme of my lays;
My Mary's asleep by thy murmuring stream,
Flow gently, sweet Afton, disturb not her dream.

1789   1789

WILLIE BREW'D A PECK O' MAUT

The air is Masterton's; the song mine. The occasion of it was this:—Mr. Wm. Nicol of the High School, Edinburgh, during the autumn vacation being at Moffat, honest Allan (who was at that time on a visit to Dalswinton) and I went to pay Nicol a visit. We had such a joyous meeting that Mr. Masterton and I agreed, each in our own way, that we should celebrate the business.— (Burns, in Interleaved Copy.)

CHORUS

We are na fou,[1] we're nae that fou,
  But just a drappie[2] in our e'e!
The cock may craw, the day may daw,
  And ay we'll taste the barley-bree![3]

O, Willie brew'd a peck o' maut,
  And Rob and Allan cam to see;
Three blyther hearts, that lee-lang[4] night,
  Ye wad na found in Christendie.

Here are we met, three merry boys,
  Three merry boys, I trow, are we;   10
And monie a night we've merry been,
  And monie mae[5] we hope to be!

It is the moon, I ken her horn,
  That's blinkin in the lift[6] sae hie;
She shines sae bright to wyle[7] us hame,
  But, by my sooth, she'll wait a wee!

Wha first shall rise to gang awa,
  A cuckold, coward loun is he!
Wha first beside his chair shall fa',
  He is the King amang us three!   20

1789   1790

CA' THE YOWES

CHORUS

Ca' the yowes to the knowes,
  Ca' them where the heather grows,

---

1 sweetheart.   2 unwrinkled.
3 bald.   4 head.   5 happy.
1 birch.

1 full: drunk.   2 small drop.
3 barley-brew.   4 live-long.
5 more.   6 sky.
7 lure.

Ca'them where the burnie rows,
   My bonnie dearie.

Hark! the mavis' evening sang
Sounding Clouden's woods amang;
Then a-faulding let us gang,
   My bonnie dearie.

We'll gae down by Clouden side,
Thro' the hazels spreading wide   10
O'er the waves that sweetly glide
   To the moon sae clearly.

Yonder's Clouden's silent towers,
Where at moonshine midnight hours,
O'er the dewy-bending flowers,
   Fairies dance sae cheery.

Ghaist nor bogle shalt thou fear;
Thou'rt to Love and Heav'n sae dear,
Nocht of ill may come thee near,
   My bonnie dearie.   20

Fair and lovely as thou art,
Thou hast stown my very heart;
I can die—but canna part,
   My bonnie dearie.

   1789   1790

MY HEART'S IN THE HIGHLANDS

The first half stanza of this song is old; the rest is mine.
—(Burns, in Interleaved Copy.)

CHORUS

MY heart's in the Highlands, my heart is not
      here;
My heart's in the Highland's a-chasing the
      deer;
A-chasing the wild deer, and following the
      roe—
My heart's in the Highlands, wherever I go!

Farewell to the Highlands, farewell to the North,
The birthplace of valour, the country of worth;
Wherever I wander, wherever I rove,
The hills of the Highlands forever I love.

Farewell to the mountains, high-cover'd with
      snow;
Farewell to the straths[1] and green valleys   10
      below;
Farewell to the forests and wild-hanging woods;
Farewell to the torrents and loud-pouring floods!

   1789   1790

---

1 broad valleys.

THOU LING'RING STAR

[On a Sunday in May 1786, by the banks of Ayr, Burns
took his farewell of Mary Campbell, his Highland sweetheart, whom he had promised to marry and who was
leaving for her home in Clyde to arrange for the wedding. In October of the same year, at Greenock on her
way to meet Burns, she died of a fever before he even
heard of her illness. In this famous lament Burns professes 'undying love' for his Highland Mary and reveals
the bitter remorse occasioned by her death.]

THOU ling'ring star with less'ning ray,
   That lov'st to greet the early morn,
Again thou usher'st in the day
   My Mary from my soul was torn.
O Mary, dear departed shade!
   Where is thy place of blissful rest?
See'st thou thy lover lowly laid?
   Hear'st thou the groans that rend his breast?

That sacred hour can I forget,
   Can I forget the hallow'd grove,   10
Where, by the winding Ayr, we met
   To live one day of parting love?
Eternity cannot efface
   Those records dear of transports past,
Thy image at our last embrace—
   Ah! little thought we 'twas our last!

Ayr, gurgling, kiss'd his pebbl'd shore,
   O'erhung with wild woods, thickening green;
The fragrant birch and hawthorn hoar
   Twin'd amorous round the raptur'd scene;   20
The flowers sprang wanton to be prest,
   The birds sang love on every spray,
Till too, too soon, the glowing west
   Proclaim'd the speed of wingèd day.

Still o'er these scenes my mem'ry wakes
   And fondly broods with miser-care.
Time but th' impression stronger makes,
   As streams their channels deeper wear.
O Mary, dear departed shade!
   Where is thy place of blissful rest?   30
See'st thou thy lover lowly laid?
   Hear'st thou the groans that rend his breast?

   October 1789   1790

TAM O' SHANTER

A TALE

Of Brownyis and of Bogillis full is this Buke.
                           —GAWIN DOUGLAS

[When Burns wrote his masterpiece, Alloway Kirk,
whose site was less than a mile from the poet's birthplace,
had long been in ruins and many legends and witch

stories had gathered round it. Among the liveliest and
best known was that of Douglas Graham, a tenant farmer
of Shanter noted for his convivial habits, whose experience probably gave Burns the suggestion for this poem.]

WHEN chapman billies[1] leave the street,
And drouthy[2] neibors neibors meet,
As market-days are wearing late,
An' folk begin to tak the gate;
While we sit bousing at the nappy,[3]
An' getting fou and unco happy,
We think na on the lang Scots miles,
The mosses, waters, slaps,[4] and styles,
That lie between us and our hame,
Where sits our sulky sullen dame,   10
Gathering her brows like gathering storm,
Nursing her wrath to keep it warm.

This truth fand honest Tam o' Shanter,
As he frae Ayr ae night did canter—
(Auld Ayr, wham ne'er a town surpasses
For honest men and bonnie lasses).

O Tam! hadst thou but been sae wise
As ta'en thy ain wife Kate's advice!
She tauld thee weel thou was a skellum,[5]
A bletherin', blusterin', drunken blellum;[6]   20
That frae November till October,
Ae market-day thou was na sober;
That ilka melder[7] wi' the miller
Thou sat as lang as thou had siller;
That ev'ry naig was ca'd a shoe on,[8]
The smith and thee gat roarin' fou on;
That at the Lord's house, even on Sunday,
Thou drank wi' Kirkton Jean till Monday.
She prophesied that, late or soon,
Thou would be found deep drown'd in Doon;   30
Or catch'd wi' warlocks in the mirk[9]
By Alloway's auld haunted kirk.

Ah, gentle dames! it gars me greet[10]
To think how mony counsels sweet,
How mony lengthen'd sage advices,
The husband frae the wife despises!

But to our tale: Ae market night,
Tam had got planted unco right,
Fast by an ingle, bleezing finely,
Wi' reaming swats,[11] that drank divinely;   40
And at his elbow, Souter[12] Johnny,
His ancient, trusty, drouthy crony;

Tam lo'ed him like a very brither;
They had been fou for weeks thegither.
The night drave on wi' sangs and clatter.
And aye the ale was growing better:
The landlady and Tam grew gracious,
Wi' favours secret, sweet, and precious;
The Souter tauld his queerest stories;
The landlord's laugh was ready chorus: 50
The storm without might rair and rustle,
Tam did na mind the storm a whistle.

Care, mad to see a man sae happy,
E'en drown'd himsel amang the nappy.
As bees flee hame wi' lades o' treasure,
The minutes wing'd their way wi' pleasure;
Kings may be blest, but Tam was glorious,
O'er a' the ills o' life victorious!

But pleasures are like poppies spread—
You seize the flow'r, its bloom is shed;   60
Or like the snow falls in the river—
A moment white, then melts for ever;
Or like the borealis race,
That flit ere you can point their place;
Or like the rainbow's lovely form
Evanishing amid the storm.
Nae man can tether time nor tide;
The hour aproaches Tam maun ride;
That hour, o' night's black arch the key-stane,
That dreary hour, he mounts his beast in;   70
And sic a night he taks the road in,
As ne'er poor sinner was abroad in.

The wind blew as 'twad blawn its last;
The rattling show'rs rose on the blast;
The speedy gleams the darkness swallow'd;
Loud, deep, and lang, the thunder bellow'd:
That night, a child might understand,
The Deil had business on his hand.

Weel mounted on his gray mare, Meg,
A better never lifted leg,   80
Tam skelpit[13] on thro' dub[14] and mire,
Despising wind, and rain, and fire;
Whiles holding fast his gude blue bonnet;
Whiles crooning o'er some auld Scots sonnet;[15]
Whiles glow'ring round wi' prudent cares,
Lest bogles[16] catch him unawares.
Kirk-Alloway was drawing nigh,
Whare ghaists and houlets[17] nightly cry.

By this time he was cross the ford,
Where in the snaw the chapman smoor'd;[18]

---

1 pedlar fellows.   2 thirsty.
3 ale.   4 gates.
5 good-for-nothing.   6 babbler.
7 every grinding of grain.   8 every time a horse was shod.
9 dark.   10 makes me weep.
11 foaming ale.   12 cobbler.

---

13 clattered.   14 puddle.   15 song.
16 goblins.   17 ghosts and owls.   18 smothered.

And past the birks[19] and meikle[20] stane,
Where drunken Charlie brak's neck-bane;
And thro' the whins,[21] and by the cairn,[22]
Where hunters fand the murder'd bairn;
And near the thorn, aboon the well,
Where Mungo's mither hang'd hersel.
Before him Doon pours all his floods;
The doubling storm roars thro' the woods;
The lightnings flash from pole to pole;
Near and more near the thunders roll: 100
When, glimmering thro' the groaning trees,
Kirk-Alloway seem'd in a bleeze;
Thro' ilka bore[23] the beams were glancing,
And loud resounded mirth and dancing.

Inspiring bold John Barleycorn!
What dangers thou canst make us scorn!
Wi' tippenny,[24] we fear nae evil;
Wi' usquebae,[25] we'll face the devil!
The swats sae ream'd[26] in Tammie's noddle,
Fair play, he car'd na deils a boddle![27]   110
But Maggie stood right sair astonish'd,
Till, by the heel and hand admonish'd,
She ventur'd forward on the light;
And, vow! Tam saw an unco sight!

Warlocks and witches in a dance!
Nae cotillon brent new frae France,
But hornpipes, jigs, strathspeys, and reels,
Put life and mettle in their heels.
A winnock-bunker[28] in the east,
There sat auld Nick, in shape o' beast—   120
A touzie tyke,[29] black, grim, and large!
To gie them music was his charge:
He screw'd the pipes and gart them skirl,[30]
Till roof and rafters a' did dirl.[31]
Coffins stood round like open presses,
That shaw'd the dead in their last dresses;
And by some devilish cantraip[32] sleight
Each in its cauld hand held a light,
By which heroic Tam was able
To note upon the haly table   130
A murderer's banes in gibbet-airns;
Twa span-lang, wee, unchristen'd bairns;
A thief new-cutted frae the rape—
Wi' his last gasp his gab[33] did gape;
Five tomahawks, wi' blude red rusted;
Five scymitars, wi' murder crusted;
A garter, which a babe had strangled;

A knife, a father's throat had mangled,
Whom his ain son o' life bereft—
The grey hairs yet stack to the heft;   140
Wi' mair of horrible and awfu',
Which even to name wad be unlawfu'.

As Tammie glowr'd, amaz'd, and curious,
The mirth and fun grew fast and furious:
The piper loud and louder blew;
The dancers quick and quicker flew;
They reel'd, they set, they cross'd, they cleekit,[34]
Till ilka carlin[35] swat and reekit,
And coost her duddies[36] to the wark,
And linkit at it in her sark![37]   150

Now Tam, O Tam! had thae been queans,[38]
A' plump and strapping in their teens;
Their sarks, instead o' creeshie[39] flannen,
Been snaw-white seventeen hunder linen![40]
Thir breeks o' mine, my only pair,
That ance were plush, o' gude blue hair,
I wad hae gi'en them off my hurdies,[41]
For ae blink o' the bonnie burdies!

But wither'd beldams, auld and droll,
Rigwoodie[42] hags wad spean[43] a foal,   160
Louping and flinging on a crummock,[44]
I wonder didna turn thy stomach.

But Tam kent what was what fu' brawlie[45]
There was ae winsome wench and walie[46]
That night enlisted in the core,[47]
Lang after kent on Carrick[48] shore!
(For mony a beast to dead she shot,
And perish'd mony a bonnie boat,
And shook baith meikle corn and bear,[49]
And kept the country-side in fear.)   170
Her cutty sark,[50] o' Paisley harn,[51]
That while a lassie she had worn,
In longitude tho' sorely scanty,
It was her best, and she was vauntie.[52]
Ah! little kent thy reverend grannie
That sark she coft[53] for her wee Nannie
Wi' twa pund Scots ('twas a' her riches)
Wad ever grac'd a dance of witches!

---

19 birches.	20 great.
21 furze.	22 heap of stones.
23 every crevice.	24 twopenny ale.
25 whiskey.	26 ale so foamed.
27 farthing.	28 window-seat.
29 shaggy cur.	30 made them shriek.
31 ring.	32 magic.
33 mouth.	

34 linked arms.	35 every old hag.
36 threw off her clothes.	37 tripped it in her shirt.
38 young women.	39 greasy.
40 fine linen with seventeen hundred threads to a width.	
41 hips.	42 bony.
43 wean.	44 crooked staff.
45 perfectly.	46 buxom.
47 company.	48 the southern district of Ayrshire.
49 barley.	50 short skirt.
51 coarse linen.	52 vain.
53 bought.	

But here my muse her wing maun cour;[54]
Sic flights are far beyond her pow'r—   180
To sing how Nannie lap and flang,
(A souple jade she was, and strang);
And how Tam stood, like ane bewitch'd,
And thought his very een enrich'd;
Even Satan glowr'd, and fidg'd fu' fain,
And hotch'd[55] and blew wi' might and main:
Til first ae caper, syne anither,
Tam tint[56] his reason a' thegither,
And roars out 'Weel done, Cutty-sark!'
And in an instant all was dark!   190
And scarcely had he Maggie rallied,
When out the hellish legion sallied.

As bees bizz out wi' angry fyke[57]
When plundering herds[58] assail their byke.[59]
As open pussie's[60] mortal foes
When pop! she starts before their nose,
As eager runs the market-crowd,
When 'Catch the thief! resounds aloud.
So Maggie runs; the witches follow,
Wi' mony an eldritch[61] skriech and hollow.   200

Ah, Tam! ah, Tam! thou'll get thy fairin'![62]
In hell they'll roast thee like a herrin'!
In vain thy Kate awaits thy comin'!
Kate soon will be a woefu' woman!
Now do thy speedy utmost, Meg,
And win the key-stane o' the brig:[63]
There at them thou thy tail may toss,
A running stream they darena cross.
But ere the key-stane she could make,
The fient[64] a tail she had to shake!   210
For Nannie, far before the rest,
Hard upon noble Maggie prest,
And flew at Tam wi' furious ettle;[65]
But little wist she Maggie's mettle!
Ae spring brought off her master hale,
But left behind her ain grey tail:
The carlin claught her by the rump,
And left poor Maggie scarce a stump.

Now, wha this tale o' truth shall read,
Each man and mother's son, take heed;   220
Whene'er to drink you are inclin'd,
Or cutty-sarks rin in your mind,
Think! ye may buy the joys o'er dear;
Remember Tam o' Shanter's mare.

1790   1791

---

54 lower.   55 hitched.
56 lost.   57 fury.
58 shepherds.   59 hive.
60 the hare's.   61 unearthly.
62 reward.   63 bridge.
64 devil.   65 intent.

YE FLOWERY BANKS

YE flowery banks o' bonnie Doon.
 How can ye blume sae fair?
How can ye chant, ye litle birds,
 And I sae fu' o' care.

Thou'll break my heart, thou bonnie bird,
 That sings upon the bough;
Thou minds me o' the happy days,
 When my fause luve was true.

Thou'll break my heart, thou bonnie bird,
 That sings beside thy mate;   10
For sae I sat, and sae I sang,
 And wist na o' my fate.

Aft hae I rov'd by bonnie Doon,
 To see the wood-bine twine,
And ilka[1] bird sang o' its love,
 And sae did I o' mine.

Wi' lightsome heart I pu'd a rose
 Frae off its thorny tree:
But my fause luver staw[2] my rose,
 And left the thorn wi' me.   20

1791   1792

AE FOND KISS

[This poem was addressed to 'Clarinda' (Mrs. Mc-Lehose) on the occasion of her departure from Edinburgh in January 1792 to join her husband in the West Indies.]

AE fond kiss, and then we sever!
Ae fareweel, alas, for ever!
Deep in heart-wrung tears I'll pledge thee,
Warring sighs and groans I'll wage[1] thee.
Who shall say that Fortune grieves him
While the star of hope she leaves him?
Me, nae cheerfu' twinkle lights me,
Dark despair around benights me.

I'll ne'er blame my partial fancy,
Naething could resist my Nancy;   10
But to see her was to love her,
Love but her, and love for ever.
Had we never lov'd sae kindly,
Had we never lov'd sae blindly,
Never met—or never parted—
We had ne'er been broken-hearted.

Fare thee weel, thou first and fairest!
Fare thee weel, thou best and dearest!
Thine be ilka[2] joy and treasure,

---

1 every.   2 stole.
1 pledge.   2 every.

Peace, Enjoyment, Love, and Pleasure.   20
Ae fond kiss, and then we sever;
Ae fareweel, alas, for ever!
Deep in heart-wrung tears I'll pledge thee,
Warring sighs and groans I'll wage thee.

1791   1792

HIGHLAND MARY[1]

YE banks, and braes,[2] and streams around
    The castle o' Montgomery,
Green be your woods, and fair your flowers,
    Your waters never drumlie![3]
There Simmer first unfauld her robes,
    And there the langest tarry;
For there I took the last fareweel
    O' my sweet Highland Mary.

How sweetly bloom'd the gay green birk,[4]
    How rich the hawthorn's blossom,   10
As underneath their fragrant shade
    I clasp'd her to my bosom!
The golden hours on angel wings
    Flew o'er me and my dearie;
For dear to me as light and life
    Was my sweet Highland Mary.

Wi' mony a vow, and lock'd embrace,
    Our parting was fu' tender;
And, pledging aft to meet again,
    We tore oursels asunder;   20
But oh! fell Death's untimely frost,
    That nipt my flower sae early!
Now green 's the sod, and cauld 's the clay,
    That wraps my Highland Mary!

O pale, pale now, those rosy lips,
    I aft have kiss'd sae fondly!
And closed for aye the sparkling glance,
    That dwelt on me sae kindly!
And mould'ring now in silent dust,
    That heart that lo'ed me dearly!   30
But still within my bosom's core
    Shall live my Highland Mary.

1792   1799

SCOTS WHA HAE

ROBERT BRUCE'S ADDRESS TO HIS ARMY, BEFORE
THE BATTLE OF BANNOCKBURN[1]

SCOTS, wha hae wi' Wallace bled,
    Scots, wham Bruce has aften led,

---

1 Mary Campbell. See the headnote to *Thou Ling'ring Star.*
2 hillsides.   3 muddy.   4 birch.

1 The battle was fought on 24 June 1314, near the village of Bannockburn, about three miles south of Stirling. Here the Scots
under Bruce, numbering about thirty thousand, totally defeated
the English under Edward II, whose force was more than three
times that of the enemy.

Welcome to your gory bed,
    Or to victorie!

Now 's the day, and now 's the hour;
See the front o' battle lour!
See approach proud Edward's power—
    Chains and slaverie!

Wha will be a traitor knave?
Wha can fill a coward's grave?   10
Wha sae base as be a slave?
    Let him turn and flee!

Wha for Scotland's King and law
Freedom's sword will strongly draw,
Freeman stand, or freeman fa'
    Let him follow me!

By Oppression's woes and pains!
By your sons in servile chains!
We will drain our dearest veins,
    But they shall be free!   20

Lay the proud usurpers low!
Tyrants fall in every foe!
Liberty 's in every blow!
    Let us do or die!

1793   1794

IT WAS A' FOR OUR RIGHTFU' KING

IT was a' for our rightfu' King,
    We left fair Scotland's strand;
It was a' for our rightfu' King,
    We e'er saw Irish land,
            My dear—
    We e'er saw Irish land.

Now a' is done that men can do,
    And a' is done in vain;
My Love and Native Land farewell,   10
    For I maun cross the main,
            My dear—
    For I maun cross the main.

He turn'd him right and round about
    Upon the Irish shore;
And gae his bridle-reins a shake,
    With adieu for evermore,
            My dear—
    Adieu for evermore.

The sodger from the wars returns,
    The sailor frae the main;   20
But I hae parted frae my love,

Never to meet again,
　　My dear—
Never to meet again.

When day is gane, and night is come,
　And a' folk boune to sleep,
I think on him that's far awa',
　The lee-lang night, and weep,
　　My dear—
　The lee-lang night, and weep.　　30

　c. 1794　　　　　　　　　1796

MY LUVE IS LIKE A RED, RED ROSE

O, MY luve is like a red, red rose
　That's newly sprung in June:
O, my luve is like the melodie
　That's sweetly play'd in tune.

So fair art thou, my bonnie lass,
　So deep in luve am I:
And I will luve thee still, my dear,
　Till a' the seas gang dry.

Till a' the seas gang dry, my dear,
　And the rocks melt wi' the sun :　10
And I will luve thee still, my dear,
　While the sands o' life shall run.

And fare thee weel, my only luve,
　And fare thee weel awhile!
And I will come again, my luve,
　Tho' it were ten thousand mile.

1794　　　　　　　　　　　1796

IS THERE FOR HONEST POVERTY

Is there for honest poverty,
　That hings his head, an' a' that?
The coward slave, we pass him by—
　We dare be poor for a' that!
For a' that, an' a' that,
　Our toils obscure, an' a' that,
The rank is but the guinea's stamp;
　The man 's the gowd[1] for a' that.

What though on hamely fare we dine,
　Wear hoddin grey[2] an' a' that?　10
Gie fools their silks, and knaves their wine—
　A man's a man for a' that!
For a' that, an' a' that,
　Their tinsel show, an' a' that,
The honest man, tho' e'er sae poor,
　Is king o' men for a' that.

Ye see yon birkie,[3] ca'd 'a lord.'
　Wha struts, an' stares, an' a' that?
Tho' hundreds worship at his word,
　He's but a cuif[4] for a' that:　　20
For a' that, an' a' that,
　His ribband, star, an' a' that,
The man o' independent mind,
　He looks an' laughs at a' that.

A prince can mak a belted knight,
　A marquis, duke, an' a' that;
But an honest man's aboon his might—
　Guid faith, he mauna fa'[5] that!
For a' that, an' a' that,
　Their dignities, an' a' that.　　30
The pith o' sense, an' pride o' worth,
　Are higher rank than a' that.

Then let us pray that come it may,
　As come it will for a' that,
That Sense and Worth, o'er a' the earth,
　Shall bear the gree[6] an' a' that;
For a' that, an' a' that,
　It's comin yet for a' that,
That man to man, the world o'er,
　Shall brithers be for a' that!　　40

1794　　　　　　　　　　　1795

O, WERT THOU IN THE CAULD BLAST

[This poem was written during Burns's last illness in honor of Jessie Lewars, his eighteen-year-old nurse and companion, after she had played for him the melody 'The Robin Came to the Wren's Nest.']

O, WERT thou in the cauld blast
　On yonder lea, on yonder lea,
My plaidie to the angry airt,[1]
　I'd shelter thee, I'd shelter thee.
Or did Misfortune's bitter storms
　Around thee blaw, around thee blaw,
Thy bield[2] should be my bosom,
　To share it a', to share it a'.

Or were I in the wildest waste,
　Sae black and bare, sae black and bare,　10
The desert were a Paradise,
　If thou wert there, if thou wert there.
Or were I Monarch o' the globe,
　Wi' thee to reign, wi' thee to reign,
The brightest jewel in my crown
　Wad be my Queen, wad be my Queen.

1796　　　　　　　　　　　1800

---

1 gold.　　　　2 coarse woolen cloth.

3 conceited fellow.　4 blockhead.
5 claim.　　　　　6 prize.
1 direction of the wind.　2 shelter.

1737 · THOMAS PAINE · 1809

1737   Born at Thetford in Norfolk, England, son of a Quaker. Educated at Thetford Grammar School.

1750–74   Served as a sailor; worked for a time at his father's trade, corset making; was twice appointed to and twice dismissed from the excise.

1774–6   Sold out as a bankrupt; left England carrying a letter of introduction from Franklin; secured employment in Philadelphia with the *Pennsylvania Magazine.*

1776   Published *Common Sense,* an anonymous pamphlet advocating American independence.

1776–87   Ably supported the cause of the colonies by a series of tracts called *The Crisis,* and by other public services.

1787–1802   Returned to Europe, to enter the political battle there raging; wrote *The Rights of Man* (1791) as a reply to Burke; indicted for treason in England, but escaped to France, where he was for a time in high favor with the Revolutionists; sentenced to death for remonstrating against violence to the King, but saved from the guillotine by the intervention of the American ambassador.

1794–6   Published *The Age of Reason,* a defense of eighteenth-century deism.

1802   Returned to America.

1809   Died in New Rochelle, New York.

WORLD-CITIZEN Tom Paine has been described in extreme language of condemnation and of praise: by his revilers as 'a coarse-grained fanatic'; by his partisans as 'the great Commoner of Mankind.' He expounded radical Republicanism in England, America, and France and for a generation was listened to on both sides of the ocean with fear or with admiration, but rarely with indifference. However qualifiedly Britishers may evaluate Paine's contribution to their country's welfare, the genuine service he rendered to the cause of American independence is now generally recognized. Written on the eve of the American Revolution, *Common Sense* had a powerful effect in setting the minds and hearts of the colonists against the mother country. In the fateful year 1775, 170,000 copies of this pamphlet were sold in three months, probably half a million in all. In England his *Rights of Man,* prepared as a reply to Burke's *Reflections on the French Revolution,* won for Paine an immediate and universal notoriety. To the man in the streets it became a popular textbook of Republican principles. To the conservatives, who at the time stood in terror of the Revolution, it came as a crowning offense, condemned alike by the church, the professions, trade, and good society. Paine was labeled as a dangerous and treasonable agitator and was outlawed by his government. It is still difficult to be dispassionate in judging the *Rights of Man:* one historian has called it 'demagogic violence'; another has labeled it 'a superb statement of the philosophy of democracy.'

Whatever judgment may be passed upon Paine and his writings, all agree that he had an amazing power to attract and hold the masses. He addressed them as he would have harangued them on the streets, with direct, driving sentences pointed up with invective, ridicule, irony, or humor, and made vivid with simple, homely illustrations. Combined with his extraordinary forensic power was a notable ability to turn a phrase and, as the basis for all his writing, a sound sense and clarity of expression. 'I bring reason to your ears,' he wrote, 'and in language as plain as A, B, C, hold up truths to your eyes.'

Paine's last important work, *Age of Reason,* a rough but forcible defense of deism, by its seemingly irreverent handling of the Bible cost him many friends. He died in the land of his adoption a lonely and embittered man.

From THE RIGHTS OF MAN[1]

AMONG the incivilities by which nations or individuals provoke and irritate each other, Mr. Burke's pamphlet on the French Revolution[2] is an extrordinary instance. Neither the people of France nor the National Assembly were troubling themselves about the affairs of England or the English Parliament; and why Mr. Burke should commence an unprovoked attack upon them, both in parliament and in public, is a conduct that cannot be pardoned on the score of manners, nor justified on that of policy.

There is scarcely an epithet of abuse to be found in the English language with which Mr. Burke has not loaded the French nation and the National Assembly. Everything which rancour, prejudice, ignorance, or knowledge could suggest, are poured forth in the copious fury of near four hundred pages. In the strain and on the plan Mr. Burke was writing, he might have wrote on to as many thousands. When the tongue or the pen is let loose in a phrenzy of passion, it is the man and not the subject that becomes exhausted.

Hitherto Mr. Burke has been mistaken and disappointed in the opinions he had formed of the affairs of France; but such is the ingenuity of his hope, or the malignancy of his despair, that it furnishes him with new pretenses to go on. There was a time when it was impossible to make Mr. Burke believe there would be any revolution in France. His opinion then was that the French had neither spirit to undertake it nor fortitude to support it; and now that there is one, he seeks an escape by condemning it.

Not sufficiently content with abusing the National Assembly, a great part of his work is taken up with abusing Dr. Price[3] (one of the best-hearted men that exists) and the two societies in

England, known by the name of the Revolution and the Constitutional societies.

Dr. Price had preached a sermon on the 4th of November, 1789, being the anniversary of what is called in England the Revolution, which took place in 1688. Mr. Burke, speaking of this sermon, says, 'the political Divine proceeds dogmatically to assert that, by the principles of the Revolution, the people of England have acquired three fundamental rights:

1. To choose our own governors.
2. To cashier them for misconduct,
3. To frame a government for ourselves.'

Dr. Price does not say that the right to do these things exists in this or in that person, or in this or in that description of persons, but that it exists in the *whole*—that it is a right resident in the nation. Mr. Burke, on the contrary, denies that such a right exists in the nation, either in whole or in part, or that it exists anywhere; and what is still more strange and marvellous, he says that 'the people of England utterly disclaim such a right, and that they will resist the practical assertion of it with their lives and fortunes.' That men should take up arms and spend their lives and fortunes *not* to maintain their rights, but to maintain that they have *not* rights, is an entire new species of discovery, and suited to the paradoxical genius of Mr. Burke.

The method which Mr. Burke takes to prove that the people of England have no such rights, and that such rights do not now exist in the nation, either in whole or in part, or anywhere at all, is of the same marvellous and monstrous kind with what he has already said; for his arguments are that the persons, or the generation of persons, in whom they did exist are dead, and with them the right is dead also. To prove this, he quotes a declaration made by parliament about a hundred years ago to William and Mary in these words: 'The Lords spiritual and temporal, and Commons, do, in the name of the people aforesaid (meaning the people of England

---

1 The text is the first English edition, 1791.
2 Edmund Burke, *Reflections on the Revolution in France,* 1790.
3 Richard Price, 1723-91, English philosophical writer whose approbation of the French Revolution was attacked by Burke.

then living) most humbly and faithfully *submit* themselves, their *heirs* and *posterities,* FOR-EVER.' He also quotes a clause of another act of parliament made in the same reign, the terms of which, he says, 'binds us (meaning the people of that day), our *heirs* and our *posterity, to them,* their *heirs* and *posterity,* to the end of time.'

Mr. Burke conceives his point sufficiently established by producing those clauses, which he enforces by saying that they exclude the right of the nation *forever:* and not yet content with making such declarations, repeated over and over again, he further says 'that if the people of England possessed such a right before the Rev-olution' (which he acknowledges to have been the case, not only in England, but throughout Europe, at an early period), 'yet that the *Eng-lish nation* did, at the time of the Revolution, most solemnly renounce and abdicate it, for themselves, and *for all their posterity forever.'*

As Mr. Burke occasionally applies the poison drawn from his horrid principles (if it is not a profanation to call them by the name of princi-ples) not only to the English nation, but to the French Revolution and the National Assembly, and charges that august, illuminated and illu-minating body of men with the epithet of *usurp-ers,* I shall, *sans cérémonie,* place another system of principles in opposition to his.

The English Parliament of 1688 did a certain thing which for themselves and their constituents they had a right to do, and which it appeared right should be done; but in addition to this right, which they possessed by delegation, *they set up another right by assumption,* that of binding and controlling posterity to the end of time. The case, therefore, divides itself into two parts; the right which they possessed by delegation, and the right which they set up by assumption. The first is admitted; but with respect to the second, I reply:

There never did, there never will, and there never can exist a parliament, or any description of men, or any generation of men, in any coun-try, possessed of the right or the power of bind-ing and controlling posterity to the *'end of time,'* or of commanding forever how the world shall be governed, or who shall govern it; and there-fore all such clauses, acts, or declarations, by which the makers of them attempt to do what they have neither the right nor the power to do, nor the power to execute, are in themselves null and void. Every age and generation must be as free to act for itself, *in all cases,* as the ages and generations which preceded it. The vanity and presumption of governing beyond the grave is the most ridiculous and insolent of all tyrannies. Man has no property in man; neither has any generation a property in the generations which are to follow. The parliament or the people of 1688, or of any other period, had no more right to dispose of the people of the present day, or to bind or to control them *in any shape whatever,* than the parliament or the people of the present day have to dispose of, bind, or control those who are to live a hundred or a thousand years hence. Every generation is and must be compe-tent to all the purposes which its occasions re-quire. It is the living and not the dead that are to be accommodated. When man ceases to be, his power and his wants cease with him; and having no longer any participation in the con-cerns of this world, he has no longer any authority in directing who shall be its governors, or how its government shall be organized, or how administered.

I am not contending for, nor against, any form of government, nor for nor against any party, here or elsewhere. That which a whole nation chooses to do, it has a right to do. Mr. Burke says, No. Where then *does* the right exist? I am contending for the right of the *living,* and against their being willed away, and controlled and con-tracted for, by the manuscript-assumed authority of the dead; and Mr. Burke is contending for the authority of the dead over the rights and freedom of the living. There was a time when kings disposed of their crowns by will upon their deathbeds, and consigned the people, like beasts of the field, to whatever successor they ap-pointed. This is now so exploded as scarcely to be remembered, and so monstrous as hardly to be believed; but the parliamentary clauses upon which Mr. Burke builds his political church are of the same nature.

The laws of every country must be analogous to some common principle. In England, no par-ent or master, nor all the authority of parlia-ment, omnipotent as it has called itself, can bind or control the personal freedom even of an indi-vidual beyond the age of twenty-one years: On what ground of right then could the parliament of 1688, or any other parliament, bind all poster-ity forever? . . .

'We have seen (says Mr. Burke) the French rebel against a mild and lawful Monarch with more fury, outrage, and insult than any people has been known to raise against the most illegal usurper, or the most sanguinary tyrant.' This is one among a thousand other instances in which

Mr. Burke shews that he is ignorant of the springs and principles of the French Revolution.

It was not against Louis XVI but against the despotic principles of the government that the nation revolted. These principles had not their origin in him, but in the original establishment, many centuries back; and they were become too deeply rooted to be removed, and the Augean stable[4] of parasites and plunderers too abominably filthy to be cleansed, by anything short of a complete and universal revolution.

When it becomes necessary to do a thing, the whole heart and soul should go into the measure, or not attempt it. That crisis was then arrived, and there remained no choice but to act with determined vigour or not to act at all. The King was known to be the friend of the nation, and this circumstance was favourable to the enterprise. Perhaps no man bred up in the style of an absolute King ever possessed a heart so little disposed to the exercise of that species of power as the present King of France. But the principles of the government itself still remained the same. The Monarch and the Monarchy were distinct and separate things; and it was against the established despotism of the latter, and not against the person or principles of the former, that the revolt commenced, and the revolution has been carried on.

Mr. Burke does not attend to the distinction between *men* and *principles,* and therefore he does not see that a revolt may take place against the despotism of the latter, while there lies no charge of despotism against the former.

The natural moderation of Louis XVI contributed nothing to alter the hereditary despotism of the monarchy. All the tyrannies of former reigns, acted under that hereditary despotism, were still liable to be revived in the hands of a successor. It was not the respite of a reign that would satisfy France, enlightened as she was then become. A casual discontinuance of the *practice* of despotism is not a discontinuance of its *principles;* the former depends on the virtue of the individual who is in immediate possession of the power; the latter on the virtue and fortitude of the nation. In the case of Charles I and James II of England, the revolt was against the personal despotism of the men; whereas in France it was against the hereditary despotism of the established government. But men who can consign over the rights of posterity forever on the authority of a mouldy parchment, like Mr.

Burke, are not qualified to judge of this revolution. It takes in a field too vast for their views to explore, and proceeds with a mightiness of reason they cannot keep pace with.

But there are many points of view in which this revolution may be considered. When despotism has established itself for ages in a country, as in France, it is not in the person of the King only that it resides. It has the appearance of being so in show, and in nominal authority; but it is not so in practice and in fact. It has its standard everywhere. Every office and department has its despotism, founded upon custom and usage. Every place has its Bastille,[5] and every Bastille its despot. The original hereditary despotism resident in the person of the king divides and subdivides itself into a thousand shapes and forms, till at last the whole of it is acted by deputation. This was the case in France; and against this species of despotism, proceeding on through an endless labyrinth of office till the source of it is scarcely perceptible, there is no mode of redress. It strengthens itself by assuming the appearance of duty, and tyrannizes under the pretense of obeying.

When a man reflects on the condition which France was in from the nature of her government, he will see other causes for revolt than those which immediately connect themselves with the person or character of Louis XVI. There were, if I may so express it, a thousand despotisms to be reformed in France, which had grown up under the hereditary despotism of the monarchy, and become so rooted as to be in a great measure independent of it. Between the monarchy, the parliament, and the church, there was a *rivalship* of despotism, besides the feudal despotism operating locally, and the ministerial despotism operating everywhere. But Mr. Burke, by considering the King as the only possible object of a revolt, speaks as if France was a village in which everything that passed must be known to its commanding officer and no oppression could be acted but what he could immediately control. Mr. Burke might have been in the Bastille his whole life, as well under Louis XVI as Louis XIV, and neither the one nor the other have known that such a man as Mr. Burke existed. The despotic principles of the government were the same in both reigns, though the dispositions of the men were as remote as tyranny and benevolence.

What Mr. Burke considers as a reproach to

---

4 the filthy stable of King Augeas cleansed by Hercules in a day by diverting two rivers to flow through it.

5 the French national prison, stormed and destroyed by the populace, 14 July 1789.

the French Revolution, (that of bringing it forward under a reign more mild than the preceding ones), is one of its highest honours. The revolutions that have taken place in European countries have been excited by personal hatred. The rage was against the man, and he became the victim. But, in the instance of France, we see a revolution generated in the rational contemplation of the rights of man, and distinguishing from the beginning between persons and principles.

But Mr. Burke appears to have no idea of principles, when he is contemplating governments. 'Ten years ago,' says he, 'I could have felicitated France on her having a government, without inquiring what the nature of that government was, or how it was administered.' Is this the language of a rational man? Is it the language of a heart feeling as it ought to feel for the rights and happiness of the human race? On this ground Mr. Burke must compliment every government in the world, while the victims who suffer under them, whether sold into slavery or tortured out of existence, are wholly forgotten. It is power and not principles that Mr. Burke venerates; and under this abominable depravity he is disqualified to judge between them. Thus much for his opinion as to the occasions of the French Revolution. I now proceed to other considerations.

I know a place in America called Point-no-Point; because as you proceed along the shore, gay and flowery as Mr. Burke's language, it continually recedes and presents itself at a distance ahead;and when you have got as far as you can go, there is no point at all. Just thus is it with Mr. Burke's three hundred and fifty-six pages. It is therefore difficult to reply to him. But as the points that he wishes to establish may be inferred from what he abuses, it is in his paradoxes that we must look for his arguments.

As to the tragic paintings by which Mr. Burke has outraged his own imagination and seeks to work upon that of his readers, they are very well calculated for theatrical representation, where facts are manufactured for the sake of show and accommodated to produce, through the weakness of sympathy, a weeping effect. But Mr. Burke should recollect that he is writing History, and not *Plays;* and that his readers will expect truth, and not the spouting rant of high-toned exclamation.

When we see a man dramatically lamenting, in a publication intended to be believed, that '*The age of chivalry is gone*'; that '*the glory of*

Europe is extinguished forever!' that '*the unbought grace of life* (if anyone knows what it is), *the cheap defense of nations, the nurse of manly sentiment and heroic enterprise is gone!*'—and all this because the Quixote age of chivalric nonsense is gone; what opinion can we form of his judgment, or what regard can we pay to his facts? In the rhapsody of his imagination he has discovered a world of windmills, and his sorrows are that there are no Quixotes to attack them. But if the age of aristocracy, like that of chivalry, should fall, and they had originally some connection, Mr. Burke, the trumpeter of the Order, may continue his parody to the end, and finish with exclaiming—'*Othello's occupation's gone!*'

Notwithstanding Mr. Burke's horrid paintings, when the French Revolution is compared with that of other countries the astonishment will be that it is marked with so few sacrifices; but this astonishment will cease when we reflect that it was *principles,* and not *persons,* that were the meditated objects of destruction. The mind of the nation was acted upon by a higher stimulus than what the consideration of persons could inspire, and sought a higher conquest than could be produced by the downfall of an enemy. Among the few who fell, there do not appear to be any that were intentionally singled out. They all of them had their fate in the circumstances of the moment, and were not pursued with that long, cold-blooded, unabated revenge which pursued the unfortunate Scotch in the affair of 1745.[6]

Through the whole of Mr. Burke's book I do not observe that the Bastille is mentioned more than once, and that with a kind of implication as if he were sorry it is pulled down, and wished it were built up again. 'We have rebuilt Newgate (says he) and tenanted the mansion; and we have prisons almost as strong as the Bastille for those who dare to libel the Queens of France.' As to what a madman, like the person called Lord George Gordon, might say, and to whom Newgate is rather a bedlam than a prison, it is unworthy a rational consideration. It was a madman that libelled—and that is sufficient apology, and it afforded an opportunity for confining him, which was the thing that was wished for; but certain it is that Mr. Burke, who does not call himself a madman, whatever other people may do, has libelled, in the most unprovoked manner and in the grossest style of the most vulgar abuse, the whole representative authority of France; and yet Mr. Burke takes his seat in the

---

6 Parliament enacted a series of repressive laws penalizing the Highland clans for their participation in the Jacobite rebellion.

British House of Commons! From his violence and his grief, his silence on some points and his excess on others, it is difficult not to believe that Mr. Burke is sorry, extremely sorry, that arbitrary power, the power of the Pope and the Bastille, are pulled down.

Not one glance of compassion, not one commiserating reflection, that I can find throughout his book, has he bestowed on those who lingered out the most wretched of lives, a life without hope, in the most miserable of prisons. It is painful to behold a man employing his talents to corrupt himself. Nature has been kinder to Mr. Burke than he is to her. He is not affected by the reality of distress touching upon his heart, but by the showy resemblance of it striking his imagination. He pities the plumage, but forgets the dying bird. Accustomed to kiss the artistocratical hand that hath purloined him from himself, he degenerates into a composition of art, and the genuine soul of nature forsakes him. His hero or his heroine must be a tragedy-victim, expiring in show, and not the real prisoner of misery, sliding into death in the silence of a dungeon. . . .

Before anything can be reasoned upon to a conclusion, certain facts, principles, or data, to reason from, must be established, admitted, or denied. Mr. Burke, with his usual outrage, abuses the *Declaration of the Rights of Man,* published by the National Assembly of France as the basis on which the constitution of France is built. This he calls 'paltry and blurred sheets of paper about the rights of man.' Does Mr. Burke mean to deny that *man* has any rights? If he does, then he must mean that there are no such things as rights anywhere, and that he has none himself; for who is there in the world but man? But if Mr. Burke means to admit that man has rights, the question then will be, What are those rights, and how came man by them originally?

The error of those who reason by precedents drawn from antiquity, respecting the rights of man, is that they do not go far enough into antiquity. They do not go the whole way. They stop in some of the intermediate stages of an hundred or a thousand years, and produce what was then done as a rule for the present day. This is no authority at all. If we travel still farther into antiquity, we shall find a directly contrary opinion and practice prevailing; and if antiquity is to be authority, a thousand such authorities may be produced, successively contradicting each other: But if we proceed on, we shall at last come out right; we shall come to the time when man came from the hand of his Maker. What was he then? Man. Man was his high and only title, and a higher cannot be given him. But of titles I shall speak hereafter.

We have now arrived at the origin of man, and at the origin of his rights. As to the manner in which the world has been governed from that day to this, it is no farther any concern of ours than to make a proper use of the errors or the improvements which the history of it presents. Those who lived an hundred or a thousand years ago were then moderns as we are now. They had *their* ancients and those ancients had others, and we also shall be ancients in our turn. If the mere name of antiquity is to govern in the affairs of life, the people who are to live an hundred or a thousand years hence may as well take us for a precedent, as we make a precedent of those who lived an hundred or a thousand years ago. The fact is that portions of antiquity, by proving everything, establish nothing. It is authority against authority all the way till we come to the divine origin of the rights of man at the creation. Here our inquiries find a resting-place, and our reason finds a home. If a dispute about the rights of man had arisen at the distance of an hundred years from the creation, it is to this source of authority they must have referred, and it is to the same source of authority that we must now refer.

Though I mean not to touch upon any sectarian principle of religion, yet it may be worth observing that the genealogy of Christ is traced to Adam. Why then not trace the rights of man to the creation of man? I will answer the question. Because there have been an upstart of governments, thrusting themselves between, and presumptuously working to *un-make* man.

If any generation of men ever possessed the right of dictating the mode by which the world should be governed forever, it was the first generation that existed; and if that generation did not do it, no succeeding generation can shew any authority for doing it, nor set any up. The illuminating and divine principle of the equal rights of man (for it has its origin from the Maker of man) relates, not only to the living individuals, but to generations of men succeeding each other. Every generation is equal in rights to the generations which preceded it, by the same rule that every individual is born equal in rights with his co-temporary.

Every history of the creation, and every traditionary account, whether from the lettered or unlettered world, however they may vary in their opinion or belief of certain particulars, all agree in establishing one point, *the unity of man;* by which I mean that man is all of *one degree,* and consequently that all men are born equal and with equal natural rights, in the same manner as if posterity had been continued by *creation* instead of *generation,* the latter being only the mode by which the former is carried forward; and consequently every child born into the world must be considered as deriving its existence from God. The world is as new to him as it was to the first man that existed, and his natural right in it is of the same kind.

The Mosaic account of the creation, whether taken as divine authority, or merely historical, is fully up to this point, *the unity or equality of man.* The expressions admit of no controversy. 'And God said, Let us make man in our own image. In the image of God created he him; male and female created he them.' The distinction of sexes is pointed out, but no other distinction is even implied. If this be not divine authority, it is at least historical authority, and shews that the equality of man, so far from being a modern doctrine, is the oldest upon record.

It is also to be observed that all the religions known in the world are founded, so far as they relate to man, on the *unity of man* as being all of one degree. Whether in heaven or in hell or in whatever state man may be supposed to exist hereafter, the good and the bad are the only distinctions. Nay, even the laws of governments are obliged to slide into this principle by making degrees to consist in crimes and not in persons.

It is one of the greatest of all truths, and of the highest advantage to cultivate. By considering man in this light, and by instructing him to consider himself in this light, it places him in a close connection with all his duties, whether to his Creator, or to the creation of which he is a part; and it is only when he forgets his origin or, to use a more fashionable phrase, his *birth and family,* that he becomes dissolute. It is not among the least of the evils of the present existing governments in all parts of Europe, that man, considered as man, is thrown back to a vast distance from his Maker, and the artificial chasm filled up by a succession of barriers, or a sort of turnpike gates, through which he has to pass. I will quote Mr. Burke's catalogue of barriers that he has set up between man and his Maker. Putting himself in the character of a herald, he says, 'We fear God—we look with *awe* to kings—with affection to parliaments—with duty to magistrates—with reverence to priests, and with respect to nobility.' Mr. Burke has forgot to put in 'chivalry.' He has also forgot to put in Peter.

The duty of man is not a wilderness of turnpike gates through which he is to pass by tickets from one to the other. It is plain and simple, and consists but of two points. His duty to God, which every man must feel; and with respect to his neighbour, to do as he would be done by. If those to whom power is delegated do well, they will be respected; if not they will be despised; and with regard to those to whom no power is delegated, but who assume it, the rational world can know nothing of them.

Hitherto we have spoken only (and that but in part) of the natural rights of man. We have now to consider the civil rights of man, and to shew how the one originates out of the other. Man did not enter into society to become *worse* than he was before, nor to have less rights than he had before, but to have those rights better secured. His natural rights are the foundation of all his civil rights. But in order to pursue this distinction with more precision, it will be necessary to mark the different qualities of natural and civil rights.

A few words will explain this. Natural rights are those which appertain to man in right of his existence. Of this kind are all the intellectual rights, or rights of the mind, and also all those rights of acting as an individual for his own comfort and happiness, which are not injurious to the rights of others. Civil rights are those which appertain to man in right of his being a member of society. Every civil right has for its foundation some natural rights pre-existing in the individual, but to which his individual power is not, in all cases, sufficiently competent. Of this kind are all those which relate to security and protection.

From this short review, it will be easy to distinguish between that class of natural rights which man retains after entering into society and those which he throws into common stock as a member of society.

The natural rights which he retains are all those in which the power to execute is as perfect in the individual as the right itself. Among this class, as is before mentioned, are all the intellectual rights, or rights of the mind: consequently, religion is one of those rights. The natural rights which are not retained are all those in which, though the right is perfect in the individual, the power to execute them is defective. They answer not his purpose. A man, by natural right, has a right to judge in his own cause; and so far as the right of the mind is concerned, he never surrenders it: But what availeth it him to judge, if he has not power to redress? He therefore deposits this right in the common stock of society, and takes the arm of society, of which he is a part, in preference and in addition to his own. Society *grants* him nothing. Every man is a proprietor in society, and draws on the capital as a matter of right.

From these premises, two or three certain conclusions will follow.

First, That every civil right grows out of a natural right; or, in other words, is a natural right exchanged.

Secondly, That civil power, properly considered as such, is made up of the aggregate of that class of the natural rights of man which becomes defective in the individual in point of power, and answers not his purpose, but when collected to a focus, becomes competent to the purpose of everyone.

Thirdly, That the power produced by the aggregate of natural rights, imperfect in power in the individual, cannot be applied to invade the natural rights which are retained in the individual, and in which the power to execute is as perfect as the right itself.

We have now, in a few words, traced man from a natural individual to a member of society, and shewn, or endeavoured to shew, the quality of the natural rights retained and of those which are exchanged for civil rights. Let us now apply those principles to governments.

In casting our eyes over the world, it is extremely easy to distinguish the governments which have arisen out of society, or out of the social compact, from those which have not: but to place this in a clearer light than what a single glance may afford, it will be proper to take a review of the several sources from which governments have arisen and on which they have been founded.

They may be all comprehended under three heads. First, Superstition. Secondly, Power. Thirdly, the common interest of society, and the common rights of man.

The first was a government of priestcraft, the second of conquerors, and the third of reason.

When a set of artful men pretended, through the medium of oracles, to hold intercourse with the Deity as familiarly as they now march up the back-stairs in European courts, the world was completely under the government of superstition. The oracles were consulted, and whatever they were made to say became the law; and this sort of government lasted as long as this sort of superstition lasted.

After these a race of conquerors arose, whose government, like that of William the Conqueror, was founded in power, and the sword assumed the name of a sceptre. Governments thus established last as long as the power to support them lasts; but that they might avail themselves of every engine in their favour, they united fraud to force, and set up an idol which they called *Divine Right,* and which, in imitation of the Pope who affects to be spiritual and temporal, and in contradiction to the Founder of the Christian religion, twisted itself afterwards into an idol of another shape, called *Church and State.* The key of St. Peter and the key of the Treasury became quartered on one another, and the wondering, cheated multitude, worshipped the invention.

When I contemplate the natural dignity of man; when I feel (for Nature has not been kind enough to me to blunt my feelings) for the honour and happiness of its character, I become irritated at the attempt to govern mankind by force and fraud as if they were all knaves and fools, and can scarcely avoid disgust at those who are thus imposed upon.

We have now to review the governments which arise out of society, in contradistinction to those which arose out of superstition and conquest.

It has been thought a considerable advance towards establishing the principles of Freedom, to say that government is a compact between those who govern and those who are governed: but this cannot be true, because it is putting the effect before the cause; for as man must have existed before governments existed, there necessarily was a time when governments did not exist, and consequently there could originally exist no governors to form such a compact with. The fact therefore must be that the *individuals themselves,* each in his own personal and sovereign right, *entered into a compact with each other* to produce a government: and this is the only mode in which governments have a right to arise, and the only principle on which they have a right to exist.

1756 · WILLIAM GODWIN · 1836

1756   Born, the son of a Dissenting minister.

1763–81   Educated for the ministry and served as minister in several parishes. Through friendship with the radical, Joseph Fawcett, became imbued with French revolutionary philosophy.

1782   Went to London to regenerate society through his writing.

1783–5   Published a biography and a volume of sermons; began contributing to the *Annual Register* and other periodicals.

1793   Published the *Enquiry concerning Political Justice*.

1794   Published the sociological novel, *Caleb Williams*.

1797   Married Mary Wollstonecraft, who died after the birth of a daughter, Mary, the future wife of Shelley.

1799   Published his second novel, *St. Leon*.

1801   Married a widow, Mrs. Clairmont, mother of Jane ('Claire') Clairmont.

1800–1834   Tried miscellaneous writing and publishing without much success; for many years struggled with pecuniary difficulties.

1836   Died.

'No work in our time,' wrote Hazlitt, 'gave such a blow to the philosophical mind of the country as the celebrated *Enquiry concerning Political Justice*.' It carried away many among the younger generation of liberals, including Southey and Coleridge (quickening their schemes for a Pantisocratic society) and, to a lesser degree, Wordsworth, upon whom for a brief period it worked its spell. Its influence on Shelley was profound and its influence was considerable even in America, especially among the New England transcendentalists. So wide was the renown of *Political Justice* in the last decade of the eighteenth century that Godwin became the universally acknowledged representative of the revolutionary spirit in England at that critical time.

Godwin is the most extreme of the revolutionary philosophers. His system is derived from Locke's sensationalistic theory of knowledge and is built upon the dogma of metaphysical determinism. Man, says Godwin, is a creature of external conditions, but primarily of those conditions he may hope to modify through education. 'Sound reasoning and truth when adequately communicated must always be victorious over error. Truth is omnipotent.' Vice is an error in judgment. A society founded upon reason will enjoy the full rights of justice and liberty. In the eye of reason all men will be equal and equality will make men frank and ingenuous. The great obstacle to this golden return of justice is the existence of government. Government is the evil of which the less we have the better. Particularly are monarchy and aristocracy false and corrupt: 'To make men serfs it is indispensably necessary to make them brutes.' Of all forms of government democracy most nearly conforms with the nature of man. The ultimate goal, however, in Godwin's view, was to be rid completely of government with all its consequences of law, restrictions, and punishments. Thus Godwinian logic led to anarchism, but Godwin condemned the use of violence against government as well as by government. Man is perfectible, but the way to a better world was not by force but by continuous peaceful discussion and gradual steady enlightenment. According to the law of Necessity, in which Godwin optimistically believed, there are powers operating in the physical universe, in history, and in the human mind which make for inevitable continuous progress in all three realms.

At the turn of the century, when conservatism set in, Godwin's fame faded rapidly, though he continued to exert an influence. His second marriage proved to be unfortunate and he suffered hardships in the latter part of his life; nevertheless, he possessed to the end an unquenchable optimism for society's regeneration.

Godwin's system is an odd assortment of doctrine, much of it borrowed and marred by inconsistencies and contradictions. Yet more than a century after his death students of political theory still turn with inquiring minds to the writings of the philosopher described by Herbert Read as 'the first and most eloquent prophet of libertarian socialism.'

ENQUIRY CONCERNING POLITICAL JUSTICE

From BOOK II: PRINCIPLES OF SOCIETY

CHAPTER VI: OF THE RIGHT OF PRIVATE JUDGMENT

THERE can be no doubt, that the proper way of conveying to my understanding a truth of which I am ignorant, or of impressing upon me a firmer persuasion of a truth with which I am acquainted, is by an appeal to my reason. Even an angry expostulation with me upon my conduct, will but excite similar passions in me, and cloud, instead of illuminate, my understanding. There is certainly a way of expressing truth, with such benevolence as to command attention, and such evidence as to enforce conviction in all cases whatever.

Punishment inevitably excites in the sufferer, and ought to excite, a sense of injustice. Let its purpose be to convince me of the truth of a position which I at present believe to be false. It is not, abstractedly considered, of the nature of an argument, and therefore it cannot begin with producing conviction. Punishment is a comparatively specious name; but is in reality nothing more than force put upon one being, by another who happens to be stronger. But strength apparently does not constitute justice. The case of punishment, in the view in which we now consider it, is the case of you and me differing in opinon, and your telling me that you must be right, since you have a more brawny arm, or have applied your mind more to the acquiring skill in your weapons than I have.

But let us suppose that I am convinced of my error, but that my conviction is superficial and fluctuating, and the object you propose is to ren-

der it durable and profound. Ought it to be thus durable and profound? There are no doubt arguments and reasons calculated to render it so. Is the subject in reality problematical, and do you wish by the weight of your blows to make up for the deficiency of your logic? This can never be defended. An appeal to force must appear to both parties, in proportion to the soundness of their understanding, to be a concession of imbecility. He that has recourse to it would have no occasion for this expedient, if he were sufficiently acquainted with the powers of that truth it is his office to communicate. If there be any man who, in suffering punishment, is not conscious of injury, he must have had his mind previously debased by slavery, and his sense of moral right and wrong blunted by a series of oppressions.

If there be any truth more unquestionable than the rest, it is, that every man is bound to the exertion of his faculties in the discovery of right, and to the carrying into effect all the right with which he is acquainted. It may be granted that an infallible standard, if it could be discovered, would be considerably beneficial. But this infallible standard itself would be of little use in human affairs, unless it had the property of reasoning as well as deciding, of enlightening the mind as well as constraining the body. If a man be in some cases obliged to prefer his own judgment, he is in all cases obliged to consult that judgment, before he can determine whether the matter in question be of the sort provided for or no. So that from this reasoning it ultimately appears, that the conviction of a man's individual understanding, is the only legitimate principle, imposing on him the duty of adopting any species of conduct.

Such are the genuine principles of human society. Such would be the unconstrained condition of its members in a state where every individual within the society, and every neighbour without, was capable of listening with sobriety to the dictates of reason. We shall not fail to be impressed with considerable regret, if, when we descend to the present mixed characters of mankind, we find ourselves obliged in any degree to depart from so simple and grand a principle. The universal exercise of private judgment is a doctrine so unspeakably beautiful, that the true politician will certainly feel infinite reluctance in admitting the idea of interfering with it.

From BOOK III: PRINCIPLES OF GOVERNMENT

CHAPTER VII: OF FORMS OF GOVERNMENT

DIFFERENT forms of government, are best adapted to the condition of different nations. Yet there is one form, in itself considered, better than any other form. Every other mode of society, except that which conduces to the best and most pleasurable state of the human species, is at most only an object of toleration. It must of necessity be ill in various respects; it must entail mischiefs; it must foster unsocial and immoral prejudices. Yet upon the whole, it may be, like some excrescences and defects in the human frame, it cannot immediately be removed without introducing something worse. In the machine of human society all the wheels must move together. He that should violently attempt to raise any one part into a condition more exalted than the rest, or force it to start away from its fellows would be the enemy, and not the benefactor, of his contemporaries.

It follows, however, from the principles already detailed that the interests of the human species require a gradual, but uninterrupted change. He who should make these principles the regulators of his conduct, would not rashly insist upon the instant abolition of all existing abuses. But he would not nourish them with false praise. He would show no indulgence to their enormities. He would tell all the truth he could discover, in relation to the genuine interests of mankind. Truth delivered in a spirit of universal kindness with no narrow resentments or angry invective, can scarcely be dangerous, or fail, so far as relates to its own operation, to communicate a similar spirit to the hearer. Truth, however unreserved be the mode of its enunciation, will be sufficiently gradual in its progress. It will be fully comprehended, only by slow degrees, by its most assiduous votaries; and the degrees will be still more temperate by which it will pervade so considerable a portion of the community as to render them mature for a change of their common institutions.

Again: if conviction of the understanding be the compass which is to direct our proceedings in the general affairs, we shall have many reforms, but no revolutions. As it is only in a gradual manner that the public can be instructed, a violent explosion in the community is by no means the most likely to happen as the result of instruction. Revolutions are the produce of passion, not of sober and tranquil reason. There must be an obstinate resistance to improvement on the one side to engender a furious determination of realizing a system at a stroke on the other. The reformers must have suffered from incessant counteraction, till, inflamed by the treachery and art of their opponents, they are wrought up to the desperate state of imagining that all must be secured in the first favourable crisis, as the only alternative for its being ever secured. It would seem, therefore, that the demand of the effectual ally of the public happiness, upon those who enjoy the privileges of the state, would be, 'Do not give us too soon; do not give us too much; but act under the incessant influence of a disposition to give us something.'

Government, under whatever point of view we examine this topic, is unfortunately pregnant with motives to censure and complaint. Incessant change, everlasting innovation, seem to be dictated by the true interests of mankind. But government is the perpetual enemy of change. What was admirably observed of a particular system of government, is in a great degree true of all: They 'lay their hand on the spring there is in society, and put a stop to its motion.' Their tendency is to perpetuate abuse. Whatever was once thought right and useful, they undertake to entail to the latest posterity. They reverse the genuine propensities of man, and, instead of suffering us to proceed, teach us to look backward for perfection. They prompt us to seek the public welfare, not in alteration and improvement, but in a timid reverence for the decisions of our ancestors, as if it were the nature of the human mind, always to degenerate, and never to advance.

Man is in a state of perpetual mutation. He must grow either better or worse, either correct his habits or confirm them. The government under which we are placed, must either increase our passions and prejudices by fanning the flame, or, by gradually discouraging, tend to extirpate them. In reality, it is impossible to conceive a government that shall have the latter tendency. By its very nature positive institution has a tendency to suspend the elasticity and progress of mind. Every scheme for embodying imperfection must be injurious. That which is today a considerable melioration, will at some future period, if preserved unaltered, appear a defect and disease in the body politic. It is earnestly to be desired, that each man should be wise enough to govern himself, without the intervention of any compulsory restraint; and since government, even in its best state, is an evil, the object principally to be aimed at is that we should have as little of it as the general peace of human society will permit.

From BOOK IV: MISCELLANEOUS PRINCIPLES

CHAPTER VII: OF FREE WILL AND NECESSITY

... Let us proceed to apply these reasonings concerning matter to the illustration of the theory of mind. Is it possible in this latter theory, as in the former subject, to discover any general principles? Can intellect be made a topic of science? Are we able to reduce the multiplied phenomena of mind to any certain standard of reasoning? If the affirmative of these questions be conceded, the inevitable consequence appears to be that mind as well as matter exhibits a constant conjunction of events, and furnishes all the ground that any subject will afford for an opinion of necessity. It is of no importance that we cannot see the ground of that necessity, or imagine how sensations, pleasurable or painful, when presented to the mind of a percipient being are able to generate volition and animal motion; for, if there be any truth in the above statement, we are equally incapable of perceiving a ground of connection between any two events in the material universe, the common and received opinion, that we do perceive such ground of connection, being in reality nothing more than a vulgar prejudice.

That mind is a topic of science may be argued from all those branches of literature and enquiry which have mind for their subject. What species of amusement or instruction would history afford, if there were no ground of inference from moral antecedents to their consequents, if certain temptations and inducements did not in all ages and climates introduce a certain series of actions, if we were unable to trace a method and unity of system in men's tempers, propensities, and transactions? The amusement would be inferior to that which we derive from the perusal of a chronological table where events have no order but that of time; since, however, the chronologist may neglect to mark the regularity of conjunction between successive transactions, the mind of the reader is busied in supplying that regularity from memory or imagination: but the very idea of such regularity would never have suggested itself, if we had never found the source of that idea in experience. The instruction arising from the perusal of history would be absolutely none; since instruction implies, in its very nature, the classing and generalizing of objects. But, upon the supposition on which we are arguing, all objects would be irregular and disjunct without the possibility of affording any grounds of reasoning or principles of science.

The idea correspondent to the term character inevitably includes in it the assumption of necessity and system. The character of any man is the result of a long series of impressions, communicated to his mind, and modifying it in a certain manner so as to enable us, a number of these modifications and impressions being given, to predict his conduct. Hence arise his temper and habits, respecting which we reasonably conclude that they will not be abruptly superseded and reversed; and that, if ever they be reversed, it will not be accidentally, but in consequence of some strong reason persuading, or some extraordinary event modifying his mind. If there were not this original and essential conjunction between motives and actions, and, which forms one particular branch of this principle, between men's past and future actions, there could be no such thing as character or as a ground of inference enabling us to predict what men would be from what they have been.

From the same idea of regularity and conjunction arise all the schemes of policy in consequence of which men propose to themselves by a certain plan of conduct to prevail upon others to become the tools and instruments of their purposes. All the arts of courtship and flattery, of playing upon men's hopes and fears, proceed upon the supposition that mind is subject to certain laws, and that, provided we be skilful and assiduous in applying the motive, the action will inevitably follow.

Lastly, the idea of moral discipline proceeds entirely upon this principle. If I carefully persuade, exhort, and exhibit motives to another, it is because I believe that motives have a tendency to influence his conduct. If I reward or punish him, either with a view to his own improvement, or as an example to others, it is because I have been led to believe that rewards and punishments are calculated to affect the dispositions and practices of mankind. . . .

But the regularity of events in the material universe, will not of itself afford a sufficient foundation of morality and prudence. The voluntary conduct of our neighbours enters for a share into almost all those calculations upon which our plans and determinations are founded. If voluntary conduct, as well as material impulse, were not subjected to general laws, and a legitimate topic of prediction and foresight, the certainty of events in the material universe would be productive of little benefit. But in reality the mind passes from one of these topics of speculation to the other without accurately distributing them into classes, or imagining that there is any difference in the certainty with which they are attended. Hence it appears that the most uninstructed peasant or artisan is practically a necessarian. The farmer calculates as securely upon the inclination of mankind to buy his corn when it is brought into the market, as upon the tendency of the seasons to ripen it. The labourer no more suspects that his employer will alter his mind, and not pay him his daily wages, than he suspects that his tools will refuse to perform those functions today in which they were yesterday employed with success.

Another argument in favour of the doctrine of necessity, not less clear and irresistible than that from the uniformity of conjunction of antecedents and consequents, will arise from a reference to the nature of voluntary action. The motions of the animal system distribute themselves into two great classes, voluntary and involuntary. 'Voluntary action,' as we formerly observed, 'is where the event is foreseen previously to its occurrence, and the hope or fear of that event forms the excitement, prompting our effort to forward or retard it.'

Here then the advocates of intellectual liberty have a clear dilemma proposed to their choice. They must ascribe this freedom, this imperfect conjunction of antecedents and consequents, either to our voluntary or our involuntary actions. They have already made their determination. They are aware that to ascribe freedom to that which is involuntary, even if the assumption could be maintained, would be altogether foreign to the great subjects of moral, theological, or

political enquiry. Man would not be in any degree more an agent or an accountable being, though it could be proved that all his involuntary motions sprung up in a fortuitous and capricious manner.

But on the other hand to ascribe freedom to our voluntary actions is an express contradiction in terms. No motion is voluntary any further than it is accompanied with intention and design and has for its proper antecedent the apprehension of an end to be accomplished. So far as it flows in any degree from another source, it is involuntary. The new-born infant foresees nothing; therefore all his motions are involuntary. A person arrived at maturity, takes an extensive survey of the consequences of his actions; therefore he is eminently a voluntary and rational being. If any part of my conduct be destitute of all foresight of the events to result, who is there that ascribes to it depravity and vice? Xerxes acted just as soberly as such a reasoner when he caused his attendants to inflict a thousand lashes on the waves of the Hellespont.

The truth of the doctrine of necessity will be still more evident, if we consider the absurdity of the opposite hypothesis. One of its principal ingredients is self-determination. Liberty in an imperfect and popular sense is ascribed to the motions of the animal system when they result from the foresight and deliberation of the intellect and not from external compulsion. It is in this sense that the word is commonly used in moral and political reasoning. Philosophical reasoners, therefore, who have desired to vindicate the property of freedom not only to our external motions, but to the acts of the mind have been obliged to repeat this process. Our external actions are then said to be free when they truly result from the determination of the mind. If our volitions, or internal acts, be also free, they must in like manner result from the determination of the mind, or in other words, 'the mind in adopting them' must be 'self-determined.' Now nothing can be more evident than that that [determination] in which the mind exercises its freedom must be an act of the mind. Liberty, therefore, according to this hypothesis, consists in this,—that every choice we make has been chosen by us, and every act of the mind, been preceded and produced by an act of the mind. This is so true that in reality the ultimate act is not styled free from any quality of its own, but because the mind in adopting it was self-determined, that is, because it was preceded by another act. The ultimate act resulted completely from the determination that was its precursor. It was itself necessary; and, if we would look for freedom, it must be to that preceding act. But in that preceding act also, if the mind were free, it was self-determined, that is, this volition was chosen by a preceding volition, and, by the same reasoning, this also by another antecedent to itself. All the acts except the first were necessary, and followed each other as inevitably as the links of a chain do when the first link is drawn forward. But then neither was this first act free, unless the mind in adopting it were self-determined, that is, unless this act were chosen by a preceding act. Trace back the chain as far as you please, every act at which you arrive is necessary. That act which gives the character of freedom to the whole can never be discovered; and if it could in its own nature includes a contradiction. . . .

Lastly, it may be observed upon the hypothesis of free will that the whole system is built upon a distinction where there is no difference, to wit, a distinction between the intellectual and active powers of the mind. A mysterious philosophy taught men to suppose that when an object was already felt to be desirable there was need of some distinct power to put the body in motion. But reason finds no ground for this supposition; nor is it possible to conceive (in the case of an intellectual faculty placed in an aptly organized body where preference exists, together with a sentiment, the dictate of experience, of our power to obtain the object preferred) of anything beyond this that can contribute to render a certain motion of the animal frame the necessary result. We need only attend to the obvious meaning of the terms in order to perceive that the will is merely as it has been happily termed, 'the last act of the understanding,' 'one of the different cases of the association of ideas.' What indeed is preference but a feeling of something that really inheres, or is supposed to inhere, in the objects of themselves? It is the comparison, true or erroneous, which the mind makes respecting such things as are brought into competition with each other. This is indeed the same principle as was established upon a former occasion when we undertook to prove that the voluntary actions of men originate in their opinions. But if this fact had been sufficiently attended to, the freedom of the will would never have been gravely maintained by philosophical writers; since no man ever imagined that we were free to feel or not to feel an impression made upon our organs, and to believe or not to believe a proposition demonstrated to our understanding.

CHAPTER XI: MORAL EFFECTS OF ARISTOCRACY

THE features of aristocratical institution are principally two: privilege, and an aggravated monopoly of wealth. The first of these is the essence of aristocracy; the second, that without which aristocracy can rarely be supported. They are both of them in direct opposition to all sound morality and all generous independence of character.

Inequality of wealth is perhaps the necessary result of the institution of property, in any state of progress at which the human mind has yet arrived; and cannot, till the character of the human species is essentially altered, be superseded but by a despotic and positive interference, more injurious to the common welfare than the inequality it attempted to remove. Inequality of wealth involves with it inequality of inheritance.

But the mischief of aristocracy is that it inexpressibly aggravates and embitters an evil which, in its mildest form, is deeply to be deplored. The first sentiment of an uncorrupted mind when it enters upon the theatre of human life is: Remove from me and my fellows all arbitrary hindrances; let us start fair; render all the advantages and honours of social institution accessible to every man, in proportion to his talents and exertions.

Is it true, as has often been pretended, that generous and exalted qualities are hereditary in particular lines of descent? They do not want the alliance of positive institution to secure to them their proper ascendancy, and enable them to command the respect of mankind. Is it false? Let it share the fate of exposure and detection with other impostures. If I conceived of a young person that he was destined from his earliest infancy to be a sublime poet, or a profound philosopher, should I conceive that the readiest road to the encouraging and fostering his talents was, from the moment of his birth, to put a star upon his breast, to salute him with titles of honour, and to bestow upon him, independently of all exertion, those advantages which exertion usually proposes to itself as its ultimate object of pursuit? No; I should send him to the school of man, and oblige him to converse with his fellows upon terms of equality.

Privilege is a regulation rendering a few men, and those only, by the accident of their birth, eligible to certain situations. It kills all liberal ambition in the rest of mankind by opposing to it an apparently insurmountable bar. It diminishes it in the favoured class itself by showing them the principal qualification as indefeasibly theirs. Privilege entitles a favoured few to engross to themselves gratifications which the system of the universe left at large to all her sons; it puts into the hands of these few the means of oppression against the rest of their species; it fills them with vainglory, and affords them every incitement to insolence and a lofty disregard to the feelings and interests of others.

Privilege, as we have already said, is the essence of aristocracy; and, in a rare condition of human society, such as that of the ancient Romans, privilege has been able to maintain itself without the accession of wealth and to flourish in illustrious poverty. But this can be the case only under a very singular coincidence of circumstances. In general, an aggravated monopoly of wealth has been one of the objects about which the abettors of aristocracy have been most incessantly solicitous. Hence the origin of entails, rendering property, in its own nature too averse to a generous circulation, a thousand times more stagnant and putrescent than before; of primogeniture, which disinherits every other member of a family, to heap unwholesome abundance upon one; and of various limitations, filling the courts of civilized Europe with endless litigation, and making it in many cases impossible to decide, who it is that has the right of conveying a property, and what shall amount to a legal transfer.

There is one thing, more than all the rest, of importance to the well-being of mankind,—justice. A neglect of justice is not only to be deplored for the direct evil it produces; it is perhaps still more injurious, by its effects, in perverting the understanding, overturning our calculations of the future, and thus striking at the root of moral discernment, and genuine power and decision of character.

Of all the principles of justice, there is none so material to the moral rectitude of mankind, as that no man can be distinguished but by his personal merit. When a man has proved himself a benefactor to the public, when he has already, by laudable perseverance, cultivated in himself talents, which need only encouragement and public favour to bring them to maturity, let that man be honoured. In a state of society where fictitious distinctions are unknown, it is impossible he should not be honoured. But that a man should be looked up to with servility and awe, because the king has bestowed on him a spurious name, or decorated him with a ribband; that

another should revel in luxury, because his ancestor three centuries ago bled in the quarrel of Lancaster or York; do we imagine that these iniquities can be practiced without injury?

Let those who entertain this opinion converse a little with the lower orders of mankind. They will perceive that the unfortunate wretch, who with unremitted labour finds himself incapable adequately to feed and clothe his family, has a sense of injustice rankling at his heart.

But let us suppose that their sense of injustice were less acute than is here supposed, what favourable inference can be deduced from that? Is not the injustice real? If the minds of men are so withered and stupified by the constancy with which it is practised that they do not feel the rigour that grinds them into nothing, how does that improve the picture?

Let us fairly consider, for a moment, what is the amount of injustice included in the institution of aristocracy. I am born, suppose, a Polish prince with an income of £300,000 per annum. You are born a manerial serf, or a Creolian negro, attached to the soil, and transferable, by barter or otherwise, to twenty successive lords. In vain shall be your most generous efforts, and your unwearied industry, to free yourself from the intolerable yoke. Doomed, by the law of your birth, to wait at the gates of the palace you must never enter; to sleep under a ruined, weather-beaten roof, while your master sleeps under canopies of state; to feed on putrified offals, while the world is ransacked for delicacies for his table; to labour, without moderation or limit, under a parching sun, while he basks in perpetual sloth; and to be rewarded at last with contempt, reprimand, stripes, and mutilation. In fact the case is worse than this. I could endure all that injustice or caprice could inflict, provided I possessed, in the resource of a firm mind, the power of looking down with pity on my tyrant, and of knowing that I had that within, that sacred character of truth, virtue, and fortitude which all his injustice could not reach. But a slave and a serf are condemned to stupidity and vice, as well as to calamity.

Is all this nothing? Is all this necessary for the maintenance of civil order? Let it be recollected that, for this distinction, there is not the smallest foundation in the nature of things, that, as we have already said, there is no particular mould for the construction of lords, and that they are born neither better nor worse than the poorest of their dependents. It is this structure of aristocracy, in all its sanctuaries and fragments.

against which reason and morality have declared war. It is alike unjust, whether we consider it in the casts of India; the villainage of the feudal system; or the despotism of ancient Rome, where the debtors were dragged into personal servitude, to expiate, by stripes and slavery, the usurious loans they could not repay. Mankind will never be, in an eminent degree, virtuous and happy, till each man shall possess that portion of distinction and no more to which he is entitled by his personal merits. The dissolution of aristocracy is equally the interest of the oppressor and the oppressed. The one will be delivered from the listlessness of tyranny, and the other from the brutalizing operation of servitude. How long shall we be told in vain that mediocrity of fortune is the true rampart of personal happiness?

CHAPTER XIV: GENERAL FEATURES OF DEMOCRACY

In the estimate that is usually made of democracy one of the sources of our erroneous judgment lies in our taking mankind such as monarchy and aristocracy have made them, and thence judging how fit they are to manage for themselves. Monarchy and aristocracy would be no evils, if their tendency were not to undermine the virtues and the understandings of their subjects. The thing most necessary is to remove all those restraints which prevent the human mind from attaining its genuine strength. Implicit faith, blind submission to authority, timid fear, a distrust of our powers, an inattention to our own importance and the good purposes we are able to effect—these are the chief obstacles to human improvement. Democracy restores to man a consciousness of his value, teaches him, by the removal of authority and oppression, to listen only to the suggestions of reason, gives him confidence to treat all other men with frankness and simplicity, and induces him to regard them no longer, as enemies against whom to be upon his guard, but as brethren whom it becomes him to assist. The citizen of a democratical state, when he looks upon the oppression and injustice that prevail in the countries around him, cannot but entertain an inexpressible esteem for the advantages he enjoys, and the most unalterable determination to preserve them. The influence of democracy upon the sentiments of its members is altogether of the negative sort, but its consequences are inestimable. Nothing can be more unreasonable than to argue, from men as we now find them, to men as they may hereafter be made. Strict and accurate reasoning, instead of suffering us to be surprised that Athens did so much, would at first induce us to wonder that she retained so many imperfections.

The road to the improvement of mankind is in the utmost degree simple: to speak and act the truth. If the Athenians had had more of this, it is impossible they should have been so flagrantly erroneous. To express ourselves to all men with honesty and unreserve, and to administer justice without partiality, are principles which, when once thoroughly adopted, are in the highest degree prolific. They enlighten the understanding, give decision to the judgment, and strip misrepresentation of its speciousness. In Athens, men suffered themselves to be dazzled by splendour and show. If the error in their constitution which led to this defect can be discovered, if a form of political society can be devised, in which men shall be accustomed to judge simply and soberly, and be habitually exercised to the manliness of truth, democracy will, in that society, cease from the turbulence, instability, fickleness, and violence that have too often characterized it. Nothing can be more worthy to be depended on than the omnipotence of truth, or, in other words, than the connection between the judgment and the outward behaviour. The contest between truth and falsehood is of itself too unequal for the former to stand in need of support from any political ally. The more it is discovered, especially that part of it which relates to man in society, the more simple and self-evident will it appear; and it will be found impossible any otherwise to account for its having been so long concealed than from the pernicious influence of positive institution.

CHAPTER XXIV: OF THE DISSOLUTION OF GOVERNMENT

It remains for us to consider what is the degree of authority necessary to be vested in such a modified species of national assembly as we have admitted into our system. Are they to issue their commands to the different members of the confederacy? Or is it sufficient that they should invite them to cooperate for the common advantage, and by arguments and addresses convince them of the reasonableness of the measures they propose? The former of these might at first be necessary. The latter would afterwards become sufficient. The Amphictyonic council of Greece[1]

---

[1] The council was held by the deputies of certain states bound together in a league for their mutual protection and the maintaining of worship in the temple of a deity. Of several such confederations the most famous was that of Delphi.

possessed no authority but that which flowed from its personal character. In proportion as the spirit of party was extirpated, as the restlessness of public commotion subsided, and as the political machine became simple, the voice of reason would be secure to be heard. An appeal by the assembly to the several districts would not fail to obtain the approbation of reasonable men, unless it contained in it something so evidently questionable as to make it perhaps desirable that it should prove abortive.

This remark leads us one step further. Why should not the same distinction between commands and invitations which we have just made in the case of national assemblies be applied to the particular assemblies or juries of the several districts? At first, we will suppose that some degree of authority and violence would be necessary. But this necessity does not arise out of the nature of man, but out of the institutions by which he has already been corrupted. Man is not originally vicious. He would not refuse to listen to or to be convinced by the expostulations that are addressed to him had he not been accustomed to regard them as hypocritical, and to conceive that, while his neighbour, his parent and his political governor pretended to be actuated by a pure regard to his interest, they were in reality, at the expense of his, promoting their own. Such are the fatal effects of mysteriousness and complexity. Simplify the social system in the manner which every motive but those of usurpation and ambition powerfully recommends; render the plain dictates of justice level to every capacity; remove the necessity of implicit faith; and we may expect the whole species to become reasonable and virtuous. It might then be sufficient for juries to recommend a certain mode of adjusting controversies without assuming the prerogative of dictating that adjustment. It might then be sufficient for them to invite offenders to forsake their errors. If their expostulations proved in a few instances ineffectual, the evils arising out of this circumstance would be of less importance than those which proceed from the perpetual violation of the exercise of private judgment. But in reality no evils would arise, for where the empire of reason was so universally acknowledged, the offender would either readily yield to the expostulations of authority, or, if he resisted, though suffering no personal molestation, he would feel so uneasy under the unequivocal disapprobation and observant eye of public judgment as willingly to remove to a society more congenial to his errors.

The reader has probably anticipated the ultimate conclusion from these remarks. If juries might at length cease to decide and be contented to invite, if force might gradually be withdrawn and reason trusted alone, shall we not one day find that juries themselves and every other species of public institution may be laid aside as unnecessary? Will not the reasonings of one wise man be as effectual as those of twelve? Will not the competence of one individual to instruct his neighbours be a matter of sufficient notoriety without the formality of an election? Will there be many vices to correct and much obstinacy to conquer? This is one of the most memorable stages of human improvement. With what delight must every well-informed friend of mankind look forward to the auspicious period, the dissolution of political government, of that brute engine which has been the only perennial cause of the vices of mankind, and which, as has abundantly appeared in the progress of the present work, has mischiefs of various sorts incorporated with its substance, and no otherwise removable than by its utter annihilation!

From BOOK VIII: OF PROPERTY

CHAPTER VIII: APPENDIX. OF COOPERATION, COHABITATION, AND MARRIAGE

THE subject of cohabitation is particularly interesting, as it includes in it the subject of marriage. It will therefore be proper to pursue the enquiry in greater detail. The evil of marriage, as it is practised in European countries, extends further than we have yet described. The method is for a thoughtless and romantic youth of each sex to come together, to see each other for a few times and under circumstances full of delusion, and then to vow eternal attachment. What is the consequence of this? In almost every instance they find themselves deceived. They are reduced to make the best of an irretrievable mistake. They are led to conceive it their wisest policy to shut their eyes upon realities, happy, if, by any perversion of intellect, they can persuade themselves that they were right in their first crude opinions of each other. Thus the institution of marriage is made a system of fraud; and men who carefully mislead their judgments in the daily affair of their life, must be expected to have a crippled judgment in every other concern.

Add to this, that marriage, as now understood, is a monopoly, and the worst of monopolies. So long as two human beings are forbidden, by positive institution, to follow the dictates of their own mind, prejudice will be alive and vigorous. So long as I seek, by despotic and artificial means, to maintain my possession of a woman, I am guilty of the most odious selfishness. Over this imaginary prize, men watch with perpetual jealousy; and one man finds his desire and his capacity to circumvent as much excited, as the other is excited to traverse his projects and frustrate his hopes. As long as this state of society continues philanthropy will be crossed and checked in a thousand ways, and the still augmenting stream of abuse will continue to flow.

The abolition of the present system of marriage appears to involve no evils. We are apt to represent that abolition to ourselves as the harbinger of brutal lust and depravity. But it really happens in this, as in other cases, that the positive laws which are made to restrain our vices, irritate and multiply them. Not to say that the same sentiments of justice and happiness which, in a state of equality, would destroy our relish for expensive gratifications, might be expected to decrease our inordinate appetites of every kind, and to lead us universally to prefer the pleasures of intellect to the pleasures of sense.

It is a question of some moment, whether the intercourse of the sexes in a reasonable state of society would be promiscuous, or whether each man would select for himself a partner to whom he will adhere as long as that adherence shall continue to be the choice of both parties. Probability seems to be greatly in favour of the latter.

Perhaps this side of the alternative is most favourable to population. Perhaps it would suggest itself in preference to the man who would wish to maintain the several propensities of his frame, in the order due to their relative importance, and to prevent a merely sensual appetite from engrossing excessive attention. It is scarcely to be imagined that this commerce in any state of society will be stripped of its adjuncts, and that men will as willingly hold it with a woman whose personal and mental qualities they disapprove as with one of a different description. But it is the nature of the human mind to persist for a certain length of time in its opinion or choice. The parties, therefore, having acted upon selection are not likely to forget this selection when the interview is over. Friendship, if by friendship we understand that affection for an individual which is measured singly by what we know of his worth, is one of the most exquisite gratifications, perhaps one of the most improving exercises, of a rational mind. Friendship therefore may be expected to come in aid of the sexual intercourse, to refine its grossness, and increase its delight. All these arguments are calculated to determine our judgment in favour of marriage as a salutary and respectable institution, but not of that species of marriage in which there is no room for repentance and to which liberty and hope are equally strangers.

1797

1797

1759 · MARY WOLLSTONECRAFT · 1797

1759   Born at Hoxton of well-to-do Irish parents.

1780–88   After the death of her mother and the second marriage of her improvident drunkard father, earned her own livelihood as schoolteacher, governess, and miscellaneous writer.

1789–92   Devoted herself solely to writing, undertaking translations and stories, some of which were illustrated by William Blake.

1792   Published *A Vindication of the Rights of Woman.*

1792–3   Went to Paris and formed a connection with Captain Gilbert Imlay, an American, by whom she had a daughter, Fanny.

1795   Returned to England and was deserted by Imlay.

1796–7   Met and married William Godwin, the political philosopher.

1797   Died following the birth of her daughter Mary, the future wife of Shelley.

MARY WOLLSTONECRAFT, famed in literary chronicles as the wife of William Godwin and the mother of Mary Godwin Shelley, is remembered for *A Vindication of the Rights of Woman,* a book that has been called 'perhaps the most original of its century.' The originality of *A Vindication* derived not so much from its ideas as from the vitality and authenticity of their expression. Mary Wollstonecraft spoke poignantly from her own bitter experiences of the humiliation intelligent women were made to suffer in a smug and cruel society. Her book has the marks of a work hastily written, and is full of digressions and repetitions. Its style is sometimes stilted, and often flowery and rhetorical. But for all its faults it is a book of power, courageous and impassioned, and filled with apt phrases and telling sentences. Brailsford has called it 'a landmark in the revolt against sexual sham and cant.' In the eighteenth century men were possessed of the naïve belief that woman exists only to contribute to the pleasure and comfort of man. Women were placed in intellectual fetters and denied the independence of their own personalities. Early in the century Defoe and Swift had made unheeded protests against society's inhumanities to women; and later Holbach and Condorcet had made warmhearted pleas for the improvement of women's status, without, however, attracting much attention. When Mary Wollstonecraft spoke out, she used great plainness of speech and her book aroused widespread opposition. After its publication, she was called a 'hyena in petticoats' and denounced as a social outcast. Actually her teachings seem conservative when compared to the present status of English and American women. She did not attack the institution of marriage or assail orthodox religion. Essentially her book was an appeal for the equality of sexes in education and for intellectual companionship. To a remarkable degree she was ahead of her time, her work anticipating by nearly a century the theme of Ibsen's *A Doll's House,* that a woman should be herself and lead her own life.

From A VINDICATION OF THE RIGHTS
OF WOMAN

To account for, and excuse the tyranny of man, many ingenious arguments have been brought forward to prove, that the two sexes, in the acquirement of virtue, ought to aim at attaining a very different character; or, to speak explicitly, women are not allowed to have sufficient strength of mind to acquire what really deserves the name of virtue. Yet it should seem, allowing them to have souls, that there is but one way appointed by Providence to lead *mankind* to either virtue or happiness.

If then women are not a swarm of ephemeron triflers, why should they be kept in ignorance under the specious name of innocence? Men complain, and with reason, of the follies and caprices of our sex, when they do not keenly satirise our headstrong passions and grovelling vices. Behold, I should answer, the natural effect of ignorance! The mind will ever be unstable that has only prejudices to rest on, and the current will run with destructive fury when there are no barriers to break its force. Women are told from their infancy, and taught by the example of their mothers, that a little knowledge of human weakness, justly termed cunning, softness of temper, *outward* obedience, and a scrupulous attention to a puerile kind of propriety, will obtain for them the protection of man; and should they be beautiful, everything else is needless, for at least twenty years of their lives.

Thus Milton describes our first frail mother; though when he tells us that women are formed for softness and sweet attractive grace, I cannot comprehend his meaning, unless, in the true Mahometan strain, he meant to deprive us of souls, and insinuate that we were beings only designed by sweet attractive grace, and docile blind obedience, to gratify the senses of man when he can no longer soar on the wing of contemplation.

How grossly do they insult us who thus advise us only to render ourselves gentle, domestic brutes! For instance, the winning softness so warmly and frequently recommended, that governs by obeying. What childish expressions, and how insignificant is the being—can it be an immortal one?—who will condescend to govern by such sinister methods? 'Certainly,' says Lord Bacon, 'man is of kin to the beasts by his body; and if he be not of kin to God by his spirit, he is a base and ignoble creature!'[1] Men, indeed, appear to me to act in a very unphilosophical manner, when they try to secure the good conduct of women by attempting to keep them always in a state of childhood. Rousseau was more consistent when he wished to stop the progress of reason in both sexes, for if men eat of the tree of knowledge, women will come in for a taste; but, from the imperfect cultivation which their understandings now receive, they only attain a knowledge of evil.

.   .

Consequently, the most perfect education, in my opinion, is such an exercise of the understanding as is best calculated to strengthen the body and form the heart. Or, in other words, to enable the individual to attain such habits of virtue as will render it independent. In fact, it is a farce to call any being virtuous whose virtues do not result from the exercise of its own reason. This was Rousseau's opinion respecting men; I extend it to women, and confidently assert that they have been drawn out of their sphere by false refinement, and not by an endeavour to acquire masculine qualities. Still the regal homage which they receive is so intoxicating, that until the manners of the times are changed, and formed on more reasonable principles, it may be impossible to convince them that the illegitimate power which they obtain by degrading themselves is a curse, and that they must return to nature and equality if they wish to secure the placid satisfaction that unsophisticated affections impart. But for this epoch we must wait—wait perhaps till kings and nobles, enlightened by reason, and, preferring the real dignity of man to childish state, throw off their gaudy hereditary trappings; and if then women do not resign the arbitrary power of beauty—they will prove that they have *less* mind than man.

I may be accused of arrogance; still I must declare what I firmly believe, that all the writers who have written on the subject of female education and manners, from Rousseau to Dr. Gregory,[2] have contributed to render women more artificial, weak characters, than they would otherwise have been; and consequently, more useless members of society.

Rousseau declares that a woman should never for a moment feel herself independent, that she should be governed by fear to exercise her *natural* cunning, and made a coquettish slave in order to render her a more alluring object of desire, a *sweeter* companion to man, whenever he chooses

---

1 *Of Atheism.*

2 John Gregory, 1724–73, Scottish physician, author of *A Father's Legacy to his Daughters*, 1774.

to relax himself. He carries the arguments, which he pretends to draw from the indications of nature, still further, and insinuates that truth and fortitude, the cornerstones of all human virtue, should be cultivated with certain restrictions, because, with respect to the female character, obedience is the grand lesson which ought to be impressed with unrelenting rigour.[3]

What nonsense! When will a great man arise with sufficient strength of mind to puff away the fumes which pride and sensuality have thus spread over the subject? If women are by nature inferior to men, their virtues must be the same in quality, if not in degree, or virtue is a relative idea; consequently, their conduct should be founded on the same principles, and have the same aim.

.   .   .

Women ought to endeavour to purify their heart; but can they do so when their uncultivated understandings make them entirely dependent on their senses for employment and amusement, when no noble pursuits sets them above the little vanities of the day, or enables them to curb the wild emotions that agitate a reed, over which every passing breeze has power? To gain the affections of a virtuous man, is affection necessary? Nature has given woman a weaker frame than man; but, to ensure her husband's affections, must a wife, who, by the exercise of her mind and body whilst she was discharging the duties of a daughter, wife, and mother, has allowed her constitution to retain its natural strength, and her nerves a healthy tone,—is she, I say, to condescend to use art, and feign a sickly delicacy, in order to secure her husband's affection? Weakness may excite tenderness, and gratify the arrogant pride of man; but the lordly caresses of a protector will not gratify a noble mind that pants for and deserves to be respected. Fondness is a poor substitute for friendship!

In a seraglio, I grant, that all these arts are necessary; the epicure must have his palate tickled, or he will sink into apathy; but have women so little ambition as to be satisfied with such a condition? Can they supinely dream life away in the lap of pleasure, or the languor of weariness, rather than assert their claim to pursue reasonable pleasures, and render themselves conspicuous by practising the virtues which dignify mankind? Surely she has not an immortal soul who can loiter life away merely employed

to adorn her person, that she may amuse the languid hours, and soften the cares of a fellow-creature who is willing to be enlivened by her smiles and tricks, when the serious business of life is over.

Besides, the woman who strengthens her body and exercises her mind will, by managing her family and practising various virtues, become the friend, and not the humble dependent of her husband; and if she, by possessing such substantial qualities, merit his regard, she will not find it necessary to conceal her affection, nor to pretend to an unnatural coldness of constitution to excite her husband's passions. In fact, if we revert to history, we shall find that the women who have distinguished themselves have neither been the most beautiful nor the most gentle of their sex.

.   .   .

Surely there can be but one rule of right, if morality has an eternal foundation, and whoever sacrifices virtue, strictly so called, to present convenience, or whose *duty* it is to act in such a manner, lives only for the passing day, and cannot be an accountable creature.

The poet then should have dropped his sneer when he says—

'If weak women go astray,
The stars are more in fault than they.'[4]

For that they are bound by the adamantine chain of destiny is most certain, if it be proved that they are never to exercise their own reason, never to be independent, never to rise above opinion, or to feel the dignity of a rational will that only bows to God, and often forgets that the universe contains any being but itself and the model of perfection to which its ardent gaze is turned, to adore attributes that, softened into virtues, may be imitated in kind, though the degree overwhelms the enraptured mind.

If, I say, for I would not impress by declamation when Reason offers her sober light, if they be really capable of acting like rational creatures, let them not be treated like slaves; or, like the brutes who are dependent on the reason of man, when they associate with him; but cultivate their minds, give them the salutary sublime curb of principle, and let them attain conscious dignity by feeling themselves only dependent on God. Teach them, in common with man, to submit to necessity, instead of giving, to render them more pleasing, a sex to morals.

---

3 See Rousseau's *Emile,* Book v.

4 Matthew Prior, *Hans Carvel.* 11–12.

Further, should experience prove that they cannot attain the same degree of strength of mind, perseverance, and fortitude, let their virtues be the same in kind, though they may vainly struggle for the same degree; and the superiority of man will be equally clear, if not clearer; and truth, as it is a simple principle, which admits of no modification, would be common to both. Nay the order of society, as it is at present regulated, would not be inverted, for woman would then only have the rank that reason assigned her, and arts could not be practised to bring the balance even, much less to turn it.

These may be termed Utopian dreams. Thanks to that Being who impressed them on my soul, and gave me sufficient strength of mind to dare to exert my own reason, till, becoming dependent only on Him for the support of my virtue, I view with indignation, the mistaken notions that enslave my sex.

I love man as my fellow; but his sceptre, real or usurped, extends not to me, unless the reason of an individual demands my homage; and even then the submission is to reason, and not to man. In fact, the conduct of an accountable being must be regulated by the operations of its own reason; or on what foundation rests the throne of God?

If love be the supreme good, let woman be only educated to inspire it, and let every charm be polished to intoxicate the senses; but if they be moral beings, let them have a chance to become intelligent; and let love to man be only a part of that glowing flame of universal love, which, after encircling humanity, mounts in grateful incense to God.

.   .   .

But to render her really virtuous and useful, she must not, if she discharge her civil duties, want individually the protection of civil laws; she must not be dependent on her husband's bounty for her subsistence during his life, or support after his death; for how can a being be generous who has nothing of its own? or virtuous who is not free? The wife, in the present state of things, who is faithful to her husband, and neither suckles nor educates her children, scarcely deserves the name of a wife, and has no right to that of a citizen. But take away natural rights, and duties become null.

Women then must be considered as only the wanton solace of men, when they become so weak in mind and body that they cannot exert themselves unless to pursue some frothy pleasure, or

to invent some frivolous fashion. What can be a more melancholy sight to a thinking mind, than to look into the numerous carriages that drive helter-skelter about this metropolis in a morning full of pale-faced creatures who are flying from themselves! I have often wished, with Dr. Johnson, to place some of them in a little shop with half-a-dozen children looking up to their languid countenances for support. I am much mistaken, if some latent vigour would not soon give health and spirit to their eyes, and some lines drawn by the exercise of reason on the blank cheeks, which before were only undulated by dimples, might restore lost dignity to the character, or rather enable it to attain the true dignity of its nature. Virtue is not to be acquired even by speculation, much less by the negative supineness that wealth naturally generates.

.   .   .

But what have women to do in society? I may be asked, but to loiter with easy grace; surely you would not condemn them all to suckle fools and chronicle small beer! No. Women might certainly study the art of healing, and be physicians as well as nurses. And midwifery, decency seems to allot to them, though I am afraid, the word midwife, in our dictionaries, will soon give place to *accoucheur,* and one proof of the former delicacy of the sex be effaced from the language.

They might also study politics, and settle their benevolence on the broadest basis; for the reading of history will scarcely be more useful than the perusal of romances, if read as mere biography; if the character of the times, the political improvements, arts, &c., be not observed. In short, if it be not considered as the history of man; and not of particular men, who filled a niche in the temple of fame, and dropped into the black rolling stream of time, that silently sweeps all before it, into the shapeless void called—eternity.—For shape, can it be called, 'that shape hath none'?[5]

Business of various kinds, they might likewise pursue, if they were educated in a more orderly manner, which might save many from common and legal prostitution. Women would not then marry for a support, as men accept of places under Government, and neglect the implied duties; nor would an attempt to earn their own subsistence, a most laudable one! sink them almost to the level of those poor abandoned creatures who live by prostitution. For are not milliners and mantuamakers[6] reckoned the next class? The few

---

5 *Paradise Lost,* II, 667.
6 dressmakers.

employments open to women, so far, from being liberal, are menial; and when a superior education enables them to take charge of the education of children as governesses, they are not treated like the tutors of sons, though even clerical tutors are not always treated in a manner calculated to render them respectable in the eyes of their pupils, to say nothing of the private comfort of the individual. But as women educated like gentlewomen, are never designed for the humiliating situation which necessity sometimes forces them to fill; these situations are considered in the light of a degradation; and they know little of the human heart, who need to be told, that nothing so painfully sharpens sensibility as such a fall in life.

. . .

Would men but generously snap our chains, and be content with rational fellowship instead of slavish obedience, they would find us more observant daughters, more affectionate sisters, more faithful wives, more reasonable mothers—in a word, better citizens. We should then love them with true affection, because we should learn to respect ourselves; and the peace of mind of a worthy man would not be interrupted by the idle vanity of his wife, nor the babes sent to nestle in a strange bosom, having never found a home in their mother's.

. . .

That women at present are by ignorance rendered foolish or vicious, is, I think, not to be disputed; and, that the most salutary effects tending to improve mankind might be expected from a REVOLUTION in female manners, appears, at least, with a face of probability, to rise out of the observation. For as marriage has been termed the parent of those endearing charities which draw man from the brutal herd, the corrupting intercourse that wealth, idleness, and folly, produce between the sexes, is more universally injurious to morality than all the other vices of mankind collectively considered. To adulterous lust the most sacred duties are sacrificed, because before marriage, men, by a promiscuous intimacy with women, learned to consider love as a selfish gratification —learned to separate it not only from esteem, but from the affection merely built on habit, which mixes a little humanity with it. Justice and friendship are also set at defiance, and that purity of taste is vitiated which would naturally lead a man to relish an artless display of affec-

tion rather than affected airs. But that noble simplicity of affection, which dares to appear unadorned, has few attractions for the libertine, though it be the charm, which by cementing the matrimonial tie, secures to the pledges of a warmer passion the necessary parental attention; for children will never be properly educated till friendship subsists between parents. Virtue flies from a house divided against itself—and a whole legion of devils take up their residence there.

The affection of husbands and wives cannot be pure when they have so few sentiments in common, and when so little confidence is established at home, as must be the case when their pursuits are so different. That intimacy from which tenderness should flow, will not, cannot subsist between the vicious.

Contending, therefore, that the sexual distinction which men have so warmly insisted upon, is arbitrary, I have dwelt on an observation, that several sensible men, with whom I have conversed on the subject, allowed to be well founded; and it is simply this, that the little chastity to be found amongst men, and consequent disregard of modesty, tend to degrade both sexes; and further, that the modesty of women, characterized as such, will often be only the artful veil of wantonness instead of being the natural reflection of purity, till modesty be universally respected.

From the tyranny of man, I firmly believe, the greater number of female follies proceed; and the cunning, which I allow makes at present a part of their character, I likewise have repeatedly endeavoured to prove, is produced by oppression.

. . .

Asserting the rights which women in common with men ought to contend for, I have not attempted to extenuate their faults; but to prove them to be the natural consequence of their education and station in society. If so, it is reasonable to suppose that they will change their character, and correct their vices and follies, when they are allowed to be free in a physical, moral, and civil sense.

Let woman share the rights, and she will emulate the virtues of man; for she must grow more perfect when emancipated, or justify the authority that chains such a weak being to her duty. If the latter, it will be expedient to open a fresh trade with Russia for whips: a present which a father should always make to his son-in-law on his wedding day, that a husband may keep his whole family in order by the same means; and without any violation of justice reign, wielding this sceptre, sole master of his house, because he is the only being in it who has reason:—the divine, indefeasible earthly sovereignty breathed into man by the Master of the universe. Allowing this position, women have not any·inherent rights to claim; and, by the same rule, their duties vanish, for rights and duties are inseparable.

Be just then, O ye men of understanding: and mark not more severely what women do amiss than the vicious tricks of the horse or the ass for whom ye provide provender—and allow her the privileges of ignorance, to whom ye deny the rights of reason, or ye will be worse than Egyptian taskmasters, expecting virtue where nature has not given understanding.

1792

1757   WILLIAM BLAKE · 1827

1757   Born in London, 28 November, third son of James Blake, a none-too-prosperous hosier.

1761   The faculty of 'vision' came to the poet when he was only four years old (God pressed his face to the window and set the child a-screaming); and by the time he was eight was becoming habitual (angels walked among the haymakers in a summer field; Ezekiel appeared to him and angels filled a tree). A strange and stormy child, he was spared by his father the discipline of school; but was taught at home to read and write. Showed such a precocious talent for drawing that at the age of ten was sent to Mr. Pars's drawing school in the Strand. In his twelfth year wrote the earliest of the *Poetical Sketches.*

1772-9   Was apprenticed for seven years to James Basire, engraver to the Society of Antiquaries. During the last five years of his apprenticeship was engaged in sketching monuments in Westminster Abbey and other old churches. His imagination was 'gothicized' by his long and close study of Gothic art and architecture. In his nineteenth and twentieth years wrote the last of the *Poetical Sketches.*

1778   Studied under George Moser in the Antique School of the Royal Academy. Began water-color painting with his *Penance of Jane Shore.*

1779   Began to earn his living by making engravings for London booksellers.

1780   Became acquainted with Thomas Stothard, an illustrator, and with Flaxman (his 'dear Sculptor of Eternity'), who gave him friendship and professional assistance. Another early friend was the Swiss-born painter, Henry Fuseli, a neighbor in Broad Street—'The only man that e'er I knew/Who did not make me almost spew.' Exhibited for the first time at the Royal Academy. (Continued to exhibit at the Academy up to 1808.)

1781   Fell in love with a 'lively little girl' named Polly Wood, but she rejected him. Felt so upset over the rejection that he went for a change of scene to Battersea where he stayed with a market-gardener named Boucher, whose daughter, Catherine, soon consoled Blake and won his heart.

1782   In August, married Catherine Boucher and with her set up housekeeping in Green Street, Leicester Fields. Was introduced by Flaxman to Mrs. Henry Mathew, the bluestocking wife of a minister, and became for a time a frequent visitor to her salon, where he used to recite and sometimes to sing his own poems.

1783   His earliest compositions, *Poetical Sketches,* printed at the expense of Flaxman and the Reverend Henry Mathew.

1784   After the death of his father, set up a print-seller's shop in Broad Street in partnership with James Parker, a former fellow-apprentice. His favorite brother, Robert, came to live with him and to be his pupil. Wrote *An Island in the Moon,* an explosive satire-fantasy, which was left unfinished. The manuscript contains the earliest of *Songs of Innocence.*

1787-93   Tended his brother Robert day and night during the last weeks of his fatal illness. At his death, saw Robert's soul rising into heaven and 'clapping its hands for joy.' Later, Blake tells us, his brother appeared to him and revealed in a vision the secret of illuminated printing. Gave up the print shop, dissolving the partnership with Parker, and moved to Poland Street where he lived for five years. During this period was much in the society of sympathizers with the French Revolution whom he met, for the most part, at the shop of Johnson, the radical bookseller. His circle of acquaintances included some of the most advanced thinkers of the day: Dr. Price, Dr. Joseph Priestley, Tom Paine, Mary Wollstonecraft, and William Godwin.

1788   First used the new process of relief-engraving in 'Illuminated Printing.' Engraved the tractates, *There is No Natural Religion* and *All Religions are One,* which first set forth his mature philosophy. Wrote annotations to Lavater's *Aphorisms* and Swedenborg's *Wisdom of Angels.* Wrote *Tiriel.*

1789   Engraved *Songs of Innocence* and *The Book of Thel,* works that first reveal his mystical cast of mind.

1790   Engraved *The Marriage of Heaven and Hell.*

1791   *The French Revolution,* Book I, set up in type by Johnson but not published.

1793   Engraved *Visions of the Daughters of Albion.* Moved to Hercules Buildings, Lambeth. Published a small book of engravings entitled *The Gates of Paradise.* Published *America: A Prophecy.* Met his future patron and lifelong friend, Thomas Butts.

1794   Engraved *Songs of Experience, Europe: A Prophecy, The First Book of Urizen.*

1795   Engraved *The Song of Los, The Book of Los, The Book of Ahania.* Began probably at this time to write the long mystical poem entitled *Vala,* afterward altered to *The Four Zoas.*

1796   Engaged on designs and engravings for Young's *Night Thoughts.*

1797-9   Suffered from lack of employment as engraver. Turned to designing in water color. Obtained some commissions from Thomas Butts.

1800   Was introduced by Flaxman to William Hayley, a country squire and popular versifier, who invited him to Felpham.

1800-1803   Rented a cottage near the seashore at Felpham and in a happy frame of mind settled down to painting miniatures and to executing various commissions for Hayley. Revised *The Four Zoas.* Began the composition of *Milton.* Also wrote poems in the *Rossetti MS.* and *Pickering MS.* In the third year relations with Hayley became strained and he decided to leave Felpham. An affray with a dragoon, who had entered Blake's garden, led to false accusations and a warrant for his arrest on the charge of sedition. Returned to London in September 1803. In spite of 'tame' Hayley, a damp cottage, and work unworthy of his genius, his years at Felpham were fruitful.

1804   Stood trial for treason at the Chichester Quarter Sessions and was acquitted amid the applause of the assembly. Began the composition of *Jerusalem.* His faculty of 'vision' miraculously renewed during a visit to the Truchsessian Picture Gallery.

1805   Prepared designs for Blair's *The Grave* commissioned by an ex-engraver and printseller, R. H. Cromek; but Cromek in violation of his agreement cheated Blake by passing on his drawings to another artist to be engraved.

1806-7   Cromek, again slyly seeking to profit by another's expense, after seeing Blake's design, *Canterbury Pilgrims,* commissioned Stothard to paint a picture on the same subject. When Blake saw Stothard's *Canterbury Pilgrims* exhibited, he was furious over this second act of Cromek's duplicity and attacked him in angry epigrams—'A petty, sneaking knave I knew/Oh, Mr. Cromek, how do you do!' Though Blake was not at fault, the quarrel with Cromek lost him friends and naturally affected his chances of getting work as an engraver. Entered in his notebook for January 1807: 'Between two and seven in the evening—despair.'

1807-9   Designed illustrations for *Paradise Lost;* annotated Reynolds' *Discourses;* completed the engraving of *Milton.* Exhibited his pictures in his brother's shop in Broad Street but apparently without much success. Issued *A Descriptive Catalogue.*

1810   Publication of his engraving of the *Canterbury Pilgrims.*

1811-17   Occupied with sketches and engravings.

1818   Met John Linnell, a young portrait painter, who became Blake's friend and admirer and a link with the young artists of the period. Wrote *The Everlasting Gospel.*

1820   Designed and executed woodcuts for Thornton's *Pastorals of Virgil.* Completed the engraving of *Jerusalem.* Executed water-color designs illustrating the *Book of Job* for Thomas Butts.

1821   Moved to Fountain Court, The Strand.

1822   Received a donation of £25 from the Royal Academy.

1823   Commissioned by Linnell to paint and engrave replicas of the designs for *Job.*

1825   Completed engravings for *Job.* First met Crabb Robinson, the diarist. Began designs in illustration of Dante for Linnell.

1827   Died, 12 August, welcoming death with joyful songs.

WILLIAM BLAKE, who today stands high among English artists and poets, in his own lifetime was almost unknown beyond a small circle of painters and personal friends. He lived and worked in isolation, earning a precarious livelihood as an engraver. Unfortunately in his day the craft of engraving to which he had been apprenticed was losing ground to more popular art forms; besides, Blake himself by his creative handling of assignments often alienated clients who neither understood nor appreciated his work. Thus the times and his own genius combined to deny him the measure of worldly success which should have been his. In his distress he became vehement against artists like Reynolds, who had become wealthy from painting portraits of the socially prominent, and against society at large, which he conceived was conspiring to defeat him. Personal failure drove him into a lifelong warfare with the 'world-out-there.' He fell in with a band of intellectual revolutionaries and became their most daring spokesman. No custom or institution escaped the fire of his wrath. Fiercely he decried men for their meekness and pleaded with them to cast off forever through faith and daring their 'mind-forged manacles.' By rash deeds and forthright utterance Blake condemned himself to a life of poverty. But we need not pity him for his lot nor think of him necessarily as an unhappy man. He was generously compensated for his lack of practical success by leisure to write and engrave his visions of truth. He knew the unparalleled joy of the creative artist and the confident hope of the man of faith. As a personality, he was simple-hearted, honest, sensitive, and gentle; though when roused, he could become passionately indignant or bitterly satirical. His dominant trait was a tremendous mental force, a kind of primal intelligence, which he enlisted in fighting the very limitations of the mind itself, in himself and in mankind.

Blake was a man of vision who believed he had found the original, ineffable secret. During ecstatic, supersensuous moments he experienced states of mental illumination in which he beheld ultimate truth. The region of his vision was the strange (yet familiar) region of the human mind, which for him became the region of Eternal worlds. 'I rest not from my great task!/To open the Eternal Worlds, to open the immortal Eyes/Of Man inwards into the Worlds of Thought, into Eternity.' To report the wonders of this magical, unchartered region, Blake turned from the past. 'I must Create a system or be enslaved by another man's,' he declared. 'I will not reason and compare: my business is to create.' But in undertaking to reject tradition he substituted a symbolical framework which is enormously complicated and confusing. Blake was self-educated except as an engraver and like many self-taught men fanatically learned. He soaked up vast quantities of occult, philosophical, and religious literature, including the writings of Bacon, Locke, Berkeley, Boehme, Lavater, Swedenborg, and (above all) the Holy Bible. This multifarious literature he often indiscriminately used as fuel for the conflagration that was going on in his mind. Many of Blake's ideas are in consequence automatically superstitious and a large part of his writing obscurantist and rant. Yet Blake is undeniably a poet of startling originality and unquestioned genius. His appeal is for a renewal, through vision, of faith in human integrity. Vision is for him the great secret of life. The whole of his work is an attempt to develop this faculty of vision that men may see to understand, and understanding may forgive and act rightly.

Even in his first book of verse, *Poetical Sketches,* Blake reveals something of those qualities of independence and daring that so highly characterize his later writings. Although he was still only a youth when he composed these poems, he broke with the prevalent poetic modes of the eighteenth century and revived the lyrical accents of Milton and the Elizabethans. The bulk of the *Sketches,* as might be expected, are obviously derivative: they include echoes from Collins, Chatterton, Macpherson, and other eighteenth-century favorites, as well as from earlier authors. Nevertheless, not infrequently the reader is rewarded with striking and original phrases and with not a few entire lyrics both artless and unrestrained. Pervasive throughout the work is a mental quality of unreality, which we soon identify as typically Blakean. Though Blake himself had a low opinion of this slight volume, we now recognize in its publication a signal event marking the advance of a new poetic era.

Blake's originality burst into full and magical bloom with *Songs of Innocence.* These inimitable songs were given form by a new process known as 'illuminated printing,' the secret of which Blake said was revealed to him by his dead brother in a vision. In this process the letters and decorations were written in varnish on a copper plate and were then made to stand out after an acid had lowered the surface of the plate. Impressions were taken from the raised etchings and then colored by hand. Most of Blake's famous works were produced in this way: he gave his visions substance by all the arts open to him. In *Songs of Innocence* he recovered the spontaneous joy and innocence of childhood. During moments of ecstatic vision Blake discovered that his own extreme sense of freedom and happiness was equivalent to the condition of childhood; that heaven verily lay about him in his infancy. The original state of happiness, self-enjoyment, and unity, he tells us in these poems, is in childhood; the enfranchized adult returns to it. Literally he declares: 'Lest ye become again as a little child ye cannot hope to enter the kingdom of heaven.' Thus *Songs of Innocence* is the record of a vivid, personal reaffirmation of New Testament doctrine, a fact abundantly recognized by Blake's use throughout the poems of characteristic pastoral Christian symbols (the Christ child, the lamb, the shepherd, and the flock). The language of the songs is simple and crystal clear. Blake so closely identifies himself with children that they themselves seem to be speaking. This is a rare accomplishment. The poet has left out all art, all moralizing, all pretending. The theme of loss and finding runs through the songs, and the gaiety and laughter of children fills them.

After the mystical joy of innocence, Blake's soul was shaken with a deeper passion: the state of Innocence was supplanted by the state of Experience. A bitter incident in his own life led him into an intense awareness of the evils arbitrarily created by man-made laws and institutions. Deeply stirred by what he experienced of the world's hypocrisy and cruelty, Blake spoke out indignantly in *Songs of Experience.* Innocence is Heaven; Experience is Hell. In Experience free and joyous love is crushed by cankerous selfishness ('builds a Hell in Heaven's despite'), and by the prohibitions of a tradition-ridden priesthood ('Thou shalt not' is writ over the chapel door of love). In Experience the innocent laughter of children is silenced by interfering adults, and the children's frail bodies are exploited by a hardened society. The church remains apathetic to gross abuses; the state supports the vested interests. To Blake the social evils he beheld were an intolerable national disgrace. He did not at the time see his way to a solution, but in *Songs of Experience* he bitterly voiced his indignation and compassion. These songs reverberate the intensity of his feeling in brilliant denunciatory phrases, tight rhythms, and searing imagery. The best of them are rarely to be matched elsewhere in Blake, or (for that matter) in their kind in anyone else.

'Experience' had been for Blake a state of purgation and he emerged from it with a clearer perception. He came thereafter to see Innocence and Experience as the interplaying contraries that give life meaning. The human soul, Blake now perceived, which was once a unity, under the stress of its mortal existence has become divided against itself;

but through Imagination it can be reintegrated. In *The Marriage of Heaven and Hell*, Blake shows how man's spiritual emancipation is possible. Dogma has petrified man's instinctive life into an arbitrary code of false moral values. Traditional religion has set up the dualism of good and evil. But good is only convention; and evil is the energy working in opposition to it. The true dualism is not Good and Evil, but Wisdom and Folly; not Body and Soul, but Energy and Reason. The body, which religion had condemned as corruptible, was in truth a vital part of the soul; and the senses, which religion had viewed with suspicion, were 'the chief inlets of the soul in this age.' Men of vision will follow their impulses. The senses will be purified by indulging them to the utmost: 'The Road of Excess leads to the Palace of Wisdom.' Then through Imagination the infinite will be perceived in everything and the human image will be reintegrated. In *The Marriage of Heaven and Hell* and in *A Song of Liberty* (a plea to nations to cast off their bondage) with which the marriage ends, Blake pierces through the anomalies of his age (the disintegration of personality and the overemphasis of reason) in a ringing battle call for emancipation. 'Each sentence [of the *Marriage*],' says Damon, 'seems to give the mind a push, and then leave it moving.' Blake's subsequent prophecies are but the larger working out of the fundamental doctrines of this text.

In the early 'nineties when Blake was much in the company of radicals his writing was directed almost wholly to themes of revolutionary and social prophecy. *The Marriage of Heaven and Hell* and *A Song of Liberty*, which have been discussed, fall within this framework and so do *The French Revolution*, *America*, and *Europe*. The last-mentioned deal with the contemporary political scene. They are a mixture of history, drama, and allegory exhorting men, as in *A Song of Liberty*, to rise and break their chains. Of the social prophecies the earliest, and in its theme a prelude to the rest, is *The Book of Thel*. In this lovely lyrical narrative Blake personifies Thel as a human soul, about to leave its Eden of Innocence, gazing fearfully through the gates of imagination upon the World of Generation. Thel is told that her mortality will be sanctified ('Everything that lives is holy'), but when faced with the terrors of fleshly life she flees back to her world of Innocence. (By some interpreters *The Book of Thel* is projected on the cosmic scale with Thel as a pre-existent soul unwilling to enter the grave of earthly existence; by others, notably Plowman, the drama of Thel is acted out in its entirety on the world's stage.) In *Visions of the Daughters of Albion* the soul in innocence has crossed the threshold into experience. Blake here allegorizes the tragedy for the man or woman in love who comes in conflict with the social laws which do not recognize that 'one law for the Lion and Ox is oppression.' The *Visions* is a scathing attack upon the legal bondage which brings misery to a loveless marriage. Blake believed in the innocence of instinct and the evils of repression, at one time even going so far as to preach a community of loves. Actually in practice Blake adjusted himself in his own married life to conditions that at the outset seemed to him intolerable. But he understood only too well the tragic consequences possible in ill-matched marriages for a generation in which divorce was rare and difficult to obtain.

In what have been designated as the Prophetic Lays (*The First Book of Urizen, The Book of Ahania, The Book of Los, The Song of Los*) and in the long visionary prophecy, *The Four Zoas*, Blake moves from history to cosmology, from Time to Eternity. In these prophecies he pictures the separate human faculties at war with each other. Man as a being is divided against himself; his true home is in Eternity, but he is caught up in the meshes of Time and Space. He fell from Eternity into Division. The present struggle in man is to find the true road back into Eternity, which is in the mind of every man, the Imagination. Blake believed that there was a time when the visionary and imaginative powers of men were not beguiled. He attempts to explain in the Prophetic Lays how the contraries in man arose and how the different forces within man may be brought into a state of balance. It is the familiar story of the wars of the gods that he tells, but used symbolically to represent the interior spiritual struggle in the mind of man. The chief figures in these prophetic works are Los (imagination), Urizen (reason), Luvah (passions), and Tharmas (instincts). These are the Four Zoas, or the four eternal senses of man. The general drift of the symbolism can perhaps be grasped by analyzing the central figure of Urizen. Urizen is the false god who separated himself from prime unity and set in motion the divisions of man. Politically he stands for the *ancien régime,* opposed to Orc, the spirit of Revolution; morally he is the spirit of servile obedience to law, convention, and 'positive institutions'; theologically he is Jehovah of the Old Testament, 'a jealous god enmeshing man in nets of religion and priestcraft' (Grierson); psychologically he represents the contamination of cold, logical reasoning, embodied for Blake in the analytics of Newton and the skepticism of Voltaire. Set in opposition to him is Los, the imagination, incarnate in artists like Blake himself. In *The Four Zoas* the crucial moment in the redemption of Albion occurs when the separate gods or geniuses of Heart, Mind, Body, and Spirit all recognize their subservience to the 'Human form Divine' and the futility of setting themselves up separately as dominant powers. In these prophecies, baffled by the persecutions of the world of men, Blake turned his thought inward in an attempt to create in a world of his own the harmony that he felt must exist but that he had failed to discover in the external world. It was inevitable, however, that the two revolutions which shook the world around him and were actual in his life should be actual also in his writings. Much therefore of the dissonance and confusion that he hoped to escape is transferred to his compositions. Moreover, driven by fear or disdain, or perhaps both, to hide his intentions from common men, his writing grows more complex and vaguer, the symbols ever more shifting and confusing as he advances further into his cosmic prophecy. The general impression of these poems is one of incoherent, thrashing power. Yet within the weltering chaos the counterpoint of tension between Urizen and Los at times exalts the theme to a peculiar grandeur. And not infrequently breaking through the darkness to reward the persistent reader are extended tracts of verse of striking intensity and beauty.

The mythology of the earlier prophecies is non-Christian. Man apparently by his own efforts can overthrow Urizen, cast off repressive codes, and destroy false moralities. In the later prophecies, *Milton* and *Jerusalem,* Blake passed to another form of myth which he created largely in terms of Christian doctrine as he interpreted it. Now man (Albion) himself is the guilty one. He is divided against himself. He is not yet what he has been nor what he may be, but he seeks fulfillment. The agency for his redemption is vision, vision that will burst through his contraries and restore man's prime identity. But vision, which was formerly Los, is now Jesus, the Divine Imagination. 'The Eternal Body of Man is Imagination. That is God Himself, the Divine Body, Jesus.' Innocence returns to itself greater by way of Experience. The hypocrite world will fulfill itself in its own despite. 'Error is Created. Truth is Eternal.' But man knows the one only by the other. 'To be in Error and to be cast out is a part of God's design.' Through the black night of struggle with self-hood comes the recognition of spiritual truth above the codified, rational law of men, and with this recognition emancipation and victory. The climactic teaching of the later prophecies is that of the Sermon on the Mount: love and kindness and the mutual forgiveness of sins among men. Regarded as poetry *Milton* and *Jerusalem* are not lucid and attractive as wholes. They are not meaningless, but to most readers they are 'too hazardously built and too apocalyptic.' The mental states represented in them are described in too great agitation and complexity. Blake crams too much into his myth. Before the reader has proceeded far he becomes entangled in a vast web of extravagant rhetoric. As in the earlier prophecies there are splendid fragments of lyrical beauty and passionate descriptive passages. There is an exciting sense of some elements of profound truth in them, but in the end the mind is not satisfied.

Though the commentaries are increasing year by year and little by little the light breaks through the darkness, it is unlikely that there ever will be a standard codification of Blake's thought. Blake himself often deliberately obscured his meaning: 'That which can be made Explicit to the Idiot,' he wrote, 'is not worth my care. The wisest of the Ancients consider'd what is not too Explicit as the fittest for Instruction, because it rouzes the faculties to act.' This attitude may be well intentioned, but unfortunately the strangeness and complexity in his writing which were the result have consistently repelled many readers and in his own age kept Blake virtually without influence and unknown as a poet until long after his death. The mid-nineteenth century passed before the rarer qualities of his genius were appreciated. Since then his reputation has continually advanced, until today he stands among his admirers in danger of overpraise. But when the current vogue is over, Blake will endure. His is the triumph of poetic faith. He quickens the imagination of men, tears away the shell of the earth, and reads the book of truth 'not with but through the eye.'

> A double vision my eyes do see,
> And a double vision is always with me.

Blake is both 'inspired' and 'prophetic.' He anticipates much that is accounted new in our own day. Among thinkers and writers who resemble or use him may be named Freud, Jung, Kahlil Gibran, Auden, Spender, Day Lewis, Elinor Wylie, and D. H. Lawrence. It is probable that for years to come the intellectuals will not cease to grapple with Blake's subjective world. Most readers, however, will not be most impressed by the prophetic books, but by his lucid and searching lyrics. It is here that 'thought and speech are one and passion is sublimated into vision.' Among the lyrics the last express an even more noble indignation than *Songs of Experience.* Unsurpassed for intensity are the spirited scorn of 'Mock on, mock on, Voltaire, Rousseau,' and the valiant battle-shout of 'Bring me my chariot of fire!'

From POETICAL SKETCHES

(Published 1783)

TO SPRING

O THOU with dewy locks, who lookest down
Thro' the clear windows of the morning, turn
Thine angel eyes upon our western isle,
Which in full choir hails thy approach, O Spring!

The hills tell each other, and the list'ning
Vallies hear; all our longing eyes are turned
Up to thy bright pavillions: issue forth,
And let thy holy feet visit our clime.

Come o'er the eastern hills, and let our winds
Kiss thy perfumed garments; let us taste   10
Thy morn and evening breath; scatter thy pearls
Upon our love-sick land that mourns for thee.

O deck her forth with thy fair fingers; pour
Thy soft kisses on her bosom; and put
Thy golden crown upon her languish'd head,
Whose modest tresses were bound up for thee!

TO THE EVENING STAR

THOU fair-hair'd angel of the evening,
Now, whilst the sun rests on the mountains, light
Thy bright torch of love; thy radiant crown
Put on, and smile upon our evening bed!
Smile on our loves, and, while thou drawest the
Blue curtains of the sky, scatter thy silver dew
On every flower that shuts its sweet eyes
In timely sleep. Let thy west wind sleep on
The lake; speak silence with thy glimmering eyes,

And wash the dusk with silver. Soon, full soon, 10
Dost thou withdraw; then the wolf rages wide,
And the lion glares thro' the dun forest:
The fleeces of our flocks are cover'd with
Thy sacred dew: protect them with thine influence.

TO MORNING

O HOLY virgin! clad in purest white,
Unlock heav'n's golden gates, and issue forth;
Awake the dawn that sleeps in heaven; let light
Rise from the chambers of the east, and bring
The honied dew that cometh on waking day.
O radiant morning, salute the sun,
Rouz'd like a huntsman to the chace, and, with
Thy buskin'd feet, appear upon our hills.

SONG

How sweet I roam'd from field to field,
    And tasted all the summer's pride,
'Till I the prince of love beheld,
    Who in the sunny beams did glide!

He shew'd me lilies for my hair,
    And blushing roses for my brow;
He led me through his gardens fair,
    Where all his golden pleasures grow.

With sweet May dews my wings were wet,
    And Phœbus[1] fir'd my vocal rage;   10
He caught me in his silken net,
    And shut me in his golden cage.

---

[1] Apollo, god of the sun and of poetry.

He loves to sit and hear me sing,
   Then, laughing, sports and plays with me;
Then stretches out my golden wing,
   And mocks my loss of liberty.

SONG

MY silks and fine array,
   My smiles and languish'd air,
By love are driv'n away;
   And mournful lean Despair
Brings me yew to deck my grave:
Such end true lovers have.

His face is fair as heav'n,
   When springing buds unfold;
O why to him was't giv'n,
   Whose heart is wintry cold?   10
His breast is love's all worship'd tomb,
Where all love's pilgrims come.

Bring me an axe and spade,
   Bring me a winding sheet;
When I my grave have made,
   Let winds and tempests beat:
Then down I'll lie, as cold as clay.
True love doth pass away!

SONG

LOVE and harmony combine,
And around our souls intwine,
While thy branches mix with mine,
And our roots together join.

Joys upon our branches sit,
Chirping loud, and singing sweet;
Like gentle streams beneath our feet
Innocence and virtue meet.

Thou the golden fruit dost bear,
I am clad in flowers fair;   10
Thy sweet boughs perfume the air,
And the turtle[1] buildeth there.

There she sits and feeds her young,
Sweet I hear her mournful song;
And thy lovely leaves among,
There is love: I hear his tongue.

There his charming nest doth lay,
There he sleeps the night away;
There he sports along the day,
And doth among our branches play.   20

---

[1] turtledove.

MAD SONG

THE wild winds weep,
   And the night is a-cold;
Come hither, Sleep,
   And my griefs unfold:
But lo! the morning peeps
   Over the eastern steeps,
And the rustling birds of dawn
The earth do scorn.

Lo! to the vault
   Of paved heaven,   10
With sorrow fraught
   My notes are driven:
They strike the ear of night,
   Make weep the eyes of day;
They make mad the roaring winds,
   And with tempests play.

Like a fiend in a cloud,
   With howling woe,
After night I do croud,
   And with night will go;   20
I turn my back to the east,
From whence comforts have increas'd;
For light doth seize my brain
With frantic pain.

SONG

FRESH from the dewy hill, the merry year
Smiles on my head, and mounts his flaming car;
Round my young brows the laurel wreathes a
    shade,
And rising glories beam around my head.

My feet are wing'd, while o'er the dewy lawn
I meet my maiden, risen like the morn:
Oh bless those holy feet, like angels' feet;
Oh bless those limbs, beaming with heav'nly light!

Like as an angel glitt'ring in the sky
In times of innocence and holy joy;   10
The joyful shepherd stops his grateful song
To hear the music of an angel's tongue.

So when she speaks, the voice of Heaven I hear:
So when we walk, nothing impure comes near;
Each field seems Eden, and each calm retreat;
Each village seems the haunt of holy feet.

But that sweet village, where my black-ey'd maid
Closes her eyes in sleep beneath night's shade,
Whene'er I enter, more than mortal fire
Burns in my soul, and does my song inspire.   20

TO THE MUSES

['In these lines the eighteenth century dies to music.' —Symons.]

WHETHER on Ida's shady brow,[1]
  Or in the chambers of the East,
The chambers of the sun, that now
  From antient melody have ceas'd;

Whether in Heav'n ye wander fair,
  Or the green corners of the earth,
Or the blue regions of the air,
  Where the melodious winds have birth;

Whether on chrystal rocks ye rove,
  Beneath the bosom of the sea   10
Wand'ring in many a coral grove,
  Fair Nine, forsaking Poetry!

How have you left the antient love
  That bards of old enjoy'd in you!
The languid strings do scarcely move!
  The sound is forc'd, the notes are few!

From SONGS OF INNOCENCE

(Published in 1789)

INTRODUCTION

[This song has been called by Ellis 'Blake's one great, if brief, Essay on Poetry.']

PIPING down the valleys wild,
Piping songs of pleasant glee,
On a cloud I saw a child,
And he laughing said to me:

'Pipe a song about a Lamb!'
So I piped with merry chear.
'Piper, pipe that song again;'
So I piped: he wept to hear.

'Drop thy pipe, thy happy pipe;
Sing thy songs of happy chear:'   10
So I sung the same again,
While he wept with joy to hear.

'Piper, sit thee down and write
In a book, that all may read.'
So he vanish'd from my sight,
And I pluck'd a hollow reed,

And I made a rural pen,
And I stain'd the water clear,

And I wrote my happy songs
Every child may joy to hear.   20

THE SHEPHERD

How sweet is the Shepherd's sweet lot!
From the morn to the evening he strays;
He shall follow his sheep all the day,
And his tongue shall be filled with praise.

For he hears the lamb's innocent call,
And he hears the ewe's tender reply;
He is watchful while they are in peace,
For they know when their Shepherd is nigh.

THE LAMB

[This song opens the world of poetry to Innocence and sounds the mystery of creation. *The Tiger* is its anti-type in *Songs of Experience.*]

  LITTLE Lamb, who made thee?
    Dost thou know who made thee?
  Gave thee life, & bid thee feed
  By the stream & o'er the mead;
  Gave thee clothing of delight,
  Softest clothing, wooly, bright;
  Gave thee such a tender voice,
  Making all the vales rejoice?
    Little Lamb, who made thee?
    Dost thou know who made thee?   10

  Little Lamb, I'll tell thee,
    Little Lamb, I'll tell thee:
  He is called by thy name,
  For he calls himself a Lamb.
  He is meek, & he is mild;
  He became a little child.
  I a child, & thou a lamb,
  We are called by his name.
    Little Lamb, God bless thee!
    Little Lamb, God bless thee!   20

THE LITTLE BLACK BOY

[This poem, a favorite with Coleridge, was inspired by the antislavery agitation of Blake's time.]

MY mother bore me in the southern wild,
And I am black, but O! my soul is white;
White as an angel is the English child,
But I am black, as if bereav'd of light.

My mother taught me underneath a tree,
And sitting down before the heat of day,

---

1 Mount Ida was famous in Greek legend as the place of worship of Cybele, mother of the gods.

She took me on her lap and kissed me,
And pointing to the east, began to say:

'Look on the rising sun: there God does live,
And gives his light, and gives his heat away;   10
And flowers and trees and beasts and man receive
Comfort in morning, joy in the noonday.

'And we are put on earth a little space,
That we may learn to bear the beams of love;
And these black bodies and this sunburnt face
Is but a cloud, and like a shady grove.

'For when our souls have learn'd that heat to bear,
The cloud will vanish; we shall hear his voice,
Saying: "Come out from the grove, my love & care,
And round my golden tent like lambs rejoice."'20

Thus did my mother say, and kissed me;
And thus I say to little English boy:
When I from black and he from white cloud free,
And round the tent of God like lambs we joy,

I'll shade him from the heat, till he can bear
To lean in joy upon our father's knee;
And then I'll stand and stroke his silver hair,
And be like him, and he will then love me.

THE CHIMNEY SWEEPER

[This poem was inspired by the agitation in Blake's
time to pass laws against the use of children as chimney
sweeps.]

WHEN my mother died I was very young,
And my father sold me while yet my tongue
Could scarcely cry ''weep! 'weep! 'weep! 'weep!'[1]
So your chimneys I sweep, & in soot I sleep.

There's little Tom Dacre, who cried when his head,
That curl'd like a lamb's back, was shav'd: so I said
'Hush, Tom! never mind it, for when your head's
       bare
You know that the soot cannot spoil your white
       hair.'

And so he was quiet, & that very night,
As Tom was a-sleeping, he had such a sight!   10
That thousands of sweepers, Dick, Joe, Ned,
       & Jack,
Were all of them lock'd up in coffins of black.

And by came an Angel who had a bright key,
And he open'd the coffins & set them all free;

---

1 ''Weep' is the little boy's lisping cry for 'sweep.'

Then down a green plain leaping, laughing, they
       run,
And wash in a river, and shine in the Sun.

Then naked & white, all their bags left behind,
They rise upon clouds and sport in the wind;
And the Angel told Tom, if he'd be a good boy,
He'd have God for his father, & never want joy. 20

And so Tom awoke; and we rose in the dark,
And got with our bags & our brushes to work.
Tho' the morning was cold, Tom was happy &
       warm;
So if all do their duty they need not fear harm.

THE LITTLE BOY LOST

[*The Little Boy Lost* and *The Little Boy Found* are
meant to be read as one poem. The theme, a favorite
with Blake, is the protection of Divine providence.]

'FATHER! father! where are you going?
O do not walk so fast.
Speak, father, speak to your little boy,
Or else I shall be lost.'

The night was dark, no father was there;
The child was wet with dew;
The mire was deep, & the child did weep,
And away the vapour flew.

THE LITTLE BOY FOUND

THE little boy lost in the lonely fen,
Led by the wand'ring light,
Began to cry; but God, ever nigh,
Appear'd like his father in white.

He kissed the child & by the hand led
And to his mother brought,
Who in sorrow pale, thro' the lonely dale,
Her little boy weeping sought.

LAUGHING SONG

WHEN the green woods laugh with the voice of
       joy,
And the dimpling stream runs laughing by;
When the air does laugh with our merry wit,
And the green hill laughs with the noise of it;

When the meadows laugh with lively green,
And the grasshopper laughs in the merry scene,
When Mary and Susan and Emily
With their sweet round mouths sing 'Ha, Ha, He!'

When the painted birds laugh in the shade,
Where our table with cherries and nuts is spread, 10
Come live & be merry, and join with me,
To sing the sweet chorus of 'Ha, Ha, He!'

A CRADLE SONG

SWEET dreams, form a shade
O'er my lovely infant's head;
Sweet dreams of pleasant streams
By happy, silent, moony beams.

Sweet sleep, with soft down
Weave thy brows an infant crown.
Sweet sleep, Angel mild,
Hover o'er my happy child.

Sweet smiles, in the night
Hover over my delight;   10
Sweet smiles, Mother's smiles,
All the livelong night beguiles.

Sweet moans, dovelike sighs,
Chase not slumber from thy eyes.
Sweet moans, sweeter smiles,
All the dovelike moans beguiles.

Sleep, sleep, happy child,
All creation slept and smil'd;
Sleep, sleep, happy sleep,
While o'er thee thy mother weep.   20

Sweet babe, in thy face
Holy image I can trace.
Sweet babe, once like thee,
Thy maker lay and wept for me,

Wept for me, for thee, for all,
When he was an infant small.
Thou his image ever see,
Heavenly face that smiles on thee,

Smiles on thee, on me, on all;
Who became an infant small.   30
Infant smiles are his own smiles;
Heaven & earth to peace beguiles.

THE DIVINE IMAGE

To Mercy, Pity, Peace, and Love
All pray in their distress;
And to these virtues of delight
Return their thankfulness.

For Mercy, Pity, Peace, and Love
Is God, our father dear,
And Mercy, Pity, Peace, and Love
Is Man, his child and care.

For Mercy has a human heart,
Pity a human face,   10
And Love, the human form divine,
And Peace, the human dress.

Then every man, of every clime,
That prays in his distress,
Prays to the human form divine,
Love, Mercy, Pity, Peace.

And all must love the human form,
In heathen, turk, or jew;
Where Mercy, Love & Pity dwell
There God is dwelling too.   20

HOLY THURSDAY

'TWAS on a Holy Thursday, their innocent faces
    clean,
The children walking two & two, in red & blue &
    green,
Grey-headed beadles walk'd before, with wands
    as white as snow,
Till into the high dome of Paul's[1] they like Thames'
    waters flow.

O what a multitude they seem'd, these flowers of
    London town!
Seated in companies they sit with radiance all
    their own.
The hum of multitudes was there, but multitudes
    of lambs,
Thousands of little boys & girls raising their inno-
    cent hands.

Now like a mighty wind they raise to heaven the
    voice of song,
Or like harmonious thunderings the seats of
    Heaven among.   10
Beneath them sit the aged men, wise guardians of
    the poor;
Then cherish pity, lest you drive an angel from
    your door.

NIGHT

[This poem is notable for the sheer perfection of its lyrical phrase and for 'the marvelous adaptation of exter-

---

1 Saint Paul's Cathedral, where London's orphan children congregated each Thursday for worship.

nal variations in rhythm and pattern to the inner meaning.' The world is still in Innocence, but the mood is
wistful and wild animals haunt the border regions of
human fears.]

THE sun descending in the west,
The evening star does shine;
The birds are silent in their nest,
And I must seek for mine.
The moon like a flower
In heaven's high bower,
With silent delight
Sits and smiles on the night.

Farewell, green fields and happy groves,
Where flocks have took delight.   10
Where lambs have nibbled, silent moves
The feet of angels bright;
Unseen they pour blessing
And joy without ceasing,
On each bud and blossom,
And each sleeping bosom.

They look in every thoughtless nest,
Where birds are cover'd warm;
They visit caves of every beast,
To keep them all from harm.   20
If they see any weeping
That should have been sleeping,
They pour sleep on their head,
And sit down by their bed.

When wolves and tygers howl for prey,
They pitying stand and weep;
Seeking to drive their thirst away,
And keep them from the sheep;
But if they rush dreadful,
The angels, most heedful,   30
Receive each mild spirit,
New worlds to inherit.

And there the lion's ruddy eyes
Shall flow with tears of gold,
And pitying the tender cries,
And walking round the fold,
Saying 'Wrath, by his meekness,
And by his health, sickness
Is driven away
From our immortal day.   40

'And now beside thee, bleating lamb,
I can lie down and sleep;
Or think on him who bore thy name,
Graze after thee and weep.
For, wash'd in life's river,
My bright mane for ever

Shall shine like the gold
As I guard o'er the fold.'

NURSE'S SONG

WHEN the voices of children are heard on the
    green
And laughing is heard on the hill,
My heart is at rest within my breast
And everything else is still.

'Then come home, my children, the sun is gone
    down
And the dews of night arise;
Come, come, leave off play, and let us away
Till the morning appears in the skies.'

'No, no, let us play, for it is yet day
And we cannot go to sleep;   10
Besides, in the sky the little birds fly
And the hills are all cover'd with sheep.'

'Well, well, go & play till the light fades away
And then go home to bed.'
The little ones leaped & shouted & laugh'd
And all the hills ecchoed.

A DREAM

ONCE a dream did weave a shade
O'er my Angel-guarded bed,
That an Emmet[1] lost its way
Where on grass methought I lay.

Troubled, 'wilder'd, and forlorn,
Dark, benighted, travel-worn,
Over many a tangled spray,
All heart-broke I heard her say:

'O, my children! do they cry?
Do they hear their father sigh?   10
Now they look abroad to see:
Now return and weep for me.'

Pitying, I drop'd a tear;
But I saw a glow-worm near,
Who replied: 'What wailing wight
Calls the watchman of the night?

'I am set to light the ground,
While the beetle goes his round:
Follow now the beetle's hum;
Little wanderer, hie thee home.'   20

---

1 ant.

ON ANOTHER'S SORROW

CAN I see another's woe,
And not be in sorrow too?
Can I see another's grief,
And not seek for kind relief?

Can I see a falling tear,
And not feel my sorrow's share?
Can a father see his child
Weep, nor be with sorrow fill'd?

Can a mother sit and hear
An infant groan an infant fear?   10
No, no! never can it be!
Never, never can it be!

And can he who smiles on all
Hear the wren with sorrows small,
Hear the small bird's grief & care,
Hear the woes that infants bear,

And not sit beside the nest,
Pouring pity in their breast;
And not sit the cradle near,
Weeping tear on infant's tear;   20

And not sit both night & day,
Wiping all our tears away?
O, no! never can it be!
Never, never can it be!

He doth give his joy to all;
He becomes an infant small;
He becomes a man of woe;
He doth feel the sorrow too.

Think not thou canst sigh a sigh
And thy maker is not by;   30
Think not thou canst weep a tear
And thy maker is not near.

O! he gives to us his joy
That our grief he may destroy;
Till our grief is fled & gone
He doth sit by us and moan.

From SONGS OF EXPERIENCE

(Published in 1794)

INTRODUCTION

HEAR the voice of the Bard!
Who Present, Past, & Future, sees:

Whose ears have heard
The Holy Word
That walk'd among the ancient trees,

Calling the lapsed Soul,
And weeping in the evening dew;
That might controll
The starry pole,
And fallen, fallen light renew!   10

'O Earth, O Earth, return!
Arise from out the dewy grass;
Night is worn,
And the morn
Rises from the slumberous mass.

'Turn away no more;
Why wilt thou turn away?
The starry floor,
The wat'ry shore,
Is giv'n thee till the break of day.'   20

EARTH'S ANSWER

EARTH rais'd up her head
From the darkness dread & drear.
Her light fled,
Stony dread!
And her locks cover'd with grey despair.

'Prison'd on wat'ry shore,
Starry Jealousy does keep my den:
Cold and hoar,
Weeping o'er,
I hear the father of the ancient men.   10

'Selfish father of men!
Cruel, jealous, selfish fear!
Can delight,
Chain'd in night,
The virgins of youth and morning bear?

'Does spring hide its joy
When buds and blossoms grow?
Does the sower
Sow by night
Or the plowman in darkness plow?   20

'Break this heavy chain
That does freeze my bones around.
Selfish! vain!
Eternal bane!
That free Love with bondage bound.'

THE CLOD AND THE PEBBLE

[This poem sets forth the contrary states of Innocence and Experience as expressed in unselfish and selfish love.]

'LOVE seeketh not Itself to please,
Nor for itself hath any care,
But for another gives its ease,
And builds a Heaven in Hell's despair.'

So sung a little Clod of Clay
Trodden with the cattle's feet,
But a Pebble of the brook
Warbled out these metres meet:

'Love seeketh only Self to please,
To bind another to Its delight,   10
Joys in another's loss of ease,
And builds a Hell in Heaven's despite.'

HOLY THURSDAY

Is this a holy thing to see
In a rich and fruitful land,
Babes reduc'd to misery,
Fed with cold and usurous hand?

Is that trembling cry a song?
Can it be a song of joy?
And so many children poor?
It is a land of poverty!

And their sun does never shine,
And their fields are bleak & bare,   10
And their ways are fill'd with thorns:
It is eternal winter there.

For where-e'er the sun does shine,
And where-e'er the rain does fall,
Babe can never hunger there,
Nor poverty the mind appall.

NURSE'S SONG

WHEN the voices of children are heard on the
    green
And whisp'rings are in the dale,
The days of my youth rise fresh in my mind,
My face turns green and pale.

Then come home, my children, the sun is gone
    down
And the dews of night arise;
Your spring & your day are wasted in play,
And your winter and night in disguise.

THE ANGEL

[This poem describes the tragedy of concealed love.]

I DREAMT a Dream! what can it mean?
And that I was a maiden Queen,
Guarded by an Angel mild:
Witless woe was ne'er beguil'd!

And I wept both night and day,
And he wip'd my tears away,
And I wept both day and night,
And hid from him my heart's delight.

So he took his wings and fled;
Then the morn blush'd rosy red;   10
I dried my tears, & arm'd my fears
With ten thousand shields and spears.

Soon my Angel came again:
I was arm'd, he came in vain;
For the time of youth was fled,
And grey hairs were on my head.

THE TYGER

[This is one of the very great poems in the English language and the best known of all Blake's works.]

TYGER! Tyger! burning bright
In the forests of the night,
What immortal hand or eye
Could frame thy fearful symmetry?

In what distant deeps or skies
Burnt the fire of thine eyes?
On what wings dare he aspire?
What the hand dare sieze the fire?

And what shoulder, & what art,
Could twist the sinews of thy heart?   10
And when thy heart began to beat,
What dread hand? & what dread feet?

What the hammer? what the chain?
In what furnace was thy brain?
What the anvil? what dread grasp
Dare its deadly terrors clasp?

When the stars threw down their spears,
And water'd heaven with their tears,
Did he smile his work to see?
Did he who made the Lamb make thee?   20

Tyger! Tyger! burning bright
In the forests of the night,
What immortal hand or eye,
Dare frame thy fearful symmetry?

AH, SUN-FLOWER

[The sunflower, rooted in earth, symbolizes man bound
by the flesh yet ever yearning for freedom of the spirit.]

AH, Sun-flower! weary of time,
Who countest the steps of the Sun,
Seeking after that sweet golden clime
Where the traveller's journey is done:

Where the Youth pined away with desire,
And the pale Virgin shrouded in snow
Arise from their graves, and aspire
Where my Sun-flower wishes to go.

THE GARDEN OF LOVE

[This is a characteristic poem on the sanctity of natural
love and the cruelty of religious prohibitions.]

I WENT to the Garden of Love,
And saw what I never had seen:
A Chapel was built in the midst,
Where I used to play on the green.

And the gates of this Chapel were shut,
And 'Thou shalt not' writ over the door;
So I turn'd to the Garden of Love
That so many sweet flowers bore;

And I saw it was filled with graves,
And tomb-stones where flowers should be;   10
And Priests in black gowns were walking their
        rounds,
And binding with briars my joys & desires.

LONDON

I WANDER thro' each charter'd street,
Near where the charter'd Thames does flow,
And mark in every face I meet
Marks of weakness, marks of woe.

In every cry of every Man,
In every Infant's cry of fear,
In every voice, in every ban,
The mind-forg'd manacles I hear.

How the Chimney-sweeper's cry
Every black'ning Church appalls;   10

And the hapless Soldier's sigh
Runs in blood down Palace walls.

But most thro' midnight streets I hear
How the youthful Harlot's curse
Blasts the new born Infant's tear,
And blights with plagues the Marriage hearse.

THE HUMAN ABSTRACT

PITY would be no more
If we did not make somebody Poor;
And Mercy no more could be
If all were as happy as we.

And mutual fear brings peace,
Till the selfish loves increase:
Then Cruelty knits a snare,
And spreads his baits with care.

He sits down with holy fears,
And waters the ground with tears;   10
Then Humility takes its root
Underneath his foot.

Soon spreads the dismal shade
Of Mystery over his head;
And the Catterpiller and Fly
Feed on the Mystery.

And it bears the fruit of Deceit,
Ruddy and sweet to eat;
And the Raven his nest has made
In its thickest shade.   20

The Gods of the earth and sea
Sought thro' Nature to find this Tree;
But their search was all in vain:
There grows one in the Human Brain.

A POISON TREE

[This poem treats of the terrifying consequence of suppressed anger.]

I WAS angry with my friend:
I told my wrath, my wrath did end.
I was angry with my foe:
I told it not, my wrath did grow.

And I water'd it in fears,
Night & morning with my tears;
And I sunned it with smiles,
And with soft deceitful wiles.

And it grew both day and night,
Till it bore an apple bright;   10
And my foe beheld it shine,
And he knew that it was mine,

And into my garden stole
When the night had veil'd the pole:
In the morning glad I see
My foe outstretch'd beneath the tree.

A LITTLE BOY LOST

'NOUGHT loves another as itself,
Nor venerates another so,
Nor is it possible to Thought
A greater than itself to know:

'And Father, how can I love you
Or any of my brothers more?
I love you like the little bird
That picks up crumbs around the door.'

The Priest sat by and heard the child,
In trembling zeal he siez'd his hair: 10
He led him by his little coat,
And all admir'd the Priestly care.

And standing on the altar high,
'Lo! what a fiend is here!' said he,
'One who sets reason up for judge
Of our most holy Mystery.'

The weeping child could not be heard,
The weeping parents wept in vain;
They strip'd him to his little shirt,
And bound him in an iron chain;   20

And burn'd him in a holy place,
Where many had been burn'd before:
The weeping parents wept in vain.
Are such things done on Albion's[1] shore?

TO TIRZAH

[This poem is a late addition to *Songs of Experience*.]

WHATE'ER is Born of Mortal Birth
Must be consumed with the Earth
To rise from Generation free:
Then what have I to do with thee?

The Sexes sprung from Shame & Pride,
Blow'd in the morn; in evening died;

But Mercy chang'd Death into Sleep;
The Sexes rose to work & weep.

Thou, Mother of my Mortal part,
With cruelty didst mould my Heart,   10
And with false self-decieving tears
Didst bind my Nostrils, Eyes, & Ears:

Didst close my Tongue in senseless clay,
And me to Mortal Life betray.
The Death of Jesus set me free:
Then what have I to do with thee?

THE BOOK OF THEL

[This fragile and beautiful narrative, the simplest of
Blake's longer poems, makes use of the imagery of psychological symbols such as that found throughout the
later prophecies.]

THEL'S MOTTO

Does the Eagle know what is in the pit?
Or wilt thou go ask the Mole?
Can Wisdom be put in a silver rod?
Or Love in a golden bowl?

I

THE daughters of the Seraphim led round their
      sunny flocks,
All but the youngest: she in paleness sought the
      secret air,
To fade away like morning beauty from her mor-
      tal day:
Down by the river of Adona her soft voice is
      heard,
And thus her gentle lamentation falls like morn-
      ing dew:

'O life of this our spring! why fades the lotus of
      the water,
Why fade these children of the spring, born but
      to smile & fall?
Ah! Thel is like a wat'ry bow, and like a parting
      cloud;
Like a reflection in a glass; like shadows in the
      water;
Like dreams of infants, like a smile upon an
      infant's face;   10
Like the dove's voice; like transient day; like
      music in the air.
Ah! gentle may I lay me down, and gentle rest
      my head,
And gentle sleep the sleep of death, and gentle
      hear the voice
Of him that walketh in the garden in the evening
      time.'

---

1 England's.

The Lilly of the valley, breathing in the humble
    grass,
Answer'd the lovely maid and said: 'I am a wat'ry
    weed,
And I am very small and love to dwell in lowly
    vales;
So weak, the gilded butterfly scarce perches on
    my head.
Yet I am visited from heaven, and he that smiles
    on all
Walks in the valley and each morn over me
    spreads his hand,   20
Saying, "Rejoice, thou humble grass, thou new-
    born lilly flower,
Thou gentle maid of silent valleys and of modest
    brooks;
For thou shalt be clothed in light, and fed with
    morning manna,
Till summer's heat melts thee beside the foun-
    tains and the springs
To flourish in eternal vales." Then why should
    Thel complain?
Why should the mistress of the vales of Har utter
    a sigh?'

She ceas'd & smil'd in tears, then sat down in her
    silver shrine.

Thel answer'd: 'Oh thou little virgin of the peace-
    ful valley,
Giving to those that cannot crave, the voiceless,
    the o'er-tired;
Thy breath doth nourish the innocent lamb, he
    smells thy milky garments,   30
He crops thy flowers while thou sittest smiling
    in his face,
Wiping his mild and meekin mouth from all con-
    tagious taints.
Thy wine doth purify the golden honey; thy per-
    fume,
Which thou dost scatter on every little blade of
    grass that springs,
Revives the milked cow, & tames the fire-breath-
    ing steed.
But Thel is like a faint cloud kindled at the rising
    sun:
I vanish from my pearly throne, and who shall
    find my place?'

'Queen of the vales,' the Lilly answer'd, 'ask the
    tender cloud,
And it shall tell thee why it glitters in the morn-
    ing sky,
And why it scatters its bright beauty thro' the
    humid air.   40

Descend, O little Cloud, & hover before the eyes
    of Thel.'

The Cloud descended, and the Lilly bow'd her
    modest head
And went to mind her numerous charge among
    the verdant grass.

II

'O little Cloud,' the virgin said, 'I charge thee tell
    to me
Why thou complainest not when in one hour
    thou fade away:
Then we shall seek thee, but not find. Ah! Thel
    is like to thee:
I pass away: yet I complain, and no one hears
    my voice.'

The Cloud then shew'd his golden head & his
    bright form emerg'd,
Hovering and glittering on the air before the face
    of Thel.

'O virgin, know'st thou not our steeds drink of
    the golden springs   50
Where Luvah doth renew his horses? Look'st thou
    on my youth,
And fearest thou, because I vanish and am seen
    no more,
Nothing remains? O maid, I tell thee, when I
    pass away
It is to tenfold life, to love, to peace and raptures
    holy:
Unseen descending, weigh my light wings upon
    balmy flowers,
And court the fair-eyed dew to take me to her
    shining tent:
The weeping virgin, trembling kneels before the
    risen sun,
Till we arise link'd in a golden band and never
    part,
But walk united, bearing food to all our tender
    flowers.'

'Dost thou, O little Cloud? I fear that I am not
    like thee,   60
For I walk thro' the vales of Har, and smell the
    sweetest flowers,
But I feed not the little flowers; I hear the war-
    bling birds,
But I feed not the warbling birds; they fly and
    seek their food:
But Thel delights in these no more, because I
    fade away;

And all shall say, "Without a use this shining
    woman liv'd,
Or did she only live to be at death the food of
    worms?"'

The Cloud reclin'd upon his airy throne and an-
    swer'd thus:

'Then if thou art the food of worms, O virgin of
    the skies,
How great thy use, how great thy blessing! Every
    thing that lives
Lives not alone nor for itself. Fear not, and I will
    call   70
The weak worm from its lowly bed, and thou
    shalt hear its voice.
Come forth, worm of the silent valley, to thy pen-
    sive queen.'

The helpless worm arose, and sat upon the Lilly's
    leaf,
And the bright Cloud sail'd on, to find his partner
    in the vale.

III

Then Thel astonish'd view'd the Worm upon its
    dewy bed.

'Art thou a Worm? Image of weakness, art thou
    but a Worm?
I see thee like an infant wrapped in the Lilly's
    leaf.
Ah! weep not, little voice, thou canst not speak,
    but thou canst weep.
Is this a Worm? I see thee lay helpless & naked,
    weeping,
And none to answer, none to cherish thee with
    mother's smiles.'   80

The Clod of Clay heard the Worm's voice & rais'd
    her pitying head:
She bow'd over the weeping infant, and her life
    exhal'd
In milky fondness: then on Thel she fix'd her
    humble eyes.

'O beauty of the vales of Har! we live not for
    ourselves.
Thou seest me the meanest thing, and so I am
    indeed.
My bosom of itself is cold, and of itself is dark;
But he, that loves the lowly, pours his oil upon
    my head,
And kisses me, and binds his nuptial bands
    around my breast,

And says: "Thou mother of my children, I have
    loved thee
And I have given thee a crown that none can
    take away."   90
But how this is, sweet maid, I know not, and I
    cannot know;
I ponder, and I cannot ponder; yet I live and
    love.'

The daughter of beauty wip'd her pitying tears
    with her white veil,
And said: 'Alas! I knew not this, and therefore
    did I weep.
That God would love a Worm I knew, and pun-
    ish the evil foot
That wilful bruis'd its helpless form; but that he
    cherish'd it
With milk and oil I never knew, and therefore
    did I weep;
And I complain'd in the mild air, because I fade
    away,
And lay me down in thy cold bed, and leave my
    shining lot.'

'Queen of the vales,' the matron Clay answer'd,
    'I heard thy sighs,   100
And all thy moans flew o'er my roof, but I have
    call'd them down.
Wilt thou, O Queen, enter my house? 'Tis given
    thee to enter
And to return: fear nothing, enter with thy vir-
    gin feet.'

IV

The eternal gates' terrific porter lifted the north-
    ern bar:
Thel enter'd in & saw the secrets of the land un-
    known.
She saw the couches of the dead, & where the
    fibrous roots
Of every heart on earth infixes deep its restless
    twists:
A land of sorrows & of tears where never smile
    was seen.

She wander'd in the land of clouds thro' valleys
    dark, list'ning
Dolours & lamentations; waiting oft beside a
    dewy grave   110
She stood in silence, list'ning to the voices of the
    ground,
Till to her own grave plot she came, & there she
    sat down,
And heard this voice of sorrow breathed from
    the hollow pit.

'Why cannot the Ear be closed to its own destruc-
  tion?
Or the glist'ning Eye to the poison of a smile?
Why are Eyelids stor'd with arrows ready drawn,
Where a thousand fighting men in ambush lie?
Or an Eye of gifts & graces show'ring fruits &
  coined gold?
Why a Tongue impress'd with honey from every
  wind?
Why an Ear, a whirlpool fierce to draw creations
  in?   120
Why a Nostril wide inhaling terror, trembling, &
  affright?
Why a tender curb upon the youthful burning
  boy?
Why a little curtain of flesh on the bed of our
  desire?'

The Virgin started from her seat, & with a shriek
Fled back unhinder'd till she came into the vales
  of Har.

                                                1789

THE MARRIAGE OF HEAVEN AND HELL

[*The Marriage of Heaven and Hell* is fragmentary in
character, yet it contains in essentials all of Blake's mature philosophy. The poet has brought into harmony the
seemingly irreconcilable contraries of Heaven (spiritual
life) and of Hell (instinctive life).]

RINTRAH[1] roars & shakes his fires in the burden'd air;
Hungry clouds swag on the deep.

Once meek, and in a perilous path,
The just man kept his course along
The vale of death.
Roses are planted where thorns grow,
And on the barren heath
Sing the honey bees.

Then the perilous path was planted,
And a river and a spring   10
On every cliff and tomb,
And on the bleached bones
Red clay brought forth;

Till the villain left the paths of ease,
To walk in perilous paths, and drive
The just man into barren climes.

Now the sneaking serpent walks
In mild humility,
And the just man rages in the wilds
Where lions roam.   20

Rintrah roars & shakes his fires in the burden'd
  air;
Hungry clouds swag on the deep.

As a new heaven is begun, and it is now thirty-
three years since its advent, the Eternal Hell revives. And lo! Swedenborg is the Angel sitting at
the tomb: his writings are the linen clothes folded
up.[2] Now is the dominion of Edom, & the return
of Adam into Paradise. See Isaiah xxxiv & xxxv
Chap.

Without Contraries is no progression. Attraction and Repulsion, Reason and Energy, Love
and Hate, are necessary to Human existence.

From these contraries spring what the religious
call Good & Evil. Good is the passive that obeys
Reason. Evil is the active springing from Energy.

Good is Heaven. Evil is Hell.

THE VOICE OF THE DEVIL

All Bibles or sacred codes have been the causes
of the following Errors:

1. That Man has two real existing principles:
Viz: a Body & a Soul.

2. That Energy, call'd Evil, is alone from the
Body; & that Reason, call'd Good, is alone from
the Soul.

3. That God will torment Man in Eternity for
following his Energies.

But the following Contraries to these are True:

1. Man has no Body distinct from his Soul; for
that call'd Body is a portion of Soul discern'd by
the five Senses, the chief inlets of Soul in this age.

2. Energy is the only life, and is from the Body;
and Reason is the bound or outward circumference of Energy.

3. Energy is Eternal Delight.

Those who restrain desire, do so because theirs
is weak enough to be restrained; and the restrainer
or reason usurps its place & governs the unwilling.

---

1 Rintrah is a daemon of wrath and fury. The significance of the
symbol in the present passage is obscure, but may represent the
malignity that figures as morality in the scheme of the 'Angel' in
the argument. It would thus serve usefully to stir the mental forces
of the 'Devil' (the poet).

2 Emanuel Swedenborg (1688–1772) was a Swedish scientist, philosopher, and mystic. His belief in the spiritual symbolism of the
material world and his interpretation of the Bible in accordance
with this belief had a lasting effect on Blake's thought. However,
Blake came to see limitations in his former master and in 1790
(thirty-three years after Swedenborg's announcement that 1757
was the first year of the New Age) began his *Marriage of Heaven
and Hell* in refutation of Swedenborg's more conventional views.

And being restrain'd, it by degrees becomes passive, till it is only the shadow of desire.

The history of this is written in Paradise Lost, & the Governor or Reason is call'd Messiah.

And the original Archangel, or possessor of the command of the heavenly host, is call'd the Devil or Satan, and his children are call'd Sin & Death.

But in the Book of Job, Milton's Messiah is call'd Satan.

For this history has been adopted by both parties.

It indeed appear'd to Reason as if Desire was cast out; but the Devil's account is, that the Messiah fell, & formed a heaven of what he stole from the Abyss.

This is shewn in the Gospel, where he prays to the Father to send the comforter, or Desire, that Reason may have Ideas to build on; the Jehovah of the Bible being no other than he who dwells in flaming fire.

Know that after Christ's death, he became Jehovah.

But in Milton, the Father is Destiny, the Son a Ratio of the five senses, & the Holy-ghost Vacuum!

NOTE: The reason Milton wrote in fetters when he wrote of Angels & God, and at liberty when of Devils & Hell, is because he was a true Poet and of the Devil's party without knowing it.

A MEMORABLE FANCY

As I was walking among the fires of hell, delighted with the enjoyments of Genius, which to Angels look like torment and insanity, I collected some of their Proverbs; thinking that as the sayings used in a nation mark its character, so the Proverbs of Hell show the nature of Infernal wisdom better than any description of buildings or garments.

When I came home: on the abyss of the five senses, where a flat sided steep frowns over the present world, I saw a mighty Devil folded in black clouds, hovering on the sides of the rock: with corroding fires he wrote the following sentence now percieved by the minds of men, & read by them on earth:

How do you know but ev'ry Bird that cuts the airy way,
Is an immense world of delight, clos'd by your senses five?

PROVERBS OF HELL

In seed time learn, in harvest teach, in winter enjoy.

Drive your cart and your plow over the bones of the dead.

The road of excess leads to the palace of wisdom.

Prudence is a rich, ugly old maid courted by Incapacity.

He who desires but acts not, breeds pestilence.

The cut worm forgives the plow.

Dip him in the river who loves water.

A fool sees not the same tree that a wise man sees.

He whose face gives no light, shall never become a star.

Eternity is in love with the productions of time.

The busy bee has no time for sorrow.

The hours of folly are measur'd by the clock; but of wisdom, no clock can measure.

All wholesome food is caught without a net or a trap.

Bring out number, weight & measure in a year of dearth.

No bird soars too high, if he soars with his own wings.

A dead body revenges not injuries.

The most sublime act is to set another before you.

If the fool would persist in his folly he would become wise.

Folly is the cloke of knavery.

Shame is Pride's cloke.

Prisons are built with stones of Law, Brothels with bricks of Religion.

The pride of the peacock is the glory of God.

The lust of the goat is the bounty of God.

The wrath of the lion is the wisdom of God.

The nakedness of woman is the work of God.

Excess of sorrow laughs. Excess of joy weeps.

The roaring of lions, the howling of wolves, the raging of the stormy sea, and the destructive sword, are portions of eternity, too great for the eye of man.

The fox condemns the trap, not himself.

Joys impregnate. Sorrows bring forth.

Let man wear the fell of the lion, woman the fleece of the sheep.

The bird a nest, the spider a web, man friendship.

The selfish, smiling fool, & the sullen, frowning fool shall be both thought wise, that they may be a rod.

What is now proved was once only imagin'd.

The rat, the mouse, the fox, the rabbet watch the roots; the lion, the tyger, the horse, the elephant watch the fruits.

The cistern contains: the fountain overflows.

One thought fills immensity.

Always be ready to speak your mind, and a base man will avoid you.

Every thing possible to be believ'd is an image of truth.

The eagle never lost so much time as when he submitted to learn of the crow.

The fox provides for himself, but God provides for the lion.

Think in the morning. Act in the noon. Eat in the evening. Sleep in the night.

He who has suffer'd you to impose on him, knows you.

As the plow follows words, so God rewards prayers.

The tygers of wrath are wiser than the horses of instruction.

Expect poison from the standing water.

You never know what is enough unless you know what is more than enough.

Listen to the fool's reproach! it is a kingly title!

The eyes of fire, the nostrils of air, the mouth of water, the beard of earth.

The weak in courage is strong in cunning.

The apple tree never asks the beech how he shall grow; nor the lion, the horse, how he shall take his prey.

The thankful reciever bears a plentiful harvest.

If others had not been foolish, we should be so.

The soul of sweet delight can never be defil'd.

When thou seest an Eagle, thou seest a portion of Genius; lift up thy head!

As the caterpiller chooses the fairest leaves to lay her eggs on, so the priest lays his curse on the fairest joys.

To create a little flower is the labour of ages.

Damn braces. Bless relaxes.

The best wine is the oldest, the best water the newest.

Prayers plow not! Praises reap not!

Joys laugh not! Sorrows weep not!

The head Sublime, the heart Pathos, the genitals Beauty, the hands & feet Proportion.

As the air to a bird or the sea to a fish, so is contempt to the contemptible.

The crow wish'd every thing was black, the owl that every thing was white.

Exuberance is Beauty.

If the lion was advised by the fox, he would be cunning.

Improvement makes strait roads; but the crooked roads without Improvement are roads of Genius.

Sooner murder an infant in its cradle than nurse unacted desires.

Where man is not, nature is barren.

Truth can never be told so as to be understood, and not be believ'd.

Enough! or Too much.

The ancient Poets animated all sensible objects with Gods or Geniuses, calling them by the names and adorning them with the properties of woods, rivers, mountains, lakes, cities, nations, and whatever their enlarged & numerous senses could percieve.

And particularly they studied the genius of each city & country, placing it under its mental deity;

Till a system was formed, which some took advantage of, & enslav'd the vulgar by attempting to realize or abstract the mental deities from their objects: thus began Priesthood;

Choosing forms of worship from poetic tales.

And at length they pronounc'd that the Gods had order'd such things.

Thus men forgot that All deities reside in the human breast.

A MEMORABLE FANCY

The Prophets Isaiah and Ezekiel dined with me, and I asked them how they dared so roundly to assert that God spoke to them; and whether they did not think at the time that they would be misundersood, & so be the cause of imposition.

Isaiah answer'd: 'I saw no God, nor heard any, in a finite organical perception; but my senses discover'd the infinite in everything, and as I was then perswaded, & remain confirm'd, that the voice of honest indignation is the voice of God, I cared not for consequences, but wrote.'

Then I asked: 'Does a firm perswasion that a thing is so, make it so?'

He replied: 'All poets believe that it does, & in ages of imagination this firm perswasion removed mountains; but many are not capable of a firm perswasion of any thing.'

Then Ezekiel said: 'The philosophy of the east taught the first principles of human perception: some nations held one principle for the origin, and some another: we of Israel taught that the Poetic Genius (as you now call it) was the first principle and all the others merely derivative, which was the cause of our despising the Priests & Philosophers of other countries, and prophecying that all Gods would at last be proved to originate in ours & to be the tributaries of the Poetic Genius; it was this that our great poet, King David, desired so fervently & invokes so pathetic'ly, saying by this he conquers enemies & governs kingdoms; and we so loved our God, that we cursed in his name all the deities of surrounding nations, and asserted that they had rebelled: from these opinions the vulgar came to think that all nations would at last be subject to the jews.'

'This,' said he, 'like all firm perswasions, is come to pass; for all nations believe the jews' code and worship the jews' god, and what greater subjection can be?'

I heard this with some wonder, & must confess my own conviction. After dinner I ask'd Isaiah to favour the world with his lost works; he said none of equal value was lost. Ezekiel said the same of his.

I also asked Isaiah what made him go naked and barefoot three years? he answer'd: 'the same that made our friend Diogenes, the Grecian.'

I then asked Ezekiel why he eat dung & lay so long on his right & left side? he answer'd, 'the desire of raising other men into a perception of the infinite: this the North American tribes practise, & is he honest who resists his genius or conscience only for the sake of present ease or gratification?'

The ancient tradition that the world will be consumed in fire at the end of six thousand years is true, as I have heard from Hell.

For the cherub with his flaming sword is hereby commanded to leave his guard at tree of life; and when he does, the whole creation will be consumed and appear infinite and holy, whereas it now appears finite & corrupt.

This will come to pass by an improvement of sensual enjoyment.

But first the notion that man has a body distinct from his soul is to be expunged; this I shall do by printing in the infernal method, by corrosives, which in Hell are salutary and medicinal, melting apparent surfaces away, and displaying the infinite which was hid.

If the doors of perception were cleansed every thing would appear to man as it is, infinite.

For man has closed himself up, till he sees all things thro' narrow chinks of his cavern.

A MEMORABLE FANCY

I was in a Printing house in Hell, & saw the method in which knowledge is transmitted from generation to generation.

In the first chamber was a Dragon-Man, clearing away the rubbish from a cave's mouth; within, a number of Dragons were hollowing the cave.

In the second chamber was a Viper folding round the rock & the cave, and others adorning it with gold, silver and precious stones.

In the third chamber was an Eagle with wings and feathers of air: he caused the inside of the cave to be infinite; around were numbers of Eagle-like men who built palaces in the immense cliffs.

In the fourth chamber were Lions of flaming fire, raging around & melting the metals into living fluids.

In the fifth chamber were Unnam'd forms, which cast the metals into the expanse.

There they were reciev'd by Men who occupied the sixth chamber, and took the forms of books & were arranged in libraries.

The Giants who formed this world into its sensual existence, and now seem to live in it in chains, are in truth the causes of its life & the sources of all activity; but the chains are the cunning of weak and tame minds which have power to resist energy; according to the proverb, the weak in courage is strong in cunning.

Thus one portion of being is the Prolific, the other the Devouring: to the Devourer it seems as if the producer was in his chains; but it is not so, he only takes portions of existence and fancies that the whole.

But the Prolific would cease to be Prolific unless the Devourer, as a sea, reciev'd the excess of his delights.

Some will say: 'Is not God alone the Prolific?' I answer: 'God only Acts & Is, in existing beings or Men.'

These two classes of men are always upon earth, & they should be enemies: whoever tries to reconcile them seeks to destroy existence.

Religion is an endeavour to reconcile the two.

NOTE: Jesus Christ did not wish to unite, but to separate them, as in the Parable of sheep and goats! & he says: 'I came not to send Peace, but a Sword.'

Messiah or Satan or Tempter was formerly thought to be one of the Antediluvians who are our Energies.

A MEMORABLE FANCY

An Angel came to me and said: 'O pitiable foolish young man! O horrible! O dreadful state! consider the hot burning dungeon thou art preparing for thyself to all eternity, to which thou art going in such career.'

I said: 'Perhaps you will be willing to shew me my eternal lot, & we will contemplate together upon it, and see whether your lot or mine is most desirable.'

So he took me thro' a stable & thro' a church & down into the church vault, at the end of which was a mill: thro' the mill we went, and came to a cave: down the winding cavern we groped our tedious way, till a void boundless as a nether sky appear'd beneath us, & we held by the roots of trees and hung over this immensity; but I said: 'if you please, we will commit ourselves to this void, and see whether providence is here also: if you will not, I will:' but he answer'd: 'do not presume, O young man, but as we here remain, behold thy lot which will soon appear when the darkness passes away.'

So I remain'd with him, sitting in the twisted root of an oak; he was suspended in a fungus, which hung with the head downward into the deep.

By degrees we beheld the infinite Abyss, fiery as the smoke of a burning city; beneath us, at an immense distance, was the sun, black but shining; round it were fiery tracks on which revolv'd vast spiders, crawling after their prey, which flew, or rather swum, in the infinite deep, in the most terrific shapes of animals sprung from corruption; & the air was full of them, & seem'd composed of them: these are Devils, and are called Powers of the air. I now asked my companion which was my eternal lot? he said: 'between the black & white spiders.'

But now, from between the black & white spiders, a cloud and fire burst and rolled thro' the deep, black'ning all beneath, so that the nether deep grew black as a sea, & rolled with a terrible noise; beneath us was nothing now to be seen but a black tempest, till looking east between the clouds & the waves, we saw a cataract of blood mixed with fire, and not many stones' throw from us appear'd and sunk again the scaly fold of a monstrous serpent; at last, to the east, distant about three degrees, appear'd a fiery crest above the waves; slowly it reared like a ridge of golden rocks, till we discover'd two globes of crimson fire, from which the sea fled away in clouds of smoke; and now we saw it was the head of Leviathan; his forehead was divided into streaks of green & purple like those on a tyger's forehead: soon we saw his mouth & red gills hang just above the raging foam, tinging the black deep with beams of blood, advancing toward us with all the fury of a spiritual existence.

My friend the Angel climb'd up from his station into the mill: I remain'd alone; & then this appearance was no more, but I found myself sitting on a pleasant bank beside a river by moonlight, hearing a harper, who sung to the harp; &

his theme was: 'The man who never alters his opinion is like standing water, & breeds reptiles of the mind.'

But I arose and sought for the mill, & there I found my Angel, who, surprised, asked me how I escaped?

I answer'd: 'All that we saw was owing to your metaphysics; for when you ran away, I found myself on a bank by moonlight hearing a harper. But now we have seen my eternal lot, shall I shew you yours?' he laugh'd at my proposal; but I by force suddenly caught him in my arms, & flew westerly thro' the night, till we were elevated above the earth's shadow; then I flung myself with him directly into the body of the sun; here I clothed myself in white, & taking in my hand Swedenborg's volumes, sunk from the glorious clime, and passed all the planets till we came to saturn: here I stay'd to rest, & then leap'd into the void between saturn & the fixed stars.

'Here,' said I, 'is your lot, in this space—if space it may be call'd.' Soon we saw the stable and the church, & I took him to the altar and open'd the Bible, and lo! it was a deep pit, into which I descended, driving the Angel before me; soon we saw seven houses of brick; one we enter'd; in it were a number of monkeys, baboons, & all of that species, chain'd by the middle, grinning and snatching at one another, but withheld by the shortness of their chains: however, I saw that they sometimes grew numerous, and then the weak were caught by the strong, and with a grinning aspect, first coupled with, & then devour'd, by plucking off first one limb and then another, till the body was left a helpless trunk; this, after grinning & kissing it with seeming fondness, they devour'd too; and here & there I saw one savourily picking the flesh off his own tail; as the stench terribly annoy'd us both, we went into the mill, & I in my hand brought the skeleton of a body, which in the mill was Aristotle's Analytics.

So the Angel said: 'thy phantasy has imposed upon me, & thou oughtest to be ashamed.'

I answer'd: 'we impose on one another, & it is but lost time to converse with you whose works are only Analytics.'

Opposition is true Friendship.

I have always found that Angels have the vanity to speak of themselves as the only wise; this they do with a confident insolence sprouting from systematic reasoning.

Thus Swedenborg boasts that what he writes is

new: tho' it is only the Contents or Index of already publish'd books.

A man carried a monkey about for a shew, & because he was a little wiser than the monkey, grew vain, and conciev'd himself as much wiser than seven men. It is so with Swedenborg: he shews the folly of churches, & exposes hypocrites, till he imagines that all are religious, & himself the single one on earth that ever broke a net.

Now hear a plain fact: Swedenborg has not written one new truth. Now hear another: he has written all the old falsehoods.

And now hear the reason. He conversed with Angels who are all religious, & conversed not with Devils who all hate religion, for he was incapable thro' his conceited notions.

Thus Swedenborg's writings are a recapitulation of all superficial opinions, and an analysis of the more sublime—but no further.

Have now another plain fact. Any man of mechanical talents may, from the writings of Paracelsus or Jacob Behmen, produce ten thousand volumes of equal value with Swedenborg's, and from those of Dante or Shakespear an infinite number.

But when he has done this, let him not say that he knows better than his master, for he only holds a candle in sunshine.

A MEMORABLE FANCY

Once I saw a Devil in a flame of fire, who arose before an Angel that sat on a cloud, and the Devil utter'd these words:

'The worship of God is: Honouring his gifts in other men, each according to his genius, and loving the greatest men best: those who envy or calumniate great men hate God; for there is no other God.'

The Angel hearing this became almost blue; but mastering himself he grew yellow, & at last white, pink, & smiling, and then replied:

'Thou Idolator! is not God One? & is not he visible in Jesus Christ? and has not Jesus Christ given his sanction to the law of ten commandments? and are not all other men fools, sinners, & nothings?'

The Devil answer'd: 'Bray a fool in a morter with wheat, yet shall not his folly be beaten out of him; if Jesus Christ is the greatest man, you ought to love him in the greatest degree; now hear how he has given his sanction to the law of ten commandments: did he not mock at the sabbath and so mock the sabbath's God? murder those who were murder'd because of him? turn away the law

from the woman taken in adultery? steal the labor of others to support him? bear false witness when he omitted making a defence before Pilate? covet when he pray'd for his disciples, and when he bid them shake off the dust of their feet against such as refused to lodge them? I tell you, no virtue can exist without breaking these ten commandments. Jesus was all virtue, and acted from impulse, not from rules.'

When he had so spoken, I beheld the Angel, who stretched out his arms, embracing the flame of fire, & he was consumed and arose as Elijah.

NOTE: This Angel, who is now become a Devil, is my particular friend; we often read the Bible together in its infernal or diabolical sense, which the world shall have if they behave well.

I have also The Bible of Hell, which the world shall have whether they will or no.

One Law for the Lion & Ox is Oppression.

c. 1790

A SONG OF LIBERTY

1. THE Eternal Female[1] groan'd! it was heard over all the Earth.

2. Albion's coast is sick, silent; the American meadows faint!

3. Shadows of Prophecy shiver along by the lakes and the rivers, and mutter across the ocean: France, rend down thy dungeon!

4. Golden Spain, burst the barriers of old Rome!

5. Cast thy keys, O Rome, into the deep down falling, even to eternity down falling.

6. And weep.

7. In her trembling hand she took the new born terror,[2] howling.

8. On those infinite mountains of light, now barr'd out by the atlantic sea, the new born fire stood before the starry king![3]

9. Flag'd with grey brow'd snows and thunderous visages, the jealous wings wav'd over the deep.

10. The speary hand burned aloft, unbuckled was the shield; forth went the hand of jealousy among the flaming hair, and hurl'd the new born wonder thro' the starry night.

11. The fire, the fire is falling!

12. Look up! look up! O citizen of London, enlarge thy countenance! O Jew, leave counting

---

1 The Eternal Female is Enitharmon, who in Blake's mythological system is Poetic Inspiration, also Space. As Space she is 'a manifestation of the providential purpose of temporal existence, the regeneration of man.'

2 Enitharmon's child is Orc, the Spirit of Revolt. In terms of the revolutionary movement Orc became for Blake 'the symbol and the promise of man's liberation from all forms of restraint.'

3 Urizen, the false god of convention and sterile reason.

gold! return to thy oil and wine. O African! black African! (go, winged thought, widen his forehead.)

13. The fiery limbs, the flaming hair, shot like the sinking sun into the western sea.

14. Wak'd from his eternal sleep, the hoary element roaring fled away.

15. Down rush'd, beating his wings in vain, the jealous king; his grey brow'd councellors, thunderous warriors, curl'd veterans, among helms, and shields, and chariots, horses, elephants, banners, castles, slings, and rocks.

16. Falling, rushing, ruining! buried in the ruins, on Urthona's dens;[4]

17. All night beneath the ruins; then, their sullen flames faded, emerge round the gloomy king.

18. With thunder and fire, leading his starry hosts thro' the waste wilderness, he promulgates his ten commands, glancing his beamy eyelids over the deep in dark dismay,

19. Where the son of fire in his eastern cloud, while the morning plumes her golden breast,

20. Spurning the clouds written with curses, stamps the stony law to dust, loosing the eternal horses from the dens of night crying:

EMPIRE IS NO MORE! AND NOW THE LION & WOLF
SHALL CEASE

CHORUS

Let the Priests of the Raven of dawn no longer, in deadly black, with hoarse note curse the sons of joy. Nor his accepted brethren—whom, tyrant, he calls free—lay the bound or build the roof. Nor pale religious letchery call that virginity that wishes but acts not!

For every thing that lives is Holy.

c. 1790

NEVER SEEK TO TELL THY LOVE

[This and the next two poems are from the *Rossetti MS.*]

NEVER seek to tell thy love
Love that never told can be;
For the gentle wind does move
Silently, invisibly.

I told my love, I told my love,
I told her all my heart,

---

4 Urthona's dens are the lowest part of the spirit. Urthona is the regent of the world of spirit.

Trembling, cold, in ghastly fears—
Ah, she doth depart.

Soon as she was gone from me
A traveller came by   10
Silently, invisibly—
O, was no deny.

c. 1793

I SAW A CHAPEL ALL OF GOLD

I SAW a chapel all of gold
That none did dare to enter in,
And many weeping stood without,
Weeping, mourning, worshipping.

I saw a serpent rise between
The white pillars of the door,
And he forc'd & forc'd & forc'd,
Down the golden hinges tore.

And along the pavement sweet,
Set with pearls & rubies bright,   10
All his slimy length he drew,
Till upon the altar white

Vomiting his poison out
On the bread & on the wine.
So I turn'd into a sty
And laid me down among the swine.

c. 1793

A CRADLE SONG

[This song was intended as a contrary to *A Cradle Song* in the *Songs of Innocence.*]

SLEEP, Sleep, beauty bright
Dreaming o'er the joys of night.
Sleep, Sleep: in thy sleep
Little sorrows sit & weep.

Sweet Babe, in thy face
Soft desires I can trace
Secret joys & secret smiles
Little pretty infant wiles.

As thy softest limbs I feel
Smiles as of the morning steal   10
O'er thy cheek & o'er thy breast
Where thy little heart does rest.

O, the cunning wiles that creep
In thy little heart asleep.

When thy little heart does wake,
Then the dreadful lightnings break,

From thy cheek & from thy eye
O'er the youthful harvests nigh
Infant wiles & infant smiles
Heaven & Earth of peace beguiles.   20

c. 1793

From VISIONS OF THE DAUGHTERS
OF ALBION

[TAKE THY BLISS, O MAN]

'O URIZEN![1] Creator of men! mistaken Demon
of heaven!
Thy joys are tears, thy labour vain to form men
to thine image.
How can one joy absorb another? are not different joys
Holy, eternal, infinite? and each joy is a Love.

'Does not the great mouth laugh at a gift, & the
narrow eyelids mock
At the labour that is above payment? and wilt
thou take the ape
For thy councellor, or the dog for a schoolmaster
to thy children?   120
Does he who contemns poverty and he who turns
with abhorrence
From usury feel the same passion, or are they
moved alike?
How can the giver of gifts experience the delights
of the merchant?
How the industrious citizen the pains of the husbandman?
How different far the fat fed hireling with hollow
drum,
Who buys whole corn fields into wastes, and sings
upon the heath!
How different their eye and ear! how different
the world to them!
With what sense does the parson claim the labour
of the farmer?
What are his nets & gins & traps; & how does he
surround him
With cold floods of abstraction, and with forests
of solitude,   130
To build him castles and high spires, where kings
& priests may dwell;
Till she who burns with youth, and knows no fixed
lot, is bound
In spells of law to one she loaths? and must she
drag the chain

Of life in weary lust? must chilling, murderous
thoughts obscure
The clear heaven of her eternal spring; to bear
the wintry rage
Of a harsh terror, driv'n to madness, bound to
hold a rod
Over her shrinking shoulders all the day, & all
the night
To turn the wheel of false desire, and longings
that wake her womb
To the abhorred birth of cherubs in the human
form,
That live a pestilence & die a meteor, & are no
more;   140
Till the child dwell with one he hates, and do
the deed he loaths,
And the impure scourge force his seed into its
unripe birth
Ere yet his eyelids can behold the arrows of the
day?

'Does the whale worship at thy footsteps as the
hungry dog;
Or does he scent the mountain prey because his
nostrils wide
Draw in the ocean? does his eye discern the flying cloud
As the raven's eye? or does he measure the expanse like the vulture?
Does the still spider view the cliffs where eagles
hide their young;
Or does the fly rejoice because the harvest is
brought in?
Does not the eagle scorn the earth & despise the
treasures beneath?   150
But the mole knoweth what is there, & the worm
shall tell it thee.
Does not the worm erect a pillar in the mouldering church yard
And a palace of eternity in the jaws of the hungry
grave?
Over his porch these words are written: "Take
thy bliss, O Man!
And sweet shall be thy taste, & sweet thy infant
joys renew!"'

1793

From AMERICA: A PROPHECY

[EMPIRE IS NO MORE]

'THE morning comes, the night decays, the watchmen leave their stations;
The grave is burst, the spices shed, the linen
wrapped up;

---

1 Blake's mythological character symbolizing false Reason.

The bones of death, the cov'ring clay, the sinews
    shrunk & dry'd
Reviving shake, inspiring move, breathing, awak-
    ening,   40
Spring like redeemed captives when their bonds
    & bars are burst.
Let the slave grinding at the mill run out into the
    field,
Let him look up into the heavens & laugh in the
    bright air;
Let the inchained soul, shut up in darkness and
    in sighing,
Whose face has never seen a smile in thirty weary
    years,
Rise and look out; his chains are loose, his dun-
    geon doors are open;
And let his wife and children return from the
    oppressor's scourge;
They look behind at every step & believe it is a
    dream,
Singing: "The Sun has left his blackness & has
    found a fresher morning,
And the fair Moon rejoices in the clear & cloud-
    less night;   50
For Empire is no more, and now the Lion & Wolf
    shall cease." '

In thunders ends the voice. Then Albion's Angel
    wrathful burnt
Beside the Stone of Night, and like the Eternal
    Lion's howl
In famine & war, reply'd: 'Art thou not Orc,[1] who
    serpent-form'd
Stands at the gate of Enitharmon to devour her
    children?
Blasphemous Demon, Antichrist, hater of Dig-
    nities,
Lover of wild rebellion, and transgressor of God's
    Law,
Why dost thou come to Angel's eyes in this ter-
    rific form?'

The Terror answer'd: 'I am Orc, wreath'd round
    the accursed tree:
The times are ended; shadows pass, the morning
    'gins to break;   60
The fiery joy, that Urizen perverted to ten com-
    mands,
What night he led the starry hosts thro' the wide
    wilderness,

That stony law I stamp to dust; and scatter re-
    ligion abroad
To the four winds as a torn book, & none shall
    gather the leaves;
But they shall rot on desart sands, & consume in
    bottomless deeps,
To make the desarts blossom, & the deeps shrink
    to their fountains,
And to renew the fiery joy, and burst the stony
    roof;
That pale religious letchery, seeking Virginity,
May find it in a harlot, and in coarse-clad honesty
The undefil'd, tho' ravish'd in her cradle night
    and morn;   70
For everything that lives is holy, life delights in
    life;
Because the soul of sweet delight can never be
    defil'd.
Fires inwrap the earthly globe, yet man is not
    consum'd;
Amidst the lustful fires he walks; his feet become
    like brass,
His knees and thighs like silver, & his breast and
    head like gold.'

1793

POEMS FROM BLAKE'S LETTERS TO THOMAS BUTTS[1]

I

TO MY FRIEND BUTTS I WRITE

[This verse epistle has been called by Damon, 'Blake's
clearest and most personal description of a mystical
vision.']

Felpham, 2 October, 1800

To my Friend Butts I write
My first Vision of Light,
On the yellow sands sitting.
The Sun was Emitting
His Glorious beams
From Heaven's high Streams.
Over Sea, over Land
My Eyes did Expand
Into regions of air
Away from all Care,   10
Into regions of fire
Remote from Desire;
The Light of the Morning
Heaven's Mountains adorning:
In particles bright

---

[1] Blake's mythological character symbolizing the Spirit of Youth
and Revolt. He is the child of Los (Poetic Instinct) and Enitharmon (Spiritual Beauty).

[1] patron and discerning friend who supported Blake over a
period of years.

The jewels of Light
Distinct shone & clear.
Amaz'd & in fear
I each particle gazed,
Astonish'd, Amazed;   20
For each was a Man
Human-form'd. Swift I ran,
For they beckon'd to me
Remote by the Sea,
Saying: 'Each grain of Sand,
Every Stone on the Land,
Each rock & each hill,
Each fountain & rill,
Each herb & each tree,
Mountain, hill, earth & sea,   30
Cloud, Meteor & Star,
Are Men seen Afar.'
I stood in the Streams
Of Heaven's bright beams,
And saw Felpham sweet
Beneath my bright feet
In soft Female charms;
And in her fair arms
My Shadow I knew
And my wife's shadow too,   40
And My Sister & Friend.
We like Infants descend
In our Shadows on Earth,
Like a weak mortal birth.
My Eyes more and more
Like a Sea without shore
Continue Expanding,
The Heavens commanding,
Till the Jewels of Light,
Heavenly Men beaming bright,   50
Appear'd as One Man,
Who complacent began
My limbs to infold
In his beams of bright gold;
Like dross purg'd away
All my mire & my clay.
Soft consum'd in delight
In his bosom Sun bright
I remain'd. Soft he smil'd,
And I heard his voice Mild   60
Saying: 'This is My Fold,
O thou Ram horn'd with gold,
Who awakest from Sleep
On the Sides of the Deep.
On the Mountains around
The roarings resound
Of the lion & wolf,
The loud Sea & deep gulf.
These are guards of My Fold,
O thou Ram horn'd with gold!'   70

And the voice faded mild.
I remain'd as a Child;
All I ever had known
Before me bright Shone.
I saw you & your wife
By the fountains of Life.
Such the Vision to me
Appear'd on the sea.

II

WITH HAPPINESS STRETCHED ACROSS THE HILLS

[Blake copied out this poem and sent it in a letter to
Thomas Butts with the explanation that it was composed
about a twelvemonth before, while he was walking from
Felpham to Lavant to meet his sister.]

22 November, 1802

WITH happiness stretch'd across the hills
In a cloud that dewy sweetness distills,
With a blue sky spread over with wings
And a mild sun that mounts & sings,
With trees & fields full of Fairy elves
And little devils who fight for themselves—
Rememb'ring the Verses that Hayley[2] sung
When my heart knock'd against the root of my
    tongue—
With Angels planted in Hawthorn bowers
And God himself in the passing hours,   10
With Silver Angels across my way
And Golden Demons that none can stay,
With my Father hovering upon the wind
And my Brother Robert just behind
And my Brother John, the evil one,
In a black cloud making his mone;
Tho' dead, they appear upon my path,
Notwithstanding my terrible wrath:
They beg, they intreat, they drop their tears,
Fill'd full of hopes, fill'd full of fears—   20
With a thousand Angels upon the Wind
Pouring disconsolate from behind
To drive them off, & before my way
A frowning Thistle implores my stay.
What to others a trifle appears
Fills me full of smiles or tears;
For double the vision my Eyes do see,
And a double vision is always with me.
With my inward Eye 'tis an old Man grey;
With my outward, a Thistle across my way.   30
'If thou goest back,' the thistle said,
'Thou art to endless woe betray'd;
For here does Theotormon[3] lower

2 William Hayley, 1745–1820, self-styled poet and amateur artist,
who was Blake's employer and companion for several years.
3 Theotormon is Blake's mythological character representing
Desire, one of the four Sons of Los.

And here is Enitharmon's[4] bower
And Los[5] the terrible thus hath sworn,
Because thou backward dost return,
Poverty, Envy, old age & fear
Shall bring thy Wife upon a bier;
And Butts shall give what Fuseli[6] gave,
A dark black Rock & a gloomy Cave.'   40

I struck the Thistle with my foot,
And broke him up from his delving root:
'Must the duties of life each other cross?
Must every joy be dung & dross?
Must my dear Butts feel cold neglect
Because I give Hayley his due respect?
Must Flaxman[7] look upon me as wild,
And all my friends be with doubts beguil'd?
Must my Wife live in my Sister's bane,
Or my Sister survive on my Love's pain?   50
The curses of Los, the terrible shade,
And his dismal terrors make me afraid.'

So I spoke & struck in my wrath
The old man weltering upon my path.
Then Los appear'd in all his power:
In the Sun he appear'd, descending before
My face in fierce flames; in my double sight
'Twas outward a Sun, inward Los in his might.

'My hands are labour'd day & night,
And Ease comes never in my sight.   60
My Wife has no indulgence given
Except what comes to her from heaven.
We eat little, we drink less;
This Earth breeds not our happiness.
Another Sun feeds our life's streams,
We are not warmed with thy beams;
Thou measurest not the Time to me,
Nor yet the Space that I do see;
My Mind is not with thy light array'd,
Thy terrors shall not make me afraid.'   70

When I had my Defiance given,
The Sun stood trembling in heaven;
The Moon that glow'd remote below,
Became leprous & white as snow;
And every soul of men on the Earth
Felt affliction & sorrow & sickness & dearth.
Los flam'd in my path, & the Sun was hot

With the bows of my Mind & the Arrows of
    Thought—
My bowstring fierce with Ardour breathes,
My arrows glow in their golden sheaves;   80
My brother & father march before;
The heavens drop with human gore.

Now I a fourfold vision[8] see,
And a fourfold vision is given to me;
'Tis fourfold in my supreme delight
And threefold in soft Beulah's[9] night
And twofold Always. May God us keep
From Single vision & Newton's sleep!

MOCK ON, MOCK ON, VOLTAIRE, ROUSSEAU

Mock on, Mock on, Voltaire, Rousseau:
Mock on, Mock on; 'tis all in vain!
You throw the sand against the wind,
And the wind blows it back again.

And every sand becomes a Gem
Reflected in the beams divine;
Blown back they blind the mocking Eye,
But still in Israel's paths they shine.

The Atoms of Democritus
And Newton's Particles of light   10
Are sands upon the Red sea shore,
Where Israel's tents do shine so bright.

c. 1803   1863

From THE FOUR ZOAS
[THE PRICE OF EXPERIENCE]

'I am made to sow the thistle for wheat, the nettle
    for a nourishing dainty.
I have planted a false oath in the earth; it has
    brought forth a poison tree.
I have chosen the serpent for a councellor, & the
    dog
For a schoolmaster to my children.
I have blotted out from light & living the dove
    & nightingale,
And I have caused the earth worm to beg from
    door to door.

---

4 Enitharmon is Spiritual Beauty, or Poetic Inspiration; the emanation of Los (l. 35).
5 Los is Poetic Instinct.
6 Henry Fuseli, 1741–1825, Swiss-English artist friend with whom Blake had quarreled.
7 John Flaxman, 1755–1826, famous sculptor who was a friend and admirer of Blake, though at a later time the friendship was clouded with suspicions.

8 'This is one of Blake's familiar terms and is in reality quite simple. Single vision was pure sensation, such as the scientists (Newton in particular) cultivate; twofold vision added an intellectual appreciation of the object; threefold infused the perception with its emotional value; and fourfold crowned it with mystical insight as to its place in the universe.'—(Damon.)
9 Beulah, often represented by the moon, symbolizes a 'state of repose' during which the mind is receptive to intellectual and spiritual suggestions.

'I have taught the thief a secret path into the
  house of the just.
I have taught pale artifice to spread his nets upon
  the morning.
My heavens are brass, my earth is iron, my moon
  a clod of clay,
My sun a pestilence burning at noon & a vapour
  of death in night.   10

'What is the price of Experience? do men buy it
  for a song?
Or wisdom for a dance in the street? No, it is
  bought with the price
Of all that a man hath, his house, his wife, his
  children.
Wisdom is sold in the desolate market where
  none come to buy,
And in the wither'd field where the farmer plows
  for bread in vain.

'It is an easy thing to triumph in the summer's sun
And in the vintage & to sing on the waggon loaded
  with corn.
It is an easy thing to talk of patience to the afflicted,
To speak the laws of prudence to the houseless
  wanderer,
To listen to the hungry raven's cry in wintry
  season   20
When the red blood is fill'd with wine & with the
  marrow of lambs.

'It is an easy thing to laugh at wrathful elements,
To hear the dog howl at the wintry door, the ox in
  the slaughter house moan;
To see a god on every wind & a blessing on every
  blast;
To hear sounds of love in the thunder storm that
  destroys our enemies' house;
To rejoice in the blight that covers his field, & the
  sickness that cuts off his children,
While our olive & vine sing & laugh round our
  door, & our children bring fruits & flowers.

'Then the groan & the dolor are quite forgotten,
  & the slave grinding at the mill,
And the captive in chains, & the poor in the prison,
  & the soldier in the field
When the shatter'd bone hath laid him groaning
  among the happier dead.   30

'It is an easy thing to rejoice in the tents of prosperity:
Thus could I sing & thus rejoice: but it is not so
  with me.'

1797

THE MENTAL TRAVELLER

[There have been numerous attempts to explain this
cryptic poem. W. M. Rossetti may be fairly close to the
fundamental meaning. *The Mental Traveller,* he thinks,
'indicates an explorer of mental phenomena. The mental
phenomenon here symbolized seems to be the career of
any great idea or intellectual movement—as, for instance,
Christianity, chivalry, art, etc.—represented as going
through the stages of—1, birth; 2, adversity and persecution; 3, triumph and maturity; 4, decadence through
over-ripeness; 5, gradual transformation, under new conditions, into another renovated Idea, which again has to
pass through the same stages. In other words, the poem
represents the action and reaction of ideas upon society,
and of society upon ideas.'—S. Foster Damon sees *The
Mental Traveller* as representing the five stages in the life
of the Mystic recurring in a vast cycle.]

I TRAVEL'D thro' a Land of Men,
A Land of Men & Women too,
And heard & saw such dreadful things
As cold Earth wanderers never knew.

For there the Babe is born in joy
That was begotten in dire woe;
Just as we Reap in joy the fruit
Which we in bitter tears did sow.

And if the Babe is born a Boy
He's given to a Woman Old,   10
Who nails him down upon a rock,
Catches his shrieks in cups of gold.

She binds iron thorns around his head,
She pierces both his hands & feet,
She cuts his heart out at his side
To make it feel both cold & heat.

Her fingers number every Nerve,
Just as a Miser counts his gold;
She lives upon his shrieks & cries,
And she grows young as he grows old.   20

Till he becomes a bleeding youth,
And she becomes a Virgin bright;
Then he rends up his Manacles
And binds her down for his delight.

He plants himself in all her Nerves,
Just as a Husbandman his mould;
And she becomes his dwelling place
And Garden fruitful seventy fold.

An aged Shadow, soon he fades,
Wand'ring round an Earthly Cot,   30
Full filled all with gems & gold
Which he by industry had got.

And these are the gems of the Human Soul,
The rubies & pearls of a lovesick eye,
The countless gold of the akeing heart,
The martyr's groan & the lover's sigh.

They are his meat, they are his drink;
He feeds the Beggar & the Poor
And the wayfaring Traveller:
For ever open is his door.   40

His grief is their eternal joy;
They make the roofs & walls to ring;
Till from the fire on the hearth
A little Female Babe does spring.

And she is all of solid fire
And gems & gold, that none his hand
Dares stretch to touch her Baby form,
Or wrap her in his swaddling-band.

But She comes to the Man she loves,
If young or old, or rich or poor;   50
They soon drive out the aged Host,
A Beggar at another's door.

He wanders weeping far away,
Until some other take him in;
Oft blind & age-bent, sore distrest,
Untill he can a Maiden win.

And to allay his freezing Age
The Poor Man takes her in his arms;
The Cottage fades before his sight,
The Garden & its lovely Charms.   60

The Guests are scatter'd thro' the land,
For the Eye altering alters all;
The Senses roll themselves in fear,
And the flat Earth becomes a Ball;

The stars, sun, Moon, all shrink away,
A desart vast without a bound,
And nothing left to eat or drink,
And a dark desart all around.

The honey of her Infant lips,
The bread & wine of her sweet smile,   70
The wild game of her roving Eye,
Does him to Infancy beguile;

For as he eats & drinks he grows
Younger & younger every day;
And on the desart wild they both
Wander in terror & dismay.

Like the wild Stag she flees away,
Her fear plants many a thicket wild;
While he pursues her night & day,
By various arts of Love beguil'd,   80

By various arts of Love & Hate,
Till the wide desart planted o'er
With Labyrinths of wayward Love,
Where roam the Lion, Wolf & Boar,

Till he becomes a wayward Babe,
And she a weeping Woman Old.
Then many a Lover wanders here;
The Sun & Stars are nearer roll'd.

The trees bring forth sweet Extacy
To all who in the desert roam;   90
Till many a City there is Built,
And many a pleasant Shepherd's home.

But when they find the frowning Babe,
Terror strikes thro' the region wide:
They cry 'The Babe! the Babe is Born!'
And flee away on Every side.

For who dare touch the frowning form,
His arm is wither'd to its root;
Lions, Boars, Wolves, all howling flee,
And every Tree does shed its fruit.   100

And none can touch that frowning form,
Except it be a Woman Old;
She nails him down upon the Rock,
And all is done as I have told.

c. 1803   1863

AUGURIES OF INNOCENCE

[These 'auguries' from the *Pickering MS.* are a gathering of scattered jottings condemning cruelty to animals, physical punishment, militarism, and agnosticism. They appear to be portions of an incomplete poem, which Blake doubtless intended to rearrange before publication.]

To see a World in a Grain of Sand
And a Heaven in a Wild Flower,
Hold Infinity in the palm of your hand
And Eternity in an hour.

A Robin Red breast in a Cage
Puts all Heaven in a Rage.
A dove house fill'd with doves & Pigeons
Shudders Hell thro' all its regions.
A dog starv'd at his Master's Gate

Predicts the ruin of the State.   10
A Horse misus'd upon the Road
Calls to Heaven for Human blood.
Each outcry of the hunted Hare
A fibre from the Brain does tear.
A Skylark wounded in the wing,
A Cherubim does cease to sing.
The Game Cock clip'd & arm'd for fight
Does the Rising Sun affright.
Every Wolf's & Lion's howl
Raises from Hell a Human Soul.   20
The wild deer, wand'ring here & there,
Keeps the Human Soul from Care.
The Lamb misus'd breeds Public strife
And yet forgives the Butcher's Knife.
The Bat that flits at close of Eve
Has left the Brain that won't Believe.
The Owl that calls upon the Night
Speaks the Unbeliever's fright.
He who shall hurt the little Wren
Shall never be belov'd by Men.   30
He who the Ox to wrath has mov'd
Shall never be by Woman lov'd.
The wanton Boy that kills the Fly
Shall feel the Spider's enmity.
He who torments the Chafer's sprite
Weaves a Bower in endless Night.
The Catterpiller on the Leaf
Repeats to thee thy Mother's grief.
Kill not the Moth nor Butterfly,
For the Last Judgment draweth nigh.   40
He who shall train the Horse to War
Shall never pass the Polar Bar.
The Beggar's Dog & Widow's Cat,
Feed them & thou wilt grow fat.
The Gnat that sings his Summer's song
Poison gets from Slander's tongue.
The poison of the Snake & Newt
Is the sweat of Envy's Foot.
The Poison of the Honey Bee
Is the Artist's Jealousy.   50
The Prince's Robes & Beggar's Rags
Are Toadstools on the Miser's Bags.
A truth that's told with bad intent
Beats all the Lies you can invent.
It is right it should be so;
Man was made for Joy & Woe;
And when this we rightly know
Thro' the World we safely go,
Joy & Woe are woven fine,
A Clothing for the Soul divine;   60
Under every grief & pine
Runs a joy with silken twine.
The Babe is more than Swadling Bands;

Throughout all these Human Lands
Tools were made, & Born were hands,
Every Farmer Understands.
Every Tear from Every Eye
Becomes a Babe in Eternity;
This is caught by Females bright
And return'd to its own delight.   70
The Bleat, the Bark, Bellow & Roar
Are Waves that Beat on Heaven's Shore.
The Babe that weeps the Rod beneath
Writes Revenge in realms of death.
The Beggar's Rags, fluttering in Air,
Does to Rags the Heavens tear.
The Soldier, arm'd with Sword & Gun,
Palsied strikes the Summer's Sun.
The poor Man's Farthing is worth more
Than all the Gold on Afric's Shore.   80
One Mite wrung from the Labrer's hands
Shall buy & sell the Miser's Lands:
Or, if protected from on high,
Does that whole Nation sell & buy.
He who mocks the Infant's Faith
Shall be mock'd in Age & Death.
He who shall teach the Child to Doubt
The rotting Grave shall ne'er get out.
He who respects the Infant's faith
Triumphs over Hell & Death.   90
The Child's Toys & the Old Man's Reasons
Are the Fruits of the Two seasons.
The Questioner, who sits so sly,
Shall never know how to Reply.
He who replies to words of Doubt
Doth put the Light of Knowledge out.
The Strongest Poison ever known
Came from Caesar's Laurel Crown.
Nought can deform the Human Race
Like to the Armour's iron brace.   100
When Gold & Gems adorn the Plow
To peaceful Arts shall Envy Bow.
A Riddle or the Cricket's Cry
Is to Doubt a fit Reply.
The Emmet's[1] Inch & Eagle's Mile
Make Lame Philosophy to smile.
He who Doubts from what he sees
Will ne'er Believe, do what you Please.
If the Sun & Moon should doubt,
They'd immediately Go out.   110
To be in a Passion you Good may do,
But no Good if a Passion is in you.
The Whore & Gambler, by the State
Licenc'd, build that Nation's Fate.
The Harlot's cry from Street to Street
Shall weave Old England's winding Sheet.

1 ant.

The Winner's Shout, the Loser's Curse,
Dance before dead England's Hearse.
Every Night & every Morn
Some to Misery are Born.   120
Every Morn & every Night
Some are Born to sweet delight.
Some are Born to sweet delight,
Some are Born to Endless Night.
We are led to Believe a Lie
When we see not Thro' the Eye
Which was Born in a Night to perish in a Night
When the Soul Slept in Beams of Light.
God Appears & God is Light
To those poor Souls who dwell in Night,   130
But does a Human Form Display
To those who Dwell in Realms of day.

    c. 1803   1863

From MILTON

PREFACE

THE Stolen and Perverted Writings of Homer
& Ovid, of Plato & Cicero, which all men ought
to contemn, are set up by artifice against the Sublime of the Bible; but when the New Age is at
leisure to Pronounce, all will be set right, & those
Grand Works of the more ancient & consciously
& professedly Inspired Men will hold their proper
rank, & the Daughters of Memory shall become
the Daughters of Inspiration. Shakspeare & Milton were both curb'd by the general malady &
infection from the silly Greek & Latin slaves of
the Sword.

   Rouze up, O Young Men of the New Age! set
your foreheads against the ignorant Hirelings!
For we have Hirelings in the Camp, the Court &
the University, who would, if they could, for ever
depress Mental & prolong Corporeal War. Painters! on you I call. Sculptors! Architects! Suffer
not the fashonable Fools to depress your powers
by the prices they pretend to give for contemptible works, or the expensive advertizing boasts
that they make of such works; believe Christ &
his Apostles that there is a Class of Men whose
whole delight is in Destroying. We do not want
either Greek or Roman Models if we are but
just & true to our own Imaginations, those Worlds
of Eternity in which we shall live for ever in JESUS
OUR LORD.

    And did those feet in ancient time
    Walk upon England's mountains green?
    And was the holy Lamb of God
    On England's pleasant pastures seen?

    And did the Countenance Divine
    Shine forth upon our clouded hills?
    And was Jerusalem builded here
    Among these dark Satanic Mills?

    Bring me my Bow of burning gold:
    Bring me my Arrows of desire: 10
    Bring me my Spear: O clouds unfold!
    Bring me my Chariot of fire.

    I will not cease from Mental Fight,
    Nor shall my Sword sleep in my hand
    Till we have built Jerusalem
    In England's green & pleasant Land.

'Would to God that all the Lord's people were
    Prophets.'
                     Numbers xi, 29.

[THE WINE-PRESS OF LOS]

[The agencies of Los (poetic imagination), which are
symbolized by the weeds, insects, and creatures, rejoice
and dance secure in their naked beauty about the Wine-
press (body) as they watch the war of the destroying human passions.]

... THE Wine-press of Los is eastward of Golgo-
    nooza[1] before the Seat
Of Satan: Luvah[2] laid the foundation & Urizen[3]
    finish'd it in howling woe.
How red the sons & daughters of Luvah! here
    they tread the grapes:
Laughing & shouting, drunk with odours many
    fall o'erwearied,
Drown'd in the wine is many a youth & maiden:
    those around
Lay them on skins of Tygers & of the spotted
    Leopard & the Wild Ass
Till they revive, or bury them in cool grots, mak-
    ing lamentation.

This Wine-press is call'd War on Earth: it is the
    Printing-Press
Of Los, and here he lays his words in order above
    the mortal brain,
As cogs are form'd in a wheel to turn the cogs of
    the adverse wheel.   10

Timbrels & violins sport round the Wine-presses;
    the little Seed,
The sportive Root, the Earth-worm, the gold
    Beetle, the wise Emmet[4]
Dance round the Wine-presses of Luvah: the Cen-
    tipede is there,

---

1 the City of Art.   2 love.   3 intellect.   4 ant.

The ground Spider with many eyes, the Mole
clothed in velvet,
The ambitious Spider in his sullen web, the lucky
golden Spinner,
The Earwig arm'd, the tender Maggot, emblem of
immortality,
The Flea, Louse, Bug, the Tape-Worm, all the
Armies of Disease,
Visible or invisible to the slothful vegetating Man.
The slow Slug, the Grasshopper that sings &
laughs & drinks:
Winter comes, he folds his slender bones with-
out a murmur.   20
The cruel Scorpion is there, the Gnat, Wasp,
Hornet & the Honey Bee,
The Toad & venomous Newt, the Serpent cloth'd
in gems & gold.
They throw off their gorgeous raiment: they re-
joice with loud jubilee
Around the Wine-presses of Luvah, naked &
drunk with wine.

There is the Nettle that stings with soft down,
and there
The indignant Thistle whose bitterness is bred in
his milk,
Who feeds on contempt of his neighbour: there
all the idle Weeds
That creep around the obscure places shew their
various limbs
Naked in all their beauty dancing round the Wine-
presses.
But in the Wine-presses the Human grapes sing
not nor dance: 30
They howl & writhe in shoals of torment, in fierce
flames consuming,
In chains of iron & in dungeons circled with cease-
less fires,
In pits & dens & shades of death, in shapes of tor-
ment & woe:
The plates & screws & wracks & saws & cords &
fires & cisterns,
The cruel joys of Luvah's Daughters, lacerating
with knives
And whips their Victims, & the deadly sport of
Luvah's Sons.

They dance around the dying & they drink the
howl & groan,
They catch the shrieks in cups of gold, they hand
them to one another:
These are the sports of love, & these the sweet
delights of amorous play,
Tears of the grape, the death sweat of the cluster,
the last sigh   40

Of the mild youth who listens to the lureing songs
of Luvah.

[REASON AND IMAGINATION]

THE Negation is the Spectre, the Reasoning Power
in Man:
This is a false Body, an Incrustation over my Im-
mortal
Spirit, a Selfhood which must be put off & anni-
hilated alway.
To cleanse the Face of my Spirit by Self-examina-
tion,
To bathe in the Waters of Life, to wash off the
Not Human,
I come in Self-annihilation & the grandeur of In-
spiration,
To cast off Rational Demonstration by Faith in
the Saviour,
To cast off the rotten rags of Memory by Inspira-
tion,
To cast off Bacon, Locke & Newton from Albion's
covering,
To take off his filthy garments & clothe him with
Imagination;   10
To cast aside from Poetry all that is not Inspira-
tion,
That it no longer shall dare to mock with the as-
persion of Madness
Cast on the Inspired by the tame high finisher of
paltry Blots
Indefinite, or paltry Rhymes, or paltry Harmonies,
Who creeps into State Government like a catter-
piller to destroy;
To cast off the idiot Questioner who is always
questioning
But never capable of answering, who sits with a
sly grin
Silent plotting when to question, like a thief in
a cave,
Who publishes doubt & calls it knowledge, whose
Science is Despair,
Whose pretence to knowledge is Envy, whose
whole Science is   20
To destroy the wisdom of ages to gratify raven-
ous Envy
That rages round him like a Wolf day & night
without rest:
He smiles with condescension, he talks of Bene-
volence & Virtue,
And those who act with Benevolence & Virtue
they murder time on time.
These are the destroyers of Jerusalem, these are
the murderers

Of Jesus, who deny the Faith & mock at Eternal
    Life,
Who pretend to Poetry that they may destroy
    Imagination
By imitation of Nature's Images drawn from Re-
    membrance.
These are the Sexual Garments, the Abomina-
    tion of Desolation,
Hiding the Human Lineaments as with an Ark &
    Curtains   30
Which Jesus rent & now shall wholly purge away
    with Fire
Till Generation is swallow'd up in Regeneration.

[THE CHOIR OF DAY]

THOU hearest the Nightingale begin the Song of
    Spring.
The Lark sitting upon his earthy bed, just as the
    morn
Appears, listens silent; then springing from the
    waving Cornfield, loud
He leads the Choir of Day: trill, trill, trill, trill,
Mounting upon the wings of light into the Great
    Expanse,
Reecchoing against the lovely blue & shining
    heavenly Shell,
His little throat labours with inspiration; every
    feather
On throat & breast & wings vibrates with the
    effluence Divine.
All Nature listens silent to him, & the awful Sun
Stands still upon the Mountain looking on this
    little Bird   10
With eyes of soft humility & wonder, love & awe,
Then loud from their green covert all the Birds
    begin their Song:
The Thrush, the Linnet & the Goldfinch, Robin
    & the Wren
Awake the Sun from his sweet reverie upon the
    Mountain.
The Nightingale again assays his song, & thro'
    the day
And thro' the night warbles luxuriant, every Bird
    of Song
Attending his loud harmony with admiration &
    love.
This is a Vision of the lamentation of Beulah[1]
    over Ololon.[2]

Thou percievest the Flowers put forth their pre-
    cious Odours,
And none can tell how from so small a centre
    comes such sweets,   20
Forgetting that within that Centre Eternity ex-
    pands
Its ever during doors that Og & Anak[3] fiercely
    guard.
First, e'er the morning breaks, joy opens in the
    flowery bosoms,
Joy even to tears, which the Sun rising dries;
    first the Wild Thyme
And Meadow-sweet, downy & soft waving among
    the reeds,
Light springing on the air, lead the sweet Dance:
    they wake
The Honeysuckle sleeping on the Oak; the flaunt-
    ing beauty
Revels along upon the wind; the White-thorn,
    lovely May,
Opens her many lovely eyes listening; the Rose
    still sleeps,
None dare to wake her; soon she bursts her crim-
    son curtain'd bed   30
And comes forth in the majesty of beauty; every
    Flower,
The Pink, the Jessamine, the Wall-flower, the
    Carnation,
The Jonquil, the mild Lilly, opes her heavens;
    every Tree
And Flower & Herb soon fill the air with an in-
    numerable Dance,
Yet all in order sweet & lovely. Men are sick with
    Love,
Such is a Vision of the lamentation of Beulah
    over Ololon.

From JERUSALEM

TO THE PUBLIC

WE who dwell on Earth can do nothing of ourselves; every thing is conducted by Spirits, no less
than Digestion or Sleep. . . . When this Verse was
first dictated to me, I consider'd a Monotonous
Cadence, like that used by Milton & Shakespeare
& all writers of English Blank Verse, derived from
the modern bondage of Rhyming, to be a necessary and indispensible part of Verse. But I soon
found that in the mouth of a true Orator such
monotony was not only awkward, but as much
a bondage as rhyme itself. I therefore have pro-

---

1 Beulah is next to the highest state in humanity, a place of refuge
from doubt and of repose of the spirit.
2 Ololon is one of the Eternals who dwells on the banks of the
river Eden, highest of the regions of humanity. Blake identified
Ololon with a virgin twelve years old whom he had seen in a vision
at Felpham.

3 Satanic giants symbolizing natural fears, who guard jointly the
gates of the heart and the brain.

duced a variety in every line, both of cadences & number of syllables. Every word and every letter is studied and put into its fit place; the terrific numbers are reserved for the terrific parts, the mild & gentle for the mild & gentle parts, and the prosaic for inferior parts; all are necessary to each other. Poetry Fetter'd Fetters the Human Race. Nations are Destroy'd or Flourish in proportion as Their Poetry, Painting and Music are Destroy'd or Flourish! The Primeval State of Man was Wisdom, Art and Science.

.   .   .

TO THE DEISTS

HE never can be a Friend to the Human Race who is the Preacher of Natural Morality or Natural Religion; he is a flatterer who means to betray, to perpetuate Tyrant Pride & the Laws of that Babylon which he foresees shall shortly be destroyed, with the Spiritual and not the Natural Sword. He is in the State named Rahab,[1] which State must be put off before he can be the Friend of Man.

You, O Deists, profess yourselves the Enemies of Christianity, and you are so: you are also the Enemies of the Human Race & of Universal Nature. Man is born a Spectre or Satan & is altogether an Evil, & requires a New Selfhood continually, & must continually be changed into his direct Contrary. But your Greek Philosophy (which is a remnant of Druidism) teaches that Man is Righteous in his Vegetated Spectre: an Opinion of fatal & accursed consequence to Man, as the Ancients saw plainly by Revelation, to the intire abrogation of Experimental Theory; and many believed what they saw and Prophecied of Jesus.

Man must & will have Some Religion: if he has not the Religion of Jesus, he will have the Religion of Satan & will erect the Synagogue of Satan, calling the Prince of this World, God, and destroying all who do not worship Satan under the Name of God. Will any one say, 'Where are those who worship Satan under the Name of God?' Where are they? Listen! Every Religion that Preaches Vengeance for Sin is the Religion of the Enemy & Avenger and not of the Forgiver of Sin, and their God is Satan, Named by the Divine Name. Your Religion, O Deists! Deism, is the Worship of the God of this World by the means of what you call Natural Religion and Natural Philosophy, and of Natural Morality or Self-Righteousness, the Selfish Virtues of the Natural Heart. This was the Religion of the Pharisees who murder'd Jesus. Deism is the same & ends in the same.

Voltaire, Rousseau, Gibbon, Hume, charge the Spiritually Religious with Hypocrisy; but how a Monk, or a Methodist either, can be a Hypocrite, I cannot concieve. We are Men of like passions with others & pretend not to be holier than others; therefore, when a Religious Man falls into Sin, he ought not to be call'd a Hypocrite; this title is more properly to be given to a Player who falls into Sin, whose profession is Virtue & Morality & the making Men Self-Righteous. Foote[2] in calling Whitefield,[3] Hypocrite, was himself one; for Whitefield pretended not to be holier than others, but confessed his Sins before all the World. Voltaire! Rousseau! You cannot escape my charge that you are Pharisees & Hypocrites, for you are constantly talking of the Virtues of the Human Heart and particularly of your own, that you may accuse others, & especially the Religious, whose errors you, by this display of pretended Virtue, chiefly design to expose. Rousseau thought Men Good by Nature: he found them Evil & found no friend. Friendship cannot exist without Forgiveness of Sins continually. The Book written by Rousseau call'd his Confessions, is an apology & cloke for his sin & not a confession.

But you also charge the poor Monks & Religious with being the causes of War, while you acquit & flatter the Alexanders & Caesars, the Lewis's & Fredericks, who alone are its causes & its actors. But the Religion of Jesus, Forgiveness of Sin, can never be the cause of a War nor of a single Martyrdom.

Those who Martyr others or who cause War are Deists, but never can be Forgivers of Sin. The Glory of Christianity is To Conquer by Forgiveness. All the Destruction, therefore, in Christian Europe has arisen from Deism, which is Natural Religion.

I saw a Monk of Charlemaine
Arise before my sight:
I talk'd with the Grey Monk as we stood
In beams of infernal light.

Gibbon arose with a lash of steel,
And Voltaire with a wracking wheel:

---

1 Rahab is the 'red harlot of Babylon' who has dominion over restrictive religion.

2 Samuel Foote (1720–77), English dramatist and comic actor, and an acquaintance of Reynolds.
3 George Whitefield (1714–70), English evangelical preacher.

The Schools, in clouds of learning roll'd,
Arose with War in iron & gold.

'Thou lazy Monk,' they sound afar,
'In vain condemning glorious War;   10
'And in your Cell you shall ever dwell:
Rise, War, & bind him in his Cell!'

The blood red ran from the Grey Monk's side,
His hands & feet were wounded wide,
His body bent, his arms & knees
Like to the roots of ancient trees.

When Satan first the black bow bent
And the Moral Law from the Gospel rent,
He forg'd the Law into a Sword
And spill'd the blood of mercy's Lord.   20

Titus! Constantine! Charlemaine!
O Voltaire! Rousseau! Gibbon! Vain
Your Grecian Mocks & Roman Sword
Against this image of his Lord!

For a Tear is an Intellectual thing,
And a Sigh is the Sword of an Angel King,
And the bitter groan of a Martyr's woe
Is an Arrow from the Almightie's Bow.

TO THE CHRISTIANS

I GIVE you the end of a golden string;
    Only wind it into a ball.
It will lead you in at Heaven's gate
    Built in Jerusalem's wall.

We are told to abstain from fleshly desires that
we may lose no time from the Work of the Lord:
Every moment lost is a moment that cannot be
redeemed; every pleasure that intermingles with
the duty of our station is a folly unredeemable, &
is planted like the seed of a wild flower among
our wheat: All the tortures of repentance are tortures of self-reproach on account of our leaving
the Divine Harvest to the Enemy, the struggles of
intanglement with incoherent roots. I know of no
other Christianity and of no other Gospel than
the liberty both of body & mind to exercise the
Divine Arts of Imagination, Imagination, the
real & eternal World of which this Vegetable Universe is but a faint shadow, & in which we shall
live in our Eternal or Imaginative Bodies when
these Vegetable Mortal Bodies are no more. The
Apostles knew of no other Gospel. What were all
their spiritual gifts? What is the Divine Spirit? is

the Holy Ghost any other than an Intellectual
Fountain? What is the Harvest of the Gospel &
its Labours? What is that Talent which it is a
curse to hide? What are the Treasures of Heaven
which we are to lay up for ourselves, are they any
other than Mental Studies & Performances? What
are all the Gifts of the Gospel, are they not all
Mental Gifts? Is God a Spirit who must be worshipped in Spirit & in Truth, and are not the Gifts
of the Spirit Every-thing to Man? O ye Religious,
discountenance every one among you who shall
pretend to despise Art & Science! I call upon you
in the Name of Jesus! What is the Life of Man
but Art & Science? is it Meat & Drink? is not the
Body more than Raiment? What is Mortality but
the things relating to the Body which Dies? What
is Immortality but the things relating to the Spirit
which Lives Eternally? What is the Joy of Heaven
but Improvement in the things of the Spirit?
What are the Pains of Hell but Ignorance, Bodily Lust, Idleness & devastation of the things of
the Spirit? Answer this to yourselves, & expel
from among you those who pretend to despise
the labours of Art & Science, which alone are
the labours of the Gospel. Is not this plain &
manifest to the thought? Can you think at all &
not pronounce heartily That to Labour in Knowledge is to Build up Jerusalem, and to Despise
Knowledge is to Despise Jerusalem & her Builders. And remember: He who despises & mocks a
Mental Gift in another, calling it pride & selfishness & sin, mocks Jesus the giver of every Mental
Gift, which always appear to the ignorance-loving
Hypocrite as Sins; but that which is a Sin in the
sight of cruel Man is not so in the sight of our
kind God. Let every Christian, as much as in him
lies, engage himself openly & publicly before all
the World in some Mental pursuit for the Building up of Jerusalem.

England! awake! awake! awake!
    Jerusalem thy Sister calls!
Why wilt thou sleep the sleep of death
    And close her from thy ancient walls?

Thy hills & valleys felt her feet
    Gently upon their bosoms move:
Thy gates beheld sweet Zion's ways:
    Then was a time of joy and love.

And now the time returns again:
    Our souls exult, & London's towers   10
Recieve the Lamb of God to dwell·
    In England's green & pleasant bowers.

TO THE QUEEN

[These stanzas addressed to Queen Charlotte, wife of George III, are Blake's Dedication of his 'Illustrations for Blair's *Grave*.']

THE Door of Death is made of Gold,
That Mortal Eyes cannot behold;
But, when the Mortal Eyes are clos'd,
And cold and pale the Limbs repos'd,
The Soul awakes; and, wond'ring, sees
In her mild Hand the golden Keys:
The Grave is Heaven's golden Gate,
And rich and poor around it wait;
O Shepherdess of England's Fold,
Behold this Gate of Pearl and Gold!   10

To dedicate to England's Queen
The Visions that my Soul has seen,
And, by Her kind permission, bring
What I have borne on solemn Wing
From the vast regions of the Grave,
Before Her Throne my Wings I wave;
Bowing before my Sov'reign's Feet,
'The Grave produc'd these Blossoms sweet
In mild repose from Earthly strife;
The Blossoms of Eternal Life!'   20

c. 1806   1808

SELECTIONS FROM BLAKE'S LETTERS

1 *To* the Reverend Dr. Trusler

13 Hercules Buildings,
Lambeth,
23 August, 1799

Revd. Sir,

I really am sorry that you are fall'n out with the Spiritual World, Especially if I should have to answer for it. I feel very sorry that your Ideas & Mine on Moral Painting differ so much as to have made you angry with my method of study. If I am wrong, I am wrong in good company. I had hoped your plan comprehended All Species of this Art, & Expecially that you would not regret that Species which gives Existence to Every other, namely, Visions of Eternity. You say that I want somebody to Elucidate my Ideas. But you ought to know that What is Grand is necessarily obscure to Weak men. That which can be made Explicit to the Idiot is not worth my care. The wisest of the Ancients consider'd what is not too Explicit as the fittest for Instruction, becauses it rouzes the faculties to act. I name Moses, Solomon, Esop, Homer, Plato.

But as you have favor'd me with your remarks on my Design, permit me in return to defend it against a mistaken one, which is, That I have supposed Malevolence without a Cause. Is not Merit in one a Cause of Envy in another, & Serenity & Happiness & Beauty a Cause of Malevolence? But Want of Money & the Distress of A Thief can never be alleged as the Cause of his Thieving, for many honest people endure greater hardships with Fortitude. We must therefore seek the Cause elsewhere than in want of Money, for that is the Miser's passion, not the Thief's.

I have therefore proved your Reasonings Ill proportion'd, which you can never prove my figures to be; they are those of Michael Angelo, Rafael & the Antique, & of the best living Models. I percieve that your Eye is perveted by Caricature Prints, which ought not to abound so much as they do. Fun I love, but too much Fun is of all things the most loathsom. Mirth is better than Fun, & Happiness is better than Mirth. I feel that a Man may be happy in This World. And I know that This World Is a World of Imagination & Vision. I see Every thing I paint In This World, but Every body does not see alike. To the Eyes of a Miser a Guinea is far more beautiful than the Sun, & a bag worn with the use of Money has more beautiful proportions than a Vine filled with Grapes. The tree which moves some to tears of joy is in the Eyes of others only a Green thing which stands in the way. Some see Nature all Ridicule & Deformity, & by these I shall not regulate my proportions; & some scarce see Nature at all. But to the Eyes of the Man of Imagination, Nature is Imagination itself. As a man is, so he sees. As the Eye is formed, such are its Powers. You certainly Mistake, when you say that the Visions of Fancy are not to be found in This World. To Me This World is all One continued Vision of Fancy or Imagination, & I feel Flatter'd when I am told so. What is it sets Homer, Virgil & Milton in so high a rank of Art? Why is the Bible more Entertaining & Instructive than any other book? Is it not because they are addressed to the Imagination, which is Spiritual Sensation, & but mediately to the Understanding or Reason? Such is True Painting, and such was alone valued by the Greeks & the best modern Artists. Consider what Lord Bacon says: 'Sense sends over to Imagination before Reason have judged, & Reason sends over to Imagination before the Decree can be acted.' See Advancemt. of Learning, Part 2, P. 47 of first Edition.

But I am happy to find a Great Majority of Fellow Mortals who can Elucidate My Visions,

& Particularly they have been Elucidated by Children, who have taken a greater delight in contemplating my Pictures than I even hoped. Neither Youth nor Childhood is Folly or Incapacity. Some Children are Fools & so are some Old Men. But There is a vast Majority on the side of Imagination or Spiritual Sensation.

To Engrave after another Painter is infinitely more laborious than to Engrave one's own Inventions. And of the size you require my price has been Thirty Guineas, & I cannot afford to do it for less. I had Twelve for the Head I sent you as a specimen; but after my own designs I could do at least Six times the quantity of labour in the same time, which will account for the difference of price as also that Chalk Engraving is at least six times as laborious as Aqua tinta. I have no objection to Engraving after another Artist. Engraving is the profession I was apprenticed to, & should never have attempted to live by anything else, If orders had not come in for my Designs & Paintings, which I have the pleasure to tell you are Increasing Every Day. Thus If I am a Painter it is not to be attributed to seeking after. But I am contented whether I live by Painting or Engraving.

I am, Revd. Sir, your very obedient servant,
William Blake

2   *To* Thomas Butts

Felpham, 10 January, 1802

Dear Sir,

... You have so generously & openly desired that I will divide my griefs with you, that I cannot hide what it is now become my duty to explain.—My unhappiness has arisen from a source which, if explor'd too narrowly, might hurt my pecuniary circumstances, As my dependence is on Engraving at present, & particularly on the Engravings I have in hand for Mr. H.: & I find on all hands great objections to my doing anything but the meer drudgery of business, & intimations that if I do not confine myself to this, I shall not live; this has always pursu'd me. You will understand by this the source of all my uneasiness. This from Johnson & Fuseli brought me down here, & this from Mr. H. will bring me back again; for that I cannot live without doing my duty to lay up treasures in heaven is Certain & Determined, & to this I have long made up my mind, & why this should be made an objection to Me, while Drunkenness, Lewdness, Gluttony & even Idleness itself, does not hurt other men, let Satan himself Explain. The Thing I have most at Heart—more than life, or all that seems to make life comfortable without—Is the Interest

of True Religion & Science, & whenever any thing appears to affect that Interest (Especially if I myself omit any duty to my Station as a Soldier of Christ), It gives me the greatest of torments. I am not ashamed, afraid, or averse to tell you what Ought to be Told: That I am under the direction of Messengers from Heaven, Daily & Nightly; but the nature of such things is not, as some suppose, without trouble or care. Temptations are on the right hand & left; behind, the sea of time & space roars & follows swiftly; he who keeps not right onward is lost, & if our footsteps slide in clay, how can we do otherwise than fear & tremble? but I should not have troubled You with this account of my spiritual state, unless it had been necessary in explaining the actual cause of my uneasiness, into which you are so kind as to Enquire; for I never obtrude such things on others unless question'd, & then I never disguise the truth.—But if we fear to do the dictates of our Angels, & tremble at the Tasks set before us; if we refuse to do Spiritual Acts because of Natural Fears or Natural Desires! Who can describe the dismal torments of such a state!—I too well remember the Threats I heard!—'If you, who are organised by Divine Providence for spiritual communion, Refuse, & bury your Talent in the Earth, even tho' you should want Natural Bread, Sorrow & Desperation pursues you thro' life, & after death shame & confusion of face to eternity. Every one in Eternity will leave you, aghast at the Man who was crown'd with glory & honour by his brethren, & betray'd their cause to their enemies. You will be call'd the base Judas who betray'd his Friend!'—Such words would make any stout man tremble, & how then could I be at ease? But I am now no longer in That State, & now go on again with my Task, Fearless, and tho' my path is difficult, I have no fear of stumbling while I keep it. ... Naked we came here, naked of Natural things, & naked we shall return; but while cloth'd with the Divine Mercy, we are richly cloth'd in Spiritual & suffer all the rest gladly. Pray give my Love to Mrs. Butts & your family. I am, Yours Sincerely,

William Blake

From ANNOTATIONS TO SIR JOSHUA REYNOLDS'S DISCOURSES[1]

THIS Man was Hired to Depress Art.

---

1 Sir Joshua Reynolds (1723–92) was a famous portrait painter and first president of the Royal Academy of Arts. He delivered his *Discourses* on the principles of art to the students of the academy between 1769 and 1790.

This is the Opinion of Will Blake: my Proofs of this Opinion are given in the following Notes.

.   .   .

The Arts & Sciences are the Destruction of Tyrannies or Bad Governments. Why should A Good Government endeavour to Depress what is its Chief & only Support?

The Foundation of Empire is Art & Science. Remove them or Degrade them, & the Empire is No More. Empire follows Art & Not Vice Versa as Englishmen suppose. . . .

Liberality! we want not Liberality. We want a Fair Price & Proportionate Value & a General Demand for Art.

Let not that Nation where Less than Nobility is the Reward, Pretend that Art is Encouraged by that Nation. Art is First in Intellectuals & Ought to be First in Nations. . . .

I consider Reynolds's Discourses to the Royal Academy as the Simulations of the Hypocrite who smiles particularly where he means to Betray. His Praise of Rafael is like the Hysteric Smile of Revenge. His Softness & Candour, the hidden trap & the poisoned feast. He praises Michel Angelo for Qualities which Michel Angelo abhorr'd, & He blames Rafael for the only Qualities which Rafael Valued. Whether Reynolds knew what he was doing is nothing to me: the Mischief is just the same whether a Man does it Ignorantly or Knowingly. I always consider'd True Art & True Artists to be particularly insulted & Degraded by the Reputation of these Discourses, As much as they were Degraded by the Reputation of Reynolds's Paintings, & that Such Artists as Reynolds are at all times Hired by the Satans for the Depression of Art—A Pretence of Art, To destroy Art. . . .

The Rich Men of England form themselves into a Society to Sell & Not to Buy Pictures. The Artist who does not throw his Contempt on such Trading Exhibitions, does not know either his own Interest or his Duty.

When Nations grow Old, The Arts grow Cold
And Commerce settles on every Tree,
And the Poor & the Old can live upon Gold,
For all are Born Poor, Aged Sixty three.

Reynolds's Opinion was that Genius May be Taught & that all Pretence to Inspiration is a Lie & a Deceit, to say the least of it. For if it is a Deceit, the whole Bible is Madness. This Opinion originates in the Greeks' calling the Muses Daughters of Memory.

The Enquiry in England is not whether a Man has Talents & Genius, But whether he is Passive & Polite & a Virtuous Ass & obedient to Noblemen's Opinions in Art & Science. If he is, he is a Good Man. If Not, he must be Starved.

Minute Discrimination is Not Accidental. All Sublimity is founded on Minute Discrimination.

I do not believe that Rafael taught Mich. Angelo, or that Mich. Angelo taught Rafael, any more than I believe that the Rose teaches the Lilly how to grow, or the Apple tree teaches the Pear tree how to bear Fruit. . . .

Are we to understand him to mean that Facility in Composing is a Frivolous pursuit? A Facility in Composing is the Greatest Power of Art, & Belongs to None but the Greatest Artists, the Most Minutely Discriminating & Determinate.

Mechanical Excellence is the Only Vehicle of Genius.

Execution is the Chariot of Genius. . . .

No one can ever Design till he has learn'd the Language of Art by making many Finish'd Copies both of Nature & Art & of whatever comes in his way from Earliest Childhood. The difference between a bad Artist & a Good One Is: the Bad Artist Seems to copy a Great deal. The Good one Really does Copy a Great deal. . . .

The Man who on Examining his own Mind finds nothing of Inspiration ought not to dare to be an Artist, & he is a Fool & a Cunning Knave suited to the Purposes of Evil Demons.

The Man who never in his Mind & Thoughts travel'd to Heaven Is No Artist.

Artists who are above a plain Understanding are Mock'd & Destroy'd by this President of Fools.

It is Evident that Reynolds Wish'd none but Fools to be in the Arts & in order to this, he calls all others Vague Enthusiasts or Madmen.

What has Reasoning to do with the Art of Painting? . . .

Knowledge of Ideal Beauty is Not to be Acquired. It is Born with us. Innate Ideas are in Every Man, Born with him; they are truly Himself. The Man who says that we have No Innate Ideas must be a Fool & Knave, Having no Con-Science or Innate Science.

One Central Form composed of all other Forms being Granted, it does not therefore follow that all other Forms are Deformity.

All Forms are Perfect in the Poet's Mind, but these are not Abstracted nor compounded from Nature, but are from Imagination.

The Great Bacon—he is Call'd: I call him the Little Bacon—says that Every thing must be done by Experiment; his first principle is Unbelief, and yet here he says that Art must be produc'd Without such Method. He is Like Sr Joshua, full of Self-Contradiction & Knavery. . . .

Of what consequence is it to the Arts what a Portrait Painter does? . . .

When a Man talks of Acquiring Invention & of learning how to produce Original Conception, he must expect to be call'd a Fool by Men of Understanding; but such a Hired Knave cares not for the Few. His Eye is on the Many, or, rather, the Money.

Bacon's Philosophy has Destroy'd [*word cut away*] Art & Science. The Man who says that the Genius is not Born, but Taught—Is a Knave.

O Reader, behold the Philosopher's Grave!
He was born quite a Fool, but he died quite
        a Knave.

How ridiculous it would be to see the Sheep Endeavouring to walk like the Dog, or the Ox striving to trot like the Horse; just as Ridiculous it is to see One Man Striving to Imitate Another. Man varies from Man more than Animal from Animal of different Species.

If Art was Progressive We should have had Mich. Angelos & Rafaels to Succeed & to Improve upon each other. But it is not so. Genius dies with its Possessor & Comes not again till Another is Born with It. . . .

Identities or Things are Neither Cause nor Effect. They are Eternal.

Reynolds Thinks that Man Learns all that he knows. I say on the Contrary that Man Brings All that he has or can have Into the World with him. Man is Born Like a Garden ready Planted & Sown. This World is too poor to produce one Seed.

Reynolds: The mind is but a barren soil; a soil which is soon exhausted, and will produce no crop, . . .

The mind that could have produced this Sentence must have been a Pitiful, a Pitiable Imbecillity. I always thought that the Human Mind was the most Prolific of All Things & Inexhaustible. I certainly do Thank God that I am not like Reynolds. . . .

The Ancients did not mean to Impose when they affirm'd their belief in Vision & Revelation. Plato was in Earnest: Milton was in Earnest. They believ'd that God did Visit Man Really & Truly & not as Reynolds pretends.

How very Anxious Reynolds is to Disprove & Contemn Spiritual Perception!

He states Absurdities in Company with Truths & calls both Absurd. . . .

It is not in Terms that Reynolds & I disagree. Two Contrary Opinions can never by any Language be made alike. I say, Taste & Genius are Not Teachable or Acquirable, but are born with us. Reynolds says the Contrary. . . .

God forbid that Truth should be Confined to Mathematical Demonstration!

He who does not Know Truth at Sight is unworthy of Her Notice.

Here is a great deal to do to Prove that All Truth is Prejudice, for All that is Valuable in Knowledge is Superior to Demonstrative Science, such as is Weighed or Measured.

He thinks he has proved that Genius & Inspiration are All a Hum.

He may as well say that if Man does not lay down settled Principles, The Sun will not rise in a Morning. . . .

Burke's Treatise on the Sublime & Beautiful is founded on the Opinions of Newton & Locke;

on this Treatise Reynolds has grounded many of his assertions in all his Discourses. I read Burke's Treatise when very Young; at the same time I read Locke on Human Understanding & Bacon's Advancement of Learning; on Every one of these Books I wrote my Opinions, & on looking them over find that my Notes on Reynolds in this Book are exactly Similar. I felt the Same Contempt & Abhorrence then that I do now. They mock Inspiration & Vision. Inspiration & Vision was then, & now is, & I hope will always Remain, my Element, my Eternal Dwelling place; how can I then hear it Contemned without returning Scorn for Scorn?

From ANNOTATIONS TO 'POEMS' BY WILLIAM WORDSWORTH

I SEE in Wordsworth the Natural Man rising up against the Spiritual Man Continually, & then

he is No Poet but a Heathen Philosopher at Enmity against all true Poetry or Inspiration.

There is no such Thing as Natural Piety Because The Natural Man is at Enmity with God.

I cannot think that Real Poets have any competition. None are greatest in the Kingdom of Heaven; it is so in Poetry.

Natural Objects always did & now do weaken, deaden & obliterate Imagination in Me. Wordsworth must know that what he Writes Valuable is Not to be found in Nature.

I Believe both Macpherson & Chatterton, that what they say is Ancient Is so.

I own myself an admirer of Ossian equally with any other Poet whatever, Rowley & Chatterton also.

Imagination has nothing to do with Memory.

1770 · WILLIAM WORDSWORTH · 1850

1770   Born 7 April, at Cockermouth, in Cumberland, second son of John Wordsworth and Anne (Cookson). Of sturdy north-country stock on both sides of his house; his father a lawyer, who acted as solicitor for Earl of Lonsdale. Grew up in happy childhood with his three brothers (Richard, John, and Christopher) and his sister, Dorothy, in the family mansion on the River Derwent, across from the picturesque ruins of Cockermouth Castle. Attended Anne Birkett's school at Penrith, where Mary Hutchinson, his future wife, was one of his schoolmates. When he was seven years old his mother died and the family was dispersed, Dorothy being sent to live with her grandmother at Penrith and Richard and William to school at Hawkshead in Lancashire.

1779–87   For eight years lived in Hawkshead at the house of Anne Tyson and attended the village grammar school. His schoolmaster was William Taylor, who taught him Latin, Greek, and mathematics and encouraged him in writing verses. Although the school days were long, he enjoyed complete freedom after hours and during holidays to range the open countryside, alone or with his schoolmates, hunting, trapping, nutting, or sometimes engaging in the more venturesome sport of gathering raven eggs from the crags. These years were among the happiest of his life. His sensibilities were sharpened, his sympathies enlarged, and his love of Nature confirmed. Read widely in books of his own choosing (*Arabian Nights* was a favorite) and came to know intimately by observation and association the village characters that later so prominently figure in his poetry (*Prelude* I, II). Wordsworth's father died in 1783, leaving an estate of about £5000, chiefly in claims upon Earl of Lonsdale, who thwarted a settlement during his lifetime. After the Earl's death in 1802, his successor made the Wordsworths a complete settlement with interest. The Wordsworth children were left in the guardianship of their uncles.

1787–91   Entered St. John's College, Cambridge. Found the routine of the university somewhat boring. Attended lectures and enjoyed undergraduate social life but did not 'go in for honors.' On his own read the classics, learned Italian, and read the 'moderns.' Among scientific studies, geometry especially appealed to him. Although cut off from his native hills, he experienced at times, even in the level fields of Cambridgeshire, exaltation in the presence of Nature (*Prelude* III, VI). Spent the first summer vacation at Hawkshead, where on a memorable morning he dedicated himself to a life of lofty purpose (*Prelude* IV). Spent the second summer vacation (1789) with Dorothy and Mary Hutchinson at Penrith. Composed *An Evening Walk* (1787–9). Spent the third summer vacation (1790) in a walking tour through France, Switzerland, and Italy with Robert Jones. His sympathies were aroused for the French people, celebrating the first anniversary of their newborn republic, but at that time he was far more impressed by 'the sublime and beautiful' scenery of the Alps. Took his degree in January without distinction and without plans for the future (*Prelude* VI).

1791   'Ranged at large' in London, February-May (*Prelude* VII). Visited his college friend Jones in Wales (May–September) and with him made a walking tour of the north countries. In November set out for Orléans, France, with the intention of perfecting himself in French preparatory to becoming a traveling tutor. Visited in Paris on his way south.

1792   At Orléans fell in love with Annette Vallon (a vivacious woman of good family about four years older than Wordsworth), who bore him a daughter, Caroline. Spent part of the year at Blois, where he made the acquaintance of Captain Michel Beaupuy. Became a complete convert to French Republicanism. Was back in Orléans by September. In October was in Paris and probably in close association with the Girondist leaders. A peremptory summons home in December prevented him from sharing their fate (*Prelude* IX, X, XI). Composed *Descriptive Sketches* (1791–2).

1793   Published *An Evening Walk* and *Descriptive Sketches.* May have intended to marry Annette, but in February war broke out between France and England, making his return to France impossible. He was not to see Annette or her daughter again until 1802. Was in disgrace with his relatives, who cut off further advances on his expected inheritance and even denied him admission to the house where Dorothy was living. In late summer went on a walking tour with William Calvert through the south of England, across Salisbury Plain, along the River Wye, and through North Wales. His conscience heavy with thoughts of Annette and his loyalties at conflict over his country's war with France. However, his sympathies still strongly Republican. Associated with members of London's radical circle, including William Godwin, Joseph Fawcett, Tom Paine, and Mary Wollstonecraft, and was converted to Godwin's social radicalism. Wrote a spirited letter (left unfinished and unpublished) to Richard Watson, Bishop of Llandaff, attacking him for his apostasy from the cause of liberty. Completed *Guilt and Sorrow* (1791–4).

1794   Moved about, living with relatives and friends, in the Lake District, Yorkshire, and on the Lancashire coast at Rampside near Peele Castle. Spent several delightful weeks in Dorothy's company in the Lake District, though their 'gypsying about' and lodging together at a farmhouse was prudishly frowned upon by relatives.

1795   Raisley Calvert died, leaving Wordsworth £900. In September he established a home with Dorothy at Racedown, in Dorsetshire. They took the child Edward Montagu to live with them.

1796   Plunged into extensive reading of modern European literature, especially books of travel. Began *The Borderers.*

1797   Mary Hutchinson was a guest at Racedown during the spring. In June Coleridge came down for the memorable visit which was to initiate a close and long-enduring friendship between the two poets. In July, the Wordsworths settled at Alfoxden, a country estate near Nether Stowey, in Somerset, where Coleridge lived. For the next twelve months Coleridge, Wordsworth, and Dorothy were in close communion of spirit ('we were three persons with one soul') which resulted in a great quickening of the creative powers in each. *Lyrical Ballads* begun.

1798   In January, Dorothy began her famous Journal. Hazlitt visited in the spring. The lease of Alfoxden having expired in June, the Wordsworths and Coleridge went to Bristol to arrange with Cottle about the publication of their joint volume. A walking trip along the River Wye with Dorothy resulted in the famous *Lines Written a Few Miles above Tintern Abbey. Lyrical Ballads* published in September. Wordsworth in London with Dorothy during late summer. With Dorothy and Coleridge sailed from Yarmouth for Germany, mid-September. Arrived at Goslar, after a stay in Hamburg, early October.

1799   At Goslar until late February. A bitterly cold and lonely winter (Coleridge had left for study at Göttingen University), but poetically productive. Wrote the Lucy poems, *Ruth,* and parts of *The Prelude.* Traveled in Germany and returned to England in May. Visited with the Hutchinsons at Sockburn. On a walking tour through the Lake District with Coleridge. Settled at Dove Cottage (Town-end), Grasmere, with Dorothy, 20 December (their home until 1808).

1800   One of the most prolific years: finished books I and II of *The Prelude,* the great fragment of *The Recluse,* and many other poems, including *Michael.* Dorothy faithfully recorded in her Journal the joy and beauty of their life at Grasmere. Coleridge settled near by at Keswick. Published a second, and enlarged, edition of *Lyrical Ballads,* with the famous Preface.

1801   Paid a brief visit to Scotland. Modernized several of Chaucer's poems, but Wordsworth's own creative energies were in temporary subsidence. Mary Hutchinson a guest for three months during the autumn.

1802   This year opened with a resurgence of creative power, which continued with few and short interruptions until 1807. Composed part of the great *Ode: Intimations of Immortality,* many of his best sonnets, and numerous fine lyrics. In late summer, journeyed with Dorothy to Calais and spent a month there in daily visits with Annette and Caroline. Arranged to pay £30 annually in Caroline's support. On 4 October married Mary Hutchinson.

1803   In June, shortly after the birth of his first son, John, set off with Dorothy and Coleridge on a tour of Scotland. Coleridge separated from his companions at Loch Lomond, but they continued their journey through the Highlands. On the return, they spent a week with Walter Scott. A series of poems resulted from the tour. Friendship and patronage of Sir George Beaumont began in this year and continued until Sir George's death in 1827.

1804   In the spring, re-engaged in the composition of *The Prelude.* His daughter Dora born.

1805   His brother John drowned in the wreck of his own vessel, the *Abergavenny,* 5 February. Completed *The Prelude.*

1806   Second son, Thomas, born. Lived in a farmhouse at Coleorton, Leicestershire, on the estate of Sir George Beaumont, from October 1806 to the summer of 1807.

1807   Published *Poems in Two Volumes.*

1808   Daughter Catherine born. Moved to Allan Bank, Grasmere.

1809   Published *The Convention of Cintra,* a political tract.

1810   Son William born. Became estranged from Coleridge.

1811   Moved from Allan Bank to the Rectory, Grasmere.

1812   Visited London and became reconciled with Coleridge. Death of two of his children, Catherine (in June) and Thomas (in December).

1813   Was appointed to the office of Distributor of Stamps for Westmoreland, which returned him about £400 a year. Moved to Rydal Mount, his home for the rest of his life.

1814   Made a second tour of Scotland. Published *The Excursion.*

1815   Published *Poems* and *The White Doe of Rylstone* (written in 1807).

1816   Published *A Letter to a Friend of Robert Burns* and *Thanksgiving Ode.*

1819   Published *Peter Bell* (written in 1798) and *The Waggoner* (written in 1805).

1820   Published *The River Duddon,* a series of sonnets. With his wife and sister made a tour of the continent, visiting Switzerland, the Italian lakes, and Paris.

1822   Published *Memorials of a Tour on the Continent, Ecclesiastical Sketches,* and *A Description of the Scenery of the Lakes,* a prose work.

1823   Made a tour of the Netherlands and Belgium.

1828   With Coleridge and Dora made a tour up the Rhine.

1829   Visited Ireland.

1831   Made a tour in the Highlands with Dora and a nephew. Visited Scott at Abbotsford.

1833   Made a tour of the Isle of Man and Scotland.

1835   Published *Yarrow Revisited, and Other Poems.*

1837   Made a tour through France and Italy.

1842   Published his last volume, *Poems Chiefly of Early and Late Years.* Resigned his post of Stamp Distributor and received a pension of £300 from the Civil List.

1843   Succeeded Southey as Poet Laureate. Dictated notes on his poems to Miss Fenwick.

1850   Died, 23 April, at Rydal Mount and lies buried in Grasmere Churchyard. *The Prelude,* revised in 1839, published posthumously.

WILLIAM WORDSWORTH was the most truly original genius of his age and exerted a power over the poetic destinies of his century unequaled by any of his contemporaries. The source of his strength lay within his own extraordinary powers of awareness. He saw things that other people do not see or see but dimly, and he saw them with singular frequency and vividness. His poetic impulse came to him through some perfectly familiar experience, such as beholding the rainbow or hearing the shout of the cuckoo. From an impression simply and purely sensuous there would be set up a mood of mind or feeling in which 'the object contemplated was suddenly released from the tie of custom and became a source of mysterious exaltation' (Havens). In such brief, intensely charged moments Wordsworth experienced a feeling of release; sensation blanked out, consciousness was almost completely lost, and he became 'living soul.' Through frequent repetitions of these periods of transcendent ecstasy, Wordsworth became overpoweringly aware of the reality and importance of the spiritual world. His transfiguring vision most often occurred during vigils of contemplation in natural surroundings. Nature spoke to him of the 'mystery of infinitude, of Powers, Spirits, Presences.' The divine in Nature and the divine in his own soul he felt to be one and the same thing. When Wordsworth was in his middle thirties his spiritual perceptions began to fade. The intensity of his experiences and the strenuousness of the poet's calling had burned him out early. Gradually, as age came on and inspiration slackened, the intellectual powers took over and his fibers toughened. The best of the poetry was written before half of his life was spent. But during his youth his sensibilities were keen and his impulses strong. He was then the 'trusting child of nature, the foe to conventionality, and the defiant champion of the poor' (Harper). Wordsworth was gifted with intense personal magnetism and a large capacity for friendship. But by some he was thought to be immoderately self-centered, and to many his later rigidity of opinion and ultra-conservatism have been unattractive. Under critical attack he did not always behave amiably; though as the years passed and the opposition to his poetry disappeared, he developed an improved mildness and humility. To Carlyle, who in many ways was unsympathetic to Wordsworth, the poet in his later days was a 'right good old steel-grey figure, with a fine rustic simplicity and dignity about him, and a veracious strength looking through him.' Wordsworth, like Milton, considered himself a dedicated spirit. He assumed the prophet's role to his generation, and through all his vicissitudes kept a single-minded and single-hearted devotion to his task. He put aside littleness and fixed his attention 'upon the wide spaces of earth and sky.' In favored moments the grace of vision descended upon him. Then he comprehended eternal wisdom and wrote down for the generations of men 'truths that wake, to perish never.'

Wordsworth's progress toward a settled and healthy state of genius was faltering and slow. In his early work we find him struggling in the toils of literary convention. Eventually Wordsworth was to become the major force to break the prevailing literary mode, but in his first substantial poem, *An Evening Walk,* written during his Cambridge days, he displays eighteenth-century mannerisms at their worst. And in his next important composition, *Descriptive Sketches,* there is, if possible, even more to displease. Both poems abound in personifications, hackneyed allusions, fantastic figures of speech, violent displacements, and other eccentricities of style fashionable in the mediocre poetry of the time. Yet in spite of numerous obvious and flagrant faults these earliest poems carry the marks of genius. In *An Evening Walk,* which transcribes scenes from the poet's native Lake District, his sense of truth led him to break through convention at times with a language of promising naturalness and bold simplicity. In *Descriptive Sketches,* written in France in the full tide of revolutionary fervor, there is reach and power, clarity of outline, and in a number of places fresh and striking imagery. On his return from France in December 1792, at a bewildering time for the whole of Europe and for Wordsworth personally, the poet was captivated by the radical philosophy of William Godwin. At that juncture in his affairs it was highly comforting to him to discover a ready-made philosophical system that reduced all complex problems, public and private, to the sole and simple principle of reason. The newly engrafted Godwinian doctrine he fully exploited in his next important poem, *Guilt and Sorrow*. In this work he gives glowing, though strangely perverted, expression to the sound idealism that had fired his imagination in France. He portrays the bitter sufferings of the poor through the calamities of war and exposes the vices of the penal code. *Guilt and Sorrow* is artistically freer than are *An Evening Walk* and *Descriptive Sketches,* but emotionally it is morbid and morally confused; for right and wrong do not, as Wordsworth (following Godwin) assumes, derive from the same source. In time Wordsworth came to see the dangers of doctrinaire reason when it is separated from the general impulses of heart and soul. But his deliverance from Godwinism was gradual. The *Borderers,* a five-act play which followed *Guilt and Sorrow,* is a curious mixture of Godwinism and an exposure of its dangers. Wordsworth had hoped by adopting Godwinian doctrine to free himself from remorse over his abandonment of Annette. But, though he compromised skillfully, he found that remorse clung to him. In *The Borderers* (a work of no intrinsic merit) he faced his problem honestly, exposed the warped and dangerous psychology of Godwin, and in doing so purged himself of pessimism. Freed at last from his guilt, he bade farewell forever to all systems that neglect the 'universal heart.' French Revolutionary idealism and Godwin's social humanitarianism he retained; all else that was false in Godwin's doctrine he abandoned. Fully alive to 'humble cares' and human suffering, Wordsworth was finally ready to enter into his true inheritance. The new light came to him sooner because of the reunion at Racedown in 1795 with his beloved sister, Dorothy. With her exquisite regard for common things and her cheerful, affectionate disposition she reawakened his sensibilities and softened down his over-sternness. Not long after, her good offices were augmented by that 'marvelous man' Coleridge. It was a memorable day for English poetry when, in June 1797, Coleridge saw Dorothy for the first time and her brother recited for them *The Ruined Cottage.*

By his unreserved admiration and encouragement Coleridge gave Wordsworth confidence just when he needed it most. He also importantly brought into focus Wordsworth's latent interest in the associational psychology of David Hartley. As a result of Coleridge's contagious enthusiasm for Hartley (he named his firstborn son after the philosopher) almost all of Wordsworth's work in the key years 1797–8 is rooted in the sensationistic-associationistic psychology stemming from Locke, Hume, and Hartley. According to this psychology human knowledge originates for the most part in perceptions made by the five senses. These perceptions through association are transformed to the complexes—the hopes, fears, beliefs—of mental life. All is built up from the outside; there are no innate, or inborn, ideas. There is, however, from the first an activity or motion of the human spirit which transmutes the mental complexes into their appropriate personal values. Interest in Hartleian psychology led Wordsworth often to choose peasants, children, or defectives as subjects for his study of the mind of man. He went to rustics (in much the same spirit as a scientific investigator) 'to explore the primary laws of our nature.' He was audacious in the presentation of his findings, often bringing ridicule upon himself for his rendering of the mental states of indigents or idiots. And in presenting the basic psychological problem of the 'way in which the mind of man is wedded to this goodly universe' he shocked and alarmed even Coleridge by his literal adherence to sensationistic philosophy. Wordsworth cast aside the supernatural and made for himself a naturally revealed religion. He was well pleased to recognize

> In nature and the language of the sense,
> The anchor of my purest thoughts, the nurse,
> The guide, the guardian of my heart, and soul
> Of all my moral being.

On the basis of this passage in *Tintern Abbey* and similarly unqualified expressions of sensationism, Coleridge dubbed his friend 'a semi-atheist.' Yet in spite of censure, Wordsworth consistently renounced orthodox Christianity up to 1805 and studiously avoided any use of its dogmas and symbols.

Throughout his great creative period, 1797–1807, Wordsworth owed much to Coleridge, but their first year of intimacy, when they were near neighbors in the lovely Quantocks, was the most fruitful time of all. They were then in daily companionship and in almost constant exaltation of spirits. With the fervor of high-minded youth (Coleridge was then twenty-six, Wordsworth, twenty-eight) they talked of making the world better through their poetry. They hoped in that time of national crisis and pessimism to bring to men disillusioned by the failure of the French Revolutionary Idea the secret they had discovered of a principle of joy in the universe. They would preach no political or social reform, but in order to reach men they would cast out of their writing all poetic diction and return to directness, sincerity, and basic human emotions. The older poets and the traditional ballads would be their models. In their discussions together they became absorbed with the problem of how the imagination can spread an atmosphere of the ideal world over familiar forms and incidents and how also it can give an air of reality to the marvelous. As a result of their talks a series of poems was planned in which Wordsworth was 'to give the charm of novelty to subjects of every-day life,' and 'to excite a feeling analogous to the supernatural, by awakening the mind's attention from the lethargy of custom, and directing it to the loveliness and the wonders of the world before us.' It was agreed that Coleridge's endeavors 'should be directed to persons and characters supernatural, or at least romantic; yet so as to transfer from our inward nature a human interest and a semblance of truth sufficient to procure for these shadows of imagination that willing suspension of disbelief for the moment, which constitutes poetic faith.' The program was carried out by Coleridge with 'splendid audacity' and with less success in a more difficult assignment by Wordsworth in *Lyrical Ballads,* 1798. Wordsworth's industry was greater, but his artistry was less perfect. Probably no one of his poems on human beings in this volume wholly justified his method. Yet he has presented a remarkable list of personages with sincerity and courage and with striking psychological veracity. With far-reaching charity, neither sentimental nor condescending, he has penetrated through the outward show of things to discover the 'primary laws of our nature' in the lives of homely men and women. In work soon to follow he was to continue his interpretation of humble life with greater poetic success: in *Michael, Ruth, The Brothers,* the Matthew poems, and *Resolution and Independence.*

Even more famous in the 1798 *Lyrical Ballads* was Wordsworth's group of poems, culminating in *Tintern Abbey,* in which he set forth his philosophical faith in Nature. These are the truly 'Wordsworthian' poems which give the key to his newly found solution to the riddle of the universe. With Dorothy's gentle ministry and Coleridge's philosophical guidance Wordsworth rediscovered the vitality and joy in Nature that he had known in youth. Once again all living things are to him positive, real, and good. Joy is in 'widest commonalty spread.' Even the humblest of created things shares in the universal gladness. It is his faith that 'every flower enjoys the air it breathes.' Everywhere he finds design, order, harmony, and pleasure in the universe. Thus he speaks of Nature as 'kindly,' 'fostering,' and 'holy.' Nor were these concepts for Wordsworth mere externals. The universe to him is impregnated with a free, active, moving power which he identified with deity. What Wordsworth requires is a world with God *in* it: literally to him God and Nature are one. For him there is no division between Man and Nature, as there is no division between Nature and God—all things adhere in a mighty unity. 'Each thing has a life of its own and we are all one life,' wrote Coleridge, interpreting Spinoza. This is the view Wordsworth expressed in the well-known passage in *Tintern Abbey,* called by Hazlitt the most perfect statement of pantheism ever written:

> And I have felt
> A presence that disturbs me with the joy
> Of elevated thoughts; a sense sublime
> Of something far more deeply interfused,
> Whose dwelling is the light of setting suns,

And the round ocean and the living air,
And the blue sky, and in the mind of man;
A motion and a spirit, that impels
All thinking things, all objects of all thought,
And rolls through all things.

Man's mind, Wordsworth is telling us, and all natural objects are interpenetrative, knit together as one thing in a chain of benevolent necessity. It is given to man through mystical union to participate in the spiritual Power that lies behind and activates all existence. In favored moments the divine fountain light of Spirit will flow into him and illuminate the whole of his moral world. Essentially Wordsworth was concerned in *Tintern Abbey* (and later in *The Prelude*) to show progressively how through the various age levels of our lives the beautiful objects of Nature can strengthen our character, humanize our attitude toward man, and enable us 'to see into the life of things'—that is, to give us insight into the spiritual governance of the universe. No object or experience was too slight to serve his purpose. The world of things is 'forever speaking'; we have but to listen and to look to find a 'tale in everything.' In these nature poems Wordsworth captured something of the primal impulses of Nature herself. He has rendered natural images with great clearness, 'fresh with points of morning dew.' He has given highly original and lasting expression to the romantic doctrine of Nature lifted to the realm of religious worship. He has given also a luminous personal record of how he conceived that Nature molded his character and how it may mold others who bring a 'heart that watches and receives.'

Lyrical Ballads was published anonymously by Wordsworth and Coleridge as an experiment to call in question the prevalent taste of the day and to determine how far the language of conversation of the lower and middle classes might be suited to poetical composition. On its appearance the volume almost immediately drew the fire of critics questioning the value of the experiment. In due time the young poets undertook to defend their critical position. Meanwhile, in Germany in the winter of 1798–9, Wordsworth hit upon a new kind of poetry. In one of the coldest winters on record the poet and his sister were isolated at Goslar, with no acquaintances or books, no social amenities, and few opportunities to learn the German language, the chief purpose for which they had come. Thrown back by circumstances upon his inner resources, Wordsworth entered a period of 'intense mental activity and creativeness' (Harper). He fed his imagination upon recollections of England and found within them the stuff of poetry. Reminiscence, or recollection, had already appeared in *Tintern Abbey*, but in the Lucy poems, *Nutting*, and *The Prelude I* and *II*, it was raised and intensified to a higher power. Within the recesses of his own mind Wordsworth recovered those 'spots of time'—moments that returned to consciousness out of the depth of the past, leaping 'from hiding places ten years deep.' A substantial list of fine poems, including *There Was a Boy, Lucy Gray, Two April Mornings,* and *The Fountain,* composed at Goslar, in addition to those already named, gives evidence to the rich new source of inspiration the poet had discovered. Imaginative illumination through recollection became a characteristic method in many later poems. We find a parallel, for example, in *Stepping Westward,* where a girl's wild greeting on a lonely heath touched off the 'spontaneous overflow' of reminiscence. Many sonnets and, from the two volumes of 1807, *My Heart Leaps Up, I Wandered Lonely as a Cloud, The Sparrow's Nest, To the Cuckoo,* and the great *Ode on Immortality* are built upon the indestructible germs of incident which the imagination recovers and makes into poetry. The second edition of *Lyrical Ballads,* 1800, not only contains new poems of this kind but also has a Preface to explain and defend the critical position of their author.

The famous Preface to *Lyrical Ballads,* 1800, was urged by Coleridge and written by Wordsworth to meet the challenge of critical opposition aroused by the first edition. Wordsworth began by explaining that their experiment was undertaken to combat the perverse writings—'the frantic novels, sickly and stupid German tragedies, and the deluge of idle and extravagant stories in verse'—which were then degrading the public taste. He further made clear that their poetry was distinguished from this 'gaudy verse,' by (1) being built upon incidents and situations chosen from common life related in simple language, (2) having a worthy *purpose,* and (3) having the emphasis not upon the action but upon the feeling therein developed. These principles upon which the new poetry was to be written involved actually only a few basic ideas. But they were sufficiently audacious at the time and were presented with such bluntness, and sometimes ineptness, that they stirred the anger of the critics and the resistance of readers for nearly a generation. Yet Wordsworth's doctrines were essentially sound and in line with the great tradition in English letters. Wordsworth showed good sense in striving to make feeling give rise to action and showed courage in carrying this principle into his most ambitious writing. Furthermore, he brought a renewed worthiness to English poetry by dealing directly with human passions, human characters, and human incidents. Some of his loftiest poetry rises from a profound and deeply spiritual sympathy with common, simple folk. In the matter of language Wordsworth's aim was to set up the speech of rustics and the language of Chaucer, Shakespeare, and Milton against the rhetorical eccentricities—the so-called 'poetic diction'—then fashionable. Language for him meant the real (not the perverted) language of men, rooted in accurate observation and approved by usage. Colloquial forms and phrases were to Wordsworth the most sincere expression of deep human passion. Meter, Wordsworth explained, refines and selects the passions of real life and is necessary in poetry for giving an overbalance of pleasure. In stating that there is no essential difference between poetry and prose (a much misunderstood maxim) Wordsworth meant that both are based on *reality* and should therefore be built upon identical proprieties and idioms. As a medium, he is saying, there is no essential difference between prose and verse. The word 'essential' in this connection has a wide application. Along with new theory the Preface contains remarks upon poetry in general and upon the role of the poet in society. Wordsworth describes poetry in his famous definition as 'a spontaneous overflow of powerful feelings' taking its origin from 'emotion recollected in tranquility.' It is important to observe in Wordsworth's full account that, though poetry may begin in tranquility, the original emotion or 'spot of time' is contemplated until a new emotion, kindred to the original, exists in the mind. It is at this point that feeling overflows and poetic composition begins. Wordsworth held a lofty conception of the function of the poet; his is a sacred office. Poetry is the 'breath and spirit of all knowledge'; it is as immortal as the heart of man. In practice Wordsworth was carried away by his revolt against 'poetic diction' and made too much of an issue of it. In his initial ardor he allowed his plea for simplicity (sound in and for itself and not untimely) to become a call to battle. He often applied too mechanically his principles and many times failed. Yet it is interesting to note that some of Wordsworth's greatest successes are grounded upon the same principles as his failures. *The Idiot Boy* and *Michael* represent two extreme results, yet they are built upon similarly simple subjects. And from the real and homely language of men we have the wide, unclosed gap between the clear, fresh poetry of *Lines Written in Early Spring* and the flatness and dullness of *Simon Lee.* Wordsworth found in time that he himself could not keep to 'maxims somewhat unwarily stated.' The language of 'Rolled round in earth's diurnal course,' Walter Raleigh reminds us, did not come from the sheep-walks. The language of rustics progressively disappeared from Wordsworth's poetry and this part of the theory was retained only formally. Most of Wordsworth's theories, however, were 'on the side of truth and for his own day dazzlingly new.' By a return to simple subjects and unadorned language grounded upon genuine emotion they set the way for a historic advance in English poetry.

As early as March 1798, spurred on by Coleridge's enthusiasm, Wordsworth undertook a great philosophical poem to be entitled *The Recluse: or Views on Man, on Nature, and on Human Life.* He launched into his new undertaking in high spirits, but after turning out a few hundred lines he was overwhelmed with doubts about his ability to carry through the tremendous task he had set for himself. He decided that he should review his powers to determine 'how far nature and education had qualified him to construct a literary work that might live.' The result of this self-examination is *The Prelude.* It was Wordsworth's intention to make *The Prelude* introductory to *The Recluse,* but because the new poem far outran the original scheme, ultimately reaching the great length of fourteen books and better than 8000 lines, it was deemed not suitable for that purpose. However, *The Prelude* stands independently as a memorable account of the origin and development of the poetic mind. To a considerable extent *The Prelude* is necessarily autobiographical. Yet it is not so much the story of his life that Wordsworth is telling as it is the recounting of the unusually rich imaginative experiences that were his and the tracing of the steps by which the mind absorbed and reshaped external circumstances until true knowledge and imaginative power had been attained. The poem was not carefully planned in detail in advance. It takes its shape book by book from the incidents as they unfold. Sometimes events are twisted out of their normal order; sometimes biography is lost track of; nor is the development of the mind kept consistently to the forefront. Within the smaller units *The Prelude* is clearly lacking in the niceties of architectonics; yet the larger whole is skillfully ordered. The poem begins at the end. The poet at the age of twenty-nine now 'safe in haven relates the odyssey of his soul and imagination' (de Selincourt). The poem, as de Selincourt has observed, is not unlike an epic which with its episodes, vicissitudes, and climax goes a kind of circuit. The first eight books relate how Nature quickened his sensibilities and molded his mind in childhood and youth, how he was consecrated to his great task, and how his powers progressed and expanded unchecked through early manhood. The ninth book reveals the poet at the height of a 'buoyant but untried faith.' The tenth book recounts the unsettling of his hopes and the distress of mind and the moral skepticism he suffered. The last books tell of recovery from despair, reconciliation, and the restoration of creative imagination. The spiritual cycle at the close is completed and the poet enters into his true heritage. *The Prelude* is addressed to Coleridge and was recited to him by Wordsworth in its entirety upon Coleridge's return from Malta in 1806. Coleridge was greatly moved by the recital and expressed his admiration in lines addressed to Wordsworth. But because it was a highly personal document, *The Prelude* was left unpublished until after its author's death. The manuscript was not laid aside and forgotten, however. Wordsworth went back to it during the remaining years of his life, retouching and revising, so that the poem of 1850 differs in many respects from the poem read to Coleridge in 1806. For a picture of Wordsworth's early mind the unrevised *Prelude* is generally more to be trusted than the 1850 version; as poetry the final text is, on the whole, the better one. In both texts there are faulty lines and inferior passages; yet there is a predominant strength of style which rises again and again to superb poetry. *The Prelude* was written when the poet was at the height of his powers and when the emotional recollections of early days still vividly survived. The materials are varied and pleasingly interfused: absorbing narrative, arresting description and incident come to break and to give perspective to highly reflective matter. The whole is sustained with a remarkable freshness and strength. The impressiveness of *The Prelude* derives not only from the poet's rare faculty of making the record intelligible but also from his ability to sustain a mighty spiritual exaltation. Transcendental vision predominates in the treatment of the theme. The psychological concept proclaimed in *Tintern Abbey* that knowledge is derived wholly from the senses is in *The Prelude* substantially modified. Wordsworth still makes use of the principle of association, but he far overreaches the belief formerly held that the mental processes are mechanistic. Now a glory is shed upon sensations by the mystical intuitions of the mind. Now the 'hiding places of man's power' find their abode in the living mind, the Imagination. The Imagination synthesizes, transfuses, and modifies. It reveals a sense of coherence of all being, an interdependence, interpenetration, and oneness in spiritual substance. It discloses all Nature as permeated with one spirit, beyond space and time, which is Eternal and Infinite Mind. Through the agency of Imagination, Man himself becomes a Spirit living in Time and Space far diffused, merged with this Spiritual Power, which is Itself the Great Imagination, World Soul, and 'Reason in her most exalted mood.' To participate in the creative act of perfect self-identification with the Great Imagination is to know intellectual freedom; it is to experience the very love of God himself. This creative triumph of Imagination is the 'moving soul' and climax of the poet's long labor in *The Prelude*.

The year 1802 was both outwardly and inwardly a landmark in Wordsworth's creative life. It was signalized by peace between France and England, Wordsworth's visit to Annette at Calais, his marriage to Mary, and the renewal of war. These momentous events enlarged the poet's horizon and sharpened his vision. Early in the year a newly awakened admiration for Milton's sonnets had set him to composing in a style more majestic in phrase and rich in music; it also quickened in him a new faith in the ideal of ordered liberty. His visit to Calais at the very time the French nation was granting the Consulship to Napoleon for life opened Wordsworth's eyes to the huge peril of Napoleon's tyranny for all freedom-loving European nations and particularly for England. With the cause of liberty once again brought sharply into focus (though under vastly different circumstances from the days when he had visited France as a college youth), he began a series of sonnets which were to be 'the most complete expression of larger humanity' (Herford) he ever attained. In these sonnets nature now operates with and through man in the unending struggle for freedom. Powers are at work for the hero, Toussaint L'Ouverture, whom the poet addresses:

> . . . air, earth, and skies;
> There's not a breathing of the common wind
> That will forget thee; thou hast great allies;
> Thy friends are exultations, agonies,
> And love, and man's unconquerable mind.

Upon his return to London, Wordsworth is struck by the seeming worldliness and indifference of Englishmen in the midst of the mighty conflict which engages them. At first he is openly critical of his country's backslidings (though professing deep and abiding affection for her) and invokes Milton and the revolutionary England of the Commonwealth to rally his countrymen. He warns them that 'by the soul/Only the nations shall be great and free.' Prospects of invasion, however, silenced his rebukes and called forth what was militant and heroic. Wordsworth pleads for a strengthening of the nation within by a return to moral virtue and the establishment of ordered liberty, and for the defeat abroad of the tyranny that threatens to destroy them. His ardor for freedom embraced other nations as well as England and reached out to those heroes of whatever country who had died vindicating the cause. By the universality and the intensity of his passion Wordsworth established himself through these glorious sonnets as the pre-eminent poet of English patriotism.

In *The Prelude* Wordsworth sets up the imagination as the supreme guide by which to judge the value of human actions. Imagination is regarded as the creative matrix of human freedom; the reconciler of emotion, intelligence, and volition; and a steadying influence in moral relations. However, in the spring of 1802 the realization that his own imaginative vision might be failing him, as it had failed Coleridge, led the poet to a re-examination of the role of the imagination in human existence. This crucial problem is probed and resolved in *Ode: Intimations of Immortality as Recollected from Early Childhood.* The poet opens the ode (stanzas one and two) with the cry that the ecstatic imaginative communing with Nature that once was his is gone. A momentary stay to his grief is given (stanza three) through 'a timely utterance,' probably, as Garrod first suggested, the rainbow poem. In this poem, lines from which were prefixed to the ode, the paradisal vision that was his in childhood has been recovered. In the cuckoo lyric, also, written at the same time, the bird's shout begets again that golden time when the world seemed all 'an unsubstantial faery place.' In the ode (stanzas three and four) the poet again shares, through the reassuring experience of the rainbow vision, the fullness of the bliss of the children as they go flower-gathering on a May morning. But the solace is only temporary. The visionary gleam quickly fades away and the sense of loss returns. In the middle stanzas (five through eight), Wordsworth puts forth a theoretical explanation for the loss of vision, suggested to him by Coleridge and based on the doctrine of pre-existence or reminiscence. Both of the poets had realized the profound significance of childhood in the growth of mature manhood. In considering the recovery of his imagination as recounted in *The Prelude,* Wordsworth places great emphasis upon the part played by the restorative power of imaginative moments recollected from his own childhood.

Oh! mystery of man, from what a depth
Proceed thy honors. I am lost, but see
In simple childhood something of the base
On which thy greatness stands.

(*Prelude* xii, 272–5)

Now a reading of Plato and the Neo-platonists suggested that the dream-like moments experienced in childhood were simply carry-overs from the spirit realm from which the soul descended. Gradually as the natural child grew up forgetfulness set in and the celestial brightness dimmed and finally completely faded away. Confirmation of this process was beheld in Coleridge's small son, the 'six year's darling of a pigmy size.' But the problem of the loss of ecstatic vision was left unresolved and the ode left unfinished in 1802 with the eighth stanza, because Wordsworth was unwilling to rest his case upon the presumptive evidence of pre-existence. Also, the logic of pre-existence led him to the inescapable conclusion that maturity was a time of inevitable darkness and grief—a conclusion that ran counter to human experience in its totality. When he resumed the composition of the poem two years later Wordsworth was on firmer ground. He is now convinced that the visionary splendor glimpsed in childhood is gone past recall; but he is equally certain that the indestructible elements that generate youth's vision persist in all stages of our development. These 'first affections,' whatever they may be, are the 'fountain light to all our day.' Having once been for us they must still be, and we can in thought revive them and be grateful for them. The ecstatic contemplation of Nature is past, but now in its place the philosophic mind reads the 'music of humanity' interfused everywhere through the beauty of the visible scene. Thus the child is indeed the father of the man. Childhood has the vision and manhood the wisdom, their days bound each to each by a continuous, indestructible spiritual energy. And whereas certain elements in Nature as represented earlier in the ode lay heavy upon the soul, at the poem's close, thanks to the saving power of human-heartedness, every grove and brook and stone and flower gives the poet thoughts of sublimity which 'lie too deep for tears.'

The *Ode to Duty,* composed early in 1804, ties in with the heroical last stanzas of the *Ode on Immortality.* In the *Ode to Duty,* as in the more famous ode, the poet accepts the law of life fulfilled in terms of human love and self-sacrifice as a welcome replacement for the rapturous visions and unchartered freedom of his youth. Nature still takes a prominent place in the scheme of existence, but now the supreme power that moves the sun and the other stars is identified with the moral law. Two types of character are described in the *Ode to Duty* as fulfilling duty's ordinances. First there are those (stanzas two and three) who instinctively with glad innocence do duty's work and know it not; next (stanzas four and five) those who, by transcending self, knowingly and willingly submit to duty as objective law. In a stanza included in the 1807 edition, but subsequently rejected, Wordsworth described a third situation, an ideal as yet unattained in this world, in which human desire and self-interest coincide with duty so that moral victory is always enhanced by enjoyment. But in our imperfect world persons of the second class (among whom the poet places himself) will win peace of mind by a self-imposed inner control. In this new philosophical creed of duty Wordsworth is close to Seneca (whose motto prefaces the poem) and to Kant, who values stoical autonomy as the triumph of human nature. In 1805 the tragic drowning of Wordsworth's dearly beloved brother John confirmed the predominant soberness of life expressed in the closing stanzas of the *Ode on Immortality* and the *Ode to Duty.* This devastating experience brought the poet's earlier and later moods into actual and acute antagonism. In *Elegiac Stanzas,* memorializing his brother, Wordsworth renounces forever the fond illusions of his youth and faces the harsh reality of experience with stoic valor and self-control. A second poem honoring his brother, entitled *The Happy Warrior,* a kind of personified ideal of the *Ode to Duty,* also confirms the poet's new stoic attitude. With this momentous group of poems in 1804–5, then (*Ode on Immortality, Ode to Duty, Elegiac Stanzas,* and *The Happy Warrior*), a great turning point in Wordsworth's thought is marked, as he passed from a period of sheer self-dependence to one of rigorous stoicism in later life. The new-found austerity appears in *The Song at the Feast of Brougham Castle* and in *The White Doe of Rylstone,* stories of heroic martyrdom composed in 1807. In these poems fortitude and love when put to proof in adversity are transmuted to wisdom, even to beatification.

Somewhere between 1805 and 1807 Wordsworth's poetic vitality began slowly to decline. More and more with the passing of time the conservative elements of his intellect gained dominance and he developed a disposition to fall back upon sententious and dogmatic pronouncements. His poetical method, tone, and style, also, changed considerably. These alterations in thought and expression are reflected in *The Excursion* (published in 1814), the major work of the poet's less inspired middle years. The 'argument' of the poem is the vindication of man's right to hope by the overcoming or avoidance of despondency through the re-establishment of genuine knowledge. The 'action' develops by means of argument in which the culminating moment occurs in a debate between the Wanderer and the Solitary in Book IV. The cause of Hope is thereafter supported in a series of stories intended to show how Wisdom may be attained, and finally is applied by the Wanderer to a criticism of social conditions in England. The story in Book I of Margaret's tragic desolation, which had been written at Racedown and Alfoxden, was needed to introduce the high argument for optimism. It stands as one of Wordsworth's finest achievements in his early manner. *The Excursion,* however, representing as a whole his later manner, is an impressive but not a great poem. There is a lofty, sincere purpose and a steady, sure examination of experience as the way of life. There is a grasp of social problems, and a sane insistence upon underlying ethical principles that is assuring and revealing. There are splendid bursts of imaginative eloquence in the dialogue and occasional sweet, fresh passages descriptive of the natural surroundings in the Lake Country. But taken in its entirety *The Excursion* represents an unquestioned falling away from the imaginative power of the golden years, a talking about rather than an example of elevation. After *The Excursion* there appeared very little more that was great and distinctive in Wordsworth's poetry. Yet even as inspiration declined, the poet's artistic skill and technique continued to develop. Now and then the call to stoical and Christian fortitude fostered a noble utterance. *Laodamia* is just such a poem, one of Wordsworth's rare classical studies, written in a style reminiscent of Milton and Virgil. In the mutability sonnets, the farewell to Scott, *Afterthought* in the Duddon series, and *An Evening of Extraordinary Splendour* the old poet recovered at rare moments his former power. Also among the achievements of the late years must be numbered the revisions of *The Prelude.* But when all of the accomplishments of the last forty years of the poet's life are added together they are of relatively small weight when placed in the balance against the poetry of the earlier years. It is the greater and earlier poetry that has survived.

Widespread public recognition came tardily to Wordsworth. Readers had scarcely begun to discover the *Lyrical Ballads* when Francis Jeffrey, critic-potentate of the *Edinburgh Review,* opened up an abusive attack upon the new poetry from which he did not relent during a period of two decades. Jeffrey's strenuous opposition to Wordsworth was unhappily only too effective. But by the early 1820's, by virtue of his own great strength Wordsworth had gained such headway with the public that Jeffrey found it prudent to retire from the field. Thereafter the opposition among critics and readers alike quickly faded and the poet's fame steadily rose until it reached a high point in the 1830's. In his declining years Wordsworth was acknowledged as the pre-eminent living British poet and when he died he was honored and revered by a wide public. Shortly after his death his popularity receded somewhat and reached an ebb around 1865. In the late 'seventies a highly significant essay by Leslie Stephen provoked a famous reply by Matthew Arnold, which stimulated new interest among scholars and general readers. Since Arnold's time critical studies and biographies have multiplied and readers have grown in numbers with the years. Today there are few responsible critics who would question Wordsworth's right to a place among the foremost English poets. Wordsworth does not, to be sure, meet with the ready acceptance accorded Chaucer, Shakespeare, and Milton. He wrote too much slack stuff, too much in which inspiration failed. There is a certain pedestrian tone, an unfortunate comic element of prosiness that is easy to laugh at and easy to find dull. The light touch of humor might have done much for Wordsworth, but he lacked that saving grace. Nor was he gifted with the dramatic imagination, or, in any ordinary sense, with the story-teller's art. But granting a good deal, granting even that in some of his best work there are occasional flaws that are difficult to excuse, there yet remains a substantial amount of poetry written at the height of his powers which has an immense variety of excellences and a wide appeal. The greatness of Wordsworth's best work proceeds from a calm, almost elemental, strength. He possessed a weight of character, an extraordinary emotional force and reach of intellect, and a tremendous imaginative power. He had, if poet ever had, 'the vision and the faculty divine.' This strength Wordsworth conveyed in language of matchless power and felicity. His style at its best is unsurpassed in its naked idiomatic force and its quiet unadorned beauty of word and phrase. It excels in epigrammatic power, dignity, ampleness, poignant intensity, and vigorous masculinity. Wordsworth is not at all a monotonous poet but exhibits a great variety in style, mood, and subject matter. Among the short lyrics alone there is a long roll call of perennial favorites displaying his extraordinary variety in form and range in material. He is pre-eminent for the truth of his report about Nature. He loved what was common and delighted in recording the abundant exquisite beauties of the natural world which he discovered everywhere about him. He displays a matchless ability in delineating objects. But Wordsworth is much more than a mere reporter of surface beauties. He has penetrated beneath the show of things to the realm of the universal. As a mystic he has seized upon those profound spiritual relationships that exist among man, nature, and the eternal world. Particularly he has searched the region of the human spirit for those universal laws that govern our own being. With true sympathy and profound imaginative insight he has reached into the humblest hearts and discovered in the primary affections a true source of joy and strength for living. Out of a boy's random feelings, a mother's sorrow, or a leech-gatherer's gossip about his trade he framed his songs, which from lowliest origins rise to the universality and nobility of Greek tragedy. Wordsworth's deepest concern was for the betterment of mankind through a fuller, happier realization of hidden resources within each individual. His unique experiences, particularly his residence in France during the revolution, as well as his genius, gave him an unequaled perspective for interpreting the essential thoughts and passions of his age. In the political realm he was led to hope—not mistakenly, as it proved—that his countrymen might be roused by an appeal to the ideals of freedom to a renewed sense of their strength and their responsibility. In the literary realm, his insight led him to perfect a new kind of poetry which not only stemmed the classical decay but gave a forward impetus to English and American thought and expression that has hardly yet subsided. Some of the truths advanced by Wordsworth which were startlingly new to his generation and were revered by the Victorians may no longer excite us. Some portions of his report on Nature may need qualifying. But we are not going to yield the gains he won for us. He has handed on an impressive body of philosophical speculation which stimulates thought and challenges meditation. He has answers for life's problems and consolations for the ills that beset men. There are few poets who have so much to give to our mechanistic twentieth century.

WRITTEN IN VERY EARLY YOUTH

CALM is all nature as a resting wheel.
The kine are couched upon the dewy grass;
The horse alone, seen dimly as I pass,
Is cropping audibly his later meal:
Dark is the ground; a slumber seems to steal
O'er vale, and mountain, and the starless sky.
Now, in this blank of things, a harmony,
Home-felt, and home-created, comes to heal
That grief for which the senses still supply
Fresh food; for only then, when memory   10
Is hushed, am I at rest. My Friends! restrain
Those busy cares that would allay my pain;
Oh! leave me to myself, nor let me feel
The officious touch that makes me droop again.

1802

From AN EVENING WALK

ADDRESSED TO A YOUNG LADY

Lines 86–113, 168–249, 279–314, 364–78

The young Lady to whom this was addressed was my Sister. It was composed at school, and during my two first College vacations. There is not an image in it which I have not observed; and now, in my seventy-third year, I recollect the time and place where most of them were noticed. . . . The plan of it has not been confined to a particular walk or an individual place,—a proof (of which I was unconscious at the time) of my unwillingness to submit the poetic spirit to the chains of fact and real circumstance. The country is idealized rather than described in any one of its local aspects.—(Wordsworth.)

DEAR Brook, farewell! To-morrow's noon again
Shall hide me, wooing long thy wildwood strain;
But now the sun has gained his western road,
And eve's mild hour invites my steps abroad.

While, near the midway cliff, the silvered kite 90
In many a whistling circle wheels her flight;
Slant watery lights, from parting clouds, apace
Travel along the precipice's base;
Cheering its naked waste of scattered stone,
By lichens grey, and scanty moss, o'ergrown;
Where scarce the foxglove peeps, or thistle's beard;
And restless stone-chat, all day long, is heard.

How pleasant, as the sun declines, to view
The spacious landscape change in form and hue!
Here, vanish, as in mist, before a flood   100
Of bright obscurity, hill, lawn, and wood;
There, objects, by the searching beams betrayed,
Come forth, and here retire in purple shade;
Even the white stems of birch, the cottage white,
Soften their glare before the mellow light;
The skiffs, at anchor where with umbrage wide
Yon chestnuts half the latticed boathouse hide,
Shed from their sides, that face the sun's slant beam,
Strong flakes of radiance on the tremulous stream:
Raised by yon travelling flock, a dusty cloud 110
Mounts from the road, and spreads its moving shroud;
The shepherd, all involved in wreaths of fire,
Now shows a shadowy speck, and now is lost entire.

. . .

Just where a cloud above the mountain rears
An edge all flame, the broadening sun appears;
A long blue bar its ægis orb divides,   170
And breaks the spreading of its golden tides;
And now that orb has touched the purple steep,
Whose softened image penetrates the deep.
'Cross the calm lake's blue shades the cliffs aspire,
With towers and woods, a 'prospect all on fire';[1]
While coves and secret hollows, through a ray

Of fainter gold, a purple gleam betray.
Each slip of lawn the broken rocks between
Shines in the light with more than earthly green:
Deep yellow beams the scattered stems illume, 180
Far in the level forest's central gloom:
Waving his hat, the shepherd, from the vale,
Directs his winding dog the cliffs to scale,—
The dog, loud barking, 'mid the glittering rocks,
Hunts, where his master points, the intercepted flocks.
Where oaks o'erhang the road the radiance shoots
On tawny earth, wild weeds, and twisted roots;
The druid-stones a brightened ring unfold;
And all the babbling brooks are liquid gold;
Sunk to a curve, the day-star lessens still,   190
Gives one bright glance, and drops behind the hill.[2]

In these secluded vales, if village fame,
Confirmed by hoary hairs, belief may claim;
When up the hills, as now, retired the light,
Strange apparitions mocked the shepherd's sight.

The form appears of one that spurs his steed
Midway along the hill with desperate speed;
Unhurt pursues his lengthened flight, while all
Attend, at every stretch, his headlong fall.
Anon, appears a brave, a gorgeous show   200
Of horsemen-shadows moving to and fro;
At intervals imperial banners stream,
And now the van reflects the solar beam;
The rear through iron brown betrays a sullen gleam.
While silent stands the admiring crowd below,
Silent the visionary warriors go,
Winding in ordered pomp their upward way,[3]
Till the last banner of their long array
Has disappeared, and every trace is fled
Of splendour—save the beacon's spiry head   210
Tipt with eve's latest gleam of burning red.

Now, while the solemn evening shadows sail,
On slowly-waving pinions, down the vale;
And, fronting the bright west, yon oak entwines
Its darkening boughs and leaves in stronger lines;
'Tis pleasant near the tranquil lake to stray
Where, winding on along some secret bay,
The swan uplifts his chest, and backward flings
His neck, a varying arch, between his towering wings:
The eye that marks the gliding creature sees 220

---

1 from a poem, *Sunday Thoughts,* by Moses Browne.

2 from Thomson.—(Wordsworth.)
3 See a description of an appearance of this kind in Clark's *Survey of the Lakes,* accompanied by vouchers of its veracity, that may amuse the reader.—(Wordsworth.)

How graceful, pride can be, and how majestic,
  ease.
While tender cares and mild domestic loves
With furtive watch pursue her as she moves,
The female with a meeker charm succeeds,
And her brown little-ones around her leads,
Nibbling the water lilies as they pass,
Or playing wanton with the floating grass.
She, in a mother's care, her beauty's pride
Forgetting, calls the wearied to her side;
Alternately they mount her back, and rest   230
Close by her mantling wings' embraces prest.

Long may they float upon this flood serene;
Theirs be these holms untrodden, still, and green,
Where leafy shades fence off the blustering gale,
And breathes in peace the lily of the vale!
Yon isle, which feels not even the milkmaid's feet,
Yet hears her song, 'by distance made more sweet'[4]
Yon isle conceals their home, their hut-like bower;
Green water-rushes overspread the floor;
Long grass and willows form the woven wall, 240
And swings above the roof the poplar tall.
Thence issuing often with unwieldy stalk,
They crush with broad black feet their flowery
  walk;
Or, from the neighbouring water, hear at morn
The hound, the horse's tread, and mellow horn;
Involve their serpent-necks in changeful rings,
Rolled wantonly between their slippery wings,
Or, starting up with noise and rude delight,
Force half upon the wave their cumbrous flight.

      .   .   .

Sweet are the sounds that mingle from afar,
Heard by calm lakes, as peeps the folding star, 280
Where the duck dabbles 'mid the rustling sedge,
And feeding pike starts from the water's edge,
Or the swan stirs the reeds, his neck and bill
Wetting, that drip upon the water still;
And heron, as resounds the trodden shore,
Shoots upward, darting his long neck before.

Now, with religious awe, the farewell light
Blends with the solemn colouring of night;
'Mid groves of clouds that crest the mountain's
  brow,
And round the west's proud lodge their shadows
  throw,   290
Like Una[5] shining on her gloomy way,
The half-seen form of Twilight roams astray;

---

4 from Collins, *Ode to Passions*, 60.
5 Alluding to this passage of Spenser—
            Her angel face
As the great eye of Heaven shined bright,
And made a sunshine in that shady place.—(Wordsworth.)

Shedding, through paly loop-holes mild and small,
Gleams that upon the lake's still bosom fall;
Soft o'er the surface creep those lustres pale
Tracking the motions of the fitful gale.
With restless interchange at once the bright
Wins on the shade, the shade upon the light.
No favoured eye was e'er allowed to gaze
On lovelier spectacle in faery days;   300
When gentle Spirits urged a sportive chase,
Brushing with lucid wands the water's face:
While music, stealing round the glimmering deeps,
Charmed the tall circle of the enchanted steeps.
—The lights are vanished from the watery plains:
No wreck of all the pageantry remains.
Unheeded night has overcome the vales:
On the dark earth the wearied vision fails;
The latest lingerer of the forest train,
The lone black fir, forsakes the faded plain; 310
Last evening sight, the cottage smoke, no more,
Lost in the thickened darkness, glimmers hoar;
And, towering from the sullen dark-brown mere,
Like a black wall, the mountain-steeps appear.

      .   .   .

The song of mountain-streams, unheard by day,
Now hardly heard, beguiles my homeward way.
Air listens, like the sleeping water, still,
To catch the spiritual music of the hill,
Broke only by the slow clock tolling deep,
Or shout that wakes the ferry-man from sleep, 370
The echoed hoof nearing the distant shore,
The boat's first motion—made with dashing oar;
Sound of closed gate, across the water borne,
Hurrying the timid hare through rustling corn;
The sportive outcry of the mocking owl;
And at long intervals the mill-dog's howl;
The distant forge's swinging thump profound;
Or yell, in the deep woods, of lonely hound.

    1787–9   1793

THE REVERIE OF POOR SUSAN

This arose out of my observation of the affecting music of these birds hanging in this way in the London streets during the freshness and stillness of the Spring morning. —(Wordsworth.)

At the corner of Wood Street, when daylight ap-
  pears,
Hangs a Thrush that sings loud, it has sung for
  three years:
Poor Susan has passed by the spot, and has heard
In the silence of morning the song of the Bird.

'Tis a note of enchantment; what ails her? She sees
A mountain ascending, a vision of trees;

Bright volumes of vapour through Lothbury glide,
And a river flows on through the vale of Cheap-
          side.

Green pastures she views in the midst of the dale,
Down which she so often has tripped with her
          pail;   10
And a single small cottage, a nest like a dove's,
The one only dwelling on earth that she loves.

She looks, and her heart is in heaven: but they
          fade,
The mist and the river, the hill and the shade:
The stream will not flow, and the hill will not rise,
And the colours have all passed away from her
          eyes!

1797   1800

THE OLD CUMBERLAND BEGGAR

   The class of beggars, to which the old man here described belongs, will probably soon be extinct. It consisted of poor, and, mostly, old and infirm persons, who
confined themselves to a stated round in their neighbourhood, and had certain fixed days, on which, at different
houses, they regularly received alms, sometimes in
money, but mostly in provisions.—(Wordsworth.)

I SAW an aged Beggar in my walk;
And he was seated, by the highway side,
On a low structure of rude masonry
Built at the foot of a huge hill, that they
Who lead their horses down the steep rough road
May thence remount at ease. The aged Man
Had placed his staff across the broad smooth stone
That overlays the pile; and, from a bag
All white with flour, the dole of village dames,
He drew his scraps and fragments, one by one;   10
And scanned them with a fixed and serious look
Of idle computation. In the sun,
Upon the second step of that small pile,
Surrounded by those wild unpeopled hills,
He sat, and ate his food in solitude:
And ever, scattered from his palsied hand,
That, still attempting to prevent the waste,
Was baffled still, the crumbs in little showers
Fell on the ground; and the small mountain birds,
Not venturing yet to peck their destined meal, 20
Approached within the length of half his staff.

   Him from my childhood have I known; and
          then
He was so old, he seems not older now;
He travels on, a solitary Man,
So helpless in appearance, that for him
The sauntering Horseman throws not with a slack

And careless hand his alms upon the ground,
But stops,—that he may safely lodge the coin
Within the old Man's hat; nor quits him so,
But still, when he has given his horse the rein, 30
Watches the aged Beggar with a look
Sidelong, and half-reverted. She who tends
The toll-gate, when in summer at her door
She turns her wheel, if on the road she sees
The aged Beggar coming, quits her work,
And lifts the latch for him that he may pass.
The post-boy, when his rattling wheels o'ertake
The aged Beggar in the woody lane,
Shouts to him from behind; and, if thus warned
The old man does not change his course, the boy 40
Turns with less noisy wheels to the roadside,
And passes gently by, without a curse
Upon his lips or anger at his heart.

   He travels on, a solitary Man;
His age has no companion. On the ground
His eyes are turned, and, as he moves along,
They move along the ground; and, evermore,
Instead of common and habitual sight
Of fields with rural works, of hill and dale,
And the blue sky, one little span of earth   50
Is all his prospect. Thus, from day to day,
Bow-bent, his eyes for ever on the ground,
He plies his weary journey; seeing still,
And seldom knowing that he sees, some straw,
Some scattered leaf, or marks which, in one track,
The nails of cart or chariot-wheel have left
Impressed on the white road,—in the same line,
At distance still the same. Poor Traveller!
His staff trails with him; scarcely do his feet
Disturb the summer dust; he is so still   60
In look and motion, that the cottage curs,
Ere he has passed the door, will turn away,
Weary of barking at him. Boys and girls,
The vacant and the busy, maids and youths,
And urchins newly breeched—all pass him by:
Him even the slow-paced waggon leaves behind.

   But deem not this Man useless.—Statesmen! ye
Who are so restless in your wisdom, ye
Who have a broom still ready in your hands
To rid the world of nuisances; ye proud,   70
Heart-swoln, while in your pride ye contemplate
Your talents, power, or wisdom, deem him not
A burthen of the earth! 'Tis Nature's law
That none, the meanest of created things,
Of forms created the most vile and brute,
The dullest or most noxious, should exist
Divorced from good—a spirit and pulse of good,
A life and soul, to every mode of being
Inseparably linked. Then be assured

That least of all can aught—that ever owned   80
The heaven-regarding eye and front sublime
Which man is born to—sink, howe'er depressed,
So low as to be scorned without a sin;
Without offence to God cast out of view;
Like the dry remnant of a garden-flower
Whose seeds are shed, or as an implement
Worn out and worthless. While from door to
   door,
This old Man creeps, the villagers in him
Behold a record which together binds
Past deeds and offices of charity,   90
Else unremembered, and so keeps alive
The kindly mood in hearts which lapse of years,
And that half-wisdom half-experience gives,
Make slow to feel, and by sure steps resign
To selfishness and cold oblivious cares.
Among the farms and solitary huts,
Hamlets and thinly-scattered villages,
Where'er the aged Beggar takes his rounds,
The mild necessity of use compels
To acts of love; and habit does the work   100
Of reason; yet prepares that after-joy
Which reason cherishes. And thus the soul,
By that sweet taste of pleasure unpursued,
Doth find herself insensibly disposed
To virtue and true goodness.
                              Some there are,
By their good works exalted, lofty minds,
And meditative, authors of delight
And happiness, which to the end of time
Will live, and spread, and kindle: even such minds
In childhood, from this solitary Being,   110
Or from like wanderer, haply have received
(A thing more precious far than all that books
Or the solicitudes of love can do!)
That first mild touch of sympathy and thought,
In which they found their kindred with a world
Where want and sorrow were. The easy man
Who sits at his own door,—and, like the pear
That overhangs his head from the green wall,
Feeds in the sunshine; the robust and young,
The prosperous and unthinking, they who live   120
Sheltered, and flourish in a little grove
Of their own kindred;—all behold in him
A silent monitor, which on their minds
Must needs impress a transitory thought
Of self-congratulation, to the heart
Of each recalling his peculiar boons,
His charters and exemptions; and, perchance,
Though he to no one give the fortitude
And circumspection needful to preserve
His present blessings, and to husband up   130
The respite of the reason, he, at least,
And 'tis no vulgar service, makes them felt.

Yet further.   Many, I believe, there are
Who live a life of virtuous decency,
Men who can hear the Decalogue and feel
No self-reproach; who of the moral law
Established in the land where they abide
Are strict observers; and not negligent
In acts of love to those with whom they dwell,
Their kindred, and the children of their blood.   140
Praise be to such, and to their slumbers peace!
—But of the poor man ask, the abject poor;
Go, and demand of him, if there be here
In this cold abstinence from evil deeds,
And these inevitable charities,
Wherewith to satisfy the human soul?
No—man is dear to man; the poorest poor
Long for some moments in a weary life
When they can know and feel that they have
   been,
Themselves, the fathers and the dealers-out   150
Of some small blessings; have been kind to such
As needed kindness, for this single cause,
That we have all of us one human heart.
—Such pleasure is to one kind Being known,
My neighbour, when with punctual care, each
   week,
Duly as Friday comes, though pressed herself
By her own wants, she from her store of meal
Takes one unsparing handful for the scrip
Of this old Mendicant, and, from her door
Returning with exhilarated heart,   160
Sits by her fire, and builds her hope in heaven.

   Then let him pass, a blessing on his head!
And while in that vast solitude to which
The tide of things has borne him, he appears
To breathe and live but for himself alone,
Unblamed, uninjured, let him bear about
The good which the benignant law of Heaven
Has hung around him: and, while life is his,
Still let him prompt the unlettered villagers
To tender offices and pensive thoughts.   170
—Then let him pass, a blessing on his head!
And, long as he can wander, let him breathe
The freshness of the valleys; let his blood
Struggle with frosty air and winter snows;
And let the chartered wind that sweeps the heath
Beat his grey locks against his withered face.
Reverence the hope whose vital anxiousness
Gives the last human interest to his heart.
May never HOUSE,[1] misnamed of INDUSTRY,
Make him a captive!—for that pent-up din,   180
Those life-consuming sounds that clog the
   air,
Be his the natural silence of old age!

---

1 poorhouse.

Let him be free of mountain solitudes;
And have around him, whether heard or not,
The pleasant melody of woodland birds.
Few are his pleasures; if his eyes have now
Been doomed so long to settle upon earth
That not without some effort they behold
The countenance of the horizontal sun,
Rising or setting, let the light at least   190
Find a free entrance to their languid orbs,
And let him, *where* and *when* he will, sit down
Beneath the trees, or on a grassy bank
Of highway side, and with the little birds
Share his chance-gathered meal; and, finally,
As in the eye of Nature he has lived,
So in the eye of Nature let him die!

1797   1800

A NIGHT-PIECE

Composed on the road between Nether Stowey and
Alfoxden, extempore. I distinctly recollect the very moment when I was struck, as described—'He looks up—
the clouds are split,' etc.—(Wordsworth.)

————The sky is overcast
With a continuous cloud of texture close,
Heavy and wan, all whitened by the Moon,
Which through that veil is indistinctly seen,
A dull, contracted circle, yielding light
So feebly spread that not a shadow falls,
Chequering the ground—from rock, plant, tree,
     or tower.
At length a pleasant instantaneous gleam
Startles the pensive traveller while he treads
His lonesome path, with unobserving eye   10
Bent earthwards; he looks up—the clouds are
     split
Asunder,—and above his head he sees
The clear Moon, and the glory of the heavens.
There in a black-blue vault she sails along,
Followed by multitudes of stars, that, small
And sharp, and bright, along the dark abyss
Drive as she drives: how fast they wheel away,
Yet vanish not!—the wind is in the tree,
But they are silent;—still they roll along
Immeasurably distant; and the vault,   20
Built round by those white clouds, enormous
     clouds,
Still deepens its unfathomable depth.
At length the Vision closes; and the mind,
Not undisturbed by the delight it feels,
Which slowly settles into peaceful calm,
Is left to muse upon the solemn scene.

1798   1815

WE ARE SEVEN

Written at Alfoxden in the spring of 1798, under circumstances somewhat remarkable. The little girl who is
the heroine I met within the area of Goodrich Castle in
the year 1793. Having left the Isle of Wight and crossed
Salisbury Plain, as mentioned in the Preface to *Guilt and
Sorrow,* I proceeded by Bristol up the Wye, and so on to
North Wales, to the Vale of Clwydd, where I spent my
summer under the roof of the father of my friend, Robert Jones. In reference to this poem I will here mention
one of the most remarkable facts in my own poetic history and that of Mr. Coleridge. In the spring of the year
1798, he, my sister, and myself, started from Alfoxden
pretty late in the afternoon, with a view to visit Lenton
and the valley of Stones near it; and as our united funds
were very small, we agreed to defray the expense of the
tour by writing a poem, to be sent to *The New Monthly
Magazine* set up by Phillips the bookseller, and edited
by Dr. Aikin. Accordingly we set off and proceeded
along the Quantock Hills, towards Watchet, and in the
course of this walk was planned the poem of *The Ancient
Mariner,* founded on a dream, as Mr. Coleridge said, of
his friend, Mr. Cruikshank. Much the greatest part of the
story was Mr. Coleridge's invention; but certain parts I
myself suggested:—for example, some crime was to be
committed which should bring upon the Old Navigator,
as Coleridge afterwards delighted to call him, the spectral persecution, as a consequence of that crime, and his
own wanderings. I had been reading in Shelvock's *Voyages* a day or two before that while doubling Cape Horn
they frequently saw albatrosses in that latitude, the largest sort of sea-fowl, some extending their wings twelve or
thirteen feet. 'Suppose,' said I, 'you represent him as
having killed one of these birds on entering the South
Sea, and that the tutelary Spirits of those regions take
upon them to avenge the crime.' The incident was
thought fit for the purpose and adopted accordingly. I
also suggested the navigation of the ship by the dead
men, but do not recollect that I had anything more to do
with the scheme of the poem. The Gloss with which it
was subsequently accompanied was not thought of by
either of us at the time; at least, not a hint of it was given
to me, and I have no doubt it was a gratuitous afterthought. We began the composition together on that, to
me, memorable evening. I furnished two or three lines at
the beginning of the poem, in particular:—

'And listened like a three years' child;
The Mariner had his will.'

These trifling contributions, all but one (which Mr. C.
has with unnecessary scrupulosity recorded) slipt out of
his mind as they well might. As we endeavoured to proceed conjointly (I speak of the same evening) our respective manners proved so widely different that it would
have been quite presumptuous in me to do anything but
separate from an undertaking upon which I could only
have been a clog. We returned after a few days from a
delightful tour, of which I have many pleasant, and
some of them droll-enough, recollections. We returned
by Dulverton to Alfoxden. *The Ancient Mariner* grew
and grew till it became too important for our first object,
which was limited to our expectation of five pounds, and
we began to talk of a Volume, which was to consist, as
Mr. Coleridge has told the world, of Poems chiefly on
supernatural subjects taken from common life, but
looked at, as much as might be, through an imaginative
medium. Accordingly I wrote *The Idiot Boy, Her Eyes*

Are Wild, etc., *We Are Seven, The Thorn*, and some others. To return to *We Are Seven*, the piece that called forth this note, I composed it while walking in the grove at Alfoxden. My friends will not deem it too trifling to relate that while walking to and fro I composed the last stanza first, having begun with the last line. When it was all but finished, I came in and recited it to Mr. Coleridge and my sister, and said, 'A prefatory stanza must be added, and I should sit down to our little tea-meal with greater pleasure if my task were finished.' I mentioned in substance what I wished to be expressed, and Coleridge immediately threw off the stanza thus:—

'A little child, dear brother Jem,'—

I objected to the rhyme, 'dear brother Jem,' as being ludicrous, but we all enjoyed the joke of hitching-in our friend, James T[obin]'s name, who was familiarly called Jem. He was the brother of the dramatist, and this reminds me of an anecdote which it may be worth while here to notice. The said Jem got a sight of the *Lyrical Ballads* as it was going through the press at Bristol, during which time I was residing in that city. One evening he came to me with a grave face, and said, 'Wordsworth, I have seen the volume that Coleridge and you are about to publish. There is one poem in it which I earnestly entreat you to cancel, for, if published, it will make you everlastingly ridiculous.' I answered that I felt much obliged by the interest he took in my good name as a writer, and begged to know what was the unfortunate piece he alluded to. He said, 'It is called *We Are Seven*.' —'Nay,' said I, 'that shall take its chance, however,' and he left me in despair. —(Wordsworth.)

——A SIMPLE Child,
That lightly draws its breath,
And feels its life in every limb,
What should it know of death?

I met a little cottage Girl:
She was eight years old, she said;
Her hair was thick with many a curl
That clustered round her head.

She had a rustic, woodland air,
And she was wildly clad: 10
Her eyes were fair, and very fair;
—Her beauty made me glad.

'Sisters and brothers, little maid,
How many may you be?'
'How many? Seven in all,' she said,
And wondering looked at me.

'And where are they? I pray you tell.'
She answered, 'Seven are we;
And two of us at Conway dwell,
And two are gone to sea.   20

'Two of us in the church-yard lie,
My sister and my brother;
And, in the church-yard cottage, I
Dwell near them with my mother.'

'You say that two at Conway dwell,
And two are gone to sea,
Yet ye are seven! I pray you tell,
Sweet Maid, how this may be.'

Then did the little Maid reply,
'Seven boys and girls are we;   30
Two of us in the church-yard lie,
Beneath the church-yard tree.'

'You run about, my little Maid,
Your limbs they are alive;
If two are in the church-yard laid,
Then ye are only five.'

'Their graves are green, they may be seen,'
The little Maid replied,
'Twelve steps or more from my mother's door,
And they are side by side.   40

'My stockings there I often knit,
My kerchief there I hem;
And there upon the ground I sit,
And sing a song to them.

'And often after sun-set, Sir,
When it is light and fair,
I take my little porringer,
And eat my supper there.

'The first that died was sister Jane;
In bed she moaning lay,   50
Till God released her of her pain;
And then she went away.

'So in the church-yard she was laid;
And, when the grass was dry,
Together round her grave we played,
My brother John and I.

'And when the ground was white with snow,
And I could run and slide,
My brother John was forced to go,
And he lies by her side.'   60

'How many are you, then,' said I,
'If they two are in heaven?'
Quick was the little Maid's reply,
'O Master! we are seven.'

'But they are dead; those two are dead!
Their spirits are in heaven!'
'Twas throwing words away; for still
The little Maid would have her will,
And said, 'Nay, we are seven!'

1798   1800

ANECDOTE FOR FATHERS

'Retine vim istam, falsa enim dicam, si coges.'
—EUSEBIUS. [Restrain your power, for I shall
speak falsely if you force me.]

This was suggested in front of Alfoxden. The Boy was
a son of my friend, Basil Montagu, who had been two
or three years under our care. The name of Kilve is from
a village on the Bristol Channel, about a mile from Alfoxden; and the name of Liswyn Farm was taken from a
beautiful spot on the Wye.—(Wordsworth.)

I HAVE a boy of five years old;
  His face is fair and fresh to see;
His limbs are cast in beauty's mould,
  And dearly he loves me.

One morn we strolled on our dry walk,
  Our quiet home all full in view,
And held such intermitted talk
  As we are wont to do.

My thoughts on former pleasures ran;
  I thought of Kilve's delightful shore,   10
Our pleasant home when spring began,
  A long, long year before.

A day it was when I could bear
  Some fond regrets to entertain;
With so much happiness to spare,
  I could not feel a pain.

The green earth echoed to the feet
  Of lambs that bounded through the glade,
From shade to sunshine, and as fleet
  From sunshine back to shade.   20

Birds warbled round me—and each trace
  Of inward sadness had its charm;
Kilve, thought I, was a favoured place,
  And so is Liswyn farm.

My boy beside me tripped, so slim
  And graceful in his rustic dress!
And, as we talked, I questioned him,
  In very idleness.

'Now tell me, had you rather be,'
  I said, and took him by the arm,   30
'On Kilve's smooth shore, by the green sea,
  Or here at Liswyn farm?'

In careless mood he looked at me,
  While still I held him by the arm,
And said, 'At Kilve I'd rather be
  Than here at Liswyn farm.'

'Now, little Edward, say why so:
  My little Edward, tell me why.'—
'I cannot tell, I do not know.'—
  'Why, this is strange,' said I;   40

'For here are woods, hills smooth and warm:
  There surely must some reason be
Why you would change sweet Liswyn farm
  For Kilve by the green sea.'

At this my boy hung down his head,
  He blushed with shame, nor made reply;
And three times to the child I said,
  'Why, Edward, tell me why?'

His head he raised—there was in sight,
  It caught his eye, he saw it plain—   50
Upon the house-top, glittering bright,
  A broad and gilded vane.

Then did the boy his tongue unlock,
  And eased his mind with this reply:
'At Kilve there was no weather-cock;
  And that's the reason why.'

O dearest, dearest boy! my heart
  For better lore would seldom yearn,
Could I but teach the hundredth part
  Of what from thee I learn.   60

                    1798   1798

THE THORN

Written at Alfoxden. Arose out of my observing, on
the ridge of Quantock Hill, on a stormy day, a thorn
which I had often past, in calm and bright weather, without noticing it. I said to myself, 'Cannot I by some invention do as much to make this Thorn permanently an
impressive object as the storm has made it to my eyes at
this moment?' I began the poem accordingly, and composed it with great rapidity.—(Wordsworth.)

[In a note to *Lyrical Ballads* (1800) Wordsworth explained that this poem was not supposed to be spoken in
the author's own person but by an imaginary narrator,
such as a captain of a small trading vessel, prone to superstition, retired on an annuity, and, having little to do,
becoming talkative from indolence.]

'THERE is a Thorn—it looks so old,
  In truth, you'd find it hard to say
How it could ever have been young,
  It looks so old and grey.
Not higher than a two years' child
  It stands erect, this aged Thorn;
No leaves it has, no prickly points;
  It is a mass of knotted joints,
A wretched thing forlorn.

It stands erect, and like a stone   10
With lichens it is overgrown.

'Like rock or stone, it is o'ergrown,
With lichens to the very top,
And hung with heavy tufts of moss,
A melancholy crop:
Up from the earth these mosses creep,
And this poor Thorn they clasp it round
So close, you'd say that they are bent
With plain and manifest intent
  To drag it to the ground;   20
And all have joined in one endeavour
To bury this poor Thorn for ever.

'High on a mountain's highest ridge,
Where oft the stormy winter gale
Cuts like a scythe, while through the clouds
It sweeps from vale to vale;
Not five yards from the mountain path,
This Thorn you on your left espy;
And to the left, three yards beyond,
You see a little muddy pond   30
Of water—never dry,
Though but of compass small, and bare
To thirsty suns and parching air.

'And, close beside this aged Thorn,
There is a fresh and lovely sight,
A beauteous heap, a hill of moss,
Just half a foot in height.
All lovely colours there you see,
All colours that were ever seen;
And mossy network too is there,   40
As if by hand of lady fair
The work had woven been;
And cups, the darlings of the eye,
So deep is their vermilion dye.

'Ah me! what lovely tints are there
Of olive green and scarlet bright,
In spikes, in branches, and in stars,
Green, red, and pearly white!
This heap of earth o'ergrown with moss,
Which close beside the Thorn you see,   50
So fresh in all its beauteous dyes,
Is like an infant's grave in size,
As like as like can be:
But never, never any where,
An infant's grave was half so fair.

'Now would you see this aged Thorn,
This pond, and beauteous hill of moss,
You must take care and choose your time
The mountain when to cross.

For oft there sits between the heap,   60
So like an infant's grave in size,
And that same pond of which I spoke,
A Woman in a scarlet cloak,
And to herself she cries,
"Oh misery! oh misery!
Oh woe is me! oh misery!"

'At all times of the day and night
This wretched Woman thither goes;
And she is known to every star,
And every wind that blows;   70
And there, beside the Thorn, she sits
When the blue daylight's in the skies,
And when the whirlwind's on the hill,
Or frosty air is keen and still,
And to herself she cries,
"Oh misery! oh misery!
Oh woe is me! oh misery!"

'Now wherefore, thus, by day and night,
In rain, in tempest, and in snow,
Thus to the dreary mountain-top   80
Does this poor Woman go?
And why sits she beside the Thorn
When the blue daylight's in the sky
Or when the whirlwind's on the hill,
Or frosty air is keen and still,
And wherefore does she cry?—
O wherefore? wherefore? tell me why
Does she repeat that doleful cry?

'I cannot tell; I wish I could;
For the true reason no one knows: 90
But would you gladly view the spot,
The spot to which she goes;
The hillock like an infant's grave,
The pond—and Thorn, so old and grey;
Pass by her door—'tis seldom shut—
And if you see her in her hut—
Then to the spot away!
I never heard of such as dare
Approach the spot when she is there.'

'But wherefore to the mountain-top   100
Can this unhappy Woman go,
Whatever star is in the skies,
Whatever wind may blow?'
'Full twenty years are past and gone
Since she (her name is Martha Ray)
Gave with a maiden's true good-will
Her company to Stephen Hill;
And she was blithe and gay,
While friends and kindred all approved
Of him whom tenderly she loved.   110

'And they had fixed the wedding day,
The morning that must wed them both;
But Stephen to another Maid
Had sworn another oath;
And, with this other Maid, to church
Unthinking Stephen went—
Poor Martha! on that woeful day
A pang of pitiless dismay
Into her soul was sent;
A fire was kindled in her breast,   120
Which might not burn itself to rest.

'They say, full six months after this,
While yet the summer leaves were green,
She to the mountain-top would go,
And there was often seen.
What could she seek?—or wish to hide?
Her state to any eye was plain;
She was with child, and she was mad;
Yet often was she sober sad
From her exceeding pain.   130
O guilty Father—would that death
Had saved him from that breach of faith!

'Sad case for such a brain to hold
Communion with a stirring child!
Sad case, as you may think, for one
Who had a brain so wild!
Last Christmas-eve we talked of this,
And grey-haired Wilfred of the glen
Held that the unborn infant wrought
About its mother's heart, and brought   140
Her senses back again:
And, when at last her time drew near,
Her looks were calm, her senses clear.

'More know I not, I wish I did,
And it should all be told to you;
For what became of this poor child
No mortal ever knew;
Nay—if a child to her was born
No earthly tongue could ever tell;
And if 'twas born alive or dead,   150
Far less could this with proof be said;
But some remember well
That Martha Ray about this time
Would up the mountain often climb.

'And all that winter, when at night
The wind blew from the mountain-peak,
'Twas worth your while, though in the dark,
The churchyard path to seek:
For many a time and oft were heard
Cries coming from the mountain head: 160
Some plainly living voices were;

And others, I've heard many swear,
Were voices of the dead:
I cannot think, whate'er they say,
They had to do with Martha Ray.

'But that she goes to this old Thorn,
The Thorn which I described to you,
And there sits in a scarlet cloak,
I will be sworn is true.
For one day with my telescope,   170
To view the ocean wide and bright,
When to this country first I came,
Ere I had heard of Martha's name,
I climbed the mountain's height:—
A storm came on, and I could see
No object higher than my knee.

''Twas mist and rain, and storm and rain:
No screen, no fence could I discover;
And then the wind! in sooth, it was
A wind full ten times over.   180
I looked around, I thought I saw
A jutting crag,—and off I ran,
Head-foremost, through the driving rain,
The shelter of the crag to gain;
And, as I am a man,
Instead of jutting crag I found
A Woman seated on the ground.

'I did not speak—I saw her face;
Her face!—it was enough for me;
I turned about and heard her cry,   190
"Oh misery! oh misery!"
And there she sits, until the moon
Through half the clear blue sky will go;
And when the little breezes make
The waters of the pond to shake,
As all the country know,
She shudders, and you hear her cry,
"Oh misery! oh misery!"

'But what's the Thorn? and what the pond?
And what the hill of moss to her?   200
And what the creeping breeze that comes
The little pond to stir?'
'I cannot tell; but some will say
She hanged her baby on the tree;
Some say she drowned it in the pond,
Which is a little step beyond:
But all and each agree,
The little Babe was buried there,
Beneath that hill of moss so fair.

'I've heard, the moss is spotted red   210
With drops of that poor infant's blood;

But kill a new-born infant thus,
I do not think she could!
Some say if to the pond you go,
And fix on it a steady view,
The shadow of a babe you trace,
A baby and a baby's face,
And that it looks at you;
Whene'er you look on it, 'tis plain
The baby looks at you again.   220

'And some had sworn an oath that she
Should be to public justice brought;
And for the little infant's bones
With spades they would have sought.
But instantly the hill of moss
Before their eyes began to stir!
And, for full fifty yards around,
The grass—it shook upon the ground!
Yet all do still aver
The little Babe lies buried there,   230
Beneath that hill of moss so fair.

'I cannot tell how this may be,
But plain it is the Thorn is bound
With heavy tufts of moss that strive
To drag it to the ground;
And this I know, full many a time,
When she was on the mountain high,
By day, and in the silent night,
When all the stars shone clear and bright,
That I have heard her cry,   240
"Oh misery! oh misery!
Oh woe is me! oh misery!"'

1798   1798

SIMON LEE

THE OLD HUNTSMAN;

WITH AN INCIDENT IN WHICH HE WAS
CONCERNED

This old man had been huntsman to the squires of
Alfoxden. . . . The fact was as mentioned in the poem;
and I have, after an interval of forty-five years, the image
of the old man as fresh before my eyes as if I had seen
him yesterday. The expression when the hounds were
out, 'I dearly love their voice,' was word for word from
his own lips.—(Wordsworth.)

IN the sweet shire of Cardigan,
Not far from pleasant Ivor-hall,
An old Man dwells, a little man,—
'Tis said he once was tall.
Full five-and-thirty years he lived
A running huntsman merry;

And still the centre of his cheek
Is red as a ripe cherry.

No man like him the horn could sound,
And hill and valley rang with glee   10
When Echo bandied, round and round,
The halloo of Simon Lee.
In those proud days, he little cared
For husbandry or tillage;
To blither tasks did Simon rouse
The sleepers of the village.

He all the country could outrun,
Could leave both man and horse behind;
And often, ere the chase was done,
He reeled, and was stone-blind.   20
And still there's something in the world
At which his heart rejoices;
For when the chiming hounds are out,
He dearly loves their voices!

But, oh the heavy change!—bereft
Of health, strength, friends, and kindred,
    see!
Old Simon to the world is left
In liveried poverty.
His Master's dead,—and no one now
Dwells in the Hall of Ivor;   30
Men, dogs, and horses, all are dead;
He is the sole survivor.

And he is lean and he is sick;
His body, dwindled and awry,
Rests upon ankles swoln and thick;
His legs are thin and dry.
One prop he has, and only one,
His wife, an aged woman,
Lives with him, near the waterfall,
Upon the village Common.   40

Beside their moss-grown hut of clay,
Not twenty paces from the door,
A scrap of land they have, but they
Are poorest of the poor.
This scrap of land he from the heath
Enclosed when he was stronger;
But what to them avails the land
Which he can till no longer?

Oft, working by her Husband's side,
Ruth does what Simon cannot do;   50
For she, with scanty cause for pride,
Is stouter of the two.
And, though you with your utmost skill
From labour could not wean them,

'Tis little, very little—all
That they can do between them.

Few months of life has he in store
As he to you will tell,
For still, the more he works, the more
Do his weak ankles swell.   60
My gentle Reader, I perceive
How patiently you've waited,
And now I fear that you expect
Some tale will be related.

O Reader! had you in your mind
Such stores as silent thought can bring,
O gentle Reader! you would find
A tale in every thing.
What more I have to say is short,
And you must kindly take it: 70
It is no tale; but, should you think,
Perhaps a tale you'll make it.

One summer-day I chanced to see
This old Man doing all he could
To unearth the root of an old tree,
A stump of rotten wood.
The mattock tottered in his hand;
So vain was his endeavour,
That at the root of the old tree
He might have worked for ever.   80

'You're overtasked, good Simon Lee,
Give me your tool,' to him I said;
And at the word right gladly he
Received my proffered aid.
I struck, and with a single blow
The tangled root I severed,
At which the poor old Man so long
And vainly had endeavoured.

The tears into his eyes were brought,
And thanks and praises seemed to run   90
So fast out of his heart, I thought
They never would have done.
—I've heard of hearts unkind, kind deeds
With coldness still returning;
Alas! the gratitude of men
Hath oftener left me mourning.

1798   1798

LINES WRITTEN IN EARLY SPRING

Actually composed while I was sitting by the side of
the brook that runs down from the Comb, in which stands
the village of Alford, through the grounds of Alfoxden.
It was a chosen resort of mine. The brook fell down a

sloping rock so as to make a waterfall considerable for
that country, and across the pool below had fallen a tree,
an ash, if I rightly remember, from which rose perpendicularly, boughs in search of the light intercepted by the
deep shade above. The boughs bore leaves of green that
for want of sunshine had faded into almost lily-white;
and from the underside of this natural sylvan bridge depended long and beautiful tresses of ivy which waved
gently in the breeze that might poetically speaking be
called the breath of the waterfall.—(Wordsworth.)

I HEARD a thousand blended notes,
While in a grove I sate reclined,
In that sweet mood when pleasant thoughts
Bring sad thoughts to the mind.

To her fair works did Nature link
The human soul that through me ran;
And much it grieved my heart to think
What man has made of man.

Through primrose tufts, in that green bower,
The periwinkle trailed its wreaths;   10
And 'tis my faith that every flower
Enjoys the air it breathes.

The birds around me hopped and played,
Their thoughts I cannot measure:—
But the least motion which they made,
It seemed a thrill of pleasure.

The budding twigs spread out their fan,
To catch the breezy air;
And I must think, do all I can,
That there was pleasure there.   20

If this belief from heaven be sent,
If such be Nature's holy plan,
Have I not reason to lament
What man has made of man?

1798   1798

TO MY SISTER

Composed in front of Alfoxden House. My little boy-
messenger on this occasion was the son of Basil Montagu. The larch mentioned in the first stanza was standing when I revisited the place in May 1841, more than
forty years after.—(Wordsworth.)

IT is the first mild day of March:
Each minute sweeter than before,
The redbreast sings from the tall larch
That stands beside our door.

There is a blessing in the air,
Which seems a sense of joy to yield

To the bare trees, and mountains bare,
And grass in the green field.

My sister! ('tis a wish of mine)
Now that our morning meal is done,   10
Make haste, your morning task resign;
Come forth and feel the sun.

Edward will come with you;—and, pray,
Put on with speed your woodland dress;
And bring no book: for this one day
We'll give to idleness.

No joyless forms shall regulate
Our living calendar:
We from to-day, my Friend, will date
The opening of the year.   20

Love, now a universal birth,
From heart to heart is stealing,
From earth to man, from man to earth:
—It is the hour of feeling.

One moment now may give us more
Than years of toiling reason:
Our minds shall drink at every pore
The spirit of the season.

Some silent laws our heart will make,
Which they shall long obey: 30
We for the year to come may take
Our temper from to-day.

And from the blessed power that rolls
About, below, above,
We'll frame the measure of our souls:
They shall be tuned to love.

Then come, my Sister! come, I pray,
With speed put on your woodland dress;
And bring no book: for this one day
We'll give to idleness.   40

1798   *1798*

EXPOSTULATION AND REPLY

[This and the succeeding poem 'arose out of conversation with a friend who was somewhat unreasonably attached to modern books of moral philosophy.' The friend
was William Hazlitt.]

'WHY, William, on that old grey stone,
Thus for the length of half a day,
Why, William, sit you thus alone,
And dream your time away?

'Where are your books?—that light bequeathed
To Beings else forlorn and blind!
Up! up! and drink the spirit breathed
From dead men to their kind.

'You look round on your Mother Earth,
As if she for no purpose bore you;   10
As if you were her first-born birth,
And none had lived before you!'

One morning thus, by Esthwaite lake,
When life was sweet, I knew not why,
To me my good friend Matthew spake,
And thus I made reply:

'The eye—it cannot choose but see;
We cannot bid the ear be still;
Our bodies feel, where'er they be,
Against or with our will.   20

'Nor less I deem that there are Powers
Which of themselves our minds impress;
That we can feed this mind of ours
In a wise passiveness.

'Think you, 'mid all this mighty sum
Of things for ever speaking,
That nothing of itself will come,
But we must still be seeking?

'—Then ask not wherefore, here, alone,
Conversing as I may,   30
I sit upon this old grey stone,
And dream my time away.'

1798   *1798*

THE TABLES TURNED

AN EVENING SCENE ON THE SAME SUBJECT

UP! up! my Friend, and quit your books;
Or surely you'll grow double:
Up! up! my Friend, and clear your looks;
Why all this toil and trouble?

The sun, above the mountain's head,
A freshening lustre mellow
Through all the long green fields has spread,
His first sweet evening yellow.

Books! 'tis a dull and endless strife:
Come, hear the woodland linnet,   10
How sweet his music! on my life,
There's more of wisdom in it.

And hark! how blithe the throstle sings!
He, too, is no mean preacher:
Come forth into the light of things,
Let Nature be your Teacher.

She has a world of ready wealth,
Our minds and hearts to bless—
Spontaneous wisdom breathed by health,
Truth breathed by cheerfulness.   20

One impulse from a vernal wood
May teach you more of man,
Of moral evil and of good,
Than all the sages can.

Sweet is the lore which Nature brings;
Our meddling intellect
Mis-shapes the beauteous forms of things:—
We murder to dissect.

Enough of Science and of Art;
Close up those barren leaves;   30
Come forth, and bring with you a heart
That watches and receives.

1798   1798

LINES

COMPOSED A FEW MILES ABOVE TINTERN
ABBEY, ON REVISITING THE BANKS OF
THE WYE DURING A TOUR

No poem of mine was composed under circumstances
more pleasant for me to remember than this. I began it
upon leaving Tintern, after crossing the Wye, and concluded it just as I was entering Bristol in the evening,
after a ramble of four or five days, with my Sister. Not a
line of it was altered, and not any part of it written down
till I reached Bristol. It was published almost immediately after in the little volume of which so much has been
said in these Notes [the *Lyrical Ballads*].—(Wordsworth.)

FIVE years have past; five summers, with the length
Of five long winters! and again I hear
These waters, rolling from their mountain-springs
With a soft inland murmur.[1]—Once again
Do I behold these steep and lofty cliffs,
That on a wild secluded scene impress
Thoughts of more deep seclusion; and connect
The landscape with the quiet of the sky.
The day is come when I again repose
Here, under this dark sycamore, and view   10
These plots of cottage-ground, these orchard-tufts,
Which at this season, with their unripe fruits,
Are clad in one green hue, and lose themselves

[1] The river is not affected by the tides a few miles above Tintern.
—(Wordsworth.)

'Mid groves and copses. Once again I see
These hedge-rows, hardly hedge-rows, little lines
Of sportive wood run wild: these pastoral farms,
Green to the very door; and wreaths of smoke
Sent up, in silence, from among the trees!
With some uncertain notice, as might seem
Of vagrant dwellers in the houseless woods,   20
Or of some Hermit's cave, where by his fire
The Hermit sits alone.

                    These beauteous forms,
Through a long absence, have not been to me
As is a landscape to a blind man's eye:
But oft, in lonely rooms, and 'mid the din
Of towns and cities, I have owed to them,
In hours of weariness, sensations sweet,
Felt in the blood, and felt along the heart;
And passing even into my purer mind,
With tranquil restoration:—feelings too
Of unremembered pleasure: such, perhaps,
As have no slight or trivial influence
On that best portion of a good man's life,
His little, nameless, unremembered, acts
Of kindness and of love. Nor less, I trust,
To them I may have owed another gift,
Of aspect more sublime; that blessed mood,
In which the burthen of the mystery,
In which the heavy and the weary weight
Of all this unintelligible world,
Is lightened:—that serene and blessed mood,   40
In which the affections gently lead us on,—
Until, the breath of this corporeal frame
And even the motion of our human blood
Almost suspended, we are laid asleep
In body, and become a living soul:
While with an eye made quiet by the power
Of harmony, and the deep power of joy,
We see into the life of things.
                              If this
Be but a vain belief, yet, oh! how oft—   50
In darkness and amid the many shapes
Of joyless daylight; when the fretful stir
Unprofitable, and the fever of the world,
Have hung upon the beatings of my heart—
How oft, in spirit, have I turned to thee,
O sylvan Wye! thou wanderer thro' the woods,
How often has my spirit turned to thee!

    And now, with gleams of half-extinguished
        thought,
With many recognitions dim and faint,
And somewhat of a sad perplexity,   60
The picture of the mind revives again:
While here I stand, not only with the sense
Of present pleasure, but with pleasing thoughts
That in this moment there is life and food

For future years. And so I dare to hope,
Though changed, no doubt, from what I was when
    first
I came among these hills; when like a roe
I bounded o'er the mountains, by the sides
Of the deep rivers, and the lonely streams,
Wherever nature led: more like a man   70
Flying from something that he dreads than one
Who sought the thing he loved. For nature then
(The coarser pleasures of my boyish days,
And their glad animal movements all gone by)
To me was all in all.—I cannot paint
What then I was. The sounding cataract
Haunted me like a passion: the tall rock,
The mountain, and the deep and gloomy wood,
Their colours and their forms, were then to me
An appetite; a feeling and a love,   80
That had no need of a remoter charm,
By thought supplied, nor any interest
Unborrowed from the eye.—That time is past,
And all its aching joys are now no more,
And all its dizzy raptures. Not for this
Faint I, nor mourn nor murmur; other gifts
Have followed; for such loss, I would believe,
Abundant recompense. For I have learned
To look on nature, not as in the hour
Of thoughtless youth; but hearing oftentimes 90
The still, sad music of humanity,
Nor harsh nor grating, though of ample power
To chasten and subdue. And I have felt
A presence that disturbs me with the joy
Of elevated thoughts; a sense sublime
Of something far more deeply interfused,
Whose dwelling is the light of setting suns,
And the round ocean and the living air,
And the blue sky, and in the mind of man:
A motion and a spirit, that impels   100
All thinking things, all objects of all thought,
And rolls through all things. Therefore am I still
A lover of the meadows and the woods,
And mountains; and of all that we behold
From this green earth; of all the mighty world
Of eye, and ear,—both what they half create,
And what perceive; well pleased to recognise
In nature and the language of the sense
The anchor of my purest thoughts, the nurse,
The guide, the guardian of my heart, and soul 110
Of all my moral being.
                Nor perchance,
If I were not thus taught, should I the more
Suffer my genial spirits to decay:
For thou art with me here upon the banks
Of this fair river; thou my dearest Friend,
My dear, dear Friend; and in thy voice I catch
The language of my former heart, and read

My former pleasures in the shooting lights
Of thy wild eyes. Oh! yet a little while
May I behold in thee what I was once,   120
My dear, dear Sister! and this prayer I make,
Knowing that Nature never did betray
The heart that loved her; 'tis her privilege,
Through all the years of this our life, to lead
From joy to joy: for she can so inform
The mind that is within us, so impress
With quietness and beauty, and so feed
With lofty thoughts, that neither evil tongues,
Rash judgments, nor the sneers of selfish men,
Nor greetings where no kindness is, nor all   130
The dreary intercourse of daily life,
Shall e'er prevail against us, or disturb
Our cheerful faith, that all which we behold
Is full of blessings. Therefore let the moon
Shine on thee in thy solitary walk;
And let the misty mountain-winds be free
To blow against thee: and, in after years,
When these wild ecstasies shall be matured
Into a sober pleasure; when thy mind
Shall be a mansion for all lovely forms,   140
Thy memory be as a dwelling-place
For all sweet sounds and harmonies; oh! then,
If solitude, or fear, or pain, or grief,
Should be thy portion, with what healing thoughts
Of tender joy wilt thou remember me,
And these my exhortations! Nor, perchance—
If I should be where I no more can hear
Thy voice, nor catch from thy wild eyes these
    gleams
Of past existence—wilt thou then forget
That on the banks of this delightful stream   150
We stood together; and that I, so long
A worshipper of Nature, hither came
Unwearied in that service: rather say
With warmer love—oh! with far deeper zeal
Of holier love. Nor wilt thou then forget
That after many wanderings, many years
Of absence, these steep woods and lofty cliffs,
And this green pastoral landscape, were to me
More dear, both for themselves and for thy sake!

                        1798

NUTTING

Written in Germany; intended as part of a poem on
my own life, but struck out as not being wanted there.
Like most of my school fellows I was an impassioned
nutter. For this pleasure, the vale of Esthwaite, abounding in coppice-wood, furnished a very wide range. These
verses arose out of the remembrance of feelings I had
often had when a boy, and particularly in the extensive
woods that still stretch from the side of Esthwaite Lake
towards Graythwaite, the seat of the ancient family of
Sandys.—(Wordsworth.)

——————————It seems a day
(I speak of one from many singled out)
One of those heavenly days that cannot die;
When, in the eagerness of boyish hope,
I left our cottage-threshold, sallying forth
With a huge wallet o'er my shoulders slung,
A nutting-crook in hand; and turned my steps
Tow'rd some far-distant wood, a Figure quaint,
Tricked out in proud disguise of cast-off weeds[1]
Which for that service had been husbanded,   10
By exhortation of my frugal Dame—
Motley accoutrement, of power to smile
At thorns, and brakes, and brambles,—and in
    truth
More ragged than need was! O'er pathless rocks,
Through beds of matted fern, and tangled thickets,
Forcing my way, I came to one dear nook
Unvisited, where not a broken bough
Drooped with its withered leaves, ungracious sign
Of devastation; but the hazels rose
Tall and erect, with tempting clusters hung,   20
A virgin scene!—A little while I stood,
Breathing with such suppression of the heart
As joy delights in; and with wise restraint
Voluptuous, fearless of a rival, eyed
The banquet;—or beneath the trees I sate
Among the flowers, and with the flowers I played;
A temper known to those who, after long
And weary expectation, have been blest
With sudden happiness beyond all hope.
Perhaps it was a bower beneath whose leaves   30
The violets of five seasons re-appear
And fade, unseen by any human eye;
Where fairy water-breaks[2] do murmur on
For ever; and I saw the sparkling foam,
And—with my cheek on one of those green stones
That, fleeced with moss, under the shady trees,
Lay round me, scattered like a flock of sheep—
I heard the murmur and the murmuring sound,
In that sweet mood when pleasure loves to pay
Tribute to ease; and, of its joy secure,   40
The heart luxuriates with indifferent things,
Wasting its kindliness on stocks and stones,
And on the vacant air. Then up I rose,
And dragged to earth both branch and bough,
    with crash
And merciless ravage: and the shady nook
Of hazels, and the green and mossy bower,
Deformed and sullied, patiently gave up
Their quiet being: and unless I now
Confound my present feelings with the past,
Ere from the mutilated bower I turned   50
Exulting, rich beyond the wealth of kings,
I felt a sense of pain when I beheld

---

1 clothes.   2 broken, rippling water.

The silent trees, and saw the intruding sky.—
Then, dearest Maiden, move along these shades
In gentleness of heart; with gentle hand
Touch—for there is a spirit in the woods.

1798   1800

LUCY POEMS

[Who Lucy is in these famous poems of love and grief
is not known. She may have been a purely imaginary
creature, though the poet's deeply personal sentiment
leads to the belief that the situations in the poems probably owe their origin in part at least to actual experience.
Lucy has been variously identified in real life as (1) an
unknown maiden whom the poet loved in youth, (2)
Mary Hutchinson, later his wife, (3) Annette Vallon, (4)
his sister Dorothy. Though a likely case can be made out
for one or another of these candidates, and the best of all
for Dorothy, it should be kept in mind that the poet's
Lucy need not have been derived from one source only.]

I

STRANGE fits of passion have I known:
And I will dare to tell,
But in the Lover's ear alone,
What once to me befell.

When she I loved looked every day
Fresh as a rose in June,
I to her cottage bent my way,
Beneath an evening-moon.

Upon the moon I fixed my eye,
All over the wide lea;   10
With quickening pace my horse drew nigh
Those paths so dear to me.

And now we reached the orchard-plot;
And, as we climbed the hill,
The sinking moon to Lucy's cot
Came near, and nearer still.

In one of those sweet dreams I slept,
Kind Nature's gentlest boon!
And all the while my eyes I kept
On the descending moon.   20

My horse moved on; hoof after hoof
He raised, and never stopped:
When down behind the cottage roof,
At once, the bright moon dropped.

What fond and wayward thoughts will slide
Into a Lover's head!
'O mercy!' to myself I cried,
'If Lucy should be dead!'

1799   1800

II

SHE dwelt among the untrodden ways
    Beside the springs of Dove,[1]
A Maid whom there were none to praise
    And very few to love:

A violet by a mossy stone
    Half hidden from the eye!
—Fair as a star, when only one
    Is shining in the sky.

She lived unknown, and few could know
    When Lucy ceased to be;   10
But she is in her grave, and, oh,
    The difference to me!

1799   1800

III

I TRAVELLED among unknown men,
    In lands beyond the sea;
Nor, England! did I know till then
    What love I bore to thee.

'Tis past, that melancholy dream!
    Nor will I quit thy shore
A second time; for still I seem
    To love thee more and more.

Among thy mountains did I feel
    The joy of my desire;   10
And she I cherished turned her wheel
    Beside an English fire.

Thy mornings showed, thy nights concealed,
    The bowers where Lucy played;
And thine too is the last green field
    That Lucy's eyes surveyed.

1801   1807

IV

THREE years she grew in sun and shower,
Then Nature said, 'A lovelier flower
On earth was never sown;
This Child I to myself will take;
She shall be mine, and I will make
A Lady of my own.

'Myself will to my darling be
Both law and impulse: and with me

----

[1] There has been much speculation about the identity of 'the springs of Dove.' Wordsworth knew a river Dove in Derbyshire, in Yorkshire, and in Westmoreland; but of which particular stream he was thinking we do not know.

The Girl, in rock and plain,
In earth and heaven, in glade and bower,   10
Shall feel an overseeing power
To kindle or restrain.

'She shall be sportive as the fawn
That wild with glee across the lawn
Or up the mountain springs;
And hers shall be the breathing balm,
And hers the silence and the calm
Of mute insensate things.

'The floating clouds their state shall lend
To her; for her the willow bend;   20
Nor shall she fail to see
Even in the motions of the Storm
Grace that shall mould the Maiden's form
By silent sympathy.

'The stars of midnight shall be dear
To her; and she shall lean her ear
In many a secret place
Where rivulets dance their wayward round,
And beauty born of murmuring sound
Shall pass into her face.   30

'And vital feelings of delight
Shall rear her form to stately height,
Her virgin bosom swell;
Such thoughts to Lucy I will give
While she and I together live
Here in this happy dell.'

Thus Nature spake—The work was done—
How soon my Lucy's race was run!
She died, and left to me
This heath, this calm, and quiet scene;   40
The memory of what has been,
And never more will be.

1799   1800

V

A SLUMBER did my spirit seal;
    I had no human fears:
She seemed a thing that could not feel
    The touch of earthly years.

No motion has she now, no force;
    She neither hears nor sees;
Rolled round in earth's diurnal course,
    With rocks, and stones, and trees.

1799   1800

A POET'S EPITAPH

ART thou a Statist[1] in the van
Of public conflicts trained and bred?
—First learn to love one living man;
Then may'st thou think upon the dead.

A Lawyer art thou?—draw not nigh!
Go, carry to some fitter place
The keenness of that practised eye,
The hardness of that sallow face.

Art thou a Man of purple cheer?
A rosy Man, right plump to see?   10
Approach; yet, Doctor,[2] not too near,
This grave no cushion is for thee.

Or art thou one of gallant pride,
A Soldier and no man of chaff?
Welcome!—but lay thy sword aside,
And lean upon a peasant's staff.

Physician art thou?—one, all eyes,
Philosopher!—a fingering slave,
One that would peep and botanize
Upon his mother's grave?   20

Wrapt closely in thy sensual fleece,
O turn aside,—and take, I pray,
That he below may rest in peace,
Thy ever-dwindling soul, away!

A Moralist perchance appears;
Led, Heaven knows how! to this poor sod:
And he has neither eyes nor ears;
Himself his world, and his own God;

One to whose smooth-rubbed soul can cling
Nor form, nor feeling, great or small;   30
A reasoning, self-sufficing thing,
An intellectual All-in-all!

Shut close the door; press down the latch;
Sleep in thy intellectual crust;
Nor lose ten tickings of thy watch
Near this unprofitable dust.

But who is He, with modest looks,
And clad in homely russet brown?
He murmurs near the running brooks
A music sweeter than their own.   40

He is retired as noontide dew,
Or fountain in a noon-day grove;
And you must love him, ere to you
He will seem worthy of your love.

The outward shows of sky and earth,
Of hill and valley, he has viewed;
And impulses of deeper birth
Have come to him in solitude.

In common things that round us lie
Some random truths he can impart,—   50
The harvest of a quiet eye
That broods and sleeps on his own heart.

But he is weak; both Man and Boy,
Hath been an idler in the land;
Contented if he might enjoy
The things which others understand.

—Come hither in thy hour of strength;
Come, weak as is a breaking wave!
Here stretch thy body at full length;
Or build thy house upon this grave.   60

1799   1800

THE TWO APRIL MORNINGS

WE walked along, while bright and red
Uprose the morning sun;
And Matthew stopped, he looked, and said,
'The will of God be done!'

A village schoolmaster was he,
With hair of glittering grey;
As blithe a man as you could see
On a spring holiday.

And on that morning, through the grass,
And by the steaming rills,   10
We travelled merrily, to pass
A day among the hills.

'Our work,' said I, 'was well begun,
Then from thy breast what thought,
Beneath so beautiful a sun,
So sad a sigh has brought?'

A second time did Matthew stop;
And fixing still his eye
Upon the eastern mountain-top,
To me he made reply: 20

'Yon cloud with that long purple cleft
Brings fresh into my mind

---

1 statesman.   2 a divine.

A day like this which I have left
Full thirty years behind.

'And just above yon slope of corn
Such colours, and no other,
Were in the sky, that April morn,
Of this the very brother.

'With rod and line I sued¹ the sport
Which that sweet season gave,   30
And, to the churchyard come, stopped short
Beside my daughter's grave.

'Nine summers had she scarcely seen,
The pride of all the vale;
And then she sang;—she would have been
A very nightingale.

'Six feet in earth my Emma lay;
And yet I loved her more,
For so it seemed, than till that day
I e'er had loved before.   40

'And, turning from her grave, I met,
Beside the churchyard yew,
A blooming Girl, whose hair was wet
With points of morning dew.

'A basket on her head she bare;
Her brow was smooth and white:
To see a child so very fair,
It was a pure delight!

'No fountain from its rocky cave
E'er tripped with foot so free;   50
She seemed as happy as a wave
That dances on the sea.

'There came from me a sigh of pain
Which I could ill confine;
I looked at her, and looked again:
And did not wish her mine!'

Matthew is in his grave, yet now,
Methinks, I see him stand,
As at that moment, with a bough
Of wilding² in his hand.   60

1799   1800

THE FOUNTAIN

A CONVERSATION

WE talked with open heart, and tongue
Affectionate and true,

---

¹ pursued.   ² wild apple blossoms.

A pair of friends, though I was young,
And Matthew seventy-two.

We lay beneath a spreading oak,
Beside a mossy seat;
And from the turf a fountain broke,
And gurgled at our feet.

'Now, Matthew!' said I, 'let us match
This water's pleasant tune   10
With some old border-song, or catch
That suits a summer's noon;

'Or of the church-clock and the chimes
Sing here beneath the shade,
That half-mad thing of witty rhymes
Which you last April made!'

In silence Matthew lay, and eyed
The spring beneath the tree;
And thus the dear old Man replied,
The grey-haired man of glee: 20

'No check, no stay, this Streamlet fears;
How merrily it goes!
'Twill murmur on a thousand years,
And flow as now it flows.

'And here, on this delightful day,
I cannot choose but think
How oft, a vigorous man, I lay
Beside this fountain's brink.

'My eyes are dim with childish tears,
My heart is idly stirred,   30
For the same sound is in my ears
Which in those days I heard.

'Thus fares it still in our decay:
And yet the wiser mind
Mourns less for what age takes away
Than what it leaves behind.

'The blackbird amid leafy trees,
The lark above the hill,
Let loose their carols when they please,
Are quiet when they will.   40

'With Nature never do *they* wage
A foolish strife; they see
A happy youth, and their old age
Is beautiful and free:

'But we are pressed by heavy laws;
And often, glad no more,

Solitude
& death

We wear a face of joy, because
We have been glad of yore.

'If there be one who need bemoan
His kindred laid in earth,   50
The household hearts that were his own;
It is the man of mirth.

'My days, my Friend, are almost gone,
My life has been approved,
And many love me! but by none
Am I enough beloved.'

'Now both himself and me he wrongs,
The man who thus complains!
I live and sing my idle songs
Upon these happy plains;   60

'And, Matthew, for thy children dead
I'll be a son to thee!'
At this he grasped my hand, and said,
'Alas! that cannot be.'

We rose up from the fountain-side;
And down the smooth descent
Of the green sheep-track did we glide;
And through the wood we went;

And, ere we came to Leonard's rock,
He sang those witty rhymes   70
About the crazy old church-clock,
And the bewildered chimes.

1799   1800

LUCY GRAY

OR, SOLITUDE

Written at Goslar in Germany. It was founded on a circumstance told me by my Sister, of a little girl who, not far from Halifax in Yorkshire, was bewildered in a snow-storm. Her footsteps were traced by her parents to the middle of the lock of a canal, and no other vestige of her, backward or forward, could be traced. The body, however, was found in the canal. The way in which the incident was treated and the spiritualizing of the character might furnish hints for contrasting the imaginative influences which I have endeavoured to throw over common life with Crabbe's matter of fact style of treating subjects of the same kind. This is not spoken to his disparagement, far from it, but to direct the attention of thoughtful readers, into whose hands these notes may fall, to a comparison that may both enlarge the circle of their sensibilities, and tend to produce in them a catholic judgment.—(Wordsworth.)

Oft I had heard of Lucy Gray:
And, when I crossed the wild,

I chanced to see at break of day
The solitary child.

No mate, no comrade Lucy knew;
She dwelt on a wide moor,
—The sweetest thing that ever grew
Beside a human door!

You yet may spy the fawn at play,
The hare upon the green;   10
But the sweet face of Lucy Gray
Will never more be seen.

'To-night will be a stormy night—
You to the town must go;
And take a lantern, Child, to light
Your mother through the snow.'

'That, Father! will I gladly do:
'Tis scarcely afternoon—
The minster-clock has just struck two,
And yonder is the moon!'   20

At this the Father raised his hook,
And snapped a faggot-band;
He plied his work;—and Lucy took
The lantern in her hand.

Not blither is the mountain roe:
With many a wanton stroke
Her feet disperse the powdery snow,
That rises up like smoke.

The storm came on before its time:
She wandered up and down;   30
And many a hill did Lucy climb:
But never reached the town.

The wretched parents all that night
Went shouting far and wide;
But there was neither sound nor sight
To serve them for a guide.

At day-break on a hill they stood
That overlooked the moor;
And thence they saw the bridge of wood,
A furlong from their door.   40

They wept—and, turning homeward, cried,
'In heaven we all shall meet;'
—When in the snow the mother spied
The print of Lucy's feet.

Then downwards from the steep hill's edge
They tracked the footmarks small;

And through the broken hawthorn hedge,
And by the long stone-wall;

And then an open field they crossed:
The marks were still the same;   50
They tracked them on, nor ever lost;
And to the bridge they came.

They followed from the snowy bank
Those footmarks, one by one,
Into the middle of the plank;
And further there were none!

—Yet some maintain that to this day
She is a living child;
That you may see sweet Lucy Gray
Upon the lonesome wild.   60

O'er rough and smooth she trips along,
And never looks behind;
And sings a solitary song
That whistles in the wind.

1799   1800

RUTH

Suggested by an account I had of a wanderer in Somersetshire.—(Wordsworth.)

WHEN Ruth was left half desolate,
Her Father took another Mate;
And Ruth, not seven years old,
A slighted child, at her own will
Went wandering over dale and hill,
In thoughtless freedom, bold.

And she had made a pipe of straw,
And music from that pipe could draw
Like sounds of winds and floods;
Had built a bower upon the green,   10
As if she from her birth had been
An infant of the woods.

Beneath her father's roof, alone
She seemed to live; her thoughts her own;
Herself her own delight;
Pleased with herself, nor sad, nor gay;
And, passing thus the live-long day,
She grew to woman's height.

There came a Youth from Georgia's shore—
A military casque he wore,   20
With splendid feathers drest;
He brought them from the Cherokees;

The feathers nodded in the breeze,
And made a gallant crest.

From Indian blood you deem him sprung:
But no! he spake the English tongue,
And bore a soldier's name;
And, when America was free
From battle and from jeopardy,
He 'cross the ocean came.   30

With hues of genius on his cheek
In finest tones the Youth could speak:
—While he was yet a boy,
The moon, the glory of the sun,
And streams that murmur as they run,
Had been his dearest joy.

He was a lovely Youth! I guess
The panther in the wilderness
Was not so fair as he;
And, when he chose to sport and play,   40
No dolphin ever was so gay
Upon the tropic sea.

Among the Indians he had fought,
And with him many tales he brought
Of pleasure and of fear;
Such tales as told to any maid
By such a Youth, in the green shade,
Were perilous to hear.

He told of girls—a happy rout!
Who quit their fold with dance and shout,   50
Their pleasant Indian town,
To gather strawberries all day long;
Returning with a choral song
When daylight is gone down.

He spake of plants that hourly change
Their blossoms, through a boundless range
Of intermingling hues;
With budding, fading, faded flowers
They stand the wonder of the bowers
From morn to evening dews.   60

He told of the magnolia, spread
High as a cloud, high over head!
The cypress and her spire;
—Of flowers that with one scarlet gleam
Cover a hundred leagues, and seem
To set the hills on fire.

The Youth of green savannahs spake,
And many an endless, endless lake,

With all its fairy crowds
Of islands, that together lie 70
As quietly as spots of sky
Among the evening clouds.

'How pleasant,' then he said, 'it were
A fisher or a hunter there,
In sunshine or in shade
To wander with an easy mind;
And build a household fire, and find
A home in every glade!

'What days and what bright years! Ah me!
Our life were life indeed, with thee 80
So passed in quiet bliss,
And all the while,' said he, 'to know
That we were in a world of woe,
On such an earth as this!'

And then he sometimes interwove
Fond thoughts about a father's love:
'For there,' said he, 'are spun
Around the heart such tender ties,
That our own children to our eyes
Are dearer than the sun. 90

'Sweet Ruth! and could you go with me
My helpmate in the woods to be,
Our shed at night to rear;
Or run, my own adopted bride,
A sylvan huntress at my side,
And drive the flying deer!

'Beloved Ruth!'—No more he said.
The wakeful Ruth at midnight shed
A solitary tear:
She thought again—and did agree 100
With him to sail across the sea,
And drive the flying deer.

'And now, as fitting is and right,
We in the church our faith will plight,
A husband and a wife.'
Even so they did; and I may say
That to sweet Ruth that happy day
Was more than human life.

Through dream and vision did she sink,
Delighted all the while to think 110
That on those lonesome floods,
And green savannahs, she should share
His board with lawful joy, and bear
His name in the wild woods.

But, as you have before been told,
This Stripling, sportive, gay, and bold,
And, with his dancing crest,
So beautiful, through savage lands
Had roamed about, with vagrant bands
Of Indians in the west. 120

The wind, the tempest roaring high,
The tumult of a tropic sky,
Might well be dangerous food
For him, a Youth to whom was given
So much of earth—so much of heaven,
And such impetuous blood.

Whatever in those climes he found
Irregular in sight or sound
Did to his mind impart
A kindred impulse, seemed allied 130
To his own powers, and justified
The workings of his heart.

Nor less, to feed voluptuous thought,
The beauteous forms of nature wrought,
Fair trees and gorgeous flowers;
The breezes their own languor lent;
The stars had feelings, which they sent
Into those favoured bowers.

Yet, in his worst pursuits I ween
That sometimes there did intervene 140
Pure hopes of high intent:
For passions linked to forms so fair
And stately needs must have their share
Of noble sentiment.

But ill he lived, much evil saw,
With men to whom no better law
Nor better life was known;
Deliberately, and undeceived,
Those wild men's vices he received,
And gave them back his own. 150

His genius and his moral frame
Were thus impaired, and he became
The slave of low desires:
A Man who without self-control
Would seek what the degraded soul
Unworthily admires.

And yet he with no feigned delight
Had wooed the Maiden, day and night
Had loved her, night and morn:
What could he less than love a Maid 160

Whose heart with so much nature played?
So kind and so forlorn!

Sometimes, most earnestly, he said,
'O Ruth! I have been worse than dead;
False thoughts, thoughts bold and vain,
Encompassed me on every side
When I, in confidence and pride,
Had crossed the Atlantic main.

'Before me shone a glorious world—
Fresh as a banner bright, unfurled   170
To music suddenly:
I looked upon those hills and plains,
And seemed as if let loose from chains,
To live at liberty.

'No more of this; for now, by thee
Dear Ruth! more happily set free
With nobler zeal I burn;
My soul from darkness is released,
Like the whole sky when to the east
The morning doth return.'   180

Full soon that better mind was gone:
No hope, no wish remained, not one,—
They stirred him now no more;
New objects did new pleasure give,
And once again he wished to live
As lawless as before.

Meanwhile, as thus with him it fared,
They for the voyage were prepared,
And went to the sea-shore,
But, when they thither came, the Youth   190
Deserted his poor Bride, and Ruth
Could never find him more.

God help thee, Ruth!—Such pains she had,
That she in half a year was mad,
And in a prison housed;
And there, with many a doleful song
Made of wild words, her cup of wrong
She fearfully caroused.

Yet sometimes milder hours she knew,
Nor wanted sun, nor rain, nor dew,   200
Nor pastimes of the May;
—They all were with her in her cell;
And a clear brook with cheerful knell
Did o'er the pebbles play.

When Ruth three seasons thus had lain,
There came a respite to her pain;

She from her prison fled;
But of the Vagrant none took thought;
And where it liked her best she sought
Her shelter and her bread.   210

Among the fields she breathed again:
The master-current of her brain
Ran permanent and free;
And, coming to the Banks of Tone,[1]
There did she rest; and dwell alone
Under the greenwood tree.

The engines of her pain, the tools
That shaped her sorrow, rocks and pools,
And airs that gently stir
The vernal leaves—she loved them still;   220
Nor ever taxed them with the ill
Which had been done to her.

A Barn her *winter* bed supplies;
But, till the warmth of summer skies
And summer days is gone,
(And all do in this tale agree)
She sleeps beneath the greenwood tree,
And other home hath none.

An innocent life, yet far astray!
And Ruth will, long before her day,   230
Be broken down and old:
Sore aches she needs must have! but less
Of mind than body's wretchedness,
From damp, and rain, and cold.

If she is prest by want of food,
She from her dwelling in the wood
Repairs to a road-side;
And there she begs at one steep place
Where up and down with easy pace
The horsemen-travellers ride.   240

That oaten pipe of hers is mute,
Or thrown away; but with a flute
Her loneliness she cheers:
This flute, made of a hemlock stalk,
At evening in his homeward walk
The Quantock woodman hears.

I, too, have passed her on the hills
Setting her little water-mills
By spouts and fountains wild—
Such small machinery as she turned   250
Ere she had wept, ere she had mourned,
A young and happy Child!

_____
1 a river of Somersetshire.

Farewell! and when thy days are told,
Ill-fated Ruth, in hallowed mould
Thy corpse shall buried be,
For thee a funeral bell shall ring,
And all the congregation sing
A Christian psalm for thee.

1799 1800

THE PRELUDE; OR, GROWTH OF A POET'S MIND

AN AUTOBIOGRAPHICAL POEM

ADVERTISEMENT

The following Poem was commenced in the beginning of the year 1799, and completed in the summer of 1805.

The design and occasion of the work are described by the Author in his Preface to the 'Excursion,' first published in 1814, where he thus speaks:—

'Several years ago, when the Author retired to his native mountains with the hope of being enabled to construct a literary work that might live, it was a reasonable thing that he should take a review of his own mind, and examine how far Nature and Education had qualified him for such an employment.

'As subsidiary to this preparation, he undertook to record, in verse, the origin and progress of his own powers, as far as he was acquainted with them.

'That work, addressed to a dear friend, most distinguished for his knowledge and genius, and to whom the Author's intellect is deeply indebted, has been long finished; and the result of the investigation which gave rise to it, was a determination to compose a philosophical Poem, containing views of Man, Nature, and Society, and to be entitled the "Recluse"; as having for its principal subject the sensations and opinions of a poet living in retirement.

'The preparatory poem is biographical, and conducts the history of the Author's mind to the point when he was emboldened to hope that his faculties were sufficiently matured for entering upon the arduous labour which he had proposed to himself; and the two works have the same kind of relation to each other, if he may so express himself, as the Ante-chapel has to the body of a Gothic church. Continuing this allusion, he may be permitted to add, that his minor pieces, which have been long before the public, when they shall be properly arranged, will be found by the attentive reader to have such connexion with the main work as may give them claim to be likened to the little cells, oratories, and sepulchral recesses, ordinarily included in those edifices.'

Such was the Author's language in the year 1814.

It will thence be seen, that the present Poem was intended to be introductory to the 'Recluse,' and that the 'Recluse,' if completed, would have consisted of Three Parts. Of these, the Second Part alone: viz. the 'Excursion,' was finished, and given to the world by the Author.

The First Book of the First Part of the 'Recluse' still remains in manuscript; but the Third Part was only planned. The materials of which it would have been formed have, however, been incorporated, for the most part, in the Author's other Publications, written subsequently to the 'Excursion.'

The Friend, to whom the present Poem is addressed, was the late SAMUEL TAYLOR COLERIDGE, who was resident in Malta, for the restoration of his health, when the greater part of it was composed.

Mr. Coleridge read a considerable portion of the Poem while he was abroad; and his feelings, on hearing it recited by the Author (after his return to his own country), are recorded in his Verses, addressed to Mr. Wordsworth.

Rydal Mount, 13 July 1850

BOOK FIRST

INTRODUCTION—CHILDHOOD AND SCHOOL-TIME

Lines 1–131, 261–646

OH there is blessing in this gentle breeze,
A visitant that while it fans my cheek
Doth seem half-conscious of the joy it brings
From the green fields, and from yon azure sky.
Whate'er its mission, the soft breeze can come
To none more grateful than to me; escaped
From the vast city,[1] where I long had pined
A discontented sojourner: now free,
Free as a bird to settle where I will.
What dwelling shall receive me? in what vale   10
Shall be my harbour? underneath what grove
Shall I take up my home? and what clear stream
Shall with its murmur lull me into rest?
The earth is all before me. With a heart
Joyous, nor scared at its own liberty,
I look about; and should the chosen guide
Be nothing better than a wandering cloud,
I cannot miss my way. I breathe again!
Trances of thought and mountings of the mind
Come fast upon me: it is shaken off,   20
That burthen of my own unnatural self,
The heavy weight of many a weary day
Not mine, and such as were not made for me.
Long months of peace (if such bold word accord
With any promises of human life),
Long months of ease and undisturbed delight
Are mine in prospect; whither shall I turn,
By road or pathway, or through trackless field,
Up hill or down, or shall some floating thing
Upon the river point me out my course?   30

Dear Liberty! Yet what would it avail
But for a gift that consecrates the joy?
For I, methought, while the sweet breath of heaven
Was blowing on my body, felt within
A correspondent breeze, that gently moved
With quickening virtue, but is now become
A tempest, a redundant energy,
Vexing its own creation. Thanks to both,

---

1 London.

And their congenial powers, that, while they join
In breaking up a long-continued frost,   40
Bring with them vernal promises, the hope
Of active days urged on by flying hours,—
Days of sweet leisure, taxed with patient thought
Abstruse, nor wanting punctual service high,
Matins and vespers of harmonious verse!

   Thus far, O Friend![2] did I, not used to make
A present joy the matter of a song,
Pour forth that day my soul in measured strains
That would not be forgotten, and are here
Recorded: to the open fields I told   50
A prophecy: poetic numbers came
Spontaneously to clothe in priestly robe
A renovated spirit singled out,
Such hope was mine, for holy services.
My own voice cheered me, and, far more, the
    mind's
Internal echo of the imperfect sound;
To both I listened, drawing from them both
A cheerful confidence in things to come.

   Content and not unwilling now to give
A respite to this passion, I paced on   60
With brisk and eager steps; and came, at length,
To a green shady place, where down I sate
Beneath a tree, slackening my thoughts by choice,
And settling into gentler happiness.
'Twas autumn, and a clear and placid day,
With warmth, as much as needed, from a sun
Two hours declined towards the west; a day
With silver clouds, and sunshine on the grass,
And in the sheltered and the sheltering grove
A perfect stillness. Many were the thoughts   70
Encouraged and dismissed, till choice was made
Of a known Vale,[3] whither my feet should turn,
Nor rest till they had reached the very door
Of the one cottage which methought I saw.
No picture of mere memory ever looked
So fair; and while upon the fancied scene
I gazed with growing love, a higher power
Than Fancy gave assurance of some work
Of glory there forthwith to be begun,
Perhaps too there performed. Thus long I
    mused,   80
Nor e'er lost sight of what I mused upon,
Save when, amid the stately grove of oaks,
Now here, now there, an acorn, from its cup
Dislodged, through sere leaves rustled, or at once
To the bare earth dropped with a startling sound.
From that soft couch I rose not, till the sun
Had almost touched the horizon; casting then
A backward glance upon the curling cloud

Of city smoke, by distance ruralised;
Keen as a Truant or a Fugitive,   90
But as a Pilgrim resolute, I took,
Even with the chance equipment of that hour,
The road that pointed toward the chosen Vale.
It was a splendid evening, and my soul
Once more made trial of her strength, nor lacked
Æolian visitations; but the harp
Was soon defrauded, and the banded host
Of harmony dispersed in straggling sounds,
And lastly utter silence! 'Be it so;
Why think of anything but present good?'   100
So, like a home-bound labourer, I pursued
My way beneath the mellowing sun, that shed
Mild influence; nor left in me one wish
Again to bend the Sabbath of that time
To a servile yoke. What need of many words?
A pleasant loitering journey, through three days
Continued, brought me to my hermitage.
I spare to tell of what ensued, the life
In common things—the endless store of things,
Rare, or at least so seeming, every day   110
Found all about me in one neighbourhood—
The self-congratulation, and, from morn
To night, unbroken cheerfulness serene.
But speedily an earnest longing rose
To brace myself to some determined aim,
Reading or thinking; either to lay up
New stores, or rescue from decay the old
By timely interference: and therewith
Came hopes still higher, that with outward life
I might endue some airy phantasies   120
That had been floating loose about for years,
And to such beings temperately deal forth
The many feelings that oppressed my heart.
That hope hath been discouraged; welcome
    light
Dawns from the east, but dawns to disappear
And mock me with a sky that ripens not
Into a steady morning: if my mind,
Remembering the bold promise of the past,
Would gladly grapple with some noble theme,
Vain is her wish; where'er she turns she finds 130
Impediments from day to day renewed.

       .   .   .

This is my lot; for either still I find
Some imperfection in the chosen theme,
Or see of absolute accomplishment
Much wanting, so much wanting, in myself,
That I recoil and droop, and seek repose
In listlessness from vain perplexity,
Unprofitably traveling toward the grave,
Like a false steward who hath much received
And renders nothing back.

---

2 Samuel Taylor Coleridge.   3 Racedown.

Was it for this
That one,[4] the fairest of all rivers, loved   270
To blend his murmurs with my nurse's song,
And, from his alder shades and rocky falls,
And from his fords and shallows, sent a voice
That flowed along my dreams? For this, didst thou,
O Derwent! winding among grassy holms
Where I was looking on, a babe in arms,
Make ceaseless music that composed my thoughts
To more than infant softness, giving me
Amid the fretful dwellings of mankind
A foretaste, a dim earnest, of the calm   280
That Nature breathes among the hills and groves.

When he had left the mountains and received
On his smooth breast the shadow of those towers[5]
That yet survive, a shattered monument
Of feudal sway, the bright blue river passed
Along the margin of our terrace walk;
A tempting playmate whom we dearly loved.
Oh, many a time have I, a five years' child,
In a small mill-race severed from his stream,
Made one long bathing of a summer's day;   290
Basked in the sun, and plunged and basked again
Alternate, all a summer's day, or scoured
The sandy fields, leaping through flowery groves
Of yellow ragwort; or when rock and hill,
The woods, and distant Skiddaw's lofty height,
Were bronzed with deepest radiance, stood alone
Beneath the sky, as if I had been born
On Indian plains, and from my mother's hut
Had run abroad in wantonness, to sport,
A naked savage, in the thunder shower.   300

Fair seed-time had my soul, and I grew up
Fostered alike by beauty and by fear:
Much favoured in my birthplace, and no less
In that belovèd Vale[6] to which erelong
We were transplanted—there were we let loose
For sports of wider range. Ere I had told
Ten birth-days, when among the mountain-slopes
Frost, and the breath of frosty wind, had snapped
The last autumnal crocus, 'twas my joy
With store of springes[7] o'er my shoulder hung   310
To range the open heights where woodcocks run
Among the smooth green turf. Through half the
    night,
Scudding away from snare to snare, I plied
That anxious visitation;—moon and stars
Were shining o'er my head. I was alone,
And seemed to be a trouble to the peace

That dwelt among them. Sometimes it befell
In these night wanderings, that a strong desire
O'erpowered my better reason, and the bird
Which was the captive of another's toil   320
Became my prey; and when the deed was done
I heard among the solitary hills
Low breathings coming after me, and sounds
Of undistinguishable motion, steps
Almost as silent as the turf they trod.

Nor less when spring had warmed the cultured
    Vale,
Roved we as plunderers where the mother-bird
Had in high places built her lodge; though mean
Our object and inglorious, yet the end
Was not ignoble. Oh! when I have hung   330
Above the raven's nest, by knots of grass
And half-inch fissures in the slippery rock
But ill sustained, and almost (so it seemed)
Suspended by the blast that blew amain,
Shouldering the naked crag, oh, at that time
While on the perilous ridge I hung alone,
With what strange utterance did the loud dry wind
Blow through my ear! the sky seemed not a sky
Of earth—and with what motion moved the
    clouds!

Dust as we are, the immortal spirit grows   340
Like harmony in music; there is a dark
Inscrutable workmanship that reconciles
Discordant elements, makes them cling together
In one society. How strange that all
The terrors, pains, and early miseries,
Regrets, vexations, lassitudes interfused
Within my mind, should e'er have borne a part,
And that a needful part, in making up
The calm existence that is mine when I
Am worthy of myself! Praise to the end!   350
Thanks to the means which Nature deigned to
    employ;
Whether her fearless visitings, or those
That came with soft alarm, like hurtless light
Opening the peaceful clouds; or she may use
Severer interventions, ministry
More palpable, as best might suit her aim.

One summer evening (led by her) I found
A little boat tied to a willow tree
Within a rocky cave, its usual home.
Straight I unloosed her chain, and stepping in   360
Pushed from the shore. It was an act of stealth
And troubled pleasure, nor without the voice
Of mountain-echoes did my boat move on;
Leaving behind her still, on either side,
Small circles glittering idly in the moon,

---

4 The Derwent River flows past Wordsworth's birthplace.
5 Cockermouth Castle.
6 Esthwaite vale in Lancashire, where picturesque Hawkshead,
Wordsworth's boyhood home, is located.
7 snares for catching birds.

Until they melted all into one track
Of sparkling light. But now, like one who rows,
Proud of his skill, to reach a chosen point
With an unswerving line, I fixed my view
Upon the summit of a craggy ridge,   370
The horizon's utmost boundary; for above
Was nothing but the stars and the grey sky.
She was an elfin pinnace; lustily
I dipped my oars into the silent lake,
And, as I rose upon the stroke, my boat
Went heaving through the water like a swan;
When, from behind that craggy steep till then
The horizon's bound, a huge peak, black and huge,
As if with voluntary power instinct
Upreared its head. I struck and struck again,   380
And growing still in stature the grim shape
Towered up between me and the stars, and still,
For so it seemed, with purpose of its own
And measured motion like a living thing,
Strode after me. With trembling oars I turned,
And through the silent water stole my way
Back to the covert of the willow tree;
There in her mooring-place I left my bark,—
And through the meadows homeward went, in
    grave
And serious mood; but after I had seen   390
That spectacle, for many days, my brain
Worked with a dim and undetermined sense
Of unknown modes of being; o'er my thoughts
There hung a darkness, call it solitude
Or blank desertion. No familiar shapes
Remained, no pleasant images of trees,
Of sea or sky, no colours of green fields;
But huge and mighty forms, that do not live
Like living men, moved slowly through the mind
By day, and were a trouble to my dreams.   400

Wisdom and Spirit of the universe![8]
Thou Soul that art the eternity of thought,
That givest to forms and images a breath
And everlasting motion, not in vain
By day or star-light thus from my first dawn
Of childhood didst thou intertwine for me
The passions that build up our human soul;
Not with the mean and vulgar works of man,
But with high objects, with enduring things—
With life and nature—purifying thus   410
The elements of feeling and of thought,
And sanctifying, by such discipline,
Both pain and fear, until we recognise
A grandeur in the beatings of the heart.
Nor was this fellowship vouchsafed to me

With stinted kindness. In November days,
When vapours rolling down the valley made
A lonely scene more lonesome, among woods,
At noon and 'mid the calm of summer nights,
When, by the margin of the trembling lake,   420
Beneath the gloomy hills homeward I went
In solitude, such intercourse was mine;
Mine was it in the fields both day and night,
And by the waters, all the summer long.

    And in the frosty season, when the sun
Was set, and visible for many a mile
The cottage windows blazed through twilight
    gloom,
I heeded not their summons: happy time
It was indeed for all of us—for me
It was a time of rapture! Clear and loud   430
The village clock tolled six,—I wheeled about,
Proud and exulting like an untired horse
That cares not for his home. All shod with steel,
We hissed along the polished ice in games
Confederate, imitative of the chase
And woodland pleasures,—the resounding horn,
The pack loud chiming, and the hunted hare.
So through the darkness and the cold we flew,
And not a voice was idle; with the din
Smitten, the precipices rang aloud;   440
The leafless trees and every icy crag
Tinkled like iron; while far distant hills
Into the tumult sent an alien sound
Of melancholy not unnoticed, while the stars
Eastward were sparkling clear, and in the west
The orange sky of evening died away.
Not seldom from the uproar I retired
Into a silent bay, or sportively
Glanced sideway, leaving the tumultuous throng,
To cut across the reflex of a star   450
That fled, and, flying still before me, gleamed
Upon the glassy plain; and oftentimes,
When we had given our bodies to the wind,
And all the shadowy banks on either side
Came sweeping through the darkness, spinning
    still
The rapid line of motion, then at once
Have I, reclining back upon my heels,
Stopped short; yet still the solitary cliffs
Wheeled by me—even as if the earth had rolled
With visible motion her diurnal round!   460
Behind me did they stretch in solemn train,
Feebler and feebler, and I stood and watched
Till all was tranquil as a dreamless sleep.

Ye Presences of Nature in the sky
And on the earth! Ye Visions of the hills!
And Souls of lonely places! can I think

---

8 This famous section, through line 463, was highly praised by
Coleridge. It was first published separately in *The Friend*, under
the title, 'Growth of Genius from the Influences of Natural Objects on the Imagination in Boyhood and Early Youth.'

A vulgar hope was yours when ye employed
Such ministry, when ye through many a year
Haunting me thus among my boyish sports,
On caves and trees, upon the woods and hills, 470
Impressed upon all forms the characters
Of danger or desire; and thus did make
The surface of the universal earth
With triumph and delight, with hope and fear,
Work like a sea?

           Not uselessly employed,
Might I pursue this theme through every change
Of exercise and play, to which the year
Did summon us in his delightful round.

  We were a noisy crew; the sun in heaven
Beheld not vales more beautiful than ours;   480
Nor saw a band in happiness and joy
Richer, or worthier of the ground they trod.
I could record with no reluctant voice
The woods of autumn, and their hazel bowers
With milk-white clusters hung; the rod and line,
True symbol of hope's foolishness, whose strong
And unreproved enchantment led us on
By rocks and pools shut out from every star,
All the green summer, to forlorn cascades
Among the windings hid of mountain brooks. 490
—Unfading recollections! at this hour
The heart is almost mine with which I felt,
From some hill-top on sunny afternoons,
The paper kite high among fleecy clouds
Pull at her rein like an impetuous courser;
Or, from the meadows sent on gusty days,
Beheld her breast the wind, then suddenly
Dashed headlong, and rejected by the storm.

  Ye lowly cottages wherein we dwelt,
A ministration of your own was yours;   500
Can I forget you, being as you were
So beautiful among the pleasant fields
In which ye stood? or can I here forget
The plain and seemly countenance with which
Ye dealt out your plain comforts? Yet had ye
Delights and exultations of your own.
Eager and never weary we pursued
Our home-amusements by the warm peat-fire
At evening, when with pencil, and smooth slate
In square divisions parcelled out and all   510
With crosses and with cyphers scribbled o'er,
We schemed and puzzled, head opposed to head
In strife too humble to be named in verse:
Or round the naked table, snow-white deal,
Cherry or maple, sate in close array,
And to the combat, Loo[9] or Whist, led on
A thick-ribbed army; not, as in the world,

Neglected and ungratefully thrown by
Even for the very service they had wrought,
But husbanded through many a long campaign. 520
Uncouth assemblage was it, where no few
Had changed their functions; some, plebeian
    cards
Which Fate, beyond the promise of their birth,
Had dignified, and called to represent
The persons of departed potentates,
Oh, with what echoes on the board they fell!
Ironic diamonds,—clubs, hearts, diamonds,
    spades,
A congregation piteously akin!
Cheap matter offered they to boyish wit,
Those sooty knaves, precipitated down   530
With scoffs and taunts, like Vulcan out of heaven:
The paramount ace, a moon in her eclipse,
Queens gleaming through their splendour's last
    decay,
And monarchs surly at the wrongs sustained
By royal visages. Meanwhile abroad
Incessant rain was falling, or the frost
Raged bitterly, with keen and silent tooth;
And, interrupting oft that eager game,
From under Esthwaite's[10] splitting fields of ice
The pent-up air, struggling to free itself,   540
Gave out to meadow-grounds and hills a loud
Protracted yelling, like the noise of wolves
Howling in troops along the Bothnic Main.[11]

  Nor, sedulous as I have been to trace
How Nature by extrinsic passion first
Peopled the mind with forms sublime or fair,
And made me love them, may I here omit
How other pleasures have been mine, and joys
Of subtler origin; how I have felt,
Not seldom even in that tempestuous time,   550
Those hallowed and pure motions of the sense
Which seem, in their simplicity, to own
An intellectual charm; that calm delight
Which, if I err not, surely must belong
To those first-born affinities that fit
Our new existence to existing things,
And, in our dawn of being, constitute
The bond of union between life and joy.

  Yes, I remember when the changeful earth,
And twice five summers on my mind had
    stamped   560
The faces of the moving year, even then
I held unconscious intercourse with beauty
Old as creation, drinking in a pure
Organic pleasure from the silver wreaths

---

9 a card game.

10 a lake near Hawkshead.
11 Baltic Sea.

Of curling mist, or from the level plain
Of waters coloured by impending clouds.

   The sands of Westmoreland, the creeks and bays
Of Cumbria's rocky limits,[12] they can tell
How, when the Sea threw off his evening shade
And to the shepherd's hut on distant hills   570
Sent welcome notice of the rising moon,
How I have stood, to fancies such as these
A stranger, linking with the spectacle
No conscious memory of a kindred sight,
And bringing with me no peculiar sense
Of quietness or peace; yet have I stood,
Even while mine eye hath moved o'er many a
    league
Of shining water, gathering as it seemed,
Through every hair-breadth in that field of light,
New pleasure like a bee among the flowers.   580

   Thus oft amid those fits of vulgar joy
Which, through all seasons, on a child's pursuits
Are prompt attendants, 'mid that giddy bliss
Which, like a tempest, works along the blood
And is forgotten; even then I felt
Gleams like the flashing of a shield;—the earth
And common face of Nature spake to me
Rememberable things; sometimes, 'tis true,
By chance collisions and quaint accidents
(Like those ill-sorted unions, work supposed   590
Of evil-minded fairies), yet not vain
Nor profitless, if haply they impressed
Collateral objects and appearances,
Albeit lifeless then, and doomed to sleep
Until maturer seasons called them forth
To impregnate and to elevate the mind.
—And if the vulgar joy by its own weight
Wearied itself out of the memory,
The scenes which were a witness of that joy
Remained in their substantial lineaments   600
Depicted on the brain, and to the eye
Were visible, a daily sight; and thus
By the impressive discipline of fear,
By pleasure and repeated happiness,
So frequently repeated, and by force
Of obscure feelings representative
Of things forgotten, these same scenes so bright,
So beautiful, so majestic in themselves,
Though yet the day was distant, did become
Habitually dear, and all their forms   610
And changeful colours by invisible links
Were fastened to the affections.
              I began
My story early—not misled, I trust,
By an infirmity of love for days

---

12 the Cumbrian Mountains.

Disowned by memory—ere the breath of spring
Planting my snowdrops among winter snows:
Nor will it seem to thee, O Friend! so prompt
In sympathy, that I have lengthened out
With fond and feeble tongue a tedious tale.
Meanwhile, my hope has been, that I might
    fetch   620
Invigorating thoughts from former years;
Might fix the wavering balance of my mind,
And haply meet reproaches too, whose power
May spur me on, in manhood now mature,
To honourable toil. Yet should these hopes
Prove vain, and thus should neither I be taught
To understand myself, nor thou to know
With better knowledge how the heart was framed
Of him thou lovest; need I dread from thee
Harsh judgments, if the song be loth to quit   630
Those recollected hours that have the charm
Of visionary things, those lovely forms
And sweet sensations that throw back our life,
And almost make remotest infancy
A visible scene, on which the sun is shining?

   One end at least hath been attained; my mind
Hath been revived, and if this genial mood
Desert me not, forthwith shall be brought down
Through later years the story of my life.
The road lies plain before me;—'tis a theme   640
Single and of determined bounds; and hence
I choose it rather at this time, than work
Of ampler or more varied argument,
Where I might be discomfited and lost:
And certain hopes are with me, that to thee
This labour will be welcome, honoured Friend!

BOOK SECOND

SCHOOL-TIME (*Continued*)

Lines 175–97, 265–451

Thus were my sympathies enlarged, and thus
Daily the common range of visible things
Grew dear to me: already I began
To love the sun; a boy I loved the sun,
Not as I since have loved him, as a pledge
And surety of our earthly life, a light   180
Which we behold and feel we are alive;
Nor for his bounty to so many worlds—
But for this cause, that I had seen him lay
His beauty on the morning hills, had seen
The western mountain touch his setting orb,
In many a thoughtless hour, when, from excess
Of happiness, my blood appeared to flow
For its own pleasure, and I breathed with joy.
And, from like feelings, humble though intense,

To patriotic and domestic love 190
Analogous, the moon to me was dear;
For I could dream away my purposes,
Standing to gaze upon her while she hung
Midway between the hills, as if she knew
No other region, but belonged to thee,
Yea, appertained by a peculiar right
To thee and thy grey huts, thou one dear Vale!

           From early days,
Beginning not long after that first time
In which, a Babe, by intercourse of touch
I held mute dialogues with my Mother's heart,
I have endeavoured to display the means
Whereby this infant sensibility, 270
Great birthright of our being, was in me
Augmented and sustained. Yet is a path
More difficult before me; and I fear
That in its broken windings we shall need
The chamois' sinews, and the eagle's wing:
For now a trouble came into my mind
From unknown causes. I was left alone
Seeking the visible world, nor knowing why.
The props of my affections were removed,
And yet the building stood, as if sustained 280
By its own spirit! All that I beheld
Was dear, and hence to finer influxes
The mind lay open, to a more exact
And close communion. Many are our joys
In youth, but oh! what happiness to live
When every hour brings palpable access
Of knowledge, when all knowledge is delight,
And sorrow is not there! The seasons came,
And every season wheresoe'er I moved
Unfolded transitory qualities, 290
Which, but for this most watchful power of love,
Had been neglected; left a register
Of permanent relations, else unknown.
Hence life, and change, and beauty, solitude
More active even than 'best society'—
Society made sweet as solitude
By silent inobtrusive sympathies,
And gentle agitations of the mind
From manifold distinctions, difference
Perceived in things, where, to the unwatchful
    eye, 300
No difference is, and hence, from the same source,
Sublimer joy; for I would walk alone,
Under the quiet stars, and at that time
Have felt whate'er there is of power in sound
To breathe an elevated mood, by form
Or image unprofaned; and I would stand,
If the night blackened with a coming storm,
Beneath some rock, listening to notes that are
The ghostly language of the ancient earth,

Or make their dim abode in distant winds. 310
Thence did I drink the visionary power;
And deem not profitless those fleeting moods
Of shadowy exultation: not for this,
That they are kindred to our purer mind
And intellectual life; but that the soul,
Remembering how she felt, but what she felt
Remembering not, retains an obscure sense
Of possible sublimity, whereto
With growing faculties she doth aspire,
With faculties still growing, feeling still 320
That whatsoever point they gain, they yet
Have something to pursue.

              And not alone,
'Mid gloom and tumult, but no less 'mid fair
And tranquil scenes, that universal power
And fitness in the latent qualities
And essences of things, by which the mind
Is moved with feelings of delight, to me
Came strengthened with a superadded soul,
A virtue not its own. My morning walks
Were early;—oft before the hours of school 330
I travelled round our little lake, five miles
Of pleasant wandering. Happy time! more dear
For this, that one was by my side, a Friend,[13]
Then passionately loved; with heart how full
Would he peruse these lines! For many years
Have since flowed in between us, and, our minds
Both silent to each other, at this time
We live as if those hours had never been.
Nor seldom did I lift our cottage latch
Far earlier, ere one smoke-wreath had risen 340
From human dwelling, or the vernal thrush
Was audible; and sate among the woods
Alone upon some jutting eminence,
At the first gleam of dawn-light, when the Vale,
Yet slumbering, lay in utter solitude.
How shall I seek the origin? where find
Faith in the marvellous things which then I felt?
Oft in these moments such a holy calm
Would overspread my soul, that bodily eyes
Were utterly forgotten, and what I saw 350
Appeared like something in myself, a dream,
A prospect in the mind.

              'Twere long to tell
What spring and autumn, what the winter snows,
And what the summer shade, what day and night,
Evening and morning, sleep and waking thought,
From sources inexhaustible, poured forth
To feed the spirit of religious love
In which I walked with Nature. But let this
Be not forgotten, that I still retained
My first creative sensibility; 360
That by the regular action of the world

---

13 the Reverend John Fleming of Windermere.

My soul was unsubdued. A plastic power
Abode with me; a forming hand, at times
Rebellious, acting in a devious mood;
A local spirit of his own, at war
With general tendency, but, for the most,
Subservient strictly to external things
With which it communed. An auxiliar light
Came from my mind, which on the setting sun
Bestowed new splendour; the melodious birds, 370
The fluttering breezes, fountains that run on
Murmuring so sweetly in themselves, obeyed
A like dominion, and the midnight storm
Grew darker in the presence of my eye:
Hence my obeisance, my devotion hence,
And hence my transport.
                    Nor should this, perchance,
Pass unrecorded, that I still had loved
The exercise and produce of a toil,
Than analytic industry to me
More pleasing, and whose character I deem   380
Is more poetic as resembling more
Creative agency. The song would speak
Of that interminable building reared
By observation of affinities
In objects where no brotherhood exists
To passive minds. My seventeenth year was come;
And, whether from this habit rooted now
So deeply in my mind, or from excess
In the great social principle of life
Coercing all things into sympathy,   390
To unorganic natures were transferred
My own enjoyments; or the power of truth
Coming in revelation, did converse
With things that really are; I, at this time,
Saw blessings spread around me like a sea.
Thus while the days flew by, and years passed on,
From Nature and her overflowing soul
I had received so much, that all my thoughts
Were steeped in feeling; I was only then
Contented, when with bliss ineffable   400
I felt the sentiment of Being spread
O'er all that moves and all that seemeth still;
O'er all that, lost beyond the reach of thought
And human knowledge, to the human eye
Invisible, yet liveth to the heart;
O'er all that leaps and runs, and shouts and sings,
Or beats the gladsome air; o'er all that glides
Beneath the wave, yea, in the wave itself,
And mighty depth of waters. Wonder not
If high the transport, great the joy I felt   410
Communing in this sort through earth and
     heaven
With every form of creature, as it looked
Towards the Uncreated with a countenance
Of adoration, with an eye of love.

One song they sang, and it was audible,
Most audible, then, when the fleshly ear,
O'ercome by humblest prelude of that strain,
Forgot her functions, and slept undisturbed.

If this be error, and another faith
Find easier access to the pious mind,   420
Yet were I grossly destitute of all
Those human sentiments that make this earth
So dear, if I should fail with grateful voice
To speak of you, ye mountains, and ye lakes
And sounding cataracts, ye mists and winds
That dwell among the hills where I was born.
If in my youth I have been pure in heart,
If, mingling with the world, I am content
With my own modest pleasures, and have lived
With God and Nature communing, removed   430
From little enmities and low desires,
The gift is yours; if in these times of fear
This melancholy waste of hopes o'erthrown,
If, 'mid indifference and apathy,
And wicked exultation when good men
On every side fall off, we know not how,
To selfishness, disguised in gentle names
Of peace and quiet and domestic love,
Yet mingled not unwillingly with sneers
On visionary minds; if, in this time   440
Of dereliction and dismay, I yet
Despair not of our nature, but retain
A more than Roman confidence, a faith
That fails not, in all sorrow my support,
The blessing of my life; the gift is yours,
Ye winds and sounding cataracts! 'tis yours,
Ye mountains! thine, O Nature! Thou hast fed
My lofty speculations; and in thee,
For this uneasy heart of ours, I find
A never-failing principle of joy   450
And purest passion.

BOOK THIRD

RESIDENCE AT CAMBRIDGE

Lines 46–169

The Evangelist St. John my patron was:[14]
Three Gothic courts are his, and in the first
Was my abiding-place, a nook obscure;
Right underneath, the College kitchens made
A humming sound, less tuneable than bees,   50
But hardly less industrious; with shrill notes
Of sharp command and scolding intermixed.
Near me hung Trinity's loquacious clock,

_____
14 Wordsworth entered St. John's College, Cambridge, in October
1787.

Who never let the quarters, night or day,
Slip by him unproclaimed, and told the hours
Twice over with a male and female voice.
Her pealing organ was my neighbour too;
And from my pillow, looking forth by light
Of moon or favouring stars, I could behold
The antechapel where the statue stood   60
Of Newton with his prism and silent face,
The marble index of a mind for ever
Voyaging through strange seas of Thought,
    alone.

added this in old age

Of College labours, of the Lecturer's room
All studded round, as thick as chairs could stand,
With loyal students faithful to their books,
Half-and-half idlers, hardy recusants,
And honest dunces—of important days,
Examinations, when the man was weighed
As in a balance! of excessive hopes,   70
Tremblings withal and commendable fears,
Small jealousies, and triumphs good or bad—
Let others that know more speak as they know.
Such glory was but little sought by me,
And little won. Yet from the first crude days
Of settling time in this untried abode,
I was disturbed at times by prudent thoughts,
Wishing to hope without a hope, some fears
About my future worldly maintenance
And, more than all, a strangeness in the mind, 80
A feeling that I was not for that hour,
Nor for that place. But wherefore be cast down?
For (not to speak of Reason and her pure
Reflective acts to fix the moral law
Deep in the conscience, nor of Christian Hope,
Bowing her head before her sister Faith
As one far mightier), hither I had come,
Bear witness Truth, endowed with holy powers
And faculties, whether to work or feel.
Oft when the dazzling show no longer new   90
Had ceased to dazzle, oftimes did I quit
My comrades, leave the crowd, buildings and
    groves,
And as I paced alone the level fields
Far from those lovely sights and sounds sublime
With which I had been conversant, the mind
Drooped not; but there into herself returning,
With prompt rebound seemed fresh as hereto-
    fore.
At least I more distinctly recognised
Her native instincts: let me dare to speak
A higher language, say that now I felt   100
What independent solaces were mine,
To mitigate the injurious sway of place
Or circumstance, how far soever changed
In youth, or *to* be changed in manhood's prime;

Or for the few who shall be called to look
On the long shadows in our evening years,
Ordained precursors to the night of death.
As if awakened, summoned, roused, constrained,
I looked for universal things; perused
The common countenance of earth and sky: 110
Earth, nowhere unembellished by some trace
Of that first Paradise whence man was driven;
And sky, whose beauty and bounty are expressed
By the proud name she bears—the name of
    Heaven.
I called on both to teach me what they might;
Or turning the mind in upon herself,
Pored, watched, expected, listened, spread my
    thoughts
And spread them with a wider creeping; felt
Incumbencies more awful, visitings
Of the Upholder of the tranquil soul,   120
That tolerates the indignities of Time,
And, from the centre of Eternity
All finite motions overruling, lives
In glory immutable. But peace! enough
Here to record that I was mounting now
To such community with highest truth—
A track pursuing, not untrod before,
From strict analogies by thought supplied
Or consciousnesses not to be subdued,
To every natural form, rock, fruit, or flower, 130
Even the loose stones that cover the highway,
I gave a moral life: I saw them feel,
Or linked them to some feeling: the great mass
Lay bedded in a quickening soul, and all
That I beheld respired with inward meaning.
Add that whate'er of Terror or of Love
Or Beauty, Nature's daily face put on
From transitory passion, unto this
I was as sensitive as waters are
To the sky's influence; in a kindred mood   140
Of passion was obedient as a lute
That waits upon the touches of the wind.
Unknown, unthought of, yet I was most rich—
I had a world about me—'twas my own;
I made it, for it only lived to me,
And to the God who sees into the heart.
Such sympathies, though rarely, were betrayed
By outward gestures and by visible looks;
Some called it madness—so indeed it was,
If child-like fruitfulness in passing joy,   150
If steady moods of thoughtfulness matured
To inspiration, sort with such a name;
If prophecy be madness; if things viewed
By poets in old time, and higher up
By the first men, earth's first inhabitants,
May in these tutored days no more be seen
With undisordered sight. But leaving this,

It was no madness, for the bodily eye
Amid my strongest workings evermore
Was searching out the lines of difference   160
As they lie hid in all external forms,
Near or remote, minute or vast; an eye
Which, from a tree, a stone, a withered leaf,
To the broad ocean and the azure heavens
Spangled with kindred multitudes of stars,
Could find no surface where its power might
    sleep;
Which spake perpetual logic to my soul,
And by an unrelenting agency
Did bind my feelings even as in a chain.

BOOK FOURTH

SUMMER VACATION

Lines 137–90, 276–338, 354–469

　　　　　When first I made
Once more the circuit of our little lake,
If ever happiness hath lodged with man,
That day consummate happiness was mine,   140
Wide-spreading, steady, calm, contemplative.
The sun was set, or setting, when I left
Our cottage door,[15] and evening soon brought on
A sober hour, not winning or serene,
For cold and raw the air was, and untuned;
But as a face we love is sweetest then
When sorrow damps it, or, whatever look
It chance to wear, is sweetest if the heart
Have fulness in herself; even so with me
It fared that evening. Gently did my soul   150
Put off her veil, and, self-transmuted, stood
Naked, as in the presence of her God.
While on I walked, a comfort seemed to touch
A heart that had not been disconsolate:
Strength came where weakness was not known to
    be,
At least not felt; and restoration came
Like an intruder knocking at the door
Of unacknowledged weariness. I took
The balance, and with firm hand weighed myself.
—Of that external scene which round me lay,   160
Little, in this abstraction, did I see;
Remembered less; but I had inward hopes
And swellings of the spirit, was rapt and soothed,
Conversed with promises, had glimmering views
How life pervades the undecaying mind;
How the immortal soul with God-like power
Informs, creates, and thaws the deepest sleep
That time can lay upon her; how on earth
Man, if he do but live within the light

15 the cottage of Anne Tyson, the 'kind and motherly' old Dame
with whom Wordsworth lived during his Hawkshead school days.

Of high endeavours, daily spreads abroad   170
His being armed with strength that cannot
    fail,
Nor was there want of milder thoughts, of love,
Of innocence, and holiday repose;
And more than pastoral quiet, 'mid the stir
Of boldest projects, and a peaceful end
At last, or glorious, by endurance won.
Thus musing, in a wood I sate me down
Alone, continuing there to muse: the slopes
And heights meanwhile were slowly overspread
With darkness, and before a rippling breeze   180
The long lake lengthened out its hoary line,
And in the sheltered coppice where I sate,
Around me from among the hazel leaves,
Now here, now there, moved by the straggling
    wind,
Came ever and anon a breath-like sound,
Quick as the pantings of the faithful dog,
The off and on companion of my walk;
And such, at times, believing them to be,
I turned my head to look if he were there;
Then into solemn thought I passed once
    more.   190

　　　　　　　　　　　　Yet in spite
Of pleasure won, and knowledge not withheld,
There was an inner falling off—I loved,
Loved deeply all that had been loved before,
More deeply even than ever: but a swarm   280
Of heady schemes jostling each other, gawds,
And feast and dance, and public revelry,
And sports and games (too grateful in them-
    selves,
Yet in themselves less grateful, I believe,
Than as they were a badge glossy and fresh
Of manliness and freedom) all conspired
To lure my mind from firm habitual quest
Of feeding pleasures, to depress the zeal
And damp those yearnings which had once been
    mine—
A wild, unworldly-minded youth, given up   290
To his own eager thoughts. It would demand
Some skill, and longer time than may be spared,
To paint these vanities, and how they wrought
In haunts where they, till now, had been un-
    known,
It seemed the very garments that I wore
Preyed on my strength, and stopped the quiet
    stream
Of self-forgetfulness.
　　　　　　　　　　　Yes, that heartless chase
Of trivial pleasures was a poor exchange
For books and nature at that early age.

Doesn't feel quite right about having a good time.

'Tis true, some casual knowledge might be
　　gained　　　　　　　　　　　　　　　300
Of character or life; but at that time,
Of manners put to school I took small note,
And all my deeper passions lay elsewhere.
Far better had it been to exalt the mind
By solitary study, to uphold
Intense desire through meditative peace;
And yet, for chastisement of these regrets,
The memory of one particular hour
Doth here rise up against me. 'Mid a throng
Of maids and youths, old men, and matrons
　　staid,　　　　　　　　　　　　　　310
A medley of all tempers, I had passed
The night in dancing, gaiety, and mirth,
With din of instruments and shuffling feet,
And glancing forms, and tapers glittering,
And unaimed prattle flying up and down;
Spirits upon the stretch, and here and there
Slight shocks of young love-liking interspersed,
Whose transient pleasure mounted to the head,
And tingled through the veins. Ere we retired,
The cock had crowed, and now the eastern
　　sky　　　　　　　　　　　　　　320
Was kindling, nor unseen, from humble copse
And open field, through which the pathway
　　wound,
And homeward led my steps. Magnificent
The morning rose, in memorable pomp,
Glorious as e'er I had beheld—in front,
The sea lay laughing at a distance; near,
The solid mountains shone, bright as the clouds,
Grain-tinctured,[16] drenched in empyrean light;
And in the meadows and the lower grounds
Was all the sweetness of a common dawn—　330
Dews, vapours, and the melody of birds,
And labourers going forth to till the fields.
Ah! need I say, dear Friend! that to the brim
My heart was full; I made no vows, but vows
Were then made for me; bond unknown to me
Was given, that I should be, else sinning greatly,
A dedicated Spirit. On I walked
In thankful blessedness, which yet survives.

　　When from our better selves we have too long
Been parted by the hurrying world, and droop,
‧k of its business, of its pleasures tired,
‧ gracious, how benign, is Solitude;
.1ow potent a mere image of her sway;
Most potent when impressed upon the mind
With an appropriate human centre—hermit,　360
Deep in the bosom of the wilderness;
Votary (in vast cathedral, where no foot

16 crimson.

Is treading, where no other face is seen)
Kneeling at prayers; or watchman on the top
Of lighthouse, beaten by Atlantic waves;
Or as the soul of that great Power is met
Sometimes embodied on a public road,
When, for the night deserted, it assumes
A character of quiet more profound
Than pathless wastes.
　　　　　　　Once, when those　　370
　　summer months
Were flown, and autumn brought its annual
　　show
Of oars with oars contending, sails with sails,
Upon Winander's spacious breast, it chanced
That—after I had left a flower-decked room
(Whose in-door pastime, lighted up, survived
To a late hour), and spirits overwrought
Were making night do penance for a day
Spent in a round of strenuous idleness—
My homeward course led up a long ascent,
Where the road's watery surface, to the top　380
Of that sharp rising, glittered to the moon
And bore the semblance of another stream
Stealing with silent lapse to join the brook
That murmured in the vale. All else was still;
No living thing appeared in earth or air,
And, save the flowing water's peaceful voice,
Sound there was none—but, lo! an uncouth
　　shape,
Shown by a sudden turning of the road,
So near that, slipping back into the shade
Of a thick hawthorn, I could mark him well,　390
Myself unseen. He was of stature tall,
A span above man's common measure, tall,
Stiff, lank, and upright; a more meagre man
Was never seen before by night or day.
Long were his arms, pallid his hands; his mouth
Looked ghastly in the moonlight: from behind,
A mile-stone propped him; I could also ken
That he was clothed in military garb,
Though faded, yet entire. Companionless,
No dog attending, by no staff sustained　　400
He stood, and in his very dress appeared
A desolation, a simplicity,
To which the trappings of a gaudy world
Make a strange back-ground. From his lips, ere
　　long,
Issued low muttered sounds, as if of pain
Or some uneasy thought; yet still his form
Kept the same awful steadiness—at his feet
His shadow lay, and moved not. From self-blame
Not wholly free, I watched him thus; at length
Subduing my heart's specious cowardice,　　410
I left the shady nook where I had stood
And hailed him. Slowly from his resting-place

He rose, and with a lean and wasted arm
In measured gesture lifted to his head
Returned my salutation; then resumed
His station as before; and when I asked
His history, the veteran, in reply,
Was neither slow nor eager; but, unmoved,
And with a quiet uncomplaining voice,
A stately air of mild indifference,　　　　420
He told in few plain words a soldier's tale—
That in the Tropic Islands he had served,
Whence he had landed scarcely three weeks past;
That on his landing he had been dismissed,
And now was travelling towards his native home.
This heard, I said, in pity, 'Come with me.'
He stooped, and straightway from the ground
　　　took up
An oaken staff by me yet unobserved—
A staff which must have dropt from his slack
　　　hand
And lay till now neglected in the grass.　　　430
Though weak his step and cautious, he appeared
To travel without pain, and I beheld,
With an astonishment but ill suppressed,
His ghostly figure moving at my side;
Nor could I, while we journeyed thus, forbear
To turn from present hardships to the past,
And speak of war, battle, and pestilence,
Sprinkling this talk with questions, better spared,
On what he might himself have seen or felt.
He all the while was in demeanour calm,　　　440
Concise in answer; solemn and sublime
He might have seemed, but that in all he said
There was a strange half-absence, as of one
Knowing too well the importance of his theme,
But feeling it no longer. Our discourse
Soon ended, and together on we passed
In silence through a wood gloomy and still.
Up-turning, then, along an open field,
We reached a cottage. At the door I knocked,
And earnestly to charitable care　　　450
Commended him as a poor friendless man,
Belated and by sickness overcome.
Assured that now the traveller would repose
In comfort, I entreated that henceforth
He would not linger in the public ways,
But ask for timely furtherance and help
Such as his state required. At this reproof,
With the same ghastly mildness in his look,
He said, 'My trust is in the God of Heaven,
And in the eye of him who passes me!'　　　460

The cottage door was speedily unbarred,
And now the soldier touched his hat once more
With his lean hand, and in a faltering voice,
Whose tone bespake reviving interests

Till then unfelt, he thanked me; I returned
The farewell blessing of the patient man,
And so we parted. Back I cast a look,
And lingered near the door a little space,
Then sought with quiet heart my distant home.

BOOK FIFTH

BOOKS
Lines 347–425, 491–533

　These mighty workmen of our later age,
Who, with a broad highway, have overbridged
The froward chaos of futurity,
Tamed to their bidding; they who have the skill 350
To manage books, and things, and make them act
On infant minds as surely as the sun
Deals with a flower; the keepers of our time,
The guides and wardens of our faculties,
Sages who in their prescience would control
All accidents, and to the very road
Which they have fashioned would confine us down,
Like engines; when will their presumption learn,
That in the unreasoning progress of the world
A wiser spirit is at work for us,　　　360
A better eye than theirs, most prodigal
Of blessings, and most studious of our good,
Even in what seem our most unfruitful hours?

　There was a Boy: ye knew him well, ye cliffs
And islands of Winander!—many a time
At evening, when the earliest stars began
To move along the edges of the hills,
Rising or setting, would he stand alone
Beneath the trees or by the glimmering lake,
And there, with fingers interwoven, both hands 370
Pressed closely palm to palm, and to his mouth
Uplifted, he, as through an instrument,
Blew mimic hootings to the silent owls,
That they might answer him; and they would shout
Across the watery vale, and shout again,
Responsive to his call, with quivering peals,
And long halloos and screams, and echoes loud,
Redoubled and redoubled, concourse wild
Of jocund din; and, when a lengthened pause
Of silence came and baffled his best skill,　　　380
Then sometimes, in that silence while he hung
Listening, a gentle shock of mild surprise
Has carried far into his heart the voice
Of mountain torrents; or the visible scene
Would enter unawares into his mind,
With all its solemn imagery, its rocks,
Its woods, and that uncertain heaven, received
Into the bosom of the steady lake.

This Boy was taken from his mates, and died
In childhood, ere he was full twelve years old, 390
Fair is the spot, most beautiful the vale
Where he was born; the grassy churchyard hangs
Upon a slope above the village school,
And through that churchyard when my way has led
On summer evenings, I believe that there
A long half hour together I have stood
Mute, looking at the grave in which he lies!
Even now appears before the mind's clear eye
That self-same village church; I see her sit
(The thronèd Lady whom erewhile we hailed) 400
On her green hill, forgetful of this Boy
Who slumbers at her feet,—forgetful, too,
Of all her silent neighbourhood of graves,
And listening only to the gladsome sounds
That, from the rural school ascending, play
Beneath her and about her. May she long
Behold a race of young ones like to those
With whom I herded!—(easily, indeed,
We might have fed upon a fatter soil
Of arts and letters—but be that forgiven)— 410
A race of real children; not too wise,
Too learned, or too good; but wanton, fresh
And bandied up and down by love and hate;
Not unresentful where self-justified;
Fierce, moody, patient, venturous, modest, shy;
Mad at their sports like withered leaves in
      winds;
Though doing wrong and suffering, and full oft
Bending beneath our life's mysterious weight
Of pain, and doubt, and fear, yet yielding not
In happiness to the happiest upon earth. 420
Simplicity in habit, truth in speech,
Be these the daily strengtheners of their minds;
May books and Nature be their early joy!
And knowledge, rightly honoured with that
      name—
Knowledge not purchased by the loss of power!

. . .

A gracious spirit o'er this earth presides,
And o'er the heart of man: invisibly
It comes, to works of unreproved delight,
And tendency benign, directing those
Who care not, know not, think not what they do.
The tales that charm away the wakeful night
In Araby, romances; legends penned
For solace by dim light of monkish lamps;
Fictions, for ladies of their love, devised
By youthful squires; adventures endless, spun 500
By the dismantled warrior in old age,
Out of the bowels of those very schemes
In which his youth did first extravagate;
These spread like day, and something in the shape

Of these will live till man shall be no more.
Dumb yearnings, hidden appetites, are ours,
And *they must* have their food. Our childhood sits,
Our simple childhood, sits upon a throne
That hath more power than all the elements.
I guess not what this tells of Being past, 510
Nor what it augurs of the life to come;
But so it is, and, in that dubious hour,
That twilight when we first begin to see
This dawning earth, to recognise, expect,
And, in the long probation that ensues,
The time of trial, ere we learn to live
In reconcilement with our stinted powers;
To endure this state of meagre vassalage,
Unwilling to forego, confess, submit,
Uneasy and unsettled, yoke-fellows 520
To custom, mettlesome, and not yet tamed
And humbled down;—oh! then we feel, we feel,
We know where we have friends. Ye dreamers,
      then,
Forgers of daring tales! we bless you then,
Impostors, drivellers, dotards, as the ape
Philosophy will call you: *then* we feel
With what, and how great might ye are in league,
Who make our wish our power, our thought a
      deed,
An empire, a possession,—ye whom time
And seasons serve; all Faculties;—to whom 530
Earth crouches, the elements are potter's clay,
Space like a heaven filled up with northern lights,
Here, nowhere, there, and everywhere at once.

BOOK SIXTH

CAMBRIDGE AND THE ALPS

Lines 42–94, 322–408, 489–99, 562–640, 754–78

The Poet's soul was with me at that time;
Sweet meditations, the still overflow
Of present happiness, while future years
Lacked not anticipations, tender dreams,
No few of which have since been realised;
And some remain, hopes for my future life.
Four years and thirty, told this very week,
Have I been now a sojourner on earth,
By sorrow not unsmitten; yet for me 50
Life's morning radiance hath not left the hills,
Her dew is on the flowers. Those were the days
Which also first emboldened me to trust
With firmness, hitherto but lightly touched
By such a daring thought, that I might leave
Some monument behind me which pure hearts
Should reverence. The instinctive humbleness,
Maintained even by the very name and thought

Of printed books and authorship, began
To melt away; and further, the dread awe   60
Of mighty names was softened down and seemed
Approachable, admitting fellowship
Of modest sympathy. Such aspect now,
Though not familiarly, my mind put on,
Content to observe, to achieve, and to enjoy.

All winter long, whenever free to choose,
Did I by night frequent the College groves
And tributary walks; the last, and oft
The only one, who had been lingering there
Through hours of silence, till the porter's bell, 70
A punctual follower on the stroke of nine,
Rang with its blunt unceremonious voice,
Inexorable summons! Lofty elms,
Inviting shades of opportune recess,
Bestowed composure on a neighbourhood
Unpeaceful in itself. A single tree
With sinuous trunk, boughs exquisitely wreathed,
Grew there; an ash which Winter for himself
Decked as in pride, and with outlandish grace:
Up from the ground, and almost to the top,   80
The trunk and every master branch were green
With clustering ivy, and the lightsome twigs
And outer spray profusely tipped with seeds
That hung in yellow tassels, while the air
Stirred them, not voiceless. Often have I stood
Foot-bound uplooking at this lovely tree
Beneath a frosty moon. The hemisphere
Of magic fiction, verse of mine perchance
May never tread; but scarcely Spenser's self
Could have more tranquil visions in his youth, 90
Or could more bright appearances create
Of human forms with superhuman powers,
Than I beheld loitering on calm clear nights
Alone, beneath this fairy work of earth.

.   .   .

When the third summer freed us from restraint,
A youthful friend,[17] he too a mountaineer,
Not slow to share my wishes, took his staff,
And sallying forth, we journeyed side by side,
Bound to the distant Alps. A hardy slight
Did this unprecedented course imply
Of college studies and their set rewards;
Nor had, in truth, the scheme been formed by me
Without uneasy forethought of the pain,   330
The censures, and ill-omening of those
To whom my worldly interests were dear.
But Nature then was sovereign in my mind,
And mighty forms, seizing a youthful fancy,
Had given a charter to irregular hopes.

In any age of uneventful calm
Among the nations, surely would my heart
Have been possessed by similar desire;
But Europe at that time was thrilled with joy,
France standing on the top of golden hours, 340
And human nature seeming born again.

Lightly equipped, and but a few brief looks
Cast on the white cliffs of our native shore
From the receding vessel's deck, we chanced
To land at Calais on the very eve
Of that great federal day;[18] and there we saw,
In a mean city, and among a few,
How bright a face is worn when joy of one
Is joy for tens of millions. Southward thence
We held our way, direct through hamlets,
          towns,   350
Gaudy with reliques of that festival,
Flowers left to wither on triumphal arcs,
And window-garlands. On the public roads,
And, once, three days successively, through paths
By which our toilsome journey was abridged,
Among sequestered villages we walked
And found benevolence and blessedness
Spread like a fragrance everywhere, when spring
Hath left no corner of the land untouched:
Where elms for many and many a league in files 360
With their thin umbrage, on the stately roads
Of that great kingdom, rustled o'er our heads,
For ever near us as we paced along:
How sweet at such a time, with such delight
On every side, in prime of youthful strength,
To feed a Poet's tender melancholy
And fond conceit of sadness, with the sound
Of undulations varying as might please
The wind that swayed them; once, and more than
          once,
Unhoused beneath the evening star we saw   370
Dances of liberty, and, in late hours
Of darkness, dances in the open air
Deftly prolonged, though grey-haired lookers on
Might waste their breath in chiding.
                              Under hills—
The vine-clad hills and slopes of Burgundy,
Upon the bosom of the gentle Saone
We glided forward with the flowing stream.
Swift Rhone! thou wert the *wings* on which we cut
A winding passage with majestic ease
Between thy lofty rocks. Enchanting show   380
Those woods and farms and orchards did present,
And single cottages and lurking towns,
Reach after reach, succession without end
Of deep and stately vales! A lonely pair

17 Robert Jones, a college mate, to whom Wordsworth afterward
dedicated *Descriptive Sketches*, memorials of their tour.

18 i.e. on 13 July 1790, the eve of the day when the king was to
swear fidelity to the new constitution.

Of strangers, till day closed, we sailed along,
Clustered together with a merry crowd
Of those emancipated, a blithe host
Of travellers, chiefly delegates returning
From the great spousals newly solemnized
At their chief city, in the sight of Heaven.   390
Like bees they swarmed, gaudy and gay as bees;
Some vapoured in the unruliness of joy,
And with their swords flourished as if to fight
The saucy air. In this proud company
We landed[19]—took with them our evening meal,
Guests welcome almost as the angels were
To Abraham of old. The supper done,
With flowing cups elate and happy thoughts
We rose at signal given, and formed a ring
And, hand in hand, danced round and round the
     board;   400
All hearts were open, every tongue was loud
With amity and glee; we bore a name
Honoured in France, the name of Englishmen,
And hospitably did they give us hail,
As their forerunners in a glorious course;
And round and round the board we danced again.
With these blithe friends our voyage we renewed
At early dawn.

          .   .

'Tis not my present purpose to retrace
That variegated journey step by step.   490
A march it was of military speed,
And Earth did change her images and forms
Before us, fast as clouds are changed in heaven.
Day after day, up early and down late,
From hill to vale we dropped, from vale to hill
Mounted—from province on to province swept,
Keen hunters in a chase of fourteen weeks,[20]
Eager as birds of prey, or as a ship
Upon the stretch, when winds are blowing fair:

When from the Vallais we had turned, and clomb
Along the Simplon's steep and rugged road,
Following a band of muleteers, we reached
A halting-place, where all together took
Their noon-tide meal. Hastily rose our guide,
Leaving us at the board; awhile we lingered,
Then paced the beaten downward way that led
Right to a rough stream's edge, and there broke
     off;
The only track now visible was one   570
That from the torrent's further brink held forth
Conspicuous invitation to ascend
A lofty mountain. After brief delay

Crossing the unbridged stream, that road we took,
And clomb with eagerness, till anxious fears
Intruded, for we failed to overtake
Our comrades gone before. By fortunate chance,
While every moment added doubt to doubt,
A peasant met us, from whose mouth we learned
That to the spot which had perplexed us first   580
We must descend, and there should find the road,
Which in the stony channel of the stream
Lay a few steps, and then along its banks;
And, that our future course, all plain to sight,
Was downwards, with the current of that stream.
Loth to believe what we so grieved to hear,
For still we had hopes that pointed to the clouds,
We questioned him again, and yet again;
But every word that from the peasant's lips
Came in reply, translated by our feelings,   590
Ended in this,—*that we had crossed the Alps.*

Imagination—here the Power so called
Through sad incompetence of human speech,
That awful Power rose from the mind's abyss
Like an unfathered vapour that enwraps,
At once, some lonely traveller. I was lost;
Halted without an effort to break through;
But to my conscious soul I now can say—
'I recognise thy glory': in such strength
Of usurpation, when the light of sense   600
Goes out, but with a flash that has revealed
The invisible world, doth greatness make abode,
There harbours; whether we be young or old,
Our destiny, our being's heart and home,
Is with infinitude, and only there;
With hope it is, hope that can never die,
Effort, and expectation, and desire,
And something evermore about to be.
Under such banners militant, the soul
Seeks for no trophies, struggles for no spoils   610
That may attest her prowess, blest in thoughts
That are their own perfection and reward,
Strong in herself and in beatitude
That hides her, like the mighty flood of Nile
Poured from his fount of Abyssinian clouds
To fertilise the whole Egyptian plain.

The melancholy slackening that ensued
Upon those tidings by the peasant given
Was soon dislodged. Downwards we hurried fast,
And, with the half-shaped road which we had
     missed,   620
Entered a narrow chasm.[21] The brook and road
Were fellow-travellers in this gloomy strait,
And with them did we journey several hours
At a slow pace. The immeasurable height

[handwritten top margin: to suggest the contradictions of the Apocalypse.]

[handwritten left margin: very seat picture of nature tremendous of opposites conventions of opposites come together]

Of woods decaying, never to be decayed,
The stationary blasts of waterfalls,
And in the narrow rent at every turn
Winds thwarting winds, bewildered and forlorn,
The torrents shooting from the clear blue sky,
The rocks that muttered close upon our ears, 630
Black drizzling crags that spake by the way-side
As if a voice were in them, the sick sight
And giddy prospect of the raving stream,
The unfettered clouds and region of the Heavens,
Tumult and peace, the darkness and the light—
Were all like workings of one mind, the features
Of the same face, blossoms upon one tree;
Characters of the great Apocalypse,
The types and symbols of Eternity,
Of first, and last, and midst, and without end. 640

       .   .   .

    Oh, most belovèd Friend! a glorious time,
A happy time that was; triumphant looks
Were then the common language of all eyes;
As if awaked from sleep, the Nations hailed
Their great expectancy: the fife of war
Was then a spirit-stirring sound indeed,
A blackbird's whistle in a budding grove.   760
We left the Swiss exulting in the fate
Of their near neighbours; and, when shortening
     fast
Our pilgrimage, nor distant far from home,
We crossed the Brabant armies on the fret
For battle in the cause of Liberty.[22]
A stripling, scarcely of the household then
Of social life, I looked upon these things
As from a distance; heard, and saw, and felt,
Was touched, but with no intimate concern;
I seemed to move along them, as a bird   770
Moves through the air, or as a fish pursues
Its sport, or feeds in its proper element;
I wanted not that joy, I did not need
Such help; the ever-living universe,
Turn where I might, was opening out its glories,
And the independent spirit of pure youth
Called forth, at every season, new delights
Spread round my steps like sunshine o'er green
     fields.

BOOK SEVENTH

RESIDENCE IN LONDON

Lines 486–543, 619–49

    Pass we from entertainments, that are such
Professedly, to others titled higher,

---

[22] Republican troops of the Belgian Province of Brabant preparing to oppose infringement of their inherited rights by King Leopold II.

Yet, in the estimate of youth at least,
More near akin to those than names imply,—
I mean the brawls of lawyers in their courts   490
Before the ermined judge, or that great stage[23]
Where senators, tongue-favoured men, perform,
Admired and envied. Oh! the beating heart,
When one among the prime of these rose up,—
One, of whose name from childhood we had
     heard
Familiarly, a household term, like those,
The Bedfords, Glosters, Salisburys, of old
Whom the fifth Harry talks of.   Silence! hush!
This is no trifler, no short-flighted wit,
No stammerer of a minute, painfully   500
Delivered. No! the Orator hath yoked
The Hours, like young Aurora, to his car:
Thrice welcome Presence! how can patience e'er
Grow weary of attending on a track
That kindles with such glory! All are charmed,
Astonished; like a hero in romance,
He winds away his never-ending horn;
Words follow words, sense seems to follow sense:
What memory and what logic! till the strain
Transcendent, superhuman as it seemed,   510
Grows tedious even in a young man's ear.

    Genius of Burke! forgive the pen seduced
By specious wonders, and too slow to tell
Of what the ingenuous, what bewildered men,
Beginning to mistrust their boastful guides,
And wise men, willing to grow wiser, caught,
Rapt auditors! from thy most eloquent tongue—
Now mute, for ever mute in the cold grave.
I see him,—old, but vigorous in age,—
Stand like an oak whose stag-horn branches
     start   520
Out of its leafy brow, the more to awe
The younger brethren of the grove. But some—
While he forewarns, denounces, launches forth,
Against all systems built on abstract rights,
Keen ridicule; the majesty proclaims
Of Institutes and Laws, hallowed by time;
Declares the vital power of social ties
Endeared by Custom; and with high disdain,
Exploding upstart Theory, insists
Upon the allegiance to which men are born— 530
Some—say at once a froward multitude—
Murmur (for truth is hated, where not loved)
As the winds fret within the Æolian cave,
Galled by their monarch's chain. The times were
     big
With ominous change, which, night by night,
     provoked

---

[23] parliament.

Keen struggles, and black clouds of passion
    raised;
But memorable moments intervened,
When Wisdom like the Goddess from Jove's
    brain,
Broke forth in armour of resplendent words,
Startling the Synod. Could a youth, and one 540
In ancient story versed, whose breast had heaved
Under the weight of classic eloquence,
Sit, see, and hear, unthankful, uninspired?

    .   .   .

  As the black storm upon the mountain-top
Sets off the sunbeam in the valley, so   620
That huge fermenting mass of human-kind
Serves as a solemn background, or relief,
To single forms and objects, whence they draw,
For feeling and contemplative regard,
More than inherent liveliness and power.
How oft, amid those overflowing streets,
Have I gone forward with the crowd, and said
Unto myself, 'The face of every one
That passes by me is a mystery!'
Thus have I looked, nor ceased to look,
    oppressed   630
By thoughts of what and whither, when and how,
Until the shapes before my eyes became
A second-sight procession, such as glides
Over still mountains, or appears in dreams;
And once, far-travelled in such mood, beyond
The reach of common indication, lost
Amid the moving pageant, I was smitten
Abruptly, with the view (a sight not rare)
Of a blind Beggar, who, with upright face,
Stood, propped against a wall, upon his chest 640
Wearing a written paper, to explain
His story, whence he came, and who he was.
Caught by the spectacle my mind turned round
As with the might of waters; an apt type
This label seemed of the utmost we can know,
Both of ourselves and of the universe;
And, on the shape of that unmoving man,
His steadfast face and sightless eyes, I gazed,
As if admonished from another world.

BOOK EIGHTH

RETROSPECT—LOVE OF NATURE LEADING TO LOVE
OF MAN

Lines 1–339

WHAT sounds are those, Helvellyn, that are heard
Up to thy summit, through the depth of air
Ascending, as if distance had the power
To make the sounds more audible? What crowd

Covers, or sprinkles o'er, yon village green?
Crowd seems it, solitary hill! to thee,
Though but a little family of men,
Shepherds and tillers of the ground—betimes
Assembled with their children and their wives,
And here and there a stranger interspersed.   10
They hold a rustic fair—a festival,
Such as, on this side now, and now on that,
Repeated through his tributary vales,
Helvellyn, in the silence of his rest,
Sees annually, if clouds towards either ocean
Blown from their favourite resting-place, or mists
Dissolved, have left him an unshrouded head.
Delightful day it is for all who dwell
In this secluded glen, and eagerly
They give it welcome. Long ere heat of noon, 20
From byre[24] or field the kine were brought; the
    sheep
Are penned in cotes; the chaffering[25] is begun.
The heifer lows, uneasy at the voice
Of a new master; bleat the flocks aloud.
Booths are there none; a stall or two is here;
A lame man or a blind, the one to beg,
The other to make music; hither, too,
From far, with basket, slung upon her arm,
Of hawker's wares—books, pictures, combs, and
    pins—
Some aged woman finds her way again,   30
Year after year, a punctual visitant!
There also stands a speech-maker by rote,
Pulling the strings of his boxed raree-show;
And in the lapse of many years may come
Prouder itinerant, mountebank, or he
Whose wonders in a covered wain lie hid.
But one there is, the loveliest of them all,
Some sweet lass of the valley, looking out
For gains, and who that sees her would not buy?
Fruits of her father's orchard are her wares, 40
And with the ruddy produce she walks round
Among the crowd, half pleased with, half
    ashamed
Of her new office, blushing restlessly.
The children now are rich, for the old today
Are generous as the young; and, if content
With looking on, some ancient wedded pair
Sit in the shade together, while they gaze,
'A cheerful smile unbends the wrinkled brow,
The days departed start again to life,
And all the scenes of childhood reappear, 50
Faint, but more tranquil, like the changing sun
To him who slept at noon and wakes at eve.'[26]
Thus gaiety and cheerfulness prevail,

---

24 cow barn.
25 bargaining.
26 from *Malvern Hills* by Joseph Cottle.

Spreading from young to old, from old to young,
And no one seems to want his share.—Immense
Is the recess, the circumambient world
Magnificent, by which they are embraced:
They move about upon the soft green turf:
How little they, they and their doings, seem,
And all that they can further or obstruct!　60
Through utter weakness pitiably dear,
As tender infants are: and yet how great!
For all things serve them; them the morning light
Loves, as it glistens on the silent rocks;
And them the silent rocks, which now from high
Look down upon them; the reposing clouds;
The wild brooks prattling from invisible haunts;
And old Helvellyn, conscious of the stir
Which animates this day their calm abode.

With deep devotion, Nature, did I feel,　70
In that enormous City's turbulent world
Of men and things, what benefit I owed
To thee, and those domains of rural peace,
Where to the sense of beauty first my heart
Was opened; tract more exquisitely fair
Than that famed paradise of ten thousand trees,
Or Gehol's matchless gardens,[27] for delight
Of the Tartarian dynasty composed
(Beyond that mighty wall, not fabulous,
China's stupendous mound) by patient toil　80
Of myriads and boon nature's lavish help;
There, in a clime from widest empire chosen,
Fulfilling (could enchantment have done more?)
A sumptuous dream of flowery lawns, with
　　domes
Of pleasure sprinkled over, shady dells
For eastern monasteries, sunny mounts
With temples crested, bridges, gondalos,
Rocks, dens, and groves of foliage taught to melt
Into each other their obsequious hues,
Vanished and vanishing in subtle chase,　90
Too fine to be pursued; or standing forth
In no discordant opposition, strong
And gorgeous as the colours side by side
Bedded among rich plumes of tropic birds;
And mountains over all, embracing all;
And all the landscape, endlessly enriched
With waters running, falling, or asleep.

But lovelier far than this, the paradise
Where I was reared; in Nature's primitive gifts
Favoured no less, and more to every sense　100
Delicious, seeing that the sun and sky,
The elements, and seasons as they change,
Do find a worthy fellow-labourer there—
Man free, man working for himself, with choice

27 Hanging Gardens of Babylon.

Of time, and place, and object; by his wants,
His comforts, native occupations, cares,
Cheerfully led to individual ends
Or social, and still followed by a train
Unwooed, unthought-of even—simplicity,
And beauty, and inevitable grace.　110

Yea, when a glimpse of those imperial bowers
Would to a child be transport over-great,
When but a half-hour's roam through such a
　　place
Would leave behind a dance of images,
That shall break in upon his sleep for weeks;
Even then the common haunts of the green earth,
And ordinary interests of man,
Which they embosom, all without regard
As both may seem, are fastening on the heart
Insensibly, each with the other's help.　120
For me, when my affections first were led
From kindred, friends, and playmates, to partake
Love for the human creature's absolute self,
That noticeable kindliness of heart
Sprang out of fountains, there abounding most,
Where sovereign Nature dictated the tasks
And occupations which her beauty adorned,
And Shepherds were the men that pleased me
　　first;
Not such as Saturn ruled 'mid Latian wilds,
With arts and laws so temptered, that their　130
　　lives
Left, even to us toiling in this late day,
A bright tradition of the golden age;
Not such as, 'mid Arcadian fastnesses
Sequestered, handed down among themselves
Felicity, in Grecian song renowned;
Nor such as—when an adverse fate had driven,
From house and home, the courtly band whose
　　fortunes
Entered, with Shakspeare's genius, the wild woods
Of Arden—amid sunshine or in shade
Culled the best fruits of Time's uncounted
　　hours,　140
Ere Phœbe sighed for the false Ganymede;[28]
Or there where Perdita and Florizel
Together danced, Queen of the feast, and King,[29]
Nor such as Spenser fabled. True it is,
That I had heard (what he perhaps had seen)
Of maids at sunrise bringing in from far
Their May-bush, and along the street in flocks
Parading with a song of taunting rhymes,
Aimed at the laggards slumbering within doors;
Had also heard, from those who yet remem-
　　bered,　150

28 in *As You Like It.*
29 in *The Winter's Tale.*

Tales of the May-pole dance, and wreaths that
   decked
Porch, door-way, or kirk-pillar; and of youths,
Each with his maid, before the sun was up,
By annual custom, issuing forth in troops,
To drink the waters of some sainted well,
And hang it round with garlands. Love survives;
But, for such purpose, flowers no longer grow:
The times, too sage, perhaps too proud, have
   dropped
These lighter graces; and the rural ways
And manners which my childhood looked upon 160
Were the unluxuriant produce of a life
Intent on little but substantial needs,
Yet rich in beauty, beauty that was felt.
But images of danger and distress,
Man suffering among awful Powers and Forms;
Of this I heard, and saw enough to make
Imagination restless; nor was free
Myself from frequent perils; nor were tales
Wanting,—the tragedies of former times,
Hazards and strange escapes, of which the
   rocks   170
Immutable, and everflowing streams,
Where'er I roamed, were speaking monuments.

   Smooth life had flock and shepherd in old time,
Long springs and tepid winters, on the banks
Of delicate Galesus;[30] and no less
Those scattered along Adria's[31] myrtle shores:
Smooth life had herdsman, and his snow-white
   herd
To triumphs and to sacrificial rites
Devoted, on the inviolable stream
Of rich Clitumnus,[32] and the goat-herd lived 180
As calmly, underneath the pleasant brows
Of cool Lucretilis,[33] where the pipe was heard
Of Pan, Invisible God, thrilling the rocks
With tutelary music, from all harm
The fold protecting. I myself, mature
In manhood then, have seen a pastoral tract[34]
Like one of these, where Fancy might run wild,
Though under skies less generous, less serene:
There, for her own delight had Nature framed
A pleasure-ground, diffused a fair expanse 190
Of level pasture, islanded with groves
And banked with woody risings; but the Plain
Endless, here opening widely out, and there
Shut up in lesser lakes or beds of lawn
And intricate recesses, creek or bay
Sheltered within a shelter, where at large

The shepherd strays, a rolling hut his home.
Thither he comes with spring-time, there abides
All summer, and at sunrise ye may hear
His flageolet to liquid notes of love   200
Attuned, or sprightly fife resounding far.
Nook is there none, nor tract of that vast space
Where passage opens, but the same shall have
In turn its visitant, telling there his hours
In unlaborious pleasure, with no task
More toilsome than to carve a beechen bowl
For spring or fountain, which the traveller finds,
When through the region he pursues at will
His devious course. A glimpse of such sweet life
I saw when, from the melancholy walls   210
Of Goslar, once imperial I renewed
My daily walk along that wide champaign,
That, reaching to her gates, spreads east and west,
And northwards, from beneath the mountainous
   verge
Of the Hercynian forest.[35] Yet, hail to you
Moors, mountains, headlands, and ye hollow vales,
Ye long deep channels for the Atlantic's voice,
Powers of my native region! Ye that seize
The heart with firmer grasp! Your snows and
   streams
Ungovernable, and your terrifying winds,   220
That howl so dismally for him who treads
Companionless your awful solitudes!
There, 'tis the shepherd's task the winter long
To wait upon the storms: of their approach
Sagacious, into sheltering coves he drives
His flock, and thither from the homestead bears
A toilsome burden up the craggy ways,
And deals it out, their regular nourishment
Strewn on the frozen snow. And when the spring
Looks out, and all the pastures dance with
   lambs,   230
And when the flock, with warmer weather, climbs
Higher and higher, him his office leads
To watch their goings, whatsoever track
The wanderers choose. For this he quits his home
At day-spring, and no sooner doth the sun
Begin to strike him with a fire-like heat,
Than he lies down upon some shining rock,
And breakfasts with his dog. When they have
   stolen,
As is their wont, a pittance from strict time,
For rest not needed or exchange of love,   240
Then from his couch he starts; and now his feet
Crush out a livelier fragrance from the flowers
Of lowly thyme, by Nature's skill enwrought
In the wild turf: the lingering dews of morn

---

30 a river in Italy.
31 the Adriatic Sea.
32 a river tributary to the Tiber.
33 a mountain visible from Horace's Sabine farm.
34 at Goslar, Germany.

---

35 The Hercynian (Hartz) forest in ancient times stretched over a vast mountainous track in South and Central Germany near the Rhine.

Smoke round him, as from hill to hill he hies,
His staff protending like a hunter's spear,
Or by its aid leaping from crag to crag,
And o'er the brawling beds of unbridged streams.
Philosophy, methinks, at Fancy's call,
Might deign to follow him through what he
        does   250
Or sees in his day's march; himself he feels
In those vast regions where his service lies,
A freeman, wedded to his life of hope
And hazard, and hard labour interchanged
With that majestic indolence so dear
To native man. A rambling schoolboy, thus
I felt his presence in his own domain,
As of a lord and master, or a power,
Or genius, under Nature, under God,
Presiding; and severest solitude   260
Had more commanding looks when he was there.
When up the lonely brooks on rainy days
Angling I went, or trod the trackless hills
By mists bewildered, suddenly mine eyes
Have glanced upon him distant a few steps,
In size a giant, stalking through thick fog,
His sheep like Greenland bears; or, as he stepped
Beyond the boundary line of some hill-shadow,
His form hath flashed upon me, glorified
By the deep radiance of the setting sun: 270
Or him have I descried in distant sky,
A solitary object and sublime,
Above all height! like an aerial cross
Stationed alone upon a spiry rock
Of the Chartreuse,[36] for worship. Thus was man
Ennobled outwardly before my sight,
And thus my heart was early introduced
To an unconscious love and reverence
Of human nature; hence the human form
To me became an index of delight,   280
Of grace and honour, power and worthiness.
Meanwhile this creature—spiritual almost
As those of books, but more exalted far;
Far more of an imaginative form
Than the gay Corin of the groves, who lives
For his own fancies, or to dance by the hour,
In coronal,[37] with Phyllis in the midst—
Was, for the purposes of kind, a man
With the most common; husband, father;
        learned,
Could teach, admonish; suffered with the rest 290
From vice and folly, wretchedness and fear;
Of this I little saw, cared less for it,
But something must have felt.
                    Call ye these appearances—
Which I beheld of shepherds in my youth,

This sanctity of Nature given to man—
A shadow, a delusion, ye who pore
On the dead letter, miss the spirit of things;
Whose truth is not a motion or a shape
Instinct with vital functions, but a block
Or waxen image which yourselves have made, 300
And ye adore! But blessèd be the God
Of Nature and of Man that this was so;
That men before my inexperienced eyes
Did first present themselves thus purified,
Removed, and to a distance that was fit;
And so we all of us in some degree
Are led to knowledge, wheresoever led,
And howsoever; were it otherwise,
And we found evil fast as we find good
In our first years, or think that it is found,   310
How could the innocent heart bear up and live!
But doubly fortunate my lot; not here
Alone, that something of a better life
Perhaps was round me than it is the privilege
Of most to move in, but that first I looked
At man through objects that were great or fair;
First communed with him by their help. And thus
Was founded a sure safeguard and defence
Against the weight of meanness, selfish cares,
Coarse manners, vulgar passions, that beat in 320
On all sides from the ordinary world
In which we traffic. Starting from this point
I had my face turned toward the truth, began
With an advantage furnished by that kind
Of prepossession, without which the soul
Receives no knowledge that can bring forth good,
No genuine insight ever comes to her.
From the restraint of over-watchful eyes
Preserved, I moved about, year after year,
Happy, and now most thankful that my walk 330
Was guarded from too early intercourse
With the deformities of crowded life,
And those ensuing laughters and contempts,
Self-pleasing, which, if we would wish to think
With a due reverence on earth's rightful lord,
Here placed to be the inheritor of heaven,
Will not permit us; but pursue the mind,
That to devotion willingly would rise,
Into the temple and the temple's heart.

BOOK NINTH

RESIDENCE IN FRANCE

Lines 288–417, 431–532

Among that band of Officers was one,[38]
Already hinted at, of other mould—

---

36 mountains near Grenoble in France, upon the tops of which
crosses were placed by the Carthusian monks.
37 crowned with wreaths of flowers.

38 Michel Beaupuy, Republican general, stationed at Orleans at
the time Wordsworth was resident there. He was of a noble family, but his sympathy was entirely with the revolutionary cause;
he was, moreover, a student and widely read in the philosophy of
the eighteenth century.

A patriot, thence rejected by the rest,   290
And with an oriental loathing spurned,
As of a different caste. A meeker man
Than this lived never, nor a more benign,
Meek though enthusiastic. Injuries
Made *him* more gracious, and his nature then
Did breathe its sweetness out most sensibly,
As aromatic flowers on Alpine turf,
When foot hath crushed them. He through the
     events
Of that great change wandered in perfect faith,
As through a book, an old romance, or tale 300
Of Fairy, or some dream of actions wrought
Behind the summer clouds. By birth he ranked
With the most noble, but unto the poor
Among mankind he was in service bound,
As by some tie invisible, oaths professed
To a religious order. Man he loved
As man; and, to the mean and the obscure,
And all the homely in their homely works,
Transferred a courtesy which had no air
Of condescension; but did rather seem   310
A passion and a gallantry, like that
Which he, a soldier, in his idler day
Had paid to woman: somewhat vain he was,
Or seemed so, yet it was not vanity,
But fondness, and a kind of radiant joy
Diffused around him, while he was intent
On works of love or freedom, or revolved
Complacently the progress of a cause,
Whereof he was a part: yet this was meek
And placid, and took nothing from the man   320
That was delightful. Oft in solitude
With him did I discourse about the end
Of civil government, and its wisest forms;
Of ancient loyalty, and chartered rights,
Custom and habit, novelty and change;
Of self-respect, and virtue in the few
For patrimonial honour set apart,
And ignorance in the labouring multitude.
For he, to all intolerance indisposed,
Balanced these contemplations in his mind;   330
And I, who at that time was scarcely dipped
Into the turmoil, bore a sounder judgment
Than later days allowed; carried about me,
With less alloy to its integrity,
The experience of past ages, as, through help
Of books and common life, it makes sure way
To youthful minds, by objects over near
Not pressed upon, nor dazzled or misled
By struggling with the crowd for present ends.

But though not deaf, nor obstinate to find   340
Error without excuse upon the side
Of them who strove against us, more delight

We took, and let this freely be confessed,
In painting to ourselves the miseries
Of royal courts, and that voluptuous life
Unfeeling, where the man who is of soul
The meanest thrives the most; where dignity,
True personal dignity, abideth not;
A light, a cruel, and vain world cut off
From the natural inlet of just sentiment,   350
From lowly sympathy and chastening truth:
Where good and evil interchange their names,
And thirst for bloody spoils abroad is paired
With vice at home. We added dearest themes—
Man and his noble nature, as it is
The gift which God has placed within his power,
His blind desires and steady faculties
Capable of clear truth, the one to break
Bondage, the other to build liberty
On firm foundations, making social life,   360
Through knowledge spreading and imperishable,
As just in regulation, and as pure
As individual in the wise and good.

We summoned up the honourable deeds
Of ancient Story, thought of each bright spot,
That would be found in all recorded time,
Of truth preserved and error passed away;
Of single spirits that catch the flame from Heaven,
And how the multitudes of men will feed
And fan each other; thought of sects, how keen 370
They are to put the appropriate nature on,
Triumphant over every obstacle
Of custom, language, country, love, or hate,
And what they do and suffer for their creed;
How far they travel, and how long endure;
How quickly mighty Nations have been formed,
From least beginnings; how, together locked
By new opinions, scattered tribes have made
One body, spreading wide as clouds in heaven.
To aspirations then of our own minds   380
Did we appeal; and, finally, beheld
A living confirmation of the whole
Before us, in a people from the depth
Of shameful imbecility uprisen,
Fresh as the morning star. Elate we looked
Upon their virtues; saw, in rudest men,
Self-sacrifice the firmest; generous love,
And continence of mind, and sense of right,
Uppermost in the midst of fiercest strife.

Oh, sweet it is, in academic groves,   390
Or such retirement, Friend! as we have known
In the green dales beside our Rotha's stream,
Greta, or Derwent, or some nameless rill,
To ruminate, with interchange of talk,
On rational liberty, and hope in man,

Justice and peace. But far more sweet such toil—
Toil, say I, for it leads to thoughts abstruse—
If nature then be standing on the brink
Of some great trial, and we hear the voice
Of one devoted,—one whom circumstance   400
Hath called upon to embody his deep sense
In action, give it outwardly a shape,
And that of benediction, to the world.
Then doubt is not, and truth is more than truth,—
A hope it is, and a desire; a creed
Of zeal, by an authority Divine
Sanctioned, of danger, difficulty, or death.
Such conversation, under Attic shades,
Did Dion[39] hold with Plato; ripened thus
For a deliverer's glorious task,—and such   410
He, on that ministry already bound,
Held with Eudemus and Timonides,
Surrounded by adventurers in arms,
When those two vessels with their daring freight,
For the Sicilian Tyrant's overthrow,
Sailed from Zacynthus,—philosophic war,
Led by Philosophers.

    Along that very Loire, with festal mirth
Resounding at all hours, and innocent yet
Of civil slaughter, was our frequent walk;
Or in wide forests of continuous shade,
Lofty and over-arched, with open space
Beneath the trees, clear footing many a mile—
A solemn region. Oft amid those haunts,
From earnest dialogues I slipped in thought,
And let remembrance steal to other times,
When o'er those interwoven roots, moss-clad, 440
And smooth as marble or a waveless sea,
Some Hermit, from his cell forth-strayed, might
    pace
In sylvan meditation undisturbed;
As on the pavement of a Gothic church
Walks a lone Monk, when service hath expired,
In peace and silence. But if e'er was heard,—
Heard, though unseen,—a devious traveller,
Retiring or approaching from afar
With speed and echoes loud of trampling hoofs
From the hard floor reverberated, then   450
It was Angelica[40] thundering through the woods
Upon her palfrey, or that gentle maid
Erminia,[41] fugitive as fair as she.

Sometimes methought I saw a pair of knights
Joust underneath the trees, that as in storm
Rocked high above their heads; anon, the din
Of boisterous merriment, and music's roar,
In sudden proclamation, burst from haunt
Of Satyrs in some viewless glade, with dance
Rejoicing o'er a female in the midst,   460
A mortal beauty, their unhappy thrall.
The width of those huge forests, unto me
A novel scene, did often in this way
Master my fancy while I wandered on
With that revered companion. And sometimes—
When to a convent in a meadow green,
By a brook-side, we came, a roofless pile,
And not by reverential touch of Time
Dismantled, but by violence abrupt—
In spite of those heart-bracing colloquies,   470
In spite of real fervour, and of that
Less genuine and wrought up within myself—
I could not but bewail a wrong so harsh,
And for the Matin-bell to sound no more
Grieved, and the twilight taper, and the cross
High on the topmost pinnacle, a sign
(How welcome to the weary traveller's eyes!)
Of hospitality and peaceful rest.
And when the partner of those varied walks
Pointed upon occasion to the site   480
Of Romorentin,[42] home of ancient kings,
To the imperial edifice of Blois,
Or to that rural castle, name now slipped
From my remembrance, where a lady[43] lodged,
By the first Francis wooed, and bound to him
In chains of mutual passion, from the tower,
As a tradition of the country tells,
Practised to commune with her royal knight
By cressets and love-beacons, intercourse
'Twixt her high-seated residence and his   490
Far off at Chambord[44] on the plain beneath;
Even here, though less than with the peaceful
    house
Religious, 'mid those frequent monuments
Of Kings, their vices and their better deeds,
Imagination, potent to inflame
At times with virtuous wrath and noble scorn,
Did also often mitigate the force
Of civic prejudice, the bigotry,
So call it, of a youthful patriot's mind;
And on these spots with many gleams I looked 500
Of chivalrous delight. Yet not the less,
Hatred of absolute rule, where will of one
Is law for all, and of that barren pride
In them who, by immunities unjust,

---

39 Dion was an admirer and pupil of Plato's. He induced Plato
to assist him in the reformation of his dissolute brother-in-law,
Dionysius, tyrant of Syracuse. For his pains he was exiled and his
property confiscated. In retaliation, Dion, joined by the philosophers Eudemus and Timonides, assembled a force at Zacynthus,
one of the Cyclades, whence he sailed for Syracuse and deposed
Dionysius.
40 heroine in *Orlando Furioso* of Ariosto.
41 heroine of Tasso's *Jerusalem Delivered.*

42 capital of Sologne.
43 Claude, daughter of Louis XII.
44 a small château, twenty-five miles from Blois.

Between the sovereign and the people stand,
His helper and not theirs, laid stronger hold
Daily upon me, mixed with pity too
And love; for where hope is, there love will be
For the abject multitude. And when we chanced
One day to meet a hunger-bitten girl,   510
Who crept along fitting her languid gait
Unto a heifer's motion, by a cord
Tied to her arm, and picking thus from the lane
Its sustenance, while the girl with pallid hands
Was busy knitting in a heartless mood
Of solitude, and at the sight my friend
In agitation said, ''Tis against *that*
That we are fighting,' I with him believed
That a benignant spirit was abroad
Which might not be withstood, that poverty   520
Abject as this would in a little time
Be found no more, that we should see the earth
Unthwarted in her wish to recompense
The meek, the lowly, patient child of toil,
All institutes for ever blotted out
That legalised exclusion, empty pomp
Abolished, sensual state and cruel power,
Whether by edict of the one or few;
And finally, as sum and crown of all,
Should see the people having a strong hand   530
In framing their own laws; whence better days
To all mankind.

BOOK TENTH

RESIDENCE IN FRANCE—*(Continued)*

Lines 48–93, 133–208, 356–415, 437–80

Cheered with this hope, to Paris I returned,
And ranged, with ardour heretofore unfelt,
The spacious city, and in progress passed   50
The prison where the unhappy Monarch lay,[45]
Associate with his children and his wife
In bondage; and the palace, lately stormed
With roar of cannon by a furious host.
I crossed the square (an empty area then!)
Of the Carrousel,[46] where so late had lain
The dead, upon the dying heaped, and gazed
On this and other spots, as doth a man
Upon a volume whose contents he knows
Are memorable, but from him locked up,   60
Being written in a tongue he cannot read,
So that he questions the mute leaves with pain,

---

45 When Wordsworth returned to Paris in October 1792, the city
was seething with strife and unrest. In August the king had been
deposed and imprisoned 'for his own security.' Then, when the
Princes threatened military violence by the allied forces, in retaliation the committee of the Commune, under the leadership of
Robespierre, ordered the September massacres, in which over
3000 Royalist suspects were guillotined.
46 Place de Carrousel, a public square.

And half upbraids their silence. But that night
I felt most deeply in what world I was,
What ground I trod on, and what air I breathed.
High was my room and lonely, near the roof
Of a large mansion or hotel, a lodge
That would have pleased me in more quiet times;
Nor was it wholly without pleasure then.
With unextinguished taper I kept watch,   70
Reading at intervals; the fear gone by
Pressed on me almost like a fear to come.
I thought of those September massacres,
Divided from me by one little month,
Saw them and touched: the rest was conjured up
From tragic fictions or true history,
Remembrances and dim admonishments.
The horse is taught his manage, and no star
Of wildest course but treads back his own steps;
For the spent hurricane the air provides   80
As fierce a successor; the tide retreats
But to return out of its hiding-place
In the great deep; all things have second birth;
The earthquake is not satisfied at once;
And in this way I wrought upon myself,
Until I seemed to hear a voice that cried,
To the whole city, 'sleep no more.' The trance
Fled with the voice to which it had given birth;
But vainly comments of a calmer mind
Promised soft peace and sweet forgetfulness.   90
The place, all hushed and silent as it was,
Appeared unfit for the repose of night,
Defenceless as a wood where tigers roam.

My inmost soul
Was agitated; yea, I could almost
Have prayed that throughout earth upon all men,
By patient exercise of reason made
Worthy of liberty, all spirits filled
With zeal expanding in Truth's holy light,
The gift of tongues might fall, and power arrive
From the four quarters of the winds to do   140
For France, what without help she could not do,
A work of honour; think not that to this
I added, work of safety; from all doubt
Or trepidation for the end of things
Far was I, far as angels are from guilt.

Yet did I grieve, nor only grieved, but thought
Of opposition and of remedies:
An insignificant stranger and obscure,
And one, moreover, little graced with power
Of eloquence even in my native speech,   150
And all unfit for tumult or intrigue,
Yet would I at this time with willing heart
Have undertaken for a cause so great

Service however dangerous. I revolved,
How much the destiny of Man had still
Hung upon single persons; that there was,
Transcendent to all local patrimony,
One nature, as there is one sun in heaven;
That objects, even as they are great, thereby
Do come within the reach of humblest eyes;   160
That Man is only weak through his mistrust
And want of hope where evidence divine
Proclaims to him that hope should be most sure;
Nor did the inexperience of my youth
Preclude conviction, that a spirit strong
In hope, and trained to noble aspirations,
A spirit thoroughly faithful to itself,
Is for Society's unreasoning herd
A domineering instinct, serves at once
For way and guide, a fluent receptacle   170
That gathers up each petty straggling rill
And vein of water, glad to be rolled on
In safe obedience; that a mind, whose rest
Is where it ought to be, in self-restraint,
In circumspection and simplicity,
Falls rarely in entire discomfiture
Below its aim, or meets with, from without,
A treachery that foils it or defeats;
And, lastly, if the means on human will,
Frail human will, dependent should betray   180
Him who too boldly trusted them, I felt
That 'mid the loud distractions of the world
A sovereign voice subsists within the soul,
Arbiter undisturbed of right and wrong,
Of life and death, in majesty severe
Enjoining, as may best promote the aims
Of truth and justice, utter sacrifice,
From whatsoever region of our cares
Or our infirm affections Nature pleads,
Earnest and blind, against the stern decree.   190

On the other side, I called to mind those truths
That are the commonplaces of the schools—
(A theme for boys, too hackneyed for their
     sires,)
Yet, with a revelation's liveliness,
In all their comprehensive bearings known
And visible to philosophers of old,
Men who, to business of the world untrained,
Lived in the shade; and to Harmodius known
And his composer Aristogiton, known
To Brutus—that tyrannic power is weak,   200
Hath neither gratitude, nor faith, nor love,
Nor the support of good or evil men
To trust in; that the godhead which is ours
Can never utterly be charmed or stilled;
That nothing hath a natural right to last
But equity and reason; that all else

Meets foes irreconcilable, and at best
Lives only by variety of disease.

.   .   .

Domestic carnage[47] now filled the whole year
With feast-days; old men from the chimney-
     nook,
The maiden from the bosom of her love,
The mother from the cradle of her babe,
The warrior from the field—all perished,
     all—   360
Friends, enemies, of all parties, ages, ranks,
Head after head, and never heads enough
For those that bade them fall. They found their
     joy,
They made it proudly, eager as a child,
(If like desires of innocent little ones
May with such heinous appetites be compared)
Pleased in some open field to exercise
A toy that mimics with revolving wings
The motion of a wind-mill; though the air
Do of itself blow fresh, and make the vanes   370
Spin in his eyesight, *that* contents him not,
But, with the plaything at arm's length, he sets
His front against the blast, and runs amain.
That it may whirl the faster.
                                   Amid the depth
Of those enormities, even thinking minds
Forgot, at seasons, whence they had their being;
Forgot that such a sound was ever heard
As Liberty upon earth: yet all beneath
Her innocent authority was wrought,
Nor could have been, without her blessèd
     name.   380
The illustrious wife of Roland,[48] in the hour
Of her composure, felt that agony,
And gave it vent in her last words. O Friend!
It was a lamentable time for man,
Whether a hope had e'er been his or not;
A woeful time for them whose hopes survived
The shock; most woeful for those few who still
Were flattered, and had trust in human kind:
They had the deepest feeling of the grief.
Meanwhile the Invaders fared as they
     deserved: 390
The Herculean Commonwealth had put forth her
     arms,
And throttled with an infant godhead's might
The snakes about her cradle; that was well,
And as it should be; yet no cure for them

---

47 The 'Reign of Terror' began in July 1793. Robespierre was executed the following summer.
48 Madame Roland, wife of the minister of the interior. Her last
words on the scaffold were 'O Liberty, what crimes are committed in thy name!' Following her execution, her husband killed
himself.

Whose souls were sick with pain or what would
    be
Hereafter brought in charge against mankind.
Most melancholy at that time, O Friend!
Were my day-thoughts,—my nights were miser-
    able;
Through months, through years, long after the
    last beat
Of those atrocities, the hour of sleep   400
To me came rarely charged with natural gifts,
Such ghastly visions had I of despair
And tyranny, and implements of death;
And innocent victims sinking under fear,
And momentary hope, and worn-out prayer,
Each in his separate cell, or penned in crowds
For sacrifice, and struggling with forced mirth
And levity in dungeons, where the dust
Was laid with tears. Then suddenly the scene
Changed, and the unbroken dream entangled
    me   410
In long orations, which I strove to plead
Before unjust tribunals—with a voice
Labouring, a brain confounded, and a sense,
Death-like, of treacherous desertion, felt
In the last place of refuge—my own soul.

.   .   .

But as the ancient Prophets, borne aloft
In vision, yet constrained by natural laws
With them to take a troubled human heart,
Wanted not consolations, nor a creed   440
Of reconcilement, then when they denounced,
On towns and cities, wallowing in the abyss
Of their offences, punishment to come;
Or saw, like other men, with bodily eyes,
Before them, in some desolated place,
The wrath consummate and the threat fulfilled;
So, with devout humility be it said,
So, did a portion of that spirit fall
On me uplifted from the vantage-ground
Of pity and sorrow to a state of being   450
That through the time's exceeding fierceness saw
Glimpses of retribution, terrible,
And in the order of sublime behests:
But, even if that were not, amid the awe
Of unintelligible chastisement,
Not only acquiescences of faith
Survived, but daring sympathies with power,
Motions not treacherous or profane, else why
Within the folds of no ungentle breast
Their dread vibration to this hour prolonged? 460
Wild blasts of music thus could find their way
Into the midst of turbulent events;
So that worst tempests might be listened to.

Then was the truth received into my heart,
That, under heaviest sorrow earth can bring,
If from the affliction somewhere do not grow
Honour which could not else have been, a faith,
An elevation, and a sanctity,
If new strength be not given nor old restored,
The blame is ours, not Nature's. When a taunt 470
Was taken up by scoffers in their pride,
Saying, 'Behold the harvest that we reap
From popular government and equality,'
I clearly saw that neither these nor aught
Of wild belief engrafted on their names
By false philosophy had caused the woe,
But a terrific reservoir of guilt
And ignorance filled up from age to age,
That could no longer hold its loathsome charge,
But burst and spread in deluge through the
    land.   480

BOOK ELEVENTH

FRANCE—(*Concluded*)

Lines 75–222, 270–356

            It hath been told
That I was led to take an eager part
In arguments of civil polity,
Abruptly, and indeed before my time:
I had approached, like other youths, the shield
Of human nature from the golden side,   80
And would have fought, even to the death, to attest
The quality of the metal which I saw.
What there is best in individual man,
Of wise in passion, and sublime in power,
Benevolent in small societies,
And great in large ones, I had oft revolved,
Felt deeply, but not thoroughly understood
By reason: nay, far from it; they were yet,
As cause was given me afterwards to learn,
Not proof against the injuries of the day;   90
Lodged only at the sanctuary's door,
Not safe within its bosom. Thus prepared,
And with such general insight into evil,
And of the bounds which sever it from good,
As books and common intercourse with life
Must needs have given—to the inexperienced
    mind,
When the world travels in a beaten road,
Guide faithful as is needed—I began
To meditate with ardour on the rule
And management of nations; what it is   100
And ought to be; and strove to learn how far
Their power or weakness, wealth or poverty,
Their happiness or misery, depends
Upon their laws, and fashion of the State.

O pleasant exercise of hope and joy!
For mighty were the auxiliars which then stood
Upon our side, us who were strong in love!
Bliss was it in that dawn to be alive,
But to be young was very Heaven! O times,
In which the meagre, stale, forbidding ways　110
Of custom, law, and statute, took at once
The attraction of a country in romance!
When Reason seemed the most to assert her rights
When most intent on making of herself
A prime enchantress—to assist the work,
Which then was going forward in her name!
Not favoured spots alone, but the whole Earth,
The beauty wore of promise—that which sets
(As at some moments might not be unfelt
Among the bowers of Paradise itself)　120
The budding rose above the rose full blown.
What temper at the prospect did not wake
To happiness unthought of? The inert
Were roused, and lively natures rapt away!
They who had fed their childhood upon dreams,
The play-fellows of fancy, who had made
All powers of swiftness, subtilty, and strength
Their ministers,—who in lordly wise had stirred
Among the grandest objects of the sense,
And dealt with whatsoever they found there　130
As if they had within some lurking right
To wield it;—they, too, who of gentle mood
Had watched all gentle motions, and to these
Had fitted their own thoughts, schemers more mild,
And in the region of their peaceful selves;—
Now was it that *both* found, the meek and lofty
Did both find, helpers to their hearts' desire,
And stuff at hand, plastic as they could wish,—
Were called upon to exercise their skill,
Not in Utopia,—subterranean fields,—　140
Or some secreted island, Heaven knows where!
But in the very world, which is the world
Of all of us,—the place where, in the end,
We find our happiness, or not at all!

Why should I not confess that Earth was then
To me, what an inheritance, new-fallen,
Seems, when the first time visited, to one
Who thither comes to find in it his home?
He walks about and looks upon the spot
With cordial transport, moulds it and remoulds, 150
And is half pleased with things that are amiss,
'Twill be such joy to see them disappear.

An active partisan, I thus convoked
From every object pleasant circumstance
To suit my ends; I moved among mankind
With genial feelings still predominant;
When erring, erring on the better part,

And in the kinder spirit; placable,
Indulgent, as not uninformed that men
See as they have been taught—Antiquity　160
Gives rights to error; and aware, no less,
That throwing off oppression must be work
As well of License as of Liberty;
And above all—for this was more than all—
Not caring if the wind did now and then
Blow keen upon an eminence that gave
Prospect so large into futurity;
In brief, a child of Nature, as at first,
Diffusing only those affections wider
That from the cradle had grown up with me,　170
And losing, in no other way than light
Is lost in light, the weak in the more strong.

In the main outline, such it might be said
Was my condition, till with open war
Britain opposed the liberties of France.[49]
This threw me first out of the pale of love;
Soured and corrupted, upwards to the source,
My sentiments; was not, as hitherto,
A swallowing up of lesser things in great,
But change of them into their contraries;　180
And thus a way was opened for mistakes
And false conclusions, in degree as gross,
In kind more dangerous. What had been a pride,
Was now a shame; my likings and my loves
Ran in new channels, leaving old ones dry;
And hence a blow that, in maturer age,
Would but have touched the judgment, struck
　　　more deep
Into sensations near the heart: meantime,
As from the first, wild theories were afloat,
To whose pretensions, sedulously urged,　190
I had but lent a careless ear, assured
That time was ready to set all things right,
And that the multitude, so long oppressed,
Would be oppressed no more.
　　　　　　　　　　　　But when events
Brought less encouragement, and unto these
The immediate proof of principles no more
Could be entrusted, while the events themselves,
Worn out in greatness, stripped of novelty,
Less occupied the mind, and sentiments
Could through my understanding's natural
　　　growth　　　　　　　　　　　　　200
No longer keep their ground, by faith maintained
Of inward consciousness, and hope that laid
Her hand upon her object—evidence
Safer, of universal application, such
As could not be impeached, was sought elsewhere.

But now, become oppressors in their turn,

---

49 in 1793.

Frenchmen had changed a war of self-defence
For one of conquest, losing sight of all
Which they had struggled for: up mounted now,
Openly in the eye of earth and heaven,   210
The scale of liberty. I read her doom,
With anger vexed, with disappointment sore,
But not dismayed, nor taking to the shame
Of a false prophet. While resentment rose
Striving to hide, what nought could heal, the
          wounds
Of mortified presumption, I adhered
More firmly to old tenets, and, to prove
Their temper, strained them more; and thus, in
          heat
Of contest, did opinions every day
Grow into consequence, till round my mind 220
They clung, as if they were its life, nay more,
The very being of the immortal soul.

          .   .   .

          A strong shock   270
Was given to old opinions; all men's minds
Had felt its power, and mine was both let loose,
Let loose and goaded. After what hath been
Already said of patriotic love,
Suffice it here to add, that, somewhat stern
In temperament, withal a happy man,
And therefore bold to look on painful things,
Free likewise of the world, and thence more bold,
I summoned my best skill, and toiled, intent
To anatomise the frame of social life;   280
Yea, the whole body of society
Searched to its heart. Share with me, Friend! the
          wish
That some dramatic tale, endued with shapes
Livelier, and flinging out less guarded words
Than suit the work we fashion, might set forth
What then I learned, or think I learned, of truth,
And the errors into which I fell, betrayed
By present objects, and by reasonings false
From their beginnings, inasmuch as drawn
Out of a heart that had been turned aside   290
From Nature's way by outward accidents,
And which was thus confounded, more and more
Misguided, and misguiding. So I fared,
Dragging all precepts, judgments, maxims, creeds,
Like culprits to the bar; calling the mind,
Suspiciously, to establish in plain day
Her titles and her honours; now believing,
Now disbelieving; endlessly perplexed
With impulse, motive, right and wrong, the ground
Of obligation, what the rule and whence   300
The sanction; till, demanding formal *proof*,
And seeking it in everything, I lost
All feeling of conviction, and, in fine,

Sick, wearied out with contrarieties,
Yielded up moral questions in despair.

This was the crisis of that strong disease,
This the soul's last and lowest ebb; I drooped,
Deeming our blessèd reason of least use
Where wanted most: 'The lordly attributes
Of will and choice,' I bitterly exclaimed,   310
'What are they but a mockery of a Being
Who hath in no concerns of his a test
Of good and evil; knows not what to fear
Or hope for, what to covet or to shun;
And who, if those could be discerned, would yet
Be little profited, would see, and ask
Where is the obligation to enforce?
And, to acknowledged law rebellious, still,
As selfish passion urged, would act amiss;
The dupe of folly, or the slave of crime.'   320

Depressed, bewildered thus, I did not walk
With scoffers, seeking light and gay revenge
From indiscriminate laughter, nor sate down
In reconcilement with an utter waste
Of intellect; such sloth I could not brook,
(Too well I loved, in that my spring of life,
Pains-taking thoughts, and truth, their dear re-
          ward)
But turned to abstract science, and there sought
Work for the reasoning faculty enthroned
Where the disturbances of space and time— 330
Whether in matter's various properties
Inherent, or from human will and power
Derived—find no admission. Then it was—
Thanks to the bounteous Giver of all good!—
That the belovèd Sister in whose sight
Those days were passed, now speaking in a voice
Of sudden admonition—like a brook
That did but *cross* a lonely road, and now
Is seen, heard, felt, and caught at every turn,
Companion never lost through many a
          league—   340
Maintained for me a saving intercourse
With my true self; for, though bedimmed and
          changed
Much, as it seemed, I was no further changed
Than as a clouded and a waning moon:
She whispered still that brightness would return,
She, in the midst of all, preserved me still
A Poet, made me seek beneath that name,
And that alone, my office upon earth;
And, lastly, as hereafter will be shown,
If willing audience fail not, Nature's self,   350
By all varieties of human love
Assisted, led me back through opening day
To those sweet counsels between head and heart

Whence grew that genuine knowledge, fraught
   with peace,
Which, through the later sinkings of this cause,
Hath still upheld me, and upholds me now.

BOOK TWELFTH

IMAGINATION AND TASTE, HOW IMPAIRED AND RESTORED

Lines 1–43, 174–335

LONG time have human ignorance and guilt
Detained us, on what spectacles of woe
Compelled to look, and inwardly oppressed
With sorrow, disappointment, vexing thoughts,
Confusion of the judgment, zeal decayed,
And, lastly, utter loss of hope itself
And things to hope for! Not with these began
Our song, and not with these our song must end.—
Ye motions of delight, that haunt the sides
Of the green hills; ye breezes and soft airs,   10
Whose subtle intercourse with breathing flowers,
Feelingly watched, might teach Man's haughty
   race
How without injury to take, to give
Without offence; ye who, as if to show
The wondrous influence of power gently used,
Bend the complying heads of lordly pines,
And, with a touch, shift the stupendous clouds
Through the whole compass of the sky; ye brooks,
Muttering along the stones, a busy noise
By day, a quiet sound in silent night;   20
Ye waves, that out of the great deep steal forth
In a calm hour to kiss the pebbly shore,
Not mute, and then retire, fearing no storm;
And you, ye groves, whose ministry it is
To interpose the covert of your shades,
Even as a sleep, between the heart of man
And outward troubles, between man himself,
Not seldom, and his own uneasy heart:
Oh! that I had a music and a voice
Harmonious as your own, that I might tell   30
What ye have done for me. The morning shines,
Nor heedeth Man's perverseness; Spring returns,—
I saw the Spring return, and could rejoice,
In common with the children of her love,
Piping on boughs, or sporting on fresh fields,
Or boldly seeking pleasure nearer heaven
On wings that navigate cerulean skies.
So neither were complacency, nor peace,
Nor tender yearnings, wanting for my good
Through these distracted times; in Nature still   40
Glorying, I found a counterpoise in her,
Which, when the spirit of evil reached its height,
Maintained for me a secret happiness.

. . . . .

          Before I was called forth
From the retirement of my native hills,
I loved whate'er I saw: nor lightly loved,
But most intensely; never dreamt of aught
More grand, more fair, more exquisitely framed
Than those few nooks to which my happy feet
Were limited. I had not at that time   180
Lived long enough, nor in the least survived
The first diviner influence of this world,
As it appears to unaccustomed eyes.
Worshipping then among the depth of things,
As piety ordained; could I submit
To measured admiration, or to aught
That should preclude humility and love?
I felt, observed, and pondered; did not judge,
Yea, never thought of judging; with the gift
Of all this glory filled and satisfied.   190
And afterwards, when through the gorgeous Alps
Roaming, I carried with me the same heart:
In truth, the degradation—howsoe'er
Induced, effect, in whatsoe'er degree,
Of custom that prepares a partial scale
In which the little oft outweighs the great;
Or any other cause that hath been named;
Or lastly, aggravated by the times
And their impassioned sounds, which well might
   make
The milder, minstrelsies of rural scenes   200
Inaudible—was transient; I had known
Too forcibly, too early in my life,
Visitings of imaginative power
For this to last: I shook the habit off
Entirely and for ever, and again
In Nature's presence stood, as now I stand,
A sensitive being, a *creative* soul.

    There are in our existence spots of time,
That with distinct pre-eminence retain
A renovating virtue, whence, depressed
By false opinion and contentious thought,
Or aught of heavier or more deadly weight,
In trivial occupations, and the round
Of ordinary intercourse, our minds
Are nourished and invisibly repaired;
A virtue, by which pleasure is enhanced,
That penetrates, enables us to mount,
When high, more high, and lifts us up when fallen.
This efficacious spirit chiefly lurks
Among those passages of life that give   220
Profoundest knowledge to what point, and how,
The mind is lord and master—outward sense
The obedient servant of her will. Such moments
Are scattered everywhere, taking their date
From our first childhood. I remember well,
That once, while yet my inexperienced hand

Could scarcely hold a bridle, with proud hopes
I mounted, and we journeyed towards the hills:
An ancient servant of my father's house
Was with me, my encourager and guide: 230
We had not travelled long, ere some mischance
Disjoined me from my comrade; and, through fear
Dismounting, down the rough and stony moor
I led my horse, and, stumbling on, at length
Came to a bottom, where in former times
A murderer had been hung in iron chains.
The gibbet-mast had mouldered down, the bones
And iron case were gone; but on the turf,
Hard by, soon after that fell deed was wrought,
Some unknown hand had carved the murderer's
    name. 240
The monumental letters were inscribed
In times long past; but still, from year to year,
By superstition of the neighbourhood,
The grass is cleared away, and to this hour
The characters are fresh and visible:
A casual glance had shown them, and I fled,
Faltering and faint, and ignorant of the road:
Then, reascending the bare common, saw
A naked pool that lay beneath the hills,
The beacon on the summit, and, more near, 250
A girl, who bore a pitcher on her head,
And seemed with difficult steps to force her way
Against the blowing wind. It was, in truth,
An ordinary sight; but I should need
Colours and words that are unknown to man,
To paint the visionary dreariness
Which, while I looked all round for my lost guide,
Invested moorland waste, and naked pool,
The beacon crowning the lone eminence,
The female and her garments vexed and tossed 260
By the strong wind. When, in the blessèd hours
Of early love, the loved one at my side,
I roamed, in daily presence of this scene,
Upon the naked pool and dreary crags,
And on the melancholy beacon, fell
A spirit of pleasure and youth's golden gleam;
And think ye not with radiance more sublime
For these remembrances, and for the power
They had left behind? So feeling comes in aid
Of feeling,[50] and diversity of strength 270
Attends us, if but once we have been strong.
Oh! mystery of man, from what a depth
Proceed thy honours. I am lost, but see
In simple childhood something of the base
On which thy greatness stands; but this I feel,
That from thyself it comes, that thou must give,

Else never canst receive. The days gone by
Return upon me almost from the dawn
Of life: the hiding-places of man's power
Open; I would approach them, but they close. 280
I see by glimpses now; when age comes on,
May scarcely see at all; and I would give,
While yet we may, as far as words can give,
Substance and life to what I feel, enshrining,
Such is my hope, the spirit of the Past
For future restoration.—Yet another
Of these memorials:—

         One Christmas-time,[51]
On the glad eve of its dear holidays,
Feverish, and tired, and restless, I went forth
Into the fields, impatient for the sight 290
Of those led palfreys that should bear us home;
My brothers and myself. There rose a crag,
That, from the meeting-point of two highways
Ascending, overlooked them both, far stretched;
Thither, uncertain on which road to fix
My expectation, thither I repaired,
Scout-like, and gained the summit; 'twas a day
Tempestuous, dark, and wild, and on the grass
I sate half-sheltered by a naked wall;
Upon my right hand crouched a single sheep, 300
Upon my left a blasted hawthorn stood;
With those companions at my side, I watched,
Straining my eyes intensely, as the mist
Gave intermitting prospect of the copse
And plain beneath. Ere we to school returned,—
That dreary time,—ere we had been ten days
Sojourners in my father's house, he died,
And I and my three brothers, orphans then,
Followed his body to the grave. The event,
With all the sorrow that it brought, appeared 310
A chastisement; and when I called to mind
That day so lately past, when from the crag
I looked in such anxiety of hope;
With trite reflections of morality,
Yet in the deepest passion, I bowed low
To God, Who thus corrected my desires;
And, afterwards, the wind and sleety rain,
And all the business of the elements,
The single sheep, and the one blasted tree,
And the bleak music from that old stone wall, 320
The noise of wood and water, and the mist
That on the line of each of those two roads
Advanced in such indisputable shapes;
All these were kindred spectacles and sounds
To which I oft repaired, and thence would drink,
As at a fountain; and on winter nights,
Down to this very time, when storm and rain
Beat on my roof, or, haply, at noon day,
While in a grove I walk, whose lofty trees,

---

50 Lines 269–86 are, says de Selincourt, 'a statement of the central
point of Wordsworth's creed, that poetry "takes its origin from
emotion recollected in tranquillity," drawing its inspiration and
its material from the great moments of the past, especially from
the scenes of childhood and early youth, when feeling is strongest.'

51 in 1783.

Laden with summer's thickest foliage, rock   330
In a strong wind, some working of the spirit,
Some inward agitations thence are brought,
Whate'er their office, whether to beguile
Thoughts over busy in the course they took,
Or animate an hour of vacant ease.

BOOK THIRTEENTH

IMAGINATION AND TASTE, HOW IMPAIRED AND

RESTORED—(*Concluded*)

Lines 1–278

FROM Nature doth emotion come, and moods
Of calmness equally are Nature's gift:
This is her glory; these two attributes
Are sister horns that constitute her strength.
Hence Genius, born to thrive by interchange
Of peace and excitation, finds in her
His best and purest friend; from her receives
That energy by which he seeks the truth,
From her that happy stillness of the mind
Which fits him to receive it when unsought.   10

Such benefit the humblest intellects
Partake of, each in their degree; 'tis mine
To speak, what I myself have known and felt;
Smooth task! for words find easy way, inspired
By gratitude, and confidence in truth.
Long time in search of knowledge did I range
The field of human life, in heart and mind
Benighted; but, the dawn beginning now
To re-appear, 'twas proved that not in vain
I had been taught to reverence a Power   20
That is the visible quality and shape
And image of right reason; that matures
Her processes by steadfast laws; gives birth
To no impatient or fallacious hopes,
No heat of passion or excessive zeal,
No vain conceits; provokes to no quick turns
Of self-applauding intellect; but trains
To meekness, and exalts by humble faith;
Holds up before the mind intoxicate
With present objects, and the busy dance   30
Of things that pass away, a temperate show
Of objects that endure; and by this course
Disposes her, when over-fondly set
On throwing off incumbrances, to seek
In man, and in the frame of social life,
Whate'er there is desirable and good
Of kindred permanence, unchanged in form
And function, or, through strict vicissitude
Of life and death, revolving. Above all
Were re-established now those watchful
      thoughts   40

Which, seeing little worthy or sublime
In what the Historian's pen so much delights
To blazon—power and energy detached
From moral purpose—early tutored me
To look with feelings of fraternal love
Upon the unassuming things that hold
A silent station in this beauteous world.

Thus moderated, thus composed, I found
Once more in Man an object of delight,
Of pure imagination, and of love;   50
And, as the horizon of my mind enlarged,
Again I took the intellectual eye
For my instructor, studious more to see
Great truths, than touch and handle little ones.
Knowledge was given accordingly; my trust
Became more firm in feelings that had stood
The test of such a trial; clearer far
My sense of excellence—of right and wrong:
The promise of the present time retired
Into its true proportion; sanguine schemes,   60
Ambitious projects, pleased me less; I sought
For present good in life's familiar face,
And built thereon my hopes of good to come.

With settling judgments now of what would last
And what would disappear; prepared to find
Presumption, folly, madness, in the men
Who thrust themselves upon the passive world
As Rulers of the world; to see in these,
Even when the public welfare is their aim,
Plans without thought, or built on theories   70
Vague and unsound; and having brought the
      books
Of modern statists to their proper test,
Life, human life, with all its sacred claims
Of sex and age, and heaven-descended rights,
Mortal, or those beyond the reach of death;
And having thus discerned how dire a thing
Is worshipped in that idol proudly named
'The Wealth of Nations,'[52] *where* alone that wealth
Is lodged, and how increased; and having gained
A more judicious knowledge of the worth   80
And dignity of individual man,
No composition of the brain, but man
Of whom we read, the man whom we behold
With our own eyes—I could not but enquire—
Not with less interest than heretofore,
But greater, though in spirit more subdued—
Why is this glorious creature to be found
One only in ten thousand? What one is,
Why may not millions be? What bars are thrown
By Nature in the way of such a hope?   90
Our animal appetites and daily wants,

52 famous treatise on political economy by Adam Smith, 1776.

Are these obstructions insurmountable?
If not, then others vanish into air.
'Inspect the basis of the social pile:
Enquire,' said I, 'how much of mental power
And genuine virtue they possess who live
By bodily toil, labour exceeding far
Their due proportion, under all the weight
Of that injustice which upon ourselves
Ourselves entail.' Such estimate to frame   100
I chiefly looked (what need to look beyond?)
Among the natural abodes of men,
Fields with their rural works; recalled to mind
My earliest notices; with these compared
The observations made in later youth,
And to that day continued —For, the time
Had never been when throes of mighty Nations
And the world's tumult unto me could yield,
How far soe'er transported and possessed,
Full measure of content; but still I craved   110
An intermingling of distinct regards
And truths of individual sympathy
Nearer ourselves. Such often might be gleaned
From the great City, else it must have proved
To me a heart-depressing wilderness;
But much was wanting: therefore did I turn
To you, ye pathways, and ye lonely roads;
Sought you enriched with everything I prized,
With human kindnesses and simple joys.

Oh! next to one dear state of bliss,
    vouchsafed   120
Alas! to few in this untoward world,
The bliss of walking daily in life's prime
Through field or forest with the maid we love,
While yet our hearts are young, while yet we
    breathe
Nothing but happiness, in some lone nook,
Deep vale, or anywhere, the home of both,
From which it would be misery to stir:
Oh! next to such enjoyment of our youth,
In my esteem, next to such dear delight,
Was that of wandering on from day to day   130
Where I could meditate in peace, and cull
Knowledge that step by step might lead me on
To wisdom; or, as lightsome as a bird
Wafted upon the wind from distant lands,
Sing notes of greeting to strange fields or groves,
Which lacked not voice to welcome me in
    turn:
And, when that pleasant toil had ceased to
    please,
Converse with men, where if we meet a face
We almost meet a friend, on naked heaths
With long long ways before, by cottage bench, 140
Or well-spring where the weary traveller rests.

Who doth not love to follow with his eye
The windings of a public way? the sight,
Familiar object as it is, hath wrought
On my imagination since the morn
Of childhood, when a disappearing line,
One daily present to my eyes, that crossed
The naked summit of a far-off hill
Beyond the limits that my feet had trod,
Was like an invitation into space   150
Boundless, or guide into eternity.
Yes, something of the grandeur which invests
The mariner who sails the roaring sea
Through storm and darkness, early in my mind
Surrounded, too, the wanderers of the earth;
Grandeur as much, and loveliness far more.
Awed have I been by strolling Bedlamites;
From many other uncouth vagrants (passed
In fear) have walked with quicker step; but why
Take note of this? When I began to enquire,   160
To watch and question those I met, and speak
Without reserve to them, the lonely roads
Were open schools in which I daily read
With most delight the passions of mankind,
Whether by words, looks, sighs, or tears, revealed;
There saw into the depth of human souls,
Souls that appear to have no depth at all
To careless eyes. And—now convinced at heart
How little those formalities, to which
With overweening trust alone we give   170
The name of Education, have to do
With real feeling and just sense; how vain
A correspondence with the talking world
Proves to the most; and called to make good search
If man's estate, by doom of Nature yoked
With toil, be therefore yoked with ignorance;
If virtue be indeed so hard to rear,
And intellectual strength so rare a boon—
I prized such walks still more, for there I found
Hope to my hope, and to my pleasure peace   180
And steadiness, and healing and repose
To every angry passion. There I heard,
From mouths of men obscure and lowly, truths
Replete with honour; sounds in unison
With loftiest promises of good and fair.

There are who think that strong affection, love
Known by whatever name, is falsely deemed
A gift, to use a term which they would use,
Of vulgar nature; that its growth requires
Retirement, leisure, language purified   190
By manners studied and elaborate;
That whoso feels such passion in its strength
Must live within the very light and air
Of courteous usages refined by art.
True is it, where oppression worse than death

Salutes the being at his birth, where grace
Of culture hath been utterly unknown,
And poverty and labour in excess
From day to day pre-occupy the ground
Of the affections, and to Nature's self   200
Oppose a deeper nature; there, indeed,
Love cannot be; nor does it thrive with ease
Among the close and overcrowded haunts
Of cities, where the human heart is sick,
And the eye feeds it not, and cannot feed.
—Yes, in those wanderings deeply did I feel
How we mislead each other; above all,
How books mislead us, seeking their reward
From judgments of the wealthy Few, who see
By artificial lights; how they debase   210
The Many for the pleasure of those Few;
Effeminately level down the truth
To certain general notions, for the sake
Of being understood at once, or else
Through want of better knowledge in the heads
That framed them; flattering self-conceit with
     words,
That, while they most ambitiously set forth
Extrinsic differences, the outward marks
Whereby society has parted man
From man, neglect the universal heart.   220

Here, calling up to mind what then I saw,
A youthful traveller, and see daily now
In the familiar circuit of my home,
Here might I pause, and bend in reverence
To Nature, and the power of human minds,
To men as they are men within themselves.
How oft high service is performed within,
When all the external man is rude in show,—
Not like a temple rich with pomp and gold,
But a mere mountain-chapel, that protects   230
Its simple worshippers from sun and shower.
Of these, said I, shall be my song; of these,
If future years mature me for the task,
Will I record the praises, making verse
Deal boldly with substantial things; in truth
And sanctity of passion, speak of these,
That justice may be done, obeisance paid
Where it is due: thus haply shall I teach,
Inspire; through unadulterated ears
Pour rapture, tenderness, and hope,—my
     theme   240
No other than the very heart of man,
As found among the best of those who live—
Not unexalted by religious faith,
Nor uninformed by books, good books, though
     few—
In Nature's presence: thence may I select
Sorrow, that is not sorrow, but delight;

And miserable love, that is not pain
To hear of, for the glory that redounds
Therefrom to human kind, and what we are.
Be mine to follow with no timid step   250
Where knowledge leads me: it shall be my pride
That I have dared to tread this holy ground,
Speaking no dream, but things oracular;
Matter not lightly to be heard by those
Who to the letter of the outward promise
Do read the invisible soul; by men adroit
In speech, and for communion with the world
Accomplished; minds whose faculties are then
Most active when they are most eloquent,
And elevated most when most admired.   260
Men may be found of other mould than these,
Who are their own upholders, to themselves
Encouragement, and energy, and will,
Expressing liveliest thoughts in lively words
As native passion dictates. Others, too,
There are among the walks of homely life
Still higher, men for contemplation framed,
Shy, and unpractised in the strife of phrase:
Meek men, whose very souls perhaps would sink
Beneath them, summoned to such intercourse: 270
Theirs is the language of the heavens, the power,
The thought, the image, and the silent joy:
Words are but under-agents in their souls;
When they are grasping with their greatest strength,
They do not breathe among them: this I speak
In gratitude to God, Who feeds our hearts
For His own service; knoweth, loveth us,
When we are unregarded by the world.

BOOK FOURTEENTH

CONCLUSION

Lines 1–129, 162–205

IN one of those excursions (may they ne'er
Fade from remembrance!) through the Northern
     tracts
Of Cambria, ranging with a youthful friend,[53]
I left Bethgelert's huts at couching-time,
And westward took my way, to see the sun
Rise, from the top of Snowdon. To the door
Of a rude cottage at the mountain's base
We came, and roused the shepherd who attends
The adventurous stranger's steps, a trusty guide;
Then, cheered by short refreshment, sallied
     forth.   10

It was a close, warm, breezeless summer night,
Wan, dull, and glaring, with a dripping fog
Low-hung and thick that covered all the sky;

---

53 Jones, his college friend, whom he was visiting in the summer
of 1793.

But, undiscouraged, we began to climb
The mountain-side. The mist soon girt us round,
And, after ordinary travellers' talk
With our conductor, pensively we sank
Each into commerce with his private thoughts:
Thus did we breast the ascent, and by myself
Was nothing either seen or heard that checked 20
Those musings or diverted, save that once
The shepherd's lurcher, who, among the crags,
Had to his joy unearthed a hedgehog, teased
His coiled-up prey with barkings turbulent.
This small adventure, for even such it seemed
In that wild place and at the dead of night,
Being over and forgotten, on we wound
In silence as before. With forehead bent
Earthward, as if in opposition set
Against an enemy, I panted up 30
With eager pace, and not less eager thoughts.
Thus might we wear a midnight hour away,
Ascending at loose distance each from each,
And I, as chanced, the foremost of the band;
When at my feet the ground appeared to brighten,
And with a step or two seemed brighter still;
Nor was time given to ask or learn the cause,
For instantly a light upon the turf
Fell like a flash, and lo! as I looked up,
The Moon hung naked in a firmament 40
Of azure without cloud, and at my feet
Rested a silent sea of hoary mist.
A hundred hills their dusky backs upheaved
All over this still ocean; and beyond,
Far, far beyond, the solid vapours stretched,
In headlands, tongues, and promontory shapes,
Into the main Atlantic, that appeared
To dwindle, and give up his majesty,
Usurped upon far as the sight could reach.
Not so the ethereal vault; encroachment none 50
Was there, nor loss; only the inferior stars
Had disappeared, or shed a fainter light
In the clear presence of the full-orbed Moon,
Who, from her sovereign elevation, gazed
Upon the billowy ocean, as it lay
All meek and silent, save that through a rift—
Not distant from the shore whereon we stood,
A fixed, abysmal, gloomy, breathing-place—
Mounted the roar of waters, torrents, streams
Innumerable, roaring with one voice! 60
Heard over earth and sea, and, in that hour,
For so it seemed, felt by the starry heavens.

When into air had partially dissolved
That vision, given to spirits of the night
And three chance human wanderers, in calm
    thought
Reflected, it appeared to me the type

Of a majestic intellect, its acts
And its possessions, what it has and craves,
What in itself it is, and would become.
There I beheld the emblem of a mind 70
That feeds upon infinity, that broods
Over the dark abyss, intent to hear
Its voices issuing forth to silent light
In one continuous stream; a mind sustained
By recognitions of transcendent power,
In sense conducting to ideal form,
In soul of more than mortal privilege.
One function, above all, of such a mind
Had Nature shadowed there, by putting forth,
'Mid circumstances awful and sublime, 80
That mutual domination which she loves
To exert upon the face of outward things,
So moulded, joined, abstracted, so endowed
With interchangeable supremacy,
That men, least sensitive, see, hear, perceive,
And cannot choose but feel. The power, which all
Acknowledge when thus moved, which Nature
    thus
To bodily sense exhibits, is the express
Resemblance of that glorious faculty
That higher minds bear with them as their own. 90
This is the very spirit in which they deal
With the whole compass of the universe:
They from their native selves can send abroad
Kindred mutations; for themselves create
A like existence; and, whene'er it dawns
Created for them, catch it, or are caught
By its inevitable mastery,
Like angels stopped upon the wing by sound
Of harmony from Heaven's remotest spheres.
Them the enduring and the transient both 100
Serve to exalt; they build up greatest things
From least suggestions; ever on the watch,
Willing to work and to be wrought upon,
They need not extraordinary calls
To rouse them; in a world of life they live,
By sensible impressions not enthralled,
But by their quickening impulse made more
    prompt
To hold fit converse with the spiritual world,
And with the generations of mankind
Spread over time, past, present, and to come, 110
Age after age, till Time shall be no more.
Such minds are truly from the Deity,
For they are Powers; and hence the highest bliss
That flesh can know is theirs—the consciousness
Of Whom they are, habitually infused
Through every image and through every thought,
And all affections by communion raised
From earth to heaven, from human to divine;
Hence endless occupation for the Soul,

Whether discursive or intuitive;   120
Hence cheerfulness for acts of daily life,
Emotions which best foresight need not fear,
Most worthy then of trust when most intense.
Hence, amid ills that vex and wrongs that crush
Our hearts—if here the words of Holy Writ
May with fit reverence be applied—that peace
Which passeth understanding, that repose
In moral judgments which from this pure source
Must come, or will by man be sought in vain.

                    To fear and love,
To love as prime and chief, for there fear ends,
Be this ascribed; to early intercourse,
In presence of sublime or beautiful forms,
With the adverse principles of pain and joy—
Evil as one is rashly named by men
Who know not what they speak. By love subsists
All lasting grandeur, by pervading love;
That gone, we are as dust.—Behold the fields   170
In balmy spring-time full of rising flowers
And joyous creatures; see that pair, the lamb
And the lamb's mother, and their tender ways
Shall touch thee to the heart; thou callest this love,
And not inaptly so, for love it is,
Far as it carries thee. In some green bower
Rest, and be not alone, but have thou there
The One who is thy choice of all the world:
There linger, listening, gazing, with delight
Impassioned, but delight how pitiable!   180
Unless this love by a still higher love
Be hallowed, love that breathes not without awe;
Love that adores, but on the knees of prayer,
By heaven inspired; that frees from chains the
          soul,
Lifted, in union with the purest, best,
Of earth-born passions, on the wings of praise
Bearing a tribute to the Almighty's Throne.

    This spiritual Love acts not nor can exist
Without Imagination, which, in truth,
Is but another name for absolute power   190
And clearest insight, amplitude of mind,
And Reason in her most exalted mood.
This faculty hath been the feeding source
Of our long labour: we have traced the stream
From the blind cavern whence is faintly heard
Its natal murmur; followed it to light
And open day; accompanied its course
Among the ways of Nature, for a time
Lost sight of it bewildered and engulphed;
Then given it greeting as it rose once more   200
In strength, reflecting from its placid breast
The works of man and face of human life;

And lastly, from its progress have we drawn
Faith in life endless, the sustaining thought
Of human Being, Eternity, and God.

1798–1805   1850

MICHAEL
A PASTORAL POEM

    Written at Town-end, Grasmere, about the same time as *The Brothers*. The Sheepfold, on which so much of the poem turns, remains, or rather the ruins of it. The character and circumstances of Luke were taken from a family to whom had belonged, many years before, the house we lived in at Town-end, along with some fields and woodlands on the eastern shore of Grasmere. The name of the Evening Star was not in fact given to this house, but to another on the same side of the valley, more to the north.—(Wordsworth.)

    [To his friend, Thomas Poole, Wordsworth wrote of this poem: 'I have attempted to give a picture of a man, of strong mind and lively sensibility, agitated by two of the most powerful affections of the human heart: the parental affection, and the love of property (*landed* property), including the feelings of inheritance, home, and personal and family independence. . . . In writing it I had your character often before my eyes.']

IF from the public way you turn your steps
Up the tumultuous brook of Green-head Ghyll,[1]
You will suppose that with an upright path
Your feet must struggle; in such bold ascent
The pastoral mountains front you, face to face.
But, courage! for around that boisterous brook
The mountains have all opened out themselves,
And made a hidden valley of their own.
No habitation can be seen; but they
Who journey thither find themselves alone   10
With a few sheep, with rocks and stones, and kites
That overhead are sailing in the sky.
It is in truth an utter solitude;
Nor should I have made mention of this Dell
But for one object which you might pass by,
Might see and notice not. Beside the brook
Appears a straggling heap of unhewn stones!
And to that simple object appertains
A story—unenriched with strange events,
Yet not unfit, I deem, for the fireside,   20
Or for the summer shade. It was the first
Of those domestic tales that spake to me
Of Shepherds, dwellers in the valleys, men
Whom I already loved;—not verily
For their own sakes, but for the fields and hills
Where was their occupation and abode.
And hence this Tale, while I was yet a Boy
Careless of books, yet having felt the power

1 A Ghyll is a steep, narrow valley with a stream running through it.—(Wordsworth.)

Of Nature, by the gentle agency
Of natural objects, led me on to feel   30
For passions that were not my own, and think
(At random and imperfectly indeed)
On man, the heart of man, and human life.
Therefore, although it be a history
Homely and rude, I will relate the same
For the delight of a few natural hearts;
And, with yet fonder feeling, for the sake
Of youthful Poets, who among these hills
Will be my second self when I am gone.

    Upon the forest-side in Grasmere Vale   40
There dwelt a Shepherd, Michael was his name;
An old man, stout of heart, and strong of limb.
His bodily frame had been from youth to age
Of an unusual strength: his mind was keen,
Intense, and frugal, apt for all affairs,
And in his shepherd's calling he was prompt
And watchful more than ordinary men.
Hence had he learned the meaning of all winds,
Of blasts of every tone; and oftentimes,
When other heeded not, He heard the South   50
Make subterraneous music, like the noise
Of bagpipers on distant Highland hills.
The Shepherd, at such warning, of his flock
Bethought him, and he to himself would say,
'The winds are now devising work for me!'
And, truly, at all times, the storm, that drives
The traveller to a shelter, summoned him
Up to the mountains: he had been alone
Amid the heart of many thousand mists,
That came to him, and left him, on the heights. 60
So lived he till his eightieth year was past.
And grossly that man errs, who should suppose
That the green valleys, and the streams and rocks,
Were things indifferent to the Shepherd's thoughts.
Fields, where with cheerful spirits he had breathed
The common air; hills, which with vigorous step
He had so often climbed; which had impressed
So many incidents upon his mind
Of hardship, skill or courage, joy or fear;
Which, like a book, preserved the memory   70
Of the dumb animals, whom he had saved,
Had fed or sheltered, linking to such acts
The certainty of honourable gain;
Those fields, those hills—what could they less? had laid
Strong hold on his affections, were to him
A pleasurable feeling of blind love,
The pleasure which there is in life itself.

    His days had not been passed in singleness.
His Helpmate was a comely matron, old—
Though younger than himself full twenty years. 80

She was a woman of a stirring life,
Whose heart was in her house: two wheels she had
Of antique form; this large, for spinning wool;
That small, for flax; and, if one wheel had rest,
It was because the other was at work.
The Pair had but one inmate in their house,
An only Child, who had been born to them
When Michael, telling o'er his years, began
To deem that he was old,—in shepherd's phrase,
With one foot in the grave. This only Son,   90
With two brave sheep-dogs tried in many a storm,
The one of an inestimable worth,
Made all their household. I may truly say,
That they were as a proverb in the vale
For endless industry. When day was gone,
And from their occupations out of doors
The Son and Father were come home, even then,
Their labour did not cease; unless when all
Turned to the cleanly supper-board, and there,
Each with a mess of pottage and skimmed milk, 100
Sat round the basket piled with oaten cakes,
And their plain home-made cheese. Yet when the meal
Was ended, Luke (for so the Son was named)
And his old Father both betook themselves
To such convenient work as might employ
Their hands by the fire-side; perhaps to card
Wool for the Housewife's spindle, or repair
Some injury done to sickle, flail, or scythe,
Or other implement of house or field.

    Down from the ceiling, by the chimney's edge,   110
That in our ancient uncouth country style
With huge and black projection overbrowed
Large space beneath, as duly as the light
Of day grew dim the Housewife hung a lamp;
An aged utensil, which had performed
Service beyond all others of its kind.
Early at evening did it burn—and late,
Surviving comrade of uncounted hours,
Which, going by from year to year, had found,
And left, the couple neither gay perhaps   120
Nor cheerful, yet with objects and with hopes,
Living a life of eager industry.
And now, when Luke had reached his eighteenth year,
There by the light of this old lamp they sate,
Father and Son, while far into the night
The Housewife plied her own peculiar work,
Making the cottage through the silent hours
Murmur as with the sound of summer flies.
This light was famous in its neighbourhood,
And was a public symbol of the life   130
That thrifty Pair had lived. For, as it chanced,

Their cottage on a plot of rising ground
Stood single, with large prospect, north and south,
High into Easedale, up to Dunmail-Raise,
And westward to the village near the lake;
And from this constant light, so regular,
And so far seen, the House itself, by all
Who dwelt within the limits of the vale,
Both old and young, was named THE EVENING
    STAR.

   Thus living on through such a length of
    years   140
The Shepherd, if he loved himself, must needs
Have loved his Helpmate; but to Michael's heart
This son of his old age was yet more dear—
Less from instinctive tenderness, the same
Fond spirit that blindly works in the blood of all—
Than that a child, more than all other gifts
That earth can offer to declining man,
Brings hope with it, and forward-looking thoughts,
And stirrings of inquietude, when they
By tendency of nature needs must fail.   150
Exceeding was the love he bare to him,
His heart and his heart's joy! For oftentimes
Old Michael, while he was a babe in arms,
Had done him female service, not alone
For pastime and delight, as is the use
Of fathers, but with patient mind enforced
To acts of tenderness; and he had rocked
His cradle, as with a woman's gentle hand.

   And in a later time, ere yet the Boy
Had put on boy's attire, did Michael love,   160
Albeit of a stern, unbending mind,
To have the Young-one in his sight, when he
Wrought in the field, or on his shepherd's stool
Sate with a fettered sheep before him stretched
Under the large old oak, that near his door
Stood single, and, from matchless depth of shade,
Chosen for the Shearer's covert from the sun,
Thence in our rustic dialect was called
The CLIPPING TREE,[2] a name which yet it bears,
There, while they two were sitting in the shade. 170
With others round them, earnest all and blithe,
Would Michael exercise his heart with looks
Of fond correction and reproof bestowed
Upon the Child, if he disturbed the sheep
By catching at their legs, or with his shouts
Scared them, while they lay still beneath the
    shears.

   And when by Heaven's good grace the boy
    grew up

A healthy Lad, and carried in his cheek
Two steady roses that were five years old;
Then Michael from a winter coppice cut   180
With his own hand a sapling, which he hooped
With iron, making it throughout in all
Due requisites a perfect shepherd's staff,
And gave it to the Boy; wherewith equipt
He as a watchman oftentimes was placed
At gate or gap, to stem or turn the flock;
And, to his office prematurely called,
There stood the urchin, as you will divine,
Something between a hindrance and a help;
And for this cause not always, I believe,   190
Receiving from his Father hire of praise;
Though nought was left undone which staff, or
    voice,
Or looks, or threatening gestures, could perform.

   But soon as Luke, full ten years old, could stand
Against the mountain blasts; and to the heights,
Not fearing toil, nor length of weary ways,
He with his Father daily went, and they
Were as companions, why should I relate
That objects which the Shepherd loved before
Were dearer now? that from the Boy there
    came   200
Feelings and emanations—things which were
Light to the sun and music to the wind;
And that the old Man's heart seemed born again?

   Thus in his Father's sight the Boy grew up:
And now, when he had reached his eighteenth
    year,
He was his comfort and his daily hope.

   While in this sort the simple household lived
From day to day, to Michael's ear there came
Distressful tidings. Long before the time
Of which I speak, the Shepherd had been
    bound   210
In surety for his brother's son, a man
Of an industrious life, and ample means;
But unforeseen misfortunes suddenly
Had prest upon him; and old Michael now
Was summoned to discharge the forfeiture,
A grievous penalty, but little less
Than half his substance. This unlooked-for claim,
At the first hearing, for a moment took
More hope out of his life than he supposed
That any old man ever could have lost.   220
As soon as he had armed himself with strength
To look his trouble in the face, it seemed
The Shepherd's sole resource to sell at once
A portion of his patrimonial fields.
Such was his first resolve; he thought again,

2 Clipping is the word used in the North of England for shearing.
—(Wordsworth.)

And his heart failed him. 'Isabel,' said he,
Two evenings after he had heard the news,
'I have been toiling more than seventy years,
And in the open sunshine of God's love
Have we all lived; yet, if these fields of ours 230
Should pass into a stranger's hand, I think
That I could not lie quiet in my grave.
Our lot is a hard lot; the sun himself
Has scarcely been more diligent than I;
And I have lived to be a fool at last
To my own family. An evil man
That was, and made an evil choice, if he
Were false to us; and, if he were not false,
There are ten thousand to whom loss like this
Had been no sorrow. I forgive him;—but 240
'Twere better to be dumb than to talk thus.

When I began, my purpose was to speak
Of remedies and of a cheerful hope.
Our Luke shall leave us, Isabel; the land
Shall not go from us, and it shall be free;
He shall possess it, free as is the wind
That passes over it. We have, thou know'st,
Another kinsman—he will be our friend
In this distress. He is a prosperous man,
Thriving in trade—and Luke to him shall go, 250
And with his kinsman's help and his own thrift
He quickly will repair this loss, and then
He may return to us. If here he stay,
What can be done? Where every one is poor,
What can be gained?'
                    At this the old Man paused,
And Isabel sat silent, for her mind
Was busy, looking back into past times.
There's Richard Bateman, thought she to herself,
He was a parish-boy—at the church-door
They made a gathering for him, shillings,
       pence, 260
And halfpennies, wherewith the neighbours
       bought
A basket, which they filled with pedlar's wares;
And, with this basket on his arm, the lad
Went up to London, found a master there,
Who, out of many, chose the trusty boy
To go and overlook his merchandise
Beyond the seas; where he grew wondrous rich,
And left estates and monies to the poor,
And, at his birth-place, built a chapel floored
With marble, which he sent from foreign
       lands. 270
These thoughts, and many others of like sort,
Passed quickly through the mind of Isabel,
And her face brightened. The old Man was glad,
And thus resumed:—'Well, Isabel! this scheme
These two days has been meat and drink to me.

Far more than we have lost is left us yet.
—We have enough—I wish indeed that I
Were younger;—but this hope is a good hope.
Make ready Luke's best garments, of the best
Buy for him more, and let us send him forth 280
To-morrow, or the next day, or to-night:
       If he *could* go, the Boy should go tonight.'

       Here Michael ceased, and to the fields went
              forth
With a light heart. The Housewife for five days
Was restless morn and night, and all day long
Wrought on with her best fingers to prepare
Things needful for the journey of her son.
But Isabel was glad when Sunday came
To stop her in her work: for, when she lay
By Michael's side, she through the last two
       nights 290
Heard him, how he was troubled in his sleep:
And when they rose at morning she could see
That all his hopes were gone. That day at noon
She said to Luke, while they two by themselves
Were sitting at the door, 'Thou must not go:
We have no other Child but thee to lose,
None to remember—do not go away,
For if thou leave thy Father he will die.'
The Youth made answer with a jocund voice;
And Isabel, when she had told her fears, 300
Recovered heart. That evening her best fare
Did she bring forth, and all together sat
Like happy people round a Christmas fire.

       With daylight Isabel resumed her work;
And all the ensuing week the house appeared
As cheerful as a grove in Spring: at length
The expected letter from their kinsman came,
With kind assurances that he would do
His utmost for the welfare of the Boy;
To which, requests were added, that
       forthwith 310
He might be sent to him. Ten times or more
The letter was read over; Isabel
Went forth to show it to the neighbours round;
Nor was there at that time on English land
A prouder heart than Luke's. When Isabel
Had to her house returned, the old Man said,
'He shall depart to-morrow.' To this word
The Housewife answered, talking much of things
Which, if at such short notice he should go,
Would surely be forgotten. But at length 320
She gave consent, and Michael was at ease.

       Near the tumultuous brook of Green-head
              Ghyll,
In that deep valley, Michael had designed

To build a Sheep-fold; and, before he heard
The tidings of his melancholy loss,
For this same purpose he had gathered up
A heap of stones, which by the streamlet's edge
Lay thrown together, ready for the work.
With Luke that evening thitherward he walked:
And soon as they had reached the place he
    stopped   330
And thus the old Man spake to him:—'My son,
To-morrow thou wilt leave me: with full heart
I look upon thee, for thou art the same
That wert a promise to me ere thy birth,
And all thy life hast been my daily joy.
I will relate to thee some little part
Of our two histories; 'twill do thee good
When thou art from me, even if I should touch
On things thou canst not know of.——After thou
First cam'st into the world—as oft befalls   340
To new-born infants—thou didst sleep away
Two days, and blessings from thy Father's tongue
Then fell upon thee. Day by day passed on,
And still I loved thee with increasing love.
Never to living ear came sweeter sounds
Than when I heard thee by our own fireside
First uttering, without words, a natural tune;
While thou, a feeding babe, didst in thy joy
Sing at thy Mother's breast. Month followed
    month,
And in the open fields my life was passed   350
And on the mountains; else I think that thou
Hadst been brought up upon thy Father's knees.
But we were playmates, Luke: among these hills,
As well thou knowest, in us the old and young
Have played together, nor with me didst thou
Lack any pleasure which a boy can know.'
Luke had a manly heart; but at these words
He sobbed aloud. The old Man grasped his hand,
And said, 'Nay, do not take it so—I see
That these are things of which I need not
    speak.   360
—Even to the utmost I have been to thee
A kind and a good Father: and herein
I but repay a gift which I myself
Received at others' hands; for, though now old
Beyond the common life of man, I still
Remember them who loved me in my youth.
Both of them sleep together: here they lived,
As all their Forefathers had done; and, when
At length their time was come, they were not loth
To give their bodies to the family mould.   370
I wished that thou shouldst live the life they
    lived,
But 'tis a long time to look back, my Son,
And see so little gain from threescore years.

Till I was forty years of age, not more
Than half of my inheritance was mine.
I toiled and toiled; God blessed me in my work,
And till these three weeks past the land was free
—It looks as if it never could endure
Another Master. Heaven forgive me, Luke,   380
If I judge ill for thee, but it seems good
That thou should'st go.'
                  At this the old Man paused;
Then, pointing to the stones near which they
    stood,
Thus, after a short silence, he resumed:
'This was a work for us; and now, my Son,
It is a work for me. But, lay one stone—
Here, lay it for me, Luke, with thine own hands.
Nay, Boy, be of good hope;—we both may live
To see a better day. At eighty-four
I still am strong and hale;—do thou thy part;   390
I will do mine.—I will begin again
With many tasks that were resigned to thee:
Up to the heights, and in among the storms,
Will I without thee go again, and do
All works which I was wont to do alone,
Before I knew thy face.—Heaven bless thee, Boy!
Thy heart these two weeks has been beating fast
With many hopes; it should be so—yes—yes—
I knew that thou couldst never have a wish
To leave me, Luke: thou hast been bound to
    me   400
Only by links of love: when thou art gone,
What will be left to us!—But I forget
My purposes. Lay now the corner-stone,
As I requested; and hereafter, Luke,
When thou art gone away, should evil men
Be thy companions, think of me, my Son,
And of this moment; hither turn thy thoughts,
And God will strengthen thee: amid all fear
And all temptation, Luke, I pray that thou
May'st bear in mind the life thy Fathers
    lived,   410
Who, being innocent, did for that cause
Bestir them in good deeds. Now, fare thee well—
When thou return'st, thou in this place wilt see
A work which is not here: a covenant
'Twill be between us; but, whatever fate
Befall thee, I shall love thee to the last,
And bear thy memory with me to the grave.'

    The Shepherd ended here; and Luke stooped
    down,
And, as his Father had requested, laid
The first stone of the Sheep-fold. At the
    sight   420
The old Man's grief broke from him; to his heart

He pressed his Son, he kissèd him and wept;
And to the house together they returned.
—Hushed was that House in peace, or seeming
    peace,
Ere the night fell:—with morrow's dawn the Boy
Began his journey, and, when he had reached
The public way, he put on a bold face;
And all the neighbours, as he passed their doors,
Came forth with wishes and with farewell
    prayers,
That followed him till he was out of sight.   430

A good report did from their Kinsman come,
Of Luke and his well-doing: and the Boy
Wrote loving letters, full of wondrous news,
Which, as the Housewife phrased it, were
    throughout
'The prettiest letters that were ever seen.'
Both parents read them with rejoicing hearts.
So, many months passed on: and once again
The Shepherd went about his daily work
With confident and cheerful thoughts, and
    now
Sometimes when he could find a leisure
    hour   440
He to the valley took his way, and there
Wrought at the Sheep-fold. Meantime Luke be-
    gan
To slacken in his duty; and, at length,
He in the dissolute city gave himself
To evil courses: ignominy and shame
Fell on him, so that he was driven at last
To seek a hiding-place beyond the seas.

There is a comfort in the strength of love;
'Twill make a thing endurable, which else
Would overset the brain, or break the heart;   450
I have conversed with more than one who
    well
Remember the old Man, and what he was
Years after he had heard this heavy news.
His bodily frame had been from youth to age
Of an unusual strength. Among the rocks
He went, and still looked up to sun and cloud,
And listened to the wind; and, as before,
Performed all kinds of labour for his sheep,
And for the land, his small inheritance.
And to that hollow dell from time to time   460
Did he repair, to build the Fold of which
His flock had need. 'Tis not forgotten yet
The pity which was then in every heart
For the old Man—and 'tis believed by all
That many and many a day he thither went,
And never lifted up a single stone.

There, by the Sheep-fold, sometimes was he
    seen
Sitting alone, or with his faithful Dog,
Then old, beside him, lying at his feet.
The length of full seven years, from time to
    time,   470
He at the building of this Sheep-fold wrought,
And left the work unfinished when he died.
Three years, or little more, did Isabel
Survive her Husband: at her death the estate
Was sold, and went into a stranger's hand.
The Cottage which was named THE EVENING
    STAR
Is gone—the ploughshare has been through the
    ground
On which it stood; great changes have been
    wrought
In all the neighbourhood:—yet the oak is left
That grew beside their door; and the remains 480
Of the unfinished Sheep-fold may be seen
Beside the boisterous brook of Green-head
    Ghyll.

1800   1800

'TIS SAID THAT SOME HAVE DIED FOR LOVE

'TIS said that some have died for love:
And here and there a churchyard grave is found
In the cold north's unhallowed ground,
Because the wretched man himself had slain,
His love was such a grievous pain.
And there is one whom I five years have known;
He dwells alone
Upon Helvellyn's side:
He loved—the pretty Barbara died;
And thus he makes his moan: 10
Three years had Barbara in her grave been laid
When thus his moan he made:

'Oh, move, thou Cottage, from behind that oak!
Or let the aged tree uprooted lie,
That in some other way yon smoke
May mount into the sky!
The clouds pass on; they from the heavens de-
    part:
I look—the sky is empty space;
I know not what I trace;
But when I cease to look, my hand is on my
    heart.   20

'O! what a weight is in these shades! Ye leaves,
That murmur once so dear, when will it cease?
Your sound my heart of rest bereaves,

It robs my heart of peace.
Thou Thrush, that singest loud—and loud and
    free,
Into yon row of willows flit,
Upon that alder sit;
Or sing another song, or choose another tree.

'Roll back, sweet Rill! back to thy mountain-
    bounds,
And there for ever be thy waters chained!   30
For thou dost haunt the air with sounds
That cannot be sustained;
If still beneath that pine-tree's ragged bough
Headlong yon waterfall must come,
Oh let it then be dumb!
Be anything, sweet Rill, but that which thou art
    now.

'Thou Eglantine, so bright with sunny showers,
Proud as a rainbow spanning half the vale,
Thou one fair shrub, oh! shed thy flowers,
And stir not in the gale.   40
For thus to see thee nodding in the air
To see thy arch thus stretch and bend,
Thus rise and thus descend,—
Disturbs me till the sight is more than I can bear.'

The Man who makes this feverish complaint
Is one of giant stature, who could dance
Equipped from head to foot in iron mail.
Ah gentle Love! if ever thought was thine
To store up kindred hours for me, thy face
Turn from me, gentle Love! nor let me walk   50
Within the sound of Emma's voice, nor know
Such happiness as I have known to-day.

1800   1800

THE SPARROW'S NEST

Written in the Orchard, Town-end, Grasmere. At the
end of the garden of my father's house at Cockermouth
was a high terrace that commanded a fine view of the
river Derwent and Cockermouth Castle. This was our
favourite play-ground. The terrace-wall, a low one, was
covered with closely-clipped privet and roses, which gave
an almost impervious shelter to birds that built their
nests there. The latter of these stanzas alludes to one of
those nests.—(Wordsworth.)

BEHOLD, within the leafy shade,
Those bright blue eggs together laid!
On me the chance-discovered sight
Gleamed like a vision of delight.
I started—seeming to espy
The home and sheltered bed,

The Sparrow's dwelling, which, hard by
My Father's house, in wet or dry
My sister Emmeline and I
    Together visited.   10

She looked at it and seemed to fear it;
Dreading, tho' wishing, to be near it:
Such heart was in her, being then
A little Prattler among men.
The Blessing of my later years
Was with me when a boy:
She gave me eyes, she gave me ears;
And humble cares, and delicate fears;
A heart, the fountain of sweet tears;
    And love, and thought, and joy.   20

1800   1800

LOUISA[1]

AFTER ACCOMPANYING HER ON A MOUNTAIN EXCURSION

I MET Louisa in the shade,
And, having seen that lovely Maid,
Why should I fear to say
That, nymph-like, she is fleet and strong,
And down the rocks can leap along
Like rivulets in May?

And she hath smiles to earth unknown;
Smiles, that with motion of their own
Do spread, and sink, and rise;
That come and go with endless play,   10
And ever, as they pass away,
Are hidden in her eyes.

She loves her fire, her cottage-home;
Yet o'er the moorland will she roam
In weather rough and bleak;
And, when against the wind she strains,
Oh! might I kiss the mountain rains
That sparkle on her cheek.

Take all that's mine 'beneath the moon,'
If I with her but half a noon   20
May sit beneath the walls
Of some old cave, or mossy nook,
When up she winds along the brook
To hunt the waterfalls.

1801   1807

1 Mary Hutchinson, the poet's wife, and Joanna Hutchinson, her
sister, have each been identified as the original of Louisa. De Selincourt thinks it is most probable that *Louisa* and *To a Young
Lady* are in part fancy pictures, but that Dorothy was chiefly in
Wordsworth's thoughts as he wrote.

TO A YOUNG LADY

WHO HAD BEEN REPROACHED FOR TAKING LONG
WALKS IN THE COUNTRY

Composed at the same time and on the same view as
'I met Louisa in the shade': indeed they were designed
to make one piece.—(Wordsworth.)

DEAR Child of Nature, let them rail!
—There is a nest in a green dale,
A harbour and a hold;
Where thou, a Wife and Friend, shalt see
Thy own heart-stirring days, and be
A light to young and old.

There, healthy as a shepherd boy,
And treading among flowers of joy
Which at no season fade,
Thou, while thy babes around thee cling,   10
Shalt show us how divine a thing
A Woman may be made.

Thy thoughts and feelings shall not die,
Nor leave thee, when grey hairs are nigh,
A melancholy slave;
But an old age serene and bright,
And lovely as a Lapland night,
Shall lead thee to thy grave.

1801   1802

TO THE CUCKOO

Composed in the orchard, Town-end, Grasmere.—
(Wordsworth.)

O BLITHE New-comer! I have heard,
I hear thee and rejoice.
O Cuckoo! shall I call thee Bird,
Or but a wandering Voice?

While I am lying on the grass
Thy twofold shout I hear;
From hill to hill it seems to pass
At once far off, and near.

Though babbling only to the Vale,
Of sunshine and of flowers,   10
Thou bringest unto me a tale
Of visionary hours.

Thrice welcome, darling of the Spring!
Even yet thou art to me
No bird, but an invisible thing,
A voice, a mystery;

The same whom in my schoolboy days
I listend to; that Cry
Which made me look a thousand ways
In bush, and tree, and sky.   20

To seek thee did I often rove
Through woods and on the green;
And thou wert still a hope, a love;
Still longed for, never seen.

And I can listen to thee yet;
Can lie upon the plain
And listen, till I do beget
That golden time again.

O blessèd Bird! the earth we pace
Again appears to be   30
An unsubstantial, faery place;
That is fit home for Thee!

1802   1807

MY HEART LEAPS UP WHEN I BEHOLD

Written at Town-end, Grasmere.—(Wordsworth.)

My heart leaps up when I behold
    A rainbow in the sky:
So was it when my life began;
So is it now I am a man;
So be it when I shall grow old,
    Or let me die!
The Child is father of the Man;
And I could wish my days to be
Bound each to each by natural piety.

26 March, 1802   1807

WRITTEN IN MARCH

WHILE RESTING ON THE BRIDGE AT THE
FOOT OF BROTHER'S WATER

[Dorothy records in her *Journal* for 16 April (Good
Friday) the circumstances under which this poem was
composed: 'When we came to the foot of Brother's
Water, I left William sitting on the bridge. . . . When I
returned I found William writing a poem descriptive of
the sights and sounds we saw and heard. There was the
gentle flowing of the stream, the glittering, lively lake,
green fields without a living creature to be seen on them,
behind us, a flat pasture with forty-two cattle feeding.
. . . The people were at work ploughing, harrowing,
and sowing; lasses working, a dog barking now and then;
cocks crowing, birds twittering; the snow in patches at
the top of the highest hills. . . . William finished the poem
before we got to the foot of Kirkstone.']

THE Cock is crowing,
The stream is flowing,

The small birds twitter,
The lake doth glitter,
The green field sleeps in the sun;
The oldest and youngest
Are at work with the strongest;
The cattle are grazing,
Their heads never raising;
There are forty feeding like one!   10

Like an army defeated
The snow hath retreated,
And now doth fare ill
On the top of the bare hill;
The Ploughboy is whooping—anon—anon:
There's joy in the mountains;
There's life in the fountains;
Small clouds are sailing,
Blue sky prevailing;
The rain is over and gone!   20

1802   1807

TO A BUTTERFLY

Written in the orchard, Town-end, Grasmere. My
sister and I were parted immediately after the death of
our mother, who died in 1778, both being very young.—
(Wordsworth.)

I

STAY near me—do not take thy flight!
A little longer stay in sight!
Much converse did I find in thee,
Historian of my infancy!
Float near me; do not yet depart!
Dead times revive in thee:
Thou bring'st, gay creature as thou art!
A solemn image to my heart,
My father's family!

Oh! pleasant, pleasant were the days,   10
The time, when in our childish plays,
My sister Emmeline and I
Together chased the butterfly!
A very hunter did I rush
Upon the prey;—with leaps and springs
I followed on from brake to bush;
But she, God love her! feared to brush
The dust from off its wings.

II

I'VE watched you now a full half-hour,
Self-poised upon that yellow flower;
And, little Butterfly! indeed
I know not if you sleep or feed.

How motionless!—not frozen seas
More motionless! and then
What joy awaits you, when the breeze
Hath found you out among the trees,
And calls you forth again!

This plot of orchard-ground is ours;   10
My trees they are, my Sister's flowers;
Here rest your wings when they are weary;
Here lodge as in a sanctuary!
Come often to us, fear no wrong;
Sit near us on the bough!
We'll talk of sunshine and of song,
And summer days, when we were young;
Sweet childish days, that were as long
As twenty days are now.

1802   1807

TO THE SMALL CELANDINE[1]

Written at Town-end, Grasmere. It is remarkable that
this flower, coming out so early in the spring as it does,
and so bright and beautiful, and in such profusion, should
not have been noticed earlier in English verse. What adds
much to the interest that attends it is its habit of shutting
itself up and opening out according to the degree of light
and temperature of the air.—(Wordsworth.)

PANSIES, lilies, kingcups, daisies,
Let them live upon their praises;
Long as there's a sun that sets,
Primroses will have their glory;
Long as there are violets,
They will have a place in story:
There's a flower that shall be mine,
'Tis the little Celandine.

Eyes of some men travel far
For the finding of a star;   10
Up and down the heavens they go,
Men that keep a mighty rout!
I'm as great as they, I trow,
Since the day I found thee out,
Little Flower—I'll make a stir,
Like a sage astronomer.

What love they bore each other.
Modest, yet withal an Elf
Bold, and lavish of thyself;
Since we needs must first have met
I have seen thee, high and low,   20
Thirty years or more, and yet
'Twas a face I did not know;

---

[1] common pilewort, a European herb with flowers resembling a
buttercup.

Thou hast now, go where I may,
Fifty greetings in a day.

Ere a leaf is on a bush,
In the time before the thrush
Has a thought about her nest,
Thou wilt come with half a call,
Spreading out thy glossy breast
Like a careless Prodigal;   30
Telling tales about the sun,
When we've little warmth, or none.

Poets, vain men in their mood!
Travel with the multitude:
Never heed them; I aver
That they all are wanton wooers;
But the thrifty cottager,
Who stirs little out of doors,
Joys to spy thee near her home;
Spring is coming, Thou art come!   40

Comfort have thou of thy merit,
Kindly, unassuming Spirit!
Careless of thy neighbourhood,
Thou dost show thy pleasant face
On the moor, and in the wood,
In the lane;—there's not a place,
Howsoever mean it be,
But 'tis good enough for thee.

Ill befall the yellow flowers,
Children of the flaring hours!   50
Buttercups, that will be seen,
Whether we will see or no;
Others, too, of lofty mien;
They have done as worldlings do,
Taken praise that should be thine,
Little, humble Celandine.

Prophet of delight and mirth,
Ill-requited upon earth;
Herald of a mighty band,
Of a joyous train ensuing,   60
Serving at my heart's command,
Tasks that are no tasks renewing,
I will sing, as doth behove,
Hymns in praise of what I love!

1802   1807

TO THE SAME FLOWER

PLEASURES newly found are sweet
When they lie about our feet:
February last, my heart

First at sight of thee was glad;
All unheard of as thou art,
Thou must needs, I think, have had,
Celandine! and long ago,
Praise of which I nothing know.

I have not a doubt but he,
Whosoe'er the man might be,   10
Who the first with pointed rays
(Workman worthy to be sainted)
Set the sign-board in a blaze,
When the rising sun he painted,
Took the fancy from a glance
At thy glittering countenance.

Soon as gentle breezes bring
News of winter's vanishing,
And the children build their bowers,
Sticking 'kerchief-plots of mould   20
All about with full-blown flowers,
Thick as sheep in shepherd's fold!
With the proudest thou art there,
Mantling in the tiny square.

Often have I sighed to measure
By myself a lonely pleasure,
Sighed to think I read a book
Only read, perhaps, by me;
Yet I long could overlook
Thy bright coronet and Thee,   30
And thy arch and wily ways,
And thy store of other praise.

Blithe of heart, from week to week
Thou dost play at hide-and-seek;
While the patient primrose sits
Like a beggar in the cold,
Thou, a flower of wiser wits,
Slip'st into thy sheltering hold;
Liveliest of the vernal train
When ye all are out again.   40

Drawn by what peculiar spell,
By what charm of sight or smell,
Does the dim-eyed curious Bee,
Labouring for her waxen cells,
Fondly settle upon Thee
Prized above all buds and bells
Opening daily at thy side,
By the season multiplied?

Thou art not beyond the moon,
But a thing 'beneath our shoon';   50
Let the bold Discoverer thrid

In his bark the polar sea;
Rear who will a pyramid;
Praise it is enough for me,
If there be but three or four
Who will love my little Flower.

1802   1807

STANZAS

WRITTEN IN MY POCKET COPY OF THOMSON'S 'CASTLE OF INDOLENCE'

[Dorothy stated that these stanzas were about Coleridge and her brother.]

WITHIN our happy Castle there dwelt One
Whom without blame I may not overlook;
For never sun on living creature shone
Who more devout enjoyment with us took:
Here on his hours he hung as on a book,
On his own time here would he float away,
As doth a fly upon a summer brook;
But go to-morrow, or belike to-day,
Seek for him,—he is fled; and whither none can
     say.

Thus often would he leave our peaceful home, 10
And find elsewhere his business or delight;
Out of our Valley's limits did he roam:
Full many a time, upon a stormy night,
His voice came to us from the neighbouring height:
Oft could we see him driving full in view
At mid-day when the sun was shining bright;
What ill was on him, what he had to do,
A mighty wonder bred among our quiet crew.

Ah! piteous sight it was to see this Man
When he came back to us, a withered flower,— 20
Or like a sinful creature, pale and wan.
Down would he sit; and without strength or power
Look at the common grass from hour to hour:
And oftentimes, how long I fear to say,
Where apple-trees in blossom made a bower,
Retired in that sunshiny shade he lay;
And, like a naked Indian, slept himself away.

Great wonder to our gentle tribe it was
Whenever from our Valley he withdrew;
For happier soul no living creature has   30
Than he had, being here the long day through.
Some thought he was a lover, and did woo:
Some thought far worse of him, and judged him
     wrong;
But verse was what he had been wedded to;
And his own mind did like a tempest strong
Come to him thus, and drove the weary Wight
     along.

With him there often walked in friendly guise,
Or lay upon the moss by brook or tree,
A noticeable Man with large grey eyes,
And a pale face that seemed undoubtedly   40
As if a blooming face it ought to be;
Heavy his low-hung lip did oft appear,
Deprest by weight of musing Phantasy;
Profound his forehead was, though not severe;
Yet some did think that he had little business here:

Sweet heaven forefend! his was a lawful right;
Noisy he was, and gamesome as a boy;
His limbs would toss about him with delight,
Like branches when strong winds the trees annoy.
Nor lacked his calmer hours device or toy   50
To banish listlessness and irksome care; ·
He would have taught you how you might employ
Yourself; and many did to him repair,—
And certes not in vain; he had inventions rare.

Expedients, too, of simplest sort he tried:
Long blades of grass, plucked round him as he lay,
Made, to his ear attentively applied,
A pipe on which the wind would deftly play;
Glasses he had, that little things display,
The beetle panoplied in gems and gold,   60
A mailèd angel on a battle-day;
The mysteries that cups of flowers enfold,
And all the gorgeous sights which fairies do be-
     hold.

He would entice that other Man to hear
His music, and to view his imagery:
And, sooth, these two were each to the other dear:
No livelier love in such a place could be:
There did they dwell—from earthly labour free,
As happy spirits as were ever seen;
If but a bird, to keep them company,   70
Or butterfly sate down, they were, I ween,
As pleased as if the same had been a Maiden-
     queen.

1802   1815

RESOLUTION AND INDEPENDENCE

Written at Town-end, Grasmere. This old Man I met
a few hundred yards from my cottage; and the account
of him is taken from his own mouth. I was in the state of
feeling described in the beginning of the poem, while
crossing over Barton Fell from Mr. Clarkson's, at the
foot of Ullswater, toward Askham. The image of the
hare I then observed on the ridge of the Fell.—(Wordsworth.)
[Dorothy records in her *Journal* (3 October 1800) the
incident upon which the poem was founded: 'When

William and I returned, we met an old man almost double. . . . He was of Scotch parents, but had been born in
the army. He had had a wife, and "she was a good
woman, and it pleased God to bless us with ten children."
All these were dead but one, of whom he had not heard
for many years, a sailor. His trade was to gather leeches,
but now leeches were scarce, and he had not strength for
it. He lived by begging, and was making his way to Carlisle, where he should buy a few godly books to sell. He
said leeches were very scarce, partly owing to this dry
season, but many years they have been scarce. . . . He
had been hurt in driving a cart, his leg broken, his body
driven over, his skull fractured. He felt no pain till he recovered from his first insensibility. . . . It was then late in
the evening when the light was just going away.']

THERE was a roaring in the wind all night;
The rain came heavily and fell in floods;
But now the sun is rising calm and bright;
The birds are singing in the distant woods;
Over his own sweet voice the Stock-dove broods;
The Jay makes answer as the Magpie chatters;
And all the air is filled with pleasant noise of
    waters.

All things that love the sun are out of doors;
The sky rejoices in the morning's birth;
The grass is bright with rain-drops;—on the
    moors   10
The hare is running races in her mirth;
And with her feet she from the plashy earth
Raises a mist; that, glittering in the sun,
Runs with her all the way, wherever she doth run.

I was a Traveller then upon the moor;
I saw the hare that raced about with joy;
I heard the woods and distant waters roar;
Or heard them not, as happy as a boy:
The pleasant season did my heart employ:
My old remembrances went from me wholly; 20
And all the ways of men, so vain and melancholy.

But, as it sometimes chanceth, from the might
Of joy in minds that can no further go,
As high as we have mounted in delight
In our dejection do we sink as low;
To me that morning did it happen so;
And fears and fancies thick upon me came;
Dim sadness—and blind thoughts, I knew not,
    nor could name.

I heard the sky-lark warbling in the sky;
And I bethought me of the playful hare: 30
Even such a happy Child of earth am I;
Even as these blissful creatures do I fare;
Far from the world I walk, and from all care;
But there may come another day to me—
Solitude, pain of heart, distress, and poverty.

My whole life I have lived in pleasant thought,
As if life's business were a summer mood;
As if all needful things would come unsought
To genial faith, still rich in genial good;
But how can He expect that others should 40
Build for him, sow for him, and at his call
Love him, who for himself will take no heed at all?

I thought of Chatterton, the marvellous Boy,
The sleepless Soul that perished in his pride;
Of Him[1] who walked in glory and in joy
Following his plough, along the mountain-side:
By our own spirits are we deified:
We Poets in our youth begin in gladness;
But thereof come in the end despondency and
    madness.

Now, whether it were by peculiar grace, 50
A leading from above, a something given,
Yet it befell that, in this lonely place,
When I with these untoward thoughts had striven,
Beside a pool bare to the eye of heaven
I saw a Man before me unawares:
The oldest man he seemed that ever wore grey
    hairs.

As a huge stone is sometimes seen to lie
Couched on the bald top of an eminence;
Wonder to all who do the same espy,
By what means it could thither come, and
    whence; 60
So that it seems a thing endued with sense:
Like a sea-beast crawled forth, that on a shelf
Of rock or sand reposeth, there to sun itself;

Such seemed this Man, not all alive nor dead,
Nor all asleep—in his extreme old age:
His body was bent double, feet and head
Coming together in life's pilgrimage;
As if some dire constraint of pain, or rage
Of sickness felt by him in times long past,
A more than human weight upon his frame
    had cast. 70

Himself he propped, limbs, body, and pale face,
Upon a long grey staff of shaven wood:
And, still as I drew near with gentle pace,
Upon the margin of that moorish flood
Motionless as a cloud the old Man stood,
That heareth not the loud winds when they call;
And moveth all together, if it move at all.

At length, himself unsettling, he the pond
Stirred with his staff, and fixedly did look

[1] Robert Burns.

Upon the muddy water, which he conned,   80
As if he had been reading in a book:
And now a stranger's privilege I took;
And, drawing to his side, to him did say,
'This morning gives us promise of a glorious day.'

A gentle answer did the old Man make,
In courteous speech which forth he slowly drew:
And him with further words I thus bespake,
'What occupation do you there pursue?
This is a lonesome place for one like you.'
Ere he replied, a flash of mild surprise   90
Broke from the sable orbs of his yet-vivid eyes.

His words came feebly, from a feeble chest,
But each in solemn order followed each,
With something of a lofty utterance drest—
Choice word and measured phrase, above the
      reach
Of ordinary men; a stately speech;
Such as grave Livers do in Scotland use,
Religious men, who give to God and man their
      dues.

He told, that to these waters he had come
To gather leeches, being old and poor: 100
Employment hazardous and wearisome!
And he had many hardships to endure:
From pond to pond he roamed, from moor to
      moor;
Housing, with God's good help, by choice or
      chance;
And in this way he gained an honest maintenance.

The old Man still stood talking by my side;
But now his voice to me was like a stream
Scarce heard; nor word from word could I divide;
And the whole body of the Man did seem
Like one whom I had met with in a dream;   110
Or like a man from some far region sent,
To give me human strength, by apt admonish-
      ment.

My former thoughts returned: the fear that kills;
And hope that is unwilling to be fed;
Cold, pain, and labour, and all fleshly ills;
And mighty Poets in their misery dead.
—Perplexed, and longing to be comforted,
My question eagerly did I renew,
'How is it that you live, and what is it you do?'

He with a smile did then his words repeat;   120
And said that, gathering leeches, far and wide
He travelled; stirring thus about his feet
The waters of the pools where they abide.

'Once I could meet with them on every side;
But they have dwindled long by slow decay;
Yet still I persevere, and find them where I may.'

While he was talking thus, the lonely place,
The old Man's shape, and speech—all troubled
      me:
In my mind's eye I seemed to see him pace
About the weary moors continually,   130
Wandering about alone and silently.
While I these thoughts within myself pursued,
He, having made a pause, the same discourse re-
      newed.

And soon with this he other matter blended,
Cheerfully uttered, with demeanour kind,
But stately in the main; and, when he ended,
I could have laughed myself to scorn to find
In that decrepit Man so firm a mind.
'God,' said I, 'be my help and stay secure;
I'll think of the Leech-gatherer on the lonely
      moor!'   140

1802   1807

I GRIEVED FOR BUONAPARTÉ

I GRIEVED for Buonaparté, with a vain
And an unthinking grief! The tenderest mood
Of that Man's mind—what can it be? what food
Fed his first hopes? what knowledge could *he*
      gain?
'Tis not in battles that from youth we train
The Governor who must be wise and good,
And temper with the sternness of the brain
Thoughts motherly, and meek as womanhood.
Wisdom doth live with children round her knees:
Books, leisure, perfect freedom, and the talk   10
Man holds with week-day man in the hourly walk
Of the mind's business: these are the degrees
By which true Sway doth mount; this is the stalk
True Power doth grow on; and her rights are these.

1802   1802

COMPOSED UPON WESTMINSTER
BRIDGE

3 SEPTEMBER, 1802[1]

EARTH has not anything to show more fair:
Dull would he be of soul who could pass by

---

1 This sonnet actually was composed 31 July on the way to
France. Dowden suggests that Wordsworth could hardly have forgotten either the occasion or the date, and that possibly he considered July with its 'fierce light' less in harmony with the sonnet
than the more subdued light of September. For an account of the
composition of this and the next two sonnets see Dorothy's *Journal* for July 1802, text, p. 453.

A sight so touching in its majesty:
This City now doth, like a garment, wear
The beauty of the morning; silent, bare,
Ships, towers, domes, theatres, and temples lie
Open unto the fields, and to the sky;
All bright and glittering in the smokeless air.
Never did sun more beautifully steep
In his first splendour, valley, rock, or hill;   16
Ne'er saw I, never felt, a calm so deep!
The river glideth at his own sweet will:
Dear God! the very houses seem asleep;
And all that mighty heart is lying still!

1802   1807

COMPOSED BY THE SEA-SIDE,
NEAR CALAIS, August 1802

Fair Star of evening, Splendour of the west,
Star of my Country!—on the horizon's brink
Thou hangest, stooping, as might seem, to sink
On England's bosom; yet well pleased to rest,
Meanwhile, and be to her a glorious crest
Conspicuous to the Nations. Thou, I think,
Shouldst be my Country's emblem; and shouldst
    wink,
Bright Star! with laughter on her banners, drest
In thy fresh beauty. There! that dusky spot
Beneath thee, that is England; there she lies.   10
Blessings be on you both! one hope, one lot,
One life, one glory!—I, with many a fear
For my dear Country, many heartfelt sighs,
Among men who do not love her, linger here.

1802   1807

IT IS A BEAUTEOUS EVENING
CALM AND FREE

This was composed on the beach near Calais, in the
autumn of 1802.—(Wordsworth.)

It is a beauteous evening, calm and free,
The holy time is quiet as a Nun
Breathless with adoration; the broad sun
Is sinking down in its tranquillity;
The gentleness of heaven broods o'er the Sea:
Listen! the mighty Being is awake,
And doth with his eternal motion make
A sound like thunder—everlastingly.
Dear Child![1] dear Girl! that walkest with me here,
If thou appear untouched by solemn thought,   10
Thy nature is not therefore less divine:
Thou liest in Abraham's bosom all the year;

---

1 Wordsworth's French daughter, Caroline.

And worshipp'st at the Temple's inner shrine,
God being with thee when we know it not.

1802   1807

ON THE EXTINCTION OF THE
VENETIAN REPUBLIC[1]

Once did She hold the gorgeous east in fee;
And was the safeguard of the west: the worth
Of Venice did not fall below her birth,
Venice, the eldest Child of Liberty.
She was a maiden City, bright and free;
No guile seduced, no force could violate;
And, when she took unto herself a Mate,
She must espouse the everlasting Sea.[2]
And what if she had seen those glories fade,
Those titles vanish, and that strength decay;   10
Yet shall some tribute of regret be paid
When her long life hath reached its final day:
Men are we, and must grieve when even the Shade
Of that which once was great is passed away.

1802   1807

TO TOUSSAINT L'OUVERTURE[1]

Toussaint, the most unhappy man of men!
Whether the whistling Rustic tend his plough
Within thy hearing, or thy head be now
Pillowed in some deep dungeon's earless den;—
O miserable Chieftain! where and when
Wilt thou find patience! Yet die not; do thou
Wear rather in thy bonds a cheerful brow:
Though fallen thyself, never to rise again,
Live, and take comfort. Thou hast left behind
Powers that will work for thee; air, earth, and
    skies;   10
There's not a breathing of the common wind
That will forget thee; thou hast great allies;
Thy friends are exultations, agonies,
And love, and man's unconquerable mind.

1802   1803

---

1 The Venetian republic in 997 became an independent state remaining powerful and free for centuries, the center of prosperous
trade. Its long independence was ended when in 1797 Napoleon
occupied the city and dissolved the republic.
2 In the twelfth century the custom arose whereby the Doge of
Venice wed the Adriatic sea to symbolize the mastery of the city
over it. This annual ceremony, which became one of much magnificence, was performed by a naval procession and the casting of
a gold ring into the water.

---

1 Toussaint, surnamed L'Ouverture, the Opener, was a Negro
slave who freed Haiti from Spanish domination and abolished
slavery there. Later he was treacherously arrested by Napoleon's
order and taken to France, where he died in a dungeon, 1803.

NEAR DOVER

SEPTEMBER 1802

INLAND, within a hollow vale, I stood;
And saw, while sea was calm and air was clear,
The coast of France—the coast of France how
    near!
Drawn almost into frightful neighbourhood.
I shrunk; for verily the barrier flood
Was like a lake, or river bright and fair,
A span of waters; yet what power is there!
What mightiness for evil and for good!
Even so doth God protect us if we be
Virtuous and wise. Winds blow, and waters roll, 10
Strength to the brave, and Power, and Deity;
Yet in themselves are nothing! One decree
Spake laws to *them,* and said that by the soul
Only, the Nations shall be great and free.

1802   1807

IN LONDON, SEPTEMBER 1802

This was written immediately after my return from
France to London, when I could not but be struck, as
here described, with the vanity and parade of our own
country, especially in great towns and cities, as contrasted
with the quiet, and I may say the desolation, that the revolution had produced in France. This must be borne in
mind, or else the reader may think that in this and the
succeeding Sonnets I have exaggerated the mischief engendered and fostered among us by undisturbed wealth.
It would not be easy to conceive with what a depth of
feeling I entered into the struggle carried on by the
Spaniards for their deliverance from the usurped power
of the French. Many times have I gone from Allan Bank
in Grasmere vale, where we were then residing, to the
top of the Raise-gap as it is called, so late as two o'clock
in the morning, to meet the carrier bringing the newspaper from Keswick. Imperfect traces of the state of
mind in which I then was may be found in my Tract on
the Convention of Cintra, as well as in these Sonnets.—
(Wordsworth.)

O FRIEND! I know not which way I must look
For comfort, being, as I am, opprest,
To think that now our life is only drest
For show; mean handy-work of craftsman, cook,
Or groom!—We must run glittering like a brook
In the open sunshine, or we are unblest:
The wealthiest man among us is the best:
No grandeur now in nature or in book
Delights us. Rapine, avarice, expense,
This is idolatry; and these we adore: 10
Plain living and high thinking are no more:
The homely beauty of the good old cause
Is gone; our peace, our fearful innocence,
And pure religion breathing household laws.

1802   1807

LONDON, 1802

MILTON! thou shouldst be living at this hour:
England hath need of thee: she is a fen
Of stagnant waters: altar, sword, and pen,
Fireside, the heroic wealth of hall and bower,
Have forfeited their ancient English dower
Of inward happiness. We are selfish men;
Oh! raise us up, return to us again;
And give us manners, virtue, freedom, power.
Thy soul was like a Star, and dwelt apart;
Thou hadst a voice whose sound was like the
    sea: 10
Pure as the naked heavens, majestic, free,
So didst thou travel on life's common way,
In cheerful godliness; and yet thy heart
The lowliest duties on herself did lay.

1802   1807

GREAT MEN HAVE BEEN AMONG US

GREAT men have been among us; hands that
    penned
And tongues that uttered wisdom—better none:
The later Sidney, Marvel, Harrington,
Young Vane, and others who called Milton friend.
These moralists could act and comprehend:
They knew how genuine glory was put on;
Taught us how rightfully a nation shone
In splendour: what strength was, that would not
    bend
But in magnanimous meekness. France, 'tis
    strange,
Hath brought forth no such souls as we had
    then.   10
Perpetual emptiness! unceasing change!
No single volume paramount, no code,
No master spirit, no determined road;
But equally a want of books and men!

1802   1807

IT IS NOT TO BE THOUGHT OF

IT is not to be thought of that the Flood
Of British freedom, which, to the open sea
Of the world's praise, from dark antiquity
Hath flowed, 'with pomp of waters, unwithstood,'
Roused though it be full often to a mood
Which spurns the check of salutary bands,
That this most famous Stream in bogs and sands
Should perish; and to evil and to good
Be lost for ever. In our halls is hung
Armoury of the invincible Knights of old: 10
We must be free or die, who speak the tongue
That Shakspeare spake; the faith and morals hold

Which Milton held.—In every thing we are sprung
Of Earth's first blood, have titles manifold.

1802 or 1803   1803

WHEN I HAVE BORNE IN MEMORY

WHEN I have borne in memory what has tamed
Great Nations, how ennobling thoughts depart
When men change swords for ledgers, and desert
The student's bower for gold, some fears unnamed
I had, my Country—am I to be blamed?
Now, when I think of thee, and what thou art,
Verily, in the bottom of my heart,
Of those unfilial fears I am ashamed.
For dearly must we prize thee; we who find
In thee a bulwark for the cause of men;   10
And I by my affection was beguiled:
What wonder if a Poet now and then,
Among the many movements of his mind,
Felt for thee as a lover or a child!

1802 or 1803   1803

THE WORLD IS TOO MUCH WITH US

THE world is too much with us; late and soon,
Getting and spending, we lay waste our powers:
Little we see in Nature that is ours;
We have given our hearts away, a sordid boon!
This Sea that bares her bosom to the moon;
The winds that will be howling at all hours,
And are up-gathered now like sleeping flowers;
For this, for everything, we are out of tune;
It moves us not.—Great God! I'd rather be
A Pagan suckled in a creed outworn;   10
So might I, standing on this pleasant lea,
Have glimpses that would make me less forlorn;
Have sight of Proteus rising from the sea;
Or hear old Triton blow his wreathèd horn.

c. 1802   1807

TO H. C.[1]

SIX YEARS OLD

O THOU! whose fancies from afar are brought;
Who of thy words dost make a mock apparel,
And fittest to unutterable thought
The breeze-like motion and the self-born carol;
Thou faery voyager! that dost float
In such clear water, that thy boat
May rather seem
To brood on air than on an earthly stream;
Suspended in a stream as clear as sky,
Where earth and heaven do make one imagery;   10

---
[1] Hartley Coleridge, son of Samuel Taylor Coleridge.

O blessèd vision! happy child!
Thou art so exquisitely wild,
I think of thee with many fears
For what may be thy lot in future years.

I thought of times when Pain might be thy
      guest,
Lord of thy house and hospitality;
And Grief, uneasy lover! never rest
But when she sate within the touch of thee.
O too industrious folly!
O vain and causeless melancholy!   20
Nature will either end thee quite;
Or, lengthening out thy season of delight,
Preserve for thee, by individual right,
A young lamb's heart among the full-grown
      flocks.
What hast thou to do with sorrow,
Or the injuries of to-morrow?
Thou art a dew-drop which the morn brings forth,
Ill fitted to sustain unkindly shocks,
Or to be trailed along the soiling earth;
A gem that glitters while it lives,   30
And no forewarning gives;
But, at the touch of wrong, without a strife
Slips in a moment out of life.

1802   1807

TO THE DAISY

'Her divine skill taught me this,
That from every thing I saw
I could some instruction draw,
And raise pleasure to the height
Through the meanest object's sight.
By the murmur of a spring
Or the least bough's rustelling;
By a Daisy whose leaves spread
Shut when Titan goes to bed;
Or a shady bush or tree;
She could more infuse in me
Than all Nature's beauties can
In some other wiser man.'

                              G. WITHER

IN youth from rock to rock I went,
From hill to hill in discontent
Of pleasure high and turbulent,
      Most pleased when most uneasy;
But now my own delights I make,—
My thirst at every rill can slake,
And gladly Nature's love partake
      Of Thee, sweet Daisy!

Thee Winter in the garland wears
That thinly decks his few grey hairs;   10
Spring parts the clouds with softest airs,
　That she may sun thee;
Whole Summer-fields are thine by right;
And Autumn, melancholy Wight!
Doth in thy crimson[1] head delight
　When rains are on thee.

In shoals and bands, a morrice train,[2]
Thou greet'st the traveller in the lane;
Pleased at his greeting thee again;
　Yet nothing daunted,   20
Nor grieved if thou be set at nought:
And oft alone in nooks remote
We meet thee, like a pleasant thought,
　When such are wanted.

Be violets in their secret mews[3]
The flowers the wanton Zephyrs choose;
Proud be the rose, with rains and dews
　Her head impearling,
Thou liv'st with less ambitious aim,
Yet has not gone without thy fame;   30
Thou art indeed by many a claim
　The Poet's darling.

If to a rock from rains he fly,
Or, some bright day of April sky,
Imprisoned by hot sunshine lie
　Near the green holly,
And wearily at length should fare;
He needs but look about, and there
Thou art!—a friend at hand, to scare
　His melancholy.   40

A hundred times, by rock or bower,
Ere thus I have lain couched an hour,
Have I derived from thy sweet power
　Some apprehension;
Some steady love; some brief delight;
Some memory that had taken flight;
Some chime of fancy wrong or right;
　Or stray invention.

If stately passions in me burn,
And one chance look to Thee should turn,   50
I drink out of an humbler urn
　A lowlier pleasure;
The homely sympathy that heeds

The common life our nature breeds;
A wisdom fitted to the needs
　Of hearts at leisure.

Fresh-smitten by the morning ray,
When thou art up, alert and gay,
Then, cheerful Flower! my spirits play
　With kindred gladness: 60
And when, at dusk, by dews opprest
Thou sink'st, the image of thy rest
Hath often eased my pensive breast
　Of careful sadness.

And all day long I number yet,
All seasons through, another debt,
Which I, wherever thou art met,
　To thee am owing;
An instinct call it, a blind sense;
A happy, genial influence,   70
Coming one knows not how, nor whence,
　Nor wither going.

Child of the Year! that round dost run
Thy pleasant course,—when day's begun
As ready to salute the sun
　As lark or leveret,[4]
Thy long-lost praise thou shalt regain;
Nor be less dear to future men
Than in old time;—thou not in vain
　Art Nature's favourite.[5]

1802　　　　　　　　　　　　　　　1807

TO THE SAME FLOWER

With little here to do or see
Of things that in the great world be,
Daisy! again I talk to thee,
　For thou art worthy,
Thou unassuming Common-place
Of Nature, with that homely face,
And yet with something of a grace
　Which love makes for thee!

Oft on the dappled turf at ease
I sit, and play with similes,   10
Loose types of things through all degrees,
　Thoughts of thy raising:
And many a fond and idle name
I give to thee, for praise or blame,

---

1 The English daisy is smaller than the American daisy and has reddish rays.
2 A morris was a rustic dance; a morris train, a procession of morris dancers.
3 hiding places.

4 a young hare.
5 See, in Chaucer and the elder Poets, the honours formerly paid to the flower.—(Wordsworth.)

As is the humour of the game,
  While I am gazing.

A nun demure of lowly port;
Or sprightly maiden, of Love's court,
In thy simplicity the sport
  Of all temptations;   20
A queen in crown of rubies drest;
A starveling in a scanty vest;
Are all, as seems to suit thee best,
  Thy appellations.

A little Cyclops with one eye
Staring to threaten and defy.
That thought comes next—and instantly
  The freak is over,
The shape will vanish—and behold
A silver shield with boss of gold,   30
That spreads itself, some faery bold
  In fight to cover!

I see thee glittering from afar—
And then thou art a pretty star;
Not quite so fair as many are
  In heaven above thee!
Yet like a star, with glittering crest,
Self-poised in air thou seem'st to rest;—
May peace come never to his nest,
  Who shall reprove thee!   40

Bright *Flower!* for by that name at last,
When all my reveries are past,
I call thee, and to that cleave fast,
  Sweet silent creature!
That breath'st with me in sun and air,
Do thou, as thou art wont, repair
My heart with gladness, and a share
  Of thy meek nature!

1802   1807

TO THE DAISY

    This and the other Poems addressed to the same flower were composed at Town-end, Grasmere, during the earlier part of my residence there. I have been censured for the last line but one—'thy function apostolical' —as being little less than profane. How could it be thought so? The word is adopted with reference to its derivation, implying something sent on a mission; and assuredly this little flower, especially when the subject of verse, may be regarded, in its humble degree, as administering both to moral and spiritual purposes.—(Wordsworth.)

BRIGHT Flower! whose home is everywhere,
Bold in maternal Nature's care,

And all the long year through the heir
  Of joy and sorrow;
Methinks that there abides in thee
Some concord with humanity,
Given to no other flower to see
  The forest thorough!

Is it that Man is soon deprest?
A thoughtless Thing! who, once unblest,   10
Does little on his memory rest,
  Or on his reason,
And Thou wouldst teach him how to find
A shelter under every wind,
A hope for times that are unkind
  And every season?

Thou wander'st the wide world about,
Unchecked by pride or scrupulous doubt
With friends to greet thee, or without,
  Yet pleased and willing;   20
Meek, yielding to the occasion's call,
And all things suffering from all,
Thy function apostolical
  In peace fulfilling.

1802   1807

THE GREEN LINNET

BENEATH these fruit-tree boughs that shed
Their snow-white blossoms on my head,
With brightest sunshine round me spread
  Of spring's unclouded weather,
In this sequestered nook how sweet
To sit upon my orchard-seat!
And birds and flowers once more to greet,
  My last year's friends together.

One have I marked, the happiest guest
In all this covert of the blest: 10
Hail to Thee, far above the rest
  In joy of voice and pinion!
Thou, Linnet! in thy green array,
Presiding Spirit here to-day,
Dost lead the revels of the May;
  And this is thy dominion.

While birds, and butterflies, and flowers,
Make all one band of paramours,
Thou, ranging up and down the bowers,
  Art sole in thy employment: 20
A Life, a Presence like the Air,
Scattering thy gladness without care,
Too blest with any one to pair;
  Thyself thy own enjoyment.

Amid yon tuft of hazel trees,
That twinkle to the gusty breeze,
Behold him perched in ecstasies,
    Yet seeming still to hover;
There! where the flutter of his wings
Upon his back and body flings   30
Shadows and sunny glimmerings,
    That cover him all over.

My dazzled sight he oft deceives,
A Brother of the dancing leaves;
Then flits, and from the cottage eaves
    Pours forth his song in gushes;
As if by that exulting strain
He mocked and treated with disdain
The voiceless Form he chose to feign,
    While fluttering in the bushes.   40

1803   1807

YEW-TREES

Written at Grasmere. These yew-trees are still standing, but the spread of that at Lorton is much diminished
by mutilation. I will here mention that a little way up the
hill, on the road leading from Rosthwaite to Stonethwaite
(in Borrowdale), lay the trunk of a yew-tree, which appeared as you approached, so vast was its diameter, like
the entrance of a cave, and not a small one. Calculating
upon what I have observed of the slow growth of this
tree in rocky situations, and of its durability, I have
often thought that the one I am describing must have
been as old as the Christian era. The tree lay in the line
of a fence. Great masses of its ruins were strewn about,
and some had been rolled down the hillside and lay near
the road at the bottom. As you approached the tree, you
were struck with the number of shrubs and young plants,
ashes, etc., which had found a bed upon the decayed
trunk and grew to no inconsiderable height, forming, as
it were, a part of the hedgerow. In no part of England, or
of Europe, have I ever seen a yew-tree at all approaching
this in magnitude, as it must have stood. By the bye, Hut-
ton, the old guide, of Keswick, had been so impressed
with the remains of this tree, that he used gravely to tell
strangers that there could be no doubt of its having been
in existence before the flood.—(Wordsworth.)

THERE is a Yew-tree, pride of Lorton Vale,
Which to this day stands single, in the midst
Of its own darkness, as it stood of yore:
Not loth to furnish weapons for the bands
Of Umfraville or Percy ere they marched
To Scotland's heaths; or those that crossed the
        sea
And drew their sounding bows at Azincour,
Perhaps at earlier Crecy, or Poictiers.
Of vast circumference and gloom profound
This solitary Tree! a living thing   10
Produced too slowly ever to decay;
Of form and aspect too magnificent

To be destroyed. But worthier still of note
Are those fraternal Four of Borrowdale,
Joined in one solemn and capacious grove;
Huge trunks! and each particular trunk a growth
Of intertwisted fibres serpentine
Up-coiling, and inveterately convolved;
Nor uninformed with Phantasy, and looks
That threaten the profane; a pillared shade,   20
Upon whose grassless floor of red-brown hue,
By sheddings from the pining[1] umbrage tinged
Perennially—beneath whose sable roof
Of boughs, as if for festal purpose decked
With unrejoicing berries—ghostly Shapes
May meet at noontide; Fear and trembling Hope,
Silence and Foresight; Death the Skeleton
And Time the Shadow;—there to celebrate,
As in a natural temple scattered o'er
With altars undisturbed of mossy stone,   30
United worship; or in mute repose
To lie, and listen to the mountain flood
Murmuring from Glaramara's inmost caves.

1803   1815

AT THE GRAVE OF BURNS

SEVEN YEARS AFTER HIS DEATH

[This and the next four poems are connected with
Wordsworth's tour of Scotland in 1803. Dorothy has told
in her *Journal* for 18 August of a visit to the churchyard
where Burns is buried and how she and her brother
'looked at Burns's grave with melancholy and painful reflections repeating to each other his own verses.' Wordsworth's tribute to Burns is written in the Scottish poet's
favorite stanza and includes quotations from his *To a
Mountain Daisy* and *A Bard's Epitaph*.]

I SHIVER, Spirit fierce and bold,
At thought of what I now behold:
As vapours breathed from dungeons cold
        Strike pleasure dead,
So sadness comes from out the mould
        Where Burns is laid.

And have I then thy bones so near,
And thou forbidden to appear?
As if it were thyself that's here
        I shrink with pain;   10
And both my wishes and my fear
        Alike are vain.

Off weight—nor press on weight!—away
Dark thoughts!—they came, but not to stay;
With chastened feelings would I pay
        The tribute due

---

1 languishing, dying.

To him, and aught that hides his clay
    From mortal view.

Fresh as the flower, whose modest worth
He sang, his genius 'glinted' forth,   20
Rose like a star that touching earth,
    For so it seems,
Doth glorify its humble birth
    With matchless beams.

The piercing eye, the thoughtful brow,
The struggling heart, where be they now?—
Full soon the Aspirant of the plough,
    The prompt, the brave,
Slept, with the obscurest, in the low
    And silent grave.   30

I mourned with thousands, but as one
More deeply grieved, for He was gone
Whose light I hailed when first it shone,
    And showed my youth
How Verse may build a princely throne
    On humble truth.

Alas! where'er the current tends,
Regret pursues and with it blends,—
Huge Criffel's hoary top ascends
    By Skiddaw seen,—   40
Neighbours we were, and loving friends
    We might have been;

True friends though diversely inclined;
But heart with heart and mind with mind,
Where the main fibres are entwined,
    Through Nature's skill,
May even by contraries be joined
    More closely still.

The tear will start, and let it flow;
Thou 'poor Inhabitant below,'   50
At this dread moment—even so—
    Might we together
Have sate and talked where gowans[1] blow,
    Or on wild heather.

What treasures would have then been placed
Within my reach; of knowledge graced
By fancy what a rich repast!
    But why go on?—
Oh! spare to sweep, thou mournful blast,
    His grave grass-grown.   60

There, too, a Son, his joy and pride,
(Not three weeks past the Stripling died,)

Lies gathered to his Father's side,
    Soul-moving sight!
Yet one to which is not denied
    Some sad delight.

For *he* is safe, a quiet bed
Hath early found among the dead,
Harboured where none can be misled,
    Wronged, or distrest;   70
And surely here it may be said
    That such are blest.

And oh for Thee, by pitying grace
Checked oft-times in a devious race,
May He, who halloweth the place
    Where Man is laid,
Receive thy Spirit in the embrace
    For which it prayed!

Sighing I turned away; but ere
Night fell I heard, or seemed to hear,   80
Music that sorrow comes not near,
    A ritual hymn,
Chanted in love that casts out fear
    By Seraphim.

1803   1842

TO A HIGHLAND GIRL

AT INVERSNEYDE, UPON LOCH LOMOND

    This delightful creature and her demeanour are particularly described in my Sister's Journal.[1] The sort of prophecy with which the verses conclude has, through God's goodness, been realized; and now, approaching the close of my 73rd year, I have a most vivid remembrance of her and the beautiful objects with which she was surrounded. She is alluded to in the Poem of 'The Three Cottage Girls' among my Continental Memorials. In illustration of this class of poems I have scarcely anything to say beyond what is anticipated in my Sister's faithful and admirable Journal.—(Wordsworth.)

Sweet Highland Girl, a very shower
Of beauty is thy earthly dower!
Twice seven consenting years have shed
Their utmost bounty on thy head:
And these grey rocks; that household lawn;
Those trees, a veil just half withdrawn;
This fall of water that doth make
A murmur near the silent lake;
This little bay; a quiet road
That holds in shelter thy Abode—   10
In truth together do ye seem
Like something fashioned in a dream;
Such Forms as from their covert peep

---

1 daisies.

1 See Dorothy's *Journal* for 28 August 1803, text, p. 456.

When earthly cares are laid asleep!
But, O fair Creature! in the light
Of common day, so heavenly bright,
I bless Thee, Vision as thou art,
I bless thee with a human heart;
God shield thee to thy latest years!
Thee, neither know I, nor thy peers;   20
And yet my eyes are filled with tears.

With earnest feeling I shall pray
For thee when I am far away:
For never saw I mien, or face,
In which more plainly I could trace
Benignity and home-bred sense
Ripening in perfect innocence.
Here scattered, like a random seed,
Remote from men, Thou dost not need
The embarrassed look of shy distress,   30
And maidenly shamefacedness:
Thou wear'st upon thy forehead clear
The freedom of a Mountaineer:
A face with gladness overspread!
Soft smiles, by human kindness bred!
And seemliness complete, that sways
Thy courtesies, about thee plays;
With no restraint, but such as springs
From quick and eager visitings
Of thoughts that lie beyond the reach   40
Of thy few words of English speech:
A bondage sweetly brooked, a strife
That gives thy gestures grace and life!
So have I, not unmoved in mind,
Seen birds of tempest-loving kind—
Thus beating up against the wind.

What hand but would a garland cull
For thee who art so beautiful?
O happy pleasure! here to dwell
Beside thee in some heathy dell;   50
Adopt your homely ways, and dress,
A Shepherd, thou a Shepherdess!
But I could frame a wish for thee
More like a grave reality:
Thou art to me but as a wave
Of the wild sea; and I would have
Some claim upon thee, if I could,
Though but of common neighbourhood.
What joy to hear thee, and to see!
Thy elder Brother I would be,   60
Thy Father—anything to thee!

Now thanks to Heaven! that of its grace
Hath led me to this lonely place.
Joy have I had; and going hence
I bear away my recompense.

In spots like these it is we prize
Our Memory, feel that she hath eyes:
Then, why should I be loth to stir?
I feel this place was made for her;
To give new pleasure like the past,   70
Continued long as life shall last.
Nor am I loth, though pleased at heart,
Sweet Highland Girl! from thee to part;
For I, methinks, till I grow old,
As fair before me shall behold,
As I do now, the cabin small,
The lake, the bay, the waterfall;
And Thee, the Spirit of them all!

1803   1807

STEPPING WESTWARD

While my Fellow-traveller and I were walking by the
side of Loch Ketterine, one fine evening after sunset, in
our road to a Hut where, in the course of our Tour, we
had been hospitably entertained some weeks before, we
met, in one of the loneliest parts of that solitary region,
two well-dressed Women, one of whom said to us, by
way of greeting, 'What, you are stepping westward?'—
(Wordsworth.)

'*What, you are stepping westward?*'—'*Yea.*'
—'Twould be a *wildish* destiny,
If we, who thus together roam
In a strange Land, and far from home,
Were in this place the guests of Chance:
Yet who would stop, or fear to advance,
Though home or shelter he had none,
With such a sky to lead him on?

The dewy ground was dark and cold;
Behind, all gloomy to behold;   10
And stepping westward seemed to be
A kind of *heavenly* destiny:
I liked the greeting; 'twas a sound
Of something without place or bound;
And seemed to give me spiritual right
To travel through that region bright.

The voice was soft, and she who spake
Was walking by her native lake:
The salutation had to me
The very sound of courtesy: 20
Its power was felt; and while my eye
Was fixed upon the glowing Sky,
The echo of the voice enwrought
A human sweetness with the thought
Of travelling through the world that lay
Before me in my endless way.

1803   1807

THE SOLITARY REAPER

It was harvest-time, and the fields were quietly—might I be allowed to say pensively?—enlivened by small companies of reapers. It is not uncommon in the more lonely parts of the Highlands to see a single person so employed. The following poem was suggested to William by a beautiful sentence in Thomas Wilkinson's *Tour in Scotland.*[1]
—(Dorothy Wordsworth.)

BEHOLD her, single in the field,
Yon solitary Highland Lass!
Reaping and singing by herself;
Stop here, or gently pass!
Alone she cuts and binds the grain,
And sings a melancholy strain;
O listen! for the Vale profound
Is overflowing with the sound.

No Nightingale did ever chaunt
More welcome notes to weary bands   10
Of travellers in some shady haunt,
Among Arabian sands:
A voice so thrilling ne'er was heard
In spring-time from the Cuckoo-bird,
Breaking the silence of the seas
Among the farthest Hebrides.

Will no one tell me what she sings?—
Perhaps the plaintive numbers flow
For old, unhappy, far-off things,
And battles long ago: 20
Or is it some more humble lay,
Familiar matter of to-day?
Some natural sorrow, loss, or pain,
That has been, and may be again?

Whate'er the theme, the Maiden sang
As if her song could have no ending;
I saw her singing at her work,
And o'er the sickle bending;
I listened, motionless and still;
And, as I mounted up the hill,   30
The music in my heart I bore,
Long after it was heard no more.

1805   1807

YARROW UNVISITED

FROM Stirling castle we had seen
The mazy Forth unravelled;
Had trod the banks of Clyde, and Tay,
And with the Tweed had travelled;
And when we came to Clovenford,
Then said my '*winsome Marrow*,'[1]
'Whate'er betide, we'll turn aside,
And see the Braes of Yarrow.'

'Let Yarrow folk, *frae* Selkirk town,
Who have been buying, selling,   10
Go back to Yarrow, 'tis their own;
Each maiden to her dwelling!
On Yarrow's banks let herons feed,
Hares couch, and rabbits burrow! ·
But we will downward with the Tweed,
Nor turn aside to Yarrow.

'There's Galla Water, Leader Haughs,
Both lying right before us;
And Dryborough, where with chiming Tweed
The lintwhites[2] sing in chorus;   20
There's pleasant Tiviot-dale, a land
Made blithe with plough and harrow:
Why throw away a needful day
To go in search of Yarrow?

'What's Yarrow but a river bare,
That glides the dark hills under?
There are a thousand such elsewhere
As worthy of your wonder.'
—Strange words they seemed of slight and
          scorn;
My True-love sighed for sorrow;   30
And looked me in the face, to think
I thus could speak of Yarrow!

'Oh! green,' said I, 'are Yarrow's holms,
And sweet is Yarrow flowing!
Fair hangs the apple frae the rock,
But we will leave it growing.
O'er hilly path, and open Strath,[3]
We'll wander Scotland thorough;
But, though so near, we will not turn
Into the dale of Yarrow.   40

'Let beeves and home-bred kine partake
The sweets of Burn-mill meadow;
The swan on still St. Mary's Lake
Float double, swan and shadow!
We will not see them; will not go,
To-day, nor yet to-morrow;

---

1 The passage referred to in Wilkinson is as follows: 'Passed by a female who was reaping alone, she sung in Erse as she bended over her sickle, the sweetest human voice I ever heard. Her strains were tenderly melancholy, and felt delicious long after they were heard no more.'

---

1 Marrow is a mate or companion; here referring, of course, to Dorothy.
2 linnets.
3 a wide river valley.

Enough if in our hearts we know
There's such a place as Yarrow.

'Be Yarrow stream unseen, unknown!
It must, or we shall rue it: 50
We have a vision of our own;
Ah! why should we undo it?
The treasured dreams of times long past,
We'll keep them, winsome Marrow!
For when we're there, although 'tis fair,
'Twill be another Yarrow!

'If Care with freezing years should come,
And wandering seem but folly,—
Should we be loth to stir from home,
And yet be melancholy;   60
Should life be dull, and spirits low,
'Twill soothe us in our sorrow,
That earth hath something yet to show,
The bonny holms of Yarrow!'

          1803   1807

OCTOBER 1803

[This sonnet was inspired by the expectations of an invasion of England by the French in 1803.]

WHEN, looking on the present face of things,
I see one man,[1] of men the meanest too!
Raised up to sway the world, to do, undo,
With mighty Nations for his underlings,
The great events with which old story rings
Seem vain and hollow; I find nothing great:
Nothing is left which I can venerate;
So that a doubt almost within me springs
Of Providence, such emptiness at length
Seems at the heart of all things. But, great
     God!   10
I measure back the steps which I have trod;
And tremble, seeing whence proceeds the
     strength
Of such poor Instruments, with thoughts sublime
I tremble at the sorrow of the time.

          1803   1807

SHE WAS A PHANTOM
OF DELIGHT

Written at Town-end, Grasmere. The germ of this
poem was four lines composed as a part of the verses on
the Highland Girl. Though beginning in this way, it was
written from my heart, as is sufficiently obvious.—
(Wordsworth.)

---

1 Napoleon.

SHE[1] was a Phantom of delight
When first she gleamed upon my sight;
A lovely Apparition, sent
To be a moment's ornament;
Her eyes as stars of Twilight fair;
Like Twilight's, too, her dusky hair;
But all things else about her drawn
From May-time and the cheerful Dawn;
A dancing Shape, an Image gay,
To haunt, to startle, and way-lay.   10

I saw her upon nearer view,
A Spirit, yet a Woman too!
Her household motions light and free,
And steps of virgin-liberty;
A countenance in which did meet
Sweet records, promises as sweet;
A Creature not too bright or good
For human nature's daily food;
For transient sorrows, simple wiles,
Praise, blame, love, kisses, tears, and smiles. 20

And now I see with eye serene
The very pulse of the machine;[2]
A Being breathing thoughtful breath,
A Traveller between life and death;
The reason firm, the temperate will,
Endurance, foresight, strength, and skill;
A perfect Woman, nobly planned,
To warn, to comfort, and command;
And yet a Spirit still, and bright
With something of angelic light.   30

          1804   1807

I WANDERED LONELY AS A CLOUD

Written at Town-end, Grasmere. The Daffodils grew
and still grow on the margin of Ullswater, and probably
may be seen to this day as beautiful in the month of
March, nodding their golden heads beside the dancing
and foaming waves.—(Wordsworth.)[1]

---

1 Mary Hutchinson, the poet's wife.
2 The word 'machine' (which has been criticized for its prosaic
suggestion) is perhaps intended, Dowden thinks, to apply, not to
the body but to 'the whole woman with all her household routine
conceived of as an organism of which the thoughtful soul is the
animating principle.' In support of this interpretation Dowden
quotes from Bartram's *Travels* (a book used by Wordsworth in
his *Ruth*) the following interesting passage: 'At the return of the
morning, by the powerful influence of light, the *pulse* of nature
becomes more active, and the universal vibration of life insensibly
and irresistibly moves the wondrous *machine*.' (*Poems by Wordsworth*, 1897, p. 435.) Cf. also Hamlet's 'Thine evermore most dear
lady, whilst this machine is to him' (*Hamlet*, II, ii, 124).

---

1 See also Dorothy's *Journal* account for 15 April 1802, text, p. 452.

I WANDERED lonely as a cloud
That floats on high o'er vales and hills,
When all at once I saw a crowd,
A host, of golden daffodils;
Beside the lake, beneath the trees,
Fluttering and dancing in the breeze.

Continuous as the stars that shine
And twinkle on the milky way,
They stretched in never-ending line
Along the margin of a bay: 10
Ten thousand saw I at a glance,
Tossing their heads in sprightly dance.

The waves beside them danced; but they
Out-did the sparkling waves in glee:
A poet could not but be gay,
In such a jocund company:
I gazed—and gazed—but little thought
What wealth the show to me had brought:

For oft, when on my couch I lie
In vacant or in pensive mood,   20
They flash upon that inward eye
Which is the bliss of solitude;
And then my heart with pleasure fills,
And dances with the daffodils.

1804   1807

THE AFFLICTION OF MARGARET

Written at Town-end, Grasmere. This was taken from
the case of a poor widow who lived in the town of Penrith. Her sorrow was well known to Mrs. Wordsworth, to
my Sister, and, I believe, to the whole town. She kept a
shop, and when she saw a stranger passing by, she was
in the habit of going out into the street to inquire of him
after her son.—(Wordsworth.)

WHERE art thou, my beloved Son,
Where art thou, worse to me than dead?
Oh find me, prosperous or undone!
Or, if the grave be now thy bed,
Why am I ignorant of the same
That I may rest; and neither blame
Nor sorrow may attend thy name?

Seven years, alas! to have received
No tidings of an only child;
To have despaired, have hoped, believed,
And been for evermore beguiled;   10
Sometimes with thoughts of very bliss!
I catch at them, and then I miss;
Was ever darkness like to this?

He was among the prime in worth,
An object beauteous to behold;
Well born, well bred; I sent him forth
Ingenuous, innocent, and bold:
If things ensued that wanted grace,
As hath been said, they were not base;   20
And never blush was on my face.

Ah! little doth the young-one dream,
When full of play and childish cares,
What power is in his wildest scream,
Heard by his mother unawares!
He knows it not, he cannot guess:
Years to a mother bring distress;
But do not make her love the less.

Neglect me! no, I suffered long
From that ill thought; and, being blind,   30
Said, 'Pride shall help me in my wrong:
Kind mother have I been, as kind
As ever breathed': and that is true;
I've wet my path with tears like dew,
Weeping for him when no one knew.

My Son, if thou be humbled, poor,
Hopeless of honour and of gain,
Oh! do not dread thy mother's door;
Think not of me with grief and pain:
I now can see with better eyes;   40
And worldly grandeur I despise,
And fortune with her gifts and lies.

Alas! the fowls of heaven have wings,
And blasts of heaven will aid their flight;
They mount—how short a voyage brings
The wanderers back to their delight!
Chains tie us down by land and sea;
And wishes, vain as mine, may be
All that is left to comfort thee.

Perhaps some dungeon hears thee groan,   50
Maimed, mangled by inhuman men;
Or thou upon a desert thrown
Inheritest the lion's den;
Or hast been summoned to the deep,
Thou, thou and all thy mates, to keep
An incommunicable sleep.

I look for ghosts; but none will force
Their way to me: 'tis falsely said
That there was ever intercourse
Between the living and the dead;   60
For, surely, then I should have sight
Of him I wait for day and night,
With love and longings infinite.

My apprehensions come in crowds;
I dread the rustling of the grass;
The very shadows of the clouds
Have power to shake me as they pass:
I question things and do not find
One that will answer to my mind;
And all the world appears unkind.　　　70

Beyond participation lie
My troubles, and beyond relief:
If any chance to heave a sigh,
They pity me, and not my grief.
Then come to me, my Son, or send
Some tidings that my woes may end;
I have no other earthly friend!

　　1804　　　　　　　　　　　1807

ODE TO DUTY

Jam non consilio bonus, sed more eō perductus, ut non tantum rectē facere possim, sed nisi rectē facere non possim.[1] This ode is on the model of Gray's *Ode to Adversity* which is copied from Horace's *Ode to Fortune.*—(Wordsworth.)

Stern Daughter of the Voice of God!
O Duty! if that name thou love
Who art a light to guide, a rod
To check the erring, and reprove;
Thou, who art victory and law
When empty terrors overawe;
From vain temptations dost set free;
And calm'st the weary strife of frail humanity!

There are who ask not if thine eye
Be on them; who, in love and truth,　　　10
Where no misgiving is, rely
Upon the genial sense of youth:
Glad Hearts! without reproach or blot;
Who do thy work, and know it not:
Oh! if through confidence misplaced
They fail, thy saving arms, dread Power! around
　　them cast.

Serene will be our days and bright,
And happy will our nature be,
When love is an unerring light,
And joy its own security.　　　20
And they a blissful course may hold
Even now, who, not unwisely bold,

Live in the spirit of this creed;
Yet seek thy firm support, according to their
　　need.

I, loving freedom, and untried;
No sport of every random gust,
Yet being to myself a guide,
Too blindly have reposed my trust:
And oft, when in my heart was heard
Thy timely mandate, I deferred　　　30
The task, in smoother walks to stray;
But thee I now would serve more strictly, if I
　　may.

Through no disturbance of my soul,
Or strong compunction in me wrought,
I supplicate for thy control;
But in the quietness of thought:
Me this unchartered freedom tires;
I feel the weight of chance-desires:
My hopes no more must change their name,
I long for a repose that ever is the same.[2]　　　40

Stern Lawgiver! yet thou dost wear
The Godhead's most benignant grace;
Nor know we anything so fair
As is the smile upon thy face:
Flowers laugh before thee on their beds
And fragrance in thy footing treads:
Thou dost preserve the stars from wrong;
And the most ancient heavens, through Thee, are
　　fresh and strong.

To humbler functions, awful Power!
I call thee: I myself commend　　　50
Unto thy guidance from this hour;
Oh, let my weakness have an end!
Give unto me, made lowly wise,
The spirit of self-sacrifice;
The confidence of reason give;
And in the light of truth thy Bondman let me
　　live!

　　1804　　　　　　　　　　　1807

---

1 'Now I am urged on, not by good resolution, but rather by custom; so that it is not that I am able to do right, but that I am able to do no wrong.'—Adapted from Seneca, *Moral Epistles*, CXX, 10.

2 The published text of 1807 includes a stanza between the fifth and sixth stanzas, omitted from subsequent editions, which links the thought and serves as a valuable extension of Wordsworth's philosophy.

Yet not the less would I throughout
Still act according to the voice
Of my own wish; and feel past doubt
That my submissiveness was choice:
Not seeking in the school of pride
For 'precepts over dignified,'
Denial and restraint I prize
No farther than they breed a second Will more wise.

ODE

INTIMATIONS OF IMMORTALITY FROM RECOLLECTIONS OF EARLY CHILDHOOD

This was composed during my residence at Town-end, Grasmere. Two years at least passed between the writing of the four first stanzas and the remaining part. To the attentive and competent reader the whole sufficiently explains itself; but there may be no harm in adverting here to particular feelings or *experiences* of my own mind on which the structure of the poem partly rests. Nothing was more difficult for me in childhood than to admit the notion of death as a state applicable to my own being. I have said elsewhere—

'A simple child,
That lightly draws its breath,
And feels its life in every limb,
What should it know of death!—'

But it was not so much from feelings of animal vivacity that *my* difficulty came as from a sense of the indomitableness of the Spirit within me. I used to brood over the stories of Enoch and Elijah, and almost to persuade myself that, whatever might become of others, I should be translated, in something of the same way, to heaven. With a feeling congenial to this, I was often unable to think of external things as having external existence, and I communed with all that I saw as something not apart from, but inherent in, my own immaterial nature. Many times while going to school have I grasped at a wall or tree to recall myself from this abyss of idealism to the reality. At that time I was afraid of such processes. In later periods of life I have deplored, as we have all reason to do, a subjugation of an opposite character, and have rejoiced over the remembrances, as is expressed in the lines—

'Obstinate questionings
Of sense and outward things,
Fallings from us, vanishings;' etc.

To that dream-like vividness and splendour which invest objects of sight in childhood, every one, I believe, if he would look back, could bear testimony, and I need not dwell upon it here: but having in the poem regarded it as presumptive evidence of a prior state of existence, I think it right to protest against a conclusion, which has given pain to some good and pious persons, that I meant to inculcate such a belief. It is far too shadowy a notion to be recommended to faith, as more than an element in our instincts of immortality. But let us bear in mind that, though the idea is not advanced in revelation, there is nothing there to contradict it, and the fall of Man presents an analogy in its favour. Accordingly, a preëxistent state has entered into the popular creeds of many nations; and, among all persons acquainted with classic literature, is known as an ingredient in Platonic philosophy. Archimedes said that he could move the world if he had a point whereon to rest his machine. Who has not felt the same aspirations as regards the world of his own mind? Having to wield some of its elements when I was impelled to write this poem on the 'Immortality of the Soul,' I took hold of the notion of preëxistence as having sufficient foundation in humanity for authorizing me to make for my purpose the best use of it I could as a poet.

—(Wordsworth.)

The Child is Father of the Man;
And I could wish my days to be
Bound each to each by natural piety.

I

THERE was a time when meadow, grove, and
stream,
The earth, and every common sight,
To me did seem
Apparelled in celestial light,
The glory and the freshness of a dream.
It is not now as it hath been of yore;—
Turn wheresoe'er I may,
By night or day,
The things which I have seen I now can see no
more.

II

The Rainbow comes and goes,   10
And lovely is the Rose.
The Moon doth with delight
Look round her when the heavens are bare.
Waters on a starry night
Are beautiful and fair;
The sunshine is a glorious birth;
But yet I know, where'er I go,
That there hath past away a glory from the earth.

III

Now, while the birds thus sing a joyous song,
And while the young lambs bound   20
As to the tabor's sound,
To me alone there came a thought of grief:
A timely utterance gave that thought relief,
And I again am strong:
The cataracts blow their trumpets from the steep;
No more shall grief of mine the season wrong;
I hear the Echoes through the mountains throng,
The Winds come to me from the fields of sleep,
And all the earth is gay;
Land and sea   30
Give themselves up to jollity,
And with the heart of May
Doth every Beast keep holiday;—
Thou Child of Joy,
Shout round me, let me hear thy shouts, thou
happy Shepherd-boy!

IV

Ye blessèd Creatures, I have heard the call
Ye to each other make; I see

ode formal, elevated, turning away from the love & simplicity in the Lyrical Ballads

The heavens laugh with you in your jubilee;
  My heart is at your festival,
    My head hath its coronal,
The fulness of your bliss, I feel—I feel it all.   40
    Oh evil day! if I were sullen
    While Earth herself is adorning,
      This sweet May-morning
    And the Children are culling
      On every side,
    In a thousand valleys far and wide,
    Fresh flowers; while the sun shines warm,
And the Babe leaps up on his Mother's arm:—
    I hear, I hear, with joy I hear!   50
    —But there's a Tree, of many, one,
A single Field which I have looked upon,
Both of them speak of something that is
      gone:
    The Pansy at my feet
    Doth the same tale repeat:
Whither is fled the visionary gleam?
Where is it now, the glory and the dream?

V

Our birth is but a sleep and a forgetting:
The Soul that rises with us, our life's Star,
    Hath had elsewhere its setting,   60
      And cometh from afar:
    Not in entire forgetfulness,
    And not in utter nakedness,
But trailing clouds of glory do we come
    From God, who is our home:
Heaven lies about us in our infancy!
Shades of the prison-house begin to close
    Upon the growing Boy,
But He beholds the light, and whence it flows,
    He sees it in his joy;   70
The Youth, who daily farther from the east
    Must travel, still is Nature's Priest,
    And by the vision splendid
    Is on his way attended;
At length the Man perceives it die away,
And fade into the light of common day.

VI

Earth fills her lap with pleasures of her own;
Yearnings she hath in her own natural kind,
And, even with something of a Mother's
      mind,
    And no unworthy aim,
    The homely Nurse doth all she can   80
To make her Foster-child, her Inmate Man,
    Forget the glories he hath known,
And that imperial palace whence he came.

VII

Behold the Child among his new-born blisses,
A six years' Darling of a pigmy size!
See, where 'mid work of his own hand he lies,
Fretted by sallies of his mother's kisses,
With light upon him from his father's eyes!
See, at his feet, some little plan or chart,   90
Some fragment from his dream of human life,
Shaped by himself with newly-learned art;
    A wedding or a festival,
    A mourning or a funeral;
    And this hath now his heart,
    And unto this he frames his song:
    Then will he fit his tongue
To dialogues of business, love, or strife;
    But it will not be long
    Ere this be thrown aside,   100
    And with new joy and pride
The little Actor cons another part;
Filling from time to time his 'humorous stage'
With all the Persons, down to palsied Age,
That Life brings with her in her equipage;
    As if his whole vocation
    Were endless imitation.

VIII

Thou, whose exterior semblance doth belie Thy
    Soul's immensity;
Thou best Philosopher, who yet dost keep   110
Thy heritage, thou Eye among the blind,
That, deaf and silent, read'st the eternal deep,
Haunted for ever by the eternal mind,—
    Mighty Prophet! Seer blest!
    On whom those truths do rest,
Which we are toiling all our lives to find,
In darkness lost, the darkness of the grave;
Thou, over whom thy Immortality
Broods like the Day, a Master o'er a Slave,
A Presence which is not to be put by;[1]   120
Thou little Child, yet glorious in the might
Of heaven-born freedom on thy being's height,
Why with such earnest pains dost thou provoke
The years to bring the inevitable yoke,
Thus blindly with thy blessedness at strife?
Full soon thy Soul shall have her earthly freight,
And custom lie upon thee with a weight,
Heavy as frost, and deep almost as life!

---

1 The following insert appeared from 1807-15 after line 120:

        To whom the grave
  Is but a lonely bed without the sense or sight
      Of day or the warm light,
  A place of thought where we in waiting lie;

IX

O joy! that in our embers
    Is something that doth live,   130
That nature yet remembers
    What was so fugitive!
The thought of our past years in me doth breed
Perpetual benediction: not indeed
For that which is most worthy to be blest;
Delight and liberty, the simple creed
Of Childhood, whether busy or at rest,
With new-fledged hope still fluttering in his
      breast:—
    Not for these I raise
    The song of thanks and praise;   140
  But for those obstinate questionings
  Of sense and outward things,
  Fallings from us, vanishings;
  Blank misgivings of a Creature
Moving about in worlds not realised,
High instincts before which our mortal Nature
Did tremble like a guilty Thing surprised:
    But for those first affections,
    Those shadowy recollections,
  Which, be they what they may,   150
Are yet the fountain-light of all our day,
Are yet a master-light of all our seeing;
  Uphold us, cherish, and have power to make
Our noisy years seem moments in the being
Of the eternal Silence: truths that wake,
    To perish never:
Which neither listlessness, nor mad endeavour,
    Nor Man nor Boy,
Nor all that is at enmity with joy,
Can utterly abolish or destroy!   160
  Hence in a season of calm weather
    Though inland far we be,
Our Souls have sight of that immortal sea
    Which brought us hither,
    Can in a moment travel thither,
And see the Children sport upon the shore,
And hear the mighty waters rolling evermore.

X

Then sing, ye Birds, sing, sing a joyous song!
    And let the young Lambs bound
    As to the tabor's sound!   170
We in thought will join your throng,
    Ye that pipe and ye that play,
    Ye that through your hearts today
    Feel the gladness of the May!
What though the radiance which was once so
    bright
Be now for ever taken from my sight,

Though nothing can bring back the hour
Of splendour in the grass, of glory in the flower;
    We will grieve not, rather find
    Strength in what remains behind;   180
    In the primal sympathy
    Which having been must ever be;
    In the soothing thoughts that spring
    Out of human suffering;
    In the faith that looks through death,
In years that bring the philosophic mind.

XI

And O, ye Fountains, Meadows, Hills, and
    Groves,
Forbode not any severing of our loves!
Yet in my heart of hearts I feel your might;
I only have relinquished one delight   190
To live beneath your more habitual sway.
I love the Brooks which down their channels fret,
Even more than when I tripped lightly as they;
The innocent brightness of a new-born Day
    Is lovely yet;
The Clouds that gather round the setting sun
Do take a sober colouring from an eye
That hath kept watch o'er man's mortality;
Another race hath been, and other palms are
    won.
Thanks to the human heart by which we live. 200
Thanks to its tenderness, its joys, and fears,
To me the meanest flower that blows can give
Thoughts that do often lie too deep for tears.

1802–4   1807

ELEGIAC STANZAS

SUGGESTED BY A PICTURE OF PEELE CASTLE,[1] IN A
STORM, PAINTED BY SIR GEORGE BEAUMONT

[These stanzas had their origin in bereavement over
the tragic death of the poet's dearly beloved brother
John, who went down with his ship on 5 February 1805.]

I WAS thy neighbour once, thou rugged Pile!
Four summer weeks[2] I dwelt in sight of thee:
I saw thee every day; and all the while
Thy Form was sleeping on a glassy sea.

So pure the sky, so quiet was the air!
So like, so very like, was day to day!

---

1 situated on a small island by the same name off the coast of
Lancashire.
2 During the month of August, 1794, Wordsworth visited his
cousin Elizabeth Wordsworth (Mrs. Barker), who lived at Rampside near Peele Castle.

Whene'er I looked, thy Image still was there;
It trembled, but it never passed away.

How perfect was the calm! it seemed no sleep;
No mood, which season takes away, or brings: 10
I could have fancied that the mighty Deep
Was even the gentlest of all gentle Things.

Ah! then, if mine had been the Painter's hand,
To express what then I saw; and add the gleam,
The light that never was, on sea or land,
The consecration, and the Poet's dream;

I would have planted thee, thou hoary Pile
Amid a world how different from this!
Beside a sea that could not cease to smile;
On tranquil land, beneath a sky of bliss.   20

Thou shouldst have seemed a treasure-house
       divine
Of peaceful years; a chronicle of heaven;—
Of all the sunbeams that did ever shine
The very sweetest had to thee been given.

A Picture had it been of lasting ease,
Elysian quiet, without toil or strife;
No motion but the moving tide, a breeze,
Or merely silent Nature's breathing life.

Such, in the fond illusion of my heart,
Such Picture would I at that time have made: 30
And seen the soul of truth in every part,
A steadfast peace that might not be betrayed.

So once it would have been,—'tis so no more;
I have submitted to a new control:
A power is gone, which nothing can restore;
A deep distress hath humanised my Soul.

Not for a moment could I now behold
A smiling sea, and be what I have been:
The feeling of my loss will ne'er be old;
This, which I know, I speak with mind serene. 40

Then, Beaumont, Friend! who would have been
       the Friend,
If he had lived, of Him whom I deplore,
This work of thine I blame not, but commend;
This sea in anger, and that dismal shore.

O 'tis a passionate Work!—yet wise and well,
Well chosen is the spirit that is here;
That Hulk which labours in the deadly swell,
This rueful sky, this pageantry of fear!

And this huge Castle, standing here sublime,
I love to see the look with which it braves,   50
Cased in the unfeeling armour of old time,
The lightning, the fierce wind, and trampling
       waves.

Farewell, farewell the heart that lives alone,
Housed in a dream, at distance from the Kind![3]
Such happiness, wherever it be known,
Is to be pitied; for 'tis surely blind.

But welcome fortitude, and patient cheer,
And frequent sights of what is to be borne!
Such sights, or worse, as are before me here.—
Not without hope we suffer and we mourn.   60

1805   1807

CHARACTER OF THE HAPPY WARRIOR

[Some of the features of this noble poem honoring 'the
military character' were suggested by the life and heroic
death of Nelson; others, Wordsworth tells us, were found
in his brother John, who perished by shipwreck. Still
others may have been suggested by the character of the
poet's French friend, Michel Beaupuy, who was killed in
battle.]

WHO is the happy Warrior? Who is he
That every man in arms should wish to be?
—It is the generous Spirit, who, when brought
Among the tasks of real life, hath wrought
Upon the plan that pleased his boyish thought:
Whose high endeavours are an inward light
That makes the path before him always bright:
Who, with a natural instinct to discern
What knowledge can perform, is diligent to learn;
Abides by this resolve, and stops not there,   10
But makes his moral being his prime care;
Who, doomed to go in company with Pain,
And Fear, and Bloodshed, miserable train!
Turns his necessity to glorious gain;
In face of these doth exercise a power
Which is our human nature's highest dower;
Controls them and subdues, transmutes, bereaves
Of their bad influence, and their good receives:
By objects, which might force the soul to abate
Her feeling, rendered more compassionate;   20
Is placable—because occasions rise
So often that demand such sacrifice;
More skilful in self-knowledge, even more pure,
As tempted more; more able to endure,
As more exposed to suffering and distress;
Thence, also, more alive to tenderness.
—'Tis he whose law is reason; who depends

_____
3 mankind.

Upon that law as on the best of friends;
Whence, in a state where men are tempted still
To evil for a guard against worse ill,   30
And what in quality or act is best
Doth seldom on a right foundation rest.
He labours good on good to fix, and owes
To virtue every triumph that he knows:
—Who, if he rise to station of command,
Rises by open means; and there will stand
On honourable terms, or else retire,
And in himself possess his own desire;
Who comprehends his trust, and to the same
Keeps faithful with a singleness of aim;   40
And therefore does not stoop, nor lie in wait
For wealth, or honours, or for worldly state;
Whom they must follow; on whose head must
          fall,
Like showers of manna, if they come at all:
Whose powers shed round him in the common
          strife,
Or mild concerns of ordinary life,
A constant influence, a peculiar grace;
But who, if he be called upon to face
Some awful moment to which Heaven has joined
Great issues, good or bad for human kind,   50
Is happy as a Lover; and attired
With sudden brightness, like a Man inspired;
And, through the heat of conflict, keeps the law
In calmness made, and sees what he foresaw;
Or if an unexpected call succeed,
Come when it will, is equal to the need:
—He who, though thus endued as with a sense
And faculty for storm and turbulence,
Is yet a Soul whose master-bias leans
To homefelt pleasures and to gentle scenes;   60
Sweet images! which, wheresoe'er he be,
Are at his heart; and such fidelity
It is his darling passion to approve;
More brave for this, that he hath much to
          love:——
'Tis, finally, the Man, who, lifted high,
Conspicuous object in a Nation's eye,
Or left unthought-of in obscurity,—
Who, with a toward or untoward lot,
Prosperous or adverse, to his wish or not—
Plays, in the many games of life, that one   70
Where what he most doth value must be won:
Whom neither shape of danger can dismay,
Nor thought of tender happiness betray;
Who, not content that former worth stand fast,
Looks forward, persevering to the last,
From well to better, daily self-surpast:
Who, whether praise of him must walk the earth

For ever, and to noble deeds give birth,
Or he must fall, to sleep without his fame,
And leave a dead unprofitable name—   80
Finds comfort in himself and in his cause;
And, while the mortal mist is gathering, draws
His breath in confidence of Heaven's applause:
This is the happy Warrior; this is He
That every Man in arms should wish to be.

1805–6   1807

YES, IT WAS THE MOUNTAIN ECHO

Written at Town-end, Grasmere. The echo came from
Nab-scar, when I was walking on the opposite side of
Rydal Mere.—(Wordsworth.)

YES, it was the mountain Echo,
Solitary, clear, profound,
Answering to the shouting Cuckoo,
Giving to her sound for sound!

Unsolicited reply
To a babbling wanderer sent;
Like her ordinary cry,
Like—but oh, how different!

Hears not also mortal Life?
Hear not we, unthinking Creatures!   10
Slaves of folly, love, or strife—
Voices of two different natures?

Have not *we* too?—yes, we have
Answers, and we know not whence;
Echoes from beyond the grave,
Recognised intelligence!

Such rebounds our inward ear
Catches sometimes from afar—
Listen, ponder, hold them dear;
For of God,—of God they are.   20

1806   1807

NUNS FRET NOT AT THEIR CONVENT'S
NARROW ROOM

In the cottage, Town-end, Grasmere, one afternoon in
1801, my sister read to me the Sonnets of Milton. I had
long been well acquainted with them, but I was particularly struck on that occasion with the dignified simplicity
and majestic harmony that runs through most of them,
—in character so totally different from the Italian, and
still more so from Shakespeare's fine Sonnets. I took fire,
if I may be allowed to say so, and produced three Sonnets the same afternoon, the first I ever wrote except an
irregular one at school. Of these three, the only one I
distinctly remember is—'I grieved for Buonaparté.' One
was never written down: the third, which was, I believe,
preserved, I cannot particularize.—(Wordsworth.)

NUNS fret not at their convent's narrow room;
And hermits are contented with their cells;
And students with their pensive citadels;
Maids at the wheel, the weaver at his loom,
Sit blithe and happy; bees that soar for bloom,
High as the highest Peak of Furness-fells,
Will murmur by the hour in foxglove bells:
In truth the prison, unto which we doom
Ourselves, no prison is: and hence for me,
In sundry moods, 'twas pastime to be bound   10
Within the Sonnet's scanty plot of ground;
Pleased if some Souls (for such there needs must
      be)
Who have felt the weight of too much liberty,
Should find brief solace there, as I have found.

                                      1807

PERSONAL TALK

Written at Town-end, Grasmere. The last line but two
[of the first sonnet] stood, at first, better and more characteristically, thus:

'By my half-kitchen and half-parlour fire.'

My Sister and I were in the habit of having the tea-kettle
in our little sitting-room; and we toasted the bread ourselves, which reminds me of a little circumstance not
unworthy of being set down among these minutiæ. Happening both of us to be engaged a few minutes one morning when we had a young prig of a Scotch lawyer to
breakfast with us, my dear Sister, with her usual simplicity, put the toasting-fork with a slice of bread into the
hands of this Edinburgh genius. Our little book-case
stood on one side of the fire. To prevent loss of time, he
took down a book, and fell to reading, to the neglect of
the toast, which was burned to a cinder. Many a time
have we laughed at this circumstance, and other cottage
simplicities of that day. By the bye, I have a spite at one
of this series of Sonnets (I will leave the reader to discover which) as having been the means of nearly putting
off forever our acquaintance with dear Miss Fenwick,
who has always stigmatized one line of it as vulgar, and
worthy only of having been composed by a country
squire.—(Wordsworth.)

I

I AM not One who much or oft delight
To season my fireside with personal talk,—
Of friends, who live within an easy walk,
Or neighbours, daily, weekly, in my sight:
And, for my chance-acquaintance, ladies bright,
Sons, mothers, maidens withering on the stalk,
These all wear out of me, like Forms with chalk
Painted on rich men's floors, for one feast-night.
Better than such discourse doth silence long,
Long, barren silence, square with my desire;   10
To sit without emotion, hope, or aim,
In the loved presence of my cottage-fire,

And listen to the flapping of the flame,
Or kettle whispering its faint under-song.

II

'Yet life,' you say, 'is life; we have seen and see,
And with a living pleasure we describe;
And fits of sprightly malice do but bribe
The languid mind into activity.
Sound sense, and love itself, and mirth and glee
Are fostered by the comment and the gibe.'   20
Even be it so: yet still among your tribe,
Our daily world's true Worldlings, rank not me!
Children are blest, and powerful; their world lies
More justly balanced; partly at their feet,
And part far from them:—sweetest melodies
Are those that are by distance made more sweet;
Whose mind is but the mind of his own eyes,
He is a Slave; the meanest we can meet!

III

Wings have we,—and as far as we can go
We may find pleasure: wilderness and wood,   30
Blank ocean and mere sky, support that mood
Which with the lofty sanctifies the low.
Dreams, books, are each a world; and books, we
      know,
Are a substantial world, both pure and good:
Round these, with tendrils strong as flesh and
      blood,
Our pastime and our happiness will grow.
There find I personal themes, a plenteous store,
Matter wherein right voluble I am,
To which I listen with a ready ear;
Two shall be named, pre-eminently dear,—   40
The gentle Lady[1] married to the Moor;
And heavenly Una[2] with her milk-white Lamb.

IV

Nor can I not believe but that hereby
Great gains are mine; for thus I live remote
From evil-speaking; rancour, never sought,
Comes to me not; malignant truth, or lie.
Hence have I genial seasons, hence have I
Smooth passions, smooth discourse, and joyous
      thought:
And thus from day to day my little boat
Rocks in its harbour, lodging peaceably.   50
Blessings be with them—and eternal praise,
Who gave us nobler loves, and nobler cares—
The Poets, who on earth have made us heirs

---

1 Desdemona, wife of Othello.
2 the lovely lady personifying Truth in Spenser's *Faerie Queene*.

Of truth and pure delight by heavenly lays!
Oh! might my name be numbered among theirs,
Then gladly would I end my mortal days.

1806   1807

WHERE LIES THE LAND

WHERE lies the Land to which yon Ship must go?
Fresh as a lark mounting at break of day,
Festively she puts forth in trim array;
Is she for tropic suns, or polar snow?
What boots the enquiry?—Neither friend nor foe
She cares for; let her travel where she may,
She finds familiar names, a beaten way
Ever before her, and a wind to blow.
Yet still I ask, what haven is her mark?
And, almost as it was when ships were rare   10
(From time to time, like Pilgrims, here and there
Crossing the waters) doubt, and something dark,
Of the old Sea some reverential fear,
Is with me at thy farewell, joyous Bark!

1807

WITH SHIPS THE SEA WAS SPRINKLED

WITH Ships the sea was sprinkled far and nigh,
Like stars in heaven, and joyously it showed;
Some lying fast at anchor in the road,
Some veering up and down, one knew not why.
A goodly Vessel did I then espy
Come like a giant from a haven broad;
And lustily along the bay she strode,
Her tackling rich, and of apparel high.
This Ship was nought to me, nor I to her,
Yet I pursued her with a Lover's look;   10
This Ship to all the rest did I prefer:
When will she turn, and whither? She will brook
No tarrying; where She comes the winds must stir:
On went She, and due north her journey took.

1807

TO SLEEP

A FLOCK of sheep that leisurely pass by,
One after one; the sound of rain, and bees
Murmuring; the fall of rivers, winds and seas,
Smooth fields, white sheets of water, and pure sky;
I have thought of all by turns, and yet do lie
Sleepless! and soon the small birds' melodies
Must hear, first uttered from my orchard trees;
And the first cuckoo's melancholy cry.
Even thus last night, and two nights more, I lay
And could not win thee, Sleep! by any stealth: 10
So do not let me wear to-night away:

Without Thee what is all the morning's wealth?
Come, blessed barrier between day and day,
Dear mother of fresh thoughts and joyous health!

1807

THOUGHT OF A BRITON ON THE SUBJUGATION OF SWITZERLAND

Two Voices[1] are there; one is of the sea,
One of the mountains; each a mighty Voice:
In both from age to age thou didst rejoice,
They were thy chosen music, Liberty!
There came a Tyrant,[2] and with holy glee
Thou fought'st against him; but hast vainly
    striven;
Thou from thy Alpine holds at length art driven,
Where not a torrent murmurs heard by thee.
Of one deep bliss thine ear hath been bereft:
Then cleave, O cleave to that which still is left; 10
For, high-souled Maid, what sorrow would it be
That Mountain floods should thunder as before,
And Ocean bellow from his rocky shore,
And neither awful Voice be heard by thee!

1807   1807

SONG AT THE FEAST OF BROUGHAM CASTLE

UPON THE RESTORATION OF LORD CLIFFORD,[1] THE
SHEPHERD, TO THE ESTATES AND HONOURS
OF HIS ANCESTORS

HIGH in the breathless Hall the Minstrel sate,
And Emont's[2] murmur mingled with the Song.—
The words of ancient time I thus translate,
A festal strain that hath been silent long:—

'From town to town, from tower to tower,
The red rose[3] is a gladsome flower.
Her thirty years of winter[4] past,
The red rose is revived at last;
She lifts her head for endless spring,
For everlasting blossoming: 10
Both roses flourish, red and white:
In love and sisterly delight
The two that were at strife are blended,[5]

---

1 England and Switzerland.
2 Napoleon; his forces overran Switzerland in February 1798.

---

1 In the War of the Roses, young Henry Lord Clifford, the subject of the poem, was deprived of his possessions by the Yorkists and forced for twenty-four years to live in hiding as a shepherd. He was restored to his estates in the reign of Henry VII.
2 the river Emont, beside which Brougham castle is situated.
3 The red rose was the sign of the House of Lancaster.
4 from the first battle of St. Albans, 1455, to the battle of Bosworth, 1485.
5 by the marriage of Henry VII with Elizabeth of York.

And all old troubles now are ended.—
Joy! joy to both! but most to her
Who is the flower of Lancaster!
Behold her how She smiles to-day
On this great throng, this bright array!
Fair greeting doth she send to all
From every corner of the hall;   20
But chiefly from above the board
Where sits in state our rightful Lord,
A Clifford to his own restored!

 'They came with banner, spear, and shield;
And it was proved in Bosworth-field.
Not long the Avenger was withstood—
Earth helped him with the cry of blood:
St. George was for us, and the might
Of blessed Angels crowned the right.
Loud voice the Land has uttered forth,   30
We loudest in the faithful north:
Our fields rejoice, our mountains ring,
Our streams proclaim a welcoming;
Our strong-abodes and castles see
The glory of their loyalty.

 'How glad is Skipton[6] at this hour—
Though lonely, a deserted Tower;
Knight, squire, and yeoman, page and groom:
We have them at the feast of Brough'm.
How glad Pendragon[7]—though the sleep   40
Of years be on her!—She shall reap
A taste of this great pleasure, viewing
As in a dream her own renewing.
Rejoiced is Brough,[8] right glad, I deem,
Beside her little humble stream;
And she[9] that keepeth watch and ward
Her statelier Eden's course to guard;
They both are happy at this hour,
Though each is but a lonely Tower:—
But here is perfect joy and pride   ,50
For one fair House by Emont's side,
This day, distinguished without peer,
To see her Master and to cheer—
Him, and his Lady-mother dear!

 'Oh! it was a time forlorn
When the fatherless was born—
Give her wings that she may fly,
Or she sees her infant die!
Swords that are with slaughter wild
Hunt the Mother and the Child.   60
Who will take them from the light?
—Yonder is a man in sight—

Yonder is a house—but where?
No, they must not enter there.
To the caves, and to the brooks,
To the clouds of heaven she looks;
She is speechless, but her eyes
Pray in ghostly agonies.
Blissful Mary, Mother mild,
Maid and Mother undefiled,   70
Save a Mother and her Child!

 'Now Who is he that bounds with joy
On Carrock's[10] side, a Shepherd-boy?
No thoughts hath he but thoughts that pass
Light as the wind along the grass.
Can this be He who hither came
In secret, like a smothered flame?
O'er whom such thankful tears were shed
For shelter, and a poor man's bread!
God loves the Child; and God hath willed   80
That those dear words should be fulfilled,
The Lady's words, when forced away
The last she to her Babe did say:
"My own, my own, thy Fellow-guest
I may not be; but rest thee, rest,
For lowly shepherd's life is best!"

 'Alas! when evil men are strong
No life is good, no pleasure long.
The Boy must part from Mosedale's[11] groves,
And leave Blencathara's rugged coves,   90
And quit the flowers that summer brings
To Glenderamakin's lofty springs;
Must vanish, and his careless cheer
Be turned to heaviness and fear.
—Give Sir Lancelot Threlkeld[12] praise!
Hear it, good man, old in days!
Thou tree of covert and of rest
For this young Bird that is distrest;
Among thy branches safe he lay,
And he was free to sport and play,   100
When falcons were abroad for prey.

 'A recreant harp, that sings of fear
And heaviness in Clifford's ear!
I said, when evil men are strong,
No life is good, no pleasure long.
A weak and cowardly untruth!
Our Clifford was a happy Youth,
And thankful through a weary time,
That brought him up to manhood's prime.
—Again he wanders forth at will,   110
And tends a flock from hill to hill:
His garb is humble; ne'er was seen

---

6 a castle in Yorkshire comprised in the Clifford estates.
7 another castle of the Cliffords.
8 still another castle of the Cliffords.
9 Appleby Castle.

10 in Cumberland.
11 The places mentioned are in Cumberland.
12 He concealed the boy Clifford on his estates.

Such garb with such a noble mien;
Among the shepherd-grooms no mate
Hath he, a Child of strength and state!
Yet lacks not friends for simple glee,
Nor yet for higher sympathy.
To his side the fallow-deer
Came, and rested without fear;
The eagle, lord of land and sea,   120
Stooped down to pay him fealty;
And both the undying fish[13] that swim
Through Bowscale-tarn did wait on him;
The pair were servants of his eye
In their immortality;
And glancing, gleaming, dark or bright,
Moved to and fro, for his delight.
He knew the rocks which Angels haunt
Upon the mountains visitant;
He hath kenned them taking wing: 130
And into caves where Faeries sing
He hath entered; and been told
By Voices how men lived of old.
Among the heavens his eye can see
The face of thing that is to be;
And, if that men report him right,
His tongue could whisper words of might.
—Now another day is come,
Fitter hope, and nobler doom;
He hath thrown aside his crook,   140
And hath buried deep his book;
Armour rusting in his halls
On the blood of Clifford calls;[14]—
"Quell the Scot," exclaims the Lance—
Bear me to the heart of France,
Is the longing of the Shield—
Tell thy name, thou trembling Field;
Field of death, where'er thou be,
Groan thou with our victory!
Happy day, and mighty hour,   150
When our Shepherd in his power,
Mailed and horsed, with lance and sword,
To his ancestors restored
Like a re-appearing Star,
Like a glory from afar,
First shall head the flock of war!'

Alas! the impassioned minstrel did not know
How, by Heaven's grace, this Clifford's heart was
   framed:

How he, long forced in humble walks to go,
Was softened into feeling, soothed, and tamed. 160

Love had he found in huts where poor men lie;
His daily teachers had been woods and rills,
The silence that is in the starry sky,
The sleep that is among the lonely hills.

In him the savage virtue of the Race,
Revenge, and all ferocious thoughts were dead:
Nor did he change; but kept in lofty place
The wisdom which adversity had bred.

Glad were the vales, and every cottage-hearth;
The Shepherd-lord was honoured more and
   more;   170
And, ages after he was laid in earth,
'The good Lord Clifford' was the name he bore.

    1807   1807

HERE PAUSE: THE POET CLAIMS AT LEAST THIS PRAISE

HERE pause: the poet claims at least this praise,
That virtuous Liberty hath been the scope
Of his pure song, which did not shrink from hope
In the worst moment of these evil days;
From hope, the paramount *duty* that Heaven
   lays,
For its own honour, on man's suffering heart.
Never may from our souls one truth depart—
That an accursed thing it is to gaze
On prosperous tyrants with a dazzled eye;
Nor—touched with due abhorrence of *their*
   guilt   10
For whose dire ends tears flow, and blood is spilt,
And justice labours in extremity—
Forget thy weakness, upon which is built,
O wretched man, the throne of tyranny!

    1811   1815

From THE EXCURSION

PROSPECTUS

The title-page announces that this is only a portion of
a poem; and the Reader must be here apprised that it
belongs to the second part of a long and laborious Work,
[The Recluse], which is to consist of three parts,[1] . . . [the
first and third parts] of meditations in the Author's own
person; and that in the intermediate part (*The Excursion*)
the intervention of characters speaking is employed, and
something of a dramatic form adopted.

---

13 It is imagined by the people in the country that there are two
immortal Fish, inhabitants of this Tarn, which lies in the mountains not far from Threlkeld.—(Wordsworth.)
14 The martial character of the Cliffords is well known to the
readers of English history; but it may not be improper here to say,
by way of comment on these lines and what follows, that besides
several others who perished in the same manner, the four immediate Progenitors of the Person in whose hearing this is supposed
to be spoken all died in the Field.—(Wordsworth.)

---

1 Of these three parts the second alone (that is, *The Excursion*)
was completed. A first book of the first part of *The Recluse* was
left by Wordsworth in manuscript except for the passage beginning 'On Man, on Nature, and on Human Life.'

It is not the Author's intention formally to announce a system: it was more animating to him to proceed in a different course; and if he shall succeed in conveying to the mind clear thoughts, lively images, and strong feelings, the Reader will have no difficulty in extracting the system for himself. And in the meantime the following passage, taken from the conclusion of the first book of *The Recluse,* may be acceptable as a kind of Prospectus of the design and scope of the whole Poem. [From 'Preface to the Edition of 1814.']

'On Man, on Nature, and on Human Life,
Musing in solitude, I oft perceive
Fair trains of imagery before me rise,
Accompanied by feelings of delight
Pure, or with no unpleasing sadness mixed.
And I am conscious of affecting thoughts
And dear remembrances, whose presence soothes
Or elevates the Mind, intent to weigh
The good and evil of our mortal state.
—To these emotions, whencesoe'er they come, 10
Whether from breath of outward circumstance,
Or from the Soul—an impulse to herself—
I would give utterance in numerous verse.
Of Truth, of Grandeur, Beauty, Love, and Hope,
And melancholy Fear subdued by Faith;
Of blessèd consolations in distress;
Of moral strength, and intellectual Power;
Of joy in widest commonalty spread;
Of the individual Mind that keeps her own
Inviolate retirement, subject there   20
To Conscience only, and the law supreme
Of that Intelligence which governs all—
I sing:—"fit audience let me find though few!"

'So prayed, more gaining than he asked, the Bard—
In holiest mood. Urania, I shall need
Thy guidance, or a greater Muse, if such
Descend to earth or dwell in highest heaven!
For I must tread on shadowy ground, must sink
Deep—and, aloft ascending, breathe in worlds
To which the heaven of heavens is but a veil.   30
All strength—all terror, single or in bands,
That ever was put forth in personal form—
Jehovah—with his thunder, and the choir
Of shouting Angels, and the empyreal thrones—
I pass them unalarmed. Not Chaos, not
The darkest pit of lowest Erebus,
Nor aught of blinder vacancy, scooped out
By help of dreams—can breed such fear and awe
As fall upon us often when we look
Into our Minds, into the Mind of Man—   40
My haunt, and the main region of my song.
—Beauty—a living Presence of the earth,
Surpassing the most fair ideal Forms

Which craft of delicate Spirits hath composed
From earth's materials—waits upon my steps;
Pitches her tents before me as I move,
An hourly neighbour. Paradise, and groves
Elysian, Fortunate Fields—like those of old
Sought in the Atlantic Main—why should they be
A history only of departed things,   50
Or a mere fiction of what never was?
For the discerning intellect of Man,
When wedded to this goodly universe
In love and holy passion, shall find these
A simple produce of the common day.
—I, long before the blissful hour arrives,
Would chant, in lonely peace, the spousal verse
Of this great consummation:—and, by words
Which speak of nothing more than what we are,
Would I arouse the sensual from their sleep   60
Of Death, and win the vacant and the vain
To noble raptures; while my voice proclaims
How exquisitely the individual Mind
(And the progressive powers perhaps no less
Of the whole species) to the external World
Is fitted:—and how exquisitely, too—
Theme this but little heard of among men—
The external World is fitted to the Mind;
And the creation (by no lower name
Can it be called) which they with blended might   70
Accomplish:—this is our high argument.
—Such grateful haunts foregoing, if I oft
Must turn elsewhere—to travel near the tribes
And fellowships of men, and see ill sights
Of madding passions mutually inflamed;
Must hear Humanity in fields and groves
Pipe solitary anguish; or must hang
Brooding above the fierce confederate storm
Of sorrow, barricadoed evermore
Within the walls of cities—may these sounds   80
Have their authentic comment; that even these
Hearing, I be not downcast or forlorn!—
Descend, prophetic Spirit! that inspir'st
The human Soul of universal earth,
Dreaming on things to come; and dost possess
A metropolitan temple in the hearts
Of mighty Poets: upon me bestow
A gift of genuine insight; that my Song
With star-like virtue in its place may shine,
Shedding benignant influence, and secure,   90
Itself, from all malevolent effect
Of those mutations that extend their sway
Throughout the nether sphere!—And if with this
I mix more lowly matter; with the thing
Contemplated, describe the Mind and Man

Contemplating; and who, and what he was—
The transitory Being that beheld
This Vision; when and where, and how he
    lived;—
Be not this labour useless. If such theme
May sort with highest objects, then—dread
    Power!   100
Whose gracious favour is the primal source
Of all illumination,—may my Life
Express the image of a better time,
More wise desires, and simpler manners;—nurse
My Heart in genuine freedom:—all pure
    thoughts
Be with me;—so shall thy unfailing love
Guide, and support, and cheer me to the end!'

                  1814

BOOK FIRST

THE WANDERER

Lines 1–37, 108–243, 340–81, 434–970

A summer forenoon.—The Author reaches a ruined
Cottage upon a Common, and there meets with a revered Friend, the Wanderer, of whose education and
course of life he gives an account.—The Wanderer, while
resting under the shade of the Trees that surround the
Cottage, relates the History of its last Inhabitant.

'TWAS summer, and the sun had mounted high:
Southward the landscape indistinctly glared
Through a pale steam; but all the northern
    downs,
In clearest air ascending, showed far off
A surface dappled o'er with shadows flung
From brooding clouds; shadows that lay in spots
Determined and unmoved, with steady beams
Of bright and pleasant sunshine interposed;
To him most pleasant who on soft cool moss
Extends his careless limbs along the front   10
Of some huge cave, whose rocky ceiling casts
A twilight of its own, an ample shade,
Where the wren warbles, while the dreaming
    man,
Half conscious of the soothing melody,
With side-long eye looks out upon the scene,
By power of that impending covert, thrown
To finer distance. Mine was at that hour
Far other lot, yet with good hope that soon
Under a shade as grateful I should find
Rest, and be welcomed there to livelier joy.   20
Across a bare wide Common I was toiling
With languid steps that by the slippery turf
Were baffled; nor could my weak arm disperse
The host of insects gathering round my face,
And ever with me as I paced along.

Upon that open moorland stood a grove,
The wished-for port to which my course was
    bound.
Thither I came, and there, amid the gloom
Spread by a brotherhood of lofty elms,
Appeared a roofless Hut; four naked walls   30
That stared upon each other!—I looked round,
And to my wish and to my hope espied
The Friend I sought; a Man of reverend age,
But stout and hale, for travel unimpaired.
There was he seen upon the cottage-bench,
Recumbent in the shade, as if asleep;
An iron-pointed staff lay at his side.

         .   .   .

[THE WANDERER][1]

  Among the hills of Athol he was born;
Where, on a small hereditary farm,
An unproductive slip of rugged ground,   110
His Parents, with their numerous offspring,
    dwelt;
A virtuous household, though exceeding poor!
Pure livers were they all, austere and grave,
And fearing God; the very children taught
Stern self-respect, a reverence for God's word,
And an habitual piety, maintained
With strictness scarcely known on English
    ground.

  From his sixth year, the Boy of whom I speak,
In summer, tended cattle on the hills;
But, through the inclement and the perilous
    days   120
Of long-continuing winter, he repaired,
Equipped with satchel, to a school, that stood
Sole building on a mountain's dreary edge,
Remote from view of city spire, or sound
Of minster clock! From that bleak tenement
He, many an evening, to his distant home
In solitude returning, saw the hills
Grow larger in the darkness; all alone
Beheld the stars come out above his head,
And travelled through the wood, with no one
    near   130
To whom he might confess the things he saw.

  So the foundations of his mind were laid.
In such communion, not from terror free,
While yet a child, and long before his time,

---

1 In creating the person of the Wanderer, Wordsworth has attributed to him many of the features of character and education that
had marked his own development under the fostering influence
of Nature and of books. The Wanderer is, in fact, another Wordsworth.

Had he perceived the presence and the power
Of greatness; and deep feelings had impressed
So vividly great objects that they lay
Upon his mind like substances, whose presence
Perplexed the bodily sense. He had received
A precious gift; for, as he grew in years,   140
With these impressions would he still compare
All his remembrances, thoughts, shapes, and
      forms;
And, being still unsatisfied with aught
Of dimmer character, he thence attained
An active power to fasten images
Upon his brain; and on their pictured lines
Intensely brooded, even till they acquired
The liveliness of dreams. Nor did he fail,
While yet a child, with a child's eagerness
Incessantly to turn his ear and eye   150
On all things which the moving seasons brought
To feed such appetite—nor this alone
Appeased his yearning:—in the after-day
Of boyhood, many an hour in caves forlorn,
And 'mid the hollow depths of naked crags
He sate, and even in their fixed lineaments,
Or from the power of a peculiar eye,
Or by creative feeling overborne,
Or by predominance of thought oppressed,
Even in their fixed and steady lineaments   160
He traced an ebbing and a flowing mind,
Expression ever varying!
                              Thus informed,
He had small need of books; for many a tale
Traditionary round the mountains hung,
And many a legend, peopling the dark woods,
Nourished Imagination in her growth,
And gave the Mind that apprehensive power
By which she is made quick to recognise
The moral properties and scope of things.
But eagerly he read, and read again,   170
Whate'er the minister's old shelf supplied;
The life and death of martyrs, who sustained,
With will inflexible, those fearful pangs
Triumphantly displayed in records left
Of persecution, and the Covenant—times
Whose echo rings through Scotland to this hour!
And there, by lucky hap, had been preserved
A straggling volume, torn and incomplete,
That left half-told the preternatural tale,
Romance of giants, chronicle of fiends,   180
Profuse in garniture of wooden cuts
Strange and uncouth; dire faces, figures dire,
Sharp-kneed, sharp-elbowed, and lean-ankled
      too,
With long and ghostly shanks—forms which
      once seen

Could never be forgotten!
                              In his heart,
Where Fear sate thus, a cherished visitant,
Was wanting yet the pure delight of love
By sound diffused, or by the breathing air,
Or by the silent looks of happy things,
Or flowing from the universal face   190
Of earth and sky. But he had felt the power
Of Nature, and already was prepared,
By his intense conceptions, to receive
Deeply the lesson deep of love which he,
Whom Nature, by whatever means, has taught
To feel intensely, cannot but receive.

    Such was the Boy—but for the growing Youth
What soul was his, when, from the naked top
Of some bold headland, he beheld the sun
Rise up, and bathe the world in light!
            He looked—   200
Ocean and earth, the solid frame of earth
And ocean's liquid mass, in gladness lay
Beneath him:—Far and wide the clouds were
      touched,
And in their silent faces could he read
Unutterable love. Sound needed none,
Nor any voice of joy; his spirit drank
The spectacle: sensation, soul, and form,
All melted into him; they swallowed up
His animal being; in them did he live,
And by them did he live; they were his life.   210
In such access of mind, in such high hour
Of visitation from the living God,
Thought was not; in enjoyment it expired.
No thanks he breathed, he proffered no request;
Rapt into still communion that transcends
The imperfect offices of prayer and praise,
His mind was a thanksgiving to the power
That made him; it was blessedness and love!

    A Herdsman on the lonely mountain-tops,
Such intercourse was his, and in this sort   220
Was his existence oftentimes *possessed*.
O then how beautiful, how bright, appeared
The written promise! Early had he learned
To reverence the volume that displays
The mystery, the life which cannot die;
But in the mountains did he *feel* his faith.
All things, responsive to the writing, there
Breathed immortality, revolving life,
And greatness still revolving; infinite:
There littleness was not; the least of things   230
Seemed infinite; and there his spirit shaped
Her prospects, nor did he believe,—he *saw*.
What wonder if his being thus became

Sublime and comprehensive! Low desires,
Low thoughts had there no place; yet was his
    heart
Lowly; for he was meek in gratitude,
Oft as he called those ecstasies to mind,
And whence they flowed; and from them he ac-
    quired
Wisdom, which works thro' patience; thence he
    learned
In oft-recurring hours of sober thought   240
To look on Nature with a humble heart,
Self-questioned where it did not understand,
And with a superstitious eye of love.

                From his native hills   340
He wandered far; much did he see of men,
Their manners, their enjoyments, and pursuits,
Their passions and their feelings; chiefly those
Essential and eternal in the heart,
That, 'mid the simpler forms of rural life,
Exist more simple in their elements,
And speak a plainer language. In the woods,
A lone Enthusiast, and among the fields,
Itinerant in this labour, he had passed
The better portion of his time; and there   350
Spontaneously had his affections thriven
Amid the bounties of the year, the peace
And liberty of nature; there he kept
In solitude and solitary thought
His mind in a just equipoise of love.
Serene it was, unclouded by the cares
Of ordinary life; unvexed, unwarped
By partial bondage. In his steady course,
No piteous revolutions had he felt,
No wild varieties of joy and grief.   360
Unoccupied by sorrow of its own,
His heart lay open; and, by nature tuned
And constant disposition of his thoughts
To sympathy with man, he was alive
To all that was enjoyed where'er he went,
And all that was endured; for, in himself
Happy, and quiet in his cheerfulness,
He had no painful pressure from without
That made him turn aside from wretchedness
With coward fears. He could *afford* to suffer 370
With those whom he saw suffer. Hence it
    came
That in our best experience he was rich,
And in the wisdom of our daily life.
For hence, minutely, in his various rounds,
He had observed the progress and decay
Of many minds, of minds and bodies too;
The history of many families;

How they had prospered; how they were o'er-
    thrown
By passion or mischance, or such misrule
Among the unthinking masters of the earth   380
As makes the nations groan.

       .   .

[MARGARET, OR THE RUINED COTTAGE][2]

   So was He framed; and such his course of life
Who now, with no appendage but a staff,
The prized memorial of relinquished toils,
Upon that cottage-bench reposed his limbs,
Screened from the sun. Supine the Wanderer lay,
His eyes as if in drowsiness half shut,
The shadows of the breezy elms above   440
Dappling his face. He had not heard the sound
Of my approaching steps, and in the shade
Unnoticed did I stand some minutes' space.
At length I hailed him, seeing that his hat
Was moist with water-drops, as if the brim
Had newly scooped a running stream. He rose,
And ere our lively greeting into peace
Had settled, ' 'Tis,' said I, 'a burning day:
My lips are parched with thirst, but you, it seems,
Have somewhere found relief.' He, at the
    word,   450
Pointing towards a sweet-briar, bade me climb
The fence where that aspiring shrub looked out
Upon the public way. It was a plot
Of garden ground run wild, its matted weeds
Marked with the steps of those, whom, as they
    passed,
The gooseberry trees that shot in long lank slips,
Or currants, hanging from their leafless stems,
In scanty strings, had tempted to o'erleap
The broken wall. I looked around, and there,
Where two tall hedge-rows of thick alder
    boughs   460
Joined in a cold damp nook, espied a well
Shrouded with willow-flowers and plumy fern.
My thirst I slaked, and, from the cheerless spot
Withdrawing, straightway to the shade returned
Where sate the old Man on the cottage-bench;
And, while, beside him, with uncovered head,
I yet was standing, freely to respire,
And cool my temples in the fanning air,
Thus did he speak. 'I see around me here

---

2 Wordsworth began the story of Margaret in 1795 and substantially completed it in 1798. He seems originally to have designed it
for a separate poem. At the time of Coleridge's memorable visit
at Racedown in June 1797, William read his new poem, *The Ruined
Cottage*, Dorothy tells us, to Coleridge, who was 'much delighted'
with it.

Things which you cannot see: we die, my
    Friend,   470
Nor we alone, but that which each man loved
And prized in his peculiar nook of earth
Dies with him, or is changed; and very soon
Even of the good is no memorial left.
—The Poets, in their elegies and songs
Lamenting the departed, call the groves,
They call upon the hills and streams to mourn,
And senseless rocks; nor idly; for they speak,
In these their invocations, with a voice
Obedient to the strong creative power   480
Of human passion. Sympathies there are
More tranquil, yet perhaps of kindred birth,
That steal upon the meditative mind,
And grow with thought. Beside yon spring
    I stood,
And eyed its waters till we seemed to feel
One sadness, they and I. For them a bond
Of brotherhood is broken: time has been
When, every day, the touch of human hand
Dislodged the natural sleep that binds them up
In mortal stillness; and they ministered   490
To human comfort. Stooping down to drink,
Upon the slimy foot-stone I espied
The useless fragment of a wooden bowl,
Green with the moss of years, and subject only
To the soft handling of the elements:
There let it lie—how foolish are such thoughts!
Forgive them;—never—never did my steps
Approach this door but she who dwelt within
A daughter's welcome gave me, and I loved her
As my own child. Oh, Sir! the good die first, 500
And they whose hearts are dry as summer dust
Burn to the socket. Many a passenger
Hath blessed poor Margaret for her gentle looks,
When she upheld the cool refreshment drawn
From that forsaken spring; and no one came
But he was welcome; no one went away
But that it seemed she loved him. She is dead,
The light extinguished of her lonely hut,
The hut itself abandoned to decay,
And she forgotten in the quiet grave.   510
    'I speak,' continued he, 'of One whose stock
Of virtues bloomed beneath this lowly roof.
She was a Woman of a steady mind,
Tender and deep in her excess of love;
Not speaking much, pleased rather with the joy
Of her own thoughts; by some especial care
Her temper had been framed, as if to make
A Being, who by adding love to peace
Might live on earth a life of happiness.
Her wedded Partner lacked not on his side 520
The humble worth that satisfied her heart:

Frugal, affectionate, sober, and withal
Keenly industrious. She with pride would tell
That he was often seated at his loom,
In summer, ere the mower was abroad
Among the dewy grass,—in early spring,
Ere the last star had vanished.—They who passed
At evening, from behind the garden fence
Might hear his busy spade, which he would ply,
After his daily work, until the light   530
Had failed, and every leaf and flower were lost
In the dark hedges. So their days were spent
In peace and comfort; and a pretty boy
Was their best hope, next to the God in heaven.

    'Not twenty years ago, but you I think
Can scarcely bear it now in mind, there came
Two blighting seasons, when the fields were left
With half a harvest. It pleased Heaven to add
A worse affliction in the plague of war:
This happy Land was stricken to the heart! 540
A Wanderer then among the cottages,
I, with my freight of winter raiment, saw
The hardships of that season: many rich
Sank down, as in a dream, among the poor;
And of the poor did many cease to be,
And their place knew them not. Meanwhile,
    abridged
Of daily comforts, gladly reconciled
To numerous self-denials, Margaret
Went struggling on through those calamitous
    years
With cheerful hope, until the second autumn, 550
When her life's Helpmate on a sick-bed lay,
Smitten with perilous fever. In disease
He lingered long; and, when his strength returned,
He found the little he had stored, to meet
The hour of accident or crippling age,
Was all consumed. A second infant now
Was added to the troubles of a time
Laden, for them and all of their degree,
With care and sorrow: shoals of artisans
From ill-requited labour turned adrift   560
Sought daily bread from public charity,
They, and their wives and children—happier far
Could they have lived as do the little birds
That peck along the hedge-rows, or the kite
That makes her dwelling on the mountain rocks!

    'A sad reverse it was for him who long
Had filled with plenty, and possessed in peace,
This lonely Cottage. At the door he stood,
And whistled many a snatch of merry tunes
That had no mirth in them; or with his knife 570
Carved uncouth figures on the heads of sticks—
Then, not less idly, sought, through every nook
In house or garden, any casual work

Of use or ornament; and with a strange,
Amusing, yet uneasy, novelty,
He mingled, where he might, the various tasks
Of summer, autumn, winter, and of spring.
But this endured not; his good humour soon
Became a weight in which no pleasure was;
And poverty brought on a petted mood   580
And a sore temper: day by day he drooped,
And he would leave his work—and to the town
Would turn without an errand his slack steps;
Or wander here and there among the fields.
One while he would speak lightly of his babes,
And with a cruel tongue: at other times
He tossed them with a false unnatural joy:
And 'twas a rueful thing to see the looks
Of the poor innocent children. "Every smile,"
Said Margaret to me, here beneath these trees, 590
"Made my heart bleed."'
                    At this the Wanderer paused;
And, looking up to those enormous elms,
He said, ''Tis now the hour of deepest noon.
At this still season of repose and peace,
This hour when all things which are not at rest
Are cheerful; while this multitude of flies
With tuneful hum is filling all the air;
Why should a tear be on an old Man's cheek?
Why should we thus, with an untoward mind,
And in the weakness of humanity,   600
From natural wisdom turn our hearts away;
To natural comfort shut our eyes and ears;
And, feeding on disquiet, thus disturb
The calm of nature with our restless thoughts?'

———————

He spake with somewhat of a solemn tone:
But, when he ended, there was in his face
Such easy cheerfulness, a look so mild,
That for a little time it stole away
All recollection; and that simple tale
Passed from my mind like a forgotten sound.   610
A while on trivial things we held discourse,
To me soon tasteless. In my own despite,
I thought of that poor Woman as of one
Whom I had known and loved. He had rehearsed
Her homely tale with such familiar power,
With such an active countenance, an eye
So busy, that the things of which he spake
Seemed present; and, attention now relaxed,
A heart-felt chillness crept along my veins.
I rose; and, having left the breezy shade,   620
Stood drinking comfort from the warmer sun,
That had not cheered me long—ere, looking
     round
Upon that tranquil Ruin, I returned,
And begged of the old Man that, for my sake,
He would resume his story.

                              He replied,
'It were a wantonness, and would demand
Severe reproof, if we were men whose hearts'
Could hold vain dalliance with the misery
Even of the dead; contented thence to draw
A momentary pleasure, never marked   630
By reason, barren of all future good.
But we have known that there is often found
In mournful thoughts, and always might be
     found,
A power to virtue friendly; were 't not so,
I am a dreamer among men, indeed
An idle dreamer! 'Tis a common tale,
An ordinary sorrow of man's life,
A tale of silent suffering, hardly clothed
In bodily form.—But without further bidding
I will proceed.
                    While thus it fared with them, 640
To whom this cottage, till those hapless years,
Had been a blessèd home, it was my chance
To travel in a country far remote;
And when these lofty elms once more appeared
What pleasant expectations lured me on
O'er the flat Common!—With quick step I reached
The threshold, lifted with light hand the latch;
But, when I entered, Margaret looked at me
A little while; then turned her head away
Speechless,—and, sitting down upon a chair, 650
Wept bitterly. I wist not what to do,
Nor how to speak to her. Poor Wretch! at last
She rose from off her seat, and then,—O Sir!
I cannot *tell* how she pronounced my name:—
With fervent love, and with a face of grief
Unutterably helpless, and a look
That seemed to cling upon me, she enquired
If I had seen her husband. As she spake
A strange surprise and fear came to my heart,
Nor had I power to answer ere she told   660
That he had disappeared—not two months gone.
He left his house: two wretched days had past,
And on the third, as wistfully she raised
Her head from off her pillow, to look forth,
Like one in trouble, for returning light,
Within her chamber-casement she espied
A folded paper, lying as if placed
To meet her waking eyes. This tremblingly
She opened—found no writing, but beheld
Pieces of money carefully enclosed,   670
Silver and gold. "I shuddered at the sight,"
Said Margaret, "for I knew it was his hand
That must have placed it there; and ere that day
Was ended, that long anxious day, I learned,
From one who by my husband had been sent
With the sad news, that he had joined a troop
Of soldiers, going to a distant land.

—He left me thus—he could not gather heart
To take a farewell of me; for he feared
That I should follow with my babes, and sink 680
Beneath the misery of that wandering life.''

'This tale did Margaret tell with many tears:
And, when she ended, I had little power
To give her comfort, and was glad to take
Such words of hope from her own mouth as served
To cheer us both. But long we had not talked
Ere we built up a pile of better thoughts,
And with a brighter eye she looked around
As if she had been shedding tears of joy.
We parted.—'Twas the time of early spring; 690
I left her busy with her garden tools;
And well remember, o'er that fence she looked,
And, while I paced along the foot-way path,
Called out, and sent a blessing after me,
With tender cheerfulness, and with a voice
That seemed the very sound of happy thoughts.

'I roved o'er many a hill and many a dale,
With my accustomed load; in heat and cold,
Through many a wood and many an open ground,
In sunshine and in shade, in wet and fair, 700
Drooping or blithe of heart, as might befall;
My best companions now the driving winds,
And now the "trotting brooks" and whispering
trees.
And now the music of my own sad steps,
With many a short-lived thought that passed be-
tween,
And disappeared.
I journeyed back this way,
When, in the warmth of midsummer, the wheat
Was yellow; and the soft and bladed grass,
Springing afresh, had o'er the hay-field spread
Its tender verdure. At the door arrived, 710
I found that she was absent. In the shade,
Where now we sit, I waited her return.
Her cottage, then a cheerful object, wore
Its customary look,—only, it seemed,
The honeysuckle, crowding round the porch,
Hung down in heavier tufts; and that bright weed,
The yellow stone-crop, suffered to take root
Along the window's edge, profusely grew
Blinding the lower panes. I turned aside,
And strolled into her garden. It appeared 720
To lag behind the season, and had lost
Its pride of neatness. Daisy-flowers and thrift
Had broken their trim border-lines, and straggled
O'er paths they used to deck: carnations, once
Prized for surpassing beauty, and no less
For the peculiar pains they had required,
Declined their languid heads, wanting support.

The cumbrous bind-weed, with its wreaths and
bells,
Had twined about her two small rows of peas,
And dragged them to the earth.
Ere this an hour 730
Was wasted.—Back I turned my restless steps;
A stranger passed; and, guessing whom I sought,
He said that she was used to ramble far.—
The sun was sinking in the west; and now
I sate with sad impatience. From within
Her solitary infant cried aloud;
Then, like a blast that dies away self-stilled,
The voice was silent. From the bench I rose;
But neither could divert nor soothe my thoughts.
The spot, though fair, was very desolate— 740
The longer I remained, more desolate:
And, looking round me, now I first observed
The corner stones, on either side the porch,
With dull red stains discoloured, and stuck o'er
With tufts and hairs of wool, as if the sheep,
That fed upon the Common, thither came
Familiarly, and found a couching-place
Even at her threshold. Deeper shadows fell
From these tall elms; the cottage-clock struck
eight:—
I turned, and saw her distant a few steps. 750
Her face was pale and thin—her figure, too,
Was changed. As she unlocked the door, she
said,
"It grieves me you have waited here so long,
But, in good truth, I've wandered much of late;
And, sometimes—to my shame I speak—have
need
Of my best prayers to bring me back again."
While on the board she spread our evening meal,
She told me—interrupting not the work
Which gave employment to her listless hands—
That she had parted with her elder child; 760
To a kind master on a distant farm
Now happily apprenticed.—"I perceive
You look at me, and you have cause; to-day
I have been travelling far; and many days
About the fields I wander, knowing this
Only, that what I seek I cannot find;
And so I waste my time: for I am changed;
And to myself," said she, "have done much
wrong
And to this helpless infant. I have slept
Weeping, and weeping have I waked; my tears 770
Have flowed as if my body were not such
As others are; and I could never die.
But I am now in mind and in my heart
More easy; and I hope," said she, "that God
Will give me patience to endure the things
Which I behold at home.''

It would have grieved
Your very soul to see her. Sir, I feel
The story linger in my heart; I fear
'Tis long and tedious; but my spirit clings
To that poor Woman:—so familiarly   780
Do I perceive her manner, and her look,
And presence; and so deeply do I feel
Her goodness, that, not seldom, in my walks
A momentary trance comes over me;
And to myself I seem to muse on One
By sorrow laid asleep; or borne away,
A human being destined to awake
To human life, or something very near
To human life, when he shall come again
For whom she suffered. Yes, it would have
     grieved   790
Your very soul to see her: evermore
Her eyelids drooped, her eyes downward were
     cast;
And, when she at her table gave me food,
She did not look at me. Her voice was low,
Her body was subdued. In every act
Pertaining to her house-affairs, appeared
The careless stillness of a thinking mind
Self-occupied; to which all outward things
Are like an idle matter. Still she sighed,
But yet no motion of the breast was seen,   800
No heaving of the heart. While by the fire
We sate together, sighs came on my ear,
I knew not how, and hardly whence they came.

'Ere my departure, to her care I gave,
For her son's use, some tokens of regard,
Which with a look of welcome she received;
And I exhorted her to place her trust
In God's good love, and seek his help by prayer.
I took my staff, and, when I kissed her babe,
The tears stood in her eyes. I left her then   810
With the best hope and comfort I could give:
She thanked me for my wish;—but for my hope
It seemed she did not thank me.
                    I returned,
And took my rounds along this road again
When on its sunny bank the primrose flower
Peeped forth, to give an earnest of the Spring.
I found her sad and drooping: she had learned
No tidings of her husband; if he lived,
She knew not that he lived; if he were dead,
She knew not he was dead. She seemed the
     same   820
In person and appearance; but her house
Bespake a sleepy hand of negligence;
The floor was neither dry nor neat, the hearth
Was comfortless, and her small lot of books,
Which, in the cottage-window, heretofore

Had been piled up against the corner panes
In seemly order, now, with straggling leaves
Lay scattered here and there, open or shut,
As they had chanced to fall. Her infant Babe
Had from its mother caught the trick of grief, 830
And sighed among its playthings. I withdrew,
And once again entering the garden saw,
More plainly still, that poverty and grief
Were now come nearer to her: weeds defaced
The hardened soil, and knots of withered grass:
No ridges there appeared of clear black mould,
No winter greenness; of her herbs and flowers,
It seemed the better part were gnawed away
Or trampled into earth; a chain of straw,
Which had been twined about the slender
     stem   840
Of a young apple-tree, lay at its root;
The bark was nibbled round by truant sheep.
—Margaret stood near, her infant in her arms,
And, noting that my eye was on the tree,
She said, "I fear it will be dead and gone
Ere Robert come again." When to the House
We had returned together, she enquired
If I had any hope:—but for her babe
And for her little orphan boy, she said,
She had no wish to live, that she must die   850
Of sorrow. Yet I saw the idle loom
Still in its place; his Sunday garments hung
Upon the self-same nail; his very staff
Still undisturbed behind the door.
                    And when,
In bleak December, I retraced this way,
She told me that her little babe was dead,
And she was left alone. She now, released
From her maternal cares, had taken up
The employment common through these wilds,
     and gained,
By spinning hemp, a pittance for herself;   860
And for this end had hired a neighbour's boy
To give her needful help. That very time
Most willingly she put her work aside,
And walked with me along the miry road,
Heedless how far; and, in such piteous sort
That any heart had ached to hear her, begged
That, wheresoe'er I went, I still would ask
For him whom she had lost. We parted then—
Our final parting; for from that time forth
Did many seasons pass ere I returned   870
Into this tract again.
                    Nine tedious years;
From their first separation, nine long years,
She lingered in unquiet widowhood;
A Wife and Widow. Needs must it have been
A sore heart-wasting! I have heard, my Friend,
That in yon arbour oftentimes she sate

Alone, through half the vacant sabbath day;
And, if a dog passed by, she still would quit
The shade, and look abroad. On this old bench
For hours she sate; and evermore her eye　　880
Was busy in the distance, shaping things
That made her heart beat quick. You see that path,
Now faint,—the grass has crept o'er its grey line;
There, to and fro, she paced through many a day
Of the warm summer, from a belt of hemp
That girt her waist, spinning the long-drawn thread
With backward steps. Yet ever as there passed
A man whose garments showed the soldier's red,
Or crippled mendicant in sailor's garb,
The little child who sate to turn the wheel　　890
Ceased from his task; and she with faltering voice
Made many a fond enquiry; and when they,
Whose presence gave no comfort, were gone by,
Her heart was still more sad. And by yon gate,
That bars the traveller's road, she often stood,
And when a stranger horseman came, the latch
Would lift, and in his face look wistfully:
Most happy, if, from aught discovered there
Of tender feeling, she might dare repeat
The same sad question. Meanwhile her poor Hut　　900
Sank to decay; for he was gone, whose hand,
At the first nipping of October frost,
Closed up each chink, and with fresh bands of straw
Chequered the green-grown thatch. And so she lived
Through the long winter, reckless and alone;
Until her house by frost, and thaw, and rain,
Was sapped; and while she slept, the nightly damps
Did chill her breast; and in the stormy day
Her tattered clothes were ruffled by the wind,
Even at the side of her own fire. Yet still　　910
She loved this wretched spot, nor would for worlds
Have parted hence; and still that length of road,
And this rude bench, one torturing hope endeared,
Fast rooted at her heart: and here, my Friend,—
In sickness she remained; and here she died;
Last human tenant of these ruined walls!'

　The old Man ceased: he saw that I was moved;
From that low bench, rising instinctively
I turned aside in weakness, nor had power
To thank him for the tale which he had told.　920
I stood, and leaning o'er the garden wall
Reviewed that Woman's sufferings; and it seemed
To comfort me while with a brother's love

I blessed her in the impotence of grief.
Then towards the cottage I returned; and traced
Fondly, though with an interest more mild,
That secret spirit of humanity
Which, 'mid the calm oblivious tendencies
Of nature, 'mid her plants, and weeds, and flowers,
And silent overgrowings, still survived.　　930
The old Man, noting this, resumed, and said,
'My Friend! enough to sorrow you have given,
The purposes of wisdom ask no more:
Nor more would she have craved as due to One
Who, in her worst distress, had ofttimes felt
The unbounded might of prayer; and learned, with soul
Fixed on the Cross, that consolation springs,
From sources deeper far than deepest pain,
For the meek Sufferer. Why then should we read
The forms of things with an unworthy eye?　940
She sleeps in the calm earth, and peace is here.
I well remember that those very plumes,
Those weeds, and the high spear-grass on that wall,
By mist and silent rain-drops silvered o'er,
As once I passed, into my heart conveyed
So still an image of tranquillity,
So calm and still, and looked so beautiful
Amid the uneasy thoughts which filled my mind,
That what we feel of sorrow and despair
From ruin and from change, and all the grief　950
That passing shows of Being leave behind,
Appeared an idle dream, that could maintain,
Nowhere, dominion o'er the enlightened spirit
Whose meditative sympathies repose
Upon the breast of Faith. I turned away,
And walked along my road in happiness.'

　He ceased. Ere long the sun declining shot
A slant and mellow radiance, which began
To fall upon us, while, beneath the trees,
We sate on that low bench: and now we felt,　960
Admonished thus, the sweet hour coming on.
A linnet warbled from those lofty elms,
A thrush sang loud, and other melodies,
At distance heard, peopled the milder air.
The old Man rose, and, with a sprightly mien
Of hopeful preparation, grasped his staff;
Together casting then a farewell look
Upon those silent walls, we left the shade;
And, ere the stars were visible, had reached
A village-inn,—our evening resting-place.　970

BOOK SECOND

THE SOLITARY

Lines 691–725, 828–77

View, from the window, of two mountain summits;
and the Solitary's description of the companionship they
afford him. . . . Description of a grand spectacle upon the
mountains, with its effect upon the Solitary's mind.

I COULD not, ever and anon, forbear
To glance an upward look on two huge Peaks,[1]
That from some other vale peered into this.
'Those lusty twins,' exclaimed our host, 'if here
It were your lot to dwell, would soon become
Your prized companions.—Many are the notes
Which, in his tuneful course, the wind draws forth
From rocks, woods, caverns, heaths, and dashing
    shores;
And well those lofty brethren bear their part
In the wild concert—chiefly when the storm   700
Rides high; then all the upper air they fill
With roaring sound, that ceases not to flow,
Like smoke, along the level of the blast,
In mighty current; theirs, too, is the song
Of stream and headlong flood that seldom fails;
And, in the grim and breathless hour of noon,
Methinks that I have heard them echo back
The thunder's greeting. Nor have nature's laws
Left them ungifted with a power to yield
Music of finer tone; a harmony,   710
So do I call it, though it be the hand
Of silence, though there be no voice;—the clouds,
The mist, the shadows, light of golden suns,
Motions of moonlight, all come thither—touch,
And have an answer—thither come, and shape
A language not unwelcome to sick hearts
And idle spirits:—there the sun himself,
At the calm close of summer's longest day,
Rests his substantial orb;—between those heights
And on the top of either pinnacle,   720
More keenly than elsewhere in night's blue vault,
Sparkle the stars, as of their station proud.
Thoughts are not busier in the mind of man
Than the mute agents stirring there:—alone
Here do I sit and watch.—'

.   .   .

           'Homeward the
  shepherds moved
Through the dull mist, I following—when a step,
A single step, that freed me from the skirts   830
Of the blind vapour, opened to my view
Glory beyond all glory ever seen
By waking sense or by the dreaming soul!

---

[1] the Langdale Pikes.

The appearance, instantaneously disclosed,
Was of a mighty city—boldly say
A wilderness of building, sinking far
And self-withdrawn into a boundless depth,
Far sinking into splendour—without end!
Fabric it seemed of diamond and of gold,
With alabaster domes, and silver spires,   840
And blazing terrace upon terrace, high
Uplifted; here, serene pavilions bright,
In avenues disposed; there, towers begirt
With battlements that on their restless fronts
Bore stars—illumination of all gems!
By earthly nature had the effect been wrought
Upon the dark materials of the storm
Now pacified; on them, and on the coves
And mountain-steeps and summits, whereunto
The vapours had receded, taking there   850
Their station under a cerulean sky.
Oh, 'twas an unimaginable sight!
Clouds, mists, streams, watery rocks and emerald
    turf,
Clouds of all tincture, rocks and sapphire sky,
Confused, commingled, mutually inflamed,
Molten together, and composing thus,
Each lost in each, that marvellous array
Of temple, palace, citadel, and huge
Fantastic pomp of structure without name,
In fleecy folds voluminous, enwrapped.   860
Right in the midst, where interspace appeared
Of open court, an object like a throne
Under a shining canopy of state
Stood fixed; and fixed resemblances were seen
To implements of ordinary use,
But vast in size, in substance glorified;
Such as by Hebrew Prophets were beheld
In vision—forms uncouth of mightiest power
For admiration and mysterious awe.
This little Vale, a dwelling-place of Man,   870
Lay low beneath my feet; 'twas visible—
I saw not, but I felt that it was there.
That which I *saw* was the revealed abode
Of Spirits in beatitude: my heart
Swelled in my breast.—"I have been dead," I
    cried,
"And now I live! Oh! wherefore *do* I live?"
And with that pang I prayed to be no more!—'

BOOK FOURTH

DESPONDENCY CORRECTED

Lines 1106–1270

Wanderer points out how to commune with Nature.

          'As men from men
Do, in the constitution of their souls,
Differ, by mystery not to be explained;

And as we fall by various ways, and sink
One deeper than another, self-condemned   1110
Through manifold degrees of guilt and shame;
So manifold and various are the ways
Of restoration, fashioned to the steps
Of all infirmity, and tending all
To the same point, attainable by all—
Peace in ourselves, and union with our God.
For you, assuredly, a hopeful road
Lies open: we have heard from you a voice
At every moment softened in its course
By tenderness of heart; have seen your eye,   1120
Even like an altar lit by fire from heaven,
Kindle before us.—Your discourse this day,
That, like the fabled Lethe, wished to flow
In creeping sadness, through oblivious shades
Of death and night, has caught at every turn
The colours of the sun. Access for you
Is yet preserved to principles of truth,
Which the imaginative Will upholds
In seats of wisdom, not to be approached
By the inferior Faculty that moulds,   1130
With her minute and speculative pains,
Opinion, ever changing!

                I have seen
A curious child, who dwelt upon a tract
Of inland ground, applying to his ear
The convolutions of a smooth-lipped shell;
To which, in silence hushed, his very soul
Listened intensely; and his countenance soon
Brightened with joy; for from within were heard
Murmurings, whereby the monitor expressed
Mysterious union with its native sea.   1140
Even such a shell the universe itself
Is to the ear of Faith; and there are times,
I doubt not, when to you it doth impart
Authentic tidings of invisible things;
Of ebb and flow, and ever-during power;
And central peace, subsisting at the heart
Of endless agitation. Here you stand,
Adore, and worship, when you know it not;
Pious beyond the intention of your thought;
Devout above the meaning of your will.   1150
—Yes, you have felt, and may not cease to feel.
The estate of man would be indeed forlorn
If false conclusions of the reasoning power
Made the eye blind, and closed the passages
Through which the ear converses with the heart.
Has not the soul, the being of your life,
Received a shock of awful consciousness,
In some calm season, when these lofty rocks
At night's approach bring down the unclouded
    sky,
To rest upon their circumambient walls;   1160
A temple framing of dimensions vast,

And yet not too enormous for the sound
Of human anthems,—choral song, or burst
Sublime of instrumental harmony,
To glorify the Eternal! What if these
Did never break the stillness that prevails
Here,—if the solemn nightingale be mute,
And the soft woodlark here did never chant
Her vespers,—Nature fails not to provide
Impulse and utterance. The whispering air   1170
Sends inspiration from the shadowy heights,
And blind recesses of the caverned rocks;
The little rills, and waters numberless,
Inaudible by daylight, blend their notes
With the loud streams: and often, at the hour
When issue forth the first pale stars, is heard,
Within the circuit of this fabric huge,
One voice—the solitary raven, flying
Athwart the concave of the dark blue dome,
Unseen, perchance above all power of
    sight—   1180
An iron knell! with echoes from afar
Faint—and still fainter—as the cry, with which
The wanderer accompanies her flight
Through the calm region, fades upon the ear,
Diminishing by distance till it seemed
To expire; yet from the abyss is caught again,
And yet again recovered!

                But descending
From these imaginative heights, that yield
Far-stretching views into eternity,
Acknowledge that to Nature's humbler
    power   1190
Your cherished sullenness is forced to bend
Even here, where her amenities are sown
With sparing hand. Then trust yourself abroad
To range her blooming bowers, and spacious
    fields,
Where on the labours of the happy throng
She smiles, including in her wide embrace
City, and town, and tower,—and sea with ships
Sprinkled;—be our Companion while we track
Her rivers populous with gliding life;
While, free as air, o'er printless sands we
    march,   1200
Or pierce the gloom of her majestic woods;
Roaming, or resting under grateful shade
In peace and meditative cheerfulness;
Where living things, and things inanimate,
Do speak, at Heaven's command, to eye and ear,
And speak to social reason's inner sense,
With inarticulate language.

                For, the Man—
Who, in this spirit, communes with the Forms
Of nature, who with understanding heart

Both knows and loves such objects as excite 1210
No morbid passions, no disquietude,
No vengeance, and no hatred—needs must feel
The joy of that pure principle of love
So deeply, that, unsatisfied with aught
Less pure and exquisite, he cannot choose
But seek for objects of a kindred love
In fellow-natures and a kindred joy.
Accordingly he by degrees perceives
His feelings of aversion softened down;
A holy tenderness pervade his frame. 1220
His sanity of reason not impaired,
Say rather, all his thoughts now flowing clear,
From a clear fountain flowing, he looks round
And seeks for good; and finds the good he seeks:
Until abhorrence and contempt are things
He only knows by name; and, if he hear,
From other mouths, the language which they
 speak,
He is compassionate; and has no thought,
No feeling, which can overcome his love.

'And further; by contemplating these
 Forms 1230
In the relations which they bear to man,
He shall discern, how, through the various means
Which silently they yield, are multiplied
The spiritual presences of absent things.
Trust me, that for the instructed, time will come
When they shall meet no object but may teach
Some acceptable lesson to their minds
Of human suffering, or of human joy.
So shall they learn, while all things speak of man,
Their duties from all forms; and general
 laws, 1240
And local accidents, shall tend alike
To rouse, to urge; and, with the will, confer
The ability to spread the blessings wide
Of true philanthropy. The light of love
Not failing, perseverance from their steps
Departing not, for them shall be confirmed
The glorious habit by which sense is made
Subservient still to moral purposes,
Auxiliar to divine. That change shall clothe
The naked spirit, ceasing to deplore 1250
The burthen of existence. Science then
Shall be a precious visitant; and then,
And only then, be worthy of her name:
For then her heart shall kindle; her dull eye,
Dull and inanimate, no more shall hang
Chained to its object in brute slavery;
But taught with patient interest to watch
The processes of things, and serve the cause
Of order and distinctness, not for this

Shall it forget that its most noble use, 1260
Its most illustrious province, must be found
In furnishing clear guidance, a support
Not treacherous, to the mind's *excursive* power.
—So build we up the Being that we are;
Thus deeply drinking-in the soul of things,
We shall be wise perforce; and, while inspired
By choice, and conscious that the Will is free,
Shall move unswerving, even as if impelled
By strict necessity, along the path
Of order and of good.' 1270

BOOK NINTH

DISCOURSE OF THE WANDERER, AND AN EVENING VISIT TO THE LAKE

Lines 1–26, 419–73

Wanderer asserts an active principle pervades the Universe; its noblest seat the human soul. . . Walk to the Lake.—Grand spectacle from the side of a hill.

'To every Form of being is assigned,'
Thus calmly spake the venerable Sage,
'An *active* Principle:—howe'er removed
From sense and observation, it subsists
In all things, in all natures; in the stars
Of azure heaven, the unenduring clouds,
In flower and tree, in every pebbly stone
That paves the brooks, the stationary rocks,
The moving waters, and the invisible air.
Whate'er exists hath properties that spread 10
Beyond itself, communicating good,
A simple blessing, or with evil mixed;
Spirit that knows no insulated spot,
No chasm, no solitude; from link to link
It circulates, the Soul of all the worlds.
This is the freedom of the universe;
Unfolded still the more, more visible,
The more we know; and yet is reverenced least,
And least respected in the human Mind,
Its most apparent home. The food of hope 20
Is meditated action; robbed of this
Her sole support, she languishes and dies.
We perish also; for we live by hope
And by desire; we see by the glad light
And breathe the sweet air of futurity;
And so we live, or else we have no life.

'Behold the shades of afternoon have fallen
Upon this flowery slope; and see—beyond— 420
The silvery lake is streaked with placid blue;
As if preparing for the peace of evening.
How temptingly the landscape shines! The air

Breathes invitation; easy is the walk
To the lake's margin, where a boat lies moored
Under a sheltering tree.'—Upon this hint
We rose together: all were pleased; but most
The beauteous girl, whose cheek was flushed with
    joy.
Light as a sunbeam glides along the hills
She vanished—eager to impart the scheme   430
To her loved brother and his shy compeer.
—Now was there bustle in the Vicar's house
And earnest preparation.—Forth we went,
And down the vale along the streamlet's edge
Pursued our way, a broken company,
Mute or conversing, single or in pairs.
Thus having reached a bridge, that overarched
The hasty rivulet where it lay becalmed
In a deep pool, by happy chance we saw
A twofold image; on a grassy bank   440
A snow-white ram, and in the crystal flood
Another and the same! Most beautiful,
On the green turf, with his imperial front
Shaggy and bold, and wreathèd horns superb,
The breathing creature stood; as beautiful,
Beneath him, showed his shadowy counterpart.
Each had his glowing mountains, each his sky,
And each seemed centre of his own fair world:
Antipodes unconscious of each other,
Yet, in partition, with their several spheres,   450
Blended in perfect stillness, to our sight!

    'Ah! what a pity were it to disperse,
Or to disturb, so fair a spectacle,
And yet a breath can do it!'
                    These few words
The Lady whispered, while we stood and gazed
Gathered together, all in still delight,
Not without awe. Thence passing on, she said
In like low voice to my particular ear,
'I love to hear that eloquent old Man
Pour forth his meditations, and descant   460
On human life from infancy to age.
How pure his spirit! in what vivid hues
His mind gives back the various forms of things,
Caught in their fairest, happiest, attitude!
While he is speaking, I have power to see
Even as he sees; but when his voice hath ceased,
Then, with a sigh, sometimes I feel, as now,
That combinations so serene and bright
Cannot be lasting in a world like ours,
Whose highest beauty, beautiful as it is,   470
Like that reflected in yon quiet pool,
Seems but a fleeting sunbeam's gift, whose peace
The sufferance only of a breath of air!'

1795–1814   1814

LAODAMÍA [1]

    Written at Rydal Mount. The incident of the trees
growing and withering put the subject into my thoughts,
and I wrote with the hope of giving it a loftier tone than,
so far as I know, has been given to it by any of the ancients who have treated of it. It cost me more trouble
than almost anything of equal length I have ever written.
—(Wordsworth.)

'WITH sacrifice before the rising morn
Vows have I made by fruitless hope inspired;
And from the infernal Gods, 'mid shades forlorn
Of night, my slaughtered Lord have I required:
Celestial pity I again implore;—
Restore him to my sight—great Jove, restore!'

So speaking, and by fervent love endowed
With faith, the Suppliant heavenward lifts her
    hands;
While, like the sun emerging from a cloud,
Her countenance brightens—and her eye ex-
    pands;   10
Her bosom heaves and spreads, her stature
    grows;
And she expects the issue in repose.

O terror! what hath she perceived?—O joy!
What doth she look on?—whom doth she be-
    hold?
Her Hero slain upon the beach of Troy?
His vital presence? his corporeal mould?
It is—if sense deceive her not—'tis He!
And a God leads him, wingèd Mercury!

Mild Hermes spake—and touched her with his
    wand
That calms all fear; 'Such grace hath crowned
    thy prayer,   20
Laodamía! that at Jove's command
Thy Husband walks the paths of upper air:
He comes to tarry with thee three hours' space;
Accept the gift, behold him face to face!'

Forth sprang the impassioned Queen her Lord to
    clasp;
Again that consummation she essayed;
But unsubstantial Form eludes her grasp
As often as that eager grasp was made.
The Phantom parts—but parts to re-unite,
And re-assume his place before her sight.   30

'Protesiláus, lo! thy guide is gone!
Confirm, I pray, the vision with thy voice:
This is our palace,—yonder is thy throne;

1 Laodamia was the wife of Protesiláus, the first Greek to die in
the siege of Troy.

Speak, and the floor thou tread'st on will rejoice.
Not to appal me have the gods bestowed
This precious boon; and blest a sad abode.'

'Great Jove, Laodamía! doth not leave
His gifts imperfect:—Spectre though I be,
I am not sent to scare thee or deceive;
But in reward of thy fidelity.   40
And something also did my worth obtain;
For fearless virtue bringeth boundless gain.

'Thou knowest, the Delphic oracle foretold
That the first Greek who touched the Trojan
   strand
Should die; but me the threat could not with-
   hold:
A generous cause a victim did demand;
And forth I leapt upon the sandy plain;
A self-devoted chief—by Hector slain.'

'Supreme of Heroes—bravest, noblest, best!
Thy matchless courage I bewail no more,   50
Which then, when tens of thousands were de-
   prest
By doubt, propelled thee to the fatal shore;
Thou found'st—and I forgive thee—here thou
   art—
A nobler counsellor than my poor heart.

'But thou, though capable of sternest deed,
Wert kind as resolute, and good as brave;
And he, whose power restores thee, hath decreed
Thou shouldst elude the malice of the grave:
Redundant are thy locks, thy lips as fair
As when their breath enriched Thessalian air. 60

'No Spectre greets me,—no vain Shadow this;
Come, blooming Hero, place thee by my side!
Give, on this well-known couch, one nuptial
   kiss
To me, this day, a second time thy bride!'
Jove frowned in heaven: the conscious Parcæ[2]
   threw
Upon those roseate lips a Stygian hue.

'This visage tells thee that my doom is past:
Nor should the change be mourned, even if the
   joys
Of sense were able to return as fast
And surely as they vanish. Earth destroys   70
Those raptures duly—Erebus[3] disdains:
Calm pleasures there abide—majestic pains.

'Be taught, O faithful Consort, to control
Rebellious passion: for the Gods approve
The depth, and not the tumult, of the soul;
A fervent, not ungovernable, love.
Thy transports moderate; and meekly mourn
When I depart, for brief is my sojourn—'

'Ah wherefore?—Did not Hercules by force
Wrest from the guardian Monster of the
   tomb[4]   80
Alcestis, a reanimated corse,
Given back to dwell on earth in vernal bloom?
Medea's spells dispersed the weight of years,
And Æson stood a youth 'mid youthful peers.[5]

'The Gods to us are merciful—and they
Yet further may relent: for mightier far
Than strength of nerve and sinew, or the sway
Of magic potent over sun and star,
Is love, though oft to agony distrest,
And though his favourite seat be feeble woman's
   breast.   90

'But if thou goest, I follow—' 'Peace!' he said,—
She looked upon him and was calmed and
   cheered;
The ghastly colour from his lips had fled;
In his deportment, shape, and mien, appeared
Elysian beauty, melancholy grace,
Brought from a pensive though a happy place.

He spake of love, such love as Spirits feel
In worlds whose course is equable and pure;
No fears to beat away—no strife to heal—
The past unsighed for, and the future sure;   100
Spake of heroic arts in graver mood
Revived, with finer harmony pursued;

Of all that is most beauteous—imaged there
In happier beauty; more pellucid streams,
An ampler ether, a diviner air,
And fields invested with purpureal gleams;
Climes which the sun, who sheds the brightest
   day
Earth knows, is all unworthy to survey.

Yet there the Soul shall enter which hath earned
That privilege by virtue.—'Ill,' said he,   110
'The end of man's existence I discerned,
Who from ignoble games and revelry
Could draw, when we had parted, vain delight,

---

2 the Fates.   3 a region of the lower world.

4 Cerberus, guard at the entrance to Hades.
5 Æson, father of Jason, was restored to youth by Medea's art.

While tears were thy best pastime, day and
    night;

'And while my youthful peers before my eyes
(Each hero following his peculiar bent)
Prepared themselves for glorious enterprise
By martial sports,—or, seated in the tent,
Chieftains and kings in council were detained;
What time the fleet at Aulis[6] lay enchained.   120

'The wished-for wind was given:—I then re-
    volved
The oracle, upon the silent sea;
And, if no worthier led the way, resolved
That, of a thousand vessels, mine should be
The foremost prow in pressing to the strand,—
Mine the first blood that tinged the Trojan
    sand.

'Yet bitter, oft-times bitter, was the pang
When of thy loss I thought, belovèd Wife!
On thee too fondly did my memory hang,
And on the joys we shared in mortal life,—   130
The paths which we had trod—these fountains,
    flowers;
My new-planned cities, and unfinished towers.

'But should suspense permit the Foe to cry,
"Behold they tremble!—haughty their array,
Yet of their number no one dares to die?"
In soul I swept the indignity away:
Old frailties then recurred:—but lofty thought,
In act embodied, my deliverance wrought.

'And Thou, though strong in love, art all too
    weak
In reason, in self-government too slow;   140
I counsel thee by fortitude to seek
Our blest re-union in the shades below.
The invisible world with thee hath sympathised;
Be thy affections raised and solemnised.

'Learn, by a mortal yearning, to ascend—
Seeking a higher object. Love was given,
Encouraged, sanctioned, chiefly for that end;
For this the passion to excess was driven—
That self might be annulled: her bondage prove
The fetters of a dream opposed to love.'—   150

Aloud she shrieked! for Hermes reappears!
Round the dear Shade she would have clung—
    'tis vain:

---

6 a port in Boeotia where the Greek fleet was detained until Artemis was appeased by the sacrifice of Iphigenia.

The hours are past—too brief had they been
    years;
And him no mortal effort can detain:
Swift, toward the realms that know not earthly
    day,
He through the portal takes his silent way,
And on the palace-floor a lifeless corse She lay.

Thus, all in vain exhorted and reproved,
She perished; and, as for a wilful crime,
By the just Gods whom no weak pity moved, 160
Was doomed to wear out her appointed time,
Apart from happy Ghosts, that gather flowers
Of blissful quiet 'mid unfading bowers.

—Yet tears to human suffering are due;
And mortal hopes defeated and o'erthrown
Are mourned by man, and not by man alone,
As fondly he believes.—Upon the side
Of Hellespont (such faith was entertained)
A knot of spiry trees for ages grew
From out the tomb of him for whom she
    died;   170
And ever, when such stature they had gained
That Ilium's walls were subject to their view,
The trees' tall summits withered at the sight;
A constant interchange of growth and blight!

     1814   1815

YARROW VISITED

SEPTEMBER 1814

   As mentioned in my verses on the death of the Ettrick
Shepherd, my first visit to Yarrow was in his company.
We had lodged the night before at Traquhair, where
Hogg had joined us and also Dr. Anderson, the Editor
of the British Poets, who was on a visit at the Manse. Dr.
A. walked with us till we came in view of the Vale of
Yarrow, and, being advanced in life, he then turned back.
. . . I seldom read or think of this poem without regretting that my dear Sister was not of the party, as she
would have had so much delight in recalling the time
when, travelling together in Scotland, we declined going
in search of this celebrated stream, not altogether, I will
frankly confess, for the reasons assigned in the poem on
the occasion.—(Wordsworth.)

AND is this—Yarrow?—*This* the Stream
Of which my fancy cherished,
So faithfully, a waking dream?
An image that hath perished!
O that some Minstrel's harp were near,
To utter notes of gladness,
And chase this silence from the air,
That fills my heart with sadness!

Yet why?—a silvery current flows
With uncontrolled meanderings;   10
Nor have these eyes by greener hills
Been soothed, in all my wanderings.
And, through her depths, Saint Mary's Lake
Is visibly delighted;
For not a feature of those hills
Is in the mirror slighted.

A blue sky bends o'er Yarrow vale,
Save where that pearly whiteness
Is round the rising sun diffused,
A tender hazy brightness;   20
Mild dawn of promise! that excludes
All profitless dejection;
Though not unwilling here to admit
A pensive recollection.

Where was it that the famous Flower
Of Yarrow Vale lay bleeding?[1]
His bed perchance was yon smooth mound
On which the herd is feeding:
And haply from this crystal pool,
Now peaceful as the morning,   30
The Water-wraith ascended thrice—
And gave his doleful warning.

Delicious is the Lay that sings
The haunts of happy Lovers,
The path that leads them to the grove,
The leafy grove that covers:
And Pity sanctifies the Verse
That paints, by strength of sorrow,
The unconquerable strength of love;
Bear witness, rueful Yarrow!   40

But thou, that didst appear so fair
To fond imagination,
Dost rival in the light of day
Her delicate creation:
Meek loveliness is round thee spread,
A softness still and holy;
The grace of forest charms decayed,
And pastoral melancholy.

That region left, the vale unfolds
Rich groves of lofty stature,   50
With Yarrow winding through the pomp
Of cultivated nature;
And, rising from those lofty groves,

Behold a Ruin hoary!
The shattered front of Newark's Towers,
Renowned in Border story.

Fair scenes for childhood's opening bloom,
For sportive youth to stray in;
For manhood to enjoy his strength;
And age to wear away in!   60
Yon cottage seems a bower of bliss,
A covert for protection
Of tender thoughts, that nestle there—
The brood of chaste affection.

How sweet, on this autumnal day,
The wild-wood fruits to gather,
And on my True-love's forehead plant
A crest of blooming heather!
And what if I enwreathed my own!
'Twere no offence to reason;   70
The sober Hills thus deck their brows
To meet the wintry season.

I see—but not by sight alone,
Loved Yarrow, have I won thee;
A ray of fancy still survives—
Her sunshine plays upon thee!
Thy ever-youthful waters keep
A course of lively pleasure;
And gladsome notes my lips can breathe,
Accordant to the measure.   80

The vapours linger round the Heights,
They melt, and soon must vanish;
One hour is theirs, nor more is mine—
Sad thought, which I would banish,
But that I know, where'er I go,
Thy genuine image, Yarrow!
Will dwell with me—to heighten joy,
And cheer my mind in sorrow.

1814   1815

WEAK IS THE WILL OF MAN, HIS
JUDGMENT BLIND

'WEAK is the will of Man, his judgment blind;
Remembrance persecutes, and Hope betrays;
Heavy is woe;—and joy, for human-kind,
A mournful thing, so transient is the blaze!'
Thus might *he* paint our lot of mortal days
Who wants the glorious faculty assigned
To elevate the more-than-reasoning Mind,
And colour life's dark cloud with orient rays.

---

1 The famous 'Flower of Yarrow' was Mary Scott of Dryhope;
but here Wordsworth doubtless is following Logan's 'Braes of
Yarrow,' where the lady laments her lover and calls him 'the flower of Yarrow.'

Imagination is that sacred power,
Imagination lofty and refined: 10
'Tis hers to pluck the amaranthine flower
Of Faith, and round the sufferer's temples bind
Wreaths that endure affliction's heaviest shower,
And do not shrink from sorrow's keenest wind.

    c. 1815   1815

SURPRISED BY JOY—IMPATIENT AS THE WIND

SURPRISED by joy—impatient as the Wind
I turned to share the transport—Oh! with whom
But Thee,[1] deep buried in the silent tomb,
That spot which no vicissitude can find?
Love, faithful love, recalled thee to my mind—
But how could I forget thee? Through what
    power,
Even for the least division of an hour,
Have I been so beguiled as to be blind
To my most grievous loss!—That thought's re-
    turn
Was the worst pang that sorrow ever bore,   10
Save one, one only, when I stood forlorn,
Knowing my heart's best treasure was no more;
That neither present time, nor years unborn
Could to my sight that heavenly face restore.

    After 1812   1815

COMPOSED UPON AN EVENING OF EXTRAORDINARY SPLENDOUR AND BEAUTY

    Felt and in a great measure composed upon the little mount in front of our abode at Rydal.—(Wordsworth.)

I

HAD this effulgence disappeared
With flying haste, I might have sent,
Among the speechless clouds, a look
Of blank astonishment;
But 'tis endued with power to stay,
And sanctify one closing day,
That frail Mortality may see—
What is?—ah no, but what *can* be!
Time was when field and watery cove
With modulated echoes rang,   10
While choirs of fervent Angels sang
Their vespers in the grove;
Or, crowning, star-like, each some sovereign
    height,

Warbled, for heaven above and earth below,
Strains suitable to both.—Such holy rite,
Methinks, if audibly repeated now
From hill or valley, could not move
Sublimer transport, purer love,
Than doth this silent spectacle—the gleam—
The shadow—and the peace supreme!   20

II

No sound is uttered,—but a deep
And solemn harmony pervades
The hollow vale from steep to steep,
And penetrates the glades.
Far-distant images draw nigh,
Called forth by wondrous potency
Of beamy radiance, that imbues
Whate'er it strikes with gem-like hues!
In vision exquisitely clear,
Herds range along the mountain side;   30
And glistening antlers are descried;
And gilded flocks appear.
Thine is the tranquil hour, purpureal Eve!
But long as god-like wish, or hope divine,
Informs my spirit, ne'er can I believe
That this magnificence is wholly thine!
—From worlds not quickened by the sun
A portion of the gift is won;
An intermingling of Heaven's pomp is spread
On ground which British shepherds tread!   40

III

And if there be whom broken ties
Afflict, or injuries assail,
Yon hazy ridges to their eyes
Present a glorious scale,
Climbing suffused with sunny air,
To stop—no record hath told where!
And tempting Fancy to ascend,
And with immortal Spirits blend!
—Wings at my shoulders seem to play;
But, rooted here, I stand and gaze   50
On those bright steps that heavenward raise
Their practicable way.[1]
Come forth, ye drooping old men, look abroad,
And see to what fair countries ye are bound!
And if some traveller, weary of his road,
Hath slept since noon-tide on the grassy ground,
Ye Genii! to his covert speed;
And wake him with such gentle heed
As may attune his soul to meet the dower
Bestowed on this transcendent hour!   60

---

[1] the poet's daughter, Catherine, who died 4 June 1812.

[1] a kind of Jacob's ladder produced by the sunny haze, which may be climbed to heaven.

IV

Such hues from their celestial Urn
Were wont to stream before mine eye,
Where'er it wandered in the morn
Of blissful infancy.
This glimpse of glory, why renewed?
Nay, rather speak with gratitude;
For, if a vestige of those gleams
Survived, 'twas only in my dreams.
Dread Power! whom peace and calmness serve
No less than Nature's threatening voice,   70
If aught unworthy be my choice,
From THEE if I would swerve;
Oh, let Thy grace remind me of the light
Full early lost, and fruitlessly deplored;
Which, at this moment, on my waking sight
Appears to shine, by miracle restored;
My soul, though yet confined to earth,
Rejoices in a second birth!
—'Tis past, the visionary splendour fades;
And night approaches with her shades.[2]

1818   1820

AFTER-THOUGHT

THE RIVER DUDDON[1] SONNETS, NO. 34

I first became acquainted with the Duddon, as I have
good reason to remember, in early boyhood. Upon the
banks of the Derwent I had learnt to be very fond of
angling. Fish abound in that large river; not so in the
small streams in the neighbourhood of Hawkshead; and
I fell into the common delusion that the farther from
home the better sport would be had. Accordingly, one
day I attached myself to a person living in the neighbourhood of Hawkshead, who was going to try his fortune as
an angler near the source of the Duddon. We fished a
great part of the day with very sorry success, the rain
pouring torrents, and long before we got home I was
worn out with fatigue; and, if the good man had not carried me on his back, I must have lain down under the
best shelter I could find. Little did I think then it would
be my lot to celebrate, in a strain of love and admiration,
the stream which for many years I never thought of without recollections of disappointment and distress.—
(Wordsworth in his prefatory note to the series.)

I THOUGHT of Thee, my partner and my guide,
As being past away.—Vain sympathies!
For, backward, Duddon! as I cast my eyes,
I see what was, and is, and will abide;
Still glides the Stream, and shall forever glide;

2 Allusions to the Ode entitled 'Intimations of Immortality' pervade the last stanza.—(Wordsworth.)

1 The River Duddon rises upon Wrynose Fell, on the confines of
Westmoreland, Cumberland, and Lancashire; and, having served
as a boundary to the two last Counties for the space of about
twenty-five miles, enters the Irish Sea, between the Isle of Walney
and the Lordship of Millum.—(Wordsworth.)

The Form remains, the Function never dies;
While we, the brave, the mighty, and the wise,
We Men, who in our morn of youth defied
The elements, must vanish;—be it so!
Enough, if something from our hands have
      power   10
To live, and act, and serve the future hour;
And if, as toward the silent tomb we go,
Through love, through hope, and faith's tran-
      scendent dower,
We feel that we are greater than we know.

1819   1820

MUTABILITY

ECCLESIASTICAL SONNETS, NO. 34

FROM low to high doth dissolution climb,
And sink from high to low, along a scale
Of awful notes, whose concord shall not fail;
A musical but melancholy chime,
Which they can hear who meddle not with crime,
Nor avarice, nor over-anxious care.
Truth fails not; but her outward forms that bear
The longest date do melt like frosty rime,
That in the morning whitened hill and plain
And is no more; drop like the tower sublime   10
Of yesterday, which royally did wear
His crown of weeds, but could not even sustain
Some casual shout that broke the silent air,
Or the unimaginable touch of Time.

1821   1822

INSIDE OF KING'S COLLEGE CHAPEL, CAMBRIDGE

ECCLESIASTICAL SONNETS, NO. 43

TAX not the royal Saint[1] with vain expense,
With ill-matched aims the Architect who
      planned—
Albeit labouring for a scanty band
Of white-robed Scholars only—this immense
And glorious Work of fine intelligence!
Give all thou canst; high Heaven rejects the lore
Of nicely-calculated less or more;
So deemed the man who fashioned for the sense
These lofty pillars, spread that branching roof
Self-poised, and scooped into ten thousand
      cells,   10
Where light and shade repose, where music
      dwells
Lingering—and wandering on as loth to die;

1 Henry VI.

Like thoughts whose very sweetness yieldeth
    proof
That they were born for immortality.

1821   1822

TO A SKY-LARK

ETHEREAL minstrel! pilgrim of the sky!
Dost thou despise the earth where cares abound?
Or, while the wings aspire, are heart and eye
Both with thy nest upon the dewy ground?
Thy nest which thou canst drop into at will,
Those quivering wings composed, that music
    still!

Leave to the nightingale her shady wood;
A privacy of glorious light is thine;
Whence thou dost pour upon the world a flood
Of harmony, with instinct more divine;   10
Type of the wise who soar, but never roam;
True to the kindred points of Heaven and Home!

1825   1827

SCORN NOT THE SONNET

SCORN not the Sonnet; Critic, you have frowned,
Mindless of its just honours; with this key
Shakspeare unlocked his heart; the melody
Of this small lute gave ease to Petrarch's wound;[1]
A thousand times this pipe did Tasso sound;
With it Camöens soothed an exile's grief;[2]
The Sonnet glittered a gay myrtle leaf
Amid the cypress[3] with which Dante crowned
His visionary brow: a glow-worm lamp,
It cheered mild Spenser, called from Faery-
    land   10
To struggle through dark ways; and when a
    damp
Fell round the path of Milton, in his hand
The Thing became a trumpet; whence he blew
Soul-animating strains—alas, too few!

                  1827

YARROW REVISITED

The following Stanzas are a memorial of a day passed with Sir Walter Scott and other Friends visiting the Banks of Yarrow under his guidance, immediately after his departure from Abbotsford, for Naples.

---

[1] referring to the hopelessness of Petrarch's love for Laura or to his grief at her death.
[2] Camöens was banished from Lisbon because of his love for Donna Caterina; he lamented her death in his sonnets.
[3] Myrtle is the symbol of love; cypress of death.

The title *Yarrow Revisited* will stand in no need of explanation for Readers acquainted with the Author's previous poems suggested by that celebrated Stream.—(Wordsworth.)

THE gallant Youth, who may have gained,
    Or seeks, a 'winsome Marrow,'
Was but an Infant in the lap
    When first I looked on Yarrow;
Once more, by Newark's Castle-gate
    Long left without a warder,
I stood, looked, listened, and with Thee,
    Great Minstrel of the Border!

Grave thoughts ruled wide on that sweet day,
    Their dignity installing   10
In gentle bosoms, while sere leaves
    Were on the bough, or falling;
But breezes played, and sunshine gleamed—
    The forest to embolden;
Reddened the fiery hues, and shot
    Transparence through the golden.

For busy thoughts the Stream flowed on
    In foamy agitation;
And slept in many a crystal pool
    For quiet contemplation: 20
No public and no private care
    The freeborn mind enthralling,
We made a day of happy hours,
    Our happy days recalling.

Brisk Youth appeared, the Morn of Youth,
    With freaks of graceful folly,—
Life's temperate Noon, her sober Eve,
    Her Night not melancholy;
Past, present, future, all appeared
    In harmony united,   30
Like guests that meet, and some from far,
    By cordial love invited.

And if, as Yarrow, through the woods
    And down the meadow ranging,
Did meet us with unaltered face,
    Though we were changed and changing;
If, *then,* some natural shadows spread
    Our inward prospect over,
The soul's deep valley was not slow
    Its brightness to recover.   40

Eternal blessings on the Muse,
    And her divine employment!
The blameless Muse, who trains her Sons
    For hope and calm enjoyment;
Albeit sickness, lingering yet,

Has o'er their pillow brooded;
And Care waylays their steps—a Sprite
  Not easily eluded.

For thee, O SCOTT! compelled to change
  Green Eildon-hill and Cheviot   50
For warm Vesuvio's vine-clad slopes;
  And leave thy Tweed and Tiviot
For mild Sorento's breezy waves;
  May classic Fancy, linking
With native Fancy her fresh aid,
  Preserve thy heart from sinking!

Oh! while they minister to thee,
  Each vying with the other,
May Health return to mellow Age,
  With Strength, her venturous brother;   60
And Tiber, and each brook and rill
  Renowned in song and story,
With unimagined beauty shine,
  Nor lose one ray of glory!

For Thou, upon a hundred streams,
  By tales of love and sorrow,
Of faithful love, undaunted truth,
  Hast shed the power of Yarrow;
And streams unknown, hills yet unseen,
  Wherever they invite Thee,   70
At parent Nature's grateful call,
  With gladness must requite Thee.

A gracious welcome shall be thine,
  Such looks of love and honour
As thy own Yarrow gave to me
  When first I gazed upon her;
Beheld what I had feared to see,
  Unwilling to surrender
Dreams treasured up from early days,
  The holy and the tender.   80

And what, for this frail world, were all
  That mortals do or suffer,
Did no responsive harp, no pen,
  Memorial tribute offer?
Yea, what were mighty Nature's self?
  Her features, could they win us,
Unhelped by the poetic voice
  That hourly speaks within us?

Nor deem that localised Romance
  Plays false with our affections;   90
Unsanctifies our tears—made sport
  For fanciful dejections:
Ah, no! the visions of the past

Sustain the heart in feeling
Life as she is—our changeful Life,
  With friends and kindred dealing.

Bear witness, Ye, whose thoughts that day
  In Yarrow's groves were centred;
Who through the silent portal arch
  Of mouldering Newark entered;   100
And clomb the winding stair that once
  Too timidly was mounted
By the 'last Minstrel,' (not the last!)
  Ere he his Tale recounted.

Flow on for ever, Yarrow Stream!
  Fulfil thy pensive duty,
Well pleased that future Bards should chant
  For simple hearts thy beauty;
To dream-light dear while yet unseen,
  Dear to the common sunshine,   110
And dearer still, as now I feel,
  To memory's shadowy moonshine!

1831   1835

ON THE DEPARTURE OF SIR WALTER SCOTT FROM ABBOTSFORD, FOR NAPLES

In the autumn of 1831 my daughter and I set off from Rydal to visit Sir Walter Scott before his departure for Italy. . . . How sadly changed did I find him from the man I had seen so healthy, gay, and hopeful, a few years before, when he said at the inn at Paterdale, in my presence: 'I mean to live till I am *eighty,* and shall write as long as I live.' . . . On Tuesday morning Sir Walter Scott accompanied us and most of the party to Newark Castle on the Yarrow. When we alighted from the carriages he walked pretty stoutly, and had great pleasure in revisiting those his favourite haunts. Of that excursion the verses *Yarrow Revisited* are a memorial. Notwithstanding the romance that pervades Sir Walter's works and attaches to many of his habits, there is too much pressure of fact for these verses to harmonize as much as I could wish with other poems. On our return in the afternoon we had to cross the Tweed directly opposite Abbotsford. The wheels of our carriage grated upon the pebbles in the bed of the stream, that there flows somewhat rapidly; a rich but sad light of rather a purple than a golden hue was spread over the Eildon hills at that moment; and, thinking it probable that it might be the last time Sir Walter would cross the stream, I was not a little moved, and expressed some of my feelings in the sonnet beginning—'A trouble, not of clouds, or weeping rain.'—(Wordsworth in Preface to *Yarrow Revisited and Other Poems,* 1831.)

A TROUBLE, not of clouds, or weeping rain,
  Nor of the setting sun's pathetic light
Engendered, hangs o'er Eildon's triple height:
Spirits of Power, assembled there, complain
For kindred Power departing from their sight;

While Tweed, best pleased in chanting a blithe
   strain,
Saddens his voice again, and yet again.
Lift up your hearts, ye Mourners! for the might
Of the whole world's good wishes with him goes;
Blessings and prayers in nobler retinue   10
Than sceptred king or laurelled conqueror
   knows,
Follow this wondrous Potentate. Be true,
Ye winds of ocean, and the midland sea,[1]
Wafting your Charge to soft Parthenope![2]

1831   1835

IF THOU INDEED DERIVE THY LIGHT FROM HEAVEN

These verses were written some time after we had become residents at Rydal Mount, and I will take occasion
from them to observe upon the beauty of that situation,
as being backed and flanked by lofty fells, which bring
the heavenly bodies to touch, as it were, the earth upon
the mountain-tops, while the prospect in front lies open
to a length of level valley, the extended lake, and a terminating ridge of low hills; so that it gives an opportunity to the inhabitants of the place of noticing the stars in
both the positions here alluded to, namely, on the tops
of the mountains, and as winter-lamps at a distance
among the leafless trees.—(Wordsworth.)

If thou indeed derive thy light from Heaven,
Then, to the measure of that heaven-born light,
Shine, Poet! in thy place, and be content:—
The stars pre-eminent in magnitude,
And they that from the zenith dart their beams,
(Visible though they be to half the earth,
Though half a sphere be conscious of their
   brightness)
Are yet of no diviner origin,
No purer essence, than the one that burns,
Like an untended watch-fire, on the ridge   10
Of some dark mountain; or than those which
   seem
Humbly to hang, like twinkling winter lamps,
Among the branches of the leafless trees;
All are the undying offspring of one Sire:
Then, to the measure of the light vouchsafed,
Shine, Poet! in thy place, and be content.

1832   1836

MOST SWEET IT IS WITH UNUPLIFTED EYES

Most sweet it is with unuplifted eyes
To pace the ground, if path be there or none,

---

[1] the Mediterranean.
[2] a siren who drowned herself when she failed to attract Ulysses
with her songs.

While a fair region round the traveller lies
Which he forbears again to look upon;
Pleased rather with some soft ideal scene,
The work of Fancy, or some happy tone
Of meditation, slipping in between
The beauty coming and the beauty gone.
If Thought and Love desert us, from that day
Let us break off all commerce with the Muse: 10
With Thought and Love companions of our way,
Whate'er the senses take or may refuse,
The Mind's internal heaven shall shed her dews
Of inspiration on the humblest lay.

1833   1835

A POET!—HE HATH PUT HIS HEART TO SCHOOL

I was impelled to write this Sonnet by the disgusting
frequency with which the word *artistical,* imported with
other impertinences from the Germans, is employed by
writers of the present day: for artistical let them substitute artificial, and the poetry written on this system, both
at home and abroad, will be for the most part much
better characterized.—(Wordsworth.)

A Poet!—He hath put his heart to school,
Nor dares to move unpropped upon the staff
Which Art hath lodged within his hand—must
   laugh
By precept only, and shed tears by rule.
Thy Art be Nature; the live current quaff,
And let the groveller sip his stagnant pool,
In fear that else, when Critics grave and cool
Have killed him, Scorn should write his epitaph.
How does the Meadow-flower its bloom unfold?
Because the lovely little flower is free   10
Down to its root, and, in that freedom, bold;
And so the grandeur of the Forest-tree
Comes not by casting in a formal mould,
But from its *own* divine vitality.

1842?   1842

SO FAIR, SO SWEET, WITHAL SO SENSITIVE

So fair, so sweet, withal so sensitive,
Would that the little Flowers were born to live,
Conscious of half the pleasure which they give;

That to this mountain-daisy's self were known
The beauty of its star-shaped shadow, thrown
On the smooth surface of this naked stone!

And what if hence a bold desire should mount
High as the Sun, that he could take account
Of all that issues from his glorious fount!

So might he ken how by his sovereign aid   10
These delicate companionships are made;
And how he rules the pomp of light and shade;

And were the Sister-power that shines by night
So privileged, what a countenance of delight
Would through the clouds break forth on human
    sight!

Fond fancies! wheresoe'er shall turn thine eye
On earth, air, ocean, or the starry sky,
Converse with Nature in pure sympathy;

All vain desires, all lawless wishes quelled,
Be Thou to love and praise alike impelled,   20
Whatever boon is granted or withheld.

                1845

PREFACE TO THE *LYRICAL BALLADS*

THE first Volume of these Poems has already been submitted to general perusal. It was published, as an experiment, which, I hoped, might be of some use to ascertain, how far, by fitting to metrical arrangement a selection of the real language of men in a state of vivid sensation, that sort of pleasure and that quantity of pleasure may be imparted, which a Poet may rationally endeavour to impart.

I had formed no very inaccurate estimate of the probable effect of those Poems: I flattered myself that they who should be pleased with them would read them with more than common pleasure: and, on the other hand, I was well aware, that by those who should dislike them, they would be read with more than common dislike. The result has differed from my expectation in this only, that a greater number have been pleased than I ventured to hope I should please.

.   .   .

Several of my Friends are anxious for the success of these Poems, from a belief, that, if the views with which they were composed were indeed realised, a class of Poetry would be produced, well adapted to interest mankind permanently, and not unimportant in the quality, and in the multiplicity of its moral relations: and on this account they have advised me to prefix a systematic defence of the theory upon which the Poems were written. But I was unwilling to undertake the task, knowing that on this occasion the Reader would look coldly upon my arguments, since I might be suspected of having been principally influenced by the selfish and foolish hope of *reasoning* him into an approbation of these particular Poems: and I was still more unwilling to undertake the task, because, adequately to display the opinions, and fully to enforce the arguments, would require a space wholly disproportionate to a preface. For, to treat the subject with the clearness and coherence of which it is susceptible, it would be necessary to give a full account of the present state of the public taste in this country, and to determine how far this taste is healthy or depraved; which, again, could not be determined, without pointing out in what manner language and the human mind act and re-act on each other, and without retracing the revolutions, not of literature alone, but likewise of society itself. I have therefore altogether declined to enter regularly upon this defence; yet I am sensible, that there would be something like impropriety in abruptly obtruding upon the Public, without a few words of introduction, Poems so materially different from those upon which general approbation is at present bestowed.

It is supposed, that by the act of writing in verse an Author makes a formal engagement that he will gratify certain known habits of association; that he not only thus apprises the Reader that certain classes of ideas and expressions will be found in his book, but that others will be carefully excluded. This exponent or symbol held forth by metrical language must in different eras of literature have excited very different expectations: for example, in the age of Catullus, Terence, and Lucretius, and that of Statius or Claudian; and in our own country, in the age of Shakspeare and Beaumont and Fletcher, and that of Donne and Cowley, or Dryden, or Pope. I will not take upon me to determine the exact import of the promise which, by the act of writing in verse, an Author in the present day makes to his reader: but it will undoubtedly appear to many persons that I have not fulfilled the terms of an engagement thus voluntarily contracted. They who have been accustomed to the gaudiness and inane phraseology of many modern writers, if they persist in reading this book to its conclusion, will, no doubt, frequently have to struggle with feelings of strangeness and awkwardness: they will look round for poetry, and will be induced to inquire by what species of courtesy these attempts can be permitted to assume that title. I hope therefore the reader will not censure me for attempting to state what I have proposed to myself to perform; and also (as far as the limits of a preface will permit) to explain some of the chief reasons which have determined me in the choice of my purpose: that at least he may be spared any unpleasant feeling of disappointment, and that I myself may be protected from one of the most dishonourable accusations which can be brought against an Author; namely, that of an indolence which prevents him from endeavouring to ascertain what is his duty, or, when his duty is ascertained, prevents him from performing it.

The principal object, then, proposed in these Poems was to choose incidents and situations from common life, and to relate or describe them, throughout, as far as was possible in a selection of language really used by men, and, at the same time, to throw over them a certain colouring of imagination, whereby ordinary things should be presented to the mind in an unusual aspect; and, further, and above all, to make these incidents and situations interesting by tracing in them, truly though not ostentatiously, the primary laws of our nature: chiefly, as far as regards the manner in which we associate ideas in a state of excitement. Humble and rustic life was generally chosen, because, in that condition, the essential passions of the heart find a better soil in which they can attain their maturity, are less under restraint, and speak a plainer and more emphatic language; because in that condition of life our elementary feelings coexist in a state of greater simplicity, and, consequently, may be more accurately contemplated, and more forcibly communicated; because the manners of rural life germinate from those elementary feelings, and, from the necessary character of rural occupations, are more easily comprehended, and are more durable; and, lastly, because in that condition the passions of men are incorporated with the beautiful and permanent forms of nature. The language, too, of these men has been adopted (purified indeed from what appear to be its real defects, from all lasting and rational causes of dislike or disgust) because such men hourly communicate with the best objects from which the best part of language is originally derived; and because, from their rank in society and the sameness and narrow circle of their intercourse, being less under the influence of social vanity, they convey their feelings and notions in simple and unelaborated expressions. Accordingly, such a language, arising out of repeated experience and regular feelings, is a more permanent, and a far more philosophical language, than that which is frequently substituted for it by Poets, who think that they are conferring honour upon themselves and their art, in proportion as they separate themselves from the sympathies of men, and indulge in arbitrary and capricious habits of expression, in order to furnish food for fickle tastes, and fickle appetites, of their own creation.[1]

I cannot, however, be insensible to the present outcry against the triviality and meanness, both of thought and language, which some of my contemporaries have occasionally introduced into their metrical compositions; and I acknowledge that this defect, where it exists, is more dishonourable to the Writer's own character than false refinement or arbitrary innovation, though I should contend at the same time, that it is far less pernicious in the sum of its consequences. From such verses the Poems in these volumes will be found distinguished at least by one mark of difference, that each of them has a worthy *purpose*. Not that I always began to write with a distinct purpose formally conceived; but habits of meditation have, I trust, so prompted and regulated my feelings, that my descriptions of such objects as strongly excite those feelings, will be found to carry along with them a *purpose*. If this opinion be erroneous, I can have little right to the name of a Poet. For all good poetry is the spontaneous overflow of powerful feelings: and though this be true, Poems to which any value can be attached were never produced on any variety of subjects but by a man who, being possessed of more than usual organic sensibility, had also thought long and deeply. For our continued influxes of feeling are modified and directed by our thoughts, which are indeed the representatives of all our past feelings; and, as by contemplating the relation of these general representatives to each other, we discover what is really important to men, so, by the repetition and continuance of this act, our feelings will be connected with important subjects, till at length, if we be originally possessed of much sensibility, such habits of mind will be produced, that, by obeying blindly and mechanically the impulses of those habits, we shall describe objects, and utter sentiments, of such a nature, and in such connection with each other, that

---

[1] It is worth while here to observe that the affecting parts of Chaucer are almost always expressed in language pu;e and universally intelligible even to this day.—(Wordsworth.)

the understanding of the Reader must necessarily be in some degree enlightened, and his affections strengthened and purified.

It has been said that each of these poems has a purpose. Another circumstance must be mentioned which distinguishes these Poems from the popular Poetry of the day; it is this, that the feeling therein developed gives importance to the action and situation, and not the action and situation to the feeling.

A sense of false modesty shall not prevent me from asserting, that the Reader's attention is pointed to this mark of distinction, far less for the sake of these particular Poems than from the general importance of the subject. The subject is indeed important! For the human mind is capable of being excited without the application of gross and violent stimulants; and he must have a very faint perception of its beauty and dignity who does not know this, and who does not further know, that one being is elevated above another, in proportion as he possesses this capability. It has therefore appeared to me, that to endeavour to produce or enlarge this capability is one of the best services in which, at any period, a Writer can be engaged; but this service, excellent at all times, is especially so at the present day. For a multitude of causes, unknown to former times, are now acting with a combined force to blunt the discriminating powers of the mind, and, unfitting it for all voluntary exertion, to reduce it to a state of almost savage torpor. The most effective of these causes are the great national events which are daily taking place, and the increasing accumulation of men in cities, where the uniformity of their occupations produces a craving for extraordinary incident, which the rapid communication of intelligence hourly gratifies. To this tendency of life and manners the literature and theatrical exhibitions of the country have conformed themselves. The invaluable works of our elder writers, I had almost said the works of Shakspeare and Milton, are driven into neglect by frantic novels, sickly and stupid German Tragedies, and deluges of idle and extravagant stories in verse.—When I think upon this degrading thirst after outrageous stimulation, I am almost ashamed to have spoken of the feeble endeavour made in these volumes to counteract it; and, reflecting upon the magnitude of the general evil, I should be oppressed with no dishonourable melancholy, had I not a deep impression of certain inherent and indestructible qualities of the human mind, and likewise of certain powers in the great and permanent objects that act upon it, which are equally inherent and indestructible; and were there not added to this impression a belief, that the time is approaching when the evil will be systematically opposed, by men of greater powers, and with far more distinguished success.

Having dwelt thus long on the subjects and aim of these Poems, I shall request the Reader's permission to apprise him of a few circumstances relating to their *style*, in order, among other reasons, that he may not censure me for not having performed what I never attempted. The Reader will find that personifications of abstract ideas rarely occur in these volumes; and are utterly rejected, as an ordinary device to elevate the style, and raise it above prose. My purpose was to imitate, and, as far as possible, to adopt the very language of men; and assuredly such personifications do not make any natural or regular part of that language. They are, indeed, a figure of speech occasionally prompted by passion, and I have made use of them as such; but have endeavoured utterly to reject them as a mechanical device of style, or as a family language which Writers in metre seem to lay claim to by prescription. I have wished to keep the Reader in the company of flesh and blood, persuaded that by so doing I shall interest him. Others who pursue a different track will interest him likewise; I do not interfere with their claim, but wish to prefer a claim of my own. There will also be found in these volumes little of what is usually called poetic diction; as much pains has been taken to avoid it as is ordinarily taken to produce it; this has been done for the reason already alleged, to bring my language near to the language of men; and further, because the pleasure which I have proposed to myself to impart, is of a kind very different from that which is supposed by many persons to be the proper object of poetry. Without being culpably particular, I do not know how to give my Reader a more exact notion of the style in which it was my wish and intention to write, than by informing him that I have at all times endeavoured to look steadily at my subject; consequently, there is I hope in these Poems little falsehood of description, and my ideas are expressed in language fitted to their respective importance. Something must have been gained by this practice, as it is friendly to one property of all good poetry, namely, good sense: but it has necessarily cut me off from a large portion of phrases and figures of speech which from father to son have long been regarded as the common inheritance of Poets. I have also thought it expedient to restrict myself still further, having abstained from the use of many expressions, in themselves proper and beautiful, but which have been foolishly repeated by bad Poets, till such feelings of disgust are connected with them as it is scarcely possible by any art of association to overpower.

If in a poem there should be found a series of lines, or even a single line, in which the language, though naturally arranged, and according to the strict laws of metre, does not differ from that of prose, there is a numerous class of critics, who, when they stumble upon these prosaisms, as they call them, imagine that they have made a notable discovery, and exult over the Poet as over a man ignorant of his own profession. Now these men would establish a canon of criticism which the Reader will conclude he must utterly reject, if he wishes to be pleased with these volumes. And it would be a most easy task to prove to him, that not only the language of a large portion of every good poem, even of the most elevated character, must necessarily, except with reference to the metre, in no respect differ from that of good prose, but likewise that some of the most interesting parts of the best poems will be found to be strictly the language of prose when prose is well written. The truth of this assertion might be demonstrated by innumerable passages from almost all the poetical writings, even of Milton himself. To illustrate the subject in a general manner, I will here adduce a short composition of Gray, who was at the head of those who, by their reasonings, have attempted to widen the space of separation betwixt Prose and Metrical composition, and was more than any other man curiously elaborate in the structure of his own poetic diction.

'In vain to me the smiling mornings shine,
And reddening Phoebus lifts his golden fire:
The birds in vain their amorous descant join,
Or cheerful fields resume their green attire.
These ears, alas! for other notes repine;
A different object do these eyes require;
My lonely anguish melts no heart but mine;
And in my breast the imperfect joys expire;
Yet morning smiles the busy race to cheer,
And new-born pleasure brings to happier men;
The fields to all their wonted tribute bear;

To warm their little loves the birds complain.
I fruitless mourn to him that cannot hear,
And weep the more because I weep in vain.'

It will easily be perceived, that the only part of this Sonnet which is of any value is the lines printed in Italics; it is equally obvious, that, except in the rhyme, and in the use of the single word 'fruitless' for fruitlessly, which is so far a defect, the language of these lines does in no respect differ from that of prose.

By the foregoing quotation it has been shown that the language of Prose may yet be well adapted to Poetry; and it was previously asserted, that a large portion of the language of every good poem can in no respect differ from that of good Prose. We will go further. It may be safely affirmed, that there neither is, nor can be, any *essential* difference between the language of prose and metrical composition. We are fond of tracing the resemblance between Poetry and Painting, and, accordingly, we call them Sisters: but where shall we find bonds of connection sufficiently strict to typify the affinity betwixt metrical and prose composition? They both speak by and to the same organs; the bodies in which both of them are clothed may be said to be of the same substance, their affections are kindred, and almost identical, not necessarily differing even in degree; Poetry[2] sheds no tears 'such as Angels weep,' but natural and human tears; she can boast of no celestial ichor that distinguishes her vital juices from those of prose; the same human blood circulates through the veins of them both.

If it be affirmed that rhyme and metrical arrangement of themselves constitute a distinction which overturns what has just been said on the strict affinity of metrical language with that of prose, and paves the way for other artificial distinctions which the mind voluntarily admits, I answer that the language of such Poetry as is here recommended is, as far as is possible, a selection of the language really spoken by men; that this selection, wherever it is made with true taste and feeling, will of itself form a distinction far greater than would at first be imagined, and

---

2 I here use the word *poetry* (though against my own judgment) as opposed to the word *prose*, and synonymous with metrical composition. But much confusion has been introduced into criticism by this contradistinction of *poetry* and *prose*, instead of the more philosophical one of *poetry* and *matter of fact*, or *science*. The only strict antithesis to *prose* is *metre*; nor is this, in truth, a *strict* antithesis, because lines and passages of metre so naturally occur in writing prose that it would be scarcely possible to avoid them, even were it desirable.—(Wordsworth.)

will entirely separate the composition from the vulgarity and meanness of ordinary life; and, if metre be superadded thereto, I believe that a dissimilitude will be produced altogether sufficient for the gratification of a rational mind. What other distinction would we have? Whence is it to come? And where is it to exist? Not, surely, where the Poet speaks through the mouths of his characters: it cannot be necessary here, either for elevation of style, or any of its supposed ornaments: for, if the Poet's subject be judiciously chosen, it will naturally, and upon fit occasion, lead him to passions the language of which, if selected truly and judiciously, must necessarily be dignified and variegated, and alive with metaphors and figures. I forbear to speak of an incongruity which would shock the intelligent Reader, should the Poet interweave any foreign splendour of his own with that which the passion naturally suggests: it is sufficient to say that such addition is unnecessary. And, surely, it is more probable that those passages, which with propriety abound with metaphors and figures, will have their due effect, if, upon other occasions where the passions are of a milder character, the style also be subdued and temperate.

But, as the pleasure which I hope to give by the Poems now presented to the Reader must depend entirely on just notions upon this subject, and, as it is in itself of high importance to our taste and moral feelings, I cannot content myself with these detached remarks. And if, in what I am about to say, it shall appear to some that my labour is unnecessary, and that I am like a man fighting a battle without enemies, such persons may be reminded, that, whatever be the language outwardly holden by men, a practical faith in the opinions which I am wishing to establish is almost unknown. If my conclusions are admitted, and carried as far as they must be carried if admitted at all, our judgments concerning the works of the greatest Poets both ancient and modern will be far different from what they are at present, both when we praise, and when we censure: and our moral feelings influencing and influenced by these judgments will, I believe, be corrected and purified.

Taking up the subject, then, upon general grounds, let me ask, what is meant by the word Poet? What is a Poet? To whom does he address himself? And what language is to be expected from him?—He is a man speaking to men: a man, it is true, endowed with more lively sensibility, more enthusiasm and tenderness, who has a greater knowledge of human nature, and a more comprehensive soul, than are supposed to be common among mankind; a man pleased with his own passions and volitions, and who rejoices more than other men in the spirit of life that is in him; delighting to contemplate similar volitions and passions as manifested in the goings-on of the Universe, and habitually impelled to create them where he does not find them. To these qualities he has added a disposition to be affected more than other men by absent things as if they were present; an ability of conjuring up in himself passions, which are indeed far from being the same as those produced by real events, yet (especially in those parts of the general sympathy which are pleasing and delightful) do more nearly resemble the passions produced by real events, than anything which, from the motions of their own minds merely, other men are accustomed to feel in themselves:—whence, and from practice, he has acquired a greater readiness and power in expressing what he thinks and feels, and especially those thoughts and feelings which, by his own choice, or from the structure of his own mind, arise in him without immediate external excitement.

But whatever portion of this faculty we may suppose even the greatest Poet to possess, there cannot be a doubt that the language which it will suggest to him, must often, in liveliness and truth, fall short of that which is uttered by men in real life, under the actual pressure of those passions, certain shadows of which the Poet thus produces, or feels to be produced, in himself.

However exalted a notion we would wish to cherish of the character of a Poet, it is obvious, that while he describes and imitates passions, his employment is in some degree mechanical, compared with the freedom and power of real and substantial action and suffering. So that it will be the wish of the Poet to bring his feelings near to those of the persons whose feelings he describes, nay, for short spaces of time, perhaps, to let himself slip into an entire delusion, and even confound and identify his own feelings with theirs; modifying only the language which is thus suggested to him by a consideration that he describes for a particular purpose, that of giving pleasure. Here, then, he will apply the principle of selection which has been already insisted upon. He will depend upon this for removing what would otherwise be painful or disgusting in the passion; he will feel that there is no necessity to trick out or to elevate nature: and, the more industriously he applies this principle, the deeper will be his faith that no words, which *his* fancy or imagination can suggest, will be to be compared with those which are the emanations of reality and truth.

But it may be said by those who do not object to the general spirit of these remarks, that, as it is impossible for the Poet to produce upon all occasions language as exquisitely fitted for the passion as that which the real passion itself suggests, it is proper that he should consider himself as in the situation of a translator, who does not scruple to substitute excellencies of another kind for those which are unattainable by him; and endeavours occasionally to surpass his original, in order to make some amends for the general inferiority to which he feels that he must submit. But this would be to encourage idleness and unmanly despair. Further, it is the language of men who speak of what they do not understand; who talk of Poetry as of a matter of amusement and idle pleasure; who will converse with us as gravely about a *taste* for Poetry, as they express it, as if it were a thing as indifferent as a taste for rope-dancing, or Frontiniac[3] or Sherry. Aristotle, I have been told, has said, that Poetry is the most philosophic of all writing: it is so: its object is truth, not individual and local, but general, and operative; not standing upon external testimony, but carried alive into the heart by passion; truth which is its own testimony, which gives competence and confidence to the tribunal to which it appeals, and receives them from the same tribunal. Poetry is the image of man and nature. The obstacles which stand in the way of the fidelity of the Biographer and Historian, and of their consequent utility, are incalculably greater than those which are to be encountered by the Poet who comprehends the dignity of his art. The Poet writes under one restriction only, namely, the necessity of giving immediate pleasure to a human Being possessed of that information which may be expected from him, not as a lawyer, a physician, a mariner, an astronomer, or a natural philosopher, but as a Man. Except this one restriction, there is no object standing between the Poet and the image of things; between this, and the Biographer and Historian, there are a thousand.

Nor let this necessity of producing immediate pleasure be considered as a degradation of the Poet's art. It is far otherwise. It is an ac-

3 a kind of wine.

knowledgment of the beauty of the universe, an acknowledgment the more sincere, because not formal, but indirect; it is a task light and easy to him who looks at the world in the spirit of love: further, it is a homage paid to the native and naked dignity of man, to the grand elementary principle of pleasure, by which he knows, and feels, and lives, and moves. We have no sympathy but what is propagated by pleasure: I would not be misunderstood; but wherever we sympathise with pain, it will be found that the sympathy is produced and carried on by subtle combinations with pleasure. We have no knowledge, that is, no general principles drawn from the contemplation of particular facts, but what has been built up by pleasure, and exists in us by pleasure alone. The Man of science, the Chemist and Mathematician, whatever difficulties and disgusts they may have had to struggle with, know and feel this. However painful may be the objects with which the Anatomist's knowledge is connected, he feels that his knowledge is pleasure; and where he has no pleasure he has no knowledge. What then does the Poet? He considers man and the objects that surround him as acting and re-acting upon each other, so as to produce an infinite complexity of pain and pleasure; he considers man in his own nature and in his ordinary life as contemplating this with a certain quantity of immediate knowledge, with certain convictions, intuitions, and deductions, which from habit acquire the quality of intuitions; he considers him as looking upon this complex scene of ideas and sensations, and finding everywhere objects that immediately excite in him sympathies which, from the necessities of his nature, are accompanied by an over-balance of enjoyment.

To this knowledge which all men carry about with them, and to these sympathies in which, without any other discipline than that of our daily life, we are fitted to take delight, the Poet principally directs his attention. He considers man and nature as essentially adapted to each other, and the mind of man as naturally the mirror of the fairest and most interesting properties of nature. And thus the Poet, prompted by this feeling of pleasure, which accompanies him through the whole course of his studies, converses with general nature, with affections akin to those, which, through labour and length of time, the Man of science has raised up in himself, by conversing with those particular parts of nature which are the objects of his studies.

The knowledge both of the Poet and the Man of science is pleasure; but the knowledge of the one cleaves to us as a necessary part of our existence, our natural and unalienable inheritance; the other is a personal and individual acquisition, slow to come to us, and by no habitual and direct sympathy connecting us with our fellow-beings. The Man of science seeks truth as a remote and unknown benefactor; he cherishes and loves it in his solitude: the Poet, singing a song in which all human beings join with him, rejoices in the presence of truth as our visible friend and hourly companion. Poetry is the breath and finer spirit of all knowledge; it is the impassioned expression which is in the countenance of all Science. Emphatically may it be said of the Poet, as Shakspeare hath said of man, 'that he looks before and after.' He is the rock of defence for human nature; an upholder and preserver, carrying everywhere with him relationship and love. In spite of difference of soil and climate, of language and manners, of laws and customs: in spite of things silently gone out of mind, and things violently destroyed; the Poet binds together by passion and knowledge the vast empire of human society, as it is spread over the whole earth, and over all time. The objects of the Poet's thoughts are everywhere; though the eyes and senses of man are, it is true, his favourite guides, yet he will follow wheresoever he can find an atmosphere of sensation in which to move his wings. Poetry is the first and last of all knowledge—it is as immortal as the heart of man. If the labours of Men of science should ever create any material revolution, direct or indirect, in our condition, and in the impressions which we habitually receive, the Poet will sleep then no more than at present; he will be ready to follow the steps of the Man of science, not only in those general indirect effects, but he will be at his side, carrying sensation into the midst of the objects of the science itself. The remotest discoveries of the Chemist, the Botanist, or Mineralogist, will be as proper objects of the Poet's art as any upon which it can be employed, if the time should ever come when these things shall be familiar to us, and the relations under which they are contemplated by the followers of these respective sciences shall be manifestly and palpably material to us as enjoying and suffering beings. If the time should ever come when what is now called science, thus familiarised to men, shall be ready to put on, as it were, a form of flesh and blood, the Poet will lend his divine spirit to aid the transfiguration, and will welcome the Being thus produced, as a dear and genuine inmate of the household of man.—It is not, then, to be supposed that any one, who holds that sublime notion of Poetry which I have attempted to convey, will break in upon the sanctity and truth of his pictures by transitory and accidental ornaments, and endeavour to excite admiration of himself by arts, the necessity of which must manifestly depend upon the assumed meanness of his subject.

What has been thus far said applies to Poetry in general; but especially to those parts of composition where the Poet speaks through the mouths of his characters; and upon this point it appears to authorise the conclusion that there are few persons of good sense, who would not allow that the dramatic parts of composition are defective, in proportion as they deviate from the real language of nature, and are coloured by a diction of the Poet's own, either peculiar to him as an individual Poet or belonging simply to Poets in general; to a body of men who, from the circumstance of their compositions being in metre, it is expected will employ a particular language.

It is not, then, in the dramatic parts of composition that we look for this distinction of language; but still it may be proper and necessary where the Poet speaks to us in his own person and character. To this I answer by referring the Reader to the description before given of a Poet. Among the qualities there enumerated as principally conducing to form a Poet, is implied nothing differing in kind from other men, but only in degree. The sum of what was said is, that the Poet is chiefly distinguished from other men by a greater promptness to think and feel without immediate external excitement, and a greater power in expressing such thoughts and feelings as are produced in him in that manner. But these passions and thoughts and feelings are the general passions and thoughts and feelings of men. And with what are they connected? Undoubtedly with our moral sentiments and animal sensations, and with the causes which excite these; with the operations of the elements, and the appearances of the visible universe; with storm and sunshine, with the revolutions of the seasons, with cold and heat, with loss of friends and kindred, with injuries and resentments, gratitude and hope, with fear and sorrow. These, and the like, are the sensations and objects which the Poet describes, as they are the sensations of other men, and the objects which interest them. The Poet thinks and feels in the spirit of human passions. How, then, can his language differ in any material degree from that of all other men who feel vividly and see clearly? It might be *proved* that it is impossible. But supposing that this were not the case, the Poet might then be allowed to use a peculiar language when expressing his feelings for his own gratification, or that of men like himself. But Poets do not write for Poets alone, but for men. Unless therefore we are advocates for that admiration which subsists upon ignorance, and that pleasure which arises from hearing what we do not understand, the Poet must descend from this supposed height; and, in order to excite rational sympathy, he must express himself as other men express themselves. To this it may be added, that while he is only selecting from the real language of men, or, which amounts to the same thing, composing accurately in the spirit of such selection, he is treading upon safe ground, and we know what we are to expect from him. Our feelings are the same with respect to metre; for, as it may be proper to remind the Reader, the distinction of metre is regular and uniform, and not, like that which is produced by what is usually called POETIC DICTION, arbitrary, and subject to infinite caprices upon which no calculation whatever can be made. In the one case, the Reader is utterly at the mercy of the Poet, respecting what imagery or diction he may choose to connect with the passion; whereas, in the other, the metre obeys certain laws, to which the Poet and Reader both willingly submit because they are certain, and because no interference is made by them with the passion, but such as the concurring testimony of ages has shown to heighten and improve the pleasure which coexists with it.

It will now be proper to answer an obvious question, namely, Why, professing these opinions, have I written in verse? To this, in addition to such answer as is included in what has been already said, I reply, in the first place, Because, however I may have restricted myself, there is still left open to me what confessedly constitutes the most valuable object of all writing, whether in prose or verse; the great and universal passions of men, the most general and interesting of their occupations, and the entire world of nature before me—to supply endless combinations of forms and imagery. Now, supposing for a moment that whatever is interesting in these objects may be as vividly described in prose, why should I be condemned for attempting to superadd to such description the charm which, by the consent of all nations, is acknowledged to exist in metrical language? To this, by such as are yet unconvinced, it may be answered that a very small part of the pleasure given by Poetry depends upon the metre, and that it is injudicious to write in metre, unless it be accompanied with the other artificial distinctions of style with which metre is usually accompanied, and that, by such deviation, more will be lost from the shock which will thereby be given to the Reader's associations than will be counterbalanced by any pleasure which he can derive from the general power of numbers. In answer to those who still contend for the necessity of accompanying metre with certain appropriate colours of style in order to the accomplishment of its appropriate end, and who also, in my opinion, greatly underrate the power of metre in itself, it might, perhaps, as far as relates to these Volumes, have been almost sufficient to observe, that poems are extant, written upon more humble subjects, and in a still more naked and simple style, which have continued to give pleasure from generation to generation. Now, if nakedness and simplicity be a defect, the fact here mentioned affords a strong presumption that poems somewhat less naked and simple are capable of affording pleasure at the present day; and, what I wished *chiefly* to attempt, at present, was to justify myself for having written under the impression of this belief.

But various causes might be pointed out why, when the style is manly, and the subject of some importance, words metrically arranged will long continue to impart such a pleasure to mankind as he who proves the extent of that pleasure will be desirous to impart. The end of Poetry is to produce excitement in co-existence with an overbalance of pleasure; but, by the supposition, excitement is an unusual and irregular state of the mind; ideas and feelings do not, in that state, succeed each other in accustomed order. If the words, however, by which this excitement is produced be in themselves powerful, or the images and feelings have an undue proportion of pain connected with them, there is some danger that the excitement may be carried beyond its proper bounds. Now the co-presence of something regular, something to which the mind has been accustomed in various moods and in a less excited state, cannot but have great efficacy in tempering and restraining the passion by an intertexture of ordinary feeling, and of feeling not strictly and necessarily connected with the passion. This is unquestionably true; and hence, though the opinion will at first appear paradoxical, from the tendency of metre to divest language, in a certain degree, of its reality, and thus to throw a sort of half-consciousness of unsubstantial existence over the whole composition, there can be little doubt but that more pathetic situations and sentiments, that is, those which have a greater proportion of pain connected with them, may be endured in metrical composition, especially in rhyme, than in prose. The metre of the old ballads is very artless; yet they contain many passages which would illustrate this opinion; and, I hope, if the following Poems be attentively perused, similar instances will be found in them. This opinion may be further illustrated by appealing to the Reader's own experience of the reluctance with which he comes to the re-perusal of the distressful parts of 'Clarissa Harlowe,'[4] or the 'Gamester';[5] while Shakspeare's writings, in the most pathetic scenes, never act upon us, as pathetic, beyond the bounds of pleasure— an effect which, in a much greater degree than might at first be imagined, is to be ascribed to small, but continual and regular impulses of pleasurable surprise from the metrical arrangement.—On the other hand (what it must be allowed will much more frequently happen) if the Poet's words should be incommensurate with the passion, and inadequate to raise the Reader to a height of desirable excitement, then, (unless the Poet's choice of his metre has been grossly injudicious) in the feelings of pleasure which the Reader has been accustomed to connect with metre in general, and in the feeling, whether cheerful or melancholy, which he has been accustomed to connect with that particular movement of metre, there will be found something which will greatly contribute to impart passion to the words, and to effect the complex end which the Poet proposes to himself.

If I had undertaken a SYSTEMATIC defence of the theory here maintained, it would have been my duty to develope the various causes upon which the pleasure received from metrical language depends. Among the chief of these causes is to be reckoned a principle which must be well known to those who have made any of the Arts the object of accurate reflection; namely, the

pleasure which the mind derives from the perception of similitude in dissimilitude. This principle is the great spring of the activity of our minds, and their chief feeder. From this principle the direction of the sexual appetite, and all the passions connected with it, take their origin: it is the life of our ordinary conversation; and upon the accuracy with which similitude in dissimilitude, and dissimilitude in similitude are perceived, depend our taste and our moral feelings. It would not be a useless employment to apply this principle to the consideration of metre, and to show that metre is hence enabled to afford much pleasure, and to point out in what manner that pleasure is produced. But my limits will not permit me to enter upon this subject, and I must content myself with a general summary.

I have said that poetry is the spontaneous overflow of powerful feelings: it takes its origin from emotion recollected in tranquillity: the emotion is contemplated till, by a species of reaction, the tranquillity gradually disappears, and an emotion, kindred to that which was before the subject of contemplation, is gradually produced, and does itself actually exist in the mind. In this mood successful composition generally begins, and in a mood similar to this it is carried on; but the emotion, of whatever kind, and in whatever degree, from various causes, is qualified by various pleasures, so that in describing any passions whatsoever, which are voluntarily described, the mind will, upon the whole, be in a state of enjoyment. If Nature be thus cautious to preserve in a state of enjoyment a being so employed, the Poet ought to profit by the lesson held forth to him, and ought especially to take care, that, whatever passions he communicates to his Reader, those passions, if his Reader's mind be sound and vigorous, should always be accompanied with an overbalance of pleasure. Now the music of harmonious metrical language, the sense of difficulty overcome, and the blind association of pleasure which has been previously received from works of rhyme or metre of the same or similar construction, an indistinct perception perpetually renewed of language closely resembling that of real life, and yet, in the circumstance of metre, differing from it so widely —all these imperceptibly make up a complex feeling of delight, which is of the most important use in tempering the painful feeling always found intermingled with powerful descriptions of the deeper passions. This effect is always pro-

4 famous novel by Samuel Richardson.
5 an eighteenth-century prose tragedy by Edward Moore.

duced in pathetic and impassioned poetry; while, in lighter compositions, the ease and gracefulness with which the Poet manages his numbers are themselves confessedly a principal source of the gratification of the Reader. All that it is *necessary* to say, however, upon this subject, may be effected by affirming, what few persons will deny, that, of two descriptions, either of passions, manners, or characters, each of them equally well executed, the one in prose and the other in verse, the verse will be read a hundred times where the prose is read once.

Having thus explained a few of my reasons for writing in verse, and why I have chosen subjects from common life, and endeavoured to bring my language near to the real language of men, if I have been too minute in pleading my own cause, I have at the same time been treating a subject of general interest; and for this reason a few words shall be added with reference solely to these particular poems, and to some defects which will probably be found in them. I am sensible that my associations must have sometimes been particular instead of general, and that, consequently, giving to things a false importance, I may have sometimes written upon unworthy subjects; but I am less apprehensive on this account, than that my language may frequently have suffered from those arbitrary connections of feelings and ideas with particular words and phrases, from which no man can altogether protect himself. Hence I have no doubt, that, in some instances, feelings, even of the ludicrous, may be given to my Readers by expressions which appeared to me tender and pathetic. Such faulty expressions, were I convinced they were faulty at present, and that they must necessarily continue to be so, I would willingly take all reasonable pains to correct. But it is dangerous to make these alterations on the simple authority of a few individuals, or even of certain classes of men; for where the understanding of an Author is not convinced, or his feelings altered, this cannot be done without great injury to himself: for his own feelings are his stay and support; and, if he set them aside in one instance, he may be induced to repeat this act till his mind shall lose all confidence in itself, and become utterly debilitated. To this it may be added, that the critic ought never to forget that he is himself exposed to the same errors as the Poet, and, perhaps, in a much greater degree: for there can be no presumption in saying of most readers, that it is not probable they will be so well acquainted

with the various stages of meaning through which words have passed, or with the fickleness or stability of the relations of particular ideas to each other; and, above all, since they are so much less interested in the subject, they may decide lightly and carelessly.

Long as the Reader has been detained, I hope he will permit me to caution him against a mode of false criticism which has been applied to Poetry, in which the language closely resembles that of life and nature. Such verses have been triumphed over in parodies, of which Dr. Johnson's stanza is a fair specimen:—

> 'I put my hat upon my head
> And walked into the Strand,
> And there I met another man
> Whose hat was in his hand.'

Immediately under these lines let us place one of the most justly-admired stanzas of the 'Babes in the Wood.'

> 'These pretty Babes with hand in hand
> Went wandering up and down;
> But never more they saw the Man
> Approaching from the Town.'

In both these stanzas the words, and the order of the words, in no respect differ from the most unimpassioned conversation. There are words in both, for example, 'the Strand,' and 'the Town,' connected with none but the most familiar ideas; yet the one stanza we admit as admirable, and the other as a fair example of the superlatively contemptible. Whence arises this difference? Not from the metre, not from the language, not from the order of the words; but the *matter* expressed in Dr. Johnson's stanza is contemptible. The proper method of treating trivial and simple verses, to which Dr. Johnson's stanza would be a fair parallelism, is not to say, this is a bad kind of poetry, or, this is not poetry; but, this wants sense; it is neither interesting in itself, nor can *lead* to anything interesting; the images neither originate in that sane state of feeling which arises out of thought, nor can excite thought or feeling in the Reader. This is the only sensible manner of dealing with such verses. Why trouble yourself about the species till you have previously decided upon the genus? Why take pains to prove that an ape is not a Newton, when it is self-evident that he is not a man?

One request I must make of my reader, which is, that in judging these Poems he would decide by his own feelings genuinely, and not by reflection upon what will probably be the judgment of others. How common is it to hear a person say, I myself do not object to this style of composition, or this or that expression, but, to such and such classes of people it will appear mean or ludicrous! This mode of criticism, so destructive of all sound unadulterated judgment, is almost universal: let the Reader then abide, independently, by his own feelings, and, if he finds himself affected, let him not suffer such conjectures to interfere with his pleasure.

If an Author, by any single composition, has impressed us with respect for his talents, it is useful to consider this as affording a presumption, that on other occasions where we have been displeased, he, nevertheless, may not have written ill or absurdly; and further, to give him so much credit for this one composition as may induce us to review what has displeased us, with more care than we should otherwise have bestowed upon it. This is not only an act of justice, but, in our decisions upon poetry especially, may conduce, in a high degree, to the improvement of our own taste; for an *accurate* taste in poetry, and in all the other arts, as Sir Joshua Reynolds has observed, is an *acquired* talent, which can only be produced by thought and a long-continued intercourse with the best models of composition. This is mentioned, not with so ridiculous a purpose as to prevent the most inexperienced Reader from judging for himself, (I have already said that I wish him to judge for himself;) but merely to temper the rashness of decision, and to suggest, that, if Poetry be a subject on which much time has not been bestowed, the judgment may be erroneous; and that, in many cases, it necessarily will be so.

Nothing would, I know, have so effectually contributed to further the end which I have in view, as to have shown of what kind the pleasure is, and how that pleasure is produced, which is confessedly produced by metrical composition essentially different from that which I have here endeavoured to recommend: for the Reader will say that he has been pleased by such composition; and what more can be done for him? The power of any art is limited; and he will suspect, that, if it be proposed to furnish him with new friends, that can be only upon condition of his abandoning his old friends. Besides, as I have said, the Reader is himself conscious of the pleasure which he has received from such composition, composition to which he has peculiarly attached the endearing name of Poetry; and all men feel an habitual gratitude, and something of an honourable bigotry, for the objects which have long continued to please them: we not only wish to be pleased, but to be pleased in that particular way in which we have been accustomed to be pleased. There is in these feelings enough to resist a host of arguments; and I should be the less able to combat them successfully, as I am willing to allow, that, in order entirely to enjoy the Poetry which I am recommending, it would be necessary to give up much of what is ordinarily enjoyed. But, would my limits have permitted me to point out how this pleasure is produced, many obstacles might have been removed, and the Reader assisted in perceiving that the powers of language are not so limited as he may suppose; and that it is possible for poetry to give other enjoyments, of a purer, more lasting, and more exquisite nature. This part of the subject has not been altogether neglected, but it has not been so much my present aim to prove, that the interest excited by some other kinds of poetry is less vivid, and less worthy of the nobler powers of the mind as to offer reasons for presuming, that if my purpose were fulfilled, a species of poetry would be produced, which is genuine poetry; in its nature well adapted to interest mankind permanently, and likewise important in the multiplicity and quality of its moral relations.

From what has been said, and from a perusal of the Poems, the Reader will be able clearly to perceive the object which I had in view: he will determine how far it has been attained; and, what is a much more important question, whether it be worth attaining: and upon the decision of these two questions will rest my claim to the approbation of the Public.

1800   1800

APPENDIX TO THE *LYRICAL BALLADS*

PERHAPS, as I have no right to expect that attentive perusal, without which, confined, as I have been, to the narrow limits of a preface, my meaning cannot be thoroughly understood, I am anxious to give an exact notion of the sense in which the phrase poetic diction has been used; and for this purpose, a few words shall here be added, concerning the origin and characteristics of the phraseology, which I have condemned under that name.

The earliest poets of all nations generally wrote from passion excited by real events; they wrote naturally, and as men: feeling powerfully as they did, their language was daring, and figurative. In succeeding times, Poets, and Men ambitious of the fame of Poets, perceiving the influence of such language, and desirous of producing the same effect without being animated by the same passion, set themselves to a mechanical adoption of these figures of speech, and made use of them, sometimes with propriety, but much more frequently applied them to feelings and thoughts with which they had no natural connection whatsoever. A language was thus insensibly produced, differing materially from the real language of men in *any situation*. The Reader or Hearer of this distorted language found himself in a perturbed and unusual state of mind: when affected by the genuine language of passion he had been in a perturbed and unusual state of mind also: in both cases he was willing that his common judgment and understanding should be laid asleep, and he had no instinctive and infallible perception of the true to make him reject the false; the one served as a passport for the other. The emotion was in both cases delightful, and no wonder if he confounded the one with the other, and believed them both to be produced by the same, or similar causes. Besides, the Poet spake to him in the character of a man to be looked up to, a man of genius and authority. Thus, and from a variety of other causes, this distorted language was received with admiration; and Poets, it is probable, who had before contented themselves for the most part with misapplying only expressions which at first had been dictated by real passion, carried the abuse still further, and introduced phrases composed apparently in the spirit of the original figurative language of passion, yet altogether of their own invention, and characterised by various degrees of wanton deviation from good sense and nature.

It is indeed true, that the language of the earliest Poets was felt to differ materially from ordinary language, because it was the language of extraordinary occasions; but it was really spoken by men, language which the Poet himself had uttered when he had been affected by the events which he described, or which he had heard uttered by those around him. To this language it is probable that metre of some sort or other was early superadded. This separated the genuine language of Poetry still further from common life, so that whoever read or heard the poems of these earliest Poets felt himself moved in a way in which he had not been accustomed to be moved in real life, and by causes manifestly different from those which acted upon him in real life. This was the great temptation to all the corruptions which have followed: under the protection of this feeling succeeding Poets constructed a phraseology which had one thing, it is true, in common with the genuine language of poetry, namely, that it was not heard in ordinary conversation; that it was unusual. But the first Poets, as I have said, spake a language which, though unusual, was still the language of men. This circumstance, however, was disregarded by their successors; they found that they could please by easier means: they became proud of modes of expression which they themselves had invented, and which were uttered only by themselves. In process of time metre became a symbol or promise of this unusual language, and whoever took upon him to write in metre, according as he possessed more or less of true poetic genius, introduced less or more of this adulterated phraseology into his compositions, and the true and the false were inseparably interwoven until, the taste of men becoming gradually perverted, this language was received as a natural language: and at length, by the influence of books upon men, did to a certain degree really become so. Abuses of this kind were imported from one nation to another, and with the progress of refinement this diction became daily more and more corrupt, thrusting out of sight the plain humanities of nature by a motley masquerade of tricks, quaintnesses, hieroglyphics, and enigmas.

It would not be uninteresting to point out the causes of the pleasure given by this extravagant and absurd diction. It depends upon a great variety of causes, but upon none, perhaps, more than its influence in impressing a notion of the peculiarity and exaltation of the Poet's character, and in flattering the Reader's self-love by bringing him nearer to a sympathy with that character; an effect which is accomplished by unsettling ordinary habits of thinking, and thus assisting the Reader to approach to that perturbed and dizzy state of mind in which if he does not find himself, he imagines that he is *balked* of a peculiar enjoyment which poetry can and ought to bestow.

The sonnet quoted from Gray, in the Preface,

except the lines printed in Italics, consists of little else but this diction, though not of the worst kind; and indeed, if one may be permitted to say so, it is far too common in the best writers both ancient and modern. Perhaps in no way, by positive example, could more easily be given a notion of what I mean by the phrase *poetic diction* than by referring to a comparison between the metrical paraphrase which we have of passages in the Old and New Testament, and those passages as they exist in our common Translation. See Pope's 'Messiah' throughout; Prior's 'Did sweeter sounds adorn my flowing tongue,' &c. &c. 'Though I speak with the tongues of men and of angels,' &c. &c. 1st Corinthians, chap. xiii. By way of immediate example take the following of Dr. Johnson:—

'Turn on the prudent Ant thy heedless eyes,
Observe her labours, Sluggard, and be wise;
No stern command, no monitory voice,
Prescribes her duties, or directs her choice;
Yet, timely provident, she hastes away
To snatch the blessings of a plenteous day;
When fruitful Summer loads the teeming plain,
She crops the harvest, and she stores the grain.
How long shall sloth usurp thy useless hours,
Unnerve thy vigour, and enchain thy powers?
While artful shades thy downy couch enclose,
And soft solicitation courts repose,
Amidst the drowsy charms of dull delight,
Year chases year with unremitted flight,
Till Want now following, fraudulent and slow,
Shall spring to seize thee, like an ambush'd foe.'

From this hubbub of words pass to the original. 'Go to the Ant, thou Sluggard, consider her ways, and be wise: which having no guide, overseer, or ruler, provideth her meat in the summer, and gathereth her food in the harvest. How long wilt thou sleep, O Sluggard? when wilt thou arise out of thy sleep? Yet a little sleep, a little slumber, a little folding of the hands to sleep. So shall thy poverty come as one that travelleth, and thy want as an armed man.' Proverbs, chap. vi.

One more quotation, and I have done. It is from Cowper's Verses supposed to be written by Alexander Selkirk[1]:—

'Religion! what treasure untold
Resides in that heavenly word!
More precious than silver and gold,

Or all that this earth can afford.
But the sound of the church-going bell
These valleys and rocks never heard,
Ne'er sighed at the sound of a knell,
Or smiled when a sabbath appeared.

'Ye winds, that have made me your sport
Convey to this desolate shore
Some cordial endearing report
Of a land I must visit no more.
My Friends, do they now and then send
A wish or a thought after me?
O tell me I yet have a friend,
Though a friend I am never to see.'

This passage is quoted as an instance of three different styles of composition. The first four lines are poorly expressed; some Critics would call the language prosaic; the fact is, it would be bad prose, so bad, that it is scarcely worse in metre. The epithet 'church-going' applied to a bell, and that by so chaste a writer as Cowper, is an instance of the strange abuses which Poets have introduced into their language, till they and their Readers take them as matters of course, if they do not single them out expressly as objects of admiration. The two lines 'Ne'er sighed at the sound,' &c., are, in my opinion, an instance of the language of passion wrested from its proper use, and, from the mere circumstance of the composition being in metre, applied upon an occasion that does not justify such violent expressions; and I should condemn the passage, though perhaps few Readers will agree with me, as vicious poetic diction. The last stanza is throughout admirably expressed: it would be equally good whether in prose or verse, except that the Reader has an exquisite pleasure in seeing such natural language so naturally connected with metre. The beauty of this stanza tempts me to conclude with a principle which ought never to be lost sight of, and which has been my chief guide in all I have said,—namely, that in works of *imagination and sentiment,* for of these only have I been treating, in proportion as ideas and feelings are valuable, whether the composition be in prose or in verse, they require and exact one and the same language. Metre is but adventitious to composition, and the phraseology for which that passport is necessary, even where it may be graceful at all, will be little valued by the judicious.

1802

LETTER TO LADY BEAUMONT

Coleorton, 21 May 1807

My dear Lady Beaumont,

Though I am to see you so soon, I cannot but write a word or two, to thank you for the interest you take in my Poems, as evinced by your solicitude about their immediate reception. I write partly to thank you for this, and to express the pleasure it has given me, and partly to remove any uneasiness from your mind which the disappointments you sometimes meet with in this labour of love may occasion. I see that you have many battles to fight for me,—more than in the ardour and confidence of your pure and elevated mind you had ever thought of being summoned to; but be assured that this opposition is nothing more than what I distinctly foresaw that you and my other friends would have to encounter. I say this, not to give myself credit for an eye of prophecy, but to allay any vexatious thoughts on my account which this opposition may have produced in you.

It is impossible that any expectations can be lower than mine concerning the immediate effect of this little work upon what is called the public. I do not here take into consideration the envy and malevolence, and all the bad passions which always stand in the way of a work of any merit from a living poet; but merely think of the pure, absolute, honest ignorance in which all worldlings of every rank and situation must be enveloped, with respect to the thoughts, feelings, and images, on which the life of my poems depends. The things which I have taken, whether from within or without,—what have they to do with routs, dinners, morning calls, hurry from door to door, from street to street, on foot or in carriage; with Mr. Pitt or Mr. Fox, Mr. Paul or Sir Francis Burdett, the Westminster election or the borough of Honiton? In a word—for I cannot stop to make my way through the hurry of images that present themselves to me—what have they to do with endless talking about things nobody cares anything for except as far as their own vanity is concerned, and this with persons they care nothing for but as their vanity or *selfishness* is concerned?—what have they to do (to say all at once) with a life without love? In such a life there can be no thought; for we have no thought (save thoughts of pain) but as far as we have love and admiration.

It is an awful truth, that there neither is, nor can be, any genuine enjoyment of poetry among nineteen out of twenty of those persons who live, or wish to live, in the broad light of the world— among those who either are, or are striving to make themselves, people of consideration in society. This is a truth, and an awful one, because to be incapable of a feeling of poetry, in my sense of the word, is to be without love of human nature and reverence for God.

Upon this I shall insist elsewhere; at present let me confine myself to my object, which is to make you, my dear friend, as easy-hearted as myself with respect to these poems. Trouble not yourself upon their present reception; of what moment is that compared with what I trust is their destiny?—to console the afflicted; to add sunshine to daylight, by making the happy happier; to teach the young and the gracious of every age to see, to think, and feel, and, therefore, to become more actively and securely virtuous; this is their office, which I trust they will faithfully perform, long after we (that is, all that is mortal of us) are mouldered in our graves. I am well aware how far it would seem to many I overrate my own exertions, when I speak in this way, in direct connexion with the volume I have just made public.

I am not, however, afraid of such censure, insignificant as probably the majority of those poems would appear to very respectable persons. I do not mean London wits and witlings, for these have too many bad passions about them to be respectable, even if they had more intellect than the benign laws of Providence will allow to such a heartless existence as theirs is; but grave, kindly-natured, worthy persons, who would be pleased if they could. I hope that these volumes are not without some recommendations, even for readers of this class: but their imagination has slept; and the voice which is the voice of my poetry, without imagination, cannot be heard. Leaving these, I was going to say a word to such readers as Mr. Rogers. Such!— how would he be offended if he knew I considered him only as a representative of a class, and not an unique! 'Pity,' says Mr. R. 'that so many trifling things should be admitted to obstruct the view of those that have merit.' Now, let this candid judge take, by way of example, the sonnets, which, probably, with the exception of two or three other poems, for which I will not contend, appear to him the most trifling, as they are the shortest. I would say to him, omitting things of higher consideration, there is one thing which must strike you at once, if you will only read these poems,—that those to Liberty, at least, have a connexion with, or a bearing upon, each other; and, therefore, if individually they want weight, perhaps, as a body, they may not be so deficient. At least, this ought to induce you to suspend your judgment, and qualify it so far as to allow that the writer aims at least at comprehensiveness.

But, dropping this, I would boldly say at once, that these sonnets, while they each fix the attention upon some important sentiment, separately considered, do, at the same time, collectively make a poem on the subject of civil liberty and national independence, which, either for simplicity of style or grandeur of moral sentiment, is, alas! likely to have few parallels in the poetry of the present day. Again, turn to the 'Moods of my own Mind.' There is scarcely a poem here of above thirty lines, and very trifling these poems will appear to many; but, omitting to speak of them individually, do they not, taken collectively, fix the attention upon a subject eminently poetical, viz., the interest which objects in nature derive from the predominance of certain affections, more or less permanent, more or less capable of salutary renewal in the mind of the being contemplating these objects? This is poetic, and essentially poetic. And why? Because it is creative.

But I am wasting words, for it is nothing more than you know; and if said to those for whom it is intended, it would not be understood.

I see by your last letter, that Mrs. Fermor has entered into the spirit of these 'Moods of my own Mind.' Your transcript from her letter gave me the greatest pleasure; but I must say that even she has something yet to receive from me. I say this with confidence, from her thinking that I have fallen below myself in the sonnet, beginning,

> With ships the sea was sprinkled far and
> nigh.[1]

As to the other which she objects to, I will only observe, that there is a misprint in the last line but two,

> And *though* this wilderness

for

> And *through* this wilderness,

that makes it unintelligible. This latter sonnet, for many reasons (though I do not abandon it), I will not now speak of; but upon the other, I could say something important in conversation, and will attempt now to illustrate it by a comment, which, I feel, will be inadequate to convey my meaning. There is scarcely one of my poems which does not aim to direct the attention to some moral sentiment, or to some general principle, or law of thought, or of our intellectual constitution. For instance, in the present case, who is there that has not felt that the mind can have no rest among a multitude of objects, of which it either cannot make one whole, or from which it cannot single out one individual whereupon may be concentrated the attention, divided among or distracted by a multitude? After a certain time, we must either select one image or object, which must put out of view the rest wholly, or must subordinate them to itself while it stands forth as a head:

> How glowed the firmament
> With living sapphires! Hesperus, that *led*
> The starry host, rode brightest; till the Moon,
> Rising in clouded majesty, at length,
> Apparent *Queen,* unveiled *her peerless* light,
> And o'er the dark her silver mantle threw.[2]

Having laid this down as a general principle, take the case before us. I am represented in the sonnet as casting my eyes over the sea, sprinkled with a multitude of ships, like the heavens with stars. My mind may be supposed to float up and down among them, in a kind of dreamy indifference with respect either to this or that one, only in a pleasurable state of feeling with respect to the whole prospect. 'Joyously it showed.' This continued till that feeling may be supposed to have passed away, and a kind of comparative listlessness or apathy to have succeeded, as at this line,

> Some veering up and down, one knew not why.

All at once, while I am in this state, comes forth an object, an individual; and my mind, sleepy and unfixed, is awakened and fastened in a moment.

> Hesperus, that *led*
> The starry host

is a poetical object, because the glory of his own nature gives him the pre-eminence the moment he appears. He calls forth the poetic faculty, re-

---

[1] See text, p. 333.

[2] *Paradise Lost*, iv, 604–9.

ceiving its exertions as a tribute. But this ship in the sonnet may, in a manner still more appropriate, be said to come upon a mission of the poetic spirit, because, in its own appearance and attributes, it is barely sufficiently distinguished to rouse the creative faculty of the human mind, to exertions at all times welcome, but doubly so when they come upon us when in a state of remissness. The mind being once fixed and rouzed, all the rest comes from itself; it is merely a lordly ship, nothing more:

> This ship was nought to me, nor I to her,
> Yet I pursued her with a lover's look.

My mind wantons with grateful joy in the exercise of its own powers, and, loving its own creation,

> This ship to all the rest I did prefer,

making her a sovereign or a regent, and thus giving body and life to all the rest; mingling up this idea with fondness and praise—

> where she comes the winds must stir;

and concluding the whole with,

> On went She, and due north her journey took;

thus taking up again the reader with whom I began, letting him know how long I must have watched this favourite vessel, and inviting him to rest his mind as mine is resting.

Having said so much upon mere fourteen lines, which Mrs. Fermor did not approve, I cannot but add a word or two upon my satisfaction in finding that my mind has so much in common with hers, and that we participate so many of each other's pleasures. I collect this from her having singled out the two little Poems, 'The Daffodils,' and 'The Rock crowned with Snowdrops.' I am sure that whoever is much pleased with either of these quiet and tender delineations must be fitted to walk through the recesses of my poetry with delight, and will there recognize, at every turn, something or other in which, and over which, it has that property and right which knowledge and love confer. The line,

> Come, blessed barrier, etc.,

in the 'Sonnet upon Sleep,' which Mrs. F. points out, had before been mentioned to me by Cole-

ridge, and, indeed, by almost everybody who had heard it, as eminently beautiful. My letter (as this second sheet, which I am obliged to take, admonishes me) is growing to an enormous length; and yet, saving that I have expressed my calm confidence that these poems will live, I have said nothing which has a particular application to the object of it, which was to remove all disquiet from your mind on account of the condemnation they may at present incur from that portion of my contemporaries who are called the public. I am sure, my dear Lady Beaumont, if you attach any importance to it, it can only be from an apprehension that it may affect me, upon which I have already set you at ease; or from a fear that this present blame is ominous of their future or final destiny. If this be the case, your tenderness for me betrays you. Be assured that the decision of these persons has nothing to do with the question; they are altogether incompetent judges. These people, in the senseless hurry of their idle lives, do not *read* books, they merely snatch a glance at them, that they may talk about them. And even if this were not so, never forget what, I believe, was observed to you by Coleridge, that every great and original writer, in proportion as he is great or original, must himself create the taste by which he is to be relished; he must teach the art by which he is to be seen; this, in a certain degree, even to all persons, however wise and pure may be their lives, and however unvitiated their taste. But for those who dip into books in order to give an opinion of them, or talk about them to take up an opinion—for this multitude of unhappy, and misguided, and misguiding beings, an entire regeneration must be produced; and if this be possible, it must be a work *of time*. To conclude, my ears are stone-dead to this idle buzz, and my flesh as insensible as iron to these petty stings; and, after what I have said, I am sure yours will be the same. I doubt not that you will share with me an invincible confidence that my writings (and among them these little poems) will co-operate with the benign tendencies in human nature and society, wherever found; and that they will, in their degree, be efficacious in making men wiser, better, and happier. Farewell! I will not apologize for this letter, though its length demands an apology.

Most affectionately yours,

Wm. Wordsworth

1772 Born 21 October at Ottery St. Mary, Devonshire, youngest son of the Reverend John Coleridge (a man known for his remarkable scholarship and simplicity of character) and his second wife, Anne Bowdon (a woman of great good sense). A precocious and imaginative child. Shunned the society of other children, preferring the make-believe world of *Arabian Nights* or the companionship of his learned and eccentric father.

1782–91 Following the death of his father was sent to Christ's Hospital in London. Became a Grecian under headmaster Boyer, who bred him up an excellent Latin and Greek scholar and molded his poetical preference for the better classical and English writers. Was a voracious reader of highly imaginative and of difficult and abstruse works. Established a lifelong friendship with Charles Lamb. Imagined himself in love with Mary Evans, sister of one of his schoolmates. Permanently injured his health by swimming the New River in his clothes and letting them dry on his back. Under the stimulus of the *Sonnets* of Bowles became a poet.

1791–3 Won a scholarship and entered Jesus College, Cambridge. At first applied himself and earned the approval of his superiors. Won the Browne Gold Medal and competed for the Craven scholarship. Found himself more and more in the society of men holding radical opinions; under the influence of William Frend became a unitarian and a democrat. Becoming hopelessly involved in debt and despairing over his love for Mary Evans, rushed off to London and enlisted in the King's Light Dragoons under the name 'Silas Tomkin Comberbach.'

1794 His brothers purchased his discharge from the army and he returned to Cambridge. On a visit to Oxford met Robert Southey and roused him to an acceptance of the Utopian scheme of 'Pantisocracy.' Made a walking tour of Wales and visited Southey at his home in Bristol where the two continued discussions of their ideal community. In the flush of enthusiasm for the success of the scheme became engaged to Sara Fricker, the sister of Southey's fiancée. Wrote with Southey a crude tragedy, *The Fall of Robespierre*. Met and established a friendship with Thomas Poole, a well-to-do tanner of Stowey. Returned to Cambridge, but his head was too full of Pantisocracy and he left the university without taking a degree. Avowed his love to Mary Evans, but too late; she had become engaged to marry another.

1795 Lived with Southey in Bristol and became acquainted with the publisher Cottle. Delivered lectures on politics. Quarreled with Southey; as a consequence Pantisocracy went on the rocks. First met Wordsworth. Married Sara Fricker (4 October) and settled first at Clevedon, near Bristol, then in Bristol.

1796 Projected a periodical called *The Watchman* and made a tour of the north to enlist subscribers. (*The Watchman* endured for a brief two months.) Published *Poems on Various Subjects*. To gain relief from a violent attack of neuralgia, began at about this time the fatal habit of taking opium.

1797 Wrote a play, *Osorio*, which was rejected by Sheridan. In June visited William and Dorothy Wordsworth at Racedown. In July the Wordsworths moved to Alfoxden close to Nether Stowey to be near Coleridge. The intimate association of the two poets, which began in this year, awakened in each the best of his genius. An attempted collaboration, soon abandoned, in writing the *Ancient Mariner* led to the inception of a joint volume, the now famous *Lyrical Ballads* (published 1798). Wrote *The Rime of the Ancient Mariner, Christabel* (part one), and *Kubla Khan.* Published *Poems,* second edition.

1798   Preached in the Unitarian chapel at Shrewsbury and was offered the pastorate; but upon being granted an annuity by Thomas and Josiah Wedgwood, gave up his reluctantly formed intention of becoming a minister. Decided to visit Germany and in September accompanied by Wordsworth and his sister left England for Hamburg. Soon left the Wordsworths and spent his time at Ratzeburg and Göttingen mastering the German language and absorbing the new intellectual tendencies then stirring in Germany. After a ten months' absence returned to Stowey.

1799   Visited at Sockburn where Wordsworth was staying with the Hutchinsons. Met and fell in love with Sarah Hutchinson, the sister of Wordsworth's future wife. Contributed to the *Morning Post* and translated Schiller's *Wallenstein.*

1800–1804   Settled with his family in Greta Hall, Keswick, some thirteen miles from the Wordsworths at Grasmere. Waged an unsuccessful battle against broken health, marital strife, and a dangerous overindulgence in opium. Found some consolation from his miseries by absorbing himself in metaphysical studies. Started out with William and Dorothy Wordsworth on a tour of Scotland (August 1803), but parted their company at Loch Lomond.

1804–6   Made a trip to Malta and the Mediterranean in search of health. Served for some months as secretary to the military governor of Malta and resided in Naples and Rome. Unfortunately suffered from homesickness and returned to England in worse health than when he had left two years earlier. Opium now an inveterate habit. Visited the Wordsworths at Coleorton (December 1806–January 1807).

1807   Separated from his wife. Met De Quincey in Bristol and accepted a gift from him of £300.

1808   Delivered his first course of lectures on literature at the Royal Institution. Went to live with the Wordsworths at Grasmere.

1809   Launched *The Friend,* 'a literary, moral, and political weekly paper,' which appeared at irregular intervals for twenty-seven numbers (June 1809–March 1810); published *The Friend* in book form in 1812 and in a revised edition in 1818.

1810   Soon after leaving Grasmere for London, quarreled with Wordsworth. The immediate cause of the rift was the inadvertent repetition and probable exaggeration by Basil Montagu of Wordsworth's well-meant criticism of Coleridge's temperament and habits. Later their differences were patched up, but the two men had inevitably grown apart. The 'glad morning friendship' of their youth could never be renewed again.

1811–12   Josiah Wedgwood withdrew his share of the annuity. Delivered the second and third course of literary lectures. Drudged at newspaper hackwork.

1813   Revised *Osorio* and saw it produced with some success as *Remorse.*

1813–16   In Bristol lectured on Shakespeare. Suffered financial distress. Began work on *Biographia Literaria.* April 1816, bearing the proof sheets of *Christabel* in his hand, placed himself under the medical care of Dr. Gillman at Highgate. A stay planned for one month lasted for eighteen years, ending only with his death. During these last years found comparative happiness and health. Published *Christabel, Kubla Khan, Pains of Sleep* (June 1816).

1817   Published *Lay Sermons, Biographia Literaria, Sibylline Leaves, Zapolya.* Suffered abusive criticism from Hazlitt and the *Edinburgh Review.*

1818–23   Delivered further lectures and began to attract young disciples such as J. H. Green, Thomas Allsop, and John Sterling.

1824 Enjoyed an Indian Summer of fame as the 'Oracle of Highgate.' Published *Aids to Reflection* (1825), a theological work which was well received. Toured Germany with the Wordsworths. Published *Constitution of Church and State* (1830).

1834 Died, 25 July.

SAMUEL TAYLOR COLERIDGE possessed one of the most extraordinary intellects of his generation. In his mental explorations he 'touched nearly every shore of thought.' He pioneered in the fields of metaphysics, politics, and religion and profoundly influenced his epoch by great original poetry and advanced critical theory. There was something about him like his own Ancient Mariner that arrested men's attention. He was a wonderful talker, giving forth his ideas in an inexhaustible stream of speech. 'Charles, did you ever hear me preach?' he once asked Lamb. 'I never heard you do anything else,' was his friend's reply. His mind's expression was chiefly vocal 'whether in conversation, sermon, leading article, written treatise, or flowing address.' The famous lectures on letters in 1818 were 'scarcely different from a kind of exalted monologue' (Shawcross). But whether in conversation or in the written word the 'endlessly fertilizing shower' of his mind and the charm of his benevolent nature were widely felt. 'He was the only *wonderful* man I ever met,' said Wordsworth, who more than any other knew the quickening stimulus of Coleridge's genius. Yet his towering and incessantly active intellect left only scattered fragments of its performance. For Coleridge was irresolute in character and incapable of integrating the extraordinary powers within him. The history of his life is one of designs largely unfulfilled. He drifted from speculation to speculation, squandering his time in vague reverie over vast works never begun. Chronic ill-health, domestic unhappiness, and self-distrust early impaired his genius. He took to opium first as a relief from physical pain; then as the awareness of continued failure weighed upon him, he began to use the drug to allay his sense of weakness. Opium soon paralyzed his intellect and his will, confirmed his indolence, undermined his self-respect, and made him by the time he was thirty incapable of sustained creative effort. The waste of Coleridge's talents is greatly to be regretted. What is important to remember, however, is that in the fabric of his character, with the less attractive traits, were woven the rarer powers of genius. He was endowed with an acute susceptibility to sense impressions, a tenacious memory, and a unique kind of detached and delicate visionariness. It was from a combination of these faculties under the stimulus of opium that the most strikingly original creations of his genius were produced. At the outset of his poetic career, however, opium was not a factor.

Coleridge's early verse was nourished on dreams of love, revolutionary zeal, and the abstractions of metaphysics and theology. Up to the time of his association with Wordsworth his poetry is characterized by youthful sentimentality and expansiveness. There are, to be sure, some intimations of promise in these early pieces. In *The Eolian Harp* and *Reflections on Having Left a Place of Retirement,* for example, we have a highly satisfactory handling of conversational blank verse (a form in which Coleridge was to become a master) and extended passages of delicately sensuous description. But in the early poetry the interest lies chiefly in the promise shown, not in the promise fulfilled. It was with the arrival of Wordsworth and his 'exquisite' sister, Dorothy, as near neighbors at Alfoxden that a magical transformation was wrought. Under the stimulation of their friendship Coleridge's genius suddenly 'bloomed as it had not bloomed before and as it never was to bloom again' (Grierson). During one short season, from June 1797 through September 1798, Coleridge was supreme as a lyric poet, and only fitfully thereafter. This 'wonder year,' as it has been called, was a time for him not only of exciting mental activity but one as well of almost unbroken personal happiness. The mere presence of Wordsworth exalted his conception of the role of poetry. He was fascinated, moreover, by the passion (kindled and enthusiastically shared by his companions) of observing the minute goings-on of Nature. Reflecting this new delight, Coleridge's verse of the great year abounds in precise descriptions clearly derived from an immediate contact with the object. Nature is evoked in word pictures, with a myriad of delicate details (as beautiful and strange as they are exact), and (with a gift no less rare than that of careful observation) embodied in sharp, memorable diction. The result is a group of blank-verse poems (*This Lime-tree Bower, Frost at Midnight, Fears in Solitude,* and *The Nightingale*) 'Wordsworthian in their representation of nature, yet warmed by personal happiness and shrouded in a mystic, faery beauty that mark them uniquely as Coleridge's own.' In this year, also, Coleridge reached the highest point of eloquence on the political theme with *France: an Ode,* the direct result of a recent, unprovoked French invasion of Switzerland. The ode is an impassioned recantation of his belief in France and marks the acceptance of the conservatism which thereafter he held throughout his life.

The rarest magic of the wonder year is to be found in *The Rime of the Ancient Mariner, Christabel,* and *Kubla Khan,* three poems sufficient in themselves to rank their author among the very greatest of English poets. In the longest and most famous of the three, *The Rime of the Ancient Mariner,* the exact and exquisite recording of the intricacies of Nature, which distinguished the conversational pieces, remains a chief ingredient but with a difference. The emphasis now is upon the mystic and shadowy in nature, the unique and wonderful—upon lightning and thunder-fit, tropical calm, journeying moon, 'a thousand slimy things,' and 'a hundred fire-flags sheen.' Animistic beliefs and supernatural fancies such as belong to remote times pervade the narrative. The mariner, in the words of Coleridge's marginal gloss, 'heareth sounds and seeth strange sights and commotions in the sky and the element.' Many of these features of strangeness and wonder were drawn from the poet's capacious memory, abundantly stocked with all manner of miraculous things gathered from his omnivorous reading. Professor Lowes has brilliantly demonstrated in *The Road to Xanadu* Coleridge's fabulous coverage of scientific and pseudo-scientific lore and travel literature. He has shown also in his book how Coleridge's memory tenaciously fastened upon numberless details, and how from the poet's subconscious mind a thousand ideas and images welled up, and how memory after memory was controlled and directed by the waking mind and active imagination to shape the poem. Professor Lowes minimizes the role of opium in the *Ancient Mariner,* but it seems probable that opium was a stimulant to Coleridge's imagination in the creation of this poem as it doubtless was also in *Christabel* and admittedly was in *Kubla Khan. Kubla Khan* by Coleridge's own account is an opium dream. The *Ancient Mariner* is a kind of waking dream: Coleridge gave it at one time the subtitle *A Poet's Reverie.* We are transported to a region of enchantment, a wonder world of dream-reality. The poet's success lies in the conviction he brings in telling us of the impossible, in spinning a yarn as fantastic as a dream yet as consistent within itself as reality. The rime is 'a triumph of enchantment made real.' It is an allegory of such psychological states, moral values, or illusions as we have experienced in our own actions or dreams. The simplest matters of heart and head are blended with the strangest visions of the senses without losing credence for either. On the artistic side the narrative is a marvel of construction. The central figure, the mariner, draws the complex pattern of the story to him and brings the most divergent elements into a seemingly simple whole. He tells his story, but meanwhile a wedding is going on; and there is the wedding guest, who in spite of himself becomes involved in the moral lesson of salvation. For the speed and directness of his narrative Coleridge owed a debt to the folk ballad. He fell heir to the simple ballad style and stanza, which were becoming fashionable at the time, and imitated the rude traditional four-line stanza, the repetitive features, and the narrative objectivity. He sometimes extended the four-line stanza to five, six, even nine lines, and he often enriched the lines with inner rhyme, alliteration, and assonance. Although his narrative is several times longer than the average folk ballad, none of the swiftness and force of the original ballad meter is lost, while a new richness and subtlety is gained. Moreover, all the old charm and stray beauties of the antique ballad diction are retained; while to these Coleridge added new magic in strong and luminous colors and in 'the shooting lights of far-off scenery.' The moral lesson of salvation for the slayer of the albatross through a love for all living things is not, as some have argued, intrusive. When Coleridge said that the poem had too much moral he was only replying to Mrs. Barbauld who said it had none. The moral is embedded in the poem. Without it the narrative would have lacked articulation and become a mere phantasmagoria. The lesson it carries is true to the intrinsic human values of charity, pity, and remorse. That Coleridge could successfully amalgamate the moral reality of men with the world of phantasy is part of the miracle. But it is only a part. *The Rime of the Ancient Mariner* has been called 'the most sustained piece of imaginative writing in English poetry.' For gorgeous meter and color and rhythmical harmony there surely had been 'nothing like it for one hundred years, nothing as *new*' (Grierson).

Christabel is more remote from human life and passions than the *Ancient Mariner*. It is a 'piece of pure witchcraft,' a marvelous fragment of enchantment, needing no further explanation than the fact of its existence. A literal spell hovers over the first part and most of the second. Innumerable touches of inward magic are skillfully woven into the fabric of the poem, so that we are won over to the marvelous, not by direct description but by subtle emotional stresses. The omens, good and bad, are the characteristic superstitions of old ballads and romance but they are given a modern psychological significance. The dramatic suspense, the wealth of rich, delicate detail, the beauty of diction and melody, the imaginative control of thought and sentiment have combined to produce poetry of the highest order. The second part is less original than the first, though it is a fine poem in its way and contains the famous passage on broken friendship. More than any other poem *Christabel* represents 'the fruitful collaboration between Coleridge and Dorothy Wordsworth.' A number of images recorded in Dorothy's *Journal* appear in the poem: among them, the 'one, red leaf,' the 'slowly advancing spring,' the 'howl of the mastiff,' and the 'white, thin cloud.' Coleridge believed the verse of *Christabel* (which has four accents to the line with feet of varying length and stress) was conceived on a new principle. Actually the invention was not new, for there are medieval poems and a poem by Spenser which have a similar prosody; but no poet has used syncopation and resolution in this pattern with more delicate skill. In *Kubla Khan* the mastery of cadence changes and verbal music reaches a point of flawlessness. In this magical dream fragment Coleridge has captured for a few short bars the heavenly accents of Israfel. However, it is his own history that he sings:

> For he on honey dew hath fed,
> And drunk the milk of Paradise.

A break in Coleridge's poetic activity came in September 1798, with his departure from Nether Stowey for Germany. He separated from Wordsworth and his sister shortly after their arrival on the Continent and as the force of their influence waned his poetic powers waned with it. Though never thereafter entirely forsaken by inspiration, Coleridge was never again the poet of that glorious morning-time. In Germany he intensely occupied himself with the study of philosophy, with the result that his imaginative faculties were overborne and supplanted by the speculative and critical. After his return from Germany ill-health, marital estrangement, and opium further contributed to the destruction of his creative powers. He himself was painfully conscious of a growing sterility and failure. 'The poet is dead in me,' he wrote to Godwin in 1801. Though not quite literally true, Coleridge's self-judgment was nearly so. With *Dejection: an Ode* in 1802 his poetic career is virtually ended. *Dejection* is not the last fine poem, but it is the last of his greater ones. A handful of poems beautiful and moving may be gathered from the later years. Among them will be found a few revivals of something like the old magic in brief dramatic or poignantly personal lyrics. But most of the later poems are nostalgic laments for lost youth and vanished hopes, fragments from the broken dream of life, not wanting in poetic charm, but lacking in the superlative minstrelsy of the great year.

The cardinal fact of Coleridge's poetic life is the sudden emergence of great creative faculties during his year of close association with Wordsworth and his sister and the almost as sudden deterioration of his powers after that time. Considering this circumstance it is not surprising that Coleridge should parallel Wordsworth in extended areas of his poetry in sensitively reporting Nature's external features. Nature was for Coleridge, as it was for his fellow poet, an animated body informed and made expressive by indwelling intelligence. The universe to him was alive and mysteriously divine. He penetrated to the silent and unseen processes and brought to men the world of Nature as if it were newly created in living, evanescent detail. Nature reciprocally induced in him subjective moods, so that a large proportion of his Nature poetry is autobiographical or about his friends or his family. In the greatest poems (and some of the lesser ones) Nature is transplanted to the world of dreams. In almost all of his supreme things, Coleridge takes not only the substance but the manner from the dream-state. It is noteworthy that even his expressed poetic faith—'a willing suspension of disbelief'—is merely a transference of the condition of the dream-state to the realm of poetic experience. In poetic practice Coleridge transposes into his waking hours, the unconscious technique of his dreams. This is not to deny Coleridge the genius of craftsmanship, for to satisfy the reader the romance of dreams must be disciplined by vigorous laws of beauty and structure. As Professor Lowes has abundantly demonstrated, this is precisely the triumph of *The Rime of the Ancient Mariner*. In the great pieces a constructive and impersonal art is at work, in combination with romantic beauty and fascination and, at times, moral intensity. Coleridge's poetic genius, it must be admitted, was involved in a field of somewhat narrow range. But by virtue of a small handful of poems of exceptional qualities of beauty and imagination distinctly his own Coleridge stands in the highest ranks among men of creative imagination. In 'the magically suggestive treatment of the supernatural' he stands almost alone.

When Coleridge ceased to create in poetry he fell back upon philosophical speculation and literary study. Throughout the later years he was occupied in soaking up quantities of erudition and in giving forth in prose and talk a great bulk of thought. He dreamed up many an ambitious undertaking, but was constitutionally incapable of carrying through his projects on a great scale. His prose for the most part is an aggregate of disjointed discourses, often fragmentary and obscure, which have to be pieced together to make consecutive sense. Nevertheless, though he is unsystematic and sometimes mutable, he has delivered in a wide diversity of fields and in prose of distinction 'a great bounty of pronouncements often stimulating and ingenious.' In spite of obvious limitations, Coleridge is unquestionably one of the foremost critics of modern times. His most solid performance as a critic of letters is *Biographia Literaria*. This volume is scarcely 'a masterpiece of hard thought.' There is much cloudy theorizing about the distinction between Fancy and Imagination and a quantity of 'irritating moonshiny rhetoric.' Coleridge often breaks the forward progress of the argument and wanders like a hound. Yet in some chapters he drives hard toward general principles in an attempt to ground his criticism in philosophy and to apply it as a literary touchstone. He often goes astray in attempting generalizations, but when testing out Wordsworth's doctrine he is accurate and luminous. His sword play on poetic diction is masterly. Likewise he is unerring in his particular judgments on Wordsworth's poems. He reveals insight, good taste, and sure intuitive judgment. Coleridge's enumeration in *Biographia Literaria* of Wordsworth's faults and excellences is still the best balanced pronouncement on that poet. Next in importance to *Biographia Literaria*, though less full and detailed, is Coleridge's criticism of Shakespeare and the other dramatists of Shakespeare's time. Here again his writings are uneven, fragmentary, and discontinuous. They are represented by a heterogeneous mass of notes and germinal ideas recorded in notebooks, marginalia, reports of lectures, meager and incomplete and often imperfectly recorded. There is much dross mixed with gold, but taken in the mass Coleridge's Shakespearian criticism is of great value. Historically he broke down the inveterate neo-classical dogma on Shakespeare and although he fell into the error of

a kind of German idolatry, he must be credited with initiating and establishing the nineteenth-century tradition of English Shakespearian criticism. He made numerous attempts,
some of them rewarding, to probe the essences of Shakespeare's ideas to discover the laws
that a great work of art creates within itself. However, his best dramatic criticism is in the
particular analyses of Shakespeare's characters, among which perhaps the most revealing
is that on Hamlet. There are limitations in scope and proportion in Coleridge's literary
criticism and innumerable flaws in detail; nevertheless, to Coleridge must be credited the
most fundamental philosophy of literary criticism that has yet been attempted. He laid
the groundwork of ideas on the nature of poetic expression and tried to answer the question 'What is poetry?' His attempt remains only fragmentary, but Coleridge was himself
a poet as well as a critic and knew his way. What the author of the *Ancient Mariner* and
Christabel has to tell us about poetry is nearly always worth our attention.

Coleridge was actively interested in politics and for two periods in his life was regularly employed to write editorials and articles in leading London newspapers. His own
periodicals, *The Watchman* and *The Friend*, and in later years, *Lay Sermons* and *Constitution of Church and State*, were largely occupied with political problems. In these undertakings Coleridge proved himself to be a shrewd political observer. But of more lasting
value than his contributions to political theory are those to philosophy and religion. In
philosophy Coleridge must be reckoned as the chief force in bringing about the abrupt
discard of the prevailing rationalistic doctrines of Locke and Hartley and the substitution
for them in contemporary English thought of German transcendentalism. Though he
failed to create a satisfactory system, Coleridge had a lifelong enthusiasm to reconstruct
philosophy and theology on an idealistic basis. Moreover, he became a great stimulator
through his scattered writings and even more by his talk. He did much to widen English
thought in his lifetime and exerted a marked influence over many young men like Sterling
who in the next generation were to be the spiritual leaders in the great ecclesiastical revival known as the Oxford Movement.

LIFE

As late I journey'd o'er the extensive plain
  Where native Otter sports his scanty stream,
Musing in torpid woe a Sister's pain,
  The glorious prospect woke me from the
  dream.

At every step it widen'd to my sight—
  Wood, Meadow, verdant Hill, and dreary
  Steep,
Following in quick succession of delight,—
  Till all—at once—did my eye ravish'd sweep!

May this (I cried) my course through Life por-
  tray!
New scenes of Wisdom may each step display, 10
  And Knowledge open as my days advance!
Till what time Death shall pour the undarken'd
  ray,
  My eye shall dart thro' infinite expanse,
And thought suspended lie in Rapture's blissful
  trance.

1789   1834

PANTISOCRACY[1]

No more my visionary soul shall dwell
On joys that were; no more endure to weigh
The shame and anguish of the evil day,
Wisely forgetful! O'er the ocean swell
Sublime of Hope, I seek the cottag'd dell
Where Virtue calm with careless step may
  stray,
And dancing to the moonlight roundelay,
The wizard Passions weave an holy spell.
Eyes that have ach'd with Sorrow! Ye shall
  weep
Tears of doubt-mingled joy, like theirs who
  start   10
From Precipices of distemper'd sleep,
On which the fierce-eyed Fiends their revels
  keep,
And see the rising Sun, and feel it dart
New rays of pleasance trembling to the heart.

1794   1849

---

1 The ideal social state that Coleridge and Southey planned to
establish in America.

ON A DISCOVERY MADE TOO LATE

[Coleridge discovered too late that Mary Evans, whom
he loved, had become engaged to another.]

THOU bleedest, my poor Heart! and thy distress
Reasoning I ponder with a scornful smile
And probe thy sore wound sternly, though the
    while
Swoln be mine eye and dim with heaviness.
Why didst thou listen to Hope's whisper bland?
Or, listening, why forget the healing tale,
When Jealousy with feverous fancies pale
Jarr'd thy fine fibres with a maniac's hand?
Faint was that Hope, and rayless!—Yet 'twas fair
And sooth'd with many a dream the hour of
    rest: 10
Thou should'st have lov'd it most, when most
    opprest,
And nurs'd it with an agony of care,
Even as a mother her sweet infant heir
That wan and sickly droops upon her breast!

1794   1796

TO A YOUNG ASS

ITS MOTHER BEING TETHERED NEAR IT

POOR little Foal of an oppressèd race!
I love the languid patience of thy face:
And oft with gentle hand I give thee bread,
And clap thy ragged coat, and pat thy head.
But what thy dulled spirits hath dismay'd,
That never thou dost sport along the glade?
And (most unlike the nature of things young)
That earthward still thy moveless head is
    hung?
Do thy prophetic fears anticipate,
Meek Child of Misery! thy future fate?   10
The starving meal, and all the thousand aches
'Which patient Merit of the Unworthy takes'?[1]
Or is thy sad heart thrill'd with filial pain
To see thy wretched mother's shorten'd chain?
And truly, very piteous is *her* lot—
Chain'd to a log within a narrow spot,
Where the close-eaten grass is scarcely seen,
While sweet around her waves the tempting
    green!

Poor Ass! thy master should have learnt to show
Pity—best taught by fellowship of Woe!   20
For much I fear me that *He* lives like thee,

---

[1] *Hamlet*, III, i, 74.

Half famish'd in a land of Luxury!
How *askingly* its footsteps hither bend?
It seems to say, 'And have I then *one* friend?'
Innocent foal! thou poor despis'd forlorn!
I hail thee *Brother*—spite of the fool's scorn!
And fain would take thee with me, in the Dell
Of Peace and mild Equality to dwell,[2]
Where Toil shall call the charmer Health his
    bride,
And Laughter tickle Plenty's ribless side!   30
How thou wouldst toss thy heels in gamesome
    play,
And frisk about, as lamb or kitten gay!
Yea! and more musically sweet to me
Thy dissonant harsh bray of joy would be,
Than warbled melodies that soothe to rest
The aching of pale Fashion's vacant breast!

1794   1794

LA FAYETTE[1]

As when far off the warbled strains are heard
    That soar on Morning's wing the vales among;
    Within his cage the imprison'd Matin Bird
Swells the full chorus with a generous song:

He bathes no pinion in the dewy light,
    No Father's joy, no Lover's bliss he shares,
    Yet still the rising radiance cheers his sight—
His fellows' Freedom soothes the Captive's
    cares!

Thou, FAYETTE! who didst wake with startling
    voice
    Life's better Sun from that long wintry
    night,   10
    Thus in thy Country's triumphs shalt rejoice
And mock with raptures high the Dungeon's
    might:

For lo! the Morning struggles into Day,
And Slavery's spectres shriek and vanish from
    the ray!

1794   1794

---

[2] On the banks of the Susquehanna where Coleridge and Southey
planned to establish their Pantisocratic society.

---

[1] Marquis de La Fayette, 1757–1834, was the celebrated French
general who gave his support to the American Revolution and
later to the French Revolution. In 1792 he left France to escape
persecution by the extremists and was made a political prisoner
by the Prussians and Austrians. He escaped prison shortly after
Coleridge wrote this sonnet.

KOSKIUSKO[1]

O WHAT a loud and fearful shriek was there,
  As though a thousand souls one death-groan
    pour'd!
  Ah me! they saw beneath a Hireling's sword
Their KOSKIUSKO fall! Through the swart air
(As pauses the tir'd Cossac's barbarous yell
  Of Triumph) on the chill and midnight gale
  Rises with frantic burst or sadder swell
The dirge of murder'd Hope! while Freedom
    pale
Bends in such anguish o'er her destin'd bier,
  As if from eldest time some Spirit meek   10
  Had gather'd in a mystic urn each tear
That ever on a Patriot's furrow'd cheek
Fit channel found; and she had drain'd the bowl
In the mere wilfulness, and sick despair of soul!

1794   *1794*

TO THE REVEREND W. L. BOWLES[1]

  I had just entered on my seventeenth year, when the sonnets of Mr. Bowles, twenty in number, and just then published in a quarto pamphlet, were first made known and presented to me, by a schoolfellow who had quitted us for the University, and who, during the whole time that he was in our first form (or in our school language a Grecian,) had been my patron and protector. I refer to Dr. Middleton, the truly learned, and every way excellent Bishop of Calcutta. . . .
  It was a double pleasure to me, and still remains a tender recollection, that I should have received from a friend so reverend the first knowledge of a poet, by whose works, year after year, I was so enthusiastically delighted and inspired. My earliest acquaintances will not have forgotten the undisciplined eagerness and impetuous zeal, with which I laboured to make proselytes, not only of my companions, but of all with whom I conversed, of whatever rank, and in whatever place. As my school finances did not permit me to purchase copies, I made, within less than a year and a half, more than forty transcriptions, as the best presents I could offer to those, who had in any way won my regard. And with almost equal delight did I receive the three or four following publications of the same author.—(Coleridge from *Biographia Literaria,* chapter I.)

MY heart has thank'd thee, BOWLES! for those
  soft strains
  Whose sadness soothes me, like the murmur-
    ing
  Of wild-bees in the sunny showers of spring!
For hence not callous to the mourner's pains

---

1 Thaddeus Koskiusko, 1746–1817, was a famous Polish patriot and general who took part in the American Revolution. In 1794 he led the Polish insurrection against the Russians but was defeated and taken prisoner.

1 See text, p. 121.

Through Youth's gay prime and thornless paths
  I went:
  And when the mightier Throes of mind began,
  And drove me forth, a thought-bewilder'd
    man,
Their mild and manliest melancholy lent

A mingled charm, such as the pang consign'd
  To slumber, though the big tear it renew'd; 10
  Bidding a strange mysterious PLEASURE brood
Over the wavy and tumultuous mind,

As the great SPIRIT erst with plastic sweep
Mov'd on the darkness of the unform'd deep.

1794   *1794*

THE EOLIAN HARP

COMPOSED AT CLEVEDON, SOMERSETSHIRE

MY pensive Sara![1] thy soft cheek reclined
Thus on mine arm, most soothing sweet it is
To sit beside our Cot, our Cot o'ergrown
With white-flower'd Jasmin, and the broad-
  leav'd Myrtle,
(Meet emblems they of Innocence and Love!)
And watch the clouds, that late were rich with
  light,
Slow saddening round, and mark the star of eve
Serenely brilliant (such should Wisdom be)
Shine opposite! How exquisite the scents
Snatch'd from yon bean-field! and the world *so*
  hush'd!   10
The stilly murmur of the distant Sea
Tells us of silence.

              And that simplest Lute,
Placed length-ways in the clasping casement,
  hark!
How by the desultory breeze caress'd,
Like some coy maid half yielding to her lover,
It pours such sweet upbraiding, as must needs
Tempt to repeat the wrong! And now, its strings
Boldlier swept, the long sequacious notes
Over delicious surges sink and rise,
Such a soft floating witchery of sound   20
As twilight Elfins make, when they at eve
Voyage on gentle gales from Fairy-Land,
Where Melodies round honey-dropping flowers,
Footless and wild, like birds of Paradise,
Nor pause, nor perch, hovering on untam'd wing!
O! the one Life within us and abroad,

---

1 Sara Fricker, whom Coleridge married soon after this poem was written.

an anticipation of
Coleridge's interest in the
supernatural

Which meets all motion and becomes its soul,
A light in sound, a sound-like power in light,
Rhythm in all thought, and joyance every
    where—
Methinks, it should have been impossible   30
Not to love all things in a world so fill'd;
Where the breeze warbles, and the mute still air
Is Music slumbering on her instrument.

    And thus, my Love! as on the midway slope
Of yonder hill I stretch my limbs at noon,
Whilst through my half-clos'd eye-lids I behold
The sunbeams dance, like diamonds, on the
    main,
And tranquil muse upon tranquillity;
Full many a thought uncall'd and undetain'd,
And many idle flitting phantasies,   40
Traverse my indolent and passive brain,
As wild and various as the random gales
That swell and flutter on this subject Lute!
    And what if all of animated nature
Be but organic Harps diversely fram'd,
That tremble into thought, as o'er them sweeps
Plastic and vast, one intellectual breeze,
At once the Soul of each, and God of all?
    But thy more serious eye a mild reproof
Darts, O belovéd Woman! nor such thoughts   50
Dim and unhallow'd dost thou not reject,
And biddest me walk humbly with my God.
Meek Daughter in the family of Christ!
Well hast thou said and holily disprais'd
These shapings of the unregenerate mind;
Bubbles that glitter as they rise and break
On vain Philosophy's aye-babbling spring.
For never guiltless may I speak of him,
The Incomprehensible! save when with awe
I praise him, and with Faith that inly *feels*;   60
Who with his saving mercies healéd me,
A sinful and most miserable man,
Wilder'd and dark, and gave me to possess
Peace, and this Cot, and thee, heart-honour'd
    Maid!

    20 August, 1793   1795

REFLECTIONS ON HAVING LEFT A PLACE OF RETIREMENT[1]

Low was our pretty Cot: our tallest Rose
Peep'd at the chamber-window. We could hear
At silent noon, and eve, and early morn,
The Sea's faint murmur. In the open air

---

[1] A cottage at Clevedon, near Bristol, where Coleridge and his
bride spent three happy months following their marriage.

Our Myrtles blossom'd; and across the porch
Thick Jasmins twined: the little landscape round
Was green and woody, and refresh'd the eye.
It was a spot which you might aptly call
The Valley of Seclusion! Once I saw
(Hallowing his Sabbath-day by quietness)   10
A wealthy son of Commerce saunter by,
Bristowa's citizen: methought, it calm'd
His thirst of idle gold, and made him muse
With wiser feelings: for he paus'd, and look'd
With a pleas'd sadness, and gaz'd all around
Then eyed our Cottage, and gaz'd round again,
And sigh'd, and said, it was a Blesséd Place.
And we *were* bless'd. Oft with patient ear
Long-listening to the viewless sky-lark's note
(Viewless, or haply for a moment seen   20
Gleaming on sunny wings) in whisper'd tones
I've said to my Belovéd, 'Such, sweet Girl!
The inobtrusive song of Happiness,
Unearthly minstrelsy! then only heard
When the Soul seeks to hear; when all is hush'd,
And the Heart listens!'

                  But the time, when first
From that low Dell, steep up the stony Mount
I climb'd with perilous toil and reach'd the top,
Oh! what a goodly scene! *Here* the bleak mount,
The bare bleak mountain speckled thin with
    sheep;   30
Grey clouds, that shadowing spot the sunny
    fields;
And river, now with bushy rocks o'er-brow'd,
Now winding bright and full, with naked banks;
And seats, and lawns, the Abbey and the wood,
And cots, and hamlets, and faint city-spire;
The Channel *there,* the Islands and white sails,
Dim coasts, and cloud-like hills, and shoreless
    Ocean—
It seem'd like Omnipresence! God, methought,
Had built him there a Temple: the whole World
Seem'd *imag'd* in its vast circumference: 40
No *wish* profan'd my overwhelméd heart.
Blest hour! It was a luxury,—to be!

    Ah! quiet Dell! dear Cot, and Mount sublime!
I was constrain'd to quit you. Was it right,
While my unnumber'd brethren toil'd and bled,
That I should dream away the entrusted hours
On rose-leaf beds, pampering the coward heart
With feelings all too delicate for use?
Sweet is the tear that from some Howard's[2] eye
Drops on the cheek of one he lifts from earth: 50

---

[2] John Howard, 1726-90, was a famous philanthropist and prison
reformer.

And he that works me good with unmov'd face,
Does it but half; he chills me while he aids,
My benefactor, not my brother man!
Yet even this, this cold beneficence
Praise, praise it, O my Soul! oft as thou scann'st
The sluggard Pity's vision-weaving tribe!
Who sigh for Wretchedness, yet shun the Wretched,
Nursing in some delicious solitude
Their slothful loves and dainty sympathies!
I therefore go, and join head, heart, and hand, 60
Active and firm, to fight the bloodless fight
Of Science, Freedom, and the Truth in Christ.

Yet oft when after honourable toil
Rests the tir'd mind, and waking loves to dream,
My spirit shall revisit thee, dear Cot!
Thy Jasmin and thy window-peeping Rose,
And Myrtles fearless of the mild sea-air.
And I shall sigh fond wishes—sweet Abode!
Ah!—had none greater! And that all had such!
It might be so—but the time is not yet. 70
Speed it, O Father! Let thy Kingdom come!

1795   1796

From RELIGIOUS MUSINGS

A DESULTORY POEM,

WRITTEN ON THE CHRISTMAS EVE OF 1794

ARGUMENT

Introduction. Person of Christ. His prayer on the Cross. The process of his Doctrines on the mind of the Individual. Character of the Elect. Superstition. Digression to the present War. Origin and Uses of Government and Property. The present State of Society. The French Revolution. Millennium Universal Redemption. Conclusion.

Lines 28–45, 105–16, 198–end

LOVELY was the death
Of Him whose life was Love! Holy with power
He on the thought-benighted Sceptic beamed 30
Manifest Godhead, melting into day
What floating mists of dark idolatry
Broke and misshaped the omnipresent Sire;[1]
And first by Fear uncharmed the drowsèd Soul.
Till of its nobler nature it 'gan feel
Dim recollections; and thence soared to Hope.
Strong to believe whate'er of mystic good
The Eternal dooms for His immortal sons.

---

1 Τὸ Νοητὸν διηρήκασιν εἰς πολλῶν Θεῶν ἰδιότητας

DAMAS. DE MYST. AEGYPT.
[Men have divided the Knowing One into the peculiarities of the many gods.]—(Coleridge.)

From Hope and firmer Faith to perfect Love
Attracted and absorbed: and centered there   40
God only to behold, and know, and feel,
Till by exclusive consciousness of God
All self-annihilated it shall make[2]
God its Identity: God all in all!
We and our Father one!

There is one Mind, one omnipresent Mind,
Omnific. His most holy name is Love.
Truth of subliming import! with the which
Who feeds and saturates his constant soul,
He from his small particular orbit flies
With blest outstarting! From himself he flies, 110
Stands in the sun, and with no partial gaze
Views all creation; and he loves it all,
And blesses it, and calls it very good!
This is indeed to dwell with the Most High!
Cherubs and rapture-trembling Seraphim
Can press no nearer to the Almighty's throne.

In the primeval age a dateless while
The vacant Shepherd wander'd with his flock,
Pitching his tent where'er the green grass
    waved.   200
But soon Imagination conjured up
An host of new desires: with busy aim,
Each for himself, Earth's eager children toiled.
So Property began, twy-streaming fount,
Whence Vice and Virtue flow, honey and gall.
Hence the soft couch, and many-coloured robe,
The timbrel, and arched dome and costly feast,
With all the inventive arts, that nursed the soul
To forms of beauty, and by sensual wants
Unsensualised the mind, which in the means 210
Learnt to forget the grossness of the end,
Best pleasured with its own activity.
And hence Disease that withers manhood's arm,
The daggered Envy, spirit-quenching Want,
Warriors, and Lords, and Priests—all the sore
    ills[3]
That vex and desolate our mortal life.
Wide-wasting ills! yet each the immediate source

---

2 See this *demonstrated* by Hartley, vol. 1, p. 114, and vol. 2, p. 329. See it likewise proved, and freed from the charge of Mysticism, by Pistorius in his Notes and Additions to part second of Hartley on Man.—(Coleridge.)

3 By a Priest I mean a man who holding the scourge of power in his right hand and a bible (translated by authority) in his left, doth necessarily cause the bible and the scourge to be associated ideas, and so produces that temper of mind which leads to Infidelity—Infidelity which judging of Revelation by the doctrines and practices of established Churches honours God by rejecting Christ.—(Coleridge.)

Of mightier good. Their keen necessities
To ceaseless action goading human thought
Have made Earth's reasoning animal her
    Lord;   220
And the pale-featured Sage's trembling hand
Strong as an host of arméd Deities,
Such as the blind Ionian[4] fabled erst.

From Avarice thus, from Luxury and War
Sprang heavenly Science; and from Science
    Freedom.
O'er waken'd realms Philosophers and Bards
Spread in concentric circles: they whose souls,
Conscious of their high dignities from God,
Brook not Wealth's rivalry! and they, who long
Enamoured with the charms of order, hate   230
The unseemly disproportion: and whoe'er
Turn with mild sorrow from the Victor's car
And the low puppetry of thrones, to muse
On that blest triumph, when the Patriot Sage[5]
Called the red lightnings from the o'er-rushing
    cloud
And dashed the beauteous terrors on the earth
Smiling majestic. Such a phalanx ne'er
Measured firm paces to the calming sound
Of Spartan flute! These on the fated day,
When, stung to rage by Pity, eloquent men   240
Have roused with pealing voice the unnumbered
    tribes
That toil and groan and bleed, hungry and
    blind—
These, hush'd awhile with patient eye serene,
Shall watch the mad careering of the storm;
Then o'er the wild and wavy chaos rush
And tame the outrageous mass, with plastic
    might
Moulding Confusion to such perfect forms,
As erst were wont,—bright visions of the day!—
To float before them, when, the summer noon,
Beneath some arched romantic rock reclined   250
They felt the sea-breeze lift their youthful locks;
Or in the month of blossoms, at mild eve,
Wandering with desultory feet inhaled
The wafted perfumes, and the flocks and woods
And many-tinted streams and setting sun
With all his gorgeous company of clouds
Ecstatic gazed! then homeward as they strayed
Cast the sad eye to earth, and inly mused
Why there was misery in a world so fair.

Ah! far removed from all that glads the sense,   260
From all that softens or ennobles Man,

The wretched Many! Bent beneath their loads
They gape at pageant Power, nor recognise
Their cots' transmuted plunder! From the tree
Of Knowledge, ere the vernal sap had risen
Rudely disbranchéd! Blessed Society!
Fitliest depictured by some sun-scorched waste,
Where oft majestic through the tainted noon
The Simoom sails, before whose purple pomp[6]
Who falls not prostrate dies! And where by
    night,   270
Fast by each precious fountain on green herbs
The lion couches: or hyaena dips
Deep in the lucid stream his bloody jaws;
Or serpent plants his vast moon-glittering bulk,
Caught in whose monstrous twine Behemoth[7]
    yells,
His bones loud-crashing!

                O ye numberless,
Whom foul Oppression's ruffian gluttony
Drives from Life's plenteous feast! O thou poor
    Wretch
Who nursed in darkness and made wild by want,
Roamest for prey, yea thy unnatural hand   280
Dost lift to deeds of blood! O pale-eyed form,
The victim of seduction, doomed to know
Polluted nights and days of blasphemy;
Who in loathed orgies with lewd wassailers
Must gaily laugh, while thy remembered Home
Gnaws like a viper at thy secret heart!
O agéd Women! ye who weekly catch
The morsel tossed by law-forced charity,
And die so slowly, that none call it murder!
O loathly suppliants! ye, that unreceived   290
Totter heart-broken from the closing gates
Of the full Lazar-house; or, gazing, stand,
Sick with despair! O ye to Glory's field
Forced or ensnared, who, as ye gasp in death,
Bleed with new wounds beneath the vulture's
    beak!
O thou poor widow, who in dreams dost view
Thy husband's mangled corse, and from short
    doze
Start'st with a shriek; or in thy half-thatched cot
Waked by the wintry night-storm, wet and cold
Cow'rst o'er thy screaming baby! Rest awhile 300
Children of Wretchedness! More groans must
    rise,

---

4 Homer.
5 Benjamin Franklin.

6 In a footnote to line 269 Coleridge quotes a passage from
Bruce's *Travels* describing the ominous purple haze and suffocating heat which accompany the tropical desert windstorm, or
simoom.
7 Behemoth, in Hebrew, signifies wild beasts in general. Some
believe it is the Elephant, some the Hippopotamus; some affirm
it is the Wild Bull. Poetically, it designates any large Quadruped.
—(Coleridge.)

More blood must stream, or ere your wrongs be
full.
Yet is the day of Retribution nigh:
The Lamb of God hath opened the fifth seal;[8]
And upward rush on swiftest wing of fire
The innumerable multitude of wrongs
By man on man inflicted! Rest awhile,
Children of Wretchedness! The hour is nigh
And lo! the Great, the Rich, the Mighty Men,
The Kings and the Chief Captains of the
World,   310
With all that fixed on high like stars of Heaven
Shot baleful influence, shall be cast to earth,
Vile and down-trodden, as the untimely fruit
Shook from the fig-tree by a sudden storm.
Even now the storm begins;[9] each gentle name,
Faith and meek Piety, with fearful joy
Tremble far-off—for lo! the Giant Frenzy
Uprooting empires with his whirlwind arm
Mocketh high Heaven; burst hideous from the
cell
Where the old Hag, unconquerable, huge,   320
Creation's eyeless drudge, black Ruin, sits
Nursing the impatient earthquake.

                              O return!
Pure Faith! meek Piety! The abhorréd Form[10]
Whose scarlet robe was stiff with earthly pomp,
Who drank iniquity in cups of gold,
Whose names were many and all blasphemous,
Hath met the horrible judgment! Whence that
cry?
The mighty army of foul Spirits shrieked
Disherited of earth! For she hath fallen
On whose black front was written Mystery;   330
She that reeled heavily, whose wine was blood;
She that worked whoredom with the Daemon
Power,
And from the dark embrace all evil things
Brought forth and nurtured: mitred Atheism!
And patient Folly who on bended knee
Gives back the steel that stabbed him; and pale
Fear
Haunted by ghastlier shapings than surround

Moon-blasted Madness when he yells at mid-
night!
Return pure Faith! return meek Piety!
The kingdoms of the world are your's: each
heart   340
Self-governed, the vast family of Love
Raised from the common earth by common
toil
Enjoy the equal produce. Such delights
As float to earth, permitted visitants!
When in some hour of solemn jubilee
The massy gates of Paradise are thrown
Wide open, and forth come in fragments wild
Sweet echoes of unearthly melodies,
And odours snatched from beds of Amaranth,
And they, that from the crystal river of life   350
Spring up on freshened wing, ambrosial gales!
The favoured good man in his lonely walk
Perceives them, and his silent spirit drinks
Strange bliss which he shall recognise in heaven.
And such delights, such strange beatitudes
Seize on my young anticipating heart
When that blest future rushes on my view!
For in his own and in his Father's might
The Saviour comes! While as the Thousand
Years[11]
Lead up their mystic dance, the Desert
shouts!   360
Old Ocean claps his hands! The mighty Dead
Rise to new life, whoe'er from earliest time
With conscious zeal had urged Love's wondrous
plan,
Coadjutors of God. To Milton's trump
The high groves of the renovated Earth
Unbosom their glad echoes: inly hushed,
Adoring Newton his serener eye
Raises to heaven: and he of mortal kind
Wisest, he[12] first who marked the ideal tribes
Up the fine fibres through the sentient brain.   370
Lo! Priestley[13] there, patriot, and saint, and
sage,

---

8 See the sixth chapter of the Revelation of St. John the Divine.
—(Coleridge.)

9 This passage alludes to the French Revolution: and the subsequent paragraph to the downfall of Religious Establishments. I
am convinced that the Babylon of the Apocalypse does not apply
to Rome exclusively; but to the union of Religion with Power and
Wealth, wherever it is found.—(Coleridge.)

10 And there came one of the seven Angels which had the seven
vials, and talked with me, saying unto me, come hither! I will
show unto thee the judgement of the great Whore, that sitteth
upon many waters; with whom the kings of the earth have committed fornication, &c. Revelation of St. John the Divine, chapter the seventeenth.—(Coleridge.)

11 The Millennium:—in which I suppose, that Man will continue
to enjoy the highest glory, of which his human nature is capable.
—That all who in past ages have endeavoured to ameliorate the
state of man will rise and enjoy the fruits and flowers, the imperceptible seeds of which they had sown in their former Life: and
that the wicked will during the same period, be suffering the remedies adapted to their several bad habits. I suppose that this
period will be followed by the passing away of this Earth and by
our entering the state of pure intellect, when all Creation shall rest
from its labours.—(Coleridge.)

12 David Hartley, 1705-57, English materialistic philosopher and
founder of associational psychology.

13 Joseph Priestley, 1733-1804, English clergyman and natural
philosopher, celebrated as the discoverer of oxygen. For sympathizing with the French Revolution he was attacked in 1791 by a
mob; his house was burned and his manuscripts and instruments
were destroyed. In 1794 he left England for America.

Him, full of years, from his loved native land
Statesmen blood-stained and priests idolatrous
By dark lies maddening the blind multitude
Drove with vain hate. Calm, pitying he retired,
And mused expectant on these promised years.

O Years! the blest pre-eminence of Saints!
Ye sweep athwart my gaze, so heavenly bright,
The wings that veil the adoring Seraphs' eyes,
What time they bend before the Jasper
    Throne[14]   380
Reflect no lovelier hues! Yet ye depart,
And all beyond is darkness! Heights most
    strange,
Whence Fancy falls, fluttering her idle wing.
For who of woman born may paint the hour,
When seized in his mid course, the Sun shall
    wane
Making noon ghastly! Who of woman born
May image in the workings of his thought,
How the black-visaged, red-eyed Fiend out-
    stretched[15]
Beneath the unsteady feet of Nature groans,
In feverous slumbers—destined then to wake, 390
When fiery whirlwinds thunder his dread
    name
And Angels shout, Destruction! How his arm
The last great Spirit lifting high in air
Shall swear by Him, the ever-living One,
Time is no more!

            Believe thou, O my soul,[16]
Life is a vision shadowy of Truth;
And vice, and anguish, and the wormy grave,
Shapes of a dream! The veiling clouds retire,
And lo! the Throne of the redeeming God
Forth flashing unimaginable day   400
Wraps in one blaze earth, heaven, and deepest
    hell.

Contemplant Spirits! ye that hover o'er
With untired gaze the immeasurable fount
Ebullient with creative Deity!
And ye of plastic power, that interfused
Roll through the grosser and material mass
In organizing surge! Holies of God!
(And what if Monads of the infinite mind?)
I haply journeying my immortal course

Shall sometime join your mystic choir! Till
    then   410
I discipline my young and novice thought
In ministeries of heart-stirring song,
And aye on Meditation's heaven-ward wing
Soaring aloft I breathe the empyreal air
Of Love, omnific, omnipresent Love,
Whose day-spring rises glorious in my soul
As the great Sun, when he his influence
Sheds on the frost-bound waters—The glad
    stream
Flows to the ray and warbles as it flows.

1794–6   *1796*

From THE DESTINY OF NATIONS

Lines 13–88

    FOR what is Freedom, but the unfettered use
Of all the powers which God for use had given?
But chiefly this, him First, him Last to view
Through meaner powers and secondary things
Effulgent, as through clouds that veil his blaze.
For all that meets the bodily sense I deem
Symbolical, one mighty alphabet
For infant minds; and we in this low world   20
Placed with our backs to bright Reality,
That we may learn with young unwounded
    ken
The substance from its shadow. Infinite Love,
Whose latence[1] is the plenitude of All,
Thou with retracted beams, and self-eclipse
Veiling, revealest thine eternal Sun.

    But some there are who deem themselves most
    free
When they within this gross and visible sphere
Chain down the wingéd thought, scoffing ascent,
Proud in their meanness: and themselves they
    cheat   30
With noisy emptiness of learnéd phrase,
Their subtle fluids, impacts, essences,
Self-working tools, uncaused effects, and all
Those blind Omniscients, those Almighty Slaves,
Untenanting creation of its God.

    But Properties are God: the naked mass
(If mass there be, fantastic guess or ghost)
Acts only by its inactivity.
Here we pause humbly. Others boldlier think
That as one body seems the aggregate   40

---

14 Revelation, iv. 2–3.—And immediately I was in the Spirit; and, behold, a Throne was set in Heaven and one sat on the Throne. And he that sat was to look upon like a jasper and a sardine stone: &c.—(Coleridge.)
15 The final Destruction impersonated.—(Coleridge.)
16 This paragraph is intelligible to those, who, like the Author, believe and feel the sublime system of Berkeley; and the doctrine of the final Happiness of all men.—(Coleridge.)

1 concealed existence.

Of atoms numberless, each organized;
So by a strange and dim similitude
Infinite myriads of self-conscious minds
Are one all-conscious Spirit, which informs
With absolute ubiquity of thought
(His one eternal self-affirming act!)
All his involvéd Monads, that yet seem
With various province and apt agency
Each to pursue its own self-centering end.
Some nurse the infant diamond in the mine;   50
Some roll the genial juices through the oak;
Some drive the mutinous clouds to clash in
    air,
And rushing on the storm with whirlwind speed,
Yoke the red lightnings to their volleying car.
Thus these pursue their never-varying course,
No eddy in their stream. Others, more wild,
With complex interests weaving human fates,
Duteous or proud, alike obedient all,
Evolve the process of eternal good.

  And what if some rebellious, o'er dark
    realms   60
Arrogate power? yet these train up to God,
And on the rude eye, unconfirmed for day,
Flash meteor-lights better than total gloom.
As ere from Lieule-Oaive's vapoury head
The Laplander beholds the far-off Sun
Dart his slant beam on unobeying snows,
While yet the stern and solitary Night
Brooks no alternate sway, the Boreal Morn
With mimic lustre substitutes its gleam,
Guiding his course or by Niemi lake   70
Or Balda Zhiok, or the mossy stone
Of Solfar-kapper, while the snowy blast
Drifts arrowy by, or eddies round his sledge,
Making the poor babe at its mother's back
Scream in its scanty cradle: he the while
Wins gentle solace as with upward eye
He marks the streamy banners of the North,
Thinking himself those happy spirits shall
    join
Who there in floating robes of rosy light
Dance sportively. For Fancy is the power   80
That first unsensualises the dark mind,
Giving it new delights; and bids it swell
With wild activity; and peopling air,
By obscure fears of Beings invisible,
Emancipates it from the grosser thrall
Of the present impulse, teaching Self-control,
Till Superstition with unconscious hand
Seat Reason on her throne.

1796   1817

ODE TO THE DEPARTING YEAR

> Ἰοὺ ἰού, ὦ ὦ κακά.
> Ὑπ' αὖ με δεινὸς ὀρθομαντείας πόνος
> Στροβεῖ, ταράσσων φροιμίοις δυσφροιμίοις.
>
> Τὸ μέλλον ἥξει. Καὶ σύ μ' ἐν τάχει παρὼν
> Ἄγαν ἀληθόμαντιν οἰκτείρας ἐρεῖς.

AESCHYL. *Agam.* 1173-5; 1199-1200.

[Cassandra: Woe for me, woe! Again the
    agony—
Dread pain that sees the future all too well
With ghastly preludes whirls and racks my soul.

Nay, then, believe me not: what skills belief
Or disbelief? Fate works its will—and thou
Wilt see and say in ruth, *Her tale was true.*

MORSHEAD.]

ARGUMENT

The Ode commences with an address to the Divine
Providence that regulates into one vast harmony all the
events of time, however calamitous some of them may
appear to mortals. The second Strophe calls on men to
suspend their private joys and sorrows, and devote them
for a while to the cause of human nature in general. The
first Epode speaks of the Empress of Russia, who died of
an apoplexy on the 17th of November 1796; having just
concluded a subsidiary treaty with the Kings combined
against France. The first and second Antistrophes describe the Image of the Departing Year, etc., as in a
vision. The second Epode prophesies, in anguish of
spirit, the downfall of this country.

I

SPIRIT who sweepest the wild Harp of Time!
  It is most hard, with an untroubled ear
    Thy dark inwoven harmonies to hear!
Yet, mine eye fix'd on Heaven's unchanging
    clime
Long had I listen'd, free from mortal fear,
  With inward stillness, and a bowéd mind;
    When lo! its folds far waving on the wind,
I saw the train of the Departing Year!
  Starting from my silent sadness
    Then with no unholy madness,   10
Ere yet the enter'd cloud foreclos'd my sight,
I rais'd the impetuous song, and solemnis'd his
    flight.

II

  Hither, from the recent tomb,
  From the prison's direr gloom,
  From Distemper's midnight anguish;
And thence, where Poverty doth waste and lan-
    guish;

Or where, his two bright torches blending,
    Love illumines Manhood's maze;
Or where o'er cradled infants bending,
    Hope has fix'd her wishful gaze;   20
    Hither, in perplexéd dance,
Ye Woes! ye young-eyed Joys! advance!
By Time's wild harp, and by the hand
    Whose indefatigable sweep
    Raises its fateful strings from sleep,
I bid you haste, a mix'd tumultuous band!
    From every private bower,
        And each domestic hearth,
    Haste for one solemn hour;
And with a loud and yet a louder voice,   30
O'er Nature struggling in portentous birth,
        Weep and rejoice!
Still echoes the dread Name that o'er the earth[1]
Let slip the storm, and woke the brood of Hell:
    And now advance in saintly Jubilee
Justice and Truth! They too have heard thy spell,
They too obey thy name, divinest Liberty!

III

I mark'd Ambition in his war-array!
    I heard the mailéd Monarch's troublous
        cry—
'Ah! wherefore does the Northern Conqueress
        stay!'[2]   40
Groans not her chariot on its onward way?'
    Fly, mailéd Monarch, fly!
    Stunn'd by Death's twice mortal mace,
    No more on Murder's lurid face
The insatiate Hag shall gloat with drunken
    eye!
    Manes of the unnumber'd slain!
    Ye that gasp'd on Warsaw's plain!
    Ye that erst at Ismail's tower,
When human ruin choked the streams,

Fell in Conquest's glutted hour,   50
Mid women's shrieks and infants' screams!
    Spirits of the uncoffin'd slain,
    Sudden blasts of triumph swelling,
    Oft, at night, in misty train,
    Rush around her narrow dwelling!
The exterminating Fiend is fled—
    (Foul her life, and dark her doom)
Mighty armies of the dead
    Dance, like death-fires, round her tomb!
Then with prophetic song relate,   60
Each some Tyrant-Murderer's fate!

IV

Departing Year! 'twas on no earthly shore
    My soul beheld thy Vision![3] Where alone,
    Voiceless and stern, before the cloudy throne,
Aye Memory sits: thy robe inscrib'd with
        gore,
With many an unimaginable groan
    Thou storied'st thy sad hours! Silence ensued,
    Deep silence o'er the ethereal multitude,
Whose locks with wreaths, whose wreaths with
        glories shone.
    Then, his eye wild ardours glancing,   70
    From the choiréd gods advancing,
The Spirit of the Earth made reverence meet,
And stood up, beautiful, before the cloudy seat.

V

    Throughout the blissful throng,
    Hush'd were harp and song:
Till wheeling round the throne the Lampads
    seven,
    (The mystic Words of Heaven)
    Permissive signal make:
The fervent Spirit bow'd, then spread his wings
    and spake!
    'Thou in stormy blackness throning   80
    Love and uncreated Light,
By the Earth's unsolaced groaning,
    Seize thy terrors, Arm of might!
By Peace with proffer'd insult scared,
    Masked Hate and envying Scorn!
    By years of Havoc yet unborn!
And Hunger's bosom to the frost-winds bared!
    But chief by Afric's wrongs,
        Strange, horrible, and foul!
    By what deep guilt belongs   90
    To the deaf Synod, 'full of gifts and lies!'[4]

---

1 The Name of Liberty, which at the commencement of the French Revolution was both the occasion and the pretext of un-numbered crimes and horrors.—(Coleridge.)

2 A subsidiary Treaty had been just concluded: and Russia was to have furnished more effectual aid than that of pious manifestoes to the Powers combined against France. I rejoice—not over the deceased Woman (I never dared figure the Russian Sovereign to my imagination under the dear and venerable Character of WOMAN—WOMAN, that complex term for Mother, Sister, Wife!) I rejoice, as at the disenshrining of a Daemon! I rejoice, as at the extinction of the evil Principle impersonated! This very day, six years ago, the Massacre of Ismail was perpetrated. THIRTY THOU-SAND HUMAN BEINGS, MEN, WOMEN, AND CHILDREN, murdered in cold blood, for no other crime than that their garrison had de-fended the place with perseverance and bravery. Why should I recall the poisoning of her husband, her iniquities in Poland, or her late unmotived attack on Persia, the desolating ambition of her public life, or the libidinous excesses of her private hours! I have no wish to qualify myself for the office of Historiographer to the King of Hell—!—(Coleridge.)

---

3 Thy Image in a vision.—(Coleridge.)
4 Gifts used in Scripture for corruption.—(Coleridge.)

By Wealth's insensate laugh! by Torture's howl!
    Avenger, rise!
For ever shall the thankless Island scowl,
  Her quiver full, and with unbroken bow?
Speak! from thy storm-black Heaven O speak
  aloud!
    And on the darkling foe
Open thine eye of fire from some uncertain
  cloud!
O dart the flash! O rise and deal the blow!
The Past to thee, to thee the Future cries! 100
  Hark! how wide Nature joins her groans be-
    low!
    Rise, God of Nature! rise.'

VI

The voice had ceas'd, the Vision fled;
Yet still I gasp'd and reel'd with dread.
And ever, when the dream of night
Renews the phantom to my sight,
Cold sweat-drops gather on my limbs;
  My ears throb hot; my eye-balls start;
My brain with horrid tumult swims;
  Wild is the tempest of my heart; 110
And my thick and struggling breath
Imitates the toil of death!
No stranger agony confounds
  The Soldier on the war-field spread,
When all foredone with toil and wounds,
  Death-like he dozes among heaps of
    dead!
(The strife is o'er, the day-light fled,
  And the night-wind clamours hoarse!
See! the starting wretch's head
  Lies pillow'd on a brother's corse!) 120

VII

Not yet enslaved, not wholly vile,
O Albion! O my mother Isle!
Thy valleys, fair as Eden's bowers
Glitter green with sunny showers;
Thy grassy uplands' gentle swells
  Echo to the bleat of flocks;
(Those grassy hills, those glittering dells
  Proudly ramparted with rocks)
And Ocean mid his uproar wild
Speaks safety to his Island-child! 130
Hence for many a fearless age
Has social Quiet lov'd thy shore;
Nor ever proud Invader's rage
Or sack'd thy towers, or stain'd thy fields with
  gore.

VIII

Abandon'd of Heaven![5] mad Avarice thy guide,
At cowardly distance, yet kindling with pride—
Mid thy herds and thy corn-fields secure thou
    hast stood,
And join'd the wild yelling of Famine and Blood!
The nations curse thee! They with eager wonder-
    ing
  Shall hear Destruction, like a vulture,
    scream! 140
  Strange-eyed Destruction! who with many a
    dream
Of central fires through nether seas up-thunder-
    ing
  Soothes her fierce solitude; yet as she lies
  By livid fount, or red volcanic stream,
  If ever to her lidless dragon-eyes,
  O Albion! thy predestin'd ruins rise,
The fiend-hag on her perilous couch doth leap,
Muttering distemper'd triumph in her charméd
    sleep.

IX

    Away, my soul, away!
  In vain, in vain the Birds of warning
    sing— 150
And hark! I hear the famish'd brood of prey
Flap their lank pennons on the groaning wind!
    Away, my soul, away!
  I unpartaking of the evil thing,
    With daily prayer and daily toil
    Soliciting for food my scanty soil,

---

5 The poet from having considered the peculiar advantages, which this country has enjoyed, passes in rapid transition to the uses, which we have made of these advantages. We have been preserved by our insular situation, from suffering the actual horrors of war ourselves, and we have shown our gratitude to Providence for this immunity by our eagerness to spread those horrors over nations less happily situated. In the midst of plenty and safety we have raised or joined the yell for famine and blood. Of the one hundred and seven last years, fifty have been years of war. Such wickedness cannot pass unpunished. We have been proud and confident in our alliances and our fleets—but God has prepared the cankerworm, and will smite the *gourds* of our pride. 'Art thou better than populous No, that was situate among the rivers, that had the waters round about it, whose rampart was the Sea? Ethiopia and Egypt were her strength and it was infinite: Put and Lubim were her helpers. Yet she was carried away, she went into captivity: and they cast lots for her honourable men, and all her great men were bound in chains. Thou also shalt be drunken: all thy strongholds shall be like fig trees with the first ripe figs; if they be shaken, they shall even fall into the mouth of the eater. Thou has multiplied thy merchants above the stars of heaven. Thy crowned are as the locusts; and thy captains as the great grasshoppers which camp in the hedges in the cool-day; but when the sun ariseth they flee away, and their place is not known where they are. There is no healing of thy bruise; thy wound is grievous: all, that hear the report of thee, shall clap hands over thee: for upon whom hath not thy wickedness passed continually?' *Nahum*, chap. iii.—(Coleridge.)

Have wail'd my country with a loud La-
    ment.
Now I recentre my immortal mind
    In the deep Sabbath of meek self-content;
Cleans'd from the vaporous passions that
        bedim   160
God's Image, sister of the Seraphim.[6]

1796   1796

SONNET

TO A FRIEND[1] WHO ASKED, HOW I FELT WHEN
THE NURSE FIRST PRESENTED MY INFANT TO ME

CHARLES! my slow heart was only sad, when first
    I scann'd that face of feeble infancy:
For dimly on my thoughtful spirit burst
    All I had been, and all my child might be!
But when I saw it on its mother's arm,
    And hanging at her bosom (she the while
    Bent o'er its features with a tearful smile)
Then I was thrill'd and melted, and most warm
Impress'd a father's kiss: and all beguil'd
    Of dark remembrance and presageful fear,   10
    I seem'd to see an angel-form appear—
'Twas even thine, belovéd woman mild!
    So for the mother's sake the child was dear,
And dearer was the mother for the child.

1796   1797

THIS LIME-TREE BOWER MY PRISON

ADDRESSED TO CHARLES LAMB, OF THE INDIA
HOUSE, LONDON

In the June of 1797 some long-expected friends paid a
visit to the author's cottage; and on the morning of their
arrival, he met with an accident, which disabled him
from walking during the whole time of their stay. One
evening, when they had left him for a few hours, he composed the following lines in the garden-bower.—(Coleridge.)

WELL, they are gone, and here must I remain,
This lime-tree bower my prison! I have lost
Beauties and feelings, such as would have been
Most sweet to my remembrance even when age
Had dimm'd mine eyes to blindness! They,
    meanwhile,

---

6 Let it not be forgotten during the perusal of this Ode that it was
written many years before the abolition of the Slave Trade by the
British Legislature, likewise before the invasion of Switzerland by
the French Republic, which occasioned the Ode that follows
[*France: an Ode.*]—(Coleridge.)

---

1 Probably Charles Lloyd.

Friends,[1] whom I never more may meet again,
On springy heath, along the hill-top edge,
Wander in gladness, and wind down, perchance,
To that still roaring dell, of which I told;
The roaring dell, o'erwooded, narrow, deep,   10
And only speckled by the mid-day sun;
Where its slim trunk the ash from rock to rock
Flings arching like a bridge;—that branchless
    ash,
Unsunn'd and damp, whose few poor yellow
    leaves
Ne'er tremble in the gale, yet tremble still,
Fann'd by the water-fall! and there my friends
Behold the dark green file of long lank weeds,
That all at once (a most fantastic sight!)
Still nod and drip beneath the dripping edge
Of the blue clay-stone.

                        Now, my friends emerge 20
Beneath the wide wide Heaven—and view again
The many-steepled tract magnificent
Of hilly fields and meadows, and the sea,
With some fair bark, perhaps, whose sails light
    up
The slip of smooth clear blue betwixt two Isles
Of purple shadow! Yes! they wander on
In gladness all; but thou, methinks, most glad,
My gentle-hearted Charles! for thou hast pined
And hunger'd after Nature, many a year,
In the great City pent, winning thy way   30
With sad yet patient soul, through evil and pain
And strange calamity! Ah! slowly sink
Behind the western ridge, thou glorious Sun!
Shine in the slant beams of the sinking orb,
Ye purple heath-flowers! richlier burn, ye clouds!
Live in the yellow light, ye distant groves!
And kindle, thou blue Ocean! So my friend
Struck with deep joy may stand, as I have stood,
Silent with swimming sense; yea, gazing round
On the wide landscape, gaze till all doth
    seem   40
Less gross than bodily; and of such hues
As veil the Almighty Spirit, when yet he makes
Spirits perceive his presence.

                        A delight
Comes sudden on my heart, and I am glad
As I myself were there! Nor in this bower,
This little lime-tree bower, have I not mark'd
Much that has sooth'd me. Pale beneath the
    blaze
Hung the transparent foliage; and I watch'd
Some broad and sunny leaf, and lov'd to see

---

1 Charles Lamb, and Dorothy and William Wordsworth.

The shadow of the leaf and stem above   50
Dappling its sunshine! And that walnut-tree
Was richly ting'd, and a deep radiance lay
Full on the ancient ivy, which usurps
Those fronting elms, and now, with blackest
     mass
Makes their dark branches gleam a lighter hue
Through the late twilight: and though now the
     bat
Wheels silent by, and not a swallow twitters,
Yet still the solitary humble-bee
Sings in the bean-flower! Henceforth I shall
     know
That Nature ne'er deserts the wise and pure;   60
No plot so narrow, be but Nature there,
No waste so vacant, but may well employ
Each faculty of sense, and keep the heart
Awake to Love and Beauty! and sometimes
'Tis well to be bereft of promis'd good,
That we may lift the soul, and contemplate
With lively joy the joys we cannot share.
My gentle-hearted Charles! when the last rook
Beat its straight path along the dusky air
Homewards, I blest it! deeming its black wing 70
(Now a dim speck, now vanishing in light)
Had cross'd the mighty Orb's dilated glory,
While thou stood'st gazing; or, when all was still,
Flew creeking o'er thy head, and had a charm
For thee, my gentle-hearted Charles, to whom
No sound is dissonant which tells of Life.

1797   1800

KUBLA KHAN: OR, A VISION IN A DREAM

A FRAGMENT

In the summer of the year 1797[1] the Author, then in ill-health, had retired to a lonely farm-house between Porlock and Linton, on the Exmoor confines of Somerset and Devonshire. In consequence of a slight indisposition, an anodyne had been prescribed, from the effect of which he fell asleep in his chair at the moment he was reading the following sentence, or words of the same substance, in Purchas's *Pilgrimage*: 'Here the Khan Kubla commanded a palace to be built, and a stately garden thereunto: and thus ten miles of fertile ground were inclosed with a wall.' The Author continued for about three hours in a profound sleep, at least of the external senses, during which time he has the most vivid confidence, that he could not have composed less than from two to three hundred lines; if that indeed can be called composition in which all the images rose up before him as *things*, with a parallel production of the correspondent expressions, without any sensation or consciousness of effort. On awaking he appeared to himself to have a distinct recollection of the whole, and taking his pen, ink, and paper, instantly and eagerly wrote down the lines that are here preserved. At this moment he was unfortunately called out by a person on business from Porlock, and detained by him above an hour, and on his return to his room, found, to his no small surprise and mortification, that though he still retained some vague and dim recollection of the general purport of the vision, yet, with the exception of some eight or ten scattered lines and images, all the rest had passed away like the images on the surface of a stream into which a stone had been cast, but, alas! without the after restoration of the latter:

> Then all the charm
> Is broken—all that phantom-world so fair,
> Vanishes, and a thousand circlets spread,
> And each mis-shape the other. Stay awhile,
> Poor youth! who scarcely dar'st lift up thine eyes—
> The stream will soon renew its smoothness, soon
> The visions will return! And lo! he stays,
> And soon the fragments dim of lovely forms
> Come trembling back, unite, and now once more
> The pool becomes a mirror.[2]

Yet from the still surviving recollections in his mind, the Author has frequently purposed to finish for himself what had been originally, as it were, given to him Αὔριον ἄδιον ἄσω:[3] but the to-morrow is yet to come.

IN Xanadu did Kubla Khan[4]
A stately pleasure-dome decree:
Where Alph, the sacred river, ran
Through caverns measureless to man
   Down to a sunless sea.
So twice five miles of fertile ground
With walls and towers were girdled round:
And there were gardens bright with sinuous rills,
Where blossomed many an incense-bearing tree;
And here were forests ancient as the hills,   10
Enfolding sunny spots of greenery.

But oh! that deep romantic chasm which slanted
Down the green hill athwart a cedarn cover!
A savage place! as holy and enchanted
As e'er beneath a waning moon was haunted
By woman wailing for her demon-lover!
And from this chasm, with ceaseless turmoil
     seething,
As if this earth in fast thick pants were breathing,
A mighty fountain momently was forced:
Amid whose swift half-intermitted burst   20
Huge fragments vaulted like rebounding hail,
Or chaffy grain beneath the thresher's flail:
And 'mid these dancing rocks at once and ever
It flung up momently the sacred river.

1 Coleridge's dating has been thought to be a mistake for 1798, but see E. K. Chambers' persuasive argument for confirming 1797 as the year of composition. (*Coleridge*, pp. 100–103.)

2 from Coleridge's *The Picture*, 91–100.
3 'Tomorrow to sing a sweeter song'—(Theocritus, Idyl I.)
4 Mongol emperor of the thirteenth century and grandson of Ghengis Khan, who founded the Mongol dynasty in China.

Five miles meandering with a mazy motion
Through wood and dale the sacred river ran,
Then reached the caverns measureless to man,
And sank in tumult to a lifeless ocean:
And 'mid this tumult Kubla heard from far
Ancestral voices prophesying war!   30
    The shadow of the dome of pleasure
    Floated midway on the waves;
    Where was heard the mingled measure
    From the fountain and the caves.
It was a miracle of rare device,
A sunny pleasure-dome with caves of ice!

A damsel with a dulcimer
In a vision once I saw:
It was an Abyssinian maid,
And on her dulcimer she played,   40
Singing of Mount Abora.
Could I revive within me
Her symphony and song,
To such a deep delight 'twould win me,
That with music loud and long,
I would build that dome in air,
That sunny dome! those caves of ice!
And all who heard should see them there,
And all should cry, Beware! Beware!
His flashing eyes, his floating hair!   50
Weave a circle round him thrice,
And close your eyes with holy dread,
For he on honey-dew hath fed,
And drunk the milk of Paradise.

1797   1816

THE RIME OF THE ANCIENT MARINER

[For the origin of this poem see Coleridge's *Biographia
Literaria,* Chapter XIV, text, p. 424, and Wordsworth's
note to *We Are Seven,* text, p. 251. An additional statement by Wordsworth was reported to H. N. Coleridge
by the Reverend Alexander Dyce: '*The Ancient Mariner*
was founded on a strange dream, which a friend of Coleridge had, who fancied he saw a skeleton ship, with figures in it. We had both determined to write some poetry
for a monthly magazine, the profits of which were to defray the expenses of a little excursion we were to make
together. *The Ancient Mariner* was intended for this periodical, but was too long. I had very little share in the
composition of it, for I soon found that the style of Coleridge and myself would not assimilate. Besides the lines
(in the fourth part):

    "And thou art long, and lank, and brown,
    As is the ribbed sea-sand"—

I wrote the stanza (in the first part):

    "He holds him with his glittering eye—
    The Wedding-Guest stood still,
    And listens like a three-years' child:
    The Mariner hath his will"—

and four or five lines more in different parts of the poem,
which I could not now point out. The idea of "*shooting
an albatross*" was mine; *for I had been reading Shelvocke's
Voyages, which probably Coleridge never saw.* I also suggested the reanimation of the dead bodies, to work the
ship.'

    The final form of *The Ancient Mariner* differs in sev-
eral notable respects from that which first appeared in
1798. In the revision Coleridge dropped many archaic
words and spellings, modified some lines and stanzas,
and added the Latin motto and the prose narrative in
the margin.]

IN SEVEN PARTS

    Facile credo, plures esse Naturas invisibiles quam visi-
biles in rerum universitate. Sed horum omnium familiam
quis nobis enarrabit? et gradus et cognationes et dis-
crimina et singulorum munera? Quid agunt? quae loca
habitant? Harum rerum notitiam semper ambivit ingen-
ium humanum, nunquam attigit. Juvat, interea, non
diffiteor, quandoque in animo, tanquam in tabula, ma-
joris et melioris mundi imaginem contemplari: ne mens
assuefacta hodiernae vitae minutiis se contrahat nimis,
et tota subsidat in pusillas cogitationes. Sed veritati interea in vigilandum est, modusque servandus, ut certa
ab incertis, diem a nocte, distinguamus—T. Burnet, *Ar-
chæol. Phil.* P. 68.

[I readily believe that there are more invisible than visible beings in the universe. But who will tell us the family, the ranks, the relationships, the differences, the
respective functions of all these beings? What do they
do? Where do they dwell? The human mind has circled
around this knowledge, but has never reached it. Still, it
is pleasant, I have no doubt, to contemplate sometimes
in one's mind, as in a picture, the image of a bigger and
better world; lest the mind, accustomed to the details of
daily life, be too narrowed and settle down entirely on
trifling thoughts. Meanwhile, however, we must be on
the lookout for truth and observe restraint, in order that
we may distinguish the certain from the uncertain, day
from night.]

ARGUMENT

    How a Ship having passed the Line was driven by
storms to the cold Country towards the South Pole; and
how from thence she made her course to the tropical
Latitude of the Great Pacific Ocean; and of the strange
things that befell: and in what manner the Ancyent Marinere came back to his own Country.

PART I

It is an ancient Mariner,   *An ancient*
And he stoppeth one of three.   *Mariner meet-*
'By thy long grey beard and glit- *eth three Gal-*
    tering eye,   *lants bidden*
                                to a wedding-
Now wherefore stopp'st thou me? *feast, and de-*
                                taineth one.

The Bridegroom's doors are opened wide,
And I am next of kin;
The guests are met, the feast is set:
May'st hear the merry din.'

He holds him with his skinny hand,
'There was a ship,' quoth he.   10
'Hold off! unhand me, grey-beard loon!'
Eftsoons[1] his hand dropt he.

He holds him with his glittering
   eye—
The Wedding-Guest stood still,
And listens like a three years'
   child:
The Mariner hath his will.

      The Wedding-Guest is spell-bound by the eye of the old seafaring man, and con-strained to hear his tale.

The Wedding-Guest sat on a stone:
He cannot choose but hear;
And thus spake on that ancient man,
The bright-eyed Mariner.   20

'The ship was cheered, the harbour cleared,
Merrily did we drop
Below the kirk, below the hill,
Below the lighthouse top.

      The Mariner tells how the ship sailed southward with a good wind and fair weather, till it reached the line.

The Sun came up upon the left,
Out of the sea came he!
And he shone bright, and on the
   right
Went down into the sea.

Higher and higher every day,
Till over the mast at noon—'   30
The Wedding-Guest here beat his breast,
For he heard the loud bassoon.

The bride hath paced into the
   hall,
Red as a rose is she;
Nodding their heads before her
   goes
The merry minstrelsy.

      The Wedding-Guest heareth the bridal music; but the Mariner continueth his tale.

The Wedding-Guest he beat his breast,
Yet he cannot choose but hear;
And thus spake on that ancient man,
The bright-eyed Mariner.   40

'And now the STORM-BLAST
   came, and he
Was tyrannous and strong:
He struck with his o'ertaking wings,
And chased us south along.

      The ship driven by a storm towards the south pole.

With sloping masts and dipping prow,
As who pursued with yell and blow

Still treads the shadow of his foe,
And forward bends his head,
The ship drove fast, loud roared the blast,
And southward aye we fled.   50

And now there came both mist and snow,
And it grew wondrous cold:
And ice, mast-high, came floating by,
As green as emerald.

And through the drifts the snowy
   clifts
Did send a dismal sheen:
Nor shapes of men nor beasts we
   ken—
The ice was all between.

      The land of ice, and of fearful sounds where no living thing was to be seen.

The ice was here, the ice was there,
The ice was all around: 60
It cracked and growled, and roared and howled,
Like noises in a swound![2]

At length did cross an Albatross,
Thorough the fog it came;
As if it had been a Christian soul,
We hailed it in God's name.

It ate the food it ne'er had eat,
And round and round it flew.
The ice did split with a thunder-
   fit;
The helmsman steered us through!   70

      Till a great sea-bird, called the Albatross, came through the snow-fog, and was received with great joy and hospitality.

And a good south wind sprung
   up behind;
The Albatross did follow,
And every day, for food or play,
Came to the mariner's hollo!

In mist or cloud, on mast or
   shroud,[3]
It perched for vespers nine;
Whiles all the night, through fog-smoke white,
Glimmered the white Moon-shine.'

      And lo! the Albatross proveth a bird of good omen, and followeth the ship as it returned northward through fog and floating ice.

'God save thee, ancient Mariner!
From the fiends, that plague thee
   thus!—
Why look'st thou so?'—With
   my cross-bow
I shot the ALBATROSS.

      The ancient Mariner inhospitably killeth the pious bird of good omen.   80

---

1 immediately.

2 swoon.

3 rope supporting the masthead.

PART II

The Sun now rose upon the right:
Out of the sea came he,
Still hid in mist, and on the left
Went down into the sea.

And the good south wind still blew behind,
But no sweet bird did follow,
Nor any day for food or play
Came to the mariners' hollo!   90

And I had done a hellish thing,   His shipmates
And it would work 'em woe: cry out against
For all averred, I had killed the   the ancient
bird   Mariner, for
That made the breeze to blow.   killing the
Ah wretch! said they, the bird to   bird of good
slay,   luck.
That made the breeze to blow!

Nor dim nor red, like God's own   But when the
head,   fog cleared
The glorious Sun uprist: off, they
Then all averred, I had killed the   justify the
bird   same, and
That brought the fog and mist.   thus make
'Twas right, said they, such birds   themselves
to slay,   accomplices   100
That bring the fog and mist.   in the crime.

The fair breeze blew, the white   The fair breeze
foam flew,   continues;
The furrow followed free;   the ship enters
We were the first that ever burst   the Pacific
Into that silent sea.   Ocean, and
                                       sails north-
                                       ward, even
                                       till it reaches
                                       the Line.

Down dropt the breeze, the sails
dropt down,
'Twas sad as sad could be;
And we did speak only to   The ship hath
break   been suddenly
The silence of the sea!   becalmed.
                                                     110

All in a hot and copper sky,
The bloody Sun, at noon,
Right up above the mast did stand,
No bigger than the Moon.

Day after day, day after day,
We stuck, nor breath nor motion;
As idle as a painted ship
Upon a painted ocean.

Water, water, every where   And the Alba-
And all the boards did   tross begins to
shrink;   be avenged.
Water, water, every where,   120
Nor any drop to drink.

The very deep did rot: O Christ!
That ever this should be!
Yea, slimy things did crawl with legs
Upon the slimy sea.

About, about, in reel and rout
The death-fires[4] danced at night;
The water, like a witch's oils,
Burnt green, and blue and white.   130

And some in dreams assuréd   A Spirit had
were   followed them;
Of the Spirit that plagued us   one of the in-
so;   visible inhabi-
Nine fathom deep he had fol-   tants of this
lowed us   planet, neither
From the land of mist and snow.   departed souls nor
                                    angels; concerning
                                    whom the learned
                                    Jew, Josephus, and
                                    the Platonic Con-
And every tongue, through utter   stantinopolitan, Mi-
drought,   chael Psellus, may
Was withered at the root;   be consulted. They
We could not speak, no more   are very numerous,
than if   and there is no
We had been choked with soot.   climate or element
                                    without one or
                                    more.

Ah! well a-day! what evil looks   The shipmates,
Had I from old and young!   in their sore   140
Instead of the cross, the Alba-   distress, would
tross   fain throw the
About my neck was hung.   whole guilt on
                                    the ancient
                                    Mariner: in sign
          PART III   whereof they
                                    hang the dead sea-
                                    bird round his
There passed a weary time. Each   neck.
throat
Was parched, and glazed each eye.
A weary time! a weary time!
How glazed each weary eye,
When looking westward, I be-   The ancient
held   Mariner be-
A something in the sky.   holdeth a sign
                                    in the element
                                    afar off.

At first it seemed a little speck,
And then it seemed a mist;   150

---

4 phosphorescent gleams on the ship's riggings believed by sailors to foretell disaster.

It moved and moved, and took at last
A certain shape, I wist.[5]

A speck, a mist, a shape, I wist!
And still it neared and neared:
As if it dodged a water-sprite,
It plunged and tacked and veered.

With throats unslaked, with
    black lips baked,
We could nor laugh nor wail;
Through utter drought all dumb
    we stood!
I bit my arm, I sucked the blood,
And cried, A sail! a sail!

At its nearer approach, it seemeth him to be a ship; and at a dear ransom he freeth his speech from the bonds of thirst. 160

With throats unslaked, with black lips baked,
Agape they heard me call:
Gramercy! they for joy did grin,
And all at once their breath drew
    in,
As they were drinking all.

A flash of joy.

See! see! (I cried) she tacks no
    more!
Hither to work us weal;
Without a breeze, without a tide,
She steadies with upright keel!

And horror follows. For can it be a ship that comes onward without wind or tide? 170

The western wave was all a-flame.
The day was well nigh done!
Almost upon the western wave
Rested the broad bright Sun;
When that strange shape drove suddenly
Betwixt us and the Sun.

And straight the Sun was flecked
    with bars,
(Heaven's Mother send us grace!)
As if through a dungeon-grate
    he peered
With broad and burning face.   180

It seemeth him but the skeleton of a ship.

Alas! (thought I, and my heart
    beat loud)
How fast she nears and nears!
Are those *her* sails that glance in
    the Sun,
Like restless gossameres?

And its ribs are seen as bars on the face of the setting Sun.

Are those *her* ribs through which
    the Sun

Did peer, as through a grate?
And is that Woman all her crew?
Is that a DEATH? and are there
    two?
Is DEATH that woman's mate?

The Spectre-Woman and her Death-mate, and no other on board the skeleton ship.

Her lips were red, *her* looks were
    free,
Her locks were yellow as gold:
Her skin was as white as leprosy,
The Night-mare LIFE-IN-DEATH
    was she,
Who thicks man's blood with
    cold.

Like vessel, like crew! 190

Death and Life-in-Death have diced for the ship's crew, and she (the latter) winneth the ancient Mariner.

The naked hulk alongside came,
And the twain were casting dice;
'The game is done! I've won!
    I've won!'
Quoth she, and whistles thrice.

The Sun's rim dips; the stars
    rush out:
At one stride comes the dark;
With far-heard whisper, o'er the sea,
Off shot the spectre-bark.

No twilight within the courts of the Sun. 200

We listened and looked sideways
    up!
Fear at my heart, as at a cup,
My life-blood seemed to sip!
The stars were dim, and thick the night,
The steersman's face by his lamp gleamed white;
From the sails the dew did drip—
Till clomb above the eastern bar
The hornéd Moon, with one bright star
Within the nether tip.

At the rising of the Moon,

210

One after one, by the star-dogged
    Moon,[6]
Too quick for groan or sigh,
Each turned his face with a ghastly pang,
And cursed me with his eye.

One after another,

Four times fifty living men,
(And I heard nor sigh nor groan)
With heavy thump, a lifeless lump,
They dropped down one by one.

His shipmates drop down dead.

The souls did from their bodies
    fly,—   220

---

[5] knew.

6 It is a common superstition among sailors that something evil is about to happen whenever a star dogs the moon.—(Coleridge, in a manuscript note.)

They fled to bliss or woe!
And every soul, it passed me by,
Like the whizz of my cross-bow!

But Life-in-Death begins her work on the ancient Mariner.

PART IV

'I fear thee, ancient Mariner!
I fear thy skinny hand!
And thou art long, and lank, and brown,
As is the ribbed sea-sand.[7]

The Wedding-Guest feareth that a Spirit is talking to him;

I fear thee and thy glittering eye,
And thy skinny hand, so brown.'—
Fear not, fear not, thou Wedding-Guest!
This body dropt not down.

But the ancient Ma- 230 *riner assureth him of his bodily life, and proceedeth to relate his horrible penance.*

Alone, alone, all, all alone,
Alone on a wide wide sea!
And never a saint took pity on
My soul in agony.

The many men, so beautiful!
And they all dead did lie:
And a thousand thousand slimy things
Lived on; and so did I.

He despiseth the creatures of the calm,

I looked upon the rotting sea,
And drew my eyes away;
I looked upon the rotting deck,
And there the dead men lay.

And envi- 240 *eth that they should live, and so many be dead.*

I looked to heaven, and tried to pray;
But or ever a prayer had gusht,
A wicked whisper came, and made
My heart as dry as dust.

I closed my lids, and kept them close,
And the balls like pulses beat;
For the sky and the sea, and the sea and the sky
Lay like a load on my weary eye,
And the dead were at my feet.

250

The cold sweat melted from their limbs,
Nor rot nor reek did they:

But the curse liveth for him in the eye of the dead men.

The look with which they looked on me
Had never passed away.

An orphan's curse would drag to hell
A spirit from on high;
But oh! more horrible than that
Is the curse in a dead man's eye!
Seven days, seven nights, I saw that curse,
And yet I could not die.

260

The moving Moon went up the sky,
And no where did abide:
Softly she was going up,
And a star or two beside—

In his loneliness and fixedness he yearneth towards the journeying Moon, and the stars that still sojourn, yet still move onward; and every where the blue sky belongs to them, and is their appointed rest, and their native country and their own natural homes, which they enter unan- 270 *nounced, as lords that are certainly expected and yet there is a silent joy at their arrival.*

Her beams bemocked the sultry main,
Like April hoar-frost spread;
But where the ship's huge shadow lay,
The charméd water burnt alway
A still and awful red.

Beyond the shadow of the ship,
I watched the water-snakes:
They moved in tracks of shining white,
And when they reared, the elfish light
Fell off in hoary flakes.

By the light of the Moon he beholdeth God's creatures of the great calm.

Within the shadow of the ship
I watched their rich attire:
Blue, glossy green, and velvet black,
They coiled and swam; and every track
Was a flash of golden fire.

280

O happy living things! no tongue
Their beauty might declare:
A spring of love gushed from my heart,
And I blessed them unaware:
Sure my kind saint took pity on me,
And I blessed them unaware.

Their beauty and their happiness.

He blesseth them in his heart.

The self-same moment I could pray;
And from my neck so free
The Albatross fell off, and sank
Like lead into the sea.

290

The spell begins to break.

---

7 For the last two lines of this stanza, I am indebted to Mr. Wordsworth. It was on a delightful walk from Nether Stowey to Dulverton, with him and his sister, in the Autumn of 1797, that this poem was planned, and in part composed.—(Coleridge.)

PART V

Oh sleep! it is a gentle thing,
Beloved from pole to pole!
To Mary Queen the praise be given!
She sent the gentle sleep from Heaven,
That slid into my soul.

The silly[8] buckets on the deck,   *By grace of*
That had so long remained,   *the holy*
I dreamt that they were filled   *Mother, the*
   with dew;   *ancient*
                                   Mariner is
And when I awoke, it rained.   *refreshed with*
                               rain.   300

My lips were wet, my throat was cold,
My garments all were dank;
Sure I had drunken in my dreams,
And still my body drank.

I moved, and could not feel my limbs:
I was so light—almost
I thought that I had died in sleep,
And was a blessèd ghost.

And soon I heard a roaring wind: *He heareth*
It did not come anear;   *sounds and*
But with its sound it shook the   *seeth strange* 310
   sails,   *sights and*
                               commotions in
That were so thin and sere.   *the sky and*
                               the element.

The upper air burst into life!
And a hundred fire-flags[9] sheen,[10]
To and fro they were hurried about!
And to and fro, and in and out,
The wan stars danced between.

And the coming wind did roar more loud,
And the sails did sigh like sedge;
And the rain poured down from one black
   cloud;   320
The Moon was at its edge.

The thick black cloud was cleft, and still
The Moon was at its side:
Like waters shot from some high crag,
The lightning fell with never a jag,
A river steep and wide.

The loud wind never reached   *The bodies of*
   the ship,   *the ship's crew*
                               are inspired
Yet now the ship moved on!   *[inspirited]*
                               and the ship

---

8 empty, useless.
9 perhaps the Polar Lights, known in the Northern Hemisphere
as the Aurora Borealis.
10 bright, beautiful.

Beneath the lightning and the
   Moon
The dead men gave a groan.   330

They groaned, they stirred, they all uprose,
Nor spake, nor moved their eyes;
It had been strange, even in a dream,
To have seen those dead men rise.

The helmsman steered, the ship moved on;
Yet never a breeze up-blew;
The mariners all 'gan work the ropes,
Where they were wont to do;
They raised their limbs like lifeless tools—
We were a ghastly crew.   340

The body of my brother's son
Stood by me, knee to knee:
The body and I pulled at one rope,
But he said nought to me.

'I fear thee, ancient Mariner!'   *But not by the*
Be calm, thou Wedding-Guest!   *souls of the*
'Twas not those souls that fled in   *men, nor by*
   pain,   *dæmons of*
Which to their corses came   *earth or*
   again,   *middle air, but*
But a troop of spirits blest: *by a blessed*
                               troop of
                               angelic spirits,
For when it dawned—they   *sent down by*
   dropped their arms,   *the invocation*
                              of the guar-
And clustered round the mast;   *dian saint.* 350
Sweet sounds rose slowly through
   their mouths,
And from their bodies passed.

Around, around, flew each sweet sound,
Then darted to the Sun;
Slowly the sounds came back again,
Now mixed, now one by one.

Sometimes a-dropping from the sky
I heard the sky-lark sing;
Sometimes all little birds that are,   360
How they seemed to fill the sea and air
With their sweet jargoning!

And now 'twas like all instruments,
Now like a lonely flute;
And now it is an angel's song,
That makes the heavens be mute.

It ceased; yet still the sails made on
A pleasant noise till noon,

A noise like of a hidden brook
In the leafy month of June,   370
That to the sleeping woods all night
Singeth a quiet tune.

Till noon we quietly sailed on,
Yet never a breeze did breathe:
Slowly and smoothly went the ship,
Moved onward from beneath.

Under the keel nine fathom deep,
From the land of mist and snow,
The spirit slid: and it was he
That made the ship to go.
The sails at noon left off their
        tune,
And the ship stood still also.

The lonesome Spirit from the south pole carries on the ship as far as the Line, in obedience to the angelic troop, but still requireth vengeance.

The Sun, right up above the
        mast,
Had fixed her to the ocean:
But in a minute she 'gan stir,
With a short uneasy motion—
Backwards and forwards half her length
With a short uneasy motion.

Then like a pawing horse let go,
She made a sudden bound: 390
It flung the blood into my head,
And I fell down in a swound.

How long in that same fit I lay,
I have not to declare;
But ere my living life returned,
I heard and in my soul discerned
Two voices in the air.

The Polar Spirit's fellow-dæmons, the invisible inhabitants of the element, take part in his wrong; and two of them relate, one to the other, that penance long and heavy for the ancient Mariner hath been accorded to the Polar Spirit, who returneth southward.

'Is it he?' quoth one, 'Is this the
        man?
By him who died on cross,
With his cruel bow he laid full
        low
The harmless Albatross.

The spirit who bideth by himself
In the land of mist and snow,
He loved the bird that loved the
        man
Who shot him with his bow.'

The other was a softer voice,
As soft as honey-dew:
Quoth he, 'The man hath penance done,
And penance more will do.'

PART VI

FIRST VOICE

'But tell me, tell me! speak again,   410
Thy soft response renewing—
What makes that ship drive on so fast?
What is the ocean doing?'

SECOND VOICE

'Still as a slave before his lord,
The ocean hath no blast;
His great bright eye most silently
Up to the Moon is cast—

If he may know which way to go;
For she guides him smooth or grim.
See, brother, see! how graciously   420
She looketh down on him.'

FIRST VOICE

'But why drives on that ship so
        fast,
Without or wave or wind?'

The Mariner hath been cast into a trance; for the angelic power causeth the vessel to drive northward faster than human life could endure.

SECOND VOICE

'The air is cut away before,
And closes from behind.

Fly, brother, fly! more high,
        more high!
Or we shall be belated:
For slow and slow that ship will go,
When the Mariner's trance is abated.'

I woke, and we were sailing on
As in a gentle weather:
'Twas night, calm night, the
        moon was high;
The dead men stood together.

The supernatural motion is retarded; the Mariner awakes, and his penance begins anew.   430

All stood together on the deck,
For a charnel-dungeon fitter:
All fixed on me their stony eyes,
That in the Moon did glitter.

The pang, the curse, with which they died,
Had never passed away:
I could not draw my eyes from theirs,   440
Nor turn them up to pray.

And now this spell was snapt: *The curse is*
   once more   *finally ex-*
I viewed the ocean green,   *piated.*
And looked far forth, yet little saw
Of what had else been seen—

Like one, that on a lonesome road
Doth walk in fear and dread,
And having once turned round walks on,
And turns no more his head;
Because he knows, a frightful fiend   450
Doth close behind him tread.

But soon there breathed a wind on me,
Nor sound nor motion made:
Its path was not upon the sea,
In ripple or in shade.

It raised my hair, it fanned my cheek
Like a meadow-gale of spring—
It mingled strangely with my fears,
Yet it felt like a welcoming.

Swiftly, swiftly flew the ship,   460
Yet she sailed softly too:
Sweetly, sweetly blew the breeze—
On me alone it blew.

Oh! dream of joy! is this indeed   *And the*
The light-house top I see?   *ancient*
Is this the hill? is this the kirk?   *Mariner be-*
Is this mine own countree?   *holdeth his*
                              native country.

We drifted o'er the harbour-bar,
And I with sobs did pray—
O let me be awake, my God!   470
Or let me sleep alway.

The harbour-bay was clear as glass,
So smoothly it was strewn!
And on the bay the moonlight lay,
And the shadow of the Moon.

The rock shone bright, the kirk no less,
That stands above the rock:
The moonlight steeped in silentness
The steady weathercock.

And the bay was white with silent
   light,   480
Till rising from the same,   *The angelic*
Full many shapes, that shadows *spirits leave*
   were,   *the dead*
In crimson colours came.   *bodies,*

A little distance from the prow   *And appear in*
Those crimson shadows were: *their own*
I turned my eyes upon the deck— *forms of light.*
Oh, Christ! what saw I there!

Each corse lay flat, lifeless and flat,
And, by the holy rood![11]
A man all light, a seraph-man,   490
On every corse there stood.

This seraph-band, each waved his hand:
It was a heavenly sight!
They stood as signals to the land,
Each one a lovely light;

This seraph-band, each waved his hand,
No voice did they impart—
No voice; but oh! the silence sank
Like music on my heart.

But soon I heard the dash of oars,   500
I heard the Pilot's cheer;
My head was turned perforce away
And I saw a boat appear.

The Pilot and the Pilot's boy,
I heard them coming fast:
Dear Lord in Heaven! it was a joy
The dead men could not blast.

I saw a third—I heard his voice:
It is the Hermit good!
He singeth loud his godly hymns   510
That he makes in the wood.
He'll shrieve my soul, he'll wash away
The Albatross's blood.

PART VII

This Hermit good lives in that   *The Hermit of*
   wood   *the Wood,*
Which slopes down to the sea.
How loudly his sweet voice he rears!
He loves to talk with marineres
That come from a far countree.

He kneels at morn, and noon, and eve—
He hath a cushion plump: 520
It is the moss that wholly hides
The rotted old oak-stump.

The skiff-boat neared: I heard them talk,
'Why, this is strange, I trow!

11 *cross.*

Where are those lights so many and fair,
That signal made but now?'

'Strange, by my faith!' the Her-   Approacheth
    mit said—   the ship with
'And they answered not our   wonder.
    cheer!
The planks looked warped! and see those
    sails,
How thin they are and sere!   530
I never saw aught like to them,
Unless perchance it were

Brown skeletons of leaves that lag
My forest-brook along;
When the ivy-tod[12] is heavy with snow,
And the owlet whoops to the wolf below,
That eats the she-wolf's young.'

'Dear Lord! it hath a fiendish look—
(The Pilot made reply)
I am a-feared'—'Push on, push on!'   540
Said the Hermit cheerily.

The boat came closer to the ship,
But I nor spake nor stirred;
The boat came close beneath the ship,
And straight a sound was heard.

Under the water it rumbled on,   The ship
Still louder and more dread: suddenly
It reached the ship, it split the   sinketh.
    bay;
The ship went down like lead.

Stunned by that loud and dread-   The ancient
    ful sound,   Mariner is
Which sky and ocean smote,   saved in the 550
Like one that hath been seven   Pilot's boat.
    days drowned
My body lay afloat;
But swift as dreams, myself I found
Within the Pilot's boat.

Upon the whirl, where sank the ship,
The boat spun round and round;
And all was still, save that the hill
Was telling of the sound.

I moved my lips—the Pilot shrieked   560
And fell down in a fit;
The holy Hermit raised his eyes,
And prayed where he did sit.

I took the oars: the Pilot's boy,
Who now doth crazy go,
Laughed loud and long, and all the while
His eyes went to and fro.
'Ha! ha!' quoth he, 'full plain I see,
The Devil knows how to row.'

And now, all in my own countree,   570
I stood on the firm land!
The Hermit stepped forth from the boat,
And scarcely he could stand.

'O shrieve me, shrieve me, holy   The ancient
    man!'   Mariner
The Hermit crossed his brow.[13]   earnestly en-
'Say quick,' quoth he, 'I bid thee   treateth the
    say—   Hermit to
What manner of man art thou?'   shrieve him;
                                     and the
                                     penance of
                                     life falls on
                                     him.

Forthwith this frame of mine
    was wrenched
With a woful agony,
Which forced me to begin my tale;   580
And then it left me free.

Since then, at an uncertain hour,   And ever and
That agony returns: anon through
And till my ghastly tale is told,   out his future
This heart within me burns.   life an agony
                                      constraineth
                                      him to travel
                                      from land to
I pass, like night, from land to   land;
    land;
I have strange power of speech;
That moment that his face I see,
I know the man that must hear me:
To him my tale I teach.   590

What loud uproar bursts from that door!
The wedding-guests are there:
But in the garden-bower the bride
And bride-maids singing are:
And hark the little vesper bell,
Which biddeth me to prayer!

O Wedding-Guest! this soul hath been
Alone on a wide wide sea:
So lonely 'twas, that God himself
Scarce seeméd there to be.   600

O sweeter than the marriage-feast,
'Tis sweeter far to me,
To walk together to the kirk
With a goodly company!—

_____
12 ivy-bush.

_____
13 made the sign of the cross on his brow.

To walk together to the kirk,
And all together pray,
While each to his great Father bends,
Old men, and babes, and loving friends
And youths and maidens gay!

Farewell, farewell! but this I tell
To thee, thou Wedding-Guest!
He prayeth well, who loveth well
Both man and bird and beast.

And to teach, 610
by his own
example, love
and reverence
to all things
that God made
and loveth.

He prayeth best, who loveth best
All things both great and small;
For the dear God who loveth us,
He made and loveth all.

The Mariner, whose eye is bright,
Whose beard with age is hoar,
Is gone: and now the Wedding-Guest 620
Turned from the bridegroom's door.

He went like one that hath been stunned,
And is of sense forlorn:
A sadder and a wiser man,
He rose the morrow morn.

1797–8   1798

CHRISTABEL

PREFACE

The first part of the following poem was written in the year 1797, at Stowey, in the county of Somerset. The second part, after my return from Germany, in the year 1800, at Keswick, Cumberland. It is probable that if the poem had been finished at either of the former periods, or if even the first and second part had been published in the year 1800, the impression of its originality would have been much greater than I dare at present expect. But for this I have only my own indolence to blame. The dates are mentioned for the exclusive purpose of precluding charges of plagiarism or servile imitation from myself. For there is amongst us a set of critics, who seem to hold, that every possible thought and image is traditional; who have no notion that there are such things as fountains in the world, small as well as great; and who would therefore charitably derive every rill they behold flowing, from a perforation made in some other man's tank. I am confident, however, that as far as the present poem is concerned, the celebrated poets[1] whose writings I might be suspected of having imitated, either in particular passages, or in the tone and the spirit of the whole, would be among the first to vindicate me from the charge, and who, on any striking coincidence, would permit me to address them in this doggerel version of two monkish Latin hexameters.

1 Scott and Byron.

'Tis mine and it is likewise yours;
But an if this will not do;
Let it be mine, good friend! for I
Am the poorer of the two.

I have only to add that the metre of Christabel is not, properly speaking, irregular, though it may seem so from its being founded on a new principle: namely, that of counting in each line the accents, not the syllables. Though the latter may vary from seven to twelve, yet in each line the accents will be found to be only four. Nevertheless, this occasional variation in number of syllables is not introduced wantonly, or for the mere ends of convenience, but in correspondence with some transition in the nature of the imagery or passion.—(Coleridge.)

[*Christabel* was originally intended for publication in *Lyrical Ballads,* 1800, but it was never completed. Coleridge had a plan for finishing the poem, but feared he 'could not carry on with equal success the execution of the idea, an extremely subtle and difficult one.' *Christabel* was first published with *Kubla Khan* and *The Pains of Sleep* in 1816.]

PART I

'TIS the middle of night by the castle clock,
And the owls have awakened the crowing cock;
Tu—whit!——Tu—whoo!
And hark, again! the crowing cock,
How drowsily it crew.

Sir Leoline, the Baron rich,
Hath a toothless mastiff bitch;
From her kennel beneath the rock
She maketh answer to the clock,
Four for the quarters, and twelve for the
    hour;   10
Ever and aye, by shine and shower,
Sixteen short howls, not over loud;
Some say, she sees my lady's shroud.

Is the night chilly and dark?
The night is chilly, but not dark.
The thin gray cloud is spread on high,
It covers but not hides the sky.
The moon is behind, and at the full;
And yet she looks both small and dull.
The night is chill, the cloud is gray: 20
'Tis a month before the month of May,
And the Spring comes slowly up this way.

The lovely lady, Christabel,
Whom her father loves so well,
What makes her in the wood so late,
A furlong from the castle gate?
She had dreams all yesternight
Of her own betrothéd knight;
And she in the midnight wood will pray
For the weal of her lover that's far away.   30

She stole along, she nothing spoke,
The sighs she heaved were soft and low,
And naught was green upon the oak
But moss and rarest mistletoe:
She kneels beneath the huge oak tree,
And in silence prayeth she.

The lady sprang up suddenly,
The lovely lady, Christabel!
It moaned as near, as near can be,
But what it is she cannot tell.—   40
On the other side it seems to be,
Of the huge, broad-breasted, old oak tree.

The night is chill; the forest bare;
Is it the wind that moaneth bleak?
There is not wind enough in the air
To move away the ringlet curl
From the lovely lady's cheek—
There is not wind enough to twirl
The one red leaf, the last of its clan,
That dances as often as dance it can,   50
Hanging so light, and hanging so high,
On the topmost twig that looks up at the sky.

Hush, beating heart of Christabel!
Jesu, Maria, shield her well!
She folded her arms beneath her cloak,
And stole to the other side of the oak.
         What sees she there?

There she sees a damsel bright,
Drest in a silken robe of white,
That shadowy in the moonlight shone: 60
The neck that made that white robe wan,
Her stately neck, and arms were bare;
Her blue-veined feet unsandal'd were,
And wildly glittered here and there
The gems entangled in her hair.
I guess, 'twas frightful there to see
A lady so richly clad as she—
Beautiful exceedingly!

Mary mother, save me now!
(Said Christabel,) And who art thou?   70

The lady strange made answer meet,
And her voice was faint and sweet:—
Have pity on my sore distress,
I scarce can speak for weariness:
Stretch forth thy hand, and have no fear!
Said Christabel, How camest thou here?
And the lady, whose voice was faint and sweet,
Did thus pursue her answer meet:—

My sire is of a noble line,
And my name is Geraldine: 80
Five warriors seized me yestermorn,
Me, even me, a maid forlorn:
They choked my cries with force and fright,
And tied me on a palfrey white.
The palfrey was as fleet as wind,
And they rode furiously behind.

They spurred amain, their steeds were white:
And once we crossed the shade of night.
As sure as Heaven shall rescue me,
I have no thought what men they be;   90
Nor do I know how long it is
(For I have lain entranced I wis)
Since one, the tallest of the five,
Took me from the palfrey's back,
A weary woman, scarce alive.
Some muttered words his comrades spoke:
He placed me underneath this oak;
He swore they would return with haste;
Whither they went I cannot tell—
I thought I heard, some minutes past,   100
Sounds as of a castle bell.
Stretch forth thy hand (thus ended she),
And help a wretched maid to flee.

Then Christabel stretched forth her hand,
And comforted fair Geraldine:
O well, bright dame! may you command
The service of Sir Leoline;
And gladly our stout chivalry
Will he send forth and friends withal
To guide and guard you safe and free   110
Home to your noble father's hall.

She rose: and forth with steps they passed
That strove to be, and were not, fast.
Her gracious stars the lady blest,
And thus spake on sweet Christabel:
All our household are at rest,
The hall as silent as the cell;
Sir Leoline is weak in health,
And may not well awakened be,
But we will move as if in stealth,   120
And I beseech your courtesy,
This night, to share your couch with me.

They crossed the moat, and Christabel
Took the key that fitted well;
A little door she opened straight,
All in the middle of the gate;
The gate that was ironed within and without,
Where an army in battle array had marched out.

The lady sank, belike through pain,
And Christabel with might and main   130
Lifted her up, a weary weight,
Over the threshold of the gate:
Then the lady rose again,
And moved, as she were not in pain.[2]

So free from danger, free from fear,
They crossed the court: right glad they were.
And Christabel devoutly cried
To the lady by her side,
Praise we the Virgin all divine
Who hath rescued thee from thy distress!   140
Alas, alas! said Geraldine,
I cannot speak for weariness.
So free from danger, free from fear,
They crossed the court: right glad they were.

Outside her kennel, the mastiff old
Lay fast asleep, in moonshine cold.
The mastiff old did not awake,
Yet she an angry moan did make!
And what can ail the mastiff bitch?
Never till now she uttered yell   150
Beneath the eye of Christabel.
Perhaps it is the owlet's scritch:
For what can ail the mastiff bitch?[3]

They passed the hall, that echoes still,
Pass as lightly as you will!
The brands were flat, the brands were dying,
Amid their own white ashes lying;
But when the lady passed, there came
A tongue of light, a fit of flame;
And Christabel saw the lady's eye,   160
And nothing else saw she thereby,
Save the boss of the shield of Sir Leoline tall,
Which hung in a murky old niche in the wall.
O softly tread, said Christabel,
My father seldom sleepeth well.

Sweet Christabel her feet doth bare,
And jealous of the listening air
They steal their way from stair to stair,
Now in glimmer, and now in gloom,
And now they pass the Baron's room,   170
As still as death, with stifled breath!
And now have reached her chamber door;
And now doth Geraldine press down
The rushes of the chamber floor.

2 Geraldine pretended helplessness because, being an evil spirit, she could not cross a threshold that had been blessed except by being carried over.
3 Animals were believed to have a keen sense of the presence of supernatural beings.

The moon shines dim in the open air,
And not a moonbeam enters here.
But they without its light can see
The chamber carved so curiously,
Carved with figures strange and sweet,
All made out of the carver's brain,   180
For a lady's chamber meet:
The lamp with twofold silver chain
Is fastened to an angel's feet.

The silver lamp burns dead and dim;
But Christabel the lamp will trim.
She trimmed the lamp, and made it bright,
And left it swinging to and fro,
While Geraldine, in wretched plight,
Sank down upon the floor below.

O weary lady, Geraldine,   190
I pray you, drink this cordial wine!
It is a wine of virtuous powers;
My mother made it of wild flowers.

And will your mother pity me,
Who am a maiden most forlorn?
Christabel answered—Woe is me!
She died the hour that I was born.
I have heard the grey-haired friar tell
How on her death-bed she did say,
That she should hear the castle-bell   200
Strike twelve upon my wedding-day.
O mother dear! that thou wert here!
I would, said Geraldine, she were!

But soon with altered voice, said she—
'Off, wandering mother! Peak and pine!
I have power to bid thee flee.'
Alas! what ails poor Geraldine?
Why stares she with unsettled eye?
Can she the bodiless dead espy?
And why with hollow voice cries she,   210
'Off, woman, off! this hour is mine—
Though thou her guardian spirit be,
Off, woman, off! 'tis given to me.'

Then Christabel knelt by the lady's side,
And raised to heaven her eyes so blue—
Alas! said she, this ghastly ride—
Dear lady! it hath wildered you!
The lady wiped her moist cold brow,
And faintly said, ''tis over now!'

Again the wild-flower wine she drank: 220
Her fair large eyes 'gan glitter bright,
And from the floor whereon she sank,

The lofty lady stood upright:
She was most beautiful to see,
Like a lady of a far countrée.

And thus the lofty lady spake—
'All they who live in the upper sky,
Do love you, holy Christabel!
And you love them, and for their sake
And for the good which me befel,   230
Even I in my degree will try,
Fair maiden, to requite you well.
But now unrobe yourself; for I
Must pray, ere yet in bed I lie.'

Quoth Christabel, So let it be!
And as the lady bade, did she.
Her gentle limbs did she undress,
And lay down in her loveliness.

But through her brain of weal and woe
So many thoughts moved to and fro,   240
That vain it were her lids to close;
So half-way from the bed she rose,
And on her elbow did recline
To look at the lady Geraldine.

Beneath the lamp the lady bowed,
And slowly rolled her eyes around;
Then drawing in her breath aloud,
Like one that shuddered, she unbound
The cincture from beneath her breast:
Her silken robe, and inner vest,   250
Dropt to her feet, and full in view,
Behold! her bosom and half her side——
A sight to dream of, not to tell!
O shield her! shield sweet Christabel!

Yet Geraldine nor speaks nor stirs;
Ah! what a stricken look was hers!
Deep from within she seems half-way
To lift some weight with sick assay,
And eyes the maid and seeks delay;
Then suddenly, as one defied,   260
Collects herself in scorn and pride,
And lay down by the Maiden's side!—
And in her arms the maid she took,
                    Ah wel-a-day!
And with low voice and doleful look
These words did say:
'In the touch of this bosom there worketh a
    spell,
Which is lord of thy utterance, Christabel!
Thou knowest to-night, and wilt know to-mor-
    row,

This mark of my shame, this seal of my
    sorrow;   270
        But vainly thou warrest,
        For this is alone in
        Thy power to declare,
        That in the dim forest
        Thou heard'st a low moaning,
And found'st a bright lady, surpassingly fair;
And didst bring her home with thee in love and
    in charity,
To shield her and shelter her from the damp air.'

THE CONCLUSION TO PART I

It was a lovely sight to see
The lady Christabel, when she   280
Was praying at the old oak tree.
        Amid the jaggéd shadows
        Of mossy leafless boughs,
        Kneeling in the moonlight,
        To make her gentle vows;
Her slender palms together prest,
Heaving sometimes on her breast;
Her face resigned to bliss or bale—
Her face, oh call it fair not pale,
And both blue eyes more bright than
    clear,   290
Each about to have a tear.

With open eyes (ah woe is me!)
Asleep, and dreaming fearfully,
Fearfully dreaming, yet, I wis,
Dreaming that alone, which is—
O sorrow and shame! Can this be she,
The lady, who knelt at the old oak tree?
And lo! the worker of these harms,
That holds the maiden in her arms,
Seems to slumber still and mild,   300
As a mother with her child.

A star hath set, a star hath risen,
O Geraldine! since arms of thine
Have been the lovely lady's prison.
O Geraldine! one hour was thine—
Thou'st had thy will! By tairn and rill,
The night-birds all that hour were still.
But now they are jubilant anew,
From cliff and tower, tu—whoo! tu—
    whoo!
Tu—whoo! tu—whoo! from wood and
    fell!   310

And see! the lady Christabel
Gathers herself from out her trance;

Her limbs relax, her countenance
Grows sad and soft; the smooth thin lids
Close o'er her eyes; and tears she sheds—
Large tears that leave the lashes bright!
And oft the while she seems to smile
As infants at a sudden light!

Yea, she doth smile, and she doth weep,
Like a youthful hermitess,   320
Beauteous in a wilderness,
Who, praying always, prays in sleep.
And, if she move unquietly,
Perchance, 'tis but the blood so free
Comes back and tingles in her feet.
No doubt, she hath a vision sweet.
What if her guardian spirit 'twere,
What if she knew her mother near?
But this she knows, in joys and woes,
That saints will aid if men will call: 330
For the blue sky bends over all!

PART II

Each matin bell, the Baron saith,
Knells us back to a world of death.
These words Sir Leoline first said,
When he rose and found his lady dead:
These words Sir Leoline will say
Many a morn to his dying day!

And hence the custom and law began
That still at dawn the sacristan,
Who duly pulls the heavy bell,   340
Five and forty beads must tell
Between each stroke—a warning knell,
Which not a soul can choose but hear
From Bratha Head to Wyndermere.

Saith Bracy the bard, So let it knell!
And let the drowsy sacristan
Still count as slowly as he can!
There is no lack of such, I ween,
As well fill up the space between.
In Langdale Pike and Witch's Lair,[4]   350

And Dungeon-ghyll so foully rent,
With ropes of rock and bells of air
Three sinful sextons' ghosts are pent,
Who all give back, one after t'other,
The death-note to their living brother;

And oft too, by the knell offended,
Just as their one! two! three! is ended,
The devil mocks the doleful tale
With a merry peal from Borodale.

The air is still! through mist and cloud   360
That merry peal comes ringing loud;
And Geraldine shakes off her dread,
And rises lightly from the bed;
Puts on her silken vestments white,
And tricks her hair in lovely plight,[5]
And nothing doubting of her spell
Awakens the lady Christabel.
'Sleep you, sweet lady Christabel?
I trust that you have rested well.'

And Christabel awoke and spied   370
The same who lay down by her side—
O rather say, the same whom she
Raised up beneath the old oak tree!
Nay, fairer yet! and yet more fair!
For she belike hath drunken deep
Of all the blessedness of sleep!
And while she spake, her looks, her air
Such gentle thankfulness declare,
That (so it seemed) her girded vests
Grew tight beneath her heaving breasts.   380
'Sure I have sinn'd!' said Christabel,
'Now heaven be praised if all be well!'
And in low faltering tones, yet sweet,
Did she the lofty lady greet
With such perplexity of mind
As dreams too lively leave behind.

So quickly she rose, and quickly arrayed
Her maiden limbs, and having prayed
That He, who on the cross did groan,
Might wash away her sins unknown,   390
She forthwith led fair Geraldine
To meet her sire, Sir Leoline.

The lovely maid and the lady tall
Are pacing both into the hall,
And pacing on through page and groom,
Enter the Baron's presence-room.

The Baron rose, and while he prest
His gentle daughter to his breast,
With cheerful wonder in his eyes
The lady Geraldine espies,   400
And gave such welcome to the same,
As might beseem so bright a dame!

---

4 The places referred to in this and the following lines of the
poem are located in the Lake country, though of course the true
setting of *Christabel* is in the world of enchantment.

5 archaic for *plait*.

But when he heard the lady's tale,
And when she told her father's name,
Why waxed Sir Leoline so pale,
Murmuring o'er the name again,
Lord Roland de Vaux of Tryermaine?

Alas! they had been friends in youth;[6]
But whispering tongues can poison truth;
And constancy lives in realms above;   410
And life is thorny; and youth is vain;
And to be wroth with one we love
Doth work like madness in the brain.
And thus it chanced, as I divine,
With Roland and Sir Leoline.
Each spake words of high disdain
And insult to his heart's best brother:
They parted—ne'er to meet again!
But never either found another
To free the hollow heart from paining—   420
They stood aloof, the scars remaining,
Like cliffs which had been rent asunder;
A dreary sea now flows between;—
But neither heat, nor frost, nor thunder,
Shall wholly do away, I ween,
The marks of that which once hath been.

Sir Leoline, a moment's space,
Stood gazing on the damsel's face:
And the youthful Lord of Tryermaine
Came back upon his heart again.   430

O then the Baron forgot his age,
His noble heart swelled high with rage;
He swore by the wounds in Jesu's side
He would proclaim it far and wide,
With trump and solemn heraldry,
That they, who thus had wronged the dame,
Were base as spotted infamy!
'And if they dare deny the same,
My herald shall appoint a week,
And let the recreant traitors seek   440
My tourney court—that there and then
I may dislodge their reptile souls
From the bodies and forms of men!'
He spake: his eye in lightning rolls!
For the lady was ruthlessly seized; and he
    kenned
In the beautiful lady the child of his friend!

And now the tears were on his face,
And fondly in his arms he took

---

6 Coleridge called lines 408–26 'the best and sweetest' he had ever written. They may have been given added poignancy by his estrangement from Southey or, possibly, from a temporary alienation from Charles Lamb.

Fair Geraldine, who met the embrace,
Prolonging it with joyous look.   450
Which when she viewed, a vision fell
Upon the soul of Christabel,
The vision of fear, the touch and pain!
She shrunk and shuddered, and saw again—
(Ah, woe is me! Was it for thee,
Thou gentle maid! such sights to see?)

Again she saw that bosom old,
Again she felt that bosom cold,
And drew in her breath with a hissing
    sound:
Whereat the Knight turned wildly round,   460
And nothing saw, but his own sweet maid
With eyes upraised, as one that prayed.

The touch, the sight, had passed away,
And in its stead that vision blest,
Which comforted her after-rest
While in the lady's arms she lay,
Had put a rapture in her breast,
And on her lips and o'er her eyes
Spread smiles like light!
                   With new surprise,
'What ails then my belovéd child?'   470
The Baron said—His daughter mild
Made answer, 'All will yet be well!'
I ween, she had no power to tell
Aught else: so mighty was the spell.

Yet he, who saw this Geraldine,
Had deemed her sure a thing divine:
Such sorrow with such grace she blended,
As if she feared she had offended
Sweet Christabel, that gentle maid!
And with such lowly tones she prayed   480
She might be sent without delay
Home to her father's mansion.
                      'Nay!
Nay, by my soul!' said Leoline.
'Ho! Bracy the bard, the charge be thine!
Go thou, with music sweet and loud,
And take two steeds with trappings proud,
And take the youth whom thou lov'st best
To bear thy harp, and learn thy song,
And clothe you both in solemn vest,
And over the mountains haste along,   490
Lest wandering folk, that are abroad,
Detain you on the valley road.

'And when he has crossed the Irthing flood,
My merry bard! he hastes, he hastes
Up Knorren Moor, through Halegarth Wood,

And reaches soon that castle good
Which stands and threatens Scotland's wastes.

'Bard Bracy! bard Bracy! your horses are fleet,
Ye must ride up the hall, your music so sweet,
More loud than your horses' echoing feet!   500
And loud and loud to Lord Roland call,
Thy daughter is safe in Langdale hall!
Thy beautiful daughter is safe and free—
Sir Leoline greets thee thus through me!
He bids thee come without delay
With all thy numerous array
And take thy lovely daughter home:
And he will meet thee on the way
With all his numerous array
White with their panting palfreys' foam: 510
And, by mine honour! I will say,
That I repent me of the day
When I spake words of fierce disdain
To Roland de Vaux of Tryermaine!—
—For since that evil hour hath flown,
Many a summer's sun hath shone;
Yet ne'er found I a friend again
Like Roland de Vaux of Tryermaine.'

The lady fell, and clasped his knees,
Her face upraised, her eyes o'erflowing;   520
And Bracy replied, with faltering voice,
His gracious Hail on all bestowing!—
'Thy words, thou sire of Christabel,
Are sweeter than my harp can tell;
Yet might I gain a boon of thee,
This day my journey should not be,
So strange a dream hath come to me,
That I had vowed with music loud
To clear yon wood from thing unblest,
Warned by a vision in my rest!   530
For in my sleep I saw that dove,
That gentle bird, whom thou dost love,
And call'st by thy own daughter's name—
Sir Leoline! I saw the same
Fluttering, and uttering fearful moan,
Among the green herbs in the forest alone.
Which when I saw and when I heard,
I wonder'd what might ail the bird;
For nothing near it could I see,
Save the grass and green herbs underneath the
    old tree.   540

'And in my dream methought I went
To search out what might there be found;
And what the sweet bird's trouble meant,
That thus lay fluttering on the ground.
I went and peered, and could descry

No cause for her distressful cry;
But yet for her dear lady's sake
I stooped, methought, the dove to take,
When lo! I saw a bright green snake
Coiled around its wings and neck.   550
Green as the herbs on which it couched,
Close by the dove's its head it crouched;
And with the dove it heaves and stirs,
Swelling its neck as she swelled hers!
I woke; it was the midnight hour,
The clock was echoing in the tower;
But though my slumber was gone by,
This dream it would not pass away—
It seems to live upon my eye!
And thence I vowed this self-same day   560
With music strong and saintly song
To wander through the forest bare,
Lest aught unholy loiter there.'

Thus Bracy said: the Baron, the while,
Half-listening heard him with a smile;
Then turned to Lady Geraldine,
His eyes made up of wonder and love;
And said in courtly accents fine,
'Sweet maid, Lord Roland's beauteous dove,
With arms more strong than harp or song,   570
Thy sire and I will crush the snake!'
He kissed her forehead as he spake,
And Geraldine in maiden wise
Casting down her large bright eyes,
With blushing cheek and courtesy fine
She turned her from Sir Leoline;
Softly gathering up her train,
That o'er her right arm fell again;
And folded her arms across her chest,
And couched her head upon her breast,   580
And looked askance at Christabel——
Jesu, Maria, shield her well!

A snake's small eye blinks dull and shy;
And the lady's eyes they shrunk in her head,
Each shrunk up to a serpent's eye,
And with somewhat of malice, and more of
    dread,
At Christabel she looked askance!—
One moment—and the sight was fled!
But Christabel in dizzy trance
Stumbling on the unsteady ground   590
Shuddered aloud, with a hissing sound;
And Geraldine again turned round,
And like a thing, that sought relief,
Full of wonder and full of grief,
She rolled her large bright eyes divine
Wildly on Sir Leoline.

The maid, alas! her thoughts are gone,
She nothing sees—no sight but one!
The maid, devoid of guile and sin,
I know not how, in fearful wise,   600
So deeply had she drunken in
That look, those shrunken serpent eyes,
That all her features were resigned
To this sole image in her mind:
And passively did imitate
That look of dull and treacherous hate!
And thus she stood, in dizzy trance,
Still picturing that look askance
With forced unconscious sympathy
Full before her father's view——   610
As far as such a look could be
In eyes so innocent and blue!

And when the trance was o'er, the maid
Paused awhile, and inly prayed:
Then falling at the Baron's feet,
'By my mother's soul do I entreat
That thou this woman send away!'
She said: and more she could not say:
For what she knew she could not tell,
O'er-mastered by the mighty spell.   620

Why is thy cheek so wan and wild,
Sir Leoline? Thy only child
Lies at thy feet, thy joy, thy pride,
So fair, so innocent, so mild;
The same, for whom thy lady died!
O by the pangs of her dear mother
Think thou no evil of thy child!
For her, and thee, and for no other,
She prayed the moment ere she died:
Prayed that the babe for whom she died,   630
Might prove her dear lord's joy and pride!
   That prayer her deadly pangs beguiled,
      Sir Leoline!
   And wouldst thou wrong thy only child,
      Her child and thine?

Within the Baron's heart and brain
If thoughts, like these, had any share,
They only swelled his rage and pain,
And did but work confusion there.
His heart was cleft with pain and rage,   640
His cheeks they quivered, his eyes were wild,
Dishonoured thus in his old age;
Dishonoured by his only child,
And all his hospitality
To the wronged daughter of his friend
By more than woman's jealousy
Brought thus to a disgraceful end—

He rolled his eye with stern regard
Upon the gentle minstrel bard,
And said in tones abrupt, austere—   650
'Why, Bracy! dost thou loiter here?
I bade thee hence!' The bard obeyed;
And turning from his own sweet maid,
The agéd knight, Sir Leoline,
Led forth the lady Geraldine!

THE CONCLUSION TO PART II[7]

A little child, a limber elf,
Singing, dancing to itself,
A fairy thing with red round cheeks,
That always finds, and never seeks,
Makes such a vision to the sight   660
As fills a father's eyes with light;
And pleasures flow in so thick and fast
Upon his heart, that he at last
Must needs express his love's excess
With words of unmeant bitterness.
Perhaps 'tis pretty to force together
Thoughts so all unlike each other;
To mutter and mock a broken charm,
To dally with wrong that does no harm.
Perhaps 'tis tender too and pretty   670
At each wild word to feel within
A sweet recoil of love and pity.
And what, if in a world of sin
(O sorrow and shame should this be true!)
Such giddiness of heart and brain
Comes seldom save from rage and pain,
So talks as it's most used to do.

1797–1800   1816

FROST AT MIDNIGHT

THE Frost performs its secret ministry,
Unhelped by any wind. The owlet's cry
Came loud—and hark, again! loud as before.
The inmates of my cottage, all at rest,
Have left me to that solitude, which suits
Abstruser musings: save that at my side
My cradled infant[1] slumbers peacefully.
'Tis calm indeed! so calm, that it disturbs
And vexes meditation with its strange
And extreme silentness. Sea, hill, and wood,   10
This populous village! Sea, and hill, and wood,

---

7 The lines of the Conclusion to Part II have no apparent relation
to the poem. They were originally enclosed in a letter to Southey
expressing anxiety over the state of young Hartley Coleridge's
health.

1 his son Hartley.

With all the numberless goings-on of life,
Inaudible as dreams! the thin blue flame
Lies on my low-burnt fire, and quivers not;
Only that film, which fluttered on the grate,[2]
Still flutters there, the sole unquiet thing.
Methinks, its motion in this hush of nature
Gives it dim sympathies with me who live,
Making it a companionable form,
Whose puny flaps and freaks the idling Spirit 20
By its own moods interprets, every where
Echo or mirror seeking of itself,
And makes a toy of Thought.

                    But O! how oft,
How oft, at school, with most believing mind,
Presageful have I gazed upon the bars,
To watch that fluttering *stranger!* and as oft
With unclosed lids, already had I dreamt
Of my sweet birth-place, and the old church-
    tower,
Whose bells, the poor man's only music, rang
From morn to evening, all the hot Fair-day, 30
So sweetly, that they stirred and haunted me
With a wild pleasure, falling on mine ear
Most like articulate sounds of things to come!
So gazed I, till the soothing things, I dreamt,
Lulled me to sleep, and sleep prolonged my
    dreams!
And so I brooded all the following morn,
Awed by the stern preceptor's face, mine eye
Fixed with mock study on my swimming book;
Save if the door half opened, and I snatched
A hasty glance, and still my heart leaped up, 40
For still I hoped to see the *stranger's* face,
Townsman, or aunt, or sister more beloved,
My play-mate when we both were clothed alike!

    Dear Babe, that sleepest cradled by my side,
Whose gentle breathings, heard in this deep
    calm,
Fill up the interspersèd vacancies
And momentary pauses of the thought!
My babe so beautiful! it thrills my heart
With tender gladness, thus to look at thee,
And think that thou shalt learn far other lore, 50
And in far other scenes! For I was reared
In the great city, pent 'mid cloisters dim,
And saw nought lovely but the sky and stars.
But *thou,* my babe! shalt wander like a breeze
By lakes and sandy shores, beneath the crags
Of ancient mountain, and beneath the clouds,

2 In all parts of the kingdom these films are called *strangers* and
supposed to portend the arrival of some absent friend.—(Coleridge.)

Which image in their bulk both lakes and shores
And mountain crags: so shalt thou see and hear
The lovely shapes and sounds intelligible
Of that eternal language, which thy God 60
Utters, who from eternity doth teach
Himself in all, and all things in himself,
Great universal Teacher! he shall mould
Thy spirit, and by giving make it ask.

    Therefore all seasons shall be sweet to thee,
Whether the summer clothe the general earth
With greenness, or the redbreast sit and sing
Betwixt the tufts of snow on the bare branch
Of mossy apple-tree, while the nigh thatch
Smokes in the sun-thaw; whether the eave-drops
    fall 70
Heard only in the trances of the blast,
Or if the secret ministry of frost
Shall hang them up in silent icicles,
Quietly shining to the quiet Moon.

1798   1798

FRANCE: AN ODE

ARGUMENT

First Stanza. An invocation to those objects in Nature
the contemplation of which had inspired the Poet with a
devotional love of Liberty. *Second Stanza.* The exultation of the Poet at the commencement of the French
Revolution, and his unqualified abhorrence of the Alliance against the Republic. *Third Stanza.* The blasphemies
and horrors during the domination of the Terrorists regarded by the Poet as a transient storm. . . . *Fourth
Stanza.* Switzerland, and the Poet's recantation. *Fifth
Stanza.* An address to Liberty, in which the Poet expresses his conviction that those feelings and that grand
ideal of Freedom . . . belong to the individual man, so
far as he is pure, and inflamed with the love and adoration of God in Nature.—(Coleridge.)

I

YE Clouds! that far above me float and pause,
    Whose pathless march no mortal may con-
      troul!
Ye Ocean-Waves! that, whereso'er ye roll,
Yield homage only to eternal laws!
Ye Woods! that listen to the night-birds sing-
    ing,
    Midway the smooth and perilous slope re-
      clined,
Save when your own imperious branches
    swinging,
    Have made a solemn music of the wind!
Where, like a man beloved of God,
Through glooms, which never woodman
    trod, 10
    How oft, pursuing fancies holy,

My moonlight way o'er flowering weeds I
    wound,
    Inspired, beyond the guess of folly,
By each rude shape and wild unconquerable
    sound!
O ye loud Waves! and O ye Forest high!
    And O ye Clouds that far above me soared!
Thou rising Sun! thou blue rejoicing Sky!
    Yea, every thing that is and will be free!
    Bear witness for me, wheresoe'er ye be,
    With what deep worship I have still
        adored   20
        The spirit of divinest Liberty.

Byron wrote English Bards.

When France in wrath her giant-limbs upreared,
    And with that oath, which smote air, earth,
        and sea,
    Stamped her strong foot and said she would be
        free,
Bear witness for me, how I hoped and feared!
With what a joy my lofty gratulation
    Unawed I sang, amid a slavish band:
And when to whelm the disenchanted nation,
    Like fiends embattled by a wizard's wand,
    The Monarchs¹ marched in evil day,   30
    And Britain joined the dire array;
    Though dear her shores and circling ocean,
Though many friendships, many youthful loves
    Had swoln the patriot emotion
And flung a magic light o'er all her hills and
    groves;
Yet still my voice, unaltered, sang defeat
    To all that braved the tyrant-quelling lance,
And shame too long delayed and vain retreat!
For ne'er, O Liberty! with partial aim
I dimmed thy light or damped thy holy flame; 40
    But blessed the paeans of delivered France,
And hung my head and wept at Britain's name.

III

'And what,' I said, 'though Blasphemy's loud
    scream
    With that sweet music of deliverance strove!
    Though all the fierce and drunken passions
        wove
A dance more wild than e'er was maniac's dream!
    Ye storms, that round the dawning East assem-
        bled,
The Sun was rising, though ye hid his light!'
    And when, to soothe my soul, that hoped and
        trembled,

¹ Of Austria and Prussia against whom France declared war in
1792. England joined the alliance against France in 1793.

The dissonance ceased, and all seemed calm and
    bright;   50
    When France her front deep-scarr'd and gory
    Concealed with clustering wreaths of glory;
        When, insupportably advancing,
    Her arm made mockery of the warrior's ramp;
        While timid looks of fury glancing.
    Domestic treason, crushed beneath her fatal
        stamp,
Writhed like a wounded dragon in his gore;
    Then I reproached my fears that would not
        flee;
'And soon,' I said, 'shall Wisdom teach her lore
In the low huts of them that toil and groan!   60
And, conquering by her happiness alone,
    Shall France compel the nations to be free,
Till Love and Joy look round, and call the Earth
    their own.'

IV

Forgive me, Freedom! O forgive those dreams!
    I hear thy voice, I hear thy loud lament.
    From bleak Helvetia's icy caverns sent—
I hear thy groans upon her blood-stained streams!
    Heroes, that for your peaceful country per-
        ished,
    And ye that, fleeing, spot your mountain-snows
        With bleeding wounds; forgive me, that I cher-
            ished   70
One thought that ever blessed your cruel foes!
    To scatter rage, and traitorous guilt,
    Where Peace her jealous home had built;
        A patriot-race to disinherit
Of all that made their stormy wilds so dear;
        And with inexpiable spirit
To taint the bloodless freedom of the moun-
    taineer—
O France, that mockest Heaven, adulterous,
    blind,
    And patriot only in pernicious toils!
Are these thy boasts, Champion of human
    kind?   80
    To mix with Kings in the low lust of sway,
Yell in the hunt, and share the murderous prey;
To insult the shrine of Liberty with spoils
    From freemen torn; to tempt and to betray?

V

    The Sensual and the Dark rebel in vain,
    Slaves by their own compulsion! In mad game
    They burst their manacles and wear the name
        Of Freedom, graven on a heavier chain!
    O Liberty! with profitless endeavour
Have I pursued thee, many a weary hour;   90
    But thou nor swell'st the victor's strain, nor ever

Didst breathe thy soul in forms of human power.
  Alike from all, howe'er they praise thee,
  (Nor prayer, nor boastful name delays thee)
    Alike from Priestcraft's harpy minions,
  And factious Blasphemy's obscener slaves,
    Thou speedest on thy subtle pinions,
The guide of homeless winds, and playmate of
    the waves!
And there I felt thee!—on that sea-cliff's verge,
  Whose pines, scarce travelled by the breeze
    above,   100
Had made one murmur with the distant surge!
Yes, while I stood and gazed, my temples bare,
And shot my being through earth, sea, and air,
  Possessing all things with intensest love,
  O Liberty! my spirit felt thee there.

1798   *1798*

LEWTI

OR THE CIRCASSIAN[1] LOVE-CHANT

AT midnight by the stream I roved,
To forget the form I loved.
Image of Lewti! from my mind
Depart; for Lewti is not kind.
The Moon was high, the moonlight gleam
  And the shadow of a star
Heaved upon Tamaha's stream;
  But the rock shone brighter far,
The rock half sheltered from my view
By pendent boughs of tressy yew.—   10
So shines my Lewti's forehead fair,
Gleaming through her sable hair.
Image of Lewti! from my mind
Depart; for Lewti is not kind.

I saw a cloud of palest hue,
  Onward to the moon it passed;
Still brighter and more bright it grew,
With floating colours not a few,
  Till it reached the moon at last:
Then the cloud was wholly bright,   20
With a rich and amber light!
And so with many a hope I seek,
  And with such joy I find my Lewti;
And even so my pale wan cheek
  Drinks in as deep a flush of beauty!
Nay, treacherous image! leave my mind,
If Lewti never will be kind.

The little cloud—it floats away,
  Away it goes; away so soon!
Alas! it has no power to stay: 30

Its hues are dim, its hues are grey—
  Away it passes from the moon!
How mournfully it seems to fly,
  Ever fading more and more,
To joyless regions of the sky—
  And now 'tis whiter than before!
As white as my poor cheek will be,
  When, Lewti! on my couch I lie,
A dying man for love of thee.
Nay, treacherous image! leave my mind—   40
And yet, thou didst not look unkind.

I saw a vapour in the sky,
  Thin, and white, and very high;
I ne'er beheld so thin a cloud:
  Perhaps the breezes that can fly
  Now below and now above,
Have snatched aloft the lawny shroud
  Of Lady fair—that died for love.
For maids, as well as youths, have perished
From fruitless love too fondly cherished.   50
Nay, treacherous image! leave my mind—
For Lewti never will be kind.

Hush! my heedless feet from under
  Slip the crumbling banks for ever:
Like echoes to a distant thunder,
  They plunge into the gentle river.
The river-swans have heard my tread,
And startle from their reedy bed.
O beauteous birds! methinks ye measure
  Your movements to some heavenly tune!   60
O beauteous birds! 'tis such a pleasure
  To see you move beneath the moon,
I would it were your true delight
To sleep by day and wake all night.

I know the place where Lewti lies,
When silent night has closed her eyes:
  It is a breezy jasmine-bower,
The nightingale sings o'er her head:
  Voice of the Night! had I the power
That leafy labyrinth to thread,   70
And creep, like thee, with soundless tread,
I then might view her bosom white
Heaving lovely to my sight,
As these two swans together heave
On the gently-swelling wave.

Oh! that she saw me in a dream,
  And dreamt that I had died for care;
All pale and wasted I would seem,
  Yet fair withal, as spirits are!
I'd die indeed, if I might see

---

1 Circassia was the name formerly given to a region northwest of
the Caucasus Mountains, and now part of Russia.

Her bosom heave, and heave for me!
Soothe, gentle image! soothe my mind!
To-morrow Lewti may be kind.

1798   1798

FEARS IN SOLITUDE

WRITTEN IN APRIL 1798, DURING THE ALARM OF
AN INVASION[1]

A GREEN and silent spot, amid the hills,
A small and silent dell! O'er stiller place
No singing sky-lark ever poised himself.
The hills are heathy, save that swelling slope,
Which hath a gay and gorgeous covering on,
All golden with the never-bloomless furze,
Which now blooms most profusely: but the dell,
Bathed by the mist, is fresh and delicate
As vernal corn-field, or the unripe flax,
When, through its half-transparent stalks, at
      eve,   10
The level sunshine glimmers with green light.
Oh! 'tis a quiet spirit-healing nook!
Which all, methinks, would love; but chiefly he,
The humble man, who, in his youthful years,
Knew just so much of folly, as had made
His early manhood more securely wise!
Here he might lie on fern or withered heath,
While from the singing lark (that sings unseen
The minstrelsy that solitude loves best),
And from the sun, and from the breezy air,   20
Sweet influences trembled o'er his frame;
And he, with many feelings, many thoughts,
Made up a meditative joy, and found
Religious meanings in the forms of Nature!
And so, his senses gradually wrapt
In a half sleep, he dreams of better worlds,
And dreaming hears thee still, O singing lark,
That singest like an angel in the clouds!

   My God! it is a melancholy thing
For such a man, who would full fain preserve 30
His soul in calmness, yet perforce must feel
For all his human brethren—O my God!
It weighs upon the heart, that he must think
What uproar and what strife may now be stirring
This way or that way o'er these silent hills—
Invasion, and the thunder and the shout,
And all the crash of onset; fear and rage,
And undetermined conflict—even now,
Even now, perchance, and in his native isle:

Carnage and groans beneath this blessed sun! 40
We have offended, Oh! my countrymen!
We have offended very grievously,
And been most tyrannous. From east to west
A groan of accusation pierces Heaven!
The wretched plead against us; multitudes
Countless and vehement, the sons of God,
Our brethren! Like a cloud that travels on,
Steamed up from Cairo's swamps of pestilence,
Even so, my countrymen! have we gone forth
And borne to distant tribes slavery and
      pangs,   50
And, deadlier far, our vices, whose deep taint
With slow perdition murders the whole man,
His body and his soul! Meanwhile, at home,
All individual dignity and power
Engulfed in Courts, Committees, Institutions,
Associations and Societies,
A vain, speech-mouthing, speech-reporting
      Guild,
One Benefit-Club for mutual flattery,
We have drunk up, demure as at a grace,
Pollutions from the brimming cup of wealth; 60
Contemptuous of all honourable rule,
Yet bartering freedom and the poor man's life
For gold, as at a market! The sweet words
Of Christian promise, words that even yet
Might stem destruction, were they wisely
      preached,
Are muttered o'er by men, whose tones proclaim
How flat and wearisome they feel their trade:
Rank scoffers some, but most too indolent
To deem them falsehoods or to know their truth.
Oh! blasphemous! the Book of Life is made 70
A superstitious instrument, on which
We gabble o'er the oaths we mean to break,
For all must swear—all and in every place,
College and wharf, council and justice-court;
All, all must swear, the briber and the bribed,
Merchant and lawyer, senator and priest,
The rich, the poor, the old man and the young;
All, all make up one scheme of perjury,
That faith doth reel; the very name of God
Sounds like a juggler's charm; and, bold with
      joy,   80
Forth from his dark and lonely hiding-place,
(Portentous sight!) the owlet Atheism,
Sailing on obscene wings athwart the noon,
Drops his blue-fringéd lids, and holds them close,
And hooting at the glorious sun in Heaven,
Cries out, 'Where is it?'

                           Thankless too for peace,
(Peace long preserved by fleets and perilous seas)

---

1 There were rumors of a projected invasion of England in 1798,
which may or may not have been spread by the French to divert
attention from Napoleon's attack on Egypt.

Secure from actual warfare, we have loved
To swell the war-whoop, passionate for war!
Alas! for ages ignorant of all 90
Its ghastlier workings, (famine or blue plague,
Battle, or siege, or flight through wintry snows,)
We, this whole people, have been clamorous
For war and bloodshed; animating sports,
The which we pay for as a thing to talk of,
Spectators and not combatants! No guess
Anticipative of a wrong unfelt,
No speculation on contingency,
However dim and vague, too vague and dim
To yield a justifying cause; and forth, 100
(Stuffed out with big preamble, holy names,
And adjurations of the God in Heaven,)
We send our mandates for the certain death
Of thousands and ten thousands! Boys and girls,
And women, that would groan to see a child
Pull off an insect's leg, all read of war,
The best amusement for our morning meal!
The poor wretch, who has learnt his only prayers
From curses, who knows scarcely words enough
To ask a blessing from his Heavenly Father, 110
Becomes a fluent phraseman, absolute
And technical in victories and defeats,
And all our dainty terms for fratricide;
Terms which we trundle smoothly o'er our
  tongues
Like mere abstractions, empty sounds to which
We join no feeling and attach no form!
As if the soldier died without a wound;
As if the fibres of this godlike frame
Were gored without a pang; as if the wretch,
Who fell in battle, doing bloody deeds, 120
Passed off to Heaven, translated and not killed;
As though he had no wife to pine for him,
No God to judge him! Therefore, evil days
Are coming on us, O my countrymen!
And what if all-avenging Providence,
Strong and retributive, should make us know
The meaning of our words, force us to feel
The desolation and the agony
Of our fierce doings?

                    Spare us yet awhile,
Father and God! O! spare us yet awhile! 130
Oh! let not English women drag their flight
Fainting beneath the burthen of their babes,
Of the sweet infants, that but yesterday
Laughed at the breast! Sons, brothers, husbands,
  all
Who ever gazed with fondness on the forms
Which grew up with you round the same fire-side,
And all who ever heard the sabbath-bells

Without the infidel's scorn, make yourselves
  pure!
Stand forth! be men! repel an impious foe,
Impious and false, a light yet cruel race, 140
Who laugh away all virtue, mingling mirth
With deeds of murder; and still promising
Freedom, themselves too sensual to be free,
Poison life's amities, and cheat the heart
Of faith and quiet hope, and all that soothes,
And all that lifts the spirit! Stand we forth;
Render them back upon the insulted ocean,
And let them toss as idly on its waves
As the vile sea-weed, which some mountain-blast
Swept from our shores! And oh! may we
  return 150
Not with a drunken triumph, but with fear,
Repenting of the wrongs with which we stung
So fierce a foe to frenzy!

                    I have told,
O Britons! O my brethren! I have told
Most bitter truth, but without bitterness.
Nor deem my zeal or factious or mistimed;
For never can true courage dwell with them,
Who, playing tricks with conscience, dare not
  look
At their own vices. We have been too long
Dupes of a deep delusion! Some, belike, 160
Groaning with restless enmity, expect
All change from change of constituted power;
As if a Government had been a robe,
On which our vice and wretchedness were tagged
Like fancy-points and fringes, with the robe
Pulled off at pleasure. Fondly these attach
A radical causation to a few
Poor drudges of chastising Providence,
Who borrow all their hues and qualities
From our own folly and rank wickedness, 170
Which gave them birth and nursed them. Others,
  meanwhile,
Dote with a mad idolatry; and all
Who will not fall before their images,
And yield them worship, they are enemies
Even of their country!

                    Such have I been deemed.—
But, O dear Britain! O my Mother Isle!
Needs must thou prove a name most dear and
  holy
To me, a son, a brother, and a friend,
A husband, and a father! who revere
All bonds of natural love, and find them all 180
Within the limits of thy rocky shores.
O native Britain! O my Mother Isle!

How shouldst thou prove aught else but dear and
   holy
To me, who from thy lakes and mountain-hills,
Thy clouds, thy quiet dales, thy rocks and seas,
Have drunk in all my intellectual life,
All sweet sensations, all ennobling thoughts,
All adoration of the God in nature,
All lovely and all honourable things,
Whatever makes this mortal spirit feel   190
The joy and greatness of its future being?
There lives nor form nor feeling in my soul
Unborrowed from my country! O divine
And beauteous island! thou hast been my sole
And most magnificent temple, in the which
I walk with awe, and sing my stately songs,
Loving the God that made me!—

                              May my fears,
My filial fears, be vain! and may the vaunts
And menace of the vengeful enemy
Pass like the gust, that roared and died away 200
In the distant tree: which heard, and only heard
In this low dell, bowed not the delicate grass.

   But now the gentle dew-fall sends abroad
The fruit-like perfume of the golden furze:
The light has left the summit of the hill,
Though still a sunny gleam lies beautiful,
Aslant the ivied beacon. Now farewell,
Farewell, awhile, O soft and silent spot!
On the green sheep-track, up the heathy hill,
Homeward I wind my way; and lo! recalled   210
From bodings that have well-nigh wearied me,
I find myself upon the brow, and pause
Startled! And after lonely sojourning
In such a quiet and surrounding nook,
This burst of prospect, here the shadowy main,
Dim-tinted, there the mighty majesty
Of that huge amphitheatre of rich
And elmy fields, seems like society—
Conversing with the mind, and giving it
A livelier impulse and a dance of thought!   220
And now, belovéd Stowey! I behold
Thy church-tower, and, methinks, the four huge
   elms
Clustering, which mark the mansion of my
   friend;[2]
And close behind them, hidden from my view,
Is my own lowly cottage, where my babe
And my babe's mother dwell in peace! With light
And quickened footsteps thitherward I tend,
Remembering thee, O green and silent dell!
And grateful, that by nature's quietness

---

[2] Thomas Poole.

And solitary musings, all my heart   230
Is softened, and made worthy to indulge
Love, and the thoughts that yearn for human
   kind.

        Nether Stowey, 20 April 1798   1798

THE NIGHTINGALE

No cloud, no relique of the sunken day
Distinguishes the West, no long thin slip
Of sullen light, no obscure trembling hues.
Come, we will rest on this old mossy bridge!
You see the glimmer of the stream beneath,
But hear no murmuring: it flows silently,
O'er its soft bed of verdure. All is still,
A balmy night! and though the stars be dim,
Yet let us think upon the vernal showers
That gladden the green earth, and we shall find 10
A pleasure in the dimness of the stars.
And hark! the Nightingale begins its song,
'Most musical, most melancholy'[1] bird!
A melancholy bird? Oh! idle thought!
In Nature there is nothing melancholy.
But some night-wandering man whose heart was
   pierced
With the remembrance of a grievous wrong,
Or slow distemper, or neglected love,
(And so, poor wretch! filled all things with him-
   self,
And made all gentle sounds tell back the tale   20
Of his own sorrow) he, and such as he,
First named these notes a melancholy strain.
And many a poet echoes the conceit;
Poet who hath been building up the rhyme
When he had better far have stretched his limbs
Beside a brook in mossy forest-dell,
By sun or moon-light, to the influxes
Of shapes and sounds and shifting elements
Surrendering his whole spirit, of his song
And of his fame forgetful! so his fame   30
Should share in Nature's immortality,
A venerable thing! and so his song
Should make all Nature lovelier, and itself
Be loved like Nature! But 'twill not be so;
And youths and maidens most poetical,
Who lose the deepening twilights of the spring
In ball-rooms and hot theatres, they still
Full of meek sympathy must heave their sighs
O'er Philomela's pity-pleading strains.

My Friend, and thou, our Sister![2] we have
   learnt   40

---

[1] *Il Penseroso*, 62.
[2] William and Dorothy Wordsworth.

A different lore: we may not thus profane
Nature's sweet voices, always full of love
And joyance! 'Tis the merry Nightingale
That crowds, and hurries, and precipitates
With fast thick warble his delicious notes,
As he were fearful that an April night
Would be too short for him to utter forth
His love-chant, and disburthen his full soul
Of all its music!

          And I know a grove
Of large extent, hard by a castle huge,   50
Which the great lord inhabits not; and so
This grove is wild with tangling underwood,
And the trim walks are broken up, and grass,
Thin grass and king-cups grow within the paths.
But never elsewhere in one place I knew
So many nightingales; and far and near,
In wood and thicket, over the wide grove,
They answer and provoke each other's song,
With skirmish and capricious passagings,
And murmurs musical and swift jug jug,   60
And one low piping sound more sweet than all—
Stirring the air with such a harmony,
That should you close your eyes, you might al-
    most
Forget it was not day! On moonlight bushes,
Whose dewy leaflets are but half-disclosed,
You may perchance behold them on the twigs,
Their bright, bright eyes, their eyes both bright
    and full,
Glistening, while many a glow-worm in the shade
Lights up her love-torch.

             A most gentle Maid,
Who dwelleth in her hospitable home   70
Hard by the castle, and at latest eve
(Even like a Lady vowed and dedicate
To something more than Nature in the grove)
Glides through the pathways; she knows all their
    notes,
That gentle Maid! and oft, a moment's space,
What time the moon was lost behind a cloud,
Hath heard a pause of silence; till the moon
Emerging, hath awakened earth and sky
With one sensation, and those wakeful birds
Have all burst forth in choral minstrelsy,   80
As if some sudden gale had swept at once
A hundred airy harps! And she hath watched
Many a nightingale perch giddily
On blossomy twig still swinging from the breeze,
And to that motion tune his wanton song
Like tipsy Joy that reels with tossing head.

Farewell, O Warbler! till to-morrow eve,
And you, my friends! farewell, a short farewell!
We have been loitering long and pleasantly,
And now for our dear homes.—That strain
    again!   90
Full fain it would delay me! My dear babe,[3]
Who, capable of no articulate sound,
Mars all things with his imitative lisp,
How he would place his hand beside his ear,
His little hand, the small forefinger up,
And bid us listen! And I deem it wise
To make him Nature's play-mate. He knows well
The evening-star; and once, when he awoke
In most distressful mood (some inward pain
Had made up that strange thing, an infant's
    dream—)   100
I hurried with him to our orchard-plot,
And he beheld the moon, and, hushed at once,
Suspends his sobs, and laughs most silently,
While his fair eyes, that swam with undropped
    tears,
Did glitter in the yellow moon-beam! Well!—
It is a father's tale: But if that Heaven
Should give me life, his childhood shall grow up
Familiar with these songs, that with the night
He may associate joy.—Once more, farewell,
Sweet Nightingale! once more, my friends!
    farewell.   110

1798   1798

THE BALLAD OF THE DARK LADIÉ

A FRAGMENT

BENEATH yon birch with silver bark,
And boughs so pendulous and fair,
The brook falls scatter'd down the rock:
    And all is mossy there!

And there upon the moss she sits,
The Dark Ladié in silent pain;
The heavy tear is in her eye,
    And drops and swells again.

Three times she sends her little page
Up the castled mountain's breast,   10
If he might find the Knight that wears
    The Griffin for his crest.

The sun was sloping down the sky,
And she had linger'd there all day,
Counting moments, dreaming fears—
    Oh wherefore can he stay?

---
3 his son Hartley.

She hears a rustling o'er the brook,
She sees far off a swinging bough!
' 'Tis He! 'Tis my betrothéd Knight!
    Lord Falkland, it is Thou!'   20

She springs, she clasps him round the neck,
She sobs a thousand hopes and fears,
Her kisses glowing on his cheeks
    She quenches with her tears.

      *   *   *

'My friends with rude ungentle words
They scoff and bid me fly to thee!
O give me shelter in thy breast!
    O shield and shelter me!

'My Henry, I have given thee much,
I gave what I can ne'er recall,   30
I gave my heart, I gave my peace,
    O Heaven! I gave thee all.'

The Knight made answer to the Maid,
While to his heart he held her hand,
'Nine castles hath my noble sire,
    None statelier in the land.

'The fairest one shall be my love's,
The fairest castle of the nine!
Wait only till the stars peep out,
    The fairest shall be thine: 40

'Wait only till the hand of eve
Hath wholly closed yon western bars,
And through the dark we two will steal
    Beneath the twinkling stars!'—

'The dark? the dark? No! not the dark?
The twinkling stars? How, Henry? How?'
O God! 'twas the eye of noon
    He pledged his sacred vow!

And in the eye of noon my love,
Shall lead me from my mother's door,   50
Sweet boys and girls all clothed in white
    Strewing flowers before:

But first the nodding minstrels go
With music meet for lordly bowers,
The children next in snow-white vests.
    Strewing buds and flowers!

And then my love and I shall pace,
My jet black hair in pearly braids,

Between our comely bachelors
    And blushing bridal maids.

      *   *   *

1798   1834

LOVE

[This poem was first published in the *Morning Post* 21
December, 1799, as *Introduction to the Tale of the Dark
Ladie*. It was inspired by Coleridge's love for Sarah
Hutchinson.]

ALL thoughts, all passions, all delights,
Whatever stirs this mortal frame,
All are but ministers of Love,
    And feed his sacred flame.

Oft in my waking dreams do I
Live o'er again that happy hour,
When midway on the mount I lay,
    Beside the ruined tower.

The moonshine, stealing o'er the scene
Had blended with the lights of eve;   10
And she was there, my hope, my joy,
    My own dear Genevieve!

She leant against the arméd man,
The statue of the arméd knight;
She stood and listened to my lay,
    Amid the lingering light.

Few sorrows hath she of her own,
My hope! my joy! my Genevieve!
She loves me best, whene'er I sing
    The songs that make her grieve.   20

I played a soft and doleful air,
I sang an old and moving story—
An old rude song, that suited well
    That ruin wild and hoary.

She listened with a flitting blush,
With downcast eyes and modest grace;
For well she knew, I could not choose
    But gaze upon her face.

I told her of the Knight that wore
Upon his shield a burning brand;   30
And that for ten long years he wooed
    The Lady of the Land.

I told her how he pined: and ah!
The deep, the low, the pleading tone
With which I sang another's love,
    Interpreted my own.

She listened with a flitting blush,
With downcast eyes, and modest grace;
And she forgave me, that I gazed
    Too fondly on her face!   40

But when I told the cruel scorn
That crazed that bold and lovely Knight,
And that he crossed the mountain-woods,
    Nor rested day nor night;

That sometimes from the savage den,
And sometimes from the darksome shade,
And sometimes starting up at once
    In green and sunny glade,—

There came and looked him in the face
An angel beautiful and bright;   50
And that he knew it was a Fiend,
    This miserable Knight!

And that unknowing what he did,
He leaped amid a murderous band,
And saved from outrage worse than death
    The Lady of the Land!

And how she wept, and clasped his knees;
And how she tended him in vain—
And ever strove to expiate
    The scorn that crazed his brain:—   60

And that she nursed him in a cave;
And how his madness went away,
When on the yellow forest-leaves
    A dying man he lay;—

His dying words—but when I reached
That tenderest strain of all the ditty,
My faultering voice and pausing harp
    Disturbed her soul with pity!

All impulses of soul and sense
Had thrilled my guileless Genevieve;   70
The music and the doleful tale,
    The rich and balmy eve;

And hopes, and fears that kindle hope,
An undistinguishable throng,
And gentle wishes long subdued,
    Subdued and cherished long!

She wept with pity and delight,
She blushed with love, and virgin-shame;
And like the murmur of a dream,
    I heard her breathe my name.   80

Her bosom heaved—she stepped aside,
As conscious of my look she stepped—
Then suddenly, with timorous eye
    She fled to me and wept.

She half enclosed me with her arms,
She pressed me with a meek embrace;
And bending back her head, looked up,
    And gazed upon my face.

'Twas partly love, and partly fear,
And partly 'twas a bashful art,   90
That I might rather feel, than see,
    The swelling of her heart.

I calmed her fears, and she was calm,
And told her love with virgin pride;
And so I won my Genevieve,
    My bright and beauteous Bride.

1799   1799

APOLOGIA PRO VITA SUA[1]

THE poet in his lone yet genial hour
Gives to his eyes a magnifying power:
Or rather he emancipates his eyes
From the black shapeless accidents of size—
In unctuous cones of kindling coal,
Or smoke upwreathing from the pipe's trim bole,
    His gifted ken[2] can see
    Phantoms of sublimity.

1800   1822

DEJECTION: AN ODE

Late, late yestreen I saw the new Moon,
With the old Moon in her arms:
And I fear, I fear, my Master dear!
We shall have a deadly storm.

BALLAD OF SIR PATRICK SPENCE.

[This poem was originally addressed to Sarah Hutchinson. In its first published form, which appeared in the
Morning Post on Wordsworth's wedding day, 4 October
1802, 'Sarah' was changed to 'Edmund' (having first
been changed in MS. to 'William'). In later editions 'Edmund' was changed to 'Lady,' and to 'Otway' in l. 120.]

I

WELL! If the Bard was weather-wise, who made
    The grand old ballad of Sir Patrick Spence,
    This night, so tranquil now, will not go hence
Unroused by winds, that ply a busier trade
Than those which mould yon cloud in lazy flakes,

---

1 'Apology for His Life.'
2 insight.

Samuel Taylor Coleridge

Or the dull sobbing draft, that moans and rakes
Upon the strings of this Æolian lute,
 Which better far were mute.
.For lo! the New-moon winter-bright!
And overspread with phantom light,   10
(With swimming phantom light o'erspread
But rimmed and circled by a silver thread)
I see the old Moon in her lap, foretelling
The coming-on of rain and squally blast.
And oh! that even now the gust were swelling,
 And the slant night-shower driving loud and
  fast!
Those sounds which oft have raised me, whilst
  they awed,
 And sent my soul abroad,
Might now perhaps their wonted impulse give,
Might startle this dull pain, and make it move
 and live!   20

II

A grief without a pang, void, dark, and drear,
 A stifled, drowsy, unimpassioned grief,
 Which finds no natural outlet, no relief,
  In word, or sigh, or tear—
O Lady! in this wan and heartless mood,
To other thoughts by yonder throstle woo'd,
 All this long eve, so balmy and serene,
Have I been gazing on the western sky,
 And its peculiar tint of yellow green:
And still I gaze—and with how blank an eye!   30
And those thin clouds above, in flakes and bars,
That give away their motion to the stars;
Those stars, that glide behind them or between,
Now sparkling, now bedimmed, but always seen:
Yon crescent Moon, as fixed as if it grew
In its own cloudless, starless lake of blue;
I see them all so excellently fair,
I see, not feel, how beautiful they are!

III

 My genial spirits fail;
 And what can these avail   40
To lift the smothering weight from off my breast?
 It were a vain endeavour,
 Though I should gaze for ever
On that green light that lingers in the west:
I may not hope from outward forms to win
The passion and the life, whose fountains are
 within.

IV

O Lady! we receive but what we give,
And in our life alone does Nature live:

Ours is her wedding garment, ours her shroud!
 And would we aught behold, of higher
  worth,
Than that inanimate cold world allowed
To the poor loveless ever-anxious crowd,
 Ah! from the soul itself must issue forth
A light, a glory, a fair luminous cloud
 Enveloping the Earth—
And from the soul itself must there be sent
 A sweet and potent voice, of its own birth,
Of all sweet sounds the life and element!

V

O pure of heart! thou need'st not ask of me
What this strong music in the soul may be!   60
What, and wherein it doth exist,
This light, this glory, this fair luminous mist,
This beautiful and beauty-making power.
 Joy, virtuous Lady! Joy that ne'er was given,
Save to the pure, and in their purest hour,
Life, and Life's effluence, cloud at once and
  shower,
Joy, Lady! is the spirit and the power,
Which wedding Nature to us gives in dower
 A new Earth and new Heaven,
Undreamt of by the sensual and the proud— 70
Joy is the sweet voice, Joy the luminous cloud—
 We in ourselves rejoice!
And thence flows all that charms or ear or sight,
 All melodies the echoes of that voice,
All colours a suffusion from that light.

VI

There was a time when, though my path was
  rough,
 This joy within me dallied with distress,
And all misfortunes were but as the stuff
 Whence Fancy made me dreams of happiness:
For hope grew round me, like the twining vine, 80
And fruits, and foliage, not my own, seemed
  mine.
But now afflictions bow me down to earth;
Nor care I that they rob me of my mirth;
 But oh! each visitation
Suspends what nature gave me at my birth,
 My shaping spirit of Imagination.
For not to think of what I needs must feel,
 But to be still and patient, all I can;
And haply by abstruse research to steal
 From my own nature all the natural man— 90
 This was my sole resource, my only plan:
Till that which suits a part infects the whole,
And now is almost grown the habit of my soul.

Mood suddenly changes like the weather

VII

Hence, viper thoughts, that coil around my
    mind,
    Reality's dark dream!
I turn from you, and listen to the wind,
    Which long has raved unnoticed. What a
    scream
Of agony by torture lengthened out
That lute sent forth! Thou Wind, that rav'st
    without,
    Bare crag, or mountain-tairn,[1] or blasted
    tree,   100
Or pine-grove whither woodman never clomb,
Or lonely house, long held the witches' home,
    Methinks were fitter instruments for thee,
Mad Lutanist! who in this month of showers,
Of dark-brown gardens, and of peeping flowers,
Mak'st Devils' yule, with worse than wintry song,
The blossoms, buds, and timorous leaves among.
    Thou Actor, perfect in all tragic sounds!
Thou mighty Poet, e'en to frenzy bold!
    What tell'st thou now about?   110
    'Tis of the rushing of an host in rout,
With groans, of trampled men, with smarting
    wounds—
At once they groan with pain, and shudder with
    the cold!
But hush! there is a pause of deepest silence!
    And all that noise, as of a rushing crowd,
With groans, and tremulous shudderings—all is
    over—
    It tells another tale, with sounds less deep and
    loud!
    A tale of less affright,
    And tempered with delight,
As Otway's self[2] had framed the tender lay,— 120
    'Tis of a little child[3]
    Upon a lonesome wild,
Not far from home, but she hath lost her way:
And now moans low in bitter grief and fear,
And now screams loud, and hopes to make her
    mother hear.

VIII

'Tis midnight, but small thoughts have I of sleep:
Full seldom may my friend such vigils keep!
Visit her, gentle Sleep! with wings of healing,
    And may this storm be but a mountain-birth,
May all the stars hang bright above her
    dwelling,   130

Silent as though they watched the sleeping
    Earth!
    With light heart may she rise,
    Gay fancy, cheerful eyes,
Joy lift her spirit, joy attune her voice;
To her may all things live, from pole to pole,
Their life the eddying of her living soul!
    O simple spirit, guided from above,
Dear Lady! friend devoutest of my choice,
Thus mayest thou ever, evermore rejoice.

    1802   1802

HYMN BEFORE SUNRISE, IN THE VALE OF CHAMOUNI[1]

Besides the Rivers, Arve and Arveiron, which have
their sources in the foot of Mont Blanc, five conspicuous
torrents rush down its sides; and within a few paces of
the glaciers, the Gentiana Major grows in immense numbers, with its 'flowers of loveliest blue.'—(Coleridge.)
[Coleridge never actually visited the Vale of Chamouni.
His poem has been shown to be based upon a translation of an *Ode to Chamouny* by Friederika Brun.]

HAST thou a charm to stay the morning-star
In his steep course? So long he seems to pause
On thy bald awful head, O sovran BLANC,
The Arve and Arveiron at thy base
Rave ceaselessly; but thou, most awful Form!
Risest from forth thy silent sea of pines,
How silently! Around thee and above
Deep is the air and dark, substantial, black,
An ebon mass: methinks thou piercest it,
As with a wedge! But when I look again,   10
It is thine own calm home, thy crystal shrine,
Thy habitation from eternity!
O dread and silent Mount! I gazed upon thee,
Till thou, still present to the bodily sense,
Didst vanish from my thought: entranced in
    prayer
I worshipped the Invisible alone.

    Yet, like some sweet beguiling melody,
So sweet, we know not we are listening to it,
Thou, the meanwhile, wast blending with my
    Thought,
Yea, with my Life and Life's own secret joy: 20
Till the dilating Soul, enrapt, transfused,
Into the mighty vision passing—there
As in her natural form, swelled vast to Heaven!

---

1 Tairn is a small lake, generally if not always applied to the lakes
up in the mountains and which are the feeders of those in the valleys.—(Coleridge.)
2 'Edmund's self' in an earlier version.
3 Wordsworth's Lucy Gray.

---

1 Chamouni is one of the highest mountain valleys of the Barony
of Faucigny in the Savoy Alps; and exhibits a kind of fairy world,
in which the wildest appearances (I had almost said horrors) of
nature alternate with the softest and most beautiful.—(From
Coleridge's introductory note to the poem when first published in
The Morning Post, 11 September 1802.)

Awake, my soul! not only passive praise
Thou owest! not alone these swelling tears,
Mute thanks and secret ecstasy! Awake,
Voice of sweet song! Awake, my heart, awake!
Green vales and icy cliffs, all join my Hymn.

Thou first and chief, sole sovereign of the
    Vale!
O struggling with the darkness all the night,   30
And visited all night by troops of stars,
Or when they climb the sky or when they sink:
Companion of the morning-star at dawn,
Thyself Earth's rosy star, and of the dawn
Co-herald: wake, O wake, and utter praise!
Who sank thy sunless pillars deep in Earth?
Who filled thy countenance with rosy light?
Who made thee parent of perpetual streams?

And you, ye five wild torrents fiercely glad!
Who called you forth from night and utter
    death,   40
From dark and icy caverns called you forth,
Down those precipitous, black, jaggéd rocks,
For ever shattered and the same for ever?
Who gave you your invulnerable life,
Your strength, your speed, your fury, and your
    joy,
Unceasing thunder and eternal foam?
And who commanded (and the silence came),
Here let the billows stiffen, and have rest?

Ye Ice-falls! ye that from the mountain's brow
Adown enormous ravines slope amain—   50
Torrents, methinks, that heard a mighty voice,
And stopped at once amid their maddest plunge!
Motionless torrents! silent cataracts!
Who made you glorious as the Gates of Heaven
Beneath the keen full moon? Who bade the
    sun
Clothe you with rainbows? Who, with living
    flowers
Of loveliest blue, spread garlands at your feet?—
GOD! let the torrents, like a shout of nations,
Answer! and let the ice-plains echo, GOD!
GOD! sing ye meadow-streams with gladsome
    voice!   60
Ye pine-groves, with your soft and soul-like
    sounds!
And they too have a voice, yon piles of snow,
And in their perilous fall shall thunder, GOD!

Ye living flowers that skirt the eternal frost!
Ye wild goats sporting round the eagle's nest!
Ye eagles, play-mates of the mountain-storm!
Ye lightnings, the dread arrows of the clouds!

Ye signs and wonders of the element!
Utter forth God, and fill the hills with praise!

Thou too, hoar Mount! with thy sky-pointing
    peaks,   70
Oft from whose feet the avalanche, unheard,
Shoots downward, glittering through the pure
    serene
Into the depth of clouds, that veil thy breast—
Thou too again, stupendous Mountain! thou
That as I raise my head, awhile bowed low
In adoration, upward from thy base
Slow travelling with dim eyes suffused with tears,
Solemnly seemest, like a vapoury cloud,
To rise before me—Rise, O ever rise,
Rise like a cloud of incense from the Earth!   80
Thou kingly Spirit throned among the hills,
Thou dread ambassador from Earth to Heaven,
Great Hierarch! tell thou the silent sky,
And tell the stars, and tell yon rising sun
Earth, with her thousand voices, praises GOD.

1802   1802

ANSWER TO A CHILD'S QUESTION

Do you ask what the birds say? The Sparrow, the
    Dove,
The Linnet and Thrush say, 'I love and I love!'
In the winter they're silent—the wind is so
    strong;
What it says, I don't know, but it sings a loud
    song.
But green leaves, and blossoms, and sunny warm
    weather,
And singing, and loving—all come back to-
    gether.
But the Lark is so brimful of gladness and love,
The green fields below him, the blue sky above,
That he sings, and he sings; and for ever sings
    he—
'I love my Love, and my Love loves me!'   10

1802   1802

THE PAINS OF SLEEP

[Coleridge sent this poem in a letter to Southey, September 1803, with the following comment: 'I do not know how I came to scribble down these verses to you—my heart was aching, my head all confused—but they are, doggerel as they may be, a true portrait of my nights. What to do, I am at a loss; for it is hard thus to be withered, having the faculties and attainments which I have.']

ERE on my bed my limbs I lay,
It hath not been my use to pray
With moving lips or bended knees;
But silently, by slow degrees,
My spirit I to Love compose,
In humble trust mine eye-lids close,
With reverential resignation,
No wish conceived, no thought exprest,
Only a sense of supplication;
A sense o'er all my soul imprest   10
That I am weak, yet not unblest,
Since in me, round me, every where
Eternal Strength and Wisdom are.

But yester-night I prayed aloud
In anguish and in agony,
Up-starting from the fiendish crowd
Of shapes and thoughts that tortured me:
A lurid light, a trampling throng,
Sense of intolerable wrong,
And whom I scorned, those only strong!   20
Thirst of revenge, the powerless will
Still baffled, and yet burning still!
Desire with loathing strangely mixed
On wild or hateful objects fixed.
Fantastic passions! maddening brawl!
And shame and terror over all!
Deeds to be hid which were not hid,
Which all confused I could not know
Whether I suffered, or I did:
For all seemed guilt, remorse or woe,   30
My own or others still the same
Life-stifling fear, soul-stifling shame.

So two nights passed: the night's dismay
Saddened and stunned the coming day.
Sleep, the wide blessing, seemed to me
Distemper's worst calamity.
The third night, when my own loud scream
Had waked me from the fiendish dream,
O'ercome with sufferings strange and wild,
I wept as I had been a child;   40
And having thus by tears subdued
My anguish to a milder mood,
Such punishments, I said, were due
To natures deepliest stained with sin,—
For aye entempesting anew
The unfathomable hell within,
The horror of their deeds to view,
To know and loathe, yet wish and do!
Such griefs with such men well agree,
But wherefore, wherefore fall on me?   50
To be beloved is all I need,
And whom I love, I love indeed.

1803   1816

TO WILLIAM WORDSWORTH

COMPOSED ON THE NIGHT AFTER HIS RECITATION
OF A POEM[1] ON THE GROWTH OF
AN INDIVIDUAL MIND

FRIEND of the wise! and Teacher of the Good!
Into my heart have I received that Lay
More than historic, that prophetic Lay
Wherein (high theme by thee first sung aright)
Of the foundations and the building up
Of a Human Spirit thou hast dared to tell
What may be told, to the understanding mind
Revealable; and what within the mind
By vital breathings secret as the soul
Of vernal growth, oft quickens in the heart   10
Thoughts all too deep for words!—

                              Theme hard as high!
Of smiles spontaneous, and mysterious fears
(The first-born they of Reason and twin-birth),
Of tides obedient to external force,
And currents self-determined, as might seem,
Or by some inner Power; of moments awful,
Now in thy inner life, and now abroad,
When power streamed from thee, and thy soul
      received
The light reflected, as a light bestowed—
Of fancies fair, and milder hours of youth,   20
Hyblean[2] murmurs of poetic thought
Industrious in its joy, in vales and glens
Native or outland, lakes and famous hills!
Or on the lonely high-road, when the stars
Were rising; or by secret mountain-streams,
The guides and the companions of thy way!

Of more than Fancy, of the Social Sense
Distending wide, and man beloved as man,
Where France in all her towns lay vibrating
Like some becalméd bark beneath the burst   30
Of Heaven's immediate thunder, when no cloud
Is visible, or shadow on the main.
For thou wert there, thine own brows garlanded,
Amid the tremor of a realm aglow,
Amid a mighty nation jubilant,
When from the general heart of human kind
Hope sprang forth like a full-born Deity!
——Of that dear Hope afflicted and struck
      down,
So summoned homeward, thenceforth calm and
      sure
From the dread watch-tower of man's absolute
      self,   40
With light unwaning on her eyes, to look

---
1 *The Prelude.*
2 honeyed; flowing sweetly.

Far on—herself a glory to behold,
The Angel of the vision! Then (last strain)
Of Duty, chosen Laws controlling choice,
Action and joy!—An Orphic[3] song indeed,
A song divine of high and passionate thoughts
To their own music chaunted!

                O great Bard!
Ere yet that last strain dying awed the air,
With stedfast eye I viewed thee in the choir
Of ever-enduring men. The truly great   50
Have all one age, and from one visible space
Shed influence! They, both in power and act,
Are permanent, and Time is not with them,
Save as it worketh for them, they in it.
Nor less a sacred Roll, than those of old,
And to be placed, as they, with gradual fame
Among the archives of mankind, thy work
Makes audible a linkéd lay of Truth,
Of Truth profound a sweet continuous lay,
Not learnt, but native, her own natural notes! 60
Ah! as I listened with a heart forlorn,
The pulses of my being beat anew:
And even as Life returns upon the drowned,
Life's joy rekindling roused a throng of pains—
Keen pangs of Love, awakening as a babe
Turbulent, with an outcry in the heart;
And fears self-willed, that shunned the eye of
    Hope;
And Hope that scarce would know itself from
    Fear;
Sense of past Youth, and Manhood come in vain,
And Genius given, and Knowledge won in
    vain;   70
And all which I had culled in wood-walks wild,
And all which patient toil had reared, and all,
Commune with thee had opened out—but flow-
    ers
Strewed on my corse, and borne upon my bier
In the same coffin, for the self-same grave!

    That way no more! and ill beseems it me,
Who came a welcomer in herald's guise,
Singing of Glory, and Futurity,
To wander back on such unhealthful road,
Plucking the poisons of self-harm! And ill   80
Such intertwine beseems triumphal wreaths
Strew'd before thy advancing!

                Nor do thou,
Sage Bard! impair the memory of that hour
Of thy communion with my nobler mind
By pity or grief, already felt too long!

---

3 like music ascribed to Orpheus.

Nor let my words import more blame than needs.
The tumult rose and ceased: for Peace is nigh
Where Wisdom's voice has found a listening
    heart.
Amid the howl of more than wintry storms,
The Halcyon[4] hears the voice of vernal hours 90
Already on the wing.

             Eve following eve,
Dear tranquil time, when the sweet sense of
    Home
Is sweetest! moments for their own sake hailed
And more desired, more precious, for thy song,
In silence listening, like a devout child,
My soul lay passive, by thy various strain
Driven as in surges now beneath the stars,
With momentary stars of my own birth,
Fair constellated foam,[5] still darting off
Into the darkness; now a tranquil sea,   100
Outspread and bright, yet swelling to the moon.

And when—O Friend! my comforter and guide!
Strong in thyself, and powerful to give strength!—
Thy long sustainéd Song finally closed,
And thy deep voice had ceased—yet thou thyself
Wert still before my eyes, and round us both
That happy vision of belovéd faces—
Scarce conscious, and yet conscious of its close
I sate, my being blended in one thought
(Thought was it? or aspiration? or resolve?) 110
Absorbed, yet hanging still upon the sound—
And when I rose, I found myself in prayer.

1806   *1817*

TIME, REAL AND IMAGINARY

AN ALLEGORY

By imaginary Time, I meant the state of a school boy's
mind when on his return to school he projects his being
in his day dreams, and lives in his next holidays, six
months hence; and this I contrasted with real Time.
                    —(Coleridge.)

ON the wide level of a mountain's head,
(I knew not where, but 'twas some faery place)
Their pinions, ostrich-like, for sails out-spread,
Two lovely children run an endless race,
    A sister and a brother!
    This far outstripp'd the other;
    Yet ever runs she with reverted face,

---

4 a kingfisher which was fabled to nest at sea about the time of
the winter solstice and to calm the waves.
5 A beautiful white cloud of Foam at momentary intervals coursed
by the side of the Vessel with a Roar, and little stars of flame
danced and sparkled and went out in it: and every now and then
light detachments of this white cloud-like foam dashed off from
the vessel's side, each with its own small constellation, over the
Sea, and scoured out of sight like a Tartar Troop over a wilderness.—(Coleridge.)

And looks and listens for the boy behind:
 For he, alas! is blind!
O'er rough and smooth with even step he
 passed,   10
And knows not whether he be first or last.

1812   1817

THE KNIGHT'S TOMB

WHERE is the grave of Sir Arthur O'Kellyn?
Where may the grave of that good man be?—
By the side of a spring, on the breast of Helvellyn,
Under the twigs of a young birch tree!
The oak that in summer was sweet to hear,
And rustled its leaves in the fall of the year,
And whistled and roared in the winter alone,
Is gone,—and the birch in its stead is grown.—
The Knight's bones are dust,
 And his good sword rust:—   10
His soul is with the saints, I trust.

?1817   1834

YOUTH AND AGE

VERSE, a breeze mid blossoms straying,
Where Hope clung feeding, like a bee—
Both were mine! Life went a-maying
  With Nature, Hope, and Poesy,
    When I was young!

When I was young?—Ah, woful When!
Ah! for the change 'twixt Now and Then!
This breathing house not built with hands,
This body that does me grievous wrong,
O'er aery cliffs and glittering sands, 10
How lightly then it flashed along:—
Like those trim skiffs, unknown of yore,
On winding lakes and rivers wide,
That ask no aid of sail or oar,
That fear no spite of wind or tide!
Nought cared this body for wind or weather
When Youth and I lived in't together.

Flowers are lovely; Love is flower-like;
Friendship is a sheltering tree;
O! the joys, that came down shower-like, 20
Of Friendship, Love, and Liberty,
    Ere I was old!

Ere I was old? Ah woful Ere,
Which tells me, Youth's no longer here!
O Youth! for years so many and sweet,
'Tis known, that Thou and I were one,
I'll think it but a fond conceit—

It cannot be that Thou art gone!
Thy vesper-bell hath not yet toll'd:—
And thou wert aye a masker bold! 30
What strange disguise hast now put on,
To make believe, that thou art gone?
I see these locks in silvery slips,
This drooping gait, this altered size:
But Spring-tide blossoms on thy lips,
And tears take sunshine from thine eyes!
Life is but thought: so think I will
That Youth and I are house-mates still.

Dew-drops are the gems of morning,
But the tears of mournful eve! 40
Where no hope is, life's a warning
That only serves to make us grieve,
    When we are old:

That only serves to make us grieve
With oft and tedious taking-leave,
Like some poor nigh-related guest,
That may not rudely be dismist;
Yet hath outstay'd his welcome while,
And tells the jest without the smile.

1823–32   1834

WORK WITHOUT HOPE

LINES COMPOSED 21ST FEBRUARY 1825

ALL Nature seems at work. Slugs leave their
 lair—
The bees are stirring—birds are on the wing—
And Winter slumbering in the open air,
Wears on his smiling face a dream of Spring!
And I the while, the sole unbusy thing,
Nor honey make, nor pair, nor build, nor sing.

 Yet well I ken the banks where amaranths
  blow,
Have traced the fount whence streams of nectar
  flow.
Bloom, O ye amaranths! bloom for whom ye
  may,
For me ye bloom not! Glide, rich streams,
  away!   10
With lips unbrightened, wreathless brow, I stroll:
And would you learn the spells that drowse my
  soul?
Work without Hope draws nectar in a sieve,
And Hope without an object cannot live.

1825   1828

PHANTOM OR FACT

A DIALOGUE IN VERSE

AUTHOR

A LOVELY form there sate beside my bed,
And such a feeding calm its presence shed,
A tender love so pure from earthly leaven,
That I unnethe[1] the fancy might control,
'Twas my own spirit newly come from heaven,
Wooing its gentle way into my soul!
But ah! the change—It had not stirr'd, and yet—
Alas! that change how fain would I forget!
That shrinking back, like one that had mistook!
That weary, wandering, disavowing look!   10
'Twas all another, feature, look, and frame,
And still, methought, I knew, it was the same!

FRIEND

This riddling tale, to what does it belong?
Is't history? vision? or an idle song?
Or rather say at once, within what space
Of time this wild disastrous change took place?

AUTHOR

Call it a moment's work (and such it seems)
This tale's a fragment from the life of dreams;
But say, that years matur'd the silent strife,
And 'tis a record from the dream of life.   20

1830   1834

LOVE'S APPARITION AND EVANISHMENT

AN ALLEGORIC ROMANCE

LIKE a lone Arab, old and blind,
Some caravan had left behind,
Who sits beside a ruin'd well,
Where the shy sand-asps bask and swell;
And now he hangs his agéd head aslant,
And listens for a human sound—in vain!
And now the aid, which Heaven alone can grant,
Upturns his eyeless face from Heaven to gain;—
Even thus, in vacant mood, one sultry hour,
Resting my eye upon a drooping plant,   10
With brow low-bent, within my garden-bower,
I sate upon the couch of camomile;[1]
And—whether 'twas a transient sleep, perchance,

---

[1] with difficulty.

[1] a plant having strong-scented foliage from which oil is extracted for medicinal use.

Flitted across the idle brain, the while
I watch'd the sickly calm with aimless scope,
In my own heart; or that, indeed a trance,
Turn'd my eye inward—thee, O genial Hope,
Love's elder sister! thee did I behold,
Drest as a bridesmaid, but all pale and cold,
With roseless cheek, all pale and cold and dim, 20
   Lie lifeless at my feet!
And then came Love, a sylph in bridal trim,
   And stood beside my seat;
She bent, and kiss'd her sister's lips,
   As she was wont to do;—
Alas! 'twas but a chilling breath
Woke just enough of life in death
   To make Hope die anew.

L'ENVOY

In vain we supplicate the Powers above;
There is no resurrection for the Love   30
That, nursed in tenderest care, yet fades away
In the chill'd heart by gradual self-decay.

1833   1834

EPITAPH

STOP, Christian passer-by!—Stop, child of God,
And read with gentle breast. Beneath this sod
A poet lies, or that which once seem'd he.
O, lift one thought in prayer for S. T. C.;
That he who many a year with toil of breath
Found death in life, may here find life in death!
Mercy for praise—to be forgiven for fame
He ask'd, and hoped, through Christ. Do thou
   the same!

1833   1834

From BIOGRAPHIA LITERARIA

CHAPTER XIV

Occasion of the *Lyrical Ballads,* and the objects originally proposed—Preface to the second edition—The ensuing controversy, its causes and acrimony—Philosophic definitions of a poem and poetry with scholia.[1]

DURING the first year that Mr. Wordsworth and I were neighbours our conversations turned frequently on the two cardinal points of poetry, the power of exciting the sympathy of the reader by a faithful adherence to the truth of nature, and the power of giving the interest of novelty by the modifying colours of imagination. The sudden charm, which accidents of light and shade, which moonlight or sunset diffused over a known and

---

[1] explanatory comments.

familiar landscape, appeared to represent the practicability of combining both. These are the poetry of nature. The thought suggested itself (to which of us I do not recollect) that a series of poems might be composed of two sorts. In the one, the incidents and agents were to be, in part at least, supernatural; and the excellence aimed at was to consist in the interesting of the affections by the dramatic truth of such emotions as would naturally accompany such situations, supposing them real. And real in *this* sense they have been to every human being who, from whatever source of delusion, has at any time believed himself under supernatural agency. For the second class, subjects were to be chosen from ordinary life; the characters and incidents were to be such as will be found in every village and its vicinity, where there is a meditative and feeling mind to seek after them, or to notice them when they present themselves.

In this idea originated the plan of the *Lyrical Ballads;* in which it was agreed, that my endeavours should be directed to persons and characters supernatural, or at least romantic; yet so as to transfer from our inward nature a human interest and a semblance of truth sufficient to procure for these shadows of imagination that willing suspension of disbelief for the moment, which constitutes poetic faith. Mr. Wordsworth, on the other hand, was to propose to himself as his object, to give the charm of novelty to things of every day, and to excite a feeling analogous to the supernatural, by awakening the mind's attention from the lethargy of custom, and directing it to the loveliness and the wonders of the world before us; an inexhaustible treasure, but for which, in consequence of the film of familiarity and selfish solicitude we have eyes, yet see not, ears that hear not, and hearts that neither feel nor understand.

With this view I wrote *The Ancient Mariner,* and was preparing, among other poems, *The Dark Ladie,* and the *Christabel,* in which I should have more nearly realized my ideal than I had done in my first attempt. But Mr. Wordsworth's industry had proved so much more successful, and the number of his poems so much greater, that my compositions, instead of forming a balance, appeared rather an interpolation of heterogeneous matter. Mr. Wordsworth added two or three poems written in his own character, in the impassioned, lofty, and sustained diction, which is characteristic of his genius. In this form the *Lyrical Ballads* were published; and were presented by him, as an *experiment,* whether subjects, which from their nature rejected the usual ornaments and extra-colloquial style of poems in general, might not be so managed in the language of ordinary life as to produce the pleasurable interest, which it is the peculiar business of poetry to impart. To the second edition he added a preface of considerable length, in which, notwithstanding some passages of apparently a contrary import, he was understood to contend for the extension of this style to poetry of all kinds, and to reject as vicious and indefensible all phrases and forms of style that were not included in what he (unfortunately, I think, adopting an equivocal expression) called the language of *real* life. From this preface, prefixed to poems in which it was impossible to deny the presence of original genius, however mistaken its direction might be deemed, arose the whole long-continued controversy. For from the conjunction of perceived power with supposed heresy I explain the inveteracy and in some instances, I grieve to say, the acrimonious passions, with which the controversy has been conducted by the assailants.

Had Mr. Wordsworth's poems been the silly, the childish things, which they were for a long time described as being; had they been really distinguished from the compositions of other poets merely by meanness of language and inanity of thought; had they indeed contained nothing more than what is found in the parodies and pretended imitations of them; they must have sunk at once, a dead weight, into the slough of oblivion, and have dragged the preface along with them. But year after year increased the number of Mr. Wordsworth's admirers. They were found, too, not in the lower classes of the reading public, but chiefly among young men of strong sensibility and meditative minds; and their admiration (inflamed perhaps in some degree by opposition) was distinguished by its intensity, I might almost say, by its *religious* fervour. These facts, and the intellectual energy of the author, which was more or less consciously felt, where it was outwardly and even boisterously denied, meeting with sentiments of aversion to his opinions, and of alarm at their consequences, produced an eddy of criticism, which would of itself have borne up the poems by the violence with which it whirled them round and round. With many parts of this preface, in the sense attributed to them, and which the words undoubtedly seem to authorize, I never concurred; but on the contrary objected to them as erroneous in principle, and as contradictory (in appearance at least) both to other parts of the same preface, and to the author's own practice in the greater number of the poems themselves. Mr. Wordsworth in his recent collection has, I find, degraded this prefatory disquisition to the end of his second volume, to be read or not at the reader's choice. But he has not, as far as I can discover, announced any change in his poetic creed. At all events, considering it as the source of a controversy, in which I have been honoured more than I deserve by the frequent conjunction of my name with his, I think it expedient to declare once for all, in what points I coincide with his opinions, and in what points I altogether differ. But in order to render myself intelligible I must previously, in as few words as possible, explain my ideas, first, of a *poem;* and secondly, of *poetry* itself, in *kind,* and in *essence.*

The office of philosophical *disquisition* consists in just *distinction;* while it is the privilege of the philosopher to preserve himself constantly aware, that distinction is not division. In order to obtain adequate notions of any truth, we must intellectually separate its distinguishable parts; and this is the technical *process* of philosophy. But having so done, we must then restore them in our conceptions to the unity, in which they actually co-exist; and this is the *result* of philosophy. A poem contains the same elements as a prose composition; the difference therefore must consist in a different combination of them, in consequence of a different object being proposed. According to the difference of the object will be the difference of the combination. It is possible that the object may be merely to facilitate the recollection of any given facts or observations by artificial arrangement; and the composition will be a poem, merely because it is distinguished from prose by metre, or by rhyme, or by both conjointly. In this, the lowest sense, a man might attribute the name of a poem to the well-known enumeration of the days in the several months:

Thirty days hath September,
April, June, and November, &c.

and others of the same class and purpose. And as a particular pleasure is found in anticipating the recurrence of sounds and quantities, all compositions that have this charm superadded, whatever be their contents, *may* be entitled poems.

So much for the superficial *form.* A difference of object and contents supplies an additional ground of distinction. The immediate purpose may be the communication of truths; either of

truth absolute and demonstrable, as in works of science; or of facts experienced and recorded, as in history. Pleasure, and that of the highest and most permanent kind, may *result* from the *attainment* of the end; but it is not itself the immediate end. In other works the communication of pleasure may be the immediate purpose; and though truth, either moral or intellectual, ought to be the *ultimate* end, yet this will distinguish the character of the author, not the class to which the work belongs. Blest indeed is that state of society, in which the immediate purpose would be baffled by the perversion of the proper ultimate end; in which no charm of diction or imagery could exempt the *Bathyllus* even of an Anacreon, or the *Alexis* of Virgil, from disgust and aversion!

But the communication of pleasure may be the immediate object of a work not metrically composed; and that object may have been in a high degree attained, as in novels and romances. Would then the mere superaddition of metre, with or without rhyme, entitle *these* to the name of poems? The answer is, that nothing can permanently please, which does not contain in itself the reason why it is so, and not otherwise. If metre be superadded, all other parts must be made consonant with it. They must be such as to justify the perpetual and distinct attention to each part, which an exact correspondent recurrence of accent and sound are calculated to excite. The final definition then, so deduced, may be thus worded. A poem is that species of composition, which is opposed to works of science, by proposing for its *immediate* object pleasure, not truth; and from all other species (having *this* object in common with it) it is discriminated by proposing to itself such delight from the *whole,* as is compatible with a distinct gratification from each component *part.*

Controversy is not seldom excited in consequence of the disputants attaching each a different meaning to the same word; and in few instances has this been more striking, than in disputes concerning the present subject. If a man chooses to call every composition a poem, which is rhyme, or measure, or both, I must leave his opinion uncontroverted. The distinction is at least competent to characterize the writer's intention. If it were subjoined, that the whole is likewise entertaining or affecting, as a tale, or as a series of interesting reflections, I of course admit this as another fit ingredient of a poem, and an additional merit. But if the definition sought for be that of a *legitimate* poem, I answer, it must be one the parts of which mutually support and explain each other; all in their proportion harmonizing with, and supporting the purpose and known influences of metrical arrangement. The philosophic critics of all ages coincide with the ultimate judgement of all countries, in equally denying the praises of a just poem, on the one hand, to a series of striking lines or distiches, each of which, absorbing the whole attention of the reader to itself, disjoins it from its context, and makes it a separate whole, instead of an harmonizing part; and on the other hand, to an unsustained composition, from which the reader collects rapidly the general result, unattracted by the component parts. The reader should be carried forward, not merely or chiefly by the mechanical impulse of curiosity, or by a restless desire to arrive at the final solution; but by the pleasurable activity of mind excited by the attractions of the journey itself. Like the motion of a serpent, which the Egyptians made the emblem of intellectual power; or like the path of sound through the air; at every step he pauses and half recedes, and from the retrogressive movement collects the force which again carries him onward. *Præcipitandus est liber spiritus,*[2] says Petronius Arbiter most happily. The epithet, *liber,* here balances the preceding verb; and it is not easy to conceive more meaning condensed in fewer words.

But if this should be admitted as a satisfactory character of a poem, we have still to seek for a definition of poetry. The writings of Plato, and Bishop Taylor,[3] and the *Theoria Sacra* of Burnet,[4] furnish undeniable proofs that poetry of the highest kind may exist without metre, and even without the contradistinguishing objects of a poem. The first chapter of *Isaiah* (indeed a very large portion of the whole book) is poetry in the most emphatic sense; yet it would be not less irrational than strange to assert, that pleasure, and not truth, was the immediate object of the prophet. In short, whatever *specific* import we attach to the word, poetry, there will be found involved in it, as a necessary consequence, that a poem of any length neither can be, nor ought to be, all poetry. Yet if an harmonious whole is to be produced, the remaining parts must be preserved *in keeping* with the poetry; and this can be no otherwise effected than by such a studied selection and artificial arrangement as will partake of *one,* though not a *peculiar* property of poetry. And this again can be no other than the property

of exciting a more continuous and equal attention than the language of prose aims at, whether colloquial or written.

My own conclusions on the nature of poetry, in the strictest use of the word, have been in part anticipated in the preceding disquisition on the fancy and imagination. What is poetry? is so nearly the same question with, what is a poet? that the answer to the one is involved in the solution of the other. For it is a distinction resulting from the poetic genius itself, which sustains and modifies the images, thoughts, and emotions of the poet's own mind.

The poet, described in *ideal* perfection, brings the whole soul of man into activity, with the subordination of its faculties to each other according to their relative worth and dignity. He diffuses a tone and spirit of unity, that blends, and (as it were) *fuses,* each into each, by that synthetic and magical power, to which we have exclusively appropriated the name of imagination. This power, first put in action by the will and understanding, and retained under their irremissive, though gentle and unnoticed, control (*laxis effertur habenis*[5]) reveals itself in the balance or reconciliation of opposite or discordant qualities: of sameness, with difference; of the general, with the concrete; the idea, with the image; the individual, with the representative; the sense of novelty and freshness, with old and familiar objects; a more than usual state of emotion, with more than usual order; judgement ever awake and steady self-possession, with enthusiasm and feeling profound or vehement; and while it blends and harmonizes the natural and the artificial, still subordinates art to nature; the manner to the matter; and our admiration of the poet to our sympathy with the poetry. 'Doubtless,' as Sir John Davies observes[6] of the soul (and his words may with slight alteration be applied, and even more appropriately, to the poetic imagination),—

Doubtless this could not be, but that she turns
   Bodies to spirit by sublimation strange,
As fire converts to fire the things it burns,
   As we our food into our nature change.

From their gross matter she abstracts their
    forms,
   And draws a kind of quintessence from
    things;
Which to her proper nature she transforms,
   To bear them light on her celestial wings.

Thus does she, when from individual states

---

2 'The free spirit should be impelled forward.'
3 Jeremy Taylor, 1613–67.
4 Thomas Burnet, 1635–1715.

5 'is carried along with loose reins.'
6 in his poem *Of the Soul of Man,* section 6.

She doth abstract the universal kinds;
Which then re-clothed in divers names and
    fates
Steal access through our senses to our minds.

Finally, good sense is the body of poetic genius,
fancy its drapery, motion its life, and imagination
the soul that is everywhere, and in each; and
forms all into one graceful and intelligent whole.

CHAPTER XVII

Examination of the tenets peculiar to Mr. Wordsworth—Rustic life (above all, *low* and rustic life) especially unfavourable to the formation of a human diction
—The best parts of language the product of philosophers,
not of clowns or shepherds—Poetry essentially ideal and
generic—The language of Milton as much the language
of *real* life, yea, incomparably more so than that of the
cottager.

As far, then, as Mr. Wordsworth in his preface
contended, and most ably contended, for a reformation in our poetic diction, as far as he has
evinced the truth of passion, and the *dramatic*
propriety of those figures and metaphors in the
original poets, which, stripped of their justifying reasons, and converted into mere artifices of
connexion or ornament, constitute the characteristic falsity in the poetic style of the moderns;
and as far as he has, with equal acuteness and
clearness, pointed out the process by which this
change was effected, and the resemblances between that state into which the reader's mind is
thrown by the pleasurable confusion of thought
from an unaccustomed train of words and
images, and that state which is induced by the
natural language of impassioned feeling; he undertook a useful task, and deserves all praise,
both for the attempt and for the execution. The
provocations to this remonstrance in behalf of
truth and nature were still of perpetual recurrence before and after the publication of this
preface. I cannot likewise but add, that the comparison of such poems of merit, as have been
given to the public within the last ten or twelve
years, with the majority of those produced previously to the appearance of that preface, leave no
doubt on my mind, that Mr. Wordsworth is fully
justified in believing his efforts to have been by
no means ineffectual. Not only in the verses of
those who have professed their admiration of his
genius, but even of those who have distinguished
themselves by hostility to his theory, and depre-
ciation of his writings, are the impressions of his
principles plainly visible. It is possible that with
these principles others may have been blended,
which are not equally evident; and some which

are unsteady and subvertible from the narrowness or imperfection of their basis. But it is more
than possible that these errors of defect or exaggeration, by kindling and feeding the controversy, may have conduced not only to the wider
propagation of the accompanying truths, but
that, by their frequent presentation to the mind
in an excited state, they may have won for them a
more permanent and practical result. A man will
borrow a part from his opponent the more easily,
if he feels himself justified in continuing to reject
a part. While there remain important points in
which he can still feel himself in the right, in
which he still finds firm footing for continued resistance, he will gradually adopt those opinions,
which were the least remote from his own convictions, as not less congruous with his own theory
than with that which he reprobates. In like manner with a kind of instinctive prudence, he will
abandon by little and little his weakest posts, till
at length he seems to forget that they had ever
belonged to him, or affects to consider them at
most as accidental and 'petty annexments,' the
removal of which leaves the citadel unhurt and
unendangered.

My own differences from certain supposed
parts of Mr. Wordsworth's theory ground themselves on the assumption that his words had been
rightly interpreted, as purporting that the proper
diction for poetry in general consists altogether
in a language taken, with due exceptions, from
the mouths of men in real life, a language which
actually constitutes the natural conversation of
men under the influence of natural feelings. My
objection is, first, that in *any* sense this rule is applicable only to *certain* classes of poetry; secondly, that even to these classes it is not applicable, except in such a sense, as hath never by
any one (as far as I know or have read) been denied or doubted; and lastly, that as far as, and in
that degree in which it is *practicable*, yet, as a *rule*,
it is useless, if not injurious, and therefore either
need not or ought not to be practised. The poet
informs his reader that he had generally chosen
low and rustic life; but not *as* low and rustic, or in
order to repeat that pleasure of doubtful moral
effect, which persons of elevated rank and of superior refinement oftentimes derive from a happy
imitation of the rude unpolished manners and
discourse of their inferiors. For the pleasure so
derived may be traced to three exciting causes.
The first is the naturalness, in *fact*, of the things
represented. The second is the apparent naturalness of the *representation*, as raised and qualified
by an imperceptible infusion of the author's own

knowledge and talent, which infusion does, indeed, constitute it an *imitation* as distinguished from a mere *copy*. The third cause may be found in the reader's conscious feeling of his superiority, awakened by the contrast presented to him; even as for the same purpose the kings and great barons of yore retained sometimes *actual* clowns and fools, but more frequently shrewd and witty fellows in that *character*. These, however, were not Mr. Wordsworth's objects. *He* chose low and rustic life, 'because in that condition the essential passions of the heart find a better soil, in which they can attain their maturity, are less under restraint, and speak a plainer and more emphatic language; because in that condition of life our elementary feelings coexist in a state of greater simplicity, and consequently may be more accurately contemplated, and more forcibly communicated; because the manners of rural life germinate from those elementary feelings; and from the necessary character of rural occupations are more easily comprehended, and are more durable; and lastly, because in that condition the passions of men are incorporated with the beautiful and permanent forms of nature.'

Now it is clear to me that in the most interesting of the poems, in which the author is more or less dramatic, as *The Brothers, Michael, Ruth, The Mad Mother,* etc., the persons introduced are by no means taken *from low or rustic life* in the common acceptation of those words; and it is not less clear that the sentiments and language, as far as they can be conceived to have been really transferred from the minds and conversation of such persons, are attributable to causes and circumstances not necessarily connected with 'their occupations and abode.' The thoughts, feelings, language, and manners of the shepherd-farmers in the vales of Cumberland and Westmorland, as far as they are actually adopted in those poems, may be accounted for from causes, which will and do produce the same results in *every* state of life, whether in town or country. As the two principal I rank that independence which raises a man above servitude, or daily toil for the profit of others, yet not above the necessity of industry and a frugal simplicity of domestic life; and the accompanying unambitious, but solid and religious, education which has rendered few books familiar but the Bible and the liturgy or hymn book. To this latter cause, indeed, which is so far *accidental* that it is the blessing of particular countries and a particular age, not the product of particular places or employments, the poet owes the show of probability, that his personages might really feel, think, and talk with any tolerable resemblance to his representation. It is an excellent remark of Dr. Henry More's, . . . that 'a man of confined education, but of good parts, by constant reading of the Bible, will naturally form a more winning and commanding rhetoric than those that are learned, the intermixture of tongues and of artificial phrases debasing *their* style.'[7]

It is, moreover, to be considered that to the formation of healthy feelings and a reflecting mind, *negations* involve impediments not less formidable than sophistication and vicious intermixture. I am convinced that for the human soul to prosper in rustic life a certain vantage-ground is prerequisite. It is not every man that is likely to be improved by a country life or by country labours. Education, or original sensibility, or both, must pre-exist, if the changes, forms, and incidents of nature are to prove a sufficient stimulant. And where these are not sufficient, the mind contracts and hardens by want of stimulants; and the man becomes selfish, sensual, gross, and hard-hearted. Let the management of the Poor Laws in Liverpool, Manchester, or Bristol be compared with the ordinary dispensation of the poor rates in agricultural villages, where the *farmers* are the overseers and guardians of the poor. If my own experience have not been particularly unfortunate, as well as that of the many respectable country clergymen with whom I have conversed on the subject, the result would engender more than skepticism concerning the desirable influences of low and rustic life in and for itself. Whatever may be concluded on the other side, from the stronger local attachments and enterprising spirit of the Swiss, and other mountaineers, applies to a particular mode of pastoral life, under forms of property that permit and beget manners truly republican, not to rustic life in general, or to the absence of artificial cultivation. On the contrary, the mountaineers, whose manners have been so often eulogized, are in general better educated and greater readers than men of equal rank elsewhere. But where this is not the case, as among the peasantry of North Wales, the ancient mountains, with all their terrors and all their glories, are pictures to the blind, and music to the deaf.

I should not have entered so much into detail upon this passage, but here seems to be the point to which all the lines of difference converge as to their source and centre. (I mean, as far as, and in whatever respect, my poetic creed *does* differ

7 *Enthusiasmus Triumphatus*, section 35.

from the doctrines promulgated in this preface.) I adopt with full faith the principle of Aristotle, that poetry as poetry is essentially *ideal,* that it avoids and excludes all *accident;* that its apparent individualities of rank, character, or occupation must be *representative* of a class; and that the *persons* of poetry must be clothed with *generic* attributes, with the *common* attributes of the class; not with such as one gifted individual might *possibly* possess, but such as from his situation it is most probable before-hand that he *would* possess. If my premises are right and my deductions legitimate, it follows that there can be no *poetic* medium between the swains of Theocritus and those of an imaginary golden age.

The characters of the vicar and the shepherd-mariner in the poem of *The Brothers,* and that of the shepherd of Greenhead Ghyll in the *Michael,* have all the verisimilitude and representative quality that the purposes of poetry can require. They are persons of a known and abiding class, and their manners and sentiments the natural product of circumstances common to the class. . . . On the other hand, in the poems which are pitched at a lower note, as the *Harry Gill, The Idiot Boy,* the *feelings* are those of human nature in general; though the poet has judiciously laid the *scene* in the country, in order to place *himself* in the vicinity of interesting images, without the necessity of ascribing a sentimental perception of their beauty to the persons of his drama. In *The Idiot Boy,* indeed, the mother's character is not so much a real and native product of a 'situation where the essential passions of the heart find a better soil, in which they can attain their maturity and speak a plainer and more emphatic language,' as it is an impersonation of an instinct abandoned by judgement. Hence the two following charges seem to me not wholly groundless; at least, they are the only plausible objections which I have heard to that fine poem. The one is, that the author has not, in the poem itself, taken sufficient care to preclude from the reader's fancy the disgusting images of *ordinary morbid idiocy,* which yet it was by no means his intention to represent. He has even by the 'burr, burr, burr,' uncounteracted by any preceding description of the boy's beauty, assisted in recalling them. The other is, that the idiocy of the *boy* is so evenly balanced by the folly of the *mother,* as to present to the general reader rather a laughable burlesque on the blindness of anile dotage, than an analytic display of maternal affection in its ordinary workings.

In *The Thorn,* the poet himself acknowledges in a note the necessity of an introductory poem, in which he should have portrayed the character of the person from whom the words of the poem are supposed to proceed: a superstitious man moderately imaginative, of slow faculties and deep feelings, 'a captain of a small trading vessel, for example, who, being past the middle age of life, had retired upon an annuity, or small independent income, to some village or country town of which he was not a native, or in which he had not been accustomed to live. Such men having nothing to do become credulous and talkative from indolence.' But in a poem, still more in a lyric poem (and the Nurse in Shakespeare's *Romeo and Juliet* alone prevents me from extending the remark even to dramatic *poetry,* if indeed the Nurse itself can be deemed altogether a case in point) it is not possible to imitate truly a dull and garrulous discourser, without repeating the effects of dullness and garrulity. However this may be, I dare assert that the parts (and these form the far larger portion of the whole) which might as well or still better have proceeded from the poet's own imagination, and have been spoken in his own character, are those which have given, and which will continue to give, universal delight; and that the passages exclusively appropriate to the supposed narrator, such as the last couplet of the third stanza, the seven last lines of the tenth, and the five following stanzas, with the exception of the four admirable lines at the commencement of the fourteenth, are felt by many unprejudiced and unsophisticated hearts, as sudden and unpleasant sinkings from the height to which the poet had previously lifted them, and to which he again re-elevates both himself and his reader.

If then I am compelled to doubt the theory, by which the choice of *characters* was to be directed, not only *a priori,* from grounds of reason, but both from the few instances in which the poet himself *need* be supposed to have been governed by it, and from the comparative inferiority of those instances; still more must I hesitate in my assent to the sentence which immediately follows the former citation, and which I can neither admit as particular fact, or as general rule. 'The language too of these men is adopted (purified indeed from what appear to be its real defects, from all lasting and rational causes of dislike or disgust) because such men hourly communicate with the best objects from which the best part of language is originally derived; and because, from their rank in society and the sameness and narrow circle of their intercourse, being less under the action of social vanity, they convey their feelings and notions in simple and unelaborated expressions.' To this I reply that a rustic's language, purified from all provincialism and grossness, and so far reconstructed as to be made consistent with the rules of grammar (which are in essence no other than the laws of universal logic, applied to psychological materials) will not differ from the language of any other man of common sense, however learned or refined he may be, except as far as the notions, which the rustic has to convey, are fewer and more indiscriminate. This will become still clearer, if we add the consideration (equally important though less obvious) that the rustic, from the more imperfect development of his faculties, and from the lower state of their cultivation, aims almost solely to convey *insulated facts,* either those of his scanty experience or his traditional belief; while the educated man chiefly seeks to discover and express those *connexions* of things, or those relative *bearings* of fact to fact, from which some more or less general law is deducible. For *facts* are valuable to a wise man, chiefly as they lead to the discovery of the indwelling *law,* which is the true *being* of things, the sole solution of their modes of existence, and in the knowledge of which consists our dignity and our power.

As little can I agree with the assertion that from the objects with which the rustic hourly communicates, the best part of language is formed. For first, if to communicate with an object implies such an acquaintance with it as renders it capable of being discriminately reflected on, the distinct knowledge of an uneducated rustic would furnish a very scanty vocabulary. The few things and modes of action requisite for his bodily conveniences would alone be individualized; while all the rest of nature would be expressed by a small number of confused general terms. Secondly, I deny that the words and combinations of words derived from the objects with which the rustic is familiar, whether with distinct or confused knowledge, can be justly said to form the *best* part of language. It is more than probable that many classes of the brute creation possess discriminating sounds, by which they can convey to each other notices of such objects as concern their food, shelter, or safety. Yet we hesitate to call the aggregate of such sounds a language, otherwise than metaphorically. The best part of human language, properly so called, is derived from reflection on the acts of the mind itself. It is formed by a voluntary appropriation of fixed symbols to internal acts, to processes and

results of imagination, the greater part of which have no place in the consciousness of uneducated man; though in civilized society, by imitation and passive remembrance of what they hear from their religious instructors and other superiors, the most uneducated share in the harvest which they neither sowed [n]or reaped. If the history of the phrases in hourly currency among our peasants were traced, a person not previously aware of the fact would be surprised at finding so large a number which three or four centuries ago were the exclusive property of the universities and the schools, and at the commencement of the Reformation had been transferred from the school to the pulpit, and thus gradually passed into common life. The extreme difficulty, and often the impossibility, of finding words for the simplest moral and intellectual processes of the languages of uncivilized tribes has proved perhaps the weightiest obstacle to the progress of our most zealous and adroit missionaries. Yet these tribes are surrounded by the same nature as our peasants are, but in still more impressive forms; and they are, moreover, obliged to *particularize* many more of them. When, therefore, Mr. Wordsworth adds, 'accordingly, such a language' (meaning, as before, the language of rustic life purified from provincialism) 'arising out of repeated experience and regular feelings, is a more permanent, and a far more philosophical language, than that which is frequently substituted for it by poets, who think they are conferring honour upon themselves and their art in proportion as they indulge in arbitrary and capricious habits of expression,' it may be answered that the language which he has in view can be attributed to rustics with no greater right than the style of Hooker or Bacon to Tom Brown[8] or Sir Roger L'Estrange.[9] Doubtless, if what is peculiar to each were omitted in each, the result must needs be the same. Further, that the poet who uses an illogical diction, or a style fitted to excite only the low and changeable pleasure of wonder by means of groundless novelty, substitutes a language of *folly* and *vanity,* not for that of the *rustic,* but for that of *good sense* and *natural feeling.*

Here let me be permitted to remind the reader that the positions which I controvert are contained in the sentences—'a *selection of the real language of men';*—'the *language of these men'* (i.e. men in low and rustic life) '*I propose to my-*

8 a pamphleteer and satirist, 1663–1704, who produced worthless imitations of the ancients.
9 a journalist, 1616–1704, whose writings were noted for their scurrility.

self to imitate, and, as far as is possible, to adopt the very language of men.' 'Between the language of prose and that of metrical composition, there neither is, nor can be, any essential difference.' It is against these exclusively that my opposition is directed.

I object, in the very first instance, to an equivocation in the use of the word 'real.' Every man's language varies according to the extent of his knowledge, the activity of his faculties, and the depth or quickness of his feelings. Every man's language has, first, its *individualities;* secondly, the common properties of the *class* to which he belongs; and thirdly, words and phrases of *universal* use. The language of Hooker, Bacon, Bishop Taylor, and Burke differs from the common language of the learned class only by the superior number and novelty of the thoughts and relations which they had to convey. The language of Algernon Sidney[10] differs not at all from that which every well-educated gentleman would wish to write, and (with due allowances for the undeliberateness, and less connected train, of thinking natural and proper to conversation), such as he would wish to talk. Neither one nor the other differ half so much from the general language of cultivated society, as the language of Mr. Wordsworth's homeliest composition differs from that of a common peasant. For 'real,' therefore, we must substitute *ordinary,* or *lingua communis.* And this, we have proved, is no more to be found in the phraseology of low and rustic life than in that of any other class. Omit the peculiarities of each, and the result of course must be common to all. And assuredly the omissions and changes to be made in the language of rustics, before it could be transferred to any species of poem, except the drama or other professed imitation, are at least as numerous and weighty as would be required in adapting to the same purpose the ordinary language of tradesmen and manufacturers. Not to mention that the language so highly extolled by Mr. Wordsworth varies in every county, nay, in every village, according to the accidental character of the clergyman, the existence or non-existence of schools; or even, perhaps, as the exciseman, publican, or barber happen to be, or not to be, zealous politicians and readers of the weekly newspaper *pro bono publico.* Anterior to cultivation, the *lingua communis* of every country, as Dante has well observed, exists everywhere in parts, and nowhere as a whole.

Neither is the case rendered at all more tenable by the addition of the words, *in a state of excitement.* For the nature of a man's words, where he is strongly affected by joy, grief, or anger, must necessarily depend on the number and quality of the general truths, conceptions, and images, and of the words expressing them, with which his mind had been previously stored. For the property of passion is not to *create,* but to set in increased activity. At least, whatever new connexions of thoughts or images, or (which is equally, if not more than equally, the appropriate effect of strong excitement) whatever generalizations of truth or experience the heat of passion may produce, yet the terms of their conveyance must have pre-existed in his former conversations, and are only collected and crowded together by the unusual stimulation. It is indeed very possible to adopt in a poem the unmeaning repetitions, habitual phrases, and other blank counters, which an unfurnished or confused understanding interposes at short intervals, in order to keep hold of his subject, which is still slipping from him, and to give him time for recollection; or, in mere aid of vacancy, as in the scanty companies of a country stage the same player pops backwards and forwards, in order to prevent the appearance of empty spaces, in the procession of *Macbeth,* or *Henry VIII.* But what assistance to the poet, or ornament to the poem, these can supply, I am at a loss to conjecture. Nothing assuredly can differ either in origin or in mode more widely from the *apparent* tautologies of intense and turbulent feeling, in which the passion is greater and of longer endurance than to be exhausted or satisfied by a single representation of the image or incident exciting it. Such repetitions I admit to be a beauty of the highest kind, as illustrated by Mr. Wordsworth himself from the song of Deborah. *'At her feet he bowed, he fell, he lay down: at her feet he bowed, he fell: where he bowed, there he fell down dead.'*[11]

From CHAPTER XVIII

Language of metrical composition, why and wherein essentially different from that of prose. . . .

I conclude, therefore, that the attempt is impracticable; and that, were it not impracticable, it would still be useless. For the very power of making the selection implies the previous possession of the language selected. Or where can the poet have lived? And by what rules could he direct his choice, which would not have enabled

---

10 English politician and patriot, 1622–83, the grandnephew of Sir Philip Sidney.

11 Judges, V, 27.

him to select and arrange his words by the light of his own judgement? We do not adopt the language of a class by the mere adoption of such words exclusively as that class would use, or at least understand; but likewise by following the *order* in which the words of such men are wont to succeed each other. Now this order, in the intercourse of uneducated men, is distinguished from the diction of their superiors in knowledge and power, by the greater *disjunction* and *separation* in the component parts of that, whatever it be, which they wish to communicate. There is a want of that prospectiveness of mind, that *surview*, which enables a man to foresee the whole of what he is to convey, appertaining to any one point; and by this means so to subordinate and arrange the different parts according to their relative importance, as to convey it at once, and as an organized whole.

Now I will take the first stanza, on which I have chanced to open, in the *Lyrical Ballads*. It is one of the most simple and the least peculiar in its language:

In distant countries have I been,
And yet I have not often seen
A healthy man, a man full grown,
Weep in the public roads, alone.
But such a one, on English ground,
And in the broad highway, I met;
Along the broad highway he came,
His cheeks with tears were wet:
Sturdy he seemed, though he was sad;
And in his arms a Lamb he had.[12]

The words here are doubtless such as are current in all ranks of life; and of course not less so in the hamlet and cottage than in the shop, manufactory, college, or palace. But is this the *order*, in which the rustic would have placed the words? I am grievously deceived, if the following less *compact* mode of commencing the same tale be not a far more faithful copy. 'I have been in a many parts, far and near, and I don't know that I ever saw before a man crying by himself in the public road; a grown man I mean, that was neither sick nor hurt,' etc., etc. But when I turn to the following stanza in *The Thorn:*

At all times of the day and night
This wretched Woman thither goes;
And she is known to every star,
And every wind that blows:
And there, beside the Thorn, she sits,
When the blue day-light's in the skies;

And when the whirlwind's on the hill,
Or frosty air is keen and still;
And to herself she cries
'Oh misery! Oh misery!
Oh woe is me! Oh misery!'

and compare this with the language of ordinary men, or with that which I can conceive at all likely to proceed, in *real* life, from *such* a narrator as is supposed in the note to the poem—compare it either in the succession of the images or of the sentences—I am reminded of the sublime prayer and hymn of praise which Milton, in opposition to an established liturgy, presents as a fair *specimen* of common extemporary devotion, and such as we might expect to hear from every self-inspired minister of a conventicle! And I reflect with delight, how little a mere theory, though of his own workmanship, interferes with the processes of genuine imagination in a man of true poetic genius, who possesses, as Mr. Wordsworth, if ever man did, most assuredly does possess,

The Vision and the Faculty divine.[13]

One point then alone remains, but that the most important; its examination having been, indeed, my chief inducement for the preceding inquisition. '*There neither is* [n]*or can be any essential difference between the language of prose and metrical composition.*' Such is Mr. Wordsworth's assertion. Now prose itself, at least in all argumentative and consecutive works, differs, and ought to differ, from the language of conversation; even as reading ought to differ from talking. Unless, therefore, the difference denied be that of the mere *words*, as materials common to all styles of writing, and not of the *style* itself in the universally admitted sense of the term, it might be naturally presumed that there must exist a still greater between the ordonnance of poetic composition and that of prose, than is expected to distinguish prose from ordinary conversation. . . .

The question is not, whether there may not occur in prose an order of words which would be equally proper in a poem, nor whether there are not beautiful lines and sentences of frequent occurrence in good poems, which would be equally becoming as well as beautiful in good prose; for neither the one nor the other has ever been either denied or doubted by anyone. The true question must be, whether there are not

---

12 *The Last of the Flock*, first stanza.

13 *The Excursion*, I, 79.

modes of expression, a *construction,* and an *order* of sentences, which are in their fit and natural place in a serious prose composition, but would be disproportionate and heterogeneous in metrical poetry; and, vice versa, whether in the language of a serious poem there may not be an arrangement both of words and sentences, and a use and selection of (what are called) *figures of speech,* both as to their kind, their frequency, and their occasions, which on a subject of equal weight would be vicious and alien in correct and manly prose. I contend that in both cases this unfitness of each for the place of the other frequently will and ought to exist.

From CHAPTER XXII

The characteristic defects of Wordsworth's poetry, with the principles from which the judgement, that they are defects, is deduced—Their proportion to the beauties —For the greatest part characteristic of his theory only.

If Mr. Wordsworth has set forth principles of poetry which his arguments are insufficient to support, let him and those who have adopted his sentiments be set right by the confutation of these arguments, and by the substitution of more philosophical principles. And still let the due credit be given to the portion and importance of the truths which are blended with his theory; truths, the too exclusive attention to which had occasioned its errors by tempting him to carry those truths beyond their proper limits. If his mistaken theory have at all influenced his poetic compositions, let the effects be pointed out, and the instances given. But let it likewise be shown, how far the influence has acted; whether diffusively, or only by starts; whether the number and importance of the poems and passages thus infected be great or trifling compared with the sound portion; and lastly, whether they are inwoven into the texture of his works, or are loose and separable. The result of such a trial would evince beyond a doubt, what it is high time to announce decisively and aloud, that the *supposed* characteristics of Mr. Wordsworth's poetry, whether admired or reprobated; whether they are simplicity or simpleness; faithful adherence to essential nature, or wilful selections from human nature of its meanest forms and under the least attractive associations; are as little the *real* characteristics of his poetry at large, as of his genius and the constitution of his mind.

In a comparatively small number of poems, he chose to try an experiment; and this experiment we will suppose to have failed. Yet even in these poems it is impossible not to perceive that the natural tendency of the poet's mind is to great objects and elevated conceptions. The poem entitled *Fidelity* is for the greater part written in language as unraised and naked as any perhaps in the two volumes. Yet take the following stanza and compare it with the preceding stanzas of the same poem.

> There sometimes doth a leaping fish
> Send through the tarn a lonely cheer;
> The crags repeat the raven's croak,
> In symphony austere;
> Thither the rainbow comes—the cloud—
> And mists that spread the flying shroud;
> And sun-beams; and the sounding blast,
> That, if it could, would hurry past;
> But that enormous barrier holds it fast.

Or compare the four last lines of the concluding stanza with the former half.

> Yes, proof was plain that, since the day
> On which the Traveller thus had died,
> The Dog had watched about the spot,
> Or by his master's side:
> *How nourished there through such long time*
> *He knows, who gave that love sublime,*
> *And gave that strength of feeling, great*
> *Above all human estimate!*

Can any candid and intelligent mind hesitate in determining which of these best represents the tendency and native character of the poet's genius? Will he not decide that the one was written because the poet *would* so write, and the other because he could not so entirely repress the force and grandeur of his mind, but that he must in some part or other of every composition write otherwise? In short, that his only disease is the being out of his element; like the swan, that, having amused himself, for a while, with crushing the weeds on the river's bank, soon returns to his own majestic movements on its reflecting and sustaining surface. Let it be observed that I am here supposing the imagined judge, to whom I appeal, to have already decided against the poet's theory, as far as it is different from the principles of the art, generally acknowledged.

I cannot here enter into a detailed examination of Mr. Wordsworth's works; but I will attempt to give the main results of my own judgement, after an acquaintance of many years, and repeated perusals. And though to appreciate the defects of a great mind it is necessary to understand previously its characteristic excellences, yet I have already expressed myself with sufficient fulness to preclude most of the ill effects that might arise from my pursuing a contrary arrangement. I will therefore commence with what I deem the prominent *defects* of his poems hitherto published.

The first characteristic, though only occasional defect, which I appear to myself to find in these poems is the *inconstancy* of the style. Under this name I refer to the sudden and unprepared transitions from lines or sentences of peculiar felicity (at all events striking and original) to a style, not only unimpassioned but undistinguished. He sinks too often and too abruptly to that style which I should place in the second division of language, dividing it into the three species; first, that which is peculiar to poetry; second, that which is only proper in prose; and third, the neutral or common to both. There have been works, such as Cowley's *Essay on Cromwell,* in which prose and verse are intermixed (not as in the *Consolation* of Boetius,[14] or the *Argenis* of Barclay,[15] by the insertion of poems supposed to have been spoken or composed on occasions previously related in prose, but) the poet passing from one to the other, as the nature of the thoughts or his own feelings dictated. Yet this mode of composition does not satisfy a cultivated taste. There is something unpleasant in the being thus obliged to alternate states of feeling so dissimilar, and this too in a species of writing, the pleasure from which is in part derived from the preparation and previous expectation of the reader. A portion of that awkwardness is felt which hangs upon the introduction of songs in our modern comic operas; and to prevent which the judicious Metastasio[16] (as to whose exquisite taste there can be no hesitation, whatever doubts may be entertained as to his poetic genius) uniformly placed the *aria* at the end of the scene, at the same time that he almost always raises and impassions the style of the recitative immediately preceding. Even in real life, the difference is great and evident between words used as the arbitrary marks of thought, our smooth market-coin of intercourse, with the image and superscription worn out by currency; and those which convey pictures either borrowed from one outward object to enliven and particularize some other; or used allegorically to body forth the inward state of the person speaking; or such as are at least the exponents of his peculiar turn and unusual extent of faculty. So much so

indeed, that in the social circles of private life we often find a striking use of the latter put a stop to the general flow of conversation, and by the excitement arising from concentered attention produce a sort of damp and interruption for some minutes after. But in the perusal of works of literary art, we prepare ourselves for such language; and the business of the writer, like that of a painter whose subject requires unusual splendour and prominence, is so to raise the lower and neutral tints, that what in a different style would be the commanding colours, are here used as the means of that gentle *degradation* requisite in order to produce the effect of a whole. Where this is not achieved in a poem, the metre merely reminds the reader of his claims in order to disappoint them; and where this defect occurs frequently, his feelings are alternately startled by anticlimax and hyperclimax.

I refer the reader to the exquisite stanzas cited for another purpose from *The Blind Highland Boy;* and then annex, as being in my opinion instances of this *disharmony* in style, the two following:

> And one, the rarest, was a Shell,
> Which he, poor Child, had studied well:
> The Shell of a green Turtle, thin
> And hollow;—you might sit therein,
>   It was so wide, and deep.

> Our Highland Boy oft visited
> The house which held this prize; and, led
> By choice or chance, did thither come
> One day, when no one was at home,
>   And found the door unbarred. . . .

The second defect I can generalize with tolerable accuracy, if the reader will pardon an uncouth and new-coined word. There is, I should say, not seldom a *matter-of-factness* in certain poems. This may be divided into, first, a laborious minuteness and fidelity in the representation of objects, and their positions, as they appeared to the poet himself; secondly, the insertion of accidental circumstances, in order to the full explanation of his living characters, their dispositions and actions, which circumstances might be necessary to establish the probability of a statement in real life, where nothing is taken for granted by the hearer, but appear superfluous in poetry, where the reader is willing to believe for his own sake. To this *accidentality* I object, as contravening the essence of poetry, which Aristotle pronounces to be σπουδαιότατον καὶ φιλοσοφώτατον γένος, the most intense, weighty and philo-

---

14 Roman philosopher of the sixth century of the Christian era.
15 John Barclay, Scottish poet, 1582-1621.
16 Pietro Metastasio, a popular Italian poet of the eighteenth century.

sophical product of human art; adding, as the reason, that it is the most catholic and abstract. The following passage from Davenant's prefatory letter to Hobbes[17] well expresses this truth. 'When I considered the actions which I meant to describe (those inferring the persons), I was again persuaded rather to choose those of a former age, than the present; and in a century so far removed, as might preserve me from their improper examinations,who know not the requisites of a poem, nor how much pleasure they lose (and even the pleasures of heroic poesy are not unprofitable) who take away the liberty of a poet, and fetter his feet in the shackles of an historian. For why should a poet doubt in story to mend the intrigues of fortune by more delightful conveyances of probable fictions, because austere historians have entered into bond to truth? An obligation, which were in poets as foolish and unnecessary, as is the bondage of false martyrs, who lie in chains for a mistaken opinion. *But by this I would imply that truth, narrative and past, is the idol of historians (who worship a dead thing), and truth operative, and by effects continually alive, is the mistress of poets, who hath not her existence in matter, but in reason.*'

For this minute accuracy in the painting of local imagery, the lines in *The Excursion*, pp. 96, 97, and 98,[18] may be taken, if not as a striking instance, yet as an illustration of my meaning. It must be some strong motive (as, for instance, that the description was necessary to the intelligibility of the tale) which could induce me to describe in a number of verses what a draughtsman could present to the eye with incomparably greater satisfaction by half a dozen strokes of his pencil, or the painter with as many touches of his brush. Such descriptions too often occasion in the mind of a reader, who is determined to understand his author, a feeling of labour not very dissimilar to that with which he would construct a diagram, line by line, for a long geometrical proposition. It seems to be like taking the pieces of a dissected map out of its box. We first look at one part, and then at another, then join and dovetail them; and when the successive acts of attention have been completed, there is a retrogressive effort of mind to behold it as a whole. The poet should paint to the imagination, not to the fancy; and I know no happier case to exemplify the distinction between these two faculties. Masterpieces of the former mode of poetic

painting abound in the writings of Milton, for example:

> The fig-tree; not that kind for fruit renown'd,
> But such as at this day, to Indians known,
> In Malabar or Decan spreads her arms
> Branching so broad and long, that in the ground
> The bended twigs take root, *and daughters grow
> About the mother tree, a pillar'd shade
> High over-arch'd and* ECHOING WALKS BETWEEN:
> *There oft the Indian herdsman, shunning heat,
> Shelters in cool, and tends his pasturing herds
> At loopholes cut through thickest shade.*[19]

This is creation rather than painting, or if painting, yet such, and with such co-presence of the whole picture flashed at once upon the eye, as the sun paints in a camera obscura. But the poet must likewise understand and command what Bacon calls the *vestigia communia*[20] of the senses, the latency of all in each, and more especially as by a magical *penna duplex*,[21] the excitement of vision by sound and the exponents of sound. Thus, 'The echoing walks between,' may be almost said to reverse the fable in tradition of the head of Memnon,[22] in the Egyptian statue. Such may be deservedly entitled the *creative words* in the world of imagination.

The second division respects an apparent minute adherence to *matter-of-fact* in character and incidents; *a biographical* attention to probability, and an *anxiety* of explanation and retrospect. Under this head I shall deliver, with no feigned diffidence, the results of my best reflection on the great point of controversy between Mr. Wordsworth and his objectors; namely, on *the choice of his characters*. I have already declared and, I trust, justified, my utter dissent from the mode of argument which his critics have hitherto employed. To *their* question, Why did you choose such a character, or a character from such a rank of life? the poet might, in my opinion, fairly retort: Why with the conception of my character did you make wilful choice of mean or ludicrous associations not furnished by me, but supplied from your own sickly and fastidious feelings? How was it, indeed, probable that such arguments could have any weight with an author whose plan, whose guiding principle, and main object it was to attack and subdue that state of association which leads us to place the

---

17 Sir William Davenant's *Preface before Gondibert. To His much honoured friend, Mr. Hobbes,* 2 January 1650.
18 Book iii. 5off.

19 *Paradise Lost,* ix, 1101ff.
20 'common tracks.'
21 'double wing.'
22 It was fabled that when touched by the rays of the rising sun the statue of Memnon gave forth a sound.

chief value on those things in which man differs from man, and to forget or disregard the high dignities, which belong to human nature, the sense and the feeling, which may be, and ought to be, found in all ranks? The feelings with which, as Christians, we contemplate a mixed congregation rising or kneeling before their common Maker, Mr. Wordsworth would have us entertain at all times, as men, and as readers; and by the excitement of this lofty, yet prideless impartiality in poetry, he might hope to have encouraged its continuance in real life. The praise of good men be his! In real life, and, I trust, even in my imagination, I honour a virtuous and wise man, without reference to the presence or absence of artificial advantages. Whether in the person of an armed baron, a laurelled bard, or of an old pedlar, or still older leech-gatherer, the same qualities of head and heart must claim the same reverence. And even in poetry I am not conscious that I have ever suffered my feelings to be disturbed or offended by any thoughts or images which the poet himself has not presented.

But yet I object, nevertheless, and for the following reasons. First, because the object in view, as an *immediate* object, belongs to the moral philosopher, and would be pursued, not only more appropriately, but in my opinion with far greater probability of success, in sermons or moral essays, than in an elevated poem. It seems, indeed, to destroy the main fundamental distinction, not only between a poem and prose, but even between philosophy and works of fiction, inasmuch as it proposes *truth* for its immediate object, instead of *pleasure*. Now till the blessed time shall come, when truth itself shall be pleasure, and both shall be so united, as to be distinguishable in words only, not in feeling, it will remain the poet's office to proceed upon that state of association, which actually exists as general; instead of attempting first to make it what it ought to be, and then to let the pleasure follow. But here is unfortunately a small *hysteron-proteron.*[23] For the communication of pleasure is the introductory means by which alone the poet must expect to moralize his readers. Secondly: though I were to admit, for a moment, *this* argument to be groundless: yet how is the moral effect to be produced, by merely attaching the name of some low profession to powers which are *least* likely, and to qualities which are assuredly not *more* likely, to be found in it? The poet, speaking in his own person, may at once delight and improve us by sentiments which teach us the independence

of goodness, of wisdom, and even of genius, on the favours of fortune. And having made a due reverence before the throne of Antonine,[24] he may bow with equal awe before Epictetus[25] among his fellow-slaves—

> and rejoice
> In the plain presence of his dignity.[26]

. . . All the admirable passages interposed in this narration [*The Excursion*], might, with trifling alterations, have been far more appropriately, and with far greater verisimilitude, told of a poet in the character of a poet;[27] and without incurring another defect which I shall now mention, and a sufficient illustration of which will have been here anticipated.

Third; an undue predilection for the *dramatic* form in certain poems, from which one or other of two evils result. Either the thoughts and diction are different from that of the poet, and then there arises an incongruity of style; or they are the same and indistinguishable, and then it presents a species of ventriloquism, where two are represented as talking, while in truth one man only speaks.

The fourth class of defects is closely connected with the former; but yet are such as arise likewise from an intensity of feeling disproportionate to such knowledge and value of the objects described, as can be fairly anticipated of men in general, even of the most cultivated classes; and with which therefore few only, and those few particularly circumstanced, can be supposed to sympathize. In this class, I comprise occasional prolixity, repetition, and an eddying, instead of progression, of thought. As instances, see pages 27, 28, and 62 of the Poems, Vol. I., and the first eighty lines of the Sixth Book of *The Excursion*.

Fifth and last; thoughts and images too great for the subject. This is an approximation to what might be called mental bombast, as distinguished from verbal: for, as in the latter there is a disproportion of the expressions to the thoughts, so in this there is a disproportion of thought to the circumstance and occasion. This, by the bye, is a fault of which none but a man of genius is capable. It is the awkwardness and strength of Hercules with the distaff of Omphale.[28]

It is a well-known fact that bright colours in motion both make and leave the strongest im-

---

23 an inversion of the natural order of logic.
24 Roman emperor and stoic philosopher.
25 Greek stoic philosopher born a slave.
26 *The Excursion*, I, 76.
27 Wordsworth cast his leading character in *The Excursion* in the role of a peddler.
28 a queen of Lydia who was Hercules' mistress.

pressions on the eye. Nothing is more likely too, than that a vivid image or visual spectrum, thus originated, may become the link of association in recalling the feelings and images that had accompanied the original impression. But if we describe this in such lines as

> They flash upon that inward eye,
> Which is the bliss of solitude![29]

in what words shall we describe the joy of retrospection, when the images and virtuous actions of a whole well-spent life pass before that conscience which is indeed the *inward* eye: which is indeed *'the bliss of solitude'*? Assuredly we seem to sink most abruptly, not to say burlesquely, and almost as in a medley, from this couplet to—

> And then my heart with pleasure fills,
> And dances with the daffodils. . . .

The last instance of this defect (for I know no other than these already cited) is from the *Ode*, page 351, Vol. II, where, speaking of a child, 'a six years' darling of a pigmy size,' he thus addresses him:

> Thou best Philosopher, who yet dost keep
> Thy heritage! Thou Eye among the blind,
> That, deaf and silent, read'st the eternal deep,
> Haunted forever by the Eternal Mind,—
> Mighty Prophet! Seer blest!
> On whom those truths do rest,
> Which we are toiling all our lives to find!
> Thou, over whom thy Immortality
> Broods like the Day, a Master o'er a Slave,
> A Presence which is not to be put by!

Now here, not to stop at the daring spirit of metaphor which connects the epithets 'deaf and silent,' with the apostrophized *eye*: or (if we are to refer it to the preceding word, 'philosopher') the faulty and equivocal syntax of the passage; and without examining the propriety of making a 'master *brood* o'er a slave,' or 'the *day*' brood *at all;* we will merely ask, What does all this mean? In what sense is a child of that age a *philosopher?* In what sense does he *read* 'the eternal deep'? In what sense is he declared to be *'forever haunted'* by the supreme being? or so inspired as to deserve the splendid titles of a *mighty prophet, a blessed seer*? By reflection? by knowledge? by conscious intuition? or by *any* form or modification of consciousness? These would be tidings indeed; but such as would presuppose an immediate revelation to the inspired communicator, and

29 *I Wandered Lonely as a Cloud.*

require miracles to authenticate his inspiration. Children at this age give us no such information of themselves; and at what time were we dipped in the Lethe, which has produced such utter oblivion of a state so god-like? . . .

To these defects which, as appears by the extracts, are only occasional, I may oppose, with far less fear of encountering the dissent of any candid and intelligent reader, the following (for the most part correspondent) excellences. First, an austere purity of language both grammatically and logically; in short a perfect appropriateness of the words to the meaning. Of how high value I deem this, and how particularly estimable I hold the example at the present day, has been already stated: and in part, too, the reasons on which I ground both the moral and intellectual importance of habituating ourselves to a strict accuracy of expression. It is noticeable how limited an acquaintance with the masterpieces of art will suffice to form a correct and even a sensitive taste, where none but masterpieces have been seen and admired: while, on the other hand, the most correct notions, and the widest acquaintance with the works of excellence of all ages and countries, will not perfectly secure us against the contagious familiarity with the far more numerous offspring of tastelessness or of a perverted taste. If this be the case, as it notoriously is, with the arts of music and painting, much more difficult will it be to avoid the infection of multiplied and daily examples in the practice of an art which uses words, and words only, as its instruments. In poetry, in which every line, every phrase, may pass the ordeal of deliberation and deliberate choice, it is possible, and barely possible, to attain that ultimatum which I have ventured to propose as the infallible test of a blameless style,—its *untranslatableness* in words of the same language without injury to the meaning. Be it observed, however, that I include in the *meaning* of a word not only its correspondent object, but likewise all the associations which it recalls. For language is framed to convey not the object alone, but likewise the character, mood, and intentions of the person who is representing it. In poetry it *is* practicable to preserve the diction uncorrupted by the affectations and misappropriations which promiscuous authorship, and reading not promiscuous only because it is disproportionately most conversant with the compositions of the day, have rendered general. Yet even to the poet, composing in his own province, it is an arduous work: and as the result and pledge of a watchful good sense, of fine and luminous distinction, and of complete self-possession, may justly claim all the honour which belongs to an attainment equally difficult and valuable, and the more valuable for being rare. It is at *all* times the proper food of the understanding; but in an age of corrupt eloquence it is both food and antidote.

In prose I doubt whether it be even possible to preserve our style wholly unalloyed by the vicious phraseology which meets us everywhere, from the sermon to the newspaper, from the harangue of the legislator to the speech from the convivial chair, announcing a *toast* or sentiment. Our chains rattle, even while we are complaining of them. The poems of Boetius rise high in our estimation when we compare them with those of his contemporaries, as Sidonius Apollinarius, &c. They might even be referred to a purer age, but that the prose in which they are set, as jewels in a crown of lead or iron, betrays the true age of the writer. Much however, may be effected by education. I believe not only from grounds of reason, but from having in great measure assured myself of the fact by actual though limited experience, that, to a youth led from his first boyhood to investigate the meaning of every word and the reason of its choice and position, logic presents itself as an old acquaintance under new names.

On some future occasion, more especially demanding such disquisition, I shall attempt to prove the close connection between veracity and habits of mental accuracy; the beneficial aftereffects of verbal precision in the preclusion of fanaticism, which masters the feelings more especially by indistinct watchwords; and to display the advantages which language alone, at least which language with incomparably greater ease and certainty than any other means, presents to the instructor of impressing modes of intellectual energy so constantly, so imperceptibly, and, as it were, by such elements and atoms, as to secure in due time the formation of a second nature. When we reflect that the cultivation of the judgement is a positive command of the moral law, since the reason can give the *principle* alone, and the conscience bears witness only to the *motive,* while the application and effects must depend on the judgement: when we consider that the greater part of our success and comfort in life depends on distinguishing the similar from the same, that which is peculiar in each thing from that which it has in common with others, so as still to select the most probable, instead of the merely possible or positively unfit, we shall learn to value earnestly and with

a practical seriousness a mean, already prepared for us by nature and society, of teaching the young mind to think well and wisely by the same unremembered process and with the same neverforgotten results, as those by which it is taught to speak and converse. Now how much warmer the interest is, how much more genial the feelings of reality and practicability, and thence how much stronger the impulses to imitation are, which a *contemporary* writer, and especially a contemporary *poet,* excites in youth and commencing manhood, has been treated of in the earlier pages of these sketches. I have only to add that all the praise which is due to the exertion of such influence for a purpose so important, joined with that which must be claimed for the infrequency of the same excellence in the same perfection, belongs in full right to Mr. Wordsworth. I am far, however, from denying that we have poets whose *general* style possesses the same excellence, as Mr. Moore, Lord Byron, Mr. Bowles, and, in all his later and more important works, our laurel-honouring Laureate.[30] But there are none in whose works I do not appear to myself to find *more* exceptions than in those of Wordsworth. Quotations or specimens would here be wholly out of place, and must be left for the critic who doubts and would invalidate the justice of this eulogy so applied.

The second characteristic excellence of Mr. W[ordsworth]'s work is: a correspondent weight and sanity of the thoughts and sentiments, won, not from books, but from the poet's own meditative observation. They are *fresh* and have the dew upon them. His muse, at least when in her strength of wing, and when she hovers aloft in her proper element,

> Makes audible a linkèd lay of truth,
> Of truth profound a sweet continuous lay,
> Not learnt, but native, her own natural notes![31]
>
> S. T. C.

Even throughout his smaller poems there is scarcely one which is not rendered valuable by some just and original reflection. . . .

Both in respect of this and of the former excellence, Mr. Wordsworth strikingly resembles Samuel Daniel, one of the golden writers of our golden Elizabethan age, now most causelessly neglected: Samuel Daniel, whose diction bears no mark of time, no distinction of age, which has been, and as long as our language shall last, will be so far the language of the today and for-

---

30 Southey.
31 Coleridge's *To William Wordsworth,* 58–60.

ever, as that it is more intelligible to us than the transitory fashions of our own particular age. A similar praise is due to his sentiments. No frequency of perusal can deprive them of their freshness. For though they are brought into the full daylight of every reader's comprehension, yet are they drawn up from depths which few in any age are privileged to visit, into which few in any age have courage or inclination to descend. If Mr. Wordsworth is not equally with Daniel alike intelligible to all readers of average understanding in all passages of his works, the comparative difficulty does not arise from the greater impurity of the ore, but from the nature and uses of the metal. A poem is not necessarily obscure because it does not aim to be popular. It is enough if a work be perspicuous to those for whom it is written, and

> Fit audience find, though few.

To the *Ode on the Intimation[s] of Immortality from Recollections of Early Childhood* the poet might have prefixed the lines which Dante addresses to one of his own Canzoni—

> Canzon, io credo, che saranno radi
> Che tua ragione intendan bene,
> Tanto lor sei faticoso ed alto.

> O lyric song, there will be few, think I,
> Who may thy import understand aright:
> Thou art for *them* so arduous and so high!

But the ode was intended for such readers only as had been accustomed to watch the flux and reflux of their inmost nature, to venture at times into the twilight realms of consciousness, and to feel a deep interest in modes of inmost being, to which they know that the attributes of time and space are inapplicable and alien, but which yet can not be conveyed, save in symbols of time and space. For such readers the sense is sufficiently plain, and they will be as little disposed to charge Mr. Wordsworth with believing the Platonic pre-existence, in the ordinary interpretation of the words, as I am to believe that Plato himself ever meant or taught it. . . .

Third (and wherein he soars far above Daniel), the sinewy strength and originality of single lines and paragraphs: the frequent *curiosa felicitas* of his diction, of which I need not here give specimens, having anticipated them in a preceding page. This beauty, and as eminently characteristic of Wordsworth's poetry, his rudest assailants have felt themselves compelled to acknowledge and admire.

Fourth, the perfect truth of nature in his images and descriptions, as taken immediately from nature, and proving a long and genial intimacy with the very spirit which gives the physiognomic expression to all the works of nature. Like a green field reflected in a calm and perfectly transparent lake, the image is distinguished from the reality only by its greater softness and lustre. Like the moisture or the polish on a pebble, genius neither distorts nor false-colours its objects; but on the contrary brings out many a vein and many a tint, which escapes the eye of common observation, thus raising to the rank of gems what had been often kicked away by the hurrying foot of the traveller on the dusty high road of custom. . . .

Fifth, a meditative pathos, a union of deep and subtle thought with sensibility; a sympathy with man as a man; the sympathy indeed of a contemplator, rather than a fellow-sufferer or co-mate (*spectator, haud particeps*),[32] but of a contemplator, from whose view no difference of rank conceals the sameness of the nature; no injuries of wind or weather, or toil, or even of ignorance, wholly disguise the human face divine. The superscription and the image of the Creator still remain legible to *him* under the dark lines with which guilt or calamity had cancelled or cross-barred it. Here the man and the poet lose and find themselves in each other, the one as glorified, the latter as substantiated. In this mild and philosophic pathos, Wordsworth appears to be without a compeer. Such as he *is:* so he *writes*. . . .

Last, and pre-eminently, I challenge for this poet the gift of Imagination in the highest and strictest sense of the word. In the play of *fancy*, Wordsworth, to my feelings, is not always graceful, and sometimes *recondite*. The *likeness* is occasionally too strange, or demands too peculiar a point of view, or is such as appears the creature of predetermined research, rather than spontaneous presentation. Indeed, his fancy seldom displays itself as mere and unmodified fancy. But in imaginative power he stands nearest of all modern writers to Shakespeare and Milton; and yet in a kind perfectly unborrowed and his own. To employ his own words, which are at once an instance and an illustration, he does indeed to all thoughts and to all objects—

> add the gleam,
> The light that never was, on sea or land,
> The consecration, and the poet's dream. . . .[33]

---

32 'an observer, not a partaker.'
33 *Elegiac Stanzas Suggested by a Picture of Peele Castle*, 14–16.

The following analogy will, I am apprehensive, appear dim and fantastic, but in reading Bartram's *Travels* I could not help transcribing the following lines as a sort of allegory, or connected simile and metaphor of Wordsworth's intellect and genius.—'The soil is a deep, rich, dark mould, on a deep stratum of tenacious clay; and that on a foundation of rocks, which often break through both strata, lifting their back above the surface. The trees which chiefly grow here are the gigantic black oak, magnolia magniflora, fraximus excelsior, platane, and a few stately tulip trees.' What Mr. Wordsworth *will* produce, it is not for me to prophesy: but I could pronounce with the liveliest convictions what he is capable of producing. It is the FIRST GENUINE PHILOSOPHIC POEM.

1815–16 1817

From SHAKESPEAREAN CRITICISM

[Coleridge did not publish his lectures on Shakespeare. However, after his death they were edited by H. N. Coleridge and appeared as *Literary Remains* (1840). An authoritative and accurate text has been prepared from contemporary shorthand reports of Coleridge's oral lectures, and from his MSS. and notebooks by T. M. Raysor in *Coleridge's Shakespearean Criticism* (1930). Excerpts are reprinted from this text by permission of the Harvard University Press.]

HAMLET

WE will now pass to *Hamlet* in order to obviate some of the general prejudices against the author, in reference to the character of the hero. Much has been objected to, which ought to have been praised, and many beauties of the highest kind have been neglected, because they are somewhat hidden.

The first question we should ask ourselves is—What did Shakespeare mean when he drew the character of Hamlet? He never wrote any thing without design, and what was his design when he sat down to produce this tragedy? My belief is, that he always regarded his story, before he began to write, much in the same light as a painter regards his canvas, before he begins to paint—as a mere vehicle for his thoughts—as the ground upon which he was to work. What then was the point to which Shakespeare directed himself in Hamlet? He intended to portray a person, in whose view the external world, and all its incidents and objects, were comparatively dim, and of no interest in themselves, and which began to interest only, when they were reflected in the mirror of his mind. Hamlet beheld external things in the same way that a man of vivid imagination, who shuts his eyes, sees what has previously made an impression on his organs.

The poet places him in the most stimulating circumstances that a human being can be placed in. He is the heir apparent of a throne; his father dies suspiciously; his mother excludes her son from his throne by marrying his uncle. This is not enough; but the Ghost of the murdered father is introduced, to assure the son that he was put to death by his own brother. What is the effect upon the son?—instant action and pursuit of revenge? No: endless reasoning and hesitating—constant urging and solicitation of the mind to act, and as constant an escape from action; ceaseless reproaches of himself for sloth and negligence, while the whole energy of his resolution evaporates in these reproaches. This, too, not from cowardice, for he is drawn as one of the bravest of his time—not from want of forethought or slowness of apprehension, for he sees through the very souls of all who surround him, but merely from that aversion to action, which prevails among such as have a world in themselves.

How admirable, too, is the judgement of the poet! Hamlet's own disordered fancy has not conjured up the spirit of his father; it has been seen by others: he is prepared by them to witness its re-appearance, and when he does see it, Hamlet is not brought forward as having long brooded on the subject. The moment before the Ghost enters, Hamlet speaks of other matters: he mentions the coldness of the night, and observes that he has not heard the clock strike, adding, in reference to the custom of drinking, that it is

More honour'd in the breach than the
  observance.[1]

Owing to the tranquil state of his mind, he indulges in some moral reflections. Afterwards, the Ghost suddenly enters.

Hor.   Look, my lord! it comes.
Ham. Angels and ministers of grace defend us![2]

The same thing occurs in *Macbeth*: in the dagger-scene, the moment before the hero sees it, he has his mind applied to some indifferent matters; 'Go, tell thy mistress,' etc. Thus, in both cases, the preternatural appearance has all the effect of abruptness, and the reader is totally divested of the notion, that the figure is a vision of a highly wrought imagination.

Here Shakespeare adapts himself so admirably

---

[1] I, iv, 16.
[2] I, iv, 38–9.

to the situation—in other words, so puts himself into it—that, though poetry, his language is the very language of nature. No terms, associated with such feelings, can occur to us so proper as those which he has employed, especially on the highest, the most august, and the most awful subjects that can interest a human being in this sentient world. That this is no mere fancy, I can undertake to establish from hundreds, I might say thousands, of passages. No character he has drawn, in the whole list of his plays, could so well and fitly express himself as in the language Shakespeare has put into his mouth.

There is no indecision about Hamlet, as far as his own sense of duty is concerned; he knows well what he ought to do, and over and over again he makes up his mind to do it. The moment the players, and the two spies set upon him, have withdrawn, of whom he takes leave with a line so expressive of his contempt,

Ay so; good-bye you.—Now I am alone,[3]

he breaks out into a delirium of rage against himself for neglecting to perform the solemn duty he had undertaken, and contrasts the factitious and artificial display of feeling by the player with his own apparent indifference;

What's Hecuba to him, or he to Hecuba,
That he should weep for her?[4]

Yet the player did weep for her, and was in an agony of grief at her sufferings, while Hamlet is unable to rouse himself to action, in order that he may perform the command of his father, who had come from the grave to incite him to revenge:—

     This is most brave!
That I, the son of a dear father murder'd,
Prompted to my revenge by heaven and hell,
Must, like a whore, unpack my heart with words,
And fall a cursing like a very drab,
A scullion.[5]

It is the same feeling, the same conviction of what is his duty, that makes Hamlet exclaim in a subsequent part of the tragedy:

How all occasions do inform against me,
And spur my dull revenge! What is a man,
If his chief good, and market of his time,
Be but to sleep and feed? A beast, no more. . . .
   . . . I do not know
Why yet I live to say—'this thing's to do,'

Sith I have cause and will and strength
  and means
To do't.[6]

Yet with all this strong conviction of duty, and with all this resolution arising out of strong conviction, nothing is done. This admirable and consistent character, deeply acquainted with his own feelings, painting them with such wonderful power and accuracy, and firmly persuaded that a moment ought not to be lost in executing the solemn charge committed to him, still yields to the same retiring from reality, which is the result of having, what we express by the terms, a world within himself.

Such a mind as Hamlet's is near akin to madness. Dryden has somewhere said,

Great wit to madness nearly is allied,[7]

and he was right; for he means by 'wit' that greatness of genius, which led Hamlet to a perfect knowledge of his own character, which, with all strength of motive, was so weak as to be unable to carry into act his own most obvious duty.

With all this he has a sense of imperfectness, which becomes apparent when he is moralising on the skull in the churchyard. Something is wanting to his completeness—something is deficient which remains to be supplied, and he is therefore described as attached to Ophelia. His madness is assumed, when he finds that witnesses have been placed behind the arras to listen to what passes, and when the heroine has been thrown in his way as a decoy.

Another objection has been taken by Dr. Johnson, and Shakespeare has been taxed very severely. I refer to the scene where Hamlet enters and finds his uncle praying, and refuses to take his life, excepting when he is in the height of his iniquity. To assail him at such a moment of confession and repentance, Hamlet declares,

Why, this is hire and salary, not revenge.[8]

He therefore forbears, and postpones his uncle's death, until he can catch him in some act

That has no relish of salvation in't.[9]

This conduct, and this sentiment, Dr. Johnson has pronounced to be so atrocious and horrible, as to be unfit to be put into the mouth of a human being. The fact, however, is that Dr. Johnson did not understand the character of

---

3 II, ii, 575.
4 II, ii, 585.
5 II, ii, 610–15.

6 IV, iv, 32–5, 43–5.
7 'Great wits are sure to madness near allied.'—*Absolom and Achitophel*, 163.
8 III, iii, 79.
9 III, iii, 92.

Hamlet, and censured accordingly: the determination to allow the guilty King to escape at such a moment is only part of the indecision and irresoluteness of the hero. Hamlet seizes hold of a pretext for not acting, when he might have acted so instantly and effectually: therefore, he again defers the revenge he was bound to seek, and declares his determination to accomplish it at some time,

> When he is drunk, asleep, or in his rage,
> Or in th' incestuous pleasures of his bed.[10]

This, allow me to impress upon you most emphatically, was merely the excuse Hamlet made to himself for not taking advantage of this particular and favourable moment for doing justice upon his guilty uncle, at the urgent instance of the spirit of his father.

Dr. Johnson farther states, that in the voyage to England, Shakespeare merely follows the novel as he found it, as if the poet had no other reason for adhering to his original; but Shakespeare never followed a novel, because he found such and such an incident in it, but because he saw that the story, as he read it, contributed to enforce, or to explain some great truth inherent in human nature. He never could lack invention to alter or improve a popular narrative; but he did not wantonly vary from it, when he knew that, as it was related, it would so well apply to his own great purpose. He saw at once how consistent it was with the character of Hamlet, that after still resolving, and still deferring, still determining to execute, and still postponing execution, he should finally, in the infirmity of his disposition, give himself up to his destiny, and hopelessly place himself in the power, and at the mercy of his enemies.

Even after the scene with Osrick, we see Hamlet still indulging in reflection, and hardly thinking of the task he has just undertaken: he is all dispatch and resolution, as far as words and present intentions are concerned, but all hesitation and irresolution, when called upon to carry his words and intentions into effect; so that, resolving to do everything, he does nothing. He is full of purpose, but void of that quality of mind which accomplishes purpose.

Anything finer than this conception, and working out of a great character, is merely impossible. Shakespeare wished to impress upon us the truth, that action is the chief end of existence—that no faculties of intellect, however brilliant, can be considered valuable, or indeed otherwise than as misfortunes, if they withdraw us from, or render us repugnant to action, and lead us to think and think of doing, until the time has elapsed when we can do anything effectually.

In enforcing this moral truth, Shakespeare has shown the fullness and force of his powers: all that is amiable and excellent in nature is combined in Hamlet, with the exception of one quality. He is a man living in meditation, called upon to act by every motive human and divine, but the great object of his life is defeated by continually resolving to do, yet doing nothing but resolve.

SHAKESPEARE'S JUDGEMENT EQUAL TO HIS GENIUS

Shakespeare appears, from his poems alone, apart from his great works, to have possessed all the conditions of a true poet, and by this proof to do away, as far as may [be] in my power, the popular notion that he was a great dramatist by a sort of instinct, immortal in his own despite, and sinking below men of second or third-rate character when he attempted aught beside the drama—even as bees construct their cells and manufacture their honey to admirable perfection, but would in vain attempt to build a nest. Now this mode of reconciling a compelled sense of inferiority with a feeling of pride, began in a few pedants, who having read that Sophocles was the great model of tragedy, and Aristotle the infallible dictator, and finding that the *Lear, Hamlet, Othello,* and the rest, were neither in imitation of Sophocles, nor in obedience to Aristotle—and not having (with one or two exceptions) the courage to affirm that the delight which their country received from generation to generation, in defiance of the alterations of circumstances and habits, was wholly groundless—it was a happy medium and refuge, to talk of Shakespeare as a sort of beautiful *lusus naturae*,[11] a delightful monster, —wild, indeed, without taste or judgement, but like the inspired idiots so much venerated in the East, uttering, amid the strangest follies, the sublimest truths. In nine places out of ten in which I find his awful name mentioned, it is with some epithet of 'wild,' 'irregular,' 'pure child of nature,' etc., etc., etc. If all this be true, we must submit to it; though to a thinking mind it cannot but be painful to find any excellence, merely human, thrown out of all human analogy, and thereby leaving us neither rules for imitation, nor motives to imitate. But if false, it is a dangerous falsehood; for it affords a refuge to secret self-conceit,—enables a vain man at once to escape

---

10 III, iii, 89-90.

11 freak of nature.

his reader's indignation by general swollen pane-gyrics on Shakespeare, merely by his *ipse dixit* to treat what he has not intellect enough to compre-hend, or soul to feel, as contemptible, without as-signing any reason, or referring his opinion to any demonstrated principle; and so has left Shakespeare as a sort of Tartarian Dalai Lama,[12] adored indeed, and his very excrescences prized as relics, but with no authority, no real influence. I grieve that every late voluminous edition of his works would enable me to substantiate the pres-ent charge with a variety of facts one tenth of which would of themselves exhaust the time al-lotted to me. Every critic, who has or has not made a collection of black letter books—in itself a useful and respectable amusement—puts on the seven-league boots of self-opinion and strides at once from an illustrator into a supreme judge, and blind and deaf, fills his three-ounce phial at the waters of Niagara—and determines positively the greatness of the cataract to be neither more nor less than his three-ounce phial has been able to receive.

THE CHARACTERISTICS OF SHAKESPEARE

1. Expectation in preference to surprise. 'God said, let there be *light,* and there was *light,*'—not there *was* light. As the feeling with which we startle at a shooting star, compared with that of watching the sunrise at the pre-established mo-ment, such and so low is surprise compared with expectation.

2. Signal adherence to the great law of nature that opposites tend to attract and temper each other. Passion in Shakespeare displays, libertin-ism involves, morality. The exception [is] char-acteristic [of the individual], independent of the intrinsic value, as the farewell precepts of the parent, and having some end beyond even the parental relation. Thus the Countess's beautiful precepts to Bertram,[13] by elevating her charac-ter, elevate that of Helena, her favourite, and soften down the point in her which Shakespeare does not mean us not to see, but to see and for-give, and at length to justify. So Polonius, who is the personified *memory* of wisdom no longer actually possessed.

So again folly, dullness itself, the vehicles of wisdom. As all the deities of Homer were in armour, even Venus, etc., so all in Shakespeare strong. No difficulty in being a fool to imitate a fool; but to be, remain, and speak like a wise

man, and yet so as to give a vivid representation of a fool, *hic labor, hoc opus.*[14] Dogberry,[15] etc.

3. Independence of the interest on the plot. The plot interests us on account of the charac-ters, not *vice versa;* it is the canvas only. Justifi-cation of the same stratagem in Benedict and Beatrice—same vanity, etc. Take away from *Much Ado About Nothing* all that which is [not] indispensable to the plot, either as having little to do with it, or at best, like Dogberry and his comrades, forced into the service when any other less ingeniously absurd watchmen and night-constables would have answered; take away Benedict, Beatrice, Dogberry, and the reaction of the former on the character of Hero, and what will remain? In other writers the main agent of the plot is always the prominent character. In Shakespeare so or not so, as the character is in itself calculated or not calculated to form the plot. So Don John, the mainspring of the plot, is merely shown and withdrawn.

4. Independence of the interest on *the story* as the ground-work of the plot. Hence Shakespeare did not take the trouble of inventing stories. It was enough for him to select from those that had been invented or recorded such as had one or other, or both, of two recommendations, namely, suitableness to his purposes, and sec-ond, their being already parts of popular tradi-tion—names we had often heard of, and of their fortunes, and we should like to see the *man* him-self. It is the man himself that Shakespeare for the first time makes us acquainted with. *Lear* (omit the first scene, yet all remains). So Shylock.

5. The interfusion of the lyrical, of that which in its very essence is poetical, not only with the dramatic, as in the plays of Metastasio,[16] where at the end of the scene comes the aria, as the exit speech of the character. Now songs in Shake-speare are introduced as *songs,* and just as songs are in real life, beautifully as they are often made characteristic of the person who has called for them, [as] Desdemona and the Count in *As You Like It;* [they are introduced] not only with the dramatic, but as a part of the dramatic. The whole *Midsummer Night's Dream* is one con-tinued specimen of the lyrical dramatized. But take [also] the beginning of the third act of [the] first part of *Henry IV.*; represent the [speech of] Hotspur,—

Marry, and I'm glad on't with all my heart:
I had rather be a kitten and cry mew—

---

12 Grand Lama, or high priest.
13 *All's Well,* I, i, 70–79.
14 'This is the task, this is the work.'
15 in *Much Ado.*
16 Italian poet, 1698–1782.

and then [the transition of the lyrical speech of] Mortimer—

> I understand thy looks: that pretty Welsh
> Which thou pour'st down from these swelling
>   heavens
> I am too perfect in.[17]

6. Closely connected with this is that Shakespeare's characters are like those in life, to be *inferred* by the reader, not *told to him*. Of this excellence I know no other instance; and it has one mark of real life—that Shakespeare's characters have been as generally misunderstood and from precisely the same causes [as real persons]. If you take what his friends say, you may be deceived— still more so, if his enemies; and the character himself sees himself through the medium of his character, not exactly as it is. But the clown or the fool will suggest a shrewd hint; and take all together, and the impression is right, and all [the spectators] have it. And it may be given as soon as the true Idea is given, and then all the speeches receive the light and attest by reflecting it.

GENERAL CHARACTERISTICS OF SHAKESPEARE

Great as was the genius of Shakespeare, his judgement was at least equal. Of this we shall be convinced, if we look round on the age, and compare the nature of the respective dramas of Greece and England, differing from the necessary dissimilitude of circumstances by which they are modified and influenced. The Greek stage had its origin in the ceremonies of a sacrifice, such as the goat to Bacchus. It were erroneous to call him only the jolly god of wine; among the ancients he was venerable; he was the symbol of that power which acts without our consciousness from the vital energies of nature, as Apollo was the symbol of our intellectual consciousness. Their heroes under his influence performed more than human actions; hence tales of their favourite champions soon passed into dialogue. On the Greek stage the chorus was always before the audience—no curtain dropt. *Change of place* was impossible; the absurd idea of its improbability was not indulged. The scene cannot be an exact copy of nature, but only an imitation. If we can believe ourselves at Thebes in one act, we can believe ourselves at Athens in the next. There seems to be no just boundary but what the feelings prescribe. In Greece, however, great judgement was necessary where the same persons were perpetually before the audi-

ence. If a story lasted twenty-four hours or twenty-four years, it was equally improbable. They never attempted to impose on the senses, by bringing places to men, though they could bring men to places.

Unity of time was not necessary, where no offence was taken at its lapse between the acts, or between scene and scene, for where there were no acts or scenes it was impossible rigidly to observe its laws. To overcome these difficulties the judgement and great genius of the ancients supplied music, and with the charms of their poetry filled up the vacuity. In the story of the *Agamemnon* of Aeschylus, the taking of Troy was supposed to be announced by the lighting of beacons on the Asiatic shore: the mind being beguiled by the narrative ode of the chorus, embracing the events of the siege, hours passed as minutes, and no improbability was felt at the return of Agamemnon; and yet examined rigidly he must have passed over from Troy in less than fifteen minutes. Another fact here presented itself, seldom noticed: with the ancients three plays were performed in one day; they were called trilogies. In Shakespeare we may fancy these trilogies connected into one representation. If *Lear* were divided into three, each part would be a play with the ancients. Or take the three plays of Agamemnon, and divide them into acts, they would form one play. . . .

Contrast the stage of the ancients with that of the time of Shakespeare, and we shall be struck with his genius: with them, it had the trappings of royal and religious ceremony; with him, it was a naked room, a blanket for a curtain; but with his vivid appeals the imagination figured it out

> A field for monarchs.

After the rupture of the Northern nations, the Latin language, blended with the modern, produced the *Romaunt* tongue, the language of the minstrels: to which term, as distinguishing their songs and fabliaux, we owe the word and the species of *romance*. The romantic may be considered as opposed to the antique, and from this change of manners, those of Shakespeare take their colouring. He is not to be tried by ancient and classic rules, but by the standard of his age. That law of unity which has its foundation, not in factitious necessity of custom, but in nature herself, is instinctively observed by Shakespeare.

A *unity of feeling* pervades the whole of his plays. In *Romeo and Juliet* all is youth and spring—it is youth with its follies, its virtues, its

---

17 *1 Henry IV*, III, i, 128–9, 200–202.

precipitancies; it is spring with its odours, flowers, and transiency:—the same feeling commences, goes through, and ends the play. The old men, the Capulets and Montagues, are not common old men; they have an eagerness, a hastiness, a precipitancy—the effect of spring. With Romeo his precipitate change of passion, his hasty marriage, and his rash death, are all the effects of youth. With Juliet love has all that is tender and melancholy in the nightingale, all that is voluptuous in the rose, with whatever is sweet in the freshness of spring; but it ends with a long deep sigh, like the breeze of the evening. This unity of character pervades the whole of his dramas.

Of that species of writing termed *tragi-comedy,* too much has been produced, but it has been doomed to the shelf. With Shakespeare his comic constantly reacted on his tragic characters. Lear, wandering amidst the tempest, had all his feelings of distress increased by the overflowings of the wild wit of the Fool, as vinegar poured upon wounds exacerbates their pain; thus even his comic humour tends to the developments of tragic passion.

The next character belonging to Shakespeare as Shakespeare, was the *keeping at all times the high road of life.* With him there were no innocent adulteries; he never rendered that amiable which religion and reason taught us to detest; he never clothed vice in the garb of virtue, like Beaumont and Fletcher, the Kotzebues[18] of his day: his fathers were roused by ingratitude, his husbands were stung by unfaithfulness; the affections were wounded in those points where all may and all must feel. Another evidence of exquisite judgement in Shakespeare was that he seized hold of popular tales. *Lear* and the *Merchant of Venice* were popular tales, but so excellently managed, that both were the representation of men in all ages and at all times.

His dramas do not arise absolutely out of some one extraordinary circumstance; the scenes may stand independently of any such one connecting incident, as faithful reflections of men and manners. In his *mode of drawing characters* there were no pompous descriptions of a man by himself; his character was to be drawn as in real life, from the whole course of the play, or out of the mouths of his enemies or friends. This might be exemplified in the character of Polonius, which actors have often misrepresented. Shakespeare never intended to represent him as a buffoon. It was natural that Hamlet, a young man of genius and

fire, detesting formality, and disliking Polonius for political reasons, as imagining that he had assisted his uncle in his usurpation, should express himself satirically; but Hamlet's words should not be taken as Shakespeare's conception of him. In Polonius a certain induration of character arose from long habits of business; but take his advice to Laertes, the reverence of his memory by Ophelia, and we shall find that he was a statesman of business, though somewhat past his faculties. One particular feature which belonged to his character was, that his recollections of past life were of wisdom, and showed a knowledge of human nature, whilst what immediately passed before, and escaped from him, was emblematical of weakness.

Another excellence in Shakespeare, and in which no other writer equalled him, was in the *language of nature.* So correct was it that we could see ourselves in all he wrote; his style and manner had also that felicity, that not a sentence could be read without its being discovered if it were *Shakespearean.* In observations of living character, such as of landlords and postilions, Fielding had great excellence; but in drawing from his own heart, and depicting that species of character which no observation could teach, he failed in comparison with Richardson, who perpetually placed himself, as it were, in a daydream. But Shakespeare excelled in both; witness an accuracy of character in the Nurse of Juliet. On the other hand, [consider] the great characters of Othello, Iago, Hamlet, and Richard III.; as he never could have witnessed anything similar, he appears invariably to have asked himself, How should I act or speak in such circumstances? His comic characters were also peculiar. A drunken constable was not uncommon; but he could make folly a vehicle for wit, as in Dogberry. Everything was as a substratum on which his creative genius might erect a superstructure.

To distinguish what is *legitimate* in Shakespeare from what does not belong to him, we must observe his varied images symbolical of moral truth, thrusting by and seeming to trip up each other, from an impetuosity of thought, producing a metre which is always flowing from one verse into the other, and seldom closing with the tenth syllable of the line—an instance of which may be found in the play of *Pericles,* written a century before, but which Shakespeare altered, and where his alteration may be recognized even to half a line. This was the case not merely in his later plays, but in his early dramas, such as *Love's*

---

18 August Von Kotzebue, 1761-1819, was a prolific German playwright whose melodramas were popular in England.

Labour's Lost. The same perfection in the flowing continuity of interchangeable metrical pauses is constantly perceptible.

Lastly, contrast his *morality* with the writers of his own or the succeeding age, or with those of the present day, who boast of their superiority. He never, as before observed, deserted the high road of life; he never made his lovers openly gross or profane; for common candour must allow that his images were incomparably less so than those of his contemporaries. Even the letters of females in high life were coarser than his writings. The writings of Beaumont and Fletcher bear no comparison; the grossest passages of Shakespeare were purity to theirs; and it should be remembered that though he might occasionally disgust a sense of delicacy, he never injured the mind: he caused no excitement of passion which he flattered to degrade, never used what was faulty for a faulty purpose; carried on no warfare against virtue, by which wickedness may be made to appear as not wickedness, and where our sympathy was to be entrapped by the misfortunes of vice; with him vice never walked, as it were, in twilight. He never inverted the order of nature and propriety, like some modern writers, who suppose every magistrate to be a glutton or a drunkard, and every poor man humane and temperate; with him we had no benevolent braziers or sentimental rat-catchers. Nothing was purposely out of place. . . . Shakespeare was a writer of all others the most calculated to make his readers better as well as wiser.

Delivered 1812–13   1930

1771 · DOROTHY WORDSWORTH · 1855

1771   Born at Cockermouth, only sister of the poet William Wordsworth, who was one year her senior.

1777–87   Following the death of her mother, was placed under the care of a cousin, Elizabeth Threlkeld, at Halifax.

1787–93   Lived for a year with her maternal grandparents at Penrith, where she was not very happy, and afterward for six years with an uncle at Forncett, in Norfolk.

1794–5   Visited 'Aunt' Threlkeld and joined William in a walking tour through the Lakes.

1795   Took up her abode with William at Racedown in Dorsetshire.

1797   Moved to a large manor house, Alfoxden, in the Quantock Hills, where she and her brother became neighbors of Coleridge, who was living at Nether Stowey.

1798–9   On 20 January began her invaluable Alfoxden *Journal.* With her brother and Coleridge visited Germany, keeping a journal account of their experiences. On the return from Germany, settled with William at Dove Cottage, Grasmere.

1800–1803   On 14 May 1800, started her Grasmere *Journal,* which was continued until 11 January 1803. (MSS. covering nine months in 1802 have been lost.)

1803   Composed *Recollections of a Tour in Scotland* after her return from an excursion with her brother and Coleridge.

1805   Took a walking trip to Ullswater with her brother, and preserved a record of it in *Excursion on the Banks of Ullswater.*

1820   Made a tour of the Continent with members of the family and

1822   A second tour of Scotland, without her brother, but accompanied by Joanna Hutchinson. Kept journal records of both tours.

1829   Suffered a complete breakdown and was never again in good health.

1836   Lost her mental faculties, and until her death remained a pathetic member of the Wordsworth household.

1855   Died at Grasmere.

AT A CRITICAL TIME in the life of William Wordsworth, at Racedown, 1795, when he was bewildered over the failure of the French Revolution and despairing over his affair with Annette Vallon, his sister, Dorothy, with extraordinary sympathy and utter selflessness, devoted herself to his recovery. In their daily rambles together she reawakened his delight in the out-of-doors, and through her 'exquisite regard for common things' she revived his perceptions and helped him to transform mere observation, 'the tyranny of the eye,' into imaginative creation. She saved his poetic soul alive; and he fully realized it, and tells us so in *The Prelude.* Throughout his poetry he has left us many beautiful tributes to her benign and joyous companionship. As for Dorothy, she lived intensely in and for her brother all her days. She faithfully chronicled his observations, guided the bent of his poetic mind, furnished him encouragement and vision, supplied through her journals raw materials for his compositions, inspired many poems, was their first critic, and often helped to give them their final form.

The value of the records Dorothy preserved, especially during the early years, is hardly to be overestimated. Through her exquisite feminine presence we can observe daily and hourly the New Poetry as it is being fashioned by Wordsworth and Coleridge at the close of the eighteenth century. But it is not merely for the historical and biographical value of her notes that Dorothy Wordsworth lays claim upon us. She deserves an independent place in literary history as one of the finest of English descriptive writers. The companionship with her brother no doubt quickened her observations and the pages of her wonderful journal certainly contain a record of Wordsworth's remarks as well as her own. But she 'would have discovered wonders anywhere, and the literary form, which it would be difficult to praise too highly, is hers' (Harper). She makes no pretense of setting herself up as author, but without reflection she acutely noted down the fugitive beauty of the homely country sights and sounds around her. She has the happy gift for the inevitable word, and a genuine charm of phrase which springs from complete and unaffected simplicity. The Grasmere Journal is more intimate than the Alfoxden; it has 'more of the nebular stuff of poetry in it' and is a more personal revelation of Dorothy herself. *The Recollections of a Tour in Scotland* was written expressly for 'the sake of a few friends, who, it seemed, ought to have been with us.' It does not have, therefore, like the Grasmere Journal, the character of the purely private diary, but was more carefully composed for a wider audience. Yet the events are set down in natural and vivid language. The result is a masterpiece for Dorothy and one of the most enjoyable of all books of travel.

It is to be seriously doubted that Dorothy suffered from a frustrated passion for Coleridge. She was devoted to him, but her love for William precluded any love for another (de Selincourt). The fervent intensity of her spirit, her extraordinary capacity for sympathy, her 'brave, voiceless' surrender at the time of her brother's marriage, the wear and tear of bringing up his family are contributing factors which may partially explain her ultimate breakdown.

From JOURNALS

Alfoxden,[1] *January 20th, 1798.*—The green paths down the hillsides are channels for streams. The young wheat is streaked by silver lines of water running between the ridges, the sheep are gathered together on the slopes. After the wet dark days, the country seems more populous. It peoples itself in the sunbeams. The garden, mimic of spring, is gay with flowers. The purple-starred hepatica spreads itself in the sun, and the clustering snow-drops put forth their white heads, at first upright, ribbed with green, and like a rosebud when completely opened, hanging their heads downwards, but slowly lengthening their slender stems. The slanting woods of an unvarying brown, showing the light through the thin network of their upper boughs. Upon the highest ridge of that round hill covered with planted oaks, the shafts of the trees show in the light like the columns of a ruin.

January 23rd.—Bright sunshine, went out at 3 o'clock. The sea perfectly calm blue, streaked with deeper colour by the clouds, and tongues or points of sand; on our return of a gloomy red. The sun gone down. The crescent moon, Jupiter, and Venus. The sound of the sea distinctly heard on the tops of the hills, which we could never hear in summer. We attribute this partly to the bareness of the trees, but chiefly to the absence of the singing of birds, the hum of insects, that noiseless noise which lives in the summer air. The villages marked out by beautiful beds of smoke. The turf fading into the mountain road. The scarlet flowers of the moss.

February 1st.—About two hours before dinner, set forward towards Mr. Bartholomew's.[2] The wind blew so keen in our faces that we felt ourselves inclined to seek the covert of the wood. There we had a warm shelter, gathered a burthen of large rotten boughs blown down by the wind

---

[1] a large and beautiful country-house leased by Wordsworth, situated in Somersetshire about four miles from the village of Nether Stowey.

[2] Mr. Bartholomew rented Alfoxden and sublet the house to Wordsworth.

of the preceding night. The sun shone clear, but all at once a heavy blackness hung over the sea. The trees almost *roared,* and the ground seemed in motion with the multitudes of dancing leaves, which made a rustling sound, distinct from that of the trees. Still the asses pastured in quietness under the hollies, undisturbed by these forerunners of the storm. The wind beat furiously against us as we returned. Full moon. She rose in uncommon majesty over the sea, slowly ascending through the clouds. Sat with the window open an hour in the moonlight.

February 3rd.—A mild morning, the windows open at breakfast, the redbreasts singing in the garden. Walked with Coleridge over the hills. The sea at first obscured by vapour; that vapour afterwards slid in one mighty mass along the seashore; the islands and one point of land clear beyond it. The distant country (which was purple in the clear dull air), overhung by straggling clouds that sailed over it, appeared like the darker clouds, which are often seen at a great distance apparently motionless, while the nearer ones pass quickly over them, driven by the lower winds. I never saw such a union of earth, sky, and sea. The clouds beneath our feet spread themselves to the water, and the clouds of the sky almost joined them. Gathered sticks in the wood; a perfect stillness. The redbreasts sang upon the leafless boughs. Of a great number of sheep in the field, only one standing. Returned to dinner at five o'clock. The moonlight still and warm as a summer's night at nine o'clock.

February 17th.—A deep snow upon the ground. Wm. and Coleridge walked to Mr. Bartholomew's, and to Stowey. Wm. returned, and we walked through the wood into the Coombe[3] to fetch some eggs. The sun shone bright and clear. A deep stillness in the thickest part of the wood, undisturbed except by the occasional dropping of the snow from the holly boughs; no other sound but that of the water, and the slender notes of a redbreast, which sang at intervals on the outskirts of the southern side of the wood. There the bright green moss was bare at the roots of the trees, and the little birds were upon it. The whole appearance of the wood was enchanting; and each tree, taken singly, was beautiful. The branches of the hollies pendent with their white burden, but still showing their bright red berries, and their glossy green leaves. The bare branches of the oaks thickened by the snow.

February 26th.—Coleridge came in the morning, and Mr. and Mrs. Cruikshank,[4] walked with Coleridge nearly to Stowey after dinner. A very clear afternoon. We lay sidelong upon the turf, and gazed on the landscape till it melted into more than natural loveliness. The sea very uniform, of a pale greyish blue, only one distant bay, bright and blue as a sky; had there been a vessel sailing up it, a perfect image of delight. Walked to the top of a high hill to see a fortification. Again sat down to feed upon the prospect; a magnificent scene, *curiously* spread out for even minute inspection, though so extensive that the mind is afraid to calculate its bounds. A winter prospect shows every cottage, every farm, and the forms of distant trees, such as in summer have no distinguishing mark. On our return, Jupiter and Venus before us. While the twilight still overpowered the light of the moon, we were reminded that she was shining bright above our heads, by our faint shadows going before us. We had seen her on the tops of the hills, melting into the blue sky. Poole[5] called while we were absent.

March 1st.—We rose early. A thick fog obscured the distant prospect entirely, but the shapes of the nearer trees and the dome of the wood dimly seen and dilated. It cleared away between ten and eleven. The shapes of the mist, slowly moving along, exquisitely beautiful; passing over the sheep they almost seemed to have more of life than those quiet creatures. The unseen birds singing in the mist.

March 7th.—William and I drank tea at Coleridge's. A cloudy sky. Observed nothing particularly interesting—the distant prospect obscured. One only leaf upon the top of a tree—the sole remaining leaf—danced round and round like a rag blown by the wind.

March 23rd.—Coleridge dined with us. He brought his ballad[6] finished. We walked with him to the Miner's house. A beautiful evening, very starry, the horned moon.

April 6th.—Went a part of the way home with Coleridge. A pleasant warm morning, but a showery day. Walked a short distance up the lesser Coombe, with an intention of going to the

---

3 a narrow ravine-like valley.

4 residents of Nether Stowey.
5 Thomas Poole was a wealthy young tanner who lived in Nether Stowey. He and Wordsworth were lifelong friends.
6 *The Rime of the Ancient Mariner.*

source of the brook, but the evening closing in, cold prevented us. The Spring still advancing very slowly. The horse-chestnuts budding, and the hedgerows beginning to look green, but nothing fully expanded.

May 6th, Sunday.—Expected the painter, and Coleridge. A rainy morning—very pleasant in the evening. Met Coleridge as we were walking out. Went with him to Stowey; heard the nightingale; saw a glow-worm.

[*Grasmere,*[7] *May 16th, 1800*] *Friday Morning.*— Warm and mild, after a fine night of rain. . . . The woods extremely beautiful with all autumnal variety and softness. I carried a basket for mosses, and gathered some wild plants. Oh! that we had a book of botany. All flowers now are gay and deliciously sweet. The primrose still pre-eminent among the later flowers of the spring. Foxgloves very tall, with their heads budding. I went forward round the lake at the foot of Loughrigg Fell.[8] I was much amused with the business of a pair of stone-chats; their restless voices as they skimmed along the water following each other, their shadows under them, and their returning back to the stones on the shore, chirping with the same unwearied voice. Could not cross the water, so I went round by the stepping-stones. . . . Rydale[9] was very beautiful, with spear-shaped streaks of polished steel. . . . Grasmere[10] was very solemn in the last glimpse of twilight; it calls home the heart to quietness.

[*August*] *31st, Sunday.* . . . A great deal of corn is cut in the vale, and the whole prospect, though not tinged with a general autumnal yellow, yet softened down into a mellowness of colouring, which seems to impart softness to the forms of hills and mountains. At 11 o'clock Coleridge came, when I was walking in the still clear moonshine in the garden. He came over Helvellyn.[11] Wm. was gone to bed, and John also, worn out with his ride round Coniston.[12] We sat and chatted till half-past three. . . . Coleridge read us a part of *Christabel*. Talked much about the mountains, etc., etc. . . .

October 3rd, Friday.—Very rainy all the morn-

ing. . . . Wm. walked to Ambleside[13] after dinner. I went with him part of the way. He talked much about the object of his essay for the second volume of 'L. B.' . . . Amos Cottle's[14] death in the *Morning Post*.

N.B.—When William and I returned from accompanying Jones,[15] we met an old man almost double. He had on a coat, thrown over his shoulders, above his waistcoat and coat. Under this he carried a bundle, and had an apron on and a night-cap. His face was interesting. He had dark eyes and a long nose. John, who afterwards met him at Wytheburn,[16] took him for a Jew. He was of Scotch parents, but had been born in the army. He had had a wife, and 'a good woman, and it pleased God to bless us with ten children.' All these were dead but one, of whom he had not heard for many years, a sailor. His trade was to gather leeches, but now leeches are scarce, and he had not strength for it. He lived by begging, and was making his way to Carlisle, where he should buy a few godly books to sell. He said leeches were very scarce, partly owing to this dry season, but many years they have been scarce—he supposed it owing to their being much sought after, that they did not breed fast, and were of slow growth. Leeches were formerly 2s. 6d. per 100; they are now 30s. He had been hurt in driving a cart, his leg broke, his body driven over, his skull fractured. He felt no pain till he recovered from his first insensibility. It was then late in the evening, when the light was just going away.

[*November*] *24th* [*1801*] *Tuesday.* . . . It was very windy, and we heard the wind everywhere about us as we went along the lane, but the walls sheltered us. John Green's house looked pretty under Silver How.[17] As we were going along we were stopped at once, at the distance perhaps of 50 yards from our favourite birch tree. It was yielding to the gusty wind with all its tender twigs. The sun shone upon it, and it glanced in the wind like a flying sunshiny shower. It was a tree in shape, with stem and branches, but it was like a Spirit of water. The sun went in, and it resumed its purplish appearance, the twigs still yielding to the wind, but not so visibly to us. The

7 a village in the center of the beautiful Lake Country where the Wordsworths went to live in 1800.
8 a mountain overlooking Rydal and its vicinity.
9 Rydal Water.
10 Grasmere Lake.
11 Coleridge came over the mountain road from Keswick where he was then residing.
12 Coniston Water is ten miles south of Grasmere.
13 a town about three miles from Grasmere located on the north end of Lake Windermere.
14 Amos Cottle was the brother of Joseph Cottle, Bristol bookseller and publisher for Wordsworth, Coleridge, and Southey.
15 Robert Jones was a college mate and lifelong friend. He accompanied Wordsworth on his tour through the Alps and often visited him in later years.
16 a village five miles north of Grasmere.
17 a mountain west of Grasmere.

other birch trees that were near it looked bright and cheerful, but it was a creature by its own self among them. . . . We went through the wood—it became fair. There was a rainbow which spanned the lake from the island-house to the foot of Bainriggs.[18] The village looked populous and beautiful. Catkins are coming out; palm trees budding; the alder, with its plum-coloured buds. We came home over the stepping-stones. The lake was foamy with white waves. I saw a solitary butter-flower in the wood. . . .

March 18th, 1802, Thursday.—Rydale vale was full of life and motion. The wind blew briskly, and the lake was covered all over with bright silver waves, that were there each the twinkling of an eye, then others rose up and took their place as fast as they went away. The rocks glittered in the sunshine, the crows and the ravens were busy, and the thrushes and little birds sang. I went through the fields, and sat half an hour afraid to pass a cow. The cow looked at me, and I looked at the cow, and whenever I stirred the cow gave over eating. . . . A parcel came in from Birmingham, with Lamb's play[19] for us, and for C. . . . As we came along Ambleside vale in the twilight, it was a grave evening. There was something in the air that compelled me to serious thought—the hills were large, closed in by the sky. . . . Night was come on, and the moon was overcast. But, as I climbed the Moss,[20] the moon came out from behind a mountain mass of black clouds. O, the unutterable darkness of the sky, and the earth below the moon! and the glorious brightness of the moon itself! There was a vivid sparkling streak of light at this end of Rydale water, but the rest was very dark, and Loughrigg Fell and Silver How were white and bright, as if they were covered with hoar frost. The moon retired again, and appeared and disappeared several times before I reached home. Once there was no moonlight to be seen but upon the island-house and the promontory of the island where it stands. 'That needs must be a holy place,'[21] etc. etc. I had many very exquisite feelings, and when I saw this lowly Building in the waters, among the dark and lofty hills, with that bright, soft light upon it, it made me more than half a poet.

April 15th, Thursday.—It was a threatening,

misty morning, but mild. We set off after dinner from Eusemere.[22] Mrs. Clarkson went a short way with us, but turned back. The wind was furious, and we thought we must have returned. We first rested in the large boathouse, then under a furze bush opposite Mr. Clarkson's. Saw the plough going in the field. The wind seized our breath. The lake was rough. There was a boat by itself floating in the middle of the bay below Water Millock.[23] We rested again in the Water Millock Lane. The hawthorns are black and green, the birches here and there greenish, but there is yet more of purple to be seen on the twigs. We got over into a field to avoid some cows—people working. A few primroses by the roadside—woodsorrel flower, the anemone, scentless violets, strawberries, and that starry, yellow flower which Mrs. C. calls pile wort. When we were in the woods beyond Gowbarrow Park[24] we saw a few daffodils close to the waterside. We fancied that the lake had floated the seeds ashore, and that the little colony had so sprung up. But as we went along there were more and yet more; and at last, under the boughs of the trees, we saw that there was a long belt of them along the shore, about the breadth of a country turnpike road. I never saw daffodils so beautiful. They grew among the mossy stones about and about them; some rested their heads upon these stones as on a pillow for weariness; and the rest tossed and reeled and danced, and seemed as if they verily laughed with the wind, that blew upon them over the lake; they looked so gay, ever glancing, ever changing. This wind blew directly over the lake to them. There was here and there a little knot, and a few stragglers a few yards higher up; but they were so few as not to disturb the simplicity, unity, and life of that one busy highway.

May 6th, Thursday.—A sweet morning. We have put the finishing stroke to our bower, and here we are sitting in the orchard. It is one o'clock. We are sitting upon a seat under the wall, which I found my brother building up, when I came to him. . . . He had intended that it should have been done before I came. It is a nice, cool, shady spot. The small birds are singing, lambs bleating, cuckoo calling, the thrush sings by fits, Thomas Ashburner's axe is going quietly (without passion) in the orchard, hens

18 a wooded hill rising from the east shore of Grasmere Lake.
19 *John Woodvil,* a tragedy by Charles Lamb, 1802.
20 White Moss Common.
21 This quotation has not been identified.

22 The home of the Clarksons situated at the northern end of Ullswater. Thomas Clarkson was active in the abolitionist movement.
23 a village on the north shore of Ullswater.
24 an estate on the north shore of Ullswater.

are cackling, flies humming, the women talking together at their doors, plum and pear trees are in blossom—apple trees greenish—the opposite woods green, the crows are cawing. We have heard ravens. The ash trees are in blossom, birds flying all about us. The stitchwort is coming out, there is one budding lychnis, the primroses are passing their prime, celandine, violets, and wood sorrel forevermore, little geraniums and pansies on the wall. We walked in the evening to Tail End,[25] to inquire about hurdles for the orchard shed. . . . When we came in we found a magazine, and review, and a letter from Coleridge with verses to Hartley, and Sara H.[26] We read the review, etc. The moon was a perfect boat, a silver boat, when we were out in the evening. The birch tree is all over green in *small* leaf, more light and elegant than when it is full out. It bent to the breezes, as if for the love of its own delightful motions. Sloethorns and hawthorns in the hedges.

June 20th, Sunday.—We were in the orchard a great part of the morning. After tea we walked upon our own path for a long time. We talked sweetly together about the disposal of our riches. We lay upon the sloping turf. Earth and sky were so lovely that they melted our very hearts. The sky to the north was of a chastened yet rich yellow, fading into pale blue, and streaked and scattered over with steady islands of purple, melting away into shades of pink. It made my heart almost feel like a vision to me. . . .

[*July 1802.*]—On Thursday morning, 29th, we arrived in London. Wm. left me at the Inn. . . . After various troubles and disasters, we left London on Saturday morning at half-past five or six, the 31st of July. . . . We mounted the Dover coach at Charing Cross. It was a beautiful morning. The city, St. Paul's, with the river and a multitude of little boats, made a most beautiful sight as we crossed Westminster Bridge. The houses were not overhung by their cloud of smoke, and they were spread out endlessly, yet the sun shone so brightly, with such a fierce light, that there was even something like the purity of one of nature's own grand spectacles.

We rode on cheerfully, now with the Paris diligence before us, now behind. We walked up the steep hills, a beautiful prospect everywhere, till we even reached Dover. At first the rich, populous, wide-spreading, woody country about London, then the River Thames, ships sailing, chalk cliffs, trees, little villages. Afterwards Canterbury, situated on a plain, rich and woody, but the city and cathedral disappointed me. . . .

We saw the castle of Dover, and the sea beyond, four or five miles before we reached D[over]. We looked at it through a long vale, the castle being upon an eminence, as it seemed, at the end of this vale, which opened to the sea. . . . It was near dark when we reached Dover. We were told that the packet was about to sail, so we went down to the custom-house in half-an-hour—had our luggage examined, etc. etc., and then we drank tea with the Honourable Mr. Knox and his tutor. We arrived at Calais at four o'clock on Sunday morning, the 1st of August. We stayed in the vessel till half-past seven; then William went for letters; at about half-past eight or nine we found out Annette and C[27] chez Madame Avril dans la Rue de la Tete d'or. We lodged opposite two ladies, in tolerable decent-sized rooms, but badly furnished. . . . The weather was very hot. We walked by the seashore almost every evening with Annette and Caroline, or William and I alone. I had a bad cold, and could not bathe at first, but William did. It was a pretty sight to see, as we walked upon the sands when the tide was low, perhaps a hundred people bathing about a quarter of a mile distant from us. And we had delightful walks after the heat of the day was passed away—seeing far off in the west the coast of England like a cloud crested with Dover castle, which was but like the summit of the cloud—the evening star and the glory of the sky. The reflections in the water were more beautiful than the sky itself, purple waves brighter than precious stones, forever melting away upon the sands. The fort, a wooden building, at the entrance of the harbour at Calais, when the evening twilight was coming on, and we could not see anything of the building but its shape, which was far more distinct than in perfect daylight, seemed to be reared upon pillars of ebony, between which pillars the sea was seen in the most beautiful colours that can be conceived. Nothing in romance was ever half so beautiful. Now came in view, as the evening star sank down, and the colours of the west faded away, the two lights of England, lighted up by Englishmen in our country, to warn vessels off rocks or sands. These we used to see from the pier, when we could see no other distant

---

25 a dwelling on the west side of Grasmere Lake.
26 Sara Hutchinson, whose sister became Wordsworth's wife.

27 Caroline, Wordsworth's French daughter. Annette Vallon was her mother.

objects but the clouds, the sky, and the sea itself:
All was dark behind. The town of Calais seemed
deserted of the light of heaven, but there was always light and life and joy upon the sea. One
night, though, I shall never forget—the day had
been very hot, and William and I walked alone
together upon the pier. The sea was gloomy, for
there was a blackness over all the sky, except
when it was overspread with lightning, which
often revealed to us a distant vessel. Near us the
waves roared and broke against the pier, and
they were interfused with greenish fiery light.
The more distant sea always black and gloomy.
It was also beautiful, on the calm hot night, to
see the little boats row out of harbour with wings
of fire, and the sail boats with the fiery track
which they cut as they went along, and which
closed up after them with a hundred thousand
sparkles, balls, shootings and stream of glow-
worm light. Caroline was delighted.

From RECOLLECTIONS OF A TOUR MADE IN SCOTLAND, 1803

Saturday, August 27th.—We found the ferryman at work in the field above his hut, and he
was at liberty to go with us, but, being wet and
hungry, we begged that he would let us sit by
his fire till we had refreshed ourselves. This was
the first genuine Highland hut we had been in.
We entered by the cow-house, the house-door
being within, at right angles to the outer door.
The woman was distressed that she had a bad
fire, but she heaped up some dry peats and
heather, and, blowing it with her breath, in a
short time raised a blaze that scorched us into
comfortable feelings. A small part of the smoke
found its way out of the hole of the chimney,
the rest through the open window-places, one
of which was within the recess of the fireplace,
and made a frame to a little picture of the restless lake and the opposite shore, seen when the
outer door was open. The woman of the house
was very kind: whenever we asked her for anything it seemed a fresh pleasure to her that she
had it for us; she always answered with a sort
of softening down of the Scotch exclamation,
'Hoot!' 'Ho! yes, ye'll get that,' and hied to her
cupboard in the spence.[28] We were amused with
the phrase 'Ye'll get that' in the Highlands, which
appeared to us as if it came from a perpetual feeling of the difficulty with which most things are
procured. We got oatmeal, butter, bread and

28 pantry.

milk, made some porridge, and then departed.
It was rainy and cold, with a strong wind. . . .

We left the hut, retracing the few yards of road
which we had climbed; our boat lay at anchor
under the rock in the last of all the compartments of the lake, a small oblong pool, almost
shut up within itself, as several others had appeared to be, by jutting points of rock. It was
the termination of a long out-shooting of the
water, pushed up between the steeps of the main
shore (where the huts stand) and a broad promontory which, with its hillocks and points and
lesser promontories, occupies the centre of the
foot of the lake. A person sailing through the
lake up the middle of it, would just as naturally
suppose that the outlet was here as on the other
side; and so it might have been, with the most
trifling change in the disposition of the ground,
for at the end of this slip of water the lake is confined only by a gentle rising of a few yards
towards an opening between the hills, a narrow
pass or valley through which the river might have
flowed. The road is carried through this valley,
which only differs from the lower part of the vale
of the lake in being excessively narrow, and without water; it is enclosed by mountains, rocky
mounds, hills and hillocks scattered over with
birch trees, and covered with Dutch myrtle and
heather, even surpassing what we had seen before. Our mother Eve had no fairer, though a
more diversified garden, to tend, than we found
within this little close valley. It rained all the
time, but the mists and calm air made us ample
amends for a wetting.

At the opening of the pass we climbed up a
low eminence, and had an unexpected prospect
suddenly before us—another lake, small compared with Loch Ketterine, though perhaps four
miles long, but the misty air concealed the end
of it. The transition from the solitary wildness
of Loch Ketterine and the narrow valley or pass
to this scene was very delightful: it was a gentle
place, with lovely open bays, one small island,
corn fields, woods, and a group of cottages. This
vale seemed to have been made to be tributary
to the comforts of man, Loch Ketterine for the
lonely delight of Nature, and kind spirits delighting in beauty. The sky was grey and heavy,
—floating mists on the hill-sides, which softened
the objects, and where we lost sight of the lake it
appeared so near to the sky that they almost
touched one another, giving a visionary beauty
to the prospect. While we overlooked this quiet
scene we could hear the stream rumbling among

the rocks between the lakes, but the mists concealed any glimpse of it which we might have had. This small lake is called Loch Achray.

We returned, of course, by the same road. Our guide repeated over and over again his lamentations that the day was so bad, though we had often told him—not indeed with much hope that he would believe us—that we were glad of it. As we walked along he pulled a leafy twig from a birch tree, and, after smelling it, gave it to me, saying, how 'sweet and halesome' it was, and that it was pleasant and very halesome on a fine summer's morning to sail under the banks where the birks are growing. This reminded me of the old Scotch songs, in which you continually hear of the 'pu'ing the birks.' Common as birches are in the north of England, I believe their sweet smell is a thing unnoticed among the peasants. We returned again to the huts to take a farewell look. We had shared our food with the ferryman and a traveller whom we had met here, who was going up the lake, and wished to lodge at the ferry-house, so we offered him a place in the boat. Coleridge chose to walk. We took the same side of the lake as before, and had much delight in visiting the bays over again; but the evening began to darken, and it rained so heavily before we had gone two miles that we were completely wet. It was dark when we landed, and on entering the house I was sick with cold.

The good woman had provided, according to her promise, a better fire than we had found in the morning; and indeed when I sat down in the chimney-corner of her smoky biggin' I thought I had never been more comfortable in my life. Coleridge had been there long enough to have a pan of coffee boiling for us, and having put our clothes in the way of drying, we all sat down, thankful for a shelter. We could not prevail upon the man of the house to draw near the fire, though he was cold and wet, or to suffer his wife to get him dry clothes till she had served us which she did, though most willingly, not very expeditiously. A Cumberland man of the same rank would not have had such a notion of what was fit and right in his own house, or if he had, one would have accused him of servility; but in the Highlander it only seemed like politeness (however erroneous and painful to us) naturally growing out of the dependence of the inferiors of the clan upon their laird; he did not, however, refuse to let his wife bring out the whisky-bottle at our request: 'she keeps a dram,' as the phrase is; indeed, I believe there is scarcely

a lonely house by the wayside in Scotland where travellers may not be accommodated with a dram. We asked for sugar, butter, barley-bread, and milk, and with a smile and a stare more of kindness than wonder, she replied, 'Ye'll get that,' bringing each article separately.

We caroused our cups of coffee, laughing like children at the strange atmosphere in which we were: the smoke came in gusts, and spread along the walls and above our heads in the chimney, where the hens were roosting like light clouds in the sky. We laughed and laughed again, in spite of the smarting of our eyes, yet had a quieter pleasure in observing the beauty of the beams and rafters gleaming between the clouds of smoke. They had been crusted over and varnished by many winters, till, where the firelight fell upon them, they were as glossy as black rocks on a sunny day cased in ice. When we had eaten our supper we sat about half an hour, and I think I had never felt so deeply the blessing of a hospitable welcome and a warm fire. The man of the house repeated from time to time that we should often tell of this night when we got to our homes, and interposed praises of this, his own lake, which he had more than once, when we were returning in the boat, ventured to say was 'bonnier than Loch Lomond.'

Our companion from the Trossachs,[29] who it appeared was an Edinburgh drawing-master going during the vacation on a pedestrian tour to Johnny Groat's House, was to sleep in the barn with William and Coleridge, where the man said he had plenty of dry hay. I do not believe that the hay of the Highlands is often very dry, but this year it had a better chance than usual: wet or dry, however, the next morning they said they had slept comfortably. When I went to bed, the mistress, desiring me to 'go *ben*,' attended me with a candle, and assured me that the bed was dry, though not 'sic as I had been used to.' It was of chaff; there were two others in the room, a cupboard and two chests, on one of which stood the milk in wooden vessels covered over; I should have thought that milk so kept could not have been sweet, but the cheese and butter were good. The walls of the whole house were of stone unplastered. It consisted of three apartments,— the cow-house at one end, the kitchen or house in the middle, and the spence at the other end. The rooms were divided, not up to the rigging, but only to the beginning of the roof, so that there

29 a beautifully wooded valley between lakes Achray and Katrine in Perthshire, Scotland.

was a free passage for light and smoke from one end of the house to the other.

I went to bed sometime before the family. The door was shut between us, and they had a bright fire, which I could not see; but the light it sent up among the varnished rafters and beams, which crossed each other in almost as intricate and fantastic a manner as I have seen the under-boughs of a large beech-tree withered by the depth of the shade above, produced the most beautiful effect that can be conceived. It was like what I should suppose an underground cave or temple to be, with a dripping or moist roof, and the moonlight entering in upon it by some means or other, and yet the colours were more like the colour of melted gems. I lay looking up till the light of the fire faded away, and the man and his wife and child had crept into their bed at the other end of the room. I did not sleep much, but passed a comfortable night, for my bed, though hard, was warm and clean: the unusualness of my situation prevented me from sleeping. I could hear the waves beat against the shore of the lake; a little *syke*[30] close to the door made a much louder noise; and when I sat up in my bed I could see the lake through an open window-place at the bed's head. Add to this, it rained all night. I was less occupied by remembrance of the Trossachs, beautiful as they were, than the vision of the Highland hut, which I could not get out of my head. I thought of the Fairyland of Spenser, and what I had read in romance at other times, and then, what a feast would it be for a London pantomimemaker, could he but transplant it to Drury Lane, with all its beautiful colours!

August 28th, Sunday.—When beginning to descend the hill towards Loch Lomond, we overtook two girls, who told us we could not cross the ferry till evening, for the boat was gone with a number of people to church. One of the girls was exceedingly beautiful; and the figures of both of them, in grey plaids falling to their feet, their faces only being uncovered, excited our attention before we spoke to them; but they answered us so sweetly that we were quite delighted, at the same time that they stared at us with an innocent look of wonder. I think I never heard the English language sound more sweetly than from the mouth of the elder of these girls, while she stood at the gate answering our inquiries, her face flushed with the rain; her pronunciation was clear and distinct: without difficulty, yet slow,

like that of a foreign speech. They told us we might sit in the ferry-house till the return of the boat, went in with us, and made a good fire as fast as possible to dry our wet clothes. We learned that the taller was the sister of the ferryman, and had been left in charge with the house for the day, and the other was his wife's sister, and was come with her mother on a visit,—an old woman, who sat in a corner beside the cradle, nursing her little grand-child. We were glad to be housed, with our feet upon a warm hearthstone; and our attendants were so active and good-humoured that it was pleasant to have to desire them to do anything. The younger was a delicate and unhealthy-looking girl; but there was an uncommon meekness in her countenance, with an air of premature intelligence, which is often seen in sickly young persons. The other made me think of Peter Bell's Highland Girl:

> As light and beauteous as a squirrel,
> As beauteous and as wild![31]

She moved with unusual activity, which was chastened very delicately by a certain hesitation in her looks when she spoke being able to understand us but imperfectly. They were both exceedingly desirous to get me what I wanted to make me comfortable. I was to have a gown and petticoat of the mistress's; so they turned out her whole wardrobe upon the parlour floor, talking Erse to one another, and laughing all the time. It was long before they could decide which of the gowns I was to have; they chose at last, no doubt thinking that it was the best, a light-coloured sprigged cotton, with long sleeves, and they both laughed while I was putting it on, with the blue linsey petticoat, and one or the other, or both together, helped me to dress, repeating at least half a dozen times, 'You never had on the like of that before.' They held a consultation of several minutes over a pair of coarse woolen stockings, gabbling Erse as fast as their tongues could move, and looked as if uncertain what to do: at last, with great diffidence, they offered them to me, adding, as before, that I had never worn 'the like of them.' When we entered the house we had been not a little glad to see a fowl stewing in barley-broth; and now when the wettest of our clothes were stripped off, began again to recollect that we were hungry, and asked if we could have dinner. 'Oh yes, ye may get that,' the elder replied, pointing to the pan on the fire.

Conceive what a busy house it was—all our

---

30 brook.

31 *Peter Bell*, iii, 154-5.

wet clothes to be dried, dinner prepared and set out for us four strangers, and a second cooking for the family; add to this, two rough *callans,* as they called them, boys about eight years old, were playing beside us; the poor baby was fretful all the while; the old woman sang soleful Erse songs rocking it in its cradle the more violently the more it cried; then there were a dozen cookings of porridge, and it could never be fed without the assistance of all three. The hut was after the Highland fashion, but without anything beautiful except its situation; the floor was rough, and wet with the rain that came in at the door, so that the lasses' bare feet were as wet as if they had been walking through street puddles, in passing from one room to another; the windows were open, as at the other hut; but the kitchen had a bed in it, and was much smaller, and the shape of the house was like that of a common English cottage, without its comfort; yet there was no appearance of poverty—indeed, quite the contrary. The peep out of the open door-place across the lake made some amends for the want of the long roof and elegant rafters of our boatman's cottage, and all the while the waterfall, which we could not see, was roaring at the end of the hut, which seemed to serve as a sounding-board for its noise, so that it was not unlike sitting in a house where a mill is going. The dashing of the waves against the shore could not be distinguished; yet in spite of my knowledge of this I could not help fancying that the tumult and storm came from the lake, and went out several times to see if it was possible to row over in safety. . . .

After long waiting, the girls, who had been on the lookout, informed us that the boat was coming. I went to the water-side, and saw a cluster of people on the opposite shore; but being yet a distance, they looked more like soldiers surrounding a carriage than a group of men and women; red and green were the distinguishable colours. We hastened to get ourselves ready as soon as we saw the party approach, but had longer to wait than we expected, the lake being wider than it appears to be. As they drew near we could distinguish men in tartan plaids, women in scarlet cloaks, and green umbrellas by the half-dozen. The landing was as pretty a sight as ever I saw. The bay, which had been so quiet two days before, was all in motion with small waves, while the swoln waterfall roared in our ears. The boat came steadily up, being pressed almost to the water's edge by the weight of its cargo; perhaps twenty

people landed, one after another. It did not rain much, but the women held up their umbrellas; they were dressed in all the colours of the rainbow, and, with their scarlet cardinals, the tartan plaids of the men, and Scotch bonnets, made a gay appearance. There was a joyous bustle surrounding the boat, which even imparted something of the same character to the waterfall in its tumult, and the restless grey waves; the young men laughed and shouted, the lasses laughed, and the elder folks seemed to be in a bustle to be away. I remember well with what haste the mistress of the house where we were ran up to seek after her child, and seeing us, how anxiously and kindly she inquired how we had fared, if we had had a good fire, had been well waited upon, etc. etc. All this in three minutes—for the boatman had another party to bring from the other side and hurried us off.

The hospitality we had met with at the two cottages and Mr. Macfarlane's gave us very favourable impressions on this our first entrance into the Highlands, and at this day the innocent merriment of the girls, with their kindness to us, and the beautiful figure and face of the elder, come to my mind whenever I think of the ferryhouse and waterfall of Loch Lomond, and I never think of the two girls but the whole image of that romantic spot is before me, a living image, as it will be to my dying day. . . .

We were rowed over speedily by the assistance of two youths, who went backwards and forwards for their own amusement, helping at the oars, and pulled as if they had strength and spirits to spare for a year to come. We noticed that they had uncommonly fine teeth, and that they and the boatman were very handsome people. Another merry crew took our place in the boat.

We had three miles to walk to Tarbet.[32] It rained, but not heavily; the mountains were not concealed from us by the mists, but appeared larger and more grand; twilight was coming on, and the obscurity under which we saw the objects, with the sounding of the torrents, kept our minds alive and wakeful; all was solitary and huge—sky, water, and mountains mingled together. While we were walking forward, the road leading us over the top of a brow, we stopped suddenly at the sound of a half-articulate Gaelic hooting from the field close to us; it came from a little boy, whom we could see on the hill between us and the lake, wrapped up in a grey plaid; he was

---

32 a village on the western shore of Loch Lomond.

probably calling home the cattle for the night. His appearance was in the highest degree moving to the imagination: mists were on the hillsides, darkness shutting in upon the huge avenue of mountains, torrents roaring, no house in sight to which the child might belong; his dress, cry, and appearance all different from anything we had been accustomed to. It was a text, as William has since observed to me, containing in itself the whole history of the Highlander's life—his melancholy, his simplicity, his poverty, his superstition, and above all, that visionariness which results from a communion with the unworldliness of nature.

1775 · HENRY CRABB ROBINSON · 1867

1775   Born at Bury St. Edmunds, the son of a tanner.

1796   Entered the office of a solicitor.

1800–1805   After inheriting a sum of money, traveled on the Continent chiefly in Germany where he met Goethe and Schiller; spent three years as a student at the University of Jena.

1807   Became foreign correspondent of *The Times* in Altona, and subsequently foreign editor and its special correspondent in the Peninsular War.

1810–12   Read for the bar at the Middle Temple.

1813–28   Practiced law.

1828–67   Traveled extensively, read omnivorously, met and talked with people everywhere.

1867   Died.

HENRY CRABB ROBINSON—successful lawyer, man of business, and diarist—was a tolerant, eminently sociable bachelor possessed of an abundance of physical vitality. He enjoyed mixing with all sorts of people and was never too busy to do someone a good turn. To be sure, he had his crotchets and he could be dull and self-assertive; but he liked people. He was a great traveler, an inveterate theater-goer, a voracious devourer of books, and a capital talker. He had a remarkable memory and a wide range of anecdotes. His writings cover eighty-five years of literary recollections beginning with a reference to *John Gilpin* (1782) for learning which by heart he was given sixpence, to the last entry in his diary, five days before his death in 1867, referring to Matthew Arnold's *Function of Criticism*. Edith Morley thinks it no exaggeration to say that between those dates Crabb Robinson read every important book in English and German and knew and often was friendly with most of their writers. His *Diary*, begun in 1811, is the long record of his numberless friends and their talk, and of the thoughts of the times. In its pages the diarist reveals himself as a receptive rather than an originative thinker; nevertheless, he has a mind of his own capable of biting off sturdy and pointed critical judgments on the worth of new works. More important, he has a genuine gift for characterization and the ability to relate with extraordinary vividness the daily record of his experiences. He writes in a straightforward, unassuming style but with a steady-flowing enthusiasm for his subject. 'Crabb,' as he was called by his friends, is best known for his association with Wordsworth, Coleridge, and Lamb. He was one of Wordsworth's earliest admirers and defenders and has left an invaluable account of Coleridge's lectures, which reveal his deep admiration for Coleridge but which allow place 'for adverse judgments full of good sense.' Though he does not understand Blake, 'his account of interviews with Blake is the most revealing contemporary interpretation which we have of that poet' (Morley).

459

From DIARY AND REMINISCENCES

Nov. 15th., 1810. A very delightful evening at Charles Lamb's; Coleridge, Morgan,[1] Mr. Burney,[2] etc., there. Coleridge very eloquent on German metaphysics and poetry, Wordsworth, and Spanish politics.

Of Wordsworth he spoke with great warmth of praise, but objected to some of his poems. Wishing to avoid an undue regard to the high and genteel in society, Wordsworth had unreasonably attached himself to the low, so that he himself erred at last. He should have recollected that verse being the language of passion, and passion dictating energetic expressions, it became him to make his subjects and style accord. One asks why tales so simple were not in prose. With *malice prepense* he fixes on objects of reflection, which do not naturally excite it. Coleridge censured the disproportion in the machinery of the poem on the Gypsies. Had the whole world been standing idle, more powerful arguments to expose the evil could not have been brought forward. . . .

Dec. 20th. Met Coleridge by accident with Charles and Mary Lamb. As I entered, he was apparently arguing in favour of Christianity. At the same time contending that miracles were not an essential in the Christian system, he insisted that they were not brought forward as proofs; that miracles were acknowledged as having been performed by others as well as the true believers. Pharaoh's magicians wrought miracles also, though those of Moses were more powerful. In the New Testament the appeal is made to the knowledge which the believer has of the truths of his religion, not to the wonders wrought to make him believe. Of Jesus Christ he asserted that he was a Platonic philosopher, and when Christ spoke of his identity with the Father, he spoke in a Spinozistic or Pantheistic sense, according to which he could truly say that his transcendental sense was *one* with God, while his empirical sense retained its finite nature. . . .

Dec. 23rd. Coleridge dined with the Colliers,[3] talked a vast deal, and delighted every one. Politics, Kantian philosophy, and Shakespeare successively,—and at last a playful exposure of some bad poets. His remarks on Shakespeare were singularly ingenious. Shakespeare, he said, delighted in portraying characters in which the intellectual powers are found in a preeminent degree, while the moral faculties are wanting, at the same time that he taught the superiority of moral greatness. Such is the contrast exhibited in Iago and Othello. Iago's most marked feature is his delight in governing by fraud and superior understanding the noble-minded and generous Moor. In Richard III cruelty is less the prominent trait than pride, to which a sense of personal deformity gave a deadly venom. Coleridge, however, asserted his belief that Shakespeare wrote hardly anything of this play except the character of Richard: he found the piece a stock play and rewrote the parts which developed the hero's character: he certainly did not write the scenes in which Lady Anne yielded to the usurper's solicitations. He considered *Pericles* as illustrating the way in which Shakespeare handled a piece he had to refit for representation. At first he proceeded with indifference, only now and then troubling himself to put in a thought or an image, but as he advanced he interested himself in his employment, and the last two acts are almost entirely by him.

Hamlet he considered in a point of view which seems to agree very well with the representation given in *Wilhelm Meister*.[4] Hamlet is a man whose ideal and internal images are so vivid that all real objects are faint and dead to him. This we see in his soliloquies on the nature of man and his disregard of life: hence also his vacillation, and the purely convulsive energies he displayed. He acts only by fits and snatches. He manifests a strong inclination to suicide. On my observing that it appeared strange Shakespeare did not make suicide the termination of his piece, Coleridge replied that Shakespeare wished to show how even such a character is at last obliged to be the sport of chance,—a salutary moral doctrine. But I thought this the suggestion of the moment only, and not a happy one, to obviate a seeming objection. Hamlet remains at last the helpless, unpractical being, though every inducement to activity is given which the very appearance of the spirit of his murdered father could bring with it.

Coleridge also considered Falstaff as an instance of the predominance of intellectual power. He is content to be thought both a liar and a coward in order to obtain influence over the minds of his associates. His aggravated lies about

---

1 John James Morgan, a friend and benefactor of Coleridge.
2 Martin Burney, barrister, a faithful attendant at the Lambs' Wednesday evening gatherings.
3 John Payne Collier, 1789-1883, was a dramatic critic and literary forger.
4 *William Meister's Apprenticeship* by Goethe, Book IV, ch. 13.

the robbery are conscious and purposed, not inadvertent untruths. On my observing that this account seemed to justify Cooke's[5] representation, according to which a foreigner imperfectly understanding the character would fancy Falstaff the designing knave who does actually outwit the Prince, Coleridge answered that, in his *own* estimation, Falstaff is the superior, who cannot easily be convinced that the Prince has escaped him; but that, as in other instances, Shakespeare has shown us the defeat of mere intellect by a noble feeling; the Prince being the superior moral character, who rises above his insidious companion.

Jan. 8th., 1811. Spent part of the evening with Charles Lamb (unwell) and his sister. . . . We spoke of Wordsworth and Coleridge. Lamb, to my surprise, asserted Coleridge to be the greater man. He preferred the *Mariner* to anything Wordsworth had written. Wordsworth, he thought, is narrow and confined in his views compared with Coleridge. He does not, like Shakespeare, become everything he pleases, but forces the reader to submit to his individual feelings. This, I observe, lies very much in the lyrical character, and Lamb concluded by expressing high admiration of Wordsworth. He had read many of his things with great pleasure indeed, especially the sonnets, which I had before spoken of as my favourites.

March 29th. Spent evening with W. Hazlitt. Smith, his wife and son, Hume,[6] Coleridge, and afterwards Lamb were there. Coleridge philosophized as usual. . . . We talked of politics. It was amusing to observe how Coleridge blundered against Scotchmen and Frenchmen. He represented the *Edinburgh Review* as being a concentration of all the smartness of all Scotland. Edinburgh is a talking town, and whenever in their conversaziones a single spark is elicited, it is instantly caught, preserved, and brought to the *Review*. He denied humour to the nation. . . . Before Lamb came, Coleridge had spoken with warmth of his excellent and serious conversation. Hazlitt imputed his puns to humility.

June 21st. Charles and Mary Lamb, Dr. and Mrs. Adams, Barron Field,[7] Wright,[8] and M. An-

drews spent the evening. At whist, which I enjoyed.

We sat up late. Lamb was very merry; his puns were more numerous than select; he made one good pun. Field had said: 'Whoever puns will steal. I always button my pockets when in company with a punster.' Someone said: 'Punsters have no pocket.' 'No,' said Lamb, 'they have no pocket; they carry only a ridicule.'[9] . . .

July 24th. Returned late to Charles Lamb's. Found a very large party there. Southey had been with Blake, and admired both his designs and his poetic talents, at the same time that he held him for a decided madman. Blake, he says, spoke of his visions with the diffidence that is usual with such people, and did not seem to expect that he should be believed. He showed Southey a perfectly mad poem called *Jerusalem.* . . .

Nov. 29th. Of course you have already heard of the lectures on poetry which Coleridge is now delivering, and I fear have begun to think me inattentive in not sending you some account of them, or rather I should say, of his success in the undertaking. Yesterday he delivered the fourth, and I could not before, form anything like an opinion of the probable result. Indeed it is hardly otherwise now with me, but were I to wait till I could form a judgement, the very subject itself might escape from observation. Coleridge has about 150 hearers on an average and I fear the number is rather likely to diminish than increase. . . . [The lectures] have been brilliant, that is, in passages, but I doubt much his capacity to render them popular. Or rather I should say I doubt any man's power to render a system of philosophy popular which supposes so much unusual attention and rare faculties of thinking in the hearer. The majority of what are called sensible and thinking men have, to borrow a phrase from Coleridge, 'the passion of clear ideas' and as all poets have a very opposite passion, that of warm feelings, and delight in musing over conceptions, and imaginings beyond the reach of the analytic faculty, no wonder there is a sort of natural hostility between these classes of minds. This will ever be a bar to Coleridge's popularity; besides which he has certain unfortunate habits, which he *will* not, (perhaps *can* not) correct, very detrimental to his interests: I mean the vice of apologising, anticipating and repeating. We have had four lectures, and are still in the prolegomena

---

5 George Frederick Cooke, 1756–1811, was an eminent Shakespearean actor.
6 Joseph Hume, M. P.
7 Barron Field, 1786–1846, lawyer and miscellaneous writer.
8 Waller R. Wright, poet.

9 the pun is on *reticule*, a small workbag carried by women.

to the Shakespearian drama; When we are to begin Milton I have no idea. With all these defects there will always be a small circle who will listen with delight to his eloquent effusions (for that is the appropriate expression). I have not missed a lecture and have always left the room with the satisfaction which the hearkening to the display of truth in a beautiful form always gives. I have a German friend who attends also and who is delighted to find the logic and the rhetoric of his country delivered in a foreign language. There is no doubt that Coleridge's mind is much more German than English. My friend has pointed out striking analogies between Coleridge and German authors whom he has never seen. . . .

Dec. 5th. Accompanied Mrs. Rutt to Coleridge's lecture. In this he surpassed himself in the art of talking very amusingly without speaking at all on the subject to which the audience were especially invited. According to advertisement, Coleridge was to lecture on *Romeo and Juliet* and Shakespeare's female characters. Instead, he began with a defence of school flogging, at least in preference to Lancaster's[10] mode of punishing, without pretending to find the least connexion between that topic and poetry. Afterwards he remarked on the character of the age of Elizabeth and James I at the commencement in which intellect predominated, over that of Charles I, in which moral feeling prevailed. He distinguished between wit and fancy, not very clearly; he discoursed on the character of the different languages of Europe, attacked the fashionable notion concerning poetic diction, and abused Johnson's lines, '[Let] Observation with extensive view,'[11] etc., ridiculing the tautology. And he commented on the alleged impurity of Shakespeare, and vindicated him against the charge with warmth!

The man is absolutely incorrigible. But his *vitia*[12] are, indeed, *splendida*. I would have reported for the *Morning Chronicle* but it was too late. While Coleridge was so irrelevantly commenting on Lancaster's mode of punishing boys, Charles Lamb whispered: 'It is a pity he did not leave this till he got to *Henry VI* and then he might say he could not help taking part against the Lancastrians.' And afterwards, when Cole-

ridge was so extravagantly running from topic to topic without any guide whatever, Charles Lamb said: 'This is not so much amiss. Coleridge said in his advertisement he would speak about the nurse in *Romeo and Juliet,* and so he is delivering the lecture in the character of the nurse.' . . .

May 13th., 1812. . . . I will continue my anticipation and say here all that occurs to me about the *Edinburgh Review* which I do the more readily because these Reminiscences will probably not be brought down so low as to include what I wish to say.

The scornful treatment of my friends *Wordsworth, Lamb,* etc., etc., always incensed me against the *Edinburgh Review*. Wordsworth always thought that he was robbed of his just fame and consequently of his just emolument by the *Edinburgh Review* and many years afterwards he told Serjeant Talfourd[13] that he might say to his friend Mr. Jeffrey that but for *him,* (Jeffrey), Wordsworth would have gone to Rome twenty years before he did. Talfourd never reported to Wordsworth what Jeffrey replied to this. Nor did he to me but he told me this,—That he obtained from Jeffrey a frank confession that he was conscious he was wrong in the judgement he had formed of Lamb, whom he *then* admired. But he adhered to his original judgement of Wordsworth and could acquire no taste for him more than he had at first. This is evidenced by the reprinting in the collected papers even of the silly review of the *Rejected Addresses* in which the tale of Nancy Lake is declared to be 'rather a favourable specimen' of W. W. I believe no one of the articles on Lamb [is] retained.

I once only met Jeffrey by dining with him at Talfourd's. I managed to introduce the subject and obtained from him the strange assertion: 'I was always an admirer of Wordsworth.' 'Indeed,' I answered, 'The *Edinburgh Review* had a strange way of expressing admiration.' But Jeffrey intimated the same sort of thing to Coleridge. Such declarations are worse than foolish.

May 24th. A very interesting day. Rose late; at half-past ten joined Wordsworth in Oxford Road, and we then got into the fields and walked to Hampstead. We talked of Lord Byron. Wordsworth allowed him power, but denied his style to be English. Of his moral qualities we think the same. He adds that there is insanity in Lord By-

---

10 Joseph Lancaster, 1778–1838, founded a system of education based 'on general Christian principles' in schools organized on the monitorial system.
11 *The Vanity of Human Wishes,* 1.
12 faults.

13 Sir Thomas N. Talfourd, 1795–1854, judge and author.

ron's family, and that he believes Lord Byron to be somewhat cracked. I read Wordsworth some of Blake's poems; he was pleased with some of them, and considered Blake as having the elements of poetry a thousand times more than either Byron or Scott; but Scott he thinks superior to Campbell.

May 31st. A day of great enjoyment. . . . At Hamond's[14] found Wordsworth demonstrating to Hamond some of the points of his philosophical theory. Speaking of his own poems, Wordsworth said he principally valued them as being *a new power* in the literary world. Hamond's friend, Miller, esteemed Wordsworth for the pure morality of his works. Wordsworth said he himself looked to the powers of the mind his poems call forth, and the energies they presuppose and excite, as the standard by which they are to be estimated. . . . Wordsworth spoke in defence of Church establishment, and on the usual grounds said he would shed his blood for it. He declared himself not virtuous enough for a clergyman. Confessed he knew not when he had been in a church at home—'All our ministers are such vile creatures'—and he allowed us to laugh at this droll concession from a staunch advocate for the establishment.

June 11th. An unexpected call from Wordsworth. He had received the information of the death of a daughter (Catharine) of the age of four and he was going down immediately to Wales to Mrs. Wordsworth. He seemed deeply affected. I called with him on a Mr. De Quincey, a friend who had been lately in Westmoreland and was much attached to the little child. De Quincey burst into tears on seeing Mr. Wordsworth as if *he* had been the father. Miss Wordsworth had written to him. This was the first time I had seen De Quincey. I had heard of him only as a literary friend of Wordsworth of whose talents as a writer Wordsworth thought highly. He has since acquired celebrity as the Opium Eater and has lived a sad example of the wretchedness that attends the life of a man of superior intellect whose conduct is the sport of ill-regulated passions. His history is a curious one. . . .

I used occasionally to see him in London. For some years I was the depository of a large collection of books which were kept in my chambers to save warehouse rent, till they were sold to supply

his wants. They were classical works and I believe of value. His *Confessions of an Opium Eater* acquired celebrity, but it is the only work of his which did. He became an unsuccessful hanger-on of the booksellers and took up his residence in Scotland: in London he could not possibly maintain himself. I saw him occasionally there as a shiftless man. He had a wretchedly invalid countenance: his skin looked like mother-of-pearl. He had a very delicate hand and a voice more soft than a woman's, but his conversation was highly intelligent and interesting. He was near being a very attractive man, as he was always an object of compassion. I have not seen him for many years and as a writer, it is only in periodicals that I am acquainted with him. He wore out the patience of *Blackwood* and of the *Edinburgh Review,* obtaining from the publishers prepayment for papers which, being paid for, were not to be had. It has been latterly only in *Tait's Magazine* that I have read his papers, and Tait, I hear, never pays till he has the article in hand. Those which I have read with most interest have been the papers entitled *Autobiography of the Opium Eater,* and these are rendered entertaining because they are full of anecdotes of the great poets of the Lakes. But to create this interest, he has had recourse to the most unworthy expedients. Outraging all decency, he betrays private confidence without the slightest scruple, relating the most confidential conversations, even reporting the unkind words uttered by one friend of another and utterly regardless of all delicacy. I was with Wordsworth one day when the advertisement of one of his papers was read. He said with great earnestness: 'I beg that no friend of mine will ever tell me a word of the contents of those papers' and I dare say he was substantially obeyed. It was a year or two afterwards (for these papers went on for a long time and were very amusing) however, that I ventured to say: 'I cannot help telling one thing De Quincey says in his last number in these very words—that Mrs. Wordsworth is a better wife than you deserve.' 'Did he say that?' Wordsworth exclaimed in a tone of unusual vehemence, 'Did he say that? That is *so* true that I can forgive him almost anything else he says.' Yet writing of Mrs. Wordsworth in terms of the most extravagant eulogy, he could not refrain from concluding: '*But she squints.*'

Dec. 16th., 1813. . . . Returned to Lamb's. Hazlitt was there, and overbearing and rude. Dis-

---

14 Elton Hamond was a young acquaintance of H. C. R. who within a few years of this meeting took his own life.

puted with him on politics. He mixes passion and ill-humour and personal feelings in his judgements on public events and characters more than any man I know, and this infinitely detracts from the value of his opinions, which, possessing as he does rare talents, would be otherwise very valuable. He always vindicates Buonaparte, not because he is insensible to his enormous crimes, but out of spite to the Tories of this country and the friends of the war of 1792.

July 3rd., 1814. A day of great pleasure. Charles Lamb and I walked to Enfield by Southgate, after an early breakfast in his chambers. We were most hospitably received by Anthony Robinson[15] and wife, and after tea, at which we were joined by the Freemans,[16] Lamb and I returned. The whole day most delightfully fine, and the scenery very agreeable. Lamb enjoyed the walk more than the scenery, for the enjoyment of which he seems to have no great susceptibility. His great delight, even in preference to a country walk, is a stroll in London. The shops and the busy streets, such as Thames Street, Bank Side, etc., are his great favourites. He for the same reason has no relish for landscape painting. But his relish for historic painting is exquisite. Lamb's peculiarities are very interesting. We had not much conversation. He hummed tunes, I repeated Wordsworth's *Daffodils,* of which I am become very fond.

Dec. 4th. Went to Dr. Aikin's,[17] with whom I dined and made a very comfortable visit. I read *Christabel* to them. Miss Aikin appeared to enjoy it. The doctor could not relish a fragment which was so entirely unintelligible, and what Miss Aikin called high flights of poetry he thought akin to absurdity. Miss Aikin, however, lost whatever credit her tolerance of *Christabel* might procure for her by being insensible to the merits of THE POEM [*The Excursion*]. She was not able to read it through! . . .

Sept. 11th., 1816. . . . Mr. Wordsworth came to me, and between three and four o'clock we set out on our journey, he on horseback, I on foot. We set out during a heavy shower, which thoroughly wetted me, and from which I did not entirely recover the whole evening. The rain continued with but little intermission during a great part of the afternoon. . . . In the close and interesting conversation we kept up, Mr. Wordsworth was not quite attentive to the road . . . and it was late before we reached the Globe at Cockermouth. . . . If this were the place, and if my memory were good, I could enrich my journal by one valuable page in retailing Wordsworth's conversation. He is an eloquent speaker, and he talked upon his own art and his own works very feelingly and very profoundly, but I cannot venture to state more than a few intelligible results, for I own that much of what he said was above my comprehension. He stated, what I had before taken for granted, that most of his *Lyrical Ballads* were founded on some incident he had witnessed or had heard of, and in order to illustrate how facts are turned into poetry he mentioned the origin of several poems; *Lucy Gray,* that tender and pathetic narrative of a child mysteriously lost on a common, was occasioned by the death of a child who fell into the lock of a canal. He removed from his poem all that pertained to art, and it being his object to exhibit poetically entire *solitude,* he represents his child as observing the day-*moon* which no town or village girl would ever notice. The Leech Gatherer he did actually meet near Grasmere, except that he gave to his poetic character powers of mind which his original did not possess.

Dec. 22nd. It was on Sunday, the 22d of December, the day after this conversation with Coleridge, that I broke altogether with Hazlitt. I had read in the morning's *Examiner,* a paper, manifestly by Hazlitt, abusing Wordsworth for his writings in favour of the King, I rather think especially the sonnet expressing the wish that the king could be restored for an instant to his faculties in order to be aware of the victory gained by the nation over Buonaparte. 'I recollected,' he said,—(I quote from memory)—'hearing this gentleman say "I should wish to see every member of the House of Commons hanged." I put in a word in favour of Charles Fox and Sheridan. But he said: "No. There is not one of them fit to live." And then he referred to what he called their tergiversation.'[18] This evening I took tea at Basil Montagu's.[19] Hazlitt on coming in, offered me his hand which I refused. And during the evening I took an opportunity to say; 'Nothing should induce me to continue an ac-

15 a lifelong friend of H. C. R.
16 Enfield friends of Lamb.
17 John Aikin, M. D.

18 turning against a cause formerly supported; political trimming.
19 Basil Montagu, 1770-1851, was a legal and miscellaneous writer, intimate in his youth with Coleridge and Wordsworth.

quaintance with the writer of an article in today's *Examiner*.' Hazlitt said coolly, 'I am not in the habit of defending everything I write. I do not say that all I have written is just.' And on my especially remarking on the breach of confidence, he said, 'It may be indelicate, but I must write an article every week, and I have not time to be delicate.' On which I repeated the anecdote of the French minister to the libeller: 'Je n'en vois pas la necessite.'[20] He then made a distinction: 'I would never take advantage of a slip in a man's conversation, who might say *once* what was not his real habitual opinion and a repetition would be a substantial falsehood. But what I published was an often repeated sentiment, not said to me alone but many. And such things might be repeated.' I replied, 'One aggravation is wanting in this case and your vindication amounts to this: "Though I won't lie, I will betray." ' He said he thought it useful to expose persons who would otherwise gain credit by canting. I admitted that the attack on Southey's *Carmen Nuptiale* was unexceptionable and he said he still believed Southey was an honest man.

After this evening I never to my recollection exchanged a word with Hazlitt. I often met him at Lamb's but we never spoke. He lived twelve years afterwards and many years before his death he said to Mary Lamb, 'Robinson cuts me, but in spite of that I shall always have a kind feeling towards him, for he was the first person that ever found out there was anything in me.' That is true, for when I became acquainted with him at Bury, he was living with his elder brother a miniature painter. And I admired him when no one else thought anything of him and before he had printed anything.

Dec. 30th. I dined with the Colliers and spent the evening at Lamb's. I found a large party collected round the two poets, but Coleridge had the larger body. Talfourd only had fixed himself by Wordsworth and remained by his side all the evening. There was, however, scarcely any conversation beyond a whisper. Coleridge was philosophising in his rambling way to Monkhouse,[21] who listened attentively; to Manning,[22] who sometimes smiled as if he thought Coleridge had no right to metaphysicise on chemistry without any knowledge on the subject; to Martin Burney,

who was eager to interpose, and Alsager,[23] who was content to be a listener; while Wordsworth was for a great part of the time engaged tête-à-tête with Talfourd. I could catch scarcely anything of the conversation; but I heard at one time Coleridge quoting Wordsworth's verses, and Wordsworth quoting—*not* Coleridge's but his own.

April 18th. . . . to Lamb's again. There was a large party—the greater part of those who are usually there, but also Hunt and his wife—she a very disgusting woman; he, though a man I very much dislike, did not displease me this evening. He has improved in manliness and healthfulness since I saw him last, some years ago. There was a glee about him which evinced high spirits, if not perfect health, and I envied his vivacity. He imitated Hazlitt capitally, Wordsworth not so well. Talfourd was there, and injudiciously loquacious, quoting verses without mercy. He threw away Wordsworth's fine lines on scorners. Hunt, who did not sympathise with Talfourd, opposed him playfully, and that I liked him for. . . .

Dec. 15th., 1820. I read Keats's *Pot of Basil*— a pathetic tale delightfully told. I afterwards read the story in Boccaccio, each in his way excellent. I am greatly mistaken if Keats do not very soon take a high place among our poets. There is great feeling and a powerful imagination in this little volume.

Dec. 10th., 1825. Dined with Aders,[24] a very remarkable and interesting evening. The party Blake the painter and Linnell, also a painter and engraver. . . .

BLAKE

I will put down as they occur to me without method all I can recollect of the conversation of this remarkable man. Shall I call him artist or genius—or mystic—or madman? Probably he is all. He has a most interesting appearance. He is now old—pale, with a Socratic countenance and an expression of great sweetness, but bordering on weakness except when his features are animated by expression, and then he has an air of inspiration about him. The conversation was on art and on poetry and on religion; but it was my object—and I was successful— in drawing him out and in so getting from him an avowal

20 'I do not see the necessity.'
21 Thomas Monkhouse, 1785–1825, London merchant, friend and benefactor of authors. He was a kinsman of Wordsworth's wife.
22 Thomas Manning, 1772–1840, one of Lamb's most intimate friends.
23 Thomas M. Alsager was City Correspondent to the London *Times*.
24 Charles Aders.

of his *peculiar* sentiments. I was aware before of the nature of his impressions or I should at times have been at a loss to understand him. He was shown soon after he entered the room some compositions of Mrs. Aders, which he cordially praised, and he brought with him an engraving of his Canterbury Pilgrims for Aders. One of the figures resembled one in one of Aders's pictures. 'They say I stole it from this picture, but I did it twenty years before I knew of the picture. However, in my youth I was always studying this kind of painting; no wonder there is a resemblance.' In this he seemed to explain *humanly* what he had done; but he at another time spoke of his paintings as being what he had seen in his visions, and when he said '*my visions*' it was in the ordinary unemphatic tone in which we speak of trivial matters that every one understands and cares nothing about. In the same tone he said repeatedly: 'The Spirit told me.' I took occasion to say: 'You use the same word as Socrates used. What resemblance do you suppose is there between your spirit and the spirit of Socrates?' 'The same as between our countenances.' He paused and added: 'I *was* Socrates,' and then, as if correcting himself, 'a sort of brother. I must have had conversations with him, so I had with Jesus Christ. I have an obscure recollection of having been with both of them.' It was before this that I had suggested on very obvious philosophical grounds the *impossibility* of supposing an immortal being created—an eternity *a parte post* without an eternity *a parte ante*. This is an obvious truth I have been many (perhaps thirty) years fully aware of. His eye brightened on my saying this, and he eagerly concurred: 'To be sure it is impossible; we are all co-existent with God, members of the divine body; we are all partakers of the divine nature. In this, by the bye, Blake has but adopted an ancient Greek idea, Query of Plato? As connected with this idea I will mention here (though it formed part of our talk walking homeward), that on my asking in what light he viewed the great question concerning the divinity of Jesus Christ, he said: 'He is the only God'; but then he added: 'and so am I and so are you.' Now he had just before (and that occasioned my question) been speaking of the errors of Jesus Christ: 'He was wrong in suffering himself to be crucified, he should not have attacked the government, he had no business with such matters.' On my inquiring how he reconciled this with the sanctity and divine qualities of Jesus, he said: 'He was not then become the Father.' Connecting as well as one can these fragmentary sentiments it would be hard to fix Blake's station between Christianity, Platonism, and Spinozaism, yet he professes to be very hostile to Plato and reproaches Wordsworth with being not a Christian but a Platonist.

It is one of the subtle remarks of Hume on certain religious speculations that the tendency of them is to make men indifferent to whatever takes place by destroying all ideas of good and evil. I took occasion to apply this remark to something Blake said. 'If so,' I said, 'there is no use in discipline or education, no difference between good and evil.' He hastily broke in on me: 'There is no use in education—I hold it wrong—it is the great sin—it is eating of the tree of knowledge of good and evil. That was the fault of Plato: he knew of nothing but of the Virtues and Vices and Good and Evil. There is nothing in all that. Everything is good in God's eyes.' On my putting the obvious question, "Is there nothing absolutely evil in what men do.' 'I am no judge of that—perhaps not in God's eyes.' Though on this and other occasions he spoke as if he denied altogether the existence of evil and as if we had nothing to do with right and wrong, it being sufficient to consider all things as alike the work of God. I interposed with the German word objectivity, which he approved of, yet at other times he spoke of error as being in heaven. I asked about the *moral* character of Dante in writing his *Vision*— was he *pure?*—'*Pure?*' said Blake. 'Do you think there is any purity in God's eyes; the angels in heaven are no more so than we. He chargeth his angels with folly.' He afterwards extended this to the Supreme Being. 'Did he not repent him that he had made Nineveh?'[25] It is easier to repeat the personal remarks of Blake than these metaphysical speculations so nearly allied to the most opposite systems. He spoke with seeming complacency of himself, said he acted by command; the Spirit said to him: 'Blake, be an artist and nothing else. In this there is felicity.' His eye glistened when he spoke of the joy of devoting himself solely to divine art. Art is inspiration—When Michael Angelo or Raphael or Mr. Flaxman[26] does any of his fine things he does them in the spirit. Blake said: 'I should be sorry if I had any earthly fame, for whatever natural glory a man has is so much detracted from his spiritual glory. I wish to do nothing for profit. I wish to live for art. I want nothing whatever. I am quite happy.'

Among the unintelligible sentiments which he

25 See Nahum, ii–iii.
26 John Flaxman, 1775–1826, English sculptor and engraver.

was continually expressing is his distinction between the natural and spiritual world. The natural world must be consumed. Incidentally Swedenborg was spoken of. 'He was a divine teacher; he has done much and will do much good; he has corrected many errors of Popery, and also of Luther and Calvin.' Yet he also said that Swedenborg was wrong in endeavouring to explain to the *rational* faculty what the reason cannot comprehend; he should have left that. As Blake mentioned Swedenborg and Dante together I wished to know whether he considered their visions of the same kind. As far as I could recollect he does. Dante, he said, was the greater poet —he had political objects; yet this, though wrong, does not appear in Blake's mind to affect the truth of the vision. Strangely inconsistent with this was the language of Blake about Wordsworth. Wordsworth, he thinks, is no Christian, but a Platonist. He asked me: 'Does he believe in the Scriptures?' On my answering in the affirmative he said he had been much pained by reading the introduction to *The Excursion*—it brought on a fit of illness. The passage was produced and read:

Jehovah—with his thunder and the choir
Of shouting angels, and the empyreal
    thrones—
I pass them unalarmed.

This *pass them unalarmed* greatly offended Blake. 'Does Mr. Wordsworth think his mind can surpass Jehovah?' I tried to twist this passage into a sense corresponding with Blake's own theories, but failed, and Wordsworth was finally set down as a Pagan, but still with great praise as the greatest poet of the age. . . . I feel great admiration and respect for [Blake]; he is certainly a most amiable man, a good creature, and of his poetical and pictorial genius there is no doubt, I believe, in the minds of judges. . . .

I regret that I have been unable to do more than set down these seeming idle and rambling sentences. The tone and manner are incommunicable. There is a natural sweetness and gentility about Blake which are delightful, and when he is not referring to his visions he talks sensibly and acutely.

Aug. 2nd., 1829. A golden day! But I feel ashamed at my inability to leave a memorial at all worthy of it. . . . It was between ten and eleven when I left my card at Goethe's house for his daughter-in-law, and we proceeded then to the small house in the park, where we were at once admitted to the Great Man. I was oppressed by the cordial reception, and as the cordiality increased during two most interesting conversations, the sense of unworthiness is but increased and now disturbs the otherwise delightful feelings which several hours' conversation has produced. . . . We spoke of Lord Byron and I mentioned *The Vision of Judgment*. He called it sublime and laughed while he referred to the summoning of Junius and Wilkes as witnesses and to the letting of the king slip into heaven, etc., as admirable hits. He said: '*Es sind keine Flickwörter im Gedichte,*'[27] and he compared the brilliancy and clearness of his style to a metal wire drawn through a steel plate!

Aug. 16th., 1830. Mr. Landor stepped in to whom I was introduced as a friend of Wordsworth and after a long talk Landor intimated a wish to be further acquainted. . . . Landor is altogether different from what I had imagined him to be. He is a florid man with large eyes, an animated air, having the look of a country gentleman and an officer. He talks decisively and freely, even cynically. He is said to be a man whom it is difficult to keep on good terms with, being apt to take offence.

Dec. 30th., 1834. This day I shall long recollect. . . . I have been lounging over books but my mind has been wandering from them. I read in the morning papers that *Charles Lamb died on Saturday*—one of the most amiable of men and an admirable genius.

---

27 'There are no superfluities in his poetry.'

1774 · ROBERT SOUTHEY · 1843

1774   Born in Bristol, son of a linen draper.

1788–92   Entered Westminster School; after four years there was expelled for a precocious essay against flogging.

1793   Matriculated at Balliol College, Oxford, but gained little from the university and left without taking a degree.

1794   At Oxford met Coleridge and was fired by his dreams of an American Utopia on the banks of the Susquehanna. Published *Poems,* with Coleridge and Lovell.

1795   As part of the 'pantisocratic' scheme, married Edith Fricker, whose sister became the wife of Coleridge. Met the publisher Cottle who bought his epic *Joan of Arc* and published it the following year.

1796–1801   Visited Portugal. On his return to England tried studying law, but gave it up for the serious pursuit of literature. Lived for a time at Bristol and made a second trip to Portugal.

1803   Took up his residence at Greta Hall, Keswick, which he and his family shared with the Coleridges.

1801–5   Published *Thalaba* and *Metrical Tales* and *Madoc.*

1808   Became a regular contributor to the Tory *Quarterly Review.*

1810   Published *The Curse of Kehama,*

1810–19   *History of Brazil,* and

1813   *Life of Nelson.* Was appointed Poet Laureate after Scott's refusal of the office.

1814   Published *Roderick, the Last of the Goths.*

1817   Was embarrassed by the piratical publication of *Wat Tyler,* a drama of extreme radical enthusiasm written during Oxford days.

1820   Published *Life of Wesley* and

1821   *A Vision of Judgement,* which caused a flare-up of his smoldering controversy with Byron.

1825   Published *A Tale of Paraguay,*

1823–32   *History of the Peninsular War,*

1824   *The Book of the Church,*

1829   *Colloquies on Society,*

1833–7   *Works of Cowper,* and

1834–47   *The Doctor,* a humorous prose miscellany.

1835–7   Was offered, but refused, a baronetcy. Was afflicted with domestic sorrows.

1839   Married his second wife, Caroline Bowles, a writer of verse and a friend of long standing.

1843   Died at Greta Hall literally worn out by brain labor.

IF UNREMITTING TOIL could produce literary masterpieces, Robert Southey would have a just claim to be among the immortals. His output, always founded upon immense reading, was enormous. His collected verse alone, with its explanatory notes, fills ten volumes and his prose about forty more, not including the unfinished history of Portugal, the most ambitious of all his projects. Southey built a high contemporary reputation for himself and had not the slightest doubt but that he would be recognized as a great poet by posterity. Yet the vast epics upon which he staked his hopes for fame, even in his own time ceased to be read and since then the blight of neglect has spread to all but an infinitesimal fragment of his total verse. Fatally lacking in imagination and poetic sympathy, he is now remembered by only a few short pieces: the ballad on Bishop Hatto and some other similar comic-grotesque ballads, for which he had a special talent; *The Holly Tree* and the lines about his books, with their pungent homeliness; and above anything else, the ironical *Battle of Blenheim*. There is not much more worth saving.

Southey's prose is better than his verse; even so, comparatively little of it has lived. In the mass his prose, like his poetry, is 'lacking in any exquisite qualities of passion or magic.' But if Southey is not a great prose writer, he is a sound and good one, and not infrequently an entertaining one. He developed a prose style that has been much admired—lucid, perspicuous, flexible, and never obtruding itself between the reader and the subject. His highest achievement was in biography. In this field his admirable *Life of Nelson* is the single work that has won him the greatest acclaim. The exploits of England's naval hero are told simply and directly with a skillful interweaving of the historical and biographical parts into an absorbing narrative. The biographies of Cowper and Wesley, though not on a level with that of Nelson, are both nevertheless excellent. Southey's letters have been praised for their naturalness and charm; yet superior to the letters for humor and leisurely reflection are the *Colloquies* and *The Doctor*. That delightful story of the three bears known to every child first appeared in *The Doctor* and was one of Southey's real successes.

Southey's life touched at many points the lives of other notable men of the age. He was the brother-in-law of Coleridge, the neighbor of Wordsworth, the close editorial associate of Scott, and the lifelong friend of Landor. Like Wordsworth and Coleridge he started out as a liberal in the early years of the French Revolution and lived to distrust popular government and to become the strenuous defender of institutions of the past. His quasi-epical enterprises (portions of his gigantic scheme of turning the great mythologies of the world into heroic poems) illustrate the desire of the romanticists to reach out to distant continents and exotic legends. But Southey's romantic impulses were nourished by reading and by study rather than by inward experience; and although he associated with some of the greatest geniuses of his time, his life was self-contained and closed to all passions but that of self-culture. Rogers called him a 'cold man' who was 'never happy except when reading a book or making one.' Within the limits of his pedestrian talents he did his work well. He lived a busy and honorable life of letters, supporting not only his own household but the widow of Lovell and the wife and family of Coleridge by his incessant literary labors. But his industry alone has proved to be an insufficient substitute for genius that was denied him.

THE BATTLE OF BLENHEIM

[In the Battle of Blenheim, 1704, the English and Austrians under the Duke of Marlborough and Prince Eugene won a decisive victory over the French and Bavarian armies. This 'famous victory' dealt a heavy blow to Louis XIV's ambition to establish a French universal monarchy in Europe.]

IT was a summer evening,
  Old Kaspar's work was done,

And he before his cottage door
  Was sitting in the sun,
And by him sported on the green
His little grandchild Wilhelmine.

She saw her brother Peterkin
  Roll something large and round,
Which he beside the rivulet
  In playing there had found;   10

He came to ask what he had found,
That was so large, and smooth, and round.

Old Kaspar took it from the boy,
  Who stood expectant by;
And then the old man shook his head,
  And, with a natural sigh,
''Tis some poor fellow's skull,' said he,
'Who fell in the great victory.

'I find them in the garden,
  For there's many here about;   20
And often when I go to plough,
  The ploughshare turns them out!
For many thousand men,' said he,
'Were slain in that great victory.'

'Now tell us what 'twas all about,'
  Young Peterkin, he cries;
And little Wilhelmine looks up
  With wonder-waiting eyes;
'Now tell us all about the war,
And what they fought each other for.'   30

'It was the English,' Kaspar cried,
  'Who put the French to rout;
But what they fought each other for,
  I could not well make out;
But everybody said,' quoth he,
  'That 'twas a famous victory.

'My father lived at Blenheim then,
  Yon little stream hard by;
They burnt his dwelling to the ground,
  And he was forced to fly;   40
So with his wife and child he fled,
Nor had he where to rest his head.

'With fire and sword the country round
  Was wasted far and wide,
And many a childing mother then,
  And new-born baby died;
But things like that, you know, must be
At every famous victory.

'They say it was a shocking sight
  After the field was won;   50
For many thousand bodies here
  Lay rotting in the sun;
But things like that, you know, must be
After a famous victory.

'Great praise the Duke of Marlbro' won,
  And our good Prince Eugene.'

'Why 'twas a very wicked thing!'
  Said little Wilhelmine.
'Nay, nay, my little girl,' quoth he,
'It was a famous victory.   60

'And everybody praised the Duke
  Who this great fight did win.'
'But what good came of it at last?'
  Quoth little Peterkin.
'Why that I cannot tell,' said he,
'But 'twas a famous victory.'

1798   1798

THE HOLLY TREE

O READER! hast thou ever stood to see
    The Holly Tree?
The eye that contemplates it well perceives
    Its glossy leaves
Order'd by an intelligence so wise,
As might confound the Atheist's sophistries.

Below, a circling fence, its leaves are seen
    Wrinkled and keen;
No grazing cattle through their prickly round
    Can reach to wound;   10
But as they grow where nothing is to fear,
Smooth and unarm'd the pointless leaves appear.

I love to view these things with curious eyes,
    And moralise:
And in this wisdom of the Holly Tree
    Can emblems see
Wherewith perchance to make a pleasant rhyme,
One which may profit in the after time.

Thus, though abroad perchance I might appear
    Harsh and austere,   20
To those who on my leisure would intrude
    Reserved and rude,
Gentle at home amid my friends I'd be
Like the high leaves upon the Holly Tree.

And should my youth, as youth is apt I know,
    Some harshness show,
All vain asperities I day by day
    Would wear away,
Till the smooth temper of my age should be
Like the high leaves upon the Holly Tree.   30

And as when all the summer trees are seen
    So bright and green,

The Holly leaves a sober hue display
    Less bright than they,
But when the bare and wintry woods we see,
What then so cheerful as the Holly Tree?

So serious should my youth appear among
    The thoughtless throng,
So would I seem amid the young and gay
    More grave than they,   40
That in my age as cheerful I might be
As the green winter of the Holly Tree.

    1798   *1799*

GOD'S JUDGEMENT ON A WICKED
BISHOP

[Southey prefaced his ballad with the legendary history of Hatto, Archbishop of Mentz, as given in *Coryat's
Crudities*. According to this account, the events happened in the year 914, a time of 'an exceeding great famine' in Germany.]

THE summer and autumn had been so wet,
That in winter the corn was growing yet,
'Twas a piteous sight to see all around
The grain lie rotting on the ground.

Every day the starving poor
Crowded around Bishop Hatto's door,
For he had a plentiful last-year's store,
And all the neighbourhood could tell
His granaries were furnish'd well.

At last Bishop Hatto appointed a day   10
To quiet the poor without delay;
He bade them to his great Barn repair,
And they should have food for the winter there.

Rejoiced such tidings good to hear,
The poor folk flock'd from far and near;
The great Barn was full as it could hold
Of women and children, and young and old.

Then when he saw it could hold no more,
Bishop Hatto he made fast the door;
And while for mercy on Christ they call,   20
He set fire to the Barn and burnt them all.

'I'faith 'tis an excellent bonfire!' quoth he,
'And the country is greatly obliged to me,
For ridding it in these times forlorn,
Of Rats that only consume the corn.'

So then to his palace returned he,
And he sat down to supper merrily,
And he slept that night like an innocent man;
But Bishop Hatto never slept again.

In the morning as he enter'd the hall   30
Where his picture hung against the wall,
A sweat like death all over him came,
For the Rats had eaten it out of the frame.

As he look'd there came a man from his
    farm—
He had a countenance white with alarm;
'My Lord, I open'd your granaries this morn,
And the Rats had eaten all your corn.'

Another came running presently,
And he was pale as pale could be,
'Fly! my Lord Bishop, fly,' quoth he,   40
'Ten thousand Rats are coming this way,—
The Lord forgive you for yesterday!'

'I'll go to my tower on the Rhine,' replied he,
''Tis the safest place in Germany;
The walls are high and the shores are steep,
And the stream is strong and the water deep.'

Bishop Hatto fearfully hasten'd away,
And he crost the Rhine without delay,
And reach'd his tower, and barr'd with care
All the windows, doors, and loop-holes there.   50

He laid him down and closed his eyes;
But soon a scream made him arise,
He started and saw two eyes of flame
On his pillow from whence the screaming came.

He listen'd and look'd;—it was only the Cat;
But the Bishop he grew more fearful for that,
For she sat screaming, mad with fear
At the Army of Rats that were drawing near.

For they have swum over the river so deep,
And they have climb'd the shores so steep,   60
And up the Tower their way is bent,
To do the work for which they were sent.

They are not to be told by the dozen or score,
By thousands they come, and by myriads and
    more,
Such numbers had never been heard of before,
Such a judgement had never been witness'd of
    yore.

Down on his knees the Bishop fell,
And faster and faster his beads did he tell,

As louder and louder drawing near
The gnawing of their teeth he could hear.　　70

And in at the windows and in at the door,
And through the walls helter-skelter they pour,
And down from the ceiling and up through the
　　floor,
From the right and the left, from behind and
　　before,
From within and without, from above and below,
And all at once to the Bishop they go.

They have whetted their teeth against the stones,
And now they pick the Bishop's bones;
They gnaw'd the flesh from every limb,
For they were sent to do judgement on him!　　80

1799　　　　　　　　　　　　　　　1799

MY DAYS AMONG THE DEAD ARE PAST

[Southey was a great lover of books and in his lonely
life at Keswick spent more and more time in his library,
which at his death comprised some fourteen thousand
well-selected volumes.]

MY days among the dead
　　Are past; around me I behold,
Where'er these casual eyes are cast,
　　The mighty minds of old;
My never-failing friends are they,
With whom I converse day by day.

With them I take delight in weal,
　　And seek relief in woe;
And while I understand and feel
　　How much to them I owe,
My cheeks have often been bedew'd　　10
With tears of thoughtful gratitude.

My thoughts are with the dead, with them
　　I live in long-past years,
Their virtues love, their faults condemn,
　　Partake their hopes and fears,
And from their lessons seek and find
Instruction with an humble mind.

My hopes are with the dead, anon
　　My place with them will be,　　20
And I with them shall travel on
　　Through all futurity;
Yet leaving here a name, I trust,
That will not perish in the dust.

1818　　　　　　　　　　　　　　1823

From A VISION OF JUDGEMENT

(PART VI)

THE ABSOLVERS

[This unlucky poem in hexameters, commemorating
the death of King George III, was written by Southey in
the perfunctory fulfillment of his duty as Poet Laureate.
It is remembered now chiefly by way of Byron's brilliant
travesty, *The Vision of Judgment* (text, p. 913). In the
following episode George Washington exonerates
George III from dishonorable motives in the war with
the colonies.]

Ho! he[1] exclaim'd, King George of England
　　standeth in judgement!
Hell hath been dumb in his presence. Ye who on
　　earth arraign'd him,
Come ye before him now, and here accuse or ab-
　　solve him!
For injustice hath here no place.

　　　　　　　　　From the Souls of the Blessed
Some were there then who advanced; and more
　　from the skirts of the meeting—
Spirits who had not yet accomplish'd their purifi-
　　cation,
Yet, being cleansed from pride, from faction and
　　error deliver'd,
Purged of the film wherewith the eye of the mind
　　is clouded,
They, in their better state, saw all things clear;
　　and discerning
Now, in the light of truth, what tortuous views
　　had deceived them,　　10
They acknowledged their fault, and own'd the
　　wrong they had offer'd;
Not without ingenuous shame, and a sense of
　　compunction,
More or less, as each had more or less to atone
　　for.
One alone remain'd,[2] when the rest had retired to
　　their station:
Silently he had stood, and still unmoved and in
　　silence,
With a steady mien, regarded the face of the
　　Monarch.
Thoughtful awhile he gazed; severe, but serene,
　　was his aspect;
Calm, but stern; like one whom no compassion
　　could weaken,
Neither could doubt deter, nor violent impulses
　　alter;

---

1 the Archangel Michael, who was conducting the trial of the
king before the gates of heaven.
2 Washington.

Lord of his own resolves,—of his own heart absolute master.   20
Awful Spirit; his place was with ancient sages
   and heroes;
Fabius, Aristides, and Solon, and Epaminondas.

   Here then at the Gate of Heaven we are met!
   said the Spirit;
King of England! albeit in life opposed to each
   other,
Here we meet at last. Not unprepared for the
   meeting
Ween I; for we had both outlived all enmity, ren-
   dering
Each to each that justice which each from each
   had withholden.
In the course of events, to thee I seem'd as a
   Rebel,
Thou a Tyrant to me;—so strongly doth circum-
   stance rule men
During evil days, when right and wrong are con-
   founded.   30

Left to our hearts we were just. For me, my actions have spoken,
That not for lawless desires, nor goaded by desperate fortunes,
Nor for ambition, I chose my part; but observant of duty,
Self-approved. And here, this witness I willingly
   bear thee,—
Here, before Angels and Men, in the awful hour
   of judgement,—
Thou too didst act with upright heart, as befitted
   a Sovereign
True to his sacred trust, to his crown, his kingdom, and people.
Heaven in these things fulfill'd its wise, though
   inscrutable purpose,
While we work'd its will, doing each in his place
   as became him.

Washington! said the Monarch, well hast thou
   spoken and truly,   40
Just to thyself and to me. On them is the guilt of
   the contest,
Who for wicked ends, with foul arts of faction
   and falsehood,
Kindled and fed the flame; but verily they have
   their guerdon.
Thou and I are free from offense. And would
   that the nations,
Learning of us, would lay aside all wrongful resentment,

All injurious thought, and, honouring each in the
   other
Kindred courage and virtue, and cognate knowledge and freedom,
Live in brotherhood wisely conjoin'd. We set the
   example.
They who stir up strife, and would break that
   natural concord,
Evil they sow, and sorrow will they reap for their
   harvest.   50
1820   1821

IMITATED FROM THE PERSIAN

Lᴏʀᴅ! who art merciful as well as just,
Incline thine ear to me, a child of dust!
Not what I would, O Lord! I offer thee,
   Alas! but what I can.
Father Almighty, who hast made me man,
And bade me look to Heaven, for Thou art
   there,
Accept my sacrifice and humble prayer.
Four things which are not in thy treasury,
I lay before thee, Lord, with this petition:—
   My nothingness, my wants,   10
   My sins, and my contrition.

Lowther Castle, 1828   1828

THE LIFE OF NELSON

CHAPTER IX

[ᴛʜᴇ ʙᴀᴛᴛʟᴇ ᴏꜰ ᴛʀᴀꜰᴀʟɢᴀʀ ᴀɴᴅ ᴛʜᴇ ᴅᴇᴀᴛʜ ᴏꜰ ɴᴇʟsᴏɴ]

Uɴʀᴇᴍɪᴛᴛɪɴɢ exertions were made to equip
the ships which he [Nelson] had chosen, and
especially to refit the *Victory,* which was once
more to bear his flag. Before he left London he
called at his upholsterer's, where the coffin which
Captain Hallowell had given him was deposited,
and desired that its history might be engraven
upon the lid, saying it was highly probable he
might want it on his return. He seemed, indeed,
to have been impressed with an expectation that
he should fall in the battle. In a letter to his
brother, written immediately after his return, he
had said: 'We must not talk of Sir Robert Cal-
der's[1] battle. I might not have done so much with
my small force. If I had fallen in with them you
might probably have been a lord before I wished,
for I know they meant to make a dead set at the

---

[1] a British admiral who several weeks previously had fought a
disappointingly indecisive battle against the French fleet.

Victory.' Nelson had once regarded the prospect of death with gloomy satisfaction; it was when he anticipated the upbraidings of his wife and the displeasure of his venerable father.[2] The state of his feelings now was expressed in his private journal in these words: 'Friday night (Sept. 13th), at half-past ten, I drove from dear, dear Merton,[3] where I left all which I hold dear in this world, to go to serve my king and country. May the great God whom I adore enable me to fulfil the expectations of my country! And, if it is His good pleasure that I should return, my thanks will never cease being offered up to the throne of His mercy. If it is His good providence to cut short my days upon earth, I bow with the greatest submission; relying that He will protect those so dear to me, whom I may leave behind! His will be done. Amen! Amen! Amen!'

Early on the following morning he reached Portsmouth; and, having despatched his business on shore, endeavoured to elude the populace by taking a byway to the beach; but a crowd collected in his train, pressing forward to obtain a sight of his face;—many were in tears, and many knelt down before him, and blessed him as he passed. England has had many heroes, but never one who so entirely possessed the love of his fellow-countrymen as Nelson. All men knew that his heart was as humane as it was fearless; that there was not in his nature the slightest alloy of selfishness or cupidity; but that, with perfect and entire devotion, he served his country with all his heart, and with all his soul, and with all his strength; and, therefore, they loved him as truly and as fervently as he loved England. They pressed upon the parapet to gaze after him when his barge pushed off, and he was returning their cheers by waving his hat. The sentinels, who endeavoured to prevent them from trespassing upon this ground, were wedged among the crowd; and an officer, who, not very prudently upon such an occasion, ordered them to drive the people down with their bayonets, was compelled speedily to retreat; for the people would not be debarred from gazing, till the last moment, upon the hero—the darling hero of England. . . .

At daybreak[4] the combined fleets were distinctly seen from the *Victory's* deck, formed in a close line of battle ahead, on the starboard tack, about twelve miles to leeward, and stand-ing to the south. Our fleet consisted of twenty-seven sail of the line and four frigates; theirs of thirty-three and seven large frigates. Their superiority was greater in size and weight of metal than in numbers. They had four thousand troops on board; and the best riflemen who could be procured, many of them Tyrolese, were dispersed through the ships. Little did the Tyrolese, and little did the Spaniards at that day, imagine what horrors the wicked tyrant whom they served was preparing for their country.[5]

Soon after daylight Nelson came upon deck. The 21st of October was a festival in his family, because on that day his uncle, Captain Suckling, in the *Dreadnought,* with two other line-of-battle ships, had beaten off a French squadron of four sail of the line and three frigates. Nelson, with that sort of superstition from which few persons are entirely exempt, had more than once expressed his persuasion that this was to be the day of his battle also; and he was well pleased at seeing his prediction about to be verified. The wind was now from the west,—light breezes, with a long heavy swell. Signal was made to bear down upon the enemy in two lines; and the fleet set all sail. Collingwood, in the *Royal Sovereign,* led the lee-line[6] of thirteen ships; the *Victory* led the weather-line of fourteen. Having seen that all was as it should be, Nelson retired to his cabin, and wrote this prayer:

'May the Great God, whom I worship, grant to my country, and for the benefit of Europe in general, a great and glorious victory; and may no misconduct in any one tarnish it! and may humanity after victory be the predominant feature in the British fleet! For myself individually, I commit my life to Him that made me, and may His blessing alight on my endeavours for serving my country faithfully! To Him I resign myself, and the just cause which is intrusted to me to defend. Amen, Amen, Amen.' . . .

Blackwood went on board the *Victory* about six. He found him in good spirits, but very calm; not in that exhilaration which he had felt upon entering into battle at Aboukir and Copenhagen; he knew that his own life would be particularly aimed at, and seems to have looked for death with almost as sure an expectation as for victory. His whole attention was fixed upon the enemy. They tacked to the northward, and formed

---

2 because of Nelson's liaison with the beautiful Lady Hamilton, wife of the British envoy at Naples.

3 a village in Surrey, England, where Nelson had been living with Lady Hamilton.

4 on 21 October 1805, the day of the battle.

5 In 1808, after victories over the Spaniards, Napoleon made his brother Joseph, King of Spain. In 1809 he ruthlessly crushed the Tirolese.

6 the line farthest from the direction from which the wind blows; the weather line is the opposite.

their line on the larboard tack; thus bringing the shoals of Trafalgar and St. Pedro under the lee of the British, and keeping the port of Cadiz open for themselves. This was judiciously done: and Nelson, aware of all the advantages which it gave them, made signal to prepare to anchor.

Villeneuve[7] was a skilful seaman, worthy of serving a better master and a better cause. His plan of defence was as well conceived, and as original, as the plan of attack. He formed the fleet in a double line, every alternate ship being about a cable's length to windward of her second ahead and astern. Nelson, certain of a triumphant issue to the day, asked Blackwood what he should consider as a victory. That officer answered that, considering the handsome way in which battle was offered by the enemy, their apparent determination for a fair trial of strength, and the situation of the land, he thought it would be a glorious result if fourteen were captured. He replied: 'I shall not be satisfied with less than twenty.' Soon afterwards he asked him if he did not think there was a signal wanting. Captain Blackwood made answer that he thought the whole fleet seemed very clearly to understand what they were about. These words were scarcely spoken before that signal was made which will be remembered as long as the language or even the memory of England shall endure—Nelson's last signal: 'ENGLAND EXPECTS EVERY MAN TO DO HIS DUTY!' It was received throughout the fleet with a shout of answering acclamation, made sublime by the spirit which it breathed and the feeling which it expressed. 'Now,' said Lord Nelson, 'I can do no more. We must trust to the great Disposer of all events and the justice of our cause. I thank God for this great opportunity of doing my duty.'

He wore that day, as usual, his Admiral's frock-coat, bearing on the left breast four stars of the different orders with which he was invested. Ornaments which rendered him so conspicuous a mark for the enemy were beheld with ominous apprehension by his officers. It was known that there were riflemen on board the French ships, and it could not be doubted but that his life would be particularly aimed at. They communicated their fears to each other, and the surgeon, Mr. Beatty,[8] spoke to the chaplain, Dr. Scott, and to Mr. Scott, the public secretary, desiring that some person would entreat him to change his dress or cover the stars; but they knew that such a request would highly displease him. 'In honour I gained them,' he had said when such a thing had been hinted to him formerly, 'and in honour I will die with them.' Mr. Beatty, however, would not have been deterred by any fear of exciting his displeasure from speaking to him himself upon a subject in which the weal of England, as well as the life of Nelson, was concerned; but he was ordered from the deck before he could find an opportunity. This was a point upon which Nelson's officers knew that it was hopeless to remonstrate or reason with him, but both Blackwood and his own captain, Hardy, represented to him how advantageous to the fleet it would be for him to keep out of action as long as possible; and he consented at last to let the *Leviathan* and the *Téméraire,* which were sailing abreast of the *Victory,* be ordered to pass ahead. Yet even here the last infirmity of this noble mind was indulged; for these ships could not pass ahead if the *Victory* continued to carry all her sail; and so far was Nelson from shortening sail, that it was evident he took pleasure in pressing on, and rendering it impossible for them to obey his own orders. A long swell was setting into the Bay of Cadiz: our ships, crowding all sail, moved majestically before it, with light winds from the southwest. The sun shone on the sails of the enemy; and their well-formed line, with their numerous three-deckers, made an appearance which any other assailants would have thought formidable; but the British sailors only admired the beauty and the splendour of the spectacle; and, in full confidence of winning what they saw, remarked to each other, what a fine sight yonder ships would make at Spithead![9]

The French admiral, from the *Bucentaure,* beheld the new manner in which his enemy was advancing—Nelson and Collingwood each leading his line; and, pointing them out to his officers, he is said to have exclaimed that such conduct could not fail to be successful. Yet Villeneuve had made his own dispositions with the utmost skill, and the fleets under his command waited for the attack with perfect coolness. Ten minutes before twelve they opened their fire. Eight or nine of the ships immediately ahead of the *Victory,* and across her bows, fired single guns at her, to ascertain whether she was yet within their range. As

---

7 Admiral in command of the French fleet.
8 In this part of the work I have chiefly been indebted to this gentleman's *Narrative of Lord Nelson's Death*—a document as interesting as it is authentic.—(Southey.)

9 a strait off Portsmouth, England, principal anchorage for the British navy and the scene of many splendid naval pageants.

soon as Nelson perceived that their shot passed over him, he desired Blackwood and Captain Prowse, of the *Sirius*, to repair to their respective frigates, and on their way to tell all the captains of the line-of-battle ships that he depended on their exertions, and that, if by the prescribed mode of attack they found it impracticable to get into action immediately, they might adopt whatever they thought best, provided it led them quickly and closely alongside an enemy. As they were standing on the front of the poop, Blackwood took him by the hand, saying he hoped soon to return and find him in possession of twenty prizes. He replied, 'God bless you, Blackwood; I shall never see you again.'

Nelson's column was steered about two points more to the north than Collingwood's, in order to cut off the enemy's escape into Cadiz. The lee line, therefore, was first engaged. 'See,' cried Nelson, pointing to the *Royal Sovereign,* as she steered right for the centre of the enemy's line, cut through it astern of the *Santa Anna,* three-decker, and engaged her at the muzzle of her guns on the starboard side; 'see how that noble fellow Collingwood carries his ship into action!' Collingwood, delighted at being first in the heat of the fire, and knowing the feelings of his Commander and old friend, turned to his captain and exclaimed, 'Rotherham, what would Nelson give to be here!' Both these brave officers perhaps at this moment thought of Nelson with gratitude for a circumstance which had occurred on the preceding day. Admiral Collingwood, with some of the captains, having gone on board the *Victory* to receive instructions, Nelson inquired of him where his captain was, and was told in reply that they were not upon good terms with each other. 'Terms!' said Nelson, 'good terms with each other!' Immediately he sent a boat for Captain Rotherham, led him, as soon as he arrived, to Collingwood, and saying, 'Look, yonder are the enemy!' bade them shake hands like Englishmen.

The enemy continued to fire a gun at a time at the *Victory* till they saw that a shot had passed through her main-top-gallant sail; then they opened their broadsides, aiming chiefly at her rigging, in the hope of disabling her before she could close with them. Nelson, as usual, had hoisted several flags, lest one should be shot away. The enemy showed no colours till late in the action, when they began to feel the necessity of having them to strike.[10] For this reason the *Santissima Trinidad*—Nelson's old acquaintance, as he used to call her—was distinguishable only by her four decks; and to the bow of this opponent he ordered the *Victory* to be steered. Meantime an incessant raking fire was kept up upon the *Victory*. The admiral's secretary was one of the first who fell: he was killed by a cannon-shot, while conversing with Hardy. Captain Adair, of the marines, with the help of a sailor, endeavoured to remove the body from Nelson's sight, who had a great regard for Mr. Scott; but he anxiously asked, 'Is that poor Scott that's gone?' and being informed that it was indeed so, exclaimed, 'Poor fellow!' Presently a double-headed shot struck a party of marines, who were drawn up on the poop, and killed eight of them: upon which Nelson immediately desired Captain Adair to disperse his men round the ship, that they might not suffer so much from being together. A few minutes afterwards a shot struck the forebrace bits[11], on the quarter-deck, and passed between Nelson and Hardy, a splinter from the bit tearing off Hardy's buckle and bruising his foot. Both stopped and looked anxiously at each other, each supposing the other to be wounded. Nelson then smiled, and said, 'This is too warm work, Hardy, to last long.'

The *Victory* had not yet returned a single gun: fifty of her men had been by this time killed or wounded, and her main-top-mast, with all her studding-sails and their booms, shot away. Nelson declared that, in all his battles, he had seen nothing which surpassed the cool courage of his crew on this occasion. At four minutes after twelve she opened her fire from both sides of her deck. It was not possible to break the enemy's line without running on board one of their ships; Hardy informed him of this, and asked him which he would prefer. Nelson replied: 'Take your choice, Hardy, it does not signify much.' The master was then ordered to put the helm to port, and the *Victory* ran on board the *Redoubtable,* just as her tiller ropes were shot away. The French ship received her with a broadside, then instantly let down her lower-deck ports for fear of being boarded through them, and never afterwards fired a great gun during the action. Her tops, like those of all the enemy's ships, were filled with riflemen. Nelson never placed musketry in his tops; he had a strong dislike to the practice, not merely because it endangers setting fire to the sails, but also because it is a murderous sort of warfare, by which individuals may suffer,

---

10 to lower, in surrender.

11 spars to which the ropes of the foresail were fastened.

and a commander now and then be picked off, but which never can decide the fate of a general engagement.

Captain Harvey, in the *Téméraire,* fell on board the *Redoubtable* on the other side; another enemy was in like manner on board the *Téméraire;* so that these four ships formed as compact a tier as if they had been moored together, their heads lying all the same way. The lieutenants of the *Victory,* seeing this, depressed their guns of the middle and lower decks, and fired with a diminished charge, lest the shot should pass through and injure the *Téméraire;* and because there was danger that the *Redoubtable* might take fire from the lower-deck guns, the muzzles of which touched her side when they were run out, the fireman of each gun stood ready with a bucket of water, which, as soon as the gun was discharged, he dashed into the hole made by the shot. An incessant fire was kept up from the *Victory* from both sides; her larboard guns playing upon the *Bucentaure* and the huge *Santissima Trinidad.*

It had been part of Nelson's prayer that the British fleet might be distinguished by humanity in the victory which he expected. Setting an example himself, he twice gave orders to cease firing upon the *Redoubtable,* supposing that she had struck,[12] because her great guns were silent; for, as she carried no flag, there was no means of instantly ascertaining the fact. From this ship, which he had thus twice spared, he received his death. A ball fired from her mizzen-top, which, in the then situation of the two vessels, was not more than fifteen yards from that part of the deck where he was standing, struck the epaulette on his left shoulder,—about a quarter after one, just in the heat of the action. He fell upon his face, on the spot which was covered with his poor secretary's blood. Hardy, who was a few steps from him, turning round, saw three men raising him up. 'They have done for me at last, Hardy!' said he. 'I hope not!' cried Hardy. 'Yes,' he replied; 'my back bone is shot through.' Yet even now, not for a moment losing his presence of mind, he observed, as they were carrying him down the ladder, that the tiller ropes, which had been shot away, were not yet replaced, and ordered that new ones should be rove[13] immediately. Then, that he might not be seen by the crew, he took out his handkerchief, and covered his face and his stars. Had he but concealed these badges of honour from the enemy, England, per-

haps, would not have had cause to receive with sorrow the news of the battle of Trafalgar.

The cockpit was crowded with wounded and dying men, over whose bodies he was with some difficulty conveyed, and laid upon a pallet in the midshipmen's berth. It was soon perceived, upon examination, that the wound was mortal. This, however, was concealed from all, except Captain Hardy, the chaplain, and the medical attendants. He himself being certain, from the sensation in his back, and the gush of blood which he felt momently within his breast, that no human care could avail him, insisted that the surgeon should leave him, and attend to those to whom he might be useful. 'For,' said he, 'you can do nothing for me.' All that could be done was to fan him with paper, and frequently to give him lemonade to alleviate his intense thirst. He was in great pain, and expressed much anxiety for the event of the action, which now began to declare itself. As often as a ship struck, the crew of the *Victory* hurrahed, and at every hurrah a visible expression of joy gleamed in the eyes and marked the countenance of the dying hero. But he became impatient to see Captain Hardy; and as that officer, though often sent for, could not leave the deck, Nelson feared that some fatal cause prevented him, and repeatedly cried: 'Will no one bring Hardy to me? He must be killed! He is surely dead!' An hour and ten minutes elapsed from the time when Nelson received his wound before Hardy could come to him. They shook hands in silence; Hardy in vain struggling to suppress the feelings of that most painful and yet sublimest moment. 'Well, Hardy,' said Nelson, 'how goes the day with us?'—'Very well,' replied Hardy, 'ten ships have struck, but five of their van have tacked, and show an intention of bearing down upon the *Victory.* I have called two or three of our fresh ships round, and have no doubt of giving them a drubbing.'—'I hope,' said Nelson, 'none of our ships have struck?' Hardy answered, 'There was no fear of that.' Then, and not till then, Nelson spoke of himself. 'I am a dead man, Hardy,' said he; 'I am going fast; it will be all over with me soon. Come nearer to me. Let my dear Lady Hamilton have my hair; and all other things belonging to me.' Hardy observed that he hoped Mr. Beatty could yet hold out some prospect of life. 'Oh no!' he replied, 'it is impossible; my back is shot through. Beatty will tell you so.' Captain Hardy then once more shook hands with him, and with a heart almost bursting, hastened upon deck.

12 surrendered.
13 drawn through the eye-holes of the tiller.

By this time all feeling below the breast was gone; and Nelson, having made the surgeon ascertain this, said to him: 'You know I am gone. I know it. I feel something rising in my breast'—putting his hand on his left side—'which tells me so.' And upon Beatty's inquiring whether his pain was very great, he replied, 'So great that he wished he was dead. Yet,' said he in a lower voice, 'one would like to live a little longer too!' And after a few minutes, in the same under-tone, he added: 'What would become of poor Lady Hamilton if she knew my situation!' Next to his country she occupied his thoughts.

Captain Hardy, some fifty minutes after he had left the cockpit, returned, and again taking the hand of his dying friend and Commander, congratulated him on having gained a complete victory. How many of the enemy were taken he did not know, as it was impossible to perceive them distinctly, but fourteen or fifteen at least. 'That's well!' cried Nelson, 'but I bargained for twenty.' And then in a stronger voice he said: 'Anchor, Hardy, anchor.' Hardy upon this hinted that Admiral Collingwood would take upon himself the direction of affairs. 'Not while I live, Hardy,' said the dying Nelson, ineffectually endeavouring to raise himself from the bed. 'Do you anchor.' His previous order for preparing to anchor had shown how clearly he foresaw the necessity of this. Presently, calling Hardy back, he said to him, in a low voice, 'Don't throw me overboard'; and he desired that he might be buried by his parents, unless it should please the king to order otherwise. Then, reverting to private feelings: 'Take care of my dear Lady Hamilton, Hardy; take care of poor Lady Hamilton.—Kiss me, Hardy,' said he. Hardy knelt down, and kissed his cheek; and Nelson said, 'Now I am satisfied. Thank God, I have done my duty.' Hardy stood over him in silence for a moment or two, then knelt again, and kissed his forehead. 'Who is that?' said Nelson; and being informed, he replied, 'God bless you, Hardy.' And Hardy then left him—forever.

Nelson now desired to be turned upon his right side, and said: 'I wish I had not left the deck; for I shall soon be gone.' Death was, indeed, rapidly approaching. He said to the chaplain: 'Doctor, I have *not* been a *great* sinner'; and, after a short pause, 'Remember that I leave Lady Hamilton, and my daughter Horatia, as a legacy to my country.' His articulation now became difficult; but he was distinctly heard to say, 'Thank God, I have done my duty!' These words he repeatedly pronounced; and they were the last words he uttered. He expired at thirty minutes after four,—three hours and a quarter after he had received his wound. . . .

Once, amidst his sufferings, Nelson had expressed a wish that he were dead; but immediately the spirit subdued the pains of death, and he wished to live a little longer; doubtless that he might hear the completion of the victory which he had seen so gloriously begun. That consolation—that joy—that triumph, was afforded him. He lived to know that the victory was decisive; and the last guns which were fired at the flying enemy were heard a minute or two before he expired. . . .

It is almost superfluous to add that all the honours which a grateful country could bestow were heaped upon the memory of Nelson. His brother was made an earl, with a grant of £6,000 per year; £10,000 were voted to each of his sisters; and £100,000 for the purchase of an estate. A public funeral was decreed, and a public monument. Statues and monuments also were voted by most of our principal cities. The leaden coffin in which he was brought home, was cut in pieces, which were distributed as relics of Saint Nelson,—so the gunner of the *Victory* called them,—and when, at his interment, his flag was about to be lowered into the grave, the sailors who assisted at the ceremony, with one accord rent it in pieces, that each might preserve a fragment while he lived.

The death of Nelson was felt in England as something more than a public calamity; men started at the intelligence, and turned pale, as if they had heard of the loss of a dear friend. An object of our admiration and affection, of our pride and of our hopes, was suddenly taken from us; and it seemed as if we had never, till then, known how deeply we loved and reverenced him. What the country had lost in its great naval hero—the greatest of our own, and of all former times—was scarcely taken into the account of grief. So perfectly, indeed, had he performed his part, that the maritime war, after the battle of Trafalgar, was considered at an end; the fleets of the enemy were not merely defeated, but destroyed; new navies must be built, and a new race of seamen reared for them, before the possibility of their invading our shores could again be contemplated. It was not, therefore, from any selfish reflection upon the magnitude of our loss that we mourned for him: the general sorrow was of a higher character. The people of England grieved that funeral ceremonies, public monuments, and posthumous rewards, were all which they could now bestow upon him, whom the king, the legislature, and the nation, would alike have delighted to honour; whom every tongue would have blessed; whose presence in every village through which he might have passed would have wakened the church bells, have given school-boys a holiday, have drawn children from their sports to gaze upon him, and 'old men from the chimney corner,' to look upon Nelson ere they died. The victory of Trafalgar was celebrated, indeed, with the usual forms of rejoicing, but they were without joy; for such already was the glory of the British navy, through Nelson's surpassing genius, that it scarcely seemed to receive any addition from the most signal victory that ever was achieved upon the seas; and the destruction of this mighty fleet, by which all the maritime schemes of France were totally frustrated, hardly appeared to add to our security or strength; for while Nelson was living, to watch the combined squadrons of the enemy, we felt ourselves as secure as now, when they were no longer in existence.

There was reason to suppose, from the appearances upon opening the body, that in the course of nature he might have attained, like his father, to a good old age. Yet he cannot be said to have fallen prematurely whose work was done, nor ought he to be lamented who died so full of honours and at the height of human fame. The most triumphant death is that of the martyr; the most awful that of the martyred patriot; the most splendid that of the hero in the hour of victory; and if the chariot and the horses of fire had been vouchsafed for Nelson's translation, he could scarcely have departed in a brighter blaze of glory. He has left us, not indeed his mantle of inspiration, but a name and an example which are at this hour inspiring hundreds of the youth of England—a name which is our pride, and an example which will continue to be our shield and our strength. Thus it is that the spirits of the great and the wise continue to live and to act after them, verifying in this sense the language of the old mythologist:

Τοὶ μὲν δαίμονες εἰσί, Διὸς μεγάλου διὰ βουλάς.
Ἐσθλοὶ, ἐπιχθόνιοι, φύλακες θνητῶν ἀνθρώπων.[14]

1808–13   1813

---

14 'They are spirits, by the will of great Zeus. Kindly, haunting the earth, they are the guardians of mortal men.'—Hesiod, *Works and Days*, 122-3.

1775 · WALTER SAVAGE LANDOR · 1864

1775   Born, 30 January, at Warwick, the eldest son of a well-to-do physician. Involved in trouble throughout his life by a headstrong temper.

1783–94   Educated at Rugby and at Trinity College, Oxford. Was rusticated for firing a gun against the shutters of another student's room for whom he had taken a dislike.

1795   Published a volume of juvenile poems.

1796–1803   Lived for three years in Swansea, South Wales, for the most part in studious seclusion; subsequently at London, Swansea, Oxford, and Paris.

1798   Published *Gebir*.

1802   Published *Poems*.

1803–7   Lived mainly at Bath. Met Ianthe (Sophia Jane Swifte). Upon his father's death came into possession of an independent fortune.

1808   Met Southey at Bristol; ever afterward they were the closest of friends. Made an expedition to Spain where he campaigned against Napoleon at the head of a regiment equipped at his own expense. After Cintra the regiment melted away and Landor, having quarreled with his allies and his officers, recrossed the channel to continue his denunciation of everyone in political office directing the nation's affairs. His Spanish experiences served him in the composition of the tragedy, *Count Julian* (published 1812).

1811–14   Married Julia Thuillier, nineteen years younger than himself. (The marriage proved to be anything but a happy one.) Went to live at Llanthony Abbey in Monmouthshire. After sinking a fortune in his estate, fled England to escape his creditors.

1815–35   Lived in Italy, chiefly in Florence and Fiesole. Deserted his wife and family (though he provided for them liberally) and returned to Bath, England.

1824–9   Published *Imaginary Conversations*.

1834   *The Citation and Examination of William Shakespeare*.

1836   *Pericles and Aspasia*.

1837   *The Pentameron*.

1839–40   *Andrea of Hungary, Giovanna of Naples*, and *Fra Rupert*, an historical trilogy.

1847   *The Hellenics*.

1853   *The Last Fruit Off an Old Tree*.

1858   *Dry Sticks, Fagoted*.

1858–64   Fled England again, this time from the disastrous results of an ignoble libel and returned, combative as ever, to the Italian home he had left twenty-three years before! Domestic distractions were to some extent alleviated by the exertions of his good friend and neighbor, Robert Browning. In 1859, however, Landor left his family never to rejoin them.

1863   Published *Heroic Idylls*.

1864   Died at Florence on 17 September.

WALTER SAVAGE LANDOR has been described as 'a classic writing in a romantic age.' He possessed from his earliest youth a strong attachment to classical languages and literatures, and habitually turned to Greek and Latin models for his style and not infrequently for the sources of his inspiration. He often first composed in Latin, then translating into English, preserved in the English version the classical qualities of the original. His longest single work, *Pericles and Aspasia,* considered by some critics his masterpiece, was a studied attempt to revive for a modern audience the glory of Athens' golden age. On every page of his voluminous works the 'chastened expression and noble restraint typical of classical writing is unmistakable and pervasive.' Yet Landor could not escape from being the child of his own time. Born into a revolutionary era and by temperament an extreme individualist, he was all his days an ardent lover of personal liberty. He was similarly, in keeping with fashion, a worshiper of nature and a chivalrous defender of the helpless. Actually the contrast between the classicist and the romanticist in him is not as striking as may perhaps first appear. In his prose and verse, as in the man, there is a mingling of opposites: order and vehemence, dignity and sensitiveness, magnanimity and irresponsible self-will. In his art Landor was, it is true, comparatively isolated from his generation. He sincerely professed not to care for a wide popularity. 'I shall dine late,' he said, 'but the dining room will be well-lighted, the guests few and select.' Though he may not have much influenced them, or have been influenced by them, he was, nevertheless, not unappreciated by his more notable contemporaries, among them Wordsworth, Carlyle, Dickens, Browning, and Swinburne.

Landor gave the first twenty-six years of his literary career almost wholly to verse, of which *Gebir,* written during two years of solitude in Wales, is the earliest work of consequence. It is an epic in seven books recounting the adventures of the mythic founder of Gibraltar, based on an Arabian tale found in a book lent him by his friend Rose Aylmer. Published in 1798, the year of *Lyrical Ballads,* it marks an advance of its own in English literature by the introduction of an elevated style and a cadenced blank verse suggestive of Milton and classical authors, among whom Pindar was Landor's chief model. Though admired by a few discriminating contemporaries, *Gebir* was totally lacking in characterization and story interest, and was therefore neglected by the general reader. Its successes were in scattered beautiful passages, what Coleridge described as 'eminences excessively bright and all the ground around and between them in darkness.'

The Hellenics were imaginary dialogues of moderate length in verse. They keep close to classical models; in fact they were, like parts of *Gebir,* frequently written first in Latin. For these sketches Landor chose statuesque scenes of dramatic import, placed his figures in relief—harmoniously arranged—then carefully guarding proportion and purity, austerely worked out his design. The results more often resemble 'the sedate coolness of sculpture than the intensity of drama.' As in the tragic *Iphigeneia* or the idyllic *Hamadryad,* however, human emotion may be felt throbbing beneath the chiseled beauty. Except for several 'closet' dramas, of which *Count Julian* was the most nearly successful, but none of which quite came off, almost all of Landor's remaining poetry, and his best, was in the form of occasional lyrics. He has left us some hundreds of verses of the occasional kind, more perhaps than any English poet since Herrick, which he threw off happily and incessantly over a period of more than a half a century. They form a record 'of cheerful friendly hours and knightly gallantry and of controlled affections,' or else the 'harmonious sadness of retrospect' (Symons). Among these lyrics are the immortal successes, *Rose Aylmer* (which Lamb was never tired of quoting) and *Dirce,* 'jewels in verse,' and many more of their kind of incomparable charm, and by their side no inconsiderable number of 'playful trivialities, graceful compliments, and roguish or sentimental trifles.' Landor rarely succeeds in being spontaneous and he sometimes completely misses the mark. Yet he possesses sensitiveness, exquisiteness and beauty of phrase, an extraordinary fecundity of imagery, and nearly everywhere grace and dignity and fastidiousness.

'Poetry,' Landor tells us in a famous statement, 'was always my amusement, prose my study and business.' In Italy during the fruitful middle years of his life he concentrated his powers upon writing his *Imaginary Conversations*, the voluminous prose work upon which his fame most securely rests. These conversations are carried on between characters of all ages and cover a wide range from classical times to the author's own. Characteristically they focus upon a moment of intense passion preceding the climax of an action, as when some great resolution is about to be fulfilled. The bulk of the *Imaginary Conversations* is great, filling well over half of the volumes of Landor's total collected works. Their value is exceedingly unequal. The style at its best is unsurpassed and remarkably uniform throughout. However, a sense of monotony is inescapable in the conversations, resulting largely from a failure to draw distinct dramatic differentiations. At other times, an 'ill-tempered satirical slanting often with a political bias,' will render a dialogue almost completely worthless. But Landor's intimate familiarity with and enthusiasm for the characters and background of ancient Greece and Rome, of Renaissance Italy, and of his native England, gave felicity and value to a score or more of his character delineations. It has been said that the turmoil of Landor's outward life is absent from his literary creations. To a degree this is apparently true, for the restraint and purity of his workmanship covers the human passion with an external sculpturesque calm. Yet Landor's fierce contempt for tyranny and brutal selfishness, and his tender sympathy with helpless innocence may be felt throughout such a dialogue as *Leofric and Godiva*. Moreover, Landor's heroic passions found successful expression in rendering characters of noble stature either in action or in suffering as, for example, in the magnificent colloquy on the battlefield between the conquering Hannibal and the dying Marcellus. A vein of anticlerical irony comes out in the conversation between Bossuet and Duchess Fontanges, in a high strain of comedy, 'unlike but worthy of Molière.' Landor's most congenial subject and his best sustained long prose work is *Pericles and Aspasia*, a creative romance of the Golden Age of Athens. The characters are never entirely or perfectly natural, yet the narrative moves straight forward in a clear, simple, and dignified way and frequently with charm and grace. The *Pentameron* reveals Landor's delight in Boccaccio. In the concluding visions of Boccaccio and Petrarch, the author is supreme in his own kind of harmony. The emotional prose 'never over-reaches itself.' It is infinitely varied in modulation, precise in imagery, tender in feeling, and warmly passionate in its very restraint.

Landor falls short of the highest genius. As a poet he must be ranked below his contemporaries Blake, Wordsworth, Coleridge, Byron, Shelley, and Keats; as a prose writer below Lamb, Hazlitt, De Quincey, and Scott. He has left a few perfect short poems, but nothing, perhaps, among the 'indispensable masterpieces of prose.' Yet he enlarged the domain of English prose and had 'an undeniable genius for elaborate style of great charm.'

From GEBIR

BOOK I

TAMAR'S WRESTLING

[Tamar is the younger brother of Gebir, a shepherd. His narrative tells how he lost a sheep from his flock.]

'Twas evening, though not sun-set, and spring-
    tide
Level with these green meadows, seem'd still
    higher;
'Twas pleasant: and I loosen'd from my neck
The pipe you gave me, and began to play.
O that I ne'er had learnt the tuneful art!   120
It always brings us enemies or love!

Well, I was playing—when above the waves
Some swimmer's head methought I saw ascend;
I, sitting still, survey'd it, with my pipe
Awkwardly held before my lips half-clos'd.
Gebir! it was a nymph! a nymph divine!
I cannot wait describing how she came,
How I was sitting, how she first assum'd
The sailor: of what happened, there remains
Enough to say, and too much to forget.   130
The sweet deceiver stept upon this bank
Before I was aware; for, with surprize
Moments fly rapid as with love itself.
Stooping to tune afresh the hoarsen'd reed,
I heard a rustling; and where that arose
My glance first lighted on her nimble feet.

Her feet resembled those long shells explored
By him who to befriend his steeds' dim sight
Would blow the pungent powder in their eye.—
Her eyes too! O immortal Gods! her eyes 140
Resembled—what could they resemble—what
Ever resemble those! E'en her attire
Was not of wonted woof nor vulgar art:
Her mantle shew'd the yellow samphire-pod,
Her girdle, the dove-colour'd wave serene.
'Shepherd,' said she, 'and will you wrestle now,
And with the sailor's hardier race engage?'
I was rejoiced to hear it, and contrived
How to keep up contention;—could I fail
By pressing not too strongly, still to press. 150
'Whether a shepherd, as indeed you seem,
Or whether of the hardier race you boast,
I am not daunted, no: I will engage.'
'But first,' said she, 'what wager will you lay?'
'A sheep,' I answered, 'add whate'er you will.'
'I cannot,' she replied, 'make that return:
Our hided vessels, in their pitchy round,
Seldom, unless from rapine, hold a sheep.
But I have sinuous shells, of pearly hue
Within, and they that lustre have imbibed 160
In the sun's palace porch; where, when unyoked,
His chariot wheel stands midway in the wave.
Shake one, and it awakens; then apply
Its polished lips to your attentive ear,
And it remembers its august abodes,
And murmurs as the ocean murmurs there.
And I have others given me by the nymphs,
Of sweeter sound than any pipe you have.—
But we, by Neptune, for no pipe contend;
This time a sheep I win, a pipe the next.' 170
Now came she forward, eager to engage;
But, first her dress, her bosom then, survey'd,
And heav'd it, doubting if she could deceive.
Her bosom seem'd, inclos'd in haze like heav'n,
To baffle touch; and rose forth undefined.
Above her knees she drew the robe succinct,
Above her breast, and just below her arms:
'This will preserve my breath, when tightly
    bound,
If struggle and equal strength should so con-
    strain.'
Thus, pulling hard to fasten it, she spoke, 180
And, rushing at me, closed. I thrill'd throughout
And seem'd to lessen and shrink up with cold.
Again, with violent impulse gushed my blood;
And hearing nought external, thus absorb'd,
I heard it, rushing through each turbid vein,
Shake my unsteady swimming sight in air.
Yet with unyielding though uncertain arms,
I clung around her neck; the vest beneath

Rustled against our slippery limbs entwined:
Often mine, springing with eluded force, 190
Started aside, and trembled, till replaced.
And when I most succeeded, as I thought,
My bosom and my throat felt so comprest
That life was almost quivering on my lips,
Yet nothing was there painful! these are signs
Of secret arts, and not of human might,
What arts I cannot tell: I only know
My eyes grew dizzy, and my strength decay'd,
I was indeed o'ercome!—with what regret,
And more, with what confusion, when I
    reached 200
The fold, and yielding up the sheep, she cried,
'This pays a shepherd to a conquering maid.'
She smil'd, and more of pleasure than disdain
Was in her dimpled chin, and liberal lip,
And eyes that languished, lengthening,—just like
    love.
She went away: I, on the wicker gate
Lean'd, and could follow with my eyes alone.
The sheep she carried easy as a cloak.
But when I heard its bleating, as I did,
And saw, she hastening on, its hinder feet 210
Struggle, and from her snowy shoulder slip,
(One shoulder its poor efforts had unveil'd,)
Then, all my passions mingling fell in tears!
Restless then ran I to the highest ground
To watch her; she was gone; gone down the tide;
And the long moon-beam on the hard wet sand
Lay like a jaspar column half uprear'd.

1798

ROSE AYLMER

[Rose Aylmer, born 1779, was the daughter of Henry,
Baron Aylmer, with whose family Landor established a
warm friendship during his early years in Wales. This
unforgettable elegy was written after hearing the news
of her untimely death in India in 1800.]

AH what avails the sceptred race,
    Ah what the form divine!
What every virtue, every grace!
    Rose Aylmer, all were thine.
Rose Aylmer, whom these wakeful eyes
    May weep, but never see,
A night of memories and of sighs
    I consecrate to thee.

1806

ABSENCE

[Sophia Jane Swifte was Landor's early sweetheart
and for a time his mistress. She was twice married and
for many years lived with her second husband in Paris.

Verses to or about Ianthe over a long period of time reveal a passionate attachment which Landor never ceased to regard as the strongest in his life.]

IANTHE! you resolve to cross the sea!
    A path forbidden *me!*
Remember, while the Sun his blessing sheds
    Upon the mountain-heads,
How often we have watcht him laying down
    His brow, and dropt our own
Against each other's, and how faint and short
    And sliding the support!
What will succede it now? Mine is unblest,
    Ianthe! nor will rest   10
But on the very thought that swells with pain.
    O bid me hope again!
O give me back what Earth, what (without you)
    Not Heaven itself can do—
One of the golden days that we have past,
    And let it be my last!
Or else the gift would be, however sweet,
    Fragile and incomplete.

                 1831

PAST RUIN'D ILION

PAST ruin'd Ilion Helen[1] lives,
    Alcestis[2] rises from the shades;
Verse calls them forth; 'tis verse that gives
    Immortal youth to mortal maids.

Soon shall Oblivion's deepening veil
    Hide all the peopled hills you see,
The gay, the proud, while lovers hail
    In distant ages you and me.

The tear for fading beauty check,
    For passing glory cease to sigh;   10
One form shall rise above the wreck,
    One name, Ianthe, shall not die.

                 1831

FIESOLAN IDYL

HERE,[1] where precipitate Spring with one light
    bound
Into hot Summer's lusty arms expires;
And where go forth at morn, at eve, at night,
Soft airs, that want the lute to play with them,

---

1 Helen, wife of Menelaus, King of Sparta, was carried off by Paris to Troy (Ilion). After the defeat of the Trojans, she returned to her husband.
2 Alcestis sacrificed her life to save her husband from a mortal sickness. Later her life was restored.

---

1 Fiesole, where Landor lived for some years, is a beautiful old cathedral town near Florence, Italy.

And softer sighs, that know not what they want;
Under a wall, beneath an orange-tree
Whose tallest flowers could tell the lowlier ones
Of sights in Fiesole right up above,
While I was gazing a few paces off
At what they seemed to show me with their
    nods,   10
Their frequent whispers and their pointing
    shoots,
A gentle maid came down the garden-steps
And gathered the pure treasure in her lap.
I heard the branches rustle, and stept forth
To drive the ox away, or mule, or goat,
(Such I believed it must be); for sweet scents
Are the swift vehicles of still sweeter thoughts,
And nurse and pillow the dull memory
That would let drop without them her best stores.
They bring me tales of youth and tones of
    love,   20
And 'tis and ever was my wish and way
To let all flowers live freely, and all die,
Whene'er their Genius bids their souls depart,
Among their kindred in their native place.
I never pluck the rose; the violet's head
Hath shaken with my breath upon its bank
And not reproacht me; the ever-sacred cup
Of the pure lily hath between my hands
Felt safe, unsoil'd, nor lost one grain of gold.
I saw the light that made the glossy leaves   30
More glossy; the fair arm, the fairer cheek
Warmed by the eye intent on its pursuit;
I saw the foot, that, altho half-erect
From its grey slipper, could not lift her up
To what she wanted: I held down a branch
And gather'd her some blossoms, since their hour
Was come, and bees had wounded them, and flies
Of harder wing were working their way thro
And scattering them in fragments under foot.
So crisp were some, they rattled unevolved,   40
Others, ere broken off, fell into shells,
For such appear the petals when detacht,
Unbending, brittle, lucid, white like snow,
And like snow not seen thro, by eye or sun:
Yet every one her gown received from me
Was fairer than the first . . I thought not so,
But so she praised them to reward my care.
I said: *you find the largest.*
                    This indeed,
Cried she, *is large and sweet.*
                        She held one forth,
Whether for me to look at or to take   50
She knew not, nor did I; but taking it
Would best have solved (and this she felt) her
    doubts.
I dared not touch it; for it seemed a part

Of her own self; fresh, full, the most mature
Of blossoms, yet a blossom; with a touch
To fall, and yet unfallen.
                              She drew back
The boon she tendered, and then, finding not
The ribbon at her waist to fix it in,
Dropt it, as loth to drop it, on the rest.

1831

DIRCE[1]

STAND close around, ye Stygian set,[2]
    With Dirce in one boat conveyed!
Or Charon,[3] seeing, may forget
    That he is old and she a shade.

1831

ON LUCRETIA BORGIA'S HAIR

BORGIA,[1] thou once were almost too august,
And high for adoration;—now thou 'rt dust!
All that remains of thee these plaits infold—
Calm hair, meand'ring with pellucid gold!

1837

TO ROBERT BROWNING

THERE is delight in singing, though none hear
Beside the singer; and there is delight
In praising, though the praiser sit alone
And see the prais'd far off him, far above.
Shakspeare is not *our* poet, but the world's,
Therefore on him no speech; and short for thee,
Browning! Since Chaucer was alive and hale,
No man hath walk'd along our roads with step
So active, so inquiring eye, or tongue
So varied in discourse. But warmer climes[1]   10
Give brighter plumage, stronger wing; the breeze
Of Alpine heights thou playest with, borne on
Beyond Sorrento and Amalfi,[2] where
The Siren waits thee, singing song for song.

1845

THE DEATH OF ARTEMIDORA

[This poem is from the second edition of *Pericles and Aspasia*, Letter 85. The dying Artemidora is betrothed to Elpenor.]

---

1 the beautiful wife of Lycus, King of Thebes, who was put to death by the sons of Lycus' divorced wife.
2 inhabitants of the infernal regions.
3 the ferryman in Hades who transported the souls of the dead over the River Styx.

---

1 Duchess of Ferrara, 1480–1519, who was famed for her great beauty, her patronage of the arts, and her wickedness.

---

1 Browning moved to Italy just after marrying Elizabeth Barrett.
2 seaports a few miles south of Naples.

'ARTEMIDORA! Gods invisible,
While thou art lying faint along the couch,
Have tied the sandal to thy veined feet,
And stand beside thee, ready to convey
Thy weary steps where other rivers flow.
Refreshing shades will waft thy weariness
Away, and voices like thine own come nigh,
Soliciting, nor vainly, thy embrace.'
    Artemidora sigh'd, and would have press'd
The hand now pressing hers, but was too
    weak.   10
Fate's shears were over her dark hair unseen
While thus Elpenor spake: he look'd into
Eyes that had given light and life erewhile
To those above them, those now dim with tears
And watchfulness. Again he spake of joy
Eternal. At that word, that sad word, *joy*,
Faithful and fond her bosom heav'd once more,
Her head fell back: one sob, one loud deep sob
Swell'd through the darkened chamber; 'twas not
    hers:
With her that old boat incorruptible,   20
Unwearied, undiverted in its course,
Had plash'd the water up the farther strand.[1]

1846

MOTHER, I CANNOT MIND MY WHEEL

MOTHER, I cannot mind my wheel;
    My fingers ache, my lips are dry:
Oh! if you felt the pain I feel!
    But oh, who ever felt as I?
No longer could I doubt him true;
    All other men may use deceit:
He always said my eyes were blue,
    And often swore my lips were sweet.

1846

YES: I WRITE VERSES

YES: I write verses now and then
But blunt and flaccid is my pen,
No longer talked of by young men
        As rather clever.
In the last quarter are my eyes,
You see it by their form and size:
Is it not time then to be wise?
        Or now or never!

Fairest that ever sprang from Eve!
While Time allows the short reprieve,   10
Just look at me! would you believe
        'Twas once a lover?

---

1 In a later version Landor omitted the last three lines.

I cannot clear the five-bar gate,
But, trying first its timbers' state,
Climb stiffly up, take breath, and wait
          To trundle over.

Thro' gallopade[1] I cannot swing
The entangling blooms of Beauty's spring;
I cannot say the tender thing,
          Be't true or false: 20
And am beginning to opine
Those girls are only half-divine
Whose waists yon wicked boys entwine
          In giddy waltz.

I fear that arm above that shoulder;
I wish them wiser, graver, older,
Sedater, and no harm if colder
          And panting less.
Ah! people were not half so wild
In former days, when, starchly mild,   30
Upon her high-heel'd Essex smiled
          The brave Queen Bess.

                                        1846

I KNOW NOT WHETHER I AM PROUD

I KNOW not whether I am proud,
But this I know, I hate the crowd:
Therefore pray let me disengage
My verses from the motley page,
Where others far more sure to please
Pour out their choral song with ease.
And yet perhaps, if some should tire
With too much froth or too much fire,
There is an ear that may incline
Even to words so dull as mine.   10

                                        1846

ALAS, HOW SOON THE HOURS

ALAS, how soon the hours are over,
Counted us out to play the lover!
And how much narrower is the stage,
Allotted us to play the sage!
But when we play the fool, how wide
The theatre expands; beside,
How long the audience sits before us!
How many prompters! what a chorus!

                                        1846

----

1 a lively dance.

VARIOUS THE ROADS OF LIFE

VARIOUS the roads of life; in one
          All terminate, one lonely way.
We go; and 'Is he gone?'
          Is all our best friends say.

                                        1846

DO YOU REMEMBER ME?

'Do you remember me? or are you proud?'
Lightly advancing thro' her star-trimm'd crowd,
          Ianthe said, and lookt into my eyes.
'A *yes*, a *yes*, to both: for Memory
Where you but once have been must ever be,
          And at your voice Pride from his throne must
          rise.'

                                        1846

From THE HELLENICS

[Landor originated the term 'Hellenics' to describe a
series of short tales or dialogues in verse treating Greek
mythological or idyllic themes.]

I

ON THE HELLENICS

COME back, ye wandering Muses, come back
          home,
Ye seem to have forgotten where it lies:
Come, let us walk upon the silent sands
Of Simois,[1] where deep footmarks show long
          strides;
Thence we may mount, perhaps, to higher
          ground,[2]
Where Aphroditè from Athenè won
The golden apple, and from Herè too,
And happy Ares shouted far below.
          Or would ye rather choose the grassy vale
Where flows Anapos[3] thro' anemones,
Hyacinths, and narcissuses, that bend
To show their rival beauty in the stream?
          Bring with you each her lyre, and each in turn
Temper a graver with a lighter song.

                                        1859

II

IPHIGENEIA

[When the Greek fleet at Aulis was prevented from
sailing against Troy by adverse winds raised in anger by

----

1 a river near ancient Troy.
2 Mount Ida, where the three goddesses contested before Paris for
the prize of beauty. Ares, god of war, is happy because he knows
the judgment of Paris will bring on the Trojan War.
3 a river in Sicily.

Artemis, the soothsayer Calchas declared that the only
way to calm the wind was to appease the goddess by sacrificing Iphigeneia, daughter of the Commander in Chief,
Agamemnon. This was a fearful judgment, but Agamemnon yielded. The tragic moment is imagined in Landor's
poem to come when Iphigeneia, alone with her father,
pleads with him that her life might be spared.]

IPHIGENEIA, when she heard her doom
At Aulis, and when all beside the king
Had gone away, took his right-hand, and said,
'O father! I am young and very happy.
I do not think the pious Calchas heard
Distinctly what the Goddess spake. Old age
Obscures the senses. If my nurse, who knew
My voice so well, sometimes misunderstood,
While I was resting on her knee both arms
And hitting it to make her mind my words,   10
And looking in her face, and she in mine,
Might not he also hear one word amiss,
Spoken from so far off, even from Olympus?'
The father placed his cheek upon her head,
And tears dropt down it, but the king of men
Replied not. Then the maiden spake once more.
'O father! sayst thou nothing? Hear'st thou not
Me, whom thou ever hast, until this hour,
Listen'd to fondly, and awaken'd me
To hear my voice amid the voice of birds,   20
When it was inarticulate as theirs,
And the down deadened it within the nest?'
He moved her gently from him, silent still,
And this, and this alone, brought tears from her,
Altho' she saw fate nearer: then with sighs,
'I thought to have laid down my hair before
Benignant Artemis, and not have dimm'd
Her polisht altar with my virgin blood;
I thought to have selected the white flowers
To please the Nymphs, and to have askt of
    each   30
By name, and with no sorrowful regret,
Whether, since both my parents will'd the
    change,
I might at Hymen's feet bend my clipt brow;
And (after these who mind us girls the most)
Adore our own Athena, that she would
Regard me mildly with her azure eyes.
But father! to see you no more, and see
Your love, O father! go ere I am gone!'
Gently he moved her off, and drew her back,
Bending his lofty head far over her's,   40
And the dark depths of nature heaved and burst.
He turn'd away; not far, but silent still.
She now first shudder'd; for in him, so nigh,
So long a silence seem'd the approach of death,
And like it. Once again she rais'd her voice.
'O father! if the ships are now detain'd,

And all your vows move not the Gods above,
When the knife strikes me there will be one
    prayer
The less to them: and purer can there be
Any, or more fervent than the daughter's
    prayer   50
For her dear father's safety and success?'
A groan that shook him shook not his resolve.
An aged man now enter'd, and without
One word, stept slowly on, and took the wrist
Of the pale maiden. She lookt up, and saw
The fillet of the priest and calm cold eyes.
Then turn'd she where her parent stood, and
    cried
'O father! grieve no more: the ships can sail.'

                                               1846

                        III

                THE HAMADRYAD[1]

RHAICOS was born amid the hills wherefrom
Gnidos[2] the light of Caria is discern'd,
And small are the white-crested that play near,
And smaller onward are the purple waves.
Thence festal choirs were visible, all crown'd
With rose and myrtle if they were inborn;
If from Pandion[3] sprang they, on the coast
Where stern Athenè raised her citadel,
Then olive was intwined with violets
Cluster'd in bosses,[4] regular and large.   10
For various men wore various coronals;
But one was their devotion; 'twas to her[5]
Whose laws all follow, her whose smile with-
    draws
The sword from Ares, thunderbolt from Zeus,
And whom in his chill caves the mutable
Of mind, Poseidon, the sea-king, reveres,
And whom his brother, stubborn Dis,[6] hath
    pray'd
To turn in pity the averted cheek
Of her[7] he bore away, with promises,
Nay, with loud oath before dread Styx[8] itself, 20
To give her daily more and sweeter flowers
Than he made drop from her on Enna's dell.[9]

---

1 a nymph inhabiting a tree, whose life began and ended with
that of the tree of which she was the spirit.
2 an ancient city of Caria, a division of Ancient Minor.
3 i.e. from Athens where Pandion was a legendary king.
4 raised ornaments.
5 Venus or Aphrodite.
6 Pluto, god of the lower world.
7 Proserpine.   8 principal river of Hades.
9 where Proserpine, daughter of Ceres, was gathering flowers
when Pluto carried her off and made her queen of the lower world.

Rhaicos was looking from his father's door
At the long trains that hastened to the town
From all the valleys, like bright rivulets
Gurgling with gladness, wave outrunning wave,
And thought it hard he might not also go
And offer up one prayer, and press one hand,
He knew not whose. The father call'd him in,
And said, 'Son Rhaicos! those are idle games; 30
Long enough I have lived to find them so.'
And ere he ended sighed; as old men do
Always, to think how idle such games are.
'I have not yet,' thought Rhaicos in his heart,
And wanted proof.
          'Suppose thou go and help
Echeion at the hill, to bark yon oak
And lop its branches off, before we delve
About the trunk and ply the root with axe:
This we may do in winter.'
                Rhaicos went;
For thence he could see farther, and see more 40
Of those who hurried to the city-gate.
Echeion he found there with naked arm
Swart-hair'd, strong-sinew'd, and his eyes intent
Upon the place where first the axe should fall:
He held it upright. 'There are bees about,
Or wasps, or hornets,' said the cautious eld,
'Look sharp, O son of Thallinos!' The youth
Inclined his ear, afar, and warily,
And cavern'd in his hand. He heard a buzz
At first, and then the sound grew soft and
    clear, 50
And then divided into what seem'd tune,
And there were words upon it, plaintive words.
He turn'd, and said, 'Echeion! do not strike
That tree: it must be hollow; for some god
Speaks from within. Come thyself near.' Again
Both turn'd towards it: and behold! there sat
Upon the moss below, with her two palms
Pressing it, on each side, a maid in form.
Downcast were her long eyelashes, and pale
Her cheek, but never mountain-ash display'd 60
Berries of colour like her lip so pure,
Nor were the anemones about her hair
Soft, smooth and wavering like the face beneath.
  'What dost thou here?' Echeion, half-afraid,
Half-angry cried. She lifted up her eyes,
But nothing spake she. Rhaicos drew one step
Backward, for fear came likewise over him,
But not such fear: he panted, gasp'd, drew in
His breath, and would have turn'd it into words,
But could not into one.
             'O send away 70
That sad old man!' said she. The old man went
Without a warning from his master's son,

Glad to escape, for sorely he now fear'd,
And the axe shone behind him in their eyes.
  Hamad. And wouldst thou too shed the most
    innocent
Of blood? No vow demands it; no god wills
The oak to bleed.
  Rhaicos.   Who art thou? whence? why here?
And whither wouldst thou go? Among the robed
In white or saffron, or the hue that most
Resembles dawn or the clear sky, is none 80
Array'd as thou art. What so beautiful
As that grey robe which clings about thee close,
Like moss to stones adhering, leaves to trees,
Yet lets thy bosom rise and fall in turn,
As, touch'd by zephyrs, fall and rise the boughs
Of graceful platan by the river-side.
  Hamad. Lovest thou well thy father's house?
  Rhaicos. Indeed
I love it, well I love it, yet would leave
For thine, where'er it be, my father's house,
With all the marks upon the door, that show 90
My growth at every birthday since the third,
And all the charms, o'erpowering evil eyes,
My mother nail'd for me against my bed,
And the Cydonian[10] bow (which thou shalt see)
Won in my race last spring from Eutychos.
  Hamad. Bethink thee what it is to leave a
    home
Thou never yet has left, one night, one day.
  Rhaicos. No, 'tis not hard to leave it; 'tis not
    hard
To leave, O maiden, that paternal home,
If there be one on earth whom we may love 100
First, last, for ever; one who says that she
Will love for ever too. To say which words,
Only to say it, surely is enough . .
It shows such kindness . . if 'twere possible
We at the moment think she would indeed.
  Hamad. Who taught thee all this folly at thy
    age?
  Rhaicos. I have seen lovers and have learnt to
    love.
  Hamad. But wilt thou spare the tree?
  Rhaicos. My father wants
The bark; the tree may hold its place awhile.
  Hamad. Awhile! thy father numbers then my
    days? 110
  Rhaicos. Are there no others where the moss
    beneath
Is quite as tufty? Who would send thee forth
Or ask thee why thou tarriest? Is thy flock
Anywhere near?

---

10 from the ancient city of Cydonia in Crete, famous for its
archery.

Hamad. I have no flock: I kill
Nothing that breathes, that stirs, that feels the
 air,
The sun, the dew. Why should the beautiful
(And thou art beautiful) disturb the source
Whence springs all beauty? Hast thou never
 heard
Of Hamadryads?
 Rhaicos. Heard of them I have:
Tell me some tale about them. May I sit   120
Beside thy feet? Art thou not tired? The herbs
Are very soft; I will not come too nigh;
Do but sit there, nor tremble so, nor doubt.
Stay, stay an instant: let me first explore
If any acorn of last year be left
Within it; thy thin robe too ill protects
Thy dainty limbs against the harm one small
Acorn may do. Here's none. Another day
Trust me; till then let me sit opposite.
 Hamad. I seat me; be thou seated, and con-
 tent.   130
 Rhaicos. O sight for gods! ye men below!
 adore
The Aphroditè. *Is* she there below?
Or sits she here before me? as she sate
Before the shepherd[11] on those heights that shade
The Hellespont, and brought his kindred woe.
 Hamad. Reverence the higher Powers; nor
 deem amiss
Of her who pleads to thee, and would repay—
Ask not how much—but very much. Rise not;
No, Rhaicos, no! Without the nuptial vow
Love is unholy. Swear to me that none   140
Of mortal maids shall ever taste thy kiss,
Then take thou mine; then take it, not before.
 Rhaicos. Hearken, all gods above! O Aphro-
 ditè!
O Herè! Let my vow be ratified!
But wilt thou come into my father's house?
 Hamad. Nay; and of mine I cannot give thee
 part.
 Rhaicos. Where is it?
 Hamad.   In this oak.
 Rhaicos.   Ay; now begins
The tale of Hamadryad; tell it through.
 Hamad. Pray of thy father never to cut down
My tree; and promise him, as well thou
 mayst,   150
That every year he shall receive from me
More honey than will buy him nine fat sheep,
More wax than he will burn to all the gods.
Why fallest thou upon thy face? Some thorn

11 Paris, whose award of the golden apple to Aphrodite brought
on the Trojan War.

May scratch it, rash young man! Rise up; for
 shame!
 Rhaicos. For a shame I cannot rise. O pity me!
I dare not sue for love . . but do not hate!
Let me once more behold thee . . not once more,
But many days: let me love on . . unloved!
I aimed too high: on my head the bolt   160
Falls back, and pierces to the very brain.
 Hamad. Go . . rather go, than make me say I
 love.
 Rhaicos. If happiness is immortality,
(And whence enjoy it else the gods above?)
I am immortal too: my vow is heard:
Hark! on the left . . Nay, turn not from me now,
I claim my kiss.
 Hamad. Do men take first, then claim?
Do thus the seasons run their course with them?

—Her lips were seal'd, her head sank on his
 breast.
'Tis said that laughs were heard within the
 wood: 170
But who should hear them? . . and whose laughs?
 and why?

Savoury was the smell, and long past noon,
Thallinos! in thy house: for marjoram,
Basil and mint, and thyme and rosemary,
Were sprinkled on the kid's well roasted length,
Awaiting Rhaicos. Home he came at last
Not hungry, but pretending hunger keen.
With head and eyes just o'er the maple plate.
'Thou seest but badly, coming from the sun,
Boy Rhaicos!' said the father. 'That oak's
 bark   180
Must have been tough, with little sap between;
It ought to run; but it and I are old.'
Rhaicos, although each morsel of the bread
Increased by chewing, and the meat grew cold
And tasteless to his palate, took a draught
Of gold-bright wine, which, thirsty as he was,
He thought not of until his father fill'd
The cup, averring water was amiss,
But wine had been at all times pour'd on kid,
It was religion.
   He thus fortified   190
Said, not quite boldly, and not quite abashed,
'Father, that oak is Zeusis' own; that oak
Year after year will bring thee wealth from wax
And honey. There is one who fears the gods
And the gods love—that one.'
    (He blushed, nor said
What one)
 'Has promised this, and may do more.

We have not many moons to wait until
The bees have done their best; if then there come
Nor wax nor honey, let the tree be hewn.'
'Zeus hath bestow'd on thee a prudent
        mind.'   200
Said the glad sire: 'but look thou often there,
And gather all the honey thou canst find
In every crevice, over and above
What hath been promist; would they reckon
        that?

Rhaicos went daily; but the nymph as oft,
Invisible. To play at love, she knew,
Stopping its breathings when it breathes most
        soft,
Is sweeter than to play on any pipe.
She play'd on his: she fed upon his sighs;
They pleas'd her when they gently waved her
        hair,   210
Cooling the pulses of her purple veins,
And when her absence brought them out, they
        pleas'd.
Even among the fondest of them all,
What mortal or immortal maid is more
Content with giving happiness than pain?
One day he was returning from the wood
Despondently. She pitied him, and said
'Come back!' and twined her fingers in the hem
Above his shoulder. Then she led his steps
To a cool rill that ran o'er level sand   220
Through lentisk[12] and through oleander,[12] there
Bathed she his feet, lifting them on her lap
When bathed, and drying them in both her
        hands.
He dared complain; for those who most are
        loved
Most dare it; but not harsh was his complaint.
'O thou inconstant!' said he, 'if stern law
Bind thee, or will, stronger than sternest law
O, let me know henceforward when to hope
The fruit of love that grows for me but here.'
He spake; and pluck'd it from its pliant stem. 230
'Impatient Rhaicos! Why thus intercept
The answer I would give? There is a bee
Whom I have fed, a bee who knows my thoughts
And executes my wishes: I will send
That messenger. If ever thou art false,
Drawn by another, own it not, but drive
My bee away; then shall I know my fate,
And—for thou must be wretched—weep at thine.
But often as my heart persuades to lay
Its cares on thine and throb itself to rest,   240

_____
12 varieties of sweet-smelling shrubs.

Expect her with thee, whether it be morn
Or eve, at any time when woods are safe.'
    Day after day the Hours beheld them blest,
And season after season: years had past,
Blest were they still. He who asserts that Love
Ever is sated of sweet things, the same
Sweet things he fretted for in earlier days,
Never, by Zeus! loved he a Hamadryad.
    The nights had now grown longer, and perhaps
The Hamadryads find them lone and dull   250
Among their woods; one did, alas! She called
Her faithful bee: 'twas when all bees should
        sleep,
And all did sleep but hers. She was sent forth
To bring that light which never wintry blast
Blows out, nor rain nor snow extinguishes,
The light that shines from loving eyes upon
Eyes that love back, till they can see no more.

    Rhaicos was sitting at his father's hearth;
Between them stood the table, not o'erspread
With fruits which autumn now profusely
        bore,   260
Nor anise cakes, nor odorous wine; but there
The draft-board was expanded; at which game
Triumphant sat old Thallinos; the son
Was puzzled, vext, discomfited, distraught.
A buzz was at his ear: up went his hand,
And it was heard no longer. The poor bee
Return'd (but not until the morn shone bright)
And found the Hamadryad with her head
Upon her aching wrist, and showed one wing
Half-broken off, the other's meshes marr'd,   270
And there were bruises which no eye could see
Saving a Hamadryad's.
                              At this sight
Down fell the languid brow, both hands fell
        down,
A shriek was carried to the ancient hall
Of Thallinos: he heard it not: his son
Heard it, and ran forthwith into the wood.
No bark was on the tree, no leaf was green,
The trunk was riven through. From that day
        forth
Nor word nor whisper sooth'd his ear, nor sound
Even of insect wing; but loud laments   280
The woodmen and the shepherds one long year
Heard day and night; for Rhaicos would not
        quit
The solitary place, but moan'd and died.

Hence milk and honey wonder not, O guest,
To find set duly on the hollow stone.
                                                                    1842

GOD SCATTERS BEAUTY

GOD scatters beauty as he scatters flowers
O'er the wide earth, and tells us all are ours.
A hundred lights in every temple burn,
And at each shrine I bend my knee in turn.

                                              1853

DEATH STANDS ABOVE ME

DEATH stands above me, whispering low
    I know not what into my ear:
Of his strange language all I know
    Is, there is not a word of fear.

                                              1853

TO YOUTH

WHERE art thou gone, light-ankled Youth?
    With wing at either shoulder,
And smile that never left thy mouth
    Until the Hours grew colder:

Then somewhat seem'd to whisper near
    That thou and I must part;
I doubted it: I felt no fear,
    No weight upon the heart:

If aught befell it, Love was by
    And roll'd it off again;
So, if there ever was a sigh,   10
    'Twas not a sigh of pain.

I may not call thee back; but thou
    Returnest when the hand
Of gentle Sleep waves o'er my brow
    His poppy-crested wand;

Then smiling eyes bend over mine,
    Then lips once pressed invite;
But sleep hath given a silent sign,
    And both, alas! take flight.   20

                                              1852

TO AGE

WELCOME, old friend! These many years
    Have we lived door by door:
The Fates have laid aside their shears
    Perhaps for some few more.

I was indocil at an age
    When better boys were taught,
But thou at length hast made me sage,
    If I am sage in aught.

Little I know from other men,
    Too little they from me,   10
But thou hast pointed well the pen
    That writes these lines to thee.

Thanks for expelling Fear and Hope,
    One vile, the other vain;
One's scourge, the other's telescope,
    I shall not see again:

Rather what lies before my feet
    My notice shall engage . . .
He who hath braved Youth's dizzy heat
    Dreads not the frost of Age.   20

                                              1852

SO THEN, I FEEL NOT DEEPLY!

So then, I feel not deeply! if I did,
I should have seized the pen and pierced there-
    with
The passive world!
                    And thus thou reasonest?
Well hast thou known the lover's, not so well
The poet's heart: while that heart bleeds, the
    hand
Presses it close. Grief must run on and pass
Into near Memory's more quiet shade
Before it can compose itself in song.
He who is agonized and turns to show
His agony to those who sit around,   10
Seizes the pen in vain: thought, fancy, power,
Rush back into his bosom; all the strength
Of genius can not draw them into light
From under mastering Grief; but Memory,
The Muse's mother, nurses, rears them up,
Informs, and keeps them with her all her days.

                                              1853

I STROVE WITH NONE[1]

I STROVE with none, for none was worth my strife:
    Nature I loved, and, next to Nature, Art:
I warm'd both hands before the fire of Life;
    It sinks; and I am ready to depart.

                                              1849

HEARTS-EASE

THERE is a flower I wish to wear,
    But not until first worne by you . .

---

[1] Written by Landor on his seventy-fourth birthday, 30 January
1849, and published that year in the *Examiner* under the title of
Dying Speech of an Old Philosopher.

Hearts-ease . . of all Earth's flowers most rare:
Bring it; and bring enough for two.

1858

THERE ARE SWEET FLOWERS

THERE are sweet flowers that only blow by night,
And sweet tears are there that avoid the light;
No mortal sees them after day is born,
They, like the dew, drop trembling from their
    thorn.

1863

TO MY NINTH DECADE

To my ninth decade I have totter'd on,
  And no soft arm bends now my steps to steady;
She, who once led me where she would, is gone,
  So when he calls me, Death shall find me ready.

1863

From IMAGINARY CONVERSATIONS

MARCELLUS AND HANNIBAL

[Hannibal, famous Carthaginian general, in the third
century B.C. overcame Marcellus in southern Italy and
almost conquered Rome. Appian and Plutarch, Roman
historians who give the facts upon which the following
scene is based, report Marcellus already dead when Hannibal comes up. Landor, characteristically adapting history to his purpose, has Marcellus survive his death-
wound long enough to reveal the resolute pride of the
Roman and the generosity of his victorious foe.]

Hannibal. Could a Numidian horseman[1] ride
no faster? Marcellus! ho! Marcellus! He moves
not—he is dead. Did he not stir his fingers? Stand
wide, soldiers—wide, forty paces—give him air—
bring water—halt! Gather those broad leaves,
and all the rest, growing under the brushwood—
unbrace his armour. Loose the helmet first—his
breast rises. I fancied his eyes were fixed on me—
they have rolled back again. Who presumed to
touch my shoulder? This horse? It was surely the
horse of Marcellus! Let no man mount him. Ha!
ha! the Romans, too, sink into luxury: here is
gold about the charger.

Gaulish Chieftain. Execrable thief! The golden
chain of our king under a beast's grinders! The
vengeance of the gods hath overtaken the impure——

Hannibal. We will talk about vengeance when
we have entered Rome, and about purity among
the priests, if they will hear us. Sound for the sur-

geon. That arrow may be extracted from the side,
deep as it is.—The conqueror of Syracuse lies before me.—Send a vessel off to Carthage. Say
Hannibal is at the gates of Rome.—Marcellus,
who stood alone between us, fallen. Brave man!
I would rejoice and cannot. How awfully serene
a countenance! Such as we hear are in the Islands
of the Blessed.[2] And how glorious a form and
stature! Such too was theirs! They also once lay
thus upon the earth wet with their blood—few
other enter there. And what plain armour!

Gaulish Chieftain. My party slew him—indeed
I think I slew him myself. I claim the chain: it
belongs to my king; the glory of Gaul requires
it. Never will she endure to see another take it:
rather would she lose her last man. We swear!
we swear!

Hannibal. My friend, the glory of Marcellus
did not require him to wear it. When he suspended the arms of your brave king in the temple, he thought such a trinket unworthy of himself
and of Jupiter. The shield he battered down, the
breast-plate he pierced with his sword—these he
showed to the people and to the gods; hardly his
wife and little children saw this, ere his horse
wore it.

Gaulish Chieftain. Hear me, O Hannibal!

Hannibal. What! when Marcellus lies before
me? when his life may perhaps be recalled?
when I may lead him in triumph to Carthage?
when Italy, Sicily, Greece, Asia, wait to obey
me? Content thee! I will give thee mine own
bridle, worth ten such.

Gaulish Chieftain. For myself?

Hannibal. For thyself.

Gaulish Chieftain. And these rubies and emeralds, and that scarlet——

Hannibal. Yes, yes.

Gaulish Chieftain. O glorious Hannibal! unconquerable hero! O my happy country! to have
such an ally and defender. I swear eternal gratitude—yes, gratitude, love, devotion, beyond eternity.

Hannibal. In all treaties we fix the time: I
could hardly ask a longer. Go back to thy station.—I would see what the surgeon is about, and
hear what he thinks. The life of Marcellus! the
triumph of Hannibal! what else has the world in
it? Only Rome and Carthage: these follow.

Surgeon. Hardly an hour of life is left.

Marcellus. I must die then? The gods be
praised! The commander of a Roman army is
no captive.

---

1 one of Hannibal's cavalry.

2 where heroes favored by the gods dwell in eternal joy.

Hannibal (to the Surgeon). Could not he bear a sea-voyage? Extract the arrow.

Surgeon. He expires that moment.

Marcellus. It pains me: extract it.

Hannibal. Marcellus, I see no expression of pain on your countenance, and never will I consent to hasten the death of an enemy in my power. Since your recovery is hopeless, you say truly you are no captive.

(To the Surgeon.) Is there nothing, man, that can assuage the mortal pain? for, suppress the signs of it as he may, he must feel it. Is there nothing to alleviate and allay it?

Marcellus. Hannibal, give me thy hand—thou hast found it and brought it me, compassion.

(To the Surgeon.) Go, friend; others want thy aid; several fell around me.

Hannibal. Recommend to your country, O Marcellus, while time permits it, reconciliation and peace with me, informing the Senate of my superiority in force, and the impossibility of resistance. The tablet is ready: let me take off this ring—try to write, to sign it, at least. Oh, what satisfaction I feel at seeing you able to rest upon the elbow, and even to smile!

Marcellus. Within an hour or less, with how severe a brow would Minos[3] say to me, 'Marcellus, is this thy writing?'

Rome loses one man: she hath lost many such, and she still hath many left.

Hannibal. Afraid as you are of falsehood, say you this? I confess in shame the ferocity of my countrymen. Unfortunately, too, the nearer posts are occupied by Gauls, infinitely more cruel. The Numidians are so in revenge: the Gauls both in revenge and in sport. My presence is required at a distance, and I apprehend the barbarity of one or other, learning, as they must do, your refusal to execute my wishes for the common good, and feeling that by this refusal you deprive them of their country, after so long an absence.

Marcellus. Hannibal, thou art not dying.

Hannibal. What then? What mean you?

Marcellus. That thou mayest, and very justly, have many things yet to apprehend: I can have none. The barbarity of thy soldiers is nothing to me: mine would not dare be cruel. Hannibal is forced to be absent; and his authority goes away with his horse. On this turf lies defaced the semblance of a general; but Marcellus is yet the regulator of his army. Dost thou abdicate a power conferred on thee by thy nation? Or wouldst thou

acknowledge it to have become, by thy own sole fault, less plenary than thy adversary's?

I have spoken too much: let me rest: this mantle oppresses me.

Hannibal. I placed my mantle on your head when the helmet was first removed, and while you were lying in the sun. Let me fold it under, and then replace the ring.

Marcellus. Take it, Hannibal. It was given me by a poor woman who flew to me at Syracuse, and who covered it with her hair, torn off in desperation that she had no other gift to offer. Little thought I that her gift and her words should be mine. How suddenly may the most powerful be in the situation of the most helpless! Let that ring and the mantle under my head be the exchange of guests at parting. The time may come, Hannibal, when thou (and the gods alone know whether as conqueror or conquered) mayest sit under the roof of my children, and in either case it shall serve thee. In thy adverse fortune, they will remember on whose pillow their father breathed his last; in thy prosperous (Heaven grant it may shine upon thee in some other country!), it will rejoice thee to protect them. We feel ourselves the most exempt from affliction when we relieve it, although we are then the most conscious that it may befall us.

There is one thing here which is not at the disposal of either.

Hannibal. What?

Marcellus. This body.

Hannibal. Whither would you be lifted? Men are ready.

Marcellus. I meant not so. My strength is failing. I seem to hear rather what is within than what is without. My sight and my other senses are in confusion. I would have said—This body, when a few bubbles of air shall have left it, is no more worthy of thy notice than of mine; but thy glory will not let thee refuse it to the piety of my family.

Hannibal. You would ask something else. I perceive an inquietude not visible till now.

Marcellus. Duty and Death make us think of home sometimes.

Hannibal. Thitherward the thoughts of the conqueror and of the conquered fly together.

Marcellus. Hast thou any prisoners from my escort?

Hannibal. A few dying lie about—and let them lie—they are Tuscans. The remainder I saw at a distance, flying, and but one brave man among

---

3 judge in the lower world.

them—he appeared a Roman—a youth who turned back, though wounded. They surrounded and dragged him away, spurring his horse with their swords. These Etrurians measure their courage carefully, and tack it well together before they put it on, but throw it off again with lordly ease.

Marcellus, why think about them? or does aught else disquiet your thoughts?

Marcellus. I have suppressed it long enough. My son—my beloved son!

Hannibal. Where is he? Can it be? Was he with you?

Marcellus. He would have shared my fate— and has not. Gods of my country! beneficent throughout life to me, in death surpassingly beneficent: I render you, for the last time, thanks.

1828

LEOFRIC AND GODIVA

[This conversation is based upon the legend contained in the annals of Coventry that about the middle of the eleventh century Leofric, Earl of Mercia, agreed to relieve the city of a burdensome tax on condition that his wife, Godiva, should ride naked through the market place. This she did veiled only by her luxuriant hair. To this day her festival is celebrated in Coventry.]

Godiva. There is a dearth in the land, my sweet Leofric! Remember how many weeks of drought we have had, even in the deep pastures of Leicestershire; and how many Sundays we have heard the same prayers for rain, and supplications that it would please the Lord in his mercy to turn aside his anger from the poor pining cattle. You, my dear husband, have imprisoned more than one malefactor for leaving his dead ox in the public way; and other hinds[1] have fled before you out of the traces, in which they and their sons and their daughters, and haply their old fathers and mothers, were dragging the abandoned wain homeward. Although we were accompanied by many brave spearmen and skilful archers, it was perilous to pass the creatures which the farm-yard dogs, driven from the hearth by the poverty of their masters, were tearing and devouring; while others, bitten and lamed, filled the air either with long and deep howls or sharp and quick barkings, as they struggled with hunger and feebleness or were exasperated by heat and pain. Nor could the thyme from the heath, nor the bruised branches of the fir-tree, extinguish or abate the foul odour.

----
1 peasants.

Leofric. And now, Godiva my darling, thou art afraid we should be eaten up before we enter the gates of Coventry; or perchance that in the gardens there are no roses to greet thee, no sweet herbs for thy mat and pillow.

Godiva. Leofric, I have no such fears. This is the month of roses: I find them everywhere since my blessed marriage: they, and all other sweet herbs, I know not why, seem to greet me wherever I look at them, as though they knew and expected me. Surely they cannot feel that I am fond of them.

Leofric. O light laughing simpleton! But what wouldst thou? I came not hither to pray; and yet if praying would satisfy thee, or remove the drought, I would ride up straightway to Saint Michael's and pray until morning.

Godiva. I would do the same, O Leofric! but God hath turned away his ear from holier lips than mine. Would my own dear husband hear me, if I implored him for what is easier to accomplish? what he can do like God.

Leofric. How! what is it?

Godiva. I would not, in the first hurry of your wrath, appeal to you, my loving lord, in behalf of these unhappy men who have offended you.

Leofric. Unhappy! is that all?

Godiva. Unhappy they must surely be, to have offended you so grievously. What a soft air breathes over us! how quiet and serene and still an evening! how calm are the heavens and the earth! shall none enjoy them? not even we, my Leofric? The sun is ready to set: let it never set, O Leofric, on your anger. These are not my words; they are better than mine; should they lose their virtue from my unworthiness in uttering them?

Leofric. Godiva, wouldst thou plead to me for rebels?

Godiva. They have then drawn the sword against you! Indeed I knew it not.

Leofric. They have omitted to send me my dues, established by my ancestors, well knowing of our nuptials, and of the charges and festivities they require, and that in a season of such scarcity my own lands are insufficient.

Godiva. If they were starving, as they said they were . .

Leofric. Must I starve too? Is it not enough to lose my vassals?

Godiva. Enough! O God! too much! too much! may you never lose them! Give them life, peace, comfort, contentment. There are those among them who kissed me in my infancy, and who blessed me at the baptismal font. Leofric, Leofric! the first old man I meet I shall think is one of those; and I shall think on the blessing he gave, and (ah me!) on the blessing I bring back to him. My heart will bleed, will burst . . and he will weep at it! he will weep, poor soul! for the wife of a cruel lord who denounces vengeance on him, who carries death into his family.

Leofric. We must hold solemn festivals.

Godiva. We must indeed.

Leofric. Well then.

Godiva. Is the clamorousness that succeeds the death of God's dumb creatures, are crowded halls, are slaughtered cattle, festivals? are maddening songs and giddy dances, and hireling praises from parti-coloured coats? Can the voice of a minstrel tell us better things of ourselves than our own internal one might tell us; or can his breath make our breath softer in sleep? O my beloved! let everything be a joyance to us: it will, if we will. Sad is the day, and worse must follow, when we hear the blackbird in the garden and do not throb with joy. But, Leofric, the high festival is strown by the servant of God upon the heart of man. It is gladness, it is thanksgiving; it is the orphan, the starveling, pressed to the bosom, and bidden as its first commandment to remember its benefactor. We will hold this festival; the guests are ready: we may keep it up for weeks, and months, and years together, and always be the happier and the richer for it. The beverage of this feast, O Leofric, is sweeter than bee or flower or vine can give us: it flows from heaven; and in heaven will it abundantly be poured out again, to him who pours it out here unsparingly.

Leofric. Thou art wild.

Godiva. I have indeed lost myself. Some Power, some good kind Power, melts me (body and soul and voice) into tenderness and love. O, my husband, we must obey it. Look upon me! look upon me! lift your sweet eyes from the ground! I will not cease to supplicate; I dare not.

Leofric. We may think upon it.

Godiva. Never say that! What! think upon goodness when you can be good? Let not the infants cry for sustenance! The mother of our blessed Lord will hear them; us never, never afterward.

Leofric. Here comes the bishop: we are but one mile from the walls. Why dismountest thou? no bishop can expect it. Godiva! my honour and

rank among men are humbled by this: Earl Godwin will hear of it: up! up! the bishop hath seen it: he urgeth his horse onward: dost thou not hear him now upon the solid turf behind thee?

Godiva. Never, no never will I rise, O Leofric, until you remit this most impious tax, this tax on hard labour, on hard life.

Leofric. Turn round: look how the fat nag canters, as to the tune of a sinner's psalm, slow and hard-breathing. What reason or right can the people have to complain, while their bishop's steed is so sleek and well caparisoned? Inclination to change, desire to abolish old usages. . . Up! up! for shame! They shall smart for it, idlers! Sir bishop, I must blush for my young bride.

Godiva. My husband, my husband! will you pardon the city?

Leofric. Sir bishop! I could not think you would have seen her in this plight. Will I pardon? yea, Godiva, by the holy rood,[2] will I pardon the city, when thou ridest naked at noontide through the streets.

Godiva. O my dear cruel Leofric, where is the heart you gave me! It was not so! can mine have hardened it?

Bishop. Earl, thou abashest thy spouse; she turneth pale and weepeth. Lady Godiva, peace be with thee.

Godiva. Thanks, holy man! peace will be with me when peace is with your city. Did you hear my lord's cruel word?

Bishop. I did, lady.

Godiva. Will you remember it, and pray against it?

Bishop. Wilt *thou* forget it, daughter?

Godiva. I am not offended.

Bishop. Angel of peace and purity!

Godiva. But treasure it up in your heart: deem it an incense, good only when it is consumed and spent, ascending with prayer and sacrifice. And now what was it?

Bishop. Christ save us! that he will pardon the city when thou ridest naked through the streets at noon.

Godiva. Did he not swear an oath?

Bishop. He sware by the holy rood.

Godiva. My Redeemer! thou hast heard it! save the city!

Leofric. We are now upon the beginning of the pavement: these are the suburbs: let us think

2 cross.

of feasting: we may pray afterward: to-morrow we shall rest.

Godiva. No judgements then to-morrow, Leofric?

Leofric. None: we will carouse.

Godiva. The saints of heaven have given me strength and confidence: my prayers are heard: the heart of my beloved is now softened.

Leofric (aside). Ay, ay . . they shall smart, though.

Godiva. Say, dearest Leofric, is there indeed no other hope, no other mediation?

Leofric. I have sworn: beside, thou hast made me redden and turn my face away from thee, and all the knaves have seen it: this adds to the city's crime.

Godiva. I have blushed too, Leofric, and was not rash nor obdurate.

Leofric. But thou, my sweetest, art given to blushing; there is no conquering it in thee. I wish thou hadst not alighted so hastily and roughly: it hath shaken down a sheaf of thy hair: take heed thou sit not upon it, lest it anguish thee. Well done! it mingleth now sweetly with the cloth of gold upon the saddle, running here and there, as if it had life and faculties and business, and were working thereupon some newer and cunninger device. O my beauteous Eve! there is a Paradise about thee! the world is refreshed as thou movest and breathest on it. I cannot see or think of evil where thou art. I could throw my arms even here about thee. No signs for me! no shaking of sunbeams! no reproof or frown or wonderment . . I *will* say it . . now then for worse . . I could close with my kisses thy half-open lips, ay, and those lovely and loving eyes, before the people.

Godiva. To-morrow you shall kiss me, and they shall bless you for it. I shall be very pale, for to-night I must fast and pray.

Leofric. I do not hear thee; the voices of the folk are so loud under this archway.

Godiva (to herself). God help them! good kind souls! I hope they will not crowd about me so to-morrow. O Leofric! could my name be forgotten! and yours alone remembered! But perhaps my innocence may save me from reproach! and how many as innocent are in fear and famine! No eye will open on me but fresh from tears. What a young mother for so large a family! Shall my youth harm me! Under God's hand it gives me courage. Ah, when will the morning come! ah, when will the noon be over!

1829

BOSSUET AND THE DUCHESS DE FONTANGES[1]

Bossuet. Mademoiselle, it is the king's desire that I compliment you on the elevation you have attained.

Fontanges. O Monseigneur, I know very well what you mean. His Majesty is kind and polite to everybody. The last thing he said to me was, 'Angélique! do not forget to compliment Monseigneur the bishop on the dignity I have conferred upon him, of almoner[2] to the Dauphiness. I desired the appointment for him, only that he might be of rank sufficient to confess you, now you are duchess. Let him be your confessor, my little girl. He has fine manners.'

Bossuet. I dare not presume to ask you, mademoiselle, what was your gracious reply to the condescension of our royal master.

Fontanges. O yes, you may. I told him I was almost sure I should be ashamed of confessing such naughty things to a person of high rank, who writes like an angel.

Bossuet. The observation was inspired, mademoiselle, by your goodness and modesty.

Fontanges. You are so agreeable a man, monseigneur, I will confess to you directly, if you like.

Bossuet. Have you brought yourself to a proper frame of mind, young lady?

Fontanges. What is that?

Bossuet. Do you hate sin?

Fontanges. Very much.

Bossuet. Are you resolved to leave it off?

Fontanges. I have left it off entirely since the king began to love me. I have never said a spiteful word of anybody since.

Bossuet. In your opinion, mademoiselle, are there no other sins than malice?

Fontanges. I never stole anything; I never committed adultery; I never coveted my neighbour's wife; I never killed any person: though several have told me they should die for me.

Bossuet. Vain, idle talk! did you listen to it?

Fontanges. Indeed I did, with both ears; it seemed so funny.

Bossuet. You have something to answer for then.

Fontanges. No, indeed I have not, monsigneur. I have asked many times after them, and found they were all alive: which mortified me.

---

1 The Duchess of Fontanges was a mistress of Louis XIV. In a note Landor quotes a contemporary who said that she was 'as beautiful as an angel, but as stupid as a basket.'
2 dispenser of alms for another.

Bossuet. So then! you would really have them die for you?

Fontanges. Oh no, no!——But I wanted to see whether they were in earnest or told me fibs; for if they told me fibs I would never trust them again. I do not care about them; for the king told me I was only to mind *him.*

Bossuet. Lowest and highest, we all owe to his Majesty our duty and submission.

Fontanges. I am sure he has mine: so you need not blame me or question me on that. At first, indeed, when he entered the folding-doors, I was in such a flurry I could hear my heart beat across the chamber: by degrees I cared little about the matter: and at last, when I grew used to it, I liked it rather than not. Now, if this is not confession, what is?

Bossuet. We must abstract the soul from every low mundane thought. Do you hate the world, mademoiselle?

Fontanges. A good deal of it: all Picardy for example, and all Sologne: nothing is uglier,—— and, oh my life, what frightful men and women!

Bossuet. I would say, in plain language, do you hate the flesh and the devil?

Fontanges. Who does not hate the devil? If you will hold my hand the while, I will tell him so ——I hate you, beast! There now. As for flesh, I never could bear a fat man. Such people can neither dance nor hunt, nor do anything that I know of.

Bossuet. Mademoiselle Marie-Angélique de Scoraille de Rousille, Duchess de Fontanges! do you hate titles and dignities and yourself?

Fontanges. Myself! does any one hate me? why should I be the first? Hatred is the worst thing in the world: it makes one so very ugly.

Bossuet. To love God, we must hate our-selves. We must detest our bodies if we would save our souls.

Fontanges. That is hard: how can I do it? I see nothing so detestable in mine, do you? To love is easier. I love God whenever I think of him; he has been so very good to me. But I can-not hate myself, if I would. As God hath not hated me, why should I? Besides, it was he who made the king to love me; for I heard you say in a sermon that the hearts of kings are in his rule and governance. As for titles and dignities, I do not care much about them while his Maj-esty loves me, and calls me his Angélique. They make people more civil about us; and therefore it must be a simpleton who hates or disregards them, and a hypocrite who pretends it. I am glad

to be a duchess. Manon and Lisette have never tied my garter so as to hurt me since, nor has the mischievous old La Grange said anything cross or bold; on the contrary, she told me what a fine colour and what a plumpness it gave me. Would not you be rather a duchess than a waiting-maid or a nun, if the king gave you your choice?

Bossuet. Pardon me, Mademoiselle, I am con-founded at the levity of your question.

Fontanges. I am in earnest, as you see.

Bossuet. Flattery will come before you in other and more dangerous forms; you will be com-mended for excellences which do not belong to you; and this you will find as injurious to your re-pose as to your virtue. An ingenuous mind feels in unmerited praise the bitterest reproof. If you reject it you are unhappy, if you accept it you are undone. The compliments of a king are of them-selves sufficient to pervert your intellect.

Fontanges. There you are mistaken twice over. It is not my person that pleases him so greatly; it is my spirit, my wit, my talents, my genius, and that very thing which you have mentioned—— (what was it?) my intellect. He never compli-mented me the least upon my beauty. Others have said that I am the most beautiful young creature under heaven; a blossom of Paradise, a nymph, an angel; worth (let me whisper it in your ear——(do I lean too hard?) a thousand Montespans.[3] But his Majesty never said more on the occasion than that I was *imparagonable!*[4] (what is that?) and that he adored me; holding my hand and sitting quite still, when he might have romped with me and kissed me.

Bossuet. I would aspire to the glory of con-verting you.

Fontanges. You may do anything with me but convert me: you must not do that: I am a Cath-olic born. M. de Turenne and Mademoiselle de Duras[5] were heretics: you did right there. The king told the chancellor that he prepared them, that the business was arranged for you, and that you had nothing to do but to get ready the ar-guments and responses, which you did gallantly, did not you? And yet Mademoiselle de Duras was very awkward for a long while afterwards in crossing herself, and was once remarked to beat her breast in the litany with the points of two fingers at a time, when everyone is taught to use only the second, whether it has a ring upon

3 Marquise de Montespan, 1641-1707, was the favorite mistress of Louis XIV. She bore him seven children.

4 a malapropism for *incomparable.*

5 Henry, Vicomte de Turenne, 1611-75, celebrated French mar-shal, and his sister, Elizabeth, Duchess of Duras, abjured Prot-estantism and joined the Roman Catholic Church in 1668.

it or not. I am sorry she did so; for people might think her insincere in her conversion, and pretend that she kept a finger for each religion.

Bossuet. It would be as uncharitable to doubt the conviction of Mademoiselle de Duras as that of M. le Marcéchal.

Fontanges. I have heard some fine verses, I can assure you, monseigneur, in which you are called the conqueror of Turenne. I should like to have been his conqueror myself, he was so great a man. I understand that you have lately done a much more difficult thing.

Bossuet. To what do you refer, mademoiselle?

Fontanges. That you have overcome quietism.[6] Now, in the name of wonder, how could you manage that?

Bossuet. By the grace of God.

Fontanges. Yes, indeed; but never until now did God give any preacher so much of his grace as to subdue this pest.

Bossuet. It has appeared among us but lately.

Fontanges. O dear me! I have always been subject to it dreadfully, from a child.

Bossuet. Really! I never heard so.

Fontanges. I checked myself as well as I could, although they constantly told me I looked well in it.

Bossuet. In what, mademoiselle?

Fontanges. In quietism; that is, when I fell asleep at sermon-time. I am ashamed that such a learned and pious man as M. de Fénelon[7] should incline to it, as they say he does.

Bossuet. Mademoiselle, you quite mistake the matter.

Fontanges. Is not then M. de Fénelon thought a very pious and learned person?

Bossuet. And justly.

Fontanges. I have read a great way in a romance he has begun, about a knight-errant in search of a father.[8] The king says there are many such about his court; but I never saw them, nor heard of them before. The marchioness de la Motte, his relative, brought it to me, written out in a charming hand, as much as the copy-book would hold, and I got through I know not how far. If he had gone on with the nymphs in the grotto I never should have been tired of him; but he quite forgot his own story, and left them at once; in a hurry (I suppose) to set out upon

his mission to Saintonge in the *pays d'Aunis,*[9] where the king has promised him a famous *heretic-hunt.* He is, I do assure you, a wonderful creature; he understands so much Latin and Greek, and knows all the tricks of the sorceresses. Yet you keep him under.

Bossuet. Mademoiselle, if you really have anything to confess, and if you desire that I should have the honour of absolving you, it would be better to proceed in it, than to oppress me with unmerited eulogies on my humble labours.

Fontanges. You must first direct me, monseigneur: I have nothing particular. The king assures me there is no harm whatever in his love towards me.

Bossuet. That depends on your thoughts at the moment. If you abstract the mind from the body, and turn your heart towards heaven——

Fontanges. O monseigneur, I always did so—— every time but once——you quite make me blush. Let us converse about something else, or I shall grow too serious, just as you made me the other day at the funeral sermon. And now let me tell you, my lord, you compose such pretty funeral-sermons, I hope I shall have the pleasure of hearing you preach, mine.

Bossuet. Rather let us hope, mademoiselle, that the hour is yet far distant when so melancholy a service will be performed for you. May he who is unborn be the sad announcer of your departure hence![10] May he indicate to those around him many virtues not perhaps yet full-blown in you, and point triumphantly to many faults and foibles checked by you in their early growth, and lying dead on the open road you shall have left behind you! To me the painful duty will, I trust, be spared: I am advanced in age: you are a child.

Fontanges. O no, I am seventeen.

Bossuet. I should have supposed you younger by two years at least. But do you collect nothing from your own reflection, which raises so many in my breast? You think it possible that I, aged as I am, may preach a sermon on your funeral. Alas, it is so! such things have been! There is, however, no funeral so sad to follow as the funeral of our own youth, which we have been pampering with fond desires, ambitious hopes,

---

6 religious mysticism as practiced by a sect founded in the seventeenth century.

7 a celebrated French prelate, 1651–1715.

8 *Télémaque,* published in 1699, in which the adventures of the son of Ulysses are made into a political novel.

9 In 1685, Fénelon was sent on a mission to convert the Protestants of Saintonge, a district near the famous Huguenot citadel of La Rochelle.

10 Bossuet was in his fifty-fourth year: Mademoiselle de Fontanges died in childbed the year following; he survived her twenty-three [years].—(Landor.)

and all the bright berries that hang in poisonous clusters over the path of life.

Fontanges. I never minded them; I like peaches better; and one a day is quite enough for me.

Bousset. We say that our days are few; and, saying it, we say too much. Marie-Angélique, we have but one: the past are not ours, and who can promise us the future? This in which we live is ours only while we live in it; the next moment may strike it off from us; the next sentence I would utter may be broken and fall between us. The beauty that has made a thousand hearts to beat at one instant, at the succeeding has been without pulse and colour, without admirer, friend, companion, follower. She by whose eyes the march of victory shall have been directed, whose name shall have animated armies at the extremities of the earth, drops into one of its crevices and mingles with its dust. Duchess de Fontanges! think on this! Lady! so live as to think on it undisturbed.

Fontanges. O God! I am quite alarmed. Do not talk thus gravely. It is in vain that you speak to me in so sweet a voice. I am frightened even at the rattle of the beads about my neck; take them off, and let us talk on other things. What was it that dropped on the floor as you were speaking? It seemed to shake the room, though it sounded like a pin or button.

Bossuet. Never mind it: leave it there: I pray you, I implore you, madame!

Fontanges. Why do you rise? why do you run? why not let me? I am nimbler. So, your ring fell from your hand, my lord bishop! How quick you are! Could not you have trusted me to pick it up?

Bossuet. Madame is too condescending: had this happened, I should have been overwhelmed with confusion. My hand is shrivelled; the ring has ceased to fit it. A mere accident may draw us into perdition: a mere accident may bestow on us the means of grace. A pebble has moved you more than my words.

Fontanges. It pleases me vastly: I admire rubies: I will ask the king for one exactly like it. This is the time he usually comes from the chase. I am sorry you cannot be present to hear how prettily I shall ask him. But that is impossible, you know; for I shall do it just when I am certain he would give me anything. He said so himself; he said but yesterday

Such a sweet creature is worth a world;
and no actor on the stage was ever more like a king than his Majesty was when he spoke it, if he had but kept his wig and robe on. And yet you know he is rather stiff and wrinkled for so great a monarch; and his eyes, I am afraid, are beginning to fail him; he looks so close at things.

Bossuet. Mademoiselle, such is the duty of a prince who desires to conciliate our regard and love.

Fontanges. Well, I think so too; though I did not like it in him at first. I am sure he will order the ring for me, and I will confess to you with it upon my finger. But first I must be cautious and particular to know of him how much it is his royal will that I should say.

1828

From PERICLES AND ASPASIA

[In his longest single work Landor aimed to represent the spirit of the Golden Age of Pericles through a series of imaginary letters supposed to pass between Pericles, his mistress Aspasia, and their friends. In his final letter Pericles, about to die, names over those great men of Greece whom he remembers.]

LETTER CCXXXV: PERICLES TO ASPASIA

IT is right and orderly, that he who has partaken so largely in the prosperity of the Athenians, should close the procession of their calamities. The fever that has depopulated our city returned upon me last night, and Hippocrates and Acron tell me that my end is near.

When we agreed, O Aspasia, in the beginning of our loves, to communicate our thoughts by writing, even while we were both in Athens, and when we had many reasons for it, we little foresaw the more powerful one that has rendered it necessary of late. We never can meet again: the laws forbid it, and love itself enforces them. Let wisdom be heard by you as imperturbably, and affection as authoritatively, as ever: and remember that the sorrow of Pericles can arise but from the bosom of Aspasia. There is only one word of tenderness we could say, which we have not said oftentimes before; and there is no consolation in it. The happy never say, and never hear said, farewell.

Reviewing the course of my life, it appears to me at one moment as if we met but yesterday; at another as if centuries had passed within it; for within it have existed the greater part of those who, since the origin of the world, have been the luminaries of the human race. Damon called me from my music to look at Aristides on his way to exile: and my father pressed the wrist by which he was leading me along, and whispered in my ear,

'Walk quickly by; glance cautiously; it is there Miltiades is in prison.'

In my boyhood Pindar took me up in his arms, when he brought to our house the dirge he had composed for the funeral of my grandfather: in my adolescence I offered the rights of hospitality to Empedocles: not long afterward I embraced the neck of Æschylus, about to abandon his country. With Sophocles I have argued on eloquence; with Euripides on polity and ethics; I have discoursed, as became an inquirer, with Protagoras and Democritus, with Anaxagoras and Meton. From Herodotus I have listened to the most instructive history, conveyed in a language the most copious and the most harmonious; a man worthy to carry away the collected suffrages of universal Greece; a man worthy to throw open the temples of Egypt, and to celebrate the exploits of Cyrus. And from Thucydides, who alone can succeed to him, how recently did my Aspasia hear with me the energetic praises of his just supremacy!

As if the festival of life were incomplete, and wanted one great ornament to crown it, Phidias placed before us, in ivory and gold, the tutelary Deity of this land, and the Zeus of Homer and Olympus.

To have lived with such men, to have enjoyed their familiarity and esteem, overpays all labours and anxieties. I were unworthy of the friendships I have commemorated, were I forgetful of the latest. Sacred it ought to be, formed as it was under the portico of Death, my friendship with the most sagacious, the most scientific, the most beneficent of philosophers, Acron and Hippocrates. If mortal could war against Pestilence and Destiny, they had been victorious. I leave them in the field; unfortunate he who finds them among the fallen!

And now, at the close of my day, when every light is dim and every guest departed, let me own that these wane before me, remembering, as I do in the pride and fulness of my heart, that Athens confided her glory, and Aspasia her happiness, to me.

Have I been a faithful guardian? do I resign them to the custody of the Gods undiminished and unimpaired? Welcome then, welcome, my last hour! After enjoying for so great a number of years, in my public and my private life, what I believe has never been the lot of any other, I now extend my hand to the urn, and take without reluctance or hesitation what is the lot of all.

1836

From THE PENTAMERON

[*The Pentameron* consists of a series of five conversations held on successive days between Giovanni Boccaccio and Francesco Petrarca, celebrated Italian poets of the fourteenth century. The following selection, from the fifth day, gives Boccaccio's vision of his beloved Fiametta.]

THE DREAM OF BOCCACCIO

Boccaccio. I prayed; and my breast, after some few tears, grew calmer. Yet sleep did not ensue until the break of morning, when the dropping of soft rain on the leaves of the fig-tree at the window, and the chirping of a little bird, to tell another there was shelter under them, brought me repose and slumber. Scarcely had I closed my eyes, if indeed time can be reckoned any more in sleep than in heaven, when my Fiametta seemed to have led me into the meadow. You will see it below you: turn away that branch: gently! gently! do not break it; for the little bird sat there.

Petrarca. I think, Giovanni, I can divine the place. Although this fig-tree, growing out of the wall between the cellar and us, is fantastic enough in its branches, yet that other which I see yonder, bent down and forced to crawl along the grass by the prepotency of the young shapely walnut-tree, is much more so. It forms a seat, about a cubit above the ground, level and long enough for several.

Boccacio. Ha! you fancy it must be a favourite spot with me, because of the two strong forked stakes wherewith it is propped and supported!

Petrarca. Poets know the haunts of poets at first sight; and he who loved Laura—O Laura! did I say he who *loved* thee?—hath whisperings where those feet would wander which have been restless after Fiametta.

Boccaccio. It is true, my imagination has often conducted her thither; but here in this chamber she appeared to me more visibly in a dream.

'Thy prayers have been heard, O Giovanni,' said she.

I sprang to embrace her.

'Do not spill the water! Ah! you have spilt a part of it.'

I then observed in her hand a crystal vase. A few drops were sparkling on the sides and running down the rim: a few were trickling from the base and from the hand that held it.

'I must go down to the brook,' said she, 'and fill it again as it was filled before.'

What a moment of agony was this to me! Could I be certain how long might be her absence? She went: I was following: she made a sign for me to turn back: I disobeyed her only an instant: yet my sense of disobedience, increasing my feebleness and confusion, made me lose sight of her. In the next moment she was again at my side, with the cup quite full. I stood motionless: I feared my breath might shake the water over. I looked her in the face for her commands—and to see it—to see it so calm, so beneficent, so beautiful. I was forgetting what I had prayed for, when she lowered her head, tasted of the cup, and gave it me. I drank; and suddenly sprang forth before me many groves and palaces and gardens, and their statues and their avenues, and their labyrinths of alaternus and bay, and alcoves of citron, and watchful loopholes in the retirements of impenetrable pomegranate. Farther off, just below where the fountain slipt away from its marble hall and guardian gods, arose, from their beds of moss and drosera and darkest grass, the sisterhood of oleanders, fond of tantalising with their bosomed flowers and their moist and pouting blossoms the little shy rivulet, and of covering its face with all the colours of the dawn. My dream expanded and moved forward. I trod again the dust of Posilipo, soft as the feathers in the wings of Sleep. I emerged on Baia; I crossed her innumerable arches; I loitered in the breezy sunshine of her mole; I trusted the faithful seclusion of her caverns, the keepers of so many secrets; and I reposed on the buoyancy of her tepid sea. Then Naples, and her theatres and her churches, and grottoes and dells and forts and promontories, rushed forward in confusion, now among soft whispers, now among sweetest sounds, and subsided, and sank, and disappeared. Yet a memory seemed to come fresh from every one: each had time enough for its tale, for its pleasure, for its reflection, for its pang. As I mounted with silent steps the narrow staircase of the old palace, how distinctly did I feel against the palm of my hand the coldness of that smooth stonework, and the greater of the cramps of iron in it!

'Ah me! is this forgetting?' cried I anxiously to Fiametta.

'We must recall these scenes before us,' she replied: 'such is the punishment of them. Let us hope and believe that the apparition, and the compunction which must follow it, will be accepted as the full penalty, and that both will pass away almost together.'

I feared to lose anything attendant on her presence: I feared to approach her forehead with my lips: I feared to touch the lily on its long wavy leaf in her hair, which filled my whole heart with fragrance. Venerating, adoring, I bowed my head at last to kiss her snow-white robe, and trembled at my presumption. And yet the effulgence of her countenance vivified while it chastened me. I loved her—I must not say *more* than ever—*better* than ever; it was Fiametta who had inhabited the skies. As my hand opened toward her.

'Beware!' said she, faintly smiling; 'beware, Giovanni! Take only the crystal; take it, and drink again.'

'Must all be then forgotten?' said I sorrowfully.

'Remember your prayer and mine, Giovanni? Shall both have been granted—O how much worse than in vain?'

I drank instantly; I drank largely. How cool my bosom grew; how could it grow so cool before her? But it was not to remain in its quiescency; its trials were not yet over. I will not, Francesco! no, I may not commemorate the incidents she related to me, nor which of us said, 'I blush for having loved *first*'; nor which of us replied, 'Say *least,* say *least,* and blush again.'

The charm of the words (for I felt not the encumbrance of the body nor the acuteness of the spirit) seemed to possess me wholly. Although the water gave me strength and comfort, and somewhat of celestial pleasure, many tears fell around the border of the vase as she held it up before me, exhorting me to take courage, and inviting me with more than exhortation to accomplish my deliverance. She came nearer, more tenderly, more earnestly; she held the dewy globe with both hands, leaning forward, and sighed and shook her head, drooping at my pusillanimity. It was only when a ringlet had touched the rim, and perhaps the water (for a sunbeam on the surface could never have given it such a golden hue) that I took courage, clasped it, and exhausted it. Sweet as was the water, sweet as was the serenity it gave me—alas! that also which it moved away from me was sweet!

'This time you can trust me alone,' said she, and parted my hair, and kissed my brow. Again she went toward the brook: again my agitation, my weakness, my doubt, came over me: nor could I see her while she raised the water, nor knew I whence she drew it. When she returned, she was close to me at once: she smiled: her smile pierced me to the bones: it seemed an angel's. She sprinkled the pure water on me; she looked most fondly; she took my hand; she suffered me to press hers to my bosom; but, whether by design I cannot tell, she let fall a few drops of the chilly element between.

'And now, O my beloved!' said she, 'we have consigned to the bosom of God our earthly joys and sorrows. The joys cannot return, let not the sorrows. These alone would trouble my repose among the blessed.'

'Trouble thy repose! Fiametta! Give me the chalice!' cried I—'not a drop will I leave in it, not a drop.'

'Take it!' said that soft voice. 'O now most dear Giovanni! I know thou hast strength enough; and there is but little—at the bottom lies our first kiss.'

'Mine! didst thou say, beloved one? and is that left thee still?'

'*Mine,*' said she, pensively; and as she abased her head, the broad leaf of the lily hid her brow and her eyes; the light of heaven shone through the flower.

'O Fiametta! Fiametta!' cried I in agony, 'God is the God of mercy, God is the God of love—can I, can I ever?' I struck the chalice against my head, unmindful that I held it; the water covered my face and my feet. I started up, not yet awake, and I heard the name of Fiametta in the curtains.

1837

THE DREAM OF PETRARCA[1]

An Allegory of Love, Sleep, and Death

WEARIED with the length of my walk over the mountains, and finding a soft old molehill, covered with grey grass, by the way-side, I laid my head upon it, and slept. I cannot tell how long it was before a species of dream or vision came over me.

Two beautiful youths appeared beside me; each was winged; but the wings were hanging down, and seemed ill adapted to flight. One of them, whose voice was the softest I ever heard, looking at me frequently, said to the other,

'He is under my guardianship for the present: do not awaken him with that feather.'

Methought, hearing the whisper, I saw something like the feather on an arrow; and then the arrow itself; the whole of it, even to the point; although he carried it in such a manner that it was difficult at first to discover more than a palm's length of it: the rest of the shaft, and the whole of the barb, was behind his ankles.

'This feather never awakens any one,' replied

he, rather petulantly; 'but it brings more of confident security, and more of cherished dreams, than you without me are capable of imparting.'

'Be it so!' answered the gentler—'none is less inclined to quarrel or dispute than I am. Many whom you have wounded grievously, call upon me for succour. But so little am I disposed to thwart you, it is seldom I venture to do more for them than to whisper a few words of comfort in passing. How many reproaches on these occasions have been cast upon me for indifference and infidelity! Nearly as many, and nearly in the same terms, as upon you!'

'Odd enough that we, O Sleep! should be thought so alike!' said Love, contemptuously. 'Yonder is he who bears a nearer resemblance to you: the dullest have observed it.' I fancied I turned my eyes to where he was pointing, and saw at a distance the figure he designated. Meanwhile the contention went on uninterruptedly. Sleep was slow in asserting his power or his benefits. Love recapitulated them; but only that he might assert his own above them. Suddenly he called on me to decide, and to choose my patron. Under the influence, first of the one, then of the other, I sprang from repose to rapture, I alighted from rapture on repose—and knew not which was sweetest. Love was very angry with me, and declared he would cross me throughout the whole of my existence. Whatever I might on other occasions have thought of his veracity, I now felt too surely the conviction that he would keep his word. At last, before the close of the altercation, the third Genius had advanced, and stood near us. I cannot tell how I knew him, but I knew him to be the Genius of Death. Breathless as I was at beholding him, I soon became familiar with his features. First they seemed only calm; presently they grew contemplative; and lastly beautiful: those of the Graces themselves are less regular, less harmonious, less composed. Love glanced at him unsteadily, with a countenance in which there was somewhat of anxiety, somewhat of disdain; and cried, 'Go away! go away! nothing that thou touchest, lives.'

'Say rather, child!' replied the advancing form, and advancing grew loftier and statelier, 'Say rather that nothing of beautiful or of glorious lives its own true life until my wing hath passed over it.'

Love pouted, and rumpled and bent down with his forefinger the stiff short feathers on his arrowhead; but replied not. Although he frowned worse than ever, and at me, I dreaded

---

1 This selection concludes *The Pentameron.*

him less and less, and scarcely looked towards him. The milder and calmer Genius, the third in proportion as I took courage to contemplate him, regarded me with more and more complacency. He held neither flower nor arrow, as the others did; but, throwing back the clusters of dark curls that overshadowed his countenance, he presented to me his hand, openly and benignly. I shrank on looking at him so near, and yet I sighed to love him. He smiled, not without an expression of pity, at perceiving my diffidence, my timidity: for I remembered how soft was the hand of Sleep, how warm and entrancing was Love's. By degrees, I became ashamed of my ingratitude; and turning my face away, I held out my arms, and felt my neck within his. Composure strewed and allayed all the throbbings of my bosom; the coolness of freshest morning breathed around; the heavens seemed to open above me; while the beautiful cheek of my deliverer rested on my head. I would now have looked for those others; but knowing my intention by my gesture, he said consolatorily,

'Sleep is on his way to the Earth, where many are calling him; but it is not to these he hastens; for every call only makes him fly farther off. Sedately and gravely as he looks, he is nearly as capricious and volatile as the more arrogant and ferocious one.'

'And Love!' said I, 'whither is he departed? If not too late, I would propitiate and appease him.'

'He who cannot follow me, he who cannot overtake and pass me,' said the Genius, 'is unworthy of the name, the most glorious in earth or heaven. Look up! Love is yonder, and ready to receive thee.'

I looked: the earth was under me: I saw only the clear blue sky, and something brighter above it.

1837

1754 · GEORGE CRABBE · 1832

1754   Born at Aldeborough in Suffolk, the son of a salt-tax collector.

1768–79   After a brief elementary schooling, was apprenticed to an apothecary, or surgeon, and worked as a quay laborer. Served as parish doctor of Aldeborough, but found the work uncongenial, and eventually abandoned it for a precarious literary livelihood.

1780   Visited London with such poems as he had in MS. to solicit publishers and patrons. Was saved from nearly starving in Grub Street by gifts from his boyhood sweetheart, Sarah Elmy. At length was befriended by Edmund Burke, who advised the publication of *The Library* (1781).

1781   Took orders and was appointed chaplain to the Duke of Rutland at Belvoir Castle.

1783   Published *The Village* and married Sarah Elmy.

1785   Published *The Newspaper*. Following this somewhat uninteresting publication, for twenty-two years gave up writing to devote his attention to parish affairs. Resided at Muston parsonage, Leicestershire, and during a long interval at several villages in Suffolk.

1807   Published *The Parish Register,* which first revealed the author's gift as a narrative poet.

1810   Published *The Borough,* a poem in twenty-four 'letters,' which illustrated by various stories the life in a country town.

1812   Published *Tales in Verse,* a collection of twenty-one narratives.

1814   Following the death of his wife, was appointed vicar of Trowbridge, Wiltshire. Was prosperous during the last years of his life; a constant visitor to London, was in friendship with most of the literary celebrities of the time, including Rogers, Campbell, and Moore.

1819   Published *Tales of the Hall.*

1822   Visited Sir Walter Scott at Edinburgh.

1832   Died at Trowbridge. A number of posthumous *Tales* were published by his son in the collected works (1834).

GEORGE CRABBE, who was born and bred among the poor, learned first-hand from his own poverty-stricken youth of the vast range of actions, passions, and sufferings of the English peasantry. A man of strong prejudices and somewhat stern disposition himself (though he mellowed greatly in the latter part of his life), he fearlessly set down human nature as he saw it. As a young author he came forward to expose the sentimentality of traditional Arcadianism, which still lingered in conventional polite literature. With conscious antagonism to what he conceived to be unrealities in Goldsmith's idyllic picture of Auburn, Crabbe described his own harsh and desolate fishing village of Aldeborough. 'I paint the cot as Truth will paint it and as bards will not,' he declared, and carried the rendering to the opposite extreme. In *The Village* he remorselessly traced with stern veracity every dull and sordid detail: the barren landscape, the sterile soil, the weeds, the half-starved inhabitants amid their smuggling surroundings, their sufferings concealed by pride or suppressed by necessity, the hopelessness of their dreary lives which end in loneliness and misery in the workhouse.

In *The Village,* with its perfection perhaps aided in part by the revisions of Johnson and Burke, Crabbe reached a point in poetic workmanship which he never surpassed. The poem justly earned for its author a speedy and wide popularity. After a long silence, Crabbe again took up the old text—'the Auburns and the Edens can be found no more' —and with a series of notable works established himself as a satiric verse novelist of country life. In these later tales his materials are taken for the most part from the Suffolk coastal region near Aldeborough, with additions drawn from his clerical experiences. He follows the same realistic method, with the same harsh nudity of description, as in *The Village,* but he adds memorable episodes of individual lives. He illustrates in these bare narratives the peculiar temptations and perils to which the poor are exposed. With unrelenting exactitude he traces in their frustrated lives the slow mutation and degeneration of character. In *Peter Grimes* (to take for illustration a story revived in fame by Britten's opera) the author pursues the gradual breakdown of the sadist Grimes, haunted by the spirits of the boys he has murdered and the sight of his father, whose life he threatened but had not taken, to his final agony of delirium and lonely death.

Crabbe was hostile to the novel of sentiment and Gothic adventure. His greatest admiration was for Pope, and more than any other poet Crabbe carried into the nineteenth century the traditions of the eighteenth. He was an isolated figure living through a great literary revolution but with little traceable influence of the new matter or spirit in his own work. Like Wordsworth he resolutely discarded conventional imagery and stock phrasing, but he has nothing of Wordsworth's vision and 'none of the grace of the new dispensation.' A flat monotony and drabness characterize Crabbe's language and style, and there is a certain obscurity of expression from which he never quite freed himself. These are the limitations of his genius. But his prosaic verse was a fitting garb for his feeling and his themes, nor is the style always flat and the verse monotonous. When he is deeply moved his narrative breaks free with clean and rapid strokes and his language glows with an enkindled fervor. His passion was the observation of man and especially of the darker side of man's character and lot. He minutely observes and records the scenes, objects, and manners in the bitter struggles of human nature. For most men, Crabbe tells us, life is a progressive disillusionment; happiness, an exception. His psychology is hard, firm, and persistent—but subtle as well. Perhaps there is too much of the psychologist and the preacher in Crabbe. He is persistently didactic; yet one remembers not so much the moral but the inevitability of what he has related. His compassion for human misery is deep and true and his humor genuine. He uses his realism in the cause of humanity. His point of view is thus the point of view of Zola or of Dreiser. Crabbe held his own for a long period. He was praised by Jeffrey and Scott, and appreciated by Wordsworth. To Byron he was 'nature's sternest painter and her best.' Thomas Hardy acknowledged Crabbe's influence on the realism of his novels. His works no longer attract wide public interest. But he enlarged the scope of poetry by refusing to draw delusively pleasing pictures. His was the 'realist's implicit sense of the richness of common things and the drama of homely life.'

From THE VILLAGE

BOOK I

THE village life, and every care that reigns
O'er youthful peasants and declining swains;
What labour yields, and what, that labour past,
Age, in its hour of languor, finds at last;
What form the real picture of the poor,
Demand a song—the Muse can give no more.

Fled are those times, when, in harmonious strains,
The rustic poet praised his native plains:
No shepherds now, in smooth alternate verse,
Their country's beauty or their nymphs' rehearse;   10
Yet still for these we frame the tender strain,
Still in our lays fond Corydons[1] complain,

---

1 a conventional name for lovers in pastoral poetry.

And shepherds' boys their amorous pains reveal,
The only pains, alas! they never feel.
    On Mincio's banks,[2] in Cæsar's bounteous reign,
If Tityrus[3] found the Golden Age again,
Must sleepy bards the flattering dream prolong,
Mechanic echoes of the Mantuan song?
From Truth and Nature shall we widely stray,
Where Virgil, not where Fancy, leads the way? 20
    Yes, thus the Muses sing of happy swains,
Because the Muses never knew their pains:
They boast their peasants' pipes; but peasants now
Resign their pipes and plod behind the plough;
And few, amid the rural-tribe, have time
To number syllables, and play with rhyme;
Save honest Duck,[4] what son of verse could share
The poet's rapture, and the peasant's care?
Or the great labours of the field degrade,
With the new peril of a poorer trade? 30
    From this chief cause these idle praises spring,
That themes so easy few forbear to sing;
For no deep thought the trifling subjects ask;
To sing of shepherds is an easy task:
The happy youth assumes the common strain,
A nymph his mistress, and himself a swain;
With no sad scenes he clouds his tuneful prayer,
But all, to look like her, is painted fair.
    I grant indeed that fields and flocks have charms
For him that grazes or for him that farms; 40
But when amid such pleasing scenes I trace
The poor laborious natives of the place,
And see the mid-day sun, with fervid ray,
On their bare heads and dewy temples play;
While some, with feebler heads and fainter hearts,
Deplore their fortune, yet sustain their parts:
Then shall I dare these real ills to hide
In tinsel trappings of poetic pride?
    No; cast by Fortune on a frowning coast,
Which neither groves nor happy valleys boast, 50
Where other cares than those the Muse relates,
And other shepherds dwell with other mates,
By such examples taught, I paint the cot,
As Truth will paint it, and as bards will not:
Nor you, ye poor, of letter'd scorn complain,
To you the smoothest song is smooth in vain;
O'ercome by labour, and bow'd down by time.
Feel you the barren flattery of a rhyme?

Can poets soothe you, when you pine for bread,
By winding myrtles round your ruin'd shed? 60
Can their light tales your weighty griefs o'er-power,
Or glad with airy mirth the toilsome hour?
    Lo! where the heath with withering brake grown o'er,
Lends the light turf that warms the neighbouring poor;
From thence a length of burning sand appears,
Where the thin harvest waves its wither'd ears;
Rank weeds, that every art and care defy,
Reign o'er the land, and rob the blighted rye:
There thistles stretch their prickly arms afar,
And to the ragged infant threaten war; 70
There poppies nodding, mock the hope of toil;
There the blue bugloss paints the sterile soil;
Hardy and high, above the slender sheaf,
The slimy mallow waves her silky leaf;
O'er the young shoot the charlock throws a shade,
And clasping tares cling round the sickly blade;
With mingled tints the rocky coasts abound,
And a sad splendour vainly shines around.
So looks the nymph whom wretched arts adorn,
Betray'd by man, then left for man to scorn; 80
Whose cheek in vain assumes the mimic rose,
While her sad eyes the troubled breast disclose;
Whose outward splendour is but folly's dress,
Exposing most, whom most it gilds distress.
    Here joyless roam a wild amphibious race,
With sullen woe display'd in every face;
Who, far from civil arts and social fly,
And scowl at strangers with suspicious eye.
    Here too the lawless merchant of the main[5]
Draws from his plough th' intoxicated swain; 90
Want only claim'd the labour of the day,
But vice now steals his nightly rest away.
    Where are the swains, who, daily labour done,
With rural games play'd down the setting sun;
Who struck with matchless force the bounding hall,
Or made the pond'rous quoit obliquely fall;
While some huge Ajax, terrible and strong,
Engaged some artful stripling of the throng,
And fell beneath him, foil'd, while far around
Hoarse triumph rose, and rocks return'd the sound? 100
Where now are these?—Beneath yon cliff they stand,
To show the freighted pinnace where to land,
To load the ready steed with guilty haste,
To fly in terror o'er the pathless waste,

---

2 a reference to the banks of the Mincius, a river flowing into the Po below Mantua, the home of Virgil.
3 the name of one of the two speakers in Virgil's first Eclogue.
4 Stephen Duck, 1705–56, the thresher poet, who was pensioned by Queen Caroline.

---

5 smuggler.

Or, when detected, in their straggling course,
To foil their foes by cunning or by force;
Or, yielding part (which equal knaves demand),
To gain a lawless passport through the land.
 Here, wand'ring long, amid these frowning
  fields,
I sought the simple life that Nature yields; 110
Rapine and Wrong and Fear usurp'd her place,
And a bold, artful, surly, savage race,
Who, only skill'd to take the finny tribe,
The yearly dinner, or septennial bribe,[6]
Wait on the shore, and, as the waves run high,
On the tost vessel bend their eager eye,
Which to their coast directs its vent'rous way,
Theirs, or the ocean's, miserable prey.
 As on their neighbouring beach yon swallows
  stand,
And wait for favouring winds to leave the
  land, 120
While still for flight the ready wing is spread,
So waited I the favouring hour, and fled—
Fled from these shores where guilt and famine
  reign,
And cried, 'Ah! hapless they who still remain;
Who still remain to hear the ocean roar,
Whose greedy waves devour the lessening shore;
Till some fierce tide, with more imperious
  sway,
Sweeps the low hut and all it holds away:
When the sad tenant weeps from door to door,
And begs a poor protection from the poor!' 130
But these are scenes where Nature's niggard
  hand
Gave a spare portion to the famish'd land;
Hers is the fault, if here mankind complain
Of fruitless toil and labour spent in vain;
But yet in other scenes more fair in view,
Where Plenty smiles—alas! she smiles for few—
And those who taste not, yet behold her store,
Are as the slaves that dig the golden ore,—
The wealth around them makes them doubly
  poor.
 Or will you deem them amply paid in
  health, 140
Labour's fair child, that languishes with wealth?
Go then! and see them rising with the sun,
Through a long course of daily toil to run;
See them beneath the dog-star's raging heat,
When the knees tremble and the temples beat;
Behold them, leaning on their scythes, look o'er
The labour past, and toils to come explore;
See them alternate suns and showers engage,
And hoard up aches and anguish for their age;

6 bribe given by candidates for Parliament.

Through fens and marshy moors their steps
  pursue, 150
When their warm pores imbibe the evening
  dew;
Then own that labour may as fatal be
To these thy slaves, as thine excess to thee.
 Amid this tribe too oft a manly pride
Strives in strong toil the fainting heart to hide;
There may you see the youth of slender frame
Contend with weakness, weariness, and shame;
Yet, urged along, and proudly loth to yield,
He strives to join his fellows of the field,
Till long-contending nature droops at last, 160
Declining health rejects his poor repast,
His cheerless spouse the coming danger sees,
And mutual murmurs urge the slow disease.
 Yet grant them health, 'tis not for us to tell,
Though the head droops not, that the heart is
  well;
Or will you praise that homely, healthy fare,
Plenteous and plain, that happy peasants share!
Oh! trifle not with wants you cannot feel,
Nor mock the misery of a stinted meal;
Homely, not wholesome, plain, not plenteous,
  such 170
As you who praise would never deign to touch.
 Ye gentle souls, who dream of rural ease,
Whom the smooth stream and smoother sonnet
  please;
Go! if the peaceful cot your praises share,
Go look within, and ask if peace be there;
If peace be his—that drooping weary sire,
Or theirs, that offspring round their feeble fire;
Or hers, that matron pale, whose trembling hand
Turns on the wretched hearth th' expiring brand!
 Nor yet can Time itself obtain for these 180
Life's latest comforts, due respect and ease;
For yonder see that hoary swain, whose age
Can with no cares except his own engage;
Who, propp'd on that rude staff, looks up to see
The bare arms broken from the withering tree,
On which, a boy, he clim'd the loftiest bough,
Then his first joy, but his sad emblem now.
 He once was chief in all the rustic trade;
His steady hand the straightest furrow made;
Full many a prize he won, and still is proud 190
To find the triumphs of his youth allow'd;
A transient pleasure sparkles in his eyes,
He hears and smiles, then thinks again and sighs:
For now he journeys to his grave in pain;
The rich disdain him; nay, the poor disdain:
Alternate masters now their slave command,
Urge the weak efforts of his feeble hand,
And, when his age attempts its task in vain,
With ruthless taunts, of lazy poor complain.

Oft may you see him, when he tends the
    sheep,   200
His winter-charge, beneath the hillock weep;
Oft hear him murmur to the winds that blow
O'er his white locks and bury them in snow,
When, roused by rage and muttering in the morn,
He mends the broken hedge with icy thorn:—
    'Why do I live, when I desire to be
At once from life and life's long labour free?
Like leaves in spring, the young are blown away,
Without the sorrows of a slow decay;
I, like yon wither'd leaf, remain behind,   210
Nipp'd by the frost, and shivering in the wind;
There it abides till younger buds come on,
As I, now all my fellow-swains are gone;
Then, from the rising generation thrust,
It falls, like me, unnoticed, to the dust.
    'These fruitful fields, these numerous flocks
    I see,
Are others' gain, but killing cares to me;
To me the children of my youth are lords,
Cool in their looks, but hasty in their words:
Wants of their own demand their care; and
    who   220
Feels his own want and succours others too?
A lonely, wretched man, in pain I go,
None need my help, and none relieve my woe;
Then let my bones beneath the turf be laid,
And men forget the wretch they would not aid.'
    Thus groan the old, till, by disease oppress'd,
They taste a final woe, and then they rest.
    Theirs is yon house that holds the parish-poor,
Whose walls of mud scarce bear the broken door;
There, where the putrid vapours, flagging,
    play,   230
And the dull wheel[7] hums doleful through the
    day;—
There children dwell who know no parents' care;
Parents who know no children's love, dwell
    there!
Heartbroken matrons on their joyless bed,
Forsaken wives, and mothers never wed,
Dejected widows with unheeded tears,
And crippled age with more than childhood
    fears;
The lame, the blind, and, far the happiest they!
The moping idiot and the madman gay.
Here too the sick their final doom receive,   240
Here brought, amid the scenes of grief, to grieve,
Where the loud groans from some sad chamber
    flow,
Mix'd with the clamours of the crowd below;
Here, sorrowing, they each kindred sorrow scan,
And the cold charities of man to man:

Whose laws indeed for ruin'd age provide,
And strong compulsion plucks the scrap from
    pride;
But still that scrap is bought with many a sigh,
And pride embitters what it can't deny.
    Say ye, oppress'd by some fantastic woes,   250
Some jarring nerve that baffles your repose;
Who press the downy couch, while slaves ad-
    vance
With timid eye, to read the distant glance;
Who with sad prayers the weary doctor tease,
To name the nameless ever-new disease;
Who with mock patience dire complaints endure,
Which real pain and that alone can cure;
How would ye bear in real pain to lie,
Despised, neglected, left alone to die?
How would ye bear to draw your latest
    breath,   260
Where all that's wretched paves the way for
    death?
    Such is that room which one rude beam di-
    vides,
And naked rafters form the sloping sides;
Where the vile bands that bind the thatch are
    seen,
And lath and mud are all that lie between,
Save one dull pane, that, coarsely patch'd, gives
    way
To the rude tempest, yet excludes the day:
Here, on a matted flock,[8] with dust o'erspread,
The drooping wretch reclines his languid head;
For him no hand the cordial cup applies,   270
Or wipes the tear that stagnates in his eyes;
No friends with soft discourse his pain beguile,
Or promise hope till sickness wears a smile.
    But soon a loud and hasty summons calls,
Shakes the thin roof, and echoes round the walls;
Anon, a figure enters, quaintly neat,
All pride and business, bustle and conceit;
With looks unalter'd by these scenes of woe,
With speed that, entering, speaks his haste to go,
He bids the gazing throng around him fly,   280
And carries fate and physic in his eye:
A potent quack, long versed in human ills,
Who first insults the victim whom he kills;
Whose murd'rous hand a drowsy Bench protect,
And whose most tender mercy is neglect.
    Paid by the parish for attendance here,
He wears contempt upon his sapient sneer;
In haste he seeks the bed where Misery lies,
Impatience mark'd in his averted eyes;
And, some habitual queries hurried o'er,   290
Without reply, he rushes on the door:
His drooping patient, long inured to pain,

---

7 spinning wheel.

8 bed filled with coarse wool.

And long unheeded, knows remonstrance vain;
He ceases now the feeble help to crave
Of man; and silent sinks into the grave.

But ere his death some pious doubts arise,
Some simple fears, which 'bold bad' men despise;
Fain would he ask the parish-priest to prove
His title certain to the joys above:
For this he sends the murmuring nurse, who
    calls   300
The holy stranger to these dismal walls:
And doth not he, the pious man, appear,
He, 'passing rich with forty pounds a year'?[9]
Ah! no; a shepherd of a different stock,
And far unlike him, feeds this little flock:
A jovial youth, who thinks his Sunday's task
As much as God or man can fairly ask;
The rest he gives to loves and labours light,
To fields the morning, and to feasts the night;
None better skill'd the noisy pack to guide,   310
To urge their chase, to cheer them or to chide;
A sportsman keen, he shoots through half the
    day,
And, skill'd at whist, devotes the night to play:
Then, while such honours bloom around his head,
Shall he sit sadly by the sick man's bed,
To raise the hope he feels not, or with zeal
To combat fears that e'en the pious feel?

Now once again the gloomy scene explore,
Less gloomy now; the bitter hour is o'er,
The man of many sorrows sighs no more.   320
Up yonder hill, behold how sadly slow
The bier moves winding from the vale below;
There lie the happy dead, from trouble free,
And the glad parish pays the frugal fee:
No more, O Death! thy victim starts to hear
Churchwarden stern, or kingly overseer;
No more the farmer claims his humble bow,
Thou art his lord, the best of tyrants thou!

Now to the church behold the mourners come,
Sedately torpid and devoutly dumb;   330
The village children now their games suspend,
To see the bier that bears their ancient friend;
For he was one in all their idle sport,
And like a monarch ruled their little court.
The pliant bow he form'd, the flying ball,
The bat, the wicket, were his labours all;
Him now they follow to his grave, and stand
Silent and sad, and gazing, hand in hand;
While bending low, their eager eyes explore
The mingled relics of the parish poor: 340
The bell tolls late, the moping owl flies round,
Fear marks the flight and magnifies the sound;
The busy priest, detain'd by weightier care,
Defers his duty till the day of prayer;

And, waiting long, the crowd retire distress'd,
To think a poor man's bones should lie unbless'd.

1780–83   1783

From THE BOROUGH

LETTER XXII

PETER GRIMES

Old Peter Grimes made fishing his employ;
His wife he cabin'd with him and his boy,
And seem'd that life laborious to enjoy.
To town came quiet Peter with his fish,
And had of all a civil word and wish.
He left his trade upon the Sabbath-day,
And took young Peter in his hand to pray;
But soon the stubborn boy from care broke loose,
At first refused, then added his abuse;
His father's love he scorn'd, his power defied,   10
But, being drunk, wept sorely when he died.

Yes! then he wept, and to his mind there came
Much of his conduct, and he felt the shame:—
How he had oft the good old man reviled,
And never paid the duty of a child;
How, when the father in his Bible read,
He in contempt and anger left the shed;
'It is the word of life,' the parent cried;
'This is the life itself,' the boy replied;
And while old Peter in amazement stood,   20
Gave the hot spirit to his boiling blood;—
How he, with oath and furious speech, began
To prove his freedom and assert the man;
And when the parent check'd his impious rage,
How he had cursed the tyranny of age;—
Nay, once had dealt the sacrilegious blow
On his bare head, and laid his parent low;
The father groan'd—'If thou art old,' said he,
'And hast a son—thou wilt remember me;
Thy mother left me in a happy time,   30
Thou kill'dst not her—Heav'n spares the double
    crime.'
On an inn-settle, in his maudlin grief,
This he revolved, and drank for his relief.
Now lived the youth in freedom, but debarr'd
From constant pleasure, and he thought it hard;
Hard that he could not every wish obey,
But must awhile relinquish ale and play;
Hard! that he could not to his cards attend,
But must acquire the money he would spend.

With greedy eye he look'd on all he saw;   40
He knew not justice, and he laugh'd at law;
On all he mark'd he stretch'd his ready hand;
He fish'd by water, and he filch'd by land.
Oft in the night has Peter dropp'd his oar,
Fled from his boat and sought for prey on shore;

---

9 Goldsmith, *The Deserted Village*, 142.

Oft up the hedge-row glided, on his back
Bearing the orchard's produce in a sack,
Or farm-yard load, tugg'd fiercely from the stack;
And as these wrongs to greater numbers rose,
The more he look'd on all men as his foes.   50

He built a mud-wall'd hovel, where he kept
His various wealth, and there he oft-times slept;
But no success could please his cruel soul,
He wish'd for one to trouble and control;
He wanted some obedient boy to stand
And bear the blow of his outrageous hand;
And hoped to find in some propitious hour
A feeling creature subject to his power.

Peter had heard there were in London then—
Still have they being!—workhouse-clearing
     men,   60
Who, undisturb'd by feelings just or kind,
Would parish-boys to needy tradesmen bind;
They in their want a trifling sum would take,
And toiling slaves of piteous orphans make.

Such Peter sought, and, when a lad was found,
The sum was dealt him, and the slave was bound.
Some few in town observed in Peter's trap·
A boy, with jacket blue and woolen cap;
But none inquired how Peter used the rope,
Or what the bruise, that made the stripling
     stoop;   70
None could the ridges on his back behold,
None sought him shiv'ring in the winter's cold;
None put the question—'Peter, dost thou give
The boy his food?—What, man! the lad must
     live:
Consider, Peter, let the child have bread,
He'll serve thee better if he's stroked and fed.'
None reason'd thus—and some, on hearing cries,
Said calmly, 'Grimes is at his exercise.'

Pinn'd, beaten, cold, pinch'd, threaten'd, and
     abused—
His efforts punish'd and his food refused—   80
Awake tormented—soon aroused from sleep—
Struck if he wept, and yet compell'd to weep:
The trembling boy dropp'd down and strove to
     pray,
Received a blow, and trembling turn'd away,
Or sobb'd and hid his piteous face;—while he,
The savage master, grinn'd in horrid glee:
He'd now the power he ever loved to show,
A feeling being subject to his blow.

Thus lived the lad, in hunger, peril, pain,
His tears despised, his supplications vain.   90
Compell'd by fear to lie, by need to steal,
His bed uneasy and unbless'd his meal,
For three sad years the boy his tortures bore;
And then his pains and trials were no more.

'How died he, Peter?' when the people said,

He growl'd—'I found him lifeless in his bed';
Then tried for softer tone, and sigh'd, 'Poor Sam
     is dead.'
Yet murmurs were there, and some questions
     ask'd—
How he was fed, how punish'd, and how task'd?
Much they suspected, but they little proved,   100
And Peter pass'd untroubled and unmoved.

Another boy with equal ease was found,
The money granted, and the victim bound;
And what his fate?—One night, it chanced he fell
From the boat's mast and perish'd in her well,
Where fish were living kept, and where the boy
(So reason'd men) could not himself destroy.—

'Yes! so it was,' said Peter; 'in his play,
(For he was idle both by night and day,)
He climb'd the main-mast and then fell
     below';—   110
Then show'd his corpse and pointed to the
     blow—
What said the jury?'—They were long in doubt;
But sturdy Peter faced the matter out:
So they dismiss'd him, saying at the time,
'Keep fast your hatchway, when you've boys who
     climb.'
This hit the conscience, and he colour'd more
Than for the closest questions put before.

Thus all his fears the verdict set aside,
And at the slave-shop Peter still applied.

Then came a boy, of manners soft and
     mild—   120
Our seamen's wives with grief beheld the child;
All thought (the poor themselves) that he was one
Of gentle blood, some noble sinner's son,
Who had, belike, deceived some humble maid,
Whom he had first seduced and then betray'd.—
However this, he seem'd a gracious lad,
In grief submissive and with patience sad.

Passive he labour'd, till his slender frame
Bent with his loads, and he at length was lame;—
Strange that a frame so weak could bear so
     long   130
The grossest insult and the foulest wrong;
But there were causes—in the town they gave
Fire, food, and comfort, to the gentle slave;
And though stern Peter, with a cruel hand,
And knotted rope, enforced the rude command,
Yet he consider'd what he'd lately felt,
And his vile blows with selfish pity dealt.

One day such draughts the cruel fisher made
He could not vend them in his borough-trade,
But sail'd for London-mart; the boy was ill,   140
But ever humbled to his master's will;
And on the river, where they smoothly sail'd,

He strove with terror and awhile prevail'd;
But, new to danger on the angry sea,
He clung affrighten'd to his master's knee.
The boat grew leaky and the wind was strong,
Rough was the passage and the time was long;
His liquor fail'd, and Peter's wrath arose—
No more is known—the rest we must suppose,
Or learn of Peter;—Peter says, he 'spied   150
The stripling's danger and for harbour tried;
Meantime the fish, and then th' apprentice
      died.'
    The pitying women raised a clamour round,
And weeping said, 'Thou hast thy 'prentice
      drown'd.'
    Now the stern man was summon'd to the hall,
To tell his tale before the burghers all.
He gave th' account; profess'd the lad he loved,
And kept his brazen features all unmoved.
    The mayor himself with tone severe replied,—
'Henceforth with thee shall never boy abide;   160
Hire thee a freeman, whom thou durst not beat,
But who, in thy despite, will sleep and eat.
Free thou art now!—again shouldst thou appear,
Thou'lt find thy sentence, like thy soul, severe.'
    Alas! for Peter not a helping hand,
So was he hated, could he now command;
Alone he row'd his boat; alone he cast
His nets beside, or made his anchor fast;
To hold a rope or hear a curse was none—
He toil'd and rail'd; he groan'd and swore
      alone.   170
    Thus by himself compell'd to live each day,
To wait for certain hours the tide's delay;
At the same time the same dull views to see,
The bounding marsh-bank and the blighted tree;
The water only when the tides were high;
When low, the mud half-cover'd and half-dry;
The sun-burnt tar that blisters on the planks,
And bank-sides stakes in their uneven ranks;
Heaps of entangled weeds that slowly float,
As the tide rolls by the impeded boat.   180
    When tides were neap,[1] and, in the sultry day,
Through the tall bounding mud-banks made
      their way,
Which on each side rose swelling, and below
The dark warm flood ran silently and slow:
There anchoring, Peter chose from man to hide,
There hang his head, and view the lazy tide
In its hot slimy channel slowly glide;
Where the small eels that left the deeper way
For the warm shore, within the shallows play;
Where gaping muscles, left upon the mud,   190
Slope their slow passage to the fallen flood:—

Here dull and hopeless he'd lie down and trace
How sidelong crabs had scrawl'd their crooked
      race;
Or sadly listen to the tuneless cry
Of fishing gull or clanging golden-eye;
What time the sea-birds to the marsh would
      come,
And the loud bittern, from the bull-rush home,
Gave from the salt-ditch side the bellowing
      boom.
He nursed the feelings these dull scenes produce,
And loved to stop beside the opening sluice;   200
Where the small stream, confined in narrow
      bound,
Ran with a dull, unvaried, sadd'ning sound;
Where all presented to the eye or ear
Oppress'd the soul with misery, grief, and fear.
    Besides these objects, there were places three,
Which Peter seem'd with certain dread to see;
When he drew near them he would turn from
      each,
And loudly whistle till he pass'd the reach.[2]
    A change of scene to him brought no relief;
In town, 'twas plain, men took him for a
      thief: 210
The sailors' wives would stop him in the street,
And say, 'Now, Peter, thou'st no boy to beat';
Infants at play, when they perceived him, ran,
Warning each other—'That's the wicked man';
He growl'd an oath, and in an angry tone
Cursed the whole place and wish'd to be alone.
    Alone he was, the same dull scenes in view,
And still more gloomy in his sight they grew.
Though man he hated, yet employ'd alone
At bootless labour, he would swear and
      groan,   220
Cursing the shoals that glided by the spot,
And gulls that caught them when his arts could
      not.
    Cold nervous tremblings shook his sturdy
      frame,
And strange disease—he couldn't say the name;
Wild were his dreams, and oft he rose in fright,
Waked by his view of horrors in the night—
Horrors that would the sternest minds amaze,
Horrors that demons might be proud to raise;
And, though he felt forsaken, grieved at heart,
To think he lived from all mankind apart;   230
Yet, if a man approach'd, in terrors he would
      start.
    A winter pass'd since Peter saw the town,
And summer-lodgers were again come down;
These, idly curious, with their glasses spied

---

1 lowest.

2 a straight course between two bends of a navigable river.

The ships in bay as anchor'd for the tide—
The river's craft—the bustle of the quay—
And sea-port views, which landmen love to see.
 One, up the river, had a man and boat
Seen day by day, now anchor'd, now afloat;
Fisher he seem'd, yet used no net nor hook; 240
Of sea-fowl swimming by no heed he took,
But on the gliding waves still fix'd his lazy look;
At certain stations he would view the stream,
As if he stood bewilder'd in a dream,
Or that some power had chain'd him for a time,
To feel a curse or meditate on crime.
 This known, some curious, some in pity went,
And others question'd—'Wretch, dost thou re-
    pent?'
He heard, he trembled, and in fear resign'd
His boat; new terror fill'd his restless mind; 250
Furious he grew, and up the country ran,
And there they seized him—a distemper'd
    man.—
Him we received; and to a parish-bed,
Follow'd and cursed, the groaning man was led.
 Here when they saw him, whom they used to
    shun,
A lost, lone man, so harass'd and undone,
Our gentle females, ever prompt to feel,
Perceived compassion on their anger steal;
His crimes they could not from their memories
    blot;
But they were grieved, and trembled at his
    lot.   260
 A priest too came, to whom his words are told;
And all the signs they shudder'd to behold.
 'Look! look!' they cried; 'his limbs with hor-
    ror shake,
And as he grinds his teeth, what noise they make!
How glare his angry eyes, and yet he's not awake.
See! what cold drops upon his forehead stand,
And how he clenches that broad bony hand.'
 The priest, attending, found he spoke at times
As one alluding to his fears and crimes:
'It was the fall,' he mutter'd, 'I can show 270
The manner how—I never struck a blow';—
And then aloud—'Unhand me, free my chain;
On oath, he fell—it struck him to the brain;—
Why ask my father?—that old man will swear
Against my life; besides, he wasn't there;—
What, all agreed?—Am I to die to-day?—
My Lord, in mercy, give me time to pray.'
 Then, as they watch'd him, calmer he became,
And grew so weak he couldn't move his frame,
But murmuring spake—while they could see and
    hear   280
The start of terror and the groan of fear;

See the large dew-beads on his forehead rise,
And the cold death-drop glaze his sunken eyes;
Nor yet he died, but with unwonted force
Seem'd with some fancied being to discourse.
He knew not us, or with accustom'd art
He hid the knowledge, yet exposed his heart;
'Twas part confession and the rest defence,
A madman's tale, with gleams of waking sense.
 'I'll tell you all,' he said; 'the very day 290
When the old man first placed them in my way:
My father's spirit—he who always tried
To give me trouble, when he lived and died—
When he was gone, he could not be content
To see my days in painful labour spent,
But would appoint his meetings, and he made
Me watch at these, and so neglect my trade.
 ' 'Twas one hot noon, all silent, still, serene;
No living being had I lately seen;
I paddled up and down and dipp'd my net, 300
But (such his pleasure) I could nothing get—
A father's pleasure, when his toil was done,
To plague and torture thus an only son!
And so I sat and look'd upon the stream,
How it ran on, and felt as in a dream—
But dream it was not; no!—I fix'd my eyes
On the mid stream and saw the spirits rise;
I saw my father on the water stand,
And hold a thin pale boy in either hand;
And there they glided ghastly on the top 310
Of the salt flood, and never touch'd a drop.
I would have struck them, but they knew th'
    intent,
And smiled upon the oar, and down they went.
 'Now, from that day, whenever I began
To dip my net, there stood the hard old man—
He and those boys; I humbled me and pray'd
They would be gone;—they heeded not, but
    stay'd.
Nor could I turn, nor would the boat go by,
But gazing on the spirits, there was I;
They bade me leap to death, but I was loth to
    die.   320
And every day, as sure as day arose,
Would these three spirits meet me ere the
    close:
To hear and mark them daily was my doom,
And "Come," they said, with weak, sad voices,
    "come."
To row away with all my strength I try'd;
But there were they, hard by me in the tide,
The three unbodied forms—and "Come," still
    "come," they cried.
 'Fathers should pity—but this old man shook
His hoary locks, and froze me by a look.

Thrice, when I struck them, through the water
    came   330
A hollow groan that weaken'd all my frame;
"Father!" said I, "have mercy!"—He replied,
I know not what—the angry spirit lied,—
"Didst thou not draw thy knife?" said he;—
    'Twas true,
But I had pity and my arm withdrew;
He cried for mercy which I kindly gave,
But he has no compassion in his grave.
   'There were three places, where they ever
    rose;—
The whole long river has not such as those—
Places accursed, where, if a man remain,   340
He'll see the things which strike him to the brain;
And there they made me on my paddle lean,
And look at them for hours—accursed scene!
When they would glide to that smooth eddy-
    space,
Then bid me leap and join them in the place;
And at my groans each little villain sprite
Enjoy'd my pains and vanish'd in delight.
   'In one fierce summer-day, when my poor
    brain
Was burning hot and cruel was my pain,
Then came this father-foe; and there he
    stood   350
With his two boys again upon the flood;
There was more mischief in their eyes, more glee

In their pale faces when they glared at me.
Still did they force me on the oar to rest,
And when they saw me fainting and oppress'd,
He, with his hand, the old man, scoop'd the flood,
And there came flame about him, mix'd with
    blood;
He bade me stoop and look upon the place,
Then flung the hot-red liquor in my face;
Burning it blazed, and then I roar'd for pain, 360
I thought the demons would have turn'd my
    brain.
   'Still there they stood, and forced me to behold
A place of horrors—they cannot be told—
Where the flood open'd, there I heard the shriek
Of tortured guilt no earthly tongue can speak:
"All days alike! for ever!" did they say,
"And unremitted torments every day!"—
Yes, so they said;'—but here he ceased and
    gazed
On all around, affrighten'd and amazed;
And still he tried to speak, and look'd in
    dread   370
Of frighten'd females gathering round his bed;
Then dropp'd exhausted and appear'd at rest,
Till the strong foe the vital powers possess'd;
Then with an inward, broken voice he cried,
'Again they come,' and mutter'd as he died.

                                  1810

1771 · SIR WALTER SCOTT · 1832

1771 Born 15 August in Edinburgh, of Scottish parents of middle class society—his father, a lawyer; his mother, the daughter of a medical professor in the University. His line of ancestry, in which he prided himself, reached back to Scott of Harden, a famous hero in Border warfare.

1773 Suffered an attack of infantile paralysis which left him sickly as a child and permanently lame. His boyhood spent at his grandfather's farm at Sandyknowe in the famous border region, where he drank in the romantic songs and tales of his clan with which his grandmother and aunt beguiled the winter evenings.

1778–91 His early education irregular; but, possessing extraordinary assimilative powers, by the time he was strong enough to attend high school he had acquired an unusual store of miscellaneous knowledge. Was a favorite because of his gift for storytelling. After high school, attended Edinburgh University, and was apprenticed to his father in his law office.

1792–9 Admitted to the bar; was active in debating societies and in the Edinburgh volunteer cavalry. Spent his holidays scouring the country in search of ballads and other relics of antiquity; found also and treasured against future use many traits of living manners and many a lively sketch and story. Began his literary career with the anonymous publication of *The Chase* and *William and Helen* (1796), translated from the German. Fell in love with Williamina Stuart and proposed marriage, but she refused him. On Christmas Eve, 1797, married Charlotte Carpenter, daughter of a French royalist refugee, and took up his residence at Lasswade, about six miles from Edinburgh. Was appointed Sheriff of Selkirkshire.

1801 Contributed *Glenfinlas* and *The Eve of St. John* to Lewis's *Tales of Wonder*.

1802 Published *Minstrelsy of the Scottish Border,* a collection of ballads.

1804 Moved to a rented house at Ashetiel on the upper Tweed.

1805 Published *The Lay of the Last Minstrel,* his first considerable original work, which at once set him up as the most popular poet of the day. Entered into a secret partnership in the printing business with James Ballantyne, a schoolfellow.

1806 Collected and published his *Ballads and Lyrical Pieces.* Was appointed permanent Clerk of Session at Edinburgh.

1808 Published *The Works of Dryden* and *Marmion,* which, though severely reviewed by Jeffrey, was even more popular than the Lay.

1809 Set up the publishing house of John Ballantyne and Co., to be managed by John Ballantyne, James's younger brother, with Scott as a silent partner. The publishing venture was a wild folly, leading eventually to financial ruin for all concerned. Promoted the founding of the Tory *Quarterly Review.*

1810 Published *The Lady of the Lake,* which was received with universal acclaim.

1812 Removed to a cottage at Abbotsford on the Tweed and began his schemes for building a castle and for reviving the life-ways of a feudal laird.

1813 Published *The Bridal of Triermain* and *Rokeby.* Was rescued from the threat of bankruptcy by the publisher Constable, who was eager to obtain the author's services. In the midst of financial embarrassments, chanced upon the manuscript of the opening chapter of *Waverley*, which he had written in 1805. Knowing that his meridian as a poet was passed, resolved to complete the story. Declined the offer of the laureateship and recommended Southey to the honor.

1814   Published *Waverley* anonymously and the *Works of Swift*.

1815   Published his second novel, *Guy Mannering*, and *The Lord of the Isles*, his sixth verse romance. Made a visit to London and to the battlefield at Waterloo and to other points of interest in France and the Low Countries. Dined with the Prince Regent; met the Duke of Wellington and most of the crowned heads of Europe. Became acquainted with Byron.

1816   Published *Paul's Letters to his Kinsfolk* based on his continental trip, and the novels, *The Antiquary*, *The Black Dwarf*, and *Old Mortality*. Acquired more land and further extended and furnished Abbotsford.

1817   Published *Rob Roy* and *Harold the Dauntless*, his last long poem.

1818   Published *The Heart of Midlothian*.

1819   Published *The Bride of Lammermoor*, *The Legend of Montrose*, and *Ivanhoe*. This year marked the height of his popularity as a novelist.

1820   Published *The Monastery* and *The Abbot*. Was made a baronet.

1821   Published *Kenilworth* and *The Pirate*, and

1822   *The Fortunes of Nigel*. Was master of ceremonies during a visit of George IV of England.

1823   Published *Peveril of the Peak*, *Quentin Durward*, *St. Ronan's Well*,

1824   *Redgauntlet*,

1825   *Tales of the Crusaders*, *The Betrothed*, and *The Talisman*. Began his *Journal* in the midst of financial anxieties.

1826   Published *Woodstock*. Following the great commercial crash of 1825—partly through his own improvident borrowing, partly through the mismanagement of James Ballantyne, his partner—Scott found himself and Ballantyne and Constable involved in ruin, and personally liable for some £130,000. Desiring to save Abbotsford for his family, he heroically set himself the task of clearing off this enormous debt by his pen. He succeeded, but shortened his life by his strenuous efforts. During this year his wife died and he suffered other bereavements.

1827   Published *Chronicles of the Canongate*, a series of short stories (a second series, appeared the following year), and *The Life of Napoleon Buonaparte*. Avowed his authorship of the novels.

1828   Published *The Fair Maid of Perth* and *Tales of a Grandfather*, a history of Scotland begun for the amusement of his small grandson, Hugh Lockhart.

1829   Published *Anne of Geierstein*.

1830   As a result of overtaxing his strength, suffered a stroke of apoplexy; but persuasions of friends and physicians could not induce him to take a rest.

1831   In failing health, cruised about the Mediterranean in a government vessel put at his disposal, visiting places of interest for about a year. *Count Robert of Paris* and *Castle Dangerous* were published.

1832   Died 21 September at Abbotsford, and lies buried at Dryburgh Abbey.

S COTT was called by Carlyle 'as fine a piece of sterling and healthy manhood as had ever been put together in Scotland.' This esteem of the author of *Waverley* by his fellow-countryman was universally shared both north and south of the Tweed and abroad wherever Scott's works were read and their author was known. For Sir Walter won a firm hold upon the affections of men not only by the wide pleasure his writings gave but perhaps equally by the strength and range of his sympathies and by his generosity and simple ways. Scott had no self-deception about the transcendent value of literature. Amazing success did not spoil him and financial disaster when it came did not subdue his fine courage. The weak spot in his character was the desire for splendor and power. His aim was to amass a fortune by which he might lay the foundation for a family of Abbotsford Scotts. Translating into fact this romantic and feudal dream was the dominating principle of his life and in the end proved to be his ruin. Scott idealized the old order; along with Burke he resisted the destructive side of the Revolution. Toryism was an important bias of his mind and colored his whole view of life, but his massive common sense kept him from being a mere exponent of narrow nationalism. By temperament he was not romantic, resembling more the literary men of the eighteenth century than Coleridge, Byron, and Shelley. But of certain romantic elements he was master. He loved Scotland, her scenes and her people, and he raised his imagination in an ever-widening horizon towards her past.

Scott's first stimulus to write came from the translation and imitation of German romances. But he soon turned to native tradition and found himself as a poet in the process of preparing an edition of Border ballads, which he published under the title *Minstrelsy of the Scottish Border.* In this work Scott began by combining, correcting, and improving old ballads and ended by writing a dozen or so stirring, though imperfect, imitations of the originals. Having reached full stride as an editor and poet with this collection, Scott came forth as an original writer in *The Lay of the Last Minstrel,* an expanded ballad of Border enchantment and warfare. For this and other poetical lays or tales, of which he wrote seven in all, Scott went to the metrical romances of the middle ages. To make a poem he took a Border raid, a Highland foray, a Flodden Field or Bannockburn, laid the action amid scenes that he knew and loved—the Border, the Trossachs, the country around Tantallon Castle—made ready his characters in appropriate costume dress, then 'launched his story in swinging tetrameter verse.' For the free meter of *The Lay of the Last Minstrel,* Scott was indebted to Coleridge's *Christabel,* which he had heard recited; unfortunately, as he went on, he fell back on the easy facility of the regular tetrameter couplet. Nevertheless, the *Lay* was an original, fresh, and spontaneous poem which established Scott as the most popular storyteller in verse of his day. *Marmion,* the story of the overthrow of Scottish knighthood at Flodden, followed soon after and was even more successful. Of all the romances this is the most grimly romantic. The Gothic trappings of disguise and horrid death, and the dark passions and cynical egoism of Marmion 'echo Mrs. Radcliffe and foretell Byron.' In *The Lady of the Lake,* which came next, the theatrical quality is not diminished but the tone is completely altered. The new poem is sunnily romantic, an 'idyllic thing drawn straight out of tradition,' and 'a fountain spring of original, creative poetry.' In it Scott gave a picturesque transcription of Highland manners and customs against the scenic background of the lakes and mountains and projected the chivalric story of a monarch in disguise among his foes. It is the most perfectly executed of the lays and contains some of Scott's finest descriptions and lyrics. After 1812, at which time Byron began to feed the public taste for adventure on 'a more piquant diet than Scott could provide,' Scott's popularity as a poet declined. He made several trials to recapture the magic of his early successes, but with the exception of some fine lyrics in *Rokeby* and the novels and a fitful splendor in *The Lord of the Isles,* Scott's best work in verse was done. By 1814 Scott discovered 'the better way for him' of romance in prose.

Scott's romantic lays upon which he established his extraordinary fame as a poet have faults that are perhaps more obvious to us than they were to his contemporary audience. His stories now seem commonplace, the love interest wearisome, the drama not seldom melodrama, the splendor of his descriptions often surface glitter, and the characters pasteboard figures. The plots are more often than not faulty in execution; only *The Lady of the Lake* and *Lord of the Isles* hold up under analysis. Blemishes in language and phrasing are common and redundancies frequent, resulting in part from Scott's over-facile and sometimes hurried composition. Finally, there is 'an astonishingly light weight of thought' in the metrical histories. Yet it would be a mistake to pass Scott off merely as a clever and spirited improvisator. He had essentially the balladist's mind, and knew how with bold and free strokes to tell a tale. Moreover, he made picturesque the natural scenery of his country and dramatized her history. He was at his best in describing rapid movement, especially that of large groups of men and horse, as in the superb battle-piece in *Marmion* or in the stirring chase in *The Lady of the Lake.* Airy romance, chivalric sentiment and melancholy, the minstrel's haunting sense of a romantic past that has vanished—these are in the lays if we wish to seek them out. The verse romances should be read primarily by young people, 'uncritically and for what they are, stories in verse.'

If Scott's long narrative poems have fallen in critical esteem, the ballads and songs have risen. Many fine short pieces are scattered in the lays and the novels. These poems, like the songs in Shakespeare's plays, are inserted for a particular dramatic situation; still they stand and survive by themselves as expressions of objective and universal experience. Sir Herbert Grierson thinks that, of all his poetry, Scott reached the highest expression of his genius in the songs. One large group is joyous and cordial, either with the chivalric gaiety of *Waken, Lords and Ladies Gay,* or with the dashing, galloping anapests of *Lochinvar,* or the ringing military rhythm of *Bonny Dundee.* In songs such as these Scott shows his power 'to externalize the true passion of the hunt, combat, sport, or adventure.' In another group, more perfect in workmanship or in the power to move, he deals with 'the mysteries of life, not its gallant bustle, and the supreme mystery of death' (Grierson). Of such is the plaintive song, *Where Shall the Lover Rest?,* or the sorrow of the clan laid bare in public lamentation in the *Coronach;* such is *Proud Maisie,* which 'gives the essence in sixteen lines of all that needs to be said about the dying of a young girl' (Grierson).

As a poet, Scott's genius did not incline him to the expression of deep meditation or intense passion; moreover, he lacked certain of the rarer qualities demanded in the poet's art. Measured by the lyrical magic of Shelley or Keats, his poetry is likely to seem conventional and commonplace. Indeed, his poetry never has attracted much attention from the greater poets. But from the days of its creation it has given immeasurable pleasure to hosts of unsophisticated and, particularly, young readers. For Scott himself the poetry served as a 'superb training ground to exercise and define his imagination' in preparation for writing the novels.

When Scott gave up verse for prose and sat down to finish *Waverley* in 1814, he had already proved himself master of dramatic narrative, scenic painting, and the delineation of a wide variety of characters and situations. Hence his powers as romancer in prose were displayed full-blown in this first novel, and *Waverley,* compounded of stirring Jacobite intrigue laid amid the picturesque setting of the Highlands, achieved an immediate and universal success. Gratified with the reception of *Waverley* and encouraged by the public's demand for more, Scott busied himself for the next fifteen years in writing similar romances, twenty-seven in all, as well as two series of short stories. Mystery was added to excitement as each new novel made its appearance, for to his public the author of *Waverley* was 'the Great Unknown' until in 1827 Scott finally avowed his authorship. None of the novels dealt with manners strictly contemporaneous with publication. All dipped into the past and some into the remote past. Those most recent in time are *St. Ronan's Well* and *The Antiquary,* which portray English and Scottish society around 1800. From that date, with some breaks, Scott traversed English and Scottish history back to the crusades. The largest number, eleven in all, deal with Scottish life during the eighteenth century; six with Scottish life during an earlier epoch; seven with English history before the eighteenth century; and three with countries beyond England and Scotland. The most distinctly historical deal with the reigns of Elizabeth and James I of England, and with the protectorate of Cromwell. Scott has been called the apologist and glorifier of medievalism. This obviously is an exaggeration. Only half a dozen of the novels are strictly concerned with that period and only three of these are successful. His favorite period and the one in which he achieved the greatest success is the eighteenth century. Taken together the *Waverley* novels offer 'the most splendid series of historical scenes fiction has yet produced' (Buchan).

In Scott all the lines of romantic adventure converged: the sentimental-romantic from Mackenzie's *Man of Feeling,* the grimly Gothic from the romances of Mrs. Radcliffe and 'Monk' Lewis, the heroic from the mass of border literature that had been collecting for half a century. Quickly and easily Scott assimilated all these floating impulses of the romantic tradition; moreover, he was proud of his Border ancestors, and the lure of adventure stirred in his blood. Consequently, when he worked with chronicle or history, fact was likely to be transformed to high romance. He shrank, for example, from exposing his characters to the full storm of life and showed a marked preference for a happy ending. The wicked often disappear or perish, but 'the light is not turned full on them.' Exceptions to the pattern occur in *The Bride of Lammermoor, St. Ronan's Well,* and *Kenilworth.* But for the most part innocence is protected and goodness rewarded. Historical events are compressed and their order changed, and events are introduced which never occurred at all and for which there was no authority in his chronicle. *Ivanhoe,* which may be censured on the score of historic truth, is 'a glowingly romantic affair,' a triumph as sheer romance and one of the most popular of his novels. Scott genuinely admired the antiquities of history, even though he did not always reverence literal fact, but as a creative artist his sympathies were on the side of romance. Yet more and more it is coming to be recognized that the most valuable element in Scott's work is the realism with which he portrayed Scotland from his own intimate knowledge and sympathy. Ostensibly going to the past, and to some extent borrowing its circumstances, he had in reality gone 'straight to men and women of the world, of life, of time in general.' Beneath the borrowed garments and trappings of other times and climes, his characters are true flesh and blood. Scott in fact created a new synthesis in fiction. He gathered up the threads of romance, combined them with Fielding's realism, and delighted his readers by giving them the same sense of real life as found in the eighteenth-century novelists but with a romantic setting of place and time, and with more varied and exciting characters. Thackeray, Mark Twain, and others rebelled against what they called Scott's romantic nonsense. But these critics have failed to grasp the substantial reality of the novels. Beneath a casing of romance there is a core of realism.

The true power of Scott's novels, then, and that which keeps them of perennial interest, derives ultimately not from their romance, or their historical background, or their picturesqueness, but from their rich and full humanity. His pages swarm with a vast crowd of Scots peasants, farmers, shepherds, freebooters, gypsies, Highlanders, Edinburgh lawyers, soldiers, and lairds—a representation of humankind more numerous and varied, and whose voices ring truer, than those of any novelist but Balzac. All ranks and conditions of men from the lowest to the highest move through his stories 'in all the associated web of legend, chronicle, superstition, custom, law, and dialect.' At the upper level of society there is a great succession of portraits of nobles and statesmen, soldiers and kings, paralleling in a degree the *dramatis personae* of Shakespeare's famous histories. The most impressive of this class are the regal portraits appearing in *The Abbot, Kenilworth, The Fortunes of Nigel,* and *Quentin Durward* of Mary Queen of Scots, Elizabeth of England, James I, and a masterly drawing of Louis XI of France. From middle-class society, Scott excels in his drawing of theologians and lairds, and of the advocates and judges whose living tones and faces he faithfully reported from lifelong association and observation in the courts of law. Scott's greatest success, however, comes in his portraiture of the humble ranks of society, of those gypsies, ruffians, bandits, outcasts, mendicants, freebooters, and the like, who, the author confessed, won his heart in spite of himself. These lowly men and women Scott draws with realism, often with humorous exaggeration, but he never distorts their lives merely for the sake of laughing at them. Nor does he label his characters as did Dickens 'by gesture and phrase repeated *ad nauseum.*' He displays perhaps his greatest skill in portraying the superstitious, the fanatical, and the insane. He has drawn, for example, a powerful picture of malignant hatred and religious fanaticism in Habbakkuk Mucklewrath in *Old Mortality.* And he has epitomized the wildest superstitions of the North in Madge Wildfire and Norma of the Fitful Head, at the same time rendering their insanity with remarkable fidelity and true pathos.

Most of Scott's heroes and heroines, it has long been recognized, are somewhat colorless and conventional. Scott realized himself that he was a 'bad hand at depicting a hero.' But this shortcoming is not universal. For example, *Ivanhoe* is mainly an exciting adventure story, but the greater success of the novel is the Jewess Rebecca, one of Scott's finest creations of a woman. And there are other notable exceptions: the tragic heroine, Lucy Ashton, Bride of Lammermoor, for example, and Jeanie Deans, the peasant lass of St. Leonard's Crags. The finest shades and subtler phases of character escape Scott. 'His young men are inferior to his old, his gentles to his professionals, his heroes and heroines to his rogues' (Elton). He had hardly any sense for character development. His characters have a brilliant fixity with simple strongly marked traits and humors. He does not go deeply into the motives or the reactions of his characters. The world of humanity existed for him as a wonderful play and what he saw he reproduced as it appeared to exist in and for itself. Hasty critics have detected a shallowness in his rendering. But if he drew the surface of life, he did not draw it superficially. Nothing is more difficult, Grierson reminds us, than to draw the surface in this way except to go deeper still in Shakespeare's way. The clatter of the market place, the buzz of the law courts, the unceasing stir of the open country live in the *Waverley* novels as they do in reality. 'Scott is nature's secretary,' wrote Hazlitt, 'he neither adds to nor takes away from her book and that makes him what he is, the most popular writer living.' It is by the mass and excellence of his reporting from Nature's book that Scott even today maintains his supremacy among fiction writers.

Scott by general admission ranks with the great storytellers of the world, yet he was hardly a master at plot. He confessed that he could never keep to a plot; indeed, he seems hardly to have tried. He worked instinctively, his stories unfolding as he progressed. When he really felt his story his workmanship within the episode transcended his management of the whole. The end result was more often than not an episodic rather than an organic pattern, though as a rule the novels do achieve something like an artistic unity.

Scott's style is often commonplace, charmless, pedestrian, sometimes stilted. It is rarely surprising or felicitous, 'never precious or an end in itself.' Scott was not given to revising or filing, and was seemingly constitutionally incapable of giving minute attention to the details of composition. Yet the staple of his style is workmanlike, and improves as the story quickens. At its best 'it is simple, direct, vigorous, at times rising to eloquence' (Elton). There is a complete rightness in the dialogue of his Scots characters. Whatever their occupation or rank, their speech is always natural and in perfect dramatic keeping. Except for his high-born lovers, who talk 'a genteel rhetoric,' his characters speak the language of the heart and their words carry the accents of living speech.

Carlyle complained of the absence of high moral purpose or mission in the *Waverley* novels. But the complaint is hardly justified. Scott, like Shakespeare, keeps to the 'high-road of life.' He affirms the dignity of household virtues and the enduring wisdom of 'goodness.' And if he is not chiefly concerned with the highest raptures of love or devotion, he has given in Jeanie Deans and Rebecca two examples of characters exalted by moral fervor and self-sacrifice.

Scott was the first writer to unite the great events of history with the dim unchronicled lives of ordinary mortals. He had the power of giving life to historical movements and of broadly delineating large chapters of history. He was not always historically accurate. He made his most conspicuous historical mistakes in those novels that take the reader off Scottish soil—*The Talisman, Ivanhoe, Quentin Durward, Kenilworth*. In these novels the interest focuses upon the story and the characters; the period background and history are secondary. Scott found no difficulty in reproducing the language and habits of his own people in the eighteenth century, which still had thirty years to run when he was born. Scott declared that his aim was to throw the force of his narrative 'upon the characters and passions of the actors—those passions common to men in all stages of society, and which alike have agitated the human heart, whether it throbbed under the steel corslet of the fifteenth century or any later costume.' He reviewed the picture of life in different ages by giving a certain coloring, but not too much, to the descriptive setting, the costume, the manners, and the language of the time. Some later writers have excelled Scott in the accuracy of their historical detail but few have matched him in his power of communicating life to persons, story, and dialogue or in his spontaneity and abundance of invention.

　　Scott is the most potent creative force that has yet appeared in English fiction. Through one great fertile idea he tremendously enlarged the boundaries of the novel and caused his influence to be felt throughout the entire Western literary world. His vogue was enormous. In England nearly every major fiction writer of the nineteenth century—including Bulwer-Lytton, Dickens, Thackeray, Kinsley, Reade, and George Eliot—aspired to write at least one masterpiece in historical form. On the Continent, Balzac, the elder Dumas, Hugo, de Vigny, Freytag, Manzoni, and many others, and in the United States, Cooper, Hawthorne and Melville fell under the fascination of Scott's magical formula. Even the twentieth century has felt the influence of his historical method. Many a current best seller and not seldom, more noteworthy novel owe allegiance to the 'wizard of Abbotsford.'

WILLIAM AND HELEN

IMITATED FROM THE *Lenore* OF BÜRGER

FROM heavy dreams fair Helen rose,
　　And eyed the dawning red:
'Alas, my love, thou tarriest long!
　　O art thou false or dead?'

With gallant Fred'rick's[1] princely power
　　He sought the bold Crusade;
But not a word from Judah's wars
　　Told Helen how he sped.

With Paynim and with Saracen
　　At length a truce was made,　　　　　　10
And every knight return'd to dry
　　The tears his love had shed.

Our gallant host was homeward bound
　　With many a song of joy;
Green waved the laurel in each plume,
　　The badge of victory.

And old and young, and sire and son,
　　To meet them crowd the way,
With shouts, and mirth, and melody,
　　The debt of love to pay.　　　　　　　20

Full many a maid her true-love met,
　　And sobb'd in his embrace,
And flutt'ring joy in tears and smiles
　　Array'd full many a face.

Nor joy nor smile for Helen sad;
　　She sought the host in vain;

For none could tell her William's fate,
　　If faithless, or if slain.

The martial band is past and gone;
　　She rends her raven hair,　　　　　　30
And in distraction's bitter mood
　　She weeps with wild despair.

'O rise, my child,' her mother said,
　　'Nor sorrow thus in vain;
A perjured lover's fleeting heart
　　No tears recall again.'

'O mother, what is gone, is gone,
　　What's lost for ever lorn:
Death, death alone can comfort me;
　　O had I ne'er been born!　　　　　　40

'O break, my heart—O break at once!
　　Drink my life-blood, Despair!
No joy remains on earth for me,
　　For me in heaven no share.'

'O enter not in judgment, Lord!'
　　The pious mother prays;
'Impute not guilt to thy frail child!
　　She knows not what she says.

'O say thy pater noster, child!
　　O turn to God and grace!　　　　　　50
His will, that turn'd thy bliss to bale,
　　Can change thy bale to bliss.'

'O mother, mother, what is bliss?
　　O mother, what is bale?
My William's love was heaven on earth,
　　Without it earth is hell.

---

1 Frederick Barbarossa, noted Emperor of the Holy Roman Empire and King of Germany, who joined the Third Crusade in 1189.

'Why should I pray to ruthless Heaven,
　Since my loved William's slain?
I only pray'd for William's sake,
　And all my prayers were vain.'   60

'O take the sacrament, my child,
　And check these tears that flow;
By resignation's humble prayer,
　O hallow'd be thy woe!'

'No sacrament can quench this fire,
　Or slake this scorching pain;
No sacrament can bid the dead
　Arise and live again.

'O break, my heart—O break at once!
　Be thou my god, Despair!   70
Heaven's heaviest blow has fallen on me,
　And vain each fruitless prayer.'

'O enter not in judgment, Lord,
　With thy frail child of clay!
She knows not what her tongue has spoke;
　Impute it not, I pray!

'Forbear, my child, this desperate woe,
　And turn to God and grace;
Well can devotion's heavenly glow
　Convert thy bale to bliss.'   80

'O mother, mother, what is bliss?
　O mother, what is bale?
Without my William what were heaven,
　Or with him what were hell?'

Wild she arraigns the eternal doom,
　Upbraids each sacred power,
Till, spent, she sought her silent room,
　All in the lonely tower.

She beat her breast, she wrung her hands,
　Till sun and day were o'er,   90
And through the glimmering lattice shone
　The twinkling of the star.

Then, crash! the heavy drawbridge fell
　That o'er the moat was hung;
And, clatter! clatter! on its boards
　The hoof of courser rung.

The clank of echoing steel was heard
　As off the rider bounded;
And slowly on the winding stair
　A heavy footstep sounded.   100

And hark! and hark! a knock—tap! tap!
　A rustling stifled noise;
Door-latch and tinkling staples ring;
　At length a whispering voice:

'Awake, awake, arise, my love!
　How, Helen, dost thou fare?
Wak'st thou, or sleep'st? laugh'st thou, or
　　weep'st?
　Hast thought on me, my fair?'

'My love! my love!—so late by night!
　I waked, I wept for thee: 110
Much have I borne since dawn of morn;
　Where, William, couldst thou be?'

'We saddle late—from Hungary
　I rode since darkness fell;
And to its bourne we both return
　Before the matin-bell.'

'O rest this night within my arms,
　And warm thee in their fold!
Chill howls through hawthorn bush the wind:
　My love is deadly cold.'   120

'Let the wind howl through hawthorn bush!
　This night we must away;
The steed is wight,[2] the spur is bright;
　I cannot stay till day.

'Busk, busk, and boune![3] thou mount'st be-
　　hind
　Upon my black barb[4] steed:
O'er stock and stile, a hundred miles,
　We haste to bridal bed.'

'To-night—to-night a hundred miles?
　O dearest William, stay!   130
The bell strikes twelve—dark, dismal hour!
　O wait, my love, till day!'

'Look here, look here—the moon shines clear—
　Full fast I ween we ride;
Mount and away! for ere the day
　We reach our bridal bed.

'The black barb snorts, the bridle rings;
　Haste, busk, and boune, and seat thee!
The feast is made, the chamber spread,
　The bridal guests await thee.'   140

---

2 strong; powerful.
3 dress and make ready for the journey.
4 Barbary.

Strong love prevail'd. She busks, she bounes,
　　She mounts the barb behind,
And round her darling William's waist
　　Her lily arms she twined.

And, hurry! hurry! off they rode,
　　As fast as fast might be;
Spurn'd from the courser's thundering heels
　　The flashing pebbles flee.

And on the right, and on the left,
　　Ere they could snatch a view,　　　150
Fast, fast each mountain, mead, and plain,
　　And cot, and castle flew.

'Sit fast—dost fear? The moon shines clear;
　　Fleet goes my barb—keep hold!
Fear'st thou?' 'O no!' she faintly said;
　　'But why so stern and cold?

'What yonder rings? what yonder sings?
　　Why shrieks the owlet grey?'
' 'Tis death-bells' clang, 'tis funeral song,
　　The body to the clay.　　　160

'With song and clang, at morrow's dawn,
　　Ye may inter the dead:
To-night I ride, with my young bride,
　　To deck our bridal bed.

'Come with thy choir, thou coffin'd guest,
　　To swell our nuptial song!
Come, priest, to bless our marriage feast!
　　Come all, come all along!'

Ceased clang and song; down sunk the bier;
　　The shrouded corpse arose:　　　170
And, hurry! hurry! all the train
　　The thundering steed pursues.

And, forward! forward! on they go;
　　High snorts the straining steed;
Thick pants the rider's labouring breath,
　　As headlong on they speed.

'O William, why this savage haste?
　　And where thy bridal bed?'
' 'Tis distant far, low, damp, and chill,
　　And narrow, trustless maid.'　　　180

'No room for me?' 'Enough for both;
　　Speed, speed, my barb, thy course!'
O'er thundering bridge, through boiling surge
　　He drove the furious horse.

Tramp! tramp! along the land they rode,
　　Splash! splash! along the sea;
The scourge is wight, the spur is bright,
　　The flashing pebbles flee.

Fled past on right and left how fast
　　Each forest, grove, and bower!　　　190
On right and left fled past how fast
　　Each city, town, and tower!

'Dost fear? dost fear? The moon shines clear,
　　Dost fear to ride with me?
Hurrah! hurrah! the dead can ride!'
　　'O William, let them be!'

'See there, see there! What yonder swings,
　　And creaks 'mid whistling rain?'
'Gibbet and steel, th' accursed wheel;
　　A murderer in his chain.　　　200

'Hollo! thou felon, follow here:
　　To bridal bed we ride;
And thou shalt prance a fetter dance
　　Before me and my bride.'

And, hurry! hurry! clash! clash! clash!
　　The wasted form descends;
And fleet as wind through hazel bush
　　The wild career attends.

Tramp! tramp! along the land they rode,
　　Splash! splash! along the sea;　　　210
The scourge is red, the spur drops blood,
　　The flashing pebbles flee.

How fled what moonshine faintly show'd!
　　How fled what darkness hid!
How fled the earth beneath their feet,
　　The heaven above their head!

'Dost fear? dost fear? The moon shines clear,
　　And well the dead can ride;
Does faithful Helen fear for them?'
　　'O leave in peace the dead!'　　　220

'Barb! barb! methinks I hear the cock;
　　The sand will soon be run:
Barb! barb! I smell the morning air;
　　The race is wellnigh done.'

Tramp! tramp! along the land they rode,
　　Splash! splash! along the sea;
The scourge is red, the spur drops blood,
　　The flashing pebbles flee.

'Hurrah! hurrah! well ride the dead;
  The bride, the bride is come;   230
And soon we reach the bridal bed,
  For, Helen, here's my home.'

Reluctant on its rusty hinge
  Revolved an iron door,
And by the pale moon's setting beam
  Were seen a church and tower.

With many a shriek and cry, whiz round
  The birds of midnight, scared;
And rustling like autumnal leaves
  Unhallow'd ghosts were heard.   240

O'er many a tomb and tombstone pale
  He spurr'd the fiery horse,
Till sudden at an open grave
  He check'd the wondrous course.

The falling gauntlet quits the rein,
  Down drops the casque of steel,
The cuirass leaves his shrinking side,
  The spur his gory heel.

The eyes desert the naked skull,
  The mould'ring flesh the bone,   250
Till Helen's lily arms entwine
  A ghastly skeleton.

The furious barb snorts fire and foam,
  And, with a fearful bound,
Dissolves at once in empty air,
  And leaves her on the ground.

Half seen by fits, by fits half heard,
  Pale spectres flit along,
Wheel round the maid in dismal dance,
  And howl the funeral song;   260

'E'en when the heart's with anguish cleft,
  Revere the doom of Heaven!
Her soul is from her body reft;
  Her spirit be forgiven!'

1795   1796

THE VIOLET

[This poem refers to Scott's ill-starred romance with
Williamina Stuart, whose fickleness in throwing him over
for his rival resulted momentarily in bitter disappointment for the young poet.]

THE violet in her greenwood bower,
  Where birchen boughs with hazels mingle,
May boast itself the fairest flower
  In glen, or copse, or forest dingle.

Though fair her gems of azure hue,
  Beneath the dewdrop's weight reclining;
I've seen an eye of lovelier blue,
  More sweet through wat'ry lustre shining.

The summer sun that dew shall dry,
  Ere yet the day be past its morrow;   10
Nor longer in my false love's eye
  Remain'd the tear of parting sorrow.

1796   1810

THE EVE OF SAINT JOHN

... *The Eve of St. John,* in which Scott repeoples the
tower of Smailholm, the awe-inspiring haunt of his infancy; and here he touches, for the first time, the one
superstition which can still be appealed to with full and
perfect effect; the only one which lingers in minds long
since weaned from all sympathy with the machinery of
witches and goblins. And surely this mystery was never
touched with more thrilling skill than in that noble ballad. It is the first of his original pieces, too, in which he
uses the measure of his own favourite Minstrels; a measure which the monotony of mediocrity had long and successfully been labouring to degrade, but in itself adequate to the expression of the highest thoughts, as well
as the gentlest emotions; and capable, in fit hands, of as
rich a variety of music as any other of modern times.
This was written at Mertoun-house in the autumn of
1799.—(Lockhart.)

THE Baron of Smaylho'me rose with day,
  He spurr'd his courser on,
Without stop or stay, down the rocky way,
  That leads to Brotherstone.

He went not with the bold Buccleuch,
  His banner broad to rear;
He went not 'gainst the English yew
  To lift Scottish spear.

Yet his plate-jack[1] was braced, and his helmet
    was laced,
  And his vaunt-brace[2] of proof he wore;   10
At his saddle-gerthe was a good steel sperthe,[3]
  Full ten pound weight and more.

The Baron return'd in three days' space,
  And his looks were sad and sour;
And weary was his courser's pace,
  As he reach'd his rocky tower.

---

1 coat armor.
2 armor for the forearm.
3 battle-ax.

He came not from where Ancram Moor[4]
   Ran red with English blood;
Where the Douglas true and the bold Buccleuch
   'Gainst keen Lord Evers stood.   20

Yet was his helmet hack'd and hew'd,
   His acton[5] pierced and tore,
His axe and his dagger with blood imbrued,—
   But it was not English gore.

He lighted at the Chapellage,
   He held him close and still;
And he whistled thrice for his little foot-page,
   His name was English Will.

'Come thou hither, my little foot-page,
   Come hither to my knee;   30
Though thou art young, and tender of age,
   I think thou art true to me.

'Come, tell me all that thou hast seen,
   And look thou tell me true!
Since I from Smaylho'me tower have been,
   What did thy lady do?'

'My lady each night sought the lonely light
   That burns on the wild Watchfold;
For, from height to height, the beacons bright
   Of the English foemen told.   40

'The bittern clamour'd from the moss,
   The wind blew loud and shrill;
Yet the craggy pathway she did cross
   To the eiry Beacon Hill.

'I watch'd her steps, and silent came
   Where she sat her on a stone;
No watchman stood by the dreary flame,
   It burnèd all alone.

'The second night I kept her in sight
   Till to the fire she came,   50
And, by Mary's might! an armed Knight
   Stood by the lonely flame.

'And many a word that warlike lord
   Did speak to my lady there;
But the rain fell fast, and loud blew the blast,
   And I heard not what they were.

'The third night there the sky was fair,
   And the mountain-blast was still,

As again I watch'd the secret pair
   On the lonesome Beacon Hill.   60

'And I heard her name the midnight hour,
   And name this holy eve,
And say "Come this night to thy lady's bower;
   Ask no bold Baron's leave.

' "He lifts his spear with the bold Buccleuch;
   His lady is all alone;
The door she'll undo to her knight so true
   On the eve of good Saint John."

' "I cannot come, I must not come,
   I dare not come to thee;   70
On the eve of Saint John I must wander alone,
   In thy bower I may not be."

' "Now out on thee, fainthearted knight!
   Thou shouldst not say me nay;
For the eve is sweet, and when lovers meet
   Is worth the whole summer's day.

' "And I'll chain the blood-hound, and the warder
     shall not sound,
   And rushes shall be strew'd on the stair;
So, by the black rood-stone,[6] and by holy Saint
     John,
   I conjure thee, my love, to be there!"   80

' "Though the blood-hound be mute, and the rush
     beneath my foot,
   And the warder his bugle should not blow,
Yet there sleepeth a priest in the chamber to the
     east,
   And my footstep he would know.

' "O fear not the priest, who sleepeth to the east,
   For to Dryburgh the way he has ta'en;
And there to say mass, till three days do pass,
   For the soul of a knight that is slayne."

'He turn'd him around, and grimly he frown'd,
   Then he laugh'd right scornfully—   90
"He who says the mass-rite for the soul of that
     knight
   May as well say mass for me.

' "At the lone midnight hour, when bad spirits
     have power,
   In thy chamber will I be."
With that he was gone, and my lady left alone,
   And no more did I see.'

---

4 near Jedburgh, Scotland, where in 1545 the Scots under Earl of
Angus and Scott of Buccleuch decisively defeated the invading
English under Lord Evers, who with his son and more than 800
others was slain.
5 jacket plated with steel.

6 The black-rood of Melrose was a crucifix of black marble, and
of superior sanctity.—(Scott.)

Then changed, I trow, was that bold Baron's
    brow,
  From the dark to the blood-red high—
'Now tell me the mien of the knight thou hast
    seen,
  For, by Mary, he shall die!'   100

'His arms shone full bright in the beacon's red
    light;
  His plume it was scarlet and blue;
On his shield was a hound in a silver leash
    bound,
  And his crest was a branch of the yew.'

'Thou liest, thou liest, thou little foot-page,
  Loud dost thou lie to me!
For that knight is cold, and low laid in the mould,
  All under the Eildon-tree.' [7]

'Yet hear but my word, my noble lord!
  For I heard her name his name;   110
And that lady bright, she called the knight
  Sir Richard of Coldinghame.'

The bold Baron's brow then changed, I trow,
  From high blood-red to pale—
'The grave is deep and dark, and the corpse is
    stiff and stark,
  So I may not trust thy tale.

'Where fair Tweed flows round holy Melrose,
  And Eildon slopes to the plain,
Full three nights ago, by some secret foe,
  That gay gallant was slain.   120

'The varying light deceived thy sight,
  And the wild winds drown'd the name;
For the Dryburgh bells ring and the white monks
    do sing
  For Sir Richard of Coldinghame!'

He pass'd the court-gate, and he oped the tower-
    grate,
  And he mounted the narrow stair
To the bartizan-seat,[8] where, with maids that on
    her wait
  He found his lady fair.

That lady sat in mournful mood,
  Look'd over hill and vale,   130

Over Tweed's fair flood and Mertoun's wood
  And all down Teviotdale.

'Now hail, now hail, thou lady bright!'
  'Now hail, thou Baron true!
What news, what news from Ancram fight?
  What news from the bold Buccleuch?'

'The Ancram Moor is red with gore,
  For many a southron fell;
And Buccleuch has charged us evermore
  To watch our beacons well.'   140

The lady blush'd red, but nothing she said;
  Nor added the Baron a word.
Then she stepp'd down the stair to her chamber
    fair,
  And so did her moody lord.

In sleep the lady mourn'd, and the Baron toss'd
    and turn'd,
  And oft to himself he said,
'The worms around him creep, and his bloody
    grave is deep—
  It cannot give up the dead!'

It was near the ringing of matin-bell,
  The night was wellnigh done,   150
When a heavy sleep on that Baron fell,
  On the eve of good Saint John.

The lady look'd through the chamber fair,
  By the light of a dying flame;
And she was aware of a knight stood there—
  Sir Richard of Coldinghame!

'Alas! away, away!' she cried,
  'For the holy Virgin's sake!'
'Lady, I know who sleeps by thy side;
  But, lady, he will not awake.   160

'By Eildon-tree, for long nights three,
  In bloody grave have I lain;
The mass and the death-prayer are said for me,
  But, lady, they are said in vain.

'By the Baron's brand, near Tweed's fair strand,
  Most foully slain I fell;
And my restless sprite on the beacon's height
  For a space is doom'd to dwell.

'At our trysting-place, for a certain space,
  I must wander to and fro;   170
But I had not had power to come to thy bower
  Had'st thou not conjured me so.'

---

7 Eildon is a high hill, terminating in three conical summits, immediately above the town of Melrose, where are the admired ruins of a magnificent monastery. Eildon-tree is said to be the spot where Thomas the Rhymer uttered his prophecies.—(Scott.)
8 seat in a small overhanging battlement above the castle gateway.

Love master'd fear; her brow she cross'd—
  'How, Richard, hast thou sped?
And art thou saved, or art thou lost?'
  The vision shook his head!

'Who spilleth life shall forfeit life;
  So bid thy lord believe:
That lawless love is guilt above,
  This awful sign receive.'   180

He laid his left palm on an oaken beam,
  His right upon her hand—
The lady shrunk, and fainting sunk,
  For it scorch'd like a fiery brand.

The sable score of fingers four
  Remains on that board impress'd;
And for evermore that lady wore
  A covering on her wrist.

There is a nun in Dryburgh bower,
  Ne'er looks upon the sun;   190
There is a monk in Melrose tower,
  He speaketh word to none;

That nun who ne'er beholds the day,
  That monk who speaks to none—
That nun was Smaylho'me's Lady gay,
  That monk the bold Baron.

    1799   1801

From THE LAY OF THE LAST MINSTREL, CANTO 6

BREATHES THERE THE MAN

BREATHES there the man, with soul so dead,
Who never to himself hath said,
  This is my own, my native land!
Whose heart hath ne'er within him burn'd,
As home his footsteps he hath turn'd,
  From wandering on a foreign strand!
If such there breathe, go, mark him well;
For him no Minstrel raptures swell;
High though his titles, proud his name,
Boundless his wealth as wish can claim;   10
Despite those titles, power, and pelf,[1]
The wretch, concentred all in self,
Living, shall forfeit fair renown,
And, doubly dying, shall go down
To the vile dust, from whence he sprung,
Unwept, unhonour'd, and unsung.

---

[1] ill-gotten wealth; plunder.

O Caledonia![2] stern and wild,
Meet nurse for a poetic child!
Land of brown heath and shaggy wood,
Land of the mountain and the flood,   20
Land of my sires! what mortal hand
Can e'er untie the filial band,
That knits me to thy rugged strand!
Still as I view each well-known scene,
Think what is now, and what hath been,
Seems as, to me, of all bereft,
Sole friends thy woods and streams were left;
And thus I love them better still,
Even in extremity of ill.
By Yarrow's stream still let me stray,   30
Though none should guide my feeble way;
Still feel the breeze down Ettrick break,
Although it chill my wither'd cheek;
Still lay my head by Teviot Stone,
Though there, forgotten and alone,
The Bard may draw his parting groan.

    1802–4   1805

SONG OF ALBERT GRÆME

IT was an English ladye bright,
  (The sun shines fair on Carlisle wall,)
And she would marry a Scottish knight,
  For Love will still be lord of all.

Blithely they saw the rising sun,
  When he shone fair on Carlisle wall;
But they were sad ere day was done,
  Though Love was still the lord of all.

Her sire gave brooch and jewel fine,
  Where the sun shines fair on Carlisle wall;   10
Her brother gave but a flask of wine,
  For ire that Love was lord of all.

For she had lands, both meadow and lea,
  Where the sun shines fair on Carlisle wall;
And he swore her death ere he would see
  A Scottish knight the lord of all!

That wine she had not tasted well,
  (The sun shines fair on Carlisle wall,)
When dead in her true love's arms she fell,
  For Love was still the lord of all!   20

He pierc'd her brother to the heart,
  Where the sun shines fair on Carlisle wall:
So perish all would true love part,
  That Love may still be lord of all!

---

[2] Scotland.

And then he took the cross divine,
  (Where the sun shines fair on Carlisle wall,)
And died for her sake in Palestine;
  So Love was still the lord of all.

Now all ye lovers that faithful prove,
  (The sun shines fair on Carlisle wall,)   30
Pray for their souls who died for love,
  For Love shall still be lord of all!

                    1805

HAROLD'S SONG: ROSABELLE

O LISTEN, listen, ladies gay!
  No haughty feat of arms I tell;
Soft is the note, and sad the lay,
  That mourns the lovely Rosabelle.[1]

—'Moor, moor the barge, ye gallant crew!
  And, gentle ladye, deign to stay!
Rest thee in Castle Ravensheuch,[2]
  Nor tempt the stormy firth to-day.

'The blackening wave is edg'd with white;
  To inch[3] and rock the sea-mews fly;   10
The fishers have heard the Water-Sprite,
  Whose screams forebode that wreck is nigh.

'Last night the gifted Seer did view
  A wet shroud swathed round ladye gay;
Then stay thee, Fair, in Ravensheuch:
  Why cross the gloomy firth to-day?'

' 'Tis not because Lord Lindesay's heir
  To-night at Roslin[4] leads the ball,
But that my ladye-mother there
  Sits lonely in her castle-hall.   20

' 'Tis not because the ring they ride,[5]
  And Lindesay at the ring rides well,
But that my sire the wine will chide,
  If 'tis not fill'd by Rosabelle.'

O'er Roslin all that dreary night
  A wondrous blaze was seen to gleam;
'Twas broader than the watch-fire's light,
  And redder than the bright moon-beam.

It glar'd on Roslin's castled rock,
  It ruddied all the copse-wood glen;   30
'Twas seen from Dryden's groves of oak,
  And seen from cavern'd Hawthorn-den.

Seem'd all on fire that chapel proud,
  Where Roslin's chiefs uncoffin'd lie,
Each Baron, for a sable shroud,
  Sheath'd in his iron panoply.

Seem'd all on fire within, around,
  Deep sacristy and altar's pale,[6]
Shone every pillar foliage-bound,
  And glimmer'd all the dead men's mail.   40

Blaz'd battlement and pinnet[7] high,
  Blaz'd every rose-carved buttress fair—
So still they blaze when fate is nigh
  The lordly line of high St. Clair.

There are twenty of Roslin's barons bold
  Lie buried within that proud chapelle;
Each one the holy vault doth hold—
  But the sea holds lovely Rosabelle!

And each St. Clair was buried there,
  With candle, with book, and with knell;   50
But the sea-caves rung, and the wild winds sung,
  The dirge of lovely Rosabelle.

                    1805

THE MAID OF NEIDPATH

  There is a tradition in Tweeddale that, when Neidpath Castle, near Peebles, was inhabited by the Earls of March, a mutual passion subsisted between a daughter of that noble family and a son of the Laird of Tushielaw, in Ettrick Forest. As the alliance was thought unsuitable by her parents, the young man went abroad. During his absence the lady fell into a consumption; and at length, as the only means of saving her life, her father consented that her lover should be recalled. On the day when he was expected to pass through Peebles, on the road to Tushielaw, the young lady, though much exhausted, caused herself to be carried to the balcony of a house in Peebles belonging to the family, that she might see him as he rode past. Her anxiety and eagerness gave such a force to her organs, that she is said to have distinguished his horse's footsteps at an incredible distance. But Tushielaw, unprepared for the change in her appearance, and not expecting to see her in that place, rode on without recognizing her, or even slackening his pace. The lady was unable to support the shock; and, after a short struggle, died in the arms of her attendants.—(Scott.)

O LOVERS' eyes are sharp to see,
  And lovers' ears in hearing;

---

1 This was a family name in the house of St. Clair. Henry St. Clair, the second of the line, married Rosabelle, fourth daughter of the Earl of Stratherne.—(Scott.)
2 a large and strong castle on the Firth of Forth, Fifeshire, Scotland, given to Sir William St. Clair by King James III of Scotland in 1471.
3 island.
4 the family seat of the St. Clairs in the county of Edinburgh, Scotland.
5 It was a favorite sport of mounted riders to gallop at full speed past a suspended ring and attempt to carry it off on the point of a lance.

---

6 enclosure.
7 pinnacle.

And love, in life's extremity,
　　Can lend an hour of cheering.
Disease had been in Mary's bower,
　　And slow decay from mourning,
Though now she sits on Neidpath's tower,
　　To watch her love's returning.

All sunk and dim her eyes so bright,
　　Her form decay'd by pining,   10
Till through her wasted hand, at night,
　　You saw the taper shining;
By fits, a sultry hectic hue
　　Across her cheek was flying;
By fits, so ashy pale she grew,
　　Her maidens thought her dying.

Yet keenest powers to see and hear
　　Seem'd in her frame residing;
Before the watch-dog prick'd his ear
　　She heard her lover's riding;   20
Ere scarce a distant form was ken'd,
　　She knew, and waved to greet him;
And o'er the battlement did bend,
　　As on the wing to meet him.

He came—he pass'd—an heedless gaze,
　　As o'er some stranger glancing;
Her welcome, spoke in faltering phrase,
　　Lost in his courser's prancing.
The castle arch, whose hollow tone
　　Returns each whisper spoken,   30
Could scarcely catch the feeble moan
　　Which told her heart was broken.

1806

HUNTING SONG

WAKEN, lords and ladies gay,
On the mountain dawns the day,
All the jolly chase is here,
With hawk, and horse, and hunting-spear!
Hounds are in their couples¹ yelling,
Hawks are whistling, horns are knelling,
Merrily, merrily, mingle they,
'Waken, lords and ladies gay.'

Waken, lords and ladies gay,
The mist has left the mountain grey,   10
Springlets in the dawn are steaming,
Diamonds on the brake are gleaming:
And foresters have busy been,
To track the buck in thicket green;
Now we come to chant our lay,
'Waken, lords and ladies gay.'

---
¹ The hounds are coupled together on leashes.

Waken, lords and ladies gay,
To the greenwood haste away;
We can show you where he lies,
Fleet of foot, and tall of size;   20
We can show the marks he made,
When 'gainst the oak his antlers fray'd;
You shall see him brought to bay,
'Waken, lords and ladies gay.'

Louder, louder chant the lay,
Waken, lords and ladies gay!
Tell them youth, and mirth, and glee,
Run a course as well as we;
Time, stern huntsman! who can baulk,
Stanch as hound, and fleet as hawk: 30
Think of this, and rise with day,
Gentle lords and ladies gay.

1808

From MARMION

CANTO 3

WHERE SHALL THE LOVER REST

WHERE shall the lover rest,
　　Whom the fates sever
From his true maiden's breast,
　　Parted for ever?
Where, through groves deep and high,
　　Sounds the far billow,
Where early violets die,
　　Under the willow.

Chorus

Eleu loro, &c. Soft shall be his pillow.

There, through the summer day,   10
　　Cool streams are laving;
There, while the tempests sway,
　　Scarce are boughs waving;
There, thy rest shalt thou take,
　　Parted for ever,
Never again to wake,
　　Never, O never!

Chorus

Eleu loro, &c. Never, O never!

Where shall the traitor rest,
　　He, the deceiver,   20
Who could win maiden's breast,
　　Ruin, and leave her?
In the lost battle,
　　Borne down by the flying,

Where mingles war's rattle
  With groans of the dying.

Chorus

Eleu loro, &c. There shall he be lying.

Her wing shall the eagle flap
  O'er the false-hearted;
His warm blood the wolf shall lap,   30
  Ere life be parted.
Shame and dishonour sit
  By his grave ever;
Blessing shall hallow it,
  Never, O never!

Chorus

Eleu loro, &c. Never, O never!

1808

Canto 5

LOCHINVAR

O, YOUNG Lochinvar is come out of the west,
Through all the wide Border his steed was the
  best;
And save his good broadsword he weapons had
  none,
He rode all unarm'd, and he rode all alone.
So faithful in love, and so dauntless in war,
There never was knight like the young Lochinvar.

He staid not for brake, and he stopp'd not for
  stone,
He swam the Eske river where ford there was
  none;
But ere he alighted at Netherby gate,
The bride had consented, the gallant came
  late: 10
For a laggard in love, and a dastard in war,
Was to wed the fair Ellen of brave Lochinvar.

So boldly he enter'd the Netherby Hall,
Among bride's-men, and kinsmen, and brothers,
  and all:
Then spoke the bride's father, his hand on his
  sword,
(For the poor craven bridegroom said never a
  word,)
'O come ye in peace here, or come ye in war,
Or to dance at our bridal, young Lord Lochin-
  var?'

'I long woo'd your daughter, my suit you denied;—

Love swells like the Solway, but ebbs like its
  tide—   20
And now am I come, with this lost-love of mine,
To lead but one measure, drink one cup of wine.
There are maidens in Scotland more lovely by
  far,
That would gladly be bride to the young Lochin-
  var.'

The bride kiss'd the goblet: the knight took it
  up,
He quaff'd off the wine, and he threw down the
  cup.
She look'd down to blush, and she look'd up to
  sigh,
With a smile on her lips, and a tear in her eye.
He took her soft hand, ere her mother could
  bar,—
'Now tread we a measure!' said young
  Lochinvar.   30

So stately his form, and so lovely her face,
That never a hall such a galliard did grace;
While her mother did fret, and her father did
  fume,
And the bridegroom stood dangling his bonnet
  and plume;
And the bride-maidens whisper'd, ''Twere bet-
  ter by far,
To have match'd our fair cousin with young
  Lochinvar.'

One touch to her hand, and one word in her
  ear,
When they reach'd the hall-door, and the charger
  stood near;
So light to the croupe the fair lady he swung,
So light to the saddle before her he sprung!   40
'She is won! we are gone, over bank, bush, and
  scaur;'[1]
They'll have fleet steeds that follow,' quoth young
  Lochinvar.

There was mounting 'mong Græmes of the Neth-
  erby clan;
Forsters, Fenwicks, and Musgraves, they rode
  and they ran:
There was racing and chasing on Cannobie Lee,
But the lost bride of Netherby ne'er did they see.
So daring in love, and so dauntless in war,
Have ye e'er heard of gallant like young Lochin-
  var?—

1808

---

1 rock.

Canto 6

THE BATTLE

Lines 380–471, 551–932, 993–1066

[The story of Marmion, a fictitious character in the service of Henry VIII, culminates in the historic Battle of Flodden Field, 9 September 1513. Here an invading Scottish army under King James IV was met and defeated by an English host led by the Earl of Surrey. An account of the battle is given in Scott's note to line 682.]

NOT far advanc'd was morning day,   380
When Marmion did his troop array
    To Surrey's camp to ride;
He had safe conduct for his band,
Beneath the royal seal and hand,
    And Douglas[1] gave a guide:
The ancient Earl, with stately grace,
Would Clara[2] on her palfrey place,
And whisper'd in an under tone,
'Let the hawk stoop, his prey is flown.'
The train from out the castle drew,   390
But Marmion stopp'd to bid adieu:—
    'Though something I might 'plain,' he said,
'Of cold respect to stranger guest,
Sent hither by your King's behest,
    While in Tantallon's towers I staid;
Part we in friendship from your land,
And, noble Earl, receive my hand.'
But Douglas round him drew his cloak,
Folded his arms, and thus he spoke:
'My manors, halls, and bowers, shall still   400
Be open, at my Sovereign's will,
To each one whom he lists, howe'er
Unmeet to be the owner's peer.
My castles are my King's alone,
From turret to foundation-stone—
The hand of Douglas is his own;
And never shall in friendly grasp
The hand of such as Marmion clasp.'

Burn'd Marmion's swarthy cheek like fire,
And shook his very frame for ire,   410
    And 'This to me!' he said;
'An 'twere not for thy hoary beard,
Such hand as Marmion's had not spar'd
    To cleave the Douglas' head!
And, first, I tell thee, haughty Peer,
He, who does England's message here,
Although the meanest in her state,
May well, proud Angus, be thy mate:
And, Douglas, more I tell thee here,
    Even in thy pitch of pride,   420

Here in thy hold, thy vassals near—
(Nay, never look upon your lord,
And lay your hands upon your sword!)
    I tell thee, thou'rt defied!
And if thou said'st I am not peer
To any lord in Scotland here,
Lowland or Highland, far or near,
    Lord Angus, thou hast lied!'
On the Earl's cheek the flush of rage
O'ercame the ashen hue of age: 430
Fierce he broke forth, 'And dar'st thou
        then
To beard the lion in his den,
    The Douglas in his hall?
And hop'st thou hence unscathed to go
No, by Saint Bride of Bothwell, no!
Up drawbridge, grooms—what, warder, ho!
    Let the portcullis fall.'
Lord Marmion turn'd,—well was his need,
And dash'd the rowels in his steed,
Like arrow through the archway sprung,   440
The ponderous grate behind him rung:
To pass there was such scanty room,
The bars, descending, razed his plume.

The steed along the drawbridge flies,
Just as it trembled on the rise;
Nor lighter does the swallow skim
Along the smooth lake's level brim:
And when Lord Marmion reach'd his band,
He halts, and turns with clenched hand,
And shout of loud defiance pours,   450
And shook his gauntlet at the towers.
'Horse! horse!' the Douglas cried, 'and chase!'
But soon he rein'd his fury's pace:
'A royal messenger he came,
Though most unworthy of the name.—
A letter forged! Saint Jude to speed!
Did ever knight so foul a deed!
At first in heart it liked me ill,
When the King prais'd his clerkly skill.
Thanks to Saint Bothan, son of mine,   460
Save Gawain, ne'er could pen a line:
So swore I, and I swear it still,
Let my boy-bishop fret his fill.
Saint Mary mend my fiery mood!
Old age ne'er cools the Douglas blood,
I thought to slay him where he stood.
'Tis pity of him too,' he cried:
'Bold can he speak, and fairly ride,
I warrant him a warrior tried.'
With this his mandate he recalls,   470
And slowly seeks his castle halls.

---

1 Douglas, Earl of Angus, who has entertained Marmion in his castle while on an official mission for the English crown.
2 Lady Clare, who in the story is affianced to Sir Ralph de Wilton, Marmion's rival.

Next morn the Baron climb'd the tower,
To view afar the Scottish power,
   Encamp'd on Flodden edge:
The white pavilions made a show,
Like remnants of the winter snow,
   Along the dusky ridge.
Long Marmion look'd: at length his eye
Unusual movement might descry
   Amid the shifting lines:
The Scottish host drawn out appears,   560
For, flashing on the hedge of spears
   The eastern sunbeam shines.
Their front now deepening, now extending;
Their flank inclining, wheeling, bending,
Now drawing back, and now descending,
The skilful Marmion well could know
They watch'd the motions of some foe,
Who travers'd on the plain below.

Even so it was. From Flodden ridge
   The Scots beheld the English host   570
   Leave Barmore-wood, their evening post,
   And heedful watch'd them as they cross'd
The Till by Twisel Bridge.[3]
   High sight it is, and haughty, while
   They dive into the deep defile;
   Beneath the cavern'd cliff they fall,
   Beneath the castle's airy wall;
By rock, by oak, by hawthorn-tree,
   Troop after troop are disappearing;
   Troop after troop their banners rearing,   580
Upon the eastern bank you see;
Still pouring down the rocky den,
   Where flows the sullen Till,
And rising from the dim-wood glen,
Standards on standards, men on men,
   In slow succession still,
And, sweeping o'er the Gothic arch,
And pressing on, in ceaseless march,
   To gain the opposing hill.

That morn, to many a trumpet clang,   590
Twisel! thy rock's deep echo rang;
And many a chief of birth and rank,
Saint Helen! at thy fountain drank.
Thy hawthorn glade, which now we see
In spring-tide bloom so lavishly,
Had then from many an axe its doom,
To give the marching columns room.

And why stands Scotland idly now,
Dark Flodden! on thy airy brow,
Since England gains the pass the while,   600
And struggles through the deep defile?
What checks the fiery soul of James?
Why sits that champion of the dames
   Inactive on his steed,
And sees, between him and his land,
Between him and Tweed's southern strand,
   His host Lord Surrey lead?
What 'vails the vain knight-errant's brand?
O, Douglas,[4] for thy leading wand!
   Fierce Randolph,[4] for thy speed!   610
O for one hour of Wallace[5] wight,[6]
Or well-skill'd Bruce,[7] to rule the fight,
And cry 'Saint Andrew and our right!'
Another sight had seen that morn,
From Fate's dark book a leaf been torn,
And Flodden had been Bannockbourne![8]
The precious hour has pass'd in vain,
And England's host has gain'd the plain;
Wheeling their march, and circling still,
Around the base of Flodden hill.   620

Ere yet the bands met Marmion's eye
Fitz-Eustace shouted loud and high,
'Hark! hark! my lord, an English drum!
And see ascending squadrons come
   Between Tweed's river and the hill,
Foot, horse, and cannon: hap what hap,
My basnet[9] to a prentice[10] cap,
   Lord Surrey's o'er the Till!
Yet more! yet more!—how far array'd
They file from out the hawthorn shade,   630
   And sweep so gallant by!
With all their banners bravely spread,
   And all their armour flashing high,

---

3 On the evening previous to the memorable battle of Flodden, Surrey's headquarters were at Barmoor Wood, and King James held an inaccessible position on the ridge of Flodden Hill, one of the last and lowest eminences detached from the ridge of Cheviot. The Till, a deep and slow river, winded between the armies. On the morning of the 9th September, 1513, Surrey marched in a north-westerly direction, and crossed the Till, with his van and artillery, at Twisel Bridge, nigh where that river joins the Tweed, his rear-guard column passing about a mile higher, by a ford. This movement had the double effect of placing his army between King James and his supplies from Scotland, and of striking the Scottish monarch with surprise, as he seems to have relied on the depth of the river in his front. But as the passage, both over the bridge and through the ford, was difficult and slow, it seems possible that the English might have been attacked to great advantage while struggling with these natural obstacles. I know not if we are to impute James's forbearance to want of military skill, or to the romantic declaration which Pitscottie puts in his mouth, 'that he was determined to have his enemies before him on a plain field,' and therefore would suffer no interruption to be given, even by artillery, to their passing the river.—(Scott.)

4 Douglas and Randolph were famous lieutenants of Bruce at the battle of Bannockburn.
5 Sir William Wallace, c.1274-1305, a Scottish patriot and national hero.
6 brave, valiant.
7 Robert I, 'The Bruce,' 1274-1329, King of Scotland and one of the heroes of his country.
8 the battle of Bannockburn in Stirlingshire, 24 June 1314, where the Scots under Robert Bruce totally defeated the English.
9 a light helmet.
10 cap worn by one serving an apprenticeship.

Saint George might waken from the dead,
  To see fair England's standards fly.'
'Stint in thy prate,' quoth Blount, 'thou 'dst best,
And listen to our lord's behest.'
With kindling brow Lord Marmion said,
'This instant be our band array'd;
The river must be quickly cross'd,   640
That we may join Lord Surrey's host.
If fight King James,—as well I trust,
That fight he will, and fight he must,—
The Lady Clare behind our lines
Shall tarry, while the battle joins.'

Himself he swift on horseback threw,
Scarce to the Abbot bade adieu;
Far less would listen to his prayer
To leave behind the helpless Clare.
Down to the Tweed his band he drew,   650
And mutter'd as the flood they view,
'The pheasant in the falcon's claw,[11]
He scarce will yield to please a daw:
Lord Angus may the Abbot awe,
  So Clare shall bide with me.'
Then on that dangerous ford, and deep,
Where to the Tweed Leat's[12] eddies creep,
  He ventured desperately:
And not a moment will he bide,
Till squire, or groom, before him ride;   660
Headmost of all he stems the tide,
  And stems it gallantly.
Eustace held Clare upon her horse,
  Old Hubert led her rein,
Stoutly they brav'd the current's course,
And, though far downward driven per force,
  The southern bank they gain;
Behind them, straggling, came to shore,
  As best they might, the train:
Each o'er his head his yew-bow bore,   670
  A caution not in vain;
Deep need that day that every string,
By wet unharm'd, should sharply ring.
A moment then Lord Marmion staid,
And breath'd his steed, his men array'd,
  Then forward mov'd his band,
Until, Lord Surrey's rear-guard won,
He halted by a Cross of Stone,
That, on a hillock standing lone,
  Did all the field command.   680

Hence might they see the full array
Of either host, for deadly fray;[13]

Their marshall'd lines stretch'd east and west,
  And fronted north and south,
And distant salutation pass'd
  From the loud cannon mouth;
Not in the close successive rattle,
That breathes the voice of modern battle,
  But slow and far between.
The hillock gain'd, Lord Marmion staid: 690

Flodden; but, so far as is necessary to understand the romance, I beg to remind him, that, when the English army, by their skilful countermarch, were fairly placed between King James and his own country, the Scottish monarch resolved to fight; and, setting fire to his tents, descended from the ridge of Flodden to secure the neighbouring eminence of Brankstone, on which that village is built. Thus the two armies met, almost without seeing each other, when, according to the old poem of *Flodden Field,*

    The English line stretched east and west,
      And southward were their faces set;
    The Scottish northward proudly prest,
      And manfully their foes they met.

The English army advanced in four divisions. On the right, which first engaged, were the sons of Earl Surrey, namely, Thomas Howard, the Admiral of England, and Sir Edmund, the Knight Marshal of the army. Their divisions were separated from each other; but, at the request of Sir Edmund, his brother's battalion was drawn very near to his own. The centre was commanded by Surrey in person; the left wing by Sir Edward Stanley, with the men of Lancashire, and of the palatinate of Chester. Lord Dacres, with a large body of horse, formed a reserve. When the smoke, which the wind had driven between the armies, was somewhat dispersed, they perceived the Scots, who had moved down the hill in a similar order of battle, and in deep silence. The Earls of Huntly and of Home commanded their left wing, and charged Sir Edmund Howard with such success, as entirely to defeat his part of the English right wing. Sir Edmund's banner was beaten down, and he himself escaped with difficulty to his brother's division. The Admiral, however, stood firm; and Dacre advancing to his support with the reserve of cavalry, probably between the interval of the divisions commanded by the brothers Howard, appears to have kept the victors in effectual check. Home's men, chiefly Borderers, began to pillage the baggage of both armies; and their leader is branded, by the Scottish historians, with negligence or treachery. On the other hand, Huntly, on whom they bestow many encomiums, is said, by the English historians, to have left the field after the first charge. Meanwhile the Admiral, whose flank these chiefs ought to have attacked, availed himself of their inactivity, and pushed forward against another large division of the Scottish army in his front, headed by the Earls of Crawford and Montrose, both of whom were slain, and their forces routed. On the left, the success of the English was yet more decisive; for the Scottish right wing, consisting of undisciplined Highlanders, commanded by Lennox and Argyle, was unable to sustain the charge of Sir Edward Stanley, and especially the severe execution of the Lancashire archers. The King and Surrey, who commanded the respective centres of their armies, were meanwhile engaged in close and dubious conflict. James, surrounded by the flower of his kingdom, and impatient of the galling discharge of arrows, supported also by his reserve under Bothwell, charged with such fury, that the standard of Surrey was in danger. At that critical moment, Stanley, who had routed the left wing of the Scottish, pursued his career of victory, and arrived on the right flank, and in the rear of James's division, which, throwing itself into a circle, disputed the battle till night came on. Surrey then drew back his forces; for the Scottish centre not having been broken, and their left wing being victorious, he yet doubted the event of the field. The Scottish army, however, felt their loss, and abandoned the field of battle in disorder, before dawn. They lost, perhaps, from eight to ten thousand men; but that included the very prime of their nobility, gentry, and even clergy. Scarce a family of eminence but has an ancestor killed at Flodden; and there is no province in Scotland, even at this day, where the battle is mentioned without a sensation of terror and sorrow.—(Scott.)

---

11 Marmion's crest was a falcon.
12 The Leat River was a small tributary to the Tweed.
13 The reader cannot here expect a full account of the Battle of

'Here, by this Cross,' he gently said,
'You well may view the scene.
Here shalt thou tarry, lovely Clare:
O! think of Marmion in thy prayer!
Thou wilt not?—well, no less my care
Shall, watchful, for thy weal prepare.
You, Blount and Eustace, are her guard,
With ten pick'd archers of my train;
With England if the day go hard,
To Berwick speed amain. 700
But if we conquer, cruel maid,
My spoils shall at your feet be laid,
When here we meet again.'
He waited not for answer there,
And would not mark the maid's despair,
Nor heed the discontented look
From either squire; but spurr'd amain,
And, dashing through the battle plain,
His way to Surrey took.

'The good Lord Marmion, by my life! 710
Welcome to danger's hour!
Short greeting serves in time of strife:
Thus have I rang'd my power:
Myself will rule this central host,
Stout Stanley fronts their right,
My sons command the vaward post,
With Brian Tunstall, stainless knight;
Lord Dacre, with his horsemen light,
Shall be in rearward of the fight,
And succour those that need it most. 720
Now, gallant Marmion, well I know
Would gladly to the vanguard go;
Edmund, the Admiral, Tunstall there,
With thee their charge will blithely share;
There fight thine own retainers too,
Beneath De Burg, thy steward true.'
'Thanks, noble Surrey!' Marmion said,
Nor farther greeting there he paid;
But, parting like a thunderbolt,
First in the vanguard made a halt, 730
Where such a shout there rose
Of Marmion! Marmion! that the cry,
Up Flodden mountain shrilling high,
Startled the Scottish foes.

Blount and Fitz-Eustace rested still
With Lady Clare upon the hill!
On which (for far the day was spent),
The western sunbeams now were bent.
The cry they heard, its meaning knew,
Could plain their distant comrades view: 740
Sadly to Blount did Eustace say,
'Unworthy office here to stay!

No hope of gilded, spurs to-day.
But see! look up—on Flodden bent
The Scottish foe has fired his tent.'
And sudden, as he spoke,
From the sharp ridges of the hill,
All downward to the banks of Till,
Was wreath'd in sable smoke.
Volum'd and fast, and rolling far, 750
The cloud envelop'd Scotland's war,
As down the hill they broke;
Nor martial shout, nor minstrel tone,
Announc'd their march; their tread alone,
At times one warning trumpet blown,
At times a stifled hum,
Told England, from his mountain-throne
King James did rushing come.
Scarce could they hear, or see their foes,
Until at weapon-point they close. 760
They close, in clouds of smoke and dust,
With sword-sway, and with lance's thrust;
And such a yell was there,
Of sudden and portentous birth,
As if men fought upon the earth,
And fiends in upper air;
O life and death were in the shout,
Recoil and rally, charge and rout,
And triumph and despair.
Long look'd the anxious squires; their eye 770
Could in the darkness nought descry.

At length the freshening western blast
Aside the shroud of battle cast;
And, first, the ridge of mingled spears
Above the brightening cloud appears;
And in the smoke the pennons flew,
As in the storm the white sea-mew.
Then mark'd they, dashing broad and far,
The broken billows of the war,
And plumed crests of chieftains brave, 780
Floating like foam upon the wave;
But nought distinct they see:
Wide rag'd the battle on the plain;
Spears shook, and falchions flash'd amain;
Fell England's arrow-flight like rain;
Crests rose, and stoop'd, and rose again,
Wild and disorderly.
Amid the scene of tumult, high
They saw Lord Marmion's falcon fly:
And stainless Tunstall's banner white, 790
And Edmund Howard's lion bright,
Still bear them bravely in the fight:
Although against them come,
Of gallant Gordons many a one,
And many a stubborn Badenoch-man,

And many a rugged Border clan,
  With Huntly, and with Home.

Far on the left, unseen the while,
Stanley broke Lennox and Argyle;
Though there the western mountaineer   800
Rush'd with bare bosom on the spear,
And flung the feeble targe aside,
And with both hands the broadsword plied.
'Twas vain:—But Fortune, on the right,
With fickle smile, cheer'd Scotland's fight.
Then fell that spotless banner white,
  The Howard's lion fell;
Yet still Lord Marmion's falcon flew
With wavering flight, while fiercer grew
  Around the battle-yell.   810
The Border slogan rent the sky!
A Home! a Gordon! was the cry:
  Loud were the clanging blows;
Advanc'd, forc'd back, now low, now high,
  The pennon sunk and rose;
As bends the bark's mast in the gale,
When rent are rigging, shrouds, and sail,
  It waver'd 'mid the foes.
No longer Blount the view could bear:
'By Heaven, and all its saints! I swear   820
  I will not see it lost!
Fitz-Eustace, you wish Lady Clare
May bid your beads, and patter prayer,—
  I gallop to the host.'
And to the fray he rode amain,
Follow'd by all the archer train.
The fiery youth, with desperate charge,
Made, for a space, an opening large,
  The rescued banner rose,
But darkly clos'd the war around,   830
Like pine-tree, rooted from the ground,
  It sunk among the foes.
Then Eustace mounted too:—yet staid
As loath to leave the helpless maid,
  When, fast as shaft can fly,
Bloodshot his eyes, his nostrils spread,
The loose rein dangling from his head,
Housing and saddle bloody red,
  Lord Marmion's steed rush'd by;
And Eustace, maddening at the sight,   840
  A look and sign to Clara cast
  To mark he would return in haste,
Then plung'd into the fight.

Ask me not what the maiden feels,
  Left in that dreadful hour alone:
Perchance her reason stoops, or reels;
Perchance a courage, not her own,
Braces her mind to desperate tone.
The scatter'd van of England wheels;
  She only said, as loud in air   850
  The tumult roar'd, 'Is Wilton there?'
They fly, or, madden'd by despair,
  Fight but to die,—'Is Wilton there?'
With that, straight up the hill there rode
  Two horsemen drench'd with gore,
And in their arms, a helpless load,
  A wounded knight they bore.
His hand still strain'd the broken brand;
His arms were smear'd with blood and sand:
Dragg'd from among the horses' feet,   860
With dinted shield, and helmet beat,
The falcon-crest and plumage gone,
Can that be haughty Marmion!
Young Blount his armour did unlace,
And, gazing on his ghastly face,
  Said, 'By Saint George, he's gone!
That spear-wound has our master sped,
And see the deep cut on his head!
  Good-night to Marmion.'
'Unnurtur'd Blount! thy brawling cease: 870
He opes his eyes,' said Eustace; 'peace!'

When doff'd his casque, he felt free air,
Around 'gan Marmion wildly stare:—
'Where's Harry Blount? Fitz-Eustace where?
Linger ye here, ye hearts of hare!
Redeem my pennon,—charge again!
Cry "Marmion to the rescue!"—Vain!
Last of my race, on battle-plain
That shout shall ne'er be heard again!
Yet my last thought is England's; fly,   880
  To Dacre bear my signet-ring:
  Tell him his squadrons up to bring.
Fitz-Eustace, to Lord Surrey hie;
  Tunstall lies dead upon the field,
  His life-blood stains the spotless shield:
  Edmund is down:—my life is reft;
  The Admiral alone is left.
  Let Stanley charge with spur of fire,—
  With Chester charge, and Lancashire,
  Full upon Scotland's central host,   890
  Or victory and England's lost.
  Must I bid twice?—hence, varlets! fly!
  Leave Marmion here alone—to die.'
They parted, and alone he lay;
Clare drew her from the sight away,
Till pain wrung forth a lowly moan,
And half he murmur'd, 'Is there none,
  Of all my halls have nurst,
Page, squire, or groom, one cup to bring

Of blessed water from the spring,   900
  To slake my dying thirst!'

O Woman! in our hours of ease,
Uncertain, coy, and hard to please,
And variable as the shade
By the light quivering aspen made;
When pain and anguish wring the brow,
A ministering angel thou!
Scarce were the piteous accents said,
When, with the Baron's casque, the maid
  To the nigh streamlet ran: 910
Forgot were hatred, wrongs, and fears;
The plaintive voice alone she hears,
  Sees but the dying man.
She stoop'd her by the runnel's side,
  But in abhorrence backward drew;
For, oozing from the mountain's side,
Where raged the war, a dark-red tide
  Was curdling in the streamlet blue.
Where shall she turn?—behold her mark
  A little fountain cell,   920
Where water, clear as diamond-spark,
  In a stone basin fell.
Above, some half-worn letters say,
𝔇rink . weary . pilgrim . drink . and . pray.
𝔉or . the . kind . soul . of . 𝔖ybil . 𝔊rey.
  𝔚ho . built . this . cross . and . well.[14]
She fill'd the helm, and back she hied,
And with surprise and joy espied
  A monk supporting Marmion's head:
A pious man, whom duty brought   930
To dubious verge of battle fought,
  To shrieve the dying, bless the dead.

. . .

By this though deep the evening fell,
Still rose the battle's deadly swell,
For still the Scots, around their King,
Unbroken, fought in desperate ring.
Where's now their victor vaward wing,
  Where Huntly, and where Home?—
O, for a blast of that dread horn,
On Fontarabian echoes borne,   1000
  That to King Charles did come,
When Rowland brave, and Olivier,
And every paladin and peer,
  On Roncesvalles died![15]

---

14 The fountain and Sibyl Grey are not historic.
15 At Roncesvalles near Fontarabia, in Spain, Roland and Oliver,
with the others of the famous twelve peers, forming the rearguard
to King Charlemagne's army, fought off an overwhelming force
of Saracens. When the Saracens had retreated and Roland alone,
though mortally wounded, survived on the field of battle, he blew
his mighty horn summoning Charlemagne, who pursued and destroyed the enemy.

Such blast might warn them, not in vain,
To quit the plunder of the slain,
And turn the doubtful day again,
  While yet on Flodden side,
Afar, the Royal Standard flies,
And round it toils, and bleeds, and dies,   1010
  Our Caledonian pride!
In vain the wish—for far away,
While spoil and havoc mark their way,
Near Sybil's Cross the plunderers stray.
'O, Lady,' cried the Monk, 'away!'
  And plac'd her on her steed,
And led her to the chapel fair,
  Of Tilmouth upon Tweed.
There all the night they spent in prayer,
And at the dawn of morning, there   1020
She met her kinsman, Lord Fitz-Clare.

But as they left the dark'ning heath,
More desperate grew the strife of death.
The English shafts in volleys hail'd,
In headlong charge their horse assail'd;
Front, flank, and rear, the squadrons sweep
To break the Scottish circle deep,
  That fought around their King.
But yet, though thick the shafts as snow,
Though charging knights like whirlwinds go,   1030
Though bill-men ply the ghastly blow,
  Unbroken was the ring;
The stubborn spear-men still made good
Their dark impenetrable wood,
Each stepping where his comrade stood,
  The instant that he fell.
No thought was there of dastard flight;
Link'd in the serried phalanx tight,
Groom fought like noble, squire like knight,
  As fearlessly and well;   1040
Till utter darkness closed her wing
O'er their thin host and wounded King.
Then skilful Surrey's sage commands
Led back from strife his shatter'd bands;
  And from the charge they drew,
As mountain-waves, from wasted lands,
  Sweep back to ocean blue.
Then did their loss his foemen know;
Their King, their Lords, their mightiest low,
They melted from the field as snow,   1050
When streams are swoln and south winds blow,
  Dissolves in silent dew.
Tweed's echoes heard the ceaseless plash,
  While many a broken band,
Disorder'd, through her currents dash,
  To gain the Scottish land;

To town and tower, to town and dale,
To tell red Flodden's dismal tale,
And raise the universal wail.
Tradition, legend, tune, and song,   1060
Shall many an age that wail prolong:
Still from the sire the son shall hear
Of the stern strife, and carnage drear,
  Of Flodden's fatal field,
Where shiver'd was fair Scotland's spear,
  And broken was her shield!

                                                  1808

From THE LADY OF THE LAKE

The ancient manners, the habits, and customs of the
aboriginal race by whom the Highlands of Scotland were
inhabited, had always appeared to me peculiarly adapted
to poetry. The change in their manners, too, had taken
place almost within my own time, or at least I had
learned many particulars concerning the ancient state of
the Highlands from the old men of the last generation. I
had always thought the old Scottish Gael highly adapted
for poetical composition. The feuds, and political dissen-
sions, which, half a century earlier, would have rendered
the richer and wealthier part of the kingdom indisposed
to countenance a poem, the scene of which was laid in
the Highlands, were now sunk in the generous compassion which the English, more than any other nation, feel
for the misfortunes of an honourable foe. The poems of
Ossian had, by their popularity, sufficiently shown, that
if writings on Highland subjects were qualified to interest the reader, mere national prejudices were, in the
present day, very unlikely to interfere with their success.

I had also read a great deal, seen much, and heard
more, of that romantic country, where I was in the habit
of spending some time every autumn; and the scenery of
Loch Katrine was connected with the recollection of
many a dear friend and merry expedition of former
days. This poem, the action of which lay among scenes
so beautiful, and so deeply imprinted on my recollection,
was a labor of love; and it was no less so to recall the
manners and incidents introduced.—(From Scott's 'Introduction,' April 1830.)

The scene of the following poem is laid chiefly in the
vicinity of Loch Katrine, in the Western Highlands of
Perthshire.—(Scott.)

Canto 1

THE CHASE

Harp of the North! that mouldering long hast
    hung
  On the witch-elm[1] that shades Saint Fillan's
    spring,
And down the fitful breeze thy numbers flung,
  Till envious ivy did around thee cling,
Muffling with verdant ringlet every string—
  O minstrel Harp, still must thine accents
    sleep?

'Mid rustling leaves and fountains murmuring,
  Still must thy sweeter sounds their silence
    keep,
Nor bid a warrior smile, nor teach a maid to
    weep?

Not thus, in ancient days of Caledon,[2]   10
  Was thy voice mute amid the festal crowd,
When lay of hopeless love, or glory won,
  Aroused the fearful, or subdued the proud.
At each according pause was heard aloud
  Thine ardent symphony sublime and high!
Fair dames and crested chiefs attention bow'd;
  For still the burden of thy minstrelsy
Was Knighthood's dauntless deed, and Beauty's
    matchless eye.

O wake once more! how rude soe'er the hand
  That ventures o'er thy magic maze to stray; 20
O wake once more! though scarce my skill com-
    mand
  Some feeble echoing of thine earlier lay:
Though harsh and faint, and soon to die away,
  And all unworthy of thy nobler strain,
Yet if one heart throb higher at its sway,
  The wizard note has not been touch'd in vain.
Then silent be no more! Enchantress, wake
    again!

I

The stag at eve had drunk his fill,
Where danced the moon on Monan's rill,
And deep his midnight lair had made   30
In lone Glenartney's hazel shade;
But, when the sun his beacon red
Had kindled on Benvoirlich's head,
The deep-mouth'd bloodhound's heavy bay
Resounded up the rocky way,
And faint, from farther distance borne,
Were heard the clanging hoof and horn.

II

As Chief, who hears his warder call,
'To arms! the foemen storm the wall,'
The antler'd monarch of the waste   40
Sprung from his heathery couch in haste.
But, ere his fleet career he took,
The dew-drops from his flanks he shook;
Like crested leader proud and high,
Toss'd his beam'd frontlet to the sky;
A moment gazed adown the dale,
A moment snuff'd the tainted gale,

_____
1 the broad-leaved elm.

2 Scotland.

A moment listen'd to the cry,
That thicken'd as the chase drew nigh;
Then, as the headmost foes appear'd,   50
With one brave bound the copse he clear'd,
And, stretching forward free and far,
Sought the wild heaths of Uam-Var.[3]

III

Yell'd on the view the opening pack;
Rock, glen, and cavern, paid them back;
To many a mingled sound at once
The awaken'd mountain gave response.
A hundred dogs bay'd deep and strong,
Clatter'd a hundred steeds along,
Their peal the merry horns rung out,   60
A hundred voices join'd the shout;
With hark and whoop and wild halloo,
No rest Benvoirlich's echoes knew.
Far from the tumult fled the roe,
Close in her covert cower'd the doe;
The falcon, from her cairn on high,
Cast on the rout a wondering eye,
Till far beyond her piercing ken
The hurricane had swept the glen.
Faint and more faint, its failing din   70
Return'd from cavern, cliff, and linn,[4]
And silence settled, wide and still,
On the lone wood and mighty hill.

IV

Less loud the sounds of silvan war
Disturb'd the heights of Uam-Var,
And roused the cavern, where, 'tis told,
A giant made his den of old;
For ere that steep ascent was won,
High in his pathway hung the sun,
And many a gallant, stay'd perforce,   80
Was fain to breathe his faltering horse,
And of the trackers of the deer,
Scarce half the lessening pack was near;
So shrewdly[5] on the mountain side
Had the bold burst their mettle tried.

V

The noble stag was pausing now
Upon the mountain's southern brow,
Where broad extended, far beneath,

---

3 Ua-var, as the name is pronounced, or more properly *Uaigh-mor*, is a mountain to the northeast of the village of Callander, in Menteith, deriving its name, which signifies the great den, or cavern, from a sort of retreat among the rocks on the south side, said, by tradition, to have been the abode of a giant. In latter times, it was the refuge of robbers and banditti, who have been only extirpated within these forty or fifty years.—(Scott.)
4 steep ravine.
5 severely.

The varied realms of fair Menteith.
With anxious eye he wander'd o'er   90
Mountain and meadow, moss and moor,
And ponder'd refuge from his toil
By far Lochard or Aberfoyle.
But nearer was the copsewood grey,
That waved and wept on Loch-Achray,
And mingled with the pine-trees blue
On the bold cliffs of Benvenue.
Fresh vigour with the hope return'd,
With flying foot the heath he spurn'd,
Held westward with unwearied race,   100
And left behind the panting chase.

VI

'Twere long to tell what steeds gave o'er,
As swept the hunt through Cambusmore:
What reins were tighten'd in despair,
When rose Benledi's ridge in air;
Who flagg'd upon Bochastle's heath,
Who shunn'd to stem the flooded Teith,—
For twice that day, from shore to shore,
The gallant stag swam stoutly o'er.
Few were the stragglers, following far,   110
That reach'd the lake of Vennachar;
And when the Brigg of Turk was won,
The headmost horseman rode alone.

VII

Alone, but with unbated zeal,
That horseman plied the scourge and steel;
For jaded now, and spent with toil,
Emboss'd with foam, and dark with soil,
While every gasp with sobs he drew,
The labouring stag strain'd full in view.
Two dogs of black Saint Hubert's breed,   120
Unmatch'd for courage, breath, and speed,
Fast on his flying traces came,
And all but won that desperate game;
For, scarce a spear's length from his haunch,
Vindictive toil'd the bloodhounds stanch;
Nor nearer might the dogs attain,
Nor farther might the quarry strain.
Thus up the margin of the lake,
Between the precipice and brake,
O'er stock and rock their race they take.   130

VIII

The Hunter mark'd that mountain high,
The lone lake's western boundary,
And deem'd the stag must turn to bay,
Where that huge rampart barr'd the way;
Already glorying in the prize,
Measured his antlers with his eyes;
For the death-wound and death-halloo,

Muster'd his breath, his whinyard[6] drew;—
But thundering as he came prepared,
With ready arm and weapon bared,   140
The wily quarry shunn'd the shock,
And turn'd him from the opposing rock;
Then, dashing down a darksome glen,
Soon lost to hound and hunter's ken,
In the deep Trosachs' wildest nook
His solitary refuge took.
There, while close couch'd, the thicket shed
Cold dews and wild-flowers on his head,
He heard the baffled dogs in vain
Rave through the hollow pass amain,   150
Chiding the rocks that yell'd again.

IX

Close on the hounds the hunter came,
To cheer them on the vanish'd game;
But, stumbling in the rugged dell,
The gallant horse exhausted fell.
The impatient rider strove in vain
To rouse him with the spur and rein,
For the good steed, his labours o'er,
Stretch'd his stiff limbs, to rise no more;
Then, touch'd with pity and remorse,   160
He sorrow'd o'er the expiring horse:
'I little thought, when first thy rein
I slack'd upon the banks of Seine,
That Highland eagle e'er should feed
On thy fleet limbs, my matchless steed!
Woe worth the chase, woe worth the day,
That costs thy life, my gallant grey!'

X

Then through the dell his horn resounds,
From vain pursuit to call the hounds.
Back limp'd, with slow and crippled pace,   170
The sulky leaders of the chase;
Close to their master's side they press'd,
With drooping tail and humbled crest;
But still the dingle's hollow throat
Prolong'd the swelling bugle-note.
The owlets started from their dream,
The eagles answer'd with their scream,
Round and around the sounds were cast,
Till echo seem'd an answering blast;
And on the hunter hied his way,   180
To join some comrades of the day,
Yet often paused, so strange the road,
So wondrous were the scenes it show'd.

XI

The western waves of ebbing day
Roll'd o'er the glen their level way;

Each purple peak, each flinty spire,
Was bathed in floods of living fire.
But not a setting beam could glow
Within the dark ravines below,
Where twined the path in shadow hid,   190
Round many a rocky pyramid,
Shooting abruptly from the dell
Its thunder-splinter'd pinnacle;
Round many an insulated mass,
The native bulwarks of the pass,
Huge as the tower which builders vain
Presumptuous piled on Shinar's plain.[7]
The rocky summits, split and rent,
Form'd turret, dome, or battlement,
Or seem'd fantastically set   200
With cupola or minaret,[8]
Wild crests as pagod[9] ever deck'd,
Or mosque of Eastern architect.
Nor were these earth-born castles bare,
Nor lack'd they many a banner fair;
For, from their shiver'd brows display'd,
Far o'er the unfathomable glade,
All twinkling with the dewdrop sheen,
The brier-rose fell in streamers green,
And creeping shrubs, of thousand dyes,   210
Waved in the west-wind's summer sighs.

XII

Boon nature scatter'd, free and wild,
Each plant or flower, the mountain's child.
Here eglantine embalm'd the air,
Hawthorn and hazel mingled there;
The primrose pale, and violet flower,
Found in each cliff a narrow bower;
Fox-glove and night-shade, side by side,
Emblems of punishment and pride,
Group'd their dark hues with every stain   220
The weather-beaten crags retain.
With boughs that quaked at every breath,
Grey birch and aspen wept beneath;
Aloft, the ash and warrior oak
Cast anchor in the rifted rock;
And, higher yet, the pine-tree hung
His shatter'd trunk, and frequent flung,
Where seem'd the cliffs to meet on high,
His boughs athwart the narrow'd sky.
Highest of all, where white peaks glanced,   230
Where glist'ning streamers waved and danced,
The wanderer's eye could barely view
The summer heaven's delicious blue;
So wondrous wild, the whole might seem
The scenery of a fairy dream.

---

6 huntsman's short sword or dagger.

7 the Tower of Babel. See *Genesis*, xi, 1–9.
8 a lofty tower with balconies.
9 pagoda, an oriental temple with tower-like structure.

XIII

Onward, amid the copse 'gan peep
A narrow inlet, still and deep,
Affording scarce such breadth of brim
As served the wild duck's brood to swim.
Lost for a space, through thickets veering,   240
But broader when again appearing,
Tall rocks and tufted knolls their face
Could on the dark-blue mirror trace;
And farther as the hunter stray'd,
Still broader sweep its channels made.
The shaggy mounds no longer stood,
Emerging from entangled wood,
But, wave-encircled, seem'd to float,
Like castle girdled with its moat;
Yet broader floods extending still   250
Divide them from their parent hill,
Till each, retiring, claims to be
An islet in an inland sea.

XIV

And now, to issue from the glen,
No pathway meets the wanderer's ken,
Unless he climb, with footing nice,
A far projecting precipice.
The broom's tough roots his ladder made,
The hazel saplings lent their aid;
And thus an airy point he won,   260
Where, gleaming with the setting sun,
One burnish'd sheet of living gold,
Loch Katrine lay beneath him roll'd;
In all her length far winding lay,
With promontory, creek, and bay,
And islands that, empurpled bright,
Floated amid the livelier light,
And mountains, that like giants stand,
To sentinel enchanted land.
High on the south, huge Benvenue   270
Down to the lake in masses threw
Crags, knolls, and mounds, confusedly hurl'd,
The fragments of an earlier world;
A wildering forest feather'd o'er
His ruin'd sides and summit hoar,
While on the north, through middle air,
Ben-an heaved high his forehead bare.

XV

From the steep promontory gazed
The stranger, raptured and amazed.
And, 'What a scene were here,' he cried,   280
'For princely pomp, or churchman's pride!
On this bold brow, a lordly tower;
In that soft vale, a lady's bower;
On yonder meadow, far away,
The turrets of a cloister grey;
How blithely might the bugle-horn
Chide, on the lake, the lingering morn!
How sweet, at eve, the lover's lute
Chime, when the groves were still and mute!
And, when the midnight moon should lave   290
Her forehead in the silver wave,
How solemn on the ear would come
The holy matins' distant hum,
While the deep peal's commanding tone
Should wake, in yonder islet lone,
A sainted hermit from his cell,
To drop a bead with every knell—
And bugle, lute, and bell, and all,
Should each bewilder'd stranger call
To friendly feast, and lighted hall.   300

XVI

'Blithe were it then to wander here!
But now,—beshrew yon nimble deer,—
Like that same hermit's, thin and spare,
The copse must give my evening fare;
Some mossy bank my couch must be,
Some rustling oak my canopy.
Yet pass we that; the war and chase
Give little choice of resting-place;—
A summer night, in greenwood spent,
Were but to-morrow's merriment: 310
But hosts may in these wilds abound,
Such as are better miss'd than found;
To meet with Highland plunderers here[10]
Were worse than loss of steed or deer.—
I am alone;—my bugle-strain
May call some straggler of the train;
Or, fall the worst that may betide,
Ere now this falchion[11] has been tried.'

XVII

But scarce again his horn he wound,
When lo! forth starting at the sound,   320
From underneath an aged oak,
That slanted from the islet rock,
A damsel guider of its way,
A little skiff shot to the bay,
That round the promontory steep
Led its deep line in graceful sweep,
Eddying, in almost viewless wave,
The weeping willow-twig to lave,
And kiss, with whispering sound and slow,
The beach of pebbles bright as snow.   330
The boat had touch'd this silver strand,

---

10 The clans who inhabited the romantic regions in the neighbourhood of Loch Katrine were, even until a late period, much addicted to predatory excursions upon their Lowland neighbors.
—(Scott.)
11 sword.

Just as the Hunter left his stand,
And stood conceal'd amid the brake,
To view this Lady of the Lake.
The maiden paused, as if again
She thought to catch the distant strain.
With head up-raised, and look intent,
And eye and ear attentive bent,
And locks flung back, and lips apart,
Like monument of Grecian art,   340
In listening mood, she seem'd to stand,
The guardian Naiad of the strand.

XVIII

And ne'er did Grecian chisel trace
A Nymph, a Naiad, or a Grace
Of finer form, or lovelier face!
What though the sun, with ardent frown,
Had slightly tinged her cheek with brown;
The sportive toil, which, short and light,
Had dyed her glowing hue so bright,
Served too in hastier swell to show   350
Short glimpses of a breast of snow:
What though no rule of courtly grace
To measured mood had train'd her pace;
A foot more light, a step more true,
Ne'er from the heath-flower dash'd the dew;
E'en the slight harebell raised his head,
Elastic from her airy tread:
What though upon her speech there hung
The accents of the mountain tongue;
Those silver sounds, so soft, so dear,   360
The listener held his breath to hear!

XIX

A Chieftain's daughter seem'd the maid;
Her satin snood, her silken plaid,
Her golden brooch, such birth betray'd.
And seldom was a snood amid
Such wild luxuriant ringlets hid,
Whose glossy black to shame might bring
The plumage of the raven's wing;
And seldom o'er a breast so fair,
Mantled a plaid with modest care,   370
And never brooch the folds combin'd
Above a heart more good and kind.
Her kindness and her worth to spy,
You need but gaze on Ellen's eye;
Not Katrine, in her mirror blue,
Gives back the shaggy banks more true,
Than every free-born glance confess'd
The guileless movements of her breast;
Whether joy danced in her dark eye,
Or woe or pity claim'd a sigh,   380

Or filial love was glowing there,
Or meek devotion pour'd a prayer,
Or tale of injury call'd forth
The indignant spirit of the North.
One only passion unreveal'd,
With maiden pride the maid conceal'd,
Yet not less purely felt the flame;—
O need I tell that passion's name?

XX

Impatient of the silent horn,
Now on the gale her voice was borne:—   390
'Father!' she cried; the rocks around
Loved to prolong the gentle sound.
A while she paused, no answer came;
'Malcolm, was thine the blast?' the name
Less resolutely utter'd fell;
The echoes could not catch the swell.
'A stranger I,' the Huntsman said,
Advancing from the hazel shade.
The maid, alarm'd, with hasty oar,
Push'd her light shallop from the shore,   400
And when a space was gain'd between,
Closer she drew her bosom's screen;
(So forth the startled swan would swing,
So turn to prune his ruffled wing.)
Then safe, though flutter'd and amazed,
She paused, and on the stranger gazed.
Not his the form, nor his the eye,
That youthful maidens wont to fly.

XXI

On his bold visage middle age
Had slightly press'd its signet sage,   410
Yet had not quench'd the open truth
And fiery vehemence of youth;
Forward and frolic glee was there,
The will to do, the soul to dare,
The sparkling glance, soon blown to fire,
Of hasty love, or headlong ire.
His limbs were cast in manly mould,
For hardy sports or contest bold;
And though in peaceful garb array'd,
And weaponless, except his blade,   420
His stately mien as well implied
A high-born heart, a martial pride,
As if a Baron's crest he wore,
And sheathed in armour trode the shore.
Slightly the petty need he show'd,
He told of his benighted road;
His ready speech flow'd fair and free,
In phrase of gentlest courtesy;
Yet seem'd that tone, and gesture bland,
Less used to sue than to command.   430

XXII

A while the maid the stranger eyed,
And, reassured, at length replied,
That Highland halls were open still
To wilder'd wanderers of the hill.
'Nor think you unexpected come
To yon lone isle, our desert home;
Before the heath had lost the dew,
This morn, a couch was pull'd for you;
On yonder mountain's purple head
Have ptarmigan[12] and heath-cock[12] bled,   440
And our broad nets have swept the mere,
To furnish forth your evening cheer.'
'Now, by the rood,[13] my lovely maid,
Your courtesy has err'd,' he said;
'No right have I to claim, misplaced,
The welcome of expected guest.
A wanderer, here by fortune tost,
My way, my friends, my courser lost,
I ne'er before, believe me, fair,
Have ever drawn your mountain air,   450
Till on this lake's romantic strand
I found a fay in fairy land!'

XXIII

'I well believe,' the maid replied,
As her light skiff approach'd the side,
'I well believe that ne'er before
Your foot has trod Loch Katrine's shore;
But yet, as far as yesternight,
Old Allan-Bane foretold your plight,—
A grey-hair'd sire, whose eye intent
Was on the vision'd future bent.   460
He saw your steed, a dappled grey,
Lie dead beneath the birchen way;
Painted exact your form and mien,
Your hunting suit of Lincoln green,
That tassell'd horn so gaily gilt,
That falchion's crooked blade and hilt,
That cap with heron plumage trim,
And yon two hounds so dark and grim.
He bade that all should ready be
To grace a guest of fair degree;   470
But light I held his prophecy,
And deem'd it was my father's horn
Whose echoes o'er the lake were borne.'

XXIV

The stranger smiled: 'Since to your home
A destined errant-knight I come,
Announced by prophet sooth and old,
Doom'd, doubtless, for achievement bold,

I'll lightly front each high emprise
For one kind glance of those bright eyes.
Permit me, first, the task to guide   480
Your fairy frigate o'er the tide.'
The maid, with smile suppress'd and sly,
The toil unwonted saw him try;
For seldom sure, if e'er before,
His noble hand had grasp'd an oar:
Yet with main strength his strokes he drew,
And o'er the lake the shallop flew;
With heads erect, and whimpering cry,
The hounds behind their passage ply.
Nor frequent does the bright oar break   490
The dark'ning mirror of the lake,
Until the rocky isle they reach,
And moor their shallop on the beach.

XXV

The stranger view'd the shore around;
'Twas all so close with copsewood bound,
Nor track nor pathway might declare
That human foot frequented there,
Until the mountain-maiden show'd
A clambering unsuspected road,
That winded through the tangled screen,   500
And open'd on a narrow green,
Where weeping birch and willow round
With their long fibres swept the ground.
Here, for retreat in dangerous hour,[14]
Some chief had framed a rustic bower.

XXVI

It was a lodge of ample size,
But strange of structure and device;
Of such materials, as around
The workman's hand had readiest found;
Lopp'd off their boughs, their hoar trunks
         bared,   510
And by the hatchet rudely squared.
To give the walls their destined height
The sturdy oak and ash unite;
While moss and clay and leaves combin'd
To fence each crevice from the wind.
The lighter pine-trees, over-head,
Their slender length for rafters spread,
And wither'd heath and rushes dry
Supplied a russet canopy.
Due westward, fronting to the green,   520
A rural portico was seen,
Aloft on native pillars borne,
Of mountain fir, with bark unshorn,

---

12 a kind of game bird.
13 by the cross.

14 The Celtic chieftains, whose lives were continually exposed to peril, had usually, in the most retired spot of their domains, some place of retreat for the hour of necessity, which, as circumstances would admit, was a tower, a cavern, or a rustic hut, in a strong and secluded situation.—(Scott.)

Where Ellen's hand had taught to twine
The ivy and Idaean vine,[15]
The clematis, the favour'd flower
Which boasts the name of virgin-bower,
And every hardy plant could bear
Loch Katrine's keen and searching air.
An instant in this porch she staid,   530
And gaily to the stranger said,
'On heaven and on thy lady call,
And enter the enchanted hall!'

XXVII

'My hope, my heaven, my trust must be,
My gentle guide, in following thee.'
He cross'd the threshold—and a clang
Of angry steel that instant rang.
To his bold brow his spirit rush'd,
But soon for vain alarm he blush'd
When on the floor he saw display'd,   540
Cause of the din, a naked blade
Dropp'd from the sheath, that careless flung,
Upon a stag's huge antlers swung;
For all around, the walls to grace,
Hung trophies of the fight or chase:
A target there, a bugle here,
A battle-axe, a hunting-spear,
And broadswords, bows, and arrows store,
With the tusk'd trophies of the boar.
Here grins the wolf as when he died,   550
And there the wild-cat's brindled hide
The frontlet of the elk adorns,
Or mantles o'er the bison's horns;
Pennons and flags defaced and stain'd,
That blackening streaks of blood retain'd,
And deer-skins, dappled, dun, and white,
With otter's fur and seal's unite,
In rude and uncouth tapestry all,
To garnish forth the silvan hall.

XXVIII

The wondering stranger round him gazed,   560
And next the fallen weapon raised:
Few were the arms whose sinewy strength
Sufficed to stretch it forth at length;
And as the brand he poised and sway'd,
'I never knew but one,' he said,
'Whose stalwart arm might brook to wield
A blade like this in battle-field.'
She sigh'd, then smiled and took the word:
'You see the guardian champion's sword;
As light it trembles in his hand,   570
As in my grasp a hazel wand;
My sire's tall form might grace the part

Of Ferragus or Ascabart;[16]
But in the absent giant's hold
Are women now, and menials old.'

XXIX

The mistress of the mansion came,
Mature of age, a graceful dame;[17]
Whose easy step and stately port
Had well become a princely court;
To whom, though more than kindred knew,   580
Young Ellen gave a mother's due.
Meet welcome to her guest she made,
And every courteous rite was paid
That hospitality could claim,
Though all unask'd his birth and name.[18]
Such then the reverence to a guest,
That fellest foe might join the feast,
And from his deadliest foeman's door
Unquestion'd turn, the banquet o'er.
At length his rank the stranger names,   590
'The Knight of Snowdoun, James Fitz-James;
Lord of a barren heritage,
Which his grave sires, from age to age,
By their good swords had held with toil;
His sire had fallen in such turmoil,
And he, God wot, was forced to stand
Oft for his right with blade in hand.
This morning, with Lord Moray's train,
He chased a stalwart stag in vain,
Outstripp'd his comrades, miss'd the deer,   600
Lost his good steed, and wander'd here.'

XXX

Fain would the Knight in turn require
The name and state of Ellen's sire.
Well show'd the elder lady's mien,
That courts and cities she had seen;
Ellen, though more her looks display'd
The simple grace of silvan maid,
In speech and gesture, form and face,
Show'd she was come of gentle race.
'Twere strange, in ruder rank to find   610
Such looks, such manners, and such mind.
Each hint the Knight of Snowdoun gave,
Dame Margaret heard with silence grave;
Or Ellen, innocently gay,
Turn'd all inquiry light away—
'Weird women we! by dale and down

---

16 giants celebrated in medieval fable.
17 She was the maternal aunt of Ellen.
18 The Highlanders, who carried hospitality to a punctilious excess, are said to have considered it as churlish to ask a stranger his name or lineage before he had taken refreshment. Feuds were so frequent among them, that a contrary rule would in many cases have produced the discovery of some circumstance which might have excluded the guest from the benefit of the assistance he stood in need of.—(Scott.)

---

15 *Idaean* is from *Ida,* a mountain near ancient Troy famous for its vines.

We dwell, afar from tower and town.
We stem the flood, we ride the blast,
On wandering knights our spells we cast;
While viewless minstrels touch the string,   620
'Tis thus our charmed rhymes we sing.'
She sung, and still a harp unseen
Fill'd up the symphony between.

XXXI

Song

'Soldier, rest! thy warfare o'er,
   Sleep the sleep that knows not breaking;
Dream of battled fields no more,
   Days of danger, nights of waking.
In our isle's enchanted hall,
   Hands unseen thy couch are strewing,
Fairy strains of music fall,   630
   Every sense in slumber dewing.
Soldier, rest! thy warfare o'er,
Dream of fighting fields no more;
Sleep the sleep that knows not breaking,
Morn of toil, nor night of waking.

'No rude sound shall reach thine ear,
   Armour's clang, or war-steed champing,
Trump nor pibroch[19] summon here
   Mustering clan, or squadron tramping.
Yet the lark's shrill fife may come   640
   At the day-break from the fallow,
And the bittern sound his drum,
   Booming from the sedgy shallow.
Ruder sounds shall none be near,
Guards nor warders challenge here,
Here's no war-steed's neigh and champing,
Shouting clans, or squadrons stamping.'

XXXII

She paused—then, blushing, led the lay
To grace the stranger of the day.
Her mellow notes awhile prolong   650
The cadence of the flowing song,
Till to her lips in measured frame
The minstrel verse spontaneous came:—

Song Continued

'Huntsman, rest! thy chase is done;
   While our slumbrous spells assail ye,
Dream not, with the rising sun,
   Bugles here shall sound reveillé.
Sleep! the deer is in his den;
   Sleep! thy hounds are by thee lying;
Sleep! nor dream in yonder glen,   660
   How thy gallant steed lay dying.

---

19 martial music played on the bagpipe.

Huntsman, rest! thy chase is done,
   Think not of the rising sun,
For at dawning to assail ye,
   Here no bugles sound reveillé.'

XXXIII

The hall was clear'd—the stranger's bed
Was there of mountain heather spread,
Where oft a hundred guests had lain,
And dream'd their forest sports again.
But vainly did the heath-flower shed   670
Its moorland fragrance round his head;
Not Ellen's spell had lull'd to rest
The fever of his troubled breast.
In broken dreams the image rose
Of varied perils, pains, and woes:
His steed now flounders in the brake,
Now sinks his barge upon the lake;
Now leader of a broken host,
His standard falls, his honour's lost.
Then,—from my couch may heavenly might   680
Chase that worst phantom of the night!—
Again return'd the scenes of youth,
Of confident undoubting truth;
Again his soul he interchanged
With friends whose hearts were long estranged.
They come, in dim procession led,
The cold, the faithless, and the dead;
As warm each hand, each brow as gay,
As if they parted yesterday.
And doubt distracts him at the view—   690
O were his senses false or true?
Dream'd he of death, or broken vow,
Or is it all a vision now?

XXXIV

At length, with Ellen in a grove
He seem'd to walk, and speak of love;
She listen'd with a blush and sigh,
His suit was warm, his hopes were high.
He sought her yielded hand to clasp,
And a cold gauntlet met his grasp:
The phantom's sex was changed and gone,   700
Upon its head a helmet shone;
Slowly enlarged to giant size,
With darken'd cheek and threatening eyes,
The grisly visage, stern and hoar,
To Ellen still a likeness bore.
He woke, and, panting with affright,
Recall'd the vision of the night.
The hearth's decaying brands were red,
And deep and dusky lustre shed,
Half showing, half concealing, all   710
The uncouth trophies of the hall.
'Mid those the stranger fix'd his eye,

Where that huge falchion hung on high,
And thoughts on thoughts, a countless throng,
Rush'd, chasing countless thoughts along,
Until, the giddy whirl to cure,
He rose, and sought the moonshine pure.

XXXV

The wild-rose, eglantine, and broom,
Wasted around their rich perfume;
The birch-trees wept in fragrant balm,   720
The aspens slept beneath the calm;
The silver light, with quivering glance,
Play'd on the water's still expanse:
Wild were the heart whose passion's sway
Could rage beneath the sober ray!
He felt its calm, that warrior guest,
While thus he communed with his breast:
'Why is it, at each turn I trace
Some memory of that exiled race?
Can I not mountain-maiden spy,   730
But she must bear the Douglas eye?
Can I not view a Highland brand,
But it must match the Douglas hand?
Can I not frame a fever'd dream,
But still the Douglas is the theme?
I'll dream no more; by manly mind
Not even in sleep is will resign'd.
My midnight orisons said o'er,
I'll turn to rest, and dream no more.'
His midnight orisons he told,   740
A prayer with every bead of gold,
Consign'd to heaven his cares and woes,
And sunk in undisturb'd repose;
Until the heath-cock shrilly crew,
And morning dawn'd on Benvenue.

1809–10   1810

CANTO 2

HAIL TO THE CHIEF WHO IN TRIUMPH ADVANCES!

[The song] is intended as an imitation of the *jorrams,*
or boat songs, of the Highlanders, which were usually
composed in honour of a favourite chief. They are so
adapted as to keep time with the sweep of the oars, and
it is easy to distinguish between those intended to be
sung to the oars of a galley, where the stroke is lengthened and doubled, as it were, and those which were
timed to the rowers of an ordinary boat.—(Scott.)

'HAIL to the Chief who in triumph advances!
    Honour'd and bless'd be the evergreen Pine!
Long may the tree, in his banner that glances,
    Flourish, the shelter and grace of our line!
        Heaven send it happy dew,
        Earth lend it sap anew,
Gayly to bourgeon, and broadly to grow,

While every Highland glen
    Sends our shout back agen,
Roderigh Vich Alpine dhu, ho! ieroe![1]   10

Ours is no sapling, chance-sown by the fountain,
    Blooming at Beltane,[2] in winter to fade;
When the whirlwind has stripp'd every leaf on
    the mountain,
    The more shall Clan-Alpine exult in her shade,
        Moor'd in the rifted rock,
        Proof to the tempest's shock,
Firmer he roots him the ruder it blow;
        Menteith and Breadalbane, then,
        Echo his praise agen,
Roderigh Vich Alpine dhu, ho! ieroe!   20

'Proudly our pibroch has thrill'd in Glen Fruin,
    And Bannochar's groans to our slogan replied;
Glen Luss and Ross-dhu, they are smoking in
    ruin,
    And the best of Loch Lomond lie dead on her
    side.
        Widow and Saxon maid
        Long shall lament our raid,
Think of Clan-Alpine with fear and with woe;
        Lennox and Leven-glen
        Shake when they hear agen,
Roderigh Vich Alpine dhu, ho! iero!   30

'Row, vassals, row, for the pride of the High-
    lands!
    Stretch to your oars, for the evergreen Pine!
O! that the rose-bud that graces yon islands
    Were wreathed in a garland around him to
    twine!
        O that some seedling gem,
        Worthy such noble stem,
Honour'd and bless'd in their shadow might
    grow!
        Loud should Clan-Alpine then
        Ring from her deepmost glen,
Roderigh Vich Alpine dhu, ho! ieroe!'   40

                                          1810

CANTO 3

CORONACH

The *Coronach* of the Highlanders, like the *Ulalatus* of
the Romans, and the *Ululoo* of the Irish, was a wild expression of lamentation, poured forth by the mourners

---

1 The line signifies. 'Black Roderick, the descendant of Alpine.'
—(Scott.)
2 May Day.

over the body of a departed friend. When the words of it were articulate, they expressed the praises of the deceased, and the loss the clan would sustain by his death. ... The coronach has for some years past been superseded at funerals by the use of the bagpipe; and that also is, like many other Highland peculiarities, falling into disuse, unless in remote districts.—(Scott.)

'HE is gone on the mountain,
 He is lost to the forest,
Like a summer-dried fountain,
 When our need was the sorest.
The font, reappearing,
 From the rain-drops shall borrow,
But to us comes no cheering,
 To Duncan no morrow!

The hand of the reaper
 Takes the ears that are hoary,   10
But the voice of the weeper
 Wails manhood in glory.
The autumn winds rushing
 Waft the leaves that are searest,
But our flower was in flushing,[1]
 When blighting was nearest.

Fleet foot on the correi,[2]
 Sage counsel in cumber,[3]
Red hand in the foray,
 How sound is thy slumber!   20
Like the dew on the mountain,
 Like the foam on the river,
Like the bubble on the fountain,
 Thou art gone, and for ever!'

                1810

CANTO 3

HYMN TO THE VIRGIN

'AVE Maria! maiden mild!
 Listen to a maiden's prayer!
Thou canst hear though from the wild,
 Thou canst save amid despair.
Safe may we sleep beneath thy care,
 Though banish'd, outcast, and reviled;
Maiden! hear a maiden's prayer—
 Mother, hear a suppliant child!
                Ave Maria!

Ave Maria! undefiled!   10
 The flinty couch we now must share
Shall seem with down of eider piled,
 If thy protection hover there.
The murky cavern's heavy air

Shall breathe of balm if thou hast smiled;
Then, Maiden! hear a maiden's prayer;
 Mother, list a suppliant child!
                Ave Maria!

Ave Maria! stainless styled!
 Foul demons of the earth and air,   20
From this their wonted haunt exiled,
 Shall flee before thy presence fair.
We bow us to our lot of care,
 Beneath thy guidance reconciled;
Hear for a maid a maiden's prayer,
 And for a father hear a child!
                Ave Maria!'

                1810

CANTO 4

THE TOILS ARE PITCHED

'THE toils[1] are pitch'd, and the stakes are set,
 Ever sing merrily, merrily;
The bows they bend, and the knives they whet,
 Hunters live so cheerily.

'It was a stag, a stag of ten,[2]
 Bearing its branches sturdily;
He came stately down the glen,
 Ever sing hardily, hardily.

'It was there he met with a wounded doe,
 She was bleeding deathfully;   10
She warn'd him of the toils below,
 O, so faithfully, faithfully!

'He had an eye, and he could heed,
 Ever sing warily, warily;
He had a foot, and he could speed—
 Hunters watch so narrowly.'

                1810

From ROKEBY

CANTO 3

BRIGNALL BANKS[1]

O, BRIGNAL banks are wild and fair,
 And Greta woods are green,

---

1 in full bloom.   2 a hillside where game lies hidden.
3 trouble.

1 nets.   2 Having ten branches on his antlers.—(Scott.)

1 The banks of the Greta [a river in Yorkshire], below Rutherford Bridge, abound in seams of greyish slate, which are wrought in some places to a very great depth under ground, thus forming artificial caverns, which, when the seam has been exhausted, are gradually hidden by the underwood which grows in profusion upon the romantic banks of the river. In times of public confusion, they might be well adapted to the purposes of banditti.—(Scott.)

And you may gather garlands there
  Would grace a summer queen.
And as I rode by Dalton-hall,
  Beneath the turrets high,
A maiden on the castle wall
  Was singing merrily,—
'O, Brignal banks are fresh and fair,
  And Greta woods are green;   10
I'd rather rove with Edmund there,
  Than reign our English queen.'

'If, maiden, thou wouldst wend with me,
  To leave both tower and town,
Thou first must guess what life lead we,
  That dwell by dale and down.
And if thou canst that riddle read,
  As read full well you may,
Then to the greenwood shalt thou speed,
  As blithe as Queen of May.'   20
Yet sung she, 'Brignal banks are fair,
  And Greta woods are green;
I'd rather rove with Edmund there,
  Than reign our English queen.

'I read you, by your bugle-horn,
  And by your palfrey good,
I read you for a ranger sworn,
  To keep the king's greenwood.'
'A ranger, lady, winds his horn,
  And 'tis at peep of light;   30
His blast is heard at merry morn,
  And mine at dead of night.'
Yet sung she, 'Brignal banks are fair,
  And Greta woods are gay;
I would I were with Edmund there,
  To reign his Queen of May!

'With burnish'd brand and musketoon,[2]
  So gallantly you come,
I read you for a bold dragoon,
  That lists the tuck of drum.'   40
'I list no more the tuck of drum,
  No more the trumpet hear;
But when the beetle sounds his hum,
  My comrades take the spear.
And O! though Brignal banks be fair,
  And Greta woods be gay,
Yet mickle must the maiden dare,
  Would reign my Queen of May!

'Maiden! a nameless life I lead,
  A nameless death I'll die;   50
The fiend, whose lantern lights the mead,

  Were better mate than I!
And when I'm with my comrades met
  Beneath the greenwood bough,
What once we were we all forget,
  Nor think what we are now.
Yet Brignal banks are fresh and fair,
  And Greta woods are green,
And you may gather garlands there
  Would grace a summer queen.'   60
1812   1813

Canto 3

ALLEN-A-DALE

ALLEN-A-DALE has no fagot for burning,
Allen-a-Dale has no furrow for turning,
Allen-a-Dale has no fleece for the spinning,
Yet Allen-a-Dale has red gold for the winning.
Come, read me my riddle! come, hearken my
  tale!
And tell me the craft of bold Allen-a-Dale.

The Baron of Ravensworth prances in pride,
And he views his domains upon Arkindale side;
The mere[1] for his net, and the land for his game,
The chase for the wild, and the park for the
  tame;   10
Yet the fish of the lake, and the deer of the vale,
Are less free to Lord Dacre than Allen-a-Dale!

Allen-a-Dale was ne'er belted a knight,
Though his spur be as sharp, and his blade be as
  bright;
Allen-a-Dale is no baron, or lord,
Yet twenty tall yeomen will draw at his word;
And the best of our nobles his bonnet will vail,[2]
Who at Rere-cross on Stanmore meets Allen-a-
  Dale.

Allen-a-Dale to his wooing is come;
The mother, she ask'd of his household and
  home: 20
'Though the castle of Richmond stand fair on the
  hill,
My hall,' quoth bold Allen, 'shows gallanter still;
'Tis the blue vault of heaven, with its crescent so
  pale,
And with all its bright spangles!' said Allen-a-
  Dale.

The father was steel, and the mother was stone;
They lifted the latch, and they bade him be
  gone;

---

2 short musket.   1 lake.   2 take off.

But loud, on the morrow, their wail and their
    cry:
He had laugh'd on the lass with his bonny black
    eye,
And she fled to the forest to hear a love-tale,
And the youth it was told by was Allen-a-
    Dale!   30

                    1830

From WAVERLEY

CHAPTER 12

HIE AWAY, HIE AWAY

[The voice of Davie Gellatley, a simple-minded youth,
is heard in a court singing to his two large deer grey-
hounds.]

HIE away, hie away,
Over bank and over brae,
Where the copsewood is the greenest,
Where the fountains glisten sheenest,
Where the lady-fern grows strongest,
Where the morning dew lies longest,
Where the black-cock sweetest sips it,
Where the fairy latest trips it:
Hie to haunts right seldom seen,
Lovely, lonesome, cool, and green.   10
Over bank and over brae,
Hie away, hie away.

                    1814

From GUY MANNERING

CHAPTER 4

TWIST YE, TWINE YE! EVEN SO

[Sung by Meg Merrilies, a gypsy, as she spins her
charm over a newborn child.]

TWIST ye, twine ye! even so
Mingle shades of joy and woe,
Hope, and fear, and peace, and strife,
In the thread of human life.

While the mystic twist is spinning,
And the infant's life beginning,
Dimly seen through twilight bending,
Lo, what varied shapes attending!

Passions wild, and follies vain,
Pleasures soon exchanged for pain;   10
Doubt, and jealousy, and fear,
In the magic dance appear.

Now they wax, and now they dwindle,
Whirling with the whirling spindle.

Twist ye, twine ye! even so
Mingle human bliss and woe.

                    1815

CHAPTER 27

WASTED, WEARY, WHEREFORE STAY

[A prayer, or spell, sung by Meg Merrilies to speed the
passage of a dying smuggler, *Guy Mannering,* Chapter
27.]

WASTED, weary, wherefore stay,
Wrestling thus with earth and clay?
From the body pass away;—
    Hark! the mass is singing.

From thee doff thy mortal weed,
Mary Mother be thy speed,
Saints to help thee at thy need;—
    Hark! the knell is ringing.

Fear not snowdrift driving fast,
Sleet, or hail, or levin[1] blast;   10
Soon the shroud shall lap thee fast,
And the sleep be on thee cast
    That shall ne'er know waking.

Haste thee, haste thee, to be gone,
Earth flits fast, and time draws on,—
Gasp thy gasp, and groan thy groan,
    Day is near the breaking.

                    1815

LULLABY OF AN INFANT CHIEF

AIR—'*Cadul gu lo*'[1]

O HUSH thee, my babie, thy sire was a knight,
Thy mother a lady, both lovely and bright;
The woods and the glens, from the towers which
    we see,
They all are belonging, dear babie, to thee.
    O ho ro, i ri ri, cadul gu lo,
    O ho ro, i ri ri, &c.

O fear not the bugle, though loudly it blows,
It calls but the warders that guard thy repose;
Their bows would be bended, their blades would
    be red,
Ere the step of a foeman drew near to thy
    bed.   10
    O ho ro, i ri ri, &c.

---

1 lightning.

---

1 'Sleep on till day.'

O hush thee, my babie, the time soon will come
When thy sleep shall be broken by trumpet and
    drum;
Then hush thee, my darling, take rest while you
    may,
For strife comes with manhood, and waking with
    day.
        O ho ro, i ri ri, &c.

                      1815

JOCK OF HAZELDEAN

[The first stanza is from an old Scotch ballad.]

'WHY weep ye by the tide, ladie?
    Why weep ye by the tide?
I'll wed ye to my youngest son,
    And ye sall be his bride:
And ye sall be his bride, ladie,
    Sae comely to be seen'—
But aye she loot the tears down fa'
    For Jock of Hazeldean.

'Now let this wilfu' grief be done,
    And dry that cheek so pale;   10
Young Frank is chief of Errington,
    And lord of Langley-dale;
His step is first in peaceful ha','[1]
    His sword in battle keen'—
But aye she loot the tears down fa'
    For Jock of Hazeldean.

'A chain of gold ye sall not lack,
    Nor braid to bind your hair;
Nor mettled[2] hound, nor managed[3] hawk,
    Nor palfrey fresh and fair;   20
And you, the foremost o' them a',
    Shall ride our forest queen'—
But aye she loot the tears down fa'
    For Jock of Hazeldean.

The kirk was deck'd at morning-tide,
    The tapers glimmer'd fair;
The priest and bridegroom wait the bride,
    And dame and knight are there.
They sought her baith by bower and ha';
    The ladie was not seen!   30
She's o'er the Border, and awa'
    Wi' Jock of Hazeldean.

                      1816

---

1 hall.
2 spirited.
3 trained.

PIBROCH OF DONUIL DHU

This is a very ancient pibroch belonging to Clan Mac-
Donald, and supposed to refer to the expedition of Donald Balloch, who, in 1431, launched from the Isles with a
considerable force, invaded Lochaber, and at Inverlochy
defeated and put to flight the Earls of Mar and Caithness, though at the head of an army superior to his own.
—(Scott.)

PIBROCH[1] of Donuil Dhu,
    Pibroch of Donuil,
Wake thy wild voice anew,
    Summon Clan-Conuil.
Come away, come away,
    Hark to the summons!
Come in your war array,
    Gentles and commons.

Come from deep glen, and
    From mountain so rocky,   10
The war-pipe and pennon
    Are at Inverlochy.
Come every hill-plaid, and
    True heart that wears one,
Come every steel blade, and
    Strong hand that bears one.

Leave untended the herd,
    The flock without shelter;
Leave the corpse uninterr'd,
    The bride at the altar;   20
Leave the deer, leave the steer,
    Leave nets and barges
Come with your fighting gear,
    Broadswords and targes.

Come as the winds come, when
    Forests are rended,
Come as the waves come, when
    Navies are stranded:
Faster come, faster come,
    Faster and faster,   30
Chief, vassal, page and groom,
    Tenant and master.

Fast they come, fast they come;
    See how they gather!
Wide waves the eagle plume,
    Blended with heather.
Cast your plaids, draw your blades,
    Forward, each man, set!
Pibroch of Donuil Dhu,
    Knell for the onset!   40

                      1816

---

1 wild, heart-stirring music of the bagpipe.

From THE ANTIQUARY

CHAPTER 10

WHY SIT'ST THOU BY THAT RUIN'D HALL

'WHY sit'st thou by that ruin'd hall,
    Thou aged carle so stern and grey?
Dost thou its former pride recall,
    Or ponder how it pass'd away?'—

'Know'st thou not me?' the Deep Voice[1] cried;
    'So long enjoy'd, so oft misused—
Alternate, in thy fickle pride,
    Desired, neglected, and accused!

'Before my breath, like blazing flax,
    Man and his marvels pass away!   10
And changing empires wane and wax,
    Are founded, flourish, and decay.

'Redeem mine hours—the space is brief—
    While in my glass the sand-grains shiver,
And measureless thy joy or grief
    When TIME and thou shalt part for ever!'
                                        1816

From OLD MORTALITY

CHAPTER 19

AND WHAT THOUGH WINTER WILL PINCH SEVERE

[Sung by Major Bellenden, in a time of adversity.]

AND what though winter will pinch severe
    Through locks of grey and a cloak that's old,
Yet keep up thy heart, bold cavalier,
    For a cup of sack shall fence the cold.

For time will rust the brightest blade,
    And years will break the strongest bow;
Was never wight so starkly made,
    But time and years would overthrow.
                                        1816

From THE HEART OF MIDLOTHIAN

CHAPTER 40

PROUD MAISIE

[Sung by the crazed Madge Wildfire as she lay dying.]

PROUD Maisie is in the wood,
    Walking so early;
Sweet Robin sits on the bush,
    Singing so rarely.

---
1 The 'Deep Voice' is that of Time.

'Tell me, thou bonny bird,
    When shall I marry me?'
'When six braw[1] gentlemen
    Kirkward shall carry ye.'

'Who makes the bridal bed,
    Birdie, say truly?'   10
'The grey-headed sexton
    That delves the grave duly.

'The glow-worm o'er grave and stone
    Shall light thee steady.
The owl from the steeple sing,
    "Welcome, proud lady." '
                                        1818

From THE BRIDE OF LAMMERMOOR

CHAPTER 3

LUCY ASHTON'S SONG: 'LOOK NOT THOU ON BEAUTY'S CHARMING'

LOOK not thou on beauty's charming,
Sit thou still when kings are arming,
Taste not when the wine-cup glistens,
Speak not when the people listens,
Stop thine ear against the singer,
From the red gold keep thy finger;
Vacant heart and hand and eye,
Easy live and quiet die.
                                        1819

From THE LEGEND OF MONTROSE

CHAPTER 6

ANNOT LYLE'S SONG: 'BIRDS OF OMEN'

BIRDS of omen dark and foul,
Night-crow, raven, bat, and owl,
Leave the sick man to his dream—
All night long he heard your scream.
Haste to cave and ruin'd tower,
Ivy tod,[1] or dingled-bower,[2]
There to wink and mope, for, hark!
In the mild air sings the lark.

Hie to moorish gills and rocks,
Prowling wolf and wily fox;   10
Hie ye fast, nor turn your view,
Though the lamb bleats to the ewe.
Couch your trains, and speed your flight,

---
1 brave; handsome.

---
1 ivy bush.
2 a bower secluded in a valley.

Safety parts with parting night;
And on distant echo borne,
Comes the hunter's early horn.

The moon's wan crescent scarcely gleams,
Ghost-like she fades in morning beams:
Hie hence, each peevish imp and fay
That scare the pilgrim on his way.   20
Quench, kelpie! [3] quench, in bog and fen,
Thy torch, that cheats benighted men;
Thy dance is o'er, thy reign is done,
For Ben-y-glow hath seen the sun.

Wild thoughts that, sinful, dark, and deep,
O'erpower the passive mind in sleep,
Pass from the slumberer's soul away,
Like night-mists from the brow of day:
Foul hag, whose blasted visage grim
Smothers the pulse, unnerves the limb,   30
Spur thy dark palfrey, and begone!
Thou dar'st not face the godlike sun.

                                                      1819

From IVANHOE

CHAPTER 39

REBECCA'S HYMN

WHEN Israel, of the Lord beloved,
   Out from the land of bondage came,
Her fathers' God before her moved,
   An awful guide in smoke and flame.
By day, along the astonish'd lands
   The cloudy pillar glided slow;
By night, Arabia's crimson'd sands
   Return'd the fiery column's glow.

There rose the choral hymn of praise,
   And trump and timbrel answer'd keen,   10
And Zion's daughters pour'd their lays,
   With priest's and warrior's voice between.
No portents now our foes amaze,
   Forsaken Israel wanders lone:
Our fathers would not know Thy ways,
   And Thou hast left them to their own.

But present still, though now unseen!
   When brightly shines the prosperous day,
Be thoughts of Thee a cloudy screen
   To temper the deceitful ray.   20
And oh, when stoops on Judah's path
   In shade and storm the frequent night,

Be Thou, long-suffering, slow to wrath,
   A burning and a shining light!

Our harps we left by Babel's[1] streams,
   The tyrant's jest, the Gentile's scorn;
No censer round our altar beams,
   And mute are timbrel, harp, and horn.
But Thou hast said, The blood of goat,
   The flesh of rams I will not prize;   30
A contrite heart, a humble thought,
   Are mine accepted sacrifice.

                                                      1819

From THE MONASTERY

CHAPTER 25

BORDER MARCH

MARCH, march, Ettrick and Teviotdale,
   Why the deil dinna ye march forward in order?
March, march, Eskdale and Liddesdale,
   All the Blue Bonnets are bound for the Border.
      Many a banner spread,
      Flutters above your head,
   Many a crest that is famous in story.
      Mount and make ready then,
      Sons of the mountain glen,
   Fight for the Queen[1] and the old Scottish
      glory.   10

Come from the hills where your hirsels[2] are
      grazing,
   Come from the glen of the buck and the roe;
Come to the crag where the beacon is blazing,
   Come with the buckler, the lance, and the bow.
      Trumpets are sounding,
      War-steeds are bounding,
   Stand to your arms then, and march in good
      order;
      England shall many a day
      Tell of the bloody fray,
   When the Blue Bonnets came over the
      Border.   20

                                                      1820

From THE DOOM OF DEVORGOIL

ACT II, SCENE 2

BONNY DUNDEE

[Bonny Dundee was John Graham of Claverhouse,
Viscount Dundee, a staunch supporter of the Stuart

---

3 water spirit.

1 Babylonia's.

1 Mary Stuart, Queen of Scots, 1542-89.   2 herds; flocks.

kings, Charles II and James II. After James's flight into
France, Dundee supported his cause even to defying the
Scottish Parliament (the 'Lords of Convention'), who
had accepted William. After attempting without success
to persuade the Duke of Gordon to hold Edinburgh
Castle for James, he retired to the Highlands, where he
organized the chiefs against the government. In the battle of Killiecrankie the Highlanders won a victory over
William, but in the act of encouraging his men Dundee
was mortally wounded and died on the night of the battle.]

To the Lords of Convention 'twas Claver'se who
    spoke,
'Ere the King's crown shall fall there are crowns
    to be broke;
So let each Cavalier who loves honour and me,
Come follow the bonnet of Bonny Dundee.

    'Come fill up my cup, come fill up my can,
    Come saddle your horses, and call up your
      men;
    Come open the West Port, and let me gang
      free,
    And it's room for the bonnets of Bonny Dun-
      dee!'

Dundee he is mounted, he rides up the street,
The bells are rung backward,[1] the drums they are
    beat;   10
But the Provost, douce[2] man, said, 'Just e'en let
    him be,
The Gude Town is weel quit of that Deil of
    Dundee.'
    Come fill up my cup, &c.

As he rode down the sanctified bends of the
    Bow,[3]
Ilk carline[4] was flyting[5] and shaking her pow;[6]
But the young plants of grace they look'd couthie
    and slee,[7]
Thinking, 'Luck to thy bonnet, thou Bonny
    Dundee!'
    Come fill up my cup, &c.

With sour-featured Whigs the Grass-market[8]
    was cramm'd
As if half the West had set tryst to be hang'd; 20
There was spite in each look, there was fear in
    each e'e,

As they watch'd for the bonnets of Bonny Dun-
    dee.
    Come fill up my cup, &c.

These cowls of Kilmarnock[9] had spits[10] and had
    spears,
And lang-hafted gullies[11] to kill Cavaliers;
But they shrunk to close-heads,[12] and the cause-
    way was free,
At the toss of the bonnet of Bonny Dundee.
    Come fill up my cup, &c.

He spurr'd to the foot of the proud Castle rock,[13]
And with the gay Gordon he gallantly spoke; 30
'Let Mons Meg[14] and her marrows[15] speak twa
    words or three,
For the love of the bonnet of Bonny Dundee.'
    Come fill up my cup, &c.

The Gordon demands of him which way he
    goes—
'Where'er shall direct me the shade of Mont-
    rose![16]
Your Grace in short space shall hear tidings of
    me,
Or that low lies the bonnet of Bonny Dundee.
    Come fill up my cup, &c.

'There are hills beyond Pentland, and lands be-
    yond Forth,
If there's lords in the Lowlands, there's chiefs in
    the North;   40
There are wild Duniewassals,[17] three thousand
    times three,
Will cry *hoigh!* for the bonnet of Bonny Dundee.
    Come fill up my cup, &c.

'There's brass on the target[18] of barken'd bull-
    hide;[19]
There's steel in the scabbard that dangles beside;
The brass shall be burnish'd, the steel shall flash
    free,
At a toss of the bonnet of Bonny Dundee.
    Come fill up my cup, &c.

---

1 The chimes are rung backward in sign of alarm.
2 serene; prudent.
3 the windings of Bow Street, called sanctified because they were occupied mainly by Covenanters.
4 every old woman.   5 scolding.
6 head.   7 loving and sly.
8 a public square in Edinburgh where executions formerly took place.

9 hooded garments made at Kilmarnock, worn by the Presby-terians.
10 swords.   11 long-handled knives.
12 blind alleys.   13 Edinburgh castle.
14 nickname of a huge cannon. 15 companions.
16 The Marquis of Montrose, a royalist supporter, who was cap-tured and executed by the Covenanters in 1650.
17 Highlandmen in the service of the chiefs.
18 shield.   19 hide tanned with bark.

'Away to the hills, to the caves, to the rocks—
Ere I own an usurper, I'll couch with the fox; 50
And tremble, false Whigs, in the midst of your
     glee,
You have not seen the last of my bonnet and
     me!'

Come fill up my cup, &c.

He waved his proud hand, and the trumpets were
     blown,
The kettle-drums clash'd, and the horsemen rode
     on,
Till on Ravelston's cliffs and on Clermiston's lee,
Died away the wild war-notes of Bonny Dundee.

Come fill up my cup, come fill up my can,
Come saddle the horses and call up the men,
Come open your gates, and let me gae free, 60
For it's up with the bonnets of Bonny Dundee!

1825   1830

From REDGAUNTLET

CHAPTER 11

WANDERING WILLIE'S TALE

[*Redgauntlet*, 1824, is an historical novel centering
around an apocryphal return of the Stuart pretender,
Charles Edward, to England some years after 1745 to try
once more his cause, an attempt that ends in failure. The
leader of the movement is Mr. Redgauntlet, a fanatical
Jacobite and a descendant of the Redgauntlet in *Wandering Willie's Tale*. His nephew, Darsie Latimer, is the
hero of the novel and, unknown to himself, head of the
house of Redgauntlet. Wandering Willie, a blind fiddler
and ballad singer, tells his tale to Darsie as the two
tramp across a downs to a village frolic near the ancestral home. The Steenie Steenson of the story is the grandfather of Wandering Willie; hence the events of the narrative relate to the families of both men.

The proof sheets of *Wandering Willie's Tale* show that
Scott made many amendments of the original, an indication of the exceptional pains he took with it. As a result
of this care, the finished product is generally accounted
among the author's highest achievements in the supernatural and one of the best stories of its kind in the
world. Especially noteworthy is the adroitness with
which Scott seemingly eliminates the border line between the real and the occult world. John Buchan has
pointed out how Wandering Willie in telling the tale
gives two different versions of the crucial incident of the
receipt, 'one which allows for prosaic explanation and a
second, in flat contradiction and full of excited detail,
which transports the whole affair into the realm of the
occult.' The attentive reader will easily discover other
examples that reveal Scott's acute observation of human
psychology and his consummate art as a storyteller.]

YE maun[1] have heard of Sir Robert Redgauntlet of that Ilk,[2] who lived in these parts before the
dear years.[3] The country will lang mind him;
and our fathers used to draw breath thick if ever
they heard him named. He was out wi' the Hie-
landmen in Montrose's time; and again he was
in the hills wi' Glencairn in the sixteen hundred and fifty-twa; and sae when King Charles
the Second came in, wha was in sic favour as
the Laird of Redgauntlet?[4] He was knighted at
London court, wi' the King's ain sword; and
being a redhot prelatist,[5] he came down here,
rampauging like a lion, with commissions of
lieutenancy, (and of lunacy, for what I ken,) to
put down a' the Whigs and Covenanters in the
country. Wild wark they made of it; for the
Whigs were as dour[6] as the Cavaliers were fierce,
and it was which should first tire the other. Redgauntlet was aye for the strong hand, and his
name is kend[7] as wide in the country as Claverhouse's[8] or Tam Dalyell's.[9] Glen, nor dargle,[10]
nor mountain, nor cave, could hide the puir
hill-folk when Redgauntlet was out with bugle
and bloodhound after them, as if they had been
sae mony deer. And troth, when they fand them,
they didna mak muckle[11] mair ceremony than a
Hielandman wi' a roebuck—It was just, 'Will ye
tak the test?'[12]—if not, 'Make ready—present—
fire!'—and there lay the recusant.[13]

Far and wide was Sir Robert hated and feared.
Men thought he had a direct compact with Satan
—that he was proof against steel—and that bullets happed aff his buff-coat like hailstanes from
a hearth—that he had a mear that would turn a
hare on the   side of Carrifra-gawns[14]—and
muckle to the same purpose, of whilk[15] mair
anon. The best blessing they wared on him was,
'Deil scowp[16] wi' Red-gauntlet!' He wasna a bad
master to his ain folk though, and was weel
aneugh liked by his tenants; and as for the
lackies[17] and troopers that raid out wi' him to the

---

1 must.   2 same name.
3 hard times.
4 Sir Robert was a Cavalier fighting with Montrose and Glencairn against the Puritans; accordingly he was rewarded when the
Stuarts were restored.
5 supporter of the Church of England.
6 stubborn.   7 known.
8 Col. John Graham of Claverhouse, afterward Viscount Dundee. See Scott's *Bonny Dundee*, text p. 550.
9 Thomas Dalyell, 1599–1685, was a British general, who participated in the Royalist rebellion in the highlands of Scotland in
1654.
10 dell.   11 much.
12 take the oath of loyalty to Church and King.
13 dissenter; nonconformist.
14 A precipitous side of a mountain in Moffatdale.—(Scott.)
15 which.   16 make away.
17 camp followers.

persecutions, as the Whigs caa'd those killing times, they wad hae drunken themsells blind to his health at ony time.

Now you are to ken that my gudesire lived on Redgauntlet's grund—they ca' the place Primrose-Knowe. We had lived on the grund, and under the Redgauntlets, since the riding days,[18] and lang before. It was a pleasant bit; and I think the air is callerer[19] and fresher there than ony where else in the country. It's a' deserted now; and I sat on the broken door-cheek three days since, and was I glad I couldna see the plight the place was in; but that's a' wide o' the mark. There dwelt my gudesire, Steenie Steenson, a rambling, rattling chiel'[20] he had been in his young days, and could play weel on the pipes; he was famous at 'Hoopers and Girders'—a' Cumberland couldna touch him at 'Jockie Lattin'—and he had the finest finger for the back-lilt between Berwick and Carlisle. The like o' Steenie wasna the sort that they made Whigs o'. And so he became a Tory, as they ca' it, which we now ca' Jacobites, just out of a kind of needcessity, that he might belang to some side or other. He had nae ill-will to the Whig bodies, and liked little to see the blude rin, though, being obliged to follow Sir Robert in hunting and hosting,[21] watching and warding, he saw muckle mischief, and maybe did some, that he couldna avoid.

Now Steenie was a kind of favourite with his master, and kend a' the folks about the castle, and was often sent for to play the pipes when they were at their merriment. Auld Dougal MacCallum, the butler, that had followed Sir Robert through gude and ill, thick and thin, pool and stream, was specially fond of the pipes, and aye gae[22] my gudesire his gude word wi' the Laird; for Dougal could turn his master round his finger.

Weel, round came the Revolution, and it had like to have broken the hearts baith of Dougal and his master. But the change was not a'thegether sae great as they feared, and other folk thought for. The Whigs made an unco crawing[23] what they wad do with their auld enemies, and in special wi' Sir Robert Redgauntlet. But there were ower mony great folks dipped in the same doings, to make a spick and span new warld. So Parliament passed it a'ower easy; and Sir Robert, bating[24] that he was held to hunting foxes

instead of Covenanters, remained just the man he was. His revel was as loud, and his hall as weel lighted, as ever it had been, though maybe he lacked the fines of the nonconformists, that used to come to stock his larder and cellar; for it is certain he began to be keener about the rents than his tenants used to find him before, and they behoved to be prompt to the rent-day, or else the Laird wasna pleased. And he was sic an awsome body that naebody cared to anger him; for the oaths he swore, and the rage that he used to get into, and the looks that he put on, made men sometimes think him a devil incarnate.

Weel, my gudesire was nae manager—no that he was a very great misguider,—but he hadna the saving gift, and he got twa terms' rent in arrear. He got the first brash[25] at Whitsunday put ower wi' fair word and piping; but when Martinmas came, there was a summons from the grund-officer[26] to come wi' the rent on a day preceese, or else Steenie behoved to flit. Sair wark he had to get the siller; but he was weel-freended, and at last he got the haill scraped thegither—a thousand merks—the maist of it was from a neighbour they caa'd Laurie Lapraik—a sly tod.[27] Laurie had walth o' gear[28]— could hunt wi' the hound and rin wi' the hare— and be Whig or Tory, saunt or sinner, as the wind stood. He was a professor[29] in this Revolution warld; but he liked an orra sough[30] of this warld, and a tune on the pipes weel aneugh at a by time; and abune a',[31] he thought he had gude security for the siller he lent my gudesire ower the stocking at Primrose-Knowe.

Away trots my gudesire to Redgauntlet Castle wi' a heavy purse and a light heart, glad to be out of the Laird's danger. Weel, the first thing he learned at the Castle was, that Sir Robert had fretted himsell into a fit of the gout, because he did not appear before twelve o'clock. It wasna a'thegether for sake of the money, Dougal thought, but because he didna like to part wi' my gudesire aff the grund. Dougal was glad to see Steenie, and brought him into the great oak parlour, and there sat the Laird his leesome lane,[32] excepting that he had beside him a great, ill-favoured jackanape,[33] that was a special pet of his; a cankered beast it was, and mony an ill-natured trick it played—ill to please it was, and

18 persecution times. 19 cooler. 20 fellow. 21 military mustering. 22 always gave. 23 uncommon crawing. 24 except. 25 outburst of anger. 26 overseer. 27 fox. 28 property. 29 that is, he pretended to be religious. 30 other tune. 31 above all. 32 all alone. 33 monkey.

easily angered—ran about the haill castle, chattering and yowling, and pinching, and biting folk, specially before ill-weather or disturbances in the state. Sir Robert caa'd it Major Weir,[34] after the warlock that was burnt; and few folk liked either the name or the conditions of the creature—they thought there was something in it by ordinar[35]—and my gudesire was not just easy in his mind when the door shut on him, and he saw himself in the room wi' naebody but the Laird, Dougal MacCallum, and the Major, a thing that hadna chanced to him before.

Sir Robert sat, or I should say, lay, in a great armed chair, wi' his grand velvet gown, and his feet on a cradle; for he had baith gout and gravel, and his face looked as gash[36] and ghastly as Satan's. Major Weir sat opposite to him, in a red laced coat, and the Laird's wig on his head; and aye as Sir Robert girned[37] wi' pain, the jackanape girned too, like a sheep's-head between a pair of tangs—an ill-faur'd,[38] fearsome couple they were. The Laird's buff-coat was hung on a pin behind him, and his broadsword and his pistols within reach; for he keepit up the auld fashion of having the weapons ready, and a horse saddled day and night, just as he used to do when he was able to loup[39] on horse-back, and away after ony of the hill-folk he could get speerings[40] of. Some said it was for fear of the Whigs taking vengeance, but I judge it was just his auld custom—he wasna gien to fear ony thing. The rental-book, wi' its black cover and brass clasps, was lying beside him; and a book of sculduddry sangs[41] was put betwixt the leaves, to keep it open at the place where it bore evidence against the Goodman of Primrose-Knowe, as behind the hand with his mails[42] and duties. Sir Robert gave my gudesire a look, as if he would have withered his heart in his bosom. Ye maun ken he had a way of bending his brows, that men saw the visible mark of a horse-shoe in his forehead, deep-dinted, as if it had been stamped there.

Are ye come light-handed, ye son of a toom[43] whistle?' said Sir Robert. 'Zounds! if you are ____'

My gudesire, with as gude a countenance as he could put on, made a leg, and placed the bag of money on the table wi' a dash, like a man that does something clever. The Laird drew it to him hastily—'Is it all here, Steenie, man?'

'Your honour will find it right,' said my gudesire.

'Here, Dougal,' said the Laird, 'gie Steenie a tass of brandy downstairs, till I count the siller and write the receipt.'

But they werena weel out of the room, when Sir Robert gied a yelloch that garr'd[44] the Castle rock. Back ran Dougal—in flew the livery-men—yell on yell gied the Laird, ilk ane mair awfu' than the ither. My gudesire knew not whether to stand or flee, but he ventured back into the parlour, where a' was gaun hirdy-girdie—naebody to say 'come in' or 'gae out.' Terribly the Laird roared for cauld water to his feet, and wine to cool his throat; and Hell, hell, hell, and its flames, was aye the word in his mouth. They brought him water, and when they plunged his swoln feet into the tub, he cried out it was burning; and folk said that it *did* bubble and sparkle like a seething caldron. He flung the cup at Dougal's head, and said he had given him blood instead of burgundy; and, sure aneugh, the lass washed clotted blood aff the carpet the neist day. The jackanape they caa'd Major Weir, it jibbered and cried as if it was mocking its master; my gudesire's head was like to turn—he forgot baith siller and receipt, and downstairs he banged; but as he ran, the shrieks came faint and fainter; there was a deep-drawn shivering groan; and word gaed through the Castle that the Laird was dead.

Weel, away came my gudesire, wi' his finger in his mouth, and his best hope was, that Dougal had seen the money-bag, and heard the Laird speak of writing the receipt. The young Laird, now Sir John, came from Edinburgh, to see things put to rights. Sir John and his father never gree'd weel. Sir John had been bred an advocate, and afterwards sat in the last Scots Parliament and voted for the Union, having gotten, it was thought, a rug[45] of the compensations—if his father could have come out of his grave, he would have brained him for it on his awn hearthstane. Some thought it was easier counting with the auld rough Knight than the fair-spoken young ane—but mair of that anon.

Dougal MacCallum, poor body, neither grat nor graned,[46] but gaed about the house looking like a corpse, but directing, as was his duty, a' the order of the grand funeral. Now, Dougal

---

34 A celebrated wizard, executed at Edinburgh for sorcery and other crimes.—(Scott.)
35 out of the ordinary.
36 dismal-looking.
37 grimaced; showed his teeth.
38 ill-favored.
39 leap.
40 tidings.
41 ribald songs.
42 rents.
43 empty.

44 jarred.
45 good share.
46 wept nor groaned.

looked aye waur[47] and waur when night was coming, and was aye the last to gang to his bed, whilk was in a little round just opposite the chamber of dais,[48] whilk his master occupied while he was living, and where he now lay in state, as they caa'd it, weel-a-day! The night before the funeral, Dougal could keep his awn counsel nae langer; he came doun with his proud spirit, and fairly asked auld Hutcheon to sit in his room with him for an hour. When they were in the round, Dougal took ae tass of brandy to himsell, and gave another to Hutcheon, and wished him all health and lang life, and said that, for himsell, he wasna lang for this world; for that, every night since Sir Robert's death, his silver call had sounded from the state chamber, just as it used to do at nights in his lifetime, to call Dougal to help to turn him in his bed. Dougal said, that being alone with the dead on that floor of the tower, (for naebody cared to wake[49] Sir Robert Redgauntlet like another corpse,) he had never daured to answer the call, but that now his conscience checked him for neglecting his duty; for, 'though death breaks service,' said MacCallum, 'it shall never break my service to Sir Robert; and I will answer his next whistle, so be you will stand by me, Hutcheon.'

Hutcheon had nae will to the wark, but he had stood by Dougal in battle and broil, and he wad not fail him at this pinch; so down the carles sat ower a stoup of brandy, and Hutcheon, who was something of a clerk, would have read a chapter of the Bible; but Dougal would hear naething but a blaud[50] of Davie Lindsay,[51] whilk was the waur preparation.

When midnight came, and the house was quiet as the grave, sure enough the silver whistle sounded as sharp and shrill as if Sir Robert was blowing it, and up got the twa auld serving-men, and tottered into the room where the dead man lay. Hutcheon saw aneugh at the first glance; for there were torches in the room, which shewed him the foul fiend,[52] in his ain shape, sitting on the Laird's coffin! Ower he cowped[53] as if he had been dead. He could not tell how lang he lay in a trance at the door, but when he gathered himself, he cried on his neighbour, and getting nae answer, raised the house, when Dougal was found lying dead within two steps of the bed where his master's coffin was placed. As for the whistle, it was gaen anes and aye[54]; but mony a

time was it heard at the top of the house on the bartizan,[55] and amang the auld chimneys and turrets where the howlets[56] have their nests. Sir John hushed the matter up, and the funeral passed over without mair bogle-wark.[57]

But when a' was ower, and the Laird was beginning to settle his affairs, every tenant was called up for his arrears, and my gudesire for the full sum that stood against him in the rental-book. Weel, away he trots to the Castle, to tell his story, and there he is introduced to Sir John, sitting in his father's chair, in deep mourning, with weepers[58] and hanging cravat, and a small walking rapier by his side, instead of the auld broadsword that had a hundred-weight of steel about it, what with blade, chape,[59] and basket-hilt. I have heard their communing so often tauld ower that I almost think I was there mysell, though I couldna be born at the time. (In fact, Alan, my companion mimicked, with a good deal of humour, the flattering, conciliating tone of the tenant's address, and the hypocritical melancholy of the Laird's reply. His grandfather, he said, had, while he spoke, his eye fixed on the rental-book, as if it were a mastiff-dog that he was afraid would spring up and bite him.)

'I wuss[60] ye joy, sir, of the head seat, and the white loaf, and the braid lairdship. Your father was a kind man to friends and followers; muckle grace to you, Sir John, to fill his shoon[61]—his boots, I suld say, for he seldom wore shoon, unless it were muils[62] when he had the gout.'

'Ay, Steenie,' quoth the laird, sighing deeply, and putting his napkin to his een, 'his was a sudden call, and he will be missed in the country; no time to set his house in order—weel prepared Godward, no doubt, which is the root of the matter—but left us behind a tangled hesp[63] to wind, Steenie.—Hem! hem! We maun go to business, Steenie; much to do, and little time to do it in.'

Here he opened the fatal volume. I have heard of a thing they call Doomsdaybook—I am clear it has been a rental of back-ganging tenants.

'Stephen,' said Sir John, still in the same soft, sleekit[64] tone of voice—'Stephen Stevenson, or Steenson, ye are down here for a year's rent behind the hand—due at last term.'

---

47 worse.
48 room of state.
49 watch over the dead.
50 ballad.
51 Sir David Lindsay, c.1490–1555, whose poems contained unsanctified lines.
52 the Devil.   53 fell.   54 once for all.

55 small overhanging tower.
56 small owls.
57 ghost work.
58 a white sleeve band worn in token of mourning.
59 the loop by which the scabbard is attached.
60 wish.   61 shoes.
62 slippers.   63 hank of yarn.
64 smooth.

Stephen. 'Please your honour, Sir John, I paid it to your father.'

Sir John. 'Ye took a receipt then, doubtless, Stephen, and can produce it?'

Stephen. 'Indeed I hadna time, an it like your honour; for nae sooner had I set doun the siller, and just as his honour Sir Robert, that's gaen, drew it till him to count it, and write out the receipt, he was ta'en wi' the pains that removed him.'

'That was unlucky,' said Sir John, after a pause. 'But ye maybe paid it in the presence of somebody. I want but a *talis qualis*⁶⁵ evidence, Stephen. I would go ower strictly to work with no poor man.'

Stephen. 'Troth, Sir John, there was naebody in the room but Dougal MacCallum the butler. But, as your honour kens, he has e'en followed his auld master.'

'Very unlucky again, Stephen,' said Sir John, without altering his voice a single note. 'The man to whom ye paid the money is dead—and the man who witnessed the payment is dead too —and the siller, which should have been to the fore, is neither seen nor heard tell of in the repositories. How am I to believe a' this?'

Stephen. 'I dinna ken, your honour; but there is a bit memorandum note of the very coins; for, God help me! I had to borrow out of twenty purses; and I am sure that ilka⁶⁶ man there set down will take his grit oath for what purpose I borrowed the money.'

Sir John. 'I have little doubt ye *borrowed* the money, Steenie. It is the *payment* to my father that I want to have some proof of.'

Stephen. 'The siller maun be about the house, Sir John. And since your honour never got it, and his honour that was canna have taen it wi' him, maybe some of the family may have seen it.'

Sir John. 'We will examine the servants, Stephen; that is but reasonable.'

But lackey and lass, and page and groom, all denied stoutly that they had ever seen such a bag of money as my gudesire described. What was waur, he had unluckily not mentioned to any living soul of them his purpose of paying his rent. Ae quean⁶⁷ had noticed something under his arm, but she took it for the pipes.

Sir John Redgauntlet ordered the servants out of the room, and then said to my gudesire, 'Now, Steenie, ye see ye have fair play; and, as I have little doubt ye ken better where to find the siller than ony other body, I beg, in fair terms, and for

your own sake, that you will end this fasherie;⁶⁸ for, Stephen, ye maun pay or flit.'

'The Lord forgie your opinion,' said Stephen, driven almost to his wit's end—'I am an honest man.'

'So am I, Stephen,' said his honour; 'and so are all the folks in the house, I hope. But if there be a knave amongst us, it must be he that tells the story he cannot prove.' He paused, and then added, mair sternly, 'If I understand your trick, sir, you want to take advantage of some malicious reports concerning things in this family, and particularly respecting my father's sudden death, thereby to cheat me out of the money, and perhaps take away my character, by insinuating that I have received the rent I am demanding.— Where do you suppose this money to be?—I insist upon knowing.'

My gudesire saw every thing look so muckle against him, that he grew nearly desperate—however, he shifted from one foot to another, looked to every corner of the room, and made no answer.

'Speak out, sirrah,' said the Laird, assuming a look of his father's, a very particular ane, which he had when he was angry—it seemed as if the wrinkles of his frown made that self-same fearful shape of a horse's shoe in the middle of his brow; —'Speak out, sir! I *will* know your thoughts;—do you suppose that I have this money?'

'Far be it frae me to say so,' said Stephen.

'Do you charge any of my people with having taken it?'

'I wad be laith⁶⁹ to charge them that may be innocent,' said my gudesire; 'and if there be any one that is guilty, I have nae proof.'

'Somewhere the money must be, if there is a word of truth in your story,' said Sir John. 'I ask where you think it is—and demand a correct answer?'

'In hell, if you *will* have my thoughts of it,' said my gudesire, driven to extremity,—'in hell! with your father, his jackanape, and his silver whistle.'

Down the stairs he ran, (for the parlour was nae place for him after such a word,) and he heard the Laird swearing blood and wounds, behind him, as fast as ever did Sir Robert, and roaring for the bailie and the baron-officer.

Awaye rode my gudesire to his chief creditor, (him they caa'd Laurie Lapraik,) to try if he could make ony thing out of him; but when he tauld his story, he got but the worst word in his wame⁷⁰—thief, beggar, and dyvour,⁷¹ were the

---

65 such as it is; acceptable.   66 every.   67 woman.

68 nonsense.   69 loath; reluctant.
70 belly.   71 bankrupt.

saftest terms; and to the boot of these hard terms, Laurie brought up the auld story of his dipping his hand in the blood of Gad's saunts,[72] just as if a tenant could have helped riding with the Laird, and that a laird like Sir Robert Redgauntlet. My gudesire way by this time far beyond the bounds of patience, and, while he and Laurie were at deil speed the liars, he was wanchancie[73] aneugh to abuse Lapraik's doctrine as weel as the man, and said things that garr'd folks' flesh grue[74] that heard them;—he wasna just himsell, and he had lived wi' a wild set in his day.

At last they parted, and my gudesire was to ride hame through the wood of Pitmurkie, that is a' fou of black firs, as they say.—I ken the wood, but the firs may be black or white for what I can tell.—At the entry of the wood there is a wild common, and on the edge of the common, a little lonely changehouse,[75] that was keepit then by an ostler-wife, they suld hae caa'd[76] her Tibbie Faw, and there puir Steenie cried for a mutchkin[77] of brandy, for he had had no refreshment the haill day. Tibbie was earnest wi' him to take a bite of meat, but he couldna think o't, nor would he take his foot out of the stirrup, and took off the brandy wholely at two draughts, and named a toast at each:—the first was, the memory of Sir Robert Redgauntlet, and might he never lie quiet in his grave till he had righted his poor bond-tenant; and the second was, a health to Man's Enemy, if he would but get him back the pock[78] of siller, or tell him what came o't, for he saw the haill world was like to regard him as a thief and a cheat, and he took that waur than even the ruin of his house and hauld.[79]

On he rode, little caring where. It was a dark night turned, and the trees made it yet darker, and he let the beast take its ain road through the wood; when all of a sudden, from tired and wearied\ that it was before, the nag began to spring, and flee, and stend,[80] that my gudesire could hardly keep the saddle.—Upon the whilk, a horseman, suddenly riding up beside him, said, 'That's a mettle beast of yours, freend; will you sell him?'—So saying, he touched the horse's neck with his riding-wand, and it fell into its auld heigh-ho of a stumbling trot. 'But his spunk's soon out of him, I think,' continued the stranger, 'and that is like mony a man's courage, that

thinks he wad do great things till he come to the proof.'

My gudesire scarce listened to this, but spurred his horse, with 'Gude e'en to you, freend.'

But it's like the stranger was ane that doesna lightly yield his point; for, ride as Steenie liked, he was aye beside him at the self-same pace. At last my gudesire, Steenie Steenson, grew half angry; and, to say the truth, half feared.

'What is it that ye want with me, freend?' he said. 'If ye be a robber, I have nae money; if ye be a leal[81] man, wanting company, I have nae heart to mirth or speaking; and if ye want to ken the road, I scarce ken it mysell.'

'If you will tell me your grief,' said the stranger, 'I am one that, though I have been sair miscaa'd in the world, am the only hand for helping my freends.'

So my gudesire, to ease his ain heart, mair than from any hope of help, told him the story from beginning to end.

'It's a hard pinch,' said the stranger; 'but I think I can help you.'

'If you could lend the money, sir, and take a lang day—I ken nae other help on earth,' said my gudesire.

'But there may be some under the earth,' said the stranger. 'Come, I'll be frank wi' you; I could lend you the money on bond, but you would maybe scruple my terms. Now, I can tell you that your auld Laird is disturbed in his grave by your curses, and the wailing of your family, and if ye daur venture to go to see him, he will give you the receipt.'

My gudesire's hair stood on end at this proposal, but he thought his companion might be some humorsome chield that was trying to frighten him, and might end with lending him the money. Besides, he was bauld wi' brandy, and desperate wi' distress, and he said he had courage to go to the gate of hell, and a step farther, for that receipt.—The stranger laughed.

Weel, they rode on through the thickest of the wood, when, all of a sudden, the horse stopped at the door of a great house; and, but that he knew the place was ten miles off, my father would have thought he was at Redgauntlet Castle. They rode into the outer court-yard, through the muckle faulding yetts,[82] and aneath the auld portcullis; and the whole front of the house was lighted, and there were pipes and fiddles, and as much dancing and deray[83] within as used to be in Sir Robert's house at Pace and Yule,[84] and such high sea-

---

72 saints; that is, covenanter martyrs.
73 unlucky.
74 creep.
75 small alehouse.
76 are said to have called.
77 about a pint.
78 bag.
79 hold.
80 rear up.
81 loyal; honest.
82 folding gates.
83 disorderly merrymaking.
84 Easter and Christmas.

sons. They lap off, and my gudesire, as seemed to him, fastened his horse to the very ring he had tied him to that morning, when he gaed to wait on the young Sir John.

'God!' said my gudesire, 'if Sir Robert's death be but a dream!'

He knocked at the ha' door just as he was wont, and his auld acquaintance, Dougal Mac-Callum, just after his wont, too—came to open the door, and said, 'Piper Steenie, are ye there, lad? Sir Robert has been crying for you.'

My gudesire was like a man in a dream—he looked for the stranger, but he was gane for the time. At last he just tried to say, 'Ha! Dougal Driveower, are ye living? I thought ye had been dead.'

'Never fash[85] yoursell wi' me,' said Dougal, 'but look to yourself; and see ye tak naething frae ony body here, neither meat, drink, or siller, except just the receipt that is your ain.'

So saying, he led the way out through halls and trances[86] that were weel kend to my gudesire, and into the auld oak parlour; and there was as much singing of profane sangs, and birling[87] of red wine, and speaking blasphemy and sculduddry,[88] as had ever been in Redgauntlet Castle when it was at the blithest.

But, Lord take us in keeping, what a set of ghastly revellers they were that sat around that table![89]—My gudesire kend mony that had long before gane to their place, for often had he piped to the most part in the hall of Redgauntlet. There was the fierce Middleton, and the dissolute Rothes, and the crafty Lauderdale; and Dalyell, with his bald head and a beard to his girdle; and Earlshall, with Cameron's blude on his hand; and wild Bonshaw, that tied blessed Mr. Car-gill's limbs till the blude sprung; and Dunbarton Douglas, the twice-turned traitor baith to coun-try and king. There was the Bluidy Advocate MacKenyie, who, for his worldly wit and wis-dom, had been to the rest as a god. And there was Claverhouse, as beautiful as when he lived, with his long, dark, curled locks streaming down over his laced buff-coat, and his left hand always on his right spule-blade,[90] to hide the wound that the silver bullet[91] had made. He sat apart from them all, and looked at them with a melancholy, haughty countenance; while the rest hallooed,

and sung, and laughed, that the room rang. But their smiles were fearfully contorted from time to time; and their laugh passed into such wild sounds, as made my gudesire's very nails grow blue, and chilled the marrow in his banes.

They that waited at the table were just the wicked serving-men and troopers, that had done their work and cruel bidding on earth. There was the Lang Lad of the Nethertown, that helped to take Argyle; and the Bishop's summoner, that they called the Deil's Rattle-bag; and the wicked guardsmen in their laced coats; and the savage Highland Amorites, that shed blood like water; and many a proud serving-man, haughty of heart and bloody of hand, cringing to the rich, and making them wickeder than they would be; grinding the poor to powder, when the rich had broken them to fragments. And mony, mony mair were coming and ganging, a' as busy in their vocation as if they had been alive.

Sir Robert Redgauntlet, in the midst of a' this fearful riot, cried, wi' a voice like thunder, on Steenie Piper to come to the board-head where he was sitting; his legs stretched out before him, and swathed up with flannel, with his holster pistols aside him, while the great broadsword rested against his chair, just as my gudesire had seen him the last time upon earth. The very cushion for the jackanape was close to him, but the creature itsell was not there—it wasna its hour, it's likely; for he heard them say as he came forward, 'Is not the Major come yet?' And an-other answered, 'The jackanape will be here be-times the morn.' And when my gudesire came forward, Sir Robert, or his ghaist, or the deevil in his likeness, said, 'Weel, piper, hae ye settled wi' my son for the year's rent?'

With much ado my father gat breath to say, that Sir John would not settle without his hon-our's receipt.

'Ye shall hae that for a tune of the pipes, Steenie,' said the appearance of Sir Robert.— 'Play us up "Weel hoddled, Luckie."'

Now this was a tune my gudesire learned frae a warlock, that heard it when they were wor-shipping Satan at their meetings; and my gude-sire had sometimes played it at the ranting sup-pers in Redgauntlet Castle, but never very will-ingly; and now he grew cauld at the very name of it, and said, for excuse, he hadna his pipes wi' him.

'MacCallum, ye limb of Beezlebub,' said the fearfu' Sir Robert, 'bring Steenie the pipes that I am keeping for him!'

MacCallum brought a pair of pipes might have

---

85 trouble.
86 passageways.
87 drinking.
88 ribaldry.
89 The passage that follows—accounted one of Scott's finest—describes the notorious persecutors of the Covenanters.
90 shoulder blade.
91 Claverhouse was shot with a silver bullet, as this was believed to have the power of killing a person possessed of the devil.

served the piper of Donald of the Isles. But he gave my gudesire a nudge as he offered them; and looking secretly and closely, Steenie saw that the chanter[92] was of steel, and heated to a white heat; so he had fair warning not to trust his fingers with it. So he excused himself again, and said, he was faint and frightened, and had not wind aneugh to fill the bag.

'Then ye maun eat and drink, Steenie,' said the figure; 'for we do little else here, and it's ill speaking between a fou man[93] and a fasting.'

Now these were the very words that the bloody Earl of Douglas said to keep the king's messenger in hand, while he cut the head off MacLellan of Bombie, at the Threave Castle;[94] and that put Steenie mair and mair on his guard. So he spoke up like a man, and said he came neither to eat, or drink, or make minstrelsy; but simply for his ain —to ken what was come o' the money he had paid, and to get a discharge for it; and he was so stout-hearted by this time that he charged Sir Robert for conscience-sake—(he had no power to say the holy Name) and—as he hoped for peace and rest, to spread no snares for him, but just to give his ain.

The appearance gnashed its teeth and laughed, but it took from a large pocket-book the receipt, and handed it to Steenie. 'There is your receipt, ye pitiful cur; and for the money, my dog-whelp of a son may go look for it in the Cat's Cradle.'

My gudesire uttered mony thanks, and was about to retire, when Sir Robert roared aloud, 'Stop though, thou sack-doudling[95] son of a whore! I am not done with thee. HERE we do nothing for nothing; and you must return on this very day twelvemonth, to pay your master the homage that you owe me for my protection.'

My father's tongue was loosed of a suddenty, and he said aloud, 'I refer mysell to God's pleasure, and not to yours.'

He had no sooner uttered the word than all was dark around him; and he sunk on the earth with such a sudden shock, that he lost both breath and sense.

How lang Steenie lay there, he could not tell, but when he came to himsell, he was lying in the auld kirkyard of Redgauntlet parochine[96] just at the door of the family aisle, and the skutcheon of the auld knight, Sir Robert, hanging over his head. There was a deep morning fog on grass and gravestane around him, and his horse was feeding quietly beside the minister's two cows. Steenie would have thought the whole was a dream, but he had the receipt in his hand, fairly written and signed by the auld Laird; only the last letters of his name were a little disorderly, written like one seized with sudden pain.

Sorely troubled in his mind, he left that dreary place, rode through the mist to Redgauntlet Castle, and with much ado he got speech of the Laird.

'Well, you dyvour bankrupt,' was the first word, 'have you brought me my rent?'

'No,' answered my gudesire, 'I have not; but I have brought your honour Sir Robert's receipt for it.'

'How, sirrah?—Sir Robert's receipt!—You told me he had not given you one.'

'Will your honour please to see if that bit line is right?'

Sir John looked at every line, and at every letter, with much attention; and at last at the date, which my gudesire had not observed. *'From my appointed place,'* he read, *'this twenty-fifth of November.'* 'What—That is yesterday!—Villain, thou must have gone to hell for this!'

'I got it from your honour's father—whether he be in heaven or hell, I know not,' said Steenie.

'I will delate[97] you for a warlock to the Privy Council!' said Sir John. 'I will send you to your master, the devil, with the help of a tar-barrel and a torch!'

'I intend to delate mysell to the Presbytery,' said Steenie, 'and tell them all I have seen last night, whilk are things fitter for them to judge of than a borrel[98] man like me.'

Sir John paused, composed himsell, and desired to hear the full history; and my gudesire told it him from point to point, as I have told it you—word for word, neither more nor less.

Sir John was silent again for a long time, and at last he said, very composedly, 'Steenie, this story of yours concerns the honour of many a noble family besides mine; and if it be a leasing-making,[99] to keep yourself out of my danger, the least you can expect is to have a redhot iron driven through your tongue, and that will be as bad as scauding your fingers wi' a redhot chanter. But yet it may be true, Steenie; and if the money cast up, I shall not know what to think of it.—But where shall we find the Cat's Cradle? There are cats enough about the old house, but I think they kitten without the ceremony of bed or cradle.'

---

92 finger pipe.   93 madman.
94 The reader is referred for particulars to Pitscottie's *History of Scotland.*—(Scott.)
95 bagpiping.   96 parish.

---

97 accuse.   98 rough; common.
99 lying.   100 knocked.

'We were best ask Hutcheon,' said my gude-sire; 'he kens a' the odd corners about as weel as—another serving-man that is now gane, and that I wad not like to name.'

Aweel, Hutcheon, when he was asked, told them that a ruinous turret, lang disused, next to the clock-house, only accessible by a ladder, for the opening was on the outside, and far above the battlements, was called of old the Cat's Cradle.

'There will I go immediately,' said Sir John; and he took (with what purpose Heaven kens) one of his father's pistols from the hall-table, where they had lain since the night he died, and hastened to the battlements.

It was a dangerous place to climb, for the ladder was auld and frail, and wanted ane or two rounds. However, up got Sir John, and entered at the turret door, where his body stopped the only little light that was in the bit turret. Something flees at him wi' a vengeance, maist dang[100] him back over—bang gaed the knight's pistol, and Hutcheon, that held the ladder, and my gudesire that stood beside him, hears a loud skel-loch.[101] A minute after, Sir John flings the body of the jackanape down to them, and cries that the siller is fund, and that they should come up and help him. And there was the bag of siller sure aneugh, and mony orra things besides, that had been missing for mony a day. And Sir John, when he had riped[102] the turret weel, led my gudesire into the dining-parlour, and took him by the hand, and spoke kindly to him, and said he was sorry he should have doubted his word, and that he would hereafter be a good master to him, to make amends.

'And now, Steenie,' said Sir John, 'although this vision of yours tends, on the whole, to my father's credit, as an honest man, that he should, even after his death, desire to see justice done to a poor man like you, yet you are sensible that ill-dispositioned men might make bad constructions upon it, concerning his soul's health. So, I think, we had better lay the haill dirdum[103] on that ill-deedie creature, Major Weir, and say naething about your dream in the wood of Pitmurkie. You had taken ower muckle brandy to be very certain about ony thing; and, Steenie, this receipt,' (his hand shook while he held it out,)—'it's but a queer kind of document, and we will do best, I think, to put it quietly in the fire.'

'Od, but for as queer as it is, it's a' the voucher I have for my rent,' said my gudesire, who was afraid, it may be, of losing the benefit of Sir Robert's discharge.

'I will bear the contents to your credit in the rental-book, and give you a discharge under my own hand,' said Sir John, 'and that on the spot. And, Steenie, if you can hold your tongue about this matter, you shall sit, from this term downward, at an easier rent.'

'Mony thanks to your honour,' said Steenie, who saw easily in what corner the wind was; 'doubtless I will be conformable to all your honour's commands; only I would willingly speak wi' some powerful minister on the subject, for I do not like the sort of soumons of appointment whilk your honour's father——'

'Do not call the phantom my father!' said Sir John, interrupting him.

'Weel, then, the thing that was so like him,' said my gudesire; 'he spoke of my coming back to see him this time twelvemonth, and it's a weight on my conscience.'

'Aweel, then,' said Sir John, 'if you be so much distressed in mind, you may speak to our minister of the parish. He is a douce[104] man, regards the honour of our family, and the mair that he may look for some patronage from me.'

Wi' that, my gudesire readily agreed that the receipt should be burnt, and the Laird threw it into the chimney with his ain hand. Burn it would not for them, though; but away it flew up the lum,[105] wi' a lang train of sparks at its tail, and a hissing noise like a squib.

My gudesire gaed down to the Manse, and the minister, when he had heard the story, said it was his real opinion that, though my gudesire had gaen very far in tampering with dangerous matters, yet, as he had refused the devil's arles,[106] (for such was the offer of meat and drink,) and had refused to do homage by piping at his bidding, he hoped, that if he held a circumspect walk hereafter, Satan could take little advantage by what was come and gane. And, indeed, my gudesire, of his ain accord, lang foreswore baith the pipes and the brandy—it was not even till the year was out, and the fatal day past, that he would so much as take the fiddle, or drink usque-baugh or tippenny.[107]

Sir John made up his story about the jacka-nape as he liked himsell; and some believe till this day there was no more in the matter than the filching nature of the brute. Indeed, ye'll no

---

hinder some to threap,[108] that it was nane o' the auld Enemy that Dougal and my gudesire saw in the Laird's room, but only that wanchancy creature, the Major, capering on the coffin; and that, as to the blawing on the Laird's whistle that was heard after he was dead, the filthy brute could do that as well as the Laird himsell, if no better. But Heaven kens the truth, whilk first came out by the minister's wife, after Sir John and her ain gudeman were baith in the moulds. And then my gudesire, wha was failed in his limbs, but not in his judgment or memory—at least nothing to speak of—was obliged to tell the real narrative to his freends, for the credit of his good name. He might else have been charged for a warlock.

108 hint.

1824

1794 · JOHN GIBSON LOCKHART · 1854

1794   Born in Cambusnethan, Lanarkshire, Scotland, the son of a minister.

1800–1813   Attended public schools in Glasgow and Balliol College, Oxford, where he graduated with first honors in classics.

1814–16   Studied and began to practice law in Edinburgh.

1817   Joined the staff of *Blackwood's Magazine.*

1819   Published *Peter's Letters to His Kinsfolk.*

1820   Married Scott's eldest daughter, Sophia.

1821–4   Published four novels of some merit.

1825   Accepted the editorship of the *Quarterly Review,* a post which he held until a year before his death.

1828   Published *Life of Burns.*

1837–8   Published *Life of Sir Walter Scott,* his chief work.

1854   Died at Abbotsford.

JOHN GIBSON LOCKHART, Scott's son-in-law and biographer, was a gifted linguist and a brilliant scholar. By temperament he was sardonic with an unfortunate penchant for caricaturing his acquaintances. His talent was that of the reporter observing and describing real people, as in his once popular *Peter's Letters to His Kinsfolk,* which are deftly-etched characterizations, full of pungent humor, of Edinburgh and Glasgow personages of his day. Some verse written in his youth and a batch of novels attest to imaginative gifts never realized. But the truth is that Lockhart's peculiar powers were not primarily creative but intellectual. These powers, in evidence rather consistently from the first, eventually were to find their fullest scope in the fields of literary criticism and biography.

In the years of his association with *Blackwood's,* Lockhart's faculty for malicious satire earned him the nickname of 'The Scorpion.' Among the numerous targets of his barbed language were the rival *Edinburgh Review,* Whig politics and literature, and the poetry of Leigh Hunt and Keats. The much-discussed onslaught against Hunt and Keats in the Cockney School articles may be charged perhaps to politics or to the proverbial rowdyism of the reviews, perhaps to Lockhart's youthful vanity in the public display of his satirical powers. Whatever the explanation, the point has been made that the article on Keats is not, on the whole, savage or vindictive, but is written rather in a vein of playful raillery (See G. Macbeth, *Lockhart,* p. 113). In any event, the mature Lockhart, editor of the *Quarterly,* was a different man from the brilliant, free-lance critic of *Blackwood's.* The passing years, which brought with them family sorrows and the intimate life at Abbotsford, mellowed and deepened his character; in time the latent qualities of fair-mindedness and dignity became predominant. On occasion even as a youthful critic Lockhart had displayed qualities of discretion. He was one of the early defenders of Wordsworth and Coleridge, and he had praised Byron discriminately and had championed Shelley. It is as biographer, however, that Lockhart holds his highest claim to distinction. His short *Life of Burns* has remarkable merit; his enduring *Life of Scott* is generally regarded, after Boswell's *Johnson*, as most admirable biography in the language.

MEMOIRS OF SIR WALTER SCOTT

From CHAPTER IX

SCOTT IN THE HEY-DAY OF HIS FAME

AT this moment,[1] [Scott's] position, take it for all in all, was, I am inclined to believe, what no other man had ever won for himself by the pen alone. His works were the daily food, not only of his countrymen, but of all educated Europe. His society was courted by whatever England could show of eminence. Station, power, wealth, beauty, and genius, strove with each other in every demonstration of respect and worship, and —a few political fanatics and envious poetasters apart—wherever he appeared in town or country, whoever had Scotch blood in him, 'gentle or simple,' felt it move more rapidly through his veins when he was in the presence of Scott. To descend to what many looked on as higher things, he considered himself, and was considered by all about him, as rapidly consolidating a large fortune:— the annual profits of his novels alone had, for several years, been not less than £10,000; his domains were daily increased—his castle was rising—and perhaps few doubted that ere long he might receive from the just favour of his Prince some distinction in the way of external rank, such as had seldom before been dreamt of as the possible consequences of a mere literary celebrity. It was about this time that the compiler of these pages first had the opportunity of observing the plain easy modesty which had survived the many temptations of such a career; and the kindness of heart pervading, in all circumstances, his gentle deportment, which made him the rare, perhaps the solitary, example of a man signally elevated from humble beginnings, and loved more and more by his earliest friends and connections, in proportion as he had fixed on himself the homage of the great and the wonder of the world.

It was during the sitting of the General Assembly of the Kirk in May 1818, that I first had the honour of meeting him in private society: the party was not a large one, at the house of a much-valued common friend—Mr. Home Drummond, the grandson of Lord Kames. Mr. Scott, ever apt to consider too favourably the literary efforts of others, and more especially of very young persons, received me, when I was presented to him, with a cordiality which I had not been prepared to expect from one filling a station so exalted. This, however, is the same story that every individual, who ever met him under similar circumstances, has had to tell. When the ladies retired from the dinner-table, I happened to sit next him; and he, having heard that I had lately returned from a tour in Germany, made that country and its recent literature the subject of some conversation. In the course of it, I told him that when, on reaching the inn at Weimar, I asked the waiter whether Goethe was then in the town, the man stared as if he had not heard the name before; and that on my repeating the question, adding *Goethe der grosse Dichter* (the great poet), he shook his head as doubtfully as before—until the landlady solved our difficulties, by suggesting that perhaps the traveller might mean 'the *Herr Geheimer-Rath* (Privy Councillor) *Von Goethe.'*—Scott seemed amused with this, and said, 'I hope you will come one of these days and see me at Abbotsford: and when you reach Selkirk or Melrose, be sure you ask even the landlady for nobody but *the sheriff.'* He appeared particularly interested when I described Goethe as I first saw him, alighting from a carriage crammed with wild plants and herbs which he had picked up in the course of his morning's botanising among the hills above Jena. 'I am glad,' said he, 'that my old master has pursuits somewhat akin to my own. I am no botanist, properly speaking; and though a dweller on the banks of the Tweed, shall never be knowing about Flora's beauties; but how I should like to have a talk with him about trees!' I mentioned how much any one must be struck with the majestic beauty of Goethe's countenance—the noblest certainly by far that I have ever yet seen—'Well,' said he, 'the grandest demigod I ever saw was Dr. Carlyle,[2] minister of Musselburgh, commonly called *Jupiter Carlyle,* from having sat more than once for the king of gods

---

1 February 1818, coincident with the enthusiastic public reception of *Rob Roy.*

2 the Reverend Alexander Carlyle, 1722-1805, leader of the Scottish Broad Church party.

and men to Gavin Hamilton[3]—and a shrewd, clever old carle was he, no doubt, but no more a poet than his precentor.[4] As for poets, I have seen, I believe, all the best of our own time and country—and though Burns had the most glorious eyes imaginable, I never thought any of them would come up to an artist's notion of the character, except Byron.' Principal Nicol of St. Andrews expressed his regret that he had never seen Lord Byron. 'And the prints,' resumed Scott, 'give one no impression of him—the lustre is there, Doctor, but it is not lighted up. Byron's countenance is *a thing to dream of.* A certain fair lady,[5] whose name has been too often mentioned in connection with his, told a friend of mine, that when she first saw Byron, it was in a crowded room, and she did not know who it was, but her eyes were instantly nailed, and she said to herself, *that pale face is my fate.* And, poor soul, if a godlike face and godlike powers could have made any excuse for devilry, to be sure she had one.' In the course of this talk, Sir P. Murray of Ochtertyre, an old friend and schoolfellow of Scott's, asked him, across the table, if he had any faith in the antique busts of Homer. 'No, truly,' he answered, smiling, 'for if there had been either limners or stuccoyers worth their salt in those days, the owner of such a headpiece would never have had to trail the poke.[6] They would have alimented[7] the honest man decently among them for a lay-figure.'[8]

A few days after this, I received a communication from the Messrs. Ballantyne,[9] to the effect that Mr. Scott's various avocations had prevented him from fulfilling his agreement with them as to the historical department of the Edinburgh Annual Register for 1816, and that it would be acceptable to him as well as them, if I could undertake to supply it in the course of the autumn. This proposal was agreed to, and I had consequently occasion to meet him pretty often during that summer session. He told me, that if the war had gone on, he should have liked to do the historical summary as before; but that the prospect of having no events to record but radical riots, and the passing or rejecting of corn bills and poor bills, sickened him; that his health was no longer what it had been; and that though he did not mean to give over writing altogether—(here he smiled significantly, and glanced his eye towards a pile of MS. on the desk by him)—he

thought himself now entitled to write nothing but what would rather be an amusement than a fatigue to him—'*Juniores ad labores.*'[10]

He at this time occupied as his *den* a small square room, behind the dining parlour in Castle Street. It had but a single Venetian window, opening on a patch of turf not much larger than itself, and the aspect of the place was on the whole sombrous. The walls were entirely clothed with books; most of them folios and quartos, and all in that complete state of repair which at a glance reveals a tinge of bibliomania. A dozen volumes or so, needful for immediate purposes of reference, were placed close by him on a small movable frame—something like a dumb-waiter. All the rest were in their proper niches, and wherever a volume had been lent, its room was occupied by a wooden block of the same size, having a card with the name of the borrower and date of the loan, tacked on its front. The old bindings had obviously been retouched and regilt in the most approved manner; the new, when the books were of any mark, were rich, but never gaudy— a large proportion of blue morocco—all stamped with his *device* of the portcullis, and its motto, *clausus tutus ero*[11]—being an anagram of his name in Latin. Every case and shelf was accurately lettered, and the works arranged systematically: history and biography on one side— poetry and the drama on another—law books and dictionaries behind his own chair. The only table was a massive piece of furniture which he had had constructed on the model of one at Rokeby; with a desk and all its appurtenances on either side, that an amanuensis might work opposite to him when he chose; and with small tiers of drawers, reaching all round to the floor. The top displayed a goodly array of session papers, and on the desk below were, besides the MS. at which he was working, sundry parcels of letters, proof-sheets, and so forth, all neatly done up with red tape. His own writing apparatus was a very handsome old box, richly carved, lined with crimson velvet, and containing ink-bottles, taper-stand, &c., in silver—the whole in such order that it might have come from the silversmith's window half an hour before. Besides his own huge elbow-chair, there were but two others in the room, and one of these seemed, from its position, to be reserved exclusively for the amanuensis. I observed, during the first evening I spent with him in this *sanctum,* that while he talked, his hands were hardly ever idle; sometimes he folded

---

3 citizen of Mauchline, Ayrshire; a friend of Burns.
4 choir master.
5 Lady Caroline Lamb.
6 carry a beggar's pouch. 7 supported.
8 artist's model. 9 Scott's publishers.

10 'the younger men for labors.'
11 'kept closed, I shall be safe.'

letter-covers—sometimes he twisted paper into matches, performing both tasks with great mechanical expertness and nicety; and when there was no loose paper fit to be so dealt with, he snapped his fingers, and the noble Maida aroused himself from his lair on the hearth-rug, and laid his head across his master's knees, to be caressed and fondled. The room had no space for pictures except one, a portrait of Claverhouse,[12] which hung over the chimneypiece, with a Highland target on either side, and broadswords and dirks (each having its own story) disposed star-fashion round them. A few green tinboxes, such as solicitors keep title-deeds in, were piled over each other on one side of the window; and on the top of these lay a fox's tail, mounted on an antique silver handle, wherewith, as often as he had occasion to take down a book, he gently brushed the dust off the upper leaves before opening it. I think I have mentioned all the furniture of the room except a sort of ladder, low, broad, well carpeted, and strongly guarded with oaken rails, by which he helped himself to books from his higher shelves. On the top step of this convenience, Hinse of Hinsfeldt (so called from one of the German *Kinder-Märchen*), a venerable tom-cat, fat and sleek, and no longer very locomotive, usually lay watching the proceedings of his master and Maida with an air of dignified equanimity; but when Maida chose to leave the party, he signified his inclinations by thumping the door with his huge paw, as violently as ever a fashionable footman handled a knocker in Grosvenor Square; the Sheriff rose and opened it for him with courteous alacrity, —and then Hinse came down purring from his perch, and mounted guard by the footstool, *vice*[13] Maida absent upon furlough. Whatever discourse might be passing, was broken every now and then by some affectionate apostrophe to these four-footed friends. He said they understood everything he said to them—and I believe they did understand a great deal of it. But at all events, dogs and cats, like children, have some infallible tact for discovering at once who is, and who is not, really fond of their company; and I venture to say, Scott was never five minutes in any room before the little pets of the family, whether dumb or lisping, had found out his kindness for all their generation.

1838

COCKNEY SCHOOL OF POETRY[1]

NO. IV

—of Keats,
The Muses' son of promise, and what feats
He yet may do, &c.

CORNELIUS WEBB

OF all the manias of this mad age, the most incurable, as well as the most common, seems to be no other than the *Metromanie*. The just celebrity of Robert Burns and Miss Baillie has had the melancholy effect of turning the heads of we know not how many farm-servants and unmarried ladies; our very footmen compose tragedies, and there is scarcely a superannuated governess in the island that does not leave a roll of lyrics behind her in her bandbox. To witness the disease of any human understanding, however feeble, is distressing; but the spectacle of an able mind reduced to a state of insanity is of course ten times more afflicting. It is with such sorrow as this that we have contemplated the case of Mr. John Keats. This young man appears to have received from nature talents of an excellent, perhaps even of a superior order—talents which, devoted to the purposes of any useful profession, must have rendered him a respectable, if not an eminent citizen. His friends, we understand, destined him to the career of medicine, and he was bound apprentice some years ago to a worthy apothecary in town. But all has been undone by a sudden attack of the malady to which we have alluded. Whether Mr. John had been sent home with a diuretic or composing draught to some patient far gone in the poetical mania, we have not heard. This much is certain, that he has caught the infection, and that thoroughly. For some time we were in hopes that he might get off with a violent fit or two; but of late the symptoms are terrible. The phrenzy of the *Poems* was bad enough in its way; but it did not alarm us half so seriously as the calm, settled, imperturbable, drivelling idiocy of *Endymion*. We hope, however, that in so young a person, and with a constitution originally so good, even now the disease is not utterly incurable. Time, firm treatment, and rational restraint, do much for many apparently hopeless invalids; and if Mr. Keats should happen, at some interval of reason, to cast his eye upon our pages, he may perhaps be convinced

---

of the existence of his malady, which, in such cases, is often all that is necessary to put the patient in a fair way of being cured.

The readers of the *Examiner* newspaper were informed, some time ago, by a solemn paragraph, in Mr. Hunt's best style, of the appearance of two new stars of glorious magnitude and splendour in the poetical horizon of the land of Cockaigne. One of these turned out, by and by, to be no other than Mr. John Keats. This precocious adulation confirmed the wavering apprentice in his desire to quit the gallipots, and at the same time excited in his too susceptible mind a fatal admiration for the character and talents of the most worthless and affected of all the versifiers of our time. . . .

The old story of the moon falling in love with a shepherd, so prettily told by a Roman Classic, and so exquisitely enlarged and adorned by one of the most elegant of German poets, has been seized upon by Mr. John Keats, to be done with as might seem good unto the sickly fancy of one who never read a single line either of Ovid or of Wieland. If the quantity, not the quality, of the verses dedicated to the story is to be taken into account, there can be no doubt that Mr. John Keats may now claim Endymion entirely to himself. To say the truth, we do not suppose either the Latin or the German poet would be very anxious to dispute about the property of the hero of the 'Poetic Romance.' Mr. Keats has thoroughly appropriated the character, if not the name. His Endymion is not a Greek shepherd, loved by a Grecian goddess; he is merely a young Cockney rhymester, dreaming a phantastic dream at the full of the moon. Costume, were it worth while to notice such a trifle, is violated in every page of this goodly octavo. From his prototype Hunt, John Keats has acquired a sort of vague idea, that the Greeks were a most tasteful people, and that no mythology can be so finely adapted for the purposes of poetry as theirs. It is amusing to see what a hand the two Cockneys make of this mythology; the one confesses that he never read the Greek Tragedians, and the other knows Homer only from

Chapman; and both of them write about Apollo, Pan, Nymphs, Muses, and Mysteries, as might be expected from persons of their education. We shall not, however, enlarge at present upon this subject, as we mean to dedicate an entire paper to the classical attainments and attempts of the Cockney poets. As for Mr. Keats' *Endymion*, it has just as much to do with Greece as it has with 'old Tartary the fierce'; no man, whose mind has ever been imbued with the smallest knowledge or feeling of classical poetry or classical history, could have stooped to profane and vulgarise every association in the manner which has been adopted by this 'son of promise.' Before giving any extracts, we must inform our readers, that this romance is meant to be written in English heroic rhyme. To those who have read any of Hunt's poems, this hint might indeed be needless. Mr. Keats has adopted the loose, nerveless versification, and Cockney rhymes of the poet of Rimini; but in fairness to that gentleman, we must add, that the defects of the system are tenfold more conspicuous in his disciple's work than in his own. Mr. Hunt is a small poet, but he is a clever man. Mr. Keats is a still smaller poet, and he is only a boy of pretty abilities, which he has done every thing in his power to spoil. . . .

And now, good-morrow to 'the Muses' son of Promise'; as for 'the feats he yet may do,' as we do not pretend to say, like himself, 'Muse of my native land am I inspired,' we shall adhere to the safe old rule of *pauca verba*. We venture to make one small prophecy, that his bookseller will not a second time venture £50 upon any thing he can write. It is a better and a wiser thing to be a starved apothecary than a starved poet; so back to the shop Mr. John, back to 'plasters, pills, and ointment boxes,' &c. But, for Heaven's sake, young Sangrado,[2] be a little more sparing of extenuatives and soporifics in your practice than you have been in your poetry.

                                    Z.

                              1818

---

[2] a doctor in Le Sage's *Gil Blas* whose treatment consisted of profuse bloodletting and of drinking quantities of hot water.

1784 · ALLAN CUNNINGHAM · 1842

1784   Born in Dumfriesshire, Scotland.

1800–1810   Practiced the trade of stonemason.

1810   Supplied R. H. Cromek with most of the pieces (mainly fabricated by himself) for Cromek's *Remains of Nithsdale and Galloway Song*.

1810   Went to London where he supported himself by newspaper reporting.

1814   Became manager of the works of Francis Chantrey, sculptor, in whose employ he remained until 1841.

1822   Published *Traditional Tales of the English and Scottish Peasantry*, and

1825   *Songs of Scotland, Ancient and Modern*.

1842   Died.

'ONEST' ALLAN CUNNINGHAM was a capable man of all work and an industrious author. He wrote voluminously in prose and verse, but both are over-ornate and full of mannerisms. Some of his short songs and ballads, however, gained a deserved popularity in his own time. Today Cunningham is chiefly remembered for his *Wet Sheet and a Flowing Sea*, one of the best sea songs in the language.

A WET SHEET AND A FLOWING SEA

A WET sheet and a flowing sea,
  A wind that follows fast,
And fills the white and rustling sail
  And bends the gallant mast;
And bends the gallant mast, my boys,
  While, like the eagle free,
Away the good ship flies, and leaves
  Old England on the lee.

'O for a soft and gentle wind!'
  I heard a fair one cry;   10
But give to me the snoring breeze
  And white waves heaving high;

And white waves heaving high, my lads,
  The good ship tight and free,—
The world of waters is our home,
  And merry men are we.

There's tempest in yon hornéd moon,
  And lightning in yon cloud;
But hark the music, mariners!
  The wind is piping loud;   20
The wind is piping loud, my boys,
  The lightning flashes free,—
While the hollow oak our palace is,
  Our heritage the sea.

                                    1825

567

1773 · FRANCIS JEFFREY · 1850

1773   Born at Edinburgh.

1787–92   Attended Glasgow and Edinburgh universities and Queens College, Oxford.

1794   Admitted to the Scottish bar.

1802   With Sydney Smith, H. P. Brougham, and others, founded the *Edinburgh Review,* and after the third number was appointed editor.

1806   Because of strictures on the morality of Moore's poems, was called out by Moore in a duel; the proceedings were interrupted, however, by the police and the affair led eventually to a warm friendship between the critic and the poet.

1829   Resigned the editorship of the *Edinburgh Review.*

1830–32   Served in Parliament.

1834   Was elevated to the judicial bench as Lord Jeffrey.

1844   Published *Contributions to the Edinburgh Review.*

1850   Died.

THE 'ONCE-NOTED DESPOT OF LETTERS,' Francis Jeffrey, in his day an eminently successful advocate and judge, produced in the intervals of leisure and often with little opportunity for preparation some two hundred review articles on literature and the public issues of the day. As the leading contributor, and as editor and guiding spirit for more than a quarter of a century of the famous and influential *Edinburgh Review,* he was popularly taken as the last court of appeals in letters. Both by temperament and by professional training, the 'great Jamfray,' as he was called, was eminently fitted to play the role he had assumed of critic-journalist for his generation, perhaps not the least by his very superficialities and adroitness. Yet he possessed talents of a very high order. Carlyle speaks of his ingenuity, sagacity, and opulent brilliancy of mind. Lockhart, too, pays a debt of admiration to his fertile, teeming intellect; and his conversation 'one of the most remarkable things in the·world.' Certainly no journalist up to his day ever held such influence to raise or depress an author in the public's esteem. A most notorious injury to Wordsworth, for example, resulted from Jeffrey's discreditable abuse of his dictatorial powers. Beginning with his first contribution to the *Edinburgh Review* and for twenty years at frequent intervals whenever opportunity offered, Jeffrey hammered home his charges against Wordsworth. In reviewing Wordsworth's poetry of 1807 he described the daisy poem as 'very flat, feeble, affected,' the *Ode to Duty* as 'a very paragon of silliness and affectation,' *The Ode on Intimations of Immortality* as of all the pieces the 'most illegible and unintelligible.' Throughout the years Jeffrey's settled order of attack upon Wordsworth was fixed upon broad, predetermined ridicule and abuse. In his review of *The Excursion,* with a caustic and crashing 'This will never do!' he proclaimed his intent once and for all to crush Wordsworth. As Southey said, he might as well have sat on Skiddaw and tried to crush the mountain. Nevertheless, at the time Jeffrey's influence over the reading public was such that even as late as 1825 not a single copy of Wordsworth's works was to be procured in all Edinburgh. Fundamentally the split between Wordsworth and Jeffrey derived from their diverse applications of the principles of taste. But Jeffrey's love of popularity and gain led him into unfair practices; thus unhappily as with Wordsworth—and as not infrequently with other authors—whenever Jeffrey assumed primarily the role of faultfinder instead of the critic of literature he became the scourge of authors. As a critic he was not insensitive to the energy of Byron nor to the rich imagery of Keats; yet he could ignore Shelley, while praising the half-hearted and elegant romanticism of Rogers and Campbell. On the credit side, Jeffrey may be said to have invented the modern review article and to have made criticism a profession. He created a 'public' and prepared the way for greater critics who came after him.

From CRABBE'S POEMS

WE receive the proofs of Mr. Crabbe's poetical existence, which are contained in this volume,[1] with the same sort of feeling that would be excited by tidings of an ancient friend, whom we no longer expected to hear of in this world. We rejoice in his resurrection, both for his sake and for our own; but we feel also a certain movement of self-condemnation, for having been remiss in our inquiries after him, and somewhat too negligent of the honours which ought, at any rate, to have been paid to his memory.

It is now, we are afraid, upwards of twenty years since we were first struck with the vigour, originality, and truth of description of *The Village;* and since, we regretted that an author who could write so well should have written so little. From that time to the present, we have heard little of Mr. Crabbe; and fear that he has been in a great measure lost sight of by the public, as well as by us. With a singular, and scarcely pardonable indifference to fame, he has remained, during this long interval, in patient or indolent repose; and, without making a single movement to maintain or advance the reputation he had acquired, has permitted others to usurp the attention which he was sure of commanding, and allowed himself to be nearly forgotten by a public, which reckons upon being reminded of all the claims which the living have on its favour. His former publications, though of distinguished merit, were perhaps too small in volume to remain long the objects of general attention, and seem, by some accident, to have been jostled aside in the crowd of more clamorous competitors.

Yet, though the name of Crabbe has not hitherto been very common in the mouths of our poetical critics, we believe there are few real lovers of poetry to whom some of his sentiments and descriptions are not secretly familiar. There is a truth and a force in many of his delineations of rustic life, which is calculated to sink deep into the memory; and, being confirmed by daily observation, they are recalled upon innumerable occasions, when the ideal pictures of more fanciful authors have lost all their interest. For ourselves at least, we profess to be indebted to Mr. Crabbe for many of these strong impressions; and have known more than one of our unpoetical acquaintances, who declared they could never pass by a parish workhouse without thinking of the description of it they had read at school in the *Poetical Extracts.* The volume before us will renew, we trust, and extend many such impressions. It contains all the former productions of the author, with about double their bulk of new matter, most of it in the same taste and manner of composition with the former, and some of a kind of which we have had no previous example in this author. The whole, however, is of no ordinary merit, and will be found, we have little doubt, a sufficient warrant for Mr. Crabbe to take his place as one of the most original, nervous, and pathetic poets of the present century.

His characteristic, certainly, is force, and truth of description, joined for the most part to great selection and condensation of expression,—that kind of strength and originality which we meet with in Cowper, and that sort of diction and versification which we admire in *The Deserted Village* of Goldsmith, or *The Vanity of Human Wishes* of Johnson. If he can be said to have imitated the manner of any author, it is Goldsmith, indeed, who has been the object of his

---

[1] an edition of Crabbe's poems, published in October 1807.

imitation; and yet his general train of thinking, and his views of society, are so extremely opposite, that, when *The Village* was first published, it was commonly considered as an antidote or an answer to the more captivating representations of *The Deserted Village.* Compared with this celebrated author, he will be found, we think, to have more vigour and less delicacy; and while he must be admitted to be inferior in the fine finish and uniform beauty of his composition, we cannot help considering him as superior, both in the variety and the truth of his pictures. Instead of that uniform tint of pensive tenderness which overspreads the whole poetry of Goldsmith, we find in Mr. Crabbe many gleams of gaiety and humour. Though his habitual views of life are more gloomy than those of his rival, his poetical temperament seems far more cheerful; and when the occasions of sorrow and rebuke are gone by, he can collect himself for sarcastic pleasantry, or unbend in innocent playfulness. His diction, though generally pure and powerful, is sometimes harsh, and sometimes quaint; and he has occasionally admitted a couplet or two in a state so unfinished as to give a character of inelegance to the passages in which they occur. With a taste less disciplined and less fastidious than that of Goldsmith, he has, in our apprehension, a keener eye for observation, and a readier hand for the delineation of what he has observed. There is less poetical keeping in his whole performance; but the groups of which it consists are conceived, we think, with equal genius, and drawn with greater spirit as well as far greater fidelity.

It is not quite fair, perhaps, thus to draw a detailed parallel between a living poet, and one whose reputation has been sealed by death, and by the immutable sentence of a surviving generation. Yet there are so few of his contemporaries to whom Mr. Crabbe bears any resemblance that we can scarcely explain our opinion of his merit without comparing him to some of his predecessors. There is one set of writers, indeed, from whose works those of Mr. Crabbe might receive all that elucidation which results from contrast, and from an entire opposition in all points of taste and opinion. We allude now to the Wordsworths, and the Southeys, and Coleridges, and all that ambitious fraternity, that, with good intentions and extraordinary talents, are labouring to bring back our poetry to the fantastical oddity and puling childishness

of Withers, Quarles, or Marvel.[2] These gentlemen write a great deal about rustic life, as well as Mr. Crabbe; and they even agree with him in dwelling much on its discomforts; but nothing can be more opposite than the views they take of the subject, or the manner in which they execute their representations of them.

Mr. Crabbe exhibits the common people of England pretty much as they are, and as they must appear to every one who will take the trouble of examining into their condition, at the same time that he renders his sketches in a very high degree interesting and beautiful by selecting what is most fit for description, by grouping them into such forms as must catch the attention or awake the memory, and by scattering over the whole such traits of moral sensibility, of sarcasm, and of deep reflection, as every one must feel to be natural, and own to be powerful. The gentlemen of the new school, on the other hand, scarcely ever condescend to take their subjects from any description of persons at all known to the common inhabitants of the world; but invent for themselves certain whimsical and unheard-of beings, to whom they impute some fantastical combination of feelings, and then labour to excite our sympathy for them, either by placing them in incredible situations, or by some strained and exaggerated moralisation of a vague and tragical description. Mr. Crabbe, in short, shows us something which we have all seen, or may see, in real life; and draws from it such feelings and such reflections as every human being must acknowledge that it is calculated to excite. He delights us by the truth, and vivid and picturesque beauty of his representations, and by the force and pathos of the sensations with which we feel that they are connected. Mr. Wordsworth and his associates, on the other hand, introduce us to beings whose existence was not previously suspected by the acutest observers of nature; and excite an interest for them—where they do excite any interest—more by an eloquent and refined analysis of their own capricious feelings, than by any obvious or intelligible ground of sympathy in their situation.

Those who are acquainted with the *Lyrical Ballads,* or the more recent publications of Mr. Wordsworth, will scarcely deny the justice of this representation; but in order to vindicate it to such as do not enjoy that advantage, we must beg leave to make a few hasty references to the

2 seventeenth-century English poets.

former, and by far the least exceptionable of those productions.

A village schoolmaster, for instance, is a pretty common poetical character. Goldsmith has drawn him inimitably;[3] so has Shenstone, with the slight change of sex;[4] and Mr. Crabbe, in two passages, has followed their footsteps.[5] Now, Mr. Wordsworth has a village schoolmaster also, a personage who makes no small figure in three or four of his poems.[6] But by what traits is this worthy old gentleman delineated by the new poet? No pedantry, no innocent vanity of learning, no mixture of indulgence with the pride of power, and of poverty with the consciousness of rare acquirements. Every feature which belongs to the situation, or marks the character in common apprehension, is scornfully discarded by Mr. Wordsworth, who represents his gray-haired rustic pedagogue as a sort of half crazy, sentimental person, overrun with fine feelings, constitutional merriment, and a most humorous melancholy. Here are the two stanzas in which this consistent and intelligible character is portrayed. The diction is at least as new as the conception.

The sighs which Matthew heav'd were sighs
  Of one tir'd out with *fun* and *madness;*
The tears which came to Matthew's eyes
  Were tears of light—*the oil of gladness.*

Yet sometimes, when the secret cup
  Of still and serious thought went round
He seem'd as if he *drank it up,*
  He felt with spirit so profound.
Thou *soul* of God's best *earthly mould,*[7] etc.

A frail damsel again is a character common enough in all poems, and one upon which many fine and pathetic lines have been expended. Mr. Wordsworth has written more than three hundred on the subject; but, instead of new images of tenderness, or delicate representation of intelligible feelings, he has contrived to tell us nothing whatever of the unfortunate fair one, but that her name is Martha Ray, and that she goes up to the top of a hill, in a red cloak, and cries, 'O misery!' All the rest of the poem[8] is filled with a description of an old thorn and a pond, and of the silly stories which the neighbouring old women told about them.

The sports of childhood, and the untimely death of promising youth, is also a common topic of poetry. Mr. Wordsworth has made some blank verse about it; but, instead of the delightful and picturesque sketches with which so many authors of moderate talents have presented us on this inviting subject, all that he is pleased to communicate of *his* rustic child is, that he used to amuse himself with shouting to the owls, and hearing them answer. To make amends for this brevity, the process of his mimicry is most accurately described.

——With fingers interwoven, both hands
Press'd closely palm to palm, and to his mouth
Uplifted, he, as through an instrument,
Blew mimic hootings to the silent owls,
That they might answer him.[9]

This is all we hear of him; and for the sake of this one accomplishment, we are told that the author has frequently stood mute, and gazed on his grave for half an hour together!

Love, and the fantasies of lovers, have afforded an ample theme to poets of all ages. Mr. Wordsworth, however, has thought fit to compose a piece, illustrating this copious subject by one single thought. A lover trots away to see his mistress one fine evening, gazing all the way on the moon; when he comes to her door,

O mercy! to myself I cried,
  If Lucy should be dead![10]

And there the poem ends!

Now, we leave it to any reader of common candour and discernment to say whether these representations of character and sentiment are drawn from that eternal and universal standard of truth and nature, which every one is knowing enough to recognise, and no one great enough to depart from with impunity; or whether they are not formed, as we have ventured to allege, upon certain fantastic and affected peculiarities in the mind or fancy of the author, into which it is most improbable that many of his readers will enter, and which cannot, in some cases, be comprehended without much effort and explanation. Instead of multiplying instances of these wide and wilful aberrations from ordinary nature, it may be more satisfactory to produce the author's own admis-

---

3 *The Deserted Village,* 193–218.
4 *The Schoolmistress.*
5 *The Village,* II, 296–317.
6 *Matthew, The Two April Mornings,* and *The Fountain.*
7 *Matthew,* 21ff.
8 *The Thorn.*

---

9 *The Boy of Winander* (*Prelude,* v, 364ff.)
10 *Strange Fits of Passion Have I Known.*

sion of the narrowness of the plan upon which he writes, and of the very extraordinary circumstances which he himself sometimes thinks it necessary for his readers to keep in view, if they would wish to understand the beauty or propriety of his delineations.

A pathetic tale of guilt or superstition may be told, we are apt to fancy, by the poet himself, in his general character of poet, with full as much effect as by any other person. An old nurse, at any rate, or a monk or parish clerk, is always at hand to give grace to such a narration. None of these, however, would satisfy Mr. Wordsworth. He has written a long poem of this sort,[11] in which he thinks it indispensably necessary to apprise the reader, that he has endeavoured to represent the language and sentiments of a particular character—of which character, he adds, 'the reader will have a general notion, if he has ever known a man, *a captain of a small trading vessel,* for example, who being *past the middle age of life,* has retired upon an *annuity, or small independent income,* to some *village* or country town, of which he was *not a native,* or in which he had not been accustomed to live!'[12]

Now, we must be permitted to doubt whether, among all the readers of Mr. Wordsworth (few or many), there is a single individual who has had the happiness of knowing a person of this very peculiar description; or who is capable of forming any sort of conjecture of the particular disposition and turn of thinking which such a combination of attributes would be apt to produce. To us, we will confess, the *annonce*[13] appears as ludicrous and absurd as it would be in the author of an ode or an epic to say, 'Of this piece the reader will necessarily form a very erroneous judgement unless he is apprised that it was written by a pale man in a green coat—sitting cross-legged on an oaken stool—with a scratch on his nose, and a spelling dictionary on the table.'

From these childish and absurd affectations, we turn with pleasure to the manly sense and correct picturing of Mr. Crabbe; and, after being dazzled and made giddy with the elaborate raptures and obscure originalities of these new artists, it is refreshing to meet again with the spirit and nature of our old masters, in the nervous pages of the author now before us. . . .

1808

---

11 *The Thorn.*
12 quoted from Wordsworth's note to *The Thorn.*
13 announcement.

From ALISON'S ESSAYS ON THE NATURE AND PRINCIPLES OF TASTE

POEMS and other compositions in words are beautiful in proportion as they are conversant with beautiful objects—or as they suggest to us, in a more direct way, the moral and social emotions on which the beauty of all objects depends. Theorems and demonstrations, again, are beautiful according as they excite in us emotions of admiration for the genius and intellectual power of their inventors, and images of the magnificent and beneficial ends to which such discoveries may be applied;—and mechanical contrivances are beautiful when they remind us of similar talents and ingenuity, and at the same time impress us with a more direct sense of their vast utility to mankind, and of the great additional conveniences with which life is consequently adorned. In all cases, therefore, there is the suggestion of some interesting conception or emotion associated with a present perception, in which it is apparently confounded and embodied—and this, according to the whole of the preceding deduction, is the distinguishing characteristic of beauty.

Having now explained, as fully as we think necessary, the grounds of that opinion as to the nature of beauty which appears to be most conformable to the truth, we have only to add a word or two as to the necessary consequences of its adoption upon several other controversies of a kindred description.

In the first place, then, we conceive that it establishes the substantial identity of the sublime, the beautiful, and the picturesque; and consequently puts an end to all controversy that is not purely verbal, as to the difference of those several qualities. Every material object that interests us, without actually hurting or gratifying our bodily feelings, must do so, according to this theory, in one and the same manner,—that is, by suggesting or recalling some emotion or affection of ourselves or some other sentient being, and presenting, to our imagination at least, some natural object of love, pity, admiration, or awe. The interest of material objects, therefore, is always *the same;* and arises, in every case, not from any physical qualities they may possess, but from their association with some idea of emotion. But though material objects have but one means of exciting emotion, the emotions they do excite are infinite. They are mirrors that may reflect all shades and all colours, and, in point of fact, do seldom reflect the same hues twice. No two interesting objects, perhaps, whether known by the name of beautiful, sublime, or picturesque, ever produced exactly the same emotion in the beholder; and no one object, it is most probable, ever moved any two persons to the very same conceptions. As they may be associated with all the feelings and affections of which the human mind is susceptible, so they may suggest those feelings in all their variety, and, in fact, do daily excite all sorts of emotions—running through every gradation, from extreme gaiety and elevation to the borders of horror and disgust.

Now it is certainly true that all the variety of emotions raised in this way on the single basis of association may be classed, in a rude way, under the denominations of sublime, beautiful, and picturesque, according as they partake of awe, tenderness, or admiration; and we have no other objection to this nomenclature except its extreme imperfection, and the delusions to which we know that it has given occasion. If objects that interest by their association with ideas of power and danger and terror are to be distinguished by the peculiar name of the sublime, why should there not be a separate name also for objects that interest by associations of mirth and gaiety—another for those that please by suggestions of softness and melancholy—another for such as are connected with impressions of comfort and tranquillity—and another for those that are related to pity and admiration and love and regret and all the other distinct emotions and affections of our nature? These are not in reality less distinguishable from each other than from the emotions of awe and veneration that confer the title of sublime on *their* representatives; and while all the former are confounded under the comprehensive appellation of beauty, this partial attempt at distinction is only apt to mislead us into an erroneous opinion of our accuracy, and to make us believe, both that there is a greater conformity among the things that pass under the same name, and a greater difference between those that pass under different names, than is really the case. We have seen already that the radical error of almost all preceding inquirers has lain in supposing that everything that passed under the name of beautiful must have some real and inherent quality in common with everything else that obtained that name. And it is scarcely necessary for us to observe that it has been almost as general an opinion that sublimity was not only something

radically different from beauty, but actually opposite to it; whereas the fact is, that it is far more nearly related to some sorts of beauty than many sorts of beauty are to each other; and that both are founded exactly upon the same principle of suggesting some past or possible emotion of some sentient being.

Upon this important point we are happy to find our opinions confirmed by the authority of Mr. Stewart, who, in his *Essay on the Beautiful,* already referred to, has observed, not only that there appears to him to be no inconsistency or impropriety in such expressions as the *sublime beauties* of nature, or of the sacred Scriptures;—but has added in express terms that 'to oppose the beautiful to the sublime or to the picturesque strikes him as something analogous to a contrast between the beautiful and the comic—the beautiful and the tragic—the beautiful and the pathetic—or the beautiful and the romantic.'

The only other advantage which we shall specify as likely to result from the general adoption of the theory we have been endeavouring to illustrate is, that it seems calculated to put an end to all these perplexing and vexatious questions about the standard of taste, which have given occasion to so much impertinent and so much elaborate discussion. If things are not beautiful in themselves, but only as they serve to suggest interesting conceptions to the mind, then everything which does in point of fact suggest such a conception to any individual, *is beautiful* to that individual; and it is not only quite true that there is no room for disputing about tastes, but that all tastes are equally just and correct, in so far as each individual speaks only of his own emotions. When a man calls a thing beautiful, however, he may indeed mean to make two very different assertions;—he may mean that it gives *him* pleasure by suggesting to him some interesting emotion; and, in this sense, there can be no doubt that, if he merely speak truth, the thing is beautiful; and that it pleases him precisely in the same way that all other things please those to whom they appear beautiful. But if he mean farther to say that the thing possesses some quality which should make it appear beautiful to every other person, and that it is owing to some prejudice or defect in them if it appear otherwise, then he is as unreasonable and absurd as he would think those who should attempt to convince him that he felt no emotion of beauty.

All tastes, then, are equally just and true, in

so far as concerns the individual whose taste is in question; and what a man feels distinctly to be beautiful, *is beautiful* to him, whatever other people may think of it. All this follows clearly from the theory now in question: but it does not follow, from it, that all tastes are equally good or desirable, or that there is any difficulty in describing that which is really the best, and the most to be envied. The only use of the faculty of taste is to afford an innocent delight, and to assist in the cultivation of a finer morality; and that man certainly will have the most delight from this faculty, who has the most numerous and most powerful perceptions of beauty. But, if beauty consist in the reflection of our affections and sympathies, it is plain that *he* will always see the most beauty whose affections are the warmest and most exercised—whose imagination is the most powerful, and who has most accustomed himself to attend to the objects by which he is surrounded. In so far as mere feeling and enjoyment are concerned, therefore, it seems evident that the best taste must be that which belongs to the best affections, the most active fancy, and the most attentive habits of observation. It will follow pretty exactly, too, that all men's perceptions of beauty will be nearly in proportion to the degree of their sensibility and social sympathies; and that those who have no affections towards sentient beings, will be as certainly insensible to beauty in external objects, as he, who cannot hear the sound of his friend's voice, must be deaf to its echo.

In so far as the sense of beauty is regarded as a mere source of enjoyment, this seems to be the only distinction that deserves to be attended to; and the only cultivation that taste should ever receive, with a view to the gratification of the individual, should be through the indirect channel of cultivating the affections and powers of observation. If we aspire, however, to be *creators,* as well as observers of beauty, and place any part of our happiness in ministering to the gratification of others—as artists, or poets, or authors of any sort—then, indeed, a new distinction of tastes, and a far more laborious system of cultivation, will be necessary. A man who pursues only his own delight, will be as much charmed with objects that suggest powerful emotions in consequence of personal and accidental associations, as with those that introduce similar emotions by means of associations that are universal and indestructible. To him, all objects of the former class are really as beautiful as those

of the latter—and for his own gratification, the creation of that sort of beauty is just as important an occupation: but if he conceive the ambition of creating beauties for the admiration of others, he must be cautious to employ only such objects as are the *natural* signs, or the *inseparable* concomitants of emotions, of which the greater part of mankind are susceptible; and his taste will *then* deserve to be called bad and false, if he obtrude upon the public, as beautiful, objects that are not likely to be associated in common minds with any interesting impressions.

For a man himself, then, there is no taste that is either bad or false; and the only difference worthy of being attended to, is that between a great deal and a very little. Some who have cold affections, sluggish imaginations, and no habits of observation, can with difficulty discern beauty in anything; while others, who are full of kindness and sensibility, and who have been accustomed to attend to all the objects around them, feel it almost in everything. It is no matter what other people may think of the objects of their admiration; nor ought it to be any concern of theirs that the public would be astonished or offended, if they were called upon to join in that admiration. So long as no such call is made, this anticipated discrepancy of feeling need give *them* no uneasiness; and the suspicion of it should produce no contempt in any other persons. It is a strange aberration indeed of vanity that makes us despise persons for being happy—for having sources of enjoyment in which we cannot share:—and yet this is the true source of the ridicule which is so generally poured upon individuals who seek only to enjoy their peculiar tastes unmolested:—for, if there be any truth in the theory we have been expounding, no taste is bad for any other reason than because it is peculiar —as the objects in which it delights must actually serve to suggest to the individual those common emotions and universal affections upon which the sense of beauty is everywhere founded. The misfortune is, however, that we are apt to consider all persons who make known their peculiar relishes, and especially all who create any objects for their gratification, as in some measure dictating to the public, and setting up an idol for general adoration; and hence this intolerant interference with almost all peculiar perceptions of beauty, and the unsparing derision that pursues all deviations from acknowledged standards. This intolerance, we admit, is often provoked by something of a spirit of *proselytism* and arrogance, in those who mistake their own casual associations for natural or universal relations; and the consequence is, that mortified vanity ultimately dries up, even for them, the fountain of their peculiar enjoyment; and disenchants, by a new association of general contempt or ridicule, the scenes that had been consecrated by some innocent but accidental emotion.

As all men must have some peculiar associations, all men must have some peculiar notions of beauty, and, of course, to a certain extent, a taste that the public would be entitled to consider as false or vitiated. For those who make no demands on public admiration, however, it is hard to be obliged to sacrifice this source of enjoyment; and, even for those who labour for applause, the wisest course, perhaps, if it were only practicable, would be to have *two* tastes—one to enjoy, and one to work by—one founded upon universal associations, according to which they finished those performances for which they challenged universal praise—and another guided by all casual and individual associations, through which they might still look fondly upon nature, and upon the objects of their secret admiration.

1811

From WORDSWORTH'S THE EXCURSION[1]

THIS will never do! It bears no doubt the stamp of the author's heart and fancy; but unfortunately not half so visibly as that of his peculiar system. His former poems were intended to recommend that system, and to bespeak favour for it by their individual merit; but this, we suspect, must be recommended by the system, and can only expect to succeed where it has been previously established. It is longer, weaker, and tamer than any of Mr. Wordsworth's other productions, with less boldness of originality, and less even of that extreme simplicity and lowliness of tone which wavered so prettily, in the *Lyrical Ballads,* between silliness and pathos. We have imitations of Cowper, and even of Milton here, engrafted on the natural drawl of the Lakers[2]—and all diluted into harmony by that profuse and irrepressible wordiness which deluges all the blank verse of this school of poetry, and lubricates and weakens the whole structure of their style.

Though it fairly fills four hundred and twenty good quarto pages, without note, vignette, or any sort of extraneous assistance, it is stated in the title—with something of an imprudent candour—to be but 'a portion' of a larger work; and in the preface, where an attempt is rather unsuccessfully made to explain the whole design, it is still more rashly disclosed that it is but '*a part of the second part,* of a *long* and laborious work'—which is to consist of three parts!

What Mr. Wordsworth's ideas of length are, we have no means of accurately judging. But we

[1] I have spoken in many places rather too bitterly and confidently of the faults of Mr. Wordsworth's poetry; and forgetting that, even on my own view of them, they were but faults of taste, or venial self-partiality, have sometimes visited them, I fear, with an asperity which should be reserved for objects of moral reprobation. If I were now to deal with the whole question of his poetical merits, though my judgement might not be substantially different, I hope I should repress the greater part of these *vivacités* of expression: and indeed so strong has been my feeling in this way, that, considering how much I have always loved many of the attributes of his genius, and how entirely I respect his character, it did at first occur to me whether it was quite fitting that, in my old age and his, I should include in this publication any of those critiques which may have formerly given pain or offence, to him or his admirers. But, when I reflected that the mischief, if there really ever was any, was long ago done, and that I still retain, in substance, the opinions which I should now like to have seen more gently expressed, I felt that to omit all notice of them on the present occasion, might be held to import a retraction which I am as far as possible from intending; or even be represented as a very shabby way of backing out of sentiments which should either be manfully persisted, in, or openly renounced, and abandoned as untenable.

I finally resolved, therefore, to reprint my review of *The Excursion,* which contains a pretty full view of my griefs and charges against Mr. Wordsworth; set forth too, I believe, in a more temperate strain than most of my other inculpations,—and of which I think I may now venture to say farther that if the faults are unsparingly noted, the beauties are not penuriously or grudgingly allowed, but commended to the admiration of the reader with at least as much heartiness and good-will.

But I have also reprinted a short paper on the same author's *White Doe of Rylstone,*—in which there certainly is no praise, or notice of beauties, to set against the very unqualified censures of which it is wholly made up. I have done this, however, not merely because I adhere to these censures, but chiefly because it seemed necessary to bring me fairly to issue with those who may not concur in them. I can easily understand that many whose admiration of *The Excursion,* or the *Lyrical Ballads,* rests substantially on the passages which I too should join in admiring, may view with greater indulgence than I can do, the tedious and flat passages with which they are interspersed, and may consequently think my censure of these works a great deal too harsh and uncharitable. Between such persons and me, therefore, there may be no radical difference of opinion, or contrariety as to principles of judgement. But if there be any who actually admire this *White Doe of Rylstone,* or *Peter Bell the Waggoner,* or the *Lamentations of Martha Rae,* or the *Sonnets on the Punishment of Death,* there can be no such ambiguity, or means of reconcilement. Now I have been assured not only that there are such persons, but that almost all those who seek to exalt Mr. Wordsworth as the founder of a new school of poetry, consider these as by far his best and most characteristic productions, and would at once reject from their communion anyone who did not acknowledge in them the traces of a high inspiration. Now I wish it to be understood, that when I speak with general intolerance or impatience of the school of Mr. Wordsworth, it is to the school holding these tenets, and applying these tests, that I refer, and I really do not see how I could better explain the grounds of my dissent from their doctrines, than by republishing my remark on this *White Doe.*—(Jeffrey's note in the collected edition of his works, 1844.)

[2] The label fastened by Jeffrey upon Wordsworth, Coleridge, and Southey because of their residence in the lake district of England.

cannot help suspecting that they are liberal, to a degree that will alarm the weakness of most modern readers. As far as we can gather from the preface, the entire poem—or one of them (for we really are not sure whether there is to be one or two) is of a biographical nature, and is to contain the history of the author's mind, and of the origin and progress of his poetical powers, up to the period when they were sufficiently matured to qualify him for the great work on which he has been so long employed. Now, the quarto before us contains an account of one of his youthful rambles in the vales of Cumberland, and occupies precisely the period of three days! So that, by the use of a very powerful *calculus,* some estimate may be formed of the probable extent of the entire biography.

This small specimen, however, and the statements with which it is prefaced, have been sufficient to set our minds at rest in one particular. The case of Mr. Wordsworth, we perceive, is now manifestly hopeless; and we give him up as altogether incurable, and beyond the power of criticism. We cannot indeed altogether omit taking precautions now and then against the spreading of the malady; but for himself, though we shall watch the progress of his symptoms as a matter of professional curiosity and instruction, we really think it right not to harass him any longer with nauseous remedies, but rather to throw in cordials and lenitives, and wait in patience for the natural termination of the disorder. In order to justify this desertion of our patient, however, it is proper to state why we despair of the success of a more active practice.

A man who has been for twenty years at work on such matter as is now before us, and who comes complacently forward with a whole quarto of it, after all the admonitions he has received, cannot reasonably be expected to 'change his hand, or check his pride,' upon the suggestion of far weightier monitors than we can pretend to be. Inveterate habit must now have given a kind of sanctity to the errors of early taste; and the very powers of which we lament the perversion, have probably become incapable of any other application. The very quantity, too, that he has written, and is at this moment working up for publication upon the old pattern, makes it almost hopeless to look for any change of it. All this is so much capital already sunk in the concern, which must be sacrificed if that be abandoned; and no man likes to give up for lost the

time and talent and labour which he has embodied in any permanent production. We were not previously aware of these obstacles to Mr. Wordsworth's conversion; and, considering the peculiarities of his former writings merely as the result of certain wanton and capricious experiments on public taste and indulgence, conceived it to be our duty to discourage their repetition by all the means in our power. We now see clearly, however, how the case stands; and, making up our minds, though with the most sincere pain and reluctance, to consider him as finally lost to the good cause of poetry, shall endeavour to be thankful for the occasional gleams of tenderness and beauty which the natural force of his imagination and affections must still shed over all his productions, and to which we shall ever turn with delight, in spite of the affectation and mysticism and prolixity, with which they are so abundantly contrasted.

Long habits of seclusion, and an excessive ambition of originality, can alone account for the disproportion which seems to exist between this author's taste and his genius; or for the devotion with which he has sacrificed so many precious gifts at the shrine of those paltry idols which he has set up for himself among his lakes and his mountains. Solitary musings, amidst such scenes, might no doubt be expected to nurse up the mind to the majesty of poetical conception, (though it is remarkable that all the greater poets lived, or had lived, in the full current of society); but the collision of equal minds—the admonition of prevailing impressions—seems necessary to reduce its redundancies, and repress that tendency to extravagance or puerility, into which the self-indulgence and self-admiration of genius is so apt to be betrayed, when it is allowed to wanton, without awe or restraint, in the triumph and delight of its own intoxication. That its flights should be graceful and glorious in the eyes of men, it seems almost to be necessary that they should be made in the consciousness that men's eyes are to behold them, and that the inward transport and vigour by which they are inspired should be tempered by an occasional reference to what will be thought of them by those ultimate dispensers of glory. An habitual and general knowledge of the few settled and permanent maxims which form the canon of general taste in all large and polished societies—a certain tact, which informs us at once that many things, which we still love, and are moved by in secret, must necessarily be despised as childish, or derided as absurd, in all such societies—though it will not stand in the place of genius, seems necessary to the success of its exertions; and though it will never enable any one to produce the higher beauties of art, can alone secure the talent which does produce them from errors that must render it useless. Those who have most of the talent, however, commonly acquire this knowledge with the greatest facility; and if Mr. Wordsworth, instead of confining himself almost entirely to the society of the dalesmen and cottagers, and little children, who form the subjects of his book, had condescended to mingle a little more with the people that were to read and judge of it, we cannot help thinking that its texture might have been considerably improved. At least it appears to us to be absolutely impossible that any one who had lived or mixed familiarly with men of literature and ordinary judgement in poetry (of course we exclude the coadjutors and disciples of his own school) could ever have fallen into such gross faults, or so long mistaken them for beauties. His first essays[3] we looked upon in a good degree as poetical paradoxes,—maintained experimentally, in order to display talent, and court notoriety;—and so maintained, with no more serious belief in their truth than is usually generated by an ingenious and animated defence of other paradoxes. But when we find that he has been for twenty years exclusively employed upon articles of this very fabric, and that he has still enough of raw material on hand to keep him so employed for twenty years to come, we cannot refuse him the justice of believing that he is a sincere convert to his own system, and must ascribe the peculiarities of his composition, not to any transient affectation, or accidental caprice of imagination, but to a settled perversity of taste or understanding, which has been fostered, if not altogether created, by the circumstances to which we have alluded.

The volume before us, if we were to describe it very shortly, we should characterise as a tissue of moral and devotional ravings, in which innumerable changes are rung upon a very few simple and familiar ideas—but with such an accompaniment of long words, long sentences, and unwieldy phrases, and such a hubbub of strained raptures and fantastical sublimities, that it is often difficult for the most skilful and attentive student to obtain a glimpse of the author's meaning—and altogether impossible for an ordinary

reader to conjecture what he is about. Moral and religious enthusiasm, though undoubtedly poetical emotions, are at the same time but dangerous inspirers of poetry, nothing being so apt to run into interminable dulness or mellifluous extravagance without giving the unfortunate author the slightest intimation of his danger. His laudable zeal for the efficacy of his preachments, he very naturally mistakes for the ardour of poetical inspiration; and, while dealing out the high words and glowing phrases which are so readily supplied by themes of this description, can scarcely avoid believing that he is eminently original and impressive. All sorts of commonplace notions and expressions are sanctified in his eyes by the sublime ends for which they are employed; and the mystical verbiage of the Methodist pulpit is repeated till the speaker entertains no doubt that he is the chosen organ of divine truth and persuasion. But if such be the common hazards of seeking inspiration from those potent fountains, it may easily be conceived what chance Mr. Wordsworth had of escaping their enchantment, with his natural propensities to wordiness, and his unlucky habit of debasing pathos with vulgarity. The fact accordingly is, that in this production he is more obscure than a Pindaric poet of the seventeenth century,[4] and more verbose 'than even himself of yore'; while the wilfulness with which he persists in choosing his examples of intellectual dignity and tenderness exclusively from the lowest ranks of society, will be sufficiently apparent, from the circumstance of his having thought fit to make his chief prolocutor[5] in this poetical dialogue, and chief advocate of Providence and Virtue, *an old Scotch Pedlar*, retired indeed from business, but still rambling about in his former haunts, and gossiping among his old customers, without his pack on his shoulders. The other persons of the drama are a retired military chaplain, who has grown half an atheist and half a misanthrope, the wife of an unprosperous weaver, a servant girl with her natural child, a parish pauper, and one or two other personages of equal rank and dignity.

The character of the work is decidedly didactic; and more than nine-tenths of it are occupied with a species of dialogue, or rather a series of long sermons or harangues which pass between the pedlar, the author, the old chaplain, and a worthy vicar, who entertains the whole party at

---

3 attempts; referring to Wordsworth's poems in *Lyrical Ballads*, 1798.

4 Abraham Cowley, who imitated the elaborate odes of the Greek poet Pindar.

5 spokesman.

dinner on the last day of their excursion. The incidents which occur in the course of it are as few and trifling as can well be imagined; and those which the different speakers narrate in the course of their discourses, are introduced rather to illustrate their arguments or opinions, than for any interest they are supposed to possess of their own. The doctrine which the work is intended to enforce, we are by no means certain that we have discovered. In so far as we can collect, however, it seems to be neither more nor less than the old familiar one, that a firm belief in the providence of a wise and beneficent Being must be our great stay and support under all afflictions and perplexities upon earth; and that there are indications of his power and goodness in all the aspects of the visible universe, whether living or inanimate, every part of which should therefore be regarded with love and reverence, as exponents of those great attributes. We can testify, at least, that these salutary and important truths are inculcated at far greater lengths, and with more repetitions, than in any ten volumes of sermons that we ever perused. It is also maintained, with equal conciseness and originality, that there is frequently much good sense, as well as much enjoyment, in the humbler conditions of life; and that, in spite of great vices and abuses, there is a reasonable allowance both of happiness and goodness in society at large. If there be any deeper or more recondite doctrines in Mr. Wordsworth's book, we must confess that they have escaped us; and, convinced as we are of the truth and soundness of those to which we have alluded, we cannot help thinking that they might have been better enforced with less parade and prolixity. His effusions on what may be called the physiognomy of external nature, or its moral and theological expression, are eminently fantastic, obscure, and affected. It is quite time, however, that we should give the reader a more particular account of this singular performance.

It opens with a picture of the author toiling across a bare common in a hot summer day, and reaching at last a ruined hut surrounded with tall trees, where he meets by appointment with a hale old man, with an iron-pointed staff lying beside him. Then follows a retrospective account of their first acquaintance—formed, it seems, when the author was at a village school, and his aged friend occupied 'one room—the fifth part of a house'[6]—in the neighbourhood. After this, we have the history of this reverend person at no small length. He was born, we are happy to find,

in Scotland—among the hills of Athol; and his mother, after his father's death, married the parish schoolmaster—so that he was taught his letters betimes. But then, as it is here set forth with much solemnity,

> From his sixth year, the boy of whom I speak,
> In summer tended cattle on the hills![7]

And again, a few pages after, that there may be no risk of mistake as to a point of such essential importance—

> From early childhood, even, as hath been said,
> From his *sixth year,* he had been sent abroad,
> *In summer*—to tend herds! Such was his task![8]

In the course of this occupation it is next recorded that he acquired such a taste for rural scenery and the open air, that when he was sent to teach a school in a neighbouring village, he found it 'a misery to him,'[9] and determined to embrace the more romantic occupation of a pedlar—or, as Mr. Wordsworth more musically expresses it,

> A vagrant merchant, bent beneath his load;[10]

—and in the course of his peregrinations had acquired a very large acquaintance, which, after he had given up dealing, he frequently took a summer ramble to visit.

The author, on coming up to this interesting personage, finds him sitting with his eyes half shut,—and not being quite sure whether he is asleep or awake, stands 'some minutes' space'[11] in silence beside him.—'At length,' says he, with his own delightful simplicity—

> At length I hail'd him—*seeing that his hat*
> *Was moist* with water-drops, as if the brim
> Had newly scoop'd a running stream!—
>
>   *   *   **
>
> —''Tis,' said I, 'a burning day!
> My lips are parched with thirst;—but you, I
>   guess,
> Have somewhere found relief!'[12]

Upon this, the benevolent old man points him out, not a running stream, but a well in a corner, to which the author repairs, and after minutely describing its situation, beyond a broken wall, and between two alders that 'grew in a cold damp nook,'[13] he thus faithfully chronicles the process of his return:—

---

6 I, 57.

7 I, 118–19.   8 I, 197–9.   9 I, 314.
10 I, 324.   11 I, 443.
12 I, 444–50.   13 I, 461.

My thirst I slak'd, and from the cheerless spot
Withdrawing, straightway to the shade re-
turn'd,
Where sat the old man on the cottage bench.[14]

The Pedlar then gives an account of the last inhabitants of the deserted cottage beside them.
These were a good industrious weaver and his
wife and children. They were very happy for
awhile, till sickness and want of work came upon
them, and then the father enlisted as a soldier,
and the wife pined in that lonely cottage—growing every year more careless and desponding, as
her anxiety and fears for her absent husband, of
whom no tidings ever reached her, accumulated.
Her children died and left her cheerless and
alone; and at last she died also; and the cottage
fell to decay. We must say that there is very considerable pathos in the telling of this simple story,
and that they who can get over the repugnance
excited by the triteness of its incidents, and the
lowness of its objects, will not fail to be struck
with the author's knowledge of the human heart,
and the power he possesses of stirring up its
deepest and gentlest sympathies. His prolixity,
indeed, it is not so easy to get over. This little
story fills about twenty-five quarto pages, and
abounds, of course, with mawkish sentiment and
details of preposterous minuteness. When the
tale is told, the travellers take their staffs and end
their first day's journey, without further adventure, at a little inn. . . .

[The review includes at this point a résumé of the
poem, book by book.]

Our abstract of the story has been so extremely
concise that it is more than usually necessary for
us to lay some specimens of the work itself before our readers. Its grand staple, as we have already said, consists of a kind of mystical morality: and the chief characteristics of the style are
that it is prolix, and very frequently unintelligible: and though we are sensible that no great
gratification is to be expected from the exhibition of those qualities, yet it is necessary to give
our readers a taste of them, both to justify the
sentence we have passed, and to satisfy them
that it was really beyond our power to present
them with any abstract or intelligible account of
those long conversations which we have had so
much occasion to notice in our brief sketch of
its contents. We need give ourselves no trouble,
however, to select passages for this purpose.
Here is the first that presents itself to us on open-

ing the volume; and if our readers can form the
slightest guess at its meaning, we must give them
credit for a sagacity to which we have no pretension.

But by the storms of *circumstance* unshaken,
And subject neither to eclipse or wane,
Duty exists;—immutably survive,
For our support, the measures and the forms,
Which an abstract Intelligence supplies;
Whose kingdom is where Time and Space are not:
Of other converse, which mind, soul, and heart,
Do, with united urgency, require,
What more, that may not perish?[15]

'Tis, by comparison, an easy task
Earth to despise; but to converse with Heav'n,
This is not easy:—to relinquish all
We have, or hope, of happiness and joy,—
And stand in freedom loosen'd from this world;
I deem not arduous!—but must needs confess
That 'tis a thing impossible to frame
Conceptions equal to the Soul's desires.[16]

This is a fair sample of that rapturous mysticism which eludes all comprehension, and fills
the despairing reader with painful giddiness and
terror. . . .

There is no beauty, we think, it must be admitted, in these passages, and so little either of
interest or curiosity in the incidents they disclose,
that we can scarcely conceive that any man to
whom they had actually occurred should take
the trouble to recount them to his wife and children by his idle fireside; but that man or child
should think them worth writing down in blank
verse and printing in magnificent quarto, we
should certainly have supposed altogether impossible, had it not been for the ample proofs
which Mr. Wordsworth has afforded to the contrary.

Sometimes their silliness is enhanced by a paltry attempt at effect and emphasis, as in the following account of that very touching and extraordinary occurrence of a lamb bleating among
the mountains. The poet would actually persuade
us that he thought the mountains themselves
were bleating, and that nothing could be so
grand or impressive. 'List!' cries the old Pedlar,
suddenly breaking off in the middle of one of his
daintiest ravings—

—'List!—I heard,
From yon huge breast of rock, *a solemn bleat!*
Sent forth as if it were the mountain's voice!
As if the visible mountain made the cry!

14 I, 463–5.   15 IV, 71–9.   16 IV, 130–37.

Again!'—The effect upon the soul was such
As he express'd; for, from the mountain's heart
The solemn bleat appear'd to come! There was
No other—and the region all around
Stood silent, empty of all shape of life.
—*It was a Lamb*—left somewhere to itself![17]

What we have now quoted will give the reader a notion of the taste and spirit in which this volume is composed: and yet if it had not contained something a good deal better, we do not know how we should have been justified in troubling him with any account of it. But the truth is that Mr. Wordsworth, with all his perversities, is a person of great powers; and has frequently a force in his moral declamations, and a tenderness in his pathetic narratives, which neither his prolixity nor his affectation can altogether deprive of their effect. . . .

Nobody can be more disposed to do justice to the great powers of Mr. Wordsworth than we are; and, from the first time that he came before us, down to the present moment, we have uniformly testified in their favour, and assigned indeed our high sense of their value as the chief ground of the bitterness with which we resented their perversion. That perversion, however, is now far more visible than their original dignity; and while we collect the fragments, it is impossible not to mourn over the ruins from which we are condemned to pick them. If any one should doubt of the existence of such a perversion, or be disposed to dispute about the instances we have hastily brought forward, we would just beg leave to refer him to the general plan and character of the poem now before us. Why should Mr. Wordsworth have made his hero a superannuated pedlar? What but the most wretched affectation, or provoking perversity of taste, could induce any one to place his chosen advocate of wisdom and virtue in so absurd and fantastic a condition? Did Mr. Wordsworth really imagine that his favourite doctrines were likely to gain anything in point of effect or authority by being put into the mouth of a person accustomed to higgle about tape or brass sleeve-buttons? Or is it not plain that, independent of the ridicule and disgust which such a personification must excite in many of his readers, its adoption exposes his work throughout to the charge of revolting incongruity and utter disregard of probability or nature? For, after he has thus wilfully debased his moral teacher by a low occupation, is there one word that he puts into his

17 IV, 402–11.

mouth, or one sentiment of which he makes him the organ, that has the most remote reference to that occupation? Is there anything in his learned, abstract and logical harangues that savours of the calling that is ascribed to him? Are any of their materials such as a pedlar could possibly have dealt in? Are the manners, the diction, the sentiments in any, the very smallest degree, accommodated to a person in that condition? or are they not eminently and conspicuously such as could not by possibility belong to it? A man who went about selling flannel and pocket-handkerchiefs in this lofty diction would soon frighten away all his customers; and would infallibly pass either for a madman or for some learned and affected gentleman, who, in a frolic, had taken up a character which he was peculiarly ill qualified for supporting.

The absurdity in this case, we think, is palpable and glaring; but it is exactly of the same nature with that which infects the whole substance of the work, a puerile ambition of singularity engrafted on an unlucky predilection for truisms, and an affected passion for simplicity and humble life, most awkwardly combined with a taste for mystical refinements, and all the gorgeousness of obscure phraseology. His taste for simplicity is evinced by sprinkling up and down his interminable declamations a few descriptions of baby-houses, and of old hats with wet brims; and his amiable partiality for humble life, by assuring us that a wordy rhetorician, who talks about Thebes, and allegorizes all the heathen mythology, was once a pedlar—and making him break in upon his magnificent orations with two or three awkward notices of something that he had seen when selling winter raiment about the country—or of the changes in the state of society, which had almost annihilated his former calling.

1814

From KEATS' ENDYMION AND POEMS, 1820

WE had never happened to see either of these volumes till very lately—and have been exceedingly struck with the genius they display, and the spirit of poetry which breathes through all their extravagance. That imitation of our older writers, and especially of our older dramatists, to which we cannot help flattering ourselves that we have somewhat contributed, has brought on, as it were, a second spring in our poetry;—and few of its blossoms are either more profuse of sweetness, or richer in promise, than this which is now before us. Mr. Keats, we understand, is still a very young man; and his whole works, indeed, bear evidence enough of the fact. They are full of extravagance and irregularity, rash attempts at originality, interminable wanderings, and excessive obscurity. They manifestly require, therefore, all the indulgence that can be claimed for a first attempt:—But we think it no less plain that they deserve it: For they are flushed all over with the rich lights of fancy; and so coloured and bestrewn with the flowers of poetry, that even while perplexed and bewildered in their labyrinths, it is impossible to resist the intoxication of their sweetness, or to shut our hearts to the enchantments they so lavishly present. The models upon which he has formed himself, in the *Endymion,* the earliest and by much the most considerable of his poems, are obviously *The Faithful Shepherdess* of Fletcher, and *The Sad Shepherd* of Ben Jonson;—the exquisite metres and inspired diction of which he has copied with great boldness and fidelity—and, like his great originals, has also contrived to impart to the whole piece that true rural and poetical air —which breathes only in them, and in Theocritus—which is at once homely and majestic, luxurious and rude, and sets before us the genuine sights and sounds and smells of the country, with all the magic and grace of Elysium. His subject has the disadvantage of being mythological; and in this respect, as well as on account of the raised and rapturous tone it consequently assumes, his poem, it may be thought, would be better compared to the *Comus* and the *Arcades* of Milton, of which, also, there are many traces of imitation. The great distinction, however, between him and these divine authors, is, that imagination in them is subordinate to reason and judgement, while, with him, it is paramount and supreme—that their ornaments and images are employed to embellish and recommend just sentiments, engaging incidents, and natural characters, while his are poured out without measure or restraint, and with no apparent design but to unburden the breast of the author, and give vent to the overflowing vein of his fancy. The thin and scanty tissue of his story is merely the light framework on which his florid wreaths are suspended, and while his imaginations go rambling and entangling themselves everywhere, like wild honeysuckles, all idea of sober reason, and plan, and consistency, is utterly forgotten, and 'strangled in their waste fertility.' A great part of the work, indeed, is written in the strangest and most fantastical manner that can be imagined.

It seems as if the author had ventured everything that occurred to him in the shape of a glittering image or striking expression—taken the first word that presented itself to make up a rhyme, and then made that word the germ of a new cluster of images—a hint for a new excursion of the fancy—and so wandered on, equally forgetful whence he came, and heedless whither he was going, till he had covered his pages with an interminable arabesque of connected and incongruous figures, that multiplied as they extended, and were only harmonized by the brightness of their tints, and the graces of their forms. In this rash and headlong career he has of course many lapses and failures. There is no work, accordingly, from which a malicious critic could cull more matter for ridicule, or select more obscure, unnatural, or absurd passages. But we do not take *that* to be our office;—and must beg leave, on the contrary, to say, that any one who, on this account, would represent the whole poem as despicable, must either have no notion of poetry, or no regard to truth.

It is, in truth, at least as full of genius as of absurdity; and he who does not find a great deal in it to admire and to give delight, cannot in his heart see much beauty in the two exquisite dramas to which we have already alluded; or find any great pleasure in some of the finest creations of Milton and Shakespeare. There are very many such persons, we verily believe, even among the reading and judicious part of the community— correct scholars, we have no doubt, many of them, and, it may be, very classical composers in prose and in verse—but utterly ignorant, on our view of the matter, of the true genius of English poetry, and incapable of estimating its appropriate and most exquisite beauties. With that spirit we have no hesitation in saying that Mr. Keats is deeply imbued—and of those beauties he has presented us with many striking examples. We are very much inclined indeed to add, that we do not know any book which we would sooner employ as a test to ascertain whether anyone had in him a native relish for poetry, and a genuine sensibility to its intrinsic charm. . . .

Mr. Keats has unquestionably a very beautiful imagination, a perfect ear for harmony, and a great familiarity with the finest diction of English poetry; but he must learn not to misuse or misapply these advantages; and neither to waste the good gifts of nature and study on intractable themes, nor to luxuriate too recklessly on such as are more suitable.

1820

1775 · CHARLES LAMB · 1834

1775   Born 10 February in Crown Office Row, Inner Temple, London, in which place his father, John Lamb, was the clerk and confidential attendant of Samuel Salt, a lawyer.

1782–9   Educated at Christ's Hospital, where he formed an enduring friendship with his schoolmate S. T. Coleridge.

1791–1825   After a few months' employment at the South Sea House, was appointed clerk in the East India House, where during thirty-three years of employment the hundred official folios of what he facetiously called his true 'works' were produced.

1794–5   Joined Coleridge in writing sonnets for the *Morning Post;* assisted James White in the composition of *Original Letters of Sir John Falstaff;* was briefly confined to an asylum for the insane, probably as the result of an unsuccessful love affair with Ann Simmons.

1796   His mother was stabbed to death by his sister, Mary, in a fit of insanity. Following the tragedy, Lamb undertook the responsibility of his sister's safe keeping, and although she repaid him with intelligent and affectionate companionship, she remained subject to periodic seizures. The whole future course of his domestic life was lived under the cursed shadow of madness. Contributed four sonnets to a volume of *Poems on Various Subjects* by Coleridge and some pieces of blank verse in a second edition (1797).

1797   Spent his short summer holiday with Coleridge at Nether Stowey, where he met the Wordsworths, William and Dorothy, and established a warm friendship with both.

1798   Published, with Charles Lloyd, *Blank Verse* and a tragic prose tale, *Rosamund Gray*.

1799   On the death of his father, Mary Lamb came to live again with her brother, their home then being at Pentonville, London.

1801   Settled at Mitre Court Buildings, Temple, London; began to contribute to the newspapers.

1802   Published *John Woodvil,* a blank-verse tragedy in the Elizabethan style.

1806   A farce, *Mr. H.,* produced at Drury Lane, which did not survive the night of its first appearance.

1807   Published, with Mary Lamb, *Tales from Shakespeare,* which has become a juvenile classic.

1808   Published *Adventures of Ulysses,* another book for children, and *Specimens of the English Dramatic Poets.*

1809   Moved to Inner Temple Lane, Temple, London. Published, with Mary Lamb, *Poetry for Children* and *Mrs. Leicester's School.*

1810–11   Contributed to Leigh Hunt's quarterly *The Reflector.*

1817   Moved to Great Russell Street, Covent Garden, London.

1818   Published *Works,* a collection of his miscellaneous writings in prose and verse.

1819   Proposed marriage to Fanny Kelly, the actress; but was refused.

1820–23   Contributed to the *London Magazine* the first series of the *Essays of Elia.*

1823   Published *Essays of Elia* in a separate volume. Adopted Emma Isola. Moved to Colebrook Row, Islington, London.

1825   Retired on a pension of £450 per year.

1827   Moved to the quiet of the country at Enfield to aid his sister's health.

1830   Published *Album Verses*.

1833   Published *Last Essays of Elia*. Moved to Edmonton, so that his sister might be under the continual care of a Mr. and Mrs. Walden. Emma Isola married Edward Moxon, leaving Lamb more alone than ever.

1834   Died 27 December at Edmonton.

CHARLES LAMB is 'the prince of English essayists.' His greatest companions, Bacon, Thomas Browne, Steele and Addison, Goldsmith, and Hazlitt, share many characteristics with him—exquisite humor, lofty eloquence, human kindliness, and heart-touching pathos—but there is 'no other who has so firm a hold upon our affection.' Lamb was a man of great charity and incomparable gentleness of disposition. From the day of his mother's tragic death until his own, he patiently and uncomplainingly devoted himself to the care of his sister. The sacrifice, instead of making him bitter, only served to enlarge his sympathies, especially for 'fireside happiness and for children.' It is this boundless charity that irradiates from the pages of his essays and letters and endears him to us. He takes us intimately into his confidence. To an almost unparalleled degree in English literature Lamb is personal and autobiographical. He had an exquisite sense of make-believe, an irrepressible sense of humor, a sweet and reasonable sanity. He was a Londoner all his days and London was his recreation and delight, 'particularly all that was expressive of its *human* side, present or past.'

Like many another author, Lamb tried his hand at various types of writing with only partial success before he discovered his own best medium of expression. His first published writings were poetry, when he was only twenty-two. He was, truthfully, not much of a poet, there being apparently some native deficiency in 'the accomplishment of verse.' Many pleasant things, however, tender and youthfully sentimental, are to be found in his early volumes; and at least two poems, *Hester* and *The Old Familiar Faces,* have become as famous as his essays. Lamb's first book of criticism, *Specimens of the English Dramatic Poets,* though following the poetry by something over a decade, also appeared fairly early in his career. In his critical commentaries in this volume on the plays of Middleton, Webster, Tourneur, Ford, and other Elizabethan dramatists he discerned in 'brief, essential words' the true spirit of the originals. Like Coleridge, Lamb excelled 'not only in supreme aesthetic divination, but also in the recreative power to communicate it.' This power he showed pre-eminently in his protest against the acting of Shakespeare's tragedies. Tragic 'essences,' he maintained—with ample justification, it would seem—are beyond even the greatest actors and are to be captured only by silent, thoughtful reading. Much of Lamb's criticism is casual and unaspiring to be found in the margins of books, in letters, and elsewhere. Nevertheless, his critical observations form an important part of the progressive body of literary theory in his day. With Coleridge and Hazlitt, he helped measurably to enlarge the province of English criticism.

Between 1811 and 1820 Lamb played whist and entertained his friends at his famous Wednesday and Thursday evenings, but he wrote very little. In 1818, he gathered together and published his *Works,* in two volumes, no doubt believing that with this event his literary career was virtually ended. Yet the essays, and in particular the *Essays of Elia,* upon which his fame almost entirely rests were still to be written. Lamb had made some trials and successes in the essay, when he was thirty-five, but did not find ease in his manner until he was forty-five. It was then, in 1820, that he began his now celebrated contributions to the *London Magazine* under the pseudonym of Elia. Lamb borrowed the name from a fellow-clerk at the South Sea House, and apparently enjoying the freedom that anonymity gave him and the joke of mystifying his readers, retained the disguise throughout the five-year period that the series was continued. When in 1825, the *London Magazine,* through faulty management, was disrupted, Lamb dissociated himself from the journal. Following this break, his enthusiasm faded rapidly—no doubt, too, the mine of reminiscence had been pretty thoroughly worked out—with the result that there is a decided falling-off in the quality of all his writing after Elia. But in the *Essays of Elia* he is supreme.

These essays taken all together are not very numerous, but they afford a surprising variety of subject matter and of treatment. They range from the vision of lovely children that were never to be to the ironical jesting upon borrowers evoked by S. T. C.'s depredations upon Lamb's library, from the mock-serious rebellion against poor relations to the poetically sublime memories of Mackery End, where hardly one person 'was not a cousin there.' They sustain throughout an intimate and self-revealing quality 'from the child Elia's small and magic world of The Temple sundials and fountains to the man's superannuation from his daily work of year on year' (Blunden). Over and over again we share Lamb's delight in familiar places and their old associations, in simple things and simple people—in 'hearty, homely, loving Hertfordshire,' in the feasting chimney-sweeps of Smithfield, in the gray-headed beggar on London bridge, in the runaway scholar at Christ's Hospital—in all the tender, melancholy, humorous thought evoked by recollection—in his speculations too, 'Sun and sky, and breeze, and solitary walks, and summer holidays, and the greenness of fields, and the delicious juices of meats and fishes, and society, and the cheerful glass, and fire-side conversations, and innocent vanities, and jests, and *irony* itself—do these things go out with life?' Wisdom is the greatest of Lamb's powers and the foundation of his sincerity. Never is there in him a show of self-pity or false pathos. He offers his ideas tentatively, half-apologetically. The essays are full of those 'surmises, guesses, misgivings, half-intuitions, semi-consciousnesses, partial illuminations, dim instincts, embryo conceptions,' which he upholds in *Imperfect Sympathies*. By an instinctive sureness of taste and an ineradicable humility he 'woos and wins us.' Next to wisdom, humor is a foremost quality; humor of infinite jest; humor mellowed and made droll through whimsical retrospect and in combination with delicate pathos; humor charged 'with poetry and kindliness, with imagination and with love, with airiest romance and profoundest good sense' (Elwin).

The essays unfold informally, following the lead of the author's fancy or his boyish good spirits into a 'far-ranging train of new and fertile thoughts'; but they never go astray or are diffuse. For all their apparent ease and spontaneity, they are not hasty things thrown off in a moment; rather they are careful and elaborate studies in structure and style. Lamb had a characteristic fondness for 'whatever was rich and fantastic in an old-fashioned way.' Innate congeniality drew him to the early dramatists and to the seventeenth-century prose masters such as Burton of *The Anatomy of Melancholy*, Fuller, Donne, and most of all, Sir Thomas Browne. In Lamb there flowered again the 'beautiful obliquities' of the old masters side by side with the most conversational expressions of his own day. A great range and variety of quaint and rambling allusions from these and other writers enhance and give an antique flavor to his style. They come forth naturally out of the deeps of his amply stored and resourceful memory—quoted or misquoted—expertly adapted, compact, pregnant. They are not artificially engrafted upon his thought; they are his thought. The same may be said for Lamb's use of quaint and unusual words, his archaisms, his word coinage, his long and learned words, his antique phrases, and his paradoxes. The same may be said for his sentence structure which with its impressive changes of length and stress, its floating parallelism and quaint embroideries, its rich and labyrinthine rhythm is, like other features of his style, highly original. If the occasion called for it, Lamb could and did write with purity and plainness; more often 'he chose not to be plain at all, but characteristically decked out his thoughts in quaint and sumptuous pageantry.'

In Lamb's letters, of which an unusually large number have been preserved, we have perhaps the most complete and fascinating disclosure of a personality in English literature. The letters from the first to the last, with 'absolute spontaneity and utter lack of restraint, give Lamb as he really was' (French). Some in a nonsensical mood are the most delightful buffoonery ever captured in words; many for their sheer unreserve are a joy to the reader. The letters are also of interest to the scholar, not merely for their biographical value but as the first expression of ideas which later develop into essays. *The Dissertation on Roast Pig* and *The Two Races of Men,* among others, first took shape in the letters. But for the general reader the letters, like the essays, are their own excuse for being.

CHILDHOOD FLED

WE were two pretty babes, the youngest she,
The youngest, and the loveliest far, I ween,
And Innocence her name. The time has been,
We two did love each other's company;
Time was, we two had wept to have been apart.
But when, by show of seeming good beguiled,
I left the garb and manners of a child,
And my first love for man's society,
Defiling with the world my virgin heart—
My loved companion dropped a tear, and fled,   10
And hid in deepest shades her awful head.
Beloved, who shall tell me where thou art—
In what delicious Eden to be found—
That I may seek thee, the wide world around?

1795   1796

THE OLD FAMILIAR FACES

WHERE are they gone, the old familiar faces?
I had a mother, but she died, and left me,
Died prematurely in a day of horrors—[1]
All, all are gone, the old familiar faces.

I have had playmates, I have had companions,
In my days of childhood, in my joyful school-
days—
All, all are gone, the old familiar faces.

I have been laughing, I have been carousing,
Drinking late, sitting late, with my bosom
cronies—
All, all are gone, the old familiar faces.   10

I loved a love once, fairest among women;[2]
Closed are her doors on me, I must not see her—
All, all are gone, the old familiar faces.

I have a friend,[3] a kinder friend has no man;
Like an ingrate, I left my friend abruptly;
Left him, to muse on the old familiar faces.

Ghost-like, I paced round the haunts of my
childhood.
Earth seem'd a desert I was bound to traverse,
Seeking to find the old familiar faces.

Friend of my bosom,[4] thou more than a
brother,   20
Why wert not thou born in my father's dwelling?
So might we talk of the old familiar faces.

How some they have died, and some they have
left me,
And some are taken from me;[5] all are departed;
All, all are gone, the old familiar faces.

January 1798   1798

HESTER

[Hester Savory was the daughter of a Quaker gold-smith. She died in her twenty-sixth year a few months after her marriage. In a letter to Manning enclosing these lines Lamb said that he had been in love with her for some years though he had never spoken a word to her in his life.]

WHEN maidens such as Hester die,
Their place ye may not well supply,
Though ye among a thousand try,
    With vain endeavour.

A month or more hath she been dead,
Yet cannot I by force be led
To think upon the wormy bed,
    And her together.

A springy motion in her gait,
A rising step, did indicate   10
Of pride and joy no common rate,
    That flush'd her spirit.

I know not by what name beside
I shall it call:—if 'twas not pride,
It was a joy to that allied,
    She did inherit.

Her parents held the Quaker rule,
Which doth the human feeling cool,
But she was train'd in Nature's school,
    Nature had blest her.   20

---

1 alluding to the day his sister, Mary, went insane and killed their mother.
2 Ann Simmons of Blenheims. She is Alice W——n in *Dream Children.*
3 Charles Lloyd, between whom and Lamb some coolness had arisen over their joint volumes of poetry.

---

4 Coleridge.
5 As a result of a second attack of insanity in January 1798, his sister was taken back to the asylum.

A waking eye, a prying mind,
A heart that stirs, is hard to bind,
A hawk's keen sight ye cannot blind,
    Yet could not Hester.

My sprightly neighbour, gone before
To that unknown and silent shore,
Shall we not meet, as heretofore,
    Some summer morning,

When from thy cheerful eyes a ray
Hath struck a bliss upon the day,   30
A bliss that would not go away,
    A sweet forewarning?

1803   1818

WRITTEN AT CAMBRIDGE

I was not train'd in Academic bowers,
And to those learned streams I nothing owe
Which copious from those twin fair founts do
    flow;
Mine have been anything but studious hours.
Yet I can fancy, wandering 'mid thy towers,
Myself a nursling, Granta, of thy lap;
My brow seems tightening with the Doctor's cap,
And I walk *gowned;* feel unusual powers.
Strange forms of logic clothe my admiring
    speech,

Old Ramus' [1] ghost is busy at my brain;   10
And my skull teems with notions infinite.
Be still, ye reeds of Camus, while I teach
Truths, which transcend the searching School-
    men's vein,
And half had staggered that stout Stagirite! [2]

August 1819   1819

From ON THE TRAGEDIES OF SHAKE-SPEARE, CONSIDERED WITH REFERENCE TO THEIR FITNESS FOR STAGE REPRESENTATION

It may seem a paradox, but I cannot help being of opinion that the plays of Shakespeare are less calculated for performance on a stage, than those of almost any other dramatist whatever. Their distinguished excellence is a reason that they should be so. There is so much in them which comes not under the province of acting, with which eye, and tone, and gesture, have nothing to do.

The glory of the scenic art is to personate passion, and the turns of passion; and the more coarse and palpable the passion is, the more hold upon the eyes and ears of the spectators the performer obviously possesses. For this reason, scolding scenes, scenes where two persons talk themselves into a fit of fury, and then in a surprising manner talk themselves out of it again, have always been the most popular upon our stage. And the reason is plain, because the spectators are here most palpably appealed to; they are the proper judges in this war of words; they are the legitimate ring that should be formed round such 'intellectual prize-fighters.' Talking is the direct object of the imitation here. But in all the best dramas, and in Shakespeare above all, how obvious it is that the form of *speaking,* whether it be in soliloquy or dialogue, is only a medium, and often a highly artificial one, for putting the reader or spectator into possession of that knowledge of the inner structure and workings of mind in a character, which he could otherwise never have arrived at *in that form of composition* by any gift short of intuition. We do here as we do with novels written in the *epistolary form.* How many improprieties, perfect solecisms in letter-writing, do we put up with in *Clarissa* [1] —and other books, for the sake of the delight with which that form upon the whole gives us.

But the practice of stage representation reduces everything to a controversy of elocution. Every character, from the boisterous blasphemings of Bajazet [2] to the shrinking timidity of womanhood, must play the orator. The love-dialogues of Romeo and Juliet, their silver-sweet sounds of lovers' tongues by night; the more intimate and sacred sweetness of nuptial colloquy between an Othello or a Posthumus with their married wives, all those delicacies which are so delightful in the reading, as when we read of those youthful dalliances in Paradise—

                  As beseem'd
Fair couple link'd in happy nuptial league
Alone; [3]

by the inherent fault of stage representation, how are these things sullied and turned from their very nature by being exposed to a large assembly; when such speeches as Imogen addresses to her lord, [4] come drawling out of the mouth of a hired actress, whose courtship, though nominally

---

1 Petrus Ramus, 1515-72, a French logician noted for his writings directed against Aristotelianism.
2 Aristotle, the celebrated Greek philosopher, who was born in Stagira, a city in Macedonia.

1 Richardson's *Clarissa,* 1748.
2 a ranting character in Marlowe's *Tamburlaine.*
3 *Paradise Lost,* IV, 338-40.
4 *Cymbeline,* I, i,

addressed to the personated Posthumus, is manifestly aimed at the spectators, who are to judge of her endearments and her returns of love.

The character of Hamlet is perhaps that by which, since the days of Betterton,[5] a succession of popular performers have had the greatest ambition to distinguish themselves. The length of the part may be one of their reasons. But for the character itself, we find it in a play, and therefore we judge it a fit subject of dramatic representation. The play itself abounds in maxims and reflections beyond any other, and therefore we consider it as a proper vehicle for conveying moral instruction. But Hamlet himself—what does he suffer meanwhile by being dragged forth as a public schoolmaster, to give lectures to the crowd! Why, nine parts in ten of what Hamlet does are transactions between himself and his moral sense; they are the effusions of his solitary musings, which he retires to holes and corners and the most sequestered parts of the palace to pour forth; or rather, they are the silent meditations with which his bosom is bursting, reduced to *words* for the sake of the reader, who must else remain ignorant of what is passing there. These profound sorrows, these light-and-noise-abhorring ruminations, which the tongue scarce dares utter to deaf walls and chambers, how can they be represented by a gesticulating actor, who comes and mouths them out before an audience, making four hundred people his confidants at once? I say not that it is the fault of the actor so to do; he must pronounce them *ore rotundo*,[6] he must accompany them with his eye, he must insinuate them into his auditory by some trick of the eye, tone, or gesture, or he fails. *He must be thinking all the while of his appearance, because he knows that all the while the spectators are judging of it.* And this is the way to represent the shy, negligent, retiring Hamlet.

It is true that there is no other mode of conveying a vast quantity of thought and feeling to a great portion of the audience, who otherwise would never earn it for themselves by reading, and the intellectual acquisition gained this way may, for aught I know, be inestimable; but I am not arguing that Hamlet should not be acted, but how much Hamlet is made another thing by being acted. I have heard much of the wonders which Garrick[7] performed in this part; but as I never saw him, I must have leave to doubt

whether the representation of such a character came within the province of his art. Those who tell me of him, speak of his eye, of the magic of his eye, and of his commanding voice: physical properties, vastly desirable in an actor, and without which he can never insinuate meaning into an auditory,—but what have they to do with Hamlet? what have they to do with intellect? In fact, the things aimed at in theatrical representation are to arrest the spectator's eye upon the form and the gesture, and so to gain a more favourable hearing to what is spoken: it is not what the character is, but how he looks; not what he says, but how he speaks it. I see no reason to think that if the play of *Hamlet* were written over again by some such writer as Banks or Lillo,[8] retaining the process of the story, but totally omitting all the poetry of it, all the divine features of Shakespeare, his stupendous intellect, and only taking care to give us enough of passionate dialogue, which Banks or Lillo were never at a loss to furnish,—I see not how the effect could be much different upon an audience, nor how the actor has it in his power to represent Shakespeare to us differently from his representation of Banks or Lillo. Hamlet would still be a youthful accomplished prince, and must be gracefully personated; he might be puzzled in his mind, wavering in his conduct, seemingly-cruel to Ophelia; he might see a ghost, and start at it, and address it kindly when he found it to be his father; all this in the poorest and most homely language of the servilest creeper after nature that ever consulted the palate of an audience, without troubling Shakespeare for the matter: and I see not but there would be room for all the power which an actor has, to display itself. All the passions and changes of passion might remain: for those are much less difficult to write or act than is thought; it is a trick easy to be attained; it is but rising or falling a note or two in the voice, a whisper with a significant foreboding look to announce its approach, and so contagious the counterfeit appearance of any emotion is that, let the words be what they will, the look and tone shall carry it off and make it pass for deep skill in the passions.

It is common for people to talk of Shakespeare's plays being *so natural;* that everybody can understand him. They are natural indeed; they are grounded deep in nature, so deep that the depth of them lies out of the reach of most of us. You shall hear the same persons say that

---

5 Thomas Betterton, 1635-1710, a great actor of Dryden's age.
6 'with rotund voice'—Horace, *Ars Poetica*, 323.
7 David Garrick, 1717-79, a celebrated English actor.

8 John Banks, *c.*1650-96, and George Lillo, 1693-1739, were authors of popular, melodramatic plays.

George Barnwell[9] is very natural, and *Othello* very natural, that they are both very deep; and to them they are the same kind of thing. At the one they sit and shed tears, because a good sort of young man is tempted by a naughty woman to commit *a trifling peccadillo,* the murder of an uncle or so, that is all, and so comes to an untimely end, which is *so moving;* and at the other, because a blackamoor in a fit of jealousy kills his innocent white wife: and the odds are that ninety-nine out of a hundred would willingly behold the same catastrophe happen to both the heroes, and have thought the rope more due to Othello than to Barnwell. For of the texture of Othello's mind, the inward construction marvellously laid open with all its strengths and weaknesses, its heroic confidences and its human misgivings, its agonies of hate springing from the depths of love, they see no more than the spectators at a cheaper rate, who pay their pennies apiece to look through the man's telescope in Leicester-fields, see into the inward plot and topography of the moon. Some dim thing or other they see; they see an actor personating a passion, of grief or anger, for instance, and they recognize it as a copy of the usual external effects of such passions; for at least as being true to *that symbol of the emotion which passes current at the theatre for it,* for it is often no more than that: but of the grounds of the passion, its correspondence to a great or heroic nature, which is the only worthy object of tragedy,—that common auditors know anything of this, or can have any such notions dinned into them by the mere strength of an actor's lungs,—that apprehensions foreign to them should be thus infused into them by storm, I can neither believe, nor understand how it can be possible.

We talk of Shakespeare's admirable observation of life, when we should feel, that not from a petty inquisition into those cheap and every-day characters which surrounded him, as they surround us, but from his own mind, which was, to borrow a phrase of Ben Jonson's the very 'sphere of humanity,'[10] he fetched those images of virtue and of knowledge, of which every one of us recognizing a part, think we comprehend in our natures the whole, and oftentimes mistake the powers which he positively creates in us, for nothing more than indigenous faculties of our own minds which only waited the application of

9 a sentimental tragedy by George Lillo in which the hero, George Barnwell, is led on by his courtesan lover to rob his employer and murder his uncle.
10 *A Pindaric Ode to Sir Lucius Cary and Sir H. Morrison,* ii, 20.

corresponding virtues in him to return a full and clear echo of the same.

To return to Hamlet.—Among the distinguishing features of that wonderful character, one of the most interesting (yet painful) is that soreness of mind which makes him treat the intrusions of Polonius with harshness, and that asperity which he puts on in his interviews with Ophelia. These tokens of an unhinged mind (if they be not mixed in the latter case with a profound artifice of love, to alienate Ophelia by affected discourtesies, so to prepare her mind for the breaking off of that loving intercourse, which can no longer find a place amidst business so serious as that which he has to do) are parts of his character, which to reconcile with our admiration of Hamlet, the most patient consideration of his situation is no more than necessary; they are what we *forgive afterwards,* and explain by the whole of his character, but *at the time* they are harsh and unpleasant. Yet such is the actor's necessity of giving strong blows to the audience, that I have never seen a player in this character who did not exaggerate and strain to the utmost these ambiguous features,—these temporary deformities in the character. They make him express a vulgar scorn at Polonius, which utterly degrades his gentility, and which no explanation can render palatable; they make him show contempt, and curl up the nose at Ophelia's father,—contempt in its very grossest and most hateful form; but they get applause by it: it is natural, people say; that is, the words are scornful, and the actor expresses scorn, and that they can judge of: but why so much scorn, and of that sort, they never think of asking.

So to Ophelia.—All the Hamlets that I have ever seen, rant and rave at her as if she had committed some great crime, and the audience are highly pleased, because the words of the part are satirical, and they are enforced by the strongest expression of satirical indignation of which the face and voice are capable. But then, whether Hamlet is likely to have put on such brutal appearances to a lady whom he loved so dearly, is never thought on. The truth is that in all such deep affections as had subsisted between Hamlet and Ophelia, there is a stock of *supererogatory love* (if I may venture to use the expression), which in any great grief of heart, especially where that which preys upon the mind cannot be communicated, confers a kind of indulgence upon the grieved party to express itself, even to its heart's dearest object, in the language of a temporary alienation; but it is not alienation, it is a distraction purely, and so it always makes itself to be felt by that object: it is not anger, but grief assuming the appearance of anger,—love awkwardly counterfeiting hate, as sweet countenances when they try to frown: but such sternness and fierce disgust as Hamlet is made to show is no counterfeit, but the real face of absolute aversion,—of irreconcilable alienation. It may be said he puts on the madman; but then he should only so far put on this counterfeit lunacy as his own real distraction will give him leave; that is, incompletely, imperfectly; not in that confirmed practised way, like a master of his art, or, as Dame Quickly would say, 'like one of those harlotry players.'[11] . . .

The truth is, the characters of Shakespeare are so much the objects of meditation rather than of interest or curiosity as to their actions, that while we are reading any of his great criminal characters,—Macbeth, Richard, even Iago,—we think not so much of the crimes which they commit, as of the ambition, the aspiring spirit, the intellectual activity, which prompts them to overleap those moral fences. Barnwell is a wretched murderer; there is a certain fitness between his neck and the rope; he is the legitimate heir to the gallows; nobody who thinks at all can think of any alleviating circumstances in his case to make him a fit object of mercy. Or to take an instance from the higher tragedy, what else but a mere assassin is Glenalvon![12] Do we think of anything but of the crime which he commits, and the rack which he deserves? That is all which we really think about him. Whereas in corresponding characters in Shakespeare so little do the actions comparatively affect us, that while the impulses, the inner mind in all its perverted greatness, solely seems real and is exclusively attended to, the crime is comparatively nothing. But when we see these things represented, the acts which they do are comparatively everything, their impulses nothing. The state of sublime emotion into which we are elevated by those images of night and horror which Macbeth is made to utter, that solemn prelude with which he entertains the time till the bell shall strike which is to call him to murder Duncan,—when we no longer read it in a book, when we have given up that vantage-ground of abstraction which reading possesses over seeing, and come to see a man in his bodily shape before our eyes actually preparing to commit a murder, if the acting be true and impressive, as I have witnessed it in Mr. K.'s[13] performance of that part, the painful anxiety about the act, the natural longing to prevent it while it yet seems unperpetrated, the too close pressing semblance of reality, give a pain and an uneasiness which totally destroy all the delight which the words in the book convey, where the deed doing never presses upon us with the painful sense of presence: it rather seems to belong to history,—to something past and inevitable, if it has anything to do with time at all. The sublime images, the poetry alone, is that which is present to our minds in the reading.

So to see Lear acted,—to see an old man tottering about the stage with a walking-stick, turned out of doors by his daughters in a rainy night, has nothing in it but what is painful and disgusting. We want to take him into shelter and relieve him. That is all the feeling which the acting of Lear ever produced in me. But the Lear of Shakespeare cannot be acted. The contemptible machinery by which they mimic the storm which he goes out in, is not more inadequate to represent the horrors of the real elements, than any actor can be to represent Lear: they might more easily propose to personate the Satan of Milton upon a stage, or one of Michael Angelo's terrible figures. The greatness of Lear is not in corporal dimension, but in intellectual: the explosions of his passion are terrible as a volcano: they are storms turning up and disclosing to the bottom that sea, his mind, with all its vast riches. It is his mind which is laid bare. This case of flesh and blood seems too insignificant to be thought on; even as he himself neglects it. On the stage we see nothing but corporal infirmities and weakness, the impotence of rage; while we read it, we see not Lear, but we are Lear,—we are in his mind, we are sustained by a grandeur which baffles the malice of daughters and storms; in the aberrations of his reason, we discover a mighty irregular power of reasoning, immethodized from the ordinary purposes of life, but exerting its powers, as the wind blows where it listeth, at will upon the corruptions and abuses of mankind. What have looks, or tones, to do with that sublime identification of his age with that of the *heavens themselves*, when in his reproaches to them for conniving at the injustice of his children, he reminds them that 'they themselves are old'?[14] What gesture shall we appropriate to

---

11 *I Henry IV*, II, iv, 437.
12 a character in *Douglas*, by John Home, 1722–1808.

13 John Philip Kemble, 1757–1823, eminent Shakespearean actor.
14 *King Lear*, II, iv, 194.

this? What has the voice or the eye to do with such things? But the play is beyond all art, as the tamperings with it show: it is too hard and stony; it must have love-scenes, and a happy ending. It is not enough that Cordelia is a daughter; she must shine as a lover too. Tate[15] has put his hook in the nostrils of this Leviathan, for Garrick and his followers, the showmen of the scene, to draw the mighty beast about more easily. A happy ending!—as if the living martyrdom that Lear had gone through,—the flaying of his feelings alive, did not make a fair dismissal from the stage of life the only decorous thing for him. If he is to live and be happy after, if he could sustain this world's burden after, why all this pudder and preparation,—why torment us with all this unnecessary sympathy? As if the childish pleasure of getting his gilt robes and sceptre again could tempt him to act over again his misused station,—as if at his years, and with his experience, anything was left but to die.

1811

CHRIST'S HOSPITAL FIVE AND THIRTY YEARS AGO[1]

In Mr. Lamb's 'Works,' published a year or two since, I find a magnificent eulogy on my old school,[2] such as it was, or now appears to him to have been, between the years 1782 and 1789. It happens, very oddly, that my own standing at Christ's was nearly corresponding with his; and, with all gratitude to him for his enthusiasm for the cloisters, I think he has contrived to bring together whatever can be said in praise of them, dropping all the other side of the argument most ingeniously.

I remember L. at school; and can well recollect that he had some peculiar advantages, which I and others of his schoolfellows had not. His friends lived in town, and were near at hand; and he had the privilege of going to see them, almost as often as he wished, through some invidious distinction, which was denied to us. The present worthy sub-treasurer[3] to the Inner Temple can explain how that happened. He had his tea and

hot rolls in a morning, while we were battening upon our quarter of a penny loaf—our *crug*[4]—moistened with attenuated small beer, in wooden piggins,[5] smacking of the pitched leathern jack it was poured from. Our Monday's milk porritch, blue and tasteless, and the pease soup of Saturday, coarse and choking, were enriched for him with a slice of 'extraordinary bread and butter,' from the hot-loaf of the Temple. The Wednesday's mess of millet, somewhat less repugnant (we had three banyan[6] to four meat days in the week), was endeared to his palate with a lump of double-refined, and a smack of ginger (to make it go down the more glibly) or the fragrant cinnamon. In lieu of our *half-pickled* Sundays, or *quite fresh* boiled beef on Thursdays (strong as *caro equina*[7]), with detestable marigolds floating in the pail to poison the broth—our scanty mutton crags[8] on Fridays—and rather more savoury, but grudging, portions of the same flesh, rotten-roasted or rare, on the Tuesdays (the only dish which excited our appetites, and disappointed our stomachs, in almost equal proportion)—he had his hot plate of roast veal, or the more tempting griskin[9] (exotics unknown to our palates), cooked in the paternal kitchen (a great thing), and brought him daily by his maid or aunt! I remember the good old relative (in whom love forbade pride) squatting down upon some odd stone in a by-nook of the cloisters, disclosing the viands (of higher regale than those cates[10] which the ravens ministered to the Tishbite[11]); and the contending passions of L. at the unfolding. There was love for the bringer; shame for the thing brought, and the manner of its bringing; sympathy for those who were too many to share in it; and, at top of all, hunger (eldest, strongest of the passions!) predominant, breaking down the stony fences of shame, and awkwardness, and a troubling over-consciousness.

I was a poor friendless boy.[12] My parents and those who should care for me, were far away. Those few acquaintances of theirs, which they could reckon upon being kind to me in the great city, after a little forced notice, which they had the grace to take of me on my first arrival in town, soon grew tired of my holiday visits. They seemed to them to recur too often, though I

---

15 Nahum Tate, 1652-1715, wrote an adaptation of *King Lear* in which Lear and Cordelia survive, and Cordelia marries Edgar.

1 Christ's Hospital was the old Blue Coat School, founded in 1552 by Edward VI. It was removed from London to Horsham, Sussex, in 1902. In the essay Lamb blends his own schoolboy experiences with those of Coleridge and others.

2 *Recollections of Christ's Hospital.*—(Lamb.)

3 Randal Norris, an old friend of Lamb's father.

4 slang for 'bread.'

5 small pails.

6 meatless.

7 'horse flesh.'

8 necks.

9 pork loin.

10 delicacies.

11 Elijah. See I Kings, xvii, 6.

12 Here Lamb writes as though he were Coleridge.

thought them few enough; and one after another, they all failed me, and I felt myself alone among six hundred playmates.

O the cruelty of separating a poor lad from his early homestead! The yearnings which I used to have towards it in those unfledged years! How, in my dreams, would my native town (far in the west) come back, with its church, and trees, and faces! How I would wake weeping, and in the anguish of my heart exclaim upon sweet Calne in Wiltshire![13]

To this late hour of my life, I trace impressions left by the recollection of those friendless holidays. The long warm days of summer never return but they bring with them a gloom from the haunting memory of those *whole-day-leaves,* when, by some strange arrangement, we were turned out, for the live-long day, upon our own hands, whether we had friends to go to, or none. I remember those bathing-excursions to the New-River, which L. recalls with such relish, better, I think, than he can—for he was a home-seeking lad, and did not much care for such water-pastimes. How merrily we would sally forth into the fields; and strip under the first warmth of the sun; and wanton like young dace in the streams; getting us appetites for noon, which those of us that were pennyless (our scanty morning crust long since exhausted) had not the means of allaying—while the cattle, and the birds, and the fishes, were at feed about us, and we had nothing to satisfy our cravings—the very beauty of the day, and the exercise of the pastime, and the sense of liberty, setting a keener edge upon them!—How faint and languid, finally, we would return, towards nightfall, to our desired morsel, half-rejoicing, half-reluctant, that the hours of our uneasy liberty had expired!

It was worse in the days of winter, to go prowling about the streets objectless—shivering at cold windows of print-shops, to extract a little amusement; or haply, as a last resort, in the hope of a little novelty, to pay a fifty-times repeated visit (where our individual faces should be as well known to the warden as those of his own charges) to the Lions in the Tower—to whose levée[14] by courtesy immemorial, we had a prescriptive title to admission.

L.'s governor[15] (so we called the patron who presented us to the foundation) lived in a manner under his paternal roof. Any complaint which he had to make was sure of being attended to. This was understood at Christ's, and was an effectual screen to him against the severity of masters, or worse tyranny of the monitors. The oppressions of these young brutes are heart-sickening to call to recollection. I have been called out of my bed, and *waked for the purpose,* in the coldest winter nights—and this not once, but night after night—in my shirt, to receive the discipline of a leathern thong, with eleven other sufferers, because it pleased my callow overseer, when there has been any talking heard after we were gone to bed, to make the six last beds in the dormitory, where the youngest children of us slept, answerable for an offense they neither dared to commit, nor had the power to hinder. The same execrable tyranny drove the younger part of us from the fires, when our feet were perishing with snow; and, under the cruelest penalties, forbad the indulgence of a drink of water, when we lay in sleepless summer nights, fevered with the season, and the day's sports.

There was one H——, who, I learned, in after days was seen expiating some maturer offense in the hulks.[16] (Do I flatter myself in fancying that this might be the planter of that name, who suffered—at Nevis,[17] I think, or St. Kits,[17]—some few years since? My friend Tobin was the benevolent instrument of bringing him to the gallows.) This petty Nero actually branded a boy, who had offended him, with a red hot iron; and nearly starved forty of us, with exacting contributions, to the one-half of our bread, to pamper a young ass, which, incredible as it may seem, with the connivance of the nurse's daughter (a young flame of his) he had contrived to smuggle in, and keep upon the leads[18] of the *ward,* as they called our dormitories. This game went on for better than a week, till the foolish beast, not able to fare well but he must cry roast meat[19]—happier than Caligula's minion,[20] could he have kept his own counsel—but, foolisher, alas! than any of his species in the fables—waxing fat, and kicking, in the fulness of bread, one unlucky minute would needs proclaim his good fortune to the world below; and, laying out his simple throat, blew such a ram's-horn blast, as (toppling down the walls of his own Jericho[21] set concealment any longer at defiance. The client was dismissed,

13 a masquerade for Coleridge's home, Ottery St. Mary, in Devonshire.
14 reception.
15 Samuel Salt, d. 1792, a lawyer of the Inner Temple. He arranged for Lamb to attend Christ's Hospital.
16 prison ship.
17 islands in the British West Indies.
18 the roof.
19 that is, publish his good fortune.
20 the horse that the Roman Emperor Caligula kept in a marble stable and made a Roman consul.
21 Joshua, vi, 5.

with certain attentions, to Smithfield; but I never understood that the patron underwent any censure on the occasion. This was in the stewardship of L.'s admired Perry.

Under the same *facile* administration, can L. have forgotten the cool impunity with which the nurses used to carry away openly, in open platters, for their own tables, one out of two of every hot joint, which the careful matron had been seeing scrupulously weighed out for our dinners? These things were daily practised in that magnificent apartment, which L. (grown connoisseur since, we presume) praises so highly for the grand paintings 'by Verrio,[22] and others,' with which it is 'hung round and adorned.' But the sight of sleek well-fed blue-coat boys in pictures was, at that time, I believe, little consolatory to him, or us, the living ones, who saw the better part of our provisions carried away before our faces by harpies; and ourselves reduced (with the Trojan[23] in the hall of Dido)

To feed our mind with idle portraiture.[24]

L. has recorded the repugnance of the school to *gags,* or the fat of fresh beef boiled; and sets it down to some superstition. But these unctuous morsels are never grateful to young palates (children are universally fat-haters) and in strong, coarse, boiled meats, *unsalted,* are detestable. A *gag-eater* in our time was equivalent to a *goul* and held in equal detestation.——suffered under the imputation:

——— 'Twas said
He ate strange flesh.[25]

He was observed, after dinner, carefully to gather up the remnants left at his table (not many, nor very choice fragments, you may credit me)—and, in an especial manner, these disreputable morsels, which he would convey away and secretly stow in the settle that stood at his bedside. None saw when he ate them. It was rumoured that he privately devoured them in the night. He was watched, but no traces of such midnight practices were discoverable. Some reported that, on leave-days, he had been seen to carry out of the bounds a large blue check handkerchief, full of something. This then must be the accursed thing. Conjecture next was at work to imagine how he could dispose of it. Some said he

sold it to the beggars. This belief generally prevailed. He went about moping. None spake to him. No one would play with him. He was excommunicated; put out of the pale of the school. He was too powerful a boy to be beaten, but he underwent every mode of that negative punishment, which is more grievous than many stripes. Still he persevered. At length he was observed by two of his schoolfellows, who were determined to get at the secret, and had traced him one leave-day for that purpose, to enter a large worn-out building, such as there exist specimens of in Chancery-lane, which are let out to various scales of pauperism with open door, and a common staircase. After him they silently slunk in, and followed by stealth up four flights, and saw him tap at a poor wicket, which was opened by an aged woman, meanly clad. Suspicion was now ripened into certainty. The informers had secured their victim. They had him in their toils. Accusation was formally preferred, and retribution most signal was looked for. Mr. Hathaway, the then steward (for this happened a little after my time), with that patient sagacity which tempered all his conduct, determined to investigate the matter, before he proceeded to sentence. The result was that the supposed mendicants, the receivers or purchasers of the mysterious scraps, turned out to be the parents of ——, an honest couple come to decay,—whom this seasonable supply had, in all probability, saved from mendicancy; and that this young stork, at the expense of his own good name, had all this while been only feeding the old birds!—The governors on this occasion, much to their honour, voted a present relief to the family of ——, and presented him with a silver medal. The lesson which the steward read upon RASH JUDGEMENT, on the occasion of publicly delivering the medal to ——, I believe, would not be lost upon his auditory. I had left school then, but I well remember ——. He was a tall, shambling youth, with a cast in his eye, not at all calculated to conciliate hostile prejudices. I have since seen him carrying a baker's basket. I think I heard he did not do quite so well by himself, as he had done by the old folks.

I was a hypochondriac lad;[26] and the sight of a boy in fetters, upon the day of my first putting on the blue clothes, was not exactly fitted to assuage the natural terrors of initiation. I was of tender years, barely turned of seven; and had

---

22 Antonio Verrio, 1639–1707, Italian mural painter known for his decorations of Windsor palace and Hampton Court.
23 Aeneas.
24 *Aeneid,* I, 464.
25 *Antony and Cleopatra,* I, iv, 67.

26 Lamb here assumes his own character.

only read of such things in books, or seen them but in dreams. I was told he had *run away.* This was the punishment for the first offence. As a novice I was soon after taken to see the dungeons. These were little, square, Bedlam cells, where a boy could just lie at his length upon straw and a blanket—a mattress, I think, was afterwards substituted—with a peep of light, let in askance, from a prison-orifice at top, barely enough to read by. Here the poor boy was locked in by himself all day, without sight of any but the porter who brought him his bread and water—who *might not speak to him;*—or of the beadle, who came twice a week to call him out to receive his periodical chastisement, which was almost welcome, because it separated him for a brief interval from solitude:—and here he was shut by himself *of nights,* out of the reach of any sound, to suffer whatever horrors the weak nerves, and superstition incident to his time of life, might subject him to.[27] This was the penalty for the second offence.—Wouldst thou like, reader, to see what became of him in the next degree?

The culprit, who had been a third time an offender, and whose expulsion was at this time deemed irreversible, was brought forth, as at some solemn *auto da fe,*[28] arrayed in uncouth and most appalling attire—all trace of his late 'watchet weeds'[29] carefully effaced, he was exposed in a jacket, resembling those which London lamplighters formerly delighted in, with a cap of the same. The effect of this divestiture was such as the ingenious devisers of it could have anticipated. With his pale and frighted features, it was as if some of those disfigurements in Dante[30] had seized upon him. In this disguisement he was brought into the hall *(L.'s favourite state-room),* where awaited him the whole number of his school-fellows, whose joint lessons and sports he was thenceforth to share no more; the awful presence of the steward, to be seen for the last time; of the executioner beadle, clad in his state robe for the occasion; and of two faces more, of direr import, because never but in these extremities visible. These were governors; two of

whom, by choice, or charter, were always accustomed to officiate at these *Ultima Supplicia,*[31] not to mitigate (so at least we understood it), but to enforce the uttermost stripe. Old Bamber Gascoigne, and Peter Aubert, I remember, were colleagues on one occasion, when the beadle turning rather pale, a glass of brandy was ordered to prepare him for the mysteries. The scourging was, after the old Roman fashion, long and stately. The lictor accompanied the criminal quite round the hall. We were generally too faint with attending to the previous disgusting circumstances, to make accurate report with our eyes of the degree of corporal punishment inflicted. Report, of course, gave out the back knotty and livid. After scourging, he was made over, in his *San Benito,*[32] to his friends, if he had any (but commonly such poor runagates were friendless), or to his parish officer, who, to enhance the effect of the scene, had his station allotted to him on the outside of the hall gate.

These solemn pageantries were not played off so often as to spoil the general mirth of the community. We had plenty of exercise and recreation *after* school hours; and, for myself, I must confess, that I was never happier, than *in* them. The Upper and Lower Grammar Schools were held in the same room; and an imaginary line only divided their bounds. Their character was as different as that of the inhabitants of the two sides of the Pyrenees. The Rev. James Boyer was the Upper Master; but the Rev. Matthew Field presided over that portion of the apartment of which I had the good fortune to be a member. We lived a life as careless as birds. We talked and did just what we pleased, and nobody molested us. We carried an accidence, or a grammar, for form; but for any trouble it gave us, we might take two years in getting through the verbs deponent, and another two in forgetting all that we had learned about them. There was now and then the formality of saying a lesson, but if you had not learned it, a brush across the shoulders (just enough to disturb a fly) was the sole remonstrance. Field never used the rod; and in truth he wielded the cane with no great good will—holding it 'like a dancer.' It looked in his hands rather like an emblem than an instrument of authority; and an emblem, too, he was ashamed of. He was a good easy man, that did not care to ruffle his own peace, nor perhaps set any great

27 One or two instances of lunacy, or attempted suicide, accordingly, at length convinced the governors of the impolicy of this part of the sentence, and the midnight torture of the spirits was dispensed with. This fancy of dungeons for children was a sprout of Howard's brain, for which (saving the reverence due to Holy Paul) methinks I could willingly spit upon his statue.—(Lamb.)
28 literally 'act of faith;' applied to the execution of judgment upon condemned heretics under the Spanish Inquisition.
29 blue clothes.
30 in the *Inferno.*

31 extreme punishments.
32 the garment worn by persons condemned by the Inquisition when brought forth for execution.

consideration upon the value of juvenile time. He came among us, now and then, but often staid away whole days from us; and when he came, it made no difference to us—he had his private room to retire to, the short time he staid, to be out of the sound of our noise. Our mirth and uproar went on. We had classics of our own, without being beholden to 'insolent Greece or haughty Rome,'[33] that passed current among us —*Peter Wilkins—The Adventures of the Hon. Capt. Robert Boyle—The Fortunate Blue Coat Boy*[34]—and the like. Or we cultivated a turn for mechanic or scientific operations; making little sun-dials of paper; or weaving those ingenious parentheses, called *cat-cradles;* or making dry pease to dance upon the end of a tin pipe; or studying the art military over that laudable game 'French and English,' and a hundred other such devices to pass away the time—mixing the useful with the agreeable—as would have made the souls of Rousseau and John Locke chuckle to have seen us.[35]

Matthew Field belonged to that class of modest divines who affect to mix in equal proportion the *gentleman,* the *scholar,* and the *Christian;* but, I know not how, the first ingredient is generally found to be the predominating dose in the composition. He was engaged in gay parties, or with his courtly bow at some episcopal levée, when he should have been attending upon us. He had for many years the classical charge of a hundred children, during the four or five first years of their education; and his very highest form seldom proceeded further than two or three of the introductory fables of Phædrus. How things were suffered to go on thus, I cannot guess. Boyer, who was the proper person to have remedied these abuses, always affected, perhaps felt, a delicacy in interfering in a province not strictly his own. I have not been without my suspicions that he was not altogether displeased at the contrast we presented to his end of the school. We were a sort of Helots to his young Spartans.[36] He would sometimes, with ironic deference, send to borrow a rod of the Under Master, and then, with sardonic grin, observe to one of his upper

boys, 'how neat and fresh the twigs looked.' While his pale students were battering their brains over Xenophon and Plato, with a silence as deep as that enjoined by the Samite,[37] we were enjoying ourselves at our ease in our little Goshen.[38] We saw a little into the secrets of his discipline, and the prospect did but the more reconcile us to our lot. His thunders rolled innocuous for us; his storms came near, but never touched us; contrary to Gideon's miracle,[39] while all around were drenched, our fleece was dry. His boys turned out the better scholars; we, I suspect, have the advantage in temper. His pupils cannot speak of him without something of terror allaying their gratitude; the remembrance of Field comes back with all the soothing images of indolence, and summer slumbers, and work like play, and innocent idleness, and Elysian exemptions, and life itself a 'playing holiday.'

Though sufficiently removed from the jurisdiction of Boyer, we were near enough (as I have said) to understand a little of his system. We occasionally heard sounds of the *Ululantes,*[40] and caught glances of Tartarus.[41] B. was a rabid pedant. His English style was crampt to barbarism. His Easter anthems (for his duty obliged him to those periodical flights) were grating as *scrannel*[42] *pipes.*[43] He would laugh, ay, and heartily, but then it must be at Flaccus's quibble about *Rex*[44] —— or at the *tristis severitas in vultu,* or *inspicere in patinas,*[45] of Terence—thin jests, which at their first broaching could hardly have had *vis*[46] enough to move Roman muscle.—He had two wigs, both pedantic, but of differing

---

33 Jonson, *To the Memory of My Beloved Master, William Shakespeare,* 39.
34 eighteenth-century popular adventure-stories.
35 the reference is to the educational theories of these two philosophers, who advocated combining the practical with the theoretical.
36 It was a practice of the Spartans to exhibit a drunken Helot, or slave, as a warning to their sons.
37 Pythagoras, the Greek philosopher, sixth century B.C., who, it is said, forbade his pupils to speak until they had listened to his lectures for five years.
38 that part of Egypt in which the Hebrews lived while in bondage.
39 Judges, vi, 37-8.
40 howling sufferers.
41 the infernal regions.
42 harsh. See *Lycidas,* 124.
43 In this and everything B. was the antipodes of his coadjutor. While the former was digging his brains for crude anthems, worth a pignut, F. would be recreating his gentlemanly fancy in the more flowery walks of the Muses. A little dramatic effusion of his, under the name of *Vertumnus and Pomona,* is not yet forgotten by the chroniclers of that sort of literature. It was accepted by Garrick, but the town did not give it their sanction. B. used to say of it, in a way of half-compliment, half-irony, that it was *too classical for representation.*—(Lamb.)
44 Horace Flaccus, i.e. the Roman poet, in his *Satires,* I, vii, 35, plays on the double meaning of 'King' as the name of a man, and 'King' as a monarch.
45 'sad severity of his countenance,' spoken of a cunning rogue in Terence's *Andrea;* 'to look into the stewpans,' said by a servant in Terence's *The Adelphi,* in mockery of a father who has advised his son to look into men's lives as into a mirror.
46 strength.

omen. The one serene, smiling, fresh powdered, betokening a mild day. The other, an old discoloured, unkempt, angry caxon,[47] denoting frequent and bloody execution. Woe to the school, when he made his morning appearance in his *passy,* or *passionate wig.* No comet expounded surer.—J. B. had a heavy hand. I have known him double his knotty fist at a poor trembling child (the maternal milk hardly dry upon its lips) with a 'Sirrah, do you presume to set your wits at me?'—Nothing was more common than to see him make a headlong entry into the schoolroom, from his inner recess, or library, and, with turbulent eye, singling out a lad, roar out, 'Od's my life, Sirrah' (his favourite adjuration), 'I have a great mind to whip you,'—then, with as sudden a retracting impulse, fling back into his lair—and, after a cooling lapse of some minutes (during which all but the culprit had totally forgotten the context) drive headlong out again, piecing out his imperfect sense, as if it had been some Devil's Litany, with the expletory yell—'*and I* WILL, *too.*'—In his gentler moods, when the *rabidus furor*[48] was assuaged, he had resort to an ingenious method, peculiar, for what I have heard, to himself, of whipping the boy, and reading the Debates, at the same time; a paragraph, and a lash between; which in those times, when parliamentary oratory was most at a height and flourishing in these realms, was not calculated to impress the patient with a veneration for the diffuser graces of rhetoric.

Once, and but once, the uplifted rod was known to fall ineffectual from his hand—when droll squinting W—— having been caught putting the inside of the master's desk to a use for which the architect had clearly not designed it, to justify himself, with great simplicity averred, that *he did not know that the thing had been forewarned.* This exquisite irrecognition of any law antecedent to the *oral or declaratory,* struck so irresistibly upon the fancy of all who heard it (the pedagogue himself not excepted) that remission was unavoidable.

L. has given credit to B's great merits as an instructor. Coleridge, in his *Literary Life,* has pronounced a more intelligible and ample encomium on them. The author of *The Country Spectator*[49] doubts not to compare him with the ablest teachers of antiquity. Perhaps we cannot

dismiss him better than with the pious ejaculation of C—— when he heard that his old master was on his death-bed—'Poor J. B.!—may all his faults be forgiven; and may he be wafted to bliss by little cherub boys, all head and wings, with no *bottoms* to reproach his sublunary infirmities.'

Under him were many good and sound scholars bred.—First Grecian[50] of my time was Lancelot Pepys Stevens, kindest of boys and men, since Co-grammar-master (and inseparable companion) with Dr. T——e.[51] What an edifying spectacle did this brace of friends present to those who remembered the anti-socialities of their predecessors!—You never met the one by chance in the street without a wonder, which was quickly dissipated by the almost immediate sub-appearance of the other. Generally arm in arm, these kindly coadjutors lightened for each other the toilsome duties of their profession, and when, in advanced age, one found it convenient to retire, the other was not long in discovering that it suited him to lay down the fasces[52] also. Oh, it is pleasant, as it is rare, to find the same arm linked in yours at forty, which at thirteen helped it to turn over the *Cicero De Amicitia,*[53] or some tale of Antique Friendship, which the young heart even then was burning to anticipate!—Co-Grecian with S. was Th——,[54] who has since executed with ability various diplomatic functions at the Northern courts. Th—— was a tall, dark, saturnine youth, sparing of speech, with raven locks. Thomas Fanshaw Middleton followed him (now Bishop of Calcutta) a scholar and a gentleman in his teens. He has the reputation of an excellent critic; and is author (besides *The Country Spectator*) of *A Treatise on the Greek Article, against Sharpe.*—M. is said to bear his mitre in India, where the *regni novitas*[55] (I dare say) sufficiently justifies the bearing. A humility quite as primitive as that of Jewel or Hooker[56] might not be exactly fitted to impress the minds of those Anglo-Asiatic diocesans with a reverence for home institutions, and the church which those fathers watered. The manners of M. at school, though firm, were mild, and unassuming.—Next

---

47 a wig.
48 furious rage.
49 Thomas Fanshaw Middleton, 1769–1822.
50 the name given to the boys in the highest class.
51 Arthur William Trollope, who succeeded Boyer as headmaster.
52 the bundle of rods carried by the Roman lictors as a symbol of authority.
53 Cicero's *Essay Concerning Friendship.*
54 Sir Edward Thornton, 1766–1852, diplomatist.
55 'newness of the rule.'
56 noted English theologians of the sixteenth century.

to M. (if not senior to him) was Richards, author of *The Aboriginal Britons,* the most spirited of the Oxford Prize Poems; a pale, studious Grecian.—Then followed poor S——,[57] ill-fated M——![58] of these the Muse is silent.

> Finding some of Edward's race
> Unhappy pass their annals by.[59]

Come back into memory, like as thou wert in the day-spring of thy fancies, with hope like a fiery column before thee[60]—the dark pillar not yet turned—Samuel Taylor Coleridge—Logician, Metaphysician, Bard!—How have I seen the casual passer through the Cloisters stand still, intranced with admiration (while he weighed the disproportion between the *speech* and the *garb* of the young Mirandula[61]), to hear thee unfold, in thy deep and sweet intonations, the mysteries of Jamblichus, or Plotinus[62] (for even in those years thou waxedst not pale at such philosophic draughts), or reciting Homer in his Greek, or Pindar——while the walls of the old Grey Friars re-echoed to the accents of the *inspired charity-boy!* —Many were the 'wit-combats' (to dally awhile with the words of old Fuller[63]), between him and C. V. LeG——,[64] 'which two I behold like a Spanish great galleon, and an English man of war; Master Coleridge, like the former, was built far higher in learning, solid, but slow in his performances. C. V. L., with the English man of war, lesser in bulk, but lighter in sailing, could turn with all tides, tack about, and take advantage of all winds, by the quickness of his wit and invention.'

Nor shalt thou, their compeer, be quickly forgotten, Allen, with the cordial smile, and still more cordial laugh, with which thou wert wont to make the old Cloisters shake in thy cognition of some poignant jest of theirs; or the anticipation of some more material, and, peradventure, practical one, of thine own. Extinct are those smiles, with that beautiful countenance, with which (for thou wert the *Nireus formosus*[65] of the school), in the days of thy maturer waggery, thou didst disarm the wrath of infuriated town-damsel, who, incensed by provoking pinch, turning tigress-like round, suddenly converted by thy angel-look, exchanged the half-formed terrible '*bl*——,' for a gentler greeting—'*bless thy handsome face!*'

Next follow two, who ought to be now alive, the friends of Elia—the junior LeG——[66] and F——;[67] who impelled, the former by a roving temper, the latter by too quick a sense of neglect —ill capable of enduring the slights poor sizars[68] are sometimes subject to in our seats of learning—exchanged their Alma Mater for the camp; perishing, one by climate, and one on the plains of Salamanca:—LeG——, sanguine, volatile, sweet-natured; F——, dogged, faithful, anticipative of insult, warm-hearted, with something of the old Roman height about him.

Fine, frank-hearted Fr——,[69] the present master of Hertford, with Marmaduke T——,[70] mildest of missionaries—and both my good friends still—close the catalogue of Grecians in my time.

1820

THE TWO RACES OF MEN

THE human species, according to the best theory I can form of it, is composed of two distinct races, *the men who borrow,* and *the men who lend.* To these two original diversities may be reduced all those impertinent classifications of Gothic and Celtic tribes, white men, black men, red men. All the dwellers upon earth, 'Parthians, and Medes, and Elamites,'[1] flock hither, and do naturally fall in with one or other of these primary distinctions. The infinite superiority of the former, which I choose to designate as the *great race,* is discernible in their figure, port, and a certain instinctive sovereignty. The latter are born degraded. 'He shall serve his brethren.'[2] There is something in the air of one of this cast, lean and suspicious; contrasting with the open, trusting, generous manners of the other.

Observe who have been the greatest borrowers

---

57 identified by Lamb as Scott, a student who died in a hospital for the insane.
58 identified by Lamb as Maunde, who was dismissed from school.
59 Prior, *Carmen Seculare* for the year 1700, viii, 4-5.
60 Exodus, xiv, 21-2.
61 Pico della Mirandola, 1463-94, an Italian humanist and writer.
62 Greek neo-platonic philosopher of the third century of the Christian era.
63 Thomas Fuller, 1608-61, whose words Lamb here adapts from his account of the wit combat between Shakespeare and Jonson.
64 Charles Valentine Le Grice.
65 'comely Nireus'—said to be the handsomest Greek at the siege of Troy.

66 Samuel Le Grice, who became a soldier and died in the West Indies.
67 Joseph Favell. He is the 'poor W——' of Lamb's *Poor Relations.*
68 students exempted from college fees.
69 Frederick William Franklin.
70 Marmaduke Thompson.

---

1 Acts, ii, 9.
2 Genesis, ix, 25.

of all ages—Alcibiades[3]—Falstaff[4]—Sir Richard Steele[5]—our late incomparable Brinsley[6]—what a family likeness in all four!

What a careless, even deportment hath your borrower! what rosy gills! what a beautiful reliance on Providence doth he manifest,—taking no more thought than lilies![7] What contempt for money,—accounting it (yours and mine especially) no better than dross. What a liberal confounding of those pedantic distinctions of *meum* and *tuum*![8] or rather, what a noble simplification of language (beyond Tooke[9]), resolving these supposed opposites into one clear, intelligible pronoun adjective!—What near approaches doth he make to the primitive *community*,[10]—to the extent of one half of the principle at least!

He is the true taxer, who 'calleth all the world up to be taxed';[11] and the distance is as vast between him and *one of us*, as subsisted betwixt the Augustan Majesty and the poorest obolary[12] Jew that paid it tribute-pittance at Jerusalem!— His exactions, too, have such a cheerful, voluntary air! So far removed from your sour parochial or state-gatherers,—those ink-horn varlets, who carry their want of welcome in their faces! He cometh to you with a smile, and troubleth you with no receipt; confining himself to no set season. Every day is his Candlemas, or his Feast of Holy Michael.[13] He applieth the *lene tormentum*[14] of a pleasant look to your purse,—which to that gentle warmth expands her silken leaves, as naturally as the cloak of the traveller, for which sun and wind contended![15] He is the true Propontic[16] which never ebbeth! The sea which taketh handsomely at each man's hand. In vain the victim, whom he delighteth to honour, struggles with destiny; he is in the net. Lend therefore cheerfully, O man ordained to lend—that thou lose not in the end, with thy worldly penny, the

reversion promised.[17] Combine not preposterously in thine own person the penalties of Lazarus and of Dives![18]—but, when thou seest the proper authority coming, meet it smilingly, as it were half-way. Come, a handsome sacrifice! See how light *he* makes of it! Strain not courtesies with a noble enemy.

Reflections like the foregoing were forced upon my mind by the death of my old friend, Ralph Bigod, Esq.,[19] who departed this life on Wednesday evening, dying, as he had lived, without much trouble. He boasted himself a descendant from mighty ancestors of that name, who heretofore held ducal dignities in this realm. In his actions and sentiments he belied not the stock to which he pretended. Early in life he found himself invested with ample revenues, which, with that noble disinterestedness which I have noticed as inherent in men of the *great race,* he took almost immediate measures entirely to dissipate and bring to nothing: for there is something revolting in the idea of a king holding a private purse; and the thoughts of Bigod were all regal. Thus furnished, by the very act of disfurnishment; getting rid of the cumbersome luggage of riches, more apt (as one sings)

To slacken virtue, and abate her edge,
Than prompt her to do aught may merit praise;[20]

he set forth, like some Alexander, upon his great enterprise, 'borrowing and to borrow'![21]

In his periegesis,[22] or triumphant progress throughout this island, it has been calculated that he laid a tythe[23] part of the inhabitants under contribution. I reject this estimate as greatly exaggerated:—but having had the honour of accompanying my friend, divers times, in his perambulations about this vast city, I own I was greatly struck at first with the prodigious number of faces we met who claimed a sort of respectful acquaintance with us. He was one day so obliging as to explain the phenomenon. It seems, these were his tributaries; feeders of his exchequer; gentlemen, his good friends (as he was pleased to express himself), to whom he had occasionally been beholden for a loan. Their multitudes did no way disconcert him. He rather took a pride in numbering them; and, with Co-

---

3 a brilliant but dissolute Athenian statesman, fifth century B.C.
4 a famous character in Shakespeare's *Henry IV.*
5 English essayist, 1672-1729, who founded *The Tatler* and contributed to *The Spectator.* Steele was a moralist and a generous spendthrift.
6 Richard Brinsley Sheridan, 1751-1816, noted dramatist, orator, and politician. He, too, was a great spendthrift.
7 Matthew, vi, 28.
8 mine and thine.
9 John Horne Tooke, 1736-1812, politician and philologist.
10 Acts, ii, 44.
11 Luke, ii, 1.
12 impoverished.
13 quarter-days on which rents fell due.
14 'gentle torment'—Horace, *Odes.*
15 in one of Æsop's fables.
16 Ancient name for the Sea of Marmora, between European and Asiatic Turkey. It is not subject to tides.

17 Proverbs, xix, 17.
18 Luke, xvi, 20-31.
19 John Fenwick, editor of the *Albion* to which Lamb contributed.
20 *Paradise Regained.* II, 455.
21 Revelation, vi, 2.
22 tour.
23 tenth.

mus, seemed pleased to be 'stocked with so fair a herd.'[24]

With such sources, it was a wonder how he contrived to keep his treasury always empty. He did it by force of an aphorism, which he had often in his mouth, that 'money kept longer than three days stinks.' So he made use of it while it was fresh. A good part he drank away (for he was an excellent toss-pot), some he gave away, the rest he threw away, literally tossing and hurling it violently from him—as boys do burrs, or as if it had been infectious,—into ponds, or ditches, or deep holes,—inscrutable cavities of the earth; —or he would bury it (where he would never seek it again) by a river's side under some bank, which (he would facetiously observe) paid no interest—but out away from him it must go peremptorily, as Hagar's offspring[25] into the wilderness, while it was sweet. He never missed it. The streams were perennial which fed his fisc.[26] When new supplies became necessary, the first person that had the felicity to fall in with him, friend or stranger, was sure to contribute to the deficiency. For Bigod had an *undeniable* way with him. He had a cheerful, open exterior, a quick jovial eye, a bald forehead, just touched with gray (*cana fides*[27]). He anticipated no excuse, and found none. And, waiving for a while my theory as to the *great race,* I would put it to the most untheorizing reader, who may at times have disposable coin in his pocket, whether it is not more repugnant to the kindliness of his nature to refuse such a one as I am describing, than to say *no* to a poor petitionary rogue (your bastard borrower) who, by his mumping visnomy,[28] tells you, that he expects nothing better, and, therefore, whose preconceived notions and expectations you do in reality so much less shock in the refusal.

When I think of this man; his fiery glow of heart; his swell of feeling, how magnificent, how *ideal* he was; how great at the midnight hour; and when I compare with him the companions with whom I have associated since, I grudge the saving of a few idle ducats, and think that I am fallen into the society of *lenders,* and *little* men.

To one like Elia, whose treasures are rather cased in leather covers than closed in iron coffers, there is a class of alienators more formidable than that which I have touched upon; I mean your *borrowers of books*—*those* mutilators of collections, spoilers of the symmetry of shelves, and creators of odd volumes. There is Comberbatch,[29] matchless in his depredations!

That foul gap in the bottom shelf facing you, like a great eye-tooth knocked out (you are now with me in my little back study in Bloomsbury,[30] reader!), with the huge Switzer-like[31] tomes on each side (like the Guildhall giants,[32] in their reformed posture, guardant of nothing), once held the tallest of my folios, *Opera Bonaventuræ,*[33] choice and massy divinity, to which its two supporters (school divinity also, but of a lesser calibre,—Bellarmine,[34] and Holy Thomas[35]), showed but as dwarfs,—itself an Ascapart![36]—*that* Comberbatch abstracted upon the faith of a theory he holds, which is more easy, I confess, for me to suffer by than to refute, namely, that 'the title to property in a book (my Bonaventure, for instance) is in exact ratio to the claimant's powers of understanding and appreciating the same.' Should he go on acting upon this theory, which of our shelves is safe?

The slight vacuum in the left-hand case—two shelves from the ceiling—scarcely distinguishable but by the quick eye of a loser—was whilom the commodious resting-place of Browne[37] on *Urn Burial*. C. will hardly allege that he knows more about that treatise than I do, who introduced it to him, and was indeed the first (of the moderns) to discover its beauties—but so have I known a foolish lover to praise his mistress in the presence of a rival more qualified to carry her off than himself.—Just below, Dodsley's dramas[38] want their fourth volume, where *Vittoria Corombona*[39] is! The remainder nine are as distasteful as Priam's refuse sons, when the Fates borrowed *Hector*.[40] Here stood *The Anatomy of*

---

24 *Comus,* 152.

25 Ishmael, Genesis xxi.

26 royal treasury.

27 'hoary fidelity'—that is, inspiring respect because of white hair. *Aeneid,* I, 292.

28 mumbling countenance: *mumping* is a coinage from the old word *mumper,* meaning a beggar.

29 Silas Tomkyn Comberback was the pseudonym under which Coleridge enlisted in the dragoons.

30 When Lamb wrote this he was living in Great Russell Street, Covent Garden, not far from Bloomsbury.

31 that is, tall, like the giant men of the Swiss Guard.

32 two colossal wooden figures that stood at the entrance to the council hall of London.

33 the works of St. Bonaventura, an Italian theologian of the thirteenth century.

34 Roberto Bellarmino, 1542-1621, a noted Italian cardinal and Jesuit theologian.

35 St. Thomas Aquinas, famous scholastic philosopher and theologian of the thirteenth century.

36 a giant in the old romance of *Bevis of Hampton*.

37 Sir Thomas Browne, 1605-82, English physician and author.

38 a collection of *Old English Plays* in twelve volumes, 1744, edited by Robert Dodsley.

39 *The White Devil,* a tragedy by John Webster, early seventeenth-century dramatist.

40 After the death of Priam's favorite son, Hector, nine of his sons were left alive. *Iliad,* XXIV, 248ff.

Melancholy,[41] in sober state.—There loitered *The Complete Angler,*[42] quiet as in life, by some stream side.—In yonder nook, *John Buncle,* a widower-volume, with 'eyes closed,' mourns his ravished mate.[43]

One justice I must do my friend, that if he sometimes, like the sea, sweeps away a treasure, at another time, sea-like, he throws up as rich an equivalent to match it. I have a small under-collection of this nature (my friend's gatherings in his various calls), picked up, he has forgotten at what odd places, and deposited with as little memory at mine. I take in these orphans, the twice-deserted. These proselytes of the gate[44] are welcome as the true Hebrews. There they stand in conjunction; natives, and naturalized. The latter seem as little disposed to inquire out their true lineage as I am.—I charge no warehouse-room for these deodands,[45] nor shall ever put myself to the ungentlemanly trouble of advertising a sale of them to pay expenses.

To lose a volume to C. carries some sense and meaning in it. You are sure that he will make one hearty meal on your viands, if he can give no account of the platter after it. But what moved thee, wayward, spiteful K.,[46] to be so importunate to carry off with thee, in spite of tears and adjurations to thee to forbear, the *Letters* of that princely woman, the thrice noble Margaret Newcastle?[47]—knowing at the time, and knowing that I knew also, thou most assuredly wouldst never turn over one leaf of the illustrious folio:—what but the mere spirit of contradiction, and childish love of getting the better of thy friend?—Then, worst cut of all! to transport it with thee to the Gallican land—

Unworthy land to harbour such a sweetness,
A virtue in which all ennobling thoughts dwelt,
Pure thoughts, kind thoughts, high thoughts, her
    sex's wonder!

——hadst thou not thy play-books, and books of jests and fancies, about thee, to keep thee merry, even as thou keepest all companies with thy quips and mirthful tales?—Child of the Green-room,[48] it was unkindly done of thee. Thy wife, too, that part-French, better-part Englishwoman!—that *she* could fix upon no other treatise to bear away, in kindly token of remembering us, than the works of Fulke Greville, Lord Brooke[49]—of which no Frenchman, nor woman of France, Italy, or England, was ever by nature constituted to comprehend a tittle! *Was there not Zimmerman on Solitude?*[50]

Reader, if haply thou art blessed with a moderate collection, be shy of showing it; or if thy heart overfloweth to lend them, lend thy books; but let it be to such a one as S. T. C.[51]—he will return them (generally anticipating the time appointed) with usury; enriched with annotations, tripling their value. I have had experience. Many are these precious MSS. of his—(in *matter* oftentimes, and almost in *quantity* not unfrequently vying with the originals)—in no very clerkly hand—legible in my Daniel;[52] in old Burton; in Sir Thomas Browne; and those abstruser cogitations of the Greville, now, alas! wandering in Pagan lands.—I counsel thee, shut not thy heart, nor thy library, against S. T. C.

1820

MRS. BATTLE'S OPINIONS ON WHIST

'A CLEAR fire, a clean hearth, and the rigor of the game.' This was the celebrated *wish* of old Sarah Battle[1] (now with God) who, next to her devotions, loved a good game at whist. She was none of your lukewarm gamesters, your half-and-half players, who have no objection to take a hand, if you want one to make up a rubber; who affirm that they have no pleasure in winning; that they like to win one game, and lose another; that they can while away an hour very agreeably at a card-table, but are indifferent whether they play or no; and will desire an adversary, who has slipt a wrong card, to take it up and play another. These insufferable triflers are the curse of a table. One of these flies will spoil a whole pot. Of such it may be said, that they do not play at cards, but only play at playing at them.

Sarah Battle was none of that breed. She de-

41 by Robert Burton, published in 1621.
42 by Izaak Walton, published in 1653.
43 *The Life of John Buncle,* by Thomas Amory, published 1756–66, in which the hero, after the death of one of his seven wives, remained four days with his eyes shut.
44 converts to Judaism who were not governed by the strict Mosaic law. Leviticus, xix, 33–4.
45 gifts; from the old legal term meaning anything forfeited to the crown.
46 James Kenny, 1780–1849, dramatist.
47 Margaret Cavendish, Duchess of Newcastle, d. 1674, poet and writer of miscellaneous works.

48 the stage.
49 poet and statesman in the court of Queen Elizabeth.
50 Johann G. von Zimmerman, a Swiss philosopher and physician, who wrote *On Solitude,* 1755.
51 the initials of Coleridge.
52 Samuel Daniel, 1562–1619, English poet and historian.

1 Mrs. Battle is believed to be more or less a portrait of Sarah Burney, the wife of Lamb's friend Captain James Burney, with the addition of a few traits from Lamb's grandmother Field. Lamb himself was a great whist player.

tested them, as I do, from her heart and soul; and would not, save upon a striking emergency, willingly seat herself at the same table with them. She loved a thorough-paced partner, a determined enemy. She took, and gave, no concessions. She hated favours. She never made a revoke, nor ever passed it over in her adversary without exacting the utmost forfeiture. She fought a good fight: cut and thrust. She held not her good sword (her cards) 'like a dancer.' She sate bolt upright; and neither showed you her cards, nor desired to see yours. All people have their blind side—their superstitions; and I have heard her declare, under the rose,[2] that Hearts was her favourite suit.

I never in my life—and I knew Sarah Battle many of the best years of it—saw her take out her snuff-box when it was her turn to play; or snuff a candle in the middle of a game; or ring for a servant, till it was fairly over. She never introduced, or connived at, miscellaneous conversation during its process. As she emphatically observed, cards were cards: and if I ever saw unmingled distaste in her fine last-century countenance, it was at the airs of a young gentleman of a literary turn, who had been with difficulty persuaded to take a hand; and who, in his excess of candour, declared that he thought there was no harm in unbending the mind now and then, after serious studies, in recreations of that kind! She could not bear to have her noble occupation, to which she wound up her faculties, considered in that light. It was her business, her duty, the thing she came into the world to do,—and she did it. She unbent her mind afterwards—over a book.

Pope was her favourite author: his *Rape of the Lock* her favourite work. She once did me the favour to play over with me (with the cards) his celebrated game of ombre[3] in that poem; and to explain to me how far it agreed with, and in what points it would be found to differ from, tradrille. Her illustrations were apposite and poignant; and I had the pleasure of sending the substance of them to Mr. Bowles,[4] but I suppose they came too late to be inserted among his ingenious notes upon that author.

Quadrille, she has often told me, was her first love; but whist had engaged her maturer esteem. The former, she said, was showy and specious, and likely to allure young persons. The uncer-

tainty and quick shifting of partners—a thing which the constancy of whist abhors;—the dazzling supremacy and regal investiture of Spadille[5]—absurd, as she justly observed, in the pure aristocracy of whist, where his crown and garter gave him no proper power above his brothernobility of the Aces;—the giddy vanity, so taking to the inexperienced, of playing alone:—above all, the overpowering attractions of a *Sans Prendre Vole,*[6]—to the triumph of which there is certainly nothing parallel or approaching, in the contingencies of whist:—all these, she would say, make quadrille a game of captivation to the young and enthusiastic. But whist was the *soldier* game: that was her word. It was a long meal; not, like quadrille, a feast of snatches. One or two rubbers might co-extend in duration with an evening. They gave time to form rooted friendships, to cultivate steady enmities. She despised the chance-started, capricious, and ever fluctuating alliances of the other. The skirmishes of quadrille, she would say, reminded her of the petty ephemeral embroilments of the little Italian states, depicted by Machiavel;[7] perpetually changing postures and connexions; bitter foes today, sugared darling tomorrow; kissing and scratching in a breath;—but the wars of whist were comparable to the long, steady, deeprooted, rational antipathies of the great French and English nations.

A grave simplicity was what she chiefly admired in her favourite game. There was nothing silly in it, like the nob[8] in cribbage—nothing superfluous. No *flushes*—that most irrational of all pleas that a reasonable being can set up:—that any one should claim four by virtue of holding cards of the same mark and colour, without reference to the playing of the game, or the individual worth or pretensions of the cards themselves! She held this to be a solecism; as pitiful an ambition at cards as alliteration is in authorship. She despised superficiality, and looked deeper than the colours of things.—Suits were soldiers, she would say, and must have a uniformity of array to distinguish them: but what should we say to a foolish squire, who should claim a merit from dressing up his tenantry in red jackets, that never were to be marshalled—never to take the field?—She even wished that whist were more simple than it is; and, in my

---

2 *sub rosa,* in confidence.
3 a Spanish card game, modified in England in the two varieties of tradrille and quadrille.
4 W. L. Bowles published his edition of Pope in 1806.

5 the ace of spades.
6 taking all the tricks without the aid of a partner.
7 Niccolo Machiavelli, 1469-1527, Florentine statesman and political writer.
8 the knave of trumps, counting one point for the holder.

mind, would have stript it of some appendages, which, in the state of human frailty, may be venially, and even commendably allowed of. She saw no reason for the deciding of the trump by the turn of the card. Why not one suit always trumps?—Why two colours, when the mark of the suits would have sufficiently distinguished them without it?—

'But the eye, my dear Madam, is agreeably refreshed with the variety. Man is not a creature of pure reason—he must have his senses delightfully appealed to. We see it in Roman Catholic countries, where the music and the paintings draw in many to worship, whom your quaker spirit of unsensualizing would have kept out.—You, yourself, have a pretty collection of paintings—but confess to me, whether, walking in your gallery at Sandham, among those clear Vandykes,[9] or among the Paul Potters[10] in the anteroom, you ever felt your bosom glow with an elegant delight, at all comparable to *that* you have in your power to experience most evenings over a well-arranged assortment of the court cards?—the pretty antic habits, like heralds in a procession—the gay triumph-assuring scarlets—the contrasting deadly-killing sables—the 'hoary majesty of spades,'[11] Pam[12] in all his glory!—

'All these might be dispensed with; and, with their naked names upon the drab pasteboard, the game might go on very well, picture-less. But the *beauty* of cards would be extinguished forever. Stripped of all that is imaginative in them, they must degenerate into mere gambling.—Imagine a dull deal board, or drum head, to spread them on, instead of that nice verdant carpet (next to nature's), fittest arena for those courtly combatants to play their gallant jousts and turneys in!—Exchange those delicately-turned ivory markers—(work of Chinese artist, unconscious of their symbol,—or as profanely slighting their true application as the arrantest Ephesian journeyman that turned out those little shrines for the goddess[13])—exchange them for little bits of leather (our ancestors' money) or chalk and a slate!'—

The old lady, with a smile, confessed the soundness of my logic; and to her approbation of my arguments on her favourite topic that evening, I have always fancied myself indebted for the legacy of a curious cribbage board, made of

the finest Sienna marble, which her maternal uncle (old Walter Plumer, whom I have elsewhere celebrated[14]) brought with him from Florence:—this, and a trifle of five hundred pounds, came to me at her death.

The former bequest (which I do not least value) I have kept with religious care; though she herself, to confess a truth, was never greatly taken with cribbage. It was an essentially vulgar game, I have heard her say,—disputing with her uncle, who was very partial to it. She could never heartily bring her mouth to pronounce '*go*'—or '*that's a go.*'[15] She called it an ungrammatical game. The pegging teased her. I once knew her to forfeit a rubber (a five dollar stake), because she would not take advantage of the turn-up knave, which would have given it her, but which she must have claimed by the disgraceful tenure of declaring '*two for his heels.*' There is something extremely genteel in this sort of self-denial. Sarah Battle was a gentlewoman born.

Piquet she held the best game at the cards for two persons, though she would ridicule the pedantry of the terms—such as pique—repique—the capot—they savoured (she thought) of affectation. But games for two, or even three, she never greatly cared for. She loved the quadrate, or square. She would argue thus:—Cards are warfare: the ends are gain, with glory. But cards are war, in disguise of a sport: when single adversaries encounter, the ends proposed are too palpable. By themselves, it is too close a fight; with spectators, it is not much bettered. No looker-on can be interested, except for a bet, and then it is a mere affair of money; he cares not for your luck *sympathetically,* or for your play.—Three are still worse; a mere naked war of every man against every man, as in cribbage, without league or alliance; or a rotation of petty and contradictory interests, a succession of heartless leagues, and not much more hearty infractions of them, as in tradrille.—But in square games (*she meant whist*) all that is possible to be attained in card-playing is accomplished. There are the incentives of profit with honour, common to every species—though the *latter* can be but very imperfectly enjoyed in those other games, where the spectator is only feebly a participator. But the parties in whist are spectators and principals too. They are a theatre to themselves, and a looker-on is not wanted. He is rather worse than nothing, and an impertinence. Whist abhors neutrality, or interests beyond its

---

9 Sir Anthony Vandyke, 1599-1641, a famous Flemish portrait painter.
10 Paul Potter, 1625-54, a noted Dutch painter of cattle and landscapes.
11 Pope, *The Rape of the Lock*, iii, 56.
12 the knave of clubs.
13 Ephesus was famous for its temple of Diana.

14 in *The South-Sea House,* the first of Lamb's *Essays of Elia.*
15 a failure to play, counting one point for the opponent.

sphere. You glory in some surprising stroke of skill or fortune, not because a cold—or even an interested—bystander witnesses it, but because your *partner* sympathizes in the contingency. You win for two. You triumph for two. Two are exalted. Two again are mortified; which divides their disgrace, as the conjunction doubles (by taking off the invidiousness) your glories. Two losing to two are better reconciled, than one to one in that close butchery. The hostile feeling is weakened by multiplying the channels. War becomes a civil game.—By such reasonings as these the old lady was accustomed to defend her favourite pastime.

No inducement could ever prevail upon her to play at any game, where chance entered into the composition, *for nothing*. Chance, she would argue—and here again, admire the subtlety of her conclusion!—chance is nothing, but where something else depends upon it. It is obvious, that cannot be *glory*. What rational cause of exultation could it give to a man to turn up size ace[16] a hundred times together by himself? or before spectators, where no stake was depending? —Make a lottery of a hundred thousand tickets with but one fortunate number—and what possible principle of our nature, except stupid wonderment, could it gratify to gain that number as many times successively, without a prize?— Therefore she disliked the mixture of chance in backgammon, where it was not played for money. She called it foolish, and those people idiots, who were taken with a lucky hit under such circumstances. Games of pure skill were as little to her fancy. Played for a stake, they were a mere system of over-reaching. Played for glory, they were a mere setting of one man's wit,—his memory, or combination-faculty rather—against another's; like a mock-engagement at a review, bloodless and profitless.—She could not conceive a *game* wanting the spritely infusion of chance,— the handsome excuses of good fortune. Two people playing at chess in a corner of a room, whilst whist was stirring in the centre, would inspire her with insufferable horror and ennui. Those well-cut similitudes of Castles, and Knights, the *imagery* of the board, she would argue (and I think in this case justly), were entirely misplaced and senseless. Those hard head-contests can in no instance ally with the fancy. They reject form and colour. A pencil and dry slate (she used to say) were the proper arena for such combatants.

To those puny objectors against cards, as nur-

turing the bad passions, she would retort that man is a gaming animal. He must be always trying to get the better in something or other:—that this passion can scarcely be more safely expended than upon a game at cards; that cards are a temporary illusion; in truth, a mere drama; for we do but *play* at being mightily concerned, where a few idle shillings are at stake, yet, during the illusion, we *are* as mightily concerned as those whose stake is crowns and kingdoms. They are a sort of dream-fighting; much ado; great battling, and little bloodshed; mighty means for disproportioned ends; quite as diverting, and a great deal more innoxious, than many of those more serious *games* of life, which men play, without esteeming them to be such.

With great deference to the old lady's judgement on these matters, I think I have experienced some moments in my life, when playing at cards *for nothing* has even been agreeable. When I am in sickness, or not in the best spirits, I sometimes call for the cards, and play a game at piquet *for love* with my cousin Bridget—Bridget Elia.[17]

I grant there is something sneaking in it; but with a tooth-ache, or a sprained ancle,—when you are subdued and humble,—you are glad to put up with an inferior spring of action.

There is such a thing in nature, I am convinced, as *sick whist*.

I grant it is not the highest style of man—I deprecate the manes[18] of Sarah Battle—she lives not, alas! to whom I should apologize.

At such times, those *terms* which my old friend objected to, come in as something admissible—I love to get a tierce or a quatorze,[19] though they mean nothing. I am subdued to an inferior interest. Those shadows of winning amuse me.

That last game I had with my sweet cousin (I capotted[20] her)—(dare I tell thee, how foolish I am?)—I wished it might have lasted forever, though we gained nothing, and lost nothing, though it was a mere shade of play: I would be content to go on in that idle folly forever. The pipkin[21] should be ever boiling, that was to prepare the gentle lenitive to my foot, which Bridget was doomed to apply after the game was over: and, as I do not much relish appliances, there it should ever bubble. Bridget and I should be ever playing.

1821

16 six and one on the dice.

17 Mary Lamb.
18 shade; spirit.
19 a sequence of three or four cards in the same suit.
20 won all the tricks from.
21 a small earthenware pot.

MACKERY END, IN HERTFORDSHIRE

BRIDGET Elia[1] has been my housekeeper for many a long year. I have obligations to Bridget, extending beyond the period of memory. We house together, old bachelor and maid, in a sort of double singleness; with such tolerable comfort, upon the whole, that I, for one, find in myself no sort of disposition to go out upon the mountains, with the rash king's offspring,[2] to bewail my celibacy. We agree pretty well in our tastes and habits—yet so, as 'with a difference.'[3] We are generally in harmony, with occasional bickerings —as it should be among near relations. Our sympathies are rather understood, than expressed; and once, upon my dissembling a tone in my voice more kind than ordinary, my cousin burst into tears, and complained that I was altered. We are both great readers in different directions. While I am hanging over (for the thousandth time) some passage in old Burton,[4] or one of his strange contemporaries, she is abstracted in some modern tale, or adventure, whereof our common reading-table is daily fed with assiduously fresh supplies. Narrative teases me. I have little concern in the progress of events. She must have a story—well, ill, or indifferently told—so there be life stirring in it, and plenty of good or evil accidents. The fluctuations of fortune in fiction— and almost in real life—have ceased to interest, or operate but dully upon me. Out-of-the-way humours and opinions—heads with some diverting twist in them—the oddities of authorship please me most. My cousin has a native disrelish of anything that sounds odd or bizarre. Nothing goes down with her, that is quaint, irregular, or out of the road of common sympathy. She 'holds Nature more clever.'[5] I can pardon her blindness to the beautiful obliquities of the *Religio Medici*;[6] but she must apologize to me for certain disrespectful insinuations, which she has been pleased to throw out latterly, touching the intellectuals of a dear favourite of mine, of the last century but one—the thrice noble, chaste, and virtuous,—but again somewhat fantastical, and original-brain'd, generous Margaret Newcastle.[7]

It has been the lot of my cousin, oftener perhaps than I could have wished, to have had for her associates and mine, free-thinkers[8]—leaders, and disciples, of novel philosophies and systems; but she neither wrangles with, nor accepts, their opinions. That which was good and venerable to her, when a child, retains its authority over her mind still. She never juggles or plays tricks with her understanding.

We are both of us inclined to be a little too positive; and I have observed the result of our disputes to be almost uniformly this,—that in matters of fact, dates, and circumstances, it turns out that I was in the right, and my cousin in the wrong. But where we have differed upon moral points; upon something proper to be done, or let alone; whatever heat of opposition, or steadiness of conviction, I set out with, I am sure always, in the long run, to be brought over to her way of thinking.

I must touch upon the foibles of my kinswoman with a gentle hand, for Bridget does not like to be told of her faults. She hath an awkward trick (to say no worse of it) of reading in company: at which times she will answer *yes* or *no* to a question, without fully understanding its purport—which is provoking, and derogatory in the highest degree to the dignity of the putter of the said question. Her presence of mind is equal to the most pressing trials of life, but will sometimes desert her upon trifling occasions. When the purpose requires it, and is a thing of moment, she can speak to it greatly; but in matters which are not stuff of the conscience, she hath been known sometimes to let slip a word less seasonably.

Her education in youth was not much attended to; and she happily missed all that train of female garniture, which passeth by the name of accomplishments. She was tumbled early, by accident or design, into a spacious closet of good old English reading,[9] without much selection or prohibition, and browsed at will upon that fair and wholesome pasturage. Had I twenty girls, they should be brought up exactly in this fashion. I know not whether their chance in wedlock might not be diminished by it; but I can answer for it, that it makes (if the worst come to the worst) most incomparable old maids.

In a season of distress, she is the truest comforter; but in the teasing accidents, and minor

---

1 Lamb's sister, Mary.   2 Jephthah's daughter, Judges, xi, 38.
3 *Hamlet*, IV, v, 183.
4 Robert Burton, 1577–1640, author of *The Anatomy of Melancholy*, a work admired and imitated by Lamb.
5 Gay, *Epitaph of Bywords*.
6 by Sir Thomas Browne, 1605–82, English physician and author. Lamb was fond of his odd ideas and elaborately curious style.
7 Margaret Cavendish, Duchess of Newcastle, d. 1674, poet and author of a celebrated memoir of her husband.

8 William Godwin, Leigh Hunt, William Hazlitt, and Thomas Holcroft were among Lamb's close acquaintances.
9 This was in the library of Samuel Salt of the Inner Temple.

perplexities, which do not call out the *will* to meet them, she sometimes maketh matters worse by an excess of participation. If she does not always divide your trouble, upon the pleasanter occasions of life, she is sure always to treble your satisfaction. She is excellent to be at play with, or upon a visit; but best, when she goes a journey with you.

We made an excursion together a few summers since, into Hertfordshire, to beat up the quarters of some of our less-known relations in that fine corn[10] country.

The oldest thing I remember is Mackery End; or Mackerel End, as it is spelt, perhaps more properly, in some old maps of Hertfordshire; a farm-house,—delightfully situated within a gentle walk from Wheathampstead. I can just remember having been there, on a visit to a great-aunt, when I was a child, under the care of Bridget, who, as I have said, is older than myself by some ten years. I wish that I could throw into a heap the remainder of our joint existences, that we might share them in equal division. But that is impossible. The house was at that time in the occupation of a substantial yeoman, who had married my grandmother's sister. His name was Gladman. My grandmother was a Bruton, married to a Field. The Gladmans and the Brutons are still flourishing in that part of the county, but the Fields are almost extinct. More than forty years had elapsed since the visit I speak of; and, for the greater portion of that period, we had lost sight of the other two branches also. Who or what sort of persons inherited Mackery End —kindred or strange folk—we were afraid almost to conjecture, but determined some day to explore.

By somewhat a circuitous route, taking the noble park at Luton in our way from Saint Alban's,[11] we arrived at the spot of our anxious curiosity about noon. The sight of the old farmhouse, though every trace of it was effaced from my recollection, affected me with a pleasure which I had not experienced for many a year. For though *I* had forgotten it, *we* had never forgotten being there together, and we had been talking about Mackery End all our lives, till memory on my part became mocked with a phantom of itself, and I thought I knew the aspect of a place, which, when present, O how

unlike it was to *that*, which I had conjured up so many times instead of it!

Still the air breathed balmily about it; the season was in the 'heart of June,' and I could say with the poet,

> But thou, that didst appear so fair
>   To fond imagination,
> Dost rival in the light of day
>   Her delicate creation![12]

Bridget's was more a waking bliss than mine, for she easily remembered her old acquaintance again—some altered features, of course, a little grudged at. At first, indeed, she was ready to disbelieve for joy; but the scene soon reconfirmed itself in her affections—and she traversed every out-post of the old mansion, to the wood-house, the orchard, the place where the pigeon-house had stood (house and birds were alike flown)— with a breathless impatience of recognition, which was more pardonable perhaps than decorous at the age of fifty odd. But Bridget in some things is behind her years.

The only thing left was to get into the house —and that was a difficulty which to me singly would have been insurmountable; for I am terribly shy in making myself known to strangers and out-of-date kinsfolk. Love, stronger than scruple, winged my cousin in without me; but she soon returned with a creature that might have sat to a sculptor for the image of Welcome. It was the youngest of the Gladmans; who, by marriage with a Bruton, had become mistress of the old mansion. A comely brood are the Brutons. Six of them, females, were noted as the handsomest young women in the county. But this adopted Bruton, in my mind, was better than they all— more comely. She was born too late to have remembered me. She just recollected in early life to have had her cousin Bridget once pointed out to her, climbing a stile. But the name of kindred, and of cousinship, was enough. Those slender ties, that prove slight as gossamer in the rending atmosphere of a metropolis, bind faster, as we found it, in hearty, homely, loving Hertfordshire. In five minutes we were as thoroughly acquainted as if we had been born and bred up together; were familiar, even to the calling each other by our Christian names. So Christians should call one another. To have seen Bridget, and her—it was like the meeting of the two scrip-

10 wheat.
11 a city in Hertfordshire, twenty miles northwest of London.

12 Wordsworth, *Yarrow Visited,* 41-4.

tural cousins![13] There was a grace and dignity, an amplitude of form and stature, answering to her mind, in this farmer's wife, which would have shined in a palace—or so we thought it. We were made welcome by husband and wife equally—we, and our friend that was with us—I had almost forgotten him—but B. F.[14] will not so soon forget that meeting, if peradventure he shall read this on the far distant shores where the kangaroo haunts. The fatted calf was made ready, or rather was already so, as if in anticipation of our coming, and, after an appropie glass of native wine, never let me forget with what honest pride this hospitable cousin made us proceed to Wheathampstead, to introduce us (as some new-found rarity) to her mother and sister Gladmans, who did indeed know something more of us, at a time when she almost knew nothing.—With what corresponding kindness we were received by them also—how Bridget's memory, exalted by the occasion, warmed into a thousand half-obliterated recollections of things and persons, to my utter astonishment, and her own—and to the astoundment of B. F., who sat by, almost the only thing that was not a cousin there,—old effaced images of more than half-forgotten names and circumstances still crowding back upon her, as words written in lemon come out upon exposure to a friendly warmth,—when I forget all this, then may my country cousins forget me; and Bridget no more remember, that in the days of weakling infancy I was her tender charge—as I have been her care in foolish manhood since—in those pretty pastoral walks, long ago, about Mackery End, in Hertfordshire.

1821

DREAM-CHILDREN[1]

A REVERIE

CHILDREN love to listen to stories about their elders when *they* were children; to stretch their imagination to the conception of a traditionary great-uncle, or grandame whom they never saw. It was in this spirit that my little ones crept about me the other evening to hear about their great-grandmother Field, who lived in a great house in Norfolk[2] (a hundred times bigger than that in which they and papa lived) which had been the scene—so at least it was generally believed in that part of the country—of the tragic incidents which they had lately become familiar with from the ballad of *The Children in the Wood*. Certain it is that the whole story of the children and their cruel uncle was to be seen fairly carved out in wood upon the chimney-piece of the great hall, the whole story down to the Robin Redbreasts, till a foolish rich person pulled it down to set up a marble one of modern invention in its stead, with no story upon it. Here Alice put out one of her dear mother's looks, too tender to be called upbraiding. Then I went on to say how religious and how good their great-grandmother Field was, how beloved and respected by everybody, though she was not indeed the mistress of this great house, but had only the charge of it (and yet in some respects she might be said to be the mistress of it too) committed to her by the owner, who preferred living in a newer and more fashionable mansion which he had purchased somewhere in the adjoining county; but still she lived in it in a manner as if it had been her own, and kept up the dignity of the great house in a sort while she lived, which afterwards came to decay, and was nearly pulled down, and all its old ornaments stripped and carried away to the owner's other house, where they were set up, and looked as awkward as if some one were to carry away the old tombs they had seen lately at the Abbey, and stick them up in Lady C.'s tawdry gilt drawing-room. Here John smiled, as much as to say, 'that would be foolish indeed.' And then I told how, when she came to die, her funeral was attended by a concourse of all the poor, and some of the gentry too, of the neighbourhood for many miles round, to show their respect for her memory, because she had been such a good and religious woman; so good indeed that she knew all the Psaltery, by heart, ay, and a great part of the Testament besides. Here little Alice spread her hands. Then I told what a tall, upright, graceful person their great-grandmother Field once was; and how in her youth she was esteemed the best dancer—here Alice's little right foot played an involuntary movement, till, upon my looking grave, it desisted—the best

13 Mary and Elizabeth, Luke, i, 39–40.
14 Barron Field, English barrister and friend of the Lambs, who at this time was living in Australia.

1 The death of Lamb's brother John on 26 October 1821, is believed to have inspired the tender vein of reminiscence and reverie in *Dream-Children*, an essay justly regarded as one of Lamb's most exquisite prose pieces.

2 Lamb's grandmother, Mary Field, was housekeeper for more than fifty years at Blakesmore in Hertfordshire.

dancer, I was saying, in the county, till a cruel disease, called a cancer, came, and bowed her down with pain; but it could never bend her good spirits, or make them stoop, but they were still upright, because she was so good and religious. Then I told how she was used to sleep by herself in a lone chamber of the great lone house; and how she believed that an apparition of two infants was to be seen at midnight gliding up and down the great staircase near where she slept, but she said 'those innocents would do her no harm'; and how frightened I used to be, though in those days I had my maid to sleep with me, because I was never half so good or religious as she—and yet I never saw the infants. Here John expanded all his eye-brows and tried to look courageous. Then I told how good she was to all her grand-children, having us to the great-house in the holydays, where I in particular used to spend many hours by myself, in gazing upon the old busts of the Twelve Cæsars, that had been Emperors of Rome, till the old marble heads would seem to live again, or I to be turned into marble with them; how I never could be tired with roaming about that huge mansion, with its vast empty rooms, with their worn-out hangings, fluttering tapestry, and carved oaken panels, with the gilding almost rubbed out—sometimes in the spacious old-fashioned gardens, which I had almost to myself, unless when now and then a solitary gardening man would cross me—and how the nectarines and peaches hung upon the walls, without my ever offering to pluck them, because they were forbidden fruit, unless now and then, —and because I had more pleasure in strolling about among the old melancholy-looking yew trees, or the firs, and picking up the red berries, and the fir apples, which were good for nothing but to look at—or in lying about upon the fresh grass, with all the fine garden smells around me —or basking in the orangery, till I could almost fancy myself ripening too along with the oranges and the limes in that grateful warmth—or in watching the dace that darted to and fro in the fish-pond, at the bottom of the garden, with here and there a great sulky pike hanging midway down the water in silent state, as if it mocked at their impertinent friskings,—I had more pleasure in these busy-idle diversions than in all the sweet flavours of peaches, nectarines, oranges, and such like common baits of children. Here John slyly deposited back upon the plate a bunch of grapes, which, not unobserved by Alice, he had meditated dividing with her, and both seemed willing to relinquish them for the present as irrelevant. Then in somewhat a more heightened tone, I told how, though their great-grand-mother Field loved all her grand-children, yet in an especial manner she might be said to love their uncle, John L——, because he was so handsome and spirited a youth, and a king to the rest of us; and, instead of moping about in solitary corners, like some of us, he would mount the most mettlesome horse he could get, when but an imp no bigger than themselves, and make it carry him half over the county in a morning, and join the hunters when there were any out—and yet he loved the old great house and gardens too, but had too much spirit to be always pent up within their boundaries—and how their uncle grew up to man's estate as brave as he was handsome, to the admiration of every body, but of their great-grandmother Field especially; and how he used to carry me upon his back when I was a lame-footed boy—for he was a good bit older than me—many a mile when I could not walk for pain;—and how in after life he became lame-footed too, and I did not always (I fear) make allowances enough for him when he was impatient, and in pain, nor remember sufficiently how considerate he had been to me when I was lame-footed; and how when he died, though he had not been dead an hour, it seemed as if he had died a great while ago, such a distance there is betwixt life and death; and how I bore his death as I thought pretty well at first, but afterwards it haunted and haunted me; and though I did not cry or take it to heart as some do, and as I think he would have done if I had died, yet I missed him all day long, and knew not till then how much I had loved him. I missed his kindness, and I missed his crossness, and wished him to be alive again, to be quarrelling with him (for we quarrelled sometimes) rather than not have him again, and was as uneasy without him, as he their poor uncle must have been when the doctor took off his limb.[3] Here the children fell a-crying, and asked if their little mourning which they had on was not for uncle John, and they looked up, and prayed me not to go on about their uncle, but to tell them some stories about their pretty dead mother. Then I told how for seven long years, in hope sometimes, sometimes in despair, yet

3 This is a detail supplied by Lamb's imagination.

persisting ever, I courted the fair Alice W———n;[4] and, as much as children could understand, I explained to them what coyness, and difficulty, and denial meant in maidens—when suddenly, turning to Alice, the soul of the first Alice looked out at her eyes with such a reality of re-presentment, that I became in doubt which of them stood there before me, or whose that bright hair was; and while I stood gazing, both the children gradually grew fainter to my view, receding, and still receding till nothing at last but two mournful features were seen in the uttermost distance, which, without speech, strangely impressed upon me the effects of speech: 'We are not of Alice, nor of thee, nor are we children at all. The children of Alice called Bartrum[5] father. We are nothing; less than nothing, and dreams. We are only what might have been, and must wait upon the tedious shores of Lethe[6] millions of ages before we have existence, and a name'———and immediately awaking, I found myself quietly seated in my bachelor arm-chair, where I had fallen asleep, with the faithful Bridget unchanged by my side—but John L. (or James Elia) was gone forever.

1822

THE PRAISE OF CHIMNEY-SWEEPERS

I LIKE to meet a sweep—understand me—not a grown sweeper—old chimney-sweepers are by no means attractive—but one of those tender novices, blooming through their first nigritude, the maternal washings not quite effaced from the cheek—such as come forth with the dawn, or somewhat earlier, with their little professional notes sounding like the *peep peep* of a young sparrow; or liker to the matin lark should I pronounce them, in their aerial ascents not seldom anticipating the sun-rise?

I have a kindly yearning towards these dim specks—poor blots—innocent blacknesses—

I reverence these young Africans of our own growth—these almost clergy imps, who sport their cloth without assumption; and from their little pulpits (the tops of chimneys), in the nipping air of a December morning, preach a lesson of patience to mankind.

When a child, what a mysterious pleasure it was to witness their operation! to see a chit no bigger than one's self enter, one knew not by what process, into what seemed the *fauces Averni*[1]—to pursue him in imagination, as he went sounding on through so many dark stifling caverns, horrid shades!—to shudder with the idea that 'now, surely, he must be lost for ever!' —to revive at hearing his feeble shout of discovered daylight—and then (O fulness of delight) running out of doors, to come just in time to see the sable phenomenon emerge in safety, the brandished weapon of his art victorious like some flag waved over a conquered citadel! I seem to remember having been told that a bad sweep was once left in a stack with his brush, to indicate which way the wind blew. It was an awful spectacle certainly; not much unlike the old stage direction in *Macbeth*, where the 'Apparition of a child crowned with a tree in his hand rises.'

Reader, if thou meetest one of these small gentry in thy early rambles, it is good to give him a penny. It is better to give him twopence. If it be starving weather, and to the proper troubles of his hard occupation, a pair of kibed[2] heels (no unusual accompaniment) be superadded, the demand on thy humanity will surely rise to a tester.[3]

There is a composition, the groundwork of which I have understood to be the sweet wood yclept sassafras. This wood boiled down to a kind of tea, and tempered with an infusion of milk and sugar, hath to some tastes a delicacy beyond the China luxury. I know not how thy palate may relish it; for myself, with every deference to the judicious Mr. Read, who hath time out of mind kept open a shop (the only one he avers in London) for the vending of this 'wholesome and pleasant beverage,' on the south side of Fleet Street, as thou approachest Bridge Street—*the only Salopian house,*[4]—I have never yet adventured to dip my own particular lip in a basin of his commended ingredients—cautious premonition to the olfactories constantly whispering to me that my stomach must infallibly, with all due courtesy, decline it. Yet I have seen palates, otherwise not uninstructed in dietetical elegances, sup it up with avidity.

I know not by what particular conformation of the organ it happens, but I have always found

4 Alice Winterton, a feigned name, possibly to be identified with Ann Simmons, Lamb's early sweetheart.
5 Ann Simmons married a London merchant named Bartram.
6 the river of oblivion in Hades.

1 'jaws of Hades'—*Aeneid*, VI, 201.
2 chapped or swollen with chilblains.
3 sixpence.
4 a place for the sale of *saloop*, a drink made of sassafras and other ingredients.

that this composition is surprisingly gratifying to the palate of a young chimney-sweeper—whether the oily particles (sassafras is slightly oleaginous) do attenuate and soften the fuliginous concretions,[5] which are sometimes found (in dissections) to adhere to the roof of the mouth in these unfledged practitioners; or whether Nature, sensible that she had mingled too much of bitter wood in the lot of these raw victims, caused to grow out of the earth her sassafras for a sweet lenitive—but so it is, that no possible taste or odour to the senses of a young chimney-sweeper can convey a delicate excitement comparable to this mixture. Being penniless, they will yet hang their black heads over the ascending steam, to gratify one sense, if possible, seemingly no less pleased than those domestic animals—cats—when they purr over a new-found sprig of valerian.[6] There is something more in these sympathies than philosophy can inculcate.

Now albeit Mr. Read boasteth, not without reason, that his is the *only Salopian house;* yet be it known to thee, reader—if thou art one who keepest what is called good hours, thou art happily ignorant of the fact—he hath a race of industrious imitators, who from stalls, and under open sky, dispense the same savoury mess to humbler customers, at the dead time of the dawn, when (as extremes meet) the rake, reeling home from his midnight cups, and the hard-handed artisan leaving his bed to resume the premature labours of the day, jostle, not unfrequently to the manifest disconcerting of the former, for the honours of the pavement. It is the time when, in summer, between the expired and the not yet relumined kitchen-fires, the kennels of our fair metropolis give forth their least satisfactory odours. The rake who wisheth to dissipate his o'ernight vapours in more grateful coffee, curses the ungenial fume, as he passeth; but the artisan stops to taste, and blesses the fragrant breakfast.

This is *Saloop*—the precocious herb-woman's darling—the delight of the early gardener, who transports his smoking cabbages by break of day from Hammersmith to Covent Garden's[7] famed piazzas—the delight, and, oh I fear, too often the envy, of the unpennied sweep. Him shouldst thou haply encounter, with his dim visage pendent over the grateful steam, regale him with a sumptuous basin (it will cost thee but three halfpennies) and a slice of delicate bread and butter (an added halfpenny); so may thy culinary fires, eased of the o'ercharged secretions from thy worse-placed hospitalities, curl up a lighter volume to the welkin—so may the descending soot never taint thy costly well-ingredienced soups—nor the odious cry, quick-reaching from street to street, of the *fired chimney,* invite the rattling engines from ten adjacent parishes to disturb for a casual scintillation thy peace and pocket!

I am by nature extremely susceptible of street affronts; the jeers and taunts of the populace; the low-bred triumph they display over the casual trip, or splashed stocking, of a gentleman. Yet can I endure the jocularity of a young sweep with something more than forgiveness. In the last winter but one, pacing along Cheapside with my accustomed precipitation when I walk westward, a treacherous slide brought me upon my back in an instant. I scrambled up with pain and shame enough—yet outwardly trying to face it down, as if nothing had happened—when the roguish grin of one of these young wits encountered me. There he stood, pointing me out with his dusky finger to the mob, and to a poor woman (I suppose his mother) in particular, till the tears for the exquisiteness of the fun (so he thought it) worked themselves out at the corners of his poor red eyes, red from many a previous weeping, and soot-inflamed, yet twinkling through all with such a joy, snatched out of desolation, that Hogarth[8]——but Hogarth has got him already (how could he miss him?) in 'The March to Finchley,' grinning at the pie-man——there he stood, as he stands in the picture, irremovable, as if the jest was to last for ever—with such a maximum of glee, and minimum of mischief, in his mirth—for the grin of a genuine sweep hath absolutely no malice in it—that I could have been content, if the honour of a gentleman might endure it, to have remained his butt and his mockery till midnight.

I am by theory obdurate to the seductiveness of what are called a fine set of teeth. Every pair of rosy lips (the ladies must pardon me) is a casket presumably holding such jewels; but, methinks, they should take leave to 'air' them as frugally as possible. The fine lady, or fine gentleman, who show me their teeth, show me bones. Yet must I confess that from the mouth of a true

---

5 sooty deposits.

6 a pungent herb.

7 Hammersmith was a suburb of London famed for its market gardens; the piazzas of Covent Garden were (and still are) the chief market place of the city.

8 William Hogarth, 1697-1764, a noted English painter and engraver whose studies of eighteenth-century life were greatly admired by Lamb.

sweep a display (even to ostentation) of those white and shining ossifications, strikes me as an agreeable anomaly in manners, and an allowable piece of foppery. It is, as when

A sable cloud
Turns forth her silver lining on the night.[9]

It is like some remnant of gentry not quite extinct; a badge of better days; a hint of nobility: —and, doubtless, under the obscuring darkness and double night of their forlorn disguisement, oftentimes lurketh good blood, and gentle conditions, derived from lost ancestry, and a lapsed pedigree. The premature apprenticements of these tender victims give but too much encouragement, I fear, to clandestine and almost infantile abductions; the seeds of civility and true courtesy, so often discernible in these young grafts (not otherwise to be accounted for) plainly hint at some forced adoptions; many noble Rachels mourning[10] for their children, even in our days, countenance the fact; the tales of fairy-spiriting may shadow a lamentable verity, and the recovery of the young Montagu[11] be but a solitary instance of good fortune, out of many irreparable and hopeless *defiliations*.[12]

In one of the state-beds at Arundel Castle,[13] a few years since—under a ducal canopy—(that seat of the Howards is an object of curiosity to visitors, chiefly for its beds, in which the late Duke was especially a connoisseur)—encircled with curtains of delicatest crimson, with starry coronets inwoven—folded between a pair of sheets whiter and softer than the lap where Venus lulled Ascanius[14]—was discovered by chance, after all methods of search had failed, at noon-day, fast asleep, a lost chimney-sweeper. The little creature, having somehow confounded his passage among the intricacies of those lordly chimneys, by some unknown aperture had alighted upon this magnificent chamber; and, tired with his tedious explorations, was unable to resist the delicious invitement to repose, which he there saw exhibited; so, creeping between the sheets very quietly, laid his black head upon the pillow, and slept like a young Howard.

Such is the account given to the visitors at the Castle.—But I cannot help seeming to perceive a confirmation of what I have just hinted at in this story. A high instinct was at work in the case, or I am mistaken. Is it probable that a poor child of that description, with whatever weariness he might be visited, would have ventured, under such a penalty as he would be taught to expect, to uncover the sheets of a Duke's bed, and deliberately to lay himself down between them, when the rug, or the carpet, presented an obvious couch, still far above his pretensions—is this probable, I would ask, if the great power of nature, which I contend for, had not been manifested within him, prompting to the adventure? Doubtless this young nobleman (for such my mind misgives me that he must be) was allured by some memory, not amounting to full consciousness, of his condition in infancy, when he was used to be lapt by his mother, or his nurse, in just such sheets as he there found, into which he was now but creeping back as into his proper *incunabula*[15] and resting place. By no other theory, than by this sentiment of a pre-existent state (as I may call it), can I explain a deed so venturous, and, indeed, upon any other system, so indecorous, in this tender, but unseasonable, sleeper.

My pleasant friend Jem White[16] was so impressed with a belief of metamorphoses like this frequently taking place, that in some sort to reverse the wrongs of fortune in these poor changelings, he instituted an annual feast of chimney-sweepers, at which it was his pleasure to officiate as host and waiter. It was a solemn supper held in Smithfield, upon the yearly return of the fair of St. Bartholomew.[17] Cards were issued a week before to the master-sweeps in and about the metropolis, confining the invitation to their younger fry. Now and then an elderly stripling would get in among us, and be good-naturedly winked at; but our main body were infantry. One unfortunate wight, indeed, who, relying upon his dusky suit, had intruded himself into our party, but by tokens was providentially discovered in time to be no chimney-sweeper (all is not soot which looks so), was quoited out of the presence with universal indignation, as not having on the wedding garment,[18] but in gen-

---

9 *Comus*, 221-2.
10 Jeremiah, xxxi, 15.
11 Edward Wortley Montagu, 1713-76, son of Lady Mary Montagu, once ran away from school and became a chimney-sweep.
12 losses of sons.
13 in Sussex county, the ancestral seat of the Howards, Dukes of Norfolk.
14 the young son of Aeneas, *Aeneid*, I, 691.

15 cradle clothes.
16 James White, 1775-1820, a schoolmate of Lamb's at Christ's Hospital and author of *Falstaff's Letters*, 1796.
17 The great national fair formerly held at Smithfield on 3 September. It was abolished in 1855.
18 Matthew, xxii, 11-13.

eral the greatest harmony prevailed. The place chosen was a convenient spot among the pens, at the north side of the fair, not so far distant as to be impervious to the agreeable hubbub of that vanity, but remote enough not to be obvious to the interruption of every gaping spectator in it. The guests assembled about seven. In those little temporary parlours three tables were spread with napery, not so fine as substantial, and at every board a comely hostess presided with her pan of hissing sausages. The nostrils of the young rogues dilated at the savour. James White, as head waiter, had charge of the first table; and myself, with our trusty companion Bigod,[19] ordinarily ministered to the other two. There was clambering and jostling, you may be sure, who should get at the first table—for Rochester[20] in his maddest days could not have done the humours of the scene with more spirit than my friend. After some general expression of thanks for the honour the company had done him, his inaugural ceremony was to clasp the greasy waist of old dame Ursula[21] (the fattest of the three), that stood frying and fretting, half-blessing, half-cursing, 'the gentleman,' and imprint upon her chaste lips a tender salute, whereat the universal host would set up a shout that tore the concave,[22] while hundreds of grinning teeth startled the night with their brightness. O it was a pleasure to see the sable younkers lick in the unctuous meat, with *his* more unctuous sayings—how he would fit the tit-bits to the puny mouths, reserving the lengthier links for the seniors—how he would intercept a morsel even in the jaws of some young desperado, declaring it 'must to the pan again to be browned, for it was not fit for a gentleman's eating'—how he would recommend this slice of white bread, or that piece of kissing-crust,[23] to a tender juvenile, advising them all to have a care of cracking their teeth, which were their best patrimony,—how genteelly he would deal about the small ale, as if it were wine, naming the brewer, and protesting, if it were not good, he should lose their custom; with a special recommendation to wipe the lip before drinking. Then we had our toasts—'The King,'—the 'Cloth,'[24]—which, whether they understood or

not, was equally diverting and flattering;—and for a crowning sentiment, which never failed, 'May the Brush supersede the Laurel.' All these, and fifty other fancies, which were rather felt than comprehended by his guests, would he utter, standing upon tables, and prefacing every sentiment with a 'Gentlemen, give me leave to propose so and so,' which was a prodigious comfort to those young orphans; and every now and then stuffing into his mouth (for it did not do to be squeamish on these occasions) indiscriminate pieces of those reeking sausages, which pleased them mightily, and was the savouriest part, you may believe, of the entertainment.

> Golden lads and lasses must,
> As chimney-sweepers, come to dust.[25]

James White is extinct, and with him these suppers have long ceased. He carried away with him half the fun of the world when he died—of my world at least. His old clients look for him among the pens; and, missing him, reproach the altered feast of St. Bartholomew, and the glory of Smithfield departed forever.

1822

A DISSERTATION UPON ROAST PIG[1]

MANKIND, says a Chinese manuscript, which my friend M. was obliging enough to read and explain to me, for the first seventy thousand ages ate their meat raw, clawing or biting it from the living animal, just as they do in Abyssinia to this day. This period is not obscurely hinted at by their great Confucius in the second chapter of his *Mundane Mutations,* where he designates a kind of golden age by the term Cho-fang, literally the Cooks' Holiday. The manuscript goes on to say, that the art of roasting, or rather broiling (which I take to be the elder brother) was accidentally discovered in the manner following. The swineherd, Ho-ti, having gone out into the woods one morning, as his manner was, to collect mast[2] for his hogs, left his cottage in the care of his eldest son Bo-bo, a great lubberly boy, who being fond of playing with fire, as younkers of his age commonly are, let some sparks escape into a

---

19 John Fenwick, a journalist friend of Lamb's.
20 Second Earl of Rochester, 1648-80, a poet and courtier noted for his madcap escapades.
21 the allusion is to a fat pig woman in Ben Jonson's *Bartholomew Fair.*
22 Cf. *Paradise Lost,* I, 541-2.
23 the overhanging crust of a loaf that touches another loaf while baking.
24 the clergy.

25 *Cymbeline,* IV, ii, 262-3.
1 Lamb doubtless obtained the story of the discovery of roast pig, as he says, from his friend Thomas Manning, who had traveled in China. Similar stories, however, have been found to be rather widely scattered in early literature. Except for the historical figure of Confucius, the details in Lamb's account are all fictitious.
2 nuts and acorns.

bundle of straw, which kindling quickly, spread the conflagration over every part of their poor mansion till it was reduced to ashes. Together with the cottage (a sorry antediluvian make-shift of a building, you may think it), what was of much more importance, a fine litter of new-far-rowed pigs, no less than nine in number, per-ished. China pigs have been esteemed a luxury all over the East from the remotest periods that we read of. Bo-bo was in the utmost consterna-tion, as you may think, not so much for the sake of the tenement, which his father and he could easily build up again with a few dry branches, and the labour of an hour or two, at any time, as for the loss of the pigs. While he was think-ing what he should say to his father, and wring-ing his hands over the smoking remnants of one of those untimely sufferers, an odour assailed his nostrils, unlike any scent which he had before ex-perienced. What could it proceed from?—not from the burnt cottage—he had smelt that smell before—indeed this was by no means the first accident of the kind which had occurred through the negligence of this unlucky young fire-brand. Much less did it resemble that of any known herb, weed, or flower. A premonitory moistening at the same time overflowed his nether lip. He knew not what to think. He next stooped down to feel the pig, if there were any signs of life in it. He burnt his fingers, and to cool them he ap-plied them in his booby fashion to his mouth. Some of the crumbs of the scorched skin had come away with his fingers, and for the first time in his life (in the world's life indeed, for before him no man had known it) he tasted—*crackling!*[3] Again he felt and fumbled at the pig. It did not burn him so much now, still he licked his fingers from a sort of habit. The truth at length broke into his slow understanding, that it was the pig that smelt so, and the pig that tasted so deli-cious; and, surrendering himself up to the new-born pleasure, he fell to tearing up whole handfuls of the scorched skin with the flesh next it, and was cramming it down his throat in his beastly fashion, when his sire entered amid the smoking rafters, armed with retributory cudgel, and finding how affairs stood, began to rain blows upon the young rogue's shoulders, as thick as hail-stones, which Bo-bo heeded not any more than if they had been flies. The tickling pleasure, which he experienced in his lower regions, had rendered him quite callous to any inconveniences

3 the crisp skin of roast pork.

he might feel in those remote quarters. His father might lay on, but he could not beat him from his pig, till he had fairly made an end of it, when, be-coming a little more sensible of his situation, something like the following dialogue ensued.

'You graceless whelp, what have you got there devouring? Is it not enough that you have burnt me down three houses with your dog's tricks, and be hanged to you, but you must be eating fire, and I know not what—what have you got there, I say?'

'O father, the pig, the pig, do come and taste how nice the burnt pig eats.'

The ears of Ho-ti tingled with horror. He cursed his son, and he cursed himself that ever he should beget a son that should eat burnt pig.

Bo-bo, whose scent was wonderfully sharp-ened since morning, soon raked out another pig, and fairly rending it asunder, thrust the lesser half by main force into the fists of Ho-ti, still shouting out 'Eat, eat, eat the burnt pig, father, only taste—O Lord,'—with such-like barbarous ejaculations, cramming all the while as if he would choke.

Ho-ti trembled in every joint while he grasped the abominable thing, wavering whether he should not put his son to death for an unnatural young monster, when the crackling scorching his fingers, as it had done his son's, and applying the same remedy to them, he in his turn tasted some of its flavour, which, make what sour mouths he would for a pretence, proved not altogether dis-pleasing to him. In conclusion (for the manu-script here is a little tedious) both father and son fairly sat down to the mess, and never left off till they had despatched all that remained of the litter.

Bo-bo was strictly enjoined not to let the se-cret escape, for the neighbours would certainly have stoned them for a couple of abominable wretches, who could think of improving upon the good meat which God had sent them. Neverthe-less, strange stories got about. It was observed that Ho-ti's cottage was burnt down now more frequently than ever. Nothing but fires from this time forward. Some would break out in broad day, others in the night-time. As often as the sow farrowed, so sure was the house of Ho-ti to be in a blaze; and Ho-ti himself, which was the more remarkable, instead of chastising his son, seemed to grow more indulgent to him than ever. At length they were watched, the terrible mystery discovered, and father and son summoned to take their trial at Pekin, then an inconsiderable assize town.[4] Evidence was given, the obnoxious food itself produced in court, and verdict about to be pronounced, when the foreman of the jury begged that some of the burnt pig, of which the culprits stood accused, might be handed into the box. He handled it, and they all handled it, and burning their fingers, as Bo-bo and his father had done before them, and nature prompting to each of them the same remedy, against the face of all the facts, and the clearest charge which judge had ever given—to the surprise of the whole court, townsfolk, strangers, reporters, and all present—without leaving the box, or any manner of consultation whatever, they brought in a simultaneous verdict of Not Guilty.

The judge, who was a shrewd fellow, winked at the manifest iniquity of the decision: and, when the court was dismissed, went privily, and bought up all the pigs that could be had for love or money. In a few days his Lordship's town house was observed to be on fire. The thing took wing, and now there was nothing to be seen but fires in every direction. Fuel and pigs grew enormously dear all over the district. The insurance offices one and all shut up shop. People built slighter and slighter every day, until it was feared that the very science of architecture would in no long time be lost to the world. Thus this custom of firing houses continued, till in process of time, says my manuscript, a sage arose, like our Locke,[5] who made a discovery, that the flesh of swine, or indeed of any other animal, might be cooked *(burnt,* as they called it) without the necessity of consuming a whole house to dress it. Then first began the rude form of a gridiron. Roasting by the string, or spit, came in a century or two later; I forget in whose dynasty. By such slow degrees, concludes the manuscript, do the most useful and seemingly the most obvious arts, make their way among mankind.

Without placing too implicit faith in the account above given, it must be agreed, that if a worthy pretext for so dangerous an experiment as setting houses on fire (especially in these days) could be assigned in favour of any culinary object, that pretext and excuse might be found in ROAST PIG.

Of all the delicacies in the whole *mundus edibilis,*[6] I will maintain it to be the most delicate—*princeps obsoniorum.*[7]

I speak not of your grown porkers—things between pig and pork—those hobbydehoys—but a young and tender suckling—under a moon old—guiltless as yet of the sty—with no original speck of the *amor immunditiæ,*[8] the hereditary failing of the first parent, yet manifest—his voice as yet not broken, but something between a childish treble, and a grumble—the mild forerunner, or *præludium,* of a grunt.

He must be roasted. I am not ignorant that our ancestors ate them seethed, or boiled—but what a sacrifice of the exterior tegument!

There is no flavour comparable, I will contend, to that of the crisp, tawny, well-watched, not over-roasted, *crackling,* as it is well called—the very teeth are invited to their share of the pleasure at this banquet in overcoming the coy, brittle resistance—with the adhesive oleaginous—O call it not fat—but an indefinable sweetness growing up to it—the tender blossoming of fat—fat cropped in the bud—taken in the shoot—in the first innocence—the cream and quintessence of the child-pig's yet pure food——the lean, no lean, but a kind of animal manna—or, rather, fat and lean (if it must be so) blended and running into each other, that both together make but one ambrosian result, or common substance.

Behold him, while he is doing—it seemeth rather a refreshing warmth, than a scorching heat, that he is so passive to. How equably he twirleth round the string!—Now he is just done. To see the extreme sensibility of that tender age, he hath wept out his pretty eyes—radiant jellies—shooting stars[9]—

See him in the dish, his second cradle, how meek he lieth!—wouldst thou have had this innocent grow up to the grossness and indocility which too often accompany maturer swinehood? Ten to one he would have proved a glutton, a sloven, an obstinate, disagreeable animal—wallowing in all manner of filthy conversation[10]—from these sins he is happily snatched away—

Ere sin could blight, or sorrow fade,
Death came with timely care[11]——

his memory is odoriferous—no clown curseth, while his stomach half rejecteth, the rank bacon—no coal heaver bolteth him in reeking sausages—he hath a fair sepulchre in the grateful

---

4 town where the circuit court sits.
5 the seventeenth-century English philosopher.
6 'world of eatables.'   7 'chief of delicacies.'
8 'love of filth.'
9 alluding to the superstition that shooting stars turned to jelly where they fell.
10 manner of life, as in II Peter, ii, 7, 'the filthy conversation of the wicked.'
11 Coleridge, *Epitaph on an Infant.*

stomach of the judicious epicure—and for such a tomb might be content to die.

He is the best of sapours.[12] Pine-apple is great. She is indeed almost too transcendent—a delight, if not sinful, yet so like to sinning, that really a tender-conscienced person would do well to pause—too ravishing for mortal taste, she woundeth and excoriateth the lips that approach her—like lovers' kisses, she biteth—she is a pleasure bordering on pain from the fierceness and insanity of her relish—but she stoppeth at the palate—she meddleth not with the appetite —and the coarsest hunger might barter her consistently for a mutton chop.

Pig—let me speak his praise—is no less provocative of the appetite, than he is satisfactory to the criticalness of the censorious palate. The strong man may batten on him, and the weakling refuseth not his mild juices.

Unlike to mankind's mixed characters, a bundle of virtues and vices, inexplicably intertwisted, and not to be unravelled without hazard, he is— good throughout. No part of him is better or worse than another. He helpeth, as far as his little means extend, all around. He is the least envious of banquets. He is all neighbours' fare.

I am one of those who freely and ungrudgingly impart a share of the good things of this life which fall to their lot (few as mine are in this kind), to a friend. I protest I take as great an interest in my friend's pleasures, his relishes, and proper satisfactions, as in mine own. 'Presents,' I often say, 'endear Absents.' Hares, pheasants, partridges, snipes, barn-door chicken (those 'tame villatic[13] fowl'), capons, plovers, brawn,[14] barrels of oysters, I dispense as freely as I receive them. I love to taste them, as it were, upon the tongue of my friend. But a stop must be put somewhere. One would not, like Lear, 'give everything.' I make my stand upon pig. Methinks it is an ingratitude to the Giver of all good flavours, to extra-domiciliate, or send out of the house, slightingly, (under pretext of friendship, or I know not what) a blessing so particularly adapted, predestined, I may say, to my individual palate.—It argues an insensibility.

I remember a touch of conscience in this kind at school. My good old aunt, who never parted from me at the end of a holiday without stuffing a sweet-meat, or some nice thing, into my pocket, had dismissed me one evening with a smoking plum-cake, fresh from the oven. In my way to school (it was over London bridge) a grey headed old beggar saluted me (I have no doubt at this time of day that he was a counterfeit). I had no pence to console him with, and in the vanity of self-denial, and the very coxcombry of charity, school-boy-like, I made him a present of—the whole cake! I walked on a little, buoyed up, as one is on such occasions, with a sweet soothing of self-satisfaction; but before I had got to the end of the bridge, my better feelings returned, and I burst into tears, thinking how ungrateful I had been to my good aunt, to go and give her good gift away to a stranger, that I had never seen before, and who might be a bad man for aught I knew; and then I thought of the pleasure my aunt would be taking in thinking that I— I myself, and not another—would eat her nice cake — and what should I say to her the next time I saw her—how naughty I was to part with her pretty present—and the odour of that spicy cake came back upon my recollection, and the pleasure and the curiosity I had taken in seeing her make it, and her joy when she sent it to the oven, and how disappointed she would feel that I had never had a bit of it in my mouth at last—and I blamed my impertinent spirit of alms giving, and out-of-place hypocrisy of goodness, and above all I wished never to see the face again of that insidious, good-for-nothing, old grey impostor.

Our ancestors were nice in their method of sacrificing these tender victims. We read of pigs whipt to death with something of a shock, as we hear of any other obsolete custom. The age of discipline is gone by, or it would be curious to inquire (in a philosophical light merely) what effect this process might have towards inteneriating and dulcifying[15] a substance, naturally so mild and dulcet as the flesh of young pigs. It looks like refining a violet. Yet we should be cautious, while we condemn the inhumanity, how we censure the wisdom of the practice. It might impart a gusto—

I remember an hypothesis, argued upon by the young students, when I was at St. Omer's,[16] and maintained with much learning and pleasantry on both sides, 'Whether, supposing that the flavour of a pig who obtained his death by whipping (*per flagellationen extremam*[17]) superadded

12 appetizers.
13 farmyard (Milton, *Samson Agonistes*.)
14 boar's flesh pickled or potted.

15 making tender and sweet.
16 A French Jesuit college: here playfully mentioned because of the reputation of Jesuits for subtle disputations on questions of morality. Lamb, of course, never attended school there.
17 'by flogging to death.'

a pleasure upon the palate of a man more intense than any possible suffering we can conceive in the animal, is man justified in using that
method of putting the animal to death?' I forget
the decision.

His sauce should be considered. Decidedly, a
few bread crumbs, done up with his liver and
brains, and a dash of mild sage. But, banish,
dear Mrs. Cook, I beseech you, the whole onion
tribe. Barbecue your whole hogs to your palate,
steep them in shalots,[18] stuff them out with plan-
tations of the rank and guilty garlic; you cannot
poison them, or make them stronger than they
are—but consider, he is a weakling—a flower.

1822

PREFACE[1]

BY A FRIEND OF THE LATE ELIA

THIS poor gentleman, who for some months
past had been in a declining way, hath at length
paid his final tribute to nature.

To say truth, it is time he were gone. The humour of the thing, if there ever was much in it,
was pretty well exhausted; and a two years' and
a half existence has been a tolerable duration for
a phantom.

I am now at liberty to confess that much which
I have heard objected to my late friend's writings
was well-founded. Crude they are, I grant you—
a sort of unlicked, incondite[2] things—villainously
pranked in an affected array of antique modes
and phrases. They had not been *his,* if they had
been other than such; and better it is, that a
writer should be natural in a self-pleasing quaintness, than to affect a naturalness (so called) that
should be strange to him. Egotistical they have
been pronounced by some who did not know
what he tells us, as of himself, was often true only
(historically) of another; as in a former essay[3] (to
save many instances)—where the *first person* (his
favourite figure) he shadows forth the forlorn
estate of a country-boy placed at a London
school, far from his friends and connections—in
direct opposition to his own early history. If it be
egotism to imply and twine with his own identity

the griefs and affections of another—making
himself many, or reducing many unto himself—
then is the skilful novelist, who all along brings
in his hero or heroine, speaking of themselves,
the greatest egotist of all; who yet has never,
therefore, been accused of that narrowness. And
how shall the intenser dramatist escape being
faulty, who, doubtless, under cover of passion
uttered by another, oftentimes gives blameless
vent to his most inward feelings, and expresses
his own story modestly?

My late friend was in many respects a singular character. Those who did not like him, hated
him; and some, who once liked him, afterwards
became his bitterest haters. The truth is, he gave
himself too little concern that he uttered, and in
whose presence. He observed neither time nor
place, and would e'en out with what came uppermost. With the severe religionist he would pass
for a free-thinker; while the other faction set
him down for a bigot, or persuaded themselves
that he belied his sentiments. Few understood
him; and I am not certain that at all times he
quite understood himself. He too much affected
that dangerous figure—irony. He sowed doubtful speeches, and reaped plain, unequivocal hatred.—He would interrupt the gravest discussion
with some light jest; and yet, perhaps, not quite
irrelevant, in ears that could understand it. Your
long and much talkers hated him. The informal
habit of his mind, joined to an inveterate impediment of speech, forbade him to be an orator; and
he seemed determined that no one else should
play that part when he was present. He was *petit*
and ordinary in his person and appearance. I
have seen him sometimes in what is called good
company, but where he has been a stranger, sit
silent, and be suspected for an odd fellow; till,
some unlucky occasion provoking it, he would
stutter out some senseless pun (not altogether
senseless perhaps, if rightly taken), which has
stamped his character for the evening. It was hit
or miss with him; but nine times out of ten, he
contrived by this device to send away a whole
company his enemies. His conceptions rose kind-
lier than his utterance, and his happiest *impromp-
tus* had the appearance of effort. He has been
accused of trying to be witty, when in truth he
was but struggling to give his poor thoughts articulation. He chose his companions for some
individuality of character which they manifested.
—Hence, not many persons of science, and few
professed *literati*, were of his councils. They were,

18 strong onions.

1 This essay first appeared in the *London Magazine* for January
1823, and was reprinted as preface to the *Last Essays*, 1833. It is 'a
notable example of Lamb's ability to understand himself and crit-
icize his own work' (Blunden). It should not, however, be accepted as literal truth throughout.
2 unpolished.
3 *Christ's Hospital Five and Thirty Years Ago.*

for the most part, persons of an uncertain fortune; and, as to such people commonly nothing is more obnoxious than a gentleman of settled (though moderate) income, he passed with most of them for a great miser. To my knowledge this was a mistake. His *intimados*[4] to confess a truth, were in the world's eye a ragged regiment. He found them floating on the surface of society; and the colour, or something else, in the weed pleased him. The burrs stuck to him—but they were good and loving burrs for all that. He never greatly cared for the society of what are called good people. If any of these were scandalized (and offences were sure to arise), he could not help it. When he has been remonstrated with for not making more concessions to the feelings of good people, he would retort by asking, what one point did these good people ever concede to him? He was temperate in his meals and diversions, but always kept a little on this side of abstemiousness. Only in the use of the Indian weed he might be thought a little excessive. He took it, he would say, as a solvent of speech. Marry—as the friendly vapour ascended, how his prattle would curl up sometimes with it! the ligaments which tongue-tied him were loosened, and the stammerer proceeded a statist![5]

I do not know whether I ought to bemoan or rejoice that my old friend is departed. His jests were beginning to grow obsolete, and his stories to be found out. He felt the approaches of age; and while he pretended to cling to life, you saw how slender were the ties left to bind him. Discoursing with him latterly on this subject, he expressed himself with a pettishness which I thought unworthy of him. In our walks about his suburban retreat (as he called it) at Shacklewell, some children belonging to a school of industry had met us, and bowed and curtseyed, as he thought, in an especial manner to *him*. 'They take me for a visiting governor,'[6] he muttered earnestly. He had a horror, which he carried to a foible, of looking like anything important and parochial. He thought that he approached nearer to that stamp daily. He had a general aversion from being treated like a grave or respectable character, and kept a wary eye upon the advances of age that should so entitle him. He herded always, while it was possible, with people younger than himself. He did not conform to the

march of time, but was dragged along in the procession. His manners lagged behind his years. He was too much of the boy-man. The *toga virilis*[7] never sate gracefully upon his shoulders. The impressions of infancy had burnt into him, and he resented the impertinence of manhood. These were weaknesses; but such as they were, they are a key to explicate some of his writings.

1823

POOR RELATIONS

A POOR relation is the most irrelevant thing in nature,—a piece of impertinent correspondency,—an odious approximation,—a haunting conscience,—a preposterous shadow, lengthening in the noontide of your prosperity,—an unwelcome remembrancer,—a perpetually recurring mortification,—a drain on your purse,—a more intolerable dun upon your pride,—a drawback upon success,—a rebuke to your rising,—a stain in your blood,—a blot on your scutcheon,—a rent in your garment,—a death's head at your banquet,—Agathocles'[1] pot,—a Mordecai in your gate,[2]—a Lazarus at your door,[3]—a lion in your path,—a frog in your chamber,—a fly in your ointment,—a mote in your eye,—a triumph to your enemy,—an apology to your friends,—the one thing not needful,—the hail in harvest,—the ounce of sour in a pound of sweet.

He is known by his knock. Your heart telleth you 'That is Mr. ——.' A rap, between familiarity and respect, that demands, and at the same time, seems to despair of entertainment. He entereth smiling, and—embarrassed. He holdeth out his hand to you to shake, and—draweth it back again. He casually looketh in about dinner time—when the table is full. He offereth to go away, seeing you have company—but is induced to stay. He filleth a chair, and your visitor's two children are accommodated at a side table. He never cometh upon open days, when your wife says with some complacency, 'My dear, perhaps Mr. —— will drop in today.' He remembereth birthdays—and professeth he is fortunate to have stumbled upon one. He declareth against fish, the turbot being small—yet suffereth himself to be importuned into a slice against his first resolution. He sticketh by the port—yet will be

4 intimate friends.
5 statesman.
6 director of the school.

7 garment of manhood.

1 Agathocles, tyrant of Syracuse, 361-289 B.C., was the son of a potter.
2 Esther, ii, 19.
3 Luke, xvi, 20.

prevailed upon to empty the remainder glass of claret, if a stranger press it upon him. He is a puzzle to the servants, who are fearful of being too obsequious, or not civil enough, to him. The guests think 'they have seen him before.' Every one speculateth upon his condition,[4] and the most part take him to be—a tide-waiter.[5] He calleth you by your Christian name, to imply that his other is the same with your own. He is too familiar by half, yet you wish he had less diffidence. With half the familiarity he might pass for a casual dependent; with more boldness he would be in no danger of being taken for what he is. He is too humble for a friend, yet taketh on him more state than befits a client. He is a worse guest than a country tenant, inasmuch as he bringeth up no rent—yet 'tis odds, from his garb and demeanour that your guests take him for one. He is asked to make one at the whist table; refuseth on the score of poverty, and—resents being left out. When the company breaks up, he proffereth to go for a coach—and lets the servant go. He recollects your grandfather; and will thrust in some mean, and quite unimportant anecdote of—the family. He knew it when it was not quite so flourishing as 'he is blest in seeing it now.' He reviveth past situations, to institute what he calleth—favourable comparisons. With a reflecting sort of congratulation, he will inquire the price of your furniture; and insults you with a special commendation of your window-curtains. He is of opinion that the urn is the more elegant shape, but, after all, there was something more comfortable about the old tea-kettle—which you must remember. He dare say you must find a great convenience in having a carriage of your own, and appealeth to your lady if it is not so. Inquireth if you have had your arms done on vellum yet; and did not know till lately that such-and-such had been the crest of the family. His memory is unseasonable; his compliments perverse; his talk a trouble; his stay pertinacious; and when he goeth away, you dismiss his chair into a corner, as precipitately as possible, and feel fairly rid of two nuisances.

There is a worse evil under the sun, and that is—a female Poor Relation. You may do something with the other; you may pass him off tolerably well; but your indigent she-relative is hopeless. 'He is an old humourist,' you may say, 'and affects to go threadbare. His circumstances are better than folks would take them to be. You are fond of having a Character at your table, and truly he is one.' But in the indications of female poverty there can be no disguise. No woman dresses below herself from caprice. The truth must out without shuffling. 'She is plainly related to the L—'s; or what does she at their house?' She is, in all probability, your wife's cousin. Nine times out of ten, at least, this is the case. Her garb is something between a gentlewoman and a beggar, yet the former evidently predominates. She is most provokingly humble and ostentatiously sensible to her inferiority. He may require to be repressed sometimes—*aliquando sufflaminandus erat*[6]—but there is no raising her. You send her soup at dinner, and she begs to be helped—after the gentlemen. Mr. —— requests the honour of taking wine with her; she hesitates between port and Madeira, and chooses the former—because he does. She calls the servant *Sir;* and insists on not troubling him to hold her plate. The housekeeper patronizes her. The children's governess takes upon her to correct her, when she has mistaken the piano for a harpsichord.

Richard Amlet,[7] Esq., in the play, is a notable instance of the disadvantages, to which this chimerical notion of *affinity constituting a claim to acquaintance,* may subject the spirit of a gentleman. A little foolish blood is all that is betwixt him and a lady of great estate. His stars are perpetually crossed by the malignant maternity of an old woman, who persists in calling him 'her son Dick.' But she has wherewithal in the end to recompense his indignities, and float him again upon the brilliant surface, under which it had been her seeming business and pleasure all along to sink him. All men, besides, are not of Dick's temperament. I knew an Amlet in real life, who, wanting Dick's buoyancy, sank indeed. Poor W——[8] was of my own standing at Christ's, a fine classic, and a youth of promise. If he had a blemish, it was too much pride; but its quality was inoffensive; it was not of that sort which hardens the heart, and serves to keep inferiors at a distance; it only sought to ward off derogation from itself. It was the principle of self-respect carried as far as it could go, without infringing upon that respect, which he would have every one else equally maintain for himself. He would have you to think alike with him on this topic. Many a quarrel have I had with him, when

---

4 social rank.
5 a minor customs officer; used here metaphorically, of course.

6 'sometimes he had to be repressed.'
7 a character in *The Confederacy,* by Sir John Vanbrugh.
8 Joseph Favell, mentioned in *Christ's Hospital Five and Thirty Years Ago.*

we were rather older boys, and our tallness made us more obnoxious to observation in the blue clothes, because I would not thread the alleys and blind ways of the town with him to elude notice, when we have been out together on a holiday in the streets of this sneering and prying metropolis. W—— went, sore with these notions, to Oxford, where the dignity and sweetness of a scholar's life, meeting with the alloy of a humble introduction, wrought in him a passionate devotion to the place, with a profound aversion from the society. The servitor's gown (worse than his school array) clung to him with Nessian venom.[9] He thought himself ridiculous in a garb, under which Latimer[10] must have walked erect; and in which Hooker,[10] in his young days, possibly flaunted in a vein of no discommendable vanity. In the depth of college shades, or in his lonely chamber, the poor student shrunk from observation. He found shelter among books, which insult not; and studies, that ask no questions of a youth's finances. He was lord of his library, and seldom cared for looking out beyond his domains. The healing influence of studious pursuits was upon him, to soothe and to abstract. He was almost a healthy man; when the waywardness of his fate broke out against him with a second and worse malignity. The father of W—— had hitherto exercised the humble profession of house-painter at N——, near Oxford. A supposed interest with some of the heads of the colleges had now induced him to take up his abode in that city, with the hope of being employed upon some public works which were talked of. From that moment I read in the countenance of the young man, the determination which at length tore him from academical pursuits forever. To a person unacquainted with our universities, the distance between the gownsmen and the townsmen, as they are called—the trading part of the latter especially—is carried to an excess that would appear harsh and incredible. The temperament of W——'s father was diametrically the reverse of his own. Old W—— was a little, busy, cringing tradesman, who, with his son upon his arm, would stand bowing and scraping, cap in hand, to anything that wore the semblance of a gown—insensible to the winks and opener remonstrances of the young man, to whose chamber-fellow, or equal in standing, perhaps, he was thus obsequiously and gratuitously ducking.

Such a state of things could not last. W—— must change the air of Oxford or be suffocated. He chose the former; and let the sturdy moralist, who strains the point of the filial duties as high as they can bear, censure the dereliction; he cannot estimate the struggle. I stood with W——, the last afternoon I ever saw him, under the eaves of his paternal dwelling. It was in the fine lane leading from the High-street to the back of —— College, where W—— kept his rooms. He seemed thoughtful, and more reconciled. I ventured to rally him—finding him in a better mood—upon a representation of the Artist Evangelist,[11] which the old man, whose affairs were beginning to flourish, had caused to be set up in a splendid sort of frame over his really handsome shop, either as a token of prosperity, or badge of gratitude to his saint. W—— looked up at the Luke, and, like Satan, 'knew his mounted sign—and fled.'[12] A letter on his father's table the next morning, announced that he had accepted a commission in a regiment about to embark for Portugal. He was among the first who perished before the walls of St. Sebastian.[13]

I do not know how, upon a subject which I began with treating half-seriously, I should have fallen upon a recital so eminently painful; but this theme of poor relationship is replete with so much matter for tragic as well as comic associations, that it is difficult to keep the account distinct without blending. The earliest impressions which I received on this matter are certainly not attended with anything painful, or very humiliating, in the recalling. At my father's table (no very splendid one) was to be found, every Saturday, the mysterious figure of an aged gentleman, clothed in neat black, of a sad yet comely appearance. His deportment was of the essence of gravity; his words few or none; and I was not to make a noise in his presence. I had little inclination to have done so—for my cue was to admire in silence. A particular elbow chair was appropriated to him, which was in no case to be violated. A peculiar sort of sweet pudding, which appeared on no other occasion, distinguished the days of his coming. I used to think him a prodigiously rich man. All I could make out of him was, that he and my father had been schoolfellows a world ago at Lincoln, and that he came from the Mint. The Mint I knew to be a place where all the money was coined—and I

---

9 The shirt poisoned by the blood of the centaur Nessus and worn by Hercules so agonized Hercules that he took his own life.
10 Latimer and Hooker, famous sixteenth-century divines, were both servitors, the former at Cambridge, the latter at Oxford.

11 St. Luke.
12 *Paradise Lost*, IV, 1013–14.
13 St. Sebastian in Spain was besieged and taken by Wellington in 1813.

thought he was the owner of all that money. Awful ideas of the Tower twined themselves about his presence. He seemed above human infirmities and passions. A sort of melancholy grandeur invested him. From some inexplicable doom I fancied him obliged to go about in an eternal suit of mourning; a captive—a stately being, let out of the Tower on Saturdays. Often have I wondered at the temerity of my father, who, in spite of an habitual general respect which we all in common manifested towards him, would venture now and then to stand up against him in some argument, touching their youthful days. The houses of the ancient city of Lincoln are divided (as most of my readers know) between the dwellers on the hill, and in the valley. This marked distinction formed an obvious division between the boys who lived above (however brought together in a common school) and the boys whose paternal residence was on the plain; a sufficient cause of hostility in the code of these young Grotiuses.[14] My father had been a leading Mountaineer; and would still maintain the general superiority, in skill and hardihood, of the *Above Boys* (his own faction) over the *Below Boys* (so were they called), of which party his contemporary had been a chieftain. Many and hot were the skirmishes on this topic—the only one upon which the old gentleman was ever brought out—and bad blood bred; even sometimes almost to the recommencement (so I expected) of actual hostilities. But my father, who scorned to insist upon advantages, generally contrived to turn the conversation upon some adroit by-commendation of the old Minster, in the general preference of which, before all other cathedrals in the island, the dweller on the hill, and the plain-born, could meet on a conciliating level, and lay down their less important differences. Once only I saw the old gentleman really ruffled, and I remember with anguish the thought that came over me: 'Perhaps he will never come here again.' He had been pressed to take another plate of the viand, which I have already mentioned as the indispensable concomitant of his visits. He had refused, with a resistance amounting to rigour—when my aunt, an old Lincolnian, but who had something of this, in common with my cousin Bridget, that she would sometimes press civility out of season—uttered the following memorable application—'Do take another slice, Mr. Billet, for you do not get pudding every day.' The old

gentleman said nothing at the time—but he took occasion in the course of the evening, when some argument had intervened between them, to utter with an emphasis which chilled the company, and which chills me now as I write it—'Woman, you are superannuated.' John Billet did not survive long, after the digesting of this affront; but he survived long enough to assure me that peace was actually restored! and, if I remember aright, another pudding was discreetly substituted in the place of that which had occasioned the offence. He died at the Mint (Anno 1781) where he had long held, what he accounted, a comfortable independence; and with five pounds, fourteen shillings, and a penny, which were found in his escrutoire after his decease, left the world, blessing God that he had enough to bury him, and that he had never been obliged to any man for a sixpence. This was—a Poor Relation.

1823

OLD CHINA

I HAVE an almost feminine partiality for old china. When I go to see any great house, I inquire for the china-closet, and next for the picture gallery. I cannot defend the order of preference, but by saying that we have all some taste or other, of too ancient a date to admit of our remembering distinctly that it was an acquired one. I can call to mind the first play, and the first exhibition, that I was taken to; but I am not conscious of a time when china jars and saucers were introduced into my imagination.

I had no repugnance then—why should I now have?—to those little, lawless, azure-tinctured grotesques, that under the notion of men and women, float about, uncircumscribed by any element, in that world before perspective—a china tea-cup.

I like to see my old friends—whom distance cannot diminish—figuring up in the air (so they appear to our optics), yet on *terra firma* still—for so we must in courtesy interpret that speck of deeper blue, which the decorous artist, to prevent absurdity, has made to spring up beneath their sandals.

I love the men with women's faces, and the women, if possible, with still more womanish expressions.

Here is a young and courtly Mandarin, handing tea to a lady from a salver—two miles off. See

---

14 Hugo Grotius, 1583-1645, was a celebrated Dutch jurist credited with founding a system of international law.

how distance seems to set off respect! And here the same lady, or another—for likeness is identity on tea-cups—is stepping into a little fairy boat, moored on the hither side of this calm garden river, with a dainty mincing foot, which in a right angle of incidence (as angles go in our world) must infallibly land her in the midst of a flowery mead—a furlong off on the other side of the same strange stream!

Farther on—if far or near can be predicated of their world—see horses, trees, pagodas, dancing the hays.[1]

Here—a cow and rabbit couchant, and co-extensive—so objects show, seen through the lucid atmosphere of fine Cathay.

I was pointing out to my cousin last evening, over our Hyson[2] (which we are old fashioned enough to drink unmixed still of an afternoon), some of these *speciosa miracula*[3] upon a set of extraordinary old blue china (a recent purchase) which we were now for the first time using; and could not help remarking, how favourable circumstances had been to us of late years, that we could afford to please the eye sometimes with trifles of this sort—when a passing sentiment seemed to over-shade the brows of my companion. I am quick at detecting these summer clouds in Bridget.[4]

'I wish the good old times would come again,' she said, 'when we were not quite so rich. I do not mean that I want to be poor; but there was a middle state';—so she was pleased to ramble on, —'in which I am sure we were a great deal happier. A purchase is but a purchase, now that you have money enough and to spare. Formerly it used to be a triumph. When we coveted a cheap luxury (and, O! how much ado I had to get you to consent in those times!) we were used to have a debate two or three days before, and to weigh the *for* and *against,* and think what we might spare it out of, and what saving we could hit upon, that should be an equivalent. A thing was worth buying then, when we felt the money that we paid for it.

'Do you remember the brown suit, which you made to hang upon you, till all your friends cried shame upon you, it grew so thread-bare—and all because of that folio Beaumont and Fletcher, which you dragged home late at night from

Barker's in Covent-garden? Do you remember how we eyed it for weeks before we could make up our minds to the purchase, and had not come to a determination till it was near ten o'clock of the Saturday night, when you set off from Islington, fearing you should be too late—and when the old bookseller with some grumbling opened his shop, and by the twinkling taper (for he was setting bedwards) lighted out the relic from his dusty treasures—and when you lugged it home, wishing it were twice as cumbersome—and when you presented it to me—and when we were exploring the perfectness of it (*collating* you called it)—and while I was repairing some of the loose leaves with paste, which your impatience would not suffer to be left till day-break—was there no pleasure in being a poor man? or can those neat black clothes which you wear now, and are so careful to keep brushed, since we have become rich and finical, give you half the honest vanity with which you flaunted it about in that overworn suit—your old corbeau[5]—for four or five weeks longer than you should have done, to pacify your conscience for the mighty sum of fifteen —or sixteen shillings was it?—a great affair we thought it then—which you had lavished on the old folio. Now you can afford to buy any book that pleases you, but I do not see that you ever bring me home any nice old purchases now.

'When you came home with twenty apologies for laying out a less number of shillings upon that print after Lionardo, which we christened the *Lady Blanch;*[6] when you looked at the purchase, and thought of the money—and thought of the money, and looked again at the picture— was there no pleasure in being a poor man? Now, you have nothing to do but to walk into Colnaghi's,[7] and buy a wilderness of Lionardos. Yet do you?

'Then, do you remember our pleasant walks to Enfield, and Potter's Bar, and Waltham, when we had a holyday—holydays, and all other fun, are gone, now we are rich—and the little hand-basket in which I used to deposit our day's fare of savoury cold lamb and salad—and how you would pry about at noon-tide for some decent house, where we might go in, and produce our store—only paying for the ale that you must call for—and speculate upon the looks of the land-

---

1 an old country dance.
2 green tea.
3 'dazzling wonders'—Horace, *Ars Poetica,* 144.
4 Lamb's sister, Mary.

5 black coat.
6 Mary Lamb had written a poem on this picture by Leonardo da Vinci.
7 the shop of the print dealer, Paul Colnaghi.

lady, and whether she was likely to allow us a table-cloth—and wish for such another honest hostess, as Izaak Walton has described[8] many a one on the pleasant banks of the Lea, when he went a-fishing—and sometimes they would prove obliging enough, and sometimes they would look grudgingly upon us—but we had cheerful looks still for one another, and would eat our plain food savourily, scarcely grudging Piscator[9] his Trout Hall? Now, when we go out a day's pleasuring, which is seldom moreover, we *ride* part of the way—and go into a fine inn, and order the best of dinners, never debating the expense—which, after all, never has half the relish of those chance country snaps, when we were at the mercy of uncertain usage, and a precarious welcome.

'You are too proud to see a play anywhere now but in the pit. Do you remember where it was we used to sit, when we saw *The Battle of Hexham,* and *The Surrender of Calais,*[10] and Bannister and Mrs. Bland[11] in *The Children in the Wood*[12]—when we squeezed out our shillings a-piece to sit three or four times in a season in the one-shilling gallery—where you felt all the time that you ought not to have brought me—and more strongly I felt obligation to you for having brought me—and the pleasure was the better for a little shame—and when the curtain drew up, what cared we for our place in the house, or what mattered it where we were sitting, when our thoughts were with Rosalind in Arden, or with Viola at the Court of Illyria? You used to say that the gallery was the best place of all for enjoying a play socially—that the relish of such exhibitions must be in proportion to the infrequency of going—that the company we met there, not being in general readers of plays, were obliged to attend the more, and did attend, to what was going on, on the stage—because a word lost would have been a chasm, which it was impossible for them to fill up. With such reflections we consoled our pride then—and I appeal to you, whether, as a woman, I met generally with less attention and accommodation than I have done since in more expensive situations in the house? The getting in indeed, and the crowding up those inconvenient staircases, was bad enough,—but there was still a law of civility to women recog-

nized to quite as great an extent as we ever found in the other passages—and how a little difficulty overcome heightened the snug seat, and the play, afterwards! Now we can only pay our money, and walk in. You cannot see, you say, in the galleries now. I am sure we saw, and heard too, well enough then—but sight, and all, I think, is gone with our poverty.

'There was pleasure in eating strawberries, before they became quite common—in the first dish of peas, while they were yet dear—to have them for a nice supper, a treat. What treat can we have now? If we were to treat ourselves now—that is, to have dainties a little above our means, it would be selfish and wicked. It is the very little more that we allow ourselves beyond what the actual poor can get at, that makes what I call a treat—when two people living together, as we have done, now and then indulge themselves in a cheap luxury, which both like; while each apologizes, and is willing to take both halves of the blame to his single share. I see no harm in people making much of themselves in that sense of the word. It may give them a hint how to make much of others. But now—what I mean by the word—we never do make much of ourselves. None but the poor can do it. I do not mean the veriest poor of all, but persons as we were, just above poverty.

'I know what you were going to say, that it is mighty pleasant at the end of the year to make all meet—and much ado we used to have every Thirty-first Night of December to account for our exceedings—many a long face did you make over your puzzled accounts, and in contriving to make it out how we had spent so much—or that we had not spent so much—or that it was impossible we should spend so much next year—and still we found our slender capital decreasing—but then, betwixt ways, and projects, and compromises of one sort or another, and talk of curtailing this charge, and doing without that for the future—and the hope that youth brings, and laughing spirits (in which you were never poor till now), we pocketed up our loss, and in conclusion, with "lusty brimmers"[13] (as you used to quote it out of *hearty cheerful Mr. Cotton,* as you called him), we used to welcome in the "coming guest." Now we have no reckoning at all at the end of the old year—no flattering promises about the new year doing better for us.'

8 in *The Compleat Angler.*
9 a character in Walton's *Compleat Angler,* one of whose favorite stopping places was Trout Hall, an 'honest ale-house.'
10 plays by George Colman the younger, 1762–1836.
11 a comic actor and a singer attached to Drury Lane theater.
12 a short musical play by Thomas Morton, produced in 1793.

13 pleasant cups; quoted from *The New Year* by Charles Cotton, 1630–87.

Bridget is so sparing of her speech, on most occasions, that when she gets into a rhetorical vein, I am careful how I interrupt it. I could not help, however, smiling at the phantom of wealth which her dear imagination had conjured up out of a clear income of poor——hundred pounds a year. 'It is true we were happier when we were poorer, but we were also younger, my cousin. I am afraid we must put up with the excess, for if we were to shake the superflux into the sea, we should not much mend ourselves. That we had much to struggle with, as we grew up together, we have reason to be most thankful. It strengthened, and knit our compact closer. We could never have been what we have been to each other, if we had always had the sufficiency which you now complain of. The resisting power—those natural dilations of the youthful spirit, which circumstances cannot straiten—with us are long since passed away. Competence to age is supplementary youth; a sorry supplement indeed, but I fear the best that is to be had. We must ride, where we formerly walked: live better, and lie softer—and shall be wise to do so—than we had means to do in those good old days you speak of. Yet could those days return—could you and I once more walk our thirty miles a day—could Bannister and Mrs. Bland again be young, and you and I be young to see them—could the good old one-shilling gallery days return—they are dreams, my cousin, now—but could you and I at this moment, instead of this quiet argument, by our well-carpeted fire-side, sitting on this luxurious sofa—be once more struggling up those inconvenient stair-cases, pushed about, and squeezed, and elbowed by the poorest rabble of poor gallery scramblers—could I once more hear those anxious shrieks of yours—and the delicious *Thank God, we are safe,* which always followed when the topmost stair, conquered, let in the first light of the whole cheerful theatre down beneath us—I know not the fathom line that ever touched a descent so deep as I would be willing to bury more wealth in than Crœsus had, or the great Jew R——[14] is supposed to have, to purchase it. And now do just look at that merry little Chinese waiter holding an umbrella, big enough for a bed-tester,[15] over the head of that pretty insipid half-Madonna-ish chit of a lady in that very blue summer-house.'

1823

THE SUPERANNUATED MAN[1]

Sera tamen respexit
Libertas.[2]

VIRGIL

A Clerk I was in London gay.

O'KEEFE

IF peradventure, Reader, it has been thy lot to waste the golden years of thy life—thy shining youth—in the irksome confinement of an office; to have thy prison days prolonged through middle age down to decrepitude and silver hairs, without hope of release or respite; to have lived to forget that there are such things as holidays, or to remember them but as the prerogatives of childhood; then, and then only, will you be able to appreciate my deliverance.

It is now six and thirty years since I took my seat at the desk in Mincing Lane. Melancholy was the transition at fourteen from the abundant playtime and the frequently intervening vacations of school days, to the eight, nine, and sometimes ten hours' a-day attendance at a counting-house. But time partially reconciles us to anything. I gradually became content—doggedly contented, as wild animals in cages.

It is true I had my Sundays to myself; but Sundays, admirable as the institution of them is for purposes of worship, are for that very reason the very worst adapted for days of unbending and recreation. In particular, there is a gloom for me attendant upon a city Sunday, a weight in the air. I miss the cheerful cries of London, the music, and the ballad-singers—the buzz and stirring murmur of the streets. Those eternal bells depress me. The closed shops repel me. Prints, pictures, all the glittering and endless succession of knacks and gewgaws, and ostentatiously displayed wares of tradesmen, which make a week-day saunter through the less busy parts of the metropolis so delightful—are shut out. No book-stalls deliciously to idle over—no busy faces to recreate the idle man who contemplates them ever passing by—the very face of business a charm by contrast to his temporary relaxation from it. Nothing to be seen but unhappy countenances—or half-happy at best—of emancipated 'prentices and little tradesfolks, with here and there a servant maid that has got

---

14 Nathan Meyer Rothschild, 1777–1836, a famous banker.
15 bed-canopy.

1 This essay, except for some slight disguises, is a record of autobiographical fact. Lamb retired on a pension from the India House in March 1825. 'Superannuated' means 'retired for age.'
2 'Freedom though late has thought on me.'

leave to go out, who, slaving all the week, with the habit has lost almost the capacity of enjoying a free hour, and livelily expressing the hollowness of a day's pleasuring. The very strollers in the fields on that day look anything but comfortable.

But besides Sundays I had a day at Easter, and a day at Christmas, with a full week in the summer to go and air myself in my native fields[3] of Hertfordshire. This last was a great indulgence; and the prospect of its recurrence, I believe, alone kept me up through the year, and made my durance tolerable. But when the week came round, did the glittering phantom of the distance keep touch with me? or rather was it not a series of seven uneasy days, spent in restless pursuit of pleasure, and a wearisome anxiety to find out how to make the most of them? Where was the quiet, where the promised rest? Before I had a taste of it, it was vanished. I was at the desk again, counting upon the fifty-one tedious weeks that must intervene before such another snatch would come. Still the prospect of its coming threw something of an illumination upon the darker side of my captivity. Without it, as I have said, I could scarcely have sustained my thraldom.

Independently of the rigours of attendance, I have ever been haunted with a sense (perhaps a mere caprice) of incapacity for business. This, during my latter years, had increased to such a degree that it was visible in all the lines of my countenance. My health and my good spirits flagged. I had perpetually a dread of some crisis, to which I should be found unequal. Besides my daylight servitude, I served over again all night in my sleep, and would awake with terrors of imaginary false entries, errors in my accounts, and the like. I was fifty years of age, and no prospect of emancipation presented itself. I had grown to my desk, as it were; and the wood had entered into my soul.

My fellows in the office would sometimes rally me upon the trouble legible in my countenance; but I did not know that it had raised the suspicions of any of my employers, when on the 5th of last month, a day ever to be remembered by me, L——, the junior partner in the firm, calling me on one side, directly taxed me with my bad looks, and frankly enquired the cause of them. So taxed, I honestly made confession of my infirmity, and added that I was afraid I should eventually be obliged to resign his service. He spoke some words of course to hearten me, and there the matter rested. A whole week I remained labouring under the impression that I had acted imprudently in my disclosure; that I had foolishly given a handle against myself, and had been anticipating my own dismissal. A week passed in this manner, the most anxious one, I verily believe, in my whole life, when on the evening of the 12th of April, just as I was about quitting my desk to go home (it might be about eight o'clock) I received an awful summons to attend the presence of the whole assembled firm in the formidable back parlour. I thought now my time is surely come, I have done for myself, I am going to be told that they have no longer occasion for me. L——, I could see, smiled at the terror I was in, which was a little relief to me,—when to my utter astonishment B——, the eldest partner, began a formal harangue to me on the length of my services, my very meritorious conduct during the whole of the time (the deuce, thought I, how did he find that out? I protest I never had the confidence to think as much). He went on to descant on the expediency of retiring at a certain time of life (how my heart panted!), and, asking me a few questions as to the amount of my own property, of which I have a little, ended with a proposal, to which his three partners nodded a grave assent, that I should accept from the house, which I had served so well, a pension for life to the amount of two-thirds of my accustomed salary—a magnificent offer! I do not know what I answered between surprise and gratitude, but it was understood that I accepted their proposal, and I was told that I was free from that hour to leave their service. I stammered out a bow, and at just ten minutes after eight I went home—for ever. This noble benefit—gratitude forbids me to conceal their names—I owe to the kindness of the most munificent firm in the world—the house of Boldero, Merryweather, Bosanquet, and Lacy.[4] *Esto perpetua!* [5]

For the first day or two I felt stunned, overwhelmed. I could only apprehend my felicity; I was too confused to taste it sincerely. I wandered about, thinking I was happy, and knowing that I was not. I was in the condition of a prisoner in the Old Bastile,[6] suddenly let loose after a forty years' confinement. I could scarce

---

3 Lamb was a native of London, but spent part of his boyhood in Hertfordshire.

4 the names are fictitious.
5 'May it endure forever.'
6 a state prison in Paris.

trust myself with myself. It was like passing out of Time into Eternity—for it is a sort of Eternity for a man to have his Time all to himself. It seemed to me that I had more time on my hands than I could ever manage. From a poor man, poor in Time, I was suddenly lifted up into a vast revenue; I could see no end of my possessions; I wanted some steward, or judicious bailiff, to manage my estates in Time for me. And here let me caution persons grown old in active business, not lightly, nor without weighing their own resources, to forego their customary employment all at once, for there may be danger in it. I feel it by myself, but I know that my resources are sufficient; and now that those first giddy raptures have subsided, I have a quiet home-feeling of the blessedness of my condition. I am in no hurry. Having all holidays, I am as though I had none. If Time hung heavy upon me, I could walk it away; but I do *not* walk all day long, as I used to do in those old transient holidays, thirty miles a day, to make the most of them. If Time were troublesome, I could read it away, but I do *not* read in that violent measure with which, having no Time my own but candlelight Time, I used to weary out my head and eyesight in by-gone winters. I walk, read, or scribble (as now) just when the fit seizes me. I no longer hunt after pleasure; I let it come to me. I am like the man

—that's born, and has his years come to him,
In some green desert.[7]

'Years,' you will say; 'what is this superannuated simpleton calculating upon? He has already told us he is past fifty.'

I have indeed lived nominally fifty years, but deduct out of them the hours which I have lived to other people, and not to myself, and you will find me still a young fellow. For *that* is the only true Time, which a man can properly call his own, that which he has all to himself; the rest, though in some sense he may be said to live it, is other people's time, not his. The remnant of my poor days, long or short, is at least multiplied for me threefold. My next ten years, if I stretch so far, will be as long as any preceding thirty. 'Tis a fair rule-of-three sum.

Among the strange fantasies which beset me at the commencement of my freedom, and of which all traces are not yet gone, one was, that a vast tract of time had intervened since I quit-ted the Counting House. I could not conceive of it as an affair of yesterday. The partners, and the clerks with whom I had for so many years, and for so many hours in each day of the year, been so closely associated—being suddenly removed from them—they seemed as dead to me. There is a fine passage, which may serve to illustrate this fancy, in a tragedy[8] by Sir Robert Howard, speaking of a friend's death:

——'Twas but just now he went away;
I have not since had time to shed a tear;
And yet the distance does the same appear
As if he had been a thousand years from me.
Time takes no measure in Eternity.

To dissipate this awkward feeling, I have been fain to go among them once or twice since; to visit my old desk-fellows—my co-brethren of the quill—that I had left below in the state militant. Not all the kindness with which they received me could quite restore to me that pleasant familiarity which I had heretofore enjoyed among them. We cracked some of our old jokes, but methought they went off but faintly. My old desk, the peg where I hung my hat, were appropriated to another. I knew it must be, but I could not take it kindly. D——l take me, if I did not feel some remorse—beast, if I had not—at quitting my old compeers, the faithful partners of my toils for six and thirty years, that smoothed for me with their jokes and conundrums the ruggedness of my professional road. Had it been so rugged then after all? or was I a coward simply? Well, it is too late to repent; and I also know that these suggestions are a common fallacy of the mind on such occasions. But my heart smote me. I had violently broken the bands betwixt us. It was at least not courteous. I shall be some time before I get quite reconciled to the separation. Farewell, old cronies, yet not for long, for again and again I will come among ye, if I shall have your leave. Farewell, Ch——, dry, sarcastic, and friendly! Do——, mild, slow to move, and gentlemanly! Pl——,[9] officious to do, and to volunteer, good services!—and thou, thou dreary pile, fit mansion for a Gresham[10] or a Whittington[11] of old, stately House of Merchants; with thy labyrinthine passages, and light-excluding, pent-up

---

7 Middleton, *The Mayor of Queenborough*, I, i, 133–4.

8 *The Vestal Virgin*, 1665.
9 John Chambers, Henry Dodwell, and W. D. Plumley.
10 Sir Thomas Gresham, founder of the Royal Exchange in the sixteenth century.
11 Sir Richard Whittington, d. 1423, celebrated as thrice mayor of London.

offices, where candles for one-half the year supplied the place of the sun's light; unhealthy contributor to my weal, stern fosterer of my living, farewell! In thee remain, and not in the obscure collection of some wandering bookseller, my 'works!' There let them rest, as I do from my labours, piled on thy massy shelves, more MSS. in folio than ever Aquinas[12] left, and full as useful! My mantle I bequeath among ye.—

A fortnight had passed since the date of my first communication. At that period I was approaching to tranquillity, but had not reached it. I boasted of a calm indeed, but it was comparative only. Something of the first flutter was left; an unsettling sense of novelty; the dazzle to weak eyes of unaccustomed light. I missed my old chains, forsooth, as if they had been some necessary part of my apparel. I was a poor Carthusian,[13] from strict cellular discipline suddenly by some revolution returned upon the world. I am now as if I had never been other than my own master. It is natural to me to go where I please, to do what I please. I find myself at eleven o'clock in the day in Bond Street, and it seems to me that I have been sauntering there at that very hour for years past. I digress into Soho, to explore a book-stall. Methinks I have been thirty years a collector. There is nothing strange nor new in it. I find myself before a fine picture in the morning. Was it ever otherwise? What is become of Fish Street Hill? Where is Fenchurch Street? Stones of old Mincing Lane, which I have worn with my daily pilgrimage for six and thirty years, to the footsteps of what toil-worn clerk are your everlasting flints now vocal? I indent the gayer flags of Pall Mall. It is 'Change time, and I am strangely among the Elgin marbles.[14] It was no hyperbole when I ventured to compare the change in my condition to a passing into another world. Time stands still in a manner to me. I have lost all distinction of season. I do not know the day of the week, or of the month. Each day used to be individually felt by me in its reference to the foreign post days; in its distance from, or propinquity to, the next Sunday. I had my Wednesday feelings, my Saturday nights' sensations. The genius of each day was upon me distinctly during the whole of it, affecting my appetite, spirits, &c. The phantom of the next day,

with the dreary five to follow, sate as a load upon my poor Sabbath recreations. What charm has washed the Ethiop white?[15] What is gone of Black Monday? All the days are the same. Sunday itself—that unfortunate failure of a holiday, as it too often proved, what with my sense of its fugitiveness, and overcare to get the greatest quantity of pleasure out of it—is melted down into a week day. I can spare to go to church now, without grudging the huge cantle[16] which it used to cut out of the holiday. I have Time for everything. I can visit a sick friend. I can interrupt the man of much occupation when he is busiest. I can insult over him with an invitation to take a day's pleasure with me to Windsor this fine May-morning. It is Lucretian pleasure[17] to behold the poor drudges, whom I have left behind in the world, carking and caring; like horses in a mill, drudging on in the same eternal round— and what is it all for? A man can never have too much Time to himself, nor too little to do. Had I a little son, I would christen him NOTHING-TO-DO; he should do nothing. Man, I verily believe, is out of his element as long as he is operative. I am altogether for the life contemplative. Will no kindly earthquake come and swallow up those accursed cotton mills? Take me that lumber of a desk there, and bowl it down

As low as to the fiends.[18]

I am no longer * * * * * *, clerk to the firm of, &c. I am Retired Leisure. I am to be met with in trim gardens. I am already come to be known by my vacant face and careless gesture, perambulating at no fixed pace nor with any settled purpose. I walk about; not to and from. They tell me, a certain *cum dignitate*[19] air, that has been buried so long with my other good parts, has begun to shoot forth in my person. I grow into gentility perceptibly. When I take up a newspaper it is to read the state of the opera. *Opus operatum est.*[20] I have done all that I came into this world to do. I have worked task-work, and have the rest of the day to myself.

1825

---

12 St. Thomas Aquinas, d. 1274, famous medieval theologian whose works filled seventeen folio volumes.
13 a monastic order noted for the strictness of its discipline.
14 relics of Greek sculpture brought to the British Museum by Lord Elgin.

15 See Jeremiah, xiii, 23.
16 slice.
17 a reference to the passage in Lucretius *De Rerum Natura*, II, which begins: 'It is sweet, when on the great sea the winds trouble its waters, to behold from land another's deep distress.'
18 *Hamlet*, II, ii, 519.
19 adapted from the Ciceronian phrase *otium cum dignitate*, 'ease with dignity.'
20 'My work is finished.'

SELECTIONS FROM LAMB'S LETTERS

1 *To* Samuel Taylor Coleridge

p.m. September 27, 1796

My dearest Friend,

White or some of my friends or the public papers by this time may have informed you of the terrible calamities that have fallen on our family. I will only give you the outlines. My poor dear, dearest sister in a fit of insanity has been the death of her own mother. I was at hand only time enough to snatch the knife out of her grasp. She is at present in a mad house, from whence I fear she must be moved to an hospital. God has preserved to me my senses,—I eat and drink and sleep, and have my judgement I believe very sound. My poor father was slightly wounded, and I am left to take care of him and my aunt. Mr. Norris of the Bluecoat School has been very kind to us, and we have no other friend, but thank God I am very calm and composed, and able to do the best that remains to do. Write,— as religious a letter as possible—but no mention of what is gone and done with—with me the former things are passed away, and I have something more to do than to feel—

God almighty have us all in his keeping.—

                                C. Lamb

Mention nothing of poetry. I have destroyed every vestige of past vanities of that kind. Do as you please, but if you publish, publish mine (I give free leave) without name or initial, and never send me a book, I charge you. Your own judgement will convince you not to take any notice of this yet to your dear wife.—You look after your family,—I have my reason and strength left to take care of mine. I charge you don't think of coming to see me. Write. I will not see you if you come. God almighty love you and all of us—

2 *To* Robert Lloyd[1]

November 13, 1798

My dear Robert,

One passage in your letter a little displeased me. The rest was nothing but kindness, which Robert's letters are ever brimful of. You say that 'this World to you seems drained of all its

sweets!' At first I had hoped you only meant to insinuate the high price of Sugar! but I am afraid you meant more. O Robert, I don't know what you call sweet. Honey and the honeycomb, roses and violets, are yet in the earth. The sun and moon yet reign in Heaven, and the lesser lights keep up their pretty twinklings. Meats and drinks, sweet sights and sweet smells, a country walk, spring and autumn, follies and repentance, quarrels and reconcilements, have all a sweetness by turns. Good humour and good nature, friends at home that love you, and friends abroad that miss you, you possess all these things, and more innumerable, and these are all sweet things. . . . You may extract honey from everything; do not go a gathering after gall. The Bees are wiser in their generation than the race of sonnet writers and complainers, Bowles's and Charlotte Smiths,[2] and all that tribe, who can see no joys but what are past, and fill people's heads with notions of the unsatisfying nature of Earthly comforts. I assure you I find this world a very pretty place. My kind love to all your sisters and to Thomas—he never writes to me—and tell Susanna I forgive her.

3 *To* William Wordsworth

January 30, 1801

Thanks for your Letter and Present. I had already borrowed your second volume.[3] What most please me are, the song of Lucy . . . . *Simon's sickly daughter* in 'The Sexton' made me *cry*. Next to these are the description of the continuous echoes in the story of Joanna's laugh, where the mountains and all the scenery absolutely seem alive—and that fine Shakespearian character of the Happy Man, in *The Brothers,*

—— that creeps about the fields,
Following his fancies by the hour, to bring
Tears down his cheek, or solitary smiles
Into his face, *until the Setting Sun
Write Fool upon his forehead.*[4]

I will mention one more: the delicate and curious feeling in the wish for the Cumberland Beggar, that he may have about him the melody of birds, although he hear them not. Here the mind knowingly passes a fiction upon herself, first substituting her own feelings for the Beggar's, and, in the

---

[1] Bristol bookseller and brother of Charles Lloyd, Coleridge's early associate and friend.

[2] William L. Bowles and Mrs. Charlotte Smith were popular sonnet writers of the late eighteenth century.
[3] second edition of the *Lyrical Ballads,* 1800.
[4] ll. 108–12.

same breath detecting the fallacy, will not part with the wish.—The 'Poet's Epitaph' is disfigured, to my taste by the vulgar satire upon parsons and lawyers in the beginning, and the coarse epithet of pin point in the 6th stanza. All the rest is eminently good, and your own. I will just add that it appears to me a fault in the Beggar, that the instructions conveyed in it are too direct and like a lecture: they don't slide into the mind of the reader, while he is imagining no such matter. An intelligent reader finds a sort of insult in being told, I will teach you how to think upon this subject. This fault, if I am right, is in a ten-thousandth worse degree to be found in Sterne and many many novelists and modern poets, who continually put a sign post up to show where you are to feel. They set out with assuming their readers to be stupid. Very different from *Robinson Crusoe, The Vicar of Wakefield, Roderick Random,* and other beautiful bare narratives. There is implied an unwritten compact between author and reader; I will tell you a story, and I suppose you will understand it. Modern novels 'St. Leons'[5] and the like are full of such flowers as these 'Let not my reader suppose,' 'Imagine, *if you can'*—modest!—etc.—I will here have done with praise and blame. I have written so much, only that you may not think I have passed over your book without observation.—I am sorry that Coleridge has christened his *Ancient Mariner* 'a poet's Reverie'—it is as bad as Bottom the Weaver's declaration that he is not a Lion but only the scenical representation of a Lion.[6] What new idea is gained by this title, but one subversive of all credit, which the tale should force upon us, of its truth? For me, I was never so affected with any human tale. After first reading it, I was totally possessed with it for many days—I dislike all the miraculous part of it, but the feelings of the man under the operation of such scenery dragged me along like Tom Piper's magic whistle. I totally differ from your idea that the Marinere should have had a character and profession. This is a beauty in *Gulliver's Travels,* where the mind is kept in a placid state of little wonderments; but the Ancient Mariner undergoes such trials, as overwhelm and bury all individuality or memory of what he was, like the state of a man in a bad dream, one terrible peculiarity of which is: that all consciousness of personality is gone. Your other observation is I think as well a little unfounded: the Mariner from being conversant

in supernatural events *has* acquired a supernatural and strange cast of *phrase,* eye, appearance, etc., which frighten the wedding guest. You will excuse my remarks, because I am hurt and vexed that you should think it necessary, with a prose apology, to open the eyes of dead men that cannot see. To sum up a general opinion of the second volume—I do not feel any one poem in it so forcibly as the *Ancient Mariner, The Mad Mother,* and the *Lines at Tintern Abbey* in the first.—I could, too, have wished the critical preface had appeared in a separate treatise. All its dogmas are true and just, and most of them new, *as* criticism. But they associate a *diminishing* idea with the poems which follow, as having been written for *experiment* on the public taste, more than having sprung (as they must have done) from living and daily circumstances.—I am prolix, because I am gratified in the opportunity of writing to you, and I don't well know when to leave off. I ought before this to have replied to your very kind invitation into Cumberland. With you and your sister I could gang any where. But I am afraid whether I shall ever be able to afford so desperate a journey. Separate from the pleasure of your company, I don't much care if I never see a mountain in my life. I have passed all my days in London, until I have formed as many and intense local attachments, as any of you mountaineers can have done with dead nature. The lighted shops of the Strand and Fleet Street, the innumerable trades, tradesmen and customers, coaches, waggons, playhouses, all the bustle and wickedness round about Covent Garden, the very women of the town, the watchmen, drunken scenes, rattles,—life awake, if you awake, at all hours of the night, the impossibility of being dull in Fleet Street, the crowds, the very dirt and mud, the sun shining upon houses and pavements, the print shops, the old book stalls, parsons cheap'ning[7] books, coffee houses, steams of soups from kitchens, the pantomimes, London itself a pantomime and a masquerade,—all these things work themselves into my mind and feed me, without a power of satiating me. The wonder of these sights impells me into night-walks about her crowded streets, and I often shed tears in the motley Strand from fulness of joy at so much Life.— All these emotions must be strange to you. So are your rural emotions to me. But consider, what must I have been doing all my life, not to have lent great portions of my heart with usury to such scenes?—

---

5 *St. Leon* was a novel by William Godwin.
6 *A Midsummer Night's Dream,* III, i, 40ff.

7 bargaining for.

My attachments are all local, purely local. I have no passion (or have had none since I was in love, and then it was the spurious engendering of poetry and books) to groves and vallies. The rooms where I was born, the furniture which has been before my eyes all my life, a book case which has followed me about (like a faithful dog, only exceeding him in knowledge) wherever I have moved—old chairs, old tables, streets, squares, where I have sunned myself, my old school,—these are my mistresses. Have I not enough, without your mountains? I do not envy you. I should pity you, did I not know, that the mind will make friends of any thing. Your sun and moon and skies and hills and lakes affect me no more, or scarcely come to me in more venerable characters, than as a gilded room with tapestry and tapers, where I might live with handsome visible objects. I consider the clouds above me but as a roof, beautifully painted but unable to satisfy the mind, and at last, like the pictures of the apartment of a connoisseur, unable to afford him any longer a pleasure. So fading upon me, from disuse, have been the Beauties of Nature, as they have been confinedly called; so ever fresh and green and warm are all the inventions of men and assemblies of men in this great city. I should certainly have laughed with dear Joanna.[8]

Give my kindest love, *and my sister's,* to D.[9] and your*self* and a kiss from me to little Barbara Lewthwaite.[10]

Thank you for liking my Play!![11]

C. Lamb.

4 *To* Thomas Manning[12]

February 15, 1801

I had need be cautious henceforward what opinion I give of the *Lyrical Ballads.* All the North of England are in a turmoil. Cumberland and Westmoreland have already declared a state of war. I lately received from Wordsworth a copy of the second volume, accompanied by an acknowledgement of having received from me many months since a copy of a certain tragedy, with excuses for not having made any acknowledgement sooner, it being owing to an 'almost insurmountable aversion from letter-writing.'

This letter I answered in due form and time, and enumerated several of the passages which had most affected me, adding, unfortunately, that no single piece had moved me so forcibly as the *Ancient Mariner, The Mad Mother,* or the *Lines at Tintern Abbey.* The Post did not sleep a moment. I received almost instantaneously a long letter of four sweating pages from my Reluctant Letter-Writer, the purport of which was, that he was sorry his 2d vol. had not given me more pleasure (Devil a hint did I give that it had *not pleased me*), and 'was compelled to wish that my range of sensibility was more extended, being obliged to believe that I should receive large influxes of happiness and happy thoughts' (I suppose from the L. B.)—With a deal of stuff about a certain union of tenderness and imagination, which in the sense he used imagination was not the characteristic of Shakespeare, but which Milton possessed in a degree far exceeding other poets: which union, as the highest species of poetry, and chiefly deserving that name, 'He was most proud to aspire to'; then illustrating the said union by two quotations from his own 2d vol. (which I had been so unfortunate as to miss). First specimen—a father addresses his son:

When thou
First camest into the World, as it befalls
To new-born Infants, thou didst sleep away
Two days: and *Blessings from Thy father's Tongue
Then fell upon thee.*[13]

The lines were thus undermarked, and then followed 'This Passage, as combining in an extraordinary degree that Union of Imagination and Tenderness which I am speaking of, I consider as one of the Best I ever wrote!'

Second specimen.—A youth, after years of absence, revisits his native place, and thinks (as most people do) that there has been strange alteration in his absence:—

And that the rocks
And everlasting Hills themselves were changed.[14]

You see both these are good poetry: but after one has been reading Shakespeare twenty of the best years of one's life, to have a fellow start up, and prate about some unknown quality, which Shakespeare possessed in a degree inferior to Milton and *somebody else!!* This was not to be *all* my castigation. Coleridge, who had not written to me some months before, starts up from

---

8 she of the laugh in the poem *To Joanna.*
9 Dorothy, Wordsworth's sister.
10 the heroine of Wordsworth's poem *The Pet Lamb.*
11 *John Woodvil.*
12 Thomas Manning, 1772–1840, was a tutor of mathematics at Cambridge University who became one of Lamb's most intimate friends. In 1806 he traveled to the Far East to study the language and customs of the people. He returned in 1817.

13 *Michael,* 339–43.
14 *The Brothers,* 98–9.

his bed of sickness to reprove me for my hardy presumption: four long pages, equally sweaty and more tedious, came from him; assuring me that, when the works of a man of true genius such as W. undoubtedly was, do not please me at first sight, I should suspect the fault to lie 'in me and not in them,' etc., etc., etc., etc., etc. What am I to do with such people? I certainly shall write them a very merry letter. Writing to *you*, I may say that the 2d vol. has no such pieces as the three I enumerated. It is full of original thinking and an observing mind, but it does not often make you laugh or cry.—It too artfully aims at simplicity of expression. And you sometimes doubt if Simplicity be not a cover for Poverty. The best piece in it I will send you, being *short*. I have grievously offended my friends in the North by declaring my undue preference; but I need not fear you:—

She dwelt among the untrodden ways
  Beside the Springs of Dove,
A maid whom there were few [none] to praise
  And very few to love.

A violet, by a mossy stone,
  Half hidden from the eye.
Fair as a star when only one
  Is shining in the sky.

She lived unknown; and few could know,
  When Lucy ceased to be.
But she is in the [her] grave, and oh!
  The difference to me.

This is choice and genuine, and so are many, many more. But one does not like to have 'em rammed down one's throat. 'Pray, take it—it's very good—let me help you—eat faster.' . . .

5 *To* Thomas Manning

London, September 24, 1802

My dear Manning:

Since the date of my last letter, I have been a traveller. A strong desire seized me of visiting remote regions. My first impulse was to go and see Paris. It was a trivial objection to my aspiring mind, that I did not understand a word of the language, since I certainly intend some time in my life to see Paris, and equally certainly never intend to learn the language; therefore that could be no objection. However, I am very glad I did not go, because you had left Paris (I see) before I could have set out. I believe, Stoddart promis-

ing to go with me another year prevented that plan. My next scheme, (for to my restless, ambitious mind London was become a bed of thorns) was to visit the farfamed Peak in Derbyshire, where the Devil sits, they say, without breeches. *This* my purer mind rejected as indelicate. And my final resolve was a tour of the Lakes. I set out with Mary to Keswick, without giving Coleridge any notice; for my time being precious did not admit of it. He received us with all the hospitality in the world, and gave up his time to show us all the wonders of the country. He dwells upon a small hill by the side of Keswick, in a comfortable house, quite enveloped on all sides by a net of mountains: great floundering bears and monsters they seemed, all couchant and asleep. We got in in the evening, travelling in a post-chaise from Penrith, in the midst of a gorgeous sunshine, which transmuted all the mountains into colours, purple, etc., etc. We thought we had got into Fairy Land. But that went off (as it never came again—while we stayed we had no more fine sunsets); and we entered Coleridge's comfortable study just in the dusk, when the mountains were all dark with clouds upon their heads. Such an impression I never received from objects of sight before, nor do I suppose I can ever again. Glorious creatures, fine old fellows, Skiddaw, etc. I never shall forget ye, how ye lay about that night, like an intrenchment; gone to bed, as it seemed for the night, but promising that ye were to be seen in the morning. Coleridge had got a blazing fire in his study; which is a large, antique, ill-shaped room, with an old-fashioned organ, never played upon, big enough for a church, shelves of scattered folios, an Æolian harp, and an old sofa, half-bed, etc. And all looking out upon the last fading view of Skiddaw and his broad-breasted brethren: what a night! Here we stayed three full weeks, in which time I visited Wordsworth's cottage, where we stayed a day or two with the Clarksons[15] (good people and most hospitable, at whose house we tarried one day and night), and saw Lloyd. The Wordsworths were gone to Calais. They have since been in London and passed much time with us: he is now gone into Yorkshire to be married to a girl of small fortune,[16] but he is in expectation of augmenting his own in consequence of the death of Lord Lonsdale, who kept him out of his own in conformity with a plan my lord had taken up in

15 Thomas Clarkson, 1760–1846, the anti-slavery agitator.
16 Wordsworth married Mary Hutchinson on 4 October 1802.

early life of making everybody unhappy.[17] So we have seen Keswick, Grasmere, Ambleside, Ulswater (where the Clarksons live), and a place at the other end of Ulswater—I forget the name —to which we travelled on a very sultry day, over the middle of Helvellyn. We have clambered up to the top of Skiddaw, and I have waded up the bed of Lodore.[18] In fine, I have satisfied myself, that there is such a thing as that which tourists call *romantic*, which I very much suspected before: they make such a spluttering about it, and toss their splendid epithets around them, till they give as dim a light as at four o'clock next morning the lamps do after an illumination. Mary was excessively tired, when she got about half-way up Skiddaw, but we came to a cold rill (than which nothing can be imagined more cold, running over cold stones), and with the reinforcement of a draught of cold water she surmounted it most manfully. Oh, its fine black head, and the bleak air atop of it, with a prospect of mountains all about, and about, making you giddy; and then Scotland afar off, and the border countries so famous in song and ballad! It was a day that will stand out, like a mountain, I am sure, in my life. But I am returned (I have now been come home near three weeks—I was a month out), and you cannot conceive the degradation I felt at first, from being accustomed to wander free as air among mountains, and bathe in rivers without being controlled by any one, to come home and *work*. I felt very *little*. I had been dreaming I was a very great man. But that is going off, and I find I shall conform in time to that state of life to which it has pleased God to call me. Besides, after all, Fleet-Street and the Strand are better places to live in for good and all than among Skiddaw. Still, I turn back to those great places where I wandered about, participating in their greatness. After all, I could not *live* in Skiddaw. I could spend a year—two, three years— among them, but I must have a prospect of seeing Fleet-Street at the end of that time, or I should mope and pine away, I know. Still, Skiddaw is a fine creature. My habits are changing, I think: *i.e.* from drunk to sober. Whether I shall be happier or not remains to be proved. I shall certainly be more happy in a morning; but whether I shall not sacrifice the fat, and the marrow, and the kidneys, *i.e.* the night, the glorious care-drowning night, that heals all our wrongs, pours wine into our mortifications, changes the scene from indifferent and flat to bright and brilliant!—O Manning, if I should have formed a diabolical resolution, by the time you come to England, of not admitting any spirituous liquors into my house, will you be my guest on such shameworthy terms? Is life, with such limitations, worth trying? The truth is, that my liquors bring a nest of friendly harpies about my house, who consume me. This is a pitiful tale to be read at St. Gothard;[19] but it is just now nearest my heart. Fenwick[20] is a ruined man. He is hiding himself from his creditors, and has sent his wife and children into the country. Fell, my other drunken companion (that has been: nam hic caestus artemque repono[21]), is turned editor of a 'Naval Chronicle.' Godwin (with a pitiful artificial wife) continues a steady friend, though the same facility does not remain of visiting him often. That Bitch has detached Marshall from his house, Marshall the man who went to sleep when the *Ancient Mariner* was reading: the old, steady, unalterable friend of the Professor. Holcroft[22] is not yet come to town. I expect to see him, and will deliver your message. How I hate *this part* of a letter. Things come crowding in to say, and no room for 'em. Some things are too little to be told, *i.e.* to have a preference; some are too big and circumstantial. Thanks for yours, which was most delicious. Would I had been with you, benighted etc. I fear my head is turned with wandering. I shall never be the same acquiescent being. Farewell; write again quickly, for I shall not like to hazard a letter, not knowing where the fates have carried you. Farewell, my dear fellow.

6 *To* Thomas Manning

February 19, 1803

My dear Manning,

The general scope of your letter afforded no indications of insanity, but some particular points raised a scruple. For God's sake don't think any more of 'Independent Tartary.' What

---

17 James Lowther, Earl of Lonsdale, 1736–1802, owed large sums of money to Wordsworth's father but had repudiated the debt. After the earl's death, however, his heir paid the Wordsworths in full with interest.
18 a famous cataract in Cumberlandshire.

19 the St. Gothard pass in Switzerland, where Manning was studying at that time.
20 John Fenwick, owner and editor of the *Albion*, to which Lamb contributed.
21 'For here I lay down my boxing gloves and the game.'—*Aeneid*, v, 484.
22 Thomas Holcroft, 1745–1809, a writer of miscellaneous works, best known for his autobiography, *Memoirs*, edited and completed by Hazlitt.

have you to do among such Ethiopians? Is there no *lineal descendant* of Prester John?[23]

Is the chair empty? Is the sword unswayed?—depend upon't they'll never make you their king, as long as any branch of that great stock is remaining. I tremble for your Christianity. They'll certainly circumcise you. Read Sir John Mandevil's travels to cure you, or come over to England. There is a Tartarman now exhibiting at Exeter Change. Come and talk with him, and hear what he says first. Indeed, he is no very favourable specimen of his Countrymen! But perhaps the best thing you can do, is to *try* to get the idea out of your head. For this purpose repeat to yourself every night, after you have said your prayers, the words Independent Tartary, Independent Tartary, two or three times, and associate with them the *idea of oblivion* ('tis Hartley's method[24] with obstinate memories), or say, Independent, Independent, have I not already got an *Independence?* That was a clever way of the old puritans—pun-divinity. My dear friend, think what a sad pity it would be to bury such *parts* in heathen countries, among nasty, unconversable, horse-belching, Tartar people! Some say, they are Cannibals; and then conceive a Tartar-fellow *eating* my friend, and adding the *cool malignity* of mustard and vinegar! I am afraid 'tis the reading of Chaucer has misled you; his foolish stories about Cambuscan and the ring, and the horse of brass.[25] Believe me, there's no such things, 'tis all the poet's *invention*; but if there were such *darling* things as old Chaucer sings, I would *up* behind you on the Horse of Brass, and frisk off for Prester John's Country. But these are all tales; a Horse of Brass never flew, and a King's daughter never talked with Birds! The Tartars, really, are a cold, insipid, smouchey set. You'll be sadly moped (if you are not eaten) among them. Pray *try* and cure yourself. Take Hellebore (the counsel is Horace's, 'twas none of my thought *originally*). Shave yourself oftener. Eat no saffron, for saffron-eaters contract a terrible Tartar-like yellow. Pray, to avoid the fiend. Eat nothing that gives the heart-burn. *Shave the upper lip.* Go about like an European. Read no books of voyages (they're nothing but lies): only now and then a romance, to keep the fancy *under*. Above all, don't go to any sights of *wild beasts. That has been your ruin.* Accustom yourself to

write familiar letters on common subjects to your friends in England, such as are of a moderate understanding. And think about common things more. There's your friend Holcroft now, has written a play. You used to be fond of the drama. Nobody went to see it. Notwithstanding this, with an audacity perfectly original, he faces the town down in a preface, that they *did like* it very much. I have heard a waspish punster say, 'Sir, why did you not laugh at my jest?' But for a man boldly to face me out with, 'Sir, I maintain it, you did laugh at my jest,' is a little too much. I have seen H. but once. He spoke of you to me in honourable terms. H. seems to me to be drearily dull. Godwin is dull, but then he has a dash of affectation, which smacks of the coxcomb, and your coxcombs are always agreeable. I supped last night with Rickman,[26] and met a merry *natural* captain, who pleases himself vastly with once having made a Pun at Otaheite in the O. language. 'Tis the same man who said Shakespeare he liked, because he was so *much of the Gentleman.* Rickman is a man 'absolute in all numbers.' I think I may one day bring you acquainted, if you do not go to Tartary first; for you'll never come back. Have a care, my dear friend, of Anthropophagi![27] their stomachs are always craving. But if you do go among [them] pray contrive to *stink* as soon as you can that you may [not] hang a [on hand] at the Butcher's. 'Tis terrible to be weighed out for 5d. a-pound. To sit at table (the reverse of fishes in Holland),[28] not as a guest, but as a meat.

God bless you: do come to England. Air and exercise may do great things. Talk with some Minister. Why not your father?

God dispose all for the best. I have discharged my duty.

Your sincere friend,

C. Lamb.

7 *To* Thomas Manning

December 25th, 1815

Dear old Friend and Absentee,

This is Christmas Day 1815 with us; what it may be with you I don't know, the 12th of June next year perhaps; and if it should be the conse-

23 the name given by early writers to the King of Ethiopia.
24 David Hartley, 1705–57, English philosopher, developed the theory of associational psychology.
25 In Chaucer's *Squire's Tale,* Cambuscan, King of Sarra, in Tartary, is conveyed on his horse of brass wherever he chooses to go; and his daughter is enabled by a magic ring to talk to birds.

26 John Rickman, 1771–1840, eminent statistician and lifelong friend of Southey's.
27 man-eaters.
28 The allusion is to Andrew Marvell's whimsical satire on the Dutch:

> The fish ofttimes the burgher dispossessed
> And sat not as a meat but as a guest.

crated season with you, I don't see how you can keep it. You have no turkeys; you would not desecrate the festival by offering up a withered Chinese bantam, instead of the savoury grand Norfolcian[29] holocaust, that smokes all around my nostrils at this moment from a thousand firesides. Then what puddings have you? Where will you get holly to stick in your churches, or churches to stick your dried tea-leaves (that must be the substitute) in? What memorials you can have of the holy time, I see not. A chopped missionary or two may keep up the thin idea of Lent and the wilderness; but what standing evidence have you of the Nativity?—'tis our rosy-cheeked, homestalled divines, whose faces shine to the tune of *unto us a child;* faces fragrant with the mince-pies of half a century, that alone can authenticate the cheerful mystery—I feel.

I feel my bowels refreshed with the holy tide —my zeal is great against the unedified heathen. Down with the Pagodas—down with the idols— Ching-chong-fo and his foolish priesthood! Come out of Babylon, O my friend! for her time is come, and the child that is native, and the Proselyte of her gates, shall kindle and smoke together! And in sober sense what makes you so long from among us, Manning? You must not expect to see the same England again which you left.

Empires have been overturned, crowns trodden into dust, the face of the western world quite changed; your friends have all got old—those you left blooming—myself (who am one of the few that remember you) those golden hairs which you recollect my taking a pride in, turned to silvery and grey. Mary has been dead and buried many years—she desired to be buried in the silk gown you sent her. Rickman, that you remember active and strong, now walks out supported by a servant-maid and a stick. Martin Burney is a very old man. The other day an aged woman knocked at my door, and pretended to my acquaintance; it was long before I had the most distant cognition of her; but at last together we made her out to be Louisa, the daughter of Mrs. Topham, formerly Mrs. Morton, who had been Mrs. Reynolds, formerly Mrs. Kenney, whose first husband was Holcroft, the dramatic writer of the last century. St. Paul's Church is a heap of ruins; the Monument isn't half so high as you knew it, divers parts being successively taken down which the ravages of time had rendered dangerous; the

horse at Charing Cross is gone, no one knows whither,—and all this has taken place while you have been settling whether Ho-hing-tong should be spelt with a —— or a ——. For aught I see you had almost as well remain where you are, and not come like a Struldbug[30] into a world where few were born when you went away. Scarce here and there one will be able to make out your face; all your opinions will be out of date, your jokes obsolete, your puns rejected with fastidiousness as wit of the last age. Your way of mathematics has already given way to a new method, which after all is I believe the old doctrine of Maclaurin,[31] new-vamped up with what he borrowed of the negative quantity of fluxions from Euler.[32]

Poor Godwin! I was passing his tomb the other day in Cripplegate churchyard. There are some verses upon it written by Miss Hayes, which if I thought good enough I would send you. He was one of those who would have hailed your return, not with boisterous shouts and clamours, but with the complacent gratulations of a philosopher anxious to promote knowledge as leading to happiness—but his systems and his theories are ten feet deep in Cripplegate mould. Coleridge is just dead, having lived just long enough to close the eyes of Wordsworth, who paid the debt to nature but a week or two before. Poor Col., but two days before he died he wrote to a bookseller proposing an epic poem on the 'Wanderings of Cain,' in twenty-four books. It is said he has left behind him more than forty thousand treatises in criticism and metaphysics, but few of them in a state of completion. They are now destined, perhaps, to wrap up spices. You see what mutations the busy hand of Time has produced, while you have consumed in foolish voluntary exile that time which might have gladdened your friends—benefited your country; but reproaches are useless. Gather up the wretched reliques, my friend, as fast as you can, and come to your old home. I will rub my eyes and try to recognise you. We will shake withered hands together, and talk of old things—of St. Mary's Church and the barber's opposite, where the young students in mathematics used to assemble. Poor Crisp, that kept it afterwards, set up a fruiterer's shop in Trumpington-street, and for aught I know, resides there still, for I saw the name up in the last

---

29 Norfolk supplied choice Christmas turkeys to the London market.

30 the Struldbrugs, in *Gulliver's Travels,* were wretched old people who could not die.

31 Colin Maclaurin, 1698–1746, was a celebrated Scottish mathematician.

32 Leonhard Euler, 1707–83, was a famous Swiss mathematician.

journey I took there with my sister just before she died. I suppose you heard that I had left the India House, and gone into the Fishmongers' Alms-houses over the bridge. I have a little cabin there, small and homely; but you shall be welcome to it. You like oysters, and to open them yourself; I'll get you some if you come in oyster time. Marshall, Godwin's old friend, is still alive, and talks of the faces you used to make.

Come as soon as you can.

8 *To* Samuel Taylor Coleridge

[Autumn 1820]

Dear C.,

Why will you make your visits, which should give pleasure, matter of regret to your friends? You never come but you take away some folio that is part of my existence. With a great deal of difficulty I was made to comprehend the extent of my loss. My maid Becky brought me a dirty bit of paper, which contained her description of some book which Mr. Coleridge had taken away. It was 'Luster's Tables,'[33] which, for some time, I could not make out. 'What! has he carried away any of the *tables,* Becky?' 'No, it wasn't any tables, but it was a book that he called Luster's Tables.' I was obliged to search personally among my shelves, and a huge fissure suddenly disclosed to me the true nature of the damage I had sustained. That book, C., you should not have taken away, for it is not mine; it is the property of a friend, who does not know its value, nor indeed have I been very sedulous in explaining to him the estimate of it; but was rather contented in giving a sort of corroboration to a hint that he let fall, as to its being suspected to be not genuine, so that in all probability it would have fallen to me as a deodand;[34] not but I am as sure it is Luther's as I am sure that Jack Bunyan wrote the Pilgrim's Progress'; but it was not for me to pronounce upon the validity of testimony that had been disputed by learneder clerks than I. So I quietly let it occupy the place it had usurped upon my shelves, and should never have thought of issuing an ejectment against it; for why should I be so bigoted as to allow rites of hospitality to none but my own books, children, etc.?—a species of egotism I abhor from my heart. No; let 'em all snug together, Hebrews and Prose-lytes of the gate; no selfish partiality of mine shall make distinction between them; I charge no warehouse-room for my friends' commodities; they are welcome to come and stay as long as they like, without paying rent. I have several such strangers that I treat with more than Arabian courtesy; there's a copy of More's fine poem,[35] which is none of mine; but I cherish it as my own; I am none of those churlish landlords that advertise the goods to be taken away in ten days' time, or then to be sold to pay expenses. So you see I had no right to lend you that book; I may lend you my own books, because it is at my own hazard, but it is not honest to hazard a friend's property; I always make that distinction. I hope you will bring it with you, or send it by Hartley; or he can bring that, and you the 'Polemical Discourses,'[36] and come and eat some atoning mutton with us one of these days shortly. We are engaged two or three Sundays deep, but always dine at home on week-days at half-past four. So come all four—men and books I mean—my third shelf (northern compartment) from the top has two devilish gaps, where you have knocked out its two eye-teeth.

Your wronged friend,

C. Lamb.

9 *To* Samuel Taylor Coleridge

March 9th, 1822

Dear C.,

It gives me great satisfaction to hear that the pig turned out so well—they are interesting creatures at a certain age—what a pity such buds should blow out into the maturity of rank bacon! You had all some of the crackling—and brain sauce—did you remember to rub it with butter, and gently dredge it a little, just before the crisis? Did the eyes come away kindly with no Œdipean avulsion?[37] Was the crackling the colour of the ripe pomegranate? Had you no complement of boiled neck of mutton before it, to blunt the edge of delicate desire? Did you flesh maiden teeth in it? Not that I sent the pig, or can form the remotest guess what part Owen[38] could play in the business. I never knew him give any-

---

33 Luther's *Table Talk.*
34 a gift; old legal phraseology for anything forfeited to the crown.
35 *Psychozoia Platonica,* by Henry More, seventeenth-century Platonist.
36 by Jeremy Taylor, the noted seventeenth-century divine.
37 violent tearing out; referring to the legend that Oedipus, King of Thebes, in a passion of grief, tore out his eyes.
38 Lamb's landlord.

thing away in my life. He would not begin with strangers. I suspect the pig, after all, was meant for me; but at the unlucky juncture of time being absent, the present somehow went round to Highgate.[39] To confess an honest truth, a pig is one of those things I could never think of sending away. Teals, wigeons,[40] snipes, barn-door fowl, ducks, geese—your tame villatic[41] things—Welsh mutton, collars of brawn, sturgeon, fresh or pickled, your potted char,[42] Swiss cheeses, French pies, early grapes, muscadines,[43] I impart as freely unto my friends as to myself. They are but self-extended; but pardon me if I stop somewhere—where the fine feeling of benevolence giveth a higher smack than the sensual rarity—there my friends (or any good man) may command me; but pigs are pigs, and I myself therein am nearest to myself. Nay, I should think it an affront, an undervaluing done to Nature who bestowed such a boon upon me, if in a churlish mood I parted with the precious gift. One of the bitterest pangs of remorse I ever felt was when a child—when my kind old aunt had strained her pocket-strings to bestow a sixpenny whole plum-cake upon me. In my way home through the Borough, I met a venerable old man, not a mendicant, but thereabouts—a look-beggar, not a verbal petitionist; and in the coxcombry of taught-charity I gave away the cake to him. I walked on a little in all the pride of an Evangelical peacock, when of a sudden my old aunt's kindness crossed me—the sum it was to her—the pleasure she had a right to expect that I—not the old impostor—should take in eating her cake—the cursed ingratitude by which, under the colour of a Christian virtue, I had frustrated her cherished purpose. I sobbed, wept, and took it to heart so grievously, that I think I never suffered the like—and I was right. It was a piece of unfeeling hypocrisy, and proved a lesson to me ever after. The cake has long been masticated, consigned to the dunghill with the ashes of that unseasonable pauper.

But when Providence, who is better to us all than our aunts, gives me a pig, remembering my temptation and my fall, I shall endeavour to act towards it more in the spirit of the donor's purpose.

Yours (short of pig) to command in everything.

10 *To* Bernard Barton[44]

January 9th, 1824

Dear B. B.,

Do you know what it is to succumb under an insurmountable day mare—whoreson lethargy,[45] Falstaff calls it—an indisposition to do any thing, or to be any thing—a total deadness and distaste—a suspension of vitality—an indifference to locality—a numb soporifical goodfornothingness—an ossification all over—an oysterlike insensibility to the passing events—a mind-stupor,—a brawny defiance to the needles of a thrusting-in conscience—did you ever have a very bad cold with a total irresolution to submit to water gruel processes?—this has been for many weeks my lot, and my excuse—my fingers drag heavily over this paper, and to my thinking it is three and twenty furlongs from here to the end of this demi-sheet—I have not a thing to say—nothing is of more importance than another—I am flatter than a denial or a pancake—emptier than Judge Park's[46] wig when the head is in it—duller than a country stage when the actors are off it—a cypher—an 0—I acknowledge life at all, only by an occasional convulsional cough, and a permanent phlegmatic pain in the chest—I am weary of the world—Life is weary of me—My day is gone into Twilight and I don't think it worth the expense of candles—my wick hath a thief in it, but I can't muster courage to snuff it—I inhale suffocation—I can't distinguish veal from mutton—nothing interests me—'tis 12 o'clock and Thurtell is just now coming out upon the New Drop[47]—Jack Ketch[48] alertly tucking up his greasy sleeves to do the last office of mortality, yet cannot I elicit a groan or a moral reflection—if you told me the world will be at end tomorrow, I should just say, 'will it?'—I have not volition enough to dot my i's—much less to comb my EYEBROWS—my eyes are set in my head—my brains are gone out to see a poor relation in Moorfields, and they did not say when they'd come back again—my scull is a Grub street Attic, to let—not so much as a joint stool or a cracked jordan left in it—my hand writes, not I, from habit, as chickens run about a little when their heads are off—O for a vigorous fit of gout, cholic, tooth

---

39 where Coleridge was living with the Gilmans.
40 a kind of small wild duck.
41 farmyard.
42 a delicious kind of trout.
43 a large, musky grape.

44 Quaker banker and poet, 1784–1849.
45 *II Henry IV*, I, ii, 127.
46 Sir James A. Park was the judge who tried the notorious murderer Thurtell.
47 Thurtell was hanged at Hertford on 9 January 1824.
48 'dynastic' name of English hangman, after John Ketch, who had beheaded Monmouth.

ache—an earwig in my auditory, a fly in my visual organs—pain is life—the sharper, the more evidence of life—but this apathy, this death—did you ever have an obstinate cold, a six or seven weeks' unintermitting chill and suspension of hope, fear, conscience, and every thing—yet do I try all I can to cure it. I try wine, and spirits, and smoking, and snuff in unsparing quantities, but they all only seem to make me worse, instead of better—I sleep in a damp room, but it does me no good; I come home late o' nights, but do not find any visible amendment.

Who shall deliver me from the body of this death?[49]

It is just fifteen minutes after twelve. Thurtell is by this time a good way on his journey, baiting at Scorpion[50] perhaps, Ketch is bargaining for his cast coat and waistcoat,[51] the Jew demurs at first at three half crowns, but on consideration that he may get somewhat by showing 'em in the Town, finally closes.—

11 *To* Dr. Jacob Vale Asbury[52]

[No date]

Dear Sir,

It is an observation of a wise man that 'moderation is best in all things.' I cannot agree with him 'in liquor.' There is a smoothness and oiliness in wine that makes it go down by a natural channel, which I am positive was made for that descending. Else, why does not wine choke us? Could Nature have made that sloping lane, not to facilitate the down-going? She does nothing in vain. You know that better than I. You know how often she has helped you at a dead lift, and how much better entitled she is to a fee than yourself sometimes, when you carry off the credit. Still there is something due to manners and customs, and I should apologise to you and Mrs. Asbury for being absolutely carried home upon a man's shoulders through Silver Street, up Parson's Lane, by the Chapels (which might have taught me better), and then to be deposited like a dead log at Gaffar Westwood's, who it seems does not 'insure' against intoxication. Not that the mode of conveyance is objectionable.

On the contrary, it is more easy than a one-horse chaise. Ariel in the 'Tempest' says

> On a bat's back do I fly,
> After sunset merrily.

Now I take it that Ariel must sometimes have stayed out late of nights. Indeed, he pretends that 'where the bee sucks, there lurks he,' as much as to say that his suction is as innocent as that little innocent (but damnably stinging when he is provoked) winged creature. But I take it, that Ariel was fond of metheglin,[53] of which the Bees are notorious Brewers. But then you will say: What a shocking sight to see a middle-aged gentleman-and-a-half riding a Gentleman's back up Parson's Lane at midnight. Exactly the time for that sort of conveyance, when nobody can see him, nobody but Heaven and his own conscience; now Heaven makes fools, and don't expect much from her own creation; and as for conscience, She and I have long since come to a compromise. I have given up false modesty, and she allows me to abate a little of the true. I like to be liked, but I don't care about being respected. I don't respect myself. But, as I was saying, I thought he would have let me down just as we got to Lieutenant Barker's Coal-shed (or emporium) but by a cunning jerk I eased myself, and righted my posture. I protest, I thought myself in a palanquin,[54] and never felt myself so grandly carried. It was a slave under me. There was I, all but my reason. And what is reason? and what is the loss of it? and how often in a day do we do without it, just as well? Reason is only counting, two and two makes four. And if on my passage home, I thought it made five, what matter? Two and two will just make four, as it always did, before I took the finishing glass that did my business. My sister has begged me to write an apology to Mrs. A. and you for disgracing your party; now it does seem to me, that I rather honoured your party, for every one that was not drunk (and one or two of the ladies, I am sure, were not) must have been set off greatly in the contrast to me. I was the scapegoat. The soberer they seemed. By the way is magnesia good on these occasions? *iii* pol: med: sum: ante noct: in rub: can:.[55] I am no licentiate, but know enough of simples to beg you to send me a draught after this model. But still you'll say (or the men and maids at your house will say) that it

49 Romans, vii, 24.

50 the zodiacal sign, en route to the next world.

51 the executed man's clothes were the perquisites of the hangman.

52 an Enfield physician.

53 a fermented beverage made of honey and water.

54 an enclosed litter such as is used in the Orient.

55 'three medium pills taken before night,' etc.

is not a seemly sight for an old gentleman to go home pick-a-back. Well, may be it is not. But I have never studied grace. I take it to be a mere superficial accomplishment. I regard more the internal acquisitions. The great object after supper is to get home, and whether that is obtained in a horizontal posture or perpendicular (as foolish men and apes affect for dignity) I think is little to the purpose. The end is always greater than the means. Here I am, able to compose a sensible rational apology, and what signifies how I got here? I have just sense enough to remember I was very happy last night, and to thank our kind host and hostess, and that's sense enough, I hope.

Charles Lamb

N.B.—What is good for a desperate head-ache? Why, Patience, and a determination not to mind being miserable all day long. And that I have made my mind up to.

So, here goes. It is better than not being alive at all, which I might have been, had your man toppled me down at Lieut. Barker's Coal-shed. My sister sends her sober compliments to Mrs. A. She is not much the worse.

12 *To* Edward Moxon[56]

p.m. July 24th, 1833

For god's sake, give Emma no more watches. *One* has turned her head. She is arrogant, and insulting. She said something very unpleasant to our old Clock in the passage, as if he did not keep time, and yet he had made her no appointment. She takes it out every instant to look at the moment-hand. She lugs us out into the fields, because there the bird-boys ask you 'Pray, Sir, can you tell us what's a Clock,' and she answers them punctually. She loses all her time looking 'what the time is.' I overheard her whispering, 'Just so many hours, minutes, etc., to Tuesday—I think St. George's goes too slow'—This little present of Time, why, 'tis Eternity to her—

What can make her so fond of a gingerbread watch?

She has spoiled some of the movements. Between ourselves, she has kissed away 'half past 12,' which I suppose to be the canonical hour in Hanover Sq.

Well, if 'love me, love my watch,' answers, she will keep time to you—

It goes right by the Horse Guards—

[On the next page:]

Emma has kissed this yellow wafer—a hint.

Dearest M.—Never mind opposite nonsense. She does not love you for the watch, but the watch for you.

I will be at the wedding, and keep the 30 July as long as my poor months last me, as a festival gloriously.

Yours *ever,*

Elia

We have not heard from Cambridge. I will write the moment we do.

Edmonton, 24th July, 3:20 post meridian minutes, 4 instants by Emma's watch.

13 *To* Mrs. George Dyer[57]

Dec. 22nd, 1834

Dear Mrs. Dyer,

I am very uneasy about a Book which I either have lost or left at your house on Thursday. It was the book I went out to fetch from Miss Buffam's, while the tripe was frying. It is called Phillip's *Theatrum Poetarum;* but it is an English book. I think I left it in the parlour. It is Mr. Cary's book, and I would not lose it for the world. Pray, if you find it, book it at the Swan, Snow Hill, by an Edmonton stage immediately, directed to Mr. Lamb, Church-street, Edmonton, or write to say you cannot find it. I am quite anxious about it. If it is lost, I shall never like tripe again.

With kindest love to Mr. Dyer and all,

Yours truly,

C. Lamb.

---

56 Edward Moxon, 1801-58, publisher. He married Lamb's adopted daughter, Emma Isola.

57 Mrs. Dyer was the wife of George Dyer, 1755-1841, eccentric poet and friend of Lamb.

1778 · WILLIAM HAZLITT · 1830

1778   Born 10 April, at Maidstone, the son of a Unitarian minister.

1792   Except for four years when his father took the family to America, he grew up and had his schooling in the village of Wem in Shropshire.

1793–8   Was sent to Hackney Theological College in London, but having no inclination for the ministry gave up his course after about three years; returned to Wem and spent his time in reading, painting, and philosophizing. In January 1798, made the acquaintance of Coleridge, who was spending the night at the Hazlitts, and heard him preach at Shrewsbury. In the spring visited Coleridge at Nether Stowey and became acquainted with Wordsworth.

1799–1802   In London became acquainted with many literary men and established a friendship with Charles and Mary Lamb, which lasted for his lifetime. Studied painting under his brother John.

1802–5   Went to Paris where he spent four months copying portraits at the Louvre. On his return to England visited Wordsworth, Coleridge, and Southey in the Lake country. Tried portrait painting, but realizing a lack of ability to excel in his art, gave it up for writing.

1805   Published his first book, *An Essay on the Principles of Human Action.*

1806–7   Abridged Tucker's *Light of Nature Pursued;* began political pamphleteering with *Free Thoughts on Public Affairs;* tilted against Sterling of the *Times;* wrote a 'reply' to Malthus; compiled *The Eloquence of the British Senate.*

1808–12   Married Sarah Stoddart, a friend of Mary Lamb, and settled at Winterslow, Salisbury, on a small estate Mrs. Hazlitt had inherited. Published *A New and Improved Grammar of the English Tongue* (1810). Finished a *Life of Holcroft* (published in 1816).

1812   Delivered a course of lectures at the Russell Institution on the *Rise and Progress of Modern Philosophy.*

1813–17   Launched himself on a journalistic career; was Parliamentary reporter and subsequently dramatic critic for the *Morning Chronicle;* contributed to the *Champion, The Times, The Edinburgh Review,* and the *Examiner.*

1818   Published a collection of periodical articles entitled *A View of the English Stage.*

1817–19   Delivered courses of lectures on *Characters of Shakespeare's Plays, English Poets,* and *English Comic Writers.*

1819   Separated from his wife and went to live in Southampton Building; his marriage dissolved in consequence of his infatuation for his lodging-housekeeper's daughter, Sarah Walker. Gave to the world in *Liber Amoris* (1823) an indiscreetly frank account of his thwarted and half-insane love. Published *Letter to William Gifford,* a spirited reply to scurrilous attacks by the editor of the *Quarterly Review.*

1820   Became a contributor to the *London Magazine.* Delivered and published Lectures on the *Dramatic Literature of the Age of Elizabeth.*

1821–2 Collected and published *Table Talk, or Original Essays on Men and Manners.*

1824 Married a Mrs. Bridgewater and spent a leisurely honeymoon traveling through France, Switzerland, and Italy. At the end of the trip, which lasted for about a year, the second Mrs. Hazlitt left him. Contributed a series of letters on his tour to the *Morning Chronicle.* On his return, a friendship with the painter Northcote resulted in *The Conversations of James Northcote, R.A.* (published 1830).

1825 Published *The Spirit of the Age; or Contemporary Portraits.*

1826 Published a collection of essays under the title *The Plain Speaker: Opinions on Books, Men, and Things.*

1828–30 Published *The Life of Napoleon Buonaparte,* in four volumes, a work which was to have crowned his literary reputation, but which has next to no value.

1830 Died 18 September in solitude, except for the comforting presence of his son and Charles Lamb. Posthumous volumes published include *Literary Remains* (1836), *Sketches and Essays* (1839), and *Winterslow* (1850).

WILLIAM HAZLITT, lecturer, critic, essayist, found himself comparatively late, having spent his life up to his middle thirties for the most part in metaphysical speculation, portrait painting, and miscellaneous political and editorial journeywork. He was early disappointed in his ideals and, being unable to make allowances or to adjust himself, he tended to find his pleasures in isolation and to look with misanthropic eyes upon 'corrupted' society. He always had a relish for what was original and strong, and a peculiar hatred for what was insipid and affected; but whether hating or admiring, passion was his element. A sort of furious intensity characterized his every experience from playing tennis and studying philosophy to writing and quarreling. His political convictions, which he maintained with a fierce and blind consistency, were always getting him into trouble. He championed the unpopular Revolutionary cause during the years of the Tory reaction, seeing in it the perpetual struggle of freedom against tyranny, and he poured rabid satires on all autocrats except, oddly enough, on Napoleon whom he forever defended as 'the crusher of kings who crushed the people.' For his beliefs he was savagely attacked by the Tory journals, the *Quarterly* and *Blackwood's;* and for a time, in consequence, the sale of his writings was blighted and he was discredited with his publishers. Maddened by the deliberately malicious abuse of the reviewers, Hazlitt retaliated in kind, and proved himself more than a match in hard-hitting political pamphleteering. Unfortunately he quarreled furiously with his friends as well as with his political enemies. He became estranged from his early friends, the Lake poets, for what he regarded as their political apostasy, to him a sacrilegious betrayal. His perverse wrongheadedness alienated him for a time even from the sincere gentleness of Charles Lamb and the geniality of Leigh Hunt. Someone has remarked that Hazlitt needed all the compensations that art and literature could give him. Yet his last words were, 'Well, I've had a happy life.' He loved a combat. Whetted by the intense zest of his nature, life with all its loves and hates had been an exciting adventure. This feeling of excitement sweeps over the pages of his essays and gives 'an edge to his writing.'

Hazlitt's essays divide into two classes: literary criticism and essays on miscellaneous subjects, and in both spheres Hazlitt holds a high place. In his criticism he is distinguished above all for insight and virility. He brings a contagious spirit of enjoyment into literature. With wit and gusto he leads the reader on to sharing and to accepting his impressionistic judgments founded on a taste rarely at fault. In a great series of discourses, he has left an extensive body of criticism from Elizabethan times to his own day, more panoramic in range, and more catholic and vital in its commentary on English literature than any since Dryden. Of these critical essays, those on the *Characters of Shakespeare's Plays,* though perhaps not regarded by the professional critic as the most rewarding, are to the general reader the best known. The analyses of Hamlet, Lear, and Falstaff are characteristic instances of his powers of reasoning and of his felicitous and incisive style. Hazlitt throws the salient features of the plays into brilliant relief, concentrating upon Shakespeare's characters, and does not, like Coleridge, penetrate into the unobtrusive and inmost obscurities. His grasp of a subject is strenuous, rarely profound; he exhibits rather than reveals the beauties of an author. But his judgments are sure and he makes us feel the genius of Shakespeare. Making allowances for his lack of the power of divination, which Saintsbury reminds us is 'the highest and rarest of critical powers,' Hazlitt is hardly to be surpassed as a critic of Elizabethan literature unless perhaps by Coleridge and Lamb. In contemporary criticism Hazlitt's only serious rival is Coleridge. Hazlitt's *Spirit of the Age,* though marred at times by prejudice and ill-temper and other accidental inadequacies, is a remarkably discriminating series of contemporary portraits.

Hazlitt is even better in his miscellaneous essays than he is in his criticism. Like Leigh Hunt and De Quincey, he lived by writing articles, and in addition to his lectures, has left more than a hundred essays on a wide variety of subjects—on politics, books of all sorts, sports and games, pictures, the out-of-doors, and play-acting—to name only general classifications. Hazlitt knew his subjects thoroughly, was absorbed by them, and had á passion 'for bringing out the unnoticed sides of familiar truth.' He is unreservedly autobiographical, revealing frankly his prejudices along with his interests, and pursuing both with full-hearted zest. An infectious enthusiasm for any subject that 'takes' him is perhaps his most characteristic quality. However, sentiment is always kept in bounds by a sinewy intellectual control. Enthusiasm comes out well in the essay *On Going a Journey,* and in *My First Acquaintance with Poets,* in which 'the remembered order of hero worship is touched with the sub-acid of disillusionment' (Elton). The best of the later writing has a note of meditative reminiscence, which at times, as in *On the Feeling of Immortality in Youth,* could reach 'the height of tragic, and not merely poetic, utterance.'

Hazlitt's style 'resembles a kind of talk.' It is spontaneous, animated, challenging, cheerfully dogmatic and personal, and entirely free from pose. It abounds in striking images, apt quotations, and picturesque phrases. It scintillates with epigrammatic brilliance and agile paradox. Yet at no time do his adornments or displays of wit seem intrusive or hackneyed. They are as much a part of his mental furnishings as his words. His sentences march in military array, 'curt, pellet-like, uncompounded.' His diction is 'a well of native English undefiled.' Stevenson, who along with a number of other nineteenth-century writers fell under the influence of Hazlitt's nervous and manly prose style, paid him a craftsman's tribute. 'We are mighty fine fellows nowadays,' he declared, 'but we cannot write like William Hazlitt.' Though modern prose writers no longer try particularly to ape Hazlitt's style as Stevenson once did, neither has anyone yet challenged Stevenson's eulogy. By general consent Hazlitt's place among English essayists is beside the greatest.

From CHARACTERS OF SHAKESPEARE'S PLAYS

HAMLET

THIS is that Hamlet the Dane, whom we read of in our youth, and whom we may be said almost to remember in our after-years; he who made that famous soliloquy on life, who gave the advice to the players, who thought 'this goodly frame, the earth, a steril promontory, and this brave o'erhanging firmament, the air, this majestical roof fretted with golden fire, a foul and pestilent congregation of vapours'; whom 'man delighted not, nor woman neither'; he who talked with the grave-diggers, and moralized on Yorick's skull; the schoolfellow of Rosencrans and Guildenstern at Wittenberg; the friend of Horatio; the lover of Ophelia; he that was mad and sent to England; the slow avenger of his father's death; who lived at the court of Horwendillus five hundred years before we were born, but all whose thoughts we seem to know as well as we do our own, because we have read them in Shakespeare.

Hamlet is a name; his speeches and sayings but the idle coinage of the poet's brain. What then, are they not real? They are as real as our own thoughts. Their reality is in the reader's mind. It is *we* who are Hamlet. This play has a prophetic truth, which is above that of history. Whoever has become thoughtful and melancholy through his own mishaps or those of others; whoever has borne about with him the clouded brow of reflection, and thought himself 'too much i' th' sun'; whoever has seen the golden lamp of day dimmed by envious mists rising in his own breast, and could find in the world before him only a dull blank with nothing left remarkable in it; whoever has known 'the pangs of despised love, the insolence of office, or the spurns which patient merit of the unworthy takes'; he who has felt his mind sink within him, and sadness cling to his heart like a malady, who has had his hopes blighted and his youth staggered by the apparitions of strange things; who cannot be well at ease, while he sees evil hovering near him like a spectre; whose powers of action have been eaten up by thought, he to whom the universe seems infinite, and himself nothing; whose bitterness of soul makes him careless of consequences, and who goes to a play as his best resource to shove off, to a second remove, the evils of life by a mock representation of them—this is the true Hamlet.

We have been so used to this tragedy that we hardly know how to criticise it any more than we should know how to describe our own faces. But we must make such observations as we can. It is the one of Shakespeare's plays that we think of the oftenest, because it abounds most in striking reflections on human life, and because the distresses of Hamlet are transferred, by the turn of his mind, to the general account of humanity. Whatever happens to him we apply to ourselves, because he applies it to himself as a means of general reasoning. He is a great moralizer; and what makes him worth attending to is that he moralizes on his own feelings and experience. He is not a common-place pedant. If *Lear* is distinguished by the greatest depth of passion, *Hamlet* is the most remarkable for the ingenuity, originality, and unstudied development of character. Shakespeare had more magnanimity than any other poet, and he has shewn more of it in this play than in any other. There is no attempt to force an interest: everything is left for time and circumstances to unfold. The attention is excited without effort, the incidents succeed each other as matters of course, the characters think and speak and act just as they might do, if left entirely to themselves. There is no set purpose, no

straining at a point. The observations are suggested by the passing scene—the gusts of passion come and go like sounds of music borne on the wind. The whole play is an exact transcript of what might be supposed to have taken place at the court of Denmark, at the remote period of time fixed upon, before the modern refinements in morals and manners were heard of. It would have been interesting enough to have been admitted as a by-stander in such a scene, at such a time, to have heard and witnessed something of what was going on. But here we are more than spectators. We have not only 'the outward pageants and the signs of grief'; but 'we have that within which passes shew.' We read the thoughts of the heart, we catch the passions living as they rise. Other dramatic writers give us very fine versions and paraphrases of nature: but Shakespeare, together with his own comments, gives us the original text, that we may judge for ourselves: This is a very great advantage.

The character of Hamlet stands quite by itself. It is not a character marked by strength of will or even of passion, but by refinement of thought and sentiment. Hamlet is as little of the hero as a man can well be: but he is a young and princely novice, full of high enthusiasm and quick sensibility—the sport of circumstances, questioning with fortune and refining on his own feelings, and forced from the natural bias of his disposition by the strangeness of his situation. He seems incapable of deliberate action, and is only hurried into extremities on the spur of the occasion, when he has no time to reflect, as in the scene where he kills Polonius, and again, where he alters the letters which Rosencrans and Guildenstern are taking with them to England, purporting his death. At other times, when he is most bound to act, he remains puzzled, undecided, and skeptical, dallies with his purposes, till the occasion is lost, and finds out some pretence to relapse into indolence and thoughtfulness again. For this reason he refuses to kill the King when he is at his prayers, and by a refinement in malice, which is in truth only an excuse for his own want of resolution, defers his revenge to a more fatal opportunity, when he shall be engaged in some act 'that has no relish of salvation in it.'

He kneels and prays,
And now I'll do 't, and so he goes to heaven,
And so am I reveng'd; *that would be scann'd;*
He kill'd my father, and for that,
I, his sole son, send him to heaven.

Why this is reward, not revenge.
Up sword and know thou a more horrid time,
When he is drunk, asleep, or in a rage.[1]

He is the prince of philosophical speculators;
and because he cannot have his revenge perfect,
according to the most refined idea his wish can
form, he declines it altogether. So he scruples to
trust the suggestions of the Ghost, contrives the
scene of the play to have surer proof of his uncle's
guilt, and then rests satisfied with this confirmation of his suspicions, and the success of his experiment, instead of acting upon it. Yet he is
sensible of his own weakness, taxes himself with
it, and tries to reason himself out of it.

How all occasions do inform against me,
And spur my dull revenge! What is a man,
If his chief good and market of his time
Be but to sleep and feed? A beast; no more.
Sure he that made us with such large discourse,
Looking before and after, gave us not
That capability and god-like reason
To rust in us unus'd: now whether it be
Bestial oblivion, or some craven scruple
Of thinking too precisely on th' event,—
A thought which quarter'd, hath but one part
        wisdom,
And ever three parts coward;—I do not know
Why yet I live to say, this thing's to do;
Sith I have cause, and will, and strength,
        and means
To do it. Examples gross as earth exhort me:
Witness this army of such mass and charge,
Led by a delicate and tender prince,
Whose spirit with divine ambition puff'd,
Makes mouths at the invisible event,
Exposing what is mortal and unsure
To all that fortune, death and danger dare,
Even for an egg-shell. 'Tis not to be great
Never to stir without great argument;
But greatly to find quarrel in a straw,
When honour's at the stake. How stand I then,
That have a father kill'd, a mother stain'd,
Excitements of my reason and my blood,
And let all sleep, while to my shame I see
The imminent death of twenty thousand
        men,
That for a fantasy and trick of fame,
Go to their graves like beds, fight for a plot
Whereon the numbers cannot try the cause,
Which is not tomb enough and continent

To hide the slain?—O, from this time forth,
My thoughts be bloody or be nothing worth.[2]

Still he does nothing; and this very speculation
on his own infirmity only affords him another
occasion for indulging it. It is not for any want
of attachment to his father or abhorrence of his
murder that Hamlet is thus dilatory, but it is
more to his taste to indulge his imagination in
reflecting upon the enormity of the crime and
refining on his schemes of vengeance, than to
put them into immediate practice. His ruling passion is to think, not to act: and any vague pretext
that flatters this propensity instantly diverts him
from his previous purposes.

The moral perfection of this character has been
called in question, we think, by those who did not
understand it. It is more interesting than according to rules; amiable, though not faultless. The
ethical delineations of 'that noble and liberal
casuist'[3] (as Shakespeare has been well called)
do not exhibit the drab-coloured quakerism of
morality. His plays are not copied either from
The Whole Duty of Man[4] or from *The Academy
of Compliments*![5] We confess we are a little
shocked at the want of refinement in those who
are shocked at the want of refinement in Hamlet.
The neglect of punctilious exactness in his behaviour either partakes of the 'license of the
time,' or else belongs to the very excess of intellectual refinement in the character, which makes
the common rules of life, as well as his own purposes, sit loose upon him. He may be said to be
amenable only to the tribunal of his own
thoughts, and is too much taken up with the airy
world of contemplation to lay as much stress as
he ought on the practical consequences of things.
His habitual principles of action are unhinged
and out of joint with the time. His conduct to
Ophelia is quite natural in his circumstances. It
is that of assumed severity only. It is the effect
of disappointed hope, of bitter regrets, of affection suspended, not obliterated, by the distractions of the scene around him! Amidst the natural and preternatural horrors of his situation,
he might be excused in delicacy from carrying
on a regular courtship. When 'his father's spirit
was in arms,' it was not a time for the son to

---

1 III, iii, 73–9, 88–9.

2 IV, iv, 32–66.
3 Lamb refers to the Elizabethan dramatists Middleton and
Rowley as 'those noble and liberal casuists' in his *Characters of
Dramatic Writers.*
4 a once-popular ethical treatise by Richard Allestree, 1619–81,
published in 1658.
5 a popular treatise on the art of courtship published in the seventeenth century.

make love in. He could neither marry Ophelia, nor wound her mind by explaining the cause of his alienation, which he durst hardly trust himself to think of. It would have taken him years to have come to a direct explanation on the point. In the harassed state of his mind, he could not have done much otherwise than he did. His conduct does not contradict what he says when he sees her funeral,

> I loved Ophelia: forty thousand brothers
> Could not with all their quantity of love
> Make up my sum.[6]

Nothing can be more affecting or beautiful than the Queen's apostrophe to Ophelia on throwing the flowers into the grave.

> —Sweets to the sweet, farewell.
> I hop'd thou should'st have been my Hamlet's wife:
> I thought thy bride-bed to have deck'd, sweet maid,
> And not have strew'd thy grave.[7]

Shakespeare was thoroughly a master of the mixed motives of human character, and he here shews us the Queen, who was so criminal in some respects, not without sensibility and affection in other relations of life.—Ophelia is a character almost too exquisitely touching to be dwelt upon. Oh, rose of May, oh, flower too soon faded! Her love, her madness, her death, are described with the truest touches of tenderness and pathos. It is a character which nobody but Shakespeare could have drawn in the way that he has done, and to the conception of which there is not even the smallest approach, except in some of the old romantic ballads. Her brother, Laertes, is a character we do not like so well: he is too hot and choleric, and somewhat rhodomontade. Polonius is a perfect character in its kind; nor is there any foundation for the objections which have been made to the consistency of this part. It is said that he acts very foolishly and talks very sensibly. There is no inconsistency in that. Again, that he talks wisely at one time and foolishly at another; that his advice to Laertes is very excellent, and his advice to the King and Queen on the subject of Hamlet's madness very ridiculous. But he gives the one as a father, and is sincere in it; he gives the other as a mere courtier, a busy-body, and is accordingly officious, garrulous, and impertinent. In short, Shakespeare has been accused of inconsistency in this and other characters, only because he has kept up the distinction which there is in nature, between the understandings and the moral habits of men, between the absurdity of their ideas and the absurdity of their motives. Polonius is not a fool, but he makes himself so. His folly, whether in his actions or speeches, comes under the head of impropriety of intention.

We do not like to see our author's plays acted, and least of all, *Hamlet.* There is no play that suffers so much in being transferred to the stage. Hamlet himself seems hardly capable of being acted. Mr. Kemble[8] unavoidably fails in this character from a want of ease and variety. The character of Hamlet is made up of undulating lines; it has the yielding flexibility of 'a wave o' th' sea.'[9] Mr. Kemble plays it like a man in armour, with a determined inveteracy of purpose, in one undeviating straight line, which is as remote from the natural grace and refined susceptibility of the character, as the sharp angles and abrupt starts which Mr. Kean[10] introduces into the part. Mr. Kean's Hamlet is as much too splenetic and rash as Mr. Kemble's is too deliberate and formal. His manner is too strong and pointed. He throws a severity, approaching .o virulence, into the common observations and answers. There is nothing of this in Hamlet. He is, as it were, wrapped up in his reflections, and only *thinks aloud.* There should therefore be no attempt to impress what he says upon others by a studied exaggeration of emphasis or manner; no *talking at* his hearers. There should be as much of the gentleman and scholar as possible infused into the part, and as little of the actor. A pensive air of sadness should sit reluctantly upon his brow, but no appearance of fixed and sullen gloom. He is full of weakness and melancholy, but there is no harshness in his nature. He is the most amiable of misanthropes.

LEAR

We wish that we could pass this play over, and say nothing about it. All that we can say must fall far short of the subject; or even of what we ourselves conceive of it. To attempt to give a description of the play itself or of its effect upon the mind, is mere impertinence: yet we must say something.—It is then the best of all Shakespeare's plays, for it is the one in which he was the most in earnest. He was here fairly caught

6 V, i, 292-4.
7 V, i, 266-9.

8 John Philip Kemble, 1757-1823, eminent Shakespearean actor.
9 *The Winter's Tale,* IV, iv, 141.
10 Edmund Kean, 1787-1833, celebrated actor.

in the web of his own imagination. The passion which he has taken as his subject is that which strikes its root deepest into the human heart; of which the bond is the hardest to be unloosed; and the cancelling and tearing to pieces of which gives the greatest revulsion to the frame. This depth of nature, this force of passion, this tug and war of the elements of our being, this firm faith in filial piety, and the giddy anarchy and whirling tumult of the thoughts at finding this prop failing it, the contrast between the fixed, immovable basis of natural affection, and the rapid, irregular starts of imagination, suddenly wrenched from all its accustomed holds and resting-places in the soul, this is what Shakespeare has given, and what nobody else but he could give. So we believe.—The mind of Lear, staggering between the weight of attachment and the hurried movements of passion, is like a tall ship driven about by the winds, buffetted by the furious waves, but that still rides above the storm, having its anchor fixed in the bottom of the sea; or it is like the sharp rock circled by the eddying whirlpool that foams and beats against it, or like the solid promontory pushed from its basis by the force of an earthquake.

The character of Lear itself is very finely conceived for the purpose. It is the only ground on which such a story could be built with the greatest truth and effect. It is his rash haste, his violent impetuosity, his blindness to everything but the dictates of his passions or affections, that produces all his misfortunes, that aggravates his impatience of them, that enforces our pity for him. The part which Cordelia bears in the scene is extremely beautiful: the story is almost told in the first words she utters. We see at once the precipice on which the poor old king stands from his own extravagant and credulous importunity, the indiscreet simplicity of her love (which, to be sure, has a little of her father's obstinacy in it) and the hollowness of her sisters' pretensions. Almost the first burst of that noble tide of passion, which runs through the play, is in the remonstrance of Kent to his royal master on the injustice of his sentence against his youngest daughter—'Be Kent unmannerly, when Lear is mad!'[1] This manly plainness, which draws down on him the displeasure of the unadvised king, is worthy of the fidelity with which he adheres to his fallen fortunes. The true character of the two eldest daughters, Regan and Gonerill (they are so thoroughly hateful that we do not even like to repeat their names) breaks out in their answer to Cordelia who desires them to treat their father well—'Prescribe not us our duties'[2]—their hatred of advice being in proportion to their determination to do wrong, and to their hypocritical pretensions to do right. Their deliberate hypocrisy adds the last finishing to the odiousness of their characters. It is the absence of this detestable quality that is the only relief in the character of Edmund the Bastard, and that at times reconciles us to him. We are not tempted to exaggerate the guilt of his conduct, when he himself gives it up as a bad business, and writes himself down 'plain villain.' Nothing more can be said about it. His religious honesty in this respect is admirable. One speech of his is worth a million. His father, Gloster, whom he has just deluded with a forged story of his brother Edgar's designs against his life, accounts for his unnatural behaviour and the strange depravity of the times from the late eclipses in the sun and moon. Edmund, who is in the secret, says when he is gone —'This is the excellent foppery of the world, that when we are sick in fortune (often the surfeits of our own behaviour) we make guilty of our disasters the sun, the moon, and stars: as if we were villains on necessity; fools by heavenly compulsion; knaves, thieves, and treacherous by spherical predominance; drunkards, liars, and adulterers by an enforced obedience of planetary influence; and all that we are evil in, by a divine thrusting on. An admirable evasion of whoremaster man, to lay his goatish disposition on the charge of a star! My father compounded with my mother under the Dragon's tail, and my nativity was under Ursa Major: so that it follows, I am rough and lecherous. Tut! I should have been what I am, had the maidenliest star in the firmament twinkled on my bastardising.'[3]—The whole character, its careless, lighthearted villainy, contrasted with the sullen, rancorous malignity of Regan and Gonerill, its connection with the conduct of the under-plot, in which Gloster's persecution of one of his sons and the ingratitude of another, form a counterpart to the mistakes and misfortunes of Lear,—his double amour with the two sisters, and the share which he has in bringing about the fatal catastrophe, are all managed with an uncommon degree of skill and power.

It has been said, and we think justly, that the third act of *Othello* and the first three acts of *Lear*, are Shakespeare's great masterpieces in

---

[1] I, i, 146-7.

[2] I, i, 279.

[3] I, ii, 132-49.

the logic of passion: that they contain the highest examples not only of the force of individual passion but of its dramatic vicissitudes and striking effects arising from the different circumstances and characters of the persons speaking. We see the ebb and flow of the feeling, its pauses and feverish starts, its impatience of opposition, its accumulating force when it has time to recollect itself, the manner in which it avails itself of every passing word or gesture, its haste to repel insinuation, the alternate contraction and dilatation of the soul, and all 'the dazzling fence of controversy'[4] in this mortal combat with poisoned weapons, aimed at the heart, where each wound is fatal. We have seen in *Othello,* how the unsuspecting frankness and impetuous passions of the Moor are played upon and exasperated by the artful dexterity of Iago. In the present play, that which aggravates the sense of sympathy in the reader, and of uncontrollable anguish in the swoln heart of Lear, is the petrifying indifference, the cold, calculating, obdurate selfishness of his daughters. His keen passions seem whetted on their stony hearts. The contrast would be too painful, the shock too great, but for the intervention of the Fool, whose well-timed levity comes in to break the continuity of feeling when it can no longer be borne, and to bring into play again the fibres of the heart just as they are growing rigid from over-strained excitement. The imagination is glad to take refuge in the half-comic, half-serious comments of the Fool, just as the mind under the extreme anguish of a surgical operation vents itself in sallies of wit. The character was also a grotesque ornament of the barbarous times, in which alone the tragic groundwork of the story could be laid. In another point of view it is indispensable, inasmuch as while it is a diversion to the too great intensity of our disgust, it carries the pathos to the highest pitch of which it is capable, by shewing the pitiable weakness of the old king's conduct and its irretrievable consequences in the most familiar point of view. Lear may well 'beat at the gate which let his folly in,'[5] after, as the Fool says, 'he has made his daughters his mothers.'[6] The character is dropped in the third act to make room for the entrance of Edgar as Mad Tom, which well accords with the increasing bustle and wildness of the incidents; and nothing can be more complete than the distinction between Lear's real and Edgar's assumed madness, while the resemblance in the cause of their distresses, from the severing of the nearest

ties of natural affection, keeps up a unity of interest. Shakespeare's mastery over his subject, if it was not art, was owing to a knowledge of the connecting links of the passions, and their effect upon the mind still more wonderful than any systematic adherence to rules, and that anticipated and outdid all the efforts of the most refined art not inspired and rendered instinctive by genius. . . .

HENRY IV

[Falstaff]

If Shakespeare's fondness for the ludicrous sometimes led to faults in his tragedies (which was not often the case) he has made us amends by the character of Falstaff. This is perhaps the most substantial comic character that ever was invented. Sir John carries a most portly presence in the mind's eye; and in him, not to speak it profanely, 'we behold the fulness of the spirit of wit and humour bodily.'[1] We are as well acquainted with his person as his mind, and his jokes come upon us with double force and relish from the quantity of flesh through which they make their way, as he shakes his fat sides with laughter, or 'lards the lean earth as he walks along.'[2] Other comic characters seem, if we approach and handle them, to resolve themselves into air, 'into thin air';[3] but this is embodied and palpable to the grossest apprehension: it lies 'three fingers deep upon the ribs,'[4] it plays about the lungs and the diaphragm with all the force of animal enjoyment. His body is like a good estate to his mind, from which he receives rents and revenues of profit and pleasure in kind, according to its extent, and the richness of the soil. Wit is often a meagre substitute for pleasurable sensation; an effusion of spleen and petty spite at the comforts of others, from feeling none in itself. Falstaff's wit is an emanation of a fine constitution; an exuberance of good-humour and good-nature; an overflowing of his love of laughter and good-fellowship; a giving vent to his heart's ease, and over-contentment with himself and others. He would not be in character, if he were not so fat as he is; for there is the greatest keeping in the boundless luxury of his imagination and the pampered self-indulgence of his physical appetites. He manures and nourishes his mind with

---

4 Cf. *Comus,* 790–91.   5 I, iv, 294–5.   6 I, iv, 189.

1 Cf, Colossians, ii, 9.
2 *I Henry IV,* II, ii, 116.
3 *The Tempest,* IV, i, 150.
4 *I Henry IV,* IV, ii, 81.

jests, as he does his body with sack and sugar. He carves out his jokes, as he would a capon or a haunch of venison, where there is *cut and come again;* and pours out upon them the oil of gladness. His tongue drops fatness, and in the chambers of his brain 'it snows of meat and drink.'[5] He keeps up perpetual holiday and open house, and we live with him in a round of invitations to a rump and dozen.—Yet we are not to suppose that he was a mere sensualist. All this is as much in imagination as in reality. His sensuality does not engross and stupify his other faculties, but 'ascends me into the brain, clears away all the dull, crude vapours that environ it, and makes it full of nimble, fiery, and delectable shapes.'[6] His imagination keeps up the ball after his senses have done with it. He seems to have even a greater enjoyment of the freedom from restraint, of good cheer, of his ease, of his vanity, in the ideal exaggerated description which he gives of them, than in fact. He never fails to enrich his discourse with allusions to eating and drinking, but we never see him at table. He carries his own larder about with him, and he is himself 'a tun of man.'[7] His pulling out the bottle in the field of battle is a joke to shew his contempt for glory accompanied with danger, his systematic adherence to his Epicurean philosophy in the most trying circumstances. Again, such is his deliberate exaggeration of his own vices, that it does not seem quite certain whether the account of his hostess's bill, found in his pocket, with such an out-of-the-way charge for capons and sack with only one halfpenny worth of bread, was not put there by himself as a trick to humour the jest upon his favourite propensities, and as a conscious caricature of himself. He is represented as a liar, a braggart, a coward, a glutton, etc. and yet we are not offended but delighted with him; for he is all these as much to amuse others as to gratify himself. He openly assumes all these characters to shew the humourous part of them. The unrestrained indulgence of his own ease, appetites, and convenience, has neither malice nor hypocrisy in it. In a word, he is an actor in himself almost as much as upon the stage, and we no more object to the character of Falstaff in a moral point of view than we should think of bringing an excellent comedian, who should represent him to the life, before one of the police offices. We only consider the number of pleasant lights in which he puts certain foibles (the more pleasant as they are opposed to the received rules and necessary restraints of society) and do not trouble ourselves about the consequences resulting from them for no mischievous consequences do result. Sir John is old as well as fat, which gives a melancholy retrospective tinge to the character; and by the disparity between his inclinations and his capacity for enjoyment, makes it still more ludicrous and fantastical.

The secret of Falstaff's wit is for the most part a masterly presence of mind, an absolute self-possession, which nothing can disturb. His repartees are involuntary suggestions of his self-love; instinctive evasions of everything that threatens to interrupt the career of his triumphant jollity and self-complacency. His very size floats him out of all his difficulties in a sea of rich conceits; and he turns round on the pivot of his convenience, with every occasion and at a moment's warning. His natural repugnance to every unpleasant thought or circumstance, of itself makes light of objections, and provokes the most extravagant and licentious answers in his own justification. His indifference to truth puts no check upon his invention, and the more improbable and unexpected his contrivances are, the more happily does he seem to be delivered of them, the anticipation of their effect acting as a stimulus to the gaiety of his fancy. The success of one adventurous sally gives him spirits to undertake another: he deals always in round numbers, and his exaggerations and excuses are 'open, palpable, monstrous as the father that begets them.'[8]

1817

POLITICAL ESSAYS WITH SKETCHES OF PUBLIC CHARACTERS

PREFACE

I AM no politician, and still less can I be said to be a party-man: but I have a hatred of tyranny, and a contempt for its tools; and this feeling I have expressed as often and as strongly as I could. I cannot sit quietly down under the claims of barefaced power, and I have tried to expose the little arts of sophistry by which they are defended. I have no mind to have my person made a property of, nor my understanding made a dupe of. I deny that liberty and slavery are convertible terms, that right and wrong, truth and falsehood, plenty and famine, the com-

---

5 *Prologue to the Canterbury Tales*, 345.
6 *II Henry IV*, IV, iii, 105-8.
7 *I Henry IV*, iv, 494.

8 *I Henry IV*, II, iv, 249-51.

forts or wretchedness of a people, are matters of perfect indifference. That is all I know of the matter; but on these points I am likely to remain incorrigible, in spite of any arguments that I have seen used to the contrary. It needs no sagacity to discover that two and two make four; but to persist in maintaining this obvious position, if all the fashion, authority, hypocrisy, and venality of mankind were arrayed against it, would require a considerable effort of personal courage, and would soon leave a man in a very formidable minority. Again, I am no believer in the doctrine of *divine right*, either as it regards the Stuarts or the Bourbons;[1] nor can I bring myself to approve of the enormous waste of blood and treasure wilfully incurred by a family[2] that supplanted the one in this country to restore the others in France. It is to my mind a piece of sheer impudence. The question between natural liberty and hereditary slavery, whether men are born free or slaves, whether kings are the servants of the people, or the people the property of kings (whatever we may think of it in the abstract, or debate about it in the schools)—in this country, in Old England, and under the succession of the House of Hanover, is not a question of theory, but has been long since decided by certain facts and feelings, to call which in question would be equally inconsistent with proper respect to the people, or common decency towards the throne.[3] An English subject cannot call this principle in question without renouncing his country; an English prince cannot call it in question without disclaiming his title to the crown, which was placed by our ancestors on the head of his ancestors, on no other ground and for no other possible purpose than to vindicate this sacred principle in their own persons, and to hold it out as an example to posterity and to the world. An Elector of Hanover, called over here to be made king of England,[4] in contempt and to the exclusion of the claims of the old, hereditary possessors and pretenders to the throne, on any other plea except that of his being the chosen representative and appointed guardian of the rights and liberties of the people (the consequent pledge and guarantee of the rights and liberties of other nations) would indeed be a solecism more absurd and contemptible than any to be found in history. What! Send for a petty Elector of a petty foreign state to reign over us from respect to *his* right to the throne of these realms, in defiance of the legitimate heir to the crown, and 'in contempt of the choice of the people!'[5] Oh monstrous fiction! Miss Flora Mac Ivor[6] would not have heard of such a thing: the author of Waverley has well answered Mr. Burke's 'Appeal from the New to the Old Whigs.'[7] Let not our respect for our ancestors, who fought and bled for their own freedom, and to aid (not to stifle) the cause of freedom in other nations, suffer us to believe this poor idiot calumny of them. Let not our shame at having been inveigled into crusades and Holy Alliances against the freedom of mankind, suffer us to be made the dupes of it ourselves, in thought, in word, or deed. The question of genuine liberty or of naked slavery, if put in words, should be answered by Englishmen with scorn: if put in any other shape than words, it must be answered in a different way, unless they would lose the name of Englishmen! An Englishman has no distinguishing virtue but honesty; he has and can have no privilege or advantage over other nations but liberty. If he is not free, he is the worst of slaves, for he is nothing else. If he feels that he has wrongs and dare not say so, he is the mean-

---

1 The Stuarts were the ruling house of England from 1603 to 1714; and the Bourbons were the royal house of France from the sixteenth century until the Revolution, and from the fall of Napoleon until 1830.

2 the House of Hanover.

3 By the Act of Settlement, 1701, legal provision was made that in the event Anne and William III should die without heirs the crown of England should pass to the Electress of Hanover and her heirs 'being Protestant.' All the sovereigns of England since Queen Anne have held their crowns by virtue of this act.

4 George I, 1714-27, son of Electress Sophia, of Hanover, great-grandson of James I.

5 Burke, *Reflections on the French Revolution*, 1790.

6 the heroine of Scott's *Waverley*.

7 Mr. Burke pretends in this Jesuitical Appeal, that a nation has a right to insist upon and revert to old establishments and prescriptive privileges, but not to lay claim to new ones; in a word, to change its governors, if refractory, but not its form of government, however bad. Thus he says we had a right to cashier James II, because he wished to alter the laws and religion as they were then established. By what right did we emancipate ourselves from popery and arbitrary power a century before? He defends his consistency in advocating the American Revolution, though the rebels, in getting rid of the reigning branch of the Royal Family, did not send for the next of kin to rule over them 'in contempt of their choice,' but prevented all such equivocations by passing at once from a viceroyalty to a republic. He also extols the Polish Revolution as a monument of wisdom and virtue (I suppose because it had not succeeded), though this also was a total and absolute change in the frame and principles of the government, to which the people were in this case bound by no feudal tenure or divine right. But he insists that the French Revolution was stark-naught, because the people here did the same thing, passed from slavery to liberty, from an arbitrary to a constitutional government, to which they had, it seems, no prescriptive right, and therefore, according to the appellant, no right at all. Oh nice professor of humanity! We had a right to turn off James II because he broke a compact with the people. The French had no right to turn off Louis XVI. because he broke no compact with them, for he had none to break; in other words, because he was an arbitrary despot, tied to no laws, and they a herd of slaves, and therefore they were bound, by every law divine and human, always to remain so, in perpetuity and by the grace of God! Oh unanswerable logician!—(Hazlitt.)

est of hypocrites; for it is certain that he cannot be contented under them.—This was once a free, a proud, and happy country, when under a constitutional monarchy and a Whig king, it had just broken the chains of tyranny that were prepared for it, and successfully set at defiance the menaces of an hereditary pretender; when the monarch still felt what he owed to himself and the people, and in the opposite claims which were set up to it, saw the real tenure on which he held his crown; when civil and religious liberty were the watchwords by which good men and true subjects were known to one another, not by the cant of legitimacy; when the reigning sovereign stood between you and the polluted touch of a bigot and a despot who stood ready to seize upon you and yours as his lawful prey; when liberty and loyalty went hand in hand, and the Tory principles of passive obedience and non-resistance were more unfashionable at court than in the country; when to uphold the authority of the throne, it was not thought necessary to undermine the privileges or break the spirit of the nation; when an Englishman felt that his name was another name for independence, 'the envy of less happier lands,'[8] when it was his pride to be born, and his wish that other nations might become free; before a sophist and an apostate had dared to tell him that he had no share, no merit, no free agency, in the glorious Revolution of 1688, and that he was bound to lend a helping hand to crush all others, that implied a right in the people to choose their own form of government; before he was become sworn brother to the Pope, familiar to the Holy Inquisition, an encourager of the massacres of his Protestant brethren, a patron of the Bourbons, and jailor to the liberties of mankind! Ah, John Bull! John Bull! thou art not what thou wert in the days of thy friend, Arbuthnot![9] Thou wert an honest fellow then: now thou art turned bully and coward.

This is the only politics I know; the only patriotism I feel. The question with me is, whether I and all mankind are born slaves or free. That is the one thing necessary to know and to make good: the rest is *flocci, nauci, nihili, pili.*[10] Secure this point, and all is safe: lose this, and all is lost. There are people who cannot understand a principle; nor perceive how a cause can be connected with an individual, even in spite of himself, nor how the salvation of mankind can be bound up with the success of one man. It is in vain that I address to them what follows.—'One fate attends the altar and the throne.' So sings Mr. Southey.[11] I say, that one fate attends the people and the assertor of the people's rights against those who say they have no rights, that they are their property, their goods, their chattels, the livestock on the estate of Legitimacy. This is what kings at present tell us with their swords, and poets with their pens. He who tells me this deprives me not only of the right, but of the very heart and will to be free, takes the breath out of the body of liberty, and leaves it a dead and helpless corse, destroys 'at one fell swoop'[12] the dearest hopes, and blasts the fairest prospects of mankind through all ages and nations, sanctifies slavery, binds it as a spell on the understanding, and makes freedom a mockery, and the name a bye-word. The poor wretch immured in the dungeons of the Inquisition may breathe a sigh to liberty, may repeat its name, may think of it as a blessing, if not to himself, to others; but the wretch imprisoned in the dungeon of Legitimacy, the very tomb of freedom, that 'painted sepulchre, white without, but full of ravening and all uncleanness within,'[13] must not even think of it, must not so much as dream of it, but as a thing forbid: it is a profanation to his lips, an impiety to his thoughts; his very imagination is enthralled, and he can only look forward to the never-ending flight of future years, and see the same gloomy prospect of abject wretchedness and hopeless desolation spread out for himself and his species. They who bow to thrones and hate mankind may here feast their eyes with blight, mildew, the blue pestilence and glittering poison of slavery, 'bogs, dens, and shades of death—a universe of death.'[14] This is that true moral atheism, the equal blasphemy against God and man, the sin against the Holy Ghost, that lowest deep of debasement and despair to which there is no lower deep. He who saves me from this conclusion, who makes a mock of this doctrine, and sets at naught its power, is to me not less than the God of my idolatry, for he has left one drop of comfort in my soul. The plague-spot has not tainted me quite; I am not leprous all over, the lie of Legitimacy does not fix its mortal sting in my inmost soul, nor, like an ugly spider, entangle me in its

---

8 *Richard II*, II, i, 49.
9 John Arbuthnot, 1667–1735, physician and man of letters, whose pamphlet *The History of John Bull* appeared in 1712.
10 The beginning of a rule in the old Latin grammars which brings together a number of words meaning 'of little or no account.'

11 in *Carmen Nuptiale*, st. 51.
12 *Macbeth*, IV, iii, 218.
13 Cf. Matthew, xxiii, 27.
14 *Paradise Lost*, II, 621–2.

slimy folds; but is kept off from me, and broods on its own poison. He who did this for me, and for the rest of the world, and who alone could do it, was Buonaparte. He withstood the inroads of this new Jaggernaut,[15] this foul Blatant Beast,[16] as it strode forward to its prey over the bodies and minds of a whole people, and put a ring in its nostrils, breathing flame and blood, and led it in triumph, and played with its crowns and sceptres, and wore them in its stead, and tamed its crested pride, and made it a laughing-stock and a mockery to the nations. He, one man, did this, and as long as he did this, (how, or for what end, is nothing to the magnitude of this mighty question) he saved the human race from the last ignominy, and that foul stain that had so long been intended, and was at last, in an evil hour and by evil hands, inflicted on it. He put his foot upon the neck of kings, who would have put their yoke upon the necks of the people: he scattered before him with fiery execution millions of hired slaves, who came at the bidding of their masters to deny the right of others to be free. The monument of greatness and of glory he erected, was raised on ground forfeited again and again to humanity—it reared its majestic front on the ruins of the shattered hopes and broken faith of the common enemies of mankind. If he could not secure the freedom, peace, and happiness of his country, he made her a terror to those who by sowing civil dissension and exciting foreign wars, would not let her enjoy those blessings. They who had trampled upon Liberty could not at least triumph in her shame and her despair, but themselves became objects of pity and derision. Their determination to persist in extremity of wrong only brought on themselves repeated defeat, disaster, and dismay: the accumulated aggressions their infuriated pride and disappointed malice meditated against others, returned in just and aggravated punishment upon themselves: they heaped coals of fire upon their own heads; they drank deep and long, in gall and bitterness, of the poisoned chalice they had prepared for others: the destruction with which they had threatened a people daring to call itself free, hung suspended over their heads, like a precipice ready to fall upon and crush them. 'Awhile they stood abashed,'[17] abstracted from their evil purposes, and felt how awful freedom is, its power how dreadful. Shrunk

from the boasted pomp of royal state into their littleness as men, defeated of their revenge, baulked of their prey, their schemes stripped of their bloated pride, and with nothing left but the deformity of their malice, not daring to utter a syllable or move a finger, the lords of the earth, who had looked upon men as of an inferior species, born for their use, and devoted to be their slaves, turned an imploring eye to the people, and with coward hearts and hollow tongues invoked the name of Liberty, thus to get the people once more within their unhallowed gripe, and to stifle the name of Liberty forever. I never joined the vile and treacherous cry of spurious humanity in favour of those who have from the beginning of time, and will to the end of it, make a butt of humanity, and its distresses their sport. I knew that shameful was this new alliance between kings and people; fatal this pretended league: that 'never can true reconcilement grow where wounds of deadly hate have pierced so deep.'[18] I was right in this respect. I knew my friends from my foes. So did Lord Castlereagh:[19] so did not Benjamin Constant.[20] Did any of the Princes of Europe ever regard Buonaparte as anything more than the child and champion of Jacobinism? Why then should I: for on that point I bow to their judgements as infallible. Passion speaks truer than reason. If Buonaparte was a conqueror, he conquered the grand conspiracy of kings against the abstract right of the human race to be free; and I, as a man, could not be indifferent which side to take. If he was ambitious, his greatness was not founded on the unconditional, avowed surrender of the rights of human nature. But with him, the state of man rose exalted too. If he was arbitrary and a tyrant, first France as a country was in a state of military blockade, on garrison duty, and not to be defended by mere paper bullets of the brain; secondly, but chief, he was not, nor he could not become, a tyrant by right divine. Tyranny in him was not sacred: it was not eternal: it was not instinctively bound in league of amity with other tyrannies; it was not sanctioned by all the laws of religion and morality. There was an end of it with the individual: there was an end of it with the temporary causes, which gave it birth, and of which it was only the too necessary reaction. But there are persons of that low and inordinate ap-

---

15 a form of Vishnu, Hindu deity worshiped with blind devotion and ruthless sacrifice.
16 a foul monster in Spenser's *Faerie Queene*, the personification of vile slander.
17 Cf. *Paradise Lost*, IV, 846.

18 Ibid. IV, 98.
19 Robert Stewart, 1769–1822, British statesman who became Viscount Castlereagh and afterward Earl of Londonderry. He was noted for his contempt for all persons who did not belong to the aristocracy.
20 a French liberal politician, 1767–1830.

petite for servility, that they cannot be satisfied with anything short of that sort of tyranny that has lasted forever, and is likely to last forever; that is strengthened and made desperate by the superstitions and prejudices of ages; that is enshrined in traditions, in laws, in usages, in the outward symbols of power, in the very idioms of language; that has struck its roots into the human heart, and clung round the human understanding like a nightshade; that overawes the imagination, and disarms the will to resist it, by the very enormity of the evil; that is cemented with gold and blood; guarded by reverence, guarded by power; linked in endless succession to the principle by which life is transmitted to the generations of tyrants and slaves, and destroying liberty with the first breath of life; that is absolute, unceasing, unerring, fatal, unutterable, abominable, monstrous. These true devotees of superstition and despotism cried out Liberty and Humanity in their desperate frenzy at Buonaparte's sudden elevation and incredible successes against their favourite idol, 'that Harlot old, the same that is, that was, and is to be,'[21] but we have heard no more of their triumph of Liberty and their *douce humanité,*[22] since they clapped down the hatches upon us again, like wretches in a slave-ship who have had their chains struck off and pardon promised them to fight the common enemy; and the poor Reformers who were taken in to join the cry, because they are as fastidious in their love of liberty as their opponents are inveterate in their devotion to despotism, continue in vain to reproach them with their temporary professions, woeful grimaces, and vows made in pain, which ease has recanted; but to these reproaches the legitimate professors of Liberty and Humanity do not even deign to return the answer of a smile at their credulity and folly. Those who did not see this result at the time were, I think, weak; those who do not acknowledge it now are, I am sure, hypocrites.—To this pass have we been brought by the joint endeavours of Tories, Whigs, and Reformers; and as they have all had a hand in it, I shall here endeavour to ascribe to each their share of merit in this goodly piece of work. . . .

A Reformer is not a gregarious animal. Speculative opinion leads men different ways, each according to his particular fancy:—it is prejudice or interest that drives before it the herd of mankind. That *which is,* with all its confirmed abuses and 'tickling commodities,'[23] is alone solid and certain: that *which may be* or *ought to be,* has a thousand shapes and colours, according to the eye that sees it, is infinitely variable and evanescent in its effects. Talk of mobs as we will, the only true mob is that incorrigible mass of knaves and fools in every country, who never think at all, and who never feel for any one but themselves. I call any assembly of people a mob (be it the House of Lords or House of Commons) where each person's opinion on any question is governed by what others say of it, and by what he can get by it. . . . Every corporate body, or casual concourse of people, is nothing more than a collection of prejudices, and the only arguments current with them, a collection of watchwords. You may ring the changes forever on the terms Bribery and Corruption with the people in Palace-yard, as they do in the Room over the way on Religion, Loyalty, Public Credit, and Social Order. There is no difference whatever in this respect between the Great Vulgar and the Small, who are managed just in the same way by their different leaders. To procure unanimity, to get men to act in *corps,* we must appeal for the most part to gross and obvious motives, to authority and passion, to their vices, not their virtues: we must discard plain truth and abstract justice as doubtful and inefficient pleas, retaining only the names and the pretext as a convenient salvo for hypocrisy! He is the best leader of a party who can find out the greatest number of commonplaces faced with the public good; and he will be the stoutest partisan who can best turn the lining to account.—Tory sticks to Tory: Whig sticks to Whig: the Reformer sticks neither to himself nor to anybody else. It is no wonder he comes to the ground with all his schemes and castle-building. A house divided against itself cannot stand. It is a pity, but it cannot be helped. A Reformer is necessarily and naturally a Marplot,[24] for the foregoing and the following reasons. First, he does not very well know what he would be at. Secondly, if he did, he does not care very much about it. Thirdly, he is governed habitually by a spirit of contradiction, and is always wise beyond what is practicable. He is a bad tool to work with; a part of a machine that never fits its place; he cannot be trained to discipline, for he follows his own idle humours, or drilled into an obedience to orders, for the first principle of

---

21 Southey, *Carmen Nuptiale,* st. 52.
22 'sweet humanity'—Burke's phrase.

23 Cf. *King John,* II, i, 573.
24 one who by his officious interference mars or frustrates any undertaking.

his mind is the supremacy of conscience, and the independent right of private judgement. A man to be a Reformer must be more influenced by imagination and reason than by received opinions or sensible impressions. With him ideas bear sway over things; the possible is of more value than the real; that which is not, is better than that which is. He is by the supposition a speculative (and somewhat fantastical) character; but there is no end of possible speculations, of imaginary questions, and nice distinctions; or if there were, he would not willingly come to it; he would still prefer living in the world of his own ideas, be for raising some new objection, and starting some new chimera, and never be satisfied with any plan that he found he could realize. Bring him to a fixed point, and his occupation would be gone. A Reformer never is— but always to be blest, in the accomplishment of his airy hopes and shifting schemes of progressive perfectibility. Let him have the plaything of his fancy, and he will spoil it, like the child that makes a hole in its drum: set some brilliant illusion before his streaming eyes, and he will lay violent hands upon it, like little wanton boys that play with air-bubbles. Give him one thing, and he asks for another; like the dog in the fable, he loses the substance for the shadow: offer him a great good, and he will not stretch out his hand to take it, unless it were the greatest possible good. And then who is to determine what is the greatest possible good? Among a thousand pragmatical speculators, there will be a thousand opinions on this subject; and the more they differ, the less will they be inclined to give way or compromise the matter. With each of these, his self-opinion is the first thing to be attended to; his understanding must be satisfied in the first place, or he will not budge an inch; he cannot for the world give up a principle to a party. He would rather have slavery than liberty, unless it is a liberty precisely after his own fashion: he would sooner have the Bourbons than Buonaparte; for he truly is for a Republic, and if he cannot have that, is indifferent about the rest. . . . Instead of making his option between two things, a good or an evil, within his reach, our exquisite Sir sets up a third thing as the object of his choice, with some impossible condition annexed to it,—to dream, to talk, to write, to be meddlesome and troublesome about, to serve him for a topic of captious discontent or vague declamation, and which if he saw any hopes of cordial agreement or prac-

tical cooperation to carry it into effect, he would instantly contrive to mar, and split it into a thousand fractions, doubts, and scruples to make it an impossibility for anything ever to be done for the good of mankind, which is merely the plaything of his theoretical imbecility and active impertinence! The Goddess of his idolatry is and will always remain a cloud, instead of a Juno.[25] One of these virtuosos, these Nicolas Gimcracks[26] of Reform, full of intolerable and vain conceit, sits smiling in the baby-house of his imagination, 'pleased with a feather, tickled with a straw,'[27] trimming the balance of power in the lookingglass of his own self-complacency, having everything his own way at a word's speaking, making the 'giant-mass'[28] of things only a reflection of his personal pretensions, approving everything that is right, condemning everything that is wrong, in compliment to his own character, considering how what he says will affect not the cause, but himself; keeping himself aloof from party spirit, and from everything that can cast a shade on the fancied delicacy of his own breast, and thus letting the cause of Liberty slip through his fingers, and be spilt like water on the ground: —while another, more bold than he, in a spirit of envy and ignorance, quarrels with all those who are labouring at the same oar, lays about him like mad, runs amuck at every one who has done, or is likely to do, anything to promote the common object, and with his desperate club dashes out his neighbour's brains, and thinks he has done a good piece of service to the cause, because he has glutted his own ill-humour and self-will, which he mistakes for the love of liberty and a zeal for truth! Others, not able to do mischief enough singly, club their senseless contradictions and unmanageable humours together, turn their attention to cabal and chicane, get into committees, makes speeches, move or second resolutions, dictate to their followers, set up for the heads of a party, in opposition to another party; abuse, vilify, expose, betray, counteract and undermine each other in every way, and throw the game into the hands of the common enemy, who laughs in his sleeve, and watches them and their little perverse, pettifogging passions at work for him, from the high

25 a reference to the Greek legend concerning Ixion, King of Thessaly, who in the form of a cloud made love to Hera, and fathered the Centaurs.
26 Sir Nicolas Gimcrack was the virtuoso in Shadwell's comedy by that name remarkable for his 'scientific' vagaries.
27 Pope, *Essay on Man*, II, 276.
28 Shakespeare, *Troilus and Cressida*, I, iii, 345.

tower of his pride and strength! If an honest and able man arises among them, they grow jealous of him, and would rather, in the petty ostracism of their minds, that their cause should fail, than that another should have the credit of bringing it to a triumphant conclusion. They criticise his conduct, carp at his talents, denounce his friends, suspect his motives, and do not rest, till by completely disgusting him with the name of Reform and Reformers, they have made him what they wish, a traitor and deserter from a cause that no man can serve! This is just what they like—they satisfy their malice, they have to find out a new leader, and the cause is to begin again! So it was, and so it will be, while man remains the little, busy, mischievous animal described in *Gulliver's Travels!*—A pretty hopeful set to make head against their opponents—a rope of sand against a rock of marble—with no centre of gravity, but a collection of atoms whirled about in empty space by their own levity, or jostling together by numberless points of repulsion, and tossed with all their officious projects and airy predictions, by the first breath of caprice or shock of power, into that Limbo of Vanity, where embryo statesmen and drivelling legislators dance the hays of Reform, 'perpetual circle, multiform and mix, and hinder all things,'[29] proud of the exclusive purity of their own motives, and the unattainable perfection of their own plans!—How different from the self-centred, well-knit, inseparable phalanx of power and authority opposed to their impotent and abortive designs!

A Tory is one who is governed by sense and habit alone. He considers not what is possible, but what is real; he gives might the preference over right. He cries Long Life to the conqueror, and is ever strong upon the stronger side—the side of corruption and prerogative. He says what others say; he does as he is prompted by his own advantage. He knows on which side his bread is buttered, and that St. Peter is well at Rome. He is for going with Sancho to Camacho's wedding, and not for wandering with Don Quixote in the desert, after the mad lover.[30] Strait is the gate and narrow the way that leadeth to Reform, but broad is the way that leadeth to Corruption, and multitudes there are that walk therein. The Tory is sure to be in the thickest of them. His principle

is to follow the leader; and this is the infallible rule to have numbers and success on your side, to be on the side of success and numbers. Power is the rock of his salvation; priestcraft is the second article of his implicit creed. He does not trouble himself to inquire which is the best form of government—but he knows that the reigning monarch is 'the best of kings.'[31] He does not, like a fool, contest for modes of faith; but like a wise man, swears by that which is by law established. He has no principles himself, nor does he profess to have any, but will cut your throat for differing with any of his bigoted dogmas, or for objecting to any act of power that he supposes necessary to his interest. He will take his Bible oath that black is white, and that whatever is, is right, if it is for his convenience. He is for having a slice in the loan, a share in a borough, a situation in the church or state, or for standing well with those who have. He is not for empty speculations, but for full pockets. He is for having plenty of beef and pudding, a good coat to his back, a good house over his head, and for cutting a respectable figure in the world. He is *Epicuri de grege porcus*[32]—not a man but a beast. He is styled in his prejudices—he wallows in the mire of his senses—he cannot get beyond the trough of his sordid appetites, whether it is of gold or wood. Truth and falsehood are to him, something to buy and sell; principle and conscience, something to eat and drink. He tramples on the plea of Humanity, and lives, like a caterpillar, on the decay of public good. Beast as he is, he knows that the King is the fountain of honour, that there are good things to be had in the Church, treats the cloth with respect, bows to a magistrate, lies to the tax-gatherer, nicknames the Reformers, and 'blesses the Regent and the Duke of York.'[33] He treads the primrose path of preferment; 'when a great wheel goes up a hill, holds fast by it; and when it rolls down, lets it go.'[34] He is not an enthusiast, a Utopian philosopher or a Theophilanthropist,[35] but a man of business and the world, who minds the main chance, does as other people do, and takes his wife's advice to get on in the world, and set up a coach for her to ride in, as fast as possible. This fellow is in the right, and 'wiser in his gen-

29 *Paradise Lost*, v, 182–3.
30 The reference is to an episode in Cervantes' *Don Quixote* in which Sancho Panza, the worldly-wise squire, remains to enjoy a great wedding feast which Camacho, a rich but unfortunate man, has provided only to find himself at the last moment cheated out of his bride. See the Second Part, Book II, chaps. xx and xxi.

31 a phrase applied to Ferdinand VII of Spain in official documents.
32 'a pig from Epicurus' herd'—Horace, *Epistles*, I, iv, 16.
33 through the instrumentality of the clergy.
34 *King Lear*, II, iv, 73.
35 member of a deistical society established by Tom Paine in Paris in 1797.

eration than the children of the light.'[36] The 'servile slaves'[37] of wealth and power have a considerable advantage over the independent and the free. How much easier is it to smell out a job than to hit upon a scheme for the good of mankind! How much safer is it to be the tool of the oppressor than the advocate of the oppressed! How much more fashionable to fall in with the opinion of the world, to bow the knee to Baal,[38] than to seek for obscure and obnoxious truth! How strong are the ties that bind men together for their own advantage, compared with those that bind them to the good of their country or of their kind! For as the Reformer has no guide to his conclusions but speculative reason, which is a source not of unanimity or certainty, but of endless doubt and disagreement, so he has no ground of attachment to them but a speculative interest, which is too often liable to be warped by sinister motives, and is a flimsy barrier against the whole weight of worldly and practical interests opposed to it. He either tires and grows lukewarm after the first gloss of novelty is over, and is thrown into the hands of the adverse party, or to keep alive an interest in it, he makes it the stalking-horse of his ambition, of his personal enmity, of his conceit or love of gossiping; as we have seen. An opinion backed by power and prejudice, riveted and mortised to the throne, is of more force and validity than all the abstract reason in the world, without power and prejudice. A cause centred in an individual, which is strengthened by all the ties of passion and self-interest, as in the case of a king against a whole people, is more likely to prevail than that of a scattered multitude, who have only a common and divided interest to hold them together, and 'screw their courage to the sticking-place,'[39] against an influence, that is never distracted or dissipated; that neither slumbers nor sleeps; that is never lulled into security, nor tamed by adversity; that is intoxicated with the insolence of success, and infuriated with the rage of disappointment; that eyes its one sole object of personal agrandizement, moves unremittingly to it, and carries after it millions of its slaves and trainbearers. Can you persuade a king to hear reason, to submit his pretensions to the tribunal of the people, to give up the most absurd and mischievous of his prerogatives? No: he is always true to himself, he grasps at power and hugs it close, as it is exorbitant or invidious, or likely to be torn from him; and his followers stick to him, and never boggle at any lengths they are forced to go, because they know what they have to trust to in the good faith of kings to themselves and one another. Power then is fixed and immovable, for this reason, because it is lodged in an individual who is driven to madness by the undisputed possession, or apprehended loss of it; his self-will is the keystone that supports the tottering arch of corruption, steadfast as it leans on him:—liberty is vacillating, transient, and hunted through the world, because it is entrusted to the breasts of many, who care little about it, and quarrel in the execution of their trust. Too many cooks spoil the broth. The principle of tyranny is in fact identified with a man's pride and the servility of others in the highest degree; the principle of liberty abstracts him from himself, and has to contend in its feeble course with all his own passions, prejudices, interests, and those of the world and of his own party; the cavils of Reformers, the threats of Tories, and the sneers of Whigs.

A modern Whig is but a fag-end of a Tory. The old Whigs[40] were in principle what the modern Jacobins are, Anti-Jacobites, that is, opposers of the doctrine of divine right, the one in the soil of England, the other by parity of reasoning, in the soil of France. But the Opposition have pressed so long against the Ministry without effect, that being the softer substance, and made of more yielding materials, they have been moulded into their image and superscription, spelt backwards, or they differ as concave and convex, or they go together like substantive and adjective, or like man and wife, they two have become one flesh. A Tory is the indispensable prop to the doubtful sense of self-importance, and peevish irritability of negative success, which mark the life of a Whig leader or underling. They 'are subdued even to the very quality'[41] of the Lords of the Treasury Bench, and have quarrelled so long that they would be quite at a loss without the ordinary food of political contention. To interfere between them is as dangerous as to interfere in a matrimonial squabble. To overturn the one is to trip up the heels of the other. Their hostility is not directed against things at all, nor

---

36 St. Luke, xvi, 8.
37 *The Faerie Queene*, II, vii, 33.
38 the supreme divinity of ancient Semitic peoples, conceived as the productive power of fertility and worshiped as the sun-god.
39 *Macbeth*, I, vii, 60.

40 The 'Old' Whigs followed Fox in opposition to the War with France.
41 *Othello*, I, iii, 112.

to effectual and decisive opposition to men, but to that sort of petty warfare and parliamentary *tracasserie,*[42] of which there is neither end nor use, except making the parties concerned of consequence in their own eyes, and contemptible in those of the nation. They will not allow Ministers to be severely handled by anyone but themselves, nor even that: but they say civil things of them in the House of Commons, and whisper scandal against them at Holland House.[43] This shews gentlemanly refinement and good breeding; while my Lord Erskine[44] 'calls us untaught knaves, unmannerly to come betwixt the wind and his nobility.'[45] But the leaden bullets and steel bayonets, the *ultima ratio regum,*[46] by which these questions are practically decided, do their business in another-guess manner; they do not stand on the same ceremony. Soft words and hard blows are a losing game to play at: and this, one would think, the Opposition, if they were sincere, must have found out long ago. But they rather wish to screen the Ministry, as their *locum tenens*[47] in the receipt of the perquisites of office and the abuse of power, of which they themselves expect the reversion.

Strange that such difference should be
Twixt Tweedledum and Tweedledee.[48]

The distinction between a great Whig and Tory Lord is laughable. For Whigs to Tories 'nearly are allied, and thin partitions do their bounds divide.'[49] So I cannot find out the different drift (as far as politics are concerned) of the ＊＊＊＊＊＊and ＊＊＊＊＊＊Reviews,[50] which remind one of Opposition coaches, that raise a great dust or spatter one another with mud, but both travel the same road and arrive at the same destination. When the Editor of a respectable Morning Paper reproached me with having called Mr. Gifford a cat's-paw,[51] I did not tell him that he was a glove upon that cat's-paw. I might have done so. There is a difference between a sword and a foil. The Whigs do not at all relish that ugly thing, a knock-down blow; which is so dif-

ferent from their endless see-saw way of going about a question. They are alarmed 'lest the courtiers offended should be';[52] for they are so afraid of their adversaries, that they dread the reaction even of successful opposition to them, and will neither attempt it themselves, nor stand by anyone that does. Any writer who is not agreeable to the Tories, becomes obnoxious to the Whigs; he is disclaimed by them as a dangerous colleague, merely for having 'done the cause some service'; is considered as having the malicious design to make a breach of the peace, and to interrupt with most admired disorder the harmony and mutual good understanding which subsists between Ministers and the Opposition, and on the adherence to which they are alone suffered to exist, or to have a shadow of importance in the state. They are, in fact, a convenient medium to break the force of popular feeling, and to transmit the rays of popular indignation against the influence and power of the crown, blunted and neutralized by as many qualifications and refractions as possible. A Whig is properly what is called a Trimmer—that is, a coward to both sides of a question, who dare not be a knave nor an honest man, but is a sort of whiffling, shuffling, cunning, silly, contemptible, unmeaning negation of the two. He is a poor purblind creature, who halts between two opinions and complains that he cannot get any two people to think alike. He is a cloak for corruption, and a mar-plot to freedom. He will neither do anything himself, nor let anyone else do it. He is on bad terms with the Government, and not on good ones with the people. He is an impertinence and a contradiction in the state. If he has a casting weight, for fear of overdoing the mark, he throws it into the wrong scale. He is a person of equally feeble understanding and passions. He has some notion of what is right, just enough to hinder him from pursuing his own interest: he has selfish and worldly prudence enough, not to let him embark in any bold or decided measure for the advancement of truth and justice. He is afraid of his own conscience, which will not let him lend his unqualified support to arbitrary measures: he stands in awe of the opinion of the world, which will not let him express his opposition to those measures with warmth and effect. His politics are a strange mixture of cross-purposes. He is wedded to forms and appearances, impeded by every petty ob-

---

42 quarrel.
43 the mansion house in Kensington, London, of Henry Richard Fox, third Baron Holland, famed as a social gathering-place of the Whigs.
44 Thomas Erskine, 1750–1823, Whig advocate, and Lord Chancellor, 1806–7.
45 *I Henry IV*, I, iii, 43.
46 'the last resort of kings'—Richelieu's maxim.
47 deputy.
48 John Byrom, *On the Feuds between Handel and Bononcini.*
49 Dryden, *Absalom and Achitophel*, I, 163–4.
50 *The Edinburgh* and *The Quarterly.*
51 *A Letter to William Gifford*, published in March 1819.

52 Gay, *The Beggar's Opera*, II, x.

stacle and pretext of difficulty, more tenacious of the means than the end—anxious to secure all suffrages by which he secures none—hampered not only by the ties of friendship to his actual associates, but to all those that he thinks may become so; and unwilling to offer arguments to convince the reason of his opponents lest he should offend their prejudices, by shewing them how much they are in the wrong; 'letting I dare not wait upon I would, like the poor cat in the adage';[53] stickling for the letter of the Constitution, with the affectation of a prude, and abandoning its principles with the effrontery of a prostitute to any shabby Coalition he can patch up with its deadly enemies. This is very pitiful work; and, I believe, the public with me are tolerably sick of the character. At the same time, he hurls up his cap with a foolish face of wonder and incredulity at the restoration of the Bourbons, and affects to chuckle with secret satisfaction over the last act of the Revolution, which reduced him to perfect insignificance. We need not wonder at the results, when it comes to the push between parties so differently constituted and unequally matched. We have seen what those results are. I cannot do justice to the picture, but I find it done to my hands in those prophetic lines of Pope, where he describes the last Triumph of Corruption:—

But 'tis the fall degrades her to a whore:
Let greatness own her, and she's mean no more.
Her birth, her beauty, crowds and courts confess;
Chaste matrons praise her, and grave bishops bless:
In golden chains the willing world she draws,
And her's the Gospel is, and her's the Laws;
Mounts the tribunal, lifts her scarlet head,
And sees pale virtue carted in her stead.
Lo! at the wheels of her triumphal car,
Old England's genius, rough with many a scar,
Dragg'd in the dust! his arms hang idly round,
His flag inverted trails along the ground:
Our youth, all liveried o'er with foreign gold,
Before her dance, behind her crawl the old!
See thronging millions to the Pagod run,
And offer country, parent, wife, or son!
Hear her black trumpet thro' the land proclaim,
That *not to be corrupted is the shame.*
In soldier, churchman, patriot, man in power,
'Tis avarice all, ambition is no more!
See all our nobles begging to be slaves!
See all our fools aspiring to be knaves!

---

53 *Macbeth*, I, vii, 45.

All, all look up with reverential awe
At crimes that 'scape or triumph o'er the law;
While truth, worth, wisdom daily they decry:
'Nothing is sacred now but villainy.'
Yet may this verse (if such a verse remain)
Shew there was one who held it in disdain.[54]

1819

ON THE PLEASURE OF PAINTING

'There is a pleasure in painting which none but painters know.'[1] In writing, you have to contend with the world; in painting, you have only to carry on a friendly strife with Nature. You sit down to your task, and are happy. From the moment that you take up the pencil, and look Nature in the face, you are at peace with your own heart. No angry passions rise to disturb the silent progress of the work, to shake the hand, or dim the brow; no irritable humours are set afloat: you have no absurd opinions to combat, no point to strain, no adversary to crush, no fool to annoy —you are actuated by fear or favour to no man. There is 'no juggling here,' no sophistry, no intrigue, no tampering with the evidence, no attempt to make black white, or white black: but you resign yourself into the hands of a greater power, that of Nature, with the simplicity of a child, and the devotion of an enthusiast—'study with joy her manner, and with rapture taste her style.'[2] The mind is calm, and full at the same time. The hand and eye are equally employed. In tracing the commonest object, a plant or the stump of a tree, you learn something every moment. You perceive unexpected differences, and discover likenesses where you looked for no such thing. You try to set down what you see—find out your error, and correct it. You need not play tricks, or purposely mistake: with all your pains, you are still far short of the mark. Patience grows out of the endless pursuit, and turns it into a luxury. A streak in a flower, a wrinkle in a leaf, a tinge in a cloud, a stain in an old wall or ruin grey, are seized with avidity as the *spolia optima*[3] of this sort of mental warfare, and furnish out labour for another half day. The hours pass away untold, without chagrin, and without weariness; nor would you ever wish to pass them otherwise.

---

54 Pope, *Epilogue to the Satires*, I, 143 ff.

1 adapted from Dryden, *The Spanish Friar*: 'There is a pleasure, sure, in being mad, which none but madmen know.'
2 Cowper, *The Task*, III, 227–8.
3 richest spoils.

Innocence is joined with industry, pleasure with business; and the mind is satisfied, though it is not engaged in thinking or in doing harm.

I have not much pleasure in writing these Essays, or in reading them afterwards; though I own I now and then meet with a phrase that I like, or a thought that strikes me as a true one. But after I begin them, I am only anxious to get to the end of them, which I am not sure I shall do, for I seldom see my way a page or even a sentence beforehand; and when I have as by a miracle escaped, I trouble myself little more about them. I sometimes have to write them twice over: then it is necessary to read the *proof,* to prevent mistakes by the printer; so that by the time they appear in a tangible shape, and one can con them over with a conscious, sidelong glance to the public approbation, they have lost their gloss and relish, and become 'more tedious than a twice-told tale.' For a person to read his own works over with any great delight, he ought first to forget that he ever wrote them. Familiarity naturally breeds contempt. It is, in fact, like poring fondly over a piece of blank paper; from repetition, the words convey no distinct meaning to the mind, are mere idle sounds, except that our vanity claims an interest and property in them. I have more satisfaction in my own thoughts than in dictating them to others: words are necessary to explain the impression of certain things upon me to the reader, but they rather weaken and draw a veil over than strengthen it to myself. However, I might say with the poet, 'My mind to me a kingdom is,'[4] yet I have little ambition 'to set a throne or chair of state in the understandings of other men.'[5] The ideas we cherish most, exist best in a kind of shadowy abstraction,

> Pure in the last recesses of the mind;[6]

and derive neither force nor interest from being exposed to public view. They are old established acquaintance, and any change in them, arising from the adventitious ornaments of style or dress, is hardly to their advantage. After I have once written on a subject, it goes out of my mind: my feelings about it have been melted down into words, and *them* I forget. I have, as it were, discharged my memory of its old habitual reckoning, and rubbed out the score of real sentiment.

In future, it exists only for the sake of others.— But I cannot say, from my own experience, that the same process takes place in transferring our ideas to canvas; they gain more than they lose in the mechanical transformation. One is never tired of painting, because you have to set down not what you knew already, but what you have just discovered. In the former case, you translate feelings into words; in the latter, names into things. There is a continual creation out of nothing going on. With every stroke of the brush, a new field of inquiry is laid open; new difficulties arise, and new triumphs are prepared over them. By comparing the imitation with the original, you see what you have done, and how much you have still to do. The test of the senses is severer than that of fancy, and an over-match even for the delusions of our self-love. One part of a picture shames another, and you determine to paint up to yourself, if you cannot come up to Nature. Every object becomes lustrous from the light thrown back upon it by the mirror of art: and by the aid of the pencil we may be said to touch and handle the objects of sight. The air-drawn visions that hover on the verge of existence have a bodily presence given them on the canvas: the form of beauty is changed into a substance: the dream and the glory of the universe is made 'palpable to feeling as to sight.'[7]—And see! a rainbow starts from the canvas, with all its humid train of glory, as if it were drawn from its cloudy arch in heaven. The spangled landscape glitters with drops of dew after the shower. The 'fleecy fools' show their coats in the gleams of the setting sun. The shepherds pipe their farewell notes in the fresh evening air. And is this bright vision made from a dead dull blank, like a bubble reflecting the mighty fabric of the universe? Who would think this miracle of Ruben's pencil possible to be performed? Who, having seen it, would not spend his life to do the like? See how the rich fallows, the bare stubble-field, the scanty harvest-home, drag in Rembrandt's landscapes! How often have I looked at them and Nature, and tried to do the same, till the very 'light thickened,'[8] and there was an earthiness in the feeling of the air! There is no end of the refinements of art and Nature in this respect. One may look at the misty glimmering horizon till the eye dazzles and the imagination is lost, in hopes to transfer the whole interminable expanse at one blow upon can-

4 The first line of the well-known poem attributed to Sir Edward Dyer, d. 1607.
5 Bacon, *Advancement of Learning*, I, viii, 3.
6 Dryden, *Satires of Persius*, II, 133.

7 *Macbeth*, II, i, 36–7.
8 *Macbeth*, III, ii, 50.

vas. Wilson[9] said, he endeavoured to paint the effect of the motes dancing in the setting sun. At another time, a friend coming into his painting-room when he was sitting on the ground in a melancholy posture, observed that his picture looked like a landscape after a shower: he started up with the greatest delight, and said, 'That is the effect I intended to represent, but thought I had failed.' Wilson was neglected; and, by degrees, neglected his art to apply himself to brandy. His hand became unsteady, so that it was only by repeated attempts that he could reach the place, or produce the effect he aimed at; and when he had done a little to a picture, he would say to any acquaintance who chanced to drop in, 'I have painted enough for one day: come let us go somewhere.' It was not so Claude[10] left his pictures, or his studies on the banks of the Tiber, to go in search of other enjoyments, or ceased to gaze upon the glittering sunny vales and distant hills; and while his eye drank in the clear sparkling hues and lovely forms of Nature, his hand stamped them on the lucid canvas to remain there forever!—One of the most delightful parts of my life was one fine summer, when I used to walk out of an evening to catch the last light of the sun, gemming the green slopes or russet lawns, and gilding tower or tree, while the blue sky gradually turning to purple and gold, or skirted with dusky grey, hung its broad marble pavement over all, as we see it in the great master of Italian landscape. But to come to a more particular explanation of the subject.

The first head I ever tried to paint was an old woman with the upper part of the face shaded by her bonnet, and I certainly laboured it with great perseverance. It took me numberless sittings to do it. I have it by me still, and sometimes look at it with surprise, to think how much pains were thrown away to little purpose,—yet not altogether in vain, if it taught me to see good in everything, and to know that there is nothing vulgar in Nature seen with the eye of science or of true art. Refinement creates beauty everywhere: it is the grossness of the spectator that discovers nothing but grossness in the object. Be this as it may, I spared no pains to do my best. If art was long, I thought that life was so too at that moment. I got in the general effect the first day; and pleased and surprised enough I was at my success. The rest was a work of time—of weeks and months (if need were) of patient toil and careful finishing. I had seen an old head by Rembrandt at Burleigh House,[11] and if I could produce a head at all like Rembrandt in a year, in my life-time, it would be glory and felicity, and wealth and fame enough for me! The head I had seen at Burleigh was an exact and wonderful facsimile of Nature, and I resolved to make mine (as nearly as I could) an exact facsimile of Nature. I did not then, nor do I now believe, with Sir Joshua,[12] that the perfection of art consists in giving general appearances without individual details, but in giving general appearances with individual details. Otherwise, I had done my work the first day. But I saw something more in Nature than general effect, and I thought it worth my while to give it in the picture. There was a gorgeous effect of light and shade: but there was a delicacy as well as depth in the *chiaro scuro*,[13] which I was bound to follow into all its dim and scarce perceptible variety of tone and shadow. Then I had to make the transition from a strong light to as dark a shade, preserving the masses, but gradually softening off the intermediate parts. It was so in Nature: the difficulty was to make it so in the copy. I tried, and failed again and again; I strove harder, and succeeded, as I thought. The wrinkles in Rembrandt were not hard lines; but broken and irregular. I saw the same appearance in Nature, and strained every nerve to give it. If I could hit off this crumbling appearance, and insert the reflected light in the furrows of old age in half a morning, I did not think I had lost a day. Beneath the shrivelled yellow parchment look of the skin, there was here and there a streak of the blood—colour tinging the face; this I made a point of conveying, and did not cease to compare what I saw with what I did (with jealous lynx-eyed watchfulness) till I succeeded to the best of my ability and judgement. How many revisions were there! How many attempts to catch an expression which I had seen the day before! How often did we strive to get the old position, and wait for the return of the same light! There was a puckering up of the lips, a cautious introversion of the eye under the shadow of the bonnet, indicative of the feebleness and suspicion of old age, which at last we managed, after many trials

---

9 Richard Wilson, 1714–82, noted English landscape painter, one of the original members of the Royal Academy.
10 Claude Lorrain, 1600–82, celebrated French landscape painter.

11 Seat of the titled Cecil family, in Stamford, Lincolnshire. Hazlitt is supposed to have made his first visit to Burleigh House in 1795 when he was seventeen,
12 Sir Joshua Reynolds, 1723–92.
13 light and shade.

and some quarrels, to a tolerable nicety. The picture was never finished, and I might have gone on with it to the present hour. I used to set it on the ground when my day's work was done, and saw revealed to me with swimming eyes the birth of new hopes, and of a new world of objects. The painter thus learns to look at Nature with different eyes. He before saw her 'as in a glass darkly, but now face to face.'[14] He understands the texture and meaning of the visible universe, and 'sees into the life of things,'[15] not by the help of mechanical instruments, but of the improved exercise of his faculties, and an intimate sympathy with Nature. The meanest thing is not lost upon him, for he looks at it with an eye to itself, not merely to his own vanity or interest, or the opinion of the world. Even where there is neither beauty nor use—if that ever were—still there is truth, and a sufficient source of gratification in the indulgence of curiosity and activity of mind. The humblest painter is a true scholar; and the best of scholars—the scholar of Nature. For myself, and for the real comfort and satisfaction of the thing, I had rather have been Jan Steen[16] or Gerard Dow[17] than the greatest casuist or philologer that ever lived. The painter does not view things in clouds or 'mist, the common gloss of theologians,'[18] but applies the same standard of truth and disinterested spirit of inquiry, that influence his daily practice, to other subjects. He perceives form; he distinguishes character. He reads men and books with an intuitive glance. He is a critic as well as a connoisseur. The conclusions he draws are clear and convincing, because they are taken from actual experience. He is not a fanatic, a dupe, or a slave; for the habit of seeing for himself also disposes him to judge for himself. The most sensible men I know (taken as a class) are painters; that is, they are the most lively observers of what passes in the world about them, and the closest observers of what passes in their own minds. From their profession they in general mix more with the world than authors; and if they have not the same fund of acquired knowledge, are obliged to rely more on individual sagacity. I might mention the names of Opie,[19] Fuseli,[20] Northcote,[21] as persons distin-

guished for striking description and acquaintance with the subtle traits of character. Painters in ordinary society, or in obscure situations where their value is not known, and they are treated with neglect and indifference, have sometimes a forward self-sufficiency of manner: but this is not so much their fault as that of others. Perhaps their want of regular education may also be in fault in such cases. Richardson, who is very tenacious of the respect in which the profession ought to be held, tells a story[22] of Michael Angelo, that after a quarrel between him and Pope Julius II, 'upon account of a slight the artist conceived the pontiff had put upon him, Michael Angelo was introduced by a bishop, who, thinking to serve the artist by it, made it an argument that the Pope should be reconciled to him, because men of his profession were commonly ignorant, and of no consequence otherwise: his holiness, enraged at the bishop, struck him with his staff, and told him, it was he that was the blockhead, and affronted the man himself would not offend; the prelate was driven out of the chamber, and Michael Angelo had the Pope's benediction accompanied with presents. This bishop had fallen into the vulgar error, and was rebuked accordingly.'

Besides the employment of the mind, painting exercises the body. It is a mechanical as well as a liberal art. To do anything, to dig a hole in the ground, to plant a cabbage, to hit a mark, to move a shuttle, to work a pattern,—in a word, to attempt to produce any effect, and to *succeed*, has something in it that gratifies the love of power, and carries off the restless activity of the mind of man. Indolence is a delightful but distressing state: we must be doing something to be happy. Action is no less necessary than thought to the instinctive tendencies of the human frame; and painting combines them both incessantly. The hand furnishes a practical test of the correctness of the eye; and the eye, thus admonished, imposes fresh tasks of skill and industry upon the hand. Every stroke tells, as the verifying of a new truth; and every new observation, the instant it is made, passes into an act and emanation of the will. Every step is nearer what we wish, and yet there is always more to do. In spite of the facility, the fluttering grace, the evanescent hues, that play round the pencil of Rubens and Vandyke, however I may admire, I do not envy them this power so much as I do the slow, patient, la-

14 I Corinthians, xiii, 12.
15 Wordsworth, *Lines Composed a Few Miles above Tintern Abbey*, 50.
16 a famous Flemish figure painter, 1626–79.
17 a celebrated Flemish painter, 1613–75.
18 *Paradise Lost*, v, 435–6.
19 John Opie, 1761–1807, historical and portrait painter.
20 Henry Fuseli, 1741–1825, Swiss-English painter and art critic.
21 James Northcote, 1746–1831, historical and portrait painter.

22 Jonathan Richardson, 1665-1745, painter and author, in his *Essays*, pp. 297-8 of 1773 ed.

bourious execution of Correggio, Leonardo da Vinci, and Andrea del Sarto, where every touch appears conscious of its charge, emulous of truth, and where the painful artist has so distinctly wrought,

That you might almost say his picture thought![23]

In the one case, the colours seem breathed on the canvas as by magic, the work and the wonder of a moment: in the other, they seem inlaid in the body of the work, and as if it took the artist years of unremitting labour, and of delightful never-ending progress to perfection. Who would wish ever to come to the close of such works,— not to dwell on them, to return to them, to be wedded to them to the last? Rubens, with his florid, rapid style, complained that when he had just learned his art, he should be forced to die. Leonardo, in the slow advances of his, had lived long enough!

Painting is not, like writing, what is properly understood by a sedentary employment. It requires not indeed a strong, but a continued and steady exertion of muscular power. The precision and delicacy of the manual operation makes up for the want of vehemence,—as to balance himself for any time in the same position the ropedancer must strain every nerve. Painting for a whole morning gives one as excellent an appetite for one's dinner, as old Abraham Tucker[24] acquired for his by riding over Banstead Downs.[25] It is related of Sir Joshua Reynolds, that 'he took no other exercise than what he used in his painting-room,'—the writer means, in walking backwards and forwards to look at his picture; but the act of painting itself, of laying on the colours in the proper place and proper quantity, was a much harder exercise than this alternate receding from and returning to the picture. The last would be rather a relaxation and relief than an effort. It is not to be wondered at, that an artist like Sir Joshua, who delighted so much in the sensual and practical part of his art, should have found himself at a considerable loss when the decay of his sight precluded him, for the last year or two of his life, from the following up of his profession,—'the source,' according to his own remark, 'of thirty years' uninterrupted enjoyment and prosperity to him.' It is only those who never think at all, or else who have accus-

tomed themselves to brood invariably on abstract ideas, that never feel *ennui*.

To give one instance more, and then I will have done with this rambling discourse. One of my first attempts was a picture of my father, who was then in a green old age with strong-marked features, and scarred with the small-pox. I drew it with a broad light crossing the face, looking down, with spectacles on, reading. The book was Shaftesbury's *Characteristics*, in a fine old binding, with Gribelin's etchings.[26] My father would as lieve it had been any other book; but for him to read was to be content, was 'riches fineless.'[27] The sketch promised well; and I set to work to finish it, determined to spare no time nor pains. My father was willing to sit as long as I pleased; for there is a natural desire in the mind of man to sit for one's picture, to be the object of continued attention, to have one's likeness multiplied; and besides his satisfaction in the picture, he had some pride in the artist, though he would rather I should have written a sermon than painted like Rembrandt or like Raphael. Those winter days, with the gleams of sunshine coming through the chapel-windows, and cheered by the notes of the robin-redbreast in our garden (that 'ever in the haunch of winter sings'[28])—as my afternoon's work drew to a close,—were among the happiest of my life. When I gave the effect I intended to any part of the picture for which I had prepared my colours, when I imitated the roughness of the skin by a lucky stroke of the pencil, when I hit the clear pearly tone of a vein, when I gave the ruddy complexion of health, the blood circulating under the broad shadows of one side of the face, I thought my fortune made; or rather it was already more than made, in my fancying that I might one day be able to say with Correggio, '*I also am a painter!*' It was an idle thought, a boy's conceit; but it did not make me less happy at the time. I used regularly to set my work in the chair to look at it through the long evenings; and many a time did I return to take leave of it, before I could go to bed at night. I remember sending it with a throbbing heart to the Exhibition, and seeing it hung up there by the side of one of the Honourable Mr. Skeffington (now Sir George).[29] There was nothing in common be-

---

23 Donne, *An Anatomy of the World, Second Anniversary*, 246.

24 an English philosopher, 1705-74, whose *The Light of Nature Pursued* was abridged by Hazlitt.

25 the old name for Epsom Downs, famous English race course fifteen miles southwest of London.

26 The second (1714) and subsequent editions of Shaftesbury's famous work were illustrated by the well-known engraver Simon Gribelin, 1661-1733.

27 *Othello*, II, iii, 173.

28 *II Henry IV*, IV, iv, 92.

29 Sir Lumley St. George Skeffington, 1771-1850, author of *The Sleeping Beauty* and other plays.

tween them, but that they were the portraits of two very good-natured men. I think, but am not sure, that I finished this portrait (or another afterwards) on the same day that the news of the battle of Austerlitz[30] came; I walked out in the afternoon, and, as I returned, saw the evening star set over a poor man's cottage with other thoughts and feelings than I shall ever have again. Oh for the revolution of the great Platonic year, that those times might come over again! I could sleep out the three hundred and sixty-five thousand intervening years very contentedly!—The picture is left: the table, the chair, the window where I learned to construe Livy, the chapel where my father preached, remain where they were; but he himself is gone to rest, full of years, of faith, of hope, and charity![31]

1820

ON FAMILIAR STYLE

IT is not easy to write a familiar style. Many people mistake a familiar for a vulgar style, and suppose that to write without affectation is to write at random. On the contrary, there is nothing that requires more precision, and, if I may so say, purity of expression, than the style I am speaking of. It utterly rejects not only all unmeaning pomp, but all low, cant phrases, and loose, unconnected, *slipshod* allusions. It is not to take the first word that offers, but the best word in common use; it is not to throw words together in any combinations we please, but to follow and avail ourselves of the true idiom of the language. To write a genuine familiar or truly English style, is to write as any one would speak in common conversation, who had a thorough command and choice of words, or who could discourse with ease, force, and perspicuity, setting aside all pedantic and oratorical flourishes. Or to give another illustration, to write naturally is the same thing in regard to common conversation, as to read naturally is in regard to common speech. It does not follow that it is an easy thing to give the true accent and inflection to the words you utter, because you do not attempt to rise above the level of ordinary life and colloquial speaking. You do not assume indeed the solemnity of the pulpit, or the tone of stage-declamation; neither are you at liberty to gabble on at a venture, without emphasis or discretion, or to resort to vulgar dialect or clownish pronunciation. You must steer a middle course. You are tied down to a given and appropriate articulation, which is determined by the habitual associations between sense and sound, and which you can only hit by entering into the author's meaning, as you must find the proper words and style to express yourself by fixing your thoughts on the subject you have to write about. Any one may mouth out a passage with a theatrical cadence, or get upon stilts to tell his thoughts: but to write or speak with propriety and simplicity is a more difficult task. Thus it is easy to affect a pompous style, to use a word twice as big as the thing you want to express: it is not so easy to pitch upon the very word that exactly fits it. Out of eight or ten words equally common, equally intelligible, with nearly equal pretensions, it is a matter of some nicety and discrimination to pick out the very one, the preferableness of which is scarcely perceptible, but decisive. The reason why I object to Dr. Johnson's style is, that there is no discrimination, no selection, no variety in it. He uses none but 'tall, opaque words,'[1] taken from the 'first row of the rubric'[2]:—words with the greatest number of syllables, or Latin phrases with merely English terminations. If a fine style depended on this sort of arbitrary pretension, it would be fair to judge of an author's elegance by the measurement of his words, and the substitution of foreign circumlocutions (with no precise associations) for the mother-tongue.[3] How simple it is to be dignified without ease, to be pompous without meaning! Surely, it is but a mechanical rule for avoiding what is low to be always pedantic and affected. It is clear you cannot use a vulgar English word, if you never use a common English word at all. A fine tact is shewn in adhering to those which are perfectly common, and yet never falling into any expressions which are debased by disgusting circumstances, or which owe their significance and point to technical or professional allusions. A truly natural or familiar style can never be quaint or vulgar, for this reason, that it is of universal force and applicability, and that quaintness and vulgarity arise out of the immediate connection of certain words with coarse and disagreeable, or with con-

---

1 Sterne, *Tristram Shandy*, III, xx, Author's Preface.
2 *Hamlet*, II, ii, 448.
3 I have heard of such a thing as an author who makes it a rule never to admit a monosyllable into his vapid verse. Yet the charm and sweetness of Marlow's lines depended often on their being made up almost entirely of monosyllables.—(Hazlitt.)

fined ideas. The last form what we understand by *cant* or *slang* phrases.—To give an example of what is not very clear in the general statement. I should say that the phrase *To cut with a knife,* or *To cut a piece of wood,* is perfectly free from vulgarity, because it is perfectly common: but to *cut an acquaintance* is not quite unexceptionable, because it is not perfectly common or intelligible, and has hardly yet escaped out of the limits of slang phraseology. I should hardly therefore use the word in this sense without putting it in italics as a license of expression, to be received *cum grano salis.*[4] All provincial or bye-phrases come under the same mark of reprobation—all such as the writer transfers to the page from his fireside or a particular *coterie,* or that he invents for his own sole use and convenience. I conceive that words are like money, not the worse for being common, but that it is the stamp of custom alone that gives them circulation or value. I am fastidious in this respect, and would almost as soon coin the currency of the realm as counterfeit the King's English. I never invented or gave a new and unauthorized meaning to any word but one single one (the term *impersonal* applied to feelings) and that was in an abstruse metaphysical discussion to express a very difficult distinction. I have been (I know) loudly accused of revelling in vulgarisms and broken English. I cannot speak to that point: but so far I plead guilty to the determined use of acknowledged idioms and common elliptical expressions. I am not sure that the critics in question know the one from the other, that is, can distinguish any medium between formal pedantry and the most barbarous solecism. As an author, I endeavour to employ plain words and popular modes of construction, as were I a chapman and dealer, I should common weights and measures.

The proper force of words lies not in the words themselves, but in their application. A word may be a fine-sounding word, of an unusual length, and very imposing from its learning and novelty, and yet in the connection in which it is introduced, may be quite pointless and irrelevant. It is not pomp or pretension, but the adaptation of the expression to the idea that clenches a writer's meaning:—as it is not the size or glossiness of the materials, but their being fitted each to its place, that gives strength to the arch; or as the pegs and nails are as necessary to the support of the building as the larger timbers, and more so

than the mere shewy, unsubstantial ornaments. I hate anything that occupies more space than it is worth. I hate to see a load of band-boxes go along the street, and I hate to see a parcel of big words without anything in them. A person who does not deliberately dispose of all his thoughts alike in cumbrous draperies and flimsy disguises, may strike out twenty varieties of familiar everyday language, each coming somewhat nearer to the feeling he wants to convey, and at last not hit upon that particular and only one, which may be said to be identical with the exact impression in his mind. This would seem to shew that Mr. Cobbett[5] is hardly right in saying that the first word that occurs is always the best. It may be a very good one; and yet a better may present itself on reflection or from time to time. It should be suggested naturally, however, and spontaneously, from a fresh and lively conception of the subject. We seldom succeed by trying at improvement, or by merely substituting one word for another that we are not satisfied with, as we cannot recollect the name of a place or person by merely plaguing ourselves about it. We wander farther from the point by persisting in a wrong scent; but it starts up accidentally in the memory when we least expected it, by touching some link in the chain of previous association.

There are those who hoard up and make a cautious display of nothing but rich and rare phraseology;—ancient medals, obscure coins, and Spanish pieces of eight. They are very curious to inspect; but I myself would neither offer nor take them in the course of exchange. A sprinkling of archaisms is not amiss: but a tissue of obsolete expressions is more fit *for keep than wear.* I do not say I would not use any phrase that had been brought into fashion before the middle or the end of the last century; but I should be shy of using any that had not been employed by any approved author during the whole of that time. Words, like clothes, get old-fashioned, or mean and ridiculous, when they have been for some time laid aside. Mr. Lamb is the only imitator of old English style I can read with pleasure; and he is so thoroughly imbued with the spirit of his authors, that the idea of imitation is almost done away. There is an inward unction, a marrowy vein both in the thought and feeling, an intuition, deep and lively, of his subject, that carries off any quaintness or awkwardness arising from an antiquated style and dress. The matter is com-

---

4 with a grain of salt.

5 William Cobbett, 1763–1835. English political writer.

pletely his own, though the manner is assumed. Perhaps his ideas are altogether so marked and individual as to require their point and pungency to be neutralised by the affectation of a singular but traditional form of conveyance. Tricked out in the prevailing costume, they would probably seem more startling and out of the way. The old English authors, Burton, Fuller, Coryate, Sir Thomas Brown,[6] are a kind of mediators between us and the more eccentric and whimsical modern, reconciling us to his peculiarities. I do not, however, know how far this is the case or not, till he condescends to write like one of us. I must confess that what I like best of his papers under the signature of 'Elia' (still I do not presume, amidst such excellence, to decide what is most excellent) is the account of *Mrs. Battle's Opinions on Whist,* which is also the most free from obsolete allusions and turns of expression—

A well of native English undefiled.[7]

To those acquainted with his admired prototypes, these *Essays* of the ingenious and highly gifted author have the same sort of charm and relish, that Erasmus's *Colloquies*[8] or a fine piece of modern Latin have to the classical scholar. Certainly, I do not know any borrowed pencil that has more power or felicity of execution than the one of which I have here been speaking.

It is as easy to write a gaudy style without ideas, as it is to spread a pallet of shewy colours, or to smear in a flaunting transparency. 'What do you read?'—'Words, words, words.'—'What is the matter?'[9]—'*Nothing,*' it might be answered. The florid style is the reverse of the familiar. The last is employed as an unvarnished medium to convey ideas; the first is resorted to as a spangled veil to conceal the want of them. When there is nothing to be set down but words, it costs little to have them fine. Look through the dictionary, and cull out a *florilegium,*[10] rival the *tulippomania.*[11] *Rouge* high enough, and never mind the natural complexion. The vulgar, who are not in the secret, will admire the look of preternatural health and vigour; and the fashionable, who regard only appearances, will be delighted with the imposition. Keep to your sounding generali-

ties, your tinkling phrases, and all will be well. Swell out an unmeaning truism to a perfect tympany of style. A thought, a distinction is the rock on which all this brittle cargo of verbiage splits at once. Such writers have merely *verbal* imaginations, that retain nothing but words. Or their puny thoughts have dragon-wings, all green and gold. They soar far above the vulgar failing of the *Sermo humi obrepens*[12]—their most ordinary speech is never short of an hyperbole, splendid, imposing, vague, incomprehensible, magniloquent, a cento[13] of sounding commonplaces. If some of us, whose 'ambition is more lowly,'[14] pry a little too narrowly into nooks and corners to pick up a number of 'unconsidered trifles,'[15] they never once direct their eyes or lift their hands to seize on any but the most gorgeous, tarnished, thread-bare patch-work set of phrases, the left-off finery of poetic extravagance, transmitted down through successive generations of barren pretenders. If they criticise actors and actresses, a huddled phantasmagoria of feathers, spangles, floods of light, and oceans of sound float before their morbid sense, which they paint in the style of Ancient Pistol.[16] Not a glimpse can you get of the merits or defects of the performers: they are hidden in a profusion of barbarous epithets and wilful rhodomontade. Our hypercritics are not thinking of these little fantoccini beings[17]—

That strut and fret their hour upon the stage[18]—

but of tall phantoms of words, abstractions, *genera* and *species,* sweeping clauses, periods that unite the poles, forced alliterations, astounding antitheses—

And on their pens *Fustian* sits plumed.[19]

If they describe kings and queens, it is an Eastern pageant. The Coronation at either House is nothing to it. We get at four repeated images—a curtain, a throne, a sceptre, and a foot-stool. These are with them the wardrobe of a lofty imagination; and they turn their servile strains to servile uses. Do we read a description of pictures? It is not a reflection of tones and hues which 'nature's

---

6 seventeenth-century authors who influenced the formation of Lamb's style.

7 Spenser, *The Faerie Queene,* IV, ii, 32.

8 *Colloquia,* 1519, by Desiderius Erasmus, [?1466–1536] famous Dutch classicist and theologian.

9 *Hamlet,* II, ii, 193.

10 descriptive list of flowers.

11 craze for growing tulips.

12 'speech which creeps on the ground'—Horace, *Epistles,* II, i, 250–51.

13 patchwork.

14 Cf. *The Tempest,* I, ii, 481–2.

15 *The Winter's Tale,* IV, iii, 26.

16 a braggart in Shakespeare's *Henry IV, Henry V,* and *The Merry Wives of Windsor.*

17 puppets.

18 *Macbeth,* V, v, 5.

19 an adaptation from *Paradise Lost,* IV, 988–9.

own sweet and cunning hand laid on,'[20] but piles of precious stones, rubies, pearls, emeralds, Golconda's mines, and all the blazonry of art. Such persons are in fact besotted with words, and their brains are turned with the glittering, but empty and sterile phantoms of things. Personifications, capital letters, seas of sunbeams, visions of glory, shining inscriptions, the figures of a transparency, Britannia with her shield, or Hope leaning on an anchor, make up their stock in trade. They may be considered as *hieroglyphical* writers. Images stand out in their minds isolated and important merely in themselves, without any ground-work of feeling—there is no context in their imaginations. Words affect them in the same way, by the mere sound, that is, by their possible, not by their actual application to the subject in hand. They are fascinated by first appearances, and have no sense of consequences. Nothing more is meant by them than meets the ear: they understand or feel nothing more than meets their eye. The web and texture of the universe, and of the heart of man, is a mystery to them: they have no faculty that strikes a chord in unison with it. They cannot get beyond the daubings of fancy, the varnish of sentiment. Objects are not linked to feelings, words to things, but images revolve in splendid mockery, words represent themselves in their strange rhapsodies. The categories of such a mind are pride and ignorance—pride in outside show, to which they sacrifice everything, and ignorance of the true worth and hidden structure both of words and things. With a sovereign contempt for what is familiar and natural, they are the slaves of vulgar affectation—of a routine of high-flown phrases. Scorning to imitate realities, they are unable to invent anything, to strike out one original idea. They are not copyists of nature, it is true: but they are the poorest of all plagiarists, the plagiarists of words. All is far-fetched, dear-bought, artificial, oriental in subject and allusion: all is mechanical, conventional, vapid, formal, pedantic in style and execution. They startle and confound the understanding of the reader, by the remoteness and obscurity of their illustrations: they soothe the ear by the monotony of the same everlasting round of circuitous metaphors. They are the *mock-school* in poetry and prose. They flounder about between fustian in expression, and bathos in sentiment. They tantalise the fancy, but never reach the head nor touch the heart. Their Temple of Fame

is like a shadowy structure raised by Dulness to Vanity, or like Cowper's description of the Empress of Russia's palace of ice, as 'worthless as in shew 'twas glittering'—

> It smiled, and it was cold![21]

1821

ON GOING A JOURNEY

ONE of the pleasantest things in the world is going a journey; but I like to go by myself. I can enjoy society in a room; but out of doors, nature is company enough for me. I am then never less alone than when alone.

> The fields his study, nature was his book.[1]

I cannot see the wit of walking and talking at the same time. When I am in the country, I wish to vegetate like the country. I am not for criticising hedge-rows and black cattle. I go out of town in order to forget the town and all that is in it. There are those who for this purpose go to watering-places, and carry the metropolis with them. I like more elbow-room, and fewer incumbrances. I like solitude, when I give myself up to it, for the sake of solitude; nor do I ask for

> A friend in my retreat,
> Whom I may whisper, solitude is sweet.[2]

The soul of a journey is liberty, perfect liberty, to think, feel, do, just as one pleases. We go a journey chiefly to be free of all impediments and of all inconveniences; to leave ourselves behind, much more to get rid of others. It is because I want a little breathing-space to muse on indifferent matters, where Contemplation

> May plume her feathers and let grow her wings,
> That in the various bustle of resort
> Were all too ruffled, and sometimes impair'd,[3]

that I absent myself from the town for awhile, without feeling at a loss the moment I am left by myself. Instead of a friend in a post-chaise or in a Tilbury,[4] to exchange good things with, and vary the same stale topics over again, for once let me have a truce with impertinence. Give me the clear blue sky over my head, and the green turf beneath my feet, a winding road be-

---

20 *Twelfth Night*, I, v, 258.

21 Cowper, *The Task*, v, 173-6.

---

1 Robert Bloomfield, *The Farmer's Boy, Spring,* 32.
2 Cowper, *Retirement,* 741-2.
3 Milton, *Comus,* 378-80.
4 a gig, or a two-wheeled open carriage.

fore me, and a three hours' march to dinner—and then to thinking! It is hard if I cannot start some game on these lone heaths. I laugh, I run, I leap, I sing for joy. From the point of yonder rolling cloud, I plunge into my past being, and revel there, as the sunburnt Indian plunges headlong into the wave that wafts him to his native shore. Then long-forgotten things, like 'sunken wrack and sumless treasuries,'[5] burst upon my eager sight, and I begin to feel, think, and be myself again. Instead of an awkward silence, broken by attempts at wit or dull common-places, mine is that undisturbed silence of the heart which alone is perfect eloquence. No one likes puns, alliterations, antitheses, argument, and analysis better than I do; but I sometimes had rather be without them. 'Leave, oh, leave me to my repose!'[6] I have just now other business in hand, which would seem idle to you, but is with me the 'very stuff of the conscience.'[7] Is not this wild rose sweet without a comment? Does not this daisy leap to my heart set in its coat of emerald? Yet if I were to explain to you the circumstance that has so endeared it to me, you would only smile. Had I not better then keep it to myself, and let it serve me to brood over, from here to yonder craggy point, and from thence onward to the far-distant horizon? I should be but bad company all that way, and therefore prefer being alone. I have heard it said that you may, when the moody fit comes on, walk or ride on by yourself, and indulge your reveries. But this looks like a breach of manners, a neglect of others, and you are thinking all the time that you ought to rejoin your party. 'Out upon such half-faced fellowship,'[8] say I. I like to be either entirely to myself, or entirely at the disposal of others; to talk or be silent, to walk or sit still, to be sociable or solitary. I was pleased with an observation of Mr. Cobbett's[9] that 'he thought it a bad French custom to drink our wine with our meals, and that an Englishman ought to do only one thing at a time.' So I cannot talk and think, or indulge in melancholy musing and lively conversation by fits and starts. 'Let me have a companion of my way,' says Sterne, 'were it but to remark how the shadows lengthen as the sun goes down.'[10] It is beautifully said: but in my opinion, this continual comparing of notes interferes with the involuntary impression of things upon the mind, and hurts the sentiment. If you only hint what you feel in a kind of dumb show, it is insipid: if you have to explain it, it is making a toil of a pleasure. You cannot read the book of nature, without being perpetually put to the trouble of translating it for the benefit of others. I am for the synthetical method on a journey, in preference to the analytical. I am content to lay in a stock of ideas then, and to examine and anatomise them afterwards. I want to see my vague notions float like the down of the thistle before the breeze, and not to have them entangled in the briars and thorns of controversy. For once, I like to have it all my own way; and this is impossible unless you are alone, or in such company as I do not covet. I have no objection to argue a point with anyone for twenty miles of measured road, but not for pleasure. If you remark the scent of a bean-field crossing the road, perhaps your fellow-traveller has no smell. If you point to a distant object, perhaps he is short-sighted, and has to take out his glass to look at it. There is a feeling in the air, a tone in the colour of a cloud which hits your fancy, but the effect of which you are unprepared to account for. There is then no sympathy, but an uneasy craving after it, and a dissatisfaction which pursues you on the way, and in the end probably produces ill humour. Now I never quarrel with myself, and take all my own conclusions for granted till I find it necessary to defend them against objections. It is not merely that you may not be of accord on the objects and circumstances that present themselves before you—they may recall a number of ideas, and lead to associations too delicate and refined to be possibly communicated to others. Yet these I love to cherish, and sometimes still fondly clutch them, when I can escape from the throng to do so. To give way to our feelings before company, seems extravagance or affectation; on the other hand, to have to unravel this mystery of our being at every turn, and to make others take an equal interest in it (otherwise the end is not answered) is a task to which few are competent. We must 'give it an understanding, but no tongue.'[11] My old friend C——,[12] however, could do both. He could go on in the most delightful explanatory way over hill and dale, a summer's day, and convert a landscape into a didactic poem or a Pindaric ode. 'He talked far above singing.'[13] If I could so

5 Shakespeare, *Henry V*, I, ii, 165.
6 Gray, *The Descent of Odin*, 55.
7 *Othello*, I, ii, 2.
8 *I Henry IV*, I, iii, 208.
9 William Cobbett, 1763–1835, essayist and political reformer.
10 Laurence Sterne, *Sermons*, 1760.

11 *Hamlet*, I, ii, 250.
12 Coleridge.
13 Beaumont and Fletcher, *Philaster*, V, v, 165-6.

clothe my ideas in sounding and flowing words, I might perhaps wish to have some one with me to admire the swelling theme; or I could be more content, were it possible for me still to hear his echoing voice in the woods of All-Foxden.[14] They had 'that fine madness in them which our first poets had';[15] and if they could have been caught by some rare instrument, would have breathed such strains as the following:

Here be woods as green
As any, air likewise as fresh and sweet
As when smooth Zephyrus plays on the fleet
Face of the curled streams, with flow'rs as many
As the young spring gives, and as choice as any;
Here be all new delights, cool streams and wells,
Arbors o'ergrown with woodbine, caves and
        dells;
Choose where thou wilt, whilst I sit by and sing,
Or gather rushes, to make many a ring
For thy long fingers; tell thee tales of love:
How the pale Phœbe, hunting in a grove,
First saw the boy Endymion, from whose eyes
She took eternal fire that never dies;
How she convey'd him softly in a sleep,
His temples bound with poppy, to the steep
Head of old Latmos, where she stoops each night,
Gilding the mountain with her brother's light,
To kiss her sweetest,[16]

Had I words and images at command like these, I would attempt to wake the thoughts that lie slumbering on golden ridges in the evening clouds: but at the sight of nature my fancy, poor as it is, droops and closes up its leaves, like flowers at sunset. I can make nothing out on the spot: —I must have time to collect myself.—

In general, a good thing spoils out-of-door prospects: it should be reserved for Table-talk. L——[17] is for this reason, I take it, the worst company in the world out of doors; because he is the best within. I grant, there is one subject on which it is pleasant to talk on a journey; and that is, what one shall have for supper when we get to our inn at night. The open air improves this sort of conversation or friendly altercation, by setting a keener edge on appetite. Every mile of the road heightens the flavour of the viands we expect at the end of it. How fine it is to enter some old town, walled and turreted just at approach of nightfall, or to come to some straggling vil-

lage, with the lights streaming through the surrounding gloom; and then after inquiring for the best entertainment that the place affords, to 'take one's ease at one's inn!'[18] These eventful moments in our lives are in fact too precious, too full of solid, heart-felt happiness to be frittered and dribbled away in imperfect sympathy. I would have them all to myself, and drain them to the last drop: they will do to talk of or to write about afterwards. What a delicate speculation it is, after drinking whole goblets of tea,

The cups that cheer, but not inebriate,[19]

and letting the fumes ascend into the brain, to sit considering what we shall have for supper—eggs and a rasher, a rabbit smothered in onions, or an excellent veal-cutlet! Sancho in such a situation, once fixed upon cow-heel;[20] and his choice, though he could not help it, is not to be disparaged. Then, in the intervals of pictured scenery and Shandean[21] contemplation, to catch the preparation and the stir in the kitchen—*Procul, O procul este profani!*[22] These hours are sacred to silence and to musing, to be treasured up in the memory, and to feed the source of smiling thoughts hereafter. I would not waste them in idle talk; or if I must have the integrity of fancy broken in upon, I would rather it were by a stranger than a friend. A stranger takes his hue and character from the time and place; he is a part of the furniture and costume of an inn. If he is a Quaker, or from the West Riding of Yorkshire,[23] so much the better. I do not even try to sympathise with him, and he breaks no squares. I associate nothing with my travelling companion but present objects and passing events. In his ignorance of me and my affairs, I in a manner forget myself. But a friend reminds me of other things, rips up old grievances, and destroys the abstraction of the scene. He comes in ungraciously between us and our imaginary character. Something is dropped in the course of conversation that gives a hint of your profession and pursuits; or from having someone with you that knows the less sublime portions of your history, it seems that other people do. You are no longer a citizen of the world: but your 'unhoused free condition is

14 the residence of Wordsworth in Somersetshire in 1797.
15 Michael Drayton, *To Henry Reynolds*, 109.
16 John Fletcher, *The Faithful Shepherdess*, I, iii, 27-43.
17 Lamb.
18 *I Henry IV*, III, iii, 93.
19 Cowper, *The Task*, IV, 39-40.
20 Don Quixote's squire in Cervantes' romance, *Don Quixote*, II, lix.
21 whimsically discursive, in the manner of Walter Shandy in Sterne's novel, *Tristram Shandy*.
22 'Retire hence, ye uninitiated'—*Aeneid*, VI, 258.
23 one of the 'ridings' or administrative divisions of Yorkshire, which was then an extreme provincial district.

put into circumscription and confine.'[24] The *incognito* of an inn is one of its striking privileges —'lord of one's self, uncumber'd with a name.'[25] Oh! it is great to shake off the trammels of the world and of public opinion—to lose our importunate, tormenting, everlasting personal identity in the elements of nature, and become the creature of the moment, clear of all ties—to hold to the universe only by a dish of sweet-breads, and to owe nothing but the score of the evening —and no longer seeking for applause and meeting with contempt, to be known by no other title than *the Gentleman in the parlour*! One may take one's choice of all characters in this romantic state of uncertainty as to one's real pretensions, and become indefinitely respectable and negatively right-worshipful. We baffle prejudice and disappoint conjecture; and from being so to others, begin to be objects of curiosity and wonder even to ourselves. We are no more those hackneyed commonplaces that we appear in the world: an inn restores us to the level of nature, and quits scores with society! I have certainly spent some enviable hours at inns—sometimes when I have been left entirely to myself, and have tried to solve some metaphysical problem, as once at Witham-common,[26] where I found out the proof that likeness is not a case of the association of ideas—at other times, when there have been pictures in the room, as at St. Neot's[26] (I think it was), where I first met with Gribelin's engravings of the Cartoons,[27] into which I entered at once, and at a little inn on the borders of Wales, where there happened to be hanging some of Westall's[28] drawings, which I compared triumphantly (for a theory that I had, not for the admired artist) with the figure of a girl who had ferried me over the Severn,[29] standing up in a boat between me and the fading twilight—at other times I might mention luxuriating in books, with a peculiar interest in this way, as I remember sitting up half the night to read *Paul and Virginia*,[30] which I picked up at an inn at Bridgewater, after being drenched in the rain all day; and at the same place I got through two volumes of Madame D'Arblay's *Camilla*.[31] It was

on the 10th of April, 1798, that I sat down to a volume of *The New Eloise*,[32] at the inn at Llangollen,[33] over a bottle of sherry and a cold chicken. The letter[34] I chose was that in which St. Preux describes his feelings as he first caught a glimpse from the heights of the Jura of the Pays de Vaud,[35] which I had brought with me as a *bonne bouch*[36] to crown the evening with. It was my birthday, and I had for the first time come from a place in the neighbourhood to visit this delightful spot. The road to Llangollen turns off between Chirk and Wrexham,[37] and on passing a certain point, you come all at once upon the valley, which opens like an amphitheatre, broad, barren hills rising in majestic state on either side, with 'green upland swells that echo to the bleat of the flocks'[38] below, and the river Dee[39] babbling over its stony bed in the midst of them. The valley at this time 'glittered green with sunny showers,'[40] and a budding ash-tree dipped its tender branches in the chiding stream. How proud, how glad I was to walk along the high road that commanded the delicious prospect, repeating the lines which I have just quoted from Mr. Coleridge's poems! But besides the prospect which opened beneath my feet, another also opened to my inward sight, a heavenly vision, on which were written, in letters large as Hope could make them, these four words, LIBERTY, GENIUS, LOVE, VIRTUE, which have since faded into the light of common day,[41] or mock my idle gaze.

The beautiful is vanished and returns not.[42]

Still I would return some time or other to this enchanted spot; but I would return to it alone. What other self could I find to share that influx of thoughts, of regret, and delight, the traces of which I could hardly conjure up to myself, so much have they been broken and defaced! I could stand on some tall rock, and overlook the precipice of years that separates me from what I then was. I was at that time going shortly to visit the poet whom I have above named. Where is he now?[43] Not only I myself have changed;

24 *Othello*, I, ii, 26.
25 Dryden, *To my Honour'd Kinsman*, 18.
26 a town within twenty miles of London.
27 Simon Gribelin's engravings of the religious drawings of Raphael were published in 1707.
28 Richard Westall, 1765-1836, a prominent English historical painter.
29 a river in the west of England.
30 a romance by Bernardin de St. Pierre, published in 1788.
31 a novel by Frances Burney published in 1796.

32 *La Nouvelle Héloise*, 1761, by Jean Jacques Rousseau.
33 a town in northern Wales.
34 Part IV, letter xvii.
35 a canton in Switzerland.
36 choice morsel.
37 towns in northern Wales.
38 Coleridge, *Ode on the Departing Year*, 125-6.
39 flows through Chester to the Irish Sea.
40 *Ode to the Departing Year*, 124.
41 Wordsworth, *Ode on Intimations of Immortality*, 77.
42 Coleridge, *The Death of Wallenstein*, V, i, 62.
43 Hazlitt has reference to Coleridge's politics, which had shifted from the radical liberalism of his youth.

the world, which was then new to me, has become old and incorrigible. Yet will I turn to thee in thought, O sylvan Dee, as then thou wert, in joy, in youth and gladness; and thou shalt always be to me the river of Paradise, where I will drink of the waters of life freely!

There is hardly anything that shows the short-sightedness or capriciousness of the imagination more than travelling does. With change of place we change our ideas; nay, our opinions and feelings. We can by an effort indeed transport ourselves to old and long-forgotten scenes, and then the picture of the mind revives again; but we forget those that we have just left. It seems that we can think but of one place at a time. The canvas of the fancy has only a certain extent, and if we paint one set of objects upon it, they immediately efface every other. We cannot enlarge our conceptions, we only shift our point of view. The landscape bares its bosom to the enraptured eye, we take our fill of it, and seem as if we could form no other image of beauty or grandeur. We pass on, and think no more of it: the horizon that shuts it from our sight, also blots it from our memory like a dream. In travelling through a wild barren country, I can form no idea of a woody and cultivated one. It appears to me that all the world must be barren, like what I see of it. In the country we forget the town, and in town, we despise the country. 'Beyond Hyde Park,' says Sir Fopling Flutter, 'all is a desert.'[44] All that part of the map that we do not see before us is a blank. The world in our conceit of it is not much bigger than a nutshell. It is not one prospect expanded into another, county joined to county, kingdom to kingdom, lands to seas, making an image voluminous and vast;—the mind can form no larger idea of space than the eye can take in at a single glance. The rest is a name written on a map, a calculation of arithmetic. For instance, what is the true signification of that immense mass of territory and population, known by the name of China to us? An inch of pasteboard on a wooden globe, of no more account than a China orange! Things near us are seen of the size of life: things at a distance are diminished to the size of the understanding. We measure the universe by ourselves, and even comprehend the texture of our own being only piecemeal. In this way, however, we remember an infinity of things and places. The mind is like a mechanical instrument that plays a great variety of tunes, but it

must play them in succession. One idea recalls another, but it at the same time excludes all others. In trying to renew old recollections, we cannot as it were unfold the whole web of our existence; we must pick out the single threads. So in coming to a place where we have formerly lived and with which we have intimate associations, everyone must have found that the feeling grows more vivid the nearer we approach the spot, from the mere anticipation of the actual impression: we remember circumstances, feelings, persons, faces, names that we had not thought of for years; but for the time all the rest of the world is forgotten!—To return to the question I have quitted above.

I have no objection to go to see ruins, aqueducts, pictures, in company with a friend or a party, but rather the contrary, for the former reason reversed. They are intelligible matters, and will bear talking about. The sentiment here is not tacit, but communicable and overt. Salisbury Plain is barren of criticism, but Stonehenge[45] will bear a discussion antiquarian, picturesque, and philosophical. In setting out on a party of pleasure, the first consideration always is where we shall go to: in taking a solitary ramble, the question is what we shall meet with by the way. 'The mind there is its own place';[46] nor are we anxious to arrive at the end of our journey. I can myself do the honours indifferently well to works of art and curiosity. I once took a party to Oxford with no mean *éclat*[47]—shewed them the seat of the Muses at a distance,

With glistering spires and pinnacles adorn'd[48]—

descanted on the learned air that breathes from the grassy quadrangles and stone walls of halls and colleges—was at home in the Bodleian;[49] and at Blenheim[50] quite superseded the powdered Ciceroni[51] that attended us, and that pointed in vain with his wand to commonplace beauties in matchless pictures.—As another exception to the above reasoning, I should not feel confident in venturing on a journey in a foreign country without a companion. I should want at intervals to hear the sound of my own language. There is an involuntary antipathy in the mind

44 in *The Man of Mode*, 1676, by Sir George Etherege, v, ii.

45 a famous group of prehistoric monumental stones on Salisbury Plain in Wiltshire.
46 *Paradise Lost*, I, 254.
47 Hazlitt refers to the time he took Charles and Mary Lamb on a visit to Oxford in 1810.
48 *Paradise Lost*, III, 550.
49 the great library at Oxford.
50 the seat of the Duke of Marlborough, near Oxford.
51 guides.

of an Englishman to foreign manners and notions that requires the assistance of social sympathy to carry it off. As the distance from home increases, this relief, which was at first a luxury, becomes a passion and an appetite. A person would almost feel stifled to find himself in the deserts of Arabia without friends and countrymen: there must be allowed to be something in the view of Athens or old Rome that claims the utterance of speech; and I own that the Pyramids are too mighty for any single contemplation. In such situations, so opposite to all one's ordinary train of ideas, one seems a species by one's-self, a limb torn off from society, unless one can meet with instant fellowship and support.—Yet I did not feel this want or craving very pressing once, when I first set my foot on the laughing shores of France.[52] Calais was peopled with novelty and delight. The confused, busy murmur of the place was like oil and wine poured into my ears; nor did the mariners' hymn, which was sung from the top of an old crazy vessel in the harbour, as the sun went down, send an alien sound into my soul. I breathed the air of general humanity. I walked over 'the vine-covered hills and gay regions of France,'[53] erect and satisfied; for the image of man was not cast down and chained to the foot of arbitrary thrones: I was at no loss for language, for that of all the great schools of painting was open to me. The whole is vanished like a shade. Pictures, heroes, glory, freedom, all are fled; nothing remains but the Bourbons[54] and the French people!—There is undoubtedly a sensation in travelling into foreign parts that is to be had nowhere else: but it is more pleasing at the time than lasting. It is too remote from our habitual associations to be a common topic of discourse or reference, and, like a dream or another state of existence, does not piece into our daily modes of life. It is an animated but a momentary hallucination. It demands an effort to exchange our actual for our ideal identity; and to feel the pulse of our old transports revive very keenly, we must 'jump' all our present comforts and connexions. Our romantic and itinerant character is not to be domesticated. Dr. Johnson remarked how little foreign travel added to the facilities of conversation in those who had been abroad.[55] In fact, the time we have spent there is both delightful and in one sense instructive; but it appears to be cut out of our substantial, downright existence, and never to join kindly on to it. We are not the same, but another, and perhaps more enviable individual, all the time we are out of our own country. We are lost to ourselves, as well as to our friends. So the poet somewhat quaintly sings,

Out of my country and myself I go.[56]

Those who wish to forget painful thoughts, do well to absent themselves for a while from the ties and objects that recall them: but we can be said only to fulfil our destiny in the place that gave us birth. I should on this account like well enough to spend the whole of my life in travelling abroad, if I could anywhere borrow another life to spend afterwards at home!

1822

MY FIRST ACQUAINTANCE WITH POETS

MY father was a Dissenting Minister at W——m[1] in Shropshire; and in the year 1798 (the figures that compose that date are to me like the 'dreaded name of Demogorgon'[2]) Mr. Coleridge came to Shrewsbury, to succeed Mr. Rowe in the spiritual charge of a Unitarian congregation there. He did not come till late on the Saturday afternoon before he was to preach; and Mr. Rowe, who himself went down to the coach in a state of anxiety and expectation, to look for the arrival of his successor, could find no one at all answering the description but a round-faced man in a short black coat (like a shooting-jacket) which hardly seemed to have been made for him, but who seemed to be talking at a great rate to his fellow-passengers. Mr. Rowe had scarce returned to give an account of his disappointment, when the round-faced man in black entered, and dissipated all doubts on the subject by beginning to talk. He did not cease while he staid; nor has he since, that I know of. He held the good town of Shrewsbury in delightful suspense for three weeks that he remained there, 'fluttering the *proud Salopians* like an eagle in a dove-cote';[3] and the Welsh mountains that skirt the horizon

---

52 in 1802, when Hazlitt was on his way to Paris to study at the Louvre.

53 William Roscoe, *Song*, 1791.

54 the French royal house, which ruled continuously from the sixteenth century until the Revolution, and from the fall of Napoleon until 1830.

55 Boswell, *The Life of Samuel Johnson*. III, 352 (Hill's ed.).

56 This quotation has not been identified.

1 Wem.

2 *Paradise Lost*, II, 964-5.

3 *Coriolanus*, V, vi, 115. A *Salopian* is an inhabitant of Salop, or Shropshire.

with their tempestuous confusion, agree to have heard no such mystic sounds since the days of High-born Hoel's harp or soft Llewellyn's lay![4] As we passed along between W——m and Shrewsbury, and I eyed their blue tops seen through the wintry branches, or the red rustling leaves of the sturdy oak-trees by the roadside, a sound was in my ears as of a Siron's song; I was stunned, startled with it, as from deep sleep; but I had no notion then that I should ever be able to express my admiration to others in motley imagery or quaint allusion, till the light of his genius shone into my soul, like the sun's rays glittering in the puddles of the road. I was at that time dumb, inarticulate, helpless, like a worm by the way-side, crushed, bleeding, lifeless; but now, bursting from the deadly bands that 'bound them,'

With Styx nine times round them,[5]

my ideas float on winged words, and as they expand their plumes, catch the golden light of other years. My soul has indeed remained in its original bondage, dark, obscure, with longings infinite and unsatisfied; my heart, shut up in the prison-house of this rude clay, has never found, nor will it ever find, a heart to speak to; but that my understanding also did not remain dumb and brutish, or at length found a language to express itself, I owe to Coleridge. But this is not to my purpose.

My father lived ten miles from Shrewsbury, and was in the habit of exchanging visits with Mr. Rowe, and with Mr. Jenkins of Whitchurch (nine miles farther on) according to the custom of Dissenting Ministers in each other's neighbourhood. A line of communication is thus established, by which the flame of civil and religious liberty is kept alive, and nourishes its smouldering fire unquenchable, like the fires in the *Agamemnon* of Æschylus, placed at different stations, that waited for ten long years to announce with their blazing pyramids the destruction of Troy. Coleridge had agreed to come over to see my father, according to the courtesy of the country, as Mr. Rowe's probable successor; but in the meantime I had gone to hear him preach the Sunday after his arrival. A poet and a philosopher getting up into a Unitarian pulpit to preach the Gospel, was a romance in these degenerate days, a sort of revival of the primitive spirit of Christianity, which was not to be resisted.

It was in January, 1798, that I rose one morning before daylight, to walk ten miles in the mud, and went to hear this celebrated person preach. Never, the longest day I have to live, shall I have such another walk as this cold, raw, comfortless one, in the winter of the year 1798. *Il y a des impressions que ni le tems ni les circonstances peuvent effacer. Dusse-je vivre des siècles entiers, le doux tems de ma jeunesse ne peut renaître pour moi, ni s'effacer jamais dans ma mémoire.*[6] When I got there, the organ was playing the 100th Psalm, and, when it was done, Mr. Coleridge rose and gave out his text, 'And he went up into the mountain to pray, HIMSELF, ALONE.'[7] As he gave out this text, his voice 'rose like a steam of rich distilled perfumes,'[8] and when he came to the two last words, which he pronounced loud, deep, and distinct, it seemed to me, who was then young, as if the sounds had echoed from the bottom of the human heart, and as if that prayer might have floated in solemn silence through the universe. The idea of St. John came into mind, 'of one crying in the wilderness, who had his loins girt about, and whose food was locusts and wild honey.'[9] The preacher then launched into his subject, like an eagle dallying with the wind. The sermon was upon peace and war; upon church and state—not their alliance, but their separation—on the spirit of the world and the spirit of Christianity, not as the same, but as opposed to one another. He talked of those who had 'inscribed the cross of Christ on banners dripping with human gore.' He made a poetical and pastoral excursion,—and to shew the fatal effects of war, drew a striking contrast between the simple shepherd boy, driving his team afield, or sitting under the hawthorn, piping to his flock, 'as though he should never be old,'[10] and the same poor country-lad, crimped, kidnapped, brought into town, made drunk at an ale-house, turned into a wretched drummer-boy, with his hair sticking on end with powder and pomatum, a long cue at his back, and tricked out in the loathsome finery of the profession of blood.

Such were the notes our once-lov'd poet sung.[11]

---

4 Gray, *The Bard,* 28.
5 Pope, *Ode for Music on St. Cecilia's Day,* 90–91.

6 There are impressions which neither times nor circumstances can efface. Were I enabled to live entire ages, the sweet days of my youth could not return for me, nor ever be obliterated from my memory.—Rousseau, *Confessions.*
7 St. John, vi, 15.   8 *Comus,* 556.
9 Matthew, iii, 3–4.
10 Sidney, *Arcadia,* 1, 2.
11 Pope, *Epistle to Robert Earl of Oxford,* 1.

And for myself, I could not have been more delighted if I had heard the music of the spheres. Poetry and Philosophy had met together. Truth and Genius had embraced, under the eye and with the sanction of Religion. This was even beyond my hopes. I returned home well satisfied. The sun that was still labouring pale and wan through the sky, obscured by thick mists, seemed an emblem of the *good cause;* and the cold dank drops of dew that hung half melted on the beard of the thistle, had something genial and refreshing in them; for there was a spirit of hope and youth in all nature, that turned everything into good. The face of nature had not then the brand of Jus Divinum[12] on it:

Like to that sanguine flower inscrib'd with woe.[13]

On the Tuesday following, the half-inspired speaker came. I was called down into the room where he was, and went half-hoping, half-afraid. He received me very graciously, and I listened for a long time without uttering a word. I did not suffer in his opinion by my silence. 'For those two hours,' he afterwards was pleased to say, 'he was conversing with W. H.'s forehead!' His appearance was different from what I had anticipated from seeing him before. At a distance, and in the dim light of the chapel, there was to me a strange wildness in his aspect, a dusky obscurity, and I thought him pitted with the small-pox. His complexion was at that time clear, and even bright—

As are the children of yon azure sheen.[14]

His forehead was broad and high, light as if built of ivory, with large projecting eyebrows, and his eyes rolling beneath them like a sea with darkened lustre. 'A certain tender bloom his face o'erspread,'[15] a purple tinge as we see it in the pale thoughtful complexions of the Spanish portrait-painters, Murillo and Velasquez. His mouth was gross, voluptuous, open, eloquent; his chin good-humoured and round; but his nose, the rudder of the face, the index of the will, was small, feeble, nothing—like what he has done. It might seem that the genius of his face as from a height surveyed and projected him (with sufficient capacity and huge aspiration) into the world unknown of thought and imagination, with nothing to support or guide his veering purpose, as if Columbus had launched his adventurous course for the New World in a scallop, without oars or compass. So at least I comment on it after the event. Coleridge in his person was rather above the common size, inclining to the corpulent, or like Lord Hamlet, 'somewhat fat and pursy.'[16] His hair (now, alas! grey) was then black and glossy as the raven's, and fell in smooth masses over his forehead. This long pendulous hair is peculiar to enthusiasts, to those whose minds tend heavenward; and is traditionally inseparable (though of a different colour) from the pictures of Christ. It ought to belong, as a character, to all who preach *Christ crucified,* and Coleridge was at that time one of those!

It was curious to observe the contrast between him and my father, who was a veteran in the cause, and then declining into the vale of years. He had been a poor Irish lad, carefully brought up by his parents, and sent to the University of Glasgow (where he studied under Adam Smith[17]) to prepare him for his future destination. It was his mother's proudest wish to see her son a Dissenting Minister. So if we look back to past generations (as far as eye can reach) we see the same hopes, fears, wishes, followed by the same disappointments, throbbing in the human heart; and so we may see them (if we look forward) rising up forever, and disappearing, like vapourish bubbles, in the human breast! After being tossed about from congregation to congregation in the heats of the Unitarian controversy, and squabbles about the American war, he had been relegated to an obscure village, where he was to spend the last thirty years of his life, far from the only converse that he loved, the talk about disputed texts of Scripture and the cause of civil and religious liberty. Here he passed his days, repining but resigned, in the study of the Bible, and the perusal of the Commentators,—huge folios, not easily got through, one of which would outlast a winter! Why did he pore on these from morn to night (with the exception of a walk in the fields or a turn in the garden to gather broccoli-plants or kidney-beans of his own rearing, with no small degree of pride and pleasure)? Here were 'no figures nor no fantasies,'[18]—neither poetry nor philosophy—nothing to dazzle, nothing to excite modern curiosity; but to his lack-lustre eyes there appeared, within the pages of the ponderous, unwieldy, neglected tomes, the sacred name of JEHOVAH in Hebrew capitals: pressed down by the weight of the style, worn

---

12 divine right (of kings).
13 *Lycidas,* 106.
14 Thomson, *The Castle of Indolence,* II, 295.
15 Ibid. I, 507.

16 *Hamlet,* III, iv, 153. *pursy* means *scant of breath.*
17 the celebrated political economist, 1723–90.
18 *Julius Caesar,* II, i, 231.

to the last fading thinness of the understanding, there were glimpses, glimmering notions of the patriarchal wanderings, with palm-trees hovering in the horizon, and processions of camels at the distance of three thousand years; there was Moses with the Burning Bush, the number of the Twelve Tribes, types, shadows, glosses on the law and the prophets; there were discussions (dull enough) on the age of Methuselah, a mighty speculation! there were outlines, rude guesses at the shape of Noah's Ark and of the riches of Solomon's Temple; questions as to the date of the creation, predictions of the end of all things; the great lapses of time, the strange mutations of the globe were unfolded with the voluminous leaf, as it turned over; and though the soul might slumber with an hieroglyphic veil of inscrutable mysteries drawn over it, yet it was in a slumber ill-exchanged for all the sharpened realities of sense, wit, fancy, or reason. My father's life was comparatively a dream; but it was a dream of infinity and eternity, of death, the resurrection, and a judgement to come!

No two individuals were ever more unlike than were the host and his guest. A poet was to my father a sort of nondescript: yet whatever added grace to the Unitarian cause was to him welcome. He could hardly have been more surprised or pleased, if our visitor had worn wings. Indeed, his thoughts had wings; and as the silken sounds rustled round our little wainscotted parlour, my father threw back his spectacles over his forehead, his white hairs mixing with its sanguine hue; and a smile of delight beamed across his rugged cordial face, to think that Truth had found a new ally in Fancy![19] Besides, Coleridge seemed to take considerable notice of me, and that of itself was enough. He talked very familiarly, but agreeably, and glanced over a variety of subjects. At dinner-time he grew more animated, and dilated in a very edifying manner on Mary Wolstonecraft[20] and Mackintosh.[21] The last, he said, he considered (on my father's speaking of his *Vindiciæ Gallicæ* as a capital performance) as a clever scholastic man—a master of the topics,—or as the ready warehouseman of letters, who knew exactly where to lay his hand on what he wanted, though the goods were not his own. He thought him no match for Burke, either in style or matter. Burke was a metaphysician, Mackintosh a mere logician. Burke was an orator (almost a poet) who reasoned in figures, because he had an eye for nature: Mackintosh, on the other hand, was a rhetorician, who had only an eye to commonplaces. On this I ventured to say that I had always entertained a great opinion of Burke, and that (as far as I could find) the speaking of him with contempt might be made the test of a vulgar democratical mind. This was the first observation I ever made to Coleridge, and he said it was a very just and striking one. I remember the leg of Welsh mutton and the turnips on the table that day had the finest flavour imaginable. Coleridge added that Mackintosh and Tom Wedgwood[22] (of whom, however, he spoke highly) had expressed a very indifferent opinion of his friend Mr. Wordsworth, on which he remarked to them—'He strides on so far before you, that he dwindles in the distance!' Godwin had once boasted to him of having carried on an argument with Mackintosh for three hours with dubious success; Coleridge told him—'If there had been a man of genius in the room, he would have settled the question in five minutes.' He asked me if I had ever seen Mary Wolstonecraft, and I said, I had once for a few moments, and that she seemed to me to turn off Godwin's objections to something she advanced with quite a playful, easy air. He replied, that 'this was only one instance of the ascendancy which people of imagination exercised over those of mere intellect.' He did not rate Godwin very high[23] (this was caprice or prejudice, real or affected) but he had a great idea of Mrs. Wolstonecraft's powers of conversation, none at all of her talent for book-making. We talked a little about Holcroft.[24] He had been asked if he was not much struck *with* him, and he said, he thought himself in more danger of being struck *by* him. I complained that he would not let me get on at all, for he required a definition of even the commonest word, exclaiming, 'What do you mean by a *sensation*, Sir? What do you mean by an *idea*?' This, Coleridge said, was barricadoing the road to truth:—it was setting up a turnpike-gate at every

19 My father was one of those who mistook his talent after all. He used to be very much dissatisfied that I preferred his Letters to his Sermons. The last were forced and dry; the first came naturally from him. For ease, half-plays on words, and a supine, monkish, indolent pleasantry, I have never seen them equalled. —(Hazlitt.)

20 author of *Vindication of the Rights of Woman*, 1792. See text, p. 187.

21 Sir James Mackintosh, 1765–1832, philosopher and historian, who wrote *Vindiciae Gallicae*, 1791, in answer to Burke's attack on the French Revolution.

22 second son, 1771–1805, of the famous potter Josiah Wedgwood.

23 He complained in particular of the presumption of his attempting to establish the future immortality of man, 'without' (as he said) 'knowing what Death was, or what Life was'—and the tone in which he pronounced these two words seemed to convey a complete image of both.—(Hazlitt.)

24 Thomas Holcroft, 1745–1809, actor and dramatist.

step we took. I forget a great number of things, many more than I remember; but the day passed off pleasantly, and the next morning Mr. Coleridge was to return to Shrewsbury. When I came down to breakfast, I found that he had just received a letter from his friend, T. Wedgwood, making him an offer of £150 a year if he chose to waive his present pursuit, and devote himself entirely to the study of poetry and philosophy. Coleridge seemed to make up his mind to close with this proposal in the act of tying on one of his shoes. It threw an additional damp on his departure. It took the wayward enthusiast quite from us to cast him into Deva's[25] winding vales, or by the shores of old romance. Instead of living at ten miles distance, of being the pastor of a Dissenting congregation at Shrewsbury, he was henceforth to inhabit the Hill of Parnassus, to be a Shepherd on the Delectable Mountains.[26] Alas! I knew not the way thither, and felt very little gratitude for Mr. Wedgwood's bounty. I was presently relieved from this dilemma; for Mr. Coleridge asking for a pen and ink, and going to a table to write something on a bit of card, advanced towards me with undulating step, and giving me the precious document, said that that was his address, *Mr. Coleridge, Nether-Stowey, Somersetshire;* and that he should be glad to see me there in a few weeks' time, and, if I chose, would come half-way to meet me. I was not less surprised than the shepherd-boy (this simile is to be found in *Cassandra*)[27] when he sees a thunder-bolt fall close at his feet. I stammered out my acknowledgements and acceptance of this offer (I thought Mr. Wedgwood's annuity a trifle to it) as well as I could; and this mighty business being settled, the poet-preacher took leave, and I accompanied him six miles on the road. It was a fine morning in the middle of winter, and he talked the whole way. The scholar in Chaucer is described as going

Sounding on his way.[28]

So Coleridge went on his. In digressing, in dilating, in passing from subject to subject, he appeared to me to float in air, to slide on ice. He told me in confidence (going along) that he should have preached two sermons before he accepted the situation at Shrewsbury, one on Infant Baptism, the other on the Lord's Supper, shewing that he could not administer either, which would have effectually disqualified him for the object in view. I observed that he continually crossed me on the way by shifting from one side of the foot-path to the other. This struck me as an odd movement; but I did not at that time connect it with any instability of purpose or involuntary change of principle, as I have done since. He seemed unable to keep on in a straight line. He spoke slightingly of Hume[29] (whose *Essay on Miracles* he said was stolen from an objection started in one of South's Sermons[30]—*Credat Judœus Apella*![31]). I was not very much pleased at this account of Hume, for I had just been reading, with infinite relish, that completest of all metaphysical *choke-pears,* his *Treatise on Human Nature,* to which the *Essays,* in point of scholastic subtlety and close reasoning, are mere elegant trifling, light summer-reading. Coleridge even denied the excellence of Hume's general style, which I think betrayed a want of taste or candour. He however made me amends by the manner in which he spoke of Berkeley.[32] He dwelt particularly on his *Essay on Vision* as a masterpiece of analytical reasoning. So it undoubtedly is. He was exceedingly angry with Dr. Johnson for striking the stone with his foot, in allusion to this author's *Theory of Matter and Spirit,* and saying, 'Thus I confute him, Sir.'[33] Coleridge drew a parallel (I don't know how he brought about the connection) between Bishop Berkeley and Tom Paine. He said the one was an instance of a subtle, the other of an acute, mind, than which no two things could be more distinct. The one was a shop-boy's quality, the other the characteristic of a philosopher. He considered Bishop Butler[34] as a true philosopher, a profound and conscientious thinker, a genuine reader of nature and of his own mind. He did not speak of his *Analogy,* but of his *Sermons at the Rolls' Chapel,* of which I had never heard. Coleridge somehow always contrived to prefer the *unknown* to the *known.* In this instance he was right. The *Analogy* is a tissue of sophistry, of wire-drawn, theological special-pleading; the *Sermons* (with the Preface to them) are in a fine vein of deep, matured reflection, a candid appeal to our

---

25 the ancient Latin name for the Dee, a river which flows through Chester to the Irish Sea.

26 in *Pilgrim's Progress* Christian and Hopeful come to the Shepherds of the Delectable Mountains after their escape from Giant Despair.

27 a French heroic romance, popular in the seventeenth century.

28 Chaucer, *Prologue to the Canterbury Tales,* 307.

29 David Hume, 1711-76, famous Scottish philosopher and historian.

30 Robert South, 1634-1716, noted English theologian.

31 'Let the Jew Apella believe it'—Horace, *Satires,* I, v, 100.

32 George Berkeley, 1685-1753, Irish bishop and philosopher whose *Essay on Vision* was published in 1709.

33 See Boswell's *Life* (Hill's ed.), I, 471.

34 Joseph Butler, 1692-1752, English divine and philosopher.

observation of human nature, without pedantry and without bias. I told Coleridge I had written a few remarks, and was sometimes foolish enough to believe that I had made a discovery on the same subject (the *Natural Disinterestedness of the Human Mind*[35])—and I tried to explain my view of it to Coleridge, who listened with great willingness, but I did not succeed in making myself understood. I sat down to the task shortly afterwards for the twentieth time, got new pens and paper, determined to make clear work of it, wrote a few meagre sentences in the skeleton-style of a mathematical demonstration, stopped half-way down the second page; and, after trying in vain to pump up any words, images, notions, apprehensions, facts, or observations, from that gulf of abstraction in which I had plunged myself for four or five years preceding, gave up the attempt as labour in vain, and shed tears of helpless despondency on the blank unfinished paper. I can write fast enough now. Am I better than I was then? Oh no! One truth discovered, one pang of regret at not being able to express it, is better than all the fluency and flippancy in the world. Would that I could go back to what I then was! Why can we not revive past times as we can revisit old places? If I had the quaint Muse of Sir Philip Sidney to assist me, I would write a *Sonnet to the Road between W——m and Shrewsbury,* and immortalise every step of it by some fond enigmatical conceit. I would swear that the very milestones had ears, and that Harmer-hill stooped with all its pines, to listen to a poet, as he passed! I remember but one other topic of discourse in this walk. He mentioned Paley,[36] praised the naturalness and clearness of his style, but condemned his sentiments, thought him a mere time-serving casuist, and said that 'the fact of his work on *Moral and Political Philosophy* being made a text-book in our Universities was a disgrace to the national character.' We parted at the six-mile stone; and I returned homewards, pensive but much pleased. I had met with unexpected notice from a person, whom I believed to have been prejudiced against me. 'Kind and affable to me had been his condescension, and should be honoured ever with suitable regard.'[37] He was the first poet I had known, and he certainly answered to that inspired name. I had heard a great deal of his powers of conversation, and was not disappointed. In fact, I never met with anything at all like them, either before or since. I could easily credit the accounts which were circulated of his holding forth to a large party of ladies and gentlemen, an evening or two before, on the Berkeleian Theory, when he made the whole material universe look like a transparency of fine words; and another story (which I believe he has somewhere told himself)[38]—of his being asked to a party at Birmingham, of his smoking tobacco and going to sleep after dinner on a sofa, where the company found him, to their no small surprise, which was increased to wonder when he started up of a sudden, and rubbing his eyes, looked about him, and launched into a three-hours' description of the third heaven, of which he had had a dream, very different from Mr. Southey's *Vision of Judgement* and also from that other *Vision of Judgment*,[39] which Mr. Murray, the Secretary of the Bridgestreet Junto,[40] has taken into his especial keeping!

On my way back, I had a sound in my ears, it was the voice of Fancy: I had a light before me, it was the face of Poetry. The one still lingers there, the other has not quitted my side! Coleridge in truth met me half-way on the ground of philosophy, or I should not have been won over to his imaginative creed. I had an uneasy, pleasurable sensation all the time, till I was to visit him. During those months the chill breath of winter gave me a welcoming; the vernal air was balm and inspiration to me. The golden sunsets, the silver star of evening, lighted me on my way to new hopes and prospects. *I was to visit Coleridge in the spring.* This circumstance was never absent from my thoughts, and mingled with all my feelings. I wrote to him at the time proposed, and received an answer postponing my intended visit for a week or two, but very cordially urging me to complete my promise then. This delay did not damp, but rather increased, my ardour. In the meantime I went to Llangollen Vale,[41] by way of initiating myself in the mysteries of natural scenery; and I must say I was enchanted with it. I had been reading Coleridge's description of England, in his fine *Ode on the Departing Year,* and I applied it, *con amore,* to the objects before me. That valley was to me (in a manner) the cradle of a new existence: in the river that winds through it, my spirit was baptized in the waters of Helicon!

I returned home, and soon after set out on my

---

35 published by Hazlitt in 1805.
36 William Paley, 1743–1805, English theologian and philosopher.
37 *Paradise Lost,* VIII, 648–50.
38 *Biographia Literaria,* chap. x.
39 by Lord Byron (text, p. 913).
40 The Tory *Quarterly Review* was published by Murray in Bridge Street, London,
41 in Wales, about forty miles from Wem.

journey with unworn heart and untried feet. My way lay through Worcester and Gloucester, and by Upton, where I thought of Tom Jones and the adventure of the muff.[42] I remember getting completely wet through one day, and stopping at an inn (I think it was at Tewkesbury) where I sat up all night to read *Paul and Virginia*.[43] Sweet were the showers in early youth that drenched my body, and sweet the drops of pity that fell upon the books I read! I recollect a remark of Coleridge's upon this very book, that nothing could shew the gross indelicacy of French manners and the entire corruption of their imagination more strongly than the behaviour of the heroine in the last fatal scene, who turns away from a person on board the sinking vessel, that offers to save her life, because he has thrown off his clothes to assist him in swimming. Was this a time to think of such a circumstance? I once hinted to Wordsworth, as we were sailing in his boat on Grasmere lake, that I thought he had borrowed the idea of his *Poems on the Naming of Places* from the local inscriptions of the same kind in *Paul and Virginia*. He did not own the obligation, and stated some distinction without a difference, in defence of his claim to originality. Any the slightest variation would be sufficient for this purpose in his mind; for whatever *he* added or omitted would inevitably be worth all that any one else had done, and contain the marrow of the sentiment. I was still two days before the time fixed for my arrival, for I had taken care to set out early enough. I stopped these two days at Bridgewater, and when I was tired of sauntering on the banks of its muddy river, returned to the inn, and read *Camilla*.[44] So have I loitered my life away, reading books, looking at pictures, going to plays, hearing, thinking, writing on what pleased me best. I have wanted only one thing to make me happy; but wanting that, have wanted everything!

I arrived, and was well received. The country about Nether Stowey is beautiful, green and hilly, and near the seashore. I saw it but the other day, after an interval of twenty years, from a hill near Taunton. How was the map of my life spread out before me, as the map of the country lay at my feet! In the afternoon Coleridge took me over to All-Foxden, a romantic old family-mansion of the St. Aubins, where Wordsworth lived. It was then in the possession of a friend of the poet's, who gave him the free use of it.[45] Somehow that period (the time just after the French Revolution) was not a time when *nothing was given for nothing*. The mind opened, and a softness might be perceived coming over the heart of individuals, beneath 'the scales that fence' our self-interest. Wordsworth himself was from home, but his sister kept house, and set before us a frugal repast; and we had free access to her brother's poems, the *Lyrical Ballads*, which were still in manuscript, or in the form of *Sybilline Leaves*. I dipped into a few of these with great satisfaction, and with the faith of a novice. I slept that night in an old room with blue hangings, and covered with the round-faced family-portraits of the age of George I and II and from the wooded declivity of the adjoining park that overlooked my window, at the dawn of day, could

Hear the loud stag speak.[46]

In the outset of life (and particularly at this time I felt it so) our imagination has a body to it. We are in a state between sleeping and waking, and have indistinct but glorious glimpses of strange shapes, and there is always something to come better than what we see. As in our dreams the fulness of the blood gives warmth and reality to the coinage of the brain, so in youth our ideas are clothed, and fed, and pampered with our good spirits; we breathe thick with thoughtless happiness, the weight of future years presses on the strong pulses of the heart, and we repose with undisturbed faith in truth and good. As we advance, we exhaust our fund of enjoyment and of hope. We are no longer wrapped in *lamb's-wool*, lulled in Elysium. As we taste the pleasures of life, their spirit evaporates, the sense palls; and nothing is left but the phantoms, the lifeless shadows of what *has been!*

That morning, as soon as breakfast was over, we strolled out into the park, and seating ourselves on the trunk of an old ash-tree that stretched along the ground, Coleridge read aloud with a sonorous and musical voice *The Ballad of Betty Foy*. I was not critically or skeptically inclined. I saw touches of truth and nature, and took the rest for granted. But in *The Thorn, The Mad Mother,* and *The Complaint of a Poor Indian Woman,* I felt that deeper power and pathos which have been since acknowledged,

---

42 in Fielding's *Tom Jones*, x, v.
43 an idyllic French romance by Bernardin de Saint Pierre.
44 the novel by Fanny Burney.

45 Wordsworth paid a rental of £23 for the year he occupied Alfoxden.
46 Ben Jonson, *To Sir Robert Wroth*.

In spite of pride, in erring reason's spite,[47]

as the characteristics of this author; and the sense of a new style and a new spirit in poetry came over me. It had to me something of the effect that arises from the turning up of the fresh soil, or of the first welcome breath of spring:

While yet the trembling year is unconfirmed.[48]

Coleridge and myself walked back to Stowey that evening, and his voice sounded high

Of Providence, foreknowledge, will, and fate,
Fix'd fate, free-will, foreknowledge absolute,[49]

as we passed through echoing grove, by fairy stream or waterfall, gleaming in the summer moonlight! He lamented that Wordsworth was not prone enough to believe in the traditional superstitions of the place, and that there was a something corporeal, a *matter-of-fact-ness*, a clinging to the palpable, or often to the petty, in his poetry, in consequence. His genius was not a spirit that descended to him through the air; it sprung out of the ground like a flower, or unfolded itself from a green spray, on which the gold-finch sang. He said, however (if I remember right) that this objection must be confined to his descriptive pieces, that his philosophic poetry had a grand and comprehensive spirit in it, so that his soul seemed to inhabit the universe like a palace, and to discover truth by intuition, rather than by deduction. The next day Wordsworth arrived from Bristol at Coleridge's cottage. I think I see him now. He answered in some degree to his friend's description of him, but was more gaunt and Don Quixote-like. He was quaintly dressed (according to the *costume* of that unconstrained period) in a brown fustian jacket and striped pantaloons. There was something of a roll, a lounge, in his gait, not unlike his own Peter Bell. There was a severe, worn pressure of thought about his temples, a fire in his eye (as if he saw something in objects more than the outward appearance), an intense high narrow forehead, a Roman nose, cheeks furrowed by strong purpose and feeling, and a convulsive inclination to laughter about the mouth, a good deal at variance with the solemn, stately expression of the rest of his face. Chantry's bust[50] wants the marking traits; but he was teazed into making it

regular and heavy: Haydon's head[51] of him, introduced into *The Entrance of Christ into Jerusalem,* is the most like his drooping weight of thought and expression. He sat down and talked very naturally and freely, with a mixture of clear, gushing accents in his voice, a deep guttural intonation, and a strong tincture of the northern *burr,*[52] like the crust on wine. He instantly began to make havoc of the half of a Cheshire cheese on the table, and said triumphantly that 'his marriage with experience had not been so unproductive as Mr. Southey's in teaching him a knowledge of the good things of this life.' He had been to see *The Castle Spectre,*[53] by Monk Lewis, while at Bristol, and described it very well. He said 'it fitted the taste of the audience like a glove.' This *ad captandum*[54] merit was however by no means a recommendation of it, according to the severe principles of the new school, which reject rather than court popular effect. Wordsworth, looking out of the low, latticed window, said, 'How beautifully the sun sets on that yellow bank!' I thought within myself, 'With what eyes these poets see nature!' and ever after, when I saw the sunset stream upon the objects facing it, conceived I had made a discovery, or thanked Mr. Wordsworth for having made one for me! We went over to All-Foxden again the day following, and Wordsworth read us the story of *Peter Bell* in the open air; and the comment made upon it by his face and voice was very different from that of some later critics! Whatever might be thought of the poem, 'his face was as a book where men might read strange matters,'[55] and he announced the fate of his hero in prophetic tones. There is a *chaunt* in the recitation both of Coleridge and Wordsworth, which acts as a spell upon the hearer, and disarms the judgement. Perhaps they have deceived themselves by making habitual use of this ambiguous accompaniment. Coleridge's manner is more full, animated, and varied; Wordsworth's more equable, sustained, and internal. The one might be termed more *dramatic,* the other more *lyrical.* Coleridge has told me that he himself liked to compose in walking over uneven ground, or breaking through the straggling branches of a copsewood; whereas Wordsworth always wrote

---

47 Pope, *An Essay on Man,* I, 293.
48 Thomson, *The Seasons, Spring,* 18.
49 *Paradise Lost,* II, 559–60.
50 Sir Francis Chantrey, 1781–1842, executed a bust of Wordsworth in 1820.

51 the famous painting by Benjamin Robert Haydon, 1786–1846, exhibited in 1820, included, among others, portraits of Hazlitt, Keats, and Wordsworth.
52 that is, he rolled his *r*'s.
53 produced at Drury Lane in 1797.
54 designed to win popular applause.
55 *Macbeth,* I, v, 63.

(if he could) walking up and down a straight gravel-walk, or in some spot where the continuity of his verse met with no collateral interruption. Returning that same evening, I got into a meta-physical argument with Wordsworth, while Cole-ridge was explaining the different notes of the nightingale to his sister, in which we neither of us succeeded in making ourselves perfectly clear and intelligible. Thus I passed three weeks at Nether Stowey and in the neighbourhood, gener-ally devoting the afternoons to a delightful chat in an arbour made of bark by the poet's friend Tom Poole, sitting under two fine elm-trees, and listening to the bees humming round us, while we quaffed our *flip*.[56] It was agreed, among other things, that we should make a jaunt down the Bristol-Channel, as far as Linton. We set off to-gether on foot, Coleridge, John Chester, and I. This Chester was a native of Nether Stowey, one of those who were attracted to Coleridge's dis-course as flies are to honey, or bees in swarming-time to the sound of a brass pan. He 'followed in the chase like a dog who hunts, not like one that made up the cry.'[57] He had on a brown cloth coat, boots, and corduroy breeches, was low in stature, bow-legged, had a drag in his walk like a drover, which he assisted by a hazel switch, and kept on a sort of trot by the side of Cole-ridge, like a running footman by a state coach, that he might not lose a syllable or sound, that fell from Coleridge's lips. He told me his private opinion, that Coleridge was a wonderful man. He scarcely opened his lips, much less offered an opinion the whole way: yet of the three, had I to choose during that journey, I would be John Chester. He afterwards followed Coleridge into Germany, where the Kantean philosophers were puzzled how to bring him under any of their cate-gories. When he sat down at table with his idol, John's felicity was complete; Sir Walter Scott's or Mr. Blackwood's, when they sat down at the same table with the King,[58] was not more so. We passed Dunster on our right, a small town be-tween the brow of a hill and the sea. I remem-ber eying it wistfully as it lay below us: con-trasted with the woody scene around, it looked as clear, as pure, as *embrowned* and ideal as any landscape I have seen since, of Gasper Poussin's or Domenichino's.[59] We had a long day's march

—(our feet kept time to the echoes of Cole-ridge's tongue)—through Minehead and by the Blue Anchor, and on to Linton, which we did not reach till near midnight, and where we had some difficulty in making a lodgment. We however knocked the people of the house up at last, and we were repaid for our apprehensions and fa-tigue by some excellent rashers of fried bacon and eggs. The view in coming along had been splendid. We walked for miles and miles on dark brown heaths overlooking the channel, with the Welsh hills beyond, and at times descended into little sheltered valleys close by the sea-side, with a smuggler's face scowling by us, and then had to ascend conical hills with a path winding up through a coppice to a barren top, like a monk's shaven crown, from one of which I pointed out to Coleridge's notice the bare masts of a vessel on the very edge of the horizon and within the red-orbed disk of the setting sun, like his own spectre-ship in *The Ancient Mariner*. At Linton the character of the sea-coast becomes more marked and rugged. There is a place called *The Valley of Rocks* (I suspect this was only the poetical name for it) bedded among precipices overhanging the sea, with rocky caverns beneath, into which the waves dash, and where the sea-gull forever wheels its screaming flight. On the tops of these are huge stones thrown transverse, as if an earthquake had tossed them there, and behind these is a fretwork of perpendicular rocks, something like *The Giant's Causeway*.[60] A thunder-storm came on while we were at the inn, and Coleridge was running out bareheaded to en-joy the commotion of the elements in *The Valley of Rocks,* but as if in spite, the clouds only mut-tered a few angry sounds, and let fall a few re-freshing drops. Coleridge told me that he and Wordsworth were to have made this place the scene of a prose-tale, which was to have been in the manner of, but far superior to, *The Death of Abel,*[61] but they had relinquished the design. In the morning of the second day, we breakfasted luxuriously in an old-fashioned parlour, on tea, toast, eggs, and honey, in the very sight of the bee-hives from which it had been taken, and a garden full of thyme and wild flowers that had produced it. On this occasion Coleridge spoke of Virgil's *Georgics,* but not well. I do not think he had much feeling for the classical or elegant. It was in this room that we found a little worn-out

56 hot spiced liquor.
57 *Othello,* II, iii, 370.
58 probably a reference to the banquet given by the magistrates of Edinburgh to George IV, 24 August 1822.
59 Gasper Poussin, 1613–75, French landscape painter; Domenico Zampieri, 1581–1641, noted Italian painter.

60 a celebrated rock formation on the north coast of Ireland.
61 by Solomon Gessner, 1730–88, a Swiss idyllic poet and land-scape painter.

copy of *The Seasons,* lying in a window-seat, on which Coleridge exclaimed, '*That* is true fame!' He said Thomson was a great poet, rather than a good one; his style was as meretricious as his thoughts were natural. He spoke of Cowper as the best modern poet. He said the *Lyrical Ballads* were an experiment about to be tried by him and Wordsworth, to see how far the public taste would endure poetry written in a more natural and simple style than had hitherto been attempted; totally discarding the artifices of poetical diction, and making use only of such words as had probably been common, in the most ordinary language since the days of Henry II. Some comparison was introduced between Shakespeare and Milton. He said 'he hardly knew which to prefer. Shakespeare appeared to him a mere stripling in the art; he was as tall and as strong, with infinitely more activity than Milton, but he never appeared to have come to man's estate; or if he had, he would not have been a man, but a monster.' He spoke with contempt of Gray, and with intolerance of Pope. He did not like the versification of the latter. He observed that 'the ears of these couplet-writers might be charged with having short memories, that could not retain the harmony of whole passages.' He thought little of Junius[62] as a writer; he had a dislike of Dr. Johnson; and a much higher opinion of Burke as an orator and politician, than of Fox or Pitt. He however thought him very inferior in richness of style and imagery to some of our elder prose-writers, particularly Jeremy Taylor. He liked Richardson, but not Fielding; nor could I get him to enter into the merits of *Caleb Williams.*[63] In short, he was profound and discriminating with respect to those authors whom he liked, and where he gave his judgement fair play; capricious, perverse, and prejudiced in his antipathies and distastes. We loitered on the 'ribbed sea-sands,'[64] in such talk as this, a whole morning, and I recollect met with a curious sea-weed, of which John Chester told us the country name! A fisherman gave Coleridge an account of a boy that had been drowned the day before, and that they had tried to save him at the risk of their own lives. He said 'he did not know how it was that they ventured, but, sir, we have a *nature* towards one another.' This expression, Coleridge remarked to me, was a fine illustration of that theory of disinterestedness which I (in common with Butler) had adopted. I

broached to him an argument of mine to prove that *likeness* was not mere association of ideas. I said that the mark in the sand put one in mind of a man's foot, not because it was part of a former impression of a man's foot (for it was quite new) but because it was like the shape of a man's foot. He assented to the justness of this distinction (which I have explained at length elsewhere, for the benefit of the curious), and John Chester listened; not from any interest in the subject, but because he was astonished that I should be able to suggest anything to Coleridge that he did not already know. We returned on the third morning, and Coleridge remarked the silent cottage-smoke curling up the valleys where, a few evenings before, we had seen the lights gleaming through the dark.

In a day or two after we arrived at Stowey, we set out, I on my return home, and he for Germany. It was a Sunday morning, and he was to preach that day for Dr. Toulmin of Taunton. I asked him if he had prepared anything for the occasion? He said he had not even thought of the text, but should as soon as we parted. I did not go to hear him,—this was a fault,—but we met in the evening at Bridgewater. The next day we had a long day's walk to Bristol, and sat down, I recollect, by a well-side on the road, to cool ourselves and satisfy our thirst, when Coleridge repeated to me some descriptive lines of his tragedy of *Remorse,* which I must say became his mouth and that occasion better than they, some years after, did Mr. Elliston's and the Drury-lane boards,—

Oh memory! shield me from the world's poor strife,
And give those scenes thine everlasting life.

I saw no more of him for a year or two, during which period he had been wandering in the Hartz Forest in Germany; and his return was cometary, meteorous, unlike his setting out. It was not till some time after that I knew his friends Lamb and Southey. The last always appears to me (as I first saw him) with a common-place-book under his arm, and the first with a *bon-mot* in his mouth. It was at Godwin's that I met him with Holcroft and Coleridge, where they were disputing fiercely which was the best—*Man as he was, or man as he is to be.* 'Give me,' says Lamb, 'man as he is *not* to be.' This saying was the beginning of a friendship between us, which I believe still continues.— Enough of this for the present.

---

62 pseudonym of an unknown writer of a series of political pamphlets attacking the government of George III.
63 famous political novel by William Godwin, published in 1794.

64 *The Rime of the Ancient Mariner,* 227.

But there is matter for another rhyme,
And I to this may add a second tale.[65]

1823

ON THE FEELING OF IMMORTALITY IN YOUTH

Life is a pure flame, and we live by an invisible sun within us.—SIR THOMAS BROWNE.[1]

No young man believes he shall ever die. It was a saying of my brother's,[2] and a fine one. There is a feeling of Eternity in youth, which makes us amends for everything. To be young is to be as one of the Immortal Gods. One half of time indeed is flown—the other half remains in store for us with all its countless treasures; for there is no line drawn, and we see no limit to our hopes and wishes. We make the coming age our own.—

The vast, the unbounded prospect lies before us.[3]

Death, old age, are words without a meaning, that pass by us like the idle air which we regard not. Others may have undergone, or may still be liable to them—we 'bear a charmed life,'[4] which laughs to scorn all such sickly fancies. As in setting out on a delightful journey, we strain our eager gaze forward—

Bidding the lovely scenes at distance hail,[5]—

and see no end to the landscape, new objects presenting themselves as we advance; so, in the commencement of life, we set no bounds to our inclinations, nor to the unrestricted opportunities of gratifying them. We have as yet found no obstacle, no disposition to flag; and it seems that we can go on so forever. We look round in a new world, full of life, and motion, and ceaseless progress; and feel in ourselves all the vigour and spirit to keep pace with it, and do not foresee from any present symptoms how we shall be left behind in the natural course of things, decline into old age, and drop into the grave. It is the simplicity, and as it were *abstractedness* of our feelings in youth, that (so to speak) identifies us with nature, and (our experience being slight and our passions strong) deludes us into a belief of being immortal like it. Our short-lived con-

nexion with existence, we fondly flatter ourselves, is an indissoluble and lasting union—a honeymoon that knows neither coldness, jar, nor separation. As infants smile and sleep, we are rocked in the cradle of our wayward fancies, and lulled into security by the roar of the universe around us—we quaff the cup of life with eager haste without draining it, instead of which it only overflows the more—objects press around us, filling the mind with their magnitude and with the throng of desires that wait upon them, so that we have no room for the thoughts of death. From that plenitude of our being, we cannot change all at once to dust and ashes, we cannot imagine 'this sensible, warm motion, to become a kneaded clod'[6]—we are too much dazzled by the brightness of the waking dream around us to look into the darkness of the tomb. We no more see our end than our beginning: the one is lost in oblivion and vacancy, as the other is hid from us by the crowd and hurry of approaching events. Or the grim shadow is seen lingering in the horizon, which we are doomed never to overtake, or whose last, faint, glimmering outline touches upon Heaven and translates us to the skies! Nor would the hold that life has taken of us permit us to detach our thoughts from present objects and pursuits, even if we would. What is there more opposed to health, than sickness; to strength and beauty, than decay and dissolution; to the active search of knowledge than mere oblivion? Or is there none of the usual advantage to bar the approach of Death, and mock his idle threats; Hope supplies their place, and draws a veil over the abrupt termination of all our cherished schemes. While the spirit of youth remains unimpaired, ere the 'wine of life is drank up,'[7] we are like people intoxicated or in a fever, who are hurried away by the violence of their own sensations: it is only as present objects begin to pall upon the sense, as we have been disappointed in our favourite pursuits, cut off from our closest ties, that passion loosens its hold upon the breast, that we by degrees become weaned from the world, and allow ourselves to contemplate, 'as in a glass, darkly,'[8] the possibility of parting with it for good. The example of others, the voice of experience, has no effect upon us whatever. Casualties we must avoid: the slow and deliberate advances of age we can play at *hide-and-seek* with. We think ourselves too lusty and too nimble for that blear-eyed decrepit old gentleman to catch

---

65 Wordsworth, *Hart-leap Well*, 95–6.

1 *Hydriotaphia: Urn Burial,* chap. V.
2 John Hazlitt, the painter.
3 Addison, *Cato,* V, i, 13.
4 *Macbeth,* V, viii, 12.
5 Collins, *The Passions,* 32.

6 *Measure for Measure,* III, i, 120.
7 *Macbeth,* II, iii, 100.
8 I Corinthians, xiii, 12.

us. Like the foolish fat scullion, in Sterne,[9] when she hears that Master Bobby is dead, our only reflection is—'So am not I!' The idea of death, instead of staggering our confidence, rather seems to strengthen and enhance our possession and our enjoyment of life. Others may fall around us like leaves, or be mowed down like flowers by the scythe of Time: these are but tropes and figures to the unreflecting ears and overweening presumption of youth. It is not till we see the flowers of Love, Hope, and Joy, withering around us, and our own pleasures cut up by the roots, that we bring the moral home to ourselves, that we abate something of the wanton extravagance of our pretensions, or that the emptiness and dreariness of the prospect before us reconciles us to the stillness of the grave!

> Life! thou strange thing, thou hast a power to feel
> Thou art, and to perceive that others are.[10]

Well might the poet begin his indignant invective against an art, whose professed object is its destruction, with this animated apostrophe to life. Life is indeed a strange gift, and its privileges are most miraculous. Nor is it singular that when the splendid boon is first granted us, our gratitude, our admiration, and our delight should prevent us from reflecting on our own nothingness, or from thinking it will ever be recalled. Our first and strongest impressions are taken from the mighty scene that is opened to us, and we very innocently transfer its durability as well as magnificence to ourselves. So newly found, we cannot make up our minds to parting with it yet and at least put off that consideration to an indefinite term. Like a clown at a fair, we are full of amazement and rapture, and have no thoughts of going home, or that it will soon be night. We know our existence only from external objects, and we measure it by them. We can never be satisfied with gazing; and nature will still want us to look on and applaud. Otherwise, the sumptuous entertainment, 'the feast of reason and the flow of soul,'[11] to which we were invited, seems little better than a mockery and a cruel insult. We do not go from a play till the scene is ended, and the lights are ready to be extinguished. But the fair face of things still shines on; shall we be called away, before the curtain falls, or ere we have scarce had a glimpse of what is going on?

Like children, our step-mother Nature holds us up to see the raree-show[12] of the universe; and then, as if life were a burthen to support, lets us instantly down again. Yet in that short interval, what 'brave sublunary things'[13] does not the spectacle unfold; like a bubble, at one minute reflecting the universe, and the next, shook to air!—To see the golden sun and the azure sky, the outstretched ocean, to walk upon the green earth, and to be lord of a thousand creatures, to look down giddy precipices or over distant flowery vales, to see the world spread out under one's finger in a map, to bring the stars near, to view the smallest insects in a microscope, to read history, and witness the revolutions of empires and the succession of generations, to hear of the glory of Sidon and Tyre, of Babylon and Susa, as of a faded pageant, and to say all these were, and are now nothing, to think that we exist in such a point of time, and in such a corner of space, to be at once spectators and a part of the moving scene, to watch the return of the seasons of spring and autumn, to hear

> The stockdove plain amid the forest deep,
> That drowsy rustles to the sighing gale[14]—

to traverse desert wildernesses, to listen to the midnight choir, to visit lighted halls, or plunge into the dungeon's gloom, or sit in crowded theatres and see life itself mocked, to feel heat and cold, pleasure and pain, right and wrong, truth and falsehood, to study the works of art and refine the sense of beauty to agony, to worship fame and to dream of immortality, to have read Shakespeare and belong to the same species as Sir Isaac Newton;[15] to be and to do all this, and

---

9 *Tristram Shandy*, v, vii.
10 *The Art of War*, 1795, by Joseph Fawcett, dissenting minister and early influential friend of Hazlitt.
11 Pope, *Imitations of Horace*, Satire I, 128.

12 cheap street show.
13 Drayton, *To Henry Reynolds*, 106.
14 Thomson, *The Castle of Indolence*, I, 33–4.
15 Lady Wortley Montagu says, in one of her letters, that 'she would much rather be a rich *effendi*,[a] with all his ignorance, than Sir Isaac Newton, with all his knowledge.' This was not perhaps an impolitic choice, as she had a better chance of becoming one than the other, there being many rich effendis to one Sir Isaac Newton. The wish was not a very intellectual one. The same petulance of rank and sex breaks out everywhere in these *Letters*. She is constantly reducing the poets or philosophers who have the misfortune of her acquaintance, to the figure they might make at her Ladyship's levee or toilette, not considering that the public mind does not sympathize with this process of a fastidious imagination. In the same spirit, she declares of Pope and Swift, that 'had it not been for the *good-nature* of mankind, these two superior beings were entitled, by their birth and hereditary fortune, to be only a couple of link-boys.'[b] *Gulliver's Travels*, and *The Rape of the Lock*, go for nothing in this critical estimate, and the world raised the authors to the rank of superior beings, in spite of their disadvantages of birth and fortune, *out of pure good-nature!* So again, she says of Richardson, that he had never got beyond the servant's hall, and was utterly unfit to describe the manners of people of quality; till in the capricious workings of her vanity, she persuades herself that Clarissa is very like what she was at her

then in a moment to be nothing, to have it all snatched from one like a juggler's ball or a phantasmagoria; there is something revolting and in-

age, and that Sir Thomas and Lady Grandison strongly resembled what she had heard of her mother and remembered of her father. It is one of the beauties and advantages of literature, that it is the means of abstracting the mind from the narrowness of local and personal prejudices, and of enabling us to judge of truth and excellence by their inherent merits alone. Woe be to the pen that would undo this fine illusion (the only reality), and teach us to regulate our notions of genius and virtue by the circumstances in which they happen to be placed! You would not expect a person whom you saw in a servant's hall, or behind a counter, to write *Clarissa;* but after he had written the work, to *pre-judge* it from the situation of the writer, is an unpardonable piece of injustice and folly. His merit could only be the greater from the contrast. If literature is an elegant accomplishment, which none but persons of birth and fashion should be allowed to excel in, or to exercise with advantage to the public, let them by all means take upon them the task of enlightening and refining mankind; if they decline this responsibility as too heavy for their shoulders, let those who do the drudgery in their stead, however inadequately, for want of their polite example, receive the meed that is their due, and not be treated as low pretenders who have encroached upon the provinces of their betters. Suppose Richardson to have been acquainted with the great man's steward, or valet, instead of the great man himself, I will venture to say that there was more difference between him who lived in an *ideal world,* and had the genius and felicity to open that world to others, and his friend the steward, than between the lacquey and the mere lord, or between those who lived in different rooms of the same house, who dined on the same luxuries at different tables, who rode outside or inside of the same coach, and were proud of wearing or of bestowing the same tawdry livery. If the lord is distinguished from his valet by anything else, it is by education and talent, which he has in common with the author. But if the latter shows these in the highest degree, it is asked What are his pretensions? Not birth or fortune, for neither of these would enable him to write *Clarissa.* One man is born with a title and estate, another with genius. That is sufficient; and we have no right to question the genius for want of the *gentility,* unless the former ran in families, or could be bequeathed with a fortune, which is not the case. Were it so, the flowers of literature, like jewels and embroidery, would be confined to the fashionable circles; and there would be no pretenders to taste or elegance but those whose names were found in the court list. No one objects to Claude's Landscapes as the work of a pastry-cook, or withholds from Raphael the epithet of *divine,* because his parents were not rich. This impertinence is confined to men of letters; the evidence of the senses baffles the envy and foppery of mankind. No quarter ought to be given to this *aristocratic* tone of criticism whenever it appears. People of quality are not contented with carrying all the external advantages for their own share, but would persuade you that all the intellectual ones are packed up in the same bundle. Lord Byron was a later instance of this double and unwarrantable style of pretension—*monstrum ingens, biforme.*[c] He could not endure a wit who was not a wit, nor a poet who was not a lord. Nobody but himself answered to his own standard of perfection. Mr. Moore carries a proxy in his pocket from some noble persons to estimate literary merit by the same rule. Lady Mary calls Fielding names, but she afterwards makes atonement by doing justice to his frank, free, hearty nature, where she says 'his spirits gave him raptures with his cookmaid, and cheerfulness when he was starving in a garret, and his happy constitution made him forget everything when he was placed before a venison-pasty or over a flask of champagne.' She does not want shrewdness and spirit when her petulance and conceit do not get the better of her, and she has done ample and merited execution on Lord Bolingbroke. She is, however, very angry at the freedoms taken with the Great; *smells a rat* in this indiscriminate scribbling, and the familiarity of writers with the reading public; and inspired by her Turkish costume, foretells a French and English revolution as the consequence of transferring the patronage of letters from the *quality* to the mob, and of supposing that ordinary writers or readers can have any notions in common with their superiors.—(Hazlitt.)

[[a] a Turkish term of respect; [b] torchbearers; [c] 'a huge, shapeless monster.']

credible to sense in the transition, and no wonder that, aided by youth and warm blood, and the flush of enthusiasm, the mind contrives for a long time to reject it with disdain and loathing as a monstrous and improbable fiction, like a monkey on a housetop, that is loath, amidst its fine discoveries and specious antics, to be tumbled headlong into the street, and crushed to atoms, the sport and laughter of the multitude!

The change, from the commencement to the close of life, appears like a fable, after it has taken place; how should we treat it otherwise than as a chimera before it has come to pass. There are some things that happened so long ago, places or persons we have formerly seen, of which such dim traces remain, we hardly know whether it was sleeping or waking they occurred; they are like dreams within the dream of life, a mist, a film before the eye of memory, which, as we try to recall them more distinctly, elude our notice altogether. It is but natural that the lone interval that we thus look back upon, should have appeared long and endless in prospect. There are others so distinct and fresh, they seem but of yesterday—their very vividness might be deemed a pledge of their permanence. Then, however far back our impressions may go, we find others still older (for our years are multiplied in youth); descriptions of scenes that we had read, and people before our time, Priam[16] and the Trojan war; and even then, Nestor[17] was old and dwelt delighted on his youth, and spoke of the race, of heroes that were no more;—what wonder that, seeing this long line of being pictured in our minds, and reviving as it were in us, we should give ourselves involuntary credit for an indeterminate period of existence? In the Cathedral at Peterborough there is a monument to Mary, Queen of Scots, at which I used to gaze when a boy, while the events of the period, all that had happened since, passed in review before me. If all this mass of feeling and imagination could be crowded into a moment's compass, what might not the whole of life be supposed to contain? We are heirs of the past; we count upon the future as our natural reversion. Besides, there are some of our early impressions so exquisitely tempered, it appears that they must always last—nothing can add to or take away from their sweetness and purity—the first breath of spring, the hyacinth dipped in the dew, the mild lustre of the evening-star, the rainbow after a storm—while we have the full enjoyment

16　King Priam of Troy.
17　counselor of the Greeks in the Trojan War.

of these, we must be young; and what can ever alter us in this respect? Truth, friendship, love, books, are also proof against the canker of time; and while we live, but for them, we can never grow old. We take out a new lease of existence from the objects on which we set our affections, and become abstracted, impassive, immortal in them. We cannot conceive how certain sentiments should ever decay or grow cold in our breasts; and, consequently, to maintain them in their first youthful glow and vigour, the flame of life must continue to burn as bright as ever, or rather, they are the fuel that feed the sacred lamp, that kindle 'the purple light of love,'[18] and spread a golden cloud around our heads! Again, we not only flourish and survive in our affections (in which we will not listen to the possibility of a change, any more than we foresee the wrinkles on the brow of a mistress), but we have a farther guarantee against the thoughts of death in our favourite studies and pursuits and in their continual advance. Art we know is long; life, we feel, should be so too. We see no end of the difficulties we have to encounter: perfection is slow of attainment, and we must have time to accomplish it in. Rubens complained that when he had just learned his art, he was snatched away from it: we trust we shall be more fortunate! A wrinkle in an old head takes whole days to finish it properly: but to catch 'the Raphael grace, the Guido air,'[19] no limit should be put to our endeavours. What a prospect for the future! What a task we have entered upon! and shall we be arrested in the middle of it? We do not reckon our time thus employed lost, or our pains thrown away, or our progress slow—we do not droop or grow tired, but 'gain new vigour at our endless task';[20]—and shall Time grudge us the opportunity to finish what we have auspiciously begun, and have formed a sort of compact with nature to achieve? The fame of the great names we look up to is also imperishable; and shall not we, who contemplate it with such intense yearnings, imbibe a portion of ethereal fire, the *divinæ particula auræ,*[21] which nothing can extinguish? I remember to have looked at a print of Rembrandt for hours together, without being conscious of the flight of time, trying to resolve it into its component parts, to connect its strong and sharp gradations, to learn the secret of its reflected lights, and found neither satiety nor

pause in the prosecution of my studies. The print over which I was poring would last long enough; why should the idea of my mind, which was finer, more impalpable, perish before it? At this, I redoubled the ardour of my pursuit, and by the very subtlety and refinement of my inquiries, seemed to bespeak for them an exemption from corruption and the rude grasp of Death.[22]

Objects, on our first acquaintance with them, have that singleness and integrity of impression that it seems as if nothing could destroy or obliterate them, so firmly are they stamped and riveted on the brain. We repose on them with a sort of voluptuous indolence, in full faith and boundless confidence. We are absorbed in the present moment, or return to the same point—idling away a great deal of time in youth, thinking we have enough and to spare. There is often a local feeling in the air, which is as fixed as if it were of marble; we loiter in dim cloisters, losing ourselves in thought and in their glimmering arches; a winding road before us seems as long as the journey of life, and as full of events. Time and experience dissipate this illusion; and by reducing them to detail, circumscribe the limits of our expectations. It is only as the pageant of life passes by and the masques turn their backs upon us, that we see through the deception, or believe that the train will have an end. In many cases, the slow progress and monotonous texture of our lives, before we mingle with the world and are embroiled in its affairs, has a tendency to aid the same feeling. We have a difficulty, when left to ourselves, and without the resource of books or some more lively pursuit, to 'beguile the slow and creeping hours of time,'[23] and argue that if it moves on always at this tedious snail's-pace, it can never come to an end. We are willing to skip over certain portions of it that separate us from favourite objects, that irritate ourselves at the unnecessary delay. The young are prodigal of life from a superabundance of it; the old are tenacious on the same score, because they have little left, and cannot enjoy even what remains of it.

For my part, I set out in life with the French Revolution, and that event had considerable influence on my early feelings, as on those of others. Youth was then doubly such. It was the dawn of a new era, a new impulse had been given

---

18 Gray, *The Progress of Poesy,* 41.
19 Pope, *Moral Essays,* VIII, 36.
20 Cowper, *Charity,* 104.
21 'portions of the divine breath.'

22 Is it not this that frequently keeps artists alive so long, *viz.,* the constant occupation of their minds with vivid images, with little of the *wear-and-tear* of the body?—(Hazlitt.)
23 *As You Like It,* II, vii, 112.

to men's minds, and the sun of Liberty rose upon the sun of Life in the same day, and both were proud to run their race together. Little did I dream, while my first hopes and wishes went hand in hand with those of the human race, that long before my eyes should close, that dawn would be overcast, and set once more in the night of despotism— 'total eclipse!' Happy that I did not. I felt for years, and during the best part of my existence, *heart-whole* in that cause, and triumphed in the triumphs over the enemies of man! At that time, while the fairest aspirations of the human mind seemed about to be realised, ere the image of man was defaced and his breast mangled in scorn, philosophy took a higher, poetry could afford a deeper range. At that time, to read *The Robbers,*[24] was indeed delicious, and to hear

> From the dungeon of the tower time-rent,
> That fearful voice, a famish'd father's cry[25]

could be borne only amidst the fulness of hope, the crash of the fall of the strongholds of power, and the exulting sounds of the march of human freedom. What feelings the death-scene in *Don Carlos*[26] sent into the soul! In that headlong career of lofty enthusiasm, and the joyous opening of the prospects of the world and our own, the thought of death crossing it, smote doubly cold upon the mind; there was a stifling sense of oppression and confinement, an impatience of our present knowledge, a desire to grasp the whole of our existence in one strong embrace, to sound the mystery of life and death, and in order to put an end to the agony of doubt and dread, to burst through our prison-house, and confront the King of Terrors in his grisly palace!—As I was writing out this passage, my miniature picture when a child lay on the mantle-piece, and I took it out of the case to look at it. I could perceive few traces of myself in it; but there was the same placid brow, the dimpled mouth, the same timid, inquisitive glance as ever. But its careless smile did not seem to reproach me with having become recreant to the sentiments that were then sown in my mind, or with having written a sentence that could call up a blush in this image of ingenuous youth!

'That time is past with all its giddy raptures.'[27] Since the future was barred to my progress, I have turned for consolation to the past, gathering up the fragments of my early recollections, and putting them into a form that might live. It is thus, that when we find our personal and substantial identity vanishing from us, we strive to gain a reflected and substituted one in our thoughts: we do not like to perish wholly, and wish to bequeath our names at least to posterity. As long as we can keep alive our cherished thoughts and nearest interests in the minds of others, we do not appear to have retired altogether from the stage, we still occupy a place in the estimation of mankind, exercise a powerful influence over them, and it is only our bodies that are trampled into dust or dispersed to air. Our darling speculations still find favour and encouragement, and we make as good a figure in the eyes of our descendants, nay, perhaps, a better than we did in our life-time. This is one point gained; the demands of our self-love are so far satisfied. Besides, if by the proofs of intellectual superiority we survive ourselves in this world, by exemplary virtue or unblemished faith, we are taught to ensure an interest in another and a higher state of being, and to anticipate at the same time the applauses of men and angels.

> Even from the tomb the voice of nature cries;
> Even in our ashes live their wonted fires.[28]

As we advance in life, we acquire a keener sense of the value of time. Nothing else, indeed, seems of any consequence; and we become misers in this respect. We try to arrest its few last tottering steps, and to make it linger on the brink of the grave. We can never leave off wondering how that which has ever been should cease to be, and would still live on, that we may wonder at our own shadow, and when 'all the life of life is flown,'[29] dwell on the retrospect of the past. This is accompanied by a mechanical tenaciousness of whatever we possess, by a distrust and a sense of fallacious hollowness in all we see. Instead of the full, pulpy feeling of youth, everything is flat and insipid. The world is a painted witch, that puts us off with false shews and tempting appearances. The ease, the jocund gaiety, the unsuspecting security of youth are fled: nor can we, without flying in the face of common sense,

> From the last dregs of life, hope to receive
> What its first sprightly runnings could not give.[30]

---

24 a revolutionary drama by Schiller, 1759–1805.
25 Coleridge, *Sonnet to Schiller.*
26 Schiller's play, 1787.
27 Wordsworth, *Tintern Abbey,* 83–5.

28 Gray, *Elegy,* 91–2.
29 Burns, *Lament for James, Earl of Glencairn,* st. 6.
30 Dryden, *Aurengzebe,* IV, i, 41–2.

If we can slip out of the world without notice or mischance, can tamper with bodily infirmity, and frame our minds to the becoming composure of *still-life*, before we sink into total insensibility, it is as much as we ought to expect. We do not in the regular course of nature die all at once: we have mouldered away gradually long before; faculty after faculty, attachment after attachment, we are torn from ourselves piece-meal while living; year after year takes something from us; and death only consigns the last remnant of what we were to the grave. The revulsion is not so great, and a quiet *euthanasia*[31] is a winding-up of the plot, that is not out of reason or nature.

That we should thus in a manner outlive ourselves, and dwindle imperceptibly into nothing, is not surprising, when even in our prime the strongest impressions leave so little traces of themselves behind, and the last object is driven out by the succeeding one. How little effect is produced on us at any time by the books we have read, the scenes we have witnessed, the sufferings we have gone through! Think only of the variety of feelings we experience in reading an interesting romance, or being present at a fine play—what beauty, what sublimity, what soothing, what heart-rending emotions! You would suppose these would last forever, or at least subdue the mind to a correspondent tone and harmony—while we turn over the page, while the scene is passing before us, it seems as if nothing could ever after shake our resolution, that 'treason domestic, foreign levy, nothing could touch us farther!'[32] The first splash of mud we get, on entering the street, the first pettifogging shopkeeper that cheats us out of two-pence, and the whole vanishes clean out of our remembrance, and we become the idle prey of the most petty and annoying circumstances. The mind soars by an effort to the grand and lofty: it is at home, in the grovelling, the disagreeable, and the little. This happens in the height and hey-day of our existence, when novelty gives a stronger impulse to the blood and takes a faster hold of the brain, (I have known the impression on coming out of a gallery of pictures then last half a day)—as we grow old, we become more feeble and querulous, every object 'reverbs its own hollowness,'[33] and both worlds are not enough to satisfy the peevish importunity and extravagant presumption of our desires! There are a few superior, happy beings, who are born with a temper exempt from every trifling annoyance. This spirit sits serene and smiling as in its native skies, and a divine harmony (whether heard or not) plays around them. This is to be at peace. Without this, it is in vain to fly into deserts, or to build a hermitage on the top of rocks, if regret and ill-humour follow us there: and with this, it is needless to make the experiment. The only true retirement is that of the heart; the only true leisure is the repose of the passions. To such persons it makes little difference whether they are young or old; and they die as they have lived, with graceful resignation.

1827

---

31 mode of dying.

32 *Macbeth*, III, ii, 24-6.
33 *King Lear*, I, i, 156.

1785 · THOMAS DE QUINCEY · 1859

1785   Born 15 August at Manchester, son of a well-to-do merchant. Suffered several bereavements early in life, including the death of his father.

1797–1803   His schooling intermittent and irregular. At seventeen, ran away from the Manchester Grammar School, wandered through Wales, and passed a year in vagabondage in London, hiding out from his relatives and guardians.

1803–8   Was reconciled to his guardians and sent to Worcester College, Oxford, where his knowledge of Greek astonished the examiners. Made the acquaintanceship of Wordsworth and Coleridge.

1809–21   Left Oxford without taking a degree, and for a time led an unsettled life. Upon deciding on a literary career, took a lease on Dove Cottage, at Grasmere, after Wordsworth left it. Enjoyed the companionship of Wordsworth, Southey, and Wilson, though following his marriage in 1816 to a 'dalesman's daughter' he became estranged from Wordsworth.

1821–8   Removed to London to become a member of the staff of the *London Magazine,* for which he wrote *Confessions of an English Opium-Eater* (published in book form in 1822), *On the Knocking at the Gate in Macbeth,* and many other articles.

1828–59   Settled in Edinburgh, where he was associated with *Blackwood's Magazine,* the *Edinburgh Literary Gazette,* and *Tait's Edinburgh Magazine.* Contributed *Suspiria de Profundis, The English Mail Coach, On Murder Considered as One of the Fine Arts, Autobiographic Sketches, Literary Reminiscences,* et cetera. Published a novel, *Klosterheim* (1832), and *The Logic of Political Economy* (1844). After the death of his wife, lived his last twenty years in uneventful and eccentric solitude.

1859   Died 8 December in Edinburgh.

THOMAS DE QUINCEY was a scholar and a recluse with gentle habits and simple tastes, but ludicrously lacking in a grasp of practical considerations. After his marriage he had constant debts and pecuniary difficulties; and although he was always a great reader, it is doubtful whether he would ever have turned author except from necessity. But finding himself in his thirty-sixth year with a family to support he was compelled to write for bread and began accordingly the *Confessions of an English Opium-Eater* for the *London Magazine;* thenceforth he contributed an almost endless succession of articles to the magazines until his death. He turned out in all some 215 separate essays on a wide variety of subjects, for the most part historical, philosophical, and critical in character. His critical writings include estimates of Pope, Richter, Wordsworth, Coleridge, Lamb, and others; but except for his famous paper *On the Knocking at the Gate in Macbeth* and the classic paragraphs in the essay on Pope distinguishing between the literature of knowledge and the literature of power, he has not left us one other criticism that is quite satisfactory. Among the historical essays *The Revolt of the Tartars* and *Joan of Arc* are the best and are still good reading. But by far the greater part of De Quincey's voluminous writings on erudite subjects deserve the fate of neglect that has overtaken them. Their author's short-comings are those that are common to the magazine writer. He is chronically discursive and intricate, and lacking in any sustained effort of construction. He has an irritating habit of digression and of making a show of his learning. His humor is constantly degenerating into triviality or forced jocoseness. And he can be dull for pages. Yet his attainments were extensive, and his powers of mind extraordinary. After nine tenths of his work is set aside, there remains a comparatively large and distinct body of prose, chiefly autobiographical, upon which De Quincey may lay a just claim to greatness.

In a group of essays, or portions of essays, which may be designated dream rhapsodies or fantasies, De Quincey attempted to clothe in words his sensations, the tumults of his brain, and those impressions of the real and the ideal world which were blended and transfigured in his opium dreams. For him the psychological experiences of deep suffering or joy first attained their fullness of experience when reverberated from his dreams. He spoke of these self-revelations 'as a far higher class of writing than his philosophical or historical writings,' and, declaring for their originality, claimed them to be, unlike the matter-of-fact memoirs of Rousseau or St. Augustine, 'modes of impassioned prose, ranging under no precedents that I am aware of in any literature.' The dreams were not due to opium, though they were magnified and made beautiful by it. They were released by it and made recognizable as typical fragments of human experience, but without having any forced connection or allegorical meaning. Working from the dream world of unrelated images De Quincey aimed at a conscious reconstruction at once of the dream and its remembered causes. The dream fantasies taken altogether represent a modest bulk, but they opened up a totally new kind of art and marked the highest reach of De Quincey's genius. A few of the fantasies, such as *Savannah-la-Mar*, are more strictly in the nature of prose poems. But the best rise out of matter-of-fact, and not infrequently long, preparation, as in the Dream Fugue, where the slow-paced and infinitely detailed preparation of the first incident rises gradually but inevitably to the climactic vision of sudden death, then swells to the gorgeous and shattering heavenly revelation in the fugue itself. *Levana* belongs to this same pattern, with its starting point the prosaic discussion of the derivation and meaning of a word.

Apart from the dream rhapsodies De Quincey's genius shows itself best in narrative and reminiscence. In the *Autobiographic Sketches* and in the *Confessions* and the body of memoirs that surround these works we are given an absorbing picture of the author's early life. We are led far back into memories of his childhood and the brink of dreams to behold the molding of the dreamer and his idiosyncracies. In a series of related studies he has apotheosized childhood—'the glory of innocence made perfect.' There is more in the *Confessions* than in any other work of the elusive personality of the Opium Eater; of his fondness for isolation and secretiveness; his impracticality; his proneness to whims; his wide human fellow-feeling; his gentleness, honesty, and generosity; his lithe, active mind; his love of books, among which he unobtrusively let pass the 'hypocritic days.'

De Quincey developed a style that deliberately exalts its subject matter; a style not intended for constant use, but for use when passion and imagination required it. A master of rhetorical ingenuity, he uses with consummate skill every known device to achieve the peculiar splendor of his majestic prose harmonies. The sentences are for the most part periodic, holding the attention in suspense, with involutions and parentheses, 'cycle on epicycle,' until the 'full-orbed' close. The vocabulary is predominantly Latinized, rich and well-modulated, but also variegated, daring, and gorgeous. Personifications are used continually, as well as elaborate similes and vivid metaphors; and there is an overflowing fullness of allusion and illustration. Rhythms full and flexible beat through the paragraphs with elaborate and stately cadences. Sometimes the structure of his style becomes overladen with an 'unwieldy comprehensiveness,' and then falls to the level of sham-sublime, or near it. At other times, De Quincey's irresistible temptation to wander destroys unity. But discounting these and other occasional imperfections, for his successes we must accord De Quincey top place among the romantics as a writer of rhetorical prose. His only serious rival is Landor, but of the two, De Quincey is the less artificial and more spontaneous. In his wide-awake moods he could expound and describe the real world admirably and narrate skillfully. He displays broad sympathies, subtle humor, and rare pathos. But most of all he excels in soaring imagination. He is, without peer, the 'prince of dreamers.'

CONFESSIONS OF AN ENGLISH OPIUM-EATER

From PRELIMINARY CONFESSIONS

I HAVE often been asked how I came to be a regular opium-eater; and have suffered, very unjustly, in the opinion of my acquaintance, from being reputed to have brought upon myself all the sufferings which I shall have to record, by a long course of indulgence in this practice purely for the sake of creating an artificial state of pleasurable excitement. This, however, is a misrepresentation of my case. True it is, that for nearly ten years I did occasionally take opium for the sake of the exquisite pleasure it gave me: but, so long as I took it with this view, I was effectually protected from all material bad consequences by the necessity of interposing long intervals between the several acts of indulgence, in order to renew the pleasurable sensations. It was not for the purpose of creating pleasure, but of mitigating pain in the severest degree, that I first began to use opium as an article of daily diet. In the twenty-eighth year of my age, a most painful affection of the stomach, which I had first experienced about ten years before, attacked me in great strength. This affection had originally been caused by extremities of hunger, suffered in my boyish days. During the season of hope and redundant happiness which succeeded (that is, from eighteen to twenty-four) it had slumbered: for the three following years it had revived at intervals: and now, under unfavourable circumstances, from depression of spirits, it attacked me with a violence that yielded to no remedies but opium. As the youthful sufferings which first produced this derangement of the stomach, were interesting in themselves, and in the circumstances that attended them, I shall here briefly retrace them.

My father died when I was about seven years old, and left me to the care of four guardians. I was sent to various schools,[1] great and small, and was very early distinguished for my classical attainments, especially for my knowledge of Greek. At thirteen I wrote Greek with ease: and at fifteen my command of that language was so great that I not only composed Greek verses in lyric metres, but could converse in Greek fluently, and without embarrassment—an accomplishment which I have not since met with in any scholar of my times, and which, in my case, was owing to the practice of daily reading off the newspapers into the best Greek I could furnish *extempore:* for the necessity of ransacking my memory and invention for all sorts and combinations of periphrastic expressions, as equivalents for modern ideas, images, relations of things, etc., gave me a compass of diction which would never have been called out by a dull translation of moral essays, etc. 'That boy,' said one of my masters,[2] pointing the attention of a stranger to me, 'that boy could harangue an Athenian mob better than you or I could address an English one.' He who honoured me with this eulogy, was a scholar, 'and a ripe and good one'[3]: and, of all my tutors, was the only one whom I loved or reverenced. Unfortunately for me (and, as I afterwards learned, to this worthy man's great indignation), I was transferred to the care, first of a blockhead,[4] who was in a perpetual panic lest I should expose his ignorance; and finally, to that of a respectable scholar,[5] at the head of a great school on an ancient foundation. This man had been appointed to his situation by [Brasenose] College, Oxford; and was a sound, well-built scholar, but, like most men whom I have known from that college, coarse, clumsy, and inelegant. A miserable contrast he presented, in my eyes, to the Etonian brilliancy of my favourite master: and, besides, he could not disguise from my hourly notice the poverty and meagreness of his understanding. It is a bad thing for a boy to be, and to know himself, far beyond his tutors, whether in knowledge or in power of mind. This was the case, so far as regarded knowledge at

---

1 at Bath, at Winkfield, and at Manchester.
2 Dr. Morgan, of Bath Grammar School.
3 Shakespeare, *Henry VIII,* IV, ii, 51.
4 Mr. Spencer, master of Winkfield School.
5 Mr. Lawson, the head of Manchester Grammar School.

least, not with myself only: for the two boys, who jointly with myself composed the first form, were better Grecians than the head-master, though not more elegant scholars, nor at all more accustomed to sacrifice to the graces. When I first entered, I remember that we read Sophocles; and it was a constant matter of triumph to us, the learned triumvirate of the first form, to see our *Archididascalus,*[6] as he loved to be called, conning our lesson before we went up, and laying a regular train, with lexicon and grammar, for blowing up and blasting, as it were, any difficulties he found in the choruses; whilst *we* never condescended to open our books until the moment of going up, and were generally employed in writing epigrams upon his wig, or some such important matter. My two class-fellows were poor, and dependent for their future prospects at the university, on the recommendation of the head-master: but I, who had a small patrimonial property, the income of which was sufficient to support me at college, wished to be sent thither immediately. I made earnest representations on the subject to my guardians, but all to no purpose. One, who was more reasonable, and had more knowledge of the world than the rest, lived at a distance: two of the other three resigned all their authority into the hands of the fourth;[7] and this fourth, with whom I had to negotiate, was a worthy man in his way, but haughty, obstinate, and intolerant of all opposition to his will. After a certain number of letters and personal interviews, I found that I had nothing to hope for, not even a compromise of the matter, from my guardian; unconditional submission was what he demanded: and I prepared myself, therefore, for other measures. Summer was now coming on with hasty steps, and my seventeenth birthday was fast approaching, after which day I had sworn within myself that I would no longer be numbered amongst schoolboys. Money being what I chiefly wanted, I wrote to a woman of high rank,[8] who, though young herself, had known me from a child, and had latterly treated me with great distinction, requesting that she would 'lend' me five guineas. For upwards of a week no answer came; and I was beginning to despond, when, at length, a servant put into my hands a double letter, with a coronet on the seal. The letter was kind and obliging: the fair writer was on the sea-coast, and

in that way the delay had arisen: she enclosed double of what I had asked, and good-naturedly hinted that if I should *never* repay her it would not absolutely ruin her. Now, then, I was prepared for my scheme: ten guineas, added to about two which I had remaining from my pocket money, seemed to me sufficient for an indefinite length of time: and at that happy age, if no *definite* boundary can be assigned to one's power, the spirit of hope and pleasure makes it virtually infinite.

It is a just remark of Dr. Johnson's, and, what cannot often be said of his remarks, it is a very feeling one, that we never do anything consciously for the last time—of things, that is, which we have long been in the habit of doing—without sadness of heart.[9] This truth I felt deeply, when I came to leave [Manchester], a place which I did not love, and where I had not been happy. On the evening before I left [Manchester] forever, I grieved when the ancient and lofty school-room resounded with the evening service, performed for the last time in my hearing; and at night, when the muster-roll of names was called over, and mine, as usual, was called first, I stepped forward, and, passing the head-master, who was standing by, I bowed to him, and looked earnestly in his face, thinking to myself, 'He is old and infirm, and in this world I shall not see him again.' I was right: I never *did* see him again, nor ever shall. He looked at me complacently, smiled good-naturedly, returned my salutation, or rather my valediction, and we parted, though he knew it not, forever. I could not reverence him intellectually: but he had been uniformly kind to me, and had allowed me many indulgences: and I grieved at the thought of the mortification I should inflict upon him.

The morning came which was to launch me into the world, and from which my whole succeeding life has, in many important points, taken its colouring. I lodged in the head-master's house, and had been allowed, from my first entrance, the indulgence of a private room, which I used both as a sleeping-room and as a study. At half after three I rose, and gazed with deep emotion at the ancient towers of [the Collegiate Church], 'dressed in earliest light,' and beginning to crimson with the radiant lustre of a cloudless July morning. I was firm and immovable in my purpose: but yet agitated by anticipation of uncertain danger and troubles; and, if I could have

---

6 Greek for 'chief teacher.'
7 the Rev. Samuel Hall, curate at Salford near Manchester.
8 Lady Carbery, a friend of De Quincey's mother.

9 *The Idler,* No. 103.

foreseen the hurricane and perfect hail-storm of affliction which soon fell upon me, well might I have been agitated. To this agitation the deep peace of the morning presented an affecting contrast, and in some degree a medicine. The silence was more profound than that of midnight: and to me the silence of a summer morning is more touching than all other silence, because, the light being broad and strong, as that of noon-day at other seasons of the year, it seems to differ from perfect day chiefly because man is not yet abroad; and thus the peace of nature, and of the innocent creatures of God, seems to be secure and deep, only so long as the presence of man, and his restless and unquiet spirit, are not there to trouble its sanctity. I dressed myself, took my hat and gloves, and lingered a little in the room. For the last year and a half this room had been my 'pensive citadel'[10]: here I had read and studied through all the hours of night: and, though true it was that for the latter part of this time I, who was framed for love and gentle affections, had lost my gaiety and happiness, during the strife and fever of contention with my guardian; yet, on the other hand, as a boy so passionately fond of books, and dedicated to intellectual pursuits, I could not fail to have enjoyed many happy hours in the midst of general dejection. I wept as I looked round on the chair, hearth, writing-table, and other familiar objects, knowing too certainly that I looked upon them for the last time. Whilst I write this, it is eighteen years ago: and yet, at this moment, I see distinctly as if it were yesterday the lineaments and expression of the object on which I fixed my parting gaze: it was a picture of the lovely ———,[11] which hung over the mantle-piece; the eyes and mouth of which were so beautiful, and the whole countenance so radiant with benignity and divine tranquillity, that I had a thousand times laid down my pen or my book, to gather consolation from it, as a devotee from his patron saint. Whilst I was yet gazing upon it, the deep tones of [Manchester] clock proclaimed that it was four o'clock. I went up to the picture, kissed it, and then gently walked out, and closed the door forever!

*   *   *

So blended and intertwined in this life are occasions of laughter and of tears, that I cannot yet recall, without smiling, an incident which oc-

curred at that time, and which had nearly put a stop to the immediate execution of my plan. I had a trunk of immense weight; for, besides my clothes, it contained nearly all my library. The difficulty was to get this removed to a carrier's: my room was at an aerial elevation in the house, and (what was worse) the staircase, which communicated with this angle of the building, was accessible only by a gallery which passed the head-master's chamber-door. I was a favourite with all the servants; and, knowing that any of them would screen me, and act confidentially, I communicated my embarrassment to a groom of the head-master's. The groom swore he would do anything I wished; and, when the time arrived, went up stairs to bring the trunk down. This I feared was beyond the strength of any one man: however, the groom was a man—

> Of Atlantean shoulders, fit to bear
> The weight of mightiest monarchies[12]

and had a back as spacious as Salisbury plain.[13] Accordingly, he persisted in bringing down the trunk alone, whilst I stood waiting at the foot of the last flight, in anxiety for the event. For some time I heard him descending with slow and firm steps but, unfortunately, from his trepidation as he drew near the dangerous quarter, within a few steps of the gallery, his foot slipped; and the mighty burden, falling from his shoulders, gained such increase of impetus at each step of the descent, that, on reaching the bottom, it tumbled, or rather leaped, right across, with the noise of twenty devils, against the very bedroom door of the Archididascalus. My first thought was that all was lost, and that my only chance for executing a retreat was to sacrifice my baggage. However, on reflection, I determined to abide the issue. The groom was in the utmost alarm, both on his own account and on mine: but, in spite of this, so irresistibly had the sense of the ludicrous, in this unhappy *contretemps*,[14] taken possession of his fancy, that he sang out a long, loud, and canorous[15] peal of laughter, that might have wakened the Seven Sleepers.[16] At the sound of this resonant merriment, within the very ears of insulted authority, I could not myself forbear join-

10 Wordsworth, *Nuns' Fret Not,* 3.
11 The portrait was thought to be a copy from one of the old masters.
12 *Paradise Lost,* II, 305–7.
13 a wide undulating expanse in Wiltshire.
14 mishap.
15 ringing.
16 The Seven Sleepers of Ephesus were, according to legend, seven young Christians who hid themselves in a cave during the persecution under Decius, A.D. 201–51, and did not awaken until two centuries later.

ing in it: subdued to this, not so much by the unhappy *étourderie*[17] of the trunk, as by the effect it had upon the groom. We both expected, as a matter of course, that Dr. [Lawson] would sally out of his room: for, in general, if but a mouse stirred, he sprang out like a mastiff from his kennel. Strange to say, however, on this occasion, when the noise of laughter had ceased, no sound, or rustling even, was to be heard in the bedroom. Dr. [Lawson] had a painful complaint, which, sometimes keeping him awake, made his sleep, perhaps, when it *did* come, the deeper. Gathering courage from the silence, the groom hoisted his burden again, and accomplished the remainder of his descent without accident. I waited until I saw the trunk placed on a wheel-barrow, and on its road to the carrier's: then, 'with Providence my guide,'[18] I set off on foot,—carrying a small parcel, with some articles of dress, under my arm; a favourite English poet in one pocket; and a small 12mo volume, containing about nine plays of Euripides, in the other.

·   ·   ·

Soon after this, I contrived, by means which I must omit for want of room, to transfer myself to London. And now began the latter and fiercer stage of my long sufferings; without using a disproportionate expression, I might say, of my agony. For I now suffered, for upwards of sixteen weeks, the physical anguish of hunger in various degrees of intensity; but as bitter, perhaps, as ever any human being can have suffered who has survived it. I would not needlessly harass my reader's feelings by a detail of all that I endured: for extremities such as these, under any circumstances of heaviest misconduct or guilt, cannot be contemplated even in description without a rueful pity that is painful to the natural goodness of the human heart. Let it suffice, at least on this occasion, to say that a few fragments of bread from the breakfast-table of one individual,[19] who supposed me to be ill, but did not know of my being in utter want, and these at uncertain intervals, constituted my whole support. During the former part of my sufferings, that is, generally in Wales, and always for the first two months in London, I was houseless, and very seldom slept under a roof. To this constant exposure to the open air I ascribe it mainly that

I did not sink under my torments. Latterly, however, when colder and more inclement weather came on, and when, from the length of my sufferings, I had begun to sink into a more languishing condition, it was, no doubt, fortunate for me that the same person to whose breakfast-table I had access allowed me to sleep in a large unoccupied house, of which he was tenant. Unoccupied, I call it, for there was no household or establishment in it; nor any furniture indeed, except for a table and a few chairs. But I found, on taking possession of my new quarters, that the house already contained one single inmate, a poor friendless child, apparently ten years old; but she seemed hunger-bitten; and sufferings of that sort often make children look older than they are. From this forlorn child I learned that she had slept and lived there alone for some time before I came: and great joy the poor creature expressed, when she found that I was, in future, to be her companion through the hours of darkness. The house was large; and, from the want of furniture, the noise of the rats made a prodigious echoing on the spacious staircase and hall; and, amidst the real fleshly ills of cold, and, I fear, hunger, the forsaken child had found leisure to suffer still more, it appeared, from the self-created one of ghosts. I promised her protection against all ghosts whatsoever: but, alas! I could offer her no other assistance. We lay upon the floor, with a bundle of cursed law papers for a pillow: but with no other covering than a sort of large horseman's cloak: afterwards, however, we discovered, in a garret, an old sofa-cover, a small piece of rug, and some fragments of other articles, which added a little to our warmth. The poor child crept close to me for warmth, and for security against her ghostly enemies. When I was not more than usually ill, I took her into my arms, so that, in general, she was tolerably warm, and often slept when I could not: for, during the last two months of my sufferings, I slept much in the day-time, and was apt to fall into transient dozing at all hours. But my sleep distressed me more than my watching: for, besides the tumultuousness of my dreams, which were only not so awful as those which I shall have to describe hereafter as produced by opium, my sleep was never more than what is called *dogsleep;* so that I could hear myself moaning, and was often, as it seemed to me, wakened suddenly by my own voice; and, about this time, a hideous sensation began to haunt me as soon as I fell into a slum-

17 blunder.
18 *Paradise Lost,* XII, 647.
19 a Mr. Brunell, recommended to him by a money-lender named Dell.

ber, which has since returned upon me at differ-ent periods of my life, *viz.*, a sort of twitching, I know not where, but apparently about the re-gion of the stomach, which compelled me vio-lently to throw out my feet for the sake of reliev-ing it. This sensation coming on as soon as I began to sleep, and the effort to relieve it con-stantly awaking me, at length I slept only from exhaustion; and from increasing weakness, as I said before, I was constantly falling asleep, and constantly awaking. Meantime, the master of the house sometimes came in upon us suddenly, and very early, sometimes not till ten o'clock, some-times not at all. He was in constant fear of bailiffs: improving on the plan of Cromwell,[20] every night he slept in a different quarter of Lon-don; and I observed that he never failed to ex-amine through a private window the appearance of those who knocked at the door, before he would allow it to be opened. He breakfasted alone: indeed, his tea equipage would hardly have admitted of his hazarding an invitation to a second person—any more than the quantity of esculent[21] *matériel,* which for the most part, was little more than a roll, or a few biscuits, which he had bought on his road from the place where he had slept. Or, if he *had* asked a party, as I once learnedly and facetiously observed to him—the several members of it must have *stood* in the re-lation to each other (not *sat* in any relation what-ever) of succession, as the metaphysicians have it, and not of co-existence; in the relation of the parts of time, and not of the parts of space. Dur-ing his breakfast, I generally contrived a reason for lounging in; and, with an air of as much in-difference as I could assume, took up such frag-ments as he had left—sometimes, indeed, there were none at all. In doing this, I committed no robbery except upon the man himself, who was thus obliged, I believe, now and then to send out at noon for an extra biscuit; for, as to the poor child, *she* was never admitted into his study, if I may give that name to his chief depository of parchments, law writings, etc.; that room was to her the Bluebeard room of the house, being regu-larly locked on his departure to dinner, about six o'clock, which usually was his final departure for the night. Whether this child were an illegitimate daughter of Mr. [Brunell], or only a servant, I could not ascertain; she did not herself know;

but certainly she was treated altogether as a me-nial servant. No sooner did Mr. [Brunell] make his appearance, than she went below stairs, brushed his shoes, coat, etc.; and, except when she was summoned to run an errand, she never emerged from the dismal Tartarus[22] of the kitch-ens, etc., to the upper air, until my welcome knock at night called up her little trembling foot-steps to the front door. Of her life during the day-time, however, I knew little but what I gathered from her own account at night; for, as soon as the hours of business commenced, I saw that my ab-sence would be acceptable; and, in general, there-fore, I went off, and sat in the parks, or elsewhere, until nightfall. . . .

Except the Bluebeard room, which the poor child believed to be haunted, all others, from the attics to the cellars, were at our service; 'the world was all before us';[23] and we pitched our tent for the night in any spot we chose. This house I have already described as a large one; it stands in a conspicuous situation, and in a well-known part of London. Many of my readers will have passed it, I doubt not, within a few hours of reading this. For myself, I never fail to visit it when business draws me to London; about ten o'clock, this very night, August 15, 1821, being my birthday,—I turned aside from my evening walk, down Oxford Street, purposely to take a glance at it: it is now occupied by a respectable family; and, by the lights in the front drawing-room, I observed a domestic party, assembled perhaps at tea, and apparently cheerful and gay. Marvellous contrast in my eyes to the darkness —cold—silence—and desolation of that same house eighteen years ago, when its nightly occu-pants were one famishing scholar, and a neg-lected child.—Her, by the bye, in after years, I vainly endeavoured to trace. Apart from her sit-uation, she was not what would be called an interesting child: she was neither pretty, nor quick in understanding, nor remarkably pleasing in manners. But, thank God! even in those years I needed not the embellishments of novel acces-sories to conciliate my affections; plain human nature, in its humblest and most homely apparel, was enough for me: and I loved the child because she was my partner in wretchedness. If she is now living, she is probably a mother, with children of her own; but, as I have said, I could never trace her.

---

20 Royalist Tory historians spread the story that after the dissolu-tion of his last parliament Cromwell out of fear for his life lodged scarcely two nights together in the same place.
21 edible.

---

22 infernal region.
23 *Paradise Lost,* XII, 646.

This I regret, but another person there was at that time, whom I have since sought to trace with far deeper earnestness, and with far deeper sorrow at my failure. This person was a young woman, and one of that unhappy class who subsist upon the wages of prostitution. I feel no shame, nor have any reason to feel it, in avowing that I was then on familiar and friendly terms with many women in that unfortunate condition. The reader needs neither smile at this avowal, nor frown. For, not to remind my classical readers of the old Latin proverb—'*Sine Cerere,*'[24] etc., it may well be supposed that in the existing state of my purse my connexion with such women could not have been an impure one. But the truth is, that at no time of my life have I been a person to hold myself polluted by the touch or approach of any creature that wore a human shape: on the contrary, from my very earliest youth it has been my pride to converse familiarly, *more Socratico,*[25] with all human beings, man, woman, and child, that chance might fling in my way: a practice which is friendly to the knowledge of human nature, to good feelings, and to that frankness of address which becomes a man who would be thought a philosopher. For a philosopher should not see with the eyes of the poor limitary creature calling himself a man of the world, and filled with narrow and self-regarding prejudices of birth and education, but should look upon himself as a catholic creature, and as standing in an equal relation to high and low—to educated and uneducated, to the guilty and the innocent. Being myself at that time of necessity a peripatetic, or a walker of the streets, I naturally fell in more frequently with those female peripatetics who are technically called street-walkers. Many of these women had occasionally taken my part against watchmen who wished to drive me off the steps of houses where I was sitting. But one amongst them, the one on whose account I have at all introduced this subject—yet no! let me not class thee, oh noble-minded Ann ——, with that order of women; let me find, if it be possible, some gentler name to designate the condition of her to whose bounty and compassion, ministering to my necessities when all the world had forsaken me, I owe it that I am at this time alive. —For many weeks I had walked at nights with this poor friendless girl up and down Oxford Street, or had rested with her on steps and under the shelter of porticoes. She could not be so old as myself: she told me, indeed, that she had not completed her sixteenth year. By such questions as my interest about her prompted, I had gradually drawn forth her simple history. Hers was a case of ordinary occurrence (as I have since had reason to think), and one in which, if London beneficence had better adapted its arrangements to meet it, the power of the law might oftener be interposed to protect, and to avenge. But the stream of London charity flows in a channel which, though deep and mighty, is yet noiseless and underground; not obvious or readily accessible to poor houseless wanderers; and it cannot be denied that the outside air and frame-work of London society is harsh, cruel, and repulsive. In any case, however, I saw that part of her injuries might easily have been redressed; and I urged her often and earnestly to lay her complaint before a magistrate: friendless as she was, I assured her that she would meet with immediate attention; and that English justice, which was no respecter of persons, would speedily and amply avenge her on the brutal ruffian who had plundered her little property. She promised me often that she would; but she delayed taking the steps I pointed out from time to time: for she was timid and dejected to a degree which showed how deeply sorrow had taken hold of her young heart: and perhaps she thought justly that the most upright judge, and the most righteous tribunals, could do nothing to repair her heaviest wrongs. Something, however, would perhaps have been done: for it had been settled between us at length, but unhappily on the very last time but one that I was ever to see her, that in a day or two we should go together before a magistrate, and that I should speak on her behalf. This little service it was destined, however, that I should never realize. Meantime, that which she rendered to me, and which was greater than I could ever have repaid her, was this:—One night, when we were pacing slowly along Oxford Street, and after a day when I had felt more than usually ill and faint, I requested her to turn off with me into Soho Square; thither we went; and we sat down on the steps of a house, which, to this hour, I never pass without a pang of grief, and an inner act of homage to the spirit of that unhappy girl, in memory of the noble action which she there performed. Suddenly, as we sat, I grew much worse: I had been leaning my head against her bosom;

24 *Sine Cerere et Baccho friget Venus* [Without food and wine love grows cold].—Terence, *Eunuchus,* IV, v, 6.
25 'after the manner of Socrates.'

and all at once I sank from her arms and fell backwards on the step. From the sensations I then had, I felt an inner conviction of the liveliest kind that without some powerful and reviving stimulus, I should either have died on the spot—or should at least have sunk to a point of exhaustion from which all re-ascent under my friendless circumstances would soon have become hopeless. Then it was, at this crisis of my fate, that my poor orphan companion—who had herself met with little but injuries in this world—stretched out a saving hand to me. Uttering a cry of terror, but without a moment's delay, she ran off into Oxford Street, and in less time than could be imagined, returned to me with a glass of port wine and spices, that acted upon my empty stomach (which at that time would have rejected all solid food) with an instantaneous power of restoration: and for this glass the generous girl without a murmur paid out of her own humble purse at a time—be it remembered!—when she had scarcely wherewithal to purchase the bare necessaries of life, and when she could have no reason to expect that I should ever be able to reimburse her.——Oh! youthful benefactress! how often in succeeding years, standing in solitary places, and thinking of thee with grief of heart and perfect love, how often have I wished that, as in ancient times the curse of a father was believed to have a supernatural power, and to pursue its object with a fatal necessity of self-fulfilment,—even so the benediction of a heart oppressed with gratitude might have a like prerogative; might have power given it from above to chase—to haunt—to way-lay—to overtake—to pursue thee into the central darkness of a London brothel, or, if it were possible, into the darkness of the grave—there to awaken thee with an authentic message of peace and forgiveness, and of final reconciliation!

I do not often weep: for not only do my thoughts on subjects connected with the chief interests of man daily, nay hourly, descend a thousand fathoms 'too deep for tears,'[26] not only does the sternness of my habits of thought present an antagonism to the feelings which prompt tears—wanting of necessity to those who, being protected usually by their levity from any tendency to meditative sorrow, would by that same levity be made incapable of resisting it on any casual access of such feelings:—but also, I believe that all minds which have contemplated such objects as deeply as I have done, must, for their own protection from utter despondency, have early encouraged and cherished some tranquilizing belief as to the future balances and the hieroglyphic meanings of human sufferings. On these accounts, I am cheerful to this hour; and, as I have said, I do not often weep. Yet some feelings, though not deeper or more passionate, are more tender than others; and often, when I walk at this time in Oxford Street by dreamy lamp-light, and hear those airs played on a barrel-organ which years ago solaced me and my dear companion, as I must always call her, I shed tears, and muse with myself at the mysterious dispensation which so suddenly and so critically separated us forever.

.   .   .

From THE PLEASURES OF OPIUM

It is so long since I first took opium that if it had been a trifling incident in my life I might have forgotten its date: but cardinal events are not to be forgotten; and from circumstances connected with it I remember that it must be referred to the autumn of 1804. During that season I was in London, having come thither for the first time since my entrance at college. And my introduction to opium arose in the following way. From an early age I had been accustomed to wash my head in cold water at least once a day: being suddenly seized with tooth-ache, I attributed it to some relaxation caused by an accidental intermission of that practice; jumped out of bed; plunged my head into a basin of cold water; and with hair thus wetted went to sleep. The next morning, as I need hardly say, I awoke with excruciating rheumatic pains of the head and face, from which I had hardly any respite for about twenty days. On the twenty-first day, I think it was, and on a Sunday, that I went out into the streets, rather to run away, if possible, from my torments, than with any distinct purpose. By accident I met a college acquaintance who recommended opium. Opium! dread agent of unimaginable pleasure and pain! I had heard of it as I had of manna or of ambrosia, but no further: how unmeaning a sound was it at that time! what solemn chords does it now strike upon my heart! what heart-quaking vibrations of sad and happy remembrances! Reverting for a moment to these, I feel a mystic importance attached to the minutest circumstances connected with the place and the time, and the man, if man he was,

26 *Ode on Intimations of Immortality,* last line.

that first laid open to me the Paradise of Opium-eaters. It was a Sunday afternoon, wet and cheerless: and a duller spectacle this earth of ours has not to show than a rainy Sunday in London. My road homewards lay through Oxford Street; and near 'the *stately* Pantheon,'[27] as Mr. Wordsworth has obligingly called it, I saw a druggist's shop. The druggist, unconscious minister of celestial pleasures!—as if in sympathy with the rainy Sunday, looked dull and stupid, just as any mortal druggist might be expected to look on a Sunday; and, when I asked for the tincture of opium, he gave it to me as any other man might do: and furthermore, out of my shilling, returned me what seemed to be real copper halfpence, taken out of a real wooden drawer. Nevertheless, in spite of such indications of humanity, he has ever since existed in my mind as the beatific vision of an immortal druggist, sent down to earth on a special mission to myself. And it confirms me in this way of considering him, that, when I next came up to London, I sought him near the stately Pantheon, and found him not: and thus to me, who knew not his name (if indeed he had one), he seemed rather to have vanished from Oxford Street than to have removed in any bodily fashion. The reader may choose to think of him as, possibly, no more than a sublunary druggist: it may be so: but my faith is better: I believe him to have evanesced,[28] or evaporated. So unwillingly would I connect any mortal remembrances with that hour, and place, and creature, that first brought me acquainted with the celestial drug.

Arrived at my lodgings, it may be supposed that I lost not a moment in taking the quantity prescribed. I was necessarily ignorant of the whole art and mystery of opium-taking: and, what I took, I took under every disadvantage. But I took it:—and in an hour, oh! heavens! what a revulsion! what an upheaving, from its lowest depths, of the inner spirit! what an apocalypse of the world within me! That my pains had

vanished, was now a trifle in my eyes:—this negative effect was swallowed up in the immensity of those positive effects which had opened before me—in the abyss of divine enjoyment thus suddenly revealed. Here was a panacea—a φάρμακον νηπενθές [29] for all human woes; here was the secret of happiness, about which philosophers had disputed for so many ages, at once discovered: happiness might now be bought for a penny, and carried in the waistcoat pocket: portable ecstasies might be had corked up in a pint bottle: and peace of mind could be sent down in gallons by the mail-coach. But, if I talk in this way, the reader will think I am laughing: and I can assure him, that nobody will laugh long who deals much with opium: its pleasures even are of a grave and solemn complexion; and in his happiest state, the opium-eater cannot present himself in the character of 'L'Allegro'[30]: even then, he speaks and thinks as becomes 'Il Penseroso.'[30] Nevertheless, I have a very reprehensible way of jesting at times in the midst of my own misery: and, unless when I am checked by some more powerful feelings, I am afraid I shall be guilty of this indecent practice even in these annals of suffering or enjoyment. The reader must allow a little to my infirm nature in this respect: and with a few indulgences of that sort, I shall endeavour to be as grave, if not drowsy, as fits a theme like opium, so antimercurial as it really is, and so drowsy as it is falsely reputed. . . .

Certainly, opium is classed under the head of narcotics; and some such effect it may produce in the end: but the primary effects of opium are always, and in the highest degree, to excite and stimulate the system: this first stage of its action always lasted with me, during my noviciate, for upwards of eight hours: so that it must be the fault of the opium-eater himself if he does not so time his exhibition of the dose, to speak medically, as that the whole weight of its narcotic influence may descend upon his sleep. Turkish opium-eaters, it seems, are absurd enough to sit, like so many equestrian statues, on logs of wood as stupid as themselves. But that the reader may judge of the degree in which opium is likely to stupify the faculties of an Englishman, I shall, by way of treating the question illustratively, rather than argumentatively, describe the way in which I myself often passed an opium evening in Lon-

---

27 At the time De Quincey wrote, the Pantheon was a great concert hall.

28 This way of going off the stage of life appears to have been well known in the seventeenth century, but at that time to have been considered a peculiar privilege of blood-royal, and by no means to be allowed to druggists. For about the year 1686, a poet of rather ominous name (and who, by the by, did ample justice to his name)—*viz.,* Mr. *Flatman,* in speaking of the death of Charles II, expresses his surprise that any prince should commit so absurd an act as dying: because, says he,

> 'Kings should disdain to die, and only
> *disappear.*'

They should *abscond,* that is, into the other world.—(De Quincey.)

29 'drug banishing sorrow'—Homer, *Odyssey,* IV, 220.

30 *L'Allegro* and *Il Penseroso* are well-known descriptive poems by Milton. *L'Allegro* means 'the cheerful man,' and *Il Penseroso* 'the thoughtful man.'

don, during the period between 1804 and 1812. It will be seen that at least opium did not move me to seek solitude, and much less to seek inactivity, or the torpid state of self-involution ascribed to the Turks. I give this account at the risk of being pronounced a crazy enthusiast or visionary: but I regard *that* little: I must desire my reader to bear in mind that I was a hard student, and at severe studies for all the rest of my time: and certainly I had a right occasionally to relaxations as well as other people: these, however, I allowed myself but seldom.

The late Duke of [Norfolk] used to say, 'Next Friday, by the blessing of Heaven, I purpose to be drunk'; and in like manner I used to fix beforehand how often, within a given time, and when, I would commit a debauch of opium. This was seldom more than once in three weeks: for at that time I could not have ventured to call every day (as I did afterwards) for *'a glass of laudanum negus,*[31] *warm, and without sugar.'* No: as I have said, I seldom drank laudanum, at that time, more than once in three weeks: this was usually on a Tuesday or a Saturday night; my reason for which was this. In those days Grassini[32] sang at the Opera: and her voice was delightful to me beyond all that I had ever heard. I know not what may be the state of the Opera-house now, having never been within its walls for seven or eight years, but at that time it was by much the most pleasant place of public resort in London for passing an evening. Five shillings admitted one to the gallery, which was subject to far less annoyance than the pit of the theatres: the orchestra was distinguished by its sweet and melodious grandeur from all English orchestras, the composition of which, I confess, is not acceptable to my ear, from the predominance of the clangorous instruments, and the absolute tyranny of the violin. The choruses were divine to hear: and when Grassini appeared in some interlude, as she often did, and poured forth her passionate soul as Andromache at the tomb of Hector,[33] etc., I question whether any Turk, of all that ever entered the paradise of opium-eaters, can have had half the pleasure I had. But, indeed, I honour the Barbarians too much by supposing them capable of any pleasures approaching to the intellectual ones of an Englishman. For mu-

sic is an intellectual or a sensual pleasure, according to the temperament of him who hears it. And, by the by, with the exception of the fine extravaganza on that subject in *Twelfth Night,*[34] I do not recollect more than one thing said adequately on the subject of music in all literature; it is a passage in the *Religio Medici*[35] of Sir T. Brown; and, though chiefly remarkable for its sublimity, has also a philosophic value, inasmuch as it points to the true theory of musical effects. The mistake of most people is to suppose that it is by the ear they communicate with music, and, therefore, that they are purely passive to its effects. But this is not so: it is by the reaction of the mind upon the notices of the ear (the *matter* coming by the senses, the *form* from the mind) that the pleasure is constructed: and therefore it is that people of equally good ear differ so much in this point from one another. Now opium, by greatly increasing the activity of the mind generally, increases, of necessity, that particular mode of its activity by which we are able to construct out of the raw material of organic sound an elaborate intellectual pleasure. But, says a friend, a succession of musical sounds is to me like a collection of Arabic characters: I can attach no ideas to them. Ideas! my good sir? there is no occasion for them: all that class of ideas which can be available in such a case has a language of representative feelings. But this is a subject foreign to my present purpose: it is sufficient to say that a chorus, etc., of elaborate harmony, displayed before me, as in a piece of arras work, the whole of my past life—not as if recalled by an act of memory, but as if present and incarnated in the music; no longer painful to dwell upon: but the detail of its incidents removed, or blended in some hazy abstraction; and its passions exalted, spiritualized, and sublimed. All this was to be had for five shillings. And over and above the music of the stage and the orchestra, I had all around me, in the intervals of the performance, the music of the Italian language talked by Italian women: for the gallery was usually crowded with Italians: and I listened with a pleasure such as that with which Weld the traveller lay and listened, in Canada, to the sweet laughter of Indian women;[36] for the less you understand of a lan-

---

31 a hot beverage of wine, water, sugar, nutmeg, and lemon.

32 Josephina Grassini, 1773–1850, an Italian contralto who was a reigning London favorite at the opening of the century.

33 In Grétry's *Andromaque*, which was produced at Paris in 1780. Andromache was the wife of Hector, leader of the Trojans.

34 I, i, 1–7.

35 I have not the book at this moment to consult; but I think the passage begins—'And even that tavern music, which makes one man merry, another mad in me strikes a deep fit of devotion,' etc. —(De Quincey.) [The passage appears in Part II, sec. 9.]

36 The incident is recorded by I. Weld, Jr., in his *Travels through the States of North Carolina and the Provinces of Canada*, 1799, p. 411.

guage the more sensible you are to the melody or harshness of its sounds; for such a purpose, therefore, it was an advantage to me that I was a poor Italian scholar, reading it but little, and not speaking it at all, nor understanding a tenth part of what I heard spoken.

These were my Opera pleasures: but another pleasure I had which, as it could be had only on a Saturday night, occasionally struggled with my love of the Opera; for, at that time, Tuesday and Saturday were the regular Opera nights. On this subject I am afraid I shall be rather obscure, but, I can assure the reader, not at all more so than Marinus in his *Life of Proclus*,[37] or many other biographers and autobiographers of fair reputation. This pleasure, I have said, was to be had only on a Saturday night. What then was Saturday night to me more than any other night? I had no labours that I rested from; no wages to receive: what needed I to care for Saturday night, more than as it was a summons to hear Grassini? True, most logical reader: what you say is unanswerable. And yet so it was and is, that, whereas different men throw their feelings into different channels, and most are apt to show their interest in the concerns of the poor, chiefly by sympathy, expressed in some shape or other, with their distresses and sorrows, I, at that time, was disposed to express my interest by sympathizing with their pleasures. The pains of poverty I had lately seen too much of; more than I wished to remember: but the pleasures of the poor, their consolations of spirit, and their reposes from bodily toil, can never become oppressive to contemplate. Now Saturday night is the season for the chief, regular, and periodic return of rest to the poor: in this point the most hostile sects unite, and acknowledge a common link of brotherhood: almost all Christendom rests from its labours. It is a rest introductory to another rest: and divided by a whole day and two nights from the renewal of toil. On this account I feel always, on a Saturday night, as though I also were released from some yoke of labour, had some wages to receive, and some luxury of repose to enjoy. For the sake, therefore, of witnessing, upon as large a scale as possible, a spectacle with which my sympathy was so entire, I used often, on Saturday nights, after I had taken opium, to wander forth, without much regarding the direction or the distance, to all the markets and other parts of London to which the poor resort on a Saturday night for lay-

ing out their wages. Many a family party, consisting of a man, his wife, and sometimes one or two of his children, have I listened to, as they stood consulting on their ways and means, or the strength of their exchequer, or the price of household articles. Gradually I became familiar with their wishes, their difficulties, and their opinions. Sometimes there might be heard murmurs of discontent: but far oftener expressions on the countenance, or uttered in words, of patience, hope, and tranquility. And taken generally, I must say that, in this point at least, the poor are far more philosophic than the rich—that they show a more ready and cheerful submission to what they consider as irremediable evils, or irreparable losses. Whenever I saw occasion, or could do it without appearing to be intrusive, I joined their parties; and gave my opinion upon the matter in discussion, which, if not always judicious, was always received indulgently. If wages were a little higher, or expected to be so, or the quartern loaf[38] a little lower, or it was reported that onions and butter were expected to fall, I was glad: yet, if the contrary were true, I drew from opium some means of consoling myself. For opium, like the bee, that extracts its materials indiscriminately from roses and from the soot of chimneys, can overrule all feelings into a compliance with the master key. Some of these rambles led me to great distances: for an opium-eater is too happy to observe the motion of time. And sometimes in my attempts to steer homewards upon nautical principles, by fixing my eye on the pole-star, and seeking ambitiously for a northwest passage, instead of circumnavigating all the capes and headlands I had doubled in my outward voyage, I came suddenly upon such knotty problems of alleys, such enigmatical entries, and such sphinx's riddles of streets without thoroughfares, as must, I conceive, baffle the audacity of porters, and confound the intellects of hackney-coachmen. I could almost have believed, at times, that I must be the first discoverer of some of these *terræ incognitæ*,[39] and doubted whether they had yet been laid down in the modern charts of London. For all this, however, I paid a heavy price in distant years, when the human face tyrannized over my dreams, and the perplexities of my steps in London came back and haunted my sleep with the feeling of perplexities, moral or intellectual, that brought confu-

---

37 Marinus of Flavia Neapolis in Palestine was a disciple of the celebrated Neoplatonist philosopher Proclus, A.D. 410–85.

38 a loaf of bread weighing about four pounds.
39 unknown lands.

sion to the reason, or anguish and remorse to the conscience.

Thus I have shown that opium does not, of necessity, produce inactivity or torpor; but that, on the contrary, it often led me into markets and theatres. Yet, in candour, I will admit that markets and theatres are not the appropriate haunts of the opium-eater, when in the divinest state incident to his enjoyment. In that state, crowds become an oppression to him; music even, too sensual and gross. He naturally seeks solitude and silence, as indispensable conditions of those trances and profoundest reveries which are the crown or consummation of what opium can do for human nature. I, whose disease it was to meditate too much, and to observe too little, and who upon my first entrance at college was nearly falling into a deep melancholy from brooding too much on the sufferings which I had witnessed in London, was sufficiently aware of the tendencies of my own thoughts to do all I could to counteract them.—I was, indeed, like a person who, according to the old legend, had entered the cave of Trophonius;[40] and the remedies I sought were to force myself into society, and to keep my understanding in continual activity upon matters of science. But for these remedies, I should certainly have become hypochondriacally melancholy. In after years, however, when my cheerfulness was more fully re-established, I yielded to my natural inclination for a solitary life. And, at that time, I often fell into these reveries upon taking opium; and more than once it has happened to me, on a summer night, when I have been at an open window, in a room from which I could overlook the sea at a mile below me, and could command a view of the great town of L[iverpool], at about the same distance, that I have sat, from sunset to sun-rise, motionless, and without wishing to move.

I shall be charged with mysticism, Behmenism,[41] quietism, etc., but *that* shall not alarm me. Sir H. Vane, the Younger,[42] was one of our wisest men: and let my readers see if he, in his philosophical works, be half as unmystical as I am.— I say, then, that it has often struck me that the scene itself was somewhat typical of what took place in such a reverie. The town of L[iverpool] represented the earth, with its sorrows and its graves left behind, yet not out of sight, nor wholly forgotten. The ocean, in everlasting but gentle agitation, and brooded over by a dove-like calm, might not unfitly typify the mind and the mood which then swayed it. For it seemed to me as if then first I stood at a distance, and aloof from the uproar of life, as if the tumult, the fever, and the strife, were suspended; a respite granted from the secret burthens of the heart; a sabbath of repose; a resting from human labours. Here were the hopes which blossom in the paths of life, reconciled with the peace which is in the grave; motions of the intellect as unwearied as the heavens, yet for all anxieties a halcyon calm;[43] a tranquility that seemed no product of inertia, but as if resulting from mighty and equal antagonisms; infinite activities, infinite repose.

Oh! just, subtle, and mighty opium! that to the hearts of poor and rich alike, for the wounds that will never heal, and for 'the pangs that tempt the spirit to rebel,'[44] bringest an assuaging balm; eloquent opium! that with thy potent rhetoric stealest away the purposes of wrath; and to the guilty man for one night givest back the hopes of his youth, and hands washed pure from blood; and to the proud man a brief oblivion for

Wrongs unredress'd and insults unavenged;[45]

that summonest to the chancery of dreams, for the triumphs of suffering innocence, false witnesses; and confoundest perjury; and dost reverse the sentences of unrighteous judges:—thou buildest upon the bosom of darkness, out of the fantastic imagery of the brain, cities and temples beyond the art of Phidias and Praxiteles[46]—beyond the splendour of Babylon and Hekatompylos:[47] and 'from the anarchy of dreaming sleep,'[48] callest into sunny light the faces of long-buried beauties, and the blessed household countenances, cleansed from the 'dishonors of the grave.'[49] Thou only givest these gifts to man; and thou hast the keys of Paradise, oh, just, subtle, and mighty opium![50]

---

40 It was supposed that a visitor to the oracle in this cave never smiled again.

41 a type of religious mysticism derived from the teachings of the Lutheran philosopher, Jakob Böhme, 1575-1624.

42 Puritan statesman and patriot, 1613-62.

43 The halcyon was a bird fabled to nest on the sea and to calm the waves.

44 Wordsworth, *The White Doe of Rylstone*, Dedication, 36.

45 Wordsworth, *The Excursion*, III, 374.

46 celebrated Greek sculptors.

47 Hekatompylos, i.e. 'the hundred-gated,' is De Quincey's epithet for Thebes, ancient Egyptian capital of imposing temples and tombs. Babylon was famed for its Hanging Gardens, regarded as one of the seven wonders of the world.

48 Wordsworth, *Excursion*, IV, 87.

49 I Corinthians, xv, 43.

50 Adapted from the apostrophe to Death with which Walter Raleigh concludes his *History of the World:* 'O, eloquent, just, and mighty Death!' etc.

From INTRODUCTION TO THE PAINS OF OPIUM

If any man, poor or rich, were to say that he would tell us what had been the happiest day in his life, and the why, and the wherefore, I suppose that we should all cry out—Hear him! Hear him!—As to the happiest *day,* that must be very difficult for any wise man to name: because any event, that could occupy so distinguished a place in a man's retrospect of his life, or be entitled to have shed a special felicity on any one day, ought to be of such an enduring character, as that, accidents apart, it should have continued to shed the same felicity, or one not distinguishably less, on many years together. To the happiest *lustrum,*[51] however, or even to the happiest *year,* it may be allowed to any man to point without discountenance from wisdom. This year, in my case, reader, was the one which we have now reached,[52] though it stood, I confess, as a parenthesis between years of a gloomier character. It was a year of brilliant water, to speak after the manner of jewelers, set as it were, and insulated, in the gloom and cloudy melancholy of opium. Strange as it may sound, I had a little before this time descended suddenly, and without any considerable effort, from 320 grains of opium (*i.e.,* eight thousand drops of laudanum[53]) per day, to forty grains, or one-eighth part. Instantaneously, and as if by magic, the cloud of profoundest melancholy which rested upon my brain, like some black vapours that I have seen roll away from the summits of mountains, drew off in one day ($νυχθήμερον$ [54]); passed off with its murky banners as simultaneously as a ship that has been stranded, and is floated off by a spring tide—

That moveth altogether, if it move at all.[55]

Now, then, I was again happy: I now took only 1000 drops of laudanum per day: and what was that? A latter spring had come to close up the season of youth; my brain performed its functions as heathily as ever before: I read Kant

again; and again I understood him, or fancied that I did. Again my feelings of pleasure expanded themselves to all around me: and if any man from Oxford or Cambridge, or from neither, had been announced to me in my unpretending cottage, I should have welcomed him with as sumptuous a reception as so poor a man could offer. Whatever else was wanting to a wise man's happiness,—of laudanum I would have given him as much as he wished, and in a golden cup. And, by the way, now that I speak of giving laudanum away, I remember, about this time, a little incident, which I mention, because, trifling as it was, the reader will soon meet it again in my dreams, which it influenced more fearfully than could be imagined. One day a Malay knocked at my door.[56] What business a Malay could have to transact amongst English mountains, I cannot conjecture: but possibly he was on his road to a seaport about forty miles distant.

The servant who opened the door to him was a young girl born and bred amongst the mountains, who had never seen an Asiatic dress of any sort: his turban, therefore, confounded her not a little: and, as it turned out that his attainments in English were exactly of the same extent as hers in the Malay, there seemed to be an impassable gulf fixed between all communication of ideas, if either party had happened to possess any. In this dilemma, the girl, recollecting the reputed learning of her master, and doubtless giving me credit for a knowledge of all the languages of the earth, besides, perhaps, a few of the lunar ones, came and gave me to understand that there was a sort of demon below, whom she clearly imagined that my art could exorcise from the house. I did not immediately go down: but, when I did, the group which presented itself, arranged as it was by accident, though not very elaborate, took hold of my fancy and my eye in a way that none of the statuesque attitudes exhibited in the ballets at the Opera-house, though so ostentatiously complex, had ever done. In a cottage kitchen, but panelled on the wall with dark wood that from age and rubbing resembled oak, and looking more like a rustic hall of entrance than a kitchen, stood the Malay—his turban and loose trousers of dingy white relieved upon the dark panelling: he had placed himself nearer to the girl than she seemed to relish; though her native spirit of mountain intrepidity contended with the feeling of simple awe which her countenance expressed as she gazed upon the tiger-cat before her. And a more

51 period of five years.
52 that is, 1816.
53 I here reckon twenty-five drops of laudanum as equivalent to one grain of opium, which, I believe, is the common estimate. However, as both may be considered variable quantities (the crude opium varying much in strength, and the tincture still more), I suppose that no infinitesimal accuracy can be had in such a calculation. Tea-spoons vary as much in size as opium in strength. Small ones hold about 100 drops; so that 8000 drops are about eighty times a tea-spoonful. The reader sees how much I kept within Dr. Buchan's indulgent allowance.—(De Quincey.)
54 'a night and a day.'
55 Wordsworth, *Resolution and Independence,* 77.

56 This Malay has been thought by some to be fictitious.

striking picture there could not be imagined, than the beautiful English face of the girl, and its exquisite fairness, together with her erect and independent attitude, contrasted with the sallow and bilious skin of the Malay, enamelled or veneered with mahogany, by marine air, his small, fierce, restless eyes, thin lips, slavish gestures and adorations. Half-hidden by the ferocious looking Malay was a little child from a neighbouring cottage who had crept in after him, and was now in the act of reverting its head, and gazing upwards at the turban and the fiery eyes beneath it, whilst with one hand he caught at the dress of the young woman for protection. My knowledge of the Oriental tongues is not remarkably extensive, being indeed confined to two words—the Arabic word for barley, and the Turkish for opium (madjoon), which I have learnt from Anastasius.[57] And, as I had neither a Malay dictionary, nor even Adelung's *Mithridates,*[58] which might have helped me to a few words, I addressed him in some lines from the *Iliad,* considering that, of such languages as I possessed, Greek, in point of longitude, came geographically nearest to an Oriental one. He worshipped me in a most devout manner, and replied in what I suppose was Malay. In this way I saved my reputation with my neighbours for the Malay had no means of betraying the secret. He lay down upon the floor for about an hour, and then pursued his journey. On his departure, I presented him with a piece of opium. To him, as an Orientalist, I concluded that opium must be familiar: and the expression of his face convinced me that it was. Nevertheless, I was struck with some little consternation when I saw him suddenly raise his hand to his mouth, and, in the schoolboy phrase, bolt the whole, divided into three pieces, at one mouthful. The quantity was enough to kill three draggoons and their horses: and I felt some alarm for the poor creature: but what could be done? I had given him the opium in compassion for his solitary life, on recollecting that if he had travelled on foot from London it must be nearly three weeks since he could have exchanged a thought with any human being. I could not think of violating the laws of hospitality by having him seized and drenched with an emetic, and thus frightening him into a notion that we were going to sacrifice him to some English idol. No: there was clearly no help for it:—he took his leave: and

for some days I felt anxious: but as I never heard of any Malay being found dead, I became convinced that he was used[59] to opium: and that I must have done him the service I designed, by giving him one night of respite from the pains of wandering.

This incident I have digressed to mention, because this Malay, partly from the picturesque exhibition he assisted to frame, partly from the anxiety I connected with his image for some days, fastened afterwards upon my dreams, and brought other Malays with him worse than himself, that ran 'a-muck'[60] at me, and led me into a world of troubles.—But to quit this episode, and to return to my intercalary[61] year of happiness. I have said already, that on a subject so important to us all as happiness, we should listen with pleasure to any man's experience or experiments, even though he were but a plough-boy, who cannot be supposed to have ploughed very deep into such an intractable soil as that of human pains and pleasures, or to have conducted his researches upon any very enlightened principles. But I, who have taken happiness, both in a solid and a liquid shape, both boiled and unboiled, both East India and Turkey—who have conducted my experiments upon this interesting subject with a sort of galvanic battery—and have, for the general benefit of the world, inoculated myself, as it were, with the poison of 8000 drops of laudanum per day (just for the same reason as a French surgeon inoculated himself lately with cancer—an English one, twenty years ago, with plague—and a third, I know not of what nation, with hydrophobia),—I, it will be admitted, must surely know what happiness is, if anybody does. And, therefore, I will here lay down an analysis of happiness; and as the most interesting mode of communicating it, I will give it, not didactically, but wrapt up and involved in a picture of one evening, as I spent every evening during

---

57 Title of a once popular novel by Thomas Hope, published in 1819.
58 a treatise on the Asiatic languages by J. C. Adelung, 1732–1806, a German philologist.

59 This, however, is not a necessary conclusion; the varieties of effect produced by opium on different constitutions are infinite. A London Magistrate (Harriott's *Struggles through Life,* vol. iii, p. 391, Third Edition) has recorded that, on the first occasion of his trying laudanum for the gout, he took *forty* drops, the next night *sixty,* and on the fifth night *eighty,* without any effect whatever; and this at an advanced age. I have an anecdote from a country surgeon, however, which sinks Mr. Harriott's case into a trifle; and in my projected medical treatise on opium, which I will publish, provided the College of Surgeons will pay me for enlightening their benighted understandings upon this subject, I will relate it; but it is far too good a story to be published gratis.—(De Quincey.)
60 See the common accounts in any Eastern traveller or voyager of the frantic excesses committed by Malays who have taken opium, or are reduced to desperation by ill luck at gambling.—(De Quincey.)
61 inserted among others in the calendar.

the intercalary year when laudanum, though taken daily, was to me no more than the elixir of pleasure. This done, I shall quit the subject of happiness altogether, and pass to a very different one—*the pains of opium.*

Let there be a cottage, standing in a valley, eighteen miles from any town—no spacious valley, but about two miles long, by three-quarters of a mile in average width, the benefit of which provision is that all the families resident within its circuit will compose, as it were, one larger household personally familiar to your eye, and more or less interesting to your affections. Let the mountains be real mountains, between three and four thousand feet high; and the cottage, a real cottage,[62] not, as a witty author has it, 'a cottage, with a double coach-house'[63]: let it be, in fact—for I must abide by the actual scene—a white cottage, embowered with flowering shrubs, so chosen as to unfold a succession of flowers upon the walls, and clustering round the windows through all the months of spring, summer, and autumn—beginning, in fact, with May roses, and ending with jasmine. Let it, however, *not* be spring, nor summer, nor autumn—but winter, in his sternest shape. This is a most important point in the science of happiness. And I am surprised to see people overlook it, and think it matter of congratulation that winter is going; or, if coming, is not likely to be a severe one. On the contrary, I put up a petition annually for as much snow, hail, frost, or storm, of one kind or other, as the skies can possibly afford us. Surely everybody is aware of the divine pleasures which attend a winter fire-side: candles at four o'clock, warm hearth-rugs, tea, a fair tea-maker, shutters closed, curtains flowing in ample draperies on the floor, whilst the wind and rain are raging audibly without,

> And at the doors and windows seemed to call,
> As heav'n and earth they would together mell:
> Yet the least entrance find they none at all:
> Whence sweeter grows our rest secure in massy
> hall.[64]

All these are items in the description of a winter evening, which must surely be familiar to everybody born in a high latitude. And it is evident that most of these delicacies, like ice-cream, require a very low temperature of the atmosphere to produce them: they are fruits which cannot be ripened without weather stormy or inclement, in some way or other. I am not '*particular,*' as people say, whether it be snow, or black frost, or wind so strong that (as Mr. [Anti-Slavery Clarkson[65]] says) 'you may lean your back against it like a post.' I can put up even with rain, provided it rains cats and dogs: but something of the sort I must have: and, if I have it not, I think myself in a manner ill-used: for why am I called on to pay so heavily for winter, in coals, and candles, and various privations that will occur even to gentlemen, if I am not to have the article good of its kind? No: a Canadian winter for my money: or a Russian one, where every man is but a co-proprietor with the north wind in the fee-simple[66] of his own ears. Indeed, so great an epicure am I in this matter, that I cannot relish a winter night fully if it be much past St. Thomas's day,[67] and have degenerated into disgusting tendencies to vernal appearances: no: it must be divided by a thick wall of dark nights from all return of light and sunshine.—From the latter weeks of October to Christmas-eve, therefore, is the period during which happiness is in season, which, in my judgement, enters the room with the tea-tray: for tea, though ridiculed by those who are naturally of coarse nerves, or are become so from wine-drinking, and are not susceptible of influence from so refined a stimulant, will always be the favourite beverage of the intellectual: and, for my part, I would have joined Dr. Johnson in a *bellum internecinum*[68] against Jonas Hanway,[69] or any other impious person who should presume to disparage it.—But here, to save myself the trouble of too much verbal description, I will introduce a painter, and give him directions for the rest of the picture. Painters do not like white cottages, unless a good deal weather-stained: but as the reader now understands that it is a winter night, his services will not be required, except for the inside of the house.

Paint me, then, a room seventeen feet by twelve, and not more than seven and a half feet high. This, reader, is somewhat ambitiously

---

62 The cottage and the valley concerned in this description were not imaginary: the valley was the lovely one, *in those days*, of Grasmere; and the cottage was occupied for more than twenty years by myself, as immediate successor, in the year 1809, to Wordsworth.—(De Quincey's note, in enlarged *Confessions*.)

63 Coleridge, *The Devil's Thoughts*, 21.

64 Thomson, *The Castle of Indolence*, I, 383-7.

65 Thomas Clarkson, 1760–1846, philanthropist devoted to the abolition of the slave trade.

66 unrestricted ownership; literally, in law *fee simple* implies ownership without condition or restriction regarding heirs.

67 21 December.

68 civil war.

69 philanthropist and tourist, 1712–86, who attacked tea drinking and became involved in a controversy on that subject with Dr. Johnson, an inveterate tea drinker.

styled, in my family, the drawing-room: but being contrived 'a double debt to pay,'[70] it is also, and more justly, termed the library; for it happens that books are the only article of property in which I am richer than my neighbours. Of these, I have about five thousand, collected gradually since my eighteenth year. Therefore, painter, put as many as you can into this room. Make it populous with books: and, furthermore, paint me a good fire; and furniture, plain and modest, befitting the unpretending cottage of a scholar. And, near the fire, paint me a tea-table; and, as it is clear that no creature can come to see one such a stormy night, place only two cups and saucers on the tea-tray: and, if you know how to paint such a thing symbolically, or otherwise, paint me an eternal tea-pot—eternal *a parte ante,* and *a parte post*;[71] for I usually drink tea from eight o'clock at night to four o'clock in the morning. And, as it is very unpleasant to make tea, or to pour it out for oneself, paint me a lovely young woman, sitting at the table. Paint her arms like Aurora's, and her smiles like Hebe's.—But no, dear M[argaret],[72] not even in jest let me insinuate that thy power to illuminate my cottage rests upon a tenure so perishable as mere personal beauty; or that the witch-craft of angelic smiles lies within the empire of any earthly pencil. Pass, then, my good painter, to something more within its power: and the next article brought forward should naturally be myself—a picture of the Opium-eater with his 'little golden receptacle of the pernicious drug,'[73] lying beside him on the table. As to the opium, I have no objection to see a picture of *that,* though I would rather see the original: you may paint it, if you choose; but I apprise you, that no 'little' receptacle would, even in 1816, answer *my* purpose, who was at a distance from the 'stately Pantheon,'[74] and all druggists (mortal or otherwise). No: you may as well paint the real receptacle, which was not of gold, but of glass, and as much like a wine-decanter as possible. Into this you may put a quart of ruby-coloured laudanum: that, and a book of German metaphysics placed by its side, will sufficiently attest my being in the neighbourhood; but, as to myself, —there I demur.

From THE PAINS OF OPIUM

I now pass to what is the main subject of these latter confessions, to the history and journal of what took place in my dreams; for these were the immediate and proximate cause of my acutest suffering.

The first notice I had of any important change going on in this part of my physical economy, was from the reawakening of a state of eye generally incident to childhood, or exalted states of irritability. I know not whether my reader is aware that many children, perhaps most, have a power of painting, as it were, upon the darkness, all sorts of phantoms; in some, that power is simply a mechanic affection of the eye; others have a voluntary, or a semi-voluntary power to dismiss or to summon them; or, as a child once said to me when I questioned him on this matter, 'I can tell them to go, and they go; but sometimes they come when I don't tell them to come.' Whereupon I told him that he had almost as unlimited command over apparitions as a Roman centurion over his soldiers.—In the middle of 1817, I think it was, that this faculty became positively distressing to me: at night, when I lay awake in bed, vast processions passed along in mournful pomp; friezes of never-ending stories, that to my feelings were as sad and solemn as if they were stories drawn from times before Œdipus or Priam—before Tyre—before Memphis.[75] And, at the same time, a corresponding change took place in my dreams; a theatre seemed suddenly opened and lighted up within my brain, which presented nightly spectacles of more than earthly splendour. And the four following facts may be mentioned, as noticeable at this time:

1. That, as the creative state of the eye increased, a sympathy seemed to arise between the waking and the dreaming states of the brain in one point—that whatsoever I happened to call up and to trace by a voluntary act upon the darkness was very apt to transfer itself to my dreams; so that I feared to exercise this faculty; for, as Midas turned all things to gold, that yet baffled his hopes and defrauded his human desires, so whatever things capable of being visually represented I did but think of in the darkness, immediately shaped themselves into phantoms of the eye; and, by a process apparently no less inevitable, when thus once traced in faint and visionary colours, like writings in sympathetic ink,[76]

70 Goldsmith, *The Deserted Village,* 229.
71 'from the part before and the part after.'
72 De Quincey's wife.
73 quoted from *Anastasius,* a picaresque novel of Oriental adventure. Cf. note 57.
74 See note 27.

75 These names call up successively great civilizations of the past —of Greece, of Phoenicia, of Egypt.
76 a colorless fluid used for writing; it becomes visible when heated.

they were drawn out by the fierce chemistry of my dreams, into insufferable splendour that fretted my heart.

2. For this and all other changes in my dreams were accompanied by deep-seated anxiety and gloomy melancholy, such as are wholly incommunicable by words. I seemed every night to descend, not metaphorically, but literally to descend, into chasms and sunless abysses, depths below depths, from which it seemed hopeless that I could ever reascend. Nor did I, by waking, feel that I *had* reascended. This I do not dwell upon; because the state of gloom which attended these gorgeous spectacles, amounting at least to utter darkness, as of some suicidal despondency, cannot be approached by words.

3. The sense of space, and in the end, the sense of time, were both powerfully affected. Buildings, landscapes, etc., were exhibited in proportions so vast as the bodily eye is not fitted to receive. Space swelled, and was amplified to an extent of unutterable infinity. This, however, did not disturb me so much as the vast expansion of time; I sometimes seemed to have lived for 70 or 100 years in one night; nay, sometimes had feelings representative of a millennium passed in that time, or, however, of a duration far beyond the limits of any human experience.

4. The minutest incidents of childhood, or forgotten scenes of later years, were often revived: I could not be said to recollect them; for if I had been told of them when waking, I should not have been able to acknowledge them as parts of my past experience. But placed as they were before me, in dreams like intuitions, and clothed in all their evanescent circumstances and accompanying feelings, I *recognized* them instantaneously. I was once told by a near relative of mine, that having in her childhood fallen into a river, and being on the very verge of death but for the critical assistance which reached her, she saw in a moment her whole life, in its minutest incidents, arrayed before her simultaneously as in a mirror; and she had a faculty developed as suddenly for comprehending the whole and every part. This, from some opium experiences of mine, I can believe; I have, indeed, seen the same thing asserted twice in modern books, and accompanied by a remark which I am convinced is true; *viz.*, that the dread book of account[77] which the Scriptures speak of is, in fact, the mind itself of each individual. Of this, at least, I feel assured, that there is no such thing as *forgetting*

possible to the mind; a thousand accidents may and will interpose a veil between our present consciousness and the secret inscriptions on the mind; accidents of the same sort will also rend away this veil; but alike, whether veiled or unveiled, the inscription remains forever; just as the stars seem to withdraw before the common light of day, whereas, in fact, we all know that it is the light which is drawn over them as a veil —and that they are waiting to be revealed, when the obscuring daylight shall have withdrawn.

. . .

May 1818

The Malay has been a fearful enemy for months. I have been every night, through his means, transported into Asiatic scenes. I know not whether others share in my feelings on this point; but I have often thought that if I were compelled to forego England, and to live in China, and among Chinese manners and modes of life and scenery, I should go mad. The causes of my horror lie deep and some of them must be common to others. Southern Asia, in general, is the seat of awful images and associations. As the cradle of the human race, it would alone have a dim and reverential feeling connected with it. But there are other reasons. No man can pretend that the wild, barbarous, and capricious superstitions of Africa, or of savage tribes elsewhere, affect him in the way that he is affected by the ancient, monumental, cruel, and elaborate religions of Indostan, etc. The mere antiquity of Asiatic things, of their institutions, histories, modes of faith, etc., is so impressive, that to me the vast age of the race and name overpowers the sense of youth in the individual. A young Chinese seems to me an antediluvian man renewed. Even Englishmen, though not bred in any knowledge of such institutions, cannot but shudder at the mystic sublimity of *castes* that have flowed apart, and refused to mix, through such immemorial tracts of time; nor can any man fail to be awed by the names of the Ganges or the Euphrates. It contributes much to these feelings that southern Asia is, and has been for thousands of years, the part of the earth most swarming with human life; the great *officina gentium*.[78] Man is a weed in those regions. The vast empires also, into which the enormous population of Asia has always been cast, give a further sublimity to the feelings associated with all Oriental names or images. In China, over and above what it has in common

---

77 Revelation, xx, 12.

78 beehive of nations.

with the rest of southern Asia, I am terrified by the modes of life, by the manners, and the barrier of utter abhorrence, and want of sympathy, placed between us by feelings deeper than I can analyse. I could sooner live with lunatics, or brute animals. All this, and much more than I can say, or have time to say, the reader must enter into before he can comprehend the unimaginable horror which these dreams of Oriental imagery, and mythological tortures, impressed upon me. Under the connecting feeling of tropical heat and vertical sunlights, I brought together all creatures, birds, beasts, reptiles, all trees and plants, usages and appearances, that are found in all tropical regions, and assembled them together in China or Indostan. From kindred feelings, I soon brought Egypt and all her gods under the same law. I was stared at, hooted at, grinned at, chattered at, by monkeys, by paroquets, by cockatoos. I ran into pagodas: and was fixed for centuries at the summit, or in secret rooms; I was the idol; I was the priest; I was worshipped; I was sacrificed. I fled from the wrath of Brama through all the forests of Asia. Vishnu hated me: Seeva laid wait for me. I came suddenly upon Isis and Osiris.[79] I had done a deed, they said, which the ibis and the crocodile trembled at. I was buried for a thousand years in stone coffins, with mummies and sphinxes, in narrow chambers at the heart of eternal pyramids. I was kissed, with cancerous kisses, by crocodiles; and laid, confounded with all unutterable slimy things, amongst reeds and Nilotic mud.

I thus give the reader some slight abstraction of my Oriental dreams, which always filled me with such amazement at the monstrous scenery, that horror seemed absorbed, for a while, in sheer astonishment. Sooner or later, came a reflux of feeling that swallowed up the astonishment, and left me, not so much in terror, as in hatred and abomination of what I saw. Over every form, and threat, and punishment, and dim sightless incarceration, brooded a sense of eternity and infinity that drove me into an oppression as of madness. Into these dreams only, it was, with one or two slight exceptions, that any circumstances of physical horror entered. All before had been moral and spiritual terrors. But here the main agents were ugly birds, or snakes, or crocodiles;

especially the last. The cursed crocodile became to me the object of more horror than almost all the rest. I was compelled to live with him; and (as was always the case almost in my dreams) for centuries. I escaped sometimes, and found myself in Chinese houses, with cane tables, etc. All the feet of the tables, sofas, etc., soon became instinct with life: the abominable head of the crocodile, and his leering eyes, looked out at me, multiplied into a thousand repetitions: and I stood loathing and fascinated. And so often did this hideous reptile haunt my dreams, that many times the very same dream was broken up in the very same way: I heard gentle voices speaking to me (I hear everything when I am sleeping); and instantly I awoke: it was broad noon; and my children were standing, hand in hand, at my bedside; come to show me their coloured shoes, or new frocks, or to let me see them dressed for going out. I protest that so awful was the transition from the damned crocodile, and the other unutterable monsters and abortions of my dreams, to the sight of innocent *human* natures and of infancy, that, in the mighty and sudden revulsion of mind, I wept, and could not forbear it, as I kissed their faces.

June 1819

I have had occasion to remark, at various periods of my life, that the deaths of those whom we love, and indeed the contemplation of death generally, is (*cæteris paribus*[80]) more affecting in summer than in any other season of the year. And the reasons are these three, I think: first, that the visible heavens in summer appear far higher, more distant, and (if such a solecism may be excused) more infinite; the clouds, by which chiefly the eye expounds the distance of the blue pavilion stretched over our heads, are in summer more voluminous, massed, and accumulated in far grander and more towering piles: secondly, the light and the appearances of the declining and the setting sun are much more fitted to be types and characters of the Infinite: and, thirdly, which is the main reason, the exuberant and riotous prodigality of life naturally forces the mind more powerfully upon the antagonist thought of death, and the wintry sterility of the grave. For it may be observed, generally, that wherever two thoughts stand related to each other by a law of antagonism, and exist, as it were, by mutual repulsion, they are apt to suggest each other. On

---

79 Brahma, the evolver of the universe, Vishnu its maintainer, and Siva its destroyer compose the so-called Triad of the Hindu religion of Brahmanism. Isis and Osiris are deities of Egyptian mythology.

80 'other conditions remaining the same.'

these accounts it is that I find it impossible to banish the thought of death when I am walking alone in the endless days of summer; and any particular death, if not more affecting, at least haunts my mind more obstinately and besiegingly in that season. Perhaps this cause, and a slight incident which I omit, might have been the immediate occasions of the following dream, to which, however, a predisposition must always have existed in my mind; but having been once roused, it never left me, and split into a thousand fantastic varieties, which often suddenly reunited, and composed again the original dream.

I thought that it was a Sunday morning in May, that it was Easter Sunday, and as yet very early in the morning. I was standing, as it seemed to me, at the door of my own cottage. Right before me lay the very scene which could really be commanded from that situation, but exalted, as was usual, and solemnized by the power of dreams. There were the same mountains, and the same lovely valley at their feet; but the mountains were raised to more than Alpine height, and there was interspace far larger between them of meadows and forest lawns; the hedges were rich with white roses; and no living creature was to be seen, excepting that in the green churchyard there were cattle tranquilly reposing upon the verdant graves, and particularly round about the grave of a child whom I had tenderly loved,[81] just as I had really beheld them, a little before sunrise in the same summer, when that child died. I gazed upon the well-known scene, and I said aloud (as I thought) to myself, 'It yet wants much of sunrise; and it is Easter Sunday; and that is the day on which they celebrate the first-fruits of resurrection. I will walk abroad; old griefs shall be forgotten today; for the air is cool and still, and the hills are high, and stretch away to heaven; and the forest-glades are as quiet as the churchyard; and with the dew I can wash the fever from my forehead, and then I shall be unhappy no longer.' And I turned, as if to open my garden gate; and immediately I saw upon the left a scene far different; but which yet the power of dreams had reconciled into harmony with the other. The scene was an Oriental one; and there also it was Easter Sunday, and very early in the morning. And at a vast distance were visible, as a stain upon the horizon, the domes and cupolas of a great city—an image or faint abstraction, caught perhaps in childhood from some pictures of Jerusalem. And not a bowshot from me, upon a stone, and shaded by Judean palms, there sat a woman; and I looked; and it was—Ann! She fixed her eyes upon me earnestly; and I said to her at length: 'So then I have found you at last.' I waited: but she answered me not a word. Her face was the same as when I saw it last, and yet again how different! Seventeen years ago, when the lamplight fell upon her face, as for the last time I kissed her lips (lips, Ann, that to me were not polluted), her eyes were streaming with tears: the tears were now wiped away; she seemed more beautiful than she was at that time, but in all other points the same, and not older. Her looks were tranquil, but with unusual solemnity of expression; and I now gazed upon her with some awe, but suddenly her countenance grew dim, and, turning to the mountains, I perceived vapours rolling between us; in a moment, all had vanished; thick darkness came on; and, in the twinkling of an eye, I was far away from mountains, and by lamplight in Oxford Street, walking again with Ann—just as we walked seventeen years before, when we were both children.

As a final specimen, I cite one of a different character, from 1820.

The dream commenced with a music which now I often heard in dreams—a music of preparation and of awakening suspense; a music like the opening of the Coronation Anthem, and which, like *that,* gave the feeling of a vast march —of infinite cavalcades filing off—and the tread of innumerable armies. The morning was come of a mighty day—a day of crisis and of final hope for human nature, then suffering some mysterious eclipse, and labouring in some dread extremity. Somewhere, I knew not where—somehow, I knew not how—by some beings, I knew not whom—a battle, a strife, an agony, was conducting,—was evolving like a great drama, or piece of music; with which my sympathy was the more insupportable from my confusion as to its place, its cause, its nature, and its possible issue. I, as is usual in dreams (where, of necessity, we make ourselves central to every movement), had the power, and yet had not the power, to decide it. I had the power, if I could raise myself, to will it, and yet again had not the power, for the weight of twenty Atlantics was upon me, or the oppression of inexpiable guilt. 'Deeper than ever plummet sounded,'[82] I lay inactive. Then, like a chorus, the passion deepened. Some greater in-

---

81 Catherine Wordsworth.

82 *The Tempest*, V, i, 56.

terest was at stake; some mightier cause than ever yet the sword had pleaded, or trumpet had proclaimed. Then came sudden alarms: hurryings to and fro: trepidations of innumerable fugitives, I knew not whether from the good cause or the bad: darkness and lights: tempest and human faces: and at last, with the sense that all was lost, female forms, and the features that were worth all the world to me, and but a moment allowed,—and clasped hands, and heartbreaking partings, and then—everlasting farewells! and with a sigh, such as the caves of hell sighed when the incestuous mother[83] uttered the abhorred name of death, the sound was reverberated—everlasting farewells! and again, and yet again reverberated—everlasting farewells!

And I awoke in struggles, and cried aloud— 'I will sleep no more!'[84]

1822

ON THE KNOCKING AT THE GATE IN MACBETH

From my boyish days I had always felt a great perplexity on one point in *Macbeth*. It was this: —the knocking at the gate which succeeds to the murder of Duncan produced to my feelings an effect for which I never could account. The effect was that it reflected back upon the murderer a peculiar awfulness and a depth of solemnity; yet, however obstinately I endeavoured with my understanding to comprehend this, for many years I never could see *why* it should produce such an effect.

Here I pause for one moment to exhort the reader never to pay any attention to his understanding when it stands in opposition to any other faculty of his mind. The mere understanding, however useful and indispensable, is the meanest faculty in the human mind and the most to be distrusted; and yet the great majority of people trust to nothing else,—which may do for ordinary life, but not for philosophical purposes. Of this, out of ten thousand instances that I might produce, I will cite one. Ask of any person whatsoever who is not previously prepared for the demand by a knowledge of perspective, to draw in the rudest way the commonest appearance which depends upon the laws of that science,—as, for instance, to represent the effect of two walls standing at right angles to each other, or the appearance of the houses on each side of a street, as seen by a person looking down the street from one extremity. Now, in all cases, unless the person has happened to observe in pictures how it is that artists produce these effects, he will be utterly unable to make the smallest approximation to it. Yet why? For he has actually seen the effect every day of his life. The reason is that he allows his understanding to overrule his eyes. His understanding, which includes no intuitive knowledge of the laws of vision, can furnish him with no reason why a line which is known and can be proved to be a horizontal line should not *appear* a horizontal line: a line that made any angle with the perpendicular less than a right angle would seem to him to indicate that his houses were all tumbling down together. Accordingly he makes the line of his houses a horizontal line, and fails of course to produce the effect demanded. Here then is one instance out of many in which not only the understanding is allowed to overrule the eyes, but where the understanding is positively allowed to obliterate the eyes, as it were; for not only does the man believe the evidence of his understanding in opposition to that of his eyes, but (what is monstrous) the idiot is not aware that his eyes ever gave such evidence. He does not know that he has seen (and therefore, *quoad,* his consciousness has *not* seen) that which he *has* seen every day of his life.

But to return from this digression,—my understanding could furnish no reason why the knocking at the gate in *Macbeth* should produce any effect, direct or reflected. In fact, my understanding said positively that it could *not* produce any effect. But I knew better; I felt that it did; and I waited and clung to the problem until further knowledge should enable me to solve it. At length, in 1812, Mr. Williams made his *début* on the stage of Ratcliffe Highway,[1] and executed those unparalleled murders which have procured for him such a brilliant and undying reputation. On which murders, by the way, I must observe, that in one respect they have had an ill effect, by making the connoisseur in murder very fastidious in his taste, and dissatisfied with anything that has been since done in that line. All other murders

---

83 Sin. See *Paradise Lost*, II, 787ff.
84 Cf. *Macbeth*, II, ii, 35.

1 In December 1811, John Williams, an English seaman, committed the first of a series of sensational 'hammer' murders at no. 29 Ratcliffe Highway, in the disreputable nautical quarter of London.

look pale by the deep crimson of his; and, as an amateur once said to me in a querulous tone, 'There has been absolutely nothing *doing* since his time, or nothing that's worth speaking of.' But this is wrong, for it is unreasonable to expect all men to be great artists, and born with the genius of Mr. Williams. Now it will be remembered that in the first of these murders (that of the Marrs) the same incident (of a knocking at the door soon after the work of extermination was complete) did actually occur which the genius of Shakespeare has invented; and all good judges, and the most eminent dilettanti, acknowledged the felicity of Shakespeare's suggestion as soon as it was actually realized. Here then was a fresh proof that I had been right in relying on my own feeling in opposition to my understanding; and again I set myself to study the problem. At length I solved it to my own satisfaction; and my solution is this:—Murder, in ordinary cases, where the sympathy is wholly directed to the case of the murdered person, is an incident of coarse and vulgar horror; and for this reason—that it flings the interest exclusively upon the natural but ignoble instinct by which we cleave to life: an instinct which, as being indispensable to the primal law of self-preservation, is the same in kind (though different in degree) amongst all living creatures. This instinct, therefore, because it annihilates all distinctions, and degrades the greatest of men to the level of 'the poor beetle that we tread on,'[2] exhibits human nature in its most abject and humiliating attitude. Such an attitude would little suit the purposes of the poet. What then must he do? He must throw the interest on the murderer. Our sympathy must be with *him* (of course I mean a sympathy of comprehension, a sympathy by which we enter into his feelings, and are made to understand them—not a sympathy of pity or approbation).[3] In the murdered person all strife of thought, all flux and reflux of passion and of purpose, are crushed by one overwhelming panic; the fear of instant death smites him 'with its petrific[4] mace.' But in

the murderer, such a murderer as a poet will condescend to, there must be raging some great storm of passion—jealousy, ambition, vengeance, hatred—which will create a hell within him; and into this hell we are to look.

In *Macbeth,* for the sake of gratifying his own enormous and teeming faculty of creation, Shakespeare has introduced two murderers: and, as usual in his hands, they are remarkably discriminated: but—though in Macbeth the strife of mind is greater than in his wife, the tiger spirit not so awake, and his feelings caught chiefly by contagion from her—yet, as both were finally involved in the guilt of murder, the murderous mind of necessity is finally to be presumed in both. This was to be expressed; and on its own account, as well as to make it a more proportionable antagonist to the unoffending nature of their victim, 'the gracious Duncan,'[5] and adequately to expound 'the deep damnation of his taking off,'[6] this was to be expressed with peculiar energy. We were to be made to feel that the human nature,—*i.e.,* the divine nature of love and mercy, spread through the hearts of all creatures, and seldom utterly withdrawn from man—was gone, vanished, extinct, and that the fiendish nature had taken its place. And, as this effect is marvellously accomplished in the *dialogues* and *soliloquies* themselves, so it is finally consummated by the expedient under consideration; and it is to this that I now solicit the reader's attention. If the reader has ever witnessed a wife, daughter, or sister, in a fainting fit, he may chance to have observed that the most affecting moment in such a spectacle is *that* in which a sigh and a stirring announce the recommencement of suspended life. Or, if the reader has ever been present in a vast metropolis on the day when some great national idol was carried in funeral pomp to his grave, and, chancing to walk near the course through which it passed, has felt powerfully, in the silence and desertion of the streets and in the stagnation of ordinary business, the deep interest which at that moment was possessing the heart of man—if all at once he should hear the death-like stillness broken up by the sound of wheels rattling away from the scene, and making known that the transitory vision was dissolved, he will be aware that at no moment was his sense of the complete suspension and pause in ordinary human concerns so full and affecting as at that moment when the

---

2 *Measure for Measure,* III, i, 79.

3 It seems almost ludicrous to guard and explain my use of a word in a situation where it would naturally explain itself. But it has become necessary to do so, in consequence of the unscholarlike use of the word *sympathy*, at present so general, by which, instead of taking it in its proper sense, as the act of reproducing in our minds the feelings of another, whether for hatred, indignation, love, pity, or approbation, it is made a mere synonym of the word *pity;* and hence, instead of saying 'sympathy *with* another,' many writers adopt the monstrous barbarism of 'sympathy *for* another.' —(De Quincey.)

4 petrifying (*Paradise Lost,* X, 294).

5 III, i, 66.

6 I, vii, 20.

suspension ceases, and the goings-on of human life are suddenly resumed. All action in any direction is best expounded, measured, and made apprehensible, by reaction. Now apply this to the case in *Macbeth*. Here, as I have said, the retiring of the human heart and the entrance of the fiendish heart was to be expressed and made sensible. Another world has stepped in; and the murderers are taken out of the region of human things, human purposes, human desires. They are transfigured: Lady Macbeth is 'unsexed'; Macbeth has forgot that he was born of woman; both are conformed to the image of devils; and the world of devils is suddenly revealed. But how shall this be conveyed and made palpable? In order that a new world may step in, this world must for a time disappear. The murderers, and the murder, must be insulated—cut off by an immeasurable gulf from the ordinary tide and succession of human affairs—locked up and sequestered in some deep recess; we must be made sensible that the world of ordinary life is suddenly arrested—laid asleep—tranced—racked into a dread armistice; time must be annihilated; relation to things without abolished; and all must pass self-withdrawn into a deep syncope[7] and suspension of earthly passion. Hence it is that, when the deed is done, when the work of darkness is perfect, then the world of darkness passes away like a pageantry in the clouds: the knocking at the gate is heard, and it makes known audibly that the reaction has commenced; the human has made its reflux upon the fiendish: the pulses of life are beginning to beat again; and the re-establishment of the goings-on of the world in which we live first makes us profoundly sensible of the awful parenthesis that had suspended them.

O mighty poet! Thy works are not as those of other men, simply and merely great works of art, but are also like the phenomena of nature, like the sun and the sea, the stars and the flowers, like frost and snow, rain and dew, hail-storm and thunder, which are to be studied with entire submission of our own faculties, and in the perfect faith that in them there can be no too much or too little, nothing useless or inert, but that, the farther we press in our discoveries, the more we shall see proofs of design and self-supporting arrangement where the careless eye had seen nothing but accident!

1823

---

7 cessation.

From SUSPIRIA DE PROFUNDIS[1]

LEVANA AND OUR LADIES OF SORROW

OFTENTIMES at Oxford I saw Levana in my dreams. I knew her by her Roman symbols. Who is Levana? Reader, that do not pretend to have leisure for very much scholarship, you will not be angry with me for telling you. Levana was the Roman goddess that performed for the new-born infant the earliest office of ennobling kindness,—typical, by its mode, of that grandeur which belongs to man everywhere, and of that benignity in powers invisible which even in Pagan worlds sometimes descends to sustain it. At the very moment of birth, just as the infant tasted for the first time the atmosphere of our troubled planet, it was laid on the ground. *That* might bear different interpretations. But immediately, lest so grand a creature should grovel there for more than one instant, either the paternal hand, as proxy for the goddess Levana, or some near kinsman, as proxy for the father, raised it upright, bade it look erect as the king of all this world, and presented its forehead to the stars, saying, perhaps, in his heart, 'Behold what is greater than yourselves!' This symbolic act represented the function of Levana. And that mysterious lady, who never revealed her face (except to me in dreams), but always acted by delegation, had her name from the Latin verb (as still it is the Italian verb) *levare,* to raise aloft.

This is the explanation of Levana. And hence it has arisen that some people have understood by Levana the tutelary[2] power that controls the education of the nursery. She, that would not suffer at his birth even a prefigurative or mimic degradation for her awful ward, far less could be supposed to suffer the real degradation attaching to the non-development of his powers. She therefore watches over human education. Now, the word *educo,* with the penultimate short, was derived (by a process often exemplified in the crystallization of languages) from the word *educo,* with the penultimate long. Whatsoever *educes,* or develops, *educates.* By the education of Levana, therefore, is meant,—not the poor

---

1 'Sighs from the Depths.' *Suspiria de Profundis* was planned as a series of dream-sketches, a kind of sequel to *Confessions of an English Opium-Eater.* 'It was, in fact,' says DeQuincey, 'a legend recurring in sleep, most of which I had myself silently written or sculptured in my daylight reveries.' Of the four parts originally projected, Part I, entitled *The Affliction of Childhood,* was completed. This was published as a series of papers in *Blackwood's Magazine* during the spring of 1845, being concluded in the June number with four short pieces, of which *Levana and Our Ladies of Sorrow* was the second and *Savannah-la-Mar* the fourth.
2 guardian.

machinery that moves by spelling-books and grammars, but that mighty system of central forces hidden in the deep bosom of human life, which by passion, by strife, by temptation, by the energies of resistance, works forever upon children,—resting not day or night, any more than the mighty wheel of day and night themselves, whose moments, like restless spokes, are glimmering[3] forever as they revolve.

If, then, *these* are the ministries by which Levana works, how profoundly must she reverence the agencies of grief! But you, reader, think that children generally are not liable to grief such as mine. There are two senses in the word *generally*,—the sense of Euclid,[4] where it means *universally* (or in the whole extent of the *genus*), and a foolish sense of this word, where it means *usually*. Now, I am far from saying that children universally are capable of grief like mine. But there are more than you ever heard of who die of grief in this island of ours. I will tell you a common case. The rules of Eton require that a boy on the *foundation*[5] should be there twelve years: he is superannuated at eighteen; consequently he must come at six. Children torn away from mothers and sisters at that age not unfrequently die. I speak of what I know. The complaint is not entered by the registrar as grief; but *that* it is. Grief of that sort, and at that age, has killed more than ever have been counted amongst its martyrs.

Therefore it is that Levana often communes with the powers that shake man's heart; therefore it is that she dotes upon grief. 'These ladies,' said I softly to myself, on seeing the ministers with whom Levana was conversing, 'these are the Sorrows; and they are three in number: as the *Graces* are three, who dress man's life with beauty; the *Parcæ*[6] are three, who weave the dark arras of man's life in their mysterious loom always with colours sad in part, sometimes angry with tragic crimson and black; the *Furies* are three, who visit with retributions called from the other side of the grave offences that walk upon this; and once even the *Muses* were but three, who fit the harp, the trumpet, or the lute, to the great burdens of man's impassioned creations. These are the Sorrows; all three of whom I know.' The last words I say *now;* but in Oxford I said, 'one of whom I know, and the others too surely I *shall* know.' For already, in my fervent youth, I saw (dimly relieved upon the dark background of my dreams) the imperfect lineaments of the awful Sisters.

These Sisters—by what name shall we call them? If I say simply 'The Sorrows,' there will be a chance of mistaking the term; it might be understood of individual sorrow,—separate cases of sorrow,—whereas I want a term expressing the mighty abstractions that incarnate themselves in all individual sufferings of man's heart, and I wish to have these abstractions presented as impersonations,—that is, as clothed with human attributes of life, and with functions pointing to flesh. Let us call them, therefore, *Our Ladies of Sorrow*.

I know them thoroughly, and have walked in all their kingdoms. Three sisters they are, of one mysterious household; and their paths are wide apart; but of their dominion there is no end. Them I saw often conversing with Levana, and sometimes about myself. Do they talk, then? O no! Mighty phantoms like these disdain the infirmities of language. They may utter voices through the organs of man when they dwell in human hearts, but amongst themselves is no voice nor sound; eternal silence reigns in *their* kingdoms. They spoke not as they talked with Levana; they whispered not; they sang not; though oftentimes methought they *might* have sung: for I upon earth had heard their mysteries oftentimes deciphered by harp and timbrel, by dulcimer and organ. Like God, whose servants they are, they utter their pleasure not by sounds that perish, or by words that go astray, but by signs in heaven, by changes on earth, by pulses in secret rivers, heraldries painted on darkness, and hieroglyphics written on the tablets of the brain. *They* wheeled in mazes; *I* spelled the steps. *They* telegraphed[7] from afar; *I* read the signals. *They* conspired together; and on the mirrors of darkness *my* eye traced the plots. *Theirs* were the symbols; *mine* are the words.

What is it the Sisters are? What is it that they do? Let me describe their form and their pres-

---

3 As I have never allowed myself to covet any man's ox nor his ass, nor anything that is his, still less would it become a philosopher to covet other people's images or metaphors. Here, therefore, I restore to Mr. Wordsworth this fine image of the revolving wheel and the glimmering spokes, as applied by him to the flying successions of day and night. I borrowed it for one moment in order to point my own sentence; which being done, the reader is witness that I now pay it back instantly by a note made for that sole purpose. On the same principle I often borrow their seals from young ladies, when closing my letters, because there is sure to be some tender sentiment upon them about 'memory,' or 'hope,' or 'roses,' or 'reunion,' and my correspondent must be a sad brute who is not touched by the eloquence of the seal, even if his taste is so bad that he remains deaf to mine.—(De Quincey.)

4 famous Greek geometer of the third century B.C.

5 that is, holding a scholarship provided for by endowment,

6 goddesses of fate.

7 signaled.

ence, if form it were that still fluctuated in its outline, or presence it were that forever advanced to the front or forever receded amongst shades.

The eldest of the three is named *Mater Lachrymarum,* Our Lady of Tears. She it is that night and day raves and moans, calling for vanished faces. She stood in Rama, where a voice was heard of lamentation,—Rachel weeping for her children,[8] and refusing to be comforted. She it was that stood in Bethlehem on the night when Herod's sword swept its nurseries of Innocents,[9] and the little feet were stiffened forever which, heard at times as they trotted along floors overhead, woke pulses of love in household hearts that were not unmarked in heaven. Her eyes are sweet and subtle, wild and sleepy, by turns; oftentimes rising to the clouds, oftentimes challenging the heavens. She wears a diadem round her head. And I knew by childish memories that she could go abroad upon the winds, when she heard the sobbing of litanies, or the thundering of organs, and when she beheld the mustering of summer clouds. This Sister, the elder, it is that carries keys more than papal at her girdle,[10] which open every cottage and every palace. She, to my knowledge, sat all last summer by the bedside of the blind beggar, him that so often and so gladly I talked with, whose pious daughter, eight years old, with the sunny countenance, resisted the temptations of play and village mirth, to travel all day long on dusty roads with her afflicted father. For this did God send her a great reward. In the springtime of the year, and whilst yet her own spring was budding, He recalled her to himself. But her blind father mourns forever over *her*: still he dreams at midnight that the little guiding hand is locked within his own; and still he wakens to a darkness that is *now* within a second and a deeper darkness. This *Mater Lachrymarum* also has been sitting all this winter of 1844–5 within the bedchamber of the Czar,[11] bringing before his eyes a daughter (not less pious) that vanished to God not less suddenly, and left behind her a darkness not less profound. By the power of the keys it is that Our Lady of Tears glides, a ghostly intruder, into the chambers of sleepless men, sleepless women, sleepless children, from Ganges to the Nile, from Nile to Mississippi. And her, because she is the first-born of her house, and has the

widest empire, let us honour with the title of 'Madonna.'

The second Sister is called *Mater Suspiriorum,* Our Lady of Sighs. She never scales the clouds, nor walks abroad upon the winds. She wears no diadem. And her eyes, if they were ever seen, would be neither sweet nor subtle; no man could read their story; they would be found filled with perishing dreams, and with wrecks of forgotten delirium. But she raises not her eyes; her head, on which sits a dilapidated turban, droops forever, forever fastens on the dust. She weeps not. She groans not. But she sighs inaudibly at intervals. Her sister, Madonna, is oftentimes stormy and frantic, raging in the highest against heaven, and demanding back her darlings. But Our Lady of Sighs never clamours, never defies, dreams not of rebellious aspirations. She is humble to abjectness. Hers is the meekness that belongs to the hopeless. Murmur she may, but it is in her sleep. Whisper she may, but it is to herself in the twilight. Mutter she does at times, but it is in solitary places that are desolate as she is desolate, in ruined cities, and when the sun has gone down to his rest. This Sister is the visitor of the Pariah,[12] of the Jew, of the bondsman to the oar in the Mediterranean galleys; of the English criminal in Norfolk Island,[13] blotted out from the books of remembrance in sweet far-off England; of the baffled penitent reverting his eyes forever upon a solitary grave, which to him seems the altar overthrown of some past and bloody sacrifice, on which altar no oblations can now be availing, whether towards pardon that he might implore, or towards reparation that he might attempt. Every slave that at noonday looks up to the tropical sun with timid reproach, as he points with one hand to the earth, our general mother, but for *him* a stepmother, as he points with the other hand to the Bible, our general teacher, but against *him* sealed and sequestered;[14] every woman sitting in darkness, without love to shelter her head, or hope to illumine her solitude, because the heaven-born instincts kindling in her nature germs of holy affections, which God implanted in her womanly bosom, having been stifled by social necessities, now burn sullenly to

---

8 Jeremiah, xxxi, 15; Matthew, ii, 18.   9 Matthew, ii, 18.
10 Matthew, xv, 18–19.
11 Nicholas I, whose daughter, the Princess Alexandria, died when she was nineteen.

12 member of a low caste society in India.
13 penal colony in the South Pacific.
14 This, the reader will be aware, applies chiefly to the cotton and tobacco States of North America; but not to them only: on which account I have not scrupled to figure the sun which looks down upon slavery as *tropical,*—no matter if strictly within the tropics, or simply so near to them as to produce a similar climate.—(De Quincey.)

waste, like sepulchral lamps amongst the ancients; every nun defrauded of her unreturning May-time by wicked kinsman, whom God will judge; every captive in every dungeon; all that are betrayed, and all that are rejected; outcasts by traditionary law, and children of *hereditary* disgrace: all these walk with Our Lady of Sighs. She also carries a key; but she needs it little. For her kingdom is chiefly amongst the tents of Shem,[15] and the houseless vagrant of every clime. Yet in the very highest ranks of man she finds chapels of her own; and even in glorious England there are some that, to the world, carry their heads as proudly as the reindeer, who yet secretly have received her mark upon their foreheads.

But the third Sister, who is also the youngest——! Hush! whisper whilst we talk of *her!* Her kingdom is not large, or else no flesh should live; but within that kingdom all power is hers. Her head, turreted like that of Cybele,[16] rises almost beyond the reach of sight. She droops not; and her eyes, rising so high, *might* be hidden by distance. But, being what they are, they cannot be hidden: through the treble veil of crape which she wears the fierce light of a blazing misery, that rests not for matins or for vespers, for noon of day or noon of night, for ebbing or for flowing tide, may be read from the very ground. She is the defier of God. She also is the mother of lunacies, and the suggestress of suicides. Deep lie the roots of her power; but narrow is the nation that she rules. For she can approach only those in whom a profound nature has been upheaved by central convulsions; in whom the heart trembles and the brain rocks under conspiracies of tempest from without and tempest from within. Madonna moves with uncertain steps, fast or slow, but still with tragic grace. Our Lady of Sighs creeps timidly and stealthily. But this youngest Sister moves with incalculable motions, bounding, and with tiger's leaps. She carries no key; for, though coming rarely amongst men, she storms all doors at which she is permitted to enter at all. And *her* name is *Mater Tenebrarum,*—Our Lady of Darkness.

These were the *Semnai Theai* or Sublime Goddesses,[17] these were the *Eumenides* or Gracious Ladies (so called by antiquity in shuddering propitiation), of my Oxford dreams. Madonna spoke. She spoke by her mysterious hand. Touching my head, she beckoned to Our Lady of Sighs; and *what* she spoke, translated out of the signs which (except in dreams) no man reads, was this:—

'Lo! here is he whom in childhood I dedicated to my altars. This is he that once I made my darling. Him I led astray, him I beguiled; and from heaven I stole away his young heart to mine. Through me did he become idolatrous; and through me it was, by languishing desires, that he worshipped the worm, and prayed to the wormy grave. Holy was the grave to him; lovely was its darkness; saintly its corruption. Him, this young idolater, I have seasoned for thee, dear gentle Sister of Sighs! Do thou take him now to *thy* heart, and season him for our dreadful sister. And thou,' —turning to the *Mater Tenebrarum,* she said,— 'wicked sister, that temptest and hatest, do thou take him from *her.* See that thy sceptre lie heavy on his head. Suffer not woman and her tenderness to sit near him in his darkness. Banish the frailties of hope: wither the relenting of love; scorch the fountains of tears; curse him as only *thou* canst curse. So shall he be accomplished in the furnace; so shall he see the things that ought *not* to be seen, sights that are abominable, and secrets that are unutterable. So shall he read elder truths, sad truths, grand truths, fearful truths. So shall he rise again *before* he dies. And so shall our commission be accomplished which from God we had,—to plague his heart until we had unfolded the capacities of his spirit.'

1845

SAVANNAH-LA-MAR[1]

God smote Savannah-la-mar, and in one night, by earthquake, removed her, with all her towers standing and population sleeping, from the steadfast foundations of the shore to the coral floors of ocean. And God said,—'Pompeii did I bury and conceal from men through seventeen centuries; this city I will bury, but not conceal. She shall be a monument to men of my mysterious anger, set in azure light through generations to come; for I will enshrine her in a crystal dome of my tropic

---

15 that is, among outcasts. See Genesis, ix, 27.

16 mother of the Olympian gods, usually represented with a tower-like crown.

17 '*Sublime Goddesses*':—The word σεμνος is usually rendered *venerable* in dictionaries,—not a very flattering epithet for females. But I am disposed to think that it comes nearest to our idea of the *sublime,*—as near as a Greek word *could* come.—(De Quincey.)

---

1 'Plain of the Sea.' Savannah-la-Mar is a small coast town in Jamaica. In that island De Quincey's brother Richard was lost during a hunting trip.

seas.' This city, therefore, like a mighty galleon with all her apparel mounted, streamers flying, and tackling perfect, seems floating along the noiseless depths of ocean; and oftentimes in glassy calms, through the translucid atmosphere of water that now stretches like an air-woven awning above the silent encampment, mariners from every clime look down into her courts and terraces, count her gates, and number the spires of her churches. She is one ample cemetery, and *has* been for many a year; but, in the mighty calms that brood for weeks over tropic latitudes, she fascinates the eye with a *Fata-Morgana*[2] revelation, as of human life still subsisting in submarine asylums sacred from the storms that torment our upper air.

Thither, lured by the loveliness of cerulean depths, by the peace of human dwellings privileged from molestation, by the gleam of marble altars sleeping in everlasting sanctity, oftentimes in dreams did I and the Dark Interpreter cleave the watery veil that divided us from her streets. We looked into the belfries, where the pendulous bells were waiting in vain for the summons which should awaken their marriage peals; together we touched the mighty organ-keys, that sang no *jubilates*[3] for the ear of heaven, that sang no requiems for the ear of human sorrow; together we searched the silent nurseries, where the children were all asleep, and *had* been asleep through five generations. 'They are waiting for the heavenly dawn,' whispered the Interpreter to himself: 'and, when *that* comes, the bells and organs will utter a *jubilate* repeated by the echoes of Paradise.' Then, turning to me, he said,— 'This is sad, this is piteous; but less would not have sufficed for the purpose of God. Look here. Put into a Roman clepsydra[4] one hundred drops of water; let these run out as the sands in an hour glass, every drop measuring the hundredth part of a second, so that each shall represent but the three-hundred-and-sixty-thousandth part of an hour. Now, count the drops as they race along; and, when the fiftieth of the hundred is passing, behold! forty-nine are not, because already they have perished, and fifty are not, because they are yet to come. You see, therefore, how narrow, how incalculably narrow, is the true and actual present. Of that time which we call the present, hardly a hundredth part but belongs either to a past which has fled, or to a future which is still on the wing. It has perished, or it is not born. It was, or it is not. Yet even this approximation to the truth is *infinitely* false. For again subdivide that solitary drop, which only was found to represent the present, into a lower series of similar fractions, and the actual present which you arrest measures now but the thirty-six-millionth of an hour; and so by infinite declensions the true and very present, in which only we live and enjoy, will vanish into a mote of a mote, distinguishable only by a heavenly vision. Therefore the present, which only man possesses, offers less capacity for his footing than the slenderest film that ever spider twisted from her womb. Therefore, also, even this incalculable shadow from the narrowest pencil of moonlight is more transitory than geometry can measure, or thought of angel can overtake. The time which *is* contracts into a mathematic point; and even that point perishes a thousand times before we can utter its birth. All is finite in the present; and even that finite is infinite in its velocity of flight towards death. But in God there is nothing finite; but in God there is nothing transitory; but in God there *can* be nothing that tends to death. Therefore it follows that for God there can be no present. The future is the present of God, and to the future it is that he sacrifices the human present. Therefore it is that he works by earthquake. Therefore it is that he works by grief. O, deep is the ploughing of earthquake! O, deep' —(and his voice swelled like a *sanctus*[5] rising from a choir of a cathedral)—'O, deep is the ploughing of grief! But oftentimes less would not suffice for the agriculture of God. Upon a night of earthquake he builds a thousand years of pleasant habitations for man. Upon the sorrow of an infant he raises oftentimes from human intellects glorious vintages that could not else have been. Less than these fierce ploughshares would not have stirred the stubborn soil. The one is needed for Earth, our planet,—for Earth itself as the dwelling-place of man; but the other is needed yet oftener for God's mightiest instrument,—yes,' (and he looked solemnly at myself), 'is needed for the mysterious children of the Earth!'

1845

---

2 that is, mirage-like; so-called after Morgana the Fairy, famous necromancer of medieval legend.
3 hymns of rejoicing.
4 water clock.

---

5 hymn; beginning with the Latin *Sanctus, sanctus, sanctus* (Holy, holy, holy).

From THE POETRY OF POPE

WHAT is it that we mean by *literature*? Popularly, and amongst the thoughtless, it is held to include everything that is printed in a book. Little logic is required to disturb *that* definition. The most thoughtless person is easily made aware that in the idea of *literature* one essential element is,—some relation to a general and common interest of man, so that what applies only to a local or professional or merely personal interest, even though presenting itself in the shape of a book, will not belong to literature. So far the definition is easily narrowed; and it is as easily expanded. For not only is much that takes a station in books not literature, but, inversely, much that really *is* literature never reaches a station in books. The weekly sermons of Christendom, that vast pulpit literature which acts so extensively upon the popular mind—to warn, to uphold, to renew, to comfort, to alarm—does not attain the sanctuary of libraries in the ten-thousandth part of its extent. The drama, again, as for instance the finest of Shakespeare's plays in England and all leading Athenian plays in the noontide of the Attic stage, operated as a literature on the public mind, and were (according to the strictest letter of that term) *published* through the audiences that witnessed[1] their representation, some time before they were published as things to be read; and they were published in this scenical mode of publication with much more effect than they could have had as books during ages of costly copying or of costly printing.

Books, therefore, do not suggest an idea co-extensive and interchangeable with the idea of literature, since much literature, scenic, forensic, or didactic (as from lecturers and public orators), may never come into books, and much that *does* come into books may connect itself with no literary interest. But a far more important correction, applicable to the common vague idea of literature, is to be sought, not so much in a better definition of literature, as in a sharper distinction of the two functions which it fulfills. In that great social organ which, collectively, we call literature, there may be distinguished two separate offices,

that may blend and often *do* so, but capable, severally, of a severe insulation, and naturally fitted for reciprocal repulsion. There is, first, the literature of *knowledge,* and, secondly, the literature of *power.* The function of the first is to *teach;* the function of the second is to *move:* the first is a rudder; the second an oar or a sail. The first speaks to the *mere* discursive understanding; the second speaks ultimately, it may happen, to the higher understanding, or reason, but always *through* affections of pleasure and sympathy. Remotely it may travel towards an object seated in what Lord Bacon calls *dry* light; but proximately it does and must operate—else it ceases to be a literature of *power*—on and through that *humid* light which clothes itself in the mists and glittering *iris*[2] of human passions, desires, and genial emotions. Men have so little reflected on the higher functions of literature as to find it a paradox if one should describe it as a mean or subordinate purpose of books to give information. But this is a paradox only in the sense which makes it honourable to be paradoxical. Whenever we talk in ordinary language of seeking information or gaining knowledge, we understand the words as connected with something of absolute novelty. But it is the grandeur of all truth which *can* occupy a very high place in human interests that it is never absolutely novel to the meanest of minds: it exists eternally, by way of germ or latent principle, in the lowest as in the highest, needing to be developed but never to be planted. To be capable of transplantation is the immediate criterion of a truth that ranges on a lower scale. Besides which, there is a rarer thing than truth, namely, *power,* or deep sympathy with truth. What is the effect, for instance, upon society, of children? By the pity, by the tenderness, and by the peculiar modes of admiration, which connect themselves with the helplessness, with the innocence, and with the simplicity of children, not only are the primal affections strengthened and continually renewed, but the qualities which are dearest in the sight of heaven —the frailty, for instance, which appeals to forbearance, the innocence which symbolises the heavenly, and the simplicity which is most alien from the worldly—are kept up in perpetual remembrance, and their ideals are continually refreshed. A purpose of the same nature is answered by the higher literature, *viz.,* the literature of power. What do you learn from *Paradise*

1 Charles I, for example, when Prince of Wales, and many others in his father's court, gained their known familiarity with Shakespeare—not through the original quartos, so slenderly diffused, nor through the first folio of 1623, but through the court representations of his chief dramas at Whitehall.—(De Quincey.)

2 rainbow.

Lost? Nothing at all. What do you learn from a cookery-book? Something new, something that you did not know before, in every paragraph. But would you therefore put the wretched cookery-book on a higher level of estimation than the divine poem? What you owe to Milton is not any knowledge, of which a million separate items are still but a million of advancing steps on the same earthly level; what you owe is *power,* that is, exercise and expansion to your own latent capacity of sympathy with the infinite, where every pulse and each separate influx is a step upwards, a step ascending as upon a Jacob's ladder[3] from earth to mysterious altitudes above the earth. *All* the steps of knowledge, from first to last, carry you further on the same plane, but could never raise you one foot above your ancient level of earth; whereas the very *first* step in power is a flight, is an ascending movement into another element where earth is forgotten.

Were it not that human sensibilities are ventilated and continually called out into exercise by the great phenomena of infancy, or of real life as it moves through chance and change, or of literature as it recombines these elements in the mimicries of poetry, romance, etc., it is certain that, like any animal power or muscular energy falling into disuse, all such sensibilities would gradually droop and dwindle. It is in relation to these great *moral* capacities of man that the literature of power, as contra-distinguished from that of knowledge, lives and has its field of action. It is concerned with what is highest in man; for the Scriptures themselves never condescended to deal by suggestion or co-operation with the mere discursive understanding: when speaking of man in his intellectual capacity, the Scriptures speak, not of the understanding, but of *'the understanding heart,'*[4] making the heart,—that is, the great *intuitive* (or non-discursive) organ, to be the interchangeable formula for man in his highest state of capacity for the infinite. Tragedy, romance, fairy tale, or epopee,[5] all alike restore to man's mind the ideals of justice, of hope, of truth, of mercy, of retribution, which else (left to the support of daily life in its realities) would languish for want of sufficient illustration. What is meant, for instance, by *poetic justice?* It does not mean a justice that differs by its object from the ordinary justice of human jurisprudence, for then it must

be confessedly a very bad kind of justice; but it means a justice that differs from common forensic justice by the degree in which it *attains* its object, a justice that is more omnipotent over its own ends, as dealing, not with the refractory elements of earthly life, but with the elements of its own creation and with materials flexible to its own purest preconceptions. It is certain that, were it not for the literature of power, these ideals would often remain amongst us as mere arid notional forms; whereas, by the creative forces of man put forth in literature, they gain a vernal life of restoration and germinate into vital activities. The commonest novel, by moving in alliance with human fears and hopes, with human instincts of wrong and right, sustains and quickens those affections. Calling them into action, it rescues them from torpor. And hence the pre-eminency, over all authors that merely *teach,* of the meanest that moves, or that teaches, if at all, indirectly *by* moving. The very highest work that has ever existed in the literature of knowledge is but a provisional work, a book upon trial and sufferance, and *quamdiu bene se gesserit.*[6] Let its teaching be even partially revised, let it be but expanded, nay, even let its teaching be but placed in a better order, and instantly it is superseded. Whereas the feeblest works in the literature of power, surviving at all, survive as finished and unalterable among men. For instance, the *Principia* of Sir Isaac Newton was a book *militant* on earth from the first.[7] In all stages of its progress it would have to fight for its existence: first, as regards absolute truth; secondly, when that combat was over, as regards its form, or mode of presenting the truth. And as soon as a La Place,[8] or anybody else, builds higher upon the foundations laid by this book, effectually he throws it out of the sunshine into decay and darkness; by weapons won from this book he superannuates and destroys this book, so that soon the name of Newton remains as a mere *nominis umbra,*[9] but his book, as a living power, has transmigrated into other forms. Now, on the contrary, the *Iliad,* the *Prometheus* of Æschylus, the *Othello* or *King Lear,* the *Hamlet* or *Macbeth,* and the *Paradise Lost* are not militant but triumphant forever, as long as the languages exist in which they speak or can be taught to speak. They never

---

3 Genesis, xxviii, 12.
4 I Kings, iii, 12.
5 epic.

6 'during good behavior.'
7 Published in 1687, the *Principia* was a landmark in scientific thought.
8 French astronomer and mathematician, 1749–1827.
9 'shadow of a name.'

can transmigrate into new incarnations. To reproduce these in new forms or variations, even if in some things they should be improved, would be to plagiarise. A good steam-engine is properly superseded by a better. But one lovely pastoral valley is not superseded by another, nor a statue of Praxiteles[10] by a statue of Michael Angelo.[11] These things are separated, not by imparity, but by disparity. They are not thought of as unequal under the same standard, but as different in *kind,* and, if otherwise equal, as equal under a different standard. Human works of immortal beauty and works of nature in one respect stand on the same footing: they never absolutely repeat each other, never approach so near as not to differ; and they differ not as better and worse, or simply by more and less; they differ by undecipherable and incommunicable differences, that cannot be caught by mimicries, that cannot be reflected in the mirror of copies, that cannot become ponderable in the scales of vulgar comparison. . . . At this hour, five hundred years since their creation, the tales of Chaucer, never equalled on this earth for their tenderness, and for life of picturesqueness, are read familiarly by many in the charming language of their natal day, and by others in the modernisations of Dryden, of Pope, and Wordsworth. At this hour one thousand eight hundred years since their creation, the Pagan tales of Ovid, never equalled on this earth for the gaiety of their movement and the capricious graces of their narrative, are read by all Christendom. This man's people and their monuments are dust; but *he* is alive: he has survived them, as he told us that he had it in his commission to do, by a thousand years; 'and *shall* a thousand more.'

All the literature of knowledge builds only ground nests, that are swept away by floods, or confounded by the plough; but the literature of power builds nests in aërial altitudes of temples sacred from violation, or of forests inaccessible to fraud. *This* is a great prerogative of the *power* literature; and it is a greater which lies in the mode of its influence. The *knowledge* literature, like the fashion of this world, passeth away. An Encyclopædia is its abstract; and, in this respect, it may be taken for its speaking symbol, that, before one generation has passed, an Encyclopædia is superannuated; for it speaks through the dead memory and unimpassioned understanding, which have not the repose of higher faculties, but are continually enlarging and varying their phylacteries. But all literature, properly so called—literature *κατ' ἐξοχην*,[12] for the very same reason that it is so much more durable than the literature of knowledge—is (and by the very same proportion it is) more intense and electrically searching in its impressions. The directions in which the tragedy of this planet has trained our human feelings to play, and the combinations into which the poetry of this planet has thrown our human passions of love and hatred, of admiration and contempt, exercise a power bad or good over human life, that cannot be contemplated, when stretching through many generations, without a sentiment allied to awe. And of this let every one be assured—that he owes to the impassioned books which he has read, many a thousand more of emotions than he can consciously trace back to them. Dim by their origination, these emotions yet arise in him and mould him through life like forgotten incidents of his childhood. . . .

1848

From THE ENGLISH MAIL-COACH

I. GOING DOWN WITH VICTORY

But the grandest chapter of our experience within the whole mail-coach service was on those occasions when we went down from London with the news of victory. A period of about ten years stretched from Trafalgar to Waterloo; the second and third years of which period (1806 and 1807) were comparatively sterile; but the other nine (from 1805 to 1815 inclusively) furnished a long succession of victories, the least of which, in such a contest of Titans, had an inappreciable[1] value of position: partly for its absolute interference with the plans of our enemy, but still more from its keeping alive through central Europe the sense of a deep-seated vulnerability in France. Even to tease the coasts of our enemy, to mortify them by continual blockades, to insult them by capturing if it were but a baubling[2] schooner under the eyes of their arrogant armies, repeated from time to time a sullen proclamation of power lodged in one quarter to which the hopes of Christendom turned in secret. How much more

---

10 Greek sculptor of the fourth century B.C.
11 Michelangelo Buonarroti, 1475–1564, famous Florentine sculptor, painter, architect, and poet.

---

12 'pre-eminently.'

---

1 inestimable.   2 trifling.

loudly must this proclamation have spoken in the audacity of having bearded the *élite* of their troops, and having beaten them in pitched battles! Five years of life it was worth paying down for the privilege of an outside place on a mail-coach, when carrying down the first tidings of any such event. And it is to be noted that, from our insular situation, and the multitude of our frigates disposable for the rapid transmission of intelligence, rarely did any unauthorized rumour steal away a prelibation[3] from the first aroma of the regular despatches. The government news was generally the earliest news.

From eight p.m. to fifteen or twenty minutes later imagine the mails assembled on parade in Lombard Street; where, at that time,[4] and not in St. Martin's-le-Grand, was seated the General Post-Office. In what exact strength we mustered I do not remember; but, from the length of each separate *attelage,*[5] we filled the street, though a long one, and though we were drawn up in double file. On *any* night the spectacle was beautiful. The absolute perfection of all the appointments about the carriages and the harness, their strength, their brilliant cleanliness, their beautiful simplicity—but, more than all, the royal magnificence of the horses—were what might first have fixed the attention. Every carriage on every morning in the year was taken down to an official inspector for examination: wheels, axles, linchpins, pole, glasses, lamps, were all critically probed and tested. Every part of every carriage had been cleaned, every horse had been groomed, with as much rigour as if they belonged to a private gentleman; and that part of the spectacle offered itself always. But the night before us is a night of victory; and, behold! to the ordinary display what a heart-shaking addition! —horses, men, carriages, all are dressed in laurels and flowers, oak-leaves and ribbons. The guards, as being officially his Majesty's servants, and of the coachmen such as are within the privilege of the post-office, wear the royal liveries of course; and, as it is summer (for all the *land* victories were naturally won in summer), they wear, on this fine evening, these liveries exposed to view, without any covering of upper coats. Such a costume, and the elaborate arrangement of the laurels in their hats, dilate their hearts, by giving to them openly a personal connexion with the great news in which already they have the gen-

eral interest of patriotism. That great national sentiment surmounts and quells all sense of ordinary distinctions. Those passengers who happen to be gentlemen are now hardly to be distinguished as such except by dress; for the usual reserve of their manner in speaking to the attendants has on this night melted away. One heart, one pride, one glory, connects every man by the transcendent bond of his national blood. The spectators, who are numerous beyond precedent, express their sympathy with these fervent feelings by continual hurrahs. Every moment are shouted aloud by the post-office servants, and summoned to draw up, the great ancestral names of cities known to history through a thousand years—Lincoln, Winchester, Portsmouth, Gloucester, Oxford, Bristol, Manchester, York, Newcastle, Edinburgh, Glasgow, Perth, Sterling, Aberdeen—expressing the grandeur of the empire by the antiquity of its towns, and the grandeur of the mail establishment by the diffusive radiation of its separate missions. Every moment you hear the thunder of lids locked down upon the mail-bags. That sound to each individual mail is the signal for drawing off, which process is the finest part of the entire spectacle. Then come the horses into play. Horses! can these be horses that bound off with the action and gestures of leopards? What stir!—what sea-like ferment! —what a thundering of wheels!—what a tramping of hoofs!—what a sounding of trumpets!— what farewell cheers—what redoubling peals of brotherly congratulation, connecting the name of the particular mail—'Liverpool forever!'—with the name of the particular victory—'Badajoz forever!' or 'Salamanca forever!' The half-slumbering consciousness that all night long, and all the next day—perhaps for even a longer period— many of these mails, like fire racing along a train of gunpowder, will be kindling at every instant new successions of burning joy, has an obscure effect of multiplying the victory itself, by multiplying to the imagination into infinity the stages of its progressive diffusion. A fiery arrow seems to be let loose, which from that moment is destined to travel, without intermission, westwards for three hundred miles[6]—northwards for six

---

3 foretaste.   4 the era before Waterloo.
5 team and coach.

6 Of necessity, this scale of measurement, to an American, if he happens to be a thoughtless man, must sound ludicrous. Accordingly, I remember a case in which an American writer indulges himself in the luxury of a little fibbing, by ascribing to an Englishman a pompous account of the Thames, constructed entirely upon American ideas of grandeur, and concluding in something like these terms:—'And sir, arriving at London, this mighty father of rivers attains a breadth of at least two furlongs, having, in its winding course, traversed the astonishing distance of one hundred

hundred; and the sympathy of our Lombard Street friends at parting is exalted a hundredfold by a sort of visionary sympathy with the yet slumbering sympathies which in so vast a succession we are going to awake.

Liberated from the embarrassments of the city, and issuing into the broad uncrowded avenues of the northern suburbs, we soon begin to enter upon our natural pace of ten miles an hour. In the broad light of the summer evening, the sun, perhaps, only just at the point of setting, we are seen from every storey of every house. Heads of every age crowd to the windows; young and old understand the language of our victorious symbols; and rolling volleys of sympathising cheers run along us, behind us, and before us. The beggar, rearing himself against the wall, forgets his lameness—real or assumed—thinks not of his whining trade, but stands erect, with bold exulting smiles, as we pass him. The victory has healed him, and says, Be thou whole![7] Women and children, from garrets alike and cellars, through infinite London, look down or look up with loving eyes upon our gay ribbons and our martial laurels; sometimes kiss their hands; sometimes hang out, as signals of affection, pocket-handkerchiefs, aprons, dusters, anything that, by catching the summer breezes, will express an aerial jubilation. On the London side of Barnet[8] to which we draw near within a few minutes after nine, observe that private carriage which is approaching us. The weather being so warm, the glasses are all down; and one may read, as on the stage of a theatre, everything that goes on within. It contains three ladies—one likely to be 'mamma,' and two of seventeen or eighteen, who are probably her daughters. What lovely animation, what beautiful unpremeditated pantomime, explaining to us every syllable that passes, in these ingenuous girls! By the sudden

start and raising of the hands on first discovering our laurelled equipage, by the sudden movement and appeal to the elder lady from both of them, and by the heightened colour on their animated countenances, we can almost hear them saying, 'See, see! Look at their laurels! Oh, mamma! there has been a great battle in Spain; and it has been a great victory.' In a moment we are on the point of passing them. We passengers—I on the box, and the two on the roof behind me—raise our hats to the ladies; the coachman makes his professional salute with the whip; the guard even, though punctilious on the matter of his dignity as an officer under the crown, touches his hat. The ladies move to us, in return, with a winning graciousness of gesture; all smile on each side in a way that nobody could misunderstand, and that nothing short of a grand national sympathy could so instantaneously prompt. Will these ladies say that we are nothing to *them?* Oh no; they will not say *that.* They cannot deny—they do not deny—that for this night they are our sisters; gentle or simple, scholar or illiterate servant, for twelve hours to come, we on the outside have the honour to be their brothers. Those poor women, again, who stop to gaze upon us with delight at the entrance of Barnet, and seem, by their air of weariness, to be returning from labour—do you mean to say that they are washerwomen and charwomen? Oh, my poor friend, you are quite mistaken. I assure you they stand in a far higher rank; for this one night they feel themselves by birthright to be daughters of England, and answer to no humbler title.

Every joy, however, even rapturous joy—such is the sad law of earth—may carry with it grief, or fear of grief, to some. Three miles beyond Barnet, we see approaching us another private carriage, nearly repeating the circumstances of the former case. Here, also, the glasses are all down; here, also, is an elderly lady seated; but the two daughters are missing; for the single young person sitting by the lady's side seems to be an attendant—so I judge from her dress, and her air of respectful reserve. The lady is in mourning; and her countenance expresses sorrow. At first she does not look up; so that I believe she is not aware of our approach, until she hears the measured beating of our horses' hoofs. Then she raises her eyes to settle them painfully on our triumphal equipage. Our decorations explain the case to her at once; but she beholds them with apparent anxiety, or even with terror.

and seventy miles.' And this the candid American thinks it fair to contrast with the scale of the Mississippi. Now, it is hardly worth while to answer a pure fiction gravely; else one might say that no Englishman out of Bedlam ever thought of looking in an island for the rivers of a continent, nor, consequently, could have thought of looking for the peculiar grandeur of the Thames in the length of its course, or in the extent of soil which it drains. Yet, if he *had* been so absurd, the American might have recollected that a river, not to be compared with the Thames even as to volume of water—*viz.*, the Tiber—has contrived to make itself heard of in this world for twenty-five centuries to an extent not reached as yet by any river, however corpulent, of his own land. The glory of the Thames is measured by the destiny of the population to which it ministers, by the commerce which it supports, by the grandeur of the empire in which, though far from the largest, it is the most influential stream.—(De Quincey.)

7 Luke, viii, 48.

8 a Hertfordshire village, eleven miles north of London.

Some time before this, I, finding it difficult to hit a flying mark when embarrassed by the coachman's person and reins intervening, had given to the guard a *Courier* evening paper, containing the gazette,[9] for the next carriage that might pass. Accordingly he tossed it in, so folded that the huge capitals expressing some such legend as GLORIOUS VICTORY might catch the eye at once. To see the paper, however, at all, interpreted as it was by our ensigns of triumph, explained everything; and, if the guard were right in thinking the lady to have received it with a gesture of horror, it could not be doubtful that she had suffered some deep personal affliction in connexion with this Spanish war.

Here, now, was the case of one who, having formerly suffered, might, erroneously perhaps, be distressing herself with anticipations of another similar suffering. That same night, and hardly three hours later, occurred the reverse case. A poor woman, who too probably would find herself, in a day or two, to have suffered the heaviest of afflictions by the battle, blindly allowed herself to express an exultation so unmeasured in the news and its details as gave to her the appearance which amongst Celtic Highlanders is called *fey*.[10] This was at some little town where we changed horses an hour or two after midnight. Some fair or wake had kept the people up out of their beds, and had occasioned a partial illumination of the stalls and booths, presenting an unusual but very impressive effect. We saw many lights moving about as we drew near; and perhaps the most striking scene on the whole route was our reception at this place. The flashing of torches and the beautiful radiance of blue lights (technically, Bengal lights) upon the heads of our horses; the fine effect of such a showery and ghostly illumination falling upon our flowers and glittering laurels;[11] whilst all around ourselves, that formed a centre of light, the darkness gathered on the rear and flanks in massy blackness: these optical splendours together with the prodigious enthusiasm of the people composed a picture at once scenical and affecting, theatrical and holy. As we stayed for three or four minutes, I alighted; and immediately from a dismantled stall in the street, where

no doubt she had been presiding through the earlier part of the night, advanced eagerly a middle-aged woman. The sight of my newspaper it was that had drawn her attention upon myself. The victory which we were carrying down to the provinces on *this* occasion was the imperfect one of Talavera[12]—imperfect for its results, such was the virtual treachery[13] of the Spanish general, Cuesta, but not imperfect in its ever-memorable heroism. I told her the main outline of the battle. The agitation of her enthusiasm had been so conspicuous when listening, and when first applying for information, that I could not but ask her if she had not some relative in the Peninsular army. Oh yes; her only son was there. In what regiment? He was a trooper in the 23d Dragoons. My heart sank within me as she made that answer. This sublime regiment, which an Englishman should never mention without raising his hat to their memory, had made the most memorable and effective charge recorded in military annals. They leaped their horses—*over* a trench where they could; *into* it, and with the result of death or mutilation, when they could *not*. What proportion cleared the trench is nowhere stated. Those who *did* closed up and went down upon the enemy with such divinity of fervour (I use the word *divinity* by design: the inspiration of God must have prompted this movement for those even then He was calling to His presence) that two results followed. As regarded the enemy, this 23d Dragoons, not, I believe, originally three hundred and fifty strong, paralysed a French column six thousand strong, then ascended the hill, and fixed the gaze of the whole French army. As regarded themselves, the 23d were supposed at first to have been barely not annihilated; but eventually, I believe, about one in four survived. And this, then, was the regiment— a regiment already for some hours glorified and hallowed to the ear of all London, as lying stretched, by a large majority, upon one bloody aceldama[14]—in which the young trooper served whose mother was now talking in a spirit of such joyous enthusiasm. Did I tell her the truth? Had I the heart to break up her dreams? No. Tomorrow, said I to myself—tomorrow, or the next day, will publish the worst. For one night more wherefore should she not sleep in peace? After tomor-

---

9 an official paper listing appointments, honors, names of bankrupts, etc.

10 a state of feeling excited by a premonition of approaching death or some other calamity.

11 I must observe that the color of *green* suffers almost a spiritual change and exaltation under the effect of Bengal lights.—(De Quincey.)

12 Near this Spanish town, in 1809, the English and Spanish forces under Wellington and Cuesta defeated the French under King Joseph.

13 The 'virtual treachery' of Cuesta consisted of his refusal to follow Wellington's advice in making battle preparations.

14 field of blood.

row the chances are too many that peace will forsake her pillow. This brief respite, then, let her owe to *my* gift and *my* forbearance. But, if I told her not of the bloody price that had been paid, not therefore was I silent on the contributions from her son's regiment to that day's service and glory. I showed her not the funeral banners under which the noble regiment was sleeping. I lifted not the overshadowing laurels from the bloody trench in which horse and rider lay mangled together. But I told her how these dear children of England, officers and privates, had leaped their horses over all obstacles as gaily as hunters to the morning's chase. I told her how they rode their horses into the midst of death,—saying to myself, but not saying to *her,* 'and laid down their young lives for thee, O mother England! as willingly—poured out their noble blood as cheerfully—as ever, after a long day's sport, when infants, they had rested their weary heads upon their mother's knees, or had sung to sleep in her arms.' Strange it is, yet true, that she seemed to have no fears for her son's safety, even after this knowledge that the 23d Dragoons had been memorably engaged; but so much was she enraptured by the knowledge that *his* regiment, and therefore that *he,* had rendered conspicuous service in the dreadful conflict—a service which had actually made them, within the last twelve hours, the foremost topic of conversation in London—so absolutely was fear swallowed up in joy —that, in the mere simplicity of her fervent nature, the poor woman threw her arms round my neck, as she thought of her son, and gave to *me* the kiss which secretly was meant for *him.*

II. THE VISION OF SUDDEN DEATH

What is to be taken as the predominant opinion of man, reflective and philosophic, upon SUDDEN DEATH? It is remarkable that, in different conditions of society, sudden death has been variously regarded as the consummation of an earthly career most fervently to be desired, or, again, as that consummation which is with most horror to be deprecated. Cæsar the Dictator, at his last dinner-party *(cœna),* on the very evening before his assassination, when the minutes of his earthly career were numbered, being asked what death, in *his* judgment, might be pronounced the most eligible, replied 'That which should be most sudden.'[15] On the other hand, the divine Litany of our English Church, when breathing forth supplications, as if in some representative character, for the whole human race prostrate before God, places such a death in the very van of horrors: 'From lightning and tempest; from plague, pestilence, and famine; from battle and murder, and from SUDDEN DEATH—*Good Lord, deliver us.*' Sudden death is here made to crown the climax in a grand ascent of calamities; it is ranked among the last of curses; and yet by the noblest of Romans it was ranked as the first of blessings. In that difference most readers will see little more than the essential difference between Christianity and Paganism. But this, on consideration, I doubt. The Christian Church may be right in its estimate of sudden death; and it is a natural feeling, though after all it may also be an infirm one, to wish for a quiet dismissal from life, as that which *seems* most reconcilable with meditation, with penitential retrospects, and with the humilities of farewell prayer. There does not, however, occur to me any direct scriptural warrant for this earnest petition of the English Litany, unless under a special construction of the word *sudden.* It seems a petition indulged rather and conceded to human infirmity than exacted from human piety. It is not so much a doctrine built upon the eternities of the Christian system as a plausible opinion built upon special varieties of physical temperament. Let that, however, be as it may, two remarks suggest themselves as prudent restraints upon a doctrine which else *may* wander, and *has* wandered, into an uncharitable superstition. The first is this: that many people are likely to exaggerate the horror of a sudden death from the disposition to lay a false stress upon words or acts simply because by an accident they have become *final* words or acts. If a man dies, for instance, by some sudden death when he happens to be intoxicated, such a death is falsely regarded with peculiar horror, as though the intoxication were suddenly exalted into a blasphemy. But *that* is unphilosophic. The man was or he was not, *habitually* a drunkard. If not, if his intoxication were a solitary accident, there can be no reason for allowing special emphasis to this act simply because through misfortune it became his final act. Nor, on the other hand, if it were no accident, but one of his *habitual* transgressions, will it be the more habitual or the more a transgression because some sudden calamity, surprising him, has caused this habitual transgression to be also a final one. Could the man have had any reason even dimly to foresee his own sudden death,

---

15 This incident is related by Suetonius in his *Life of Julius Caesar,* ch. 87.

there would have been a new feature in his act of intemperance—a feature of presumption and irreverence, as in one that, having known himself drawing near to the presence of God, should have suited his demeanour to an expectation so awful. But this is no part of the case supposed. And the only new element in the man's act is not any element of special immorality, but simply of special misfortune.

The other remark has reference to the meaning of the word *sudden.* Very possibly Cæsar and the Christian Church do not differ in the way supposed,—that is, do not differ by any difference of doctrine as between Pagan and Christian views of the moral temper appropriate to death; but perhaps they are contemplating different cases. Both contemplate a violent death, a βιαθάνατος —death that is βίαιος, or, in other words, death that is brought about, not by internal and spontaneous change, but by active force having its origin from without. In this meaning the two authorities agree. Thus far they are in harmony. But the difference is that the Roman by the word *sudden* means *unlingering,* whereas the Christian Litany by *sudden death* means a *death without warning,* consequently without any available summons to religious preparation. The poor mutineer who kneels down to gather into his heart the bullets from twelve firelocks of his pitying comrades dies by a most sudden death in Cæsar's sense; one shock, one mighty spasm, one (possibly *not* one) groan, and all is over. But, in the sense of the Litany, the mutineer's death is far from sudden: his offence originally, his imprisonment, his trial, the interval between his sentence and its execution, having all furnished him with separate warnings of his fate—having all summoned him to meet it with solemn preparation.

Here at once, in this sharp verbal distinction, we comprehend the faithful earnestness with which a holy Christian Church pleads on behalf of her poor departing children that God would vouchsafe to them the last great privilege and distinction possible on a death-bed—*viz.,* the opportunity of untroubled preparation for facing this mighty trial. Sudden death, as a mere variety in the modes of dying where death in some shape is inevitable, proposes a question of choice which, equally in the Roman and the Christian sense, will be variously answered according to each man's variety of temperament. Meantime, one aspect of sudden death there is, one modification, upon which no doubt can arise, that of all mar-

tyrdoms it is the most agitating—*viz.,* where it surprises a man under circumstances which offer (or which seem to offer) some hurrying, flying, inappreciably minute chance of evading it. Sudden as the danger which it affronts must be any effort by which such an evasion can be accomplished. Even *that,* even the sickening necessity for hurrying in extremity where all hurry seems destined to be vain,—even that anguish is liable to a hideous exasperation in one particular case: *viz.,* where the appeal is made not exclusively to the instinct of self-preservation, but to the conscience, on behalf of some other life besides your own, accidentally thrown upon *your* protection. To fail, to collapse in a service merely your own, might seem comparatively venial; though, in fact, it is far from venial. But to fail in a case where Providence has suddenly thrown into your hands the final interests of another,—a fellow-creature shuddering between the gates of life and death: this, to a man of apprehensive conscience, would mingle the misery of an atrocious criminality with the misery of a bloody calamity. You are called upon, by the case supposed, possibly to die, but to die at the very moment when, by any even partial failure or effeminate collapse of your energies, you will be self-denounced as a murderer. You had but the twinkling of an eye for your effort, and that effort might have been unavailing; but to have risen to the level of such an effort would have rescued you, though not from dying, yet from dying as a traitor to your final and farewell duty.

The situation here contemplated exposes a dreadful ulcer, lurking far down in the depths of human nature. It is not that men generally are summoned to face such awful trials. But potentially, and in shadowy outline, such a trial is moving subterraneously in perhaps all men's natures. Upon the secret mirror of our dreams such a trial is darkly projected, perhaps, to every one of us. That dream, so familiar to childhood, of meeting a lion, and, through languishing prostration in hope and the energies of hope, that constant sequel of lying down before the lion publishes the secret frailty of human nature—reveals its deep-seated falsehood to itself—records its abysmal treachery. Perhaps not one of us escapes that dream; perhaps, as by some sorrowful doom of man, that dream repeats for every one of us, through every generation, the original temptation in Eden. Every one of us, in this dream, has a bait offered to the infirm places of his own individual will; once again a snare is presented for tempting him into captivity to a luxury of ruin; once again, as in aboriginal Paradise, the man falls by his own choice; again, by infinite iteration, the ancient earth groans to Heaven, through her secret caves, over the weakness of her child. 'Nature, from her seat, sighing through all her works,' again 'gives signs of woe that all is lost';[16] and again the counter-sigh is repeated to the sorrowing heavens for the endless rebellion against God. It is not without probability that in the world of dreams every one of us ratifies for himself the original transgression. In dreams, perhaps under some secret conflict of the midnight sleeper, lighted up to the consciousness at the time, but darkened to the memory as soon as all is finished, each several child of our mysterious race completes for himself the treason of the aboriginal fall.

The incident, so memorable in itself by its features of horror, and so scenical by its grouping for the eye, which furnished the text for this reverie upon *Sudden Death* occurred to myself in the dead of night, as a solitary spectator, when seated on the box of the Manchester and Glasgow mail, in the second or third summer after Waterloo. I find it necessary to relate the circumstances, because they are such as could not have occurred unless under a singular combination of accidents. In those days, the oblique and lateral communications with many rural post-offices were so arranged, either through necessity or through defect of system, as to make it requisite for the main north-western mail (*i.e.,* the *down* mail) on reaching Manchester to halt for a number of hours; how many, I do not remember; six or seven, I think; but the result was that, in the ordinary course, the mail recommenced its journey northwards about midnight. Wearied with the long detention at a gloomy hotel, I walked out about eleven o'clock at night for the sake of fresh air; meaning to fall in with the mail and resume my seat at the post-office. The night, however, being yet dark, as the moon had scarcely risen, and the streets being at that hour empty, so as to offer no opportunities for asking the road, I lost my way, and did not reach the post-office until it was considerably past midnight; but, to my great relief (as it was important for me to be in Westmoreland by the morning), I saw in the huge saucer eyes of the mail, blazing through the gloom, an evidence that my chance was not yet lost. Past the time it was; but, by some rare accident, the mail was not even yet

ready to start. I ascended to my seat on the box, where my cloak was still lying as it had lain at the Bridgewater Arms. I had left it there in imitation of a nautical discoverer, who leaves a bit of bunting on the shore of his discovery, by way of warning off the ground the whole human race, and notifying to the Christian and the heathen worlds, with his best compliments, that he has hoisted his pocket-handkerchief once and forever upon that virgin soil: thenceforward claiming the *jus dominii*[17] to the top of the atmosphere above it, and also the right of driving shafts to the centre of the earth below it; so that all people found after this warning either aloft in upper chambers of the atmosphere, or groping in subterraneous shafts, or squatting audaciously on the surface of the soil, will be treated as trespassers—kicked, that is to say, or decapitated, as circumstances may suggest, by their very faithful servant, the owner of the said pocket-handkerchief. In the present case, it is probable that my cloak might not have been respected, and the *jus gentium*[18] might have been cruelly violated in my person—for, in the dark, people commit deeds of darkness, gas being a great ally of morality; but it so happened that on this night there was no other outside passenger; and thus the crime, which else was but too probable, missed fire for want of a criminal.

Having mounted the box, I took a small quantity of laudanum, having already travelled two hundred and fifty miles—*viz.,* from a point seventy miles beyond London. In the taking of laudanum there was nothing extraordinary. But by accident it drew upon me the special attention of my assessor on the box, the coachman. And in *that* also there was nothing extraordinary. But by accident, and with great delight, it drew my own attention to the fact that this coachman was a monster in point of bulk, and that he had but one eye. In fact, he had been foretold by Virgil as

Monstrum horrendum, informe, ingens, cui
    lumen ademptum.[19]

He answered to the conditions in every one of the items:—1, a monster he was; 2, dreadful; 3, shapeless; 4, huge; 5, who had lost an eye. But why should *that* delight *me?* Had he been one of the Calendars[20] in *The Arabian Nights,* and had

---

16 *Paradise Lost,* IX, 782–4.

17 'law of ownership.'   18 'law of nations.'

19 'a horrible deformed immense monster with one eye'—(*Æneid* III, 658).

20 an order of mendicant friars founded in Arabia in the fourteenth century.

paid down his eye as the price of his criminal curiosity, what right had *I* to exult in his misfortune? I did *not* exult; I delighted in no man's punishment, though it were even merited. But these personal distinctions (Nos. 1, 2, 3, 4, 5) identified in an instant an old friend of mine whom I had known in the south for some years as the most masterly of mail-coachmen. He was the man in all Europe that could (if *any* could) have driven six-in-hand full gallop over *Al Sirat*[21] —that dreadful bridge of Mahomet, with no side battlements, and of *extra* room not enough for a razor's edge—leading right across the bottomless gulf. Under this eminent man, whom in Greek I cognominated Cyclops *Diphrélates* (Cyclops the Charioteer), I, and others known to me, studied the Diphrelatic art. Excuse, reader, a word too elegant to be pedantic. As a pupil, though I paid extra fees, it is to be lamented that I did not stand high in his esteem. It showed his dogged honesty (though, observe, not his discernment) that he could not see my merits. Let us excuse his absurdity in this particular by remembering his want of an eye. Doubtless *that* made him blind to my merits. In the art of conversation, however, he admitted that I had the whip-hand of him. On this present occasion great joy was at our meeting. But what was Cyclops doing here? Had the medical men recommended northern air, or how? I collected, from such explanations as he volunteered, that he had an interest at stake in some suit-at-law now pending at Lancaster; so that probably he had got himself transferred to this station for the purpose of connecting with his professional pursuits an instant readiness for the calls of his law-suit.

Meantime, what are we stopping for? Surely we have now waited long enough. Oh, this procrastinating mail, and this procrastinating post-office! Can't they take a lesson upon that subject from *me?* Some people have called *me* procrastinating. Yet you are witness, reader, that I was here kept waiting for the post-office. Will the post-office lay its hand on its heart, in its moments of sobriety, and assert that ever it waited for me? What are they about? The guard tells me that there is a large extra accumulation of foreign mails this night, owing to irregularities caused by war, by wind, by weather, in the packet service, which as yet does not benefit at all by steam. For an *extra* hour, it seems, the post-office has been engaged in threshing out the pure wheaten correspondence of Glasgow, and winnowing it from the chaff of all baser intermediate towns. But at last all is finished. Sound your horn, guard! Manchester, good-bye! we've lost an hour by your criminal conduct at the post-office: which, however, though I do not mean to part with a serviceable ground of complaint, and one which really *is* such for the horses, to me secretly is an advantage, since it compels us to look sharply for this lost hour amongst the next eight or nine, and to recover it (if we can) at the rate of one mile extra per hour. Off we are at last, and at eleven miles an hour; and for the moment I detect no changes in the energy or in the skill of Cyclops.

From Manchester to Kendal, which virtually (though not in law) is the capital of Westmoreland, there were at this time seven stages of eleven miles each. The first five of these, counting from Manchester, terminate in Lancaster; which is therefore fifty-five miles north of Manchester, and the same distance exactly from Liverpool. The first three stages terminate in Preston (called, by way of distinction from other towns of that name, *Proud* Preston), at which place it is that the separate roads from Liverpool and from Manchester to the north become confluent.[22] Within these first three stages lay the foundation, the progress, and termination of our night's adventure. During the first stage, I found out that Cyclops was mortal: he was liable to the shocking affection of sleep—a thing which previously I had never suspected. If a man indulges in the vicious habit of sleeping, all the skill in aurigation[23] of Apollo himself, with the horses of Aurora to execute his notions, avails him nothing. 'Oh, Cyclops!' I exclaimed, 'thou are mortal. My friend, thou snorest.' Through the first eleven miles, however, this infirmity—which I grieve to say that he shared with the whole Pagan Pantheon[24]—betrayed itself only by brief snatches. On waking up, he made an apology for himself which, instead of mending matters, laid open a gloomy vista of coming disasters. The summer assizes, he reminded me, were now going on at Lancaster: in consequence of which for three nights and three days he had not lain down in a bed. During the day he was waiting for his own

---

21 the bridge the width of a sword's edge over which souls must pass from Hades to Paradise.

22 Suppose a capital Y (the Pythagorean letter): Lancaster is at the foot of this letter; Liverpool at the top of the *right* branch; Manchester at the top of the *left;* Proud Preston at the centre, where the two branches unite. It is thirty-three miles along either of the two branches; it is twenty-two miles along the stem,—*viz.,* from Preston in the middle to Lancaster at the root. There's a lesson in geography for the reader.—(De Quincey.)

23 the act of driving a chariot.

24 that is, all the gods put together.

summons as a witness on the trial in which he was interested, or else, lest he should be missing at the critical moment, was drinking with the other witnesses under the pastoral surveillance of the attorneys. During the night, or that part of it which at sea would form the middle watch, he was driving. This explanation certainly accounted for his drowsiness, but in a way which made it much more alarming; since now, after several days' resistance to this infirmity, at length he was steadily giving way. Throughout the second stage he grew more and more drowsy. In the second mile of the third stage he surrendered himself finally and without a struggle to his perilous temptation. All his past resistance had but deepened the weight of this final oppression. Seven atmospheres of sleep rested upon him; and, to consummate the case, our worthy guard, after singing *Love Amongst the Roses* for perhaps thirty times, without invitation and without applause, had in revenge moodily resigned himself to slumber—not so deep, doubtless, as the coachman's, but deep enough for mischief. And thus at last, about ten miles from Preston, it came about that I found myself left in charge of his Majesty's London and Glasgow mail, then running at the least twelve miles an hour.

What made this negligence less criminal than else it must have been thought was the condition of the roads at night during the assizes. At that time, all the law business of populous Liverpool, and also of populous Manchester, with its vast cincture[25] of populous rural districts, was called up by ancient usage to the tribunal of Lilliputian Lancaster. To break up this old traditional usage required, 1, a conflict with powerful established interests; 2, a large system of new arrangements, and 3, a new parliamentary statute. But as yet this change was merely in contemplation. As things were at present, twice in the year[26] so vast a body of business rolled northwards from the southern quarter of the county that for a fortnight at least it occupied the severe exertions of two judges in its despatch. The consequence of this was that every horse available for such a service, along the whole line of road, was exhausted in carrying down the multitudes of people who were parties to the different suits. By sunset, therefore, it usually happened that, through utter exhaustion amongst men and horses, the road sank into profound silence. Ex-

cept the exhaustion in the vast adjacent county of York from a contested election, no such silence succeeding to no such fiery uproar was ever witnessed in England.

On this occasion the usual silence and solitude prevailed along the road. Not a hoof nor a wheel was to be heard. And, to strengthen this false luxurious confidence in the noiseless roads, it happened also that the night was one of peculiar solemnity and peace. For my own part, though slightly alive to the possibilities of peril, I had so far yielded to the influence of the mighty calm as to sink into a profound reverie. The month was August; in the middle of which lay my own birthday—a festival to every thoughtful man suggesting solemn and often sigh-born[27] thoughts. The county was my own native county[28]—upon which, in its southern section, more than upon any equal area known to man past or present, had descended the original curse of labour in its heaviest form, not mastering the bodies only of men, as of slaves, or criminals in mines, but working through the fiery will. Upon no equal space of earth was, or ever had been, the same energy of human power put forth daily. At this particular season also of the assizes, that dreadful hurricane of flight and pursuit, as it might have seemed to a stranger, which swept to and from Lancaster all day long, hunting the county up and down, and regularly subsiding back into silence about sunset, could not fail (when united with this permanent distinction of Lancashire as the very metropolis and citadel of labour) to point the thoughts pathetically upon that counter-vision of rest, of saintly repose from strife and sorrow, towards which, as to their secret haven, the profounder aspirations of man's heart are in solitude continually travelling. Obliquely upon our left we were nearing the sea; which also must, under the present circumstances, be repeating the general state of halcyon[29] repose. The sea, the atmosphere, the light, bore each an orchestral part in this universal lull. Moonlight and the first timid tremblings of the dawn were by this time blending; and the blendings were brought into a still more exquisite state of unity by a slight silvery mist, motionless and dreamy, that covered the woods and fields, but with a veil of equable transparency. Except the feet of our own horses,—which, running on a sandy margin

---

25 encirclement.

26 There were at that time only two assizes even in the most populous counties—*viz.*, the Lent Assizes and the Summer Assizes.—(De Quincey.)

27 I owe the suggestion of this word to an obscure remembrance of a beautiful phrase in Giraldus Cambrensis—*viz., suspiriosæ cogitationes.*—(De Quincey.)

28 Lancashire, celebrated for its coal production, commerce, and manufactures.

29 calm; peaceful.

of the road, made but little disturbance,—there was no sound abroad. In the clouds and on the earth prevailed the same majestic peace; and, in spite of all that the villain of a schoolmaster has done for the ruin of our sublimer thoughts, which are the thoughts of our infancy, we still believe in no such nonsense as a limited atmosphere. Whatever we may swear with our false feigning lips, in our faithful hearts we still believe, and must forever believe, in fields of air traversing the total gulf between earth and the central heavens. Still, in the confidence of children that tread without fear *every* chamber in their father's house, and to whom no door is closed, we, in that Sabbatic[30] vision which sometimes is revealed for an hour upon nights like this, ascend with easy steps from the sorrow-stricken fields of earth upwards to the sandals of God.

Suddenly, from thoughts like these I was awakened to a sullen sound, as of some motion on the distant road. It stole upon the air for a moment; I listened in awe; but then it died away. Once roused, however, I could not but observe with alarm the quickened motion of our horses. Ten years' experience had made my eye learned in the valuing of motion; and I saw that we were now running thirteen miles an hour. I pretend to no presence of mind. On the contrary, my fear is that I am miserably and shamefully deficient in that quality as regards action. The palsy of doubt and distraction hangs like some guilty weight of dark unfathomed remembrances upon my energies when the signal is flying for *action.* But, on the other hand, this accursed gift I have, as regards *thought,* that in the first step towards the possibility of a misfortune I see its total evolution; in the radix[31] of the series I see too certainly and too instantly its entire expansion; in the first syllable of the dreadful sentence I read already the last. It was not that I feared for ourselves. *Us* our bulk and impetus charmed against peril in any collision. And I had ridden through too many hundreds of perils that were frightful to approach, that were matter of laughter to look back upon, the first face of which was horror, the parting face a jest—for any anxiety to rest upon *our* interests. The mail was not built, I felt assured, nor bespoke, that could betray *me* who trusted to its protection. But any carriage that we could meet would be frail and light in comparison of ourselves. And I remarked this ominous accident of our situation,—we were on the wrong

side of the road. But then, it may be said, the other party, if other there was, might also be on the wrong side; and two wrongs might make a right. *That* was not likely. The same motive which had drawn *us* to the right-hand side of the road—*viz.,* the luxury of the soft beaten sand as contrasted with the paved centre—would prove attractive to others. The two adverse carriages would therefore, to a certainty, be travelling on the same side; and from this side, as not being ours in law, the crossing over to the other would, of course, be looked for from *us.*[32] Our lamps, still lighted, would give the impression of vigilance on our part. And every creature that met us would rely upon *us* for quartering.[33] All this, and if the separate links of the anticipation had been a thousand times more, I saw, not discursively, or by effort, or by succession, but by one flash of horrid simultaneous intuition.

Under this steady though rapid anticipation of the evil which *might* be gathering ahead, ah! what a sullen mystery of fear, what a sigh of woe, was that which stole upon the air, as again the far-off sound of a wheel was heard! A whisper it was—a whisper from, perhaps, four miles off —secretly announcing a ruin that, being foreseen, was not the less inevitable; that, being known, was not therefore healed. What could be done—who was it that could do it—to check the storm-flight of these maniacal horses? Could I not seize the reins from the grasp of the slumbering coachman? You, reader, think that it would have been in *your* power to do so. And I quarrel not with your estimate of yourself. But, from the way in which the coachman's hand was viced between his upper and lower thigh, this was impossible. Easy was it? See, then, that bronze equestrian statue. The cruel rider has kept the bit in his horses's mouth for two centuries. Unbridle him for a minute, if you please, and wash his mouth with water. Easy was it? Unhorse me, then, that imperial rider; knock me those marble feet from those marble stirrups of Charlemagne.

The sounds ahead strengthened, and were now too clearly the sounds of wheels. Who and what could it be? Was it industry in a taxed cart? Was it youthful gaiety in a gig? Was it sorrow that loitered, or joy that raced? For as yet the snatches

---

30 holy; so-called from the Sabbath, day of rest and worship.
31 original source or cause.

32 It is true that, according to the law of the case as established by legal precedents, all carriages were required to give way before royal equipages, and therefore before the mail as one of them. But this only increased the danger, as being a regulation very imperfectly made known, very unequally enforced, and therefore often embarrassing the movements on both sides.—(De Quincey.)
33 This is the technical word, and, I presume, derived from the French *cartayer,* to evade a rut or any obstacle.—(De Quincey.)

of sound were too intermitting, from distance, to decipher the character of the motion. Whoever were the travellers, something must be done to warn them. Upon the other party rests the active responsibility, but upon *us*—and, woe is me! that *us* was reduced to my frail opium-shattered self—rests the responsibility of warning. Yet, how should this be accomplished? Might I not sound the guard's horn? Already, on the first thought, I was making my way over the roof to the guard's seat. But this, from the accident which I have mentioned, of the foreign mails being piled upon the roof, was a difficult and even dangerous attempt to one cramped by nearly three hundred miles of outside travelling. And, fortunately, before I had lost much time in the attempt, our frantic horses swept round an angle of the road which opened upon us that final stage where the collision must be accomplished and the catastrophe sealed. All was apparently finished. The court was sitting; the case was heard; the judge had finished; and only the verdict was yet in arrear.

Before us lay an avenue straight as an arrow, six hundred yards, perhaps, in length; and the umbrageous trees, which rose in a regular line from either side, meeting high overhead, gave to it the character of a cathedral aisle. These trees lent a deeper solemnity to the early light; but there was still light enough to perceive, at the further end of this Gothic aisle, a frail reedy gig, in which were seated a young man, and by his side a young lady. Ah, young sir! what are you about? If it is requisite that you should whisper your communications to this young lady—though really I see nobody, at an hour and on a road so solitary, likely to overhear you—is it therefore requisite that you should carry your lips forward to hers? The little carriage is creeping on at one mile an hour; and the parties within it, being thus tenderly engaged, are naturally bending down their heads. Between them and eternity, to all human calculation, there is but a minute and a half. Oh heavens! what is it that I shall do? Speaking or acting, what help can I offer? Strange it is, and to a mere auditor of the tale might seem laughable, that I should need a suggestion from the *Iliad* to prompt the sole resource that remained. Yet so it was. Suddenly I remembered the shout of Achilles, and its effect.[34] But could I pretend to shout like the son of Peleus, aided by Pallas? No: but then I

needed not the shout that should alarm all Asia militant; such a shout would suffice as might carry terror into the hearts of two thoughtless young people and one gig-horse. I shouted—and the young man heard me not. A second time I shouted—and now he heard me, for now he raised his head.

Here, then, all had been done that, by me, *could* be done; more on *my* part was not possible. Mine had been the first step; the second was for the young man; the third was for God. If, said I, this stranger is a brave man, and if indeed he loves the young girl at his side—or, loving her not, if he feels the obligation, pressing upon every man worthy to be called a man, of doing his utmost for a woman confided to his protection—he will at least make some effort to save her. If *that* fails, he will not perish the more, or by a death more cruel, for having made it; and he will die as a brave man should, with his face to the danger, and with his arm about the woman that he sought in vain to save. But, if he makes no effort,—shrinking without a struggle from his duty,—he himself will not the less certainly perish for this baseness of poltroonery.[35] He will die no less: and why not? Wherefore should we grieve that there is one craven less in the world? No; *let* him perish, without a pitying thought of ours wasted upon him; and, in that case, all our grief will be reserved for the fate of the helpless girl who now, upon the least shadow of failure in *him,* must by the fiercest of translations—must without time for a prayer—must within seventy seconds—stand before the judgment-seat of God.

But craven he was not: sudden had been the call upon him, and sudden was his answer to the call. He saw, he heard, he comprehended, the ruin that was coming down: already its gloomy shadow darkened above him; and already he was measuring his strength to deal with it. Ah! what a vulgar thing does courage seem when we see nations buying it and selling it for a shilling a-day;[36] ah! what a sublime thing does courage seem when some fearful summons on the great deeps of life carries a man, as if running before a hurricane, up to the giddy crest of some tumultuous crisis from which lie two courses, and a voice says to him audibly, 'One way lies hope; take the other, and mourn forever!' How grand a triumph if, even then, amidst the raving of all around him, and the frenzy of the danger, the man is able to confront his situation—is able to

---

34 The shout of Achilles spread terror among the Trojans. See *Iliad*, XVIII, 217-31.

35 cowardliness.
36 referring to the practice of hiring mercenary soldiers.

retire for a moment into solitude with God, and to seek his counsel from *Him!*

For seven seconds, it might be, of his seventy, the stranger settled his countenance stedfastly upon us, as if to search and value every element in the conflict before him. For five seconds more of his seventy he sat immovably, like one that mused on some great purpose. For five more, perhaps, he sat with eyes upraised, like one that prayed in sorrow, under some extremity of doubt, for light that should guide him to the better choice. Then suddenly he rose; stood upright; and, by a powerful strain upon the reins, raising his horse's fore-feet from the ground, he slewed him round on the pivot of his hind-legs, so as to plant the little equipage in a position nearly at right angles to ours. Thus far his condition was not improved; except as a first step had been taken towards the possibility of a second. If no more were done, nothing was done; for the little carriage still occupied the very centre of our path, though in an altered direction. Yet even now it may not be too late: fifteen of the seventy seconds may still be unexhausted; and one almighty bound may avail to clear the ground. Hurry, then, hurry! for the flying moments—*they* hurry. Oh, hurry, hurry, my brave young man! for the cruel hoofs of our horses—*they* also hurry! Fast are the flying moments, faster are the hoofs of our horses. But fear not for *him,* if human energy can suffice; faithful was he that drove to his terrific duty; faithful was the horse to *his* command. One blow, one impulse given with voice and hand, by the stranger, one rush from the horse, one bound as if in the act of rising to a fence, landed the docile creature's fore-feet upon the crown or arching centre of the road. The larger half of the little equipage had then cleared our overtowering shadow: *that* was evident even to my own agitated sight. But it mattered little that one wreck should float off in safety if upon the wreck that perished were embarked the human freightage. The rear part of the carriage—was *that* certainly beyond the line of absolute ruin? What power could answer the question? Glance of eye, thought of man, wing of angel, which of these had speed enough to sweep between the question and the answer, and divide the one from the other? Light does not tread upon the steps of light more indivisibly than did our all-conquering arrival upon the escaping efforts of the gig. *That* must the young man have felt too plainly. His back was now turned to us; not by sight could he any longer communicate

with the peril; but, by the dreadful rattle of our harness, too truly had his ear been instructed that all was finished as regarded any effort of *his.* Already in resignation he had rested from his struggle; and perhaps in his heart he was whispering, 'Father, which art in heaven, do Thou finish above what I on earth have attempted.' Faster than ever mill-race we ran past them in our inexorable flight. Oh, raving of hurricanes that must have sounded in their young ears at the moment of our transit! Even in that moment the thunder of collision spoke aloud. Either with the swingle-bar,[37] or with the haunch of our near leader, we had struck the off-wheel of the little gig, which stood rather obliquely, and not quite so far advanced as to be accurately parallel with the near-wheel. The blow, from the fury of our passage, resounded terrifically. I rose in horror, to gaze upon the ruins we might have caused. From my elevated station I looked down, and looked back upon the scene; which in a moment told its own tale, and wrote all its records on my heart forever.

Here was the map of the passion that now had finished. The horse was planted immovably, with his fore-feet upon the paved crest of the central road. He of the whole party might be supposed untouched by the passion of death. The little cany carriage—partly, perhaps, from the violent torsion of the wheels in its recent movement, partly from the thundering blow we had given to it—as if it sympathised with human horror, was all alive with tremblings and shiverings. The young man trembled not, nor shivered. He sat like a rock. But *his* was the steadiness of agitation frozen into rest by horror. As yet he dared not to look round; for he knew that, if anything remained to do, by him it could no longer be done. And as yet he knew not for certain if their safety were accomplished. But the lady——

But the lady——! Oh, heavens! will that spectacle ever depart from my dreams, as she rose and sank upon her seat, sank and rose, threw up her arms wildly to heaven, clutched at some visionary object in the air, fainting, praying, raving, despairing? Figure to yourself, reader, the elements of the case; suffer me to recall before your mind the circumstances of that unparalleled situation. From the silence and deep peace of this saintly summer night—from the pathetic blending of this sweet moonlight, dawnlight, dreamlight—from the manly tenderness of this flattering, whispering, murmuring love—sud-

---

37 whippletree.

denly as from the woods and fields—suddenly as from the chambers of the air opening in revelation—suddenly as from the ground yawning at her feet, leaped upon her, with the flashing of cataracts, Death the crowned phantom, with all the equipage of his terrors, and the tiger roar of his voice.

The moments were numbered; the strife was finished; the vision was closed. In the twinkling of an eye, our flying horses had carried us to the termination of the umbrageous aisle; at the right angles we wheeled into our former direction; the turn of the road carried the scene out of my eyes in an instant, and swept it into my dreams forever.

III. DREAM-FUGUE:

FOUNDED ON THE PRECEDING THEME OF SUDDEN DEATH

Whence the sound
Of instruments, that made melodious chime,
Was heard, of harp and organ; and who moved
Their stops and chords was seen; his volant touch
Instinct through all proportions, low and high,
Fled and pursued transverse the resonant fugue.
—PARADISE LOST, BK. 11 [558-63].

Tumultuosissimamente

Passion of sudden death! that once in youth I read and interpreted by the shadows of thy averted signs![38]—rapture of panic taking the shape (which amongst tombs in churches I have seen) of woman bursting her sepulchral bonds—of woman's Ionic form[39] bending forward from the ruins of her grave with arching foot, with eyes upraised, with clasped adoring hands—waiting, watching, trembling, praying for the trumpet's call to rise from dust forever! Ah, vision too fearful of shuddering humanity on the brink of almighty abysses!—vision that didst start back, that didst reel away, like a shrivelling scroll from before the wrath of fire racing on the wings of the wind! Epilepsy so brief of horror, wherefore is it that thou canst not die? Passing so suddenly into darkness, wherefore is it that still thou sheddest thy sad funeral blights upon the gorgeous mosaics of dreams? Fragment of music too passionate, heard once, and heard no more, what aileth thee, that thy deep rolling chords come up

at intervals through all the worlds of sleep, and after forty years have lost no element of horror?

1

Lo, it is summer—almighty summer! The everlasting gates of life and summer are thrown open wide, and on the ocean, tranquil and verdant as a savannah, the unknown lady from the dreadful vision and I myself are floating—she upon a fairy pinnace, and I upon an English three-decker. Both of us are wooing gales of festal happiness within the domain of our common country, within that ancient watery park, within the pathless chase of ocean, where England takes her pleasure as a huntress through winter and summer, from the rising to the setting sun. Ah, what a wilderness of floral beauty was hidden, or was suddenly revealed, upon the tropic islands through which the pinnace moved! And upon her deck what a bevy of human flowers: young women how lovely, young men how noble, that were dancing together, and slowly drifting towards *us* amidst music and incense, amidst blossoms from forests and gorgeous corymbi[40] from vintages, amidst natural carolling, and the echoes of sweet girlish laughter. Slowly the pinnace nears us, gaily she hails us, and silently she disappears beneath the shadow of our mighty bows. But then, as at some signal from heaven, the music, and the carols, and the sweet echoing of girlish laughter—all are hushed. What evil has smitten the pinnace, meeting or overtaking her? Did ruin to our friends couch within our own dreadful shadow? Was our shadow the shadow of death? I looked over the bow for an answer, and behold! the pinnace was dismantled; the revel and the revellers were found no more; the glory of the vintage was dust; and the forests with their beauty were left without a witness upon the seas. 'But where,' and I turned to our crew—'where are the lovely women that danced beneath the awning of flowers and clustering corymbi? Whither have fled the noble young men that danced with *them*?' Answer there was none. But suddenly the man at the mast-head, whose countenance darkened with alarm, cried out, 'Sail on the weather beam! Down she comes upon us: in seventy seconds she also will founder.'

2

I looked to the weather side, and the summer had departed. The sea was rocking, and shaken

---

38 I read the course and changes of the lady's agony in the succession of her involuntary gestures; but it must be remembered that I read all this from the rear, never once catching the lady's full face, and even her profile imperfectly.—(De Quincey.)
39 delicate and graceful form such as that which characterizes Ionic architecture.

40 clusters of fruit or flowers.

with gathering wrath. Upon its surface sat mighty mists, which grouped themselves into arches and long cathedral aisles. Down one of these, with the fiery pace of a quarrel[41] from a cross-bow, ran a frigate right athwart our course. 'Are they mad?' some voice exclaimed from our deck. 'Do they woo their ruin?' But in a moment, as she was close upon us, some impulse of a heady current or local vortex gave a wheeling bias to her course, and off she forged without a shock. As she ran past us, high aloft amongst the shrouds stood the lady of the pinnace. The deeps opened ahead in malice to receive her, towering surges of foam ran after her, the billows were fierce to catch her. But far away she was borne into desert spaces of the sea: whilst still by sight I followed her, as she ran before the howling gale, chased by angry sea-birds and by maddening billows; still I saw her, as at the moment when she ran past us, standing amongst the shrouds, with her white draperies streaming before the wind. There she stood, with hair dishevelled, one hand clutched amongst the tackling—rising, sinking, fluttering, trembling, praying; there for leagues I saw her as she stood, raising at intervals one hand to heaven, amidst the fiery crests of the pursuing waves and the raving of the storm; until at last, upon a sound from afar of malicious laughter and mockery, all was hidden forever in driving showers; and afterwards, but when I knew not, nor how.

3

Sweet funeral bells from some incalculable distance, wailing over the dead that die before the dawn, awakened me as I slept in a boat moored to some familiar shore. The morning twilight even then was breaking; and, by the dusky revelations which it spread, I saw a girl, adorned with a garland of white roses about her head for some great festival, running along the solitary strand in extremity of haste. Her running was the running of panic; and often she looked back as to some dreadful enemy in the rear. But, when I leaped ashore, and followed on her steps to warn her of a peril in front, alas! from me she fled as from another peril, and vainly I shouted to her of quicksands that lay ahead. Faster and faster she ran; round a promontory of rocks she wheeled out of sight; in an instant I also wheeled round it, but only to see the treacherous sands gathering above her head. Already her person was buried; only the fair young head and the dia-

dem of white roses around it were still visible to the pitying heavens; and, last of all, was visible one white marble arm. I saw by the early twilight this fair young head, as it was sinking down to darkness—saw this marble arm, as it rose above her head and her treacherous grave, tossing, faltering, rising, clutching, as at some false deceiving hand stretched out from the clouds—saw this marble arm uttering her dying hope, and then uttering her dying despair. The head, the diadem, the arm—these all had sunk; at last over these also the cruel quicksand had closed; and no memorial of the fair young girl remained on earth, except my own solitary tears, and the funeral bells from the desert seas, that, rising again more softly, sang a requiem over the grave of the buried child, and over her blighted dawn.

I sat, and wept in secret the tears that men have ever given to the memory of those that died before the dawn, and by the treachery of earth, our mother. But suddenly the tears and funeral bells were hushed by a shout as of many nations, and by a roar as from some great king's artillery, advancing rapidly along the valleys, and heard afar by echoes from the mountains. 'Hush!' I said, as I bent my ear earthwards to listen—'hush!—this either is the very anarchy of strife, or else'—and then I listened more profoundly, and whispered as I raised my head—'or else, oh heavens! it is *victory* that is final, victory that swallows up all strife.'

4

Immediately, in trance, I was carried over land and sea to some distant kingdom, and placed upon a triumphal car, amongst companions crowned with laurel. The darkness of gathering midnight, brooding over all the land, hid from us the mighty crowds that were weaving restlessly about ourselves as a centre: we heard them, but saw them not. Tidings had arrived, within an hour, of a grandeur that measured itself against centuries; too full of pathos they were, too full of joy, to utter themselves by other language than by tears, by restless anthems, and *Te Deums*[42] reverberated from the choirs and orchestras of earth. These tidings we that sat upon the laurelled car had it for our privilege to publish amongst all nations. And already, by signs audible through the darkness, by snortings and tramplings, our angry horses, that knew no fear of

---

41 an arrow having a four-edged head.

42 hymns of praise; so-called from the opening words of the celebrated Christian hymn, *Te Deum laudamus* (We Praise Thee, O God).

fleshly weariness, upbraided us with delay. Wherefore *was* it that we delayed? We waited for a secret word, that should bear witness to the hope of nations as now accomplished forever. At midnight the secret word arrived; which word was— *Waterloo and Recovered Christendom!* The dreadful word shone by its own light; before us it went; high above our leaders' heads it rode, and spread a golden light over the paths which we traversed. Every city, at the presence of the secret word, threw open its gates. The rivers were conscious as we crossed. All the forests, as we ran along their margins, shivered in homage to the secret word. And the darkness comprehended it.[43]

Two hours after midnight we approached a mighty Minster. Its gates, which rose to the clouds, were closed. But, when the dreadful word that rode before us reached them with its golden light, silently they moved back upon their hinges; and at a flying gallop our equipage entered the grand aisle of the cathedral. Headlong was our pace; and at every altar, in the little chapels and oratories to the right hand and left of our course, the lamps, dying or sickening, kindled anew in sympathy with the secret word that was flying past. Forty leagues we might have run in the cathedral, and as yet no strength of morning light had reached us, when before us we saw the aerial galleries of organ and choir. Every pinnacle of the fretwork, every station of advantage amongst the traceries, was crested by white-robed choristers that sang deliverance; that wept no more tears, as once their fathers had wept; but at intervals that sang together to the generations, saying,

'Chant the deliverer's praise in every tongue,'

and receiving answers from afar,

'Such as once in heaven and earth were sung.'

And of their chanting was no end; of our headlong pace was neither pause nor slackening.

Thus as we ran like torrents—thus as we swept with bridal rapture over the Campo Santo[44] of the cathedral graves—suddenly we became aware of a vast necropolis rising upon the far-off horizon—a city of sepulchres, built within the saintly cathedral for the warrior dead that rested from their feuds on earth. Of purple granite was the necropolis; yet, in the first minute, it lay like a

purple stain upon the horizon, so mighty was the distance. In the second minute it trembled through many changes, growing into terraces and towers of wondrous altitude, so mighty was the pace. In the third minute already, with our dreadful gallop, we were entering its suburbs. Vast sarcophagi[45] rose on every side, having towers and turrets that, upon the limits of the central aisle, strode forward with haughty intrusion, that ran back with mighty shadows into answering recesses. Every sarcophagus showed many bas-reliefs—bas-reliefs of battles and of battle-fields; battles from forgotten ages, battles from yesterday; battle-fields that, long since, nature had healed and reconciled to herself with the sweet oblivion of flowers; battle-fields that were yet angry and crimson with carnage. Where the terraces ran, there did *we* run; where the towers curved, there did *we* curve. With the flight of swallows our horses swept round every angle. Like rivers in flood wheeling round headlands, like hurricanes that ride into the secrets of forests, faster than ever light unwove the mazes of darkness, our flying equipage carried earthly passions, kindled warrior instincts, amongst the dust that lay around us—dust oftentimes of our noble fathers that had slept in God from Créci to Trafalgar.[46] And now had we reached the last sarcophagus, now were we abreast of the last bas-relief, already had we recovered the arrow-like flight of the illimitable central aisle, when coming up this aisle to meet us we beheld afar off a female child, that rode in a carriage as frail as flowers. The mists which went before her hid the fawns that drew her, but could not hide the shells and tropic flowers with which she played —but could not hide the lovely smiles by which she uttered her trust in the mighty cathedral, and in the cherubim that looked down upon her from the mighty shafts of its pillars. Face to face she was meeting us; face to face she rode, as if danger there were none. 'Oh, baby!' I exclaimed, 'shalt thou be the ransom for Waterloo? Must we, that carry tidings of great joy to every people, be messengers of ruin to thee!' In horror I rose at the thought; but then also, in horror at the thought, rose one that was sculptured on a bas-relief—a Dying Trumpeter. Solemnly from the field of battle he rose to his feet; and, unslinging his stony trumpet, carried it, in his dying anguish, to his stony lips—sounding once, and yet once

---

43 John, i, 5.
44 The cemetery at Pisa, composed of earth brought from Jerusalem from a bed of sanctity.—(De Quincey.)

45 tombs of stone.
46 The battle of Crécy was fought in 1346; the battle of Trafalgar, in 1805.

again; proclamation that, in *thy* ears, oh baby! spoke from the battlements of death. Immediately deep shadows fell between us, and aboriginal silence. The choir had ceased to sing. The hoofs of our horses, the dreadful rattle of our harness, the groaning of our wheels, alarmed the graves no more. By horror the bas-relief had been unlocked unto life. By horror we, that were so full of life, we men and our horses, with their fiery fore-legs rising in mid air to their everlasting gallop, were frozen to a bas-relief. Then a third time the trumpet sounded; the seals were taken off all pulses; life, and the frenzy of life, tore into their channels again; again the choir burst forth in sunny grandeur, as from the muffling of storms and darkness; again the thunderings of our horses carried temptation into the graves. One cry burst from our lips, as the clouds, drawing off from the aisle, showed it empty before us. —'Whither has the infant fled?—is the young child caught up to God?' Lo! afar off, in a vast recess, rose three mighty windows to the clouds; and on a level with their summits, at height insuperable to man, rose an altar of purest alabaster. On its eastern face was trembling a crimson glory. A glory was it from the reddening dawn that now streamed *through* the windows? Was it from the crimson robes of the martyrs painted *on* the windows? Was it from the bloody bas-reliefs of earth? There suddenly, within that crimson radiance, rose the apparition of a woman's head, and then of a woman's figure. The child it was—grown up to woman's height. Clinging to the horns of the altar, voiceless she stood—sinking, rising, raving, despairing; and behind the volume of incense that, night and day, streamed upwards from the altar, dimly was seen the fiery font, and the shadow of that dreadful being who should have baptized her with the baptism of death. But by her side was kneeling her better angel, that hid his face with wings; that wept and pleaded for *her;* that prayed when *she* could *not;* that fought with Heaven by tears for *her* deliverance; which also, as he raised his immortal countenance from his wings, I saw, by the glory in his eye, that from Heaven he had won at last.

5

Then was completed the passion of the mighty fugue. The golden tubes of the organ, which as yet had but muttered at intervals—gleaming amongst clouds and surges of incense—threw up, as from fountains unfathomable, columns of heart-shattering music. Choir and anti-choir were filling fast with unknown voices. Thou also, Dying Trumpeter, with thy love that was victorious, and thy anguish that was finishing, didst enter the tumult; trumpet and echo—farewell love, and farewell anguish—rang through the dreadful *sanctus.*[47] Oh, darkness of the grave! that from the crimson altar and from the fiery font wert visited and searched by the effulgence in the angel's eye—were these indeed thy children? Pomps of life, that, from the burials of centuries, rose again to the voice of perfect joy, did ye indeed mingle with the festivals of Death? Lo! as I looked back for seventy leagues through the mighty cathedral, I saw the quick and the dead that sang together to God, together that sang to the generations of man. All the hosts of jubilation, like armies that ride in pursuit, moved with one step. Us, that, with laurelled heads, were passing from the cathedral, they overtook, and, as with a garment, they wrapped us round with thunders greater than our own. As brothers we moved together; to the dawn that advanced, to the stars that fled, rendering thanks to God in the highest—that, having hid His face through one generation behind thick clouds of War, once again was ascending, from the Campo Santo of Waterloo was ascending, in the visions of Peace; rendering thanks for thee, young girl! whom having overshadowed with His ineffable passion of death, suddenly did God relent, suffered thy angel to turn aside His arm, and even in thee, sister unknown! shown to me for a moment only to be hidden forever, found an occasion to glorify His goodness. A thousand times, amongst the phantoms of sleep, have I seen thee entering the gates of the golden dawn, with the secret word riding before thee, with the armies of the grave behind thee,—seen thee sinking, rising, raving, despairing; a thousand times in the worlds of sleep have seen thee followed by God's angel through storms, through desert seas, through the darkness of quicksands, through dreams and the dreadful revelations that are in dreams; only that at the last, with one sling of His victorious arm, He might snatch thee back from ruin, and might emblazon in thy deliverance the endless resurrections of His love!

1849

---

47 the hymn, 'Holy, Holy, Holy, Lord God of Hosts.'

1780 · JOHN WILSON CROKER · 1857

1780–1800   Born in Ireland, son of the surveyor-general of customs; educated at Trinity College, Dublin.

1800–1807   Studied at Lincoln's Inn and began the practice of law.

1808–37   Entered Parliament and was appointed secretary to the Admiralty; was an active and capable Tory politician for more than twenty years.

1809–50   Contributed to the *Quarterly Review* with which he was associated from its founding.

1831   Edited Boswell's *Life of Johnson,* his chief work.

1857   Died.

JOHN WILSON CROKER was a capable public servant, an accurate investigator, and a vigorous though sometimes unscrupulous party debater. He was possessed of a strong spirit of Toryism which he carried with him into the arena of literary criticism. In a series of acrimonious articles on Leigh Hunt and the 'Cockney School' in the *Quarterly Review,* Croker eventually brought Keats under critical assault. It was Croker's unjust and brutal criticism of the young poet that was supposed at the time to have caused Keats's early death.

ENDYMION: A POETIC ROMANCE

BY JOHN KEATS

REVIEWERS have been sometimes accused of not reading the works which they affected to criticise. On the present occasion we shall anticipate the author's complaint, and honestly confess that we have not read his work. Not that we have been wanting in our duty—far from it; indeed, we have made efforts almost as superhuman as the story itself appears to be, to get through it; but with the fullest stretch of our perseverance, we are forced to confess that we have not been able to struggle beyond the first of the four books of which this 'Poetic Romance' consists. We should extremely lament this want of energy, or whatever it may be, on our parts, were it not for one consolation—namely, that we are no better acquainted with the meaning of the book through which we have so painfully toiled, than we are with that of the three which we have not looked into.

It is not that Mr. Keats (if that be his real name, for we almost doubt that any man in his senses would put his real name to such a rhapsody), it is not, we say, that the author has not powers of language, rays of fancy, and gleams of genius—he has all these; but he is unhappily a disciple of the new school of what has been somewhere called Cockney poetry,[1] which may be defined to consist of the most incongruous ideas in the most uncouth language.

Of this school, Mr. Leigh Hunt, as we observed in a former Number, aspires to be the hierophant. Our readers will recollect the pleasant recipes for harmonious and sublime poetry which he gave us

---

[1] a nickname applied by Lockhart and other Tory critics to the poetry of Leigh Hunt, Shelley, and Keats.

in his Preface to *Rimini*, and the still more facetious instances of his harmony and sublimity in
the verses themselves; and they will recollect
above all the contempt of Pope, Johnson, and
such poetasters and pseudo-critics, which so forcibly contrasted itself with Mr. Leigh Hunt's self-
complacent approbation of

—all the things itself had wrote,
Of special merit though of little note.

This author is a copyist of Mr. Hunt; but he
is more unintelligible, almost as rugged, twice
as diffuse, and ten times more tiresome and absurd than his prototype, who, though he impu-
dently presumed to seat himself in the chair of
criticism, and to measure his own poetry by his
own standard, yet generally had a meaning. But
Mr. Keats had advanced no dogmas which he
was bound to support by examples; his nonsense,
therefore, is quite gratuitous; he writes it for its
own sake; and, being bitten by Mr. Leigh Hunt's
insane criticism, more than rivals the insanity of
his poetry.

Mr. Keats's Preface hints that his poem was
produced under peculiar circumstances.

Knowing within myself (he says) the manner
in which this poem has been produced, it is not
without a feeling of regret that I make it public.
—What manner I mean, will be *quite clear* to
the reader, who must soon perceive great inexperience, immaturity, and every error denoting
a feverish attempt, rather than a deed accomplished.—*Preface,* p. vii.

We humbly beg his pardon, but this does not
appear to us to be *quite so clear*—we really do
not know what he means—but the next passage
is more intelligible.

The two first books, and indeed the two last,
I feel sensible are not of such completion[2] as to
warrant their passing the press.—*Preface,* p. vii.

Thus 'the two first books' are, even in his own
judgement, unfit to appear, and 'the two last'
are, it seems, in the same condition—and as two
and two make four, and as that is the whole number of books, we have a clear and, we believe, a
very just estimate of the entire work.

Mr. Keats, however, deprecates criticism on
this 'immature and feverish work' in terms which
are themselves sufficiently feverish; and we confess that we should have abstained from inflict-

ing upon him any of the tortures of the *'fierce
hell'* of criticism, which terrify his imagination,
if he had not begged to be spared in order that
he might write more; if we had not observed
in him a certain degree of talent which deserves
to be put in the right way, or which, at least,
ought to be warned of the wrong; and if, finally,
he had not told us that he is of an age and temper which imperiously require mental discipline.

Of the story we have been able to make out
but little; it seems to be mythological, and probably relates to the loves of Diana and Endymion;
but of this, as the scope of the work has altogether escaped us, we cannot speak with any degree of certainty; and must therefore content
ourselves with giving some instances of its diction and versification; and here again we are perplexed and puzzled. At first it appeared to us that
Mr. Keats had been amusing himself and wearying his readers with an immeasurable game at
bouts-rimés;[3] but, if we recollect rightly, it is an
indispensable condition at this play, that the
rhymes when filled up shall have a meaning; and
our author, as we have already hinted, has no
meaning. He seems to us to write a line at random, and then he follows not the thought excited by this line, but that suggested by the
rhyme with which it concludes. There is hardly a
complete couplet inclosing a complete idea in the
whole book. He wanders from one subject to another, from the association, not of ideas but of
sounds, and the work is composed of hemistichs[4]
which, it is quite evident, have forced themselves
upon the author by the mere force of the catch-
words on which they turn.

We shall select, not as the most striking instance, but as that least liable to suspicion, a
passage from the opening of the poem.

——Such the sun, the moon,
Trees old and young, sprouting a shady boon
For simple sheep; and such are daffodils
With the green world they live in; and clear rills
That for themselves a cooling covert make
'Gainst the hot season; the mid-forest brake,
Rich with a sprinkling of fair musk-rose blooms;
And such, too, is the grandeur of the dooms
We have imagined for the mighty dead; etc., etc.
                                        [ll. 13–21]

Here it is clear that the word, and not the idea,
moon produces the simple sheep and their shady

---

2 perfection.

3 rhyming words used to fill out verses.
4 incomplete verses.

boon, and that 'the *dooms* of the mighty dead' would never have intruded themselves but for the *'fair musk-rose blooms.'*

Again.

For 'twas the morn: Apollo's upward fire
Made every eastern cloud a silvery pyre
Of brightness so unsullied, that therein
A melancholy spirit well might win
Oblivion, and melt out his essence fine
Into the winds: rain-scented eglantine
Gave temperate sweets to the well-wooing sun;
The lark was lost in him; cold springs had run
To warm their chilliest bubbles in the grass;
Man's voice was on the mountains; and the mass
Of nature's lives and wonders puls'd tenfold,
To feel this sun-rise and its glories old.
[ll. 95–106]

Here Apollo's *fire* produces a *pyre,* a silvery pyre of clouds, *wherein* a spirit might *win* oblivion and melt his essence *fine,* and scented *eglantine* gives sweets to the *sun,* and cold springs had *run* into the *grass,* and then the pulse of the *mass* pulsed *tenfold* to feel the glories *old* of the newborn day, etc.

One example more.

Be still the unimaginable lodge
For solitary thinkings, such as dodge
Conception to the very bourne of heaven,
Then leave the naked brain: be still the leaven,
That spreading in this dull and clodded earth
Gives it a touch ethereal—a new birth.
[ll. 293–298]

Lodge, dodge—heaven, leaven—earth, birth; such, in six words, is the sum and substance of six lines.

We come now to the author's taste in versification. He cannot indeed write a sentence, but perhaps he may be able to spin a line. Let us see. The following are specimens of his prosodial notions of our English heroic metre.

Dear as the temple's self, so does the moon,
The passion poesy, glories infinite.—[ll. 28, 29]

So plenteously all weed-hidden roots.—[l. 65]

Of some strange history, potent to send.—[l. 324]

Before the deep intoxication.—[l. 502]

Her scarf into a fluttering pavilion.—[l. 628]

The stubborn canvas for my voyage prepared.
[l. 772]

'Endymion! the cave is secreter
Than the isle of Delos. Echo hence shall stir
No sighs but sigh-warm kisses, or light noise
Of thy combing hand, the while it travelling cloys
And trembles through my labyrinthine hair.'
—[ll. 965–969]

By this time our readers must be pretty well satisfied as to the meaning of his sentences and the structure of his lines. We now present them with some of the new words with which, in imitation of Mr. Leigh Hunt, he adorns our language.

We are told that 'turtles *passion* their voices' [l. 248]; that an 'arbour was *nested'* [l. 431]; and a lady's locks *'gordian'd up'* [l. 614]; and to supply the place of the nouns thus verbalized, Mr. Keats, with great fecundity, spawns new ones; such as 'men-slugs and human *serpentry'* [l. 821]; the *'honey-feel of bliss'* [l. 903]; 'wives prepare *needments'* [l. 208]—and so forth.

Then he has formed new verbs by the process of cutting off their natural tails, the adverbs, and affixing them to their foreheads; thus, 'the wine out-sparkled' [l. 154]; the 'multitude up-followed' [l. 164]; and 'night up-took' [l. 561]. 'The wind up-blows' [l. 627]; and the 'hours are down-sunken' [l. 708].

But if he sinks some adverbs in the verbs, he compensates the language with adverbs and adjectives which he separates from the parent stock. Thus, a lady 'whispers *pantingly* and close' [l. 407], makes *'hushing* signs' [l. 409], and steers her skiff into a *'ripply* cove' [l. 430]; a shower falls *'refreshfully'* [l. 898]; and a vulture has a *'spreaded* tail' [l. 867].

But enough of Mr. Leigh Hunt and his simple neophyte. If any one should be bold enough to purchase this 'Poetic Romance,' and so much more patient than ourselves as to get beyond the first book, and so much more fortunate as to find a meaning, we entreat him to make us acquainted with his success; we shall then return to the task which we now abandon in despair, and endeavour to make all due amends to Mr. Keats and to our readers.

1818

1763 · WILLIAM COBBETT · 1835

1763   Born at Farnham, the son of a farmer and innkeeper. Self-educated.

1784–91   Served in the army in Nova Scotia and New Brunswick.

1791–2   Obtained a discharge on his return to England; his liberty threatened, as the result of his bringing charges of peculation against some of his former officers, he retired to France.

1792–1800   Resided in America where he authored numerous virulent pro-British, anti-French, and anti-Republican pamphlets under the pseudonym 'Peter Porcupine.'

1800–1802   Ruined by libel suits, he returned to England; became a Tory journalist, inaugurating *Cobbett's Weekly Political Register* (continued until his death).

1804–20   Veered gradually from supporting the Tories to adopting radical opinions; published numerous pamphlets and books on a wide variety of subjects.

1805–35   Farmed in Hampstead and subsequently in Surrey.

1810–12   Served a prison term for an article attacking military flogging.

1817–19   Under stress of financial difficulties, absconded to America.

1820–30   Returned to England and entered into his period of greatest literary activity; published *History of the Protestant Reformation in England and Ireland* (1824), *The English Gardener* (1829), *Advice to Young Men* (1829), and *Rural Rides* (1830), reprinted from the *Register*.

1832   Elected to parliament.

1835   Died.

WILLIAM COBBETT was the most powerful and truculent radical of his time. With utter recklessness he assailed privilege and pleaded the cause of reform until he became 'the most popular and best-hated man in England.' Coleridge described him as 'the rhinoceros of politicians . . . with a horn of brute strength on the nose of scorn and hate.' Personal prejudices and the spirit of combativeness too often misled him into wholly irrational or contradictory positions. Yet in spite of a colossal one-sidedness, Cobbett had a keen insight into the economic malady of his country, and for the most part he was right. He was one of England's great journalists, not unworthy to be named with Defoe or Swift, who with a mastery of popular style 'unremittently dinned his homely truths into all men's ears.' *Rural Rides* are today the most interesting and picturesque of his writings. They form a living chronicle of their author's journeying over the beloved rural England that he knew how to see. Through his rugged but wonderfully varied and singular mind and character, we become aware—amidst the jangling of a thousand diatribes—of the quiet beauty of the land, of its fertility and diversity, of the robust pageantry of its country manners, of wild flowers and the songs of birds, and of a wistful longing for the England that was, before THE THING had fastened tentacles upon it threatening its life.

From RURAL RIDES

Old Hall, Saturday night, 10 November, 1821.

Went to Hereford this morning. It was market-day. My arrival became known, and, I am sure, I cannot tell how. A sort of *buz* got about. I could perceive here, as I always have elsewhere, very ardent friends and very bitter enemies; but all full of curiosity. One thing could not fail to please me exceedingly; my friends were *gay* and my enemies *gloomy:* the former smiled, and the latter, in endeavouring to screw their features into a sneer, could get them no further than the half sour and half sad: the former seemed, in their looks to say, 'Here he is,' and the latter to respond, 'Yes, G—d——him!'—I went into the market-place, amongst the farmers, with whom, in general, I was very much pleased. If I were to live in the county two months, I should be acquainted with every man of them. The country is very fine all the way from Ross to Hereford. The soil is always a red loam upon a bed of stone. The trees are very fine, and certainly winter comes later here than in Middlesex. Some of the oak trees are still perfectly green, and many of the ashes as green as in September.—In coming from Hereford to this place, which is the residence of Mrs. Palmer and that of her two younger sons, Messrs. Philip and Walter Palmer, who with their brother, had accompanied me to Hereford; in coming to this place, which lies at about two miles distance from the great road, and at about an equal distance from Hereford and from Ross, we met with something, the sight of which pleased me exceedingly; it was that of a very pretty pleasant-looking lady (and *young* too) with two beautiful children, riding in a little sort of chaise-cart, drawn by *an ass,* which she was driving in reins. She appeared to be well known to my friends, who drew up and spoke to her, calling her Mrs. *Lock,* or *Locky* (I hope it was not *Lockart)* or some such name. Her husband, who is, I suppose, some young farmer of the neighbourhood, may well call himself Mr. *Lucky;* for to have such a wife, and for such a wife to have the good sense to put up with an ass-cart, in order to avoid, as much as possible, feeding those cormorants who gorge on the taxes, is a blessing that falls, I am afraid, to the lot of very few rich farmers. Mrs. *Lock* (if that be her name) is a real *practical radical.* Others of us resort to radical coffee and radical tea; and she has a radical carriage. This is a very effectual way of assailing the thing, and peculiarly well suited for the practice of the female sex. But the self-denial ought not to be imposed on the wife only: the husband ought to set the example: and, let me hope, that *Mr. Lock* does not indulge in the use of wine and spirits, while Mrs. Lock and her children ride in a jack-ass gig; for, if he do, he wastes, in this way, the means of keeping her a chariot and pair. If there be to be any expense not absolutely necessary; if there be to be anything bordering on extravagance, surely it ought to be for the pleasure of that part of the family, who have the least number of objects of enjoyment; and for a husband to indulge himself in the guzzling of expensive, unnecessary, and really injurious drink, to the tune, perhaps, of 50 or 100 pounds a year, while he preaches economy to his wife, and, with a face as long as my arm, talks of the low price of corn, and wheedles her out of a curricle into a jack-ass cart, is not only unjust but *unmanly.*

Friday, 16 November, 1821.

A whole day most delightfully passed a hare-hunting, with a pretty pack of hounds kept here by Messrs. Palmer. They put me upon a horse that seemed to have been made on purpose for me, strong, tall, gentle and bold; and that carried me either over or through everything. I, who am just the weight of a four-bushel sack of good wheat, actually sat on his back from daylight in the morning to dusk (about nine hours), without once setting my foot on the ground. Our ground was at Orcop, a place about four miles distance from this place. We found a hare in a few minutes after throwing off; and in the course of the day, we had to find four, and were never more than ten minutes in finding. A steep and naked ridge, lying between two flat valleys, having a mixture of pretty large fields and small woods, formed our ground. The hares crossed the ridge forwards and backwards, and gave us numerous views and very fine sport.—I never rode on such steep ground before; and, really, in going up and down some of the craggy places, where the rains had washed the earth from the rocks, I did think, once or twice, of my neck, and how Sidmouth[1] would like to see me.—As to the *cruelty,* as some pretend, of this sport, that point I have, I think, settled, in one of the chapters of my *Year's Residence in America.* As to the expense, a pack, even

---

[1] Henry Addington, first Viscount Sidmouth, 1757–1844, English politician, who as Home Secretary (1812–22) was noted for his repressive measures.

a full pack of harriers, like this, costs less than two bottles of wine a day with their inseparable concomitants. And as to the *time* thus spent, hunting is inseparable from *early rising;* and with habits of early rising, who ever wanted time for any business?

Farnham, Surrey, Thursday, 27 October, 1825.

We came over the heath from Thursley, this morning, on our way to Winchester. Mr. Wyndham's fox-hounds are coming to Thursley on Saturday. More than three-fourths of all the interesting talk in that neighbourhood, for some days past, has been about this anxiously looked-for event. I have seen no man, or boy, who did not talk about it. There had been a false report about it; the hounds did *not come;* and the anger of the disappointed people was very great. At last, however, the *authentic* intelligence came, and I left them all as happy as if all were young and all just going to be married. An abatement of my pleasure, however, on this joyous occasion was, that I brought away with me *one,* who was as eager as the best of them. Richard, though now only 11 years and 6 months old, had, it seems, one fox-hunt, in Herefordshire, last winter; and he actually has begun to talk rather contemptuously of hare hunting. To show me that he is in no *danger,* he has been leaping his horse over banks and ditches by the road side, all our way across the country from Reigate; and he joined with such glee in talking of the expected arrival of the foxhounds that I felt some little pain at bringing him away. My engagement at Winchester is for Saturday; but if it had not been so, the deep and hidden ruts in the heath, in a wood in the midst of which the hounds are sure to find, and the immense concourse of horsemen that is sure to be assembled, would have made me bring him away. Upon the high, hard and open countries I should not be afraid for him, but here the danger would have been greater than it would have been right for me to suffer him to run.

We came hither by the way of Waverley Abbey and Moore Park. On the commons I showed Richard some of my old hunting scenes, when I was of his age, or younger, reminding him that I was obliged to hunt on foot. We got leave to go and see the grounds at Waverley where all the old monks' garden walls are totally gone, and where the spot is become a sort of lawn. I showed him the spot where the strawberry garden was, and where I, when sent to gather *hautboys,*[2] used to eat every remarkably fine one, instead of letting it go to be eaten by Sir Robert Rich. I showed him a tree, close by the ruins of the Abbey, from a limb of which I once fell into the river, in an attempt to take the nest of a *crow,* which had artfully placed it upon a branch so far from the trunk as not to be able to bear the weight of a boy eight years old. I showed him an old elm tree, which was hollow even then, into which I, when a very little boy, once saw a cat go, that was as big as a middle-sized spaniel dog, for relating which I got a great scolding, for standing to which I, at last, got a beating; but stand to which I still did. I have since many times repeated it; and I would take my oath of it to this day. When in New Brunswick I saw the great wild grey cat, which is there called a *Lucifee;* and it seemed to me to be just such a cat as I had seen at Waverley. I found the ruins not very greatly diminished; but it is strange how small the mansion, and ground, and everything but the trees, appeared to me. They were all great to my mind when I saw them last; and that early impression had remained, whenever I had talked or thought of the spot; so that, when I came to see them again, after seeing the sea and so many other immense things, it seemed as if they had all been made small. This was not the case with regard to the trees, which are nearly as big here as they are anywhere else; and the old cat-elm, for instance, which Richard measured with his whip, is about 16 or 17 feet round.

From Waverley we went to Moore Park, once the seat of Sir William Temple, and when I was a very little boy, the seat of a lady, or a Mrs. Temple. Here I showed Richard Mother Ludlum's Hole; but, alas! it is not the enchanting place that I knew it, nor that which Grose describes in his Antiquities![3] The semicircular paling is gone; the basins, to catch the never ceasing little stream, are gone; the iron cups, fastened by chains, for people to drink out of, are gone; the pavement all broken to pieces; the seats for people to sit on, on both sides of the cave, torn up are gone; the stream that ran down a clean paved channel now making a dirty gutter; and the ground opposite, which was a grove, chiefly of laurels, intersected by closely mowed grass-walks, now become a poor, ragged-looking alder-coppice. Near the mansion, I showed Richard the

---

2 strawberries.
3 Francis Grose, *The Antiquities of England and Wales,* 1773–87.

hill upon which Dean Swift tells us he used to run for exercise, while he was pursuing his studies here; and I would have showed him the garden-seat, under which Sir William Temple's heart was buried, agreeably to his will; but the seat was gone, also the wall at the back of it; and the exquisitely beautiful little lawn in which the seat stood was turned into a parcel of divers-shaped cockney-clumps, planted according to the strictest rules of artificial and refined vulgarity.

At Waverley, Mr. Thompson, a merchant of some sort, has succeeded (after the monks) the Orby Hunters and Sir Robert Rich. At Moore Park, a Mr. Laing, a West India planter or merchant, has succeeded the Temples; and at the castle of Farnham, which you see from Moore Park, Bishop Prettyman Tomline has, at last, after perfectly regular and due gradations, succeeded William of Wykham! In coming up from Moore Park to Farnham town, I stopped opposite the door of a little old house, where there appeared to be a great parcel of children. 'There Dick,' said I, 'when I was just such a little creature as that whom you see in the doorway, I lived in this very house with my grandmother Cobbett.' He pulled up his horse, and looked *very hard at it,* but said nothing, and on we came.

Burchclere, Monday Morning, 31 October 1825.

We had, or I had, resolved not to breakfast at Winchester yesterday: and yet we were detained till nearly noon. But at last off we came, *fasting.* The turnpike-road from Winchester to this place comes through a village called Sutton Scotney, and then through Whitchurch, which lies on the Andover and London road, through Basingstoke. We did not take the cross-turnpike till we came to Whitchurch. We went to King's Worthy; that is about two miles on the road from Winchester to London; and then, turning short to our left, came up upon the downs to the north of Winchester race-course. Here, looking back at the city and at the fine valley above and below it, and at the many smaller valleys that run down from the high ridges into that great and fertile valley, I could not help admiring the taste of the ancient kings, who made this city (which once covered all the hill round about, and which contained 92 churches and chapels) a chief place of their residence. There are not many finer spots in England; and if I were to take in a circle of eight or ten miles of semi-diameter, I should say that I believe there is not one so fine. Here are hill, dell, water, meadows, woods, corn-fields, downs: and all of them very fine and very beautifully disposed. This country does not present to us that sort of beauties which we see about Guildford and Godalming, and round the skirts of Hindhead and Blackdown, where the ground lies in the form that the surface-water in a boiling copper would be in, if you could, by word of command, *make it be still,* the variously-shaped bubbles all sticking up; and really, to look at the face of the earth, who can help imagining that some such process has produced its present form? Leaving this matter to be solved by those who laugh at mysteries, I repeat, that the country round Winchester does not present to us beauties of *this sort;* but of a sort which I like a great deal better. Arthur Young calls the vale between Farnham and Alton *the finest ten miles in England.* Here is a river with fine meadows on each side of it, and with rising grounds on each outside of the meadows, those grounds having some hop-gardens and some pretty woods. But, though I was born in this vale, I must confess that the ten miles between Maidstone and Tunbridge (which the Kentish folks call the *Garden of Eden*) is a great deal finer; for here, with a river three times as big, and a vale three times as broad, there are, on rising grounds six times as broad, not only hop-gardens and beautiful woods, but immense orchards of apples, pears, plums, cherries and filberts, and these, in many cases, with gooseberries and currants and raspberries beneath; and, all taken together, the vale is really worthy of the appellation which it bears. But even this spot, which I believe to be the very finest, as to fertility and diminutive beauty, in this whole world, I, for my part, do not like so well; nay, as a spot to *live on,* I think nothing at all of it, compared with a country where high downs prevail, with here and there a large wood on the top or the side of a hill, and where you see, in the deep dells, here and there a farmhouse, and here and there a village, the buildings sheltered by a group of lofty trees.

This is my taste, and here, in the north of Hampshire, it has its full gratification. I like to look at the winding side of a great down, with two or three numerous flocks of sheep on it, belonging to different farms; and to see, lower down, the folds, in the fields, ready to receive them for the night. We had, when we got upon the downs, after leaving Winchester, this sort of country all the way to Whitchurch. Our point of destination was this village of Burghclere, which lies close under the north side of the lofty hill at Highclere, which is called Beacon-hill, and on the top of which there are still the marks of a Roman encampment. We saw this hill as soon as we got on Winchester downs; and without any regard to *roads,* we *steered* for it, as sailors do for a land-mark. Of these 13 miles (from Winchester to Whitchurch) we rode about eight or nine upon the *green-sward,* or over fields equally smooth. And here is one great pleasure of living in coun-tries of this sort: no sloughs, no ditches, no nasty dirty lanes, and the hedges, where there are any, are more for boundary marks than for fences. Fine for hunting and coursing: no impediments; no gates to open; nothing to impede the dogs, the horses, or the view. The water is not *seen running;* but the great bed of chalk *holds it,* and the sun draws it up for the benefit of the grass and the corn; and whatever inconvenience is experienced from the necessity of deep wells, and of driving sheep and cattle far to water, is amply made up for by the goodness of the water, and by the com-plete absence of floods, of drains, of ditches and of water-furrows. As *things now are,* however, these countries have one great drawback: the poor day-labourers suffer from the want of fuel, and they have nothing but their *bare pay.* For these reasons they are greatly worse off than those of the woodland *countries;* and it is really surprising what a difference there is between the faces that you see here, and the round, red faces that you see in the *wealds* and the *forests,* particu-larly in Sussex, where the labourers *will* have a *meat-pudding* of some sort or other; and where they *will* have a *fire* to sit by in the winter.

After steering for some time, we came down to a very fine farmhouse, which we stopped a little to admire; and I asked Richard whether *that* was not a place to be happy in. The village, which we found to be Stoke-Charity, was about a mile lower down this little vale. Before we got to it, we overtook the owner of the farm, who knew me, though I did not know him; but when I found it was Mr. Hinton Bailey, of whom and whose farm I had heard so much, I was not at all surprised at the fineness of what I had just seen. I told him that the word *charity,* making, as it did, part of the name of this place, had nearly inspired me with boldness enough to go to the farmhouse, in the ancient style, and ask for something to eat; for that we had not yet breakfasted. He asked us to go back; but at Burghclere we were *resolved to dine.* After, however, crossing the vil-

lage, and beginning again to ascend the downs, we came to a labourer's (*once a farmhouse*), where I asked the man whether he had any *bread and cheese,* and was not a little pleased to hear him say '*Yes.*' Then I asked him to give us a bit, pro-testing that we had not yet broken our fast. He answered in the affirmative, at once, though I did not talk of payment. His wife brought out the cut loaf, and a piece of Wiltshire cheese, and I took them in hand, gave Richard a good hunch, and took another for myself. I verily believe that all the pleasure of eating enjoyed by all the feeders in London in a whole year does not equal that which we enjoyed in gnawing this bread and cheese, as we rode over this cold down, whip and bridle-reins in one hand, and the hunch in the other. Richard, who was purse bearer, gave the woman, by my direction, about enough to buy two quartern loaves: for she told me that they had to buy their bread *at the mill,* not being able to bake themselves for *want of fuel;* and this, as I said before, is one of the drawbacks in this sort of country. I wish every one of these people had an *American fireplace.* Here they might then, even in these bare countries, have comfortable warmth. Rubbish of any sort would, by this means, give them warmth. I am now, at six o'clock in the morning, sitting in a room where one of these fireplaces, with very light *turf* in it, gives as good and steady a warmth as it is possible to feel, and which room has, too, been *cured of smoking* by this fireplace.

Before we got this supply of bread and cheese, we, though in ordinary times a couple of singu-larly jovial companions, and seldom going a hun-dred yards (except going very fast) without one or the other speaking, began to grow *dull,* or rather *glum.* The way seemed long; and, when I had to speak in answer to Richard, the speaking was as brief as might be. Unfortunately, just at this critical period, one of the loops that held the straps of Richard's little portmanteau broke; and it became necessary (just before we overtook Mr. Bailey) for me to fasten the portmanteau on be-fore me, upon my saddle. This, which was not the work of more than five minutes, would, had I had *a breakfast,* have been nothing at all, and, indeed, matter of laughter. But, *now,* it was *something.* It was his '*fault*' for capering and jerking about '*so.*' I jumped off, saying, '*Here!* I'll carry it *myself.*' And then I began to take off the remaining strap, pulling with great violence and in great haste. Just at this time my eyes met his, in which I saw *great surprise;* and, feeling the just rebuke, feeling heartily ashamed of myself, I instantly changed my tone and manner, cast the blame upon the saddler, and talked of the effectual means which we would take to prevent the like in future.

Now, if such was the effect produced upon me by the want of food for only two or three hours; me, who had dined well the day before and eaten toast and butter the over-night; if the missing of only one breakfast, and that, too, from my own whim, while I had money in my pocket, to get one at any public house, and while I could get one only for asking for at any farmhouse; if the not having breakfasted could, and under such circumstances, make me what you may call *'cross'* to a child like this, whom I must necessarily love so much, and to whom I never speak but in the very kindest manner; if this mere absence of a breakfast could thus put me *out of temper,* how great are the allowances that we ought to make for the poor creatures who, in this once happy and now miserable country, are doomed to lead a life of constant labour and of half-starvation. I suppose that, as we rode away from the cottage, we gnawed up, between us, a pound of bread and a quarter of a pound of cheese. Here was about *five-pence* worth at present prices. Even this, which was only a mere *snap,* a mere *stay-stomach,* for us, would, for us two, come to 3*s.* a week all but a penny. How, then, gracious God! is a labouring man, his wife, and, perhaps, four or five small children, to exist upon 8*s.* or 9*s.* a week! Aye, and to find house-rent, clothing, bedding and fuel out of it? Richard and I ate here, at his snap, more, and much more, than the average of labourers, their wives and children, have to eat in a whole day, and that the labourer has to *work* on too!

East Everley, Monday Morning,
5 o'clock, 28 August 1826.

A very fine morning; a man, *eighty-two years of age,* just beginning to mow the short-grass, in the garden; I thought it, even when I was young, the *hardest work* that man had to do. To *look on,* this work seems nothing; but it tries every sinew in your frame, if you go upright and do your work well. This old man never knew how to do it well, and he stoops, and he hangs his scythe wrong; but, with all this, it must be a surprising man to mow short-grass, as well as he does, at *eighty. I wish I* may be able to mow short-grass at eighty! That's all I have to say of the matter. I am just setting off for the source of the Avon, which runs from near Marlborough to Salisbury, and thence to the sea; and I intend to pursue it as far as Sal-

isbury. In the distance of thirty miles, here are, I see by the books, more than thirty churches. I wish to see, with my own eyes, what evidence there is that those thirty churches were built without hands, without money, and without a congregation; and, thus, to find matter, if I can, to justify the mad wretches, who, from Committee-Rooms and elsewhere, are bothering this half-distracted nation to death about a 'surplus popalashon, mon.'[4]

My horse is ready; and the rooks are just gone off to the stubble-fields. These rooks rob the pigs; but, they have *a right* to do it. I wonder (upon my soul I do) that there is no lawyer, Scotchman, or Parson-Justice, to propose a law to punish the rooks for *trespass.*

Stroud, Gloucestershire, Tuesday Forenoon,
12 September, 1826.

I set off from Malmsbury this morning at 6 o'clock, in as sweet and bright a morning as ever came out of the heavens, and leaving behind me as pleasant a house and as kind hosts as I ever met with in the whole course of my life, either in England or America; and that is saying a great deal indeed. This circumstance was the more pleasant, as I had never before either seen or heard of these kind, unaffected, sensible, *sans-façons,*[5] and most agreeable friends. From Malmsbury I first came, at the end of five miles, to Tutbury, which is in Gloucestershire, there being here a sort of dell, or ravine, which, in this place, is the boundary line of the two counties, and over which you go on a bridge, one-half of which belongs to each county. And now, before I take my leave of Wiltshire, I must observe that, in the whole course of my life (days of *courtship* excepted, of course), I never passed seventeen pleasanter days than those which I have just spent in Wiltshire. It is, especially in the southern half, just the sort of country that I like; the weather has been pleasant; I have been in good houses and amongst good and beautiful gardens; and, in *every* case, I have not only been most kindly entertained, but my entertainers have been of just the stamp that I like.

I saw again, this morning, large flocks of *gold-finches* feeding on the thistle-seed on the road-side. The French call this bird by a name derived from the thistle, so notorious has it always

4 A reference to the political economist T. R. Malthus, 1766–1834, and his followers, who held that population tends to increase out of proportion to the means of subsistence and that unless it can be checked suffering and crime will be inevitable.

5 without ceremony; informal.

been that they live upon this seed. *Thistle* is, in French, *chardon;* and the French call this beautiful little bird *chardonaret.* I never could have supposed that such flocks of these birds would ever be seen in England. But it is a great year for all the feathered race, whether wild or tame: naturally so, indeed; for everyone knows that it is the *wet,* and not the *cold,* that is injurious to the breeding of birds of all sorts, whether land-birds or water-birds. They say that there are, this year, double the usual quantity of ducks and geese: and, really, they do seem to swarm in the farmyards, wherever I go. It is a great mistake to suppose that ducks and geese *need* water, except to drink. There is, perhaps, no spot in the world, in proportion to its size and population, where so many of these birds are reared and fatted as in Long Island; and it is not in one case out of ten that they have any ponds to go to, or that they ever see any water other than water that is drawn up out of a well.

A little way before I got to Tutbury I saw a woman digging some potatoes in a strip of ground making part of a field nearly an oblong square, and which field appeared to be laid out in strips. She told me that the field was part of a farm (to the homestead of which she pointed); that it was, by the farmer, *let out* in strips to labouring people; that each strip contained a rood (or quarter of a statute acre); that each married labourer rented one strip; and that the annual rent was *a pound* for the strip. Now the taxes being all paid by the farmer; the fences being kept in repair by him; and, as appeared to me, the land being exceedingly good: all these things considered, the rent does not appear to be too high.—This fashion is certainly a *growing* one; it is a little step towards a coming back to the ancient small life and leaseholds and common-fields! This field of strips was, in fact, a sort of common-field; and the 'agriculturists,' as the conceited asses of landlords call themselves, at their clubs and meetings, might, and they would if their skulls could admit any thoughts except such as relate to high prices and low wages; they might, and they would, begin to suspect that the 'dark age' people were not so very foolish when they had so many common-fields, and when almost every man that had a family had also a bit of land, either large or small. It is a very curious thing that the enclosing of commons, that the shutting out of the labourers *from all share* in the land; that the prohibiting of them to look at a wild animal, almost at a lark or a frog; it is

curious that this hard-hearted system should have gone on until at last it has produced effects so injurious and so dangerous to the grinders themselves that they have, of their own accord and for their own safety, begun to make a step towards the ancient system, and have, in the manner I have observed, made the labourers sharers, in some degree, in the uses, at any rate, of the soil. The far greater part of these strips of land have potatoes growing in them; but in some cases they have borne wheat, and in others barley, this year; and these have now turnips; very young most of them, but in some places very fine, and in every instance nicely hoed out. The land that will bear 400 bushels of potatoes to the acre will bear 40 bushels of wheat; and the ten bushels of wheat to the quarter of an acre would be a crop far more valuable than a hundred bushels of potatoes, as I have proved many times in the *Register.*

Just before I got into Tutbury I was met by a good many people, in twos, threes, or fives, some running, and some walking fast, one of the first of whom asked me if I had met an 'old man' some distance back. I asked what *sort* of a man: 'A *poor* man.' 'I don't recollect, indeed; but what are you all pursuing him for?' 'He has been *stealing.*' 'What has he been stealing?' 'Cabbages.' 'Where?' 'Out of Mr. Glover, the hatter's, garden.' 'What! do you call that *stealing;* and would you punish a man, a poor man, and therefore, in all likelihood, a hungry man too, and moreover an old man; do you set up a hue-and-cry after, and would you punish, such a man for taking a few cabbages, when that Holy Bible, which, I dare say, you profess to believe in, and perhaps assist to circulate, teaches you that the hungry man may, without committing any offence at all, go into his neighbour's vineyard and eat his fill of grapes, one bunch of which is worth a sackfull of cabbages?' 'Yes; but he is a very bad character.' 'Why, my friend, very poor and almost starved people are apt to be "bad characters"; but the Bible, in both Testaments, commands us to be merciful to the poor, to feed the hungry, to have compassion on the aged; and it makes no exception as to the "character" of the parties.' Another group or two of the pursuers had come up by this time; and I, bearing in mind the fate of Don Quixote when he interfered in somewhat similar cases, gave my horse the hint, and soon got away; but though doubtless I made no converts, I, upon looking back, perceived that I had slackened the pursuit! The pursuers went more slowly; I could see that they got to talking; it was now the step of deliberation rather than that of decision; and though I did not like to call upon Mr. Glover, I hope he was merciful. It is impossible for me to witness scenes like this; to hear a man called *a thief* for such a cause; to see him thus eagerly and vindictively pursued for having taken some cabbages in a garden: it is impossible for me to behold such a scene, without calling to mind the practice in the United States of America, where, if a man were even to talk of prosecuting another (especially if that other were poor or old) for taking from the land, or from the trees, any part of a growing crop, for his own personal and immediate use; if any man were even to talk of prosecuting another for such an act, such talker would be held in universal abhorrence: people would hate him, and, in short, if rich as Ricardo[6] or Baring,[7] he might live by himself; for no man would look upon him as a neighbour.

Tutbury is a very pretty town, and has a beautiful ancient church. The country is high along here for a mile or two towards Avening, which begins a long and deep and narrow valley, that comes all the way down to Stroud. When I got to the end of the high country, and the lower country opened to my view, I was at about three miles from Tutbury, on the road to Avening, leaving the Minchinghampton road to my right. Here I was upon the edge of the high land, looking right down upon the village of Avening, and seeing, just close to it, a large and fine mansion-house, a beautiful park, and, making part of the park, one of the finest, most magnificent woods (of 200 acres, I dare say), lying facing me, going from a valley up a gently-rising hill. While I was sitting on my horse, admiring this spot, a man came along with some tools in his hand, as if going somewhere to work as plumber. 'Whose beautiful place is that?' said I. 'One 'Squire Ricardo, I think they call him, but . . .'—You might have 'knocked me down with a feather,' as the old women say . . . 'but' (continued the plumber) 'the Old Gentleman's dead, and . . .' 'God——the old gentleman and the young gentleman too!' said I; and, giving my horse a blow, instead of a word, on I went down the hill. Before I got to the bottom, my reflections on the present state of the 'market' and on the probable results of 'watching the turn of it,' had made me

6 David Ricardo, 1772–1823, wealthy political economist and member of parliament, noted for his treatises on taxation and rents.

7 Sir Francis Baring, 1740–1810, English financier.

better humoured; and as one of the first objects that struck my eye in the village was the sign of the Cross, and of the Red, or Bloody, Cross too, I asked the landlord some questions, which began a series of joking and bantering that I had with the people, from one end of the village to the other. I set them all a laughing; and though they could not know my name, they will remember me for a long while.—This estate of Gatcomb belonged, I am told, to a Mr. Shepperd, and to his fathers before him. I asked where this Shepperd was now? A tradesman-looking man told me that he did not know where he was; but that he had heard that he was living somewhere near to Bath! Thus they go! Thus they are squeezed out of existence. The little ones are gone; and the big ones have nothing left for it but to resort to the bands of holy matrimony with the turn of the market watchers and their breed. This the big ones are now doing apace; and there is this comfort at any rate; namely, that the connexion cannot make them baser than they are, a borough-monger being, of all God's creatures, the very basest.

From Avening I came on through Nailsworth, Woodchester, and Rodborough to this place. These villages lie on the sides of a narrow and deep valley, with a narrow stream of water running down the middle of it, and this stream turns the wheels of a great many mills and sets of machinery for the making of *woollen-cloth*. The factories begin at Avening, and are scattered all the way down the valley. There are steam engines as well as water powers. The work and the trade is so flat that in, I should think, much more than a hundred acres of ground, which I have seen to-day, covered with rails or racks, for the drying of cloth, I do not think that I have seen one single acre where the racks had cloth upon them. The workmen do not get half wages; great numbers are thrown on the parish; but overseers and magistrates in this part of England do not presume that they are to leave anybody to starve to death; there is law here; this is in England, and not in 'the north,' where those who ought to see that the poor do not suffer, talk of their dying with hunger as Irish 'squires do; aye, and applaud them for their patient resignation!

The Gloucestershire people have no notion of dying with hunger; and it is with great pleasure that I remark that I have seen no woe-worn creature this day. The subsoil here is a yellowish ugly stone. The houses are all built with this; and it being ugly, the stone is made *white* by a wash of some sort or other. The land on both sides of the valley, and all down the bottom of it, has plenty of trees on it; it is chiefly pasture land, so that the green and the white colours, and the form and great variety of the ground, and the water, and altogether make this a very pretty ride. Here are a series of spots, every one of which a lover of landscapes would like to have painted. Even the buildings of the factories are not ugly. The people seem to have been constantly well off. A pig in almost every cottage sty; that is the infallible mark of a happy people. At present this valley suffers; and though cloth will always be wanted, there will yet be much suffering even here, while at Uly and other places they say the suffering is great indeed.

Stanford Park,
Wednesday Morning, 27 September 1826.

In a letter which I received from Sir Thomas Winnington (one of the members for this county) last year, he was good enough to request that I would call upon him if I ever came into Worcestershire, which I told him I would do; and accordingly here we are in his house, situated, certainly, in one of the finest spots in all England. We left Worcester yesterday about ten o'clock, crossed the Severn, which runs close by the town, and came on to this place, which lies in a northwestern direction from Worcester, at 14 miles distance from that city, and at about six from the borders of Shropshire. About four miles back we passed by the park and through the estate of Lord Foley, to whom is due the praise of being a most indefatigable and successful *planter of trees.* He seems to have taken uncommon pains in the execution of this work; and he has the merit of disinterestedness, the trees being chiefly oaks, which he is *sure* he can never see grow to timber. We crossed the Teme river just before we got here. Sir Thomas was out shooting; but he soon came home, and gave us a very polite reception. I had time, yesterday, to see the place, to look at trees, and the like, and I wished to get away early this morning; but being prevailed on to stay to breakfast, here I am, at six o'clock in the morning, in one of the best and best-stocked private libraries that I ever saw; and, what is more, the owner, from what passed yesterday, when he brought me hither, convinced me that he was acquainted with the *insides* of the books. I asked, and shall ask, no questions about who got these books together; but the collection is such as, I am sure, I never saw before in a private house.

The house and stables and courts are such as they ought to be for the great estate that surrounds them; and the park is everything that is beautiful. On one side of the house, looking over a fine piece of water, you see a distant valley, opening between lofty hills: on another side the ground descends a little at first, then goes gently rising for a while, and then rapidly, to the distance of a mile perhaps, where it is crowned with trees in irregular patches, or groups, single and most magnificent trees being scattered all over the whole of the park; on another side, there rise up beautiful little hills, some in the form of barrows on the downs, only forty or a hundred times as large, one or two with no trees on them, and others topped with trees; but on one of these little hills, and some yards higher than the lofty trees which are on this little hill, you see rising up the tower of the parish church, which hill is, I think, taken all together, amongst the most delightful objects that I ever beheld.

'Well, then,' says the devil of laziness, 'and could you not be contented to live here all the rest of your life; and never again pester yourself with the cursed politics?' 'Why, I think I have laboured enough. Let others work now. And such a pretty place for coursing and for hare-hunting and woodcock shooting, I dare say; and then those pretty wild ducks in the water, and the flowers and the grass and the trees and all the birds in spring and the fresh air, and never, never again to be stifled with the smoke that from the infernal Wen[8] ascendeth forevermore and that every easterly wind brings to choke me at Kensington!' The *last word* of this soliloquy carried me back, slap, to my own study (very much unlike that which I am in), and bade me think of the Gridiron;[9] bade me think of the complete triumph that I have yet to enjoy: promised me the pleasure of seeing a million of trees of my own, and sown by my own hands this very year. Ah! but the hares and the pheasants and the wild ducks! Yes, but the delight of seeing Prosperity Robinson[10] hang his head for shame: the delight of beholding the tormenting embarrassments of those who have so long retained crowds of base

---

8 a name often applied by Cobbett to London.

9 On the passage of Peel's Bill in 1819, providing for a return to the gold standard, which Cobbett stoutly opposed, he offered, if he was mistaken in his prophecies about the ill effects of the bill, to give Castlereagh leave—'to put me on the fire and broil me alive.' During the subsequent 'paper against gold' struggle Cobbett made much of his gridiron gesture, and maintained to the end of his life that his prognostications on the currency bill had been correct.

10 Frederick John Robinson, 1782-1859, English statesman.

miscreants to revile me; the delight of ousting spitten-upon Stanley[11] and bound-over Wood![12] Yes, but, then, the flowers and the birds and the sweet air! What, then, shall Canning[13] never again hear of the 'revered and ruptured Ogden!'[14] Shall he go into his grave without being again reminded of 'driving at the whole herd, in order to get at the *ignoble animal!'* Shall he never again be told of Six-Acts[15] and of his wish 'to ex-tinguish that *accursed torch of discord forever!'* Oh! God forbid! farewell hares and dogs and birds! What, shall Sidmouth, then, never again hear of his *Power of Imprisonment Bill,* of his *Circular,* of his *Letter of Thanks to the Manchester Yeomanry!*[16] I really jumped up when this thought came athwart my mind, and, without thinking of the breakfast, said to George who was sitting by me, 'Go, George, and tell them to saddle the horses'; for it seemed to me that I had been meditating some crime. Upon George asking me whether I would not stop to breakfast? I bade him not order the horses out yet; and here we are, waiting for breakfast.

1830

11 Edward G. S. Stanley, 1799–1869, English statesman. He entered parliament in 1822.
12 John Wood, M. P. for Preston in 1826, and afterward chairman of the Board of Taxes.
13 George Canning, 1770–1827, foreign secretary and prime minister. Canning was thoroughly disliked by Cobbett and was blamed by him for much of England's misfortune.
14 William Ogden, 1753–1822, radical reformer imprisoned in 1817 for sedition.
15 An act that subjected certain publications to the duties of stamps upon newspapers. It practically destroyed Cobbett's chief financial resource.

16 illiberal documents that brought Sidmouth into disrepute among the reformers.

1791 · CHARLES WOLFE · 1823

1791–1817   Irish poet, educated in English schools and at Trinity College, Dublin, where he attained scholastic distinction and carried off undergraduate prizes in versification.

1817   Entered the ministry and held the curacy in Down.

1821   Forced to give up his work because of failing health.

1823   Died at Cork.

WOLFE is remembered almost solely for his famous poem on the burial of Sir John Moore, which he composed in 1816 in the room of a college friend and circulated privately in manuscript until it made an obscure appearance in an Ulster newspaper over the initials 'C. W.' The elegy was copied by various papers in England where it won an instant popularity being wrongly attributed, among others, to Byron, who praised it but regretfully repudiated its authorship.

THE BURIAL OF SIR JOHN MOORE AT CORUNNA

[Sir John Moore, 1761–1809, was an English general in command of the operations against France in Spain in 1808–9. He was killed at Corunna and according to his wishes was buried in the citadel where he fell. Wolfe's poem is based upon Southey's prose account of the event as it was reported in the Edinburgh *Annual Register*.]

Not a drum was heard, not a funeral note,
  As his corse to the rampart we hurried;
Not a soldier discharged his farewell shot
  O'er the grave where our hero we buried.

We buried him darkly at dead of night,
  The sods with our bayonets turning;
By the struggling moonbeam's misty light,
  And the lantern dimly burning.

No useless coffin enclosed his breast,
  Not in sheet nor in shroud we wound him, 10
But he lay like a warrior taking his rest
  With his martial cloak around him.

Few and short were the prayers we said,
  And we spoke not a word of sorrow;

But we stedfastly gazed on the face that was dead,
  And we bitterly thought of the morrow.

We thought as we hollowed his narrow bed,
  And smoothed down his lonely pillow,
That the foe and the stranger would tread o'er his head,
  And we far away on the billow! 20

Lightly they'll talk of the spirit that's gone,
  And o'er his cold ashes upbraid him,—
But little he'll reck, if they let him sleep on
  In the grave where a Briton has laid him.

But half of our weary task was done
  When the clock struck the hour for retiring;
And we heard the distant random gun
  That the foe was sullenly firing.

Slowly and sadly we laid him down,
  From the field of his fame fresh and gory; 30
We carved not a line, and we raised not a stone—
  But we left him alone with his glory.

1816   1817

1777 · THOMAS CAMPBELL · 1844

1777   Scottish poet, born at Glasgow, son of a merchant.

1794–1800   Educated at Glasgow University; spent a long vacation in the western Island of Mull where he enriched his imagination with the savage beauty of the island and its lonely inhabitants; studied law in Edinburgh and became acquainted with Scott, Jeffrey, and others.

1799   Published *The Pleasures of Hope*.

1800   Traveled on the Continent. Was present at the battle of Ratisbon and saw the Danish fleet captured at Altona.

1802   Settled in London and made literature his profession.

1809   Published *Gertrude of Wyoming*.

1819   Published his *Specimens of the British Poets*.

1820   Accepted the editorship of the *New Monthly Magazine*.

1824   Published *Theodric and Other Poems*.

1822–9   Actively shared in the founding of the University of London and became lord rector of Glasgow University.

1844   Died at Boulogne and was buried in Westminster Abbey.

THOMAS CAMPBELL is a writer who achieved high fame in his own generation but upon whom a later age has passed a more discriminating judgment. He won an early success with *The Pleasures of Hope*, a rhetorical didactic poem in the Augustan tradition. By a lucky combination of the conventional manner and a timely selection of topics (the French Revolution, the partition of Poland, negro slavery, et cetera), the author had perfectly measured popular taste. Four editions of his work were called for in one month and on the strength of its reputation, Campbell held for half a century a top position among the major romantic poets. Today the shortcomings of *The Pleasures of Hope, Gertrude of Wyoming* (a genteel romance with an American setting), and Campbell's other long-short poems, are patent. Campbell was a prim Scotchman with lifelong habits of reclusion, qualities of character which showed themselves in his poetry as a kind of 'spruced-up' elegance and a timid sensibility. Moreover, he was excessively slow and fastidious in composition. Scott complained that he polished his verses until all the ruggedness appropriate to the subject was smoothed away. His passion for freedom has alone lifted some fragment of his work to near greatness. Not only was Campbell a lover of England—his patriotism quickened by his love of ships and the sea—but his enthusiasm for freedom was broad enough to include all oppressed nations. He was an ardent revolutionist who had watched the triumph of liberty in France and its defeat in Poland. It was after this passion had been brought to a focus by the most significant episode of his life (a trip to the Continent in 1800), when he saw men dead and dying on the battlefield and heard the cannonading of Hohenlinden, that Campbell felt and expressed 'the terrible sublimity of battle.' Three splendid war songs, *Ye*

Mariners of England, Hohenlinden, and *The Battle of the Baltic,* represent a notable achievement. In spite of some touches of false poetizing, these battle hymns, full of martial energy and kindling enthusiasm, rank with the best war poetry in English. On a lower level than the war songs are *Lochiel's Warning* and *Lord Ullin's Daughter* and his other ballads and lyrics which, however, occasionally show 'adroit manipulation to an impressive result.' The lurid *Last Man* is powerful if unpoetical, and the *Dead Eagle* a very good traveler's sketch.

From THE PLEASURES OF HOPE

Lines 1–100, 349–418

AT summer eve, when Heaven's ethereal bow
Spans with bright arch the glittering hills below,
Why to yon mountain turns the musing eye,
Whose sunbright summit mingles with the sky?
Why do those cliffs of shadowy tint appear
More sweet than all the landscape smiling near?
'Tis distance lends enchantment to the view,
And robes the mountain in its azure hue.

Thus, with delight, we linger to survey
The promised joys of life's unmeasured way;   10
Thus, from afar, each dim-discover'd scene
More pleasing seems than all the past hath been;
And every form, that Fancy can repair
From dark oblivion, glows divinely there.

What potent spirit guides the raptured eye
To pierce the shades of dim futurity?
Can Wisdom lend, with all her heavenly power,
The pledge of Joy's anticipated hour?
Ah, no! she darkly sees the fate of man—
Her dim horizon bounded to a span;   20
Or, if she hold an image to the view,
'Tis Nature pictured too severely true.

With thee, sweet Hope! resides the heavenly light
That pours remotest rapture on the sight:
Thine is the charm of life's bewilder'd way,
That calls each slumbering passion into play.
Waked by thy touch, I see the sister band,
On tiptoe watching, start at thy command,
And fly where'er thy mandate bids them steer,
To Pleasure's path or Glory's bright career.   30

Primeval Hope, the Aönian Muses[1] say,
When Man and Nature mourn'd their first decay;
When every form of death, and every woe,
Shot from malignant stars to earth below;
When Murder bared his arm, and rampant War
Yoked the red dragons of her iron car;
When Peace and Mercy, banish'd from the plain,
Sprung on the viewless winds to heaven again;

All, all forsook the friendless, guilty mind,
But Hope, the charmer, linger'd still behind.[2]   40

Thus, while Elijah's burning wheels prepare
From Carmel's height to sweep the fields of air,
The prophet's mantle, ere his flight began,
Dropt on the world—a sacred gift to man.[3]

Auspicious Hope! in thy sweet garden grow
Wreaths for each toil, a charm for every woe:
Won by their sweets, in Nature's languid hour
The way-worn pilgrim seeks thy summer
        bower;
There, as the wild bee murmurs on the wing,
What peaceful dreams thy handmaid spirits
        bring!   50
What viewless forms the Aeolian organ[4] play,
And sweep the furrow'd lines of anxious thought
        away!

Angel of life! thy glittering wings explore
Earth's loneliest bounds, and Ocean's wildest
        shore.
Lo! to the wintry winds the pilot yields
His bark careering o'er unfathom'd fields;
Now on the Atlantic waves he rides afar,
Where Andes, giant of the western star,
With meteor-standard to the winds unfurl'd,[5]
Looks from his throne of clouds o'er half the
        world.   60

Now far he sweeps, where scarce a summer
        smiles
On Behring's rocks,[6] or Greenland's naked isles:
Cold on his midnight watch the breezes blow
From wastes that slumber in eternal snow,

---

1 the muses of Aonia, an ancient district in Boetia, Greece.

2 The gods in revenge for the theft of fire from heaven by Prometheus, presented Pandora, the first woman, with a box but forbade her ever to open it. One day out of curiosity she lifted the lid and out flew plagues, sorrow, and mischief for mankind. Only one good remained in the box—Hope, which is to this day mankind's sole comfort.
3 See I Kings, ii, 8–15.
4 aeolian harp or lyre, a wooden frame having strings which, when made to vibrate by the wind, produce musical tones.
5 The Andes, principal mountain range of South America, contains many celebrated volcanoes.
6 Bering is the most westerly of the Aleutian Islands, situated in the North Pacific Ocean.

And waft, across the wave's tumultuous roar,
The wolf's long howl from Oonalaska's[7] shore.

Poor child of danger, nursling of the storm,
Sad are the woes that wreck thy manly form!
Rocks, waves, and winds the shatter'd bark de-
      lay;
Thy heart is sad, thy home is far away.   70

But HOPE can here her moonlight vigils keep,
And sing to charm the spirit of the deep:
Swift as yon streamer lights the starry pole,
Her visions warm the watchman's pensive soul;
His native hills that rise in happier climes,
The grot that heard his song of other times,
His cottage home, his bark of slender sail,
His glassy lake, and broomwood-blossom'd vale,
Rush on his thought; he sweeps before the wind,
Treads the lov'd shore he sigh'd to leave
      behind;   80
Meets at each step a friend's familiar face,
And flies at last to Helen's long embrace;
Wipes from her cheek the rapture-speaking tear,
And clasps, with many a sigh, his children dear!
While, long neglected, but at length caress'd,
His faithful dog salutes the smiling guest,
Points to his master's eyes (where'er they roam)
His wistful face, and whines a welcome home.

Friend of the brave! in peril's darkest hour
Intrepid Virtue looks to thee for power;   90
To thee the heart its trembling homage yields
On stormy floods, and carnage-covered fields,
When front to front the banner'd hosts combine,
Halt ere they close, and form the dreadful line.
When all is still on Death's devoted soil,
The march-worn soldier mingles for the toil;
As rings his glittering tube, he lifts on high
The dauntless brow, and spirit-speaking eye,
Hails in his heart the triumph yet to come,
And hears thy stormy music in the drum!   100

      .   .   .

Oh! sacred Truth! thy triumph ceased a while,
And Hope, thy sister, ceased with thee to
      smile,   350
When leagued Oppression[8] pour'd to Northern
      wars
Her whiskered pandoors[9] and her fierce hussars,[10]
Waved her dread standard to the breeze of morn,

Peal'd her loud drum, and twang'd her trumpet
      horn;
Tumultuous horror brooded o'er her van,
Presaging wrath to Poland—and to man!

Warsaw's last champion[11] from her height sur-
      vey'd,
Wide o'er the fields, a waste of ruin laid,
'Oh! Heaven!' he cried, 'my bleeding country
      save!
Is there no hand on high to shield the brave? 360
Yet, though destruction sweep those lovely
      plains,
Rise, fellow-men! our country yet remains!
By that dread name, we wave the sword on high!
And swear for her to live!—with her to die!'

He said, and on the rampart-heights array'd
His trusty warriors, few, but undismay'd;
Firm-paced and slow, a horrid front they form,
Still as the breeze, but dreadful as the storm;
Low murmuring sounds along their banners fly,
Revenge, or death,—the watchword and reply; 370
Then peal'd the notes, omnipotent to charm,
And the loud, tocsin[12] toll'd their last alarm!—

In vain, alas! in vain, ye gallant few!
From rank to rank your volley'd thunder flew:—
Oh, bloodiest picture in the book of Time,
Sarmatia[13] fell, unwept, without a crime;
Found not a generous friend, a pitying foe,
Strength in her arms, nor mercy in her woe!
Dropp'd from her nerveless grasp the shatter'd
      spear,
Closed her bright eye, and curb'd her high
      career;—   380
Hope, for a season, bade the world farewell,
And Freedom shriek'd as Kosciusko fell!

The sun went down, nor ceased the carnage
      there,
Tumultuous Murder shook the midnight air;
On Prague's proud arch the fires of ruin glow,
His blood-dyed waters murmuring far below;
The storm prevails, the rampart yields a way,
Bursts the wide cry of horror and dismay!
Hark, as the smouldering piles with thunder fall,
A thousand shrieks for hopeless mercy call!   390
Earth shook—red meteors flash'd along the sky,
And conscious Nature shudder'd at the cry!

---

7 largest of the Aleutian Islands, Alaska.
8 In 1792 and 1794, Russia, Prussia and Austria formed a military alliance for the partition of Poland.
9 Austrian soldiers dreaded for their courage and cruelties.
10 light cavalrymen.

11 Thaddeus Kosciusko, 1746–1817, famous Polish patriot and
general. In 1794 he led the Polish insurrection against Russia but
was defeated and taken prisoner.
12 alarm bell.
13 the ancient name for Poland.

Oh! righteous Heaven; ere Freedom found a
grave,
Why slept the sword, omnipotent to save?
Where was thine arm, O Vengeance! where thy
rod,
That smote the foes of Zion and of God,[14]
That crush'd proud Ammon, when his iron car
Was yoked in wrath, and thunder'd from afar?[15]
Where was the storm that slumber'd till the host
Of blood-stain'd Pharaoh left their trembling
coast;   400
Then bade the deep in wild commotion flow,
And heaved an ocean on their march below?[16]

Departed spirits of the mighty dead!
Ye that at Marathon and Leuctra[17] bled!
Friends of the world! restore your swords to man,
Fight in his sacred cause, and lead the van!
Yet for Sarmatia's tears of blood atone,
And make her arm puissant as your own!
Oh! once again to Freedom's cause return
The patriot Tell[18]—the Bruce of Bannock-
burn![19]   410

Yes! thy proud lords, unpitied land, shall see
That man hath yet a soul—and dare be free!
A little while, along thy saddening plains,
The starless night of Desolation reigns;
Truth shall restore the light by Nature given,
And, like Prometheus, bring the fire of Heaven!
Prone to the dust Oppression shall be hurl'd,
Her name, her nature, wither'd from the world!

1796–9   1799

YE MARINERS OF ENGLAND[1]

A NAVAL ODE

Ye Mariners of England
That guard our native seas,
Whose flag has braved, a thousand years,
The battle and the breeze—
Your glorious standard launch again
To match another foe!
And sweep through the deep,

While the stormy winds do blow,—
While the battle rages loud and long,
And the stormy winds do blow.   10

The spirits of your fathers
Shall start from every wave!
For the deck it was their field of fame,
And Ocean was their grave,
Where Blake[2] and mighty Nelson[3] fell,
Your manly hearts shall glow,
As ye sweep through the deep,
While the stormy winds do blow,—
While the battle rages loud and long,
And the stormy winds do blow.   20

Britannia needs no bulwarks,
No towers along the steep;
Her march is o'er the mountain-waves,
Her home is on the deep.
With thunders from her native oak,
She quells the floods below,
As they roar on the shore,
When the stormy winds do blow,—
When the battle rages loud and long,
And the stormy winds do blow.   30

The meteor flag of England
Shall yet terrific burn,
Till danger's troubled night depart,
And the star of peace return.
Then, then, ye ocean-warriors!
Our song and feast shall flow
To the fame of your name,
When the storm has ceased to blow,—
When the fiery fight is heard no more,
And the storm has ceased to blow.   40

1799–1800   1801

HOHENLINDEN[1]

On Linden, when the sun was low,
All bloodless lay the untrodden snow,
And dark as winter was the flow
Of Iser, rolling rapidly.

But Linden saw another sight
When the drum beat at dead of night,

---

14 See Isaiah, li, 7–10.
15 See Judges, xi, 8–33.
16 See Exodus, xiv.
17 the scenes of famous victories in ancient Greece.
18 William Tell, legendary hero of Switzerland.
19 Robert Bruce, 1274–1329, King of Scotland, who defeated Edward II of England at Bannockburn in 1314.

---

1 This 'naval ode' is said to have been composed on the prospect
of war with Russia. The patriotic ardor may be explained partly
by the fact of its being written abroad and partly by reason of recent naval victories over the French in the battles of Cape St.
Vincent, 1797, and of the Nile, 1798.

---

2 Robert Blake, famous English admiral of the Commonwealth,
died at sea in 1657.
3 Horatio Nelson, first of English admirals, 'fell' sorely wounded
at the battle of Copenhagen, April 1801. He was killed at Trafalgar
in 1805.

---

1 Hohenlinden, an Upper Bavarian village east of Munich, was
the scene of a decisive victory of the French over the Austrians in
December 1800.

Commanding fires of death to light
The darkness of her scenery.

By torch and trumpet fast arrayed,
Each horseman drew his battle-blade,   10
And furious every charger neighed
To join the dreadful revelry.

Then shook the hills with thunder riven,
Then rushed the steed to battle driven,
And louder than the bolts of heaven
Far flashed the red artillery.

But redder yet that light shall glow
On Linden's hills of stainèd snow,
And bloodier yet the torrent flow
Of Iser, rolling rapidly.   20

'Tis morn; but scarce yon level sun
Can pierce the war-clouds, rolling dun,
Where furious Frank and fiery Hun
Shout in their sulphurous canopy.

The combat deepens. On, ye brave,
Who rush to glory, or the grave!
Wave, Munich! all thy banners wave,
And charge with all thy chivalry!

Few, few shall part where many meet!
The snow shall be their winding-sheet,   30
And every turf beneath their feet
Shall be a soldier's sepulchre.

1802

LOCHIEL'S WARNING

[Donald Cameron of Lochiel, a Highland chieftain, joined the Young Pretender, Charles Stuart, in the Scottish rebellion of 1745. Cameron was wounded at Culloden, April 1746, in a battle against an English army led by the Duke of Cumberland, and fled to France where he died two years later. In the poem the wizard is warning 'Lochiel' of the disaster which is to befall him.]

WIZARD

Lochiel, Lochiel! beware of the day
When the Lowlands shall meet thee in battle array!
For a field of the dead rushes red on my sight,
And the clans of Culloden are scatter'd in fight.
They rally, they bleed, for their kingdom and crown;
Woe, woe to the riders that trample them down!
Proud Cumberland prances, insulting the slain,
And their hoof-beaten bosoms are trod to the plain.

But hark! through the fast-flashing lightning of war,
What steed to the desert flies frantic and far?   10
'Tis thine, oh Glenullin! whose bride shall await,
Like a love-lighted watch-fire, all night at the gate.
A steed comes at morning: no rider is there;
But its bridle is red with the sign of despair.
Weep, Albin![1] to death and captivity led!
Oh weep, but thy tears cannot number the dead;
For a merciless sword on Culloden shall wave,
Culloden! that reeks with the blood of the brave.

LOCHIEL

Go, preach to the coward, thou death-telling seer!
Or, if gory Culloden so dreadful appear,   20
Draw, dotard, around thy old wavering sight
This mantle, to cover the phantoms of fright.

WIZARD

Ha! laugh'st thou, Lochiel, my vision to scorn?
Proud bird of the mountain, thy plume shall be torn!
Say, rush'd the bold eagle exultingly forth,
From his home, in the dark-rolling clouds of the north?
Lo! the death-shot of foemen, outspeeding, he rode
Companionless, bearing destruction abroad;
But down let him stoop from his havoc on high!
Ah! home let him speed, for the spoiler is nigh!   30
Why flames the far summit? Why shoot to the blast
Those embers, like stars from the firmament cast?
'Tis the fire-shower of ruin, all dreadfully driven
From his eyrie, that beacons the darkness of heaven!
Oh, crested Lochiel! the peerless in might,
Whose banners arise on the battlements' height,
Heaven's fire is around thee, to blast and to burn;
Return to thy dwelling! all lonely return!
For the blackness of ashes shall mark where it stood,
And a wild mother scream o'er her famishing brood.   40

LOCHIEL

False Wizard, avaunt! I have marshall'd my clan;
Their swords are a thousand, their bosoms are one!

_____
1 Gaelic name for Scotland.

They are true to the last of their blood and their
   breath,
And like reapers descend to the harvest of death.
Then welcome be Cumberland's steed to the
   shock!
Let him dash his proud foam like a wave on the
   rock!
But woe to his kindred, and woe to his cause,
When Albin her claymore² indignantly draws;
When her bonneted chieftains to victory crowd,
Clanranald the dauntless, and Moray the
   proud,   50
All plaided and plumed in their tartan array——

WIZARD

Lochiel, Lochiel! beware of the day;
For, dark and despairing, my sight I may seal,
But man cannot cover what God would reveal.
'Tis the sunset of life gives me mystical lore,
And coming events cast their shadows before.
I tell thee, Culloden's dread echoes shall ring
With the bloodhounds that bark for thy fugitive
   king.
Lo! anointed by Heaven with the vials of wrath,
Behold where he flies on his desolate path!   60
Now in darkness and billows, he sweeps from my
   sight:
Rise, rise! ye wild tempests, and cover his flight!
'Tis finish'd. Their thunders are hush'd on the
   moors:
Culloden is lost, and my country deplores.
But where is the iron-bound prisoner? Where?
For the red eye of battle is shut in despair.
Say, mounts he the ocean-wave, banish'd, for-
   lorn,
Like a limb from his country cast bleeding and
   torn?
Ah no! for a darker departure is near;
The war-drum is muffled, and black is the bier; 70
His death-bell is tolling: oh! mercy, dispel
Yon sight, that it freezes my spirit to tell!
Life flutters convulsed in his quivering limbs,
And his blood-streaming nostril in agony swims.
Accursed be the fagots that blaze at his feet,
Where his heart shall be thrown, ere it ceases to
   beat,
With the smoke of its ashes to poison the
   gale——

LOCHIEL

Down, soothless insulter! I trust not the tale:
For never shall Albin a destiny meet

So black with dishonour, so foul with retreat. 80
Tho' my perishing ranks should be strew'd in
   their gore,
Like ocean-weeds heap'd on the surf-beaten
   shore,
Lochiel, untainted by flight or by chains,
While the kindling of life in his bosom remains,
Shall victor exult, or in death be laid low,
With his back to the field, and his feet to the foe!
And leaving in battle no blot on his name,
Look proudly to Heaven from the deathbed of
   fame.

1802

LORD ULLIN'S DAUGHTER

[The scene of this ballad is the west coast of Scotland
on the Island of Mull, one of the Hebrides, where the
poet spent several months in 1795.]

A CHIEFTAIN to the Highlands bound
   Cries, 'Boatman, do not tarry!
And I'll give thee a silver pound
   To row us o'er the ferry.'

'Now who be ye, would cross Lochgyle,
   This dark and stormy water?'
'O, I'm the chief of Ulva's isle,
   And this Lord Ullin's daughter.

'And fast before her father's men
   Three days we've fled together,   10
For should he find us in the glen,
   My blood would stain the heather.

'His horsemen hard behind us ride;
   Should they our steps discover,
Then who will cheer my bonny bride
   When they have slain her lover?'

Out spoke the hardy Highland wight,
   'I'll go, my chief; I'm ready;
It is not for your silver bright,
   But for your winsome lady.   20

'And by my word! the bonny bird
   In danger shall not tarry;
So though the waves are raging white,
   I'll row you o'er the ferry.'

By this the storm grew loud apace
   The water wraith¹ was shrieking;
And in the scowl of heaven each face
   Grew dark as they were speaking.

---

² a large two-edged sword.

¹ a spirit supposed to preside over the waters.

But still, as wilder blew the wind,
  And as the night grew drearer,   30
Adown the glen rode armed men—
  Their trampling sounded nearer.

'O haste thee, haste!' the lady cries,
  'Though tempests round us gather;
I'll meet the raging of the skies,
  But not an angry father.'

The boat has left a stormy land,
  A stormy sea before her,—
When, oh! too strong for human hand,
  The tempest gathered o'er her.   40

And still they row'd amidst the roar
  Of waters fast prevailing:
Lord Ullin reach'd that fatal shore—
  His wrath was changed to wailing.

For sore dismay'd, through storm and shade,
  His child he did discover:
One lovely hand she stretch'd for aid,
  And one was round her lover.

'Come back! come back!' he cried in grief,
  'Across the stormy water;   50
And I'll forgive your Highland chief,
  My daughter! oh, my daughter!'

'Twas vain: the loud waves lash'd the shore,
  Return or aid preventing;
The waters wild went o'er his child,
  And he was left lamenting.
          1804-5   1809

THE SOLDIER'S DREAM

OUR bugles sang truce—for the night-cloud had
    lowered,
  And the sentinel stars set their watch in the
    sky;
And thousands had sunk on the ground over-
    powered,
  The weary to sleep, and the wounded to die.

When reposing that night on my pallet of straw,
  By the wolf-scaring faggot that guarded the
    slain,
At the dead of the night a sweet vision I saw,
  And thrice ere the morning I dreamt it again.

Methought from the battle-field's dreadful array
  Far, far I had roamed on a desolate track: 10

'Twas autumn,—and sunshine arose on the way
  To the home of my fathers, that welcomed me
    back.

I flew to the pleasant fields, traversed so oft
  In life's morning march when my bosom was
    young;
I heard my own mountain-goats bleating aloft,
  And knew the sweet strain that the corn-reap-
    ers sung.

Then pledged we the wine-cup, and fondly I
    swore
  From my home and my weeping friends never
    to part;
My little ones kissed me a thousand times o'er,
  And my wife sobbed aloud in her fulness of
    heart.   20

'Stay, stay with us,—rest, thou art weary and
    worn!'
  And fain was their war-broken soldier to stay;
But sorrow returned with the dawning of morn,
  And the voice in my dreaming ear melted
    away.
                              1804

THE BATTLE OF THE BALTIC

[The Battle of Copenhagen, between the English fleet
and the Danish land and naval forces, was fought on
2 April 1801. Sir Hyde Parker, a 'commonplace' admiral
in command of the English, remained with eight ships in
reserve and sent Nelson with twelve to the attack. When
the English appeared in distress, the frightened Parker
signaled Nelson to retire, but Nelson, applying his blind
eye to the telescope, declared he could not see the signal,
ordered his fleet to close in, and won a brilliant victory.]

OF NELSON and the North
Sing the glorious day's renown,
When to battle fierce came forth
All the might of Denmark's crown,
And her arms along the deep proudly shone,—
By each gun the lighted brand
In a bold determined hand;
And the Prince of all the land
Led them on.

Like leviathans afloat   10
Lay their bulwarks on the brine,
While the sign of battle flew
On the lofty British line:
It was ten of April morn by the chime:

As they drifted on their path,
There was silence deep as death,
And the boldest held his breath
For a time.

But the might of England flushed
To anticipate the scene;   20
And her van the fleeter rushed
O'er the deadly space between.
'Hearts of oak!' our captain cried; when each
          gun
From its adamantine lips
Spread a death-shade round the ships,
Like the hurricane eclipse
Of the sun.

Again! again! again!
And the havoc did not slack,
Till a feeble cheer the Dane   30
To our cheering sent us back:
Their shots along the deep slowly boom;
Then ceased—and all is wail
As they strike the shattered sail,
Or in conflagration pale
Light the gloom.

Out spoke the victor then
As he hailed them o'er the wave,
'Ye are brothers! ye are men!
And we conquer but to save;   40
So peace instead of death let us bring:
But yield, proud foe, thy fleet
With the crews at England's feet,
And make submission meet
To our King.'

Then Denmark blessed our chief
That he gave her wounds repose;
And the sounds of joy and grief
From her people wildly rose,
As death withdrew his shades from the day;   50
While the sun looked smiling bright
O'er a wide and woful sight,
Where the fires of funeral light
Died away.

Now joy, Old England, raise
For the tidings of thy might
By the festal cities' blaze,
While the wine-cup shines in light;
And yet, amidst that joy and uproar,
Let us think of them that sleep,   60
Full many a fathom deep,

By thy wild and stormy steep,
Elsinore![1]

Brave hearts! to Britain's pride
Once so faithful and so true,
On the deck of fame that died
With the gallant good Riou;[2]
Soft sigh the winds of Heaven o'er their grave!
While the billow mournful rolls
And the mermaid's song condoles,   70
Singing glory to the souls
Of the brave!

          1804–5   1809

THE LAST MAN

ALL worldly shapes shall melt in gloom,
     The Sun himself must die,
Before this mortal shall assume
     Its Immortality!
I saw a vision in my sleep
That gave my spirit strength to sweep
     Adown the gulf of Time!
I saw the last of human mould
That shall Creation's death behold,
     As Adam saw her prime!   10

The Sun's eye had a sickly glare,
     The Earth with age was wan,
The skeletons of nations were
     Around that lonely man!
Some had expired in fight—the brands
Still rusted in their bony hands;
     In plague and famine some!
Earth's cities had no sound nor tread;
And ships were drifting with the dead
     To shores where all was dumb!   20

Yet, prophet-like, that lone one stood
     With dauntless words and high,
That shook the sere leaves from the wood
     As if a storm passed by,
Saying, 'We are twins in death, proud Sun!
Thy face is cold, thy race is run,
     'Tis Mercy bids thee go;
For thou ten thousand thousand years
Hast seen the tide of human tears,
     That shall no longer flow.   30

'What though beneath thee man put forth
     His pomp, his pride, his skill,

---

1 the seaport near Copenhagen at the entrance to the sound
where the battle was fought.
2 Captain Edward Riou, who commanded a squadron of smaller
vessels of the English line, was killed in action.

And arts that made fire, flood, and earth,
    The vassals of his will?
Yet mourn I not thy parted sway,
Thou dim discrowned king of day.
    For all those trophied arts
And triumphs that beneath thee sprang
Healed not a passion or a pang
    Entailed on human hearts.   40

'Go, let oblivion's curtain fall
    Upon the stage of men,
Nor with thy rising beams recall
    Life's tragedy again.
Its piteous pageants bring not back,
Nor waken flesh upon the rack
    Of pain anew to writhe—
Stretched in disease's shapes abhorred,
    Or mown in battle by the sword
Like grass beneath the scythe.   50

'Even I am weary in yon skies
    To watch thy fading fire;
Test of all sumless agonies,
    Behold not me expire!
My lips that speak thy dirge of death—
Their rounded gasp and gurgling breath
    To see thou shalt not boast;
The eclipse of Nature spreads my pall,—
The majesty of Darkness shall
    Receive my parting ghost!   60

'This spirit shall return to Him
    Who gave its heavenly spark;
Yet think not, Sun, it shall be dim
    When thou thyself art dark!
No! it shall live again, and shine
In bliss unknown to beams of thine,
    By him recalled to breath
Who captive led captivity,
Who robbed the grave of Victory,
    And took the sting from Death!   70

'Go, Sun, while Mercy holds me up
    On Nature's awful waste
To drink this last and bitter cup
    Of grief that man shall taste—
Go, tell the night that hides thy face
Thou saw'st the last of Adam's race
    On Earth's sepulchral clod
The darkening universe defy
To quench his immortality
    Or shake his trust in God!'   80

1823

THE DEAD EAGLE

WRITTEN AT ORAN[1]

FALLEN as he is, this king of birds still seems
Like royalty in ruins. Though his eyes
Are shut, that look undazzled on the sun,
He was the sultan of the sky, and earth
Paid tribute to his eyry. It was perched
Higher than human conqueror ever built
His bannered fort. Where Atlas' top looks o'er
Zahara's desert to the equator's line:
From thence the wingèd despot mark'd his prey,
Above th' encampments of the Bedouins, ere   10
Their watchfires were extinct, or camels knelt
To take their loads, or horsemen scoured the
    plain;
And there he dried his feathers in the dawn,
Whilst yet th' unwakened world was dark below.

There's such a charm in natural strength and
    power
That human fancy has forever paid
Poetic homage to the bird of Jove.
Hence, 'neath his image, Rome arrayed her
    turms[2]
And cohorts for the conquest of the world.
And figuring his flight, the mind is fill'd   20
With thoughts that mock the pride of wingless
    man.
True, the carred aeronaut[3] can mount as high;
But what's the triumph of his volant art?
A rash intrusion on the realms of air,
His helmless vehicle a silken toy,
A bubble bursting in the thunder-cloud;
His course has no volition, and he drifts
The passive plaything of the winds. Not such
Was this proud bird: he clove the adverse storm,
And cuffed it with his wings. He stopped his
    flight   30
As easily as the Arab reigns his steed,
And stood at pleasure 'neath Heaven's zenith,
    like
A lamp suspended from its azure dome,
Whilst underneath him the world's mountains lay
Like molehills, and her streams like lucid threads.
Then downward, faster than a falling star,
He neared the earth, until his shape distinct
Was blackly shadow'd on the sunny ground;
And deeper terror hushed the wilderness,
To hear his nearer whoop. Then up again   40

---

1 in Algeria, northern Africa.
2 troops of cavalry.
3 balloonist.

He soared and wheeled. There was an air of scorn
In all his movements, whether he threw round
His crested head to look behind him; or
Lay vertical and sportively displayed
The inside whiteness of his wing declined,
In gyres and undulations full of grace,
An object beautifying Heaven itself.

He—reckless who was victor, and above
The hearing of their guns—saw fleets engaged
In flaming combat. It was nought to him   50
What carnage, Moor or Christian, strewed their
     decks.
But if his intellect had matched his wings,
Methinks he would have scorned man's vaunted
     power
To plough the deep. His pinions bore him down
To Algiers the warlike, or the coral groves
That blush beneath the green of Bona's[4] waves;
And traversed in an hour a wider space
Than yonder gallant ship, with all her sails
Wooing the winds, can cross from morn till eve.
His bright eyes were his compass, earth his
     chart,   60
His talons anchored on the stormiest cliff,
And on the very light-house rock he perch'd,
When winds churned white the waves.
                              The earthquake's self
Disturbed not him that memorable day
When o'er yon tableland, where Spain had built
Cathedrals, cannoned forts, and palaces,
A palsy stroke of Nature shook Oran,[5]
Turning her city to a sepulchre,
And strewing into rubbish all her homes;
Amidst whose traceable foundations now,   70

Of streets and squares, the hyæna hides himself.
That hour beheld him fly as careless o'er
The stifled shrieks of thousands buried quick
As lately when he pounced the speckled snake,
Coil'd in yon mallows and wide-nettle fields
That mantle o'er the dead old Spanish town.

Strange is the imagination's dread delight
In objects linked with danger, death, and pain!
Fresh from the luxuries of polished life,
The echo of these wilds enchanted me;   80
And my heart beat with joy when first I heard
A lion's roar come down the Lybian wind
Across yon long, wide, lonely inland lake,
Where boat ne'er sails from homeless shore to
     shore.

And yet Numidia's landscape has its spots
Of pastoral pleasantness—though far between.
The village planted near the Maraboot's
Round roof has aye its feathery palm trees
Paired, for in solitude they bear no fruits.
Here nature's hues all harmonise—fields
     white   90
With alasum or blue with bugloss—banks
Of glossy fennel, blent with tulips wild
And sunflowers like a garment prankt with gold;
Acres and miles of opal asphodel,
Where sports and couches the black-eyed gazelle.
Here, too, the air's harmonious—deep-toned
     doves
Coo to the fife-like carol of the lark;
And when they cease, the holy nightingale
Winds up his long, long shakes of ecstasy,
With notes that seem but the protracted
     sounds   100
Of glassy runnels bubbling over rocks.

c.1835

---

4 the Gulf of Bona, entrance to the seaport of Bona, in Algeria.
5 In 1790 Oran was destroyed by an earthquake, and six thousand
of its inhabitants were buried under the ruins.

1779 · THOMAS MOORE · 1852

1779   Irish poet, born in Dublin, son of a prosperous grocer and wine merchant.

1794–8   Educated at Trinity College, Dublin; shared the friendship of the Irish patriot Robert Emmet.

1798–1800   Entered at the Middle Temple; rapidly became a social success in London.

1801   Issued *Poems of Thomas Little, Esq.*

1803   Received the appointment of admiralty registrar in Bermuda, but soon tiring of the monotonous life, transferred the post to a deputy and returned to England by way of the United States and Canada.

1806   Published *Epistles, Odes and other Poems.* Challenged Jeffrey to a duel for attacking the immorality of this volume; the proceedings were interrupted, however, by the police and the ludicrous affair ended in a fast friendship between the poet and his critic.

1807   First number of *Irish Melodies* appeared; others followed at intervals up to 1835.

1813   Published *The Twopenny Post Bag,* a volume of political satires directed against the Regent. Other volumes of political satire followed, including *The Fudge Family* (1818) and *Fables for a Holy Alliance* (1823).

1817   Published the Oriental romance, *Lalla Rookh.*

1818   First number of *National Airs* appeared; followed by others in 1820, 1822, 1826, and 1827.

1818–22   Owing to the defalcation of his deputy in Bermuda, became responsible for a debt of £6000; went abroad to avoid a demand for payment he could not meet and returned after a settlement had been arranged; visited Byron in Italy and lived in Paris.

1822   Published *The Loves of the Angels,* his second Oriental poem.

1825   Published *Life of Sheridan,* and

1830   *Life of Lord Byron.*

1830–46   Labored at writing a *History of Ireland,* of which four volumes were published but which met with no success.

1852   Died.

Thomas Moore wrote a great quantity of verse in a considerable variety of types and attained to a universal popularity during his lifetime. A pleasant-tempered, irresistible Irishman, he conquered London with the accomplished singing of his own songs. He was praised as a lyric poet by Shelley; adulated by crowds and esteemed by critics; he was highly paid, and pensioned and decorated; and on the appearance of his *Irish Melodies* he was lifted in popularity to a place next to Byron. Yet in his own time a fashion set in of regarding him as a 'mere melodious trifler,' and today the songs seem to many readers 'like last season's fashions, melancholy in their faded prettiness.' They have been censured as 'too facile and too shallow,' as 'poor in execution, limited in range and tawdry in sentiment.'

Even as an interpreter of Irish nationalism (a role in which Moore prided himself), present-day Dublin scholars place Moore below his Irish contemporary, Clarence Mangan. But Tom Moore should have his due. He was a born and well-trained musician who pioneered the use of a great variety of bright and varied measures and rhyming patterns. His biographer, H. M. Jones, while admitting some faults in the *Irish Melodies,* makes high claims for their metrical skill. 'They offer,' he states, 'a wealth of prosodic invention, a treasury of technical resource which neither Byron nor Wordsworth ever acquired, which as sheer craftsmanship must place Moore on a plane with Shelley and Coleridge and Keats in technique, and which, in the management of pause and metrical fingering within the line, sometimes go beyond anything that any other romanticist has to show.' It should be kept in mind that Moore was primarily a melodist creating lyrics that let themselves be sung. Among his innumerable songs, a score or more—elegiac laments for his country, love songs glowing and fanciful, homely sentimental lyrics—are, in their genre, essentially 'right.' Besides the songs, Moore did a pseudo-Oriental romance, *Lalla Rookh,* which brought him fame and fortune. This work is still readable; though it has 'the faults of bookishness and a kind of rococo prettiness that were once fashionable' (Saintsbury). For Moore's satires it is difficult at the present day to stir up much enthusiasm; nevertheless the gift for satirical improvisation must be granted him. He was adept at caricature and the humorous squib; and his generation, which was in on the fun, harkened to his gaiety with great enjoyment. In biography, Moore's *Life of Byron* was eminently worthy of its subject. In the final reckoning, however, out of a great bulk of writing, it is upon a handful of rememberable songs that the Irish singer's fame must mainly rest.

From IRISH MELODIES

(Published 1807–34)

OH, BREATHE NOT HIS NAME!

[The subject of this poem is Robert Emmet, famous Irish patriot executed in 1803 because of his part in leading a rebellion in Dublin against English rule.]

OH, BREATHE not his name! let it sleep in the
    shade,
Where cold and unhonour'd his relics are laid;
Sad, silent, and dark be the tears that we shed,
As the night-dew that falls on the grass o'er his
    head.

But the night-dew that falls, though in silence it
    weeps,
Shall brighten with verdure the grave where he
    sleeps;
And the tear that we shed, though in secret it rolls,
Shall long keep his memory green in our souls.

THE HARP THAT ONCE THROUGH TARA'S HALLS

THE harp that once through Tara's halls[1]
    The soul of music shed,

---
1 Tara, near Dublin, was an ancient stronghold of Irish kings.

Now hangs as mute on Tara's walls
    As if that soul were fled.—
So sleeps the pride of former days,
    So glory's thrill is o'er,
And hearts that once beat high for praise
    Now feel that pulse no more.

No more to chiefs and ladies bright
    The harp of Tara swells;   10
The chord alone that breaks at night
    Its tale of ruin tells.
Thus Freedom now so seldom wakes,
    The only throb she gives
Is when some heart indignant breaks,
    To shew that still she lives.

LET ERIN REMEMBER THE DAYS OF OLD

LET Erin remember the days of old,
    Ere her faithless sons betray'd her;
When Malachi wore the collar of gold,[1]
    Which he won from her proud invader,
When her kings, with standard of green unfurl'd,
    Led the Red-Branch Knights[2] to danger;—
Ere the emerald gem of the western world
    Was set in the crown of a stranger.

---
1 Malachi, an Irish king of the tenth century, slew a Danish invader and took from his neck a collar of gold.
2 a legendary order of Irish chivalry.

On Lough Neagh's bank as the fisherman strays,
  When the clear cold eve's declining,   10
He sees the round towers of other days
  In the wave beneath him shining;[3]
Thus shall memory often, in dreams sublime,
  Catch a glimpse of the days that are over;
Thus, sighing, look through the waves of time
  For the long-faded glories they cover.

BELIEVE ME, IF ALL THOSE ENDEARING YOUNG CHARMS

BELIEVE me, if all those endearing young charms,
  Which I gaze on so fondly to-day,
Were to change by to-morrow, and fleet in my
    arms,
  Like fairy gifts fading away,
Thou wouldst still be adorn'd, as this moment
    thou art,
  Let thy loveliness fade as it will,
And around the dear ruin each wish of my heart
  Would entwine itself verdantly still.

It is not while beauty and youth are thine own,
  And thy cheeks unprofan'd by a tear,   10
That the fervour and faith of a soul can be
    known,
  To which time will but make thee more dear;
No, the heart that has truly lov'd never forgets,
  But as truly loves on to the close,
As the sunflower turns on her god, when he sets,
  The same look which she turn'd when he rose.

SHE IS FAR FROM THE LAND

SHE[1] is far from the land where her young hero
    sleeps,
  And lovers are round her, sighing:
But coldly she turns from their gaze, and weeps,
  For her heart in his grave is lying.

She sings the wild song of her dear native plains,
  Every note which he lov'd awaking;—
Ah! little they think who delight in her strains
  How the heart of the Minstrel is breaking.

He had liv'd for his love, for his country he died,
  They were all that to life had entwin'd him;   10

---

3 Lough Neagh, in Antrim county, was supposed originally to
have been a fountain and to have overflowed its banks and in-
undated an entire region.

1 Sarah Curran, fiancée of the Irish patriot, Robert Emmet, commemorated in *Oh, Breathe Not His Name*.

Nor soon shall the tears of his country be dried,
  Nor long will his love stay behind him.

Oh, make her a grave where the sunbeams rest,
  When they promise a glorious morrow;
They'll shine o'er her sleep, like a smile from the
    West,
  From her own lov'd island of sorrow.

THE YOUNG MAY MOON

THE young May moon is beaming, love,
The glow-worm's lamp is gleaming, love,
    How sweet to rove
    Through Morna's grove,
When the drowsy world is dreaming, love!
Then awake!—the heavens look bright, my dear,
'Tis never too late for delight, my dear,
    And the best of all ways
    To lengthen our days,
Is to steal a few hours from the night, my
  dear!   10

Now all the world is sleeping, love,
But the Sage, his star-watch keeping, love,
    And I, whose star,
    More glorious far,
Is the eye from that casement peeping, love.
Then awake!—till rise of sun, my dear,
The Sage's glass we'll shun, my dear,
    Or, in watching the flight
    Of bodies of light,
He might happen to take thee for one, my
  dear.   20

THE TIME I'VE LOST IN WOOING

THE time I've lost in wooing,
In watching and pursuing
    The light that lies
    In woman's eyes,
Has been my heart's undoing.
Though Wisdom oft has sought me,
I scorn'd the lore she brought me,
    My only books
    Were woman's looks,
And folly's all they've taught me.   10

Her smile when Beauty granted,
I hung with gaze enchanted,
    Like him, the Sprite,
    Whom maids by night
Oft meet in glen that's haunted.
Like him, too, Beauty won me,

But while her eyes were on me;
   If once their ray
   Was turn'd away,
Oh! winds could not outrun me.   20

And are those follies going?
And is my proud heart growing
   Too cold or wise
   For brilliant eyes
Again to set it glowing?
No, vain, alas! th' endeavour
From bonds so sweet to sever;
   Poor Wisdom's chance
   Against a glance
Is now as weak as ever.   30

COME, REST IN THIS BOSOM

COME, rest in this bosom, my own stricken deer,
Though the herd have fled from thee, thy home is
   still here;
Here still is the smile, that no cloud can o'ercast,
And a heart and a hand all thy own to the last.

O, what was love made for, if 'tis not the same
Through joy and through torment, through glory
   and shame?
I know not, I ask not, if guilt's in that heart,
I but know that I love thee, whatever thou art.

Thou hast call'd me thy Angel in moments of
   bliss,
And thy Angel I'll be, 'mid the horrors of
   this,—   10
Through the furnace, unshrinking, thy steps to
   pursue,
And shield thee, and save thee,—or perish there
   too!

DEAR HARP OF MY COUNTRY

DEAR Harp of my Country! in darkness I found
   thee,
   The cold chain of silence had hung o'er thee
   long,
When proudly, my own Island Harp, I unbound
   thee,
   And gave all thy chords to light, freedom, and
   song!
The warm lay of love and the light note of gladness

Have waken'd thy fondest, thy liveliest thrill;
But, so oft hast thou echo'd the deep sigh of sadness,
   That even in thy mirth it will steal from thee
   still.

Dear Harp of my Country! farewell to thy num-
   bers,
   This sweet wreath of song is the last we shall
   twine!   10
Go, sleep with the sunshine of Fame on thy slum-
   bers,
   Till touch'd by some hand less unworthy than
   mine;
If the pulse of the patriot, soldier, or lover,
   Have throbb'd at our lay, 'tis thy glory alone;
I was but as the wind, passing heedlessly over,
   And all the wild sweetness I waked was thy
   own.

From NATIONAL AIRS

(Published 1815)

OH, COME TO ME WHEN DAYLIGHT SETS

VENETIAN AIR

OH, come to me when daylight sets;
   Sweet! then come to me,
When smoothly go our gondolets
   O'er the moonlight sea.
When Mirth's awake, and Love begins,
   Beneath that glancing ray,
With sound of lutes and mandolins,
   To steal young hearts away.
Then, come to me when daylight sets;
   Sweet! then come to me,   10
When smoothly go our gondolets
   O'er the moonlight sea.

Oh, then's the hour for those who love,
   Sweet! like thee and me;
When all's so calm below, above,
   In Heav'n and o'er the sea.
When maidens sing sweet barcarolles
   And Echo sings again
So sweet, that all with ears and souls
   Should love and listen then.   20
So, come to me when daylight sets;
   Sweet! then come to me,
When smoothly go our gondolets
   O'er the moonlight sea.

OFT, IN THE STILLY NIGHT

SCOTCH AIR

OFT, in the stilly night,
   Ere Slumber's chain has bound me,
Fond Memory brings the light
   Of other days around me;
      The smiles, the tears,
      Of boyhood's years,
   The words of love then spoken;
      The eyes that shone,
      Now dimm'd and gone,
   The cheerful hearts now broken!   10
Thus, in the stilly night,
   Ere Slumber's chain has bound me,
Sad Memory brings the light
   Of other days around me.

When I remember all
   The friends, so link'd together,
I've seen around me fall,
   Like leaves in wintry weather;
      I feel like one
      Who treads alone   20
   Some banquet-hall deserted,
      Whose lights are fled,
      Whose garlands dead,
   And all but he departed!
Thus, in the stilly night,
   Ere Slumber's chain has bound me,
Sad Memory brings the light
   Of other days around me.

HARK! THE VESPER HYMN IS STEALING

RUSSIAN AIR

HARK! the vesper hymn is stealing
   O'er the waters soft and clear;
Nearer yet and nearer pealing,
   And now bursts upon the ear:
      Jubilate, Amen.
Farther now, now farther stealing,
   Soft it fades upon the ear:
      Jubilate, Amen.

Now, like moonlight waves retreating
   To the shore, it dies along;   10
Now, like angry surges meeting,
   Breaks the mingled tide of song:
      Jubilate, Amen.
Hush! again, like waves, retreating
   To the shore, it dies along:
      Jubilate, Amen.

From LALLA ROOKH[1]

THE LIGHT OF THE HARAM

Lines 1–119

WHO has not heard of the Vale of Cashmere,
   With its roses the brightest that earth ever
      gave,
Its temples, and grottos, and fountains as clear
   As the love-lighted eyes that hang over their
      wave?
Oh! to see it at sunset, when warm o'er the lake
   Its splendour at parting a summer eve throws,
Like a bride, full of blushes, when lingering to
      take
   A last look of her mirror at night ere she goes!
When the shrines through the foliage are gleam-
      ing half shown,
And each hallows the hour by some rites of its
      own.   10
Here the music of prayer from a minaret[2] swells,
   Here the Magian his urn, full of perfume, is
      swinging,
And here, at the altar, a zone of sweet bells
   Round the waist of some fair Indian dancer is
      ringing.
Or to see it by moonlight, when mellowly shines
The light o'er its palaces, gardens, and shrines;
When the waterfalls gleam, like a quick fall of
      stars,
And the nightingale's hymn from the Isle of
      Chenars
Is broken by laughs and light echoes of feet
From the cool, shining walks where the young
      people meet: 20
Or at morn, when the magic of daylight awakes
A new wonder each minute, as slowly it breaks,—
Hills, cupolas, fountains, called forth every one
Out of darkness, as if but just born of the
      Sun.
When the Spirit of Fragrance is up with the day,
From his Haram of night-flowers stealing away;
And the wind, full of wantonness, woos like a
      lover
The young aspen-trees, till they tremble all over.
When the East is as warm as the light of first
      hopes,
   And Day, with his banner of radiance un-
      furl'd,   30

---

1 This work consists of a series of four Oriental tales recited for
the Indian Princess, Lalla Rookh, as she journeys from Delhi, India, to her betrothed, who lives in the Vale of Cashmere, a district
north of India.
2 a slender tower of a mosque, with balconies from which the
muezzin cries the call to prayer.

Shines in through the mountainous portal that
    opes,
  Sublime, from that valley of bliss to the world!

But never yet, by night or day,
In dew of spring or summer's ray,
Did the sweet valley shine so gay
As now it shines—all love and light,
Visions by day and feasts by night!
A happier smile illumes each brow,
  With quicker spread each heart uncloses,
And all is ecstasy, for now   40
  The valley holds its Feast of Roses;
The joyous time, when pleasures pour
Profusely round and, in their shower,
Hearts open, like the season's rose,—
  The floweret of a hundred leaves,
Expanding while the dew-fall flows,
  And every leaf its balm receives.

'Twas when the hour of evening came
  Upon the lake, serene and cool,
When Day had hid his sultry flame   50
  Behind the palms of Baramoule,
When maids began to lift their heads,
Refresh'd from their embroider'd beds,
Where they had slept the sun away,
And waked to moonlight and to play.
All were abroad—the busiest hive
On Bela's hills is less alive,
When saffron beds are full in flower,
Than look'd the valley in that hour.
A thousand restless torches play'd   60
Through every grove and island shade;
A thousand sparkling lamps were set
On every dome and minaret;
And fields and pathways, far and near,
Were lighted by a blaze so clear,
That you could see, in wandering round,
The smallest rose-leaf on the ground.
Yet did the maids and matrons leave
Their veils at home, that brilliant eve;
And there were glancing eyes about,   70
And cheeks, that would not dare shine out
  In open day, but thought they might
Look lovely then, because 'twas night.
  And all were free, and wandering,
    And all exclaim'd to all they met,
That never did the summer bring
  So gay a Feast of Roses yet;
The moon had never shed a light
  So clear as that which bless'd them there;
The roses ne'er shone half so bright,   80
  Nor they themselves look'd half so fair.

And what a wilderness of flowers!
It seem'd as though from all the bowers
And fairest fields of all the year,
The mingled spoil were scatter'd here.
The lake, too, like a garden breathes,
  With the rich buds that o'er it lie,—
As if a shower of fairy wreaths
  Had fallen upon it from the sky!
And then the sounds of joy:—the beat   90
Of tabors and of dancing feet;
The minaret-crier's[3] chant of glee
Sung from his lighted gallery,
And answered by a ziraleet[4]
From neighbouring Haram, wild and sweet;
The merry laughter, echoing
From gardens, where the silken swing
Wafts some delighted girl above
The top leaves of the orange-grove;
Or, from those infant groups at play   100
Among the tents that line the way,
Flinging, unawed by slave or mother,
Handfuls of roses at each other.

Then the sounds from the lake:—the low whis-
    p'ring in boats,
  As they shoot through the moonlight; the dip-
    ping of oars;
And the wild, airy warbling that everywhere
    floats,
Through the groves, round the islands, as if all the
    shores,
Like those of Kathay,[5] utter'd music, and gave
An answer in song to the kiss of each wave.
  But the gentlest of all are those sounds, full of
    feeling,   110
That soft from the lute of some lover are steal-
    ing,
Some lover, who knows all the heart-touching
    power
Of a lute and a sigh in this magical hour.
Oh! best of delights as it everywhere is
To be near the loved *One,*—what a rapture is his
Who in moonlight and music thus sweetly may
    glide
O'er the Lake of Cashmere, with that *One* by his
    side!
If woman can make the worst wilderness dear,
Think, think what a heaven she must make of
    Cashmere!

    1814–17   1817

---

3 priest.
4 joyous chorus.
5 poetical name for China.

1784 · LEIGH HUNT · 1859

1784   Born at Southgate, Middlesex, son of a West-Indian father, a clergyman, and a Philadelphian Quaker mother. Christened James Henry Leigh Hunt.

1791–1807   Educated at Christ's Hospital; employed as a government clerk.

1807   Wrote for the newspapers and published a volume of theatrical criticisms.

1808   With his brother John established *The Examiner,* a weekly radical newspaper which won an immediate wide popularity.

1810–11   Edited a quarterly magazine, the *Reflector,* for which he wrote *The Feasts of the Poets,* a satire.

1813   For libelous statements on the Prince Regent (later George IV), was fined heavily and sentenced to spend two years in jail. The cheerful courage with which he bore his imprisonment brought him admiration and visits from many friends and influential persons.

1815–21   Following his release from prison, went to live in the 'Vale of Health' in suburban Hampstead; his home became the gathering place for a circle of literary friends including Shelley, Keats, Hazlitt, Lamb, and Reynolds.

1816   Published *The Story of Rimini.*

1819–21   Published *Hero and Leander* and started the *Indicator,* in which some of his best essays appeared.

1821–2   Left England in November for Italy to establish with Shelley and Byron a liberal quarterly magazine; his arrival was retarded until July by storm, sickness, and misadventure.

1822–3   Following Shelley's tragic death, Hunt was stranded with a large and troublesome family virtually a dependent upon Byron. After four numbers of the *Liberal* had been issued, Byron set sail for Greece, and Hunt was left at Genoa to shift for himself.

1825   Returned to England.

1828   Published *Lord Byron and some of his Contemporaries,* an ill-natured book which caused offence by its too candid exposure of humiliations suffered under Byron.

1830–32   Issued the *Tatler,* a daily devoted to literary and dramatic criticism, and

1834–5   Edited the *Monthly Repository.*

1837–8   *Leigh Hunt's London Journal.*

1835   Published *Captain Sword and Captain Pen,* a poem depicting the horrors of war.

1840   A play, *Legend of Florence,* successfully produced at Covent Garden.

1842   Published a narrative poem, *The Palfrey.*

1840–47   Contributed to the *Edinburgh Review;* received an annuity from Shelley's family estates and a crown pension.

1844   Published *Imagination and Fancy,*

1846 *Wit and Humour* (a selection from the English poets) and *Stories from Italian Poets,*

1847 *Men, Women, and Books,*

1848 *The Town* and *A Jar of Honey,*

1849 *A Book for a Corner,*

1850 *Autobiography,*

1851 *Table Talk,* and

1855 *The Old Court Suburb.*

1859 Died at Putney.

OVER A LONG STRETCH of years Leigh Hunt supported his large family by a never-ceasing production of miscellaneous writing. For the most part his work suffers the defects common to journalism. Hunt had gifts much above the average workaday author, however, and made his mark as a courageous editor, an indefatigable contributor and critic, a familiar essayist, a skillful translator, and a poet of more than ordinary ability. In personality he was an amiable, improvident sort of man whose 'light externals of character' were rather unfairly magnified in Dickens' caricature of him as Harold Skimpole. Like Cobbett and Hazlitt and other outspoken radicals of the time, he earned for himself great unpopularity in espousing 'lost causes.'

Hunt's only long poem of consequence, *The Story of Rimini,* was written in prison under the spell of the Italian romances. Historically it is important because it inaugurated a free handling of the heroic couplet and a colloquial style developed and made famous by Shelley and Keats. It is marred by trivial fluency and a general lack of taste. In the dramatic scenes particularly there are glaring faults. The chatty colloquial dialogue and the touches of feminine lusciousness (in which Keats at first outdid his master) are wholly out of keeping with the dignity of the tragic theme. Yet for all its shortcomings, which have been commonly noted, *Rimini* is an original and meritorious achievement in poetical narrative. There are descriptive passages of a fresh and sensuous beauty—intermittent, to be sure, but undeniable—luxuriously perceived and rendered, and episodes 'which move forward in an admirably staple narrative style.'

If Hunt lacked the stamina and creative imagination for sustained flights in poetry, he did some smaller delightful things that now and then attain to beauty and artistic finish. The Hampstead sonnet may be named, and the Nile sonnet, which he wrote in competition with Shelley and Keats and in which, in this one instance, he surpassed his betters. The perennial household favorite, *Abou Ben Adhem,* shows a masterly narrative control and has few superiors in its scale. The delightful rondeau *Jenny Kissed Me* and the quaintly humorous *The Fish, the Man, and the Spirit* are also excellent in every way.

The lack of taste which too often blighted Hunt's poetry is also to be found in his prose but it is less harmful there. For out of the mass of his miscellaneous writing, much of it effusive and loose in treatment and often done with a facile pen to support his hand-to-mouth existence, there flows a stream of 'bright, warm-hearted, voluble' prose, full of kindliness and shrewd observation done with a charming grace of style quite his own. It radiates a cheerful enjoyment in familiar and pleasant things and is rarely without attractiveness. The manner and method derive from the *Spectator,* but the intimacy of treatment prepares the way for Lamb and Hazlitt. In his day, Hunt was an influential critic of the drama, and as a critic in general literature he was almost unique for the comprehensiveness and catholicity of his judgment. He was, be it noted, one of the first to recognize the genius of Shelley and Keats. He loved literature passionately and humbly, made an extensive study of the Italian poets, and directed the attention of younger men to Italian literature. His *Autobiography,* in one sense Hunt's only *book,* 'reveals his wit, gaiety, and abiding good nature to the best advantage.' It is, on a full scale, the most vivid and delightful of his works.

From THE STORY OF RIMINI[1]

The following story is founded on a passage in Dante, the substance of which is contained in the concluding paragraph of the second [fifth] Canto. For the rest of the incidents, generally speaking, the praise or blame remains with myself. The passage in question—the episode of Paulo and Francesca—has long been admired by the readers of Italian poetry, and is indeed the most cordial and refreshing one in the whole of that singular poem the *Inferno*. . . .

The interest of the passage is greatly increased by its being founded on acknowledged matter of fact. Even the particular circumstance which Dante describes as having hastened the fall of the lovers,—the perusal of *Launcelot of the Lake*,—is most likely a true anecdote; for he himself, not long after the event, was living at the court of Guido Novella da Polenta, the heroine's father; and indeed the very circumstance of his having related it at all, considering its nature, is a warrant of its authenticity. —(From Hunt's Preface.)

CANTO III

Lines 382–end

A NOBLE range it was, of many a rood,
Walled round with trees, and ending in a wood:
Indeed the whole was leafy; and it had
A winding stream about it, clear and glad,
That danced from shade to shade, and on its way
Seemed smiling with delight to feel the day.
There was the pouting rose, both red and white,
The flamy heart's-ease, flushed with purple light,
Blush-hiding strawberry, sunny-coloured
    box,   390
Hyacinth, handsome with his clustering locks,
The lady lily, looking gently down,
Pure lavender, to lay in bridal gown,
The daisy, lovely on both sides,—in short,
All the sweet cups to which the bees resort,
With plots of grass, and perfumed walks between
Of citron, honeysuckle and jessamine,
With orange, whose warm leaves so finely suit,
And look as if they'd shade a golden fruit;
And midst the flowers, turfed round beneath a
    shade   400
Of circling pines, a babbling fountain played,
And 'twixt their shafts you saw the water bright,
Which through the darksome tops glimmered
    with showering light.
So now you walked beside an odorous bed
Of gorgeous hues, white, azure, golden, red;

[1] Francesca, beautiful daughter of Guido da Polenta, lord of Ravenna, was given in marriage to Giovanni Malatesta of Rimini, a brave but deformed and ill-tempered man. But Paulo, his handsome young brother, had won Francesca's heart and the two lovers being surprised by Giovanni were both murdered by him on the spot. The episode occurred late in the thirteenth century.
The text is that of the 1816 edition.

And now turned off into a leafy walk,
Close and continuous, fit for lovers' talk;
And now pursued the stream, and as you trod
Onward and onward o'er the velvet sod,
Felt on your face an air, watery and sweet,   410
And a new sense in your soft-lighting feet;
And then perhaps you entered upon shades,
Pillowed with dells and uplands 'twixt the
    glades,
Through which the distant palace, now and then,
Looked lordly forth with many-windowed ken;
A land of trees, which reaching round about,
In shady blessing stretching their old arms out,
With spots of sunny opening, and with nooks,
To lie and read in, sloping into brooks,
Where at her drink you started the slim deer, 420
Retreating lightly with a lovely fear.
And all about, the birds kept leafy house,
And sung and sparkled in and out the boughs;
And all about, a lovely sky of blue
Clearly was felt, or down the leaves laughed
    through.
And here and there, in every part, were seats,
Some in the open walks, some in retreats;
With bowering leaves o'erhead, to which the eye
Looked up half sweetly and half awfully,—
Places of nestling green, for poets made,   430
Where when the sunshine struck a yellow shade,
The slender trunks, to inward peeping sight
Thronged in dark pillars up the gold green light.

But 'twixt the wood and flowery walks, halfway,
And formed of both, the loveliest portion lay,
A spot, that struck you like enchanted ground:—
It was a shallow dell, set in a mound
Of sloping shrubs, that mounted by degrees,
The birch and poplar mixed with heavier trees;
From under which, sent through a marble
    spout,   440
Betwixt the dark wet green, a rill gushed out,
Whose low sweet talking seemed as if it said
Something eternal to that happy shade:
The ground within was lawn, with plots of flowers
Heaped towards the centre, and with citron
    bowers;
And in the midst of all, clustered about
With bay and myrtle, and just gleaming-out,
Lurked a pavilion,—a delicious sight,
Small, marble, well-proportioned, mellowy white
With yellow vine-leaves sprinkled,—but no
    more—   450
And a young orange either side the door.
The door was to the wood, forward, and square,

The rest was domed at top, and circular;
And through the dome the only light came in,
Tinged, as it entered, with the vine-leaves thin.

It was a beauteous piece of ancient skill,
Spared from the rage of war, and perfect still;
By most supposed the work of fairy hands,
Famed for luxurious taste, and choice of lands,—
Alcina, or Morgana,[2]—who from fights   460
And errant fame inveigled amorous knights,
And lived with them in a long round of blisses,
Feasts, concerts, baths, and bower-enshaded
       kisses.

But 'twas a temple, as its sculpture told,
Built to the nymphs that haunted there of old;
For o'er the door was carved a sacrifice
By girls and shepherds brought, with reverent
       eyes,
Of sylvan drinks and foods, simple and sweet,
And goats with struggling horns and planted feet:
And on a line with this ran round about   470
A like relief, touched exquisitely out,
That shewed, in various scenes, the nymphs
       themselves;
Some by the water side on bowery shelves
Leaning at will,—some in the water sporting
With sides half swelling forth, and looks of court-
       ing,—
Some in a flowery dell, hearing a swain
Play on his pipe, till the hills ring again,—
Some tying up their long moist hair,—some
       sleeping
Under the trees, with fauns and satyrs peeping,—
Or, sidelong-eyed, pretending not to see   480
The latter in the brakes come creepingly,
While their forgotten urns, lying about
In the green herbage, let the water out.
Never, be sure, before or since was seen
A summer-house so fine in such a nest of green.

All the green garden, flower-bed, shade, and plot,
Francesca loved, but most of all this spot.
Whenever she walked forth, wherever went
About the grounds, to this at last she bent:
Here she had brought a lute and a few books; 490
Here would she lie for hours, with grateful looks,
Thanking at heart the sunshine and the leaves,
The summer rain-drops counting from the eaves,
And all that promising, calm smile we see
In nature's face, when we look patiently.
Then would she think of heaven; and you might
       hear

Sometimes, when every thing was hushed and
       clear,—
Her gentle voice from out those shades emerg-
       ing,
Singing the evening anthem to the Virgin.
The gardeners and the rest, who served the
       place,   500
And blest whenever they beheld her face,
Knelt when they heard it, bowing and uncov-
       ered,
And felt as if in air some sainted beauty hovered.

One day,—'twas on a summer afternoon,
When airs and gurgling brooks are best in tune,
And grasshoppers are loud, and day-work done,
And shades have heavy outlines in the sun,—
The princess came to her accustomed bower
To get her, if she could, a soothing hour,
Trying, as she was used, to leave her cares   510
Without, and slumberously enjoy the airs,
And the low-talking leaves, and that cool light
The vines let in, and all that hushing sight
Of closing wood seen through the opening door.
And distant plash of waters tumbling o'er,
And smell of citron blooms, and fifty luxuries
       more.

She tried, as usual, for the trial's sake,
For even that diminished her heart-ache;
And never yet, how ill soe'er at ease,
Came she for nothing 'midst the flowers and
       trees.   520
Yet somehow or another, on that day,
She seemed to feel too highly borne away,—
Too much relieved,—too much inclined to draw
A careless joy from every thing she saw,
And looking round her with a new-born eye,
As if some tree of knowledge had been nigh,
To taste of nature, primitive and free,
And bask at ease in her heart's liberty.

Painfully clear those rising thoughts appeared,
With something dark at bottom that she
       feared;   530
And snatching from the fields her thoughtful
       look,
She reached o'er-head, and took her down a
       book,
And fell to reading with as fixed an air,
As though she had been wrapt since morning
       there.

'Twas Launcelot of the Lake, a bright romance,
That like a trumpet, made young pulses dance,

---

2 fays in the Italian romances of Boiardo and Ariosto.

Yet had a softer note that shook still more;—
She had begun it but the day before,
And read with a full heart, half sweet, half sad,
How old King Ban was spoiled of all he had   540
But one fair castle: how one summer's day
With his fair queen and child he went away
To ask the great King Arthur for assistance;
How reaching by himself a hill at distance
He turned to give his castle a last look,
And saw its far white face: and how a smoke,
As he was looking, burst in volumes forth,
And good King Ban saw all that he was worth,
And his fair castle, burning to the ground,
So that his wearied pulse felt over-wound,   550
And he lay down, and said a prayer apart
For those he loved, and broke his poor old heart.
Then read she of the queen with her young child,
How she came up, and nearly had gone wild,
And how in journeying on in her despair,
She reached a lake and met a lady there,
Who pities her, and took the baby sweet
Into her arms, when lo, with closing feet
She sprang up all at once, like bird from brake,
And vanished with him underneath the lake. 560
The mother's feelings we as well may pass:—
The fairy of the place that lady was,
And Launcelot (so the boy was called) became
Her inmate, till in search of knightly fame
He went to Arthur's court, and played his part
So rarely, and displayed so frank a heart,
That what with all his charms of look and limb,
The queen Geneura fell in love with him:—
And here, with growing interest in her reading,
The princess, doubly fixed, was now proceed-
    ing.   570

Ready she sat with one hand to turn o'er
The leaf, to which her thoughts ran on before,
The other propping her white brow, and throwing
Its ringlets out, under the skylight glowing.
So sat she fixed; and so observed was she
Of one, who at the door stood tenderly,—
Paulo,—who from a window seeing her
Go straight across the lawn, and guessing where,
Had thought she was in tears, and found, that
    day,
His usual efforts vain to keep away.   580
'May I come in?' said he:—it made her start,—
That smiling voice;—she coloured, pressed her
    heart
A moment, as for breath, and then with free
And usual tone said, 'O yes,—certainly.'
There's apt to be, at conscious times like these,
An affectation of a bright-eyed ease,

An air of something quite serene and sure,
As if to seem so, was to be, secure:
With this the lovers met, with this they spoke,
With this they sat down to the self-same
    book,   590
And Paulo, by degrees, gently embraced
With one permitted arm her lovely waist;
And both their cheeks, like peaches on a tree,
Leaned with a touch together, thrillingly;
And o'er the book they hung, and nothing said,
And every lingering page grew longer as they
    read.

As thus they sat, and felt with leaps of heart
Their colour change, they came upon the part
Where fond Geneura, with her flame long nurst,
Smiled upon Launcelot when he kissed her
    first:—   600
That touch, at last, through every fibre slid;
And Paulo turned, scarce knowing what he did,
Only he felt he could no more dissemble,
And kissed her, mouth to mouth, all in a tremble.
Sad were those hearts, and sweet was that long
    kiss:
Sacred be love from sight, whate'er it is.
The world was all forgot, the struggle o'er,
Desperate the joy.—That day they read no more.
    1812–16   1816

TO HAMPSTEAD[1]

WRITTEN DURING THE AUTHOR'S IMPRISONMENT,
AUGUST 1813

SWEET upland, to whose walks, with fond repair,
Out of thy western slope I took my rise
Day after day, and on these feverish eyes
Met the moist fingers of the bathing air;—
If health, unearned of thee, I may not share,
Keep it, I pray thee, where my memory lies,
In thy green lanes, brown dells, and breezy skies,
Till I return, and find thee doubly fair.

Wait then my coming, on that lightsome land,
Health, and the joy that out of nature springs,   10
And Freedom's air-blown locks;—but stay with
    me,
Friendship, frank entering with the cordial hand,
And Honour, and the Muse with growing wings,
And Love Domestic, smiling equably.
                              1813

---

1 a borough in northwestern London; Hunt's home and the gathering-place for his circle of literary friends.

TO THE GRASSHOPPER AND THE CRICKET

[This sonnet was written impromptu in friendly competition with Keats. For Keats's *On the Grasshopper and Cricket* see text p. 1136.]

GREEN little vaulter in the sunny grass,
  Catching your heart up at the feel of June,
  Sole voice that's heard amidst the lazy noon,
When ev'n the bees lag at the summoning
    brass;—
And you, warm little housekeeper, who class
  With those who think the candles come too
    soon,
  Loving the fire, and with your tricksome
    tune
Nick the glad silent moments as they pass;—

Oh, sweet and tiny cousins, that belong,
  One to the fields, the other to the hearth,   10
Both have your sunshine; both, though small, are
    strong
  At your clear hearts; and both were sent on
    earth
To sing in thoughtful ears this natural song—
  In doors and out,—summer and winter,—
    Mirth.
    1816   1817

THE NILE

IT FLOWS through old hushed Egypt and its
    sands,
Like some grave mighty thought threading a
    dream,
And times and things, as in that vision, seem
Keeping along it their eternal stands,—
Caves, pillars, pyramids, the shepherd bands
That roamed through the young world, the glory
    extreme
Of high Sesostris,[1] and that southern beam,
The laughing queen[2] that caught the world's great
    hands.

Then comes a mightier silence, stern and strong,
As of a world left empty of its throng,   10
And the void weighs on us; and then we wake,
And hear the fruitful stream lapsing along
'Twixt villages, and think how we shall take
Our own calm journey on for human sake.
                                          1818

---

1 a legendary king of Egypt said to have conquered the world.
2 Cleopatra.

THE FISH, THE MAN, AND THE SPIRIT

TO A FISH

YOU strange, astonished-looking, angle-faced,
Dreary-mouthed, gaping wretches of the sea,
Gulping salt-water everlastingly,
Cold-blooded, though with red your blood be
    graced,
And mute, though dwellers in the roaring waste;
And you, all shapes beside, that fishy be,—
Some round, some flat, some long, all devilry,
Legless, unloving, infamously chaste:—

O scaly, slippery, wet, swift, staring wights,
What is't ye do? what life lead? eh, dull gog-
    gles?   10
How do ye vary your vile days and nights?
How pass your Sundays? Are ye still but joggles
In ceaseless wash? Still nought but gapes and
    bites,
And drinks, and stares, diversified with boggles?

A FISH ANSWERS

Amazing monster! that, for aught I know,
With the first sight of thee didst make our race
Forever stare! Oh flat and shocking face,
Grimly divided from the breast below!
Thou that on dry land horribly dost go
With a split body and most ridiculous pace,   20
Prong after prong, disgracer of all grace,
Long-useless-finned, haired, upright, unwet,
    slow!

O breather of unbreathable, sword-sharp air,
How canst exist? How bear thyself, thou dry
And dreary sloth? What particle canst share
Of the only blessed life, the watery?
I sometimes see of ye an actual *pair*
Go by! linked fin by fin! most odiously.

THE FISH TURNS INTO A MAN, AND THEN INTO A SPIRIT, AND AGAIN SPEAKS

Indulge thy smiling scorn, if smiling still,
O man! and loathe, but with a sort of love: 30
For difference must its use by difference prove,
And, in sweet clang, the spheres with music fill.
One of the spirits am I, that at his will
Live in whate'er has life—fish, eagle, dove—
No hate, no pride, beneath nought, nor above,
A visitor of the rounds of God's sweet skill.

Man's life is warm, glad, sad, 'twixt loves and
    graves,

Boundless in hope, honoured with pangs aus-
        tere,
Heaven-gazing; and his angel-wings he craves:
The fish is swift, small-needing, vague yet
        clear,   40
A cold, sweet, silver life, wrapped in round
        waves,
Quickened with touches of transporting fear.

                                        1836

RONDEAU

JENNY kissed me when we met,[1]
    Jumping from the chair she sat in;
Time, you thief, who love to get
    Sweets into your list, put that in:
Say I'm weary, say I'm sad,
    Say that health and wealth have missed me,
Say I'm growing old, but add,
    Jenny kissed me.

                                        1838

ABOU BEN ADHEM

[This poem is based upon an anecdote taken from
D'Herbelot's *Bibliothèque Orientale*, 1697.]

ABOU BEN ADHEM, may his tribe increase!
Awoke one night from a deep dream of peace,
And saw, within the moonlight in his room,
Making it rich, and like a lily in bloom,
An angel writing in a book of gold:—

Exceeding peace had made Ben Adhem bold,
And to the presence in the room he said,
'What writest thou?'—The vision raised its head,
And with a look made of all sweet accord,
Answered, 'The names of those who love the
        Lord.'   10
'And is mine one?' said Abou. 'Nay, not so,'
Replied the angel. Abou spoke more low,
But cheerly still; and said, 'I pray thee then,
Write me as one that loves his fellow-men.'[1]

    The angel wrote, and vanished. The next night
It came again with a great wakening light,
And showed the names whom love of God had
        blessed,
And lo! Ben Adhem's name led all the rest.

                                        1838

---

1 The kiss that so enraptured Hunt is said to have been bestowed
by Mrs. Thomas (Jane) Carlyle in a moment of joy upon Hunt's
announcement that a publisher had accepted her husband's *Frederick the Great*.

1 This line is inscribed over Hunt's grave.

THE OLD LADY

IF the old lady is a widow and lives alone, the
manners of her condition and time of life are so
much the more apparent. She generally dresses in
plain silks, that make a gentle rustling as she
moves about the silence of her room; and she
wears a nice cap with a lace border, that comes
under the chin. In a placket at her side is an old
enamelled watch, unless it is locked up in a
drawer of her toilet, for fear of accidents. Her
waist is rather tight and trim than otherwise, as
she had a fine one when young; and she is not
sorry if you see a pair of her stockings on a table,
that you may be aware of the neatness of her leg
and foot. Contented with these and other evident
indications of a good shape, and letting her
young friends understand that she can afford to
obscure it a little, she wears pockets, and uses
them well too. In the one is her handkerchief,
and any heavier matter that is not likely to come
out with it, such as the change of a sixpence; in
the other is a miscellaneous assortment, consisting of a pocket-book, a bunch of keys, a needle-
case, a spectacle-case, crumbs of biscuit, a nutmeg and grater, a smelling-bottle, and, according
to the season, an orange or apple, which after
many days she draws out, warm and glossy, to
give to some little child that has well behaved
itself. She generally occupies two rooms, in the
neatest condition possible. In the chamber is a
bed with a white coverlet, built up high and
round, to look well, and with curtains of a pastoral pattern, consisting alternately of large
plants, and shepherds and shepherdesses. On the
mantelpiece are more shepherds and shepherdesses, with dot-eyed sheep at their feet, all in coloured ware: the man, perhaps, in a pink jacket
and knots of ribbons at his knees and shoes, holding his crook lightly in one hand, and with the
other at his breast, turning his toes out and looking tenderly at the shepherdess; the woman holding a crook, also, and modestly returning his
look, with a gipsy-hat jerked up behind, a very
slender waist, with petticoat and hips to *counteract*, and the petticoat pulled up through the
pocket-holes, in order to show the trimness of
her ankles. But these patterns, of course, are
various. The toilet is ancient, carved at the edges,
and tied about with a snow-white drapery of muslin. Beside it are various boxes, mostly japan; and
the set of drawers are exquisite things for a little
girl to rummage, if ever little girl be so bold,—
containing ribbons and laces of various kinds;

linen smelling of lavender, of the flowers of which there is always dust in the corners; a heap of pocketbooks for a series of years; and pieces of dress long gone by, such as head-fronts, stomachers, and flowered satin shoes, with enormous heels. The stock of letters are under especial lock and key. So much for the bedroom. In the sitting-room is rather a spare assortment of shining old mahogany furniture, or carved arm-chairs equally old, with chintz draperies down to the ground; a folding or other screen, with Chinese figures, their round, little-eyed, meek faces perking sideways; a stuffed bird, perhaps in a glass case (a living one is too much for her); a portrait of her husband over the mantelpiece, in a coat with frog-buttons, and a delicate frilled hand lightly inserted in the waistcoat; and opposite him on the wall, is a piece of embroidered literature, framed and glazed, containing some moral distich or maxim, worked in angular capital letters with two trees or parrots below, in their proper colours; the whole concluding with an ABC and numerals, and the name of the fair industrious, expressing it to be 'her work, Jan. 14, 1762.' The rest of the furniture consists of a looking-glass with carved edges, perhaps a settee, a hassock for the feet, a mat for the little dog, and a small set of shelves, in which are *The Spectator* and *Guardian, The Turkish Spy,*[1] a *Bible* and *Prayer Book,* Young's *Night Thoughts* with a piece of lace in it to flatten, Mrs. Rowe's *Devout Exercises of the Heart,* Mrs. Glasse's *Cookery,* and perhaps *Sir Charles Grandison,* and *Clarissa.*[2] *John Buncle*[3] is in the closet among the pickles and preserves. The clock is on the landing-place between the two room doors, where it ticks audibly but quietly; and the landing-place, as well as the stairs, is carpeted to a nicety. The house is most in character, and properly coeval, if it is in a retired suburb, and strongly built, with wainscot rather than paper inside, and lockers in the windows. Before the windows should be some quivering poplars. Here the Old Lady receives a few quiet visitors to tea, and perhaps an early game at cards: or you may see her going out on the same kind of visit herself, with a light umbrella running up into a stick and crooked ivory handle, and her little dog, equally famous for his love to her and captious antipathy to strangers. Her grandchil-

dren dislike him on holidays, and the boldest sometimes ventures to give him a sly kick under the table. When she returns at night, she appears, if the weather happens to be doubtful, in a calash;[4] and her servant in pattens follows half behind and half at her side, with a lantern.

Her opinions are not many nor new. She thinks the clergyman a nice man. The Duke of Wellington, in her opinion, is a very great man; but she has a secret preference for the Marquis of Granby.[5] She thinks the young women of the present day too forward, and the men not respectful enough; but hopes her grandchildren will be better; though she differs with her daughter in several points respecting their management. She sets little value on the new accomplishments; is a great though delicate connoisseur in butcher's meat and all sorts of housewifery; and if you mention waltzes, expatiates on the grace and fine breeding of the minuet. She longs to have seen one danced by Sir Charles Grandison, whom she almost considers as a real person. She likes a walk of a summer's evening, but avoids the new streets, canals, etc., and sometimes goes through the churchyard, where her other children and her husband lie buried, serious, but not melancholy. She has had three great epochs in her life:—her marriage, her having been at court to see the King and Queen and Royal Family, and a compliment on her figure she once received, in passing, from Mr. Wilkes,[6] whom she describes as a sad, loose man, but engaging. His plainness she thinks much exaggerated. If anything takes her at a distance from home, it is still the court; but she seldom stirs, even for that. The last time but one that she went, was to see the Duke of Wirtemberg; and most probably for the last time of all, to see the Princess Charlotte and Prince Leopold. From this beatific vision she returned with the same admiration as ever for the fine comely appearance of the Duke of York and the rest of the family, and great delight at having had a near view of the Princess, whom she speaks of with smiling pomp and lifted mittens, clasping them as passionately as she can together, and calling her, in a transport of mixed loyalty and self-love, a fine royal young creature, and 'Daughter of England.'

1816

---

1 an Italian romance, of which Defoe wrote a continuation.
2 famous sentimental novels by Samuel Richardson.
3 a sentimental, amorous novel by Thomas Amory, d. 1788.
4 a hood that can be drawn over the head.
5 handsome British general twice painted by Reynolds.
6 Jack Wilkes, the political agitator and reformer.

GETTING UP ON COLD MORNINGS

An Italian author, Giulio Cordara, a Jesuit, has written a poem upon insects, which he begins by insisting, that those troublesome and abominable little animals were created for our annoyance, and that they were certainly not inhabitants of Paradise. We of the north may dispute this piece of theology; but on the other hand, it is as clear as the snow on the house-tops, that Adam was not under the necessity of shaving; and that when Eve walked out of her delicious bower, she did not step upon ice three inches thick.

Some people say it is a very easy thing to get up of a cold morning. You have only, they tell you, to take the resolution; and the thing is done. This may be very true; just as a boy at school has only to take a flogging, and the thing is over. But we have not at all made up our minds upon it; and we find it a very pleasant exercise to discuss the matter, candidly, before we get up. This, at least, is not idling, though it may be lying. It affords an excellent answer to those who ask how lying in bed can be indulged in by a reasoning being,— a rational creature. How! Why, with the argument calmly at work in one's head, and the clothes over one's shoulder. Oh! it is a fine way of spending a sensible, impartial half-hour.

If these people would be more charitable, they would get on with their argument better. But they are apt to reason so ill, and to assert so dogmatically, that one could wish to have them stand round one's bed of a bitter morning, and *lie* before their faces. They ought to hear both sides of the bed, the inside and out. If they cannot entertain themselves with their own thoughts for half-an-our or so, it is not the fault of those who can. If their will is never pulled aside by the enticing arms of imagination, so much the luckier for the stage-coachman.

Candid inquiries into one's decumbency,[1] besides the greater or less privileges to be allowed a man in proportion to his ability of keeping early hours, the work given his faculties, etc., will at least concede their due merits to such representations as the following. In the first place, says the injured but calm appealer, I have been warm all night, and find my system in a state perfectly suitable to a warm-blooded animal. To get out of this state into the cold—besides the inharmonious and uncritical abruptness of the transition, is so unnatural to such a creature, that the

poets, refining upon the tortures of the damned, make one of their greatest agonies consist in being suddenly transported from heat to cold, from fire to ice. They are 'haled' out of their 'beds,' says Milton, by 'harpy-footed furies,'—fellows who come to call them. On my first movement towards the anticipation of getting up I find that such parts of the sheets and bolster as are exposed to the air of the room are stone-cold. On opening my eyes, the first thing that meets them is my own breath rolling forth, as if in the open air, like smoke out of a cottage chimney. Think of this symptom. Then I turn my eyes sideways and see the window all frozen over. Think of that. Then the servant comes in. 'It is very cold this morning, is it not?'—'Very cold, sir.'—'Very cold indeed, isn't it?'—'Very cold indeed, sir.'— 'More than usually so, isn't it, even for this weather?' (Here the servant's wit and good-nature are put to a considerable test, and the inquirer lies on thorns for the answer.) 'Why, sir,—•I think it *is*.' (Good creature! There is not a better or more truth-telling servant going.) 'I must rise, however—get me some warm water.' —Here comes a fine interval between the departure of the servant and the arrival of the hot water, during which, of course, it is of 'no use' to get up. The hot water comes. 'Is it quite hot?'— 'Yes, sir.'—'Perhaps too hot for shaving; I must wait a little?'—'No, sir, it will just do.' (There is an over-nice propriety sometimes, an officious zeal of virtue, a little troublesome.) 'Oh—the shirt—you must air my clean shirt;—linen gets very damp this weather.'—'Yes, sir.' Here another delicious five minutes. A knock at the door. 'Oh, the shirt—very well. My stockings—I think the stockings had better be aired too.'—'Very well, sir.'—Here another interval. At length everything is ready, except myself. I now, continues our incumbent (a happy word, by-the-bye, for a country vicar)—I now cannot help thinking a good deal—who can?—upon the unnecessary and villainous custom of shaving; it is a thing so unmanly (here I nestle closer)—so effeminate (here I recoil from an unlucky step into the colder part of the bed).—No wonder that the Queen of France[2] took part with the rebels against that degenerate King, her husband, who first affronted her smooth visage with a face like her own. The Emperor Julian never showed the luxuriancy of his genius to better advantage

---

1 act of lying down.

2 Eleanor of Aquitaine, wife of Louis VII, c.1122–1204. The king shaved off his beard in compliance with an ecclesiastical order.

than in reviving the flowing beard. Look at Cardinal Bembo's picture—at Michael Angelo's—at Titian's—at Shakespeare's—at Fletcher's—at Spenser's—at Chaucer's—at Alfred's—at Plato's—I could name a great man for every tick of my watch.—Look at the Turks, a grave and otiose people.—Think of Haroun Al Raschid and Bedridden Hassan.—Think of Wortley Montague, the worthy son of his mother,[3] a man above the prejudice of his time.—Look at the Persian gentlemen, whom one is ashamed of meeting about the suburbs, their dress and appearance are so much finer than our own.—Lastly, think of the razor itself—how totally opposed to every sensation of bed—how cold, how edgy, how hard! how utterly different from anything like the warm and circling amplitude, which

> Sweetly recommends itself
> Unto our gentle senses.[4]

Add to this, benumbed fingers, which may help you to cut yourself, a quivering body, a frozen towel, and a ewer full of ice; and he that says there is nothing to oppose in all this, only shows, at any rate, that he has no merit in opposing it.

Thomson, the poet, who exclaims in his *Seasons*—

> Falsely luxurious! Will not man awake?

used to lie in bed till noon, because he said he had no motive in getting up. He could imagine the good of rising; but then he could also imagine the good of lying still; and his exclamation, it must be allowed, was made upon summer-time, not winter. We must proportion the argument to the individual character. A money-getter may be drawn out of his bed by three or four pence; but this will not suffice for a student. A proud man may say, 'What shall I think of myself, if I don't get up?' but the more humble one will be content to waive this prodigious notion of himself out of respect to his kindly bed. The mechanical man shall get up without any ado at all; and so shall the barometer. An ingenious lier-in-bed will find hard matter of discussion even on the score of health and longevity. He will ask us for our proofs and precedents of the ill effects of lying later in cold weather; and sophisticate much on the advantages of an even temperature of body; of the natural propensity (pretty universal) to have one's way; and of the animals that roll themselves up and sleep all the winter. As to longevity, he will ask whether the longest life is of necessity the best; and whether Holborn[5] is the handsomest street in London.

1820

A 'NOW'

DESCRIPTIVE OF A HOT DAY

The paper that was most liked by Keats, if I remember, was the one on a hot summer's day, entitled *A Now*. He was with me when I was writing and reading it to him, and contributed one or two of the passages.—(Hunt, in *Autobiography*, chapter 16.)

Now the rosy- (and lazy-) fingered Aurora, issuing from her saffron house, calls up the moist vapours to surround her, and goes veiled with them as long as she can; till Phœbus, coming forth in his power, looks everything out of the sky, and holds sharp, uninterrupted empire from his throne of beams. Now the mower begins to make his sweeping cuts more slowly, and resorts oftener to the beer. Now the carter sleeps a-top of his load of hay, or plods with double slouch of shoulder, looking out with eyes winking under his shading hat, and with a hitch upwards of one side of his mouth. Now the little girl at her grandmother's cottage-door watches the coaches that go by, with her hand held up over her sunny forehead. Now labourers look well resting in their white shirts at the doors of rural alehouses. Now an elm is fine there, with a seat under it; and horses drink out of the trough, stretching their yearning necks with loosened collars; and the traveller calls for his glass of ale, having been without one for more than ten minutes; and his horse stands wincing at the flies, giving sharp shivers of his skin, and moving to and fro his ineffectual docked tail; and now Miss Betty Wilson, the host's daughter, comes streaming forth in a flowered gown and earrings, carrying with four of her beautiful fingers the foaming glass, for which, after the traveller has drank it, she receives with an indifferent eye, looking another way, the lawful twopence. . . . Now grasshoppers 'fry,' as Dryden says.[1] Now cattle stand in water, and ducks are envied. Now boots, and shoes, and trees by the road-side, are thick with dust; and dogs, rolling in it, after issuing out of the water, into which they have been thrown to fetch sticks,

---

3 Lady Mary Wortley Montagu, 1689-1762, brilliant member of Pope's literary circle famed for her letter writing.
4 *Macbeth*, I, vi, 2.

5 then one of the longest streets in London, which ran through a district notorious for its dirt and poverty.

1 See his translation of Virgil's *Eclogues*, ii, 13.

come scattering horror among the legs of the spectators. Now a fellow who finds he has three miles further to go in a pair of tight shoes is in a pretty situation. Now rooms with the sun upon them become intolerable; and the apothecary's apprentice, with a bitterness beyond aloes, thinks of the pond he used to bathe in at school. Now men with powdered heads (especially if thick) envy those that are unpowdered, and stop to wipe them up hill, with countenances that seem to expostulate with destiny. Now boys assemble round the village pump with a ladle to it, and delight to make a forbidden splash and get wet through the shoes. Now also they make suckers of leather, and bathe all day long in rivers and ponds, and make mighty fishings for 'tittle-bats.'[2] Now the bee, as he hums along, seems to be talking heavily of the heat. Now doors and brick-walls are burning to the hand; and a walled lane, with dust and broken bottles in it, near a brick-field, is a thing not to be thought of. Now a green lane, on the contrary, thick-set with hedgerow elms, and having the noise of a brook 'rumbling in pebblestone,'[3] is one of the pleasantest things in the world.

Now, in town, gossips talk more than ever to one another, in rooms, in doorways, and out of window, always beginning the conversation with saying that the heat is overpowering. Now blinds are let down, and doors thrown open, and flannel waistcoats left off, and cold meat preferred to hot, and wonder expressed why tea continues so refreshing, and people delight to sliver lettuces into bowls, and apprentices water doorways with tin canisters that lay several atoms of dust. Now the water-cart, jumbling along the middle of the street, and jolting the showers out of its box of water, really does something. Now fruiterers' shops and dairies look pleasant, and ices are the only things to those who can get them. Now ladies loiter in baths; and people make presents of flowers; and wine is put into ice; and the after-dinner lounger recreates his head with applications of perfumed water out of long-necked bottles. Now the lounger, who cannot resist riding his new horse, feels his boots burn him. Now buckskins are not the lawn of Cos.[4] Now jockeys, walking in great-coats to lose flesh, curse inwardly. Now five fat people in a stagecoach hate the sixth fat one who is coming in, and think he has no right to be so large. Now clerks in office do nothing but drink soda-water and spruce-beer, and read the newspaper. Now the old-clothesman drops his solitary cry more deeply into the areas on the hot and forsaken side of the street; and bakers look vicious; and cooks are aggravated; and the steam of a tavern-kitchen catches hold of us like the breath of Tartarus.[5] Now delicate skins are beset with gnats; and boys make their sleeping companion start up, with playing a burning-glass on his hand; and blacksmiths are super-carbonated; and cobblers in their stalls almost feel a wish to be transplanted; and butter is too easy to spread; and the dragoons wonder whether the Romans liked their helmets; and old ladies, with their lappets unpinned, walk along in a state of dilapidation; and the servant maids are afraid they look vulgarly hot; and the author, who has a plate of strawberries brought him, finds that he has come to the end of his writing.

1820

From COACHES

THE carriage, as it is indifferently called (as if nothing less genteel could carry anyone), is a more decided thing than the chaise; it may be swifter even than the mail, leaves the stage at a still greater distance in every respect, and (forgetting what it may come to itself) darts by the poor old lumbering hackney with immeasurable contempt. It rolls with a prouder ease than any other vehicle. It is full of cushions and comfort; elegantly coloured inside and out; rich, yet neat; light and rapid, yet substantial. The horses seem proud to draw it. The fat and fair-wigged coachman 'lends his sounding lash,' his arm only in action, and that but little, his body well set with its own weight. The footman, in the pride of his nonchalance, holding by the straps behind, and glancing down sideways betwixt his cocked-hat and neckcloth, stands swinging from east to west upon his springy toes. The horses rush along amidst their glancing harness. Spotted dogs leap about them, barking with a princely superfluity of noise. The hammer-cloth[1] trembles through all its fringe. The paint flashes in the sun. We, contemptuous of everything less convenient, bow backwards and forwards with a certain indifferent air of gentility, infinitely

---

2 sticklebacks: a species of small fish.
3 Spenser, *Virgil's Gnat*, 163.
4 a kind of fine linen made in the Island of Cos in the Aegean.

5 the lowest part of Hades.

1 the cloth covering the driver's seat.

predominant. Suddenly, with a happy mixture of turbulence and truth, the carriage dashes up by the curbstone to the very point desired, and stops with a lordly wilfulness of decision. The coachman looks as if nothing had happened. The footman is down in an instant; the knocker reverberates into the farthest corner of the house; doors, both carriage and house, are open;—we descend, casting a matter-of-course eye at the by-standers; and the moment we touch the pavement, the vehicle, as if conscious of what it has carried, and relieved from the weight of our importance, recovers from its sidelong inclination with a jerk, tossing and panting, as it were, for very breath, like the proud heads of the horses. . . .

A post-chaise involves the idea of travelling, which in the company of those we love is home in motion. The smooth running along the road, the fresh air, the variety of scene, the leafy roads, the bursting prospects, the clatter through a town, the gaping gaze of a village, the hearty appetite, the leisure (your chaise waiting only upon your own movements), even the little contradictions to home-comfort and the expedients upon which they set us, all put the animal spirits at work, and throw a novelty over the road of life. . . .

The pleasure to be had in a mail-coach is not so much at one's command, as that in a post-chaise. There is generally too little room in it, and too much hurry out of it. The company must not lounge over their breakfast, even if they are all agreed. It is an understood thing that they are to be uncomfortably punctual. They must get in at seven o'clock, though they are all going upon business they do not like or care about, or will have to wait till nine before they can do anything. Some persons know how to manage this haste, and breakfast and dine in the cracking of a whip. They stick with their fork, they joint, they sliver, they bolt. Legs and wings vanish before them like a dragon's before a knight-errant. But if one is not a clergyman or a regular jolly fellow, one has no chance this way. To be diffident or polite is fatal. It is a merit easily acknowledged, and as quickly set aside. At last you begin upon a leg, and are called off.

A very troublesome degree of science is necessary for being well settled in the coach. We remember travelling in our youth, upon the north road with an orthodox elderly gentleman of venerable peruke, who talked much with a grave-looking young man about universities, and won our inexperienced heart with a notion that he was deep in Horace and Virgil. He was deeper in his wig. Towards evening, as he seemed restless, we asked with much diffidence whether a change, even for the worse, might not relieve him; for we were riding backwards, and thought that all elderly people disliked that way. He insinuated the very objection; so we recoiled from asking him again. In a minute or two, however, he insisted that we were uneasy ourselves, and that he must relieve us for our own sake. We protested as filially as possible against this; but at last, out of mere shame of disputing the point with so benevolent an elder, we changed seats with him. After an interval of bland meditation, we found the evening sun full in our face.—His new comfort set him dozing; and every now and then he jerked his wig in our eyes, till we had the pleasure of seeing him take out a nightcap and look very ghastly.—The same person, and his serious young companion, tricked us out of a good bed we happened to get at the inn.

The greatest peculiarity attending a mail-coach arises from its travelling at night. The gradual decline of talk, the incipient snore, the rustling and shifting of legs and nightcaps, the cessation of other noises on the road—the sound of the wind or rain, of the moist circuit of the wheels, and of the time-beating tread of the horses—all dispose the traveller, who cannot sleep, to a double sense of the little that is left him to observe. The coach stops, the door opens, a rush of cold air announces the demands and merits of the guard, who is taking his leave, and is anxious to remember us. The door is clapped to again; the sound of everything outside becomes dim; and voices are heard knocking up the people of the inn, and answered by issuing yawns and excuses. Wooden shoes clog heavily about. The horses' mouths are heard, swilling up the water out of tubs. All is still again, and someone in the coach takes a long breath. The driver mounts, and we resume our way. It happens that we can sleep anywhere except in a mail-coach; so that we hate to see a prudent, warm, old fellow, who has been eating our fowls and intercepting our toast, put on his nightcap in order to settle himself till morning. We rejoice in the digs that his neighbour's elbow gives him, and hail the long-legged traveller that sits opposite. A passenger of our wakeful description must try to content himself with listening to the sounds above mentioned; or thinking of his friends; or turning verses, as Sir Richard Blackmore[2] did, 'to the rumbling of his coach's wheels.'

The stagecoach is a great and unpretending accommodation. It is a chief substitute, notwithstanding all its eighteen-penny and two-and-sixpenny temptations, for keeping a carriage or a horse; and we really think, in spite of its gossiping, is no mean help to village liberality; for its passengers are so mixed, so often varied, so little yet so much together, so compelled to accommodate, so willing to pass a short time pleasantly, and so liable to the criticism of strangers, that it is hard if they do not get a habit of speaking, or even thinking more kindly of one another than if they mingled less often, or under other circumstances. The old and infirm are treated with reverence; the ailing sympathised with; the healthy congratulated; the rich not distinguished; the poor well met; the young, with their faces conscious of ride, patronised, and allowed to be extra. Even the fiery, nay the fat, learn to bear with each other; and if some high thoughted persons will talk now and then of their great acquaintances, or their preference of a carriage, there is an instinct which tells the rest, that they would not make such appeals to their good opinion, if they valued it so little as might be supposed. Stoppings and dust are not pleasant, but the latter may be had on grander occasions; and if anyone is so unlucky as never to keep another stopping himself, he must be content with the superiority of his virtue.

The mail or stage-coachman, upon the whole, is no inhuman mass of great-coat, gruffiness, civility, and old boots. The latter is the politer, from the smaller range of acquaintance, and his necessity for preserving them. His face is red, and his voice rough, by the same process of drink and catarrh. He has a silver watch with a steel chain, and plenty of loose silver in his pocket, mixed with halfpence. He serves the houses he goes by for a clock. He takes a glass at every alehouse; for thirst, when it is dry, and for warmth when it is wet. He likes to show the judicious reach of his whip, by twigging a dog or a goose on the road, or children that get in the way. His tenderness to descending old ladies is particular. He touches his hat to Mr. Smith. He gives 'the young woman' a ride, and lends her his box-coat in the rain. His liberality in imparting his knowledge to anyone that has the good fortune to ride on the box with him, is a happy mixture of defer-

ence, conscious possession, and familiarity. His information chiefly lies in the occupancy of houses on the road, prize-fighters, Bow Street runners, and accidents. He concludes that you know Dick Sams, or Old Joey, and proceeds to relate some of the stories that relish his pot and tobacco in the evening. If any of the four-in-hand gentry go by, he shakes his head, and thinks they might find something better to do. His contempt for them is founded on modesty. He tells you that his off-hand horse is as pretty a goer as ever was, but that Kitty—'Yeah, now there, Kitty, can't you be still? Kitty's a devil, Sir, for all you wouldn't think it.' He knows that the boys on the road admire him, and gives the horses an indifferent lash with his whip as they go by. If you wish to know what rain and dust can do, you should look at his old hat. There is an indescribably placid and paternal look in the position of his corduroy knees and old top-boots on the footboard, with their pointed toes and never-cleaned soles. His *beau-idéal* of appearance is a frockcoat, with mother-o'-pearl buttons, a striped yellow waistcoat, and a flower in his mouth.

A hackney-coach always appeared to us the most quiescent of moveables. Its horses and it, slumbering on a stand, are an emblem of all the patience in creation, animate and inanimate. The submission with which the coach takes every variety of the weather, dust, rain, and wind, never moving but when some eddying blast makes its old body shiver, is only surpassed by the vital patience of the horses. Can anything better illustrate the poet's line about

—Years that bring the philosophic mind,[3]

than the still-hung head, the dim indifferent eye, the dragged and blunt-cornered mouth, and the gaunt imbecility of body dropping its weight on three tired legs in order to give repose to the lame one? When it has blinkers on, they seem to be shutting up its eyes for death, like the windows of a house. Fatigue and the habit of suffering have become as natural to the creature as the bit to its mouth. Once in half an hour it moves the position of its leg, or shakes its drooping ears. The whip makes it go, more from habit than from pain. Its coat has become almost callous to minor stings. The blind and staggering fly in autumn might come to die against its cheek.

Of a pair of hackney-coach horses, one so much resembles the other that it seems unneces-

2 physician to Queen Anne whose poetry was once praised by Dr. Johnson.

3 Wordsworth, *Ode on Intimations of Immortality,* 187.

sary for them to compare notes. They have that within them, which is beyond the comparative. They no longer bend their heads towards each other, as they go. They stand together as if unconscious of one another's company. But they are not. An old horse misses his companion, like an old man. The presence of an associate, who has gone through pain and suffering with us, need not say anything. It is talk, and memory, and everything. Something of this it may be to our old friends in harness. What are they thinking of, while they stand motionless in the rain? Do they remember? Do they dream? Do they still, unperplexed as their old blood is by too many foods, receive a pleasure from the elements; a dull refreshment from the air and sun? Have they yet a palate for the hay which they pull so feebly? or for the rarer grain, which induces them to perform their only voluntary gesture of any vivacity, and toss up the bags that are fastened on their mouths to get at its shallow feast? . . .

We wish the hackney-coachman were as interesting a machine as either his coach or horses; but it must be owned, that of all the driving species he is the least agreeable specimen. This is partly to be attributed to the life which has most probably put him into his situation; partly to his want of outside passengers to cultivate his gentility; and partly to the disputable nature of his fare, which always leads him to be lying and cheating. The waterman of the stand, who beats him in sordidness of appearance, is more respectable. He is less of a vagabond, and cannot cheat you. Nor is the hackney-coachman only disagreeable in himself, but, like Falstaff reversed, the cause of disagreeableness in others; for he sets people upon disputing with him in pettiness and ill-temper. He induces the mercenary to be violent, and the violent to seem mercenary. A man whom you took for a pleasant laughing fellow, shall all of a sudden put on an irritable look of calculation, and vow that he will be charged with a constable, rather than pay the sixpence. Even fair woman shall waive her all-conquering softness, and sound a shrill trumpet in reprobation of the extortionate charioteer, whom, if she were a man, she says, she would expose. . . .

The stage-coachman likes the boys on the road, because he knows they admire him. The hackney-coachman knows that they cannot admire him, and that they can get up behind his coach, which makes him very savage. The cry of 'Cut behind!' from the malicious urchins on the pavement, wounds at once his self-love and his interest. He would not mind overloading his master's horses for another sixpence, but to do it for nothing is what shocks his humanity. He hates the boy for imposing upon him, and the boys for reminding him that he has been imposed upon; and he would willingly twinge the cheeks of all nine. The cut of his whip over the coach is malignant. He has a constant eye to the road behind him. He has also an eye to what may be left in the coach. He will undertake to search the straw for you, and miss the half-crown on purpose. He speculates on what he may get above his fare, according to your manners or company; and knows how much to ask for driving faster or slower than usual. He does not like wet weather so much as people suppose; for he says it rots both his horses and harness, and he takes parties out of town when the weather is fine, which produces good payments in a lump. Lovers, late supper-eaters, and girls going home from boarding-school, are his best pay. He has a rascally air of remonstrance when you dispute half the overcharge, and according to the temper he is in, begs you to consider his bread, hopes you will not make such a fuss about a trifle; or tells you, you may take his number or sit in the coach all night. . . . He only is at the mercy of every call and every casualty; he only is dragged, without notice, like the damned in Milton, into the extremities of wet and cold, from his alehouse fire to the freezing rain; he only must go anywhere, at what hour and to whatever place you choose, his old rheumatic limbs shaking under his weight of rags, and the snow and sleet beating into his puckered face, through streets which the wind scours like a channel.

1820

From ON THE REALITIES OF IMAGINATION

WE may say of the love of nature what Shakespeare says of another love, that it

Adds a special seeing to the eye.[1]

And we may say also, upon the like principle, that it adds a precious hearing to the ear. This and imagination, which ever follows upon it, are the two purifiers of our sense, which rescue us from the deafening babble of common cares, and enable us to hear all the affectionate voices of

---

1 *Love's Labour's Lost,* IV, iii, 333.

earth and heaven. The starry orbs, lapsing about in their smooth and sparkling dance, sing to us. The brooks talk to us of solitude. The birds are the animal spirits of nature, carolling in the air, like a careless lass.

> The gentle gales,
> Fanning their odoriferous wings, dispense
> Native perfumes; and whisper whence they
>   stole
> Those balmy spoils.—*Paradise Lost,* iv, 156–9.

The poets are called creators, ποιηταί, makers), because with their magical words they bring forth to our eyesight the abundant images and beauties of creation. They put them there, if the reader pleases; and so are literally creators. But whether put there or discovered, whether *created* or *invented* (for invention means nothing but finding out), there they are. If they touch us, they exist to as much purpose as anything else which touches us. If a passage in *King Lear* brings the tears into our eyes, it is as real as the touch of a sorrowful hand. If the flow of a song of Anacreon's intoxicates us, it is as true to a pulse within us as the wine he drank. We hear not their sounds with ears, nor see their sights with eyes; but we hear and see both so truly, that we are moved with pleasure; and the advantage, nay even the test, of seeing and hearing, at any time, is not in the seeing and hearing, but in the ideas we realise, and the pleasure we derive. Intellectual objects, therefore, inasmuch as they come home to us, are as true a part of the stock of nature as visible ones; and they are infinitely more abundant. Between the tree of a country clown and the tree of a Milton or Spenser, what a difference in point of productiveness! Between the plodding of a sexton through a churchyard and the walk of a Gray, what a difference! What a difference between the Bermudas of a shipbuilder and the Bermoothes of Shakespeare! the isle

> Full of noises,
> Sounds, and sweet airs, that give delight, and
>   hurt not;[2]

the isle of elves and fairies, that chased the tide to and fro on the sea-shore; of coral-bones and the knells of sea-nymphs; of spirits dancing on the sands, and singing amidst the hushes of the wind; of Caliban, whose brute nature enchantment had made poetical; of Ariel, who lay in cowslip bells,

and rode upon the bat; of Miranda, who wept when she saw Ferdinand work so hard, and begged him to let her help; telling him,

> I am your wife, if you will marry me;
> If not, I'll die your maid. To be your fellow
> You may deny me; but I'll be your servant,
> Whether you will or no.[3]

Such are the discoveries which the poets make for us; worlds to which that of Columbus was but a handful of brute matter. America began to be richer for us the other day, when Humboldt[4] came back and told us of its luxuriant and gigantic vegetation; of the myriads of shooting lights, which revel at evening in the southern sky; and of that grand constellation, at which Dante seems to have made so remarkable a guess (*Purgatorio,* cant., I, 5, 22). The natural warmth of the Mexican and Peruvian genius, set free from despotism, will soon do all the rest for it; awaken the sleeping riches of its eyesight, and call forth the glad music of its affections.

Imagination enriches everything. A great library contains not only books, but

> The assembled souls of all that men held wise.
> — DAVENANT.

The moon is Homer's and Shakespeare's moon, as well as the one we look at. The sun comes out of his chamber in the east, with a sparkling eye, 'rejoicing like a bridegroom.' The commonest thing becomes like Aaron's rod, that budded.[5] Pope called up the spirits of the Cabala[6] to wait upon a lock of hair, and justly gave it the honours of a constellation;[7] for he has hung it, sparkling forever in the eyes of posterity. A common meadow is a sorry thing to a ditcher or a coxcomb; but by the help of its dews from imagination and the love of nature, the grass brightens for us, the air soothes us, we feel as we did in the daisied hours of childhood. Its verdures, its sheep, its hedge-row elms,—all these, and all else which sight, and sound, and associations can give it, are made to furnish a treasure of pleasant thoughts. Even brick and mortar are vivified, as of old, at the harp of Orpheus. A metropolis becomes no longer a mere collection of houses or

---

2 *The Tempest,* III, ii, 144ff.

3 Ibid. III, i, 83ff.
4 Friedrich Alexander von Humboldt, 1769–1859, celebrated German naturalist and traveler.
5 Numbers, xvii, 8.
6 mystical or secret art.
7 See *The Rape of the Lock.*

of trades. It puts on all the grandeur of its history, and its literature; its towers, and rivers; its art, and jewelry, and foreign wealth; its multitude of human beings all intent upon excitement, wise or yet to learn; the huge and sullen dignity of its canopy of smoke by day; the wide gleam upwards of its lighted lustre at night-time; and the noise of its many chariots, heard at the same hour, when the wind sets gently towards some quiet suburb.

1820

From WHAT IS POETRY?

POETRY, strictly and artistically so called, that is to say, considered not merely as poetic feeling, which is more or less shared by all the world, but as the operation of that feeling, such as we see it in the poet's book, is the utterance of a passion for truth, beauty, and power, embodying and illustrating its conceptions by imagination and fancy, and modulating its language on the principle of variety in uniformity. Its means are whatever the universe contains; and its ends, pleasure and exaltation. Poetry stands between nature and convention, keeping alive among us the enjoyment of the external and the spiritual world; it has constituted the most enduring fame of nations and, next to Love and Beauty which are its parents, is the greatest proof to man of the pleasure to be found in all things, and of the probable riches of infinitude.

Poetry is a passion, because it seeks the deepest impressions; and because it must undergo, in order to convey them.

It is a passion for truth, because without truth the impression would be false or defective.

It is a passion for beauty, because its office is to exalt and refine by means of pleasure, and because beauty is nothing but the loveliest form of pleasure.

It is a passion for power, because power is impression triumphant, whether over the poet as desired by himself, or over the reader as affected by the poet.

It embodies and illustrates its impressions by imagination, or images of the objects of which it treats, and other images brought in to throw light on those objects, in order that it may enjoy and impart the feeling of their truth in its utmost conviction and affluence.

It illustrates them by fancy, which is a lighter play of imagination or the feeling of analogy coming short of seriousness, in order that it may laugh with what it loves, and show how it can decorate it with fairy ornament.

It modulates what it utters because in running the whole round of beauty it must needs include beauty of sound, and because, in the height of its enjoyment, it must show the perfection of its triumph, and make difficulty itself become part of its facility and joy.

And lastly, Poetry shapes this modulation into uniformity for its outline and variety for its parts, because it thus realizes the last idea of beauty itself, which includes the charm of diversity within the flowing round of habit and ease.

Poetry is imaginative passion. The quickest and subtlest test of the possession of its essence is in expression; the variety of things to be expressed shows the amount of its resources; and the continuity of the song completes the evidence of its strength and greatness. He who has thought, feeling, expression, imagination, action, character, and continuity, all in the largest amount and highest degree, is the greatest poet.

Poetry includes whatsoever of painting can be made visible to the mind's eye, and whatsoever of music can be conveyed by sound and proportion without singing or instrumentation. But it far surpasses those divine arts in suggestiveness, range, and intellectual wealth;—the first, in expression of thought, combination of images, and the triumph over space and time; the second, in all that can be done by speech apart from the tones and modulations of pure sound. Painting and music, however, include all those portions of the gift of poetry that can be expressed and heightened by the visible and melodious. Painting, in a certain apparent manner, is things themselves; music, in a certain audible manner, is their very emotion and grace. Music and painting are proud to be related to poetry, and poetry loves and is proud of them.

Poetry begins where matter of fact or of science ceases to be merely such and to exhibit a further truth, that is to say, the connection it has with the world of emotion, and its power to produce imaginative pleasure. Inquiring of a gardener, for instance, what flower it is we see yonder, he answers, 'A lily.' This is matter of fact. The botanist pronounces it to be of the order of 'Hexandria monogynia.' This is matter of science. It is the 'lady' of the garden, says Spenser; and here we begin to have a poetical sense of its fairness and grace. It is

The plant and flower of *light*,

says Ben Jonson; and poetry then shows us the beauty of the flower in all its mystery and splendour.

If it be asked how we know perceptions like these to be true, the answer is, by the fact of their existence—by the consent and delight of poetic readers. And as feeling is the earliest teacher, and perception the only final proof of things the most demonstrable by science, so the remotest imaginations of the poets may often be found to have the closest connexion with matter of fact; perhaps might always be so, if the subtlety of our perceptions were a match for the causes of them. Consider this image of Ben Jonson's—of a lily being the flower of light. Light, undecomposed, is white; and as the lily is white, and light is white, and whiteness itself is nothing *but* light, the two things, so far, are not merely similar, but identical. A poet might add, by an anology drawn from the connection of light and colour, that there is a 'golden dawn' issuing out of the white lily in the rich yellow of the stamens. I have no desire to push this similarity farther than it may be worth. Enough has been stated to show that, in poetical as well as in other analogies, 'the same feet of Nature,' as Bacon says, may be seen 'treading in different paths'; and that the most scornful, that is to say, dullest disciple of fact, should be cautious how he betrays the shallowness of his philosophy by discerning no poetry in its depths.

But the poet is far from dealing only with these subtle and analogical truths. Truth of every kind belongs to him, provided it can bud into any kind of beauty, or is capable of being illustrated and impressed by the poetic faculty. Nay, the simplest truth is often so beautiful and impressive of itself that one of the greatest proofs of his genius consists in his leaving it to stand alone, illustrated by nothing but the light of its own tears or smiles, its own wonder, might, or playfulness. Hence the complete effect of many a simple passage in our old English ballads and romances, and of the passionate sincerity in general of the greatest early poets, such as Homer and Chaucer, who flourished before the existence of a 'literary world,' and were not perplexed by a heap of notions and opinions, or by doubts how emotion ought to be expressed. The greatest of their successors never write equally to the purpose, except when they can dismiss everything from their minds but the like simple truth. In the beautiful poem of *Sir Eger, Sir Graham, and Sir Gray-Steel* (see it in Ellis's *Specimens* or Laing's *Early Metrical Tales),* a knight thinks himself disgraced in the eyes of his mistress:—

> Sir Eger said, 'If it be so,
> Then wot I well I must forego
> Love-liking, and manhood, all clean!'
> *The water rushed out of his een!*

Sir Gray-Steel is killed:—

> Gray-Steel into his death thus thraws
> He *walters and the grass up draws;*
>
> .   .
>
> *A little while then lay he still
> (Friends that him saw, liked full ill)
> And bled into his armour bright.*

The abode of Chaucer's Reve, or Steward, in the *Canterbury Tales,* is painted in two lines which nobody ever wished longer:—

> His wonning was full fair upon an heath,
> With greeny trees yshadowed was his place.

Every one knows the words of Lear, 'most *matter-of-fact,* most melancholy':—

> Pray, do not mock me;
> I am a very foolish fond old man,
> Fourscore and upwards:
> Not an hour more, nor less; and, to deal plainly,
> I fear I am not in my perfect mind.

It is thus by exquisite pertinence, melody, and the implied power of writing with exuberance, if need be, that beauty and truth become identical in poetry, and that pleasure, or at the very worst, a balm in our tears, is drawn out of pain.

It is a great and rare thing, and shows a lovely imagination when the poet can write a commentary, as it were, of his own on such sufficing passages of nature, and be thanked for the addition. There is an instance of this kind in Warner, an old Elizabethan poet, than which I know nothing sweeter in the world. He is speaking of Fair Rosamond and of a blow given her by Queen Eleanor:—

> With that she dashed her on the lips,
> *So dyèd double red:*
> *Hard was the heart that gave the blow,*
> *Soft were those lips that bled.*

There are different kinds and degrees of imagination, some of them necessary to the formation of every true poet, and all of them possessed by the greatest. Perhaps they may be enumerated as follows: first, that which presents to the mind any object or circumstance in everyday life, as when we imagine a man holding a sword, or looking out of a window; second, that which presents real, but not everyday circumstances, as King Alfred tending the loaves, or Sir Philip Sidney giving up the water to the dying soldier; third, that which combines character and events directly imitated from real life, with imitative realities of its own invention, as the probable parts of the histories of Priam[1] and Macbeth, or what may be called natural fiction as distinguished from supernatural; fourth, that which conjures up things and events not to be found in nature, as Homer's gods and Shakespeare's witches, enchanted horses and spears, Ariosto's hippogriff,[2] &c.; fifth, that which, in order to illustrate or aggravate one image, introduces another: sometimes in simile, as when Homer compares Apollo descending in his wrath at noon-day to the coming of night-time; sometimes in metaphor, or simile comprised in a word, as in Milton's 'motes that *people* the sunbeams';[3] sometimes in concentrating into a word the main history of any person or thing, past or even future, as in the 'starry Galileo' of Byron,[4] and that ghastly foregone conclusion of the epithet 'murdered' applied to the yet living victim in Keats's story · from Boccaccio,—

So the two brothers and their *murdered* man
Rode towards fair Florence;—[5]

sometimes in the attribution of a certain representative quality which makes one circumstance stand for others, as in Milton's grey-fly winding its '*sultry horn,*'[6] which epithet contains the heat of a summer's day; sixth, that which reverses this process, and makes a variety of circumstances take colour from one, like nature seen with jaundiced or glad eyes, or under the influence of storm or sunshine; as when in *Lycidas,* or the Greek pastoral poets, the flowers and the flocks are made to sympathise with a man's death; or, in the Italian poet, the river flowing by the sleeping Angelica seems talking of love—

Parea che l'erba le fiorisse intorno,
E d'amor ragionasse quella riva![7]
    Orlando Innamorato, Canto iii.

or in the voluptuous homage paid to the sleeping Imogen by the very light in the chamber and the reaction of her own beauty upon itself;[8] or in the 'witch element' of the tragedy of *Macbeth* and the May-day night of *Faust;*[9] seventh, and last, that which by a single expression, apparently of the vaguest kind, not only meets but surpasses in its effect the extremest force of the most particular description; as in that exquisite passage of Coleridge's *Christabel* where the unsuspecting object of the witch's malignity is bidden to go to bed:—

Quoth Christabel, So let it be!
And as the lady bade, did she.
Her gentle limbs did she undress,
And lay down in her loveliness;—

a perfect verse surely, both for feeling and music. The very smoothness and gentleness of the limbs is in the series of the letter l's.

I am aware of nothing of the kind surpassing that most lovely inclusion of physical beauty in moral, neither can I call to mind any instances of the imagination that turns accompaniments into accessories, superior to those I have alluded to. Of the class of comparison, one of the most touching (many a tear must it have drawn from parents and lovers) is in a stanza which has been copied into the *Friar of Orders Grey*[10] out of Beaumont and Fletcher:—

Weep no more, lady, weep no more,
    Thy sorrow is in vain;
For violets plucked the sweetest showers
    Will ne'er make grow again.

And Shakespeare and Milton abound in the very grandest; such as Antony's likening his changing fortunes to the cloud-rack; Lear's appeal to the old age of the heavens; Satan's appearance in the horizon, like a fleet 'hanging in the clouds'; and the comparisons of him with the comet and the eclipse. Nor unworthy of this glorious company for its extraordinary combination of delicacy and vastness is that enchanting one of Shelley's in the *Adonais:*—

---

1 King of Troy.
2 fabulous winged animal, half horse and half griffin.
3 *Il Penseroso,* 8.
4 *Childe Harold,* canto iv, st. 54.
5 *Isabella,* st. 27.
6 *Lycidas,* 28.

7 'It seemed as though the grass round her was sprinkled with flowers, and that that bank was discoursing on love.'
8 *Cymbeline,* II, ii, 19ff.
9 usually referred to as the *Walpurgis-Night's Dream.*
10 by Bishop Percy.

Life, like a dome of many-coloured glass,
Stains the white radiance of eternity.[11]

I multiply these particulars in order to impress upon the reader's mind the great importance of imagination in all its phases as a constituent part of the highest poetic faculty.

The happiest instance I remember of imaginative metaphor is Shakespeare's moonlight 'sleeping' on a bank;[12] but half his poetry may be said to be made up of it, metaphor indeed being the common coin of discourse. Of imaginary creatures, none out of the pale of mythology and the East are equal, perhaps, in point of invention to Shakespeare's Ariel and Caliban, though poetry may grudge to prose the discovery of a Winged Woman, especially such as she has been described by her inventor in the story of *Peter Wilkins*,[13] and, in point of treatment, the Mammon and Jealousy of Spenser, some of the monsters in Dante, particularly his Nimrod, his interchangements of creatures into one another, and (if I am not presumptuous in anticipating what I think will be the verdict of posterity) the Witch in Coleridge's *Christabel* may rank even with the creations of Shakespeare. It may be doubted, indeed, whether Shakespeare had bile and nightmare enough in him to have thought of such detestable horrors as those of the interchanging adversaries (now serpent, now man), or even of the huge, half-blockish enormity of Nimrod,—in Scripture, the 'mighty hunter' and builder of the tower of Babel,—in Dante, a tower of a man in his own person, standing with some of his brother giants up to the middle in a pit in hell, blowing a horn to which a thunderclap is a whisper, and hallooing after Dante and his guide in the jargon of a lost tongue! . . .

Imagination belongs to Tragedy, or the serious muse; Fancy to the comic. *Macbeth, Lear, Paradise Lost,* the poem of Dante, are full of imagination: the *Midsummer Night's Dream* and the *Rape of the Lock,* of fancy: *Romeo and Juliet, The Tempest, The Faerie Queene* and the *Orlando Furioso,* of both. The terms were formerly identical, or used as such; and neither is the best that might be found. The term Imagination is too confined: often too material. It presents too invariably the idea of a solid body;—of 'images' in the sense of the plaster-cast cry about the streets. Fancy, on the other hand, while it

means nothing but a spiritual image or apparition ($\phi\acute{a}\nu\tau a\sigma\mu a$, appearance, *phantom*), has rarely that freedom from visibility which is one of the highest privileges of imagination. Viola, in *Twelfth Night,* speaking of some beautiful music, says:—

> It gives a very echo to the seat
> Where Love is throned.

In this charming thought, fancy and imagination are combined; yet the fancy, the assumption of Love's sitting on a throne, is the image of a solid body; while the imagination, the sense of sympathy between the passion of love and impassioned music, presents us no image at all. Some new term is wanting to express the more spiritual sympathies of what is called Imagination.

One of the teachers of Imagination is Melancholy; and like Melancholy, as Albert Dürer[14] has painted her, she looks out among the stars, and is busied with spiritual affinities and the mysteries of the universe. Fancy turns her sister's wizard instruments into toys. She takes a telescope in her hand, and puts a mimic star on her forehead, and sallies forth as an emblem of astronomy. Her tendency is to the child-like and sportive. She chases butterflies, while her sister takes flight with angels. She is the genius of fairies, of gallantries, of fashions; of whatever is quaint and light, showy and capricious; of the poetical part of wit. She adds wings and feelings to the images of wit; and delights as much to people nature with smiling ideal sympathies, as wit does to bring antipathies together, and make them strike light on absurdity. Fancy, however, is not incapable of sympathy with Imagination. She is often found in her company; always, in the case of the greatest poets; often in that of less, though with them she is the greater favourite. Spenser has great imagination and fancy too, but more of the latter; Milton both also, the very greatest, but with imagination predominant; Chaucer the strongest imagination of real life, beyond any writers but Homer, Dante, and Shakespeare, and in comic painting inferior to none; Pope has hardly any imagination, but he has a great deal of fancy; Coleridge little fancy, but imagination exquisite. Shakespeare alone, of all poets that ever lived, enjoyed the regard of both in equal perfection.

1844

---

11 st. 52.   12 *Merchant of Venice,* v, i, 54.
13 a fantastic romance by Robert Paltock, published in 1751.

14 celebrated German painter and engraver, 1471-1528.

From AUTOBIOGRAPHY

CHAPTER XIV

IMPRISONMENT[1]

THE tipstaves prepared me for a singular character in my gaoler. His name was Ives. I was told he was a very self-willed personage, not the more accommodating for being in a bad state of health; and that he called everybody *Mister*. 'In short,' said one of the tipstaves, 'he is one as may be led, but he'll never be *druv.'*

The sight of the prison gate and the high wall was a dreary business. I thought of my horseback and the downs of Brighton; but congratulated myself, at all events, that I had come thither with a good conscience. After waiting in the prison yard as long as if it had been the ante-room of a minister, I was ushered into the presence of the great man. He was in his parlour, which was decently furnished, and he had a basin of broth before him, which he quitted on my appearance, and rose with much solemnity to meet me. He seemed about fifty years of age. He had a white nightcap on, as if he was going to be hanged, and a great red face, which looked as if he had been hanged already, or were ready to burst with blood. Indeed, he was not allowed by his physician to speak in a tone above a whisper.

The first thing which this dignified person said was, 'Mister, I'd ha' given a matter of a hundred pounds, that you had not come to this place—a hundred pounds!' The emphasis which he laid on the word 'hundred' was ominous.

I forget what I answered. I endeavoured to make the best of the matter; but he recurred over and over again to the hundred pounds; and said he wondered, for his part, what the Government meant by sending me there, for the prison was not a prison fit for a gentleman. He often repeated this opinion afterwards, adding, with a peculiar nod of his head, 'And, Mister, they knows it.'

I said, that if a gentleman deserved to be sent to prison, he ought not to be treated with a greater nicety than any one else: upon which he corrected me, observing very properly (though, as the phrase is, it was one word for the gentleman and two for the letter of prison-lodgings), that a person who had been used to a better mode of living than 'low people' was not treated with

the same justice, if forced to lodge exactly as they did.

I told him his observation was very true; which gave him a favourable opinion of my understanding; for I had many occasions of remarking, that he looked upon nobody as his superior, speaking even of members of the royal family as persons whom he knew very well, and whom he estimated at no higher rate than became him. One royal duke had lunched in his parlour, and another he had laid under some polite obligation. 'They knows me,' said he, 'very well, Mister; and, Mister, I knows them.' This concluding sentence he uttered with great particularity and precision.

He was not proof, however, against a Greek Pindar, which he happened to light upon one day among my books. Its unintelligible character gave him a notion that he had got somebody to deal with, who might really know something which he did not. Perhaps the gilt leaves and red morocco binding had their share in the magic. The upshot was, that he always showed himself anxious to appear well with me, as a clever fellow, treating me with great civility on all occasions but one, when I made him very angry by disappointing him in a money amount. The Pindar was a mystery that staggered him. I remember very well, that giving me a long account one day of something connected with his business, he happened to catch with his eye the shelf that contained it, and, whether he saw it or not, abruptly finished by observing, 'But, Mister, you knows all these things as well as I do.'

Upon the whole, my new acquaintance was as strange a person as I ever met with. A total want of education, together with a certain vulgar acuteness, conspired to render him insolent and pedantic. Disease sharpened his tendency to fits of passion, which threatened to suffocate him; and then in his intervals of better health he would issue forth, with his cock-up-nose and his hat on one side, as great a fop as a jockey. I remember his coming to my rooms, about the middle of my imprisonment, as if on purpose to insult over my ill health with the contrast of his convalescence, putting his arms in a gay manner akimbo, and telling me I should never live to go out, whereas he was riding about as stout as ever, and had just been in the country. He died before I left prison.

The word *jail,* in deference to the way in which it is sometimes spelt, this accomplished individual pronounced *gole;* and Mr. Brougham[2] he al-

---

1 The circumstances of Hunt's imprisonment are given in the biographical sketch, text, p. 757.

2 Henry Peter, Baron Brougham, 1778–1868, celebrated British statesman.

ways spoke of as Mr. *Bruffam.* He one day apologized for this mode of pronunciation, or rather gave a specimen of vanity and self-will, which will show the reader the high notions a jailer may entertain of himself. 'I find,' said he, 'that they calls him *Broom;* but, Mister' (assuming a look from which there was to be no appeal), '*I* calls him *Bruffam!*'

Finding that my host did not think the prison fit for me, I asked if he could let me have an apartment in his house. He pronounced it impossible; which was a trick to enhance the price. I could not make an offer to please him; and he stood out so long, and, as he thought, so cunningly, that he subsequently overreached himself by his trickery, as the reader will see. His object was to keep me among the prisoners, till he could at once sicken me of the place, and get the permission of the magistrates to receive me into his house; which was a thing he reckoned upon as a certainty. He thus hoped to secure himself in all quarters; for his vanity was almost as strong as his avarice. He was equally fond of getting money in private, and of the approbation of the great men whom he had to deal with in public; and it so happened, that there had been no prisoner, above the poorest condition, before my arrival, with the exception of Colonel Despard.[3] From abusing the prison, he then suddenly fell to speaking well of it, or rather of the room occupied by the colonel; and said, that another corresponding with it would make me a capital apartment. 'To be sure,' said he, 'there is nothing but bare walls, and I have no bed to put in it.' I replied, that of course I should not be hindered from having my own bed from home. He said, 'No; and if it rains,' observed he, 'you have only to put up with want of light for a time.' 'What!' exclaimed I, 'are there no windows?' 'Windows, Mister!' cried he; 'no windows in a prison of this sort; no glass, Mister: but excellent shutters.'

It was finally agreed, that I should sleep for a night or two in a garret of the gaoler's house, till my bed could be got ready in the prison and the windows glazed. A dreary evening followed, which, however, let me completely into the man's character, and showed him in a variety of lights, some ludicrous, and others as melancholy. There was a full-length portrait in the room, of a little girl, dizened out in her best. This, he told me, was

his daughter, whom he had disinherited for her disobedience. I tried to suggest a few reflections, capable of doing her service; but disobedience, I found, was an offence doubly irritating to his nature, on account of his sovereign habits as a gaoler; and seeing his irritability likely to inflame the plethora of his countenance, I desisted. Though not allowed to speak above a whisper, he was extremely willing to talk; but at an early hour I pleaded my own state of health, and retired to bed. . . .

I now applied to the magistrates for permission to have my wife and children constantly with me, which was granted. Not so my request to move into the gaoler's house. Mr. Holme Sumner, on occasion of a petition from a subsequent prisoner, told the House of Commons that my room had a view over the Surrey hills, and that I was very well content with it. I could not feel obliged to him for this postliminous[4] piece of enjoyment, especially when I remembered that he had done all in his power to prevent my removal out of the room, precisely (as it appeared to us) because it looked upon nothing but the felons, and because I was *not* contented. In fact, you could not see out of the windows at all, without getting on a chair; and then, all that you saw was the miserable men whose chains had been clanking from daylight. The perpetual sound of these chains wore upon my spirits in a manner to which my state of health allowed me reasonably to object. The yard, also, in which I took exercise, was very small. The gaoler proposed that I should be allowed to occupy apartments in his house, and walk occasionally in the prison garden; adding, that I should certainly die if I did not; and his opinion was seconded by that of the medical man. Mine host was sincere in this, if in nothing else. Telling us, one day, how warmly he had put it to the magistrates, and how he insisted that I should not survive, he turned round upon me, and, to the doctor's astonishment, added, 'Nor, Mister, will you.' I believe it was the opinion of many; but Mr. Holme Sumner argued otherwise; perhaps from his own sensations, which were sufficiently iron. Perhaps he concluded, also, like a proper old Tory, that if I did not think fit to flatter the magistrates a little, and play the courtier, my wants could not be very great. At all events, he came up one day with the rest of them, and after bowing to my wife, and piteously pinching the

---

3 Edward Marcus Despard, 1751–1803, Irish conspirator who was hanged for plotting against the government.

4 gratuitous: *postliminous* is from the legal term *jus postlimini,* referring to the right of persons taken in war to have restored to them those rights which they possessed before capture.

cheek of an infant in her arms, went down and did all he could to prevent our being comfortably situated.

The doctor then proposed that I should be removed into the prison infirmary; and this proposal was granted. Infirmary had, I confess, an awkward sound, even to my ears. I fancied a room shared with other sick persons, not the best fitted for companions; but the good-natured doctor (his name was Dixon) undeceived me. The infirmary was divided into four wards, with as many small rooms attached to them. The two upper wards were occupied, but the two on the floor had never been used: and one of these, not very providently (for I had not yet learned to think of money), I turned into a noble room. I papered the walls with a trellis of roses; I had the ceiling coloured with clouds and sky; the barred windows I screened with Venetian blinds; and when my bookcases were set up with their busts, and flowers and a pianoforte made their appearance, perhaps there was not a handsomer room on that side the water. I took a pleasure, when a stranger knocked at the door, to see him come in and stare about him. The surprise on issuing from the Borough, and passing through the avenues of a gaol, was dramatic. Charles Lamb declared there was no other such room, except in a fairy tale.

But I possessed another surprise; which was a garden. There was a little yard outside the room, railed off from another belonging to the neighbouring ward. This yard I shut in with green palings, adorned it with a trellis, bordered it with a thick bed of earth from a nursery, and even contrived to have a grassplot. The earth I filled with flowers and young trees. There was an apple tree, from which we managed to get a pudding the second year. As to my flowers, they were allowed to be perfect. Thomas Moore, who came to see me with Lord Byron, told me he had seen no such heart's-ease. I bought the *Parnaso Italiano*[5] while in prison, and used often to think of a passage in it, while looking at this miniature piece of horticulture:—

Mio picciol orto,
A me sei vigna, e campo, e selva, e prato.
                                                            —Baldi.
My little garden,
To me thou'rt vineyard, field, and meadow, and
     wood.

_____
5 an anthology of Italian poetry in fifty-six volumes.

Here I wrote and read in fine weather, sometimes under an awning. In autumn, my trellises were hung with scarlet-runners, which added to the flowery investment. I used to shut my eyes in my arm-chair, and affect to think myself hundreds of miles off.

But my triumph was in issuing forth of a morning. A wicket out of the garden led into the large one belonging to the prison. The latter was only for vegetables; but it contained a cherry-tree, which I saw twice in blossom. I parcelled out the ground in my imagination into favourite districts. I made a point of dressing myself as if for a long walk; and then, putting on my gloves, and taking my book under my arm, stepped forth, requesting my wife not to wait dinner if I was too late. My eldest little boy, to whom Lamb addressed some charming verses on the occasion, was my constant companion, and we used to play all sorts of juvenile games together. It was, probably, in dreaming of one of these games (but the words had a more touching effect on my ear) that he exclaimed one night in his sleep, 'No: I'm not lost; I'm found.' Neither he nor I were very strong at that time; but I have lived to see him a man of eight and forty; and wherever he is found, a generous hand and a great understanding will be found together.

I entered prison the 3rd of February, 1813, and removed to my new apartments the 16th of March, happy to get out of the noise of the chains. When I sat amidst my books, and saw the imaginary sky overhead, and my paper roses about me, I drank in the quiet at my ears, as if they were thirsty. The little room was my bedroom. I afterwards made the two rooms change characters, when my wife lay in. Permission for her continuance with me at that period was easily obtained of the magistrates, among whom a newcomer made his appearance. This was another good-natured man, Lord Leslie, afterwards Earl of Rothes. He heard me with kindness; and his actions did not belie his countenance. My eldest girl (now, alas! no more) was born in prison. She was beautiful, and for the greatest part of an existence of thirty years, she was happy. She was christened Mary after my mother, and Florimel after one of Spenser's heroines. But Mary we called her. Never shall I forget my sensations when she came into the world; for I was obliged to play the physician myself, the hour having taken us by surprise. But her mother found many unexpected comforts: and during the whole time of her confinement, which happened to be in very fine weather, the garden door was set open, and she looked upon trees and flowers. A thousand recollections rise within me at every fresh period of my imprisonment, such as I cannot trust myself with dwelling upon.

These rooms, and the visits of my friends, were the bright side of my captivity. I read verses without end, and wrote almost as many. I had also the pleasure of hearing that my brother had found comfortable rooms in Coldbath-fields,[6] and a host who really deserved that name as much as a gaoler could. The first year of my imprisonment was a long pull up-hill; but never was metaphor so literally verified, as by the sensation at the turning of the second. In the first year, all the prospect was that of the one coming: in the second, the days began to be scored off, like those of children at school preparing for a holiday. When I was fairly settled in my new apartments, the gaoler could hardly give sufficient vent to his spleen at my having escaped his clutches, his astonishment was so great. Besides, though I treated him handsomely, he had a little lurking fear of the *Examiner* upon him; so he contented himself with getting as much out of me as he could, and boasting of the grand room which he would fain have prevented my enjoying.

My friends were allowed to be with me till ten o'clock at night, when the underturnkey, a young man with his lantern, and much ambitious gentility of deportment, came to see them out. I believe we scattered an urbanity about the prison, till then unknown. Even William Hazlitt, who there first did me the honour of a visit, would stand interchanging amenities at the threshold, which I had great difficulty in making him pass. I know not which kept his hat off with the greater pertinacity of deference, I to the diffident cutter-up of Tory dukes and kings, or he to the amazing prisoner and invalid who issued out of a bower of roses. There came my old friends and schoolfellows, Pitman, whose wit and animal spirits have still kept him alive; Mitchell, now no more, who translated Aristophanes; and Barnes, gone too, who always reminded me of Fielding. It was he that introduced me to the late Mr. Thomas Alsager, the kindest of neighbours, a man of business, who contrived to be a scholar and a musician. Alsager loved his leisure, and yet would start up at a moment's notice to do the least of a prisoner's biddings.

My now old friend, Cowden Clarke, with his ever young and wise heart, was good enough to be his own introducer, paving his way like a proper investor of prisons, with baskets of fruit.

The Lambs came to comfort me in all weathers, hail or sunshine, in daylight and in darkness, even in the dreadful frost and snow of the beginning of 1814. . . .

I must not omit a visit from the venerable Bentham,[7] who was justly said to unite the wisdom of a sage with the simplicity of a child. I had had the honour of one from him before my imprisonment, when he came, he said, to make my acquaintance, because the *Examiner* had spoken well of a new weekly paper. On the present occasion he found me playing at battledore, in which he took a part; and, with his usual eye towards improvement, suggested an amendment in the constitution of shuttlecocks. I remember the surprise of the governor at his local knowledge and his vivacity. 'Why, Mister,' said he, 'his eye is everywhere at once.'

All these comforts were embittered by unceasing ill-health, and by certain melancholy reveries, which the nature of the place did not help to diminish. During the first six weeks the sound of the felons' chains, mixed with what I took for horrid execrations or despairing laughter, was never out of my ears. When I went into the infirmary, which stood between the gaol and the prison walls, gallowses were occasionally put in order by the side of my windows, and afterwards set up over the prison gates, where they remained visible. The keeper one day with an air of mystery took me into the upper ward for the purpose, he said, of gratifying me with a view of the country from the roof. Something prevented his showing me this; but the spectacle he did show me I shall never forget. It was a stout country girl, sitting in an absorbed manner, her eyes fixed on the fire. She was handsome, and had a little hectic spot in either cheek, the effect of some gnawing emotion. He told me in a whisper that she was there for the murder of her bastard child. I could have knocked the fellow down for his unfeelingness in making a show of her; but, after all, she did not see us. She heeded us not. There was no object before her but what produced the spot in her cheek. The gallows, on which she was executed, must have been brought out within her hearing; but, perhaps, she heard that as little. . . .

---

6 a goverment prison in Middlesex.

7 Jeremy Bentham, 1748-1832, the utilitarian philosopher and reformer.

On the 3rd of February, 1815, I was free. . . . It was now thought that I should dart out of my cage like a bird, and feel no end in the delight of ranging. But, partly from ill-health, and partly from habit, the day of my liberation brought a good deal of pain with it. An illness of a long standing, which required very different treatment, had by this time been burnt in upon me by the iron that enters into the soul of the captive, wrap it in flowers as he may; and I am ashamed to say, that after stopping a little at the house of my friend Alsager, I had not the courage to continue looking at the shoals of people passing to and fro, as the coach drove up the Strand. The whole business of life seemed a hideous impertinence. The first pleasant sensation I experienced was when the coach turned into the New Road, and I beheld the old hills of my affection standing where they used to do, and breathing me a welcome.

It was very slowly that I recovered anything like a sensation of health. The bitterest evil I suffered was in consequence of having been confined so long in one spot. The habit stuck to me on my return home in a very extraordinary manner; and, I fear, some of my friends thought me ungrateful. They did me an injustice; but it was not their fault; nor could I wish them the bitter experience which alone makes us acquainted with the existence of strange things. This weakness I outlived; but I have never thoroughly recovered the shock given my constitution. My natural spirits, however, have always struggled hard to see me reasonably treated. Many things give me exquisite pleasure which seem to affect other men in a very minor degree; and I enjoyed, after all, such happy moments with my friends, even in prison, that in the midst of the beautiful climate which I afterwards visited, I was sometimes in doubt whether I would not rather have been in gaol than in Italy.

1850

1788 · GEORGE NOEL GORDON, · 1824
LORD BYRON

1788   Born, 22 January, George Gordon Byron, in London, only son of Captain John 'Mad Jack' Byron ('a dazzlingly handsome but dissolute King's guardsman') and his second wife, Catherine Gordon Byron (a proud and capricious Scottish heiress of Gight). Of noble descent on both sides of his family, his ancestry could be traced through his father to followers of William the Conqueror and through his mother to James I of Scotland. His grandfather was Admiral 'Foulweather Jack' Byron and his granduncle, William 'the Wicked Lord,' Fifth Baron Byron, who in a duel had killed his neighbor, Mr. Chaworth, with whose grandniece, Mary, the poet was later to fall in love.

1794–8   At Aberdeen attended the grammar school. Reveled in the literature of Oriental romance and travel and was captivated by the Old Testament. Was treated inexpertly for his 'twisted' foot, with which he had been born. Following an attack of scarlet fever, sojourned in the Highlands to benefit his health in the summers of 1796, 1797. On the death of his granduncle (May 1798), became heir to the family title and estates. With his mother and his nurse, May Gray, visited Newstead.

1799–1801   At Dr. Glennie's academy in Dulwich.

1801–5   Attended Harrow School and spent vacations at Newstead, Annesley, and Southwell. Formed friendships at Harrow with the headmaster, Dr. Joseph Drury, and his son Henry, Lord Clare, Lord Delawarr, Long, and Wildman. 'My school-friendships were passions with me.' In spite of his lameness, became a good swimmer and boxer, and enough of a cricketer to play against Eton, with another boy running for him. A ringleader in mischief; incorrigibly lazy and not a good scholar, but a wide reader whose abilities were recognized by the masters. In the summer of 1803, fell headlong in love with Mary Chaworth, who lived with her mother at Annesley Hall three miles from Newstead. Two years older than Byron and already engaged to Mr. John Musters, a neighboring squire, she dallied with her boy lover. Her farewell and marriage in 1805 affected him deeply. She remained to Byron 'the bright morning Star Annesley' and was the subject of at least five of Byron's early poems. At Southwell stayed with his mother, whose temper at times verged on madness. Made friends there with John Pigot and his sister Elizabeth— 'No society but old parsons and old maids.' Corresponded with his half sister Augusta, who came down to Harrow on Speech Day and heard him declaim from *King Lear*.

1805–6   In October entered Trinity College, Cambridge. Squandered his large allowance and went heavily into debt. Took boxing and fencing instruction and increased his reputation as a swimmer. Following the Easter term (1806) was absent from Cambridge for a year. Spent his time at Southwell and London in flirtations and poetizing. *Fugitive Pieces*, 1806, his first volume, was suppressed on the advice of his friend, the Reverend John Becher.

1807   In January *Poems on Various Occasions* appeared, which was an expurgated and revised selection of his juvenile poems. In June this became *Hours of Idleness* with Byron's name for the first time on the title page. In London struck up a friendship with his

781

cousin, R. C. Dallas. Returned to Cambridge and to his list of college friends added C. S. Matthews, J. C. Hobhouse, Scrope Davies, and Francis Hodgson.

1808–9   In January his *Hours of Idleness* was sarcastically reviewed in *The Edinburgh Review*. Took his M.A. degree in July. After leaving Cambridge spent much of his time at Newstead.

1809   On attaining his majority was in debt by about £12,000. Took his seat in the House of Lords. In March published anonymously *English Bards and Scotch Reviewers*. Entertained his cronies at Newstead—masquerading, pistol shooting, drinking bouts. Alone and in more abstemious moods gave himself over to study and writing. 'My library is rather extensive and . . . I am a mighty scribbler.' In July set sail from Falmouth with a suite of three servants, and Hobhouse as his companion, for a tour of the Mediterranean. Visited Lisbon, Cadiz, Gibraltar, and Malta. Made a trip through the interior of Albania and there met Ali Pasha. In Athens by December, where he finished the first canto of *Childe Harold*. Lived in Athens with Madam Macri and her three daughters.

1810   Remained at Athens until March. Finished the second canto of *Childe Harold*. Visited Constantinople and swam the Hellespont—'in imitation of Leander, though without his lady.' Except for an excursion into the Morea, where he was seriously ill with malarial fever at Patras, he stayed in Athens until May 1811, living in a Franciscan convent.

1811   Returned in May to England, via Malta, reaching London in July. In August Mrs. Byron died quite suddenly before Byron could reach Newstead to see her alive. Within a short time he lost by death two of his most cherished friends, Charles Matthews and John Wingfield. For some months his life seemed a dreary void. By late October, he was back in London arranging with John Murray for the publication of *Childe Harold, I and II*. At a famous dinner at Samuel Rogers established a friendship with Tom Moore, which was to last for life.

1812   In February delivered his maiden speech in the House of Lords in behalf of the laborers of Nottingham against the Frame-work Bill, which would make the offense of framebreaking a capital crime. In early March published *Childe Harold, I and II*. Became the courted favorite of London society. Among his new acquaintances at this time were Sheridan, Southey, Leigh Hunt, Madame de Staël, 'Monk' Lewis, and Jane Porter; also Lady Melbourne, her daughter-in-law Caroline Lamb and her niece Anne Isabella Milbanke. Entered into liaisons with Caroline Lamb and Jane Elizabeth Lady Oxford. Tried to sell Newstead at auction but failed—a later abortive transaction with a defaulting purchaser brought Byron £25,000. Newstead was ultimately sold in 1817 for £94,500.

1813   Continued with his London intrigues and dissipation. Augusta, his half sister, visited him, June-September. Engaged in a transient flirtation with Lady Frances Webster at Astor Hall, September-October. Published *The Giaour* and *The Bride of Abydos*.

1814   Published *The Corsair* (13,000 copies sold on the day of publication). Addressed a contemptuous ode to Napoleon on his abdication. Published *Lara*. On 15 September his engagement to Anne Isabella Milbanke was announced. The day after Christmas he set off for Seaham with Hobhouse who was to be his best man—'the bridegroom more and more *less* impatient.'

1815   Married on 2 January at Seaham. Settled at 13 Piccadilly Terrace, London. Was in straitened financial circumstances. Published *Hebrew Melodies*. Met Sir Walter Scott. Took an active part in the management of Drury Lane Theatre. His and Lady Byron's daughter, Augusta Ada, born 10 December.

1816   In January, Lady Byron at Byron's request left London with Ada for her father's newly acquired estate of Kirby Mallory. In February, her father Sir Ralph sent a letter proposing separation. Published *The Siege of Corinth* and *Parisina*. Deed of separation favorable to Byron drawn up. Byron ostracized in London, in spite of Lady Jersey's attempt to make a stand for him at a ball honoring him and Augusta. On 25 April, with Hobhouse and Davies to see him off, he sailed from Dover never again to return to England.

Accompanied by three servants including the perennial Fletcher, and also a traveling physician named Polidori, landed at Ostend and made his way by slow stages through Antwerp, Brussels (visited the battlefield at Waterloo), and by way of the Rhine River, to Geneva. Met Shelley there (it is supposed for the first time) with whom were Mary Godwin and her stepsister, Claire Clairmont, who had entered into an intrigue with Byron a short time before he left England. Rented the Villa Diodati and enjoyed the daily companionship of Shelley, who was living close by. Toured Lake Geneva with him in June, and in September toured the Bernese Alps with Hobhouse. Shelley took back to England the manuscript of *Childe Harold III, The Prisoner of Chillon,* et cetera. These poems were published by Murray in November and December. 'What you have published before is nothing to this effort.' With Hobhouse went to Venice in November where he took lodgings.

1817   Applied himself to learning Armenian—'My mind needed something craggy to break upon'—and enjoyed the carnival. At the end of April visited Rome where he met Hobhouse again. Back at Venice he took a country villa at La Mira on the Brenta. In June, Murray published *Manfred* and *The Lament of Tasso.*

1818   *Beppo* and *Childe Harold IV* published in February and April. By March, he established himself in the Mocenigo Palace on the Grand Canal. In April, the Shelleys, with Claire and Allegra (Byron's child by Claire), returned to Italy. Byron met Shelley in Venice and offered the Shelleys, and Claire, the use of a villa he had taken at Este. Rode with Shelley, and often with Hoppner, the British consul, on the Lido. Began *Don Juan* in July.

1819   In April renewed an acquaintance with Teresa, seventeen-year-old daughter of Count Gamba of Ravenna, and wife of the sixty-year-old Count Guiccioli, and for a time was with her almost daily. In October Tom Moore made a five-day visit, staying at the Mocenigo Palace. In November, when Teresa fell ill, Byron moved to Ravenna in December to be with her. *Ode on Venice* and *Mazeppa* published in June and *Don Juan, I and II* in July.

1820   Rented a magnificent apartment in the Guiccioli Palace. Became involved with Teresa and the Gambas in the Carbonari plot against Austria. Teresa was granted a separation from her husband by Papal decree. Extraordinary literary and social activity.

1821   Published the *Prophecy of Dante, Marino Faliero, Don Juan III, IV, V.* Left Ravenna in October and settled with Teresa at Pisa. The Pisan group included the Gambas, the Shelleys, Medwin, Edward and Jane Williams, Irish Count Taaffe, and the Greek leader Mavrocordato. Byron entertained this set of individualists and got himself involved in troubles with the local authorities. Kept at his poetry and pistol shooting. Published *Cain, Sardanapalus,* and *The Two Foscari.*

1822   In January Edward J. Trelawny joined the Pisan group. In April Allegra died at the Bagnacavallo convent near Ravenna. Leigh Hunt and his large family arrived in June to join Byron and Shelley in establishing a literary journal, *The Liberal.* In July, Shelley and Williams were drowned off Leghorn and their bodies burned on the shore by Trelawny, Hunt, and Byron. *The Liberal* was abandoned after only four numbers; nevertheless, Byron subsidized Hunt to the extent of £500 and other generosities. Published *The Vision of Judgment.* Teresa ordered by the Papal decree to reside with her father. When the Gambas removed to Genoa in September, Byron accompanied them.

1823   Published *Werner, Heaven and Earth, The Age of Bronze, The Blues, The Island,* and *Don Juan, VI-XIV.* On terms of some intimacy with Lord and Lady Blessington, and Count D'Orsay, April-June. Elected to the London Greek Committee and asked by that body to go to Greece to lend his aid and prestige to the cause. Chartered the 120-ton brig *Hercules,* and with Trelawny, Pietro Gamba, Dr. Bruno, as physician, and Fletcher among the party, left Genoa, 16 July, and reached Argostoli in Cephalonia, 3 August. Threw his energies into the campaign. Advanced large sums to the Greek Government; was distracted with the incompetence, indolence, and rapacity all around him. Suffered from convulsions during an expedition to Ithaca. Lived for a time with Gamba and Bruno on the island of Mataxata.

In December crossed over to Missolonghi and was received with full military honors by Mavrocordato, head of the Greek staff.

1824 *Don Juan XV, XVI* appeared in March. The country around Missolonghi was a fever-ridden morass and the weather bad. Byron's health rapidly declined and he died on 19 April. His body was returned to England and interred at Hucknall Torkard near Newstead.

To his contemporaries Lord Byron was 'a personality first and a poet afterwards.' Goethe described him as 'a personality of eminence such as has never been and is not likely to come again.' At twenty-four he was the most talked about and sought after poet of his time. His person caught and held the popular attention of the whole of Europe. His triumph was both spectacular and unique, and was matched only by the extreme condemnation with which a few seasons after he was cast off by his countrymen. Byron was credited equally with 'abnormal genius and abnormal wickedness.' He himself declared 'My good and evil are at perpetual war.' He was a strange mixture of opposites—of courage and self-pity, sincerity and posing, faith and cynicism, serious thought and flippant action. Throughout his life his temperamental sensitiveness and reserve tended to make him withdraw from his fellows. He was always seeking escape: first as a young wanderer to the Mediterranean, later as a disillusioned popular idol to Switzerland and Italy. After the domestic crisis with his wife his feeling of isolation developed into a sense of almost fatal ostracism. He tried desperately then to escape from his own 'wretched identity' (witness *Childe Harold III* and *Manfred*). Eventually in Italy he achieved a final secure position of detachment from which he 'leveled a cool glance at the world from which he felt estranged.' This emancipation was his personal triumph and the basis for his triumph as a literary artist. There is no denying that Byron was at times arrogant and rebellious, that he was capable of tempestuous and haughty moods. But for all his flashes of vulgarity, his unworthy intrigues, his intellectual caprices, Byron was 'a man of daring, tenderness, and candor, and one of the most generous spirits of his age' (Mayne).

Byron's first poetic venture, *Hours of Idleness*, was derivative and juvenile, giving no hint of its author's spirited assault on the new poets and reviewers which was shortly afterward to be precipitated by Brougham's contemptuous article in the *Edinburgh Review*. But as soon as *English Bards and Scotch Reviewers* made its appearance it was agreed that here was a new literary force to be reckoned with. When Byron put together his satire he was in too high a temper to be just and discriminating. He was repeatedly wrong-headed and unfair (later he repented many of his gibes); yet so extraordinary were his powers of malicious statement and bristling epigram that for all its errors in taste *English Bards and Scotch Reviewers* was immediately hailed as a triumph.

It was not until after he returned from his two years' visit to the Mediterranean, however, that Byron sprang into fame. From boyhood on he had read eagerly everything he could lay his hands on that pertained to the Near East. He had lived there and gained firsthand knowledge of the scenes and customs he was to describe. His wanderings had emancipated him from English insularity, so that when he reported in *Childe Harold, I and II,* of the world beyond the Channel it was with an untrammeled mind. In his poem he describes the picturesque and romantic scenes of Spain, Greece, and the Near East. To his readers his work was at once a book of travels, a chapter of frontline reporting from the seat of war, and the diary of a new Timon in the person of a young lord. The moment for Byron's appearance in the role of poet could not have been better chosen. The public in 1812 was growing a little weary of Scott's romantic convention and was prepared to be delighted with the new and exotic fare of 'the youth with ancient name.' *Childe Harold, I and II,* is by no means a masterpiece; but to Byron's contemporaries it was exciting fare, even though somewhat highly flavored. Upon its publication Byron awoke one morning, as he tells us, to find himself famous.

But if *Childe Harold, I and II,* was the first work to attract a wider fame for its author, it was the tales in verse which followed that lifted Byron to his greatest height of popularity. In these tales, written in headlong haste in the intervals between distracting gaities in his London life, Byron entered directly into rivalry with Scott. Where Scott had gone to the past for romance, Byron found it in the strangeness and picturesqueness of the present. He transferred the scene of action from Britain to the South and East and replaced Scott's hackneyed romance of border chivalry with 'the more intense melodrama of passion and crime.' Byron's typical hero-villain in these narratives was a direct descendant of the 'satanic' personage found in the Gothic tale of terror. But Byron 'darkened the colouring and sharpened the drawing as to make of his Conrad or his Lara figures so much more impressive than his predecessors that they seemed something new' (Elton). He liked to imagine himself in the role of his hero, harried by memories of follies or crimes, and to write into these romances pages out of his own book of adventure. As had been the case with *Childe Harold, I and II,* his readers detected the self-portrait and were eager to unravel in each new tale the mysterious secrets of this lonely, misanthropic poet. To the fever pitch of curiosity about Byron himself were added his disregard of custom, his darkly hinted suggestions of unlawful passion, his strong drawing of strange adventure—all features providing 'the jaded taste of a very worldly society with the kind of poetry it could respond to' (Bredvold). The tales, accordingly, were received by his contemporary audience with uncritical admiration and acclaim. Their charm has since faded. They are slipshod in workmanship and much of them is gross melodrama; on the other hand, they have pace, a tremendous flow of life, and superb egotism. But they are not great literature. The metrical tales were for Byron the artist, even more so than with Scott, a mere prelude.

When Byron quitted England in April 1816, cast off by his country 'like a weed from the rock,' the 'violent and tragic severance' roused in him a storm of conflicting passions. He had felt himself an isolated man and 'better than his kind.' Now he was faced with public disaster, angered and mortified by his sudden downfall. His fury was roused against his wife and her family and against the 'fickle breath of popular applause.' He sought expression in poems 'intended to wound his enemies or shock the organized hypocrisy which he conceived English society to be' (Bredvold). In Switzerland he spent the greater part of the summer in almost daily association with Shelley through whose more sensitive appreciation for Nature (and the help of Wordsworth's poetry) he quickly gained a nobler insight into the glories of lake and mountain. Under the impact of these circumstances Byron's poetic energy increased tenfold. The third canto of *Childe Harold* rapidly took shape. 'I was half mad,' Byron wrote afterward, 'between metaphysics, mountains, lakes, love inextinguishable and thoughts unutterable, and the nightmare of my own delinquencies.' Into its stanzas he poured the disquiet of his personal suffering, attempting in some measure a psychological justification of himself, and pleading his case before all Europe. Confession, travel, the pageant of history, the worship of high mountains appear in a rapidly shifting pattern of many moods. In this third canto Byron is now in 'the full exercise of his ripened powers.' No longer is there any question of his courage or sincerity. His command of verse is superb; his rhetoric magnificent. Some old faults still cling—an occasional looseness of phrase, some carelessness in the choice of words, cacophonies—but these blemishes now hardly disturb the 'full-volumed mastery.'

The lyrical drama *Manfred* was a second major work of the Swiss summer, its first two acts having been written in the Alps and the third a few months afterward in Venice. Its scenic background is the 'sublime solitudes' of the Staubach and the Jungfrau; its theme the poet's personal remorse for his own inexpiable crime. 'My pang shall have a voice,' wrote Byron. And it did have; and, as Ethel Mayne has pointed out, for the last time. For with this cry of authentic remorse for a real crime Byron wrote himself out of the heroic mood. The 'Byronic' hero never again takes the stage. But in *Manfred* he is 'more startling and distinct, and more gigantic than in any previous rendering' (Mayne). He is Byron himself, forced by destiny to do spiritual murder. He has eaten the forbidden fruit; and 'the fruit of the tree of knowledge was sorrow, and was death.' The spiritual agony was genuine and his own:

The thorns which I have reaped are of the tree I planted.

'Thus the pang,' says Miss Mayne, 'had all its bitterness' and Byron could 'feel his imagination emancipated at last by the measure of its knowledge and its suffering.'

In the spring of 1817 Byron invoked the memories of Venice and of Rome in *Childe Harold, canto IV*. As in *canto III* and in *Manfred* he again projects his emotional context into his stanzas, but now his emancipation from a sense of personal guilt is apparent; for his driving passions are not inward and bitter remorse for his own wrongdoing as in *Manfred*, but outward revenge and scorn for his enemies. In *Childe Harold IV* in his interpretations of ancient monuments he seizes upon the human and pathetic aspects, and again he proves himself by his energy.

In Italy Byron learned from the Italian Renaissance writers of comic-epics a new style in which he was to achieve his greatest and most characteristic work. The Italian poets—chief among them Pulci, Berni, and Ariosto—had developed in the highly flexible *ottava rima* stanza a manner admirably suited to constant variations in mood and changing levels of style. Taking a hint from Frere, an Englishman who had imitated the Italians, Byron left off his rhetoric and, by way of the banter and mockery of the Italian medley-poem, in *Beppo* hit upon an entirely new manner in what was to prove for him his truest medium. In writing this lighthearted carnival comedy he discovered that he could use words in poetry as he would use them in talking and in exactly the same order and construction. *Ottava rima* permitted him to join words, style, language, and subject: to use the colloquial manner of ready talk or, if he chose or occasion demanded, a higher level of what Goethe has described as a 'classically elegant comic style.' Well-satisfied with his first experiment in jocose poetry, a few months after he had completed *Beppo* Byron began to revolve plans for a satiric epic of modern life on a vast scale. As he proceeded he determined upon a plan of making his poem a comic exposure of the social and political corruptions of the ruling castes of all Europe. *Don Juan,* Byron's masterpiece, is the tangible result of his planning. It is a very long poem running to sixteen cantos and part of a seventeenth, and remains unfinished. Following the pattern set by *Beppo,* the ground-tone of *Don Juan* is maintained in 'observation and free and cheery irony.' The story opens with the high-spirited comic intrigue of Donna Julia, continues with the ruthless, grim realism of the shipwreck, and rises to the tragical idyll of Haidée. Subsequent cantos include an intrigue with a sultana in Constantinople, an exciting battle scene, the hero's capture and dispatch to the Russian court at St. Petersburg, his favor with Empress Catherine, and, at the last, scenes in England where he has been sent on a political mission. After the fifth canto Byron becomes by degrees more militant in his satire. In the last cantos (xi-xvii), which give a caustic picture of fashionable English life, he creates in effect a new poem, a sequel to the preceding cantos, but which has a more ruthless intention.

Don Juan has seemed too long to some readers. It has its weak periods, as Byron himself confessed, yet it is without question one of the greatest comic poems in the language. Goethe called it 'a work of boundless genius'; Shelley described it as 'something wholly new and relative to the age, and yet surpassingly beautiful.' *Don Juan* is a clear mirror of Byron himself, a perfect vehicle of all his 'passion, irony, and knowledge of the world, . . . the fullest and final expression of the man' (Elton). The indomitable energy, the variety and zest, the rich fertility of invention, the seemingly inexhaustible resources of meter and diction are truly wonderful. The form Byron perfected enabled him to write on whatever level he chose; and the limitless scope of the poem permitted him to shift its moods as rapidly as his own. The result is an amazing medley of wit, pathos, roguery, cynicism, beauty, satire, and ribaldry. Everything goes into *Don Juan:* stolen glances, Lord Londonderry, chamber pots, a rainbow spanning the dark sea, hock and soda water, Southey. Changefulness is an inherent trait of the poem; yet *Don Juan* is more than a string of passages. The narrative moves forward without effort. Our eyes are on the hero—on the panorama of life that his adventures unfold. And never far off is the self-conscious mockery of the author enfolding and containing the unending variety and giving a final unity to the massive epic.

When we view Byron's work in perspective, two manners among several stand clearly distinguished: the early romantic manner of the lyrics, the pseudo-romances, *Childe Harold,* and *Manfred;* and the later satiric manner of *Beppo, Don Juan,* and *The Vision of Judgment.* Byron found himself late. Scarcely anything that he wrote before his final departure from England is an altogether satisfactory expression of his genius. In the lyric he lacks the magic of phrase and the music of his greatest contemporaries. His best lyrical efforts appear prosaic beside those of Shelley and Keats. In technique he never really goes far beyond *Hours of Idleness.* The last noble stanzas at Missolonghi are 'firmer and graver in substance,' but metrically they are written on the same principle as 'Well! thou art happy' (1808). Byron possessed technical ingenuity in rhyme and phrase in abundance; nevertheless, in the romantic manner his voice is eloquent rather than lyric. Of the earlier poems written in exile parts of *Childe Harold III & IV* and *Manfred* are in Byron's best oratorical style and offer many purple passages. It was only after he had recovered his composure and began the poems in *ottava rima,* however, that Byron discovered a full and responsive medium to express exactly what he felt in the tone he wished to convey it. The style he so skillfully adapted from the Italians gave him just what he required. He could be gay, eloquent, boisterous, pensively lyrical, or cynical at will; or, if he felt like it, he could break into a personality sketch or level off with his swift-moving narrative. This later poetic style approaches remarkably near to the prose of his inimitable letters written in Italy. His most faultless style is in these letters, 'so full of common sense, brilliant observation, naked sincerity, wit, insolence—all in the voice of genius' (Quennell). The closer Byron comes to prose in his poetry the nearer he comes to humanity and the real world he knew; and, paradoxical though it may sound, the closer he comes to poetry. 'To read his prose and his prose-like poetry is to approach the nearest to the fountain-springs of his power' (Bredvold). In this style Byron is an acknowledged master and admits no serious rival in English poetry. It would be pointless to deny that Byron has stylistic faults, some of them so gross as to repel fastidious readers. He was a superficial scholar, lacked responsiveness to the subtler demands of rhythm, and had no magic in words. In practice he could be diffuse and slovenly. He seemingly was wanting at times in the determination to write as well as he could. He affected to be incapable of revision and proudly professed that 'no one had done more than he to corrupt the English language.' His attitude was partly pose, and partly genuine distrust of the professional artist. If he chose, he could and did revise, as his manuscripts abundantly show. By habit, however, he was a rapid writer, like Sir Walter Scott, and his work like Scott's often betrays the marks of hurried composition. But if Byron's writings have faults they also have compensating virtues. The *ottava rima* poems, particularly, possess an exhilarating effect resulting largely from suppleness and speed. Spontaneity here compensates for the nicer refinements of verse. Byron's light-limbered improvisation, capricious and mobile, races along with the ease of ready conversation. The result is a simplicity and largeness and a sustaining power in the vivid depiction of incidents and passions. And when Byron hits his mark with barbed missiles of satire, speed drives the shafts home. With all of its artistic limitations, Byron's work has the 'great merit of effectiveness.' What he lacks in requisiteness and refinement he makes amends for in energy, directness, intellectual daring, inexhaustible variety—great personal force. He arouses an instantaneous sympathy. He is the poet of splendid excitement, of invective, of passion. 'The great object of life is sensation,' he declared, 'to feel that we exist even though in pain.' For him poetry is at once the relief and the expression; it is 'the lava of the imagination, whose eruption prevents an earthquake.' By the measure of his titanic energy and his impassioned self-assertion Byron has given us a more potent expression of 'raw and naked humanity' than all the other romantic poets put together. Byron could not get out of himself, it is true, but as P. E. More has so excellently said, his emotions are so strong, his passions so vigorous that he accomplishes more than many whose vision is wider. He has given us masterly pictures of love, hate, patriotism, honor, disdain, revenge, remorse, despair, awe, mockery. Passion does not exclude intellect. On the contrary, the elemental passions stimulate in Byron an intense activity of mind. He has a firm hold upon himself and the world. He is intellectually dauntless and fundamentally sincere. It is as a fearless mocking commentator on life that he is greatest. In *Don Juan* he sought to depict life in the comic spirit, to strip off the tinsel of sentiment and illusion. In the reactionary period in Europe after the Battle of Waterloo he became the spokesman and champion of a new era. He was the poet of *The Isles of Greece,* the hero of Missolonghi, the prophet of liberalism. He was a powerful agent in the revolt against the arrogance and hypocrisy of the ruling classes. Byron was no democrat in politics—he was 'for the people, not of them'—but he hated the intellectual oppression that tyranny fostered. His satire was so astringent because it went 'to the roots of human society.' It has been said that Byron did not have a constructive, positive philosophy. Possibly so—yet his transfiguring humor can dissolve fanaticism, stimulate the intellect, preserve our sanity.

Byron's personality has always to some extent gotten mixed up with the evaluation of his poetry. This was especially true during his own lifetime when violent contrarieties in public opinion followed closely the rise and fall of his popularity. In the early years of his career the excited identification by his readers of Byron himself as the hero of wild and irregular adventures, perhaps crimes, in *Childe Harold I and II* and the Eastern romances, probably served more than any single circumstance to lift him to sudden fame. Other factors of course were involved—the new and authentic note of passion in these poems, their cosmopolitan background, their spirit of revolt, their breadth and splendor and superficiality—but these qualities were outshone by public curiosity about the personal life of the author himself. His popularity was sudden and extraordinary. There had hitherto been positively nothing to equal it. He became overnight 'the grand Napoleon of the realms of rhyme' whose voice carried across all Europe. He was the contemporary force in poetry most to be reckoned with; the obviously outstanding figure. When, however, upon the breakup of his unfortunate marriage he left England in voluntary exile, resentment against his personal conduct broke out in fury. Byron was denounced as a moral renegade and his poetry was attacked as vicious and corrupting. Reports of the 'rich harvest of scandal' coming from across the Channel further damaged his reputation, though much more in England than on the Continent. As his name faded in England it grew in other nations. He was widely translated abroad and in time many Continental writers were numbered among his disciples, among them Victor Hugo, Lamartine, Heine, and Pushkin. At home, however, his fall from fame was almost as swift as his amazing rise. The moral British, who declined to discriminate between life and poetry, in one of their periodical fits of self-righteousness, cast off the man and his poetry together. After his death Byron's poetic fame in England underwent a rapid eclipse. The loftier poetry of Wordsworth, Shelley, and Keats began to reach a wider audience, and the sturdy influence of Carlyle began to make inroads against Byron's cynicism. The finished artistry and moral earnestness of Tennyson likewise told heavily against Byron's loose workmanship and lack of ethical cogency. His heroics came to appear to the Victorians as a false light. By the 1870's his reputation as a poet reached a low ebb. Arnold in a famous essay, though admitting Byron's faults, had praised his 'unperishable excellence of sincerity and strength' and admitted his great contribution to the cause of liberalism. But Swinburne led such a devastating attack on Byron's art that Byron was all but forsaken in the closing years of the century. With the opening of the twentieth century, however, there was a critical shift in emphasis to the satires, especially to *Don Juan* and *The Vision of Judgment.* By World War I a revival of interest in Byron was well under way. Since then he has maintained, if not the highest station among the romantics, at least a commanding position. Present-day readers are finding Byron's motley style strikingly like that which some of our better modern poets (Eliot and Auden, for example) have come to cultivate. We are also discovering in Byron an accurate expression of our own twentieth century disillusionment and cynicism. Through detachment from the traditions and petty ambitions of his own age, Byron was able to judge its values and to see it in perspective. That is why he makes us feel so much at home in his world and why we still find him so absorbing.

FAREWELL! IF EVER FONDEST PRAYER

FAREWELL! if ever fondest prayer
  For other's weal avail'd on high,
Mine will not all be lost in air,
  But waft thy name beyond the sky.
'Twere vain to speak, to weep, to sigh:
  Oh! more than tears of blood can tell,
When wrung from guilt's expiring eye,
  Are in that word—Farewell!—Farewell!

These lips are mute, these eyes are dry;
  But in my breast and in my brain,   10
Awake the pangs that pass not by,
  The thought that ne'er shall sleep again.
My soul nor deigns nor dares complain,
  Though grief and passion there rebel;
I only know we loved in vain—
  I only feel—Farewell!—Farewell!

1808   1814

WHEN WE TWO PARTED

WHEN we two parted
  In silence and tears,
Half broken-hearted
  To sever for years,
Pale grew thy cheek and cold,
  Colder thy kiss;
Truly that hour foretold
  Sorrow to this.

The dew of the morning
  Sunk chill on my brow—   10
It felt like the warning
  Of what I feel now.
Thy vows are all broken,
  And light is thy fame:
I hear thy name spoken,
  And share in its shame.

They name thee before me,
  A knell to mine ear;
A shudder comes o'er me—
  Why wert thou so dear?   20
They know not I knew thee,
  Who knew thee too well:—
Long, long shall I rue thee,
  Too deeply to tell.

In secret we met—
  In silence I grieve,
That thy heart could forget,
  Thy spirit deceive.

If I should meet thee
  After long years,   30
How should I greet thee?
  With silence and tears.

1808?   1816

From ENGLISH BARDS AND SCOTCH
REVIEWERS

A SATIRE

All my friends, learned and unlearned, have urged me
not to publish this Satire with my name. If I were to be
'turned from the career of my humour by quibbles quick,
and paper bullets of the brain,' I should have complied
with their counsel. But I am not to be terrified by abuse,
or bullied by reviewers, with or without arms. I can
safely say that I have attacked none personally, who did
not commence on the offensive. An author's works are
public property: he who purchases may judge, and publish his opinion if he pleases; and the authors I have endeavoured to commemorate may do by me as I have
done by them. I dare say they will succeed better in condemning my scribblings, than in mending their own. But
my object is not to prove that I can write well, but, if possible, to make others write better.—From Byron's Preface to the second edition.)

Lines 143–264, 438–505

BEHOLD! in various throngs the scribbling
      crew,
For notice eager, pass in long review:
Each spurs his jaded Pegasus apace,
And rhyme and blank maintain an equal race;
Sonnets on sonnets crowd, and ode on ode;
And tales of terror jostle on the road;
Immeasurable measures move along;
For simpering folly loves a varied song,   150
To strange mysterious dulness still the friend,
Admires the strain she cannot comprehend.
Thus Lays of Minstrels[1]—may they be the last!—
On half-strung harps whine mournful to the blast.
While mountain spirits prate to river sprites,
That dames may listen to the sound at nights;
And goblin brats, of Gilpin Horner's brood,
Decoy young border-nobles through the wood,
And skip at every step, Lord knows how high,
And frighten foolish babes, the Lord knows
      why;   160
While high-born ladies in their magic cell,
Forbidding knights to read who cannot spell,
Despatch a courier to a wizard's grave,
And fight with honest men to shield a knave.

---

[1] Scott's *The Lay of the Last Minstrel*, which grew out of the
suggestion for a ballad on the old Border Legend of Gilpin
Horner.

Next view in state, proud prancing on his roan,
The golden-crested haughty Marmion,
Now forging scrolls, now foremost in the fight,
Not quite a felon, yet but half a knight,
The gibbet or the field prepared to grace;
A mighty mixture of the great and base.   170
And think'st thou, Scott! by vain conceit perchance,
On public taste to foist thy stale romance,
Though Murray with his Miller² may combine
To yield thy muse just half-a-crown per line?
No! when the sons of song descend to trade,
Their bays are sear, their former laurels fade.
Let such forego the poet's sacred name,
Who rack their brains for lucre, not for fame:
Still for stern Mammon may they toil in vain!
And sadly gaze on gold they cannot gain!   180
Such be their meed, such still the just reward
Of prostituted muse and hireling bard!
For this we spurn Apollo's venal son,³
And bid a long 'good night to Marmion.'⁴

    These are the themes that claim our plaudits
          now;
These are the bards to whom the muse must bow;
While Milton, Dryden, Pope, alike forgot,
Resign their hallow'd bays to Walter Scott.

    The time has been, when yet the muse was
          young,
When Homer swept the lyre, and Maro sung, 190
An epic scarce ten centuries could claim,
While awe-struck nations hail'd the magic name:
The work of each immortal bard appears
The single wonder of a thousand years.
Empires have moulder'd from the face of earth,
Tongues have expired with those who gave them
          birth,
Without the glory such a strain can give,
As even in ruin bids the language live.
Not so with us, though minor bards, content
On one great work a life of labour spent: 200
With eagle pinion soaring to the skies,
Behold the ballad-monger Southey rise!
To him let Camoëns, Milton, Tasso yield,
Whose annual strains, like armies, take the field.
First in the ranks see Joan of Arc⁵ advance,
The scourge of England and the boast of France!
Though burnt by wicked Bedford for a witch,

Behold her statue placed in glory's niche;
Her fetters burst, and just released from prison,
A virgin phœnix from her ashes risen.   210
Next see tremendous Thalaba⁶ come on,
Arabia's monstrous, wild, and wondrous son:
Domdaniel's dread destroyer, who o'erthrew
More mad magicians than the world e'er knew.
Immortal hero! all thy foes o'ercome,
For ever reign—the rival of Tom Thumb!
Since startled metre fled before thy face,
Well wert thou doom'd the last of all thy race!
Well might triumphant genii bear thee hence,
Illustrious conqueror of common sense!   220
Now, last and greatest, Madoc⁷ spreads his sails,
Cacique⁸ in Mexico, and prince in Wales;
Tells us strange tales, as other travellers do,
More old than Mandeville's, and not so true,
Oh! Southey! Southey! cease thy varied song!
A bard may chant too often and too long:
As thou art strong in verse, in mercy, spare!
A fourth, alas! were more than we could bear.
But if, in spite of all the world can say,
Thou still wilt verseward plod thy weary
          way;   230
If still in Berkley ballads most uncivil,⁹
Thou wilt devote old women to the devil,
The babe unborn thy dread intent may rue:
'God help thee,' Southey, and thy readers too.

    Next comes the dull disciple of thy school,
That mild apostate from poetic rule,
The simple Wordsworth, framer of a lay
As soft as evening in his favourite May,
Who warns his friend 'to shake off toil and
          trouble,
And quit his books, for fear of growing
          double';¹⁰   240
Who, both by precept and example, shows
That prose is verse, and verse is merely prose;
Convincing all, by demonstration plain,
Poetic souls delight in prose insane;
And Christmas stories tortured into rhyme
Contain the essence of the true sublime.
Thus, when he tells the tale of Betty Foy,
The idiot mother of 'an idiot boy';
A moon-struck, silly lad, who lost his way,
And, like his bard, confounded night with
          day;   250

---

2 *Marmion* was published by Constable, Murray, and Miller.
3 the god of poetry's mercenary son, i.e. Scott, who was paid
£1000 for *Marmion.*
4 The pathetic and also prophetic exclamation of Henry Blount,
Esquire, on the death of honest Marmion.—(Byron.)
5 Southey's first epic, published in 1796.

6 *Thalaba the Destroyer,* 1801.
7 *Madoc,* 1805.
8 native chief or petty king.
9 See 'The Old Woman of Berkeley,' a ballad, by Mr. Southey,
wherein an aged gentleman is carried away by Beelzebub, on a
'high-trotting horse.'—(Byron.)
10 'The Tables Turned,' first stanza.

So close on each pathetic part he dwells,
And each adventure so sublimely tells,
That all who view the 'idiot in his glory'
Conceive the bard the hero of the story.

    Shall gentle Coleridge pass unnoticed here,
To turgid ode and tumid stanza dear?
Though themes of innocence amuse him best,
Yet still obscurity's a welcome guest.
If Inspiration should her aid refuse
To him who takes a pixy for a muse,[11]   260
Yet none in lofty numbers can surpass
The bard who soars to elegise an ass.[12]
So well the subject suits his noble mind,
He brays the laureat of the long-ear'd kind.

       .   .   .

    Health to immortal Jeffrey! once, in name,
England could boast a judge[13] almost the same;
In soul so like, so merciful, yet just,   440
Some think that Satan has resign'd his trust,
And given the spirit to the world again,
To sentence letters, as he sentenced men.
With hand less mighty, but with heart as black,
With voice as willing to decree the rack;
Bred in the courts betimes, though all that
    law
As yet hath taught him is to find a flaw;
Since well instructed in the patriot school
To rail at party, though a party tool,
Who knows, if chance his patrons should
    restore   450
Back to the sway they forfeited before,
His scribbling toils some recompense may meet,
And raise this Daniel to the judgement-seat?
Let Jeffreys' shade indulge the pious hope,
And greeting thus, present him with a rope:
'Heir to my virtues! man of equal mind!
Skill'd to condemn as to traduce mankind,
This cord receive, for thee reserved with care,
To wield in judgement, and at length to wear.'

    Health to great Jeffrey! Heaven preserve his
    life,   460
To flourish on the fertile shores of Fife,[14]
And guard it sacred in its future wars,
Since authors sometimes seek the field of Mars!
Can none remember that eventful day,
That ever-glorious, almost fatal fray,

When Little's leadless pistol met his eye.[15]
And Bow-street myrmidons[16] stood laughing by?
Oh, day disastrous! on her firm-set rock,
Dunedin's[17] castle felt a secret shock;
Dark roll'd the sympathetic waves of Forth,[18] 470
Low groan'd the startled whirlwinds of the north;
Tweed[19] ruffled half his waves to form a tear,
The other half pursued its calm career;
Arthur's steep summit[20] nodded to its base,
The surly Tolbooth[21] scarcely kept her place.
The Tolbooth felt—for marble sometimes can,
On such occasions, feel as much as man—
The Tolbooth felt defrauded of his charms,
If Jeffrey died, except within her arms:
Nay last, not least, on that portentous morn, 480
The sixteenth story, where himself was born,
His patrimonial garret, fell to ground,
And pale Edina[22] shudder'd at the sound:
Strew'd were the streets around with milk-white
    reams,
Flow'd all the Canongate[23] with inky streams;
This of his candour seem'd the sable dew,
That of his valour show'd the bloodless hue;
And all with justice deem'd the two combined
The mingled emblems of his mighty mind.
But Caledonia's[24] goddess hover'd o'er   490
The field, and saved him from the wrath of
    Moore;
From either pistol snatch'd the vengeful lead,
And straight restored it to her favourite's head;
That head, with greater than magnetic power,
Caught it, as Danaë[25] caught the golden shower,
And, though the thickening dross will scarce re-
    fine,
Augments its ore, and is itself a mine.
'My son,' she cried, 'ne'er thirst for gore again,
Resign the pistol and resume the pen;
O'er politics and poesy preside,   500
Boast of thy country, and Britannia's guide!

---

11 a reference to Coleridge's *Songs of the Pixies*.
12 a reference to Coleridge's *To a Young Ass*.
13 George Jeffreys, first Baron Jeffreys, 1648–89, Chief Justice under James II, whose conduct of the 'bloody assizes' branded his name with indelible infamy.
14 a county on the east coast of Scotland.

15 In 1806, Messrs. Jeffrey and Moore met at Chalk-Farm. The duel was prevented by the interference of the magistracy; and, on examination, the balls of the pistols were found to have evaporated. This incident gave occasion to much waggery in the daily prints.—(Byron.) This account of the duel was later disavowed by Byron. As a matter of fact, Jeffrey's pistol was the one found to be empty.
16 police officers from Bow Street (London).
17 Dunedin is poetic for Edinburgh.
18 The Firth of Forth, a bay in eastern Scotland on whose south shore Edinburgh is situated.
19 a river marking the boundary between Scotland and England.
20 Ben Arthur, a mountain in Argyllshire, Scotland.
21 principal prison of Edinburgh.
22 Edinburgh.
23 principal thoroughfare of Old Edinburgh.
24 Scotland's
25 Princess of Argos, mother of Perseus by Zeus, who visited her in the form of a golden shower in the tower where her father had imprisoned her.

For long as Albion's heedless sons submit,
Or Scottish taste decides on English wit,
So long shall last thine unmolested reign,
Nor any dare to take thy name in vain.'

1807–9   1809

MAID OF ATHENS,[1] ERE WE PART

Ζωή μου, σᾶς ἀγαπῶ. [2]

MAID of Athens, ere we part,
Give, oh give me back my heart!
Or, since that has left my breast,
Keep it now, and take the rest!
Hear my vow before I go,
Ζωή μου, σᾶς ἀγαπῶ.

By those tresses unconfined,
Woo'd by each Ægean wind;
By those lids whose jetty fringe
Kiss thy soft cheeks' blooming tinge;   10
By those wild eyes like the roe,
Ζωή μου, σᾶς ἀγαπῶ.

By that lip I long to taste;
By that zone-encircled waist;
By all the token-flowers that tell
What words can never speak so well;
By love's alternate joy and woe,
Ζωή μου, σᾶς ἀγαπῶ.

Maid of Athens! I am gone:
Think of me, sweet! when alone.   20
Though I fly to Istambol,
Athens holds my heart and soul:
Can I cease to love thee? No!
Ζωή μου, σᾶς ἀγαπῶ.

1810   1812

SHE WALKS IN BEAUTY

SHE[1] walks in beauty, like the night
Of cloudless climes and starry skies;
And all that's best of dark and bright
Meet in her aspect and her eyes:

Thus mellow'd to that tender light
Which heaven to gaudy day denies.

One shade the more, one ray the less,
Had half impair'd the nameless grace
Which waves in every raven tress,
Or softly lightens o'er her face;   10
Where thoughts serenely sweet express
How pure, how dear their dwelling-place.

And on that cheek, and o'er that brow,
So soft, so calm, yet eloquent,
The smiles that win, the tints that glow,
But tell of days in goodness spent,
A mind at peace with all below,
A heart whose love is innocent!

12 June 1814   1815

OH! SNATCH'D AWAY IN BEAUTY'S BLOOM

OH! snatch'd away in beauty's bloom,
On thee shall press no ponderous tomb;
But on thy turf shall roses rear
Their leaves, the earliest of the year;
And the wild cypress wave in tender gloom:

And oft by yon blue gushing stream
Shall Sorrow lean her drooping head,
And feed deep thought with many a dream,
And lingering pause and lightly tread;
Fond wretch! as if her step disturb'd the
dead!   10

Away! we know that tears are vain,
That death nor heeds nor hears distress:
Will this unteach us to complain?
Or make one mourner weep the less?
And thou—who tell'st me to forget,
Thy looks are wan, thine eyes are wet.

1814   1815

THE DESTRUCTION OF SENNACHERIB[1]

THE Assyrian came down like the wolf on the
fold,
And his cohorts were gleaming in purple and
gold;
And the sheen of their spears was like stars on
the sea,
When the blue wave rolls nightly on deep Galilee.

---

1 The Maid of Athens was Teresa Macri, eldest daughter of the widow of an English consular official. Byron wrote to Drury: 'I am dying for love of three Greek girls at Athens, sisters. I lived in the same house. Teresa, Mariana, and Katinka are the names of these divinities—all of them under fifteen.'
2 Romaic expression of tenderness. It means 'My life, I love you!' —(Byron.)

---

1 Lady Wilmot Horton, Byron's cousin by marriage, who appeared at an evening party in mourning with spangles on her dress.

1 Assyrian king, 705–681 B.C., whose forces were decimated before Jerusalem by plague. The Biblical story is told in II Kings, xix, 20–37.

Like the leaves of the forest when Summer is green,
That host with their banners at sunset were seen:
Like the leaves of the forest when Autumn hath blown,
That host on the morrow lay wither'd and strown.

For the Angel of Death spread his wings on the blast,
And breathed in the face of the foe as he pass'd;   10
And the eyes of the sleepers wax'd deadly and chill,
And their hearts but once heaved, and for ever grew still!

And there lay the steed with his nostril all wide,
But through it there roll'd not the breath of his pride;
And the foam of his gasping lay white on the turf,
And cold as the spray of the rock-beating surf.

And there lay the rider distorted and pale,
With the dew on his brow, and the rust on his mail:
And the tents were all silent, the banners alone,
The lances unlifted, the trumpet unblown.   20

And the widows of Ashur[2] are loud in their wail,
And the idols are broke in the temple of Baal;[3]
And the might of the Gentile, unsmote by the sword,
Hath melted like snow in the glance of the Lord!

17 February 1815   1815

STANZAS FOR MUSIC

THERE'S not a joy the world can give like that it takes away,
When the glow of early thought declines in feeling's dull decay;
'Tis not on youth's smooth cheek the blush alone, which fades so fast,
But the tender bloom of heart is gone, ere youth itself be past.

Then the few whose spirits float above the wreck of happiness
Are driven o'er the shoals of guilt or ocean of excess:

The magnet of their course is gone, or only points in vain
The shore to which their shiver'd sail shall never stretch again.

Then the mortal coldness of the soul like death itself comes down;
It cannot feel for others' woes, it dare not dream its own;   10
That heavy chill has frozen o'er the fountain of our tears,
And though the eye may sparkle still, 'tis where the ice appears.

Though wit may flash from fluent lips, and mirth distract the breast,
Through midnight hours that yield no more their former hope of rest;
'Tis but as ivy-leaves around the ruin'd turret wreath,
All green and wildly fresh without, but worn and grey beneath.

Oh could I feel as I have felt,—or be what I have been,
Or weep as I could once have wept o'er many a vanish'd scene;
As springs in deserts found seem sweet, all brackish though they be,
So, midst the wither'd waste of life, those tears would flow to me.   20

March 1815   1816

SONNET ON CHILLON[1]

ETERNAL Spirit of the chainless Mind!
Brightest in dungeons, Liberty! thou art,
For there thy habitation is the heart—
The heart which love of thee alone can bind;
And when thy sons to fetters are consign'd—
To fetters, and the damp vault's dayless gloom,
Their country conquers with their martyrdom,
And Freedom's fame finds wings on every wind.
Chillon! thy prison is a holy place,
And thy sad floor an altar—for 'twas trod,   10
Until his very steps have left a trace
Worn, as if thy cold pavement were a sod,
By Bonnivard! May none those marks efface!
For they appeal from tyranny to God.

June 1816   1816

---

2 Assyria.   3 the Assyrian God.

1 castle situated on the shore of Lake Geneva, in which the patriot Bonnivard was imprisoned.

THE PRISONER OF CHILLON

A FABLE

[The subject of Byron's poem is the historic prisoner of Chillon, François Bonnivard, 1493–1571, prelate to a small monastery near Geneva and patriot leader of the Genevese against the rule of Duke Charles III of Savoy. The Duke twice had Bonnivard cast into prison, the second time in the dungeon of Chillon where he was confined for six years. He was freed by the Bernese, made a member of the Council of Geneva, and awarded a house and pension of 200 crowns a year. Bonnivard in actuality was a troublesome and somewhat libertine character, but to later ages through legendary sanctification he became a martyr of liberty. Byron himself called his poem a fable. It should not, therefore, be regarded as historical truth, either in the depiction of the character of Bonnivard or in the detailed circumstances, but rather it should be regarded as an ideal, representative account of those patriot heroes who in any generation have suffered persecution in liberty's name.]

I

My hair is grey, but not with years,
  Nor grew it white
  In a single night,
As men's have grown from sudden fears:
My limbs are bow'd, though not with toil,
  But rusted with a vile repose,
For they have been a dungeon's spoil,
  And mine has been the fate of those
To whom the goodly earth and air
Are bann'd, and barr'd—forbidden fare: 10
But this was for my father's faith
I suffer'd chains and courted death;
That father perish'd at the stake
For tenets he would not forsake;
And for the same his lineal race
In darkness found a dwelling-place;
We were seven—who now are one,
  Six in youth, and one in age,
Finish'd as they had begun,
  Proud of Persecution's rage;   20
One in fire, and two in field,
Their belief with blood have seal'd,
Dying as their father died,
For the God their foes denied;
Three were in a dungeon cast,
Of whom this wreck is left the last.

II

There are seven pillars of Gothic mould,
In Chillon's dungeons deep and old,
There are seven columns, massy and grey,
Dim with a dull imprison'd ray,   30
A sunbeam which hath lost its way,

And through the crevice and the cleft
Of the thick wall is fallen and left;
Creeping o'er the floor so damp,
Like a marsh's meteor lamp:
And in each pillar there is a ring,
  And in each ring there is a chain;
That iron is a cankering thing,
  For in these limbs its teeth remain,
With marks that will not wear away,   40
Till I have done with this new day,
Which now is painful to these eyes,
Which have not seen the sun so rise
For years—I cannot count them o'er,
I lost their long and heavy score,
When my last brother droop'd and died,
And I lay living by his side.

III

They chain'd us each to a column stone,
And we were three—yet, each alone;
We could not move a single pace,   50
We could not see each other's face,
But with that pale and livid light
That made us strangers in our sight:
And thus together—yet apart,
Fetter'd in hand, but join'd in heart,
'Twas still some solace, in the dearth
Of the pure elements of earth,
To hearken to each other's speech,
And each turn comforter to each
With some new hope, or legend old,   60
Or song heroically bold;
But even these at length grew cold.
Our voices took a dreary tone,
An echo of the dungeon stone,
  A grating sound, not full and free,
  As they of yore were wont to be:
  It might be fancy, but to me
They never sounded like our own.

IV

I was the eldest of the three,
  And to uphold and cheer the rest   70
  I ought to do—and did my best—
And each did well in his degree.
  The youngest, whom my father loved,
Because our mother's brow was given
To him, with eyes as blue as heaven—
  For him my soul was sorely moved;
And truly might it be distress'd
To see such bird in such a nest;
For he was beautiful as day—
  (When day was beautiful to me   80

As to young eagles, being free)—
A polar day, which will not see
A sunset till its summer's gone,
The snow-clad offspring of the sun:
    And thus he was as pure and bright,
And in his natural spirit gay,
With tears for nought but others' ills,
And then they flow'd like mountain rills,
Unless he could assuage the woe   90
Which he abhorr'd to view below.

V

The other was as pure of mind,
But form'd to combat with his kind;
Strong in his frame, and of a mood
Which 'gainst the world in war had stood,
And perish'd in the foremost rank
    With joy:—but not in chains to pine:
His spirit wither'd with their clank,
    I saw it silently decline—
    And so perchance in sooth did mine: 100
But yet I forced it on to cheer
Those relics of a home so dear.
He was a hunter of the hills,
    Had follow'd there the deer and wolf;
    To him his dungeon was a gulf,
And fetter'd feet the worst of ills.

VI

Lake Leman[1] lies by Chillon's walls:
A thousand feet in depth below
Its massy waters meet and flow;
Thus much the fathom-line was sent   110
From Chillon's snow-white battlement,
    Which round about the wave inthrals:
A double dungeon wall and wave
Have made—and like a living grave
Below the surface of the lake
The dark vault lies wherein we lay,[2]
We heard it ripple night and day;
    Sounding o'er our heads it knock'd;
And I have felt the winter's spray
Wash through the bars when winds were
        high   120
And wanton in the happy sky;
    And then the very rock hath rock'd,
    And I have felt it shake, unshock'd,
Because I could have smiled to see
The death that would have set me free.

---

1 Lake Geneva.
2 The vault was not actually below the level of the lake.

VII

I said my nearer brother pined,
I said his mighty heart declined,
He loathed and put away his food;
It was not that 'twas coarse and rude,
For we were used to hunter's fare,   130
And for the like had little care:
The milk drawn from the mountain goat
Was changed for water from the moat,
Our bread was such as captives' tears
Have moisten'd many a thousand years,
Since man first pent his fellow men
Like brutes within an iron den;
But what were these to us or him?
These wasted not his heart or limb;
My brother's soul was of that mould   140
Which in a palace had grown cold,
Had his free breathing been denied
The range of the steep mountain's side;
But why delay the truth?—he died.
I saw, and could not hold his head,
Nor reach his dying hand—nor dead.—
Though hard I strove, but strove in vain,
To rend and gnash my bonds in twain.
He died, and they unlock'd his chain,
And scoop'd for him a shallow grave   150
Even from the cold earth of our cave.
I begg'd them as a boon to lay
His corse in dust whereon the day
Might shine—it was a foolish thought,
But then within my brain it wrought,
That even in death his freeborn breast
In such a dungeon could not rest.
I might have spared my idle prayer—
They coldly laugh'd, and laid him there:
The flat and turfless earth above   160
The being we so much did love;
His empty chain above it leant,
Such murder's fitting monument!

VIII

But he, the favourite and the flower,
Most cherish'd since his natal hour,
His mother's image in fair face,
The infant love of all his race.
His martyr'd father's dearest thought,
My latest care, for whom I sought
To hoard my life, that his might be   170
Less wretched now, and one day free;
He, too, who yet had held untired
A spirit natural or inspired—
He, too, was struck, and day by day
Was wither'd on the stalk away,
Oh, God! it is a fearful thing

To see the human soul take wing
In any shape, in any mood:
I've seen it rushing forth in blood,
I've seen it on the breaking ocean
Strive with a swoln convulsive motion,
I've seen the sick and ghastly bed
Of Sin delirious with its dread;
But these were horrors—this was woe
Unmix'd with such—but sure and slow:
He faded, and so calm and meek,
So softly worn, so sweetly weak,
So tearless, yet so tender, kind,
And grieved for those he left behind;
With all the while a cheek whose bloom   190
Was as a mockery of the tomb,
Whose tints as gently sunk away
As a departing rainbow's ray;
An eye of most transparent light,
That almost made the dungeon bright,
And not a word of murmur, not
A groan o'er his untimely lot,—
A little talk of better days,
A little hope my own to raise,
For I was sunk in silence—lost   200
In this last loss, of all the most;
And then the sighs he would suppress
Of fainting nature's feebleness,
More slowly drawn, grew less and less:
I listen'd, but I could not hear;
I call'd, for I was wild with fear;
I knew 'twas hopeless, but my dread
Would not be thus admonished;
I call'd, and thought I heard a sound—
I burst my chain with one strong bound,   210
And rush'd to him:—I found him not,
I only stirr'd in this black spot,
I only lived, *I* only drew
The accursed breath of dungeon-dew;
The last, the sole, the dearest link
Between me and the eternal brink,
Which bound me to my failing race,
Was broken in this fatal place.
One on the earth, and one beneath—
My brothers—both had ceased to breathe: 220
I took that hand which lay so still,
Alas! my own was full as chill;
I had not strength to stir, or strive,
But felt that I was still alive—
A frantic feeling, when we know
That what we love shall ne'er be so.
    I know not why
    I could not die,
I had no earthly hope but faith,
And that forbade a selfish death.   230

IX

What next befell me then and there
    I know not well—I never knew—
First came the loss of light, and air,
    And then of darkness too:
I had no thought, no feeling—none—
Among the stones I stood a stone,
And was, scarce conscious what I wist,
As shrubless crags within the mist;
For all was blank, and bleak, and grey;
It was not night, it was not day;   240
It was not even the dungeon-light,
So hateful to my heavy sight,
But vacancy absorbing space,
And fixedness without a place;
There were no stars, no earth, no time,
No check, no change, no good, no crime,
But silence, and a stirless breath
Which neither was of life nor death;
A sea of stagnant idleness,
Blind, boundless, mute, and motionless!   250

X

A light broke in upon my brain,—
    It was the carol of a bird;
It ceased, and then it came again,
    The sweetest song ear ever heard,
And mine was thankful till my eyes
Ran over with the glad surprise,
And they that moment could not see
I was the mate of misery;
But then by dull degrees came back
My senses to their wonted track;   260
I saw the dungeon walls and floor
Close slowly round me as before,
I saw the glimmer of the sun
Creeping as it before had done,
But through the crevice where it came
That bird was perch'd, as fond and tame,
    And tamer than upon the tree;
A lovely bird, with azure wings,
And song that said a thousand things,
    And seem'd to say them all for me!   270
I never saw its like before,
I ne'er shall see its likeness more:
It seem'd like me to want a mate,
But was not half so desolate,
And it was come to love me when
None lived to love me so again,
And cheering from my dungeon's brink,
Had brought me back to feel and think.
I know not if it late were free,
    Or broke its cage to perch on mine,   280

But knowing well captivity,
 Sweet bird! I could not wish for thine!
Or if it were, in winged guise,
A visitant from Paradise;
For—Heaven forgive that thought! the while
Which made me both to weep and smile—
I sometimes deem'd that it might be
My brother's soul come down to me;
But then at last away it flew,
And then 'twas mortal well I knew,   290
For he would never thus have flown,
And left me twice so doubly lone,
Lone as the corse within its shroud,
Lone as a solitary cloud,—
 A single cloud on a sunny day,
While all the rest of heaven is clear,
A frown upon the atmosphere,
That hath no business to appear
 When skies are blue, and earth is gay.

              XI

A kind of change came in my fate,
My keepers grew compassionate;   300
I know not what had made them so,
They were inured to sights of woe,
But so it was:—my broken chain
With links unfasten'd did remain,
And it was liberty to stride
Along my cell from side to side,
And up and down, and then athwart,
And tread it over every part;
And round the pillars one by one,
Returning where my walk begun,   310
Avoiding only, as I trod,
My brothers' graves without a sod;
For if I thought with heedless tread
My step profaned their lowly bed,
My breath came gaspingly and thick,
And my crush'd heart felt blind and sick.

              XII

I made a footing in the wall,
 It was not therefrom to escape,
For I had buried one and all   320
 Who loved me in a human shape;
And the whole earth would henceforth be
A wider prison unto me:
No child, no sire, no kin had I,
No partner in my misery;
I thought of this, and I was glad,
For thought of them had made me mad;
But I was curious to ascend
To my barr'd windows, and to bend

Once more, upon the mountains high,   330
The quiet of a loving eye.

              XIII

I saw them, and they were the same,
They were not changed like me in frame;
I saw their thousand years of snow
On high—their wide long lake below,
And the blue Rhone in fullest flow;
I heard the torrents leap and gush
O'er channell'd rock and broken bush;
I saw the white-wall'd distant town,
And whiter sails go skimming down;   340
And then there was a little isle,
Which in my very face did smile,
 The only one in view;
A small green isle, it seem'd no more,
Scarce broader than my dungeon floor,
But in it there were three tall trees,
And o'er it blew the mountain breeze,
And by it there were waters flowing,
And on it there were young flowers growing,
 Of gentle breath and hue.   350
The fish swam by the castle wall,
And they seem'd joyous each and all;
The eagle rode the rising blast,
Methought he never flew so fast
As then to me he seem'd to fly;
And then new tears came in my eye,
And I felt troubled—and would fain
I had not left my recent chain;
And when I did descend again,
The darkness of my dim abode   360
Fell on me as a heavy load;
It was as is a new-dug grave,
Closing o'er one we sought to save,—
And yet my glance, too much opprest,
Had almost need of such a rest.

              XIV

It might be months, or years, or days,
 I kept no count, I took no note,
I had no hope my eyes to raise,
 And clear them of their dreary mote;
At last men came to set me free;   370
 I ask'd not why, and reck'd not where;
It was at length the same to me,
Fetter'd or fetterless to be,
 I learn'd to love despair.
And thus when they appear'd at last,
And all my bonds aside were cast,
These heavy walls to me had grown
A hermitage—and all my own!

And half I felt as they were come
To tear me from a second home: 380
With spiders I had friendship made,
And watch'd them in their sullen trade,
Had seen the mice by moonlight play,
And why should I feel less than they?
We were all inmates of one place,
And I, the monarch of each race,
Had power to kill—yet, strange to tell!
In quiet we had learn'd to dwell;
My very chains and I grew friends,
So much a long communion tends   390
To make us what we are:—even I
Regain'd my freedom with a sigh.

    June 1816   1816

DARKNESS

I HAD a dream, which was not all a dream.
The bright sun was extinguish'd, and the stars
Did wander darkling in the eternal space,
Rayless, and pathless, and the icy earth
Swung blind and blackening in the moonless air;
Morn came and went—and came, and brought
   no day,
And men forgot their passions in the dread
Of this their desolation; and all hearts
Were chill'd into a selfish prayer for light:
And they did live by watchfires—and the
   thrones,   10
The palaces of crowned kings—the huts,
The habitations of all things which dwell,
Were burnt for beacons; cities were consumed,
And men were gather'd round their blazing
   homes
To look once more into each other's face;
Happy were those who dwelt within the eye
Of the volcanos, and their mountain-torch:
A fearful hope was all the world contain'd;
Forests were set on fire—but hour by hour
They fell and faded—and the crackling trunks 20
Extinguish'd with a crash—and all was black.
The brows of men by the despairing light
Wore an unearthly aspect, as by fits
The flashes fell upon them; some lay down
And hid their eyes and wept; and some did rest
Their chins upon their clenched hands, and
   smiled;
And others hurried to and fro, and fed
Their funeral piles with fuel, and look'd up
With mad disquietude on the dull sky,
The pall of a past world; and then again   30
With curses cast them down upon the dust,

And gnash'd their teeth and howl'd: the wild
   birds shriek'd
And, terrified, did flutter on the ground,
And flap their useless wings; the wildest brutes
Came tame and tremulous; and vipers crawl'd
And twined themselves among the multitude,
Hissing, but stingless—they were slain for food.
And War, which for a moment was no more,
Did glut himself again:—a meal was bought
With blood, and each sate sullenly apart   40
Gorging himself in gloom: no love was left;
All earth was but one thought—and that was
   death
Immediate and inglorious; and the pang
Of famine fed upon all entrails—men
Died, and their bones were tombless as their
   flesh;
The meagre by the meagre were devour'd,
Even dogs assail'd their masters, all save one,
And he was faithful to a corse, and kept
The birds and beasts and famish'd men at bay,
Till hunger clung[1] them, or the dropping dead 50
Lured their lank jaws; himself sought out no
   food,
But with a piteous and perpetual moan,
And a quick desolate cry, licking the hand
Which answer'd not with a caress—he died.
The crowd was famish'd by degrees; but two
Of an enormous city did survive,
And they were enemies: they met beside
The dying embers of an altar-place
Where had been heap'd a mass of holy things
For an unholy usage; they raked up,   60
And shivering scraped with their cold skeleton
   hands
The feeble ashes, and their feeble breath
Blew for a little life, and made a flame
Which was a mockery; then they lifted up
Their eyes as it grew lighter, and beheld
Each other's aspects—saw, and shriek'd, and
   died—
Even of their mutual hideousness they died,
Unknowing who he was upon whose brow
Famine had written Fiend. The world was void,
The populous and the powerful was a lump,   70
Seasonless, herbless, treeless, manless, lifeless,
A lump of death—a chaos of hard clay.
The rivers, lakes, and ocean all stood still,
And nothing stirr'd within their silent depths;
Ships sailorless lay rotting on the sea,
And their masts fell down piecemeal: as they
   dropp'd
They slept on the abyss without a surge—

---

1 shriveled.

The waves were dead; the tides were in their
    grave,
The moon, their mistress, had expired before;
The winds were wither'd in the stagnant air,   80
And the clouds perish'd; Darkness had no need
Of aid from them—She was the Universe.

    Diodati, July 1816   1816

CHILDE HAROLD'S PILGRIMAGE

[*Childe Harold* is the best-known and the best travel
poem in the language, written, Byron tells us, for the
most part amid the scenes it attempts to describe. Cantos
I and II relate in a medley of many moods the author's
observations during his Mediterranean tour of 1810–11.
In the *Preface*, Byron expressly states that Childe Harold
is the child of imagination and not a real personage.
When, however, in 1816 'self-exiled' Harold wanders
forth again, he is undeniably Byron himself 'trailing the
pageant of his bleeding heart across Europe.' Canto III
was written in Switzerland amidst the Alps in the companionship of Shelley 'who dosed him with Wordsworth.' The tone is dramatic and memorable for the impassioned portrayal of historical events and figures as
well as for the striking vigor of its nature descriptions.
Canto IV, written in 1818 in Venice, is less a continuation of Canto III than a different poem and 'treats more
of works of art than Nature.' It was inspired by the antiquarian studies of Hobhouse. It portrays the decaying
glories of Venice and the imperial ruins of Rome, and
concludes with the famous apostrophe to ocean.]

*A fin que cette application vous forçât à penser à
autre chose: il n'y a en vérité de remède que celui-
là et le temps.*[1]
LETTRE DU ROI DE PRUSSE A D'ALEMBERT, 7 SEPT., 1776.

CANTO THE THIRD

I

Is thy face like thy mother's, my fair child!
ADA! sole daughter of my house and heart?
When last I saw thy young blue eyes they
    smiled,
And then we parted,—not as now we part,
But with a hope.[2]—
                Awaking with a start,
The waters heave around me; and on high
The winds lift up their voices: I depart,
Whither I know not; but the hour's gone by,
When Albion's[3] lessening shores could grieve or
    glad mine eye.

II

Once more upon the waters! yet once
    more!   10
And the waves bound beneath me as a steed
That knows his rider. Welcome to their roar!
Swift be their guidance, wheresoe'er it lead!
Though the strain'd mast should quiver as a
    reed,
And the rent canvas fluttering strew the gale,
Still must I on; for I am as a weed,
Flung from the rock, on Ocean's foam to sail
Where'er the surge may sweep, the tempest's
    breath prevail.

III

In my youth's summer I did sing of One,[4]
The wandering outlaw of his own dark
    mind;
Again I seize the theme, then but begun,   20
And bear it with me, as the rushing wind
Bears the cloud onwards: in that Tale I find
The furrows of long thought, and dried-up
    tears,
Which, ebbing, leave a sterile track behind,
O'er which all heavily the journeying years
Plod the last sands of life,—where not a flower
    appears.

IV

Since my young days of passion—joy, or pain,
Perchance my heart and harp have lost a string,
And both may jar: it may be, that in vain   30
I would essay as I have sung to sing.
Yet, though a dreary strain, to this I cling;
So that it wean me from the weary dream
Of selfish grief or gladness—so it fling
Forgetfulness around me—it shall seem
To me, though to none else, a not ungrateful
    theme.

V

He, who grown aged in this world of woe,
In deeds, not years, piercing the depths of life,
So that no wonder waits him; nor below
Can love or sorrow, fame, ambition, strife,   40
Cut to his heart again with the keen knife
Of silent, sharp endurance: he can tell
Why thought seeks refuge in lone caves, yet
    rife

---

1 'In order that this work may force you to think of something
else: there is in truth no remedy but that and time.'

2 When Byron last saw his five-weeks-old daughter, Augusta
Ada, it was with the hope of seeing her again and of effecting a
reconciliation with his wife. However, that hope proved groundless; he never saw his daughter again.

3 England's.

---

4 Childe Harold, the imaginary character in Cantos I and II of
the poem through whose person in rather thin disguise Byron reflects his own reactions to the scenes of his early wanderings.

With airy images, and shapes which dwell
Still unimpair'd, though old, in the soul's haunted
    cell.

VI

'Tis to create, and in creating live
A being more intense, that we endow
With form our fancy, gaining as we give
The life we image, even as I do now.
What am I? Nothing: but not so art thou,   50
Soul of my thought! with whom I traverse
    earth,
Invisible but gazing, as I glow
  Mix'd with thy spirit, blended with thy birth,
And feeling still with thee in my crush'd feelings'
    dearth.

VII

Yet must I think less wildly:—I *have* thought
Too long and darkly, till my brain became,
In its own eddy boiling and o'erwrought,
A whirling gulf of phantasy and flame:
And thus, untaught in youth my heart to tame,
My springs of life were poison'd. 'Tis too
    late!   60
Yet am I changed; though still enough the
    same
In strength to bear what time cannot abate,
And feed on bitter fruits without accusing Fate.

VIII

Something too much of this:—but now 'tis
    past,
And the spell closes with its silent seal.
Long absent HAROLD re-appears at last;
He of the breast which fain no more would feel,
Wrung with the wounds which kill not, but
    ne'er heal;
Yet Time, who changes all, had alter'd him
In soul and aspect as in age: years steal   70
Fire from the mind as vigour from the limb;
And life's enchanted cup but sparkles near the
    brim.

IX

His had been quaff'd too quickly, and he found
The dregs were wormwood;[5] but he fill'd again,
And from a purer fount, on holier ground,[6]
And deem'd its spring perpetual; but in vain!
Still round him clung invisibly a chain
Which gall'd for ever, fettering though unseen,

And heavy though it clank'd not; worn with
    pain
Which pined although it spoke not, and grew
    keen,   80
Entering with every step he took through many
    a scene.

X

Secure in guarded coldness, he had mix'd
Again in fancied safety with his kind,
And deem'd his spirit now so firmly fix'd
And sheath'd with an invulnerable mind,
That, if no joy, no sorrow lurk'd behind;
And he, as one, might 'midst the many stand
Unheeded, searching through the crowd to find
Fit speculation such as in strange land
He found in wonder-works of God and Nature's
    hand.   90

XI

But who can view the ripen'd rose, nor seek
To wear it? who can curiously behold
The smoothness and the sheen of beauty's
    cheek,
Nor feel the heart can never all grow old?
Who can contemplate Fame through clouds
    unfold
The star which rises o'er her steep, nor climb?
Harold, once more within the vortex, roll'd
On with the giddy circle, chasing Time,
Yet with a nobler aim than in his youth's fond[7]
    prime.

XII

But soon he knew himself the most unfit   100
Of men to herd with Man; with whom he held
Little in common; untaught to submit
His thoughts to others, though his soul was
    quell'd
In youth by his own thoughts; still uncom-
    pell'd,
He would not yield dominion of his mind
To spirits against whom his own rebell'd;
Proud though in desolation; which could find
A life within itself, to breathe without mankind.

XIII

Where rose the mountains, there to him were
    friends;
Where roll'd the ocean, thereon was his
    home;   110

---

5 bitter. Wormwood is a plant of very bitter taste.
6 Greece.

7 foolish.

Where a blue sky, and glowing clime, extends,
He had the passion and the power to roam;
The desert, forest, cavern, breaker's foam,
Were unto him companionship; they spake
A mutual language, clearer than the tome
Of his land's tongue, which he would oft for-
sake
For Nature's pages glass'd by sunbeams on the
lake.

XIV

Like the Chaldean, he could watch the stars,
Till he had peopled them with beings bright
As their own beams; and earth, and earthborn
jars,   120
And human frailties, were forgotten quite:
Could he have kept his spirit to that flight
He had been happy; but this clay will sink
Its spark immortal, envying it the light
To which it mounts, as if to break the link
That keeps us from yon heaven which woos us to
its brink.

XV

But in Man's dwellings he became a thing
Restless and worn, and stern and wearisome,
Droop'd as a wild-born falcon with clipt
wing,
To whom the boundless air alone were
home: 130
Then came his fit again,[8] which to o'ercome,
As eagerly the barr'd-up bird will beat
His breast and beak against his wiry dome
Till the blood tinge his plumage, so the heat
Of his impeded soul would through his bosom
eat.

XVI

Self-exiled Harold wanders forth again,
With nought of hope left, but with less of
gloom;
The very knowledge that he lived in vain,
That all was over on this side the tomb,
Had made Despair a smilingness assume,   140
Which, though 'twere wild,—as on the plun-
der'd wreck
When mariners would madly meet their doom
With draughts intemperate on the sinking
deck,—
Did yet inspire a cheer, which he forbore to
check.

XVII

Stop!—for thy tread is on an Empire's dust!
An Earthquake's spoil is sepulchred below!
Is the spot mark'd with no colossal bust?
Nor column trophied for triumphal show?
None;[9] but the moral's truth tells simpler so,
As the ground was before, thus let it be;—   150
How that red rain hath made the harvest
grow!
And is this all the world has gain'd by thee,
Thou first and last of fields! king-making Vic-
tory?[10]

XVIII

And Harold stands upon this place of skulls,
The grave of France, the deadly Waterloo!
How in an hour the power which gave annuls
Its gifts, transferring fame as fleeting too!
In 'pride of place'[11] here last the eagle[12] flew,
Then tore with bloody talon the rent plain,
Pierced by the shaft of banded nations
through;   160
Ambition's life and labours all were vain;
He wears the shatter'd links of the world's
broken chain.

XIX

Fit retribution! Gaul may champ the bit
And foam in fetters;—but is Earth more free?
Did nations combat to make *One* submit;
Or league to teach all kings true sovereignty?
What! shall reviving Thraldom again be
The patch'd-up idol of enlighten'd days?
Shall we, who struck the Lion down, shall we
Pay the Wolf homage? proffering lowly
gaze   170
And servile knees to thrones? No; *prove* before ye
praise!

XX

If not, o'er one fallen despot boast no more!
In vain fair cheeks were furrow'd with hot
tears
For Europe's flowers long rooted up before
The trampler of her vineyards; in vain years
Of death, depopulation, bondage, fears,
Have all been borne, and broken by the accord

---

8 His mood returned—an echo of 'Then comes my fit again,'
Macbeth, III, iv, 21.

9 The monuments at Waterloo had not yet been erected when
Byron visited that historic ground less than a year after the battle.
10 Byron saw ironically that Waterloo only secured Europe's
monarchs more firmly upon their thrones.
11 Pride of place is a term of falconry, and means the highest
pitch of flight.—(Byron.) See *Macbeth*, II, iv, 12.
12 Napoleon.

Of roused-up millions; all that most endears
Glory, is when the myrtle wreathes a sword
Such as Harmodius[13] drew on Athens' tyrant
 lord.   180

XXI

There was a sound of revelry by night,
And Belgium's capital had gather'd then
Her Beauty and her Chivalry, and bright
The lamps shone o'er fair women and brave
 men;[14]
A thousand hearts beat happily; and when
Music arose with its voluptuous swell,
Soft eyes look'd love to eyes which spake again,
And all went merry as a marriage bell;
But hush! hark! a deep sound strikes like a rising
 knell!

XXII

Did ye not hear it?—No; 'twas but the
 wind,   190
Or the car rattling o'er the stony street;
On with the dance! let joy be unconfined;
No sleep till morn, when Youth and Pleasure
 meet
To chase the glowing Hours with flying feet—
But hark!—that heavy sound breaks in once
 more,
As if the clouds its echo would repeat;
And nearer, clearer, deadlier than before!
Arm! Arm! it is—it is—the cannon's opening
 roar!

XXIII

Within a window'd niche of that high hall
Sate Brunswick's fated chieftain;[15] he did
 hear   200
That sound the first amidst the festival,
And caught its tone with Death's prophetic
 ear;
And when they smiled because he deem'd it
 near,
His heart more truly knew that peal too well
Which stretch'd his father on a bloody bier,

And roused the vengeance blood alone could
 quell;
He rush'd into the field, and, foremost fighting,
 fell.

XXIV

Ah! then and there was hurrying to and fro,
And gathering tears, and tremblings of dis-
 tress,
And cheeks all pale, which but an hour ago 210
Blush'd at the praise of their own loveliness;
And there were sudden partings, such as press
The life from out young hearts, and choking
 sighs
Which ne'er might be repeated; who could
 guess
If ever more should meet those mutual eyes,
Since upon night so sweet such awful morn could
 rise!

First waltz in 1812

XXV

And there was mounting in hot haste: the
 steed,
The mustering squadron, and the clattering
 car,
Went pouring forward with impetuous speed,
And swiftly forming in the ranks of war; 220
And the deep thunder peal on peal afar;
And near, the beat of the alarming drum
Roused up the soldier ere the morning star;
While throng'd the citizens with terror dumb,
Or whispering, with white lips—'The foe! they
 come! they come!'

XXVI

And wild and high the 'Cameron's gathering'[16]
 rose!
The war-note of Lochiel,[17] which Albyn's[18]
 hills
Have heard, and heard, too, have her Saxon
 foes:—
How in the noon of night that pibroch[19] thrills,
Savage and shrill! But with the breath which
 fills   230
Their mountain-pipe, so fill the mountaineers
With the fierce native daring which instils
The stirring memory of a thousand years,

---

13 Harmodius and Aristogiton with daggers concealed in myrtle
assassinated the Athenian tyrant Hipparchus during a religious
festival, 514 B.C.
14 The Duchess of Richmond's famous ball, 15 June, 1815, on
the eve of the battle of Quatre-Bras and three days before Waterloo.
15 The Duke of Brunswick, fighting in the front line at Quatre-
Bras, was one of the first to fall. His father had been killed at the
battle of Auerstädt in 1806.

16 war song of the Cameron clan.
17 Chief of the Highland clan of the Camerons.
18 Scotland's.
19 martial bagpipe music.

And Evan's, Donald's[20] fame rings in each clans-
man's ears!

XXVII

And Ardennes[21] waves above them her green
  leaves,
Dewy with nature's tear-drops as they pass,
Grieving, if aught inanimate e'er grieves,
Over the unreturning brave,—alas!
Ere evening to be trodden like the grass
Which now beneath them, but above shall
  grow   240
In its next verdure, when this fiery mass
Of living valour, rolling on the foe
And burning with high hope shall moulder cold
  and low.

XXVIII

Last noon beheld them full of lusty life,
Last eve in Beauty's circle proudly gay,
The midnight brought the signal-sound of
  strife,
The morn the marshalling in arms,—the day
Battle's magnificently stern array!
The thunder-clouds close o'er it, which when
  rent
The earth is cover'd thick with other clay, 250
Which her own clay shall cover, heap'd and
  pent,
Rider and horse,—friend, foe,—in one red burial
  blent!

XXIX

Their praise is hymn'd by loftier harps than
  mine:
Yet one[22] I would select from that proud
  throng,
Partly because they blend me with his line,
And partly that I did his sire some wrong,
And partly that bright names will hallow song;
And his was of the bravest, and when shower'd
The death-bolts deadliest the thinn'd files
  along,
Even where the thickest of war's tempest
  lower'd,   260
They reach'd no nobler breast than thine, young
  gallant Howard!

XXX

There have been tears and breaking hearts for
  thee,
And mine were nothing had I such to give;
But when I stood beneath the fresh green tree,
Which living waves where thou didst cease to
  live,
And saw around me the wide field revive
With fruits and fertile promise, and the Spring
Came forth her work of gladness to contrive,
With all her reckless birds upon the wing,
I turn'd from all she brought to those she could
  not bring.[23]   270

XXXI

I turn'd to thee, to thousands, of whom each
And one as all a ghastly gap did make
In his own kind and kindred, whom to teach
Forgetfulness were mercy for their sake;
The Archangel's trump, not Glory's, must
  awake
Those whom they thirst for; though the sound
  of Fame
May for a moment soothe, it cannot slake
The fever of vain longing, and the name
So honour'd but assumes a stronger, bitterer
  claim.

XXXII

They mourn, but smile at length; and, smiling,
  mourn;   280
The tree will wither long before it fall;
The hull drives on, though mast and sail be
  torn;
The roof-tree sinks, but moulders on the hall
In massy hoariness; the ruin'd wall
Stands when its wind-worn battlements are
  gone;
The bars survive the captive they enthral;
The day drags through, though storms keep
  out the sun;
And thus the heart will break, yet brokenly live
  on:

XXXIII

Even as a broken mirror, which the glass
In every fragment multiplies; and makes   290

---

20 Sir Evan Cameron, and his descendant, Donald, the 'gentle
Lochiel' of the forty-five.—(Byron.)
21 The wood of Soignies . . . a remnant of the forest of Ardennes.
—(Byron.)
22 Major Frederick Howard, Byron's second cousin, whose
father, the Earl of Carlisle, Byron had satirized in *English Bards
and Scotch Reviewers*.

23 My guide from Mount St. Jean over the field seemed intelligent and accurate. .The place where Major Howard fell was not
far from two tall and solitary trees. . . . Beneath these he died
and was buried. The body has since been removed to England. A
small hollow for the present marks where it lay, but will probably soon be effaced; the plough has been upon it, and the grain
is.—(Byron.)

A thousand images of one that was,
The same, and still the more, the more it
      breaks;
And thus the heart will do which not forsakes,
Living in shatter'd guise; and still, and cold,
And bloodless, with its sleepless sorrow aches,
Yet withers on till all without is old,
Showing no visible sign, for such things are
      untold.

XXXIV

There is a very life in our despair,
Vitality of poison,—a quick root
Which feeds these deadly branches; for it
      were   300
As nothing did we die; but Life will suit
Itself to Sorrow's most detested fruit,
Like to the apples[24] on the Dead Sea's shore,
All ashes to the taste: Did man compute
Existence by enjoyment, and count o'er
Such hours 'gainst years of life,—say, would he
      name threescore?

XXXV

The Psalmist number'd out the years of man:
They are enough; and if thy tale be *true,*
Thou, who didst grudge him even that fleeting
      span,
More than enough, thou fatal Waterloo!   310
Millions of tongues record thee, and anew
Their children's lips shall echo them, and say—
'Here, where the sword united nations drew,
Our countrymen were warring on that day!'
And this is much, and all which will not pass
      away.

XXXVI

There sunk the greatest,[25] nor the worst of men,
Whose spirit, antithetically mixt,
One moment of the mightiest, and again
On little objects with like firmness fixt;
Extreme in all things! hadst thou been be-
      twixt,   320
Thy throne had still been thine, or never been;
For daring made thy rise as fall: thou seek'st
Even now to re-assume the imperial mien,
And shake again the world, the Thunderer of the
      scene!

---

24 The (fabled) apples on the brink of the lake Asphaltites were
said to be fair without, and, within, ashes.—(Byron.)
25 Napoleon.

XXXVII

Conqueror and captive of the earth art thou!
She trembles at thee still, and thy wild name
Was ne'er more bruited in men's minds than
      now
That thou art nothing, save the jest of Fame,
Who woo'd thee once, thy vassal, and became
The flatterer of thy fierceness, till thou wert 330
A god unto thyself; nor less the same
To the astounded kingdoms all inert,
Who deem'd thee for a time whate'er thou didst
      assert.

XXXVIII

Oh, more or less than man—in high or low,
Battling with nations, flying from the field;
Now making monarchs' necks thy footstool,
      now
More than thy meanest soldier taught to yield;
An empire thou couldst crush, command, re-
      build,
But govern not thy pettiest passion, nor,
However deeply in men's spirits skill'd,   340
Look through thine own, nor curb the lust of
      war,
Nor learn that tempted Fate will leave the loftiest
      star.

XXXIX

Yet well thy soul hath brook'd the turning tide
With that untaught innate philosophy,
Which, be it wisdom, coldness, or deep pride,
Is gall and wormwood to an enemy.
When the whole host of hatred stood hard by,
To watch and mock thee shrinking, thou hast
      smiled
With a sedate and all-enduring eye;—
When Fortune fled her spoil'd and favourite
      child,   350
He stood unbow'd beneath the ills upon him
      piled.

XL

Sager than in thy fortunes; for in them
Ambition steel'd thee on too far to show
That just habitual scorn, which could contemn
Men and their thoughts; 'twas wise to feel, not
      so
To wear it ever on thy lip and brow,
And spurn the instruments thou wert to use
Till they were turn'd unto thine overthrow:
'Tis but a worthless world to win or lose;

So hath it proved to thee, and all such lot who
    choose.   360

XLI

If, like a tower upon a headland rock,
Thou hadst been made to stand or fall alone,
Such scorn of man had help'd to brave the
    shock;
But men's thoughts were the steps which
    paved thy throne,
Their admiration thy best weapon shone;
The part of Philip's son[26] was thine, not then
(Unless aside thy purple had been thrown)
Like stern Diogenes[27] to mock at men;
For sceptred cynics[28] earth were far too wide a
    den.

XLII

But quiet to quick bosoms is a hell,   370
And *there* hath been thy bane; there is a fire
And motion of the soul which will not dwell
In its own narrow being, but aspire
Beyond the fitting medium of desire;
And, but once kindled, quenchless evermore,
Preys upon high adventure, nor can tire
Of aught but rest; a fever at the core,
Fatal to him who bears, to all who ever bore.

XLIII

This makes the madmen who have made men
    mad
By their contagion; Conquerors and
    Kings,   380
Founders of sects and systems, to whom add
Sophists, Bards, Statesmen, all unquiet things
Which stir too strongly the soul's secret
    springs,
And are themselves the fools to those they fool;
Envied, yet how unenviable! what stings
Are theirs! One breast laid open were a school
Which would unteach mankind the lust to shine
    or rule:

26 Alexander the Great.
27 the Greek cynic philosopher who sought in vain for an honest man.
28 The great error of Napoleon, 'if we have writ our annals true,' was a continued obtrusion on mankind of his want of all community of feeling for or with them; perhaps more offensive to human vanity than the active cruelty of more trembling and suspicious tyranny. Such were his speeches to public assemblies as well as individuals; and the single expression which he is said to have used on returning to Paris after the Russian winter had destroyed his army, rubbing his hands over a fire. 'This is pleasanter than Moscow,' would probably alienate more favour from his cause than the destruction and reverses which led to the remark.
—(Byron.)

XLIV

Their breath is agitation, and their life
A storm whereon they ride, to sink at last,
And yet so nursed and bigoted to strife,   390
That should their days, surviving perils past,
Melt to calm twilight, they feel overcast
With sorrow and supineness, and so die;
Even as a flame unfed, which runs to waste
With its own flickering, or a sword laid by,
Which eats into itself, and rusts ingloriously.

XLV

He who ascends to mountain-tops, shall find
The loftiest peaks most wrapt in clouds and
    snow;
He who surpasses or subdues mankind,
Must look down on the hate of those
    below.   400
Though high *above* the sun of glory glow,
And far *beneath* the earth and ocean spread,
Round him are icy rocks, and loudly blow
Contending tempests on his naked head,
And thus reward the toils which to those sum-
    mits led.

XLVI

Away with these! true Wisdom's world will be
Within its own creation, or in thine,
Maternal Nature! for who teems like thee,
Thus on the banks of thy majestic Rhine?
There Harold gazes on a work divine,   410
A blending of all beauties; streams and dells,
Fruit, foliage, crag, wood, cornfield, mountain,
    vine,
And chiefless castles breathing stern farewells
From grey but leafy walls, where Ruin greenly
    dwells.

XLVII

And there they stand, as stands a lofty mind,
Worn, but unstooping to the baser crowd,
All tenantless, save to the crannying wind,
Or holding dark communion with the cloud.
There was a day when they were young and
    proud;
Banners on high, and battles[29] pass'd
    below;   420
But they who fought are in a bloody shroud,
And those which waved are shredless dust ere
    now,
And the bleak battlements shall bear no future
    blow.

29 battalions.

XLVIII

Beneath those battlements, within those walls,
Power dwelt amidst her passions; in proud
state
Each robber chief upheld his armed halls,
Doing his evil will, nor less elate
Than mightier heroes of a longer date.
What want these outlaws conquerors should
have[30]
But history's purchased page to call them
great?   430
A wider space, an ornamental grave?
Their hopes were not less warm, their souls were
full as brave.

XLIX

In their baronial feuds and single fields,
What deeds of prowess unrecorded died!
And Love, which lent a blazon to their shields,
With emblems well devised by amorous pride,
Through all the mail of iron hearts would
glide;
But still their flame was fierceness, and drew
on
Keen contest and destruction near allied,
And many a tower for some fair mischief
won,   440
Saw the discolour'd Rhine beneath its ruin run.

L

But Thou, exulting and abounding river!
Making thy waves a blessing as they flow
Through banks whose beauty would endure
for ever
Could man but leave thy bright creation so,
Nor its fair promise from the surface mow
With the sharp scythe of conflict,—then to see
Thy valley of sweet waters, were to know
Earth paved like Heaven; and to seem such to
me,
Even now what wants thy stream?—that it
should Lethe be.   450

LI

A thousand battles have assail'd thy banks,
But these and half their fame have pass'd away,
And Slaughter heap'd on high his weltering
ranks;

Their very graves are gone, and what are they?
Thy tide wash'd down the blood of yesterday,
And all was stainless, and on thy clear stream
Glass'd, with its dancing light, the sunny ray;
But o'er the blacken'd memory's blighting
dream
Thy waves would vainly roll, all sweeping as they
seem.

LII

Thus Harold inly said, and pass'd along,   460
Yet not insensible to all which here
Awoke the jocund birds to early song
In glens which might have made even exile
dear:
Though on his brow were graven lines austere,
And tranquil sternness, which had ta'en the
place
Of feelings fierier far but less severe,
Joy was not always absent from his face,
But o'er it in such scenes would steal with tran-
sient trace.

LIII

Nor was all love shut from him, though his
days
Of passion had consumed themselves to
dust.   470
It is in vain that we would coldly gaze
On such as smile upon us; the heart must
Leap kindly back to kindness, though disgust
Hath wean'd it from all worldlings: thus he
felt,
For there was soft remembrance, and sweet
trust
In one fond breast,[31] to which his own would
melt,
And in its tenderer hour on that his bosom dwelt.

LIV

And he had learn'd to love,—I know not why,
For this in such as him seems strange of
mood,—
The helpless looks of blooming infancy,   480
Even in its earliest nurture; what subdued,
To change like this, a mind so far imbued
With scorn of man, it little boots to know;
But thus it was; and though in solitude
Small power the nipp'd affections have to
grow,

---

30   'What wants that knave
          That a King should have?'
was King James's question on meeting Johnny Armstrong and
his followers in full accoutrement.—(Byron.)

31 Byron's half sister, Augusta Leigh.

In him this glow'd when all beside had ceased to
  glow.

LV

And there was one soft breast, as hath been
  said,
Which unto his was bound by stronger ties
Than the church links withal; and, though
  unwed,
That love was pure, and, far above dis-
  guise,   490
Had stood the test of mortal enmities
Still undivided, and cemented more
By peril, dreaded most in female eyes;
But this was firm, and from a foreign shore
Well to that heart might his these absent greet-
  ings pour!

1

The castled crag of Drachenfels[32]
Frowns o'er the wide and winding Rhine,
Whose breast of waters broadly swells
Between the banks which bear the vine,
And hills all rich with blossom'd trees,   500
And fields which promise corn and wine,
And scatter'd cities crowning these,
Whose far white walls along them shine,
Have strew'd a scene, which I should see
With double joy wert *thou* with me.

2

And peasant girls, with deep blue eyes,
And hands which offer early flowers,
Walk smiling o'er this paradise;
Above, the frequent feudal towers
Through green leaves lift their walls of
  gray;   510
And many a rock which steeply lowers,
And noble arch in proud decay,
Look o'er this vale of vintage-bowers;
But one thing want these banks of Rhine,—
Thy gentle hand to clasp in mine!

3

I send the lilies given to me:
Though long before thy hand they touch,
I know that they must wither'd be,
But yet reject them not as such;
For I have cherish'd them as dear,   520

Because they yet may meet thine eye,
And guide thy soul to mine even here,
When thou behold'st them drooping nigh,
And know'st them gather'd by the Rhine,
And offer'd from my heart to thine!

4

The river nobly foams and flows,
The charm of this enchanted ground,
And all its thousand turns disclose
Some fresher beauty varying round:
The haughtiest breast its wish might
  bound   530
Through life to dwell delighted here;
Nor could on earth a spot be found
To nature and to me so dear,
Could thy dear eyes in following mine
Still sweeten more these banks of Rhine!

LVI

By Coblentz, on a rise of gentle ground,
There is a small and simple pyramid,
Crowning the summit of the verdant mound;
Beneath its base are heroes' ashes hid,
Our enemy's,—but let not that forbid   540
Honour to Marceau![33] o'er whose early tomb
Tears, big tears, gush'd from the rough sol-
  dier's lid,
Lamenting and yet envying such a doom,
Falling for France, whose rights he battled to
  resume.

LVII

Brief, brave, and glorious was his young ca-
  reer,—
His mourners were two hosts, his friends and
  foes;
And fitly may the stranger lingering here
Pray for his gallant spirit's bright repose;
For he was Freedom's champion, one of
  those,
The few in number, who had not o'erstept   550
The charter to chastise which she bestows
On such as wield her weapons; he had kept
The whiteness of his soul, and thus men o'er him
  wept.

---

32 The castle of Drachenfels stands on the highest summit of
'the Seven Mountains,' over the Rhine banks; it is in ruins, and
connected with some singular traditions.—(Byron.)

33 The monument of the young and lamented General Marceau
(killed by a rifle-ball at Alterkirchen, on the last day of the fourth
year of the French Republic) still remains as described. The inscriptions on his monument are rather too long, and not required:
his name was enough; France adored, and her enemies admired;
both wept over him. His funeral was attended by the generals and
detachments from both armies.—(Byron.)

LVIII

Here Ehrenbreitstein,[34] with her shatter'd wall
Black with the miner's blast, upon her height
Yet shows of what she was, when shell and ball
Rebounding idly on her strength did light:
A tower of victory! from whence the flight
Of baffled foes was watch'd along the plain:
But Peace destroy'd what War could never
    blight,   560
And laid those proud roofs bare to Summer's
    rain—
On which the iron shower for years had pour'd
    in vain.

LIX

Adieu to thee, fair Rhine! How long delighted
The stranger fain would linger on his way!
Thine is a scene alike where souls united
Or lonely Contemplation thus might stray;
And could the ceaseless vultures cease to prey
On self-condemning bosoms, it were here,
Where Nature, nor too sombre nor too gay,
Wild but not rude, awful yet not austere,   570
Is to the mellow Earth as Autumn to the year.

LX

Adieu to thee again! a vain adieu!
There can be no farewell to scene like thine;
The mind is colour'd by thy every hue;
And if reluctantly the eyes resign
Their cherish'd gaze upon thee, lovely Rhine!
'Tis with the thankful heart of parting praise;
More mighty spots may rise, more glaring
    shine,
But none unite in one attaching maze
The brilliant, fair, and soft,—the glories of old
    days.   580

LXI

The negligently grand, the fruitful bloom
Of coming ripeness, the white city's sheen,
The rolling stream, the precipice's gloom,
The forest's growth, and Gothic walls between,
The wild rocks shaped as they had turrets been,
In mockery of man's art; and these withal
A race of faces happy as the scene,
Whose fertile bounties here extend to all,
Still springing o'er thy banks, though Empires
    near them fall.

LXII

But these recede. Above me are the Alps,   590
The palaces of Nature, whose vast walls
Have pinnacled in clouds their snowy scalps,
And throned Eternity in icy halls
Of cold sublimity, where forms and falls
The avalanche—the thunderbolt of snow!
All that expands the spirit, yet appals,
Gather around these summits, as to show
How Earth may pierce to Heaven, yet leave vain
    man below.

LXIII

But ere these matchless heights I dare to scan,
There is a spot should not be pass'd in
    vain,—   600
Morat![35] the proud, the patriot field! where
    man
May gaze on ghastly trophies of the slain,
Nor blush for those who conquer'd on that
    plain;
Here Burgundy bequeath'd his tombless host,
A bony heap, through ages to remain,
Themselves their monument;—the Stygian
    coast
Unsepulchred they roam'd, and shriek'd each
    wandering ghost.

LXIV

While Waterloo with Cannæ's[36] carnage vies,
Morat and Marathon twin names shall stand;
They were true Glory's stainless victories,   610
Won by the unambitious heart and hand
Of a proud, brotherly, and civic band,
All unbought champions in no princely cause
Of vice-entail'd Corruption; they no land
Doom'd to bewail the blasphemy of laws
Making kings' rights divine, by some Draconic[37]
    clause.

LXV

By a lone wall a lonelier column rears
A grey and grief-worn aspect of old days;
'Tis the last remnant of the wreck of years,

---

34 Ehrenbreitstein, *i.e.,* 'the broad stone of honour,' one of the strongest fortresses in Europe, was dismantled and blown up by the French at the truce of Leoben. It had been, and could only be, reduced by famine or treachery. It yielded to the former, aided by surprise.—(Byron.)

35 Near the small town of Morat is the battlefield where in 1476 the Swiss with great slaughter defeated an invading army of Burgundians and retained their independence. The site of the battle was marked by a pyramid of bones and for years some of these grisly relics lay scattered around.
36 battleground where Hannibal annihilated the Roman army sent to destroy him, in the Second Punic War, 216 B.C.
37 The code of Draco, Athenian lawmaker of the seventh century, provided so freely for the death penalty that it was said to have been written in blood.

And looks as with the wild-bewilder'd gaze 620
Of one to stone converted by amaze,
Yet still with consciousness; and there it stands
Making a marvel that it not decays,
When the coeval pride of human hands,
Leven'd Adventicum,[38] hath strew'd her subject
  lands.

LXVI

And there—oh! sweet and sacred be the
  name!—
Julia[39]—the daughter, the devoted—gave
Her youth to Heaven; her heart, beneath a
  claim
Nearest to Heaven's, broke o'er a father's
  grave.
Justice is sworn 'gainst tears, and hers would
  crave 630
The life she lived in; but the judge was just,
And then she died on him she could not save.
Their tomb was simple, and without a bust,
And held within their urn one mind, one heart,
  one dust.

LXVII

But these are deeds which should not pass
  away,
And names that must not wither, though the
  earth
Forgets her empires with a just decay,
The enslavers and the enslaved, their death
  and birth;
The high, the mountain-majesty of worth
Should be, and shall, survivor of its woe, 640
And from its immortality look forth
In the sun's face, like yonder Alpine snow,
Imperishably pure beyond all things below.

LXVIII

Lake Leman[40] woos me with its crystal face,
The mirror where the stars and mountains view
The stillness of their aspect in each trace
Its clear depth yields of their far height and
  hue:
There is too much of man here, to look
  through

With a fit mind the might which I behold;
But soon in me shall Loneliness renew 650
Thoughts hid, but not less cherish'd than of
  old,
Ere mingling with the herd had penn'd me in
  their fold.

LXIX

To fly from, need not be to hate, mankind:
All are not fit with them to stir and toil,
Nor is it discontent to keep the mind
Deep in its fountain, lest it overboil
In the hot throng, where we become the spoil
Of our infection, till too late and long
We may deplore and struggle with the coil,
In wretched interchange of wrong for
  wrong 660
Midst a contentious world, striving where none
  are strong.

LXX

There, in a moment we may plunge our years
In fatal penitence, and in the blight
Of our own soul turn all our blood to tears,
And colour things to come with hues of Night;
The race of life becomes a hopeless flight
To those that walk in darkness; on the sea
The boldest steer but where their ports invite;
But there are wanderers o'er Eternity
Whose bark drives on and on, and anchor'd ne'er
  shall be. 670

LXXI

Is it not better, then, to be alone,
And love Earth only for its earthly sake?
By the blue rushing of the arrowy Rhone,
Or the pure bosom of its nursing lake,
Which feeds it as a mother who doth make
A fair but froward infant her own care,
Kissing its cries away as these awake;—
Is it not better thus our lives to wear,
Than join the crushing crowd, doom'd to inflict
  or bear?

LXXII

I live not in myself, but I become 680
Portion of that around me; and to me
High mountains are a feeling, but the hum
Of human cities torture: I can see
Nothing to loathe in nature, save to be
A link reluctant in a fleshly chain,

---

38 ancient Roman capital of Helvetia, reduced to ruins.
39 Julia Alpinula, a young Aventian priestess, who, according to
a Latin inscription, vainly tried to save her father from death on
the charge of treason and who died soon after. The epitaph from
which Byron derived his information has since been proved a
sixteenth-century forgery.
40 Lake Geneva.

Class'd among creatures, when the soul can
  flee,
And with the sky, the peak, the heaving plain
Of ocean, or the stars, mingle, and not in vain.

LXXIII

And thus I am absorb'd, and this is life:
I look upon the peopled desert past,   690
As on a place of agony and strife,
Where, for some sin, to sorrow I was cast,
To act and suffer, but remount at last
With a fresh pinion; which I feel to spring,
Though young, yet waxing vigorous as the
  blast
Which it would cope with, on delighted wing,
Spurning the clay-cold bonds which round our
  being cling.

LXXIV

And when, at length, the mind shall be all free
From what it hates in this degraded form,
Reft of its carnal life, save what shall be   700
Existent happier in the fly and worm,—
When elements to elements conform,
And dust is as it should be, shall I not
Feel all I see, less dazzling, but more warm?
The bodiless thought? the Spirit of each spot?
Of which, even now, I share at times the immor-
  tal lot?

LXXV

Are not the mountains, waves, and skies, a part
Of me and of my soul, as I of them?
Is not the love of these deep in my heart
With a pure passion? should I not contemn   710
All objects, if compared with these? and stem
A tide of suffering, rather than forego
Such feelings for the hard and worldly phlegm
Of those whose eyes are only turn'd below,
Gazing upon the ground, with thoughts which
  dare not glow?

LXXVI

But this is not my theme; and I return
To that which is immediate, and require
Those who find contemplation in the urn,
To look on One,[41] whose dust was once all fire,
A native of the land where I respire   720
The clear air for a while—a passing guest,
Where he became a being,—whose desire

Was to be glorious; 'twas a foolish quest,
The which to gain and keep, he sacrificed all rest.

LXXVII

Here the self-torturing sophist, wild Rousseau,
The apostle of affliction, he who threw
Enchantment over passion, and from woe
Wrung overwhelming eloquence, first drew
The breath which made him wretched: yet he
  knew
How to make madness beautiful, and cast   730
O'er erring deeds and thoughts a heavenly hue
Of words, like sunbeams, dazzling as they past
The eyes, which o'er them shed tears feelingly
  and fast.

LXXVIII

His love was passion's essence:—as a tree
On fire by lightning, with ethereal flame
Kindled he was, and blasted; for to be
Thus, and enamour'd, were in him the same.
But his was not the love of living dame,
Nor of the dead who rise upon our dreams,
But of ideal beauty, which became   740
In him existence, and o'erflowing teems
Along his burning page, distemper'd though it
  seems.

LXXIX

This breathed itself to life in Julie,[42] *this*
Invested her with all that's wild and sweet;
This hallow'd, too, the memorable kiss[43]
Which every morn his fever'd lip would greet,
From hers, who but with friendship his would
  meet;
But to that gentle touch through brain and
  breast
Flash'd the thrill'd spirit's love-devouring
  heat;
In that absorbing sigh perchance more
  blest   750
Than vulgar minds may be with all they seek
  possest.

---

41 Jean Jacques Rousseau, 1712–78, the famous Swiss-French philosopher, was born at Geneva and spent his youth there.

42 heroine of Rousseau's *La Nouvelle Héloïse.*
43 This refers to the account, in his *Confessions,* of his passion for
the Comtesse d'Houdetot (the mistress of St. Lambert), and his
long walk every morning, for the sake of the single kiss which was
the common salutation of French acquaintance. Rousseau's description of his feelings on this occasion may be considered as the
most passionate, yet not impure, description and expression of
love that ever kindled into words; which, after all, must be felt,
from their very force, to be inadequate to the delineation; a painting can give no sufficient idea of the ocean.—(Byron.)

LXXX

His life was one long war with self-sought foes,
Or friends by him self-banish'd; for his mind
Had grown Suspicion's sanctuary, and chose,
For its own cruel sacrifice, the kind,
'Gainst whom he raged with fury strange and
    blind.
But he was phrensied,—wherefore, who may
    know?
Since cause might be which skill could never
    find;
But he was phrensied by disease or woe,
To that worst pitch of all, which wears a reason-
    ing show.   760

LXXXI

For then he was inspired, and from him came,
As from the Pythian's mystic cave[44] of yore,
Those oracles which set the world in flame,
Nor ceased to burn till kingdoms were no
    more:
Did he not this for France? which lay before
Bow'd to the inborn tyranny of years?
Broken and trembling to the yoke she bore,
Till by the voice of him and his compeers
Roused up to too much wrath, which follows
    o'ergrown fears?

LXXXII

They made themselves a fearful monu-
    ment!   770
The wreck of old opinions—things which grew,
Breathed from the birth of time: the veil they
    rent,
And what behind it lay, all earth shall view.
But good with ill they also overthrew,
Leaving but ruins, wherewith to rebuild
Upon the same foundation, and renew
Dungeons and thrones, which the same hour
    refill'd
As heretofore, because ambition was self-will'd.

LXXXIII

But this will not endure, nor be endured!
Mankind have felt their strength, and made it
    felt.   780
They might have used it better, but, allured
By their new vigour, sternly have they dealt
On one another; pity ceased to melt
With her once natural charities. But they,

44 oracle of Apollo at Delphi which was presided over by a
prophetess called Pythia.

Who in oppression's darkness caved had dwelt,
They were not eagles, nourish'd with the day;
What marvel then, at times, if they mistook their
    prey?

LXXXIV

What deep wounds ever closed without a scar?
The heart's bleed longest, and but heal to wear
That which disfigures it; and they who war 790
With their own hopes, and have been van-
    quish'd, bear
Silence, but not submission: in his lair
Fix'd Passion holds his breath, until the hour
Which shall atone for years; none need
    despair:
It came, it cometh, and will come,—the power
To punish or forgive—in *one* we shall be slower.

LXXXV

Clear, placid Leman! thy contrasted lake,
With the wild world I dwelt in, is a thing
Which warns me, with its stillness, to forsake
Earth's troubled waters for a purer spring, 800
This quiet sail is as a noiseless wing
To waft me from distraction; once I loved
Torn ocean's roar, but thy soft murmuring
Sounds sweet as if a Sister's voice reproved,
That I with stern delights should e'er have been
    so moved.

LXXXVI

It is the hush of night, and all between
Thy margin and the mountains, dusk, yet clear,
Mellow'd and mingling, yet distinctly seen,
Save darken'd Jura, whose capt heights ap-
    pear
Precipitously steep; and drawing near, 810
There breathes a living fragrance from the
    shore,
Of flowers yet fresh with childhood; on the ear
Drops the light drip of the suspended oar,
Or chirps the grasshopper one good-night carol
    more;

LXXXVII

He is an evening reveller, who makes
His life an infancy, and sings his fill;
At intervals, some bird from out the brakes
Starts into voice a moment, then is still.
There seems a floating whisper on the hill,
But that is fancy, for the starlight dews 820
All silently their tears of love instil,

Weeping themselves away, till they infuse
Deep into nature's breast the spirit of her hues.

LXXXVIII

Ye stars! which are the poetry of heaven!
If in your bright leaves we would read the fate
Of men and empires,—'tis to be forgiven,
That in our aspirations to be great,
Our destinies o'erleap their mortal state,
And claim a kindred with you; for ye are
A beauty and a mystery, and create   830
In us such love and reverence from afar,
That fortune, fame, power, life, have named
    themselves a star.

LXXXIX

All heaven and earth are still—though not in
    sleep,
But breathless, as we grow when feeling most;
And silent, as we stand in thoughts too deep:—
All heaven and earth are still: From the high
    host
Of stars, to the lull'd lake and mountain-coast,
All is concenter'd in a life intense,
Where not a beam, nor air, nor leaf is lost,
But hath a part of being, and a sense   840
Of that which is of all Creator and defence.

XC

Then stirs the feeling infinite, so felt
In solitude, where we are *least* alone;
A truth, which through our being then doth
    melt,
And purifies from self: it is a tone,
The soul and source of music, which makes
    known
Eternal harmony, and sheds a charm
Like to the fabled Cytherea's zone,[45]
Binding all things with beauty;—'twould dis-
    arm
The spectre Death, had he substantial power to
    harm.   850

XCI

Not vainly did the early Persian make
His altar the high places, and the peak
Of earth-o'ergazing mountains,[46] and thus take

A fit and unwall'd temple, there to seek
The Spirit, in whose honour shrines are weak,
Uprear'd of human hands. Come, and com-
    pare
Columns and idol-dwellings, Goth or Greek,
With Nature's realms of worship, earth and
    air,
Nor fix on fond abodes to circumscribe thy
    pray'r!

XCII

The sky is changed![47]—and such a change! Oh
    night,   860
And storm, and darkness, ye are wondrous
    strong,
Yet lovely in your strength, as is the light
Of a dark eye in woman! Far along,
From peak to peak, the rattling crags among
Leaps the live thunder! Not from one lone
    cloud,
But every mountain now hath found a tongue,
And Jura answers, through her misty shroud,
Back to the joyous Alps, who call to her aloud!

XCIII

And this is in the night:—Most glorious night!
Thou wert not sent for slumber! let me be   870
A sharer in thy fierce and far delight,—
A portion of the tempest and of thee!
How the lit lake shines, a phosphoric sea,
And the big rain comes dancing to the earth!
And now again 'tis black,—and now, the
    glee
Of the loud hills shakes with its mountain-
    mirth,
As if they did rejoice o'er a young earthquake's
    birth.

progress of what is called Methodism to be attributed to any cause
beyond the enthusiasm excited by its vehement faith and doctrines (the truth or error of which I presume neither to canvass
nor to question), I should venture to ascribe it to the practice of
preaching in the *fields,* and the unstudied and extemporaneous
effusions of its teachers. The Mussulmans, whose erroneous devotion (at least in the lower orders) is most sincere, and therefore impressive, are accustomed to repeat their prescribed orisons and prayers, wherever they may be, at the stated hours—of
course, frequently in the open air, kneeling upon a light mat
(which they carry for the purpose of a bed or cushion as required);
the ceremony lasts some minutes, during which they are totally
absorbed, and only living in their supplication: nothing can disturb them. On me the simple and entire sincerity of these men,
and the spirit which appeared to be within and upon them, made
a far greater impression than any general rite which was ever performed in places of worship.—(Byron.)

45 the girdle of the Cytherean Venus which endowed the wearer
with magical power to inspire love.
46 It is to be recollected that the most beautiful and impressive
doctrines of the divine Founder of Christianity were delivered,
not in the *Temple,* but on the *Mount.* . . . Were the early and rapid

47 The thunder-storm to which these lines refer occurred on the
13th of June, 1816, at midnight. I have seen, among the Acroceraunian mountains of Chimari, several more terrible, but none more
beautiful.—(Byron.)

XCIV

Now, where the swift Rhone cleaves his way
     between
Heights which appear as lovers who have
     parted
In hate, whose mining depths so inter-
     vene,   880
That they can meet no more, though broken-
     hearted;
Though in their souls, which thus each other
     thwarted,
Love was the very root of the fond rage
Which blighted their life's bloom, and then de-
     parted:
Itself expired, but leaving them an age
Of years all winters,—war within themselves to
     wage.

XCV

Now, where the quick Rhone thus hath cleft his
     way,
The mightiest of the storms hath ta'en his
     stand;
For here, not one, but many, make their play,
And fling their thunder-bolts from hand to
     hand,   890
Flashing and cast around; of all the band,
The brightest through these parted hills hath
     fork'd
His lightnings,—as if he did understand,
That in such gaps as desolation work'd,
There the hot shaft should blast whatever therein
     lurk'd.

XCVI

Sky, mountains, river, winds, lake, lightnings!
     ye!
With night, and clouds, and thunder, and a
     soul
To make these felt and feeling, well may be
Things that have made me watchful; the far
     roll
Of your departing voices, is the knoll[48]   900
Of what in me is sleepless,—if I rest.
But where of ye, O tempests! is the goal?
Are ye like those within the human breast?
Or do ye find, at length, like eagles, some high
     nest?

XCVII

Could I embody and unbosom now
That which is most within me,—could I wreak

My thoughts upon expression, and thus throw
Soul, heart, mind, passions, feelings, strong or .
     weak,
All that I would have sought, and all I seek,
Bear, know, feel, and yet breathe—into *one*
     word,   910
And that one word were Lightning, I would
     speak;
But as it is, I live and die unheard,
With a most voiceless thought, sheathing it as a
     sword.

XCVIII

The morn is up again, the dewy morn,
With breath all incense, and with cheek all
     bloom,
Laughing the clouds away with playful scorn,
And living as if earth contain'd no tomb,—
And glowing into day: we may resume
The march of our existence: and thus I,
Still on thy shores, fair Leman! may find
     room   920
And food for meditation, nor pass by
Much, that may give us pause, if ponder'd fit-
     tingly.

XCIX

Clarens! sweet Clarens,[49] birthplace of deep
     Love!
Thine air is the young breath of passionate
     thought;
Thy trees take root in Love; the snows above
The very Glaciers have his colours caught,
And sun-set into rose-hues sees them
     wrought[50]
By rays which sleep there lovingly: the rocks,
The permanent crags, tell here of Love, who
     sought
In them a refuge from the worldly shocks,   930
Which stir and sting the soul with hope that
     woos, then mocks.

48 knell.

49 a village on Lake Geneva celebrated as the scene of Rousseau's
La Nouvelle Héloïse.
50 Byron in a note quotes a passage from *La Nouvelle Héloïse* as
authority for the rose-hues on the glacier snows and then has this
to say of the locality: The feeling with which all around Clarens,
and the opposite rocks of Meillerie, is invested, is of a still higher
and more comprehensive order than the mere sympathy with individual passion; it is a sense of the existence of love in its most
extended and sublime capacity, and of our own participation of
its good and of its glory; it is the great principle of the universe,
which is there more condensed, but not less manifested; and of
which, though knowing ourselves a part, we lose our individuality, and mingle in the beauty of the whole.—If Rousseau had
never written, nor lived, the same associations would not less
have belonged to such scenes. He has added to the interest of his
works by their adoption; he has shown his sense of their beauty
by the selection; but they have done that for him which no human
being could do for them.

C

Clarens! by heavenly feet thy paths are trod,—
Undying Love's, who here ascends a throne
To which the steps are mountains; where the
    god
Is a pervading life and light,—so shown
Not on those summits solely, nor alone
In the still cave and forest; o'er the flower
His eye is sparkling, and his breath hath blown,
His soft and summer breath, whose tender
    power
Passes the strength of storms in their most deso-
    late hour.   940

CI

All things are here of *him;* from the black
    pines,
Which are his shade on high, and the loud roar
Of torrents, where he listeneth, to the vines
Which slope his green path downward to the
    shore,
Where the bow'd waters meet him, and adore,
Kissing his feet with murmurs; and the wood,
The covert of old trees, with trunks all hoar,
But light leaves, young as joy, stands where it
    stood,
Offering to him, and his, a populous solitude.

CII

A populous solitude of bees and birds,   950
And fairy-form'd and many-colour'd things,
Who worship him with notes more sweet than
    words,
And innocently open their glad wings,
Fearless and full of life: the gush of springs,
And fall of lofty fountains, and the bend
Of stirring branches, and the bud which brings
The swiftest thought of beauty, here extend,
Mingling, and made by Love, unto one mighty
    end.

CIII

He who hath loved not, here would learn that
    lore,
And make his heart a spirit; he who knows 960
That tender mystery, will love the more;
For this is Love's recess, where vain men's
    woes,
And the world's waste, have driven him far
    from those,
For 'tis his nature to advance or die;
He stands not still, but or decays, or grows

Into a boundless blessing, which may vie
With the immortal lights, in its eternity!

CIV

'Twas not for fiction chose Rousseau this
    spot,
Peopling it with affections; but he found
It was the scene which Passion must allot   970
To the Mind's purified beings; 'twas the
    ground
Where early Love[51] his Psyche's zone unbound,
And hallow'd it with loveliness: 'tis lone,
And wonderful, and deep, and hath a sound,
And sense, and sight of sweetness; here the
    Rhone
Hath spread himself a couch, the Alps have
    rear'd a throne.

CV

Lausanne! and Ferney! ye have been the
    abodes
Of names[52] which unto you bequeath'd a
    name;
Mortals, who sought and found, by dangerous
    roads,
A path to perpetuity of fame: 980
They were gigantic minds, and their steep
    aim
Was, Titan-like, on daring doubts to pile
Thoughts which should call down thunder, and
    the flame
Of Heaven again assail'd, if Heaven the while
On man and man's research could deign do more
    than smile.

CVI

The one[53] was fire and fickleness, a child
Most mutable in wishes, but in mind
A wit as various,—gay, grave, sage, or wild,—
Historian, bard, philosopher, combined;
He multiplied himself among mankind,   990
The Proteus[54] of their talents: But his own
Breathed most in ridicule,—which, as the
    wind,
Blew where it listed, laying all things prone,—
Now to o'erthrow a fool, and now to shake a
    throne.

---

51 Cupid.
52 Voltaire and Gibbon. Gibbon lived at Lausanne and there, in
1788, finished his *Decline and Fall of the Roman Empire.* Voltaire
lived at Ferney the nine years before his death in 1778.
53 Voltaire.
54 the sea god who had the power to assume different shapes.

CVII

The other,[55] deep and slow, exhausting
    thought,
And living wisdom with each studious year,
In meditation dwelt, with learning wrought,
And shaped his weapon with an edge severe,
Sapping a solemn creed with solemn sneer;
The lord of irony,—that master-spell,   1000
Which stung his foes to wrath, which grew
    from fear,
And doom'd him to the zealot's ready Hell,
Which answers to all doubts so eloquently well.

CVIII

Yet, peace be with their ashes,—for by them,
If merited, the penalty is paid;
It is not ours to judge,—far less condemn;
The hour must come when such things shall be
    made
Known unto all, or hope and dread allay'd
By slumber, on one pillow, in the dust,
Which, thus much we are sure, must lie de-
    cay'd;   1010
And when it shall revive, as is our trust,
'Twill be to be forgiven, or suffer what is just.

CIX

But let me quit man's works, again to read
His Maker's, spread around me, and suspend
This page, which from my reveries I feed,
Until it seems prolonging without end.
The clouds above me to the white Alps tend,
And I must pierce them, and survey whate'er
May be permitted, as my steps I bend
To their most great and growing region,
    where   1020
The earth to her embrace compels the powers of
    air.

CX

Italia! too, Italia! looking on thee,
Full flashes on the soul the light of ages,
Since the fierce Carthaginian[56] almost won
    thee,
To the last halo of the chiefs and sages
Who glorify thy consecrated pages;
Thou wert the throne and grave of empires;
    still,
The fount at which the panting mind assuages
Her thirst of knowledge, quaffing there her fill,

Flows from the eternal source of Rome's imperial
    hill.   1030

CXI

Thus far have I proceeded in a theme
Renew'd with no kind auspices:—to feel
We are not what we have been, and to deem
We are not what we should be, and to steel
The heart against itself; and to conceal,
With a proud caution, love, or hate, or
    aught,—
Passion or feeling, purpose, grief or zeal,—
Which is the tyrant spirit of our thought,
Is a stern task of soul:—No matter,—it is taught.

CXII

And for these words, thus woven into
    song,   1040
It may be that they are a harmless wile,—
The colouring of the scenes which fleet along,
Which I would seize, in passing, to beguile
My breast, or that of others, for a while.
Fame is the thirst of youth, but I am not
So young as to regard men's frown or smile,
As loss or guerdon of a glorious lot;
I stood and stand alone,—remember'd or forgot.

CXIII

I have not loved the world, nor the world me;
I have not flatter'd its rank breath, nor
    bow'd   1050
To its idolatries a patient knee,
Nor coin'd my cheek to smiles, nor cried aloud
In worship of an echo: in the crowd
They could not deem me one of such; I stood
Among them, but not of them; in a shroud
Of thoughts which were not their thoughts, and
    still could,
Had I not filed[57] my mind, which thus itself sub-
    dued.

CXIV

I have not loved the world, nor the world me,—
But let us part fair foes; I do believe,
Though I have found them not, that there may
    be   1060
Words which are things, hopes which will not
    deceive,
And virtues which are merciful, nor weave
Snares for the failing; I would also deem

---

55 Gibbon.
56 Hannibal.

57 defiled.

O'er others' griefs[58] that some sincerely grieve;
That two, or one, are almost what they seem,
That goodness is no name, and happiness no
    dream.

CXV

My daughter! with thy name this song begun;
My daughter! with thy name thus much shall
    end;
I see thee not, I hear thee not, but none
Can be so wrapt in thee; thou art the
    friend   1070
To whom the shadows of far years extend:
Albeit my brow thou never shouldst behold,
My voice shall with thy future visions blend,
And reach into thy heart, when mine is cold,
A token and a tone, even from thy father's mould.

CXVI

To aid thy mind's development, to watch
Thy dawn of little joys, to sit and see
Almost thy very growth, to view thee catch
Knowledge of objects,—wonders yet to thee!
To hold thee lightly on a gentle knee,   1080
And print on thy soft cheek a parent's kiss—
This, it should seem, was not reserved for me;
Yet this was in my nature: as it is,
I know not what is there, yet something like to
    this.

CXVII

Yet, though dull Hate as duty should be
    taught,[59]
I know that thou wilt love me; though my
    name
Should be shut from thee, as a spell still
    fraught
With desolation, and a broken claim:
Though the grave closed between us,—'twere
    the same,
I know that thou wilt love me; though to
    drain   1090
My blood from out thy being were an aim,
And an attainment,—all would be in vain,—
Still thou wouldst love me, still that more than
    life retain.

---

58 It is said by Rochefoucault, that 'there is *always* something in
the misfortunes of men's best friends not displeasing to them.—
(Byron.)
59 Lady Byron protested that the poet's allusions to her in *Childe
Harold* were cruel and cold, but with such a semblance as to make
her appear so, and so to attract sympathy to himself. She denied
that the insinuations had any foundation of truth.

CXVIII

The child of love, though born in bitterness,
And nurtured in convulsion. Of thy sire
These were the elements, and thine no less.
As yet such are around thee, but thy fire
Shall be more temper'd, and thy hope far
    higher.
Sweet be thy cradled slumbers! O'er the sea
And from the mountains where I now
    respire,   1100
Fain would I waft such blessing upon thee,
As, with a sigh, I deem thou might'st have been
    to me.
    May, June 1816   1816

From Canto the Fourth
*Stanzas i-x, xiii-xxix, lxxviii-lxxxi, xcv-xcviii, cvii-cxii,
cxxviii-cxlv, clxxv-clxxxvi*

I

I stood in Venice, on the Bridge of Sighs;[1]
A palace and a prison on each hand:
I saw from out the wave her structures rise
As from the stroke of the enchanter's wand:
A thousand years their cloudy wings expand
Around me, and a dying Glory smiles
O'er the far times, when many a subject land
Look'd to the winged Lion's marble piles,[2]
Where Venice sate in state, throned on her hun-
    dred isles!

II

She looks a sea Cybele,[3] fresh from ocean, 10
Rising with her tiara of proud towers
At airy distance, with majestic motion,
A ruler of the waters and their powers:
And such she was;—her daughters had their
    dowers
From spoils of nations, and the exhaustless
    East
Pour'd in her lap all gems in sparkling showers.
In purple was she robed, and of her feast
Monarchs partook, and deem'd their dignity in-
    creased.

---

1 The Bridge of Sighs (*i.e., Ponte dei Sospi)* is that which divides,
or rather joins the palace of the Doge to the prison of the state. It
has two passages: the criminal went by the one to judgment, and
returned by the other to death, being strangled in a chamber adjoining, where there was a mechanical process for the purpose.—
(Byron, in Letter to Murray, 1 July 1817.)
2 Several statues of the winged lion of St. Mark, patron saint of
Venice, stand in the city placed on top of pillars of marble. The
most notable of these and the one Byron has especially in mind is
in the Piazzetta di San Marco and near to the ducal palace.
3 Cybele, 'mother of the gods,' was regularly represented wearing a crown of towers.

III

In Venice Tasso's echoes are no more,
And silent rows the songless gondolier;[4]   20
Her palaces are crumbling to the shore,
And music meets not always now the ear:
Those days are gone—but Beauty still is here.
States fall, arts fade—but Nature doth not die,
Nor yet forget how Venice once was dear,
The pleasant place of all festivity,
The revel of the earth, the masque of Italy!

IV

But unto us she hath a spell beyond
Her name in story, and her long array
Of mighty shadows, whose dim forms despond   30
Above the dogeless city's vanish'd sway;[5]
Ours is a trophy which will not decay
With the Rialto,[6] Shylock and the Moor,[7]
And Pierre,[8] cannot be swept or worn away—
The keystones of the arch! though all were o'er,
For us repeopled were the solitary shore.

V

The beings of the mind are not of clay;
Essentially immortal, they create
And multiply in us a brighter ray
And more beloved existence: that which Fate   40
Prohibits to dull life, in this our state
Of mortal bondage, by these spirits supplied,
First exiles, then replaces what we hate;
Watering the heart whose early flowers have died,
And with a fresher growth replenishing the void.

VI

Such is the refuge of our youth and age,
The first from Hope, the last from Vacancy;
And this worn feeling peoples many a page,
And, may be, that which grows beneath mine eye:
Yet there are things whose strong reality   50
Outshines our fairy-land; in shape and hues
More beautiful than our fantastic sky,
And the strange constellations which the Muse
O'er her wild universe is skilful to diffuse:

VII

I saw or dream'd of such,—but let them go,—
They came like truth, and disappear'd like dreams;
And whatsoe'er they were—are now but so:
I could replace them if I would; still teems
My mind with many a form which aptly seems
Such as I sought for, and at moments found;   60
Let these too go—for waking Reason deems
Such overweening phantasies unsound,
And other voices speak, and other sights surround.

VIII

I've taught me other tongues, and in strange eyes
Have made me not a stranger; to the mind
Which is itself, no changes bring surprise;
Nor is it harsh to make, nor hard to find
A country with—ay, or without mankind;
Yet was I born where men are proud to be,—
Not without cause; and should I leave behind   70
The inviolate island of the sage and free,
And seek me out a home by a remoter sea,

IX

Perhaps I loved it well: and should I lay
My ashes in a soil which is not mine,
My spirit shall resume it—if we may
Unbodied choose a sanctuary. I twine
My hopes of being remember'd in my line
With my land's language: if too fond and far
These aspirations in their scope incline,—
If my fame should be, as my fortunes are,   80
Of hasty growth and blight, and dull Oblivion bar

X

My name from out the temple where the dead
Are honour'd by the nations—let it be—
And light the laurels on a loftier head!
And be the Spartan's epitaph on me—
'Sparta hath many a worthier son than he.'[9]

4 The well-known song of the gondoliers, of alternate stanzas from Tasso's *Jerusalem*, has died with the independence of Venice. Editions of the poem, with the original on one column, and the Venetian variations on the other, as sung by the boatmen, were once common, and are still to be found.—(Hobhouse's note.)
5 The last doge (ruler of Venice) was deposed by Napoleon in 1797.
6 principal island of Venice and until the sixteenth century the center of commerce and exchange. Byron, of course, uses the word symbolically.
7 Shakespeare's Shylock and Othello.
8 tragic character in Otway's *Venice Preserved*, a play admired by Byron.
9 The answer of the mother of Brasidas, the Lacedaemonian general, to the strangers who praised the memory of her son.—(Byron.)

Meantime I seek no sympathies, nor need;
The thorns which I have reap'd are of the tree
I planted: they have torn me, and I bleed:
I should have known what fruit would spring
    from such a seed.   90

XIII

Before St. Mark still glow his steeds of brass,
Their gilded collars glittering in the sun; 110
But is not Doria's menace come to pass?[10]
Are they not bridled?—Venice, lost and won,
Her thirteen hundred years of freedom done,
Sinks, like a seaweed, into whence she rose!
Better be whelm'd beneath the waves, and
    shun,
Even in destruction's depth, her foreign foes,
From whom submission wrings an infamous re-
    pose.

XIV

In youth she was all glory,—a new Tyre;[11]
Her very by-word sprung from victory,
The 'Planter of the Lion,'[12] which through
    fire   120
And blood she bore o'er subject earth and sea;
Though making many slaves, herself still free,
And Europe's bulwark 'gainst the Ottomite;[13]
Witness Troy's rival, Candia![14] Vouch it, ye
Immortal waves that saw Lepanto's[15] fight!
For ye are names no time nor tyranny can blight.

XV

Statues of glass—all shiver'd—the long file
Of her dead Doges are declined to dust;
But where they dwelt, the vast and sumptuous
    pile

Bespeaks the pageant of their splendid
    trust;   130
Their sceptre broken, and their sword in rust,
Have yielded to the stranger: empty halls,
Thin streets, and foreign aspects, such as must
Too oft remind her who and what enthrals,
Have flung a desolate cloud o'er Venice's lovely
    walls.

XVI

When Athens' armies fell at Syracuse,
And fetter'd thousands bore the yoke of war,
Redemption rose up in the Attic Muse,
Her voice their only ransom from afar;[16]
See! as they chant the tragic hymn, the car 140
Of the o'ermaster'd victor stops, the reins
Fall from his hands, his idle scimitar
Starts from its belt—he rends his captive's
    chains,
And bids him thank the bard for freedom and his
    strains.

XVII

Thus, Venice, if no stronger claim were thine,
Were all thy proud historic deeds forgot,
Thy choral memory of the Bard divine,
Thy love of Tasso,[17] should have cut the knot
Which ties thee to thy tyrants; and thy lot
Is shameful to the nations,—most of all, 150
Albion![18] to thee: the Ocean queen should not
Abandon Ocean's children; in the fall
Of Venice think of thine, despite thy watery wall.

XVIII

I loved her from my boyhood; she to me
Was as a fairy city of the heart,
Rising like water-columns from the sea,
Of joy the sojourn, and of wealth the mart;
And Otway, Radcliffe, Schiller, Shakespeare's
    art,[19]
Had stamp'd her image in me, and even so,
Although I found her thus, we did not
    part;   160
Perchance even dearer in her day of woe,

---

10 After the loss of the battle of Pola, and the taking of Chiog-gia in 1379, the Venetians sued for peace and received this reply from Peter Doria, the Genoese commander: 'On God's faith, gentlemen of Venice, ye shall have no peace from the Signor of Padua, nor from our commune of Genoa, until we have first put a rein upon those unbridled horses of yours, that are upon the porch of your evangelist St. Mark. When we have bridled them, we shall keep you quiet.'—(Hobhouse's note.)
11 the most famous city of ancient Phoenicia, noted at one time for its luxury and magnificence.
12 The winged lion of Saint Mark was the emblem of Venice.
13 Turk.
14 Long after she had yielded other eastern possessions Venice retained her hold upon Crete (Candia). In 1669 it was given up to the Turks but only after an heroic defense that lasted more than twenty years.
15 At the naval battle of Lepanto, 1571, off the west coast of Greece, in which the Spanish and Italian fleets joined forces, the Venetians earned the chief glory for a decisive victory over the Turks.

16 Plutarch relates that when the Athenians were defeated and captured at Syracuse, 413 B.C., some of the prisoners gained the favor of their captors by reciting Euripides.
17 Torquoto Tasso, 1544-95, celebrated Italian epic poet. Stanzas from his *Jerusalem Delivered* were sung by the Venetian gondoliers.
18 England.
19 Otway's *Venice Preserved;* Mrs. Radcliffe's novel, *The Mysteries of Udolpho;* Schiller's *Der Geisterseher;* The Merchant of Venice and *Othello.*

Than when she was a boast, a marvel, and a
  show.

XIX

I can repeople with the past—and of
The present there is still for eye and thought,
And meditation chasten'd down, enough;
And more, it may be, than I hoped or sought;
And of the happiest moments which were
  wrought
Within the web of my existence, some
From thee, fair Venice! have their colours
  caught:
There are some feelings Time cannot
  benumb,   170
Nor Torture shake, or mine would now be cold
  and dumb.

XX

But from their nature will the Tannen[20] grow
Loftiest on loftiest and least shelter'd rocks,
Rooted in barrenness, where nought below
Of soil supports them 'gainst the Alpine shocks
Of eddying storms; yet springs the trunk, and
  mocks
The howling tempest, till its height and frame
Are worthy of the mountains from whose
  blocks
Of bleak, gray granite into life it came,
And grew a giant tree;—the mind may grow the
  same.   180

XXI

Existence may be borne, and the deep root
Of life and sufferance make its firm abode
The bare and desolated bosoms: mute
The camel labours with the heaviest load,
And the wolf dies in silence,—not bestow'd
In vain should such example be; if they,
Things of ignoble or of savage mood,
Endure and shrink not, we of nobler clay
May temper it to bear,—it is but for a day.

XXII

All suffering doth destroy, or is destroy'd, 190
Even by the sufferer; and, in each event,
Ends:—Some, with hope replenish'd and re-
  buoy'd,
Return to whence they came—with like intent,
And weave their web again; some, bow'd and
  bent,

---

20 *Tannen* is the plural of *tanne,* a species of fir peculiar to the
Alps, which only thrives in very rocky parts.—(Byron.)

Wax grey and ghastly, withering ere their time,
And perish with the reed on which they leant;
Some seek devotion, toil, war, good or crime,
According as their souls were form'd to sink or
  climb.

XXIII

But ever and anon of griefs subdued
There comes a token like a scorpion's
  sting,   200
Scarce seen, but with fresh bitterness imbued;
And slight withal may be the things which
  bring
Back on the heart the weight which it would
  fling
Aside for ever: it may be a sound—
A tone of music—summer's eve—or spring—
A flower—the wind—the ocean—which shall
  wound,
Striking the electric chain wherewith we are
  darkly bound;

XXIV

And how and why we know not, nor can trace
Home to its cloud this lightning of the mind,
But feel the shock renew'd, nor can efface 210
The blight and blackening which it leaves be-
  hind,
Which out of things familiar, undesign'd,
When least we deem of such, calls up to view
The spectres whom no exorcism can bind,—
The cold, the changed, perchance the dead—
  anew,
The mourn'd, the loved, the lost—too many! yet
  how few!

XXV

But my soul wanders; I demand it back
To meditate amongst decay, and stand
A ruin amidst ruins; there to track
Fall'n states and buried greatness, o'er a
  land   220
Which *was* the mightiest in its old command,
And *is* the loveliest, and must ever be
The master-mould of Nature's heavenly hand;
Wherein were cast the heroic and the free,
The beautiful, the brave, the lords of earth and
  sea,

XXVI

The commonwealth of kings, the men of
Rome!

And even since, and now, fair Italy!
Thou art the garden of the world, the home
Of all Art yields, and Nature can decree;
Even in thy desert, what is like to thee?   230
Thy very weeds are beautiful, thy waste
More rich than other climes' fertility;
Thy wreck a glory, and thy ruin graced
With an immaculate charm which cannot be de-
  faced.

XXVII

The moon is up, and yet it is not night;
Sunset divides the sky with her; a sea
Of glory streams along the Alpine height
Of blue Friuli's mountains;[21] Heaven is free
From clouds, but of all colours seems to be,—
Melted to one vast Iris of the West,—   240
Where the Day joins the past Eternity,
While, on the other hand, meek Dian's crest
Floats through the azure air—an island of the
  blest![22]

XXVIII

A single star is at her side, and reigns
With her o'er half the lovely heaven; but still
Yon sunny sea heaves brightly, and remains
Roll'd o'er the peak of the far Rhætian hill,[23]
As Day and Night contending were, until
Nature reclaim'd her order:—gently flows
The deep-dyed Brenta,[24] where their hues
  instil   250
The odorous purple of a new-born rose,
Which streams upon her stream, and glass'd
  within it glows,

XXIX

Fill'd with the face of heaven, which, from
  afar,
Comes down upon the waters; all its hues,
From the rich sunset to the rising star,
Their magical variety diffuse:
And now they change; a paler shadow strews

Its mantle o'er the mountains; parting day
Dies like the dolphin, whom each pang imbues
With a new colour as it gasps away—   260
The last still loveliest,—till—'tis gone—and all is
  grey,

LXXVIII

Oh Rome! my country! city of the soul!
The orphans of the heart must turn to thee,
Lone mother of dead empires! and control
In their shut breasts their petty misery.
What are our woes and sufferance? Come and
  see
The cypress, hear the owl, and plod your way
O'er steps of broken thrones and temples,
  Ye!   700
Whose agonies are evils of a day—
A world is at our feet as fragile as our clay.

LXXIX

The Niobe[25] of nations! there she stands,
Childless and crownless, in her voiceless woe;
An empty urn within her wither'd hands,
Whose holy dust was scatter'd long ago;
The Scipios' tomb[26] contains no ashes now;
The very sepulchres lie tenantless
Of their heroic dwellers: dost thou flow,
Old Tiber! through a marble wilderness?
Rise, with thy yellow waves, and mantle her dis-
  tress.

LXXX

The Goth, the Christian, Time, War, Flood,
  and Fire,
Have dealt upon the seven-hill'd city's pride;
She saw her glories star by star expire,
And up the steep barbarian monarchs ride,
Where the car climb'd the Capitol; far and
  wide
Temple and tower went down, nor left a site:
Chaos of ruins! who shall trace the void,
O'er the dim fragments cast a lunar light,
And say, 'here was, or is,' where all is doubly
  night?   720

---

21 the Julian Alps, which lie to the north of Trieste and northeast of Venice.
22 The above description may seem fantastical or exaggerated
to those who have never seen an Oriental or Italian sky, yet is
but a literal and hardly sufficient delineation of an August evening (the eighteenth), as contemplated in one of many rides along
the banks of the Brenta, near La Mira.—(Byron.)
23 Rhaetia was the name of an ancient Roman province in Northern Italy. S. C. Chew identifies 'Rhaetian Hill' as Monte Grappa
beyond Bassano, northwest of La Mira.
24 The Brenta river rises in Tyrol and flows past Padua into the
Gulf of Venice.

25 Niobe, proud of her six daughters and six sons, boasted of her
superiority to her friend Latona, the mother of only two children.
As a punishment, the gods slew all her children; then out of pity
for her grief changed Niobe to stone but her tears continued to
flow.
26 This tomb on the Appian Way near Rome was discovered
plundered in 1780.

LXXXI

The double night of ages, and of her,
Night's daughter, Ignorance, hath wrapt and
    wrap
All round us: we but feel our way to err:
The ocean hath its chart, the stars their map,
And Knowledge spreads them on her ample
    lap;
But Rome is as the desert, where we steer
Stumbling o'er recollections; now we clap
Our hands, and cry 'Eureka!' it is clear—
When but some false mirage of ruin rises near.

. . .

XCV

I speak not of men's creeds—they rest between
Man and his Maker—but of things allow'd,
Averr'd, and known, and daily, hourly seen—
The yoke that is upon us doubly bow'd,   850
And the intent of tyranny avow'd,
The edict of Earth's rulers, who are grown
The apes of him[27] who humbled once the
    proud,
And shook them from their slumbers on the
    throne:
Too glorious, were this all his mighty arm had
    done.

XCVI

Can tyrants but by tyrants conquer'd be,
And Freedom find no champion and no child
Such as Columbia[28] saw arise when she
Sprung forth a Pallas,[29] arm'd and undefiled?
Or must such minds be nourish'd in the
    wild   860
Deep in the unpruned forest, 'midst the roar
Of cataracts, where nursing Nature smiled
On infant Washington? Has Earth no more
Such seeds within her breast, or Europe no such
    shore?

XCVII

But France got drunk with blood to vomit
    crime,
And fatal have her Saturnalia[30] been

To Freedom's cause, in every age and clime;
Because the deadly days which we have seen,
And vile Ambition, that built up between
Man and his hopes an adamantine wall,   870
And the base pageant last upon the scene,
Are grown the pretext for the eternal thrall
Which nips life's tree, and dooms man's worst—
    his second fall.

XCVIII

Yet, Freedom! yet thy banner, torn, but flying,
Streams like the thunder-storm *against* the
    wind;
Thy trumpet voice, though broken now and
    dying,
The loudest still the tempest leaves behind;
Thy tree hath lost its blossoms, and the rind,
Chopp'd by the axe, looks rough and little
    worth,
But the sap lasts,—and still the seed we
    find   880
Sown deep, even in the bosom of the North[31]
So shall a better spring less bitter fruit bring
    forth.

. . .

CVII

Cypress and ivy, weed and wallflower grown,
Matted and mass'd together, hillocks heap'd
On what were chambers, arch crush'd, column
    strown
In fragments, choked up vaults, and frescos
    steep'd
In subterranean damps, where the owl peep'd,
Deeming it midnight:—Temples, baths, or
    halls?   960
Pronounce who can; for all that Learning
    reap'd
From her research hath been, that these are
    walls—
Behold the Imperial Mount![32] 'tis thus the mighty
    falls.[33]

---

27 Napoleon.
28 poetical for America.
29 Olympian goddess, pre-eminent in civic wisdom and the arts of war.
30 Swiftly reviewed are France's criminal excesses ('her Saturnalia') beginning with the Reign of Terror, l. 865, continuing with her imperial ambitions, ll. 868-9, and closing with the despotic treaties of Vienna and Paris, l, 871.

31 Great Britain.
32 the Palatine Hill of Rome upon which according to tradition the original city was built by Romulus. Later it was the site of the palaces of the Caesars.
33 The Palatine is one mass of ruins, particularly on the side towards the Circus Maximus. The very soil is formed of crumbled brickwork. Nothing has been told—nothing can be told—to satisfy the belief of any but the Roman antiquary.—(Byron.) Systematic excavations and research have since revealed the plan of the Palatine, which in 1817 was as Byron described it, a 'mass of ruins' defying the guesses of antiquarians.

CVIII

There is the moral of all human tales;
'Tis but the same rehearsal of the past,
First Freedom, and then Glory—when that
  fails,
Wealth, vice, corruption,—barbarism at last.
And History, with all her volumes vast,
Hath but *one* page,—'tis better written here
Where gorgeous Tyranny hath thus
  amass'd   970
All treasures, all delights, that eye or ear,
Heart, soul, could seek, tongue ask—Away with
  words! draw near,

CIX

Admire, exult, despise, laugh, weep,—for here
There is such matter for all feeling:—Man!
Thou pendulum betwixt a smile and tear,
Ages and realms are crowded in this span,
This mountain, whose obliterated plan
The pyramid of empires pinnacled,
Of Glory's gewgaws shining in the van
Till the sun's rays with added flame were
  fill'd!   980
Where are its golden roofs? where those who
  dared to build?

CX

Tully[34] was not so eloquent as thou,
Thou nameless column with the buried base!
What are the laurels of the Cæsar's brow?
Crown me with ivy from his dwelling-place.
Whose arch or pillar meets me in the face,
Titus or Trajan's?[35] No—'tis that of Time:
Triumph, arch, pillar, all he doth displace
Scoffing; and apostolic statues[36] climb
To crush the imperial urn, whose ashes slept sub-
  lime,   990

CXI

Buried in air, the deep blue sky of Rome,
And looking to the stars: they had contain'd
A spirit which with these would find a home,
The last of those who o'er the whole earth
  reign'd,
The Roman globe, for after none sustain'd,

But yielded back his conquests:—he was more
Than a mere Alexander, and, unstain'd
With household blood and wine, serenely wore
His sovereign virtues—still we Trajan's name
  adore.[37]

CXII

Where is the rock of Triumph,[38] the high
  place   1000
Where Rome embraced her heroes? where the
  steep
Tarpeian? fittest goal of Treason's race,
The promontory whence the Traitor's Leap
Cured all ambition.[39] Did the conquerors heap
Their spoils here? Yes; and in yon field below,
A thousand years of silenced factions sleep—
The Forum, where the immortal accents glow,
And still the eloquent air breathes—burns with
  Cicero?

CXXVIII

Arches on arches! as it were that Rome,
Collecting the chief trophies of her line,
Would build up all her triumphs in one dome,
Her Coliseum stands; the moonbeams shine
As 'twere its natural torches, for divine
Should be the light which streams here to il-
  lume
This long-explored but still exhaustless
  mine   1150
Of contemplation; and the azure gloom
Of an Italian night, where the deep skies assume

CXXIX

Hues which have words, and speak to ye of
  heaven,
Floats o'er this vast and wondrous monument,
And shadows forth its glory. There is given
Unto the things of earth, which Time hath
  bent,
A spirit's feeling, and where he hath leant
His hand, but broke his scythe, there is a power
And magic in the ruin'd battlement,

---

34 Marcus Tullius Cicero, 106–43 B.C., celebrated Roman orator
and statesman.
35 Flavius Sabinus Vespasianus Titus, A.D. 40–81, and Marcus
Ulpius Trajanus, A.D. 53–117, were Roman emperors in whose
honor great public monuments had been erected.
36 The column of Trajan is surmounted by St. Peter; that of
Aurelius by St. Paul.—(Byron.)

37 Trajan was proverbially the best of the Roman princes; and
it would be easier to find a sovereign uniting exactly the opposite characteristics, than one possessed of all the happy qualities
ascribed to this emperor.—(Byron.)
38 the temple of Jupiter on the Capitoline Hill whose exact site
was unknown in Byron's day. Excavations some fifty years later
determined its location with reasonable certainty.
39 M. Manlius condemned on a charge of high treason, 384 B.C.,
was ordered by the tribunes to be thrown down the Tarpeian
Rock.

For which the palace of the present hour 1160
Must yield its pomp, and wait till ages are its
  dower.

CXXX

Oh Time! the beautifier of the dead,
Adorner of the ruin, comforter
And only healer when the heart hath bled;
Time! the corrector where our judgments err,
The test of truth, love—sole philosopher,
For all beside are sophists—from thy thrift,
Which never loses though it doth defer—
Time, the avenger! unto thee I lift
My hands, and eyes, and heart, and crave of thee
  a gift: 1170

CXXXI

Amidst this wreck, where thou hast made a
  shrine
And temple more divinely desolate,
Among thy mightier offerings here are mine,
Ruins of years, though few, yet full of fate:
If thou hast ever seen me too elate,
Hear me not; but if calmly I have borne
Good, and reserved my pride against the hate
Which shall not whelm me, let me not have
  worn
This iron in my soul in vain—shall *they* not
  mourn?

CXXXII

And thou, who never yet of human wrong 1180
Left the unbalanced scale, great Nemesis!
Here, where the ancient paid thee homage
  long—
Thou who didst call the Furies from the abyss,
And round Orestes[40] bade them howl and hiss
For that unnatural retribution—just,
Had it but been from hands less near—in this
Thy former realm, I call thee from the dust!
Dost thou not hear my heart?—Awake! thou
  shalt, and must.

CXXXIII

It is not that I may not have incurr'd
For my ancestral faults or mine the wound 1190
I bleed withal, and, had it been conferr'd
With a just weapon, it had flow'd unbound;
But now my blood shall not sink in the ground;
To thee I do devote it—*thou* shalt take

The vengeance, which shall yet be sought and
  found,
Which if *I* have not taken for the sake—
But let that pass—I sleep, but thou shalt yet
  awake.

CXXXIV

And if my voice break forth, 'tis not that now
I shrink from what is suffer'd: let him speak
Who hath beheld decline upon my brow, 1200
Or seen my mind's convulsion leave it weak;
But in this page a record will I seek.
Not in the air shall these my words disperse,
Though I be ashes; a far hour shall wreak
The deep prophetic fulness of this verse,
And pile on human heads the mountain of my
  curse!

CXXXV

That curse shall be Forgiveness.—Have I not—
Hear me, my mother Earth! behold it, Heaven!
Have I not had to wrestle with my lot?
Have I not suffer'd things to be forgiven? 1210
Have I not had my brain sear'd, my heart
  riven,
Hopes sapp'd, name blighted, Life's life lied
  away?
And only not to desperation driven,
Because not altogether of such clay
As rots into the souls of those whom I survey.

CXXXVI

From mighty wrongs to petty perfidy
Have I not seen what human things could do?
From the loud roar of foaming calumny
To the small whisper of the as paltry few,
And subtler venom of the reptile crew, 1220
The Janus glance[41] of whose significant eye,
Learning to lie with silence, would *seem* true,
And without utterance, save the shrug or sigh,
Deal round to happy fools its speechless obloquy.

CXXXVII

But I have lived, and have not lived in vain:
My mind may lose its force, my blood its fire,
And my frame perish even in conquering pain;
But there is that within me which shall tire
Torture and Time, and breathe when I expire;
Something unearthly, which they deem not
  of,   1230

---

40 Orestes slew his mother, Clytemnestra, and her lover to
avenge their murder of his father Agamemnon.

41 facing both directions. Janus was a Roman deity represented
with two opposite faces, seeing past and future simultaneously.

Like the remember'd tone of a mute lyre,
Shall on their soften'd spirits sink, and move
In hearts all rocky now the late remorse of love.

CXXXVIII

The seal is set.—Now welcome, thou dread
    power!
Nameless, yet thus omnipotent, which here
Walk'st in the shadow of the midnight hour
With a deep awe, yet all distinct from fear;
Thy haunts are ever where the dead walls rear
Their ivy mantles, and the solemn scene
Derives from thee a sense so deep and
    clear   1240
That we become a part of what has been,
And grow unto the spot, all-seeing but unseen.

CXXXIX

And here the buzz of eager nations ran,
In murmur'd pity, or loud-roar'd applause,
As man was slaughter'd by his fellowman.
And wherefore slaughter'd? wherefore, but be-
    cause
Such were the bloody Circus' genial laws,
And the imperial pleasure.—Wherefore not?
What matters where we fall to fill the maws
Of worms—on battle-plains or listed
    spot?[42]   1250
Both are but theatres—where the chief actors
    rot.

CXL

I see before me the Gladiator lie;[43]
He leans upon his hand—his manly brow
Consents to death, but conquers agony,
And his droop'd head sinks gradually low—
And through his side the last drops, ebbing
    slow
From the red gash, fall heavy, one by one,
Like the first of a thunder-shower; and now
The arena swims around him—he is gone,
Ere ceased the inhuman shout which hail'd the
    wretch who won.   1260

CXLI

He heard it, but he heeded not—his eyes
Were with his heart, and that was far away;
He reck'd not of the life he lost nor prize,
But where his rude hut by the Danube lay,

There were his young barbarians all at play,
There was their Dacian[44] mother—he, their
    sire,
Butcher'd to make a Roman holiday—
All this rush'd with his blood—Shall he ex-
    pire
And unavenged? Arise! ye Goths, and glut your
    ire!

CXLII

But here, where Murder breathed her bloody
    steam;   1270
And here, where buzzing nations choked the
    ways,
And roar'd or murmur'd like a mountain
    stream
Dashing or winding as its torrent strays;
Here, where the Roman million's blame or
    praise
Was death or life, the playthings of a crowd,
My voice sounds much—and fall the stars'
    faint rays
On the arena void—seats crush'd—walls
    bow'd—
And galleries, where my steps seem echoes
    strangely loud.

CXLIII

A ruin—yet what ruin! from its mass
Walls, palaces, half-cities, have been
    rear'd;   1280
Yet oft the enormous skeleton ye pass,
And marvel where the spoil could have ap-
    pear'd.
Hath it indeed been plunder'd, or but clear'd?
Alas! developed, opens the decay,
When the colossal fabric's form is near'd:
It will not bear the brightness of the day,
Which streams too much on all—years—man—
    have reft away.

CXLIV

But when the rising moon, begins to climb
Its topmost arch, and gently pauses there;
When the stars twinkle through the loops of
    time,   1290
And the low night-breeze waves along the
    air
The garland forest, which the grey walls wear,

---

42 arena.
43 Byron's famous passage on the gladiator was inspired by the
statue of the Dying Gaul now in the Capitol Museum, Rome.

44 an inhabitant of ancient Dacia, region north of the Danube
made into a Roman province, 106 B.C. Captives of Dacia were
brought to Rome and exhibited in combats for the amusement
of the people.

Like laurels on the bald first Cæsar's head;[45]
When the light shines serene but doth not
    glare,
Then in this magic circle raise the dead:
Heroes have trod this spot—'tis on their dust ye
    tread.

CXLV

'While stands the Coliseum, Rome shall stand;
When falls the Coliseum, Rome shall fall;
And when Rome falls—the World.'[46] From
    our own land
Thus spake the pilgrims o'er this mighty
    wall   1300
In Saxon times, which we are wont to call
Ancient; and these three mortal things are still
On their foundations, and unalter'd all;
Rome and her Ruin past Redemption's skill,
The World, the same wide den—of thieves, or
    what ye will.

.   .   .

CLXXV

But I forget.—My Pilgrim's shrine is won,
And he and I must part,—so let it be,—
His task and mine alike are nearly done;
Yet once more let us look upon the sea;   1570
The midland ocean[47] breaks on him and me,
And from the Alban Mount we now behold
Our friend of youth, that Ocean, which when
    we
Beheld it last by Calpe's rock[48] unfold
Those waves we follow'd on till the dark Euxine[49]
    roll'd

CLXXVI

Upon the blue Symplegades;[50] long years—
Long, though not very many—since have done
Their work on both; some suffering and some
    tears
Have left us nearly where we had begun:

45 Suetonius informs us that Julius Cæsar was particularly gratified by that decree of the senate which enabled him to wear a
wreath of laurel on all occasions. He was anxious, not to show
that he was the conqueror of the world, but to hide that he was
bald.—(Byron.)
46 This is quoted in the *Decline and Fall of the Roman Empire*,
as a proof that the Coliseum was entire, when seen by the Anglo-
Saxon pilgrims at the end of the seventh, or the beginning of the
eighth, century.—(Byron.)
47 The Mediterranean.
48 Gibraltar. Byron is recollecting his first voyage to the Levant.
49 The Black Sea.
50 two islands in the narrow passage where the Black Sea flows
into the Bosphorus.

Yet not in vain our mortal race hath run;   1580
We have had our reward, and it is here,—
That we can yet feel gladden'd by the sun,
And reap from earth, sea, joy almost as dear
As if there were no man to trouble what is clear.

CLXXVII

Oh! that the Desert were my dwelling-place,
With one fair Spirit for my minister,
That I might all forget the human race,
And hating no one, love but only her!
Ye elements!—in whose ennobling stir
I feel myself exalted—Can ye not   1590
Accord me such a being? Do I err
In deeming such inhabit many a spot?
Though with them to converse can rarely be our
    lot.

CLXXVIII

There is a pleasure in the pathless woods,
There is a rapture on the lonely shore,
There is society, where none intrudes,
By the deep Sea, and music in its roar:
I love not Man the less, but Nature more,
From these our interviews, in which I steal
From all I may be, or have been before,   1600
To mingle with the Universe, and feel
What I can ne'er express, yet cannot all conceal.

CLXXIX

Roll on, thou deep and dark blue Ocean—roll!
Ten thousand fleets sweep over thee in vain;
Man marks the earth with ruin—his control
Stops with the shore; upon the watery plain
The wrecks are all thy deed, nor doth remain
A shadow of man's ravage, save his own,
When, for a moment, like a drop of rain,
He sinks into thy depths with bubbling
    groan,   1610
Without a grave, unknell'd, uncoffin'd, and un-
    known.

CLXXX

His steps are not upon thy paths,—thy fields
Are not a spoil for him,—thou dost arise
And shake him from thee; the vile strength he
    wields
For earth's destruction thou dost all despise,
Spurning him from thy bosom to the skies,
And send'st him, shivering in thy playful spray
And howling, to his Gods, where haply lies
His petty hope in some near port or bay,

And dashest him again to earth:—there let him
  lay.   1620

CLXXXI

The armaments which thunderstrike the walls
Of rock-built cities, bidding nations quake,
And monarchs tremble in their capitals,
The oak leviathans, whose huge ribs make
Their clay creator the vain title take
Of lord of thee, and arbiter of war—
These are thy toys, and, as the snowy flake,
They melt into thy yeast of waves, which mar
Alike the Armada's pride[51] or spoils of Trafal-
  gar.[52]

CLXXXII

Thy shores are empires, changed in all save
  thee—   1630
Assyria, Greece, Rome, Carthage, what are
  they?
Thy waters wash'd them power while they were
  free,
And many a tyrant since; their shores obey
The stranger, slave, or savage; their decay
Has dried up realms to deserts:—not so
  thou;—
Unchangeable, save to thy wild waves' play,
Time writes no wrinkle on thine azure brow:
Such as creation's dawn beheld, thou rollest now.

CLXXXIII

Thou glorious mirror, where the Almighty's
  form
Glasses itself in tempests; in all time,— 1640
Calm or convulsed, in breeze, or gale, or storm,
Icing the pole, or in the torrid clime
Dark-heaving—boundless, endless, and sub-
  lime,
The image of eternity, the throne
Of the Invisible; even from out thy slime
The monsters of the deep are made; each zone
Obeys thee; thou goest forth, dread, fathomless,
  alone.

CLXXXIV

And I have loved thee, Ocean! and my joy

Of youthful sports was on thy breast to be
Borne, like thy bubbles, onward: from a
  boy   1650
I wanton'd with thy breakers—they to me
Were a delight; and if the freshening sea
Made them a terror—'twas a pleasing fear,
For I was as it were a child of thee,
And trusted to thy billows far and near,
And laid my hand upon thy mane—as I do here.

CLXXXV

My task is done, my song hath ceased, my
  theme
Has died into an echo; it is fit
The spell should break of this protracted
  dream.
The torch shall be extinguish'd which hath
  lit   1660
My midnight lamp—and what is writ, is writ;
Would it were worthier! but I am not now
That which I have been—and my visions flit
Less palpably before me—and the glow
Which in my spirit dwelt is fluttering, faint, and
  low.

CLXXXVI

Farewell! a word that must be, and hath
  been—
A sound which makes us linger;—yet—fare-
  well!
Ye! who have traced the Pilgrim to the scene
Which is his last, if in your memories dwell
A thought which once was his, if on ye
  swell   1670
A single recollection, not in vain
He wore his sandal-shoon and scallop-shell;
Farewell! with *him* alone may rest the pain,
If such there were—with *you,* the moral of his
  strain.

  1817   1818

FARE THEE WELL[1]

'Alas! they had been friends in youth:
But whispering tongues can poison truth;
And constancy lives in realms above;

---

51 pride in defeating the Armada. Over half of the mighty Spanish fleet taken by the British in 1588 was destroyed by sea-storms.
52 The gale of wind which succeeded the battle of Trafalgar destroyed the greater part (if not all) of the prizes—nineteen sail of
the line—taken on that memorable day. I should be ashamed to
specify particulars which should be known to all, did we not know
that in France the people were kept in ignorance of the event of
this most glorious victory in modern times.—(Byron.)

1 These verses were addressed to Lady Byron shortly after the
separation. Byron had them printed for private circulation among
the 'initiated,' but copies soon leaked out and the poem appeared
in the London newspapers. A clamorous outcry of condemnation
followed. Even some of his friends censured the bad taste which
sanctioned publication of these verses and looked upon the sentiment they expressed with suspicion. Since Byron's time opinion
has widely differed as to the degree of their sincerity.

And life is thorny; and youth is vain;
And to be wroth with one we love,
Doth work like madness in the brain;

But never either found another
To free the hollow heart from paining—
They stood aloof, the scars remaining,
Like cliffs which had been rent asunder;
A dreary sea now flows between,
But neither heat, nor frost, nor thunder,
Shall wholly do away, I ween,
The marks of that which once hath been.'

COLERIDGE'S *Christabel.*

FARE thee well! and if for ever,
    Still for ever, fare thee well:
Even though unforgiving, never
    'Gainst thee shall my heart rebel.

Would that breast were bared before thee
    Where thy head so oft hath lain.
While that placid sleep came o'er thee
    Which thou ne'er canst know again:

Would that breast, by thee glanced over,
    Every inmost thought could show!   10
Then thou wouldst at last discover
    'Twas not well to spurn it so.

Though the world for this commend thee—
    Though it smile upon the blow,
Even its praises must offend thee,
    Founded on another's woe:

Though my many faults defaced me,
    Could no other arm be found,
Than the one which once embraced me,
    To inflict a cureless wound?   20

Yet, oh yet, thyself deceive not;
    Love may sink by slow decay,
But by sudden wrench, believe not
    Hearts can thus be torn away:

Still thine own its life retaineth,
    Still must mine, though bleeding, beat;
And the undying thought which paineth
    Is—that we no more may meet.

These are words of deeper sorrow
    Than the wail above the dead;   30
Both shall live, but every morrow
    Wake us from a widow'd bed.

And when thou wouldst solace gather,
    When our child's first accents flow,
Wilt thou teach her to say 'Father!'
    Though his care she must forego?

When her little hands shall press thee,
    When her lip to thine is press'd,
Think of him whose prayer shall bless thee,
    Think of him thy love had bless'd!   40

Should her lineaments resemble
    Those thou never more may'st see,
Then thy heart will softly tremble
    With a pulse yet true to me.

All my faults perchance thou knowest,
    All my madness none can know;
All my hopes, where'er thou goest,
    Wither, yet with *thee* they go.

Every feeling hath been shaken;
    Pride, which not a world could bow,   50
Bows to thee—by thee forsaken,
    Even my soul forsakes me now:

But 'tis done—all words are idle—
    Words from me are vainer still;
But the thoughts we cannot bridle
    Force their way without the will.

Fare thee well! thus disunited,
    Torn from every nearer tie
Sear'd in heart, and lone, and blighted,
    More than this I scarce can die.   60

17 March 1816   1816

STANZAS FOR MUSIC

THERE be none of Beauty's daughters
    With a magic like thee;
And like music on the waters
    Is thy sweet voice to me;
When, as if its sound were causing
The charmed ocean's pausing,
The waves lie still and gleaming
And the lull'd winds seem dreaming:

And the midnight moon is weaving
    Her bright chain o'er the deep;   10
Whose breast is gently heaving,
    As an infant's asleep:
So the spirit bows before thee,
    To listen and adore thee;

With a full but soft emotion,
Like the swell of Summer's ocean.

    28 March 1816   1816

STANZAS TO AUGUSTA[1]

THOUGH the day of my destiny's over,
    And the star of my fate hath declined,
Thy soft heart refused to discover
    The faults which so many could find;
Though thy soul with my grief was acquainted,
    It shrunk not to share it with me,
And the love which my spirit hath painted
    It never hath found but in *thee*.

Then when nature around me is smiling,
    The last smile which answers to mine,   10
I do not believe it beguiling,
    Because it reminds me of thine;
And when winds are at war with the ocean,
    As the breasts I believed in with me,
If their billows excite an emotion,
    It is that they bear me from *thee*.

Though the rock of my last hope is shiver'd,
    And its fragments are sunk in the wave,
Though I feel that my soul is deliver'd
    To pain—it shall not be its slave.   20
There is many a pang to pursue me:
    They may crush, but they shall not contemn;
They may torture, but shall not subdue me;
    'Tis of *thee* that I think—not of them.

Though human, thou didst not deceive me,
    Though woman, thou didst not forsake,
Though loved, thou forborest to grieve me,
    Though slander'd, thou never couldst shake;
Though trusted, thou didst not disclaim me,
    Though parted, it was not to fly,   30
Though watchful, 'twas not to defame me,
    Nor, mute, that the world might belie.

Yet I blame not the world, nor despise it,
    Nor the war of the many with one;
If my soul was not fitted to prize it,
    'Twas folly not sooner to shun:
And if dearly that error hath cost me,
    And more than I once could foresee,

I have found that, whatever it lost me,
    It could not deprive me of *thee*.   40

From the wreck of the past, which hath perish'd,
    Thus much I at least may recall,
It hath taught me that what I most cherish'd
    Deserved to be dearest of all:
In the desert a fountain is springing,
    In the wide waste there still is a tree,
And a bird in the solitude singing,
    Which speaks to my spirit of *thee*.

    1816   1816

EPISTLE TO AUGUSTA

MY sister! my sweet sister! if a name
Dearer and purer were, it should be thine;
Mountains and seas divide us, but I claim
No tears, but tenderness to answer mine:
Go where I will, to me thou art the same—
A loved regret which I would not resign,
There yet are two things in my destiny,—
A world to roam through, and a home with thee.

The first were nothing—had I still the last,
It were the haven of my happiness;   10
But other claims and other ties thou hast,
And mine is not the wish to make them less.
A strange doom is thy father's son's, and past
Recalling, as it lies beyond redress;
Reversed for him our grandsire's fate of
    yore,—
He had no rest at sea,[1] nor I on shore.

If my inheritance of storms hath been
In other elements, and on the rocks
Of perils, overlook'd or unforeseen,
I have sustain'd my share of worldly shocks, 20
The fault was mine; nor do I seek to screen
My errors with defensive paradox;
I have been cunning in mine overthrow,
The careful pilot of my proper woe.

Mine were my faults, and mine be their re-
    ward.
My whole life was a contest, since the day
That gave me being, gave me that which
    marr'd
The gift,—a fate, or will, that walk'd astray;
And I at times have found the struggle hard,

---

1 Augusta Leigh was Byron's half sister. It was upon Byron's suspected extramarital relations with Augusta that Lady Byron based her case for separation. Byron proudly asserted the purity of his love for Augusta; she, in turn, 'loyally supported him throughout the crisis of his domestic misfortunes.'

1 Admiral John Byron, known to sailors as 'Foulweather Jack,' had a reputation of never making a voyage without encountering storms at sea.

And thought of shaking off my bonds of
    clay: 30
But now I fain would for a time survive,
If but to see what next can well arrive.

Kingdoms and empires in my little day
I have outlived, and yet I am not old;
And when I look on this, the petty spray
Of my own years of trouble, which have roll'd
Like a wild bay of breakers, melts away:
Something—I know not what—does still up-
    hold
A spirit of slight patience;—not in vain,
Even for its own sake, do we purchase pain.   40

Perhaps the workings of defiance stir
Within me—or perhaps a cold despair,
Brought on when ills habitually recur,—
Perhaps a kinder clime, or purer air,
(For even to this may change of soul refer,
And with light armour we may learn to bear,)
Have taught me a strange quiet, which was not
The chief companion of a calmer lot.

I feel almost at times as I have felt
In happy childhood; trees, and flowers, and
    brooks,   50
Which do remember me of where I dwelt
Ere my young mind was sacrificed to books,
Come as of yore upon me, and can melt
My heart with recognition of their looks;
And even at moments I could think I see
Some living thing to love—but none like thee.

Here are the Alpine landscapes which create
A fund for contemplation;—to admire
Is a brief feeling of a trivial date;
But something worthier do such scenes in-
    spire: 60
Here to be lonely is not desolate,
For much I view which I could most desire,
And, above all, a lake[2] I can behold
Lovelier, not dearer, than our own of old.[3]

Oh that thou wert but with me!—but I grow
The fool of my own wishes, and forget
The solitude which I have vaunted so
Has lost its praise in this but one regret;
There may be others which I less may show;—
I am not of the plaintive mood, and yet   70
I feel an ebb in my philosophy,
And the tide rising in my alter'd eye.

_____
2 Geneva.   3 the lake at Newstead Abbey.

I did remind thee of our own dear Lake,
By the old Hall which may be mine no more,
Leman's is fair; but think not I forsake
The sweet remembrance of a dearer shore:
Sad havoc Time must with my memory make,
Ere *that* or *thou* can fade these eyes before;
Though, like all things which I have loved, they
    are
Resign'd for ever, or divided far.   80

The world is all before me; I but ask
Of Nature that with which she will comply—
It is but in her summer's sun to bask,
To mingle with the quiet of her sky,
To see her gentle face without a mask,
And never gaze on it with apathy.
She was my early friend, and now shall be
My sister—till I look again on thee.

I can reduce all feelings but this one;
And that I would not;—for at length I see   90
Such scenes as those wherein my life begun.
The earliest—even the only paths for me—
Had I but sooner learnt the crowd to shun,
I had been better than I now can be;
The passions which have torn me would have
    slept;
I had not suffer'd, and *thou* hadst not wept.

With false Ambition what had I to do?
Little with Love, and least of all with Fame;
And yet they came unsought, and with me
    grew,
And made me all which they can make—a
    name.   100
Yet this was not the end I did pursue;
Surely I once beheld a nobler aim.
But all is over—I am one the more
To baffled millions which have gone before.

And for the future, this world's future may
From me demand but little of my care;
I have outlived myself by many a day;
Having survived so many things that were;
My years have been no slumber, but the prey
Of ceaseless vigils; for I had the share   110
Of life which might have fill'd a century,
Before its fourth in time had pass'd me by.

And for the remnant which may be to come
I am content; and for the past I feel
Not thankless,—for within the crowded sum
Of struggles, happiness at times would steal,
And for the present, I would not benumb

My feelings further.—Nor shall I conceal
That with all this I still can look around,
And worship Nature with a thought pro-
    found.   120

For thee, my own sweet sister, in thy heart
I know myself secure, as thou in mine;
We were and are—I am, even as thou art—
Beings who ne'er each other can resign;
It is the same, together or apart,
From life's commencement to its slow decline
We are entwined—let death come slow or fast,
The tie which bound the first endures the last!
    1816   1830

PROMETHEUS[1]

TITAN! to whose immortal eyes
    The sufferings of mortality,
    Seen in their sad reality,
Were not as things that gods despise;
What was thy pity's recompense?
A silent suffering, and intense;
The rock, the vulture, and the chain,
All that the proud can feel of pain,
The agony they do not show,
The suffocating sense of woe,   10
    Which speaks but in its loneliness,
And then is jealous lest the sky
Should have a listener, nor will sigh
    Until its voice is echoless.

Titan! to thee the strife was given
    Between the suffering and the will,
    Which torture where they cannot kill;
And the inexorable Heaven,
And the deaf tyranny of Fate,
The ruling principle of Hate,   20
Which for its pleasure doth create
The things it may annihilate,
Refused thee even the boon to die:
The wretched gift eternity
Was thine—and thou hast borne it well.
All that the Thunderer wrung from thee
Was but the menace which flung back

On him the torments of thy rack;
The fate thou didst so well foresee,
But would not to appease him tell;   30
And in thy Silence was his Sentence,
And in his Soul a vain repentance,
And evil dread so ill dissembled,
That in his hand the lightnings trembled.

Thy Godlike crime was to be kind,
    To render with thy precepts less
    The sum of human wretchedness,
And strengthen Man with his own mind;
But baffled as thou wert from high,
Still in thy patient energy,   40
In the endurance, and repulse
    Of thine impenetrable Spirit,
Which Earth and Heaven could not convulse,
    A mighty lesson we inherit:
Thou art a symbol and a sign
    To Mortals of their fate and force;
Like thee, Man is in part divine,
    A troubled stream from a pure source;
And Man in portions can foresee
His own funereal destiny;   50
His wretchedness, and his resistance,
And his sad unallied existence;
To which his Spirit may oppose
Itself—and equal to all woes,
    And a firm will, and a deep sense,
Which even in torture can descry
    Its own concenter'd recompense,
Triumphant where it dares defy,
And making Death a Victory.
    1816   1816

SO, WE'LL GO NO MORE A-ROVING

At present, I am on the invalid regimen myself. The Carnival—that is, the latter part of it, and sitting up late o' nights, had knocked me up a little. But it is over . . . and, though I did not dissipate much upon the whole, yet I find 'the sword wearing out the scabbard,' though I have but just turned the corner of twenty-nine.—Byron's Letter to Thomas Moore, Venice, 28 February 1817.

So, we'll go no more a-roving
    So late into the night,
Though the heart be still as loving,
    And the moon be still as bright.

For the sword outwears its sheath,
    And the soul wears out the breast,
And the heart must pause to breathe,
    And love itself have rest.

---

1 Prometheus was a Titan who angered Zeus by stealing fire from heaven and giving it to mankind. For this act Zeus had Prometheus chained to a mountain, doomed to eternal torture, and had a vulture daily consume his liver, which grew again at night. He was finally freed by Hercules, who killed the vulture.** S. C. Chew points out Byron's long-standing admiration for the *Prometheus Bound* of Aeschylus, and the Aeschylean motives—'defiance of inexorable omnipotence; beneficence towards the wretched race of men; torture as the recompense of pity; foreknowledge of the divine tyrant's doom; the will which extorts triumph from suffering.'

Though the night was made for loving,
   And the day returns too soon,
Yet we'll go no more a-roving   10
   By the light of the moon.
   1817   1830

TO THOMAS MOORE

MY boat is on the shore,
   And my bark is on the sea;
But, before I go, Tom Moore,
   Here's a double health to thee!

Here's a sigh to those who love me,
   And a smile to those who hate;
And, whatever sky's above me,
   Here's a heart for every fate.

Though the ocean roar around me,
   Yet it still shall bear me on;   10
Though a desert should surround me,
   It hath springs that may be won.

Were't the last drop in the well,
   As I gasp'd upon the brink,
Ere my fainting spirit fell,
   'Tis to thee that I would drink.

With that water, as this wine,
   The libation I would pour
Should be—peace with thine and mine,
   And a health to thee, Tom Moore.   20
   July, 1817   1821

MANFRED

A DRAMATIC POEM

'There are more things in heaven and earth,
   Horatio,
Than are dreamt of in your philosophy.'[1]

[Contemporary reviewers thought they saw resemblances in Byron's poem to Goethe's *Faustus*, Marlowe's *Dr. Faustus*, and to the *Prometheus Bound* of Aeschylus. Byron admitted the possibility of the last influence, but he denied ever having read or seen Marlowe's *Faustus*. As for Goethe, in a letter to Murray, 7 June 1820, he wrote: 'His *Faust* I never read, for I don't know German; but Matthew "Monk" Lewis, in 1816, at Coligny, translated most of it to me *viva voce*, and I was naturally much struck with it; but it was the *Staubach* and the *Jungfrau*, and something else, much more than *Faustus*, that made me write *Manfred*.' That 'something else' was a turbulent state of mind resulting from a deep sense of guilt and bitter remorse over his love affair with Augusta Leigh.]

1 *Hamlet*, I, v, 166–7.

DRAMATIS PERSONAE

MANFRED	WITCH OF THE ALPS
CHAMOIS HUNTER	ARIMANES
ABBOT OF ST. MAURICE	NEMESIS
MANUEL	THE DESTINIES
HERMAN	SPIRITS, &c

The Scene of the Drama is amongst the Higher Alps—partly in the Castle of Manfred, and partly in the Mountains.

ACT I

SCENE I.—MANFRED *alone.—Scene, a Gothic Gallery.—Time, Midnight.*

Man. The lamp must be replenish'd, but even
      then
It will not burn so long as I must watch:
My slumbers—if I slumber—are not sleep,
But a continuance of enduring thought,
Which then I can resist not: in my heart
There is a vigil, and these eyes but close
To look within; and yet I live, and bear
The aspect and the form of breathing men.
But grief should be the instructor of the wise;
Sorrow is knowledge: they who know the
      most   10
Must mourn the deepest o'er the fatal truth,
The Tree of Knowledge is not that of Life.
Philosophy and science, and the springs
Of wonder, and the wisdom of the world,
I have essay'd, and in my mind there is
A power to make these subject to itself—
But they avail not: I have done men good,
And I have met with good even among men—
But this avail'd not: I have had my foes,
And none have baffled, many fallen before
      me—   20
But this avail'd not:—Good, or evil, life,
Powers, passions, all I see in other beings,
Have been to me as rain unto the sands,
Since that all-nameless hour. I have no dread,
And feel the curse to have no natural fear,
Nor fluttering throb, that beats with hopes or
      wishes,
Or lurking love of something on the earth.
Now to my task.—
               Mysterious agency!
Ye spirits of the unbounded Universe!
Whom I have sought in darkness and in
      light—   30
Ye, who do compass earth about, and dwell
In subtler essence—ye, to whom the tops
Of mountains inaccessible are haunts,

And earth's and ocean's caves familiar things—
I call upon ye by the written charm
Which gives me power upon you—Rise! Appear!
                              [*A pause.*
They come not yet.—Now by the voice of him
Who is the first among you—by this sign,
Which makes you tremble—by the claims of him
Who is undying,—Rise! Appear!——   40
        Appear!   [*A pause.*
If it be so—Spirits of earth and air,
Ye shall not thus elude me: by a power,
Deeper than all yet urged, a tyrant-spell,
Which had its birthplace in a star condemn'd,
The burning wreck of a demolish'd world,
A wandering hell in the eternal space;
By the strong curse which is upon my soul,
The thought which is within me and around me,
I do compel ye to my will—Appear!

[*A star is seen at the darker end of the gallery: it
  is stationary; and a voice is heard singing.*

First Spirit

    Mortal! to thy bidding bow'd,   50
    From my mansion in the cloud,
    Which the breath of twilight builds,
    And the summer's sunset gilds
    With the azure and vermillion,
    Which is mix'd for my pavilion;
    Though thy quest may be forbidden,
    On a star-beam I have ridden:
    To thine adjuration bow'd,
    Mortal—be thy wish avow'd!

Voice of the Second Spirit

Mont Blanc is the monarch of mountains;   60
    They crown'd him long ago
On a throne of rocks, in a robe of clouds,
    With a diadem of snow.
Around his waist are forests braced,
    The Avalanche in his hand;
But ere it fall, that thundering ball
    Must pause for my command.
The Glacier's cold and restless mass
    Moves onward day by day;
But I am he who bids it pass,   70
    Or with its ice delay.
I am the spirit of the place,
    Could make the mountain bow
And quiver to his cavern'd base—
    And what with me wouldst *Thou?*

Voice of the Third Spirit

    In the blue depth of the waters,

Where the wave hath no strife,
Where the wind is a stranger,
    And the sea-snake hath life,
Where the Mermaid is decking   80
    Her green hair with shells,
Like the storm on the surface
    Came the sound of thy spells;
O'er my calm Hall of Coral
    The deep echo roll'd—
To the Spirit of Ocean
    Thy wishes unfold!

Fourth Spirit

Where the slumbering earthquake
    Lies pillow'd on fire,
And the lakes of bitumen   90
    Rise boilingly higher;
Where the roots of the Andes
    Strike deep in the earth,
As their summits to heaven
    Shoot soaringly forth;
I have quitted my birthplace,
    Thy bidding to bide—
Thy spell hath subdued me,
    Thy will be my guide!

Fifth Spirit

I am the Rider of the wind,   100
    The Stirrer of the storm;
The hurricane I left behind
    Is yet with lightning warm;
To speed to thee, o'er shore and sea
    I swept upon the blast:
The fleet I met sail'd well, and yet
    'Twill sink ere night be past.

Sixth Spirit

My dwelling is the shadow of the night,
Why doth thy magic torture me with light?

Seventh Spirit

The star which rules thy destiny   110
Was ruled, ere earth began, by me:
It was a world as fresh and fair
As e'er revolved round sun in air;
Its course was free and regular,
Space bosom'd not a lovelier star.
The hour arrived—and it became
A wandering mass of shapeless flame,
A pathless comet, and a curse,
The menace of the universe;
Still rolling on with innate force,   120
Without a sphere, without a course,

A bright deformity on high,
The monster of the upper sky!
And thou! beneath its influence born—
Thou worm! whom I obey and scorn—
Forced by a power (which is not thine,
And lent thee but to make thee mine)
For this brief moment to descend,
Where these weak spirits round thee bend
And parley with a thing like thee—   130
What wouldst thou, Child of Clay! with me?

The Seven Spirits

Earth, ocean, air, night, mountains, winds, thy
        star,
    Are at thy beck and bidding, Child of Clay!
Before thee at thy quest their spirits are—
    What wouldst thou with us, son of mortals—
        say?

Man. Forgetfulness——
First Spirit. Of what—of whom—and why?
Man. Of that which is within me; read it
        there—
Ye know it, and I cannot utter it.
    Spirit. We can but give thee that which we pos-
        sess:
Ask of us subjects, sovereignty, the power   140
O'er earth—the whole, or portion—or a sign
Which shall control the elements, whereof
We are the dominators,—each and all,
These shall be thine.
    Man.   Oblivion, self-oblivion
Can ye not wring from out the hidden realms
Ye offer so profusely what I ask?
    Spirit. It is not in our essence, in our skill;
But—thou may'st die.
    Man.   Will death bestow it on me?
    Spirit. We are immortal, and do not forget;
We are eternal; and to us the past   150
Is, as the future, present. Art thou answer'd?
    Man. Ye mock me—but the power which
        brought ye here
Hath made you mine. Slaves, scoff not at my will!
The mind, the spirit, the Promethean spark,
The lightning of my being, is as bright,
Pervading, and far darting as your own,
And shall not yield to yours, though coop'd in
        clay!
Answer, or I will teach you what I am.
    Spirit. We answer as we answer'd; our reply
Is even in thine own words.
    Man.   Why say ye so?   160
    Spirit. If, as thou say'st, thine essence be as
        ours,

We have replied in telling thee, the thing
Mortals call death hath nought to do with us.
    Man. I then have call'd ye from your realms
        in vain;
Ye cannot, or ye will not, aid me.
    Spirit.   Say,
What we possess we offer; it is thine:
Bethink ere thou dismiss us; ask again;
Kingdom, and sway, and strength, and length of
        days——
    Man. Accursed! what have I to do with days?
They are too long already.—Hence—begone! 170
    Spirit. Yet pause: being here, our will would
        do thee service;
Bethink thee, is there then no other gift
Which we can make not worthless in thine eyes?
    Man. No, none: yet stay—one moment, ere we
        part,
I would behold ye face to face. I hear
Your voices, sweet and melancholy sounds,
As music on the waters; and I see
The steady aspect of a clear large star;
But nothing more. Approach me as ye are,
Or one, or all, in your accustom'd forms.   180
    Spirit. We have no forms, beyond the elements
Of which we are the mind and principle:
But choose a form—in that we will appear.
    Man. I have no choice; there is no form on
        earth
Hideous or beautiful to me. Let him,
Who is most powerful of ye, take such aspect
As unto him may seem most fitting—Come!

    Seventh Spirit [*appearing in the shape of a beau-
        tiful female figure*]. Behold!
    Man. Oh God! if it be thus, and *thou*
Art not a madness and a mockery,
I yet might be most happy, I will clasp thee,   190
And we again will be——
            [*The figure vanishes.*
        My heart is crush'd!
            [MANFRED *falls senseless.*
(*A voice is heard in the Incantation which follows.*)

When the moon is on the wave,
    And the glow-worm in the grass,
And the meteor on the grave,
    And the wisp on the morass;
When the falling stars are shooting,
And the answer'd owls are hooting,
And the silent leaves are still
In the shadow of the hill,
Shall my soul be upon thine,
With a power and with a sign.   200

Though thy slumber may be deep,
Yet thy spirit shall not sleep;
There are shades which will not vanish,
There are thoughts thou canst not banish;
By a power to thee unknown,
Thou canst never be alone;
Thou art wrapt as with a shroud,
Thou art gather'd in a cloud;
And for ever shalt thou dwell   210
In the spirit of this spell.
Though thou seest me not pass by,
Thou shalt feel me with thine eye
As a thing that, though unseen,
Must be near thee, and hath been;
And when in that secret dread
Thou hast turn'd around thy head,
Thou shalt marvel I am not
As thy shadow on the spot,
And the power which thou dost feel   220
Shall be what thou must conceal.

And a magic voice and verse
Hath baptized thee with a curse;
And a spirit of the air
Hath begirt thee with a snare;
In the wind there is a voice
Shall forbid thee to rejoice;
And to thee shall night deny
All the quiet of her sky;
And the day shall have a sun,   230
Which shall make thee wish it done.

From thy false tears I did distil
An essence which hath strength to kill;
From thy own heart I then did wring
The black blood in its blackest spring;
From thy own smile I snatch'd the snake,
For there it coil'd as in a brake;
From thy own lip I drew the charm
Which gave all these their chiefest harm;
In proving every poison known,   240
I found the strongest was thine own.

By thy cold breast and serpent smile,
By thy unfathom'd gulfs of guile,
By that most seeming virtuous eye,
By thy shut soul's hypocrisy;
By the perfection of thine art
Which pass'd for human thine own heart;
By thy delight in others' pain,
And by thy brotherhood of Cain,
I call upon thee! and compel   250
Thyself to be thy proper Hell!

And on thy head I pour the vial
Which doth devote thee to this trial;
Nor to slumber, nor to die,
Shall be in thy destiny;
Though thy death shall still seem near
To thy wish, but as a fear;
Lo! the spell now works around thee,
And the clankless chain hath bound thee;
O'er thy heart and brain together   260
Hath the word been pass'd—now wither!

SCENE II.—*The Mountain of the Jungfrau.—Time,*
    Morning.—MANFRED *alone upon the Cliffs.*

  Man. The spirits I have raised abandon me,
The spells which I have studied baffle me,
The remedy I reck'd of tortured me;
I lean no more on superhuman aid;
It hath no power upon the past, and for
The future, till the past be gulf'd in darkness,
It is not of my search.—My mother Earth!
And thou fresh breaking Day, and you, ye Moun-
    tains,
Why are ye beautiful? I cannot love ye.
And thou, the bright eye of the universe,   10
That openest over all, and unto all
Art a delight—thou shin'st not on my heart.
And you, ye crags, upon whose extreme edge
I stand, and on the torrent's brink beneath
Behold the tall pines dwindled as to shrubs
In dizziness of distance; when a leap,
A stir, a motion, even a breath, would bring
My breast upon its rocky bosom's bed
To rest for ever—wherefore do I pause?
I feel the impulse—yet I do not plunge;   20
I see the peril—yet do not recede;
And my brain reels—and yet my foot is firm:
There is a power upon me which withholds,
And makes it my fatality to live,—
If it be life to wear within myself
This barrenness of spirit, and to be
My own soul's sepulchre, for I have ceased
To justify my deeds unto myself—
The last infirmity of evil. Ay,
Thou winged and cloud-cleaving minister,   30
        [*An eagle passes.*
Whose happy flight is highest into heaven,
Well may'st thou swoop so near me—I should be
Thy prey, and gorge thine eaglets; thou art gone
Where the eye cannot follow thee; but thine
Yet pierces downward, onward, or above,
With a pervading vision.—Beautiful!
How beautiful is all this visible world!
How glorious in its action and itself!

But we, who name ourselves its sovereigns, we,
Half dust, half deity, alike unfit   40
To sink or soar, with our mix'd essence make
A conflict of its elements, and breathe
The breath of degradation and of pride,
Contending with low wants and lofty will,
Till our mortality predominates,
And men are—what they name not to them-
    selves,
And trust not to each other. Hark! the note,

    [*The Shepherd's pipe in the distance is heard.*
The natural music of the mountain reed—
For here the patriarchal days are not
A pastoral fable—pipes in the liberal air,   50
Mix'd with the sweet bells of the sauntering herd;
My soul would drink those echoes. Oh, that I
    were
The viewless spirit of a lovely sound,
A living voice, a breathing harmony,
A bodiless enjoyment—born and dying
With the blest tone which made me!

    Enter from below a CHAMOIS HUNTER.

    Chamois Hunter.   Even so
This way the chamois leapt: her nimble feet
Have baffled me; my gains to-day will scarce
Repay my break-neck travail.—What is here?
Who seems not of my trade, and yet hath
    reach'd   60
A height which none even of our mountaineers,
Save our best hunters, may attain: his garb
Is goodly, his mien manly, and his air
Proud as a free-born peasant's, at this distance:
I will approach him nearer.
    Man. [*not perceiving the other*]. To be thus—
Grey-hair'd with anguish, like these blasted
    pines,
Wrecks of a single winter, barkless, branchless,
A blighted trunk upon a cursed root,
Which but supplies a feeling to decay—
And to be thus, eternally but thus,   70
Having been otherwise! Now furrow'd o'er
With wrinkles, plough'd by moments,—not by
    years,—
And hours, all tortured into ages—hours
Which I outlive!—Ye toppling crags of ice!
Ye avalanches, whom a breath draws down
In mountainous o'erwhelming, come and crush
    me!
I hear ye momently above, beneath,
Crash with a frequent conflict; but ye pass,
And only fall on things that still would live;
On the young flourishing forest, or the hut   80

And hamlet of the harmless villager.
    C. Hun. The mists begin to rise from up the
    valley;
I'll warn him to descend, or he may chance
To lose at once his way and life together.
    Man. The mists boil up around the glaciers;
    clouds
Rise curling fast beneath me, white and sulphury,
Like foam from the roused ocean of deep Hell,
Whose every wave breaks on a living shore
Heap'd with the damn'd like pebbles.—I am
    giddy.
    C. Hun. I must approach him cautiously; if
    near,   90
A sudden step will startle him, and he
Seems tottering already.
    Man.   Mountains have fallen,
Leaving a gap in the clouds, and with the shock
Rocking their Alpine brethren; filling up
The ripe green valleys with destruction's splin-
    ters;
Damming the rivers with a sudden dash,
Which crush'd the waters into mist and made
Their fountains find another channel—thus,
Thus, in its old age, did Mount Rosenberg[2]—
Why stood I not beneath it?
    C. Hun.   Friend! have a care,   100
Your next step may be fatal!—for the love
Of him who made you, stand not on that
    brink!
    Man. [*not hearing him*]. Such would have been
    for me a fitting tomb;
My bones had then been quiet in their depth;
They had not then been strewn upon the rocks
For the wind's pastime—as thus—thus they shall
    be—
In this one plunge.—Farewell, ye opening
    heavens!
Look not upon me thus reproachfully—
You were not meant for me—Earth! take these
    atoms!

    [*As* MANFRED *is in act to spring from the cliff,
    the* CHAMOIS HUNTER *seizes and retains him
    with a sudden grasp.*
    C. Hun. Hold, madman!—though a-weary of
    thy life,   110
Stain not our pure vales with thy guilty blood:
Away with me———I will not quit my hold.
    Man. I am most sick at heart—nay, grasp me
    not—
I am all feebleness—the mountains whirl

---

2 In 1806 an enormous mass of rock slipped from the face of the
Rossberg burying four villages with 457 of their inhabitants.

Spinning around me———I grow blind———What
    art thou?

   C. Hun. I'll answer that anon. Away with
    me—

The clouds grow thicker———there—now lean on
    me—

Place your foot here—here, take this staff, and
    cling

A moment to that shrub—now give me your
    hand,

And hold fast by my girdle—softly—well—   120

The Chalet will be gain'd within an hour:

Come on, we'll quickly find a surer footing,

And something like a pathway, which the torrent

Hath wash'd since winter.—Come, 'tis bravely
    done—

You should have been a hunter.—Follow me.

   [*As they descend the rocks with difficulty, the
    scene closes.*

ACT II

SCENE I.—*A Cottage amongst the Bernese Alps.*

MANFRED *and the* CHAMOIS HUNTER

   C. Hun. No, no—yet pause—thou must not yet
    go forth:

Thy mind and body are alike unfit

To trust each other, for some hours, at least;

When thou art better, I will be thy guide—

But whither?

   Man.   It imports not: I do know

My route full well, and need no further guidance.

   C. Hun. Thy garb and gait bespeak thee of high
    lineage—

One of the many chiefs, whose castled crags

Look o'er the lower valleys—which of these

May call thee lord? I only know their portals;   10

My way of life leads me but rarely down

To bask by the huge hearths of those old halls,

Carousing with the vassals; but the paths,

Which step from out our mountains to their
    doors,

I know from childhood—which of these is thine?

   Man. No matter.

   C. Hunt.   Well, sir, pardon me the ques-
    tion,

And be of better cheer. Come, taste my wine;

'Tis of an ancient vintage; many a day

'T has thaw'd my veins among our glaciers, now

Let it do thus for thine—Come, pledge me
    fairly.   20

   Man. Away, away! there's blood upon the
    brim!

Will it then never—never sink in the earth?

   C. Hun. What dost thou mean? thy senses wan-
    der from thee.

   Man. I say 'tis blood—my blood! the pure
    warm stream

Which ran in the veins of my fathers, and in ours

When we were in our youth, and had one heart,

And loved each other as we should not love,

And this was shed: but still it rises up,

Colouring the clouds, that shut me out from
    heaven,

Where thou art not—and I shall never be.   30

   C. Hun. Man of strange words, and some half-
    maddening sin,

Which makes thee people vacancy, whate'er

Thy dread and sufferance be, there's comfort
    yet—

The aid of holy men, and heavenly patience—

   Man. Patience and patience! Hence—that
    word was made

For brutes of burthen, not for birds of prey;

Preach it to mortals of a dust like thine,—

I am not of thine order.

   C. Hun.   Thanks to heaven!

I would not be of thine for the free fame

Of William Tell; but whatsoe'er thine ill,   40

It must be borne, and these wild starts are useless.

   Man. Do I not bear it?—Look on me—I live.

   C. Hun. This is convulsion, and no healthful
    life.

   Man. I tell thee, man! I have lived many years,

Many long years, but they are nothing now

To those which I must number: ages—ages—

Space and eternity—and consciousness,

With the fierce thirst of death—and still un-
    slaked!

   C. Hun. Why, on thy brow the seal of middle
    age

Hath scarce been set; I am thine elder far.   50

   Man. Think'st thou existence doth depend on
    time?

It doth; but actions are our epochs: mine

Have made my days and nights imperishable,

Endless, and all alike, as sands on the shore,

Innumerable atoms; and one desert,

Barren and cold, on which the wild waves break,

But nothing rests, save carcasses and wrecks,

Rocks, and the salt-surf weeds of bitterness.

   C. Hun. Alas! he's mad—but yet I must not
    leave him.

   Man. I would I were—for then the things I
    see   60

Would be but a distemper'd dream.

   C. Hun.   What is it

That thou dost see, or think thou look'st upon?

    Man. Myself, and thee—a peasant of the
    Alps—
Thy humble virtues, hospitable home,
And spirit patient, pious, proud, and free;
Thy self-respect, grafted on innocent thoughts;
Thy days of health, and nights of sleep; thy toils,
By danger dignified, yet guiltless; hopes
Of cheerful old age and a quiet grave,
With cross and garland over its green turf,   70
And thy grandchildren's love for epitaph;
This do I see—and then I look within—
It matters not—my soul was scorch'd already!

    C. Hun. And wouldst thou then exchange thy
    lot for mine?

    Man. No, friend! I would not wrong thee, nor
    exchange
My lot with living being: I can bear—
However wretchedly, 'tis still to bear—
In life what others could not brook to dream,
But perish in their slumber.

    C. Hun.   And with this—
This cautious feeling for another's pain,   80
Canst thou be black with evil?—say not so.
Can one of gentle thoughts have wreak'd revenge
Upon his enemies?

    Man.   Oh! no, no, no!
My injuries came down on those who loved me—
On those whom I best loved: I never quell'd
An enemy, save in my just defence—
But my embrace was fatal.

    C. Hun.   Heaven give thee rest!
And penitence restore thee to thyself;
My prayers shall be for thee.

    Man.   I need them not—
But can endure thy pity. I depart—   90
'Tis time—farewell!—Here's gold, and thanks
    for thee—
No words—it is thy due.—Follow me not—
I know my path—the mountain peril's past:
And once again I charge thee, follow not!
                   [*Exit* MANFRED.

SCENE II.—*A lower Valley in the Alps.—A*
Cataract.

Enter MANFRED.

It is not noon—the sunbow's rays[3] still arch
The torrent with the many hues of heaven,
And roll the sheeted silver's waving column

O'er the crag's headlong perpendicular,
And fling its lines of foaming light along,
And to and fro, like the pale courser's tail,
The Giant steed, to be bestrode by Death,
As told in the Apocalypse.[4] No eyes
But mine now drink this sight of loveliness;
I should be sole in this sweet solitude,   10
And with the Spirit of the place divide
The homage of these waters.—I will call her.

    [MANFRED *takes some of the water into the palm*
    of his hand, and flings it into the air, muttering
    the adjuration. After a pause, the WITCH OF
    THE ALPS *rises beneath the arch of the shadow*
    of the torrent.

Beautiful Spirit! with thy hair of light,
And dazzling eyes of glory, in whose form
The charms of earth's least mortal daughters
    grow
To an unearthly stature, in an essence
Of purer elements; while the hues of youth,—
Carnation'd like a sleeping infant's cheek,
Rock'd by the beating of her mother's heart,
Or the rose tints, which summer's twilight
    leaves   20
Upon the lofty glacier's virgin snow,
The blush of earth embracing with her
    heaven,—
Tinge thy celestial aspect, and make tame
The beauties of the sunbow which bends o'er
    thee.
Beautiful Spirit! in thy calm clear brow,
Wherein is glass'd serenity of soul,
Which of itself shows immortality,
I read that thou wilt pardon to a Son
Of Earth, whom the abstruser powers permit
At times to commune with them—if that he   30
Avail him of his spells—to call thee thus,
And gaze on thee a moment.

    Witch.   Son of Earth!
I know thee, and the powers which give thee
    power;
I know thee for a man of many thoughts,
And deeds of good and ill, extreme in both,
Fatal and fated in thy sufferings.
I have expected this—what wouldst thou with
    me?

    Man. To look upon thy beauty—nothing fur-
    ther.
The face of the earth hath madden'd me, and I
Take refuge in her mysteries, and pierce   40
To the abodes of those who govern her—
But they can nothing aid me. I have sought

---

3 This iris is formed by the rays of the sun over the lower part
of the Alpine torrents: it is exactly like a rainbow come down to
pay a visit, and so close that you may walk into it: this effect lasts
till noon.—(Byron.)

4 See Revelation, vi, 8.

From them what they could not bestow, and now
I search no further.
   Witch.   What could be the quest
Which is not in the power of the most powerful,
The rulers of the invisible?
   Man.   A boon;
But why should I repeat it? 'twere in vain.
   Witch. I know not that; let thy lips utter it.
   Man. Well, though it torture me, 'tis but the
     same;
My pang shall find a voice. From my youth up-
    wards   50
My spirit walk'd not with the souls of men,
Nor look'd upon the earth with human eyes;
The thirst of their ambition was not mine,
The aim of their existence was not mine;
My joys, my griefs, my passions, and my powers,
Made me a stranger; though I wore the form,
I had no sympathy with breathing flesh,
Nor midst the creatures of clay that girded me
Was there but one who—but of her anon.
I said with men, and with the thoughts of
    men,   60
I held but slight communion; but instead,
My joy was in the wilderness,—to breathe
The difficult air of the iced mountain's top,
Where the birds dare not build, nor insect's wing
Flit o'er the herbless granite; or to plunge
Into the torrent, and to roll along
On the swift whirl of the new breaking wave
Of river-stream, or ocean, in their flow.
In these my early strength exulted; or
To follow through the night the moving moon, 70
The stars and their development; or catch
The dazzling lightnings till my eyes grew dim;
Or to look, list'ning, on the scatter'd leaves,
While Autumn winds were at their evening song.
These were my pastimes, and to be alone;
For if the beings, of whom I was one,—
Hating to be so,—cross'd me in my path,
I felt myself degraded back to them,
And was all clay again. And then I dived,
In my lone wanderings, to the caves of death, 80
Searching its cause in its effect; and drew
From wither'd bones, and skulls, and heap'd up
    dust,
Conclusions most forbidden. Then I pass'd
The nights of years in sciences untaught,
Save in the old time; and with time and toil,
And terrible ordeal, and such penance
As in itself hath power upon the air,
And spirits that do compass air and earth,
Space, and the peopled infinite, I made
Mine eyes familiar with Eternity,   90
Such as, before me, did the Magi, and

He[5] who from out their fountain dwellings raised
Eros and Anteros, at Gadara,
As I do thee;—and with my knowledge grew
The thirst of knowledge, and the power and joy
Of this most bright intelligence, until—
   Witch. Proceed.
   Man.   Oh! I but thus prolong'd my words,
Boasting these idle attributes, because
As I approach the core of my heart's grief—
But to my task. I have not named to thee   100
Father or mother, mistress, friend, or being,
With whom I wore the chain of human ties;
If I had such, they seem'd not such to me;
Yet there was one—
   Witch.   Spare not thyself—proceed.
   Man. She was like me in lineaments; her eyes,
Her hair, her features, all, to the very tone
Even of her voice, they said were like to mine;
But soften'd all, and temper'd into beauty:
She had the same lone thoughts and wanderings,
The quest of hidden knowledge, and a mind 110
To comprehend the universe: nor these
Alone, but with them gentler powers than mine,
Pity, and smiles, and tears—which I had not;
And tenderness—but that I had for her;
Humility—and that I never had.
Her faults were mine—her virtues were her
    own—
I loved her, and destroy'd her!
   Witch.   With thy hand?
   Man. Not with my hand, but heart, which
    broke her heart;
It gazed on mine, and wither'd. I have shed
Blood, but not hers—and yet her blood was
    shed;   120
I saw—and could not stanch it.
   Witch.   And for this—
A being of the race thou dost despise,
The order, which thine own would rise above,
Mingling with us and ours,—thou dost forego
The gifts of our great knowledge, and shrink'st
    back
To recreant mortality—Away!
   Man. Daughter of Air! I tell thee, since that
    hour—
But words are breath—look on me in my sleep,
Or watch my watchings—Come and sit by me!
My solitude is solitude no more,   130
But peopled with the Furies;—I have gnash'd
My teeth in darkness till returning morn,
Then cursed myself till sunset;—I have pray'd
For madness as a blessing—'tis denied me.

---

5 The philosopher Jamblicus of the fourth century who, it is
said, raised by a magical formula Eros (Love) and Anteros
(Love's Contrary) from the springs at Gadara in Syria.

I have affronted death—but in the war
Of elements the waters shrunk from me,
And fatal things pass'd harmless; the cold hand
Of an all-pitiless demon held me back,
Back by a single hair, which would not break.
In fantasy, imagination, all   140
The affluence of my soul—which one day was
A Crœsus in creation—I plunged deep,
But, like an ebbing wave, it dash'd me back
Into the gulf of my unfathom'd thought.
I plunged amidst mankind—Forgetfulness
I sought in all, save where 'tis to be found.
And that I have to learn; my sciences,
My long-pursued and superhuman art,
Is mortal here: I dwell in my despair—
And live—and live for ever.

    Witch.   It may be   150
That I can aid thee.

    Man.   To do this thy power
Must wake the dead, or lay me low with them.
Do so—in any shape—in any hour—
With any torture—so it be the last.

    Witch. That is not in my province; but if Thou
Wilt swear obedience to my will, and do
My bidding, it may help thee to thy wishes.

    Man. I will not swear—Obey! and whom? the
       spirits
Whose presence I command, and be the slave
Of those who served me—Never!

    Witch.   Is this all? 160
Hast thou no gentler answer?—Yet bethink thee,
And pause ere thou rejectest.

    Man.   I have said it.

    Witch. Enough! I may retire then—say!

    Man.   Retire!
               [*The* WITCH *disappears*.

    Man, [*alone*]. We are the fools of time and ter-
       ror: Days
Steal on us, and steal from us; yet we live,
Loathing our life, and dreading still to die.
In all the days of this detested yoke—
This vital weight upon the struggling heart,
Which sinks with sorrow, or beats quick with
       pain,
Or joy that ends in agony or faintness—   170
In all the days of past and future, for
In life there is no present, we can number
How few—how less than few—wherein the soul
Forbears to pant for death, and yet draws back
As from a stream in winter, though the chill
Be but a moment's. I have one resource
Still in my science—I can call the dead,
And ask them what it is we dread to be:
The sternest answer can but be the Grave,

And that is nothing. If they answer not—— 180
The buried Prophet answered to the Hag
Of Endor;[6] and the Spartan Monarch drew
From the Byzantine maid's unsleeping spirit
An answer and his destiny—he slew
That which he loved, unknowing what he slew,
And died unpardon'd—though he call'd in aid
The Phyxian Jove, and in Phigalia roused
The Arcadian Evocators to compel
The indignant shadow to depose her wrath,
Or fix her term of vengeance—she replied   190
In words of dubious import, but fulfill'd.[7]
If I had never lived, that which I love
Had still been living; had I never loved,
That which I love would still be beautiful,
Happy and giving happiness. What is she?
What is she now?—a sufferer for my sins—
A thing I dare not think upon—or nothing.
Within few hours I shall not call in vain—
Yet in this hour I dread the thing I dare:
Until this hour I never shrunk to gaze   200
On spirit, good or evil—now I tremble,
And feel a strange cold thaw upon my heart.
But I can act even what I most abhor,
And champion human fears.—The night ap-
     proaches.   [*Exit*.

SCENE III.—*The Summit of the Jungfrau
Mountain.*

Enter FIRST DESTINY.

The moon is rising broad, and round, and bright;
And here on snows, where never human foot
Of common mortal trod, we nightly tread,
And leave no traces: o'er the savage sea,
The glassy ocean of the mountain ice,
We skim its rugged breakers, which put on
The aspect of a tumbling tempest's foam,
Frozen in a moment—a dead whirlpool's image:
And this most steep fantastic pinnacle,
The fretwork of some earthquake—where the
       clouds   10
Pause to repose themselves in passing by—
Is sacred to our revels, or our vigils;
Here do I wait my sisters, on our way
To the Hall of Arimanes,[8] for to-night
Is our great festival—'tis strange they come not.

6 By Saul's command the Witch of Endor called up Samuel from the grave. See I Samuel, xxviii, 8–15.

7 Pausanias, King of Sparta, by mistake killed Cleonice, his mistress, who was visiting his chamber in darkness. Thereafter, he was haunted by her image until in a temple he invoked her spirit and entreated her forgiveness. She enigmatically foretold that he would soon be delivered from all his troubles. Shortly after he was slain in Sparta.

8 abode of the Spirit of Evil, high in the air above the Jungfrau. Arimanes is 'Prince of the Powers of the Air.'

A Voice without, singing.

The Captive Usurper,
 Hurl'd down from the throne,
Lay buried in torpor,
 Forgotten and lone;
I broke through his slumbers,   20
 I shiver'd his chain,
I leagued him with numbers—
 He's Tyrant again!
With the blood of a million he'll answer my care,
With a nation's destruction—his flight and de-
 spair.

Second Voice, without.

The ship sail'd on, the ship sail'd fast,
But I left not a sail, and I left not a mast;
There is not a plank of the hull or the deck,
And there is not a wretch to lament o'er his
 wreck;
Save one, whom I held, as he swam, by the
 hair,   30
And he was a subject well worthy my care;
A traitor on land, and a pirate at sea—
But I saved him to wreak further havoc for me!

First Destiny, answering.

The city lies sleeping;
 The morn, to deplore it,
May dawn on it weeping:
 Sullenly, slowly,
The black plague flew o'er it—
 Thousands lie lowly;
Tens of thousands shall perish;   40
 The living shall fly from
The sick they should cherish;
 But nothing can vanquish
The touch that they die from.
 Sorrow and anguish,
And evil and dread,
 Envelope a nation;
The blest are the dead,
Who see not the sight
 Of their own desolation;   50
This work of a night—
This wreck of a realm—this deed of my doing—
For ages I've done, and shall still be renewing!

Enter the SECOND *and* THIRD DESTINIES.

The Three.

Our hands contain the hearts of men,
 Our footsteps are their graves:
We only give to take again
 The spirits of our slaves!

First Des. Welcome!—Where's Nemesis?
 Second Des.   At some great work;
But what I know not, for my hands were full.
 Third Des. Behold she cometh.   60

Enter NEMESIS.

 First Des.   Say, where hast thou been?
My sisters and thyself are slow to-night.
 Nem. I was detain'd repairing shatter'd
 thrones,
Marrying fools, restoring dynasties,
Avenging men upon their enemies,
And making them repent their own revenge;
Goading the wise to madness; from the dull
Shaping out oracles to rule the world
Afresh, for they were waxing out of date,
And mortals dared to ponder for themselves,
To weigh kings in the balance, and to speak 70
Of freedom, the forbidden fruit.—Away!
We have outstay'd the hour—mount we our
 clouds!   [*Exeunt.*

SCENE IV.—*The Hall of Arimanes—Arimanes on
 his Throne, a Globe of Fire, surrounded
 by the Spirits.*

Hymn of the SPIRITS.

Hail to our Master!—Prince of Earth and Air!
 Who walks the clouds and waters—in his hand
The sceptre of the elements, which tear
 Themselves to chaos at his high command!
He breatheth—and a tempest shakes the sea;
 He speaketh—and the clouds reply in thunder;
He gazeth—from his glance the sunbeams flee;
 He moveth—earthquakes rend the world
 asunder.
Beneath his footsteps the volcanoes rise;
 His shadow is the Pestilence; his path 10
The comets herald through the crackling skies;
 And planets turn to ashes at his wrath.
To him War offers daily sacrifice;
 To him Death pays his tribute: Life is his,
With all its infinite of agonies—
 And his the spirit of whatever is!

Enter the DESTINIES *and* NEMESIS.

First Des. Glory to Arimanes! on the earth
His power increaseth—both my sisters did
His bidding, nor did I neglect my duty!
 Second Des. Glory to Arimanes! we who
 bow   20
The necks of men, bow down before his throne!
 Third Des. Glory to Arimanes! we await
His nod!
 Nem. Sovereign of Sovereigns! we are thine,

And all that liveth, more or less, is ours,
And most things wholly so; still to increase
Our power, increasing thine, demands our care,
And we are vigilant. The late commands
Have been fulfill'd to the utmost.

Enter MANFRED.

 A Spirit.   What is here?
A mortal!—Thou most rash and fatal wretch,
Bow down and worship!
 Second Spirit.   I do know the man— 30
A Magian of great power, and fearful skill!
 Third Spirit. Bow down and worship, slave!—
        What, know'st thou not
Thine and our Sovereign?—Tremble, and obey!
 All the Spirits. Prostrate thyself, and thy con-
  demnèd clay,
Child of the Earth! or dread the worst.
 Man.   I know it;
And yet ye see I kneel not.
 Fourth Spirit.   'Twill be taught thee.
 Man. 'Tis taught already;—many a night on
  the earth,
On the bare ground, have I bow'd down my face,
And strew'd my head with ashes; I have known
The fulness of humiliation, for 40
I sunk before my vain despair, and knelt
To my own desolation.
 Fifth Spirit.   Dost thou dare
Refuse to Arimanes on his throne
What the whole earth accords, beholding not
The terror of his glory?—Crouch, I say.
 Man. Bid *him* bow down to that which is above
  him,
The overruling Infinite—the Maker
Who made him not for worship—let him kneel,
And we will kneel together.
 The Spirits.   Crush the worm!
Tear him in pieces!—
 First Des. Hence! avaunt!—he's mine. 50
Prince of the Powers invisible! This man
Is of no common order, as his port
And presence here denote; his sufferings
Have been of an immortal nature, like
Our own; his knowledge, and his powers and
  will,
As far as is compatible with clay,
Which clogs the ethereal essence, have been such
As clay hath seldom borne; his aspirations
Have been beyond the dwellers of the earth,
And they have only taught him what we
  know— 60
That knowledge is not happiness, and science
But an exchange of ignorance for that
Which is another kind of ignorance.

This is not all—the passions, attributes
Of earth and heaven, from which no power, nor
  being,
Nor breath from the worm upwards is exempt,
Have pierced his heart, and in their consequence
Made him a thing which I, who pity not,
Yet pardon those who pity. He is mine,
And thine, it may be; be it so, or not, 70
No other Spirit in this region hath
A soul like his—or power upon his soul.
 Nem. What doth he here then?
 First Des.   Let him answer that.
 Man. Ye know what I have known; and with-
  out power
I could not be amongst ye: but there are
Powers deeper still beyond—I come in quest
Of such, to answer unto what I seek.
 Nem. What wouldst thou?
 Man.   Thou canst not reply to me.
Call up the dead—my question is for them.
 Nem. Great Arimanes, doth thy will avouch 80
The wishes of this mortal?
 Ari.   Yea.
 Nem.   Whom wouldst thou
Uncharnel?
 Man.   One without a tomb—call up
Astarte.

Nemesis.

 Shadow! or Spirit!
  Whatever thou art,
 Which still doth inherit
  The whole or a part
 Of the form of thy birth,
  Of the mould of thy clay,
 Which return'd to the earth, 90
  Re-appear to the day!
 Bear what thou borest,
  The heart and the form,
 And the aspect thou worest
  Redeem from the worm.

 Appear!—Appear!—Appear!
 Who sent thee there requires thee here!

[*The Phantom of* ASTARTE *rises and stands in
 the midst.*

 Man. Can this be death? there's bloom upon
  her cheek;
But now I see it is no living hue,
But a strange hectic—like the unnatural red 100
Which Autumn plants upon the perish'd leaf.
It is the same! Oh, God! that I should dread
To look upon the same—Astarte!—No,
I cannot speak to her—but bid her speak—
Forgive me or condemn me.

Nemesis.

By the power which hath broken
    The grave which enthrall'd thee,
Speak to him, who hath spoken,
    Or those who have call'd thee!

    Man.   She is silent,   110
And in that silence I am more than answer'd.
    Nem. My power extends no further. Prince of
    Air!
It rests with thee alone—command her voice.
    Ari. Spirit—obey this sceptre!
    Nem.   Silent still!
She is not of our order, but belongs
To the other powers. Mortal! thy quest is vain,
And we are baffled also.
    Man.   Hear me, hear me—
Astarte! my beloved! speak to me:
I have so much endured—so much endure—
Look on me! the grave hath not changed thee
    more   120
Than I am changed for thee. Thou lovedst me
Too much, as I loved thee: we were not made
To torture thus each other, though it were
The deadliest sin to love as we have loved.
Say that thou loath'st me not—that I do bear
This punishment for both—that thou wilt be
One of the blessed—and that I shall die;
For hitherto all hateful things conspire
To bind me in existence—in a life
Which makes me shrink from immortality— 130
A future like the past. I cannot rest.
I know not what I ask, nor what I seek:
I feel but what thou art, and what I am;
And I would hear yet once before I perish
The voice which was my music—Speak to me!
For I have call'd on thee in the still night,
Startled the slumbering birds from the hush'd
    boughs,
And woke the mountain wolves, and made the
    caves
Acquainted with thy vainly echoed name,
Which answer'd me—many things answer'd
    me—   140
Spirits and men—but thou wert silent all.
Yet speak to me! I have outwatch'd the stars,
And gazed o'er heaven in vain in search of thee.
Speak to me! I have wander'd o'er the earth,
And never found thy likeness—Speak to me!
Look on the fiends around —they feel for me:
I fear them not, and feel for thee alone—
Speak to me! though it be in wrath;—but say—
I reck not what—but let me hear thee once—
This once—once more!
    Phantom of Astarte. Manfred!

    Man.   Say on, say on—   150
I live but in the sound—it is thy voice!
    Phan. Manfred! To-morrow ends thine earthly
    ills.
Farewell!
    Man. Yet one word more—am I forgiven?
    Phan. Farewell!
    Man.   Say, shall we meet again?
    Phan.   Farewell!
    Man.   One word for mercy! Say, thou lovest
    me.
    Phan. Manfred!
    [*The Spirit of* ASTARTE *disappears.*
    Nem. She's gone, and will not be recall'd;
Her words will be fulfill'd. Return to the earth.
    A Spirit. He is convulsed.—This is to be a mor-
    tal
And seek the things beyond mortality.
    Another Spirit. Yet, see, he mastereth himself,
    and makes   160
His torture tributary to his will.
Had he been one of us, he would have made
An awful spirit.
    Nem.   Hast thou further question
Of our great sovereign, or his worshippers?
    Man. None.
    Nem.   Then, for a time, farewell.
    Man. We meet then! Where? On the earth?—
Even as thou wilt: and for the grace accorded
I now depart a debtor. Fare ye well!
                      [*Exit* MANFRED.
         (*Scene closes.*)

ACT III

SCENE I.—*A Hall in the Castle of Manfred.*

MANFRED *and* HERMAN.

    Man. What is the hour?
    Her.   It wants but one till sunset,
And promises a lovely twilight.
    Man.   Say,
Are all things so disposed of in the tower
As I directed?
    Her.   All, my lord, are ready:
Here is the key and casket.
    Man.   It is well:
Thou may'st retire.   [*Exit* HERMAN.
    Man. [*alone*]. There is a calm upon me—
Inexplicable stillness! which till now
Did not belong to what I knew of life.
If that I did not know philosophy
To be of all our vanities the motliest,   10
The merest word that ever fool'd the ear
From out the schoolman's jargon, I should deem

The golden secret, the sought 'Kalon,'[9] found,
And seated in my soul. It will not last,
But it is well to have known it, though but once:
It hath enlarged my thoughts with a new sense,
And I within my tablets would note down
That there is such a feeling. Who is there?

Re-enter HERMAN.

Her. My lord, the abbot of St. Maurice craves
To greet your presence.

Enter the ABBOT OF ST. MAURICE.

Abbot. Peace be with Count Manfred!   20
Man. Thanks, holy father! welcome to these
    walls;
Thy presence honours them, and blesseth those
Who dwell within them.
Abbot.   Would it were so, Count!—
But I would fain confer with thee alone.
Man. Herman, retire.—What would my rever-
    end guest?
Abbot. Thus, without prelude:—Age and zeal,
    my office,
And good intent, must plead my privilege;
Our near, though not acquainted neighbourhood,
May also be my herald. Rumours strange,
And of unholy nature, are abroad,   30
And busy with thy name; a noble name
For centuries: may he who bears it now
Transmit it unimpair'd!
Man.   Proceed,—I listen.
Abbot. 'Tis said thou holdest converse with the
    things
Which are forbidden to the search of man;
That with the dwellers of the dark abodes,
The many evil and unheavenly spirits
Which walk the valley of the shade of death,
Thou communest. I know that with mankind,
Thy fellows in creation, thou dost rarely   40
Exchange thy thoughts, and that thy solitude
Is as an anchorite's, were it but holy.
Man. And what are they who do avouch these
    things?
Abbot. My pious brethren—the scared peas-
    antry—
Even thy own vassals—who do look on thee
With most unquiet eyes. Thy life's in peril.
Man. Take it.
Abbot. I come to save, and not destroy:
I would not pry into thy secret soul;
But if these things be sooth, there still is time
For penitence and pity: reconcile thee   50
With the true church, and through the church to
    heaven.

Man. I hear thee. This is my reply: whate'er
I may have been, or am, doth rest between
Heaven and myself. I shall not choose a mortal
To be my mediator. Have I sinn'd
Against your ordinances? prove and punish!
Abbot. My son! I did not speak of punishment,
But penitence and pardon;—with thyself
The choice of such remains—and for the last,
Our institutions and our strong belief   60
Have given me power to smooth the path from
    sin
To higher hope and better thoughts; the first
I leave to heaven,—'Vengeance is mine alone!'
So saith the Lord, and with all humbleness
His servant echoes back the awful word.
Man. Old man! there is no power in holy men,
Nor charm in prayer, nor purifying form
Of penitence, nor outward look, nor fast,
Nor agony—nor, greater than all these,
The innate tortures of that deep despair,   70
Which is remorse without the fear of hell,
But all in all sufficient to itself
Would make a hell of heaven—can exorcise
From out the unbounded spirit the quick sense
Of its own sins, wrongs, sufferance, and revenge
Upon itself; there is no future pang
Can deal that justice on the self-condemn'd
He deals on his own soul.
Abbot.   All this is well;
For this will pass away, and be succeeded
By an auspicious hope, which shall look up   80
With calm assurance to that blessed place,
Which all who seek may win, whatever be
Their earthly errors, so they be atoned:
And the commencement of atonement is
The sense of its necessity. Say on—
And all our church can teach thee shall be
    taught;
And all we can absolve thee shall be pardon'd.
Man. When Rome's sixth emperor[10] was near
    his last,
The victim of a self-inflicted wound,
To shun the torments of a public death   90
From senates once his slaves, a certain soldier,
With show of loyal pity, would have stanch'd
The gushing throat with his officious robe;
The dying Roman thrust him back, and said—
Some empire still in his expiring glance—
'It is too late—is this fidelity?'
Abbot. And what of this?
Man.   I answer with the Roman—
'It is too late!'
Abbot.   It never can be so,

---

9 Greek for the Beautiful, in a moral sense, meaning the highest good of human existence.

10 Nero.

To reconcile thyself with thy own soul,
And thy own soul with heaven. Hast thou no
    hope?   100
'Tis strange—even those who do despair above,
Yet shape themselves some fantasy on earth,
To which frail twig they cling, like drowning men.
   Man. Ay—father! I have had those earthly
    visions,
And noble aspirations in my youth,
To make my own the mind of other men,
The enlightener of nations; and to rise
I knew not whither—it might be to fall;
But fall, even as the mountain-cataract,
Which having leapt from its more dazzling
    height,   110
Even in the foaming strength of its abyss,
(Which casts up misty columns that become
Clouds raining from the re-ascended skies,)
Lies low but mighty still.—But this is past,
My thoughts mistook themselves.
   Abbot.   And wherefore so?
   Man. I could not tame my nature down; for he
Must serve who fain would sway; and soothe,
    and sue,
And watch all time, and pry into all place,
And be a living lie, who would become
A mighty thing amongst the mean, and such 120
The mass are; I disdain'd to mingle with
A herd, though to be leader—and of wolves.
The lion is alone, and so am I.
   Abbot. And why not live and act with other
    men?
   Man. Because my nature was averse from life;
And yet not cruel; for I would not make,
But find a desolation. Like the wind,
The red-hot breath of the most lone simoom,[11]
Which dwells but in the desert, and sweeps o'er
The barren sands which bear no shrubs to
    blast,   130
And revels o'er their wild and arid waves,
And seeketh not, so that it is not sought,
But being met is deadly,—such hath been
The course of my existence; but there came
Things in my path which are no more. ·
   Abbot. ·   Alas!
I 'gin to fear that thou art past all aid
From me and from my calling; yet so young,
I still would—
   Man.   Look on me! there is an order
Of mortals on the earth, who do become
Old in their youth, and die ere middle age, 140
Without the violence of warlike death;
Some perishing of pleasure, some of study,

Some worn with toil, some of mere weariness,
Some of disease, and some insanity,
And some of wither'd or of broken hearts;
For this last is a malady which slays
More than are number'd in the lists of Fate,
Taking all shapes, and bearing many names.
Look upon me! for even of all these things
Have I partaken; and of all these things,   150
One were enough; then wonder not that I
Am what I am, but that I ever was,
Or having been, that I am still on earth.
   Abbot. Yet, hear me still——
   Man.   Old man! I do respect
Thine order, and revere thine years; I deem
Thy purpose pious, but it is in vain:
Think me not churlish; I would spare thyself,
Far more than me, in shunning at this time
All further colloquy—and so—farewell.
                 [*Exit* MANFRED.
   Abbot. This should have been a noble creature:
    he   160
Hath all the energy which would have made
A goodly frame of glorious elements,
Had they been wisely mingled; as it is,
It is an awful chaos—light and darkness,
And mind and dust, and passions and pure
    thoughts
Mix'd, and contending without end or order,—
All dormant or destructive: he will perish,
And yet he must not; I will try once more.
For such are worth redemption; and my duty
Is to dare all things for a righteous end.   170
I'll follow him—but cautiously, though surely.
                 [*Exit* ABBOT.

SCENE II.—*Another Chamber.*

MANFRED *and* HERMAN.

   Her. My lord, you bade me wait on you at sun-
    set:
He sinks behind the mountain.
   Man.   Doth he so?
I will look on him. [MANFRED *advances to the*
              window of the Hall.
           Glorious Orb! the idol
Of early nature, and the vigorous race
Of undiseased mankind, the giant sons[12]
Of the embrace of angels, with a sex
More beautiful than they, which did draw down
The erring spirits who can ne'er return.—

---

11 a violent dust-laden desert wind in Arabia and Syria.

12 'And it came to pass, that the *Sons of God* saw the daughters of
men, that they were fair,' etc.—'There were giants in the earth in
those days; and also after that, when the *Sons of God* came in unto
the daughters of men, and they bare children to them, the same
became mighty men which were of old, men of renown.'—Genesis, ch. vi. verses 2 and 4.—(Byron.)

Most glorious orb! that wert a worship, ere
The mystery of thy making was reveal'd!   10
Thou earliest minister of the Almighty,
Which gladden'd, on their mountain tops, the
    hearts
Of the Chaldean shepherds, till they pour'd
Themselves in orisons! Thou material God!
And representative of the Unknown—
Who chose thee for his shadow! Thou chief star!
Centre of many stars! which mak'st our earth
Endurable, and temperest the hues
And hearts of all who walk within thy rays!
Sire of the seasons! Monarch of the climes,   20
And those who dwell in them! for near or far,
Our inborn spirits have a tint of thee
Even as our outward aspects;—thou dost rise,
And shine, and set in glory. Fare thee well!
I ne'er shall see thee more. As my first glance
Of love and wonder was for thee, then take
My latest look; thou wilt not beam on one
To whom the gifts of life and warmth have been
Of a more fatal nature. He is gone:
I follow.   [_Exit_ MANFRED.

SCENE III.—_The Mountains—The Castle of Man-_
    fred at some distance—A Terrace before' a
    Tower—Time, Twilight.

    HERMAN, MANUEL, _and other Dependants of_
                MANFRED.

  Her. 'Tis strange enough; night after night, for
    years,
He hath pursued long vigils in this tower,
Without a witness. I have been within it,—
So have we all been oft-times; but from it,
Or its contents, it were impossible
To draw conclusions absolute, of aught
His studies tend to. To be sure, there is
One chamber where none enter: I would give
The fee of what I have to come these three years,
To pore upon its mysteries.
  Manuel.   'Twere dangerous;   10
Content thyself with what thou know'st already.
  Her. Ah! Manuel! thou art elderly and wise,
And couldst say much; thou hast dwelt within
    the castle—
How many years is't?
  Manuel.   Ere Count Manfred's birth,
I served his father, whom he nought resembles.
  Her. There be more sons in like predicament.
But wherein do they differ?
  Manuel.   I speak not
Of features or of form, but mind and habits;
Count Sigismund was proud, but gay and free,—
A warrior and a reveller; he dwelt not   20

With books and solitude, nor made the night
A gloomy vigil, but a festal time,
Merrier than day; he did not walk the rocks
And forests like a wolf, nor turn aside
From men and their delights.
  Her.   Beshrew the hour,
But those were jocund times! I would that such
Would visit the old walls again; they look
As if they had forgotten them.
  Manuel.   These walls
Must change their chieftain first. Oh! I have seen
Some strange things in them, Herman.
  Her.   Come, be friendly;   30
Relate me some to while away our watch:
I've heard thee darkly speak of an event
Which happen'd hereabouts, by this same tower.
  Manuel. That was a night indeed! I do remem-
    ber
'Twas twilight, as it may be now, and such
Another evening;—yon red cloud, which rests
On Eigher's pinnacle, so rested then,—
So like that it might be the same; the wind
Was faint and gusty, and the mountain snows
Began to glitter with the climbing moon;   40
Count Manfred was, as now, within his tower,—
How occupied, we knew not, but with him
The sole companion of his wanderings
And watchings—her, whom of all earthly things
That lived, the only thing he seem'd to love,—
As he, indeed, by blood was bound to do,
The lady Astarte, his—
              Hush! who comes here?

          Enter the ABBOT.

  Abbot. Where is your master?
  Her.   Yonder in the tower.
  Abbot. I must speak with him.
  Manuel.   'Tis impossible;
He is most private, and must not be thus   50
Intruded on.
  Abbot.   Upon myself I take
The forfeit of my fault, if fault there be—
But I must see him.
  Her.   Thou hast seen him once
This eve already.
  Abbot.   Herman! I command thee,
Knock, and apprize the Count of my approach.
  Her. We dare not.
  Abbot.   Then it seems I must be herald
Of my own purpose.
  Manuel.   Reverend father, stop—
I pray you pause.
  Abbot.   Why so?
  Manuel.   But step this way.
And I will tell you further.   [_Exeunt._

SCENE IV.—*Interior of the Tower.*

Manfred alone.

The stars are forth, the moon above the tops
Of the snow-shining mountains.—Beautiful!
I linger yet with Nature, for the Night
Hath been to me a more familiar face
Than that of man; and in her starry shade
Of dim and solitary loveliness,
I learn'd the language of another world.
I do remember me, that in my youth,
When I was wandering,—upon such a night
I stood within the Coliseum's wall,   10
'Midst the chief relics of almighty Rome;
The trees which grew along the broken arches
Waved dark in the blue midnight, and the stars
Shone through the rents of ruin; from afar
The watch-dog bay'd beyond the Tiber; and
More near from out the Cæsars' palace came
The owl's long cry, and, interruptedly,
Of distant sentinels the fitful song
Begun and died upon the gentle wind.
Some cypresses beyond the time-worn
        breach   20
Appear'd to skirt the horizon, yet they stood
Within a bowshot. Where the Cæsars dwelt,
And dwell the tuneless birds of night, amidst
A grove which springs through levell'd battle-
        ments,
And twines its roots with the imperial hearths,
Ivy usurps the laurel's place of growth;
But the gladiators' bloody Circus stands,
A noble wreck in ruinous perfection,
While Cæsar's chambers, and the Augustan halls,
Grovel on earth in indistinct decay.   30
And thou didst shine, thou rolling moon, upon
All this, and cast a wide and tender light,
Which soften'd down the hoar austerity
Of rugged desolation, and fill'd up,
As 'twere anew, the gaps of centuries;
Leaving that beautiful which still was so,
And making that which was not, till the place
Became religion, and the heart ran o'er
With silent worship of the great of old,—
The dead but sceptred sovereigns, who still
        rule   40
Our spirits from their urns.
                        'Twas such a night!
'Tis strange that I recall it at this time;
But I have found our thoughts take wildest flight
Even at the moment when they should array
Themselves in pensive order.

                Enter the ABBOT.

Abbot.   My good lord!

I crave a second grace for this approach;
But yet let not my humble zeal offend
By its abruptness—all it hath of ill
Recoils on me; its good in the effect
May light upon your head—could I say
        heart—   50
Could I touch *that,* with words or prayers, I
        should
Recall a noble spirit which hath wander'd;
But is not yet all lost.
    Man.   Thou know'st me not;
My days are number'd, and my deeds recorded:
Retire, or 'twill be dangerous—Away!
    Abbot. Thou dost not mean to menace me?
    Man.   Not I;
I simply tell thee peril is at hand,
And would preserve thee.
    Abbot.   What dost thou mean?
    Man.   Look there!
What dost thou see?
    Abbot.   Nothing.
    Man.   Look there I say,
And steadfastly;—now tell me what thou
        seest?   60
    Abbot. That which should shake me, but I fear
        it not:
I see a dusk and awful figure rise,
Like an infernal god, from out the earth;
His face wrapt in a mantle, and his form
Robed as with angry clouds: he stands between
Thyself and me—but I do fear him not.
    Man. Thou hast no cause—he shall not harm
        thee—but
His sight may shock thine old limbs into palsy.
I say to thee—Retire!
    Abbot.   And I reply—
Never—till I have battled with this fiend:—   70
What doth he here?
    Man.   Why—ay—what doth he here?
I did not send for him,—he is unbidden.
    Abbot. Alas! lost mortal! what with guests like
        these
Hast thou to do? I tremble for thy sake:
Why doth he gaze on thee, and thou on him?
Ah! he unveils his aspect: on his brow
The thunder-scars are graven: from his eye
Glares forth the immortality of hell—
Avaunt!—
    Man. Pronounce—what is thy mission?
    Spirit.   Come!
    Abbot. What art thou, unknown being? an-
        swer!—speak!   80
    Spirit. The genius of this mortal.—Come! 'tis
        time.
    Man. I am prepared for all things, but deny

The power which summons me. Who sent thee
 here?
Spirit. Thou'lt know anon—Come! come!
Man.   I have commanded
Things of an essence greater far than thine,
And striven with thy masters. Get thee hence!
 Spirit. Mortal! thine hour is come—Away! I
 say.
 Man. I knew, and know my hour is come, but
 not
To render up my soul to such as thee:
Away! I'll die as I have lived—alone. 90
 Spirit. Then I must summon up my brethren.
 —Rise!
      [Other Spirits rise up.
 Abbot. Avaunt! ye evil ones!—Avaunt! I say;
Ye have no power where piety hath power,
And I do charge ye in the name——
 Spirit.   Old man!
We know ourselves, our mission, and thine or-
 der;
Waste not thy holy words on idle uses,
It were in vain: this man is forfeited.
Once more I summon him—Away! Away!
 Man. I do defy ye,—though I feel my soul
Is ebbing from me, yet I do defy ye; 100
Nor will I hence, while I have earthly breath
To breathe my scorn upon ye—earthly strength
To wrestle, though with spirits; what ye take
Shall be ta'en limb by limb.
 Spirit.   Reluctant mortal!
Is this the Magian who would so pervade
The world invisible, and make himself
Almost our equal? Can it be that thou
Art thus in love with life? the very life
Which made thee wretched!
 Man.   Thou false fiend, thou liest!
My life is in its last hour,—*that* I know, 110
Nor would redeem a moment of that hour;
I do not combat against death, but thee
And thy surrounding angels; my past power,
Was purchased by no compact with thy crew,
But by superior science—penance, daring,
And length of watching, strength of mind, and
 skill
In knowledge of our fathers—when the earth
Saw men and spirits walking side by side,
And gave ye no supremacy: I stand
Upon my strength—I do defy—deny,— 120
Spurn back, and scorn ye!—
 Spirit.   But thy many crimes
Have made thee——
 Man.   What are they to such as thee?
Must crimes be punish'd but by other crimes,
And greater criminals?—Back to thy hell!

Thou hast no power upon me, *that* I feel;
Thou never shalt possess me, *that* I know:
What I have done is done; I bear within
A torture which could nothing gain from thine:
The mind which is immortal makes itself
Requital for its good or evil thoughts,— 130
Is its own origin of ill and end—
And its own place and time: its innate sense,
When stripp'd of this mortality, derives
No colour from the fleeting things without,
But is absorb'd in sufferance or in joy,
Born from the knowledge of its own desert.
Thou didst not tempt me, and thou couldst not
 tempt me;
I have not been thy dupe, nor am thy prey—
But was my own destroyer, and will be
My own hereafter.—Back, ye baffled
 fiends!— 140
The hand of death is on me—but not yours!
      [The Demons disappear.
 Abbot. Alas! how pale thou art—thy lips are
 white—
And thy breast heaves—and in thy gasping throat
The accents rattle: Give thy prayers to heaven—
Pray—albeit but in thought,—but die not thus.
 Man. 'Tis over—my dull eyes can fix thee not;
But all things swim around me, and the earth
Heaves as it were beneath me. Fare thee well!
Give me thy hand.
 Abbot. Cold—cold—even to the heart—
But yet one prayer—Alas! how fares it with
 thee? 150
 Man. Old man! 'tis not so difficult to die.
      *[*MANFRED *expires.*
 Abbot. He's gone—his soul hath ta'en its
 earthless flight;
Whither? I dread to think—but he is gone.

 September 1816-April 1817 1817

MAZEPPA

[Byron found the chief incidents for his story in Voltaire's *Histoire de Charles XII,* from which he quotes
three excerpts to serve as preface to his poem. His Mazeppa is essentially Ivan Stepanovitch Mazeppa, 1644–
1709, a Cossack connected with the court of Poland who
achieved some political fame but was renowned chiefly
for romantic intrigue.]

I

'TWAS after dread Pultowa's day,
 When fortune left the royal Swede,[1]

---

1 Charles XII of Sweden whose forces were defeated by the
Russian army of Peter the Great at the Battle of Poltava in 1709.

Around a slaughter'd army lay,
    No more to combat and to bleed.
The power and glory of the war,
    Faithless as their vain votaries, men,
Had pass'd to the triumphant Czar,
    And Moscow's walls were safe again,
Until a day more dark and drear,[2]
And a more memorable year,   10
Should give to slaughter and to shame
A mightier host and haughtier name;
A greater wreck, a deeper fall,
A shock to one—a thunderbolt to all.

II

Such was the hazard of the die;
The wounded Charles[3] was taught to fly
By day and night through field and flood,
Stain'd with his own and subjects' blood;
For thousands fell that flight to aid:
And not a voice was heard t' upbraid   20
Ambition in his humbled hour,
When truth had nought to dread from power.
His horse was slain, and Gieta[4] gave
His own—and died the Russians' slave.
This too sinks after many a league
Of well sustain'd but vain fatigue;
And in the depth of forests, darkling
The watch-fires in the distance sparkling—
    The beacons of surrounding foes—
A king must lay his limbs at length.   30
    Are these the laurels and repose
For which the nations strain their strength?
They laid him by a savage tree,
In outworn nature's agony;
His wounds were stiff, his limbs were stark;
The heavy hour was chill and dark;
The fever in his blood forbade
A transient slumber's fitful aid:
And thus it was; but yet through all,
Kinglike the monarch bore his fall,   40
And made, in this extreme of ill,
His pangs the vassals of his will:
All silent and subdued were they,
As once the nations round him lay.

III

A band of chiefs!—alas! how few,
    Since but the fleeting of a day
Had thinn'd it; but this wreck was true
    And chivalrous: upon the clay

Each sate him down, all sad and mute,
    Beside his monarch and his steed;   50
For danger levels man and brute,
    And all are fellows in their need.
Among the rest, Mazeppa made
His pillow in an old oak's shade—
Himself as rough, and scarce less old,
The Ukraine's Hetman,[5] calm and bold;
But first, outspent with this long course,
The Cossack prince rubb'd down his horse,
And made for him a leafy bed,
    And smooth'd his fetlocks and his mane,   60
    And slack'd his girth, and stripp'd his rein,
And joy'd to see how well he fed;
For until now he had the dread
His wearied courser might refuse
To browse beneath the midnight dews:
But he was hardy as his lord,
And little cared for bed and board;
But spirited and docile too,
Whate'er was to be done, would do.
Shaggy and swift, and strong of limb,   70
All Tartar-like he carried him;
Obey'd his voice, and came to call,
And knew him in the midst of all:
Though thousands were around,—and Night,
Without a star, pursued her flight,—
That steed from sunset until dawn
His chief would follow like a fawn.

IV

This done, Mazeppa spread his cloak,
And laid his lance beneath his oak,
Felt if his arms in order good   80
The long day's march had well withstood—
If still the powder fill'd the pan,
    And flints unloosen'd kept their lock—
His sabre's hilt and scabbard felt,
And whether they had chafed his belt;
And next the venerable man,
From out his havresack and can,
    Prepared and spread his slender stock;
And to the monarch and his men
The whole or portion offer'd then   90
With far less of inquietude
Than courtiers at a banquet would.
And Charles of this his slender share
With smiles partook a moment there,
To force of cheer a greater show,
And seem above both wounds and woe;
And then he said—'Of all our band,
Though firm of heart and strong of hand,
In skirmish, march, or forage, none

2 Referring to Napoleon's Russian campaign and his disastrous retreat from Moscow in the winter of 1812.
3 Although wounded and suffering pain, Charles XII continued to direct the battle from a stretcher.
4 Colonel Gieta was a faithful officer in Charles's army who, though severely wounded, gave up his own horse to the king.

5 Cossack chieftain from the Ukraine in Russia.

Can less have said or more have done 100
Than thee, Mazeppa! on the earth
So fit a pair had never birth,
Since Alexander's days till now,
As thy Bucephalus[6] and thou:
All Scythia's fame to thine should yield
For pricking on o'er flood and field.'
Mazeppa answer'd—'Ill betide
The school wherein I learn'd to ride!'
Quoth Charles—'Old Hetman, wherefore so,
Since thou hast learn'd the art so well?' 110
Mazeppa said—' 'Twere long to tell;
And we have many a league to go,
With every now and then a blow,
And ten to one at least the foe,
Before our steeds may graze at ease
Beyond the swift Borysthenes;[7]
And, Sire, your limbs have need of rest,
    And I will be the sentinel
Of this your troop.'—'But I request,'
    Said Sweden's monarch, 'thou wilt tell 120
This tale of thine, and I may reap,
Perchance, from this the boon of sleep;
For at this moment from my eyes
The hope of present slumber flies.'

'Well, Sire, with such a hope, I'll track
My seventy years of memory back:
I think 'twas in my twentieth spring,—
Ay, 'twas,—when Casimir was king[8]—
John Casimir,—I was his page
Six summers, in my earlier age: 130
A learned monarch, faith! was he,
And most unlike your majesty;
He made no wars, and did not gain
New realms to lose them back again;
And (save debates in Warsaw's diet)
He reign'd in most unseemly quiet;
Not that he had no cares to vex;
He loved the muses and the sex;
And sometimes these so froward are,
They made him wish himself at war; 140
But soon his wrath being o'er, he took
Another mistress, or new book:
And then he gave prodigious fêtes—
All Warsaw gather'd round his gates
To gaze upon his splendid court,
And dames, and chiefs, of princely port:
He was the Polish Solomon,
So sung his poets, all but one,
Who, being unpension'd, made a satire,

And boasted that he could not flatter. 150
It was a court of jousts and mimes,
Where every courtier tried at rhymes;
Even I for once produced some verses,
And sign'd my odes "Despairing Thyrsis."
There was a certain Palatine,
    A count of far and high descent,
Rich as a salt[9] or silver mine;
And he was proud, ye may divine,
    As if from heaven he had been sent:
He had such wealth in blood and ore 160
    As few could match beneath the throne;
And he would gaze upon his store,
And o'er his pedigree would pore,
Until by some confusion led,
Which almost look'd like want of head,
    He thought their merits were his own.
His wife was not of his opinion;
    His junior she by thirty years,
Grew daily tired of his dominion;
    And, after wishes, hopes, and fears, 170
    To virtue a few farewell tears,
A restless dream or two, some glances
At Warsaw's youth, some songs, and dances,
Awaited but the usual chances,
Those happy accidents which render
The coldest dames so very tender,
To deck her Count with titles given,
'Tis said, as passports into heaven;
But, strange to say, they rarely boast
Of these, who have deserved them most. 180

V

'I was a goodly stripling then;
    At seventy years I so may say,
That there were few, or boys or men,
    Who, in my dawning time of day,
Of vassal or of knight's degree,
Could vie in vanities with me;
For I had strength, youth, gaiety,
A port, not like to this ye see,
But smooth, as all is rugged now;
    For time, and care, and war, have plough'd 190
My very soul from out my brow;
    And thus I should be disavow'd
By all my kind and kin, could they
Compare my day and yesterday;
This change was wrought, too, long ere age
Had ta'en my features for his page;
With years, ye know, have not declined
My strength, my courage, or my mind,
Or at this hour I should not be

---

6 Alexander's war horse.
7 the Dnieper, chief river of the Ukraine, which Charles fleeing southward aimed to cross.
8 John Casimir V was King of Poland from 1649 to 1668.

9 This comparison of a '*salt*' mine' may, perhaps, be permitted to a Pole, as the wealth of the country consists greatly in the salt mines.—(Byron.)

Telling old tales beneath a tree,
With starless skies my canopy.
　But let me on: Theresa's form—
Methinks it glides before me now,
Between me and yon chestnut's bough,
　The memory is so quick and warm;
And yet I find no words to tell
The shape of her I loved so well:
She had the Asiatic eye,
　Such as our Turkish neighbourhood
　Hath mingled with our Polish blood, 210
Dark as above us is the sky;
But through it stole a tender light,
Like the first moonrise of midnight;
Large, dark, and swimming in the stream,
Which seem'd to melt to its own beam;
All love, half languor, and half fire,
Like saints that at the stake expire,
And lift their raptured looks on high,
As though it were a joy to die.
A brow like a midsummer lake, 220
　Transparent with the sun therein,
When waves no murmur dare to make,
　And heaven beholds her face within.
A cheek and lip—but why proceed?
　I loved her then, I love her still;
And such as I am, love indeed
　In fierce extremes—in good and ill.
But still we love even in our rage,
And haunted to our very age
With the vain shadow of the past, 230
As is Mazeppa to the last.

VI

'We met—we gazed—I saw, and sigh'd,
She did not speak, and yet replied;
There are ten thousand tones and signs
We hear and see, but none defines—
Involuntary sparks of thought,
Which strike from out the heart o'erwrought,
And form a strange intelligence,
Alike mysterious and intense,
Which link the burning chain that binds, 240
Without their will, young hearts and minds;
Conveying, as the electric wire,
We know not how, the absorbing fire.
I saw, and sigh'd—in silence wept,
And still reluctant distance kept,
Until I was made known to her,
And we might then and there confer
Without suspicion—then, even then,
　I long'd, and was resolved to speak;
But on my lips they died again, 250
　The accents tremulous and weak,

Until one hour.—There is a game, 200
　A frivolous and foolish play,
　Wherewith we while away the day;
It is—I have forgot the name—
And we to this, it seems, were set,
By some strange chance, which I forget:
I reck'd not if I won or lost,
　It was enough for me to be
　So near to hear, and oh! to see 260
The being whom I loved the most.
I watch'd her as a sentinel,
(May ours this dark night watch as well!)
　Until I saw, and thus it was,
That she was pensive, nor perceived
Her occupation, nor was grieved
Nor glad to lose or gain; but still
Play'd on for hours, as if her will
Yet bound her to the place, though not
That hers might be the winning lot. 270
　Then through my brain the thought did pass
Even as a flash of lightning there,
That there was something in her air
Which would not doom me to despair;
And on the thought my words broke forth,
　All incoherent as they were;
Their eloquence was little worth,
But yet she listen'd—'tis enough—
　Who listens once will listen twice;
　Her heart, be sure, is not of ice, 280
And one refusal no rebuff.

VII

'I loved, and was beloved again—
　They tell me, Sire, you never knew
　Those gentle frailties; if 'tis true,
I shorten all my joy or pain;
To you 'twould seem absurd as vain;
But all men are not born to reign,
Or o'er their passions, or as you
Thus o'er themselves and nations too.
I am—or rather *was*—a prince, 290
　A chief of thousands, and could lead
　Them on where each would foremost bleed;
But could not o'er myself evince
The like control—But to resume:
　I loved, and was beloved again;
In sooth, it is a happy doom,
　But yet where happiest ends in pain.
We met in secret, and the hour
Which led me to that lady's bower
Was fiery Expectation's dower. 300
My days and nights were nothing—all
Except that hour, which doth recall,
In the long lapse from youth to age,

No other like itself: I'd give
The Ukraine back again to live
It o'er once more, and be a page,
The happy page, who was the lord
Of one soft heart, and his own sword,
And had no other gem nor wealth
Save nature's gift of youth and health.   310
We met in secret—doubly sweet,
Some say, they find it so to meet;
I know not that—I would have given
    My life but to have call'd her mine
In the full view of earth and heaven;
    For I did oft and long repine
That we could only meet by stealth.

VIII

'For lovers there are many eyes,
    And such there were on us; the devil
    On such occasions should be civil—   320
The devil!—I'm loth to do him wrong,
    It might be some untoward saint,
Who would not be at rest too long,
    But to his pious bile gave vent— ·
But one fair night, some lurking spies
Surprised and seized us both.
The Count was something more than wroth—
I was unarm'd; but if in steel,
All cap-à-pie from head to heel,
What 'gainst their numbers could I do?   330
'Twas near his castle, far away
    From city or from succour near,
And almost on the break of day;
I did not think to see another,
    My moments seem'd reduced to few;
And with one prayer to Mary Mother,
    And, it may be, a saint or two,
As I resign'd me to my fate,
They led me to the castle gate:
    Theresa's doom I never knew,   340
Our lot was henceforth separate.
An angry man, ye may opine,
Was he, the proud Count Palatine;
And he had reason good to be,
    But he was most enraged lest such
    An accident should chance to touch
Upon his future pedigree;
Nor less amazed, that such a blot
His noble 'scutcheon should have got,
While he was highest of his line;   350
    Because unto himself he seem'd
    The first of men, nor less he deem'd
In others' eyes, and most in mine.
'Sdeath! with a *page*—perchance a king
Had reconciled him to the thing;
But with a stripling of a page—
I felt, but cannot paint his rage.

IX

'"Bring forth the horse!"—the horse was
    brought;
    In truth, he was a noble steed,
    A Tartar of the Ukraine breed,   360
Who look'd as though the speed of thought
Were in his limbs; but he was wild,
    Wild as the wild deer, and untaught,
With spur and bridle undefiled—
    'Twas but a day he had been caught;
And snorting, with erected mane,
And struggling fiercely, but in vain,
In the full foam of wrath and dread
To me the desert-born was led:
They bound me on, that menial throng;   370
Upon his back with many a thong;
Then loosed him with a sudden lash—
Away!—away!—and on we dash!
Torrents less rapid and less rash.

X

'Away!—away! My breath was gone,
I saw not where he hurried on:
'Twas scarcely yet the break of day,
And on he foam'd—away!—away!
The last of human sounds which rose,
As I was darted from my foes,   380
Was the wild shout of savage laughter,
Which on the wind came roaring after
A moment from that rabble rout:
With sudden wrath I wrench'd my head,
    And snapp'd the cord, which to the mane
    Had bound my neck in lieu of rein,
And, writhing half my form about,
Howl'd back my curse; but 'midst the tread,
The thunder of my courser's speed,
Perchance they did not hear nor heed: 390
It vexes me—for I would fain
Have paid their insult back again.
I paid it well in after days:
There is not of that castle gate,
Its drawbridge and portcullis' weight,
Stone, bar, moat, bridge, or barrier left;
Nor of its fields a blade of grass,
    Save what grows on a ridge of wall,
    Where stood the hearth-stone of the hall;
And many a time ye there might pass,   400
Nor dream that e'er that fortress was.
I saw its turrets in a blaze,
Their crackling battlements all cleft,
    And the hot lead pour down like rain

From off the scorch'd and blackening roof,
Whose thickness was not vengeance-proof.
　　They little thought that day of pain,
When launch'd, as on the lightning's flash,
They bade me to destruction dash,
　　That one day I should come again,　　　410
With twice five thousand horse, to thank
　　The Count for his uncourteous ride.
They play'd me then a bitter prank,
　　When, with the wild horse for my guide,
They bound me to his foaming flank:
At length I play'd them one as frank
For time at last sets all things even—
　　And if we do but watch the hour,
　　There never yet was human power
Which could evade, if unforgiven,　　　420
The patient search and vigil long
Of him who treasures up a wrong.

XI

'Away, away, my steed and I,
　　Upon the pinions of the wind,
　　All human dwellings left behind;
We sped like meteors through the sky,
When with its crackling sound the night
Is chequer'd with the northern light:
Town—village—none were on our track
　　But a wild plain of far extent,　　　430
And bounded by a forest black;
　　And, save the scarce-seen battlement
On distant heights of some strong hold,
Against the Tartars built of old,
No trace of man. The year before
A Turkish army had march'd o'er;
And where the Spahi's[10] hoof hath trod,
The verdure flies the bloody sod:
The sky was dull, and dim, and grey,
　　And a low breeze crept moaning by—　　　440
　　I could have answer'd with a sigh—
But fast we fled, away, away,
And I could neither sigh nor pray;
And my cold sweat-drops fell like rain
Upon the courser's bristling mane;
But, snorting still with rage and fear,
He flew upon his far career:
At times I almost thought, indeed,
He must have slacken'd in his speed;
But no—my bound and slender frame　　　450
　　Was nothing to his angry might,
And merely like a spur became:
Each motion which I made to free
My swoln limbs from their agony
　　Increased his fury and affright:

_____
10 a Turkish cavalryman.

I tried my voice,—'twas faint and low,
But yet he swerved as from a blow;
And, starting to each accent, sprang
As from a sudden trumpet's clang:
Meantime my cords were wet with gore,　　　460
Which, oozing through my limbs, ran o'er;
And in my tongue the thirst became
A something fierier far than flame.

XII

'We near'd the wild wood—'twas so wide,
I saw no bounds on either side;
'Twas studded with old sturdy trees,
That bent not to the roughest breeze
Which howls down from Siberia's waste,
And strips the forest in its haste,—
But these were few and far between,　　　470
Set thick with shrubs more young and green,
Luxuriant with their annual leaves,
Ere strown by those autumnal eves
That nip the forest's foliage dead,
Discolour'd with a lifeless red,
Which stands thereon like stiffen'd gore
Upon the slain when battle's o'er,
And some long winter's night hath shed
Its frost o'er every tombless head,
So cold and stark the raven's beak　　　480
May peck unpierced each frozen cheek:
'Twas a wild waste of underwood,
And here and there a chestnut stood,
The strong oak, and the hardy pine;
　　But far apart—and well it were,
Or else a different lot were mine—
　　The boughs gave way, and did not tear
My limbs; and I found strength to bear
My wounds, already scarr'd with cold;
My bonds forbade to loose my hold.　　　490
We rustled through the leaves like wind,
Left shrubs, and trees, and wolves behind;
By night I heard them on the track,
Their troop came hard upon our back,
With their long gallop, which can tire
The hound's deep hate, and hunter's fire:
Where'er we flew they follow'd on,
Nor left us with the morning sun;
Behind I saw them, scarce a rood,
At day-break winding through the wood,　　　500
And through the night had heard their feet
Their stealing, rustling step repeat.
Oh! how I wish'd for spear or sword,
At least to die amidst the horde,
And perish—if it must be so—
At bay, destroying many a foe!
When first my courser's race begun,

I wish'd the goal already won;
But now I doubted strength and speed.
Vain doubt! his swift and savage breed   510
Had nerved him like the mountain-roe;
Nor faster falls the blinding snow
Which whelms the peasant near the door
Whose threshold he shall cross no more,
Bewilder'd with the dazzling blast,
Than through the forest-paths he pass'd—
Untired, untamed, and worse than wild;
All furious as a favour'd child
Balk'd of its wish; or fiercer still—
A woman piqued—who has her will.   520

XIII

'The wood was past; 'twas more than noon,
But chill the air, although in June;
Or it might be my veins ran cold—
Prolong'd endurance tames the bold;
And I was then not what I seem,
But headlong as a wintry stream,
And wore my feelings out before
I well could count their causes o'er:
And what with fury, fear, and wrath,
The tortures which beset my path,   530
Cold, hunger, sorrow, shame, distress,
Thus bound in nature's nakedness;
Sprung from a race whose rising blood,
When stirr'd beyond its calmer mood,
And trodden hard upon, is like
The rattle-snake's, in act to strike,
What marvel if this worn-out trunk
Beneath its woes a moment sunk?
The earth gave way, the skies roll'd round,
I seem'd to sink upon the ground;   540
But err'd, for I was fastly bound.
My heart turn'd sick, my brain grew sore,
And throbb'd awhile, then beat no more:
The skies spun like a mighty wheel;
I saw the trees like drunkards reel,
And a slight flash sprang o'er my eyes,
Which saw no farther: he who dies
Can die no more than then I died.
O'ertortured by that ghastly ride,
I felt the blackness come and go,   550
    And strove to wake; but could not make
My senses climb up from below:
I felt as on a plank at sea,
When all the waves that dash o'er thee,
At the same time upheave and whelm,
And hurl thee towards a desert realm.
My undulating life was as
The fancied lights that flitting pass
Our shut eyes in deep midnight, when

Fever begins upon the brain;   560
But soon it pass'd, with little pain,
    But a confusion worse than such:
    I own that I should deem it much,
Dying, to feel the same again;
And yet I do suppose we must
Feel far more ere we turn to dust:
No matter: I have bared my brow
Full in Death's face—before—and now.

XIV

'My thoughts came back; where was I? Cold,
    And numb, and giddy: pulse by pulse   570
Life reassumed its lingering hold,
And throb by throb,—till grown a pang
    Which for a moment would convulse,
    My blood reflow'd, though thick and chill;
My ear with uncouth noises rang,
    My heart began once more to thrill;
My sight return'd, though dim; alas!
And thicken'd, as it were, with glass.
Methought the dash of waves was nigh;
There was a gleam too of the sky,   580
Studded with stars;—it is no dream;
The wild horse swims the wilder stream!
The bright broad river's gushing tide
Sweeps, winding onward, far and wide,
And we are half-way, struggling o'er
To yon unknown and silent shore.
The waters broke my hollow trance,
And with a temporary strength
    My stiffen'd limbs were rebaptized.
My courser's broad breast proudly braves,   590
And dashes off the ascending waves,
And onward we advance!
We reach the slippery shore at length,
    A haven I but little prized,
For all behind was dark and drear,
And all before was night and fear.
How many hours of night or day
In those suspended pangs I lay,
I could not tell; I scarcely knew
If this were human breath I drew.   600

XV

'With glossy skin, and dripping mane,
    And reeling limbs, and reeking flank,
The wild steed's sinewy nerves still strain
    Up the repelling bank.
We gain the top; a boundless plain
Spreads through the shadow of the night,
    And onward, onward, onward, seems,
    Like precipices in our dreams,
To stretch beyond the sight;

And here and there a speck of white,
  Or scatter'd spot of dusky green,
In masses broke into the light,
As rose the moon upon my right:
  But nought distinctly seen
In the dim waste would indicate
The omen of a cottage gate;
No twinkling taper from afar
Stood like a hospitable star;
Not even an ignis-fatuus rose
To make him merry with my woes;   620
  That very cheat that cheer'd me then!
Although detected, welcome still,
Reminding me, through every ill,
  Of the abodes of men.

XVI

'Onward we went—but slack and slow;
  His savage force at length o'erspent,
The drooping courser, faint and low,
  All feebly foaming went.
A sickly infant had had power
To guide him forward in that hour,   630
  But useless all to me:
His new-born tameness nought avail'd—
My limbs were bound; my force had fail'd,
  Perchance, had they been free.
With feeble effort still I tried
To rend the bonds so starkly tied,
  But still it was in vain;
My limbs were only wrung the more,
And soon the idle strife gave o'er,
  Which but prolong'd their pain: 640
The dizzy race seem'd almost done,
Although no goal was nearly won:
Some streaks announced the coming sun—
  How slow, alas! he came!
Methought that mist of dawning grey
Would never dapple into day;
How heavily it roll'd away—
  Before the eastern flame
Rose crimson, and deposed the stars,
And call'd the radiance from their cars,   650
And fill'd the earth, from his deep throne,
  With lonely lustre, all his own.

XVII

'Up rose the sun; the mists were curl'd
Back from the solitary world
Which lay around, behind, before.
What booted it to traverse o'er
Plain, forest, river? Man nor brute,
Nor dint of hoof, nor print of foot,

Lay in the wild luxuriant soil;
No sign of travel, none of toil;   660
The very air was mute;
And not an insect's shrill small horn,
Nor matin bird's new voice was borne
From herb nor thicket. Many a werst,[11]
Panting as if his heart would burst,
The weary brute still stagger'd on;
And still we were—or seem'd—alone.
At length, while reeling on our way,
Methought I heard a courser neigh,
From out yon tuft of blackening firs.   670
Is it the wind those branches stirs?
No, no! from out the forest prance
  A trampling troop; I see them come!
In one vast squadron they advance!
  I strove to cry—my lips were dumb.
The steeds rush on in plunging pride;
But where are they the reins to guide?
A thousand horse, and none to ride!
With flowing tail, and flying mane,
Wide nostrils never stretch'd by pain,   680
Mouths bloodless to the bit or rein,
And feet that iron never shod,
And flanks unscarr'd by spur or rod,
A thousand horse, the wild, the free,
Like waves that follow o'er the sea,
  Came thickly thundering on,
As if our faint approach to meet;
The sight re-nerved my courser's feet,
A moment staggering, feebly fleet,
A moment, with a faint low neigh,   690
  He answer'd, and then fell;
With gasps and glazing eyes he lay,
  And reeking limbs immoveable,
  His first and last career is done!
On came the troop—they saw him stoop,
  They saw me strangely bound along
  His back with many a bloody thong:
They stop, they start, they snuff the air,
Gallop a moment here and there,
Approach, retire, wheel round and round,   700
Then plunging back with sudden bound,
Headed by one black mighty steed,
Who seem'd the patriarch of his breed,
  Without a single speck or hair
Of white upon his shaggy hide;
They snort, they foam, neigh, swerve aside,
And backward to the forest fly,
By instinct, from a human eye.
  They left me there to my despair,
Link'd to the dead and stiffening wretch,   710

11 Verst; a Russian measure equal to about two thirds of a mile.

Whose lifeless limbs beneath me stretch,
Relieved from that unwonted weight,
From whence I could not extricate
Nor him nor me—and there we lay,
   The dying on the dead!
I little deem'd another day
   Would see my houseless, helpless head.

'And there from morn to twilight bound,
I felt the heavy hours toil round,
With just enough of life to see   720
My last of suns go down on me,
In hopeless certainty of mind,
That makes us feel at length resign'd
To that which our foreboding years
Present the worst and last of fears:
Inevitable—even a boon,
Nor more unkind for coming soon,
Yet shunn'd and dreaded with such care,
As if it only were a snare
   That prudence might escape: 730
At times both wish'd-for and implored,
At times sought with self-pointed sword,
Yet still a dark and hideous close
To even intolerable woes,
   And welcome in no shape.
And, strange to say, the sons of pleasure,
They who have revell'd beyond measure
In beauty, wassail, wine, and treasure,
Die calm, or calmer, oft than he
Whose heritage was misery: 740
For he who hath in turn run through
All that was beautiful and new,
   Hath nought to hope, and nought to leave;
And, save the future, (which is view'd
Not quite as men are base or good,
But as their nerves may be endued,)
   With nought perhaps to grieve:
The wretch still hopes his woes must end,
And Death, whom he should deem his friend,
Appears, to his distemper'd eyes,   750
Arrived to rob him of his prize,
The tree of his new Paradise.
To-morrow would have given him all,
Repaid his pangs, repair'd his fall;
To-morrow would have been the first
Of days no more deplored or curst,
But bright, and long, and beckoning years,
Seen dazzling through the mist of tears,
Guerdon of many a painful hour;
To-morrow would have given him power   760
To rule, to shine, to smite, to save—
And must it dawn upon his grave?

XVIII

'The sun was sinking—still I lay
   Chain'd to the chill and stiffening steed;
I thought to mingle there our clay,
   And my dim eyes of death had need;
   No hope arose of being freed:
I cast my last looks up the sky,
   And there between me and the sun
I saw the expecting raven fly,   770
Who scarce would wait till both should die,
   Ere his repast begun;
He flew, and perch'd, then flew once more,
And each time nearer than before;
I saw his wing through twilight flit,
And once so near me he alit
   I could have smote, but lack'd the strength;
But the slight motion of my hand,
And feeble scratching of the sand,
The exerted throat's faint struggling noise,   780
Which scarcely could be called a voice,
   Together scared him off at length.
I know no more—my latest dream
   Is something of a lovely star
   Which fix'd my dull eyes from afar,
And went and came with wandering beam,
And all the cold, dull, swimming, dense
Sensation of recurring sense,
And then subsiding back to death,
And then again a little breath,   790
A little thrill, a short suspense,
   An icy sickness curdling o'er
My heart, and sparks that cross'd my brain—
A gasp, a throb, a start of pain,
   A sigh, and nothing more.

XIX

'I woke—where was I?—Do I see
A human face look down on me?
And doth a roof above me close?
Do these limbs on a couch repose?
Is this a chamber where I lie?   800
And is it mortal yon bright eye,
That watches me with gentle glance?
   I closed my own again once more,
As doubtful that my former trance
   Could not as yet be o'er.
A slender girl, long-hair'd, and tall,
Sate watching by the cottage wall;
The sparkle of her eye I caught,
Even with my first return of thought;
For ever and anon she threw   810
   A prying, pitying glance on me
   With her black eyes so wild and free:

I gazed, and gazed, until I knew
 No vision it could be,—
But that I lived, and was released
From adding to the vulture's feast:
And when the Cossack maid beheld
My heavy eyes at length unseal'd,
She smiled—and I essay'd to speak,
 But fail'd—and she approach'd, and made 820
 With lip and finger signs that said,
I must not strive as yet to break
The silence, till my strength should be
Enough to leave my accents free;
And then her hand on mine she laid,
And smooth'd the pillow for my head,
And stole along on tiptoe tread,
 And gently oped the door, and spake
In whispers—ne'er was voice so sweet!
Even music follow'd her light feet: 830
 But those she call'd were not awake,
And she went forth; but, ere she pass'd,
Another look on me she cast,
 Another sign she made, to say,
That I had nought to fear, that all
Were near, at my command or call,
 And she would not delay
Her due return:—while she was gone,
Methought I felt too much alone.

                        XX

'She came with mother and with sire—   840
What need of more?—I will not tire
With long recital of the rest,
Since I became the Cossack's guest.
They found me senseless on the plain,
 They bore me to the nearest hut,
They brought me into life again—
Me—one day o'er their realm to reign!
 Thus the vain fool who strove to glut
His rage, refining on my pain,
 Sent me forth to the wilderness,   850
Bound, naked, bleeding, and alone,
To pass the desert to a throne,—
 What mortal his own doom may guess?
 Let none despond, let none despair!
To-morrow the Borysthenes
May see our coursers graze at ease
Upon his Turkish bank, and never
Had I such welcome for a river
 As I shall yield when safely there.
Comrades, good night!'—The Hetman threw 860
 His length beneath the oak-tree shade,
 With leafy couch already made,
A bed nor comfortless nor new

To him, who took his rest whene'er
The hour arrived, no matter where:
 His eyes the hastening slumbers steep.
And if ye marvel Charles forgot
To thank his tale, *he* wonder'd not,—
 The king had been an hour asleep.

 1818   1819

DON JUAN

'*Difficile est propriè communia dicere.*'—HORACE

'*Dost thou think, because thou art virtuous, there
shall be no more cakes and ale? Yes, by Saint Anne,
and ginger shall be hot i' the mouth, too!*'—SHAKE-
SPEARE, *Twelfth Night, or What You Will.*

[Byron published no preface for *Don Juan,* but passages in his letters written during the composition of the
early cantos reveal something of his intentions for the
poem. In a letter to Moore, 19 September, 1818, he
wrote: 'I have finished the first Canto (a long one, of
about 180 octaves) of a poem in the style and manner
of *Beppo,* encouraged by the good success of the same.
It is called *Don Juan,* and is meant to be a little quietly
facetious upon everything.'
 To Murray 12 August, 1819, who had asked Byron
for the plan of his poem, he wrote: 'You ask me for the
plan of Donny Johnny: I *have* no plan—I *had* no plan;
but I had or have materials.... You are too earnest and
eager about a work never intended to be serious. Do you
suppose that I have any intention but to giggle and
make giggle?—a playful satire, with as little poetry as
could be helped, was what I meant.'
 After finishing Canto V, Byron again wrote Murray,
16 February, 1821: 'The 5th is so far from being the last
of *D. J.* that it is hardly the beginning. I meant to take
him the tour of Europe, with a proper mixture of siege,
battle, and adventure, and to make him finish as Ana-
charsis Cloots in the French Revolution. To how many
cantos this may extend, I know not, nor whether (even if
I live) I shall complete it; but this was my notion: I
meant to have him a Cavalier Servente in Italy, and a
cause for a divorce in England, and a Sentimental 'Wer-
ther-faced man' in Germany, so as to show the different
ridicules of the society in each of those countries, and to
have displayed him gradually *gâté* and *blasé* as he grew
older, as is natural. But I had not quite fixed whether to
make him end in Hell, or in an unhappy marriage, not
knowing which would be the severest. The Spanish tradition says Hell: but it is probably only an Allegory of
the other state. You are now in possession of my notions
on the subject.']

                    DEDICATION

                            I

BOB SOUTHEY! You're a poet—Poet-laureate,
 And representative of all the race;

------

1 'It is difficult to treat in your own way what is common.'—
The Art of Poetry, 128.

Don Juan

Although 'tis true that you turn'd out a Tory at
  Last,—yours has lately been a common case;
And now, my Epic Renegade! what are ye at?
  With all the Lakers,[2] in and out of place?
A nest of tuneful persons, to my eye
Like 'four and twenty Blackbirds in a pye;

II

'Which pye being open'd they began to sing'
  (This old song and new simile holds good), 10
'A dainty dish to set before the King,'
  Or Regent,[3] who admires such kind of food;—
And Coleridge, too, has lately taken wing,
  But like a hawk encumber'd with his hood,—
Explaining metaphysics to the nation—
I wish he would explain his Explanation.[4]

III

You, Bob! are rather insolent, you know,
  At being disappointed in your wish
To supersede all warblers here below,
  And be the only Blackbird in the dish; 20
And then you overstrain yourself, or so,
  And tumble downward like the flying fish
Gasping on deck, because you soar too high, Bob,
And fall, for lack of moisture quite a-dry, Bob!

IV

And Wordsworth, in a rather long 'Excursion'
  (I think the quarto holds five hundred pages),
Has given a sample from the vasty version
  Of his new system to perplex the sages;
'Tis poetry—at least by his assertion,
  And may appear so when the dog-star
    rages— 30
And he who understands it would be able
To add a story to the Tower of Babel.

V

You—Gentlemen! by dint of long seclusion
  From better company, have kept your own
At Keswick,[5] and, through still continued fusion
  Of one another's minds, at last have grown
To deem as a most logical conclusion,
  That Poesy has wreaths for you alone:
There is a narrowness in such a notion,
Which makes me wish you'd change your lakes
  for ocean. 40

VI

I would not imitate the petty thought,
  Nor coin my self-love to so base a vice,
For all the glory your conversion brought,
  Since gold alone should not have been its price.
You have your salary: was't for that you
    wrought?
  And Wordsworth has his place in the Excise.[6]
You're shabby fellows—true—but poets still,
And duly seated on the immortal hill.

VII

Your bays may hide the baldness of your brows—
  Perhaps some virtuous blushes;—let them
    go— 50
To you I envy neither fruit nor boughs—
  And for the fame you would engross below,
The field is universal, and allows
  Scope to all such as feel the inherent glow:
Scott, Rogers, Campbell, Moore, and Crabbe, will
    try
'Gainst you the question with posterity.

VIII

For me, who, wandering with pedestrian Muses,
  Contend not with you on the winged steed,
I wish your fate may yield ye, when she chooses,
  The fame you envy, and the skill you need; 60
And recollect a poet nothing loses
  In giving to his brethren their full meed
Of merit, and complaint of present days
Is not the certain path to future praise.

IX

He that reserves his laurels for posterity
  (Who does not often claim the bright rever-
    sion)
Has generally no great crop to spare it, he
  Being only injured by his own assertion;[7]
And although here and there some glorious rarity
  Arise like Titan from the sea's immersion, 70
The major part of such appellants go
To—God knows where—for no one else can
    know.

---

2 The Lake poets, chief among whom were Southey, Wordsworth, and Coleridge. All had been at one time ardent republicans, but disappointment over the excesses and failures of the
French Revolution led them to become conservative.
3 Prince of Wales, later King George IV, who was appointed
governing head of the kingdom in 1811.
4 The reference is to *Biographia Literaria*, which appeared in
1817.
5 in the lake district where Southey lived for many years.

6 Wordsworth's place may be in the Customs—it is, I think, in
that or the Excise—besides another at Lord Lonsdale's table,
where this poetical charlatan and political parasite licks up the
crumbs with a hardened alacrity; the converted Jacobin having
long subsided into the clownish sycophant of the worst prejudices
of the aristocracy.—(Byron.)
7 In the Supplementary Essay to his collected poems, 1815,
Wordsworth unwisely betrayed his resentment over popular neglect and made an appeal to posterity in language that his enemies
found easy to ridicule.

X

If, fallen in evil days on evil tongues,[8]
  Milton appealed to the Avenger, Time,
If Time, the Avenger, execrates his wrongs,
  And makes the word 'Miltonic' mean *'sublime,'*
He deign'd not to belie his soul in songs,
  Nor turn his very talent to a crime;
He did not loathe the Sire to laud the Son,
But closed the tyrant-hater he begun.   80

XI

Think'st thou, could he—the blind Old Man—
      arise,
    Like Samuel from the grave,[9] to freeze once
      more
The blood of monarchs with his prophecies,
  Or be alive again—again all hoar
With time and trials, and those helpless eyes,
  And heartless daughters[10]—worn—and pale—
      and poor;
Would *he* adore a sultan? *he* obey
The intellectual eunuch Castlereagh?[11]

XII

Cold-blooded, smooth-faced, placid miscreant!
    Dabbling its sleek young hands in Erin's
      gore,   90
And thus for wider carnage taught to pant,
  Transferr'd to gorge upon a sister shore,
The vulgarest tool that Tyranny could want,
  With just enough of talent, and no more,
To lengthen fetters by another fix'd,
And offer poison long already mix'd.

XIII

An orator of such set trash of phrase
  Ineffably—legitimately vile,
That even its grossest flatterers dare not praise,
  Nor foes—all nations—condescend to
      smile;   100

---

8 *Paradise Lost,* vii, 26.   9 See I Samuel, xxviii, 7–20.
10 'Pale, but not cadaverous':—Milton's two elder daughters are
said to have robbed him of his books, besides cheating and plaguing him in the economy of his house, etc. His feelings on such an
outrage, both as a parent and a scholar, must have been singularly
painful. Hayley compares him to Lear.—(Byron.)
11 'Would *he* subside into a hackney Laureate—A scribbling, self-
sold, soul-hired, scorn'd Iscariot?'
I doubt if 'Laureate' and 'Iscariot' be good rhymes, but must say,
as Ben Jonson did to Sylvester, who challenged him to rhyme
with—

            I, John Sylvester
            Lay with your sister.

Jonson answered,—'I, Ben Jonson, lay with your wife.' Sylvester
answered,—'That is not rhyme.'—'No,' said Ben Jonson; 'but it
is *true.'*—(Byron.) Robert Stewart, Viscount Castlereagh, was for
a number of years leader of the ultra-tory party. As the unalterable and bitter opponent to revolutionary reform he was relentlessly attacked by Byron.

Not even a sprightly blunder's spark can blaze
  From that Ixion[12] grindstone's ceaseless toil,
That turns and turns to give the world a notion
Of endless torments and perpetual motion.

XIV

A bungler even in its disgusting trade,
  And blotching, patching, leaving still behind
Something of which its masters are afraid,
    States to be curb'd and thoughts to be con-
      fined,
Conspiracy or Congress to be made—
  Cobbling at manacles for all mankind—   110
A tinkering slave-maker, who mends old chains,
With God and man's abhorrence for its gains.

XV

If we may judge of matter by the mind,
  Emasculated to the marrow *It*
Hath, but two objects, how to serve, and bind,
  Deeming the chain it wears even men may fit,
Eutropius[13] of its many masters,—blind
  To worth as freedom, wisdom as to wit,
Fearless—because *no* feeling dwells in ice,
Its very courage stagnates to a vice.   120

XVI

Where shall I turn me not to *view* its bonds,
  For I will never *feel* them;—Italy!
Thy late reviving Roman soul desponds
  Beneath the lie this State-thing breathed o'er
      thee—
Thy clanking chain, and Erin's yet green wounds,
  Have voices—tongues to cry aloud for me.
Europe has slaves, allies, kings, armies still,
And Southey lives to sing them very ill.

XVII

Meantime, Sir Laureate, I proceed to dedicate,
  In honest simple verse, this song to you.   130
And, if in flattering strains I do not predicate,
  'Tis that I still retain my 'buff and blue';[14]
My politics as yet are all to educate:
  Apostasy's so fashionable, too.
To keep *one* creed's a task grown quite Hercu-
      lean:
Is it not so, my Tory, ultra-Julian?[15]

Venice, 16 September 1818

---

12 For boasting that he made love to Hera, Ixion was punished
in hell by being bound to a ceaselessly revolving wheel.
13 a eunuch and minister at the Byzantine Court of Arcadius,
4th century A.D. 'For the character of Eutropius, see Gibbon, *Decline and Fall,* chap. xxxii.'—(Byron.)
14 colors of the Whig party.
15 The allusion is to Gibbon's hero, Julian the Apostate.

Why did Byron choose Don Juan [handwritten marginalia]

written [handwritten marginalia]

CANTO THE FIRST

I

I WANT a hero: an uncommon want,
　When every year and month sends forth a new
　　one,
Till, after cloying the gazettes with cant,
　The age discovers he is not the true one:
Of such as these I should not care to vaunt,
　I'll therefore take our ancient friend Don
　Juan—
We all have seen him, in the pantomime,
Sent to the devil somewhat ere his time.

II

Vernon, the butcher Cumberland, Wolfe,
　Hawke,
　Prince Ferdinand, Granby, Burgoyne, Keppel,
　Howe,　　　　　　　　　　　　　　　　10
Evil and good, have had their tithe of talk,
　And fill'd their sign-posts then, like Wellesley
　now;
Each in their turn like Banquo's monarchs stalk,
　Followers of fame, 'nine farrow'[1] of that sow:
France, too, had Buonaparté and Dumourier
Recorded in the Moniteur and Courier.

III

Barnave, Brissot, Condorcet, Mirabeau,
　Pétion, Clootz, Danton, Marat, La Fayette,
Were French, and famous people, as we know;
　And there were others, scarce forgotten yet,　20
Joubert, Hoche, Marceau, Lannes, Desaix,
　Moreau,
　With many of the military set,
Exceedingly remarkable at times,
But not at all adapted to my rhymes.

IV

Nelson was once Britannia's god of war,
　And still should be so, but the tide is turn'd;
There's no more to be said of Trafalgar,
　'Tis with our hero quietly inurn'd;
Because the army's grown more popular,
　At which the naval people are concerned,　30
Besides, the prince is all for the land-service,
Forgetting Duncan, Nelson, Howe, and Jervis.

V

Brave men were living before Agamemnon
　And since, exceeding valorous and sage,
A good deal like him too, though quite the same
　none;

[1] *Macbeth*, IV, i, 65.

Put down on all the people written [handwritten marginalia]

But then they shone not on the poet's page,
And so have been forgotten:—I condemn none,
But can't find any in the present age
Fit for my poem (that is, for my new one);
So, as I said, I'll take my friend Don Juan.　40

VI

Most epic poets plunge 'in medias res'[2]
　(Horace makes this the heroic turnpike road),
And then your hero tells, whene'er you please,
　What went before—by way of episode,
While seated after dinner at his ease,
　Beside his mistress in some soft abode,
　Palace, or garden, paradise, or cavern,
Which serves the happy couple for a tavern.

VII

That is the usual method, but not mine—
　My way is to begin with the beginning;　50
The regularity of my design
　Forbids all wandering as the worst of sinning,
And therefore I shall open with a line
　(Although it cost me half an hour in spinning)
Narrating somewhat of Don Juan's father,
And also of his mother, if you'd rather.

VIII

In Seville was he born, a pleasant city,
　Famous for oranges and women—he
Who has not seen it will be much to pity,
　So says the proverb—and I quite agree;　60
Of all the Spanish towns is none more pretty,
　Cadiz, perhaps—but that you soon may see:—
Don Juan's parents lived beside the river,
A noble stream, and call'd the Guadalquivir.

IX

His father's name was José—*Don,* of course,
　A true Hidalgo,[3] free from every stain
Of Moor or Hebrew blood, he traced his source
　Through the most Gothic gentlemen of Spain;[4]
A better cavalier ne'er mounted horse,
　Or, being mounted, e'er got down again,　70
Than José, who begot our hero, who
Begot—but that's to come——Well, to renew:

X

His mother was a learned lady,[5] famed

2 "in the middle of things"—Horace, *Ars Poetica.*
3 Spanish nobleman of the lower classes.
4 that is, through nobility of the purest Spanish stock descending in a direct line from the Visigoth conquerors.
5 Though Byron somewhat disingenuously denied that the satirical portraiture of Donna Inez bore resemblances to the manners and behavior of Lady Byron, the allusions are unmistakable. See particularly stanzas 12-14, and again stanzas 27-9.

For every branch of every science known—
In every Christian language ever named,
With virtues equall'd by her wit alone:
She made the cleverest people quite ashamed,
And even the good with inward envy groan,
Finding themselves so very much exceeded
In their own way by all the things that she
    did.   80

XI

Her memory was a mine; she knew by heart
  All Calderon and greater part of Lopé,
So that if any actor miss'd his part
  She could have served him for the prompter's
    copy;
For her Feinagle's[6] were an useless art,
  And he himself obliged to shut up shop—he
Could never make a memory so fine as
That which adorn'd the brain of Donna Inez.

XII

Her favourite science was the mathematical,
  Her noblest virtue was her magnanimity; 90
Her wit (she sometimes tried at wit) was Attic[7]
  all,
  Her serious sayings darken'd to sublimity;
In short, in all things she was fairly what I call
  A prodigy—her morning dress was dimity,
Her evening silk, or, in the summer, muslin,
And other stuffs, with which I won't stay puz-
  zling.

XIII

She knew the Latin—that is, 'the Lord's prayer,'
  And Greek—the alphabet—I'm nearly sure;
She read some French romances here and there,
  Although her mode of speaking was not
    pure;   100
For native Spanish she had no great care,
  At least her conversation was obscure;
Her thoughts were theorems, her words a prob-
  lem,
As if she deem'd that mystery would ennoble 'em.

XIV

She liked the English and the Hebrew tongue,
  And said there was analogy between 'em;
She proved it somehow out of sacred song,
  But I must leave the proofs to those who've
    seen 'em,
But this I heard her say, and can't be wrong,

And all may think which way their judgments
  lean 'em,   110
''Tis strange—the Hebrew noun which means
  "I am,"
The English always use to govern d—n.'

XV

Some women use their tongues—she *look'd* a lec-
  ture,
  Each eye a sermon, and her brow a homily,
An all-in-all sufficient self-director,
  Like the lamented late Sir Samuel Romilly,[8]
The Law's expounder, and the State's corrector,
  Whose suicide was almost an anomaly—
One sad example more, that 'All is vanity,'—
(The jury brought their verdict in 'Insanity.') 120

XVI

In short, she was a walking calculation,
  Miss Edgeworth's novels[9] stepping from their
    covers,
Or Mrs. Trimmer's books[10] on education,
  Or 'Cœlebs' Wife'[11] set out in quest of lovers,
Morality's prim personification,
  In which not Envy's self a flaw discovers;
To others' share let 'female errors fall,'[12]
For she had not even one—the worst of all.

XVII

Oh! she was perfect past all parallel—
  Of any modern female saint's comparison; 130
So far above the cunning powers of hell,
  Her guardian angel had given up his garrison;
Even her minutest motions went as well
  As those of the best time-piece made by Harri-
    son;[13]
In virtues nothing earthly could surpass her,
Save thine 'incomparable oil,' Macassar![14]

'XVIII

Perfect she was, but as perfection is
  Insipid in this naughty world of ours,
Where our first parents never learn'd to kiss
  Till they were exiled from their earlier
    bowers,   140

---

6 Professor Feinagle in 1812 had delivered a course of lectures
at the Royal Institution on improving the memory.
  7 classical; refined.

8 Romilly was legal counsel for Lady Byron. For Byron's comments on his suicide see text, p. 942.
9 Maria Edgeworth wrote morally edifying works such as *The
Parent's Assistant, Early Lessons,* etc.
10 Sarah Trimmer was the author of various juvenile and educational works.
11 Hannah More published *Coelebs in Search of a Wife* in 1809.
12 Pope, *The Rape of the Lock,* ii, 17.
13 John 'Longitude' Harrison, expert watchmaker and the inventor of watch compensation.
14 Macassar oil was much used in hair dressing. It was adver-
tised as having 'des vertus incomparables.'

Where all was peace, and innocence, and bliss
  (I wonder how they got through the twelve
    hours),
Don José, like a lineal son of Eve,
Went plucking various fruit without her leave.

XIX

He was a mortal of the careless kind,
  With no great love for learning, or the learn'd,
Who chose to go where'er he had a mind,
  And never dream'd his lady was concern'd;
The world, as usual, wickedly inclined
  To see a kingdom or a house o'erturn'd,   150
Whisper'd he had a mistress, some said *two,*
But for domestic quarrels *one* will do.

XX

Now Donna Inez had, with all her merit,
  A great opinion of her own good qualities;
Neglect, indeed, requires a saint to bear it,
  And such, indeed, she was in her moralities;
But then she had a devil of a spirit,
  And sometimes mix'd up fancies with realities,
And let few opportunities escape
Of getting her liege lord into a scrape.   160

XXI

This was an easy matter with a man
  Oft in the wrong, and never on his guard;
And even the wisest, do the best they can,
  Have moments, hours, and days, so un-
    prepared,
That you might 'brain them with their lady's
    fan';[15]
  And sometimes ladies hit exceeding hard,
And fans turn into falchions in fair hands,
And why and wherefore no one understands.

XXII

'Tis pity learned virgins ever wed
  With persons of no sort of education,   170
Or gentlemen, who, though well born and bred,
  Grow tired of scientific conversation;
I don't choose to say much upon this head,
  I'm a plain man, and in a single station,
But—Oh! ye lords of ladies intellectual,
Inform us truly, have they not hen-peck'd you
    all?

XXIII

Don José and his lady quarrell'd—*why,*
  Not any of the many could divine,
Though several thousand people chose to try,

15 *I Henry IV,* II, iii, 25.

'Twas surely no concern of theirs nor
    mine;   180
I loathe that low vice—curiosity;
  But if there's anything in which I shine,
'Tis in arranging all my friends' affairs,
Not having, of my own, domestic cares.

XXIV

And so I interfered, and with the best
  Intentions, but their treatment was not kind;
I think the foolish people were possess'd,
  For neither of them could I ever find,
Although their porter afterwards confess'd—
  But that's no matter, and the worst's
    behind,   190
For little Juan o'er me threw, down stairs,
A pail of housemaid's water unawares.

XXV

A little curly-headed, good-for-nothing,
  And mischief-making monkey from his birth;
His parents ne'er agreed except in doting
  Upon the most unquiet imp on earth;
Instead of quarreling, had they been but both in
  Their senses, they'd have sent young master
    forth
To school, or had him soundly whipp'd at home,
To teach him manners for the time to come.   200

XXVI

Don José and the Donna Inez led
  For some time an unhappy sort of life,
Wishing each other, not divorced, but dead;
  They lived respectably as man and wife,
Their conduct was exceedingly well-bred,
  And gave no outward signs of inward strife,
Until at length the smother'd fire broke out,
And put the business past all kind of doubt.

XXVII

For Inez call'd some druggists and physicians,
  And tried to prove her loving lord was *mad,* 210
But as he had some lucid intermissions,
  She next decided he was only *bad;*
Yet when they ask'd her for her depositions,
  No sort of explanation could be had,
Save that her duty both to man and God
Required this conduct—which seem'd very odd.

XXVIII

She kept a journal, where his faults were noted,
  And open'd certain trunks of books and let-
    ters,
All which might, if occasion served, be quoted;

And then she had all Seville for abettors,　220
Besides her good old grandmother (who doted);
　The hearers of her case became repeaters,
Then advocates, inquisitors, and judges,
Some for amusement, others for old grudges.

XXIX

And then this best and meekest woman bore
　With such serenity her husband's woes,
Just as the Spartan ladies did of yore,
　Who saw their spouses kill'd, and nobly chose
Never to say a word about them more—
　Calmly she heard each calumny that rose,　230
And saw *his* agonies with such sublimity,
That all the world exclaim'd, 'What magnanim-
　　ity!'

XXX

No doubt this patience, when the world is damn-
　　ing us,
　Is philosophic in our former friends;
'Tis also pleasant to be deem'd magnanimous,
　The more so in obtaining our own ends;
And what the lawyers call a *'malus animus'*[16]
　Conduct like this by no means comprehends:
Revenge in person's certainly no virtue,
But then 'tis not *my* fault, if *others* hurt you.　240

XXXI

And if our quarrels should rip up old stories,
　And help them with a lie or two additional,
I'm not to blame, as you well know—no more is
　Any one else—they were become traditional;
Besides, their resurrection aids our glories
　By contrast, which is what we just were wish-
　　ing all:
And science profits by this resurrection—
Dead scandals form good subjects for dissection.

XXXII

Their friends had tried at reconciliation,
　Then their relations, who made matters
　　worse,　250
('Twere hard to tell upon a like occasion
　To whom it may be best to have recourse—
I can't say much for friend or yet relation):
　The lawyers did their utmost for divorce,
But scarce a fee was paid on either side
Before, unluckily, Don José died.

XXXIII

He died: and most unluckily, because,
　According to all hints I could collect

From counsel learned in those kinds of laws
　(Although their talk's obscure and circum-
　　spect),　260
His death contrived to spoil a charming cause;
　A thousand pities also with respect
To public feeling, which on this occasion
Was manifested in a great sensation.

XXXIV

But ah! he died; and buried with him lay
　The public feeling and the lawyers' fees:
His house was sold, his servants sent away,
　A Jew took one of his two mistresses,
A priest the other—at least so they say:
　I ask'd the doctors after his disease—　270
He died of the slow fever called the tertian,
And left his widow to her own aversion.

XXXV

Yet José was an honourable man,
　That I must say, who knew him very well;
Therefore his frailties I'll no further scan,
　Indeed there were not many more to tell:
And if his passions now and then outran
　Discretion, and were not so peaceable
As Numa's (who was also named Pompilius),[17]
　He had been ill brought up, and was born
　　bilious.　280

XXXVI

Whate'er might be his worthlessness or worth,
　Poor fellow! he had many things to wound
　　him,
Let's own—since it can do no good on earth—
　It was a trying moment that which found him
Standing alone beside his desolate hearth,
　Where all his household gods lay shiver'd
　　round him:
No choice was left his feelings or his pride,
Save death or Doctors' Commons[18]—so he died.

XXXVII

Dying intestate, Juan was sole heir
　To a chancery suit, and messuages[19] and
　　lands,　290
Which, with a long minority and care,
　Promised to turn out well in proper hands:
Inez became sole guardian, which was fair,
　And answer'd but to nature's just demands;

---

16 malice aforethought.

17 Numa Pompilius, second legendary king of Rome whose reign
was long and peaceful.
18 that is, divorce. The Doctors' Commons, in London, consisted
of buildings that were used as courts having jurisdiction over marriage licenses, divorces, etc.
19 dwelling houses with their outbuildings and lands.

An only son left with an only mother
Is brought up much more wisely than another.

XXXVIII

Sagest of women, even of widows, she
   Resolved that Juan should be quite a paragon,
And worthy of the noblest pedigree:
   (His sire was of Castile, his dam from
      Aragon).   300
Then for accomplishments of chivalry,
   In case our lord the king should go to war
      again,
He learn'd the arts of riding, fencing, gunnery,
And how to scale a fortress—or a nunnery.

XXXIX

But that which Donna Inez most desired,
   And saw into herself each day before all
The learned tutors whom for him she hired,
   Was, that his breeding should be strictly moral:
Much into all his studies she inquired,
   And so they were submitted first to her, all, 310
Arts, sciences, no branch was made a mystery
To Juan's eyes, excepting natural history.

XL

The languages, especially the dead,
   The sciences, and most of all the abstruse,
The arts, at least all such as could be said
   To be the most remote from common use,
In all these he was much and deeply read:
   But not a page of anything that's loose,
Or hints continuation of the species,
Was ever suffer'd, lest he should grow vicious. 320

XLI

His classic studies made a little puzzle,
   Because of filthy loves of gods and goddesses,
Who in the earlier ages raised a bustle,
   But never put on pantaloons or bodices;
His reverend tutors had at times a tussle,
   And for their Æneids, Iliads, and Odysseys,
Were forced to make an odd sort of apology,
For Donna Inez dreaded the Mythology.

XLII

Ovid's a rake, as half his verses show him,
   Anacreon's morals are a still worse sample, 330
Catullus scarcely has a decent poem,
   I don't think Sappho's Ode a good example,
Although Longinus tells us there is no hymn
   Where the sublime soars forth on wings more
      ample;[20]

20 Longinus, *On the Sublime*, section 10.

But Virgil's songs are pure, except that horrid
   one
Beginning with 'Formosum Pastor Corydon.'[21]

XLIII

Lucretius' irreligion is too strong
   For early stomachs, to prove wholesome food;
I can't help thinking Juvenal was wrong,
   Although no doubt his real intent was
      good,   340
For speaking out so plainly in his song,
   So much indeed as to be downright rude;
And then what proper person can be partial
To all those nauseous epigrams of Martial?

XLIV

Juan was taught from out the best edition,
   Expurgated by learned men, who place,
Judiciously, from out the schoolboy's vision,
   The grosser parts; but, fearful to deface
Too much their modest bard by this omission,
   And pitying sore this mutilated case, 350
They only add them all in an appendix,[22]
Which saves, in fact, the trouble of an index;

XLV

For there we have them all 'at one fell swoop,'[23]
   Instead of being scatter'd through the pages;
They stand forth 'marshall'd in a handsome
      troop,
   To meet the ingenuous youth of future ages,
Till some less rigid editor shall stoop
   To call them back into their separate cages,
Instead of standing staring all together,
Like garden gods—and not so decent either. 360

XLVI

The Missal too (it was the family Missal)
   Was ornamented in a sort of way
Which ancient mass-books often are, and this all
   Kinds of grotesques illumined; and how they,
Who saw those figures on the margin kiss all,
   Could turn their optics to the text and pray,
Is more than I know—But Don Juan's mother
Kept this herself, and gave her son another.

XLVII

Sermons he read, and lectures he endured,
   And homilies, and lives of all the saints; 370
To Jerome and to Chrysostom[24] inured,
   He did not take such studies for restraints;

21 'Handsome Shepherd Corydon'—Virgil's *Second Eclogue.*
22 Fact! There is, or was, such an edition, with all the obnoxious
epigrams of Martial placed by themselves at the end.—(Byron.)
23 *Macbeth*, IV, iii, 219.
24 St. Jerome and St. Chrysostom were celebrated church fathers.

But how faith is acquired, and then insured,
So well not one of the aforesaid paints
As Saint Augustine in his fine Confessions,
Which make the reader envy his transgressions.[25]

XLVIII

This, too, was a seal'd book to little Juan—
I can't but say that his mamma was right,
If such an education was the true one.
She scarcely trusted him from out her
sight;   380
Her maids were old, and if she took a new one,
You might be sure she was a perfect fright,
She did this during even her husband's life—
I recommend as much to every wife.

XLIX

Young Juan wax'd in godliness and grace;
At six a charming child, and at eleven
With all the promise of as fine a face
As e'er to man's maturer growth was given.
He studied steadily and grew apace,
And seem'd, at least, in the right road to
heaven,   390
For half his days were pass'd at church, the
other
Between his tutors, confessor, and mother.

L

At six, I said, he was a charming child,
At twelve he was a fine, but quiet boy;
Although in infancy a little wild,
They tamed him down amongst them: to de-
stroy
His natural spirit not in vain they toil'd,
At least it seem'd so; and his mother's joy
Was to declare how sage, and still, and steady,
Her young philosopher was grown already. 400

LI

I had my doubts, perhaps I have them still,
But what I say is neither here nor there:
I knew his father well, and have some skill
In character—but it would not be fair
From sire to son to augur good or ill:
He and his wife were an ill sorted pair—
But scandal's my aversion—I protest
Against all evil speaking, even in jest.

LII

For my part I say nothing—nothing—but
This I will say—my reasons are my own— 410
That if I had an only son to put
To school (as God be praised that I have
none),
'Tis not with Donna Inez I would shut
Him up to learn his catechism alone,
No—no—I'd send him out betimes to college,
For there it was I pick'd up my own knowledge.

LIII

For there one learns—'tis not for me to boast,
Though I acquired—but I pass over *that,*
As well as all the Greek I since have lost:
I say that there's the place—but '*Verbum
sat,*'[26]   420
I think I pick'd up too, as well as most,
Knowledge of matters—but no matter *what*—
I never married—but, I think, I know
That sons should not be educated so.

LIV

Young Juan now was sixteen years of age,
Tall, handsome, slender, but well knit: he
seem'd
Active, though not so sprightly, as a page;
And everybody but his mother deem'd
Him almost man; but she flew in a rage
And bit her lips (for else she might have
scream'd)   430
If any said so, for to be precocious
Was in her eyes a thing the most atrocious.

LV

Amongst her numerous acquaintance, all
Selected for discretion and devotion,
There was the Donna Julia, whom to call
Pretty were but to give a feeble notion
Of many charms in her as natural
As sweetness to the flower, or salt to ocean,
Her zone to Venus, or his bow to Cupid
(But this last simile is trite and stupid), 440

LVI

The darkness of her Oriental eye
Accorded with her Moorish origin;
(Her blood was not all Spanish, by the by;
In Spain, you know, this is a sort of sin).
When proud Granada fell, and, forced to fly,
Boabdil[27] wept, of Donna Julia's kin

---

25 See his *Confessions,* I, ix. By the representation which Saint Augustine gives of himself in his youth, it is easy to see that he was what we should call a rake. He avoided the school as the plague; he loved nothing but gaming and public shows; he robbed his father of everything he could find; he invented a thousand lies to escape the rod, which they were obliged to make use of to punish his irregularities.—(Byron.)

26 'A word to the wise is sufficient.'
27 last Moorish King of Granada, attacked and defeated by Ferdinand and Isabella in 1492.

Some went to Africa, some stay'd in Spain,
Her great great grandmamma chose to remain.

LVII

She married (I forget the pedigree)
　With an Hidalgo, who transmitted down　450
His blood less noble than such blood should
　be;
　At such alliances his sires would frown,
In that point so precise in each degree
　That they bred *in and in,* as might be shown,
Marrying their cousins—nay, their aunts, and
　nieces,
Which always spoils the breed, if it increases.

LVIII

This heathenish cross restored the breed again,
　Ruin'd its blood, but much improved its flesh;
For from a root the ugliest in old Spain
　Sprung up a branch as beautiful as fresh;　460
The sons no more were short, the daughters
　plain:
　But there's a rumour which I fain would hush,
'Tis said that Donna Julia's grandmamma
Produced her Don more heirs at love than law.

LIX

However this might be, the race went on
　Improving still through every generation,
Until it centred in an only son,
　Who left an only daughter: my narration
May have suggested that this single one
　Could be but Julia (whom on this occasion　470
I shall have much to speak about), and she
Was married, charming, chaste, and twenty-
　three.

LX

Her eye (I'm very fond of handsome eyes)
　Was large and dark, suppressing half its fire
Until she spoke, then through its soft disguise
　Flash'd an expression more of pride than ire,
And love than either; and there would arise
　A something in them which was not desire,
But would have been, perhaps, but for the soul
Which struggled through and hasten'd down
　the whole.　480

LXI

Her glossy hair was cluster'd o'er a brow
　Bright with intelligence, and fair, and smooth;
Her eyebrow's shape was like the aërial bow,
　Her cheek all purple with the beam of youth,
Mounting, at times, to a transparent glow,
　As if her veins ran lightning; she, in sooth,
Possess'd an air and grace by no means common:
Her stature tall—I hate a dumpy womån.

LXII

Wedded she was some years, and to a man
　Of fifty, and such husbands are in plenty;　490
And yet, I think, instead of such a ONE
　'Twere better to have TWO of five-and-twenty,
Especially in countries near the sun:
　And now I think on't, 'mi vien in mente,'[28]
Ladies even of the most uneasy virtue
Prefer a spouse whose age is short of thirty.

LXIII

'Tis a sad thing, I cannot choose but say,
　And all the fault of that indecent sun,
Who cannot leave alone our helpless clay,
　But will keep baking, broiling, burning on,　500
That howsoever people fast and pray,
　The flesh is frail, and so the soul undone:
What men call gallantry, and gods adultery,
Is much more common where the climate's sultry.

LXIV

Happy the nations of the moral North!
　Where all is virtue, and the winter season
Sends sin, without a rag on, shivering forth
　('Twas snow that brought St. Anthony[29] to rea-
　son);
Where juries cast up what a wife is worth,
　By laying whate'er sum, in mulct,[30] they
　please on　510
The lover, who must pay a handsome price,
Because it is a marketable vice.

LXV

Alfonso was the name of Julia's lord,
　A man well looking for his years, and who
Was neither much beloved nor yet abhorr'd:
　They lived together as most people do,
Suffering each other's foibles by accord,
　And not exactly either *one* or *two;*
Yet he was jealous, though he did not show it,
For jealousy dislikes the world to know it.　520

LXVI

Julia was—yet I never could see why—
　With Donna Inez quite a favourite friend;
Between their tastes there was small sympathy,

---

28 'It comes to me.'
29 Byron was uncertain about the reference: 'I am not sure it was
not St. Francis [of Assisi] who had a wife of snow—in that case
the line must run, "St. Francis back to reason."' As a matter of
fact, it *was* St. Francis, and not his celebrated disciple, who cooled
his passion with a wife of snow.
30 in fine or penalty.

For not a line had Julia ever penn'd:
Some people whisper (but, no doubt, they lie,
    For malice still imputes some private end)
That Inez had, ere Don Alfonso's marriage,
Forgot with him her very prudent carriage;

LXVII

And that still keeping up the old connexion,
    Which time had lately render'd much more
        chaste,   530
She took his lady also in affection,
    And certainly this course was much the best:
She flatter'd Julia with her sage protection,
    And complimented Don Alfonso's taste;
And if she could not (who can?) silence scandal,
At least she left it a more slender handle.

LXVIII

I can't tell whether Julia saw the affair
    With other people's eyes, or if her own
Discoveries made, but none could be aware
    Of this, at least no symptom e'er was
        shown;   540
Perhaps she did not know, or did not care,
    Indifferent from the first, or callous grown:
I'm really puzzled what to think or say,
She kept her counsel in so close a way.

LXIX

Juan she saw, and, as a pretty child,
    Caress'd him often—such a thing might be
Quite innocently done, and harmless styled,
    When she had twenty years, and thirteen he;
But I am not so sure I should have smiled
    When he was sixteen, Julia twenty-three;   550
These few short years make wondrous altera-
    tions,
Particularly amongst sun-burnt nations.

LXX

Whate'er the cause might be, they had become
    Changed; for the dame grew distant, the youth
        shy,
Their looks cast down, their greetings almost
    dumb,
    And much embarrassment in either eye;
There surely will be little doubt with some
    That Donna Julia knew the reason why,
But as for Juan, he had no more notion
Than he who never saw the sea of ocean.   560

LXXI

Yet Julia's very coldness still was kind,
    And tremulously gentle her small hand
Withdrew itself from his, but left behind

A little pressure, thrilling, and so bland
And slight, so very slight, that to the mind
    'Twas but a doubt; but ne'er magician's wand
Wrought change with all Armida's[31] fairy art
Like what this light touch left on Juan's heart.

LXXII

And if she met him, though she smiled no more,
    She look'd a sadness sweeter than her
        smile,   570
As if her heart had deeper thoughts in store
    She must not own, but cherish'd more the
        while
For that compression in its burning core;
    Even innocence itself has many a wile,
And will not dare to trust itself with truth,
And love is taught hypocrisy from youth.

LXXIII

But passion most dissembles, yet betrays
    Even by its darkness; as the blackest sky
Foretells the heaviest tempest, it displays
    Its workings through the vainly guarded
        eye,   580
And in whatever aspect it arrays
    Itself, 'tis still the same hypocrisy:
Coldness or anger, even disdain or hate,
Are masks it often wears, and still too late.

LXXIV

Then there were sighs, the deeper for suppres-
    sion,
    And stolen glances, sweeter for the theft,
And burning blushes, though for no transgres-
    sion,
    Tremblings when met, and restlessness when
        left;
All these are little preludes to possession,
    Of which young passion cannot be bereft,   590
And merely tend to show how greatly love is
Embarrass'd at first starting with a novice.

LXXV

Poor Julia's heart was in an awkward state;
    She felt it going, and resolved to make
The noblest efforts for herself and mate,
    For honour's, pride's, religion's, virtue's sake.
Her resolutions were most truly great,
    And almost might have made a Tarquin[32]
        quake:

---

31 enchantress in Tasso's *Jerusalem Delivered* who enslaved Rin-
aldo with her magic charms.
32 Tarquinius Superbus, last of the Tarquin Kings, whose reign
was characterized by bloodshed and violence.

She pray'd the Virgin Mary for her grace,
As being the best judge of a lady's case.   600

LXXVI

She vow'd she never would see Juan more,
    And next day paid a visit to his mother,
And look'd extremely at the opening door,
    Which, by the Virgin's grace, let in another;
Grateful she was, and yet a little sore—
    Again it opens, it can be no other,
'Tis surely Juan now—No! I'm afraid
That night the Virgin was no further pray'd.

LXXVII

She now determined that a virtuous woman
    Should rather face and overcome tempta-
        tion,   610
That flight was base and dastardly, and no man
    Should ever give her heart the least sensation;
That is to say, a thought beyond the common
    Preference, that we must feel upon occasion,
For people who are pleasanter than others,
But then they only seem so many brothers.

LXXVIII

And even if by chance—and who can tell?
    The devil's so very sly—she should discover
That all within was not so very well,
    And, if still free, that such or such a lover   620
Might please perhaps, a virtuous wife can quell
    Such thoughts, and be the better when they're
        over;
And if the man should ask, 'tis but denial:
I recommend young ladies to make trial.

LXXIX

And then there are such things as love divine,
    Bright and immaculate, unmix'd and pure,
Such as the angels think so very fine,
    And matrons, who would be no less secure,
Platonic, perfect, 'just such love as mine':
    Thus Julia said—and thought so, to be
        sure;   630
And so I'd have her think, were I the man
On whom her reveries celestial ran.

LXXX

Such love is innocent, and may exist
    Between young persons without any danger:
A hand may first, and then a lip be kist;
    For my part, to such doings I'm a stranger,
But *hear* these freedoms form the utmost list
    Of all o'er which such love may be a ranger:
If people go beyond, 'tis quite a crime,
But not my fault—I tell them all in time.   640

LXXXI

Love, then, but love within its proper limits
    Was Julia's innocent determination
In young Don Juan's favour, and to him its
    Exertion might be useful on occasion;
And, lighted at too pure a shrine to dim its
    Ethereal lustre, with what sweet persuasion
He might be taught, by love and her together—
I really don't know what, nor Julia either.

LXXXII

Fraught with this fine intention, and well fenced
    In mail of proof—her purity of soul,   650
She, for the future of her strength convinced,
    And that her honour was a rock, or mole,
Exceeding sagely from that hour dispensed
    With any kind of troublesome control;
But whether Julia to the task was equal
Is that which must be mention'd in the sequel.

LXXXIII

Her plan she deem'd both innocent and feasible,
    And, surely, with a stripling of sixteen
Not scandal's fangs could fix on much that's seiz-
        able,
    Or if they did so, satisfied to mean   660
Nothing but what was good, her breast was
        peaceable:
    A quiet conscience makes one so serene!
Christians have burnt each other, quite per-
        suaded
That all the Apostles would have done as they
        did.

LXXXIV

And if in the mean time her husband died,
    But Heaven forbid that such a thought should
        cross
Her brain, though in a dream! (and then she
        sigh'd)
    Never could she survive that common loss;
But just suppose that moment should betide,
    I only say suppose it—*inter nos*.   670
(This should be *entre nous,* for Julia thought
In French, but then the rhyme would go for
        nought.)

LXXXV

I only say, suppose this supposition:
    Juan being then grown up to man's estate
Would fully suit a widow of condition,
    Even seven years hence it would not be too
        late;
And in the interim (to pursue this vision)
    The mischief, after all, could not be great,

For he would learn the rudiments of love,
I mean the seraph way of those above.　　　680

LXXXVI

So much for Julia. Now we'll turn to Juan.
　　Poor little fellow! he had no idea
Of his own case, and never hit the true one;
　　In feelings quick as Ovid's Miss Medea,[33]
He puzzled over what he found a new one,
　　But not as yet imagined it could be a
Thing quite in course, and not at all alarming,
Which, with a little patience, might grow charm-
　　　ing.

LXXXVII

Silent and pensive, idle, restless, slow,
　　His home deserted for the lonely wood,　　690
Tormented with a wound he could not know,
　　His, like all deep grief, plunged in solitude:
I'm fond myself of solitude or so,
　　But then, I beg it may be understood,
By solitude I mean a Sultan's, not
A hermit's, with a haram for a grot.

LXXXVIII

'Oh Love! in such a wilderness as this,
　　Where transport and security entwine,
Here is the empire of thy perfect bliss,
　　And here thou art a god indeed divine.'[34]　　700
The bard I quote from does not sing amiss,
　　With the exception of the second line,
For that same twining 'transport and security'
Are twisted to a phrase of some obscurity.

LXXXIX

The poet meant, no doubt, and thus appeals
　　To the good sense and senses of mankind,
The very thing which everybody feels,
　　As all have found on trial, or may find,
That no one likes to be disturb'd at meals
　　Or love.—I won't say more about 'en-
　　　twined'　　710
Or 'transport,' as we knew all that before,
But beg 'Security' will bolt the door.

XC

Young Juan wander'd by the glassy brooks,
　　Thinking unutterable things; he threw
Himself at length within the leafy nooks
　　Where the wild branch of the cork forest grew;

There poets find materials for their books,
　　And every now and then we read them
　　　through,
So that their plan and prosody are eligible,
Unless, like Wordsworth, they prove unin-
　　telligible.　　720

XCI

He, Juan (and not Wordsworth), so pursued
　　His self-communion with his own high soul,
Until his mighty heart, in its great mood,
　　Had mitigated part, though not the whole
Of its disease; he did the best he could
　　With things not very subject to control,
And turn'd, without perceiving his condition,
Like Coleridge, into a metaphysician.

XCII

He thought about himself, and the whole earth,
　　Of man the wonderful, and of the stars,　　730
And how the deuce they ever could have birth;
　　And then he thought of earthquakes, and of
　　　wars,
How many miles the moon might have in
　　girth,
　　Of air-balloons, and of the many bars
To perfect knowledge of the boundless skies;—
And then he thought of Donna Julia's eyes.

XCIII

In thoughts like these true wisdom may discern
　　Longings sublime, and aspirations high,
Which some are born with, but the most part
　　learn
　　To plague themselves withal, they know not
　　　why:　　740
'Twas strange that one so young should thus con-
　　cern
　　His brain about the action of the sky;
If *you* think 'twas philosophy that this did,
I can't help thinking puberty assisted.

XCIV

He pored upon the leaves, and on the flowers,
　　And heard a voice in all the winds; and then
He thought of wood-nymphs and immortal bow-
　　ers,
　　And how the goddesses came down to men:
He miss'd the pathway, he forgot the hours,
　　And when he look'd upon his watch again, 750
He found how much old Time had been a win-
　　ner—
He also found that he had lost his dinner.

---

33 The story of the legendary sorceress, Medea, is told by Ovid in *Metamorphoses*, VII, 9ff.
34 Byron is quoting from memory from Campbell's *Gertrude of Wyoming*.

XCV

Sometimes he turn'd to gaze upon his book,
   Boscan, or Garcilasso;[35]—by the wind
Even as the page is rustled while we look,
   So by the poesy of his own mind
Over the mystic leaf his soul was shook,
   As if 'twere one whereon magicians bind
Their spells, and give them to the passing gale
According to some good old woman's tale.   760

XCVI

Thus would he while his lonely hours away
   Dissatisfied, nor knowing what he wanted;
Nor glowing reverie, nor poet's lay,
   Could yield his spirit that for which it panted,
A bosom whereon he his head might lay,
   And hear the heart beat with the love it
     granted,
With——several other things, which I forget,
Or which, at least, I need not mention yet.

XCVII

Those lonely walks, and lengthening reveries,
   Could not escape the gentle Julia's eyes;   770
She saw that Juan was not at his ease;
   But that which chiefly may, and must surprise,
Is, that the Donna Inez did not tease
   Her only son with question or surmise;
Whether it was she did not see, or would not,
Or, like all very clever people, could not.

XCVIII

This may seem strange, but yet 'tis very common;
   For instance—gentlemen, whose ladies take
Leave to o'erstep the written rights of woman,
   And break the——Which commandment is't
     they break?   780
(I have forgot the number, and think no man
   Should rashly quote, for fear of a mistake.)
I say, when these same gentlemen are jealous,
They make some blunder, which their ladies tell
   us.

XCIX

A real husband always is suspicious,
   But still no less suspects in the wrong place,
Jealous of some one who had no such wishes,
   Or pandering blindly to his own disgrace,
By harbouring some dear friend extremely
   vicious;
   The last indeed 's infallibly the case: 790

---

35 Juan Boscan and Garcilasso de la Vega were Spanish poets of
the sixteenth century.

And when the spouse and friend are gone off
   wholly,
He wonders at their vice, and not his folly.

C

Thus parents also are at times short-sighted;
   Though watchful as the lynx, they ne'er dis-
     cover,
The while the wicked world beholds delighted,
   Young Hopeful's mistress, or Miss Fanny's
     lover,
Till some confounded escapade has blighted
   The plan of twenty years, and all is over;
And then the mother cries, the father swears,
And wonders why the devil he got heirs.   800

CI

But Inez was so anxious, and so clear
   Of sight, that I must think, on this occasion,
She had some other motive much more near
   For leaving Juan to this new temptation,
But what that motive was, I shan't say here;
   Perhaps to finish Juan's education,
Perhaps to open Don Alfonso's eyes,
In case he thought his wife too great a prize.

CII

It was upon a day, a summer's day;—
   Summer's indeed a very dangerous season, 810
And so is spring about the end of May;
   The sun, no doubt, is the prevailing reason;
But whatsoe'er the cause is, one may say,
   And stand convicted of more truth than trea-
     son,
That there are months which nature grows more
   merry in,—
March has its hares, and May must have its hero-
   ine.

CIII

'Twas on a summer's day—the sixth of June:—
   I like to be particular in dates,
Not only of the age, and year, but moon;
   They are a sort of post-house, where the
     Fates   820
Change horses, making history change its tune,
   Then spur away o'er empires and o'er states,
Leaving at last not much besides chronology,
Excepting the post-obits of theology.

CIV

'Twas on the sixth of June, about the hour
   Of half-past six—perhaps still nearer seven—
When Julia sate within as pretty a bower

As e'er held houri in that heathenish heaven
Described by Mahomet, and Anacreon Moore,[36]
    To whom the lyre and laurels have been
        given,   830
With all the trophies of triumphant song—
He won them well, and may he wear them long!

CV

She sate, but not alone; I know not well
    How this same interview had taken place,
And even if I knew, I should not tell—
    People should hold their tongues in any case;
No matter how or why the thing befell,
    But there were she and Juan, face to face—
When two such faces are so, 'twould be wise,
But very difficult, to shut their eyes.   840

CVI

How beautiful she look'd! her conscious heart
    Glow'd in her cheek, and yet she felt no wrong,
Oh Love! how perfect is thy mystic art,
    Strengthening the weak, and trampling on the
        strong!
How self-deceitful is the sagest part
    Of mortals whom thy lure hath led along!—
The precipice she stood on was immense,
So was her creed in her own innocence.

CVII

She thought of her own strength, and Juan's
        youth,
    And of the folly of all prudish fears,   850
Victorious virtue, and domestic truth,
    And then of Don Alfonso's fifty years:
I wish these last had not occurr'd, in sooth,
    Because that number rarely much endears,
And through all climes, the snowy and the sunny,
Sounds ill in love, whate'er it may in money.

CVIII

When people say, 'I've told you *fifty* times,'
    They mean to scold, and very often do;
When poets say, 'I've written *fifty* rhymes,'
    They make you dread that they'll recite them
        too;   860
In gangs of *fifty*, thieves commit their crimes;
    At *fifty* love for love is rare, 'tis true,
But then, no doubt, it equally as true is,
A good deal may be bought for *fifty* Louis.

CIX

Julia had honour, virtue, truth, and love
    For Don Alfonso; and she inly swore,

By all the vows below to powers above,
    She never would disgrace the ring she wore,
Nor leave a wish which wisdom might reprove;
    And while she ponder'd this, besides much
        more,   870
One hand on Juan's carelessly was thrown,
Quite by mistake—she thought it was her own;

CX

Unconsciously she lean'd upon the other,
    Which play'd within the tangles of her hair;
And to contend with thoughts she could not
        smother
    She seem'd, by the distraction of her air.
'Twas surely very wrong in Juan's mother
    To leave together this imprudent pair,
She who for many years had watch'd her son
        so—
I'm very certain *mine* would not have done
        so.   880

CXI

The hand which still held Juan's, by degrees
    Gently, but palpably confirm'd its grasp,
As if it said, 'Detain me, if you please';
    Yet there's no doubt she only meant to clasp
His fingers with a pure Platonic squeeze;
    She would have shrunk as from a toad, or asp,
Had she imagined such a thing could rouse
A feeling dangerous to a prudent spouse.

CXII

I cannot know what Juan thought of this,
    But what he did, is much what you would
        do;   890
His young lip thank'd it with a grateful kiss,
    And then, abash'd at its own joy, withdrew
In deep despair, lest he had done amiss,—
    Love is so very timid when 'tis new:
She blush'd, and frown'd not, but she strove to
        speak,
And held her tongue, her voice was grown so
        weak.

CXIII

The sun set, and up rose the yellow moon:
    The devil's in the moon for mischief; they
Who call'd her CHASTE, methinks, began too soon
    Their nomenclature; there is not a day,   900
The longest, not the twenty-first of June,
    Sees half the business in a wicked way,
On which three single hours of moonshine
        smile—
And then she looks so modest all the while.

---

36 Thomas Moore in his youth translated the amatory odes of
Anacreon, famous Greek lyricist.

CXIV

There is a dangerous silence in that hour,
  A stillness, which leaves room for the full soul
To open all itself, without the power
  Of calling wholly back its self-control;
The silver light which, hallowing tree and tower,
  Sheds beauty and deep softness o'er the
    whole,   910
Breathes also to the heart, and o'er it throws
A loving languor, which is not repose.

CXV

And Julia sate with Juan, half embraced
  And half retiring from the glowing arm,
Which trembled like the bosom where 'twas
    placed;
  Yet still she must have thought there was no
    harm,
Or else 'twere easy to withdraw her waist;
  But then the situation had its charm,
And then——God knows what next—I can't go
    on;
I'm almost sorry that I e'er begun.   920

CXVI

Oh Plato! Plato! you have paved the way,
  With your confounded fantasies, to more
Immoral conduct by the fancied sway
  Your system feigns o'er the controlless core
Of human hearts, than all the long array
  Of poets and romancers:—You're a bore,
A charlatan, a coxcomb—and have been,
At best, no better than a go-between.

CXVII

And Julia's voice was lost, except in sighs,
  Until too late for useful conversation;   930
The tears were gushing from her gentle eyes,
  I wish, indeed, they had not had occasion;
But who, alas! can love, and then be wise?
  Not that remorse did not oppose temptation;
A little still she strove, and much repented,
And whispering 'I will ne'er consent'—consented.

CXVIII

'Tis said that Xerxes offer'd a reward
  To those who could invent him a new pleas-
    ure.
Methinks the requisition's rather hard,
  And must have cost his majesty a treasure: 940
For my part, I'm a moderate-minded bard,
  Fond of a little love (which I call leisure);
I care not for new pleasures, as the old
Are quite enough for me, so they but hold.

CXIX

Oh Pleasure! you're indeed a pleasant thing,
  Although one must be damn'd for you, no
    doubt:
I make a resolution every spring
  Of reformation, ere the year run out,
But somehow, this my vestal vow takes wing,
  Yet still, I trust, it may be kept throughout: 950
I'm very sorry, very much ashamed,
And mean, next winter, to be quite reclaim'd.

CXX

Here my chaste Muse a liberty must take—
  Start not! still chaster reader—she'll be nice
    hence-
Forward, and there is no great cause to quake;
  This liberty is a poetic licence,
Which some irregularity may make
  In the design, and as I have a high sense
Of Aristotle and the Rules, 'tis fit
To beg his pardon when I err a bit.   960

CXXI

This licence is to hope the reader will
  Suppose from June the sixth (the fatal day
Without whose epoch my poetic skill
  For want of facts would all be thrown away),
But keeping Julia and Don Juan still
  In sight, that several months have pass'd; we'll
    say
'Twas in November, but I'm not so sure
About the day—the era's more obscure.

CXXII

We'll talk of that anon.—'Tis sweet to hear
  At midnight on the blue and moonlit deep 970
The song and oar of Adria's[37] gondolier,
  By distance mellow'd, o'er the waters sweep;
'Tis sweet to see the evening star appear;
  'Tis sweet to listen as the night-winds creep
From leaf to leaf; 'tis sweet to view on high
The rainbow, based on ocean, span the sky.

CXXIII

'Tis sweet to hear the watch-dog's honest
    bark
  Bay deep-mouth'd welcome as we draw near
    home;
'Tis sweet to know there is an eye will mark
  Our coming, and look brighter when we
    come;   980
'Tis sweet to be awaken'd by the lark,
  Or lull'd by falling waters; sweet the hum

---

37 poetic for Adriatic.

Of bees, the voice of girls, the song of birds,
The lisp of children, and their earliest words.

CXXIV

Sweet is the vintage, when the showering grapes
   In Bacchanal profusion reel to earth,
Purple and gushing; sweet are our escapes
   From civic revelry to rural mirth;
Sweet to the miser are his glittering heaps,
   Sweet to the father is his first-born's birth, 990
Sweet is revenge—especially to women,
Pillage to soldiers, prize-money to seamen.

CXXV

Sweet is a legacy, and passing sweet
   The unexpected death of some old lady
Or gentleman of seventy years complete,
   Who've made 'us youth' wait too—too long al-
    ready
For an estate, or cash, or country seat,
   Still breaking, but with stamina so steady
That all the Israelites are fit to mob its
Next owner for their double-damn'd post-
   obits.   1000

CXXVI

'Tis sweet to win, no matter how, one's laurels,
   By blood or ink; 'tis sweet to put an end
To strife; 'tis sometimes sweet to have our quar-
   rels,
   Particularly with a tiresome friend:
Sweet is old wine in bottles, ale in barrels;
   Dear is the helpless creature we defend
Against the world; and dear the schoolboy spot
We ne'er forget, though there we are forgot.

CXXVII

But sweeter still than this, than these, than all,
   Is first and passionate love—it stands
    alone,   1010
Like Adam's recollection of his fall;
   The tree of knowledge has been pluck'd—all's
    known—
And life yields nothing further to recall
   Worthy of this ambrosial sin, so shown,
No doubt in fable, as the unforgiven
Fire which Prometheus filch'd for us from
   heaven.

CXXVIII

Man's a strange animal, and makes strange use
   Of his own nature, and the various arts,
And likes particularly to produce
   Some new experiment to show his parts;   1020
This is the age of oddities let loose,
   Where different talents finds their different
    marts;
You'd best begin with truth, and when you've
    lost your
Labour, there's a sure market for imposture.

CXXIX

What opposite discoveries we have seen!
   (Signs of true genius, and of empty pockets.)
One makes new noses, one a guillotine,
   One breaks your bones, one sets them in their
    sockets;
But vaccination certainly has been
   A kind antithesis to Congreve's rockets,[38] 1030
With which the Doctor paid off an old pox,
By borrowing a new one from an ox.

CXXX

Bread has been made (indifferent) from pota-
   toes;
   And galvanism has set some corpses grin-
    ning,[39]
But has not answer'd like the apparatus
   Of the Humane Society's beginning,
By which men are unsuffocated gratis:
   What wondrous new machines have late been
    spinning!
I said the small pox has gone out of late;
Perhaps it may be follow'd by the great.   1040

CXXXI

'Tis said the great came from America;
   Perhaps it may set out on its return,—
The population there so spreads, they say
   'Tis grown high time to thin it in its turn,
With war, or plague, or famine, any way,
   So that civilisation they may learn;
And which in ravage the more loathsome evil
   is—
Their real lues, or our pseudo-syphilis?

CXXXII

This is the patent age of new inventions
   For killing bodies, and for saving souls,   1050
All propagated with the best intentions;
   Sir Humphry Davy's lantern,[40] by which coals
Are safely mined for in the mode he mentions,
   Tombuctoo travels, voyages to the Poles,
Are ways to benefit mankind, as true,
Perhaps, as shooting them at Waterloo.

---

38 Sir William Congreve invented a new kind of explosive shell;
it was used with great effect in the battle of Leipzig in 1813.
39 Galvani's nephew performed experiments in Galvanism upon
the body of a murderer in 1803.
40 Sir Humphrey Davy invented the safety lamp in 1815.

CXXXIII

Man's a phenomenon, one knows not what,
    And wonderful beyond all wondrous measure;
'Tis pity though, in this sublime world, that
    Pleasure's a sin, and sometimes sin's a
        pleasure;   1060
Few mortals know what end they would be at,
    But whether glory, power, or love, or treasure,
The path is through perplexing ways, and when
The goal is gain'd, we die, you know—and
        then——

CXXXIV

What then?—I do not know, no more do you—
    And so good night.—Return we to our story:
'Twas in November, when fine days are few,
    And the far mountains wax a little hoary,
And clap a white cape on their mantles blue;
    And the sea dashes round the promon-
        tory,   1070
And the loud breaker boils against the rock,
And sober suns must set at five o'clock.

CXXXV

'Twas, as the watchmen say, a cloudy night;
    No moon, no stars, the wind was low or loud
By gusts, and many a sparkling hearth was bright
    With the piled wood, round which the family
        crowd;
There's something cheerful in that sort of light,
    Even as a summer sky's without a cloud:
I'm fond of fire, and crickets, and all that,
A lobster salad, and champagne, and chat.   1080

CXXXVI

'Twas midnight—Donna Julia was in bed,
    Sleeping, most probably,—when at her door
Arose a clatter might awake the dead,
    If they had never been awoke before,
And that they have been so we all have read,
    And are to be so, at the least, once more;—
The door was fasten'd, but with voice and fist
First knocks were heard, then 'Madam—Madam
    —hist!

CXXXVII

'For God's sake, Madam—Madam—here's my
        master,
    With more than half the city at his back—   1090
Was ever heard of such a curst disaster!
    'Tis not my fault—I kept good watch—Alack!
Do pray undo the bolt a little faster—
    They're on the stair just now, and in a crack
Will all be here; perhaps he yet may fly—
Surely the window's not so *very* high!'

CXXXVIII

By this time Don Alfonso was arrived,
    With torches, friends, and servants in great
        number;
The major part of them had long been wived,
    And therefore paused not to disturb the slum-
        ber   1100
Of any wicked woman, who contrived
    By stealth her husband's temples to encumber;
Examples of this kind are so contagious,
Were *one* not punish'd, *all* would be outrageous.

CXXXIX

I can't tell how, or why, or what suspicion
    Could enter into Don Alfonso's head;
But for a cavalier of his condition
    It surely was exceedingly ill-bred,
Without a word of previous admonition,
    To hold a levee round his lady's bed,   1110
And summon lackeys, arm'd with fire and sword,
To prove himself the thing he most abhorr'd.

CXL

Poor Donna Julia! starting as from sleep
    (Mind—that I do not say—she had not slept),
Began at once to scream, and yawn, and weep;
    Her maid, Antonia, who was an adept,
Contrived to fling the bed-clothes in a heap,
    As if she had just now from out them crept:
I can't tell why she should take all this trouble
To prove her mistress had been sleeping
        double.   1120

CXLI

But Julia mistress, and Antonia maid,
    Appear'd like two poor harmless women, who
Of goblins, but still more of men afraid,
    Had thought one man might be deterr'd by
        two,
And therefore side by side were gently laid,
    Until the hours of absence should run through,
And truant husband should return and say,
'My dear, I was the first who came away.'

CXLII

Now Julia found at length a voice, and cried,
    'In heaven's name, Don Alfonso, what d'ye
        mean?   1130
Has madness seized you? would that I had died
    Ere such a monster's victim I had been!
What may this midnight violence betide,
    A sudden fit of drunkenness or spleen?

Dare you suspect me, whom the thought would
  kill?
Search, then, the room!'—Alfonso said, 'I will.'

CXLIII

He search'd, *they* search'd, and rummaged every-
  where,
  Closet and clothes-press, chest and window-
  seat,
And found much linen, lace, and several pair
  Of stockings, slippers, brushes, combs, com-
  plete,   1140
With other articles of ladies fair,
  To keep them beautiful, or leave them neat:
Arras they prick'd and curtains with their swords,
And wounded several shutters, and some boards.

CXLIV

Under the bed they search'd, and there they
  found—
  No matter what—it was not that they sought;
They open'd windows, gazing if the ground
  Had signs or footmarks, but the earth said
  nought;
And then they stared each other's faces round:
  'Tis odd, not one of all these seekers
  thought,   1150
And seems to me almost a sort of blunder,
Of looking *in* the bed as well as under.

CXLV

During this inquisition Julia's tongue
  Was not asleep—'Yes, search and search,' she
  cried,
'Insult on insult heap, and wrong on wrong!
  It was for this that I became a bride!
For this in silence I have suffer'd long
  A husband like Alfonso at my side;
But now I'll bear no more, nor here remain,
If there be law or lawyers in all Spain.   1160

CXLVI

'Yes, Don Alfonso! husband now no more,
  If ever you indeed deserved the name,
Is't worthy of your years?—you have three-
  score—
  Fifty, or sixty, it is all the same—
Is't wise or fitting, causeless to explore
  For facts against a virtuous woman's fame?
Ungrateful, perjured, barbarous Don Alfonso,
How dare you think your lady would go on so?

CXLVII

'Is it for this I have disdain'd to hold
  The common privileges of my sex?   1170

That I have chosen a confessor so old
  And deaf, that any other it would vex,
And never once he has had cause to scold,
  But found my very innocence perplex
So much, he always doubted I was married—
How sorry you will be when I've miscarried!

CXLVIII

'Was it for this that no Cortejo[41] e'er
  I yet have chosen from out the youth of Seville?
Is it for this I scarce went anywhere,
  Except to bull-fights, mass, play, rout, and
  revel?   1180
Is it for this, whate'er my suitors were,
  I favour'd none—nay, was almost uncivil?
Is it for this that General Count O'Reilly,
Who took Algiers,[42] declares I used him vilely?

CXLIX

'Did not the Italian Musico Cazzani
  Sing at my heart six months at least in vain?
Did not his countryman, Count Corniani,
  Call me the only virtuous wife in Spain?
Were there not also Russians, English, many?
  The Count Strongstroganoff I put in pain, 1190
And Lord Mount Coffeehouse, the Irish peer,
Who kill'd himself for love (with wine) last year.

CL

'Have I not had two bishops at my feet?
  The Duke of Ichar, and Don Fernan Nunez?
And is it thus a faithful wife you treat?
  I wonder in what quarter now the moon is:
I praise your vast forbearance not to beat
  Me also, since the time so opportune is—
Oh, valiant man! with sword drawn and cock'd
  trigger,
Now, tell me, don't you cut a pretty figure? 1200

CLI

'Was it for this you took your sudden journey,
  Under pretense of business indispensable,
With that sublime of rascals your attorney,
  Whom I see standing there, and looking sen-
  sible
Of having play'd the fool? though both I spurn,
  he
  Deserves the worst, his conduct's less defensi-
  ble,
Because, no doubt, 'twas for his dirty fee,
And not from any love to you nor me.

---

41 The Spanish *Cortejo* is much the same as the Italian *Cavalier Servente.*—(Byron.)
42 Donna Julia here made a mistake. Count O'Reilly did not take Algiers—but Algiers very nearly took him: he and his army and fleet retreated with great loss, and not much credit, from before that city, in the year 1775.—(Byron.)

CLII

'If he comes here to take a deposition,
  By all means let the gentleman proceed; 1210
You've made the apartment in a fit condition:—
  There's pen and ink for you, sir, when you
    need—
Let everything be noted with precision,
  I would not you for nothing should be fee'd—
But as my maid's undrest, pray turn your spies
    out.'
'Oh!' sobb'd Antonia, 'I could tear their eyes out.'

CLIII

'There is the closet, there the toilet, there
  The antechamber—search them under, over;
There is the sofa, there the great arm-chair,
  The chimney—which would really hold a
    lover. 1220
I wish to sleep, and beg you will take care
  And make no further noise, till you discover
The secret cavern of this lurking treasure—
And when 'tis found, let me, too, have that pleas-
    ure.

CLIV

'And now, Hidalgo! now that you have thrown
  Doubt upon me, confusion over all,
Pray have the courtesy to make it known
  Who is the man you search for? how d'ye call
Him? what's his lineage? let him but be shown—
  I hope he's young and handsome—is he-
    tall? 1230
Tell me—and be assured, that since you stain
Mine honour thus, it shall not be in vain.

CLV

'At least, perhaps, he has not sixty years,
  At that age he would be too old for slaughter,
Or for so young a husband's jealous fears—
  (Antonia! let me have a glass of water.)
I am ashamed of having shed these tears,
  They are unworthy of my father's daughter;
My mother dream'd not in my natal hour,
That I should fall into a monster's power. 1240

CLVI

'Perhaps 'tis of Antonia you are jealous,
  You saw that she was sleeping by my side,
When you broke in upon us with your fellows;
  Look where you please—we've nothing, sir, to
    hide;
Only another time, I trust, you'll tell us,
  Or for the sake of decency abide
A moment at the door, that we may be
Drest to receive so much good company.

CLVII

'And now, sir, I have done, and say no more;
  The little I have said may serve to show 1250
The guileless heart in silence may grieve o'er
  The wrongs to whose exposure it is slow:—
I leave you to your conscience as before,
  'Twill one day ask you, *why* you used me so?
God grant you feel not then the bitterest grief!
Antonia! where's my pocket-handkerchief?'

CLVIII

She ceased, and turn'd upon her pillow; pale
  She lay, her dark eyes flashing through their
    tears,
Like skies that rain and lighten; as a veil,
  Waved and o'ershading her wan cheek,
    appears 1260
Her streaming hair; the black curls strive, but
    fail,
  To hide the glossy shoulder, which uprears
Its snow through all;—her soft lips lie apart,
And louder than her breathing beats her heart.

CLIX

The Senhor Don Alfonso stood confused;
  Antonia bustled round the ransack'd room,
And, turning up her nose, with looks abused
  Her master, and his myrmidons, of whom
Not one, except the attorney, was amused;
  He, like Achates,[43] faithful to the tomb, 1270
So there were quarrels, cared not for the cause,
Knowing they must be settled by the laws.

CLX

With prying snub-nose, and small eyes, he stood,
  Following Antonia's motions here and there,
With much suspicion in his attitude;
  For reputations he had little care;
So that a suit or action were made good,
  Small pity had he for the young and fair,
And ne'er believed in negatives, till these
Were proved by competent false witnesses. 1280

CLXI

But Don Alfonso stood with downcast looks,
  And, truth to say, he made a foolish figure;
When, after searching in five hundred nooks,
  And treating a young wife with so much rigour,
He gain'd no point, except some self-rebukes,
  Added to those his lady with such vigour
Had pour'd upon him for the last half hour,
Quick, thick, and heavy—as a thunder-shower.

---

43 the faithful companion of Aeneas in Virgil's *Aeneid.*

CLXII

At first he tried to hammer an excuse,
  To which the sole reply was tears and
    sobs,   1290
And indications of hysterics, whose
  Prologue is always certain throes, and throbs,
Gasps, and whatever else the owners choose:
  Alfonso saw his wife, and thought of Job's;
He saw too, in perspective, her relations,
And then he tried to muster all his patience.

CLXIII

He stood in act to speak, or rather stammer,
  But sage Antonia cut him short before
The anvil of his speech received the hammer,
  With 'Pray, sir, leave the room, and say no
    more,   1300
Or madam dies.'—Alfonso mutter'd, 'D—n
    her,'
  But nothing else, the time of words was o'er;
He cast a rueful look or two, and did,
He knew not wherefore, that which he was bid.

CLXIV

With him retired his *'posse comitatus,'*[44]
  The attorney last, who linger'd near the door
Reluctantly, still tarrying there as late as
  Antonia let him—not a little sore
At this most strange and unexplain'd *'hiatus'*
  In Don Alfonso's facts, which just now
    wore   1310
An awkward look; as he revolved the case,
The door was fasten'd in his legal face.

CLXV

No sooner was it bolted, than—Oh shame!
  Oh sin! Oh sorrow! and Oh womankind!
How can you do such things and keep your
    fame,
  Unless this world, and t'other too, be blind?
Nothing so dear as an unfilch'd good name!
  But to proceed—for there is more behind:
With much heartfelt reluctance be it said,
Young Juan slipp'd, half-smother'd, from the
    bed.   1320

CLXVI

He had been hid—I don't pretend to say
  How, nor can I indeed describe the where—
Young, slender, and pack'd easily, he lay,
  No doubt, in little compass, round or square;
But pity him I neither must nor may
  His suffocation by that pretty pair;

'Twere better, sure, to die so, than be shut
With maudlin Clarence in his Malmsey butt.[45]

CLXVII

And, secondly, I pity not, because
  He had no business to commit a sin,   1330
Forbid by heavenly, fined by human laws;
  At least 'twas rather early to begin;
But at sixteen the conscience rarely gnaws
  So much as when we call our old debts in
At sixty years, and draw the accompts of evil,
And find a deuced balance with the devil.

CLXVIII

Of his position I can give no notion:
  'Tis written in the Hebrew Chronicle,
How the physicians, leaving pill and potion,
  Prescribed, by way of blister, a young
    belle,   1340
When old King David's blood grew dull in mo-
    tion,
  And that the medicine answer'd very well;
Perhaps 'twas in a different way applied,
For David lived, but Juan nearly died.

CLXIX

What's to be done? Alfonso will be back
  The moment he has sent his fools away.
Antonia's skill was put upon the rack,
  But no device could be brought into play—
And how to parry the renew'd attack?
  Besides, it wanted but few hours of day: 1350
Antonia puzzled; Julia did not speak,
But press'd her bloodless lip to Juan's cheek.

CLXX

He turn'd his lip to hers, and with his hand
  Call'd back the tangles of her wandering hair;
Even then their love they could not all command,
  And half forgot their danger and despair:
Antonia's patience now was at a stand—
  'Come, come, 'tis no time now for fooling
    there,'
She whisper'd, in great wrath—'I must deposit
This pretty gentleman within the closet: 1360

CLXXI

'Pray, keep your nonsense for some luckier
    night—
  Who can have put my master in this mood?
What will become on't—I'm in such a fright,
  The devil's in the urchin, and no good—
Is this a time for giggling? this a plight?

---

44 the legal term of which *posse* is the abbreviated form.

45 The Duke of Clarence, after being stabbed by his murderers, was thrown into a Malmsey butt to drown. See *Richard III*, I, iv.

Why, don't you know that it may end in blood?
You'll lose your life, and I shall lose my place,
My mistress all, for that half-girlish face.

CLXXII

'Had it but been for a stout cavalier
    Of twenty-five or thirty—(come, make
        haste)   1370
But for a child, what piece of work is here!
    I really, madam, wonder at your taste—
(Come, sir, get in)—my master must be near:
    There, for the present, at the least, he's fast,
And if we can but till the morning keep
Our counsel—(Juan, mind, you must not sleep).'

CLXXIII

Now, Don Alfonso entering, but alone,
    Closed the oration of the trusty maid:
She loiter'd, and he told her to be gone,
    An order somewhat sullenly obey'd;   1380
However, present remedy was none,
    And no great good seem'd answer'd if she
        staid;
Regarding both with slow and sidelong view,
She snuff'd the candle, curtsied, and withdrew.

CLXXIV

Alfonso paused a minute—then begun
    Some strange excuses for his late proceeding:
He would not justify what he had done,
    To say the best, it was extreme ill-breeding;
But there were ample reasons for it, none
    Of which he specified in this his pleading: 1390
His speech was a fine sample, on the whole,
Of rhetoric, which the learn'd call *'rigmarole.'*

CLXXV

Julia said nought; though all the while there rose
    A ready answer, which at once enables
A matron, who her husband's foible knows,
    By a few timely words to turn the tables,
Which, if it does not silence, still must pose,—
    Even if it should comprise a pack of fables;
'Tis to retort with firmness, and when he
Suspects with *one,* do you reproach with
        three.   1400

CLXXVI

Julia, in fact, had tolerable grounds,—
    Alfonso's loves with Inez were well known;
But whether 'twas that one's own guilt con-
        founds—
    But that can't be, as has been often shown,
A lady with apologies abounds—

It might be that her silence sprang alone
    From delicacy to Don Juan's ear,
To whom she knew his mother's fame was dear.

CLXXVII

There might be one more motive, which makes
        two,
    Alfonso ne'er to Juan had alluded,—   1410
Mentioned his jealousy, but never who
    Had been the happy lover, he concluded,
Conceal'd amongst his premises; 'tis true,
    His mind the more o'er this its mystery
        brooded
To speak of Inez now were, one may say,
Like throwing Juan in Alfonso's way.

CLXXVIII

A hint, in tender cases, is enough;
    Silence is best: besides there is a *tact*—
(That modern phrase appears to me sad stuff,
    But it will serve to keep my verse com-
        pact)—   1420
Which keeps, when push'd by questions rather
        rough,
    A lady always distant from the fact:
The charming creatures lie with such a grace,
There's nothing so becoming to the face.

CLXXIX

They blush, and we believe them, at least I
    Have always done so; 'tis of no great use,
In any case, attempting a reply,
    For then their eloquence grows quite pro-
        fuse;
And when at length they're out of breath, they
        sigh,
    And cast their languid eyes down, and let
        loose   1430
A tear or two, and then we make it up;
And then—and then—and then—sit down and
        sup.

CLXXX

Alfonso closed his speech, and begg'd her par-
        don,
    Which Julia half withheld, and then half
        granted,
And laid conditions, he thought very hard, on,
    Denying several little things he wanted:
He stood like Adam lingering near his garden,
    With useless penitence perplex'd and haunted,
Beseeching she no further would refuse,
When, lo! he stumbled o'er a pair of shoes.   1440

CLXXXI

A pair of shoes!—what then? not much, if
    they
    Are such as fit with ladies' feet, but these
(No one can tell how much I grieve to say)
    Were masculine; to see them, and to seize,
Was but a moment's act.—Ah! well-a-day!
    My teeth begin to chatter, my veins freeze—
Alfonso first examined well their fashion,
And then flew out into another passion.

CLXXXII

He left the room for his relinquish'd sword,
    And Julia instant to the closet flew.   1450
'Fly, Juan, fly! for heaven's sake—not a word—
    The door is open—you may yet slip through
The passage you so often have explored—
    Here is the garden-key—Fly—fly—Adieu!
Haste—Haste! I hear Alfonso's hurrying feet—
Day has not broke—there's no one in the
    street.'

CLXXXIII

None can say that this was not good advice,
    The only mischief was, it came too late;
Of all experience 'tis the usual price,
    A sort of income-tax laid on by fate: 1460
Juan had reach'd the room-door in a trice,
    And might have done so by the garden-gate,
But met Alfonso in his dressing-gown,
Who threaten'd death—so Juan knock'd him
    down.

CLXXXIV

Dire was the scuffle, and out went the light;
    Antonia cried out 'Rape!' and Julia 'Fire!'
But not a servant stirr'd to aid the fight.
    Alfonso, pommell'd to his heart's desire,
Swore lustily he'd be revenged this night;
    And Juan, too, blasphemed an octave
    higher;   1470
His blood was up: though young, he was a Tar-
    tar,
And not at all disposed to prove a martyr.

CLXXXV

Alfonso's sword had dropp'd ere he could draw
    it,
    And they continued battling hand to hand,
For Juan very luckily ne'er saw it;
    His temper not being under great command,
If at that moment he had chanced to claw it,
    Alfonso's days had not been in the land

Much longer.—Think of husbands', lovers' lives!
And how ye may be doubly widows—
    wives!   1480

CLXXXVI

Alfonso grappled to detain the foe,
    And Juan throttled him to get away,
And blood ('twas from the nose) began to flow;
    At last, as they more faintly wrestling lay,
Juan contrived to give an awkward blow,
    And then his only garment quite gave way;
He fled, like Joseph, leaving it; but there,
I doubt, all likeness ends between the pair.

CLXXXVII

Lights came at length, and men, and maids, who
    found
    An awkward spectacle their eyes before;   1490
Antonia in hysterics, Julia swoon'd,
    Alfonso leaning, breathless, by the door;
Some half-torn drapery scatter'd on the ground,
    Some blood, and several footsteps, but no
    more:
Juan the gate gain'd, turn'd the key about,
And liking not the inside, lock'd the out.

CLXXXVIII

Here ends this canto.—Need I sing, or say,
    How Juan, naked, favour'd by the night,
Who favours what she should not, found his way,
    And reach'd his home in an unseemly
    plight?   1500
The pleasant scandal which arose next day,
    The nine days' wonder which was brought to
    light,
And how Alfonso sued for a divorce,
Were in the English newspapers, of course.

CLXXXIX

If you would like to see the whole proceedings,
    The depositions and the cause at full,
The names of all the witnesses, the pleadings
    Of counsel to nonsuit, or to annul,
There's more than one edition, and the readings
    Are various, but they none of them are
    dull;   1510
The best is that in short-hand ta'en by Gurney,
Who to Madrid on purpose made a journey.

CXC

But Donna Inez, to divert the train
    Of one of the most circulating scandals
That had for centuries been known in Spain,
    At least since the retirement of the Vandals,

First vow'd (and never had she vow'd in vain)
  To Virgin Mary several pounds of candles;
And then, by the advice of some old ladies,
She sent her son to be shipp'd off from
    Cadiz.   1520

CXCI

She had resolved that he should travel through
  All European climes, by land or sea,
To mend his former morals, and get new,
  Especially in France and Italy
(At least this is the thing most people do).
  Julia was sent into a convent: she
Grieved, but, perhaps, her feelings may be better
Shown in the following copy of her Letter:—

CXCII

'They tell me 'tis decided you depart:
  'Tis wise—'tis well, but not the less a
    pain;   1530
I have no further claim on your young heart,
  Mine is the victim, and would be again:
To love too much has been the only art
  I used;—I write in haste, and if a stain
Be on this sheet, 'tis not what it appears;
My eyeballs burn and throb, but have no tears.

CXCIII

'I loved, I love you, for this love have lost
  State, station, heaven, mankind's, my own
    esteem,
And yet cannot regret what it hath cost,
  So dear is still the memory of that dream; 1540
Yet, if I name my guilt, 'tis not to boast,
  None can deem harshlier on me than I deem:
I trace this scrawl because I cannot rest—
I've nothing to reproach or to request.

CXCIV

'Man's love is of man's life a thing apart,
  'Tis woman's whole existence; man may range
The court, camp, church, the vessel, and the
    mart;
  Sword, gown, gain, glory, offer in exchange
Pride, fame, ambition, to fill up his heart,
  And few there are whom these cannot
    estrange;   1550
Men have all these resources, we but one,
To love again, and be again undone.

CXCV

'You will proceed in pleasure, and in pride,
  Beloved and loving many; all is o'er
For me on earth, except some years to hide

My shame and sorrow deep in my heart's core:
These I could bear, but cannot cast aside
  The passion which still rages as before,—
And so farewell—forgive me, love me—No.
That word is idle now—but let it go.   1560

CXCVI

'My breast has been all weakness, is so yet;
  But still I think I can collect my mind;
My blood still rushes where my spirit's set,
  As roll the waves before the settled wind;
My heart is feminine, nor can forget—
  To all, except one image, madly blind;
So shakes the needle, and so stands the pole,
As vibrates my fond heart to my fix'd soul.

CXCVII

'I have no more to say, but linger still,
  And dare not set my seal upon this sheet,   1570
And yet I may as well the task fulfil,
  My misery can scarce be more complete:
I had not lived till now, could sorrow kill;
  Death shuns the wretch who fain the blow
    would meet,
And I must even survive this last adieu,
And bear with life to love and pray for you!'

CXCVIII

This note was written upon gilt-edged paper
  With a neat little crow-quill, slight and new;
Her small white hand could hardly reach the
    taper,
  It trembled as magnetic needles do,   1580
And yet she did not let one tear escape her;
  The seal a sun-flower; *Elle vous suit partout,* [46]
The motto, cut upon a white cornelian; [47]
The wax was superfine, its hue vermillion.

CXCIX

This was Don Juan's earliest scrape; but whether
  I shall proceed with his adventures is
Dependent on the public altogether;
  We'll see, however, what they say to this,
Their favour in an author's cap's a feather,
  And no great mischief's done by their
    caprice;   1590
And if their approbation we experience,
Perhaps they'll have some more about a year
    hence.

CC

My poem's epic, and is meant to be

---

46 'She follows you everywhere.'
47 stone of translucent quartz.

Divided in twelve books; each book con-
taining,
With love, and war, a heavy gale at sea,
    A list of ships, and captains, and kings reign-
ing,
New characters; the episodes are three:
    A panoramic view of hell's in training,
After the style of Virgil and of Homer,
So that my name of Epic's no misnomer.   1600

CCI

All these things will be specified in time,
    With strict regard to Aristotle's rules,[48]
The *Vade Mecum*[49] of the true sublime,
    Which makes so many poets, and some fools:
Prose poets like blank-verse, I'm fond of rhyme,
    Good workmen never quarrel with their tools;
I've got new mythological machinery,
And very handsome supernatural scenery.

CCII

There's only one slight difference between
    Me and my epic brethren gone before,   1610
And here the advantage is my own, I ween
    (Not that I have not several merits more,
But this will more peculiarly be seen);
    They so embellish, that 'tis quite a bore
Their labyrinth of fables to thread through,
Whereas this story's actually true.

CCIII

If any person doubt it, I appeal
    To history, tradition, and to facts,
To newspapers, whose truth all know and feel,
    To plays in five, and operas in three acts;   1620
All these confirm my statement a good deal,
    But that which more completely faith exacts
Is, that myself, and several now in Seville,
Saw Juan's last elopement with the devil.

CCIV

If ever I should condescend to prose,
    I'll write poetical commandments, which
Shall supersede beyond all doubt all those
    That went before; in these I shall enrich
My text with many things that no one knows,
    And carry precept to the highest pitch: 1630
I'll call the work 'Longinus o'er a Bottle,
Or, Every Poet his *own* Aristotle.'

CCV

Thou shalt believe in Milton, Dryden, Pope;

Thou shalt not set up Wordsworth, Coleridge,
    Southey;
Because the first is crazed beyond all hope,
    The second drunk, the third so quaint and
mouthy:
With Crabbe it may be difficult to cope,
    And Campbell's Hippocrene is somewhat
drouthy:
Thou shalt not steal from Samuel Rogers, nor
Commit—flirtation with the muse of
    Moore.   1640

CCVI

Thou shalt not covet Mr. Sotheby's Muse,
    His Pegasus, nor anything that's his;
Thou shalt not bear false witness like 'the
    Blues'[50]—
    (There's *one,* at least, is very fond of this);
Thou shalt not write, in short, but what I choose;
    This is true criticism, and you may kiss—
Exactly as you please, or not,—the rod;
But if you don't, I'll lay it on, by G—d!

CCVII

If any person should presume to assert
    This story is not moral, first, I pray,   1650
That they will not cry out before they're hurt,
    Then that they'll read it o'er again, and say
(But, doubtless, nobody will be so pert),
    That this is not a moral tale, though gay;
Besides, in Canto Twelfth, I mean to show
The very place where wicked people go.

CCVIII

If, after all, there should be some so blind
    To their own good this warning to despise,
Let by some tortuosity of mind,
    Not to believe my verse and their own
        eyes,   1660
And cry that they 'the moral cannot find,'
    I tell him, if a clergyman, he lies;
Should captains the remark, or critics, make,
They also lie too—under a mistake.

CCIX

The public approbation I expect,
    And beg they'll take my word about the moral,
Which I with their amusement will connect
    (So children cutting teeth receive a coral);
Meantime they'll doubtless please to recollect
    My epical pretensions to the laurel: 1670

---

48 respecting the unities of time, place, and action.
49 handbook; literally, go with me.

50 the Bluestockings, i. e. club women affecting an interest in politics and literature.

For fear some prudish readers should grow skit-
tish,
I've bribed my Grandmother's Review—the
British.

CCX

I sent it in a letter to the Editor,
　Who thank'd me duly by return of post—
I'm for a handsome article his creditor;
　Yet, if my gentle Muse he please to roast,
And break a promise after having made it her,
　Denying the receipt of what it cost,
And smear his page with gall instead of honey,
All I can say is—that he had the money.　　1680

CCXI

I think that with this holy new alliance
　I may ensure the public, and defy
All other magazines of art or science,
　Daily, or monthly, or three monthly; I
Have not essay'd to multiply their clients,
　Because they tell me 'twere in vain to try,
And that the Edinburgh Review and Quarterly
Treat a dissenting author very martyrly.

CCXII

'*Non ego hoc ferrem calida juventa*
　Consule Planco,'[51] Horace said, and so　　1690
Say I; by which quotation there is meant a
　Hint that some six or seven good years ago
(Long ere I dreamt of dating from the Brenta[52])
　I was most ready to return a blow,
And would not brook at all this sort of thing
In my hot youth—when George the Third was
　King.

CCXIII

But now at thirty years my hair is grey—
　(I wonder what it will be like at forty?
I thought of a peruke the other day—)
　My heart is not much greener; and, in
　　short, I　　1700
Have squander'd my whole summer while 'twas
　May,
　And feel no more the spirit to retort; I
Have spent my life, both interest and principal,
And deem not, what I deem'd, my soul invincible.

CCXIV

No more—no more—Oh! never more on me

The freshness of the heart can fall like dew,
Which out of all the lovely things we see
　Extracts emotions beautiful and new;
Hived in our bosoms like the bag o' the bee.
　Think'st thou the honey with those objects
　　grew?　　1710
Alas! 'twas not in them, but in thy power
To double even the sweetness of a flower.

CCXV

No more—no more—Oh! never more, my heart,
　Canst thou be my sole world, my universe!
Once all in all, but now a thing apart,
　Thou canst not be my blessing or my curse;
The illusion's gone for ever, and thou art
　Insensible, I trust, but none the worse,
And in thy stead I've got a deal of judgment,
Though heaven knows how it ever found a
　lodgment.　　1720

CCXVI

My days of love are over; me no more
　The charms of maid, wife, and still less of
　　widow,
Can make the fool of which they made before,—
　In short, I must not lead the life I did do;
The credulous hope of mutual minds is o'er,
　The copious use of claret is forbid too,
So for a good old-gentlemanly vice,
I think I must take up with avarice.

CCXVII

Ambition was my idol, which was broken
　Before the shrines of Sorrow, and of Pleas-
　　ure;　　1730
And the two last have left me many a token
　O'er which reflection may be made at leisure;
Now, like Friar Bacon's brazen head, I've
　spoken,
　'Time is, Time was, Time's past';[53]—a chymic[54]
　　treasure
Is glittering youth, which I have spent betimes—
My heart in passion, and my head on rhymes.

CCXVIII

What is the end of fame? 'tis but to fill
　A certain portion of uncertain paper:
Some liken it to climbing up a hill,
　Whose summit, like all hills, is lost in
　　vapour;　　1740
For this men write, speak, preach, and heroes kill,

---

51 'I should not have borne this in the heat of my youth when
Plaucus was consul'—Horace, *Odes,* III, xiv.
52 a river in northeastern Italy which flows into the Gulf of
Venice.

53 See Robert Greene's *Friar Bacon and Friar Bungay,* sc. xi.
54 alchemic; hence, counterfeit.

And bards burn what they call their 'midnight
    taper,'
To have, when the original is dust,
A name, a wretched picture, and worse bust.

CCXIX

What are the hopes of man? Old Egypt's King
    Cheops erected the first pyramid
And largest, thinking it was just the thing
    To keep his memory whole, and mummy
      hid;
But somebody or other rummaging,
    Burglariously broke his coffin's lid: 1750
Let not a monument give you or me hopes,
Since not a pinch of dust remains of Cheops.

CCXX

But I, being fond of true philosophy,
    Say very often to myself, 'Alas!
All things that have been born were born to
    die,
    And flesh (which Death mows down to hay) is
      grass;
You've pass'd your youth not so unpleasantly,
    And if you had it o'er again—'twould pass—
So thank your stars that matters are no worse,
And read your Bible, sir, and mind your
    purse.'   1760

CCXXI

But for the present, gentle reader! and
    Still gentler purchaser! the bard—that's I—
Must, with permission, shake you by the hand,
    And so your humble servant, and goodbye!
We meet again, if we should understand
    Each other; and if not, I shall not try
Your patience further than by this short sam-
    ple—
'Twere well if others follow'd my example.

CCXXII

'Go, little book, from this my solitude!
    I cast thee on the waters—go thy ways!   1770
And if, as I believe, thy vein be good,
    The world will find thee after many days.'[55]
When Southey's read, and Wordsworth under-
    stood,
    I can't help putting in my claim to praise—
The four first rhymes are Southey's, every line:
For God's sake, reader! take them not for mine!

    1818 ————   1819

[55] Southey, *The Lay of the Laureate*, L'Envoy, ll. 1-4.

From Canto the Second

Stanzas i-xxxi, xliv-liv, xcvii-cciv

I

Oh ye! who teach the ingenuous youth of nations,
    Holland, France, England, Germany, or Spain,
I pray ye flog them upon all occasions,
    It mends their morals, never mind the pain:
The best of mothers and of educations
    In Juan's case were but employ'd in vain,
Since, in a way that's rather of the oddest, he
Became divested of his native modesty.

II

Had he but been placed at a public school,
    In the third form, or even in the fourth,   10
His daily task had kept his fancy cool,
    At least, had he been nurtured in the north;
Spain may prove an exception to the rule,
    But then exceptions always prove its worth—
A lad of sixteen causing a divorce
Puzzled his tutors very much, of course.

III

I can't say that it puzzles me at all,
    If all things be consider'd; first, there was
His lady-mother, mathematical,
    A —— never mind;—his tutor, an old ass; 20
A pretty woman—(that's quite natural,
    Or else the thing had hardly come to pass)
A husband rather old, not much in unity
With his young wife—a time, and opportunity.

IV

Well—well; the world must turn upon its axis,
    And all mankind turn with it, heads or tails,
And live and die, make love and pay our taxes,
    And as the veering wind shifts, shift our sails;
The king commands us, and the doctor quacks
    us,
    The priest instructs, and so our life
      exhales,   30
A little breath, love, wine, ambition, fame,
Fighting, devotion, dust,—perhaps a name.

V

I said, that Juan had been sent to Cadiz—
    A pretty town, I recollect it well—
'Tis there the mart of the colonial trade is,
    (Or was, before Peru learn'd to rebel,)
And such sweet girls—I mean, such graceful
    ladies,

Their very walk would make your bosom
   swell;
I can't describe it, though so much it strike,
Nor liken it—I never saw the like: 40

VI

An Arab horse, a stately stag, a barb
   New broke, a cameleopard, a gazelle,
No—none of these will do;—and then their garb,
   Their veil and petticoat—Alas! to dwell
Upon such things would very near absorb
   A canto—then their feet and ankles,—well,
Thank Heaven I've got no metaphor quite ready,
(And so, my sober Muse—come, let's be steady—

VII

Chaste Muse!—well, if you must, you must)—the
   veil
   Thrown back a moment with the glancing
     hand,   50
While the o'erpowering eye, that turns you pale,
   Flashes into the heart:—All sunny land
Of love! when I forget you, may I fail
   To ——— say my prayers—but never was there
     plann'd
A dress through which the eyes gives such
   a volley,
Excepting the Venetian Fazzioli.[1]

VIII

But to our tale: the Donna Inez sent
   Her son to Cadiz only to embark;
To stay there had not answer'd her intent,
   But why?—we leave the reader in the
     dark—   60
'Twas for a voyage the young man was meant,
   As if a Spanish ship were Noah's ark,
To wean him from the wickedness of earth,
And send him like a dove of promise forth.

IX

Don Juan bade his valet pack his things
   According to direction, then received
A lecture and some money: for four springs
   He was to travel; and though Inez grieved
(As every kind of parting has its stings),
   She hoped he would improve—perhaps
     believed: 70
A letter, too, she gave (he never read it)
Of good advice—and two or three of credit.

---

[1] *Fazzioli*—literally, little handkerchiefs—the veils most availing of St. Mark.—(Byron.)

X

In the mean time, to pass her hours away,
   Brave Inez now set up a Sunday school
For naughty children, who would rather play
   (Like truant rogues) the devil, or the fool:
Infants of three years old were taught that day,
   Dunces were whipt, or set upon a stool:
The great success of Juan's education
Spurr'd her to teach another generation.   80

XI

Juan embark'd—the ship got under way,
   The wind was fair, the water passing rough;
A devil of a sea rolls in that bay,
   As I, who've cross'd it oft, know well enough;
And, standing upon deck, the dashing spray
   Flies in one's face, and makes it weather-
     tough:
And there he stood to take, and take again,
His first—perhaps his last—farewell of Spain.

XII

I can't but say it is an awkward sight
   To see one's native land receding through   90
The growing waters; it unmans one quite,
   Especially when life is rather new:
I recollect Great Britain's coast looks white,
   But almost every other country's blue,
When gazing on them, mystified by distance,
We enter on our nautical existence.

XIII

So Juan stood, bewilder'd on the deck:
   The wind sung, cordage strain'd, and sailors
     swore,
And the ship creak'd, the town became a speck,
   From which away so fair and fast they
     bore.   100
The best of remedies is a beef-steak
   Against sea-sickness: try it, sir, before
You sneer, and I assure you this is true,
For I have found it answer—so may you.

XIV

Don Juan stood, and, gazing from the stern,
   Beheld his native Spain receding far:
First partings form a lesson hard to learn,
   Even nations feel this when they go to war;
There is a sort of unexpresst concern,
   A kind of shock that sets one's heart ajar: 110
At leaving even the most unpleasant people
And places, one keeps looking at the steeple.

XV

But Juan had got many things to leave,
  His mother, and a mistress, and no wife,
So that he had much better cause to grieve
  Than many persons more advanced in life;
And if we now and then a sigh must heave
  At quitting even those we quit in strife,
No doubt we weep for those the heart endears—
That is, till deeper griefs congeal our tears.   120

XVI

So Juan wept, as wept the captive Jews
  By Babel's waters, still remembering Sion:
I'd weep,—but mine is not a weeping Muse,
  And such light griefs are not a thing to die
    on;
Young men should travel, if but to amuse
  Themselves; and the next time their servants
    tie on
Behind their carriages their new portmanteau,
Perhaps it may be lined with this my canto.

XVII

And Juan wept, and much he sigh'd and thought,
  While his salt tears dropp'd into the salt
    sea,   130
'Sweets to the sweet'; (I like so much to quote;
  You must excuse this extract,—'tis where she,
The Queen of Denmark, for Ophelia brought
  Flowers to the grave;) and, sobbing often, he
Reflected on his present situation,
And seriously resolved on reformation.

XVIII

'Farewell, my Spain! a long farewell!' he cried,
  'Perhaps I may revisit thee no more,
But die, as many an exiled heart hath died,
  Of its own thirst to see again thy shore: 140
Farewell, where Guadalquivir's waters glide!
  Farewell, my mother! and, since all is o'er,
Farewell, too, dearest Julia!—(here he drew
Her letter out again, and read it through.)

XIX

'And oh! if e'er I should forget, I swear—
  But that's impossible, and cannot be—
Sooner shall this blue ocean melt to air,
  Sooner shall earth resolve itself to sea,
Than I resign thine image, oh, my fair!
  Or think of anything, excepting thee;   150
A mind diseased no remedy can physic—
(Here the ship gave a lurch, and he grew sea-
    sick.)

XX

'Sooner shall heaven kiss earth—(here he fell
    sicker)
  Oh, Julia! what is every other woe?—
(For God's sake let me have a glass of liquor;
  Pedro, Battista, help me down below.)
Julia, my love—(you rascal, Pedro, quicker)—
  Oh, Julia!—(this curst vessel pitches so)—
Beloved Julia, hear me still beseeching!'
(Here he grew inarticulate with retching.)   160

XXI

He felt that chilling heaviness of heart,
  Or rather stomach, which, alas! attends,
Beyond the best apothecary's art,
  The loss of love, the treachery of friends,
Or death of those we dote on, when a part
  Of us dies with them as each fond hope ends:
No doubt he would have been much more
    pathetic,
But the sea acted as a strong emetic.

XXII

Love's a capricious power: I've known it hold
  Out through a fever caused by its own
    heat,   170
But be much puzzled by a cough and cold,
  And find a quinsy[2] very hard to treat;
Against all noble maladies he's bold,
  But vulgar illnesses don't like to meet,
Nor that a sneeze should interrupt his sigh,
Nor inflammations redden his blind eye.

XXIII

But worst of all is nausea, or a pain
  About the lower region of the bowels;
Love, who heroically breathes a vein,
  Shrinks from the application of hot towels,   180
And purgatives are dangerous to his reign,
  Sea-sickness death: his love was perfect, how
    else
Could Juan's passion, while the billows roar,
Resist his stomach, ne'er at sea before?

XXIV

The ship, call'd the most holy 'Trinidada,'[3]
  Was steering duly for the port Leghorn;

---

2 acute inflammatory sore throat.
3 Byron prided himself on his knowledge of ships and wrecks
and always defended the accuracy of his account of the shipwreck
in *Don Juan*. In a letter to Murray, 23 August, 1821, he wrote:
'With regard to the charges about the Shipwreck, I think I told
you and Mr. Hobhouse, years ago, that there was not a *single
circumstance* of it *not* taken from *fact;* not, indeed, from any *single*
shipwreck, but all from *actual* facts of different wrecks.'

For there the Spanish family Moncada
    Were settled long ere Juan's sire was born:
They were relations, and for them he had a
    Letter of introduction, which the morn   190
Of his departure had been sent him by
His Spanish friends for those in Italy.

XXV

His suite consisted of three servants and
    A tutor, the licentiate[4] Pedrillo,
Who several languages did understand,
    But now lay sick and speechless on his pillow,
And, rocking in his hammock, long'd for land,
    His headache being increased by every billow;
And the waves oozing through the porthole made
His berth a little damp, and him afraid.   200

XXVI

'Twas not without some reason, for the wind
    Increased at night, until it blew a gale;
And though 'twas not much to a naval mind,
    Some landsmen would have look'd a little pale,
For sailors are, in fact, a different kind:
    At sunset they began to take in sail,
For the sky show'd it would come on to blow,
And carry away, perhaps, a mast or so.

XXVII

At one o'clock the wind with sudden shift
    Threw the ship right into the trough of the
        sea,   210
Which struck her aft, and made an awkward rift,
    Started the stern-post, also shatter'd the
Whole of her stern-frame, and, ere she could lift
    Herself from out her present jeopardy,
The rudder tore away: 'twas time to sound
The pumps, and there were four feet water found.

XXVIII

One gang of people instantly was put
    Upon the pumps, and the remainder set
To get up part of the cargo, and what not;
    But they could not come at the leak as yet;   220
At last they did get at it really, but
    Still their salvation was an even bet:
The water rush'd through in a way quite
    puzzling,
While they thrust sheets, shirts, jackets, bales of
    muslin,

XXIX

Into the opening; but all such ingredients

---

4 holder of a university degree intermediate between the bachelor's and the doctor's.

Would have been vain, and they must have
    gone down,
Despite of all their efforts and expedients,
    But for the pumps: I'm glad to make them
    known
To all the brother tars who may have need hence,
    For fifty tons of water were upthrown   230
By them per hour, and they all had been undone,
But for the maker, Mr. Mann, of London.

XXX

As day advanced the weather seem'd to abate,
    And then the leak they reckon'd to reduce,
And keep the ship afloat, though three feet yet
    Kept two hand- and one chain-pump still in
    use.
The wind blew fresh again: as it grew late
    A squall came on, and while some guns broke
    loose,
A gust—which all descriptive power transcends—
Laid with one blast the ship on her beam
    ends.   240

XXXI

There she lay, motionless, and seem'd upset;
    The water left the hold, and wash'd the decks,
And made a scene men do not soon forget;
    For they remember battles, fires, and wrecks,
Or any other thing that brings regret,
    Or breaks their hopes, or hearts, or heads, or
        necks;
Thus drownings are much talk'd of by the divers,
And swimmers, who may chance to be survivors.

· · · ·

XLIV

The ship was evidently settling now
    Fast by the head; and, all distinction gone,
Some went to prayers again, and made a vow
    Of candles to their saints—but there were none
To pay them with; and some look'd o'er the bow;
    Some hoisted out the boats; and there was
        one   350
That begg'd Pedrillo for an absolution,
Who told him to be damn'd—in his confusion.

XLV

Some lash'd them in their hammocks; some put
    on
    Their best clothes, as if going to a fair;
Some cursed the day on which they saw the sun,
    And gnash'd their teeth, and howling, tore
    their hair;

And others went on as they had begun,
　Getting the boats out, being well aware
That a tight boat will live in a rough sea,
Unless with breakers close beneath her lee.　360

XLVI

The worst of all was, that in their condition,
　Having been several days in great distress,
'Twas difficult to get out such provision
　As now might render their long suffering less:
Men, even when dying, dislike inanition;
　Their stock was damaged by the weather's
　　stress:
Two casks of biscuit, and a keg of butter,
Were all that could be thrown into the cutter.

XLVII

But in the long-boat they contrived to stow
　Some pounds of bread, though injured by the
　　wet;　370
Water, a twenty-gallon cask or so;
　Six flasks of wine: and they contrived to get
A portion of their beef up from below,
　And with a piece of pork, moreover, met,
But scarce enough to serve them for a lunch-
　eon—
Then there was rum, eight gallons in a punch-
　eon.⁵

XLVIII

The other boats, the yawl and pinnace, had
　Been stove in the beginning of the gale;
And the long-boat's condition was but bad,
　As there were but two blankets for a sail,　380
And one oar for a mast, which a young lad
　Threw in by good luck over the ship's rail;
And two boats could not hold, far less be stored,
To save one half the people then on board.

XLIX

'Twas twilight, and the sunless day went down
　Over the waste of waters; like a veil,
Which, if withdrawn, would but disclose the
　frown
　Of one whose hate is mask'd but to assail.
Thus to their hopeless eyes the night was shown,
　And grimly darkled o'er the faces pale,　390
And the dim desolate deep: twelve days had
　Fear
Been their familiar,⁶ and now Death was here.

L

Some trial had been making at a raft,

　With little hope in such a rolling sea,
A sort of thing at which one would have laugh'd,
　If any laughter at such times could be,
Unless with people who too much have quaff'd,
　And have a kind of wild and horrid glee,
Half epileptical, and half hysterical:—
Their preservation would have been a
　miracle.　　400

LI

At half-past eight o'clock, booms, hen-coops,
　spars,
　And all things, for a chance, had been cast
　　loose
That still could keep afloat the struggling tars,
　For yet they strove, although of no great use:
There was no light in heaven but a few stars,
　The boats put off o'ercrowded with their
　　crews;
She gave a heel, and then a lurch to port,
And, going down head foremost—sunk, in short.

LII

Then rose from sea to sky the wild farewell—
　Then shriek'd the timid, and stood still the
　　brave—　410
Then some leap'd overboard with dreadful
　yell,
　As eager to anticipate their grave;
And the sea yawn'd around her like a hell,
　And down she suck'd with her the whirling
　　wave,
Like one who grapples with his enemy,
And strives to strangle him before he die.

LIII

And first one universal shriek there rush'd,
　Louder than the loud ocean, like a crash
Of echoing thunder; and then all was hush'd,
　Save the wild wind and the remorseless
　　dash　420
Of billows; but at intervals there gush'd,
　Accompanied with a convulsive splash,
A solitary shriek, the bubbling cry
Of some strong swimmer in his agony.

LIV

The boats, as stated, had got off before,
　And in them crowded several of the crew;
And yet their present hope was hardly more
　Than what it had been, for so strong it blew
There was slight chance of reaching any shore;
　And then they were too many, though so
　　few—　430

Nine in the cutter, thirty in the boat,
Were counted in them when they got afloat.

    .   .   .

XCVII

As morning broke, the light wind died away,
   When he who had the watch sung out and
     swore,   770
If 'twas not land that rose with the sun's ray,
   He wish'd that land he never might see more:
And the rest rubb'd their eyes, and saw a bay,
   Or thought they saw, and shaped their course
     for shore;
For shore it was, and gradually grew
Distinct, and high, and palpable to view.

XCVIII

And then of these some part burst into tears,
   And others, looking with a stupid stare,
Could not yet separate their hopes from fears,
   And seem'd as if they had no further care; 780
While a few pray'd—(the first time for some
     years)—
And at the bottom of the boat three were
Asleep: they shook them by the hand and head,
And tried to awaken them, but found them dead.

XCIX

The day before, fast sleeping on the water,
   They found a turtle of the hawk's-bill kind,
And by good fortune, gliding softly, caught her,
   Which yielded a day's life, and to their mind
Proved even still a more nutritious matter,
   Because it left encouragement behind: 790
They thought that in such perils, more than
     chance
Had sent them this for their deliverance.

C

The land appear'd a high and rocky coast,
   And higher grew the mountains as they drew,
Set by a current, toward it: they were lost
   In various conjectures, for none knew
To what part of the earth they had been tost,
   So changeable had been the winds that blew;
Some thought it was Mount Ætna, some the
     highlands
Of Candia, Cyprus, Rhodes, or other islands. 800

CI

Meantime the current, with a rising gale,
   Still set them onwards to the welcome shore,
Like Charon's bark of spectres, dull and pale:

Their living freight was now reduced to four,
   And three dead, whom their strength could not
     avail
To heave into the deep with those before,
   Though the two sharks still follow'd them, and
     dash'd
The spray into their faces as they splash'd.

CII

Famine, despair, cold, thirst, and heat, had done
   Their work on them by turns, and thinn'd
     them to   810
Such things a mother had not known her son
   Amidst the skeletons of that gaunt crew;
By night chill'd, by day scorch'd, thus one by one
   They perish'd, until wither'd to these few.
But chiefly by a species of self-slaughter,
In washing down Pedrillo with salt water.

CIII

As they drew nigh the land, which now was seen
   Unequal in its aspect here and there,
They felt the freshness of its growing green,
   That waved in forest-tops, and smooth'd
     the air,   820
And fell upon their glazed eyes like a screen
   From glistening waves, and skies so hot and
     bare—
Lovely seem'd any object that should sweep
Away the vast, salt, dread, eternal deep.

CIV

The shore look'd wild, without a trace of man,
   And girt by formidable waves; but they
Were mad for land, and thus their course they
     ran,
   Though right ahead the roaring breakers lay:
A reef between them also now began
   To show its boiling surf and bounding
     spray,   830
But finding no place for their landing better,
They ran the boat for shore,—and overset her.

CV

But in his native stream, the Guadalquivir,
   Juan to lave his youthful limbs was wont;
And having learnt to swim in that sweet river,
   Had often turn'd the art to some account:
A better swimmer you could scarce see ever,
   He could, perhaps, have pass'd the Hellespont,
As once (a feat on which ourselves we prided)
Leander, Mr. Ekenhead, and I did.[7]   840

---

7 Byron swam the Hellespont on 3 May, 1810, in the company of
Mr. Ekenhead, a British naval officer.

CVI

So here, though faint, emaciated, and stark,
   He buoy'd his boyish limbs, and strove to ply
With the quick wave, and gain, ere it was dark,
   The beach which lay before him, high and dry:
The greatest danger here was from a shark,
   That carried off his neighbour by the thigh;
As for the other two, they could not swim,
So nobody arrived on shore but him.

CVII

Nor yet had he arrived but for the oar,
   Which, providentially for him, was
      wash'd   850
Just as his feeble arms could strike no more,
   And the hard wave o'erwhelm'd him as 'twas
      dash'd
Within his grasp; he clung to it, and sore
   The waters beat while he thereto was lash'd;
At last, with swimming, wading, scrambling, he
Roll'd on the beach, half senseless, from the sea:

CVIII

There, breathless, with his digging nails he clung
   Fast to the sand, lest the returning wave,
From whose reluctant roar his life he wrung,
   Should suck him back to her insatiate
      grave: 860
And there he lay, full length, where he was flung,
   Before the entrance of a cliff-worn cave,
With just enough of life to feel its pain,
And deem that it was saved, perhaps in vain.

CIX

With slow and staggering effort he arose,
   But sunk again upon his bleeding knee
And quivering hand; and then he look'd for
   those
Who long had been his mates upon the sea;
But none of them appear'd to share his woes,
   Save one, a corpse, from out the famish'd
      three,   870
Who died two days before, and now had found
An unknown barren beach for burial-ground.

CX

And as he gazed, his dizzy brain spun fast,
   And down he sunk; and as he sunk, the sand
Swam round and round, and all his senses pass'd:
   He fell upon his side, and his stretch'd hand
Droop'd dripping on the oar (their jury-mast),[8]
   And, like a wither'd lily, on the land

---

8 temporary mast used in an emergency.

His slender frame and pallid aspect lay,
As fair a thing as e'er was form'd of clay.   880

CXI

How long in his damp trance young Juan lay
   He knew not, for the earth was gone for him,
And time had nothing more of night nor day
   For his congealing blood, and senses dim;
And how this heavy faintness pass'd away
   He knew not, till each painful pulse and limb,
And tingling vein, seem'd throbbing back to life,
For Death, though vanquish'd, still retired with
   strife.

CXII

His eyes he open'd, shut, again unclosed,
   For all was doubt and dizziness; he
      thought   890
He still was in the boat, and had but dozed,
   And felt again with his despair o'erwrought,
And wish'd it death in which he had reposed,
   And then once more his feelings back were
      brought,
And slowly by his swimming eyes was seen
A lovely female face of seventeen.

CXIII

'Twas bending close o'er his, and the small mouth
   Seem'd almost prying into his for breath;
And chafing him, the soft warm hand of youth
   Recall'd his answering spirits back from
      death;   900
And, bathing his chill temples, tried to soothe
   Each pulse to animation, till beneath
Its gentle touch and trembling care, a sigh
To these kind efforts made a low reply.

CXIV

Then was the cordial pour'd, and mantle flung
   Around his scarce-clad limbs; and the fair arm
Raised higher the faint head which o'er it hung;
   And her transparent cheek, all pure and warm,
Pillow's his death-like forehead; then she wrung
   His dewy curls, long drench'd by every
      storm;   910
And watch'd with eagerness each throb that drew
A sigh from his heaved bosom—and hers, too.

CXV

And lifting him with care into the cave,
   The gentle girl, and her attendant,—one
Young, yet her elder, and of brow less grave,
   And more robust of figure—then begun
To kindle fire, and as the new flames gave

Light to the rocks that roof'd them, which the
    sun
Had never seen, the maid, or whatsoe'er
She was, appear'd distinct, and tall, and fair. 920

CXVI

Her brow was overhung with coins of gold,
    That sparkled o'er the auburn of her hair,
Her clustering hair, whose longer locks were
    roll'd
    In braids behind; and though her stature were
Even of the highest for a female mould,
    They nearly reach'd her heel; and in her air
There was a something which bespoke com-
    mand,
As one who was a lady in the land.

CXVII

Her hair, I said, was auburn; but her eyes
    Were black as death, their lashes the same
        hue,   930
Of downcast length, in whose silk shadow lies
    Deepest attraction; for when to the view
Forth from its raven fringe the full glance flies,
    Ne'er with such force the swiftest arrow flew;
'Tis as the snake late coil'd, who pours his length,
And hurls at once his venom and his strength.

CXVIII

Her brow was white and low, her cheek's pure
    dye
    Like twilight rosy still with the set sun;
Short upper lip—sweet lips! that make us sigh
    Ever to have seen such; for she was one   940
Fit for the model of a statuary
    (A race of mere impostors, when all's done—
I've seen much finer women, ripe and real,
Than all the nonsense of their stone ideal).

CXIX

I'll tell you why I say so, for 'tis just
    One should not rail without a decent cause:
There was an Irish lady, to whose bust
    I ne'er saw justice done, and yet she was
A frequent model; and if e'er she must
    Yield to stern Time and Nature's wrinkling
        laws,   950
They will destroy a face which mortal thought
Ne'er compass'd, nor less mortal chisel wrought.

CXX

And such was she, the lady of the cave:
    Her dress was very different from the Spanish,
Simpler, and yet of colours not so grave;

For, as you know, the Spanish women banish
Bright hues when out of doors, and yet, while
    wave
    Around them (what I hope will never vanish)
The basquina[9] and the mantilla,[10] they
Seem at the same time mystical and gay.   960

CXXI

But with our damsel this was not the case:
    Her dress was many-colour'd, finely spun;
Her locks curl'd negligently round her face,
    But through them gold and gems profusely
        shone:
Her girdle sparkled, and the richest lace
    Flow'd in her veil, and many a precious stone
Flash'd on her little hand; but, what was shock-
    ing,
Her small snow feet had slippers, but no stock-
    ing.

CXXII

The other female's dress was not unlike,
    But of inferior materials: she   970
Had not so many ornaments to strike,
    Her hair had silver only, bound to be
Her dowry; and her veil, in form alike,
    Was coarser; and her air, though firm, less
        free;
Her hair was thicker, but less long; her eyes
As black, but quicker, and of smaller size.

CXXIII

And these two tended him, and cheer'd him both
    With food and raiment, and those soft atten-
        tions,
Which are—(as I must own)—of female growth,
    And have ten thousand delicate inven-
        tions: 980
They made a most superior mess of broth,
    A thing which poesy but seldom mentions,
But the best dish that e'er was cook'd since
    Homer's
Achilles order'd dinner for new comers.[11]

CXXIV

I'll tell you who they were, this female pair,
    Lest they should seem princesses in disguise;
Besides, I hate all mystery, and that air
    Of clap-trap, which your recent poets prize;
And so, in short, the girls they really were

9 a rich outer petticoat worn by Spanish women.
10 a delicate veil covering the head and shoulders.
11 Achilles prepared a feast for Ajax, Ulysses, and Phoenix in the
Iliad, ix.

They shall appear before your curious eyes, 990
Mistress and maid; the first was only daughter
Of an old man, who lived upon the water.

CXXV

A fisherman he had been in his youth,
    And still a sort of fisherman was he;
But other speculations were, in sooth,
    Added to his connexion with the sea,
Perhaps not so respectable, in truth:
    A little smuggling, and some piracy,
Left him, at last, the sole of many masters
Of an ill-gotten million of piastres.   1000

CXXVI

A fisher, therefore, was he,—though of men,
    Like Peter the Apostle,—and he fish'd
For wandering merchant vessels, now and
        then,
    And sometimes caught as many as he wish'd;
The cargoes he confiscated, and gain
    He sought in the slave-market too, and dish'd
Full many a morsel for that Turkish trade,
By which, no doubt, a good deal may be made.

CXXVII

He was a Greek, and on his isle had built
    (One of the wild and smaller Cyclades)   1010
A very handsome house from out his guilt,
    And there he lived exceedingly at ease;
Heaven knows what cash he got, or blood he
        spilt,
    A sad old fellow was he, if you please;
But this I know, it was a spacious building,
Full of barbaric carving, paint, and gilding.

CXXVIII

He had an only daughter, call'd Haidée,
    The greatest heiress of the Eastern Isles;
Besides, so very beautiful was she,
    Her dowry was as nothing to her smiles: 1020
Still in her teens, and like a lovely tree
    She grew to womanhood, and between whiles
Rejected several suitors, just to learn
How to accept a better in his turn.

CXXIX

And walking out upon the beach, below
    The cliff,—towards sunset, on that day she
        found,
Insensible,—not dead, but nearly so,—
    Don Juan, almost famish'd, and half drown'd;
But being naked, she was shock'd, you know,
    Yet deem'd herself in common pity
        bound,   1030

As far as in her lay, 'to take him in,
A stranger'[12] dying, with so white a skin.

CXXX

But taking him into her father's house
    Was not exactly the best way to save,
But like conveying to the cat the mouse,
    Or people in a trance into their grave;
Because the good old man had so much 'νοῦς,'[13]
    Unlike the honest Arab thieves so brave,
He would have hospitably cured the stranger
And sold him instantly when out of danger. 1040

CXXXI

And therefore, with her maid, she thought it best
    (A virgin always on her maid relies)
To place him in the cave for present rest:
    And when, at last, he open'd his black eyes,
Their charity increased about their guest;
    And their compassion grew to such a size,
It open'd half the turnpike gates to heaven—
(St. Paul says, 'tis the toll which must be given).

CXXXII

They made a fire,—but such a fire as they
    Upon the moment could contrive with
        such   1050
Materials as were cast up round the bay,—
    Some broken planks, and oars, that to the
        touch
Were nearly tinder, since so long they lay,
    A mast was almost crumbled to a crutch;
But, by God's grace, here wrecks were in such
        plenty,
That there was fuel to have furnish'd twenty.

CXXXIII

He had a bed of furs, and a pelisse,[14]
    For Haidée stripp'd her sables off to make
His couch; and, that he might be more at ease,
    And warm, in case by chance he should
        awake,   1060
They also gave a petticoat apiece,
    She and her maid,—and promised by day-
        break
To pay him a fresh visit, with a dish
For breakfast, of eggs, coffee, bread, and fish.

CXXXIV

And thus they left him to his lone repose:
    Juan slept like a top, or like the dead,
Who sleep at last, perhaps (God only knows),

---

12 Matthew, xxv, 35.
13 Greek for *mind* or *spirit*.
14 a long fur coat.

Just for the present; and in his lull'd head
Not even a vision of his former woes
    Throbb'd in accursed dreams, which some-
        times spread   1070
Unwelcome visions of our former years,
Till the eye, cheated, opens thick with tears.

CXXXV

Young Juan slept all dreamless:—but the maid,
    Who smooth'd his pillow, as she left the den
Look'd back upon him, and a moment stayed,
    And turn'd, believing that he call'd again.
He slumber'd; yet she thought, at least she said
    (The heart will slip, even as the tongue and
        pen),
He had pronounced her name—but she forgot
That at this moment Juan knew it not.   1080

CXXXVI

And pensive to her father's house she went,
    Enjoining silence strict to Zoe, who
Better than her knew what, in fact, she meant,
    She being wiser by a year or two:
A year or two's an age when rightly spent,
    And Zoe spent hers, as most women do,
In gaining all that useful sort of knowledge
Which is acquired in Nature's good old college.

CXXXVII

The morn broke, and found Juan slumbering still
    Fast in his cave, and nothing clash'd upon 1090
His rest: the rushing of the neighbouring rill,
    And the young beams of the excluded sun,
Troubled him not, and he might sleep his fill;
    And need he had of slumber yet, for none
Had suffer'd more—his hardships were compar-
    ative
To those related in my grand-dad's 'Narrative.'[15]

CXXXVIII

Not so Haidée: she sadly toss'd and tumbled,
    And started from her sleep, and, turning o'er,
Dream'd of a thousand wrecks, o'er which she
    stumbled,
    And handsome corpses strew'd upon the
      shore;   1100
And woke her maid so early that she grumbled,
    And call'd her father's old slaves up, who
      swore
In several oaths—Armenian, Turk, and Greek—
They knew not what to think of such a freak.

---

15 'A Narrative of the Honourable John Byron (Commodore in a late expedition round the world), containing an account of the great distresses suffered by himself and his companions on the coast of Patagonia, from the year 1740, till their arrival in England, 1746. Written by himself. London, 1768.'

CXXXIX

But up she got, and up she made them get,
    With some pretence about the sun, that makes
Sweet skies just when he rises, or is set;
    And 'tis, no doubt, a sight to see when breaks
Bright Phœbus, while the mountains still are wet
    With mist, and every bird with him
      awakes,   1110
And night is flung off like a mourning suit
Worn for a husband,—or some other brute.

CXL

I say, the sun is a most glorious sight:
    I've seen him rise full oft, indeed of late
I have sat up on purpose all the night,
    Which hastens, as physicians say, one's fate;
And so all ye, who would be in the right
    In health and purse, begin your day to date
From daybreak, and when coffin'd at four-score
Engrave upon the plate, you rose at four.   1120

CXLI

And Haidée met the morning face to face;
    Her own was freshest, though a feverish flush
Had dyed it with the headlong blood, whose race
    From heart to cheek is curb'd into a blush,
Like to a torrent which a mountain's base,
    That overpowers some Alpine river's rush,
Checks to a lake, whose waves in circles spread;
Or the Red Sea—but the sea is not red.

CXLII

And down the cliff the island virgin came,
    And near the cave her quick light footsteps
      drew,   1130
While the sun smiled on her with his first flame,
    And young Aurora kiss'd her lips with dew,
Taking her for a sister; just the same
    Mistake you would have made on seeing the
      two,
Although the mortal, quite as fresh and fair,
Had all the advantage, too, of not being air.

CXLIII

And when into the cavern Haidée stepp'd
    All timidly, yet rapidly, she saw
That like an infant Juan sweetly slept;
    And then she stopp'd, and stood as if in
      awe   1140
(For sleep is awful), and on tiptoe crept
    And wrapt him closer, lest the air, too raw,
Should reach his blood, then o'er him still as
    death
Bent, with hush'd lips, that drank his scarce-
    drawn breath.

CXLIV

And thus like to an angel o'er the dying
  Who die in righteousness, she lean'd; and there
All tranquilly the shipwreck'd boy was lying,
  As o'er him lay the calm and stirless air:
But Zoe the meantime some eggs was frying,
  Since, after all, no doubt the youthful pair 1150
Must breakfast, and betimes—lest they should
    ask it,
She drew out her provision from the basket.

CXLV

She knew that the best feelings must have victual,
  And that a shipwreck'd youth would hungry
    be;
Besides, being less in love, she yawn'd a little,
  And felt her veins chill'd by the neighbouring
    sea;
And so, she cook'd their breakfast to a tittle;
  I can't say that she gave them any tea,
But there were eggs, fruit, coffee, bread, fish,
    honey,
With Scio wine,—and all for love, not
    money.   1160

CXLVI

And Zoe, when the eggs were ready, and
  The coffee made, would fain have waken'd
    Juan;
But Haidée stopp'd her with her quick small
    hand,
  And without word, a sign her finger drew on
Her lip, which Zoe needs must understand;
  And, the first breakfast spoilt, prepared a new
    one,
Because her mistress would not let her break
That sleep which seem'd as it would ne'er awake.

CXLVII

For still he lay, and on his thin worn cheek
  A purple hectic play'd like dying day   1170
On the snow-tops of distant hills; the streak
  Of sufferance yet upon his forehead lay,
Where the blue veins look'd shadowy, shrunk,
    and weak;
  And his black curls were dewy with the spray,
Which weigh'd upon them yet, all damp and
    salt,
Mix'd with the stony vapours of the vault.

CXLVIII

And she bent o'er him, and he lay beneath,
  Hush'd as the babe upon its mother's breast,
Droop'd as the willow when no winds can
    breathe,

Lull'd like the depth of ocean when at
    rest,   1180
Fair as the crowning rose of the whole wreath,
  Soft as the callow cygnet in its nest;
In short, he was a very pretty fellow,
Although his woes had turn'd him rather yellow.

CXLIX

He woke and gazed, and would have slept again,
  But the fair face which met his eyes forbade
Those eyes to close, though weariness and pain
  Had further sleep a further pleasure made;
For woman's face was never form'd in vain
  For Juan, so that even when he pray'd   1190
He turn'd from grisly saints, and martyrs hairy,
To the sweet portraits of the Virgin Mary.

CL

And thus upon his elbow he arose,
  And look'd upon the lady, in whose cheek
The pale contended with the purple rose,
  As with an effort she began to speak;
Her eyes were eloquent, her words would pose,
  Although she told him, in good modern Greek,
With an Ionian accent, low and sweet,
That he was faint, and must not talk, but
    eat.   1200

CLI

Now Juan could not understand a word,
  Being no Grecian; but he had an ear,
And her voice was the warble of a bird,
  So soft, so sweet, so delicately clear,
That finer, simpler music ne'er was heard;
  The sort of sound we echo with a tear,
Without knowing why—an overpowering tone,
Whence melody descends as from a throne.

CLII

And Juan gazed as one who is awoke,
  By a distant organ, doubting if he be   1210
Not yet a dreamer, till the spell is broke
  By the watchman, or some such reality,
Or by one's early valet's cursed knock;
  At least it is a heavy sound to me,
Who like a morning slumber—for the night
Shows stars and women in a better light.

CLIII

And Juan, too, was help'd out from his dream,
  Or sleep, or whatsoe'er it was, by feeling
A most prodigious appetite; the steam
  Of Zoe's cookery no doubt was stealing   1220
Upon his senses, and the kindling beam
  Of the new fire, which Zoe kept up, kneeling,

To stir her viands, made him quite awake
And long for food, but chiefly a beef-steak.

CLIV

But beef is rare within these oxless isles;
  Goat's flesh there is, no doubt, and kid, and
    mutton,
And, when a holiday upon them smiles,
  A joint upon their barbarous spits they put on:
But this occurs but seldom, between whiles,
  For some of these are rocks with scarce a hut
    on;   1230
Others are fair and fertile, among which
This, though not large, was one of the most rich.

CLV

I say that beef is rare, and can't help thinking
  That the old fable of the Minotaur[16]—
From which our modern morals, rightly shrink-
    ing,
  Condemn the royal lady's taste who wore
A cow's shape for a mask—was only (sinking
  The allegory) a mere type, no more,
That Pasiphae promoted breeding cattle,
To make the Cretans bloodier in battle.   1240

CLVI

For we all know that English people are
  Fed upon beef—I won't say much of beer,
Because 'tis liquor only, and being far
  From this my subject, has no business here;
We know, too, they are very fond of war,
  A pleasure—like all pleasures—rather dear;
So were the Cretans—from which I infer
That beef and battles both were owing to her.

CLVII

But to resume. The languid Juan raised
  His head upon his elbow, and he saw   1250
A sight on which he had not lately gazed,
  As all his latter meals had been quite raw,
Three or four things, for which the Lord he
    praised,
  And, feeling still the famish'd vulture gnaw,
He fell upon whate'er was offer'd, like
A priest, a shark, an alderman, or pike.

CLVIII

He ate, and he was well supplied; and she,
  Who watch'd him like a mother, would have
    fed

16 a monster, half man and half bull, the offspring of Queen
Pasiphae of Crete. According to the legend, Poseidon had given
a bull of great beauty to King Minos in order that Minos sacrifice
it to him. When Minos kept the bull for himself, to punish him
Poseidon caused Pasiphae to fall in love with it.

Him past all bounds, because she smiled to see
  Such appetite in one she had deem'd
    dead: 1260
But Zoe, being older than Haidée,
  Knew (by tradition, for she ne'er had read)
That famish'd people must be slowly nurst,
And fed by spoonfuls, else they always burst.

CLIX

And so she took the liberty to state,
  Rather by deeds than words, because the
    case
Was urgent, that the gentleman, whose fate
  Had made her mistress quit her bed to trace
The sea-shore at this hour, must leave his plate,
  Unless he wish'd to die upon the place—   1270
She snatch'd it, and refused another morsel,
Saying, he had gorged enough to make a horse
    ill.

CLX

Next they—he being naked, save a tatter'd
  Pair of scarce decent trowsers—went to work,
And in the fire his recent rags they scatter'd
  And dress'd him, for the present, like a Turk,
Or Greek—that is, although it not much mat-
    ter'd,
  Omitting turban, slippers, pistols, dirk,—
They furnish'd him, entire, except some stitches,
With a clean shirt, and very spacious
    breeches.   1280

CLXI

And then fair Haidée tried her tongue at speak-
    ing,
  But not a word could Juan comprehend,
Although he listen'd so that the young Greek in
  Her earnestness would ne'er have made an
    end;
And, as he interrupted not, went eking
  Her speech out to her protégé and friend,
Till pausing at the last her breath to take,
She saw he did not understand Romaic.

CLXII

And then she had recourse to nods, and signs,
  And smiles, and sparkles of the speaking
    eye,   1290
And read (the only book she could) the lines
  Of his fair face, and found, by sympathy,
The answer eloquent, where the soul shines
  And darts in one quick glance a long reply;
And thus in every look she saw exprest
A world of words, and things at which she
    guess'd.

CLXIII

And now, by dint of fingers and of eyes,
  And words repeated after her, he took
A lesson in her tongue; but by surmise,
  No doubt, less of her language than her
    look: 1300
As he who studies fervently the skies
  Turns oftener to the stars than to his book,
Thus Juan learn'd his alpha beta better
From Haidée's glance than any graven letter.

CLXIV

'Tis pleasing to be school'd in a strange tongue
  By female lips and eyes—that is, I mean,
When both the teacher and the taught are young,
  As was the case, at least, where I have been;
They smile so when one's right, and when one's
    wrong
  They smile still more, and then there
    intervene   1310
Pressure of hands, perhaps even a chaste kiss;—
I learn'd the little that I know by this:

CLXV

That is, some words of Spanish, Turk, and Greek,
  Italian not at all, having no teachers;
Much English I cannot pretend to speak,
  Learning that language chiefly from its preach-
    ers,
Barrow, South, Tillotson, whom every week
  I study, also Blair, the highest reachers
Of eloquence in piety and prose—
I hate your poets, so read none of those.   1320

CLXVI

As for the ladies, I have nought to say,
  A wanderer from the British world of fashion,
Where I, like other 'dogs, have had my day,'
  Like other men, too, may have had my pas-
    sion—
But that, like other things, has pass'd away,
  And all her fools whom I *could* lay the lash
    on:
Foes, friends, men, women, now are nought to
    me
But dreams of what has been, no more to be.

CLXVII

Return we to Don Juan. He begun
  To hear new words, and to repeat them;
    but   1330
Some feelings, universal as the sun,
  Were such as could not in his breast be shut
More than within the bosom of a nun:
  He was in love,—as you would be, no doubt,

With a young benefactress,—so was she,
Just in the way we very often see.

CLXVIII

And every day by daybreak—rather early
  For Juan, who was somewhat fond of rest—
She came into the cave, but it was merely
  To see her bird reposing in his nest;   1340
And she would softly stir his locks so curly,
  Without disturbing her yet slumbering guest,
Breathing all gently o'er his cheek and mouth,
As o'er a bed of roses the sweet south.

CLXIX

And every morn his colour freshlier came,
  And every day help'd on his convalescence;
'Twas well, because health in the human frame
  Is pleasant, besides being true love's essence,
For health and idleness to passion's flame
  Are oil and gunpowder; and some good
    lessons   1350
Are also learnt from Ceres and from Bacchus,
Without whom Venus will not long attack us.

CLXX

While Venus fills the heart (without heart really
  Love, though good always, is not quite so
    good),
Ceres presents a plate of vermicelli,—
  For love must be sustain'd like flesh and blood,
While Bacchus pours out wine, or hands a jelly;
  Eggs, oysters, too, are amatory food;
But who is their purveyor from above
Heaven knows,—it may be Neptune, Pan, or
    Jove.   1360

CLXXI

When Juan woke he found some good things
    ready,
  A bath, a breakfast, and the finest eyes
That ever made a youthful heart less steady,
  Besides her maid's, as pretty for their size;
But I have spoken of all this already—
  And repetition's tiresome and unwise,—
Well—Juan, after bathing in the sea,
Came always back to coffee and Haidée.

CLXXII

Both were so young, and one so innocent,
  That bathing pass'd for nothing: Juan
    seem'd   1370
To her, as 'twere, the kind of being sent,
  Of whom these two years she had nightly
    dream'd,
A something to be loved, a creature meant

To be her happiness, and whom she deem'd
To render happy: all who joy would win
Must share it,—Happiness was born a twin.

CLXXIII

It was such pleasure to behold him, such
   Enlargement of existence to partake
Nature with him, to thrill beneath his touch,
   To watch him slumbering, and to see him
     wake;   1380
To live with him for ever were too much;
   But then the thought of parting made her
     quake:
He was her own, her ocean-treasure, cast
Like a rich wreck—her first love, and her last.

CLXXIV

And thus a moon roll'd on, and fair Haidée
   Paid daily visits to her boy, and took
Such plentiful precautions, that still he
   Remain'd unknown within his craggy nook;
At last her father's prows put out to sea,
   For certain merchantmen upon the look, 1390
Not as of yore to carry off an Io,[17]
But three Ragusan vessels bound for Scio.

CLXXV

Then came her freedom, for she had no mother,
   So that, her father being at sea, she was
Free as a married woman, or such other
   Female, as where she likes may freely pass,
Without even the encumbrance of a brother,
   The freest she that ever gazed on glass:
I speak of Christian lands in this comparison,
Where wives, at least, are seldom kept in
     garrison.   1400

CLXXVI

Now she prolong'd her visits and her talk
   (For they must talk), and he had learnt to say
So much as to propose to take a walk,—
   For little had he wander'd since the day
On which, like a young flower snapp'd from the
     stalk,
   Drooping and dewy on the beach he lay,—
And thus they walk'd out in the afternoon,
And saw the sun set opposite the moon.

CLXXVII

It was a wild and breaker-beaten coast,
   With cliffs above, and a broad sandy
     shore,   1410
Guarded by shoals and rocks as by an host,

[17] beautiful daughter of the King of Argos, who, according to
one legend, was carried off by Phoenician traders.

   With here and there a creek, whose aspect
     wore
A better welcome to the tempest-tost;
   And rarely ceased the haughty billow's roar,
Save on the dead long summer days, which make
The outstretch'd ocean glitter like a lake.

CLXXVIII

And the small ripple spilt upon the beach
   Scarcely o'erpass'd the cream of your cham-
     pagne,
When o'er the brim the sparkling bumpers reach,
   That spring-dew of the spirit! the heart's
     rain!   1420
Few things surpass old wine; and they may
     preach
   Who please,—the more because they preach
     in vain,—
Let us have wine and women, mirth and laugh-
     ter,
Sermons and soda-water the day after.

CLXXIX

Man, being reasonable, must get drunk;
   The best of life is but intoxication:
Glory, the grape, love, gold, in these are sunk
   The hopes of all men, and of every nation;
Without their sap, how branchless were the
     trunk
   Of life's strange tree, so fruitful on
     occasion!   1430
But to return,—Get very drunk; and when
You wake with headache, you shall see what
     then.

CLXXX

Ring for your valet—bid him quickly bring
   Some hock and soda-water, then you'll
     know
A pleasure worthy Xerxes the great king;
   For not the blest sherbet, sublimed with snow,
Nor the first sparkle of the desert spring,
   Nor Burgundy in all its sunset glow,
After long travel, ennui, love, or slaughter,
Vie with that draught of hock and soda-
     water.   1440

CLXXXI

The coast—I think it was the coast that I
   Was just describing—Yes, it *was* the coast—
Lay at this period quiet as the sky,
   The sands untumbled, the blue waves untost,
And all was stillness, save the sea-bird's cry,
   And dolphin's leap, and little billow crost

By some low rock or shelve, that made it fret
Against the boundary it scarcely wet.

CLXXXII

And forth they wander'd, her sire being gone,
  As I have said, upon an expedition;   1450
And mother, brother, guardian, she had none,
  Save Zoe, who, although with due precision
She waited on her lady with the sun,
  Thought daily service was her only mission,
Bringing warm water, wreathing her long tresses,
And asking now and then for cast-off dresses.

CLXXXIII

It was the cooling hour, just when the rounded
  Red sun sinks down behind the azure hill,
Which then seems as if the whole earth it
    bounded,
  Circling all nature, hush'd, and dim, and
    still,   1460
With the far mountain-crescent half surrounded
  On one side, and the deep sea calm and chill,
Upon the other, and the rosy sky,
With one star sparkling through it like an eye.

CLXXXIV

And thus they wander'd forth, and hand in hand,
  Over the shining pebbles and the shells,
Glided along the smooth and harden'd sand,
  And in the worn and wild receptacles
Work'd by the storms, yet work'd as it were
    plann'd,
  In hollow halls, with sparry roofs and
    cells,   1470
They turn'd to rest; and, each clasp'd by an arm,
Yielded to the deep twilight's purple charm.

CLXXXV

They look'd up to the sky, whose floating glow
  Spread like a rosy ocean, vast and bright;
They gazed upon the glittering sea below,
  Whence the broad moon rose circling into
    sight;
They heard the waves splash, and the wind so
    low,
  And saw each other's dark eyes darting light
Into each other—and, beholding this,
Their lips drew near, and clung into a kiss; 1480

CLXXXVI

A long, long kiss, a kiss of youth, and love,
  And beauty, all concentrating like rays
Into one focus, kindled from above;
  Such kisses as belong to early days,

Where heart, and soul, and sense, in concert
    move,
  And the blood's lava, and the pulse a blaze,
Each kiss a heart-quake,—for a kiss's strength,
I think it must be reckon'd by its length.

CLXXXVII

By length I mean duration; theirs endured
  Heaven knows how long—no doubt they never
    reckon'd;   1490
And if they had, they could not have secured
  The sum of their sensations to a second:
They had not spoken; but they felt allured,
  As if their souls and lips each other beckon'd,
Which, being join'd, like swarming bees they
    clung—
Their hearts the flowers from whence the honey
    sprung.

CLXXXVIII

They were alone, but not alone as they
  Who shut in chambers think it loneliness;
The silent ocean, and the starlight bay,
  The twilight glow, which momently grew
    less,   1500
The voiceless sands, and dropping caves, that
    lay
  Around them, made them to each other press,
As if there were no life beneath the sky
Save theirs, and that their life could never die.

CLXXXIX

They fear'd no eyes nor ears on that lone beach,
  They felt no terrors from the night; they were
All in all to each other; though their speech
  Was broken words, they *thought* a language
    there,—
And all the burning tongues the passions teach
  Found in one sigh the best interpreter   1510
Of nature's oracle—first love,—that all
Which Eve has left her daughters since her fall.

CXC

Haidée spoke not of scruples, ask'd no vows,
  Nor offer'd any; she had never heard
Of plight and promises to be a spouse,
  Or perils by a loving maid incurr'd;
She was all which pure ignorance allows,
  And flew to her young mate like a young bird,
And never having dreamt of falsehood, she
Had not one word to say of constancy.   1520

CXCI

She loved, and was beloved—she adored,

And she was worshipp'd; after nature's
   fashion,
Their intense souls, into each other pour'd,
   If souls could die, had perish'd in that pas-
     sion,—
But by degrees their senses were restored,
   Again to be o'ercome, again to dash on;
And, beating 'gainst *his* bosom, Haidée's heart
Felt as if never more to beat apart.

CXCII

Alas! they were so young, so beautiful,
   So lonely, loving, helpless, and the hour 1530
Was that in which the heart is always full,
   And, having o'er itself no further power,
Prompts deeds eternity cannot annul,
   But pays off moments in an endless shower
Of hell-fire—all prepared for people giving
Pleasure or pain to one another living.

CXCIII

Alas! for Juan and Haidée! they were
   So loving and so lovely—till then never,
Excepting our first parents, such a pair
   Had run the risk of being damn'd for
     ever; 1540
And Haidée, being devout as well as fair,
   Had, doubtless, heard about the Stygian river,
And hell and purgatory—but forgot
Just in the very crisis she should not.

CXCIV

They look upon each other, and their eyes
   Gleam in the moonlight; and her white arm
     clasps
Round Juan's head, and his around her lies
   Half buried in the tresses which it grasps;
She sits upon his knee, and drinks his sighs,
   He hers, until they end in broken gasps; 1550
And thus they form a group that's quite antique,
Half naked, loving, natural, and Greek.

CXCV

And when those deep and burning moments
   pass'd,
   And Juan sunk to sleep within her arms,
She slept not, but all tenderly, though fast,
   Sustain'd his head upon her bosom's charms;
And now and then her eye to heaven is cast,
   And then on the pale cheek her breast now
     warms,
Pillow'd on her o'erflowing heart, which pants
With all it granted, and with all it grants. 1560

CXCVI

An infant when it gazes on a light,
   A child the moment when it drains the breast,
A devotee when soars the Host in sight,
   An Arab with a stranger for a guest,
A sailor when the prize has struck in fight,
   A miser filling his most hoarded chest,
Feel rapture; but not such true joy are reaping
As they who watch o'er what they love while
   sleeping.

CXCVII

For there it lies so tranquil, so beloved,
   All that it hath of life with us is living; 1570
So gentle, stirless, helpless, and unmoved,
   And all unconscious of the joy 'tis giving;
All it hath felt, inflicted, pass'd, and proved,
   Hush'd into depths beyond the watcher's div-
     ing;
There lies the thing we love with all its errors
And all its charms, like death without its terrors.

CXCVIII

The lady watch'd her lover—and that hour
   Of Love's, and Night's, and Ocean's solitude,
O'erflowed her soul with their united power;
   Amidst the barren sand and rocks so rude 1580
She and her wave-worn love had made their
     bower,
   Where nought upon their passion could in-
     trude,
And all the stars that crowded the blue space
Saw nothing happier than her glowing face.

CXCIX

Alas! the love of women! it is known
   To be a lovely and a fearful thing;
For all of theirs upon that die is thrown,
   And if 'tis lost, life hath no more to bring
To them but mockeries of the past alone,
   And their revenge is as the tiger's spring, 1590
Deadly, and quick, and crushing; yet, as real
Torture is theirs what they inflict they feel.

CC

They are right; for man, to man so oft unjust,
   Is always so to women; one sole bond
Awaits them, treachery is all their trust;
   Taught to conceal, their bursting hearts
     despond
Over their idol, till some wealthier lust
   Buys them in marriage—and what rests be-
     yond?

A thankless husband, next a faithless lover,
Then dressing, nursing, praying, and all's
    over.   1600

CCI

Some take a lover, some take drams or prayers,
    Some mind their household, others dissipation,
Some run away, and but exchange their cares,
    Losing the advantage of a virtuous station;
Few changes e'er can better their affairs,
    Theirs being an unnatural situation,
From the dull palace to the dirty hovel:
Some play the devil, and then write a novel.[18]

CCII

Haidée was Nature's bride, and knew not this:
    Haidée was Passion's child, born where the
      sun   1610
Showers triple light, and scorches even the kiss
    Of his gazelle-eyed daughters; she was one
Made but to love, to feel that she was his
    Who was her chosen: what was said or done
Elsewhere was nothing. She had nought to fear,
Hope, care, nor love beyond,—her heart beat
    here.

CCIII

And oh! that quickening of the heart, that
    beat!
    How much it costs us! yet each rising throb
Is in its cause as its effect so sweet,
    That Wisdom, ever on the watch to rob   1620
Joy of its alchemy, and to repeat
    Fine truths; even Conscience, too, has a tough
    job
To make us understand each good old maxim,
So good—I wonder Castlereagh don't tax 'em.

CCIV

And now 'twas done—on the lone shore were
    plighted
    Their hearts; the stars, their nuptial torches,
    shed
Beauty upon the beautiful they lighted:
    Ocean their witness, and the cave their bed,
By their own feelings hallow'd and united,
    Their priest was Solitude, and they were
    wed: 1630
And they were happy, for to their young eyes
Each was an angel, and earth paradise.

    1818–19   1819

From Canto the Third

Stanzas lxi-xciv, ci-cxi

LXI

Old Lambro pass'd unseen a private gate,
    And stood within his hall at eventide;
Meantime the lady and her lover sate
    At wassail in their beauty and their pride:
An ivory inlaid table spread with state
    Before them, and fair slaves on every side;[1]
Gems, gold, and silver, form'd the service mostly,
Mother of pearl and coral the less costly.

LXII

The dinner made about a hundred dishes;
    Lamb and pistachio nuts—in short, all
      meats,   490
And saffron soups, and sweetbreads; and the
    fishes
Were of the finest that e'er flounced in nets,
Drest to a Sybarite's[2] most pamper'd wishes;
    The beverage was various sherbets
Of raisin, orange, and pomegranate juice,
Squeezed through the rind, which makes it best
    for use.

LXIII

These were ranged round, each in its crystal
    ewer,
    And fruits, and date-bread loaves closed the
    repast,
And Mocha's berry, from Arabia pure,
    In small fine China cups, came in at last;   500
Gold cups of filigree made to secure
    The hand from burning underneath them
    placed;
Cloves, cinnamon, and saffron too were boil'd
Up with the coffee, which (I think) they spoil'd.

LXIV

The hangings of the room were tapestry, made
    Of velvet panels, each of different hue,
And thick with damask flowers of silk inlaid;
    And round them ran a yellow border too;
The upper border, richly wrought, display'd,
    Embroider'd delicately o'er with blue,   510
Soft Persian sentences, in lilac letters.
From poets, or the moralists their betters.

---

18 Lady Caroline Lamb had an affair with Byron and afterward
satirized him in her novel *Glenarvon.*

1 'Almost all *Don Juan* is *real* life, either my own, or from
people I knew. By the way, most of the description of the *furniture,* in Canto Third, is taken from Tully's *Tripoli* (pray *note this*),
and the rest from my own observation.' —Letter to Murray, 23
August 1821.

2 a voluptuary's. Inhabitants of ancient Sybaris were noted for
their love of luxury.

LXV

These Oriental writings on the wall,
  Quite common in those countries, are a kind
Of monitors adapted to recall,
  Like skulls at Memphian banquets, to the
  mind
The words which shook Belshazzar in his hall,
  And took his kingdom from him:[3] You will
  find,
Though sages may pour out their wisdom's treas-
  ure,
There is no sterner moralist than Pleasure. 520

LXVI

A beauty at the season's close grown hectic,
  A genius who has drunk himself to death,
A rake turn'd methodistic, or Eclectic—
  (For that's the name they like to pray be-
  neath)—
But most, an alderman struck apoplectic,
  Are things that really take away the breath,—
And show that late hours, wine, and love are able
To do not much less damage than the table.

LXVII

Haidée and Juan carpeted their feet
  On crimson satin, border'd with pale blue; 530
Their sofa occupied three parts complete
  Of the apartment—and appear'd quite new;
The velvet cushions (for a throne more meet)
  Were scarlet, from whose glowing centre grew
A sun emboss'd in gold, whose rays of tissue,
Meridian-like, were seen all light to issue.

LXVIII

Crystal and marble, plate and porcelain,
  Had done their work of splendour; Indian
  mats
And Persian carpets, which the heart bled to
  stain,
  Over the floors were spread; gazelles and
  cats,
And dwarfs and blacks, and such like things that
  gain 540
  Their bread as ministers and favourites—
  (that's
To say, by degradation)—mingled there
As plentiful as in a court or fair.

LXIX

There was no want of lofty mirrors, and
  The tables, most of ebony inlaid

With mother of pearl or ivory, stood at hand,
  Or were of tortoise-shell or rare woods made.
Fretted with gold or silver:—by command,
  The greater part of these were ready
  spread 550
With viands and sherbets in ice—and wine—
Kept for all comers at all hours to dine.

LXX

Of all the dresses I select Haidée's:
  She wore two jelicks[4]—one was of pale yellow;
Of azure, pink, and white was her chemise—
  'Neath which her breast heaved like a little bil-
  low,
With buttons form'd of pearls as large as peas,
  All gold and crimson shone her jelick's fellow,
And the striped white gauze baracan[5] that bound
  her,
Like fleecy clouds about the moon, flow'd round
  her. 560

LXXI

One large gold bracelet clasp'd each lovely arm,
  Lockless—so pliable from the pure gold
That the hand stretch'd and shut it without harm,
  The limb which it adorn'd its only mould;
So beautiful—its very shape would charm,
  And clinging as if loath to lose its hold,
The purest ore enclosed the whitest skin
That e'er by precious metal was held in.[6]

LXXII

Around, as princess of her father's land,
  A like gold bar above her instep roll'd[7] 570
Announced her rank; twelve rings were on her
  hand;
  Her hair was starr'd with gems; her veil's fine
  fold
Below her breast was fasten'd with a band
  Of lavish pearls, whose worth could scarce be
  told;
Her orange silk full Turkish trousers furl'd
About the prettiest ankle in the world.

LXXIII

Her hair's long auburn waves down to her heel
  Flow'd like an Alpine torrent which the sun

---

3 See Daniel v.

4 bodices.
5 a fine cloth of silk or other delicate material.
6 The dress is Moorish, and the bracelets and bar are worn in the manner described. The reader will perceive hereafter, that as the mother of Haidée was of Fez, her daughter wore the garb of the country.—(Byron.)
7 The bar of gold above the instep is a mark of sovereign rank in the women of the families of the Deys, and is worn as such by their female relatives.—(Byron.)

Dyes with his morning light,—and would conceal
  Her person[8] if allow'd at large to run,   580
And still they seem'd resentfully to feel
  The silken fillet's curb, and sought to shun
Their bonds whene'er some Zephyr caught began
To offer his young pinion as her fan.

LXXIV

Round her she made an atmosphere of life,
  The very air seem'd lighter from her eyes,
They were so soft and beautiful, and rife
  With all we can imagine of the skies,
And pure as Psyche ere she grew a wife—
  Too pure even for the purest human ties;   590
Her overpowering presence made you feel
It would not be idolatry to kneel.

LXXV

Her eyelashes, though dark as night, were tinged
  (It is the country's custom), but in vain;
For those large black eyes were so blackly
    fringed,
  The glossy rebels mock'd the jetty stain,
And in their native beauty stood avenged:
  Her nails were touch'd with henna; but again
The power of art was turn'd to nothing, for
They could not look more rosy than before.   600

LXXVI

The henna should be deeply dyed to make
  The skin relieved appear more fairly fair;
She had no need of this, day ne'er will break
  On mountain-tops more heavenly white than
    her:
The eye might doubt if it were well awake,
  She was so like a vision; I might err,
But Shakespeare also says, 'tis very silly
'To gild refined gold, or paint the lily.'[9]

LXXVII

Juan had on a shawl of black and gold,
  But a white baracan, and so transparent   610
The sparkling gems beneath you might behold,
  Like small stars through the milky way apparent;
His turban furl'd in many a graceful fold,
  An emerald aigrette[10] with Haidée's hair in't
Surmounted, as its clasp, a glowing crescent,
Whose rays shone ever trembling, but incessant.

LXXVIII

And now they were diverted by their suite,
  Dwarfs, dancing-girls, black eunuchs, and a
    poet,
Which made their new establishment complete;
  The last was of great fame, and liked to show
    it;   620
His verses rarely wanted their due feet—
  And for his theme—he seldom sung below it,
He being paid to satirise or flatter,
As the psalm says, 'inditing a good matter.'

LXXIX

He praised the present, and abused the past,
  Reversing the good custom of old days,
An Eastern anti-jacobin at last
  He turn'd, preferring pudding to *no* praise—
For some few years his lot had been o'ercast
  By his seeming independent in his lays,   630
But now he sung the Sultan and the Pacha
With truth like Southey, and with verse like
  Crashaw.

LXXX

He was a man who had seen many changes,
  And always changed as true as any needle;
His polar star being one which rather ranges,
  And not the fix'd—he knew the way to
    wheedle:
So vile he 'scaped the doom which oft avenges;
  And being fluent (save indeed when fee'd ill),
He lied with such a fervour of intention—
There was no doubt he earn'd his laureate pension.   640

LXXXI

But he had genius,—when a turncoat has it,
  The 'Vates irritabilis'[11] takes care
That without notice few full moons shall pass it;
  Even good men like to make the public
    stare:—
But to my subject—let me see—what was it?—
  Oh!—the third canto—and the pretty pair—
Their loves, and feasts, and house, and dress, and
    mode
Of living in their insular abode.

LXXXII

Their poet, a sad trimmer,[12] but no less
  In company a very pleasant fellow,   650

---

8 This is no exaggeration: there were four women whom I remember to have seen, who possessed their hair in this profusion; of these three were English, the other was a Levantine.—(Byron.)
9 *King John*, iv, ii, 11.
10 a plume-like ornament of gems.

11 irritable prophet, or poet. In the second chapter of *Biographia Literaria* Coleridge had written on the 'supposed irritability of men of genius.'
12 a compromiser of political principles.

Had been the favourite of full many a mess
  Of men, and made them speeches when half
    mellow;
And though his meaning they could rarely guess,
  Yet still they deign'd to hiccup or to bellow
The glorious meed of popular applause,
Of which the first ne'er knows the second cause.

LXXXIII

But now being lifted into high society,
  And having pick'd up several odds and ends
Of free thoughts in his travels, for variety,
  He deem'd, being in a lone isle, among
    friends,   660
That without any danger of a riot, he
  Might for long lying make himself amends;
And singing as he sung in his warm youth,
Agree to a short armistice with truth.

LXXXIV

He had travell'd 'mongst the Arabs, Turks, and
    Franks,
  And knew the self-loves of the different na-
    tions;
And having lived with people of all ranks,
  Had something ready upon most occasions—
Which got him a few presents and some thanks.
  He varied with some skill his adulations; 670
To 'do at Rome as Romans do,' a piece
Of conduct was which he observed in Greece.

LXXXV

Thus, usually, when he was asked to sing,
  He gave the different nations something na-
    tional;
'Twas all the same to him—'God save the king,'
  Or 'Ça ira,'[13] according to the fashion all:
His muse made increment of anything,
  From the high lyric down to the low rational:
If Pindar sang horse-races, what should hinder
Himself from being as pliable as Pindar? 680

LXXXVI

In France, for instance, he would write a chan-
    son;
  In England a six-canto quarto tale;
In Spain he'd make a ballad or romance on
  The last war—much the same in Portugal;
In Germany, the Pegasus he'd prance on
  Would be old Goethe's —(see what says
    De Staël);[14]

In Italy he'd ape the 'Trecentisti';[15]
In Greece, he'd sing some sort of hymn like this
    t' ye:

1

The isles of Greece, the isles of Greece!
  Where burning Sappho[16] loved and sung   690
Where grew the arts of war and peace,
  Where Delos rose, and Phœbus sprung![17]
Eternal summer gilds them yet,
But all, except their sun, is set.

2

The Scian and the Teian muse,[18]
  The hero's harp, the lover's lute,
Have found the fame your shores refuse:
  Their place of birth alone is mute
To sounds which echo further west
Than your sires' 'Islands of the Blest.'[19]   700

3

The mountains look on Marathon[20]—
  And Marathon looks on the sea;
And musing there an hour alone,
  I dream'd that Greece might still be free;
For standing on the Persians' grave,
I could not deem myself a slave.

4

A king[21] sate on the rocky brow
  Which looks o'er sea-born Salamis;[22]
And ships, by thousands, lay below,
  And men in nations;—all were his!   710
He counted them at break of day—
And when the sun set where were they?

5

And where are they? and where art thou,
  My country? On thy voiceless shore
The heroic lay is tuneless now—
  The heroic bosom beats no more!
And must thy lyre, so long divine,
Degenerate into hands like mine?

---

13 a song of the French Revolutionists.
14 Madame de Staël had said that Goethe represented the entire literature of Germany.
15 Italian writers of the fourteenth century.
16 celebrated Greek poetess, seventh century B.C.
17 The island of Delos, one of the Cyclades, is fabled to have arisen from the Aegean and become the birthplace of Phoebus Apollo.
18 Homer, according to one tradition, was born on the island of Scio; Anacreon's birthplace was Teos, Asia Minor.
19 The Μακάρων νῆσοι of the Greek poets were supposed to have been the Cape de Verde Islands, or the Canaries.—(Byron.)
20 plain that marks the site of the celebrated Greek victory which ended Persian domination, 490 B.C.
21 Xerxes, king of Persia, c. 519-465 B.C.
22 the island off Attica near which the Greeks won a decisive naval victory over the fleet of Xerxes.

6

'Tis something, in the dearth of fame,
  Though link'd among a fetter'd race,   720
To feel at least a patriot's shame,
  Even as I sing, suffuse my face;
For what is left the poet here?
For Greeks a blush—for Greece a tear.

7

Must *we* but weep o'er days more blest?
  Must *we* but blush?—Our fathers bled.
Earth! render back from out thy breast
  A remnant of our Spartan dead!
Of the three hundred grant but three,
To make a new Thermopylæ!²³   730

8

What, silent still? and silent all?
  Ah! no;—the voices of the dead
Sound like a distant torrent's fall,
  And answer, 'Let one living head,
But one arise,—we come, we come!'
'Tis but the living who are dumb.

9

In vain—in vain: strike other chords;
  Fill high the cup with Samian²⁴ wine!
Leave battles to the Turkish hordes,
  And shed the blood of Scio's vine!   740
Hark! rising to the ignoble call—
How answers each bold Bacchanal!

10

You have the Pyrrhic dance²⁵ as yet;
  Where is the Pyrrhic phalanx²⁶ gone?
Of two such lessons, why forget
  The nobler and the manlier one?
You have the letters Cadmus²⁷ gave—
Think ye he meant them for a slave?

11

Fill high the bowl with Samian wine,
  We will not think of themes like these!   750
It made Anacreon's song²⁸ divine:
  He served—but served Polycrates—

A tyrant; but our masters then
Were still, at least, our countrymen.

12

The tyrant of the Chersonese²⁹
  Was freedom's best and bravest friend;
That tyrant was Miltiades!
  Oh! that the present hour would lend
Another despot of the kind!
Such chains as his were sure to bind.   760

13

Fill high the bowl with Samian wine!
  On Suli's rock,³⁰ and Parga's shore,³¹
Exists the remnant of a line
  Such as the Doric mothers bore;
And there, perhaps, some seed is sown,
The Heracleidan blood³² might own.

14

Trust not for freedom to the Franks³³—
  They have a king who buys and sells;
In native swords, and native ranks
  The only hope of courage dwells: 770
But Turkish force, and Latin fraud,
Would break your shield, however broad.

15

Fill high the bowl with Samian wine!
  Our virgins dance beneath the shade—
I see their glorious black eyes shine;
  But gazing on each glowing maid,
My own the burning tear-drop laves,
To think such breasts must suckle slaves.

16

Place me on Sunium's marbled steep,³⁴
  Where nothing, save the waves and I,   780
May hear our mutual murmurs sweep;
  There, swan-like, let me sing and die:
A land of slaves shall ne'er be mine—
Dash down yon cup of Samian wine!

LXXXVII

Thus sung, or would, or could, or should have
    sung,
  The modern Greek, in tolerable verse;

---

23 The pass where King Leonidas and his band of Spartans made their valiant stand against the Persian hordes in 480 B.C.
24 from the island of Samos.
25 a war dance in quick time devised by the Greek general Pyrrhus, third century B.C.
26 the battle formation of infantry as used by Pyrrhus.
27 legendary founder of Thebes, reputed to have introduced from Phoenicia letters that make the Greek alphabet.
28 Anacreon sang chiefly about the pleasures of love and wine. He was court poet to the tyrant Polycrates at Samos, sixth century B.C.

29 Miltiades, who was tyrant of Chersoneus, was also a celebrated Athenian general and hero of Marathon.
30 a fortress on a height overlooking the river Suli in Albania.
31 a seaport in Albania.
32 The Heraclidae traced their descent from Hercules.
33 any European nation.
34 the promontory at the southeastern extremity of Greece, now Cape Colonna.

If not like Orpheus quite, when Greece was
    young,
    Yet in these times he might have done much
      worse:
His strain display'd some feeling—right or
    wrong;
    And feeling, in a poet, is the source   790
Of others' feeling; but they are such liars,
And take all colours—like the hands of dyers.

LXXXVIII

But words are things, and a small drop of ink,
    Falling like dew, upon a thought, produces
That which makes thousands, perhaps millions,
    think;
    'Tis strange, the shortest letter which man uses
Instead of speech, may form a lasting link
    Of ages; to what straits old Time reduces
Frail man, when paper—even a rag like this,
Survives himself, his tomb, and all that's his! 800

LXXXIX

And when his bones are dust, his grave a blank,
    His station, generation, even his nation,
Become a thing, or nothing, save to rank
    In chronological commemoration,
Some dull MS. oblivion long has sank,
    Or graven stone found in a barrack's station
In digging the foundation of a closet,
May turn his name up, as a rare deposit.

XC

And glory long has made the sages smile;
    'Tis something, nothing, words, illusion,
      wind—   810
Depending more upon the historian's style
    Than on the name a person leaves behind:
Troy owes to Homer what whist owes to Hoyle:
    The present century was growing blind
To the great Marlborough's skill in giving
    knocks,[35]
Until his late Life by Archdeacon Coxe.[36]

XCI

Milton's the prince of poets—so we say;
    A little heavy, but no less divine:
An independent being in his day—
    Learn'd, pious, temperate in love and
      wine;   820
But his life falling into Johnson's way,

We're told this great high priest of all the Nine
Was whipt at college—a harsh sire—odd spouse,
For the first Mrs. Milton left his house.

XCII

All these are, *certes,* entertaining facts,
    Like Shakespeare's stealing deer, Lord Bacon's
      bribes;
Like Titus' youth, and Cæsar's earliest acts;[37]
    Like Burns (whom Doctor Currie[38] well de-
      scribes);
Like Cromwell's pranks;[39]—but although truth
    exacts
    These amiable descriptions from the
      scribes,   830
As most essential to their hero's story,
They do not much contribute to his glory.

XCIII

All are not moralists, like Southey, when
    He prated to the world of 'Pantisocracy';[40]
Or Wordsworth unexcised, unhired, who then
    Season'd his pedlar poems with democracy;
Or Coleridge, long before his flighty pen
    Let to the Morning Post its aristocracy;[41]
When he and Southey, following the same path
Espoused two partners (milliners of Bath).[42] 840

XCIV

Such names at present cut a convict figure,
    The very Botany Bay[43] in moral geography;
Their loyal treason, renegado rigour,
    Are good manure for their more bare biog-
      raphy,
Wordsworth's last quarto, by the way, is bigger
    Than any since the birthday of typography;
A drowsy frowzy poem, call'd the 'Excursion.'
Writ in a manner which is my aversion.

CI

T' our tale.—The feast was over, the slaves gone,
    The dwarfs and dancing girls had all retired;

---

37 According to Suetonius, the youthful Titus practiced forging handwriting. Caesar, in his youth, crucified some pirates with whom he pretended to be on friendly terms.
38 James Currie, whose life of Burns, 1800, exaggerated Burns's dissipation.
39 Cromwell was said to have been skillful as a lad in robbing orchards.
40 name of the ideal social state that Southey, Coleridge, and others planned to establish in America.
41 Coleridge began writing for the *Morning Post* in 1798.
42 Southey and Coleridge married the Fricker sisters in 1795. At the time of their marriage the sisters were not milliners.
43 an inlet near Sydney, Australia, used for an English penal colony in the late eighteenth century.

---

35 the Duke of Marlborough, famous English general, defeated the French at Blenheim in 1704.
36 William Coxe, Archdeacon of Wilts, published his voluminous *Memoirs of John, Duke of Marlborough* in 1818–19.

The Arab lore and poet's song were done,
  And every sound of revelry expired;   900
The lady and her lover, left alone,
  The rosy flood of twilight's sky admired;—
Ave Maria! o'er the earth and sea,
That heavenliest hour of Heaven is worthiest
  thee!

CII

Ave Maria! blessed be the hour!
  The time, the clime, the spot, where I so oft
Have felt that moment in its fullest power
  Sink o'er the earth so beautiful and soft,
While swung the deep bell in the distant
  tower,
  Or the faint dying day-hymn stole aloft, 910
And not a breath crept through the rosy air,
And yet the forest leaves seem'd stirr'd with
  prayer.

CIII

Ave Maria! 'tis the hour of prayer!
  Ave Maria! 'tis the hour of love!
Ave Maria! may our spirits dare
  Look up to thine and to thy Son's above!
Ave Maria! oh that face so fair!
  Those downcast eyes beneath the Almighty
  dove—
What though 'tis but a pictured image?—strike,
That painting is no idol,—'tis too like.   920

CIV

Some kinder casuists are pleased to say,
  In nameless print—that I have no devotion;
But set those persons down with me to pray,
  And you shall see who has the properest notion
Of getting into heaven the shortest way;
  My altars are the mountains and the ocean,
Earth, air, stars,—all that springs from the great
  Whole,
Who hath produced, and will receive the soul.

CV

Sweet hour of twilight!—in the solitude
  Of the pine forest, and the silent shore   930
Which bounds Ravenna's immemorial wood,
  Rooted where once the Adrian wave flow'd
  o'er,
To where the last Cæsarean fortress[44] stood,
  Evergreen forest! which Boccaccio's lore

And Dryden's lay[45] made haunted ground to
  me,
How have I loved the twilight hour and thee!

CVI

The shrill cicalas, people of the pine,
  Making their summer lives one ceaseless song,
Were the sole echoes, save my steed's and mine,
  And vesper bell's that rose the boughs
  along;   940
The spectre huntsman of Onesti's line,[46]
  His hell-dogs, and their chase, and the fair
  throng
Which learn'd from this example not to fly
From a true lover,—shadow'd my mind's eye.

CVII

Oh, Hesperus! thou bringest all good things—
  Home to the weary, to the hungry cheer,
To the young bird the parent's brooding wings,
  The welcome stall to the o'erlabour'd steer;
Whate'er of peace about our hearthstone clings,
  Whate'er our household gods protect of
  dear,   950
Are gather'd round us by thy look of rest;
Thou bring'st the child, too, to the mother's
  breast.

CVIII

Soft hour! which wakes the wish and melts the
  heart
  Of those who sail the seas, on the first day
When they from their sweet friends are torn
  apart;
  Or fills with love the pilgrim on his way
As the far bell of vesper makes him start,
  Seeming to weep the dying day's decay;
Is this a fancy which our reason scorns?
Ah! surely nothing dies but something
  mourns!   960

CIX

When Nero perish'd by the justest doom
  Which ever the destroyer yet destroy'd,
Amidst the roar of liberated Rome,
  Of nations freed, and the world overjoy'd,
Some hands unseen strew'd flowers upon his
  tomb:
  Perhaps the weakness of a heart not void
Of feeling for some kindness done, when power
Had left the wretch an uncorrupted hour.

---

44 near Ravenna on the Adriatic the ancient port of Augustus and its fortifications were converted into pleasant orchards and groves in the fifth or sixth century of the Christian era.

45 Dryden's *Theodore and Honoria*, a tale adapted from Boccaccio's *Decameron.*
46 Dryden's Theodore is Boccaccio's Onesti.

CX

But I'm digressing; what on earth has Nero,
  Or any such like sovereign buffoons,   970
To do with the transactions of my hero,
  More than such madmen's fellow man—the
    moon's?
Sure my invention must be down at zero,
  And I grown one of many 'wooden spoons'
Of verse (the name with which we Cantabs[47]
  please
To dub the last of honours in degrees).

CXI

I feel this tediousness will never do—
  'Tis being *too* epic, and I must cut down
(In copying) this long canto into two;
  They'll never find it out, unless I own   980
The fact, excepting some experienced few;
  And then as an improvement 'twill be shown:
I'll prove that such the opinion of the critic is
From Aristotle *passim.*—See Ποιητικης.[48]

1819   1821

From CANTO THE FOURTH

Stanzas i-lxxiii

I

Nothing so difficult as a beginning
  In poesy, unless perhaps the end;
For oftentimes when Pegasus seems winning
  The race, he sprains a wing, and down we tend,
Like Lucifer when hurl'd from heaven for sin-
    ning;
  Our sin the same, and hard as his to mend,
Being pride, which leads the mind to soar too far,
Till our own weakness shows us what we are.

II

But time, which brings all beings to their level,
  And sharp Adversity, will teach at last   10
Man,—and, as we would hope,—perhaps the
    devil,
  That neither of their intellects are vast:
While youth's hot wishes in our red veins revel,
  We know not this—the blood flows on too
    fast:
But as the torrent widens towards the ocean,
We ponder deeply on each past emotion.

III

As boy, I thought myself a clever fellow,

And wish'd that others held the same opinion;
They took it up when my days grew more mel-
    low,
  And other minds acknowledged my do-
    minion: 20
Now my sere fancy 'falls into the yellow
  Leaf,'[1] and Imagination droops her pinion,
And the sad truth which hovers o'er my desk
Turns what was once romantic to burlesque.

IV

And if I laugh at any mortal thing,
  'Tis that I may not weep; and if I weep,
'Tis that our nature cannot always bring
  Itself to apathy, for we must steep
Our hearts first in the depths of Lethe's spring,[2]
  Ere what we least wish to behold will sleep: 30
Thetis baptized her mortal son[3] in Styx;
A mortal mother would on Lethe fix.

V

Some have accused me of a strange design
  Against the creed and morals of the land,
And trace it in this poem every line;
  I don't pretend that I quite understand
My own meaning when I would be *very* fine;
  But the fact is that I have nothing plann'd,
Unless it were to be a moment merry,
A novel word in my vocabulary.   40

VI

To the kind reader of our sober clime
  This way of writing will appear exotic;
Pulci[4] was sire of the half-serious rhyme,
  Who sang when chivalry was more Quixotic,
And revell'd in the fancies of the time,
  True knights, chaste dames, huge giant kings
    despotic:
But all these, save the last, being obsolete,
I chose a modern subject as more meet.

VII

How I have treated it, I do not know;
  Perhaps no better than they have treated
    me,   50
Who have imputed such designs as show
  Not what they saw, but what they wish'd to see;
But if it gives them pleasure, be it so,
  This is a liberal age, and thoughts are free:
Meantime Apollo plucks me by the ear,
And tells me to resume my story here.

---

47 Cantabrigians—i.e. those associated with the University of
Cambridge.
48 *Poetics.*

1 *Macbeth*, V, iii, 23.   2 the waters of forgetfulness in Hades.
3 Achilles.
4 Luigi Pulci, 1431–87, an Italian poet, wrote a burlesque epic,
Il Morgante Maggiore.

VIII

Young Juan and his lady-love were left
  To their own hearts' most sweet society;
Even Time the pitiless in sorrow cleft
  With his rude scythe such gentle bosoms;
    he   60
Sigh'd to behold them of their hours bereft,
  Though foe to love; and yet they could not be
Meant to grow old, but die in happy spring,
Before one charm or hope had taken wing.

IX

Their faces were not made for wrinkles, their
  Pure blood to stagnate, their great hearts to
    fail;
The blank grey was not made to blast their hair,
  But like the climes that know nor snow nor
    hail,
They were all summer; lightning might assail
  And shiver them to ashes, but to trail   70
A long and snake-like life of dull decay
Was not for them—they had too little clay.

X

They were alone once more; for them to be
  Thus was another Eden; they were never
Weary, unless when separate: the tree
  Cut from its forest root of years—the river
Damm'd from its fountain—the child from the
    knee
  And breast maternal wean'd at once for ever,—
Would wither less than these two torn apart;
Alas! there is no instinct like the heart—   80

XI

The heart—which may be broken: happy they!
  Thrice fortunate! who of that fragile mould,
The precious porcelain of human clay,
  Break with the first fall: they can ne'er behold
The long year link'd with heavy day on day,
  And all which must be borne, and never told;
While life's strange principle will often lie
Deepest in those who long the most to die.

XII

'Whom the gods love die young' was said of yore,
  And many deaths do they escape by this: 90
The death of friends, and that which slays even
    more—
  The death of friendship, love, youth, all that is,
Except mere breath; and since the silent shore
  Awaits at last even those who longest miss
The old archer's shafts, perhaps the early grave
Which men weep over may be meant to save.

XIII

Haidée and Juan thought not of the dead.
  The heavens, and earth, and air, seem'd made
    for them:
They found no fault with Time, save that he fled;
  They saw not in themselves aught to con-
    demn;   100
Each was the other's mirror, and but read
  Joy sparkling in their dark eyes like a gem,
And knew such brightness was but the reflection
Of their exchanging glances of affection.

XIV

The gentle pressure, and the thrilling touch,
  The least glance better understood than words,
Which still said all, and ne'er could say too
    much;
  A language, too, but like to that of birds,
Known but to them, at least appearing such
  As but to lovers a true sense affords; 110
Sweet playful phrases, which would seem absurd
To those who have ceased to hear such, or ne'er
    heard.

XV

All these were theirs, for they were children still,
  And children still they should have ever been;
They were not made in the real world to fill
  A busy character in the dull scene,
But like two beings born from out a rill,
  A nymph and her beloved, all unseen
To pass their lives in fountains and on flowers,
And never know the weight of human hours. 120

XVI

Moons changing had roll'd on, and changeless
    found
  Those their bright rise had lighted to such joys
As rarely they beheld throughout their round;
  And these were not of the vain kind which
    cloys,
For theirs were buoyant spirits, never bound
  By the mere senses; and that which destroys
Most love, possession, unto them appear'd
A thing which each endearment more endear'd.

XVII

Oh beautiful! and rare as beautiful!
  But theirs was love in which the mind
    delights   130
To lose itself, when the old world grows dull,
  And we are sick of its hack sounds and sights,
Intrigues, adventures of the common school,
  Its petty passions, marriages, and flights,

Where Hymen's torch but brands one strumpet
   more,
Whose husband only knows her not a whore.

XVIII

Hard words; harsh truth; a truth which many
   know.
   Enough.—The faithful and the fairy pair,
Who never found a single hour too slow,
   What was it made them thus exempt from
     care?   140
Young innate feelings all have felt below,
   Which perish in the rest, but in them were
Inherent; what we mortals call romantic,
And always envy, though we deem it frantic.

XIX

This is in others a factitious state,
   An opium dream of too much youth and read-
     ing,
But was in them their nature or their fate:
   No novels e'er had set their young hearts
     bleeding,
For Haidée's knowledge was by no means great,
   And Juan was a boy of saintly breeding;   150
So that there was no reason for their loves
More than for those of nightingales or doves.

XX

They gazed upon the sunset; 'tis an hour
   Dear unto all, but dearest to *their* eyes,
For it had made them what they were: the power
   Of love had first o'erwhelm'd them from such
     skies,
When happiness had been their only dower,
   And twilight saw them link'd in passion's ties;
Charm'd with each other, all things charm'd that
   brought
The past still welcome as the present
     thought.   160

XXI

I know not why, but in that hour to-night,
   Even as they gazed, a sudden tremor came,
And swept, as 'twere, across their hearts' delight,
   Like the wind o'er a harp-string, or a flame,
When one is shook in sound, and one in sight:
   And thus some boding flash'd through either
     frame,
And call'd from Juan's breast a faint low sigh,
While one new tear arose in Haidée's eye.

XXII

That large black prophet eye seem'd to dilate
   And follow far the disappearing sun,   170

As if their last day of a happy date
   With his broad, bright, and dropping orb were
     gone.
Juan gazed on her as to ask his fate—
   He felt a grief, but knowing cause for none,
His glance inquired of hers for some excuse
For feelings causeless, or at least abstruse.

XXIII

She turn'd to him, and smiled, but in that sort
   Which makes not others smile; then turn'd
     aside:
Whatever feeling shook her, it seem'd short,
   And master'd by her wisdom or her pride; 180
When Juan spoke, too—it might be in sport—
   Of this their mutual feeling, she replied—
'If it should be so,—but—it cannot be—
Or I at least shall not survive to see.'

XXIV

Juan would question further, but she press'd
   His lips to hers, and silenced him with this,
And then dismiss'd the omen from her breast,
   Defying augury with that fond kiss;
And no doubt of all methods 'tis the best:
   Some people prefer wine—'tis not amiss; 190
I have tried both; so those who would a part take
May choose between the headache and the heart-
     ache.

XXV

One of the two according to your choice,
   Woman or wine, you'll have to undergo;
Both maladies are taxes on our joys:
   But which to choose, I really hardly know;
And if I had to give a casting voice,
   For both sides I could many reasons show,
And then decide, without great wrong to either,
It were much better to have both than
     neither.   200

XXVI

Juan and Haidée gazed upon each other
   With swimming looks of speechless tenderness,
Which mix'd all feelings, friend, child, lover,
   brother;
   All that the best can mingle and express
When two pure hearts are pour'd in one another,
   And love too much, and yet cannot love less;
But almost sanctify the sweet excess
By the immortal wish and power to bless.

XXVII

Mix'd in each other's arms, and heart in heart,

Why did they not then die?—they had lived
  too long   210
Should an hour come to bid them breathe apart;
  Years could but bring them cruel things or
    wrong;
The world was not for them, nor the world's art
  For beings passionate as Sappho's song;
Love was born *with* them, *in* them, so intense,
It was their very spirit—not a sense.

XXVIII

They should have lived together deep in woods,
  Unseen as sings the nightingale; they were
Unfit to mix in these thick solitudes
  Call'd social, haunts of Hate, and Vice, and
    Care;   220
How lonely every freeborn creature broods!
  The sweetest song-birds nestle in a pair;
The eagle soars alone; the gull and crow
Flock o'er their carrion, just like men below.

XXIX

Now pillow'd cheek to cheek, in loving sleep,
  Haidée and Juan their siesta took,
A gentle slumber, but it was not deep,
  For ever and anon a something shook
Juan, and shuddering o'er his frame would creep;
  And Haidée's sweet lips murmur'd like a
    brook   230
A wordless music, and her face so fair
Stirr'd with her dream, as rose-leaves with the
  air;

XXX

Or as the stirring of a deep clear stream
  Within an Alpine hollow, when the wind
Walks o'er it, was she shaken by the dream,
  The mystical usurper of the mind—
O'erpowering us to be whate'er may seem
  Good to the soul which we no more can bind:
Strange state of being! (for 'tis still to be),
Senseless to feel, and with seal'd eyes to see. 240

XXXI

She dream'd of being alone on the sea-shore,
  Chain'd to a rock; she knew not how, but stir
She could not from the spot, and the loud roar
  Grew, and each wave rose roughly, threaten-
    ing her;
And o'er her upper lip they seem'd to pour,
  Until she sobb'd for breath, and soon they
    were
Foaming o'er her lone head, so fierce and high—
Each broke to drown her, yet she could not die.

XXXII

Anon—she was released, and then she stray'd
  O'er the sharp shingles with her bleeding
    feet,   250
And stumbled almost every step she made;
  And something roll'd before her in a sheet,
Which she must still pursue howe'er afraid:
  'Twas white and indistinct, nor stopp'd to meet
Her glance nor grasp, for still she gazed and
  grasp'd,
And ran, but it escaped her as she clasp'd.

XXXIII

The dream changed:—in a cave she stood, its
  walls
  Were hung with marble icicles; the work
Of ages on its water-fretted halls,
  Where waves might wash, and seals might
    breed and lurk;   260
Her hair was dripping, and the very balls
  Of her black eyes seem'd turn'd to tears, and
    mirk
The sharp rocks look'd below each drop they
  caught,
Which froze to marble as it fell,—she thought.

XXXIV

And wet, and cold, and lifeless at her feet,
  Pale as the foam that froth'd on his dead brow,
Which she essay'd in vain to clear, (how sweet
  Were once her cares, how idle seem'd they
    now!)
Lay Juan, nor could aught renew the beat
  Of his quench'd heart; and the sea dirges
    low   270
Rang in her sad ears like a mermaid's song,
And that brief dream appear'd a life too long.

XXXV

And gazing on the dead, she thought his face
  Faded, or alter'd into something new—
Like to her father's features, till each trace
  More like and like to Lambro's aspect grew—
With all his keen worn look and Grecian grace;
  And starting, she awoke, and what to view?
Oh! Powers of Heaven! what dark eye meets she
  there?
'Tis—'tis her father's—fix'd upon the pair! 280

XXXVI

Then shrieking, she arose, and shrieking fell,
  With joy and sorrow, hope and fear, to see
Him whom she deem'd a habitant where dwell
  The ocean-buried, risen from death, to be

Perchance the death of one she loved too well:
  Dear as her father had been to Haidée,
It was a moment of that awful kind——
I have seen such—but must not call to mind.

XXXVII

Up Juan sprang to Haidée's bitter shriek,
  And caught her falling, and from off the
    wall   290
Snatch'd down his sabre, in hot haste to wreak
  Vengeance on him who was the cause of all:
Then Lambro, who till now forbore to speak,
  Smiled scornfully, and said, 'Within my call,
A thousand scimitars await the word;
Put up, young man, put up your silly sword.'

XXXVIII

And Haidée clung around him; 'Juan, 'tis—
  'Tis Lambro—'tis my father! Kneel with me—
He will forgive us—yes—it must be—yes.
  Oh! dearest father, in this agony   300
Of pleasure and of pain—even while I kiss
  Thy garment's hem with transport, can it be
That doubt should mingle with my filial joy?
Deal with me as thou wilt, but spare this boy.'

XXXIX

High and inscrutable the old man stood,
  Calm in his voice, and calm within his eye—
Not always signs with him of calmest mood;
  He look'd upon her, but gave no reply;
Then turn'd to Juan, in whose cheek the blood
  Oft came and went, as there resolved to
    die;   310
In arms, at least, he stood, in act to spring
On the first foe whom Lambro's call might bring.

XL

'Young man, your sword'; so Lambro once more
    said:
  Juan replied, 'Not while this arm is free.'
The old man's cheek grew pale, but not with
    dread,
  And drawing from his belt a pistol, he
Replied, 'Your blood be then on your own head.'
  Then look'd close at the flint, as if to see
'Twas fresh—for he had lately used the lock—
And next proceeded quietly to cock.   320

XLI

It has a strange quick jar upon the ear,
  That cocking of a pistol, when you know
A moment more will bring the sight to bear
  Upon your person, twelve yards off, or so;
A gentlemanly distance, not too near,

If you have got a former friend for foe;
  But after being fired at once or twice,
The ear becomes more Irish, and less nice.

XLII

Lambro presented, and one instant more
  Had stopp'd this Canto, and Don Juan's
    breath,   330
When Haidée threw herself her boy before;
  Stern as her sire: 'On me,' she cried, 'let death
Descend—the fault is mine; this fatal shore
  He found—but sought not. I have pledged my
    faith;
I love him—I will die with him: I knew
Your nature's firmness—know your daughter's
    too.'

XLIII

A minute past, and she had been all tears,
  And tenderness, and infancy; but now
She stood as one who champion'd human fears—
  Pale, statue-like, and stern, she woo'd the
    blow;   340
And tall beyond her sex, and their compeers,
  She drew up to her height, as if to show
A fairer mark; and with a fix'd eye scann'd
Her father's face—but never stopp'd his hand.

XLIV

He gazed on her, and she on him; 'twas strange
  How like they look'd! the expression was the
    same;
Serenely savage, with a little change
  In the large dark eye's mutual-darted flame;
For she, too, was as one who could avenge,
  If cause should be—a lioness, though
    tame;   350
Her father's blood before her father's face
Boil'd up, and proved her truly of his race.

XLV

I said they were alike, their features and
  Their stature, differing but in sex and years:
Even to the delicacy of their hand
  There was resemblance, such as true blood
    wears;
And now to see them, thus divided, stand
  In fix'd ferocity, when joyous tears,
And sweet sensations, should have welcomed
    both,
Show what the passions are in their full
    growth.   360

XLVI

The father paused a moment, then withdrew

His weapon, and replaced it; but stood still,
And looking on her, as to look her through,
'Not *I,*' he said, 'have sought this stranger's ill;
Not *I* have made this desolation: few
    Would bear such outrage, and forbear to kill;
But I must do my duty—how thou hast
Done thine, the present vouches for the past.

XLVII

'Let him disarm; or, by my father's head,
    His own shall roll before you like a ball!'   370
He raised his whistle as the word he said,
    And blew; another answer'd to the call,
And rushing in disorderly, though led,
    And arm'd from boot to turban, one and all,
Some twenty of his train came, rank on rank;
He gave the word, 'Arrest or slay the Frank.'

XLVIII

Then, with a sudden movement, he withdrew
    His daughter; while compress'd within his
      clasp,
'Twixt her and Juan interposed the crew;
    In vain she struggled in her father's grasp— 380
His arms were like a serpent's coil: then flew
    Upon their prey, as darts an angry asp,
The file of pirates: save the foremost, who
Had fallen, with his right shoulder half cut
    through.

XLIX

The second had his cheek laid open; but
    The third, a wary, cool old sworder, took
The blows upon his cutlass, and then put
    His own well in; so well, ere you could look,
His man was floor'd, and helpless at his foot,
    With the blood running like a little brook 390
From two smart sabre gashes, deep and red—
One on the arm, the other on the head.

L

And then they bound him where he fell, and
    bore
Juan from the apartment: with a sign
Old Lambro bade them take him to the shore,
    Where lay some ships which were to sail at
    nine.
They laid him in a boat, and plied the oar
    Until they reach'd some galliots, placed in line;
On board of one of these, and under hatches,
They stow'd him, with strict orders to the
    watches.   400

LI

The world is full of strange vicissitudes,

And here was one exceedingly unpleasant:
    A gentleman so rich in the world's goods,
    Handsome and young, enjoying all the present,
Just at the very time when he least broods
    On such a thing, is suddenly to sea sent,
Wounded and chain'd, so that he cannot move,
And all because a lady fell in love.

LII

Here I must leave him, for I grow pathetic,
    Moved by the Chinese nymph of tears, green
      tea!   410
Than whom Cassandra was not more prophetic;
    For if my pure libations exceed three,
I feel my heart become so sympathetic,
    That I must have recourse to black Bohea;[5]
'Tis pity wine should be so deleterious,
For tea and coffee leave us much more serious,

LIII

Unless when qualified with thee, Cogniac![6]
    Sweet Naïad[7] of the Phlegethontic[8] rill!
Ah! why the liver wilt thou thus attack,
    And make, like other nymphs, thy lovers
      ill?   420
I would take refuge in weak punch, but *rack*[9]
    (In each sense of the word), whene'er I fill
My mild and midnight beakers to the brim,
Wakes me next morning with its synonym.

LIV

I leave Don Juan for the present, safe—
    Not sound, poor fellow, but severely wounded;
Yet could his corporal pangs amount to half
    Of those with which his Haidée's bosom
      bounded!
She was not one to weep, and rave, and chafe,
    And then give way, subdued because sur-
      rounded;   430
Her mother was a Moorish maid from Fez,
Where all is Eden, or a wilderness.

LV

There the large olive rains its amber store
    In marble fonts; there grain, and flour, and
    fruit,
Gush from the earth until the land runs o'er;
    But there, too, many a poison-tree has root,
And midnight listens to the lion's roar,
    And long, long deserts scorch the camel's foot,

---

5 inferior kind of tea.
6 a French brandy.
7 a water nymph.
8 fiery; from Phlegethon, the river of fire in Hades.
9 Rack, or 'arrack' punch; also a hangover.

Or heaving whelm the helpless caravan;
And as the soil is, so the heart of man.　　440

LVI

Afric is all the sun's, and as her earth
　　Her human clay is kindled; full of power
For good or evil, burning from its birth,
　　The Moorish blood partakes the planet's hour,
And like the soil beneath it will bring forth:
　　Beauty and love were Haidée's mother's
　　　　dower;
But her large dark eye show'd deep Passion's
　　　　force,
Though sleeping like a lion near a source.

LVII

Her daughter, temper'd with a milder ray,
　　Like summer clouds all silvery, smooth, and
　　　　fair,　　450
Till slowly charged with thunder they display
　　Terror to earth, and tempest to the air,
Had held till now her soft and milky way;
　　But overwrought with passion and despair,
The fire burst forth from her Numidian veins,
　　Even as the Simoom[10] sweeps the blasted plains.

LVIII

The last sight which she saw was Juan's gore,
　　And he himself o'ermaster'd and cut down;
His blood was running on the very floor
　　Where late he trod, her beautiful, her own;　460
Thus much she view'd an instant and no more,—
　　Her struggles ceased with one convulsive
　　　　groan;
On her sire's arm, which until now scarce held
Her writhing, fell she like a cedar fell'd.

LIX

A vein had burst, and her sweet lips' pure dyes[11]
　　Were dabbled with the deep blood which ran
　　　　o'er;
And her head droop'd, as when the lily lies
　　O'ercharged with rain: her summon'd hand-
　　　　maids bore

Their lady to her couch with gushing eyes;
　　Of herbs and cordials they produced their
　　　　store,　　470
But she defied all means they could employ,
Like one life could not hold, nor death destroy.

LX

Days lay she in that state unchanged, though
　　　　chill—
　　With nothing livid, still her lips were red;
She had no pulse, but death seem'd absent still;
　　No hideous sign proclaim'd her surely dead;
Corruption came not in each mind to kill
　　All hope; to look upon her sweet face bred
New thoughts of life, for it seem'd full of soul—
She had so much, earth could not claim the
　　　　whole.　　480

LXI

The ruling passion, such as marble shows
　　When exquisitely chisell'd, still lay there,
But fix'd as marble's unchanged aspect throws
　　O'er the fair Venus, but for ever fair;
O'er the Laocoön's[12] all eternal throes,
　　And ever-dying Gladiator's air.[13]
Their energy like life forms all their fame,
Yet looks not life, for they are still the same.

LXII

She woke at length, but not as sleepers wake,
　　Rather the dead, for life seem'd something
　　　　new,　　490
A strange sensation which she must partake
　　Perforce, since whatsoever met her view
Struck not on memory, though a heavy ache
　　Lay at her heart, whose earliest beat still true
Brought back the sense of pain without the
　　　　cause,
For, for a while, the furies made a pause.

LXIII

She look'd on many a face with vacant eye,
　　On many a token without knowing what;
She saw them watch her without asking why,
　　And reck'd not who around her pillow sat;　500
Not speechless, though she spoke not; not a sigh
　　Relieved her thoughts; dull silence and quick
　　　　chat
Were tried in vain by those who served; she gave
No sign, save breath, of having left the grave.

---

10 a hot wind of the desert.
11 This is no very uncommon effect of the violence of conflicting and different passions. The Doge Francis Foscari, on his deposition in 1457, hearing the bells of St. Mark announce the election of his successor, 'mourut subitement d'une hemorragie causée par une veine qui s'éclata dans sa poitrine.' (see Sismondi and Daru vols. i. and ii.) at the age of eighty years, when '*Who would have thought the old man had so much blood in him?*' Before I was six-teen years of age, I was witness to a melancholy instance of the same effect of mixed passions upon a young person, who, how-ever, did not die in consequence, at that time, but fell a victim some years afterwards to a seizure of the same kind, arising from causes intimately connected with agitation of mind.—(Byron.)

---

12 a sculptured group in the Vatican, Rome, shows Laocoön, with his two sons, being destroyed by two serpents.
13 See *Childe Harold*, IV, note 43 (text, p. 824).

LXIV

Her handmaids tended, but she heeded not;
  Her father watch'd, she turn'd her eyes away;
She recognised no being, and no spot,
  However dear or cherish'd in their day;
They changed from room to room, but all forgot,
  Gentle, but without memory she lay;   510
At length those eyes, which they would fain be weaning
Back to old thoughts, wax'd full of fearful meaning.

LXV

And then a slave bethought her of a harp;
  The harper came, and tuned his instrument;
At the first notes, irregular and sharp,
  On him her flashing eyes a moment bent,
Then to the wall she turn'd as if to warp
  Her thoughts from sorrow through her heart re-sent;
And he began a long low island song
Of ancient days, ere tyranny grew strong.   520

LXVI

Anon her thin wan fingers beat the wall
  In time to his old tune; he changed the theme,
And sung of love; the fierce name struck through all
  Her recollection; on her flash'd the dream
Of what she was, and is, if ye could call
  To be so being; in a gushing stream
The tears rush'd forth from her o'erclouded brain,
Like mountain mists at length dissolved in rain.

LXVII

Short solace, vain relief!—thought came too quick,
  And whirl'd her brain to madness; she arose   530
As one who ne'er had dwelt among the sick,
  And flew at all she met, as on her foes;
But no one ever heard her speak or shriek,
  Although her paroxysm drew towards its close;—
Hers was a phrensy which disdain'd to rave,
Even when they smote her, in the hope to save.

LXVIII

Yet she betray'd at times a gleam of sense;
  Nothing could make her meet her father's face,
Though on all other things with looks intense
  She gazed, but none she ever could retrace;   540
Food she refused, and raiment; no pretence
  Avail'd for either; neither change of place,
Nor time, nor skill, nor remedy, could give her
Senses to sleep—the power seem'd gone for ever.

LXIX

Twelve days and nights she wither'd thus; at last,
  Without a groan, or sigh, or glance, to show
A parting pang, the spirit from her passed:
  And they who watch'd her nearest could not know
The very instant, till the change that cast
  Her sweet face into shadow, dull and slow,   550
Glazed o'er her eyes—the beautiful, the black—
Oh! to possess such lustre—and then lack!

LXX

She died, but not alone; she held within
  A second principle of life, which might
Have dawn'd a fair and sinless child of sin;
  But closed its little being without light,
And went down to the grave unborn, wherein
  Blossom and bough lie wither'd with one blight;
In vain the dews of Heaven descend above
The bleeding flower and blasted fruit of love.   560

LXXI

Thus lived—thus died she; never more on her
  Shall sorrow light, or shame. She was not made
Through years or moons the inner weight to bear,
  Which colder hearts endure till they are laid
By age in earth: her days and pleasures were
  Brief, but delightful—such as had not stayed
Long with her destiny; but she sleeps well
By the sea-shore, whereon she loved to dwell.

LXXII

That isle is now all desolate and bare,
  Its dwellings down, its tenants pass'd away;   570
None but her own and father's grave is there,
  And nothing outward tells of human clay;
Ye could not know where lies a thing so fair,
  No stone is there to show, no tongue to say,
What was; no dirge, except the hollow sea's,
Mourns o'er the beauty of the Cyclades.

LXXIII

But many a Greek maid in a loving song

Sighs o'er her name; and many an islander
With her sire's story makes the night less long;
Valour was his, and beauty dwelt with her; 580
If she loved rashly, her life paid for wrong—
A heavy price must all pay who thus err,
In some shape; let none think to fly the danger,
For soon or late Love is his own avenger.

1819–20   1821

WHEN A MAN HATH NO FREEDOM TO FIGHT FOR AT HOME

WHEN a man hath no freedom to fight for at
   home,
  Let him combat for that of his neighbours;
Let him think of the glories of Greece and of
   Rome,
  And get knock'd on the head for his labours.
To do good to mankind is the chivalrous plan,
  And is always as nobly requited;
Then battle for freedom wherever you can,
  And, if not shot or hang'd, you'll get knighted.

1820   1824

WHO KILL'D JOHN KEATS?

WHO kill'd John Keats?
  'I,' says the Quarterly,
  So savage and Tartarly;
  ' 'Twas one of my feats.'

Who shot the arrow?[1]
  'The poet-priest Milman
  (So ready to kill man),
  Or Southey, or Barrow.'

1821   1830

THE WORLD IS A BUNDLE OF HAY

THE world is a bundle of hay,
  Mankind are the asses who pull;
Each tugs it a different way,
  And the greatest of all is John Bull.

1821   1830

---

1 The anonymous *Quarterly* article (supposed by many, including Shelley, to have killed Keats) was written by J. W. Croker, text p. 727. Henry H. Milman, 1791–1868, was Professor of Poetry at Oxford; John Barrow, 1764–1848, an English writer and traveler.

THE VISION OF JUDGMENT

BY

QUEVEDO[1] REDIVIVUS[2]

SUGGESTED BY THE COMPOSITION SO ENTITLED
BY THE AUTHOR OF 'WAT TYLER.'[3]

*'A Daniel come to judgment! yea, a Daniel!
I thank thee, Jew, for teaching me that word.'*[4]

[In *The Vision of Judgment,* which is a parody, point by point, of Southey's inflated and banal tribute to George III, Byron is at the height of his powers. The splendor, variety, and brilliant buffoonery of this travesty place it among the imperishable political satires in the language.]

PREFACE

It hath been wisely said, that 'One fool makes many;' and it hath been poetically observed—

'[That] fools rush in where angels fear to tread.'[5]

If Mr. Southey had not rushed in where he had no business, and where he never was before, and never will be again, the following poem would not have been written. It is not impossible that it may be as good as his own, seeing that it cannot, by any species of stupidity, natural or acquired, be *worse*. The gross flattery, the dull impudence, the renegado intolerance, and impious cant, of the poem by the author of 'Wat Tyler,' are something so stupendous as to form the sublime of himself—containing the quintessence of his own attributes.[6]

So much for his poem—a word on his preface. In this preface it has pleased the magnanimous Laureate to draw the picture of a supposed 'Satanic School,' the which he doth recommend to the notice of the legislature; thereby adding to his other laurels the ambition of those of an informer. If there exists anywhere, except in his imagination, such a School, is he not sufficiently armed against it by his own intense vanity? The truth is that there are certain writers whom Mr. S. imagines, like Scrub, to have 'talked of *him;* for they laughed consumedly.'[7]

I think I know enough of most of the writers to whom he is supposed to allude, to assert, that they, in their individual capacities, have done more good, in the charities of life, to their fellow-creatures, in any one year, than Mr. Southey has done harm to himself by his absurdities

---

1 Spanish humorist of the seventeenth century who wrote a satire called *Visions.*
2 alive again; brought back to life.
3 a revolutionary play by Southey written in his youth when he was a republican. Years later after he had become a complete conservative it was published much to his embarrassment.
4 *Merchant of Venice,* IV, i, 340, 341.
5 Pope's *Essay on Criticism.*
6 When George III died, in 1820, Southey as poet Laureate in duty bound had praised his virtues in *A Vision of Judgement,* text p. 472. In his Preface he went out of his way to denounce Byron as the founder of the 'Satanic school' of English poetry. Byron retorted with his own *Vision.*
7 Farquhar, *The Beaux' Stratagem,* III, ii.

in his whole life; and this is saying a great deal. But I have a few questions to ask.

1stly, is Mr. Southey the author of *Wat Tyler?*

2ndly, Was he not refused a remedy at law by the highest judge of his beloved England, because it was a blasphemous and seditious publication?

3rdly. Was he not entitled by William Smith,[8] in full parliament, 'a rancorous renegade'?

4thly, Is he not poet laureate, with his own lines on Martin the regicide staring him in the face?

And, 5thly, Putting the four preceding items together; with what conscience dare *he* call the attention of the laws to the publications of others, be they what they may?

I say nothing of the cowardice of such a proceeding, its meanness speaks for itself; but I wish to touch upon the *motive,* which is neither more nor less than that Mr. S. has been laughed at a little in some recent publications, as he was of yore in the *Antijacobin,*[9] by his present patrons. Hence all this 'skimble-scamble stuff' about 'Satanic,' and so forth. However, it is worthy of him— '*qualis ab incepto.*'

If there is anything obnoxious to the political opinions of a portion of the public in the following poem, they may thank Mr. Southey. He might have written hexameters, as he has written everything else, for aught that the writer cared—had they been upon another subject. But to attempt to canonise a monarch, who, whatever were his household virtues, was neither a successful nor a patriot king,—inasmuch as several years of his reign passed in war with America and Ireland, to say nothing of the aggression upon France,—like all other exaggeration, necessarily begets opposition. In whatever manner he may be spoken of in this new *Vision,* his *public* career will not be more favourably transmitted by history. Of his private virtues (although a little expensive to the nation) there can be no doubt.

With regard to the supernatural personages treated of, I can only say that I know as much about them, and (as an honest man) have a better right to talk of them than Robert Southey. I have also treated them more tolerantly. The way in which that poor insane creature, the Laureate, deals about his judgments in the next world, is like his own judgment in this. If it was not completely ludicrous, it would be something worse. I don't think that there is much more to say at present.

Quevedo Redivivus.

I

Saint Peter sat by the celestial gate:
　His keys were rusty, and the lock was dull,
So little trouble had been given of late;
　Not that the place by any means was full,
But since the Gallic era 'eighty-eight'[10]
　The devils had ta'en a longer, stronger pull,
And 'a pull altogether,' as they say
At sea—which drew most souls another way.

II

The angels all were singing out of tune,
　And hoarse with having little else to do,   10
Excepting to wind up the sun and moon,
　Or curb a runaway young star or two,
Or wild colt of a comet, which too soon
　Broke out of bounds o'er th' ethereal blue,
Splitting some planet with its playful tail,
As boats are sometimes by a wanton whale.

III

The guardian seraphs had retired on high,
　Finding their charges past all care below;
Terrestrial business fill'd nought in the sky
　Save the recording angel's black bureau;   20
Who found, indeed, the facts to multiply
　With such rapidity of vice and woe,
That he had stripp'd off both his wings in quills,
And yet was in arrear of human ills.

IV

His business so augmented of late years,
　That he was forced, against his will no doubt,
(Just like those cherubs, earthly ministers,)
　For some resource to turn himself about,
And claim the help of his celestial peers,
　To aid him ere he should be quite worn out   30
By the increased demand for his remarks:
Six angels and twelve saints were named his clerks.

V

This was a handsome board—at least for heaven;
　And yet they had even then enough to do,
So many conquerors' cars were daily driven,
　So many kingdoms fitted up anew;
Each day too slew its thousands six or seven,
　Till at the crowning carnage, Waterloo,
They threw their pens down in divine disgust—
The page was so besmear'd with blood and dust.   40

VI

This by the way; 'tis not mine to record
　What angels shrink from: even the very devil
On this occasion his own work, abhorr'd,
　So surfeited with the infernal revel:
Though he himself had sharpen'd every sword,
　It almost quench'd his innate thirst of evil.
(Here Satan's sole good work deserves insertion—
'Tis, that he has both generals[11] in reversion.)[12]

8 M. P. for Norwich, who attacked Southey in the House of Commons.
9 a periodical established to satirize radicalism.
10 1788 marked the last year of the *ancien régime.* The French Revolution broke out in 1789.
11 Napoleon and Wellington.
12 legally his by right of future possession.

VII

Let's skip a few short years of hollow peace,
  Which peopled earth no better, hell as
     wont,   50
And heaven none—they form the tyrant's lease,
  With nothing but new names subscribed
    upon't;
'Twill one day finish: meantime they increase,
  'With seven heads and ten horns,' and all in
    front,
Like Saint John's foretold beast;[13] but ours are
    born
Less formidable in the head than horn.

VIII

In the first year of freedom's second dawn[14]
  Died George the Third; although no tyrant,
    one
Who shielded tyrants, till each sense withdrawn
  Left him nor mental nor external sun: 60
A better farmer ne'er brush'd dew from lawn,
  A worse king never left a realm undone!
He died—but left his subjects still behind,
One half as mad—and t'other no less blind.

IX

He died! his death made no great stir on earth:
  His burial made some pomp; there was profu-
    sion
Of velvet, gilding, brass, and no great dearth
  Of aught but tears—save those shed by collu-
    sion.
For these things may be bought at their true
    worth;
  Of elegy there was the due infusion—   70
Bought also; and the torches, cloaks, and ban-
    ners,
Heralds, and relics of old Gothic manners,

X

Form'd a sepulchral melodrame. Of all
  The fools who flock'd to swell or see the
    show,
Who cared about the corpse? The funeral
  Made the attraction, and the black the woe.
There throbb'd not there a thought which pierced
    the pall;
  And when the gorgeous coffin was laid low,
It seem'd the mockery of hell to fold
The rottenness of eighty years in gold.   80

XI

So mix his body with the dust! It might
  Return to what it *must* far sooner, were
The natural compound left alone to fight
  Its way back into earth, and fire, and air;
But the unnatural balsams merely blight
  What nature made him at his birth, as bare
As the mere million's base unmummied clay—
Yet all his spices but prolong decay.

XII

He's dead—and upper earth with him has done;
  He's buried; save the undertaker's bill,   90
Or lapidary scrawl,[15] the world is gone
  For him, unless he left a German will;[16]
But where's the proctor[17] who will ask his son?
  In whom his qualities are reigning still,
Except that household virtue, most uncommon,
Of constancy to a bad, ugly woman.

XIII

'God save the king!' It is a large economy
  In God to save the like; but if he will
Be saving, all the better; for not one am I
  Of those who think damnation better still: 100
I hardly know too if not quite alone am I
  In this small hope of bettering future ill
By circumscribing, with some slight restriction,
The eternity of hell's hot jurisdiction.

XIV

I know this is unpopular; I know
  'Tis blasphemous; I know one may be damn'd
For hoping no one else may e'er be so;
  I know my catechism; I know we're cramm'd
With the best doctrines till we quite o'erflow;
  I know that all save England's church have
    shamm'd,   110
And that the other twice two hundred churches
And synagogues have made a *damn'd* bad pur-
    chase.

XV

God help us all! God help me too! I am,
  God knows, as helpless as the devil can wish,
And not a whit more difficult to damn,
  Than is to bring to land a late-hook'd fish,
Or to the butcher to purvey the lamb;
  Not that I'm fit for such a noble dish,

---

13 See Revelation, xiii.
14 The year 1820 was signalized by liberal uprisings all over
southern Europe.
15 inscription on a tombstone,
16 an allusion to the report that the late king's grandfather,
George II, of German extraction, had hidden and ignored his
father's will.
17 a law officer of the court.

As one day will be that immortal fry
Of almost everybody born to die.   120

XVI

Saint Peter sat by the celestial gate,
   And nodded o'er his keys; when, lo! there came
A wondrous noise he had not heard of late—
   A rushing sound of wind, and stream, and flame;
In short, a roar of things extremely great,
   Which would have made aught save a saint exclaim;
But he, with first a start and then a wink,
Said, 'There's another star gone out, I think!'

XVII

But ere he could return to his repose,
   A cherub flapp'd his right wing o'er his eyes—   130
At which St. Peter yawn'd, and rubb'd his nose:
   'Saint porter,' said the angel, 'prithee rise!'
Waving a goodly wing, which glow'd, as glows
   An earthly peacock's tail, with heavenly dyes:
To which the saint replied, 'Well, what's the matter?
'Is Lucifer come back with all this clatter?'

XVIII

'No,' quoth the cherub; 'George the Third is dead.'
   'And who *is* George the Third?' replied the apostle:
'*What George? what Third?*' 'The king of England,' said
   The angel. 'Well! he won't find kings to jostle   140
Him on his way; but does he wear his head?
   Because the last we saw here had a tustle,
And ne'er would have got into heaven's good graces,
Had he not flung his head in all our faces.

XIX

'He was, if I remember, king of France;[18]
   That head of his, which could not keep a crown
On earth, yet ventured in my face to advance
   A claim to those of martyrs—like my own:
If I had had my sword, as I had once
   When I cut ears off, I had cut him down;   150
But having but my *keys,* and not my brand,
I only knock'd his head from out his hand.

XX

'And then he set up such a headless howl,
   That all the saints came out and took him in;
And there he sits by St. Paul, cheek by jowl;
   That fellow Paul—the parvenù! The skin
Of St. Bartholomew,[19] which makes his cowl
   In heaven, and upon earth redeem'd his sin,
So as to make a martyr, never sped
Better than did this weak and wooden head.   160

XXI

'But had it come up here upon its shoulders,
   There would have been a different tale to tell:
The fellow-feeling in the saint's beholders
   Seems to have acted on them like a spell,
And so this very foolish head heaven solders
   Back on its trunk: it may be very well,
And seems the custom here to overthrow
Whatever has been wisely done below.'

XXII

The angel answer'd, 'Peter! do not pout:
   The king who comes has head and all entire,   170
And never knew much what it was about—
   He did as doth the puppet—by its wire,
And will be judged like all the rest, no doubt:
   My business and your own is not to inquire
Into such matters, but to mind our cue—
Which is to act as we are bid to do.'

XXIII

While thus they spake, the angelic caravan,
   Arriving like a rush of mighty wind,
Cleaving the fields of space, as doth the swan
   Some silver stream (say Ganges, Nile, or Inde,   180
Or Thames, or Tweed), and 'midst them an old man
   With an old soul, and both extremely blind,
Halted before the gate, and in his shroud
Seated their fellow traveller on a cloud.

XXIV

But bringing up the rear of this bright host
   A Spirit of a different aspect waved
His wings, like thunder-clouds above some coast
   Whose barren beach with frequent wrecks is paved;
His brow was like the deep when tempest-toss'd;
   Fierce and unfathomable thoughts engraved   190

---

18 Louis XVI, guillotined in January 1793.

19 one of the twelve apostles who, according to tradition, was flayed alive before being crucified.

Eternal wrath on his immortal face,
And *where* he gazed a gloom pervaded space.

XXV

As he drew near, he gazed upon the gate
   Ne'er to be enter'd more by him or Sin,
With such a glance of supernatural hate,
   As made Saint Peter wish himself within;
He patter'd with his keys at a great rate,
   And sweated through his apostolic skin:
Of course his perspiration was but ichor,[20]
Or some such other spiritual liquor.   200

XXVI

The very cherubs huddled all together,
   Like birds when soars the falcon; and they felt
A tingling to the tip of every feather,
   And form'd a circle like Orion's belt
Around their poor old charge; who scarce knew
      whither
   His guards had led him, though they gently
      dealt
With royal manes (for by many stories,
And true, we learn the angels all are Tories)

XXVII

As things were in this posture, the gate flew
   Asunder, and the flashing of its hinges   210
Flung over space an universal hue
   Of many-colour'd flame, until its tinges
Reach'd even our speck of earth, and made a new
   Aurora borealis spread its fringes
O'er the North Pole; the same seen, when ice-
      bound,
By Captain Parry's crew, in 'Melville's Sound.'[21]

XXVIII

And from the gate thrown open issued beaming
   A beautiful and mighty Thing of Light,
Radiant with glory, like a banner streaming
   Victorious from some world-o'erthrowing
      fight: 220
My poor comparisons must needs be teeming
   With earthly likenesses, for here the night
Of clay obscures our best conceptions, saving
Johanna Southcote,[22] or Bob Southey raving.

XXIX

'Twas the archangel Michael; all men know
   The make of angels and archangels, since

---

20 fluid that flowed in the veins of the gods.
21 described by Sir Edward Parry in his *Voyage in 1819–20*. Melville Sound is in northwestern Greenland.
22 a religious fanatic who prophesied that she would give birth to a second Messiah.

There's scarce a scribbler has not one to show,
   From the fiends' leader to the angels' prince;
There also are some altar-pieces, though
   I really can't say that they much evince   230
One's inner notions of immortal spirits;
But let the connoisseurs explain *their* merits.

XXX

Michael flew forth in glory and in good;
   A goodly work of him from whom all glory
And good arise; the portal past—he stood;
   Before him the young cherubs and saints
      hoary—
(I say *young*, begging to be understood
   By looks, not years; and should be very sorry
To state, they were not older than St. Peter,
But merely that they seem'd a little sweeter). 240

XXXI

The cherubs and the saints bow'd down before
   That arch-angelic hierarch, the first
Of essences angelical, who wore
   The aspect of a god; but this ne'er nursed
Pride in his heavenly bosom, in whose core
   No thought, save for his Master's service,
      durst
Intrude, however glorified and high;
He knew him but the viceroy of the sky.

XXXII

He and the sombre, silent Spirit met—
   They knew each other both for good and
      ill;   250
Such was their power, that neither could for-
      get
   His former friend and future foe; but still
There was a high, immortal, proud regret
   In either's eye, as if 'twere less their will
Than destiny to make the eternal years
Their date of war, and their 'champ clos'[23] the
      spheres.

XXXIII

But here they were in neutral space: we know
   From Job, that Satan hath the power to pay
A heavenly visit thrice a year or so;
   And that the 'sons of God,' like those of
      clay,   260
Must keep him company; and we might show
   From the same book, in how polite a way
The dialogue is held between the Powers
Of Good and Evil—but 'twould take up hours.

---

23 enclosed field for combat.

XXXIV

And this is not a theologic tract,
   To prove with Hebrew and with Arabic,
If Job be allegory or a fact,
   But a true narrative; and thus I pick
From out the whole but such and such an act
   As sets aside the slightest thought of trick.   270
'Tis every tittle true, beyond suspicion,
And accurate as any other vision.

XXXV

The spirits were in neutral space, before
   The gate of heaven; like eastern thresholds is
The place where Death's grand cause is argued
     o'er,[24]
   And souls despatch'd to that world or to this;
And therefore Michael and the other wore
   A civil aspect: though they did not kiss,
Yet still between his Darkness and his Brightness
There pass'd a mutual glance of great polite-
     ness.   280

XXXVI

The Archangel bow'd, not like a modern beau,
   But with a graceful Oriental bend,
Pressing one radiant arm just where below
   The heart in good men is supposed to tend;
He turn'd as to an equal, not too low,
   But kindly; Satan met his ancient friend
With more hauteur, as might an old Castilian
Poor noble meet a mushroom rich civilian.

XXXVII

He merely bent his diabolic brow
   An instant; and then raising it, he stood   290
In act to assert his right or wrong, and show
   Cause why King George by no means could or
     should
Make out a case to be exempt from woe
   Eternal, more than other kings, endued
With better sense and hearts, whom history
     mentions,
Who long have 'paved hell with their good inten-
     tions.'

XXXVIII

Michael began: 'What wouldst thou with this
     man,
   Now dead, and brought before the Lord? What
     ill
Hath he wrought since his mortal race began,

That thou canst claim him? Speak! and do thy
     will,   300
If it be just: if in this earthly span
   He hath been greatly failing to fulfil
His duties as a king and mortal, say,
And he is thine; if not, let him have way.'

XXXIX

'Michael!' replied the Prince of Air, 'even here,
   Before the Gate of him thou servest, must
I claim my subject: and will make appear
   That as he was my worshipper in dust,
So shall he be in spirit, although dear
   To thee and thine, because nor wine nor
     lust   310
Were of his weaknesses; yet on the throne
He reign'd o'er millions to serve me alone.

XL

'Look to *our* earth, or rather *mine;* it was,
   Once, more thy master's: but I triumph not
In this poor planet's conquest; nor, alas!
   Need he thou servest envy me my lot:
With all the myriads of bright worlds which pass
   In worship round him, he may have forgot
Yon weak creation of such paltry things:
I think few worth damnation save their
     kings,—
                             320

XLI

'And these but as a kind of quit-rent,[25] to
   Assert my right as lord: and even had
I such an inclination, 'twere (as you
   Well know) superfluous; they are grown so
     bad,
That hell has nothing better left to do
   Than leave them to themselves: so much more
     mad
And evil by their own internal curse,
Heaven cannot make them better, nor I worse.

XLII

'Look to the earth, I said, and say again:
   When this old, blind, mad, helpless, weak, poor
     worm
                             330
Began in youth's first bloom and flush to reign,[26]
   The world and he both wore a different form,
And much of earth and all the watery plain
   Of ocean call'd him king: through many a
     storm
His isles had floated on the abyss of time;
For the rough virtues chose them for their clime.

---

24 the gateways of Near Eastern cities were often used for public gatherings and the administration of justice.

25 a fixed rent paid by a tenant to his feudal lord.
26 George III ascended the throne in 1760 and ruled for sixty
years. During a considerable portion of this time he was insane.

XLIII

'He came to his sceptre young; he leaves it old:
    Look to the state in which he found his realm,
And left it; and his annals too behold,
    How to a minion first he gave the helm;[27]   340
How grew upon his heart a thirst for gold,
    The beggar's vice, which can but overwhelm
The meanest hearts; and for the rest, but glance
Thine eye along America and France.

XLIV

' 'Tis true, he was a tool from first to last
    (I have the workmen safe); but as a tool
So let him be consumed. From out the past
    Of ages, since mankind have known the rule
Of monarchs—from the bloody rolls amass'd
    Of sin and slaughter—from the Cæsar's
        school,   350
Take the worst pupil; and produce a reign
More drench'd with gore, more cumber'd with
        the slain.

XLV

'He ever warr'd with freedom and the free:
    Nations as men, home subjects, foreign foes,
So that they utter'd the word "Liberty!"
    Found George the Third their first opponent.
        Whose
History was ever stain'd as his will be
    With national and individual woes?
I grant his household abstinence; I grant
His neutral virtues, which most monarchs
        want;   360

XLVI

'I know he was a constant consort; own
    He was a decent sire, and middling lord,
All this is much, and most upon a throne;
    As temperance, if at Apicius'[28] board,
Is more than at an anchorite's supper shown.
    I grant him all the kindest can accord;
And this was well for him, but not for those
Millions who found him what oppression chose.

XLVII

'The New World shook him off; the Old yet
        groans
    Beneath what he and his prepared, if not   370
Completed: he leaves heirs on many thrones
    To all his vices, without what begot
Compassion for him—his tame virtues; drones

Who sleep, or despots who have now forgot
A lesson which shall be re-taught them, wake
Upon the thrones of earth; but let them quake!

XLVIII

'Five millions of the primitive,[29] who hold
    The faith which makes ye great on earth, im-
        plored
A *part* of that vast *all* they held of old,—
    Freedom to worship—not alone your
        Lord,   380
Michael, but you, and you, Saint Peter! Cold
    Must be your souls, if you have not abhorr'd
The foe to Catholic participation[30]
In all the license of a Christian nation.

XLIX

'True! he allow'd them to pray God; but as
    A consequence of prayer, refused the law
Which would have placed them upon the same
        base
    With those who did not hold the saints in awe.'
But here Saint Peter started from his place,
    And cried, 'You may the prisoner with-
        draw: 390
Ere heaven shall ope her portals to this Guelph,[31]
While I am guard, may I be damn'd myself!

L

'Sooner will I with Cerberus[32] exchange
    My office (and *his* is no sinecure)
Than see this royal Bedlam[33] bigot range
    The azure fields of heaven, of that be sure!'
'Saint!' replied Satan, 'you do well to avenge
    The wrongs he made your satellites endure;
And if to this exchange you should be given,
I'll try to coax *our* Cerberus up to heaven!'   400

LI

Here Michael interposed: 'Good saint! and devil!
    Pray, not so fast; you both outrun discretion.
Saint Peter! you were wont to be more civil!
    Satan! excuse this warmth of his expression,
And condescension to the vulgar's level:
    Even saints sometimes forget themselves in
        session.
Have you got more to say?'—'No.'—'If you
        please,
I'll trouble you to call your witnesses.'

27 Lord Bute, unpopular prime minister who was influential with
young George III.
28 a famous Roman epicure of the time of Augustus.
29 Catholics, who had been denied certain civil rights under a
settlement dating from Elizabeth.
30 George III opposed Catholic Emancipation.
31 Anti-Catholic.
32 three-headed watchdog, guardian of the entrance to Hades.
33 a London hospital for the insane—hence, any lunatic asylum.

LII

Then Satan turn'd and waved his swarthy hand,
   Which stirr'd with its electric qualities   410
Clouds farther off than we can understand,
   Although we find him sometimes in our skies;
Infernal thunder shook both sea and land
   In all the planets, and hell's batteries
Let off the artillery, which Milton mentions
As one of Satan's most sublime inventions.

LIII

This was a signal unto such damn'd souls
   As have the privilege of their damnation
Extended far beyond the mere controls
   Of worlds past, present, or to come; no
      station   420
Is theirs particularly in the rolls
   Of hell assign'd; but where their inclination
Or business carries them in search of game,
They may range freely—being damn'd the same.

LIV

They're proud of this—as very well they may,
   It being a sort of knighthood, or gilt key,[34]
Stuck in their loins; or like to an 'entré'
   Up the back stairs, or such freemasonry,
I borrow my comparisons from clay,
   Being clay myself. Let not those spirits be 430
Offended with such base low likenesses;
We know their posts are nobler far than these.

LV

When the great signal ran from heaven to hell—
   About ten million times the distance reckon'd
From our sun to its earth, as we can tell
   How much time it takes up, even to a second,
For every ray that travels to dispel
   The fogs of London, through which, dimly bea-
      con'd,
The weathercocks are gilt some thrice a year,
If that the *summer* is not too severe: 440

LVI

I say that I can tell—'twas half a minute;
   I know the solar beams take up more time
Ere, pack'd up for their journey, they begin it;
   But then their telegraph is less sublime,
And if they ran a race, they would not win it
   'Gainst Satan's couriers bound for their own
      clime.
The sun takes up some years for every ray
To reach its goal—the devil not half a day.

LVII

Upon the verge of space, about the size
   Of half-a-crown, a little speck appear'd   450
(I've seen a something like it in the skies
   In the Ægean, ere a squall); it near'd,
And, growing bigger, took another guise;
   Like an aërial ship it tack'd, and steer'd,
Or *was* steer'd (I am doubtful of the grammar
Of the last phrase, which makes the stanza stam-
      mer;—

LVIII

But take your choice): and then it grew a cloud;
   And so it was—a cloud of witnesses.
But such a cloud! No land e'er saw a crowd
   Of locusts numerous as the heavens saw
      these;   460
They shadow'd with their myriads space; their
      loud
   And varied cries were like those of wild geese
(If nations may be liken'd to a goose),
And realised the phrase of 'hell broke loose.'

LIX

Here crash'd a sturdy oath of stout John Bull,
   Who damn'd away his eyes as heretofore:
There Paddy brogued 'By Jasus!'—'What's your
      wull?'
   The temperate Scot exclaim'd: the French
      ghost swore
In certain terms I shan't translate in full,
   As the first coachman will; and 'midst the
      war,   470
The voice of Jonathan[35] was heard to express,
'*Our* president is going to war, I guess.'

LX

Besides there were the Spaniard, Dutch, and
      Dane;
   In short, an universal shoal of shades,
From Otaheite's isle to Salisbury Plain,
   Of all climes and professions, years and trades,
Ready to swear against the good king's reign,
   Bitter as clubs in cards are against spades:
All summon'd by this grand 'subpœna,' to
Try if kings mayn't be damn'd like me or you. 480

LXI

When Michael saw this host, he first grew pale,
   As angels can; next, like Italian twilight,
He turn'd all colours—as a peacock's tail,
   Or sunset streaming through a Gothic skylight
In some old abbey, or a trout not stale,

---

34 insignia of the Lord Chamberlain and of other court officials.

35 representing the typical American.

Or distant lightning on the horizon *by* night,
Or a fresh rainbow, or a grand review
Of thirty regiments in red, green, and blue.

LXII

Then he address'd himself to Satan: 'Why—
  My good old friend, for such I deem you,
    though   490
Our different parties make us fight so shy,
  I ne'er mistake you for a *personal* foe;
Our difference is *political,* and I
  Trust that, whatever may occur below,
You know my great respect for you: and this
Makes me regret whate'er you do amiss—

LXIII

'Why, my dear Lucifer, would you abuse
  My call for witnesses? I did not mean
That you should half of earth and hell produce;
  'Tis even superfluous, since two honest,
    clean,   500
True testimonies are enough: we lose
  Our time, nay, our eternity, between
The accusation and defence: if we
Hear both, 'twill stretch our immortality.'

LXIV

Satan replied, 'To me the matter is
  Indifferent, in a personal point of view:
I can have fifty better souls than this
  With far less trouble than we have gone
    through
Already; and I merely argued his
  Late majesty of Britain's case with you   510
Upon a point of form: you may dispose
Of him; I've kings enough below, God knows!'

LXV

Thus spoke the Demon (late call'd 'multi-faced'
  By multo-scribbling Southey). 'Then we'll call
One or two persons of the myriads placed
  Around our congress, and dispense with all
The rest,' quoth Michael: 'Who may be so graced
  As to speak first? there's choice enough—who
    shall
It be?' Then Satan answer'd, 'There are many;
But you may choose Jack Wilkes[36] as well as
    any.'   520

LXVI

A merry, cock-eyed, curious-looking sprite
  Upon the instant started from the throng,
Dress'd in a fashion now forgotten quite;

For all the fashions of the flesh stick long
By people in the next world; where unite
  All the costumes since Adam's, right or wrong,
From Eve's fig-leaf down to the petticoat,
Almost as scanty, of days less remote.

LXVII

The spirit look'd around upon the crowds
  Assembled, and exclaim'd, 'My friends of
    all   530
The spheres, we shall catch cold amongst these
    clouds;
  So let's to business: why this general call?
If those are freeholders I see in shrouds,
  And 'tis for an election that they bawl,
Behold a candidate with unturn'd coat!
Saint Peter, may I count upon your vote?'

LXVIII

'Sir,' replied Michael, 'you mistake; these things
  Are of a former life, and what we do
Above is more august; to judge of kings
  Is the tribunal met: so now you know.'   540
'Then I presume those gentlemen with wings,'
  Said Wilkes, 'are cherubs; and that soul be-
    low
Looks much like George the Third, but to my
    mind
A good deal older—Bless me! is he blind?'

LXIX

'He is what you behold him, and his doom
  Depends upon his deeds,' the Angel said;
'If you have aught to arraign in him, the tomb
  Gives licence to the humblest beggar's head
To lift itself against the loftiest.'—'Some,'
  Said Wilkes, 'don't wait to see them laid in
    lead,   550
For such a liberty—and I, for one,
Have told them what I thought beneath the
    sun.'

LXX

'*Above* the sun repeat, then, what thou hast
  To urge against him,' said the Archangel.
    'Why,'
Replied the spirit, 'since old scores are past,
  Must I turn evidence? In faith, not I.
Besides, I beat him hollow[37] at the last,
  With all his Lords and Commons: in the sky
I don't like ripping up old stories, since
His conduct was but natural in a prince.   560

---

36 John Wilkes, 1727–97, turbulent publicist and politician, who
headed the opposition to George III and the Tories.

37 Wilkes, who had several times been expelled from parliament,
succeeded finally in having all orders of his expulsion stricken
from the record.

LXXI

'Foolish, no doubt, and wicked, to oppress
    A poor unlucky devil without a shilling;
But then I blame the man himself much less
    Than Bute and Grafton,[38] and shall be unwill-
        ing
To see him punish'd here for their excess,
    Since they were both damn'd long ago, and still
        in
Their place below: for me, I have forgiven,
And vote his "habeas corpus" into heaven.'

LXXII

'Wilkes,' said the Devil, 'I understand all this;
    You turn'd to half a courtier ere you died,   570
And seem to think it would not be amiss
    To grow a whole one on the other side
Of Charon's ferry; you forget that *his*
    Reign is concluded; whatsoe'er betide,
He won't be sovereign more: you've lost your la-
        bour,
For at the best he will but be your neighbour.

LXXIII

'However, I knew what to think of it,
    When I beheld you in your jesting way,
Flitting and whispering round about the spit
    Where Belial, upon duty for the day,   580
With Fox's lard was basting William Pitt,[39]
    His pupil; I knew what to think, I say:
That fellow even in hell breeds farther ills;
I'll have him *gagg'd*—'twas one of his own bills.

LXXIV

'Call Junius!'[40] From the crowd a shadow stalk'd,
    And at the name there was a general squeeze,
So that the very ghosts no longer walk'd
    In comfort, at their own aërial ease,
But were all ramm'd, and jamm'd (but to be
        balk'd,
    As we shall see), and jostled hands and
        knees,   590
Like wind compress'd and pent within a bladder,
Or like a human colic, which is sadder.

LXXV

The shadow came—a tall, thin, grey-hair'd figure,
    That look'd as it had been a shade on earth;
Quick in its motions, with an air of vigour,

But nought to mark its breeding or its birth;
Now it wax'd little, then again grew bigger,
    With now an air of gloom, or savage mirth;
But as you gazed upon its features, they
Changed every instant—to *what,* none could
        say.   600

LXXVI

The more intently the ghosts gazed, the less
    Could they distinguish whose the features
        were;
The Devil himself seem'd puzzled even to guess;
    They varied like a dream—now here, now
        there;
And several people swore from out the press,
    They knew him perfectly; and one could swear
He was his father: upon which another
Was sure he was his mother's cousin's brother:

LXXVII

Another, that he was a duke, or knight,
    An orator, a lawyer, or a priest,   610
A nabob, a man-midwife; but the wight
    Mysterious changed his countenance at least
As oft as they their minds; though in full sight
    He stood, the puzzle only was increased;
The man was a phantasmagoria in
Himself—he was so volatile and thin.

LXXVIII

The moment that you had pronounced him *one,*
    Presto! his face changed, and he was another;
And when that change was hardly well put
        on,
    It varied, till I don't think his own mother   620
(If that he had a mother) would her son
    Have known, he shifted so from one to t'other;
Till guessing from a pleasure grew a task,
At this epistolary 'Iron Mask.'

LXXIX

For sometimes he like Cerberus would seem—
    'Three gentlemen at once' (as sagely says
Good Mrs. Malaprop);[41] then you might deem
    That he was not even *one;* now many rays
Were flashing round him; and now a thick steam
    Hid him from sight—like fogs on London
        days: 630
Now Burke, now Tooke, he grew to people's fan-
        cies,
And certes often like Sir Philip Francis.[42]

---

38 Tory ministers under George III.
39 Charles James Fox, 1749–1806, and William Pitt, 1759–1806, were celebrated Whig statesmen.
40 pseudonym of the unknown author who wrote a series of powerful and brilliant papers attacking the government of George III.

---

41 in Sheridan's *The Rivals.*
42 More than fifty persons have been identified as the author of the *Letters of Junius.* Though Sir Philip Francis is the most likely candidate, the authorship has never been satifactorily settled.

LXXX

I've an hypothesis—'tis quite my own;
　　I never let it out till now, for fear
Of doing people harm about the throne,
　　And injuring some minister or peer,
On whom the stigma might perhaps be blown;
　　It is—my gentle public, lend thine ear!
'Tis, that what Junius we are wont to call
Was *really, truly,* nobody at all.　　　640

LXXXI

I don't see wherefore letters should not be
　　Written without hands, since we daily view
Them written without heads; and books, we
　　see,
　　Are fill'd as well without the latter too:
And really till we fix on somebody
　　For certain sure to claim them as his due,
Their author, like the Niger's mouth, will bother
The world to say if *there* be mouth or author.

LXXXII

'And who and what art thou?' the Archangel said.
　　'For *that* you may consult my title-page,'[43]　650
Replied this mighty shadow of a shade:
　　'If I have kept my secret half an age,
I scarce shall tell it now.'—'Canst thou upbraid,'
　　Continued Michael, 'George Rex, or allege
Aught further?' Junius answer'd, 'You had
　　better
First ask him for *his* answer to my letter:

LXXXIII

'My charges upon record will outlast
　　The brass of both his epitaph and tomb.'
'Repent'st thou not,' said Michael, 'of some past
　　Exaggeration? something which may doom 660
Thyself if false, as him if true? Thou wast
　　Too bitter—is it not so?—in thy gloom
Of passion?'—'Passion!' cried the phantom dim,
'I loved my country, and I hated him.

LXXXIV

'What I have written, I have written: let
　　The rest be on his head or mine!' So spoke
Old 'Nominis Umbra'; and while speaking yet,
　　Away he melted in celestial smoke.
Then Satan said to Michael, 'Don't forget
　　To call George Washington, and John Horne
　　Tooke,[44]　　　　　　　　　　　670
And Franklin';—but at this time there was heard
A cry for room, though not a phantom stirr'd.

LXXXV

At length with jostling, elbowing, and the aid
　　Of cherubim appointed to that post,
The devil Asmodeus[45] to the circle made
　　His way, and look'd as if his journey cost
Some trouble. When his burden down he laid,
　　'What's this?' cried Michael; 'why, 'tis not a
　　ghost?'
'I know it,' quoth the incubus; 'but he
Shall be one, if you leave the affair to me.　680

LXXXVI

'Confound the renegado! I have sprain'd
　　My left wing, he's so heavy; one would think
Some of his works about his neck were chain'd.
　　But to the point; while hovering o'er the brink
Of Skiddaw[46] (where as usual it still rain'd),
　　I saw a taper, far below me, wink,
And stooping, caught this fellow at a libel—
No less on history than the Holy Bible.

LXXXVII

'The former is the devil's scripture, and
　　The latter yours, good Michael; so the
　　affair　　　　　　　　　　　690
Belongs to all of us, you understand.
　　I snatch'd him up just as you see him there,
And brought him off for sentence out of hand:
　　I've scarcely been ten minutes in the air—
At least a quarter it can hardly be:
I dare say that his wife is still at tea.'

LXXXVIII

Here Satan said, 'I know this man of old,
　　And have expected him for some time here;
A sillier fellow you will scarce behold,
　　Or more conceited in his petty sphere:　700
But surely it was not worth while to fold
　　Such trash below your wing, Asmodeus dear:
We had the poor wretch safe (without being
　　bored
With carriage) coming of his own accord.

LXXXIX

'But since he's here, let's see what he has
　　done.'
　　'Done!' cried Asmodeus, 'he anticipates
The very business you are now upon,
　　And scribbles as if head clerk to the Fates.
Who knows to what his ribaldry may run,

43　*Letters of Junius, Stat Nominis Umbra.* [He stands the shadow of a name.]
44　supporter of Wilkes and the cause of the American colonies.

45　the demon, in one of Le Sage's stories, who carries the hero through the air to a mountain top.
46　a mountain in the Lake district not far from where Southey resided.

When such an ass as this, like Balaam's,[47]
   prates?'   710
'Let's hear,' quoth Michael, 'what he has to say:
You know we're bound to that in every way.'

XC

Now the bard, glad to get an audience, which
   By no means often was his case below,
Began to cough, and hawk, and hem, and pitch
   His voice into that awful note of woe
To all unhappy hearers within reach
   Of poets when the tide of rhyme's in flow;
But stuck fast with his first hexameter,[48]
Not one of all whose gouty feet would stir.   720

XCI

But ere the spavin'd dactyls could be spurr'd
   Into recitative, in great dismay
Both cherubim and seraphim were heard
   To murmur loudly through their long array;
And Michael rose ere he could get a word
   Of all his founder'd verses under way,
And cried, 'For God's sake stop, my friend!
   'twere best—
Non Di, non homines[49]—you know the rest.'

XCII

A general bustle spread throughout the throng,
   Which seem'd to hold all verse in detesta-
   tion;   730
The angels had of course enough of song
   When upon service; and the generation
Of ghosts had heard too much in life, not long
   Before, to profit by a new occasion:
The monarch, mute till then, exclaim'd, 'What!
   what!
Pye[50] come again? No more—no more of that!'

XCIII

The tumult grew; an universal cough
   Convulsed the skies, as during a debate,
When Castlereagh has been up long enough
   (Before he was first minister of state,   740
I mean—the *slaves hear now*); some cried 'Off,
   off!'
   As at a farce; till, grown quite desperate,
The bard Saint Peter pray'd to interpose
(Himself an author) only for his prose.

---

[47] Balaam, the prophet, was rebuked by the ass he rode. See Numbers, xxii, 21–34.
[48] Southey's *A Vision of Judgement* was written in six-foot dactylic verse.
[49] 'Neither Gods nor men. . . . [will stand for mediocre poets]'— Horace, *Ars Poetica*.
[50] Henry James Pye, a mediocre writer who preceded Southey as Poet Laureate.

XCIV

The varlet[51] was not an ill-favour'd knave;
   A good deal like a vulture in the face,
With a hook nose and a hawk's eye, which gave
   A smart and sharper-looking sort of grace
To his whole aspect, which, though rather grave,
   Was by no means so ugly as his case;   750
But that, indeed, was hopeless as can be,
Quite a poetic felony *'de se.'*[52]

XCV

Then Michael blew his trump, and still'd the
   noise
   With one still greater, as is yet the mode
On earth besides; except some grumbling voice,
   Which now and then will make a slight inroad
Upon decorous silence, few will twice
   Lift up their lungs when fairly overcrow'd;
And now the bard could plead his own bad
   cause,
With all the attitudes of self-applause.   760

XCVI

He said—(I only give the heads)—he said,
   He meant no harm in scribbling; 'twas his way
Upon all topics; 'twas, besides, his bread,
   Of which he butter'd both sides; 'twould delay
Too long the assembly (he was pleased to dread),
   And take up rather more time than a day,
To name his works—he would but cite a few—
'Wat Tyler'—'Rhymes on Blenheim'—'Water-
   loo.'

XCVII

He had written praises of a regicide;
   He had written praises of all kings what-
   ever;   770
He had written for republics far and wide,
   And then against them bitterer than ever;
For pantisocracy[53] he once had cried
   Aloud, a scheme less moral than 'twas clever;
Then grew a hearty anti-jacobin[54]—
Had turn'd his coat—and would have turn'd his
   skin.

XCVIII

He had sung against all battles, and again
   In their high praise and glory; he had call'd
Reviewing 'the ungentle craft,' and then
   Become as base a critic as e'er crawl'd—   780

---

[51] Southey.
[52] upon himself.
[53] The name of the utopian state that Southey, Coleridge, and others planned to establish in America. The scheme was visionary, but not immoral.
[54] opponent to republican, or revolutionary, principles.

Fed, paid, and pamper'd by the very men
　By whom his muse and morals had been
　　maul'd:
He had written much blank verse, and blanker
　prose,
And more of both than anybody knows.

XCIX

He had written Wesley's life:—here turning
　round
　To Satan, 'Sir, I'm ready to write yours,
In two octavo volumes, nicely bound,
　With notes and preface, all that most allures
The pious purchaser; and there's no ground
　For fear, for I can choose my own
　　reviewers:　　　　　　　　　　　　790
So let me have the proper documents,
That I may add you to my other saints.'

C

Satan bow'd, and was silent. 'Well, if you,
　With amiable modesty, decline
My offer, what says Michael? There are few
　Whose memoirs could be render'd more divine.
Mine is a pen of all work; not so new
　As it was once, but I would make you shine
Like your own trumpet. By the way, my own
Has more of brass in it, and is as well blown. 800

CI

'But talking about trumpets, here's my Vision!
　Now you shall judge, all people; yes, you shall
Judge with my judgment, and by my decision
　Be guided who shall enter heaven or fall.
I settle all these things by intuition,
　Times present, past, to come, heaven, hell, and
　　all,
Like King Alfonso.[55] When I thus see double,
I save the Deity some worlds of trouble.'

CII

He ceased, and drew forth an MS.; and no
　Persuasion on the part of devils, saints,　　810
Or angels, now could stop the torrent; so
　He read the first three lines of the contents;
But at the fourth, the whole spiritual show
　Had vanish'd, with variety of scents,
Ambrosial and sulphureous, as they sprang,
Like lightning, off from his 'melodious
　　twang.'[56]

CIII

Those grand heroics acted as a spell:
　The angels stopp'd their ears and plied their
　　pinions;
The devils ran howling, deafen'd, down to hell;
　The ghosts fled, gibbering, for their own do-
　　minions—　　　　　　　　　　　　820
(For 'tis not yet decided where they dwell,
　And I leave every man to his opinions);
Michael took refuge in his trump—but, lo!
His teeth were set on edge, he could not blow!

CIV

Saint Peter, who has hitherto been known
　For an impetuous saint, upraised his keys,
And at the fifth line knock'd the poet down;
　Who fell like Phaeton,[57] but more at ease,
Into his lake, for there he did not drown;
　A different web being by the Destinies　　830
Woven for the Laureate's final wreath, whene'er
Reform shall happen either here or there.

CV

He first sank to the bottom—like his works,
　But soon rose to the surface—like himself;
For all corrupted things are buoy'd like corks,[58]
　By their own rottenness, light as an elf,
Or wisp that flits o'er a morass: he lurks,
　It may be, still, like dull books on a shelf,
In his own den, to scrawl some 'Life' or 'Vision,'
As Welborn says—'the devil turn'd pre-
　　cisian.'[59]　　　　　　　　　　　　840

CVI

As for the rest, to come to the conclusion
　Of this true dream, the telescope is gone
Which kept my optics free from all delusion,
　And show'd me what I in my turn have shown;
All I saw farther, in the last confusion,
　Was, that King George slipp'd into heaven for
　　one;
And when the tumult dwindled to a calm,
I left him practising the hundredth psalm.

1821　　　　　　　　　　　　　　1822

STANZAS WRITTEN ON THE ROAD BETWEEN FLORENCE AND PISA

OH, talk not to me of a name great in story;
The days of our youth are the days of our glory;

55　King Alfonso, speaking of the Ptolomean system, said, that 'had he been consulted at the creation of the world, he would have spared the Maker some absurdities.'—(Byron.)
56　John Aubrey, in his *Miscellanies*, 1696, tells of an apparition which disappeared 'with a curious perfume, and most melodious twang.'
57　Son of the sun-god, who being permitted by his father to drive the chariot of the sun lost control of the horses and would have set the world on fire. He was struck down by Zeus with a thunder-bolt and fell into the Po river.
58　A drowned body lies at the bottom till rotten, it then floats, as most people know.—(Byron.)
59　in Massinger's comedy, *A New Way To Pay Old Debts.*.

And the myrtle and ivy of sweet two-and-twenty
Are worth all your laurels, though ever so plenty.

What are garlands and crowns to the brow that is
    wrinkled?
'Tis but as a dead flower with May-dew be-
    sprinkled.
Then away with all such from the head that is
    hoary!
What care I for the wreaths that can *only* give
    glory!

Oh FAME!—if I e'er took delight in thy praises,
'Twas less for the sake of thy high-sounding
    phrases,   10
Than to see the bright eyes of the dear one dis-
    cover,
She thought that I was not unworthy to love her.

There chiefly I sought thee, *there* only I found
    thee;
Her glance was the best of the rays that surround
    thee;
When it sparkled o'er aught that was bright in
    my story,
I knew it was love, and I felt it was glory.

            November 1821   1830

ON THIS DAY I COMPLETE MY
THIRTY-SIXTH YEAR

'TIS time this heart should be unmoved,
    Since others it hath ceased to move:
Yet, though I cannot be beloved,
        Still let me love!

My days are in the yellow leaf;
    The flowers and fruits of love are gone;
The worm, the canker, and the grief
        Are mine alone!

The fire that on my bosom preys
    Is lone as some volcanic isle;
No torch is kindled at its blaze—   10
        A funeral pile.

The hope, the fear, the jealous care,
    The exalted portion of the pain
And power of love, I cannot share,
        But wear the chain.

But 'tis not *thus*—and 'tis not *here*—
    Such thoughts should shake my soul, nor *now,*
Where glory decks the hero's bier,
        Or binds his brow.   20

The sword, the banner, and the field,
    Glory and Greece, around me see!
The Spartan, borne upon his shield,
        Was not more free.

Awake! (not Greece—she *is* awake!)
    Awake, my spirit! Think through *whom*
Thy life-blood tracks its parent lake,
        And then strike home!

Tread those reviving passions down,
    Unworthy manhood!—unto thee   30
Indifferent should the smile or frown
        Of beauty be.

If thou regrett'st thy youth, *why live?*
    The land of honourable death
Is here:—up to the field, and give
        Away thy breath!

Seek out—less often sought than found—
    A soldier's grave, for thee the best;
Then look around, and choose thy ground,
        And take thy rest.   40

        1824   1824

SELECTIONS FROM THE LETTERS AND
JOURNALS OF LORD BYRON[1]

1 *To* Francis Hodgson[2]

Lisbon, July 16, 1809

Thus far have we pursued our route, and seen
all sorts of marvellous sights, palaces, convents,
etc.;—which, being to be heard in my friend
Hobhouse's forthcoming Book of Travels, I shall
not anticipate by smuggling any account whatsoever to you in a private and clandestine manner. I must just observe, that the village of Cintra
in Estremadura is the most beautiful, perhaps, in
the world.

I am very happy here, because I loves oranges,
and talks bad Latin to the monks, who understand it, as it is like their own,—and I goes into
society (with my pocket pistols), and I swims in
the Tagus all across at once, and I rides on an ass
or a mule, and swears Portuguese, and have got a
diarrhoea and bites from the mosquitoes. But

1 Reprinted from the text of E. H. Prothero's *Letters and Journals of Lord Byron* and from Sir John Murray's *Lord Byron's Correspondence* with the kind permission of John Murray (Publishers)
Limited.
2 the Reverend Francis Hodgson, a prolific writer, with whom
Byron became acquainted in 1807, when Hodgson was a resident
tutor at Cambridge.

what of that? Comfort must not be expected by folks that go a pleasuring.

When the Portuguese are pertinacious, I say *Carracho!*—the great oath of the grandees, that very well supplies the place of 'Damme,'—and, when dissatisfied with my neighbour, I pronounce him *Ambra di merdo*. With these two phrases, and a third, *Avra bouro,* which signifieth 'Get an ass,' I am universally understood to be a person of degree and a master of languages. How merrily we lives that travellers be!—if we had food and raiment. But, in sober sadness, anything is better than England, and I am infinitely amused with my pilgrimage as far as it has gone.

To-morrow we start to ride post near 400 miles as far as Gibraltar, where we embark for Melita and Byzantium. A letter to Malta will find me, or to be forwarded, if I am absent. Pray embrace the Drury and Dwyer, and all the Ephesians you encounter. I am writing with Butler's donative pencil, which makes my bad hand worse. Excuse illegibility.

Hodgson! send me the news, and the deaths and defeats and capital crimes and the misfortunes of one's friends; and let us hear of literary matters, and the controversies and the criticisms. All this will be pleasant—*suave mari magno,*[3] etc. Talking of that, I have been sea-sick, and sick of the sea. Adieu.

Yours faithfully, etc.

2 *To* his Mother

Prevesa, November 12, 1809

My dear Mother,

I have now been some time in Turkey: this place is on the coast, but I have traversed the interior of the province of Albania on a visit to the Pacha. I left Malta in the *Spider,* a brig of war, on the 21st of September, and arrived in eight days at Prevesa. I thence have been about 150 miles, as far as Tepaleen, his Highness's country palace, where I stayed three days. The name of the Pacha is Ali, and he is considered a man of the first abilities: he governs the whole of Albania (the ancient Illyricum), Epirus, and part of Macedonia. His son Vely Pacha, to whom he has given me letters, governs the Morea, and has great influence in Egypt; in short, he is one of the most powerful men in the Ottoman empire. When I reached Yanina, the capital, after a journey of three days over the mountains, through a country of the most picturesque beauty, I found that Ali Pacha was with his army in Illyricum, besieging Ibrahim Pacha in the castle of Berat. He had heard that an Englishman of rank was in his dominions, and had left orders in Yanina with the commandant to provide a house, and supply me with every kind of necessary *gratis;* and, though I have been allowed to make presents to the slaves, etc., I have not been permitted to pay for a single article of household consumption.

I rode out on the vizier's horses, and saw the palaces of himself and grandsons: they are splendid, but too much ornamented with silk and gold. I then went over the mountains through Zitza, a village with a Greek monastery (where I slept on my return), in the most beautiful situation (always excepting Cintra, in Portugal) I ever beheld. In nine days I reached Tepaleen. Our journey was much prolonged by the torrents that had fallen from the mountains, and intersected the roads. I shall never forget the singular scene on entering Tepaleen at five in the afternoon, as the sun was going down. It brought to my mind (with some change of *dress,* however) Scott's description of Branksome Castle in his *Lay,* and the feudal system. The Albanians, in their dresses, (the most magnificent in the world, consisting of a long *white kilt,* gold-worked cloak, crimson velvet gold-laced jacket and waistcoat, silver-mounted pistols and daggers,) the Tartars with their high caps, the Turks in their vast pelisses and turbans, the soldiers and black slaves with the horses, the former in groups in an immense large open gallery in front of the palace, the latter placed in a kind of cloister below it, two hundred steeds ready caparisoned to move in a moment, couriers entering or passing out with the despatches, the kettle-drums beating, boys calling the hour from the minaret[4] of the mosque, altogether, with the singular appearance of the building itself, formed a new and delightful spectacle to a stranger. I was conducted to a very handsome apartment, and my health inquired after by the vizier's secretary, *à-la-mode Turque!*

The next day I was introduced to Ali Pacha. I was dressed in a full suit of staff uniform, with a very magnificent sabre, etc. The vizier received me in a large room paved with marble; a fountain was playing in the centre; the apartment was

---

3 'It is sweet, when on the great sea the winds overturn the waters, from land to watch the great toil of somebody else; not because it gives joyous pleasure that some one is in distress, but because it is sweet to see the evils which you yourself have avoided.'—Lucretius, *De Rerum Natura,* book ii.

4 a lofty tower surrounded by balconies.

surrounded by scarlet ottomans. He received me standing, a wonderful compliment from a Mussulman, and made me sit down on his right hand. I have a Greek interpreter for general use, but a physician of Ali's named Femlario, who understands Latin, acted for me on this occasion. His first question was, why, at so early an age, I left my country?—(the Turks have no idea of travelling for amusement). He then said, the English minister, Captain Leake, had told him I was of a great family, and desired his respects to my mother; which I now, in the name of Ali Pacha, present to you. He said he was certain I was a man of birth, because I had small ears, curling hair, and little white hands, and expressed himself pleased with my appearance and garb. He told me to consider him as a father whilst I was in Turkey, and said he looked on me as his son. Indeed, he treated me like a child, sending me almonds and sugared sherbet, fruit and sweetmeats, twenty times a day. He begged me to visit him often, and at night, when he was at leisure. I then, after coffee and pipes, retired for the first time. I saw him thrice afterwards. It is singular that the Turks, who have no hereditary dignities, and few great families, except the Sultans, pay so much respect to birth; for I found my pedigree more regarded than my title.

To-day I saw the remains of the town of Actium, near which Antony lost the world, in a small bay, where two frigates could hardly manoeuvre: a broken wall is the sole remnant. On another part of the gulf stand the ruins of Nicopolis, built by Augustus in honour of his victory. Last night I was at a Greek marriage; but this and a thousand things more I have neither time nor *space* to describe.

His highness is sixty years old, very fat, and not tall, but with a fine face, light blue eyes, and a white beard; his manner is very kind, and at the same time he possesses that dignity which I find universal amongst the Turks. He has the appearance of anything but his real character, for he is a remorseless tyrant, guilty of the most horrible cruelties, very brave, and so good a general that they call him the Mahometan Buonaparte. Napoleon has twice offered to make him King of Epirus, but he prefers the English interest, and abhors the French, as he himself told me. He is of so much consequence, that he is much courted by both, the Albanians being the most warlike subjects of the Sultan, though Ali is only nominally dependent on the Porte; he has been a mighty warrior, but is as barbarous as he is successful,

roasting rebels, etc., etc. Buonaparte sent him a snuff-box with his picture. He said the snuff-box was very well, but the picture he could excuse, as he neither liked it nor the original. His ideas of judging of a man's birth from ears, hands, etc., were curious enough. To me he was, indeed, a father, giving me letters, guards, and every possible accommodation. Our next conversations were of war and travelling, politics and England. He called my Albanian soldier, who attends me, and told him to protect me at all hazard; his name is Viscillie, and, like all the Albanians, he is brave, rigidly honest, and faithful; but they are cruel, though not treacherous, and have several vices but no meannesses. They are, perhaps, the most beautiful race, in point of countenance, in the world; their women are sometimes handsome also, but they are treated like slaves, *beaten,* and, in short, complete beasts of burden; they plough, dig, and sow. I found them carrying wood, and actually repairing the highways. The men are all soldiers, and war and the chase their sole occupations. The women are the labourers, which after all is no great hardship in so delightful a climate. Yesterday, the 11th of November, I bathed in the sea; to-day is so hot that I am writing in a shady room of the English consul's, with three doors wide open, no fire, or even *fireplace,* in the house, except for culinary purposes.

I am going to-morrow, with a guard of fifty men, to Patras in the Morea, and thence to Athens, where I shall winter. Two days ago I was nearly lost in a Turkish ship of war, owing to the ignorance of the captain and crew, though the storm was not violent. Fletcher yelled after his wife, the Greeks called on all the saints, the Mussulmans on Alla; the captain burst into tears and ran below deck, telling us to call on God; the sails were split, the main-yard shivered, the wind blowing fresh, the night setting in, and all our chance was to make Corfu, which is in possession of the French, or (as Fletcher pathetically termed it) 'a watery grave.' I did what I could to console Fletcher, but finding him incorrigible, wrapped myself up in my Albanian capote (an immense cloak), and lay down on deck to wait the worst. I have learnt to philosophise in my travels; and if I had not, complaint was useless. Luckily the wind abated, and only drove us on the coast of Suli, on the mainland, where we landed, and proceeded, by the help of the natives, to Prevesa again; but I shall not trust Turkish sailors in future, though the Pacha had ordered one of his own galliots to take me to Patras. I am therefore going as far as Missolonghi by land, and there have only to cross a small gulf to get to Patras.

Fletcher's next epistle will be full of marvels. We were one night lost for nine hours in the mountains in a thunder-storm, and since nearly wrecked. In both cases Fletcher was sorely bewildered, from apprehensions of famine and banditti in the first, and drowning in the second instance. His eyes were a little hurt by the lightning, or crying (I don't know which), but are now recovered. When you write, address to me at Mr. Strané's, English consul, Patras, Morea.

I could tell you I know not how many incidents that I think would amuse you, but they crowd on my mind as much as they would swell my paper, and I can neither arrange them in the one, nor put them down on the other, except in the greatest confusion. I like the Albanians much; they are not all Turks; some tribes are Christians. But their religion makes little difference in their manner or conduct. They are esteemed the best troops in the Turkish service. I lived on my route, two days at once, and three days again, in a barrack at Salora, and never found soldiers so tolerable, though I have been in the garrisons of Gibraltar and Malta, and seen Spanish, French, Sicilian, and British troops in abundance. I have had nothing stolen, and was always welcome to their provision and milk. Not a week ago an Albania'n chief (every village has its chief, who is called Primate,) after helping us out of the Turkish galley in her distress, feeding us, and lodging my suite, consisting of Fletcher, a Greek, two Athenians, a Greek priest, and my companion, Mr. Hobhouse, refused any compensation but a written paper stating that I was well received; and when I pressed him to accept a few sequins, 'No,' he replied; 'I wish you to love me, not to pay me.' These are his words.

It is astonishing how far money goes in this country. While I was in the capital I had nothing to pay by the vizier's order; but since, though I have generally had sixteen horses, and generally six or seven men, the expense has not been *half* as much as staying only three weeks in Malta, though Sir A. Ball, the governor, gave me a house for nothing, and I had only *one servant*. By the by, I expect Hanson to remit regularly; for I am not about to stay in this province for ever. Let him write to me at Mr. Strané's, English consul, Patras. The fact is, the fertility of the plains is wonderful, and specie is scarce, which makes this remarkable cheapness. I am

going to Athens, to study modern Greek, which differs much from the ancient, though radically similar. I have no desire to return to England, nor shall I, unless compelled by absolute want, and Hanson's neglect; but I shall not enter into Asia for a year or two, as I have much to see in Greece, and I may perhaps cross into Africa, at least the Egyptian part. Fletcher, like all Englishmen, is very much dissatisfied, though a little reconciled to the Turks by a present of eighty piastres from the vizier, which, if you consider everything, and the value of specie here, is nearly worth ten guineas English. He has suffered nothing but from cold, heat, and vermin, which those who lie in cottages and cross mountains in a cold country must undergo, and of which I have equally partaken with himself; but he is not valiant, and is afraid of robbers and tempests. I have no one to be remembered to in England, and wish to hear nothing from it, but that you are well, and a letter or two on business from Hanson, whom you may tell to write. I will write when I can, and beg you to believe me,

Your affectionate son,

Byron.

P. S.—I have some very 'magnifiques' Albanian dresses, the only expensive articles in this country. They cost fifty guineas each, and have so much gold, they would cost in England two hundred.

I have been introduced to Hussein Bey, and Mahmout Pacha, both little boys, grandchildren of Ali, at Yanina; they are totally unlike our lads, have painted complexions like rouged dowagers, large black eyes, and features perfectly regular. They are the prettiest little animals I ever saw, and are broken into the court ceremonies already. The Turkish salute is a slight inclination of the head, with the hand on the heart; intimates always kiss. Mahmout is ten years old, and hopes to see me again; we are friends without understanding each other, like many other folks, though from a different cause. He has given me a letter to his father in the Morea, to whom I have also letters from Ali Pacha.

3 *To* his Mother

Athens, January 14, 1811

My dear Madam,

I seize an occasion to write as usual, shortly, but frequently, as the arrival of letters, where there exists no regular communication, is, of course, very precarious. I have lately made several small tours of some hundred or two miles about the Morea, Attica, etc., as I have finished my grand giro by the Troad, Constantinople, etc., and am returned down again to Athens. I believe I have mentioned to you more than once that I swam (in imitation of Leander, though without his lady) across the Hellespont, from Sestos to Abydos. Of this, and all other particulars, Fletcher, whom I have sent home with papers, etc., will apprise you. I cannot find that he is any loss; being tolerably master of the Italian and modern Greek languages, which last I am also studying with a master, I can order and discourse more than enough for a reasonable man. Besides, the perpetual lamentations after beef and beer, the stupid, bigoted contempt for everything foreign, and insurmountable incapacity of acquiring even a few words of any language, rendered him, like all other English servants, an incumbrance. I do assure you, the plague of speaking for him, the comforts he required (more than myself by far), the pilaws (a Turkish dish of rice and meat) which he could not eat, the wines which he could not drink, the beds where he could not sleep, and the long list of calamities, such as stumbling horses, want of *tea*! ! ! etc., which assailed him, would have made a lasting source of laughter to a spectator, and inconvenience to a master. After all, the man is honest enough, and, in Christendom, capable enough; but in Turkey, Lord forgive me! my Albanian soldiers, my Tartars and Jannissary, worked for him and us too, as my friend Hobhouse can testify.

It is probable I may steer homewards in spring; but to enable me to do that, I must have remittances. My own funds would have lasted me very well; but I was obliged to assist a friend, who, I know, will pay me; but, in the meantime, I am out of pocket. At present, I do not care to venture a winter's voyage, even if I were otherwise tired of travelling; but I am so convinced of the advantages of looking at mankind instead of reading about them, and the bitter effects of staying at home with all the narrow prejudices of an islander, that I think there should be a law amongst us, to set our young men abroad, for a term, among the few allies our wars have left us.

Here I see and have conversed with French, Italians, Germans, Danes, Greeks, Turks, Americans, etc., etc., etc.; and without losing sight of my own, I can judge of the countries and manners of others. Where I see the superiority of England (which, by the by, we are a good deal

mistaken about in many things), I am pleased, and where I find her inferior, I am at least enlightened. Now, I might have stayed, smoked in your towns, or fogged in your country, a century, without being sure of this, and without acquiring anything more useful or amusing at home. I keep no journal, nor have I any intention of scribbling my travels. I have done with authorship, and if, in my last production, I have convinced the critics or the world I was something more than they took me for, I am satisfied; nor will I hazard *that reputation* by a future effort. It is true I have some others in manuscript, but I leave them for those who come after me; and, if deemed worth publishing, they may serve to prolong my memory when I myself shall cease to remember. I have a famous Bavarian artist taking some views of Athens, etc., etc., for me. This will be better than scribbling, a disease I hope myself cured of. I hope, on my return, to lead a quiet, recluse life, but God knows and does best for us all; at least, so they say, and I have nothing to object, as, on the whole, I have no reason to complain of my lot. I am convinced, however, that men do more harm to themselves than ever the devil could do to them. I trust this will find you well, and as happy as we can be; you will, at least, be pleased to hear I am so, and

Yours ever.

4 *To* Scope Berdmore Davies[5]

Newstead Abbey, August 7, 1811

My dearest Davies,

Some curse hangs over me and mine. My mother lies a corpse in this house; one of my best friends[6] is drowned in a ditch. What can I say, or think, or do? I received a letter from him the day before yesterday. My dear Scrope, if you can spare a moment, do come down to me—I want a friend. Matthews's last letter was written on Friday.—on Saturday he was not. In ability, who was like Matthews? How did we all shrink before him? You do me but justice in saying, I would have risked my paltry existence to have preserved his. This very evening did I mean to write, inviting him, as I invite you, my very dear friend, to visit me. God forgive—for his apathy! What will our poor Hobhouse feel? His letters breathe but

5 one of Byron's undergraduate companions at Cambridge.
6 Charles Skinner Matthews, Scholar of Trinity College, Cambridge, a young man of extraordinary promise and Byron's intimate companion. He was drowned in the river Cam.

of Matthews. Come to me, Scrope, I am almost desolate—left almost alone in the world—I had but you, and H., and M., and let me enjoy the survivors whilst I can. Poor M., in his letter of Friday, speaks of his intended contest for Cambridge, and a speedy journey to London. Write or come, but come if you can, or one or both.

Yours ever.

5 *To* Lady Caroline Lamb[7]

[Undated. Probably late March, 1812]

I never supposed you artful: we are all selfish,—nature did that for us. But even when you attempt deceit occasionally, you cannot maintain it, which is all the better; want of success will curb the tendency. Every word you utter, every line you write, proves you to be either *sincere* or a *fool*. Now as I know you are not the one, I must believe you the other.

I never knew a woman with greater or more pleasing talents, *general* as in a woman they should be, something of everything, and too much of nothing. But these are unfortunately coupled with a total want of common conduct. For instance, the *note* to your *page*—do you suppose I delivered it? or did you mean that I should? I did not of course.

Then your heart, my poor Caro (what a little volcano!), that pours *lava* through your veins; and yet I cannot wish it a bit colder, to make a *marble slab* of, as you sometimes see (to understand my foolish metaphor) brought in vases, tables, etc., from Vesuvius, when hardened after an eruption. To drop my detestable tropes and figures, you know I have always thought you the cleverest, most agreeable, absurd, amiable, perplexing, dangerous, fascinating little being that lives now, or ought to have lived 2000 years ago. I won't talk to you of beauty; I am no judge. But our beauties cease to be so when near you, and therefore you have either some, or something better. And now, Caro, this nonsense is the first and last compliment (if it be such) I ever paid you. You have often reproached me as wanting in that respect; but others will make up the deficiency.

Come to Lord Grey's; at least do not let me keep you away. All that you so often *say*, I *feel*. Can more be said or felt? This same prudence is tiresome enough; but one *must* maintain it, or what *can* one do to be saved? Keep to it.

6 *To* Lady Caroline Lamb

May 1st, 1812

My dear Lady Caroline,

I have read over the few poems of Miss Milbanke[8] with attention. They display fancy, feeling, and a little practice would very soon induce facility of expression. Though I have an abhorrence of Blank Verse, I like the lines on Dermody so much that I wish they were in rhyme. The lines in the Cave at Seaham have a turn of thought which I cannot sufficiently commend, and here I am at least candid as my own opinions differ upon such subjects. The first stanza is very good indeed, and the others, with a few slight alterations, might be rendered equally excellent. The last are smooth and pretty. But these are all, has she no others? She certainly is a very extraordinary girl; who would imagine so much strength and variety of thought under that placid Countenance? It is not necessary for Miss M. to be an authoress, indeed I do not think publishing at all creditable either to men or women, and (though you will not believe me) very often feel ashamed of it myself; but I have no hesitation in saying that she has talents which, were it proper or requisite to indulge, would have led to distinction.

A friend of mine (fifty years old, and an author, but not *Rogers*) has just been here. As there is no name to the MSS. I showed them to him, and he was much more enthusiastic in his praises than I have been. He thinks them beautiful; I shall content myself with observing that they are better, much better, than anything of Miss M.'s protégé Blacket.[9] You will say as much of this to Miss M. as you think proper. I say all this very sincerely. I have no desire to be better acquainted with Miss Milbanke: she is too good for a fallen spirit to know, and I should like her more if she were less perfect.

Believe me, yours ever most truly.

7 *To* Miss Milbanke

Nov. 10, 1813

I perceive by part of your last letter that you are still inclined to believe me a gloomy person-

---

7 Lady Caroline was the wife of William Lamb, afterward Lord Melbourne. Her spectacular affair with Byron was the talk of London society.

8 Anne Isabella Milbanke, the future Lady Byron. See Byron's characterization in his Journal entry for 30 November 1813, text, p. 932.

9 Joseph Blacket, a shoemaker who wrote verses, befriended by Lady Milbanke and her family.

age. Those who pass so much of their time entirely alone can't be always in very high spirits; yet I don't know,—though I certainly do enjoy society to a certain extent, I never passed two hours in mixed company without wishing myself out of it again. Still I look upon myself as a facetious companion, well reputed by all the wits at whose jests I readily laugh, and whose repartees I take care never to incur by any kind of contest,—for which I feel as little qualified as I do for the more solid pursuits of demonstration.

. . .

I by no means rank poetry or poets high in the scale of intellect. This may look like affectation, but it is my real opinion. It is the lava of the imagination whose eruption prevents an earthquake. They say poets never or rarely go *mad.* Cowper and Collins are instances to the contrary (but Cowper was no poet). It is, however, to be remarked that they rarely do, but are generally so near it that I cannot help thinking rhyme is so far useful in anticipating and preventing the disorder. I prefer the talents of action—of war, or the senate, or even of science,—to all the speculations of those mere dreamers of another existence (I don't mean religiously but fancifully) and spectators of this apathy. Disgust and perhaps incapacity have rendered me now a mere spectator; but I have occasionally mixed in the active and tumultuous departments of existence, and in these alone my recollection rests with any satisfaction, though not the best parts of it.

8 Journal, November 1813—February 1814

November 23, 1813

. . . If I had any views in this country, they would probably be parliamentary. But I have no ambition; at least, if any, it would be *aut Cæsar aut nihil.*[10] My hopes are limited to the arrangement of my affairs, and settling either in Italy or the East (rather the last), and drinking deep of the languages and literature of both. Past events have unnerved me; and all I can now do is to make life an amusement, and look on while others play. After all, even the highest game of crowns and sceptres, what is it? *Vide* Napoleon's last twelvemonth. It has completely upset my system of fatalism. I thought, if crushed, he would have fallen, when *fractus illabitur orbis,*[11] and not

have been pared away to gradual insignificance; that all this was not a mere *jeu* of the gods, but a prelude to greater changes and mightier events. But men never advance beyond a certain point; and here we are, retrograding, to the dull, stupid old system,—balance of Europe—poising straws upon kings' noses, instead of wringing them off! Give me a republic, or a despotism of one, rather than the mixed government of one, two, three. A republic!—look in the history of the Earth—Rome, Greece, Venice, France, Holland, America, our short (*eheu!*)[12] Commonwealth, and compare it with what they did under masters. The Asiatics are not qualified to be republicans, but they have the liberty of demolishing despots, which is the next thing to it. To be the first man—not the Dictator—not the Sylla, but the Washington or the Aristides—the leader in talent and truth—is next to the Divinity! Franklin, Penn, and, next to these, either Brutus or Cassius—even Mirabeau—or St. Just. I shall never be anything, or rather always be nothing. The most I can hope is, that some will say, 'He might, perhaps, if he would.'

November 30, 1813

. . . Yesterday, a very pretty letter from Annabella, which I answered. What an odd situation and friendship is ours!—without one spark of love on either side, and produced by circumstances which in general lead to coldness on one side, and aversion on the other. She is a very superior woman, and very little spoiled, which is strange in an heiress—a girl of twenty—a peeress that is to be, in her own right—an only child, and a *savante,* who has always had her own way. She is a poetess—a mathematician—a metaphysician, and yet, withal, very kind, generous, and gentle, with very little pretension. Any other head would be turned with half her acquisitions, and a tenth of her advantages.

January 16, 1814

. . . I am getting rather into admiration of [Lady C. Annesley] the youngest sister of [Lady F. Webster]. A wife would be my salvation. I am sure the wives of my acquaintances have hitherto done me little good. Catherine is beautiful, but very young, and, I think, a fool. But I have not seen enough to judge; besides, I hate an *esprit* in petticoats. That she won't love me is very probable, nor shall I love her. But, on my system, and the modern system in general,

---

10 'either Caesar or nothing.'
11 'The universe breaks and falls to ruin.'—Horace, *Odes,* III, iii,

12 'alas!'

that don't signify. The business (if it came to business) would probably be arranged between papa and me. She would have her own way; I am good-humoured to women, and docile; and, if I did not fall in love with her, which I should try to prevent, we should be a very comfortable couple. As to conduct, *that* she must look to. But *if* I love, I shall be jealous;—and for that reason I will not be in love. Though, after all, I doubt my temper, and fear I should not be so patient as becomes the *bienséance*[13] of a married man in my station. Divorce ruins the poor *femme,* and damages are a paltry compensation. I do fear my temper would lead me into some of our oriental tricks of vengeance, or, at any rate, into a summary appeal to the court of twelve paces. So 'I'll none on't,' but e'en remain single and solitary;—though I should like to have somebody now and then to yawn with one.

February 18, 1814

. . . Redde a little—wrote notes and letters, and am alone, which Locke says is bad company. 'Be not solitary,' 'be not idle.'—Um!—the idleness is troublesome; but I can't see so much to regret in the solitude. The more I see of men, the less I like them. If I could but say so of women too, all would be well. Why can't I? I am now six-and-twenty; my passions have had enough to cool them; my affections more than enough to wither them,—and yet—and yet—always *yet* and *but*—'Excellent well, you are a fishmonger—get thee to a nunnery.'—'They fool me to the top of my bent.'

. . . I wonder how the deuce anybody could make such a world; for what purpose dandies, for instance, were ordained—and kings—and fellows of colleges—and women of 'a certain age' —and many men of any age—and myself, most of all!

'Divesne prisco natus ab Inacho
Nil interest, an pauper et infimâ
De gente, sub dio [*sic*] moreris,
Victima nil miserantis Orci.
Omnes eodem cogimur,' etc.[14]

Is there anything beyond?—*who* knows? *He* that can't tell. Who tells that there *is?* He who

don't know. And when shall he know? perhaps, when he don't expect, and generally when he don't wish it. In this last respect, however, all are not alike: it depends a good deal upon education,—something upon nerves and habits—but most upon digestion.

9 *To* Lady Melbourne[15]

January 16, 1814

My Dear Lady Melbourne,

Lewis[16] is just returned from Oatlands, where he has been quarrelling with Stael[17] about everything and everybody. She has not even let poor quiet *me* alone, but has discovered, first, that I am affected; and 2ndly, that I '*shut* my *eyes* during dinner!' What this last can mean I don't know, unless *she* is opposite. If I then do, she is very much obliged to me; and if at the same time I could contrive to shut my ears, she would be still more so. . . . If I really have so ludicrous a habit, will *you* tell me so—and I will try and break myself of it. In the meantime, I think the charge will amuse you. I have worse faults to find with *her* than '*shutting* her eyes'—one of which is opening her mouth too frequently.

Do not you think people are very naughty? What do you think I have this very day heard said of poor M.?[18] It provoked me beyond anything, as *he* was named as authority—why the abominable stories they circulate about Lady W., of which I can say no more. All this is owing to 'dear friend'; and yet, as far as it regards 'dear friend,' I must say I have very sufficing suspicions for believing them utterly false; at least, she must have altered strangely within this nine years—but this is the age of revolutions.

Her ascendancy always appeared to me that of a cunning mind over a weak one. But—but— why the woman is a fright, which, after all, is the best reason for not believing it.

I still mean to set off to-morrow, unless this snow adds so much to the impracticability of the roads as to render it useless. I don't mind anything but delay; and I might as well be in

13 propriety.
14 'Whether you are rich and descended from old Inachus [the first king of Argos] or tarry beneath the sky poor and of lowly birth, it makes no difference: you are the victim of pitiless Orcus [god of the lower world]. We are all being herded to the same place.'—Horace, *Odes,* II, iii, 21ff.

15 Elizabeth Lady Melbourne, aunt to Anne Isabella Milbanke and mother-in-law of Lady Caroline Lamb. Lady Melbourne was at the time of Byron's friendship sixty-two years of age and a woman of extraordinary charm. It was mainly owing to her that Byron's ill-fated marriage to her niece took place.
16 Matthew Gregory Lewis, 1775–1818, famed as the author of *The Monk.*
17 Madame de Staël, 1766–1817, a celebrated French writer.
18 Mary (Chaworth) Musters, his cousin, of Annesley, near Newstead, whom Byron once described as 'my old love of all loves.'

London as at a sordid inn, waiting for a thaw, or the subsiding of a flood and the clearing of snow.

I wonder what *your* answer will be on *Ph.'s letter.* I am growing rather partial to her younger sister; who is very pretty, but fearfully young—and I think a *fool.* A wife, you say, would be my salvation. Now I could have but one motive for marrying into that family—and even *that* might possibly only produce a scene, and spoil everything; but at all events it would in some degree be a *revenge,* and in the very face of your compliment (*ironical,* I believe) on the want of *selfishness,* I must say that I never can quite get over the '*not*' of last summer[19]—no—though it were to become 'yea' to-morrow.

I do believe that to marry would be my wisest step—but whom? I might manage this easily with '*le père,*' but I don't admire the connexion—and I have not committed myself by any attentions hitherto. But all wives would be much the same. I have no heart to spare and expect none in return; but, as Moore says, 'A pretty wife is something for the fastidious vanity of a *roué* to *retire* upon.' And mine might do as she pleased, so that she had a fair temper, and a quiet way of conducting herself, leaving me the same liberty of conscience.

What I want is a companion—a friend rather than a sentimentalist. I have seen enough of love matches—and of all matches—to make up my mind to the common lot of happy couples. The only misery would be if I fell in love afterwards—which is not unlikely, for habit has a strange power over my affections. In that case I should be jealous, and then you do not know what a devil any bad passion makes me. I should very likely *do* all that C. *threatens* in her paroxysms; and I have more reasons than you are aware of, for mistrusting myself on this point.

Heigh-ho! Good night.

Ever yours most truly.

10 *To* Thomas Moore

Hastings August 3, 1814

By the time this reaches your dwelling, I shall (God wot) be in town again probably. I have been here renewing my acquaintance with my old friend Ocean; and I find his bosom as pleasant a pillow for an hour in the morning as his

daughters of Paphos[20] could be in the twilight. I have been swimming and eating turbot, and smuggling neat brandies and silk handkerchiefs,—and listening to my friend Hodgson's raptures about a pretty wife-elect of his,—and walking on cliffs, and tumbling down hills, and making the most of the *dolce far-niente*[21] for the last fortnight. I met a son of Lord Erskine's, who says he has been married a year, and is the 'happiest of men'; and I have met the aforesaid H., who is also the 'happiest of men'; so, it is worth while being here, if only to witness the superlative felicity of these foxes, who have cut off their tails, and would persuade the rest to part with their brushes to keep them in countenance.

It rejoiceth me that you like *Lara.* Jeffrey is out with his 45th Number, which I suppose you have got. He is only too kind to me, in my share of it, and I begin to fancy myself a golden pheasant, upon the strength of the plumage wherewith he hath dedecked me. But then, 'surgit amari,' etc.[22] —the gentlemen of the *Champion,* and Perry,[23] have got hold (I know not how) of the condolatory address to Lady Jersey on the picture-abduction by our Regent,[24] and have published them—with my name, too, smack—without even asking leave, or inquiring whether or no! Damn their impudence, and damn everything. It has put me out of patience, and so, I shall say no more about it.

You shall have *Lara* and *Jacque*[25] (both with some additions) when out; but I am still demurring and delaying, and in a fuss, and so is Rogers in his way.

Newstead is to be mine again. Claughton forfeits twenty-five thousand pounds; but that don't prevent me from being very prettily ruined. I mean to bury myself there—and let my beard grow—and hate you all.

Oh! I have had the most amusing letter from Hogg, the Ettrick minstrel and shepherd. He wants me to recommend him to Murray; and, speaking of his present bookseller, whose 'bills'

---

19 Miss Milbanke had refused Byron's first proposal of marriage.

20 The ancient city of Paphos contained a temple of Aphrodite, goddess of love and beauty.
21 'sweet idleness.'
22 The reference is to a satiric treatment of love by Lucretius in *De Rerum Natura,* IV, 1134: 'Rich banquets and similar pleasures are vain, since out of the very fountain of delights there arises something bitter.'
23 James Perry, editor of the *Morning Chronicle.*
24 The Regent had removed Lady Jersey's portrait from his collection of the chief beauties. Byron's verses were printed without permission in the *Champion* and the *Morning Chronicle.*
25 *Jacqueline,* by Samuel Rogers, which was to be published in one volume with Byron's *Lara.*

are never 'lifted,' he adds, *totidem verbis,*[26] 'God damn him and them both.' I laughed, and so would you too, at the way in which this execration is introduced. The said Hogg is a strange being, but of great, though uncouth, powers. I think very highly of him, as a poet; but he, and half of these Scotch and Lake troubadours, are spoiled by living in little circles and petty societies. London and the world is the only place to take the conceit out of a man—in the milling phrase. Scott, he says, is gone to the Orkneys in a gale of wind;—during which wind, he affirms, the said Scott, he is sure, is not at his ease,—to say the best of 'it.' Lord, Lord, if these home-keeping minstrels had crossed your Atlantic or my Mediterranean, and tasted a little open boating in a white squall—or a gale in 'the Gut'—or the 'Bay of Biscay,' with no gale at all—how it would enliven and introduce them to a few of the sensations!—to say nothing of an illicit amour or two upon shore, in the way of essay upon the Passions, beginning with simple adultery, and compounding it as they went along.

I have forwarded your letter to Murray,—by the way, you had addressed it to *Miller.* Pray write to me, and say what art thou doing? 'Not finished!'—Oons! how is this?—these 'flaws and starts' must be authorised 'by your grandam,' and are unbecoming of any other author. I was sorry to hear of your discrepancy with the**s, or rather your abjuration of agreement. I don't want to be impertinent, or buffoon on a serious subject, and am therefore at a loss what to say.

I hope nothing will induce you to abate from the proper price of your poem, as long as there is a prospect of getting it. For my own part, I have *seriously* and *not whiningly* (for that is not my way—at least, it used not to be) neither hopes, nor prospects, and scarcely even wishes. I am, in some respects, happy, but not in a manner that can or ought to last,—but enough of that. The worst of it is, I feel quite enervated and indifferent. I really do not know, if Jupiter were to offer me my choice of the contents of his benevolent cask, what I would pick out of it. If I was born, as the nurses say, with a 'silver spoon in my mouth,' it has stuck in my throat, and spoiled my palate, so that nothing put into it is swallowed with much relish,—unless it be cayenne. However, I have grievances enough to occupy me that way too;—but for fear of add-

ing to yours by this pestilent long diatribe, I postpone the reading of them, *sine die.*

Ever, dear M., yours, etc.

P.S.—Don't forget my godson. You could not have fixed on a fitter porter for his sins than me, being used to carry double without inconvenience.

---

11 *To* Thomas Moore

Newstead Abbey, Sept. 20, 1814

> Here's to her who long
>   Hath waked the poet's sigh!
> The girl who gave to song
>   What gold could never buy.

My dear Moore,

I am going to be married—that is, I am accepted, and one usually hopes the rest will follow. My mother of the Gracchi (that *are* to be), *you* think too strait-laced for me, although the paragon of only children, and invested with 'golden opinions of all sorts of men,' and full of 'most blest conditions' as Desdemona herself. Miss Milbanke is the lady, and I have her father's invitation to proceed there in my elect capacity,—which, however, I cannot do till I have settled some business in London, and got a blue coat.

She is said to be an heiress, but of that I really know nothing certainly, and shall not enquire. But I do know, that she has talents and excellent qualities; and you will not deny her judgment, after having refused six suitors and taken me.

Now, if you have anything to say against this, pray do; my mind's made up, positively fixed, determined, and therefore I will listen to reason, because now it can do no harm. Things may occur to break it off, but I will hope not. In the meantime, I tell you (a secret, by the by,—at least, till I know she wishes it to be public) that I have proposed and am accepted. You need not be in a hurry to wish me joy, for one mayn't be married for months. I am going to town to-morrow: but expect to be here, on my way there, within a fortnight.

If this had not happened, I should have gone to Italy. In my way down, perhaps, you will meet me at Nottingham, and come over with me here. I need not say that nothing will give me greater pleasure. I must, of course, reform thoroughly; and, seriously, if I can contribute to her happi-

---

26 'in so many words.'

ness, I shall secure my own. She is so good a person, that—that—in short, I wish I was a better.

Ever, etc.

12 *To* Lady Melbourne

November 13, 1814

My Dear Lady Melbourne,

I delivered your letters, but have only mentioned yᵉ receipt of your last to myself.

Do you know I have grave doubts if this will be a marriage now? Her disposition is the very reverse of our imaginings. She is overrun with fine feelings, scruples about herself and her disposition (I suppose, in fact, she means mine), and to crown all, is taken ill once every three days with I know not what. But the day before, and the day after, she seems well; looks and eats well, and is cheerful and confiding, and in short like any other person in good health and spirits. A few days ago she made one *scene,* not altogether out of C.'s style; it was too long and too trifling, in fact, for me to transcribe, but it did me no good. In the article of conversation, however, she has improved with a vengeance, but I don't much admire these same agitations upon slight occasions. I don't know, but I think it by no means improbable, you will see me in town soon. I can only interpret these things one way, and merely wait to be certain, to make my obeisance and 'exit singly.' I hear of nothing but 'feeling' from morning till night, except from Sir Ralph, with whom I go on to admiration. Lady M[ilbanke] too, is pretty well; but I am never sure of A. for a moment. The least word, and you know I rattle on through thick and thin (always, however, avoiding anything I think can offend her favourite notions), if only to prevent me from yawning. The least word, or alteration of tone, has some inference drawn from it. Sometimes we are too much alike, and then again too unlike. This comes of system, and squaring her notions to the devil knows what. For my part, I have lately had recourse to the eloquence of *action* (which Demosthenes calls the first part of oratory), and find it succeeds very well, and makes her very quiet; which gives me some hopes of the efficacy of the 'calming process,' so renowned in 'our philosophy.' In fact, and *entre nous,* it is really amusing; she is like a child in that respect, and quite caressable into kindness, and good humour; though I don't think her temper *bad* at any time, but very *self* tormenting and anxious, and romantic.

In short, it is impossible to foresee how this will end *now,* any more than two years ago; if there is a break, it shall be her doing not mine.

Ever yours most truly.

13 *To* Thomas Moore

Seaham, Stockton-on-Tees,
February 2, 1815

I have heard from London that you have left Chatsworth and all the women full of 'entusymusy' about you, personally and poetically; and, in particular, that 'When first I met thee' has been quite overwhelming in its effect. I told you it was one of the best things you ever wrote, though that dog Power[27] wanted you to omit part of it. They are all regretting your absence at Chatsworth, according to my informant—'all the ladies quite,' etc., etc., etc. Stap my vitals!

Well, now you have got home again—which I dare say is as agreeable as a 'draught of cool small beer to the scorched palate of a waking sot' —now you have got home again, I say, probably I shall hear from you. Since I wrote last, I have been transferred to my father-in-law's, with my lady and my lady's maid, etc., etc., etc., and the treacle-moon is over, and I am awake, and find myself married. My spouse and I agree to—and in—admiration. Swift says 'no *wise* man ever married'; but, for a fool, I think it the most ambrosial of all possible future states. I still think one ought to marry upon *lease;* but am very sure I should renew mine at the expiration, though next term were for ninety and nine years.

I wish you would respond, for I am here *oblitusque meorum obliviscendus et illis.*[28] Pray tell me what is going on in the way of intriguery, and how the w——s and rogues of the upper Beggar's Opera go on—or rather go off—in or after marriage; or who are going to break any particular commandment. Upon this dreary coast, we have nothing but county meetings and shipwrecks: and I have this day dined upon fish, which probably dined upon the crews of several colliers lost in the late gales. But I saw the sea once more in all the glories of surf and foam,— almost equal to the Bay of Biscay, and the interesting white squalls and short seas of Archipelago memory.

My papa, Sir Ralpho, hath recently made a speech at a Durham tax-meeting; and not only

---

27 Moore's publisher.
28 'forgetting my friends and forgotten by them'—Horace, *Epistles,* I, xi, 9.

at Durham, but here, several times since after dinner. He is now, I believe, speaking it to himself (I left him in the middle) over various decanters, which can neither interrupt him nor fall asleep,—as might possibly have been the case with some of his audience.

Ever thine,

Byron.

I must go to tea—damn tea. I wish it was Kinnaird's brandy, and with you to lecture me about it.

14 *To* the Hon. Augusta Leigh

Diodati, Geneva, Sept. 8, 1816

. . . I have been in some danger on the lake (near Meillerie), but nothing to speak of; and, as to all these 'mistresses,' Lord help me—I have had but one. Now don't scold; but what could I do?—a foolish girl, in spite of all I could say or do, would come after me, or rather went before—for I found her here—and I have had all the plague possible to persuade her to go back again; but at last she went. Now, dearest, I do most truly tell thee, that I could not help this, that I did all I could to prevent it, and have at last put an end to it. I was not in love, nor have any love left for any; but I could not exactly play the Stoic with a woman, who had scrambled eight hundred miles to unphilosophize me. Besides, I had been regaled of late with so many 'two courses and a *desert*' (Alas!) of aversion, that I was fain to take a little love (if pressed particularly) by way of novelty. And now you know all that I know of that matter, and it's over. Pray write. I have heard nothing since your last, at least a month or five weeks ago. I go out very little, except into the *air*, and on journeys, and on the water, and to Copet, where Madame de Staël has been particularly kind and friendly towards me, and (I hear) fought battles without number in my very indifferent cause. It has (they say) made quite as much noise on this as the other side of *La Manche.*[29] Heaven knows why—but I seem destined to set people by the ears.

Don't hate me, but believe me, ever yours most affectionately.

15 *To* Thomas Moore

Venice, November 17, 1816

I wrote to you from Verona the other day in my progress hither, which letter I hope you will receive. Some three years ago, or it may be more, I recollect your telling me that you had received a letter from our friend Sam, dated 'On board his gondola.' *My* gondola is, at this present, waiting for me on the canal; but I prefer writing to you in the house, it being autumn—and rather an English autumn than otherwise. It is my intention to remain at Venice during the winter, probably, as it has always been (next to the East) the greenest island of my imagination. It has not disappointed me; though its evident decay would, perhaps, have that effect upon others. But I have been familiar with ruins too long to dislike desolation. Besides, I have fallen in love, which, next to falling into the canal (which would be of no use, as I can swim), is the best or the worst thing I could do. I have got some extremely good apartments in the house of a 'Merchant of Venice,' who is a good deal occupied with business, and has a wife in her twenty-second year.[30] Marianna (that is her name) is in her appearance altogether like an antelope. She has the large, black, oriental eyes, with that peculiar expression in them which is seen rarely among *Europeans*—even the Italians—and which many of the Turkish women give themselves by tinging the eyelid, —an art not known out of that country, I believe. This expression she has *naturally,*—and something more than this. In short, I cannot describe the effect of this kind of eye,—at least upon me. Her features are regular, and rather aquiline—mouth small—skin clear and soft, with a kind of hectic colour—forehead remarkably good: her hair is of the dark gloss, curl, and colour of Lady Jersey's: her figure is light and pretty, and she is a famous songstress—scientifically so: her natural voice (in conversation, I mean,) is very sweet; and the naïveté of the Venetian dialect is always pleasing in the mouth of a woman.

November 23

You will perceive that my description, which was proceeding with the minuteness of a passport, has been interrupted for several days. In the meantime.

*   *   *

December 5

Since my former dates, I do not know that I have much to add on the subject, and, luckily, nothing to take away; for I am more pleased than

---

29 the English Channel.

30 Marianna Segati, whose husband was a linen draper in the Frezzeria.

ever with my Venetian, and begin to feel very serious on that point—so much so, that I shall be silent.

* * *

By way of divertisement, I am studying daily, at an Armenian monastery, the Armenian language. I found that my mind wanted something craggy to break upon; and this—as the most difficult thing I could discover here for an amusement—I have chosen, to torture me into attention. It is a rich language, however, and would amply repay anyone the trouble of learning it. I try, and shall go on;—but I answer for nothing, least of all for my intentions or my success. There are some very curious MSS. in the monastery, as well as books; translations also from Greek originals, now lost, and from Persian and Syriac, etc., besides works of their own people. Four years ago the French instituted an Armenian professorship. Twenty pupils presented themselves on Monday morning, full of noble ardour, ingenuous youth, and impregnable industry. They persevered, with a courage worthy of the nation and of universal conquest, till Thursday; when *fifteen* of the *twenty* succumbed to the six-and-twentieth letter of the alphabet. It is, to be sure, a Waterloo of an Alphabet—that must be said for them. But it is so like these fellows, to do by it as they did by their sovereigns—abandon both; to parody the old rhymes, 'Take a thing and give a thing'—'Take a King and give a King.' They are the worst of animals, except their conquerors.

I hear that Hodgson is your neighbour, having a living in Derbyshire. You will find him an excellent-hearted fellow, as well as one of the cleverest; a little, perhaps, too much japanned by preferment in the church and the tuition of youth, as well as inoculated with the disease of domestic felicity, besides being overrun with fine feelings about woman and *constancy* (that small change of Love, which people exact so rigidly, receive in such counterfeit coin, and repay in baser metal); but, otherwise, a very worthy man, who has lately got a pretty wife, and (I suppose) a child by this time. Pray remember me to him, and say that I know not which to envy most—his neighbourhood, him, or you.

Of Venice I shall say little. You must have seen many descriptions; and they are most of them like. It is a poetical place; and classical, to us, from Shakespeare and Otway. I have not yet sinned against it in verse, nor do I know that I

shall do so, having been tuneless since I crossed the Alps, and feeling, as yet, no renewal of the *estro*. By the way, I suppose you have seen *Glenarvon*.[31] Madame de Staël lent it me to read from Copet last autumn. It seems to me that, if the authoress had written the *truth,* and nothing but the truth—the whole truth—the romance would not only have been more *romantic,* but more entertaining. As for the likeness, the picture can't be good—I did not sit long enough. When you have leisure, let me hear from and of you, believing me

Ever and truly yours most affectionately.

P.S. Oh! *your poem*—is it out? I hope Longman has paid his thousands: but don't you do as H— T—'s father did, who, having made money by a quarto tour, became a vinegar merchant; when, lo! his vinegar turned sweet (and be d—d to it) and ruined him. My last letter to you (from Verona) was enclosed to Murray—have you got it? Direct to me *here, poste restante.* There are no English here at present. There were several in Switzerland—some women; but, except Lady Dalrymple Hamilton, most of them as ugly as virtue—at least, those that I saw.

16 *To* Thomas Moore

Venice, January 28, 1817

Your letter of the 8th is before me. The remedy for your plethora is simple—abstinence. I was obliged to have recourse to the like some years ago, I mean in point of *diet,* and, with the exception of some convivial weeks and days, (it might be months, now and then), have kept to Pythagoras ever since. For all this, let me hear that you are better. You must not indulge in 'filthy beer,' nor in porter, nor eat *suppers*—the last are the devil to those who swallow dinner. . . .

I am truly sorry to hear of your father's misfortune[32]—cruel at any time, but doubly cruel in advanced life. However, you will, at least, have the satisfaction of doing your part by him, and, depend upon it, it will not be in vain. Fortune, to be sure, is a female, but not such a b * * as the rest (always excepting your wife and my sister from such sweeping terms); for she generally has some justice in the long run. I have no spite against her, though between her and Nemesis I

31 a novel by Lady Caroline Lamb in which she tells her side of her affair with Byron.
32 John Moore, the poet's father, had lost his post of barrack-master in Dublin.

have had some sore gauntlets to run—but then I have done my best to deserve no better. But to *you,* she is a good deal in arrear, and she will come round—mind if she don't; you have the vigour of life, of independence, of talent, spirit, and character all with you. What you can do for yourself, you have done and will do; and surely there are some others in the world who would not be sorry to be of use, if you would allow them to be useful, or at least attempt it.

I think of being in England in the spring. If there is a row, by the sceptre of King Ludd, but I'll be one; and if there is none, and only a continuance of 'this meek, piping time of peace,' I will take a cottage a hundred yards to the south of your abode, and become your neighbour; and we will compose such canticles, and hold such dialogues, as shall be the terror of the *Times* (including the newspaper of that name), and the wonder, and honour, and praise, of the *Morning Chronicle* and posterity.

I rejoice to hear of your forthcoming in February—though I tremble for the 'magnificence,' which you attribute to the new *Childe Harold.* I am glad you like it; it is a fine indistinct piece of poetical desolation, and my favourite. I was half mad during the time of its composition, between metaphysics, mountains, lakes, love unextinguishable, thoughts unutterable, and the nightmare of my own delinquencies. I should, many a good day, have blown my brains out, but for the recollection that it would have given pleasure to my mother-in-law; and, even *then,* if I could have been certain to haunt her—— but I won't dwell upon these trifling family matters.

Venice is in the *estro* of her carnival, and I have been up these last two nights at the ridotto[33] and the opera, and all that kind of thing. Now for an adventure. A few days ago a gondolier brought me a billet without a subscription, intimating a wish on the part of the writer to meet me either in gondola or at the island of San Lazaro, or at a third rendezvous, indicated in the note. 'I know the country's disposition well'—in Venice 'they do let Heaven see those tricks they dare not show,'[34] etc., etc.; so, for all response, I said that neither of the three places suited me; but that I would either be at home at ten at night *alone,* or be at the ridotto at midnight, where the writer might meet me masked. At ten o'clock I was at home and alone (Marianna was gone with

her husband to a conversazione), when the door of my apartment opened, and in walked a well-looking and (for an Italian) *bionda* girl of about nineteen, who informed me that she was married to the brother of my *amorosa,* and wished to have some conversation with me. I made a decent reply, and we had some talk in Italian and Romaic (her mother being a Greek of Corfu), when lo! in a very few minutes, in marches, to my very great astonishment, Marianna Segati, *in propriâ personâ,* and after making a most polite courtesy to her sister-in-law and to me, without a single word seizes her said sister-in-law by the hair, and bestows upon her some sixteen slaps, which would have made your ear ache only to hear their echo. I need not describe the screaming which ensued. The luckless visitor took flight. I seized Marianna, who, after several vain efforts to get away in pursuit of the enemy, fairly went into fits in my arms; and, in spite of reasoning, eau de Cologne, vinegar, half a pint of water, and God knows what other waters beside, continued so till past midnight.

After damning my servants for letting people in without apprizing me, I found that Marianna in the morning had seen her sister-in-law's gondolier on the stairs, and, suspecting that his apparition boded her no good, had either returned of her own accord, or been followed by her maids or some other spy of her people to the conversazione, from whence she returned to perpetrate this piece of pugilism. I had seen fits before, and also some small scenery of the same genus in and out of our island: but this was not all. After about an hour, in comes—who? why, Signor Segati, her lord and husband, and finds me with his wife fainting upon the sofa, and all the apparatus of confusion, dishevelled hair, hats, handkerchiefs, salts, smelling-bottles—and the lady as pale as ashes, without sense or motion. His first question was, 'What is all this?' The lady could not reply—so I did. I told him the explanation was the easiest thing in the world; but in the meantime it would be as well to recover his wife —at least, her senses. This came about in due time of suspiration and respiration.

You need not be alarmed—jealousy is not the order of the day in Venice, and daggers are out of fashion; while duels, on love matters, are unknown—at least, with the husbands. But, for all this, it was an awkward affair; and though he must have known that I made love to Marianna, yet I believe he was not, till that evening, aware of the extent to which it had gone. It is very well known that almost all the married women have a lover; but it is usual to keep up the forms, as in other nations. I did not, therefore, know what the devil to say. I could not out with the truth, out of regard to her, and I did not choose to lie for my sake;—besides, the thing told itself. I thought the best way would be to let her explain it as she chose (a woman being never at a loss—the devil always sticks by them)—only determining to protect and carry her off, in case of any ferocity on the part of the Signor. I saw that he was quite calm. She went to bed, and next day—how they settled it, I know not, but settle it they did. Well —then I had to explain to Marianna about this never-to-be-sufficiently-confounded sister-in-law; which I did by swearing innocence, eternal constancy, etc., etc. * * * But the sister-in-law, very much discomposed with being treated in such wise, has (not having her own shame before her eyes) told the affair to half Venice, and the servants (who were summoned by the fight and the fainting) to the other half. But, here, nobody minds such trifles, except to be amused by them. I don't know whether you will be so, but I have scrawled a long letter out of these follies.

Believe me ever, etc.

17 *To* John Murray[35]

Venice, May 30, 1817

Dear Sir,

I returned from Rome two days ago, and have received your letter; but no sign nor tidings of the parcel sent through Sir — Stuart, which you mention. After an interval of months, a packet of *Tales,* etc., found me at Rome; but this is all, and may be all that ever will find me. The post seems to be the only sane conveyance; and *that only for letters.* From Florence I sent you a poem on Tasso, and from Rome the new third act of *Manfred,* and by Dr. Polidori two pictures for my sister. I left Rome, and made a rapid journey home. You will continue to direct here as usual. Mr. Hobhouse is gone to Naples: I should have run down there too for a week, but for the quantity of English whom I heard of there. I prefer hating them at a distance; unless an earthquake, or a good real eruption of Vesuvius, were insured to reconcile me to their vicinity.

I know no other situation except Hell which I should feel inclined to participate with them— as a race, always excepting several individuals.

There were few of them in Rome, and I believe none whom you know, except that old Blue-*bore* Sotheby, who will give a fine account of Italy, in which he will be greatly assisted by his total ignorance of Italian, and yet this is the translator of Tasso.

The day before I left Rome I saw three robbers guillotined. The ceremony—including the *masqued* priests; the half-naked executioners; the bandaged criminals; the black Christ and his banner; the scaffold; the soldiery; the slow procession, and the quick rattle and heavy fall of the axe; the splash of the blood, and the ghastliness of the exposed heads—is altogether more impressive than the vulgar and ungentlemanly dirty 'new drop,' and dog-like agony of infliction upon the sufferers of the English sentence. Two of these men behaved calmly enough, but the first of the three died with great terror and reluctance, which was very horrible. He would not lie down; then his neck was too large for the aperture, and the priest was obliged to drown his exclamations by still louder exhortations. The head was off before the eye could trace the blow; but from an attempt to draw back the head, notwithstanding it was held forward by the hair, the first head was cut off close to the ears: the other two were taken off more cleanly. It is better than the oriental way, and (I should think) than the axe of our ancestors. The pain seems little; and yet the effect to the spectator, and the preparation to the criminal, are very striking and chilling. The first turned me quite hot and thirsty, and made me shake so that I could hardly hold the opera-glass (I was close, but determined to see, as one should see everything, once, with attention); the second and third (which shows how dreadfully soon things grow indifferent), I am ashamed to say, had no effect on me as a horror, though I would have saved them if I could.

It is some time since I heard from you—the 12*th April* I believe.

Yours ever truly.

18 *To* Thomas Moore

Venice, September 19, 1818

An English newspaper here would be a prodigy, and an opposition one a monster; and except some extracts *from* extracts in the vile, garbled Paris gazettes, nothing of the kind reaches the Veneto-Lombard public, who are, perhaps, the most oppressed in Europe. My cor-

---

35 Byron's publisher and the first Murray of the famous publishing house of that name.

respondences with England are mostly on business, and chiefly with my attorney, who has no very exalted notion, or extensive conception, of an author's attributes; for he once took up an *Edinburgh Review,* and, looking at it a minute, said to me, 'So, I see you have got into the "magazine," '—which is the only sentence I ever heard him utter upon literary matters, or the men thereof.

My first news of your Irish Apotheosis has, consequently, been from yourself. But, as it will not be forgotten in a hurry, either by your friends or your enemies, I hope to have it more in detail from some of the former, and, in the meantime, I wish you joy with all my heart. Such a moment must have been a good deal better than Westminster Abbey,—besides being an assurance of *that* one day (many years hence, I trust), into the bargain.

I am sorry to perceive, however, by the close of your letter, that even *you* have not escaped the *surgit amari,* etc., and that your damned deputy has been gathering such 'dew from the still *vext* Bermoothes'[36]—or rather *vexatious.* Pray, give me some items of the affair, as you say it is a serious one; and, if it grows more so, you should make a trip over here for a few months, to see how things turn out. I suppose you are a violent admirer of England by your staying so long in it. For my own part, I have passed, between the age of one-and-twenty and thirty, half the intervenient years out of it without regretting anything, except that I ever returned to it at all, and the gloomy prospect before me of business and parentage obliging me, one day, to return to it again,—at least, for the transaction of affairs, the signing of papers, and inspecting of children.

I have here my natural daughter, by name Allegra,[37]—a pretty little girl enough, and reckoned like papa. Her mamma is English,—but it is a long story, and—there's an end. She is about twenty months old. * * *

I have finished the first canto (a long one, of about 180 octaves) of a poem in the style and manner of *Beppo,* encouraged by the good success of the same. It is called *Don Juan,* and is meant to be a little quietly facetious upon everything. But I doubt whether it is not—at least, as far as it has yet gone—too free for these very modest days. However, I shall try the experiment, anonymously; and if it don't take, it will be discontinued. It is dedicated to Southey in good,

simple, savage verse, upon the Laureate's politics, and the way he got them. But the bore of copying it out is intolerable; and if I had an amanuensis he would be of no use, as my writing is so difficult to decipher.

My poem's Epic, and is meant to be
    Divided in twelve books, each book containing,
With love and war, a heavy gale at sea—
    A list of ships, and captains, and kings reigning—
New characters, etc., etc.

The above are two stanzas, which I send you as a brick of my Babel, and by which you can judge of the texture of the structure.

In writing the *Life* of Sheridan, never mind the angry lies of the humbug Whigs. Recollect that he was an Irishman and a clever fellow, and that *we* have had some very pleasant days with him. Don't forget that he was at school at Harrow, where, in my time, we used to show his name—R. B. Sheridan, 1765,—as an honour to the walls. Remember * * * Depend upon it that there were worse folks going, of that gang, than ever Sheridan was.

What did Parr[38] mean by 'haughtiness and coldness'? I listened to him with admiring ignorance, and respectful silence. What more could a talker for fame have?—they don't like to be answered. It was at Payne Knight's I met him, where he gave me more Greek than I could carry away. But I certainly meant to (and *did*) treat him with the most respectful deference.

I wish you a good night, with a Venetian benediction, '*Benedetto te, e la terra che ti fara!*'—'May you be blessed, and the *earth* which you will *make!*' is it not pretty? You would think it still prettier if you had heard it, as I did two hours ago, from the lips of a Venetian girl, with large black eyes, a face like Faustina's, and the figure of a Juno—tall and energetic as a Pythoness, with eyes flashing, and her dark hair streaming in the moonlight—one of those women who may be made anything. I am sure if I put a poniard into the hand of this one, she would plunge it where I told her,—and into *me,* if I offended her. I like this kind of animal, and am sure that I should have preferred Medea[39] to any woman that ever breathed. You may, perhaps, wonder that I don't in that case. * * * I could have forgiven the dagger

---

36 *Tempest,* I, ii, 229.
37 Her mother was Jane Clairmont.

38 Samuel Parr was a former assistant master at Harrow.
39 enchantress who when deserted by Jason sent her rival a poisoned robe, killed her own children, and fired the palace.

or the bowl,—anything, but the deliberate desolation piled upon me, when I stood alone upon
my hearth, with my household gods shivered
around me. * * *[40] Do you suppose I have forgotten it? It has comparatively swallowed up in me
every other feeling, and I am only a spectator
upon earth, till a tenfold opportunity offers. It
may come yet. There are others more to be
blamed than * * * , and it is on these that my eyes
are fixed unceasingly.

19 *To* Lady Byron

Venice, Nov. 18, 1818

Sir Samuel Romilly[41] has cut his throat for the
loss of his wife. It is now nearly three years since
he became, in the face of his compact (by a retainer—previous, and, I believe, general), the
advocate of the measures and the Approver of
the proceedings, which deprived me of mine. I
would not exactly, like Mr. Thwackum, when
Philosopher Square bit his own tongue—'saddle
him with a Judgement';[42] but

            This even-handed justice
Commends the ingredients of our poisoned
        chalice
To our own lips.[43]

This Man little thought, when he was lacerating my heart according to law, while he was
poisoning my life at its sources, aiding and abet-
ting in the blighting, branding, and exile that was
to be the result of his counsels in their indirect
effects, that in less than thirty-six moons—in the
pride of his triumph as the highest candidate for
the representation of the Sister-City of the
mightiest of Capitals—in the fullness of his professional career—in the greenness of a healthy
old age—in the radiance of fame, and the complacency of self-earned riches—that a domestic
affliction would lay him in the earth, with the
meanest of malefactors, in a cross-road with the
stake in his body, if the verdict of insanity did
not redeem his ashes from the sentence of the
laws he had lived upon by interpreting or misin-
terpreting, and died in violating.

This man had eight children, lately deprived
of their mother: could he not live? Perhaps,
previous to his annihilation, he felt a portion of
what he contributed his legal mite to make me
feel; but I have lived—lived to see him a Sexagenary Suicide.

It was not in vain that I invoked Nemesis in
the midnight of Rome from the awfullest of her
ruins.

Fare you well.

20 *To* John Murray

Venice, April 6, 1819

Dear Sir,

The Second Canto of *Don Juan* was sent, on
Saturday last, by post, in 4 packets, two of 4,
and two of three sheets each, containing in all
two hundred and seventeen stanzas, octave measure. But I will permit no curtailments, except
those mentioned about Castlereagh and the two
Bobs in the Introduction. You sha'n't make *Canticles* of my Cantos. The poem will please, if it is
lively; if it is stupid, it will fail; but I will have
none of your damned cutting and slashing. If you
please, you may publish *anonymously;* it will perhaps be better; but I will battle my way against
them all, like a Porcupine.

So you and Mr. Foscolo,[44] etc., want me to undertake what you call a 'great work?' an Epic
poem, I suppose, or some such pyramid. I'll try
no such thing; I hate tasks. And then 'seven or
eight years!' God send us all well this day three
months, let alone years. If one's years can't be
better employed than in sweating poesy, a man
had better be a ditcher. And works, too!—is
Childe Harold nothing? You have so many '*divine*' poems, is it nothing to have written a
Human one? without any of your worn-out machinery. Why, man, I could have spun the
thoughts of the four cantos of that poem into
twenty, had I wanted to book-make, and its
passion into as many modern tragedies. Since
you want *length,* you shall have enough of *Juan,*
for I'll make 50 cantos.

And Foscolo, too! Why does *he* not do something more than the *Letters of Ortis,* and a tragedy, and pamphlets? He has good fifteen years
more at his command than I have: what has he
done all that time?—proved his Genius, doubtless, but not fixed its fame, nor done his utmost.

Besides, I mean to write my best work in *Italian,* and it will take me nine years more thoroughly to master the language; and then if my
fancy exist, and I exist too, I will try what I *can*

---

40 It has been suggested that the suppressed passage must refer
to Lady Byron, whom elsewhere he styles his 'mathematical
Medea.'
41 legal counsel for Lady Byron during the divorce proceedings.
42 Fielding, *Tom Jones,* Book v, chap. ii.
43 *Macbeth,* I, vii, 10–12.
44 Ugo Foscolo, 1778–1827, an Italian patriot and author who had
settled in England.

do *really*. As to the Estimation of the English which you talk of, let them calculate what it is worth, before they insult me with their insolent condescension.

I have not written for their pleasure. If they are pleased, it is that they chose to be so; I have never flattered their opinions, nor their pride; nor will I. Neither will I make 'Ladies books' *al dilettar le femine e la plebe*.[45] I have written from the fullness of my mind, from passion, from impulse, from many motives, but not for their 'sweet voices.'

I know the precise worth of popular applause, for few Scribblers have had more of it; and if I chose to swerve into their paths, I could retain it, or resume it, or increase it. But I neither love ye, nor fear ye; and though I buy with ye and sell with ye, and talk with ye, I will neither eat with ye, drink with ye, nor pray with ye. They made me, without my search, a species of popular Idol; they, without reason or judgment, beyond the caprice of their good pleasure, threw down the Image from its pedestal; it was not broken with the fall, and they would, it seems, again replace it—but they shall not.

You ask about my health: about the beginning of the year I was in a state of great exhaustion, attended by such debility of Stomach that nothing remained upon it; and I was obliged to reform my 'way of life,' which was conducting me from the 'yellow leaf' to the Ground, with all deliberate speed. I am better in health and morals, and very much yours ever, etc.

21 *To* Douglas Kinnaird

Venice, April 24, 1819

Dear Douglas,

Damn '*the Vampire*.'[46] What do I know of Vampires? It must be some bookselling imposture; contradict it in a solemn paragraph.

I sent off on April 3rd the 2nd canto of *Don Juan* addressed to Murray, I hope it is arrived—by the Lord it is a Capo d'Opera, so 'full of pastime and prodigality,' but you sha'n't decimate nor mutilate, no—'rather than that, come critics into the list, and champion me to the uttermost.'

Nor you, nor that rugged rhinoceros Murray, have ever told me, in answer to *fifty* times the question, if he ever received the additions to

Canto *first*, entitled 'Julia's letter' and also some four stanzas for the beginning.

I have fallen in love, within the last month, with a Romagnuola Countess from Ravenna, the spouse of a year of Count Guiccioli, who is sixty—the girl twenty.

She is as fair as sunrise, and warm as noon, but she is young, and was not content with what she had done, unless it was to be turned to the advantage of the public, and so she made an éclat, which rather astonished even the Venetians, and electrified the Conversazioni of the Benzonæ, the Albrizzi, and the Michelli, and made her husband look embarrassed.

They have been gone back to Ravenna some time, but they return in the winter. She is the queerest woman I ever met with, for in general they cost one something one way or other, whereas by an odd combination of circumstances, I have proved an expense to HER, which is not *my* custom, but an accident; however it don't matter.

She is a sort of Italian Caroline Lamb, except that she is much prettier, and not so savage. But she has the same red-hot head, the same noble disdain of public opinion, with the superstructure of all that Italy can add to such natural dispositions.

She is also of the Ravenna noblesse, educated in a convent, sacrificed to wealth, filial duty, and all that.

I am damnably in love, but they are gone, for many months—and nothing but hope keeps me alive *seriously*.

Yours ever.

22 *To* John Murray

Bologna, June 7, 1819

Dear Sir,

Tell Mr. Hobhouse that I wrote to him a few days ago from Ferrara. It will therefore be idle in him or you to wait for any further answers or returns of proofs from Venice, as I have directed that no English letters be sent after me. The publication can be proceeded in without, and I am already sick of your remarks, to which I think not the least attention ought to be paid.

Tell Mr. Hobhouse that, since I wrote to him, I had availed myself of my Ferrara letters, and found the society much younger and better there than at Venice. I was very much pleased with the little the shortness of my stay permitted me to see

---

45 'for the pleasure of women and the masses.'
46 a story published in the *New Monthly Magazine* and attributed to Byron.

of the Gonfaloniere Count Mosti, and his family and friends in general.

I have been picture-gazing this morning at the famous Domenichino and Guido, both of which are superlative. I afterwards went to the beautiful Cemetery of Bologna, beyond the walls, and found, besides the superb Burial-ground, an original of a *Custode,* who reminded me of the grave-digger in Hamlet. He has a collection of Capuchins' skulls, labelled on the forehead, and taking down one of them, said, 'This was Brother Desiderio Berro, who died at forty,—one of my best friends. I begged his head of his brethren after his decease, and they gave it me. I put it in lime and then boiled it. Here it is, teeth and all, in excellent preservation. He was the merriest, cleverest fellow I ever knew. Wherever he went, he brought joy; and when any one was melancholy, the sight of him was enough to make him cheerful again. He walked so actively, you might have taken him for a dancer—he joked—he laughed—oh! he was such a Frate as I never saw before, nor ever shall again!'

He told me that he had himself planted all the Cypresses in the Cemetery; that he had the greatest attachment to them and to his dead people; that since 1801 they had buried fifty-three thousand persons. In showing some older monuments, there was that of a Roman girl of twenty, with a bust by Bernini.[47] She was a Princess Barberini, dead two centuries ago: he said that, on opening her grave, they had found her hair complete, and 'as yellow as gold.' Some of the epitaphs at Ferrara pleased me more than the more splendid monuments of Bologna; for instance:—

> Martini Luigi
> Implora pace.

> Lucrezia Picini
> Implora eterna quiete.

Can anything be more full of pathos? Those few words say all that can be said or sought: the dead had had enough of life; all they wanted was rest, and this they *'implore.'* There is all the helplessness, and humble hope, and deathlike prayer, that can arise from the grave—*'implora pace.'* I hope, whoever may survive me, and shall see me put in the foreigners' burying-ground at the Lido, within the fortress by the Adriatic, will see those two words, and no more, put over me. I trust they won't think of 'pickling, and bringing me home to Clod or Blunderbuss Hall.' I am sure my bones would not rest in an English grave, or my clay mix with the earth of that country. I believe the thought would drive me mad on my deathbed, could I suppose that any of my friends would be base enough to convey my carcass back to your soil. I would not even feed your worms, if I could help it.

So, as Shakespeare says of Mowbray, the banished Duke of Norfolk, who died at Venice (see Richard II), that he, after fighting

> Against black pagans, Turks, and Saracens,
> And toil'd with works of war, retir'd himself
> To Italy; and there, at *Venice,* gave
> His body to that *pleasant* country's earth,
> And his pure soul unto his Captain Christ,
> Under whose colours he had fought so long.

Before I left Venice, I had returned to you your late, and Mr. Hobhouse's, sheets of *Juan.* Don't wait for further answers from me, but address yours to Venice, as usual. I know nothing of my own movements; I may return there in a few days, or not for some time. All this depends on circumstances. I left Mr. Hoppner[48] very well, as well as his son and Mrs. Hoppner. My daughter Allegra was well too, and is growing pretty; her hair is growing darker, and her eyes are blue. Her temper and her ways, Mr. Hoppner says, are like mine, as well as her features: she will make, in that case, a manageable young lady.

I never hear anything of Ada, the little Electra of my Mycenae;[49] the moral Clytemnestra is not very communicative of her tidings, but there will come a day of reckoning, even if I should not live to see it.

I have at least seen Romilly shivered who was one of the assassins. When that felon, or lunatic (take your choice he must be one and might be both), was doing his worst to uproot my whole family tree, branch, and blossoms; when, after taking my retainer, he went over to them; when he was bringing desolation on my hearth and destruction on my household Gods, did he think that, in less than three years, a natural event—a severe domestic—but an expected and common domestic calamity,—would lay his carcass in a cross-road, or stamp his name in a verdict of Lunacy? Did he (who in his drivelling sexagenary dotage had not the courage to survive his Nurse —for what else was a wife to him at his time of

---

47 Giovanni Lorenzo Bernini, 1598–1680.

48 Richard Hoppner, 1786–1872, was the second son of John Hoppner, R.A. At the time of Byron's acquaintance he was English consul at Venice.

49 Electra, daughter of Agamemnon, King of Mycenae, urged her brother Orestes to avenge her father, who had been murdered by her mother, Clytemnestra, and her mother's lover.

life?)—reflect or consider what my feelings must have been, when wife, and child, and sister, and name, and fame, and country were to be my sacrifice on his legal altar—and this at a moment when my health was declining, my fortune embarrassed, and my mind had been shaken by many kinds of disappointment, while I was yet young and might have reformed what might be wrong in my conduct, and retrieved what was perplexing in my affairs. But the wretch is in his grave. I detested him living, and I will not affect to pity him dead; I still loathe him—as much as we can hate dust—but that is nothing.

What a long letter I have scribbled!

Yours truly,

Byron.

P. S. Here, as in Greece, they strew flowers on the tombs. I saw a quantity of rose-leaves, and entire roses, scattered over the graves at Ferrara. It has the most pleasing effect you can imagine.

23 *To* the Countess Guiccioli

Bologna, August 25, 1819

My Dear Teresa,

I have read this book in your garden;—my love, you were absent, or else I could not have read it. It is a favourite book of yours, and the writer was a friend of mine. You will not understand these English words, and *others* will not understand them—which is the reason I have not scrawled them in Italian. But you will recognize the handwriting of him who passionately loved you, and you will divine that, over a book which was yours, he could only think of love. In that word, beautiful in all languages, but most so in yours—*Amor mio*—is comprised my existence here and hereafter. I feel I exist here, and I fear that I shall exist hereafter,—to *what* purpose you will decide; my destiny rests with you, and you are a woman, seventeen years of age, and two out of a convent. I wish that you had stayed there, with all my heart,—or, at least, that I had never met you in your married state.

But all this is too late. I love you, and you love me,—at least, you *say so,* and *act* as if you *did* so, which last is a great consolation in all events. But *I* more than love you, and cannot cease to love you.

Think of me, sometimes, when the Alps and the ocean divide us,—but they never will, unless you *wish* it.

24 Extracts from a Diary, January-February 1821

Ravenna, January 4, 1821

'A sudden thought strikes me.' Let me begin a Journal once more. The last I kept was in Switzerland, in record of a tour made in the Bernese Alps, which I made to send to my sister in 1816, and I suppose that she has it still, for she wrote to me that she was pleased with it. Another, and longer, I kept in 1813–1814, which I gave to Thomas Moore in the same year.

This morning I gat me up late, as usual—weather bad—bad as England—worse. The snow of last week melting to the sirocco of to-day, so that there were two damned things at once. Could not even get to ride on horseback in the forest. Stayed at home all the morning—looked at the fire—wondered when the post would come. Post came at the Ave Maria, instead of half-past one o'clock, as it ought. Galignani's *Messengers,* six in number—a letter from Faenza, but none from England. Very sulky in consequence (for there ought to have been letters), and ate in consequence a copious dinner; for when I am vexed, it makes me swallow quicker—but drank very little.

I was out of spirits—read the papers—thought what *fame* was, on reading, in a case of murder, that 'Mr. Wych, grocer, at Tunbridge, sold some bacon, flour, cheese, and it is believed, some plums, to some gipsy woman accused. He had on his counter (I quote faithfully) a *book,* the Life of *Pamela,* which he was *tearing* for *waste* paper, etc., etc. In the cheese was found, etc., and a *leaf* of *Pamela wrapt round the bacon.'* What would Richardson, the vainest and luckiest of *living* authors (*i.e.* while alive)—he who, with Aaron Hill, used to prophesy and chuckle over the presumed fall of Fielding (the *prose* Homer of human nature) and of Pope (the most beautiful of poets)—what would he have said, could he have traced his pages from their place on the French prince's toilets (see Boswell's Johnson) to the grocer's counter and the gipsy-murderess's bacon!!!

What would he have said? What can anybody say, save what Solomon said long before us? After all, it is but passing from one counter to another, from the bookseller's to the other tradesman's—grocer or pastry-cook. For my part, I have met with most poetry upon trunks; so that I am apt to consider the trunk-maker as the sexton of authorship.

Wrote five letters in about half an hour, short and savage, to all my rascally correspondents. Carriage came. Heard the news of three murders at Faenza and Forli—a carabinier, a smuggler, and an attorney—all last night. The two first in a quarrel, the latter by premeditation.

Three weeks ago—almost a month—the 7th it was—I picked up the commandant, mortally wounded, out of the street; he died in my house; assassins unknown, but presumed political. His brethren wrote from Rome last night to thank me for having assisted him in his last moments. Poor fellow! it was a pity; he was a good soldier, but imprudent. It was eight in the evening when they killed him. We heard the shot; my servants and I ran out, and found him expiring, with five wounds, two whereof mortal—by slugs they seemed. I examined him, but did not go to the dissection next morning. . . .

January 5, 1821

Rose late—dull and drooping—the weather dripping and dense. Snow on the ground, and sirocco above in the sky, like yesterday. Roads up to the horse's belly, so that riding (at least for pleasure) is not very feasible. Added a postscript to my letter to Murray. Read the conclusion, for the fiftieth time (I have read all W. Scott's novels at least fifty times), of the third series of *Tales of my Landlord*—grand work—Scotch Fielding, as well as great English poet—wonderful man! I long to get drunk with him.

Dined *versus* six o' the clock. Forgot that there was a plum-pudding, (I have added, lately, *eating* to my 'family of vices,') and had dined before I knew it. Drank half a bottle of some sort of spirits—probably spirits of wine; for what they call brandy, rum, etc., etc., here is nothing but spirits of wine, coloured accordingly. Did *not* eat two apples, which were placed by way of dessert. Fed the two cats, the hawk, and the tame (but *not tamed*) crow. Read Mitford's *History of Greece*—Xenophon's *Retreat of the Ten Thousand*. Up to this present moment writing, 6 minutes before eight o' the clock—French hours, not Italian.

Hear the carriage—order pistols and great coat, as usual—necessary articles. Weather cold—carriage open, and inhabitants somewhat savage—rather treacherous and highly inflamed by politics. Fine fellows, though,—good materials for a nation. Out of chaos God made a world, and out of high passions comes a people.

Clock strikes—going out to make love. Somewhat perilous, but not disagreeable. Memorandum—a new screen put up to-day. It is rather antique, but will do with a little repair.

Thaw continues—hopeful that riding may be practicable tomorrow. Sent the papers to All'.—grand events coming.

January 6, 1821

. . . At eight went out to visit. Heard a little music—like music. Talked with Count Pietro G. of the Italian comedian Vestris, who is now at Rome—have seen him often act in Venice—a good actor—very. Somewhat of a mannerist; but excellent in broad comedy, as well as in the sentimental pathetic. He has made me frequently laugh and cry, neither of which is now a very easy matter—at least, for a player to produce in me.

Thought of the state of women under the ancient Greeks—convenient enough. Present state a remnant of the barbarism of the chivalric and feudal ages—artificial and unnatural. They ought to mind home—and be well fed and clothed—but not mixed in society. Well educated, too, in religion—but to read neither poetry nor politics—nothing but books of piety and cookery. Music—drawing—dancing—also a little gardening and ploughing now and then. I have seen them mending the roads in Epirus with good success. Why not, as well as haymaking and milking?

Came home, and read Mitford again, and played with my mastiff—gave him his supper. Made another reading to the epigram, but the turn the same. To-night at the theatre, there being a prince on his throne in the last scene of the comedy,—the audience laughed, and asked him for a *Constitution*. This shows the state of the public mind here, as well as the assassinations. It won't do. There must be an universal republic,—and there ought to be.

January 7, 1821, Sunday

. . . The Count Pietro G[amba] took me aside to say that the Patriots have had notice from Forli (twenty miles off) that to-night the government and its party mean to strike a stroke—that the Cardinal here has had orders to make several arrests immediately, and that, in consequence, the Liberals are arming, and have posted patrols in the streets, to sound the alarm and give notice to fight for it.

He asked me 'what should be done?' I answered, 'Fight for it, rather than be taken in detail'; and offered, if any of them are in immediate apprehension of arrest, to receive them in my house (which is defensible), and to defend them, with my servants and themselves (we have arms and ammunition), as long as we can,—or to try to get them away under cloud of night. On going home, I offered him the pistols which I had about me—but he refused, but said he would come off to me in case of accidents.

It wants half an hour of midnight, and rains; —as Gibbet says, 'A fine night for their enterprise—dark as hell, and blows like the devil.' If the row don't happen *now,* it must soon. I thought that their system of shooting people would soon produce a reaction—and now it seems coming. I will do what I can in the way of combat, though a little out of exercise. The cause is a good one. . . .

January 9, 1821

. . . Heard some music. At nine the usual visitors—news, *war,* or rumours of war. Consulted with P. G., etc., etc. They mean to *insurrect* here, and are to honour me with a call thereupon. I shall not fall back; though I don't think them in force or heart sufficient to make much of it. But, *onward!*—it is now the time to act, and what signifies *self,* if a single spark of that which would be worthy of the past can be bequeathed unquenchedly to the future? It is not one man, nor a million, but the *spirit* of liberty which must be spread. The waves which dash upon the shore are, one by one, broken, but yet the *ocean* conquers, nevertheless. It overwhelms the Armada, it wears the rock, and, if the *Neptunians* are to be believed, it has not only destroyed, but made a world. In like manner, whatever the sacrifice of individuals, the great cause will gather strength, sweep down what is rugged, and fertilise (for *seaweed* is *manure*) what is cultivable. And so, the mere selfish calculation ought never to be made on such occasions; and, at present, it shall not be computed by me. I was never a good arithmetician of chances, and shall not commence now.

January 13, 1821

. . . Dined—news come—the *Powers* mean to war with the peoples. The intelligence seems positive—let it be so—they will be beaten in the end. The king-times are fast finishing. There will be blood shed like water, and tears like mist; but the peoples will conquer in the end. I shall not live to see it, but I foresee it. . . .

January 21, 1821

. . . To-morrow is my birthday—that is to say, at twelve o' the clock, midnight, *i.e.* in twelve minutes, I shall have completed thirty and three years of age!!!—and I go to my bed with a heaviness of heart at having lived so long, and to so little purpose.

It is three minutes past twelve.—' 'Tis the middle of the night by the castle clock,' and I am now thirty-three!

> Eheu, fugaces, Posthume, Posthume,
> Labuntur anni;—[50]

but I don't regret them so much for what I have done, as for what I *might* have done.

> Through life's road, so dim and dirty,
> I have dragged to three-and-thirty.
> What have these years left to me?
> Nothing—except thirty-three.

January 22, 1821

> 1821.
> Here lies
> interred in the Eternity
> of the Past,
> from whence there is no
> Resurrection
> for the Days—Whatever there may be
> for the Dust—
> the Thirty-Third Year
> of an ill-spent Life,
> Which, after
> a lingering disease of many months
> sunk into a lethargy,
> and expired,
> January 22d, 1821, A. D.
> Leaving a successor
> Inconsolable
> for the very loss which
> occasioned its
> Existence.

January 25, 1821

. . . Answered Murray's letter—read—lounged. Scrawled this additional page of life's log-book. One day more is over of it and of me:—but 'which is best, life or death, the gods only know,' as Socrates said to his judges, on the breaking up of the tribunal. Two thousand years since that sage's declaration of ignorance have not enlightened us more upon this important point; for, according to the Christian dispensation, no one can know whether he is *sure* of salvation—even the most righteous—since a single slip of faith may throw him on his back, like a skater, while gliding smoothly to his paradise. Now, therefore, whatever the certainty of faith in the facts may

---

50 'Alas, Posthumus, the fleeting years slip by.'—Horace, *Odes,* II, xiv, 1.

be, the certainty of the individual as to his happiness or misery is no greater than it was under Jupiter.

It has been said that the immortality of the soul is a *grand peut-être*—but still it is a *grand* one. Everybody clings to it—the stupidest, and dullest, and wickedest of human bipeds is still persuaded that he is immortal.

January 26, 1821

On dismounting, found Lieutenant E. just arrived from Faenza. Invited him to dine with me to-morrow. Did *not* invite him for to-day, because there was a small *turbot,* (Friday, fast regularly and religiously,) which I wanted to eat all myself. Ate it.

Went out—found T. as usual—music. The gentlemen, who make revolutions and are gone on a shooting, are not yet returned. They don't return till Sunday—that is to say, they have been out for five days, buffooning, while the interests of a whole country are at stake, and even they themselves compromised.

It is a difficult part to play amongst such a set of assassins and blockheads—but, when the scum is skimmed off, or has boiled over, good may come of it. If this country could but be freed, what would be too great for the accomplishment of that desire? for the extinction of that Sigh of Ages? Let us hope. They have hoped these thousand years. The very revolvement of the chances may bring it—it is upon the dice. . . .

January 31, 1821, Midnight

I have been reading Grimm's *Correspondence.* He repeats frequently, in speaking of a poet, or a man of genius in any department, even in music, (Grétry, for instance,) that he must have *une ame qui se tourmente, un esprit violent.*[51] How far this may be true, I know not; but if it were, I should be a poet *'per excellenza';* for I have always had *une ame,* which not only tormented itself but everybody else in contact with it; and an *esprit violent,* which has almost left me without any *esprit* at all. As to defining what a poet *should* be, it is not worth while, for what are *they* worth? what have they done?

February 18, 1821

. . . To-day I have had no communication with my Carbonari cronies; but, in the meantime, my lower apartments are full of their bayonets, fusils, cartridges, and what not. I suppose that they con-

sider me as a depôt, to be sacrificed, in case of accidents. It is no great matter, supposing that Italy could be liberated, who or what is sacrificed. It is a grand object—the very *poetry* of politics. Only think—a free Italy!!! Why, there has been nothing like it since the days of Augustus. I reckon the times of Cæsar (Julius) free; because the commotions left everybody a side to take, and the parties were pretty equal at the set out. But, afterwards, it was all praetorian and legionary business—and since!—we shall see, or, at least, some will see, what card will turn up. It is best to hope, even of the hopeless. The Dutch did more than these fellows have to do, in the Seventy Years' War.

February 19, 1821

Came home *solus*—very high wind—lightning —moonshine—solitary stragglers muffled in cloaks—women in masks—white houses—clouds hurrying over the sky, like spilt milk blown out of the pail—altogether very poetical. It is still blowing hard—the tiles flying, and the house rocking—rain splashing—lightning flashing— quite a fine Swiss Alpine evening, and the sea roaring in the distance.

Visited—conversazione. All the women frightened by the squall: they *won't* go to the masquerade because it lightens—the pious reason!

Still blowing away. A. has sent me some news today. The war approaches nearer and nearer. Oh those scoundrel sovereigns! Let us but see them beaten—let the Neapolitans but have the pluck of the Dutch of old, or the Spaniards of now, or of the German Protestants, the Scotch Presbyterians, the Swiss under Tell, or the Greeks under Themistocles—*all* small and solitary nations (except the Spaniards and German Lutherans), and there is yet a resurrection for Italy, and a hope for the world.

February 20, 1821

The news of the day are, that the Neapolitans are full of energy. The public spirit *here* is certainly well kept up. The *Americani* (a patriotic society here, an under branch of the *Carbonari*) give a dinner in *the Forest* in a few days, and have invited me, as one of the C[1]. It is to be in *the Forest* of Boccacio's and Dryden's 'Huntsman's Ghost'; and, even if I had not the same political feelings, (to say nothing of my old convivial turn, which every now and then revives,) I would go as a poet, or, at least, as a lover of poetry. I shall expect to see the spectre of

---

51 'a mind which tortures itself, a turbulent spirit.'

'Ostasio degli Onesti' (Dryden has turned him into Guido Cavalcanti—an essentially different person, as may be found in Dante) come 'thundering for his prey in the midst of the festival.' At any rate, whether he does or no, I will get as tipsy and patriotic as possible.

February 24, 1821

Rode, etc., as usual. The secret intelligence arrived this morning, from the frontier to the C[1]. is as bad as possible. The *plan* has missed—the Chiefs are betrayed, military, as well as civil—and the Neapolitans not only have *not* moved, but have declared to the P. government, and to the Barbarians, that they know nothing of the matter!!!

Thus the world goes; and thus the Italians are always lost for lack of union among themselves. What is to be done *here,* between the two fires, and cut off from the N[n]. frontier, is not decided. My opinion was,—better to rise than be taken in detail; but how it will be settled now, I cannot tell. Messengers are despatched to the delegates of the other cities to learn their resolutions.

I always had an idea that it would be *bungled;* but was willing to hope, and am so still. Whatever I can do by money, means, or person, I will venture freely for their freedom; and have so repeated to them (some of the Chiefs here) half an hour ago. I have two thousand five hundred scudi, better than five hundred pounds, in the house, which I offered to begin with.

February 27, 1821

. . . Yesterday wrote two notes on the 'Bowles and Pope' controversy, and sent them off to Murray by the post. The old woman whom I relieved in the forest (she is ninety-four years of age) brought me two bunches of violets. *Nam vita gaudet mortua floribus.*[52] I was much pleased with the present. An English woman would have presented a pair of worsted stockings, at least, in the month of February. Both excellent things; but the former are more elegant. The present, at this season, reminds one of Gray's stanza, omitted from his elegy:—

Here scatter'd oft, the *earliest* of the year,
    By hands unseen, are showers of violets found;
The red-breast loves to build and warble here,
    And little footsteps lightly print the ground.

As fine a stanza as any in his elegy. I wonder that he could have the heart to omit it.

---

52 'For life when on the point of death delights in flowers.'

Last night I suffered horribly—from an indigestion, I believe. I *never* sup—that is, never at home. But, last night, I was prevailed upon by the Countess Gamba's persuasion, and the strenuous example of her brother, to swallow, at supper, a quantity of boiled cockles, and to dilute them, *not* reluctantly, with some Imola wine. When I came home, apprehensive of the consequences, I swallowed three or four glasses of spirits, which men (the venders) call brandy, rum, or hollands, but which gods would entitle spirits of wine, coloured or sugared. All was pretty well till I got to bed, when I became somewhat swollen, and considerably vertiginous. I got out, and mixing some soda-powders, drank them off. This brought on temporary relief. I returned to bed; but grew sick and sorry once and again. Took more soda-water. At last I fell into a dreary sleep. Woke, and was ill all day, till I had galloped a few miles. Query—was it the cockles, or what I took to correct them, that caused the commotion? I think both. I remarked in my illness the complete inertion, inaction, and destruction of my chief mental faculties. I tried to rouse them, and yet could not—and this is the *Soul!!!* I should believe that it was married to the body, if they did not sympathize so much with each other. If the one rose, when the other fell, it would be a sign that they longed for the natural state of divorce. But as it is, they seem to draw together like post-horses.

Let us hope the best—it is the grand possession.

25 *To* Thomas Moore

Ravenna, July 5, 1821

How could you suppose that I ever would allow anything that *could* be said on your account to weigh with *me?* I only regret that Bowles[53] had not *said* that you were the writer of that note, until afterwards, when out he comes with it, in a private letter to Murray, which Murray sends to me. D—n the controversy!

D—n Twizzle,
        D—n the bell,
And d—n the fool who rung it—Well!
From all such plagues I'll quickly be delivered.

---

53 William Lisle Bowles, who published an edition of Pope in 1806, became involved in a controversy provoked by Campbell's *Essay on English Poetry,* 1819, over the value of Pope's poetry. Byron was brought in because of his derisive lines in *English Bards and Scottish Reviewers* ridiculing Bowles's poetry. In the Bowles-Byron controversy Moore found himself in an awkward position between an old acquaintance and a friend.

I have had a friend of your Mr. Irving's[54]—a very pretty lad—a Mr. Coolidge, of Boston—only somewhat too full of poesy and 'entusymusy.' I was very civil to him during his few hours' stay, and talked with him much of Irving, whose writings are my delight. But I suspect that he did not take quite so much to me, from his having expected to meet a misanthropical gentleman, in wolf-skin breeches, and answering in fierce monosyllables, instead of a man of this world. I can never get people to understand that poetry is the expression of *excited passion,* and that there is no such thing as a life of passion any more than a continuous earthquake, or an eternal fever. Besides, who would ever *shave* themselves in such a state?

I have had a curious letter to-day from a girl in England (I never saw her), who says she is given over of a decline, but could not go out of the world without thanking me for the delight which my poesy for several years, etc., etc., etc. It is signed simply N. N. A. and has not a word of 'cant' or preachment in it upon *any* opinions. She merely says that she is dying, and that as I had contributed so highly to her existing pleasure, she thought that she might say so, begging me to *burn* her *letter*—which, by the way, I can *not* do, as I look upon such a letter in such circumstances as better than a diploma from Gottingen. I once had a letter from Drontheim in *Norway* (but not from a dying woman), in verse, on the same score of gratulation. These are the things which make one at times believe one's self a poet. But if I must believe that * * * , and such fellows, are poets also, it is better to be out of the corps.

I am now in the fifth act of *Foscari,* being the third tragedy in twelve months, besides *proses;* so you perceive that I am not at all idle. And are you, too, busy? I doubt that your life at Paris draws too much upon your time, which is a pity. Can't you divide your day, so as to combine both? I have had plenty of all sorts of worldly business on my hands last year, and yet it is not so difficult to give a few hours to the *Muses.* This sentence is so like * * * that—

Ever, etc.

If we were together, I should publish both my plays (periodically) in our *joint* journal. It should be our plan to publish all our best things in that way.

54 Washington Irving.

26 *To* Thomas Moore

Pisa, March 4, 1822

Since I wrote the enclosed, I have waited another post, and now have your answer acknowledging the arrival of the packet—a troublesome one, I fear, to you in more ways than one, both from weight external and internal.

The unpublished things in your hands, in Douglas K.'s, and Mr. John Murray's, are, *Heaven and Earth,* a lyrical kind of Drama upon the Deluge, etc.;—*Werner, now with you;*—a translation of the First Canto of the *Morgante Maggiore;*—*ditto* of an Episode in Dante;—some stanzas to the Po, June 1st, 1819;—*Hints from Horace,* written in 1811, but a good deal, *since,* to be omitted; several prose things, which may, perhaps, as well remain unpublished;—*The Vision,* etc., of Quevedo Redivivus, in verse.

Here you see is 'more matter for a May morning'; but how much of this can be published is for consideration. The Quevedo (one of my best in that line) has appalled the Row already, and must take its chance at Paris, if at all. The new Mystery is less speculative than *Cain,* and very pious; besides, it is chiefly lyrical. The *Morgante* is the *best* translation that ever was or will be made; and the rest are—whatever you please to think them.

I am sorry you think *Werner* even *approaching* to any fitness for the stage, which, with my notions upon it, is very far from my present object. With regard to the publication, I have already explained that I have no exorbitant expectations of either fame or profit in the present instances; but wish them published because they are written, which is the common feeling of all scribblers.

With respect to 'Religion,' can I never convince you that *I* have no such opinions as the characters in that drama, which seems to have frightened everybody? Yet *they* are nothing to the expressions in Goethe's *Faust* (which are ten times hardier), and not a whit more bold than those of Milton's Satan. My ideas of a character may run away with me: like all imaginative men, I, of course, embody myself with the character while I *draw* it, but not a moment after the pen is from off the paper.

I am no enemy to religion, but the contrary. As a proof, I am educating my natural daughter a strict Catholic in a convent of Romagna; for I think people can never have *enough* of religion, if they are to have any. I incline, myself, very much to the Catholic doctrines; but if I am to write a drama, I must make my characters speak as I conceive them likely to argue.

As to poor Shelley, who is another bugbear to you and the world, he is, to my knowledge, the *least* selfish and the mildest of men—a man who has made more sacrifices of his fortune and feelings for others than any I ever heard of. With his speculative opinions I have nothing in common, nor desire to have.

The truth is, my dear Moore, you live near the *stove* of society, where you are unavoidably influenced by its heat and its vapours. I did so once—and too much—and enough to give a colour to my whole future existence. As my success in society was *not* inconsiderable, I am surely not a prejudiced judge upon the subject, unless in its favour; but I think it, as now constituted, *fatal* to all great original undertakings of every kind. I never courted it *then,* when I was young and high in blood, and one of its 'curled darlings'; and do you think I would do so *now,* when I am living in a clearer atmosphere? One thing *only* might lead me back to it, and that is, to try once more if I could do any good in *politics;* but *not* in the petty politics I see now preying upon our miserable country.

Do not let me be misunderstood, however. If you speak your *own* opinions, they ever had, and will have, the greatest weight with *me.* But if you merely *echo* the *monde,* (and it is difficult not to do so, being in its favour and its ferment,) I can only regret that you should ever repeat anything to which I cannot pay attention.

But I am prosing. The gods go with you, and as much immortality of all kinds as may suit your present and all other existence.

Yours, etc.

27 *To* Lieut.-Colonel Napier

Metaxata, Sept. 9, 1823

My Dear Colonel,

I return you your somewhat desponding correspondent's epistle, with many thanks for that as for other and many kindnesses. I have had two from Blaquiere (dated Ancona and addressed to me at Genoa) in the old style, but more sanguine than Signor Pavone's. All this comes of what Mr. Braham pronounces '*Entusymusy,*' expecting too much and starting at speed; it is lucky for me so far that, fail or not fail, I

can hardly be disappointed, for I believed myself on a fool's errand from the outset, and must, therefore, like Dogberry, 'spare no wisdom.' I will at least linger on here or there till I see whether I *can* be of *any* service in *any* way; and if I doubt it, it is because I do not feel confidence in my individual capacity for this kind of beartaming, and not from a disbelief in the powers of a more active or less indifferent character to be of use to them, though I feel persuaded that that person must be a military man.

But I like the Cause at least, and will stick by it while it is not degraded nor dishonoured.

You have been so kind to me (as indeed all our compatriots have been) that any additional trouble I should give you would be in the Gospel phrase—another 'coal of fire' upon my head.

The first time I descend into the valley, I will call, and I hope whenever you come up this way you will look in and see how comfortable we are under your auspices.

Ever yours,

Noel Byron.

28 *To* the Hon. Augusta Leigh

Cephalonia, Oct. 12, 1823

My Dearest Augusta,

Your three letters on the subject of Ada's indisposition have made me very anxious to hear further of her amelioration. I have been subject to the same complaint, but not at so early an age, nor in so great a degree. Besides, it never affected my eyes but rather my hearing, and that only partially and slightly and for a short time. I had dreadful and almost periodical headaches till I was fourteen, and sometimes since; but abstinence and a habit of bathing my head in cold water every morning cured me, I think, at least I have been less molested since that period. . . . Let me know how she is. I need not say how *very* anxious I am (at this distance particularly) to hear of her welfare.

You ask why I came up amongst the Greeks? It was stated to me that my so doing might tend to their advantage in some measure in their present struggle for independence, both as an individual and as a member for the Committee now in England. How far this may be realized I cannot pretend to anticipate, but I am willing to do what I can. They have at length found leisure to quarrel among themselves, after repelling their other enemies, and it is no very easy part that I may have to play to avoid appearing partial to one or other of their factions. They have turned out Mavrocordato, who was the only *Washington* or *Kosciusko* kind of man amongst them, and they have not yet sent their deputies to London to treat for a loan, nor in short done themselves so much good as they might have done. I have written to Mr. Hobhouse three several times with a budget of documents on the subject, from which he can extract all the present information for the Committee. I have written to their government at Tripolizza and Salamis, and am waiting for instructions *where* to proceed, for things are in such a state amongst them, that it is difficult to conjecture where one could be useful to them, if at all. However, I have some hopes that they will see their own interest sufficiently not to quarrel till they have received their national independence, and then they can fight it out among them in a domestic manner—and welcome. You may suppose that I have something to *think* of at least, for you can have no idea what an intriguing cunning unquiet generation they are, and as emissaries of all parties come to me at present, and I must act impartially, it makes me exclaim, as Julian did at his military exercises, 'Oh! Plato, what a task for a Philosopher!'

However, *you* won't think much of *my philosophy; nor do I, entre nous.*

If you think this epistle or any part of it worth transmitting to Lady Byron you can send her a copy, as I suppose . . . she cannot be altogether indifferent as to my 'whereabouts' and *what-abouts.*

I am at present in a very pretty village (Metaxata in Cephalonia) between the mountains and the Sea, with a view of Zante and the Morea, waiting for some more decisive intelligence from the provisional Gov^t. in Salamis. ──But here come some visitors.

I was interrupted yesterday by Col Napier and the Captain of a King's ship now in the harbour. Col. N. is Resident or Governor here and has been extremely kind and hospitable, as indeed have been all the English here. When their visit was over a Greek arrived on business about this eternal siege of Mesalonghi (on the Coast of Acarnania or Etolia) and some convoys of provisions which we want to throw in; and after this was discussed, I got on horseback (I brought up my horses with me on board and troublesome neighbours they were in blowing weather) and road to Argostoli and back; and then I had one of my *thunder* headaches (*you* know how my head

acts like a barometer when there is electricity in the air) and I could not resume till this morning. Since my arrival in August I made a tour to Ithaca (which you will take to be Ireland, but if you look into Pope's *Odyssey,* you will discover to be the ancient name of the Isle of Wight) and also over some parts of Cephalonia.

We are pretty well in health, the Gods be thanked!

* * *

There is a clever but eccentric man here, a Dr. Kennedy, who is very pious and tries in good earnest to make converts; but his Christianity is a queer one, for he says that the priesthood of the Church of England are no more Christians than "Mahound or Termagant" are. He has made some converts, I suspect rather to the beauty of his wife (who is pretty as well as pious) than of his theology. I like what I have seen of him, of *her* I know nothing, nor desire to know, having other things to think about. *He* says that the dozen shocks of an Earthquake we had the other day are a sign of his doctrine, or a judgement on his audience, but this opinion has not acquired proselytes. One of the shocks was so prolonged that, though not very heavy, we thought the house would come down, and as we have a staircase to dismount *out* of the house (the buildings here are different from ours), it was judged expedient by the inmates (all *men* please to recollect, as if there had been females we must have helped them out or broken our heads for company) to make an expeditious retreat into the courtyard. *Who* was *first* out of the door I know not, but when I got to the bottom of the stairs I found several arrived before me, which could only have happened by their jumping out of the windows or down *over* or from the stairs (which had no balustrade or bannisters) rather than in the regular way of descent. The scene was ludicrous enough, but we had several more slight shocks in the night but stuck quietly to our beds, for it would have been of no use moving, as the house would have been down first, had it been to come down at all.

There was no great damage done in the Island (except an old house or two cracking in the middle), but the soldiers on parade were lifted up as a boat is by the tide, and you could have seen the whole line waving (though no one was in motion) by the heaving of the ground on which they were drawn up. You can't complain of this being a brief letter.

I wish you would obtain from Lady B. some account of Ada's disposition, habits, studies, moral tendencies, and temper, as well as of her personal appearance, for except from the miniature drawn five years ago (and she is now double that age nearly) I have no idea of even her aspect. When I am advised on these points, I can form some notion of her character and what way her dispositions or indispositions ought to be treated. At *her* present age I have an idea that I had many feelings and notions which people would not believe if I stated them *now,* and therefore I may as well keep them to myself. Is she social or solitary, taciturn or talkative, fond of reading or otherwise? And what is her *tic?*—I mean her foible. Is she passionate? I hope that the Gods have made her anything save *poetical*—it is enough to have one such fool in a family. You can answer all this at your leisure: address to *Genoa* as usual, the letters will be forwarded better by my Correspondents there.

Yours ever,

N. B.

P.S.—Tell Douglas Kinnaird I have only just got his letter of August 19th, and not only approve of his accepting a sum not under ten or twelve thousand pounds for the property in question, but also of his getting as much as can be gotten above that price.

29 *To* Thomas Moore

Cephalonia, December 27, 1823

I received a letter from you some time ago. I have been too much employed latterly to write as I could wish, and even now must write in haste.

I embark for Missolonghi to join Mavrocordato[55] in four-and-twenty hours. The state of parties (but it were a long story) has kept me here till *now*; but now that Mavrocordato (their Washington, or their Kosciusko) is employed again, I can act with a *safe conscience*. I carry money to pay the squadron, etc., and I have influence with the Suliotes, *supposed* sufficient to keep them in harmony with some of the dissentients;—for there are plenty of differences, but trifling.

It is imagined that we shall attempt either Patras or the castles on the Straits; and it seems, by most accounts, that the Greeks, at any rate the Suliotes, who are in affinity with me of 'bread and salt,'—except that I should march with them, and—be it even so! If anything in the way of fever, fatigue, famine, or otherwise, should cut short the middle age of a brother warbler,—like Garcilasso de la Vega, Kleist, Korner, Joukoffsky (a Russian nightingale—see Bowring's *Anthology*), or Thersander, or,—or somebody else—but never mind—I pray you to remember me in your 'smiles and wine.'

I have hopes that the cause will triumph; but whether it does or no, still 'honour must be minded as strictly as milk diet.' I trust to observe both.

Ever, etc.

---

55 Prince Alexander Mavrocordato, 1791–1865, was distinguished as a leader in the Greek war of independence, and later as minister and diplomat.

1792 · PERCY BYSSHE SHELLEY · 1822

1792   Born 4 August at Field Place, an estate near Horsham, in Sussex, eldest son of Timothy Shelley, a country squire of commonplace talents, and Elizabeth (Pilfold), a somewhat nervous, imaginative woman described as 'an excellent letter-writer but not interested in literature.' The poet's grandfather, Bysshe Shelley, was an eccentric enterprising individual, who had amassed a huge fortune by successive marriages with two heiresses. There were four younger sisters and a very much younger brother. Shelley enjoyed a happy imaginative childhood with his sisters at Field Place, playing at witches, wizards, and demons.

1798–1804   Was sent to a day school at Warnham and at the age of ten began attendance at Syon House Academy near Brentford. As a boy was extraordinarily sensitive, normally sweet-tempered and generous, but easily stirred to anger. Became the butt of the schoolyard. In the classroom, however, was a good Latin scholar, with an extremely good memory and imagination and intellectual energy far beyond his physical strength. Avidly read the 'sixpenny dreadfuls.' Developed an interest, probably through his teacher Adam Walker, in scientific experiments and speculations. During vacations at Field Place led his sisters in exploits and entertained them with extraordinary tales of supernatural wonders. At Syon Academy dedicated himself to a life of lofty idealism.

1804–10   At Eton. Rebelled against the system of fagging; in retaliation his schoolmates baited him time after time. Yet 'Mad Shelley' eventually won the respect and goodwill of his fellows. Was notorious for his lack of skill and interest in most of the popular games and in fighting, but enjoyed boating and shooting and rambling over the surrounding countryside. Indulged in boyish pranks such as setting a tree on fire with gunpowder and burning glass. Continued his enthusiasm and experiments in natural science begun at Syon House. Sought the lore of magic and witchcraft and watched all night for ghosts. His mind at this time, according to Medwin, 'ran on bandits, castles, ruined towers, wild mountains, storms and apparitions, and the terrific.' Reveled in the poetry of Southey, Chatterton, Campbell, and Scott. Was befriended by the elderly Dr. Lind, a retired physician living in near-by Windsor, in whose library he browsed and who probably introduced him to Godwin's *Political Justice.* Was actively devoted to reading in radical literature, science, and romance. Experienced a first love affair with his cousin Harriet Grove, which was terminated by the Grove family in December 1810, on account of his radical religious views. Was already a voluminous writer of letters, poems, and novels. Wrote, in 1810, *Wandering Jew, Original Poetry of Victor and Cazire* (with his sister Elizabeth), *Posthumous Fragments of Margaret Nicholson,* and two extravagant romances, *Zastrozzi* and *St. Irvyne.*

1810–11   In October took up his residence at University College, Oxford. Was bored with lectures and tutors, but gladly gave himself over to omnivorous reading, especially to the empiricists, necessitarians, and skeptics, including besides Godwin (who had become a passion with him) Hume, Locke, and Voltaire. Formed a close friendship with Thomas Jefferson Hogg, with whom he shared his new-formed political idealism founded on reason. During Christmas vacation attempted to proselytize his sisters and his father. With Hogg as co-author hastily wrote and published *The Necessity of Atheism,* which resulted in his and

Hogg's expulsion from Oxford, 25 March. Put up a bold front to hide his feelings, but was deeply hurt by his expulsion. In London made the personal acquaintanceship of Leigh Hunt, to whom in a letter he had previously avowed his sympathy and help when Hunt was being prosecuted by the government. Established a friendship with Elizabeth Hitchener, a schoolteacher, and carried on a voluminous correspondence with her. Met and fell in love with Harriet Westbrook, aged sixteen. Eloped with her and was married in Edinburgh, 28 August. Broke temporarily with Hogg. Spent several months at Keswick in the Lake country. Met Southey but was disappointed in him. Was alienated from his father over his expulsion and marriage, though finally Sir Timothy agreed to settle on his son an annuity of £200.

1812   Wrote to Godwin professing his ardent discipleship. February-April, was in Ireland speaking and writing for reform. Wrote *An Address to the Irish People* and *Proposals for an Association of Philanthropists*. April-October, resided at Nantgwillt, Lynmouth, and Tremadoc. Published *A Declaration of Rights* and *Letter to Lord Ellenborough*. Was under government suspicion as a reformer. Became disillusioned in Elizabeth Hitchener, once the 'sister of my soul,' now the 'Brown Demon.' Busily at work on *Queen Mab*. Met T. L. Peacock and William Godwin. Began advancing money to Godwin.

1813   From Tremadoc, after a brief trip to Ireland, returned to London in April. Privately printed *Queen Mab*. Daughter Ianthe born in June. In serious financial straits. Practiced vegetarianism. Established a friendship with the J. F. Newtons and through them with Mrs. Boinville and her circle. About mid-July moved to Bracknell, Berkshire, to be near the Boinvilles. October-December, went on a vacation trip to the Lakes and Edinburgh.

1814   Went to live with the Boinvilles at Bracknell in February. His incipient love affair with Cornelia Turner (Mrs. Boinville's daughter) terminated by the Boinvilles' requesting Shelley to leave. Published *A Refutation of Deism*. In May and June, frequent meetings with Mary Godwin, lovely and intelligent seventeen-year-old daughter of William Godwin and Mary Wollstonecraft. Eloped to France with Mary, 28 July, and with the lovers went Jane 'Claire' Clairmont, daughter of Godwin's second wife by her first marriage. Wrote a letter to Harriet assuring her that he was her best friend and urging her to join him and Mary and bring papers to legalize their separation. After gypsying from Paris to Switzerland, the three elopers returned to England in September by way of the Rhine country. Shelley was awakened by the tour to 'the inconstant summer of delight and beauty which invests this invisible world.' Harriet's second child, Charles Bysshe, born in November. In London many friends fell away from him because of his elopement. He also suffered financial distress, and had to move about from place to place and keep in hiding to escape imprisonment for debt.

1815   Sir Bysshe, Shelley's grandfather, died in January, relieving the poet of immediate financial worries and making him financially secure for the rest of his life. An annual income of £1000 was settled on him, of which Shelley settled £200 annually upon Harriet. Mary's first child born 22 February, but died several days after. Shelley in a state of nervous tension for nearly nine months (September 1814-May 1815). Claire, who had become a source of irritation, left the Shelleys in May. A ten-day boat excursion up the Thames with Mary, Charles Clairmont, and Peacock helped to restore the poet's health and good spirits. Residence at Bishopsgate, near Windsor, summer of 1815 to summer of 1816. Close association with Peacock. In the autumn composed *Alastor*.

1816   Mary's second child, William, born in January. *Alastor* published in March. Shelley bitterly disappointed in Godwin, who in spite of large gifts of money continued to ask for more support. Upon the failure of the lawyers to adjust their sagging financial affairs, Shelley and Mary started out in May from Dover, accompanied by Claire Clairmont, for Geneva. There they met Byron, with whom Claire had entered into an intrigue just before his departure from England. Took up residence at a cottage near Coligny. From June to September, almost daily association with Byron, who was living near by at the Villa Diodati. Boating excursion around Lake Leman with Byron. Composed *Hymn to Intellectual*

Beauty. Excursion to the Vale of Chamouni produced the poem *Mont Blanc.* Returned to England in September. Fanny Imlay, Mary's half sister, committed suicide in October. Harriet drowned herself in late November or early December. Shelley legalized his union with Mary by formal marriage, 20 December. Involved in recurrent financial entanglements with Godwin. Visited Peacock at Marlow and Leigh Hunt at Hampstead. Acquaintanceship begun with Keats, Hazlitt, and Horace Smith.

1817   Settled at Marlow and spent more than a year in busy authorship, hospitality, and beneficence to the needy. Was refused custody of his and Harriet's children by decision of Lord Chancellor Eldon. Daughter Clara born, September. Wrote *A Proposal for Putting Reform to the Vote* and *Prince Athanase,* and began *Rosalind and Helen* and *Laon and Cythna* (*The Revolt of Islam*). Close and valuable friendships with Leigh Hunt and Horace Smith. Again became involved in financial difficulties and suffered poor health.

1818   *Laon and Cythna,* the title of which was changed to *The Revolt of Islam,* was published in January. Shelley and Mary and their two children, with Claire Clairmont and Allegra (Byron's child by Claire), left England for Italy in March. Shortly after their arrival in Italy Claire relinquished control of Allegra to Byron. The party made short stays at Pisa, Leghorn, and the Baths of Lucca. Shelley accompanied Claire to Venice, as she wished to see her child there, but Shelley alone visited Byron. Daughter Clara died in Venice, September. Mary and Shelley with Byron at Este, September-November. Shelley wrote *Julian and Maddalo* and *Lines Written among the Euganean Hills,* and began *Prometheus Unbound.* Visited Rome and settled in Naples, December. In Naples, Shelley, acting at first without Mary's knowledge, adopted a daughter, baptized Elena Adelaide Shelley.

1819   Published *Rosalind and Helen.* At Rome, March-June. In solitary walks about the ruins of the Baths of Caracalla. Completed Acts II and III of *Prometheus Unbound.* Worked on *The Cenci.* Son William died in Rome, June. Mary desolate. Shelleys and Claire at the Villa Valsovano, near Leghorn, June-October. In Florence, October-January. Son Percy Florence born, November. Friendship with the Gisbornes at Leghorn and with Sophia Stacey at Florence. Composed *The Cenci, Prometheus Unbound* (Act IV), *The Masque of Anarchy;* worked on *Philosophical View of Reform* (unfinished). Grossly assailed by the *Quarterly Review* for *The Revolt of Islam.*

1820   At Pisa, January-June. Friendships with the Gisbornes, 'Mrs. Mason,' Count Taaffe, Dr. Vacca, Mavrocordato. June-August, in Leghorn; August-October, at the Baths of San Giuliano; late October again at Pisa. Thomas Medwin, Shelley's cousin and former schoolmate, joined the Shelleys at the Baths of San Giuliano. Continued financial annoyance from Godwin; increasing domestic discord between Mary and Claire. Interest in the revolution in Spain resulted in *Ode to Liberty.* Wrote *Letter to Maria Gisborne, The Sensitive Plant, Oedipus Tyrannus, The Witch of Atlas.* Met Emilia Viviani in December. Published *Prometheus Unbound* and *The Cenci.*

1821   January-February, heightened ardor for Emilia. *Epipsychidion* written probably during the first two weeks of February. Wrote *Defence of Poetry* in February and March (published 1840). Keats died in Rome, 23 February. *Adonais* begun in April; printed at Pisa in July. Edward and Jane Williams joined the Pisan circle in January. May-October, at the Baths of Giuliano. Paid a brief visit to Byron at Ravenna in mid-August. Planned with Byron to found *The Liberal* and invited Leigh Hunt to Italy as editor. Emilia Viviani married, September. Wrote *Hellas.* The Shelleys joined by Byron at Pisa, November. Shelley increasingly admired Jane Williams.

1822   Edward Trelawny, a friend of Medwin and Williams, joined the Pisan circle in January. *Hellas* published. Moved to Casa Magni, a villa near Lerici, on the Gulf of Spezzia, May. Composed lyrics to Jane and enjoyed sailing, almost daily, with Edward Williams. Worked on *The Triumph of Life* (unfinished). Met Hunt at Leghorn in June. On 8 July, was drowned with Williams in Shelley's boat, the *Ariel.* The bodies of the two friends cremated on the beach by Trelawny, Byron, and Hunt. The poet's ashes taken to the Protestant Cemetery in Rome and buried close by the grave of Keats.

Percy Bysshe Shelley was a high-minded idealist with a passion for justice and human-heartedness. Yet he was not always wise in his personal relationships. Because of his unworldliness he was sometimes strangely insensitive and impractical, and often failed to understand the motives of others. He took it for granted that the majority of his fellow-men were as altruistic and fearless as he was. When he eloped with Mary Godwin he assumed that the world would understand and accept his action. Instead he was 'exposed publicly as an unworthy person.' The elopement proved to be a fatal action, the tragic after-consequences of which colored much of his later poetry. After about 1816, 'though he generally remained an optimist so far as society was concerned, for himself he became wholly disillusioned' (White). Ill health, domestic sorrow, public indifference, and critical malignity intensified his sense of the world's persecution. In the poetry of the middle and later years a note of self-pity becomes prominent. The poet is a 'frail form,' 'a love in desolation masked,' 'fallen upon the thorns of life.' His pessimism at times expanded to include life in general. Life is the 'eclipsing curse of birth,' a 'dim vast vale of tears,' a region of 'stormy visions.' In his darkest hours he felt that the world's evils could never be overcome. In his personal relationships, however, during later years 'he developed an ability to meet the ordinary world on its own terms' (White). His sympathy, tolerance, and generosity are well attested. He never cared much for social gatherings except with close friends and came increasingly to give his time to reading. He read incessantly and voraciously. He had always had the urge and power to deal with abstract ideas, to analyze his subtlest and most profound thoughts and feelings, and to relate these to the external world and its events. More and more as he became absorbed through his reading in a world of abstractions, he came to believe in the illusory nature of reality. This abstract world carried him far away from ordinary mortals. But Shelley was very human in his passions, his errors, his failures, and his achievements. Beneath his surface eccentricities and mannerisms he was sincerely courageous and determined. Of more importance for posterity, he had the poet's penetrative, many-sided mind and soaring imagination.

Shelley's chief hope was that he might be classed among the builders of 'that great poem,' to use his own words, 'which all poets, like the co-operating thoughts of one great mind, have built up since the beginning of the world.' He thought of himself as a Promethean light-bringer whose chief business was to destroy tyrannies and establish liberty. With the combination of high sensitivity and strong-mindedness, which were his by nature, it was inevitable that the experiences of his youth should destine him for the role of spiritual emancipator. The tyrannies which as a boy he read about in Gothic fiction; the persecutions by his schoolmates at Syon House and Eton; the confirmation of his rebellious faith discovered during Eton days by his reading of Godwin's *Political Justice;* the political liberalism to which he was exposed in his home and elsewhere; the termination of his affair with Harriet Grove because of his so-called atheistical tendencies—all these influences combined to make the young poet a full-fledged radical by the time he entered Oxford, ready for life-long warfare against those oppressions which seemed to him to dominate society. While he was at Oxford a deeper reading in philosophic and religious literature led him to the modern skeptics who prepared him (with his friend Hogg's encouragement and help) to write the pamphlet, *The Necessity of Atheism.* His expulsion, which was caused by its publication, brought about 'an emotional climax in his rebelliousness.' After Oxford his life was almost completely dominated by his passion to reform society. During his life with Harriet, he engaged in many specific acts as a reformer. He became interested in practical affairs, wrote and published proselytizing pamphlets at his own expense, and made private contributions to the working class. Appalled by the misery of the Irish people, he made a quixotic effort to arouse and convert them. His *Address to the Irish*

People is a ringing manifesto of his faith. In it he calls upon all Irishmen to bring about a 'new order' of society by fortifying their minds and purifying their hearts. But the Irish peasantry was ignorant and indifferent and made Shelley soon realize that deep-rooted evils are not quickly removed by exhortations and appeals. Personal misfortunes further obstructed Shelley's efforts for reform; yet he never gave up. He remained a radical reformer to the last. After his departure for Italy he kept closely in touch with English affairs and on the occasion of the 'Peterloo massacre' let loose a series of indignant and impassioned verses dedicated to the cause of the working class. 'I always go on until I am stopped,' he once remarked, 'and I am never stopped.' Still, though his resolution was unwavering, there was some modification in his methods. As time went by he increasingly realized that reform was a long, slow process. By 1816 we find him expressing in the preface to *The Revolt of Islam* a belief in 'a slow, gradual silent change.' In *Prometheus Unbound*, written two years later, he professes an aversion to didactic poetry. Experience had taught him that 'even the noblest of human intentions is liable to error.' It is only by truth and love operating within society's individual members that we may hope for the overthrow of wrong. In the youthful *Queen Mab*, written in 1812–13, it had seemed to Shelley a relatively simple matter to cure all social ills by destroying certain institutions and freely distributing the wealth. As he grew older he came to see that no alterations, however radical in outward forms, would alone bring in the millennium of human happiness. In *Prometheus Unbound* and *Hellas* he realized that the final citadel of evil is in the human mind and that evil can be vanquished only by the enlightened will. That Shelley was not an impractical visionary is demonstrated by the soundness of his recommendations for social progress in *A Philosophical View of Reform*. The purpose of this incomplete work was to show the steps by which social change may be brought about without violence. Subsequent political and social advances in England, many of them along the lines proposed by Shelley in *A Philosophical View*, give striking confirmation to his convictions. As for the lofty idealism of the poetry, one need only look to the teachings of Socrates and Christ for their doctrinal basis, or to the successful revolution of India's masses through passive resistance led by Gandhi to observe their prophetic fulfillment.

It has been pointed out how Shelley's early failures to arouse humanity to strike off the shackles of tyranny checked the ardor of his hopes and caused him to lose confidence that the ideal was immediately attainable in this world. After his desertion of Harriet for Mary he began to be dismayed, also, over his failure to realize the fulfillment of his personal dream of ideal love. He had hoped that life with Mary would bring unimaginable delight, but instead he found himself ostracized by society, hounded by creditors, disillusioned in Godwin, and frayed in body and spirit. On the basis of a physician's report he believed he was rapidly dying of consumption. These untoward circumstances caused Shelley to brood in solitude over the predominant misery of life and to imagine his own early death. His moods and the bitter experiences of the winter of 1814–15 he records, imaginatively exalted, in the poem *Alastor*. The story is of a high-minded youth who, living a life of solitude, falls in love with a vision of his 'soul mate,' a creation of his own mind. When he awakens from his dream of love, he suddenly becomes aware of his loneliness in the midst of Nature and is driven by an irresistible passion within him to seek for the vision's prototype in the ideal world. But the consuming flames of desire age him rapidly in his vain search and finally destroy him. Two thirds of the poem, beginning with about line 300, may be interpreted as an allegory of life and death. The sea is the 'sea of life'; the leaky boat is the declining body; the winds are the storm of death and the cavern the jaws of death. The forest represents the procreation of life; the well, the mysterious source of life; the stream, the span of mortal life; the precipice over which the stream falls, the boundary marking the immeasurable void between life and the unknown region of death. The poem deals for the most part with a problem rather than with an actual person. It is a parable of such a man as Shelley himself, sensitive and idealistic, who withdraws from the harsh conflicts of life (as he was tempted to do) and loses himself in the pursuit of an ideal unattainable in earthly form. That Shelley projected his own experience into the poem and then 'read the writing on the wall' (in the preface Shelley deplored the fact that the youth tried to live without human sympathy) is confirmed by numerous autobiographical factors in the poem. These include the poet's passionate pursuit of learning; his reverence for the past; his deep sensitiveness to noble ideas; his alienation from his home; his vegetarianism; his burning curiosity to 'unveil the latent mysteries of nature'; his hopeless search for an idealized companion; his neglect of human society (at least for a time) because of his intense search for knowledge; his tendency toward self-centered seclusion; his love of boating; his fearlessness in seeking truth. The incident of the veiled maid may have been an actual experience. Shelley tells of a similar experience in an autobiographical passage in the dedication of *The Revolt of Islam*. Also the mystical elements of the vision are reminiscent of the mystical union with heavenly beauty that had exalted Shelley during his recent visit to Switzerland. *Alastor* has seemed to some readers a not altogether satisfactory poem. Some have complained of diffuseness and a lack of proper proportion or control of the materials; others see a failure to distinguish between physical lure and spiritualized passion; still others are troubled over what appears to them a basic contradiction between the preface and the poem. When Shelley was writing *Alastor* he was passionately seeking for answers to questions that are perhaps unanswerable. His philosophy at the time was in a rapid state of transition. He was still a comparatively young poet. Nevertheless, in *Alastor* he is emerging as a great artist. The poem contains magnificent descriptive passages of Swiss mountain and river scenery and of the autumnal glories of Windsor Forest, which had excited his imagination during the preceding year. It picks up the half-mystical pantheism of Wordsworth and with Wordsworth's idiom something, too, of his sincerity. It glows with a sensuous intensity of imagery and sings with a swift, lyrical power.

On his second visit to Switzerland Shelley was lifted from despondency to soaring hopefulness. Renewed study of Plato and of Wordsworth amid the almost unearthly beauty of the Alps brought about a spiritual rebirth. Two impassioned lyrics, *Hymn to Intellectual Beauty* and *Mont Blanc*, give expression to the new prophetic idealism that exalted him. Always a Platonist by temperament (he was probably never an unqualified materialist) Shelley now became one by conviction. He had early perceived that if he were to urge men to establish Utopia, man must have freedom to think and to make right choices. By way of the idealistic philosophies of Berkeley, Plato, and the Neo-Platonists, he arrived at the doctrine of Free Will. The idealism of Berkeley, broadly considered, stands opposite to the materialism of Locke espoused by the poet during his *Queen Mab* days. According to Locke the mind is built up primarily through automatic sensory responses; but according to Berkeley, the external universe assumes meaningful forms chiefly because the mind gives reality to them. Plato, like Berkeley, places true reality in the mind, ultimately in the divine mind. The general or eternal 'forms' ('ideas,' 'essences,' 'abstractions') are, by Plato's account, the only real things in the universe. The natural world partakes of the ideal world, but only as shadows of the thoughts and patterns of the eternal forms. In Platonic philosophy, co-existent with Intellectual Beauty are Truth and the Good as equal (and identical) qualities of the Absolute, the ONE, who is God, or creative mind. The ONE transcends all change. From it overflows the divine fire of energy into the world of matter. It is hidden as behind a veil from the world of the senses. Yet in auspicious moments it is given to favored individuals to pierce the veil and to come into contact (in Wordsworth's phrase, 'to see into the life of things') with the abstract reality of beauty, the ONE. Once the rapturous participation of union with the eternal archetype, or Idea, of beauty is experienced, its passing leaves the initiated with an intense awareness of the dullness and wickedness of mortal life. With Shelley, mystic illumination made him increasingly conscious of his own sufferings and, in perhaps even greater measure, the sufferings of the unnumbered multitudes of his fellow human beings. He early came to the conviction that there was a predominance of evil in the world. In *Hymn to Intellectual Beauty* he describes this world as a 'dim vast vale of tears, vacant and desolate.' In his *Essay on Christianity* he states his belief that 'according to the indisputable facts of the case, some evil spirit has dominion in this imperfect world.' Platonic philosophy and Christian doctrine alike regard this earthly existence as a poor thing—a place of 'envy and calumny and hate.' But Intellectual Beauty offers to men a measure of hope—its light alone 'gives grace and truth to life's unquiet dream.' Man can rise superior to the seductions of sense into the world of beauty, truth, and goodness where his will is free to govern his inward real self. By the new power given him he liberates himself from the tyranny of evil and becomes an agency 'to free this world from its dark slavery.' Shelley's new intuitive faith in Intellectual Beauty offered him a way to social regeneration through the freedom of the mind. It also deeply satisfied his aesthetic and moral senses.

Shelley's second Swiss poem, *Mont Blanc*, gives rhapsodic expression—though in some conflict with necessitarian doctrine—to the same philosophical idealism that animates *Hymn to Intellectual Beauty*. The mountain is made the symbol of creative mind. The stream flowing from the snow-capped mountain is likened to Divine Power flowing from Divine Mind and animating all nature. As in the *Hymn*, *Mont Blanc* is given an ethical tinge and social emphasis. Wordsworthian naturalism and ethics merge toward the close of the poem with Platonic idealism. Subsequent private sorrows increased Shelley's awareness of the irremediable sadness of life and led him in subjective lyrics into an ever more despondent utterance, but the idealistic social faith of the Alpine poems carried him in his mature period to the heroic vision and sublime poetry of *Prometheus Unbound*.

Shelley poured all his passions, beliefs, and idealisms into *Prometheus Unbound*. When the drama was completed, the poet confided to his publisher that he considered it the best thing he had ever written. It remains his masterpiece. Hints regarding the theme of *Prometheus Unbound* are provided by Mrs. Shelley in her notes to the poem. Shelley believed, she states, 'that evil is not inherent in this system of creation'; 'that mankind had only to will that there should be no evil, and there would be none'; and further 'that man could be so perfectionized as to be able to expel evil from his own nature, and from the greater part of creation.' Mrs. Shelley's statement is an oversimplification of the poet's philosophy and is open to misunderstanding, but in essentials it is correct, as will appear from a subsequent analysis of the poem. Shelley embodies his beliefs in a fable derived from Aeschylus, but he makes Aeschylus over to suit himself. Shelley's myth runs as follows: Prometheus (the regenerator and benefactor of mankind) suffers unrelenting torture at the hands of Jupiter (the Evil Principle or tyranny) until through his self-purification, Asia (the spirit of love and beauty) is empowered to move with Demogorgon (Necessity) to overthrow Jupiter; following the dethronement of Jupiter, Prometheus and Asia are joyously reunited and all living creatures made free and glad. On one level of meaning the action symbolizes man's happy reconciliation with the ideal world of love, truth, and beauty from which evil has divorced him. The stage of the drama is the world of ideas. According to the idealistic philosophy which Shelley now held and to which he was to adhere during the short remainder of his life, love, beauty, and truth exist only transcendentally. Evil also exists transcendentally, but can be expelled from the mind through an effort of will. The furies that torture Prometheus, though externalized in the drama, are the mental disturbances of which he is aware in his own mind. They are the fear, mistrust, and hate—the foul desires and distracting suspicions that torture him and tempt him to renounce his seemingly impossible task of regeneration. But when through long suffering, Prometheus has learned to cast out pride and hate and has achieved ethical victory, the spiritual side of human nature—its benevolence, self-sacrifice, wisdom, and poetic divination—comforts him. Eventually, when the time is right, he is transfigured by love and united with Asia. In his metaphysics Shelley follows Platonic idealism. Asia is Intellectual Beauty, the paragon of loveliness whose radiant steps transform the world. She is kin to the mystical idealizations found frequently in Shelley's writings: the dream vision in *Alastor,* the lady of the garden in *The Sensitive Plant,* the Witch of Atlas. She is Love, Truth, and Goodness, the supreme occult and eternal ONE. On the ethical side Shelley merges Platonic and Christian ideals. In his maturity, though never stinting in his hatred of institutional Christianity, Shelley nevertheless came wholly to admire Christ and His teaching. Ethically con-

sidered, *Prometheus Unbound* is very close to the Sermon on the Mount. Through self-purification and love Prometheus is lifted to a beatific vision like that described by Shelley in his
Essay on Christianity, illustrating the text 'Blessed are the pure in heart, for they shall see
God.' The poet's compassionate portrayal of the crucified savior in Act I is further indication of his deep sympathy and interest in Christ as a teacher of great spiritual truths. But
Prometheus Unbound is not wholly subjective. Shelley, as we know, had dedicated his life
to the cause of social reform. In his drama, through symbolical representation, he proposes
the means by which reform may be achieved in his day. On this level of meaning, Prometheus represents these idealists among men, who, Shelley felt, must assume leadership if
all hope of human progress were not to be lost. (Shelley frequently proclaimed the vital
role of poets as legislators, in foreshadowing and assisting in important social change.)
The furies are the forces by which despotic government keeps itself in power. Jupiter is
political tyranny and Thetis, his wife, 'the false hopes of despots to perpetuate their rule.'
Asia is love, the spirit of generous comradeship and brotherhood. Love has been driven
from the hearts of men by despotic rule: Asia has been separated from Prometheus by
Jupiter. Demogorgon is Necessity: 'a composite of those forces inexorably working for
the overthrow of the old order and the establishment of the new in human society' (Cameron). The Idealists (Prometheus) 'must erase all thoughts of revenge from their hearts so
that when the old order is overthrown by Necessity a new order can be built with the
help of love and brotherhood (Asia)' (Cameron). In one sense Demogorgon is Spring itself—'not the literal physical spring, but the mystical, invisible power of which spring was
the only adequate symbol' (White). It represents 'the inevitability of the resurgence of the
human spirit.' When the conditions are right the tide of change sets in as inevitably as
spring. Jupiter, as an active agent of evil, owes his power to Prometheus. 'Man makes his
gods in his own likeness.' Once they are made they tyrannize over him until the human
spirit, like Prometheus, demonstrates its worthiness by self-denial and brotherly love.
Jupiter thinks to reduce man to eternal slavery, but he has not established his supremacy
over the will of Prometheus. Jupiter is himself a slave to evil. He has bred the conditions
for his own overthrow, for 'the despotic state, once established, sets in motion forces which
will of Necessity eventually overthrow it' (Grabo). It is only through a union with love,
however, that mankind can direct the new order into channels of peaceful and constructive reform. In the third act the poet pictures this regenerated society founded on love
and freed from the shackles of political tyranny.

> The loathsome mask has fallen, the man remains
> Sceptreless, free, uncircumscribed, but man
> Equal, unclassed, tribeless, and nationless,
> Exempt from awe, worship, degree, the king
> Over himself.

The fourth act is a glorious hymning of the new order. The physical forces of the universe
which had been diverted by Jupiter to evil are now made the servants of love. 'Man having learned to control himself can learn through science to control the universe' (Grabo).
In the solvent of love Shelley has synthesized in *Prometheus Unbound* the liberal social
philosophy of the French revolutionary era, the mystical philosophy of Platonism, and
the more speculative theories of advanced science. (Shelley's fusion of science and mysticism, as Mr. Grabo has demonstrated, by identifying electricity with the divine fire of
Neo-Platonic philosophy, is one of the imaginative triumphs of the poem.) But pervasive
and fundamental throughout the drama are Christian ethics, which were also the ethics
of the best pagan philosophers. Demogorgon's closing speech shows that Shelley was 'under no deception as to the difficulty of overcoming tyrannies or of the length of time it
would take' (Cameron). He realized from his own experiences how selfish and blind men
can be and how great must be the measure of heroic fortitude to achieve victory. He concludes his 'paeans of anticipated bliss' with a reminder that good and evil are engaged in
a never-ceasing struggle, that victory is problematical, and that if it is won, there is always

the possibility of Jupiter's return. *Prometheus Unbound* is 'lyric built.' Its imagery is bold and original; its bursts of lyrical splendor are among the wonders of English poetry. White counts thirty-six different verse forms, 'all perfectly handled.' The drama has been compared to symphonic music, and indeed its total effect is very like the symphony, the four acts corresponding to the four movements of the musical form. By its combination of lyrical magic and its transporting power of thought, *Prometheus Unbound* has taken its place among the great esoteric dramas in the world's literature.

Between the composition of the third and fourth acts of *Prometheus Unbound* Shelley wrote *The Cenci,* a five-act domestic tragedy, with a view to its being acted at Covent Garden. The play was rejected, however, as too shocking to suit the taste of the times. Of the craft of the dramatist Shelley knew little by experience, though the success of his undertaking reveals that he had acquired through wide reading clear vision of the high aims of drama and how those aims should be achieved. Moral purpose, he wisely observes in his Preface to *The Cenci,* should operate in tragic drama to teach the human heart, but its teachings should be subservient and indirect. As for dramatic language, Shelley says that it should be cast in imagery adequate to carry the passions of the characters, but it should be familiar, not 'over-fastidious.' For his medium the poet fashioned a dramatic blank verse 'rigorously unadorned, yet poetic and impassioned, and cadenced to actual speech.' The language of *The Cenci* is one of its triumphs. The theme of the play is the tragic struggle of a pure and noble character against corrupted parental authority in evil alliance with religious oppression. Count Cenci is a tyrannical sadist, a man of perverted faith obsessed with the monstrous sin of violating his daughter. His prototype may be found among Elizabethan monsters of overmastering passion (Iago, Richard III, Sir Giles Overreach) and the arch-fiends of Gothic romance. Beatrice is a strong protagonist, a 'woman pure, tender, strong, and profoundly real.' She is overwhelmed by the black horror of her father's crime, yet she does not allow her misery to weaken for a moment her resolution to avenge it. Despairing of just redress by law, and being convinced that she is the chosen agency of God to make atonement, she takes it upon herself to rid the world and her family of this vile and dangerous monster. In doing so she involves herself in tragic catastrophe. As a play *The Cenci* has been generally proclaimed good 'closet' drama (that is, good tragic literature), but not good stage drama. Recent scholarship, however, has revealed that *The Cenci* has had an impressive stage history sufficient to establish it as an eminently actable play. Whenever *The Cenci* has been produced it has held the attention of its audiences. Closet critics who have depended for their evaluations solely on a reading of the drama have thought the scenes too monotonous, the speeches too long and declamatory for a successful stage play. They have argued that Count Cenci is an undramatic character because he is too horrible. They have insisted that there is too much Cenci and that after his murder in the fourth act the play falls apart. Responsible dramatic critics who have seen the play performed report, however, that Count Cenci is convincing (he is a much more complex character than has generally been realized) and that with the death of Cenci the interest deepens, not slackens. The impression of drama increases throughout as the play proceeds. The last two acts are the best and the last act the most moving of all. It is in the final act that 'the nobility of diction and the nobility of passion rise' and that 'tragic meaning flowers with complete and extraordinary beauty' (Elton). The drama reaches the 'highest facets of radiance' in the scene in which Beatrice is at bay before her judges. It is here that her patience and sorrow 'turn to warranted cunning and steely defiance.' She uses every trick open to her to throw her persecutors off the track. Her evasiveness and denial of guilt have been seen by some as inconsistent with her high-mindedness and as therefore a possible blemish in dramatic drawing. But she could deny her guilt, because guilt had no existence in her mind. She believes that she is above the law that oppresses her and has guiltlessly done the justice that the law would never have awarded. However, Shelley states his belief in the Preface that Beatrice should not have avenged her crime: 'Revenge, retaliation, atonement, are pernicious mistakes. If Beatrice had thought in this manner she would have been wiser and better; but she would never have been a tragic character.' In the final scene of the tragedy, terror, defiance, and passion dissolve in tenderness and pathos; and at the close we have in Beatrice a sense of calm suffering and of mind above fate. For the last act Shelley drew upon Webster's Vittoria as she baffled justice (*The White Devil*). He is also heavily indebted to Shakespeare, particularly for the murder scenes. But the tragic conception of Beatrice has Greek affinities as well as Elizabethan. Like Sophocles' Antigone, Shelley's heroine is destroyed by a tragic dilemma from which seemingly there can be no escape. Beatrice is one of the world's great studies of tragic women. She rightfully takes her place beside Antigone, Medea, Vittoria, and the Duchess of Malfi. To create her Shelley stepped outside his usual realm of the lyrical and the idealistic and in doing so scored another triumph.

In the winter of 1820–21 Shelley became acquainted with Emilia Viviani, the lovely nineteen-year-old daughter of the governor of Pisa, who for three years had been confined in a convent, where she was to remain until a 'marriage of convenience' should be arranged by her family. Just as Shelley had been moved to rescue Harriet Westbrook from 'durance vile' in her London boarding school, so now his sympathetic interest was quickly roused for this beautiful and intelligent young Italian girl who was being held against her will in virtual captivity. Emilia was deeply moved by Shelley's attentions, and being herself generously impulsive repaid him with warm sympathy and admiration. It was not long before a close spiritual kinship was established between the two. For a brief, intoxicating period Emilia became 'the soul out of his soul' of which Plato wrote and in which Shelley still believed. *Epipsychidion* is the record of his idealizing transport. The poem rehearses the poet's spiritual history leading to his spiritual affinity with Emilia. Outbursts of adoration interrupt the rehearsal as his flaming fancy passes back and forth between the human Emilia and the discarnate ideal of love and beauty for which she stands. Emilia is 'Spouse! Sister! Angel! Pilot of the Fate / Whose course has been so starless.' For the moment she embodies more than his wife or Claire. Yet it is reasonable, Shelley argues, that all should be beloved. Ideal love should not be centered in a particular person.

> True love in this differs from gold and clay ·
> That to divide is not to take away.

Ideal love is spiritual and non-possessive; it is the loving of all beautiful things and rises in its highest manifestation to that vision of spiritual beauty which Plato recognizes as the crown of the philosopher and lover. In the concluding portion of the poem, Shelley imagines an escape from real life with Emilia in a purely ideal elopement. As a man Shelley knew that their marriage was impossible and not desirable; as a poet he allows 'the fullest imaginative realization of their union.' Shortly after the composition of *Epipsychidion,* Shelley admitted that she whom the poem celebrated was a cloud instead of a Juno. His adventure with Emilia Viviani had been a swift, beautiful interlude of which the poem remains the magnificent record.

Shelley's great elegy, *Adonais,* was addressed to the memory of John Keats. The poem, however, cannot be considered as a deep-felt personal tribute to Keats. Shelley had been acquainted with Keats during their years of residence in England and had later shown a sympathetic interest by inviting Keats to visit him in Italy. Keats had always been cordial, but had kept his distance, thinking perhaps that the older poet might influence him unduly. Their personal relationship taken altogether had been quite limited. As for Keats's poetry, Shelley had not at first been especially impressed; though with the appearance of the 1820 volume, he had become more appreciative, even enthusiastic, especially for *Hyperion.* Yet it is problematical whether Shelley would ever have written *Adonais* (certainly not the poem we now have) if he had not been under the impression that Keats's death had been caused by the savagery of critical attacks by the reviewers. Actually the widely circulated report that the critics had killed Keats had little to support it, but it served to set Shelley off; for in his last years, as the sense of his own insignificance had grown upon him and he increasingly felt the futility of the battle with health and fame, he came to believe that it was in large measure the hostility of the reviewers that had brought about his own ruin. Therefore, though Shelley sets out in the elegy to present Keats as the innocent victim of oppression, as the poem proceeds he quite naturally merges this conception with his own idealization of himself as the neglected and misunderstood poet and 'in another's fate now wept his own.' *Adonais* opens somewhat coldly with the conventional ritual chant of the classical elegies of Bion and Moschus which Shelley was imitating—'one poet making solemn music for another.' The stanzas that follow the invocation (9–25) describe the desolation felt at the death of Adonais by all the natural and imaginative forces that he had made beautiful in poetry; the sorrow of Urania, mother of the muses; and the grief of the brother poets. Among the poet-mourners is Shelley himself—'A herd-abandoned deer struck by the hunter's dart'—presented in a famous self-portrait (stanzas 31–5). At this point (stanza 36) a curse upon the assassin reviewer breaks the sad hopelessness of lament, which has characterized the first two thirds of the elegy, to open the way to consolation and intuitive faith. With the concluding stanzas (38–55) the poem gathers intensity and, rising in a style of singular magnificence, becomes truly great. The thought of physical death as annihilation is discarded and replaced by a Platonic-Christian mystical awareness of the immortality of omnipresent spirit. For his philosophical idealization of death, in addition to the familiar Platonic and Neo-Platonic sources, Shelley drew upon Dante and Spinoza, reinforced by parallels from Petrarch's *Triumphs,* which he had recently been reading. Adonais still lives, Shelley is persuaded, 'a portion of the Eternal.' According to the grand paradox of Platonic belief, it is we, the living, on earth who are dead. We exist but in a world of illusion: 'Adonais has outsoared the shadow of our night.' The climax of Shelley's metaphysical faith is reached in the famous metaphor of stanza 52, the most powerful and beautiful definition of the philosophical dream of the ONE and the many ever penned. In the final stanzas (53–5) the poet nerves himself for still further flight. In the rapturous contemplation of the ONE the poet's despondency vanishes, his desire for personal survival ceases, and he loses all sense of self and mortality. With a glowing ardor, something like ecstasy, he is wholly united with Intellectual Beauty. At the last his spirit soars upward to join Adonais, whose soul has preceded him, in the abode of the Eternal. *Adonais* is commonly regarded as one of the two or three greatest English elegies. Shelley himself considered it his finest poem. Except for the passages of invective and the stanzas of self-pity, which some may think are blemishes, *Adonais* has all those rare qualities— sheer verse magic, impassioned beauty of imagery, and inspired intuitive conviction— such as we may ever hope to find all compact in one elegiac composition.

Shelley gave much of his time to the rapt contemplation of natural phenomena, for to him, as to Wordsworth, Nature was the garment of the Eternal, the outward manifestation through which inner, divine beauty could become known. In the infinite variety of the external world, he watched the comings and the goings of Nature's shadow, and in favored moments of inspiration believed he had identified himself with inner reality, which he called 'Light,' 'Beauty,' or 'sustaining Love.' His imagination was constantly excited by Nature and his poetry impermeated with natural metaphors and symbols. Especially numerous in his writings are figures expressive of freedom derived from the aerial and mutable forms of nature. Shelley was always fascinated with clouds, mists, winds, cataracts, rivers, and seas. The cloud, ever beautiful and transitory, is a favorite with him, representing on the physical side the cyclic mutation of water (vapor, cloud, rain, dew, vapor again) and on the intellectual side the human spirit's mutability yet permanence. 'I change but I cannot die' is the organizing sentiment of *The Cloud* on either level of meaning. The wind in Shelley's famous *Ode to the West Wind,* like the cloud, is similarly symbolic of both outer and inner Nature, matter and spirit. The West Wind, besides being the 'destroyer-preserver' of the physical, external world, is the revolutionary power inherent in the universe which, after destroying the old order of human society, with its mighty breath will quicken the establishment of the new. Shelley took great pleasure in observing and recording the evanescent lights and shadows on the face of Nature. Like the clouds and the winds, they seemed somehow to emphasize, as against our earth-bound existence, the spiritual side of reality. His poetry abounds in shimmering color words painting the wonders of moon, sun, and stars, the magic of waters, the glory of the rainbow, and the soft radiance of spring dawn and autumn twilight. Sound fascinated him even more than the miracle of light. Like Carlyle, he believed that if we go deep enough we shall find music everywhere. Each form of nature he conceived contributed its musical note to the one, vast universal symphony. But whether it is sound, light, color, or motion that he gorgeously arrays or melodiously hymns, he never forgets that they are all derived from a single source. Behind the variegated, miraculous veil of Nature lies the greater miracle of spirituality and unity.

An intense lyricism everywhere permeates Shelley's poetry, but it is a lyricism, an appreciative reader soon comes to realize, that is 'greatly enriched and given persuasive power by a firm intellectual backing.' Shelley is forever haunted by the eternal mysteries of life and death, love and hope, beauty and decay, wonder and despair. Even in the briefer lyrics the poet's ardent thought may be felt pulsating in the undying music and splendor of his verses. Yet for some readers the unearthly quality, the very abstractedness of Shelley's thought, makes much of his poetry unattractive. The poet's heightened, rarefied imagery is likely to leave ordinary mortals gasping for air in the high altitudes to which he habitually soars, and to make them want to return to comfortable earth. Shelley strained all the resources of language at his command to give form and meaning to the lofty visions revealed to him. As a consequence, especially during the earlier years, his efforts occasionally resulted in stylistic defects. Sometimes sheer lyric abandon led him into careless writing. Ineffective repetition, involved sentence structure, and annoying ambiguities in meaning are not uncommon. The poet also tends to the overfrequent use of certain favorite words and images. Used singly or sparingly they can be and often are supremely effective—words such as *daedal* or *interlunar* and images involving *veil, boat and stream, eagle and serpent,* and *moth.* Yet there is not much profit in lingering over Shelley's artistic shortcomings. Whatever defects the meticulous critic may uncover, Shelley's art on the whole is not seriously limited. There is never a mere craftsmanlike fastidiousness in Shelley, but he could and frequently did write clearly with his eye on the object. Moreover, there is increasing restraint in his later writing, so that at the last stylistic defects appear sparingly in the longer poems. The beauty and perfection of many of the shorter lyrics are beyond criticism. In the short lyric Shelley is supreme among English poets. He is the master craftsman in metrical and stanzaic patterns. With the exception of the sonnet (a form that seems not to have particularly interested him) Shelley used with assured ease and power an astonishing variety of metrical forms and invented many new ones. Only Chaucer, Spenser, and Keats can be compared to him in versatility. For lightness, melody, and grace he surpasses them all. No one has come nearer to capturing in words the inexpressible surgings of human emotion. When he is exultant his song shoots upward in a joyous flight like that of his own skylark; when he is dejected it sinks downward, expiring like his own winged words before the flame of love. But whatever his emotion—whether joy, sorrow, desire, or regret—he clothes it in vibrating, persistent, haunting overtones of song. And the world listens.

STANZAS—APRIL 1814

Away! the moor is dark beneath the moon,
  Rapid clouds have drank the last pale beam of even:
Away! the gathering winds will call the darkness soon,
  And profoundest midnight shroud the serene lights of heaven.

Pause not! The time is past! Every voice cries, Away!
  Tempt not with one last tear thy friend's ungentle mood:
Thy lover's eye, so glazed and cold, dares not entreat thy stay:
  Duty and dereliction guide thee back to solitude.

Away, away! to thy sad and silent home;
  Pour bitter tears on its desolated hearth;   10
Watch the dim shades as like ghosts they go and
    come,
  And complicate strange webs of melancholy
    mirth.

The leaves of wasted autumn woods shall float
  around thine head:
  The blooms of dewy spring shall gleam be-
    neath thy feet:
But thy soul or this world must fade in the frost
  that binds the dead,
  Ere midnight's frown and morning's smile, ere
    thou and peace may meet.

The cloud shadows of midnight possess their own
  repose,
  For the weary winds are silent, or the moon is
    in the deep:
Some respite to its turbulence unresting ocean
  knows;
  Whatever moves, or toils, or grieves, hath its
    appointed sleep.   20

Thou in the grave shalt rest—yet till the phan-
  toms flee
  Which that house and heath and garden made
    dear to thee erewhile,
Thy remembrance, and repentance, and deep
  musings are not free
  From the music of two voices and the light of
    one sweet smile.

1814   1816

TO WORDSWORTH

POET of Nature, thou hast wept to know
That things depart which never may return:
Childhood and youth, friendship and love's first
  glow,
Have fled like sweet dreams, leaving thee to
  mourn.
These common woes I feel. One loss is mine
Which thou too feel'st, yet I alone deplore.
Thou wert as a lone star, whose light did shine
On some frail bark in winter's midnight roar:
Thou hast like to a rock-built refuge stood
Above the blind and battling multitude: 10
In honoured poverty thy voice did weave
Songs consecrate to truth and liberty,—
Deserting these, thou leavest me to grieve,
Thus having been, that thou shouldst cease to be.

1815   1816

LINES: 'THE COLD EARTH SLEPT BELOW'

[Scholars are generally agreed that these lines refer to
Harriet's death by drowning, November 1816, and that
Shelley disguised the reference by dating them a year
previous to the tragedy.]

THE cold earth slept below,
  Above the cold sky shone;
And all around, with a chilling sound,
  From caves of ice and fields of snow,
  The breath of night like death did flow
    Beneath the sinking moon.

The wintry hedge was black,
  The green grass was not seen;
The birds did rest on the bare thorn's breast,
  Whose roots, beside the pathway track,   10
  Had bound their folds o'er many a crack
    Which the frost had made between.

Thine eyes glowed in the glare
  Of the moon's dying light;
As a fen-fire's beam on a sluggish stream
  Gleams dimly, so the moon shone there,
  And it yellowed the strings of thy tangled hair,
    That shook in the wind of night.

The moon made thy lips pale, beloved—
  The wind made thy bosom chill—   20
The night did shed on thy dear head
  Its frozen dew, and thou didst lie
  Where the bitter breath of the naked sky
    Might visit thee at will.

                            1823

ALASTOR

OR, THE SPIRIT OF SOLITUDE

*Nondum amabam, et amare amabam, quærebam
quid amarem, amans amare.*[1]—Confessions of St.
Augustine.

[Mrs. Shelley in her note to *Alastor* says:
'None of Shelley's poems is more characteristic than
this. The solemn spirit that reigns throughout, the worship of the majesty of nature, the broodings of a poet's
heart in solitude—the mingling of the exulting joy which
the various aspects of the visible universe inspires with
the sad and struggling pangs which human passion im-
parts—give a touching interest to the whole. The death
which he had often contemplated during the last months
as certain and near he here represented in such colours
as had, in his lonely musings, soothed his soul to peace.
The versification sustains the solemn spirit which

---

[1] 'I did not love yet, and I loved to love; I sought what I might
love, loving to love.'

breathes throughout: it is peculiarly melodious. The poem ought rather to be considered didactic than narrative: it was the outpouring of his own emotions, embodied in the purest form he could conceive, painted in the ideal hues which his brilliant imagination inspired, and softened by the recent anticipation of death.'

The title, *Alastor,* was suggested by Peacock after the poem was finished. It is a Greek word meaning an *evil genius* (Peacock's translation) or, perhaps more accurately, an *avenging fury.*]

PREFACE

The poem entitled *Alastor* may be considered as allegorical of one of the most interesting situations of the human mind. It represents a youth of uncorrupted feelings and adventurous genius led forth by an imagination inflamed and purified through familiarity with all that is excellent and majestic, to the contemplation of the universe. He drinks deep of the fountains of knowledge, and is still insatiate. The magnificence and beauty of the external world sinks profoundly into the frame of his conceptions, and affords to their modifications a variety not to be exhausted. So long as it is possible for his desires to point towards objects thus infinite and unmeasured, he is joyous, and tranquil, and self-possessed. But the period arrives when these objects cease to suffice. His mind is at length suddenly awakened and thirsts for intercourse with an intelligence similar to itself. He images to himself the Being whom he loves. Conversant with speculations of the sublimest and most perfect natures, the vision in which he embodies his own imaginations unites all of wonderful, or wise, or beautiful, which the poet, the philosopher, or the lover could depicture. The intellectual faculties, the imagination, the functions of sense, have their respective requisitions on the sympathy of corresponding powers in other human beings. The Poet is represented as uniting these requisitions, and attaching them to a single image. He seeks in vain for a prototype of his conception. Blasted by his disappointment, he descends to an untimely grave.

The picture is not barren of instruction to actual men. The Poet's self-centred seclusion was avenged by the furies of an irresistible passion pursuing him to speedy ruin. But that Power which strikes the luminaries of the world with sudden darkness and extinction, by awakening them to too exquisite a perception of its influences, dooms to a slow and poisonous decay those meaner spirits that dare to abjure its dominion. Their destiny is more abject and inglorious as their delinquency is more contemptible and pernicious. They who, deluded by no generous error, instigated by no sacred thirst of doubtful knowledge, duped by no illustrious superstitions, loving nothing on this earth, and cherishing no hopes beyond, yet keep aloof from sympathies with their kind, rejoicing neither in human joy nor mourning with human grief; these, and such as they, have their apportioned curse. They languish, because none feel with them their common nature. They are morally dead. They are neither friends, nor lovers, nor fathers, nor citizens of the world, nor benefactors of their country. Among those who attempt to exist without human sympathy, the pure and tender-hearted perish through the intensity and passion of their search after its communities, when the vacancy of their spirit suddenly makes itself felt. All else, selfish, blind, and torpid, are those unforeseeing multitudes who constitute, together with their own, the lasting misery and loneliness of the world. Those who love not their fellow-beings, live unfruitful lives, and prepare for their old age a miserable grave.

> 'The good die first,
> And those whose hearts are dry as summer dust,
> Burn to the socket!'[2]

14 December, 1815

EARTH, ocean, air, belovèd brotherhood!
If our great Mother has imbued my soul
With aught of natural piety to feel
Your love, and recompense the boon with mine;
If dewy morn, and odorous noon, and even,
With sunset and its gorgeous ministers,
And solemn midnight's tingling silentness;
If autumn's hollow sighs in the sere wood,
And winter robing with pure snow and crowns
Of starry ice the grey grass and bare boughs;   10
If spring's voluptuous pantings when she
        breathes
Her first sweet kisses, have been dear to me;
If no bright bird, insect, or gentle beast
I consciously have injured, but still loved
And cherished these my kindred; then forgive
This boast, belovèd brethren, and withdraw
No portion of your wonted favour now!

Mother of this unfathomable world!
Favour my solemn song, for I have loved
Thee ever, and thee only; I have watched   20
Thy shadow, and the darkness of thy steps,
And my heart ever gazes on the depth
Of thy deep mysteries. I have made my bed
In charnels and on coffins, where black death
Keeps record of the trophies won from thee,
Hoping to still these obstinate questionings
Of thee and thine, by forcing some lone ghost
Thy messenger, to render up the tale
Of what we are. In lone and silent hours,
When night makes a weird sound of its own
        stillness,   30
Like an inspired and desperate alchymist
Staking his very life on some dark hope,
Have I mixed awful talk and asking looks
With my most innocent love, until strange tears
Uniting with those breathless kisses, made
Such magic as compels the charmèd night
To render up thy charge: . . . and, though ne'er
        yet
Thou hast unveiled thy inmost sanctuary,
Enough from incommunicable dream,
And twilight phantasms, and deep noon-day
        thought,   40

---

2 Wordsworth, *The Excursion,* I, 500–502. The influence of Wordsworth is evident throughout *Alastor.*

Has shone within me, that serenely now
And moveless, as a long-forgotten lyre
Suspended in the solitary dome
Of some mysterious and deserted fane,
I wait thy breath, Great Parent, that my strain
May modulate with murmurs of the air,
And motions of the forests and the sea,
And voice of living beings, and woven hymns
Of night and day, and the deep heart of man.

There was a Poet whose untimely tomb   50
No human hands with pious reverence reared,
But the charmed eddies of autumnal winds
Built o'er his mouldering bones a pyramid
Of mouldering leaves in the waste wilderness:—
A lovely youth,—no mourning maiden decked
With weeping flowers, or votive cypress wreath,
The lone couch of his everlasting sleep;—
Gentle, and brave, and generous,—no lorn bard
Breathed o'er his dark fate one melodious sigh;
He lived, he died, he sung, in solitude.   60
Strangers have wept to hear his passionate notes,
And virgins, as unknown he passed, have pined
And wasted for fond love of his wild eyes.
The fire of those soft orbs has ceased to burn,
And Silence, too enamoured of that voice,
Locks its mute music in her rugged cell.

By solemn vision, and bright silver dream,
His infancy was nurtured. Every sight
And sound from the vast earth and ambient air,
Sent to his heart its choicest impulses.   70
The fountains of divine philosophy
Fled not his thirsting lips, and all of great,
Or good, or lovely, which the sacred past
In truth or fable consecrates, he felt
And knew. When early youth had passed, he left
His cold fireside and alienated home
To seek strange truths in undiscovered lands.
Many a wide waste and tangled wilderness
Has lured his fearless steps; and he has bought
With his sweet voice and eyes, from savage men,   80
His rest and food. Nature's most secret steps
He like her shadow has pursued, where'er
The red volcano overcanopies
Its fields of snow and pinnacles of ice
With burning smoke, or where bitumen lakes
On black bare pointed islets ever beat
With sluggish surge, or where the secret caves
Rugged and dark, winding among the springs
Of fire and poison, inaccessible
To avarice or pride, their starry domes   90
Of diamond and of gold expand above

Numberless and immeasurable halls,
Frequent with crystal column, and clear shrines
Of pearl, and thrones radiant with chrysolite.
Nor had that scene of ampler majesty
Than gems or gold, the varying roof of heaven
And the green earth lost in his heart its claims
To love and wonder; he would linger long
In lonesome vales, making the wild his home,
Until the doves and squirrels would partake   100
From his innocuous hand his bloodless food,
Lured by the gentle meaning of his looks,
And the wild antelope, that starts whene'er
The dry leaf rustles in the brake, suspend
Her timid steps to gaze upon a form
More graceful than her own.

His wandering step
Obedient to high thoughts, has visited
The awful ruins of the days of old:
Athens, and Tyre, and Balbec,[3] and the waste
Where stood Jerusalem, the fallen towers   110
Of Babylon, the eternal pyramids,
Memphis and Thebes, and whatsoe'er of strange
Sculptured on alabaster obelisk,
Or jasper tomb, or mutilated sphinx,
Dark Æthiopia in her desert hills
Conceals. Among the ruined temples there,
Stupendous columns, and wild images
Of more than man, where marble daemons[4]
    watch
The Zodiac's brazen mystery,[5] and dead men
Hang their mute thoughts on the mute walls
    around,   120
He lingered, poring on memorials
Of the world's youth, through the long burning
    day
Gazed on those speechless shapes, nor, when the
    moon
Filled the mysterious halls with floating shades
Suspended he that task, but ever gazed
And gazed, till meaning on his vacant mind
Flashed like strong inspiration, and he saw
The thrilling secrets of the birth of time.

Meanwhile an Arab maiden brought his food,
Her daily portion, from her father's tent,   130
And spread her matting for his couch, and stole
From duties and repose to tend his steps:—
Enamoured, yet not daring for deep awe
To speak her love:—and watched his nightly
    sleep,

---

3 a ruined ancient city of Syria, near Damascus.
4 supernatural beings of classical mythology intermediate between men and gods.
5 brazen representations of mythological creatures such as appear in the signs of the zodiac.

Sleepless herself, to gaze upon his lips
Parted in slumber, whence the regular breath
Of innocent dreams arose: then, when red morn
Made paler the pale moon, to her cold home
Wildered, and wan, and panting, she returned.

The Poet wandering on, through Arabie   140
And Persia, and the wild Carmanian waste,[6]
And o'er the aërial mountains which pour down
Indus and Oxus from their icy caves,
In joy and exultation held his way;
Till in the vale of Cashmire,[7] far within
Its loneliest dell, where odorous plants entwine
Beneath the hollow rocks a natural bower,
Beside a sparkling rivulet he stretched
His languid limbs. A vision on his sleep
There came, a dream of hopes that never yet   150
Had flushed his cheek. He dreamed a veilèd maid
Sate near him, talking in low solemn tones.
Her voice was like the voice of his own soul
Heard in the calm of thought; its music long,
Like woven sounds of streams and breezes, held
His inmost sense suspended in its web
Of many-coloured woof and shifting hues.
Knowledge and truth and virtue were her theme,
And lofty hopes of divine liberty,
Thoughts the most dear to him, and poesy,   160
Herself a poet. Soon the solemn mood
Of her pure mind kindled through all her frame
A permeating fire: wild numbers then
She raised, with voice stifled in tremulous sobs
Subdued by its own pathos: her fair hands
Were bare alone, sweeping from some strange
     harp
Strange symphony, and in their branching veins
The eloquent blood told an ineffable tale.
The beating of her heart was heard to fill
The pauses of her music, and her breath   170
Tumultuously accorded with those fits
Of intermitted song. Sudden she rose,
As if her heart impatiently endured
Its bursting burthen: at the sound he turned,
And saw by the warm light of their own life
Her glowing limbs beneath the sinuous veil
Of woven wind, her outspread arms now bare,
Her dark locks floating in the breath of night,
Her beamy bending eyes, her parted lips
Outstretched, and pale, and quivering
     eagerly.   180
His strong heart sunk and sickened with excess
Of love. He reared his shuddering limbs and
     quelled

His gasping breath, and spread his arms to meet
Her panting bosom: . . . she drew back a while,
Then, yielding to the irresistible joy,
With frantic gesture and short breathless cry
Folded his frame in her dissolving arms.
Now blackness veiled his dizzy eyes, and night
Involved and swallowed up the vision; sleep,
Like a dark flood suspended in its course,   190
Rolled back its impulse on his vacant brain.

Roused by the shock he started from his
     trance—
The cold white light of morning, the blue moon
Low in the west, the clear and garish hills,
The distinct valley and the vacant woods,
Spread round him where he stood. Whither have
     fled
The hues of heaven that canopied his bower
Of yesternight? The sounds that soothed his
     sleep,
The mystery and the majesty of Earth,
The joy, the exultation? His wan eyes   200
Gaze on the empty scene as vacantly
As ocean's moon looks on the moon in heaven.
The spirit of sweet human love has sent
A vision to the sleep of him who spurned
Her choicest gifts. He eagerly pursues
Beyond the realms of dream that fleeting shade;
He overleaps the bounds. Alas! Alas!
Were limbs, and breath, and being intertwined
Thus treacherously? Lost, lost, for ever lost,
In the wide pathless desert of dim sleep,   210
That beautiful shape! Does the dark gate of
     death
Conduct to thy mysterious paradise,
O Sleep? Does the bright arch of rainbow clouds,
And pendent mountains seen in the calm lake,
Lead only to a black and watery depth,
While death's blue vault, with loathliest vapours
     hung,
Where every shade which the foul grave exhales
Hides its dead eye from the detested day,
Conducts, O Sleep, to thy delightful realms?
This doubt with sudden tide flowed on his
     heart,   220
The insatiate hope which it awakened, stung
His brain even like despair.
                    While daylight held
The sky, the Poet kept mute conference
With his still soul. At night the passion came,
Like the fierce fiend of a distempered dream,
And shook him from his rest, and led him forth
Into the darkness.—As an eagle grasped
In folds of the green serpent, feels her breast

---

6 the desert of Kerman, in southern Persia.
7 in India, near the boundary of Tibet.

Burn with the poison, and precipitates
Through night and day, tempest, and calm, and
    cloud,   230
Frantic with dizzying anguish, her blind flight
O'er the wide aëry wilderness: thus driven
By the bright shadow of that lovely dream,
Beneath the cold glare of the desolate night,
Through tangled swamps and deep precipitous
    dells,
Startling with careless step the moonlight snake,
He fled. Red morning dawned upon his flight,
Shedding the mockery of its vital hues
Upon his cheek of death. He wandered on
Till vast Aornos[8] seen from Petra's steep[9]   240
Hung o'er the low horizon like a cloud;
Through Balk,[10] and where the desolated tombs
Of Parthian kings scatter to every wind
Their wasting dust,[11] wildly he wandered on,
Day after day a weary waste of hours,
Bearing within his life the brooding care
That ever fled on its decaying flame.
And now his limbs were lean; his scattered
    hair
Sered by the autumn of strange suffering
Sung dirges in the wind; his listless hand   250
Hung like dead bone within its withered skin;
Life, and the lustre that consumed it, shone
As in a furnace burning secretly
From his dark eyes alone. The cottagers,
Who ministered with human charity
His human wants, beheld with wondering awe
Their fleeting visitant. The mountaineer,
Encountering on some dizzy precipice
That spectral form, deemed that the Spirit of
    wind
With lightning eyes, and eager breath, and
    feet   260
Disturbing not the drifted snow, had paused
In its career: the infant would conceal
His troubled visage in his mother's robe
In terror at the glare of those wild eyes,
To remember their strange light in many a dream
Of after-times; but youthful maidens, taught
By nature, would interpret half the woe
That wasted him, would call him with false
    names
Brother, and friend, would press his pallid hand
At parting, and watch, dim through tears, the
    path   270
Of his departure from their father's door.

---

8 a mountain stronghold near the Indus, captured by Alexander
the Great in 327 B.C.
9 an ancient city in the rocky region of northwestern Arabia.
10 a region of Turkestan, in central Asia.
11 at Arbela, a city in Assyria.

At length upon the lone Chorasmian[12] shore
He paused, a wide and melancholy waste
Of putrid marshes. A strong impulse urged
His steps to the sea-shore. A swan was there,
Beside a sluggish stream among the reeds.
It rose as he approached, and with strong wings
Scaling the upward sky, bent its bright course
High over the immeasurable main.
His eyes pursued its flight.—'Thou hast a
    home,   280
Beautiful bird; thou voyagest to thine home,
Where thy sweet mate will twine her downy neck
With thine, and welcome thy return with eyes
Bright in the lustre of their own fond joy.
And what am I that I should linger here,
With voice far sweeter than thy dying notes,
Spirit more vast than thine, frame more attuned
To beauty, wasting these surpassing powers
In the deaf air, to the blind earth, and heaven
That echoes not my thoughts?' A gloomy
    smile   290
Of desperate hope wrinkled his quivering lips.
For sleep, he knew, kept most relentlessly
Its precious charge, and silent death exposed,
Faithless perhaps as sleep, a shadowy lure,
With doubtful smile mocking its own strange
    charms.

    Startled by his own thoughts he looked
      around.
There was no fair fiend near him, not a sight
Or sound of awe but in his own deep mind.
A little shallop floating near the shore
Caught the impatient wandering of his gaze.   300
It had been long abandoned, for its sides
Gaped wide with many a rift, and its frail joints
Swayed with the undulations of the tide.
A restless impulse urged him to embark
And meet lone Death on the drear ocean's waste;
For well he knew that mighty Shadow loves
The slimy caverns of the populous deep.

    The day was fair and sunny, sea and sky
Drank its inspiring radiance, and the wind
Swept strongly from the shore, blackening the
    waves.   310
Following his eager soul, the wanderer
Leaped in the boat, he spread his cloak aloft
On the bare mast, and took his lonely seat,
And felt the boat speed o'er the tranquil sea
Like a torn cloud before the hurricane.

    As one that in a silver vision floats

---

12 a desert region of Russian Turkestan.

Obedient to the sweep of odorous winds
Upon resplendent clouds, so rapidly
Along the dark and ruffled waters fled
The straining boat.—A whirlwind swept it
    on,   320
With fierce gusts and precipitating force,
Through the white ridges of the chafèd sea.
The waves arose. Higher and higher still
Their fierce necks writhed beneath the tempest's
    scourge
Like serpents struggling in a vulture's grasp.
Calm and rejoicing in the fearful war
Of wave ruining on wave, and blast on blast
Descending, and black flood on whirlpool driven
With dark obliterating course, he sate:
As if their genii were the ministers   330
Appointed to conduct him to the light
Of those belovèd eyes, the Poet sate
Holding the steady helm. Evening came on,
The beams of sunset hung their rainbow hues
High 'mid the shifting domes of sheeted spray
That canopied his path o'er the waste deep;
Twilight, ascending slowly from the east,
Entwined in duskier wreaths her braided locks
O'er the fair front and radiant eyes of day;
Night followed, clad with stars. On every side 340
More horribly the multitudinous streams
Of ocean's mountainous waste to mutual war
Rushed in dark tumult thundering, as to mock
The calm and spangled sky. The little boat
Still fled before the storm; still fled, like foam
Down the steep cataract of a wintry river;
Now pausing on the edge of the riven wave;
Now leaving far behind the bursting mass
That fell, convulsing ocean: safely fled—
As if that frail and wasted human form,   350
Had been an elemental god.
                    At midnight
The moon arose: and lo! the ethereal cliffs
Of Caucasus, whose icy summits shone
Among the stars like sunlight, and around
Whose caverned base the whirlpools and the
    waves
Bursting and eddying irresistibly
Rage and resound for ever.—Who shall save?—
The boat fled on,—the boiling torrent drove,—
The crags closed round with black and jaggèd
    arms,
The shattered mountain overhung the sea,   360
And faster still, beyond all human speed,
Suspended on the sweep of the smooth wave,
The little boat was driven. A cavern there
Yawned, and amid its slant and winding depths
Ingulfed the rushing sea. The boat fled on

With unrelaxing speed.—'Vision and Love!'
The Poet cried aloud, 'I have beheld
The path of thy departure. Sleep and death
Shall not divide us long!'

                The boat pursued
The windings of the cavern. Daylight shone   370
At length upon that gloomy river's flow;
Now, where the fiercest war among the waves
Is calm, on the unfathomable stream
The boat moved slowly. Where the mountain,
    riven,
Exposed those black depths to the azure sky,
Ere yet the flood's enormous volume fell
Even to the base of Caucasus, with sound
That shook the everlasting rocks, the mass
Filled with one whirlpool all that ample chasm;
Stair above stair the eddying waters rose,   380
Circling immeasurably fast, and laved
With alternating dash the gnarlèd roots
Of mighty trees, that stretched their giant arms
In darkness over it. I' the midst was left,
Reflecting, yet distorting every cloud,
A pool of treacherous and tremendous calm.
Seized by the sway of the ascending stream,
With dizzy swiftness, round, and round, and
    round,
Ridge after ridge the straining boat arose,
Till on the verge of the extremest curve,   390
Where, through an opening of the rocky bank,
The waters overflow, and a smooth spot
Of glassy quiet mid those battling tides
Is left, the boat paused shuddering.—Shall it sink
Down the abyss? Shall the reverting stress
Of that resistless gulf embosom it?
Now shall it fall?—A wandering stream of wind,
Breathed from the west, has caught the expanded
    sail,
And, lo! with gentle motion, between banks
Of mossy slope, and on a placid stream,   400
Beneath a woven grove it sails, and, hark!
The ghastly torrent mingles its far roar,
With the breeze murmuring in the musical
    woods.
Where the embowering trees recede, and leave
A little space of green expanse, the cove
Is closed by meeting banks, whose yellow flowers
For ever gaze on their own drooping eyes,
Reflected in the crystal calm. The wave
Of the boat's motion marred their pensive task,
Which nought but vagrant bird, or wanton
    wind,   410
Or falling spear-grass, or their own decay
Had e'er disturbed before. The Poet longed

To deck with their bright hues his withered hair,
But on his heart its solitude returned,
And he forbore. Not the strong impulse hid
In those flushed cheeks, bent eyes and shadowy
　　frame
Had yet performed its ministry: it hung
Upon his life, as lightning in a cloud
Gleams, hovering ere it vanish, ere the floods
Of night close over it.
　　　　　　　　　The noonday sun   420
Now shone upon the forest, one vast mass
Of mingling shade, whose brown magnificence
A narrow vale embosoms. There, huge caves,
Scooped in the dark base of their aëry rocks
Mocking its moans, respond and roar for ever.
The meeting boughs and implicated leaves
Wove twilight o'er the Poet's path, as led
By love, or dream, or god, or mightier Death,
He sought in Nature's dearest haunt, some bank,
Her cradle, and his sepulchre. More dark   430
And dark the shades accumulate. The oak,
Expanding its immense and knotty arms,
Embraces the light beech. The pyramids
Of the tall cedar overarching, frame
Most solemn domes within, and far below,
Like clouds suspended in an emerald sky,
The ash and the acacia floating hang
Tremulous and pale. Like restless serpents,
　　clothed
In rainbow and in fire, the parasites,
Starred with ten thousand blossoms, flow
　　around   440
The grey trunks, and, as gamesome infants' eyes,
With gentle meanings, and most innocent wiles,
Fold their beams round the hearts of those that
　　love,
These twine their tendrils with the wedded
　　boughs
Uniting their close union; the woven leaves
Make net-work of the dark blue light of day,
And the night's noontide clearness, mutable
As shapes in the weird clouds. Soft mossy lawns
Beneath these canopies extend their swells,
Fragrant with perfumed herbs, and eyed with
　　blooms   450
Minute yet beautiful. One darkest glen
Sends from its woods of musk-rose, twined with
　　jasmine,
A soul-dissolving odour, to invite
To some more lovely mystery. Through the dell,
Silence and Twilight here, twin-sisters, keep
Their noonday watch, and sail among the shades,
Like vapourous shapes half seen; beyond, a well,
Dark, gleaming, and of most translucent wave,

Images all the woven boughs above,
And each depending leaf, and every speck   460
Of azure sky, darting between their chasms;
Nor aught else in the liquid mirror laves
Its portraiture, but some inconstant star
Between one foliaged lattice twinkling fair,
Or, painted bird, sleeping beneath the moon,
Or gorgeous insect floating motionless,
Unconscious of the day, ere yet his wings
Have spread their glories to the gaze of noon.

　　Hither the Poet came. His eyes beheld
Their own wan light through the reflected
　　lines   470
Of his thin hair, distinct in the dark depth
Of that still fountain; as the human heart,
Gazing in dreams over the gloomy grave,
Sees its own treacherous likeness there. He heard
The motion of the leaves, the grass that sprung
Startled and glanced and trembled even to feel
An unaccustomed presence, and the sound
Of the sweet brook that from the secret springs
Of that dark fountain rose. A Spirit seemed
To stand beside him—clothed in no bright
　　robes   480
Of shadowy silver or enshrining light.
Borrowed from aught the visible world affords
Of grace, or majesty, or mystery;—
But, undulating woods, and silent well,
And leaping rivulet, and evening gloom
Now deepening the dark shades, for speech as-
　　suming,
Held commune with him, as if he and it
Were all that was,—only . . . when his regard
Was raised by intense pensiveness, . . . two eyes,
Two starry eyes, hung in the gloom of
　　thought,   490
And seemed with their serene and azure smiles
To beckon him.

　　　　　　　　Obedient to the light
That shone within his soul, he went, pursuing
The windings of the dell.—The rivulet
Wanton and wild, through many a green ravine
Beneath the forest flowed. Sometimes it fell
Among the moss with hollow harmony
Dark and profound. Now on the polished stones
It danced; like childhood laughing as it went:
Then, through the plain in tranquil wanderings
　　crept,   500
Reflecting every herb and drooping bud
That overhung its quietness.—'O stream!
Whose source is inaccessibly profound,
Whither do thy mysterious waters tend?
Thou imagest my life. Thy darksome stillness,

Thy dazzling waves, thy loud and hollow gulfs,
Thy searchless fountain, and invisible course
Have each their type in me: and the wide sky,
And measureless ocean may declare as soon
What oozy cavern or what wandering cloud 510
Contains thy waters, as the universe
Tell where these living thoughts reside, when
    stretched
Upon thy flowers my bloodless limbs shall waste
I' the passing wind!'

             Beside the grassy shore
Of the small stream he went; he did impress
On the green moss his tremulous step, that
    caught
Strong shuddering from his burning limbs. As
    one
Roused by some joyous madness from the couch
Of fever, he did move; yet, not like him,
Forgetful of the grave, where, when the flame 520
Of his frail exultation shall be spent,
He must descend. With rapid steps he went
Beneath the shade of trees, beside the flow
Of the wild babbling rivulet; and now
The forest's solemn canopies were changed
For the uniform and lightsome evening sky.
Grey rocks did peep from the spare moss, and
    stemmed
The struggling brook: tall spires of windlestrae[13]
Threw their thin shadows down the rugged slope,
And nought but gnarled roots of ancient
    pines 530
Branchless and blasted, clenched with grasping
    roots
The unwilling soil. A gradual change was here,
Yet ghastly. For, as fast years flow away,
The smooth brow gathers, and the hair grows
    thin
And white, and where irradiate dewy eyes
Had shone, gleam stony orbs:—so from his steps
Bright flowers departed, and the beautiful shade
Of the green groves, with all their odorous winds
And musical motions. Calm, he still pursued
The stream, that with a larger volume now 540
Rolled through the labyrinthine dell; and there
Fretted a path through its descending curves
With its wintry speed. On every side now rose
Rocks, which, in unimaginable forms,
Lifted their black and barren pinnacles
In the light of evening, and, its precipice
Obscuring the ravine, disclosed above,
Mid toppling stones, black gulfs and yawning
    caves,

---

13 a kind of grass sometimes used for plaiting baskets.

Whose windings gave ten thousand various
    tongues
To the loud stream. Lo! where the pass
    expands 550
Its stony jaws, the abrupt mountain breaks,
And seems, with its accumulated crags,
To overhang the world: for wide expand
Beneath the wan stars and descending moon
Islanded seas, blue mountains, mighty streams,
Dim tracts and vast, robed in the lustrous gloom
Of leaden-coloured even, and fiery hills
Mingling their flames with twilight, on the verge
Of the remote horizon. The near scene,
In naked and severe simplicity, 560
Made contrast with the universe. A pine,
Rock-rooted, stretched athwart the vacancy
Its swinging boughs, to each inconstant blast
Yielding one only response, at each pause
In most familiar cadence, with the howl
The thunder and the hiss of homeless streams
Mingling its solemn song, whilst the broad river,
Foaming and hurrying o'er its rugged path,
Fell into that immeasurable void
Scattering its waters to the passing winds. 570

    Yet the grey precipice and solemn pine
And torrent, were not all;—one silent nook
Was there. Even on the edge of that vast moun-
    tain,
Upheld by knotty roots and fallen rocks,
It overlooked in its serenity
The dark earth, and the bending vault of stars.
It was a tranquil spot, that seemed to smile
Even in the lap of horror. Ivy clasped
The fissured stones with its entwining arms,
And did embower with leaves for ever green, 580
And berries dark, the smooth and even space
Of its inviolated floor, and here
The children of the autumnal whirlwind bore,
In wanton sport, those bright leaves, whose
    decay,
Red, yellow, or ethereally pale,
Rivals the pride of summer. 'Tis the haunt
Of every gentle wind, whose breath can teach
The wilds to love tranquility. One step,
One human step alone, has ever broken
The stillness of its solitude:—one voice 590
Alone inspired its echoes;—even that voice
Which hither came, floating among the winds,
And led the loveliest among human forms
To make their wild haunts the depository
Of all the grace and beauty that endued
Its motions, render up its majesty,
Scatter its music on the unfeeling storm,

And to the damp leaves and blue cavern mould,
Nurses of rainbow flowers and branching moss,
Commit the colours of that varying cheek,   600
That snowy breast, those dark and drooping eyes.

    The dim and hornèd moon hung low, and
      poured
A sea of lustre on the horizon's verge
That overflowed its mountains. Yellow mist
Filled the unbounded atmosphere, and drank
Wan moonlight even to fulness: not a star
Shone, not a sound was heard; the very winds,
Danger's grim playmates, on that precipice
Slept, clasped in his embrace.—O, storm of
    death!
Whose sightless speed divides this sullen
    night: 610
And thou, colossal Skeleton,[14] that, still
Guiding its irresistible career
In thy devastating omnipotence,
Art king of this frail world, from the red field
Of slaughter, from the reeking hospital,
The patriot's sacred couch, the snowy bed
Of innocence, the scaffold and the throne,
A mighty voice invokes thee. Ruin calls
His brother Death. A rare and regal prey
He hath prepared, prowling around the
    world;   620
Glutted with which thou mayst repose, and men
Go to their graves like flowers or creeping worms,
Nor ever more offer at thy dark shrine
The unheeded tribute of a broken heart.

    When on the threshold of the green recess
The wanderer's footsteps fell, he knew that death
Was on him. Yet a little, ere it fled,
Did he resign his high and holy soul
To images of the majestic past,
That paused within his passive being now,   630
Like winds that bear sweet music, when they
    breathe
Through some dim latticed chamber. He did
    place
His pale lean hand upon the rugged trunk
Of the old pine. Upon an ivied stone
Reclined his languid head, his limbs did rest,
Diffused and motionless, on the smooth brink
Of that obscurest chasm;—and thus he lay,
Surrendering to their final impulses
The hovering powers of life. Hope and despair,
The torturers, slept; no mortal pain or fear   640
Marred his repose, the influxes of sense,
And his own being unalloyed by pain,

Yet feebler and more feeble, calmly fed
The stream of thought, till he lay breathing there
At peace, and faintly smiling:—his last sight
Was the great moon, which o'er the western line
Of the wide world her mighty horn suspended,
With whose dun beams inwoven darkness
    seemed
To mingle. Now upon the jaggèd hills
It rests, and still as the divided frame   650
Of the vast meteor sunk, the Poet's blood,
That ever beat in mystic sympathy
With nature's ebb and flow, grew feebler still:
And when two lessening points of light alone
Gleamed through the darkness, the alternate
    gasp
Of his faint respiration scarce did stir
The stagnate night:—till the minutest ray
Was quenched, the pulse yet lingered in his heart.
It paused—it fluttered. But when heaven re-
    mained
Utterly black, the murky shades involved   660
An image, silent, cold, and motionless,
As their own voiceless earth and the vacant air.
Even as a vapour fed with golden beams
That ministered on sunlight, ere the west
Eclipses it, was now that wondrous frame—
No sense, no motion, no divinity—
A fragile lute, on whose harmonious strings
The breath of heaven did wander—a bright
    stream
Once fed with many-voicèd waves—a dream
Of youth, which night and time have quenched
    for ever,   670
Still, dark, and dry, and unremembered now.

    O, for Medea's wondrous alchemy,[15]
Which wheresoe'er it fell made the earth gleam
With bright flowers, and the wintry boughs
    exhale
From vernal blooms fresh fragrance! O, that
    God,
Profuse of poisons, would concede the chalice[16]
Which but one living man[17] has drained, who
    now,
Vessel of deathless wrath, a slave that feels
No proud exemption in the blighting curse
He bears, over the world wanders for ever,   680
Lone as incarnate death! O, that the dream
Of dark magician in his visioned cave,

---

14 Death.

15 Medea, daughter of the King of Colchis, was a powerful enchantress of ancient mythology. Among other wonders, she enabled her lover Jason to obtain the golden fleece and restored
Jason's father by replacing his blood with a magic fluid.
16 of immortality.
17 the Wandering Jew, who, because he had refused Christ a
place to rest on his way to Calvary, was condemned to wander
upon earth until Christ's second coming.

Raking the cinders of a crucible
For life and power, even when his feeble hand
Shakes in its last decay, were the true law
Of this so lovely world! But thou art fled
Like some frail exhalation; which the dawn
Robes in its golden beams,—ah! thou hast fled!
The brave, the gentle, and the beautiful,
The child of grace and genius. Heartless
  things   690
Are done and said i' the world, and many worms
And beasts and men live on, and mighty Earth
From sea and mountain, city and wilderness,
In vesper low or joyous orison,
Lifts still its solemn voice:—but thou art fled—
Thou canst no longer know or love the shapes
Of this phantasmal scene, who have to thee
Been purest ministers, who are, alas!
Now thou art not. Upon those pallid lips
So sweet even in their silence, on those eyes 700
That image sleep in death, upon that form
Yet safe from the worm's outrage, let no tear
Be shed—not even in thought. Nor, when those
  hues
Are gone, and those divinest lineaments,
Worn by the senseless wind, shall live alone
In the frail pauses of this simple strain,
Let not high verse, mourning the memory
Of that which is no more, or painting's woe
Or sculpture, speak in feeble imagery
Their own cold powers. Art and eloquence, 710
And all the shows o' the world are frail and vain
To weep a loss that turns their lights to shade.
It is a woe too 'deep for tears,'[18] when all
Is reft at once, when some surpassing Spirit,
Whose light adorned the world around it, leaves
Those who remain behind, not sobs or groans,
The passionate tumult of a clinging hope;
But pale despair and cold tranquillity,
Nature's vast frame, the web of human things,
Birth and the grave, that are not as they
  were.   720
 1815   1816

HYMN TO INTELLECTUAL BEAUTY

[This poem reflects Shelley's growing interest in and
acceptance of the Platonic doctrine of Intellectual, or
Ideal, Beauty. This doctrine Shelley derived chiefly from
Plato's *Symposium,* but secondary influences include
Wordsworth and the Neo-Platonists. Within its philo-
sophical framework the *Hymn* records a personal emo-

---

18 Wordsworth, *Ode on Intimations of Immortality,* 204.

tional experience of a kind that had a profound effect
upon Shelley.
 Mrs. Shelley states in a note that the poem was conceived in the summer of 1816 on a boating trip around
Lake Geneva with Byron. Shelley wrote Leigh Hunt
that it was 'composed under the influence of feelings
which agitated me even to tears.']

I

THE awful shadow of some unseen Power
 Floats though unseen amongst us,—visiting
 This various world with an inconstant wing
As summer winds that creep from flower to
  flower,—
Like moonbeams that behind some piny moun-
  tain shower,
 It visits with inconstant glance
 Each human heart and countenance;
Like hues and harmonies of evening,—
 Like clouds in starlight widely spread,—
 Like memory of music fled,— 10
 Like aught that for its grace may be
Dear, and yet dearer for its mystery.

II

Spirit of BEAUTY, that dost consecrate
 With thine own hues all thou dost shine upon
 Of human thought or form,—where art thou
  gone?
Why dost thou pass away and leave our state,
This dim vast vale of tears, vacant and desolate?
 Ask why the sunlight not for ever
 Weaves rainbows o'er yon mountain river,
Why aught should fail and fade that once is
  shown,   20
 Why fear and dream and death and birth
 Cast on the daylight of this earth
 Such gloom,—why man has such a scope
For love and hate, despondency and hope?

III

No voice from some sublimer world hath ever
 To sage or poet these responses given—
 Therefore the names of Dæmon, Ghost, and
  Heaven,
Remain the records of their vain endeavor,
Frail spells—whose uttered charm might not
  avail to sever,
 From all we hear and all we see, 30
 Doubt, chance, and mutability.
Thy light alone—like mist o'er mountains driven,
 Or music by the night wind sent
 Through strings of some still instrument,
 Or moonlight on a midnight stream,
Gives grace and truth to life's unquiet dream.

IV

Love, Hope, and Self-esteem, like clouds depart
    And come, for some uncertain moments lent,
    Man were immortal, and omnipotent,
Didst thou, unknown and awful as thou art, 40
Keep with thy glorious train firm state within his
        heart.
    Thou messenger of sympathies,
    That wax and wane in lovers' eyes—
Thou—that to human thought art nourishment,
    Like darkness to a dying flame!
    Depart not as thy shadow came,
    Depart not—lest the grave should be,
Like life and fear, a dark reality.

V

While yet a boy I sought for ghosts, and sped
    Through many a listening chamber, cave and
        ruin, 50
    And starlight wood, with fearful steps pursuing
Hopes of high talk with the departed dead,
I called on poisonous names with which our
        youth is fed;
    I was not heard—I saw them not—
    When musing deeply on the lot
Of life, at the sweet time when winds are wooing
    All vital things that wake to bring
    News of birds and blossoming,—
    Sudden, thy shadow fell on me;
I shrieked, and clasped my hands in ecstasy! 60

VI

I vowed that I would dedicate my powers
    To thee and thine—have I not kept the vow?
    With beating heart and streaming eyes, even
        now
I call the phantoms of a thousand hours
Each from his voiceless grave: they have in vi-
        sioned bowers
    Of studious zeal or love's delight
    Outwatched with me the envious night—
They know that never joy illumined my brow
    Unlinked with hope that thou wouldst free
    This world from its dark slavery, 70
    That thou—O awful LOVELINESS,
Wouldst give whate'er these words cannot ex-
        press.

VII

The day becomes more solemn and serene
    When noon is past—there is a harmony
    In autumn, and a lustre in its sky,
Which through the summer is not heard or seen,

As if it could not be, as if it had not been!
    Thus let thy power, which like the truth
    Of nature on my passive youth
Descended, to my onward life supply   80
    Its calm—to one who worships thee,
    And every form containing thee,
    Whom, SPIRIT fair, thy spells did bind
To fear himself, and love all human kind.

1816   1817

MONT BLANC

LINES WRITTEN IN THE VALE OF CHAMOUNI

Mont Blanc was inspired by a view of that mountain, and its surrounding peaks and valleys, as he lingered on the Bridge of Arve on his way through the Valley of Chamouni. Shelley makes the following mention of this poem in his publication of the *History of a Six Weeks' Tour,* and Letters from Switzerland: 'The poem entitled *Mont Blanc* is written by the author of the two letters from Chamouni and Vevai. It was composed under the immediate impression of the deep and powerful feelings excited by the objects which it attempts to describe; and as an undisciplined overflowing of the soul, rests its claim to approbation on an attempt to imitate the un-tamable wildness and inaccessible solemnity from which these feelings sprang.'—(Mrs. Shelley.)

I

THE everlasting universe of things
Flows through the mind, and rolls its rapid
        waves,
Now dark—now glittering—now reflecting
        gloom—
Now lending splendour, where from secret
        springs
The source of human thought its tribute brings
Of waters,—with a sound but half its own,
Such as a feeble brook will oft assume
In the wild woods, among the mountains lone,
Where waterfalls around it leap for ever,
Where woods and winds contend, and a vast
        river   10
Over its rocks ceaselessly bursts and raves.

II

Thus thou, Ravine of Arve—dark, deep Ra-
        vine—
Thou many-coloured, many-voiced vale,
Over whose pines, and crags, and caverns sail
Fast cloud-shadows and sunbeams: awful scene,
Where Power in likeness of the Arve comes down
From the ice-gulfs that gird his secret throne,

Bursting through these dark mountains like the
    flame
Of lightning through the tempest;—thou dost lie,
Thy giant brood of pines around thee
    clinging,   20
Children of elder time, in whose devotion
The chainless winds still come and ever came
To drink their odours, and their mighty swinging
To hear—an old and solemn harmony;
Thine earthly rainbows stretched across the
    sweep
Of the aethereal waterfall, whose veil
Robes some unsculptured image; the strange
    sleep
Which when the voices of the desert fail
Wraps all in its own deep eternity;—
Thy caverns echoing to the Arve's commo-
    tion,   30
A loud, lone sound no other sound can tame;
Thou art pervaded with that ceaseless motion,
Thou art the path of that unresting sound—
Dizzy Ravine! and when I gaze on thee
I seem as in a trance sublime and strange
To muse on my own separate fantasy,
My own, my human mind, which passively
Now renders and receives fast influencings,
Holding an unremitting interchange
With the clear universe of things around;   40
One legion of wild thoughts, whose wandering
    wings
Now float above thy darkness, and now rest
Where that or thou art no unbidden guest,
In the still cave of the witch Poesy,
Seeking among the shadows that pass by
Ghosts of all things that are, some shade of thee,
Some phantom, some faint image; till the breast
From which they fled recalls them, thou art
    there!

III

Some say that gleams of a remoter world
Visit the soul in sleep,—that death is
    slumber,   50
And that its shapes the busy thoughts outnumber
Of those who wake and live.—I look on high;
Has some unknown omnipotence unfurled
The veil of life and death? or do I lie
In dream, and does the mightier world of sleep
Spread far around and inaccessibly
Its circles? For the very spirit fails,
Driven like a homeless cloud from steep to steep
That vanishes among the viewless gales!
Far, far above, piercing the infinite sky,   60

Mont Blanc appears,—still, snowy, and serene—
Its subject mountains their unearthly forms
Pile around it, ice and rock; broad vales between
Of frozen floods, unfathomable deeps,
Blue as the overhanging heaven, that spread
And wind among the accumulated steeps;
A desert peopled by the storms alone,
Save when the eagle brings some hunter's bone,
And the wolf tracks her there—how hideously
Its shapes are heaped around! rude, bare, and
    high,   70
Ghastly, and scarred, and riven.—Is this the
    scene
Where the old earthquake-daemon taught her
    young
Ruin? Were these their toys? or did a sea
Of fire envelop once this silent snow?
None can reply—all seems eternal now.
The wilderness has a mysterious tongue
Which teaches awful doubt, or faith so mild,
So solemn, so serene, that man may be,
But for such faith, with nature reconciled;
Thou hast a voice, great Mountain, to repeal   80
Large codes of fraud and woe; not understood
By all, but which the wise, and great, and good
Interpret, or make felt, or deeply feel.

IV

The fields, the lakes, the forests, and the streams,
Ocean, and all the living things that dwell
Within the daedal[1] earth; lightning, and rain,
Earthquake, and fiery flood, and hurricane,
The torpor of the year when feeble dreams
Visit the hidden buds, or dreamless sleep
Holds every future leaf and flower;—the
    bound   90
With which from that detested trance they leap;
The works and ways of man, their death and
    birth,
And that of him and all that his may be;
All things that move and breathe with toil and
    sound
Are born and die; revolve, subside, and swell.
Power dwells apart in its tranquillity,
Remote, serene, and inaccessible:
And *this,* the naked countenance of earth,
On which I gaze, even these primaeval mountains
Teach the adverting mind. The glaciers creep   100
Like snakes that watch their prey, from their far
    fountains,
Slow rolling on; there, many a precipice,
Frost and the Sun in scorn of mortal power

---

1 ingeniously formed.

Have piled: dome, pyramid, and pinnacle,
A city of death, distinct with many a tower
And wall impregnable of beaming ice.
Yet not a city, but a flood of ruin
Is there, that from the boundaries of the sky
Rolls its perpetual stream; vast pines are strew-
    ing
Its destined path, or in the mangled soil   110
Branchless and shattered stand; the rocks, drawn
    down
From yon remotest waste, have overthrown
The limits of the dead and living world,
Never to be reclaimed. The dwelling-place
Of insects, beasts, and birds, becomes its spoil
Their food and their retreat for ever gone,
So much of life and joy is lost. The race
Of man flies far in dread; his work and dwell-
    ing
Vanish, like smoke before the tempest's stream,
And their place is not known. Below, vast
    caves   120
Shine in the rushing torrents' restless gleam,
Which from those secret chasms in tumult well-
    ing
Meet in the vale, and one majestic River,
The breath and blood of distant lands, for
    ever
Rolls its loud waters to the ocean-waves,
Breathes its swift vapours to the circling air.

V

Mont Blanc yet gleams on high;—the power is
    there,
The still and solemn power of many sights,
And many sounds, and much of life and death.
In the calm darkness of the moonless nights,   130
In the lone glare of day, the snows descend
Upon that Mountain; none beholds them there,
Nor when the flakes burn in the sinking sun,
Or the star-beams dart through them:—Winds
    contend
Silently there, and heap the snow with breath
Rapid and strong, but silently! Its home
The voiceless lightning in these solitudes
Keeps innocently, and like vapour broods
Over the snow. The secret Strength of things
Which governs thought, and to the infinite
    dome   140
Of Heaven is as a law, inhabits thee!
And what were thou, and earth, and stars, and
    sea,
If to the human mind's imaginings
Silence and solitude were vacancy?

July 1816   1817

TO MARY[1]

DEDICATION TO *The Revolt of Islam*

So now my summer task is ended, Mary,
    And I return to thee, mine own heart's
      home;
As to his Queen some victor Knight of Faëry,
    Earning bright spoils for her enchanted
      dome;
    Nor thou disdain, that ere my fame become
A star among the stars of mortal night,
    If it indeed may cleave its natal gloom,
Its doubtful promise thus I would unite
With thy belovèd name, thou Child of love and
    light.

The toil which stole from thee so many an
    hour,   10
    Is ended,—and the fruit is at thy feet!
No longer where the woods to frame a bower
    With interlacèd branches mix and meet,
    Or where with sound like many voices sweet,
Waterfalls leap among wild islands green,
    Which framed for my lone boat a lone re-
      treat
Of moss-grown trees and weeds, shall I be
    seen:
But beside thee, where still my heart has ever
    been.

Thoughts of great deeds were mine, dear
    Friend, when first
    The clouds which wrap this world from
      youth did pass.   20
I do remember well the hour which burst
    My spirit's sleep: a fresh May-dawn it was,
    When I walked forth upon the glittering
      grass,
And wept, I knew not why; until there rose
    From the near schoolroom, voices, that,
      alas!
Were but one echo from a world of woes—
The harsh and grating strife of tyrants and of
    foes.

And then I clasped my hands and looked
    around—
    —But none was near to mock my streaming
      eyes,
Which poured their warm drops on the sunny
    ground—   30
    So, without shame, I spake:—'I will be wise,
    And just, and free, and mild, if in me lies

---

1 Mary Wollstonecraft Godwin, the poet's second wife.

Such power, for I grow weary to behold
    The selfish and the strong still tyrannise
Without reproach or check.' I then controlled
My tears, my heart grew calm, and I was meek
    and bold.

And from that hour did I with earnest thought
    Heap knowledge from forbidden mines of
    lore,
Yet nothing that my tyrants knew or taught
    I cared to learn, but from that secret store   40
    Wrought linkèd armour for my soul, before
It might walk forth to war among mankind;
    Thus power and hope were strengthened
    more and more
Within me, till there came upon my mind
A sense of loneliness, a thirst with which I pined.

Alas, that love should be a blight and snare
    To those who seek all sympathies in one!²—
Such once I sought in vain; then black despair,
    The shadow of a starless night, was thrown
    Over the world in which I moved
    alone:³—   50
Yet never found I one not false to me,
    Hard hearts, and cold, like weights of icy
    stone
Which crushed and withered mine, that could
    not be
Aught but a lifeless clod, until revived by thee.

Thou Friend, whose presence on my wintry
    heart
    Fell, like bright Spring upon some herbless
    plain;
How beautiful and calm and free thou wert
    In thy young wisdom, when the mortal chain
    Of Custom thou didst burst and rend in
    twain,⁴
And walked as free as light the clouds
    among,   60
    Which many an envious slave then breathed
    in vain
From his dim dungeon, and my spirit sprung
To meet thee from the woes which had begirt it
    long!

No more alone through the world's wilderness,
    Although I trod the paths of high intent,
I journeyed now: no more companionless,

Where solitude is like despair, I went.—
    There is the wisdom of a stern content
When Poverty can blight the just and good,
    When Infamy dares mock the innocent,   70
And cherished friends turn with the multitude
To trample: this was ours, and we unshaken
    stood!

Now has descended a screner hour,
    And with inconstant fortune, friends re-
    turn;
Though suffering leaves the knowledge and the
    power
    Which says:—Let scorn be not repaid with
    scorn.
    And from thy side two gentle babes are born
To fill our home with smiles, and thus are we
    Most fortunate beneath life's beaming morn;
And these delights, and thou, have been to
    me   80
The parents of the Song I consecrate to thee.

Is it, that now my inexperienced fingers
    But strike the prelude of a loftier strain?
Or, must the lyre on which my spirit lingers
    Soon pause in silence, ne'er to sound again,
    Though it might shake the Anarch Custom's
    reign,
And charm the minds of men to Truth's own
    sway
    Holier than was Amphion's?⁵ I would fain
Reply in hope—but I am worn away,
And Death and Love are yet contending for their
    prey.   90

And what art thou? I know, but dare not
    speak:
    Time may interpret to his silent years.
Yet in the paleness of thy thoughtful cheek,
    And in the light thine ample forehead wears,
    And in thy sweetest smiles, and in thy
    tears,
And in thy gentle speech, a prophecy
    Is whispered, to subdue my fondest fears:
And through thine eyes, even in thy soul I see
A lamp of vestal fire burning internally.

They say that thou wert lovely from thy
    birth,   100
    Of glorious parents,⁶ thou aspiring Child.
    I wonder not—for One then left this earth

---

2 The reference may be to his unhappy marriage with Harriet
Westbrook.
3 perhaps during the year before he met Mary.
4 a reference to Mary's elopement with Shelley.

5 Amphion, according to ancient legend, built the walls of Thebes
by charming the stones into place by the music of his lyre.
6 Mary Wollstonecraft Godwin and William Godwin, each the
author of influential social and political writings.

Whose life was like a setting planet mild,
Which clothed thee in the radiance undefiled
Of its departing glory;[7] still her fame
    Shines on thee, through the tempests dark
        and wild
Which shake these latter days; and thou canst
    claim
The shelter, from thy Sire, of an immortal name.

One voice came forth from many a mighty
    spirit,
    Which was the echo of three thousand
        years;   110
And the tumultuous world stood mute to hear
    it,
    As some lone man who in a desert hears
    The music of his home:—unwonted fears
Fell on the pale oppressors of our race,
    And Faith, and Custom, and low-thoughted
        cares,
Like thunder-stricken dragons, for a space
Left the torn human heart, their food and dwell-
    ing-place.

Truth's deathless voice pauses among man-
        kind!
    If there must be no response to my cry—
If men must rise and stamp with fury
        blind   120
    On his pure name who loves them,—thou
        and I,
    Sweet friend! can look from our tranquil-
        lity
Like lamps into the world's tempestuous
        night,—
    Two tranquil stars, while clouds are passing
        by
    Which wrap them from the foundering sea-
        man's sight,
That burn from year to year with unextinguished
    light.
1817   1818

TO CONSTANTIA SINGING[1]

[Constantia is Jane Clairmont, whose singing inspired
both Byron and Shelley.]

THY voice is hovering o'er my soul—it lingers
    O'ershadowing it with soft and lulling wings,
The blood and life within thy snowy fingers
    Teach witchcraft to the instrumental strings.

___
7 Mary's mother died in childbirth.

1 Text as reconstructed by Marcel Kessel and reprinted with his
kind permission.

My brain is wild—my breath comes quick—
    The blood is listening in my frame,
And thronging shadows, fast and thick,
    Fall on my overflowing eyes;
My heart is quivering like a flame;
    As morning dew, that in the sunbeam dies,   10
    I am dissolved in these consuming ecstasies.

I have no life, Constantia, but in thee
    Whilst, like the world-surrounding air, thy
        song
Flows on, and fills all things with melody,—
    Now is thy voice a tempest swift and strong,
On which, as one in trance upborne,
    Secure o'er rocks and waves I sweep,
Rejoicing like a cloud of morn.
    Now 'tis the breath of summer's night,
Which, where the starry waters sleep,   20
    Round western isles, with incense-blossoms
        bright,
    Lingering, suspends my soul in its voluptuous
        flight.

A deep and breathless awe, like the swift change
    Of dreams unseen but felt in youthful slum-
        bers,
Wild, sweet, yet uncommunicably strange,
    Thou breathest now in fast ascending num-
        bers.
The cope of heaven seems rent and cloven
    By the enchantment of thy strain,
And o'er my shoulders wings are woven,
    To follow its sublime career   30
Beyond the mighty moons that wane
    Upon the verge of Nature's utmost sphere,
    Till the world's shadowy walls are past and
        disappear.

Cease, cease—for such wild lessons madmen
        learn.
    Long thus to sink,—thus to be lost and die,
Perhaps is death indeed—Constantia turn!
    Yes! in thine eyes a power like light doth
        lie,
Even though the sounds, its voice that were
    Between thy lips, are laid to sleep—
Within thy breath, and on thy hair   40
Like odour, it is lingering yet—
    And from thy touch like fire doth leap,
    Even while I write, my burning cheeks are
        wet.
    Alas, that the torn heart can bleed, but not for-
        get.
1817   1824

OZYMANDIAS[1]

I MET a traveller from an antique land
Who said: Two vast and trunkless legs of stone
Stand in the desert . . . Near them, on the sand,
Half sunk, a shattered visage lies, whose frown,
And wrinkled lip, and sneer of cold command,
Tell that its sculptor well those passions read
Which yet survive, (stamped on these lifeless
    things,)
The hand[2] that mocked them and the heart[3] that
    fed:
And on the pedestal these words appear:
'My name is Ozymandias, king of kings: 10
Look on my works, ye Mighty, and despair!'
Nothing beside remains. Round the decay
Of that colossal wreck, boundless and bare
The lone and level sands stretch far away.

1817   1818

PROMETHEUS UNBOUND

A LYRICAL DRAMA IN FOUR ACTS

AUDISNE HAEC, AMPHIARAE, SUB TERRAM ABDITE?[1]

[Mrs. Shelley gives in her note to *Prometheus Unbound*
an excellent account of the conditions under which the
poem was composed and the general ideas it embodies:
. . . 'The first aspect of Italy enchanted Shelley; it seemed
a garden of delight placed beneath a clearer and brighter
heaven than any he had lived under before. He wrote
long descriptive letters during the first year of his residence in Italy, which, as compositions, are the most
beautiful in the world, and show how truly he appreciated and studied the wonders of Nature and Art in that
divine land.

'The poetical spirit within him speedily revived with
all the power and with more than all the beauty of his
first attempts. He meditated three subjects as the
groundwork for lyrical dramas. One was the story of
Tasso; of this a slight fragment of a song of Tasso remains. The other was one founded on the *Book of Job*,
which he never abandoned in idea, but of which no
trace remains among his papers. The third was the
Prometheus Unbound. The Greek tragedians were now
his most familiar companions in his wanderings, and
the sublime majesty of Æschylus filled him with wonder and delight. The father of Greek tragedy does not
possess the pathos of Sophocles, nor the variety and
tenderness of Euripides; the interest on which he founds
his dramas is often elevated above human vicissitudes
into the mighty passions and throes of gods and demi-

gods: such fascinated the abstract imagination of Shelley. . . .

'At first he completed the drama in three acts. It was
not till several months after, when at Florence, that he
conceived that a fourth act, a sort of hymn of rejoicing
in the fulfilment of the prophecies with regard to Prometheus, ought to be added to complete the composition.

'The prominent feature of Shelley's theory of the destiny of the human species was that evil is not inherent
in the system of the creation, but an accident that might
be expelled. This also forms a portion of Christianity:
God made earth and man perfect, till he, by his fall,

"Brought death into the world and all our woe."
                    [*Paradise Lost,* I, 3.]

Shelley believed that mankind had only to will that
there should be no evil, and there would be none. It is
not my part in these notes to notice the arguments that
have been urged against this opinion, but to mention the
fact that he entertained it, and was indeed attached to it
with fervent enthusiasm. That man could be so perfectionized as to be able to expel evil from his own nature,
and from the greater part of the creation, was the cardinal point of his system. And the subject he loved best to
dwell on was the image of One warring with the Evil
Principle, oppressed not only by it, but by all—even the
good, who were deluded into considering evil a necessary portion of humanity; a victim full of fortitude and
hope and the spirit of triumph emanating from a reliance in the ultimate omnipotence of Good. Such he had
depicted in his last poem [*The Revolt of Islam*] when he
made Laon the enemy and the victim of tyrants. He now
took a more idealized image of the same subject. He followed certain classical authorities in figuring Saturn as
the good principle, Jupiter the usurping evil one, and
Prometheus as the regenerator, who, unable to bring
mankind back to primitive innocence, used knowledge
as a weapon to defeat evil, by leading mankind, beyond
the state wherein they are sinless through ignorance, to
that in which they are virtuous through wisdom. Jupiter
punished the temerity of the Titan by chaining him to a
rock of Caucasus, and causing a vulture to devour his
still-renewed heart. There was a prophecy afloat in
heaven portending the fall of Jove, the secret of averting
which was known only to Prometheus; and the god
offered freedom from torture on condition of its being
communicated to him. According to the mythological
story, this referred to the offspring of Thetis, who was
destined to be greater than his father. Prometheus at last
bought pardon for his crime of enriching mankind with
his gifts, by revealing the prophecy. Hercules killed the
vulture, and set him free; and Thetis was married to Peleus, the father of Achilles.

'Shelley adapted the catastrophe of this story to his peculiar views. The son greater than his father, born of the
nuptials of Jupiter and Thetis, was to dethrone Evil, and
bring back a happier reign than that of Saturn. Prometheus defies the power of his enemy, and endures centuries of torture; till the hour arrives when Jove, blind to
the real event, but darkly guessing that some great good
to himself will flow, espouses Thetis. At the moment, the
Primal Power of the world drives him from his usurped
throne, and Strength, in the person of Hercules, liberates
Humanity, typified in Prometheus, from the tortures
generated by evil done or suffered. Asia, one of the
Oceanides, is the wife of Prometheus—she was, according to other mythological interpretations, the same as

---

1 Ozymandias was the Greek name for the Egyptian King Ram-
eses II. According to the historian Diodorus Siculus his statue was
reputed to be the largest in all Egypt and bore the following inscription: "I am Ozymandias, king of kings. If anyone would
know how great I am and where I lie, let him surpass any of my
works.'
2 the sculptor's.
3 Ozymandias'

1 'Do you not hear these things, Amphiaraus, down beneath
the earth?'

Venus and Nature. When the benefactor of mankind is liberated, Nature resumes the beauty of her prime, and is united to her husband, the emblem of the human race, in perfect and happy union. In the Fourth Act, the poet gives further scope to his imagination, and idealizes the forms of creation—such as we know them, instead of such as they appeared to the Greeks. Maternal Earth, the mighty parent, is superseded by the Spirit of the Earth, the guide of our planet through the realms of sky; while his fair and weaker companion and attendant, the Spirit of the Moon, receives bliss from the annihilation of Evil in the superior sphere.

'Shelley develops, more particularly in the lyrics of this drama, his abstruse and imaginative theories with regard to the Creation. It requires a mind as subtle and penetrating as his own to understand the mystic meanings scattered throughout the poem. They elude the ordinary reader by their abstraction and delicacy of distinction, but they are far from vague. It was his design to write prose metaphysical essays on the nature of man, which would have served to explain much of what is obscure in his poetry; a few scattered fragments of observations and remarks alone remain. He considered these philosophical views of mind and nature to be instinct with the intensest spirit of poetry.

'More popular poets clothe the ideal with familiar and sensible imagery. Shelley loved to idealize the real—to gift the mechanism of the material universe with a soul and a voice, and to bestow such also on the most delicate and abstract emotions and thoughts of the mind. . . .

'Through the whole poem there reigns a sort of calm and holy spirit of love; it soothes the tortured, and is hope to the expectant, till the prophecy is fulfilled, and love, untainted by any evil, becomes the law of the world. . . .

'The charm of the Roman climate helped to clothe his thoughts in greater beauty than they had ever worn before. And, as he wandered among the ruins made one with nature in their decay, or gazed on the Praxitelean shapes that throng the Vatican, the Capitol, and the palaces of Rome, his soul imbibed forms of loveliness which became a portion of itself. There are many passages in the *Prometheus* which show the intense delight he received from such studies, and give back the impression with a beauty of poetical description peculiarly his own.']

PREFACE

The Greek tragic writers, in selecting as their subject any portion of their national history or mythology, employed in their treatment of it a certain arbitrary discretion. They by no means conceived themselves bound to adhere to the common interpretation or to imitate in story as in title their rivals and predecessors. Such a system would have amounted to a resignation of those claims to preference over their competitors which incited the composition. The Agamemnonian story was exhibited in the Athenian theatre with as many variations as dramas.

I have presumed to employ a similar license. The *Prometheus Unbound* of Æschylus supposed the reconciliation of Jupiter with his victim as the price of the disclosure of the danger threatened to his empire by the consummation of his marriage with Thetis. Thetis, according to this view of the subject, was given in marriage to Peleus, and Prometheus, by the permission of Jupiter, delivered from his captivity by Hercules. Had I framed my story on this model, I should have done no more

than have attempted to restore the lost drama of Æschylus; an ambition which, if my preference to this mode of treating the subject had incited me to cherish, the recollection of the high comparison such an attempt would challenge might well abate. But, in truth, I was averse from a catastrophe so feeble as that of reconciling the champion with the oppressor of mankind. The moral interest of the fable, which is so powerfully sustained by the sufferings and endurance of Prometheus, would be annihilated if we could conceive of him as unsaying his high language and quailing before his successful and perfidious adversary. The only imaginary being resembling in any degree Prometheus, is Satan; and Prometheus is, in my judgement, a more poetical character than Satan, because, in addition to courage, and majesty, and firm and patient opposition to omnipotent force, he is susceptible of being described as exempt from the taints of ambition, envy, revenge, and a desire for personal aggrandizement, which, in the hero of *Paradise Lost,* interfere with the interest. The character of Satan engenders in the mind a pernicious casuistry which leads us to weigh his faults with his wrongs, and to excuse the former because the latter exceed all measure. In the minds of those who consider that magnificent fiction with a religious feeling it engenders something worse. But Prometheus is, as it were, the type of the highest perfection of moral and intellectual nature, impelled by the purest and the truest motives to the best and noblest ends.

This poem was chiefly written upon the mountainous ruins of the Baths of Caracalla, among the flowery glades, and thickets of odoriferous blossoming trees, which are extended in ever winding labyrinths upon its immense platforms and dizzy arches suspended in the air. The bright blue sky of Rome, and the effect of the vigorous awakening spring in that divinest climate, and the new life with which it drenches the spirits even to intoxication, were the inspiration of this drama.

The imagery which I have employed will be found, in many instances, to have been drawn from the operations of the human mind, or from those external actions by which they are expressed. This is unusual in modern poetry, although Dante and Shakespeare are full of instances of the same kind: Dante indeed more than any other poet, and with greater success. But the Greek poets, as writers to whom no resource of awakening the sympathy of their contemporaries was unknown, were in the habitual use of this power; and it is the study of their works (since a higher merit would probably be denied me) to which I am willing that my readers should impute this singularity.

One word is due in candour to the degree in which the study of contemporary writings may have tinged my composition, for such has been a topic of censure with regard to poems far more popular, and indeed more deservedly popular, than mine. It is impossible that any one who inhabits the same age with such writers as those who stand in the foremost ranks of our own, can conscientiously assure himself that his language and tone of thought may not have been modified by the study of the productions of those extraordinary intellects. It is true that, not the spirit of their genius, but the forms in which it has manifested itself, are due less to the peculiarities of their own minds than to the peculiarity of the moral and intellectual condition of the minds among which they have been produced. Thus a number of writers possess the form, whilst they want the spirit of those whom, it is alleged, they imitate; because the former is the endowment of the age in which they live, and the latter must be the uncommunicated lightning of their own mind.

The peculiar style of intense and comprehensive imagery which distinguishes the modern literature of England, has not been, as a general power, the product of the imitation of any particular writer. The mass of capabilities remains at every period materially the same; the circumstances which awaken it to action perpetually change. If England were divided into forty republics, each equal in population and extent to Athens, there is no reason to suppose but that, under institutions not more perfect than those of Athens, each would produce philosophers and poets equal to those who (if we except Shakespeare) have never been surpassed. We owe the great writers of the golden age of our literature to that fervid awakening of the public mind which shook to dust the oldest and most oppressive form of the Christian religion. We owe Milton to the progress and development of the same spirit: the sacred Milton was, let it ever be remembered, a republican, and a bold inquirer into morals and religion. The great writers of our own age are, we have reason to suppose, the companions and forerunners of some unimagined change in our social condition or the opinions which cement it. The cloud of mind is discharging its collected lightning, and the equilibrium between institutions and opinions is now restoring, or is about to be restored.

As to imitation, poetry is a mimetic art. It creates, but it creates by combination and representation. Poetical abstractions are beautiful and new, not because the portions of which they are composed had no previous existence in the mind of man or in nature, but because the whole produced by their combination has some intelligible and beautiful analogy with those sources of emotion and thought, and with the contemporary condition of them: one great poet is a masterpiece of nature which another not only ought to study but must study. He might as wisely and as easily determine that his mind should no longer be the mirror of all that is lovely in the visible universe, as exclude from his contemplation the beautiful which exists in the writings of a great contemporary. The pretence of doing it would be a presumption in any but the greatest; the effect, even in him, would be strained, unnatural, and ineffectual. A poet is the combined product of such internal powers as modify the nature of others; and of such external influences as excite and sustain these powers; he is not one, but both. Every man's mind is, in this respect, modified by all the objects of nature and art; by every word and every suggestion which he ever admitted to act upon his consciousness; it is the mirror upon which all forms are reflected, and in which they compose one form. Poets, not otherwise than philosophers, painters, sculptors, and musicians, are, in one sense, the creators, and, in another, the creations, of their age. From this subjection the loftiest do not escape. There is a similarity between Homer and Hesiod, between Æschylus and Euripides, between Virgil and Horace, between Dante and Petrarch, between Shakespeare and Fletcher, between Dryden and Pope; each has a generic resemblance under which their specific distinctions are arranged. If this similarity be the result of imitation, I am willing to confess that I have imitated.

Let this opportunity be conceded to me of acknowledging that I have, what a Scotch philosopher characteristically terms, 'a passion for reforming the world': what passion incited him to write and publish his book, he omits to explain. For my part I had rather be damned with Plato and Lord Bacon, than go to Heaven with Paley and Malthus.[2] But it is a mistake to suppose that I dedicate my poetical compositions solely to the direct enforcement of reform, or that I consider them in any degree as containing a reasoned system on the theory of human life. Didactic poetry is my abhorrence; nothing can be equally well expressed in prose that is not tedious and supererogatory in verse. My purpose has hitherto been simply to familiarize the highly refined imagination of the more select classes of poetical readers with beautiful idealisms of moral excellence; aware that until the mind can love, and admire, and trust, and hope, and endure, reasoned principles of moral conduct are seeds cast upon the highway of life which the unconscious passenger tramples into dust, although they would bear the harvest of his happiness. Should I live to accomplish what I purpose, that is, produce a systematical history of what appear to me to be the genuine elements of human society, let not the advocates of injustice and superstition flatter themselves that I should take Æschylus rather than Plato as my model.

The having spoken of myself with unaffected freedom will need little apology with the candid, and let the uncandid consider that they injure me less than their own hearts and minds by misrepresentation. Whatever talents a person may possess to amuse and instruct others, be they ever so inconsiderable, he is yet bound to exert them: if his attempt be ineffectual, let the punishment of an unaccomplished purpose have been sufficient; let none trouble themselves to heap the dust of oblivion upon his efforts; the pile they raise will betray his grave which might otherwise have been unknown.

DRAMATIS PERSONÆ

PROMETHEUS	APOLLO
DEMOGORGON	MERCURY
JUPITER	ASIA
THE EARTH	PANTHEA
OCEAN	IONE

Oceanides

HERCULES
THE PHANTASM OF JUPITER
THE SPIRIT OF THE EARTH
THE SPIRIT OF THE MOON
SPIRITS OF THE HOURS
SPIRITS, ECHOES, FAUNS, FURIES.

ACT I

SCENE.—*A Ravine of Icy Rocks in the Indian Caucasus.* PROMETHEUS *is discovered bound to the Precipice.* PANTHEA *and* IONE *are seated at his feet. Time, night. During the Scene, morning slowly breaks.*

Prometheus. MONARCH of Gods and Dæmons, and all Spirits

---

2 William Paley, 1743–1805, was an English theologian and utilitarian philosopher who proved the existence of God by logical reasoning; Thomas R. Malthus, 1766–1834, was a political economist who advanced the theory that war, famine, pestilence, and vice are necessary checks upon population.

But One,[3] who throng those bright and rolling
worlds
Which Thou and I alone of living things
Behold with sleepless eyes! regard this Earth
Made multitudinous with thy slaves, whom thou
Requitest for knee-worship, prayer, and praise,
And toil, and hecatombs[4] of broken hearts,
With fear and self-contempt and barren hope.
Whilst me, who am thy foe, eyeless in hate,
Hast thou made reign and triumph, to thy
scorn,   10
O'er mine own misery and thy vain revenge.
Three thousand years of sleep-unsheltered hours,
And moments aye divided by keen pangs
Till they seemed years, torture and solitude,
Scorn and despair,—these are mine empire:—
More glorious far than that which thou surveyest
From thine unenvied throne, O Mighty God!
Almighty, had I deigned to share the shame
Of thine ill tyranny, and hung not here
Nailed to this wall of eagle-baffling mountain, 20
Black, wintry, dead, unmeasured; without herb,
Insect, or beast, or shape or sound of life.
Ah me! alas, pain, pain ever, for ever!

No change, no pause, no hope! Yet I endure.
I ask the Earth, have not the mountains felt?
I ask yon Heaven, the all-beholding Sun,
Has it not seen? The Sea, in storm or calm,
Heaven's ever-changing Shadow, spread below,
Have its deaf waves not heard my agony?
Ah me! alas, pain, pain ever, for ever!   30

The crawling glaciers pierce me with the spears
Of their moon-freezing crystals, the bright chains
Eat with their burning cold into my bones.
Heaven's wingèd hound,[5] polluting from thy lips
His beak in poison not his own, tears up
My heart; and shapeless sights come wandering
by,
The ghastly people of the realm of dream,
Mocking me: and the Earthquake-fiends are
charged
To wrench the rivets from my quivering wounds
When the rocks split and close again behind: 40
While from their loud abysses howling throng
The genii of the storm, urging the rage
Of whirlwind, and afflict me with keen hail.
And yet to me welcome is day and night,
Whether one breaks the hoar frost of the morn,
Or starry, dim, and slow, the other climbs

---

3 Prometheus himself.
4 huge sacrifices.
5 the vulture, which according to the Greek myth daily tore out
his entrails.

The leaden-coloured east; for then they lead
The wingless, crawling hours, one among whom
—As some dark Priest hales the reluctant victim
Shall drag thee, cruel King, to kiss the blood 50
From these pale feet, which then might trample
thee
If they disdained not such a prostrate slave,
Disdain! Ah no! I pity thee. What ruin
Will hunt thee undefended through wide
Heaven!
How will thy soul, cloven to its depth with terror,
Gape like a hell within! I speak in grief,
Not exultation, for I hate no more,
As then ere misery made me wise. The curse
Once breathed on thee I would recall. Ye Moun-
tains,
Whose many-voicèd Echoes, through the
mist   60
Of cataracts, flung the thunder of that spell!
Ye icy Springs, stagnant with wrinkling frost,
Which vibrated to hear me, and then crept
Shuddering through India! Thou serenest Air,
Through which the Sun walks burning without
beams!
And ye swift Whirlwinds, who on poisèd wings
Hung mute and moveless o'er yon hushed abyss,
As thunder, louder than your own, made rock
The orbèd world! If then my words had power,
Though I am changed so that aught evil wish   70
Is dead within; although no memory be
Of what is hate, let them not lose it now!
What was that curse? for ye all heard me speak.

First Voice (from the Mountains).

Thrice three hundred thousand years
   O'er the Earthquake's couch we stood:
Oft, as men convulsed with fears,
   We trembled in our multitude.

Second Voice (from the Springs).

Thunderbolts had parched our water,
   We had been stained with bitter blood,
And had run mute, 'mid shrieks of slaugh-
ter,   80
   Thro' a city and a solitude.

Third Voice (from the Air).
I had clothed, since Earth uprose,
   Its wastes in colours not their own,
And oft had my serene repose
   Been cloven by many a rending groan.

Fourth Voice (from the Whirlwinds).

We had soared beneath these mountains
   Unresting ages; nor had thunder,

Nor yon volcano's flaming fountains,
  Nor any power above or under
  Ever made us mute with wonder.   90

              First Voice.

But never bowed our snowy crest
As at the voice of thine unrest.

              Second Voice.

Never such a sound before
To the Indian waves we bore.
A pilot asleep on the howling sea
Leaped up from the deck in agony,
And heard, and cried, 'Ah, woe is me!'
And died as mad as the wild waves be.

              Third Voice.

By such dread words from Earth to Heaven
My still realm was never riven: 100
When its wound was closed, there stood
Darkness o'er the day like blood.

              Fourth Voice.

And we shrank back: for dreams of ruin
To frozen caves our flight pursuing
Made us keep silence—thus—and thus—
Though silence is as hell to us.

The Earth. The tongueless Caverns of the
  craggy hills
Cried, 'Misery!' then; the hollow Heaven re-
  plied,
'Misery!' And the Ocean's purple waves,
Climbing the land, howled to the lashing
  winds,   110
And the pale nations heard it, 'Misery!'
  Prometheus. I heard a sound of voices: not the
  voice
Which I gave forth. Mother, thy sons and thou
Scorn him, without whose all-enduring will
Beneath the fierce omnipotence of Jove,
Both they and thou had vanished, like thin mist
Unrolled on the morning wind. Know ye not me,
The Titan? He who made his agony
The barrier to your else all-conquering foe?
Oh, rock-embosomed lawns, and snow-fed
  streams,   120
Now seen athwart frore[6] vapours, deep below,
Through whose o'ershadowing woods I wan-
  dered once
With Asia, drinking life from her loved eyes;
Why scorns the spirit which informs[7] ye, now
To commune with me? me alone, who checked,

As one who checks a fiend-drawn charioteer,
The falsehood and the force of him who reigns
Supreme, and with the groans of pining slaves
Fills your dim glens and liquid wildernesses:
Why answer ye not, still? Brethren!
  The Earth.   They dare not.   130
  Prometheus. Who dares? for I would hear that
  curse again.
Ha, what an awful whisper rises up!
'Tis scarce like sound: it tingles through the
  frame
As lightning tingles, hovering ere it strike.
Speak, Spirit! from thine inorganic voice
I only know that thou art moving near
And love. How cursed I him?
  The Earth.   How canst thou hear
Who knowest not the language of the dead?
  Prometheus. Thou art a living spirit; speak as
  they.
  The Earth. I dare not speak like life, lest
  Heaven's fell King   140
Should hear, and link me to some wheel of
  pain
More torturing than the one whereon I roll.
Subtle thou art and good, and though the Gods
Hear not this voice, yet thou art more than God,
Being wise and kind: earnestly hearken now.
  Prometheus. Obscurely through my brain, like
  shadows dim,
Sweep awful thoughts, rapid and thick. I feel
Faint, like one mingled in entwining love;
Yet 'tis not pleasure.
  The Earth.   No, thou canst not hear:
Thou art immortal, and this tongue is known 150
Only to those who die.
  Prometheus.   And what art thou,
O, melancholy Voice?
  The Earth.   I am the Earth,
Thy mother; she within whose stony veins,
To the last fibre of the loftiest tree
Whose thin leaves trembled in the frozen air,
Joy ran, as blood within a living frame,
When thou didst from her bosom, like a cloud
Of glory, arise, a spirit of keen joy!
And at thy voice her pining sons uplifted
Their prostrate brows from the polluting
  dust,   160
And our almighty Tyrant with fierce dread
Grew pale, until his thunder chained thee here.
Then, see those million worlds which burn and
  roll
Around us: their inhabitants beheld
My spherèd light wane in wide Heaven; the sea
Was lifted by strange tempest, and new fire

---

6 frozen.
7 gives you form and life.

purple — royalty (Jupiter)
blue — corruption

From earthquake-rifted mountains of bright
  snow
Shook its portentous hair beneath Heaven's
  frown;
Lightning and Inundation vexed the plains;
Blue thistles bloomed in cities; foodless toads 170
Within voluptuous chambers panting crawled:
When Plague had fallen on man, and beast, and
  worm,
And Famine; and black blight on herb and tree;
And in the corn, and vines, and meadow-grass,
Teemed ineradicable poisonous weeds
Draining their growth, for my wan breast was
  dry
With grief; and the thin air, my breath was
  stained
With the contagion of a mother's hate
Breathed on her child's destroyer; ay, I heard
Thy curse, the which, if thou rememberest
  not,   180
Yet my innumerable seas and streams,
Mountains, and caves, and winds, and yon wide
  air,
And the inarticulate people of the dead,
Preserve, a treasured spell. We meditate
In secret joy and hope those dreadful words,
But dare not speak them.
    Prometheus.   Venerable mother!
All else who live and suffer take from thee
Some comfort; flowers, and fruits, and happy
  sounds,
And love, though fleeting; these may not be mine.
But mine own words, I pray, deny me not.   190
    The Earth. They shall be told. Ere Babylon was
  dust,
The Magus Zoroaster,[8] my dead child,
Met his own image walking in the garden.
That apparition, sole of men, he saw.
For know there are two worlds of life and death:
One that which thou beholdest; but the other
Is underneath the grave, where do inhabit
The shadows of all forms that think and live
Till death unite them and they part no more;
Dreams and the light imaginings of men,   200
And all that faith creates or love desires,
Terrible, strange, sublime and beauteous shapes.
There thou art, and dost hang, a writhing shade,
'Mid whirlwind-peopled mountains; all the gods
Are there, and all the powers of nameless worlds,
Vast, sceptred phantoms; heroes, men, and
  beasts;
And Demogorgon, a tremendous gloom;

And he, the supreme Tyrant, on his throne
Of burning gold. Son, one of these shall utter
The curse which all remember. Call at will   210
Thine own ghost, or the ghost of Jupiter,
Hades or Typhon, or what mightier Gods
From all-prolific Evil, since thy ruin
Have sprung, and trampled on my prostrate sons.
Ask, and they must reply: so the revenge
Of the Supreme[9] may sweep through vacant
  shades,
As rainy wind through the abandoned gate
Of a fallen palace.
    Prometheus.   Mother, let not aught
Of that which may be evil, pass again
My lips, or those of aught resembling me.   220
Phantasm of Jupiter, arise, appear!

        Ione.

My wings are folded o'er mine ears:
  My wings are crossed o'er mine eyes:
Yet through their silver shade appears,
    And through their lulling plumes arise,
    A Shape, a throng of sounds;
      May it be no ill to thee
      O thou of many wounds!
Near whom, for our sweet sister's sake,
Ever thus we watch and wake.   230

        Panthea.

The sound is of whirlwind underground,
  Earthquake, and fire, and mountains
    cloven;
The shape is awful like the sound,
    Clothed in dark purple, star-inwoven.
  A sceptre of pale gold
    To stay steps proud, o'er the slow cloud
    His veinèd hand doth hold.
  Cruel he looks, but calm and strong,
  Like one who does, not suffers wrong.

Phantasm of Jupiter. Why have the secret pow-
  ers of this strange world   240
Driven me, a frail and empty phantom, hither
On direst storms? What unaccustomed sounds
Are hovering on my lips, unlike the voice
With which our pallid race hold ghastly talk
In darkness? And, proud sufferer, who art thou?
    Prometheus. Tremendous Image, as thou art
  must be
He whom thou shadowest forth. I am his foe,
The Titan. Speak the words which I would hear,
Although no thought inform thine empty voice.
    The Earth. Listen! And though your echoes
  must be mute,   250

8 one of the Magi and founder of the ancient Persian religion
known as Zoroastrianism.

9 Jupiter.

Grey mountains, and old woods, and haunted
    springs,
Prophetic caves, and isle-surrounding streams,
Rejoice to hear what yet ye cannot speak.
    Phantasm. A spirit seizes me and speaks
    within:
It tears me as fire tears a thunder-cloud.
    Panthea. See, how he lifts his mighty looks, the
    Heaven
Darkens above.
    Ione.   He speaks! O shelter me!
    Prometheus. I see the curse on gestures proud
    and cold,
And looks of firm defiance, and calm hate,
And such despair as mocks itself with smiles, 260
Written as on a scroll: yet speak: Oh, speak!

                    Phantasm.

    Fiend, I defy thee! with a calm, fixed mind,
        All that thou canst inflict I bid thee do;
    Foul Tyrant both of Gods and Human-kind,
        One only being shalt thou not subdue.
    Rain then thy plagues upon me here,
    Ghastly disease, and frenzying fear;
    And let alternate frost and fire
    Eat into me, and be thine ire
Lightning, and cutting hail, and legioned
        forms   270
Of furies, driving by upon the wounding
        storms.
    Ay, do thy worst. Thou art omnipotent.
        O'er all things but thyself I gave thee
        power,
    And my own will. Be thy swift mischiefs sent
        To blast mankind, from yon ethereal
        tower.
    Let thy malignant spirit move
    In darkness over those I love:
    On me and mine I imprecate
    The utmost torture of thy hate;
And thus devote to sleepless agony,   280
This undeclining head while thou must reign
    on high.

    But thou, who art the God and Lord: O,
        thou,
        Who fillest with thy soul this world of woe,
    To whom all things of Earth and Heaven do
        bow
        In fear and worship: all-prevailing foe!
    I curse thee! let a sufferer's curse
    Clasp thee, his torturer, like remorse;
    Till thine Infinity shall be
    A robe of envenomed agony;

And thine Omnipotence a crown of pain,   290
To cling like burning gold round thy dissolving
    brain.

    Heap on thy soul, by virtue of this Curse,
        Ill deeds, then be thou damned, beholding
        good;
    Both infinite as is the universe,
        And thou, and thy self-torturing solitude.
    An awful image of calm power
    Though now thou sittest, let the hour
    Come, when thou must appear to be
    That which thou art internally;
And after many a false and fruitless crime   300
Scorn track thy lagging fall through boundless
    space and time.

    Prometheus. Were these my words, O Parent?
    The Earth. They were thine.
    Prometheus. It doth repent me: words are quick
        and vain;
Grief for awhile is blind, and so was mine.
I wish no living thing to suffer pain.

                    The Earth.

    Misery, Oh misery to me,
    That Jove at length should vanquish thee.
    Wail, howl aloud, Land and Sea,
    The Earth's rent heart shall answer ye.
Howl, Spirits of the living and the dead,   310
Your refuge, your defence lies fallen and van-
    quishèd.

                    First Echo.

    Lies fallen and vanquishèd!

                    Second Echo.

    Fallen and vanquishèd!

                    Ione.

    Fear not: 'tis but some passing spasm,
        The Titan is unvanquished still.
    But see, where through the azure chasm
        Of yon forked and snowy hill
    Trampling the slant winds on high
        With golden-sandalled feet, that glow
    Under plumes of purple dye,   320
    Like rose-ensanguined ivory,
        A Shape comes now,
    Stretching on high from his right hand
    A serpent-cinctured wand.[10]

    Panthea. 'Tis Jove's world-wandering herald,
    Mercury.

---

10 the serpent-entwined staff, or caduceus, carried by Mercury.

Ione.

And who are those with hydra tresses
  And iron wings that climb the wind,
Whom the frowning God represses
  Like vapours steaming up behind,
Clanging loud, an endless crowd—   330

Panthea.

These are Jove's tempest-walking hounds,
  Whom he gluts with groans and blood,
When charioted on sulphurous cloud
  He bursts Heaven's bounds.

Ione.

Are they now led, from the thin dead
  On new pangs to be fed?

Panthea.

The Titan looks as ever, firm, not proud.

First Fury. Ha! I scent life!
Second Fury. Let me but look into his eyes!
Third Fury. The hope of torturing him smells
  like a heap
Of corpses, to a death-bird after battle.   340
First Fury. Darest thou delay, O Herald! take
  cheer, Hounds
Of Hell: what if the Son of Maia[11] soon
Should make us food and sport—who can please
  long
The Omnipotent?
Mercury.   Back to your towers of iron,
And gnash, beside the streams of fire and wail,
Your foodless teeth. Geryon, arise! and Gorgon,
Chimæra,[12] and thou Sphinx, subtlest of fiends[13]
Who ministered to Thebes Heaven's poisoned
  wine,
Unnatural love, and more unnatural hate:
These shall perform your task.
First Fury. Oh, mercy! mercy!   350
We die with our desire: drive us not back!
Mercury. Crouch then in silence.
                              Awful Sufferer!
To thee unwilling, most unwillingly
I come, by the great Father's will driven down,
To execute a doom of new revenge.
Alas! I pity thee, and hate myself
That I can do no more: aye from thy sight
Returning, for a season, Heaven seems Hell,
So thy worn form pursues me night and day,
Smiling reproach. Wise art thou, firm and
  good,   360

But vainly wouldst stand forth alone in strife
Against the Omnipotent; as yon clear lamps
That measure and divide the weary years
From which there is no refuge, long have taught
And long must teach. Even now thy Torturer
  arms
With the strange might of unimagined pains
The powers who scheme slow agonies in Hell,
And my commission is to lead them here,
Or what more subtle, foul, or savage fiends
People the abyss, and leave them to their
  task.   370
Be it not so! there is a secret known
To thee, and to none else of living things,
Which may transfer the sceptre of wide Heaven,
The fear of which perplexes the Supreme:
Clothe it in words, and bid it clasp his throne
In intercession; bend thy soul in prayer,
And like a suppliant in some gorgeous fane,
Let the will kneel within thy haughty heart:
For benefits and meek submission tame
The fiercest and the mightiest.
  Prometheus.   Evil minds   380
Change good to their own nature. I gave all
He has; and in return he chains me here
Years, ages, night and day: whether the Sun
Split my parched skin, or in the moony night
The crystal-wingèd snow cling round my hair:
Whilst my belovèd race is trampled down
By his thought-executing ministers.
Such is the tyrant's recompense: 'tis just:
He who is evil can receive no good;
And for a world bestowed, or a friend lost,   390
He can feel hate, fear, shame; not gratitude:
He but requites me for his own misdeed.
Kindness to such is keen reproach, which breaks
With bitter stings the light sleep of Revenge.
Submission, thou dost know I cannot try:
For what submission but that fatal word,
The death-seal of mankind's captivity,
Like the Sicilian's hair-suspended sword,[14]
Which trembles o'er his crown, would he accept,
Or could I yield? Which yet I will not yield. 400
Let others flatter Crime, where it sits throned
In brief Omnipotence: secure are they:
For Justice, when triumphant, will weep down
Pity, not punishment, on her own wrongs,
Too much avenged by those who err. I wait,
Enduring thus, the retributive hour
Which since we spake is even nearer now.
But hark, the hell-hounds clamour: fear delay:
Behold! Heaven lowers under thy Father's frown.
  Mercury. Oh, that we might be spared: I to
  inflict   410

---

11 Mercury.
12 fabulous monsters in Greek mythology.
13 The Sphinx devoured those who could not answer her riddles.
14 the sword of Damocles.

And thou to suffer! Once more answer me:
Thou knowest not the period of Jove's power?
   Prometheus. I know but this, that it must come.
   Mercury.   Alas!
Thou canst not count thy years to come of pain?
   Prometheus. They last while Jove must reign:
    nor more, nor less
Do I desire or fear.
   Mercury.   Yet pause, and plunge
Into Eternity, where recorded time,
Even all that we imagine, age on age,
Seems but a point, and the reluctant mind
Flags wearily in its unending flight,   420
Till it sink, dizzy, blind, lost, shelterless;
Perchance it has not numbered the slow years
Which thou must spend in torture, unreprieved?
   Prometheus. Perchance no thought can count
    them, yet they pass.
   Mercury. If thou might'st dwell among the
    Gods the while
Lapped in voluptuous joy?
   Prometheus.   I would not quit
This bleak ravine, these unrepentant pains.
   Mercury. Alas! I wonder at, yet pity thee.
   Prometheus. Pity the self-despising slaves of
    Heaven,
Not me, within whose mind sits peace serene, 430
As light in the sun, throned: how vain is talk!
Call up the fiends.
   Ione.   O, sister, look! White fire
Has cloven to the roots yon huge snow-loaded
    cedar;
How fearfully God's thunder howls behind!
   Mercury. I must obey his words and thine:
    alas!
Most heavily remorse hangs at my heart!
   Panthea. See where the child of Heaven, with
    wingèd feet,
Runs down the slanted sunlight of the dawn.
   Ione. Dear sister, close thy plumes over thine
    eyes
Lest thou behold and die: they come: they
    come   440
Blackening the birth of day with countless wings,
And hollow underneath, like death.
   First Fury.   Prometheus!
   Second Fury. Immortal Titan!
   Third Fury. Champion of Heaven's slaves!
   Prometheus. He whom some dreadful voice in-
    vokes is here,
Prometheus, the chained Titan. Horrible forms,
What and who are ye? Never yet there came
Phantasms so foul through monster-teeming Hell
From the all-miscreative brain of Jove;

Whilst I behold such execrable shapes,
Methinks I grow like what I contemplate,   450
And laugh and stare in loathsome sympathy.
   First Fury. We are the ministers of pain, and
    fear,
And disappointment, and mistrust, and hate,
And clinging crime; and as lean dogs pursue
Through wood and lake some struck and sobbing
    fawn,
We track all things that weep, and bleed, and live,
When the great King betrays them to our will.
   Prometheus. Oh! many fearful natures in one
    name,
I know ye; and these lakes and echoes know
The darkness and the clangour of your wings. 460
But why more hideous than your loathèd selves
Gather ye up in legions from the deep?
   Second Fury. We knew not that: Sisters, re-
    joice, rejoice!
   Prometheus. Can aught exult in its deformity?
   Second Fury. The beauty of delight makes lov-
    ers glad,
Gazing on one another: so are we.
As from the rose which the pale priestess kneels
To gather for her festal crown of flowers
The aëreal crimson falls, flushing her cheek,
So from our victim's destined agony   470
The shade which is our form invests us round,
Else we are shapeless as our mother Night.
   Prometheus. I laugh your power, and his who
    sent you here,
To lowest scorn. Pour forth the cup of pain.
   First Fury. Thou thinkest we will rend thee
    bone from bone,
And nerve from nerve, working like fire within?
   Prometheus. Pain is my element, as hate is
    thine;
Ye rend me now: I care not.
   Second Fury.   Dost imagine
We will but laugh into thy lidless eyes?
   Prometheus. I weigh not what ye do, but what
    ye suffer,   480
Being evil. Cruel was the power which called
You, or aught else so wretched, into light.
   Third Fury. Thou think'st we will live through
    thee, one by one,
Like animal life, and though we can obscure not
The soul which burns within, that we will dwell
Beside it, like a vain loud multitude
Vexing the self-content of wisest men:
That we will be dread thought beneath thy brain,
And foul desire round thine astonished heart,
And blood within thy labyrinthine veins   490
Crawling like agony?

Prometheus.   Why, ye are thus now;
Yet am I king over myself, and rule
The torturing and conflicting throngs within,
As Jove rules you when Hell grows mutinous.

Chorus of Furies.

From the ends of the earth, from the ends of the
          earth,
Where the night has its grave and the morning its
          birth,
               Come, come, come!
Oh, ye who shake hills with the scream of your
          mirth,
When cities sink howling in ruin; and ye
Who with wingless footsteps trample the
          sea,   500
And close upon Shipwreck and Famine's track,
Sit chattering with joy on the foodless wreck;
               Come, come, come!
     Leave the bed, low, cold, and red,
     Strewed beneath a nation dead;
     Leave the hatred, as in ashes
          Fire is left for future burning:
     It will burst in bloodier flashes
          When ye stir it, soon returning:
     Leave the self-contempt implanted   510
     In young spirits, sense-enchanted,
          Misery's yet unkindled fuel:
     Leave Hell's secrets half unchanted
     To the maniac dreamer; cruel
     More than ye can be with hate
          Is he with fear.
               Come, come, come!
We are steaming up from Hell's wide gate
And we burthen the blast of the atmosphere,
But vainly we toil till ye come here.   520
Ione. Sister, I hear the thunder of new wings.
Panthea. These solid mountains quiver with
     the sound
Even as the tremulous air: their shadows make
The space within my plumes more black than
     night.

First Fury.

     Your call was as a wingèd car
     Driven on whirlwinds fast and far;
     It rapped us from red gulfs of war.

Second Fury.

From wide cities, famine-wasted;

Third Fury.

Groans half heard, and blood untasted;

Fourth Fury.

     Kingly conclaves stern and cold,   530
     Where blood with gold is bought and sold;

Fifth Fury.

From the furnace, white and hot,
In which—

A Fury.

     Speak not: whisper not:
I know all that ye would tell,
But to speak might break the spell
Which must bend the Invincible,
     The stern of thought;
He yet defies the deepest power of Hell.

A Fury.

Tear the veil!

Another Fury.

     It is torn.

Chorus.

               The pale stars of the morn
Shine on a misery, dire to be borne.   540
Dost thou faint, mighty Titan? We laugh thee to
     scorn.
Dost thou boast the clear knowledge thou
     waken'dst for man?
Then was kindled within him a thirst which out-
     ran
Those perishing waters; a thirst of fierce fever,
Hope, love, doubt, desire, which consume him for
     ever.
     One[15] came forth of gentle worth
     Smiling on the sanguine earth;
     His words outlived him, like swift poison
          Withering up truth, peace, and pity.
          Look! where round the wide horizon 550
          Many a million-peopled city
     Vomits smoke in the bright air.
     Hark that outcry of despair!
     'Tis his mild and gentle ghost
          Wailing for the faith he kindled:
     Look again, the flames almost
          To a glow-worm's lamp have dwindled:
     The survivors round the embers
          Gather in dread.
               Joy, joy, joy!   560
Past ages crowd on thee, but each one remem-
     bers,

---

15 Christ.

And the future is dark, and the present is spread
Like a pillow of thorns for thy slumberless head.

Semichorus I.

Drops of bloody agony flow
From his white and quivering brow.
Grant a little respite now:
See a disenchanted nation
Springs like day from desolation;[16]
To Truth its state is dedicate,
And Freedom leads it forth, her mate;   570
A legioned band of linkèd brothers
Whom Love calls children—

Semichorus II.

                                    'Tis another's:
See how kindred murder kin:
'Tis the vintage-time for death and sin:
Blood, like new wine, bubbles within:
   Till Despair smothers
The struggling world, which slaves and tyrants
   win.   [*All the* FURIES *vanish, except one.*
Ione. Hark, sister! what a low yet dreadful groan
Quite unsuppressed is tearing up the heart
Of the good Titan, as storms tear the deep,   580
And beasts hear the sea moan in inland caves.
Darest thou observe how the fiends torture him?
Panthea. Alas! I looked forth twice, but will no more.
Ione. What didst thou see?
Panthea.   A woful sight: a youth
With patient looks nailed to a crucifix.
Ione. What next?
Panthea. The heaven around, the earth below
Was peopled with thick shapes of human death,
All horrible, and wrought by human hands,
And some appeared the work of human hearts,
For men were slowly killed by frowns and smiles: 590
And other sights too foul to speak and live
Were wandering by. Let us not tempt worse fear
By looking forth: those groans are grief enough.
Fury. Behold an emblem: those who do endure
Deep wrongs for man, and scorn, and chains, but heap
Thousandfold torment on themselves and him.
Prometheus. Remit the anguish of that lighted stare;

Close those wan lips; let that thorn-wounded brow
Stream not with blood; it mingles with thy tears!
Fix, fix those tortured orbs in peace and death,   600
So thy sick throes shake not that crucifix,
So those pale fingers play not with thy gore.
O, horrible! Thy name I will not speak,
It hath become a curse. I see, I see
The wise, the mild, the lofty, and the just,
Whom thy slaves hate for being like to thee,
Some hunted by foul lies from their heart's home,
An early-chosen, late-lamented home;
As hooded ounces[17] cling to the driven hind;
Some linked to corpses in unwholesome cells: 610
Some—Hear I not the multitude laugh loud?—
Impaled in lingering fire: and mighty realms
Float by my feet, like sea-uprooted isles,
Whose sons are kneaded down in common blood
By the red light of their own burning homes.
   Fury. Blood thou canst see, and fire; and canst hear groans;
Worse things, unheard, unseen, remain behind.
   Prometheus. Worse?
   Fury. In each human heart terror survives
The ravin it has gorged: the loftiest fear
All that they would disdain to think were true: 620
Hypocrisy and custom make their minds
The fanes of many a worship, now outworn.
They dare not devise good for man's estate,
And yet they know not that they do not dare.
The good want power, but to weep barren tears.
The powerful goodness want: worse need for them.
The wise want love; and those who love want wisdom;
And all best things are thus confused to ill.
Many are strong and rich, and would be just,
But live among their suffering fellow-men   630
As if none felt: they know not what they do.
   Prometheus. Thy words are like a cloud of wingèd snakes;
And yet I pity those they torture not.
   Fury. Thou pitiest them? I speak no more!
                                    [*Vanishes.*
   Prometheus.   Ah woe!
Ah woe! Alas! pain, pain ever, for ever!
I close my tearless eyes, but see more clear
Thy works within my woe-illumèd mind,
Thou subtle tyrant! Peace is in the grave.

---

16 Lines 567–77 refer to the French Revolution and its aftermath.

17 Leopards used in India for hunting deer. Like falcons they are kept hooded until the game is sighted.

The grave hides all things beautiful and good:
I am a God and cannot find it there,   640
Nor would I seek it: for, though dread revenge,
This is defeat, fierce king, not victory.
The sights with which thou torturest gird my soul
With new endurance, till the hour arrives .
When they shall be no types of things which are.
Panthea. Alas! what sawest thou more?
Prometheus. There are two woes:
To speak, and to behold; thou spare me one.
Names are there, Nature's sacred watchwords, they
Were borne aloft in bright emblazonry;[18]
The nations thronged around, and cried
     aloud,   650
As with one voice, Truth, liberty, and love!
Suddenly fierce confusion fell from heaven
Among them: there was strife, deceit, and fear:
Tyrants rushed in, and did divide the spoil.
This was the shadow of the truth I saw.
     The Earth. I felt thy torture, son; with such
     mixed joy
As pain and virtue give. To cheer thy state
I bid ascend those subtle and fair spirits,
Whose homes are the dim caves of human
     thought,
And who inhabit, as birds wing the wind,   660
Its world-surrounding aether: they behold
Beyond that twilight realm, as in a glass,
The future: may they speak comfort to thee!
     Panthea. Look, sister, where a troop of spirits
     gather,
Like flocks of clouds in spring's delightful
     weather,
Thronging in the blue air!
     Ione.   And see! more come,
Like fountain-vapours when the winds are dumb,
That climb up the ravine in scattered lines.
And, hark! is it the music of the pines?
Is it the lake? Is it the waterfall?   670
     Panthea. 'Tis something sadder, sweeter far
     than all.

Chorus of Spirits.

From unremembered ages we
Gentle guides and guardians be
Of heaven-oppressed mortality;
And we breathe, and sicken not,
The atmosphere of human thought:
Be it dim, and dank, and grey,
Like a storm-extinguished day,
Travelled o'er by dying gleams;
     Be it bright as all between   680

---

18 another reference to the French Revolution and its aftermath.

Cloudless skies and windless streams,
     Silent, liquid, and serene;
As the birds within the wind,
     As the fish within the wave,
As the thoughts of man's own mind
     Float through all above the grave;
We make there our liquid lair,
Voyaging cloudlike and unpent
Through the boundless element:
Thence we bear the prophecy   690
Which begins and ends in thee!
     Ione. More yet come, one by one: the air
     around them
Looks radiant as the air around a star.

First Spirit.

On a battle-trumpet's blast
I fled hither, fast, fast, fast,
'Mid the darkness upward cast.
From the dust of creeds outworn,
From thy tyrant's banner torn,
Gathering 'round me, onward borne,
There was mingled many a cry—   700
Freedom! Hope! Death! Victory!
Till they faded through the sky;
And one sound, above, around,
One sound beneath, around, above,
Was moving; 'twas the soul of Love;
'Twas the hope, the prophecy,
Which begins and ends in thee.

Second Spirit.

A rainbow's arch stood on the sea,
Which rocked beneath, immovably;
And the triumphant storm did flee,   710
Like a conqueror, swift and proud,
Between, with many a captive cloud,
A shapeless, dark and rapid crowd,
Each by lightning riven in half:
I heard the thunder hoarsely laugh:
Mighty fleets were strewn like chaff
And spread beneath a hell of death
O'er the white waters. I alit
On a great ship lightning-split,
And speeded hither on the sigh   720
Of one who gave an enemy
His plank, then plunged aside to die.

Third Spirit.

I sate beside a sage's bed,
And the lamp was burning red
Near the book where he had fed,
When a Dream with plumes of flame.
To his pillow hovering came,
And I knew it was the same

Which had kindled long ago
Pity, eloquence, and woe;   730
And the world awhile below
Wore the shade, its lustre made.
It has borne me here as fleet
As Desire's lightning feet:
I must ride it back ere morrow,
Or the sage will wake in sorrow.

Fourth Spirit.

On a poet's lips I slept
Dreaming like a love-adept
In the sound his breathing kept;
Nor seeks nor finds he mortal blisses, 740
But feeds on the aëreal kisses
Of shapes that haunt thought's wilder-
  nesses.
He will watch from dawn to gloom
The lake-reflected sun illume
The yellow bees in the ivy-bloom,
Nor heed nor see, what things they be;
But from these create he can
Forms more real than living man,
Nurslings of immortality!
One of these awakened me,   750
And I sped to succour thee.

Ione.

Behold'st thou not two shapes from the east
  and west
Come, as two doves to one belovèd nest,
Twin nurslings of the all-sustaining air
On swift still wings glide down the atmosphere?
And, hark! their sweet, sad voices! 'tis de-
  spair
Mingled with love and then dissolved in sound.

Panthea. Canst thou speak, sister? all my words
  are drowned.
Ione. Their beauty gives me voice. See how
  they float
On their sustaining wings of skiey grain,[19] 760
Orange and azure deepening into gold:
Their soft smiles light the air like a star's fire.

Chorus of Spirits.

Hast thou beheld the form of Love?

Fifth Spirit.

         As over wide dominions
I sped, like some swift cloud that wings the
  wide air's wildernesses,
That planet-crested shape swept by on lightning-
  braided pinions,

Scattering the liquid joy of life from his ambrosial tresses:
His footsteps paved the world with light; but as I
  passed 'twas fading,
And hollow Ruin yawned behind: great sages
  bound in madness,
And headless patriots, and pale youths who perished, unupbraiding,
Gleamed in the night. I wandered o'er, till
  thou, O King of sadness,   770
Turned by thy smile the worst I saw to recollected gladness.

Sixth Spirit.

Ah, sister! Desolation is a delicate thing:
  It walks not on the earth, it floats not on the air,
But treads with lulling footstep, and fans with si-
  lent wing
  The tender hopes which in their hearts the best
    and gentlest bear;
Who, soothed to false repose by the fanning
  plumes above
  And the music-stirring motion of its soft and
    busy feet,
Dream visions of aëreal joy, and call the monster,
  Love,
  And wake, and find the shadow Pain, as he
    whom now we greet.

Chorus.

Though Ruin now Love's shadow be, 780
Following him, destroyingly,
  On Death's white and wingèd steed,
Which the fleetest cannot flee,
  Trampling down both flower and weed,
Man and beast, and foul and fair,
Like a tempest through the air;
Thou shalt quell this horseman grim,
Woundless though in heart or limb.

Prometheus. Spirits! how know ye this shall be?

Chorus.

In the atmosphere we breathe, 790
As buds grow red when the snow-storms flee,
  From Spring gathering up beneath,
Whose mild winds shake the elder brake,
And the wandering herdsmen know
That the white-thorn soon will blow:
  Wisdom, Justice, Love, and Peace,
  When they struggle to increase,
    Are to us as soft winds be
    To shepherd boys, the prophecy
    Which begins and ends in thee. 800
Ione. Where are the Spirits fled?

---

19 color.

Panthea.   Only a sense
Remains of them, like the omnipotence
Of music, when the inspired voice and lute
Languish, ere yet the responses are mute,
Which through the deep and labyrinthine soul,
Like echoes through long caverns, wind and roll.
   Prometheus. How fair these airborn shapes!
    and yet I feel
Most vain all hope but love; and thou art far,
Asia! who, when my being overflowed,
Wert like a golden chalice to bright wine   810
Which else had sunk into the thirsty dust.
All things are still: alas! how heavily
This quiet morning weighs upon my heart;
Though I should dream I could even sleep with
   grief
If slumber were denied not. I would fain
Be what it is my destiny to be,
The saviour and the strength of suffering man,
Or sink into the original gulf of things:
There is no agony, and no solace left;
Earth can console, Heaven can torment no
   more.   820
   Panthea. Hast thou forgotten one who watches
    thee
The cold dark night, and never sleeps but when
The shadow of thy spirit falls on her?
   Prometheus. I said all hope was vain but love:
    thou lovest.
   Panthea. Deeply in truth; but the eastern star
    looks white,
And Asia waits in that far Indian vale,
The scene of her sad exile; rugged once
And desolate and frozen, like this ravine;
But now invested with fair flowers and herbs,
And haunted by sweet airs and sounds, which
   flow   830
Among the woods and waters, from the aether
Of her transforming presence, which would fade
If it were mingled not with thine. Farewell!

ACT II

SCENE I.—*Morning. A lovely Vale in the Indian
   Caucasus.* ASIA *alone.*

   Asia. From all the blasts of heaven thou hast
    descended:
Yes, like a spirit, like a thought, which makes
Unwonted tears throng to the horny eyes,
And beatings haunt the desolated heart,
Which should have learnt repose: thou hast de-
   scended
Cradled in tempests; thou dost wake, O Spring!
O child of many winds! As suddenly
Thou comest as the memory of a dream,

Which now is sad because it hath been sweet;
Like genius, or like joy which riseth up   10
As from the earth, clothing with golden clouds
The desert of our life.
This is the season, this the day, the hour;
At sunrise thou shouldst come, sweet sister mine,
Too long desired, too long delaying, come!
How like death-worms the wingless moments
   crawl!
The point of one white star is quivering still
Deep in the orange light of widening morn
Beyond the purple mountains: through a chasm
Of wind-divided mist the darker lake   20
Reflects it: now it wanes: it gleams again
As the waves fade, and as the burning threads
Of woven cloud unravel in pale air:
'Tis lost! and through yon peaks of cloud-like
   snow
The roseate sunlight quivers: hear I not
The Æolian music of her sea-green plumes
Winnowing the crimson dawn?

              [PANTHEA *enters.*

           I feel, I see
Those eyes which burn through smiles that fade
   in tears,
Like stars half quenched in mists of silver dew.
Belovèd and most beautiful, who wearest   30
The shadow of that soul by which I live,
How late thou art! the spherèd sun had climbed
The sea; my heart was sick with hope, before
The printless air felt thy belated plumes.
   Panthea. Pardon, great Sister! but my wings
    were faint
With the delight of a remembered dream,
As are the noontide plumes of summer winds
Satiate with sweet flowers. I was wont to sleep
Peacefully, and awake refreshed and calm
Before the sacred Titan's fall, and thy   40
Unhappy love, had made, through use and pity,
Both love and woe familiar to my heart
As they had grown to thine: erewhile I slept
Under the glaucous caverns of old Ocean
Within dim bowers of green and purple moss,
Our young Ione's soft and milky arms
Locked then, as now, behind my dark, moist hair,
While my shut eyes and cheek were pressed
   within
The folded depth of her life-breathing bosom:
But not as now, since I am made the wind   50
Which fails beneath the music that I bear
Of thy most wordless converse; since dissolved
Into the sense with which love talks, my rest
Was troubled and yet sweet; my waking hours
Too full of care and pain.

Asia.   Lift up thine eyes,
And let me read thy dream.
 Panthea.   As I have said
With our sea-sister at his feet I slept.
The mountain mists, condensing at our voice
Under the moon, had spread their snowy flakes,
From the keen ice shielding our linkèd sleep. 60
Then two dreams came. One, I remember not.
But in the other his pale wound-worn limbs
Fell from Prometheus, and the azure night
Grew radiant with the glory of that form
Which lives unchanged within, and his voice fell
Like music which makes giddy the dim brain,
Faint with intoxication of keen joy:
'Sister of her whose footsteps pave the world
With loveliness—more fair than aught but her,
Whose shadow thou art—lift thine eyes on
 me.'   70
I lifted them: the overpowering light
Of that immortal shape was shadowed o'er
By love; which, from his soft and flowing limbs,
And passion-parted lips, and keen, faint eyes,
Steamed forth like vaporous fire; an atmosphere
Which wrapped me in its all-dissolving power,
As the warm aether of the morning sun
Wraps ere it drinks some cloud of wandering
 dew.
I saw not, heard not, moved not, only felt
His presence flow and mingle through my
 blood   80
Till it became his life, and his grew mine,
And I was thus absorbed, until it passed,
And like the vapours when the sun sinks down,
Gathering again in drops upon the pines,
And tremulous as they, in the deep night
My being was condensed; and as the rays
Of thought were slowly gathered, I could hear
His voice, whose accents lingered ere they died
Like footsteps of weak melody: thy name
Among the many sounds alone I heard   90
Of what might be articulate; though still
I listened through the night when sound was
 none.
Ione wakened then, and said to me:
'Canst thou divine what troubles me to-night?
I always knew what I desired before,
Nor ever found delight to wish in vain.
But now I cannot tell thee what I seek;
I know not; something sweet, since it is sweet
Even to desire; it is thy sport, false sister;
Thou hast discovered some enchantment old, 100
Whose spells have stolen my spirit as I slept
And mingled it with thine: for when just now
We kissed, I felt within thy parted lips

The sweet air that sustained me, and the warmth
Of the life-blood, for loss of which I faint,
Quivered between our intertwining arms.'
I answered not, for the Eastern star grew pale,
But fled to thee.
 Asia.   Thou speakest, but thy words
Are as the air: I feel them not: Oh, lift
Thine eyes, that I may read his written soul! 110
 Panthea. I lift them though they droop beneath
 the load
Of that they would express: what canst thou see
But thine own fairest shadow imaged there?
 Asia. Thine eyes are like the deep, blue, bound-
 less heaven
Contracted to two circles underneath
Their long, fine lashes; dark, far, measureless,
Orb within orb, and line through line inwoven.
 Panthea. Why lookest thou as if a spirit
 passed?
 Asia. There is a change: beyond their inmost
 depth
I see a shade, a shape: 'tis He, arrayed   120
In the soft light of his own smiles, which spread
Like radiance from the cloud-surrounded moon.
Prometheus, it is thine! depart not yet!
Say not those smiles that we shall meet again
Within that bright pavilion which their beams
Shall build o'er the waste world? The dream is
 told.
What shape is that between us? Its rude hair
Roughens the wind that lifts it, its regard[20]
Is wild and quick, yet 'tis a thing of air,
For through its grey robe gleams the golden
 dew   130
Whose stars the noon has quenched not.
 Dream.   Follow! Follow!
 Panthea. It is mine other dream.
 Asia.   It disappears.
 Panthea. It passes now into my mind. Me-
 thought
As we sate here, the flower-infolding buds
Burst on yon lightning-blasted almond-tree,
When swift from the white Scythian wilderness
A wind swept forth wrinkling the Earth with
 frost:
I looked, and all the blossoms were blown down;
But on each leaf was stamped, as the blue bells
Of Hyacinth tell Apollo's written grief,[21]   140
O, FOLLOW, FOLLOW!
 Asia.   As you speak, your words
Fill, pause by pause, my own forgotten sleep

---

20 countenance.
21 When Apollo accidentally killed the youth Hyacinthus, from
the blood-stained grass a blue flower sprang forth, upon the petals
of which Apollo inscribed *Ai* (woe) as a memorial of his sorrow.

With shapes. Methought among these lawns to-
   gether
We wandered, underneath the young grey dawn,
And multitudes of dense white fleecy clouds
Were wandering in thick flocks along the moun-
   tains
Shepherded by the slow, unwilling wind;
And the white dew on the new-bladed grass,
Just piercing the dark earth, hung silently;
And there was more which I remember not: 150
But on the shadows of the morning clouds,
Athwart the purple mountain slope, was written
FOLLOW, O, FOLLOW! as they vanished by;
And on each herb, from which Heaven's dew had
   fallen,
The like was stamped, as with a withering fire;
A wind arose among the pines; it shook
The clinging music from their boughs, and then
Low, sweet, faint sounds, like the farewell of
   ghosts,
Were heard: O, FOLLOW, FOLLOW, FOLLOW ME!
And then I said: 'Panthea, look on me.'   160
But in the depth of those belovèd eyes
Still I saw, FOLLOW, FOLLOW!

Echo.   Follow, follow!

Panthea. The crags, this clear spring morning,
   mock our voices
As they were spirit-tongued.

Asia.   It is some being
Around the crags. What fine clear sounds! O, list!

Echoes (unseen).
Echoes we: listen!
   We cannot stay:
   As dew-stars glisten
   Then fade away—
      Child of Ocean!   170

Asia. Hark! Spirits speak. The liquid responses
Of their aërial tongues yet sound.

Panthea.   I hear.

Echoes.
O, follow, follow,
   As our voice recedeth
Through the caverns hollow,
   Where the forest spreadeth;

(More distant.)
O, follow, follow!
   Through the caverns hollow,
As the song floats thou pursue,
Where the wild bee never flew,   180
Through the noontide darkness deep,
By the odour-breathing sleep
Of faint night flowers, and the waves

At the fountain-lighted caves,
While our music, wild and sweet,
Mocks thy gently falling feet,
      Child of Ocean!

Asia. Shall we pursue the sound? It grows more
   faint
And distant.

Panthea. List! the strain floats nearer now.

Echoes.
In the world unknown   190
   Sleeps a voice unspoken;
By thy step alone
   Can its rest be broken;
      Child of Ocean!

Asia. How the notes sink upon the ebbing
   wind!

Echoes.
O, follow, follow!
   Through the caverns hollow,
As the song floats thou pursue,
By the woodland noontide dew;
By the forest, lakes, and fountains,   200
Through the many-folded mountains;
To the rents, and gulfs, and chasms,
Where the Earth reposed from spasms,
On the day when He and thou
Parted, to commingle now;
      Child of Ocean!

Asia. Come, sweet Panthea, link thy hand in
   mine,
And follow, ere the voices fade away.

SCENE II.—*A Forest, intermingled with Rocks and
Caverns.* ASIA *and* PANTHEA *pass into it. Two
young Fauns are sitting on a Rock listening.*

Semichorus I: of Spirits.
The path through which that lovely twain
   Have passed, by cedar, pine, and yew,
   And each dark tree that ever grew,
   Is curtained out from Heaven's wide blue;
Nor sun, nor moon, nor wind, nor rain,
   Can pierce its interwoven bowers,
   Nor aught, save where some cloud of dew,
Drifted along the earth-creeping breeze,
Between the trunks of the hoar trees,
   Hangs each a pearl in the pale flow-
      ers   10
   Of the green laurel, blown anew;
And bends, and then fades silently,
One frail and fair anemone:
Or when some star of many a one

That climbs and wanders through steep
    night,
Has found the cleft through which alone
Beams fall from high those depths upon
Ere it is borne away, away,
By the swift Heavens that cannot stay,   20
It scatters drops of golden light,
Like lines of rain that ne'er unite:
And the gloom divine is all around,
And underneath is the mossy ground.

Semichorus II.

There the voluptuous nightingales,
    Are awake through all the broad noon-
        day,
When one with bliss or sadness fails,
    And through the windless ivy-boughs,
    Sick with sweet love, droops dying away
On its mate's music-panting bosom;
Another from the swinging blossom,   30
    Watching to catch the languid close
Of the last strain, then lifts on high
The wings of the weak melody,
'Till some new strain of feeling bear
    The song, and all the woods are mute;
When there is heard through the dim air
The rush of wings, and rising there
    Like many a lake-surrounded flute,
Sounds overflow the listener's brain
So sweet, that joy is almost pain.   40

Semichorus I.

There those enchanted eddies play
    Of echoes, music-tongued, which draw,
    By Demogorgon's mighty law,
    With melting rapture, or sweet awe,
All spirits on that secret way;
    As inland boats are driven to Ocean
Down streams made strong with mountain-
        thaw:
    And first there comes a gentle sound
    To those in talk or slumber bound,
    And wakes the destined soft emo-
        tion,—   50
Attracts, impels them; those who saw
    Say from the breathing earth behind
    There steams a plume-uplifting wind
Which drives them on their path, while they
    Believe their own swift wings and feet
The sweet desires within obey:
And so they float upon their way,
Until, still sweet, but loud and strong,
The storm of sound is driven along,
    Sucked up and hurrying: as they fleet   60
    Behind, its gathering billows meet

And to the fatal mountain[22] bear
Like clouds amid the yielding air.
First Faun. Canst thou imagine where those
    spirits live
Which make such delicate music in the woods?
We haunt within the least frequented caves
And closest coverts, and we know these wilds,
Yet never meet them, though we hear them oft:
Where may they hide themselves?
    Second Faun.   'Tis hard to tell:
I have heard those more skilled in spirits say,   70
The bubbles, which the enchantment of the sun
Sucks from the pale faint water-flowers that pave
The oozy bottom of clear lakes and pools,
Are the pavilions where such dwell and float
Under the green and golden atmosphere
Which noontide kindles through the woven
    leaves;
And when these burst, and the thin fiery air,
The which they breathed within those lucent
    domes,
Ascends to flow like meteors through the night,
They ride on them, and rein their headlong
    speed,   80
And bow their burning crests, and glide in fire
Under the waters of the earth again.
    First Faun. If such live thus, have others other
    lives,
Under pink blossoms or within the bells
Of meadow flowers, or folded violets deep,
Or on their dying odours, when they die,
Or in the sunlight of the spherèd dew?
    Second Faun. Ay, many more which we may
    well divine.
But, should we stay to speak, noontide would
    come,
And thwart[23] Silenus find his goats undrawn,   90
And grudge to sing those wise and lovely songs
Of Fate, and Chance, and God, and Chaos old,
And Love, and the chained Titan's woful doom,
And how he shall be loosed, and make the earth
One brotherhood: delightful strains which cheer
Our solitary twilights, and which charm
To silence the unenvying nightingales.

SCENE III.—*A Pinnacle of Rock among Moun-
    tains.* ASIA *and* PANTHEA.
    Panthea. Hither the sound has borne us—to
    the realm
Of Demogorgon, and the mighty portal,
Like a volcano's meteor-breathing chasm,
Whence the oracular vapour is hurled up

---

22 The mountain of Demogorgon reached by Asia and Panthea
in the next scene.
23 cross; angry.

Which lonely men drink wandering in their
    youth,
And call truth, virtue, love, genius, or joy,
That maddening wine of life, whose dregs they
    drain
To deep intoxication; and uplift,
Like Mænads[24] who cry loud, Evoe! Evoe!
The voice which is contagion to the world.   10
    Asia. Fit throne for such a Power! Magnificent!
How glorious art thou, Earth! And if thou be
The shadow of some spirit lovelier still,
Though evil stain its work, and it should be
Like its creation, weak yet beautiful,
I could fall down and worship that and thee.
Even now my heart adoreth: Wonderful!
Look, sister, ere the vapour dim thy brain:
Beneath is a wide plain of billowy mist,
As a lake, paving in the morning sky,   20
With azure waves which burst in silver light,
Some Indian vale. Behold it, rolling on
Under the curdling winds, and islanding
The peak whereon we stand, midway, around,
Encinctured by the dark and blooming forests,
Dim twilight-lawns, and stream-illumèd caves,
And wind-enchanted shapes of wandering mist;
And far on high the keen sky-cleaving moun-
    tains
From icy spires of sun-like radiance fling
The dawn, as lifted Ocean's dazzling spray,   30
From some Atlantic islet scattered up,
Spangles the wind with lamp-like water-drops.
The vale is girdled with their walls, a howl
Of cataracts from their thaw-cloven ravines,
Satiates the listening wind, continuous, vast,
Awful as silence. Hark! the rushing snow!
The sun-awakened avalanche! whose mass,
Thrice sifted by the storm, had gathered there
Flake after flake, in heaven-defying minds
As thought by thought is piled, till some great
    truth   40
Is loosened, and the nations echo round,
Shaken to their roots, as do the mountains now.
    Panthea. Look how the gusty sea of mist is
    breaking
In crimson foam, even at our feet! it rises
As Ocean at the enchantment of the moon
Round foodless men wrecked on some oozy
    isle.
    Asia. The fragments of the cloud are scattered
    up;
The wind that lifts them disentwines my hair;
Its billows now sweep o'er mine eyes; my brain

---

24 frenzied nymphs who attended Bacchus at his festivals.

Grows dizzy; see'st thou shapes within the
    mist?   50
    Panthea. A countenance with beckoning
    smiles: there burns
An azure fire within its golden locks!
Another and another: hark! they speak!

Song of Spirits.

    To the deep, to the deep,
        Down, down!
    Through the shade of sleep,
    Through the cloudy strife
    Of Death and of Life;
    Through the veil and the bar
    Of things which seem and are   60
Even to the steps of the remotest throne,
        Down, down!

    While the sound whirls around,
        Down, down!
    As the fawn draws the hound,
    As the lightning the vapour,
    As a weak moth the taper;
    Death, despair; love, sorrow;
    Time both; to-day, to-morrow;
As steel obeys the spirit of the stone,   70
        Down, down!

    Through the gray, void abysm,
        Down, down!
    Where the air is no prism,
    And the moon and stars are not,
    And the cavern-crags wear not
    The radiance of Heaven,
    Nor the gloom to Earth given,
Where there is One pervading, One alone,
        Down, down!   80

    In the depth of the deep,
        Down, down!
    Like veiled lightning asleep,
    Like the spark nursed in embers,
    The last look Love remembers,
    Like a diamond, which shines
    On the dark wealth of mines,
A spell is treasured but for thee alone.
        Down, down!

    We have bound thee, we guide thee;   90
        Down, down!
    With the bright form beside thee;
    Resist not the weakness,
    Such strength is in meekness
    That the Eternal, the Immortal,

Must unloose through life's portal
The snake-like Doom coiled underneath his
    throne
        By that alone.

SCENE IV.—*The Cave of* DEMOGORGON. ASIA *and*
            PANTHEA.

  Panthea. What veilèd form sits on that ebon
    throne?
  Asia. The veil has fallen.
  Panthea.   I see a mighty darkness
Filling the seat of power, and rays of gloom
Dart round, as light from the meridian sun.
—Ungazed upon and shapeless; neither limb,
Nor form, nor outline; yet we feel it is
A living Spirit.
  Demogorgon. Ask what thou wouldst know.
  Asia. What canst thou tell?
  Demogorgon.   All things thou dar'st demand.
  Asia. Who made the living world?
  Demogorgon.   God.
  Asia.   Who made all
That it contains? thought, passion, reason,
    will,   10
Imagination?
  Demogorgon. God: Almighty God.
  Asia. Who made that sense which, when the
    winds of Spring
In rarest visitation, or the voice
Of one belovèd heard in youth alone,
Fills the faint eyes with falling tears which dim
The radiant looks of unbewailing flowers,
And leaves this peopled earth a solitude
When it returns no more?
  Demogorgon.   Merciful God.
  Asia. And who made terror, madness, crime,
    remorse,
Which from the links of the great chain of
    things,   20
To every thought within the mind of man
Sway and drag heavily, and each one reels
Under the load towards the pit of death;
Abandoned hope, and love that turns to hate;
And self-contempt, bitterer to drink than blood;
Pain, whose unheeded and familiar speech
Is howling, and keen shrieks, day after day;
And Hell, or the sharp fear of Hell?
  Demogorgon.   He reigns.
  Asia. Utter his name: a world pining in pain
Asks but his name: curses shall drag him
    down.   30
  Demogorgon. He reigns.
  Asia.   I feel, I know it: who?
  Demogorgon.   He reigns.

  Asia. Who reigns? There was the Heaven and
    Earth at first,
And Light and Love; then Saturn, from whose
    throne
Time fell, an envious shadow: such the state
Of the earth's primal spirits beneath his sway,
As the calm joy of flowers and living leaves
Before the wind or sun has withered them
And semivital worms; but he refused
The birthright of their being, knowledge, power,
The skill which wields the elements, the
    thought   40
Which pierces this dim universe like light,
Self-empire, and the majesty of love;
For thirst of which they fainted. Then Prome-
    theus
Gave wisdom, which is strength, to Jupiter,
And with this law alone, 'Let man be free,'
Clothed him with the dominion of wide Heaven.
To know nor faith, nor love, nor law; to be
Omnipotent but friendless is to reign;
And Jove now reigned; for on the race of man
First famine, and then toil, and then disease, 50
Strife, wounds, and ghastly death unseen before,
Fell; and the unseasonable seasons drove
With alternating shafts of frost and fire,
Their shelterless, pale tribes to mountain caves:
And in their desert hearts fierce wants he sent,
And mad disquietudes, and shadows idle
Of unreal good, which levied mutual war,
So ruining the lair wherein they raged.
Prometheus saw, and waked the legioned hopes
Which sleep within folded Elysian flowers, 60
Nepenthe, Moly, Amaranth, fadeless blooms,
That they might hide with thin and rainbow
    wings
The shape of Death; and Love he sent to bind
The disunited tendrils of that vine
Which bears the wine of life, the human heart;
And he tamed fire which, like some beast of prey,
Most terrible, but lovely, played beneath
The frown of man; and tortured to his will
Iron and gold; the slaves and signs of power,
And gems and poisons, and all subtlest forms 70
Hidden beneath the mountains and the waves.
He gave man speech, and speech created thought,
Which is the measure of the universe;
And Science struck the thrones of earth and
    heaven,
Which shook, but fell not; and the harmonious
    mind
Poured itself forth in all-prophetic song;
And music lifted up the listening spirit
Until it walked, exempt from mortal care,

Godlike, o'er the clear billows of sweet sound;
And human hands first mimicked and then
    mocked,   80
With moulded limbs more lovely than its own,
The human form, till marble grew divine;
And mothers, gazing, drank the love men see
Reflected in their race, behold, and perish.
He told the hidden power of herbs and springs,
And Disease drank and slept. Death grew like
    sleep.
He taught the implicated orbits woven
Of the wide-wandering stars; and how the sun
Changes his lair, and by what secret spell
The pale moon is transformed, when her broad
    eye   90
Gazes not on the interlunar sea:
He taught to rule, as life directs the limbs,
The tempest-wingèd chariots of the Ocean,
And the Celt knew the Indian. Cities then
Were built, and through their snow-like columns
    flowed
The warm winds, and the azure aether shone,
And the blue sea and shadowy hills were seen.
Such, the alleviations of his state,
Prometheus gave to man, for which he hangs
Withering in destined pain: but who rains
    down   100
Evil, the immedicable plague, which, while
Man looks on his creation like a God
And sees that it is glorious, drives him on,
The wreck of his own will, the scorn of earth,
The outcast, the abandoned, the alone?
Not Jove: while yet his frown shook Heaven, ay,
    when
His adversary from adamantine chains
Cursed him, he trembled like a slave. Declare
Who is his master? Is he too a slave?
    Demogorgon. All spirits are enslaved which
    serve things evil: 110
Thou knowest if Jupiter be such or no.
    Asia. Whom calledst thou God?
    Demogorgon.   I spoke but as ye speak,
For Jove is the supreme of living things.
    Asia. Who is the master of the slave?
    Demogorgon.   If the abysm
Could vomit forth its secrets. . . . But a voice
Is wanting, the deep truth is imageless;
For what would it avail to bid thee gaze
On the revolving world? What to bid speak
Fate, Time, Occasion, Chance, and Change? To
    these
All things are subject but eternal Love.   120
    Asia. So much I asked before, and my heart
    gave

The response thou hast given; and of such truths
Each to itself must be the oracle.
One more demand; and do thou answer me
As mine own soul would answer, did it know
That which I ask. Prometheus shall arise
Henceforth the sun of this rejoicing world:
When shall the destined hour arrive?
    Demogorgon.   Behold!
    Asia. The rocks are cloven, and through the
    purple night
I see cars drawn by rainbow-wingèd steeds   130
Which trample the dim winds: in each there
    stands
A wild-eyed charioteer urging their flight.
Some look behind, as fiends pursued them there,
And yet I see no shapes but the keen stars:
Others, with burning eyes, lean forth, and drink
With eager lips the wind of their own speed,
As if the thing they loved fled on before,
And now, even now, they clasped it. Their bright
    locks
Stream like a comet's flashing hair: they all
Sweep onward.
    Demogorgon. These are the immortal
    Hours,   140
Of whom thou didst demand. One waits for
    thee.
    Asia. A spirit with a dreadful countenance
Checks its dark chariot by the craggy gulf.
Unlike thy brethren, ghastly charioteer,
Who art thou? Whither wouldst thou bear me?
    Speak!
    Spirit. I am the shadow of a destiny
More dread than is my aspect: ere yon planet
Has set, the darkness which ascends with me
Shall wrap in lasting night heaven's kingless
    throne.
    Asia. What meanest thou?
    Panthea.   That terrible shadow floats   150
Up from its throne, as may the lurid smoke
Of earthquake-ruined cities o'er the sea.
Lo! it ascends the car; the coursers fly
Terrified; watch its path among the stars
Blackening the night!
    Asia.   Thus I am answered: strange!
    Panthea. See, near the verge, another chariot
    stays;
An ivory shell inlaid with crimson fire,
Which comes and goes within its sculptured
    rim
Of delicate strange tracery; the young spirit
That guides it has the dove-like eyes of hope;   160
How its soft smiles attract the soul! as light
Lures wingèd insects through the lampless air.

Spirit.

My coursers are fed with the lightning,
   They drink of the whirlwind's stream,
And when the red morning is bright'ning
   They bathe in the fresh sunbeam;
      They have strength for their swiftness I
         deem,
Then ascend with me, daughter of Ocean.
I desire: and their speed makes night kindle;
   I fear: they outstrip the Typhoon;   170
Ere the cloud piled on Atlas can dwindle
   We encircle the earth and the moon:
We shall rest from long labours at noon:
   Then ascend with me, daughter of Ocean.

SCENE V.—*The Car pauses within a Cloud on the top of a snowy Mountain.* ASIA, PANTHEA, *and the* SPIRIT OF THE HOUR.

Spirit.

On the brink of the night and the morning
   My coursers are wont to respire;
But the earth has just whispered a warning
   That their flight must be swifter than fire:
   They shall drink the hot speed of desire!

Asia. Thou breathest on their nostrils, but my
   breath
Would give them swifter speed.

Spirit.   Alas! it could not.

Panthea. Oh Spirit! pause, and tell whence is
   the light
Which fills this cloud? the sun is yet unrisen.

Spirit. The sun will rise not until noon.
                Apollo   10
Is held in heaven by wonder; and the light
Which fills this vapour, as the aëreal hue
Of fountain-gazing roses fills the water,
Flows from thy mighty sister.

Panthea.   Yes, I feel—

Asia. What is it with thee, sister? Thou art pale.

Panthea. How thou art changed! I dare not
   look on thee;
I feel but see thee not. I scarce endure
The radiance of thy beauty. Some good change
Is working in the elements, which suffer
Thy presence thus unveiled. The Nereids tell   20
That on the day when the clear hyaline[25]
Was cloven at thine uprise, and thou didst stand
Within a veinèd shell, which floated on
Over the calm floor of the crystal sea,
Among the Ægean isles, and by the shores
Which bear thy name; love, like the atmosphere
Of the sun's fire filling the living world,

---

25 ocean.

Burst from thee, and illumined earth and heaven
And the deep ocean and the sunless caves
And all that dwells within them; till grief cast 30
Eclipse upon the soul from which it came:
Such art thou now; nor is it I alone,
Thy sister, thy companion, thine own chosen one,
But the whole world which seeks thy sympathy.
Hearest thou not sounds i' the air which speak
   the love
Of all articulate beings? Feelest thou not
The inanimate winds enamoured of thee? List!
                          [*Music.*

Asia. Thy words are sweeter than aught else
   but his
Whose echoes they are: yet all love is sweet,
Given or returned. Common as light is love,   40
And its familiar voice wearies not ever.
Like the wide heaven, the all-sustaining air,
It makes the reptile equal to the God:
They who inspire it most are fortunate,
As I am now; but those who feel it most
Are happier still, after long sufferings,
As I shall soon become.

Panthea.   List! Spirits speak.

Voice in the Air, singing.

Life of Life! thy lips enkindle
   With their love the breath between them;
And thy smiles before they dwindle   50
   Make the cold air fire; then screen them
In those looks, where whoso gazes
Faints, entangled in their mazes.

Child of Light! thy limbs are burning
   Through the vest which seems to hide
      them;
As the radiant lines of morning
   Through the clouds ere they divide them;
And this atmosphere divinest
Shrouds thee wheresoe'er thou shinest.

Fair are others; none beholds thee,   60
   But thy voice sounds low and tender
Like the fairest, for it folds thee
   From the sight, that liquid splendour,
And all feel, yet see thee never,
As I feel now, lost for ever!

Lamp of Earth! where'er thou movest
   Its dim shapes are clad with brightness,
And the souls of whom thou lovest
   Walk upon the winds with lightness,
Till they fail, as I am failing,   70
Dizzy, lost, yet unbewailing!

Asia.

My soul is an enchanted boat,
    Which, like a sleeping swan, doth float
Upon the silver waves of thy sweet singing;
    And thine doth like an angel sit
    Beside a helm conducting it,
Whilst all the winds with melody are ringing.
    It seems to float ever, for ever,
    Upon that many-winding river,
    Between mountains, woods, abysses,   80
    A paradise of wildernesses!
Till, like one in slumber bound,
Borne to the ocean, I float down, around,
Into a sea profound, of ever-spreading sound:

    Meanwhile thy spirit lifts its pinions
    In music's most serene dominions;
Catching the winds that fan that happy heaven.
    And we sail on, away, afar,
    Without a course, without a star,
But, by the instinct of sweet music driven;   90
    Till through Elysian garden islets
    By thee, most beautiful of pilots,
    Where never mortal pinnace glided,
    The boat of my desire is guided:
Realms where the air we breathe is love,
Which in the winds and on the waves doth
    move,
Harmonizing this earth with what we feel
    above.

    We have passed Age's icy caves,
    And Manhood's dark and tossing waves,
And Youth's smooth ocean, smiling to
        betray: 100
    Beyond the glassy gulfs we flee
    Of shadow-peopled Infancy,
Through Death and Birth, to a diviner day;
    A paradise of vaulted bowers,
    Lit by downward-gazing flowers,
    And watery paths that wind between
    Wildernesses calm and green,
Peopled by shapes too bright to see,
And rest, having beheld; somewhat like thee;
Which walk upon the sea, and chant me-
        lodiously!   110

ACT III

SCENE I.—*Heaven.* JUPITER *on his Throne;* THETIS
and the other Deities assembled.

Jupiter. Ye congregated powers of heaven, who
        share
The glory and the strength of him ye serve,

Rejoice! henceforth I am omnipotent.
All else had been subdued to me; alone
The soul of man, like unextinguished fire,
Yet burns towards heaven with fierce reproach,
        and doubt,
And lamentation, and reluctant prayer,
Hurling up insurrection, which might make
Our antique empire insecure, though built
On eldest faith, and hell's coeval, fear;   10
And though my curses through the pendulous air,
Like snow on herbless peaks, fall flake by flake,
And cling to it; though under my wrath's night
It climbs the crags of life, step after step,
Which wound it, as ice wounds unsandalled feet,
It yet remains supreme o'er misery,
Aspiring, unrepressed, yet soon to fall:
Even now have I begotten a strange wonder,
That fatal child, the terror of the earth,
Who waits but till the destined hour arrive,   20
Bearing from Demogorgon's vacant throne
The dreadful might of ever-living limbs
Which clothed that awful spirit unbeheld,
To redescend and trample out the spark.
Pour forth heaven's wine, Idæan Ganymede,[26]
And let it fill the Dædal[27] cups like fire,
And from the flower-inwoven soil divine
Ye all-triumphant harmonies arise,
As dew from earth under the twilight stars:
Drink! be the nectar circling through your
        veins   30
The soul of joy, ye ever-living Gods,
Till exultation burst in one wide voice
Like music from Elysian winds.
                                    And thou
Ascend beside me, veilèd in the light
Of the desire which makes thee one with me,
Thetis, bright image of eternity!
When thou didst cry, 'Insufferable might!
God! Spare me! I sustain not the quick flames,
The penetrating presence; all my being,
Like him[28] whom the Numidian seps[29] did
        thaw   40
Into a dew with poison, is dissolved,
Sinking through its foundations': even then
Two mighty spirits, mingling, made a third
Mightier than either, which, unbodied now,
Between us floats, felt, although unbeheld,
Waiting the incarnation, which ascends,
(Hear ye the thunder of the fiery wheels
Griding the winds?) from Demogorgon's throne.

---

26 cup bearer of the gods on Mt. Ida.
27 marvelously shaped.
28 the Roman soldier Sabellus.
29 venomous serpent mentioned by Lucan.

Victory! victory! Feel'st thou not, O world,
The earthquake of his chariot thundering up   50
Olympus?

> [*The Car of the* HOUR *arrives.* DEMOGORGON
> *descends, and moves towards the Throne of*
> JUPITER.

          Awful shape, what art thou? Speak!
Demogorgon. Eternity. Demand no direr name.
Descend, and follow me down the abyss.
I am thy child, as thou wert Saturn's child;
Mightier than thee: and we must dwell together
Henceforth in darkness. Lift thy lightnings not.
The tyranny of heaven none may retain,
Or reassume, or hold, succeeding thee:
Yet if thou wilt, as 'tis the destiny
Of trodden worms to writhe till they are dead, 60
Put forth thy might.
    Jupiter.   Detested prodigy!
Even thus beneath the deep Titanian prisons
I trample thee! thou lingerest?
                         Mercy! mercy!
No pity, no release, no respite! Oh,
That thou wouldst make mine enemy my judge,
Even where he hangs, seared by my long revenge,
On Caucasus! he would not doom me thus.
Gentle, and just, and dreadless, is he not
The monarch of the world? What then art thou?
No refuge! no appeal!
                  Sink with me then,   70
We two will sink on the wide waves of ruin,
Even as a vulture and a snake outspent
Drop, twisted in inextricable fight,
Into a shoreless sea. Let hell unlock
Its mounded oceans of tempestuous fire,
And whelm on them into the bottomless void
This desolated world, and thee, and me,
The conqueror and the conquered, and the wreck
Of that for which they combated.
                         Ai! Ai!
The elements obey me not. I sink   80
Dizzily down, ever, for ever, down.
And, like a cloud, mine enemy above
Darkens my fall with victory! Ai, Ai!

SCENE II.—*The Mouth of a great River in the
    Island Atlantis.* OCEAN *is discovered reclining
    near the Shore;* APOLLO *stands beside him.*

  Ocean. He fell, thou sayest, beneath his con-
    queror's frown?
  Apollo. Ay, when the strife was ended which
made dim
The orb I rule, and shook the solid stars,
The terrors of his eye illumined heaven
With sanguine light, through the thick ragged
    skirts

Of the victorious darkness, as he fell:
Like the last glare of day's red agony,
Which, from a rent among the fiery clouds,
Burns far along the tempest-wrinkled deep.
  Ocean. He sunk to the abyss? To the dark
    void?   10
  Apollo. An eagle so caught in some bursting
    cloud
On Caucasus, his thunder-baffled wings
Entangled in the whirlwind, and his eyes
Which gazed on the undazzling sun, now blinded
By the white lightning, while the ponderous hail
Beats on his struggling form, which sinks at
    length
Prone, and the aëreal ice clings over it.
  Ocean. Henceforth the fields of heaven-reflect-
    ing sea
Which are my realm, will heave, unstained with
    blood,
Beneath the uplifting winds, like plains of
    corn[30]   20
Swayed by the summer air; my streams will flow
Round many-peopled continents, and round
Fortunate isles; and from their glassy thrones
Blue Proteus and his humid nymphs shall mark
The shadow of fair ships, as mortals see
The floating bark of the light-laden moon
With that white star, its sightless pilot's crest,
Borne down the rapid sunset's ebbing sea;
Tracking their path no more by blood and
    groans,
And desolation, and the mingled voice   30
Of slavery and command; but by the light
Of wave-reflected flowers, and floating odours,
And music soft, and mild, free, gentle voices,
And sweetest music, such as spirits love.
  Apollo. And I shall gaze not on the deeds which
    make
My mind obscure with sorrow, as eclipse
Darkens the sphere I guide; but list, I hear
The small, clear, silver lute of the young Spirit
That sits i' the morning star.
  Ocean.   Thou must away;
Thy steeds will pause at even, till when fare-
    well: 40
The loud deep calls me home even now to feed it
With azure calm out of the emerald urns
Which stand for ever full beside my throne.
Behold the Nereids under the green sea,
Their wavering limbs borne on the wind-like
    stream,
Their white arms lifted o'er their streaming hair
With garlands pied and starry sea-flower crowns,

---

30 wheat.

Hastening to grace their mighty sister's joy.

[*A sound of waves is heard.*

It is the unpastured sea hungering for calm.

Peace, monster; I come now. Farewell.

Apollo. Farewell 50

SCENE III.—*Caucasus.* PROMETHEUS, HERCULES,
IONE, *the* EARTH, SPIRITS, ASIA, *and* PAN-
THEA, *borne in the Car with the* SPIRIT OF THE
HOUR. HERCULES *unbinds* PROMETHEUS, *who
descends.*

Hercules. Most glorious among Spirits, thus
doth strength

To wisdom, courage, and long-suffering love,

And thee, who art the form they animate,

Minister like a slave.

Prometheus. Thy gentle words

Are sweeter even than freedom long desired

And long delayed.

Asia, thou light of life,

Shadow of beauty unbeheld: and ye,

Fair sister nymphs, who made long years of pain

Sweet to remember, through your love and care:

Henceforth we will not part. There is a cave, 10

All overgrown with trailing odorous plants,

Which curtain out the day with leaves and
flowers,

And paved with veinèd emerald, and a fountain

Leaps in the midst with an awakening sound.

From its curved roof the mountain's frozen
tears[31]

Like snow, or silver, or long diamond spires,

Hang downward, raining forth a doubtful light:

And there is heard the ever-moving air,

Whispering without from tree to tree, and birds,

And bees; and all around are mossy seats, 20

And the rough walls are clothed with long soft
grass;

A simple dwelling, which shall be our own;

Where we will sit and talk of time and change,

As the world ebbs and flows, ourselves unchanged.

What can hide man from mutability?

And if ye sigh, then I will smile; and thou,

Ione, shall chant fragments of sea-music,

Until I weep, when ye shall smile away

The tears she brought, which yet were sweet to
shed.

We will entangle buds and flowers and beams 30

Which twinkle on the fountain's brim, and make

Strange combinations out of common things,

Like human babes in their brief innocence;

And we will search, with looks and words of love,

For hidden thoughts, each lovelier than the last,

Our unexhausted spirits; and like lutes

Touched by the skill of the enamoured wind,

Weave harmonies divine, yet ever new,

From difference sweet where discord cannot be;

And hither come, sped on the charmèd winds, 40

Which meet from all the points of heaven, as bees

From every flower aëreal Enna[32] feeds,

At their known island-homes in Himera,[33]

The echoes of the human world, which tell

Of the low voice of love, almost unheard,

And dove-eyed pity's murmured pain, and music,

Itself the echo of the heart, and all

That tempers or improves man's life, now free;

And lovely apparitions,—dim at first,

Then radiant, as the mind, arising bright 50

From the embrace of beauty (whence the forms

Of which these are the phantoms) casts on them

The gathered rays which are reality—

Shall visit us, the progeny immortal

Of Painting, Sculpture, and rapt Poesy,

And arts, though unimagined, yet to be.

The wandering voices and the shadows these

Of all that man becomes, the mediators

Of that best worship love, by him and us

Given and returned; swift shapes and sounds,
which grow 60

More fair and soft as man grows wise and kind,

And, veil by veil, evil and error fall:

Such virtue has the cave and place around.

[*Turning to the* SPIRIT OF THE HOUR.

For thee, fair Spirit, one toil remains. Ione,

Give her that curvèd shell, which Proteus old

Made Asia's nuptial boon, breathing within it

A voice to be accomplished, and which thou

Didst hide in grass under the hollow rock.

Ione. Thou most desired Hour, more loved and
lovely

Than all thy sisters, this is the mystic shell; 70

See the pale azure fading into silver

Lining it with a soft yet glowing light:

Looks it not like lulled music sleeping there?

Spirit. It seems in truth the fairest shell of
Ocean:

Its sound must be at once both sweet and strange.

Prometheus. Go, borne over the cities of mankind

On whirlwind-footed coursers: once again

Outspeed the sun around the orbèd world;

And as thy chariot cleaves the kindling air,

Thou breathe into the many-folded shell, 80

Loosening its mighty music; it shall be

As thunder mingled with clear echoes: then

---

31 stalactites.

32 an ancient Sicilian town.

33 a district on the north coast of Sicily.

Return; and thou shalt dwell beside our cave.
And thou, O, Mother Earth!—
   The Earth.   I hear, I feel;
Thy lips are on me, and their touch runs down
Even to the adamantine central gloom
Along these marble nerves; 'tis life, 'tis joy,
And through my withered, old, and icy frame
The warmth of an immortal youth shoots down
Circling. Henceforth the many children fair   90
Folded in my sustaining arms; all plants,
And creeping forms, and insects rainbow-winged,
And birds, and beasts, and fish, and human
    shapes,
Which drew disease and pain from my wan
    bosom,
Draining the poison of despair, shall take
And interchange sweet nutriment; to me
Shall they become like sister-antelopes
By one fair dam, snow-white and swift as wind,
Nursed among lilies near a brimming stream.
The dew-mists of my sunless sleep shall float   100
Under the stars like balm: night-folded flowers
Shall suck unwithering hues in their repose:
And men and beasts in happy dreams shall gather
Strength for the coming day, and all its joy:
And death shall be the last embrace of her
Who takes the life she gave, even as a mother
Folding her child, says, 'Leave me not again.'
   Asia. Oh, mother! wherefore speak the name
    of death?
Cease they to love, and move, and breathe, and
    speak,
Who die?
   The Earth. It would avail not to reply: 110
Thou art immortal, and this tongue is known
But to the uncommunicating dead.
Death is the veil which those who live call life:
They sleep, and it is lifted: and meanwhile
In mild variety the seasons mild
With rainbow-skirted showers, and odorous
    winds,
And long blue meteors cleansing the dull night,
And the life-kindling shafts of the keen sun's
All-piercing bow, and the dew-mingled rain
Of the calm moonbeams, a soft influence
    mild,   120
Shall clothe the forests and the fields, ay, even
The crag-built deserts of the barren deep,
With ever-living leaves, and fruits, and flowers.
And thou! There is a cavern where my spirit
Was panted forth in anguish whilst thy pain
Made my heart mad, and those who did inhale it
Became mad too, and built a temple there,
And spoke, and were oracular, and lured

The erring nations round to mutual war,
And faithless faith, such as Jove kept with
    thee;   130
Which breath now rises, as amongst tall weeds
A violet's exhalation, and it fills
With a serener light and crimson air
Intense, yet soft, the rocks and woods around;
It feeds the quick growth of the serpent vine,
And the dark linkèd ivy tangling wild,
And budding, blown, or odour-faded blooms
Which star the winds with points of coloured
    light,
As they rain through them, and bright golden
    globes
Of fruit, suspended in their own green
    heaven,   140
And through their veinèd leaves and amber stems
The flowers whose purple and translucid bowls
Stand ever mantling with aëreal dew,
The drink of spirits: and it circles round,
Like the soft waving wings of noonday dreams,
Inspiring calm and happy thoughts, like mine,
Now thou art thus restored. This cave is thine.
Arise! Appear!
   [*A* SPIRIT *rises in the likeness of a winged child.*
               This is my torch-bearer;
Who let his lamp out in old time with gazing
On eyes from which he kindled it anew   150
With love, which is as fire, sweet daughter mine,
For such is that within thine own. Run, wayward,
And guide this company beyond the peak
Of Bacchic Nysa, Mænad-haunted mountain,
And beyond Indus and its tribute rivers,
Trampling the torrent streams and glassy lakes
With feet unwet, unwearied, undelaying,
And up the green ravine, across the vale,
Beside the windless and crystalline pool,
Where ever lies, on unerasing waves,   160
The image of a temple, built above,
Distinct with column, arch, and architrave,
And palm-like capital, and over-wrought,
And populous with most living imagery,
Praxitelean[34] shapes, whose marble smiles
Fill the hushed air with everlasting love.
It is deserted now, but once it bore
Thy name, Prometheus; there the emulous
    youths
Bore to thy honour through the divine gloom
The lamp which was thine emblem; even as
    those   170
Who bear the untransmitted torch of hope
Into the grave, across the night of life,
As thou hast borne it most triumphantly

---

34 as beautiful as the statues of the Greek sculptor Praxiteles.

To this far goal of Time. Depart, farewell.
Beside that temple is the destined cave.

SCENE IV.—*A Forest. In the Background a Cave.*
  PROMETHEUS, ASIA, PANTHEA, IONE, *and the*
  SPIRIT OF THE EARTH.

  Ione. Sister, it is not earthly: how it glides
Under the leaves! how on its head there burns
A light, like a green star, whose emerald beams
Are twined with its fair hair! how, as it moves,
The splendour drops in flakes upon the grass!
Knowest thou it?

  Panthea.   It is the delicate spirit
That guides the earth through heaven. From afar
The populous constellations call that light
The loveliest of the planets; and sometimes
It floats along the spray of the salt sea,   10
Or makes its chariot of a foggy cloud,
Or walks through fields or cities while men sleep,
Or o'er the mountain tops, or down the rivers,
Or through the green waste wilderness, as now,
Wondering at all it sees. Before Jove reigned
It loved our sister Asia, and it came
Each leisure hour to drink the liquid light
Out of her eyes, for which it said it thirsted
As one bit by a dipsas[35] and with her
It made its childish confidence, and told her   20
All it had known or seen, for it saw much,
Yet idly reasoned what it saw; and called her—
For whence it sprung it knew not, nor do I—
Mother, dear mother.

  The Spirit of the Earth (*running to* ASIA).
    Mother, dearest mother;
May I then talk with thee as I was wont?
May I then hide my eyes in thy soft arms,
After thy looks have made them tired of joy?
May I then play beside thee the long noons,
When work is none in the bright silent air?

  Asia. I love thee, gentlest being, and hence-
    forth
Can cherish thee unenvied: speak, I pray: 30
Thy simple talk once solaced, now delights.

  Spirit of the Earth. Mother, I am grown wiser,
    though a child
Cannot be wise like thee, within this day;
And happier too; happier and wiser both.
Thou knowest that toads, and snakes, and
    loathly worms,
And venomous and malicious beasts, and boughs
That bore ill berries in the woods, were ever
An hindrance to my walks o'er the green world:
And that, among the haunts of humankind,   40
Hard-featured men, or with proud, angry looks,

35 a serpent whose bite caused intolerable thirst.

Or cold, staid gait, or false and hollow smiles,
Or the dull sneer of self-loved ignorance,
Or other such foul masks, with which ill thoughts
Hide that fair being whom we spirits call man;
And women too, ugliest of all things evil,
(Though fair, even in a world where thou art fair,
When good and kind, free and sincere like thee),
When false or frowning made me sick at heart
To pass them, though they slept, and I unseen. 50
Well, my path lately lay through a great city
Into the woody hills surrounding it:
A sentinel was sleeping at the gate:
When there was heard a sound, so loud, it shook
The towers amid the moonlight, yet more sweet
Than any voice but thine, sweetest of all;
A long, long sound, as it would never end:
And all the inhabitants leaped suddenly
Out of their rest, and gathered in the streets,
Looking in wonder up to Heaven, while yet   60
The music pealed along. I hid myself
Within a fountain in the public square,
Where I lay like the reflex of the moon
Seen in a wave under green leaves; and soon
Those ugly human shapes and visages
Of which I spoke as having wrought me pain,
Passed floating through the air, and fading still
Into the winds that scattered them; and those
From whom they passed seemed mild and lovely
    forms
After some foul disguise had fallen, and all   70
Were somewhat changed, and after brief surprise
And greetings of delighted wonder, all
Went to their sleep again: and when the dawn
Came, wouldst thou think that toads, and snakes,
    and efts,
Could e'er be beautiful? yet so they were,
And that with little change of shape or hue:
All things had put their evil nature off:
I cannot tell my joy, when o'er a lake
Upon a drooping bough with nightshade twined,
I saw two azure halcyons clinging downward   80
And thinning one bright bunch of amber berries,
With quick long beaks, and in the deep there lay
Those lovely forms imaged as in a sky;
So, with my thoughts full of these happy changes,
We meet again, the happiest change of all.

  Asia. And never will we part, till thy chaste
    sister
Who guides the frozen and inconstant moon
Will look on thy more warm and equal light
Till her heart thaw like flakes of April snow
And love thee.

  Spirit of the Earth. What; as Asia loves Pro-
    metheus?
                                                          90

Asia. Peace, wanton, thou art yet not old
   enough.
Think ye by gazing on each other's eyes
To multiply your lovely selves, and fill
With spherèd fires the interlunar air?
   Spirit of the Earth. Nay, mother, while my sis-
   ·ter trims her lamp
'Tis hard I should go darkling.
   Asia.   Listen; look!
          [*The* SPIRIT OF THE HOUR *enters.*
   Prometheus. We feel what thou hast heard and
   seen; yet speak.
   Spirit of the Hour. Soon as the sound had
   ceased whose thunder filled
The abysses of the sky and the wide earth,
There was a change: the impalpable thin air   100
And the all-circling sunlight were transformed,
As if the sense of love dissolved in them
Had folded itself round the spherèd world.
My vision then grew clear, and I could see
Into the mysteries of the universe:
Dizzy as with delight I floated down,
Winnowing the lightsome air with languid
   plumes,
My coursers sought their birthplace in the sun,
Where they henceforth will live exempt from toil,
Pasturing flowers of vegetable fire;   110
And where my moonlike car will stand within
A temple, gazed upon by Phidian forms[36]
Of thee, and Asia, and the Earth, and me,
And you fair nymphs looking the love we feel,—
In memory of the tidings it has borne,—
Beneath a dome fretted with graven flowers,
Poised on twelve columns of resplendent stone,
And open to the bright and liquid sky.
Yoked to it by an amphisbaenic[37] snake
The likeness of those wingèd steeds will
   mock   120
The flight from which they find repose. Alas,
Whither has wandered now my partial tongue
When all remains untold which ye would hear?
As I have said, I floated to the earth:
It was, as it is still, the pain of bliss
To move, to breathe, to be; I wandering went
Among the haunts and dwellings of mankind,
And first was disappointed not to see
Such mighty change as I had felt within
Expressed in outward things; but soon I
   looked,   130
And behold, thrones were kingless, and men
   walked

---

36 Phidias, the most celebrated of the Greek sculptors.
37 having a head at each end and capable of moving in either direction.

One with the other even as spirits do,
None fawned, none trampled; hate, disdain, or
   fear,
Self-love or self-contempt, on human brows
No more inscribed, as o'er the gate of hell,
'All hope abandon ye who enter here';
None frowned, none trembled, none with eager
   fear
Gazed on another's eye of cold command,
Until the subject of a tyrant's will
Became, worse fate, the abject of his own,   140
Which spurred him, like an outspent horse, to
   death.
None wrought his lips in truth-entangling lines
Which smiled the lie his tongue disdained to
   speak;
None, with firm sneer, trod out in his own heart
The sparks of love and hope till there remained
Those bitter ashes, a soul self-consumed,
And the wretch crept a vampire among men,
Infecting all with his own hideous ill;
None talked that common, false, cold, hollow
   talk
Which makes the heart deny the *yes* it
   breathes,   150
Yet question that unmeant hypocrisy
With such a self-mistrust as has no name.
And women, too, frank, beautiful, and kind
As the free heaven which rains fresh light and
   dew
On the wide earth, past; gentle radiant forms,
From custom's evil taint exempt and pure;
Speaking the wisdom once they could not think,
Looking emotions once they feared to feel,
And changed to all which once they dared not
   be,
Yet being now, made earth like heaven; nor
   pride,   160
Nor jealousy, nor envy, nor ill shame,
The bitterest of those drops of treasured gall,
Spoilt the sweet taste of the nepenthe, love.

Thrones, altars, judgement-seats, and prisons;
   wherein,
And beside which, by wretched men were borne
Sceptres, tiaras, swords, and chains, and tomes
Of reasoned wrong, glozed on by ignorance,
Were like those monstrous and barbaric shapes,
The ghosts of a no-more-remembered fame,
Which, from their unworn obelisks, look
   forth   170
In triumph o'er the palaces and tombs
Of those who were their conquerors: moulder-
   ing round,

These imaged to the pride of kings and priests
A dark yet mighty faith, a power as wide
As is the world it wasted, and are now
But an astonishment; even so the tools
And emblems of its last captivity,
Amid the dwellings of the peopled earth,
Stand, not o'erthrown, but unregarded now.
And those foul shapes, abhorred by god and
    man,—   180
Which, under many a name and many a form
Strange, savage, ghastly, dark and execrable,
Were Jupiter, the tyrant of the world;
And which the nations, panic-stricken, served
With blood, and hearts broken by long hope, and
    love
Dragged to his altars soiled and garlandless,
And slain amid men's unreclaiming tears,
Flattering the thing they feared, which fear was
    hate,—
Frown, mouldering fast, o'er their abandoned
    shrines:
The painted veil, by those who were, called
    life,   190
Which mimicked, as with colours idly spread,
All men believed or hoped, is torn aside;
The loathsome mask has fallen, the man remains
Sceptreless, free, uncircumscribed, but man
Equal, unclassed, tribeless, and nationless,
Exempt from awe, worship, degree, the king
Over himself; just, gentle, wise: but man
Passionless?——no, yet free from guilt or pain,
Which were, for his will made or suffered them,
Nor yet exempt, though ruling them like
    slaves,   200
From chance, and death, and mutability,
The clogs of that which else might oversoar
The loftiest star of unascended heaven,
Pinnacled dim in the intense inane.

ACT IV

SCENE.—*A Part of the Forest near the Cave of*
PROMETHEUS. PANTHEA *and* IONE *are sleeping:*
they awaken gradually during the first Song.

    Voice of unseen Spirits.

    The pale stars are gone!
    For the sun, their swift shepherd,
    To their folds them compelling,
    In the depths of the dawn,
Hastes, in meteor-eclipsing array, and they
    flee
    Beyond his blue dwelling,
    As fawns flee the leopard.
    But where are ye?

A Train of dark Forms and Shadows passes by
    confusedly, singing.

    Here, oh, here:
    We bear the bier   10
Of the Father of many a cancelled year
    Spectres we
    Of the dead Hours be,
We bear Time to his tomb in eternity.

    Strew, oh, strew
    Hair, not yew!
Wet the dusty pall with tears, not dew!
    Be the faded flowers
    Of Death's bare bowers
Spread on the corpse of the King of
    Hours!   20

    Haste, oh, haste!
    As shades are chased,
Trembling, by day, from heaven's blue waste.
    We melt away,
    Like dissolving spray,
From the children of a diviner day,
    With the lullaby
    Of winds that die
On the bosom of their own harmony!

      Ione.

    What dark forms were they?   30

      Panthea.

The past Hours weak and grey,
With the spoil which their toil
    Raked together
From the conquest but One could foil.

      Ione.

Have they passed?

      Panthea.

        They have passed;
They outspeeded the blast,
While 'tis said, they are fled:

      Ione.

    Whither, oh, whither?

      Panthea.

To the dark, to the past, to the dead.

    Voice of unseen Spirits.

Bright clouds float in heaven,   40
Dew-stars gleam on earth,
Waves assemble on ocean,
They are gathered and driven
By the storm of delight, by the panic of
    glee!
They shake with emotion,

They dance in their mirth.
  But where are ye?

The pine boughs are singing
Old songs with new gladness,
The billows and fountains   50
Fresh music are flinging,
Like the notes of a spirit from land and from
  sea;
The storms mock the mountains
With the thunder of gladness.
  But where are ye?

Ione. What charioteers are these?
Panthea.   Where are their chariots?

Semichorus of Hours.

The voice of the Spirits of Air and of Earth
Have drawn back the figured curtain of sleep
Which covered our being and darkened our
  birth
In the deep.

A Voice.

In the deep?

Semichorus II.

            Oh, below the deep. 60

Semichorus I.

An hundred ages we had been kept
  Cradled in visions of hate and care,
And each one who waked as his brother slept,
  Found the truth—

Semichorus II.

Worse than his visions were!

Semichorus I.

We have heard the lute of Hope in sleep;
  We have known the voice of Love in dreams;
We have felt the wand of Power, and leap—

Semichorus II.

As the billows leap in the morning beams!

Chorus.

Weave the dance on the floor of the breeze,
  Pierce with song heaven's silent light,   70
Enchant the day that too swiftly flees,
  To check its flight ere the cave of Night.

Once the hungry Hours were hounds
  Which chased the day like a bleeding deer,
And it limped and stumbled with many
  wounds
  Through the nightly dells of the desert year.

But now, oh weave the mystic measure
  Of music, and dance, and shapes of light,

Let the Hours, and the spirits of might and
  pleasure,
  Like the clouds and sunbeams, unite.

A Voice.

            Unite!   80
Panthea. See, where the Spirits of the human
  mind
Wrapped in sweet sounds, as in bright veils, approach.

Chorus of Spirits.

  We join the throng
  Of the dance and the song,
By the whirlwind of gladness borne along;
  As the flying-fish leap
  From the Indian deep,
And mix with the sea-birds, half asleep.

Chorus of Hours.

Whence come ye, so wild and so fleet,
For sandals of lightning are on your feet,   90
And your wings are soft and swift as thought,
And your eyes are as love which is veilèd not?

Chorus of Spirits.

  We come from the mind
  Of human kind
Which was late so dusk, and obscene, and
  blind,
  Now 'tis an ocean
  Of clear emotion,
A heaven of serene and mighty motion.

  From that deep abyss
  Of wonder and bliss,   100
Whose caverns are crystal palaces;
  From those skiey towers
  Where Thought's crowned powers
Sit watching your dance, ye happy Hours!

  From the dim recesses
  Of woven caresses,
Where lovers catch ye by your loose tresses
  From the azure isles,
  Where sweet Wisdom smiles,
Delaying your ships with her siren wiles.   110
  From the temples high
  Of Man's ear and eye,
Roofed over Sculpture and Poesy;
  From the murmurings
  Of the unsealed springs
Where Science bedews her Dædal wings.

  Years after years,
  Through blood, and tears,

And a thick hell of hatreds, and hopes, and
    fears;
  We waded and flew,   120
  And the islets were few
Where the bud-blighted flowers of happiness
    grew.

  Our feet now, every palm,
  Are sandalled with calm,
And the dew of our wings is a rain of balm;
  And, beyond our eyes,
  The human love lies
Which makes all it gazes on Paradise.

    Chorus of Spirits and Hours.

Then weave the web of the mystic measure;
From the depths of the sky and the ends of the
    earth,   130
Come, swift Spirits of might and of pleasure,
Fill the dance and the music of mirth,
  As the waves of a thousand streams rush by
To an ocean of splendour and harmony!

    Chorus of Spirits.

  Our spoil is won,
  Our task is done,
We are free to dive, or soar, or run;
  Beyond and around,
  Or within the bound
Which clips the world with darkness
  round.   140

  We'll pass the eyes
  Of the starry skies
Into the hoar deep to colonize:
  Death, Chaos, and Night,
  From the sound of our flight,
Shall flee, like mist from a tempest's might.

  And Earth, Air, and Light,
  And the Spirit of Might,
Which drives round the stars in their fiery
    flight;
  And Love, Thought, and Breath,   150
  The powers that quell Death,
Wherever we soar shall assemble beneath.

  And our singing shall build
  In the void's loose field
A world for the Spirit of Wisdom to wield;
  We will take our plan
  From the new world of man,
And our works shall be called the Promethean.

    Chorus of Hours.

Break the dance, and scatter the song;

Let some depart, and some remain.   160
    Semichorus I.
We, beyond heaven, are driven along:
    Semichorus II.
Us the enchantments of earth retain:
    Semichorus I.
Ceaseless, and rapid, and fierce, and free,
With the Spirits which build a new earth and
    sea,
And a heaven where yet heaven could never
    be.
    Semichorus II.
Solemn, and slow, and serene, and bright,
Leading the Day and outspeeding the Night,
With the powers of a world of perfect light.
    Semichorus I.
We whirl, singing loud, round the gathering
    sphere,
Till the trees, and the beasts, and the clouds
    appear   170
From its chaos made calm by love, not fear.
    Semichorus II.
We encircle the ocean and mountains of earth,
And the happy forms of its death and birth
Change to the music of our sweet mirth.
    Chorus of Hours and Spirits.
Break the dance, and scatter the song,
  Let some depart, and some remain,
Wherever we fly we lead along
In leashes, like starbeams, soft yet strong,
  The clouds that are heavy with love's sweet
    rain.
  Panthea. Ha! they are gone!
  Ione.   Yet feel you no delight   180
From the past sweetness?
  Panthea.   As the bare green hill
When some soft cloud vanishes into rain,
Laughs with a thousand drops of sunny water
To the unpavilioned sky!
  Ione.   Even whilst we speak
New notes arise. What is that awful sound?
  Panthea. 'Tis the deep music of the rolling
    world
Kindling within the strings of the waved air
Æolian modulations.
  Ione.   Listen too,
How every pause is filled with under-notes,
Clear, silver, icy, keen, awakening tones,   190
Which pierce the sense, and live within the soul,
As the sharp stars pierce winter's crystal air
And gaze upon themselves within the sea.

Panthea. But see where through two openings
　in the forest
Which hanging branches overcanopy,
And where two runnels of a rivulet,
Between the close moss violet-inwoven,
Have made their path of melody, like sisters
Who part with sighs that they may meet in
　smiles,
Turning their dear disunion to an isle　　200
Of lovely grief, a wood of sweet sad thoughts;
Two visions of strange radiance float upon
The ocean-like enchantment of strong sound,
Which flows intenser, keener, deeper yet
Under the ground and through the windless air.
　Ione. I see a chariot like that thinnest boat,
In which the Mother of the Months[38] is borne
By ebbing light into her western cave,
When she upsprings from interlunar dreams;
O'er which is curved an orblike canopy　　210
Of gentle darkness, and the hills and woods,
Distinctly seen through that dusk aery veil,
Regard[39] like shapes in an enchanter's glass;
Its wheels are solid clouds, azure and gold,
Such as the genii of the thunderstorm
Pile on the floor of the illumined sea
When the sun rushes under it; they roll
And move and grow as with an inward wind;
Within it sits a wingèd infant, white
Its countenance, like the whiteness of bright
　snow,　　220
Its plumes are as feathers of sunny frost,
Its limbs gleam white, through the wind-flowing
　folds
Of its white robe, woof of ethereal pearl.
Its hair is white, the brightness of white light
Scattered in strings; yet its two eyes are heavens
Of liquid darkness, which the Deity
Within seems pouring, as a storm is poured
From jaggèd clouds, out of their arrowy lashes,
Tempering the cold and radiant air around,
With fire that is not brightness; in its hand　　230
It sways a quivering moonbeam, from whose
　point
A guiding power directs the chariot's prow
Over its wheelèd clouds, which as they roll
Over the grass, and flowers, and waves, wake
　sounds,
Sweet as a singing rain of silver dew.
　Panthea. And from the other opening in the
　wood
Rushes, with loud and whirlwind harmony,
A sphere,[40] which is as many thousand spheres,

Solid as crystal, yet through all its mass
Flow, as through empty space, music and
　light:　　240
Ten thousand orbs involving and involved,
Purple and azure, white, and green, and golden,
Sphere within sphere; and every space between
Peopled with unimaginable shapes,
Such as ghosts dream dwell in the lampless deep,
Yet each inter-transpicuous, and they whirl
Over each other with a thousand motions,
Upon a thousand sightless axles spinning,
And with the force of self-destroying swiftness,
Intensely, slowly, solemnly roll on,　　250
Kindling with mingled sounds, and many tones,
Intelligible words and music wild.
With mighty whirl the multitudinous orb
Grinds the bright brook into an azure mist
Of elemental subtlety, like light;
And the wild odour of the forest flowers,
The music of the living grass and air,
The emerald light of leaf-entangled beams
Round its intense yet self-conflicting speed,
Seem kneaded into one aëreal mass　　260
Which drowns the sense. Within the orb itself,
Pillowed upon its alabaster arms,
Like to a child o'erwearied with sweet toil,
On its own folded wings, and wavy hair,
The Spirit of the Earth is laid asleep,
And you can see its little lips are moving,
Amid the changing light of their own smiles,
Like one who talks of what he loves in dream.
　Ione. 'Tis only mocking the orb's harmony.
　Panthea. And from a star upon its forehead,
　shoot,　　270
Like swords of azure fire, or golden spears
With tyrant-quelling myrtle overtwined,[41]
Embleming heaven and earth united now,
Vast beams like spokes of some invisible wheel
Which whirl as the orb whirls, swifter than
　thought,
Filling the abyss with sun-like lightnings,
And perpendicular now, and now transverse,
Pierce the dark soil, and as they pierce and
　pass,
Make bare the secrets of the earth's deep heart;
Infinite mines of adamant and gold,　　280
Valueless[42] stones, and unimagined gems,
And caverns on crystalline columns poised
With vegetable silver overspread;
Wells of unfathomed fire, and water springs
Whence the great sea, even as a child is fed,

---

38 Diana, goddess of the moon.　　39 appear.
40 the earth.

41 The heroes who killed the Athenian tyrant Hipparchus concealed their swords under branches of myrtle.
42 priceless.

Whose vapours clothe earth's monarch moun-
    tain-tops
With kingly, ermine snow. The beams flash on
And make appear the melancholy ruins
Of cancelled cycles; anchors, beaks of ships;
Planks turned to marble; quivers, helms, and
    spears,   290
And gorgon-headed targes, and the wheels
Of scythèd chariots, and the emblazonry
Of trophies, standards, and armorial beasts,
Round which death laughed, sepulchred emblems
Of dead destruction, ruin within ruin!
The wrecks beside of many a city vast,
Whose population which the earth grew over
Was mortal, but not human; see, they lie,
Their monstrous works, and uncouth skeletons,
Their statues, homes and fanes; prodigious
    shapes   300
Huddled in grey annihilation, split,
Jammed in the hard, black deep; and over these,
The anatomies of unknown wingèd things,
And fishes which were isles of living scale,
And serpents, bony chains, twisted around
The iron crags, or within heaps of dust
To which the tortuous strength of their last pangs
Had crushed the iron crags; and over these
The jaggèd alligator, and the might
Of earth-convulsing behemoth, which once   310
Were monarch beasts, and on the slimy shores,
And weed-overgrown continents of earth,
Increased and multiplied like summer worms
On an abandoned corpse, till the blue globe
Wrapped deluge round it like a cloak, and they
Yelled, gasped, and were abolished; or some God
Whose throne was in a comet, passed, and cried,
'Be not!' And like my words they were no more.

The Earth.

The joy, the triumph, the delight, the madness!
  The boundless, overflowing, bursting glad-
    ness,   320
The vaporous exultation not to be confined!
  Ha! ha! the animation of delight
  Which wraps me, like an atmosphere of light,
And bears me as a cloud is borne by its own
    wind.

The Moon.

Brother mine, calm wanderer,
  Happy globe of land and air,
Some Spirit is darted like a beam from thee,
  Which penetrates my frozen frame,
  And passes with the warmth of flame,
With love, and odour, and deep melody   330
    Through me, through me!

The Earth.

Ha! ha! the caverns of my hollow mountains,
  My cloven fire-crags, sound-exulting fountains
Laugh with a vast and inextinguishable laugh-
    ter.
  The oceans, and the deserts, and the abysses,
  And the deep air's unmeasured wildernesses,
Answer from all their clouds and billows, echo-
    ing after.

  They cry aloud as I do. Sceptred curse,
  Who all our green and azure universe
Threatenedst to muffle round with black de-
    struction, sending   340
  A solid cloud to rain hot thunderstones,
  And splinter and knead down my children's
    bones,
All I bring forth, to one void mass battering and
    blending,—

  Until each crag-like tower, and storied column,
  Palace, and obelisk, and temple solemn,
My imperial mountains crowned with cloud, and
    snow, and fire;
  My sea-like forests, every blade and blossom
  Which finds a grave or cradle in my bosom,
Were stamped by thy strong hate into a lifeless
    mire:

  How art thou sunk, withdrawn, covered, drunk
    up   350
  By thirsty nothing, as the brackish cup
Drained by a desert-troop, a little drop for all!
  And from beneath, around, within, above,
  Filling thy void annihilation, love
Burst in like light on caves cloven by the thunder-
    ball.

The Moon.

The snow upon my lifeless mountains
  Is loosened into living fountains,
My solid oceans flow, and sing, and shine:
  A spirit from my heart bursts forth,
  It clothes with unexpected birth   360
My cold bare bosom: Oh! it must be thine
    On mine, on mine!

  Gazing on thee I feel, I know
  Green stalks burst forth, and bright flowers
    grow,
And living shapes upon my bosom move:
  Music is in the sea and air,
  Wingèd clouds soar here and there,
Dark with the rain new buds are dreaming of:
    'Tis love, all love!

The Earth.

It interpenetrates my granite mass,   370
  Through tangled roots and trodden clay doth
    pass
Into the utmost leaves and delicatest flowers;
  Upon the winds, among the clouds 'tis spread,
  It wakes a life in the forgotten dead,
They breathe a spirit up from their obscurest
    bowers.

And like a storm bursting its cloudy prison
  With thunder, and with whirlwind, has arisen
Out of the lampless caves of unimagined being:
  With earthquake shock and swiftness making
    shiver
  Thought's stagnant chaos, unremoved for
    ever,   380
Till hate, and fear, and pain, light-vanquished
    shadows, fleeing,

Leave Man, who was a many-sided mirror,
  Which could distort to many a shape of er-
    ror,
This true fair world of things, a sea reflecting
    love;
  Which over all his kind, as the sun's heaven
  Gliding o'er ocean, smooth, serene, and even,
Darting from starry depths radiance and life,
    doth move:

Leave Man, even as a leprous child is left,
Who follows a sick beast to some warm cleft
Of rocks, through which the might of healing
    springs is poured;   390
  Then when it wanders home with rosy smile,
  Unconscious, and its mother fears awhile
It is a spirit, then, weeps on her child restored.

Man, oh, not men! a chain of linkèd thought,
  Of love and might to be divided not,
Compelling the elements with adamantine stress;
  As the sun rules, even with a tyrant's gaze,
  The unquiet republic of the maze
Of planets, struggling fierce towards heaven's
    free wilderness.

Man, one harmonious soul of many a soul, 400
  Whose nature is its own divine control,
Where all things flow to all, as rivers to the sea;
  Familiar acts are beautiful through love;
  Labour, and pain, and grief, in life's green
    grove
Sport like tame beasts, none knew how gentle
    they could be!

His will, with all mean passions, bad delights,
  And selfish cares, its trembling satellites,
A spirit ill to guide, but mighty to obey,
  Is as a tempest-wingèd ship, whose helm
  Love rules, through waves which dare not
    overwhelm,   410
Forcing life's wildest shores to own its sovereign
    sway.

All things confess his strength. Through the
    cold mass
  Of marble and of colour his dreams pass;
Bright threads whence mothers weave the robes
    their children wear;
  Language is a perpetual Orphic song,
  Which rules with Dædal harmony a throng
Of thoughts and forms, which else senseless and
    shapeless were.

The lightning is his slave; heaven's utmost
    deep
  Gives up her stars, and like a flock of sheep
They pass before his eye, are numbered, and
    roll on!   420
  The tempest is his steed, he strides the air;
  And the abyss shouts from her depth laid bare,
Heaven, hast thou secrets? Man unveils me: I
    have none.

The Moon.

The shadow of white death has passed
  From my path in heaven at last,
A clinging shroud of solid frost and sleep;
  And through my newly-woven bowers,
  Wander happy paramours,
Less mighty, but as mild as those who keep
    Thy vales more deep.   430

The Earth.

As the dissolving warmth of dawn may fold
  A half unfrozen dew-globe, green, and gold,
And crystalline, till it becomes a wingèd mist,
  And wanders up the vault of the blue day,
  Outlives the noon, and on the sun's last ray
Hangs o'er the sea, a fleece of fire and amethyst.

The Moon.

Thou art folded, thou art lying
  In the light which is undying
Of thine own joy, and heaven's smile divine;
  All suns and constellations shower   440
  On thee a light, a life, a power
Which doth array thy sphere; thou pourest thine
    On mine, on mine!

The Earth.

I spin beneath my pyramid of night,
　Which points into the heavens dreaming de-
　　light,
Murmuring victorious joy in my enchanted sleep;
　As a youth lulled in love-dreams faintly sigh-
　　ing,
　Under the shadow of his beauty lying,
Which round his rest a watch of light and warmth
　doth keep.

The Moon.

As in the soft and sweet eclipse,　　　　　450
　When soul meets soul on lovers' lips,
High hearts are calm, and brightest eyes are dull;
　So when thy shadow falls on me,
　Then am I mute and still, by thee
Covered; of thy love, Orb most beautiful,
　　　Full, oh, too full!

Thou art speeding round the sun
　Brightest world of many a one;
Green and azure sphere which shinest
　With a light which is divinest　　　　　460
Among all the lamps of Heaven
　To whom life and light is given;
I, thy crystal paramour
　Borne beside thee by a power
Like the polar Paradise,
　Magnet-like of lovers' eyes;
I, a most enamoured maiden
　Whose weak brain is overladen
With the pleasure of her love,
　Maniac-like around thee move　　　　　470
Gazing, an insatiate bride,
　On thy form from every side
Like a Mænad, round the cup
　Which Agave[43] lifted up
In the weird Cadmæan forest.
　Brother, wheresoe'er thou soarest
I must hurry, whirl and follow
　Through the heavens wide and hollow,
Sheltered by the warm embrace
　Of thy soul from hungry space,　　　　　480
Drinking from thy sense and sight
　Beauty, majesty, and might,
As a lover or a chameleon
　Grows like what it looks upon,
As a violet's gentle eye
　Gazes on the azure sky
Until its hue grows like what it beholds,
　As a grey and watery mist

43 the daughter of Cadmus, King of Thebes. She participated in
the woodland orgies of the Bacchic women.

Glows like solid amethyst
Athwart the western mountain it enfolds,　490
　When the sunset sleeps
　　Upon its snow—

The Earth.

And the weak day weeps
　That it should be so.
Oh, gentle Moon, the voice of thy delight
Falls on me like thy clear and tender light
Soothing the seaman, borne the summer night,
　Through isles for ever calm;
Oh, gentle Moon, thy crystal accents pierce
The caverns of my pride's deep universe,　500
Charming the tiger joy, whose tramplings fierce
　Made wounds which need thy balm.
　Panthea. I rise as from a path of sparkling
　　water,
A bath of azure light, among dark rocks,
Out of the stream of sound.
　Ione.　　　　　　　　Ah me! sweet sister,
The stream of sound has ebbed away from us,
And you pretend to rise out of its wave,
Because your words fall like the clear, soft dew
Shaken from a bathing wood-nymph's limbs and
　hair.
　Panthea. Peace! peace! A mighty Power, which
　　is as darkness,　　　　　510
Is rising out of Earth, and from the sky
Is showered like night, and from within the air
Bursts, like eclipse which had been gathered up
Into the pores of sunlight: the bright visions,
Wherein the singing spirits rode and shone,
Gleam like pale meteors through a watery night.
　Ione. There is a sense of words upon mine
　　ear.
　Panthea. An universal sound like words: Oh,
　　list!

Demogorgon.

Thou, Earth, calm empire of a happy soul,
　Sphere of divinest shapes and harmonies,　520
Beautiful orb! gathering as thou dost roll
　The love which paves thy path along the skies:

The Earth.

I hear: I am as a drop of dew that dies.

Demogorgon.

Thou, Moon, which gazest on the nightly Earth
　With wonder, as it gazes upon thee;
Whilst each to men, and beasts, and the swift
　birth
　Of birds, is beauty, love, calm, harmony:

The Moon.

I hear: I am a leaf shaken by thee!

Demogorgon.

Ye Kings of suns and stars, Dæmons and Gods,
  Aetherial Dominations, who possess   530
Elysian, windless, fortunate abodes
  Beyond Heaven's constellated wilderness:

A Voice from above.

Our great Republic hears, we are blest, and
  bless.

Demogorgon.

Ye happy Dead, whom beams of brightest verse
  Are clouds to hide, not colours to portray,
Whether your nature is that universe
  Which once ye saw and suffered—

A Voice from beneath.

                             Or as they
Whom we have left, we change and pass away.

Demogorgon.

Ye elemental Genii, who have homes
  From man's high mind even to the central
    stone   540
Of sullen lead; from heaven's star-fretted domes
  To the dull weed some sea-worm battens on:

A confused Voice.

We hear: thy words waken Oblivion.

Demogorgon.

Spirits, whose homes are flesh: ye beasts and
    birds,
  Ye worms, and fish; ye living leaves and buds;
Lightning and wind; and ye untameable herds,
  Meteors and mists, which throng air's soli-
    tudes:—

A Voice.

Thy voice to us is wind among still woods.

Demogorgon.

Man, who wert once a despot and a slave;
  A dupe and a deceiver; a decay;   550
A traveller from the cradle to the grave
  Through the dim night of this immortal day:

All.

Speak: thy strong words may never pass away.

Demogorgon.

This is the day, which down the void abysm

At the Earth-born's spell[44] yawns for Heaven's
    despotism,
  And Conquest is dragged captive through the
    deep:
Love, from its awful throne of patient power
In the wise heart, from the last giddy hour
  Of dread endurance, from the slippery, steep,
And narrow verge of crag-like agony, springs 560
And folds over the world its healing wings.

Gentleness, Virtue, Wisdom, and Endurance,
These are the seals of that most firm assurance
  Which bars the pit over Destruction's strength;
And if, with infirm hand, Eternity,
Mother of many acts and hours, should free
  The serpent that would clasp her with his
    length;
These are the spells by which to reassume
An empire o'er the disentangled doom.

To suffer woes which Hope thinks infinite;   570
To forgive wrongs darker than death or night;
  To defy Power, which seems omnipotent;
To love, and bear; to hope till Hope creates
From its own wreck the thing it contemplates;
  Neither to change, nor falter, nor repent;
This, like thy glory, Titan, is to be
Good, great and joyous, beautiful and free;
This is alone Life, Joy, Empire, and Victory.

              1818–19   1820

THE CENCI

A TRAGEDY IN FIVE ACTS

[Mrs. Shelley in her note to *The Cenci* gives an excellent account of the circumstances of its composition:
  'The sort of mistake that Shelley made as to the extent
of his own genius and powers, which led him deviously
at first, but lastly into the direct track that enabled him
fully to develop them, is a curious instance of his modesty of feeling, and of the methods which the human
mind uses at once to deceive itself, and yet, in its very
delusion, to make its way out of error into the path
which Nature has marked out as its right one. He often
incited me to attempt the writing a tragedy: he conceived that I possessed some dramatic talent, and he was
always most earnest and energetic in his exhortations
that I should cultivate any talent I possessed, to the utmost. I entertained a truer estimate of my powers; and
above all (though at that time not exactly aware of the
fact) I was far too young to have any chance of succeeding, even moderately, in a species of composition that
requires a greater scope of experience in, and sympathy
with, human passion than could then have fallen to my
lot,—or than any perhaps, except Shelley, ever possessed, even at the age of twenty-six, at which he wrote
The Cenci.

---

44 the spell of Prometheus.

'On the other hand, Shelley most erroneously conceived himself to be destitute of this talent. He believed that one of the first requisites was the capacity of forming and following-up a story or plot. He fancied himself to be defective in this portion of imagination: it was that which gave him least pleasure in the writings of others, though he laid great store by it as the proper framework to support the sublimest efforts of poetry. He asserted that he was too metaphysical and abstract, too fond of the theoretical and the ideal, to succeed as a tragedian. It perhaps is not strange that I shared this opinion with himself; for he had hitherto shown no inclination for, nor given any specimen of his powers in framing and supporting the interest of a story, either in prose or verse. Once or twice, when he attempted such, he had speedily thrown it aside, as being even disagreeable to him as an occupation.

'The subject he had suggested for a tragedy was Charles I: and he had written to me: "Remember, remember Charles I. I have been already imagining how you would conduct some scenes. The second volume of *St. Leon* begins with this proud and true sentiment: 'There is nothing which the human mind can conceive which it may not execute.' Shakespeare was only a human being." These words were written in 1818, while we were in Lombardy, when he little thought how soon a work of his own would prove a proud comment on the passage he quoted. When in Rome, in 1819, a friend put into our hands the old manuscript account of the story of the Cenci. We visited the Colonna and Doria palaces, where the portraits of Beatrice were to be found; and her beauty cast the reflection of its own grace over her appalling story. Shelley's imagination became strongly excited, and he urged the subject to me as one fitted for a tragedy. More than ever I felt my incompetence; but I entreated him to write it instead; and he began, and proceeded swiftly, urged on by intense sympathy with the sufferings of the human beings whose passions, so long cold in the tomb, he revived, and gifted with poetic language. This tragedy is the only one of his works that he communicated to me during its progress. We talked over the arrangement of the scenes together. I speedily saw the great mistake we had made, and triumphed in the discovery of the new talent brought to light from that mine of wealth (never, alas, through his untimely death, worked to its depths)—his richly gifted mind.

'We suffered a severe affliction in Rome by the loss of our eldest child, who was of such beauty and promise as to cause him deservedly to be the idol of our hearts. We left the capital of the world, anxious for a time to escape a spot associated too intimately with his presence and loss.[1] Some friends of ours were residing in the neighbourhood of Leghorn, and we took a small house, Villa Valsovano, about half-way between the town and Monte Nero, where we remained during the summer. Our villa was situated in the midst of a *podere;*[2] the peasants sang as they worked beneath our windows, during the heats of a very hot season, and in the evening the water-wheel creaked as the process of irrigation went on, and the fireflies flashed from among the myrtle hedges: Nature was bright, sunshiny, and cheerful, or diversified by storms of a majestic terror, such as we had never before witnessed.

'At the top of the house there was a sort of terrace. There is often such in Italy, generally roofed: this one was very small, yet not only roofed but glazed. This Shelley made his study; it looked out on a wide prospect of fertile country, and commanded a view of the near sea. The storms that sometimes varied our day showed themselves most picturesquely as they were driven across the ocean; sometimes the dark lurid clouds dipped towards the waves, and became waterspouts that churned up the waters beneath, as they were chased onward and scattered by the tempest. At other times the dazzling sunlight and heat made it almost intolerable to every other; but Shelley basked in both, and his health and spirits revived under their influence. In this airy cell he wrote the principal part of *The Cenci*. He was making a study of Calderon at the time, reading his best tragedies with an accomplished lady living near us, to whom his letter from Leghorn was addressed during the following year. He admired Calderon, both for his poetry and his dramatic genius; but it shows his judgement and originality that, though greatly struck by his first acquaintance with the Spanish poet, none of his peculiarities crept into the composition of *The Cenci;* and there is no trace of his new studies, except in that passage to which he himself alludes as suggested by one in *El Purgatorio de San Patricio*.

'Shelley wished *The Cenci* to be acted. He was not a playgoer, being of such fastidious taste that he was easily disgusted by the bad filling-up of the inferior parts. While preparing for our departure from England, however, he saw Miss O'Neil several times. She was then in the zenith of her glory; and Shelley was deeply moved by her impersonation of several parts, and by the graceful sweetness, the intense pathos, and sublime vehemence of passion she displayed. She was often in his thoughts as he wrote: and, when he had finished, he became anxious that his tragedy should be acted, and receive the advantage of having this accomplished actress to fill the part of the heroine. . . .

'The play was accordingly sent to Mr. Harris. He pronounced the subject to be so objectionable that he could not even submit the part to Miss O'Neil for perusal, but expressed his desire that the author would write a tragedy on some other subject, which he would gladly accept. Shelley printed a small edition at Leghorn, to ensure its correctness; as he was much annoyed by the many mistakes that crept into his text when distance prevented him from correcting the press.

'Universal approbation soon stamped *The Cenci* as the best tragedy of modern times. Writing concerning it, Shelley said: "I have been cautious to avoid the introducing faults of youthful composition; diffuseness, a profusion of inapplicable imagery, vagueness, generality, and, as Hamlet says, *words, words*." There is nothing that is not purely dramatic throughout; and the character of Beatrice, proceeding, from vehement struggle, to horror, to deadly resolution, and lastly to the elevated dignity of calm suffering, joined to passionate tenderness and pathos, is touched with hues so vivid and so beautiful that the poet seems to have read intimately the secrets of the noble heart imaged in the lovely

---

[1] Such feelings haunted him when, in *The Cenci*, he makes Beatrice speak to Cardinal Camillo of

> 'that fair blue-eyed child
> Who was the lodestar of your life':—

and say—

> 'All see, since his most swift and piteous death,
> That day and night, and heaven and earth, and time,
> And all the things hoped for or done therein
> Are changed to you, through your exceeding grief.'
> —(Mrs. Shelley.)

[2] a farm consisting of several cultivated fields with a workman's house on it.

countenance of the unfortunate girl. The Fifth Act is a masterpiece. It is the finest thing he ever wrote, and may claim proud comparison not only with any contemporary, but preceding, poet. The varying feelings of Beatrice are expressed with passionate, heart-reaching eloquence. Every character has a voice that echoes truth in its tones. It is curious, to one acquainted with the written story, to mark the success with which the poet has inwoven the real incidents of the tragedy into his scenes, and yet, through the power of poetry, has obliterated all that would otherwise have shown too harsh or too hideous in the picture. His success was a double triumph; and often after he was earnestly entreated to write again in a style that commanded popular favour, while it was not less instinct with truth and genius. But the bent of his mind went the other way; and, even when employed on subjects whose interest depended on character and incident, he would start off in another direction, and leave the delineations of human passion, which he could depict in so able a manner, for fantastic creations of his fancy, or the expression of those opinions and sentiments, with regard to human nature and its destiny, a desire to diffuse which was the master passion of his soul.']

PREFACE

A Manuscript was communicated to me during my travels in Italy, which was copied from the archives of the Cenci Palace at Rome, and contains a detailed account of the horrors which ended in the extinction of one of the noblest and richest families of that city during the Pontificate of Clement VIII, in the year 1599. The story is, that an old man having spent his life in debauchery and wickedness, conceived at length an implacable hatred towards his children; which showed itself towards one daughter under the form of an incestuous passion, aggravated by every circumstance of cruelty and violence. This daughter, after long and vain attempts to escape from what she considered a perpetual contamination both of body and mind, at length plotted with her mother-in-law and brother to murder their common tyrant. The young maiden, who was urged to this tremendous deed by an impulse which overpowered its horror, was evidently a most gentle and amiable being, a creature formed to adorn and be admired, and thus violently thwarted from her nature by the necessity of circumstance and opinion. The deed was quickly discovered, and, in spite of the most earnest prayers made to the Pope by the highest persons in Rome, the criminals were put to death. The old man had during his life repeatedly bought his pardon from the Pope for capital crimes of the most enormous and unspeakable kind, at the price of a hundred thousand crowns; the death therefore of his victims can scarcely be accounted for by the love of justice. The Pope, among other motives for severity, probably felt that whoever killed the Count Cenci deprived his treasury of a certain and copious source of revenue.[3] Such a story, if told so as to present to the reader all the feelings of those who once acted it, their hopes and fears, their confidences and misgivings, their various interests, passions, and opinions, acting upon and with each other, yet all conspiring to one tremendous end, would be as

a light to make apparent some of the most dark and secret caverns of the human heart.

On my arrival at Rome I found that the story of the Cenci was a subject not to be mentioned in Italian society without awakening a deep and breathless interest; and that the feelings of the company never failed to incline to a romantic pity for the wrongs, and a passionate exculpation of the horrible deed to which they urged her, who has been mingled two centuries with the common dust. All ranks of people knew the outlines of this history, and participated in the overwhelming interest which it seems to have the magic of exciting in the human heart. I had a copy of Guido's picture of Beatrice which is preserved in the Colonna Palace, and my servant instantly recognized it as the portrait of *La Cenci*.

This national and universal interest which the story produces and has produced for two centuries and among all ranks of people in a great City, where the imagination is kept for ever active and awake, first suggested to me the conception of its fitness for a dramatic purpose. In fact it is a tragedy which has already received, from its capacity of awakening and sustaining the sympathy of men, approbation and success. Nothing remained as I imagined, but to clothe it to the apprehensions of my countrymen in such language and action as would bring it home to their hearts. The deepest and the sublimest tragic compositions, *King Lear* and the two plays in which the tale of Œdipus is told, were stories which already existed in tradition, as matters of popular belief and interest, before Shakespeare and Sophocles made them familiar to the sympathy of all succeeding generations of mankind.

This story of the Cenci is indeed eminently fearful and monstrous: anything like a dry exhibition of it on the stage would be insupportable. The person who would treat such a subject must increase the ideal, and diminish the actual horror of the events, so that the pleasure which arises from the poetry which exists in these tempestuous sufferings and crimes may mitigate the pain of the contemplation of the moral deformity from which they spring. There must also be nothing attempted to make the exhibition subservient to what is vulgarly termed a moral purpose. The highest moral purpose aimed at in the highest species of the drama, is the teaching the human heart, through its sympathies and antipathies, the knowledge of itself; in proportion to the possession of which knowledge, every human being is wise, just, sincere, tolerant and kind. If dogmas can do more, it is well: but a drama is no fit place for the enforcement of them. Undoubtedly, no person can be truly dishonoured by the act of another; and the fit return to make to the most enormous injuries is kindness and forebearance, and a resolution to convert the injurer from his dark passions by peace and love. Revenge, retaliation, atonement, are pernicious mistakes. If Beatrice had thought in this manner she would have been wiser and better; but she would never have been a tragic character: the few whom such an exhibition would have interested, could never have been sufficiently interested for a dramatic purpose, from the want of finding sympathy in their interest among the mass who surround them. It is in the restless and anatomizing casuistry with which men seek the justification of Beatrice, yet feel that she has done what needs justification; it is in the superstitious horror with which they contemplate alike her wrongs and their revenge, that the dramatic character of what she did and suffered, consists.

---

3 The Papal Government formerly took the most extraordinary precautions against the publicity of facts which offer so tragical a demonstration of its own wickedness and weakness; so that the communication of the MS. had become, until very lately, a matter of some difficulty.—(Shelley.)

I have endeavoured as nearly as possible to represent the characters as they probably were, and have sought to avoid the error of making them actuated by my own conceptions of right or wrong, false or true: thus under a thin veil converting names and actions of the sixteenth century into cold impersonations of my own mind. They are represented as Catholics, and as Catholics deeply tinged with religion. To a Protestant apprehension there will appear something unnatural in the earnest and perpetual sentiment of the relations between God and men which pervade the tragedy of the Cenci. It will especially be startled at the combination of an undoubting persuasion of the truth of the popular religion with a cool and determined perseverance in enormous guilt. But religion in Italy is not, as in Protestant countries, a cloak to be worn on particular days; or a passport which those who do not wish to be railed at carry with them to exhibit; or a gloomy passion for penetrating the impenetrable mysteries of our being, which terrifies its possessor at the darkness of the abyss to the brink of which it has conducted him. Religion coexists, as it were, in the mind of an Italian Catholic, with a faith in that of which all men have the most certain knowledge. It is interwoven with the whole fabric of life. It is adoration, faith, submission, penitence, blind admiration; not a rule for moral conduct. It has no necessary connection with any one virtue. The most atrocious villain may be rigidly devout, and without any shock to established faith, confess himself to be so. Religion pervades intensely the whole frame of society, and is according to the temper of the mind which it inhabits, a passion, a persuasion, an excuse, a refuge; never a check. Cenci himself built a chapel in the court of his Palace, and dedicated it to St. Thomas the Apostle, and established masses for the peace of his soul. Thus in the first scene of the fourth act Lucretia's design in exposing herself to the consequences of an expostulation with Cenci after having administered the opiate, was to induce him by a feigned tale to confess himself before death; this being esteemed by Catholics as essential to salvation; and she only relinquishes her purpose when she perceives that her perseverance would expose Beatrice to new outrages.

I have avoided with great care in writing this play the introduction of what is commonly called mere poetry, and I imagine there will scarcely be found a detached simile or a single isolated description, unless Beatrice's description of the chasm appointed for her father's murder should be judged to be of that nature.[4]

In a dramatic composition the imagery and the passion should interpenetrate one another, the former being reserved simply for the full development and illustration of the latter. Imagination is as the immortal God which should assume flesh for the redemption of mortal passion. It is thus that the most remote and the most familiar imagery may alike be fit for dramatic purposes when employed in the illustration of strong feeling, which raises what is low, and levels to the apprehension that which is lofty, casting over all the shadow of its own greatness. In other respects, I have written more carelessly; that is, without an over-fastidious and learned choice of words. In this respect I entirely agree with those modern critics who assert that in order to move men to true sympathy we must use the familiar language of men, and that our great ancestors the ancient English poets are the writers, a study of whom might incite us to do that for our own age which they have done for theirs. But it must be the real language of men in general and not that of any particular class to whose society the writer happens to belong. So much for what I have attempted; I need not be assured that success is a very different matter; particularly for one whose attention has but newly been awakened to the study of dramatic literature.

I endeavoured whilst at Rome to observe such monuments of this story as might be accessible to a stranger. The portrait of Beatrice at the Colonna Palace is admirable as a work of art: it was taken by Guido during her confinement in prison. But it is most interesting as a just representation of one of the loveliest specimens of the workmanship of Nature. There is a fixed and pale composure upon the features: she seems sad and stricken down in spirit, yet the despair thus expressed is lightened by the patience of gentleness. Her head is bound with folds of white drapery from which the yellow strings of her golden hair escape, and fall about her neck. The moulding of her face is exquisitely delicate; the eyebrows are distinct and arched: the lips have that permanent meaning of imagination and sensibility which suffering has not repressed and which it seems as if death scarcely could extinguish. Her forehead is large and clear; her eyes, which we are told were remarkable for their vivacity, are swollen with weeping and lustreless, but beautifully tender and serene. In the whole mien there is a simplicity and dignity which, united with her exquisite loveliness and deep sorrow, are inexpressibly pathetic. Beatrice Cenci appears to have been one of those rare persons in whom energy and gentleness dwell together without destroying one another: her nature was simple and profound. The crimes and miseries in which she was an actor and a sufferer are as the mask and the mantle in which circumstances clothed her for her impersonation on the scene of the world.

The Cenci Palace is of great extent; and though in part modernized, there yet remains a vast and gloomy pile of feudal architecture in the same state as during the dreadful scenes which are the subject of this tragedy. The Palace is situated in an obscure corner of Rome, near the quarter of the Jews, and from the upper windows you see the immense ruins of Mount Palatine half hidden under their profuse overgrowth of trees. There is a court in one part of the Palace (perhaps that in which Cenci built the Chapel to St. Thomas), supported by granite columns and adorned with antique friezes of fine workmanship, and built up, according to the ancient Italian fashion, with balcony over balcony of open-work. One of the gates of the Pallace formed of immense stones and leading through a passage, dark and lofty and opening into gloomy subterranean chambers, struck me particularly.

Of the Castle of Petrella, I could obtain no further information than that which is to be found in the manuscript.

---

4 An idea in this speech was suggested by a most sublime passage in *El Purgatorio de San Patricio* of Calderon; the only plagiarism which I have intentionally committed in the whole piece.—(Shelley.)

DRAMATIS PERSONÆ

COUNT FRANCESCO CENCI.	SAVELLA, *the Pope's Legate.*
GIACOMO ⎱ *his Sons.*	OLIMPIO ⎱ *Assassins.*
BERNARDO ⎰	MARZIO ⎰
CARDINAL CAMILLO.	ANDREA, *Servant to Cenci.*

ORSINO, *a Prelate.*   Nobles, Judges, Guards,
                                          Servants.

LUCRETIA, *Wife of* CENCI, *and Step-mother of his children.*
          BEATRICE, *his Daughter.*

The SCENE lies principally in Rome, but changes during
the Fourth Act to Petrella, a castle among the Apulian
                    Apennines.
TIME. During the Pontificate of Clement VIII.

ACT I

SCENE I.—*An Apartment in the Cenci Palace.*
Enter COUNT CENCI, *and* CARDINAL CAMILLO.

Camillo. That matter of the murder is hushed
      up
If you consent to yield his Holiness
Your fief that lies beyond the Pincian gate.[5]—
It needed all my interest in the conclave
To bend him to this point: he said that you
Bought perilous impunity with your gold;
That crimes like yours if once or twice com-
      pounded
Enriched the Church, and respited from hell
An erring soul which might repent and live:—
But that the glory and the interest   10
Of the high throne he fills, little consist
With making it a daily mart of guilt
As manifold and hideous as the deeds
Which you scarce hide from men's revolted eyes.
  Cenci. The third of my possessions—let it go!
Ay, I once heard the nephew of the Pope
Had sent his architect to view the ground,
Meaning to build a villa on my vines
The next time I compounded with his uncle:
I little thought he should outwit me so!   20
Henceforth no witness—not the lamp—shall see
That which the vassal threatened to divulge
Whose throat is choked with dust for his reward.
The deed he saw could not have rated higher
Than his most worthless life:—it angers me!
Respited me from Hell!—So may the Devil
Respite their souls from Heaven. No doubt Pope
      Clement,
And his most charitable nephews, pray
That the Apostle Peter and the Saints
Will grant for their sake that I long enjoy   30
Strength, wealth, and pride, and lust, and length
      of days
Wherein to act the deeds which are the stewards
Of their revenue.—But much yet remains
To which they show no title.
  Camillo.   Oh, Count Cenci!

---

5 on the Pincian Hill, which is located in the northern part of
Rome and extends in a long ridge east of the Tiber.

So much that thou mightst honourably live
And reconcile thyself with thine own heart
And with thy God, and with the offended world.
How hideously look deeds of lust and blood
Through those snow white and venerable
      hairs!—
Your children should be sitting round you
      now,   40
But that you fear to read upon their looks
The shame and misery you have written there.
Where is your wife? Where is your gentle daugh-
      ter?
Methinks her sweet looks, which make all things
      else
Beauteous and glad, might kill the fiend within
      you.
Why is she barred from all society
But her own strange and uncomplaining wrongs?
Talk with me, Count,—you know I mean you
      well.
I stood beside your dark and fiery youth
Watching its bold and bad career, as men   50
Watch meteors, but it vanished not—I marked
Your desperate and remorseless manhood; now
Do I behold you in dishonoured age
Charged with a thousand unrepented crimes.
Yet I have ever hoped you would amend,
And in that hope have saved your life three
      times.
  Cenci. For which Aldobrandino owes you now
My fief beyond the Pincian.—Cardinal,
One thing, I pray you, recollect henceforth,
And so we shall converse with less restraint. 60
A man you knew spoke of my wife and daugh-
      ter—
He was accustomed to frequent my house;
So the next day *his* wife and daughter came
And asked if I had seen him; and I smiled:
I think they never saw him any more.
  Camillo. Thou execrable man, beware!—
  Cenci.   Of thee?
Nay this is idle:—We should know each other.
As to my character for what men call crime
Seeing I please my senses as I list,
And vindicate that right with force or guile, 70
It is a public matter, and I care not
If I discuss it with you. I may speak
Alike to you and my own conscious heart—
For you give out that you have half reformed me,
Therefore strong vanity will keep you silent
If fear should not; both will, I do not doubt.
All men delight in sensual luxury,
All men enjoy revenge; and most exult
Over the tortures they can never feel—

Flattering their secret peace with others' pain. 80
But I delight in nothing else. I love
The sight of agony, and the sense of joy,
When this shall be another's, and that mine.
And I have no remorse and little fear,
Which are, I think, the checks of other men.
This mood has grown upon me, until now
Any design my captious fancy makes
The picture of its wish, and it forms none
But such as men like you would start to know,
Is as my natural food and rest debarred   90
Until it be accomplished.

   Camillo.   Art thou not
Most miserable?

   Cenci.   Why, miserable?—
No.—I am what your theologians call
Hardened;—which they must be in impudence,
So to revile a man's peculiar taste.
True, I was happier than I am, while yet
Manhood remained to act the thing I thought;
While lust was sweeter than revenge; and now
Invention palls:—Ay, we must all grow old—
And but that there yet remains a deed to act   100
Whose horror might make sharp an appetite
Duller than mine—I'd do—I know not what.
When I was young I thought of nothing else
But pleasure; and I fed on honey sweets:
Men, by St. Thomas! cannot live like bees,
And I grew tired:—yet, till I killed a foe,
And heard his groans, and heard his children's
   groans,
Knew I not what delight was else on earth,
Which now delights me little. I the rather
Look on such pangs as terror ill conceals,   110
The dry fixed eyeball; the pale quivering lip,
Which tell me that the spirit weeps within
Tears bitterer than the bloody sweat of Christ.
I rarely kill the body, which preserves,
Like a strong prison, the soul within my power,
Wherein I feed it with the breath of fear
For hourly pain.

   Camillo.   Hell's most abandoned fiend
Did never, in the drunkenness of guilt,
Speak to his heart as now you speak to me;
I thank my God that I believe you not.   120

           Enter ANDREA.

   Andrea. My Lord, a gentleman from Salamanca
Would speak with you.

   Cenci.   Bid him attend me in
The grand saloon.   [*Exit* ANDREA.

   Camillo.   Farewell; and I will pray
Almighty God that thy false, impious words
Tempt not his spirit to abandon thee.

                  [*Exit* CAMILLO.

   Cenci. The third of my possessions! I must use
Close husbandry, or gold, the old man's sword,
Falls from my withered hand. But yesterday
There came an order from the Pope to make
Fourfold provision for my cursèd sons;   130
Whom I had sent from Rome to Salamanca,
Hoping some accident might cut them off;
And meaning if I could to starve them there.
I pray thee, God, send some quick death upon
   them!
Bernardo and my wife could not be worse
If dead and damned:—then, as to Beatrice—
         [*Looking around him suspiciously.*
I think they cannot hear me at that door;
What if they should? And yet I need not speak
Though the heart triumphs with itself in words.
O, thou most silent air, that shalt not hear   140
What now I think! Thou, pavement, which I
   tread
Towards her chamber,—let your echoes talk
Of my imperious step scorning surprise,
But not of my intent!—Andrea!

         Enter ANDREA.

   Andrea.   My lord?

   Cenci. Bid Beatrice attend me in her chamber
This evening:—no, at midnight and alone.

                  [*Exeunt.*

SCENE II.—*A Garden of the Cenci Palace. Enter*
   BEATRICE *and* ORSINO, *as in conversation.*

   Beatrice. Pervert not truth,
Orsino. You remember where we held
That conversation;—nay, we see the spot
Even from this cypress;—two long years are past
Since, on an April midnight, underneath
The moonlight ruins of mount Palatine,
I did confess to you my secret mind.

   Orsino. You said you loved me then.

   Beatrice.   You are a Priest,
Speak to me not of love.

   Orsino.   I may obtain
The dispensation of the Pope to marry.   10
Because I am a Priest do you believe
Your image, as the hunter some struck deer,
Follows me not whether I wake or sleep?

   Beatrice. As I have said, speak to me not of
   love;
Had you a dispensation I have not;
Nor will I leave this home of misery
Whilst my poor Bernard, and that gentle lady
To whom I owe life, and these virtuous thoughts,
Must suffer what I still have strength to share.
Alas, Orsino! All the love that once   20
I felt for you, is turned to bitter pain.

Ours was a youthful contract, which you first
Broke, by assuming vows no Pope will loose.
And thus I love you still, but holily,
Even as a sister or a spirit might;
And so I swear a cold fidelity.
And it is well perhaps we shall not marry.
You have a sly, equivocating vein
That suits me not.—Ah, wretched that I am!
Where shall I turn? Even now you look on me 30
As you were not my friend, and as if you
Discovered that I thought so, with false smiles
Making my true suspicion seem your wrong.
Ah, no! forgive me; sorrow makes me seem
Sterner than else my nature might have been;
I have a weight of melancholy thoughts,
And they forbode,—but what can they forbode
Worse than I now endure?

    Orsino. All will be well.
Is the petition yet prepared? You know
My zeal for all you wish, sweet Beatrice; 40
Doubt not but I will use my utmost skill
So that the Pope attend to your complaint.

    Beatrice. Your zeal for all I wish;—Ah me, you
      are cold!
Your utmost skill . . . speak but one word . . .
    (*aside*) Alas!
Weak and deserted creature that I am,
Here I stand bickering with my only friend!
                     [*To* ORSINO.
This night my father gives a sumptuous feast,
Orsino; he has heard some happy news
From Salamanca, from my brothers there,
And with this outward show of love he mocks 50
His inward hate. 'Tis bold hypocrisy,
For he would gladlier celebrate their deaths,
Which I have heard him pray for on his knees:
Great God! that such a father should be mine!
But there is mighty preparation made,
And all our kin, the Cenci, will be there,
And all the chief nobility of Rome.
And he has bidden me and my pale Mother
Attire ourselves in festival array.
Poor lady! She expects some happy change 60
In his dark spirit from this act; I none.
At supper I will give you the petition:
Till when—farewell.

    Orsino. Farewell. (*Exit* BEATRICE.) I know the
    Pope
Will ne'er absolve me from my priestly vow
But by absolving me from the revenue
Of many a wealthy see; and, Beatrice,
I think to win thee at an easier rate.
Nor shall he read her eloquent petition:
He might bestow her on some poor relation

Of his sixth cousin, as he did her sister, 70
And I should be debarred from all access.
Then as to what she suffers from her father,
In all this there is much exaggeration:—
Old men are testy and will have their way;
A man may stab his enemy, or his vassal,
And live a free life as to wine or women,
And with a peevish temper may return
To a dull home, and rate his wife and children;
Daughters and wives call this foul tyranny.
I shall be well content if on my conscience 80
There rest no heavier sin than what they suffer
From the devices of my love—a net
From which she shall escape not. Yet I fear
Her subtle mind, her awe-inspiring gaze,
Whose beams anatomize me nerve by nerve
And lay me bare, and make me blush to see
My hidden thoughts.—Ah, no! A friendless girl
Who clings to me, as to her only hope:—
I were a fool, not less than if a panther
Were panic-stricken by the antelope's eye, 90
If she escape me.   [*Exit.*

SCENE III.—*A Magnificent Hall in the Cenci Palace. A Banquet. Enter* CENCI, LUCRETIA, BEATRICE, ORSINO, CAMILLO, NOBLES.

    Cenci. Welcome, my friends and kinsmen; wel-
    come ye,
Princes and Cardinals, pillars of the church,
Whose presence honours our festivity.
I have too long lived like an anchorite,
And in my absence from your merry meetings
An evil word is gone abroad of me;
But I do hope that you, my noble friends,
When you have shared the entertainment here,
And heard the pious cause for which 'tis given,
And we have pledged a health or two together, 10
Will think me flesh and blood as well as you;
Sinful indeed, for Adam made all so,
But tender-hearted, meek and pitiful.

    First Guest. In truth, my Lord, you seem too
      light of heart,
Too sprightly and companionable a man,
To act the deeds that rumour pins on you.
(*To his Companion.*) I never saw such blithe and
    open cheer
In any eye!

    Second Guest. Some most desired event,
In which we all demand a common joy,
Has brought us hither; let us hear it, Count. 20

    Cenci. It is indeed a most desired event.
If, when a parent from a parent's heart
Lifts from this earth to the great Father of all
A prayer, both when he lays him down to sleep,

And when he rises up from dreaming it;
One supplication, one desire, one hope,
That he would grant a wish for his two sons,
Even all that he demands in their regard—
And suddenly beyond his dearest hope
It is accomplished, he should then rejoice,   30
And call his friends and kinsmen to a feast,
And task their love to grace his merriment,—
Then honour me thus far— for I am he.
    Beatrice (to LUCRETIA). Great God! How hor-
    rible! Some dreadful ill
Must have befallen my brothers.
    Lucretia.   Fear not, Child,
He speaks too frankly.
    Beatrice.   Ah! My blood runs cold.
I fear that wicked laughter round his eye,
Which wrinkles up the skin even to the hair.
    Cenci. Here are the letters brought from Sala-
    manca;
Beatrice, read them to your mother. God!   40
I thank thee! In one night didst thou perform,
By ways inscrutable, the thing I sought.
My disobedient and rebellious sons
Are dead!—Why, dead!—What means this
    change of cheer?
You hear me not, I tell you they are dead;
And they will need no food or raiment more:
The tapers that did light them the dark way
Are their last cost. The Pope, I think, will not
Expect I should maintain them in their coffins.
Rejoice with me—my heart is wondrous glad. 50
    [LUCRETIA *sinks, half fainting;* BEATRICE
                          supports her.
    Beatrice. It is not true!—Dear lady, pray look
    up.
Had it been true, there is a God in Heaven,
He would not live to boast of such a boon.
Unnatural man, thou knowest that it is false.
    Cenci. Ay, as the word of God; whom here I
    call
To witness that I speak the sober truth;—
And whose most favouring Providence was
    shown
Even in the manner of their deaths. For Rocco
Was kneeling at the mass, with sixteen others,
When the church fell and crushed him to a
    mummy,   60
The rest escaped unhurt. Cristofano
Was stabbed in error by a jealous man,
Whilst she he loved was sleeping with his rival;
All in the self-same hour of the same night;
Which shows that Heaven has special care of me.
I beg those friends who love me, that they mark
The day a feast upon their calendars.

It was the twenty-seventh of December:
Ay, read the letters if you doubt my oath.
    [*The Assembly appears confused; several of*
                       the guests rise.
    First Guest. Oh, horrible! I will depart—
    Second Guest.   And I.—
    Third Guest.   No, stay! 70
I do believe it is some jest; though faith!
'Tis mocking us somewhat too solemnly.
I think his son has married the Infanta,
Or found a mine of gold in El Dorado;
'Tis but to season some such news; stay, stay!
I see 'tis only raillery by his smile.
    Cenci (filling a bowl of wine, and lifting it up).
Oh, thou bright wine whose purple splen-
    dour leaps
And bubbles gaily in this golden bowl
Under the lamplight, as my spirits do,
To hear the death of my accursèd sons!   80
Could I believe thou wert their mingled blood,
Then would I taste thee like a sacrament,
And pledge with thee the mighty Devil in Hell,
Who, if a father's curses, as men say,
Climb with swift wings after their children's
    souls,
And drag them from the very throne of Heaven,
Now triumphs in my triumph!—But thou art
Superfluous; I have drunken deep of joy,
And I will taste no other wine to-night.
Here, Andrea! Bear the bowl around.
    A Guest (rising).   Thou wretch! 90
Will none among this noble company
Check the abandoned villain?
    Camillo.   For God's sake
Let me dismiss the guests! You are insane,
Some ill will come of this.
    Second Guest.   Seize, silence him!
    First Guest. I will!
    Third Guest.   And I!
    Cenci (addressing those who rise with a threat-
ening gesture).
                 Who moves? Who speaks?
                 (turning to the Company)
                      'tis nothing,
Enjoy yourselves.—Beware! For my revenge
Is as the sealed commission of a king
That kills, and none dare name the murderer.
    [*The Banquet is broken up; several of the*
                     Guests are departing.
    Beatrice. I do entreat you, go not, noble guests;
What, although tyranny and impious hate   100
Stand sheltered by a father's hoary hair?
What, if 'tis he who clothed us in these limbs
Who tortures them, and triumphs? What, if we,

The desolate and the dead, were his own flesh,
His children and his wife, whom he is bound
To love and shelter? Shall we therefore find
No refuge in this merciless wide world?
O think what deep wrongs must have blotted out
First love, then reverence in a child's prone mind,
Till it thus vanquish shame and fear! O
    think!   110
I have borne much, and kissed the sacred hand
Which crushed us to the earth, and thought its
    stroke
Was perhaps some paternal chastisement!
Have excused much, doubted; and when no
    doubt
Remained, have sought by patience, love, and
    tears
To soften him, and when this could not be
I have knelt down through the long sleepless
    nights
And lifted up to God, the Father of all,
Passionate prayers: and when these were not
    heard
I have still borne,—until I meet you here,   120
Princes and kinsmen, at this hideous feast
Given at my brothers' deaths. Two yet remain,
His wife remains and I, whom if ye save not,
Ye may soon share such merriment again
As fathers make over their children's graves.
O Prince Colonna, thou art our near kinsman,
Cardinal, thou art the Pope's chamberlain,
Camillo, thou art chief justiciary,
Take us away!
    Cenci. (*He has been conversing with* CAMILLO
    during the first part of BEATRICE'S *speech; he*
    hears the conclusion, and now advances.)
            I hope my good friends here
Will think of their own daughters—or per-
    haps   130
Of their own throats—before they lend an ear
To this wild girl.
    Beatrice (*not noticing the words of Cenci*). Dare
    no one look on me?
None answer? Can one tyrant overbear
The sense of many best and wisest men?
Or is it that I sue not in some form
Of scrupulous law, that ye deny my suit?
O God! That I were buried with my brothers!
And that the flowers of this departed spring
Were fading on my grave! And that my father
Were celebrating now one feast for all!   140
    Camillo. A bitter wish for one so young and
    gentle;
Can we do nothing?
    Colonna.   Nothing that I see.

Count Cenci were a dangerous enemy:
Yet I would second any one.
    A Cardinal.   And I.
    Cenci. Retire to your chamber, insolent girl!
    Beatrice. Retire thou, impious man! Ay, hide
    thyself
Where never eye can look upon thee more!
Wouldst thou have honour and obedience
Who art a torturer? Father, never dream
Though thou mayst overbear this company,   150
But ill must come of ill.—Frown not on me!
Haste, hide thyself, lest with avenging looks
My brothers' ghosts should hunt thee from thy
    seat!
Cover thy face from every living eye,
And start if thou but hear a human step:
Seek out some dark and silent corner, there,
Bow thy white head before offended God,
And we will kneel around, and fervently
Pray that he pity both ourselves and thee.
    Cenci. My friends, I do lament this insane
    girl   160
Has spoilt the mirth of our festivity.
Good night, farewell; I will not make you longer
Spectators of our dull domestic quarrels.
Another time.—
        [*Exeunt all but* CENCI *and* BEATRICE.
               My brain is swimming round;
Give me a bowl of wine!   [*To* BEATRICE.
               Thou painted viper!
Beast that thou art! Fair and yet terrible!
I know a charm shall make thee meek and tame,
Now get thee from my sight!   [*Exit* BEATRICE.
               Here, Andrea,
Fill up this goblet with Greek wine. I said
I would not drink this evening; but I must;   170
For, strange to say, I feel my spirits fail
With thinking what I have decreed to do.
               [*Drinking the wine.*
Be thou the resolution of quick youth
Within my veins, and manhood's purpose stern,
And age's firm, cold, subtle villainy;
As if thou wert indeed my children's blood
Which I did thirst to drink! The charm works
    well;
It must be done; it shall be done, I swear!
                      [*Exit.*

ACT II

SCENE I.—*An Apartment in the Cenci Palace.*
    Enter LUCRETIA *and* BERNARDO.

    Lucretia. Weep not, my gentle boy; he struck
    but me
Who have borne deeper wrongs. In truth, if he

Had killed me, he had done a kinder deed.
O God, Almighty, do Thou look upon us,
We have no other friend but only Thee!
Yet weep not; though I love you as my own,
I am not your true mother.
    Bernardo.   O more, more,
Than ever mother was to any child,
That have you been to me! Had he not been
My father, do you think that I should weep!   10
    Lucretia. Alas! Poor boy, what else couldst
      thou have done?

              Enter BEATRICE.

    Beatrice (*in a hurried voice*). Did he pass this
      way? Have you seen him, brother?
Ah, no! that is his step upon the stairs;
'Tis nearer now; his hand is on the door;
Mother, if I to thee have ever been
A duteous child, now save me! Thou, great God,
Whose image upon earth a father is,
Dost Thou indeed abandon me? He comes;
The door is opening now; I see his face;
He frowns on others, but he smiles on me,   20
Even as he did after the feast last night.

          Enter a Servant.

Almighty God, how merciful Thou art!
'Tis but Orsino's servant.—Well, what news?
    Servant. My master bids me say, the Holy
      Father
Has sent back your petition thus unopened.
                    [*Giving a paper.*
And he demands at what hour 'twere secure
To visit you again?
    Lucretia.   At the Ave Mary.
                    [*Exit Servant.*
So, daughter, our last hope has failed; Ah me!
How pale you look; you tremble, and you stand
Wrapped in some fixed and fearful medi-
    tation,   30
As if one thought were over strong for you:
Your eyes have a chill glare; O, dearest child!
Are you gone mad? If not, pray speak to me.
    Beatrice. You see I am not mad: I speak to
    you.
    Lucretia. You talked of something that your
      father did
After that dreadful feast? Could it be worse
Than when he smiled, and cried, 'My sons are
    dead!'
And every one looked in his neighbour's face
To see if others were as white as he?
At the first word he spoke I felt the blood   40
Rush to my heart, and fell into a trance;
And when it passed I sat all weak and wild;

Whilst you alone stood up, and with strong words
Checked his unnatural pride; and I could see
The devil was rebuked that lives in him.
Until this hour thus have you ever stood
Between us and your father's moody wrath
Like a protecting presence: your firm mind
Has been our only refuge and defence:
What can have thus subdued it? What can
    now   50
Have given you that cold melancholy look,
Succeeding to your unaccustomed fear?
    Beatrice. What is it that you say? I was just
      thinking
'Twere better not to struggle any more.
Men, like my father, have been dark and bloody,
Yet never—Oh! Before worse comes of it
'Twere wise to die: it ends in that at last.
    Lucretia. Oh, talk not so, dear child! Tell me
      at once
What did your father do or say to you?
He stayed not after that accursèd feast   60
One moment in your chamber.—Speak to me.
    Bernardo. Oh, sister, sister, prithee, speak to
      us!
    Beatrice (*speaking very slowly with a forced
      calmness*). It was one word, Mother, one
      little word;
One look, one smile. (*Wildly.*) Oh! He has tram-
    pled me
Under his feet, and made the blood stream down
My pallid cheeks. And he has given us all
Ditch-water, and the fever-stricken flesh
Of buffaloes, and bade us eat or starve,
And we have eaten.—He has made me look
On my beloved Bernardo, when the rust   70
Of heavy chains has gangrened his sweet limbs,
And I have never yet despaired—but now!
What could I say?   [*Recovering herself.*
                Ah, no! 'tis nothing new.
The sufferings we all share have made me wild:
He only struck and cursed me as he passed;
He said, he looked, he did;—nothing at all
Beyond his wont, yet it disordered me.
Alas! I am forgetful of my duty,
I should preserve my senses for your sake.
    Lucretia. Nay, Beatrice; have courage, my
      sweet girl,   80
If any one despairs it should be I
Who loved him once, and now must live with him
Till God in pity call for him or me.
For you may, like your sister, find some husband,
And smile, years hence, with children round your
    knees;
Whilst I, then dead, and all this hideous coil

Shall be remembered only as a dream.
 Beatrice. Talk not to me, dear lady, of a hus-
  band.
Did you not nurse me when my mother died?
Did you not shield me and that dearest boy? 90
And had we any other friend but you
In infancy, with gentle words and looks,
To win our father not to murder us?
And shall I now desert you? May the ghost
Of my dead Mother plead against my soul
If I abandon her who filled the place
She left, with more, even, than a mother's love!
 Bernardo. And I am of my sister's mind.
  Indeed
I would not leave you in this wretchedness,
Even though the Pope should make me free to
  live 100
In some blithe place, like others of my age,
With sports, and delicate food, and the fresh air.
Oh, never think that I will leave you, Mother!
 Lucretia. My dear, dear children!

   Enter CENCI, *suddenly.*

 Cenci.   What, Beatrice here!
Come hither!
   [*She shrinks back, and covers her face.*
    Nay, hide not your face, 'tis fair;
Look up! Why, yesternight you dared to look
With disobedient insolence upon me,
Bending a stern and an inquiring brow
On what I meant; whilst I then sought to hide
That which I came to tell you—but in vain. 110
 Beatrice (*wildly, staggering towards the door*).
  O that the earth would gape! Hide me, O
  God!
 Cenci. Then it was I whose inarticulate words
Fell from my lips, and who with tottering steps
Fled from your presence, as you now from
  mine.
Stay, I command you—from this day and hour
Never again, I think, with fearless eye,
And brow superior, and unaltered cheek,
And that lip made for tenderness or scorn,
Shalt thou strike dumb the meanest of man-
  kind;
Me least of all. Now get thee to thy chamber! 120
Thou too, loathed image of thy cursèd mother.
        [*To* BERNARDO.
Thy milky, meek face makes me sick with hate!
    [*Exeunt* BEATRICE *and* BERNARDO.
 (*Aside.*) So much has passed between us as
  must make
Me bold, her fearful.—'Tis an awful thing
To touch such mischief as I now conceive:
So men sit shivering on the dewy bank,

And try the chill stream with their feet; once
  in . . .
How the delighted spirit pants for joy!
 Lucretia (*advancing timidly towards him*). O
  husband! Pray forgive poor Beatrice.
She meant not any ill.
 Cenci.   Nor you perhaps? 130
Nor that young imp, whom you have taught by
  rote
Parricide with his alphabet? Nor Giacomo?
Nor those two most unnatural sons, who stirred
Enmity up against me with the Pope?
Whom in one night merciful God cut off:
Innocent lambs! They thought not any ill.
You were not here conspiring? You said nothing
Of how I might be dungeoned as a madman;
Or be condemned to death for some offence,
And you would be the witnesses?—This
  failing, 140
How just it were to hire assassins, or
Put sudden poison in my evening drink?
Or smother me when overcome by wine?
Seeing we had no other judge but God,
And He had sentenced me, and there were none
But you to be the executioners
Of His decree enregistered in Heaven?
Oh, no! You said not this?
 Lucretia.   So help me God,
I never thought the things you charge me with!
 Cenci. If you dare speak that wicked lie
  again 150
I'll kill you. What! It was not by your counsel
That Beatrice disturbed the feast last night?
You did not hope to stir some enemies
Against me, and escape, and laugh to scorn
What every nerve of you now trembles at?
You judged that men were bolder than they are;
Few dare to stand between their grave and me.
 Lucretia. Look not so dreadfully! By my sal-
  vation
I knew not aught that Beatrice designed;
Nor do I think she designed any thing 160
Until she heard you talk of her dead brothers.
 Cenci. Blaspheming liar! You are damned for
  this!
But I will take you where you may persuade
The stones you tread on to deliver you:
For men shall there be none but those who dare
All things—not question that which I command.
On Wednesday next I shall set out: you know
That savage rock, the Castle of Petrella:
'Tis safely walled, and moated round about:
Its dungeons underground, and its thick
  towers 170

Never told tales; though they have heard and
   seen
What might make dumb things speak.—Why do
   you linger?
Make speediest preparation for the journey!
                              [*Exit* LUCRETIA.
The all-beholding sun yet shines; I hear
A busy stir of men about the streets;
I see the bright sky through the window panes:
It is a garish, broad, and peering day;
Loud, light, suspicious, full of eyes and ears,
And every little corner, nook, and hole
Is penetrated with the insolent light.   .   180
Come darkness! Yet, what is the day to me?
And wherefore should I wish for night, who do
A deed which shall confound both night and
   day?
'Tis she shall grope through a bewildering mist
Of horror: if there be a sun in heaven
She shall not dare to look upon its beams;
Nor feel its warmth. Let her then wish for night;
The act I think shall soon extinguish all
For me: I bear a darker deadlier gloom
Than the earth's shade, or interlunar air,   190
Or constellations quenched in murkiest cloud,
In which I walk secure and unbeheld
Towards my purpose.—Would that it were done!
                                    [*Exit.*

SCENE II.—*A Chamber in the Vatican. Enter*
   CAMILLO *and* GIACOMO, *in conversation.*

   Camillo. There is an obsolete and doubtful law
By which you might obtain a bare provision
Of food and clothing—
   Giacomo.   Nothing more? Alas!
Bare must be the provision which strict law
Awards, and agèd, sullen avarice pays.
Why did my father not apprentice me
To some mechanic trade? I should have then
Been trained in no highborn necessities
Which I could meet not by my daily toil.
The eldest son of a rich nobleman   10
Is heir to all his incapacities;
He has wide wants, and narrow powers. If you,
Cardinal Camillo, were reduced at once
From thrice-driven beds of down, and delicate
   food,
An hundred servants, and six palaces,
To that which nature doth indeed require?—
   Camillo. Nay, there is reason in your plea;
      'twere hard.
   Giacomo. 'Tis hard for a firm man to bear:
      but I
Have a dear wife, a lady of high birth,

Whose dowry in ill hour I lent my father   20
Without a bond or witness to the deed:
And children, who inherit her fine senses,
The fairest creatures in this breathing world;
And she and they reproach me not. Cardinal,
Do you not think the Pope would interpose
And stretch authority beyond the law?
   Camillo. Though your peculiar case is hard, I
      know
The Pope will not divert the course of law.
After that impious feast the other night
I spoke with him, and urged him then to
   check   30
Your father's cruel hand; he frowned and said,
'Children are disobedient, and they sting
Their fathers' hearts to madness and despair,
Requiting years of care with contumely.
I pity the Count Cenci from my heart;
His outraged love perhaps awakened hate,
And thus he is exasperated to ill.
In the great war between the old and young
I, who have white hairs and a tottering body,
Will keep at least blameless neutrality.'   40

              Enter ORSINO.

You, my good Lord Orsino, heard those words.
   Orsino. What words?
   Giacomo.   Alas, repeat them not again!
There then is no redress for me, at least
None but that which I may achieve myself,
Since I am driven to the brink.—But, say,
My innocent sister and my only brother
Are dying underneath my father's eye.
The memorable torturers of this land,
Galeaz Visconti, Borgia, Ezzelin,
Never inflicted on the meanest slave   50
What these endure; shall they have no protec-
   tion?
   Camillo. Why, if they would petition to the
      Pope
I see not how he could refuse it—yet
He holds it of most dangerous example
In aught to weaken the paternal power,
Being, as 'twere, the shadow of his own.
I pray you now excuse me. I have business
That will not bear delay.   [*Exit* CAMILLO.
   Giacomo.   But you, Orsino,
Have the petition: wherefore not present it?
   Orsino. I have presented it, and backed it
      with   60
My earnest prayers, and urgent interest;
It was returned unanswered. I doubt not
But that the strange and execrable deeds
Alleged in it—in truth they might well baffle
Any belief—have turned the Pope's displeasure

Upon the accusers from the criminal:
So I should guess from what Camillo said.
    Giacomo. My friend, that palace-walking devil
      Gold
Has whispered silence to his Holiness:
And we are left, as scorpions ringed with fire. 70
What should we do but strike ourselves to death?
For he who is our murderous persecutor
Is shielded by a father's holy name,
Or I would—   [*Stops abruptly.*
    Orsino. What? Fear not to speak your thought.
Words are but holy as the deeds they cover:
A priest who has forsworn the God he serves;
A judge who makes Truth weep at his decree;
A friend who should weave counsel, as I now,
But as the mantle of some selfish guile:
A father who is all a tyrant seems,   80
Were the profaner for his sacred name.
    Giacomo. Ask me not what I think; the unwill-
      ing brain
Feigns often what it would not; and we trust
Imagination with such phantasies
As the tongue dares not fashion into words,
Which have no words, their horror makes them
    dim
To the mind's eye.—My heart denies itself
To think what you demand.
    Orsino.   But a friend's bosom
Is as the inmost cave of our own mind
Where we sit shut from the wide gaze of day, 90
And from the all-communicating air.
You look what I suspected—
    Giacomo.   Spare me now!
I am as one lost in a midnight wood,
Who dares not ask some harmless passenger
The path across the wilderness, lest he,
As my thoughts are, should be—a murderer.
I know you are my friend, and all I dare
Speak to my soul that will I trust with thee.
But now my heart is heavy, and would take
Lone counsel from a night of sleepless care. 100
Pardon me, that I say farewell—farewell!
I would that to my own suspected self
I could address a word so full of peace.
    Orsino. Farewell!—Be your thoughts better or
      more bold.   [*Exit* GIACOMO.
I had disposed the Cardinal Camillo
To feed his hope with cold encouragement:
It fortunately serves my close designs
That 'tis a trick of this same family
To analyse their own and other minds.
Such self-anatomy shall teach the will   110
Dangerous secrets: for it tempts our powers,
Knowing what must be thought, and may be
    done,

Into the depth of darkest purposes:
So Cenci fell into the pit; even I,
Since Beatrice unveiled me to myself,
And made me shrink from what I cannot
    shun,
Show a poor figure to my own esteem,
To which I grow half reconciled. I'll do
As little mischief as I can; that thought
Shall fee the accuser conscience.
    (*After a pause.*)   Now what harm 120
If Cenci should be murdered?—Yet, if murdered,
Wherefore by me? And what if I could take
The profit, yet omit the sin and peril
In such an action? Of all earthly things
I fear a man whose blows outspeed his words:
And such is Cenci: and while Cenci lives
His daughter's dowry were a secret grave
If a priest wins her.—Oh, fair Beatrice!
Would that I loved thee not, or loving thee
Could but despise danger and gold and all   130
That frowns between my wish and its effect,
Or smiles beyond it! There is no escape . . .
Her bright form kneels beside me at the
    altar,
And follows me to the resort of men,
And fills my slumber with tumultuous dreams,
So when I wake my blood seems liquid fire;
And if I strike my damp and dizzy head
My hot palm scorches it: her very name,
But spoken by a stranger, makes my heart
Sicken and pant; and thus unprofitably   140
I clasp the phantom of unfelt delights
Till weak imagination half possesses
The self-created shadow. Yet much longer
Will I not nurse this life of feverous hours:
From the unravelled hopes of Giacomo
I must work out my own dear purposes.
I see, as from a tower, the end of all:
Her father dead; her brother bound to me
By a dark secret, surer than the grave;
Her mother scared and unexpostulating   150
From the dread manner of her wish achieved:
And she!—Once more take courage, my faint
    heart;
What dares a friendless maiden matched with
    thee?
I have such foresight as assures success:
Some unbeheld divinity doth ever,
When dread events are near, stir up men's
    minds
To black suggestions; and he prospers best,
Not who becomes the instrument of ill,
But who can flatter the dark spirit, that makes
Its empire and its prey of other hearts   160
Till it become his slave . . . as I will do.   [*Exit.*

ACT III

SCENE I.—*An Apartment in the Cenci Palace.*

LUCRETIA, *to her enter* BEATRICE.

Beatrice. (*She enters staggering, and speaks
    wildly.*) Reach me that handkerchief!—My
    brain is hurt;
My eyes are full of blood; just wipe them for
    me . . .
I see but indistinctly . . .
    Lucretia.   My sweet child,
You have no wound; 'tis only a cold dew
That starts from your dear brow . . . Alas! Alas!
What has befallen?
    Beatrice.   How comes this hair undone?
Its wandering strings must be what blind me so,
And yet I tied it fast.—O, horrible!
The pavement sinks under my feet! The walls
Spin round! I see a woman weeping there,   10
And standing calm and motionless, whilst I
Slide giddily as the world reels. . . . My God!
The beautiful blue heaven is flecked with blood!
The sunshine on the floor is black! The air
Is changed to vapours such as the dead breathe
In charnel pits! Pah! I am choked! There creeps
A clinging, black, contaminating mist
About me . . . 'tis substantial, heavy, thick,
I cannot pluck it from me, for it glues
My fingers and my limbs to one another,   20
And eats into my sinews, and dissolves
My flesh to a pollution, poisoning
The subtle, pure, and inmost spirit of life!
My God! I never knew what the mad felt
Before; for I am mad beyond all doubt!
(*More wildly.*) No, I am dead! These putrefying
    limbs
Shut round and sepulchre the panting soul
Which would burst forth into the wandering air!
    (*A pause.*)
What hideous thought was that I had even now?
'Tis gone; and yet its burthen remains here   30
O'er these dull eyes . . . upon this weary heart!
O, world! O, life! O, day! O, misery!
    Lucretia. What ails thee, my poor child? She
        answers not:
Her spirit apprehends the sense of pain,
But not its cause; suffering has dried away
The source from which it sprung . . .
    Beatrice (*franticly.*)   Like Parricide . . .
Misery has killed its father: yet its father
Never like mine . . . O, God! What thing am I?
    Lucretia. My dearest child, what has your
        father done?

Beatrice (*doubtfully*). Who art thou, questioner?
    I have no father   40
(*Aside.*) She is the madhouse nurse who tends on
    me,
It is a piteous office.
                [*To* LUCRETIA, *in a slow, subdued voice.*
                Do you know
I thought I was that wretched Beatrice
Men speak of, whom her father sometimes hales
From hall to hall by the entangled hair;
At others, pens up naked in damp cells
Where scaly reptiles crawl, and starves her there,
Till she will eat strange flesh. This woful story
So did I overact in my sick dreams,
That I imagined .. . . no, it cannot be!   50
Horrible things have been in this wide world,
Prodigious mixtures, and confusions strange
Of good and ill; and worse have been conceived
Than ever there was found a heart to do.
But never fancy imaged such a deed
As . . .   [*Pauses, suddenly recollecting herself.*
            Who art thou? Swear to me, ere I die
With fearful expectation, that indeed
Thou art not what thou seemest . . . Mother!
    Lucretia.   Oh!
My sweet child, know you . . .
    Beatrice.   Yet speak it not:
For then if this be truth, that other too   60
Must be a truth, a firm enduring truth,
Linked with each lasting circumstance of life,
Never to change, never to pass away.
Why so it is. This is the Cenci Palace;
Thou art Lucretia; I am Beatrice.
I have talked some wild words, but will no more.
Mother, come near me: from this point of time,
I am . . .   [*Her voice dies away faintly.*
    Lucretia. Alas! What has befallen thee, child?
What has thy father done?
    Beatrice.   What have I done?
Am I not innocent? Is it my crime   70
That one with white hair, and imperious brow,
Who tortured me from my forgotten years,
As parents only dare, should call himself
My father, yet should be!—Oh, what am I?
What name, what place, what memory shall be
    mine?
What retrospects, outliving even despair?
    Lucretia. He is a violent tyrant, surely, child:
We know that death alone can make us free;
His death or ours. But what can he have done
Of deadlier outrage or worse injury?   80
Thou art unlike thyself; thine eyes shoot forth
A wandering and strange spirit. Speak to me,

Unlock those pallid hands whose fingers twine
With one another.
   Beatrice.   'Tis the restless life
Tortured within them. If I try to speak
I shall go mad. Ay, something must be done;
What, yet I know not . . . something which shall
   make
The thing that I have suffered but a shadow
In the dread lightning which avenges it;
Brief, rapid, irreversible, destroying   90
The consequence of what it cannot cure.
Some such thing is to be endured or done:
When I know what, I shall be still and calm,
And never anything will move me more.
But now!—O blood, which art my father's blood,
Circling through these contaminated veins,
If thou, poured forth on the polluted earth,
Could wash away the crime, and punishment
By which I suffer . . . no, that cannot be!
Many might doubt there were a God above   100
Who sees and permits evil, and so die:
That faith no agony shall obscure in me.
   Lucretia. It must indeed have been some bitter
   wrong;
Yet what, I dare not guess. Oh, my lost child,
Hide not in proud impenetrable grief
Thy sufferings from my fear.
   Beatrice.   I hide them not.
What are the words which you would have me
   speak?
I, who can feign no image in my mind
Of that which has transformed me: I, whose
   thought
Is like a ghost shrouded and folded up   110
In its own formless horror: of all words,
That minister to mortal intercourse,
Which wouldst thou hear? For there is none to
   tell
My misery: if another ever knew
Aught like to it, she died as I will die,
And left it, as I must, without a name.
Death! Death! Our law and our religion call thee
A punishment and a reward . . . Oh, which
Have I deserved?
   Lucretia.   The peace of innocence;
Till in your season you be called to heaven.   120
Whate'er you may have suffered, you have done
No evil. Death must be the punishment
Of crime, or the reward of trampling down
The thorns which God has strewed upon the path
Which leads to immortality.
   Beatrice.   Ay, death . . .
The punishment of crime. I pray thee, God,

Let me not be bewildered while I judge.
If I must live day after day, and keep
These limbs, the unworthy temple of Thy spirit,
As a foul den from which what Thou
   abhorrest   130
May mock Thee, unavenged . . . it shall not be!
Self-murder . . . no, that might be no escape,
For Thy decree yawns like a Hell between
Our will and it:—O! In this mortal world
There is no vindication and no law
Which can adjudge and execute the doom
Of that through which I suffer.

                Enter ORSINO.

(*She approaches him solemnly.*) Welcome, Friend!
I have to tell you that, since last we met,
I have endured a wrong so great and strange,
That neither life nor death can give me rest.   140
Ask me not what it is, for there are deeds
Which have no form, sufferings which have no
   tongue.
   Orsino. And what is he who has thus injured
   you?
   Beatrice. The man they call my father; a dread
   name.
   Orsino. It cannot be . . .
   Beatrice.   What it can be, or not,
Forbear to think. It is, and it has been;
Advise me how it shall not be again.
I thought to die; but a religious awe
Restrains me, and the dread lest death itself
Might be no refuge from the consciousness   150
Of what is yet unexpiated. Oh, speak!
   Orsino. Accuse him of the deed, and let the law
Avenge thee.
   Beatrice.   Oh, ice-hearted counsellor!
If I could find a word that might make known
The crime of my destroyer; and that done,
My tongue should like a knife tear out the secret
Which cankers my heart's core; ay, lay all bare
So that my unpolluted fame should be
With vilest gossips a stale mouthèd story;
A mock, a byword, an astonishment:—   160
If this were done, which never shall be done,
Think of the offender's gold, his dreaded hate,
And the strange horror of the accuser's tale,
Baffling belief, and overpowering speech;
Scarce whispered, unimaginable, wrapped
In hideous hints . . . Oh, most assured redress!
   Orsino. You will endure it then?
   Beatrice.   Endure?—Orsino,
It seems your counsel is small profit.
        [*Turns from him, and speaks half to herself.*

                                        Ay,
All must be suddenly resolved and done.
What is this undistinguishable mist   170
Of thoughts, which rise, like shadow after
    shadow,
Darkening each other?
    Orsino.   Should the offender live?
Triumph in his misdeed? and make, by use,
His crime, whate'er it is, dreadful no doubt,
Thine element; until thou mayst become
Utterly lost; subdued even to the hue
Of that which thou permittest?
    Beatrice (to herself).   Mighty death!
Thou double-visaged shadow? Only judge!
Rightfullest arbiter!

                        [*She retires absorbed in thought.*
    Lucretia.   If the lightning
Of God has e'er descended to avenge . . .   180
    Orsino. Blaspheme not! His high Providence
    commits
Its glory on this earth, and their own wrongs
Into the hands of men; if they neglect
To punish crime . . .
    Lucretia.   But if one, like this wretch,
Should mock, with gold, opinion, law, and
    power?
If there be no appeal to that which makes
The guiltiest tremble? If because our wrongs,
For that they are unnatural, strange, and mon-
    strous,
Exceed all measure of belief? O God!
If, for the very reasons which should make   190
Redress most swift and sure, our injurer tri-
    umphs?
And we, the victims, bear worse punishment
Than that appointed for their torturer?
    Orsino.   Think not
But that there is redress where there is wrong,
So we be bold enough to seize it.
    Lucretia.   How?
If there were any way to make all sure,
I know not . . . but I think it might be good
To . . .
    Orsino. Why, his late outrage to Beatrice;
For it is such, as I but faintly guess,
As makes remorse dishonour, and leaves her   200
Only one duty, how she may avenge:
You, but one refuge from ills ill endured;
Me, but one counsel . . .
    Lucretia.   For we cannot hope
That aid, or retribution, or resource
Will arise thence, where every other one
Might find them with less need.

                        [BEATRICE *advances.*

    Orsino.   Then . . .
    Beatrice.   Peace, Orsino!
And, honoured Lady, while I speak, I pray,
That you put off, as garments overworn,
Forbearance and respect, remorse and fear,
And all the fit restraints of daily life,   210
Which have been borne from childhood, but
    which now
Would be a mockery to my holier plea.
As I have said, I have endured a wrong,
Which, though it be expressionless, is such
As asks atonement; both for what is past,
And lest I be reserved, day after day,
To load with crimes an overburthened soul,
And be . . . what ye can dream not. I have prayed
To God, and I have talked with my own heart,
And have unravelled my entangled will,   220
And have at length determined what is right.
Art thou my friend, Orsino? False or true?
Pledge thy salvation ere I speak.
    Orsino.   I swear
To dedicate my cunning, and my strength,
My silence, and whatever else is mine,
To thy commands.
    Lucretia.   You think we should devise
His death?
    Beatrice. And execute what is devised,
And suddenly. We must be brief and bold.
    Orsino. And yet most cautious.
    Lucretia.   For the jealous laws
Would punish us with death and infamy   230
For that which it became themselves to do.
    Beatrice. Be cautious as ye may, but prompt.
    Orsino,
What are the means?
    Orsino.   I know two dull, fierce outlaws,
Who think man's spirit as a worm's, and they
Would trample out, for any slight caprice,
The meanest or the noblest life. This mood
Is marketable here in Rome. They sell
What we now want.
    Lucretia.   To-morrow before dawn,
Cenci will take us to that lonely rock,
Petrella, in the Apulian Apennines.   240
If he arrive there . . .
    Beatrice.   He must not arrive.
    Orsino. Will it be dark before you reach the
    tower?
    Lucretia. The sun will scarce be set.
    Beatrice.   But I remember
Two miles on this side of the fort, the road
Crosses a deep ravine; 'tis rough and narrow,
And winds with short turns down the precipice;
And in its depth there is a mighty rock,

Which has, from unimaginable years,
Sustained itself with terror and with toil
Over a gulf, and with the agony   250
With which it clings seems slowly coming down;
Even as a wretched soul hour after hour,
Clings to the mass of life; yet clinging, leans;
And leaning, makes more dark the dread abyss
In which it fears to fall: beneath this crag
Huge as despair, as if in weariness,
The melancholy mountain yawns . . . below,
You hear but see not an impetuous torrent
Raging among the caverns, and a bridge
Crosses the chasm; and high above there
 grow,   260
With intersecting trunks, from crag to crag,
Cedars, and yews, and pines; whose tangled hair
Is matted in one solid roof of shade
By the dark ivy's twine. At noonday here
'Tis twilight, and at sunset blackest night.
 Orsino. Before you reach that bridge make
 some excuse
For spurring on your mules, or loitering
Until . . .
 Beatrice. What sound is that?
 Lucretia. Hark! No, it cannot be a servant's
 step
It must be Cenci, unexpectedly   270
Returned . . . Make some excuse for being here.
 Beatrice. (*To* ORSINO, *as she goes out.*) That step
 we hear approach must never pass
The bridge of which we spoke.
   [*Exeunt* LUCRETIA *and* BEATRICE.

 Orsino.   What shall I do?
Cenci must find me here, and I must bear
The imperious inquisition of his looks
As to what brought me hither: let me mask
Mine own in some inane and vacant smile.

 Enter GIACOMO, *in a hurried manner.*

How! Have you ventured hither? Know you then
That Cenci is from home?
 Giacomo.   I sought him here;
And now must wait till he returns.
 Orsino.   Great God!   280
Weigh you the danger of this rashness?
 Giacomo.   Ay!
Does my destroyer know his danger? We
Are now no more, as once, parent and child,
But man to man; the oppressor to the oppressed;
The slanderer to the slandered; foe to foe:
He has cast Nature off, which was his shield,
And Nature casts him off, who is her shame;
And I spurn both. Is it a father's throat
Which I will shake, and say, I ask not gold;
I ask not happy years; nor memories   290

Of tranquil childhood; nor home-sheltered love;
Though all these hast thou torn from me, and
 more;
But only my fair fame; only one hoard
Of peace, which I thought hidden from thy hate,
Under the penury heaped on me by thee,
Or I will . . . God can understand and pardon,
Why should I speak with man?
 Orsino.   Be calm, dear friend.
 Giacomo. Well, I will calmly tell you what he
 did.
This old Francesco Cenci, as you know,
Borrowed the dowry of my wife from me,   300
And then denied the loan; and left me so
In poverty, the which I sought to mend
By holding a poor office in the state.
It had been promised to me, and already
I bought new clothing for my raggèd babes,
And my wife smiled; and my heart knew repose.
When Cenci's intercession, as I found,
Conferred this office on a wretch, whom thus
He paid for vilest service. I returned
With this ill news, and we sate sad together   310
Solacing our despondency with tears
Of such affection and unbroken faith
As temper life's worst bitterness; when he,
As he is wont, came to upbraid and curse,
Mocking our poverty, and telling us
Such was God's scourge for disobedient sons.
And then, that I might strike him dumb with
 shame,
I spoke of my wife's dowry; but he coined
A brief yet specious tale, how I had wasted
The sum in secret riot; and he saw   320
My wife was touched, and he went smiling forth.
And when I knew the impression he had made,
And felt my wife insult with silent scorn
My ardent truth, and look averse and cold,
I went forth too: but soon returned again;
Yet not so soon but that my wife had taught
My children her harsh thoughts, and they all
 cried,
'Give us clothes, father! Give us better food!
What you in one night squander were enough
For months!' I looked, and saw that home was
 hell.   330
And to that hell will I return no more
Until mine enemy has rendered up
Atonement, or, as he gave life to me
I will, reversing Nature's law . . .
 Orsino.   Trust me,
The compensation which thou seekest here
Will be denied.
 Giacomo. Then . . . Are you not my friend?
Did you not hint at the alternative,

Upon the brink of which you see I stand,
The other day when we conversed together?
My wrongs were then less. That word
          parricide,   340
Although I am resolved, haunts me like fear.
  Orsino. It must be fear itself, for the bare word
Is hollow mockery. Mark, how wisest God
Draws to one point the threads of a just doom,
So sanctifying it: what you devise
Is, as it were, accomplished.
  Giacomo.   Is he dead?
  Orsino. His grave is ready. Know that since we
          met
Cenci has done an outrage to his daughter.
  Giacomo. What outrage?
  Orsino.   That she speaks not, but you may
Conceive such half conjectures as I do,   350
From her fixed paleness, and the lofty grief
Of her stern brow bent on the idle air,
And her severe unmodulated voice,
Drowning both tenderness and dread; and last
From this; that whilst her step-mother and I,
Bewildered in our horror, talked together
With obscure hints; both self-misunderstood
And darkly guessing, stumbling, in our talk,
Over the truth, and yet to its revenge,
She interrupted us, and with a look   360
Which told before she spoke it, he must die: . . .
  Giacomo. It is enough. My doubts are well ap-
          peased;
There is a higher reason for the act
Than mine; there is a holier judge than me,
A more unblamed avenger. Beatrice,
Who in the gentleness of thy sweet youth
Hast never trodden on a worm, or bruised
A living flower, but thou hast pitied it
With needless tears! Fair sister, thou in whom
Men wondered how such loveliness and
          wisdom   370
Did not destroy each other! Is there made
Ravage of thee? O, heart, I ask no more
Justification! Shall I wait, Orsino,
Till he return, and stab him at the door?
  Orsino. Not so; some accident might inter-
          pose
To rescue him from what is now most sure;
And you are unprovided where to fly,
How to excuse or to conceal. Nay, listen:
All is contrived; success is so assured
That . . .

              Enter BEATRICE.

  Beatrice. 'Tis my brother's voice! You know
          me not?   380
  Giacomo. My sister, my lost sister!

  Beatrice.   Lost indeed!
I see Orsino has talked with you, and
That you conjecture things too horrible
To speak, yet far less than the truth. Now, stay
          not,
He might return: yet kiss me; I shall know
That then thou hast consented to his death.
Farewell, farewell! Let piety to God,
Brotherly love, justice and clemency,
And all things that make tender hardest hearts
Make thine hard, brother. Answer not . . . fare-
          well.   390
                    [*Exeunt severally.*

SCENE II.—*A mean Apartment in* GIACOMO'S
          House. GIACOMO *alone.*

  Giacomo. 'Tis midnight, and Orsino comes not
          yet.
                [*Thunder, and the sound of a storm.*
What! can the everlasting elements
Feel with a worm like man? If so, the shaft
Of mercy-wingèd lightning would not fall
On stones and trees. My wife and children sleep:
They are now living in unmeaning dreams:
But I must wake, still doubting if that deed
Be just which is most necessary. O,
Thou unreplenished lamp! whose narrow fire
Is shaken by the wind, and on whose edge   10
Devouring darkness hovers! Thou small flame,
Which, as a dying pulse rises and falls,
Still flickerest up and down, how very soon,
Did I not feed thee, wouldst thou fail and be
As thou hadst never been! So wastes and sinks
Even now, perhaps, the life that kindled mine:
But that no power can fill with vital oil
That broken lamp of flesh. Ha! 'tis the blood
Which fed these veins that ebbs till all is cold:
It is the form that moulded mine that sinks   20
Into the white and yellow spasms of death:
It is the soul by which mine was arrayed
In God's immortal likeness which now stands
Naked before Heaven's judgement seat!
                    [*A bell strikes.*
                              One! Two!
The hours crawl on; and when my hairs are
          white,
My son will then perhaps be waiting thus,
Tortured between just hate and vain remorse;
Chiding the tardy messenger of news
Like those which I expect. I almost wish
He be not dead, although my wrongs are
          great;   30
Yet . . . 'tis Orsino's step . . .

              Enter ORSINO.
                              Speak!

Orsino.   I am come
To say he has escaped.
    Giacomo.   Escaped!
    Orsino.   And safe
Within Petrella. He passed by the spot
Appointed for the deed an hour too soon.
    Giacomo. Are we the fools of such contingen-
        cies?
And do we waste in blind misgivings thus
The hours when we should act? Then wind and
        thunder,
Which seemed to howl his knell, is the loud
        laughter
With which Heaven mocks our weakness! I
        henceforth
Will ne'er repent of aught designed or done   40
But my repentance.
    Orsino.   See, the lamp is out.
    Giacomo. If no remorse is ours when the dim
        air
Has drank this innocent flame, why should we
        quail
When Cenci's life, that light by which ill spirits
See the worst deeds they prompt, shall sink for
        ever?
No, I am hardened.
    Orsino.   Why, what need of this?
Who feared the pale intrusion of remorse
In a just deed? Although our first plan failed,
Doubt not but he will soon be laid to rest.
But light the lamp; let us not talk i' the dark.   50
    Giacomo (*lighting the lamp*). And yet once
        quenched I cannot thus relume
My father's life: do you not think his ghost
Might plead that argument with God?
    Orsino.   Once gone
You cannot now recall your sister's peace;
Your own extinguished years of youth and hope;
Nor your wife's bitter words; nor all the taunts
Which, from the prosperous, weak misfortune
        takes;
Nor your dead mother; nor . . .
    Giacomo.   O, speak no more!
I am resolved, although this very hand
Must quench the life that animated it.   60
    Orsino. There is no need of that. Listen: you
        know
Olimpio, the castellan[6] of Petrella
In old Colonna's time; him whom your father
Degraded from his post? And Marzio,
That desperate wretch, whom he deprived last
        year
Of a reward of blood, well earned and due?

---

6 warden of the castle.

Giacomo. I know Olimpio; and they say he
        hated
Old Cenci so, that in his silent rage
His lips grew white only to see him pass.
Of Marzio I know nothing.
    Orsino.   Marzio's hate   70
Matches Olimpio's. I have sent these men,
But in your name, and as at your request,
To talk with Beatrice and Lucretia.
    Giacomo. Only to talk?
    Orsino.   The moments which even now
Pass onward to to-morrow's midnight hour
May memorize their flight with death: ere then
They must have talked, and may perhaps have
        done,
And made an end . . .
    Giacomo.   Listen! What sound is that?
    Orsino. The house-dog moans, and the beams
        crack: nought else.
    Giacomo. It is my wife complaining in her
        sleep: 80
I doubt not she is saying bitter things
Of me; and all my children round her dreaming
That I deny them sustenance.
    Orsino.   Whilst he
Who truly took it from them, and who fills
Their hungry rest with bitterness, now sleeps
Lapped in bad pleasures, and triumphantly
Mocks thee in visions of successful hate
Too like the truth of day.
    Giacomo.   If e'er he wakes
Again, I will not trust to hireling hands . . .
    Orsino. Why, that were well. I must be gone;
        good-night.   90
When next we meet—may all be done!
    Giacomo.   And all
Forgotten: Oh, that I had never been!   [*Exeunt.*

ACT IV

SCENE I.—*An Apartment in the Castle of Petrella.*

Enter CENCI.

    Cenci. She comes not; yet I left her even now
Vanquished and faint. She knows the penalty
Of her delay: yet what if threats are vain?
Am I not now within Petrella's moat?
Or fear I still the eyes and ears of Rome?
Might I not drag her by the golden hair?
Stamp on her? Keep her sleepless till her brain
Be overworn? Tame her with chains and famine?
Less would suffice. Yet so to leave undone
What I most seek! No, 'tis her stubborn will   10
Which by its own consent shall stoop as low
As that which drags it down.

Enter LUCRETIA.

                                  Thou loathèd wretch!
Hide thee from my abhorrence: fly, begone!
Yet stay! Bid Beatrice come hither.
    Lucretia.   Oh,
Husband! I pray for thine own wretched sake
Heed what thou dost. A man who walks like thee
Through crimes, and through the danger of his
        crimes,
Each hour may stumble o'er a sudden grave.
And thou art old; thy hairs are hoary grey;
As thou wouldst save thyself from death and
        hell,   20
Pity thy daughter; give her to some friend
In marriage: so that she may tempt thee not
To hatred, or worse thoughts, if worse there be.
    Cenci. What! like her sister who has found a
        home
To mock my hate from with prosperity?
Strange ruin shall destroy both her and thee
And all that yet remain. My death may be
Rapid, her destiny outspeeds it. Go,
Bid her come hither, and before my mood
Be changed, lest I should drag her by the hair. 30
    Lucretia. She sent me to thee, husband. At thy
        presence
She fell, as thou dost know, into a trance;
And in that trance she heard a voice which said,
'Cenci must die! Let him confess himself!
Even now the accusing Angel waits to hear
If God, to punish his enormous crimes,
Harden his dying heart!'
    Cenci.   Why—such things are . . .
No doubt divine revealings may be made.
'Tis plain I have been favoured from above,
For when I cursed my sons they died.—Ay . . .
        so . . .   40
As to the right or wrong, that's talk . . . re-
        pentance . . .
Repentance is an easy moment's work
And more depends on God than me. Well . . .
        well . . .
I must give up the greater point, which was
To poison and corrupt her soul.
    [*A pause;* LUCRETIA *approaches anxiously, and
        then shrinks back as he speaks.*
                                  One, two;
Ay . . . Rocco and Cristofano my curse
Strangled: and Giacomo, I think, will find
Life a worse Hell than that beyond the grave:
Beatrice shall, if there be skill in hate,
Die in despair, blaspheming: to Bernardo,   50
He is so innocent, I will bequeath
The memory of these deeds, and make his youth

The sepulchre of hope, where evil thoughts
Shall grow like weeds on a neglected tomb.
When all is done, out in the wide Campagna,
I will pile up my silver and my gold;
My costly robes, paintings and tapestries;
My parchments and all records of my wealth,
And make a bonfire in my joy, and leave
Of my possessions nothing but my name;   60
Which shall be an inheritance to strip
Its wearer bare as infamy. That done,
My soul, which is a scourge, will I resign
Into the hands of him who wielded it;
Be it for its own punishment or theirs,
He will not ask it of me till the lash
Be broken in its last and deepest wound;
Until its hate be all inflicted. Yet,
Lest death outspeed my purpose, let me make
Short work and sure . . .   [*Going.*
    Lucretia. (*Stops him*). Oh, stay. It was a
        feint: 70
She had no vision, and she heard no voice.
I said it but to awe thee.
    Cenci.   That is well.
Vile palterer with the sacred truth of God,
Be thy soul choked with that blaspheming lie!
For Beatrice worse terrors are in store
To bend her to my will.
    Lucretia.   Oh! to what will?
What cruel sufferings more than she has known
Canst thou inflict?
    Cenci.   Andrea! Go call my daughter,
And if she comes not tell her that I come.
What sufferings? I will drag her, step by step, 80
Through infamies unheard of among men:
She shall stand shelterless in the broad noon
Of public scorn, for acts blazoned abroad,
One among which shall be . . . What? Canst thou
        guess?
She shall become (for what she most abhors
Shall have a fascination to entrap
Her loathing will) to her own conscious self
All she appears to others; and when dead,
As she shall die unshrived and unforgiven,
A rebel to her father and her God,   90
Her corpse shall be abandoned to the hounds;
Her name shall be the terror of the earth;
Her spirit shall approach the throne of God
Plague-spotted with my curses. I will make
Body and soul a monstrous lump of ruin.

Enter ANDREA.

    Andrea. The Lady Beatrice . . .
    Cenci.   Speak, pale slave! What
Said she?

Andrea. My Lord, 'twas what she looked; she
said:
'Go tell my father that I see the gulf
Of Hell between us two, which he may pass,
I will not.'   [*Exit* ANDREA.
   Cenci.   Go thou quick, Lucretia,   100
Tell her to come; yet let her understand
Her coming is consent: and say, moreover,
That if she come not I will curse her.
                         [*Exit* LUCRETIA.
                    Ha!
With what but with a father's curse doth God
Panic-strike armèd victory, and make pale
Cities in their prosperity? The world's Father
Must grant a parent's prayer against his child,
Be he who asks even what men call me.
Will not the deaths of her rebellious brothers
Awe her before I speak? For I on them   110
Did imprecate quick ruin, and it came.

          Enter LUCRETIA.

Well; what? Speak, wretch!
   Lucretia.   She said, 'I cannot come;
Go tell my father that I see a torrent
Of his own blood raging between us.'
   Cenci (kneeling).   God!
Hear me! If this most specious mass of flesh,
Which Thou hast made my daughter; this my
          blood,
This particle of my divided being;
Or rather, this my bane and my disease,
Whose sight infects and poisons me; this devil
Which sprung from me as from a hell, was
          meant   120
To aught good use; if her bright loveliness
Was kindled to illumine this dark world;
If nursed by Thy selectest dew of love
Such virtues blossom in her as should make
The peace of life, I pray Thee for my sake,
As Thou the common God and Father art
Of her, and me, and all; reverse that doom!
Earth, in the name of God, let her food be
Poison, until she be encrusted round
With leprous stains! Heaven, rain upon her
          head   130
The blistering drops of the Maremma's dew,[7]
Till she be speckled like a toad; parch up
Those love-enkindled lips, warp those fine limbs
To loathèd lameness! All-beholding sun,
Strike in thine envy those life-darting eyes
With thine own blinding beams!
   Lucretia.   Peace! Peace!

_____
7 The Maremma is a swampy region on the coast of Tuscany
whose noxious dews were supposed to cause malaria.

For thine own sake unsay those dreadful words.
When high God grants He punishes such pray-
          ers.
   *Cenci (leaping up, and throwing his right hand
          towards Heaven).* He does His will, I mine!
   This in addition,
That if she have a child . . .
   Lucretia.   Horrible thought! 140
   Cenci. That if she ever have a child; and thou,
Quick Nature! I adjure thee by thy God,
That thou be fruitful in her, and increase
And multiply, fulfilling his command,
And my deep imprecation! May it be
A hideous likeness of herself, that as
From a distorting mirror, she may see
Her image mixed with what she most abhors,
Smiling upon her from her nursing breast.
And that the child may from its infancy   150
Grow, day by day, more wicked and deformed,
Turning her mother's love to misery:
And that both she and it may live until
It shall repay her care and pain with hate,
Or what may else be more unnatural.
So he may hunt her through the clamorous scoffs
Of the loud world to a dishonoured grave.
Shall I revoke this curse? Go, bid her come,
Before my words are chronicled in Heaven.
                         [*Exit* LUCRETIA.
I do not feel as if I were a man,   160
But like a fiend appointed to chastise
The offences of some unremembered world.
My blood is running up and down my veins;
A fearful pleasure makes it prick and tingle:
I feel a giddy sickness of strange awe;
My heart is beating with an expectation
Of horrid joy.

          Enter LUCRETIA.

          What? Speak!
   Lucretia.   She bids thee curse;
And if thy curses, as they cannot do,
Could kill her soul . . .
   Cenci.   She would not come. 'Tis well,
I can do both: first take what I demand,   170
And then extort concession. To thy chamber!
Fly ere I spurn thee: and beware this night
That thou cross not my footsteps. It were safer
To come between the tiger and his prey.
                         [*Exit* LUCRETIA.
It must be late; mine eyes grow weary dim
With unaccustomed heaviness of sleep.
Conscience! Oh, thou most insolent of lies!
They say that sleep, that healing dew of Heaven,
Steeps not in balm the foldings of the brain

Which thinks thee an impostor. I will go   180
First to belie thee with an hour of rest,
Which will be deep and calm, I feel: and then . . .
O, multitudinous Hell, the fiends will shake
Thine arches with the laughter of their joy!
There shall be lamentation heard in Heaven
As o'er an angel fallen; and upon Earth
All good shall droop and sicken, and ill things
Shall with a spirit of unnatural life
Stir and be quickened . . . even as I am now.
                                        [*Exit.*

SCENE II.—*Before the Castle of Petrella. Enter*
BEATRICE *and* LUCRETIA *above on the Ramparts.*

    Beatrice. They come not yet.
    Lucretia.   'Tis scarce midnight.
    Beatrice.   How slow
Behind the course of thought, even sick with
        speed,
Lags leaden-footed time!
    Lucretia.   The minutes pass . . .
If he should wake before the deed is done?
    Beatrice. O, mother! He must never wake
        again.
What thou hast said persuades me that our act
Will but dislodge a spirit of deep hell
Out of a human form.
    Lucretia.   'Tis true he spoke
Of death and judgement with strange confidence
For one so wicked; as a man believing   10
In God, yet recking not of good or ill.
And yet to die without confession! . . .
    Beatrice.   Oh!
Believe that Heaven is merciful and just,
And will not add our dread necessity
To the amount of his offences.

    Enter OLIMPIO *and* MARZIO, *below.*

    Lucretia.   See,
They come.
    Beatrice. All mortal things must hasten thus
To their dark end. Let us go down.
        [*Exeunt* LUCRETIA *and* BEATRICE *from above.*
    Olimpio. How feel you to this work?
    Marzio.   As one who thinks
A thousand crowns excellent market price
For an old murderer's life. Your cheeks are
        pale.   20
    Olimpio. It is the white reflection of your own,
Which you call pale.
    Marzio.   Is that their natural hue?
    Olimpio. Or 'tis my hate and the deferred de-
        sire
To wreak it, which extinguishes their blood.

    Marzio. You are inclined then to this business?
    Olimpio.   Ay.
If one should bribe me with a thousand crowns
To kill a serpent which had stung my child,
I could not be more willing.

    Enter BEATRICE *and* LUCRETIA, *below.*

                              Noble ladies!
    Beatrice. Are ye resolved?
    Olimpio.   Is he asleep?
    Marzio.   Is all
Quiet?
    Lucretia. I mixed an opiate with his drink: 30
He sleeps so soundly . . .
    Beatrice.   That his death will be
But as a change of sin-chastising dreams,
A dark continuance of the Hell within him,
Which God extinguish! But ye are resolved?
Ye know it is a high and holy deed?
    Olimpio. We are resolved.
    Marzio.   As to the how this act
Be warranted, it rests with you.
    Beatrice.   Well, follow!
    Olimpio. Hush! Hark! What noise is that?
    Marzio.   Ha! some one comes!
    Beatrice. Ye conscience-stricken cravens, rock
        to rest
Your baby hearts. It is the iron gate,   40
Which ye left open, swinging to the wind,
That enters whistling as in scorn. Come, follow!
And be your steps like mine, light, quick and
        bold.   [*Exeunt.*

SCENE III.—*An Apartment in the Castle. Enter*
BEATRICE *and* LUCRETIA.

    Lucretia. They are about it now.
    Beatrice.   Nay, it is done.
    Lucretia. I have not heard him groan.
    Beatrice.   He will not groan.
    Lucretia. What sound is that?
    Beatrice.   List! 'tis the tread of feet
About his bed.
    Lucretia.   My God!
If he be now a cold stiff corpse . . .
    Beatrice.   O, fear not
What may be done, but what is left undone:
The act seals all.

    Enter OLIMPIO *and* MARZIO.

                              Is it accomplished?
    Marzio.   What?
    Olimpio. Did you not call?
    Beatrice.   When?
    Olimpio.   Now.

Beatrice.   I ask if all is over?
Olimpio. We dare not kill an old and sleeping
    man;
His thin gray hair, his stern and reverend
    brow,   10
His veinèd hands crossed on his heaving breast,
And the calm innocent sleep in which he lay,
Quelled me. Indeed, indeed, I cannot do it.
    Marzio. But I was bolder; for I chid Olimpio,
And bade him bear his wrongs to his own grave
And leave me the reward. And now my knife
Touched the loose wrinkled throat, when the old
    man
Stirred in his sleep, and said, 'God! hear, O, hear,
A father's curse! What, art Thou not our Father?'
And then he laughed. I knew it was the ghost   20
Of my dead father speaking through his lips,
And could not kill him.
    Beatrice.   Miserable slaves!
Where, if ye dare not kill a sleeping man,
Found ye the boldness to return to me
With such a deed undone? Base palterers!
Cowards and traitors! Why, the very conscience
Which ye would sell for gold and for revenge
Is an equivocation: it sleeps over
A thousand daily acts disgracing men;
And when a deed where mercy insults
    Heaven . . .   30
Why do I talk? [*Snatching a dagger from one of
    them and raising it.*
            Hadst thou a tongue to say,
'She murdered her own father!'—I must do it!
But never dream ye shall outlive him long!
    Olimpio. Stop, for God's sake!
    Marzio.   I will go back and kill him.
    Olimpio. Give me the weapon, we must do thy
    will.
    Beatrice. Take it! Depart! Return!
                    [*Exeunt* OLIMPIO *and* MARZIO.
                    How pale thou art!
We do but that which 'twere a deadly crime
To leave undone.
    Lucretia.   Would it were done!
    Beatrice.   Even whilst
That doubt is passing through your mind, the
    world
Is conscious of a change. Darkness and Hell   40
Have swallowed up the vapour they sent forth
To blacken the sweet light of life. My breath
Comes, methinks, lighter, and the jellied blood
Runs freely through my veins. Hark!

        Enter OLIMPIO *and* MARZIO.

                            He is . . .
    Olimpio.   Dead!

Marzio. We strangled him that there might be
    no blood;
And then we threw his heavy corpse i' the garden
Under the balcony; 'twill seem it fell.
    Beatrice (*giving them a bag of coin*). Here, take
    this gold, and hasten to your homes.
And, Marzio, because thou wast only awed
By that which made me tremble, wear thou
    this!   50
                    [*Clothes him in a rich mantle.*
It was the mantle which my grandfather
Wore in his high prosperity, and men
Envied his state: so may they envy thine.
Thou wert a weapon in the hand of God
To a just use. Live long and thrive! And, mark,
If thou hast crimes, repent: this deed is none.
                    [*A horn is sounded.*
    Lucretia. Hark, 'tis the castle horn; my God! it
    sounds
Like the last trump.
    Beatrice.   Some tedious guest is coming.
    Lucretia. The drawbridge is let down; there is a
    tramp
Of horses in the court; fly, hide yourselves!   60
                    [*Exeunt* OLIMPIO *and* MARZIO.
    Beatrice. Let us retire to counterfeit deep rest;
I scarcely need to counterfeit it now:
The spirit which doth reign within these limbs
Seems strangely undisturbed. I could even sleep
Fearless and calm: all ill is surely past.   [*Exeunt.*

SCENE IV.—*Another Apartment in the Castle. En-
    ter on one side the* LEGATE SAVELLA, *intro-
    duced by a Servant, and on the other* LUCRE-
    TIA *and* BERNARDO.

    Savella. Lady, my duty to his Holiness
Be my excuse that thus unseasonably
I break upon your rest. I must speak with
Count Cenci; doth he sleep?
    Lucretia (*in a hurried and confused manner*). I
    think he sleeps;
Yet wake him not, I pray, spare me awhile,
He is a wicked and a wrathful man;
Should he be roused out of his sleep to-night,
Which is, I know, a hell of angry dreams,
It were not well; indeed it were not well.
Wait till day break . . . (*aside*) O, I am deadly
    sick!   10
    Savella. I grieve thus to distress you, but the
    Count
Must answer charges of the gravest import,
And suddenly; such my commission is.
    Lucretia (*with increased agitation*). I dare not
    rouse him: I know none who dare . . .

'Twere perilous; . . . you might as safely waken
A serpent; or a corpse in which some fiend
Were laid to sleep.
   Savella.   Lady, my moments here
Are counted. I must rouse him from his sleep,
Since none else dare.
   Lucretia (*aside*).   O, terror! O, despair!
(*To* BERNARDO.) Bernardo, conduct you the Lord
   Legate to   20
Your father's chamber.
          [*Exeunt* SAVELLA *and* BERNARDO.

          Enter BEATRICE.

   Beatrice.   'Tis a messenger
Come to arrest the culprit who now stands
Before the throne of unappealable God.
Both Earth and Heaven, consenting arbiters,
Acquit our deed.
   Lucretia.   Oh, agony of fear!
Would that he yet might live! Even now I heard
The Legate's followers whisper as they passed
They had a warrant for his instant death.
All was prepared by unforbidden means
Which we must pay so dearly, having done.   30
Even now they search the tower, and find the
   body;
Now they suspect the truth; now they consult
Before they come to tax us with the fact;
O, horrible, 'tis all discovered!
   Beatrice.   Mother,
What is done wisely, is done well. Be bold
As thou art just. 'Tis like a truant child
To fear that others know what thou hast done,
Even from thine own strong consciousness, and
   thus
Write on unsteady eyes and altered cheeks
All thou wouldst hide. Be faithful to thyself, 40
And fear no other witness but thy fear.
For if, as cannot be, some circumstance
Should rise in accusation, we can blind
Suspicion with such cheap astonishment,
Or overbear it with such guiltless pride,
As murderers cannot feign. The deed is done,
And what may follow now regards not me.
I am as universal as the light;
Free as the earth-surrounding air; as firm
As the world's centre. Consequence, to me, 50
Is as the wind which strikes the solid rock
But shakes it not.   [*A cry within and tumult.*
   Voices.   Murder! Murder! Murder!

    Enter BERNARDO *and* SAVELLA.

   Savella (*to his followers*). Go search the castle
   round; sound the alarm;
Look to the gates that none escape!

   Beatrice.   What now?
   Bernardo. I know not what to say . . . my
   father's dead.
   Beatrice. How; dead! he only sleeps; you mis-
   take, brother.
His sleep is very calm, very like death;
'Tis wonderful how well a tyrant sleeps.
He is not dead?
   Bernardo.   Dead; murdered.
   Lucretia (*with extreme agitation*). Oh no, no,
He is not murdered though he may be dead; 60
I have alone the keys of those apartments.
   Savella. Ha! Is it so?
   Beatrice.   My Lord, I pray excuse us;
We will retire; my mother is not well.
She seems quite overcome with this strange hor-
   ror.   [*Exeunt* LUCRETIA *and* BEATRICE.
   Savella. Can you suspect who may have mur-
   dered him?
   Bernardo. I know not what to think.
   Savella.   Can you name any
Who had an interest in his death?
   Bernardo.   Alas!
I can name none who had not, and those most
Who most lament that such a deed is done;
My mother, and my sister, and myself. 70
   Savella. 'Tis strange! There were clear marks
   of violence.
I found the old man's body in the moonlight
Hanging beneath the window of his chamber,
Among the branches of a pine: he could not
Have fallen there, for all his limbs lay heaped
And effortless; 'tis true there was no blood . . .
Favour me, Sir; it much imports your house
That all should be made clear; to tell the ladies
That I request their presence.
               [*Exit* BERNARDO.

   Enter GUARDS *bringing in* MARZIO.

   Guard.   We have one.
   Officer. My Lord, we found this ruffian and
   another   80
Lurking among the rocks; there is no doubt
But that they are the murderers of Count Cenci:
Each had a bag of coin; this fellow wore
A gold-inwoven robe, which shining bright
Under the dark rocks to the glimmering moon
Betrayed them to our notice: the other fell
Desperately fighting.
   Savella.   What does he confess?
   Officer. He keeps firm silence; but these lines
   found on him
May speak.
   Savella. Their language is at least sincere.
                      [*Reads.*

'*To the Lady Beatrice.*   90

That the atonement of what my nature sickens to
conjecture may soon arrive, I send thee, at thy
brother's desire, those who will speak and do more
than I dare write. . . .

                                   Thy devoted servant, Orsino.'

Enter LUCRETIA, BEATRICE, *and* BERNARDO.

Knowest thou this writing, Lady?
    Beatrice.   No.
    Savella.   Nor thou?
    Lucretia. (*Her conduct throughout the scene is*
        marked by extreme agitation.) Where was it
        found? What is it? It should be
Orsino's hand! It speaks of that strange horror
Which never yet found utterance, but which
        made
Between that hapless child and her dead father
A gulf of obscure hatred.
    Savella.   Is it so?   100
Is it true, Lady, that thy father did
Such outrages as to awaken in thee
Unfilial hate?
    Beatrice.   Not hate, 'twas more than hate:
This is most true, yet wherefore question me?
    Savella. There is a deed demanding question
        done;
Thou hast a secret which will answer not.
    Beatrice. What sayest? My Lord, your words
        are bold and rash.
    Savella. I do arrest all present in the name
Of the Pope's Holiness. You must to Rome.
    Lucretia. O, not to Rome! Indeed we are not
        guilty.   110
    Beatrice. Guilty! Who dares talk of guilt? My
        Lord,
I am more innocent of parricide
Than is a child born fatherless . . . Dear mother,
Your gentleness and patience are no shield
For this keen-judging world, this two-edged lie,
Which seems, but is not. What! will human laws,
Rather will ye who are their ministers,
Bar all access to retribution first,
And then, when Heaven doth interpose to do
What ye neglect, arming familiar things   120
To the redress of an unwonted crime,
Make ye the victims who demanded it
Culprits? 'Tis ye are culprits! That poor wretch
Who stands so pale, and trembling, and amazed,
If it be true he murdered Cenci, was
A sword in the right hand of justest God.
Wherefore should I have wielded it? Unless
The crimes which mortal tongue dare never
        name
God therefore scruples to avenge.

    Savella.   You own
That you desired his death?
    Beatrice.   It would have been   130
A crime no less than his, if for one moment
That fierce desire had faded in my heart.
'Tis true I did believe, and hope, and pray,
Ay, I even knew . . . for God is wise and just,
That some strange sudden death hung over him.
'Tis true that this did happen, and most true
There was no other rest for me on earth,
No other hope in Heaven . . . now what of this?
    Savella. Strange thoughts beget strange deeds;
        and here are both:
I judge thee not.
    Beatrice.   And yet, if you arrest me,   140
You are the judge and executioner
Of that which is the life of life: the breath
Of accusation kills an innocent name,
And leaves for lame acquittal the poor life
Which is a mask without it. 'Tis most false
That I am guilty of foul parricide;
Although I must rejoice, for justest cause,
That other hands have sent my father's soul
To ask the mercy he denied to me.
Now leave us free; stain not a noble house   150
With vague surmises of rejected crime;
Add to our sufferings and your own neglect
No heavier sum: let them have been enough:
Leave us the wreck we have.
    Savella.   I dare not, Lady.
I pray that you prepare yourselves for Rome:
There the Pope's further pleasure will be known.
    Lucretia. O, not to Rome! O, take us not to
        Rome!
    Beatrice. Why not to Rome, dear mother?
        There as here
Our innocence is as an armèd heel
To trample accusation. God is there   160
As here, and with His shadow ever clothes
The innocent, the injured and the weak;
And such are we. Cheer up, dear Lady, lean
On me; collect your wandering thoughts. My
        Lord,
As soon as you have taken some refreshment,
And had all such examinations made
Upon the spot, as may be necessary
To the full understanding of this matter,
We shall be ready. Mother; will you come?
    Lucretia. Ha! they will bind us to the rack,
        and wrest   170
Self-accusation from our agony!
Will Giacomo be there? Orsino? Marzio?
All present; all confronted; all demanding
Each from the other's countenance the thing
Which is in every heart! O, misery!

[She faints, and is borne out.
Savella. She faints: an ill appearance this.
Beatrice.   My Lord,
She knows not yet the uses of the world.
She fears that power is as a beast which grasps
And loosens not: a snake whose look transmutes
All things to guilt which is its nutriment.   180
She cannot know how well the supine slaves
Of blind authority read the truth of things
When written on a brow of guilelessness:
She sees not yet triumphant Innocence
Stand at the judgement-seat of mortal man,
A judge and an accuser of the wrong
Which drags it there. Prepare yourself, my Lord;
Our suite will join yours in the court below.
[Exeunt.

ACT V

SCENE I.—*An Apartment in* ORSINO'S *Palace. Enter* ORSINO *and* GIACOMO.

Giacomo. Do evil deeds thus quickly come to
     end?
O, that the vain remorse which must chastise
Crimes done, had but as loud a voice to warn
As its keen sting is mortal to avenge!
O, that the hour when present had cast off
The mantle of its mystery, and shown
The ghastly form with which it now returns
When its scared game is roused, cheering the
     hounds
Of conscience to their prey! Alas! Alas!
It was a wicked thought, a piteous deed,   10
To kill an old and hoary-headed father.
     Orsino. It has turned out unluckily, in truth.
     Giacomo. To violate the sacred doors of sleep;
To cheat kind Nature of the placid death
Which she prepares for overwearied age;
To drag from Heaven an unrepentant soul
Which might have quenched in reconciling
     prayers
A life of burning crimes . . .
     Orsino.   You cannot say
I urged you to the deed.
     Giacomo.   O, had I never
Found in thy smooth and ready countenance 20
The mirror of my darkest thoughts; hadst thou
Never with hints and questions made me look
Upon the monster of my thought, until
It grew familiar to desire . . .
     Orsino.   'Tis thus
Men cast the blame of their unprosperous acts
Upon the abettors of their own resolve;
Or anything but their weak, guilty selves.
And yet, confess the truth, it is the peril

In which you stand that gives you this pale sick-
     ness
Of penitence; confess 'tis fear disguised   30
From its own shame that takes the mantle now
Of thin remorse. What if we yet were safe?
     Giacomo. How can that be? Already Beatrice,
Lucretia and the murderer are in prison.
I doubt not officers are, whilst we speak,
Sent to arrest us.
     Orsino.   I have all prepared
For instant flight. We can escape even now,
So we take fleet occasion by the hair.
     Giacomo. Rather expire in tortures, as I may.
What! will you cast by self-accusing flight   40
Assured conviction upon Beatrice?
She, who alone in this unnatural work,
Stands like God's angel ministered upon
By fiends; avenging such a nameless wrong
As turns black parricide to piety;
Whilst we for basest ends . . . I fear, Orsino,
While I consider all your words and looks,
Comparing them with your proposal now,
That you must be a villain. For what end
Could you engage in such a perilous crime,   50
Training me on with hints, and signs, and smiles,
Even to this gulf? Thou art no liar? No,
Thou art a lie! Traitor and murderer!
Coward and slave! But, no, defend thyself;
[Drawing.
Let the sword speak what the indignant tongue
Disdains to brand thee with.
     Orsino.   Put up your weapon.
Is it the desperation of your fear
Makes you thus rash and sudden with a friend,
Now ruined for your sake? If honest anger
Have moved you, know, that what I just
     proposed   60
Was but to try you. As for me, I think,
Thankless affection led me to this point,
From which, if my firm temper could repent,
I cannot now recede. Even whilst we speak
The ministers of justice wait below:
They grant me these brief moments. Now if you
Have any word of melancholy comfort
To speak to your pale wife, 'twere best to pass
Out at the postern, and avoid them so.
     Giacomo. O, generous friend! How canst thou
     pardon me?   70
Would that my life could purchase thine!
     Orsino.   That wish
Now comes a day too late. Haste; fare thee well!
Hear'st thou not steps along the corridor?
[Exit GIACOMO.
I'm sorry for it; but the guards are waiting
At his own gate, and such was my contrivance

That I might rid me both of him and them.
I thought to act a solemn comedy
Upon the painted scene of this new world,
And to attain my own peculiar ends
By some such plot of mingled good and ill   80
As others weave; but there arose a Power
Which grasped and snapped the threads of my
    device
And turned it to a net of ruin . . . Ha!
                              [*A shout is heard.*
Is that my name I hear proclaimed abroad?
But I will pass, wrapped in a vile disguise;
Rags on my back, and a false innocence
Upon my face, through the misdeeming crowd
Which judges by what seems. 'Tis easy then
For a new name and for a country new,
And a new life, fashioned on old desires,   90
To change the honours of abandoned Rome.
And these must be the masks of that within,
Which must remain unaltered . . . Oh, I fear
That what is past will never let me rest!
Why, when none else is conscious, but myself,
Of my misdeeds, should my own heart's con-
    tempt
Trouble me? Have I not the power to fly
My own reproaches? Shall I be the slave
Of . . . what? A word? which those of this false
    world
Employ against each other, not themselves;   100
As men wear daggers not for self-offence.
But if I am mistaken, where shall I
Find the disguise to hide me from myself,
As now I skulk from every other eye?   [*Exit.*

SCENE II.—*A Hall of Justice.* CAMILLO, JUDGES,
    &c., are discovered seated; MARZIO *is led in.*

    First Judge. Accused, do you persist in your
        denial?
I ask you, are you innocent, or guilty?
I demand who were the participators
In your offence? Speak truth and the whole truth.
    Marzio. My God! I did not kill him; I know
        nothing;
Olimpio sold the robe to me from which
You would infer my guilt.
    Second Judge.   Away with him!
    First Judge. Dare you, with lips yet white from
        the rack's kiss
Speak false? Is it so soft a questioner,
That you would bandy lover's talk with it   10
Till it wind out your life and soul? Away!
    Marzio. Spare me! O, spare! I will confess.
    First Judge.   Then speak.
    Marzio. I strangled him in his sleep.

    First Judge.   Who urged you to it?
    Marzio. His own son Giacomo, and the young
        prelate
Orsino sent me to Petrella; there
The ladies Beatrice and Lucretia
Tempted me with a thousand crowns, and I
And my companion forthwith murdered him.
Now let me die.
    First Judge. This sounds as bad as truth.
        Guards, there,
Lead forth the prisoner!

Enter LUCRETIA, BEATRICE, *and* GIACOMO,
            guarded.
                         Look upon this man;   20
When did you see him last?
    Beatrice.   We never saw him.
    Marzio. You know me too well, Lady Beatrice.
    Beatrice. I know thee! How? where? when?
    Marzio.   You know 'twas I
Whom you did urge with menaces and bribes
To kill your father. When the thing was done
You clothed me in a robe of woven gold
And bade me thrive: how I have thriven, you see.
You, my Lord Giacomo, Lady Lucretia,
You know that what I speak is true.
    [BEATRICE *advances towards him; he covers
            his face, and shrinks back.*
                               Oh, dart
The terrible resentment of those eyes   30
On the dead earth! Turn them away from me!
They wound: 'twas torture forced the truth. My
        Lords,
Having said this let me be led to death.
    Beatrice. Poor wretch, I pity thee: yet stay
        awhile.
    Camillo. Guards, lead him not away.
    Beatrice.   Cardinal Camillo,
You have a good repute for gentleness
And wisdom: can it be that you sit here
To countenance a wicked farce like this?
When some obscure and trembling slave is
        dragged
From sufferings which might shake the sternest
        heart   40
And bade to answer, not as he believes,
But as those may suspect or do desire
Whose questions thence suggest their own reply:
And that in peril of such hideous torments
As merciful God spares even the damned. Speak
    now
The thing you surely know, which is that you,
If your fine frame were stretched upon that
        wheel,
And you were told: 'Confess that you did poison

Your little nephew; that fair blue-eyed child
Who was the lodestar of your life':—and
   though   50
All see, since his most swift and piteous death,
That day and night, and heaven and earth, and
   time,
And all the things hoped for or done therein
Are changed to you, through your exceeding
   grief,
Yet you would say, 'I confess anything':
And beg from your tormentors, like that slave,
The refuge of dishonourable death.
I pray thee, Cardinal, that thou assert
My innocence.
   Camillo (*much moved*). What shall we think,
     my Lords?
Shame on these tears! I thought the heart was
   frozen   60
Which is their fountain. I would pledge my soul
That she is guiltless.
   Judge.   Yet she must be tortured.
   Camillo. I would as soon have tortured mine
     own nephew
(If he now lived he would be just her age;
His hair, too, was her colour, and his eyes
Like hers in shape, but blue and not so deep)
As that most perfect image of God's love
That ever came sorrowing upon the earth.
She is as pure as speechless infancy!
   Judge. Well, be her purity on your head, my
     Lord,   70
If you forbid the rack. His Holiness
Enjoined us to pursue this monstrous crime
By the severest forms of law; nay even
To stretch a point against the criminals.
The prisoners stand accused of parricide
Upon such evidence as justifies
Torture.
   Beatrice. What evidence? This man's?
   Judge.   Even so.
   Beatrice (*to* MARZIO). Come near. And who art
     thou thus chosen forth
Out of the multitude of living men
To kill the innocent?
   Marzio.   I am Marzio,   80
Thy father's vassal.
   Beatrice.   Fix thine eyes on mine;
Answer to what I ask.   [*Turning to the* JUDGES.
               I prithee mark
His countenance: unlike bold calumny
Which sometimes dares not speak the thing it
   looks,
He dares not look the thing he speaks, but bends
His gaze on the blind earth.

   (*To* MARZIO.)   What! wilt thou say
That I did murder my own father?
   Marzio.   Oh!
Spare me! My brain swims round . . . I cannot
   speak . . .
It was that horrid torture forced the truth.
Take me away! Let her not look on me!   90
I am a guilty miserable wretch;
I have said all I know; now, let me die!
   Beatrice. My Lords, if by my nature I had been
So stern, as to have planned the crime alleged,
Which your suspicions dictate to this slave,
And the rack makes him utter, do you think
I should have left this two-edged instrument
Of my misdeed; this man, this bloody knife
With my own name engraven on the heft,
Lying unsheathed amid a world of foes,   100
For my own death? That with such horrible need
For deepest silence, I should have neglected
So trivial a precaution, as the making
His tomb the keeper of a secret written
On a thief's memory? What is his poor life?
What are a thousand lives? A parricide
Had trampled them like dust; and, see, he lives!
(*Turning to* MARZIO.) And thou . . .
   Marzio.   Oh, spare me! Speak to me no more!
That stern yet piteous look, those solemn tones,
Wound worse than torture.
   (*To the* JUDGES.)   I have told it all; 110
For pity's sake lead me away to death.
   Camillo. Guards, lead him nearer the Lady
     Beatrice,
He shrinks from her regard like autumn's leaf
From the keen breath of the serenest north.
   Beatrice. O thou who tremblest on the giddy
     verge
Of life and death, pause ere thou answerest me;
So mayst thou answer God with less dismay:
What evil have we done thee? I, alas!
Have lived but on this earth a few sad years,
And so my lot was ordered, that a father   120
First turned the moments of awakening life
To drops, each poisoning youth's sweet hope;
   and then
Stabbed with one blow my everlasting soul;
And my untainted fame; and even that peace
Which sleeps within the core of the heart's heart;
But the wound was not mortal; so my hate
Became the only worship I could lift
To our great father, who in pity and love,
Armed thee, as thou dost say, to cut him off;
And thus his wrong becomes my accusation; 130
And art thou the accuser? If thou hopest
Mercy in heaven, show justice upon earth:

Worse than a bloody hand is a hard heart.
If thou hast done murders, made thy life's path
Over the trampled laws of God and man,
Rush not before thy Judge, and say: 'My maker,
I have done this and more; for there was one
Who was most pure and innocent on earth;
And because she endured what never any
Guilty or innocent endured before: 140
Because her wrongs could not be told, not
    thought;
Because thy hand at length did rescue her;
I with my words killed her and all her kin.'
Think, I adjure you, what it is to slay
The reverence living in the minds of men
Towards our ancient house, and stainless fame!
Think what it is to strangle infant pity,
Cradled in the belief of guileless looks,
Till it become a crime to suffer. Think
What 'tis to blot with infamy and blood   150
All that which shows like innocence, and is,
Hear me, great God! I swear, most innocent,
So that the world lose all discrimination
Between the sly, fierce, wild regard of guilt,
And that which now compels thee to reply
To what I ask: Am I, or am I not
A parricide?
    Marzio.   Thou art not!
    Judge.   What is this?
    Marzio. I here declare those whom I did accuse
Are innocent. 'Tis I alone am guilty.
    Judge. Drag him away to torments; let them
        be   160
Subtle and long drawn out, to tear the folds
Of the heart's inmost cell. Unbind him not
Till he confess.
    Marzio.   Torture me as ye will:
A keener pang has wrung a higher truth
From my last breath. She is most innocent!
Bloodhounds, not men, glut yourselves well with
        me;
I will not give you that fine piece of nature
To rend and ruin.   [*Exit* MARZIO, *guarded.*
    Camillo.   What say ye now, my Lords?
    Judge. Let tortures strain the truth till it be
        white
As snow thrice sifted by the frozen wind.   170
    Camillo. Yet stained with blood.
    Judge (*to* BEATRICE). Know you this paper,
        Lady?
    Beatrice. Entrap me not with questions. Who
        stands here
As my accuser? Ha! wilt thou be he,
Who art my judge? Accuser, witness, judge,
What, all in one? Here is Orsino's name;

Where is Orsino? Let his eye meet mine.
What means this scrawl? Alas! ye know not
    what,
And therefore on the chance that it may be
Some evil, will ye kill us?
                    Enter an Officer.
    Officer.   Marzio's dead.
    Judge. What did he say?
    Officer.   Nothing. As soon as we   180
Had bound him on the wheel, he smiled on us,
As one who baffles a deep adversary;
And holding his breath, died.
    Judge.   There remains nothing
But to apply the question to those prisoners,
Who yet remain stubborn.
    Camillo.   I overrule
Further proceedings, and in the behalf
Of these most innocent and noble persons
Will use my interest with the Holy Father.
    Judge. Let the Pope's pleasure then be done.
        Meanwhile
Conduct these culprits each to separate cells; 190
And be the engines ready: for this night
If the Pope's resolution be as grave,
Pious, and just as once, I'll wring the truth
Out of those nerves and sinews, groan by groan.
                                                [*Exeunt.*

SCENE III.—*The Cell of a Prison.* BEATRICE *is dis-
    covered asleep on a couch. Enter* BERNARDO.
    Bernardo. How gently slumber rests upon her
        face,
Like the last thoughts of some day sweetly spent
Closing in night and dreams, and so prolonged.
After such torments as she bore last night,
How light and soft her breathing comes. Ay me!
Methinks that I shall never sleep again.
But I must shake the heavenly dew of rest
From this sweet folded flower, thus . . . wake!
        awake!
What, sister, canst thou sleep?
    Beatrice (*awaking*).   I was just dreaming
That we were all in Paradise. Thou knowest   10
This cell seems like a kind of Paradise
After our father's presence.
    Bernardo.   Dear, dear sister,
Would that thy dream were not a dream! O God!
How shall I tell?
    Beatrice.   What wouldst thou tell, sweet
        brother?
    Bernardo. Look not so calm and happy, or
        even whilst
I stand considering what I have to say
My heart will break.

Beatrice.   See now, thou mak'st me weep:
How very friendless thou wouldst be, dear child,
If I were dead. Say what thou hast to say.
    Bernardo. They have confessed; they could en-
      dure no more   20
The tortures . . .
    Beatrice.   Ha! What was there to confess?
They must have told some weak and wicked lie
To flatter their tormentors. Have they said
That they were guilty? O white innocence,
That thou shouldst wear the mask of guilt to hide
Thine awful and serenest countenance
From those who know thee not!

    Enter JUDGE *with* LUCRETIA *and* GIACOMO,
             guarded.

                   Ignoble hearts!
For some brief spasms of pain, which are at least
As mortal as the limbs through which they pass,
Are centuries of high splendour laid in dust?   30
And that eternal honour which should live
Sunlike, above the reek of mortal fame,
Changed to a mockery and a byword? What!
Will you give up these bodies to be dragged
At horses' heels, so that our hair should sweep
The footsteps of the vain and senseless crowd,
Who, that they may make our calamity
Their worship and their spectacle, will leave
The churches and the theatres as void
As their own hearts? Shall the light multitude   40
Fling, at their choice, curses or faded pity,
Sad funeral flowers to deck a living corpse,
Upon us as we pass to pass away,
And leave . . . what memory of our having been?
Infamy, blood, terror, despair? O thou,
Who wert a mother to the parentless,
Kill not thy child! Let not her wrongs kill thee!
Brother, lie down with me upon the rack,
And let us each be silent as a corpse;
It soon will be as soft as any grave.   50
'Tis but the falsehood it can wring from fear
Makes the rack cruel.
    Giacomo.   They will tear the truth
Even from thee at last, those cruel pains:
For pity's sake say thou art guilty now.
    Lucretia. Oh, speak the truth! Let us all
      quickly die;
And after death, God is our judge, not they;
He will have mercy on us.
    Bernardo.   If indeed
It can be true, say so, dear sister mine;
And then the Pope will surely pardon you,
And all be well.

    Judge.   Confess, or I will warp   60
Your limbs with such keen tortures . . .
    Beatrice.   Tortures! Turn
The rack henceforth into a spinning-wheel!
Torture your dog, that he may tell when last
He lapped the blood his master shed . . . not me!
My pangs are of the mind, and of the heart,
And of the soul; ay, of the inmost soul,
Which weeps within tears as of burning gall
To see, in this ill world where none are true,
My kindred false to their deserted selves.
And with considering all the wretched life   70
Which I have lived, and its now wretched end,
And the small justice shown by Heaven and
    Earth
To me or mine; and what a tyrant thou art,
And what slaves these; and what a world we
    make,
The oppressor and the oppressed . . . such pangs
    compel
My answer. What is it thou wouldst with me?
    Judge. Art thou not guilty of thy father's
    death?
    Beatrice. Or wilt thou rather tax high-judging
    God
That He permitted such an act as that
Which I have suffered, and which He beheld;   80
Made it unutterable, and took from it
All refuge, all revenge, all consequence,
But that which thou hast called my father's
    death?
Which is or is not what men call a crime,
Which either I have done, or have not done;
Say what ye will. I shall deny no more.
If ye desire it thus, thus let it be,
And so an end of all. Now do your will;
No other pains shall force another word.
    Judge. She is convicted, but has not con-
    fessed.   90
Be it enough. Until their final sentence
Let none have converse with them. You, young
    Lord,
Linger not here!
    Beatrice.   Oh, tear him not away!
    Judge. Guards, do your duty.
    Bernardo (*embracing* BEATRICE). Oh! would ye
    divide
Body from soul?
    Officer.   That is the headsman's business.
    [*Exeunt all but* LUCRETIA, BEATRICE, *and*
                   GIACOMO.
    Giacomo. Have I confessed? Is it all over now?
No hope! No refuge! O weak, wicked tongue

Which hast destroyed me, would that thou hadst
   been
Cut out and thrown to dogs first! To have killed
My father first, and then betrayed my sister;   100
Ay, thee! the one thing innocent and pure
In this black guilty world, to that which I
So well deserve! My wife! my little ones!
Destitute, helpless, and I . . . Father! God!
Canst Thou forgive even the unforgiving,
When their full hearts break thus, thus! . . .
                 [*Covers his face and weeps.*
   Lucretia.   O my child!
To what a dreadful end are we all come!
Why did I yield? Why did I not sustain
Those torments? Oh, that I were all dissolved
Into these fast and unavailing tears,   110
Which flow and feel not!
   Beatrice.   What 'twas weak to do,
'Tis weaker to lament, once being done;
Take cheer! The God who knew my wrong, and
   made
Our speedy act the angel of His wrath,
Seems, and but seems, to have abandoned us.
Let us not think that we shall die for this.
Brother, sit near me; give me your firm hand,
You had a manly heart. Bear up! Bear up!
O dearest Lady, put your gentle head
Upon my lap, and try to sleep awhile: 120
Your eyes look pale, hollow and overworn,
With heaviness of watching and slow grief.
Come, I will sing you some low, sleepy tune,
Not cheerful, nor yet sad; some dull old thing,
Some outworn and unused monotony,
Such as our country gossips sing and spin,
Till they almost forget they live: lie down!
So, that will do. Have I forgot the words?
Faith! They are sadder than I thought they were.

SONG

False friend, wilt thou smile or weep   130
When my life is laid asleep?
Little cares for a smile or a tear,
The clay-cold corpse upon the bier!
   Farewell! Heigho!
   What is this whispers low?
There is a snake in thy smile, my dear;
And bitter poison within thy tear.

Sweet sleep, were death like to thee,
Or if thou couldst mortal be,
I would close these eyes of pain;   140
When to wake? Never again.
   O World! Farewell!

Listen to the passing bell!
It says, thou and I must part,
With a light and a heavy heart.
                 [*The scene closes.*

SCENE IV.—*A Hall of the Prison. Enter* CAMILLO
   and BERNARDO.

   Camillo. The Pope is stern; not to be moved
   or bent.
He looked as calm and keen as is the engine
Which tortures and which kills, exempt itself
From aught that it inflicts; a marble form,
A rite, a law, a custom: not a man.
He frowned, as if to frown had been the trick
Of his machinery, on the advocates
Presenting the defences, which he tore
And threw behind, muttering with hoarse, harsh
   voice:
'Which among ye defended their old father   10
Killed in his sleep?' Then to another: 'Thou
Dost this in virtue of thy place; 'tis well.'
He turned to me then, looking deprecation,
And said these three words, coldly: 'They must
   die.'
   Bernardo. And yet you left him not?
   Camillo.   I urged him still;
Pleading, as I could guess, the devilish wrong
Which prompted your unnatural parent's death.
And he replied: 'Paolo Santa Croce
Murdered his mother yester evening,
And he is fled. Parricide grows so rife   20
That soon, for some just cause no doubt, the
   young
Will strangle us all, dozing in our chairs.
Authority, and power, and hoary hair
Are grown crimes capital. You are my nephew,
You come to ask their pardon; stay a moment;
Here is their sentence; never see me more
Till, to the letter, it be all fulfilled.'
   Bernardo. O God, not so! I did believe indeed
That all you said was but sad preparation
For happy news. Oh, there are words and
   looks   30
To bend the sternest purpose! Once I knew
   them,
Now I forget them at my dearest need.
What think you if I seek him out, and bathe
His feet and robe with hot and bitter tears?
Importune him with prayers, vexing his brain
With my perpetual cries, until in rage
He strike me with his pastoral cross, and trample
Upon my prostrate head, so that my blood
May stain the senseless dust on which he treads,
And remorse waken mercy? I will do it!   40

Oh, wait till I return!   [*Rushes out.*
   Camillo.   Alas! poor boy!
A wreck-devoted seaman thus might pray
To the deaf sea.

Enter LUCRETIA, BEATRICE, *and* GIACOMO, *guarded.*

   Beatrice.   I hardly dare to fear
That thou bring'st other news than a just pardon.
   Camillo. May God in heaven be less inexorable
To the Pope's prayers, than he has been to mine.
Here is the sentence and the warrant.
   Beatrice (*wildly*).   O
My God! Can it be possible I have
To die so suddenly? So young to go
Under the obscure, cold, rotting, wormy
   ground!   50
To be nailed down into a narrow place;
To see no more sweet sunshine; hear no more
Blithe voice of living thing; muse not again
Upon familiar thoughts, sad, yet thus lost—
How fearful! to be nothing! Or to be . . .
What? Oh, where am I? Let me not go mad!
Sweet Heaven, forgive weak thoughts! If there
   should be
No God, no Heaven, no Earth in the void world;
The wide, gray, lampless, deep, unpeopled world!
If all things then should be . . . my father's
   spirit,   60
His eye, his voice, his touch surrounding me;
The atmosphere and breath of my dead life!
If sometimes, as a shape more like himself,
Even the form which tortured me on earth,
Masked in gray hairs and wrinkles, he should
   come
And wind me in his hellish arms, and fix
His eyes on mine, and drag me down, down,
   down!
For was he not alone omnipotent
On Earth, and ever present? Even though dead,
Does not his spirit live in all that breathe,   70
And work for me and mine still the same ruin,
Scorn, pain, despair? Who ever yet returned
To teach the laws of Death's untrodden realm?
Unjust perhaps as those which drive us now,
Oh, whither, whither?
   Lucretia.   Trust in God's sweet love,
The tender promises of Christ: ere night,
Think, we shall be in Paradise.
   Beatrice.   'Tis past!
Whatever comes my heart shall sink no more.
And yet, I know not why, your words strike chill:
How tedious, false and cold seem all things. I   80
Have met with much injustice in this world;
No difference has been made by God or man,

Or any power moulding my wretched lot,
'Twixt good or evil, as regarded me.
I am cut off from the only world I know,
From light, and life, and love, in youth's sweet
   prime.
You do well telling me to trust in God,
I hope I do trust in Him. In whom else
Can any trust? And yet my heart is cold.
   [*During the latter speeches* GIACOMO *has re-
     tired conversing with* CAMILLO, *who now
     goes out;* GIACOMO *advances.*
   Giacomo. Know you not, Mother . . . Sister,
   know you not?   90
Bernardo even now is gone to implore
The Pope to grant our pardon.
   Lucretia.   Child, perhaps
It will be granted. We may all then live
To make these woes a tale for distant years:
Oh, what a thought! It gushes to my heart
Like the warm blood.
   Beatrice.   Yet both will soon be cold.
Oh, trample out that thought! Worse than de-
   spair,
Worse than the bitterness of death, is hope:
It is the only ill which can find place
Upon the giddy, sharp and narrow hour   100
Tottering beneath us. Plead with the swift frost
That it should spare the eldest flower of spring:
Plead with awakening earthquake, o'er whose
   couch
Even now a city stands, strong, fair, and free;
Now stench and blackness yawn, like death. Oh,
   plead
With famine, or wind-walking Pestilence,
Blind lightning, or the deaf sea, not with man!
Cruel, cold, formal man; righteous in words,
In deeds a Cain. No, Mother, we must die:
Since such is the reward of innocent lives;   110
Such the alleviation of worst wrongs.
And whilst our murderers live, and hard, cold
   men,
Smiling and slow, walk through a world of
   tears
To death as to life's sleep; 'twere just the grave
Were some strange joy for us. Come, obscure
   Death,
And wind me in thine all-embracing arms!
Like a fond mother hide me in thy bosom,
And rock me to the sleep from which none wake.
Live ye, who live, subject to one another
As we were once, who now . . .

       BERNARDO *rushes in.*

   Bernardo.   Oh, horrible! 120

That tears, that looks, that hope poured forth in
   prayer,
Even till the heart is vacant and despairs,
Should all be vain! The ministers of death
Are waiting round the doors. I thought I saw
Blood on the face of one . . . What if 'twere
   fancy?
Soon the heart's blood of all I love on earth
Will sprinkle him, and he will wipe it off
As if 'twere only rain. O life! O world!
Cover me! let me be no more! To see
That perfect mirror of pure innocence   130
Wherein I gazed, and grew happy and good,
Shivered to dust! To see thee, Beatrice,
Who made all lovely thou didst look upon . . .
Thee, light of life . . . dead, dark! while I say,
   sister,
To hear I have no sister; and thou, Mother,
Whose love was as a bond to all our loves . . .
Dead! The sweet bond broken!

     Enter CAMILLO *and* GUARDS.

                They come! Let me
Kiss those warm lips before their crimson leaves
Are blighted . . . white . . . cold. Say farewell,
   before
Death chokes that gentle voice! Oh, let me
   hear   140
You speak!
  Beatrice. Farewell, my tender brother. Think
Of our sad fate with gentleness, as now:
And let mild, pitying thoughts lighten for thee
Thy sorrow's load. Err not in harsh despair,
But tears and patience. One thing more, my
   child:
For thine own sake be constant to the love
Thou bearest us; and to the faith that I,
Though wrapped in a strange cloud of crime and
   shame,
Lived ever holy and unstained. And though
Ill tongues shall wound me, and our common
   name   150
Be as a mark stamped on thine innocent brow
For men to point at as they pass, do thou
Forbear, and never think a thought unkind
Of those, who perhaps love thee in their graves.
So mayest thou die as I do; fear and pain
Being subdued. Farewell! Farewell! Farewell!
  Bernardo. I cannot say, farewell!
  Camillo.   Oh, Lady Beatrice!
  Beatrice. Give yourself no unnecessary pain,
My dear Lord Cardinal. Here, Mother, tie
My girdle for me, and bind up this hair   160
In any simple knot; ay, that does well.

And yours I see is coming down. How often
Have we done this for one another; now
We shall not do it any more. My Lord,
We are quite ready. Well, 'tis very well.

     THE END.

  1819   1820

LINES WRITTEN AMONG THE EUGANEAN HILLS

[This poem] was written after a day's excursion among those lovely mountains which surround what was once the retreat, and where is now the sepulchre, of Petrarch. If any one is inclined to condemn the insertion of the introductory lines, which image forth the sudden relief of a state of deep despondency by the radiant visions disclosed by the sudden burst of an Italian sunrise in autumn, on the highest peak of those delightful mountains, I can only offer as my excuse, that they were not erased at the request of a dear friend, with whom added years of intercourse only add to my apprehension of its value, and who would have had more right than any one to complain, that she has not been able to extinguish in me the very power of delineating sadness.—(Shelley's Preface.)

[The Euganean Hills are in northeastern Italy just off the route between Padua and Venice.]

MANY a green isle needs must be
In the deep wide sea of Misery,
Or the mariner, worn and wan,
Never thus could voyage on—
Day and night, and night and day,
Drifting on his dreary way,
With the solid darkness black
Closing round his vessel's track;
Whilst above the sunless sky,
Big with clouds, hangs heavily,   10
And behind the tempest fleet
Hurries on with lightning feet,
Riving sail, and cord, and plank,
Till the ship has almost drank
Death from the o'er-brimming deep;
And sinks down, down, like that sleep
When the dreamer seems to be
Weltering through eternity;
And the dim low line before
Of a dark and distant shore   20
Still recedes, as ever still
Longing with divided will,
But no power to seek or shun,
He is ever drifted on
O'er the unreposing wave
To the haven of the grave.
What, if there no friends will greet;
What, if there no heart will meet

His with love's impatient beat;
Wander wheresoe'er he may, 30
Can he dream before that day
To find refuge from distress
In friendship's smile, in love's caress?
Then 'twill wreak him little woe
Whether such there be or no:
Senseless is the breast, and cold,
Which relenting love would fold;
Bloodless are the veins and chill
Which the pulse of pain did fill;
Every little living nerve 40
That from bitter words did swerve
Round the tortured lips and brow,
Are like sapless leaflets now
Frozen upon December's bough.

On the beach of a northern sea
Which tempests shake eternally,
As once the wretch there lay to sleep,
Lies a solitary heap,
One white skull and seven dry bones,
On the margin of the stones, 50
Where a few gray rushes stand,
Boundaries of the sea and land:
Nor is heard one voice of wail
But the sea-mews, as they sail
O'er the billows of the gale;
Or the whirlwind up and down
Howling, like a slaughtered town,
When a king in glory rides
Through the pomp of fratricides:
Those unburied bones around 60
There is many a mournful sound;
There is no lament for him,
Like a sunless vapour, dim,
Who once clothed with life and thought
What now moves nor murmurs not.

Ay, many flowering islands lie
In the waters of wide Agony:
To such a one this morn was led,
My bark by soft winds piloted:
'Mid the mountains Euganean 70
I stood listening to the paean
With which the legioned rooks did hail
The sun's uprise majestical;
Gathering round with wings all hoar,
Through the dewy mist they soar
Like gray shades, till the eastern heaven
Bursts, and then, as clouds of even,
Flecked with fire and azure, lie
In the unfathomable sky,
So their plumes of purple grain,[1] 80

Starred with drops of golden rain,
Gleam above the sunlight woods, 90
As in silent multitudes
On the morning's fitful gale
Through the broken mist they sail,
And the vapours cloven and gleaming
Follow, down the dark steep streaming,
Till all is bright, and clear, and still,
Round the solitary hill.

Beneath is spread like a green sea 90
The waveless plain of Lombardy,
Bounded by the vaporous air,
Islanded by cities fair;
Underneath Day's azure eyes
Ocean's nursling, Venice lies,
A peopled labyrinth of walls,
Amphitrite's[2] destined halls,
Which her hoary sire[3] now paves
With his blue and beaming waves.
Lo! the sun upsprings behind, 100
Broad, red, radiant, half-reclined
On the level quivering line
Of the waters crystalline;
And before that chasm of light,
As within a furnace bright,
Column, tower, and dome, and spire,
Shine like obelisks of fire,
Pointing with inconstant motion
From the altar of dark ocean
To the sapphire-tinted skies; 110
As the flames of sacrifice
From the marble shrines did rise,
As to pierce the dome of gold
Where Apollo spoke of old.

Sun-girt City, thou hast been
Ocean's child, and then his queen;[4]
Now is come a darker day,[5]
And thou soon must be his prey,
If the power that raised thee here
Hallow so thy watery bier.[6] 120
A less drear ruin then than now,
With thy conquest-branded brow
Stooping to the slave of slaves[7]
From thy throne, among the waves
Wilt thou be, when the sea-mew
Flies, as once before it flew,

---

1 dye.
2 goddess of the sea, wife of Neptune.
3 Oceanus.
4 When Venice was a great maritime power, each year the Doge wedded the Adriatic by tossing a ring into the water.
5 In 1818 the free cities of northern Italy were under the domination of Austria.
6 It was thought that Venice was slowly sinking into the Adriatic.
7 the Austrian emperor, Francis I.

O'er thine isles depopulate,
And all is in its ancient state,
Save where many a palace gate
With green sea-flowers overgrown   130
Like a rock of Ocean's own,
Topples o'er the abandoned sea
As the tides change sullenly.
The fisher on his watery way,
Wandering at the close of day,
Will spread his sail and seize his oar
Till he pass the gloomy shore,
Lest thy dead should, from their sleep
Bursting o'er the starlight deep,
Lead a rapid masque of death   140
O'er the waters of his path.

Those who alone thy towers behold
Quivering through aëreal gold,
As I now behold them here,
Would imagine not they were
Sepulchres, where human forms,
Like pollution-nourished worms,
To the corpse of greatness cling,
Murdered, and now mouldering:
But if Freedom should awake   150
In her omnipotence, and shake
From the Celtic Anarch's[8] hold
All the keys of dungeons cold,
Where a hundred cities lie
Chained like thee, ingloriously,
Thou and all thy sister band
Might adorn this sunny land,
Twining memories of old time
With new virtues more sublime;
If not, perish thou and they!—   160
Clouds which stain truth's rising day
By her sun consumed away—
Earth can spare ye: while like flowers,
In the waste of years and hours,
From your dust new nations spring
With more kindly blossoming.

Perish—let there only be
Floating o'er thy heartless sea
As the garment of thy sky
Clothes the world immortally,   170
One remembrance, more sublime
Than the tattered pall of time,
Which scarce hides thy visage wan;—
That a tempest-cleaving Swan[9]
Of the songs of Albion,
Driven from his ancestral streams

By the might of evil dreams,
Found a nest in thee; and Ocean
Welcomed him with such emotion
That its joy grew his, and sprung   180
From his lips like music flung
O'er a mighty thunder-fit,
Chastening terror:—what though yet
Poesy's unfailing River,
Which through Albion winds forever
Lashing with melodious wave
Many a sacred Poet's grave,
Mourn its latest nursling fled?
What though thou with all thy dead
Scarce can for this fame repay   190
Aught thine own? oh, rather say
Though thy sins and slaveries foul
Overcloud a sunlike soul?
As the ghost of Homer clings
Round Scamander's[10] wasting springs;
As divinest Shakespeare's might
Fills Avon and the world with light
Like omniscient power which he
Imaged 'mid mortality;
As the love from Petrarch's urn,   200
Yet amid yon hills doth burn,
A quenchless lamp by which the heart
Sees things unearthly;—so thou art,
Mighty spirit—so shall be
The City that did refuge thee.

Lo, the sun floats up the sky
Like thought-wingèd Liberty,
Till the universal light
Seems to level plain and height;
From the sea a mist has spread,   210
And the beams of morn lie dead
On the towers of Venice now,
Like its glory long ago.
By the skirts of that gray cloud
Many-domèd Padua proud
Stands, a peopled solitude,
'Mid the harvest-shining plain,
Where the peasant heaps his grain
In the garner of his foe,
And the milk-white oxen slow   220
With the purple vintage strain,
Heaped upon the creaking wain,[11]
That the brutal Celt may swill
Drunken sleep with savage will;
And the sickle to the sword
Lies unchanged, though many a lord,
Like a weed whose shade is poison,

---

8 foreign tyrant's.
9 Byron.

10 an ancient river near Troy.
11 wagon.

Overgrows this region's foison,[12]
Sheaves of whom are ripe to come
To destruction's harvest-home: 230
Men must reap the things they sow,
Force from force must ever flow,
Or worse; but 'tis a bitter woe
That love or reason cannot change
The despot's rage, the slave's revenge.

Padua, thou within whose walls
Those mute guests at festivals,
Son and Mother, Death and Sin,
Played at dice for Ezzelin,[13]
Till Death cried, 'I win, I win!'   240
And Sin cursed to lose the wager,
But Death promised, to assuage her,
That he would petition for
Her to be made Vice-Emperor,
When the destined years were o'er,
Over all between the Po
And the eastern Alpine snow,
Under the mighty Austrian.
Sin smiled so as Sin only can,
And since that time, ay, long before,   250
Both have ruled from shore to shore,—
That incestuous pair, who follow
Tyrants as the sun the swallow,
As Repentance follows Crime,
And as changes follow Time.

In thine halls the lamp of learning,
Padua, now no more is burning;
Like a meteor, whose wild way
Is lost over the grave of day,
It gleams betrayed and to betray: 260
Once remotest nations came
To adore that sacred flame,
When it lit not many a hearth
On this cold and gloomy earth:
Now new fires from antique light
Spring beneath the wide world's might;
But their spark lies dead in thee,
Trampled out by Tyranny.
As the Norway woodman quells,
In the depth of piny dells,   270
One light flame among the brakes,
While the boundless forest shakes,
And its mighty trunks are torn
By the fire thus lowly born:
The spark beneath his feet is dead,
He starts to see the flames it fed

---

12 abundant harvest.
13 a tyrant of Padua in the thirteenth century whose name became proverbial for cruelty.

Howling through the darkened sky
With a myriad tongues victoriously,
And sinks down in fear: so thou,
O Tyranny, beholdest now   280
Light around thee, and thou hearest
The loud flames ascend, and fearest:
Grovel on the earth; ay, hide
In the dust thy purple pride!

Noon descends around me now:
'Tis the noon of autumn's glow,
When a soft and purple mist
Like a vaporous amethyst,
Or an air-dissolvèd star
Mingling light and fragrance, far   290
From the curved horizon's bound
To the point of Heaven's profound,
Fills the overflowing sky;
And the plains that silent lie
Underneath, the leaves unsodden
Where the infant Frost has trodden
With his morning-wingèd feet,
Whose bright print is gleaming yet;
And the red and golden vines,
Piercing with their trellised lines   300
The rough, dark-skirted wilderness;
The dun and bladed grass no less,
Pointing from this hoary tower
In the windless air; the flower
Glimmering at my feet; the line
Of the olive-sandalled Apennine
In the south dimly islanded;
And the Alps, whose snows are spread
High between the clouds and sun;
And of living things each one;   310
And my spirit which so long
Darkened this swift stream of song,—
Interpenetrated lie
By the glory of the sky:
Be it love, light, harmony,
Odour, or the soul of all
Which from Heaven like dew doth fall,
Or the mind which feeds this verse
Peopling the lone universe.

Noon descends, and after noon   320
Autumn's evening meets me soon,
Leading the infantine moon,
And that one star, which to her
Almost seems to minister
Half the crimson light she brings
From the sunset's radiant springs:
And the soft dreams of the morn
(Which like wingèd winds had borne
To that silent isle, which lies

Mid remembered agonies, 330
The frail bark of this lone being)
Pass, to other sufferers fleeing,
And its ancient pilot, Pain,
Sits beside the helm again.

Other flowering isles must be
In the sea of Life and Agony:
Other spirits float and flee
O'er that gulf: even now, perhaps,
On some rock the wild wave wraps,
With folded wings they waiting sit 340
For my bark, to pilot it
To some calm and blooming cove,
Where for me, and those I love,
May a windless bower be built,
Far from passion, pain, and guilt,
In a dell mid lawny hills,
Which the wild sea-murmur fills,
And soft sunshine, and the sound
Of old forests echoing round,
And the light and smell divine 350
Of all flowers that breathe and shine:
We may live so happy there,
That the Spirits of the Air,
Envying us, may even entice
To our healing Paradise
The polluting multitude;
But their rage would be subdued
By that clime divine and calm,
And the winds whose wings rain balm
On the uplifted soul, and leaves 360
Under which the bright sea heaves;
While each breathless interval
In their whisperings musical
The inspired soul supplies
With its own deep melodies,
And the love which heals all strife
Circling, like the breath of life,
All things in that sweet abode
With its own mild brotherhood:
They, not it, would change; and soon 370
Every sprite beneath the moon
Would repent its envy vain,
And the earth grow young again.

1818   1819

STANZAS

WRITTEN IN DEJECTION, NEAR NAPLES

At the time, Shelley suffered greatly in health. He put himself under the care of a medical man, who promised great things, and made him endure severe bodily pain, without any good results. Constant and poignant physical suffering exhausted him; and though he preserved the appearance of cheerfulness, and often greatly enjoyed our wanderings in the environs of Naples, and our excursions on its sunny sea, yet many hours were passed when his thoughts, shadowed by illness, became gloomy, —and then he escaped to solitude, and in verses, which he hid from fear of wounding me, poured forth morbid but too natural bursts of discontent and sadness. One looks back with unspeakable regret and gnawing remorse to such periods; fancying that, had one been more alive to the nature of his feelings, and more attentive to soothe them, such would not have existed. And yet, enjoying as he appeared to do every sight or influence of earth or sky, it was difficult to imagine that any melancholy he showed was aught but the effect of the constant pain to which he was a martyr.—(From Mrs. Shelley's note.)

THE sun is warm, the sky is clear,
    The waves are dancing fast and bright;
Blue isles and snowy mountains wear
    The purple noon's transparent might;
    The breath of the moist earth is light
Around its unexpanded buds;
    Like many a voice of one delight,
The winds, the birds, the ocean floods,
The City's voice itself, is soft like Solitude's.

I see the Deep's untrampled floor 10
    With green and purple seaweeds strown;
I see the waves upon the shore,
    Like light dissolved in star-showers, thrown:
    I sit upon the sands alone,—
The lightning of the noontide ocean
    Is flashing round me, and a tone
Arises from its measured motion,
How sweet! did any heart now share in my emotion.

Alas! I have nor hope nor health,
    Nor peace within nor calm around, 20
Nor that content surpassing wealth
    The sage in meditation found,
    And walked with inward glory crowned—
Nor fame, nor power, nor love, nor leisure.
    Others I see whom these surround—
Smiling they live, and call life pleasure;—
To me that cup has been dealt in another measure.

Yet now despair itself is mild,
    Even as the winds and waters are;
I could lie down like a tired child, 30
    And weep away the life of care
    Which I have borne and yet must bear,
Till death like sleep might steal on me,
    And I might feel in the warm air
My cheek grow cold, and hear the sea
Breathe o'er my dying brain its last monotony.

Some might lament that I were cold,
  As I, when this sweet day is gone,
Which my lost heart, too soon grown old,
  Insults with this untimely moan;   40
    They might lament—for I am one
Whom men love not,—and yet regret,
  Unlike this day, which, when the sun
Shall on its stainless glory set,
Will linger, though enjoyed, like joy in memory
    yet.
  1818   1824

SONNET: 'LIFT NOT THE PAINTED VEIL'

LIFT not the painted veil which those who live
Call Life: though unreal shapes be pictured there,
And it but mimic all we would believe
With colours idly spread,—behind, lurk Fear
And Hope, twin Destinies; who ever weave
Their shadows, o'er the chasm, sightless and
    drear.
I knew one who had lifted it—he sought,
For his lost heart was tender, things to love,
But found them not, alas! nor was there aught
The world contains, the which he could
    approve.   10
Through the unheeding many he did move,
A splendour among shadows, a bright blot
Upon this gloomy scene, a Spirit that strove
For truth, and like the Preacher found it not.
  1818   1824

THE MASK OF ANARCHY

WRITTEN ON THE OCCASION OF THE MASSACRE AT MANCHESTER[1]

Though Shelley's first eager desire to excite his countrymen to resist openly the oppressions existent during 'the good old times' had faded with early youth, still his warmest sympathies were for the people. He was a republican, and loved a democracy. He looked on all human beings as inheriting an equal right to possess the dearest privileges of our nature; the necessaries of life when fairly earned by labour, and intellectual instruction. His hatred of any despotism that looked upon the people as not to be consulted, or protected from want and ignorance, was intense. He was residing near Leghorn, at Villa Valsovano, writing *The Cenci,* when the news of the Manchester Massacre reached us; it roused in him violent emotions of indignation and compassion. The great truth that the many, if accordant and resolute, could control the few, as was shown some years after, made him long to teach his injured countrymen how to resist. Inspired by these feelings, he wrote the *Mask of Anarchy,* which he sent to his friend, Leigh Hunt, to be inserted in the *Examiner,* of which he was then the Editor.

'I did not insert it,' Leigh Hunt writes in his valuable and interesting preface to this poem, when he printed it in 1832, 'because I thought that the public at large had not become sufficiently discerning to do justice to the sincerity and kind-heartedness of the spirit that walked in this flaming robe of verse.' Days of outrage have passed away, and with them the exasperation that would cause such an appeal to the many to be injurious. Without being aware of them, they at one time acted on his suggestions, and gained the day. But they rose when human life was respected by the Minister in power; such was not the case during the Administration which excited Shelley's abhorrence.

The poem was written for the people, and is therefore in a more popular tone than usual: portions strike as abrupt and unpolished, but many stanzas are all his own. I heard him repeat, and admired, those beginning

‘My Father Time is old and grey,’

before I knew to what poem they were to belong. But the most touching passage is that which describes the blessed effects of liberty; it might make a patriot of any man whose heart was not wholly closed against his humbler fellow-creatures.—(Mrs. Shelley.)

As I lay asleep in Italy
There came a voice from over the Sea,
And with great power it forth led me
To walk in the visions of Poesy.

I met Murder on the way—
He had a mask like Castlereagh[2]—
Very smooth he looked, yet grim;
Seven blood-hounds followed him:

All were fat; and well they might
Be in admirable plight,   10
For one by one, and two by two,
He tossed them human hearts to chew
Which from his wide cloak he drew.

Next came Fraud, and he had on,
Like Eldon,[3] an ermined gown;
His big tears, for he wept well,
Turned to mill-stones as they fell.

And the little children, who
Round his feet played to and fro,
Thinking every tear a gem,   20
Had their brains knocked out by them.

Clothed with the Bible, as with light,
And the shadows of the night,

---

1 On 16 August 1819, a great reform meeting was held outside Manchester in defiance of local authorities. The militia interfered, and in the riot that followed several people were killed and scores injured.

2 Robert Stewart, Viscount Castlereagh, leader of the ultra-Tory party and unalterable opponent to revolutionary reform.
3 Lord High Chancellor, who had handed down the court decision depriving Shelley of his children.

Like Sidmouth,[4] next, Hypocrisy
On a crocodile rode by.

And many more Destructions played
In this ghastly masquerade,
All disguised, even to the eyes,
Like Bishops, lawyers, peers, or spies.

Last came Anarchy: he rode   30
On a white horse, splashed with blood;
He was pale even to the lips,
Like Death in the Apocalypse.

And he wore a kingly crown;
And in his grasp a sceptre shone;
On his brow this mark I saw—
'I AM GOD, AND KING, AND LAW!'

With a pace stately and fast,
Over English land he passed,
Trampling to a mire of blood   40
The adoring multitude.

And a mighty troop around,
With their trampling shook the ground,
Waving each a bloody sword,
For the service of their Lord.

And with glorious triumph, they
Rode through England proud and gay,
Drunk as with intoxication
Of the wine of desolation.

O'er fields and towns, from sea to sea,   50
Passed the Pageant swift and free,
Tearing up, and trampling down;
Till they came to London town.

And each dweller, panic-stricken,
Felt his heart with terror sicken
Hearing the tempestuous cry
Of the triumph of Anarchy.

For with pomp to meet him came,
Clothed in arms like blood and flame,
The hired murderers, who did sing   60
'Thou art God, and Law, and King.

'We have waited, weak and lone
For thy coming, Mighty One!
Our purses are empty, our swords are cold,
Give us glory, and blood, and gold.'

Lawyers and priests, a motley crowd,
To the earth their pale brows bowed;
Like a bad prayer not over loud,
Whispering—'Thou art Law and God.'—

Then all cried with one accord,   70
Thou art King, and God, and Lord;
Anarchy, to thee we bow,
Be thy name made holy now!'

And Anarchy, the Skeleton,
Bowed and grinned to every one,
As well as if his education
Had cost ten millions to the nation.

For he knew the Palaces
Of our Kings were rightly his;
His the sceptre, crown, and globe,   80
And the gold-inwoven robe.

So he sent his slaves before
To seize upon the Bank and Tower,[5]
And was proceeding with intent
To meet his pensioned Parliament

When one fled past, a maniac maid,
And her name was Hope, she said:
But she looked more like Despair,
And she cried out in the air:

'My father Time is weak and grey   90
With waiting for a better day;
See how idiot-like he stands,
Fumbling with his palsied hands!

'He has had child after child,
And the dust of death is piled
Over every one but me—
Misery, oh, Misery!'

Then she lay down in the street,
Right before the horses' feet,
Expecting, with a patient eye,   100
Murder, Fraud, and Anarchy.

When between her and her foes
A mist, a light, an image rose,
Small at first, and weak, and frail
Like the vapour of a vale:

Till as clouds grow on the blast,
Like tower-crowned giants striding fast,
And glare with lightnings as they fly,
And speak in thunder to the sky,

---

4 Home Secretary, noted for his repressive measures.

5 The Bank of England and the Tower of London.

It grew—a Shape arrayed in mail 110
Brighter than the viper's scale,
And upborne on wings whose grain[6]
Was as the light of sunny rain.

On its helm, seen far away,
A planet, like the Morning's, lay;
And those plumes its light rained through
Like a shower of crimson dew.

With step as soft as wind it passed
O'er the heads of men—so fast
That they knew the presence there, 120
And looked,—but all was empty air.

As flowers beneath May's footstep waken,
As stars from Night's loose hair are shaken,
As waves arise when loud winds call,
Thoughts sprung where'er that step did fall.

And the prostrate multitude
Looked—and ankle-deep in blood,
Hope, that maiden most serene,
Was walking with a quiet mien:

And Anarchy, the ghastly birth, 130
Lay dead earth upon the earth;
The Horse of Death tameless as wind
Fled, and with his hoofs did grind
To dust the murderers thronged behind.

A rushing light of clouds and splendour,
A sense awakening and yet tender
Was heard and felt—and at its close
These words of joy and fear arose

As if their own indignant Earth
Which gave the sons of England birth 140
Had felt their blood upon her brow,
And shuddering with a mother's throe

Had turnèd every drop of blood
By which her face had been bedewed
To an accent unwithstood,—
As if her heart had cried aloud:

'Men of England, heirs of Glory,
Heroes of unwritten story,
Nurslings of one mighty Mother,
Hopes of her, and one another; 150

'Rise like Lions after slumber
In unvanquishable number,

---
6 color.

Shake your chains to earth like dew
Which in sleep had fallen on you—
Ye are many—they are few.

'What is Freedom?—ye can tell
That which slavery is, too well—
For its very name has grown
To an echo of your own.

' 'Tis to work and have such pay 160
As just keeps life from day to day
In your limbs, as in a cell
For the tyrants' use to dwell,

'So that ye for them are made
Loom, and plough, and sword, and spade,
With or without your own will bent
To their defence and nourishment.

' 'Tis to see your children weak
With their mothers pine and peak,
When the winter winds are bleak,— 170
They are dying whilst I speak.

' 'Tis to hunger for such diet
As the rich man in his riot
Casts to the fat dogs that lie
Surfeiting beneath his eye;

' 'Tis to let the Ghost of Gold
Take from Toil a thousandfold
More than e'er its substance could
In the tyrannies of old.

'Paper coin—that forgery 180
Of the title-deeds, which ye
Hold to something of the worth
Of the inheritance of Earth.

' 'Tis to be a slave in soul
And to hold no strong control
Over your own wills, but be
All that others make of ye.

'And at length when ye complain
With a murmur weak and vain
'Tis to see the Tyrant's crew 190
Ride over your wives and you—
Blood is on the grass like dew.

'Then it is to feel revenge
Fiercely thirsting to exchange
Blood for blood—and wrong for wrong—
Do not thus when ye are strong.

'Birds find rest, in narrow nest
When weary of their wingèd quest;
Beasts find fare, in woody lair
When storm and snow are in the air.   200

'Asses, swine, have litter spread
And with fitting food are fed;
All things have a home but one—
Thou, Oh, Englishman, hast none!

'This is Slavery—savage men,
Or wild beasts within a den
Would endure not as ye do—
But such ills they never knew.

'What art thou Freedom? O! could slaves
Answer from their living graves   210
This demand—tyrants would flee
Like a dream's dim imagery:

'Thou art not, as impostors say,
A shadow soon to pass away,
A superstition, and a name
Echoing from the cave of Fame.

'For the labourer thou art bread,
And a comely table spread
From his daily labour come
In a neat and happy home.   220

'Thou art clothes, and fire, and food
For the trampled multitude—
No—in countries that are free
Such starvation cannot be
As in England now we see.

'To the rich thou art a check,
When his foot is on the neck
Of his victim, thou dost make
That he treads upon a snake.

'Thou art Justice—ne'er for gold   230
May thy righteous laws be sold
As laws are in England—thou
Shield'st alike the high and low.

'Thou art Wisdom—Freemen never
Dream that God will damn for ever
All who think those things untrue
Of which Priests make such ado.

'Thou art Peace—never by thee
Would blood and treasure wasted be

As tyrants wasted them, when all   240
Leagued to quench thy flame in Gaul.[7]

'What if English toil and blood
Was poured forth, even as a flood?
It availed, Oh, Liberty,
To dim, but not extinguish thee.

'Thou art Love—the rich have kissed
Thy feet, and like him[8] following Christ,
Give their substance to the free
And through the rough world follow thee,

'Or turn their wealth to arms, and make   250
War for thy belovèd sake
On wealth, and war, and fraud—whence they
Drew the power which is their prey.

'Science, Poetry, and Thought
Are thy lamps; they make the lot
Of the dwellers in a cot
So serene, they curse it not.

'Spirit, Patience, Gentleness,
All that can adorn and bless
Art thou—let deeds, not words, express   260
Thine exceeding loveliness.

'Let a great Assembly be
Of the fearless and the free
On some spot of English ground
Where the plains stretch wide around.

'Let the blue sky overhead,
The green earth on which ye tread,
All that must eternal be
Witness the solemnity.

'From the corners uttermost   270
Of the bounds of English coast;
From every hut, village, and town
Where those who live and suffer moan
For others' misery or their own,

'From the workhouse and the prison
Where pale as corpses newly risen,
Women, children, young and old
Groan for pain, and weep for cold—

'From the haunts of daily life
Where is waged the daily strife   280

7 France.
8 the wealthy man who gave up his riches to the poor. See Luke, xviii, 18–22.

With common wants and common cares
Which sows the human heart with tares—

'Lastly from the palaces
Where the murmur of distress
Echoes, like the distant sound
Of a wind alive around

'Those prison halls of wealth and fashion,
Where some few feel such compassion
For those who groan, and toil, and wail
As must make their brethren pale—   290

'Ye who suffer woes untold,
Or to feel, or to behold
Your lost country bought and sold
With a price of blood and gold—

'Let a vast assembly be,
And with great solemnity
Declare with measured words that ye
Are, as God has made ye, free—

'Be your strong and simple words
Keen to wound as sharpened swords,   300
And wide as targes let them be,
With their shade to cover ye.

'Let the tyrants pour around
With a quick and startling sound,
Like the loosening of a sea,
Troops of armed emblazonry.

'Let the charged artillery drive
Till the dead air seems alive
With the clash of clanging wheels,
And the tramp of horses' heels.   310

'Let the fixèd bayonet
Gleam with sharp desire to wet
Its bright point in English blood
Looking keen as one for food.

'Let the horsemen's scimitars
Wheel and flash, like sphereless stars
Thirsting to eclipse their burning
In a sea of death and mourning.

'Stand ye calm and resolute,
Like a forest close and mute,   320
With folded arms and looks which are
Weapons of unvanquished war,

'And let Panic, who outspeeds
The career of armèd steeds

Pass, a disregarded shade
Through your phalanx undismayed.

'Let the laws of your own land,
Good or ill, between ye stand
Hand to hand, and foot to foot,
Arbiters of the dispute,   330

'The old laws of England—they
Whose reverend heads with age are grey,
Children of a wiser day;
And whose solemn voice must be
Thine own echo—Liberty!

'On those who first should violate
Such sacred heralds in their state
Rest the blood that must ensue,
And it will not rest on you.

'And if then the tyrants dare   340
Let them ride among you there,
Slash, and stab, and maim, and hew,—
What they like, that let them do.

'With folded arms and steady eyes,
And little fear, and less surprise,
Look upon them as they slay
Till their rage has died away.

'Then they will return with shame
To the place from which they came,
And the blood thus shed will speak   350
In hot blushes on their cheek.

'Every woman in the land
Will point at them as they stand—
They will hardly dare to greet
Their acquaintance in the street.

'And the bold, true warriors
Who have hugged Danger in wars
Will turn to those who would be free,
Ashamed of such base company.

'And that slaughter to the Nation   360
Shall steam up like inspiration,
Eloquent, oracular;
A volcano heard afar.

'And these words shall then become
Like Oppression's thundered doom
Ringing through each heart and brain,
Heard again—again—again—

'Rise like Lions after slumber
In unvanquishable number—
Shake your chains to earth like dew   370
Which in sleep had fallen on you—
Ye are many—they are few.'

1819   1832

SONG TO THE MEN OF ENGLAND

[This and the following poem belong to the group of
political poems written by Shelley in 1819 under the
same impulse that led to *The Mask of Anarchy* and with
the same hope that they might aid in the great battle for
reform. None of these poems, however, was published
until after the First Reform Act had been made law.]

MEN of England, wherefore plough
For the lords who lay ye low?
Wherefore weave with toil and care
The rich robes your tyrants wear?

Wherefore feed, and clothe, and save,
From the cradle to the grave,
Those ungrateful drones who would
Drain your sweat—nay, drink your blood?

Wherefore, Bees of England, forge
Many a weapon, chain, and scourge,   10
That these stingless drones may spoil
The forced produce of your toil?

Have ye leisure, comfort, calm,
Shelter, food, love's gentle balm?
Or what is it ye buy so dear
With your pain and with your fear?

The seed ye sow, another reaps;
The wealth ye find, another keeps;
The robes ye weave, another wears;
The arms ye forge, another bears.   20

Sow seed,—but let no tyrant reap;
Find wealth,—let no impostor heap;
Weave robes,—let not the idle wear;
Forge arms,—in your defence to bear.

Shrink to your cellars, holes, and cells;
In halls ye deck another dwells.
Why shake the chains ye wrought? Ye see
The steel ye tempered glance on ye.

With plough and spade, and hoe and loom,
Trace your grave, and build your tomb,   30
And weave your winding-sheet, till fair
England be your sepulchre.

1819   1839

ENGLAND IN 1819

AN old, mad, blind, despised, and dying king;[1]
Princes, the dregs of their dull race, who flow
Through public scorn—mud from a muddy
        spring;
Rulers who neither see, nor feel, nor know,
But leech-like to their fainting country cling,
Till they drop, blind in blood, without a blow;
A people starved and stabbed in the untilled
        field;
An army, which liberticide and prey
Makes as a two-edged sword to all who wield;
Golden and sanguine laws which tempt and
        slay;   10
Religion Christless, Godless—a book sealed;
A Senate—Time's worst statute[2] unrepealed,—
Are graves, from which a glorious Phantom may
Burst to illumine our tempestuous day.

1819   1839

ODE TO THE WEST WIND

This poem was conceived and chiefly written in a
wood that skirts the Arno, near Florence, and on a day
when that tempestuous wind, whose temperature is at
once mild and animating, was collecting the vapours
which pour down the autumnal rains. They began, as I
foresaw, at sunset with a violent tempest of hail and
rain, attended by that magnificent thunder and lightning
peculiar to the Cisalpine regions.

The phenomenon alluded to at the conclusion of the
third stanza is well known to naturalists. The vegetation
at the bottom of the sea, of rivers, and of lakes, sympathizes with that of the land in the change of seasons, and
is consequently influenced by the winds which announce
it.—(Shelley.)

I

O, WILD West Wind, thou breath of Autumn's
        being,
Thou, from whose unseen presence the leaves
        dead
Are driven, like ghosts from an enchanter fleeing,

Yellow, and black, and pale, and hectic red,
Pestilence-stricken multitudes: O, thou,
Who chariotest to their dark wintry bed

The wingèd seeds, where they lie cold and low,
Each like a corpse within its grave, until
Thine azure sister of the spring shall blow

Her clarion o'er the dreaming earth, and fill   10
(Driving sweet buds like flocks to feed in air)
With living hues and odours plain and hill:

---

1 George III.
2 the acts excluding dissenters and Roman Catholics from office.

Wild Spirit, which art moving everywhere;
Destroyer and preserver; hear, oh, hear!

II

Thou on whose stream, 'mid the steep sky's commotion,
Loose clouds like earth's decaying leaves are shed,
Shook from the tangled boughs of Heaven and Ocean,

Angels[1] of rain and lightning: there are spread
On the blue surface of thine aëry surge,
Like the bright hair uplifted from the head   20

Of some fierce Mænad,[2] even from the dim verge
Of the horizon to the zenith's height
The locks of the approaching storm. Thou dirge

Of the dying year, to which this closing night
Will be the dome of a vast sepulchre,
Vaulted with all thy congregated might

Of vapors, from whose solid atmosphere
Black rain, and fire, and hail will burst: oh, hear!

III

Thou who didst waken from his summer dreams
The blue Mediterranean, where he lay,   30
Lulled by the coil of his crystalline streams,

Beside a pumice[3] isle in Baiæ's bay,[4]
And saw in sleep old palaces and towers
Quivering within the wave's intenser day,

All overgrown with azure moss and flowers
So sweet, the sense faints picturing them! Thou
For whose path the Atlantic's level powers

Cleave themselves into chasms, while far below
The sea-blooms and the oozy woods which wear
The sapless foliage of the ocean, know   40

Thy voice, and suddenly grow grey with fear,
And tremble and despoil themselves: oh, hear!

IV

If I were a dead leaf thou mightest bear;
If I were a swift cloud to fly with thee;
A wave to pant beneath thy power, and share

The impulse of thy strength, only less free
Than thou, O, uncontrollable! If even
I were as in my boyhood, and could be

The comrade of thy wanderings over heaven,
As then, when to outstrip thy skiey speed   50
Scarce seemed a vision; I would ne'er have striven

As thus with thee in prayer in my sore need,
Oh! lift me as a wave, a leaf, a cloud!
I fall upon the thorns of life! I bleed!

A heavy weight of hours has chained and bowed
One too like thee: tameless, and swift, and proud.

V

Make me thy lyre, even as the forest is:
What if my leaves are falling like its own!
The tumult of thy mighty harmonies

Will take from both a deep, autumnal tone,   60
Sweet though in sadness. Be thou, Spirit fierce,
My spirit! Be thou me, impetuous one!

Drive my dead thoughts over the universe
Like withered leaves to quicken a new birth!
And, by the incantation of this verse,

Scatter, as from an unextinguished hearth
Ashes and sparks, my words among mankind!
Be through my lips to unawakened earth

The trumpet of a prophecy! O, wind,
If Winter comes, can Spring be far behind?   70

1819   1820

THE INDIAN SERENADE

I ARISE from dreams of thee
In the first sweet sleep of night,
When the winds are breathing low,
And the stars are shining bright:
I arise from dreams of thee,
And a spirit in my feet
Hath led me—who knows how?
To thy chamber window, sweet!

The wandering airs, they faint
On the dark, the silent stream;   10
The champak[1] odours fail
Like sweet thoughts in a dream;
The nightingale's complaint,
It dies upon her heart,

---

1 messengers.
2 a frenzied female worshiper of Bacchus.
3 of light, porous volcanic lava.
4 an ancient Roman summer resort near Naples.

---

1 a kind of magnolia tree.

As I must die on thine,
　Oh, belovèd as thou art!

Oh, lift me from the grass!
　I die! I faint! I fail!
Let thy love in kisses rain
　On my lips and eyelids pale.　　　　20
My cheek is cold and white, alas!
　My heart beats loud and fast;—
Oh! press it close to thine again,
　Where it will break at last.

　　1819　　　　　　　　1822

LOVE'S PHILOSOPHY

THE fountains mingle with the river,
　And the rivers with the ocean;
The winds of heaven mix forever
　With a sweet emotion;
Nothing in the world is single;
　All things by a law divine
In one spirit meet and mingle.
　Why not I with thine?

See the mountains kiss high heaven,
　And the waves clasp one another;　　10
No sister-flower would be forgiven
　If it disdained its brother;
And the sunlight clasps the earth,
　And the moonbeams kiss the sea:
What are all these kissings worth,
　If thou kiss not me?

　　1819　　　　　　　　1819

THE SENSITIVE PLANT

PART FIRST

A SENSITIVE Plant in a garden grew,
And the young winds fed it with silver dew,
And it opened its fan-like leaves to the light,
And closed them beneath the kisses of Night.

And the Spring arose on the garden fair,
Like the Spirit of Love felt everywhere;
And each flower and herb on Earth's dark breast
Rose from the dreams of its wintry rest.

But none ever trembled and panted with bliss
In the garden, the field, or the wilderness,　　10
Like a doe in the noontide with love's sweet want,
As the companionless Sensitive Plant.

The snowdrop, and then the violet,
Arose from the ground with warm rain wet,

And their breath was mixed with fresh odour, sent
From the turf, like the voice and the instrument.

Then the pied wind-flowers[1] and the tulip tall,
And narcissi, the fairest among them all,
Who gaze on their eyes in the stream's recess,
Till they die of their own dear loveliness;　　20

And the Naiad-like lily of the vale,
Whom youth makes so fair and passion so pale
That the light of its tremulous bells is seen
Through their pavilions of tender green;

And the hyacinth purple, and white, and blue,
Which flung from its bells a sweet peal anew
Of music so delicate, soft, and intense,
It was felt like an odour within the sense;

And the rose like a nymph to the bath addressed,
Which unveiled the depth of her glowing
　　breast,　　　　　　　　　　30
Till, fold after fold, to the fainting air
The soul of her beauty and love lay bare:

And the wand-like lily, which lifted up,
As a Maenad, its moonlight-coloured cup,
Till the fiery star, which is its eye,
Gazed through clear dew on the tender sky;

And the jessamine faint, and the sweet tuberose,
The sweetest flower for scent that blows;
And all rare blossoms from every clime
Grew in that garden in perfect prime.　　40

And on the stream whose inconstant bosom
Was pranked, under boughs of embowering blossom,
With golden and green light, slanting through
Their heaven of many a tangled hue,

Broad water-lilies lay tremulously,
And starry river-buds glimmered by,
And around them the soft stream did glide and
　　dance
With a motion of sweet sound and radiance.

And the sinuous paths of lawn and of moss,
Which led through the garden along and
　　across,　　　　　　　　　　50
Some open at once to the sun and the breeze,
Some lost among bowers of blossoming trees,

Were all paved with daisies and delicate bells

---

1 anemones.

As fair as the fabulous asphodels,
And flow'rets which, drooping as day drooped
    too,
Fell into pavilions, white, purple, and blue,
To roof the glow-worm from the evening dew.

And from this undefilèd Paradise
The flowers (as an infant's awakening eyes
Smile on its mother, whose singing sweet   60
Can first lull, and at last must awaken it),

When Heaven's blithe winds had unfolded them,
As mine-lamps enkindle a hidden gem,
Shone smiling to Heaven, and every one
Shared joy in the light of the gentle sun;

For each one was interpenetrated
With the light and the odour its neighbour shed,
Like young lovers whom youth and love make
    dear
Wrapped and filled by their mutual atmosphere.

But the Sensitive Plant which could give small
    fruit   70
Of the love which it felt from the leaf to the
    root,
Received more than all, it loved more than ever,
Where none wanted but it, could belong to the
    giver,—

For the Sensitive Plant has no bright flower;
Radiance and odour are not its dower;
It loves, even like Love, its deep heart is full,
It desires what it has not, the Beautiful!

The light winds which from unsustaining wings
Shed the music of many murmurings;
The beams which dart from many a star   80
Of the flowers whose hues they bear afar;

The plumèd insects swift and free,
Like golden boats on a sunny sea,
Laden with light and odour, which pass
Over the gleam of the living grass;

The unseen clouds of the dew, which lie
Like fire in the flowers till the sun rides high,
Then wander like spirits among the spheres,
Each cloud faint with the fragrance it bears;

The quivering vapours of dim noontide,   90
Which like a sea o'er the warm earth glide,
In which every sound, and odour, and beam,
Move, as reeds in a single stream;

Each and all like ministering angels were
For the Sensitive Plant sweet joy to bear,
Whilst the lagging hours of the day went by
Like windless clouds o'er a tender sky.

And when evening descended from Heaven
    above,
And the Earth was all rest, and the air was all
    love,
And delight, though less bright, was far more
    deep,   100
And the day's veil fell from the world of sleep,

And the beasts, and the birds, and the insects
    were drowned
In an ocean of dreams without a sound;
Whose waves never mark, though they ever im-
    press
The light sand which paves it, consciousness;

(Only overhead the sweet nightingale
Ever sang more sweet as the day might fail,
And snatches of its Elysian chant
Were mixed with the dreams of the Sensitive
    Plant);—

The Sensitive Plant was the earliest   110
Upgathered into the bosom of rest;
A sweet child weary of its delight,
The feeblest and yet the favourite,
Cradled within the embrace of Night.

PART SECOND

There was a Power in this sweet place,
An Eve in this Eden; a ruling Grace
Which to the flowers, did they waken or dream,
Was as God is to the starry scheme.

A Lady, the wonder of her kind,
Whose form was upborne by a lovely mind
Which, dilating, had moulded her mien and mo-
    tion
Like a sea-flower unfolded beneath the ocean,

Tended the garden from morn to even:
And the meteors of that sublunar Heaven,   10
Like the lamps of the air when Night walks forth,
Laughed round her footsteps up from the Earth!

She had no companion of mortal race,
But her tremulous breath and her flushing face
Told, whilst the morn kissed the sleep from her
    eyes,
That her dreams were less slumber than Paradise:

As if some bright Spirit for her sweet sake
Had deserted Heaven while the stars were awake,
As if yet around her he lingering were,
Though the veil of daylight concealed him
    from her.   20

Her step seemed to pity the grass it pressed;
You might hear by the heaving of her breast,
That the coming and going of the wind
Brought pleasure there and left passion be-
    hind.

And wherever her aëry footstep trod,
Her trailing hair from the grassy sod
Erased its light vestige, with shadowy sweep,
Like a sunny storm o'er the dark green deep.

I doubt not the flowers of that garden sweet
Rejoiced in the sound of her gentle feet;   30
I doubt not they felt the spirit that came
From her glowing fingers through all their
    frame.

She sprinkled bright water from the stream
On those that were faint with the sunny beam;
And out of the cups of the heavy flowers
She emptied the rain of the thunder-showers.

She lifted their heads with her tender hands,
And sustained them with rods and osier-bands;
If the flowers had been her own infants, she
Could never have nursed them more tenderly. 40

And all killing insects and gnawing worms,
And things of obscene and unlovely forms,
She bore, in a basket of Indian woof,
Into the rough woods far aloof,—

In a basket, of grasses and wild-flowers full,
The freshest her gentle hands could pull
For the poor banished insects, whose intent,
Although they did ill, was innocent.

But the bee and the beamlike ephemeris
Whose path is the lightning's, and soft moths
    that kiss   50
The sweet lips of the flowers, and harm not, did
    she
Make her attendant angels be.

And many an antenatal tomb,
Where butterflies dream of the life to come,
She left clinging round the smooth and dark
Edge of the odorous cedar bark.

This fairest creature from earliest Spring
Thus moved through the garden ministering
All the sweet season of Summertide,
And ere the first leaf looked brown—she died! 60

PART THIRD

Three days the flowers of the garden fair,
Like stars when the moon is awakened, were,
Or the waves of Baiae,[2] ere luminous
She floats up through the smoke of Vesuvius.

And on the fourth, the Sensitive Plant
Felt the sound of the funeral chant,
And the steps of the bearers, heavy and slow,
And the sobs of the mourners, deep and low;

The weary sound and the heavy breath,
And the silent motions of passing death,   10
And the smell, cold, oppressive, and dank,
Sent through the pores of the coffin-plank;

The dark grass, and the flowers among the grass,
Were bright with tears as the crowd did pass;
From their sighs the wind caught a mournful
    tone,
And sate in the pines, and gave groan for groan.

The garden, once fair, became cold and foul,
Like the corpse of her who had been its soul,
Which at first was lovely as if in sleep,
Then slowly changed, till it grew a heap   20
To make men tremble who never weep.

Swift Summer into the Autumn flowed,
And frost in the mist of the morning rode,
Though the noonday sun looked clear and bright,
Mocking the spoil of the secret night.

The rose-leaves, like flakes of crimson snow,
Paved the turf and the moss below.
The lilies were drooping, and white, and wan,
Like the head and the skin of a dying man.

And Indian plants, of scent and hue   30
The sweetest that ever were fed on dew,
Leaf by leaf, day after day,
Were massed into the common clay.

And the leaves, brown, yellow, and grey, and red,
And white with the whiteness of what is dead,
Like troops of ghosts on the dry wind passed;
Their whistling noise made the birds aghast.

---

2 near Naples.

And the gusty winds waked the wingèd seeds,
Out of their birthplace of ugly weeds,
Till they clung round many a sweet flower's
    stem,   40
Which rotted into the earth with them.

The water-blooms under the rivulet
Fell from the stalks on which they were set;
And the eddies drove them here and there,
As the winds did those of the upper air.

Then the rain came down, and the broken stalks
Were bent and tangled across the walks;
And the leafless network of parasite bowers
Massed into ruin; and all sweet flowers.

Between the time of the wind and the snow   50
All loathliest weeds began to grow,
Whose coarse leaves were splashed with many a
    speck,
Like the water-snake's belly and the toad's back.

And thistles, and nettles, and darnels rank,
And the dock, and henbane, and hemlock dank,
Stretched out its long and hollow shank,
And stifled the air till the dead wind stank.

And plants, at whose names the verse feels loath,
Filled the place with a monstrous undergrowth,
Prickly, and pulpous, and blistering, and blue, 60
Livid, and starred with a lurid dew.

And agarics,[3] and fungi, with mildew and mould
Started like mist from the wet ground cold;
Pale, fleshy, as if the decaying dead
With a spirit of growth had been animated!

Spawn, weeds, and filth, a leprous scum,
Made the running rivulet thick and dumb,
And at its outlet flags huge as stakes
Dammed it up with roots knotted like water-
    snakes.

And hour by hour, when the air was still,   70
The vapours arose which have strength to kill;
At morn they were seen, at noon they were felt,
At night they were darkness no star could melt.

And unctuous meteors from spray to spray
Crept and flitted in broad noonday
Unseen; every branch on which they alit
By a venomous blight was burned and bit.

The Sensitive Plant, like one forbid,
Wept, and the tears within each lid
Of its folded leaves, which together grew,   80
Were changed to a blight of frozen glue.

For the leaves soon fell, and the branches soon
By the heavy axe of the blast were hewn;
The sap shrank to the root through every pore
As blood to a heart that will beat no more.

For Winter came: the wind was his whip:
One choppy finger was on his lip:
He had torn the cataracts from the hills
And they clanked at his girdle like manacles;

His breath was a chain which without a
    sound   90
The earth, and the air, and the water bound;
He came, fiercely driven, in his chariot-throne
By the tenfold blasts of the Arctic zone.

Then the weeds which were forms of living death
Fled from the frost to the earth beneath.
Their decay and sudden flight from frost
Was but like the vanishing of a ghost!

And under the roots of the Sensitive Plant
The moles and the dormice died for want:
The birds dropped stiff from the frozen air   100
And were caught in the branches naked and bare.

First there came down a thawing rain
And its dull drops froze on the boughs again;
Then there steamed up a freezing dew
Which to the drops of the thaw-rain grew;

And a northern whirlwind, wandering about
Like a wolf that had smelt a dead child out,
Shook the boughs thus laden, and heavy, and
    stiff,
And snapped them off with his rigid griff.[4]

When Winter had gone and Spring came
    back   110
The Sensitive Plant was a leafless wreck;
But the mandrakes, and toadstools, and docks,
    and darnels,
Rose like the dead from their ruined charnels.

CONCLUSION

Whether the Sensitive Plant, or that
Which within its boughs like a Spirit sat,

---

3 a type of fungus.

4 grip.

Ere its outward form had known decay,
Now felt this change, I cannot say.

Whether that Lady's gentle mind,
No longer with the form combined
Which scattered love, as stars do light,   120
Found sadness, where it left delight,

I dare not guess; but in this life
Of error, ignorance, and strife,
Where nothing is, but all things seem,
And we the shadows of the dream,

It is a modest creed, and yet
Pleasant if one considers it,
To own that death itself must be,
Like all the rest, a mockery.

That garden sweet, that lady fair,   130
And all sweet shapes and odours there,
In truth have never passed away:
'Tis we, 'tis ours, are changed; not they.

For love, and beauty, and delight,
There is no death nor change: their might
Exceeds our organs, which endure
No light, being themselves obscure.

1820   1820

THE CLOUD

I BRING fresh showers for the thirsting flowers,
  From the seas and the streams;
I bear light shade for the leaves when laid
  In their noonday dreams.
From my wings are shaken the dews that waken
  The sweet buds every one,
When rocked to rest on their mother's breast,
  As she dances about the sun.
I wield the flail of the lashing hail,
  And whiten the green plains under,   10
And then again I dissolve it in rain,
  And laugh as I pass in thunder.

I sift the snow on the mountains below,
  And their great pines groan aghast;
And all the night 'tis my pillow white,
  While I sleep in the arms of the blast.
Sublime on the towers of my skiey bowers,
  Lightning my pilot sits;
In a cavern under is fettered the thunder,
  It struggles and howls at fits;   20
Over earth and ocean, with gentle motion,
  This pilot is guiding me,
Lured by the love of the genii that move

In the depths of the purple sea;
Over the rills, and the crags, and the hills,
  Over the lakes and the plains,
Wherever he dream, under mountain or stream,
  The Spirit he loves remains;
And I all the while bask in Heaven's blue smile,
  Whilst he is dissolving in rains.   30

The sanguine Sunrise, with his meteor eyes,
  And his burning plumes outspread,
Leaps on the back of my sailing rack,
  When the morning star shines dead;
As on the jag of a mountain crag,
  Which an earthquake rocks and swings,
An eagle alit one moment may sit
  In the light of its golden wings.
And when Sunset may breathe, from the lit sea
    beneath,
  Its ardours of rest and of love,   40
And the crimson pall of eve may fall
  From the depth of Heaven above,
With wings folded I rest, on mine aëry nest,
  As still as a brooding dove.

That orbèd maiden with white fire laden,
  Whom mortals call the Moon,
Glides glimmering o'er my fleece-like floor,
  By the midnight breezes strewn;
And wherever the beat of her unseen feet,
  Which only the angels hear,   50
May have broken the woof of my tent's thin roof,
  The stars peep behind her and peer;
And I laugh to see them whirl and flee,
  Like a swarm of golden bees,
When I widen the rent in my wind-built tent,
  Till the calm rivers, lakes, and seas,
Like strips of the sky fallen through me on high,
  Are each paved with the moon and these.

I bind the Sun's throne with a burning zone,
  And the Moon's with a girdle of pearl;   60
The volcanoes are dim, and the stars reel and
    swim,
  When the whirlwinds my banner unfurl.
From cape to cape, with a bridge-like shape,
  Over a torrent sea,
Sunbeam-proof, I hang like a roof,—
  The mountains its columns be.
The triumphal arch through which I march
  With hurricane, fire, and snow,
When the Powers of the air are chained to my
    chair,
  Is the million-coloured bow;   70
The sphere-fire above its soft colours wove,
  While the moist Earth was laughing below.

I am the daughter of Earth and Water,
  And the nursling of the Sky;
I pass through the pores of the ocean and shores;
  I change, but I cannot die.
For after the rain when with never a stain
  The pavilion of Heaven is bare,
And the winds and sunbeams with their convex
    gleams
  Build up the blue dome of air,   80
I silently laugh at my own cenotaph,[1]
  And out of the caverns of rain,
Like a child from the womb, like a ghost from the
    tomb,
  I arise and unbuild it again.

      1820   1820

TO A SKYLARK

It was on a beautiful summer evening while wandering among the lanes, whose myrtle hedges were the bowers of the fireflies, that we heard the caroling of the sky-
lark, which inspired one of the most beautiful of his
poems.—(Mrs. Shelley.)

    HAIL to thee, blithe Spirit!
      Bird thou never wert,
    That from Heaven, or near it,
      Pourest thy full heart
  In profuse strains of unpremeditated art.

    Higher still and higher
      From the earth thou springest
    Like a cloud of fire;
      The blue deep thou wingest,
  And singing still dost soar, and soaring ever
    singest.   10

    In the golden lightning
      Of the sunken sun,
    O'er which clouds are bright'ning,
      Thou dost float and run;
  Like an unbodied joy whose race is just begun.

    The pale purple even
      Melts around thy flight;
    Like a star of Heaven
      In the broad daylight
  Thou art unseen, but yet I hear thy shrill
    delight,   20

    Keen as are the arrows
      Of that silver sphere,
    Whose intense lamp narrows
      In the white dawn clear,
  Until we hardly see, we feel that it is there.

---

1 empty tomb.

    All the earth and air
      With thy voice is loud,
    As, when night is bare,
      From one lonely cloud
  The moon rains out her beams, and heaven is
    overflowed.   30

    What thou art we know not;
      What is most like thee?
    From rainbow clouds there flow not
      Drops so bright to see
  As from thy presence showers a rain of mel-
    ody.

    Like a Poet hidden
      In the light of thought,
    Singing hymns unbidden,
      Till the world is wrought
  To sympathy with hopes and fears it heeded
    not—   40

    Like a high-born maiden
      In a palace tower,
    Soothing her love-laden
      Soul in secret hour
  With music sweet as love, which overflows her
    bower—

    Like a glow-worm golden
      In a dell of dew,
    Scattering unbeholden
      Its aërial hue
  Among the flowers and grass which screen it
    from the view—   50

    Like a rose embowered
      In its own green leaves,
    By warm winds deflowered,
      Till the scent it gives
  Makes faint with too much sweet these heavy-
    wingèd thieves.

    Sound of vernal showers
      On the twinkling grass,
    Rain-awakened flowers,
      All that ever was
  Joyous, and clear, and fresh, thy music doth
    surpass.   60

    Teach us, Sprite or Bird,
      What sweet thoughts are thine;
    I have never heard
      Praise of love or wine
  That panted forth a flood of rapture so di-
    vine:

Chorus Hymenæal,
    Or triumphal chaunt,
Matched with thine, would be all
    But an empty vaunt,
A thing wherein we feel there is some hidden
    want.   70

    What objects are the fountains
        Of thy happy strain?
What fields, or waves, or mountains?
        What shapes of sky or plain?
What love of thine own kind? what ignorance of
    pain?

    With thy clear keen joyance
        Languor cannot be—
Shadow of annoyance
        Never came near thee:
Thou lovest—but ne'er knew love's sad
    satiety.   80

    Waking or asleep,
        Thou of death must deem
Things more true and deep
        Than we mortals dream,
Or how could thy notes flow in such a crystal
    stream?

    We look before and after
        And pine for what is not:
    Our sincerest laughter
        With some pain is fraught;
Our sweetest songs are those that tell of saddest
    thought.   90

    Yet if we could scorn
        Hate, and pride, and fear;
If we were things born
        Not to shed a tear,
I know not how thy joy we ever should come
    near.

    Better than all measures
        Of delightful sound—
Better than all treasures
        That in books are found—
Thy skill to poet were, thou scorner of the
    ground!   100

    Teach me half the gladness
        That thy brain must know,
Such harmonious madness
        From my lips would flow,
The world should listen then—as I am listening
    now.

1820   1820

TO ——

I FEAR thy kisses, gentle maiden,
    Thou needest not fear mine;
My spirit is too deeply laden
    Ever to burthen thine.

I fear thy mien, thy tones, thy motion,
    Thou needest not fear mine;
Innocent is the heart's devotion
    With which I worship thine.

1820   1824

ARETHUSA

[Arethusa is a fountain in Ortygia, near Sicily, and Alpheus the partly subterranean river in the Peloponnesus. According to ancient Greek myth, Alpheus, the river god, became enamored of the nymph Arethusa while she bathed in his stream. She fled and Alpheus pursued her; whereupon Diana changed her into a fountain and cleft the earth so that a tunnel was made for her escape from Greece to Sicily. But Alpheus as a river followed her, and now his water mingles with hers in the Fountain of Arethusa. This poem, like the two following ones, was written for inclusion in a drama of Mrs. Shelley's. This one is sung by a nymph in *Proserpine*.]

    ARETHUSA arose
        From her couch of snows
In the Acroceraunian mountains,—
        From cloud and from crag,
        With many a jag,
Shepherding her bright fountains.
        She leapt down the rocks,
        With her rainbow locks
Streaming among the streams;—
        Her steps paved with green   10
        The downward ravine
Which slopes to the western gleams:
        And gliding and springing
        She went, ever singing,
In murmurs as soft as sleep;
        The Earth seemed to love her,
        And Heaven smiled above her,
As she lingered towards the deep.

        Then Alpheus bold,
        On his glacier cold,   20
With his trident the mountains strook
        And opened a chasm
        In the rocks;—with the spasm
All Erymanthus shook.
        And the black south wind
        It concealed behind
The urns of the silent snow,
        And earthquake and thunder
        Did rend in sunder

The bars of the springs below.   30
   The beard and the hair
   Of the River-god were
Seen through the torrent's sweep,
   As he followed the light
   Of the fleet nymph's flight
To the brink of the Dorian deep.

   'Oh, save me! Oh, guide me!
   And bid the deep hide me,
For he grasps me now by the hair!'
   The loud Ocean heard,   40
   To its blue depth stirred,
And divided at her prayer;
   And under the water
   The Earth's white daughter
Fled like a sunny beam;
   Behind her descended
   Her billows, unblended
With the brackish Dorian stream:—
   Like a gloomy stain
   On the emerald main   50
Alpheus rushed behind,—
   As an eagle pursuing
   A dove to its ruin
Down the streams of the cloudy wind.

   Under the bowers
   Where the Ocean Powers
Sit on their pearlèd thrones,
   Through the coral woods
   Of the weltering floods,
Over heaps of unvalued stones;   60
   Through the dim beams
   Which amid the streams
Weave a network of coloured light;
   And under the caves,
   Where the shadowy waves
Are as green as the forest's night:—
   Outspeeding the shark,
   And the sword-fish dark,
Under the ocean foam,
   And up through the rifts   70
   Of the mountain clifts
They passed to their Dorian home.

   And now from their fountains
   In Enna's mountains,
Down one vale where the morning basks,
   Like friends once parted
   Grown single-hearted,
They ply their watery tasks.
   At sunrise they leap
   From their cradles steep   80

In the cave of the shelving hill;
   At noontide they flow
   Through the woods below
And the meadows of asphodel;
   And at night they sleep
   In the rocking deep
Beneath the Ortygian shore;
   Like spirits that lie
   In the azure sky
When they love but live no more.   90

1820   1824

HYMN OF APOLLO

[This and the following poem were written for Mrs.
Shelley's drama, *Midas*. Apollo and Pan are contending
before Tmolus, a mountain god, for the prize in music.]

THE sleepless Hours who watch me as I lie,
   Curtained with star-inwoven tapestries,
From the broad moonlight of the sky,
   Fanning the busy dreams from my dim eyes,—
Waken me when their Mother, the grey Dawn,
Tells them that dreams and that the moon is
   gone.

Then I arise, and climbing Heaven's blue dome,
   I walk over the mountains and the waves,
Leaving my robe upon the ocean foam;
   My footsteps pave the clouds with fire; the
      caves   10
Are filled with my bright presence, and the air
Leaves the green earth to my embraces bare.

The sunbeams are my shafts, with which I kill
   Deceit, that loves the night and fears the day;
All men who do or even imagine ill
   Fly me, and from the glory of my ray
Good minds and open actions take new might,
Until diminished by the reign of night.

I feed the clouds, the rainbows and the flowers
   With their ætherial colours; the moon's
      globe   20
And the pure stars in their eternal bowers
   Are cinctured with my power as with a robe;
Whatever lamps on Earth or Heaven may shine,
Are portions of one power, which is mine.

I stand at noon upon the peak of Heaven,
   Then with unwilling steps I wander down
Into the clouds of the Atlantic even;
   For grief that I depart they weep and frown:
What look is more delightful than the smile
With which I soothe them from the western
   isle?   30

I am the eye with which the Universe
  Beholds itself and knows itself divine;
All harmony of instrument or verse,
  All prophecy, all medicine are mine,
All light of art or nature;—to my song,
Victory and praise in their own right belong.

1820   1824

HYMN OF PAN

FROM the forests and highlands
  We come, we come;
From the river-girt islands,
  Where loud waves are dumb
    Listening to my sweet pipings.
The wind in the reeds and the rushes,
  The bees on the bells of thyme,
The birds on the myrtle bushes,
  The cicale[1] above in the lime,
And the lizards below in the grass,
Were as silent as ever old Tmolus was,   10
    Listening to my sweet pipings.

Liquid Peneus[2] was flowing,
  And all dark Tempe[3] lay
In Pelion's[4] shadow, outgrowing
  The light of the dying day,
    Speeded by my sweet pipings.
The Sileni,[5] and Sylvans, and Fauns,
  And the Nymphs of the woods and waves,
To the edge of the moist river-lawns,   20
  And the brink of the dewy caves,
And all that did then attend and follow
Were silent with love, as you now, Apollo,
  With envy of my sweet pipings.

I sang of the dancing stars,
  I sang of the dædal[6] Earth,
And of Heaven—and the giant wars,
  And Love, and Death, and Birth,—
    And then I changed my pipings,—
Singing how down the vale of Menalus[7]   30
  I pursued a maiden and clasped a reed:
Gods and men, we are all deluded thus!
  It breaks in our bosom and then we bleed:
All wept, as I think both ye now would,
If envy or age had not frozen your blood,
  At the sorrow of my sweet pipings.

1820   1824

---

1 locusts.   2 a river in Thessaly.
3 a valley in Thessaly.
4 a mountain near Mount Olympus, in Thessaly.
5 satyrs and followers of Bacchus.
6 marvelously formed.
7 a mountain in Arcadia, sacred to Pan.

THE QUESTION

I DREAMED that, as I wandered by the way,
  Bare winter suddenly was changed to spring,
And gentle odours led my steps astray,
  Mixed with a sound of waters murmuring
Along a shelving bank of turf, which lay
  Under a copse, and hardly dared to fling
Its green arms round the bosom of the stream,
But kissed it and then fled, as thou mightest in
  dream.

There grew pied wind-flowers[1] and violets,
  Daisies, those pearled Arcturi[2] of the earth, 10
The constellated flower that never sets;
  Faint oxlips; tender bluebells, at whose birth
The sod scarce heaved; and that tall flower[3] that
  wets
  (Like a child, half in tenderness and mirth)
Its mother's face with heaven-collected tears,
When the low wind, its playmate's voice, it hears.

And in the warm hedge grew lush eglantine,
  Green cowbind and the moonlight-colored
  May,[4]
And cherry-blossoms, and white cups, whose
  wine
  Was the bright dew, yet drained not by the
  day;   20
And wild roses, and ivy serpentine,
  With its dark buds and leaves, wandering
  astray;
And flowers azure, black, and streaked with gold,
Fairer than any wakened eyes behold.

And nearer to the river's trembling edge
  There grew broad flag-flowers, purple prankt
  with white,
And starry river-buds among the sedge,
  And floating water-lilies, broad and bright,
Which lit the oak that overhung the hedge
  With moonlight beams of their own watery
  light;   30
And bulrushes and reeds of such deep green
As soothed the dazzled eye with sober sheen.

Methought that of these visionary flowers
  I made a nosegay, bound in such a way
That the same hues, which in their natural bow-
  ers
  Were mingled or opposed, the like array

---

1 anemones.
2 constellations.
3 probably the tulip.
4 mayflower.

Kept these imprisoned children of the Hours
  Within my hand,—and then, elate and gay,
I hastened to the spot whence I had come,
That I might there present it!—oh! to whom? 40

  1820   1822

FRAGMENT: TO THE MOON

ART thou pale for weariness
Of climbing heaven and gazing on the earth,
  Wandering companionless
Among the stars that have a different birth,—
And ever changing, like a joyless eye
That finds no object worth its constancy?

  Thou chosen sister of the spirit,
  That gazes on thee till in thee it pities . . .

  1820   1824

EPIPSYCHIDION[1]

VERSES ADDRESSED TO THE NOBLE AND UNFOR-
TUNATE LADY, EMILIA V———,[2] NOW IMPRISONED
IN THE CONVENT OF ———

[Shelley wrote of *Epipsychidion* in a letter to Ollier, his
publisher, dated 16 February 1821: 'The longer poem, I
desire, should not be considered as my own; indeed, in
a certain sense, it is a production of a portion of me already dead; and in this sense the advertisement is no fiction. It is to be published simply for the esoteric few;
and I make its author a secret to avoid the malignity of
those who turn sweet food into poison; transforming all
they touch into the corruption of their own natures.'
  In October he wrote to his friend Gisborne: 'The *Epipsychidion* is a mystery; as to real flesh and blood, you
know that I do not deal in those articles; you might as
well go to a gin-shop for a leg of mutton, as expect anything human or earthly from me.'
  In June 1822, he again wrote to Gisborne: 'The *Epipsychidion* I cannot look at; the person whom it celebrates was a cloud instead of a Juno; and poor Ixion
starts from the centaur that was the offspring of his own
embrace. If you are curious, however, to hear what I am
and have been, it will tell you something thereof. It is an
idealized history of my life and feelings. I think one is
always in love with something or other, the error, and I
confess it is not easy for spirits cased in flesh and blood
to avoid it, consists in seeking in a mortal image the likeness of what is perhaps eternal.']

ADVERTISEMENT

The Writer of the following lines died at Florence, as he
was preparing for a voyage to one of the wildest of the
Sporades, which he had bought, and where he had fitted
up the ruins of an old building, and where it was his
hope to have realized a scheme of life, suited perhaps to
that happier and better world of which he is now an inhabitant, but hardly practicable in this. His life was singular; less on account of the romantic vicissitudes which
diversified it, than the ideal tinge which it received from
his own character and feelings. The present Poem, like
the *Vita Nuova* of Dante, is sufficiently intelligible to a
certain class of readers without a matter-of-fact history
of the circumstances to which it relates; and to a certain
other class it must ever remain incomprehensible, from
a defect of a common organ of perception for the ideas
of which it treats. Not but that *gran vergogna sarebbe a
colui, che rimasse cosa sotto veste di figura, o di colore ret-
torico: e domandato non sapesse denudare le sue parole da
cotal veste, in guisa che avessero verace intendimento*.[3]
  The present poem appears to have been intended by
the Writer as the dedication to some longer one. The
stanza on the opposite page [here printed before the
poem itself] is almost a literal translation from Dante's
famous Canzone

  Voi, ch' intendendo, il terzo ciel movete, etc.

The presumptuous application of the concluding lines to
his own composition will raise a smile at the expense of
my unfortunate friend: be it a smile not of contempt, but
pity.

MY Song, I fear that thou wilt find but few
Who fitly shall conceive thy reasoning,
Of such hard matter dost thou entertain;
Whence, if by misadventure, chance should bring
Thee to base company (as chance may do),
Quite unaware of what thou dost contain,
I prithee, comfort thy sweet self again,
My last delight! tell them that they are dull,
And bid them own that thou art beautiful.

EPIPSYCHIDION

SWEET Spirit![4] Sister of that orphan one,[5]
Whose empire is the name[6] thou weepest on,
In my heart's temple I suspend to thee
These votive wreaths of withered memory.

Poor captive bird! who, from thy narrow
    cage,
Pourest such music, that it might assuage
The ruggèd hearts of those who prisoned thee,
Were they not deaf to all sweet melody;
This song shall be thy rose: its petals pale
Are dead, indeed, my adored Nightingale!   10
But soft and fragrant is the faded blossom,
And it has no thorn left to wound thy bosom.

High, spirit-wingèd Heart! who dost for ever
Beat thine unfeeling bars with vain endeavour,

---

1 a coined Greek word which means 'this soul out of my soul.'
2 Emilia Viviani, beautiful daughter of a Pisan nobleman, who
had been placed in a convent by her parents.
3 'It were a shameful thing if one should rhyme under the semblance of metaphor or rhetorical similitude, and afterwards being
questioned thereof, should be unable to rid his words of such
semblance into such guise as could be truly understood.'—From
Dante's *Vita Nuova*, xxv, translated by D. G. Rossetti.
4 Emilia.
5 Shelley's wife, Mary.
6 Shelley.

Till those bright plumes of thought, in which ar-
  rayed
It over-soared this low and worldly shade,
Lie shattered; and thy panting, wounded breast
Stains with dear blood its unmaternal nest!
I weep vain tears: blood would less bitter be, ,
Yet poured forth gladlier, could it profit thee. 20

Seraph of Heaven! too gentle to be human,
Veiling beneath that radiant form of Woman
All that is insupportable in thee
Of light, and love, and immortality!
Sweet Benediction in the eternal Curse!
Veiled Glory of this lampless Universe!
Thou Moon beyond the clouds! Thou living
  Form
Among the Dead! Thou Star above the Storm!
Thou Wonder, and thou Beauty, and thou Ter-
  ror!
Thou Harmony of Nature's art! Thou Mirror 30
In whom, as in the splendour of the Sun,
All shapes look glorious which thou gazest on!
Ay, even the dim words which obscure thee now
Flash, lightning-like, with unaccustomed glow;
I pray thee that thou blot from this sad song
All of its much mortality and wrong,
With those clear drops, which start like sacred
  dew
From the twin lights thy sweet soul darkens
  through,
Weeping, till sorrow becomes ecstasy:
Then smile on it, so that it may not die. 40

I never thought before my death to see
Youth's vision thus made perfect. Emily,
I love thee; though the world by no thin name
Will hide that love from its unvalued shame.
Would we two had been twins of the same
  mother!
Or, that the name my heart lent to another
Could be a sister's bond for her and thee,
Blending two beams of one eternity!
Yet were one lawful and the other true,
These names,[7] though dear, could paint not, as is
  due, 50
How beyond refuge I am thine. Ah me!
I am not thine: I am a part of *thee*.

Sweet Lamp! my moth-like Muse has burned
  its wings
Or, like a dying swan who soars and sings,
Young Love should teach Time, in his own grey
  style,
All that thou art. Art thou not void of guile,

A lovely soul formed to be blessed and bless?
A well of sealed and secret happiness,
Whose waters like blithe light and music are,
Vanquishing dissonance and gloom? A Star 60
Which moves not in the moving heavens, alone?
A Smile amid dark frowns? a gentle tone
Amid rude voices? a belovèd light?
A Solitude, a Refuge, a Delight?
A Lute, which those whom Love has taught to
  play
Make music on, to soothe the roughest day
And lull fond Grief asleep? a buried treasure?
A cradle of young thoughts of wingless[8] pleasure?
A violet-shrouded grave of Woe?—I measure
The world of fancies, seeking one like thee, 70
And find—alas! mine own infirmity.

She met me, Stranger, upon life's rough way,
And lured me towards sweet Death; as Night by
  Day,
Winter by Spring, or Sorrow by swift Hope,
Led into light, life, peace. An antelope,
In the suspended impulse of its lightness,
Were less aethereally light: the brightness
Of her divinest presence trembles through
Her limbs, as underneath a cloud of dew
Embodied in the windless heaven of June 80
Amid the splendour-wingèd stars, the Moon
Burns, inextinguishably beautiful:
And from her lips, as from a hyacinth full
Of honey-dew, a liquid murmur drops,
Killing the sense with passion; sweet as stops
Of planetary music[9] heard in trance.
In her mild lights the starry spirits dance,
The sunbeams of those wells which ever leap
Under the lightnings of the soul—too deep
For the brief fathom-line of thought or sense. 90
The glory of her being, issuing thence,
Stains the dead, blank, cold air with a warm
  shade
Of unentangled intermixture, made
By Love, of light and motion: one intense
Diffusion, one serene Omnipresence,
Whose flowing outlines mingle in their flowing,
Around her cheeks and utmost fingers glowing
With the unintermitted blood, which there
Quivers, (as in a fleece of snow-like air
The crimson pulse of living morning quiver,) 100
Continuously prolonged, and ending never,
Till they are lost, and in that Beauty furled
Which penetrates and clasps and fills the world;
Scarce visible from extreme loveliness.
Warm fragrance seems to fall from her light dress

---

7 sister and wife.

8 unable to take wing; hence, lasting.
9 music of the spheres.

And her loose hair; and where some heavy tress
The air of her own speed has disentwined,
The sweetness seems to satiate the faint wind;
And in the soul a wild odour is felt,
Beyond the sense, like fiery dews that melt   110
Into the bosom of a frozen bud.—
See where she stands! a mortal shape indued
With love and life and light and deity,
And motion which may change but cannot die;
An image of some bright Eternity;
A shadow of some golden dream; a Splendour
Leaving the third sphere[10] pilotless; a tender
Reflection of the eternal Moon of Love
Under whose motions life's dull billows move;
A Metaphor of Spring and Youth and
          Morning;   120
A Vision like incarnate April, warning,
With smiles and tears, Frost the Anatomy
Into his summer grave.
                    Ah, woe is me!
What have I dared? where am I lifted? how
Shall I descend, and perish not? I know
That Love makes all things equal: I have heard
By mine own heart this joyous truth averred:
The spirit of the worm beneath the sod
In love and worship, blends itself with God.

Spouse! Sister! Angel! Pilot of the Fate   130
Whose course has been so starless! O too late
Belovèd! O too soon adored, by me!
For in the fields of Immortality
My spirit should at first have worshipped thine,
A divine presence in a place divine;
Or should have moved beside it on this earth,
A shadow of that substance,[11] from its birth;
But not as now:—I love thee; yes, I feel
That on the fountain of my heart a seal
Is set, to keep its waters pure and bright   140
For thee, since in those *tears* thou hast delight.
We—are we not formed, as notes of music are,
For one another, though dissimilar;
Such difference without discord, as can make
Those sweetest sounds, in which all spirits shake
As trembling leaves in a continuous air?

Thy wisdom speaks in me, and bids me dare
Beacon the rocks on which high hearts are
          wrecked.
I never was attached to that great sect,
Whose doctrine is, that each one should
          select   150
Out of the crowd a mistress or a friend,
And all the rest, though fair and wise, commend

To cold oblivion, though it is in the code
Of modern morals, and the beaten road
Which those poor slaves with weary footsteps
          tread,
Who travel to their home among the dead
By the broad highway of the world, and so
With one chained friend, perhaps a jealous foe,
The dreariest and the longest journey go.

True Love in this differs from gold and
          clay,   160
That to divide is not to take away.
Love is like understanding, that grows bright,
Gazing on many truths; 'tis like thy light,
Imagination! which from earth and sky,
And from the depths of human fantasy,
As from a thousand prisms and mirrors, fills
The Universe with glorious beams, and kills
Error, the worm, with many a sun-like arrow
Of its reverberated lightning. Narrow
The heart that loves, the brain that contem-
          plates,   170
The life that wears, the spirit that creates
One object, and one form, and builds thereby
A sepulchre for its eternity.

Mind from its object differs most in this:
Evil from good; misery from happiness;
The baser from the nobler; the impure
And frail, from what is clear and must endure.
If you divide suffering and dross, you may
Diminish till it is consumed away;
If you divide pleasure and love and thought, 180
Each part exceeds the whole; and we know not
How much, while any yet remains unshared,
Of pleasure may be gained, of sorrow spared:
This truth is that deep well, whence sages draw
The unenvied light of hope; the eternal law
By which those live, to whom this world of life
Is as a garden ravaged, and whose strife
Tills for the promise of a later birth
The wilderness of this Elysian earth.

There was a Being[12] whom my spirit oft   190
Met on its visioned wanderings, far aloft,
In the clear golden prime of my youth's dawn,
Upon the fairy isles of sunny lawn,
Amid the enchanted mountains, and the caves
Of divine sleep, and on the air-like waves
Of wonder-level dream, whose tremulous floor
Paved her light steps;—on an imagined shore,
Under the grey beak of some promontory
She met me, robed in such exceeding glory,
That I beheld her not. In solitudes   200

---

10 the sphere of Venus, goddess of love.
11 Emily's spirit.

12 the vision of his youth.

Her voice came to me through the whispering
　　woods,
And from the fountains, and the odours deep
Of flowers, which, like lips murmuring in their
　　sleep
Of the sweet kisses which had lulled them there,
Breathed but of *her* to the enamoured air;
And from the breezes whether low or loud,
And from the rain of every passing cloud,
And from the singing of the summer-birds,
And from all sounds, all silence. In the words
Of antique verse and high romance,—in
　　form,　　　　　　　　　　　　　　　210
Sound, colour—in whatever checks that Storm
Which with the shattered present chokes the
　　past;
And in that best philosophy, whose taste
Makes this cold common hell, our life, a doom
As glorious as a fiery martyrdom;
Her Spirit was the harmony of truth.—

　　Then, from the caverns of my dreamy youth
I sprang, as one sandalled with plumes of fire,
And towards the lodestar of my one desire,
I flitted, like a dizzy moth, whose flight　　220
Is as a dead leaf's in the owlet[13] light,
When it would seek in Hesper's[14] setting sphere
A radiant death, a fiery sepulchre,
As if it were a lamp of earthly flame.—
But She, whom prayers or tears then could not
　　tame,
Passed, like a God throned on a wingèd planet,
Whose burning plumes to tenfold swiftness fan it,
Into the dreary cone of our life's shade;
And as a man with mighty loss dismayed,
I would have followed, though the grave be-
　　tween　　　　　　　　　　　　　　230
Yawned like a gulf whose spectres are unseen:
When a voice said:—'O thou of hearts the weak-
　　est,
The phantom is beside thee whom thou seekest.'
Then I—'Where?'—the world's echo answered
　　'where?'
And in that silence, and in my despair,
I questioned every tongueless wind that flew
Over my tower of mourning, if it knew
Whither 'twas fled, this soul out of my soul;
And murmured names and spells which have
　　control
Over the sightless tyrants of our fate;　　240
But neither prayer nor verse could dissipate
The night which closed on her; nor uncreate
That world within this Chaos, mine and me,

Of which she was the veiled Divinity,
The world I say of thoughts that worshipped her:
And therefore I went forth, with hope and fear
And every gentle passion sick to death,
Feeding my course with expectation's breath,
Into the wintry forest of our life;
And struggling through its error with vain
　　strife,　　　　　　　　　　　　　　250
And stumbling in my weakness and my haste,
And half bewildered by new forms, I passed,
Seeking among those untaught foresters
If I could find one form resembling hers,
In which she might have masked herself from me.
There,—One,[15] whose voice was venomed mel-
　　ody
Sate by a well, under blue nightshade bowers;
The breath of her false mouth was like faint flow-
　　ers,
Her touch was as electric poison,—flame
Out of her looks into my vitals came,　　260
And from her living cheeks and bosom flew
A killing air, which pierced like honey-dew
Into the core of my green heart, and lay
Upon its leaves; until, as hair grown grey
O'er a young brow, they hid its unblown prime
With ruins of unseasonable time.

　　In many mortal forms I rashly sought
The shadow of that idol of my thought.
And some were fair—but beauty dies away:
Others were wise—but honeyed words be-
　　tray:　　　　　　　　　　　　　　270
And One[16] was true—oh! why not true to me?
Then, as a hunted deer that could not flee,
I turned upon my thoughts, and stood at bay,
Wounded and weak and panting; the cold day
Trembled, for pity of my strife and pain.
When, like a noonday dawn, there shone again
Deliverance. One[17] stood on my path who
　　seemed
As like the glorious shape which I had dreamed
As is the Moon, whose changes ever run
Into themselves, to the eternal Sun;　　280
The cold chaste Moon, the Queen of Heaven's
　　bright isles,
Who makes all beautiful on which she smiles,
That wandering shrine of soft yet icy flame
Which ever is transformed, yet still the same,
And warms not but illumines. Young and fair
As the descended Spirit of that sphere,
She hid me, as the Moon may hide the night
From its own darkness, until all was bright

---

13 dim.
14 the evening star's.

15 a false ideal.
16 perhaps Harriet Grove.
17 Mary Shelley.

Between the Heaven and Earth of my calm mind,
And, as a cloud charioted by the wind,   290
She led me to a cave in that wild place,
And sate beside me, with her downward face
Illumining my slumbers, like the Moon
Waxing and waning o'er Endymion.
And I was laid asleep, spirit and limb,
And all my being became bright or dim
As the Moon's image in a summer sea,
According as she smiled or frowned on me;
And there I lay, within a chaste cold bed:
Alas, I then was nor alive nor dead:—   300
For at her silver voice came Death and Life,
Unmindful each of their accustomed strife,
Masked like twin babes, a sister and a brother,
The wandering hopes of one abandoned mother,
And through the cavern without wings they flew,
And cried, 'Away, he is not of our crew.'
I wept, and though it be a dream, I weep.

What storms then shook the ocean of my
    sleep,[18]
Blotting that Moon, whose pale and waning lips
Then shrank as in the sickness of eclipse;—   310
And how my soul was as a lampless sea,
And who was then its Tempest; and when She,
The Planet of that hour, was quenched, what
    frost
Crept o'er those waters, till from coast to coast
The moving billows of my being fell
Into a death of ice, immovable;—
And then—what earthquakes made it gape and
    split,
The white Moon smiling all the while on it,
These words conceal:—If not, each word would
    be
The key of staunchless tears. Weep not for
    me!   320

At length, into the obscure Forest came
The Vision I had sought through grief and shame.
Athwart that wintry wilderness of thorns
Flashed from her motion splendour like the
    Morn's,
And from her presence life was radiated
Through the grey earth and branches bare and
    dead;
So that her way was paved, and roofed above
With flowers as soft as thoughts of budding
    love;

And music from her respiration spread
Like light,—all other sounds were penetrated   330
By the small, still, sweet spirit of that sound,
So that the savage winds hung mute around;
And odours warm and fresh fell from her hair
Dissolving the dull cold in the frore[19] air:
Soft as an Incarnation of the Sun,
When light is changed to love, this glorious One
Floated into the cavern where I lay,
And called my Spirit, and the dreaming clay
Was lifted by the thing that dreamed below
As smoke by fire, and in her beauty's glow   340
I stood, and felt the dawn of my long night
Was penetrating me with living light:
I knew it was the Vision veiled from me
So many years—that it was Emily.

Twin Spheres[20] of light who rule this passive
    Earth,
This world of love, this *me;* and into birth
Awaken all its fruits and flowers, and dart
Magnetic might into its central heart;
And lift its billows and its mists, and guide
By everlasting laws, each wind and tide   350
To its fit cloud, and its appointed cave;
And lull its storms, each in the craggy grave
Which was its cradle, luring to faint bowers
The armies of the rainbow-wingèd showers;
And, as those married lights, which from the
    towers
Of Heaven look forth and fold the wandering
    globe
In liquid sleep and splendour, as a robe;
And all their many-mingled influence blend,
If equal, yet unlike, to one sweet end;—
So ye, bright regents, with alternate sway   360
Govern my sphere of being, night and day!
Thou, not disdaining even a borrowed might;
Thou, not eclipsing a remoter light;
And, through the shadow of the seasons three,
From Spring to Autumn's sere maturity,
Light it into the Winter of the tomb,
Where it may ripen to a brighter bloom.
Thou too, O Comet[21] beautiful and fierce,
Who drew the heart[22] of this frail Universe
Towards thine own; till, wrecked in that convul-
    sion,   370
Alternating attraction and repulsion,
Thine went astray and that was rent in twain;
Oh, float into our azure heaven again!

---

18 Lines 308–20, which seem to be intentionally cryptic, possibly
refer to the stormy period in Shelley's life climaxed by Harriet's
suicide and the litigation over his children. The Moon may perhaps be identified as Mary, the Tempest as Eliza Westbrook, the
Planet as Harriet.

19 frozen.
20 Mary and Emily.
21 Claire Clairmont.
22 Shelley's heart.

Be there Love's folding-star[23] at thy return;
The living Sun will feed thee from its urn
Of golden fire; the Moon will veil her horn
In thy last smiles; adoring Even and Morn
Will worship thee with incense of calm breath
And lights and shadows; as the star of Death
And Birth is worshipped by those sisters wild 380
Called Hope and Fear—upon the heart are piled
Their offerings,—of this sacrifice divine
A World shall be the altar.
                         Lady mine,
Scorn not these flowers of thought, the fading
     birth
Which from its heart of hearts that plant puts
     forth
Whose fruit, made perfect by thy sunny eyes,
Will be as of the trees of Paradise.

The day is come, and thou wilt fly with me.
To whatsoe'er of dull mortality
Is mine, remain a vestal[24] sister still;   390
To the intense, the deep, the imperishable,
Not mine but me, henceforth be thou united
Even as a bride, delighting and delighted.
The hour is come:—the destined Star has risen
Which shall descend upon a vacant prison.
The walls are high, the gates are strong, thick set
The sentinels—but true Love never yet
Was thus constrained: it overleaps all fence:
Like lightning, with invisible violence
Piercing its continents; like Heaven's free
     breath,   400
Which he who grasps can hold not; liker Death,
Who rides upon a thought, and makes his way
Through temple, tower, and palace and the array
Of arms: more strength has Love than he or they;
For it can burst his charnel, and make free
The limbs in chains, the heart in agony,
The soul in dust and chaos.
                         Emily,
A ship is floating in the harbour now,
A wind is hovering o'er the mountain's brow;
There is a path on the sea's azure floor,   410
No keel has ever ploughed that path before;
The halcyons[25] brood around the foamless isles;
The treacherous Ocean has forsworn its wiles;
The merry mariners are bold and free:
Say, my heart's sister, wilt thou sail with me?
Our bark is as an albatross, whose nest
Is a far Eden of the purple East;

And we between her wings will sit, while Night,
And Day, and Storm, and Calm, pursue their
     flight,
Our ministers, along the boundless Sea,   420
Treading each other's heels, unheededly.
It is an isle under Ionian skies,
Beautiful as a wreck of Paradise,
And, for the harbours are not safe and good,
This land would have remained a solitude
But for some pastoral people native there,
Who from the Elysian, clear, and golden air
Draw the last spirit of the age of gold,
Simple and spirited; innocent and bold.
The blue Aegean girds this chosen home,   430
With ever-changing sound and light and foam,
Kissing the sifted sands, and caverns hoar;
And all the winds wandering along the shore
Undulate with the undulating tide:
There are thick woods where sylvan forms abide;
And many a fountain, rivulet, and pond,
As clear as elemental diamond,
Or serene morning air; and far beyond,
The mossy tracks made by the goats and deer
(Which the rough shepherd treads but once a
     year)   440
Pierce into glades, caverns, and bowers, and
     halls
Built round with ivy, which the waterfalls
Illumining, with sound that never fails
Accompany the noonday nightingales;
And all the place is peopled with sweet airs;
The light clear element which the isle wears
Is heavy with the scent of lemon-flowers,
Which floats like mist laden with unseen show-
     ers,
And falls upon the eyelids like faint sleep;
And from the moss violets and jonquils
     peep,   450
And dart their arrowy odour through the brain
Till you might faint with that delicious pain.
And every motion, odour, beam, and tone,
With that deep music is in unison:
Which is a soul within the soul—they seem
Like echoes of an antenatal dream—
It is an isle 'twixt Heaven, Air, Earth, and Sea,
Cradled, and hung in clear tranquillity;
Bright as that wandering Eden Lucifer,[26]
Washed by the soft blue Oceans of young air. 460
It is a favoured place. Famine or Blight,
Pestilence, War and Earthquake, never light
Upon its mountain-peaks; blind vultures, they
Sail onward far upon their fatal way:
The wingèd storms, chanting their thunder-psalm

---

23 an evening star which rises about the time the sheep are put into their folds.
24 virgin.
25 kingfishers, said to make their nests upon the ocean and to calm the waves.

26 the morning star.

To other lands, leave azure chasms of calm
Over this isle, or weep themselves in dew,
From which its fields and woods ever renew
Their green and golden immortality.
And from the sea there rise, and from the sky   470
There fall, clear exhalations, soft and bright,
Veil after veil, each hiding some delight,
Which Sun or Moon or zephyr draw aside,
Till the isle's beauty, like a naked bride
Glowing at once with love and loveliness,
Blushes and trembles at its own excess:
Yet, like a buried lamp, a Soul no less
Burns in the heart of this delicious isle,
An atom of th' Eternal, whose own smile
Unfolds itself, and may be felt, not seen   480
O'er the grey rocks, blue waves, and forests
    green,
Filling their bare and void interstices.—
But the chief marvel of the wilderness
Is a lone dwelling, built by whom or how
None of the rustic island-people know:
'Tis not a tower of strength, though with its
    height
It overtops the woods; but, for delight,
Some wise and tender Ocean-King, ere crime
Had been invented, in the world's young prime,
Reared it, a wonder of that simple time,   490
An envy of the isles, a pleasure-house
Made sacred to his sister and his spouse.
It scarce seems now a wreck of human art,
But, as it were Titanic; in the heart
Of Earth having assumed its form, then grown
Out of the mountains, from the living stone,
Lifting itself in caverns light and high:
For all the antique and learnèd imagery
Has been erased, and in the place of it
The ivy and the wild-vine interknit   500
The volumes of their many-twining stems;
Parasite flowers illume with dewy gems
The lampless halls, and when they fade, the
    sky
Peeps through their winter-woof of tracery
With moonlight patches, or star atoms keen,
Or fragments of the day's intense serene;—
Working mosaic on their Parian[27] floors.
And, day and night, aloof, from the high tow-
    ers
And terraces, the Earth and Ocean seem
To sleep in one another's arms, and dream   510
Of waves, flowers, clouds, woods, rocks, and all
    that we
Read in their smiles, and call reality.

27 marble.

This isle and house are mine, and I have vowed
Thee to be lady of the solitude.—
And I have fitted up some chambers there
Looking towards the golden Eastern air,
And level with the living winds, which flow
Like waves above the living waves below.—
I have sent books and music there, and all
Those instruments with which high Spirits
    call   520
The future from its cradle, and the past
Out of its grave, and make the present last
In thoughts and joys which sleep, but cannot
    die,
Folded within their own eternity.
Our simple life wants little, and true taste
Hires not the pale drudge Luxury, to waste
The scene it would adorn, and therefore still,
Nature with all her children haunts the hill.
The ring-dove, in the embowering ivy, yet
Keeps up her love-lament, and the owls flit   530
Round the evening tower, and the young stars
    glance
Between the quick bats in their twilight dance;
The spotted deer bask in the fresh moonlight
Before our gate, and the slow, silent night
Is measured by the pants of their calm sleep.
Be this our home in life, and when years heap
Their withered hours, like leaves, on our decay,
Let us become the overhanging day,
The living soul of this Elysian isle,
Conscious, inseparable, one. Meanwhile   540
We two will rise, and sit, and walk together,
Under the roof of blue Ionian weather,
And wander in the meadows, or ascend
The mossy mountains, where the blue heavens
    bend
With lightest winds, to touch their paramour;
Or linger, where the pebble-paven shore,
Under the quick, faint kisses of the sea
Trembles and sparkles as with ecstasy,—
Possessing and possessed by all that is
Within that calm circumference of bliss,   550
And by each other, till to love and live
Be one:—or, at the noontide hour, arrive
Where some old cavern hoar seems yet to keep
The moonlight of the expired night asleep,
Through which the awakened day can never
    peep;
A veil for our seclusion, close as night's,
Where secure sleep may kill thine innocent
    lights;
Sleep, the fresh dew of languid love, the rain
Whose drops quench kisses till they burn again.

And we will talk, until thought's melody   560
Become too sweet for utterance, and it die
In words, to live again in looks, which dart
With thrilling tone into the voiceless heart,
Harmonizing silence without a sound.
Our breath shall intermix, our bosoms bound,
And our veins beat together; and our lips
With other eloquence than words, eclipse
The soul that burns between them, and the
     wells
Which boil under our being's inmost cells,
The fountains of our deepest life, shall be   570
Confused in Passion's golden purity,
As mountain-springs under the morning sun.
We shall become the same, we shall be one
Spirit within two frames, oh! wherefore two?
One passion in twin-hearts, which grows and
     grew,
Till like two meteors of expanding flame,
Those spheres instinct with it become the same,
Touch, mingle, are transfigured; ever still
Burning, yet ever inconsumable:
In one another's substance finding food,   580
Like flames too pure and light and unimbued
To nourish their bright lives with baser prey,
Which point to Heaven and cannot pass away:
One hope within two wills, one will beneath
Two overshadowing minds, one life, one death,
One heaven, one Hell, one immortality,
And one annihilation. Woe is me!
The wingèd words on which my soul would
     pierce
Into the height of Love's rare Universe,
Are chains of lead around its flight of fire—   590
I pant, I sink, I tremble, I expire!

Weak Verses, go, kneel at your Sovereign's
     feet,
And say:—'We are the masters of thy slave;
What wouldest thou with us and ours and thine?'
Then call your sisters from Oblivion's cave,
All singing loud: 'Love's very pain is sweet,
But its reward is in the world divine
Which, if not here, it builds beyond the grave.'
So shall ye live when I am there. Then haste
Over the hearts of men, until ye meet   600
Marina, Vanna, Primus,[28] and the rest,
And bid them love each other and be blessed:
And leave the troop which errs, and which re-
     proves,
And come and be my guest,—for I am Love's.

1821   1821

---

28 Mary Shelley, with Jane and Edward Williams.

ADONAIS

AN ELEGY ON THE DEATH OF JOHN KEATS

Ἀστὴρ πρὶν μὲν ἔλαμπες ἐνὶ ζώοισιν ἑῷος.
Νῦν δὲ θανὼν λάμπεις ἕσπερος ἐν φθιμένοις.

PLATO.[1]

[*Adonais* was first printed in Pisa, Italy, with the following preface:]

PREFACE

Φάρμακον ἦλθε, Βίων, ποτὶ σὸν στόμα,
φάρμακον εἶδες.
πῶς τευ τοῖς χείλεσσι ποτέδραμε, κοὐκ ἐγλυκάνθη;
τίς δὲ βροτὸς τοσσοῦτον ἀνάμερος, ἢ κεράσαι τοι,
ἢ δοῦναι λαλέοντι τὸ φάρμακον; ἔκφυγεν ᾠδάν.
—MOSCHUS, EPITAPH. BION.[2]

It is my intention to subjoin to the London edition of
this poem a criticism upon the claims of its lamented object to be classed among the writers of the highest genius
who have adorned our age. My known repugnance to
the narrow principles of taste on which several of his
earlier compositions were modelled prove at least that
I am an impartial judge. I consider the fragment of *Hyperion* as second to nothing that was ever produced by
a writer of the same years.

John Keats died at Rome of a consumption, in his
twenty-fourth[3] year, on the [23rd] of [Feb.], 1821; and
was buried in the romantic and lonely cemetery of the
Protestants in that city, under[4] the pyramid which is the
tomb of Cestius, and the massy walls and towers, now
mouldering and desolate, which formed the circuit of
ancient Rome. The cemetery is an open space among the
ruins, covered in winter with violets and daisies. It might
make one in love with death, to think that one should
be buried in so sweet a place.

The genius of the lamented person to whose memory
I have dedicated these unworthy verses was not less delicate and fragile than it was beautiful; and where canker-
worms abound, what wonder if its young flower was
blighted in the bud? The savage criticism on his
Endymion, which appeared in the *Quarterly Review,* produced the most violent effect on his susceptible mind;[5]
the agitation thus originated ended in the rupture of a
blood-vessel in the lungs; a rapid consumption ensued,
and the succeeding acknowledgements from more candid critics of the true greatness of his powers were ineffectual to heal the wound thus wantonly inflicted.

---

1 The Greek of Plato is translated by Shelley in a lyric entitled
To Stella:

> Thou wert the morning star among the living,
>   Ere thy fair light had fled;—
> Now, having died, thou art as Hesperus, giving
>   New splendour to the dead.

2 'Poison came, Bion, to thy mouth—thou didst know poison.
To such lips as thine did it come, and was not sweetened? What
mortal was so cruel that could mix poison for thee, or who could
give thee the venom that heard thy voice? Surely he had no music
in his soul.'—Translation by Andrew Lang.

3 actually, twenty-sixth.

4 not under, but near the pyramid.

5 Shelley shared with others the mistaken belief that Keats's life
had been 'snuffed out by an article' in the *Quarterly Review.*

It may be well said that these wretched men know not what they do. They scatter their insults and their slanders without heed as to whether the poisoned shaft lights on a heart made callous by many blows, or one, like Keats's, composed of more penetrable stuff. One of their associates is, to my knowledge, a most base and unprincipled calumniator. As to *Endymion,* was it a poem, whatever might be its defects, to be treated contemptuously by those who had celebrated with various degrees of complacency and panegyric, *Paris,* and *Woman,* and *A Syrian Tale,* and Mrs. Lefanu, and Mr. Barrett, and Mr. Howard Payne, and a long list of the illustrious obscure? Are these the men who, in their venal good-nature, presumed to draw a parallel between the Rev. Mr. Milman and Lord Byron? What gnat did they strain at here, after having swallowed all those camels? Against what woman taken in adultery dares the foremost of these literary prostitutes to cast his opprobrious stone? Miserable man! you, one of the meanest, have wantonly defaced one of the noblest specimens of the workmanship of God. Nor shall it be your excuse, that, murderer as you are, you have spoken daggers, but used none.

The circumstances of the closing scene of poor Keats's life were not made known to me until the Elegy was ready for the press. I am given to understand that the wound which his sensitive spirit had received from the criticism of *Endymion* was exasperated by the bitter sense of unrequited benefits; the poor fellow seems to have been hooted from the stage of life, no less by those on whom he had wasted the promise of his genius, than those on whom he had lavished his fortune and his care. He was accompanied to Rome, and attended in his last illness by Mr. Severn, a young artist of the highest promise, who, I have been informed, 'almost risked his own life, and sacrificed every prospect to unwearied attendance upon his dying friend.' Had I known these circumstances before the completion of my poem, I should have been tempted to add my feeble tribute of applause to the more solid recompense which the virtuous man finds in the recollection of his own motives. Mr. Severn can dispense with a reward from 'such stuff as dreams are made of.' His conduct is a golden augury of the success of his future career—may the unextinguished Spirit of his illustrious friend animate the creations of his pencil, and plead against Oblivion for his name!

I

I WEEP for Adonais[6]—he is dead!
O, weep for Adonais! though our tears
Thaw not the frost which binds so dear a head!
And thou, sad Hour, selected from all years
To mourn our loss, rouse thy obscure compeers,[7]
And teach them thine own sorrow, say: 'With me
Died Adonais; till the Future dares
Forget the Past, his fate and fame shall be
An echo and a light unto eternity!'

II

Where wert thou, mighty Mother,[8] when he lay,   10
When thy Son lay, pierced by the shaft which flies
In darkness? where was lorn Urania
When Adonais died? With veilèd eyes,
'Mid listening Echoes, in her Paradise
She sate, while one, with soft enamoured breath,
Rekindled all the fading melodies,
With which, like flowers that mock the corse beneath,
He had adorned and hid the coming bulk of Death.

III

Oh, weep for Adonais—he is dead!
Wake, melancholy Mother, wake and weep!   20
Yet wherefore? Quench within their burning bed
Thy fiery tears, and let thy loud heart keep
Like his, a mute and uncomplaining sleep;
For he is gone, where all things wise and fair
Descend;—oh, dream not that the amorous Deep
Will yet restore him to the vital air;
Death feeds on his mute voice, and laughs at our despair.

IV

Most musical of mourners, weep again!
Lament anew, Urania!—He[9] died,
Who was the Sire of an immortal strain,   30
Blind, old, and lonely, when his country's pride,
The priest, the slave, and the liberticide,
Trampled and mocked with many a loathèd rite
Of lust and blood; he went, unterrified,
Into the gulf of death; but his clear Sprite
Yet reigns o'er earth; the third[10] among the sons of light.

V

Most musical of mourners, weep anew!
Not all to that bright station dared to climb;
And happier they their happiness who knew,

---

6 a modification of Adonis, the beautiful youth loved by Aphrodite and slain by a wild boar.
7 hours less notable than that in which Keats died.
8 Urania, the Muse of Astronomy, or the spirit of heaven and the inspirer of poetry. She is the Heavenly Muse of Milton's *Paradise Lost.*
9 Milton.
10 If epic poets are meant, the other two would be Homer and Dante.

Whose tapers yet burn through that night of
  time   40
In which suns perished; others more sublime,
Struck by the envious wrath of man or god,
Have sunk, extinct in their refulgent prime;
And some yet live, treading the thorny road,
Which leads, through toil and hate, to Fame's se-
  rene abode.

VI

But now, thy youngest, dearest one, has per-
  ished—
The nursling of thy widowhood, who grew,
Like a pale flower by some sad maiden cher-
  ished,[11]
And fed with true-love tears, instead of dew;
Most musical of mourners, weep anew!   50
Thy extreme hope, the loveliest and the last,
The bloom, whose petals nipped before they
  blew
Died on the promise of the fruit, is waste;
The broken lily lies—the storm is overpast.

VII

To that high Capital,[12] where kingly Death
Keeps his pale court in beauty and decay,
He came; and bought, with price of purest
  breath,
A grave among the eternal.—Come away!
Haste, while the vault of blue Italian day
Is yet his fitting charnel-roof! while still   60
He lies, as if in dewy sleep he lay;
Awake him not! surely he takes his fill
Of deep and liquid rest, forgetful of all ill.

VIII

He will awake no more, oh, never more!—
Within the twilight chamber spreads apace
The shadow of white Death, and at the door
Invisible Corruption waits to trace
His extreme way to her dim dwelling-place;
The eternal Hunger[13] sits, but pity and awe
Soothe her pale rage, nor dares she to
  deface   70
So fair a prey, till darkness, and the law
Of change, shall o'er his sleep the mortal curtain
  draw.

IX

Oh, weep for Adonais!—The quick Dreams,
The passion-wingèd Ministers of thought,

Who were his flocks, whom near the living
  streams
Of his young spirit he fed, and whom he taught
The love which was its music, wander not,—
Wander no more, from kindling brain to brain,
But droop there, whence they sprung; and
  mourn their lot
Round the cold heart, where, after their sweet
  pain,   80
They ne'er will gather strength, nor find a home
  again.

X

And one with trembling hands clasps his cold
  head,
And fans him with her moonlight wings, and
  cries;
'Our love, our hope, our sorrow, is not dead;
See, on the silken fringe of his faint eyes,
Like dew upon a sleeping flower, there lies
A tear some Dream has loosened from his
  brain.'
Lost Angel of a ruined Paradise!
She knew not 'twas her own; as with no stain
She faded, like a cloud which had outwept its
  rain.   90

XI

One from a lucid urn of starry dew
Washed his light limbs as if embalming them;
Another clipped her profuse locks, and threw
The wreath upon him, like an anadem,[14]
Which frozen tears instead of pearls begem;
Another in her wilful grief would break
Her bow and wingèd reeds, as if to stem
A greater loss with one which was more weak;
And dull the barbèd fire against his frozen cheek.

XII

Another Splendour on his mouth alit,   100
That mouth, whence it was wont to draw the
  breath
Which gave it strength to pierce the guarded
  wit,[15]
And pass into the panting heart beneath
With lightning and with music: the damp
  death
Quenched its caress upon his icy lips;
And, as a dying meteor stains a wreath
Of moonlight vapour, which the cold night
  clips,[16]

---

11 an allusion to Keats's *Isabella*.
12 Rome.
13 Corruption.

14 garland.
15 intellect.
16 embraces.

It flushed through his pale limbs, and passed to
    its eclipse.

XIII

And others came . . . Desires and Adorations,
Wingèd Persuasions and veiled Destinies,   110
Splendours, and Glooms, and glimmering In-
    carnations
Of hopes and fears, and twilight Phantasies;
And Sorrow, with her family of Sighs,
And Pleasure, blind with tears, led by the
    gleam
Of her own dying smile instead of eyes,
Came in slow pomp;—the moving pomp might
    seem
Like pageantry of mist on an autumnal stream.

XIV

All he had loved, and moulded into thought,
From shape, and hue, and odour, and sweet
    sound,
Lamented Adonais. Morning sought   120
Her eastern watch-tower, and her hair un-
    bound,
Wet with the tears which should adorn the
    ground,
Dimmed the aëreal eyes that kindle day;
Afar the melancholy thunder moaned,
Pale Ocean in unquiet slumber lay,
And the wild Winds flew round, sobbing in their
    dismay.

XV

Lost Echo sits amid the voiceless mountains,
And feeds her grief with his remembered lay,
And will no more reply to winds or fountains,
Or amorous birds perched on the young green
    spray,   130
Or herdsman's horn, or bell at closing day;
Since she can mimic not his lips, more dear
Than those for whose disdain[17] she pined away
Into a shadow of all sounds:—a drear
Murmur, between their songs, is all the woodmen
    hear.

XVI

Grief made the young Spring wild, and she
    threw down
Her kindling buds, as if she Autumn were,
Or they dead leaves; since her delight is flown,
For whom should she have waked the sullen
    year?

To Phoebus was not Hyacinth so dear[18]   140
Nor to himself Narcissus,[19] as to both
Thou, Adonais: wan they stand and sere
Amid the faint companions of their youth,
With dew all turned to tears; odour, to sighing
    ruth.

XVII

Thy spirit's sister, the lorn nightingale
Mourns not her mate with such melodious
    pain;
Not so the eagle, who like thee could scale
Heaven, and could nourish in the sun's domain
Her mighty youth with morning, doth com-
    plain,
Soaring and screaming round her empty
    nest,   150
As Albion wails for thee; the curse of Cain
Light on his head who[20] pierced thy innocent
    breast,
And scared the angel soul that was its earthly
    guest!

XVIII

Ah, woe is me! Winter is come and gone,
But grief returns with the revolving year;
The airs and streams renew their joyous
    tone;
The ants, the bees, the swallows reappear;
Fresh leaves and flowers deck the dead Sea-
    sons' bier;
The amorous birds now pair in every brake,
And build their mossy homes in field and
    brere[21]   160
And the green lizard, and the golden snake,
Like unimprisoned flames, out of their trance
    awake.

XIX

Through wood and stream and field and hill
    and Ocean
A quickening life from the Earth's heart has
    burst
As it has ever done, with change and motion,
From the great morning of the world when first
God dawned on Chaos; in its stream im-
    mersed,
The lamps of Heaven flash with a softer light;
All baser things pant with life's sacred thirst;

---

17 Narcissus, for whose disdain Echo faded away until there was
nothing left but her voice.
18 Apollo (Phoebus) so loved the youth Hyacinthus that after his
accidental death the god caused a flower to spring up from the
blood-stained grass to memorialize his grief.
19 Narcissus fell in love with his own image and pined away until
he became a flower.
20 the reviewer of *Endymion* in the *Quarterly*.
21 briar.

Diffuse themselves; and spend in love's
    delight,   170
The beauty and the joy of their renewèd might.

XX

The leprous corpse, touched by this spirit
    tender,
Exhales itself in flowers of gentle breath;
Like incarnations of the stars, when splendour
Is changed to fragrance, they illumine death
And mock the merry worm that wakes be-
    neath;
Nought we know, dies. Shall that alone which
    knows
Be as a sword consumed before the sheath
By sightless lightning?—the intense atom[22]
    glows
A moment, then is quenched in a most cold
    repose.   180

XXI

Alas! that all we loved of him should be,
But for our grief, as if it had not been,
And grief itself be mortal! Woe is me!
Whence are we, and why are we? of what scene
The actors or spectators? Great and mean
Meet massed in death, who lends what life
    must borrow.
As long as skies are blue, and fields are green,
Evening must usher night, night urge the
    morrow,
Month follow month with woe, and year wake
    year to sorrow.

XXII

He will awake no more, oh, never more!   190
'Wake thou,' cried Misery, 'childless Mother,
    rise
Out of thy sleep, and slake, in thy heart's core,
A wound more fierce than his, with tears and
    sighs.'
And all the Dreams that watched Urania's
    eyes,
And all the Echoes whom their sister's song
Had held in holy silence, cried: 'Arise!'
Swift as a Thought by the snake Memory
    stung,
From her ambrosial rest the fading Splendour
    sprung.

XXIII

She rose like an autumnal Night, that springs
Out of the East, and follows wild and drear   200
The golden Day, which, on eternal wings,

---
22 mind; conscious spirit.

Even as a ghost abandoning a bier,
Had left the Earth a corpse. Sorrow and fear
So struck, so roused, so rapt Urania;
So saddened round her like an atmosphere
Of stormy mist; so swept her on her way
Even to the mournful place where Adonais lay.

XXIV

Out of her secret Paradise she sped,
Through camps and cities rough with stone,
    and steel,
And human hearts, which to her aery
    tread   210
Yielding not, wounded the invisible
Palms of her tender feet where'er they fell:
And barbèd tongues, and thoughts more sharp
    than they,
Rent the soft Form they never could repel,
Whose sacred blood, like the young tears of
    May,
Paved with eternal flowers that undeserving
    way.

XXV

In the death-chamber for a moment Death,
Shamed by the presence of that living Might,
Blushed to annihilation, and the breath
Revisited those lips, and Life's pale light   220
Flashed through those limbs, so late her dear
    delight.
'Leave me not wild and drear and comfortless,
As silent lightning leaves the starless night!
Leave me not!' cried Urania: her distress
Roused Death: Death rose and smiled, and met
    her vain caress.

XXVI

'Stay yet awhile! speak to me once again;
Kiss me, so long but as a kiss may live;
And in my heartless breast and burning brain
That word, that kiss, shall all thoughts else sur-
    vive,
With food of saddest memory kept alive,   230
Now thou art dead, as if it were a part
Of thee, my Adonais! I would give
All that I am to be as thou now art!
But I am chained to Time, and cannot thence
    depart!

XXVII

'O gentle child, beautiful as thou wert,
Why didst thou leave the trodden paths of
    men
Too soon, and with weak hands though mighty
    heart

Dare the unpastured dragon in his den?
Defenceless as thou wert, oh, where was then
Wisdom the mirrored shield,[23] or scorn the
    spear?   240
Or hadst thou waited the full cycle, when
Thy spirit should have filled its crescent sphere,
The monsters of life's waste had fled from thee
    like deer.

XXVIII

'The herded wolves,[24] bold only to pursue;
The obscene ravens, clamorous o'er the dead;
The vultures to the conqueror's banner true
Who feed where Desolation first has fed,
And whose wings rain contagion;—how they
    fled,
When, like Apollo, from his golden bow
The Pythian of the age[25] one arrow sped   250
And smiled!—The spoilers tempt no second
    blow,
They fawn on the proud feet that spurn them
    lying low.

XXIX

'The sun comes forth, and many reptiles
    spawn;
He sets, and each ephemeral insect then
Is gathered into death without a dawn,
And the immortal stars awake again;
So is it in the world of living men:
A godlike mind soars forth, in its delight
Making earth bare and veiling heaven, and
    when
It sinks, the swarms that dimmed or shared
    its light   260
Leave to its kindred lamps the spirit's awful
    night.'

XXX

Thus ceased she: and the mountain shepherds
    came,
Their garlands sere, their magic mantles rent;
The Pilgrim of Eternity,[26] whose fame
Over his living head like Heaven is bent,
An early but enduring monument,
Came, veiling all the lightnings of his song
In sorrow; from her wilds Ierne[27] sent
The sweetest lyrist[28] of her saddest wrong,

And Love taught Grief to fall like music from his
    tongue.   270

XXXI

Midst others of less note, came one frail
    Form,[29]
A phantom among men; companionless
As the last cloud of an expiring storm
Whose thunder is its knell; he, as I guess,
Had gazed on Nature's naked loveliness,
Actaeon-like,[30] and now he fled astray
With feeble steps o'er the world's wilderness,
And his own thoughts, along that rugged way,
Pursued, like raging hounds, their father and
    their prey.

XXXII

A pardlike[31] Spirit beautiful and swift— 280
A Love in desolation masked;—a Power
Girt round with weakness;—it can scarce
    uplift
The weight of the superincumbent hour;
It is a dying lamp, a falling shower,
A breaking billow;—even whilst we speak
Is it not broken? On the withering flower
The killing sun smiles brightly: on a cheek
The life can burn in blood, even while the heart
    may break.

XXXIII

His head was bound with pansies overblown,
And faded violets, white, and pied, and
    blue;   290
And a light spear topped with a cypress cone,
Round whose rude shaft dark ivy-tresses grew
Yet dripping with the forest's noonday dew,
Vibrated, as the ever-beating heart
Shook the weak hand that grasped it; of that
    crew
He came the last, neglected and apart;
A herd-abandoned deer struck by the hunter's
    dart.

XXXIV

All stood aloof, and at his partial[32] moan
Smiled through their tears; well knew that gen-
    tle band
Who in another's fate now wept his own,   300
As in the accents of an unknown land[33]
He sung new sorrow; sad Urania scanned

---

23 an allusion to the shield of Perseus, which enabled him to slay Medusa without meeting her fatal gaze.
24 the critics.
25 Byron, who slew the critics in *English Bards and Scotch Reviewers,* as Apollo did the Python.
26 Byron.
27 Ireland.
28 Thomas Moore.

29 Shelley himself.
30 Actaeon, having seen Diana bathing, was changed into a stag by the goddess and destroyed by his own hounds.
31 leopard-like.
32 sympathetic.
33 that is, he wrote in English, a language unknown to Urania.

The Stranger's mien, and murmured: 'Who art
  thou?'
He answered not, but with a sudden hand
Made bare his branded and ensanguined brow,
Which was like Cain's or Christ's—oh! that it
  should be so!

XXXV

What softer voice is hushed over the dead?
Athwart what brow is that dark mantle
  thrown?
What form leans sadly o'er the white death-
  bed.
In mockery of monumental stone,   310
The heavy heart heaving without a moan?
If it be He,[34] who, gentlest of the wise,
Taught, soothed, loved, honoured the departed
  one,
Let me not vex, with inharmonious sighs,
The silence of that heart's accepted sacrifice.

XXXVI

Our Adonais has drunk poison—oh!
What deaf and viperous murderer could crown
Life's early cup with such a draught of woe?
The nameless worm[35] would now itself dis-
  own:
It felt, yet could escape, the magic tone   320
Whose prelude held all envy, hate, and wrong,
But what was howling in one breast alone,
Silent with expectation of the song,
Whose master's hand is cold, whose silver lyre
  unstrung.

XXXVII

Live thou, whose infamy is not thy fame!
Live! fear no heavier chastisement from me,
Thou noteless blot on a remembered name!
But be thyself, and know thyself to be!
And ever at thy season be thou free
To spill the venom when thy fangs o'er
  flow;   330
Remorse and Self-contempt shall cling to thee;
Hot Shame shall burn upon thy secret brow,
And like a beaten hound tremble thou shalt—as
  now.

XXXVIII

Nor let us weep that our delight is fled
Far from these carrion kites that scream
  below;
He wakes or sleeps with the enduring dead;
Thou canst not soar where he is sitting now.—

34 Leigh Hunt.
35 author of the unsigned review of *Endymion* in the *Quarterly*.

Dust to the dust! but the pure spirit shall flow
Back to the burning fountain whence it came,
A portion of the Eternal, which must glow   340
Through time and change, unquenchably the
  same,
Whilst thy cold embers choke the sordid hearth
  of shame.

XXXIX

Peace, peace! he is not dead, he doth not
  sleep—
He hath awakened from the dream of life—
'Tis we, who lost in stormy visions, keep
With phantoms an unprofitable strife,
And in mad trance, strike with our spirit's
  knife
Invulnerable nothings.—*We* decay
Like corpses in a charnel; fear and grief
Convulse us and consume us day by day,   350
And cold hopes swarm like worms within our liv-
  ing clay.

XL

He has outsoared the shadow of our night;
Envy and calumny and hate and pain,
And that unrest which men miscall delight,
Can touch him not and torture not again;
From the contagion of the world's slow stain
He is secure, and now can never mourn
A heart grown cold, a head grown grey in vain;
Nor, when the spirit's self has ceased to burn,
With sparkless ashes load an unlamented
  urn.   360

XLI

He lives, he wakes—'tis Death is dead, not he;
Mourn not for Adonais.—Thou young Dawn,
Turn all thy dew to splendour, for from thee
The spirit thou lamentest is not gone;
Ye caverns and ye forests, cease to moan!
Cease, ye faint flowers and fountains, and thou
  Air,
Which like a mourning veil thy scarf hadst
  thrown
O'er the abandoned Earth, now leave it bare
Even to the joyous stars which smile on its
  despair!

XLII

He is made one with Nature: there is
  heard   370
His voice in all her music, from the moan
Of thunder, to the song of night's sweet bird;
He is a presence to be felt and known

In darkness and in light, from herb and stone,
Spreading itself where'er that Power may
    move
Which has withdrawn his being to its own;
Which wields the world with never-wearied
    love,
Sustains it from beneath, and kindles it above.

XLIII

He is a portion of the loveliness
Which once he made more lovely: he doth
    bear   380
His part, while the one Spirit's plastic stress
Sweeps through the dull dense world, com-
    pelling there,
All new successions to the forms they wear;
Torturing th' unwilling dross that checks its
    flight
To its own likeness, as each mass may bear;
And bursting in its beauty and its might
From trees and beasts and men into the Heaven's
    light.

XLIV

The splendours of the firmament of time
May be eclipsed, but are extinguished not;
Like stars to their appointed height they
    climb,   390
And death is a low mist which cannot blot
The brightness it may veil. When lofty thought
Lifts a young heart above its mortal lair,
And love and life contend in it, for what
Shall be its earthly doom, the dead live there
And move like winds of light on dark and
    stormy air.

XLV

The inheritors of unfulfilled renown
Rose from their thrones, built beyond mortal
    thought,
Far in the Unapparent. Chatterton[36]
Rose pale,—his solemn agony had not   400
Yet faded from him; Sidney, as he fought
And as he fell and as he lived and loved
Sublimely mild, a Spirit without spot,
Arose; and Lucan, by his death approved:
Oblivion as they rose shrank like a thing
    reproved.

XLVI

And many more, whose names on Earth are
    dark,

---

36 Chatterton, Sidney, and Lucan all died before the fame promised in their youth was fully attained. Sidney fell in battle; the
other two committed suicide.

But whose transmitted effluence cannot die
So long as fire outlives the parent spark,
Rose, robed in dazzling immortality.
'Thou art become as one of us,' they cry,   410
'It was for thee yon kingless sphere has long
Swung blind in unascended majesty,
Silent alone amid an Heaven of Song.
Assume thy wingèd throne, thou Vesper of our
    throng!'

XLVII

Who mourns for Adonais? Oh, come forth,
Fond wretch! and know thyself and him aright.
Clasp with thy panting soul the pendulous
    Earth;
As from a centre, dart thy spirit's light
Beyond all worlds, until its spacious might
Satiate the void circumference: then shrink 420
Even to a point within our day and night;
And keep thy heart light lest it make thee sink
When hope has kindled hope, and lured thee to
    the brink.

XLVIII

Or go to Rome, which is the sepulchre,
Oh, not of him, but of our joy: 'tis nought
That ages, empires, and religions there
Lie buried in the ravage they have wrought;
For such as he can lend,—they borrow not
Glory from those who made the world their
    prey;
And he is gathered to the kings of thought 430
Who waged contention with their time's decay,
And of the past are all that cannot pass away.

XLIX

Go thou to Rome,—at once the Paradise,
The grave, the city, and the wilderness;
And where its wrecks like shattered mountains
    rise,
And flowering weeds, and fragrant copses
    dress
The bones of Desolation's nakedness
Pass, till the spirit of the spot shall lead
Thy footsteps to a slope of green access[37]
Where, like an infant's smile, over the
    dead   440
A light of laughing flowers along the grass is
    spread;

L

And grey walls moulder round, on which dull
    Time
Feeds, like slow fire upon a hoary brand;

---

37 the Protestant cemetery at Rome where Keats was buried.

And one keen pyramid[38] with wedge sublime,
Pavilioning the dust of him who planned
This refuge for his memory, doth stand
Like flame transformed to marble; and be-
　neath,
A field is spread, on which a newer band
Have pitched in Heaven's smile their camp of
　death,
Welcoming him we lose with scarce extinguished
　breath.　　　　450

LI

Here pause: these graves are all too young as
　yet
To have outgrown the sorrow which consigned
Its charge to each; and if the seal is set,
Here, on one fountain of a mourning mind,
Break it not thou! too surely shalt thou find
Thine own well full, if thou returnest home,
Of tears and gall. From the world's bitter wind
Seek shelter in the shadow of the tomb.
What Adonais is, why fear we to become?

LII

The One remains, the many change and
　pass;　　　　460
Heaven's light forever shines, Earth's shadows
　fly;
Life, like a dome of many-coloured glass,
Stains the white radiance of Eternity,
Until Death tramples it to fragments.—Die,
If thou wouldst be with that which thou dost
　seek!
Follow where all is fled!—Rome's azure sky,
Flowers, ruins, statues, music, words, are weak
The glory they transfuse with fitting truth to
　speak.

LIII

Why linger, why turn back, why shrink, my
　Heart?
Thy hopes are gone before: from all things
　here　　　　470
They have departed; thou shouldst now de-
　part!
A light is passed from the revolving year,
And man, and woman; and what still is dear
Attracts to crush, repels to make thee wither.
The soft sky smiles,—the low wind whispers
　near:
'Tis Adonais calls! oh, hasten thither,
No more let Life divide what Death can join
　together.

---

38 the tomb of Caius Cestius.

LIV

That Light whose smile kindles the Universe,
That Beauty in which all things work and
　move,
That Benediction which the eclipsing
　Curse　　　　480
Of birth can quench not, that sustaining Love
Which through the web of being blindly wove
By man and beast and earth and air and sea,
Burns bright or dim, as each are mirrors of
The fire for which all thirst; now beams on me,
Consuming the last clouds of cold mortality.

LV

The breath whose might I have invoked in
　song
Descends on me; my spirit's bark is driven,
Far from the shore, far from the trembling
　throng
Whose sails were never to the tempest
　given;　　　　490
The massy earth and spheréd skies are riven!
I am borne darkly, fearfully, afar;
Whilst, burning through the inmost veil of
　Heaven,
The soul of Adonais, like a star,
Beacons from the abode where the Eternal are.
　1821　　　　　　　　1821

CHORUSES FROM HELLAS

Hellas was among the last of his compositions, and
is among the most beautiful. The choruses are singularly
imaginative, and melodious in their versification. There
are some stanzas that beautfully exemplify Shelley's peculiar style. . . .
　The conclusion of the last chorus is among the most
beautiful of his lyrics; the imagery is distinct and majestic; the prophecy, such as poets love to dwell upon,
the regeneration of mankind—and that regeneration reflecting back splendour on the foregone time, from
which it inherits so much of intellectual wealth, and
memory of past virtuous deeds, as must render the possession of happiness and peace of tenfold value.—(Mrs.
Shelley.)

I

LIFE may change, but it may fly not;
Hope may vanish, but can die not;
Truth be veiled, but still it burneth;
Love repulsed,—but it returneth!

Yet were life a charnel where
Hope lay coffined with Despair;
Yet were truth a sacred lie,
Love were lust—

If Liberty
Lent not life its soul of light,
Hope its iris of delight,   10
Truth its prophet's robe to wear,
Love its power to give and bear.

II

Worlds on worlds are rolling ever
    From creation to decay,
Like the bubbles on a river
    Sparkling, bursting, borne away.
    But they are still immortal
    Who, through birth's orient portal
And death's dark chasm hurrying to and fro,
    Clothe their unceasing flight
    In the brief dust and light
Gathered around their chariots as they go;   10
    New shapes they still may weave,
    New gods, new laws receive,
Bright or dim are they as the robes they last
    On Death's bare ribs had cast.

    A power from the unknown God,
    A Promethean conqueror, came;
Like a triumphal path he trod
    The thorns of death and shame.
    A mortal shape to him
    Was like the vapour dim   20
Which the orient planet animates with light;
    Hell, Sin, and Slavery came,
    Like bloodhounds mild and tame,
Nor preyed, until their lord had taken flight;
    The moon of Mahomet
    Arose, and it shall set:
While blazoned as on Heaven's immortal noon
    The cross leads generations on.

    Swift as the radiant shapes of sleep
    From one whose dreams are Paradise,   30
Fly, when the fond wretch wakes to weep,
    And Day peers forth with her blank eyes;
    So fleet, so faint, so fair,
    The Powers of earth and air
Fled from the folding-star of Bethlehem:
    Apollo, Pan, and Love,
    And even Olympian Jove
Grew weak, for killing Truth had glared on them;
    Our hills and seas and streams,
    Dispeopled of their dreams,   40
Their waters turned to blood, their dew to tears,
    Wailed for the golden years.

III

Darkness has dawned in the East
    On the noon of time:

The death-birds descend to their feast
    From the hungry clime.
Let Freedom and Peace flee far
    To a sunnier strand,
And follow Love's folding-star
    To the Evening land![1]

    The young moon has fed
    Her exhausted horn   10
        With the sunset's fire:
    The weak day is dead,
        But the night is not born;
And, like loveliness panting with wild desire
    While it trembles with fear and delight,
    Hesperus flies from awakening night,
And pants in its beauty and speed with light
    Fast-flashing, soft, and bright.
Thou beacon of love! thou lamp of the free!
        Guide us far, far away,   20
To climes where now veiled by the ardour of day
        Thou art hidden
    From waves on which weary Noon
    Faints in her summer swoon,
    Between kingless continents sinless as Eden,
    Around mountains and islands inviolably
        Pranked on the sapphire sea.

    Through the sunset of hope,
    Like the shapes of a dream,
    What Paradise islands of glory gleam!   30
        Beneath Heaven's cope,
    Their shadows more clear float by—
The sound of their oceans, the light of their sky,
The music and fragrance their solitudes breathe
Burst, like morning on dream, or like Heaven on
        death,
    Through the walls of our prison;
    And Greece, which was dead, is arisen![2]

IV

The world's great age begins anew,
    The golden years return,
The earth doth like a snake renew
    Her winter weeds outworn;
Heaven smiles, and faiths and empires gleam,
Like wrecks of a dissolving dream.

A brighter Hellas rears its mountains
    From waves serener far;
A new Peneus rolls his fountains
    Against the morning star.   10

---

1 America.
2 Greece was then fighting for her independence against the Turks.

Where fairer Tempes bloom, there sleep
Young Cyclads on a sunnier deep.

A loftier Argo cleaves the main,
    Fraught with a later prize;
Another Orpheus sings again,
    And loves, and weeps, and dies.
A new Ulysses leaves once more
Calypso for his native shore.

Oh, write no more the tale of Troy,
    If earth Death's scroll must be!   20
Nor mix with Laian rage[3] the joy
    Which dawns upon the free:
Although a subtler Sphinx renew
Riddles of death Thebes never knew.

Another Athens shall arise,
    And to remoter time
Bequeath, like sunset to the skies,
    The splendour of its prime;
And leave, if nought so bright may live,
All earth can take or Heaven can give.   30

Saturn and Love[4] their long repose
    Shall burst, more bright and good
Than all who fell, than One[5] who rose,
    Than many unsubdued:
Not gold, not blood, their altar dowers,
But votive tears and symbol flowers.

Oh, cease! must hate and death return?
    Cease! must men kill and die?
Cease! drain not to its dregs the urn
    Of bitter prophecy.   40
The world is weary of the past,
Oh, might it die or rest at last!
    1821   *1822*

TO NIGHT

SWIFTLY walk o'er the western wave,
        Spirit of Night!
Out of the misty eastern cave,
Where all the long and lone daylight,
Thou wovest dreams of joy and fear,
Which make thee terrible and dear,—
        Swift be thy flight!

Wrap thy form in a mantle grey,
        Star-inwrought!

Blind with thine hair the eyes of Day;   10
Kiss her until she be wearied out,
Then wander o'er city, and sea, and land,
Touching all with thine opiate wand—
        Come, long sought!

When I arose and saw the dawn,
        I sighed for thee;
When light rode high, and the dew was gone,
And noon lay heavy on flower and tree,
And the weary Day turned to his rest,
Lingering like an unloved guest,   20
        I sighed for thee.

Thy brother Death came, and cried,
        Wouldst thou me?
Thy sweet child Sleep, the filmy-eyed,
Murmured like a noon-tide bee,
Shall I nestle near thy side?
Wouldst thou me?—And I replied,
        No, not thee!

Death will come when thou art dead,
        Soon, too soon—   30
Sleep will come when thou art fled;
Of neither would I ask the boon
I ask of thee, belovèd Night—
Swift be thine approaching flight,
        Come soon, soon!
    1821   *1824*

TO ———

MUSIC, when soft voices die,
Vibrates in the memory;
Odours, when sweet violets sicken,
Live within the sense they quicken.

Rose leaves, when the rose is dead,
Are heaped for the belovèd's bed;
And so thy thoughts, when thou art gone,
Love itself shall slumber on.
    1821   *1824*

SONG

RARELY, rarely, comest thou,
    Spirit of Delight!
Wherefore hast thou left me now
    Many a day and night?
Many a weary night and day
'Tis since thou art fled away.

---

3 The rage of Laius, mythical king of Thebes, in a quarrel with
his son Oedipus, fulfilled the prophecy of the oracle that his own
son should slay him.
4 Saturn and Love were deities in the age of innocence.
5 Christ.

How shall ever one like me
　Win thee back again?
With the joyous and the free
　Thou wilt scoff at pain.   10
Spirit false! thou hast forgot
All but those who need thee not.

As a lizard with the shade
　Of a trembling leaf,
Thou with sorrow art dismayed;
　Even the sighs of grief
Reproach thee, that thou art not near,
And reproach thou wilt not hear.

Let me set my mournful ditty
　To a merry measure,   20
Thou wilt never come for pity,
　Thou wilt come for pleasure.
Pity then will cut away
Those cruel wings, and thou wilt stay.

I love all that thou lovest,
　Spirit of Delight!
The fresh Earth in new leaves dressed,
　And the starry night;
Autumn evening, and the morn
When the golden mists are born.   30

I love snow, and all the forms
　Of the radiant frost;
I love waves, and winds, and storms,
　Every thing almost
Which is Nature's, and may be
Untainted by man's misery.

I love tranquil solitude,
　And such society
As is quiet, wise and good;
　Between thee and me   40
What difference? but thou dost possess
The things I seek, not love them less.

I love Love—though he has wings,
　And like light can flee,
But above all other things,
　Spirit, I love thee—
Thou art love and life! O come,
Make once more my heart thy home.
1820   1824

MUTABILITY

THE flower that smiles to-day
　To-morrow dies;

All that we wish to stay
　Tempts and then flies,
What is this world's delight?
Lightning that mocks the night,
　Brief even as bright.

Virtue, how frail it is!
　Friendship how rare!
Love, how it sells poor bliss   10
　For proud despair!
But we, though soon they fall,
Survive their joy, and all
　Which ours we call.

Whilst skies are blue and bright,
　Whilst flowers are gay,
Whilst eyes that change ere night
　Make glad the day;
Whilst yet the calm hours creep,
Dream thou—and from thy sleep   20
　Then wake to weep.
1821   1824

POLITICAL GREATNESS

NOR happiness, nor majesty, nor fame,
Nor peace, nor strength, nor skill in arms or arts,
Shepherd those herds whom tyranny makes
　　tame;
Verse echoes not one beating of their hearts,
History is but the shadow of their shame,
Art veils her glass, or from the pageant starts
As to oblivion their blind millions fleet,
Staining that Heaven with obscene imagery
Of their own likeness. What are numbers knit
By force or custom? Man who man would be,   10
Must rule the empire of himself; in it
Must be supreme, establishing his throne
On vanquished will, quelling the anarchy
Of hopes and fears, being himself alone.
1821   1824

A LAMENT

O WORLD! O life! O time!
On whose last steps I climb,
　Trembling at that where I had stood before;
When will return the glory of your prime?
　No more—Oh, never more!

Out of the day and night
A joy has taken flight;
　Fresh spring, and summer, and winter hoar,
Move my faint heart with grief, but with delight
　No more—Oh, never more!   10
1821   1824

TO ———

ONE word is too often profaned
    For me to profane it,
One feeling too falsely disdained
    For thee to disdain it.
One hope is too like despair
    For prudence to smother,
And pity from thee more dear
    Than that from another.

I can give not what men call love,
    But wilt thou accept not   10
The worship the heart lifts above
    And the Heavens reject not,—
The desire of the moth for the star,
    Of the night for the morrow,
The devotion to something afar
    From the sphere of our sorrow?

1821   1824

TO ———

WHEN passion's trance is overpast,
If tenderness and truth could last,
Or live, whilst all wild feelings keep
Some mortal slumber, dark and deep,
I should not weep, I should not weep!

It were enough to feel, to see,
Thy soft eyes gazing tenderly,
And dream the rest—and burn and be
The secret food of fires unseen,
Couldst thou but be as thou hast been.   10

After the slumber of the year
The woodland violets reappear;
All things revive in field or grove,
And sky and sea, but two, which move
And form all others, life and love.

1821   1824

LINES

WHEN the lamp is shattered
The light in the dust lies dead—
    When the cloud is scattered
The rainbow's glory is shed.
    When the lute is broken,
Sweet tones are remembered not;
    When the lips have spoken,
Loved accents are soon forgot.

As music and splendour
Survive not the lamp and the lute,   10
    The heart's echoes render
No song when the spirit is mute,—
    No song but sad dirges,
Like the wind through a ruined cell,
    Or the mournful surges
That ring the dead seaman's knell.

When hearts have once mingled
Love first leaves the well-built nest,—
    The weak one is singled
To endure what it once possessed.   20
    O, Love! who bewailest
The frailty of all things here,
    Why choose you the frailest
For your cradle, your home, and your bier?

Its passions will rock thee
As the storms rock the ravens on high:
    Bright reason will mock thee,
Like the sun from a wintry sky.
    From thy nest every rafter
Will rot, and thine eagle home   30
    Leave thee naked to laughter,
When leaves fall and cold winds come.

1822   1824

WITH A GUITAR: TO JANE

[This poem is addressed to Jane Williams, who used
often to delight Shelley with music and who was the inspiration for several of his lyrics. Both she and her husband were close friends of the Shelleys during the last
year of the poet's life. Edward Williams was drowned
with Shelley.]

ARIEL[1] to Miranda;[2]—Take
This slave of Music, for the sake
Of him who is the slave of thee,
And teach it all the harmony
In which thou canst, and only thou,
Make the delighted spirit glow,
Till joy denies itself again,
And, too intense, is turned to pain;
For by permission and command
Of thine own Prince Ferdinand[3]   10
Poor Ariel sends this silent token
Of more than ever can be spoken;
Your guardian spirit, Ariel, who,
From life to life, must still pursue

---

1 the spirit in Shakespeare's *Tempest* imprisoned in the cloven
pine; here identified as Shelley himself.
2 the daughter of Prospero, who releases Ariel; here Jane Williams.
3 the lover of Miranda; here Edward Williams.

Your happiness,—for thus alone
Can Ariel ever find his own.
From Prospero's enchanted cell,
As the mighty verses tell,
To the throne of Naples, he
Lit you o'er the trackless sea,   20
Flitting on, your prow before,
Like a living meteor.
When you die, the silent Moon,
In her interlunar swoon,
Is not sadder in her cell
Than deserted Ariel.
When you live again on earth,
Like an unseen star of birth,
Ariel guides you o'er the sea
Of life from your nativity.   30
Many changes have been run
Since Ferdinand and you begun
Your course of love, and Ariel still
Has tracked your steps, and served your will;
Now, in humbler, happier lot,
This is all remembered not;
And now, alas! the poor sprite is
Imprisoned, for some fault of his,
In a body like a grave.
From you he only dares to crave,   40
For his service and his sorrow,
A smile to-day, a song to-morrow.

The artist who this idol wrought
To echo all harmonious thought,
Felled a tree, while on the steep
The woods were in their winter sleep,
Rocked in that repose divine
On the wind-swept Apennine;
And dreaming, some of autumn past,
And some of spring approaching fast,   50
And some of April buds and showers,
And some of songs in July bowers,
And all of love; and so this tree—
Oh, that such our death may be!—
Died in sleep, and felt no pain,
To live in happier form again:
From which, beneath Heaven's fairest star,
The artist wrought this loved guitar,
And taught it justly to reply,
To all who question skilfully,   60
In language gentle as thine own;
Whispering in enamoured tone
Sweet oracles of woods and dells,
And summer winds in sylvan cells;
For it had learned all harmonies
Of the plains and of the skies,
Of the forests and the mountains,

And the many-voicèd fountains;
The clearest echoes of the hills,
The softest notes of falling rills,   70
The melodies of birds and bees,
The murmuring of summer seas,
And pattering rain, and breathing dew,
And airs of evening; and it knew
That seldom-heard mysterious sound,
Which, driven on its diurnal round,
As it floats through boundless day,
Our world enkindles on its way.—
All this it knows but will not tell
To those who cannot question well   80
The Spirit that inhabits it;
It talks according to the wit
Of its companions; and no more
Is heard than has been felt before,
By those who tempt it to betray
These secrets of an elder day:
But, sweetly as its answers will
Flatter hands of perfect skill,
It keeps its highest, holiest tone
For our belovèd Jane alone.   90

1822   1832

A DIRGE

ROUGH wind, that moanest loud
    Grief too sad for song;
Wild wind, when sullen cloud
    Knells all the night long;
Sad storm, whose tears are vain,
Bare woods, whose branches strain,
Deep caves and dreary main,
    Wail, for the world's wrong!

1822   1824

From ESSAY ON CHRISTIANITY

[THE NATURE OF GOD]

THE thoughts which the word, God, suggests
to the human mind are susceptible of as many
variations as human minds themselves. The
Stoic, the Platonist, and the Epicurean,—the
Polytheist, the Dualist, and the Trinitarian, differ infinitely in their conceptions of its meaning.
They agree only in considering it the most awful
and most venerable of names, as a common term
devised to express all of mystery or majesty or
power which the invisible world contains. And
not only has every sect distinct conceptions of the
application of this name, but scarcely two indi-

viduals of the same sect, who exercise in any degree the freedom of their judgement, or yield themselves with any candour of feeling to the influencings of the visible world, find perfect coincidence of opinion to exist between them. It is interesting to enquire in what acceptation Jesus Christ employed this term.

We may conceive his mind to have been predisposed on this subject to adopt the opinions of his countrymen. Every human being is indebted for a multitude of his sentiments to the religion of his early years. Jesus Christ probably studied the historians of his country with the ardour of a spirit seeking after truth. They were undoubtedly the companions of his childish years, the food and nutriment and materials of his youthful meditations. The sublime dramatic poem entitled Job had familiarized his imagination with the boldest imagery afforded by the human mind and the material world. Ecclesiastes had diffused a seriousness and solemnity over the frame of his spirit glowing with youthful hope, and made audible to his listening heart

The still, sad music of humanity
Not harsh or grating but of ample power
To chasten and subdue.[1]

He had contemplated this name as having been prophanely perverted to the sanctioning of the most enormous and abominable crimes. We can distinctly trace in the tissue of his doctrines the persuasion that God is some universal being, differing both from man and from the mind of man. According to Jesus Christ, God is neither the Jupiter who sends rain upon the earth, nor the Venus through whom all living things are produced, nor the Vulcan who presides over the terrestrial element of fire, nor the Vesta that preserves the light which is inshrined in the sun and moon and stars. He is neither the Proteus or the Pan of the material world. But the word God, according to the acceptation of Jesus Christ, unites all the attributes which these denominations contain, and is the interfused and overruling Spirit of all the energy and wisdom included within the circle of existing things. It is important to observe that the author of the Christian system had a conception widely differing from the gross imaginations of the vulgar relatively to the ruling Power of the universe. He everywhere represents this power as something mysteriously and illimitably pervading the frame of things. Nor do his doctrines practically assume any proposition which they theoretically deny.

'Blessed are the pure in heart, for they shall see God.'[2] Blessed are those who have preserved internal sanctity of soul; who are conscious of no secret deceit; who are the same in act as they are in desire; who conceal no thought, no tendencies of thought from their own conscience; who are faithful and sincere witnesses before the tribunal of their own judgement of all that passes within their mind. Such as these shall see God. What! after death, shall their awakened eyes behold the King of Heaven? shall they stand in awe before the golden throne on which he sits, and gaze upon the venerable countenance of the paternal Monarch? Is this the reward of the virtuous and the pure? These are the idle dreams of the visionary, or the pernicious representations of impostors, who have fabricated from the very materials of wisdom a cloak for their own dwarfish or imbecile conceptions. Jesus Christ has said no more than the most excellent philosophers have felt and expressed—that virtue is its own reward. It is true that such an expression as he has used was prompted by the energy of genius; it was the overflowing enthusiasm of a poet, but it is [not] the less literally true, [because] clearly repugnant to the mistaken conceptions of the multitude. God, it has been asserted, was contemplated by Jesus Christ as every poet and every philosopher must have contemplated that mysterious principle. He considered that venerable word to express the overruling Spirit of the collective energy of the moral and material world. He affirms therefore no more than that a simple and sincere mind is an indispensable requisite of true science and true happiness. He affirms that a being of pure and gentle habits will not fail in every thought, in every object of every thought, to be aware of benignant visitings from the invisible energies by which he is surrounded. Whosoever is free from the contamination of luxury and licence may go forth to the fields and to the woods, inhaling joyous renovation from the breath of Spring, or catching from the odours and the sounds of Autumn some diviner mood of sweetest sadness, which improves the solitary heart. Whosoever is no deceiver or destroyer of his fellowmen, no liar, no flatterer, no murderer, may walk among his species, deriving from the communion with all which they contain of beautiful or of majestic,

---

1 Wordsworth, *Lines Composed above Tintern Abbey*, 91–3.

2 Matthew, v, 8.

some intercourse with the Universal God. Whoever has maintained with his own heart the strictest correspondence of confidence, who dares to examine and to estimate every imagination which suggests itself to his mind, who is that which he designs to become, and only aspires to that which the divinity of his own nature shall consider and approve—he has already seen God. We live and move and think, but we are not the creators of our own complicated nature; we are not the masters of our own imaginations and moods of mental being. There is a Power by which we are surrounded, like the atmosphere in which some motionless lyre is suspended, which visits with its breath our silent chords, at will. Our most imperial and stupendous qualities—those on which the majesty and the power of humanity is erected—are, relatively to the inferior portion of its mechanism, indeed active and imperial; but they are the passive slaves of some higher and more omnipresent Power. This Power is God. And those who have seen God, have, in the period of their purer and more perfect nature, been harmonized by their own will to so exquisite a consentaneity of powers as to give forth divinest melody when the breath of universal being sweeps over their frame.

That those who are pure in heart shall see God, and that virtue is its own reward, may be considered as equivalent assertions. . . .

God is represented by Jesus Christ as the Power from which or through which the streams of all that is excellent and delightful flow: the Power which models, as they pass, all the elements of this mixed universe to the purest and most perfect shape which it belongs to their nature to assume: Jesus Christ attributes to this power the faculty of will. How far such a doctrine in its ordinary sense may be philosophically true, or how far Jesus Christ intentionally availed himself of a metaphor easily understood, is foreign to the subject to consider. Thus much is certain that Jesus Christ represents God as the fountain of all goodness, the eternal enemy of pain and evil, the uniform and unchanging motive of the salutary operations of the material world. The supposition that this cause is excited to action by some principle analogous to the human will adds weight to the persuasion that it is foreign to its benevolent nature to inflict the slightest pain. According to Jesus Christ, and according to the indisputable facts of the case, some evil Spirit has dominion in this imperfect world. But there will come a time when the human mind shall be visited exclusively by the influences of the benignant power. Men shall die and their bodies shall rot under the ground, all the organs through which their knowledge and their feelings have flowed, or in which they have originated, shall assume other forms, and become ministrant to purposes the most foreign from their former tendencies. There is a time when we shall neither hear nor see, neither be heard or be seen by the multitude of beings like ourselves by whom we have been so long surrounded. . . . It appears that we moulder to a heap of senseless dust, a few worms that arise and perish like ourselves. Jesus Christ asserts that these appearances are fallacious, and that a gloomy and cold imagination alone suggests the conception that thought can cease to be.

Another and a more extensive state of being, rather than the complete extinction of being, will follow from that mysterious change which we call death. There shall be no misery, no pain, no fear. The empire of the evil spirit extends not beyond the boundaries of the grave. The unobscured irradiations from the fountain-fire of all goodness shall reveal all that is mysterious and unintelligible until the mutual communications of knowledge and of happiness throughout all thinking natures constitute a harmony of good that ever varies and never ends. This is Heaven, when pain and evil cease, and when the benignant principle untrammelled and uncontrolled, visits in the fulness of its power the universal frame of things. Human life with all its unreal ills and transitory hopes is as a dream which departs before the dawn leaving no trace of its evanescent hues. All that it contains of pure or of divine visits the passive mind in some serenest mood. Most holy are the affections through which our fellow-beings are rendered dear and venerable to the heart; the remembrance of their sweetness and the completion of the hopes which they did excite constitute when we awaken from the sleep of life, the fulfilment of the prophecies of its most majestic and beautiful visions. . . .

EQUALITY OF MANKIND

'The Spirit of the Lord is upon me because he hath chosen me to preach the gospel to the poor, he hath sent me to heal the broken-hearted, to preach deliverance to the captives, and recovery of sight to the blind, and to set at liberty them that are bruised' (Luke iv, v: 18).

This is an enunciation of all that Plato and Diogenes have speculated upon of the equality of mankind. They saw that the great majority of the human species were reduced to the situation of squalid ignorance, and moral imbecility, for the purpose of purveying for the luxury of a few, and contributing to the satisfaction of their thirst for power. Too mean-spirited and too feeble in resolve to attempt the conquest of their own evil passions, and of the difficulties of the material world, men sought dominion over their fellow-men as an easy method to gain that apparent majesty and power which the instinct of their nature requires. Plato wrote the scheme of a republic in which law should watch over the equal distribution of the external instruments of unequal power: honours, property, and [so forth]. Diogenes devised a nobler and more worthy system of opposition to the system of slave and tyrant. He said, It is in the power of each individual to level the inequality which is the topic of the complaint of mankind. Let him be aware of his own worth and the station which he really occupies in the scale of moral beings. Diamonds and gold, palaces and sceptres derive their value from the opinion of mankind. The only sumptuary law which can be imposed on the use and fabrication of these instruments of mischief and deceit, these symbols of successful injustice, is the law of opinion. Every man possesses the power in this respect, to legislate for himself. Let him be well aware of his own worth, and moral dignity. Let him yield in [meek reverence] to any wiser or worthier than he so long as he accords no veneration to the splendour of his apparel, the luxury of his food, the multitude of his flatterers and slaves. It is because, O mankind, ye value and seek the empty pageantry of wealth and social power that ye are enslaved to its possessions. Decrease your physical wants, learn to live, so far as nourishment and shelter are concerned like the beasts of the forest and the birds of the air; ye will need not to complain that other individuals of your species are surrounded by the diseases of luxury and the vices of subserviency. With all those who are truly wise, there will be an entire community, not only of thoughts and feelings, but also of external possessions. Insomuch therefore as ye love one another, ye may enjoy the community of whatsoever benefits arise from the inventions of civilized life. They are of value only for purposes of mental power, they are of value only as they are capable of being shared and applied to the common advantage of philosophy and—if there be no love among men, whatever institutions they may frame, must be subservient to the same purpose: to the continuance of inequality. If there be no love among men, it is best that he who sees through the hollowness of their professions, should fly from their society and suffice to his own soul. In wisdom he will thus lose nothing, in peace he will gain everything. In proportion to the love existing among men, so will be the community of property and power. Among true and real friends all is common, and were ignorance and envy, and superstition banished from the world all mankind would be as friends. The only perfect and genuine republic is that which comprehends every living being. Those distinctions which have been artificially set up of nations and cities, and families and religions are only general names expressing the abhorrence and contempt with which men blindly consider their fellow-men. I love my country, I love the city in which I was born, my parents and my wife and the children of my care, and to this city, this woman and this nation, it is incumbent on me to do all the benefit in my power. To what do these distinctions point, but to an indirect denial of the duty which humanity imposes on you of doing every possible good, to every individual, under whatever denomination he may be comprehended, to whom you have the power of doing it? You ought to love all mankind, nay, every individual of mankind; you ought not to love the individuals of your domestic circle less, but to love those who exist beyond it, more. Once make the feelings of confidence and affection universal and the distinctions of property and power will vanish; nor are they to be abolished without substituting something equivalent in mischief to them, until all mankind shall acknowledge an entire community of rights. But, as the shades of night are dispelled by the faintest glimmerings of dawn, so shall the minutest progress of the benevolent feelings disperse in some degree the gloom of tyranny and slavery, ministers of mutual suspicion and abhorrence.

Your physical wants are few, whilst those of your mind and heart cannot be numbered or described from their multitude and complication. To secure the gratification of the former, men have made themselves the bond-slaves of each other. They have cultivated these meaner wants to so great an excess as to judge nothing valuable or desirable but what relates to their gratification. Hence has arisen a system of passions which loses sight of the end which they were originally awakened to attain. Fame, power, and gold are loved for their own sakes, are worshipped with a blind and habitual idolatry. The pageantry of empire, and the fame of irresistible might is contemplated by its possessor with unmeaning complacency, without a retrospect to the properties which first made him consider them of value. It is from the cultivation of the most contemptible properties of human nature, that the discord and torpor and [indifference] by which the moral universe is disordered essentially depend. So long as these are the ties by which human society is connected, let it not be admired that they are fragile.

Before man can be free and equal and truly wise he must cast aside the chains of habit and superstition, he must strip sensuality of its pomp and selfishness of its excuses, and contemplate actions and objects as they really are. He will discover the wisdom of universal love. He will feel the meanness and the injustice of sacrificing the leisure and the liberty of his fellow-men to the indulgence of his physical appetites and becoming a party to their degradation by the consummation of his own. . . .

In proportion as mankind becomes wise, yes, in exact proportion to that wisdom should be the extinction of the unequal system under which they now subsist. Government is in fact the mere badge of their depravity. They are so little aware of the inestimable benefits of mutual love as to indulge without thought and almost without motive in the worst excesses of selfishness and malice. Hence without graduating human society into a scale of empire and subjection, its very existence has become impossible. It is necessary that universal benevolence should supersede the regulations of precedent and prescription, before these regulations can safely be abolished. Meanwhile their very subsistence depends on the system of injustice and violence which they have been devised to palliate. They suppose men endowed with the power of deliberating and determining for their equals; whilst these men as frail and as ignorant as the multitude whom they rule, possess, as a practical consequence of this power, the right which they of necessity exercise to pervert together with their own the physical and moral and intellectual nature of all mankind. It is the object of wisdom to equalize the distinctions on which this power depends; by exhibiting in their proper worthlessness the objects, a contention concerning which renders its existence a necessary evil. The evil in fact is virtually abolished wherever *justice* is practised, and it is abolished in precise proportion to the prevalence of

true virtue. The whole frame of human things is infected by the insidious poison. Hence it is that man is blind in his understanding, corrupt in his moral sense, and diseased in his physical functions. The wisest and most sublime of the ancient poets saw this truth, and embodied their conception of its value in retrospect to the earliest ages of mankind. They represented equality as the reign of Saturn,[3] and taught that mankind had gradually degenerated from the virtue which enabled them to enjoy or maintain this happy state. Their doctrine was philosophically false. Later and more correct observations have instructed us that uncivilized man is the most pernicious and miserable of beings, and that the violence and injustice, which are the genuine indications of real inequality obtain in the society of these beings without mixture and without palliation. Their imaginations of a happier state of human society were referred indeed to the [Saturnian] period, they ministered indeed to thoughts of despondency and sorrow. But they were the children of airy hope, the prophets and parents of mysterious futurity. Man was once as a wild beast; he has become a moralist, a metaphysician, a poet, and an astronomer;—Lucretius or Virgil might have referred the comparison to themselves; and as a proof of this progress of the nature of man, challenged a comparison with the cannibals of Scythia.[4] The experience of the ages which have intervened between the present period and that in which Jesus Christ taught tends to prove his doctrine and to illustrate theirs. There is more equality, because there is more justice among mankind and there is more justice because there is more universal knowledge.

To the accomplishment of such mighty hopes were the views of Jesus Christ extended; such did he believe to be the tendency of his doctrines: the abolition of artificial distinctions among mankind so far as the love which it becomes all human beings to bear towards each other, and the knowledge of truth from which that love will never fail to be produced avail to their destruction.

A young man came to Jesus Christ struck by the miraculous dignity and simplicity of his character and attracted by the words of power which he uttered. He demanded to be considered as one of the followers of his creed. 'Sell all that thou hast,' replied the philosopher; 'give it to the poor,

---

3 Roman deity fabled to have reigned during the Golden Age.
4 Jesus Christ foresaw what these poets retrospectively imagined.—(Shelley.)

and follow me.'⁵ But the young man had large possessions, and he [went away sorrowing].

1817　　　　　　　　　　　　　1859

ON LOVE

WHAT is love? Ask him who lives, what is life? ask him who adores, what is God?

I know not the internal constitution of other men, nor even thine, whom I now address. I see that in some external attributes they resemble me, but when, misled by that appearance, I have thought to appeal to something in common, and unburthen my inmost soul to them, I have found my language misunderstood, like one in a distant and savage land. The more opportunities they have afforded me for experience, the wider has appeared the interval between us, and to a greater distance have the points of sympathy been withdrawn. With a spirit ill fitted to sustain such proof, trembling and feeble through its tenderness, I have everywhere sought sympathy, and have found only repulse and disappointment.

Thou demandest what is love? It is that powerful attraction towards all that we conceive, or fear, or hope beyond ourselves, when we find within our own thoughts the chasm of an insufficient void, and seek to awaken in all things that are, a community with what we experience within ourselves. If we reason, we would be understood; if we imagine, we would that the airy children of our brain were born anew within another's; if we feel, we would that another's nerves should vibrate to our own, that the beams of their eyes should kindle at once and mix and melt into our own, that lips of motionless ice should not reply to lips quivering and burning with the heart's best blood. This is Love. This is the bond and the sanction which connects not only man with man, but with everything which exists. We are born into the world, and there is something within us which, from the instant that we live, more and more thirsts after its likeness. It is probably in correspondence with this law that the infant drains milk from the bosom of its mother; this propensity develops itself with the development of our nature. We dimly see within our intellectual nature a miniature as it were of our entire self, yet deprived of all that we condemn or despise, the ideal prototype of everything excellent or lovely that we are capable of conceiving as belonging to the nature of man. Not only the portrait of our external being, but an assemblage of the minutest particles of which our nature is composed; a mirror whose surface reflects only the forms of purity and brightness; a soul within our soul that describes a circle around its proper paradise, which pain, and sorrow, and evil dare not overleap. To this we eagerly refer all sensations, thirsting that they should resemble or correspond with it. The discovery of its antitype; the meeting with an understanding capable of clearly estimating our own; an imagination which should enter into and seize upon the subtle and delicate peculiarities which we have delighted to cherish and unfold in secret; with a frame whose nerves, like the chords of two exquisite lyres, strung to the accompaniment of one delightful voice, vibrate with the vibrations of our own; and of a combination of all these in such proportion as the type within demands; this is the invisible and unattainable point to which Love tends; and to attain which, it urges forth the powers of man to arrest the faintest shadow of that, without the possession of which there is no rest nor respite to the heart over which it rules. Hence in solitude, or in that deserted state when we are surrounded by human beings, and yet they sympathise not with us, we love the flowers, the grass, and the waters, and the sky. In the motion of the very leaves of spring, in the blue air, there is then found a secret correspondence with our heart. There is eloquence in the tongueless wind, and a melody in the flowing brooks and the rustling of the reeds beside them, which by their inconceivable relation to something within the soul, awaken the spirits to a dance of breathless rapture, and bring tears of mysterious tenderness to the eyes, like the enthusiasm of patriotic success, or the voice of one beloved singing to you alone.

1818–19　　　　　　　　　　　1829

From A PHILOSOPHICAL VIEW OF REFORM

THOSE who imagine that their personal interest is directly or indirectly concerned in maintaining the power in which they are clothed by the existing institutions of English Government do not acknowledge the necessity of a material change in those institutions. With this exception, there is no inhabitant of the British Empire of mature age and perfect understanding not fully persuaded of the necessity of Reform. . . .

What is the Reform that we desire? Before we

---

5 Matthew, xix, 21.

aspire after theoretical perfection in the amelioration of our political state, it is necessary that we possess those advantages which we have been cheated of, and to which the experience of modern times has proved that nations even under the present [conditions] are susceptible. 1st. We would regain these. 2d. We would establish some form of government which might secure us against such a series of events as have conducted us to a persuasion that the forms according to which it is now administered are inadequate to that purpose.

We would abolish the national debt.

We would disband the standing army.

We would, with every possible regard to the existing interests of the holders, abolish sinecures.

We would, with every possible regard to the existing interests of the holders, abolish tithes, and make all religions, all forms of opinion respecting the origin and government of the Universe, equal in the eye of the law.

We would make justice cheap, certain and speedy, and extend the institution of juries to every possible occasion of jurisprudence. . . .

The great principle of Reform consists in every individual of mature age and perfect understanding giving his consent to the institution and the continued existence of the social system, which is instituted for his advantage and for the advantage of others in his situation. As in a great nation this is practically impossible, masses of individuals consent to qualify other individuals, whom they delegate to superintend their concerns. These delegates have constitutional authority to exercise the functions of sovereignty; they unite in the highest degree the legislative and executive functions. A government that is founded on any other basis is a government of fraud or force and ought on the first convenient occasion to be overthrown. The broad principle of political reform is the natural equality of men, not with relation to their property but to their rights. That equality in possessions which Jesus Christ so passionately taught is a moral rather than a political truth and is such as social institutions cannot without mischief inflexibly secure. Morals and politics can only be considered as portions of the same science, with relation to a system of such absolute perfection as Christ and Plato and Rousseau and other reasoners have asserted, and as Godwin[1] has, with

irresistible eloquence, systematized and developed. Equality in possessions must be the last result of the utmost refinements of civilization; it is one of the conditions of that system of society, towards which with whatever hope of ultimate success, it is our duty to tend. We may and ought to advert to it as to the elementary principle, as to the goal, unattainable, perhaps, by us, but which, as it were, we revive in our posterity to pursue. We derive tranquility and courage and grandeur of soul from contemplating an object which is, because we will it, and may be, because we hope and desire it, and must be if succeeding generations of the enlightened sincerely and earnestly seek it. . . .

But our present business is with the difficult and unbending realities of actual life, and when we have drawn inspiration from the great object of our hopes it becomes us with patience and resolution to apply ourselves to accommodating our theories to immediate practice.

That Representative Assembly called the House of Commons ought questionless to be *immediately* nominated by the great mass of the people. The aristocracy and those who unite in their own persons the vast privileges conferred by the possession of inordinate wealth are sufficiently represented by the House of Peers and by the King. Those theorists who admire and would put into action the mechanism of what is called the British Constitution would acquiesce in this view of the question. For if the House of Peers be a permanent representation of the privileged classes, if the regal power be no more than another form, and a form still more jealously to be regarded, of the same representation, whilst the House of Commons be not chosen by the mass of the population, what becomes of that democratic element, upon the presence of which it has been supposed that the waning superiority of England over the surrounding nations has depended? . . .

If the existing government shall compel the Nation to take the task of reform into its own hands, one of the most obvious consequences of such a circumstance would be the abolition of monarchy and aristocracy. Why, it will then be argued, if the subsisting condition of social forms is to be thrown into confusion, should these things be endured? Then why do we now endure them? Is it because we think that an hereditary King is cheaper and wiser than an elected President, or a House of Lords and a Bench of Bishops are institutions modelled by the wisdom

---

1 William Godwin, 1756–1836, English political philosopher.

of the most refined and civilized periods, beyond which the wit of mortal man can furnish nothing more perfect? In case the subsisting Government should compel the people to revolt to establish a representative assembly in defiance of them, and to assume in that assembly an attitude of resistance and defence, this question would probably be answered in a very summary manner. No friend of mankind and of his country can desire that such a crisis should suddenly arrive; but still less, once having arrived, can he hesitate under what banner to array his person and his power. At the peace, the people would have been contented with strict economy and severe retrenchment, and some direct and intelligible plan for producing that equilibrium between the capitalists and the landholders which is delusively styled the payment of the national debt: had this system been adopted, they probably would have refrained from exacting Parliamentary Reform, the only secure guarantee that it would have been pursued. Two years ago it might still have been possible to have commenced a system of gradual reform. The people were then insulted, tempted and betrayed, and *the petitions of a million* of men rejected with disdain. Now they are more miserable, more hopeless, more impatient of their misery. Above all, they have become more universally aware of the true sources of their misery. It is possible that the period of conciliation is past, and that after having played with the confidence and cheated the expectations of the people, their passions will be too little under discipline to allow them to wait the slow, gradual and certain operation of such a Reform as we can imagine the constituted authorities to concede.

Upon the issue of this question depends the species of reform which a philosophical mind should regard with approbation. If Reform shall be begun by the existing government, let us be contented with a limited *beginning*, with any whatsoever opening; let the rotten boroughs be disfranchised and their rights transferred to the unrepresented cities and districts of the Nation; it is no matter how slow, gradual and cautious be the change; we shall demand more and more with firmness and moderation, never anticipating but never deferring the moment of successful opposition, so that the people may become habituated [to] exercising the functions of sovereignty, in proportion as they acquire the possession of it. If reform could begin from within the Houses of Parliament, as constituted at pres-

ent, it appears to me that what is called moderate reform, that is a suffrage whose qualification should be the possession of a certain small property, and triennial parliaments, would be principles—a system in which for the sake of obtaining without bloodshed or confusion ulterior improvements of a more important character, all reformers ought to acquiesce. Not that such are first principles, or that they would produce a system of perfect social institutions or one approaching to [such]. But nothing is more idle than to reject a limited benefit because we cannot without great sacrifices obtain an unlimited one. We might thus reject a Representative Republic, if it were obtainable, on the plea that the imagination of man can conceive of something more absolutely perfect. Towards whatsoever we regard as perfect, undoubtedly it is no less our duty than it is our nature to press forward; this is the generous enthusiasm which accomplishes not indeed the consummation after which it aspires, but one which approaches it in a degree far nearer than if the whole powers had not been developed by a delusion. It is in politics rather than in religion that faith is meritorious.

If the Houses of Parliament obstinately and perpetually refuse to concede any reform to the people, my vote is for universal suffrage and equal representation. My vote is —— but, it is asked, how shall this be accomplished, in defiance of and in opposition to the constituted authorities of the Nation, they who possess whether with or without its consent the command of a standing army and of a legion of spies and police officers, and hold all the strings of that complicated mechanism with which the hopes and fears of men are moved like puppets? They would disperse any assembly really chosen by the people, they would shoot and hew down any multitude, without regard to sex or age, as the Jews did the Canaanites, which might be collected in its defence; they would calumniate, imprison, starve, ruin and expatriate every person who wrote or acted, or thought, or might be suspected to think against them; misery and extermination would fill the country from one end to another. . . .

This question I would answer by another.

Will you endure to pay the half of your earnings to maintain in luxury and idleness the confederation of your tyrants as the reward of a successful conspiracy to defraud and oppress you? Will you make your tame cowardice and the branding record of it the everlasting inheritance of your posterity? Not only this; will you render by your torpid endurance this condition of things as permanent as the system of castes in India, by which the same horrible injustice is perpetrated under another form?

Assuredly no Englishmen by whom these propositions are understood will answer in the affirmative; and the opposite side of the alternative remains.

When the majority in any nation arrive at a conviction that it is their duty and their interest to divest the minority of a power employed to their disadvantage; and the minority are sufficiently mistaken as to believe that their superiority is tenable, a struggle must ensue.

If the majority are enlightened, united, impelled by a uniform enthusiasm and animated by a distinct and powerful apprehension of their object,—and full confidence in their undoubted power—the struggle is merely nominal. The minority perceive the approaches of the development of an irresistible force, by the influence of the public opinion of their weakness, on those political forms of which no government but an absolute despotism is devoid. They divest themselves of their usurped distinctions; the public tranquility is not disturbed by the revolution.

But these conditions may only be imperfectly fulfilled by the state of a people grossly oppressed and impotent to cast off the load. Their enthusiasm may have been subdued by the killing weight of toil and suffering; they may be panic-stricken and disunited by their oppressors, and the demagogues, the influence of fraud may have been sufficient to weaken the union of classes which compose them by suggesting jealousies, and the position of the conspirators, although it is to be forced by repeated assaults, may be tenable until the siege can be vigorously urged. The true patriot will endeavour to enlighten and to unite the nation and animate it with enthusiasm and confidence. For this purpose he will be indefatigable in promulgating political truth. He will endeavour to rally round one standard the divided friends of liberty, and make them forget the subordinate objects with regard to which they differ by appealing to that respecting which they are all agreed. He will promote such open confederations among men of principle and spirit as may tend to make their intentions and their efforts converge to a common centre. He will discourage all secret associations, which have a tendency, by making national will develop itself in a partial and premature manner, to cause tu-

mult and confusion. He will urge the necessity of exciting the people frequently to exercise their right of assembling, in such limited numbers as that all present may be actual parties to the proceedings of the day. Lastly, if circumstances had collected a more considerable number as at Manchester on the memorable 16th of August,[2] if the tyrants command their troops to fire upon them or cut them down unless they disperse, he will exhort them peaceably to risk the danger, and to expect without resistance the onset of the cavalry, and wait with folded arms the event of the fire of the artillery and receive with unshrinking bosoms the bayonets of the charging battalions. Men are every day persuaded to incur greater perils for a less manifest advantage. And this, not because active resistance is not justifiable when all other means shall have failed, but because in this instance temperance and courage would produce greater advantages than the most decisive victory. . . .

The public opinion in England ought first to be excited to action, and the durability of those forms within which the oppressors intrench themselves brought perpetually to the test of its operation. No law or institution can last if this opinion be distinctly pronounced against it. For this purpose government ought to be defied, in cases of questionable result, to prosecute for political libel. All questions relating to the jurisdiction of magistrates and courts of law respecting which any doubt could be raised ought to be agitated with indefatigable pertinacity. Some two or three of the popular leaders have shown the best spirit in this respect; they only want system and coöperation. The taxgatherer ought to be compelled in every practicable instance to distrain, whilst the right to impose taxes, as was the case in the beginning of the resistance to the tyranny of Charles the Ist[3] is formally contested by an overwhelming multitude of defendants before the courts of common law. Confound the subtlety of lawyers with the subtlety of the law. All of the nation would thus be excited to develop itself, and to declare whether it acquiesced in the existing forms of government. The manner in which all questions of this nature might be decided would develop the occasions, and afford a prognostic as to the

---

2 At a reform meeting held in St. Peter's Field, Manchester, in 1819, a charge of troops killed and wounded many of the assembly.

3 When Charles I in the early years of his reign, 1629–49, adopted questionable methods of taxation, moderate Englishmen in large numbers resisted his measures by appeals to the courts.

success, of more decisive measures. Simultaneously with this active and vigilant system of opposition, means ought to be taken of solemnly conveying the sense of large bodies and various denominations of the people in a manner the most explicit to the existing depositaries of power. Petitions, couched in the actual language of the petitioners, and emanating from distinct assemblies, ought to load the tables of the House of Commons. The poets, philosophers and artists ought to remonstrate, and the memorials entitled their petitions might show the diversity of convictions they entertain of the inevitable connection between national prosperity and freedom, and the cultivation of the imagination and the cultivation of scientific truth, and the profound development of moral and metaphysical enquiry. Suppose these memorials to be severally written by Godwin, Hazlitt, Bentham, and Hunt, they would be worthy of the age and of the cause; these, radiant and irresistible like the meridian sun would strike all but the eagles who dared to gaze upon its beams, with blindness and confusion. These appeals of solemn and emphatic argument from those who have already a predestined existence among posterity, would appal the enemies of mankind by their echoes from every corner of the world in which the majestic literature of England is cultivated; it would be like a voice from beyond the dead of those who will live in the memories of men, when they must be forgotten; it would be Eternity warning Time.

1819–20   1920

A DEFENCE OF POETRY[1]

ACCORDING to one mode of regarding those two classes of mental action, which are called reason and imagination, the former may be considered as mind contemplating the relations borne by one thought to another, however produced, and the latter as mind acting upon those thoughts so as to colour them with its own light, and composing from them, as from elements, other thoughts, each containing within itself the principle of its own integrity. The one is the τὸ ποιεῖν, or the principle of synthesis, and has for its object those forms which are common to universal nature and existence itself; the other is the τὸ λογίζειν, or principle of analysis, and its

action regards the relations of things simply as relations; considering thoughts not in their integral unity, but as the algebraical representations which conduct to certain general results. Reason is the enumeration of quantities already known; imagination is the perception of the value of those quantities, both separately and as a whole. Reason respects the differences, and imagination the similitudes of things. Reason is to imagination as the instrument to the agent, as the body to the spirit, as the shadow to the substance.

Poetry, in a general sense, may be defined to be 'the expression of the imagination'; and poetry is connate with the origin of man. Man is an instrument over which a series of external and internal impressions are driven, like the alternations of an ever-changing wind over an Æolian lyre, which move it by their motion to ever-changing melody. But there is a principle within the human being, and perhaps within all sentient beings, which acts otherwise than in the lyre, and produces not melody alone, but harmony, by an internal adjustment of the sounds or motions thus excited to the impressions which excite them. It is as if the lyre could accommodate its chords to the motions of that which strikes them, in a determined proportion of sound; even as the musician can accommodate his voice to the sound of the lyre. A child at play by itself will express its delight by its voice and motions; and every inflexion of tone and every gesture will bear exact relation to a corresponding antitype in the pleasurable impressions which awakened it; it will be the reflected image of that impression; and as the lyre trembles and sounds after the wind has died away, so the child seeks, by prolonging in its voice and motions, the duration of the effect, to prolong also a consciousness of the cause. In relation to the objects which delight a child, these expressions are what poetry is to higher objects. The savage (for the savage is to ages what the child is to years) expresses the emotions produced in him by surrounding objects in a similar manner; and language and gesture, together with plastic or pictorial imitation, become the image of the combined effect of those objects and of his apprehension of them. Man in society, with all his passions and his pleasures, next becomes the object of the passions and pleasures of man; an additional class of emotions produces an augmented treasure of expressions; and language, gesture, and the imitative arts become at once the representation and the medium, the pencil and the picture, the chisel and the statue, the

[1] Shelley wrote his essay as an antidote to Thomas Love Peacock's *Four Ages of Poetry*, an ironical and humorous attack upon the major writers of the day, in which Peacock had declared that really intellectual men were turning away from poetry.

chord and the harmony. The social sympathies, or those laws from which, as from its elements, society results, begin to develop themselves from the moment that two human beings co-exist; the future is contained within the present as the plant within the seed; and equality, diversity, unity, contrast, mutual dependence, become the principles alone capable of affording the motives according to which the will of a social being is determined to action, inasmuch as he is social; and constitute pleasure in sensation, virtue in sentiment, beauty in art, truth in reasoning, and love in the intercourse of kind. Hence men, even in the infancy of society, observe a certain order in their words and actions, distinct from that of the objects and the impressions represented by them, all expression being subject to the laws of that from which it proceeds. But let us dismiss those more general considerations which might involve an inquiry into the principles of society itself, and restrict our view to the manner in which the imagination is expressed upon its forms.

In the youth of the world, men dance and sing and imitate natural objects, observing in these actions, as in all others, a certain rhythm or order. And, although all men observe a similar, they observe not the same order in the motions of the dance, in the melody of the song, in the combinations of language, in the series of their imitations of natural objects. For there is a certain order or rhythm belonging to each of these classes of mimetic representation, from which the hearer and the spectator receive an intenser and purer pleasure than from any other; the sense of an approximation to this order has been called taste by modern writers. Every man, in the infancy of art, observes an order which approximates more or less closely to that from which this highest delight results; but the diversity is not sufficiently marked as that its gradations should be sensible, except in those instances where the predominance of this faculty of approximation to the beautiful (for so we may be permitted to name the relation between this highest pleasure and its cause) is very great. Those in whom it exists in excess are poets, in the most universal sense of the word; and the pleasure resulting from the manner in which they express the influence of society or nature upon their own minds, communicates itself to others, and gathers a sort of reduplication from that community. Their language is vitally metaphorical; that is, it marks the before unapprehended relations of things and perpetuates their apprehension, until the words, which represent them, become, through time, signs for portions or classes of thought instead of pictures of integral thoughts; and then, if no new poets should arise to create afresh the associations which have been thus disorganized, language will be dead to all the nobler purposes of human intercourse. These similitudes or relations are finely said by Lord Bacon to be 'the same footsteps of nature impressed upon the various subjects of the world'[2]—and he considers the faculty which perceives them as the storehouse of axioms common to all knowledge. In the infancy of society every author is necessarily a poet, because language itself is poetry; and to be a poet is to apprehend the true and the beautiful, in a word, the good which exists in the relation subsisting, first between existence and perception, and secondly between perception and expression. Every original language near to its source is in itself the chaos of a cyclic poem; the copiousness of lexicography and the distinctions of grammar are the works of a later age, and are merely the catalogue and the form of the creations of poetry.

But poets, or those who imagine and express this indestructible order, are not only the authors of language and of music, of the dance, and architecture, and statuary, and painting: they are the institutors of laws, and the founders of civil society, and the inventors of the arts of life, and the teachers who draw into a certain propinquity with the beautiful and the true, that partial apprehension of the agencies of the invisible world which is called religion. Hence all original religions are allegorical, or susceptible of allegory, and, like Janus, have a double face of false and true. Poets, according to the circumstances of the age and nation in which they appeared, were called, in the earlier epochs of the world, legislators or prophets; a poet essentially comprises and unites both these characters. For he not only beholds intensely the present as it is, and discovers those laws according to which present things ought to be ordered, but he beholds the future in the present, and his thoughts are the germs of the flower and the fruit of latest time. Not that I assert poets to be prophets in the gross sense of the word, or that they can foretell the form as surely as they foreknow the spirit of events; such is the pretence of superstition, which would make poetry an attribute of prophecy, rather than prophecy an attribute of poetry. A poet partici-

---

2 *De Augment. Scient.* cap. I, lib. iii.—(Shelley.)

pates in the eternal, the infinite, and the one; as far as relates to his conceptions, time and place and number are not. The grammatical forms which express the moods of time, and the difference of persons, and the distinction of place, are convertible with respect to the highest poetry without injuring it as poetry; and the choruses of Æschylus, and the *Book of Job,* and Dante's *Paradise,* would afford, more than any other writings, examples of this fact, if the limits of this essay did not forbid citation. The creations of sculpture, painting, and music are illustrations still more decisive.

Language, colour, form, and religious and civil habits of action, are all the instruments and materials of poetry; they may be called poetry by that figure of speech which considers the effect as a synonym of the cause. But poetry in a more restricted sense expresses those arrangements of language, and especially metrical language, which are created by that imperial faculty whose throne is curtained within the invisible nature of man. And this springs from the nature itself of language, which is a more direct representation of the actions and passions of our internal being, and is susceptible of more various and delicate combinations, than colour, form, or motion, and is more plastic and obedient to the control of that faculty of which it is the creation. For language is arbitrarily produced by the imagination, and has relation to thoughts alone; but all other materials, instruments, and conditions of art have relations among each other, which limit and interpose between conception and expression. The former is as a mirror which reflects, the latter as a cloud which enfeebles, the light of which both are mediums of communication. Hence the fame of sculptors, painters, and musicians, although the intrinsic powers of the great masters of these arts may yield in no degree to that of those who have employed language as the hieroglyphic of their thoughts, has never equalled that of poets in the restricted sense of the term; as two performers of equal skill will produce unequal effects from a guitar and a harp. The fame of legislators and founders of religions, so long as their institutions last, alone seems to exceed that of poets in the restricted sense; but it can scarcely be a question, whether, if we deduct the celebrity which their flattery of the gross opinions of the vulgar usually conciliates, together with that which belonged to them in their higher character of poets, any excess will remain.

We have thus circumscribed the meaning of the word *poetry* within the limits of that art which is the most familiar and the most perfect expression of the faculty itself. It is necessary, however, to make the circle still narrower, and to determine the distinction between measured and unmeasured language; for the popular division into prose and verse is inadmissible in accurate philosophy.

Sounds as well as thoughts have relation both between each other and towards that which they represent, and a perception of the order of those relations has always been found connected with a perception of the order of the relations of thoughts. Hence the language of poets has ever affected a certain uniform and harmonious recurrence of sound, without which it were not poetry, and which is scarcely less indispensable to the communication of its action than the words themselves without reference to that peculiar order. Hence the vanity of translation; it were as wise to cast a violet into a crucible that you might discover the formal principle of its colour and odour, as to seek to transfuse from one language into another the creations of a poet. The plant must spring again from its seed, or it will bear no flower—and this is the burthen of the curse of Babel.[3]

An observation of the regular mode of the recurrence of this harmony in the language of poetical minds, together with its relation to music, produced metre, or a certain system of traditional forms of harmony and language. Yet it is by no means essential that a poet should accommodate his language to this traditional form, so that the harmony, which is its spirit, be observed. The practice is indeed convenient and popular, and to be preferred especially in such composition as includes much form and action; but every great poet must inevitably innovate upon the example of his predecessors in the exact structure of his peculiar versification. The distinction between poets and prose writers is a vulgar error. The distinction between philosophers and poets has been anticipated. Plato was essentially a poet—the truth and splendour of his imagery, and the melody of his language, are the most intense that it is possible to conceive. He rejected the measure of the epic, dramatic, and lyrical forms, because he sought to kindle a harmony in thoughts divested of shape and action, and he forebore to invent any regular plan of rhythm which should include, under determinate forms, the varied pauses of his style.

---

3 See Genesis, xi, 6–9.

Cicero sought to imitate the cadence of his periods, but with little success. Lord Bacon was a poet.[4] His language has a sweet and majestic rhythm which satisfies the sense, no less than the almost superhuman wisdom of his philosophy satisfies the intellect; it is a strain which distends and then bursts the circumference of the hearer's mind, and pours itself forth together with it into the universal element with which it has perpetual sympathy. All the authors of revolutions in opinion are not only necessarily poets as they are inventors, nor even as their words unveil the permanent analogy of things by images which participate in the life of truth; but as their periods are harmonious and rhythmical, and contain in themselves the elements of verse, being the echo of the eternal music. Nor are those supreme poets, who have employed traditional forms of rhythm on account of the form and action of their subjects, less capable of perceiving and teaching the truth of things, than those who have omitted that form. Shakespeare, Dante, and Milton (to confine ourselves to modern writers) are philosophers of the very loftiest power.

A poem is the image of life expressed in its eternal truth. There is this difference between a story and a poem, that a story is a catalogue of detached facts, which have no other bond of connexion than time, place, circumstance, cause and effect; the other is the creation of actions according to the unchangeable forms of human nature, as existing in the mind of the creator, which is itself the image of all other minds. The one is partial, and applies only to a definite period of time, and a certain combination of events which can never again recur; the other is universal, and contains within itself the germ of a relation to whatever motives or actions have place in the possible varieties of human nature. Time, which destroys the beauty and the use of the story of particular facts, stript of the poetry which should invest them, augments that of Poetry, and forever develops new and wonderful applications of the eternal truth which it contains. Hence epitomes have been called the moths of just history; they eat out the poetry of it. The story of particular facts is as a mirror which obscures and distorts that which should be beautiful; Poetry is a mirror which makes beautiful that which is distorted.

The parts of a composition may be poetical, without the composition as a whole being a poem. A single sentence may be considered as a

whole, though it may be found in a series of unassimilated portions; a single word even may be a spark of inextinguishable thought. And thus all the great historians, Herodotus, Plutarch, Livy, were poets; and although the plan of these writers, especially that of Livy, restrained them from developing this faculty in its highest degree, they made copious and ample amends for their subjection, by filling all the interstices of their subjects with living images.

Having determined what is poetry, and who are poets, let us proceed to estimate its effects upon society.

Poetry is ever accompanied with pleasure: all spirits on which it falls open themselves to receive the wisdom which is mingled with its delight. In the infancy of the world, neither poets themselves nor their auditors are fully aware of the excellence of poetry, for it acts in a divine and unapprehended manner, beyond and above consciousness; and it is reserved for future generations to contemplate and measure the mighty cause and effect in all the strength and splendour of their union. Even in modern times, no living poet ever arrived at the fulness of his fame; the jury which sits in judgement upon a poet, belonging as he does to all time, must be composed of his peers; it must be impanelled by Time from the selectest of the wise of many generations. A Poet is a nightingale, who sits in darkness and sings to cheer its own solitude with sweet sounds; his auditors are as men entranced by the melody of an unseen musician, who feel that they are moved and softened, yet know not whence or why. The poems of Homer and his contemporaries were the delight of infant Greece; they were the elements of that social system which is the column upon which all succeeding civilization has reposed. Homer embodied the ideal perfection of his age in human character; nor can we doubt that those who read his verses were awakened to an ambition of becoming like to Achilles, Hector, and Ulysses; the truth and beauty of friendship, patriotism, and persevering devotion to an object, were unveiled to the depths in these immortal creations; the sentiments of the auditors must have been refined and enlarged by a sympathy with such great and lovely impersonations, until from admiring they imitated, and from imitation they identified themselves with the objects of their admiration. Nor let it be objected that these characters are remote from moral perfection, and that they can by no means be considered as edifying patterns

---

4 See the *Filum Labyrinthi* and the *Essay on Death* particularly.—(Shelley.)

for general imitation. Every epoch, under names more or less specious, has deified its peculiar errors; Revenge is the naked Idol of the worship of a semi-barbarous age; and Self-Deceit is the veiled image of unknown evil, before which luxury and satiety lie prostrate. But a poet considers the vices of his contemporaries as the temporary dress in which his creations must be arrayed, and which cover without concealing the eternal proportions of their beauty. An epic or dramatic personage is understood to wear them around his soul, as he may the ancient armour or the modern uniform around his body, whilst it is easy to conceive a dress more graceful than either. The beauty of the internal nature can not be so far concealed by its accidental vesture, but that the spirit of its form shall communicate itself to the very disguise, and indicate the shape it hides from the manner in which it is worn. A majestic form and graceful motions will express themselves through the most barbarous and tasteless costume. Few poets of the highest class have chosen to exhibit the beauty of their conceptions in its naked truth and splendour; and it is doubtful whether the alloy of costume, habit, etc., be not necessary to temper this planetary music for mortal ears.

The whole objection, however, of the immorality of poetry rests upon a misconception of the manner in which poetry acts to produce the moral improvement of man. Ethical science arranges the elements which poetry has created, and propounds schemes and proposes examples of civil and domestic life; nor is it for want of admirable doctrines that men hate, and despise, and censure, and deceive, and subjugate one another. But Poetry acts in another and diviner manner. It awakens and enlarges the mind itself by rendering it the receptacle of a thousand unapprehended combinations of thought. Poetry lifts the veil from the hidden beauty of the world, and makes familiar objects be as if they were not familiar; it reproduces all that it represents, and the impersonations clothed in its Elysian light stand thenceforward in the minds of those who have once contemplated them, as memorials of that gentle and exalted content which extends itself over all thoughts and actions with which it co-exists. The great secret of morals is love; or a going out of our own nature, and an identification of ourselves with the beautiful which exists in thought, action, or person, not our own. A man, to be greatly good, must imagine intensely and comprehensively; he must put himself in the place of another and of many others; the pains and pleasures of his species must become his own. The great instrument of moral good is the imagination; and poetry administers to the effect by acting upon the cause. Poetry enlarges the circumference of the imagination by replenishing it with thoughts of ever new delight, which have the power of attracting and assimilating to their own nature all other thoughts, and which form new intervals and interstices whose void forever craves fresh food. Poetry strengthens that faculty which is the organ of the moral nature of man, in the same manner as exercise strengthens a limb. A Poet therefore would do ill to embody his own conceptions of right and wrong, which are usually those of his place and time, in his poetical creations, which participate in neither. By this assumption of the inferior office of interpreting the effect, in which perhaps after all he might acquit himself but imperfectly, he would resign the glory in a participation in the cause. There was little danger that Homer, or any of the eternal Poets, should have so far misunderstood themselves as to have abdicated this throne of their widest dominion. Those in whom the poetical faculty, though great, is less intense, as Euripides, Lucan, Tasso, Spenser, have frequently affected a moral aim, and the effect of their poetry is diminished in exact proportion to the degree in which they compel us to advert to this purpose.

Homer and the cyclic poets were followed at a certain interval by the dramatic and lyrical Poets of Athens, who flourished contemporaneously with all that is most perfect in the kindred expressions of the poetical faculty; architecture, painting, music, the dance, sculpture, philosophy, and we may add, the forms of civil life. For although the scheme of Athenian society was deformed by many imperfections which the poetry existing in Chivalry and Christianity has erased from the habits and institutions of modern Europe, yet never at any other period has so much energy, beauty, and virtue, been developed; never was blind strength and stubborn form so disciplined and rendered subject to the will of man, or that will less repugnant to the dictates of the beautiful and the true, as during the century which preceded the death of Socrates. Of no other epoch in the history of our species have we records and fragments stamped so visibly with the image of the divinity in man. But it is Poetry alone, in form, in action, or in language, which has rendered this epoch memorable above all others, and the storehouse of examples to everlasting time. For written poetry existed at that epoch simultaneously with the other arts, and it is an idle inquiry to demand which gave and which received the light, which all, as from a common focus, have scattered over the darkest periods of succeeding ages. We know no more of cause and effect than a constant conjunction of events: Poetry is ever found to co-exist with whatever other arts contribute to the happiness and perfection of man. I appeal to what has already been established to distinguish between the cause and the effect.

It was at the period here adverted to, that the Drama had its birth; and however a succeeding writer may have equalled or surpassed those few great specimens of the Athenian drama which have been preserved to us, it is indisputable that the art itself never was understood or practised according to the true philosophy of it, as at Athens. For the Athenians employed language, action, music, painting, the dance, and religious institutions, to produce a common effect in the representation of the loftiest idealisms of passion and of power; each division in the art was made perfect in its kind by artists of the most consummate skill, and was disciplined into a beautiful proportion and unity one towards another. On the modern stage a few only of the elements capable of expressing the image of the poet's conception are employed at once. We have tragedy without music and dancing, and music and dancing without the high impersonations of which they are the fit accompaniment, and both without religion and solemnity. Religious institution has indeed been usually banished from the stage. Our system of divesting the actor's face of a mask, on which the many expressions appropriated to his dramatic character might be moulded into one permanent and unchanging expression, is favourable only to a partial and inharmonious effect; it is fit for nothing but a monologue, where all the attention may be directed to some great master of ideal mimicry. The modern practice of blending comedy with tragedy, though liable to great abuse in point of practice, is undoubtedly an extension of the dramatic circle; but the comedy should be as in *King Lear*, universal, ideal, and sublime. It is perhaps the intervention of this principle which determines the balance in favour of *King Lear* against the *Œdipus Tyrannus* or the *Agamemnon*, or, if you will, the trilogies with which they are connected; unless the intense power of the

choral poetry, especially that of the latter, should be considered as restoring the equilibrium. *King Lear,* if it can sustain this comparison, may be judged to be the most perfect specimen of the dramatic art existing in the world; in spite of the narrow conditions to which the poet was subjected by the ignorance of the philosophy of the drama which has prevailed in modern Europe. Calderon, in his religious *autos,*[5] has attempted to fulfil some of the high conditions of dramatic representation neglected by Shakespeare; such as the establishing a relation between the drama and religion, and the accommodating them to music and dancing; but he omits the observation of conditions still more important, and more is lost than gained by a substitution of the rigidly-defined and ever-repeated idealisms of a distorted superstition for the living impersonations of the truth of human passion.

But I digress. The Author of the Four Ages of Poetry has prudently omitted to dispute on the effect of the Drama upon life and manners. For, if I know the Knight by the device of his shield, I have only to inscribe Philoctetes or Agamemnon or Othello upon mine to put to flight the giant sophisms which have enchanted him, as the mirror of intolerable light though on the arm of one of the weakest of the Paladines could blind and scatter whole armies of necromancers and pagans.—The connexion of scenic exhibitions with the improvement or corruption of the manners of men, has been universally recognized: in other words, the presence or absence of poetry in its most perfect and universal form has been found to be connected with good and evil in conduct and habit. The corruption which has been imputed to the drama as an effect, begins, when the poetry employed in its constitution ends: I appeal to the history of manners whether the gradations of the growth of the one and the decline of the other have not corresponded with an exactness equal to any other example of moral cause and effect.

The drama at Athens, or wheresoever else it may have approached to its perfection, coexisted with the moral and intellectual greatness of the age. The tragedies of the Athenian poets are as mirrors in which the spectator beholds himself, under a thin disguise of circumstance, stript of all but that ideal perfection and energy which every one feels to be the internal type of

---

5 The celebrated Spanish dramatist, 1600–1681, wrote more than seventy *Autos Sacramentales,* dramatic representations of the Mystery of the Holy Communion.

all that he loves, admires, and would become. The imagination is enlarged by a sympathy with pains and passions so mighty, that they distend in their conception the capacity of that by which they are conceived; the good affections are strengthened by pity, indignation, terror, and sorrow; and an exalted calm is prolonged from the satiety of this high exercise of them into the tumult of familiar life: even crime is disarmed of half its horror and all its contagion by being represented as the fatal consequence of the unfathomable agencies of nature; error is thus divested of its wilfulness; men can no longer cherish it as the creation of their choice. In a drama of the highest order there is little food for censure or hatred; it teaches rather self-knowledge and self-respect. Neither the eye nor the mind can see itself, unless reflected upon that which it resembles. The drama, so long as it continues to express poetry, is as a prismatic and many-sided mirror, which collects the brightest rays of human nature and divides and reproduces them from the simplicity of these elementary forms, and touches them with majesty and beauty, and multiplies all that it reflects, and endows it with the power of propagating its like wherever it may fall.

But in periods of the decay of social life, the drama sympathizes with that decay. Tragedy becomes a cold imitation of the form of the great masterpieces of antiquity, divested of all harmonious accompaniment of the kindred arts; and often the very form misunderstood, or a weak attempt to teach certain doctrines, which the writer considers as moral truths, and which are usually no more than specious flatteries of some gross vice or weakness with which the author, in common with his auditors, are infected. Hence what has been called the classical and domestic drama. Addison's *Cato* is a specimen of the one; and would it were not superfluous to cite examples of the other! To such purposes poetry cannot be made subservient. Poetry is a sword of lightning, ever unsheathed, which consumes the scabbard that would contain it. And thus we observe that all dramatic writings of this nature are unimaginative in a singular degree; they affect sentiment and passion, which, divested of imagination, are other names for caprice and appetite. The period in our own history of the grossest degradation of the drama is the reign of Charles II, when all forms in which poetry had been accustomed to be expressed became hymns to the triumph of kingly power over liberty and virtue. Milton stood alone, illuminating an age unworthy of him. At such periods the calculating principle pervades all the forms of dramatic exhibition, and poetry ceases to be expressed upon them. Comedy loses its ideal universality: wit succeeds to humour; we laugh from self-complacency and triumph, instead of pleasure; malignity, sarcasm, and contempt, succeed to sympathetic merriment; we hardly laugh, but we smile. Obscenity, which is ever blasphemy against the divine beauty in life, becomes, from the very veil which it assumes, more active if less disgusting: it is a monster for which the corruption of society forever brings forth new food, which it devours in secret.

The drama being that form under which a greater number of modes of expression of poetry are susceptible of being combined than any other, the connexion of poetry and social good is more observable in the drama than in whatever other form. And it is indisputable that the highest perfection of human society has ever corresponded with the highest dramatic excellence; and that the corruption or the extinction of the drama in a nation where it has once flourished, is a mark of a corruption of manners, and an extinction of the energies which sustain the soul of social life. But, as Machiavelli says of political institutions, that life may be preserved and renewed, if men should arise capable of bringing back the drama to its principles. And this is true with respect to poetry in its most extended sense: all language, institution and form, require not only to be produced but to be sustained: the office and character of a poet participates in the divine nature as regards providence, no less than as regards creation.

Civil war, the spoils of Asia, and the fatal predominance first of the Macedonian, and then of the Roman arms, were so many symbols of the extinction or suspension of the creative faculty in Greece. The bucolic writers, who found patronage under the lettered tyrants of Sicily and Egypt, were the latest representatives of its most glorious reign. Their poetry is intensely melodious; like the odour of the tuberose, it overcomes and sickens the spirit with excess of sweetness; whilst the poetry of the preceding age was as a meadow-gale of June, which mingles the fragrance of all the flowers of the field, and adds a quickening and harmonizing spirit of its own, which endows the sense with a power of sustaining its extreme delight. The bucolic and erotic delicacy in written poetry is correlative with that softness in statuary, music, and the kindred arts, and even in manners and institutions, which distinguished the epoch to which I now refer. Nor is it the poetical faculty itself, or any misapplication of it, to which this want of harmony is to be imputed. An equal sensibility to the influence of the senses and the affections is to be found in the writings of Homer and Sophocles: the former, especially, has clothed sensual and pathetic images with irresistible attractions. Their superiority over these succeeding writers consists in the presence of those thoughts which belong to the inner faculties of our nature, not in the absence of those which are connected with the external: their incomparable perfection consists in an harmony of the union of all. It is not what the erotic poets have, but what they have not, in which their imperfection consists. It is not inasmuch as they were Poets, but inasmuch as they were not poets, that they can be considered with any plausibility as connected with the corruption of their age. Had that corruption availed so as to extinguish in them the sensibility to pleasure, passion, and natural scenery, which is imputed to them as an imperfection, the last triumph of evil would have been achieved. For the end of social corruption is to destroy all sensibility to pleasure; and therefore it is corruption. It begins at the imagination and the intellect as at the core, and distributes itself thence as a paralysing venom, through the affections into the very appetites, until all become a torpid mass in which sense hardly survives. At the approach of such a period, Poetry ever addresses itself to those faculties which are the last to be destroyed, and its voice is heard, like the footsteps of Astræa,[6] departing from the world. Poetry ever communicates all the pleasure which men are capable of receiving: it is ever still the light of life; the source of whatever of beautiful or generous or true can have place in an evil time. It will readily be confessed that those among the luxurious citizens of Syracuse and Alexandria who were delighted with the poems of Theocritus, were less cold, cruel, and sensual than the remnant of their tribe. But corruption must have utterly destroyed the fabric of human society before poetry can ever cease. The sacred links of that chain have never been entirely disjoined, which descending through the minds of many men is attached to those great minds, whence as from a magnet the invisible effluence is sent forth, which at once connects, animates, and sustains the life of all. It is the faculty which contains within itself the seeds at once of its own and of social renovation. And let us not circumscribe the effects of the bucolic and erotic poetry within the limits of the sensibility of those to whom it was addressed. They may have perceived the beauty of those immortal compositions, simply as fragments and isolated portions: those who are more finely organized, or born in a happier age, may recognize them as episodes to that great poem, which all poets, like the co-operating thoughts of one great mind, have built up since the beginning of the world.

The same revolutions within a narrower sphere had place in ancient Rome; but the actions and forms of its social life never seem to have been perfectly saturated with the poetical element. The Romans appear to have considered the Greeks as the selectest treasuries of the selectest forms of manners and of nature, and to have abstained from creating in measured language, sculpture, music, or architecture, any thing which might bear a particular relation to their own condition, whilst it might bear a general one to the universal constitution of the world. But we judge from partial evidence, and we judge perhaps partially. Ennius, Varro, Pacuvius, and Accius, all great poets, have been lost. Lucretius is in the highest, and Virgil in a very high sense, a creator. The chosen delicacy of the expressions of the latter, are as a mist of light which conceal from us the intense and exceeding truth of his conceptions of nature. Livy is instinct with poetry. Yet Horace, Catullus, Ovid, and generally the other great writers of the Virgilian age, saw man and nature in the mirror of Greece. The institutions also, and the religion of Rome, were less poetical than those of Greece, as the shadow is less vivid than the substance. Hence poetry in Rome seemed to follow, rather than accompany, the perfection of political and domestic society. The true poetry of Rome lived in its institutions; for whatever of beautiful, true and majestic, they contained, could have sprung only from the faculty which creates the order in which they consist. The life of Camillus, the death of Regulus;[7] the expectation of the Senators, in their godlike state, of the victorious Gauls: the refusal of the Republic to 'make peace with Hannibal after the battle of Cannæ, were not the consequences of a refined calculation of the probable personal ad-

---

6 the 'star' maid, goddess of Justice, who dwelt among men in the golden age, and in the brazen age was the last of the heavenly deities to leave them.

7 Camillus and Regulus were celebrated generals in early Roman history.

vantage to result from such a rhythm and order in the shews of life, to those who were at once the poets and the actors of these immortal dramas. The imagination beholding the beauty of this order, created it out of itself according to its own idea; the consequence was empire, and the reward everliving fame. These things are not the less poetry *quia carent vate sacro.*[8] They are the episodes of that cyclic poem written by Time upon the memories of men. The Past, like an inspired rhapsodist, fills the theatre of everlasting generations with their harmony.

At length the ancient system of religion and manners had fulfilled the circle of its evolutions. And the world would have fallen into utter anarchy and darkness, but that there were found poets among the authors of the Christian and chivalric systems of manners and religion, who created forms of opinion and action never before conceived; which, copied into the imaginations of men, became as generals to the bewildered armies of their thoughts. It is foreign to the present purpose to touch upon the evil produced by these systems: except that we protest, on the ground of the principles already established, that no portion of it can be attributed to the poetry they contain.

It is probable that the poetry of Moses, Job, David, Solomon, and Isaiah, had produced a great effect upon the mind of Jesus and his disciples. The scattered fragments preserved to us by the biographers of this extraordinary person, are all instinct with the most vivid poetry. But his doctrines seem to have been quickly distorted. At a certain period after the prevalence of doctrines founded upon those promulgated by him, the three forms into which Plato had distributed the faculties of mind underwent a sort of apotheosis, and became the object of the worship of Europe. Here it is to be confessed that 'Light' seems 'to thicken,' and

The crow makes wing to the rooky wood,
Good things of day begin to droop and drowse,
Whiles night's black agents to their preys do
    rouse.[9]

But mark how beautiful an order has sprung from the dust and blood of this fierce chaos! how the World, as from a resurrection, balancing itself on the golden wings of knowledge and of hope, has reassumed its yet unwearied flight into the Heaven of time. Listen to the music, unheard by outward ears, which is as a ceaseless and invisible wind, nourishing its everlasting course with strength and swiftness.

The poetry in the doctrines of Jesus Christ, and the mythology and institutions of the Celtic[10] conquerors of the Roman empire, outlived the darkness and the convulsions connected with their growth and victory, and blended themselves in a new fabric of manners and opinion. It is an error to impute the ignorance of the dark ages to the Christian doctrines or the predominance of the Celtic nations. Whatever of evil their agencies may have contained sprang from the extinction of the poetical principle, connected with the progress of despotism and superstition. Men, from causes too intricate to be here discussed, had become insensible and selfish: their own will had become feeble, and yet they were its slaves, and thence the slaves of the will of others: lust, fear, avarice, cruelty, and fraud, characterized a race amongst whom no one was to be found capable of *creating* in form, language, or institution. The moral anomalies of such a state of society are not justly to be charged upon any class of events immediately connected with them, and those events are most entitled to our approbation which could dissolve it most expeditiously. It is unfortunate for those who cannot distinguish words from thoughts, that many of these anomalies have been incorporated into our popular religion.

It was not until the eleventh century that the effects of the poetry of the Christian and Chivalric systems began to manifest themselves. The principle of equality had been discovered and applied by Plato in his *Republic,* as the theoretical rule of the mode in which the materials of pleasure and of power produced by the common skill and labour of human beings ought to be distributed among them. The limitations of this rule were asserted by him to be determined only by the sensibility of each, or the utility to result to all. Plato, following the doctrines of Timæus and Pythagoras, taught also a moral and intellectual system of doctrine, comprehending at once the past, the present, and the future condition of man. Jesus Christ divulged the sacred and eternal truths contained in these views to mankind, and Christianity, in its abstract purity, became the exoteric expression of the esoteric doctrines of the poetry and wisdom of antiquity. The incorporation of the Celtic nations with the exhausted

---

8 'Because they lack the bard divine.'—Horace, *Ode* IV.
9 *Macbeth,* III, ii, 51–3.

10 Germanic.

population of the south, impressed upon it the figure of the poetry existing in their mythology and institutions. The result was a sum of the action and reaction of all the causes included in it; for it may be assumed as a maxim that no nation or religion can supersede any other without incorporating into itself a portion of that which it supersedes. The abolition of personal and domestic slavery, and the emancipation of women from a great part of the degrading restraints of antiquity, were among the consequences of these events.

The abolition of personal slavery is the basis of the highest political hope that it can enter into the mind of man to conceive. The freedom of women produced the poetry of sexual love. Love became a religion, the idols of whose worship were ever present. It was as if the statues of Apollo and the Muses had been endowed with life and motion, and had walked forth among their worshippers; so that earth became peopled by the inhabitants of a diviner world. The familiar appearances and proceedings of life became wonderful and heavenly, and a paradise was created as out of the wrecks of Eden. And as this creation itself is poetry, so its creators were poets; and language was the instrument of their art: 'Galeotto fù il libro, e chi lo scrisse.'[11] The Provençal Trouveurs, or inventors, preceded Petrarch, whose verses are as spells, which unseal the inmost enchanted fountains of the delight which is in the grief of love. It is impossible to feel them without becoming a portion of that beauty which we contemplate: it were superfluous to explain how the gentleness and elevation of mind connected with these sacred emotions can render men more amiable, and generous and wise, and lift them out of the dull vapours of the little world of self. Dante understood the secret things of love even more than Petrarch. His *Vita Nuova* is an inexhaustible fountain of purity of sentiment and language: it is the idealized history of that period, and those intervals of his life which were dedicated to love. His apotheosis of Beatrice in Paradise, and the gradations of his own love and her loveliness, by which as by steps he feigns himself to have ascended to the throne of the Supreme Cause, is the most glorious imagination of modern poetry. The acutest critics have justly reversed the judgment of the vulgar, and the order of the great acts of the *Divina Commedia* in the measure of the ad-

miration which they accord to the Hell, Purgatory, and Paradise. The latter is a perpetual hymn of everlasting Love. Love, which found a worthy poet in Plato alone of all the ancients, has been celebrated by a chorus of the greatest writers of the renovated world; and the music has penetrated the caverns of society, and its echoes still drown the dissonance of arms and superstition. At successive intervals, Ariosto, Tasso, Shakespeare, Spenser, Calderon, Rousseau, and the great writers of our own age, have celebrated the dominion of love, planting as it were trophies in the human mind of that sublimest victory over sensuality and force. The true relation borne to each other by the sexes into which human kind is distributed, has become less misunderstood; and if the error which confounded diversity with inequality of the powers of the two sexes has become partially recognized in the opinions and institutions of modern Europe, we owe this great benefit to the worship of which Chivalry was the law, and poets the prophets.

The poetry of Dante may be considered as the bridge thrown over the stream of time, which unites the modern and ancient World. The distorted notions of invisible things which Dante and his rival Milton have idealized, are merely the mask and the mantle in which these great poets walk through eternity enveloped and disguised. It is a difficult question to determine how far they were conscious of the distinction which must have subsisted in their minds between their own creeds and that of the people. Dante at least appears to wish to mark the full extent of it by placing Riphæus,[12] whom Virgil calls *justissimus unus,* in Paradise, and observing a most heretical caprice in his distribution of rewards and punishments. And Milton's poem contains within itself a philosophical refutation of that system of which, by a strange and natural antithesis, it has been a chief popular support. Nothing can exceed the energy and magnificence of the character of Satan as expressed in *Paradise Lost.* It is a mistake to suppose that he could ever have been intended for the popular personification of evil. Implacable hate, patient cunning, and a sleepless refinement of device to inflict the extremest anguish on an enemy, these things are evil; and, although venial in a slave, are not to be forgiven in a tyrant; although redeemed by much that ennobles his defeat in one subdued, are marked by

---

11 'Galeotto was the book, and he who wrote it.'—Dante, *Inferno,* V, 137.

12 warrior 'most just among the Trojans and the strictest observer of right'—*Aeneid,* II, 426.

all that dishonours his conquest in the victor. Milton's Devil as a moral being is as far superior to his God, as One who perseveres in some purpose which he has conceived to be excellent in spite of adversity and torture, is to One who in the cold security of undoubted triumph inflicts the most horrible revenge upon his enemy, not from any mistaken notion of inducing him to repent of a perseverance in enmity, but with the alleged design of exasperating him to deserve new torments. Milton has so far violated the popular creed (if this shall be judged to be a violation) as to have alleged no superiority of moral virtue to his God over his Devil. And this bold neglect of a direct moral purpose is the most decisive proof of the supremacy of Milton's genius. He mingled as it were the elements of human nature as colours upon a single pallet, and arranged them in the composition of his great picture according to the laws of epic truth; that is, according to the laws of that principle by which a series of actions of the external universe and of intelligent and ethical beings is calculated to excite the sympathy of succeeding generations of mankind. The *Divina Commedia* and *Paradise Lost* have conferred upon modern mythology a systematic form; and when change and time shall have added one more superstition to the mass of those which have arisen and decayed upon the earth, commentators will be learnedly employed in elucidating the religion of ancestral Europe, only not utterly forgotten because it will have been stamped with the eternity of genius.

Homer was the first and Dante the second epic poet: that is, the second poet, the series of whose creations bore a defined and intelligible relation to the knowledge and sentiment and religion and politics of the age in which he lived, and of the ages which followed it: developing itself in correspondence with their development. For Lucretius had limed the wings of his swift spirit in the dregs of the sensible world; and Virgil, with a modesty that ill became his genius, had affected the fame of an imitator, even whilst he created anew all that he copied; and none among the flock of Mockbirds, though their notes were sweet, Apollonius Rhodius, Quintus Calaber, Smyrnæus Nonnus, Lucan, Statius, or Claudian,[13] have sought even to fulfil a single condition of epic truth. Milton was the third epic poet. For if the title of epic in its highest sense be refused to the *Æneid*, still less can it be conceded to the *Orlando Furioso*, the *Gerusalemme Liberata*, the *Lusiad*, or the *Fairie Queene*.[14]

Dante and Milton were both deeply penetrated with the ancient religion of the civilized world; and its spirit exists in their poetry probably in the same proportion as its forms survived in the unreformed worship of modern Europe. The one preceded and the other followed the Reformation at almost equal intervals. Dante was the first religious reformer, and Luther surpassed him rather in the rudeness and acrimony, than in the boldness of his censures of papal usurpation. Dante was the first awakener of entranced Europe; he created a language, in itself music and persuasion, out of a chaos of inharmonious barbarisms. He was the congregator of those great spirits who presided over the resurrection of learning; the Lucifer of that starry flock which in the thirteenth century shone forth from republican Italy, as from a heaven, into the darkness of the benighted world. His very words are instinct with spirit; each is as a spark, a burning atom of inextinguishable thought; and many yet lie covered in the ashes of their birth, and pregnant with a lightning which has yet found no conductor. All high poetry is infinite; it is as the first acorn, which contained all oaks potentially. Veil after veil may be undrawn, and the inmost naked beauty of the meaning never exposed. A great poem is a fountain for ever overflowing with the waters of wisdom and delight; and after one person and one age has exhausted all its divine effluence which their peculiar relations enable them to share, another and yet another succeeds, and new relations are ever developed, the source of an unforeseen and an unconceived delight.

The age immediately succeeding to that of Dante, Petrarch, and Boccaccio, was characterized by a revival of painting, sculpture, and architecture. Chaucer caught the sacred inspiration, and the superstructure of English literature is based upon the materials of Italian invention.

But let us not be betrayed from a defence into a critical history of Poetry and its influence on Society. Be it enough to have pointed out the effects of poets, in the large and true sense of the word, upon their own and all succeeding times, and to revert to the partial instances cited as illustrations of an opinion the reverse of that

---

13 minor Roman poets.

14 the respective authors are Virgil, Ariosto, Tasso, Camöens, and Spenser.

attempted to be established by the Author of the Four Ages of Poetry.

But poets have been challenged to resign the civic crown to reasoners and mechanists, on another plea. It is admitted that the exercise of the imagination is most delightful, but it is alleged that that of reason is more useful. Let us examine as the grounds of this distinction, what is here meant by utility. Pleasure or good, in a general sense, is that which the consciousness of a sensitive and intelligent being seeks, and in which, when found, it acquiesces. There are two modes or degrees of pleasure, one durable, universal and permanent; the other transitory and particular. Utility may either express the means of producing the former or the latter. In the former sense, whatever strengthens and purifies the affections, enlarges the imagination, and adds spirit to sense, is useful. But the meaning in which the Author of the Four Ages of Poetry seems to have employed the word utility, is the narrower one of banishing the importunity of the wants of our animal nature, the surrounding men with security of life, the dispersing the grosser delusions of superstition, and the conciliating such a degree of mutual forbearance among men as may consist with the motives of personal advantage.

Undoubtedly the promoters of utility, in this limited sense, have their appointed office in society. They follow the footsteps of poets, and copy the sketches of their creations into the book of common life. They make space, and give time. Their exertions are of the highest value, so long as they confine their administration of the concerns of the inferior powers of our nature within the limits due to the superior ones. But whilst the sceptic destroys gross superstitions, let him spare to deface, as some of the French writers have defaced, the eternal truths charactered upon the imaginations of men. Whilst the mechanist abridges, and the political economist combines labour, let them beware that their speculations, for want of correspondence with those first principles which belong to the imagination, do not tend, as they have in modern England, to exasperate at once the extremes of luxury and want. They have exemplified the saying, 'To him that hath, more shall be given; and from him that hath not, the little that he hath shall be taken away.'[15] The rich have become richer, and the poor have become poorer; and the vessel of the state is driven between the Scylla and Charybdis[16] of anarchy and despotism. Such are the effects which must ever flow from an unmitigated exercise of the calculating faculty.

It is difficult to define pleasure in its highest sense; the definition involving a number of apparent paradoxes. For, from an inexplicable defect of harmony in the constitution of human nature, the pain of the inferior is frequently connected with the pleasures of the superior portions of our being. Sorrow, terror, anguish, despair itself, are often the chosen expressions of an approximation to the highest good. Our sympathy in tragic fiction depends on this principle; tragedy delights by affording a shadow of the pleasure which exists in pain. This is the source also of the melancholy which is inseparable from the sweetest melody. The pleasure that is in sorrow is sweeter than the pleasure of pleasure itself. And hence the saying, 'It is better to go to the house of mourning, than to the house of mirth.'[17] Not that this highest species of pleasure is necessarily linked with pain. The delight of love and friendship, the ecstasy of the admiration of nature, the joy of the perception and still more of the creation of poetry, is often wholly unalloyed.

The production and assurance of pleasure in this highest sense is true utility. Those who produce and preserve this pleasure are Poets or poetical philosophers.

The exertions of Locke, Hume, Gibbon, Voltaire, Rousseau,[18] and their disciples, in favour of oppressed and deluded humanity, are entitled to the gratitude of mankind. Yet it is easy to calculate the degree of moral and intellectual improvement which the world would have exhibited, had they never lived. A little more nonsense would have been talked for a century or two; and perhaps a few more men, women, and children, burnt as heretics. We might not at this moment have been congratulating each other on the abolition of the Inquisition in Spain. But it exceeds all imagination to conceive what would have been the moral condition of the world if neither Dante, Petrarch, Boccaccio, Chaucer, Shakespeare, Calderon, Lord Bacon, nor Milton, had ever existed; if Raphael and Michael Angelo had never been born; if the Hebrew poetry had never

---

15 Matthew, xiii, 12.

16 The monster Scylla was fabled to inhabit a sheer rock and Charybdis a whirlpool, imperiling voyagers who entered the narrow strait of water between them.

17 Ecclesiastes, vii, 2.

18 Although Rousseau has been thus classed, he was essentially a poet. The others, even Voltaire, were mere reasoners.—(Shelley.)

been translated; if a revival of the study of Greek literature had never taken place; if no monuments of ancient sculpture had been handed down to us; and if the poetry of the religion of the ancient world had been extinguished together with its belief. The human mind could never, except by the intervention of these excitements, have been awakened to the invention of the grosser sciences, and that application of analytical reasoning to the aberrations of society, which it is now attempted to exalt over the direct expression of the inventive and creative faculty itself.

We have more moral, political and historical wisdom, than we know how to reduce into practice; we have more scientific and economical knowledge than can be accommodated to the just distribution of the produce which it multiplies. The poetry in these systems of thought, is concealed by the accumulation of facts and calculating processes. There is no want of knowledge respecting what is wisest and best in morals, government, and political economy, or at least, what is wiser and better than what men now practise and endure. But we let '*I dare not* wait upon *I would,* like the poor cat i' the adage.'[19] We want the creative faculty to imagine that which we know; we want the generous impulse to act that which we imagine; we want the poetry of life: our calculations have outrun conception; we have eaten more than we can digest. The cultivation of those sciences which have enlarged the limits of the empire of man over the external world, has, for want of the poetical faculty, proportionally circumscribed those of the internal world; and man, having enslaved the elements, remains himself a slave. To what but a cultivation of the mechanical arts in a degree disproportioned to the presence of the creative faculty, which is the basis of all knowledge, is to be attributed the abuse of all invention for abridging and combining labour, to the exasperation of the inequality of mankind? From what other cause has it arisen that these inventions which should have lightened, have added a weight to the curse imposed on Adam? Thus Poetry, and the principle of Self, of which Money is the visible incarnation, are the God and Mammon of the world.

The functions of the poetical faculty are twofold: by one it creates new materials for knowledge, and power, and pleasure; by the other it engenders in the mind a desire to reproduce and arrange them according to a certain rhythm and order which may be called the beautiful and the good. The cultivation of poetry is never more to be desired than at periods when, from an excess of the selfish and calculating principle, the accumulation of the materials of external life exceed the quantity of the power of assimilating them to the internal laws of human nature. The body has then become too unwieldy for that which animates it.

Poetry is indeed something divine. It is at once the centre and circumference of knowledge; it is that which comprehends all science, and that to which all science must be referred. It is at the same time the root and blossom of all other systems of thought; it is that from which all spring, and that which adorns all; and that which, if blighted, denies the fruit and the seed, and withholds from the barren world the nourishment and the succession of the scions of the tree of life. It is the perfect and consummate surface and bloom of things; it is as the odour and the colour of the rose to the texture of the elements which compose it, as the form and the splendour of unfaded beauty to the secrets of anatomy and corruption. What were Virtue, Love, Patriotism, Friendship; what were the scenery of this beautiful Universe which we inhabit; what were our consolations on this side of the grave, and what were our aspirations beyond it,—if Poetry did not ascend to bring light and fire from those eternal regions where the owl-winged faculty of calculation dare not ever soar? Poetry is not like reasoning, a power to be exerted according to the determination of the will. A man cannot say, 'I will compose poetry.' The greatest poet even cannot say it; for the mind in creation is as a fading coal, which some invisible influence, like an inconstant wind, awakens to transitory brightness; this power arises from within, like the colour of a flower which fades and changes as it is developed, and the conscious portions of our natures are unprophetic either of its approach or its departure. Could this influence be durable in its original purity and force, it is impossible to predict the greatness of the results; but when composition begins, inspiration is already on the decline, and the most glorious poetry that has ever been communicated to the world is probably a feeble shadow of the original conceptions of the Poet. I appeal to the great poets of the present day whether it be not an error to assert that the finest passages of poetry are produced by labour and study. The toil and the

19 *Macbeth,* I, vii, 44.

delay recommended by critics can be justly interpreted to mean no more than a careful observation of the inspired moments, and an artificial connexion of the spaces between their suggestions by the intertexture of conventional expressions—a necessity only imposed by the limitedness of the poetical faculty itself; for Milton conceived the *Paradise Lost* as a whole before he executed it in portions. We have his own authority also for the Muse having 'dictated' to him the 'unpremeditated song.' And let this be an answer to those who would allege the fifty-six various readings of the first line of the *Orlando Furioso*.[20] Compositions so produced are to poetry what mosaic is to painting. This instinct and intuition of the poetical faculty is still more observable in the plastic and pictorial arts: a great statue or picture grows under the power of the artist as a child in the mother's womb; and the very mind which directs the hands in formation, is incapable of accounting to itself for the origin, the gradations, or the media of the process.

Poetry is the record of the best and happiest moments of the happiest and best minds. We are aware of evanescent visitations of thought and feeling, sometimes associated with place or person, sometimes regarding our own mind alone, and always arising unforeseen and departing unbidden, but elevating and delightful beyond all expression; so that even in the desire and the regret they leave, there cannot but be pleasure, participating as it does in the nature of its object. It is, as it were, the interpenetration of a diviner nature through our own; but its footsteps are like those of a wind over a sea, which the coming calm erases, and whose traces remain only, as on the wrinkled sand which paves it. These and corresponding conditions of being are experienced principally by those of the most delicate sensibility and the most enlarged imagination; and the state of mind produced by them is at war with every base desire. The enthusiasm of virtue, love, patriotism, and friendship is essentially linked with these emotions; and whilst they last, self appears as what it is, an atom to a Universe. Poets are not only subject to these experiences as spirits of the most refined organization, but they can colour all that they combine with the evanescent hues of this ethereal world; a word, or a trait in the representation of a scene or a passion will touch the enchanted chord, and reanimate, in those who have ever experienced these emotions, the sleeping, the cold, the buried image of the past. Poetry thus makes immortal all that is

best and most beautiful in the world; it arrests the vanishing apparitions which haunt the interlunations of life, and veiling them or in language or in form, sends them forth among mankind, bearing sweet news of kindred joy to those with whom their sisters abide—abide, because there is no portal of expression from the caverns of the spirit which they inhabit into the universe of things. Poetry redeems from decay the visitations of the divinity in Man.

Poetry turns all things to loveliness; it exalts the beauty of that which is most beautiful, and it adds beauty to that which is most deformed; it marries exultation and horror, grief and pleasure, eternity and change; it subdues to union under its light yoke all irreconcilable things. It transmutes all that it touches, and every form moving within the radiance of its presence is changed by wondrous sympathy to an incarnation of the spirit which it breathes; its secret alchemy turns to potable gold the poisonous waters which flow from death through life; it strips the veil of familiarity from the world, and lays bare the naked and sleeping beauty which is the spirit of its forms.

All things exist as they are perceived: at least in relation to the percipient.

The mind is its own place, and of itself
Can make a Heaven of Hell, a Hell of Heaven.[21]

But poetry defeats the curse which binds us to be subjected to the accident of surrounding impressions. And whether it spreads its own figured curtain, or withdraws life's dark veil from before the scene of things, it equally creates for us a being within our being. It makes us the inhabitants of a world to which the familiar world is a chaos. It reproduces the common Universe of which we are portions and percipients, and it purges from our inward sight the film of familiarity which obscures from us the wonder of our being. It compels us to feel that which we perceive, and to imagine that which we know. It creates anew the universe, after it has been annihilated in our minds by the recurrence of impressions blunted by reiteration. It justifies [the] bold and true word of Tasso: *Non merita nome di creatore, se non Iddio ed il Poeta.*[22]

A poet, as he is the author to others of the highest wisdom, pleasure, virtue, and glory, so he ought personally to be the happiest, the best, the wisest, and the most illustrious of men. As

20 a romance by Ariosto (1474–1533).

21 *Paradise Lost*, I, 254–5.

22 'None merits the name of creator but God and the poet.'

to his glory, let Time be challenged to declare whether the fame of any other institutor of human life be comparable to that of a poet. That he is the wisest, the happiest, and the best, inasmuch as he is a poet, is equally incontrovertible; the greatest Poets have been men of the most spotless virtue, of the most consummate prudence, and, if we could look into the interior of their lives, the most fortunate of men; and the exceptions, as they regard those who possessed the imaginative faculty in a high yet inferior degree, will be found on consideration to confirm rather than destroy the rule. Let us for a moment stoop to the arbitration of popular breath, and usurping and uniting in our own persons the incompatible characters of accuser, witness, judge, and executioner, let us without trial, testimony, or form, determine that certain motives of those who are 'there sitting where we dare not soar,'[23] are reprehensible. Let us assume that Homer was a drunkard, that Virgil was a flatterer, that Horace was a coward, that Tasso was a madman, that Lord Bacon was a peculator, that Raphael was a libertine, that Spenser was a poet laureate. It is inconsistent with this division of our subject to cite living poets, but Posterity has done ample justice to the great names now referred to. Their errors have been weighed and found to have been dust in the balance; if their sins were as scarlet, they are now white as snow: they have been washed in the blood of the mediator and redeemer, Time. Observe in what a ludicrous chaos the imputations of real or fictitious crime have been confused in the contemporary calumnies against poetry and poets; consider how little is as it appears—or appears as it is; look to your own motives, and judge not, lest ye be judged.

Poetry, as has been said, in this respect differs from logic, that it is not subject to the control of the active powers of the mind, and that its birth and recurrence have no necessary connexion with consciousness or will. It is presumptuous to determine that these are the necessary conditions of all mental causation, when mental effects are experienced insusceptible of being referred to them. The frequent recurrence of the poetical power, it is obvious to suppose, may produce in the mind a habit of order and harmony correlative with its own nature and with its effects upon other minds. But in the intervals of inspiration—and they may be frequent without being durable—a poet becomes a man, and

is abandoned to the sudden reflux of the influences under which others habitually live. But as he is more delicately organized than other men, and sensible to pain and pleasure, both his own and that of others, in a degree unknown to them, he will avoid the one and pursue the other with an ardour proportioned to this difference. And he renders himself obnoxious to calumny when he neglects to observe the circumstances under which these objects of universal pursuit and flight have disguised themselves in one another's garments.

But there is nothing necessarily evil in this error, and thus cruelty, envy, revenge, avarice, and the passions purely evil, have never formed any portion of the popular imputations on the lives of poets.

I have thought it most favourable to the cause of truth to set down these remarks according to the order in which they were suggested to my mind, by a consideration of the subject itself, instead of following that of the treatise that excited me to make them public. Thus although devoid of the formality of a polemical reply; if the view they contain be just, they will be found to involve a refutation of the doctrines of the Four Ages of Poetry, so far at least as regards the first division of the subject. I can readily conjecture what should have moved the gall of the learned and intelligent author of that paper; I confess myself like him, unwilling to be stunned by the Theseids of the hoarse Codri[24] of the day. Bavius and Mævius[25] undoubtedly are, as they ever were, insufferable persons. But it belongs to a philosophical critic to distinguish rather than confound.

The first part of these remarks has related to Poetry in its elements and principles; and it has been shewn, as well as the narrow limits assigned them would permit, that what is called poetry in a restricted sense, has a common source with all other forms of order and of beauty according to which the materials of human life are susceptible of being arranged, and which is Poetry in an universal sense.

The second part will have for its object an application of these principles to the present state of the cultivation of Poetry, and a defence of the attempt to idealize the modern forms of manners and opinions, and compel them into a subordination to the imaginative and creative faculty. For the literature of England, an energetic development of which has ever preceded or accompanied

---

23 *Paradise Lost*, IV, 829.

24 Codrus was a poetaster of the first century of the Christian era, and the alleged author of a tragedy on Theseus.
25 inferior Roman poets scorned by Virgil and Horace.

a great and free development of the national will, has arisen as it were from a new birth. In spite of the low-thoughted envy which would undervalue contemporary merit, our own will be a memorable age in intellectual achievements, and we live among such philosophers and poets as surpass beyond comparison any who have appeared since the last national struggle for civil and religious liberty. The most unfailing herald, companion and follower of the awakening of a great people to work a beneficial change in opinion or institution, is Poetry. At such periods there is an accumulation of the power of communicating and receiving intense and impassioned conceptions respecting man and nature. The persons in whom this power resides may often, as far as regards many portions of their nature, have little apparent correspondence with that spirit of good of which they are the ministers. But even whilst they deny and abjure, they are yet compelled to serve the Power which is seated upon the throne of their own soul. It is impossible to read the compositions of the most celebrated writers of the present day without being startled with the electric life which burns within their words. They measure the circumference and sound the depths of human nature with a comprehensive and all-penetrating spirit, and they are themselves perhaps the most sincerely astonished at its manifestations; for it is less their spirit than the spirit of the age. Poets are the hierophants of an unapprehended inspiration; the mirrors of the gigantic shadows which futurity casts upon the present; the words which express what they understand not; the trumpets which sing to battle and feel not what they inspire; the influence which is moved not, but moves. Poets are the unacknowledged legislators of the world.

1821   1840

SELECTIONS FROM SHELLEY'S LETTERS

1 *To* Thomas Love Peacock

Naples; December 22, 1818

My dear P.,

. . . Since I last wrote to you, I have seen the ruins of Rome, the Vatican, St. Peter's, and all the miracles of ancient and modern art contained in that majestic city. The impression of it exceeds anything I have ever experienced in my travels. We stayed there only a week, intending to return at the end of February, and devote two or three months to its mines of inexhaustible contemplation, to which period I refer you for a minute account of it. We visited the Forum and the ruins of the Coliseum every day. The Coliseum is unlike any work of human hands I ever saw before. It is of enormous height and circuit, and the arches built of massy stones are piled on one another, and jut into the blue air, shattered into the forms of overhanging rocks. It has been changed by time into the image of an amphitheatre of rocky hills overgrown by the wild olive, the myrtle, and the fig tree, and threaded by little paths, which wind among its ruined stairs and immeasurable galleries: the copsewood overshadows you as you wander through its labyrinths, and the wild weeds of this climate of flowers bloom under your feet. The arena is covered with grass, and pierces, like the skirts of a natural plain, the chasms of the broken arches around. But a small part of the exterior circumference remains—it is exquisitely light and beautiful; and the effect of the perfection of its architecture, adorned with ranges of Corinthian pilasters, supporting a bold cornice, is such as to diminish the effect of its greatness. The interior is all ruin. I can scarcely believe that even when encrusted with Dorian marble and ornamented by columns of Egyptian granite, its effect could have been so sublime and so impressive as in its present state. It is open to the sky, and it was the clear and sunny weather of the end of November in this climate when we visited it, day after day.

Near it is the arch of Constantine, or rather the arch of Trajan; for the servile and avaricious senate of degraded Rome ordered that the monument of his predecessor should be demolished in order to dedicate one to the Christian reptile, who had crept among the blood of his murdered family to the supreme power. It is exquisitely beautiful and perfect. The Forum is a plain in the midst of Rome, a kind of desert full of heaps of stones and pits; and though so near the habitations of men, is the most desolate place you can conceive. The ruins of temples stand in and around it, shattered columns and ranges of others complete, supporting cornices of exquisite workmanship, and vast vaults of shattered domes distinct with regular compartments, once filled with sculptures of ivory or brass. The temples of Jupiter, and Concord, and Peace, and the Sun, and the Moon, and Vesta, are all within a short distance of this spot. Behold the wrecks of what a great nation once dedicated to the abstractions of the mind! Rome is a city, as it were, of the dead, or rather of those who cannot die, and who survive the puny generations which inhabit and pass over the spot which they have made sacred to eternity. In Rome, at least in the first enthusiasm of your recognition of ancient time, you see nothing of the Italians. The nature of the city assists the delusion, for its vast and antique walls describe a circumference of sixteen miles, and thus the population is thinly scattered over this space, nearly as great as London. Wide wild fields are enclosed within it, and there are grassy lanes and copses winding among the ruins, and a great green hill, lonely and bare, which overhangs the Tiber. The gardens of the modern palaces are like wild woods of cedar, and cypress, and pine, and the neglected walks are overgrown with weeds. The English burying-place is a green slope near the walls, under the pyramidal tomb of Cestius, and is, I think, the most beautiful and solemn cemetery I ever beheld. To see the sun shining on its bright grass, fresh, when we first visited it, with the autumnal dews, and hear the whispering of the wind among the leaves of the trees which have overgrown the tomb of Cestius, and the soil which is stirring in the sun-warm earth, and to mark the tombs, mostly of women and young people who were buried there, one might, if one were to die, desire the sleep they seem to sleep. Such is the human mind, and so it peoples with its wishes vacancy and oblivion. . . .

External nature in these delightful regions contrasts with and compensates for the deformity and degradation of humanity. We have a lodging divided from the sea by the royal gardens, and from our windows we see perpetually the blue waters of the bay, forever changing, yet forever the same, and encompassed by the mountainous island of Capreæ, the lofty peaks which overhang Salerno, and the woody hill of Posilipo, whose promontories hide from us Misenum and the lofty isle Inarime, which, with its divided summit, forms the opposite horn of the bay. From the pleasant walks of the garden we see *Vesuvius;* a smoke by day and a fire by night is seen upon its summit, and the glassy sea often reflects its light or shadow. The climate is delicious. We sit without a fire, with the windows open, and have almost all the productions of an English summer. The weather is usually like what Wordsworth calls 'the first fine day of March'; sometimes very much warmer, though perhaps it wants that 'each minute sweeter than before,' which gives an intoxicating sweetness to the awakening of the earth from its winter's sleep in England. . . .

Vesuvius is, after the Glaciers, the most impressive exhibition of the energies of nature I ever saw. It has not the immeasurable greatness, the overpowering magnificence, nor, above all, the radiant beauty of the glaciers; but it has all their character of tremendous and irresistible strength. From Resina to the hermitage you wind up the mountain, and cross a vast stream of hardened lava, which is an actual image of the waves of the sea, changed into hard black stone by enchantment. The lines of the boiling fluid seem to hang in the air, and it is difficult to believe that the billows which seem hurrying down upon you are not actually in motion. This plain was once a sea of liquid fire. From the hermitage we crossed another vast stream of lava, and then went on foot up the cone—this is the only part of the ascent in which there is any difficulty, and that difficulty has been much exaggerated. It is composed of rocks of lava, and declivities of ashes; by ascending the former and descending the latter, there is very little fatigue. On the summit is a kind of irregular plain, the most horrible chaos that can be imagined; riven into ghastly chasms, and heaped up with tumuli of great stones and cinders, and enormous rocks blackened and calcined, which had been thrown from the volcano upon one another in terrible confusion. In the midst stands the conical hill from which volumes of smoke, and the fountains of liquid fire, are rolled forth forever. The mountain is at present in a slight state of eruption; and a thick heavy white smoke is perpetually rolled out, interrupted by enormous columns of an impenetrable black bituminous vapour, which is hurled up, fold after fold, into the sky with a deep hollow sound, and fiery stones are rained down from its darkness, and a black shower of ashes fall even on where we sat. The lava, like the glacier, creeps on perpetually, with a crackling sound as of suppressed fire. There are several springs of lava, and in one place it gushes precipitously over a high crag, rolling down the half-molten rocks and its own overhanging waves; a cataract of quivering fire. We approached the extremity of one of the rivers of lava; it is about twenty feet in breadth and ten in height; and as the inclined plane was not rapid, its motion was very slow. We saw the masses of its dark exterior surface detach themselves as it moved, and betray the depth of the liquid flame. In the day the fire is but slightly seen: you only observe a tremulous motion in the air, and streams and fountains of white sulphurous smoke.

At length we saw the sun sink between Capreæ and Inarime, and, as the darkness increased, the effect of the fire became more beautiful. We were, as it were, surrounded by streams and cataracts of the red and radiant fire; and in the midst, from the column of bituminous smoke shot up into the sky, fell the vast masses of rock, white with the light of their intense heat, leaving behind them through the dark vapour trains of splendour. We descended by torchlight, and I should have enjoyed the scenery on my return, but they conducted me, I know not how, to the hermitage in a state of intense bodily suffering, the worst effect of which was spoiling the pleasure of Mary and Clare. Our guides on the occasion were complete savages. You have no idea of the horrible cries which they suddenly utter, no one knows why; the clamour, the vociferation, the tumult. Clare in her palanquin suffered most from it; and when I had gone on before, they threatened to leave her in the middle of the road, which they would have done had not my Italian servant promised them a beating, after which they became quiet. Nothing, however, can be more picturesque than the gestures and the physiognomies of these savage people. And when, in the darkness of night, they unexpectedly begin to sing in chorus some fragments of their wild but sweet national music, the effect is exceedingly fine.

Since I wrote this, I have seen the museum of this city. Such statues! There is a Venus; an ideal shape of the most winning loveliness. A Bacchus, more sublime than any living being. A Satyr making love to a youth in which the expressed life of the sculpture and the inconceivable beauty of the form of the youth overcome one's repugnance to the subject. There are multitudes of wonderfully fine statues found in Herculaneum and Pompeii. We are going to see Pompeii the first day that the sea is waveless. Herculaneum is almost filled up; no more excavations are made; the king bought the ground and built a palace upon it. . . .

 Adieu, my dear Peacock,

   Affectionately your friend,

      P.B.S.

2 *To* Leigh Hunt

Florence, November 3, 1819

My dear Friend,

The event of Carlisle's trial[1] has filled me with an indignation that will not, and ought not to be suppressed.

In the name of all we hope for in human nature what are the people of England about? Or rather how long will they, and those whose hereditary duty it is to lead them, endure the enormous outrages of which they are one day made the victim and the next the instrument? Post succeeds post, and fresh horrors are ever detailed. First we hear that a troop of the enraged master-manufacturers are let loose with sharpened swords upon a multitude of their starving dependents and in spite of the remonstrances of the regular troops that they ride over them and massacre without distinction of sex or age, and cut off women's breasts and dash the heads of infants against the stones.[2] Then comes information that a man has been found guilty of some inexplicable crime, which his prosecutors call blasphemy; one of the features of which, they inform us, is the denying that the massacring of children and the ravishing of women, was done by the immediate command of the author and preserver of all things. And thus at the same time we see on one hand men professing to act by the public authority who put in practise the trampling down and murdering an unarmed multitude without distinction of sex or age, and on the other a tribunal which punishes men for asserting that deeds of the same character, transacted in a distant age and country were not done by the command of God. If not for this, for what was Mr. Carlisle prosecuted? For impugning the Divinity of Jesus Christ? I impugn it. For denying that the whole mass of antient Hebrew literature is of divine authority? I deny it. I hope this is no blasphemy, and that I am not to be dragged home by the enmity of our political adversaries to be made a sacrifice to the superstitious fury of the ruling sect. But I am prepared both to do

---

1 Richard Carlile (1790–1843) was a radical publisher and bookseller who for more than a quarter of a century put up a vigorous battle for freedom of the press. In October 1819, he was brought to trial and sentenced to three years' imprisonment for publishing Elihu Palmer's *Principles of Nature* and Paine's *Age of Reason.* Shelley was incensed over the government's persecution of Carlile and wrote a letter of protest for publication in Leigh Hunt's *Examiner,* but it was never completed.

2 The reference is to the killing and wounding of defenseless citizens by government militia at a mass meeting of workingmen held outside the city of Manchester, August 1819.

my duty and abide by whatever consequences may be attached to its fulfilment.

It is said that Mr. Carlisle has been found guilty by a jury. Juries are frequently in cases of libel illegally and partially constituted, and whenever this can be proved the party accused has a title to a new trial. A view of the question, so simple that it is in danger of being overlooked from its very obviousness, has presented itself to me, by which, I think it will clearly appear that this illegal and partial character belonged to the jury which pronounced a verdict of guilty against Mr. Carlisle, and that he is entitled to a new trial. . . .

I hope that a subscription will be set on foot for him, as there was for Mr. Hone,[3] and that the unworthy maxim that the successful are alone entitled to reward will never prevail to prevent the one from receiving at least as much indemnification of a defeat attended by captivity and confiscation of property, as the other [receiv]ed as the reward of a victory upon which no such [—] were consequent. Let the tyrants be taught to [realize] that all their endeavours to overwhelm their victim [by] poverty and infamy, have the direct and immediate [result] of making him comfortable in his circum[stan]ces, and attracting towards him the kind attentions [of] good men. I need not ask you to visit him in [prison;] you, to soothe whose captivity respect and admiration drew the [—] characters of the nation, as compassion will draw [them] to Mr. Carlisle's. I know the value of your occu[pation] and the delicacy of your health, and I am sorry [that in] this winter time I cannot be with you to [assist] in the performance of this duty. But the great [thing] is to get him a good subscription. I will contri[bute] to the proportion of my means; I hope you will do the same, and beat up among all our friends. Let every one furnish something, no matter how little. I meant to have a master to read German with me this winter; that I will not do, but subscribe for Carlisle instead. Even penny subscriptions ought to be set to work, they are excellent expressions of popular feeling. The oppressors dream that by the condemnation of Carlisle they have obtained a partial victory to place in the balance—for such is the magic of success however wicked—against the approbation which they advised the Prince Regent to de-

clare of the execrable enormities at Manchester. Let them be instructed to know their impotence; and let those who are exposed to their rage, who occupy the vanguard of the phalanx of their opponents, see in the frank and spirited union of the advocates for Liberty, an asylum against every form in which oppression can be brought to bear against them.

These, my dear Hunt, are awful times. The tremendous question is now agitating, whether a military and judicial despotism is to be established by our present rulers, or some form of government less unfavourable to the real and permanent interests of all men is to arise from the conflict of passions now gathering to overturn them. *We* cannot hesitate which party to embrace; and whatever revolutions are to occur, though oppression should change names and names cease to be oppressions, our party will be that of liberty and of the oppressed. Whatever you may imagine to be our differences in political theory, I trust that I shall be able to prove that they are less than you imagine, by agreeing, as from my soul I do, with your principles of political practice. . . .

3 *To* John Keats

Pisa, 27 July 1820

My dear Keats,

I hear with great pain the dangerous accident that you have undergone, and Mr. Gisborne[4] who gives me the account of it, adds that you continue to wear a consumptive appearance. This consumption is a disease particularly fond of people who write such good verses as you have done, and with the assistance of an English winter it can often indulge its selection;—I do not think that young and amiable poets are at all bound to gratify its taste; they have entered into no bond with the Muses to that effect. But seriously (for I am joking on what I am very anxious about) I think you would do well to pass the winter after so tremendous an accident, in Italy, and if you think it as necessary as I do so long as you could [find] Pisa or its neighbourhood agreeable to you, Mrs. Shelley unites with myself in urging the request, that you would take up your residence with us. You might come by sea to Leghorn (France is not worth seeing, and the sea is

---

3 William Hone (1780–1842), radical author and bookseller, had been tried in 1817 for 'seditious' publications exposing the corruption of persons high in the government. Shelley contributed to the subscription raised in his behalf.

4 John Gisborne was a retired merchant who, with his wife and stepson, had joined the English colony at Leghorn.

particularly good for weak lungs), which is within a few miles of us. You ought at all events, to see Italy, and your health, which I suggest as a motive, might be an excuse to you. I spare declamation about the statues, and the paintings, and the ruins—and what is a greater piece of forbearance—about the mountain streams and the fields, the colours of the sky, and the sky itself.

I have lately read your *Endymion* again and ever with a new sense of the treasures of poetry it contains, though treasures poured forth with indistinct profusion. This, people in general will not endure, and that is the cause of the comparatively few copies which have been sold. I feel persuaded that you are capable of the greatest things, so you but will.

I always tell Ollier[5] to send you copies of my books.—*Prometheus Unbound* I imagine you will receive nearly at the same time with this letter. *The Cenci* I hope you have already received—it was studiously composed in a different style.

> 'Below the *good* how far? but far above the
> great.'[6]

In poetry I have sought to avoid system and mannerism; I wish those who excel me in genius would pursue the same plan.

Whether you remain in England, or journey to Italy,—believe that you carry with you my anxious wishes for your health, happiness and success wherever you are, or whatever you undertake, and that I am, yours sincerely,

P. B. Shelley.

4 *To* William Gifford (Editor of the
Quarterly Review)

[*Pisa, November 1820*]

Sir,

Should you cast your eye on the signature of this letter before you read the contents, you might imagine that they related to a slanderous paper which appeared in your Review some time since.[7] I never notice anonymous attacks. The wretch who wrote it has doubtless the additional reward of a consciousness of his motives, besides the thirty guineas a sheet, or whatever it is that you pay him. Of course you cannot be answerable for all the writings which you edit, and *I* certainly bear you no ill-will for having edited

the abuse to which I allude—indeed, I was too much amused by being compared to Pharaoh, not readily to forgive editor, printer, publisher, stitcher, or anyone, except the despicable writer, connected with something so exquisitely entertaining. Seriously speaking, I am not in the habit of permitting myself to be disturbed by what is said or written of me, though, I dare say, I may be condemned sometimes justly enough. But I feel, in respect to the writer in question, that 'I am there sitting, where he durst not soar.'[8]

The case is different with the unfortunate subject of this letter, the author of *Endymion,* to whose feelings and situation I entreat you to allow me to call your attention. I write considerably in the dark; but if it is Mr. Gifford that I am addressing, I am persuaded that in an appeal to his humanity and justice, he will acknowledge the *fas ab hoste doceri.*[9] I am aware that the first duty of a Reviewer is towards the public, and I am willing to confess that the *Endymion* is a poem considerably defective, and that, perhaps, it deserved as much censure as the pages of your *Review* record against it. But not to mention that there is certain contemptuousness of phraseology from which it is difficult for a critic to abstain, in the Review of *Endymion* I do not think that the writer has given it its due praise. Surely the poem with all its faults is a very remarkable production for a man of Keats's age and the promise of ultimate excellence is such as has rarely been afforded even by such as have afterwards attained high literary eminence. Look at Book 2, line 833, etc., and Book 3, line 113 to 120—read down that page, and then again from line 193. I could cite many other passages to convince you that it deserved milder usage. Why it should have been reviewed at all, excepting for the purpose of bringing its excellences into notice I cannot conceive, for it was very little read, and there was no danger that it should become a model to the age of that false taste, with which I confess that it is replenished.

Poor Keats was thrown into a dreadful state of mind by this review, which, I am persuaded, was not written with any intention of producing the effect to which it has at least greatly contributed, of embittering his existence, and inducing a disease from which there are now but faint hopes of his recovery. The first effects are described to me to have resembled insanity, and it was by assiduous watching that he was restrained from effect-

---

5 Shelley's publisher.
6 Gray, *The Progress of Poesy*, l. 123.
7 The reference is to the *Quarterly's* violent attack on Shelley's *Laon and Cythna* (*The Revolt of Islam*).

8 *Paradise Lost*, IV, 829.
9 'the justness of being taught even by an enemy'—Ovid, *Metamorphoses*, IV, 428.

ing purposes of suicide. The agony of his sufferings at length produced the rupture of a blood-vessel in the lungs, and the usual process of consumption appears to have begun. He is coming to pay me a visit in Italy; but I fear that unless his mind can be kept tranquil, little is to be hoped from the mere influence of climate.

But let me not extort anything from your pity. I have just seen a second volume published by him evidently in careless despair. I have desired my bookseller to send you a copy, and allow me to solicit your especial attention to the fragment of a poem entitled *Hyperion,* the composition of which was checked by the Review in question. The great proportion of this piece is surely in the very highest style of poetry. I speak impartially, for the canons of taste to which Keats has conformed in his other compositions are the very reverse of my own. I leave you to judge for yourself: it would be an insult to you to suppose that from motives, however honourable, you would lend yourself to a deception of the public.

[Mrs. Shelley says that this letter was never sent.]

5 *To* Thomas Love Peacock

Ravenna, c. August 10, 1821

My dear Peacock,

I received your last letter just as I was setting off from the Bagni on a visit to Lord Byron at this place. Many thanks for all your kind attention to my accursed affairs. . . .

I have sent you by the Gisbornes a copy of the *Elegy on Keats.* The subject, I know, will not please you; but the composition of the poetry, and the taste in which it is written, I do not think bad. You and the enlightened public will judge. Lord Byron is in excellent cue both of health and spirits. He has got rid of all those melancholy and degrading habits which he indulged [in] at Venice. He lives with one woman, a lady of rank here to whom he is attached, and who is attached to him, and is in every respect an altered man. He has written three more cantos of *Don Juan.* I have yet only heard the fifth, and I think that every word of it is pregnant with immortality. I have not seen his late plays, except *Marino Faliero,* which is very well, but not so transcendently fine as the *Don Juan.* Lord Byron gets up at *two.* I get up, quite contrary to my usual custom, but one must sleep or die, like Southey's sea-snake in *Kehama,* at 12. After breakfast we sit talking till six. From six till eight

we gallop through the pine forests which divide Ravenna from the sea; we then come home and dine, and sit up gossiping till six in the morning. I don't suppose this will kill me in a week or fortnight, but I shall not try it longer. Lord B.'s establishment consists, besides servants, of ten horses, eight enormous dogs, three monkeys, five cats, an eagle, a crow, and a falcon; and all these, except the horses, walk about the house, which every now and then resounds with their unarbitrated quarrels, as if they were the masters of it. Lord B. thinks you wrote a pamphlet signed 'John Bull'; he says he knew it by the style resembling *Melincourt,* of which he is a great admirer. I read it, and assured him that it could not possibly be yours. I write nothing, and probably shall write no more. It offends me to see my name classed among those who have no name. If I cannot be something better, I had rather be nothing, and the accursed cause to the downfall of which I dedicate what powers I may have had—flourishes like a cedar and covers England with its boughs. My motive was never the infirm desire of fame; and if I should continue an author, I feel that I should desire it. This cup is justly given to one only of an age; indeed, participation would make it worthless: and unfortunate they who seek it and find it not.

I congratulate you—I hope I ought to do so—on your expected stranger. He is introduced into a rough world. My regards to Hogg, and Co[u]lson if you see him.

Ever most faithfully yours,

P.B.S.

After I have sealed my letter, I find that my enumeration of the animals in this Circean Palace was defective, and that in a material point. I have just met on the grand staircase five peacocks, two guinea hens, and an Egyptian crane. I wonder who all these animals were before they were changed into these shapes.

6 *To* John Gisborne

Lerici, June 18, 1822

My dear Gisborne,

. . . I have written to Ollier to send his account to you. The *Adonais* I wished to have had a fair chance, both because it is a favourite with me and on account of the memory of Keats, who was a poet of great genius, let the classic party say what it will. *Hellas* too I liked on account of the subject—one always finds some reason or other for liking one's own composition. The *Epipsychidion* I cannot look at; the person whom it celebrates was a cloud instead of a Juno; and poor Ixion[10] starts from the centaur that was the offspring of his own embrace. If you are anxious, however, to hear what I am and have been, it will tell you something thereof. It is an idealized history of my life and feelings. I think one is always in love with something or other; the error, and I confess it is not easy for spirits cased in flesh and blood to avoid it, consists in seeking in a mortal image the likeness of what is perhaps eternal. . . .

Hunt is not yet arrived, but I expect him every day. I shall see little of Lord Byron, nor shall I permit Hunt to form the intermediate link between him and me. I detest all society—almost all, at least—and Lord Byron is the nucleus of all that is hateful and tiresome in it. He will be half mad to hear of these Memoirs. As to me, you know my supreme indifference to such affairs, except that I must confess I am sometimes amused by the ridiculous mistakes of these writers. Tell me a little of what they say of me besides my being an Atheist. One thing I regret in it, I dread lest it should injure Hunt's prospects in the establishment of the journal, for Lord Byron is so mentally capricious that the least impulse drives him from his anchorage. . . . The Williams's are now on a visit to us, and they are people who are very pleasing to me. But words are not the instruments of our intercourse. I like Jane more and more, and I find Williams the most amiable of companions. She has a taste for music, and an elegance of form and motions that compensate in some degree for the lack of literary refinement. Mrs. Gisborne knows my gross ideas of music, and will forgive me when I say that I listen the whole evening on our terrace to the simple melodies with excessive delight. I have a boat here . . . It cost me £80, and reduced me to some difficulty in point of money. However, it is swift and beautiful, and appears quite a vessel. Williams is captain, and we drive along this delightful bay in the evening wind, under the summer moon, until earth appears another world. Jane brings her guitar, and if the past and the future could be obliterated, the present would content me so well that I could say with Faust to the passing moment 'Remain, thou, thou art so beautiful.' Clare is with us, and the death of her child seems to have restored her to tran-

quility. Her character is somewhat altered. She is vivacious and talkative; and though she teases me sometimes, I like her. . . . Lord Byron is at Leghorn. He has fitted up a splendid vessel, a small schooner on the American model, and Trelawny is to be captain. How long the fiery spirit of our Pirate will accommodate itself to the caprice of the Poet remains to be seen. . . .

I write little now. It is impossible to compose except under the strong excitement of an assurance of finding sympathy in what you write. Imagine Demosthenes reciting a Philippic to the waves of the Atlantic! Lord Byron is in this respect fortunate. He touched a chord to which a million hearts responded, and the coarse music which he produced to please them disciplined him to the perfection to which he now approaches. I do not go on with *Charles the First.* I feel too little certainty of the future, and too little satisfaction with regard to the past, to undertake any subject seriously and deeply. I stand, as it were, upon a precipice, which I have ascended with great, and cannot descend without *greater,* peril, and I am content if the heaven above me is calm for the passing moment. . . .

Ever yours most affectionately,

P.B.S.

7 *To* Jane Williams

Pisa, July 4, 1822

You will probably see Williams before I can disentangle myself from the affairs with which I am now surrounded—I return to Leghorn tonight—and shall urge him to sail with the first fair wind, without expecting me. I have thus the pleasure of contributing to your happiness when deprived of every other, and of leaving you no other subject of regret, but the absence of one scarcely worth regretting. I fear you are solitary and melancholy at Villa Magni—and, in the intervals of the greater and more serious distress in which I am compelled to sympathize here, I figure to myself the countenance which has been the source of such consolation to me, shadowed by a veil of sorrow—

How soon those hours past, and how slowly they return to pass so soon again, and perhaps for ever, in which we have lived together so intimately, so happily!—Adieu, my dearest friend —I only write these lines for the pleasure of tracing what will meet your eyes.—Mary will tell you all the news.

S.

---

10 legendary king punished by Jupiter for his love for the goddess Juno by being bound on an eternally revolving wheel in Hades.

1795 · JOHN KEATS · 1821

1795 Born 31 October at the sign of the *Swan and Hoop,* Finsbury Pavement, London, eldest son of Thomas Keats, head ostler to Mr. John Jennings, and Frances Keats, only daughter of Mr. Jennings. Besides John, the poet, there were two other sons, George (born 1797), and Tom (born 1799), and a daughter, Frances (born 1803).

1803–11 Sent to the school kept by Mr. John Clarke at Enfield. Learned to read French and Latin and acquired a reputation for his quick temper, his pugnacity, his wit, and his generosity. In his last year at school developed a passionate desire to read, and carried off four prizes for his reading. Formed a lifelong friendship with Charles Cowden Clarke, his schoolmaster's son.

1804 His father killed by a fall from his horse.

1805 His mother married Will Rawlings, stablekeeper at the *Swan and Hoop,* but she left him the next year and moved with her children into the home of their grandmother, Mrs. Jennings, at Edmonton.

1810 His mother died of tuberculosis. His grandmother made a will leaving £8000 to her grandchildren, to be held in trust until the youngest boy should become of age, and appointed Messrs. Abbey and Sandell as guardians.

1811–15 Left school at Enfield and was apprenticed to an apothecary-surgeon, Mr. Thomas Hammond, at Edmonton. Plunged into reading English literature and ancient myths and finished a translation of the *Aeneid.* Was introduced by Clarke to Spenser, whose *Epithalamion* and *Faerie Queene* enthralled him and awakened his creative genius.

1815 Quarreled with Hammond and left him. Entered Guy's and St. Thomas's Hospital, London. Applied himself to his studies, but his chief delight was a rapidly growing circle of friends including the Wylies, Haslam, and Severn. Began to compose sonnets and other verses.

1816 His first poem, *To Solitude,* published in Leigh Hunt's *Examiner.* Met Hunt probably in late May or June. Passed his examinations and received a certificate from Guy's and St. Thomas's, but decided to give up medicine for literature. Resided at Margate, London, and Hampstead. By October was spending much of his time with Hunt whose enthusiasms and poetical style were influential on Keats's early writing. Wrote *I Stood Tip-Toe, Sleep and Poetry,* epistles, and more sonnets, including the famous Chapman's Homer sonnet. Met Haydon, the painter, and Hazlitt, Lamb, and Shelley.

1817 In March his *Poems,* dedicated to Hunt, was in circulation, but the volume was practically ignored, except by its author's friends. On Haydon's advice, left London in April and went to the Isle of Wight for study and self-improvement. Began *Endymion.* Moved about spending some time in the late spring and summer at Margate and Canterbury, and at Hampstead with his brothers where he met and formed friendships with C. W. Dilke and Charles A. Brown. In September paid a visit to his friend Benjamin Bailey at Oxford, with whom he studied Milton and Wordsworth. In November finished *Endymion* at Burford Bridge. In December participated in the 'Immortal Dinner' at Haydon's with Wordsworth, Lamb, and others.

1818   Spent the winter at Hampstead. Revised *Endymion* and saw it through the press. Heard Hazlitt's *Lectures on the English Poets.* In March went to Teignmouth to nurse his brother Tom who had developed tuberculosis. Wrote *Isabella* and numerous short poems. In April *Endymion* appeared. His spirits were high, but he was constantly preoccupied with George's departure for America and Tom's failing health. For rest and relief and to gain new experiences, started out late in June with Charles Brown on a walking trip into Northern England, Scotland, and Ireland. Was shocked by the misery and brutishness of the Irish peasantry, but was impressed with the mountains and Fingal's Cave. The tour ended abruptly in August when a severe sore throat (the first hint of the disease that was to kill him) caused Keats on the advice of an Inverness doctor to return by boat to London. The autumn was spent at Hampstead in constant attendance on Tom, who was slowly dying. In September two Tory journals, the *Quarterly* and *Blackwood's,* attacked *Endymion* and heaped personal abuse upon its author. Took the attack courageously and plunged into the composition of *Hyperion,* September-December. Tom died in December and Keats moved to Wentworth Place to live with Brown. In his loneliness and not knowing how fatal the state of his health was he fell deeply in love with Fanny Brawne.

1819   Gradually realized that his love for Fanny would be frustrated. Financial difficulties, anxieties about his sister, the failure of his poems, his growing illness and hopeless love—all combined to induce a winter depression of spirits. Worked at *Hyperion* but failed to get on with it. In January, his 'brooding inactivity' was broken by a trip during which he wrote *Eve of St. Agnes.* In April, reached a philosophy of tragic acceptance; whereupon his poetic genius loosed itself in *Ode to Psyche,* first of the 'great odes,' and in *La Belle Dame sans merci.* In May came the four 'great odes': *Ode on a Grecian Urn, Ode on Melancholy, Ode to a Nightingale, Ode on Indolence;* and in June-July the first part of *Lamia.* Collaborated with Brown in July-August on a versified drama, *Otho the Great.* In a bitter mood finished *Lamia* and began *Fall of Hyperion,* August-early September. At Winchester in September in a sudden calm of spirit, wrote his last great poem, *To Autumn.* After this, despair and agony thwarted his poetry. In hope of immediate financial return, wrote the historical tragedy *King Stephen,* and, with Brown, a satirical burlesque, *The Cap and Bells.*

1820   In February realized that he was doomed to an early death by tuberculosis. In March was ordered by his physician to give up all work. In May parted with Brown and during the summer lived first with the Hunts and afterward with the Brawnes. In July appeared his third volume, *Lamia, Isabella, The Eve of St. Agnes, and Other Poems.* The poems achieved a moderate success; were praised by Jeffrey in the *Edinburgh Review.* In September set sail with Severn for Italy in a desperate attempt to regain his health.

1821   Died in Rome 23 February, attended only by his faithful friend, Severn. Lies buried in the Protestant Cemetery, near the tomb of Caius Cestus. Engraved on his tombstone, as Keats desired, are the words: 'Here lies one whose name was writ in water.'

J OHN KEATS died in his twenty-sixth year. At that age Spenser had not been heard from, Milton had written only a handful of his shorter poems, and Wordsworth had done nothing more notable than *Guilt and Sorrow.* Yet even with so brief an allotted time, and with his span of years as a creative artist made briefer still by wasting disease, Keats has taken his immortal place beside the great English poets. He was not a child prodigy, but a normal, robust boy scarcely aware of the existence of poetry until he was thirteen or fourteen. He wrote very few verses before he was eighteen, and almost nothing of consequence before he was twenty. His supreme work came as 'the climax of a steady growth in emotional and intellectual power, the result of sustained mental effort and of heroic self-discipline under affliction' (de Selincourt). Keats knew only too well the vicissitudes of sickness and death, separation from his family, privation, thwarted ambition, and hopeless love. He was handicapped by perilous emotional traits—impulsive, vehement moods of depression and morbidity—inherited from his mother. But he knew his weaknesses and rarely allowed these unworthy qualities to master him. In rough going he showed plenty of courage and self-reliance. Under critical attack he reacted in a manly and generous fashion and applied himself doggedly to his task. Besides clearness of judgment, he had a fine sense of honor, a warmth of sympathy, and a sense of humor. Nor was he any stranger to happiness. He enjoyed sociability, was a favorite in company, and had an impressive list of friends. Few men have responded so cordially to friendship, or have received so much from their associates. His friends gave him encouragement and sympathy, and kindly criticism when he needed it.

But however much Keats delighted in companionship, he knew his greatest joy in solitude. He loved to take long rambles over the beautiful English countryside. Closely and eagerly he watched the goings on of nature. With a quick and sensitive responsiveness to the myriad wonders about him, he found all nature filled with a mysterious and creative joy. Intensely in his imagination he identified his being with one beautiful object after another. Ties of physical consciousness were broken, his mind was disentangled from the body, and he slipped 'into a sort of awareness' with sunset, moonlight, or mountain, or if a sparrow should come before his window, he took part in its existence and picked about the gravel. The tenderness of his nature went out to all created things. For him 'the poetry of earth is never dead.' His early verse is filled with exquisitely fresh and vivid images taken direct from nature, his later poetry with sustained passages of natural beauty and splendor.

The deep enjoyment that Keats found in nature, he found also in great literature and art. All that he saw or read he drew at once into his imaginative experience. He luxuriated in the colorful details of his favorite authors and 'seized upon their fine phrases like a lover.' ' "Sea-shouldering whales," ' he would exclaim on reading Spenser, 'what an image!' Characteristically his own poetry reflects a strong attachment to images, rather than to abstract ideas. It is simple, sensuous, and direct, abounding in phrases as rare and felicitous as any in Shakespeare or Milton, his masters. But Keats did not rest in word painting; there is 'clearance and delivery.' His brief life was fervently devoted to 'the principle of beauty in all things': beauty concrete, pictorial, and quiescent, but beauty, too, exalted with impassioned thought.

Keats's first collection of his work (*Poems*, 1817) is crowded with sentimental luxuries and a rich confusion of imagery. At this early stage he is a close disciple to the Jacobean poets and to Spenser, though as would be natural enough in so young a poet, he fails to match anything like Spenser's firmness and purity of style. A hampering, and, unfortunately, predominant influence derived from Leigh Hunt, whose facile verses and touches of vulgarity set Keats a poor example. Of the longer poems, *I Stood Tiptoe* has a pleasing atmosphere of 'dainty and luxuriant fancy,' and *Sleep and Poetry*, though marred by occasional lapses, 'radiates the young poet's aspirations and his joyous contemplation of beauty.' Scattered throughout the volume are many radiant, vigorous passages, chiefly in the sonnets, which show authentic tidings of future power. Besides the 1817 *Poems*, and surpassing anything there, is the superb Chapman's Homer sonnet, written when Keats was only nineteen, and published separately in Hunt's *Examiner*.

The modest volume of 1817 was kindly received by Keats's friends and was discriminately reviewed by Hunt; however, it failed to make an impression. But Keats wasted no time in regrets; already he had plunged headlong into the sea with *Endymion*. Out of the simple Greek myth of the poet-shepherd Endymion's love for his moon goddess ('sweetest of all songs') he was testing his powers of invention in four thousand lines of poetry. The story of Endymion's pursuit of the haunting vision of his love was to be symbolical of the pursuit of the principle of beauty by the poetic soul. As the composition progressed Keats 'soon became his own Endymion, and the poem that started out to tell the story of Endymion's search became itself a faery voyage after beauty ranging in an enchanted universe of real and imaginary loveliness and gathering along the way other legends which had no original relation to that of Endymion' (De Selincourt). The poem which resulted is rambling and confused, broken by unrelated episodes, and the moon allegory is 'never quite lucid.' The descriptive passages are over-luxuriant in detail, the style is florid and diffuse, and the loose-running couplets (patterned after Hunt's *Rimini*) are used with an excessive freedom. But in spite of numerous and fairly obvious shortcomings Keats has magically revivified the antique myths of Greece. He breaks down only when he attempts to go further than the 'realm of Flora and of Pan.' He possessed, as he was soon to realize, youthful exuberance in abundance; but he lacked vital experience and knowledge. In a modest, straightforward preface, he manfully confessed his sense of unfulfillment in *Endymion.* The Tory journals were abusive, but Keats dismissed their critical attacks with dignity. 'I have not the slightest feeling of humility towards the public,' he wrote to Reynolds before publication, 'or to anything in existence, but the eternal Being, the Principle of Beauty, and the memory of great men.' And afterward to Hessey; 'Praise or blame has but a momentary effect on the man whose love of beauty in the abstract makes him a severe critic on his own works. My own domestic criticism has given me pain without comparison beyond what Blackwood or the Quarterly could possibly inflict.' The crudities of *Endymion* offended him far more than the most slanderous criticism. When he looked back at 'this great trial of his invention' and saw that it had failed, his intellectual life awakened. Already he was plotting to try once more 'the beautiful mythology of Greece' in verses fit to live.

After *Endymion,* Keats's devotion to a 'principal of joy' yielded to a growing conception of the high demands that all worthy poetry makes upon an author's character and intellect. In his letters of 1818 Keats begins to admit to a rivalry between the hitherto absorbing passion for beauty and a desire for knowledge and action. He finds (April 1818) that he 'can have no enjoyment in this world but continual drinking in of knowledge'; and that there 'is no worthy pursuit but the idea of doing some good to the world.' His road, he decides, 'lies through application, study, and thought.' In a famous letter to Reynolds (May 1818), in which he sends the *Ode to Maia,* he holds allegiance to poetry, but poetry 'proved by larger experience, upon our pulses.' 'Until we are sick, we understand not,' he writes; and again, 'Sorrow is Wisdom.' He became absorbed in Milton, and the desire grew with him to emulate the majesty and severity of *Paradise Lost.* Throughout months of strenuous intellectual effort *Hyperion* was uppermost in his mind. In June he undertook a journey with his friend Brown through the English lakes and Scotland to 'give me more experience, rub off more Prejudice, use me to more hardship, identify finer scenes, load me with grander Mountains, and strengthen more my reach in Poetry.' Keats gained what he sought. The great rocks rising from the sea, the thunderous waterfalls, and the massive cloud-capped mountains left their traces in the colossal forms and vast aerial perspective of *Hyperion.* The austere example of Milton gave a sustained passion and grandeur to Keats's cosmic epic of the Titans; it similarly freed his style from any remaining traces of facile luxuriance, but without impairing the poetic richness of the imagery. Milton's influence strikes deep; although as the poem progresses the Miltonic mannerisms diminish, and almost disappear in Book III. Keats found Milton's manner only partly congenial; for this and for other reasons he left *Hyperion* unfinished. Later he rewrought it, but then again abandoned it. Though unfinished, *Hyperion* remains a magnificent epic fragment, 'one of the few supreme modern recreations of ancient myth,' and a poetic work unmatched in sublimity of style outside of Milton.

Keats's great artistic stride forward is accompanied by a profounder concept of the principle of beauty. Beauty is no longer merely a sensuous delight, but a symbol of power:

> for 'tis the eternal law
> That first in beauty should be first in might.

Power in beauty derives from knowledge and from struggle; it is intensified by suffering. Beauty, like Thea in *Hyperion,* is made 'more beautiful than beauty's self' by sorrow. This more mature concept of Beauty had not come to Keats from intellectual travail alone. Throughout the year 1818, sharpening adversities, culminating with his brother Tom's death and his hopeless love for Fanny Brawne, strengthened his growing belief in the supremacy of beauty born of pain. By the winter of 1818–19 a kind of fierceness and longing despair possessed him. But though his tragic passion for Fanny wrought havoc with his body it deepened his emotional power and released his energy. It opened up 'fresh vistas to his imagination' and lighted his poetic genius to a 'brief but splendid consummation' (De Selincourt).

The four tales show a progressive increase in poetical maturity and narrative craftsmanship. *Isabella*, which came first, reveals that Keats lacked at the time of its composition sufficient experience to handle the love story firmly. The love-making is marred at times by a reversion to the false taste and stylistic lushness of *Endymion*. The forward movement of the narrative, moreover, is hampered by an overabundance of rich, sensuous detail. Yet there are tender, poignant passages and after the murder there are no repellant touches in the imaginative handling of the tragic bereavement and death of Isabel. *The Eve of St. Agnes*, in contrast to *Isabella*, is a direct expression of the poet's heart, full of the passion and fire of youth, 'a great choral hymn of love,' to use Amy Lowell's excellent phrase. The narrative moves forward evenly and constantly, with skillful transitions, through a series of gorgeous scenes delineated in richly harmonious and sensuous language. The central theme of ardent young love is skillfully set off and heightened by the contrasting elements of terror and wintry torpor and of mystery in the dim half-region of enchantment. A companion piece to the *Eve of St. Agnes* is that brief, intense ballad of disillusionment *La Belle Dame sans merci* created out of the 'fire that leapt from the poet's own distracted heart.' *Lamia*, a kindred story of enchantment, is the last and within limits the most perfect of the tales. Keats handles the narrative with greater dignity and restraint than anything before it. His marvelous rich poetic expression is undiminished, but it is set forth in a new style, 'ringing and rapid,' learned from Dryden's sinewy couplets. The realistic touches have increased. The weird and remote is brought into happy union with the reality of flesh and blood. Lamia is a creature of fancy; she is also a beautiful womanly being with warm, human impulses. A parabolic meaning, not in Keats's mind when he began, arises in the latter portion of the story. In the climax the sophist's eye fixes upon Lamia and destroys her and with her the young lover dies. The action is significant. Barren philosophy, the poet seems to be telling us, will bring the destruction of all loveliness.

> Do not all charms fly
> At the mere touch of cold philosophy?

The poets's divided sympathy with his characters reflects a mind at war with itself. Already the realization that time was running out harried him. Yet this awareness only added depth and poignancy to his supreme poetry.

In the 'great odes' Keats created a new and intricate metrical texture, rich in density and sublimated by an intuitive vision of truth. The truth revealed is no mere intellectual abstraction, but a vision of beauty suffused with tenderness and made pensive by the sadness of experience. Beauty that is truth, Keats tells us, includes much of human sorrow. Yet out of discord, delight can be born, even though escape can be only temporary. The *Ode to a Nightingale* and *Ode on a Grecian Urn* share as a common starting point a mood of despondency in the contemplation of life. In the first ode the poet finds instigation and release in the loveliness of nature and comfort in meditating upon the immortal birdsong; in the second he finds consolation in the ideal eternity of Art. In the *Ode on Melancholy*, which is incomplete, Beauty and Joy are blent in 'the very temple of delight' with Melancholy; and Pleasure, even in its intensest moment, is awakened to an aching sense of its own fugitiveness. In a lighter vein, *Ode to Indolence* is a vivid record of the languid spring-fever mood in which it was conceived. *Ode to Psyche* is a hauntingly lovely return to the Endymion-like freedom of the world of legend. The last of the odes, *To Autumn*, is the most perfect. It is pensive in mood, but full of thoughtful power and 'the richest of all in sympathy and serenity.'

Keats was endowed with an exceptional gift for language. He could do with words all that the greatest poets have done. He has created unforgettable phrases charged with magical sensibility and has woven large fabrics wonderful in texture and color. His lines, perfect in the adaptation of sound and sense, are rich in musical thought—calm, deep-toned, and strongly sustained. His vocabulary is remarkable for its range and felicity. He achieves a constant effect of strangeness through the use of fine old English words. An impressive list of borrowed words can be compiled from his poetry, showing a wide and varied reading. In his early work there was a tendency to overuse antique forms and some lack of discrimination. But Keats rapidly outgrew his faults as he came to have a fuller dependence on the masters, Spenser, Shakespeare, Milton, and, to a lesser degree, on Dryden. Keats himself follows in the great tradition, but he has created, nevertheless, great passages in his own unmistakable manner. Elton names *Ode to Maia,* the two sonnets *When I have Fears* and *Bright Star,* and the description of Apollo in *Hyperion,* as in Keats's own inimitable impassioned style.

Keats displays less intellectual absorption than Shelley in political events and philosophical theories, yet he held the characteristic liberal views of his times and was impelled toward the real world of men and affairs. He had ambitions of doing the world some good and believed that poetry was incomplete if it evaded or left unexpressed 'the agonies and strife of human hearts.' Thus in the largest sense Keats shared the idealism of Shelley, but he possessed broader sympathies. He placed the highest value on aesthetic experience, reaching toward spiritual consummation through an intuitive vision of truth in beauty. Great poetry with him was a matter of perfect intuitive sympathy with mankind. It was his highest ambition to enshrine the deepest truths revealed to him in noble language. At the time of his death he was still 'straining at particles of light in the great darkness.' In the *Fall of Hyperion* he utters a bitter confession of failure to achieve his goal. He sees himself as a dreamer who 'envenoms all his days.' But Keats is too hard on himself. He had learned to look into the human heart. His letters prove that toward the end his mind was maturing rapidly. Earlier in his career and in a happier frame of mind, he thought he would be among the great English poets after his death. He has long been granted a place in that illustrious company.

IMITATION OF SPENSER

Now Morning from her orient chamber came,
And her first footsteps touch'd a verdant
    hill;
Crowning its lawny crest with amber flame,
Silv'ring the untainted gushes of its rill;
Which, pure from mossy beds, did down dis-
    till,
And after parting beds of simple flowers,
By many streams a little lake did fill,
Which round its marge reflected woven
    bowers,
And, in its middle space, a sky that never lowers.

There the king-fisher saw his plumage
    bright   10
Vieing with fish of brilliant dye below;
Whose silken fins, and golden scales' light
Cast upward, through the waves, a ruby glow:
There saw the swan his neck of arched snow,
And oar'd himself along with majesty;
Sparkled his jetty eyes; his feet did show
Beneath the waves like Afric's ebony,
And on his back a fay reclined voluptuously.

Ah! could I tell the wonders of an isle
That in that fairest lake had placed been,   20
I could e'en Dido of her grief[1] beguile;
Or rob from aged Lear his bitter teen;[2]
For sure so fair a place was never seen,
Of all that ever charm'd romantic eye:
It seem'd an emerald in the silver sheen
Of the bright waters; or as when on high,
Through clouds of fleecy white, laughs the cœru-
    lean sky.

And all around it dipp'd luxuriously
Slopings of verdure through the glossy tide,
Which, as it were in gentle amity,   30
Rippled delighted up the flowery side;
As if to glean the ruddy tears, it tried,
Which fell profusely from the rose-tree stem!
Haply it was the workings of its pride,
In strife to throw upon the shore a gem
Outvieing all the buds in Flora's diadem.

1812–13   1817

---

[1] for Aeneas, when he deserted her for the new home the gods had promised him.
[2] sorrow.

SONNET

TO A YOUNG LADY WHO SENT ME A LAUREL CROWN

FRESH morning gusts have blown away all fear
 From my glad bosom,—now from gloominess
 I mount for ever—not an atom less
Than the proud laurel shall content my bier.
No! by the eternal stars! or why sit here
 In the Sun's eye, and 'gainst my temples press
 Apollo's very leaves, woven to bless
By thy white fingers and thy spirit clear.
Lo! who dares say, 'Do this'? Who dares call
 down
 My will from its high purpose? Who say,
  'Stand,'   10
Or 'Go'? This mighty moment I would frown
 On abject Cæsars[1]—not the stoutest band
Of mailed heroes should tear off my crown:
 Yet would I kneel and kiss thy gentle hand!

  1815   1848

TO SOLITUDE

O SOLITUDE! if I must with thee dwell,
 Let it not be among the jumbled heap
 Of murky buildings; climb with me the
  steep,—
Nature's observatory—whence the dell,
Its flowery slopes, its river's crystal swell,
 May seem a span; let me thy vigils keep
 'Mongst boughs pavillion'd, where the deer's
  swift leap
Startles the wild bee from the fox-glove bell.
But though I'll gladly trace these scenes with
 thee,
 Yet the sweet converse of an innocent
  mind,   10
 Whose words are images of thoughts refin'd,
Is my soul's pleasure; and it sure must be
Almost the highest bliss of human-kind,
When to thy haunts two kindred spirits flee.

  November, 1815   1816

SONNET

ON A PICTURE OF LEANDER[1]

COME hither all sweet maidens soberly,
 Down-looking aye, and with a chasten'd light,
 Hid in the fringes of your eyelids white,
And meekly let your fair hands joined be,

---

1 probably an allusion to Mr. Richard Abbey, Keats's guardian, who objected to his becoming a poet.

1 The lover of the priestess Hero, who nightly swam the Hellespont to meet her, and who was finally drowned in a storm.

As if so gentle that ye could not see,
 Untouch'd, a victim of your beauty bright,
 Sinking away to his young spirit's night,—
Sinking bewilder'd 'mid the dreary sea:
'Tis young Leander toiling to his death;
 Nigh swooning, he doth purse his weary
  lips   10
  For Hero's cheek, and smiles against her
   smile.
 O horrid dream! see how his body dips
  Dead-heavy; arms and shoulders gleam
   awhile:
He's gone: up bubbles all his amorous breath!

  1816   1829

HOW MANY BARDS GILD THE LAPSES OF TIME!

How many bards gild the lapses of time!
 A few of them have ever been the food
 Of my delighted fancy,—I could brood
Over their beauties, earthly, or sublime:
And often, when I sit me down to rhyme,
 These will in throngs before my mind intrude:
 But no confusion, no disturbance rude
Do they occasion; 'tis a pleasing chime.
So the unnumber'd sounds that evening store;
The songs of birds—the whis'pring of the
  leaves—   10
 The voice of waters—the great bell that heaves
With solemn sound,—and thousand others more,
 That distance of recognizance bereaves,
Make pleasing music, and not wild uproar.

  1816   1817

TO ONE WHO HAS BEEN LONG IN CITY PENT

To one who has been long in city pent,
 'Tis very sweet to look into the fair
 And open face of heaven,—to breathe a prayer
Full in the smile of the blue firmament.
Who is more happy, when, with heart's content,
 Fatigued he sinks into some pleasant lair
 Of wavy grass, and reads a debonair
And gentle tale of love and languishment?
Returning home at evening, with an ear
 Catching the notes of Philomel,—an eye 10
Watching the sailing cloudlet's bright career,
 He mourns that day so soon has glided by:
E'en like the passage of an angel's tear
 That falls through the clear ether silently.

  1816   1817

TO MY BROTHER GEORGE

FULL many a dreary hour have I past,
My brain bewilder'd, and my mind o'ercast
With heaviness; in seasons when I've thought
No spherey strains by me could e'er be caught
From the blue dome, though I to dimness gaze
On the far depth where sheeted lightning plays;
Or, on the wavy grass outstretch'd supinely,
Pry 'mong the stars, to strive to think divinely:
That I should never hear Apollo's song,
Though feathery clouds were floating all
    along   10
The purple west, and, two bright streaks be-
    tween,
The golden lyre itself were dimly seen:
That the still murmur of the honey bee
Would never teach a rural song to me:
That the bright glance from beauty's eyelids
    slanting
Would never make a lay of mine enchanting,
Or warm my breast with ardour to unfold
Some tale of love and arms in time of old.

But there are times, when those that love the bay,
Fly from all sorrowing far, far away;   20
A sudden glow comes on them, naught they see
In water, earth, or air, but poesy.
It has been said, dear George, and true I hold it,
(For knightly Spenser to Libertas[1] told it,)
That when a Poet is in such a trance,
In air he sees white coursers paw, and prance,
Bestridden of gay knights, in gay apparel,
Who at each other tilt in playful quarrel,
And what we, ignorantly, sheet-lightning call,
Is the swift opening of their wide portal,   30
When the bright warder blows his trumpet clear,
Whose tones reach naught on earth but Poet's
    ear,
When these enchanted portals open wide,
And through the light the horsemen swiftly glide,
The Poet's eye can reach those golden halls,
And view the glory of their festivals:
Their ladies fair, that in the distance seem
Fit for the silv'ring of a seraph's dream;
Their rich brimm'd goblets, that incessant run
Like the bright spots that move about the sun; 40
And, when upheld, the wine from each bright jar
Pours with the lustre of a falling star.
Yet further off, are dimly seen their bowers,
Of which, no mortal eye can reach the flowers;
And 'tis right just, for well Apollo knows
'Twould make the Poet quarrel with the rose.
All that's reveal'd from that far seat of blisses,

Is, the clear fountains' interchanging kisses,
As gracefully descending, light and thin,
Like silver streaks across a dolphin's fin,   50
When he upswimmeth from the coral caves,
And sports with half his tail above the waves.

These wonders strange he sees, and many more,
Whose head is pregnant with poetic lore.
Should he upon an evening ramble fare
With forehead to the soothing breezes bare,
Would he naught see but the dark, silent blue
With all its diamonds trembling through and
    through?
Or the coy moon, when in the waviness
Of whitest clouds she does her beauty dress, 60
And staidly paces higher up, and higher,
Like a sweet nun·in holy-day attire?
Ah, yes! much more would start into his sight—
The revelries, and mysteries of night:
And should I ever see them, I will tell you
Such tales as needs must with amazement spell
    you.

These are the living pleasures of the bard:
But richer far posterity's award.
What does he murmur with his latest breath,
While his proud eye looks through the film of
    death?   70
'What though I leave this dull, and earthly
    mould, ·
Yet shall my spirit lofty converse hold
With after times.—The patriot shall feel
My stern alarum, and unsheath his steel;
Or, in the senate thunder out my numbers
To startle princes from their easy slumbers.
The sage will mingle with each moral theme
My happy thoughts sententious; he will teem
With lofty periods when my verses fire him,
And then I'll stoop from heaven to inspire
    him.   80
Lays have I left of such a dear delight
That maids will sing them on their bridal night.
Gay villagers, upon a morn of May,
When they have tired their gentle limbs with
    play,
And form'd a snowy circle on the grass,
And plac'd in midst of all that lovely lass
Who chosen is their queen,—with her fine head
Crowned with flowers purple, white, and red:
For there the lilly, and the musk-rose, sighing,
Are emblems true of hapless lovers dying; 90
Between her breasts, that never yet felt trouble,
A bunch of violets full blown, and double,
Serenely sleep:—she from a casket takes
A little book,—and then a joy awakes

---

1 Leigh Hunt.

About each youthful heart,—with stifled cries,
And rubbing of white hands, and sparkling eyes:
For she's to read a tale of hopes, and fears;
One that I foster'd in my youthful years:
The pearls, that on each glist'ning circlet sleep,
Gush ever and anon with silent creep,   100
Lured by the innocent dimples. To sweet rest
Shall the dear babe, upon its mother's breast,
Be lull'd with songs of mine. Fair world, adieu!
Thy dales, and hills, are fading from my view:
Swiftly I mount, upon wide spreading pinions,
Far from the narrow bounds of thy dominions.
Full joy I feel, while thus I cleave the air,
That my soft verse will charm thy daughters
     fair,
And warm thy sons!' Ah, my dear friend
     and brother,
Could I, at once, my mad ambition smother, 110
For tasting joys like these, sure I should be
Happier, and dearer to society.
At times, 'tis true, I've felt relief from pain
When some bright thought has darted through
     my brain:
Through all that day I've felt a greater pleasure
Than if I'd brought to light a hidden treasure.
As to my sonnets, though none else should heed
     them,
I feel delighted, still, that you should read
     them.
Of late, too, I have had much calm enjoyment,
Stretch'd on the grass at my best lov'd employ-
     ment   120
Of scribbling lines for you. These things I
     thought
While, in my face, the freshest breeze I caught.
E'en now I'm pillow'd on a bed of flowers
That crowns a lofty clift, which proudly towers
Above the ocean-waves. The stalks, and blades,
Chequer my tablet with their quivering shades.
On one side is a field of drooping oats,
Through which the poppies show their scarlet
     coats;
So pert and useless, that they bring to mind
The scarlet coats that pester human-kind.   130
And on the other side, outspread, is seen
Ocean's blue mantle streak'd with purple, and
     green.
Now 'tis I see a canvass'd ship, and now
Mark the bright silver curling round her prow.
I see the lark down-dropping to his nest,
And the broad winged sea-gull never at rest;
For when no more he spreads his feathers free,
His breast is dancing on the restless sea.
Now I direct my eyes into the west,
Which at this moment is in sunbeams drest: 140

Why westward turn? 'Twas but to say adieu!
'Twas but to kiss my hand, dear George, to you!

August, 1816   1817

TO CHARLES COWDEN CLARKE

OFT have you seen a swan superbly frowning,
And with proud breast his own white shadow
     crowning,
He slants his neck beneath the waters bright
So silently, it seems a beam of light
Come from the galaxy: anon he sports,—
With outspread wings the Naiad Zephyr courts,
Or ruffles all the surface of the lake
In striving from its crystal face to take
Some diamond water drops, and them to treasure
In milky nest, and sip them off at leisure.   10
But not a moment can he there insure them,
Nor to such downy rest can he allure them;
For down they rush as though they would be
     free,
And drop like hours into eternity.
Just like that bird am I in loss of time,
Whene'er I venture on the stream of rhyme;
With shatter'd boat, oar snapt, and canvass rent
I slowly sail, scarce knowing my intent;
Still scooping up the water with my fingers,
In which a trembling diamond never lingers.   20
By this, friend Charles, you may full plainly see
Why I have never penn'd a line to thee:
Because my thoughts were never free, and clear,
And little fit to please a classic ear;
Because my wine was of too poor a savour
For one whose palate gladdens in the flavour
Of sparkling Helicon;[1]—small good it were
To take him to a desert rude, and bare,
Who had on Baiæ's shore[2] reclin'd at ease,
While Tasso's page was floating in a breeze   30
That gave soft music from Armida's[3] bowers,
Mingled with fragrance from her rarest flowers:
Small good to one who had by Mulla's[4] stream
Fondled the maidens with the breasts of cream;
Who had beheld Belphœbe[5] in a brook,
And lovely Una[6] in a leafy nook,
And Archimago[7] leaning o'er his book:
Who had of all that's sweet tasted, and seen,

---

1 poetry; literally, a mountain in Boeotia whose springs were sacred to the muses.
2 an ancient Roman summer resort near Naples.
3 a beautiful sorceress in Tasso's *Jerusalem Delivered* who seduced Crusaders.
4 a river in Ireland not far from Kilcolman Castle, where Spenser
composed *The Faerie Queene.*
5 chaste huntress in *The Faerie Queene* representing Queen Elizabeth as a woman, as Gloriana represented her as a queen.
6 the beautiful lady in Spenser's poem, personifying Truth.
7 a magician in the same poem, the personification of hypocrisy.

From silv'ry ripple, up to beauty's queen;
From the sequester'd haunts of gay Titania,   40
To the blue dwelling of divine Urania:
One, who, of late, had ta'en sweet forest walks
With him who elegantly chats, and talks—
The wrong'd Libertas,[8]—who has told you stories
Of laurel chaplets, and Apollo's glories;
Of troops chivalrous prancing through a city,
And tearful ladies made for love, and pity:
With many else which I have never known.
Thus have I thought; and days on days have
    flown
Slowly, or rapidly—unwilling still   50
For you to try my dull, unlearned quill.
Nor should I now, but that I've known you long;
That you first taught me all the sweets of song:
The grand, the sweet, the terse, the free, the fine;
What swell'd with pathos, and what right divine:
Spenserian vowels that elope with ease,
And float along like birds o'er summer seas;
Miltonian storms, and more, Miltonian tender-
    ness;
Michael in arms, and more, meek Eve's fair slen-
    derness.
Who read for me the sonnet swelling loudly   60
Up to its climax and then dying proudly?
Who found for me the grandeur of the ode,
Growing, like Atlas, stronger from its load?
Who let me taste that more than cordial dram,
The sharp, the rapier-pointed epigram?
Show'd me that epic was of all the king,
Round, vast, and spanning all like Saturn's ring?
You too upheld the veil from Clio's[9] beauty,
And pointed out the patriot's stern duty;
The might of Alfred, and the shaft of Tell;   70
The hand of Brutus, that so grandly fell
Upon a tyrant's head. Ah! had I never seen,
Or known your kindness, what might I have
    been?
What my enjoyments in my youthful years,
Bereft of all that now my life endears?
And can I e'er these benefits forget?
And can I e'er repay the friendly debt?
No, doubly no;—yet should these rhymings
    please,
I shall roll on the grass with two-fold ease:
For I have long time been my fancy feeding   80
With hopes that you would one day think the
    reading
Of my rough verses not an hour misspent;
Should it e'er be so, what a rich content!
Some weeks have pass'd since last I saw the
    spires

In lucent Thames reflected:—warm desires
To see the sun o'erpeep the eastern dimness,
And morning shadows streaking into slimness
Across the lawny fields, and pebbly water;
To mark the time as they grow broad, and
    shorter;
To feel the air that plays about the hills,   90
And sips its freshness from the little rills;
To see high, golden corn wave in the light
When Cynthia smiles upon a summer's night,
And peers among the cloudlets jet and white,
As though she were reclining in a bed
Of bean blossoms, in heaven freshly shed.
No sooner had I stepp'd into these pleasures
Than I began to think of rhymes and measures:
The air that floated by me seem'd to say
'Write! thou wilt never have a better day.'   100
And so I did. When many lines I'd written,
Though with their grace I was not oversmitten,
Yet, as my hand was warm, I thought I'd better
Trust to my feelings, and write you a letter.
Such an attempt required an inspiration
Of a peculiar sort,—a consummation;—
Which, had I felt, these scribblings might have
    been
Verses from which the soul would never wean:
But many days have passed since last my heart
Was warm'd luxuriously by divine Mozart;   110
By Arne delighted, or by Handel madden'd;
Or by the song of Erin pierc'd and sadden'd:
What time you were before the music sitting,
And the rich notes to each sensation fitting.
Since I have walk'd with you through shady lanes
That freshly terminate in open plains,
And revel'd in a chat that ceased not
When at night-fall among your books we got:
No, nor when supper came, nor after that,—
Nor when reluctantly I took my hat;   120
No, nor till cordially you shook my hand
Mid-way between our homes:—your accents
    bland
Still sounded in my ears, when I no more
Could hear your footsteps touch the grav'ly floor.
Sometimes I lost them, and then found again;
You chang'd the footpath for the grassy plain.
In those still moments I have wish'd you joys
That well you know to honour:—'Life's very
    toys
With him,' said I, 'will take a pleasant charm;
It cannot be that aught will work him harm.'   130
These thoughts now come o'er me with all their
    might:—
Again I shake your hand,—friend Charles, good
    night.

September 1816   1817

8 Leigh Hunt.
9 the Muse of History.

ON FIRST LOOKING INTO CHAPMAN'S HOMER

[Charles Cowden Clarke and Keats spent all one October night reading over together in an old folio edition some of the finest passages of the Elizabethan Chapman's translation of Homer. To Keats, who knew no Greek, the experience was a revelation and his enthusiasm was intense. He returned home at daybreak, composed the sonnet, and sent off a copy to Clarke who found it waiting for him when he came down to breakfast.]

MUCH have I travell'd in the realms of gold,
    And many goodly states and kingdoms seen;
    Round many western islands have I been
Which bards in fealty to Apollo hold.
Oft of one wide expanse had I been told
    That deep-brow'd Homer ruled as his demesne;
    Yet did I never breathe its pure serene
Till I heard Chapman speak out loud and bold:
Then felt I like some watcher of the skies
    When a new planet swims into his ken;   10
Or like stout Cortez[1] when with eagle eyes
    He star'd at the Pacific—and all his men
Look'd at each other with a wild surmise—
    Silent, upon a peak in Darien.

        October 1816   1817

ADDRESSED TO HAYDON[1]

GREAT spirits now on earth are sojourning;
    He of the cloud, the cataract, the lake,[2]
    Who on Helvellyn's summit, wide awake,
Catches his freshness from Archangel's wing:
He of the rose, the violet, the spring,[3]
    The social smile, the chain for Freedom's sake:
    And lo!—whose stedfastness would never take
A meaner sound than Raphael's whispering.[4]
And other spirits there are standing apart
    Upon the forehead of the age to come;   10
These, these will give the world another heart,
    And other pulses. Hear ye not the hum
Of mighty workings?——
    Listen awhile ye nations, and be dumb.

        1816   1817

KEEN, FITFUL GUSTS

KEEN, fitful gusts are whisp'ring here and there
    Among the bushes half leafless, and dry;
    The stars look very cold about the sky,
And I have many miles on foot to fare.

---

[1] actually, of course, not Cortez but Balboa.

---

[1] English historical painter, 1786–1846.
[2] Wordsworth.   3 Leigh Hunt.   4 Haydon.

Yet feel I little of the cool bleak air,
    Or of the dead leaves rustling drearily,
    Or of those silver lamps that burn on high,
Or of the distance from home's pleasant lair:
For I am brimfull of the friendliness
    That in a little cottage[1] I have found;   10
Of fair-hair'd Milton's eloquent distress,
    And all his love for gentle Lycid drown'd;
Of lovely Laura in her light green dress,
    And faithful Petrarch gloriously crown'd.

    1816   1817

I STOOD TIP-TOE

'Places of nestling green for Poets made.'

                    [LEIGH HUNT] *Story of Rimini*

I STOOD tip-toe upon a little hill,
The air was cooling, and so very still,
That the sweet buds which with a modest pride
Pull droopingly, in slanting curve aside,
Their scantly leav'd, and finely tapering stems,
Had not yet lost those starry diadems
Caught from the early sobbing of the morn.
The clouds were pure and white as flocks new shorn,
And fresh from the clear brook; sweetly they slept
On the blue fields of heaven, and then there crept   10
A little noiseless noise among the leaves,
Born of the very sigh that silence heaves:
For not the faintest motion could be seen
Of all the shades that slanted o'er the green.
There was wide wand'ring for the greediest eye,
To peer about upon variety;
Far round the horizon's crystal air to skim,
And trace the dwindled edgings of its brim;
To picture out the quaint, and curious bending
Of a fresh woodland alley, never ending;   20
Or by the bowery clefts, and leafy shelves,
Guess where the jaunty streams refresh themselves.
I gazed awhile, and felt as light, and free
As though the fanning wings of Mercury
Had play'd upon my heels: I was light-hearted,
And many pleasures to my vision started;
So I straightway began to pluck a posey
Of luxuries bright, milky, soft and rosy.

A bush of May flowers with the bees about them;
Ah, sure no tasteful nook would be without them;   30

---

[1] Leigh Hunt's home in Hampstead.

And let a lush labernum oversweep them,
And let long grass grow round the roots to keep
    them
Moist, cool and green; and shade the violets,
That they may bind the moss in leafy nets.
A filbert hedge with wild briar overtwined,
And clumps of woodbine taking the soft wind
Upon their summer thrones; there too should be
The frequent chequer of a youngling tree,
That with a score of light green brethren shoots
From the quaint mossiness of aged roots: 40
Round which is heard a spring-head of clear
    waters
Babbling so wildly of its lovely daughters
The spreading blue-bells: it may haply mourn
That such fair clusters should be rudely torn
From their fresh beds, and scattered thought-
    lessly
By infant hands, left on the path to die.

Open afresh your round of starry folds,
Ye ardent marigolds!
Dry up the moisture from your golden lids,
For great Apollo bids   50
That in these days your praises should be sung
On many harps, which he has lately strung;
And when again your dewiness he kisses,
Tell him, I have you in my world of blisses:
So haply when I rove in some far vale,
His mighty voice may come upon the gale.

Here are sweet peas, on tip-toe for a flight:
With wings of gentle flush o'er delicate white,
And taper fingers catching at all things,
To bind them all about with tiny rings.   60

Linger awhile upon some bending planks
That lean against a streamlet's rushy banks,
And watch intently Nature's gentle doings:
They will be found softer than ring-dove's coo-
    ings.
How silent comes the water round that bend;
Not the minutest whisper does it send
To the o'erhanging sallows;[1] blades of grass
Slowly across the chequer'd shadows pass.

Why, you might read two sonnets, ere they reach
To where the hurrying freshnesses aye preach   70
A natural sermon o'er their pebbly beds;
Where swarms of minnows show their little
    heads,
Staying their wavy bodies 'gainst the streams,
To taste the luxury of sunny beams
Temper'd with coolness. How they ever wrestle

---

1 willows.

With their own sweet delight, and ever nestle
Their silver bellies on the pebbly sand.
If you but scantily hold out the hand,
That very instant not one will remain;
But turn your eye, and they are there again.   80
The ripples seem right glad to reach those
    cresses,
And cool themselves among the em'rald tresses;
The while they cool themselves, they freshness
    give,
And moisture, that the bowery green may live:
So keeping up an interchange of favours,
Like good men in the truth of their behaviours.
Sometimes goldfinches one by one will drop
From low hung branches; little space they stop;
But sip, and twitter, and their feathers sleek;
Then off at once, as in a wanton freak: 90
Or perhaps, to show their black, and golden
    wings,
Pausing upon their yellow flutterings.
Were I in such a place, I sure should pray
That naught less sweet, might call my thoughts
    away,
Than the soft rustle of a maiden's gown
Fanning away the dandelion's down;
Than the light music of her nimble toes
Patting against the sorrel as she goes.
How she would start, and blush, thus to be
    caught
Playing in all her innocence of thought.   100
O let me lead her gently o'er the brook,
Watch her half-smiling lips, and downward look;
O let me for one moment touch her wrist;
Let me one moment to her breathing list;
And as she leaves me may she often turn
Her fair eyes looking through her locks auburne.
What next? A tuft of evening primroses,
O'er which the mind may hover till it dozes;
O'er which it well might take a pleasant sleep,
But that 'tis ever startled by the leap   110
Of buds into ripe flowers; or by the flitting
Of diverse moths, that aye their rest are quitting;
Or by the moon lifting her silver rim
Above a cloud, and with a gradual swim
Coming into the blue with all her light.
O Maker of sweet poets, dear delight
Of this fair world, and all its gentle livers;
Spangler of clouds, halo of crystal rivers,
Mingler with leaves, and dew and tumbling
    streams,
Closer of lovely eyes to lovely dreams,   120
Lover of loneliness, and wandering,
Of upcast eye, and tender pondering!
Thee must I praise above all other glories
That smile us on to tell delightful stories.

For what has made the sage or poet write
But the fair paradise of Nature's light?
In the calm grandeur of a sober line,
We see the waving of the mountain pine;
And when a tale is beautifully staid,
We feel the safety of a hawthorn glade: 130
When it is moving on luxurious wings,
The soul is lost in pleasant smotherings:
Fair dewy roses brush against our faces,
And flowering laurel spring from diamond vases;
O'er head we see the jasmine and sweet briar,
And bloomy grapes laughing from green attire;
While at our feet, the voice of crystal bubbles
Charms us at once away from all our troubles:
So that we feel uplifted from the world,
Walking upon the white clouds wreath'd and
     curl'd.   140
So felt he, who first told, how Psyche went[2]
On the smooth wind to realms of wonderment;
What Psyche felt, and Love, when their full
     lips
First touch'd; what amorous, and fondling nips
They gave each other's cheeks; with all their
     sighs,
And how they kist each other's tremulous eyes:
The silver lamp,—the ravishment,—the won-
     der—
The darkness,—loneliness,—the fearful thunder;
Their woes gone by, and both to heaven upflown,
To bow for gratitude before Jove's throne.   150
So did he feel, who pull'd the boughs aside,
That we might look into a forest wide,
To catch a glimpse of Fauns, and Dryades
Coming with softest rustle through the trees;
And garlands woven of flowers wild, and sweet,
Upheld on ivory wrists, or sporting feet:
Telling us how fair, trembling Syrinx[3] fled
Arcadian Pan, with such a fearful dread.
Poor nymph,—poor Pan,—how he did weep to
     find,
Nought but a lovely sighing of the wind   160
Along the reedy stream; a half-heard strain,
Full of sweet desolation—balmy pain.

What first inspired a bard of old to sing
Narcissus pining o'er the untainted spring?
In some delicious ramble, he had found
A little space, with boughs all woven round;
And in the midst of all, a clearer pool
Than e'er reflected in its pleasant cool,
The blue sky here, and there, serenely peeping

Through tendril wreaths fantastically creep-
     ing.   170
And on the bank a lonely flower he spied,
A meek and forlorn flower, with naught of pride,
Drooping its beauty o'er the watery clearness,
To woo its own sad image into nearness:
Deaf to light Zephyrus it would not move;
But still would seem to droop, to pine, to love.
So while the poet stood in this sweet spot,
Some fainter gleamings o'er his fancy shot;
Nor was it long ere he had told the tale
Of young Narcissus,[4] and sad Echo's bale.   180

Where had he been, from whose warm head out-
     flew
That sweetest of all songs, that ever new,
That aye refreshing, pure deliciousness,
Coming ever to bless
The wanderer by moonlight? to him bringing
Shapes from the invisible world, unearthly sing-
     ing
From out the middle air, from flowery nests,
And from the pillowy silkiness that rests
Full in the speculation of the stars.
Ah! surely he had burst our mortal bars;   190
Into some wond'rous region he had gone,
To search for thee, divine Endymion![5]

He was a Poet, sure a lover too,
Who stood on Latmus' top, what time there blew
Soft breezes from the myrtle vale below;
And brought in faintness solemn, sweet, and slow
A hymn from Dian's temple; while upswelling,
The incense went to her own starry dwelling.
But though her face was clear as infant's eyes,
Though she stood smiling o'er the sacrifice,   200
The Poet wept at her so piteous fate,
Wept that such beauty should be desolate:
So in fine wrath some golden sounds he won,
And gave meek Cynthia her Endymion.

Queen of the wide air; thou most lovely queen
Of all the brightness that mine eyes have seen!
As thou exceedest all things in thy shine,
So every tale, does this sweet tale of thine.
O for three words of honey, that I might
Tell but one wonder of thy bridal night!   210

Where distant ships do seem to show their keels,
Phoebus awhile delay'd his mighty wheels,
And turn'd to smile upon thy bashful eyes,

---

2 The story of Cupid and Psyche is not ancient orthodox Greek
mythology, but is first told in Latin by Apuleius in his *Metamorphoses,* second century of the Christian era.
3 a nymph who fled from the wooing of Pan and was changed by
the water nymphs into a reed.

4 a beautiful youth, who rejected the nymph Echo and was punished for his self-sufficiency by falling in love with his own image
in a pool.
5 the shepherd on Mount Latmus loved by the moon goddess
Diana (or Cynthia).

Ere he his unseen pomp would solemnize.
The evening weather was so bright, and clear,
That men of health were of unusual cheer;
Stepping like Homer at the trumpet's call,
Or young Apollo on the pedestal:
And lovely women were as fair and warm,
As Venus looking sideways in alarm.   220
The breezes were ethereal, and pure,
And crept through half-closed lattices to cure
The languid sick; it cool'd their fever'd sleep,
And soothed them into slumbers full and deep.
Soon they awoke clear eyed: nor burnt with
      thirsting,
Nor with hot fingers, nor with temples bursting:
And springing up, they met the wond'ring sight
Of their dear friends, nigh foolish with delight;
Who feel their arms, and breasts, and kiss and
      stare,
And on their placid foreheads part the hair.   230
Young men, and maidens at each other gaz'd
With hands held back, and motionless, amaz'd
To see the brightness in each other's eyes;
And so they stood, fill'd with a sweet surprise,
Until their tongues were loos'd in poesy,
Therefore no lover did of anguish die:
But the soft numbers, in that moment spoken,
Made silken ties, that never may be broken.
Cynthia! I cannot tell the greater blisses,
That follow'd thine, and thy dear shepherd's
      kisses: 240
Was there a poet born?—but now no more,
My wand'ring spirit must no further soar.—

1816   1817

SLEEP AND POETRY

[This poem was conceived in Hunt's library where
Keats was 'put up' on an improvised sofa for the night.
Following an exciting evening of talk, Keats was unable
to sleep. The poem reveals his poetic aspirations, his
anxieties, and his hopes for achieving literary eminence.
Lines 181–206 contain an attack upon pseudo-classical
poetry. The closing lines describe the pictures and objects in Hunt's study.]

WHAT is more gentle than a wind in summer?
What is more soothing than the pretty hummer
That stays one moment in an open flower,
And buzzes cheerily from bower to bower?
What is more tranquil than a musk-rose blowing
In a green island, far from all men's knowing?
More healthful than the leafiness of dales?
More secret than a nest of nightingales?
More serene than Cordelia's[1] countenance?

_____
1 the youngest and best-loved daughter of King Lear, in Shakespeare's drama.

More full of visions than a high romance?   10
What, but thee Sleep? Soft closer of our eyes!
Low murmurer of tender lullabies!
Light hoverer around our happy pillows!
Wreather of poppy buds, and weeping willows!
Silent entangler of a beauty's tresses!
Most happy listener! when the morning blesses
Thee for enlivening all the cheerful eyes
That glance so brightly at the new sun-rise.

But what is higher beyond thought than thee?
Fresher than berries of a mountain tree?   20
More strange, more beautiful, more smooth,
      more regal,
Than wings of swans, than doves, than dim-seen
      eagle?
What is it? And to what shall I compare it?
It has a glory, and naught else can share it:
The thought thereof is awful, sweet, and holy,
Chasing away all worldliness and folly;
Coming sometimes like fearful claps of thunder,
Or the low rumblings earth's regions under;
And sometimes like a gentle whispering
Of all the secrets of some wond'rous thing   30
That breathes about us in the vacant air;
So that we look around with prying stare,
Perhaps to see shapes of light, aerial limning,
And catch soft floatings from a faint-heard
      hymning;
To see the laurel wreath, on high suspended,
That is to crown our name when life is ended.
Sometimes it gives a glory to the voice,
And from the heart up-springs, rejoice! rejoice!
Sounds which will reach the Framer of all
      things,
And die away in ardent mutterings.   40

No one who once the glorious sun has seen,
And all the clouds, and felt his bosom clean
For his great Maker's presence, but must know
What 'tis I mean, and feel his being glow:
Therefore no insult will I give his spirit,
By telling what he sees from native merit.

O Poesy! for thee I hold my pen
That am not yet a glorious denizen
Of thy wide heaven—Should I rather kneel
Upon some mountain-top until I feel   50
A glowing splendour round about me hung,
And echo back the voice of thine own tongue?
O Poesy! for thee I grasp my pen
That am not yet a glorious denizen
Of thy wide heaven; yet, to my ardent prayer,
Yield from thy sanctuary some clear air,
Smooth'd for intoxication by the breath

Of flowering bays, that I may die a death
Of luxury, and my young spirit follow
The morning sun-beams to the great Apollo 60
Like a fresh sacrifice; or, if I can bear
The o'erwhelming sweets, 'twill bring to me the
    fair
Visions of all places: a bowery nook
Will be elysium—an eternal book
Whence I may copy many a lovely saying
About the leaves, and flowers—about the playing
Of nymphs in woods, and fountains; and the
    shade
Keeping a silence round a sleeping maid;
And many a verse from so strange influence
That we must ever wonder how, and whence 70
It came. Also imaginings will hover
Round my fire-side, and haply there discover
Vistas of solemn beauty, where I'd wander
In happy silence, like the clear Meander
Through its lone vales; and where I found a spot
Of awfuller shade, or an enchanted grot,
Or a green hill o'erspread with chequer'd dress
Of flowers, and fearful from its loveliness,
Write on my tablets all that was permitted,
All that was for our human senses fitted. 80
Then the events of this wide world I'd seize
Like a strong giant, and my spirit teaze
Till at its shoulders it should proudly see
Wings to find out an immortality.

Stop and consider! life is but a day;
A fragile dew-drop on its perilous way
From a tree's summit; a poor Indian's sleep
While his boat hastens to the monstrous steep
Of Montmorenci.[2] Why so sad a moan?
Life is the rose's hope while yet unblown; 90
The reading of an ever-changing tale;
The light uplifting of a maiden's veil;
A pigeon tumbling in clear summer air;
A laughing school-boy, without grief or care,
Riding the springy branches of an elm.

O for ten years, that I may overwhelm
Myself in poesy; so I may do the deed
That my own soul has to itself decreed.
Then will I pass the countries that I see
In long perspective, and continually 100
Taste their pure fountains. First the realm I'll
    pass
Of Flora, and old Pan: sleep in the grass,
Feed upon apples red, and strawberries,
And choose each pleasure that my fancy sees;
Catch the white-handed nymphs in shady places,

2 a river in Quebec, Canada, known for its swift rapids and
waterfalls.

To woo sweet kisses from averted faces,—
Play with their fingers, touch their shoulders
    white
Into a pretty shrinking with a bite
As hard as lips can make it: till agreed,
A lovely tale of human life we'll read. 110
And one will teach a tame dove how it best
May fan the cool air gently o'er my rest;
Another, bending o'er her nimble tread,
Will set a green robe floating round her head,
And still will dance with ever varied ease,
Smiling upon the flowers and the trees:
Another will entice me on, and on
Through almond blossoms and rich cinnamon;
Till in the bosom of a leafy world
We rest in silence, like two gems upcurl'd 120
In the recesses of a pearly shell.

And can I ever bid these joys farewell?
Yes, I must pass them for a nobler life,
Where I may find the agonies, the strife
Of human hearts: for lo! I see afar,
O'ersailing the blue cragginess, a car
And steeds with streamy manes—the charioteer
Looks out upon the winds with glorious fear:
And now the numerous tramplings quiver lightly
Along a huge cloud's ridge; and now with
    sprightly 130
Wheel downward come they into fresher skies,
Tipt round with silver from the sun's bright eyes.
Still downward with capacious whirl they glide;
And now I see them on the green-hill's side
In breezy rest among the nodding stalks.
The charioteer with wond'rous gesture talks
To the trees and mountains; and there soon ap-
    pear
Shapes of delight, of mystery, and fear,
Passing along before a dusky space
Made by some mighty oaks: as they would
    chase 140
Some ever-fleeting music on they sweep.
Lo! how they murmur, laugh, and smile, and
    weep:
Some with upholden hand and mouth severe;
Some with their faces muffled to the ear
Between their arms; some, clear in youthful
    bloom,
Go glad and smilingly athwart the gloom;
Some looking back, and some with upward gaze;
Yes, thousands in a thousand different ways
Flit onward—now a lovely wreath of girls
Dancing their sleek hair into tangled curls; 150
And now broad wings. Most awfully intent
The driver of those steeds is forward bent,

And seems to listen: O that I might know
All that he writes with such a hurrying glow.

The visions all are fled—the car is fled
Into the light of heaven, and in their stead
A sense of real things comes doubly strong,
And, like a muddy stream, would bear along
My soul to nothingness: but I will strive
Against all doubtings, and will keep alive   160
The thought of that same chariot, and the strange
Journey it went.

          Is there so small a range
In the present strength of manhood, that the high
Imagination cannot freely fly
As she was wont of old? prepare her steeds,
Paw up against the light, and do strange deeds
Upon the clouds? Has she not shown us all?
From the clear space of ether, to the small
Breath of new buds unfolding? From the mean-
    ing
Of Jove's large eye-brow,[3] to the tender
    greening   170
Of April meadows? Here her altar shone,
E'en in this isle; and who could paragon
The fervid choir[4] that lifted up a noise
Of harmony, to where it aye will poise
Its mighty self of convoluting sound,
Huge as a planet, and like that roll round,
Eternally around a dizzy void?
Ay, in those days the Muses were nigh cloy'd
With honours; nor had any other care
Than to sing out and sooth their wavy hair.   180

Could all this be forgotten? Yes, a schism[5]
Nurtured by foppery and barbarism,
Made great Apollo blush for this his land.
Men were thought wise who could not under-
    stand
His glories: with a puling infant's force
They sway'd about upon a rocking horse,
And thought it Pegasus. Ah dismal soul'd!
The winds of heaven blew, the ocean roll'd
Its gathering waves—ye felt it not. The blue
Bared its eternal bosom, and the dew   190
Of summer nights collected still to make
The morning precious: beauty was awake!
Why were ye not awake? But ye were dead
To things ye knew not of,—were closely wed
To musty laws lined out with wretched rule
And compass vile: so that ye taught a school

Of dolts to smooth, inlay, and clip, and fit,
Till, like the certain wands of Jacob's wit,[6]
Their verses tallied. Easy was the task:
A thousand handicraftsmen wore the mask   200
Of Poesy. Ill-fated, impious race!
That blasphemed the bright Lyrist to his face,
And did not know it,—no, they went about,
Holding a poor, decrepid standard out
Mark'd with most flimsy mottos, and in large
The name of one Boileau![7]

              O ye whose charge
It is to hover round our pleasant hills!
Whose congregated majesty so fills
My boundly reverence, that I cannot trace
Your hallowed names, in this unholy place,   210
So near those common folk; did not their shames
Affright you? Did our old lamenting Thames
Delight you? Did ye never cluster round
Delicious Avon, with a mournful sound,
And weep? Or did ye wholly bid adieu
To regions where no more the laurel grew?
Or did ye stay to give a welcoming
To some lone spirits who could proudly sing
Their youth away, and die?[8] 'Twas even so:
But let me think away those times of woe: 220
Now 'tis a fairer season; ye have breathed
Rich benedictions o'er us; ye have wreathed
Fresh garlands: for sweet music has been heard
In many places;—some has been upstirr'd
From out its crystal dwelling in a lake,
By a swan's ebon bill;[9] from a thick brake,
Nested and quiet in a valley mild,
Bubbles a pipe;[10] fine sounds are floating wild
About the earth: happy are ye and glad.

These things are doubtless: yet in truth we've
    had   230
Strange thunders from the potency of song;
Mingled indeed with what is sweet and strong,
From majesty: but in clear truth the themes
Are ugly clubs, the Poets' Polyphemes[11]
Disturbing the grand sea. A drainless shower
Of light is poesy; 'tis the supreme of power;
'Tis might half slumb'ring on its own right arm.
The very archings of her eye-lids charm
A thousand willing agents to obey,

---

3 Jove's eyebrow was supposed to become particularly meaningful whenever he nodded to announce a decision.
4 the Elizabethan poets.
5 the writers of the Age of Pope.
6 alluding to the variegated rods that Jacob put in front of his
flocks and cattle to strengthen their offspring. See Genesis, xxx,
37–41.
7 the famous French critic and poet, 1636–1711, who summarized
in his *L'Art Poétique* the principles of the neo-classical school of
criticism.
8 a reference to Thomas Chatterton.
9 probably a reference to Wordsworth.
10 perhaps the reference is to Leigh Hunt.
11 one-eyed giants of Homer; here the allusion is supposedly to
Byron.

And still she governs with the mildest sway: 240
But strength alone though of the Muses born
Is like a fallen angel: trees uptorn,
Darkness, and worms, and shrouds, and sepul-
    chres
Delight it; for it feeds upon the burrs,
And thorns of life; forgetting the great end
Of poesy, that it should be a friend
To sooth the cares, and lift the thoughts of man.

Yet I rejoice: a myrtle fairer than
E'er grew in Paphos, from the bitter weeds
Lifts its sweet head into the air, and feeds   250
A silent space with ever sprouting green.
All tenderest birds there find a pleasant screen,
Creep through the shade with jaunty fluttering,
Nibble the little cupped flowers and sing.
Then let us clear away the choking thorns
From round its gentle stem; let the young fawns,
Yeaned[12] in after times, when we are flown,
Find a fresh sward beneath it, overgrown
With simple flowers: let there nothing be
More boisterous than a lover's bended knee: 260
Nought more ungentle than the placid look
Of one who leans upon a closed book;
Nought more untranquil than the grassy slopes
Between two hills. All hail delightful hopes!
As she was wont, th'imagination
Into most lovely labyrinths will be gone,
And they shall be accounted poet kings
Who simply tell the most heart-easing things.
O may these joys be ripe before I die.

Will not some say that I presumptuously   270
Have spoken? that from hastening disgrace
'Twere better far to hide my foolish face?
That whining boyhood should with reverence
    bow
Ere the dread thunderbolt could reach? How!
If I do hide myself, it sure shall be
In the very fane, the light of Poesy:
If I do fall, at least I will be laid
Beneath the silence of a poplar shade;
And over me the grass shall be smooth shaven;
And there shall be a kind memorial graven.   280
But off Despondence! miserable bane!
They should not know thee, who athirst to gain
A noble end, are thirsty every hour.
What though I am not wealthy in the dower
Of spanning wisdom; though I do not know
The shiftings of the mighty winds that blow
Hither and thither all the changing thoughts
Of man: though no great minist'ring reason sorts

Out the dark mysteries of human souls
To clear conceiving: yet there ever rolls   290
A vast idea before me, and I glean
Therefrom my liberty; thence too I've seen
The end and aim of Poesy. 'Tis clear
As anything most true; as that the year
Is made of the four seasons—manifest
As a large cross, some old cathedral's crest,
Lifted to the white clouds. Therefore should I
Be but the essence of deformity,
A coward, did my very eye-lids wink
At speaking out what I have dared to think.   300
Ah! rather let me like a madman run
Over some precipice; let the hot sun
Melt my Dedalian wings,[13] and drive me down
Convuls'd and headlong! Stay! an inward frown
Of conscience bids me be more calm awhile.
An ocean dim, sprinkled with many an isle,
Spreads awfully before me. How much toil!
How many days! what desperate turmoil!
Ere I can have explored its widenesses.
Ah, what a task! upon my bended knees,   310
I could unsay those—no, impossible!
Impossible!

For sweet relief I'll dwell
On humbler thoughts, and let this strange assay
Begun in gentleness die so away.
E'en now all tumult from my bosom fades:
I turn full hearted to the friendly aids
That smooth the path of honour; brotherhood,
And friendliness the nurse of mutual good.
The hearty grasp that sends a pleasant sonnet
Into the brain ere one can think upon it;   320
The silence when some rhymes are coming out;
And when they're come, the very pleasant rout:
The message certain to be done to-morrow.
'Tis perhaps as well that it should be to borrow
Some precious book from out its snug retreat,
To cluster round it when we next shall meet.
Scarce can I scribble on; for lovely airs
Are fluttering round the room like doves in
    pairs;
Many delights of that glad day recalling,
When first my senses caught their tender
    falling.   330
And with these airs come forms of elegance
Stooping their shoulders o'er a horse's prance,
Careless, and grand—fingers soft and round
Parting luxuriant curls;—and the swift bound
Of Bacchus from his chariot, when his eye
Made Ariadne's cheek look blushingly.

12 born.

13 presumptuously youthful. Icarus against the advice of his father, Daedalus, flew so near to the sun that the waxen wings invented by his father melted and he fell into the sea.

Thus I remember all the pleasant flow
Of words at opening a portfolio.

Things such as these are ever harbingers
To trains of peaceful images: the stirs   340
Of a swan's neck unseen among the rushes:
A linnet starting all about the bushes:
A butterfly, with golden wings broad parted,
Nestling a rose, convuls'd as though it smarted
With over pleasure—many, many more,
Might I indulge at large in all my store
Of luxuries: yet I must not forget
Sleep, quiet with his poppy coronet:
For what there may be worthy in these rhymes
I partly owe to him: and thus, the chimes   350
Of friendly voices had just given place
To as sweet a silence, when I 'gan retrace
The pleasant day, upon a couch at ease.
It was a poet's house[14] who keeps the keys
Of pleasure's temple. Round about were hung
The glorious features of the bards who sung
In other ages—cold and sacred busts
Smiled at each other. Happy he who trusts
To clear Futurity his darling fame!
Then there were fauns and satyrs taking aim   360
At swelling apples with a frisky leap
And reaching fingers, 'mid a luscious heap
Of vine-leaves. Then there rose to view a fane
Of liny marble, and thereto a train
Of nymphs approaching fairly o'er the sward:
One, loveliest, holding her white hand toward
The dazzling sun-rise: two sisters sweet
Bending their graceful figures till they meet
Over the trippings of a little child:
And some are hearing, eagerly, the wild   370
Thrilling liquidity of dewy piping.
See, in another picture, nymphs are wiping
Cherishingly Diana's timorous limbs;—
A fold of lawny mantle dabbling swims
At the bath's edge, and keeps a gentle motion
With the subsiding crystal: as when ocean
Heaves calmly its broad swelling smoothness o'er
Its rocky marge, and balances once more
The patient weeds; that now unshent by foam
Feel all about their undulating home.   380

Sappho's meek head was there half smiling down
At nothing; just as though the earnest frown
Of over thinking had that moment gone
From off her brow, and left her all alone.

Great Alfred's too, with anxious, pitying eyes,
As if he always listened to the sighs

Of the goaded world; and Kosciusko's[15] worn
By horrid suffrance—mightily forlorn.
Petrarch, outstepping from the shady green,
Starts at the sight of Laura; nor can wean   390
His eyes from her sweet face. Most happy they!
For over them was seen a free display
Of out-spread wings, and from between them
    shone
The face of Poesy: from off her throne
She overlook'd things that I scarce could tell.
The very sense of where I was might well
Keep Sleep aloof: but more than that there came
Thought after thought to nourish up the flame
Within my breast; so that the morning light
Surprised me even from a sleepless night;   400
And up I rose refresh'd, and glad, and gay,
Resolving to begin that very day
These lines; and howsoever they be done,
I leave them as a father does his son.

1816   1817

ON THE GRASSHOPPER AND CRICKET

[This sonnet was written in consequence of a friendly challenge from Leigh Hunt. For Hunt's sonnet see text, p. 762.]

THE poetry of earth is never dead:
   When all the birds are faint with the hot sun,
   And hide in cooling trees, a voice will run
From hedge to hedge about the new-mown
    mead;
That is the Grasshopper's—he takes the lead
   In summer luxury,—he has never done
   With his delights; for when tired out with fun
He rests at ease beneath some pleasant weed.
The poetry of earth is ceasing never:
   On a lone winter evening, when the frost   10
    Has wrought a silence, from the stove there
    shrills
The Cricket's song, in warmth increasing ever,
   And seems to one in drowsiness half lost,
    The Grasshopper's among some grassy hills.

30 December 1816   1817

AFTER DARK VAPOURS

AFTER dark vapours have oppress'd our plains
   For a long dreary season, comes a day
   Born of the gentle South, and clears away
From the sick heavens all unseemly stains.

14 Leigh Hunt's at Hampstead.

15 Thaddeus Kosciusko, 1746–1817, famous Polish statesman and general.

The anxious month, relieved of its pains,
   Takes as a long-lost right the feel of May;
   The eyelids with the passing coolness play
Like rose leaves with the drip of Summer rains.
The calmest thoughts come round us; as of leaves
   Budding—fruit ripening in stillness—Autumn
     suns   10
Smiling at eve upon the quiet sheaves—
Sweet Sappho's cheek—a smiling infant's
   breath—
   The gradual sand that through an hour-glass
    runs—
A woodland rivulet—a Poet's death.

   1817   1817

TO LEIGH HUNT, ESQ.

[This sonnet, said to have been written extemporaneously, is the dedication to Keats's first volume of poems.]

GLORY and loveliness have pass'd away;
   For if we wander out in early morn,
   No wreathed incense do we see upborne
Into the east, to meet the smiling day:
No crowd of nymphs soft voic'd and young, and
   gay,
   In woven baskets bringing ears of corn,
   Roses, and pinks, and violets, to adorn
The shrine of Flora in her early May.
But there are left delights as high as these,
   And I shall ever bless my destiny,   10
That in a time, when under pleasant trees
   Pan is no longer sought, I feel a free,
A leafy luxury, seeing I could please
   With these poor offerings, a man like thee.

   1817   1817

SONNET

WRITTEN AT THE END OF 'THE FLOURE AND THE LEFE'[1]

THIS pleasant tale is like a little copse:
   The honied lines do freshly interlace
   To keep the reader in so sweet a place,
So that he here and there full-hearted stops;
And oftentimes he feels the dewy drops
   Come cool and suddenly against his face,
   And by the wandering melody may trace
Which way the tender-legged linnet hops.
Oh! what a power hath white Simplicity!
   What mighty power has this gentle story!   10
   I that for ever feel athirst for glory

---

[1] a poem mistakenly ascribed to Chaucer.

Could at this moment be content to lie
   Meekly upon the grass, as those whose sob-
    bings
   Were heard of none beside the mournful
    robins.
   1817   1817

ON SEEING THE ELGIN MARBLES[1]

MY spirit is too weak—mortality
   Weighs heavily on me like unwilling sleep,
   And each imagin'd pinnacle and steep
Of godlike hardship, tells me I must die
Like a sick Eagle looking at the sky.
   Yet 'tis a gentle luxury to weep
   That I have not the cloudy winds to keep,
Fresh for the opening of the morning's eye.
Such dim-conceived glories of the brain
   Bring round the heart an undescribable
    feud;   10
So do these wonders a most dizzy pain,
   That mingles Grecian grandeur with the rude
Wasting of old Time—with a billowy main—
   A sun—a shadow of a magnitude.

   1817   1817

ON THE SEA

[Keats sent this sonnet in a letter to Reynolds, 17 April 1817. See text, p. 1207.]

IT keeps eternal whisperings around
   Desolate shores, and with its mighty swell
   Gluts twice ten thousand Caverns, till the spell
Of Hecate[1] leaves them their old shadowy sound.
Often 'tis in such gentle temper found,
   That scarcely will the very smallest shell
   Be mov'd for days from where it sometime fell,
When last the winds of Heaven were unbound.
Oh ye! who have your eye-balls vex'd and tir'd,
   Feast them upon the wideness of the Sea;   10
    Oh ye! whose ears are dinn'd with uproar
    rude,
   Or fed too much with cloying melody—
    Sit ye near some old Cavern's Mouth, and
    brood
Until ye start, as if the sea-nymphs quir'd!

   1817   1848

---

[1] The Elgin marbles are fragments of the Parthenon frieze which Lord Elgin had secured and sold to the British Museum in 1816. Haydon, who had been largely influential in their purchase by the government, was Keats's guide on his first visit to the marbles.

[1] a goddess of the moon, earth, and underworld.

[handwritten marginalia: referred to his medical studies]

[handwritten marginalia: and how interesting Keats at this stage of his development. Romantic Tales.]

ENDYMION: A POETIC ROMANCE

INSCRIBED TO THE MEMORY OF THOMAS CHATTERTON

[Keats began the actual composition of *Endymion* in late April 1817, at Carisbrooke, the Isle of Wight, and finished it at Burford Bridge in November 1817. During this interval his letters make frequent mention of the work and its progress (see especially his striking confession to Bailey, text, p. 1208). In the early part of 1818 Keats was occupied in making corrections and copying out the poem for publication. It was published by Messrs. Taylor and Hessey in April 1818, almost exactly a year from the time Keats began writing it. On its appearance, *Endymion* was bitterly attacked in reviews (mistakenly supposed to have broken Keats's heart) in *Blackwood's Edinburgh Magazine,* probably by Lockhart, and in *The Quarterly Review,* by John Wilson Croker. For these reviews see text p. 565 and p. 727.

For other references to *Endymion* see text, letters: No. 8, p. 1212; No. 10, p. 1214; No. 11, p. 1214; No. 12, p. 1216; No. 15, p. 1218.

PREFACE

Knowing within myself the manner in which this Poem has been produced, it is not without a feeling of regret that I make it public.

What manner I mean, will be quite clear to the reader, who must soon perceive great inexperience, immaturity, and every error denoting a feverish attempt, rather than a deed accomplished. The two first books, and indeed the two last, I feel sensible are not of such completion as to warrant their passing the press; nor should they if I thought a year's castigation would do them any good;— it will not: the foundations are too sandy. It is just that this youngster should die away: a sad thought for me, if I had not some hope that while it is dwindling I may be plotting, and fitting myself for verses fit to live.

This may be speaking too presumptuously, and may deserve a punishment: but no feeling man will be forward to inflict it: he will leave me alone, with the conviction that there is not a fiercer hell than the failure in a great object. This is not written with the least atom of purpose to forestall criticisms of course, but from the desire I have to conciliate men who are competent to look, and who do look with a zealous eye, to the honour of English literature.

The imagination of a boy is healthy, and the mature imagination of a man is healthy; but there is a space of life between, in which the soul is in a ferment, the character undecided, the way of life uncertain, the ambition thick-sighted: thence proceeds mawkishness, and all the thousand bitters which those men I speak of must necessarily taste in going over the following pages.

I hope I have not in too late a day touched the beautiful mythology of Greece, and dulled its brightness: for I wish to try once more, before I bid it farewell.

TEIGNMOUTH, 10 April 1818.

BOOK I

A THING of beauty is a joy for ever:
Its loveliness increases; it will never
Pass into nothingness; but still will keep
A bower quiet for us, and a sleep
Full of sweet dreams, and health, and quiet
    breathing.
Therefore, on every morrow, are we wreathing
A flowery band to bind us to the earth,
Spite of despondence, of the inhuman dearth
Of noble natures, of the gloomy days,
Of all the unhealthy and o'er-darkened ways   10
Made for our searching: yes, in spite of all,
Some shape of beauty moves away the pall
From our dark spirits. Such the sun, the moon,
Trees old, and young, sprouting a shady boon
For simple sheep; and such are daffodils
With the green world they live in; and clear rills
That for themselves a cooling covert make
'Gainst the hot season; the mid forest brake,
Rich with a sprinkling of fair musk-rose blooms:
And such too is the grandeur of the dooms   20
We have imagined for the mighty dead;
All lovely tales that we have heard or read:
An endless fountain of immortal drink,
Pouring unto us from the heaven's brink.

Nor do we merely feel these essences
For one short hour; no, even as the trees
That whisper round a temple become soon
Dear as the temple's self, so does the moon,
The passion poesy, glories infinite,
Haunt us till they become a cheering light   30
Unto our souls, and bound to us so fast,
That, whether there be shine, or gloom o'ercast,
They alway must be with us, or we die.

Therefore, 'tis with full happiness that I
Will trace the story of Endymion.
The very music of the name has gone
Into my being, and each pleasant scene
Is growing fresh before me as the green
Of our own vallies: so I will begin
Now while I cannot hear the city's din;   40
Now while the early budders are just new,
And run in mazes of the youngest hue
About old forests; while the willow trails
Its delicate amber; and the dairy pails
Bring home increase of milk. And, as the year
Grows lush in juicy stalks, I'll smoothly steer
My little boat, for many quiet hours,
With streams that deepen freshly into bowers.
Many and many a verse I hope to write,
Before the daisies, vermeil rimm'd and white,   50
Hide in deep herbage; and ere yet the bees
Hum about globes of clover and sweet peas,
I must be near the middle of my story.
O may no wintry season, bare and hoary,
See it half finish'd: but let Autumn bold,

sustained narrative poem

With universal tinge of sober gold,
Be all about me when I make an end.
And now at once, adventuresome, I send
My herald thought into a wilderness:
There let its trumpet blow, and quickly dress   60
My uncertain path with green, that I may speed
Easily onward, thorough flowers and weed.

    Upon the sides of Latmos was outspread
A mighty forest; for the moist earth fed
So plenteously all weed-hidden roots
Into o'er-hanging boughs, and precious fruits.
And it had gloomy shades, sequestered deep,
Where no man went; and if from shepherd's keep
A lamb stray'd far a-down those inmost glens,
Never again saw he the happy pens   70
Whither his brethren, bleating with content,
Over the hills at every nightfall went.
Among the shepherds, 'twas believed ever,
That not one fleecy lamb which thus did sever
From the white flock, but pass'd unworried
By angry wolf, or pard with prying head,
Until it came to some unfooted plains
Where fed the herds of Pan: aye great his gains
Who thus one lamb did lose. Paths there were
    many,
Winding through palmy fern, and rushes
    fenny,   80
And ivy banks; all leading pleasantly
To a wide lawn, whence one could only see
Stems thronging all around between the swell
Of turf and slanting branches: who could tell
The freshness of the space of heaven above,
Edg'd round with dark tree tops? through which
    a dove
Would often beat its wings, and often too
A little cloud would move across the blue.

    Full in the middle of this pleasantness
There stood a marble altar, with a tress   90
Of flowers budded newly; and the dew
Had taken fairy phantasies to strew
Daisies upon the sacred sward last eve,
And so the dawned light in pomp receive.
For 'twas the morn: Apollo's upward fire
Made every eastern cloud a silvery pyre
Of brightness so unsullied, that therein
A melancholy spirit well might win
Oblivion, and melt out his essence fine
Into the winds: rain-scented eglantine   100
Gave temperate sweets to that well-wooing
    sun;
The lark was lost in him; cold springs had run
To warm their chilliest bubbles in the grass;
Man's voice was on the mountains; and the mass

Of nature's lives and wonders puls'd tenfold,
To feel this sun-rise and its glories old.

    Now while the silent workings of the dawn
Were busiest, into that self-same lawn
All suddenly, with joyful cries, there sped
A troop of little children garlanded;   110
Who gathering round the altar, seem'd to pry
Earnestly round as wishing to espy
Some folk of holiday: nor had they waited
For many moments, ere their ears were sated
With a faint breath of music, which ev'n then
Fill'd out its voice, and died away again.
Within a little space again it gave
Its airy swellings, with a gentle wave,
To light-hung leaves, in smoothest echoes break-
    ing
Through copse-clad vallies,—ere their death,
    o'ertaking   120
The surgy murmurs of the lonely sea.

    And now, as deep into the wood as we
Might mark a lynx's eye, there glimmered light
Fair faces and a rush of garments white,
Plainer and plainer showing, till at last
Into the widest alley they all past,
Making directly for the woodland altar.
O kindly muse! let not my weak tongue faulter
In telling of this goodly company,
Of their old piety, and of their glee: 130
But let a portion of ethereal dew
Fall on my head, and presently unmew[1]
My soul; that I may dare, in wayfaring,
To stammer where old Chaucer us'd to sing.

    Leading the way, young damsels danced along,
Bearing the burden of a shepherd song;
Each having a white wicker over brimm'd
With April's tender younglings; next, well
    trimm'd,
A crowd of shepherds with as sunburnt looks
As may be read of in Arcadian books;   140
Such as sat listening round Apollo's pipe,
When the great deity, for earth too ripe,
Let his divinity o'erflowing die
In music, through the vales of Thessaly;[2]
Some idly trail'd their sheep-hooks on the
    ground,
And some kept up a shrilly mellow sound
With ebon-tipped flutes: close after these,
Now coming from beneath the forest trees,

---

1 release.
2 As a punishment for killing the Cyclops, Apollo was banished from heaven for a year and forced to tend the cattle of
King Admetus of Thessaly.

A venerable priest full soberly,
Begirt with ministring looks: alway his eye   150
Stedfast upon the matted turf he kept,
And after him his sacred vestments swept.
From his right hand there swung a vase, milk-
white,
Of mingled wine, out-sparkling generous light;
And in his left he held a basket full
Of all sweet herbs that searching eye could cull:
Wild thyme, and valley-lillies whiter still
Than Leda 's[3] love, and cresses from the rill.
His aged head, crowned with beechen wreath,
Seem'd like a poll of ivy in the teeth   160
Of winter hoar. Then came another crowd
Of shepherds, lifting in due time aloud
Their share of the ditty. After them appear'd,
Up-followed by a multitude that rear'd
Their voices to the clouds, a fair wrought car,
Easily rolling so as scarce to mar
The freedom of three steeds of dapple brown:
Who stood therein did seem of great renown
Among the throng. His youth was fully blown,
Showing like Ganymede[4] to manhood
grown;   170
And, for those simple times, his garments were
A chieftain king's: beneath his breast, half bare,
Was hung a silver bugle, and between
His nervy knees there lay a boar-spear keen.
A smile was on his countenance; he seem'd,
To common lookers on, like one who dream'd
Of idleness in groves Elysian:
But there were some who feelingly could scan
A lurking trouble in his nether lip,
And see that oftentimes the reins would slip   180
Through his forgotten hands: then would they
sigh,
And think of yellow leaves, of owlets' cry,
Of logs piled solemnly.—Ah, well-a-day,
Why should our young Endymion pine away?

Soon the assembly, in a circle rang'd,
Stood silent round the shrine: each look was
chang'd
To sudden veneration: women meek
Beckon'd their sons to silence; while each cheek
Of virgin bloom paled gently for slight fear.
Endymion too, without a forest peer,   190
Stood, wan, and pale, and with an awed face,
Among his brothers of the mountain chace.
In midst of all, the venerable priest
Eyed them with joy from greatest to the least,

And, after lifting up his aged hands,
Thus spake he: 'Men of Latmos! shepherd
bands!
Whose care it is to guard a thousand flocks:
Whether descended from beneath the rocks
That overtop your mountains; whether come
From vallies where the pipe is never dumb;   200
Or from your swelling downs, where sweet air
stirs
Blue hare-bells lightly, and where prickly furze
Buds lavish gold; or ye, whose precious charge
Nibble their fill at ocean's very marge,
Whose mellow reeds are touch'd with sounds for-
lorn
By the dim echoes of old Triton's horn:
Mothers and wives! who day by day prepare
The scrip,[5] with needments, for the mountain air;
And all ye gentle girls who foster up
Udderless lambs, and in a little cup   210
Will put choice honey for a favoured youth:
Yea, every one attend! for in good truth
Our vows are wanting to our great god Pan.
Are not our lowing heifers sleeker than
Night-swollen mushrooms? Are not our wide
plains
Speckled with countless fleeces? Have not rains
Green'd over April's lap? No howling sad
Sickens our fearful·ewes; and we have had
Great bounty from Endymion our lord.
The earth is glad: the merry lark has pour'd   220
His early song against yon breezy sky,
That spreads so clear o'er our solemnity.'

Thus ending, on the shrine he heap'd a spire
Of teeming sweets, enkindling sacred fire;
Anon he stain'd the thick and spongy sod
With wine, in honour of the shepherd-god.
Now while the earth was drinking it, and while
Bay leaves were crackling in the fragrant pile,
And gummy frankincense was sparkling bright
'Neath smothering parsley, and a hazy light   230
Spread greyly eastward, thus a chorus sang:

'O THOU,[6] whose mighty palace roof doth hang
From jagged trunks, and overshadoweth
Eternal whispers, glooms, the birth, life, death
Of unseen flowers in heavy peacefulness;
Who lov'st to see the hamadryads[7] dress
Their ruffled locks where meeting hazels darken;
And through whole solemn hours dost sit, and
hearken
The dreary melody of bedded reeds—

---

3 Leda, the mother of Helen of Troy, was wooed by Zeus in the form of a swan.
4 the beautiful Trojan youth who was carried to Olympus and made cupbearer to the gods.

---

5 knapsack.
6 Pan.
7 tree nymphs.

In desolate places, where dank moisture
   breeds   240
The pipy hemlock to strange overgrowth;
Bethinking thee, how melancholy loth
Thou wast to lose fair Syrinx[8]—do thou now,
By thy love's milky brow!
By all the trembling mazes that she ran,
Hear us, great Pan!

  'O thou, for whose soul-soothing quiet, turtles[9]
Passion their voices cooingly 'mong myrtles,
What time thou wanderest at eventide
Through sunny meadows, that outskirt the
   side   250
Of thine enmossed realms: O thou, to whom
Broad leaved fig trees even now foredoom
Their ripen'd fruitage; yellow girted bees
Their golden honeycombs; our village leas
Their fairest blossom'd beans and poppied
   corn;[10]
The chuckling linnet its five young unborn,
To sing for thee; low creeping strawberries
Their summer coolness; pent up butterflies
Their freckled wings; yea, the fresh budding year
All its completions—be quickly near,   260
By every wind that nods the mountain pine,
O forester divine!

  'Thou, to whom every faun and satyr flies
For willing service; whether to surprise
The squatted hare while in half sleeping fit;
Or upward ragged precipices flit
To save poor lambkins from the eagle's maw;
Or by mysterious enticement draw
Bewildered shepherds to their path again;
Or to tread breathless round the frothy main,   270
And gather up all fancifullest shells
For thee to tumble into Naiads'[11] cells,
And, being hidden, laugh at their out-peeping;
Or to delight thee with fantastic leaping,
The while they pelt each other on the crown
With silvery oak apples, and fir cones brown—
By all the echoes that about thee ring,
Hear us, O satyr king!

  'O Hearkener to the loud clapping shears
While ever and anon to his shorn peers   280
A ram goes bleating: Winder of the horn,
When snouted wild-boars routing tender corn
Anger our huntsmen: Breather round our farms,
To keep off mildews, and all weather harms:
Strange ministrant of undescribed sounds,

That comes a swooning over hollow grounds,
And wither drearily on barren moors:
Dread opener of the mysterious doors
Leading to universal knowledge—see,
Great son of Dryope,[12]   290
The many that are come to pay their vows
With leaves about their brows!

  'Be still the unimaginable lodge
For solitary thinkings; such as dodge
Conception to the very bourne of heaven,
Then leave the naked brain: be still the leaven,
That spreading in this dull and clodded earth
Gives it a touch ethereal—a new birth:
Be still a symbol of immensity;
A firmament reflected in a sea;   300
An element filling the space between;
An unknown—but no more: we humbly screen
With uplift hands our foreheads, lowly bending,
And giving out a shout most heaven rending,
Conjure thee to receive our humble Pæan,
Upon thy Mount Lycean!'

  Even while they brought the burden to a close,
A shout from the whole multitude arose,
That lingered in the air like dying rolls
Of abrupt thunder, when Ionian shoals   310
Of dolphins bob their noses through the brine.
Meantime, on shady levels, mossy fine,
Young companies nimbly began dancing
To the swift treble pipe, and humming string.
Aye, those fair living forms swam heavenly
To tunes forgotten—out of memory:
Fair creatures! whose young children's children
   bred
Thermopylæ[13] its heroes—not yet dead,
But in old marbles ever beautiful.
High genitors,[14] unconscious did they cull   320
Time's sweet first-fruits—they danc'd to weari-
   ness,
And then in quiet circles did they press
The hillock turf, and caught the latter end
Of some strange history, potent to send
A young mind from its bodily tenement.
Or they might watch the quoit-pitchers, intent
On either side; pitying the sad death
Of Hyacinthus, when the cruel breath
Of Zephyr slew him,[15] Zephyr penitent,

---

8 an Arcadian nymph who fled from the wooing of Pan and was
changed by the water nymphs into a reed.
9 turtle doves.
10 wheat overgrown with poppies.
11 water nymph.

12 a shepherdess, friend of the Hamadryads, who was changed
by them into a poplar.
13 the famous pass where a small band of Greeks under Leonidas
of Sparta fought off an overwhelming host of Persians, 480 B.C.
14 parents.
15 In the earliest forms of the legend, the lovely youth Hyacinth
was accidentally slain by Apollo. Keats follows later versions in
which Zephyr, jealous of Apollo's love for Hyacinth, kills the
youth.

Who now, ere Phœbus mounts the firma-
    ment,   330
Fondles the flower amid the sobbing rain.
The archers too, upon a wider plain,
Beside the feathery whizzing of the shaft,
And the dull twanging bowstring, and the raft[16]
Branch down sweeping from a tall ash top,
Call'd up a thousand thoughts to envelope
Those who would watch. Perhaps, the trembling
    knee
And frantic gape of lonely Niobe,[17]
Poor, lonely Niobe! when her lovely young
Were dead and gone, and her caressing
    tongue   340
Lay a lost thing upon her paly lip,
And very, very deadliness did nip
Her motherly cheeks. Arous'd from this sad
    mood
By one, who at a distance loud halloo'd,
Uplifting his strong bow into the air,
Many might after brighter visions stare:
After the Argonauts,[18] in blind amaze
Tossing about on Neptune's restless ways,
Until, from the horizon's vaulted side,
There shot a golden splendour far and wide,   350
Spangling those million poutings of the brine
With quivering ore: 'twas even an awful shine
From the exaltation of Apollo's bow;
A heavenly beacon in their dreary woe.
Who thus were ripe for high contemplating,
Might turn their steps towards the sober ring
Where sat Endymion and the aged priest
'Mong shepherds gone in eld, whose looks in-
    creas'd
The silvery setting of their mortal star.
There they discours'd upon the fragile bar   360
That keeps us from our homes ethereal;
And what our duties there: to nightly call
Vesper, the beauty-crest of summer weather;
To summon all the downiest clouds together
For the sun's purple couch; to emulate
In ministring the potent rule of fate
With speed of fire-tail'd exhalations;[19]
To tint her pallid cheek with bloom, who cons
Sweet poesy by moonlight: besides these,
A world of other unguess'd offices.   370
Anon they wander'd, by divine converse,
Into Elysium; vieing to rehearse
Each one his own anticipated bliss.

---

16 cleft; split.
17 Niobe, the proud mother of six daughters and six sons,
boasted of her superiority to Latona, the mother of only two
children. As a punishment the gods slew all Niobe's children.
18 the band of heroes who sailed with Jason in the ship Argo to
capture the Golden Fleece.
19 meteors.

One felt heart-certain that he could not miss
His quick gone love, among fair blossom'd
    boughs,
Where every zephyr-sigh pouts, and endows
Her lips with music for the welcoming.
Another wish'd, mid that eternal spring,
To meet his rosy child, with feathery sails,
Sweeping, eye-earnestly, through almond
    vales: 380
Who, suddenly, should stoop through the smooth
    wind,
And with the balmiest leaves his temples bind;
And, ever after, through those regions be
His messenger, his little Mercury.
Some were athirst in soul to see again
Their fellow huntsmen o'er the wide champaign
In times long past; to sit with them, and talk
Of all the chances in their earthly walk;
Comparing, joyfully, their plenteous stores
Of happiness, to when upon the moors,   390
Benighted, close they huddled from the cold,
And shar'd their famish'd scrips. Thus all out-
    told
Their fond imaginations,—saving him
Whose eyelids curtain'd up their jewels dim,
Endymion: yet hourly had he striven
To hide the cankering venom, that had riven
His fainting recollections. Now indeed
His senses had swoon'd off: he did not heed
The sudden silence, or the whispers low,
Or the old eyes dissolving at his woe,   400
Or anxious calls, or close of trembling palms,
Or maiden's sigh, that grief itself embalms:
But in the self-same fixed trance he kept.
Like one who on the earth had never stept.
Aye, even as dead still as a marble man,
Frozen in that old tale Arabian.[20]

Who whispers him so pantingly and close?
Peona, his sweet sister: of all those,
His friends, the dearest. Hushing signs she made,
And breath'd a sister's sorrow to persuade   410
A yielding up, a cradling on her care.
Her eloquence did breathe away the curse:
She led him, like some midnight spirit nurse
Of happy changes in emphatic dreams,
Along a path between two little streams,—
Guarding his forehead, with her round elbow,
From low-grown branches, and his footsteps slow
From stumbling over stumps and hillocks small;
Until they came to where these streamlets fall,
With mingled bubblings and a gentle rush,   420
Into a river, clear, brimful, and flush

---

20 The story is told in 'The Porter and the Three Ladies of Bagdad,' in *The Arabian Nights' Entertainments*.

With crystal mocking of the trees and sky.
A little shallop, floating there hard by,
Pointed its beak over the fringed bank;
And soon it lightly dipt, and rose, and sank,
And dipt again, with the young couple's
    weight,—
Peona guiding, through the water straight,
Towards a bowery island opposite:
Which gaining presently, she steered light
Into a shady, fresh, and ripply cove,   430
Where nested was an arbour, overwove
By many a summer's silent fingering;
To whose cool bosom she was used to bring
Her playmates, with their needle broidery,
And minstrel memories of times gone by.

So she was gently glad to see him laid
Under her favourite bower's quiet shade,
On her own couch, new made of flower leaves,
Dried carefully on the cooler side of sheaves
When last the sun his autumn tresses shook,   440
And the tann'd harvesters rich armfuls took.
Soon was he quieted to slumbrous rest:
But, ere it crept upon him, he had prest
Peona's busy hand against his lips,
And still, a sleeping, held her finger-tips
In tender pressure. And as a willow keeps
A patient watch over the stream that creeps
Windingly by it, so the quiet maid
Held her in peace: so that a whispering blade
Of grass, a wailful gnat, a bee bustling   450
Down in the blue-bells, or a wren light rustling
Among sere leaves and twigs, might all be heard.

O magic sleep! O comfortable bird,
That broodest o'er the troubled sea of the mind
Till it is hush'd and smooth! O unconfin'd
Restraint! imprisoned liberty! great key
To golden palaces, strange minstrelsy,
Fountains grotesque, new trees, bespangled
    caves,
Echoing grottos, full of tumbling waves
And moonlight; aye, to all the mazy world 460
Of silvery enchantment!—who, upfurl'd
Beneath thy drowsy wing a triple hour,
But renovates and lives?—Thus, in the bower,
Endymion was calm'd to life again.
Opening his eyelids with a healthier brain,
He said: 'I feel this thine endearing love
All through my bosom: thou art as a dove
Trembling its closed eyes and sleeked wings
About me; and the pearliest dew not brings
Such morning incense from the fields of
    May,   470
As do those brighter drops that twinkling stray

From those kind eyes,—the very home and haunt
Of sisterly affection. Can I want
Aught else, aught nearer heaven, than such tears?
Yet dry them up, in bidding hence all fears
That, any longer, I will pass my days
Alone and sad. No, I will once more raise
My voice upon the mountain-heights; once more
Make my horn parley from their foreheads hoar:
Again my trooping hounds their tongues shall
    loll   480
Around the breathed boar: again I'll poll[21]
The fair-grown yew tree, for a chosen bow:
And, when the pleasant sun is getting low,
Again I'll linger in a sloping mead
To hear the speckled thrushes, and see feed
Our idle sheep. So be thou cheered sweet,
And, if thy lute is here, softly intreat
My soul to keep in its resolved course.'

Hear at Peona, in their silver source,
Shut her pure sorrow drops with glad
    exclaim,   490
And took a lute, from which there pulsing came
A lively prelude, fashioning the way
In which her voice should wander. 'Twas a lay
More subtle cadenced, more forest wild
Than Dryope's lone lulling of her child;
And nothing since has floated in the air
So mournful strange. Surely some influence rare
Went, spiritual, through the damsel's hand;
For still, with Delphic emphasis,[22] she spann'd
The quick invisible strings, even though she
    saw   500
Endymion's spirit melt away and thaw
Before the deep intoxication.
But soon she came, with sudden burst, upon
Her self-possession—swung the lute aside,
And earnestly said: 'Brother, 'tis vain to hide
That thou dost know of things mysterious,
Immortal, starry; such alone could thus
Weigh down thy nature. Hast thou sinn'd in
    aught
Offensive to the heavenly powers? Caught
A Paphian dove[23] upon a message sent?   510
Thy deathful bow against some deer-herd bent
Sacred to Dian? Haply, thou hast seen
Her naked limbs among the alders green;
And that, alas! is death. No, I can trace
Something more high perplexing in thy face!'

Endymion look'd at her, and press'd her hand,
And said, 'Art thou so pale, who wast so bland

21 cut off the top.
22 inspired, like the utterances of the Delphic oracle.
23 one sent by Venus from her temple at Paphos in Cyprus.

And merry in our meadows? How is this?
Tell me thine ailment: tell me all amiss!—
Ah! thou hast been unhappy at the change 520
Wrought suddenly in me. What indeed more
    strange?
Or more complete to overwhelm surmise?
Ambition is so sluggard: 'tis no prize,
That toiling years would put within my grasp,
That I have sighed for: with so deadly gasp
No man e'er panted for a mortal love.
So all have set my heavier grief above
These things which happen. Rightly have they
    done:
I, who still saw the horizontal sun
Heave his broad shoulder o'er the edge of the
    world, 530
Out-facing Lucifer,[24] and then had hurl'd
My spear aloft, as signal for the chace—
I, who, for very sport of heart, would race
With my own steed from Araby; pluck down
A vulture from his towery perching; frown
A lion into growling, loth retire—
To lose, at once, all my toil-breeding fire,
And sink thus low! but I will ease my breast
Of secret grief, here in this bowery nest.

'This river does not see the naked sky, 540
Till it begins to progress silverly
Around the western border of the wood,
Whence, from a certain spot, its winding flood
Seems at the distance like a crescent moon:
And in that nook, the very pride of June,
Had I been used to pass my weary eves;
The rather for the sun unwilling leaves
So dear a picture of his sovereign power,
And I could witness his most kingly hour,
When he doth tighten up the golden reins, 550
And paces leisurely down amber plains
His snorting four. Now when his chariot last
Its beams against the zodiac-lion[25] cast,
There blossom'd suddenly a magic bed
Of sacred ditamy,[26] and poppies red:
At which I wondered greatly, knowing well
That but one night had wrought this flowery
    spell;
And, sitting down close by, began to muse
What it might mean. Perhaps, thought I,
    Morpheus,
In passing here, his owlet pinions shook; 560
Or, it may be, ere matron Night uptook
Her ebon urn, young Mercury, by stealth,
Had dipt his rod in it: such garland wealth

24 the morning star.
25 The sun passes through the zodiac sign of the lion in midsummer.
26 dittany, an aromatic herb.

Came not by common growth. Thus on I
    thought,
Until my head was dizzy and distraught.
Moreover, through the dancing poppies stole
A breeze, most softly lulling to my soul;
And shaping visions all about my sight
Of colours, wings, and bursts of spangly light;
The which became more strange, and strange,
    and dim, 570
And then were gulph'd in a tumultuous swim:
And then I fell asleep. Ah, can I tell
The enchantment that afterwards befel?
Yet it was but a dream: yet such a dream
That never tongue, although it overteem
With mellow utterance, like a cavern spring,
Could figure out and to conception bring
All I beheld and felt. Methought I lay
Watching the zenith, where the milky way
Among the stars in virgin splendour pours; 580
And travelling my eye, until the doors
Of heaven appear'd to open for my flight,
I became loth and fearful to alight
From such high soaring by a downward glance:
So kept me stedfast in that airy trance,
Spreading imaginary pinions wide.
When, presently, the stars began to glide,
And faint away, before my eager view:
At which I sigh'd that I could not pursue,
And dropt my vision to the horizon's verge; 590
And lo! from opening clouds, I saw emerge
The loveliest moon, that ever silver'd o'er
A shell for Neptune's goblet: she did soar
So passionately bright, my dazzled soul
Commingling with her argent spheres did roll
Through clear and cloudy, even when she went
At last into a dark and vapoury tent—
Whereat, methought, the lidless-eyed train
Of planets all were in the blue again.
To commune with those orbs, once more I
    rais'd 600
My sight right upward: but it was quite dazed
By a bright something, sailing down apace,
Making me quickly veil my eyes and face:
Again I look'd, and, O ye deities,
Who from Olympus watch our destinies!
Whence that completed form of all complete-
    ness?
Whence came that high perfection of all sweet-
    ness?
Speak, stubborn earth, and tell me where, O
    where
Hast thou a symbol of her golden hair?
Not oat-sheaves drooping in the western
    sun; 610

Not—thy soft hand, fair sister! let me shun
Such follying before thee—yet she had,
Indeed, locks bright enough to make me mad;
And they were simply gordian'd[27] up and braided,
Leaving, in naked comeliness, unshaded,
Her pearl round ears, white neck, and orbed
     brow;
The which were blended in, I know not how,
With such a paradise of lips and eyes,
Blush-tinted cheeks, half smiles, and faintest
     sighs,
That, when I think thereon, my spirit clings   620
And plays about its fancy, till the stings
Of human neighbourhood envenom all.
Unto what awful power shall I call?
To what high fane?[28]—Ah! see her hovering feet,
More bluely vein'd, more soft, more whitely
     sweet
Than those of sea-born Venus, when she rose
From out her cradle shell. The wind out-blows
Her scarf into a fluttering pavillion;
'Tis blue, and over-spangled with a million
Of little eyes, as though thou wert to shed,   630
Over the darkest, lushest blue-bell bed,
Handfuls of daisies.'—'Endymion, how strange!
Dream within dream!'—'She took an airy range,
And then, towards me, like a very maid,
Came blushing, waning, willing, and afraid,
And press'd me by the hand: Ah! 'twas too much;
Methought I fainted at the charmed touch,
Yet held my recollection, even as one
Who dives three fathoms where the waters run
Gurgling in beds of coral: for anon,   640
I felt upmounted in that region
Where falling stars dart their artillery forth,
And eagles struggle with the buffeting north
That balances the heavy meteor-stone;[29]—
Felt too, I was not fearful, nor alone,
But lapp'd and lull'd along the dangerous sky.
Soon, as it seem'd, we left our journeying high,
And straightway into frightful eddies swoop'd;
Such as aye muster where grey time has scoop'd
Huge dens and caverns in a mountain's side: 650
There hollow sounds arous'd me, and I sigh'd
To faint once more by looking on my bliss—
I was distracted; madly did I kiss
The wooing arms which held me, and did give
My eyes at once to death: but 'twas to live,
To take in draughts of life from the gold fount
Of kind and passionate looks; to count, and
     count

The moments, by some greedy help that seem'd
A second self, that each might be redeem'd
And plunder'd of its load of blessedness.   660
Ah, desperate mortal! I e'en dar'd to press
Her very cheek against my crowned lip,
And, at that moment, felt my body dip
Into a warmer air: a moment more,
Our feet were soft in flowers. There was store
Of newest joys upon that alp. Sometimes
A scent of violets, and blossoming limes,
Loiter'd around us; then of honey cells,
Made delicate from all white-flower bells;
And once, above the edges of our nest,   670
An arch face peep'd,—an Oread[30] as I guess'd.

'Why did I dream that sleep o'er-power'd me
In midst of all this heaven? Why not see,
Far off, the shadows of his pinions dark,
And stare them from me? But no, like a spark
That needs must die, although its little beam
Reflects upon a diamond, my sweet dream
Fell into nothing—into stupid sleep.
And so it was, until a gentle creep,
A careful moving caught my waking ears,   680
And up I started: Ah! my sighs, my tears,
My clenched hands;—for lo! the poppies hung
Dew-dabbled on their stalks, the ouzel[31] sung
A heavy ditty, and the sullen day
Had chidden herald Hesperus away,
With leaden looks: the solitary breeze
Bluster'd, and slept, and its wild self did teaze
With wayward melancholy; and I thought,
Mark me, Peona! that sometimes it brought
Faint fare-thee-wells, and sigh-shrilled
     adieus!—   690
Away I wander'd—all the pleasant hues
Of heaven and earth had faded: deepest shades
Were deepest dungeons; heaths and sunny glades
Were full of pestilent light; our taintless rills
Seem'd sooty, and o'er-spread with upturn's gills
Of dying fish; the vermeil rose had blown
In frightful scarlet, and its thorns out-grown
Like spiked aloe. If an innocent bird
Before my heedless footsteps stirr'd, and stirr'd
In little journeys, I beheld in it   700
A disguis'd demon, missioned to knit
My soul with under darkness; to entice
My stumblings down some monstrous precipice:
Therefore I eager followed, and did curse
The disappointment. Time, that aged nurse,
Rock'd me to patience. Now, thank gentle heaven!
These things, with all their comfortings, are given

---

27 knotted.   28 sacred place.
29 The north wind, it was supposed, could hold back a falling
meteorite.
30 woodland or mountain nymph.
31 blackbird.

To my down-sunken hours, and with thee,
Sweet sister, help to stem the ebbing sea
Of weary life.'
          Thus ended he, and both   710
Sat silent: for the maid was very loth
To answer; feeling well that breathed words
Would all be lost, unheard, and vain as swords
Against the enchased[32] crocodile, or leaps
Of grasshoppers against the sun. She weeps,
And wonders; struggles to devise some blame;
To put on such a look as would say, *Shame
On this poor weakness!* but, for all her strife,
She could as soon have crush'd away the life
From a sick dove. At length, to break the
    pause,   720
She said with trembling chance: 'Is this the
    cause?
This all? Yet it is strange, and sad, alas!
That one who through this middle earth should
    pass
Most like a sojourning demi-god, and leave
His name upon the harp-string, should achieve
No higher bard than simple maidenhood,
Singing alone, and fearfully,—how the blood
Left his young cheek; and how he used to stray
He knew not where; and how he would say, *nay,*
If any said 'twas love: and yet 'twas love;   730
What could it be but love? How a ring-dove
Let fall a sprig of yew tree in his path;
And how he died: and then, that love doth
    scathe,
The gentle heart, as northern blasts do roses;
And then the ballad of his sad life closes
With sighs, and an alas!—Endymion!
Be rather in the trumpet's mouth,—anon
Among the winds at large—that all may hearken!
Although, before the crystal heavens darken,
I watch and dote upon the silver lakes   740
Pictur'd in western cloudiness, that takes
The semblance of gold rocks and bright gold
    sands,
Islands, and creeks, and amber-fretted strands
With horses prancing o'er them, palaces
And towers of amethyst,—would I so teaze
My pleasant days, because I could not mount
Into those regions? The Morphean fount
Of that fine element that visions, dreams,
And fitful whims of sleep are made of, streams
Into its airy channels with so subtle,   750
So thin a breathing, not the spider's shuttle,
Circled a million times within the space
Of a swallow's nest-door, could delay a trace,

A tinting of its quality: how light
Must dreams themselves be; seeing they're more
    slight
Than the mere nothing that engenders them!
Then wherefore sully the entrusted gem
Of high and noble life with thoughts so sick?
Why pierce high-fronted honour to the quick
For nothing but a dream?' Hereat the youth   760
Look'd up: a conflicting of shame and ruth
Was in his plaited brow: yet, his eyelids
Widened a little, as when Zephyr bids
A little breeze to creep between the fans
Of careless butterflies: amid his pains
He seem'd to taste a drop of manna-dew,
Full palatable; and a colour grew
Upon his cheek, while thus he lifeful spake.

'Peona! ever have I long'd to slake
My thirst for the world's praises: nothing
    base,   770
No merely slumberous phantasm, could unlace
The stubborn canvas for my voyage prepar'd—
Though now 'tis tatter'd; leaving my bark bar'd
And sullenly drifting: yet my higher hope
Is of too wide, too rainbow-large a scope,
To fret at myriads of earthly wrecks.
Wherein lies happiness?[33] In that which becks
Our ready minds to fellowship divine,
A fellowship with essence; till we shine,
Full alchemiz'd, and free of space. Behold   780
The clear religion of heaven! Fold
A rose leaf round thy finger's taperness,
And soothe thy lips: hist, when the airy stress
Of music's kiss impregnates the free winds,
And with a sympathetic touch unbinds
Æolian magic from their lucid wombs:
Then old songs waken from enclouded tombs;
Old ditties sigh above their father's grave;
Ghosts of melodious prophecyings rave
Round every spot where trod Apollo's foot;   790
Bronze clarions awake, and faintly bruit,
Where long ago a giant battle was;
And, from the turf, a lullaby doth pass
In every place where infant Orpheus slept.
Feel we these things?—that moment have we
    stept

---

32 encased; armored.

33 While *Endymion* was still in press, Keats wrote to John Taylor, his publisher, in regard to the passage beginning with l. 777: 'The whole thing must, I think, have appeared to you, who are a consecutive man, as a thing almost of mere words, but I assure you that, when I wrote it, it was a regular stepping of the Imagination towards a truth. My having written that argument will perhaps be of the greatest service to me of anything I ever did. It set before me the gradations of happiness, even like a kind of pleasure thermometer, and is my first step towards the chief attempt in the drama. The playing of different natures with joy and Sorrow—'.

Into a sort of oneness, and our state
Is like a floating spirit's. But there are
Richer entanglements, enthralments far
More self-destroying, leading, by degrees,
To the chief intensity: the crown of these   800
Is made of love and friendship, and sits high
Upon the forehead of humanity.
All its more ponderous and bulky worth
Is friendship, whence there ever issues forth
A steady splendour; but at the tip-top,
There hangs by unseen film, an orbed drop
Of light, and that is love: its influence,
Thrown in our eyes, genders a novel sense,
At which we start and fret; till in the end,
Melting into its radiance, we blend,   810
Mingle, and so become a part of it,—
Nor with aught else can our souls interknit
So wingedly: when we combine therewith,
Life's self is nourish'd by its proper pith,
And we are nurtured like a pelican brood.
Aye, so delicious is the unsating food,
That men, who might have tower'd in the van
Of all the congregated world, to fan
And winnow from the coming step of time
All chaff of custom, wipe away all slime   820
Left by men-slugs and human serpentry,
Have been content to let occasion die,
Whilst they did sleep in love's elysium.
And, truly, I would rather be struck dumb,
Than speak against this ardent listlessness:
For I have ever thought that it might bless
The world with benefits unknowingly;
As does the nightingale, upperched high,
And cloister'd among cool and bunched leaves—
She sings but to her love, nor e'er conceives   830
How tiptoe Night holds back her dark-grey hood.
Just so may love, although 'tis understood
The mere commingling of passionate breath,
Produce more than our searching witnesseth:
What I know not: but who, of men, can tell
That flowers would bloom, or that green fruit
      would swell
To melting pulp, that fish would have bright
      mail,
The earth its dower of river, wood, and vale,
The meadows runnels, runnels pebble-stones,
The seed its harvest, or the lute its tones,   840
Tones ravishment, or ravishment its sweet
If human souls did never kiss and greet?

'Now, if this earthly love has power to make
Men's being mortal, immortal; to shake
Ambition from their memories, and brim
Their measure of content: what merest whim,

Seems all this poor endeavour after fame,
To one, who keeps within his stedfast aim
A love immortal, an immortal too.
Look not so wilder'd; for these things are
      true,   850
And never can be born of atomies
That buzz about our slumbers, like brain-flies,
Leaving us fancy-sick. No, no, I'm sure,
My restless spirit never could endure
To brood so long upon one luxury,
Unless it did, though fearfully, espy
A hope beyond the shadow of a dream.
My sayings will the less obscured seem,
When I have told thee how my waking sight
Has made me scruple whether that same
      night   860
Was pass'd in dreaming. Hearken, sweet Peona!
Beyond the matron-temple of Latona,
Which we should see but for these darkening
      boughs,
Lies a deep hollow, from whose ragged brows
Bushes and trees do lean all round athwart
And meet so nearly, that with wings outraught,
And spreaded tail, a vulture could not glide
Past them, but he must brush on every side.
Some moulder'd steps lead into this cool cell,
Far as the slabbed margin of a well,   870
Whose patient level peeps its crystal eye
Right upward, through the bushes, to the sky.
Oft have I brought thee flowers, on their stalks
      set
Like vestal primroses, but dark velvet
Edges them round, and they have golden pits:
'Twas there I got them, from the gaps and slits
In a mossy stone, that sometimes was my seat,
When all above was faint with mid-day heat.
And there in strife no burning thoughts to heed,
I'd bubble up the water through a reed;   880
So reaching back to boy-hood: make me ships
Of moulted feathers, touchwood,[34] alder chips,
With leaves stuck in them; and the Neptune be
Of their petty ocean. Oftener, heavily,
When love-lorn hours had left me less a child,
I sat contemplating the figures wild
Of o'er-head clouds melting the mirror through.
Upon a day, while thus I watch'd, by flew
A cloudy Cupid, with his bow and quiver;
So plainly character'd, no breeze would
      shiver   890
The happy chance: so happy, I was fain
To follow it upon the open plain,
And, therefore, was just going; when, behold!
A wonder, fair as any I have told—

---

34 punky wood used for tinder.

The same bright face I tasted in my sleep,
Smiling in the clear well. My heart did leap
Through the cool depth.—It moved as if to flee—
I started up, when lo! refreshfully,
There came upon my face in plenteous showers
Dew-drops, and dewy buds, and leaves, and
    flowers,   900
Wrapping all objects from my smothered sight,
Bathing my spirit in a new delight.
Aye, such a breathless honey-feel of bliss
Alone preserved me from the drear abyss
Of death, for the fair form had gone again.
Pleasure is oft a visitant; but pain
Clings cruelly to us, like the gnawing sloth
On the deer's tender haunches: late, and loth,
'Tis scar'd away by slow returning pleasure.
How sickening, how dark the dreadful leisure 910
Of weary days, made deeper exquisite,
By a fore-knowledge of unslumbrous night!
Like sorrow came upon me, heavier still,
Than when I wander'd from the poppy hill:
And a whole age of lingering moments crept
Sluggishly by, ere more contentment swept
Away at once the deadly yellow spleen.
Yes, thrice have I this fair enchantment seen;
Once more been tortured with renewed life.
When last the wintry gusts gave over strife   920
With the conquering sun of spring, and left the
    skies
Warm and serene, but yet with moistened eyes
In pity of the shatter'd infant buds,—
That time thou didst adorn, with amber studs,
My hunting cap, because I laugh'd and smil'd,
Chatted with thee, and many days exil'd
All torment from my breast;—'twas even then,
Straying about, yet, coop'd up in the den
Of helpless discontent,—hurling my lance
From place to place, and following at chance, 930
At last, by hap, through some young trees it
    struck,
And, plashing among bedded pebbles, stuck
In the middle of a brook,—whose silver ramble
Down twenty little falls, through reeds and bram-
    ble,
Tracing along, it brought me to a cave,
Whence it ran brightly forth, and white did lave
The nether sides of mossy stones and rock,—
'Mong which it gurgled blythe adieus, to mock
Its own sweet grief at parting. Overhead,
Hung a lush screen of drooping weeds, and
    spread   940
Thick, as to curtain up some wood-nymph's
    home.

"Ah! impious mortal, whither do I roam?"
Said I, low voic'd: "Ah, whither! 'Tis the grot
Of Proserpine, when Hell, obscure and hot,
Doth her resign; and where her tender hands
She dabbles, on the cool and sluicy sands:
Or 'tis the cell of Echo, where she sits,
And babbles thorough silence, till her wits
Are gone in tender madness, and anon,
Faints into sleep, with many a dying tone   950
Of sadness. O that she would take my vows,
And breathe them sighingly among the boughs,
To sue her gentle ears for whose fair head,
Daily, I pluck sweet flowerets from their bed,
And weave them dyingly—send honey-whispers
Round every leaf, that all those gentle lispers
May sigh my love unto her pitying!
O charitable Echo! hear, and sing
This ditty to her!—tell her"—so I stay'd
My foolish tongue, and listening, half afraid, 960
Stood stupefied with my own empty folly,
And blushing for the freaks of melancholy.
Salt tears were coming, when I heard my name
Most fondly lipp'd, and then these accents came:
"Endymion! the cave is secreter
Than the isle of Delos. Echo hence shall stir
No sighs but sigh-warm kisses, or light noise
Of thy combing hand, the while it travelling cloys
And trembles through my labyrinthine hair."
At that oppress'd I hurried in.—Ah! where   970
Are those swift moments? Whither are they
    fled?
I'll smile no more, Peona; nor will wed
Sorrow the way to death; but patiently
Bear up against it: so farewell, sad sigh;
And come instead demurest meditation,
To occupy me wholly, and to fashion
My pilgrimage for the world's dusky brink.
No more will I count over, link by link,
My chain of grief: no longer strive to find
A half-forgetfulness in mountain wind   980
Blustering about my ears: aye, thou shalt see,
Dearest of sisters, what my life shall be;
What a calm round of hours shall make my days.
There is a paly flame of hope that plays
Where'er I look: but yet, I'll say 'tis naught—
And here I bid it die. Have not I caught,
Already, a more healthy countenance?
By this the sun is setting; we may chance
Meet some of our near-dwellers with my car.'

    This said, he rose, faint-smiling like a star 990
Through autumn mists, and took Peona's hand:
They stept into the boat, and launch'd from land.

From BOOK II

Lines 1–43, 885–1023

O SOVEREIGN power of love! O grief! O balm!
All records, saving thine, come cool, and calm,
And shadowy, through the mist of passed years:
For others, good or bad, hatred and tears
Have become indolent; but touching thine,
One sigh doth echo, one poor sob doth pine,
One kiss brings honey-dew from buried days.
The woes of Troy, towers smothering o'er their
     blaze,
Stiff-holden shields, far-piercing spears, keen
     blades,
Struggling, and blood, and shrieks—all dimly
     fades   10
Into some backward corner of the brain;
Yet, in our very souls, we feel amain
The close[35] of Troilus and Cressid sweet.
Hence, pageant history! hence, gilded cheat!
Swart[36] planet in the universe of deeds!
Wide sea, that one continuous murmur breeds
Along the pebbled shore of memory!
Many old rotten-timber'd boats there be
Upon thy vaporous bosom, magnified
To goodly vessels; many a sail of pride,   20
And golden keel'd, is left unlaunch'd and dry.
But wherefore this? What care, though owl did
     fly
About the great Athenian admiral's mast?[37]
What care, though striding Alexander past
The Indus with his Macedonian numbers?
Though old Ulysses tortured from his slumbers
The glutted Cyclops, what care?—Juliet[38] leaning
Amid her window-flowers,—sighing,—weaning
Tenderly her fancy from its maiden snow,
Doth more avail than these: the silver flow   30
Of Hero's[39] tears, the swoon of Imogen,[40]
Fair Pastorella[41] in the bandit's den,
Are things to brood on with more ardency
Than the death-day of empires. Fearfully
Must such conviction come upon his head,
Who, thus far, discontent, has dared to tread,
Without one muse's smile, or kind behest,
The path of love and poesy. But rest,
In chaffing restlessness, is yet more drear

Than to be crush'd, in striving to uprear   40
Love's standard on the battlements of song.
So once more days and nights aid me along,
Like legion'd soldiers.

[After celebrating the sovereign power of love, Endymion wanders brain-sick and woeful through the
woods. His spirit is aroused by watching a butterfly that
leads him to a fountain and there disappears. But from
the bubbling waters a nymph uprises and reassures him
that he will be assisted in his quest for the mysterious
love of his dreams. From a cavern a voice calls upon him
to descend the hollows of the earth and learn its mysteries. Deep in an abysm under ground he comes upon a
lighted, magic chamber where cupids are watching over
Adonis in his winter sleep. Venus soon arrives in her
dove-drawn silver car and awakens and comforts Adonis.
She tells Endymion that one day his love will be fulfilled.
In improved spirits Endymion resumes his journey on
the back of a great eagle that bears him downward into
the gloom and lands him in a jasmine bower. Here his
mysterious love again appears to him in a dream, but
this time she becomes a reality, responds to his passion,
and vows undying love. Awakening and finding himself
once more alone, Endymion wanders on in a languid
mood until he comes to a watery grotto. The episode of
Alpheus and Arethusa, which follows, concludes Book
II.]

                    In this cool wonder
Endymion sat down, and 'gan to ponder
On all his life: his youth, up to the day
When 'mid acclaim, and feasts, and garlands gay,
He stept upon his shepherd throne: the look
Of his white palace in wild forest nook,   890
And all the revels he had lorded there:
Each tender maiden whom he once thought fair,
With every friend and fellow-woodlander—
Pass'd like a dream before him. Then the spur
Of the old bards to mighty deeds: his plans
To nurse the golden age 'mong shepherd clans:
That wondrous night: the great Pan-festival:
His sister's sorrow; and his wanderings all,
Until into the earth's deep maw he rush'd:
Then all its buried magic, till it flush'd   900
High with excessive love. 'And now,' thought he,
'How long must I remain in jeopardy
Of blank amazements that amaze no more?
Now I have tasted her sweet soul to the core[42]
All other depths are shallow: essences,
Once spiritual, are like muddy lees,
Meant but to fertilize my earthly root,
And make my branches lift a golden fruit
Into the bloom of heaven: other light,
Though it be quick and sharp enough to
     blight   910
The Olympian eagle's vision, is dark,
Dark as the parentage of chaos. Hark!

35 embrace.
36 dark.
37 An owl of good omen alighted on the rigging of Themistocles'
ship as he made ready to attack the Persians at the Battle of Salamis, 480 B.C.
38 the heroine of Shakespeare's *Romeo and Juliet*.
39 the Greek priestess, beloved by Leander.
40 the heroine of Shakespeare's *Cymbeline*.
41 in Spenser's *Faerie Queene*, vi, 12.

42 In the preceding episode Endymion has experienced sensual
love.

My silent thoughts are echoing from these shells;
Or they are but the ghosts, the dying swells
Of noises far away?—list!'—Hereupon
He kept an anxious ear. The humming tone
Came louder, and behold, there as he lay,
On either side outgush'd, with misty spray,
A copious spring; and both together dash'd
Swift, mad, fantastic round the rocks, and
    lash'd   920
Among the conchs and shells of the lofty grot,
Leaving a trickling dew. At last they shot
Down from the ceiling's height, pouring a noise
As of some breathless racers whose hopes poize
Upon the last few steps, and with spent force
Along the ground they took a winding course.
Endymion follow'd—for it seem'd that one
Ever pursued, the other strove to shun—
Follow'd their languid mazes, till well nigh
He had left thinking of the mystery,—   930
And was now rapt in tender hoverings
Over the vanish'd bliss. Ah! what is it sings
His dream away? What melodies are these?
They sound as through the whispering of trees,
Not native in such barren vaults. Give ear!

'O Arethusa, peerless nymph!43 why fear
Such tenderness as mine? Great Dian, why,
Why didst thou hear her prayer? O that I
Were rippling round her dainty fairness now,
Circling about her waist, and striving how   940
To entice her to a dive! then stealing in
Between her luscious lips and eyelids thin.
O that her shining hair was in the sun,
And I distilling from it thence to run
In amorous rillets down her shrinking form!
To linger on her lilly shoulders, warm
Between her kissing breasts, and every charm
Touch raptur'd!—See how painfully I flow:
Fair maid, be pitiful to my great woe.
Stay, stay thy weary course, and let me lead, 950
A happy wooer, to the flowery mead
Where all that beauty snar'd me.'—'Cruel god,
Desist! or my offended mistress' nod
Will stagnate all thy fountains:—teaze me not
With syren words—Ah, have I really got
Such power to madden thee? And is it true—
Away, away, or I shall dearly rue
My very thoughts: in mercy then away,
Kindest Alpheus, for should I obey
My own dear will, 'twould be a deadly bane. 960

O, Oread-Queen!44 would that thou hadst a pain
Like this of mine, then would I fearless turn
And be a criminal. Alas, I burn,
I shudder—gentle river, get thee hence.
Alpheus! thou enchanter! every sense
Of mine was once made perfect in these woods.
Fresh breezes, bowery lawns, and innocent
    floods,
Ripe fruits, and lonely couch, contentment gave;
But ever since I heedlessly did lave
In thy deceitful stream, a panting glow   970
Grew strong within me: wherefore serve me so,
And call it love? Alas, 'twas cruelty.
Not once more did I close my happy eye
Amid the thrushes' song. Away! Avaunt!
O 'twas a cruel thing.'—'Now thou dost taunt
So softly, Arethusa, that I think
If thou wast playing on my shady brink,
Thou wouldst bathe once again. Innocent maid!
Stifle thine heart no more; nor be afraid
Of angry powers: there are deities   980
Will shade us with their wings. Those fitful sighs
'Tis almost death to hear: O let me pour
A dewy balm upon them!—fear no more,
Sweet Arethusa! Dian's self must feel
Sometime these very pangs. Dear maiden, steal
Blushing into my soul, and let us fly
These dreary caverns for the open sky.
I will delight thee all my winding course,
From the green sea up to my hidden source
About Arcadian forests; and will show   990
The channels where my coolest waters flow
Through mossy rocks; where, 'mid exuberant
    green,
I roam in pleasant darkness, more unseen
Than Saturn in his exile; where I brim
Round flowery islands, and take thence a skim
Of mealy sweets, which myriads of bees
Buzz from their honey'd wings: and thou shouldst
    please
Thyself to choose the richest, where we might
Be incense-pillow'd every summer night.
Doff all sad fears, thou white deliciousness, 1000
And let us be thus comforted; unless
Thou couldst rejoice to see my hopeless stream
Hurry distracted from Sol's temperate beam,
And pour to death along some hungry sands.'—
'What can I do, Alpheus? Dian stands
Severe before me: persecuting fate!
Unhappy Arethusa! thou wast late
A huntress free in'—At this, sudden fell
Those two sad streams adown a fearful dell.
The Latmian listen'd, but he heard no more, 1010

---

43 Alpheus, a river-god, became enamoured of the nymph Arethusa while she bathed in his stream. She fled and Alpheus pursued her; whereupon, to enable Arethusa to escape him Diana
changed her into a fountain.

---

44 Diana. The oreads were mountain nymphs.

Save echo, faint repeating o'er and o'er
The name of Arethusa. On the verge
Of that dark gulph he wept, and said: 'I urge
Thee, gentle Goddess of my pilgrimage,
By our eternal hopes, to soothe, to assuage,
If thou art powerful, these lovers' pains;
And make them happy in some happy plains.'

He turn'd—there was a whelming sound—he
    stept,
There was a cooler light; and so he kept
Towards it by a sandy path, and lo!   1020
More suddenly than doth a moment go,
The visions of the earth were gone and fled—
He saw the giant sea above his head.

From BOOK III

[An induction to Book III condemns empty pride of
rank and misused power in high places. Endymion, now
under the sea, in the midst of a fervent address to his
moon goddess (in the lines quoted), sees far off a hoary
old man sitting disconsolate on a rock. The old man approaches Endymion and tells him his story. He is Glaucus, once a fisherman who forsook the life of a mortal
for life under the sea. Here he became enamoured of
the lovely, timid Scylla but she fled from his embraces.
Seeking help from the goddess Circe, he was first enchanted by her, then deserted and condemned to a thousand years of decrepit old age and servitude. Glaucus
learned, however, that if he mastered the arts of magic
and faithfully performed services for all drowned lovers
one day his deliverer would come. Recognizing Endymion as his destined helper, Glaucus instructs him
in a magic rite that breaks the spell. Glaucus regains
his youth, Scylla (who had been struck dead by Circe)
her life, and all the drowned lovers are reanimated. The
released throng move toward the palace of Neptune to
do him honor. The Sea God enters with a train of gods
and goddesses. At the sight of them Endymion collapses
because of his mortality; but the voice of his beloved
Cynthia revives him and he finds himself restored to
his own forest.]

Lines 52–102, 142–84

O MOON! the oldest shades 'mong oldest trees
Feel palpitations when thou lookest in:
O Moon! old boughs lisp forth a holier din
The while they feel thine airy fellowship.
Thou dost bless every where, with silver lip
Kissing dead things to life. The sleeping kine,
Couch'd in thy brightness, dream of fields divine:
Innumerable mountains rise, and rise,
Ambitious for the hallowing of thine eyes;   60
And yet thy benediction passeth not
One obscure hiding-place, one little spot
Where pleasure may be sent: the nested wren
Has thy fair face within its tranquil ken,
And from beneath a sheltering ivy leaf
Takes glimpses of thee; thou art a relief
To the poor patient oyster, where it sleeps

Within its pearly house.—The mighty deeps,
The monstrous sea is thine—the myriad sea!
O Moon! far-spooming[45] Ocean bows to thee, 70
And Tellus feels his forehead's cumbrous load.[46]

Cynthia! where art thou now? What far abode
Of green or silvery bower doth enshrine
Such utmost beauty? Alas, thou dost pine
For one as sorrowful: thy cheek is pale
For one whose cheek is pale: thou dost bewail
His tears, who weeps for thee. Where dost thou
    sigh?
Ah! surely that light peeps from Vesper's eye,
Or what a thing is love! 'Tis She, but lo!
How chang'd, how full of ache, how gone in
    woe!   80
She dies at the thinnest cloud; her loveliness
Is wan on Neptune's blue: yet there's a stress
Of love-spangles, just off yon cape of trees,
Dancing upon the waves, as if to please
The curly foam with amorous influence.
O, not so idle: for down-glancing thence
She fathoms eddies, and runs wild about
O'erwhelming water-courses; scaring out
The thorny sharks from hiding-holes, and fright-
    'ning
Their savage eyes with unaccustom'd light-
    ning.   90
Where will the splendour be content to reach?
O love! how potent hast thou been to teach
Strange journeyings! Wherever beauty dwells,
In gulph or aerie, mountains or deep dells,
In light, in gloom, in star or blazing sun,
Thou pointest out the way, and straight 'tis won.
Amid his toil thou gav'st Leander breath;[47]
Thou leddest Orpheus through the gleams of
    death;[48]
Thou madest Pluto bear thin element;[49]
And now, O winged Chieftain! thou hast sent 100
A moon-beam to the deep, deep water-world,
To find Endymion.

        .   .

'What is there in thee, Moon! that thou
    shouldst move
My heart so potently? When yet a child
I oft have dried my tears when thou hast smil'd.
Thou seem'dst my sister: hand in hand we went
From eve to morn across the firmament.

---

45 far-driving.
46 Tellus, goddess of the earth, feels the weight of Ocean's breakers upon her shores.
47 when each night he swam the Hellespont to visit Hero.
48 when he descended to the underworld to lead Eurydice back
to life.
49 when he came to earth to carry off Proserpine.

No apples would I gather from the tree,
Till thou hadst cool'd their cheeks deliciously:
No tumbling water ever spake romance,
But when my eyes with thine thereon could
    dance: 150
No woods were green enough, no bower divine,
Until thou liftedst up thine eyelids fine:
In sowing time ne'er would I dibble[50] take,
Or drop a seed, till thou wast wide awake;
And, in the summer tide of blossoming,
No one but thee hath heard me blythly sing
And mesh my dewy flowers all the night.
No melody was like a passing spright
If it went not to solemnize thy reign.
Yes, in my boyhood, every joy and pain   160
By thee were fashion'd to the self-same end;
And as I grew in years, still didst thou blend
With all my ardours: thou wast the deep glen;
Thou wast the mountain-top—the sage's pen—
The poet's harp—the voice of friends—the sun;
Thou wast the river—thou wast glory won;
Thou wast my clarion's blast—thou wast my
    steed—
My goblet full of wine—my topmost deed:—
Thou wast the charm of women, lovely Moon!
O what a wild and harmonized tune   170
My spirit struck from all the beautiful!
On some bright essence could I lean, and lull
Myself to immortality: I prest
Nature's soft pillow in a wakeful rest.
But, gentle Orb! there came a nearer bliss—
My strange love came—Felicity's abyss!
She came, and thou didst fade, and fade away—
Yet not entirely; no, thy starry sway
Has been an under-passion to this hour.
Now I begin to feel thine orby power   180
Is coming fresh upon me: O be kind,
Keep back thine influence, and do not blind
My sovereign vision.—Dearest love, forgive
That I can think away from thee and live!'

BOOK IV

MUSE of my native land! loftiest Muse!
O first-born on the mountains! by the hues
Of heaven on the spiritual air begot:
Long didst thou sit alone in northern grot,
While yet our England was a wolfish den;
Before our forests heard the talk of men;
Before the first of Druids was a child;—
Long didst thou sit amid our regions wild
Rapt in a deep prophetic solitude.

There came an eastern voice[51] of solemn
    mood:—   10
Yet wast thou patient. Then sang forth the
    Nine,[52]
Apollo's garland:—yet didst thou divine
Such home-bred glory,[53] that they cry'd in vain,
'Come hither, Sister of the Island!'[54] Plain
Spake fair Ausonia;[55] and once more she spake
A higher summons;[56]—still didst thou betake
Thee to thy native hopes. O thou hast won
A full accomplishment![57] The thing is done,
Which undone, these our latter days had risen
On barren souls. Great Muse, thou know'st what
    prison,   20
Of flesh and bone, curbs, and confines, and frets
Our spirit's wings: despondency besets
Our pillows; and the fresh to-morrow morn
Seems to give forth its light in very scorn
Of our dull, uninspired, snail-paced lives.
Long have I said, how happy he who shrives
To thee! But then I thought on poets gone,
And could not pray:—nor could I now—so on
I move to the end in lowliness of heart.——

'Ah, woe is me! that I should fondly part   30
From my dear native land! Ah, foolish maid!
Glad was the hour, when, with thee, myriads
    bade
Adieu to Ganges and their pleasant fields!
To one so friendless the clear freshet yields
A bitter coolness; the ripe grape is sour:
Yet I would have, great gods! but one short hour
Of native air—let me but die at home.'

Endymion to heaven's airy dome
Was offering up a hecatomb[58] of vows,
When these words reach'd him. Whereupon he
    bows   40
His head through thorny-green entanglement
Of underwood, and to the sound is bent,
Anxious as hind towards her hidden fawn.

'Is no one near to help me? No fair dawn
Of life from charitable voice? No sweet saying
To set my dull and sadden'd spirit playing?
No hand to toy with mine? No lips so sweet
That I may worship them? No eyelids meet
To twinkle on my bosom? No one dies

---

51 the voice of Hebraic literature.
52 the nine muses of Grecian song.
53 presumably a reference to Chaucer.
54 the muse of England.
55 Italy.
56 a reference to the literature of the Italian renaissance.
57 a reference to Elizabethan literature.
58 great number.

---

50 an implement used in planting.

Before me, till from these enslaving eyes   50
Redemption sparkles!—I am sad and lost.'

Thou, Carian lord, hadst better have been
   tost
Into a whirlpool. Vanish into air,
Warm mountaineer! for canst thou only bear
A woman's sigh alone and in distress?
See not her charms! Is Phœbe passionless?
Phœbe is fairer far—O gaze no more:—
Yet if thou wilt behold all beauty's store,
Behold her panting in the forest grass!
Do not those curls of glossy jet surpass   60
For tenderness the arms so idly lain
Amongst them? Feelest not a kindred pain,
To see such lovely eyes in swimming search
After some warm delight, that seems to perch
Dovelike in the dim cell lying beyond
Their upper lids?—Hist!
               'O for Hermes' wand,
To touch this flower into human shape!
That woodland Hyacinthus could escape
From his green prison, and here kneeling
   down
Call me his queen, his second life's fair
   crown!   70
Ah me, how I could love!—My soul doth melt
For the unhappy youth—Love! I have felt
So faint a kindness, such a meek surrender
To what my own full thoughts had made too ten-
   der,
That but for tears my life had fled away!—
Ye deaf and senseless minutes of the day,
And thou, old forest, hold ye this for true,
There is no lightning, no authentic dew
But in the eye of love: there's not a sound,
Melodious howsoever, can confound   80
The heavens and earth in one to such a death
As doth the voice of love: there's not a breath
Will mingle kindly with the meadow air,
Till it has panted round, and stolen a share
Of passion from the heart!'—

                Upon a bough
He leant, wretched. He surely cannot now
Thirst for another love: O impious,
That he can ever dream upon it thus!—
Thought he, 'Why am I not as are the dead,
Since to a woe like this I have been led   90
Through the dark earth, and through the won-
   drous sea?
Goddess! I love thee not the less: from thee
By Juno's smile I turn not—no, no, no—
While the great waters are at ebb and flow.—
I have a triple soul! O fond pretence—

For both, for both my love is so immense,
I feel my heart is cut for them in twain.'

And so he groan'd, as one by beauty slain.
The lady's heart beat quick, and he could see
Her gentle bosom heave tumultuously.   100
He sprang from his green covert: there she lay,
Sweet as a muskrose upon new-made hay;
With all her limbs on tremble, and her eyes
Shut softly up alive. To speak he tries.
'Fair damsel, pity me! forgive that I
Thus violate thy bower's sanctity!
O pardon me, for I am full of grief—
Grief born of thee, young angel! fairest thief!
Who stolen hast away the wings wherewith
I was to top the heavens. Dear maid, sith   110
Thou art my executioner, and I feel
Loving and hatred, misery and weal,
Will in a few short hours be nothing to me,
And all my story that much passion slew me;
Do smile upon the evening of my days:
And, for my tortur'd brain begins to craze,
Be thou my nurse; and let me understand
How dying I shall kiss that lilly hand.—
Dost weep for me? Then should I be content.
Scowl on, ye fates! until the firmament   120
Outblackens Erebus,[59] and the full-cavern'd earth
Crumbles into itself. By the cloud girth
Of Jove, those tears have given me a thirst
To meet oblivion.'—As her heart would burst
The maiden sobb'd awhile, and then replied:
'Why must such desolation betide
As that thou speak'st of? Are not these green
   nooks
Empty of all misfortune? Do the brooks
Utter a gorgon voice? Does yonder thrush,
Schooling its half-fledg'd little ones to brush   130
About the dewy forest, whisper tales?—
Speak not of grief, young stranger, or cold snails
Will slime the rose to night. Though if thou wilt,
Methinks 'twould be a guilt—a very guilt—
Not to companion thee, and sigh away
The light—the dusk—the dark—till break of
   day!'
'Dear lady,' said Endymion, ' 'tis past:
I love thee! and my days can never last.
That I may pass in patience still speak:
Let me have music dying, and I seek   140
No more delight—I bid adieu to all.
Didst thou not after other climates call,
And murmur about Indian streams?'—Then she,
Sitting beneath the midmost forest tree,
For pity sang this roundelay——

---

59 a place of gloomy darkness through which souls passed to
Hades.

'O Sorrow,
  Why dost borrow
The natural hue of health, from vermeil lips?—
    To give maiden blushes
      To the white rose bushes?   150
Or is't thy dewy hand the daisy tips?

   'O Sorrow,
  Why dost borrow
The lustrous passion from a falcon-eye?—
    To give the glow-worm light?
      Or, on a moonless night,
To tinge, on syren shores, the salt sea-spry?

   'O Sorrow,
  Why dost borrow
The mellow ditties from a mourning
    tongue?—   160
    To give at evening pale
      Unto the nightingale,
That thou mayst listen the cold dews among?

   'O Sorrow,
  Why dost borrow
Heart's lightness from the merriment of May?—
    A lover would not tread
      A cowslip on the head,
Though he should dance from eve till peep of
    day—
    Nor any drooping flower   170
      Held sacred for thy bower,
Wherever he may sport himself and play.

   'To Sorrow,
  I bade good-morrow,
And thought to leave her far away behind;
    But cheerly, cheerly,
      She loves me dearly;
She is so constant to me, and so kind:
    I would deceive her
      And so leave her,   180
But ah! she is so constant and so kind.

'Beneath my palm trees, by the river side,
I sat a weeping: in the whole world wide
There was no one to ask me why I wept,—
    And so I kept
Brimming the water-lilly cups with tears
    Cold as my fears.

'Beneath my palm trees, by the river side,
I sat a weeping: what enamour'd bride,
Cheated by shadowy wooer from the clouds,   190
    But hides and shrouds
Beneath dark palm trees by a river side?

'And as I sat, over the light blue hills
There came a noise of revellers: the rills
Into the wide stream came of purple hue—
    'Twas Bacchus and his crew!
The earnest trumpet spake, and silver thrills
From kissing cymbals made a merry din—
    'Twas Bacchus and his kin!
Like to a moving vintage down they came,   200
Crown'd with green leaves, and faces all on flame;
All madly dancing through the pleasant valley,
    To scare thee, Melancholy!
O then, O then, thou wast a simple name!
And I forgot thee, as the berried holly
By shepherds is forgotten, when, in June,
Tall chestnuts keep away the sun and moon:—
    I rush'd into the folly!

.Within his car, aloft, young Bacchus stood,
Trifling his ivy-dart, in dancing mood,   210
    With sidelong laughing;
And little rills of crimson wine imbrued
His plump white arms, and shoulders, enough
    white
    For Venus' pearly bite:
And near him rode Silenus[60] on his ass,
Pelted with flowers as he on did pass
    Tipsily quaffing.

'Whence came ye, merry Damsels! whence came
    ye!
So many, and so many, and such glee?
Why have ye left your bowers desolate,   220
    Your lutes, and gentler fate?—
"We follow Bacchus! Bacchus on the wing,
    A conquering!
Bacchus, young Bacchus! good or ill betide,
We dance before him thorough kingdoms
    wide:—
Come hither, lady fair, and joined be
    To our wild minstrelsy!"

'Whence came ye, jolly Satyrs! whence came ye!
So many, and so many, and such glee?
Why have ye left your forest haunts, why
    left   230
    Your nuts in oak-tree cleft?—
"For wine, for wine we left our kernel tree;
For wine we left our heath, and yellow brooms,
    And cold mushrooms;
For wine we follow Bacchus through the earth;
Great God of breathless cups and chirping
    mirth!—
Come hither, lady fair, and joined be
    To our mad minstrelsy!"

60 tipsy companion of Bacchus.

'Over wide streams and mountains great we went,
And, save when Bacchus kept his ivy tent,   240
Onward the tiger and the leopard pants,
      With Asian elephants:
Onward these myriads—with song and dance,
With zebras striped, and sleek Arabians' prance,
Web-footed alligators, crocodiles,
Bearing upon their scaly backs, in files,
Plump infant laughers mimicking the coil[61]
Of seamen, and stout galley-rowers' toil:
With toying oars and silken sails they glide,
      Nor care for wind and tide.   250

'Mounted on panthers' furs and lions' manes,
From rear to van they scour about the plains;
A three days' journey in a moment done:
And always, at the rising of the sun,
About the wilds they hunt with spear and horn,
      On spleenful unicorn.

'I saw Osirian Egypt kneel adown
      Before the vine-wreath crown!
I saw parch'd Abyssinia rouse and sing
      To the silver cymbals' ring!   260
I saw the whelming vintage hotly pierce
      Old Tartary the fierce!
The kings of Inde their jewel-sceptres vail,[62]
And from their treasures scatter pearled hail;
Great Brahma from his mystic heaven groans,
      And all his priesthood moans;
Before young Bacchus' eye-wing turning pale.—
Into these regions came I following him,
Sick hearted, weary—so I took a whim
To stray away into these forests drear   270
      Alone, without a peer:
And I have told thee all thou mayest hear.

      'Young stranger!
      I've been a ranger
In search of pleasure throughout every clime:
      Alas, 'tis not for me!
      Bewitch'd I sure must be,
To lose in grieving all my maiden prime.

      'Come then, Sorrow!
      Sweetest Sorrow!   280
Like an own babe I nurse thee on my breast:
      I thought to leave thee
      And deceive thee,
But now of all the world I love thee best.

      'There is not one,
      No, no, not one

But thee to comfort a poor lonely maid;
      Thou art her mother,
      And her brother,
Her playmate, and her wooer in the shade.'   290

      O what a sigh she gave in finishing,
And look, quite dead to every worldly thing!
Endymion could not speak, but gazed on her;
And listened to the wind that now did stir
About the crisped oaks full drearily,
Yet with as sweet a softness as might be
Remember'd from its velvet summer song.
At last he said: 'Poor lady, how thus long
Have I been able to endure that voice?
Fair Melody! kind Syren! I've no choice;   300
I must be thy sad servant evermore:
I cannot choose but kneel here and adore.
Alas, I must not think—by Phœbe, no!
Let me not think, soft Angel! shall it be so?
Say, beautifullest, shall I never think?
O thou could'st foster me beyond the brink
Of recollection! make my watchful care
Close up its bloodshot eyes, nor see despair!
Do gently murder half my soul, and I
Shall feel the other half so utterly!—   310
I'm giddy at that cheek so fair and smooth;
O let it blush so ever! let it soothe
My madness! let it mantle rosy-warm
With the tinge of love, panting in safe alarm.—
This cannot be thy hand, and yet it is;
And this is sure thine other softling—this
Thine own fair bosom, and I am so near!
Wilt fall asleep? O let me sip that tear!
And whisper one sweet word that I may know
This is this world—sweet dewy blossom!'—   320
      Woe!
Woe! Woe to that Endymion! Where is he?—
Even these words went echoing dismally
Through the wide forest—a most fearful tone,
Like one repenting in his latest moan;
And while it died away a shade pass'd by,
As of a thunder cloud. When arrows fly
Through the thick branches, poor ring-doves
      sleek forth
Their timid necks and tremble; so these both
Leant to each other trembling, and sat so
Waiting for some destruction—when lo,   330
Foot-feather'd Mercury appear'd sublime
Beyond the tall tree tops; and in less time
Than shoots the slanted hail-storm, down he
      dropt
Towards the ground; but rested not, nor stopt
One moment from his home: only the sward
He with his wand light touch'd, and heavenward
Swifter than sight was gone—even before

---

61 bustle.
62 lower respectfully.

The teeming earth a sudden witness bore
Of his swift magic. Diving swans appear
Above the crystal circlings white and clear;   340
And catch the cheated eye in wide surprise,
How they can dive in sight and unseen rise—
So from the turf outsprang two steeds jet-black,
Each with large dark blue wings upon his back.
The youth of Caria plac'd the lovely dame
On one, and felt himself in spleen to tame
The other's fierceness. Through the air they flew,
High as the eagles. Like two drops of dew
Exhal'd to Phœbus' lips, away they are gone,
Far from the earth away—unseen, alone,   350
Among cool clouds and winds, but that the free,
The buoyant life of song can floating be
Above their heads, and follow them untir'd.—
Muse of my native land, am I inspir'd?
This is the giddy air, and I must spread
Wide pinions to keep here; nor do I dread
Or height, or depth, or width, or any chance
Precipitous: I have beneath my glance
Those towering horses and their mournful freight.
Could I thus sail, and see, and thus await   360
Fearless for power of thought, without thine
     aid?—

There is a sleepy dusk, an odorous shade
From some approaching wonder, and behold
Those winged steeds, with snorting nostrils bold
Snuff at its faint extreme, and seem to tire,
Dying to embers from their native fire!

There curl'd a purple mist around them; soon,
It seem'd as when around the pale new moon
Sad Zephyr droops the clouds like weeping wil-
     low:
'Twas Sleep slow journeying with head on pil-
     low.   370
For the first time, since he came nigh dead born
From the old womb of night, his cave forlorn
Had he left more forlorn; for the first time,
He felt aloof the day and morning's prime—
Because into his depth Cimmerian[63]
There came a dream, showing how a young man,
Ere a lean bat could plump its wintery skin,
Would at high Jove's empyreal footstool win
An immortality, and how espouse
Jove's daughter, and be reckon'd of his house. 380
Now was he slumbering towards heaven's gate,
That he might at the threshold one hour wait
To hear the marriage melodies, and then
Sink downward to his dusky cave again.
His litter of smooth semilucent mist,

Diversely ting'd with rose and amethyst,
Puzzled those eyes that for the centre sought;
And scarcely for one moment could be caught
His sluggish form reposing motionless.
Those two on winged steeds, with all the
     stress   390
Of vision search'd for him, as one would look
Athwart the sallows of a river nook
To catch a glance at silver-throated eels,—
Or from old Skiddaw's[64] top, when fog conceals
His rugged forehead in a mantle pale,
With an eye-guess towards some pleasant vale
Descry a favourite hamlet faint and far.

These raven horses, though they foster'd are
Of earth's splenetic fire, dully drop
Their full-vein'd ears, nostrils blood wide, and
     stop;   400
Upon the spiritless mist have they outspread
Their ample feathers, are in slumber dead,—
And on those pinions, level in mid air,
Endymion sleepeth and the lady fair.
Slowly they sail, slowly as icy isle
Upon a calm sea drifting: and meanwhile
The mournful wanderer dreams. Behold! he
     walks
On heaven's pavement; brotherly he talks
To divine powers: from his hand full fain
Juno's proud birds[65] are pecking pearly grain: 410
He tries the nerve of Phœbus' golden bow,
And asketh where the golden apples grow:
Upon his arm he braces Pallas' shield,
And strives in vain to unsettle and wield
A Jovian thunderbolt: arch Hebe brings
A full-brimm'd goblet, dances lightly, sings
And tantalizes long; at last he drinks,
And lost in pleasure at her feet he sinks,
Touching with dazzled lips her starlight hand.
He blows a bugle,—an ethereal band   420
Are visible above: the Seasons four,—
Green-kyrtled Spring, flush Summer, golden
     store
In Autumn's sickle, Winter frosty hoar,
Join dance with shadowy Hours; while still the
     blast,
In swells unmitigated, still doth last
To sway their floating morris. 'Whose is this?
Whose bugle?' he inquires; they smile—'O Dis!
Why is this mortal here? Dost thou not know
Its mistress' lips? Not thou?—'Tis Dian's: lo!
She rises crescented!' He looks, 'tis she,   430
His very goddess: good-bye earth, and sea,
And air, and pains, and care, and suffering;

---

63 gloomy. The mythical people called Cimmerii dwelt in a land
of perpetual mist and gloom.
64 a mountain in the lake country.
65 peacocks.

Good-bye to all but love! Then doth he spring
Towards her, and awakes—and, strange, o'er-
    head,
Of those same fragrant exhalations bred,
Beheld awake his very dream: the gods
Stood smiling; merry Hebe laughs and nods;
And Phœbe bends towards him crescented.
O state perplexing! On the pinion bed,
Too well awake, he feels the panting side   440
Of his delicious lady. He[66] who died
For soaring too audacious in the sun,
When that same treacherous wax began to run,
Felt not more tongue-tied than Endymion.
His heart leapt up as to its rightful throne,
To that fair shadow'd passion puls'd its way—
Ah, what perplexity! Ah, well a day!
So fond, so beauteous was his bed-fellow,
He could not help but kiss her: then he grew
Awhile forgetful of all beauty save   450
Young Phœbe's, golden hair'd; and so 'gan crave
Forgiveness: yet he turn'd once more to look
At the sweet sleeper,—all his soul was shook,—
She press'd his hand in slumber; so once more
He could not help but kiss her and adore.
At this the shadow wept, melting away.
The Latmian started up: 'Bright goddess, stay!
Search my most hidden breast! By truth's own
    tongue,
I have no dædale[67] heart: why is it wrung
To desperation? Is there nought for me,   460
Upon the bourne of bliss, but misery?'

These words awoke the stranger of dark
    tresses:
Her dawning love-look rapt Endymion blesses
With 'haviour soft. Sleep yawn'd from under-
    neath.
'Thou swan of Ganges, let us no more breathe
This murky phantasm! thou contented seem'st
Pillow'd in lovely idleness, nor dream'st
What horrors may discomfort thee and me.
Ah, shouldst thou die from my heart-treachery!—
Yet did she merely weep—her gentle soul   470
Hath no revenge in it: as it is whole
In tenderness, would I were whole in love!
Can I prize thee, fair maid, all price above,
Even when I feel as true as innocence?
I do, I do.—What is this soul then? Whence
Came it? It does not seem my own, and I
Have no self-passion or identity.
Some fearful end must be: where, where is it?
By Nemesis, I see my spirit flit
Alone about the dark—Forgive me, sweet: 480

---

66 Icarus.
67 cunning; deceptive.

Shall we away?' He rous'd the steeds: they beat
Their wings chivalrous into the clear air,
Leaving old Sleep within his vapoury lair.

The good-night blush of eve was waning slow,
And Vesper, risen star, began to throe
In the dusk heavens silverly, when they
Thus sprang direct towards the Galaxy.
Nor did speed hinder converse soft and strange—
Eternal oaths and vows they interchange,
In such wise, in such temper, so aloof   490
Up in the winds, beneath a starry roof,
So witless of their doom, that verily
'Tis well nigh past man's search their hearts to
    see;
Whether they wept, or laugh'd, or griev'd, or
    toy'd—
Most like with joy gone mad, with sorrow cloy'd.

Full facing their swift flight, from ebon streak,
The moon put forth a little diamond peak,
No bigger than an unobserved star,
Or tiny point of fairy scymetar;
Bright signal that she only stoop'd to tie   500
Her silver sandals, ere deliciously
She bow'd into the heavens her timid head.
Slowly she rose, as though she would have fled,
While to his lady meek the Carian turn'd,
To mark if her dark eyes had yet discern'd
This beauty in its birth—Despair! despair!
He saw her body fading gaunt and spare
In the cold moonshine. Straight he seiz'd her
    wrist;
It melted from his grasp: her hand he kiss'd,
And, horror! kiss'd his own—he was alone.   510
Her steed a little higher soar'd, and then
Dropt hawkwise to the earth.

                  There lies a den,
Beyond the seeming confines of the space
Made for the soul to wander in and trace
Its own existence, of remotest glooms.
Dark regions are around it, where the tombs
Of buried griefs the spirit sees, but scarce
One hour doth linger weeping, for the pierce
Of new-born woe it feels more inly smart:
And in these regions many a venom'd dart   520
At random flies; they are the proper home
Of every ill: the man is yet to come
Who hath not journeyed in this native hell.
But few have ever felt how calm and well
Sleep may be had in that deep den of all.
There anguish does not sting; nor pleasure pall:
Woe-hurricanes beat ever at the gate,
Yet all is still within and desolate.

Beset with plainful gusts, within ye hear
No sound so loud as when on curtain'd bier   530
The death-watch tick is stifled. Enter none
Who strive therefore: on the sudden it is won.
Just when the sufferer begins to burn,
Then it is free to him; and from an urn,
Still fed by melting ice, he takes a draught—
Young Semele[68] such richness never quaft
In her maternal longing! Happy gloom!
Dark Paradise! where pale becomes the bloom
Of health by due; where silence dreariest
Is most articulate; where hopes infest;   540
Where those eyes are the brightest far that keep
Their lids shut longest in a dreamless sleep.
O happy spirit-home! O wondrous soul!
Pregnant with such a den to save the whole
In thine own depth. Hail, gentle Carian!
For, never since thy griefs and woes began,
Hast thou felt so content: a grievous feud
Hath led thee to this Cave of Quietude.
Aye, his lull'd soul was there, although upborne
With dangerous speed: and so he did not
         mourn   550
Because he knew not whither he was going.
So happy was he, not the aerial blowing
Of trumpets at clear parley from the east
Could rouse from that fine relish, that high feast.
They stung the feather'd horse: with fierce alarm
He flapp'd towards the sound. Alas, no charm
Could lift Endymion's head, or he had view'd
A skyey mask, a pinion'd multitude,—
And silvery was its passing: voices sweet
Warbling the while as if to lull and greet   560
The wanderer in his path. Thus warbled they,
While past the vision went in bright array.

'Who, who from Dian's feast would be away?
For all the golden bowers of the day
Are empty left? Who, who away would be
From Cynthia's wedding and festivity?
Not Hesperus: lo! upon his silver wings
He leans away for highest heaven and sings,
Snapping his lucid fingers merrily!—
Ah, Zephyrus! art here, and Flora too!   570
Ye tender bibbers of the rain and dew,
Young playmates of the rose and daffodil,
Be careful, ere ye enter in, to fill
         Your baskets high
With fennel green, and balm, and golden pines,
Savory, latter-mint, and columbines,
Cool parsley, basil sweet, and sunny thyme;
Yea, every flower and leaf of every clime,
All gather'd in the dewy morning: hie
         Away! fly, fly!—   580

68 the mother of Dionysus by Zeus.

Crystalline brother of the belt of heaven,
Aquarius![69] to whom king Jove has given
Two liquid pulse streams 'stead of feather'd
         wings,
Two fan-like fountains,—thine illuminings
         For Dian play:
Dissolve the frozen purity of air;
Let thy white shoulders silvery and bare
Show cold through watery pinions; make more
         bright
The Star-Queen's crescent on her marriage night:
         Haste, haste away!—   590
Castor has tamed the planet Lion, see!
And of the Bear has Pollux mastery:
A third is in the race! who is the third
Speeding away swift as the eagle bird?
         The ramping Centaur!
The Lion's mane's on end: the Bear how fierce!
The Centaur's arrow ready seems to pierce
Some enemy: far forth his bow is bent
Into the blue of heaven. He'll be shent,[70]
         Pale unrelentor,   600
When he shall hear the wedding lutes a play-
         ing.—
Andromeda! sweet woman! why delaying
So timidly among the stars: come hither!
Join this bright throng, and nimbly follow
         whither
         They all are going.
Danae's Son,[71] before Jove newly bow'd,
Has wept for thee, calling to Jove aloud.
Thee, gentle lady, did he disenthral:
Ye shall for ever live and love, for all
         Thy tears are flowing.—   610
By Daphne's fright, behold Apollo!—'

                                        More
Endymion heard not: down his steed him bore,
Prone to the green head of a misty hill.

         His first touch of the earth went nigh to kill.
'Alas!' said he, 'were I but always borne
Through dangerous winds, had but my footsteps
         worn
A path in hell, for ever would I bless
Horrors which nourish an uneasiness
For my own sullen conquering: to him
Who lives beyond earth's boundary, grief is
         dim,   620
Sorrow is but a shadow: now I see
The grass; I feel the solid ground—Ah, me!

69 Aquarius, the Water-Bearer, and his companion constellations in the zodiac attend the wedding of the Star-Queen, ls. 582–
611.
70 put to confusion.
71 Perseus.

It is thy voice—divinest! Where?—who? who
Left thee so quiet on this bed of dew?
Behold upon this happy earth we are;
Let us aye love each other; let us fare
On forest-fruits, and never, never go
Among the abodes of mortals here below,
Or be by phantoms duped. O destiny!
Into a labyrinth now my soul would fly,   630
But with thy beauty will I deaden it.
Where didst thou melt to? By thee will I sit
For ever: let our fate stop here—a kid
I on this spot will offer: Pan will bid
Us live in peace, in love and peace among
His forest wildernesses. I have clung
To nothing, lov'd a nothing, nothing seen
Or felt but a great dream! O I have been
Presumptuous against love, against the sky,
Against all elements, against the tie   640
Of mortals each to each, against the blooms
Of flowers, rush of rivers, and the tombs
Of heroes gone! Against his proper glory
Has my own soul conspired: so my story
Will I to children utter, and repent.
There never liv'd a mortal man, who bent
His appetite beyond his natural sphere,
But starv'd and died. My sweetest Indian, here,
Here will I kneel, for thou redeemed hast
My life from too thin breathing: gone and
          past   650
Are cloudy phantasms. Caverns lone, farewell!
And air of visions, and the monstrous swell
Of visionary seas! No, never more
Shall airy voices cheat me to the shore
Of tangled wonder, breathless and aghast.
Adieu, my daintiest Dream! although so vast
My love is still for thee. The hour may come
When we shall meet in pure elysium.
On earth I may not love thee; and therefore
Doves will I offer up, and sweetest store   660
All through the teeming year: so thou wilt shine
On me, and on this damsel fair of mine,
And bless our silver lives. My Indian bliss!
My river-lilly bud! one human kiss!
One sigh of real breath—one gentle squeeze,
Warm as a dove's nest among summer trees,
And warm with dew at ooze from living blood!
Whither didst melt? Ah, what of that!—all good
We'll talk about—no more of dreaming.—Now,
Where shall our dwelling be? Under the brow 670
Of some steep mossy hill, where ivy dun
Would hide us up, although spring leaves were
          none;
And where dark yew trees, as we rustle through,
Will drop their scarlet berry cups of dew?
O thou wouldst joy to live in such a place;

Dusk for our loves, yet light enough to grace
Those gentle limbs on mossy bed reclin'd:
For by one step the blue sky shouldst thou find,
And by another, in deep dell below,
See, through the trees, a little river go   680
All in its mid-day gold and glimmering.
Honey from out the gnarled hive I'll bring,
And apples, wan with sweetness, gather thee,—
Cresses that grow where no man may them see,
And sorrel untorn by the dew-claw'd stag:
Pipes will I fashion of the syrinx flag,[72]
That thou mayst always know whither I roam,
When it shall please thee in our quiet home
To listen and think of love. Still let me speak;
Still let me dive into the joy I seek,—   690
For yet the past doth prison me. The rill,
Thou haply mayst delight in, will I fill
With fairy fishes from the mountain tarn,[73]
And thou shalt feed them from the squirrel's
          barn.
Its bottom will I strew with amber shells,
And pebbles blue from deep enchanted wells.
Its sides I'll plant with dew-sweet eglantine,
And honeysuckles full of clear bee-wine.
I will entice this crystal rill to trace
Love's silver name upon the meadow's face.   700
I'll kneel to Vesta, for a flame of fire;
And to god Phœbus, for a golden lyre;
To Empress Dian, for a hunting spear;
To Vesper, for a taper silver-clear,
That I may see thy beauty through the night;
To Flora, and a nightingale shall light
Tame on thy finger; to the River-gods,
And they shall bring thee taper fishing-rods
Of gold, and lines of Naiads' long bright tress.
Heaven shield thee for thine utter loveliness! 710
Thy mossy footstool shall the altar be
'Fore which I'll bend, bending, dear love, to thee:
Those lips shall be my Delphos,[74] and shall speak
Laws to my footsteps, colour to my cheek,
Trembling or stedfastness to this same voice,
And of three sweetest pleasurings the choice:
And that affectionate light, those diamond things,
Those eyes, those passions, those supreme pearl
          springs,
Shall be my grief, or twinkle me to pleasure.
Say, is not bliss within our perfect seisure?   720
O that I could not doubt!'

          The mountaineer
Thus strove by fancies vain and crude to clear

---

72 reed. Syrinx was a nymph changed into a reed to escape from
the wooings of Pan.
73 lake.
74 oracle.

His briar'd path to some tranquillity.
It gave bright gladness to his lady's eye,
And yet the tears she wept were tears of sorrow;
Answering thus, just as the golden morrow
Beam'd upward from the vallies of the east:
'O that the flutter of this heart had ceas'd,
Or the sweet name of love had pass'd away.
Young feather'd tyrant! by a swift decay   730
Wilt thou devote this body to the earth:
And I do think that at my very birth
I lisp'd thy blooming titles inwardly;
For at the first, first dawn and thought of thee,
With uplift hands I blest the stars of heaven.
Art thou not cruel? Ever have I striven
To think thee kind, but ah, it will not do!
When yet a child, I heard that kisses drew
Favour from thee, and so I kisses gave
To the void air, bidding them find out love: 740
But when I came to feel how far above
All fancy, pride, and fickle maidenhood,
All earthly pleasure, all imagin'd good,
Was the warm tremble of a devout kiss,—
Even then, that moment, at the thought of this,
Fainting I fell into a bed of flowers,
And languish'd there three days. Ye milder pow-
     ers,
Am I not cruelly wrong'd? Believe, believe
Me, dear Endymion, were I to weave
With my own fancies garlands of sweet life,   750
Thou shouldst be one of all. Ah, bitter strife!
I may not be thy love: I am forbidden—
Indeed I am—thwarted, affrighted, chidden,
By things I trembled at, and gorgon wrath.
Twice hast thou ask'd whither I went: henceforth
Ask me no more! I may not utter it,
Nor may I be thy love. We might commit
Ourselves at once to vengeance; we might die;
We might embrace and die: voluptuous thought!
Enlarge not to my hunger, or I'm caught   760
In trammels of perverse deliciousness.
No, no, that shall not be: thee will I bless,
And bid a long adieu.'

         The Carian
No word return'd: both lovelorn, silent, wan,
Into the vallies green together went.
Far wandering, they were perforce content
To sit beneath a fair lone beechen tree;
Nor at each other gaz'd, but heavily
Por'd on its hazle cirque of shedded leaves.

   Endymion! unhappy! it nigh grieves   770
Me to behold thee thus in last extreme:
Ensky'd ere this, but truly that I deem
Truth the best music in a first-born song.

Thy lute-voic'd brother will I sing ere long, [75]
And thou shalt aid—hast thou not aided me?
Yes, moonlight Emperor! felicity
Has been thy meed for many thousand years;
Yet often have I, on the brink of tears,
Mourn'd as if yet thou wert a forester;—
Forgetting the old tale.

           He did not stir   780
His eyes from the dead leaves, or one small pulse
Of joy he might have felt. The spirit culls
Unfaded amaranth, [76] when wild it strays
Through the old garden-ground of boyish days.
A little onward ran the very stream
By which he took his first soft poppy dream;
And on the very bark 'gainst which he leant
A crescent he had carv'd, and round it spent
His skill in little stars. The teeming tree
Had swollen and green'd the pious charac-
     tery,   790
But not ta'en out. Why, there was not a slope
Up which he had not fear'd the antelope;
And not a tree, beneath whose rooty shade
He had not with his tamed leopards play'd:
Nor could an arrow light, or javelin,
Fly in the air where his had never been—
And yet he knew it not.

           O treachery!
Why does his lady smile, pleasing her eye
With all his sorrowing? He sees her not.
But who so stares on him? His sister sure!   800
Peona of the woods!—Can she endure—
Impossible—how dearly they embrace!
His lady smiles: delight is in her face;
It is no treachery.

          'Dear brother mine!
Endymion, weep not so! Why shouldst thou pine
When all great Latmos so exalt will be?
Thank the great gods, and look not bitterly;
And speak not one pale word, and sigh no more.
Sure I will not believe thou hast such store
Of grief, to last thee to my kiss again.   810
Thou surely canst not bear a mind in pain,
Come hand in hand with one so beautiful.
Be happy both of you! for I will pull
The flowers of autumn for your coronals.
Pan's holy priest for young Endymion calls;
And when he is restor'd, thou, fairest dame,
Shalt be our queen. Now, is it not a shame
To see ye thus,—not very, very sad?

---

75 Keats was already meditating plans for making Hyperion the
subject of his next long poem.
76 a mythical flower supposed never to fade.

Perhaps ye are too happy to be glad:
O feel as if it were a common day;   820
Free-voic'd as one who never was away.
No tongue shall ask, whence come ye? but ye
        shall
Be gods of your own rest imperial.
Not even I, for one whole month, will pry
Into the hours that have pass'd us by,
Since in my arbour I did sing to thee.
O Hermes! on this very night will be
A hymning up to Cynthia, queen of light;
For the soothsayers old saw yesternight
Good visions in the air,—whence will befal,   830
As say these sages, health perpetual
To shepherds and their flocks; and furthermore,
In Dian's face they read the gentle lore:
Therefore for her these vesper-carols are.
Our friends will all be there from nigh and far.
Many upon thy death have ditties made;
And many, even now, their foreheads shade
With cypress, on a day of sacrifice.
New singing for our maids shalt thou devise,
And pluck the sorrow from our huntsmen's
        brows.   840
Tell me, my lady-queen, how to espouse
This wayward brother to his rightful joys!
His eyes are on thee bent, as thou didst poize
His fate most goddess-like. Help me, I pray,
To lure—Endymion, dear brother, say
What ails thee?' He could bear no more, and
        so
Bent his soul fiercely like a spiritual bow,
And twang'd it inwardly, and calmly said:
'I would have thee my only friend, sweet maid!
My only visitor! not ignorant though,   850
That those deceptions which for pleasure go
'Mong men, are pleasures real as real may be:
But there are higher ones I may not see,
If impiously an earthly realm I take.
Since I saw thee, I have been wide awake
Night after night, and day by day, until
Of the empyrean I have drunk my fill.
Let it content thee, Sister, seeing me
More happy than betides mortality.
A hermit young, I'll live in mossy cave,   860
Where thou alone shalt come to me, and lave
Thy spirit in the wonders I shall tell.
Through me the shepherd realm shall prosper
        well;
For to thy tongue will I all health confide.
And, for my sake, let this young maid abide
With thee as a dear sister. Thou alone,
Peona, mayst return to me. I own
This may sound strangely: but when, dearest girl,
Thou seest it for my happiness, no pearl

Will trespass down those cheeks. Companion
        fair!   870
Wilt be content to dwell with her, to share
This sister's love with me?' Like one resign'd
And bent by circumstance, and thereby blind
In self-commitment, thus that meek unknown:
'Aye, but a buzzing by my ears has flown,
Of jubilee to Dian:—truth I heard?
Well then, I see there is no little bird,
Tender soever, but is Jove's own care.
Long have I sought for rest, and, unaware,
Behold I find it! so exalted too!   880
So after my own heart! I knew, I knew
There was a place untenanted in it:
In that same void white Chastity shall sit,
And monitor me nightly to lone slumber.
With sanest lips I vow me to the number
Of Dian's sisterhood; and, kind lady,
With thy good help, this very night shall see
My future days to her fane consecrate.'

    As feels a dreamer what doth most create
His own particular fright, so these three felt: 890
Or like one who, in after ages, knelt
To Lucifer or Baal, when he'd pine
After a little sleep: or when in mine
Far under-ground, a sleeper meets his friends
Who know him not. Each diligently bends
Towards common thoughts and things for very
        fear;
Striving their ghastly malady to cheer,
By thinking it a thing of yes and no,
That housewives talk of. But the spirit-blow
Was struck, and all were dreamers. At the
        last   900
Endymion said: 'Are not our fates all cast?
Why stand we here? Adieu, ye tender pair!
Adieu!' Whereat those maidens, with wild stare,
Walk'd dizzily away. Pained and hot
His eyes went after them, until they got
Near to a cypress grove, whose deadly maw,
In one swift moment, would what then he saw
Engulph for ever. 'Stay!' he cried, 'ah, stay!
Turn, damsels! hist! one word I have to say.
Sweet Indian, I would see thee once again.   910
It is a thing I dote on: so I'd fain,
Peona, ye should hand in hand repair
Into those holy groves, that silent are
Behind great Dian's temple. I'll be yon,
At vesper's earliest twinkle—they are gone—
But once, once, once again—' At this he press'd
His hands against his face, and then did rest

His head upon a mossy hillock green,
And so remain'd as he a corpse had been

All the long day; save when he scantly lifted   920
His eyes abroad, to see how shadows shifted
With the slow move of time,—sluggish and weary
Until the poplar tops, in journey dreary,
Had reach'd the river's brim. Then up he rose,
And, slowly as that very river flows,
Walk'd towards the temple grove with this la-
   ment:
'Why such a golden eve? The breeze is sent
Careful and soft, that not a leaf may fall
Before the serene father of them all
Bows down his summer head below the west.   930
Now am I of breath, speech, and speed possest,
But at the setting I must bid adieu
To her for the last time. Night will strew
On the damp grass myriads of lingering leaves,
And with them shall I die; nor much it grieves
To die, when summer dies on the cold sward.
Why, I have been a butterfly, a lord
Of flowers, garlands, love-knots, silly posies,
Groves, meadows, melodies, and arbour roses;
My kingdom's at its death, and just it is   940
That I should die with it: so in all this
We miscall grief, bale, sorrow, heartbreak, woe,
What is there to plain of? By Titan's foe[77]
I am but rightly serv'd.' So saying, he
Tripp'd lightly on, in sort of deathful glee;
Laughing at the clear stream and setting sun,
As though they jests had been: nor had he done
His laugh at nature's holy countenance,
Until that grove appear'd, as if perchance,
And then his tongue with sober seemlihed   950
Gave utterance as he enter'd: 'Ha! I said,
King of the butterflies; but by this gloom,
And by old Rhadamanthus'[78] tongue of doom,
This dusk religion, pomp of solitude,
And the Promethean clay[79] by thief endued,
By old Saturnus' forelock, by his head
Shook with eternal palsy, I did wed
Myself to things of light from infancy;
And thus to be cast out, thus lorn to die,
Is sure enough to make a mortal man   960
Grow impious.' So he inwardly began
On things for which no wording can be found;
Deeper and deeper sinking, until drown'd
Beyond the reach of music: for the choir
Of Cynthia he heard not, though rough briar
Nor muffling thicket interpos'd to dull
The vesper hymn, far swollen, soft and full,
Through the dark pillars of those sylvan aisles.
He saw not the two maidens, nor their smiles,
Wan as primroses gather'd at midnight   970

---

77 Jupiter.
78 a judge in the next world.
79 man, whom Prometheus made of clay and endowed with life
and for whom he stole fire from heaven.

By chilly finger'd spring. 'Unhappy wight!
Endymion!' said Peona, 'we are here!
What wouldst thou ere we all are laid on bier?'
Then he embrac'd her, and his lady's hand
Press'd, saying: 'Sister, I would have command,
If it were heaven's will, on our sad fate.'
At which that dark-eyed stranger stood elate
And said, in a new voice, but sweet as love,
To Endymion's amaze: 'By Cupid's dove,
And so thou shalt! and by the lilly truth   980
Of my own breast thou shalt, beloved youth!'
And as she spake, into her face there came
Light, as reflected from a silver flame:
Her long black hair swell'd ampler, in display
Full golden; in her eyes a brighter day
Dawn'd blue and full of love. Aye, he beheld
Phœbe, his passion! joyous she upheld
Her lucid bow, continuing thus: 'Drear, drear
Has our delaying been; but foolish fear
Withheld me first; and then decrees of fate;   990
And then 'twas fit that from this mortal state
Thou shouldst, my love, by some unlook'd for
   change
Be spiritualiz'd. Peona, we shall range
These forests, and to thee they safe shall be
As was thy cradle; hither shalt thou flee
To meet us many a time.' Next Cynthia bright
Peona kiss'd, and bless'd with fair good night:
Her brother kiss'd her too, and knelt adown
Before his goddess, in a blissful swoon.
She gave her fair hands to him, and behold,   1000
Before three swiftest kisses he had told,
They vanish'd far away!—Peona went
Home through the gloomy wood in wonderment.

1817   1818

IN A DREAR-NIGHTED DECEMBER

IN A drear-nighted December,
   Too happy, happy tree,
Thy branches ne'er remember
   Their green felicity:
   The north cannot undo them,
   With a sleety whistle through them;
   Nor frozen thawings glue them
      From budding at the prime.

In a drear-nighted December,
   Too happy, happy brook,   10
Thy bubblings ne'er remember
   Apollo's summer look;
   But with a sweet forgetting,
   They stay their crystal fretting,
   Never, never petting
      About the frozen time.

Ah! would 'twere so with many
    A gentle girl and boy!
But were there ever any
    Writh'd not at passèd joy?   20
  To know the change and feel it,
  When there is none to heal it,
  Nor numbèd sense to steel it,
    Was never said in rhyme.

    1817   1829

ON SITTING DOWN TO READ *KING LEAR* ONCE AGAIN

O GOLDEN tongued Romance, with serene lute!
  Fair plumed Syren, Queen of far-away!
  Leave melodizing on this wintry day,
Shut up thine olden pages, and be mute:
Adieu! for, once again, the fierce dispute
  Betwixt damnation and impassion'd clay
  Must I burn through; once more humbly assay
The bitter-sweet of this Shakespearian fruit:
Chief Poet! and ye clouds of Albion,
  Begetters of our deep eternal theme!   10
When through the old oak Forest I am gone,
  Let me not wander in a barren dream,
But, when I am consumed in the fire,
Give me new Phœnix wings to fly at my desire.

    1818   1848

WHEN I HAVE FEARS

WHEN I have fears that I may cease to be
  Before my pen has glean'd my teeming brain,
Before high-piled books, in charactery,
  Hold like rich garners the full ripen'd grain;
When I behold, upon the night's starr'd face,
  Huge cloudy symbols of a high romance,
And think that I may never live to trace
  Their shadows, with the magic hand of chance;
And when I feel, fair creature of an hour,
  That I shall never look upon thee more,   10
Never have relish in the faery power
  Of unreflecting love;—then on the shore
Of the wide world I stand alone, and think
Till love and fame to nothingness do sink.

    January 1818   1848

ROBIN HOOD

TO A FRIEND[1]

No! those days are gone away,
And their hours are old and gray,

[1] John Hamilton Reynolds, to whom this poem and the *Lines on the Mermaid Tavern* following were sent in a letter dated 3 February 1818. See text, p. 1213.

And their minutes buried all
Under the down-trodden pall
Of the leaves of many years:
Many times have winter's shears,
Frozen North, and chilling East,
Sounded tempests to the feast
Of the forest's whispering fleeces,
Since men knew nor rent nor leases.   10

  No, the bugle sounds no more,
And the twanging bow no more;
Silent is the ivory[2] shrill
Past the heath and up the hill;
There is no mid-forest laugh,
Where lone Echo gives the half
To some wight, amaz'd to hear
Jesting, deep in forest drear.

  On the fairest time of June
You may go, with sun or moon,   20
Or the seven stars[3] to light you,
Or the polar ray to right you;
But you never may behold
Little John, or Robin bold;
Never one, of all the clan,
Thrumming on an empty can
Some old hunting ditty, while
He doth his green way beguile
To fair hostess Merriment,
Down beside the pasture Trent;[4]   30
For he left the merry tale
Messenger for spicy ale.

  Gone, the merry morris[5] din;
Gone, the song of Gamelyn;[6]
Gone, the tough-belted outlaw
Idling in the 'grenè shawe';[7]
All are gone away and past!
And if Robin should be cast
Sudden from his turfed grave,
And if Marian should have   40
Once again her forest days,
She would weep, and he would craze:
He would swear, for all his oaks,
Fall'n beneath the dockyard strokes,
Have rotted on the briny seas;
She would weep that her wild bees
Sang not to her—strange! that honey
Can't be got without hard money!

[2] ivory whistle.
[3] the Pleiades.
[4] a river in Nottinghamshire, Robin Hood's country.
[5] a country dance in which the performers often dressed as Robin Hood, Maid Marian, and other popular characters.
[6] a medieval romance in verse closely connected with the Robin Hood stories of outlawry.
[7] green wood.

So it is: yet let us sing,
Honour to the old bow-string!   50
Honour to the bugle-horn!
Honour to the woods unshorn!
Honour to the Lincoln green![8]
Honour to the archer keen!
Honour to tight[9] little John,
And the horse he rode upon!
Honour to bold Robin Hood,
Sleeping in the underwood!
Honour to maid Marian,
And to all the Sherwood-clan!   60
Though their days have hurried by
Let us two a burden[10] try.

            1818   1820

LINES ON THE MERMAID TAVERN[1]

SOULS of Poets dead and gone,
What Elysium have ye known,
Happy field or mossy cavern,
Choicer than the Mermaid Tavern?
Have ye tippled drink more fine
Than mine host's Canary wine?
Or are fruits of Paradise
Sweeter than those dainty pies
Of venison? O generous food!
Drest as though bold Robin Hood   10
Would, with his maid Marian,
Sup and bowse from horn and can.

I have heard that on a day
Mine host's sign-board[2] flew away,
Nobody knew whither, till
An astrologer's old quill
To a sheepskin gave the story,
Said he saw you in your glory,
Underneath a new old sign
Sipping beverage divine,   20
And pledging with contented smack
The Mermaid in the Zodiac.

Souls of Poets dead and gone,
What Elysium have ye known,
Happy field or mossy cavern,
Choicer than the Mermaid Tavern?

            1818   1820

8 cloth made in Lincoln, popular with huntsmen.
9 trim.
10 chorus.

1 famous meeting place of Shakespeare, Ben Jonson, and other 'choice spirits' of the Elizabethan age.
2 The tavern's sign was a square board bearing a picture of a mermaid.

THE HUMAN SEASONS

FOUR seasons fill the measure of the year;
    There are four seasons in the mind of man:
He has his lusty Spring, when fancy clear
    Takes in all beauty with an easy span:
He has his Summer, when luxuriously
    Spring's honied cud of youthful thought he loves
To ruminate, and by such dreaming nigh
    His nearest unto heaven: quiet coves
His soul has in its Autumn, when his wings
    He furleth close; contented so to look   10
On mists in idleness—to let fair things
    Pass by unheeded as a threshold brook.
He has his Winter too of pale misfeature,
Or else he would forego his mortal nature.

            1818   1819

ISABELLA

OR

THE POT OF BASIL

A STORY, FROM BOCCACCIO[1]

I

FAIR Isabel, poor simple Isabel!
    Lorenzo, a young palmer[2] in Love's eye!
They could not in the self-same mansion dwell
    Without some stir of heart, some malady;
They could not sit at meals but feel how well
    It soothed each to be the other by;
They could not, sure, beneath the same roof sleep
But to each other dream, and nightly weep.

II

With every morn their love grew tenderer,
    With every eve deeper and tenderer still;   10
He might not in house, field, or garden stir,
    But her full shape would all his seeing fill;
And his continual voice was pleasanter
    To her, than noise of trees or hidden rill;
Her lute-string gave an echo of his name,
She spoilt her half-done broidery with the same.

III

He knew whose gentle hand was at the latch
    Before the door had given her to his eyes;
And from her chamber-window he would catch
    Her beauty farther than the falcon spies;   20

1 Keats and Reynolds made plans to put a volume of Boccaccio's tales into English verse. *Isabella*, an adaptation of the *Decameron*, iv, 5, is the only narrative which Keats completed.
2 votary; devotee.

And constant as her vespers would he watch,
  Because her face was turn'd to the same skies;
And with sick longing all the night outwear,
To hear her morning-step upon the stair.

IV

A whole long month of May in this sad plight
  Made their cheeks paler by the break of
    June:
'To-morrow will I bow to my delight,
  To-morrow will I ask my lady's boon.'—
'O may I never see another night,
  Lorenzo, if thy lips breathe not love's
    tune.'—   30
So spake they to their pillows; but, alas,
Honeyless days and days did he let pass;

V

Until sweet Isabella's untouch'd cheek
  Fell sick within the rose's just domain,
Fell thin as a young mother's, who doth seek
  By every lull to cool her infant's pain:
'How ill she is,' said he, 'I may not speak,
  And yet I will, and tell my love all plain:
If looks speak love-laws, I will drink her tears,
And at the least 'twill startle off her cares.'   40

VI

So said he one fair morning, and all day
  His heart beat awfully against his side;
And to his heart he inwardly did pray
  For power to speak; but still the ruddy tide
Stifled his voice, and puls'd resolve away—
  Fever'd his high conceit of such a bride,
Yet brought him to the meekness of a child:
Alas! when passion is both meek and wild!

VII

So once more he had wak'd and anguished
  A dreary night of love and misery,   50
If Isabel's quick eye had not been wed
  To every symbol on his forehead high;
She saw it waxing very pale and dead,
  And straight all flush'd; so, lisped tenderly,
'Lorenzo!'—here she ceas'd her timid quest,
But in her tone and look he read the rest.

VIII

'O Isabella, I can half perceive
  That I may speak my grief into thine ear;
If thou didst ever anything believe,
  Believe how I love thee, believe how near   60
My soul is to its doom: I would not grieve
  Thy hand by unwelcome pressing, would not
    fear

Thine eyes by gazing; but I cannot live
Another night, and not my passion shrive.

IX

'Love! thou art leading me from wintry cold,
  Lady! thou leadest me to summer clime,
And I must taste the blossoms that unfold
  In its ripe warmth this gracious morning time.'
So said, his erewhile timid lips grew bold,
  And poesied with hers in dewy rhyme: 70
Great bliss was with them, and great happiness
Grew, like a lusty flower in June's caress.

X

Parting they seem'd to tread upon the air,
  Twin roses by the zephyr blown apart
Only to meet again more close, and share
  The inward fragrance of each other's heart.
She, to her chamber gone, a ditty fair
  Sang, of delicious love and honey'd dart;
He with light steps went up a western hill,
And bade the sun farewell, and joy'd his fill. 80

XI

All close they met again, before the dusk
  Had taken from the stars its pleasant veil,
All close they met, all eves, before the dusk
  Had taken from the stars its pleasant veil,
Close in a bower of hyacinth and musk,
  Unknown of any, free from whispering tale.
Ah! better had it been for ever so,
Than idle ears should pleasure in their woe.

XII

Were they unhappy then?—It cannot be—
  Too many tears for lovers have been shed,   90
Too many sighs give we to them in fee,
  Too much of pity after they are dead,
Too many doleful stories do we see,
  Whose matter in bright gold were best be read;
Except in such a page where Theseus' spouse[3]
Over the pathless waves towards him bows.

XIII

But, for the general award of love,
  The little sweet doth kill much bitterness;
Though Dido silent is in under-grove,[4]
  And Isabella's was a great distress,   100
Though young Lorenzo in warm Indian clove
  Was not embalm'd, this truth is not the less—
Even bees, the little almsmen of spring-bowers,
Know there is richest juice in poison-flowers.

3 Ariadne, daughter of King Minos, who saved the life of Theseus but was later ungratefully deserted by him.
4 Queen Dido killed herself for love of Aeneas after he had abandoned her.

XIV

With her two brothers this fair lady dwelt,
  Enriched from ancestral merchandise,
And for them many a weary hand did swelt
  In torched mines and noisy factories,
And many once proud-quiver'd loins did melt
  In blood from stinging whip;—with hollow
    eyes   110
Many all day in dazzling river stood,
To take the rich-ored driftings of the flood.

XV

For them the Ceylon diver held his breath,
  And went all naked to the hungry shark;
For them his ears gush'd blood; for them in
    death
The seal on the cold ice with piteous bark
Lay full of darts; for them alone did seethe
  A thousand men in troubles wide and dark:
Half-ignorant, they turn'd an easy wheel,
That set sharp racks at work, to pinch and
    peel.   120

XVI

Why were they proud? Because their marble
    founts
  Gush'd with more pride than do a wretch's
    tears?—
Why were they proud? Because fair orange-
    mounts
  Were of more soft ascent than lazar[5] stairs?—
Why were they proud? Because red-lin'd ac-
    counts
  Were richer than the songs of Grecian years?—
Why were they proud? again we ask aloud,
Why in the name of Glory were they proud?

XVII

Yet were these Florentines as self-retired
  In hungry pride and gainful cowardice,   130
As two close Hebrews in that land inspired,
  Paled[6] in and vineyarded from beggar-spies;
The hawks of ship-mast forests[7]—the untired
  And pannier'd mules for ducats and old lies—
Quick cat's-paws on the generous stray-away,—
Great wits in Spanish, Tuscan, and Malay.

XVIII

How was it these same ledger-men could spy
  Fair Isabella in her downy nest?
How could they find out in Lorenzo's eye
  A straying from his toil? Hot Egypt's pest[8] 140

Into their vision covetous and sly!
  How could these money-bags see east and
    west?—
Yet so they did—and every dealer fair
Must see behind, as doth the hunted hare.

XIX

O eloquent and famed Boccaccio!
  Of thee we now should ask forgiving boon,
And of thy spicy myrtles as they blow,
  And of thy roses amorous of the moon,
And of thy lillies, that do paler grow
  Now they can no more hear thy ghittern's[9]
    tune,   150
For venturing syllables that ill beseem
The quiet glooms of such a piteous theme.

XX

Grant thou a pardon here, and then the tale
  Shall move on soberly, as it is meet;
There is no other crime, no mad assail
  To make old prose in modern rhyme more
    sweet:
But it is done—succeed the verse or fail—
  To honour thee, and thy gone spirit greet;
To stead thee as a verse in English tongue,
An echo of thee in the north-wind sung.   160

XXI

These brethren having found by many signs
  What love Lorenzo for their sister had,
And how she lov'd him too, each unconfines
  His bitter thoughts to other, well nigh mad
That he, the servant of their trade designs,
  Should in their sister's love be blithe and glad,
When 'twas their plan to coax her by degrees
To some high noble and his olive-trees.

XXII

And many a jealous conference had they,
  And many times they bit their lips alone,   170
Before they fix'd upon a surest way
  To make the youngster for his crime atone;
And at the last, these men of cruel clay
  Cut Mercy with a sharp knife to the bone;
For they resolved in some forest dim
To kill Lorenzo, and there bury him.

XXIII

So on a pleasant morning, as he leant
  Into the sun-rise, o'er the balustrade
Of the garden-terrace, towards him they bent
  Their footing through the dews; and to him
    said,   180

---

5 pesthouse.   6 enclosed.
7 i.e. they preyed upon the trading vessels in port.
8 swarms of flies. Exodus, viii, 21.

9 a stringed instrument.

'You seem there in the quiet of content,
　Lorenzo, and we are most loth to invade
Calm speculation; but if you are wise,
Bestride your steed while cold is in the skies.

XXIV

'To-day we purpose, aye, this hour we mount
　To spur three leagues towards the Appennine;
Come down, we pray thee, ere the hot sun count
　His dewy rosary on the eglantine.'
Lorenzo, courteously as he was wont,
　Bow'd a fair greeting to these serpents'
　　whine;　　　　　　　　　　　　　　　　190
And went in haste, to get in readiness,
With belt, and spur, and bracing huntsman's
　dress.

XXV

And as he to the court-yard pass'd along,
　Each third step did he pause, and listen'd oft
If he could hear his lady's matin-song,
　Or the light whisper of her footstep soft;
And as he thus over his passion hung,
　He heard a laugh full musical aloft;
When, looking up, he saw her features bright
Smile through an in-door lattice, all delight.　200

XXVI

'Love, Isabel!' said he, 'I was in pain
　Lest I should miss to bid thee a good morrow:
Ah! what if I should lose thee, when so fain
　I am to stifle all the heavy sorrow
Of a poor three hours' absence? but we'll gain
　Out of the amorous dark what day doth bor-
　　row.
Good bye! I'll soon be back.'—'Good bye!' said
　she:—
And as he went she chanted merrily.

XXVII

So the two brothers and their murder'd man
　Rode past fair Florence, to where Arno's
　　stream　　　　　　　　　　　　　　　　210
Gurgles through straiten'd banks, and still doth
　fan
　Itself with dancing bulrush, and the bream
Keeps head against the freshets. Sick and wan
　The brothers' faces in the ford did seem,
Lorenzo's flush with love.—They pass'd the
　water
Into a forest quiet for the slaughter.

XXVIII

There was Lorenzo slain and buried in,
　There in that forest did his great love cease;
Ah! when a soul doth thus its freedom win,

It aches in loneliness—is ill at peace　　220
　As the break-covert blood-hounds of such sin:
They dipp'd their swords in the water, and did
　tease
　Their horses homeward, with convulsed spur,
Each richer by his being a murderer.

XXIX

They told their sister how, with sudden speed,
　Lorenzo had ta'en ship for foreign lands,
Because of some great urgency and need
　In their affairs, requiring trusty hands.
Poor Girl! put on thy stifling widow's weed,
　And 'scape at once from Hope's accursed
　　bands;　　　　　　　　　　　　　　　　230
To-day thou wilt not see him, nor to-morrow,
And the next day will be a day of sorrow.

XXX

She weeps alone for pleasures not to be;
　Sorely she wept until the night came on,
And then, instead of love, O misery!
　She brooded o'er the luxury alone:
His image in the dusk she seem'd to see,
　And to the silence made a gentle moan,
Spreading her perfect arms upon the air,
And on her couch low murmuring 'Where? O
　where?'　　　　　　　　　　　　　　　　240

XXXI

But Selfishness, Love's cousin, held not long
　Its fiery vigil in her single breast;
She fretted for the golden hour, and hung
　Upon the time with feverish unrest—
Not long—for soon into her heart a throng
　Of higher occupants, a richer zest,
Came tragic; passion not to be subdued,
And sorrow for her love in travels rude.

XXXII

In the mid days of autumn, on their eves
　The breath of Winter comes from far
　　away,　　　　　　　　　　　　　　　　250
And the sick west continually bereaves
　Of some gold tinge, and plays a roundelay
Of death among the bushes and the leaves,
　To make all bare before he dares to stray
From his north cavern. So sweet Isabel
By gradual decay from beauty fell,

XXXIII

Because Lorenzo came not. Oftentimes
　She ask'd her brothers, with an eye all pale,
Striving to be itself, what dungeon climes
　Could keep him off so long? They spake a
　　tale　　　　　　　　　　　　　　　　260

Time after time, to quiet her. Their crimes
  Came on them, like a smoke from Hinnom's
    vale;[10]
And every night in dreams they groan'd aloud,
To see their sister in her snowy shroud.

XXXIV

And she had died in drowsy ignorance,
  But for a thing more deadly dark than all;
It came like a fierce potion, drunk by chance,
  Which saves a sick man from the feather'd pall
For some few gasping moments; like a lance,
  Waking an Indian from his cloudy hall   270
With cruel pierce, and bringing him again
Sense of the gnawing fire at heart and brain.

XXXV

It was a vision.—In the drowsy gloom,
  The dull of midnight, at her couch's foot
Lorenzo stood, and wept: the forest tomb
  Had marr'd his glossy hair which once could
    shoot
Lustre into the sun, and put cold doom
  Upon his lips, and taken the soft lute
From his lorn voice, and past his loamed ears
Had made a miry channel for his tears.   280

XXXVI

Strange sound it was, when the pale shadow
    spake;
  For there was striving, in its piteous tongue,
To speak as when on earth it was awake,
  And Isabella on its music hung:
Languor there was in it, and tremulous shake,
  As in a palsied Druid's harp unstrung;
And through it moan'd a ghostly under-song,
Like hoarse night-gusts sepulchral briars among.

XXXVII

Its eyes, though wild, were still all dewy bright
  With love, and kept all phantom fear aloof   290
From the poor girl by magic of their light,
  The while it did unthread the horrid woof
Of the late darken'd time,—the murderous
    spite
  Of pride and avarice,—the dark pine roof
In the forest,—and the sodden turfed dell,
Where, without any word, from stabs he fell.

XXXVIII

Saying moreover, 'Isabel, my sweet!
  Red whortle-berries droop above my head,
And a large flint-stone weighs upon my feet;

---

10 near Jerusalem, where Ahaz burnt his children as a sacrifice to
Moloch. II Chronicles, xxviii, 3.

Around me beeches and high chestnuts
    shed   300
Their leaves and prickly nuts; a sheep-fold bleat
  Comes from beyond the river to my bed:
Go, shed one tear upon my heather-bloom,
And it shall comfort me within the tomb.

XXXIX

'I am a shadow now, alas! alas!
  Upon the skirts of human-nature dwelling
Alone: I chant alone the holy mass,
  While little sounds of life are round me knell-
    ing,
And glossy bees at noon do fieldward pass,
  And many a chapel bell the hour is telling,   310
Paining me through: those sounds grow strange
    to me,
And thou art distant in Humanity.

XL

'I know what was, I feel full well what is,
  And I should rage, if spirits could go mad;
Though I forget the taste of earthly bliss,
  That paleness warms my grave, as though I
    had
A Seraph chosen from the bright abyss
  To be my spouse: thy paleness makes me glad;
Thy beauty grows upon me, and I feel
A greater love through all my essence steal.   320

XLI

The Spirit mourn'd 'Adieu!'—dissolv'd and left
  The atom darkness in a slow turmoil;
As when of healthful midnight sleep bereft,
  Thinking on rugged hours and fruitless toil,
We put our eyes into a pillowy cleft,
  And see the spangly gloom froth up and boil:
It made sad Isabella's eyelids ache,
And in the dawn she started up awake;

XLII

'Ha! ha!' said she, 'I knew not this hard life,
  I thought the worst was simple misery;   330
I thought some Fate with pleasure or with strife
  Portion'd us—happy days, or else to die;
But there is crime—a brother's bloody knife!
  Sweet Spirit, thou hast school'd my infancy:
I'll visit thee for this, and kiss thine eyes,
And greet thee morn and even in the skies.'

XLIII

When the full morning came, she had devised
  How she might secret to the forest hie;
How she might find the clay, so dearly prized,
  And sing to it one latest lullaby;   340

How her short absence might be unsurmised,
  While she the inmost of the dream would try.
Resolv'd, she took with her an aged nurse,
And went into that dismal forest-hearse.

XLIV

See, as they creep along the river side,
  How she doth whisper to that aged Dame,
And, after looking round the champaign wide,
  Shows her a knife.—'What feverous hectic
    flame
Burns in thee, child?—What good can thee be-
    tide,
  That thou should'st smile again?'—The eve-
    ning came,   350
And they had found Lorenzo's earthy bed;
The flint was there, the berries at his head.

XLV

Who hath not loiter'd in a green church-yard,
  And let his spirit, like a demon-mole,
Work through the clayey soil and gravel hard,
  To see scull, coffin'd bones, and funeral stole;
Pitying each form that hungry Death hath
    marr'd,
  And filling it once more with human soul?
Ah! this is holiday to what was felt
When Isabella by Lorenzo knelt.   360

XLVI

She gaz'd into the fresh-thrown mould, as though
  One glance did fully all its secrets tell;
Clearly she saw, as other eyes would know
  Pale limbs at bottom of a crystal well;
Upon the murderous spot she seem'd to grow,
  Like to a native lilly of the dell:
Then with her knife, all sudden, she began
To dig more fervently than misers can.

XLVII

Soon she turn'd up a soiled glove, whereon
  Her silk had play'd in purple phantasies,   370
She kiss'd it with a lip more chill than stone,
  And put it in her bosom, where it dries
And freezes utterly unto the bone
  Those dainties made to still an infant's cries:
Then 'gan she work again; nor stay'd her care,
But to throw back at times her veiling hair.

XLVIII

That old nurse stood beside her wondering,
  Until her heart felt pity to the core
At sight of such a dismal labouring,
  And so she kneeled, with her locks all
    hoar,   380
And put her lean hands to the horrid thing:

Three hours they labour'd at this travail sore;
At last they felt the kernel of the grave,
And Isabella did not stamp and rave.

XLIX

Ah! wherefore all this wormy circumstance?
  Why linger at the yawning tomb so long?
O for the gentleness of old Romance,
  The simple plaining[11] of a minstrel's song!
Fair reader, at the old tale take a glance,
  For here, in truth, it doth not well belong   390
To speak:—O turn thee to the very tale,
And taste the music of that vision pale.

L

With duller steel than the Perséan sword[12]
  They cut away no formless monster's head,
But one, whose gentleness did well accord
  With death, as life. The ancient harps have
    said,
Love never dies, but lives, immortal Lord:
  If Love impersonate was ever dead,
Pale Isabella kiss'd it, and low moan'd.
'Twas love; cold,—dead indeed, but not
    dethroned.   400

LI

In anxious secrecy they took it home,
  And then the prize was all for Isabel:
She calm'd its wild hair with a golden comb,
  And all around each eye's sepulchral cell
Pointed each fringed lash; the smeared loam
  With tears, as chilly as a dripping well,
She drench'd away:—and still she comb'd, and
    kept
Sighing all day—and still she kiss'd, and wept.

LII

Then in a silken scarf,—sweet with the dews
  Of precious flowers pluck'd in Araby,   410
And divine liquids come with odorous ooze
  Through the cold serpent-pipe refreshfully,—
She wrapp'd it up; and for its tomb did choose
  A garden-pot, wherein she laid it by,
And cover'd it with mould, and o'er it set
Sweet Basil,[13] which her tears kept ever wet.

LIII

And she forgot the stars, the moon, and sun,
  And she forgot the blue above the trees,
And she forgot the dells where waters run,
  And she forgot the chilly autumn breeze;   420
She had no knowledge when the day was done,

---

11 lament.
12 the sword used by Perseus in decapitating the Gorgon Medusa.
13 a fragrant plant, something like mint.

And the new morn she saw not: but in peace
Hung over her sweet Basil evermore,
And moisten'd it with tears unto the core.

LIV

And so she ever fed it with thin tears,
  Whence thick, and green, and beautiful it
    grew,
So that it smelt more balmy than its peers
  Of Basil-tufts in Florence; for it drew
Nurture besides, and life, from human fears,
  From the fast mouldering head there shut from
    view: 430
So that the jewel, safely casketed,
Came forth, and in perfumed leafits spread.

LV

O Melancholy, linger here awhile!
  O Music, Music, breathe despondingly!
O Echo, Echo, from some sombre isle,
  Unknown Lethean, sigh to us—O sigh!
Spirits in grief, lift up your heads, and smile;
  Lift up your heads, sweet Spirits, heavily,
And make a pale light in your cypress glooms,
Tinting with silver wan your marble tombs. 440

LVI

Moan hither, all ye syllables of woe,
  From the deep throat of sad Melpomene![14]
Through bronzed lyre in tragic order go,
  And touch the strings into a mystery;
Sound mournfully upon the winds and low;
  For simple Isabel is soon to be
Among the dead: She withers, like a palm
Cut by an Indian for its juicy balm.

LVII

O leave the palm to wither by itself;
  Let not quick Winter chill its dying
    hour!—   450
It may not be—those Baälites of pelf,[15]
  Her brethren, noted the continual shower
From her dead eyes; and many a curious elf,
  Among her kindred, wonder'd that such dower
Of youth and beauty should be thrown aside
By one mark'd out to be a Noble's bride.

LVIII

And, furthermore, her brethren wonder'd much
  Why she sat drooping by the Basil green,
And why it flourish'd, as by magic touch;
  Greatly they wonder'd what the thing might
    mean: 460

They could not surely give belief, that such
  A very nothing would have power to wean
Her from her own fair youth, and pleasures gay,
And even remembrance of her love's delay.

LIX

Therefore they watch'd a time when they might
    sift
  This hidden whim: and long they watch'd in
    vain:
For seldom did she go to chapel-shrift,
  And seldom felt she any hunger-pain;
And when she left, she hurried back, as swift
  As bird on wing to breast its eggs again;   470
And, patient as a hen-bird, sat her there
Beside her Basil, weeping through her hair.

LX

Yet they contriv'd to steal the Basil-pot,
  And to examine it in secret place;
The thing was vile with green and livid spot,
  And yet they knew it was Lorenzo's face:
The guerdon of their murder they had got,
  And so left Florence in a moment's space,
Never to turn again.—Away they went,
With blood upon their heads, to banishment. 480

LXI

O Melancholy, turn thine eyes away!
  O Music, Music, breathe despondingly!
O Echo, Echo, on some other day,
  From isles Lethean, sigh to us—O sigh!
Spirits of grief, sing not your 'Well-a-way!'
  For Isabel, sweet Isabel, will die;
Will die a death too lone and incomplete,
Now they have ta'en away her Basil sweet.

LXII

Piteous she look'd on dead and senseless things,
  Asking for her lost Basil amorously;   490
And with melodious chuckle in the strings
  Of her lorn voice, she oftentimes would cry
After the Pilgrim in his wanderings,
  To ask him where her Basil was; and why
'Twas hid from her: 'For cruel 'tis,' said she,
'To steal my Basil-pot away from me.'

LXIII

And so she pined, and so she died forlorn,
  Imploring for her Basil to the last.
No heart was there in Florence but did mourn
  In pity of her love, so overcast.   500
And a sad ditty of this story born
  From mouth to mouth through all the country
    pass'd:

---

14 the Muse of tragedy.
15 worshipers of money, like pagans who sacrificed to Baal.

Still is the burthen sung—'O cruelty,
To steal my Basil-pot away from me!'
1818   1820

FRAGMENT OF AN ODE TO MAIA, WRITTEN ON MAY DAY, 1818

MOTHER of Hermes! and still youthful Maia!
     May I sing to thee
As thou wast hymned on the shores of Baiæ?
     Or may I woo thee
In earlier Sicilian?[1] for thy smiles
Seek as they once were sought, in Grecian isles,
  By bards who died content on pleasant sward,
    Leaving great verse unto a little clan?
O, give me their old vigour, and unheard
    Save of the quiet Primrose, and the span   10
      Of heaven and few ears,
Rounded by thee, my song should die away
      Content as theirs,
. Rich in the simple worship of a day.
                    1848

TO AILSA ROCK

[While on a walking trip through Scotland, Keats records in a letter to his brother, 10 July 1818, his first viewing of Ailsa Rock: 'When we left Cairn our road lay half way up the sides of a green mountainous shore, full of clefts of verdure and eternally varying—sometimes up sometimes down, and over little bridges going across green chasms of moss, rock, and trees—winding about everywhere. After two or three miles of this we turned suddenly into a magnificent glen finely wooded in parts —seven miles long—with a mountain stream winding down the midst—full of cottages in the most happy situations—the sides of the hills covered with sheep—the effect of cattle lowing I never had so finely. At the end we had a gradual ascent and got among the tops of the mountains whence in a little time I descried in the sea Ailsa Rock 940 feet high—it was 15 miles distant and seemed close upon us. The effect of Ailsa with the peculiar perspective of the sea in connexion with the ground we stood on, and the misty rain then falling gave me a complete idea of a deluge. Ailsa struck me very suddenly—really I was a little alarmed.']

HEARKEN, thou craggy ocean pyramid!
  Give answer from thy voice, the sea-fowls'
    screams!
  When were thy shoulders mantled in huge
    streams?
When, from the sun, was thy broad forehead hid?
How long is ʼt since the mighty power bid
  Thee heave to airy sleep from fathom dreams?
  Sleep in the lap of thunder or sunbeams,

1 Baiae, near Naples, and Sicily were at one time Greek colonies.

Or when grey clouds are thy cold coverlid.
Thou answer'st not; for thou art dead asleep;
  Thy life is but two dead eternities—   10
The last in air, the former in the deep;
  First with the whales, last with the eagle-
    skies—
Drown'd wast thou till an earthquake made thee
    steep,
  Another cannot wake thy giant size.
    1818   1819

FANCY

EVER let the fancy roam,
Pleasure never is at home:
At a touch sweet Pleasure melteth,
Like to bubbles when rain pelteth;
Then let winged Fancy wander
Through the thought still spread beyond her:
Open wide the mind's cage-door,
She'll dart forth, and cloudward soar.
O sweet Fancy! let her loose;
Summer's joys are spoilt by use,   10
And the enjoying of the Spring
Fades as does its blossoming;
Autumn's red-lipp'd fruitage too,
Blushing through the mist and dew,
Cloys with tasting: What do then?
Sit thee by the ingle, when
The sear faggot blazes bright,
Spirit of a winter's night;
When the soundless earth is muffled,
And the caked snow is shuffled   20
From the ploughboy's heavy shoon;
When the Night doth meet the Noon
In a dark conspiracy
To banish Even from her sky.
Sit thee there, and send abroad,
With a mind self-overaw'd,
Fancy, high-commission'd:—send her!
She has vassals to attend her:
She will bring, in spite of frost,
Beauties that the earth hath lost;   30
She will bring thee, all together,
All delights of summer weather;
All the buds and bells of May,
From dewy sward or thorny spray;
All the heaped Autumn's wealth,
With a still, mysterious stealth;
She will mix these pleasures up
Like three fit wines in a cup,
And thou shalt quaff it:—thou shalt hear
Distant harvest-carols clear;   40
Rustle of the reaped corn;

Sweet birds antheming the morn:
And, in the same moment—hark!
'Tis the early April lark,
Or the rooks, with busy caw,
Foraging for sticks and straw.
Thou shalt, at one glance, behold
The daisy and the marigold;
White-plum'd lillies, and the first
Hedge-grown primrose that hath burst;   50
Shaded hyacinth, alway
Sapphire queen of the mid-May;
And every leaf, and every flower
Pearled with the self-same shower.
Thou shalt see the field-mouse peep
Meagre from its celled sleep;
And the snake all winter-thin
Cast on sunny bank its skin;
Freckled nest-eggs thou shalt see
Hatching in the hawthorn-tree,   60
When the hen-bird's wing doth rest
Quiet on her mossy nest;
Then the hurry and alarm
When the bee-hive casts its swarm;
Acorns ripe down-pattering,
While the autumn breezes sing.

Oh, sweet Fancy! let her loose;
Every thing is spoilt by use:
Where's the cheek that doth not fade,
Too much gaz'd at? Where's the maid   70
Whose lip mature is ever new?
Where's the eye, however blue,
Doth not weary? Where's the face
One would meet in every place?
Where's the voice, however soft,
One would hear so very oft?
At a touch sweet Pleasure melteth
Like to bubbles when rain pelteth.
Let, then, winged Fancy find
Thee a mistress to thy mind: 80
Dulcet-eyed as Ceres' daughter,[1]
Ere the God of Torment[2] taught her
How to frown and how to chide;
With a waist and with a side
White as Hebe's, when her zone[3]
Slipt its golden clasp, and down
Fell her kirtle to her feet,
While she held the goblet sweet,
And Jove grew languid.—Break the mesh
Of the Fancy's silken leash;   90
Quickly break her prison-string
And such joys as these she'll bring,—

----

1 Proserpine.
2 Pluto, who had made her queen of the lower world.
3 belt.

Let the winged Fancy roam,
Pleasure never is at home.
          1818   1820

ODE

[Keats wrote this poem in his copy of Beaumont and
Fletcher, on the blank page before the tragi-comedy *The
Fair Maid of the Inn.* He sent a copy of it, together with
the poem *Fancy,* in a letter to his brother and sister, saying: 'These are specimens of a sort of rondeau which I
think I shall become partial to—because you have one
idea amplified with greater ease and more delight and
freedom than in the sonnet.']

BARDS of Passion and of Mirth,
Ye have left your souls on earth!
Have ye souls in heaven too,
Double lived in regions new?
Yes, and those of heaven commune
With the spheres of sun and moon;
With the noise of fountains wond'rous,
And the parle of voices thund'rous;
With the whisper of heaven's trees
And one another, in soft ease   10
Seated on Elysian lawns
Brows'd by none but Dian's fawns;
Underneath large blue-bells tented,
Where the daisies are rose-scented,
And the rose herself has got
Perfume which on earth is not;
Where the nightingale doth sing
Not a senseless, tranced thing,
But divine melodious truth;
Philosophic numbers smooth;   20
Tales and golden histories
Of heaven and its mysteries.

Thus ye live on high, and then
On the earth ye live again;
And the souls ye left behind you
Teach us, here, the way to find you,
Where your other souls are joying,
Never slumber'd, never cloying.
Here, your earth-born souls still speak
To mortals, of their little week;   30
Of their sorrows and delights;
Of their passions and their spites;
Of their glory and their shame;
What doth strengthen and what maim.
Thus ye teach us, every day,
Wisdom, though fled far away.

Bards of Passion and of Mirth,
Ye have left your souls on earth!
Ye have souls in heaven too,
Double-lived in regions new!   40
          1818   1820

HYPERION[1]

A FRAGMENT

[The idea of a poem on the fall of the Titans had been in Keats's mind for some time even before the Scottish tour in the summer of 1818. However, no effective start was made on *Hyperion* until December, after Tom's death. M. R. Ridley (*Keats' Craftsmanship*, 1933, pp. 57–58) thinks that *Hyperion* was probably written in 'a continuing burst of reluctant creation' during December 1818–January 1819.

An early reference to *Hyperion* in a letter to Haydon, 23 January 1818, implies considerable previous thought about the characteristics of the poem as it was taking shape in his mind. In commenting on Haydon's remarks about some proposed illustrations for *Endymion*, Keats wrote, 'I have a complete fellow-feeling with you in this business—so much so that it would be as well to wait for a choice out of *Hyperion*—when that poem is done there will be wide range for you—in *Endymion* I think you may have many bits of the deep and sentimental cast—the nature of *Hyperion* will lead me to treat it in a more naked and Grecian manner—and the march of passion and endeavour will be undeviating—and one great contrast between them will be—that the hero of the written tale being mortal is led on, like Buonaparte, by circumstances; whereas the Apollo in *Hyperion* being a fore-seeing god will shape his actions like one.' Thus *Hyperion* was to be a far greater poem than *Endymion*, of epic proportions with a god as hero, who possessed self-knowledge and the power to shape his destiny.

In the execution, *Endymion* was, indeed, left far behind; Milton's 'full harmonics,' both directly and indirectly through the medium of Cary's *Dante,* gave to *Hyperion* a tone of elevated and sustained grandeur. But the new poem, however great, remains an experiment and a fragment. On 22 September 1819, Keats wrote to Reynolds: 'I have given up *Hyperion*—there were too many Miltonic inversions in it—Miltonic verse cannot be written but in an artful, or, rather artist's humor. I wish to give myself up to other sensations.' How Keats would have shaped the action had he gone on with the poem is, of course, a matter of conjecture.]

BOOK I

DEEP in the shady sadness of a vale
Far sunken from the healthy breath of morn,
Far from the fiery noon, and eve's one star,
Sat grey-hair'd Saturn, quiet as a stone,
Still as the silence round about his lair;
Forest on forest hung about his head
Like cloud on cloud. No stir of air was there,
Not so much life as on a summer's day
Robs not one light seed from the feather'd grass,
But where the dead leaf fell, there did it rest.   10
A stream went voiceless by, still deadened more
By reason of his fallen divinity
Spreading a shade: the Naiad 'mid her reeds
Press'd her cold finger closer to her lips.

Along the margin-sand large foot-marks went,
No further than to where his feet had stray'd,
And slept there since. Upon the sodden ground
His old right hand lay nerveless, listless, dead,
Unsceptred; and his realmless eyes were closed;
While his bow'd head seem'd list'ning to the
     Earth,   20
His ancient mother, for some comfort yet.

It seem'd no force could wake him from his
     place;
But there came one,[2] who with a kindred hand
Touch'd his wide shoulders, after bending low
With reverence, though to one who knew it not.
She was a Goddess of the infant world;
By her in stature the tall Amazon
Had stood a pigmy's height: she would have
     ta'en
Achilles by the hair and bent his neck;
Or with a finger stay'd Ixion's wheel.[3]   30
Her face was large as that of Memphian sphinx,
Pedestal'd haply in a palace court,
When sages look'd to Egypt for their lore.
But oh! how unlike marble was that face:
How beautiful, if sorrow had not made
Sorrow more beautiful than Beauty's self.
There was a listening fear in her regard,
As if calamity had but begun;
As if the vanward clouds of evil days
Had spent their malice, and the sullen rear   40
Was with its stored thunder labouring up.
One hand she press'd upon that aching spot
Where beats the human heart, as if just there,
Though an immortal, she felt cruel pain:
The other upon Saturn's bended neck
She laid, and to the level of his ear
Leaning with parted lips, some words she spake
In solemn tenour and deep organ tone:
Some mourning words, which in our feeble
     tongue
Would come in these like accents; O how frail   50
To that large utterance of the early Gods!
'Saturn, look up!—though wherefore, poor old
     King?
I have no comfort for thee, no not one:
I cannot say, "O wherefore sleepest thou?"
For heaven is parted from thee, and the earth
Knows thee not, thus afflicted, for a God;
And ocean too, with all its solemn noise,
Has from thy sceptre pass'd; and all the air
Is emptied of thine hoary majesty.
Thy thunder, conscious of the new command,   60

---

1 sun-god among the Titans and father of Helios (Apollo).

2 Thea, a Titan, the sister of Saturn and Hyperion.
3 For making love to Juno, Ixion was condemned by Jupiter to perpetual punishment by being bound on a revolving wheel of fire in Tartarus.

Rumbles reluctant o'er our fallen house;
And thy sharp lightning in unpractis'd hands
Scorches and burns our once serene domain.
O aching time! O moments big as years!
All as ye pass swell out the monstrous truth,
And press it so upon our weary griefs
That unbelief has not a space to breathe.
Saturn, sleep on:—O thoughtless, why did I
Thus violate thy slumbrous solitude?
Why should I ope thy melancholy eyes?   70
Saturn, sleep on! while at thy feet I weep.'

  As when, upon a tranced summer-night,
Those green-rob'd senators of mighty woods,
Tall oaks, branch-charmed by the earnest stars,
Dream, and so dream all night without a stir,
Save from one gradual solitary gust
Which comes upon the silence, and dies off,
As if the ebbing air had but one wave;
So came these words and went; the while in tears
She touch'd her fair large forehead to the
          ground,   80
Just where her falling hair might be outspread
A soft and silken mat for Saturn's feet.
One moon, with alteration slow, had shed
Her silver seasons four upon the night,
And still these two were postured motionless,
Like natural sculpture in cathedral cavern;
The frozen God still couchant on the earth,
And the sad Goddess weeping at his feet:
Until at length old Saturn lifted up
His faded eyes, and saw his kingdom gone,   90
And all the gloom and sorrow of the place,
And that fair kneeling Goddess; and then spake,
As with a palsied tongue, and while his beard
Shook horrid with such aspen-malady:
'O tender spouse of gold Hyperion,
Thea, I feel thee ere I see thy face;
Look up, and let me see our doom in it;
Look up, and tell me if this feeble shape
Is Saturn's; tell me, if thou hear'st the voice
Of Saturn; tell me, if this wrinkling brow,   100
Naked and bare of its great diadem,
Peers like the front of Saturn. Who had power
To make me desolate? whence came the strength?
How was it nurtur'd to such bursting forth,
 While Fate seem'd strangled in my nervous
          grasp?
But it is so; and I am smother'd up,
And buried from all godlike exercise
Of influence benign on planets pale,
Of admonitions to the winds and seas,
Of peaceful sway above man's harvesting,   110
And all those acts which Deity supreme
Doth ease its heart of love in.—I am gone

Away from my own bosom: I have left
My strong identity, my real self,
Somewhere between the throne, and where I sit
Here on this spot of earth. Search, Thea, search!
Open thine eyes eterne, and sphere them round
Upon all space: space starr'd, and lorn of light;
Space region'd with life-air; and barren void;
Spaces of fire, and all the yawn of hell.—   120
Search, Thea, search! and tell me, if thou seest
A certain shape or shadow, making way
With wings or chariot fierce to repossess
A heaven he lost erewhile: it must—it must
Be of ripe progress—Saturn must be King.
Yes, there must be a golden victory;
There must be Gods thrown down, and trumpets
          blown
Of triumph calm, and hymns of festival
Upon the gold clouds metropolitan,
Voices of soft proclaim, and silver stir   130
Of strings in hollow shells; and there shall be
Beautiful things made new, for the surprise
Of the sky-children; I will give command:
Thea! Thea! Thea! where is Saturn?'

  This passion lifted him upon his feet,
And made his hands to struggle in the air,
His Druid locks to shake and ooze with sweat,
His eyes to fever out, his voice to cease.
He stood, and heard not Thea's sobbing deep;
A little time, and then again he snatch'd   140
Utterance thus.—'But cannot I create?
Cannot I form? Cannot I fashion forth
Another world, another universe,
To overbear and crumble this to naught?
Where is another chaos? Where?'—That word
Found way unto Olympus, and made quake
The rebel three.[4]—Thea was startled up,
And in her bearing was a sort of hope,
As thus she quick-voic'd spake, yet full of awe.
'This cheers our fallen house: come to our
          friends,   150
O Saturn! come away, and give them heart;
I know the covert, for thence came I hither.'
Thus brief; then with beseeching eyes she went
With backward footing through the shade a
          space:
He follow'd, and she turn'd to lead the way
Through aged boughs, that yielded like the mist
Which eagles cleave upmounting from their nest.

  Meanwhile in other realms big tears were shed,
More sorrow like to this, and such like woe,
Too huge for mortal tongue or pen of scribe: 160

---

4 Jupiter, Neptune, and Pluto, the three sons who had rebelled
against their father Saturn and overthrown him.

The Titans fierce, self-hid, or prison-bound,
Groan'd for the old allegiance once more,
And listen'd in sharp pain for Saturn's voice.
But one of the whole mammoth-brood still kept
His sov'reignty, and rule, and majesty;—
Blazing Hyperion on his orbed fire
Still sat, still snuff'd the incense, teeming up
From man to the sun's God; yet unsecure:
For as among us mortals omens drear
Fright and perplex, so also shuddered he—   170
Not at dog's howl, or gloom-bird's hated screech,
Or the familiar visiting of one
Upon the first toll of his passing-bell,
Or prophesyings of the midnight lamp;
But horrors, portion'd to a giant nerve,
Oft made Hyperion ache. His palace bright
Bastion'd with pyramids of glowing gold,
And touch'd with shade of bronzed obelisks,
Glar'd a blood-red through all its thousand
     courts,
Arches, and domes, and fiery galleries;   180
And all its curtains of Aurorian clouds
Flush'd angerly: while sometimes eagle's wings,
Unseen before by Gods or wondering men,
Darken'd the place; and neighing steeds were
     heard,
Not heard before by Gods or wondering men.
Also, when he would taste the spicy wreaths
Of incense, breath'd aloft from sacred hills,
Instead of sweets, his ample palate took
Savour of poisonous brass and metal sick:
And so, when harbour'd in the sleepy west,   190
After the full completion of fair day,—
For rest divine upon exalted couch
And slumber in the arms of melody,
He pac'd away the pleasant hours of ease
With stride colossal, on from hall to hall;
While far within each aisle and deep recess,
His winged minions in close clusters stood,
Amaz'd and full of fear; like anxious men
Who on wide plains gather in panting troops,
When earthquakes jar their battlements and
     towers.   200
Even now, while Saturn, rous'd from icy trance,
Went step for step with Thea through the woods,
Hyperion, leaving twilight in the rear,
Came slope upon the threshold of the west;
Then, as was wont, his palace-door flew ope
In smoothest silence, save what solemn tubes,
Blown by the serious Zephyrs, gave of sweet
And wandering sounds, slow-breathed melodies;
And like a rose in vermeil tint and shape,
In fragrance soft, and coolness to the eye,   210
That inlet to severe magnificence
Stood full blown, for the God to enter in.

He enter'd, but he enter'd full of wrath;
His flaming robes stream'd out beyond his heels,
And gave a roar, as if of earthly fire,
That scar'd away the meek ethereal Hours
  And made their dove-wings tremble. On he
     flared,
From stately nave to nave, from vault to vault,
Through bowers of fragrant and enwreathed
     light,
And diamond-paved lustrous long arcades,   220
Until he reach'd the great main cupola;
  There standing fierce beneath, he stamped his
     foot,
And from the basements deep to the high towers
Jarr'd his own golden region; and before
The quavering thunder thereupon had ceas'd,
His voice leapt out, despite of godlike curb,
To this result: 'O dreams of day and night!
O monstrous forms! O effigies of pain!
O spectres busy in a cold, cold gloom!
O lank-ear'd Phantoms of black-weeded
     pools!   230
Why do I know ye? why have I seen ye? why
Is my eternal essence thus distraught
To see and to behold these horrors new?
Saturn is fallen, am I too to fall?
Am I to leave this haven of my rest,
This cradle of my glory, this soft clime,
This calm luxuriance of blissful light,
These crystalline pavilions, and pure fanes,
Of all my lucent empire? It is left
Deserted, void, nor any haunt of mine.   240
The blaze, the splendour, and the symmetry,
I cannot see—but darkness, death and darkness.
Even here, into my centre of repose,
The shady visions come to domineer,
Insult, and blind, and stifle up my pomp,—
Fall!—No, by Tellus[5] and her briny robes!
Over the fiery frontier of my realms
I will advance a terrible right arm
Shall scare that infant thunderer, rebel Jove,
And bid old Saturn take his throne again.'—   250
He spake, and ceas'd, the while a heavier threat
Held struggle with his throat but came not forth;
For as in theatres of crowded men
Hubbub increases more they call out 'Hush!'
So at Hyperion's words the Phantoms pale
Bestirr'd themselves, thrice horrible and cold;
And from the mirror'd level where he stood
A mist arose, as from a scummy marsh.
At this, through all his bulk an agony
Crept gradual from the feet unto the crown,   260
Like a lithe serpent vast and muscular
Making slow way, with head and neck convuls'd

5 the goddess of Earth.

From over-strained might. Releas'd, he fled
To the eastern gates, and full six dewy hours
Before the dawn in season due should blush,
He breath'd fierce breath against the sleepy portals,
Clear'd them of heavy vapours, burst them wide
Suddenly on the ocean's chilly streams.
The planet orb of fire, whereon he rode
Each day from east to west the heavens through,   270
Spun round in sable curtaining of clouds;
Not therefore veiled quite, blindfold, and hid,
But ever and anon the glancing spheres,
Circles, and arcs, and broad-belting colure,
Glow'd through, and wrought upon the muffling dark
Sweet-shaped lightnings from the nadir deep
Up to the zenith,—hieroglyphics old
Which sages and keen-eyed astrologers
Then living on the earth, with labouring thought
Won from the gaze of many centuries: 280
Now lost, save what we find on remnants huge
Of stone, or marble swart; their import gone,
Their wisdom long since fled.—Two wings this orb
Possess'd for glory, two fair argent wings,
Ever exalted at the God's approach:
And now, from forth the gloom their plumes immense
Rose, one by one, till all outspreaded were;
While still the dazzling globe maintain'd eclipse,
Awaiting for Hyperion's command.
Fain would he have commanded, fain took throne   290
And bid the day begin, if but for change.
He might not:—No, though a primeval God:
The sacred seasons might not be disturb'd.
Therefore the operations of the dawn
Stay'd in their birth, even as here 'tis told.
Those silver wings expanded sisterly,
Eager to sail their orb; the porches wide
Open'd upon the dusk demesnes of night;
And the bright Titan, phrenzied with new woes,
Unus'd to bend, by hard compulsion bent   300
His spirit to the sorrow of the time;
And all along a dismal rack of clouds,
Upon the boundaries of day and night,
He stretch'd himself in grief and radiance faint.
There as he lay, the Heaven with its stars
Look'd down on him with pity, and the voice
Of Cœlus,[6] from the universal space,
Thus whisper'd low and solemn in his ear.
'O brightest of my children dear, earth-born
And sky-engendered, Son of Mysteries   310

_____
6 god of the Sky.

All unrevealed even to the powers
Which met at thy creating; at whose joys
And palpitations sweet, and pleasures soft,
I, Cœlus, wonder, how they came and whence;
And at the fruits thereof what shapes they be,
Distinct, and visible; symbols divine,
Manifestations of that beauteous life
Diffus'd unseen throughout eternal space:
Of these new-form'd art thou, oh brightest child!
Of these, thy brethren and the Goddesses!   320
There is sad feud among ye, and rebellion
Of son against his sire. I saw him fall,
I saw my first-born tumbled from his throne!
To me his arms were spread, to me his voice
Found way from forth the thunders round his head!
Pale wox I, and in vapours hid my face.
Art thou, too, near such doom? vague fear there is:
For I have seen my sons most unlike Gods.
Divine ye were created, and divine
In sad demeanour, solemn, undisturb'd,   330
Unruffled, like high Gods, ye liv'd and ruled:
Now I behold in you fear, hope, and wrath;
Actions of rage and passion; even as
I see them, on the mortal world beneath,
In men who die.—This is the grief, O Son!
Sad sign of ruin, sudden dismay, and fall!
Yet do thou strive; as thou art capable,
As thou canst move about, an evident God;
And canst oppose to each malignant hour
Ethereal presence:—I am but a voice;   340
My life is but the life of winds and tides,
No more than winds and tides can I avail:—
But thou canst.—Be thou therefore in the van
Of circumstance; yea, seize the arrow's barb
Before the tense string murmur.—To the earth!
For there thou wilt find Saturn, and his woes.
Meantime I will keep watch on thy bright sun,
And of thy seasons be a careful nurse.'—
Ere half this region-whisper had come down,
Hyperion arose, and on the stars   350
Lifted his curved lids, and kept them wide
Until it ceas'd; and still he kept them wide:
And still they were the same bright, patient stars.
Then with a slow incline of his broad breast,
Like to a diver in the pearly seas,
Forward he stoop'd over the airy shore,
And plung'd all noiseless into the deep night.

BOOK II

JUST at the self-same beat of Time's wide wings
Hyperion slid into the rustled air,
And Saturn gain'd with Thea that sad place

Where Cybele[7] and the bruised Titans mourn'd.
It was a den where no insulting light
Could glimmer on their tears; where their own
      groans
They felt, but heard not, for the solid roar
Of thunderous waterfalls and torrents hoarse,
Pouring a constant bulk, uncertain where.
Crag jutting forth to crag, and rocks that
      seem'd   10
Ever as if just rising from a sleep,
Forehead to forehead held their monstrous
      horns;
And thus in thousand hugest phantasies
Made a fit roofing to this nest of woe.
Instead of thrones, hard flint they sat upon,
Couches of rugged stone, and slaty ridge
Stubborn'd with iron. All were not assembled:
Some chain'd in torture, and some wandering.
Cœus, and Gyges, and Briareüs,
Typhon, and Dolor, and Porphyrion,[8]   20
With many more, the brawniest in assault,
Were pent in regions of laborious breath;
Dungeon'd in opaque element, to keep
Their clenched teeth still clench'd, and all their
      limbs
Lock'd up like veins of metal, crampt and
      screw'd;
Without a motion, save of their big hearts
Heaving in pain, and horribly convuls'd
With sanguine feverous boiling gurge of pulse.
Mnemosyne[9] was straying in the world;
Far from her moon had Phœbe wandered;   30
And many else were free to roam abroad,
But for the main, here found they covert drear.
Scarce images of life, one here, one there,
Lay vast and edgeways; like a dismal cirque
Of Druid stones, upon a forlorn moor,
When the chill rain begins at shut of eve,
In dull November, and their chancel vault,
The Heaven itself, is blinded throughout night.
Each one kept shroud, nor to his neighbour gave
Or word, or look, or action of despair.   40
Creüs[10] was one; his ponderous iron mace
Lay by him, and a shatter'd rib of rock
Told of his rage, ere he thus sank and pined.
Iäpetus[11] another; in his grasp,
A serpent's plashy neck; its barbed tongue
Squeez'd from the gorge, and all its uncurl'd
      length
Dead; and because the creature could not spit

Its poison in the eyes of conquering Jove.
Next Cottus:[12] prone he lay, chin uppermost,
As though in pain; for still upon the flint   50
He ground severe his skull, with open mouth
And eyes at horrid working. Nearest him
Asia, born of most enormous Caf,[13]
Who cost her mother Tellus keener pangs,
Though feminine, than any of her sons:
More thought than woe was in her dusky face,
For she was prophesying of her glory;
And in her wide imagination stood
Palm-shaded temples, and high rival fanes,
By Oxus or in Ganges' sacred isles.   60
Even as Hope upon her anchor leans,
So leant she, not so fair, upon a tusk
Shed from the broadest of her elephants.
Above her, on a crag's uneasy shelve,
Upon his elbow rais'd, all prostrate else,
Shadow'd Enceladus;[14] once tame and mild
As grazing ox unworried in the meads;
Now tiger-passion'd, lion-thoughted, wroth,
He meditated, plotted, and even now
Was hurling mountains in that second war,   70
Not long delay'd, that scar'd the younger Gods
To hide themselves in forms of beast and bird.
Not far hence Atlas; and beside him prone
Phorcus, the sire of Gorgons. Neighbour'd close
Oceanus,[15] and Tethys,[16] in whose lap
Sobb'd Clymene[17] among her tangled hair.
In midst of all lay Themis,[18] at the feet
Of Ops the queen all clouded round from sight;
No shape distinguishable, more than when
Thick night confounds the pine-tops with the
      clouds: 80
And many else whose names may not be told.
For when the Muse's wings are air-ward spread,
Who shall delay her flight? And she must chaunt
Of Saturn, and his guide, who now had climb'd
With damp and slippery footing from a depth
More horrid still. Above a sombre cliff
Their heads appear'd, and up their stature grew
Till on the level height their steps found ease:
Then Thea spread abroad her trembling arms
Upon the precincts of this nest of pain,   90
And sidelong fix'd her eye on Saturn's face:
There saw she direst strife; the supreme God
At war with all the frailty of grief,
Of rage, of fear, anxiety, revenge,

---

7 wife of Saturn and mother of the Olympian gods; identical
with Ops (II, 113) and Rhea.
8 various giants and Titans.
9 the goddess of Memory; by Zeus, the mother of the Muses.
10 a Titan, a divinity of the sea.
11 another Titan, father of Prometheus.

12 a hundred-handed giant.
13 in Mohammedan mythology, a mountain said to surround the
earth.
14 a hundred-armed giant; one of the leaders in the war of the
Giants against the Olympian gods.
15 the eldest Titan, god of the stream Oceanus.
16 wife of Oceanus.
17 daughter of Oceanus and Tethys, and mother of Prometheus.
18 daughter of Saturn; by Zeus, mother of the Fates.

Remorse, spleen, hope, but most of all despair.
Against these plagues he strove in vain; for Fate
Had pour'd a mortal oil upon his head,
A disanointing poison: so that Thea,
Affrighted, kept her still, and let him pass
First onwards in, among the fallen tribe.   100

    As with us mortal men, the laden heart
Is persecuted more, and fever'd more,
When it is nighing to the mournful house
Where other hearts are sick of the same bruise;
So Saturn, as he walk'd into the midst,
Felt faint, and would have sunk among the rest,
But that he met Enceladus's eye,
Whose mightiness, and awe of him, at once
Came like an inspiration: and he shouted,
'Titans, behold your God!' at which some
    groan'd;   110
Some started on their feet; some also shouted;
Some wept, some wail'd, all bow'd with rev-
    erence:
And Ops, uplifting her black folded veil,
Show'd her pale cheeks, and all her forehead
    wan,
Her eye-brows thin and jet, and hollow eyes.
There is a roaring in the bleak-grown pines
When Winter lifts his voice; there is a noise
Among immortals when a God gives sign,
With hushing finger, how he means to load
His tongue with the full weight of utterless
    thought,   120
With thunder, and with music, and with pomp:
Such noise is like the roar of bleak-grown pines:
Which, when it ceases in this mountain'd world,
No other sound succeeds; but ceasing here,
Among these fallen, Saturn's voice therefrom
Grew up like organ, that begins anew
Its strain, when other harmonies, stopt short,
Leave the dinn'd air vibrating silverly.
Thus grew it up—'Not in my own sad breast,
Which is its own great judge and searcher
    out,   130
Can I find reason why ye should be thus:
Not in the legends of the first of days,
Studied from that old spirit-leaved book
Which starry Uranus with finger bright
Sav'd from the shores of darkness, when the
    waves
Low-ebb'd still hid it up in shallow gloom;—
And the which book ye know I ever kept
For my firm-based footstool:—Ah, infirm!
Not there, nor in sign, symbol, or portent
Of element, earth, water, air, and fire,—   140
At war, at peace, or inter-quarreling
One against one, or two, or three, or all

Each several one against the other three,
As fire with air loud warring when rain-floods
Drown both, and press them both against earth's
    face,
Where, finding sulphur, a quadruple wrath
Unhinges the poor world;—not in that strife,
Wherefrom I take strange lore, and read it deep,
Can I find reason why ye should be thus:
No, no-where can unriddle, though I search,   150
And pore on Nature's universal scroll
Even to swooning, why ye, Divinities,
The first-born of all shap'd and palpable Gods,
Should cower beneath what, in comparison,
Is untremendous might. Yet ye are here,
O'erwhelm'd, and spurn'd, and batter'd, ye are
    here!
O Titans, shall I say, "Arise!"—Ye groan:
Shall I say "Crouch!"—Ye groan. What can I
    then?
O Heaven wide! O unseen parent dear!
What can I? Tell me, all ye brethren Gods,   160
How we can war, how engine our great wrath!
O speak your counsel now, for Saturn's ear
Is all a-hunger'd. Thou, Oceanus,
Ponderest high and deep; and in thy face
I see, astonied, that severe content
Which comes of thought and musing: give us
    help!'

    So ended Saturn; and the God of the Sea,
Sophist and sage, from no Athenian grove,
But cogitation in his watery shades,
Arose, with locks not oozy, and began,   170
In murmurs, which his first-endeavouring tongue
Caught infant-like from the far-foamed sands.
'O ye, whom wrath consumes! who, passion-
    stung,
Writhe at defeat, and nurse your agonies!
Shut up your senses, stifle up your ears,
My voice is not a bellows unto ire.
Yet listen, ye who will, whilst I bring proof
How ye, perforce, must be content to stoop:
And in the proof much comfort will I give,
If ye will take that comfort in its truth.   180
We fall by course of Nature's law, not force
Of thunder, or of Jove. Great Saturn, thou
Hast sifted well the atom-universe;
But for this reason, that thou art the King,
And only blind from sheer supremacy,
One avenue was shaded from thine eyes,
Through which I wandered to eternal truth.
And first, as thou wast not the first of powers,
So art thou not the last; it cannot be:
Thou art not the beginning nor the end.   190
From chaos and parental darkness came

Light, the first fruits of that intestine broil,
That sullen ferment, which for wondrous ends
Was ripening in itself. The ripe hour came,
And with it light, and light, engendering
Upon its own producer, forthwith touch'd
The whole enormous matter into life.
Upon that very hour, our parentage,
The Heavens and the Earth, were manifest:
Then thou first born, and we the giant race,   200
Found ourselves ruling new and beauteous
     realms.
Now comes the pain of truth, to whom 'tis pain;
O folly! for to bear all naked truths,
And to envisage circumstance, all calm,
That is the top of sovereignty. Mark well!
As Heaven and Earth are fairer, fairer far
Than Chaos and blank Darkness, though once
     chiefs;
And as we show beyond that Heaven and
     Earth
In form and shape compact and beautiful,
In will, in action free, companionship,   210
And thousand other signs of purer life;
So on our heels a fresh perfection treads,
A power more strong in beauty, born of us
And fated to excel us, as we pass
In glory that old Darkness: nor are we
Thereby more conquer'd, than by us the rule
Of shapeless Chaos. Say, doth the dull soil
Quarrel with the proud forests it hath fed,
And feedeth still, more comely than itself?
Can it deny the chiefdom of green groves?   220
Or shall the tree be envious of the dove
Because it cooeth, and hath snowy wings
To wander wherewithal and find its joys?
We are such forest-trees, and our fair boughs
Have bred forth, not pale solitary doves,
But eagles golden-feather'd, who do tower
Above us in their beauty, and must reign
In right thereof; for 'tis the eternal law
That first in beauty should be first in might:
Yea, by that law, another race may drive   230
Our conquerors to mourn as we do now.
Have ye beheld the young God of the Seas,
My dispossessor? Have ye seen his face?
Have ye beheld his chariot, foam'd along
By noble winged creatures he hath made?
I saw him on the calmed waters scud,
With such a glow of beauty in his eyes,
That it enforc'd me to bid sad farewell
To all my empire: farewell sad I took,
And hither came, to see how dolorous fate   240
Had wrought upon ye; and how I might best
Give consolation in this woe extreme.
Receive the truth, and let it be your balm.'

Whether through poz'd conviction, or disdain,
They guarded silence, when Oceanus
Left murmuring, what deepest thought can tell?
But so it was, none answer'd for a space,
Save one whom none regarded, Clymene;[19]
And yet she answer'd not, only complain'd,
With hectic lips, and eyes up-looking mild,   250
Thus wording timidly among the fierce:
'O Father, I am here the simplest voice,
And all my knowledge is that joy is gone,
And this thing woe crept in among our hearts,
There to remain for ever, as I fear:
I would not bode of evil, if I thought
So weak a creature could turn off the help
Which by just right should come of mighty
     Gods;
Yet let me tell my sorrow, let me tell
Of what I heard, and how it made me weep,   260
And know that we had parted from all hope.
I stood upon a shore, a pleasant shore,
Where a sweet clime was breathed from a land
Of fragrance, quietness, and trees, and flowers.
Full of calm joy it was, as I of grief;
Too full of joy and soft delicious warmth;
So that I felt a movement in my heart
To chide, and to reproach that solitude
With songs of misery, music of our woes;
And sat me down, and took a mouthed shell   270
And murmur'd into it, and made melody—
O melody no more! for while I sang,
And with poor skill let pass into the breeze
The dull shell's echo, from a bowery strand
Just opposite, an island of the sea,
There came enchantment with the shifting wind,
That did both drown and keep alive my ears.
I threw my shell away upon the sand,
And a wave fill'd it, as my sense was fill'd
With that new blissful golden melody.   280
A living death was in each gush of sounds,
Each family of rapturous hurried notes,
That fell, one after one, yet all at once,
Like pearl beads dropping sudden from their
     string:
And then another, then another strain,
Each like a dove leaving its olive perch,
With music wing'd instead of silent plumes,
To hover round my head, and make me sick
Of joy and grief at once. Grief overcame,
And I was stopping up my frantic ears,   290
When, past all hindrance of my trembling hands,
A voice came sweeter, sweeter than all tune,
And still it cried, "Apollo! young Apollo!
The morning-bright Apollo! young Apollo!"
I fled, it follow'd me, and cried "Apollo!"

---

19 Italian goddess of fertility regarded as the wife of Saturn.

O Father, and O Brethren, had ye felt
Those pains of mine; O Saturn, hadst thou felt,
Ye would not call this too indulged tongue
Presumptuous, in thus venturing to be heard.'

    So far her voice flow'd on, like timorous
      brook   300
That, lingering along a pebbled coast,
Doth fear to meet the sea: but sea it met,
And shudder'd; for the overwhelming voice
Of huge Enceladus swallow'd it in wrath:
The ponderous syllables, like sullen waves
In the half-glutted hollows of reef-rocks,
Came booming thus, while still upon his arm
He lean'd; not rising, from supreme contempt.
'Or shall we listen to the over-wise,
Or to the over-foolish, Giant-Gods?   310
Not thunderbolt on thunderbolt, till all
That rebel Jove's whole armoury were spent,
Not world on world upon these shoulders piled,
Could agonize me more than baby-words
In midst of this dethronement horrible.
Speak! roar! shout! yell! ye sleepy Titans all.
Do ye forget the blows, the buffets vile?
Are ye not smitten by a youngling arm?
Dost thou forget, sham Monarch of the Waves,
Thy scalding in the seas? What, have I
    rous'd   320
Your spleens with so few simple words as these?
O joy! for now I see ye are not lost:
O joy! for now I see a thousand eyes
Wide-glaring for revenge!'—As this he said,
He lifted up his stature vast, and stood,
Still without intermission speaking thus:
'Now ye are flames, I'll tell you how to burn,
And purge the ether of our enemies;
How to feed fierce the crooked stings of fire,
And singe away the swollen clouds of Jove, 330
Stifling that puny essence in its tent.
O let him feel the evil he hath done;
For though I scorn Oceanus's lore,
Much pain have I for more than loss of realms:
The days of peace and slumberous calm are
    fled;
Those days, all innocent of scathing war,
When all the fair Existences of heaven
Came open-eyed to guess what we would
    speak:—
That was before our brows were taught to
    frown,
Before our lips knew else but solemn sounds; 340
That was before we knew the winged thing,
Victory, might be lost, or might be won.
And be ye mindful that Hyperion,

Our brightest brother, still is undisgraced—
Hyperion, lo! his radiance is here!'
    All eyes were on Enceladus's face,
And they beheld, while still Hyperion's name
Flew from his lips up to the vaulted rocks,
A pallid gleam across his features stern;
Not savage, for he saw full many a God   350
Wroth as himself. He look'd upon them all,
And in each face he saw a gleam of light,
But splendider in Saturn's, whose hoar locks
Shone like the bubbling foam about a keel
When the prow sweeps into a midnight cove.
In pale and silver silence they remain'd,
Till suddenly a splendour, like the morn,
Pervaded all the beetling gloomy steeps,
All the sad spaces of oblivion,
And every gulf, and every chasm old,   360
And every height, and every sullen depth,
Voiceless, or hoarse with loud tormented streams:
And all the everlasting cataracts,
And all the headlong torrents far and near,
Mantled before in darkness and huge shade,
Now saw the light and made it terrible.
It was Hyperion:—a granite peak
His bright feet touch'd, and there he stay'd to
    view
The misery his brilliance had betray'd
To the most hateful seeing of itself.   370
Golden his hair of short Numidian curl,
Regal his shape majestic, a vast shade
In midst of his own brightness, like the bulk
Of Memnon's image[20] at the set of sun
To one who travels from the dusking East:
Sighs, too, as mournful as that Memnon's harp
He utter'd, while his hands contemplative
He press'd together, and in silence stood.
Despondence seiz'd again the fallen Gods
At sight of the dejected King of Day,   380
And many hid their faces from the light:
But fierce Enceladus sent forth his eyes
Among the brotherhood; and, at their glare,
Uprose Iäpetus, and Creüs too,
And Phorcus, sea-born, and together strode
To where he towered on his eminence.
There those four shouted forth old Saturn's
    name;
Hyperion from the peak loud answered, 'Saturn!'
Saturn sat near the Mother of the Gods,
In whose face was no joy, though all the
    Gods   390
Gave from their hollow throats the name of
    'Saturn!'

---

20 According to tradition, a colossal statue of the Egyptian Memnon near Thebes gave forth musical sounds when struck by the rays of the rising sun.

BOOK III

THUS in alternate uproar and sad peace,
Amazed were those Titans utterly.
O leave them, Muse! O leave them to their woes;
For thou art weak to sing such tumults dire:
A solitary sorrow best befits
Thy lips, and antheming a lonely grief.
Leave them, O Muse! for thou anon wilt find
Many a fallen old Divinity
Wandering in vain about bewildered shores.
Meantime touch piously the Delphic harp,   10
And not a wind of heaven but will breathe
In aid soft warble from the Dorian flute;
For lo! 'tis the Father of all verse.
Flush every thing that hath a vermeil hue,
Let the rose glow intense and warm the air,
And let the clouds of even and of morn
Float in voluptuous fleeces o'er the hills;
Let the red wine within the goblet boil,
Cold as a bubbling well; let faint-lipp'd shells,
On sands, or in great deeps, vermilion turn   20
Through all their labyrinths; and let the maid
Blush keenly, as with some warm kiss surpris'd.
Chief isle of the embowered Cyclades,
Rejoice, O Delos, with thine olives green,
And poplars, and lawn-shading palms, and
        beech,
In which the Zephyr breathes the loudest song,
And hazels thick, dark-stemm'd beneath the
        shade:
Apollo is once more the golden theme!
Where was he, when the Giant of the Sun
Stood bright, amid the sorrow of his peers?   30
Together had he left his mother fair
And his twin-sister sleeping in their bower,
And in the morning twilight wandered forth
Beside the osiers of a rivulet,
Full ankle-deep in lillies of the vale.
The nightingale had ceas'd, and a few stars
Were lingering in the heavens, while the thrush
Began calm-throated. Throughout all the isle
There was no covert, no retired cave
Unhaunted by the murmurous noise of
        waves,   40
Though scarcely heard in many a green recess.
He listen'd, and he wept, and his bright tears
Went trickling down the golden bow he held.
Thus with half-shut suffused eyes he stood,
While from beneath some cumbrous boughs hard
        by
With solemn step an awful Goddess came,
And there was purport in her looks for him,
Which he with eager guess began to read
Perplex'd, the while melodiously he said:

'How cam'st thou over the unfooted sea?   50
Or hath that antique mien and robed form
Mov'd in these vales invisible till now?
Sure I have heard those vestments sweeping o'er
The fallen leaves, when I have sat alone
In cool mid-forest. Surely I have traced
The rustle of those ample skirts about
These grassy solitudes, and seen the flowers
Lift up their heads, as still the whisper pass'd.
Goddess! I have beheld those eyes before,
And their eternal calm, and all that face,   60
Or I have dream'd.'—'Yes,' said the supreme
        shape,
'Thou hast dream'd of me: and awaking up
Didst find a lyre all golden by thy side,
Whose strings touch'd by thy fingers, all the vast
Unwearied ear of the whole universe
Listen'd in pain and pleasure at the birth
Of such new tuneful wonder. Is't not strange
That thou shouldst weep, so gifted? Tell me,
        youth,
What sorrow thou canst feel; for I am sad
When thou dost shed a tear: explain thy
        griefs   70
To one who in this lonely isle hath been
The watcher of thy sleep and hours of life,
From the young day when first thy infant hand
Pluck'd witless the weak flowers, till thine arm
Could bend that bow heroic to all times.
Show thy heart's secret to an ancient Power
Who hath forsaken old and sacred thrones
For prophecies of thee, and for the sake
Of loveliness new born.'—Apollo then,
With sudden scrutiny and gloomless eyes,   80
Thus answer'd, while his white melodious throat
Throbb'd with the syllables.—'Mnemosyne!
Thy name is on my tongue, I know not how;
Why should I tell thee what thou so well seest?
Why should I strive to show what from thy lips
Would come no mystery? For me, dark, dark,
And painful vile oblivion seals my eyes:
I strive to search wherefore I am so sad,
Until a melancholy numbs my limbs;
And then upon the grass I sit, and moan,   90
Like one who once had wings.—O why should I
Feel curs'd and thwarted, when the liegeless air
Yields to my step aspirant? why should I
Spurn the green turf as hateful to my feet?
Goddess benign, point forth some unknown
        thing:
Are there not other regions than this isle?
What are the stars? There is the sun, the sun!
And the most patient brilliance of the moon!
And stars by thousands! Point me out the way

To any one particular beauteous star,   100
And I will flit into it with my lyre,
And make its silvery splendour pant with bliss.
I have heard the cloudy thunder: Where is
    power?
Whose hand, whose essence, what divinity
Makes this alarum in the elements,
While I here idle listen on the shores
In fearless yet in aching ignorance?
O tell me, lonely Goddess, by thy harp,
That waileth every morn and eventide,
Tell me why thus I rave, about these groves!   110
Mute thou remainest—mute! yet I can read
A wondrous lesson in thy silent face:
Knowledge enormous makes a God of me.
Names, deeds, grey legends, dire events, re-
    bellions,
Majesties, sovran voices, agonies,
Creations and destroyings, all at once
Pour into the wide hollows of my brain,
And deify me, as if some blithe wine
Or bright elixir peerless I had drunk,
And so become immortal.'—Thus the God,   120
While his enkindled eyes, with level glance
Beneath his white soft temples, stedfast kept
Trembling with light upon Mnemosyne.
Soon wild commotions shook him, and made
    flush
All the immortal fairness of his limbs;
Most like the struggle at the gate of death;
Or liker still to one who should take leave
Of pale immortal death, and with a pang
As hot as death's is chill, with fierce convulse
Die into life: so young Apollo anguish'd: 130
His very hair, his golden tresses famed
Kept undulation round his eager neck.
During the pain Mnemosyne upheld
Her arms as one who prophesied.—At length
Apollo shriek'd;—and lo! from all his limbs
Celestial   *   *   *   *   *   *

September 1818–April 1819   1820

THE EVE OF ST. AGNES

[Keats began *The Eve of St. Agnes* in late January
1819, and finished the first draft by the end of February.
The final draft was the result of much painstaking revision.]

I

ST. Agnes' Eve[1]—Ah, bitter chill it was!
The owl, for all his feathers, was a-cold;

---

1 20 January, proverbially one of the coldest nights of the year.
St. Agnes was a Roman virgin who suffered martyrdom in the
reign of Diocletian.

The hare limp'd trembling through the frozen
    grass,
And silent was the flock in woolly fold:
Numb were the Beadsman's fingers, while he
    told
His rosary, and while his frosted breath,
Like pious incense from a censer old,
Seem'd taking flight for heaven, without a
    death,
Past the sweet Virgin's picture, while his prayer
    he saith.

II

His prayer he saith, this patient, holy man;   10
Then takes his lamp, and riseth from his knees,
And back returneth, meagre, barefoot, wan,
Along the chapel aisle by slow degrees:
The sculptur'd dead, on each side, seem to
    freeze,
Emprison'd in black, purgatorial rails:
Knights, ladies, praying in dumb orat'ries,[2]
He passeth by; and his weak spirit fails
To think how they may ache in icy hoods and
    mails.

III

Northward he turneth through a little door,
And scarce three steps, ere Music's golden
    tongue   20
Flatter'd to tears this aged man and poor;
But no—already had his deathbell rung:
The joys of all his life were said and sung:
His was harsh penance on St. Agnes' Eve:
Another way he went, and soon among
Rough ashes sat he for his soul's reprieve,
And all night kept awake, for sinners' sake to
    grieve.

IV

That ancient Beadsman heard the prelude soft;
And so it chanc'd, for many a door was wide,
From hurry to and fro. Soon, up aloft,   30
The silver, snarling trumpets 'gan to chide:
The level chambers, ready with their pride,
Were glowing to receive a thousand guests:
The carved angels, ever eager-eyed,
Star'd, where upon their heads the cornice
    rests,
With hair blown back, and wings put cross-wise
    on their breasts.

V

At length burst in the argent revelry,
With plume, tiara, and all rich array,

---

2 small chapels for prayer.

also Byron's
Childe Harold.

Numerous as shadows haunting faerily
The brain, new stuff'd, in youth, with triumphs
   gay   40
Of old romance. These let us wish away,
And turn, sole-thoughted, to one Lady there,
Whose heart had brooded, all that wintry
   day,
On love, and wing'd St. Agnes' saintly care,
As she had heard old dames full many times de-
   clare.

VI

They told her how, upon St. Agnes' Eve,
Young virgins might have visions of delight,
And soft adorings from their loves receive
Upon the honey'd middle of the night,
If ceremonies due they did aright;   50
As, supperless to bed they must retire,
And couch supine their beauties, lilly white;
Nor look behind, nor sideways, but require
Of Heaven with upward eyes for all that they de-
   sire.

VII

Full of this whim was thoughtful Madeline:
The music, yearning like a God in pain,
She scarcely heard: her maiden eyes divine,
Fix'd on the floor, saw many a sweeping train
Pass by—she heeded not at all: in vain
Came many a tiptoe, amorous cavalier,   60
And back retir'd; not cool'd by high disdain,
But she saw not: her heart was otherwhere:
She sigh'd for Agnes' dreams, the sweetest of the
   year.

VIII

She danc'd along with vague, regardless eyes,
Anxious her lips, her breathing quick and
   short:
The hallow'd hour was near at hand: she sighs
Amid the timbrels, and the throng'd resort
Of whisperers in anger, or in sport;
'Mid looks of love, defiance, hate, and scorn,
Hoodwink'd with faery fancy; all amort,[3]   70
Save to St. Agnes and her lambs unshorn,[4]
And all the bliss to be before to-morrow morn.

IX

So, purposing each moment to retire,
She linger'd still. Meantime, across the moors,
Had come young Porphyro, with heart on fire
For Madeline. Beside the portal doors,

Buttress'd from moonlight, stands he, and im-
   plores
All saints to give him sight of Madeline,
But for one moment in the tedious hours,
That he might gaze and worship all
   unseen;   80
Perchance speak, kneel, touch, kiss—in sooth
   such things have been.

X

He ventures in: let no buzz'd whisper tell:
All eyes be muffled, or a hundred swords
Will storm his heart, Love's fev'rous citadel:
For him, those chambers held barbarian
   hordes,
Hyena foemen, and hot-blooded lords,
Whose very dogs would execrations howl
Against his lineage: not one breast affords
Him any mercy, in that mansion foul,
Save one old beldame, weak in body and in
   soul.   90

XI

Ah, happy chance! the aged creature came,
Shuffling along with ivory-headed wand,
To where he stood, hid from the torch's flame,
Behind a broad hall-pillar, far beyond
The sound of merriment and chorus bland:
He startled her; but soon she knew his face,
And grasp'd his fingers in her palsied hand,
Saying, 'Mercy, Porphyro! hie thee from this
   place:
They are all here to-night, the whole blood-
   thirsty race!

XII

'Get hence! get hence! there's dwarfish Hilde-
   brand;   100
He had a fever late, and in the fit
He cursed thee and thine, both house and
   land:
Then there's that old Lord Maurice, not a whit
More tame for his grey hairs—Alas me! flit!
Flit like a ghost away.'—'Ah, Gossip[5] dear,
We're safe enough; here in this arm-chair sit,
And tell me how'—'Good Saints! not here, not
   here;
Follow me, child, or else these stones will be thy
   bier.'

XIII

He follow'd through a lowly arched way,
Brushing the cobwebs with his lofty
   plume,   110

---

3 as if dead, lifeless.
4 On St. Agnes' day, two lambs were sacrificed at the altar during Mass. Their wool was afterward woven by the nuns. See below, l. 116.

5 godmother.

And as she mutter'd 'Well-a—well-a-day!'
He found him in a little moonlight room,
Pale, lattic'd, chill, and silent as a tomb.
'Now tell me where is Madeline,' said he,
'O tell me, Angela, by the holy loom
Which none but secret sisterhood may see,
When they St. Agnes' wool are weaving piously.'

XIV

'St. Agnes! Ah! it is St. Agnes' Eve—
Yet men will murder upon holy days:
Thou must hold water in a witch's sieve,   120
And be liege-lord of all the Elves and Fays,
To venture so: it fills me with amaze
To see thee, Porphyro!—St. Agnes' Eve!
God's help! my lady fair the conjuror plays
This very night: good angels her deceive!
But let me laugh awhile, I've mickle[6] time to
    grieve.'

XV

Feebly she laugheth in the languid moon,
While Porphyro upon her face doth look,
Like puzzled urchin on an aged crone
Who keepeth clos'd a wond'rous riddle-
    book,   130
As spectacled she sits in chimney nook.
But soon his eyes grew brilliant, when she told
His lady's purpose; and he scarce could brook
Tears, at the thought of those enchantments
    cold,
And Madeline asleep in lap of legends old.

XVI

Sudden a thought came like a full-blown rose,
Flushing his brow, and in his pained heart
Made purple riot: then doth he propose
A stratagem, that makes the beldame start:
'A cruel man and impious thou art: 140
Sweet lady, let her pray, and sleep, and dream
Alone with her good angels, far apart
From wicked men like thee. Go, go!—I deem
Thou canst not surely be the same that thou didst
    seem.'

XVII

'I will not harm her, by all saints I swear,'
Quoth Porphyro: 'O may I ne'er find grace
When my weak voice shall whisper its last
    prayer,
If one of her soft ringlets I displace,
Or look with ruffian passion in her face:
Good Angela, believe me by these tears;   150
Or I will, even in a moment's space,

Awake, with horrid shout, my foemen's ears,
And beard them, though they be more fang'd
    than wolves and bears.'

XVIII

'Ah! why wilt thou affright a feeble soul?
A poor, weak, palsy-stricken, churchyard
    thing,
Whose passing-bell may ere the midnight toll;
Whose prayers for thee, each morn and eve-
    ning,
Were never miss'd.'—Thus plaining, doth she
    bring
A gentler speech from burning Porphyro;
So woful, and of such deep sorrowing,   160
That Angela gives promise she will do
Whatever he shall wish, betide her weal or woe.

XIX

Which was, to lead him, in close secrecy,
Even to Madeline's chamber, and there hide
Him in a closet, of such privacy
That he might see her beauty unespied,
And win perhaps that night a peerless bride,
While legion'd faeries pac'd the coverlet,
And pale enchantment held her sleepy-eyed.
Never on such a night have lovers met,   170
Since Merlin paid his Demon all the monstrous
    debt.[7]

XX

'It shall be as thou wishest,' said the Dame:
All cates[8] and dainties shall be stored there
Quickly on this feast-night: by the tambour
    frame[9]
Her own lute thou wilt see: no time to spare,
For I am slow and feeble, and scarce dare
On such a catering trust my dizzy head.
Wait here, my child, with patience; kneel in
    prayer
The while: Ah! thou must needs the lady wed,
Or may I never leave my grave among the
    dead.'   180

XXI

So saying, she hobbled off with busy fear.
The lover's endless minutes slowly pass'd;
The dame return'd, and whisper'd in his ear
To follow her; with aged eyes aghast
From fright of dim espial. Safe at last,
Through many a dusky gallery, they gain

6 much.

7 The famous wizard Merlin was according to Arthurian legend
the son of a demon. He is said to have disappeared in a violent
storm raised by his own magic.
8 delicacies.
9 an embroidery frame shaped like a drum.

The maiden's chamber, silken, hush'd, and
    chaste;
Where Porphyro took covert, pleas'd amain.
His poor guide hurried back with agues in her
    brain.

XXII

Her falt'ring hand upon the balustrade,   190
Old Angela was feeling for the stair,
When Madeline, St. Agnes' charmed maid,
Rose, like a mission'd spirit, unaware:
With silver taper's light, and pious care,
She turn'd, and down the aged gossip led
To a safe level matting. Now prepare,
Young Porphyro, for gazing on that bed;
She comes, she comes again, like ring-dove
    fray'd[10] and fled.

XXIII

Out went the taper as she hurried in;
Its little smoke, in pallid moonshine, died: 200
She clos'd the door, she panted, all akin
To spirits of the air, and visions wide:
No uttered syllable, or, woe betide!
But to her heart, her heart was voluble,
Paining with eloquence her balmy side;
As though a tongueless nightingale should
    swell
Her throat in vain, and die, heart-stifled, in her
    dell.

XXIV

A casement high and triple-arch'd there was,
All garlanded with carven imag'ries
Of fruits, and flowers, and bunches of knot-
    grass,   210
And diamonded with panes of quaint device,
Innumerable of stains and splendid dyes,
As are the tiger-moth's deep-damask'd wings;
And in the midst, 'mong thousand heraldries,
And twilight saints, and dim emblazonings,
A shielded scutcheon blush'd with blood of
    queens and kings.

XXV

Full on this casement shone the wintry moon,
And threw warm gules[11] on Madeline's fair
    breast,
As down she knelt for heaven's grace and
    boon;
Rose-bloom fell on her hands, together
    prest,
And on her silver cross soft amethyst,   220

And on her hair a glory, like a saint:
She seem'd a splendid angel, newly drest,
Save wings, for heaven:—Porphyro grew faint:
She knelt, so pure a thing, so free from mortal
    taint.

XXVI

Anon his heart revives: her vespers done,
Of all its wreathed pearls her hair she frees;
Unclasps her warmed jewels one by one;
Loosens her fragrant boddice; by degrees
Her rich attire creeps rustling to her knees: 230
Half-hidden, like a mermaid in sea-weed,
Pensive awhile she dreams awake, and sees,
In fancy, fair St. Agnes in her bed,
But dares not look behind, or all the charm is
    fled.

XXVII

Soon, trembling in her soft and chilly nest,
In sort of wakeful swoon, perplex'd she lay,
Until the poppied warmth of sleep oppress'd
Her soothed limbs, and soul fatigued away;
Flown, like a thought, until the morrow-day;
Blissfully haven'd both from joy and pain;   240
Clasp'd[12] like a missal[13] where swart Paynims[14]
    pray;
Blinded alike from sunshine and from rain,
As though a rose should shut, and be a bud
    again.

XXVIII

Stol'n to this paradise, and so entranced,
Porphyro gazed upon her empty dress,
And listen'd to her breathing, if it chanced
To wake into a slumberous tenderness;
Which when he heard, that minute did
    he bless,
And breath'd himself: then from the closet
    crept,
Noiseless as fear in a wide wilderness,   250
And over the hush'd carpet, silent, stept,
And 'tween the curtains peep'd, where, lo!—how
    fast she slept.

XXIX

Then by the bed-side, where the faded moon
Made a dim, silver twilight, soft he set
A table, and, half anguish'd, threw thereon
A cloth of woven crimson, gold, and jet:—
O for some drowsy Morphean amulet![15]

---

10 frightened.
11 red (a heraldic term).
12 shut tight with clasps.
13 prayer book.
14 black pagans.
15 charm of Morpheus, god of sleep.

The boisterous, midnight, festive clarion,
The kettle-drum, and far-heard clarinet,
Affray his ears, though but in dying
    tone:—   260
The hall door shuts again, and all the noise is
    gone.

XXX

And still she slept an azure-lidded sleep,
In blanched linen, smooth, and lavender'd,
While he from forth the closet brought a heap
Of candied apple, quince, and plum, and
    gourd;
With jellies soother than the creamy curd,
And lucent syrops, tinct with cinnamon;
Manna and dates, in argosy transferr'd
From Fez; and spiced dainties, every one,
From silken Samarcand to cedar'd Lebanon. 270

XXXI

These delicates he heap'd with glowing hand
On golden dishes and in baskets bright
Of wreathed silver: sumptuous they stand
In the retired quiet of the night,
Filling the chilly room with perfume light.—
'And now, my love, my seraph fair, awake!
Thou art my heaven, and I thine eremite:[16]
Open thine eyes, for meek St. Agnes' sake,
Or I shall drowse beside thee, so my soul doth
    ache.'

XXXII

Thus whispering, his warm, unnerved arm 280
Sank in her pillow. Shaded was her dream
By the dusk curtains:—'twas a midnight
    charm
Impossible to melt as iced stream:
The lustrous salvers in the moonlight gleam;
Broad golden fringe upon the carpet lies:
It seem'd he never, never could redeem
From such a stedfast spell his lady's eyes;
So mus'd awhile, entoil'd in woofed phantasies.

XXXIII

Awakening up, he took her hollow lute,—
Tumultuous,—and, in chords that tenderest
    be,   290
He play'd an ancient ditty, long since mute,
In Provence call'd, 'La belle dame sans
    mercy':[17]
Close to her ear touching the melody;—
Wherewith disturb'd, she utter'd a soft moan:

He ceased—she panted quick—and suddenly
Her blue affrayed eyes wide open shone:
Upon his knees he sank, pale as smooth-sculp-
    tured stone.

XXXIV

Her eyes were open, but she still beheld,
Now wide awake, the vision of her sleep:
There was a painful change, that nigh
    expell'd   300
The blisses of her dream so pure and deep
At which fair Madeline began to weep,
And moan forth witless words with many a
    sigh;
While still her gaze on Porphyro would keep;
Who knelt, with joined hands and piteous eye,
Fearing to move or speak, she look'd so dream-
    ingly.

XXXV

'Ah, Porphyro!' said she, 'but even now
Thy voice was at sweet tremble in mine ear,
Made tuneable with every sweetest vow;
And those sad eyes were spiritual and
    clear: 310
How chang'd thou art! how pallid, chill, and
    drear!
Give me that voice again, my Porphyro,
Those looks immortal, those complainings
    dear!
Oh leave me not in this eternal woe,
For if thou diest, my Love, I know not where
    to go.'

XXXVI

Beyond a mortal man impassion'd far
At these voluptuous accents, he arose,
Ethereal, flush'd, and like a throbbing star
Seen mid the sapphire heaven's deep repose;
Into her dream he melted, as the rose   320
Blendeth its odour with the violet,—
Solution sweet: meantime the frost-wind blows
Like Love's alarum pattering the sharp sleet
Against the window-panes; St. Agnes' moon
    hath set.

XXXVII

'Tis dark: quick pattereth the flaw-blown[18]
    sleet:
'This is no dream, my bride, my Madeline!'
'Tis dark: the iced gusts still rave and beat:
'No dream, alas! alas! and woe is mine!
Porphyro will leave me here to fade and
    pine.—

16 hermit; devotee.
17 the title of a poem by Alain Chartier, an early fifteenth-century French poet.

18 wind-blown.

Cruel! what traitor could thee hither
   bring?   330
I curse not, for my heart is lost in thine,
Though thou forsakest a deceived thing;—
A dove forlorn and lost with sick unpruned
   wing.'

XXXVIII

'My Madeline! sweet dreamer! lovely bride!
Say, may I be for aye thy vassal blest?
Thy beauty's shield, heart-shap'd and vermeil
   dyed?
Ah, silver shrine, here will I take my rest
After so many hours of toil and quest,
A famish'd pilgrim,—sav'd by miracle.
Though I have found, I will not rob thy
   nest   340
Saving of thy sweet self; if thou think'st well
To trust, fair Madeline, to no rude infidel.

XXXIX

'Hark! 'tis an elfin-storm from faery land,
Of haggard seeming,[19] but a boon indeed:
Arise—arise! the morning is at hand;—
The bloated wassaillers will never heed:—
Let us away, my love, with happy speed;
There are no ears to hear, or eyes to see,—
Drown'd all in Rhenish[20] and the sleepy
   mead;[21]
Awake! arise! my love, and fearless be,   350
For o'er the southern moors I have a home for
   thee.'

XL

She hurried at his words, beset with fears,
For there were sleeping dragons all around,
At glaring watch, perhaps, with ready spears—
Down the wide stairs a darkling way they
   found.—
In all the house was heard no human sound.
A chain-droop'd lamp was flickering by each
   door;
The arras,[22] rich with horseman, hawk, and
   hound,
Flutter'd in the besieging wind's uproar;
And the long carpets rose along the gusty
   floor.   360

XLI

They glide, like phantoms, into the wide hall;
Like phantoms, to the iron porch, they glide;
Where lay the Porter, in uneasy sprawl,

With a huge empty flaggon by his side:
The wakeful bloodhound rose, and shook his
   hide,
But his sagacious eye an inmate owns:
By one, and one, the bolts full easy slide:—
The chains lie silent on the footworn stones;—
The key turns, and the door upon its hinges
   groans.

XLII

And they are gone: aye, ages long ago   370
These lovers fled away into the storm.
That night the Baron dreamt of many a woe,
And all his warrior-guests, with shade and
   form
Of witch, and demon, and large coffin-worm,
Were long be-nightmar'd. Angela the old
Died palsy-twitch'd, with meagre face deform;
The Beadsman, after thousand aves[23] told,
For aye unsought for slept among his ashes cold.

   1819   1820

THE EVE OF ST. MARK[1]

A FRAGMENT

[Of this poem, which he included in a journal letter to
his brother and sister begun 17 September 1819, Keats
wrote: 'The great beauty of poetry is that it makes everything in every place interesting. The palatine Venice and
the abbotine Winchester are equally interesting. Some
time since I began a poem called *The Eve of St. Mark*,
quite in the spirit of town quietude. I think it will give
you the sensation of walking about an old country town
in a coolish evening. I know not whether I shall ever finish it; I will give it as far as I have gone.']

Upon a Sabbath-day it fell;
Twice holy was the Sabbath-bell,
That call'd the folk to evening prayer;
The city streets were clean and fair
From wholesome drench of April rains;
And, on the western window panes,
The chilly sunset faintly told
Of unmatur'd green vallies cold,
Of the green thorny bloomless hedge,
Of rivers new with spring-tide sedge,   10
Of primroses by shelter'd rills,
And daisies on the aguish hills.
Twice holy was the Sabbath-bell:
The silent streets were crowded well

---

19 appearance.
20 wine from the Rhine country.
21 fermented honey and malt.
22 painted tapestry.

23 *Ave* is for *Ave Maria* (Hail Mary), a prayer in Latin.

1 A superstition connected with the Eve of St. Mark as Keats
probably intended to develop it is that if a person concealed himself near the church porch at dusk he would see enter the church
the apparitions of those persons who were to be severely ill that
year. The length of time an apparition remained in the church
signified the length and severity of the illness of the person concerned. If an apparition did not come out again, it signified death.

With staid and pious companies,
Warm from their fire-side orat'ries;
And moving, with demurest air,
To even-song, and vesper prayer.
Each arched porch, and entry low,
Was fill'd with patient folk and slow,   20
With whispers hush, and shuffling feet,
While play'd the organ loud and sweet.

The bells had ceas'd, the prayer begun,
And Bertha had not yet half done
A curious volume, patch'd and torn,
That all day long, from earliest morn,
Had taken captive her two eyes,
Among its golden broideries;
Perplex'd her with a thousand things,—
The stars of Heaven, and angels' wings,   30
Martyrs in a fiery blaze,
Azure saints in silver rays,
Moses' breastplate, and the seven
Candlesticks John saw in Heaven,
The winged Lion of Saint Mark,
And the Covenantal Ark,
With its many mysteries.
Cherubim and golden mice.

Bertha was a maiden fair,
Dwelling in the old Minster-square;   40
From her fire-side she could see,
Sidelong, its rich antiquity,
Far as the Bishop's garden-wall;
Where sycamores and elm-trees tall,
Full-leav'd, the forest had outstript,
By no sharp north-wind ever nipt,
So shelter'd by the mighty pile.
Bertha arose, and read awhile,
With forehead 'gainst the window-pane.
Again she try'd, and then again,   50
Until the dusk eve left her dark
Upon the legend of St. Mark.
From plaited lawn-frill, fine and thin,
She lifted up her soft warm chin,
With aching neck and swimming eyes,
And daz'd with saintly imageries.

All was gloom, and silent all,
Save now and then the still foot-fall
Of one returning homewards late,
Past the echoing minster-gate.   60

The clamorous daws, that all the day
Above tree-tops and towers play,
Pair by pair had gone to rest,
Each in its ancient belfry-nest,
Where asleep they fall betimes,
To music of the drowsy chimes.

All was silent, all was gloom,
Abroad and in the homely room:
Down she sat, poor cheated soul!
And struck a lamp from the dismal coal;   70
Lean'd forward, with bright drooping hair
And slant book, full against the glare.
Her shadow, in uneasy guise,
Hover'd about, a giant size,
On ceiling-beam and old oak chair,
The parrot's cage, and panel square;
And the warm angled winter screen,
On which were many monsters seen,
Call'd doves of Siam, Lima mice,
And legless birds of Paradise,   80
Macaw, and tender Avadavat,
And silken-furr'd Angora cat.
Untir'd she read, her shadow still
Glower'd about, as it would fill
The room with wildest forms and shades,
As though some ghostly queen of spades
Had come to mock behind her back,
And dance, and ruffle her garments black.
Untir'd she read the legend page,
Of holy Mark, from youth to age,   90
On land, on sea, in pagan chains,
Rejoicing for his many pains.
Sometimes the learned eremite,
With golden star, or dagger bright,
Referr'd to pious poesies
Written in smallest crow-quill size
Beneath the text; and thus the rhyme
Was parcell'd out from time to time:
——'Als² writith he of swevenis,³
Men han⁴ beforne they wake in bliss,   100
Whanne that hir friendes thinke hem bound
In crimped⁵ shroude farre under grounde;
And how a litling child mote be
A saint er⁶ its nativitie,
Gif⁷ that the modre (God her blesse!)
Kepen in solitarinesse,
And kissen devoute the holy croce.
Of Goddes love, and Sathan's force,—
He writith; and thinges many mo:
Of swiche⁸ thinges I may not show.   110
Bot I must tellen verilie
Somdel⁹ of Saintè Cicilie,
And chieflie what he auctorethe
Of Saintè Markis life and dethe':

At length her constant eyelids come
Upon the fervent martyrdom;
Then lastly to his holy shrine,

_____

2 also.   3 dreams.
4 have.   5 plaited.
6 before.   7 if.
8 such.   9 something.

Exalt amid the tapers' shine
At Venice,—

February 1819   1848

BRIGHT STAR

[Keats wrote out this sonnet for Severn in his copy of
Shakespeare one night in December 1820 on shipboard
off the coast of England while they were delayed by
storms on their way to Italy. It was believed for a long
time to have been Keats's last sonnet, but the original
version is now known to have been composed as early
as April 1819.]

BRIGHT star, would I were stedfast as thou art—
    Not in lone splendour hung aloft the night
And watching, with eternal lids apart,
    Like nature's patient, sleepless Eremite,
The moving waters at their priestlike task
    Of pure ablution round earth's human shores,
Or gazing on the new soft-fallen mask
    Of snow upon the mountains and the moors—
No—yet still stedfast, still unchangeable,
    Pillow'd upon my fair love's ripening
        breast,   10
To feel for ever its soft fall and swell,
    Awake for ever in a sweet unrest,
Still, still to hear her tender-taken breath,
And so live ever—or else swoon to death.

c.April 1819   1848

ON A DREAM

As Hermes once took to his feathers light,
    When lulled Argus,[1] baffled, swoon'd and slept,
So on a Delphic reed, my idle spright
    So play'd, so charm'd, so conquer'd, so bereft
The dragon-world of all its hundred eyes;
    And, seeing it asleep, so fled away—
Not to pure Ida with its snow-cold skies,
    Nor unto Tempe where Jove griev'd a day;
But to that second circle of sad hell,[2]
    Where 'mid the gust, the whirlwind, and the
        flaw   10
Of rain and hail-stones, lovers need not tell
    Their sorrows. Pale were the sweet lips I saw,
Pale were the lips I kiss'd, and fair the form
I floated with, about that melancholy storm.

April 1819   1820

TO SLEEP

O SOFT embalmer of the still midnight,
    Shutting, with careful fingers and benign,

1 the hundred-eyed guardian of Io, who was lulled to sleep by
the piping of Hermes and then slain by him.
2 the Inferno, where Dante's lovers, Paulo and Francesca, were
floating about amorously.

Our gloom-pleas'd eyes, embower'd from the
        light,
    Enshaded in forgetfulness divine:
O soothest Sleep! if so it please thee, close
    In midst of this thine hymn my willing eyes,
Or wait the 'Amen,' ere thy poppy throws
    Around my bed its lulling charities.
Then save me, or the passed day will shine
Upon my pillow, breeding many woes,—   10
    Save me from curious Conscience, that still
        lords
Its strength for darkness, burrowing like a mole;
    Turn the key deftly in the oiled wards,
And seal the hushed Casket of my Soul.

1819   1848

TWO SONNETS ON FAME

I

FAME, like a wayward Girl, will still be coy
    To those who woo her with too slavish knees,
But makes surrender to some thoughtless Boy,
    And dotes the more upon a heart at ease;
She is a Gipsey, will not speak to those
    Who have not learnt to be content without her;
A Jilt, whose ear was never whisper'd close,
    Who thinks they scandal her who talk about
        her;
A very Gipsey is she, Nilus-born,
    Sister-in-law to jealous Potiphar;[1]   10
Ye love-sick Bards, repay her scorn for scorn,
    Ye Artists lovelorn, madmen that ye are!
Make your best bow to her and bid adieu,
Then, if she likes it, she will follow you.

II

How fever'd is the man, who cannot look
    Upon his mortal days with temperate blood,
Who vexes all the leaves of his life's book,
    And robs his fair name of its maidenhood;
It is as if the rose should pluck herself,
    Or the ripe plum finger its misty bloom,
As if a Naiad, like a meddling elf,
    Should darken her pure grot with muddy
        gloom,
But the rose leaves herself upon the briar,
    For winds to kiss and grateful bees to feed, 10
And the ripe plum still wears its dim attire,
    The undisturbed lake has crystal space,
    Why then should man, teasing the world for
        grace,
Spoil his salvation for a fierce miscreed?

1819   1848

1 See Genesis, xxxix.

LA BELLE DAME SANS MERCI

(FIRST VERSION)

[Keats copied the original version of this poem in a journal letter to his brother and sister, February-April 1819.]

O WHAT can ail thee, Knight at arms
   Alone and palely loitering?
The sedge has withered from the Lake,
   And no birds sing!

O what can ail thee, Knight at arms,
   So haggard and so woe-begone?
The Squirrel's granary is full,
   And the harvest's done.

I see a lily on thy brow,
   With anguish moist and fever dew;   10
And on thy cheeks a fading rose
   Fast withereth too.

I met a Lady in the Meads,
   Full beautiful, a faery's child;
Her hair was long, her foot was light,
   And her eyes were wild.

I made a Garland for her head,
   And bracelets, too, and fragrant Zone;[1]
She look'd at me as she did love,
   And made sweet moan.   20

I set her on my pacing steed,
   And nothing else saw, all day long;
For sidelong would she bend, and sing
   A faery's song.

She found me roots of relish sweet,
   And honey wild, and manna dew;
And sure in language strange she said,
   'I love thee true.'

She took me to her elfin grot,
   And there she wept and sigh'd full sore;   30
And there I shut her wild, wild eyes
   With kisses four.

And there she lulled me asleep,
   And there I dreamed, ah woe betide!
The latest dream I ever dreamt,
   On the cold hill side.

I saw pale Kings, and Princes too,
   Pale warriors, death pale were they all;
They cried, 'La belle dame sans merci   40
   Thee hath in thrall!'

---

1 belt.

I saw their starv'd lips in the gloam
   With horrid warning gaped wide—
And I awoke, and found me here,
   On the cold hill's side.

And this is why I sojourn here,
   Alone and palely loitering;
Though the sedge is withered from the Lake,
   And no birds sing.

    1819   1888

ODE TO PSYCHE[1]

The following poem, the last I have written, is the first and only one with which I have taken even moderate pains; I have, for the most part, dashed off my lines in a hurry. This one I have done leisurely; I think it reads the more richly for it, and it will, I hope, encourage me to write other things in even a more peaceable and healthy spirit. You must recollect that Psyche was not embodied as a goddess before the time of Apuleius the Platonist, who lived after the Augustan age, and consequently the goddess was never worshipped or sacrificed to with any of the ancient fervour, and perhaps never thought of in the old religion. I am more orthodox than to let a heathen goddess be so neglected.—(Keats in a letter to his brother and sister, 30 April 1819.)

O GODDESS! hear these tuneless numbers, wrung
   By sweet enforcement and remembrance dear,
And pardon that thy secrets should be sung
   Even into thine own soft-conched[2] ear:
Surely I dreamt to-day, or did I see
   The winged Psyche with awaken'd eyes?
I wander'd in a forest thoughtlessly,
   And, on the sudden, fainting with surprise,
Saw two fair creatures, couched side by side
   In deepest grass, beneath the whisp'ring
       roof   10
   Of leaves and trembled blossoms, where there
       ran
       A brooklet, scarce espied:

'Mid hush'd, cool-rooted flowers, fragrant-eyed,
   Blue, silver-white, and budded Tyrian,[3]
They lay calm-breathing on the bedded grass;
   Their arms embraced, and their pinions too;
   Their lips touch'd not, but had not bade adieu,
As if disjoined by soft-handed slumber,
And ready still past kisses to outnumber
   At tender eye-dawn of aurorean love: 20
       The winged boy I knew;

---

1 In classical mythology, Psyche personifies the human soul. The story of her deification is entertainingly told by Apuleius, a Latin writer of the second century of the Christian era—how the young god Cupid, Venus' son, fell in love with the mortal princess Psyche, how Venus out of jealousy imposed many hardships upon her, and how finally Jupiter made her immortal so that the lovers could be united forever.
2 shell-shaped.
3 purple.

But who wast thou, O happy, happy dove?
   His Psyche true!

O latest born and loveliest vision far
   Of all Olympus' faded hierarchy!
Fairer than Phœbe's sapphire-region'd star,
   Or Vesper, amorous glow-worm of the sky;
Fairer than these, though temple thou hast none,
     Nor altar heap'd with flowers;
Nor virgin-choir to make delicious moan   30
     Upon the midnight hours;
No voice, no lute, no pipe, no incense sweet
   From chain-swung censer teeming;
No shrine, no grove, no oracle, no heat
   Of pale-mouth'd prophet dreaming.

O brightest! though too late for antique vows,
   Too, too late for the fond believing lyre,
When holy were the haunted forest boughs,
   Holy the air, the water, and the fire;
Yet even in these days so far retir'd   40
   From happy pieties, thy lucent fans,
   Fluttering among the faint Olympians,
I see, and sing, by my own eyes inspir'd.
So let me be thy choir, and make a moan
     Upon the midnight hours;
Thy voice, thy lute, thy pipe, thy incense sweet
   From swinged censer teeming;
Thy shrine, thy grove, thy oracle, thy heat
   Of pale-mouth'd prophet dreaming.

Yes, I will be thy priest, and build a fane⁴   50
   In some untrodden region of my mind,
Where branched thoughts, new grown with pleas-
     ant pain,
   Instead of pines shall murmur in the wind:
Far, far around shall those dark-cluster'd trees
   Fledge the wild-ridged mountains steep by
     steep;
And there by zephyrs, streams, and birds, and
     bees,
   The moss-lain Dryads shall be lull'd to sleep;
And in the midst of this wide quietness
A rosy sanctuary will I dress
With the wreath'd trellis of a working brain,   60
   With buds, and bells, and stars without a
     name,
With all the gardener Fancy e'er could feign,
   Who breeding flowers, will never breed the
     same:
And there shall be for thee all soft delight
   That shadowy thought can win,
A bright torch, and a casement ope at night,
   To let the warm Love in!

   1819   1820

---

4 temple.

ODE ON INDOLENCE

*'They toil not, neither do they spin.'*¹

[The mood and idea of this ode Keats had expressed
in admirable prose in a letter to his brother and sister,
dated 17 March 1819: 'This morning I am in a sort of
temper, indolent and supremely careless—I long after a
stanza or two of Thomson's *Castle of Indolence*—my
passions are all asleep, from my having slumbered till
nearly eleven, and weakened the animal fibre all over
me, to a delightful sensation, about three degrees on this
side of faintness. If I had teeth of pearl and the breath of
lilies I should call it languor, but as I am I must call it
laziness. In this state of effeminacy the fibres of the brain
are relaxed in common with the rest of the body, and to
such a happy degree that pleasure has no show of enticement and pain no unbearable power. Neither poetry,
nor ambition, nor love have any alertness of countenance as they pass by me; they seem rather like figures
on a Greek vase—a man and two women whom no one
but myself could distinguish in their disguisement. This
is the only happiness, and is a rare instance of the advantage of the body overpowering the mind.'
The ode was composed early in May.]

I

ONE morn before me were three figures seen,
   With bowed necks, and joined hands, side-
     faced;
And one behind the other stepp'd serene,
   In placid sandals, and in white robes graced;
They pass'd, like figures on a marble urn,
   When shifted round to see the other side;
     They came again; as when the urn once
     more
Is shifted round, the first seen shades return;
   And they were strange to me, as may betide
     With vases, to one deep in Phidian lore.² 10

II

How is it, Shadows! that I knew ye not?
   How came ye muffled in so hush a mask?
Was it a silent deep-disguised plot
   To steal away, and leave without a task
My idle days? Ripe was the drowsy hour;
   The blissful cloud of summer-indolence
     Benumb'd my eyes; my pulse grew less and
     less;
Pain had no sting, and pleasure's wreath no
     flower:
   O, why did ye not melt, and leave my sense
     Unhaunted quite of all but—nothing-
     ness?   20

III

A third time pass'd they by, and, passing, turn'd

---

1 Matthew, vi, 28.
2 lore of Phidias, celebrated Greek sculptor of the fifth century
B.C.

Each one the face a moment whiles to me;
Then faded, and to follow them I burn'd
  And ach'd for wings because I knew the three;
The first was a fair Maid, and Love her name;
  The second was Ambition, pale of cheek,
  And ever watchful with fatigued eye;
The last, whom I love more, the more of blame
  Is heap'd upon her, maiden most unmeek,—
    I knew to be my demon[3] Poesy.   30

IV

They faded, and, forsooth! I wanted wings:
  O folly! What is love! and where is it?
And for that poor Ambition! it springs
  From a man's little heart's short fever-fit;
For Poesy!—no,—she has not a joy,—
  At least for me,—so sweet as drowsy noons,
    And evenings steep'd in honied indolence;
O, for an age so shelter'd from annoy,
  That I may never know how change the
    moons,
  Or hear the voice of busy common-
    sense!   40

V

And once more came they by;—alas! where-
    fore?
  My sleep had been embroider'd with dim
    dreams;
My soul had been a lawn besprinkled o'er
  With flowers, and stirring shades, and baffled
    beams:
The morn was clouded, but no shower fell,
  Tho' in her lids hung the sweet tears of May;
    The open casement press'd a new-leav'd
      vine,
  Let in the budding warmth and throstle's lay;
O Shadows! 'twas a time to bid farewell!
  Upon your skirts had fallen no tears of
    mine.   50

VI

So, ye three Ghosts, adieu! Ye cannot raise
  My head cool-bedded in the flowery grass;
For I would not be dieted with praise,
  A pet-lamb in a sentimental farce!
Fade softly from my eyes, and be once more
  In masque-like figures on the dreamy urn;
    Farewell! I yet have visions for the night,
And for the day faint visions there is store;
    Vanish, ye Phantoms! from my idle spright,
  Into the clouds, and never more return!   60

1819   1820

---

3 guardian spirit.

ODE TO A NIGHTINGALE

[Keats was living with Charles Brown at Hampstead
at the time this poem was written. Twenty years later
Brown gave the following account of its composition:
'In the spring of 1819 a nightingale had built her nest
near my house. Keats felt a tranquil and continual joy in
her song; and one morning he took his chair from the
breakfast table to the grass-plot under a plum-tree,
where he sat for two or three hours. When he came into
the house, I perceived he had some scraps of paper in
his hand, and these he was quietly thrusting behind the
books. On inquiry, I found those scraps, four or five in
number, contained his poetic feeling on the song of our
nightingale.']

I

My heart aches, and a drowsy numbness pains
  My sense, as though of hemlock I had drunk,
Or emptied some dull opiate to the drains
  One minute past, and Lethe-wards[1] had sunk:
'Tis not through envy of thy happy lot,
  But being too happy in thine happiness,—
    That thou, light-winged Dryad of the trees,
      In some melodious plot
Of beechen green, and shadows numberless,
  Singest of summer in full-throated ease.   10

II

O, for a draught of vintage! that hath been
  Cool'd a long age in the deep-delved earth,
Tasting of Flora and the country green,
  Dance, and Provençal song, and sunburnt
    mirth!
O for a beaker full of the warm South,
  Full of the true, the blushful Hippocrene,[2]
    With beaded bubbles winking at the brim,
      And purple-stained mouth;
That I might drink, and leave the world
    unseen,
  And with thee fade away into the forest
    dim: 20

III

Fade far away, dissolve, and quite forget
  What thou among the leaves hast never
    known,
The weariness, the fever, and the fret
  Here, where men sit and hear each other
    groan;
Where palsy shakes a few, sad, last grey hairs,
  Where youth grows pale, and spectre-thin, and
    dies[3];

---

1 into forgetfulness.
2 a fountain sacred to the Muses, the waters of which inspired
poets.
3 probably an allusion to his brother Tom who died a few months
before.

Where but to think is to be full of sorrow
　　And leaden-eyed despairs,
Where Beauty cannot keep her lustrous eyes,
　　Or new Love pine at them beyond to-
　　　　morrow.　　　　　　　　　　30

IV

Away! away! for I will fly to thee,
　　Not charioted by Bacchus and his pards,[4]
But on the viewless wings of Poesy,
　　Though the dull brain perplexes and retards:
　　　　Already with thee! tender is the night,
　　　　And haply the Queen-Moon is on her throne,
　　　　　　Cluster'd around by all her starry Fays;
　　　　　　　　But here there is no light,
　　　　Save what from heaven is with the breezes
　　　　　　blown
　　　　　　Through verdurous glooms and winding
　　　　　　　　mossy ways.　　　　　　　40

V

I cannot see what flowers are at my feet,
　　Nor what soft incense hangs upon the boughs,
But, in embalmed darkness, guess each sweet
　　Wherewith the seasonable month endows
The grass, the thicket, and the fruit-tree wild;
　　White hawthorn, and the pastoral eglantine;
　　　　Fast fading violets cover'd up in leaves;
　　　　　　And mid-May's eldest child,
　　The coming musk-rose, full of dewy wine,
　　　　The murmurous haunt of flies on summer
　　　　　　eves.　　　　　　　　　　50

VI

Darkling I listen; and, for many a time
　　I have been half in love with easeful Death,
Call'd him soft names in many a mused rhyme,
　　To take into the air my quiet breath;
Now more than ever seems it rich to die,
　　To cease upon the midnight with no pain,
　　　　While thou art pouring forth thy soul
　　　　　　abroad
　　　　　　In such an ecstasy!
　　Still wouldst thou sing, and I have ears in
　　　　vain—
　　　　To thy high requiem become a sod.　　60

VII

Thou wast not born for death, immortal Bird!
　　No hungry generations tread thee down;
The voice I hear this passing night was heard
　　In ancient days by emperor and clown:
Perhaps the self-same song that found a path

Through the sad heart of Ruth,[5] when, sick for
　　home,
　　She stood in tears amid the alien corn;
　　　　The same that oft-times hath
　　Charm'd magic casements, opening on the
　　　　foam
　　　　Of perilous seas, in faery lands forlorn.　70

VIII

Forlorn! the very word is like a bell
　　To toll me back from thee to my sole self!
Adieu! the fancy cannot cheat so well
　　As she is fam'd to do, deceiving elf.
Adieu! adieu! thy plaintive anthem fades
　　Past the near meadows, over the still stream,
　　　　Up the hill-side; and now 'tis buried deep
　　　　　　In the next valley-glades:
　　Was it a vision, or a waking dream?
　　　　Fled is that music:—Do I wake or sleep?　80

1819　　　　　　　　　　　　1820

ODE ON A GRECIAN URN

[The urn of Keats's poem is not a particular urn, but
an imaginary one, shaped in the creative mind of the
poet, who drew his materials from a number of ancient
vases and sculptures, all containing scenes that might
have contributed to the total composition.]

I

Thou still unravish'd bride of quietness,
　　Thou foster-child of silence and slow time,
Sylvan historian, who canst thus express
　　A flowery tale more sweetly than our rhyme:
What leaf-fring'd legend haunts about thy shape
　　Of deities or mortals, or of both,
　　　　In Tempe or the dales of Arcady?
　　What men or gods are these? What maidens
　　　　loth?
What mad pursuit? What struggle to escape?
　　What pipes and timbrels? What wild
　　　　ecstasy?　　　　　　　　　　10

II

Heard melodies are sweet, but those unheard
　　Are sweeter; therefore, ye soft pipes, play on;
Not to the sensual ear,[1] but, more endear'd,
　　Pipe to the spirit ditties of no tone:
Fair youth, beneath the trees, thou canst not
　　leave
　　Thy song, nor ever can those trees be bare;
　　　　Bold Lover, never, never canst thou kiss,

---

4 leopards.

5 See Ruth, ii.

1 the ear of sense.

Though winning near the goal—yet, do not
   grieve;
  She cannot fade, though thou hast not thy
    bliss,
   For ever wilt thou love, and she be fair! 20

III

Ah, happy, happy boughs! that cannot shed
  Your leaves, nor ever bid the Spring adieu;
And, happy melodist, unwearied,
  For ever piping songs for ever new;
More happy love! more happy, happy love!
  For ever warm and still to be enjoy'd,
   For ever panting, and for ever young;
All breathing human passion far above,
  That leaves a heart high-sorrowful and cloy'd,
   A burning forehead, and a parching
    tongue.   30

IV

Who are these coming to the sacrifice?
  To what green altar, O mysterious priest,
Lead'st thou that heifer lowing at the skies,
  And all her silken flanks with garlands drest?
What little town by river or sea shore,
  Or mountain-built with peaceful citadel,
   Is emptied of this folk, this pious morn?
And, little town, thy streets for evermore
  Will silent be; and not a soul to tell
   Why thou art desolate, can e'er return.   40

V

O Attic shape!² Fair attitude! with brede³
  Of marble men and maidens overwrought,
With forest branches and the trodden weed;
  Thou, silent form, dost tease us out of thought
As doth eternity: Cold Pastoral!
  When old age shall this generation waste,
   Thou shalt remain, in midst of other woe
Than ours, a friend to man, to whom thou say'st,
  'Beauty is truth, truth beauty,'—that is all
   Ye know on earth, and all ye need to
    know.   50
    1819   1820

ODE ON MELANCHOLY

I

No, no, go not to Lethe,¹ neither twist
  Wolf's-bane, tight-rooted, for its poisonous
   wine;

Nor suffer thy pale forehead to be kiss'd
  By nightshade, ruby grape of Proserpine;²
Make not your rosary of yew-berries,³
  Nor let the beetle,⁴ nor the death-moth be
   Your mournful Psyche,⁵ nor the downy owl
A partner in your sorrow's mysteries;
  For shade to shade will come too drowsily,
   And drown the wakeful anguish of the
    soul.   10

II

But when the melancholy fit shall fall
  Sudden from heaven like a weeping cloud,
That fosters the droop-headed flowers all,
  And hides the green hill in an April shroud;
Then glut thy sorrow on a morning rose,
  Or on the rainbow of the salt sand-wave,
   Or on the wealth of globed peonies;
Or if thy mistress some rich anger shows,
  Emprison her soft hand, and let her rave,
   And feed deep, deep upon her peerless
    eyes.   20

III

She dwells with Beauty—Beauty that must die;
  And Joy, whose hand is ever at his lips
Bidding adieu; and aching Pleasure nigh,
  Turning to Poison while the bee-mouth sips:
Ay, in the very temple of delight
  Veil'd Melancholy has her sovran shrine,
   Though seen of none save him whose
    strenuous tongue
  Can burst Joy's grape against his palate fine;
His soul shall taste the sadness of her might,
  And be among her cloudy trophies hung.   30
    1819   1820

LAMIA

[Keats appended the following passage from Burton's
Anatomy of Melancholy as a note to the last line of his
poem: 'Philostratus, in his fourth book *de Vita Apollonii*,
hath a memorable instance in this kind, which I may not
omit, of one Menippus Lycius, a young man twenty-five
years of age, that going betwixt Cenchreas and Corinth,
met such a phantasm in the habit of a fair gentlewoman,
which, taking him by the hand, carried him home to her
house, in the suburbs of Corinth, and told him she was a
Phœnician by birth, and if he would tarry with her, he
should hear her sing and play, and drink such wine as
never any drank, and no man should molest him; but
she, being fair and lovely, would live and die with him,
that was fair and lovely to behold. The young man, a
philosopher, otherwise staid and discreet, able to mod-

---

2 Grecian. It was in Attica that Greek civilization found its
purest expression.
3 embroidery.

1 the river of forgetfulness in Hades.

2 queen of the lower regions.
3 the symbol of mourning.
4 In Egypt the sacred beetle was the symbol of resurrection, and
was placed in coffins.
5 the soul, symbolized by the butterfly or moth.

erate his passions, though not this of love, tarried with
her a while to his great content, and at last married her,
to whose wedding, amongst other guests, came Apollonius; who, by some probable conjectures, found her out
to be a serpent, a lamia; and that all her furniture was,
like Tantalus' gold, described by Homer, no substance
but mere illusions. When she saw herself descried, she
wept, and desired Apollonius to be silent, but he would
not be moved, and thereupon she, plate, house, and all
that was in it, vanished in an instant: many thousands
took notice of this fact, for it was done in the midst of
Greece.'

Lamia was begun at Hampstead in July 1819, and finished at Winchester in early September. On 18 September Keats wrote to his brother and sister that he was certain his poem had 'that sort of fire in it which must take
hold of people in some way—give them either pleasant
or unpleasant sensation.']

PART I

Upon a time, before the faery broods
Drove Nymph and Satyr from the prosperous
    woods,
Before king Oberon's bright diadem,
Sceptre, and mantle, clasp'd with dewy gem,
Frighted away the Dryads and the Fauns
From rushes green, and brakes, and cowslip'd
    lawns,
The ever-smitten Hermes empty left
His golden throne, bent warm on amorous theft:
From high Olympus had he stolen light,
On this side of Jove's clouds, to escape the
    sight   10
Of his great summoner, and made retreat
Into a forest on the shores of Crete.
For somewhere in that sacred island dwelt
A nymph, to whom all hoofed satyrs knelt;
At whose white feet the languid Tritons poured
Pearls, while on land they wither'd and adored.
Fast by the springs where she to bathe was wont,
And in those meads where sometime she might
    haunt,
Were strewn rich gifts, unknown to any Muse,
Though Fancy's casket were unlock'd to
    choose.   20
Ah, what a world of love was at her feet!
So Hermes thought, and a celestial heat
Burnt from his winged heels to either ear,
That from a whiteness, as the lilly clear,
Blush'd into roses 'mid his golden hair,
Fallen in jealous curls about his shoulders bare.

From vale to vale, from wood to wood, he flew,
Breathing upon the flowers his passion new,
And wound with many a river to its head,
To find where this sweet nymph prepar'd her se-
    cret bed: 30
In vain; the sweet nymph might nowhere be
    found,

And so he rested, on the lonely ground,
Pensive, and full of painful jealousies
Of the Wood-Gods, and even the very trees.
There as he stood, he heard a mournful voice,
Such as once heard, in gentle heart, destroys
All pain but pity: thus the lone voice spake:
'When from this wreathed tomb shall I awake!
When move in a sweet body fit for life,
And love, and pleasure, and the ruddy strife   40
Of hearts and lips! Ah, miserable me!'
The God, dove-footed, glided silently
Round bush and tree, soft-brushing, in his speed,
The taller grasses and full-flowering weed,
Until he found a palpitating snake,
Bright, and cirque-couchant¹ in a dusky brake.

She was a gordian² shape of dazzling hue,
Vermilion-spotted, golden, green, and blue;
Striped like a zebra, freckled like a pard,
Eyed like a peacock, and all crimson barr'd;   50
And full of silver moons, that, as she breathed,
Dissolv'd, or brighter shone, or interwreathed
Their lustres with the gloomier tapestries—
So rainbow-sided, touch'd with miseries,
She seem'd, at once, some penanced lady elf,
Some demon's mistress, or the demon's self.
Upon her crest she wore a wannish fire
Sprinkled with stars, like Ariadne's tiar:³
Her head was serpent, but ah, bitter-sweet!
She had a woman's mouth with all its pearls com-
    plete: 60
And for her eyes: what could such eyes do there
But weep, and weep, that they were born so fair?
As Proserpine still weeps for her Sicilian air.⁴
Her throat was serpent, but the words she spake
Came, as through bubbling honey, for Love's
    sake,
And thus; while Hermes on his pinions lay,
Like a stoop'd falcon ere he takes his prey.
  'Fair Hermes, crown'd with feathers, flutter-
    ing light,
I had a splendid dream of thee last night:
I saw thee sitting, on a throne of gold,   70
Among the Gods, upon Olympus old,
The only sad one; for thou didst not hear
The soft, lute-finger'd Muses chaunting clear,
Nor even Apollo when he sang alone,
Deaf to his throbbing throat's long, long me-
    lodious moan.
I dreamt I saw thee, robed in purple flakes,
Break amorous through the clouds, as morning
    breaks,

---

¹ coiled.
² intricately knotted.
³ Bacchus gave Ariadne a crown of seven stars, which became a
constellation after her death.
⁴ Proserpine was carried off from her home in Sicily by Pluto
and made queen of the lower world.

And, swiftly as a bright Phœbean dart,[5]
Strike for the Cretan isle; and here thou art!
Too gentle Hermes, hast thou found the
    maid?'   80
Whereat the star of Lethe[6] not delay'd
His rosy eloquence, and thus inquired:
'Thou smooth-lipp'd serpent, surely high in-
    spired!
Thou beauteous wreath, with melancholy eyes,
Possess whatever bliss thou canst devise,
Telling me only where my nymph is fled,—
Where she doth breathe!' 'Bright planet, thou
    hast said,'
Return'd the snake, 'but seal with oaths, fair
    God!'
'I swear,' said Hermes, 'by my serpent rod,
And by thine eyes, and by thy starry crown!' 90
Light flew his earnest words, among the blossoms
    blown.
Then thus again the brilliance feminine:
'Too frail of heart! for this lost nymph of thine,
Free as the air, invisibly, she strays
About these thornless wilds; her pleasant days
She tastes unseen; unseen her nimble feet
Leave traces in the grass and flowers sweet;
From weary tendrils, and bow'd branches green,
She plucks the fruit unseen, she bathes unseen:
And by my power is her beauty veil'd   100
To keep it unaffronted, unassail'd
By the love-glances of unlovely eyes,
Of Satyrs, Fauns, and blear'd Silenus'[7] sighs.
Pale grew her immortality, for woe
Of all these lovers, and she grieved so
I took compassion on her, bade her steep
Her hair in weïrd syrops, that would keep
Her loveliness invisible, yet free
To wander as she loves, in liberty.
Thou shalt behold her, Hermes, thou alone,   110
If thou wilt, as thou swearest, grant my boon!'
Then, once again, the charmed God began
An oath, and through the serpent's ears it ran
Warm, tremulous, devout, psalterian.
Ravish'd, she lifted her Circean head,
Blush'd a live damask, and swift-lisping said,
'I was a woman, let me have once more
A woman's shape, and charming as before.
I love a youth of Corinth—O the bliss!
Give me my woman's form, and place me where
    he is.   120
Stoop, Hermes, let me breathe upon thy brow,
And thou shalt see thy sweet nymph even now.'
The God on half-shut feathers sank serene,
She breath'd upon his eyes, and swift was seen

Of both the guarded nymph near-smiling on the
    green.
It was no dream; or say a dream it was,
Real are the dreams of Gods, and smoothly pass
Their pleasures in a long immortal dream.
One warm, flush'd moment, hovering, it might
    seem
Dash'd by the wood-nymph's beauty, so he
    burn'd;   130
Then, lighting on the printless verdure, turn'd
To the swoon'd serpent, and with languid arm,
Delicate, put to proof the lythe Caducean
    charm.[8]
So done, upon the nymph his eyes he bent
Full of adoring tears and blandishment,
And towards her stept: she, like a moon in wane,
Faded before him, cower'd, nor could restrain
Her fearful sobs, self-folding like a flower
That faints into itself at evening hour:
But the God fostering her chilled hand,   140
She felt the warmth, her eyelids open'd bland,
And, like new flowers at morning song of bees,
Bloom'd, and gave up her honey to the lees.
Into the green-recessed woods they flew;
Nor grew they pale, as mortal lovers do.

    Left to herself, the serpent now began
To change; her elfin blood in madness ran,
Her mouth foam'd, and the grass, therewith be-
    sprent,
Wither'd at dew so sweet and virulent;
Her eyes in torture fix'd, and anguish drear,   150
Hot, glaz'd, and wide, with lid-lashes all sear,
Flash'd phosphor and sharp sparks, without one
    cooling tear.
The colours all inflam'd throughout her train,
She writh'd about, convuls'd with scarlet pain:
A deep volcanian yellow took the place
Of all her milder-mooned body's grace;
And, as the lava ravishes the mead,
Spoilt all her silver mail, and golden brede;
Made gloom of all her frecklings, streaks and
    bars,
Eclips'd her crescents, and lick'd up her
    stars: 160
So that, in moments few, she was undrest
Of all her sapphires, greens, and amethyst,
And rubious-argent: of all these bereft,
Nothing but pain and ugliness were left.
Still shone her crown; that vanish'd, also she
Melted and disappear'd as suddenly;
And in the air, her new voice luting soft,
Cried, 'Lycius! gentle Lycius!'—Borne aloft
With the bright mists about the mountains hoar

---

5 the dart of Phoebus Apollo; sunbeam.
6 Hermes guided souls into oblivion.
7 the oldest satyr, fat, bald, jovial, and usually tipsy.

---

8 He touched her with his serpent-entwined staff, the caduceus.

These words dissolv'd: Crete's forests heard no
    more.   170

Whither fled Lamia, now a lady bright,
A full-born beauty new and exquisite?
She fled into that valley they pass o'er
Who go to Corinth from Cenchreas' shore;
And rested at the foot of those wild hills,
The rugged founts of the Peræan rills,
And of that other ridge whose barren back
Stretches, with all its mist and cloudy rack,
South-westward to Cleone. There she stood
About a young birds' flutter from a wood,   180
Fair, on a sloping green of mossy tread,
By a clear pool, wherein she passioned
To see herself escap'd from so sore ills,
While her robes flaunted with the daffodils.

Ah, happy Lycius!—for she was a maid
More beautiful than ever twisted braid,
Or sigh'd, or blush'd, or on spring-flowered lea
Spread a green kirtle to the minstrelsy:
A virgin purest lipp'd, yet in the lore
Of love deep learned to the red heart's core: 190
Not one hour old, yet of sciential brain
To unperplex bliss from its neighbour pain;
Define their pettish limits, and estrange
Their points of contact, and swift counterchange;
Intrigue with the specious chaos, and dispart
Its most ambiguous atoms with sure art;
As though in Cupid's college she had spent
Sweet days a lovely graduate, still unshent,[9]
And kept his rosy terms in idle languishment.

Why this fair creature chose so faerily   200
By the wayside to linger, we shall see;
But first 'tis fit to tell how she could muse
And dream, when in the serpent prison-house,
Of all she list, strange or magnificent:
How, ever, where she will'd, her spirit went;
Whether to faint Elysium, or where
Down through tress-lifting waves the Nereids fair
Wind into Thetis' bower by many a pearly stair;
Or where God Bacchus drains his cups divine,
Stretch'd out, at ease, beneath a glutinous
    pine;   210
Or where in Pluto's gardens palatine[10]
Mulciber's[11] columns gleam in far piazzian line.
And sometimes into cities she would send
Her dream, with feast and rioting to blend;
And once, while among mortals dreaming thus,
She saw the young Corinthian Lycius
Charioting foremost in the envious race,

Like a young Jove with calm uneager face,
And fell into a swooning love of him.
Now on the moth-time of that evening dim   220
He would return that way, as well she knew,
To Corinth from the shore; for freshly blew
The eastern soft wind, and his galley now
Grated the quaystones with her brazen prow
In port Cenchreas, from Egina isle
Fresh anchor'd; whither he had been awhile
To sacrifice to Jove, whose temple there
Waits with high marble doors for blood and in-
    cense rare,
Jove heard his vows, and better'd his desire;
For by some freakful chance he made retire   230
From his companions, and set forth to walk,
Perhaps grown wearied of their Corinth talk:
Over the solitary hills he fared,
Thoughtless at first, but ere eve's star appeared
His phantasy was lost, where reason fades,
In the calm'd twilight of Platonic shades.
Lamia beheld him coming, near, more near—
Close to her passing, in indifference drear,
His silent sandals swept the mossy green;
So neighbour'd to him, and yet so unseen   240
She stood: he pass'd, shut up in mysteries,
His mind wrapp'd like his mantle, while her eyes
Follow'd his steps, and her neck regal white
Turn'd—syllabling thus, 'Ah, Lycius bright,
And will you leave me on the hills alone?
Lycius, look back! and be some pity shown.'
He did; not with cold wonder fearingly,
But Orpheus-like at an Eurydice;[12]
For so delicious were the words she sung,
It seem'd he had lov'd them a whole summer
    long: 250
And soon his eyes had drunk her beauty up,
Leaving no drop in the bewildering cup,
And still the cup was full,—while he, afraid
Lest she should vanish ere his lip had paid
Due adoration, thus began to adore;
Her soft look growing coy, she saw his chain so
    sure;
'Leave thee alone! Look back! Ah, Goddess, see
Whether my eyes can ever turn from thee!
For pity do not this sad heart belie—
Even as thou vanishest so shall I die.   260
Stay! though a Naiad of the rivers, stay!
To thy far wishes will thy streams obey:
Stay! though the greenest woods be thy domain,
Alone they can drink up the morning rain:
Though a descended Pleiad, will not one
Of thine harmonious sisters keep in tune
Thy spheres, and as thy silver proxy shine?

---

9 innocent.
10 palatial.
11 another name for Vulcan, god of fire and metal-working.

12 After his wife Eurydice died, Orpheus was permitted to lead
her from the lower regions on condition that he should not look
around at her. He violated the condition and lost her forever.

So sweetly to these ravish'd ears of mine
Came thy sweet greeting, that if thou shouldst
    fade
Thy memory will waste me to a shade:—   270
For pity do not melt!'—'If I should stay,'
Said Lamia, 'here, upon this floor of clay,
And pain my steps upon these flowers too rough,
What canst thou say or do of charm enough
To dull the nice remembrance of my home?
Thou canst not ask me with thee here to roam
Over these hills and vales, where no joy is,—
Empty of immortality and bliss!
Thou art a scholar, Lycius, and must know
That finer spirits cannot breathe below   280
In human climes, and live: Alas! poor youth,
What taste of purer air hast thou to soothe
My essence? What serener palaces,
Where I may all my many senses please,
And by mysterious sleights a hundred thirsts ap-
    pease?
It cannot be—Adieu!' So said, she rose
Tiptoe with white arms spread. He, sick to lose
The amorous promise of her lone complain,
Swoon'd, murmuring of love, and pale with pain.
The cruel lady, without any show   290
Of sorrow for her tender favourite's woe,
But rather, if her eyes could brighter be,
With brighter eyes and slow amenity,
Put her new lips to his, and gave afresh
The life she had so tangled in her mesh:
And as he from one trance was wakening
Into another, she began to sing,
Happy in beauty, life, and love, and every thing,
A song of love, too sweet for earthly lyres,
While, like held breath, the stars drew in their
    panting fires.   300
And then she whisper'd in such trembling tone,
As those who, safe together met alone
For the first time through many anguish'd
    days,
Use other speech than looks; bidding him raise
His drooping head, and clear his soul of doubt,
For that she was a woman, and without
Any more subtle fluid in her veins
Than throbbing blood, and that the self-same
    pains
Inhabited her frail-strung heart as his.
And next she wonder'd how his eyes could
    miss   310
Her face so long in Corinth, where, she said,
She dwelt but half retir'd, and there had led
Days happy as the gold coin could invent
Without the aid of love; yet in content
Till she saw him, as once she pass'd him by,
Where 'gainst a column he lent thoughtfully
At Venus' temple porch, 'mid baskets heap'd

Of amorous herbs and flowers, newly reap'd
Late on that eve, as 'twas the night before
The Adonian feast;[13] whereof she saw no
    more,   320
But wept alone those days, for why should she
    adore?
Lycius from death awoke into amaze,
To see her still, and singing so sweet lays;
Then from amaze into delight he fell
To hear her whisper woman's lore so well;
And every word she spake entic'd him on
To unperplex'd delight and pleasure known.
Let the mad poets say whate'er they please
Of the sweets of Faeries, Peris, Goddesses,
There is not such a treat among them all,   330
Haunters of cavern, lake, and waterfall,
As a real woman, lineal indeed
From Pyrrha's pebbles[14] or old Adam's seed.
Thus gentle Lamia judg'd, and judg'd aright,
That Lycius could not love in half a fright,
So threw the goddess off, and won his heart
More pleasantly by playing a woman's part,
With no more awe than what her beauty gave,
That, while it smote, still guaranteed to save.
Lycius to all made eloquent reply,   340
Marrying to every word a twinborn sigh;
And last, pointing to Corinth, ask'd her sweet,
If 'twas too far that night for her soft feet.
The way was short, for Lamia's eagerness
Made, by a spell, the triple league decrease
To a few paces; not at all surmised
By blinded Lycius, so in her comprised.
They pass'd the city gates, he knew not how,
So noiseless, and he never thought to know.

As men talk in a dream, so Corinth all,   350
Throughout her palaces imperial,
And all her populous streets and temples lewd,
Mutter'd, like tempest in the distance brew'd,
To the wide-spreaded night above her towers.
Men, women, rich and poor, in the cool hours,
Shuffled their sandals o'er the pavement white,
Companion'd or alone; while many a light
Flared, here and there, from wealthy festivals,
And threw their moving shadows on the walls,
Or found them cluster'd in the corniced
    shade   360
Of some arch'd temple door, or dusky colon-
    nade.

Muffling his face, of greeting friends in fear,
Her fingers he press'd hard, as one came near

---

13 the midsummer festival celebrating Adonis, who was beloved
by Venus.
14 After the flood, Deucalion and Pyrrha repeopled the earth by
scattering behind them stones which grew into men.

With curl'd grey beard, sharp eyes, and smooth
    bald crown,
Slow-stepp'd, and robed in philosophic gown:
Lycius shrank closer, as they met and past,
Into his mantle, adding wings to haste,
While hurried Lamia trembled: 'Ah,' said he,
'Why do you shudder, love, so ruefully?
Why does your tender palm dissolve in
    dew?'—   370
'I'm wearied,' said fair Lamia: 'tell me who
Is that old man? I cannot bring to mind
His features:—Lycius! wherefore did you blind
Yourself from his quick eyes?' Lycius replied,
'Tis Apollonius sage, my trusty guide
And good instructor; but to-night he seems
The ghost of folly haunting my sweet dreams.'

    While yet he spake they had arrived before
A pillar'd porch, with lofty portal door,
Where hung a silver lamp, whose phosphor
    glow   380
Reflected in the slabbed steps below,
Mild as a star in water; for so new,
And so unsullied was the marble's hue,
So through the crystal polish, liquid fine,
Ran the dark veins, that none but feet divine
Could e'er have touch'd there. Sounds Æolian
Breath'd from the hinges, as the ample span
Of the wide doors disclos'd a place unknown
Some time to any, but those two alone,
And a few Persian mutes, who that same
    year   390
Were seen about the markets: none knew where
They could inhabit; the most curious
Were foil'd, who watch'd to trace them to their
    house:
And but the flitter-winged verse must tell,
For truth's sake, what woe afterwards befel,
'Twould humour many a heart to leave them
    thus,
Shut from the busy world of more incredulous.

PART II

LOVE in a hut, with water and a crust,
Is—Love, forgive us!—cinders, ashes, dust;
Love in a palace is perhaps at last
More grievous torment than a hermit's fast:—
That is a doubtful tale from faery land,
Hard for the non-elect to understand.
Had Lycius liv'd to hand his story down,
He might have given the moral a fresh frown,
Or clench'd it quite: but too short was their bliss
To breed distrust and hate, that make the soft
    voice hiss.   10
Beside, there, nightly, with terrific glare,
Love, jealous grown of so complete a pair,

Hover'd and buzz'd his wings, with fearful roar,
Above the lintel of their chamber door,
And down the passage cast a glow upon the floor.

    For all this came a ruin: side by side
They were enthroned, in the even tide,
Upon a couch, near to a curtaining
Whose airy texture, from a golden string,
Floated into the room, and let appear   20
Unveil'd the summer heaven, blue and clear,
Betwixt two marble shafts:—there they reposed,
Where use had made it sweet, with eyelids closed,
Saving a tythe which love still open kept,
That they might see each other while they almost
    slept;
When from the slope side of a suburb hill,
Deafening the swallow's twitter, came a thrill
Of trumpets—Lycius started—the sounds fled,
But left a thought, a buzzing in his head.
For the first time, since first he harbour'd in   30
That purple-lined palace of sweet sin,
His spirit pass'd beyond its golden bourn
Into the noisy world almost forsworn.
The lady, ever watchful, penetrant,
Saw this with pain, so arguing a want
Of something more, more than her empery[15]
Of joys; and she began to moan and sigh
Because he mused beyond her, knowing well
That but a moment's thought is passion's passing
    bell.
'Why do you sigh, fair creature?' whisper'd
    he: 40
'Why do you think?' return'd she tenderly:
'You have deserted me;—where am I now?
Not in your heart while care weighs on your
    brow:
No, no, you have dismiss'd me; and I go
From your breast houseless: aye, it must be so.'
He answer'd, bending to her open eyes,
Where he was mirror'd small in paradise,
'My silver planet, both of eve and morn!
Why will you plead yourself so sad forlorn,
While I am striving how to fill my heart   50
With deeper crimson, and a double smart?
How to entangle, trammel up and snare
Your soul in mine, and labyrinth you there
Like the hid scent in an unbudded rose?
Aye, a sweet kiss—you see your mighty woes.
My thoughts! shall I unveil them? Listen then!
What mortal hath a prize, that other men
May be confounded and abash'd withal,
But lets it sometimes pace abroad majestical,
And triumph, as in thee I should rejoice   60
Amid the hoarse alarm of Corinth's voice.

---

15 empire.

Let my foes choke, and my friends shout afar,
While through the thronged streets your bridal
    car
Wheels round its dazzling spokes.'—The lady's
    cheek
Trembled; she nothing said, but, pale and meek,
Arose and knelt before him, wept a rain
Of sorrows at his words; at last with pain
Beseeching him, the while his hand she wrung,
To change his purpose. He thereat was stung,
Perverse, with stronger fancy to reclaim   70
Her wild and timid nature to his aim:
Besides, for all his love, in self despite,
Against his better self, he took delight
Luxurious in her sorrows, soft and new.
His passion, cruel grown, took on a hue
Fierce and sanguineous as 'twas possible
In one whose brow had no dark veins to swell.
Fine was the mitigated fury, like
Apollo's presence when in act to strike
The serpent—Ha, the serpent! certes, she   80
Was none. She burnt, she lov'd the tyranny,
And, all subdued, consented to the hour
When to the bridal he should lead his paramour.
Whispering in midnight silence, said the youth,
'Sure some sweet name thou hast, though, by my
    truth,
I have not ask'd it, ever thinking thee
Not mortal, but of heavenly progeny,
As still I do. Hast any mortal name,
Fit appellation for this dazzling frame?
Or friends or kinsfolk on the citied earth,   90
To share our marriage feast and nuptial mirth?'
'I have no friends,' said Lamia, 'no, not one;
My presence in wide Corinth hardly known:
My parents' bones are in their dusty urns
Sepulchred, where no kindled incense burns,
Seeing all their luckless race are dead, save me,
And I neglect the holy rite for thee.
Even as you list invite your many guests;
But if, as now it seems, your vision rests
With any pleasure on me, do not bid   100
Old Apollonius—from him keep me hid.'
Lycius, perplex'd at words so blind and blank,
Made close inquiry; from whose touch she
    shrank,
Feigning a sleep; and he to the dull shade
Of deep sleep in a moment was betray'd.

It was the custom then to bring away
The bride from home at blushing shut of day,
Veil'd, in a chariot, heralded along
By strewn flowers, torches, and a marriage song,
With other pageants: but this fair unknown   110
Had not a friend. So being left alone,
(Lycius was gone to summon all his kin)

And knowing surely she could never win
His foolish heart from its mad pompousness,
She set herself, high-thoughted, how to dress
The misery in fit magnificence.
She did so, but 'tis doubtful how and whence
Came, and who were her subtle servitors.
About the halls, and to and from the doors,
There was a noise of wings, till in short space   120
The glowing banquet-room shone with wide-
    arched grace.
A haunting music, sole perhaps and lone
Supportress of the faery-roof, made moan
Throughout, as fearful the whole charm might
    fade.
Fresh carved cedar, mimicking a glade
Of palm and plantain, met from either side,
High in the midst, in honour of the bride:
Two palms and then two plantains, and so on,
From either side their stems branch'd one to
    one
All down the aisled place; and beneath all   130
There ran a stream of lamps straight on from
    wall to wall.
So canopied, lay an untasted feast
Teeming with odours. Lamia, regal drest,
Silently paced about, and as she went,
In pale contented sort of discontent,
Mission'd her viewless servants to enrich
The fretted splendour of each nook and niche.
Between the tree-stems, marbled plain at first,
Came jasper pannels; then, anon, there burst
Forth creeping imagery of slighter trees,   140
And with the larger wove in small intricacies.
Approving all, she faded at self-will,
And shut the chamber up, close, hush'd and still,
Complete and ready for the revels rude,
When dreadful guests would come to spoil her
    solitude.

The day appear'd, and all the gossip rout.
O senseless Lycius! Madman! wherefore flout
The silent-blessing fate, warm cloister'd hours,
And show to common eyes these secret bowers?
The herd approach'd; each guest, with busy
    brain,   150
Arriving at the portal, gaz'd amain,
And enter'd marvelling: for they knew the street,
Remember'd it from childhood all complete
Without a gap, yet ne'er before had seen
That royal porch, that high-built fair demesne;
So in they hurried all, maz'd, curious and keen:
Save one, who look'd thereon with eye severe,
And with calm-planted steps walk'd in austere;
'Twas Apollonius: something too he laugh'd,
As though some knotty problem, that had
    daft   160

His patient thought, had now begun to thaw,
And solve and melt:—'twas just as he foresaw.

He met within the murmurous vestibule
His young disciple. 'Tis no common rule,
Lycius,' said he, 'for uninvited guest
To force himself upon you, and infest
With an unbidden presence the bright throng
Of younger friends; yet must I do this wrong,
And you forgive me.' Lycius blush'd, and led
The old man through the inner doors broad-
    spread;   170
With reconciling words and courteous mien
Turning into sweet milk the sophist's spleen.

Of wealthy lustre was the banquet-room,
Fill'd with pervading brilliance and perfume:
Before each lucid pannel fuming stood
A censer fed with myrrh and spiced wood,
Each by a sacred tripod held aloft,
Whose slender feet wide-swerv'd upon the soft
Wool-woofed carpets: fifty wreaths of smoke
From fifty censers their light voyage took   180
To the high roof, still mimick'd as they rose
Along the mirror'd walls by twin-clouds odorous.
Twelve sphered tables, by silk seats insphered,
High as the level of a man's breast rear'd
On libbard's paws,[16] upheld the heavy gold
Of cups and goblets, and the store thrice told
Of Ceres' horn, and, in huge vessels, wine
Come from the gloomy tun with merry shine.
Thus loaded with a feast the tables stood,
Each shrining in the midst the image of a
    God.   190

When in an antichamber every guest
Had felt the cold full sponge to pleasure press'd,
By minist'ring slaves, upon his hands and feet,
And fragrant oils with ceremony meet
Pour'd on his hair, they all mov'd to the feast
In white robes, and themselves in order placed
Around the silken couches, wondering
Whence all this mighty cost and blaze of wealth
    could spring.

Soft went the music the soft air along,
While fluent Greek a vowel'd undersong   200
Kept up among the guests, discoursing low
At first, for scarcely was the wine at flow;
But when the happy vintage touch'd their brains,
Louder they talk, and louder come the strains
Of powerful instruments:—the gorgeous dyes,
The space, the splendour of the draperies,
The roof of awful richness, nectarous cheer,

Beautiful slaves, and Lamia's self, appear,
Now, when the wine has done its rosy deed,
And every soul from human trammels freed,   210
No more so strange; for merry wine, sweet wine,
Will make Elysian shades not too fair, too divine.
Soon was God Bacchus at meridian height;
Flush'd were their cheeks, and bright eyes double
    bright:
Garlands of every green, and every scent
From vales deflower'd, or forest-trees branch-
    rent,
In baskets of bright osier'd gold were brought
High as the handles heap'd, to suit the thought
Of every guest; that each, as he did please,
Might fancy-fit his brows, silk-pillow'd at his
    ease.   220

What wreath for Lamia? What for Lycius?
What for the sage, old Apollonius?
Upon her aching forehead be there hung
The leaves of willow and of adder's tongue;
And for the youth, quick, let us strip for him
The thyrsus,[17] that his watching eyes may swim
Into forgetfulness; and, for the sage,
Let spear-grass and the spiteful thistle wage
War on his temples. Do not all charms fly
At the mere touch of cold philosophy?   230
There was an awful rainbow once in heaven:
We know her woof, her texture; she is given
In the dull catalogue of common things.
Philosophy will clip an Angel's wings,
Conquer all mysteries by rule and line,
Empty the haunted air, and gnomed mine—
Unweave a rainbow, as it erewhile made
The tender-person'd Lamia melt into a shade.

By her glad Lycius sitting, in chief place,
Scarce saw in all the room another face,   240
Till, checking his love trance, a cup he took
Full brimm'd, and opposite sent forth a look
'Cross the broad table, to beseech a glance
From his old teacher's wrinkled countenance,
And pledge him. The bald-head philosopher
Had fix'd his eye, without a twinkle or stir
Full on the alarmed beauty of the bride,
Brow-beating her fair form, and troubling her
    sweet pride.
Lycius then press'd her hand, with devout touch,
As pale it lay upon the rosy couch: 250
'Twas icy, and the cold ran through his veins;
Then sudden it grew hot, and all the pains
Of an unnatural heat shot to his heart.
'Lamia, what means this? Wherefore dost thou
    start?

---

16 leopard's.

17 the wand of Bacchus entwined with grapevine and ivy.

Know'st thou that man?' Poor Lamia answer'd
   not.
He gaz'd into her eyes, and not a jot
Own'd they the lovelorn piteous appeal:
More, more he gaz'd: his human senses reel:
Some hungry spell that loveliness absorbs;
There was no recognition in those orbs.   260
'Lamia!' he cried—and no soft-toned reply.
The many heard, and the loud revelry
Grew hush; the stately music no more breathes;
The myrtle sicken'd in a thousand wreaths.
By faint degrees, voice, lute, and pleasure ceased;
A deadly silence step by step increased,
Until it seem'd a horrid presence there,
And not a man but felt the terror in his hair.
'Lamia!' he shriek'd; and nothing but the shriek
With its sad echo did the silence break.   270
'Begone, foul dream!' he cried, gazing again
In the bride's face, where now no azure vein
Wander'd on fair-spaced temples; no soft bloom
Misted the cheek; no passion to illume
The deep-recessed vision:—all was blight;
Lamia, no longer fair, there sat a deadly white.
'Shut, shut those juggling eyes, thou ruthless
   man!
Turn them aside, wretch! or the righteous ban
Of all the Gods, whose dreadful images
Here represent their shadowy presences,   280
May pierce them on the sudden with the thorn
Of painful blindness; leaving thee forlorn,
In trembling dotage to the feeblest fright
Of conscience, for their long offended might,
For all thine impious proud-heart sophistries,
Unlawful magic, and enticing lies.
Corinthians! look upon that grey-beard wretch!
Mark how, possess'd, his lashless eyelids stretch
Around his demon eyes! Corinthians, see!
My sweet bride withers at their potency.'   290
'Fool!' said the sophist, in an under-tone
Gruff with contempt; which a death-nighing
   moan
From Lycius answer'd, as heart-struck and lost,
He sank supine beside the aching ghost.
'Fool! Fool!' repeated he, while his eyes still
Relented not, nor mov'd; 'from every ill
Of life have I preserv'd thee to this day,
And shall I see thee made a serpent's prey?'
Then Lamia breath'd death breath; the sophist's
   eye,
Like a sharp spear, went through her utterly,   300
Keen, cruel, perceant, stinging: she, as well
As her weak hand could any meaning tell,
Motion'd him to be silent; vainly so.
He look'd and look'd again a level—No!
'A serpent!' echoed he; no sooner said,
Than with a frightful scream she vanished:

And Lycius' arms were empty of delight,
As were his limbs of life, from that same night.
On the high couch he lay!—his friends came
   round—
Supported him—no pulse, or breath they
   found,   310
And, in its marriage robe, the heavy body
   wound.

1819   1820

TO AUTUMN

[In a letter to Reynolds from Winchester, dated 22
September 1819, Keats enclosed a copy of his poem and
wrote as follows: 'How beautiful the season is now—
How fine the air. A temperate sharpness about it.
Really, without joking, chaste weather—Dian skies—I
never liked stubble-fields so much as now—Aye better
than the chilly green of the Spring. Somehow, a stubble-
field looks warm—in the same way that some pictures
look warm. This struck me so much in my Sunday's
walk that I composed upon it.']

SEASON of mists and mellow fruitfulness,
   Close bosom-friend of the maturing sun;
Conspiring with him how to load and bless
   With fruit the vines that round the thatch-eves
      run;
To bend with apples the moss'd cottage-trees,
   And fill all fruit with ripeness to the core;
      To swell the gourd, and plump the hazel
      shells
   With a sweet kernel; to set budding more,
And still more, later flowers for the bees,
Until they think warm days will never cease,   10
      For Summer has o'er-brimm'd their clammy
      cells.

Who hath not seen thee oft amid thy store?
   Sometimes whoever seeks abroad may find
Thee sitting careless on a granary floor,
   Thy hair soft-lifted by the winnowing wind;
Or on a half-reap'd furrow sound asleep,
   Drows'd with the fume of poppies, while thy
      hook
      Spares the next swath and all its twined
      flowers:
And sometimes like a gleaner thou dost keep
   Steady thy laden head across a brook;   20
   Or by a cyder-press, with patient look,
      Thou watchest the last oozings hours by
      hours.

Where are the songs of Spring? Ay, where are
   they?
   Think not of them, thou hast thy music too,—
While barred clouds bloom the soft-dying day,

And touch the stubble-plains with rosy hue;
Then in a wailful choir the small gnats mourn
  Among the river sallows,[1] borne aloft
  Or sinking as the light wind lives or dies;
And full-grown lambs loud bleat from hilly
    bourn;   30
  Hedge-crickets sing; and now with treble soft
  The red-breast whistles from a garden-croft;
    And gathering swallows twitter in the skies.

1819   1820

THE DAY IS GONE

THE day is gone, and all its sweets are gone!
  Sweet voice, sweet lips, soft hand, and softer
    breast,
Warm breath, light whisper, tender semi-tone,
  Bright eyes, accomplish'd shape, and lang'rous
    waist!
Faded the flower and all its budded charms,
  Faded the sight of beauty from my eyes,
Faded the shape of beauty from my arms,
  Faded the voice, warmth, whiteness, para-
    dise—
Vanish'd unseasonably at shut of eve,
  When the dusk holiday—or holinight   10
Of fragrant-curtain'd love begins to weave
  The woof of darkness thick, for hid delight;
But, as I've read love's missal through to-day,
  He'll let me sleep, seeing I fast and pray.

October 1819   1848

TO FANNY

I CRY your mercy—pity—love!—aye, love!
  Merciful love that tantalizes not,
One-thoughted, never-wandering, guileless love,
  Unmask'd, and being seen—without a blot!
O! let me have thee whole,—all—all—be mine!
  That shape, that fairness, that sweet minor
    zest
Of love, your kiss,—those hands, those eyes di-
    vine,
  That warm, white, lucent, million-pleasured
    breast,—
Yourself—your soul—in pity give me all,
  Withhold no atom's atom or I die,   10
Or living on perhaps, your wretched thrall,
  Forget, in the mist of idle misery,
Life's purposes,—the palate of my mind
Losing its gust, and my ambition blind!

November 1819   1848

---

[1] willows.

From THE FALL OF HYPERION

A DREAM

[*The Fall of Hyperion* has been considered by some critics to have been the original poem and *Hyperion* the revision. But Sidney Colvin in his *Life of Keats,* 1887, established through quite convincing evidence the priority of *Hyperion,* and since that time practically all scholars have accepted Colvin's view. M. R. Ridley (*Keats' Craftsmanship,* 1933, pp. 57–9) has argued persuasively that *The Fall of Hyperion* is virtually a new *Hyperion,* begun in August 1819, with the greater part probably completed by September.]

CANTO I

Lines 1–318

FANATICS have their dreams, wherewith they
  weave
A paradise for a sect; the savage too
From forth the loftiest fashion of his sleep
Guesses at Heaven; pity these have not
Trac'd upon vellum or wild Indian leaf
The shadows of melodious utterance.
But bare of laurel they live, dream, and die;
For Poesy alone can tell her dreams,
With the fine spell of words alone can save
Imagination from the sable chain   10
And dumb enchantment. Who alive can say,
'Thou art no Poet—may'st not tell thy dreams?'
Since every man whose soul is not a clod
Hath visions, and would speak, if he had loved,
And been well nurtured in his mother tongue.
Whether the dream now purpos'd to rehearse
Be poet's or fanatic's will be known
When this warm scribe my hand is in the grave.

Methought I stood where trees of every clime,
Palm, myrtle, oak, and sycamore, and beech, 20
With plantain, and spice-blossoms, made a
  screen;
In neighbourhood of fountains (by the noise
Soft-showering in my ears), and, (by the touch
Of scent,) not far from roses. Turning round
I saw an arbour with a drooping roof
Of trellis vines, and bells, and larger blooms,
Like floral censers, swinging light in air;
Before its wreathed doorway, on a mound
Of moss, was spread a feast of summer fruits,
Which, nearer seen, seem'd refuse of a meal 30
By angel tasted or our Mother Eve;
For empty shells were scattered on the grass,
And grape-stalks but half bare, and remnants
  more, .
Sweet-smelling, whose pure kinds I could not
  know.
Still was more plenty than the fabled horn
Thrice emptied could pour forth, at banqueting

For Proserpine return'd to her own fields,
Where the white heifers low.[1] And appetite
More yearning than on Earth I ever felt
Growing within, I ate deliciously;   40
And, after not long, thirsted, for thereby
Stood a cool vessel of transparent juice
Sipp'd by the wander'd bee, the which I took,
And, pledging all the mortals of the world,
And all the dead whose names are in our lips,
Drank. That full draught is parent of my theme.
No Asian poppy nor elixir fine
Of the soon-fading jealous Caliphat;[2]
No poison gender'd in close monkish cell,
To thin the scarlet conclave of old men,   50
Could so have rapt unwilling life away.
Among the fragrant husks and berries crush'd,
Upon the grass I struggled hard against
The domineering potion; but in vain:
The cloudy swoon came on, and down I sank,
Like a Silenus[3] on an antique vase.
How long I slumber'd 'tis a chance to guess.
When sense of life return'd, I started up
As if with wings; but the fair trees were gone,
The mossy mound and arbour were no more: 60
I look'd around upon the carved sides
Of an old sanctuary with roof august,
Builded so high, it seem'd that filmed clouds
Might spread beneath, as o'er the stars of
        heaven;
So old the place was, I remember'd none
The like upon the Earth: what I had seen
Of grey cathedrals, buttress'd walls, rent towers,
The superannuations of sunk realms,
Or Nature's rocks toil'd hard in waves and winds,
Seem'd but the faulture of decrepit things   70
To that eternal domed Monument.—
Upon the marble at my feet there lay
Store of strange vessels and large draperies,
Which needs had been of dyed asbestos wove,
Or in that place the moth could not corrupt,
So white the linen, so, in some, distinct
Ran imageries from a sombre loom.
All in a mingled heap confus'd there lay
Robes, golden tongs, censer and chafing-dish,
Girdles, and chains, and holy jewelries.   80

    Turning from these with awe, once more I
      rais'd
My eyes to fathom the space every way;
The embossed roof, the silent massy range
Of columns north and south, ending in mist
Of nothing, then to eastward, where black gates

Were shut against the sunrise evermore.—
Then to the west I look'd, and saw far off
An image, huge of feature as a cloud,
At level of whose feet an altar slept,
To be approach'd on either side by steps,   90
And marble balustrade, and patient travail
To count with toil the innumerable degrees.
Towards the altar sober-paced I went,
Repressing haste, as too unholy there;
And, coming nearer, saw beside the shrine
One minist'ring;[4] and there arose a flame.—
When in mid-way the sickening East wind
Shifts sudden to the south, the small warm rain
Melts out the frozen incense from all flowers,
And fills the air with so much pleasant
        health   100
That even the dying man forgets his shroud;—
Even so that lofty sacrificial fire,
Sending forth Maian incense, spread around
Forgetfulness of everything but bliss,
And clouded all the altar with soft smoke;
From whose white fragrant curtains thus I heard
Language pronounc'd: 'If thou canst not ascend
These steps, die on that marble where thou art.
Thy flesh, near cousin to the common dust,
Will parch for lack of nutriment—thy bones   110
Will wither in few years, and vanish so
That not the quickest eye could find a grain
Of what thou now art on that pavement cold.
The sands of thy short life are spent this hour,
And no hand in the universe can turn
Thy hourglass, if these gummed leaves be burnt
Ere thou canst mount up these immortal steps.'
I heard, I look'd: two senses both at once,
So fine, so subtle, felt the tyranny
Of that fierce threat and the hard task pro-
        posed.   120
Prodigious seem'd the toil; the leaves were yet
Burning—when suddenly a palsied chill
Struck from the paved level up my limbs,
And was ascending quick to put cold grasp
Upon those streams that pulse beside the throat:
I shriek'd, and the sharp anguish of my shriek
Stung my own ears—I strove hard to escape
The numbness; strove to gain the lowest step.
Slow, heavy, deadly was my pace: the cold
Grew stifling, suffocating, at the heart;   130
And when I clasp'd my hands I felt them not.
One minute before death, my iced foot touch'd
The lowest stair; and as it touch'd, life seem'd
To pour in at the toes: I mounted up,
As once fair angels on a ladder flew
From the green turf to Heaven—'Holy Power,'
Cried I, approaching near the horned shrine,

---

1 Proserpine, a mortal who had been made queen of the lower regions, was permitted to return to her home on earth each year in the spring for six months.
2 Caliph, a title of the sultans of Turkey.
3 drunken satyr.

4 the Roman Moneta, goddess of memory, who is to be the monitress of the poet and the interpreter of his vision.

'What am I that should so be saved from death?
What am I that another death come not
To choke my utterance sacrilegious, here?' 140
Then said the veiled shadow—'Thou hast felt
What 'tis to die and live again before
Thy fated hour, that thou hadst power to do so
Is thy own safety; thou hast dated on
Thy doom.'—'High Prophetess,' said I, 'purge off,
Benign, if so it please thee, my mind's film.'—
'None can usurp this height,' return'd that shade,
'But those to whom the miseries of the world
Are misery, and will not let them rest.
All else who find a haven in the world, 150
Where they may thoughtless sleep away their days,
If by a chance into this fane they come,
Rot on the pavement where thou rottedst half.'—
'Are there not thousands in the world,' said I,
Encourag'd by the sooth voice of the shade,
'Who love their fellows even to the death,
Who feel the giant agony of the world,
And more, like slaves to poor humanity,
Labour for mortal good? I sure should see
Other men here; but I am here alone.' 160
'Those whom thou spak'st of are no vision'ries,'
Rejoin'd that voice—'They are no dreamers weak,
They seek no wonder but the human face;
No music but a happy-noted voice—
They come not here, they have no thought to come—
And thou art here, for thou art less than they—
What benefit canst thou, or all thy tribe,
To the great world? Thou art a dreaming thing,
A fever of thyself—think of the Earth;
What bliss even in hope is there for thee? 170
What haven? every creature hath its home;
Every sole man hath days of joy and pain,
Whether his labours be sublime or low—
The pain alone; the joy alone; distinct:
Only the dreamer venoms all his days,
Bearing more woe than all his sins deserve.
Therefore, that happiness be somewhat shar'd,
Such things as thou art are admitted oft
Into like gardens thou didst pass erewhile,
And suffer'd in these temples: for that cause 180
Thou standest safe beneath this statue's knees.'
'That I am favour'd for unworthiness,
By such propitious parley medicin'd
In sickness not ignoble, I rejoice,
Aye, and could weep for love of such award.'
So answer'd I, continuing, 'If it please,
Majestic shadow, [tell me: sure not all
Those melodies sung into the World's ear

Are useless: sure a poet is a sage;
A humanist, physician to all men. 190
That I am none I feel, as vultures feel
They are no birds when eagles are abroad.
What am I then: Thou spakest of my tribe:
What tribe?' The tall shade veil'd in drooping white
Then spake, so much more earnest, that the breath
Moved the thin linen folds that drooping hung
About a golden censer from the hand
Pendent—'Art thou not of the dreamer tribe?
The poet and the dreamer are distinct,
Diverse, sheer opposite, antipodes. 200
The one pours out a balm upon the World,
The other vexes it.' Then shouted I
Spite of myself, and with a Pythia's[5] spleen
'Apollo! faded! O far flown Apollo!
Where is thy misty pestilence to creep
Into the dwellings, through the door crannies
Of all mock lyrists, large self worshippers
And careless Hectorers in proud bad verse.[6]
Though I breathe death with them it will be life
To see them sprawl before me into graves. 210
Majestic shadow][7] tell me where I am,
Whose altar this; for whom this incense curls;
What image this whose face I cannot see,
For the broad marble knees; and who thou art,
Of accent feminine so courteous?'

Then the tall shade, in drooping linens veil'd,
Spoke out, so much more earnest, that her breath
Stirr'd the thin folds of gauze that drooping hung
About a golden censer from her hand
Pendent; and by her voice I knew she shed 220
Long-treasured tears. 'This temple, sad and lone,
Is all spar'd from the thunder of a war
Foughten long since by giant hierarchy
Against rebellion: this old image here,
Whose carved features wrinkled as he fell,
Is Saturn's; I Moneta, left supreme
Sole Priestess of this desolation.'—
I had no words to answer, for my tongue,
Useless, could find about its roofed home
No syllable of a fit majesty 230
To make rejoinder to Moneta's mourn.
There was a silence, while the altar's blaze
Was fainting for sweet food: I look'd thereon,
And on the paved floor, where nigh were piled
Faggots of cinnamon, and many heaps
Of other crisped spice-wood—then again

---

5 the Python snake, slain by Apollo.
6 an attack on Byron, who is likened to swaggering Hector of the *Iliad*.
7 Lines 187–211 were omitted in the first edition. The passage is not good poetry, but is valuable as an expression of Keats's philosophy.

I look'd upon the altar, and its horns
Whiten'd with ashes, and its lang'rous flame,
And then upon the offerings again;
And so by turns—till sad Moneta cried,   240
'The sacrifice is done, but not the less
Will I be kind to thee for thy good will.
My power, which to me is still a curse,
Shall be to thee a wonder; for the scenes
Still swooning vivid through my globed brain,
With an electral changing misery,
Thou shalt with these dull mortal eyes behold,
Free from all pain, if wonder pain thee not.'
As near as an immortal's sphered words
Could to a mother's soften, were these last: 250
And yet I had a terror of her robes,
And chiefly of the veils, that from her brow
Hung pale, and curtain'd her in mysteries,
That made my heart too small to hold its blood.
This saw that Goddess, and with sacred hand
Parted the veils. Then saw I a wan face,
Not pin'd by human sorrows, but bright-blanch'd
By an immortal sickness which kills not;
It works a constant change, which happy death
Can put no end to; deathwards progressing   260
To no death was that visage; it had past
The lilly and the snow; and beyond these
I must not think now, though I saw that face—
But for her eyes I should have fled away.
They held me back, with a benignant light,
Soft mitigated by divinest lids
Half-closed, and visionless entire they seem'd
Of all external things;—they saw me not,
But in blank splendour, beam'd like the mild
     moon,
Who comforts those she sees not, who knows
     not   270
What eyes are upward cast. As I had found
A grain of gold upon a mountain's side,
And twing'd with avarice strain'd out my eyes
To search its sullen entrails rich with ore,
So at the view of sad Moneta's brow,
I ask'd to see what things the hollow brain
Behind environed: what high tragedy
In the dark secret chambers of her skull
Was acting, that could give so dread a stress
To her cold lips, and fill with such a light   280
Her planetary eyes; and touch her voice
With such a sorrow—'Shade of Memory!'—
Cried I, with act adorant at her feet,
'By all the gloom hung round thy fallen house,
By this last temple, by the golden age,
By great Apollo, thy dear Foster Child,
And by thyself, forlorn divinity,
The pale Omega of a withered race,
Let me behold, according as thou saidst,

What in thy brain so ferments to and fro!'   290
No sooner had this conjuration pass'd
My devout lips, than side by side we stood
(Like a stunt bramble by a solemn pine)
Deep in the shady sadness of a vale,[8]
Far sunken from the healthy breath of morn,
Far from the fiery noon and eve's one star.
Onward I look'd beneath the gloomy boughs,
And saw, what first I thought an image huge,
Like to the image pedestal'd so high
In Saturn's temple. Then Moneta's voice   300
Came brief upon mine ear—'So Saturn sat
When he had lost his Realms—'whereon there
     grew
A power within me of enormous ken
To see as a god sees, and take the depth
Of things as nimbly as the outward eye
Can size and shape pervade. The lofty theme
At those few words hung vast before my mind,
With half-unravell'd web. I set myself
Upon an eagle's watch, that I might see,
And seeing ne'er forget. No stir of life   310
Was in this shrouded vale, not so much air
As in the zoning of a summer's day[9]
Robs not one light seed from the feather'd grass,
But where the dead leaf fell there did it rest:
A stream went voiceless by, still deaden'd more
By reason of the fallen divinity
Spreading more shade; the Naiad 'mid her reeds
Prest her cold finger closer to her lips.

                              . . .

August 1819   1856

SELECTIONS FROM KEATS'S LETTERS

1 *To* John Hamilton Reynolds[1]

Carisbrooke[2] *April 17th–18th 1817.*

My dear Reynolds,

     Ever since I wrote to my Brothers from South-
ampton I have been in a taking, and at this moment I am about to become settled, for I have
unpacked my books, put them into a snug corner—pinned up Haydon[3]—Mary Queen of Scots,

---

8 The first version of *Hyperion* began with this line. The revision
was continued from this point for an additional 135 lines and then
abandoned.
9 as when on warm summer days the still air is divided into visible zones or layers.

---

1 John Hamilton Reynolds, 1796–1852, author and solicitor, a
kindred spirit to whom Keats wrote more freely than to any correspondent outside his family.
2 a village in the Isle of Wight.
3 Benjamin Robert Haydon, 1786–1846, historical painter, now
better known for making the nation buy the Elgin marbles than
for the excellence of his art.

and Milton with his daughters in a row. In the passage I found a head of Shakespeare which I had not before seen. It is most likely the same that George spoke so well of; for I like it extremely. Well—this head I have hung over my Books, just above the three in a row, having first discarded a French Ambassador—now this alone is a good morning's work.

Yesterday I went to Shanklin, which occasioned a great debate in my Mind whether I should live there or at Carisbrooke. Shanklin is a most beautiful place—sloping wood and meadow ground reaches round the Chine, which is a cleft between the Cliffs of the depth of nearly 300 feet at least. This cleft is filled with trees and bushes in the narrow parts; and as it widens becomes bare, if it were not for primroses on one side, which spread to the very verge of the Sea, and some fishermen's huts on the other, perched midway in the Ballustrades of beautiful green Hedges along their steps down to the sands. —But the sea, Jack, the sea—the little waterfall—then the white cliff—then St. Catherine's Hill— . . . The wind is in a sulky fit, and I feel that it would be no bad thing to be the favourite of some Fairy, who would give one the power of seeing how our Friends got on, at a Distance—I should like, of all Loves, a sketch of you and Tom and George in ink which Haydon will do if you tell him how I want them—From want of regular rest, I have been rather *narvus*—and the passage in Lear— 'Do you not hear the sea?'—has haunted me intensely. I'll tell you what—on the 23rd was Shakespeare born—now if I should receive a Letter from you and another from my Brothers on that day 'twould be a parlous good thing— Whenever you write say a Word or two on some Passage in Shakespeare that may have come rather new to you; which must be continually happening, notwithstanding that we read the same Play forty times—for instance, the following, from the Tempest, never struck me so forcibly as at present,

                    Urchins
Shall, for that vast of Night that they may work,
All exercise on thee—

How can I help bringing to your mind the Line—

In the dark backward and abysm of time.[4]

I find that I cannot exist without poetry—without eternal poetry—half the day will not do—the whole of it—I began with a little, but habit has

made me a Leviathan—I had become all in a Tremble from not having written anything of late—the Sonnet over leaf [*On the Sea*] did me some good. I slept the better last night for it— this Morning, however, I am nearly as bad again—Just now I opened Spenser, and the first Lines I saw were these.—

The noble Heart that harbours virtuous thought,
And is with Child of glorious great intent,
Can never rest, until it forth have brought
Th'eternal Brood of Glory excellent—[5]

Let me know particularly about Haydon; ask him to write to me about Hunt, if it be only ten lines—I hope all is well—I shall forthwith begin my Endymion, which I hope I shall have got some way into by the time you come, when we will read our verses in a delightful place I have set my heart upon near the Castle—Give my Love to your Sisters severally—To George and Tom—Remember me to Rice, Mr. and Mrs. Dilke and all we know—

Your sincere Friend,

John Keats

2 *To* Leigh Hunt

Margate[6] *May 10,* [*1817*]

My dear Hunt,

The little Gentleman that sometimes lurks in a gossip's bowl ought to have come in very likeness of a roasted crab and choked me outright for not having answered your Letter ere this.—However you must not suppose that I was in Town to receive it; no, it followed me to the Isle of Wight and I got it just as I was going to pack up for Margate. . . .

I went to the Isle of Wight—thought so much about Poetry so long together that I could not get to sleep at night—and moreover, I know not how it was, I could not get wholesome food. By this means in a Week or so I became not over capable in my upper Stories, and set off pell mell for Margate, at least 150 Miles—because forsooth I fancied that I should like my old Lodging here, and could contrive to do without Trees. Another thing I was too much in Solitude, and consequently was obliged to be in continual burning of thought as an only resource. However Tom is with me at present and we are very

---

4 *The Tempest,* I, ii, 50.

5 *Faerie Queene,* I, v, 1–4.
6 a seaside resort in the Isle of Thanet, Kent.

comfortable. We intend though to get among some Trees. . . . I vow that I have been down in the Mouth lately at this Work. These last two days however I have felt more confident.—I have asked myself so often why I should be a Poet more than other Men,—seeing how great a thing it is,—how great things are to be gained by it— What a thing to be in the Mouth of Fame—that at last the Idea has grown so monstrously beyond my seeming Power of attainment that the other day I nearly consented with myself to drop into a Phaeton[7]—yet 'tis a disgrace to fail even in a huge attempt, and at this moment I drive the thought from me. I began my Poem about a Fortnight since and have done some every day except travelling ones.—Perhaps I may have done a good deal for the time but it appears such a Pin's Point to me that I will not copy any out. When I consider that so many of these Pin points go to form a Bodkin point (God send I end not my Life with a bare Bodkin, in its modern sense) and that it requires a thousand bodkins to make a Spear bright enough to throw any light to posterity—I see that nothing but continual uphill Journeying! Now is there anything more unpleasant (it may come among the thousand and one) than to be so journeying and miss the Goal at last. But I intend to whistle all these cogitations into the Sea where I hope they will breed Storms violent enough to block up all exit from Russia. Does Shelley go on telling strange Stories of the Death of Kings?[8] Tell him there are strange Stories of the death of Poets—some have died before they were conceived—'How do you make that out Master Vellum?'[9] Does Mrs. S. cut Bread and Butter as neatly as ever? Tell her to procure some fatal Scissors and cut the thread of Life of all to-be-disappointed Poets. Does Mrs. Hunt tear linen in half as straight as ever? Tell her to tear from the book of Life all blank Leaves. Remember me to them all—to Miss Kent[10] and the little ones all.

> Your sincere friend,
>
> *John Keats* alias *Junkets*

You shall know where we move.

---

7 one who has failed because of rash or headstrong venturing: from *Phaethon,* son of the sun-god, who upon attempting to drive the chariot of the sun lost control and was struck down by Zeus with a thunderbolt.

8 The allusion is to a passage in Shakespeare's *Richard II:*
> For God's sake, let us sit upon the ground
> And tell sad stories of the death of Kings:
which Shelley was fond of quoting in a most startling and incongruous manner.

9 in Addison's *The Drummer or the Haunted House.*

10 Elizabeth Kent, Hunt's sister-in-law.

3 *To* Benjamin Bailey[11]

Hampstead, Wednesday, October [*8, 1817*]

My dear Bailey,

After a tolerable journey, I went from Coach to Coach to as far as Hampstead where I found my Brothers—the next Morning finding myself tolerably well I went to Lambs, Conduit Street and delivered your Parcel—Jane and Marianne[12] were greatly improved, Marianne especially; she has no unhealthy plumpness in the face—but she comes me healthy and angular to the Chin.—I did not see John.—I was extremely sorry to hear that poor Rice,[13] after having had capital Health during his tour, was very ill. I dare say you have heard from him. From No 19 I went to Hunt's and Haydon's who live now neighbours. Shelley was there. I know nothing about anything in this part of the world—everybody seems at Loggerheads. There's Hunt infatuated—there's Haydon's Picture in statu quo. There's Hunt walks up and down his painting room criticising every head most unmercifully. There's Horace Smith tired of Hunt. 'The web of our Life is of mingled Yarn.'[14] Haydon having removed entirely from Marlborough Street, Crips[15] must direct his Letter to Lisson Grove North—Paddington. Yesterday Morning while I was at Brown's[16] in came Reynolds—he was pretty bobbish. We had a pleasant day—but he would walk home at night that cursed cold distance. Mrs. Bentley's children are making a horrid row—whereby I regret I cannot be transported to your Room to write to you. I am quite disgusted with literary Men—and will never know another except Wordsworth—no, not even Byron. Here is an instance of the friendships of such. Haydon and Hunt have known each other many years—now they live *pour ainsi dire*[17] jealous Neighbours. Haydon says to me, 'Keats don't show your Lines to Hunt on any account or he will have done half for you'—so it appears Hunt wishes it to be thought. When he met Reynolds in the Theatre, John told him that I was getting on to the completion of 4000

---

11 Benjamin Bailey, 1791–1853, was an Oxford man, reading for the Church, when Keats knew him. He later became a Bishop in Ceylon.

12 sisters of Keats's friend, J. H. Reynolds.

13 James Rice trained for the law, but he was apparently known more for his wit and generosity than for any professional attainment.

14 *All's Well That Ends Well,* IV, iii, 83.

15 a young art student whom Haydon had promised to take as a pupil.

16 Charles Armitage Brown, 1786–1842, businessman and literary dilettante, was an intimate friend of Keats in the late years of his life. He accompanied Keats on the fatal walking tour in 1818.

17 'so to speak.'

Lines. Ah! says Hunt, had it not been for me they would have been 7000! If he will say this to Reynolds what would he to other People? Haydon received a Letter a little while back on this subject from some Lady—which contains a caution to me through him on this subject.— Now is not all this a most paltry thing to think about? You may see the whole of the case by the following extract from a Letter I wrote to George in the Spring: 'As to what you say about my being a Poet, I can return no answer but by saying that the high Idea I have of poetical fame makes me think I see it towering too high above me. At any rate I have no right to talk until Endymion is finished—it will be a test, a trial of my Powers of Imagination and chiefly of my invention which is a rare thing indeed—by which I must make 4000 Lines of one bare circumstance and fill them with Poetry; and when I consider that this is a great task, and that when done it will take me but a dozen paces towards the Temple of Fame—it makes me say—God forbid that I should be without such a task! I have heard Hunt say and I may be asked—why endeavour after a long Poem? To which I should answer—Do not the Lovers of Poetry like to have a little Region to wander in where they may pick and choose, and in which the images are so numerous that many are forgotten and found new in a second Reading: which may be food for a Week's stroll in the Summer? Do not they like this better than what they can read through before Mrs. Williams comes down stairs? a Morning work at most. Besides a long Poem is a test of Invention which I take to be the Polar Star of Poetry, as Fancy is the Sails, and Imagination the Rudder. Did our great Poets ever write short Pieces? I mean in the shape of Tales.—This same invention seems indeed of late Years to have been forgotten as a Poetical excellence. But enough of this; I put on no Laurels till I shall have finished Endymion, and I hope Apollo is not angered at my having made a Mockery at him at Hunt's.'

You see Bailey how independent my writing has been.—Hunt's dissuasion was of no avail— I refused to visit Shelley, that I might have my own unfettered Scope—and after all I shall have the Reputation of Hunt's elevé. His corrections and amputations will by the knowing ones be traced in the Poem. This is to be sure the vexation of a day—nor would I say so many Words about it to any but those whom I know to have my welfare and Reputation at Heart.—Haydon promised to give directions for those Casts and you may expect to see them soon—with as many

Letters. You will soon hear the dinning of Bells— never mind, you and Gleig[18] will defy the foul fiend. But do not sacrifice your health to Books; do take it kindly and not so voraciously. I am certain if you are your own Physician your Stomach will resume its proper Strength and then what great Benefits will follow. My Sister wrote a Letter to me which I think must be at your post office.—Ask Will to see. My Brothers kindest remembrances to you—we are going to dine at Brown's where I have some hopes of meeting Reynolds. The little Mercury I have taken has corrected the Poison and improved my Health—though I feel from my employment that I shall never be again secure in Robustness.— Would that you were as well as

Your sincere friend and brother,

John Keats

4 *To* Benjamin Bailey

[*London, November 3, 1817*]

My dear Bailey,

. . . There has been a flaming attack upon Hunt in the Edinburgh Magazine. I never read anything so virulent—accusing him of the greatest Crimes, depreciating his Wife, his Poetry— his Habits—his company, his Conversation. These Philippics are to come out in Numbers— called the Cockney School of Poetry. There has been but one Number published—that on Hunt to which they have prefixed a Motto from one Cornelius Webb, Poetaster—who unfortunately was of our Party occasionally at Hampstead and took it into his head to write the following— something about—'we'll talk on Wordsworth, Byron—a theme we never tire on'; and so forth, till he comes to Hunt and Keats. In the Motto they have put Hunt and Keats in large Letters. —I have no doubt that the second Number was intended for me: but have hopes of its non appearance from the following advertisement in last Sunday's Examiner. 'To Z. The writer of the Article signed Z in Blackwood's Edinburgh magazine for October, 1817 is invited to send his address to the printer of the Examiner, in order that Justice may be executed on the proper person.' I don't mind the thing much—but if he should go to such lengths with me as he has done with Hunt I must infallibly call him to an account—if he be a human being and appears in

18 George Robert Gleig, 1796–1888, army chaplain and poet, remembered as the author of *The Subaltern*.

Squares and Theatres where we might possibly meet. I don't relish his abuse. . . .

5 *To* Benjamin Bailey

[*Burford Bridge, November 22, 1817*]

My dear Bailey,

I will get over the first part of this (*unsaid*) Letter as soon as possible for it relates to the affair of poor Crips.—To a man of your nature such a Letter as Haydon's must have been extremely cutting.—What occasions the greater part of the World's Quarrels? Simply this, two Minds meet and do not understand each other time enough to prevent any shock or surprise at the conduct of either party.—As soon as I had known Haydon three days I had got enough of his character not to have been surprised at such a Letter as he has hurt you with. Nor when I knew it, was it a principle with me to drop his acquaintance although with you it would have been an imperious feeling. I wish you knew all that I think about Genius and the Heart—and yet I think you are thoroughly acquainted with my innermost breast in that respect, or you could not have known me even thus long and still hold me worthy to be your dear friend. In passing, however, I must say of one thing that has pressed upon me lately and increased my Humility and capability of submission and that is this truth—Men of Genius are great as certain ethereal Chemicals operating on the Mass of neutral intellect—but they have not any individuality, any determined Character.— I would call the top and head of those who have a proper self Men of Power.

But I am running my head into a Subject which I am certain I could not do justice to under five years Study and 3 vols octavo—and moreover long to be talking about the Imagination—so my dear Bailey do not think of this unpleasant affair if possible—do not—I defy any harm to come of it—I defy. I shall write to Crips this Week and request him to tell me all his goings on from time to time by Letter wherever I may be.—It will all go on well; so don't because you have suddenly discovered a Coldness in Haydon suffer yourself to be teased. Do not, my dear fellow. O I wish I was as certain of the end of all your troubles as that of your momentary start about the authenticity of the Imagination. I am certain of nothing but of the holiness of the Heart's affections and the truth of Imagination.—What the imagination seizes as Beauty must be truth—whether it ex-

isted before or not—for I have the same Idea of all our Passions as of Love; they are all in their sublime, creative of essential Beauty. In a Word, you may know my favourite Speculation by my first Book and the little song I sent in my last— which is a representation from the fancy of the probable mode of operating in these Matters. The Imagination may be compared to Adam's dream—he awoke and found it truth. I am the more zealous in this affair, because I have never yet been able to perceive how anything can be known for truth by consequitive reasoning—and yet it must be. Can it be that even the greatest Philosopher ever arrived at his goal without putting aside numerous objections. However it may be, O for a Life of Sensations rather than of Thoughts! It is 'a Vision in the form of Youth,' a Shadow of reality to come—and this consideration has further convinced me for it has come as auxiliary to another favourite Speculation of mine, that we shall enjoy ourselves hereafter by having what we called happiness on Earth repeated in a finer tone and so repeated. And yet such a fate can only befall those who delight in Sensation rather than hunger as you do after Truth. Adam's dream will do here and seems to be a conviction that Imagination and its empyreal reflection is the same as human Life and its Spiritual repetition. But as I was saying—the simple imaginative Mind may have its rewards in the repetition of its own silent Working coming continually on the Spirit with a fine Suddenness.—To compare great things with small— have you never by being Surprised with an old Melody—in a delicious place—by a delicious voice, felt over again your very Speculations and Surmises at the time it first operated on your Soul—do you not remember forming to yourself the singer's face more beautiful than it was possible and yet with the elevation of the Moment you did not think so—even then you were mounted on the Wings of Imagination so high— that the Prototype must be hereafter—that delicious face you will see. What a time! I am continually running away from the subject—sure this cannot be exactly the case with a complex Mind—one that is imaginative and at the same time careful of its fruits—who would exist partly on Sensation partly on thought—to whom it is necessary that years should bring the philosophic Mind—such an one I consider yours and therefore it is necessary to your eternal Happiness that you not only drink this old Wine of Heaven, which I shall call the redigestion of our most ethereal Musings on Earth; but also increase in knowledge and know all things. I am glad to hear you are in a fair way for Easter—you will soon get through your unpleasant reading and then!—but the world is full of troubles and I have not much reason to think myself pestered with many. —I think Jane or Marianne has a better opinion of me than I deserve—for really and truly I do not think my Brothers illness connected with mine.—You know more of the real Cause than they do nor have I any chance of being racked as you have been.—You perhaps at one time thought there was such a thing as Worldly Happiness to be arrived at, at certain periods of time marked out—you have of necessity from your disposition been thus led away.—I scarcely remember counting upon any Happiness.—I look not for it if it be not in the present hour—nothing startles me beyond the Moment. The setting Sun will always set me to rights—or if a Sparrow come before my Window I take part in its existence and pick about the Gravel. The first thing that strikes me on hearing a Misfortune having befallen another is this. 'Well it cannot be helped—he will have the pleasure of trying the resources of his spirit.'—And I beg now my dear Bailey that hereafter should you observe anything cold in me not to put it to the account of heartlessness but abstraction—for I assure you I sometimes feel not the influence of a Passion or affection during a whole week—and so long this sometimes continues I begin to suspect myself and the genuineness of my feelings at other times—thinking them a few barren Tragedy-tears. My Brother Tom is much improved—he is going to Devonshire—whither I shall follow him.—At present I am just arrived at Dorking to change the Scene—change the Air and give me a spur to wind up my Poem, of which there are wanting 500 Lines. I should have been here a day sooner but the Reynoldses persuaded me to stop in Town to meet your friend Christie. There were Rice and Martin[19]—we talked about Ghosts. I will have some talk with Taylor[20] and let you know—when please God I come down at Christmas. I will find that Examiner if possible. My best regards to Gleig. My Brothers to you and Mrs. Bentley.

Your affectionate friend,

John Keats

I want to say much more to you—a few hints will set me going. Direct Burford Bridge near Dorking.

---

19 John Martin, 1791–1855, member of the firm Rodwell and Martin, publishers.
20 John Taylor, 1781–1864, senior member of Keats's publishing house, Taylor and Hessey, and a critic of note.

6 *To* George and Thomas Keats

Sunday December 21, [1817]

My dear Brothers,

. . . I spent Friday evening with Wells,[21] and went next morning to see 'Death on the Pale Horse.'[22] It is a wonderful picture, when West's age is considered; But there is nothing to be intense upon; no women one feels mad to kiss, no face swelling into reality—The excellence of every art is its intensity, capable of making all disagreeables evaporate, from their being in close relationship with Beauty and Truth. Examine King Lear, and you will find this exemplified throughout; but in this picture we have unpleasantness without any momentous depth of speculation excited, in which to bury its repulsiveness —The picture is larger than 'Christ Rejected.'

I dined with Haydon the Sunday after you left, and had a very pleasant day, I dined too (for I have been out too much lately) with Horace Smith, and met his two Brothers, with Hill[23] and Kingston,[24] and one Du Bois. They only served to convince me, how superior humour is to wit in respect to enjoyment—These men say things which make one start, without making one feel; they are all alike; their manners are alike; they all know fashionables; they have a mannerism in their very eating and drinking, in their mere handling a Decanter—They talked of Kean[25] and his low company—Would I were with that Company instead of yours, said I to myself! I know such like acquaintance will never do for me, and yet I am going to Reynolds on Wednesday. Brown and Dilke[26] walked with me and back from the Christmas pantomime. I had not a dispute but a disquisition, with Dilke on various subjects; several things dove-tailed in my mind, and at once it struck me what quality went to form a Man of Achievement, especially in Literature, and which Shakespeare possessed so enormously—I mean *Negative Capability,* that is, when a man is capable of being in uncertainties, mysteries, doubts, without any irritable reaching after fact and reason—Coleridge, for instance, would let go by a fine isolated verisimilitude

---

21 Charles Wells, 1799–1879, author of *Joseph and His Brethren.*
22 by Benjamin West, P.R.A., 1738–1820. *Christ Rejected* is also by West.
23 Thomas Hill, 1760–1840, book collector and journalist.
24 John Kingston, Commissioner of Stamp Duties.
25 Edmund Kean, 1787–1833, the famous Shakespearean actor.
26 Charles Wentworth Dilke, 1789–1864, entered the Navy Pay Office as a clerk where he remained until his retirement in 1836. His interests, however, were primarily literary to which he devoted his full attention after his retirement. He was a frequent contributor to the journals and for more than a decade he was a distinguished editor of *The Athenaeum.*

caught from the Penetralium of mystery, from being incapable of remaining content with half-knowledge. This pursued through volumes would perhaps take us no further than this, that with a great poet the sense of Beauty overcomes every other consideration, or rather obliterates all consideration.

Shelley's poem[27] is out, and there are words about its being objected to as much as Queen Mab was. Poor Shelley, I think he has his Quota of good qualities, in sooth la!! Write soon to your most sincere friend and affectionate Brother

John

7 *To* Benjamin Bailey

Friday, January 23, [1818]

My dear Bailey,

Twelve days have passed since your last reached me—what has gone through the myriads of human Minds since the 12th? We talk of the immense number of Books, the Volumes ranged thousands by thousands—but perhaps more goes through the human intelligence in 12 days than ever was written. How has that unfortunate family lived through the twelve? One saying of yours I shall never forget—you may not recollect it—it being perhaps said when you were looking on the surface and seeming of Humanity alone, without a thought of the past or the future—or the deeps of good and evil—you were at the moment estranged from speculation and I think you have arguments ready for the Man who would utter it to you—this is a formidable preface for a simple thing—merely you said; 'Why should Woman suffer?' Aye. Why should she? 'By heavens I'd coin my very Soul and drop my Blood for Drachmas'![28] These things are, and he who feels how incompetent the most skyey Knight errantry is to heal this bruised fairness is like a sensitive leaf on the hot hand of thought. Your tearing, my dear friend, a spiritless and gloomy Letter up to rewrite to me is what I shall never forget—it was to me a real thing. Things have happened lately of great Perplexity. You must have heard of them. Reynolds and Haydon retorting and re-criminating—and parting forever—the same thing has happened between Haydon and Hunt —It is unfortunate—Men should bear with each other—there lives not the Man who may not be cut up, aye hashed to pieces on his weakest side.

27 *Laon and Cythna*, which was withdrawn by the publishers and converted into *The Revolt of Islam*.
28 *Julius Caesar*, IV, iii, 72–3.

The best of Men have but a portion of good in them—a kind of spiritual yeast in their frames which creates the ferment of existence—by which a Man is propelled to act and strive and buffet with Circumstance. The sure way Bailey, is first to know a Man's faults, and then be passive—if after that he insensibly draws you towards him then you have no Power to break the link. Before I felt interested in either Reynolds or Haydon— I was well read in their faults yet knowing them I have been cementing gradually with both. I have an affection for them both for reasons almost opposite—and to both must I of necessity cling— supported always by the hope that when a little time—a few years shall have tried me more fully in their esteem I may be able to bring them together—the time must come because they have both hearts—and they will recollect the best parts of each other when this gust is overblown.

. . .

I sat down to read King Lear yesterday, and felt the greatness of the thing up to the writing of a Sonnet preparatory thereto—in my next you shall have it. There were some miserable reports of Rice's health—I went and lo! Master Jemmy had been to the play the night before and was out at the time—he always comes on his Legs like a Cat—I have seen a good deal of Wordsworth. Hazlitt is lecturing on Poetry at the Surrey institution—I shall be there next Tuesday.

Your most affectionate Friend

John Keats

8 *To* George and Thomas Keats

Friday, January 23, 1818

My dear Brothers,

I was thinking what hindered me from writing so long, for I have so many things to say to you and know not where to begin. It shall be upon a thing most interesting to you—my Poem. Well! I have given the first Book to Taylor; he seemed more than satisfied with it, and to my surprise proposed publishing it in Quarto if Haydon could make a drawing of some event therein, for a Frontispiece. I called on Haydon; he said he would do anything I liked, but said he would rather paint a finished picture from it, which he seems eager to do; this in a year or two will be a glorious thing for us; and it will be, for Haydon is struck with the first Book. I left Haydon and the next day received a letter from him, proposing to make, as he says with all his might, a finished Chalk sketch of my head, to be engraved in the first style and put at the head of my Poem, saying at the same time he had never done the thing for any human being, and that it must have considerable effect as he will put the name to it. I begin today to copy my second Book—'thus far into the bowels of the Land'[29]—You shall hear whether it will be Quarto or non Quarto, picture or non Picture. Leigh Hunt I showed my first Book to. He allows it not much merit as a whole; says it is unnatural and made ten objections to it in the mere skimming over. He says the conversation is unnatural and too high-flown for Brother and Sister—says it should be simple, forgetting do ye mind that they are both overshadowed by a Supernatural Power, and of force could not speak like Francesca in the Rimini. He must first prove that Caliban's poetry is unnatural.—This with me completely overturns his objections. The fact is he and Shelley are hurt, and perhaps justly, at my not having showed them the affair officiously—and from several hints I have had they appear much disposed to dissect and anatomize, any trip or slip I may have made.—But who's afraid? Ay! Tom! Demme if I am. I went last Tuesday, an hour too late, to Hazlitt's Lecture on Poetry, got there just as they were coming out, when all these pounced upon me—Hazlitt, John Hunt and Son, Wells, Bewick, all the Landseers, Bob Harris, Rox of the Burrough, aye and more; the Landseers enquired after you particularly—I know not whether Wordsworth has left town.—But Sunday I dined with Hazlitt and Haydon, also that I took Haslam[30] with me.—I dined with Brown lately. Dilke having taken the Champion Theatricals was obliged to be in town. Fanny has returned to Walthamstow.—Mr. Abbey[31] appeared very glum the last time I went to see her, and said in an indirect way that I had no business there.—Rice has been ill, but has been mending much lately.

I think a little change has taken place in my intellect lately.—I cannot bear to be uninterested or unemployed, I, who for so long a time have been addicted to passiveness. Nothing is finer for the purposes of great productions than a very gradual ripening of the intellectual powers. . . .

I hope I have not tired you by this filling up of the dash in my last.—Constable, the bookseller, has offered Reynolds ten guineas a sheet to write for his Magazine.—It is an Edinburgh one which Blackwood's started up in opposition to. Hunt said he was nearly sure that the 'Cockney School' was written by Scott;[32] so you are right Tom!—There are no more little bits of news I can remember at present.

I remain my dear Brothers, Your very affectionate Brother,

John

9 *To* John Hamilton Reynolds

Hampstead, Tuesday [February 3, 1818]

My dear Reynolds,

I thank you for your dish of Filberts[33]—Would I could get a basket of them by way of dessert every day for the sum of two-pence. Would we were a sort of ethereal Pigs, and turned loose to feed upon spiritual Mast and Acorns—which would be merely being a squirrel and feeding upon filberts, for what is a squirrel but an airy pig, or a filbert but a sort of archangelical acorn. About the nuts being worth cracking, all I can say is that where there are a throng of delightful Images ready drawn, simplicity is the only thing. The first is the best on account of the first line, and the 'arrow—foiled of its antlered food,' and moreover (and this is the only word or two I find fault with, the more because I have had so much reason to shun it as a quicksand) the last has 'tender and true.' We must cut this, and not be rattle-snaked into any more of the like.—It may be said that we ought to read our Contemporaries—that Wordsworth, etc., should have their due from us. But, for the sake of a few fine imaginative or domestic passages, are we to be bullied into a certain Philosophy engendered in the whims of an Egotist.—Every man has his speculations, but every man does not brood and peacock over them till he makes a false coinage and deceives himself. Many a man can travel to the very bourne of Heaven, and yet want confidence to put down his half-seeing. Sancho[34] will invent a Journey heavenwards as well as anybody. We hate poetry that has a palpable design upon us—and if we do not agree, seems to put its hand in its breeches pocket. Poetry should be great and unobtrusive, a thing which enters into one's soul, and does not startle it or amaze it with itself, but with its subject.—How beautiful are the retired flowers! how would they lose their beauty were they to throng into the highway crying out, 'admire me I am a violet!—dote upon me I am a primrose!' Modern poets differ from the Eliza-

---

29 *Richard III*, v, ii, 3.
30 William Haslam, 1795–1851, one of Keats's devoted friends.
31 Richard Abbey, tea merchant of Walthamstow and Keats's guardian.

32 The paper was actually written by Lockhart, Scott's son-in-law.
33 two sonnets on Robin Hood by Reynolds.
34 the worldly-minded squire of Don Quixote.

bethans in this. Each of the moderns like an Elector of Hanover governs his petty state, and knows how many straws are swept daily from the Causeways in all his dominions and has a continual itching that all the Housewives should have their coppers well scoured: the ancients were Emperors of vast Provinces; they had only heard of the remote ones and scarcely cared to visit them.—I will cut all this—I will have no more of Wordsworth or Hunt in particular.—Why should we be of the tribe of Manasseh, when we can wander with Esau?[35] Why should we kick against the Pricks, when we can walk on Roses? Why should we be owls, when we can be Eagles? Why be teased with 'nice Eyed wagtails,'[36] when we have in sight 'the Cherub Contemplation'?[37]—Why with Wordsworth's 'Matthew with a bough of wilding in his hand,'[38] when we can have Jacques 'under an oak,' etc.?[39]—The secret of the Bough of Wilding will run through your head faster than I can write it.—Old Matthew spoke to him some years ago on some nothing, and because he happens in an Evening Walk to imagine the figure of the Old Man—he must stamp it down in black and white, and it is henceforth sacred.—I don't mean to deny Wordsworth's grandeur and Hunt's merit, but I mean to say we need not be teased with grandeur and merit when we can have them uncontaminated and unobtrusive. Let us have the old Poets, and Robin Hood. Your letter and its sonnets gave me more pleasure than will the 4th Book of Childe Harold and the whole of anybody's life and opinions. In return for your Dish of filberts, I have gathered a few Catkins; I hope they'll look pretty.

To J. H. R. In answer to his Robin Hood Sonnets. [See text, p. 1163.]

I hope you will like them—they are at least written in the Spirit of Outlawry.—Here are the Mermaid lines. [See text, p. 1164.]

I will call on you at four tomorrow and we will trudge together, for it is not the thing to be a stranger in the Land of Harpsicols.[40] I hope also to bring you my second book. In the hope that these Scribblings will be some amusement for you this evening—I remain copying on the Hill

Your sincere friend and Co-scribbler,

John Keats

35 the tribe of Manasseh inherited kingdoms and cities (Numbers, xxxii, 33); Esau was 'a cunning hunter, a man of the field' (Genesis, xxv, 27).
36 Leigh Hunt, *The Nymphs,* ii, 170.
37 Milton, *Il Penseroso,* 54.   38 *The Two April Mornings,* 59.
39 *As You Like It,* II, i. 31.   40 Harpsichords.

10 *To* John Taylor

Hampstead, February 27 [*1818*]

My dear Taylor,

Your alteration strikes me as being a great improvement—the page looks much better. And now I will attend to the Punctuations you speak of—the comma should be at *soberly,* and in the other passage the comma should follow *quiet.* I am extremely indebted to you for this attention and also for your after admonitions.—It is a sorry thing for me that anyone should have to overcome Prejudices in reading my Verses—that affects me more than any hyper-criticism on any particular Passage. In Endymion I have most likely but moved into the Go-cart from the leading strings. In Poetry I have a few Axioms, and you will see how far I am from their Centre. 1st. I think Poetry should surprise by a fine excess and not by Singularity—it should strike the Reader as a wording of his own highest thoughts, and appear almost a Remembrance.—2nd. Its touches of Beauty should never be half-way thereby making the reader breathless instead of content: the rise, the progress, the setting of imagery should like the Sun come natural to him —shine over him and set soberly, although in magnificence leaving him in the Luxury of twilight—but it is easier to think what Poetry should be than to write it—and this leads me on to another axiom. That if Poetry comes not as naturally as the Leaves to a tree it had better not come at all. However it may be with me I cannot help looking into new countries with 'O for a Muse of fire to ascend!' If Endymion serves me as a Pioneer perhaps I ought to be content. I have great reason to be content, for thank God I can read and perhaps understand Shakespeare to his depths, and I have I am sure many friends, who, if I fail, will attribute any change in my Life and Temper to Humbleness rather than to Pride —to a cowering under the Wings of great Poets rather than to a Bitterness that I am not appreciated. I am anxious to get Endymion printed that I may forget it and proceed. . . .

Your sincere and obliged friend,

John Keats

11 *To* John Hamilton Reynolds

Thursday Morning [*April 9, 1818*]

My dear Reynolds,

Since you all agree that the thing is bad, it must be so—though I am not aware there is anything like Hunt in it, (and if there is, it is my natural way, and I have something in common with Hunt) look it over again and examine into the motives, the seeds from which any one sentence sprung—I have not the slightest feel of humility towards the Public—or to anything in existence, —but the eternal Being, the Principle of Beauty, and the Memory of great Men—When I am writing for myself for the mere sake of the Moment's enjoyment, perhaps nature has its course with me—but a Preface is written to the Public; a thing I cannot help looking upon as an Enemy, and which I cannot address without feelings of Hostility—If I write a Preface in a supple or subdued style, it will not be in character with me as a public speaker—I would be subdued before my friends, and thank them for subduing me—but among Multitudes of Men—I have no feel of stooping, I hate the idea of humility to them—

I never wrote one single Line of Poetry with the least Shadow of public thought.

Forgive me for vexing you and making a Trojan horse of such a Trifle, both with respect to the matter in question, and myself—but it eases me to tell you—I could not live without the love of my friends—I would jump down Ætna for any great Public Good—but I hate a Mawkish Popularity.—I cannot be subdued before them—My glory would be to daunt and dazzle the thousand jabberers about Pictures and Books—I see swarms of Porcupines with their Quills erect 'like lime-twigs set to catch my Winged Book' and I would fright 'em away with a torch—You will say my preface is not much of a Torch. It would have been too insulting 'to begin from Jove' and I could not [set] a golden head upon a thing of clay—if there is any fault in the preface it is not affectation: but an undersong of disrespect to the Public— if I write another preface, it must be done without a thought of those people—I will think about it. If it should not reach you in four —or five days—tell Taylor to publish it without a preface, and let the dedication simply stand 'inscribed to the Memory of Thomas Chatterton.'

I had resolved last night to write to you this morning—I wish it had been about something else—something to greet you towards the close of your long illness—I have had one or two intimations of your going to Hampstead for a space; and I regret to see your confounded Rheumatism keeps you in Little Britain where I am sure the air is too confined—Devonshire continues rainy. As the drops beat against the window, they give me the same sensation as a quart of cold water offered to revive a half-drowned

devil—No feel of the clouds dropping fatness; but as if the roots of the Earth were rotten cold and drenched—I have not been able to go to Kents' Ca[ve] at Babbicum—however on one very beautiful day I had a fine Clamber over the Rocks all along as far as that place: I shall be in Town in about Ten days.—We go by way of Bath on purpose to call on Bailey. I hope soon to be writing to you about the things of the north, purposing to wayfare all over those parts. I have settled my accoutrements in my own mind, and will go to gorge wonders: However we'll have some days together before I set out—

I have many reasons for going wonder-ways: to make my winter chair free from spleen—to enlarge my vision—to escape disquisitions on Poetry and Kingston Criticism[41]—to promote di-

---

41 Stamp Commissioner Kingston achieved a capricious immortality by way of his stupid criticism at a gathering of celebrities in Haydon's studio. Haydon has left us in his *Autobiography* the following amusing account of the incident:

'On December 28th the immortal dinner came off in my painting-room, with Jerusalem towering up behind us as a background. Wordsworth was in fine cue, and we had a glorious set-to,—on Homer, Shakespeare, Milton and Virgil. Lamb got exceedingly merry, and exquisitely witty; and his fun in the midst of Wordsworth's solemn intonations of oratory was like the sarcasm and wit of the fool in the intervals of Lear's passion. He made a speech and voted me absent, and made them drink my health. "Now," said Lamb, "you old lake poet, you rascally poet, why do you call Voltaire dull?" We all defended Wordsworth, and affirmed there was a state of mind when Voltaire would be dull. "Well," said Lamb, "here's Voltaire—the Messiah of the French nation, and a very proper one too."

'He then, in a strain of humour beyond description, abused me for putting Newton's head into my picture,—"a fellow," said he, "who believed nothing unless it was as clear as the three sides of a triangle." And then he and Keats agreed he had destroyed all the poetry of the rainbow by reducing it to the prismatic colours. It was impossible to resist him, and we all drank "Newton's health, and confusion to mathematics." It was delightful to see the good-humour of Wordsworth in giving in to all our frolics without affectation and laughing as heartily as the best of us.

'By this time other friends joined, amongst them poor Ritchie who was going to penetrate by Fezzan to Timbuctoo. I introduced him to all as "a gentleman going to Africa." Lamb seemed to take no notice; but all of a sudden he roared out, "Which is the gentleman we are going to lose?" We then drank the victim's health, in which Ritchie joined.

'In the morning of this delightful day, a gentleman, a perfect stranger, had called on me. He said he knew my friends, had an enthusiasm for Wordsworth and begged I would procure him the happiness of an introduction. He told me he was a comptroller of stamps, and often had correspondence with the poet. I thought it a liberty; but still, as he seemed a gentleman, I told him he might come.

'When we retired to tea we found the comptroller. In introducing him to Wordsworth I forgot to say who he was. After a little time the comptroller looked down, looked up and said to Wordsworth, "Don't you think, sir, Milton was a great genius?" Keats looked at me, Wordsworth looked at the comptroller. Lamb who was dozing by the fire turned round and said, "Pray, sir, did you say Milton was a great genius?" "No, sir; I asked Mr. Wordsworth if he were not." "Oh," said Lamb, "then you are a silly fellow." "Charles! my dear Charles!" said Wordsworth; but Lamb, perfectly innocent of the confusion he had created, was off again by the fire.

'After an awful pause the comptroller said, "Don't you think Newton a great genius?" I could not stand it any longer. Keats

gestion and economize shoe-leather—I'll have leather buttons and belt; and if Brown holds his mind, over the Hills we go.—If my Books will help me to it,—thus will I take all Europe in turn, and see the Kingdoms of the Earth and the glory of them—Tom is getting better he hopes you may meet him at the top o' the hill—My Love to your nurses.

I am ever

Your affectionate Friend,

John Keats

12 *To* John Taylor

Teignmouth, Friday [April 24, 1818]

My dear Taylor,

I think I did very wrong to leave you to all the trouble of Endymion—but I could not help it then—another time I shall be more bent to all sorts of troubles and disagreeables.—Young Men for some time have an idea that such a thing as happiness is to be had and therefore are extremely impatient under any unpleasant restraining—in time however, of such stuff is the world about them, they know better and instead of striving from Uneasiness greet it as an habitual

---

put his head into my books. Ritchie squeezed in a laugh. Wordsworth seemed asking himself, "Who is this?" Lamb got up, and taking a candle, said, "Sir, will you allow me to look at your phrenological development?" He then turned his back on the poor man, and at every question of the comptroller he chaunted—

> "Diddle diddle dumpling, my son John
> Went to bed with his breeches on."

The man in office, finding Wordsworth did not know who he was, said in a spasmodic and half-chuckling anticipation of assured victory, "I have had the honour of some correspondence with you, Mr. Wordsworth." "With me, sir?" said Wordsworth, "not that I remember." "Don't you, sir? I am a comptroller of stamps." There was a dead silence;—the comptroller evidently thinking that was enough. While we were waiting for Wordsworth's reply, Lamb sung out

> "Hey diddle diddle,
> The cat and the fiddle."

"My dear Charles!" said Wordsworth,—

> "Diddle diddle dumpling, my son John,"

chaunted Lamb, and then rising, exclaimed, "Do let me have another look at that gentleman's organs." Keats and I hurried Lamb into the painting-room, shut the door and gave way to inextinguishable laughter. Monkhouse followed and tried to get Lamb away. We went back, but the comptroller was irreconcilable. We soothed and smiled and asked him to supper. He stayed though his dignity was sorely affected. However, being a good-natured man, we parted all in good-humour, and no ill effects followed. "All the while, until Monkhouse succeeded, we could hear Lamb struggling in the painting-room and calling at intervals, "Who is that fellow? Allow me to see his organs once more." It was indeed an immortal evening. Wordsworth's fine intonation as he quoted Milton and Virgil, Keats' eager inspired look, Lamb's quaint sparkle of lambent humour, so speeded the stream of conversation, that in my life I never passed a more delightful time.'

---

sensation, a pannier which is to weigh upon them through life.

And in proportion to my disgust at the task is my sense of your kindness and anxiety—the book pleased me much—it is very free from faults; and although there are one or two words I should wish replaced, I see in many places an improvement greatly to the purpose. . . .

I was purposing to travel over the north this Summer.—There is but one thing to prevent me —I know nothing, I have read nothing, and I mean to follow Solomon's directions of 'get Wisdom—get understanding.'—I find cavalier days are gone by. I find that I can have no enjoyment in the World but continual drinking of Knowledge.—I find there is no worthy pursuit but the idea of doing some good for the world.—Some do it with their society—some with their wit— some with their benevolence—some with a sort of power of conferring pleasure and good humour on all they meet and in a thousand ways all equally dutiful to the command of Great Nature. —There is but one way for me—the road lies through application, study, and thought. I will pursue it and to that end purpose retiring for some years. I have been hovering for some time between an exquisite sense of the luxurious and a love for Philosophy.—Were I calculated for the former I should be glad—but as I am not I shall turn all my soul to the latter.

My Brother Tom is getting better and I hope I shall see both him and Reynolds well before I retire from the World. I shall see you soon and have some talk about what Books I shall take with me.

Your very sincere friend,

John Keats

Remember me to Hessey,[42] Woodhouse[43] and Percy Street.

13 *To* John Hamilton Reynolds

Teignmouth, May 3 [1818]

My dear Reynolds,

. . . Every department of Knowledge we see excellent and calculated towards a great whole. I am so convinced of this, that I am glad at not having given away my medical Books, which I

---

42 James A. Hessey, 1785–1870, junior member of the firm Taylor and Hessey, Keats's publishers.
43 Richard Woodhouse, 1788–1834, was a young barrister who acted as literary adviser to Taylor and Hessey. His commonplace books full of materials on Keats have proved of invaluable aid to scholars.

shall again look over to keep alive the little I know thitherwards; and moreover intend through you and Rice to become a sort of pip-civilian. An extensive knowledge is needful to thinking people—it takes away the heat and fever; and helps, by widening speculation, to ease the Burden of the Mystery: a thing I begin to understand a little, and which weighed upon you in the most gloomy and true sentence in your Letter. The difference of high Sensations with and without knowledge appears to me this—in the latter case we are falling continually ten thousand fathoms deep and being blown up again without wings and with all the horror of a bare-shouldered creature—in the former case, our shoulders are fledged, and we go through the same air and space without fear.

. . . My Branchings out therefrom have been numerous: one of them is the consideration of Wordsworth's genius and as a help, in the manner of gold being the meridian Line of worldly wealth,—how he differs from Milton.—And here I have nothing but surmises, from an uncertainty whether Milton's apparently less anxiety for Humanity proceeds from his seeing further or not than Wordsworth: And whether Wordsworth has in truth epic passion, and martyrs himself to the human heart, the main region of his song.—In regard to his genius alone—we find what he says true as far as we have experienced and we can judge no further but by larger experience—for axioms in philosophy are not axioms until they are proved upon our pulses: We read fine things but never feel them to the full until we have gone the same steps as the Author.—I know this is not plain; you will know exactly my meaning when I say, that now I shall relish Hamlet more than I ever have done—or, better.—You are sensible no Man can set down Venery as a bestial or joyless thing until he is sick of it and therefore all philosophizing on it would be mere wording. Until we are sick, we understand not;—in fine, as Byron says, 'Knowledge is Sorrow'; and I go on to say that 'Sorrow is Wisdom'—and further for aught we can know for certainty 'Wisdom is folly!'

. . . I will return to Wordsworth—whether or no he has an extended vision or a circumscribed grandeur—whether he is an eagle in his nest, or on the wing.—And to be more explicit and to show you how tall I stand by the giant, I will put down a simile of human life as far as I now perceive it; that is, to the point to which I say we both have arrived at—Well—I compare human life to a large Mansion of Many Apartments, two of which I can only describe, the doors of the rest being as yet shut upon me. The first we step into we call the infant or thoughtless Chamber, in which we remain as long as we do not think.—We remain there a long while, and notwithstanding the doors of the second Chamber remain wide open, showing a bright appearance, we care not to hasten to it; but are at length imperceptibly impelled by the awakening of this thinking principle within us.—We no sooner get into the second Chamber, which I shall call the Chamber of Maiden-Thought, than we become intoxicated with the light and the atmosphere, we see nothing but pleasant wonders, and think of delaying there for ever in delight: However among the effects this breathing is father of is that tremendous one of sharpening one's vision into the heart and nature of Man—of convincing one's nerves that the world is full of Misery and Heartbreak, Pain, Sickness and Oppression—whereby this Chamber of Maiden-Thought becomes gradually darkened and at the same time on all sides of it many doors are set open—but all dark—all leading to dark passages.—We see not the balance of good and evil. We are in a Mist. *We* are now in that state—We feel the 'burden of the Mystery.' To this Point was Wordsworth come, as far as I can conceive when he wrote 'Tintern Abbey' and it seems to me that his Genius is explorative of those dark Passages. Now if we live, and go on thinking, we too shall explore them.—He is a Genius and superior to us, in so far as he can, more than we, make discoveries, and shed a light in them.—Here I must think Wordsworth is deeper than Milton—though I think it has depended more upon the general and gregarious advance of intellect, than individual greatness of Mind.—From the Paradise Lost and the other Works of Milton, I hope it is not too presuming, even between ourselves to say, that his Philosophy, human and divine, may be tolerably understood by one not much advanced in years. In his time Englishmen were just emancipated from a great superstition—and Men had got hold of certain points and resting places in reasoning which were too newly born to be doubted, and too much opposed by the Mass of Europe not to be thought ethereal and authentically divine.—Who could gainsay his ideas on virtue, vice, and Chastity in Comus, just at the time of the dismissal of Cod-pieces and a hundred other disgraces? Who would not rest satisfied with his hintings at good and evil in the Paradise Lost, when just free from the inquisition and burning in Smithfield? The Reformation produced such immediate and great benefits, that

Protestantism was considered under the immediate eye of heaven, and its own remaining Dogmas and superstitions, then, as it were, regenerated, constituted those resting places and seeming sure points of Reasoning.—From that I have mentioned, Milton, whatever he may have thought in the sequel, appears to have been content with these by his writings.—He did not think into the human heart, as Wordsworth has done. —Yet Milton as a Philosopher, had sure as great powers as Wordsworth.—What is then to be inferred? O many things:—It proves there is really a grand march of intellect;—It proves that a mighty providence subdues the mightiest Minds to the service of the time being, whether it be in human Knowledge or Religion. . . .

> Your affectionate friend,
>
> *John Keats*

14 *To* Benjamin Bailey

Inverary July 18th [*1818*]

My dear Bailey,

. . . I am sorry you are grieved at my not continuing my visits to little Britain—yet I think I have as far as a Man can do who has Books to read and subjects to think upon—for that reason I have been nowhere else except to Wentworth place so nigh at hand—moreover I have been too often in a state of health that made me think it prudent not to hazard the night Air. Yet further I will confess to you that I cannot enjoy Society small or numerous. I am certain that our fair friends are glad I should come for the mere sake of my coming; but I am certain I bring with me a Vexation they are better without—If I can possibly at any time feel my temper coming upon me I refrain even from a promised visit. I am certain I have not a right feeling towards Women— at this moment I am striving to be just to them but I cannot—Is it because they fall so far beneath my Boyish imagination? When I was a Schoolboy I thought a fair Woman a pure Goddess, my mind was a soft nest in which some one of them slept, though she knew it not—I have no right to expect more than their reality. I thought them ethereal above Men—I find them perhaps equal—great by comparison is very small. Insult may be inflicted in more ways than by Word or action—one who is tender of being insulted does not like to think an insult against another—I do not like to think insults in a Lady's Company—I commit a Crime with her which absence would have not known. Is it not extraordinary? When

among Men I have no evil thoughts, no malice, no spleen—I feel free to speak or to be silent—I can listen and from every one I can learn—my hands are in my pockets, I am free from all suspicion and comfortable. When I am among Women I have evil thoughts, malice, spleen—I cannot speak or be silent—I am full of Suspicions and therefore listen to nothing—I am in a hurry to be gone—You must be charitable and put all this perversity to my being disappointed since Boyhood. Yet with such feelings I am happier alone among Crowds of men, by myself or with a friend or two—With all this, trust me Bailey I have not the least idea that Men of different feelings and inclinations are more shortsighted than myself—I never rejoiced more than at my Brother's Marriage and shall do so at that of any of my friends—. I must absolutely get over this—but how? The only way is to find the root of evil, and so cure it 'with backward mutters of dissevering Power'[44]—that is a difficult thing; for an obstinate Prejudice can seldom be produced but from a gordian complication of feelings, which must take time to unravel and care to keep unravelled. I could say a good deal about this but I will leave it in hopes of better and more worthy dispositions—and also content that I am wronging no one, for after all I do think better of Womankind than to suppose they care whether Mister John Keats five feet high likes them or not. You appeared to wish to avoid any words on this subject—don't think it a bore my dear fellow—it shall be my Amen—I should not have consented to myself these four Months tramping in the highlands but that I thought it would give me more experience, rub off more Prejudice, use me to more hardship, identify finer scenes, load me with grander Mountains, and strengthen more my reach in Poetry, than would stopping at home among Books even though I should reach Homer. . . .

15 *To* James Augustus Hessey

[*Hampstead, October 9, 1818*]

My dear Hessey,

You are very good in sending me the letters from *The Chronicle*[45]—and I am very bad in not acknowledging such a kindness sooner. Pray forgive me. It has so chanced that I have had that paper every day—I have seen today's. I cannot but feel indebted to those Gentlemen who have

---

44 *Comus,* 817.
45 two letters to the editor of *The Morning Chronicle,* printed 3 and 8 Oct. 1818.

taken my part—As for the rest, I begin to get a little acquainted with my own strength and weakness.—Praise or blame has but a momentary effect on the man whose love of beauty in the abstract makes him a severe critic on his own Works. My own domestic criticism has given me pain without comparison beyond what Blackwood or the Quarterly could possibly inflict, and also when I feel I am right, no external praise can give me such a glow as my own solitary reperception and ratification of what is fine. J. S.[46] is perfectly right in regard to the slip-shod *Endymion*. That it is so is no fault of mine.—No!—though it may sound a little paradoxical. It is as good as I had power to make it—by myself. Had I been nervous about its being a perfect piece, and with that view asked advice, and trembled over every page, it would not have been written; for it is not in my nature to fumble—I will write independently.—I have written independently *without Judgement*. I may write independently and *with Judgement* hereafter. The Genius of Poetry must work out its own salvation in a man: It cannot be matured by law and precept, but by sensation and watchfulness in itself. That which is creative must create itself—In *Endymion* I leaped headlong into the Sea, and thereby have become better acquainted with the Soundings, the quicksands, and the rocks, than if I had stayed upon the green shore, and piped a silly pipe, and took tea and comfortable advice.—I was never afraid of failure; for I would sooner fail than not be among the greatest. But I am nigh getting into a rant. So, with remembrances to Taylor and Woodhouse, etc., I am

Yours very sincerely,

John Keats

16 *To* George and Georgiana Keats

[*October 14 or 15, 1818*]

. . . I came by ship from Inverness, and was nine days at Sea without being sick—a little Qualm now and then put me in mind of you—however as soon as you touch the shore all the horrors of Sickness are soon forgotten, as was the case with a Lady on board who could not hold her head up all the way. We had not been in the Thames an hour before her tongue began to some tune; paying off as it was fit she should all old scores. I was the only Englishman on board. There was a downright Scotchman who

hearing that there had been a bad crop of Potatoes in England had brought some triumphant specimens from Scotland—these he exhibited with national pride to all the Lightermen and Watermen from the Nore to the Bridge. I fed upon beef all the way; not being able to eat the thick Porridge which the Ladies managed to manage with large awkward horn spoons into the bargain. Severn[47] has had a narrow escape of his Life from a Typhus fever: he is now gaining strength—Reynolds has returned from a six weeks' enjoyment in Devonshire—he is well, and persuades me to publish my pot of Basil as an answer to the attacks made on me in Blackwood's Magazine and the Quarterly Review. There have been two Letters in my defence in the Chronicle and one in the Examiner, copied from the Alfred Exeter Paper, and written by Reynolds. I don't know who wrote those in the Chronicle. This is a mere matter of the moment—I think I shall be among the English Poets after my death. Even as a Matter of present interest the attempt to crush me in the Quarterly has only brought me more into notice, and it is a common expression among book men 'I wonder the Quarterly should cut its own throat.'

It does me not the least harm in Society to make me appear little and ridiculous: I know when a man is superior to me and give him all due respect—he will be the last to laugh at me and as for the rest I feel that I make an impression upon them which insures me personal respect while I am in sight whatever they may say when my back is turned. Poor Haydon's eyes will not suffer him to proceed with his picture—he has been in the Country—I have seen him but once since my return. I hurry matters together here because I do not know when the Mail sails—I shall enquire tomorrow, and then shall know whether to be particular or general in my letter—You shall have at least two sheets a day till it does sail whether it be three days or a fortnight—and then I will begin a fresh one for the next Month. The Miss Reynoldses are very kind to me, but they have lately displeased me much, and in this way—Now I am coming the Richardson. On my return the first day I called they were in a sort of taking or bustle about a Cousin of theirs who having fallen out with her Grandpapa in a serious manner was invited by Mrs. R. to take Asylum in her house. She is an East Indian and ought to be her Grandfather's Heir. At the time I called Mrs. R. was in conference with

---

46 John Scott, author of one of the letters to *The Morning Chronicle.*

47 Joseph Severn, 1793–1879, artist friend who accompanied Keats to Rome and remained with him until his death.

her upstairs, and the young Ladies were warm in her praises downstairs, calling her genteel, interesting and a thousand other pretty things to which I gave no heed, not being partial to 9 days' wonders—Now all is completely changed—they hate her, and from what I hear she is not without faults—of a real kind: but she has others which are more apt to make women of inferior charms hate her. She is not a Cleopatra, but she is at least a Charmian. She has a rich Eastern look; she has fine eyes and fine manners. When she comes into a room she makes an impression the same as the Beauty of a Leopardess. She is too fine and too conscious of herself to repulse any Man who may address her—from habit she thinks that nothing *particular*. I always find myself more at ease with such a woman; the picture before me always gives me a life and animation which I cannot possibly feel with anything inferior. I am at such times too much occupied in admiring to be awkward or in a tremble. I forget myself entirely because I live in her. You will by this time think I am in love with her; so before I go any further I will tell you I am not—she kept me awake one Night as a tune of Mozart's might do. I speak of the thing as a pastime and an amusement, than which I can feel none deeper than a conversation with an imperial woman, the very 'yes' and 'no' of whose Lips is to me a Banquet. I don't cry to take the moon home with me in my Pocket nor do I fret to leave her behind me. I like her and her like because one has no *sensations*—what we both are is taken for granted. You will suppose I have by this had much talk with her—no such thing—there are the Miss Reynoldses on the lookout. They think I don't admire her because I did not stare at her.

They call her a flirt to me—What a want of knowledge! She walks across a room in such a manner that a Man is drawn towards her with a magnetic Power. This they call flirting! they do not know things. They do not know what a Woman is. I believe though she has faults—the same as Charmian and Cleopatra might have had. Yet she is a fine thing speaking in a worldly way: for there are two distinct tempers of mind in which we judge of things—the worldly, theatrical and pantomimical; and the unearthly, spiritual and ethereal—in the former Buonaparte, Lord Byron and this Charmian hold the first place in our Minds; in the latter, John Howard,[48] Bishop Hooker[49] rocking his child's cradle and

you my dear Sister are the conquering feelings. As a Man in the world I love the rich talk of a Charmian; as an eternal Being I love the thought of you. I should like her to ruin me, and I should like you to save me. Do not think, my dear Brother, from this that my Passions are headlong, or likely to be ever of any pain to you—no

I am free from Men of Pleasure's cares,
By dint of feelings far more deep than theirs.[50]

This is Lord Byron, and is one of the finest things he has said. I have no town talk for you, as I have not been much among people—as for Politics they are in my opinion only sleepy because they will soon be too wide awake. . . .

[*Hampstead, about 25 October 1818*]

. . . I shall in a short time write you as far as I know how I intend to pass my Life—I cannot think of those things now Tom is so unwell and weak. Notwithstanding your Happiness and your recommendation I hope I shall never marry. Though the most beautiful Creature were waiting for me at the end of a Journey or a Walk; though the Carpet were of Silk, the Curtains of the morning Clouds, the chairs and Sofa stuffed with Cygnet's down; the food Manna, the Wine beyond Claret, the Window opening on Winander mere, I should not feel—or rather my Happiness would not be so fine, as my Solitude is sublime. Then instead of what I have described, there is a sublimity to welcome me home—The roaring of the wind is my wife and the Stars through the window pane are my Children. The mighty abstract Idea I have of Beauty in all things stifles the more divided and minute domestic happiness—an amiable wife and sweet Children I contemplate as a part of that Beauty, but I must have a thousand of those beautiful particles to fill up my heart. I feel more and more every day, as my imagination strengthens, that I do not live in this world alone but in a thousand worlds—No sooner am I alone than shapes of epic greatness are stationed around me, and serve my Spirit the office which is equivalent to a King's bodyguard—then 'Tragedy with sceptred pall comes sweeping by.'[51] According to my state of mind I am with Achilles shouting in the Trenches or with Theocritus in the Vales of Sicily. Or I throw my whole being into Troilus, and repeating those lines, 'I wander like a lost Soul upon the stygian Banks staying for waftage,'[52] I melt into the air with a

---

48 John Howard, ? 1726–90, philanthropist.
49 Richard Hooker, ? 1554–1600, theologian, author of *Ecclesiastical Politie*.

50 This couplet has not been found in Byron's works.
51 Cf. *Il Penseroso*, 97.
52 *Troilus and Cressida*, III, ii, 8–10.

voluptuousness so delicate that I am content to be alone. These things, combined with the opinion I have of the generality of women—who appear to me as children to whom I would rather give a sugar Plum than my time, form a barrier against Matrimony which I rejoice in.

I have written this that you might see I have my share of the highest pleasures, and that though I may choose to pass my days alone I shall be no Solitary. You see there is nothing spleenical in all this. The only thing that can ever affect me personally for more than one short passing day, is any doubt about my powers for poetry—I seldom have any, and I look with hope to the nighing time when I shall have none. I am as happy as a Man can be—that is, in myself I should be happy if Tom was well, and I knew you were passing pleasant days—Then I should be most enviable—with the yearning Passion I have for the beautiful, connected and made one with the ambition of my intellect. Think of my Pleasure in Solitude in comparison of my commerce with the world—there I am a child—there they do not know me, not even my most intimate acquaintance—I give in to their feelings as though I were refraining from irritating a little child. Some think me middling, others silly, others foolish—everyone thinks he sees my weak side against my will, when in truth it is with my will—I am content to be thought all this because I have in my own breast so great a resource. This is one great reason why they like me so: because they can all show to advantage in a room and eclipse from a certain tact one who is reckoned to be a good Poet. I hope I am not here playing tricks 'to make the angels weep': I think not: for I have not the least contempt for my species, and though it may sound paradoxical, my greatest elevations of Soul leave me every time more humbled—Enough of this—though in your Love for me you will not think it enough. . . .

17 *To* Richard Woodhouse

[*Hampstead, October 27, 1818*]

My dear Woodhouse,

Your Letter gave me a great satisfaction; more on account of its friendliness, than any relish of that matter in it which is accounted so acceptable in the 'genus irritabile.'[53] The best answer I can give you is in a clerk-like manner to make some observations on two principal points, which seem

to point like indices into the midst of the whole pro and con, about genius, and views and achievements and ambition, et cætera. 1st. As to the poetical Character itself (I mean that sort of which, if I am any thing, I am a Member; that sort distinguished from the Wordsworthian or egotistical sublime; which is a thing per se and stands alone) it is not itself—it has no self—it is everything and nothing—It has no character—it enjoys light and shade; it lives in gusto, be it foul or fair, high or low, rich or poor, mean or elevated—It has as much delight in conceiving an Iago as an Imogen. What shocks the virtuous philosopher, delights the chameleon Poet. It does no harm from its relish of the dark side of things any more than from its taste for the bright one; because they both end in speculation. A Poet is the most unpoetical of anything in existence; because he has no Identity—he is continually informing and filling some other Body—The Sun, the Moon, the Sea and Men and Women who are creatures of impulse are poetical and have about them an unchangeable attribute—the poet has none; no identity—he is certainly the most unpoetical of all God's Creatures. If then he has no self, and if I am a Poet, where is the Wonder that I should say I would write no more? Might I not at that very instant have been cogitating on the Characters of Saturn and Ops? It is a wretched thing to confess; but is a very fact that not one word I ever utter can be taken for granted as an opinion growing out of my identical nature—how can it, when I have no nature? When I am in a room with People if I ever am free from speculating on creations of my own brain, then not myself goes home to myself: but the identity of every one in the room begins to press upon me that I am in a very little time annihilated—not only among Men; it would be the same in a Nursery of children: I know not whether I make myself wholly understood: I hope enough so to let you see that no dependence is to be placed on what I said that day.

In the second place I will speak of my views, and of the life I purpose to myself. I am ambitious of doing the world some good: if I should be spared that may be the work of maturer years—in the interval I will assay to reach to as high a summit in Poetry as the nerve bestowed upon me will suffer. The faint conceptions I have of Poems to come brings the blood frequently into my forehead. All I hope is that I may not lose all interest in human affairs—that the solitary indifference I feel for applause even from the finest Spirits, will not blunt any acuteness of

53 'the irritable race of poets'—Horace, *Epistles.*

vision I may have. I do not think it will—I feel assured I should write from the mere yearning and fondness I have for the Beautiful even if my night's labours should be burnt every morning, and no eye ever shine upon them. But even now I am perhaps not speaking from myself: but from some character in whose soul I now live. I am sure however that this next sentence is from myself. I feel your anxiety, good opinion and friendliness in the highest degree, and am

Yours most sincerely,

John Keats

18 *To* George and Georgiana Keats

[*Hampstead, about December 18, 1818*]

My dear Brother and Sister,

You will have been prepared before this reaches you for the worst news you could have, nay, if Haslam's letter arrives in proper time, I have a consolation in thinking that the first shock will be past before you receive this. The last days of poor Tom were of the most distressing nature, but his last moments were not so painful, and his very last was without a pang. I will not enter into any parsonic comments on death—yet the common observations of the commonest people on death are as true as their proverbs. I have scarce a doubt of immortality of some nature or other —neither had Tom. My friends have been exceedingly kind to me every one of them—Brown detained me at his house. I suppose no one could have had their time made smoother than mine has been. During poor Tom's illness I was not able to write and since his death the task of beginning has been a hindrance to me. Within this last Week I have been everywhere—and I will tell you as nearly as possible how all go on. With Dilke and Brown I am quite thick—with Brown indeed I am going to domesticate—that is, we shall keep house together. I shall have the front parlour and he the back one, by which I shall avoid the noise of Bentley's Children—and be the better able to go on with my Studies—which have been greatly interrupted lately, so that I have not the shadow of an idea of a book in my head, and my pen seems to have grown too gouty for verse. How are you going on now? The goings on of the world make me dizzy—There you are with Birkbeck—here I am with Brown—sometimes I fancy an immense separation, and sometimes as at present, a direct communication of Spirit with you. That will be one of the grandeurs of immortality—There will be no space, and consequently the only commerce between spirits will be by their intelligence of each other—when they will completely understand each other, while we in this world merely comprehend each other in different degrees—the higher the degree of good so higher is our Love and friendship. . . .

. . . Mrs. Brawne who took Brown's house for the Summer, still resides in Hampstead. She is a very nice woman, and her daughter senior is I think beautiful and elegant, graceful, silly, fashionable and strange. We have a little tiff now and then—and she behaves a little better, or I must have sheered off. I find by a sidelong report from your Mother that I am to be invited to Miss Millar's birthday dance. Shall I dance with Miss Waldegrave? Eh! I shall be obliged to shirk a good many there. I shall be the only Dandy there—and indeed I merely comply with the invitation that the party may not be entirely destitute of a specimen of that race. I shall appear in a complete dress of purple, Hat and all—with a list of the beauties I have conquered embroidered round my Calves.

. . . Hunt has asked me to meet Tom Moore some day—so you shall hear of him. The Night we went to Novello's there was a complete set to of Mozart and punning. I was so completely tired of it that if I were to follow my own inclinations I should never meet anyone of that set again, not even Hunt, who is certainly a pleasant fellow in the main when you are with him—but in reality he is vain, egotistical, and disgusting in matters of taste and in morals. He understands many a beautiful thing; but then, instead of giving other minds credit for the same degree of perception as he himself professes—he begins an explanation in such a curious manner that our taste and self-love is offended continually. Hunt does one harm by making fine things petty, and beautiful things hateful. Through him I am indifferent to Mozart, I care not for white Busts—and many a glorious thing when associated with him becomes a nothing. This distorts one's mind—makes one's thoughts bizarre—perplexes one in the standard of Beauty. . . .

Friday [*December 25*]

I think you knew before you left England that my next subject would be 'the Fall of Hyperion.' I went on a little with it last night, but it will take some time to get into the vein again. I will not give you any extracts because I wish the whole to make an impression. I have however a few

Poems which you will like, and I will copy out on the next sheet. . . .

Shall I give you Miss Brawne? She is about my height—with a fine style of countenance of the lengthened sort—she wants sentiment in every feature—she manages to make her hair look well—her nostrils are fine—though a little painful—her mouth is bad and good—her Profile is better than her full-face which indeed is not full but pale and thin without showing any bone. Her shape is very graceful and so are her movements—her Arms are good her hands baddish—her feet tolerable. She is not seventeen—but she is ignorant—monstrous in her behaviour, flying out in all directions—calling people such names that I was forced lately to make use of the term *Minx*—this is I think not from any innate vice, but from a penchant she has for acting stylishly—I am however tired of such style and shall decline any more of it. She had a friend to visit her lately—you have known plenty such—her face is raw as if she was standing out in a frost; her lips raw and seem always ready for a Pullet—she plays the Music without one sensation but the feel of the ivory at her fingers. She is a downright Miss without one set off—We hated her and smoked her and baited her and I think drove her away. Miss B. thinks her a Paragon of fashion, and says she is the only woman she would change persons with. What a stupe—She is superior as a Rose to a Dandelion. When we went to bed Brown observed as he put out the Taper what a very ugly old woman that Miss Robinson would make—at which I must have groaned aloud for I'm sure ten minutes. I have not seen the thing Kingston again—George will describe him to you—I shall insinuate some of these Creatures into a Comedy some day—and perhaps have Hunt among them— . . .

Thursday [December 31]

. . . My thoughts have turned lately this way —The more we know the more inadequacy we find in the world to satisfy us—this is an old observation; but I have made up my Mind never to take anything for granted—but even to examine the truth of the commonest proverbs—This however is true. Mrs. Tighe and Beattie[54] once delighted me—now I see through them and can find nothing in them but weakness, and yet how many they still delight! Perhaps a superior being may look upon Shakespeare in the same light

—is it possible? No—This same inadequacy is discovered (forgive me, little George, you know I don't mean to put you in the mess) in Women with few exceptions—the Dress Maker, the blue Stocking, and the most charming sentimentalist differ but in a slight degree and are equally smokeable. But I will go no further—I may be speaking sacrilegiously—and on my word I have thought so little that I have not one opinion upon anything except in matters of taste—I never can feel certain of any truth but from a clear perception of its Beauty—and I find myself very young minded even in that perceptive power—which I hope will increase. A year ago I could not understand in the slightest degree Raphael's cartoons —now I begin to read them a little—And how did I learn to do so? By seeing something done in quite an opposite spirit—I mean a picture of Guido's in which all the Saints, instead of that heroic simplicity and unaffected grandeur which they inherit from Raphael, had each of them both in countenance and gesture all the canting, solemn, melodramatic mawkishness of Mackenzie's father Nicholas.[55] When I was last at Haydon's I looked over a Book of Prints taken from the fresco of the Church at Milan, the name of which I forget—in it are comprised Specimens of the first and second age of art in Italy. I do not think I ever had a greater treat out of Shakespeare. Full of Romance and the most tender feeling—magnificence of draperies beyond any I ever saw, not excepting Raphael's. But Grotesque to a curious pitch—yet still making up a fine whole—even finer to me than more accomplished works—as there was left so much room for Imagination. I have not heard one of this last course of Hazlitt's lectures. They were upon 'Wit and Humour,' 'the English comic writers.'

Saturday, January 2nd [1819]

Yesterday Mr. and Mrs. D. and myself dined at Mrs. Brawne's—nothing particular passed. I never intend hereafter to spend any time with Ladies unless they are handsome—you lose time to no purpose. For that reason I shall beg leave to decline going again to Redall's or Butler's or any Squad where a fine feature cannot be mustered among them all—and where all the evening's amusement consists in saying 'your good health, *your* good health, and YOUR good health—and (O I beg your pardon) yours, Miss ——,' and such things not even dull enough to keep one awake—With respect to amiable speaking I can

54 Mrs. Mary Tighe, 1772–1810, Irish poet whose *Psyche*, 1805, was an early influence on Keats. James Beattie, 1735–1803, author of *The Minstrel*.

55 Henry Mackenzie, 1745–1831, 'The Story of Father Nicholas' in *Papers from the Lounger*, 1808.

read—let my eyes be fed or I'll never go out to dinner anywhere. . . .

19 *To* Benjamin Robert Haydon

Wentworth Place [*March 8, 1819*]

My dear Haydon,

You must be wondering where I am and what I am about! I am mostly at Hampstead, and about nothing; being in a sort of qui bono temper, not exactly on the road to an epic poem. Nor must you think I have forgotten you. No, I have about every three days been to Abbey's and to the Lawyers. Do let me know how you have been getting on, and in what spirits you are.

You got out gloriously in yesterday's Examiner. What a set of little people we live amongst! I went the other day into an ironmonger's shop—without any change in my sensations—men and tin kettles are much the same in these days—they do not study like children at five and thirty—but they talk like men of twenty. Conversation is not a search after knowledge, but an endeavour at effect.

In this respect two most opposite men, Wordsworth and Hunt, are the same. A friend of mine observed the other day that if Lord Bacon were to make any remark in a party of the present day, the conversation would stop on the sudden. I am convinced of this, and from this I have come to this resolution—never to write for the sake of writing or making a poem, but from running over with any little knowledge or experience which many years of reflection may perhaps give me; otherwise I will be dumb. What imagination I have I shall enjoy, and greatly, for I have experienced the satisfaction of having great conceptions without the trouble of sonnetteering. I will not spoil my love of gloom by writing an Ode to Darkness!

With respect to my livelihood, I will not write for it,—for I will not run with that most vulgar of all crowds, the literary. Such things I ratify by looking upon myself, and trying myself at lifting mental weights, as it were. I am three and twenty, with little knowledge and middling intellect. It is true that in the height of enthusiasm I have been cheated into some fine passages; but that is not the thing.

I have not been to see you because all my going out has been to town, and that has been a great deal. Write soon.

Yours constantly,

John Keats

20 *To* George and Georgiana Keats

March 17th [*1819*]

My dear Brother and Sister,

. . . This morning I have been reading the 'False one'[56] I have been up to Mrs. Bentley's—shameful to say I was in bed at ten—I mean this morning—The Blackwood's review has committed themselves in a scandalous heresy—they have been putting up Hogg the Ettrick Shepherd against Burns—the senseless villains. I have not seen Reynolds Rice or any of our set lately—. Reynolds is completely buried in the law: he is not only reconciled to it but hobbyhorses upon it—Blackwood wanted very much to see him—the Scotch cannot manage by themselves at all —they want imagination—and that is why they are so fond of Hogg who has a little of it— . . .

This morning I am in a sort of temper indolent and supremely careless: I long after a stanza or two of Thompson's Castle of Indolence. My passions are all asleep from my having slumbered till nearly eleven and weakened the animal fibre all over me to a delightful sensation about three degrees on this side of faintness—if I had teeth of pearl and the breath of lillies I should call it languor—but as I am I must call it Laziness. In this state of effeminacy the fibres of the brain are relaxed in common with the rest of the body, and to such a happy degree that pleasure has no show of enticement and pain no unbearable frown. Neither Poetry, nor Ambition, nor Love have any alertness of countenance as they pass by me: they seem rather like three figures on a greek vase—a Man and two women whom no one but myself could distinguish in their disguisement. This is the only happiness; and is a rare instance of advantage in the body overpowering the Mind. I have this moment received a note from Haslam in which he expects the death of his Father—who has been for some time in a state of insensibility—his mother bears up he says very well—I shall go to town tomorrow to see him. This is the world—thus we cannot expect to give way many hours to pleasure—Circumstances are like Clouds continually gathering and bursting—While we are laughing, the seed of some trouble is put into the wide arable land of events—while we are laughing it sprouts it grows and suddenly bears a poison fruit which we must pluck—Even so we have leisure to reason on the misfortunes of our friends; our own touch us too nearly for words. Very few men have ever arrived at a complete disinterestedness of

---

56 by Beaumont and Fletcher.

Mind: very few have been influenced by a pure desire of the benefit of others—in the greater part of the Benefactors to Humanity some meretricious motive has sullied their greatness—some melodramatic scenery has fascinated them—From the manner in which I feel Haslam's misfortune I perceive how far I am from any humble standard of disinterestedness—Yet this feeling ought to be carried to its highest pitch as there is no fear of its ever injuring Society—which it would do I fear pushed to an extremity—For in wild nature the Hawk would lose his Breakfast of Robins and the Robin his of Worms—the Lion must starve as well as the swallow. The greater part of Men make their way with the same instinctiveness, the same unwandering eye from their purposes, the same animal eagerness as the Hawk. The Hawk wants a Mate, so does the Man—look at them both, they set about it and procure one in the same manner. They want both a nest and they both set about one in the same manner—they get their food in the same manner—The noble animal Man for his amusement smokes his pipe—the Hawk balances about the Clouds—that is the only difference of their leisures. This it is that makes the Amusement of Life—to a speculative Mind. I go among the Fields and catch a glimpse of a Stoat[57] or a field-mouse peeping out of the withered grass—the creature hath a purpose and its eyes are bright with it. I go amongst the buildings of a city and I see a Man hurrying along—to what? the Creature has a purpose and his eyes are bright with it. But then, as Wordsworth says, 'we have all one human heart'—there is an electric fire in human nature tending to purify—so that among these human creatures there is continually some birth of new heroism. The pity is that we must wonder at it: as we should at finding a pearl in rubbish. I have no doubt that thousands of people never heard of have had hearts completely disinterested: I can remember but two—Socrates and Jesus—their Histories evince it. What I heard a little time ago, Taylor observe with respect to Socrates may be said of Jesus—That he was so great a man that though he transmitted no writing of his own to posterity, we have his Mind and his sayings and his greatness handed to us by others. It is to be lamented that the history of the latter was written and revised by Men interested in the pious frauds of Religion. Yet through all this I see his splendour. Even here though I myself am pursuing the same instinctive course as the veriest human animal you can think of—I am however young, writing at random—straining at particles of light in the midst of a great darkness—without knowing the bearing of any one assertion of any one opinion. Yet may I not in this be free from sin? May there not be superior beings amused with any graceful, though instinctive attitude my mind may fall into, as I am entertained with the alertness of a Stoat or the anxiety of a Deer? Though a quarrel in the Streets is a thing to be hated, the energies displayed in it are fine; the commonest Man shows a grace in his quarrel—By a superior being our reasonings may take the same tone—though erroneous they may be fine—This is the very thing in which consists poetry; and if so it is not so fine a thing as philosophy—For the same reason that an eagle is not so fine a thing as a truth—Give me this credit—Do you not think I strive—to know myself? Give me this credit—and you will not think that on my own account I repeat Milton's lines

How charming is divine Philosophy
Not harsh and crabbed as dull fools suppose
But musical as is Apollo's lute.[58]

No—not for myself—feeling grateful as I do to have got into a state of mind to relish them properly—Nothing ever becomes real till it is experienced—Even a Proverb is no proverb to you till your Life has illustrated it. I am ever afraid that your anxiety for me will lead you to fear for the violence of my temperament continually smothered down: for that reason I did not intend to have sent you the following sonnet—but look over the two last pages and ask yourselves whether I have not that in me which will well bear the buffets of the world. It will be the best comment on my sonnet; it will show you that it was written with no Agony but that of ignorance; with no thirst of anything but Knowledge when pushed to the point though the first steps to it were through my human passions—they went away, and I wrote with my Mind—and perhaps I must confess a little bit of my heart—

Why did I laugh tonight? No voice will tell:
  No God no Deamon of severe response
Deigns to reply from heaven or from Hell.—
  Then to my human heart I turn at once—
Heart! thou and I are here sad and alone;
  Say, wherefore did I laugh? O mortal pain!
O Darkness! Darkness! ever must I moan
  To question Heaven and Hell and Heart in
    vain!
Why did I laugh? I know this being's lease

---

57 weasel.

58 *Comus*, 476–8.

My fancy to its utmost blisses spreads:
Yet could I on this very midnight cease
  And the world's gaudy ensigns see in shreds.
Verse, Fame, and Beauty are intense indeed
But Death intenser—Death is Life's high
  mead.

I went to bed, and enjoyed an uninterrupted
Sleep.

21 *To* Miss Jeffrey [of Teignmouth]

Wentworth Place, June 9, [1819]

My dear young Lady,

. . . Your advice about the Indiaman is a very
wise advice, because it just suits me, though you
are a little in the wrong concerning its destroying
the energies of Mind: on the contrary it would be
the finest thing in the world to strengthen them—
To be thrown among people who care not for
you, with whom you have no sympathies forces
the Mind upon its own resources, and leaves it
free to make its speculations of the differences
of human character and to class them with the
calmness of a Botanist. An Indiaman is a little
world. One of the great reasons that the English
have produced the finest writers in the world is,
that the English world has ill-treated them during their lives and fostered them after their
deaths. They have in general been trampled
aside into the bye paths of life and seen the fes-
terings of Society. They have not been treated
like the Raphaels of Italy. And where is the Englishman and Poet who has given a magnificent
Entertainment at the christening of one of his
Hero's Horses as Boyardo[59] did? He had a Castle in the Appenine. He was a noble Poet of Romance; not a miserable and mighty Poet of the
human Heart. The middle age of Shakespeare
was all clouded over; his days were not more
happy than Hamlet's who is perhaps more like
Shakespeare himself in his common everyday
Life than any other of his Characters—Ben Jonson was a common Soldier and in the Low countries, in the face of two armies, fought a single
combat with a French Trooper and slew him—
For all this I will not go on board an Indiaman,
nor for example's sake run my head into dark
alleys: I dare say my discipline is to come, and
plenty of it too. I have been very idle lately,
very averse to writing; both from the overpowering idea of our dead poets and from abatement
of my love of fame. I hope I am a little more of a

Philosopher than I was, consequently a little less
of a versifying Pet-lamb. I have put no more in
Print or you should have had it. You will judge
of my 1819 temper when I tell you that the thing
I have most enjoyed this year has been writing
an ode to Indolence. . . .

          Ever sincerely yours,

             John Keats

22 *To* Fanny Brawne

July 8th [1819]

My sweet Girl,

Your Letter gave me more delight, than anything in the world but yourself could do; indeed
I am almost astonished that any absent one
should have that luxurious power over my senses
which I feel. Even when I am not thinking of you
I receive your influence and a tenderer nature
stealing upon me. All my thoughts, my unhap-
piest days and nights, have I find not at all cured
me of my love of Beauty, but made it so intense
that I am miserable that you are not with me: or
rather breathe in that dull sort of patience that
cannot be called Life. I never knew before, what
such a love as you have made me feel, was; I did
not believe in it; my Fancy was afraid of it, lest it
should burn me up. But if you will fully love me,
though there may be some fire, 'twill not be more
than we can bear when moistened and bedewed
with Pleasures. You mention 'horrid people' and
ask me whether it depend upon them, whether I
see you again. Do understand me, my love, in
this. I have so much of you in my heart that I
must turn Mentor when I see a chance of harm
befalling you. I would never see anything but
Pleasure in your eyes, love on your lips, and
Happiness in your steps. I would wish to see you
among those amusements suitable to your inclinations and spirits; so that our loves might be
a delight in the midst of Pleasures agreeable
enough, rather than a resource from vexations
and cares. But I doubt much, in case of the worst,
whether I shall be philosopher enough to follow
my own Lessons: if I saw my resolution give you
a pain I could not. Why may I not speak of your
Beauty, since without that I could never have
loved you. I cannot conceive any beginning of
such love as I have for you but Beauty. There
may be a sort of love for which, without the
least sneer at it, I have the highest respect and
can admire it in others: but it has not the richness, the bloom, the full form, the enchantment
of love after my own heart. So let me speak of

---

59 Matteo Boiardo, 1434–94, whose *Orlando Innamorato* was
translated by Charles Brown.

your Beauty, though to my own endangering; if you could be so cruel to me as to try elsewhere its Power. You say you are afraid I shall think you do not love me—in saying this you make me ache the more to be near you. I am at the diligent use of my faculties here, I do not pass a day without sprawling some blank verse or tagging some rhymes; and here I must confess, that, (since I am on that subject), I love you the more in that I believe you have liked me for my own sake and for nothing else. I have met with women whom I really think would like to be married to a Poem and to be given away by a Novel. I have seen your Comet, and only wish it was a sign that poor Rice would get well whose illness makes him rather a melancholy companion: and the more so as to conquer his feelings and hide them from me, with a forced Pun. I kissed your writing over in the hope you had indulged me by leaving a trace of honey—What was your dream? Tell it me and I will tell you the interpretation thereof.

Ever yours, my love!

John Keats

Do not accuse me of delay—we have not here an opportunity of sending letters every day. Write speedily.

23 *To* Fanny Brawne

Sunday Night [July 25, 1819]

My sweet Girl,

I hope you did not blame me much for not obeying your request of a Letter on Saturday: we have had four in our small room playing at cards night and morning leaving me no undisturbed opportunity to write. Now Rice and Martin are gone I am at liberty. Brown to my sorrow confirms the account you give of your ill health. You cannot conceive how I ache to be with you: how I would die for one hour—for what is in the world? I say you cannot conceive; it is impossible you should look with such eyes upon me as I have upon you: it cannot be. Forgive me if I wander a little this evening, for I have been all day employed in a very abstract Poem and I am in deep love with you—two things which must excuse me. I have, believe me, not been an age in letting you take possession of me; the very first week I knew you I wrote myself your vassal; but burned the Letter as the very next time I saw you I thought you manifested some dislike to me. If you should ever feel for Man at the first sight what I did for you, I am lost. Yet

I should not quarrel with you, but hate myself if such a thing were to happen—only I should burst if the thing were not as fine as a Man as you are as a Woman. Perhaps I am too vehement, then fancy me on my knees, especially when I mention a part of your Letter which hurt me, you say speaking of Mr. Severn 'but you must be satisfied in knowing that I admire you much more than your friend.' My dear love, I cannot believe there ever was or ever could be anything to admire in me especially as far as sight goes—I cannot be admired, I am not a thing to be admired. You are, I love you; all I can bring you is a swooning admiration of your Beauty. I hold that place among Men which snub-nosed brunettes with meeting eyebrows do among women—they are trash to me—unless I should find one among them with a fire in her heart like the one that burns in mine. You absorb me in spite of myself—you alone: for I look not forward with any pleasure to what is called being settled in the world; I tremble at domestic cares —yet for you I would meet them, though if it would leave you the happier I would rather die than do so. I have two luxuries to brood over in my walks, your Loveliness and the hour of my death. O that I could have possession of them both in the same minute. I hate the world: it batters too much the wings of my self-will, and would I could take a sweet poison from your lips to send me out of it. From no others would I take it. I am indeed astonished to find myself so careless of all charms but yours—remembering as I do the time when even a bit of ribband was a matter of interest with me. What softer words can I find for you after this—what it is I will not read. Nor will I say more here, but in a Postscript answer anything else you may have mentioned in your Letter in so many words—for I am distracted with a thousand thoughts. I will imagine you Venus tonight and pray, pray, pray to your star like a Heathen.

Yours ever, fair Star,

John Keats

24 *To* Benjamin Bailey
Saturday 14 Aug. [1819]

We removed to Winchester for the convenience of a Library and find it an exceeding pleasant Town, enriched with a beautiful Cathedral and surrounded by a fresh-looking country. We are in tolerably good and cheap Lodgings. Within these two Months I have written 1500 Lines, most of which besides many more of prior composition you will probably see by next Winter. I have written two Tales, one from Boccaccio called the Pot of Basil; and another called St. Agnes' Eve on a popular superstition; and a third called Lamia—half finished—I have also been writing parts of my Hyperion and completed 4 Acts of a Tragedy. It was the opinion of most of my friends that I should never be able to write a scene. I will endeavour to wipe away the prejudice—I sincerely hope you will be pleased when my Labours since we last saw each other shall reach you. One of my Ambitions is to make as great a revolution in modern dramatic writing as Kean has done in acting—another to upset the drawling of the blue stocking literary world—if in the course of a few years I do these two things I ought to die content—and my friends should drink a dozen of Claret on my Tomb—I am convinced more and more every day that (excepting the human friend Philosopher) a fine writer is the most genuine Being in the World. Shakespeare and the Paradise Lost every day become greater wonders to me. I look upon fine Phrases like a Lover. I was glad to see, by a Passage in one of Brown's Letters some time ago from the north that you were in such good Spirits. Since that you have been married and in congratulating you I wish you every continuance of them. Present my Respects to Mrs. Bailey. This sounds oddly to me, and I dare say I do it awkwardly enough: but I suppose by this time it is nothing new to you—Brown's remembrances to you— As far as I know we shall remain at Winchester for a goodish while—

Ever your sincere friend,

John Keats

25 *To* Fanny Brawne

Winchester August 17th [1819]

My dear Girl—

What shall I say for myself? I have been here four days and not yet written you—'tis true I have had many teasing letters of business to dismiss—and I have been in the Claws, like a Serpent in an Eagle's, of the last act of our Tragedy.[60] This is no excuse; I know it; I do not presume to offer it. I have no right either to ask a speedy answer to let me know how lenient you are—I must remain some days in a Mist—I see you through a Mist: as I dare say you do me by this time. Believe in the first Letters I wrote you:

I assure you I felt as I wrote—I could not write so now. The thousand images I have had pass through my brain—my uneasy spirits—my unguessed fate—all spread as a veil between me and you—Remember I have had no idle leisure to brood over you—'tis well perhaps I have not. I could not have endured the throng of Jealousies that used to haunt me before I had plunged so deeply into imaginary interests. I would feign, as my sails are set, sail on without an interruption for a Brace of Months longer—I am in complete cue—in the fever; and shall in these four Months do an immense deal—This Page as my eye skims over it I see is excessively unloverlike and ungallant—I cannot help it—I am no officer in yawning quarters; no Parson-romeo. My Mind is heaped to the full; stuffed like a cricket ball— if I strive to fill it more it would burst. I know the generality of women would hate me for this; that I should have so unsoftened so hard a Mind as to forget them; forget the brightest realities for the dull imaginations of my own Brain. But I conjure you to give it a fair thinking; and ask yourself whether 'tis not better to explain my feelings to you, than write artificial Passion—Besides you would see through it. It would be vain to strive to deceive you. 'Tis harsh, harsh, I know it— My heart seems now made of iron—I could not write a proper answer to an invitation to Idalia.[61] You are my Judge: my forehead is on the ground. You seem offended at a little simple innocent childish playfulness in my last. I did not seriously mean to say that you were endeavouring to make me keep my promise. I beg your pardon for it. 'Tis but *just* your Pride should take the alarm—*seriously*. You say I may do as I please—I do not think with any conscience I can; my cash resources are for the present stopped; I fear for some time. I spend no money but it increases my debts. I have all my life thought very little of these matters—they seem not to belong to me. It may be a proud sentence; but, by heaven, I am as entirely above all matters of interest as the Sun is above the Earth—and though of my own money I should be careless; of my Friends I must be spare. You see how I go on— like so many strokes of a Hammer. I cannot help it—I am impelled, driven to it. I am not happy enough for silken Phrases, and silver sentences. I can no more use soothing words to you than if I were at this moment engaged in a charge of Cavalry—Then you will say I should not write at all —Should I not? . . . Forgive me for this flint-

---

60 *Otho the Great* on which Keats and Brown were collaborating.

61 i.e. Venus, so called from Idalium in Cyprus where she was worshiped.

worded Letter, and believe and see that I cannot think of you without some sort of energy—though *mal a propos*—Even as I leave off it seems to me that a few more moments' thought of you would uncrystallize and dissolve me. I must not give way to it—but turn to my writing again—if I fail I shall die hard. O my love, your lips are growing sweet again to my fancy—I must forget them.

Ever your affectionate

Keats

26 *To* John Taylor

Winchester, Monday morn. [August 23, 1819]

My dear Taylor—

[Brown and I] have together been engaged (this I should wish to remain secret) in a Tragedy which I have just finished; and from which we hope to share moderate Profits. . . . I feel every confidence that if I choose I may be a popular writer; that I will never be; but for all that I will get a livelihood—I equally disike the favour of the public with the love of a woman—they are both a cloying treacle to the wings of independence. I shall ever consider them (People) as debtors to me for verses, not myself to them for admiration—which I can do without. I have of late been indulging my spleen by composing a preface *at* them: after all resolving never to write a preface at all. 'There are so many verses,' would I have said to them, 'give me so much means to buy pleasure with as a relief to my hours of labour.'—You will observe at the end of this if you put down the Letter 'How a solitary life engenders pride and egotism!' True: I know it does—but this Pride and egotism will enable me to write finer things than anything else could—so I will indulge it. Just so much as I am humbled by the genius above my grasp, am I exalted and look with hate and contempt upon the literary world—A Drummer boy who holds out his hand familiarly to a field marshall—that Drummer boy with me is the good word and favour of the public. Who would wish to be among the commonplace crowd of the little-famous—who are each individually lost in a throng made up of themselves? Is this worth louting or playing the hypocrite for? To beg suffrages for a seat on the benches of a myriad-aristocracy in Letters? This is not wise—I am not a wise man—'Tis Pride. I will give you a definition of a proud Man—He is a Man who has neither vanity nor wisdom—one

filled with hatreds cannot be vain—neither can he be wise. Pardon me for hammering instead of writing—Remember me to Woodhouse, Hessey, and all in Percy street—

Ever yours sincerely,

John Keats

27 *To* John Hamilton Reynolds

Winchester, August 25 [1819]

My dear Reynolds,

By this post I write to Rice, who will tell you why we have left Shanklin; and how we like this place. I have indeed scarcely anything else to say, leading so monotonous a life, except I was to give you a history of sensations, and day-nightmares. You would not find me at all unhappy in it; as all my thoughts and feelings which are of the selfish nature, home speculations every day continue to make me more Iron. I am convinced more and more day by day that fine writing is next to fine doing, the top thing in the world; the Paradise Lost becomes a greater wonder. The more I know what my diligence may in time probably effect; the more does my heart distend with Pride and Obstinacy—I feel it in my power to become a popular Writer—I feel it in my strength to refuse the poisonous suffrage of a public. My own being which I know to be becomes of more consequence to me than the crowds of Shadows in the shape of men and women that inhabit a Kingdom. The soul is a world of itself, and has enough to do in its own home. Those whom I know already, and who have grown as it were a part of myself, I could not do without: but for the rest of mankind, they are as much a dream to me as Milton's Hierarchies. I think if I had a free and healthy and lasting organization of heart, and lungs as strong as an ox's so as to be able to bear unhurt the shock of extreme thought and sensation without weariness, I could pass my life very nearly alone though it should last eighty years. But I feel my body too weak to support me to the height; I am obliged continually to check myself and be nothing. It would be vain for me to endeavour after a more reasonable manner of writing to you. I have nothing to speak of but myself—and what can I say but what I feel? If you should have any reason to regret this state of excitement in me, I will turn the tide of your feelings in the right Channel, by mentioning that it is the only state for the best sort of Poetry—that is all I care for, all I live for. Forgive me for not filling up the whole sheet; Letters become so irksome to me that the next time I leave London I shall petition them all to be spared me. To give me credit for constancy, and at the same time waive letter writing will be the highest indulgence I can think of.

Ever your affectionate friend,

John Keats

28 *To* George and Georgiana Keats

Winchester, September [17, 1819], Friday

... I have passed my time in reading, writing, and fretting—the last I intend to give up, and stick to the other two. They are the only chances of benefit to us. Your wants will be a fresh spur to me. I assure you you shall more than share what I can get whilst I am still young. The time may come when age will make me more selfish. I have not been well treated by the world, and yet I have, capitally well. I do not know a person to whom so many purse-strings would fly open as to me, if I could possibly take advantage of them, which I cannot do, for none of the owners of these purses are rich. Your present situation I will not suffer myself to dwell upon. When misfortunes are so real, we are glad enough to escape them and the thought of them. I cannot help thinking Mr. Audubon[62] a dishonest man. Why did he make you believe that he was a man of property? How is it that his circumstances have altered so suddenly? In truth, I do not believe you fit to deal with the world, or at least the American world. But, good God! who can avoid these chances? You have done your best. Take matters as coolly as you can; and confidently expecting help from England, act as if no help were nigh. Mine, I am sure, is a tolerable tragedy; it would have been a bank to me, if just as I had finished it, I had not heard of Kean's resolution to go to America. That was the worst news I could have had. There is no actor can do the principal character besides Kean. At Covent Garden there is a great chance of its being damned. Were it to succeed even there it would lift me out of the mire; I mean the mire of a bad reputation which is continually rising against me. My name with the literary fashionables is vulgar. I am a weaver-boy to them. A tragedy would lift me out of this mess, and mess it is as far as it regards our pockets. But be not cast down any more than I am; I feel that I can bear real ills better than imaginary ones. Whenever I find myself growing vapourish, I rouse myself, wash, and put on a clean shirt, brush my hair and clothes,

tie my shoestrings neatly, and in fact adonise as I were going out. Then, all clean and comfortable, I sit down to write. This I find the greatest relief. Besides I am becoming accustomed to the privations of the pleasures of sense. In the midst of the world I live like a hermit. I have forgot how to lay plans for the enjoyment of any pleasure. I feel I can bear anything,—any misery, even imprisonment, so long as I have neither wife nor child. Perhaps you will say yours are your only comfort; they must be. I returned to Winchester the day before yesterday, and am now here alone, for Brown, some days before I left, went to Bedhampton, and there he will be for the next fortnight. ...

There is scarcely a grain of party spirit now in England. Right and wrong considered by each man abstractedly, is the fashion. I know very little of these things. I am convinced, however, that apparently small causes make great alterations. There are little signs whereby we may know how matters are going on. This makes the business about Carlisle the bookseller of great moment in my mind. He has been selling deistical pamphlets, republished Tom Paine, and many other works held in superstitious horror. He even has been selling, for some time, immense numbers of a work called 'The Deist,' which comes out in weekly numbers. For this conduct he, I think, has had about a dozen indictments issued against him, for which he has found bail to the amount of many thousand pounds. After all, they are afraid to prosecute. They are afraid of his defence; it would be published in all the papers all over the Empire. They shudder at this. The trials would light a flame they could not extinguish. Do you not think this of great import? You will hear by the papers of the proceedings at Manchester, and Hunt's triumphal entry into London. It would take me a whole day and a quire of paper to give you anything like detail. I will merely mention that it is calculated that 30,-000 people were in the streets waiting for him. The whole distance from the Angel at Islington to the Crown and Anchor was lined with multitudes. ...

You speak of Lord Byron and me. There is this great difference between us: he describes what he sees—I describe what I imagine. Mine is the hardest task; now see the immense difference. The Edinburgh Reviewers are afraid to touch upon my poem. They do not know what to make of it; they do not like to condemn it, and they will not praise it for fear. They are as shy of it as I should be of wearing a Quaker's hat. The fact is, they have no real taste. They dare not com-

---

62 Audubon, the American naturalist, it is said, sold to George Keats a boat loaded with merchandise which Audubon knew was at the bottom of the Mississippi River at the time of the sale.

promise their judgements on so puzzling a question. If on my next publication they should praise me, and so lug in Endymion. I will address them in a manner they will not at all relish. The cowardliness of the Edinburgh is worse than the abuse of the Quarterly. . . .

Tuesday [*September 21*]

You see I keep adding a sheet daily till I send the packet off, which I shall not do for a few days, as I am inclined to write a good deal; for there can be nothing so remembrancing and enchaining as a good long letter, be it composed of what it may. From the time you left me our friends say I have altered completely—am not the same person. Perhaps in this letter I am, for in a letter one takes up one's existence from the time we last met. I daresay you have altered also—every man does—our bodies every seven years are completely fresh-materiated. Seven years ago it was not this hand that clenched itself against Hammond. We are like the relict garments of a saint—the same and not the same, for the careful monks patch it and patch it till there's not a thread of the original garment left, and still they show it for St. Anthony's shirt. This is the reason why men who have been bosom friends, on being separated for any number of years meet coldly, neither of them knowing why. The fact is they are both altered.

Men who live together have a silent moulding and influencing power over each other. They interassimilate. 'Tis an uneasy thought, that in seven years the same hands cannot greet each other again. All this may be obviated by a wilful and dramatic exercise of our minds towards each other. Some think I have lost that poetic ardour and fire 'tis said I once had—the fact is, perhaps I have; but, instead of that, I hope I shall substitute a more thoughtful and quiet power. I am more frequently now contented to read and think, but now and then haunted with ambitious thoughts. Quieter in my pulse, improved in my digestion, exerting myself against vexing speculations, scarcely content to write the best verses for the fever they leave behind. I want to compose without this fever. I hope I one day shall. . . .

29 *To* Fanny Brawne

[*February 1820*]

My dear Fanny,

Do not let your mother suppose that you hurt me by writing at night. For some reason or other your last night's note was not so treasureable as former ones. I would fain that you call me *Love* still. To see you happy and in high spirits is a great consolation to me—still let me believe that you are not half so happy as my restoration would make you. I am nervous, I own, and may think myself worse than I really am; if so you must indulge me, and pamper with that sort of tenderness you have manifested towards me in different Letters. My sweet creature when I look back upon the pains and torments I have suffered for you from the day I left you to go to the Isle of Wight; the extasies in which I have passed some days and the miseries in their turn, I wonder the more at the Beauty which has kept up the spell so fervently. When I send this round I shall be in the front parlour watching to see you show yourself for a minute in the garden. How illness stands as a barrier betwixt me and you! Even if I was well—I must make myself as good a Philosopher as possible. Now I have had opportunities of passing nights anxious and awake I have found other thoughts intrude upon me. 'If I should die,' said I to myself, 'I have left no immortal work behind me—nothing to make my friends proud of my memory—but I have loved the principle of beauty in all things, and if I had had time I would have made myself remembered.' Thoughts like these came very feebly whilst I was in health and every pulse beat for you—now you divide with this (may *I* say it?) 'last infirmity of noble minds'[63] all my reflection.

God bless you, Love.

J. Keats

30 *To* Fanny Brawne

[*February 1820*]

My dearest Girl,

Indeed I will not deceive you with respect to my health. This is the fact as far as I know. I have been confined three weeks and am not yet well—this proves that there is something wrong about me which my constitution will either conquer or give way to. Let us hope for the best. Do you hear the Thrush singing over the field? I think it is a sign of mild weather—so much the better for me. Like all Sinners now I am ill I philosophize, aye out of my attachment to everything, Trees, flowers, Thrushes, Spring, Summer, Claret, etc., etc.—aye everything but you. —My sister would be glad of my company a little longer. That Thrush is a fine fellow. I hope he was fortunate in his choice this year. Do not

---

63 *Lycidas,* 71.

send any more of my Books home. I have a great pleasure in the thought of you looking on them.

Ever yours
my sweet Fanny
J.K.

31 *To* Fanny Brawne

March 1820

My dearest Fanny,

I slept well last night and am no worse this morning for it. Day by day if I am not deceived I get a more unrestrained use of my Chest. The nearer a racer gets to the Goal the more his anxiety becomes, so I lingering upon the borders of health feel my impatience increase. Perhaps on your account I have imagined my illness more serious than it is: how horrid was the chance of slipping into the ground instead of into your arms—the difference is amazing Love. Death must come at last; Man must die,[64] as Shallow says; but before that is my fate I feign would try what more pleasures than you have given, so sweet a creature as you can give. Let me have another opportunity of years before me and I will not die without being remembered. Take care of yourself dear that we may both be well in the Summer. I do not at all fatigue myself with writing, having merely to put a line or two here and there, a Task which would worry a stout state of the body and mind, but which just suits me as I can do no more.

Your affectionate
J.K.

32 *To* Fanny Brawne

Tuesday Morn.—[May 1820]

My dearest Girl,

I wrote a Letter for you yesterday expecting to have seen your mother. I shall be selfish enough to send it though I know it may give you a little pain, because I wish you to see how unhappy I am for love of you, and endeavour as much as I can to entice you to give up your whole heart to me whose whole existence hangs upon you. You could not step or move an eyelid but it would shoot to my heart—I am greedy of you. Do not think of anything but me. Do not live as if I was not existing—Do not forget me—But have I any right to say you forget me? Perhaps you think of me all day. Have I any right to wish you to be un-

happy for me? You would forgive me for wishing it, if you knew the extreme passion I have that you should love me—and for you to love me as I do you, you must think of no one but me, much less write that sentence. Yesterday and this morning I have been haunted with a sweet vision—I have seen you the whole time in your shepherdess dress. How my senses have ached at it! How my heart has been devoted to it! How my eyes have been full of Tears at it! I[n]deed I think a real Love is enough to occupy the widest heart—Your going to town alone, when I heard of it was a shock to me—yet I expected it—*promise me you will not for some time, till I get better.* Promise me this and fill the paper full of the most endearing names. If you cannot do so with good will, do my Love tell me—say what you think—confess if your heart is too much fastened on the world. Perhaps then I may see you at a greater distance, I may not be able to appropriate you so closely to myself. Were you to loose a favourite bird from the cage, how would your eyes ache after it as long as it was in sight; when out of sight you would recover a little. Perhaps if you would, if so it is, confess to me how many things are necessary to you besides me, I might be happier, by being less tantalized. Well may you exclaim, how selfish, how cruel, not to let me enjoy my youth! to wish me to be unhappy! You must be so if you love me—upon my Soul I can be contented with nothing else. If you could really what is called enjoy yourself at a Party—if you can smile in people's faces, and wish them to admire you *now,* you never have nor ever will love me. I see *life* in nothing but the certainty of your Love —convince me of it my sweetest. If I am not somehow convinced I shall die of agony. If we love we must not live as other men and women do—I cannot brook the wolfsbane of fashion and foppery and tattle. You must be mine to die upon the rack if I want you. I do not pretend to say I have more feeling than my fellows—but I wish you seriously to look over my letters kind and unkind and consider whether the Person who wrote them can be able to endure much longer the agonies and uncertainties which you are so peculiarly made to create—My recovery of bodily health will be of no benefit to me if you are not all mine when I am well. For God's sake save me—or tell me my passion is of too awful a nature for you. Again God bless you.

J.K.

No—my sweet Fanny—I am wrong. I do not want you to be unhappy—and yet I do, I must while there is so sweet a Beauty—my loveliest

64 Cf. *II Henry IV,* III, ii, 42.

my darling! Good bye! I Kiss you—O the torments!

33 *To* Fanny Brawne

[*August 1820*]

My dearest Girl,

I wish you could invent some means to make me at all happy without you. Every hour I am more and more concentrated in you; everything else tastes like chaff in my Mouth. I feel it almost impossible to go to Italy—the fact is I cannot leave you, and shall never taste one minute's content until it pleases chance to let me live with you for good. But I will not go on at this rate. A person in health as you are can have no conception of the horrors that nerves and a temper like mine go through. What Island do your friends propose retiring to? I should be happy to go with you there alone, but in company I should object to it; the backbitings and jealousies of new colonists who have nothing else to amuse themselves, is unbearable. Mr. Dilke came to see me yesterday, and gave me a very great deal more pain than pleasure. I shall never be able any more to endure the society of any of those who used to meet at Elm Cottage and Wentworth Place. The last two years taste like brass upon my Palate. If I cannot live with you I will live alone. I do not think my health will improve much while I am separated from you. For all this I am averse to seeing you—I cannot bear flashes of light and return into my glooms again. I am not so unhappy now as I should be if I had seen you yesterday. To be happy with you seems such an impossibility! it requires a luckier Star than mine! it will never be. I enclose a passage from one of your letters which I want you to alter a little—I want (if you will have it so) the matter expressed less coldly to me. If my health would bear it, I could write a Poem which I have in my head, which would be a consolation for people in such a situation as mine. I would show someone in Love as I am, with a person living in such Liberty as you do. Shakespeare always sums up matters in the most sovereign manner. Hamlet's heart was full of such Misery as mine is when he said to Ophelia 'Go to a Nunnery, go, go!' Indeed I should like to give up the matter at once—I should like to die. I am sickened at the brute world which you are smiling with. I hate men and women more. I see nothing but thorns for the future—wherever I may be next winter in Italy or nowhere Brown will be living near you with his indecencies—I see no prospect of any rest. Suppose me in Rome—well, I should there see you as in a magic glass going to and from town at all hours,——I wish you could infuse a little confidence in human nature into my heart. I cannot muster any—the world is too brutal for me—I am glad there is such a thing as the grave—I am sure I shall never have any rest till I get there. At any rate I will indulge myself by never seeing any more Dilke or Brown or any of their Friends. I wish I was either in your arms full of faith or that a Thunder bolt would strike me.

God bless you.

J.K.

34 *To* Percy Bysshe Shelley

[*Hampstead, August 1820*]

My dear Shelley,

I am very much gratified that you, in a foreign country, and with a mind almost over-occupied, should write to me in the strain of the letter beside me. If I do not take advantage of your invitation, it will be prevented by a circumstance I have very much at heart to prophesy. There is no doubt that an English winter would put an end to me, and do so in a lingering, hateful manner. Therefore, I must either voyage or journey to Italy, as a soldier marches up to a battery. My nerves at present are the worst part of me, yet they feel soothed that, come what extreme may, I shall not be destined to remain in one spot long enough to take a hatred of any four particular bedposts. I am glad you take any pleasure in my poor poem, which I would willingly take the trouble to unwrite, if possible, did I care so much as I have done about reputation. I received a copy of the Cenci, as from yourself, from Hunt. There is only one part of it I am judge of—the poetry and dramatic effect, which by many spirits nowadays is considered the Mammon. A modern work, it is said, must have a purpose, which may be the God. An artist must serve Mammon; he must have 'self-concentration'—selfishness, perhaps. You, I am sure, will forgive me for sincerely remarking that you might curb your magnanimity, and be more of an artist, and load every rift of your subject with ore. The thought of such discipline must fall like cold chains upon you, who perhaps never sat with your wings furled for six months together. And is this not extraordinary talk for the writer of Endymion, whose mind was like a pack of scattered cards? I am picked up and sorted to a pip. My imagination is a monastery, and I am its monk. I am in expectation of Prometheus every day. Could I have my own wish effected, you would have it still in manuscript, or be but now putting an end to the second act. I remember you advising me not to publish my first blights, on Hampstead Heath. I am returning advice upon your hands. Most of the poems in the volume I send you have been written above two years, and would never have been published but for hope of gain; so you see I am inclined enough to take your advice now. I must express once more my deep sense of your kindness, adding my sincere thanks and respects for Mrs. Shelley.

In the hope of soon seeing you, I remain most sincerely yours,

John Keats

35 *To* Charles Armitage Brown

Rome, November 30, 1820

My dear Brown,

'Tis the most difficult thing in the world to me to write a letter. My stomach continues so bad, that I feel it worse on opening any book,—yet I am much better than I was in quarantine. Then I am afraid to encounter the pro-ing and con-ing of anything interesting to me in England. I have an habitual feeling of my real life having passed, and that I am leading a posthumous existence. God knows how it would have been—but it appears to me—however, I will not speak of that subject. I must have been at Bedhampton nearly at the time you were writing to me from Chichester—how unfortunate—and to pass on the river too! There was my star predominant! I cannot answer anything in your letter, which followed me from Naples to Rome, because I am afraid to look it over again. I am so weak (in mind) that I cannot bear the sight of any handwriting of a friend I love so much as I do you. Yet I ride the little horse, and at my worst even in quarantine, summoned up more puns, in a sort of desperation, in one week than in any year of my life. There is one thought enough to kill me; I have been well, healthy, alert, etc., walking with her, and now—the knowledge of contrast, feeling for light and shade, all that information (primitive sense) necessary for a poem, are great enemies to the recovery of the stomach. There, you rogue, I put you to the torture; but you must bring your philosophy to bear, as I do mine, really, or how should I be able to live? Dr. Clark is very attentive to me; he says there is very little the matter with my lungs, but my stomach, he says, is very bad. I am well disappointed in hearing good news from George, for it runs in my head we shall all die young. I have not written to Reynolds yet, which he must think very neglectful; being anxious to send him a good account of my health, I have delayed it from week to week. If I recover, I will do all in my power to correct the mistakes made during sickness; and if I should not, all my faults will be forgiven. Severn is very well, though he leads so dull a life with me. Remember me to all friends, and tell Haslam I should not have left London without taking leave of him, but from being so low in body and mind. Write to George as soon as you receive this, and tell him how I am, as far as you can guess; and also a note to my sister—who walks about my imagination like a ghost—she is so like Tom. I can scarcely bid you good-bye, even in a letter. I always made an awkward bow.

God bless you!

John Keats

1785 · THOMAS LOVE PEACOCK · 1866

1785   Born the only son of a well-to-do London merchant.

1792–1803   Educated at a private school and through his own reading, chiefly in classical literature, at the British Museum; after a brief experience in business determined to devote himself to literature.

1804–14   Living on his private means, wrote a number of long poems and plays of not much merit.

1815   Became the neighbor of Shelley by the Windsor Thames where *Headlong Hall* (published 1816), the first of his satirical romances, took shape.

1817   Published *Melincourt,* a second and more elaborate satirical romance. At Great Marlow enjoyed the almost daily companionship of Shelley; wrote *Nightmare Abbey* (published 1818) and *Rhododaphne,* the best of his long poems (published 1818).

1819   Married and entered the service of the East India Company.

1822   Published *Maid Marian,*

1829   *The Misfortunes of Elphin,* and

1831   *Crochet Castle.*

1856   Retired from the East India Company on a pension, after many years of meritorious service.

1860   Published *Gryll Grange,* his last novel.

1856–64   Contributed occasional papers to *Fraser's Magazine,* including his reminiscences of Shelley.

1866   Died.

THOMAS LOVE PEACOCK, the friend of Shelley and the father-in-law of Meredith, was one of the best classical scholars of his day, though he never attended a university. He was an odd combination of sincerity, cynicism, and romance; one who was not in sympathy with the world of the romantics, though he understood it. He was a 'laughing philosopher' who ridiculed with genial mockery in his poems and novels almost every political and social foible of his time; who similarly caricatured in his pages many notable contemporaries, though directing his satire 'not so much at individuals as at crotchets.' His fantastical-satirical novels hold a unique place in English literature; they are at once scholarly, pungent, entertaining, and 'an illuminating commentary of the Romantic period upon itself.' Their style is always piquant and attractive. Shelley justly praised 'the lightness, strength, and chastity' of Peacock's diction which seems always nimbly to serve his wit. Scattered throughout the novels are admirable ballads and songs, for the most part jovial and mocking, though sometimes serious. Peacock has given us at least one love lyric of delicate tenderness; and he is an acknowledged master of the English drinking song.

BENEATH THE CYPRESS SHADE

I DUG, beneath the cypress shade,
  What well might seem an elfin's grave;
And every pledge in earth I laid,
  That erst thy false affection gave.

I pressed them down the sod beneath;
  I placed one mossy stone above;
And twined the rose's fading wreath
  Around the sepulchre of love.

Frail as thy love, the flowers were dead,
  Ere yet the evening sun was set;   10
But years shall see the cypress spread,
  Immutable as my regret.

1806

IN HIS LAST BINN SIR PETER LIES

From HEADLONG HALL

[SUNG BY MR. CHROMATIC]

IN his last binn SIR PETER lies,
  Who knew not what it was to frown:
Death took him mellow, by surprise,
  And in his cellar stopped him down.
Through all our land we could not boast
  A knight more gay, more prompt than he,
To rise and fill a bumper toast,
  And pass it round with THREE TIMES
    THREE.

None better knew the feast to sway,
  Or keep Mirth's boat in better trim;   10
For Nature had but little clay
  Like that of which she moulded him.
The meanest guest that graced his board
  Was there the freest of the free,
His bumper toast when PETER poured,
  And passed it round with THREE TIMES
    THREE.

He kept at true good humour's mark
  The social flow of pleasure's tide:
He never made a brow look dark,
  Nor caused a tear, but when he died.   20
No sorrow round his tomb should dwell:
  More pleased his gay old ghost would be,
For funeral song and passing bell,
  To hear no sound but THREE TIMES
    THREE.

1816

FOR THE SLENDER BEECH AND THE SAPLING OAK

From MAID MARIAN

FOR the slender beech and the sapling oak
  That grow by the shadowy rill,
You may cut down both at a single stroke,
  You may cut down which you will.

But this you must know, that as long as they
    grow,
  Whatever change may be,
You never can teach either oak or beech
  To be aught but a greenwood tree.

1822

THE WAR SONG OF DINAS VAWR[1]

From THE MISFORTUNES OF ELPHIN

The *War Song of Dinas Vawr* is the quintessence of all war-songs that ever were written, and the sum and substance of all appetencies, tendencies, and consequences of military.—(Peacock.)

THE mountain sheep are sweeter,
But the valley sheep are fatter;
We therefore deemed it meeter
To carry off the latter.
We made an expedition;
We met an host and quelled it;
We forced a strong position
And killed the men who held it.

On Dyfed's[2] richest valley,
Where herds of kine were browsing,   10
We made a mighty sally,
To furnish our carousing.
Fierce warriors rushed to meet us;
We met them, and o'erthrew them;
They struggled hard to beat us,
But we conquered them, and slew them.

As we drove our prize at leisure,
The king marched forth to catch us:
His rage surpassed all measure,
But his people could not match us.   20
He fled to his hall-pillars;
And, ere our force we led off,
Some sacked his house and cellars,
While others cut his head off.

We there, in strife bewildering,
Spilt blood enough to swim in:

---

1 a petty Welsh king in the time of King Arthur.
2 Dyfed was an old British name of a region in southwestern Wales (now Pembrokeshire).

We orphaned many children
And widowed many women.
The eagles and the ravens
We glutted with our foemen: 30
The heroes and the cravens,
The spearmen and the bowmen.

We brought away from battle,
And much their land bemoaned them,
Two thousand head of cattle
And the head of him who owned them:
Ednyfed, King of Dyfed,
His head was borne before us;
His wine and beasts supplied our feasts,
And his overthrow, our chorus.   40

1829

From NIGHTMARE ABBEY

[*Nightmare Abbey*, the most amusing of Peacock's novels, is a lively satire on Byronism, transcendentalism, and romantic affectation. The farcical story concerns an odd band of humorists brought together at a country house, who spend their time in matchmaking, dining, singing, and conversing. The company include Mr. Christopher Glowry, his son Scythrop, and Mr. Toobad, all pessimists of various shades; Mr. Flosky, a caricature of Coleridge, and Mr. Cypress, of Byron; and Mr. Hilary, 'a very cheerful and elastic gentleman,' who stands for Peacock's point of view. Scythrop, who cannot make up his mind to choose between one or the other of two young ladies, is a caricature of Shelley. Peacock stated in a letter to Shelley that the purpose of *Nightmare Abbey* was 'to bring into philosophical focus a few of the morbidities of modern literature, and to let in a little daylight on its atrabilious complexion.']

NIGHTMARE ABBEY, a venerable family mansion, in a highly picturesque state of semi-dilapidation, pleasantly situated on a strip of dry land between the sea and the fens, at the verge of the county of Lincoln, had the honour to be the seat of Christopher Glowry, Esquire.[1] This gentleman was naturally of an atrabilarious temperament, and much troubled with those phantoms of indigestion which are commonly called *blue devils*. He had been deceived in an early friendship: he had been crossed in love; and had offered his hand, from pique, to a lady, who accepted it from interest, and who, in so doing, violently tore asunder the bonds of a tried and youthful attachment. Her vanity was gratified by being the mistress of a very extensive, if not very lively, establishment; but all the springs of her sympathies were frozen. Riches she possessed, but that which

enriches them, the participation of affection, was wanting. All that they could purchase for her became indifferent to her, because that which they could not purchase, and which was more valuable than themselves, she had, for their sake, thrown away. She discovered, when it was too late, that she had mistaken the means for the end—that riches, rightly used, are instruments of happiness, but are not in themselves happiness. In this wilful blight of her affections, she found them valueless as means: they had been the end to which she had immolated all her affections, and were now the only end that remained to her. She did not confess this to herself as a principle of action, but it operated through the medium of unconscious self-deception, and terminated in inveterate avarice. She laid on external things the blame of her mind's internal disorder, and thus became by degrees an accomplished scold. She often went her daily rounds through a series of deserted apartments, every creature in the house vanishing at the creak of her shoe, much more at the sound of her voice, to which the nature of things affords no simile; for, as far as the voice of woman, when attuned by gentleness and love, transcends all other sounds in harmony, so far does it surpass all others in discord, when stretched into unnatural shrillness by anger and impatience.

Mr. Glowry used to say that his house was no better than a spacious kennel, for every one in it led the life of a dog. Disappointed both in love and in friendship, and looking upon human learning as vanity, he had come to a conclusion that there was but one good thing in the world, *videlicet*, a good dinner; and this his parsimonious lady seldom suffered him to enjoy: but, one morning, like Sir Leoline in *Christabel*, 'he woke and found his lady dead,' and remained a very consolate widower, with one small child.

This only son and heir Mr. Glowry had christened Scythrop, from the name of a maternal ancestor, who had hanged himself one rainy day in a fit of *taedium vitae*,[2] and had been eulogized by a coroner's jury in the comprehensive phrase of *felo de se;* on which account, Mr. Glowry held his memory in high honour, and made a punchbowl of his skull.

When Scythrop grew up, he was sent, as usual, to a public school, where a little learning was painfully beaten into him, and from thence to the university, where it was carefully taken out of him; and he was sent home like a well-threshed ear of corn,[3] with nothing in his head:

---

1 perhaps intended in some respects to resemble Sir Timothy Shelley, the poet's father.

2 ennui.   3 wheat.

having finished his education to the high satisfaction of the master and fellows of his college,
who had, in testimony of their approbation, presented him with a silver fish-slice, on which his
name figured at the head of a laudatory inscription in some semi-barbarous dialect of Anglo-
Saxonized Latin.

His fellow-students, however, who drove tan-
dem and random in great perfection, and were
connoisseurs in good inns, had taught him to
drink deep ere he departed. He had passed much
of his time with these choice spirits, and had seen
the rays of the midnight lamp tremble on many a
lengthening file of empty bottles. He passed his
vacations sometimes at Nightmare Abbey, sometimes in London, at the house of his uncle, Mr.
Hilary, a very cheerful and elastic gentleman,
who had married the sister of the melancholy
Mr. Glowry. The company that frequented his
house was the gayest of the gay. Scythrop danced
with the ladies and drank with the gentlemen,
and was pronounced by both a very accomplished charming fellow, and an honour to the
university.

At the house of Mr. Hilary, Scythrop first saw
the beautiful Miss Emily Girouette. He fell in
love; which is nothing new. He was favourably
received; which is nothing strange. Mr. Glowry
and Mr. Girouette had a meeting on the occasion, and quarrelled about the terms of the bargain; which is neither new nor strange. The
lovers were torn asunder, weeping and vowing
everlasting constancy; and, in three weeks after
this tragical event, the lady was led a smiling
bride to the altar, by the Honourable Mr. Lack-
wit; which is neither strange nor new.

Scythrop received this intelligence at Nightmare Abbey, and was half distracted on the occasion. It was his first disappointment, and
prayed deply on his sensitive spirit. His father, to
comfort him, read him a Commentary on Ecclesiastes, which he had himself composed, and which
demonstrated incontrovertibly that all is vanity. . . .

Family interests compelled Mr. Glowry to
receive occasional visits from Mr. and Mrs.
Hilary, who paid them from the same motive;
and, as the lively gentleman on these occasions
found few conductors for his exuberant gaiety,
he became like a double-charged electric jar,
which often exploded in some burst of outrageous merriment, to the signal discomposure of
Mr. Glowry's nerves.

Another occasional visitor, much more to Mr.
Glowry's taste, was Mr. Flosky, a very lachry-
mose and morbid gentleman, of some note in the
literary world, but in his own estimation of much
more merit than name. The part of his character
which recommended him to Mr. Glowry was his
very fine sense of the grim and the tearful. No
one could relate a dismal story with so many
minutiae of supererogatory wretchedness. No
one could call up a *raw head and bloody bones*
with so many adjuncts and circumstances of
ghastliness. Mystery was his mental element. He
lived in the midst of that visionary world in
which nothing is but what is not. He dreamed
with his eyes open, and saw ghosts dancing
round him at noontide. He had been in his youth
an enthusiast for liberty, and had hailed the dawn
of the French Revolution as the promise of a day
that was to banish war and slavery, and every
form of vice and misery, from the face of the
earth. Because all this was not done, he deduced
that nothing was done; and from this deduction,
according to his system of logic, he drew a conclusion that worse than nothing was done; that
the overthrow of the feudal fortresses of tyranny
and superstition was the greatest calamity that
had ever befallen mankind; and that their only
hope now was to rake the rubbish together, and
rebuild it without any of those loopholes by
which the light had originally crept in. To qualify
himself for a coadjutor in this laudable task, he
plunged into the central opacity of Kantian
metaphysics, and lay *perdu* several years in transcendental darkness, till the common daylight of
common-sense became intolerable to his eyes. He
called the sun an *ignis fatuus;* and exhorted all
who would listen to his friendly voice, which
were about as many as called 'God save King
Richard,' to shelter themselves from its delusive
radiance in the obscure haunt of Old Philosophy. This word Old had great charms for him.
The good old times were always on his lips;
meaning the days when polemic theology was
in its prime, and rival prelates beat the drum
ecclesiastic with Herculean vigour, till the
one wound up his series of syllogisms with
the very orthodox conclusion of roasting the
other.

But the dearest friend of Mr. Glowry, and his
most welcome guest, was Mr. Toobad,[4] the
Manichaean Millenarian. The twelfth verse of
the twelfth chapter of Revelation was always in
his mouth: 'Woe to the inhabiters of the earth
and of the sea! for the devil is come among you,
having great wrath, because he knoweth that he
hath but a short time.' He maintained that the supreme dominion of the world was, for wise purposes, given over for a while to the Evil Principle;

4 J. F. Newton, crackpot astrologer of Bracknell.

and that this precise period of time, commonly called the enlightened age, was the point of his plenitude of power. He used to add that by and by he would be cast down, and a high and happy order of things succeed; but he never omitted the saving clause, 'Not in our time': which last words were always echoed in doleful response by the sympathetic Mr. Glowry.

Shortly after the disastrous termination of Scythrop's passion for Miss Emily Girouette, Mr. Glowry found himself, much against his will, involved in a lawsuit, which compelled him to dance attendance on the High Court of Chancery. Scythrop was left alone at Nightmare Abbey. He was a burnt child, and dreaded the fire of female eyes. He wandered about the ample pile, or along the garden terrace, with 'his cogitative faculties immersed in cogibundity of cogitation.' The terrace terminated at the southwestern tower, which, as we have said, was ruinous and full of owls. Here would Scythrop take his evening seat on a fallen fragment of mossy stone, with his back resting against the ruined wall,—a thick canopy of ivy, with an owl in it, over his head,—and the *Sorrows of Werter*[5] in his hand. He had some taste for romance-reading before he went to the university, where, we must confess, in justice to his college, he was cured of the love of reading in all its shapes; and the cure would have been radical, if disappointment in love, and total solitude, had not conspired to bring on a relapse. He began to devour romances and German tragedies, and, by the recommendation of Mr. Flosky, to pore over ponderous tomes of transcendental philosophy, which reconciled him to the labour of studying them by their mystical jargon and necromantic imagery. In the congenial solitude of Nightmare Abbey, the distempered ideas of metaphysical romance and romantic metaphysics had ample time and space to germinate into a fertile crop of chimeras, which rapidly shot up into vigorous and abundant vegetation.

He now became troubled with the *passion for reforming the world*. He built many castles in the air, and peopled them with secret tribunals, and bands of illuminati, who were always the imaginary instruments of his projected regeneration of the human species. As he intended to institute a perfect republic, he invested himself with absolute sovereignty over these mystical dispensers of liberty. He slept with Horrid Mysteries under his pillow, and dreamed of venerable eleuther-archs[6]

and ghastly confederates holding midnight conventions in subterranean caves. He passed whole mornings in his study, immersed in gloomy reverie, stalking about the room in his nightcap, which he pulled over his eyes like a cowl, and folding his striped calico dressing-gown about him like the mantle of a conspirator.

'Action,' thus he soliloquized, 'is the result of opinion, and to new-model opinion would be to new-model society. Knowledge is power; it is in the hands of a few, who employ it to mislead the many, for their own selfish purposes of aggrandizement and appropriation. What if it were in the hands of a few who should employ it to lead the many? What if it were universal, and the multitude were enlightened? No. The many must be always in leading-strings; but let them have wise and honest conductors. A few to think, and many to act; that is the only basis of perfect society. So thought the ancient philosophers: they had their esoterical and exoterical doctrines. So thinks the sublime Kant, who delivers his oracles in language which none but the initiated can comprehend. Such were the views of those secret associations of illuminati, which were the terror of superstition and tyranny, and which, carefully selecting wisdom and genius from the great wilderness of society, as the bee selects honey from the flowers of the thorn and the nettle, bound all human excellence in a chain, which, if it had not been prematurely broken, would have commanded opinion, and regenerated the world.'

Scythrop proceeded to meditate on the practicability of reviving a confederation of regenerators. To get a clear view of his own ideas, and to feel the pulse of the wisdom and genius of the age, he wrote and published a treatise, in which his meanings were carefully wrapt up in the monk's hood of transcendental technology, but filled with hints of matter deep and dangerous, which he thought would set the whole nation in a ferment; and he awaited the result in awful expectation, as a miner who has fired a train awaits the explosion of a rock. However, he listened and heard nothing; for the explosion, if any ensued, was not sufficiently loud to shake a single leaf of the ivy on the towers of Nightmare Abbey; and some months afterwards he received a letter from his bookseller, informing him that only seven copies had been sold, and concluding with a polite request for the balance.

Scythrop did not despair. 'Seven copies,' he thought, 'have been sold. Seven is a mystical number, and the omen is good. Let me find the seven purchasers of my seven copies, and they

5 a romance by Goethe, published in 1774.
6 chiefs of an imaginary society.

shall be the seven golden candlesticks with which I will illuminate the world.'

Scythrop had a certain portion of mechanical genius, which his romantic projects tended to develop. He constructed models of cells and recesses, sliding panels and secret passages, that would have baffled the skill of the Parisian police. He took the opportunity of his father's absence to smuggle a dumb carpenter into the Abbey, and between them they gave reality to one of these models in Scythrop's tower. Scythrop foresaw that a great leader of human regeneration would be involved in fearful dilemmas, and determined, for the benefit of mankind in general, to adopt all possible precautions for the preservation of himself.

The servants, even the women, had been tutored into silence. Profound stillness reigned throughout and around the Abbey, except when the occasional shutting of a door would peal in long reverberations through the galleries, or the heavy tread of the pensive butler would wake the hollow echoes of the hall. Scythrop stalked about like the grand inquisitor, and the servants flitted past him like familiars. In his evening meditations on the terrace, under the ivy of the ruined tower, the only sounds that came to his ear were the rustling of the wind in the ivy, the plaintive voices of the feathered choristers, the owls, the occasional striking of the Abbey clock, and the monotonous dash of the sea on its low and level shore. In the meantime, he drank Madeira, and laid deep schemes for a thorough repair of the crazy fabric of human nature.

Miss Marionetta Celestina O'Carroll was a very blooming and accomplished young lady. Being a compound of the *Allegro Vivace* of the O'Carrolls, and of the *Andante Doloroso* of the Glowrys, she exhibited in her own character all the diversities of an April sky. Her hair was light-brown; her eyes hazel, and sparkling with a mild but fluctuating light; her features regular; her lips full, and of equal size; and her person surpassingly graceful. She was a proficient in music. Her conversation was sprightly, but always on subjects light in their nature and limited in their interest: for moral sympathies, in any general sense, had no place in her mind. She had some coquetry, and more caprice, liking and disliking almost in the same moment; pursuing an object with earnestness while it seemed unattainable, and rejecting it when in her power as not worth the trouble of possession.

Whether she was touched with a *penchant* for her cousin Scythrop, or was merely curious to see what effect the tender passion would have on so *outré* a person, she had not been three days in the Abbey before she threw out all the lures of her beauty and accomplishments to make a prize of his heart. Scythrop proved an easy conquest. The image of Miss Emily Girouette was already sufficiently dimmed by the power of philosophy and the exercise of reason: for to these influences, or to any influence but the true one, are usually ascribed the mental cures performed by the great physician Time. Scythrop's romantic dreams had indeed given him many *pure anticipated cognitions* of combinations of beauty and intelligence, which, he had some misgivings, were not exactly realized in his cousin Marionetta; but, in spite of these misgivings, he soon became distractedly in love; which when the young lady clearly perceived, she altered her tactics, and assumed as much coldness and reserve as she had before shown ardent and ingenuous attachment.

Marionetta observed the next day a remarkable perturbation in Scythrop, for which she could not imagine any probable cause. She was willing to believe at first that it had some transient and trifling source, and would pass off in a day or two; but, contrary to this expectation, it daily increased. She was well aware that Scythrop had a strong tendency to the love of mystery, for its own sake; that is to say, he would employ mystery to serve a purpose, but would first choose his purpose by its capability of mystery. He seemed now to have more mystery on his hands than the laws of the system allowed, and to wear his coat of darkness with an air of great discomfort. All her little playful arts lost by degrees much of their power either to irritate or to soothe; and the first perception of her diminished influence produced in her an immediate depression of spirits, and a consequent sadness of demeanour, that rendered her very interesting to Mr. Glowry; who, duly considering the improbability of accomplishing his wishes with respect to Miss Toobad (which improbability naturally increased in the diurnal ratio of that young lady's absence), began to reconcile himself by degrees to the idea of Marionetta being his daughter.

Marionetta made many ineffectual attempts to extract from Scythrop the secret of his mystery; and, in despair of drawing it from himself, began to form hopes that she might find a clue to it from Mr. Flosky, who was Scythrop's dearest friend, and was more frequently than any other person admitted to his solitary tower. Mr. Flosky, however, had ceased to be visible in a morning. He was engaged in the composition of a dismal ballad; and, Marionetta's uneasiness overcoming her scruples of decorum, she determined to seek him in the apartment which he had chosen for his study. She tapped at the door, and at the sound 'Come in,' entered the apartment. It was noon, and the sun was shining in full splendour, much to the annoyance of Mr. Flosky, who had obviated the inconvenience by closing the shutters, and drawing the window-curtains. He was sitting at his table by the light of a solitary candle, with a pen in one hand, and a muffineer[7] in the other, with which he occasionally sprinkled salt on the wick, to make it burn blue. He sate with 'his eye in a fine frenzy rolling,' and turned his inspired gaze on Marionetta as if she had been the ghostly ladie of a magical vision; then placed his hand before his eyes, with an appearance of manifest pain —shook his head—withdrew his hand—rubbed his eyes, like a waking man—and said, in a tone of ruefulness most jeremitaylorically[8] pathetic, 'To what am I to attribute this very unexpected pleasure, my dear Miss O'Carroll?'

Marionetta. I must apologise for intruding on you, Mr. Flosky; but the interest which I—you— take in my cousin Scythrop—

Mr. Flosky. Pardon me, Miss O'Carroll; I do not take any interest in any person or thing on the face of the earth; which sentiment, if you analyse it, you will find to be the quintessence of the most refined philanthropy.

Marionetta. I will take it for granted that it is so, Mr. Flosky; I am not conversant with metaphysical subleties, but—

Mr. Flosky. Subleties! my dear Miss O'Carroll. I am sorry to find you participating in the vulgar error of the *reading public,* to whom an unusual collocation of words, involving a juxtaposition of antiperistatical ideas, immediately suggests the notion of hyperoxysophistical paradoxology.

Marionetta. Indeed, Mr. Flosky, it suggests no such notion to me. I have sought you for the purpose of obtaining information.

Mr. Flosky (shaking his head). No one ever sought me for such a purpose before.

Marionetta. I think, Mr. Flosky—that is, I believe—that is, I fancy—that is, I imagine—

Mr. Flosky. The τουτεστι , the *id est,* the *cioè,* the *c'est à dire,* the *that is,* my dear Miss O'Carroll, is not applicable in this case—if you will permit me to take the liberty of saying so. Think is not synonymous with believe—for belief, in many most important particulars, results from the total absence, the absolute negation of thought, and is thereby the sane and orthodox condition of mind; and thought and belief are both essentially different from fancy, and fancy, again, is distinct from imagination. This distinction between fancy and imagination is one of the most abstruse and important points of metaphysics. I have written seven hundred pages of promise to elucidate it, which promise I shall keep as faithfully as the bank will its promise to pay.

Marionetta. I assure you, Mr. Flosky, I care no more about metaphysics than I do about the bank; and, if you will condescend to talk to a simple girl in intelligible terms—

Mr. Flosky. Say not condescend! Know you not that you talk to the most humble of men, to one who has buckled on the armour of sanctity, and clothed himself with humility as with a garment?

Marionetta. My cousin Scythrop has of late had an air of mystery about him, which gives me great uneasiness.

Mr. Flosky. That is strange: nothing is so becoming to a man as an air of mystery. Mystery is the very keystone of all that is beautiful in poetry, all that is sacred in faith, and all that is recondite in transcendental psychology. I am writing a ballad which is all mystery; it is such stuff as dreams are made of, and is, indeed, stuff made of a dream; for last night I fell asleep as usual over my book, and had a vision of pure reason. I composed five hundred lines in my sleep; so that, having had a dream of a ballad, I am now officiating as my own Peter Quince,[9] and making a ballad of my dream, and it shall be called Bottom's Dream,[10] because it has no bottom.

Marionetta. I see, Mr. Flosky, you think my intrusion unseasonable, and are inclined to punish it, by talking nonsense to me. (*Mr. Flosky gave a start at the word nonsense, which almost overturned the table.*) I assure you, I would not have intruded if I had not been very much interested in the question I wished to ask you.—(*Mr. Flosky listened in sullen dignity.*)—My cousin Scythrop seems to have some secret preying on his mind.—(*Mr. Flosky was silent.*)—He seems very unhappy— Mr. Flosky.—Perhaps you are acquainted with the cause.—(*Mr. Flosky was still silent.*)—I only wish to know—Mr. Flosky—if it is anything—

---

7 a dish for keeping muffins hot.
8 in the manner of Jeremy Taylor, seventeenth-century divine noted for the elaborate eloquence of his style.

9 a carpenter and the director of the tradesmen's play in *Midsummer Night's Dream.*
10 Nick Bottom was a weaver in the same play upon whom Puck put an ass's head.

that could be remedied by anything—that any one—of whom I know anything—could do.

Mr. Flosky (*after a pause*). There are various ways of getting at secrets. The most approved methods, as recommended both theoretically and practically in philosophical novels, are eaves-dropping at keyholes, picking the locks of chests and desks, peeping into letters, steaming wafers, and insinuating hot wire under sealing wax; none of which methods I hold it lawful to practice.

Marionetta. Surely, Mr. Flosky, you cannot suspect me of wishing to adopt or encourage such base and contemptible arts.

Mr. Flosky. Yet are they recommended, and with well-strung reasons, by writers of gravity and note, as simple and easy methods of study-ing character, and gratifying that laudable curi-osity which aims at the knowledge of man.

Marionetta. I am as ignorant of this morality which you do not approve, as of the metaphysics which you do: I should be glad to know, by your means, what is the matter with my cousin; I do not like to see him unhappy, and I suppose there is some reason for it.

Mr. Flosky. Now I should rather suppose there is no reason for it: it is the fashion to be unhappy. To have a reason for being so would be exceed-ingly commonplace: to be so without any is the province of genius: the art of being miserable for misery's sake has been brought to great perfec-tion in our days; and the ancient Odyssey, which held forth a shining example of the endurance of real misfortune, will give place to a modern one, setting out a more instructive picture of queru-lous impatience under imaginary evils.

Marionetta. Will you oblige me, Mr. Flosky, by giving me a plain answer to a plain question?

Mr. Flosky. It is impossible, my dear Miss O'Carroll. I never gave a plain answer to a ques-tion in my life.

Marionetta. Do you, or do you not, know what is the matter with my cousin?

Mr. Flosky.—To say that I do not know, would be to say that I am ignorant of something; and God forbid that a transcendental metaphysician, who has pure anticipated cognitions of every-thing, and carries the whole science of geometry in his head without ever having looked into Eu-clid, should fall into so empirical an error as to declare himself ignorant of anything: to say that I do not know, would be to pretend to positive and circumstantial knowledge touching present matter of fact, which, when you consider the na-ture of evidence, and the various lights in which the same thing may be seen—

Marionetta. I see, Mr. Flosky, that either you have no information, or are determined not to impart it; and I beg your pardon for having given you this unnecessary trouble.

Mr. Flosky. My dear Miss O'Carroll, it would have given me great pleasure to have said any-thing that would have given you pleasure; but if any person living could make report of having obtained any information on any subject from Ferdinando Flosky, my transcendental reputa-tion would be ruined forever.

.   .   .

Scythrop, attending one day the summons to dinner, found in the drawing-room his friend Mr. Cypress the poet, whom he had known at college, and who was a great favourite of Mr. Glowry. Mr. Cypress said he was on the point of leaving England, but could not think of doing so without a farewell look at Nightmare Abbey and his re-spected friends, the moody Mr. Glowry and the mysterious Mr. Scythrop, the sublime Mr. Flosky and the pathetic Mr. Listless;[11] to all of whom, and the morbid hospitality of the melancholy dwelling in which they were then assembled, he assured them he should always look back with as much affection as his lacerated spirit could feel for anything. The sympathetic condolence of their respective replies was cut short by Raven's announcement of 'dinner on table.'

The conversation that took place when the wine was in circulation, and the ladies were with-drawn, we shall report with our usual scrupulous fidelity.

Mr. Glowry. You are leaving England, Mr. Cy-press. There is a delightful melancholy in saying farewell to an old acquaintance, when the chances are twenty to one against ever meeting again. A smiling bumper to a sad parting, and let us all be unhappy together.

Mr. Cypress (*filling a bumper*). This is the only social habit that the disappointed spirit never un-learns.

The Reverend Mr. Larynx (*filling*). It is the only piece of academical learning that the finished educatee retains.

Mr. Flosky (*filling*). It is the only objective fact which the sceptic can realize.

Scythrop (*filling*). It is the only styptic for a bleeding heart.

The Honourable Mr. Listless (*filling*). It is the only trouble that is very well worth taking.

---

11 Sir Lamley Skeffington, a contemporary dandy and social ar-biter of the time.

Mr. Asterias (*filling*). It is the only key of conversational truth.

Mr. Toobad (*filling*). It is the only antidote to the great wrath of the devil.

Mr. Hilary (*filling*). It is the only symbol of perfect life. The inscription 'HIC NON BIBITUR'[12] will suit nothing but a tombstone.

Mr. Glowry. You will see many fine old ruins, Mr. Cypress; crumbling pillars, and mossy walls—many a one-legged Venus and headless Minerva—many a Neptune buried in sand—many a Jupiter turned topsy-turvy—many a perforated Bacchus doing duty as a water-pipe—many reminiscences of the ancient world, which I hope was better worth living in than the modern; though, for myself, I care not a straw more for one than the other, and would not go twenty miles to see anything that either could show.

Mr. Cypress. It is something to seek, Mr. Glowry. The mind is restless, and must persist in seeking, though to find is to be disappointed. Do you feel no aspirations towards the countries of Socrates and Cicero? No wish to wander among the venerable remains of the greatness that has passed forever?

Mr. Glowry. Not a grain.

Scythrop. It is, indeed, much the same as if a lover should dig up the buried form of his mistress, and gaze upon relics which are anything but herself, to wander among a few mouldy ruins, that are only imperfect indexes to lost volumes of glory, and meet at every step the more melancholy ruins of human nature—a degenerate race of stupid and shrivelled slaves, grovelling in the lowest depths of servility and superstition.

The Honourable Mr. Listless. It is the fashion to go abroad. I have thought of it myself, but am hardly equal to the exertion. To be sure, a little eccentricity and originality are allowable in some cases; and the most eccentric and original of all characters is an Englishman who stays at home.

Scythrop. I should have no pleasure in visiting countries that are past all hope of regeneration. There is great hope of our own; and it seems to me that an Englishman, who, either by his station in society, or by his genius, or (as in your instance, Mr. Cypress) by both, has the power of essentially serving his country in its arduous struggle with its domestic enemies, yet forsakes his country, which is still so rich in hope, to dwell in others which are only fertile in the ruins of memory, does what none of those ancients, whose fragmentary memorials you venerate, would have done in similar circumstances.

Mr. Cypress. Sir, I have quarrelled with my wife; and a man who has quarrelled with his wife is absolved from all duty to his country. I have written an ode to tell the people as much, and they may take it as they list.

Scythrop. Do you suppose, if Brutus had quarrelled with his wife, he would have given it as a reason to Cassius for having nothing to do with his enterprise? Or would Cassius have been satisfied with such an excuse?

Mr. Flosky. Brutus was a senator; so is our dear friend: but the cases are different. Brutus had some hope of political good: Mr. Cypress has none. How should he, after what we have seen in France?

Scythrop. A Frenchman is born in harness, ready saddled, bitted, and bridled, for any tyrant to ride. He will fawn under his rider one moment, and throw him and kick him to death the next; but another adventurer springs on his back, and by dint of whip and spur on he goes as before. We may, without much vanity, hope better of ourselves.

Mr. Cypress. I have no hope for myself or for others. Our life is a false nature; it is not in the harmony of things; it is an all-blasting upas, whose root is earth, and whose leaves are the skies which rain their poison-dews upon mankind. We wither from our youth; we gasp with unslaked thirst for unattainable good; lured from the first to the last by phantoms—love, fame, ambition, avarice—all idle, and all ill—one meteor of many names, that vanishes in the smoke of death.[13]

Mr. Flosky. A most delightful speech, Mr. Cypress. A most most amiable and instructive philosophy. You have only to impress its truth on the minds of all living men, and life will then, indeed, be the desert and the solitude; and I must do you, myself, and our mutual friends, the justice to observe, that let society only give fair play at one and the same time, as I flatter myself it is inclined to do, to your system of morals, and my system of metaphysics, and Scythrop's system of politics, and Mr. Listless's system of manners, and Mr. Toobad's system of religion, and the result will be as fine a mental chaos as even the immortal Kant himself could ever have hoped to see; in the prospect of which I rejoice.

Mr. Hilary. 'Certainly, ancient, it is not a thing to rejoice at': I am one of those who cannot see the good that is to result from all this mystifying and blue-devilling of society. The contrast it presents to the cheerful and solid wisdom of an-

---

12 'Here is no drinking.'

13 *Childe Harold*, IV, cxxiv, cxxvi.—(Peacock.)

tiquity is too forcible not to strike any one who has the least knowledge of classical literature. To represent vice and misery as the necessary accompaniments of genius, is as mischievous as it is false, and the feeling is as unclassical as the language in which it is usually expressed.

Mr. Toobad. It is our calamity. The devil has come among us, and has begun by taking possession of all the cleverest fellows. Yet, forsooth, this is the enlightened age. Marry, how? Did our ancestors go peeping about with dark lanterns, and do we walk at our ease in broad sunshine? Where is the manifestation of our light? By what symptoms do you recognize it? What are its signs, its tokens, its symptoms, its symbols, its categories, its conditions? What is it, and why? How, where, when is it to be seen, felt, and understood? What do we see by it which our ancestors saw not, and which at the same time is worth seeing? We see a hundred men hanged, where they saw one. We see five hundred transported, where they saw one. We see five thousand in the workhouse, where they saw one. We see scores of Bible Societies, where they saw none. We see paper, where they saw gold. We see men in stays, where they saw men in armour. We see painted faces, where they saw healthy ones. We see children perishing in manufactories, where they saw them flourishing in the fields. We see prisons, where they saw castles. We see masters, where they saw representatives. In short, they saw true men, where we see false knaves. They saw Milton, and we see Mr. Sackbut.[14]

Mr. Flosky. The false knave, sir, is my honest friend; therefore, I beseech you, let him be countenanced. God forbid but a knave should have some countenance at his friend's request.

Mr. Toobad. 'Good men and true,' was their common term, like the καλος κάγαθος[15] of the Athenians. It is so long since men have been either good or true, that it is to be questioned which is most obsolete, the fact or the phraseology.

Mr. Cypress. There is no worth nor beauty but in the mind's idea. Love sows the wind and reaps the whirlwind.[16] Confusion, thrice confounded, is the portion of him who rests even for an instant on that most brittle of reeds—the affection of a human being. The sum of our social destiny is to inflict or to endure.[17]

Mr. Hilary. Rather to bear and forbear, Mr.

Cypress—a maxim which you perhaps despise. Ideal beauty is not the mind's creation: it is real beauty, refined and purified in the mind's alembic, from the alloy which always more or less accompanies it in our mixed and imperfect nature. But still the gold exists in a very ample degree. To expect too much is a disease in the expectant, for which human nature is not responsible; and, in the common name of humanity, I protest against these false and mischievous ravings. To rail against humanity for not being abstract perfection, and against human love for not realizing all the splendid visions of the poets of chivalry, is to rail at the summer for not being all sunshine, and at the rose for not being always in bloom.

Mr. Cypress. Human love! Love is not an inhabitant of the earth. We worship him as the Athenians did their unknown God: but broken hearts are the martyrs of his faith, and the eye shall never see the form which phantasy paints, and which passion pursues through paths of delusive beauty, among flowers whose odours are agonies, and trees whose gums are poison.[18]

Mr. Hilary. You talk like a Rosicrucian, who will love nothing but a sylph, who does not believe in the existence of a sylph, and who yet quarrels with the whole universe for not containing a sylph.

Mr. Cypress. The mind is diseased of its own beauty, and fevers into false creation. The forms which the sculptor's soul has seized exist only in himself.[19]

Mr. Flosky. Permit me to discept. They are the mediums of common forms combined and arranged into a common standard. The ideal beauty of the Helen of Zeuxis was the combined medium of the real beauty of the virgins of Crotona.[20]

Mr. Hilary. But to make ideal beauty the shadow in the water, and, like the dog in the fable, to throw away the substance in catching at the shadow, is scarcely the characteristic of wisdom, whatever it may be of genius. To reconcile man as he is to the world as it is, to preserve and improve all that is good, and destroy or alleviate all that is evil, in physical and moral nature— have been the hope and aim of the greatest teachers and ornaments of our species. I will say, too, that the highest wisdom and the highest genius have been invariably accompanied with cheerfulness. We have sufficient proofs on record that

---

14 Robert Southey.
15 beauty of outward form, i. e. of persons.
16 *Childe Harold*, IV, cxxiii.—(Peacock.)
17 Ibid. III, lxxi.—(Peacock.)

18 Ibid. IV, cxxi, cxxxvi.—(Peacock.)
19 Ibid. IV, cxxii.—(Peacock.)
20 The most beautiful virgins of the Greek city of Crotona were said to have served collectively as models for the artist Zeuxis (fifth century B.C.), when he painted his celebrated picture of Helen of Troy.

Shakespeare and Socrates were the most festive of companions. But now the little wisdom and genius we have seem to be entering into a conspiracy against cheerfulness.

Mr. Toobad. How can we be cheerful with the devil among us?

The Honourable Mr. Listless. How can we be cheerful when our nerves are shattered?

Mr. Flosky. How can we be cheerful when we are surrounded by a *reading public,* that is growing too wise for its betters?

Scythrop. How can we be cheerful when our great general designs are crossed every moment by our little particular passions?

Mr. Cypress. How can we be cheerful in the midst of disappointment and despair?

Mr. Glowry. Let us all be unhappy together.

Mr. Hilary. Let us sing a catch.

Mr. Glowry. No: a nice tragical ballad. The Norfolk Tragedy to the tune of the Hundredth Psalm.

Mr. Hilary. I say a catch.

Mr. Glowry. I say no. A song from Mr. Cypress.

All. A song from Mr. Cypress.

Mr. Cypress sang—

There is a fever of the spirit,
    The brand of Cain's unresting doom,
Which in the lone dark souls that bear it
    Glows like the lamp in Tullia's tomb:
Unlike that lamp, its subtle fire
    Burns, blasts, consumes its cell, the heart,
Till, one by one, hope, joy, desire,
    Like dreams of shadowy smoke depart.

When hope, love, life itself, are only
    Dust—spectral memories—dead and cold—
The unfed fire burns bright and lonely,
    Like that undying lamp of old:
And by that drear illumination,
    Till time its clay-built home has rent,
Thought broods on feeling's desolation—
    The soul is its own monument.

Mr. Glowry. Admirable. Let us all be unhappy together.

Mr. Hilary. Now, I say again, a catch.

The Reverend Mr. Larynx. I am for you.

Mr. Hilary. 'Seamen three.'

The Reverend Mr. Larynx. Agreed. I'll be Harry Gill, with the voice of three. Begin.

Mr. Hilary and the Reverend Mr. Larynx.—

Seamen three! What men be ye?
Gotham's three wise men we be.
Whither in your bowl so free?

To rake the moon from out the sea.
The bowl goes trim. The moon doth shine.
And our ballast is old wine;
And your ballast is old wine.

Who art thou, so fast adrift?
I am he they call Old Care.
Here on board we will thee lift.
No: I may not enter there.
Wherefore so? 'Tis Jove's decree,
In a bowl Care may not be;
In a bowl Care may not be.

Fear ye not the waves that roll?
No: in charmed bowl we swim.
What the charm that floats the bowl?
Water may not pass the brim.
The bowl goes trim. The moon doth shine.
And our ballast is old wine;
And your ballast is old wine.

This catch was so well executed by the spirit and science of Mr. Hilary, and the deep triune voice of the reverend gentleman, that the whole party, in spite of themselves, caught the contagion, and joined in chorus at the conclusion, each raising a bumper to his lips:

The bowl goes trim: the moon doth shine:
And our ballast is old wine.

Mr. Cypress, having his ballast on board, stepped, the same evening, into his bowl, or travelling chariot, and departed to rake seas and rivers, lakes and canals, for the moon of ideal beauty.

.   .   .

Scythrop had dined, and was sipping his Madeira alone, immersed in melancholy musing, when Mr. Glowry entered, followed by Raven, who, having placed an additional glass and set a chair for Mr. Glowry, withdrew. Mr. Glowry sat down opposite Scythrop. After a pause, during which each filled and drank in silence, Mr. Glowry said, 'So, sir, you have played your cards well. I proposed Miss Toobad to you: you refused her. Mr. Toobad proposed you to her: she refused you. You fell in love with Marionetta, and were going to poison yourself, because, from pure fatherly regard to your temporal interests, I withheld my consent. When, at length, I offered you my consent, you told me I was too precipitate. And, after all, I find you and Miss Toobad living together in the same tower, and behaving in every respect like two plighted lovers. Now, sir, if there be any rational solution of all this absurdity, I shall be very much obliged to you for a small glimmering of information.'

'The solution, sir, is of little moment; but I will leave it in writing for your satisfaction. The crisis of my fate is come; the world is a stage, and my direction is *exit*.'

'Do not talk so, sir;—do not talk so, Scythrop. What would you have?'

'I would have my love.'

'And pray, sir, who is your love?'

'Celinda—Marionetta—either—both.'

'Both! That may do very well in a German tragedy; and the Great Mogul[21] might have found it very feasible in his lodgings at Kensington; but it will not do in Lincolnshire. Will you have Miss Toobad?'

'Yes.'

'And renounce Marionetta?'

'No.'

'But you must renounce one.'

'I cannot.'

'And you cannot have both. What is to be done?'

'I must shoot myself.'

'Don't talk so, Scythrop. Be rational, my dear Scythrop. Consider, and make a cool, calm choice, and I will exert myself in your behalf.'

'Why should I choose, sir? Both have renounced *me:* I have no hope of either.'

'Tell me which you will have, and I will plead your cause irresistibly.'

'Well, sir,—I will have—no, sir, I cannot renounce either. I cannot choose either. I am doomed to be the victim of eternal disappointments; and I have no resource but a pistol.'

'Scythrop—Scythrop;—if one of them should come to you—what then?'

'That, sir, might alter the case: but that cannot be.'

'It can be, Scythrop; it will be: I promise you it will be. Have but a little patience—but a week's patience—and it shall be.'

'A week, sir, is an age: but, to oblige you, as a last act of filial duty, I will live another week. It is now Thursday evening, twenty-five minutes past seven. At this hour and minute, on Thursday next, love and fate shall smile on me, or I will drink my last pint of port in this world.'

Mr. Glowry ordered his travelling chariot, and departed from the abbey.

.   .   .

The day after Mr. Glowry's departure was one of incessant rain, and Scythrop repented of the promise he had given. The next day was one of

---

bright sunshine: he sat on the terrace, read a tragedy of Sophocles, and was not sorry, when Raven announced dinner, to find himself alive. On the third evening, the wind blew, and the rain beat, and the owl flapped against his windows; and he put a new flint in his pistol. On the fourth day, the sun shone again; and he locked the pistol up in a drawer, where he left it undisturbed till the morning of the eventful Thursday, when he ascended the turret with a telescope, and spied anxiously along the road that crossed the fens from Claydyke: but nothing appeared on it. He watched in this manner from ten a.m. till Raven summoned him to dinner at five; when he stationed Crow at the telescope, and descended to his own funeral-feast. He left open the communications between the tower and turret, and called aloud at intervals to Crow,—'Crow, Crow, is anything coming?' Crow answered, 'The wind blows, and the windmills turn, but I see nothing coming'; and at every answer, Scythrop found the necessity of raising his spirits with a bumper. After dinner, he gave Raven his watch to set by the abbey clock. Raven brought it, Scythrop placed it on the table, and Raven departed. Scythrop called again to Crow; and Crow, who had fallen asleep, answered mechanically, 'I see nothing coming.' Scythrop laid his pistol between his watch and his bottle. The hour-hand passed the VII.—the minute-hand moved on;—it was within three minutes of the appointed time. Scythrop called again to Crow. Crow answered as before. Scythrop rang the bell: Raven appeared.

'Raven,' said Scythrop, 'the clock is too fast.'

'No, indeed,' said Raven, who knew nothing of Scythrop's intentions; 'if anything, it is too slow.'

'Villain!' said Scythrop, pointing the pistol at him; 'it is too fast.'

'Yes—yes—too fast, I meant,' said Raven, in manifest fear.

'How much too fast?' said Scythrop.

'As much as you please,' said Raven.

'How much, I say,' said Scythrop, pointing the pistol again.

'An hour, a full hour, sir,' said the terrified butler.

'Put back my watch,' said Scythrop.

Raven, with trembling hand, was putting back the watch, when the rattle of wheels was heard in the court; and Scythrop, springing down the stairs by three steps together, was at the door in sufficient time to have handed either of the young ladies from the carriage, if she had happened to be in it; but Mr. Glowry was alone.

'I rejoice to see you,' said Mr. Glowry; 'I was

fearful of being too late, for I waited to the last moment in the hope of accomplishing my promise; but all my endeavours have been vain, as these letters will show.'

Scythrop impatiently broke the seals. The contents were these:—

'Almost a stranger in England, I fled from parental tyranny, and the dread of an arbitrary marriage, to the protection of a stranger and a philosopher, whom I expected to find something better than, or at least something different from, the rest of his worthless species. Could I, after what has occurred, have expected nothing more from you than the commonplace impertinence of sending your father to treat with me, and with mine, for me? I should be a little moved in your favour, if I could believe you capable of carrying into effect the resolutions which your father says you have taken, in the event of my proving inflexible; though I doubt not you will execute them, as far as relates to the pint of wine, twice over, at least. I wish you much happiness with Miss O'Carroll. I shall always cherish a grateful recollection of Nightmare Abbey, for having been the means of introducing me to a true transcendentalist; and, though he is a little older than myself, which is all one in Germany, I shall very soon have the pleasure of subscribing myself
'CELINDA FLOSKY.'

'I hope, my dear cousin, that you will not be angry with me, but that you will always think of me as a sincere friend, who will always feel interested in your welfare; I am sure you love Miss Toobad much better than me, and I wish you much happiness with her. Mr. Listless assures me that people do not kill themselves for love nowadays, though it is still the fashion to talk about it. I shall, in a very short time, change my name and situation, and shall always be happy to see you in Berkeley Square, when, to the unalterable designation of your affectionate cousin, I shall subjoin the signature of
'MARIONETTA LISTLESS.'

Scythrop tore both the letters to atoms, and railed in good set terms against the fickleness of women.

'Calm yourself, my dear Scythrop,' said Mr. Glowry; 'there are yet maidens in England.'

'Very true, sir,' said Scythrop.

'And the next time,' said Mr. Glowry, 'have but one string to your bow.'

'Very good advice, sir,' said Scythrop.

'And, besides,' said Mr. Glowry, 'the fatal time is past, for it is now almost eight.'

'Then that villain, Raven,' said Scythrop, 'deceived me when he said that the clock was too fast; but, as you observe very justly, the time has gone by, and I have just reflected that these repeated crosses in love qualify me to take a very advanced degree in misanthropy; and there is, therefore, good hope that I may make a figure in the world. But I shall ring for the rascal Raven, and admonish him.'

Raven appeared. Scythrop looked at him very fiercely two or three minutes; and Raven, still remembering the pistol, stood quaking in mute apprehension, till Scythrop, pointing significantly towards the dining-room, said, 'Bring some Madeira.'

1817   1818

From FOUR AGES OF POETRY[1]

To the age of brass in the ancient world succeeded the dark ages, in which the light of the Gospel began to spread over Europe, and in which, by a mysterious and inscrutable dispensation, the darkness thickened with the progress of the light. The tribes that overran the Roman Empire brought back the days of barbarism, but with this difference, that there were many books in the world, many places in which they were preserved, and occasionally some one by whom they were read, who indeed (if he escaped being burned *pour l'amour de Dieu*), generally lived an object of mysterious fear, with the reputation of magician, alchymist, and astrologer. The emerging of the nations of Europe from this superinduced barbarism, and their settling into new forms of polity, was accompanied, as the first ages of Greece had been, with a wild spirit of adventure, which, co-operating with new manners and new superstitions, raised up a fresh crop of chimæras, not less fruitful, though far less beautiful, than those of Greece. The semi-deification of women by the maxims of the age of chivalry, combining with these new fables, produced the romance of the middle ages. The founders of the new line of heroes took the place of the demi-gods of Grecian poetry. Charlemagne and his Paladins, Arthur and the knights of the round table, the heroes of the iron age of chivalrous poetry, were seen through the same magnifying mist of distance, and their exploits were celebrated with

---

[1] Peacock's *Four Ages of Poetry* is an ironical attack on the major writers of the day. It provoked Shelley's more famous *A Defence of Poetry.*

even more extravagant hyperbole. These legends, combined with the exaggerated love that pervades the songs of the troubadours, the reputation of magic that attached to learned men, the infant wonders of natural philosophy, the crazy fanaticism of the crusades, the power and privileges of the great feudal chiefs, and the holy mysteries of monks and nuns, formed a state of society in which no two laymen could meet without fighting, and in which the three staple ingredients of lover, prize-fighter, and fanatic, that composed the basis of the character of every true man, were mixed up and diversified, in different individuals and classes, with so many distinctive excellencies, and under such an infinite motley variety of costume, as gave the range of a most extensive and picturesque field to the two great constituents of poetry, love and battle.

From these ingredients of the iron age of modern poetry, dispersed in the rhyme of minstrels and the songs of the troubadours, arose the golden age, in which the scattered materials were harmonized and blended about the time of the revival of learning; but with this peculiar difference, that Greek and Roman literature pervaded all the poetry of the golden age of modern poetry, and hence resulted a heterogeneous compound of all ages and nations in one picture; an infinite licence, which gave to the poet the free range of the whole field of imagination and memory. This was carried very far by Ariosto, but farthest of all by Shakespeare and his contemporaries, who used time and locality merely because they could not do without them, because every action must have its when and where: but they made no scruple of deposing a Roman Emperor by an Italian Count, and sending him off in the disguise of a French pilgrim to be shot with a blunderbuss by an English archer. This makes the old English drama very picturesque, at any rate, in the variety of costume, and very diversified in action and character; though it is a picture of nothing that ever was seen on earth except a Venetian carnival.

The greatest of English poets, Milton, may be said to stand alone between the ages of gold and silver, combining the excellencies of both; for with all the energy, and power, and freshness of the first, he united all the studied and elaborate magnificence of the second.

The silver age succeeded; beginning with Dryden, coming to perfection with Pope, and ending with Goldsmith, Collins, and Gray.

Cowper divested verse of its exquisite polish; he thought in metre, but paid more attention to his thoughts than his verse. It would be difficult to draw the boundary of prose and blank verse between his letters and his poetry.

The silver age was the reign of authority; but authority now began to be shaken, not only in poetry but in the whole sphere of its dominion. The contemporaries of Gray and Cowper were deep and elaborate thinkers. The subtle scepticism of Hume, the solemn irony of Gibbon, the daring paradoxes of Rousseau, and the biting ridicule of Voltaire, directed the energies of four extraordinary minds to shake every portion of the reign of authority. Enquiry was roused, the activity of intellect was excited, and poetry came in for its share of the general result. The changes had been rung on lovely maid and sylvan shade, summer heat and green retreat, waving trees and sighing breeze, gentle swains and amorous pains, by versifiers who took them on trust, as meaning something very soft and tender, without much caring what: but with this general activity of intellect came a necessity for even poets to appear to know something of what they professed to talk of. Thomson and Cowper looked at the trees and hills which so many ingenious gentlemen had rhymed about so long without looking at them at all, and the effect of the new operation on poetry was like the discovery of a new world. Painting shared the influence, and the principles of picturesque beauty were explored by adventurous essayists with indefatigable pertinacity. The success which attended these experiments, and the pleasure which resulted from them, had the usual effect of all new enthusiasms, that of turning the heads of a few unfortunate persons, the patriarchs of the age of brass, who, mistaking the prominent novelty for the all-important totality, seem to have ratiocinated in the following manner: 'Poetical genius is the finest of all things, and we feel that we have more of it than any one ever had. The way to bring it to perfection is to cultivate poetical impressions exclusively. Poetical impressions can be received only among natural scenes: for all that is artificial is anti-poetical. Society is artificial, therefore we will live out of society. The mountains are natural, therefore we will live in the mountains. There we shall be shining models of purity and virtue, passing the whole day in the innocent and amiable occupation of going up and down hill, receiving poetical impressions, and communicating them in immortal verse to admiring generations.' To some such perversion of intellect we owe that egregious confraternity of rhymesters, known by the name of the Lake Poets; who certainly did receive and communicate to the world some of the most extraordinary poetical impressions that were ever heard of, and ripened into models of public virtue, too splendid to need illustration. They wrote verses on a new principle; saw rocks and rivers in a new light; and remaining studiously ignorant of history, society, and human nature, cultivated the phantasy only at the expense of the memory and the reason; and contrived, though they had retreated from the world for the express purpose of seeing nature as she was, to see her only as she was not, converting the land they lived in into a sort of fairyland, which they peopled with mysticisms and chimæras. This gave what is called a new tone to poetry, and conjured up a herd of desperate imitators, who have brought the age of brass prematurely to its dotage.

The descriptive poetry of the present day has been called by its cultivators a return to nature. Nothing is more impertinent than this pretension. Poetry cannot travel out of the regions of its birth, the uncultivated lands of semi-civilized men. Mr. Wordsworth, the great leader of the returners to nature, cannot describe a scene under his own eyes without putting into it the shadow of a Danish boy or the living ghost of Lucy Gray, or some similar phantastical parturition of the moods of his own mind.

In the origin and perfection of poetry, all the associations of life were composed of poetical materials. With us it is decidedly the reverse. We know too that there are no Dryads in Hyde Park nor Naiads in the Regent's Canal. But barbaric manners and supernatural interventions are essential to poetry. Either in the scene, or in the time, or in both, it must be remote from our ordinary perceptions. While the historian and the philosopher are advancing in, and accelerating, the progress of knowledge, the poet is wallowing in the rubbish of departed ignorance, and raking up the ashes of dead savages to find gewgaws and rattles for the grown babies of the age. Mr. Scott digs up the poachers and cattle-stealers of the ancient border. Lord Byron cruises for thieves and pirates on the shores of the Morea and among the Greek islands. Mr. Southey wades through ponderous volumes of travels and old chronicles, from which he carefully selects all that is false, useless, and absurd, as being essentially poetical; and when he has a commonplace book full of monstrosities, strings them into an epic. Mr. Wordsworth picks up village legends from old women and sextons; and Mr. Coleridge, to the valuable information acquired from similar sources, superadds the dreams of crazy theologians and the mysticisms of German metaphysics, and favours the world with visions in verse, in which the quadruple elements of sexton, old woman, Jeremy Taylor, and Emanuel Kant, are harmonized into a delicious poetical compound. Mr. Moore presents us with a Persian, and Mr. Campbell with a Pennsylvanian tale, both formed on the same principle as Mr. Southey's epics, by extracting from a perfunctory and desultory perusal of a collection of voyages and travels, all that useful investigation would not seek for and that common sense would reject.

These disjointed relics of tradition and fragments of second-hand observation, being woven into a tissue of verse, constructed on what Mr. Coleridge calls a new principle (that is, no principle at all), compose a modern-antique compound of frippery and barbarism, in which the puling sentimentality of the present time is grafted on the misrepresented ruggedness of the past into a heterogeneous congeries of unamalgamating manners, sufficient to impose on the common readers of poetry, over whose understandings the poet of this class possesses that commanding advantage, which, in all circumstances and conditions of life, a man who knows something, however little, always possesses over one who knows nothing.

A poet in our times is a semi-barbarian in a civilized community. He lives in the days that are past. His ideas, thoughts, feelings, associations, are all with barbarous manners, obsolete customs, and exploded superstitions. The march of his intellect is like that of a crab, backwards. The brighter the light diffused around him by the progress of reason, the thicker is the darkness of antiquated barbarism, in which he buries himself like a mole, to throw up the barren hillocks of his Cimmerian labours. The philosophic mental tranquillity which looks round with an equal eye on all external things, collects a store of ideas, discriminates their relative value, assigns to all their proper place, and from the materials of useful knowledge thus collected, appreciated, and arranged, forms new combinations that impress the stamp of their power and utility on the real business of life, is diametrically the reverse of that frame of mind which poetry inspires, or from which poetry can emanate. The highest inspirations of poetry are resolvable into three ingredients: the rant of unregulated passion, the whine of exaggerated feeling, and the cant of factitious sentiment: and can therefore serve only to ripen a splendid lunatic like Alexander, a puling driveller like Werter,[2] or a morbid dreamer like Wordsworth. It can never make a philosopher, nor a statesman, nor in any class of life an useful or rational man. It cannot claim the slightest share in any one of the comforts and utilities of life of which we have witnessed so many and so rapid advances. But though not useful, it may be said it is highly ornamental, and deserves to be cultivated for the pleasure it yields. Even if this be granted, it does not follow that a writer of poetry in the present state of society is not a waster of his own time, and a robber of that of others. Poetry is not one of those arts which, like painting, require repetition and multiplication, in order to be diffused among society. There are more good poems already existing than are sufficient to employ that portion of life which any mere reader and recipient of poetical impressions should devote to them, and these having been produced in poetical times, are far superior in all the characteristics of poetry to the artificial reconstructions of a few morbid ascetics in unpoetical times. To read the promiscuous rubbish of the present time to the exclusion of the select treasures of the past, is to substitute the worse for the better variety of the same mode of enjoyment.

But in whatever degree poetry is cultivated, it must necessarily be to the neglect of some branch of useful study: and it is a lamentable spectacle to see minds, capable of better things, running to seed in the specious indolence of these empty aimless mockeries of intellectual exertion. Poetry was the mental rattle that awakened the attention of intellect in the infancy of civil society: but for the maturity of mind to make a serious business of the playthings of its childhood, is as absurd as for a full-grown man to rub his gums with coral, and cry to be charmed to sleep by the jingle of silver bells.

As to that small portion of our contemporary poetry, which is neither descriptive, nor narrative, nor dramatic, and which, for want of a better name, may be called ethical, the most distinguished portion of it, consisting merely of querulous, egoistical rhapsodies, to express the writer's high dissatisfaction with the world and every thing in it, serves only to confirm what has been said of the semi-barbarous character of poets, who from singing dithyrambics and 'Io Triumphe,' while society was savage, grow rabid, and out of their element, as it becomes polished and enlightened.

Now, when we consider that it is not to the thinking and studious, and scientific and philosophical part of the community, not to those whose minds are bent on the pursuit and promotion of permanently useful ends and aims, that poets must address their minstrelsy, but to that much larger portion of the reading public, whose minds are not awakened to the desire of valuable knowledge, and who are indifferent to any thing beyond being charmed, moved, excited, affected, and exalted: charmed by harmony, moved by sentiment, excited by passion, affected by pathos, and exalted by sublimity: harmony, which is language on the rack of Procrustes;[3] sentiment, which is canting egotism in the mask of refined feeling; passion, which is the commotion of a weak and selfish mind; pathos, which is the whining of an unmanly spirit; and sublimity, which is the inflation of an empty head: when we consider that the great and permanent interests of human society become more and more the main-spring of intellectual pursuit; that in proportion as they become so, the subordinacy of the ornamental to the useful will be more and more seen and acknowledged; and that therefore the progress of useful art and science, and of moral and political knowledge, will continue more and more to withdraw attention from frivolous and unconducive, to solid and conducive studies: that therefore the poetical audience will not only continually diminish in the proportion of its number to that of the rest of the reading public, but will also sink lower and lower in the comparison of intellectual acquirement: when we consider that the poet must still please his audience, and must therefore continue to sink to their level, while the rest of the community is rising above it: we may easily conceive that the day is not distant, when the degraded state of every species of poetry will be as generally recognized as that of dramatic poetry has long been: and this is not from any decrease either of intellectual power, or intellectual acquisition, but because intellectual power and intellectual acquisition have turned themselves into other and better channels, and have abandoned the cultivation and the fate of poetry to the degenerate fry of modern rhymesters, and their Olympic judges, the magazine critics, who continue to debate and promulgate oracles about poetry, as if it were still what it was in the Homeric age, the all-in-all intellectual progression, and as if there were no

---

2 morbidly romantic hero of Goethe's romance, *The Sorrows of Werther,* 1774.

3 a legendary highwayman of Attica who tied travelers on an iron bed, and stretched them or cut off their legs to fit them to its length.

such things in existence as mathematicians, astronomers, chemists, moralists, metaphysicians, historians, politicians, and political economists, who have built into the upper air of intelligence a pyramid, from the summit of which they see the modern Parnassus far beneath them, and, knowing how small a place it occupies in the comprehensiveness of their prospect, smile at the little ambition and the circumscribed perceptions with which the drivellers and mountebanks upon it are contending for the poetical palm and the critical chair.

1820

1799 · THOMAS HOOD · 1845

1799   Born in London, the son of a Scottish bookseller.

1817–21   Trained as an engraver, but because of ill-health turned to literature.

1821–4   Became sub-editor of the *London Magazine;* at the monthly dinners to contributors made the acquaintance of De Quincey, Hazlitt, Reynolds, and Lamb.

1825   Published anonymously with John Hamilton Reynolds, *Odes and Addresses to Great People,* his first volume of comic verse; followed up this success during the next two years with two volumes of *Whims and Oddities in Prose and Verse.*

1826   Married Reynolds' sister Jane.

1827   Published *The Plea of the Midsummer Fairies,* only volume of serious verse to appear in his lifetime.

1829–30   Became editor of the *Gem* and established the *Comic Annual.*

1834–40   Harassed with debt brought on by failure of a publishing house; lived on the Continent in an effort to economize.

1841   Became editor of the *New Monthly Magazine* to which he contributed some of his most brilliant pieces.

1844   Established *Hood's Magazine,* but because of a breakdown in health, was forced to give it up after a few months.

1845   Died at Hampstead.

THOMAS HOOD was a lovable and courageous writer whose life was one long story of ill-health and ceaseless struggle. A poet of at least moderate endowments, he was forced to earn his less than scanty living by playing the funnyman before a public that cared more for his comic jesting than for his serious poetry. Year in and year out he pumped up endless fun, in its total a vast quantity of humorous writing, most of which need no longer be remembered. Yet in the comic vein, Hood displayed a talent for drollery and whim and an almost boundless prodigality in punning which have justly earned for him the undisputed title of 'master among jesters.' Happily the poet in him was not altogether killed by the funnyman. His serious poems offer a much slighter bulk, but in this class nearly all are good and some truly excellent. The poet Hood, through his friendship with Reynolds, came early under the spell of Keats. During his discipleship he produced *Hero and Leander, Ode: Autumn,* and other poems steeped in fancy, and marked by a richness of phrase and imagery that often remind us of the master. He displays a rarer gift in the exquisite songs, often touched with lyrical pathos or wistful tenderness. Of a special imaginative cast is the superb tragic narrative of the crime-tortured Eugene Aram. In his last years, after a lifetime spent in jesting, Hood returned to 'themes of true and deep emotion.' He extended his personal suffering with poignant force to the compassionate *The Song of the Shirt, Bridge of Sighs,* and other humanitarian poems. Hood's variety is considerable, including much outside a strict classification of 'serious' and 'comic,' but it is chiefly for his enduring serious poetry that he has, not without cause, been called by Elton the 'truest of English poets in the years immediately preceding Tennyson.'

THE DEATH-BED

WE watched her breathing through the night,
　Her breathing soft and low,
As in her breast the wave of life
　Kept heaving to and fro.

So silently we seemed to speak,
　So slowly moved about,
As we had lent her half our powers
　To eke her living out.

Our very hopes belied our fears,
　Our fears our hopes belied—　　　　10
We thought her dying when she slept,
　And sleeping when she died.

For when the morn came dim and sad,
　And chill with early showers,
Her quiet eyelids closed—she had
　Another morn than ours.

　　　　　　　　　1825

FAITHLESS NELLY GRAY

A PATHETIC BALLAD

BEN Battle was a soldier bold,
　And used to war's alarms:
But a cannon-ball took off his legs,
　So he laid down his arms!

Now as they bore him off the field,
　Said he, 'Let others shoot,
For here I leave my second leg,
　And the Forty-second Foot!'

The army-surgeons made him limbs:
　Said he, 'They're only pegs:—　　　10
But there's as wooden members[1] quite
　As represent my legs!'

Now Ben he loved a pretty maid,
　Her name was Nelly Gray;
So he went to pay her his devours
　When he'd devoured his pay!

But when he called on Nelly Gray,
　She made him quite a scoff;

And when she saw his wooden legs,
　Began to take them off!　　　　20

'O Nelly Gray! O, Nelly Gray!
　Is this your love so warm?
The love that loves a scarlet coat
　Should be more uniform!'

Said she, 'I loved a soldier once,
　For he was blythe and brave;
But I will never have a man
　With both legs in the grave!

'Before you had those timber toes,
　Your love I did allow,　　　　30
But then, you know, you stand upon
　Another footing now!'

'O, Nelly Gray! O, Nelly Gray!
　For all your jeering speeches,
At duty's call, I left my legs
　In Badajos's *breaches*'![2]

'Why, then,' said she, 'you've lost the feet
　Of legs in war's alarms,
And now you cannot wear your shoes
　Upon your feats of arms!'　　　　40

'O, false and fickle Nelly Gray;
　I know why you refuse:—
Though I've no feet—some other man
　Is standing in my shoes!

'I wish I ne'er had seen your face;
　But, now, a long farewell!
For you will be my death;—alas!
　You will not be my *Nell*!'

Now when he went from Nelly Gray,
　His heart so heavy got—　　　　50
And life was such a burthen grown,
　It made him take a knot!

So round his melancholy neck,
　A rope he did entwine,
And, for his second time in life,
　Enlisted in the Line!

---

1 a gibe at members of Parliament.

2 Badajos was a fortress in Spain stormed by Wellington in 1812.

One end he tied around a beam,
  And then removed his pegs,
And, as his legs were off,—of course,
  He soon was off his legs!   60

And there he hung, till he was dead
  As any nail in town,—
For though distress had cut him up,
  It could not cut him down!

A dozen men sat on[3] his corpse,
  To find out why he died—
And they buried Ben in four cross-roads,
  With a *stake* in his inside![4]

                                                      1826

From HERO AND LEANDER

[In reviving the famous Greek legend of Hero and Leander, Hood has given an original treatment to the story
by adding his own incident of myth. He begins with the
separation of the lovers at dawn. As Leander toils
against the waves on his fatal return swim to Abydos,
he is embraced by a sea nymph (Scylla) who carries him
down to her home beneath the waves only to find him
dead when she reaches it. The sea nymph's sorrow and
her pitiable attempts to revive her human lover make up
the central portion of the narrative. Only at the end of
the poem does Hood return to the original tale to describe the grief and suicide of Hero.

Hood's poem contains clear echoes of Marlowe's famous poem and also of Shakespeare's *Venus and Adonis*
and of *The Rape of Lucrece;* there are also some obvious
reminiscences from Keats. The preponderant reference
is to the Elizabethans. Professor Douglas Bush sees the
poem as 'probably the most remarkable example in
modern verse of almost complete reproduction of the
narrative manner of the Elizabethan Ovidians (*Mythology and the Romantic Tradition,* p. 192).]

[THE DEATH OF LEANDER]

Lines 19–42, 91–132, 163–270

Lo! how the lark soars upward and is gone;
Turning a spirit as he nears the sky,   20
His voice is heard, though body there is none,
And rain-like music scatters from on high;
But Love would follow with a falcon spite,
To pluck the minstrel from his dewy height.

For Love hath framed a ditty of regrets,
Tuned to the hollow sobbings on the shore,
A vexing sense, that with like music frets,
And chimes this dismal burthen o'er and o'er,
Saying, Leander's joys are past and spent,
Like stars extinguished in the firmament.   30

---

3 held a jury session on.
4 According to an old custom, a suicide was generally buried at
the intersection of four roads with a stake driven through the
body.

For ere the golden crevices of morn
Let in those regal luxuries of light,
Which all the variable east adorn,
And hang rich fringes on the skirts of night,
Leander, weaning from sweet Hero's side,
Must leave a widow where he found a bride.

Hark! how the billows beat upon the sand!
Like pawing steeds impatient of delay;
Meanwhile their rider, ling'ring on the land,
Dallies with love, and holds farewell at bay
A too short span.—How tedious slow is
    grief!   40
But parting renders time both sad and brief.

So brave Leander sunders from his bride;
The wrenching pang disparts his soul in twain;
Half stays with her, half goes towards the
    tide,—
And life must ache, until they join again.
Now would'st thou know the wideness of the
    wound,
Mete every step he takes upon the ground.

And for the agony and bosom-throe,
Let it be measur'd by the wide vast air,
For that is infinite, and so is woe,
Since parted lovers breathe it every where.   100
Look how it heaves Leander's labouring chest,
Panting, at poise, upon a rocky crest!

From which he leaps into the scooping brine,
That shocks his bosom with a double chill;
Because, all hours, till the slow sun's decline,
That cold divorcer will betwixt them still;
Wherefore he likens it to Styx' foul tide,
Where life grows death upon the other side.

Then sadly he confronts his two-fold toil
Against rude waves and an unwilling mind,   110
Wishing, alas! with the stout rower's toil,
That like a rower he might gaze behind,
And watch that lonely statue he hath left
On her bleak summit, weeping and bereft!

Yet turning oft, he sees her troubled locks
Pursue him still the furthest that they may;
Her marble arms that overstretch the rocks,
And her pale passion'd hands that seem to pray
In dumb petition to the gods above:
Love prays devoutly when it prays for love!   120

Then with deep sighs he blows away the wave,
That hangs superfluous tears upon his cheek,
And bans his labour like a hopeless slave,

That, chain'd in hostile galley, faint and weak,
Plies on despairing through the restless foam,
Thoughtful of his lost love, and far-off home.

The drowsy mist before him chill and dank,
Like a dull lethargy o'erleans the sea,
Where he rows on against the utter blank,
Steering as if to dim eternity,—   130
Like Love's frail ghost departing with the dawn;
A failing shadow in the twilight drawn.

By this, the climbing sun, with rest repair'd,
Look'd through the gold embrasures of the sky,
And ask'd the drowsy world how she had
        fared;—
The drowsy world shone brighten'd in reply;
And smiling off her fogs, his slanting beam
Spied young Leander in the middle stream.

His face was pallid, but the hectic morn
Had hung a lying crimson on his cheeks,   170
And slanderous sparkles in his eyes forlorn;
So death lies ambush'd in consumptive streaks;
But inward grief was writhing o'er its task,
As heart-sick jesters weep behind the mask.

He thought of Hero and the lost delight,
Her last embracings, and the space between;
He thought of Hero and the future night,
Her speechless rapture and enamour'd mien,
When, lo! before him, scarce two galleys' space,
His thought's confronted with another face!   180

Her aspect's like a moon divinely fair,
But makes the midnight darker that it lies on;
'Tis so beclouded with her coal-black hair
That densely skirts her luminous horizon,
Making her doubly fair, thus darkly set,
As marble lies advantag'd upon jet.

She's all too bright, too argent, and too pale,
To be a woman;—but a woman's double,
Reflected on the wave so faint and frail,
She tops the billows like an air-blown bub-
        ble;   190
Or dim creation of a morning dream,
Fair as the wave-bleach'd lily of the stream.

The very rumour strikes his seeing dead:
Great beauty like great fear first stuns the sense:
He knows not if her lips be blue or red,
Nor if her eyes can give true evidence:
Like murder's witness swooning in the court,
His sight falls senseless by its own report.

Anon resuming, it declares her eyes
Are tinct with azure, like two crystal wells   200
That drink the blue complexion of the skies,
Or pearls outpeeping from their silvery shells:
Her polish'd brow, it is an ample plain,
To lodge vast contemplations of the main.

Her lips might corals seem, but corals near,
Stray through her hair like blossoms on a bower;
And o'er the weaker red still domineer,
And make it pale by tribute to more power;
Her rounded cheeks are of still paler hue,
Touch'd by the bloom of water, tender blue.   210

Thus he beholds her rocking on the water,
Under the glossy umbrage of her hair,
Like pearly Amphitrite's[1] fairest daughter,
Naiad,[2] or Nereid,[3]—or Syren[4] fair,
Mislodging music in her pitiless breast,
A nightingale within a falcon's nest.

They say there be such maidens in the deep,
Charming poor mariners, that all too near
By mortal lullabies fall dead asleep,
As drowsy men are poison'd through the ear;   220
Therefore Leander's fears begin to urge,
This snowy swan is come to sing his dirge.

At which he falls into a deadly chill,
And strains his eyes upon her lips apart;
Fearing each breath to feel that prelude shrill,
Pierce through his marrow, like a breath-blown
        dart
Shot sudden from an Indian's hollow cane,
With mortal venom fraught, and fiery pain.

Here then, poor wretch, how he begins to crowd
A thousand thoughts within a pulse's space;   230
There seem'd so brief a pause of life allow'd,
His mind stretch'd universal, to embrace
The whole wide world, in an extreme fare-
        well,—
A moment's musing—but an age to tell.

For there stood Hero, widow'd at a glance,
The foreseen sum of many a tedious fact,
Pale cheeks, dim eyes, and wither'd countenance,
A wasted ruin that no wasting lack'd;
Time's tragic consequents ere time began,
A world of sorrow in a tear-drop's span.   240

---

1 Amphitrite was the wife of Poseidon (Neptune) and goddess of
the sea.
2 a water nymph dwelling in a brook or fountain.
3 a sea nymph.
4 one of the group of sea nymphs dwelling on an island near Italy
whose singing lured sailors to their death.

A moment's thinking, is an hour in words,—
An hour of words is little for some woes;
Too little breathing a long life affords,
For love to paint itself by perfect shows;
Then let his love and grief unwrong'd lie dumb,
Whilst Fear, and that it fears, together come.

As when the crew, hard by some jutty cape,
Struck pale and panick'd by the billows' roar,
Lay by all timely measures of escape,
And let their bark go driving on the shore;   250
So fray'd⁵ Leander, drifting to his wreck,
Gazing on Scylla, falls upon her neck.

For he hath all forgot the swimmer's art,
The rower's cunning, and the pilot's skill,
Letting his arms fall down in languid part,
Sway'd by the waves, and nothing by his will
Till soon he jars against that glossy skin,
Solid like glass, though seemingly as thin.

Lo! how she startles at the warning shock,
And straightway girds him to her radiant
        breast,   260
More like his safe smooth harbour than his rock;
Poor wretch, he is so faint and toil-opprest,
He cannot loose him from his grappling foe,
Whether for love or hate, she lets not go.

His eyes are blinded with the sleety brine,
His ears are deafen'd with the wildering noise;
He asks the purpose of her fell design,
But foamy waves choke up his struggling voice;
Under the ponderous sea his body dips,
And Hero's name dies bubbling on his lips.   270

            .   .   .

[SCYLLA'S LAMENT]

Lines 535–52

'O poppy Death!—sweet poisoner of sleep!
Where shall I seek for thee, oblivious drug,
That I may steep thee in my drink, and creep
Out of life's coil. Look, Idol! how I hug
Thy dainty image in this strict embrace,
And kiss this clay-cold model of thy face!   540

'Put out, put out these sun-consuming lamps,
I do but read my sorrows by their shine,
O come and quench them with thy oozy damps,
And let my darkness intermix with thine;
Since love is blinded, wherefore should I see,
Now love is death,—death will be love to me!

---

⁵ frightened.

'Away, away, this vain complaining breath,
It does but stir the troubles that I weep,
Let it be hush'd and quieted, sweet Death,
The wind must settle ere the wave can
        sleep,—
Since love is silent, I would fain be mute,
O Death, be gracious to my dying suit!'
                                                    1827

FAIR INES

O SAW ye not fair Ines?
    She's gone into the West,
To dazzle when the sun is down,
    And rob the world of rest:
She took our daylight with her,
    The smiles that we love best,
With morning blushes on her cheek,
    And pearls upon her breast.

O turn again, fair Ines,
    Before the fall of night,   10
For fear the Moon should shine alone,
    And stars unrivall'd bright;
And blessed will the lover be
    That walks beneath their light,
And breathes the love against thy cheek
    I dare not even write!

Would I had been, fair Ines,
    That gallant cavalier,
Who rode so gaily by thy side,
    And whisper'd thee so near!—   20
Were there no bonny dames at home
    Or no true lovers here,
That he should cross the seas to win
    The dearest of the dear?

I saw thee, lovely Ines,
    Descend along the shore,
With bands of noble gentlemen,
    And banners wav'd before;
And gentle youth and maidens gay,
    And snowy plumes they wore;—   30
It would have been a beauteous dream,
    —If it had been no more!

Alas, alas, fair Ines,
    She went away with song,
With Music waiting on her steps,
    And shoutings of the throng;
But some were sad, and felt no mirth,
    But only Music's wrong,
In sounds that sang Farewell, Farewell,
    To her you've loved so long.   40

Farewell, farewell, fair Ines,
  That vessel never bore
So fair a lady on its deck,
  Nor danc'd so light before,—
Alas for pleasure on the sea,
  And sorrow on the shore!
The smile that blest one lover's heart
  Has broken many more!

1827

RUTH[1]

SHE stood breast high amid the corn,
Clasp'd by the golden light of morn,
Like the sweetheart of the sun,
Who many a glowing kiss had won.

On her cheek an autumn flush,
Deeply ripen'd;—such a blush
In the midst of brown was born,
Like red poppies grown with corn.

Round her eyes her tresses fell,
Which were blackest none could tell,   10
But long lashes veil'd a light,
That had else been all too bright.

And her hat, with shady brim,
Made her tressy forehead dim;—
Thus she stood amid the stooks,[2]
Praising God with sweetest looks:—

Sure, I said, Heav'n did not mean
Where I reap thou shouldst but glean,
Lay thy sheaf adown and come,
Share my harvest and my home.   20

1827

I REMEMBER, I REMEMBER

I REMEMBER, I remember,
  The house where I was born,
The little window where the sun
  Came peeping in at morn;
He never came a wink too soon,
  Nor brought too long a day,
But now, I often wish the night
  Had borne my breath away!

I remember, I remember,
  The roses, red and white,   10
The vi'lets, and the lily-cups,
  Those flowers made of light!

---

1 This poem is based upon the Bible story of Ruth.
2 shocks of grain.

The lilacs where the robin built,
  And where my brother set
The laburnum on his birthday,—
  The tree is living yet!

I remember, I remember,
  Where I was used to swing,
And thought the air must rush as fresh
  To swallows on the wing;   20
My spirit flew in feathers then,
  That is so heavy now,
And summer pools could hardly cool
  The fever on my brow!

I remember, I remember,
  The fir trees dark and high;
I used to think their slender tops
  Were close against the sky:
It was a childish ignorance,
  But now 'tis little joy   30
To know I'm farther off from heav'n
  Than when I was a boy.

1827

THE STARS ARE WITH THE VOYAGER

THE stars are with the voyager
  Wherever he may sail;
The moon is constant to her time;
  The sun will never fail;
But follow, follow round the world,
  The green earth and the sea;
So love is with the lover's heart,
  Wherever he may be.

Wherever he may be, the stars
  Must daily lose their light;   10
The moon will veil her in the shade;
  The sun will set at night.
The sun may set, but constant love
  Will shine when he's away;
So that dull night is never night,
  And day is brighter day.

1827

SILENCE

THERE is a silence where hath been no sound,
  There is a silence where no sound may be,
  In the cold grave—under the deep deep sea,
Or in wide desert where no life is found,
Which hath been mute, and still must sleep pro-
      found;
  No voice is hush'd—no life treads silently,
  But clouds and cloudy shadows wander free,

That never spoke, over the idle ground:
But in green ruins, in the desolate walls
    Of antique palaces, where Man hath been,   10
Though the dun fox, or wild hyena, calls,
    And owls, that flit continually between,
Shriek to the echo, and the low winds moan,
There the true Silence is, self-conscious and
    alone.

                  1827

THE DREAM OF EUGENE ARAM, THE MURDERER

    The remarkable name of Eugene Aram [1704–59], belonging to a man of unusual talents and acquirements, is unhappily associated with a deed of blood as extraordinary in its details as any recorded in our calendar of crime. In the year 1745, being then an Usher and deeply engaged in the study of Chaldee, Hebrew, Arabic, and the Celtic dialects, for the formation of a Lexicon, he abruptly turned over a still darker page in human knowledge, and the brow that learning might have made illustrious was stamped ignominious forever with the brand of Cain. To obtain a trifling property he concerted with an accomplice, and with his own hand effected, the violent death of one Daniel Clarke, a shoemaker of Knaresborough, in Yorkshire. For fourteen years nearly the secret slept with the victim in the earth of St. Robert's Cave, and the manner of its discovery would appear a striking example of the Divine Justice, even amongst those marvels narrated in that curious old volume alluded to in *The Fortunes of Nigel,* under its quaint title of *God's Revenge against Murther.*

    The accidental digging up of a skeleton, and the unwary and emphatic declaration of Aram's accomplice that it could not be that of Clarke, betraying a guilty knowledge of the true bones, he was wrought to a confession of their deposit. The learned homicide was seized and arraigned; and a trial of uncommon interest was wound up by a defence as memorable as the tragedy itself for eloquence and ingenuity—too ingenious for innocence, and eloquent enough to do credit even to that long premeditation which the interval between the deed and its discovery had afforded. That this dreary period had not passed without paroxysms of remorse, may be inferred from a fact of affecting interest. The late Admiral Burney was a scholar, at the school at Lynn in Norfolk, where Aram was an Usher, subsequent to his crime. The Admiral stated that Aram was beloved by the boys, and that he used to discourse to them of murder, not occasionally, as I have written elsewhere, but constantly, and in somewhat of the spirit ascribed to him in the poem.

    For the more imaginative part of the version I must refer back to one of those unaccountable visions, which come upon us like frightful monsters thrown up by storms from the great black deeps of slumber. A lifeless body, in love and relationship the nearest and dearest, was imposed upon my back, with an overwhelming sense of obligation—not of filial piety merely, but some awful responsibility equally vague and intense, and involving, as it seemed, inexpiable sin, horrors unutterable, torments intolerable,—to bury my dead, like Abraham, out of my sight. In vain I attempted, again and again, to obey the mysterious mandate—by some dreadful process the burthen was replaced with a more stupendous weight of injunction, and an appalling conviction of the impossibility of its fulfillment. My mental anguish was indescribable;—the mighty agonies of souls tortured on the supernatural racks of sleep are not to be penned—and if in sketching those that belong to blood-guiltiness I have been at all successful, I owe it mainly to the uninvoked inspiration of that terrible dream.—(Hood's Preface.)

'TWAS in the prime of summer time,
    An evening calm and cool,
And four-and-twenty happy boys
    Came bounding out of school:
There were some that ran and some that leapt,
    Like troutlets in a pool.

Away they sped with gamesome minds,
    And souls untouch'd by sin;
To a level mead they came, and there
    They drave the wickets in:
Pleasantly shone the setting sun   10
    Over the town of Lynn.[1]

Like sportive deer they cours'd about,
    And shouted as they ran,—
Turning to mirth all things of earth,
    As only boyhood can;
But the Usher sat remote from all,
    A melancholy man!

His hat was off, his vest apart,
    To catch heaven's blessed breeze;   20
For a burning thought was in his brow,
    And his bosom ill at ease:
So he lean'd his head on his hands, and read
    The book between his knees!

Leaf after leaf, he turn'd it o'er,
    Nor ever glanc'd aside,
For the peace of his soul he read that book
    In the golden eventide:
Much study had made him very lean,
    And pale, and leaden-ey'd.   30

At last he shut the ponderous tome,
    With a fast and fervent grasp
He strain'd the dusky covers close,
    And fix'd the brazen hasp:
'Oh God! could I so close my mind,
    And clasp it with a clasp!'

Then leaping on his feet upright,
    Some moody turns he took,—
Now up the mead, then down the mead,

---

1 a seaport in Norfolkshire.

And past a shady nook,— 40
And, lo! he saw a little boy
 That pored upon a book!

'My gentle lad, what is 't you read—
 Romance or fairy fable?
Or is it some historic page,
 Of kings and crowns unstable?'
The young boy gave an upward glance,—
 'It is *The Death of Abel*.'

The Usher took six hasty strides,
 As smit with sudden pain,— 50
Six hasty strides beyond the place,
 Then slowly back again;
And down he sat beside the lad,
 And talk'd with him of Cain;

And, long since then, of bloody men,
 Whose deeds tradition saves;
Of lonely folk cut off unseen,
 And hid in sudden graves;
Of horrid stabs, in groves forlorn,
 And murders done in caves; 60

And how the sprites of injur'd men
 Shriek upward from the sod,—
Aye, how the ghostly hand will point
 To show the burial clod;
And unknown facts of guilty acts
 Are seen in dreams from God!

He told how murderers walk the earth
 Beneath the curse of Cain,—
With crimson clouds before their eyes,
 And flames about their brain:
For blood has left upon their souls 70
 Its everlasting stain!

'And well,' quoth he, 'I know, for truth,
 Their pangs must be extreme,—
Woe, woe, unutterable woe,—
 Who spill life's sacred stream!
For why? Methought, last night, I wrought
 A murder, in a dream!

'One that had never done me wrong—
 A feeble man, and old; 80
I led him to a lonely field,—
 The moon shone clear and cold:
Now here, said I, this man shall die,
 And I will have his gold!

'Two sudden blows with a ragged stick,
 And one with a heavy stone,
One hurried gash with a hasty knife,—

And then the deed was done:
There was nothing lying at my foot
 But lifeless flesh and bone! 90

'Nothing but lifeless flesh and bone,
 That could not do me ill;
And yet I fear'd him all the more,
 For lying there so still:
There was a manhood in his look,
 That murder could not kill!

'And, lo! the universal air
 Seem'd lit with ghastly flame;—
Ten thousand thousand dreadful eyes
 Were looking down in blame: 100
I took the dead man by his hand,
 And call'd upon his name!

'Oh, God! it made me quake to see
 Such sense within the slain!
But when I touch'd the lifeless clay,
 The blood gushed out amain!
For every clot, a burning spot,
 Was scorching in my brain!

'My head was like an ardent coal,
 My heart as solid ice: 110
My wretched, wretched soul, I knew,
 Was at the Devil's price:
A dozen times I groan'd; the dead
 Had never groan'd but twice.

'And now, from forth the frowning sky
 From the Heaven's topmost height,
I heard a voice—the awful voice
 Of the blood-avenging Sprite:—
"Thou guilty man! take up thy dead,
 And hide it from my sight!" 120

'I took the dreary body up,
 And cast it in a stream,—
A sluggish water, black as ink,
 The depth was so extreme:—
My gentle Boy, remember this
 Is nothing but a dream!

'Down went the corse with a hollow plunge
 And vanish'd in the pool;
Anon I cleans'd my bloody hands,
 And wash'd my forehead cool, 130
And sat among the urchins young
 That evening in the school.

'Oh, Heaven, to think of their white souls,
 And mine so black and grim!
I could not share in childish prayer,

Nor join in Evening Hymn:
Like a Devil of the Pit, I seem'd,
    'Mid holy Cherubim!

'And Peace went with them, one and all,
    And each calm pillow spread;   140
But Guilt was my grim Chamberlain
    That lighted me to bed;
And drew my midnight curtains round
    With fingers bloody red!

'All night I lay in agony,
    In anguish dark and deep;
My fever'd eyes I dared not close,
    But stared aghast at Sleep:
For Sin had render'd unto her
    The keys of Hell to keep!   150

'All night I lay in agony,
    From weary chime to chime,
With one besetting horrid hint,
    That rack'd me all the time,—
A mighty yearning, like the first
    Fierce impulse unto crime!

'One stern tyrannic thought, that made
    All other thoughts its slave;
Stronger and stronger every pulse
    Did that temptation crave,—   160
Still urging me to go and see
    The Dead Man in his grave!

'Heavily, I rose up, as soon
    As light was in the sky,
And sought the black accursed pool
    With a wild misgiving eye;
And I saw the Dead in the river bed,
    For the faithless stream was dry!

'Merrily rose the lark, and shook
    The dew-drop from its wing;   170
But I never mark'd its morning flight,
    I never heard it sing:
For I was stooping once again
    Under the horrid thing.

'With breathless speed, like a soul in chase,
    I took him up and ran;—
There was no time to dig a grave
    Before the day began:
In a lonesome wood, with heaps of leaves,
    I hid the murder'd man!   180

'And all that day I read in school,
    But my thought was other where;

As soon as the mid-day task was done,
    In secret I was there:
And a mighty wind had swept the leaves,
    And still the corse was bare!

'Then down I cast me on my face,
    And first began to weep,
For I knew my secret then was one
    That earth refus'd to keep: 190
Or land, or sea, though he should be
    Ten thousand fathoms deep.

'So wills the fierce avenging sprite,
    Till blood for blood atones!
Ay, though he's buried in a cave,
    And trodden down with stones,
And years have rotted off his flesh,—
    The world shall see his bones!

'Oh, God! that horrid, horrid dream
    Besets me now awake!   200
Again—again, with a dizzy brain,
    The human life I take;
And my red right hand grows raging hot,
    Like Cranmer's[2] at the stake.

'And still no peace for the restless clay,
    Will wave or mould allow;
The horrid thing pursues my soul,—
    It stands before me now!'
The fearful Boy look'd up, and saw
    Huge drops upon his brow.   210

That very night, while gentle sleep
    The urchin eyelids kiss'd,
Two stern-faced men set out from Lynn,
    Through the cold and heavy mist;
And Eugene Aram walked between,
    With gyves upon his wrist.
                                        1829

DOMESTIC ASIDES; OR, TRUTH IN
PARENTHESES

'I REALLY take it very kind,
This visit, Mrs. Skinner!
I have not seen you such an age—
(The wretch has come to dinner!)

'Your daughters, too, what loves of girls—
What heads for painters' easels!

---

2 Thomas Cranmer, 1489–1556, an English Protestant divine and
reformer, was burned at the stake by Mary I.

Come here and kiss the infant, dears,—
(And give it p'rhaps the measles!)

'Your charming boys I see are home
From Reverend Mr. Russel's;   10
'Twas very kind to bring them both,—
(What boots for my new Brussels!¹)

'What! little Clara left at home?
Well now I call that shabby:
I should have lov'd to kiss her so,—
(A flabby, dabby, babby!)

'And Mr. S., I hope he's well,
Ah! though he lives so handy,
He never now drops in to sup,—
(The better for our brandy!)   20

'Come, take a seat—I long to hear
About Matilda's marriage;
You're come, of course, to spend the day!—
(Thank Heav'n, I hear the carriage!)

'What! must you go? next time I hope
You'll give me longer measure;
Nay—I shall see you down the stairs—
(With most uncommon pleasure!)

'Good-bye! good-bye! remember all
Next time you'll take your dinners!   30
(Now, David, mind I'm not at home
In future to the Skinners!)'

                                                     1839

SALLY SIMPKIN'S LAMENT

OR, JOHN JONES'S KIT-CAT-ASTROPHE

He left his body to the sea,
And made a shark his legatee.
                    —*Bryan and Perenne.*¹

'OH! what is that comes gliding in,
  And quite in middling haste?
It is the picture of my Jones,
  And painted to the waist.

'It is not painted to the life,
  For where's the trousers blue?
Oh Jones, my dear!—O dear! my Jones,
  What is become of you?'

'Oh! Sally dear, it is too true,
  The half that you remark   10

---
¹ Brussels carpet.

---
¹ a West Indian ballad.

Is come to say my other half
  Is bit off by a shark!

'Oh! Sally, sharks do things by halves,
  Yet most completely do!
A bite in one place seems enough,
  But I've been bit in two.

'You know I once was all your own,
  But now a shark must share!
But let that pass—for now to you
  I'm neither here nor there.   20

'Alas! death has a strange divorce
  Effected in the sea,
It has divided me from you,
  And even me from me!

'Don't fear my ghost will walk o' nights
  To haunt as people say;
My ghost *can't* walk, for, oh! my legs
  Are many leagues away!

'Lord! think when I am swimming round,
  And looking where the boat is,   30
A shark just snaps away a *half*,
  Without a *quarter's* notice.'²

'One half is here, the other half
  Is near Columbia placed;
Oh! Sally, I have got the whole
  Atlantic for my waist.

'But now, adieu—a long adieu!
  I've solved death's awful riddle,
And would say more, but I am doomed
  To break off in the middle.'   40

                                                     1839

THE SONG OF THE SHIRT

[This poem was inspired by an incident reported in the *Times* of 26 October 1843, which attracted widespread attention to the condition of workers in London. A poor widow, with two infant children, was charged with having pawned clothing belonging to her employer. At the trial it was brought out that this wretched woman was attempting to maintain herself and her family by making trousers at seven shillings a week, what her master called 'a very good living.' The discovery of this injustice and similar shocking conditions among poor needlewomen so aroused public sympathy, that when the *Song of the Shirt* appeared in the Christmas issue of *Punch* it 'went through the land like wild-fire.' The circulation of *Punch* was trebled and Hood became famous

---
² notice to vacate given a quarter in advance.

overnight. The *Song* was printed on handkerchiefs, sung in the streets, and read in the churches. In fulfillment of his own wish, Hood's monument bears the simple inscription 'He sang the "Song of the Shirt." ']

WITH fingers weary and worn,
  With eyelids heavy and red,
A Woman sat, in unwomanly rags,
  Plying her needle and thread—
    Stitch! stitch! stitch!
In poverty, hunger, and dirt,
    And still with a voice of dolorous pitch
She sang the 'Song of the Shirt!'

'Work! work! work!
  While the cock is crowing aloof!
And work—work—work, 10
  Till the stars shine through the roof!
It's O! to be a slave
  Along with the barbarous Turk,
Where woman has never a soul to save,
  If this is Christian work!

'Work—work—work
  Till the brain begins to swim;
Work—work—work
  Till the eyes are heavy and dim! 20
Seam, and gusset, and band,
  Band, and gusset, and seam,
Till over the buttons I fall asleep,
  And sew them on in a dream!

'O! Men with Sisters dear!
  O! Men with Mothers and Wives,
It is not linen you're wearing out,
  But human creatures' lives
Stitch—stitch—stitch,
  In poverty, hunger, and dirt, 30
Sewing at once, with a double thread,
  A Shroud as well as a Shirt.

'But why do I talk of Death?
  That Phantom of grisly bone,
I hardly fear his terrible shape,
  It seems so like my own—
It seems so like my own—
  Because of the fasts I keep,
Oh! God! that bread should be so dear,
  And flesh and blood so cheap! 40

Work—work—work!
  My labour never flags;
And what are its wages? A bed of straw,
  A crust of bread—and rags.
That shatter'd roof,—and this naked floor—
  A table—a broken chair—

And a wall so blank, my shadow I thank
  For sometimes falling there!

'Work—work—work!
  From weary chime to chime, 50
Work—work—work—
  As prisoners work for crime!
Band, and gusset, and seam,
  Seam, and gusset, and band,
Till the heart is sick, and the brain benumb'd,
  As well as the weary hand.

'Work—work—work,
  In the dull December light,
And work—work—work,
  When the weather is warm and bright— 60
While underneath the eaves
  The brooding swallows cling,
As if to show me their sunny backs
  And twit me with the spring.

'Oh! but to breathe the breath
  Of the cowslip and primrose sweet—
With the sky above my head,
  And the grass beneath my feet,
For only one short hour
  To feel as I used to feel, 70
Before I knew the woes of want
  And the walk that costs a meal!

'Oh but for one short hour!
  A respite however brief!
No blessed leisure for love or hope,
  But only time for grief!
A little weeping would ease my heart,
  But in their briny bed
My tears must stop, for every drop
  Hinders needle and thread!' 80

Seam, and gusset, and band,
  Band, and gusset, and seam,
Work, work, work,
  Like the Engine that works by Steam!
A mere machine of iron and wood
  That toils for Mammon's sake—
Without a brain to ponder and craze,
  Or a heart to feel—and break!

With fingers weary and worn,
  With eyelids heavy and red, 90
A woman sate in unwomanly rags,
  Plying her needle and thread—
    Stitch! stitch! stitch!
In poverty, hunger, and dirt,
And still with a voice of dolorous pitch,

Would that its tone could reach the Rich!—
She sang this 'Song of the Shirt!'

1843

THE BRIDGE OF SIGHS

Drown'd! drown'd!— Hamlet.

ONE more Unfortunate,
Weary of breath,
Rashly importunate,
Gone to her death!

Take her up tenderly,
Lift her with care;
Fashion'd so slenderly,
Young, and so fair!

Look at her garments
Clinging like cerements;[1]   10
Whilst the wave constantly
Drips from her clothing;
Take her up instantly,
Loving, not loathing.—

Touch her not scornfully;
Think of her mournfully,
Gently and humanly;
Not of the stains of her,
All that remains of her
Now is pure womanly.   20

Make no deep scrutiny
Into her mutiny
Rash and undutiful:
Past all dishonour
Death has left on her
Only the beautiful.

Still, for all slips of hers,
One of Eve's family—
Wipe those poor lips of hers
Oozing so clammily.   30

Loop up her tresses
Escaped from the comb,
Her fair auburn tresses;
Whilst wonderment guesses
Where was her home?

Who was her father?
Who was her mother?
Had she a sister?
Had she a brother?
Or was there a dearer one   40

1 waxed clothes used for wrapping dead bodies.

Still, and a nearer one
Yet, than all other?

Alas! for the rarity
Of Christian charity
Under the sun!
Oh! it was pitiful!
Near a whole city full,
Home she had none!

Sisterly, brotherly,
Fatherly, motherly,   50
Feelings had changed:
Love, by harsh evidence,
Thrown from its eminence;
Even God's providence
Seeming estranged.

Where the lamps quiver
So far in the river,
With many a light
From window and casement,
From garret to basement,   60
She stood, with amazement,
Houseless by night.

The bleak wind of March
Made her tremble and shiver;
But not the dark arch,
Or the black flowing river:
Mad from life's history,
Glad to death's mystery,
Swift to be hurl'd—
Anywhere, anywhere,   70
Out of the world!

In she plunged boldly,
No matter how coldly
The rough river ran,—
Over the brink of it,
Picture it—think of it,
Dissolute man!
Lave in it, drink of it,
Then, if you can!

Take her up tenderly,   80
Lift her with care;
Fashion'd so slenderly,
Young, and so fair!

Ere her limbs frigidly
Stiffen too rigidly,
Decently,—kindly,—
Smoothe and compose them:
And her eyes, close them,
Staring so blindly!

Dreadfully staring　　　　90
Thro' muddy impurity,
As when with the daring
Last look of despairing,
Fix'd on futurity.

Perishing gloomily,
Spurr'd by contumely,
Cold inhumanity,
Burning insanity,
Into her rest.—
Cross her hands humbly,　　　100
As if praying dumbly,
Over her breast!

Owning her weakness,
Her evil behaviour,
And leaving, with meekness,
Her sins to her Saviour!

　　　　　　　　　　1844

FAREWELL, LIFE

[This was Hood's last poem, written on his deathbed.]

FAREWELL, Life! My senses swim;
And the world is growing dim;
Thronging shadows cloud the light,
Like the advent of the night,—
Colder, colder, colder still
Upward steals a vapour chill—
Strong the earthy odour grows—
I smell the Mould above the Rose!

Welcome, Life! the Spirit strives!
Strength returns, and hope revives;　　　10
Cloudy fears and shapes forlorn
Fly like shadows at the morn,—
O'er the earth there comes a bloom—
Sunny light for sullen gloom,
Warm perfume for vapour cold—
I smell the Rose above the Mould!

　　　January 1845　　　　　　　　1845

1802 · WINTHROP MACKWORTH PRAED · 1839

1802   Born in London, son of an eminent barrister.

1814–22   Educated at Eton, where he founded *The Etonion* and at Trinity College, Cambridge, where he distinguished himself for brilliant scholarship and skill in versification.

1829   Admitted to the bar.

1830–39   Entered Parliament as a conservative; twice re-elected; acquired considerable reputation as a debater and a man of business.

1839   Died of tuberculosis at the age of thirty-seven.

P RAED embodies the well-bred world of Eton and Cambridge and the charmed circle of 'good society' in which he moved. His lighthearted verse, like the society it reflected, is no longer in fashion; yet such is the gaiety of Praed's good-humored, vernacular banter that the modern reader is almost immediately disarmed of his reserve and enlivened to enjoyment. His pellucid verse ripples with spontaneity, sparkling wit, and gayest rime. He reveals a fairly wide variety of styles and subject matter. Sometimes his instrument is muted to tenderness and sensitiveness to human values; at other times, he tries the serious personal lyric; or, more often, the not-at-all serious political or social satire. He has been compared to Hood, with whom he shares some traits; however, he lacks Hood's range and strength. Praed is not a great poet, but he is a consistently pleasing one and in graceful society verse he is justly acknowledged to be unequaled.

TIME'S SONG

O'er the level plains, where mountains greet me
    as I go,
O'er the desert waste, where fountains at my bid-
    ding flow,
On the boundless beam by day, on the cloud by
    night,
I am riding hence away: who will chain my
    flight?

War his weary watch was keeping,—I have
    crushed his spear;
Grief within her bower was weeping,—I have
    dried her tear;
Pleasure caught a minute's hold,—then I hurried
    by,
Leaving all her banquet cold, and her goblet dry.

Power had won a throne of glory: where is now
    his fame?
Genius said, 'I live in story': who hath heard his
    name?   10
Love beneath a myrtle bough whispered 'Why so
    fast?'
And the roses on his brow withered as I past.

I have heard the heifer lowing o'er the wild
    wave's bed;
I have seen the billow flowing where the cattle
    fed;
Where began my wandering? Memory will not
    say!
Where will rest my weary wings? Science turns
    away!

                             1826

From EVERY-DAY CHARACTERS

THE VICAR

SOME years ago, ere time and taste
　Had turned our parish topsy-turvy,
When Darnel Park was Darnel Waste,
　And roads as little known as scurvy,
The man who lost his way, between
　St. Mary's Hill and Sandy Thicket,
Was always shown across the green,
　And guided to the Parson's wicket.

Back flew the bolt of lissom lath;
　Fair Margaret, in her tidy kirtle,　　10
Led the lorn traveller up the path,
　Through clean-clipt rows of box and myrtle;
And Don and Sancho, Tramp and Tray,
　Upon the parlour steps collected,
Wagged all their tails, and seemed to say—
　'Our master knows you—you're expected.'

Uprose the Reverend Dr. Brown,
　Uprose the Doctor's winsome marrow;[1]
The lady laid her knitting down,
　Her husband clasped his ponderous Bar-
　　row;[2]　　20
Whate'er the stranger's caste or creed,
　Pundit or Papist, saint or sinner,
He found a stable for his steed,
　And welcome for himself, and dinner.

If, when he reached his journey's end,
　And warmed himself in Court or College,
He had not gained an honest friend
　And twenty curious scraps of knowledge,—
If he departed as he came,
　With no new light on love or liquor,—　　30
Good sooth, the traveller was to blame,
　And not the Vicarage, nor the Vicar.

His talk was like a stream, which runs
　With rapid change from rocks to roses:
It slipped from politics to puns,
　It passed from Mahomet to Moses;
Beginning with the laws which keep
　The planets in their radiant courses,
And ending with some precept deep
　For dressing eels, or shoeing horses.　　40

He was a shrewd and sound Divine,
　Of loud Dissent the mortal terror;
And when, by dint of page and line,
　He 'stablished Truth, or startled Error,

The Baptist found him far too deep;
　The Deist sighed with saving sorrow;
And the lean Levite went to sleep,
　And dreamed of tasting pork to-morrow.

His sermon never said or showed
　That Earth is foul, that Heaven is gracious,　　50
Without refreshment on the road
　From Jerome,[3] or from Athanasius:[4]
And sure a righteous zeal inspired
　The hand and head that penned and planned
　　them,
For all who understood admired,
　And some who did not understand them.

He wrote, too, in a quiet way,
　Small treatises, and smaller verses,
And sage remarks on chalk and clay,
　And hints to noble Lords—and nurses;　　60
True histories of last year's ghost,
　Lines to a ringlet, or a turban,
And trifles for the Morning Post,
　And nothings for Sylvanus Urban.[5]

He did not think all mischief fair,
　Although he had a knack of joking;
He did not make himself a bear,
　Although he had a taste for smoking;
And when religious sects ran mad,
　He held, in spite of all his learning,　　70
That if a man's belief is bad,
　It will not be improved by burning.

And he was kind, and loved to sit
　In the low hut or garnished cottage,
And praise the farmer's homely wit,
　And share the widow's homelier pottage!
At his approach complaint grew mild;
　And when his hand unbarred the shutter,
The clammy lips of fever smiled
　The welcome which they could not utter.　　80

He always had a tale for me
　Of Julius Caesar, or of Venus;
From him I learnt the rule of three,[6]
　Cat's cradle,[7] leap-frog,[7] and *Quae genus;*[7]
I used to singe his powdered wig,
　To steal the staff he put such trust in,
And make the puppy dance a jig,
　When he began to quote Augustine.

---

1 cheerful companion, here his wife.
2 Isaac Barrow, 1630–77, English theologian and classical scholar.
3 a father of the Latin church, d. 420.
4 one of the fathers of the Christian church, d. 373.
5 the pseudonym of the editor of the *Gentleman's Magazine.*
6 the rule for finding the fourth term of a proportion when three are given.
7 various children's games.

Alack the change! in vain I look
    For haunts in which my boyhood trifled,— 90
The level lawn, the trickling brook,
    The trees I climbed, the beds I rifled:
The church is larger than before;
    You reach it by a carriage entry;
It holds three hundred people more,
    And pews are fitted up for gentry.

Sit in the Vicar's seat: you'll hear
    The doctrine of a gentle Johnian,
Whose hand is white, whose tone is clear,
    Whose phrase is very Ciceronian. 100
Where is the old man laid?—look down,
    And construe on the slab before you,
'*Hic jacet* GVLIELMVS BROWN,
    Vir nullâ non donandus lauru.'[8]

                1829

THE BELLE OF THE BALL-ROOM

    *Il faut juger des femmes depuis la chaussure
jusqu' à la coiffure exclusivement, à peu près
comme on mesure le poisson entre queue et tête.*
—LA BRUYÈRE.

YEARS—years ago,—ere yet my dreams
    Had been of being wise or witty,—
Ere I had done with writing themes,
    Or yawned o'er this infernal Chitty;[2]—
Years—years ago,—while all my joy
    Was in my fowling-piece and filly,—
In short, while I was yet a boy,
    I fell in love with Laura Lily.

I saw her at the County Ball:
    There, when the sounds of flute and fiddle 10
Gave signal sweet in that old hall
    Of hands across and down the middle,
Hers was the subtlest spell by far
    Of all that set young hearts romancing;
She was our queen, our rose, our star;
    And then she danced—O Heaven, her danc-
        ing!

Dark was her hair, her hand was white;
    Her voice was exquisitely tender;
Her eyes were full of liquid light;
    I never saw a waist so slender! 20
Her every look, her every smile,

Shot right and left a score of arrows;
I thought 'twas Venus from her isle,
    And wondered where she'd left her sparrows.

She talked,—of politics or prayers,—
    Of Southey's prose or Wordsworth's son-
        nets,—
Of danglers—or of dancing bears,
    Of battles—or the last new bonnets,
By candlelight, at twelve o'clock,
    To me it mattered not a tittle; 30
If those bright lips had quoted Locke,[3]
    I might have thought they murmured Little.[4]

Through sunny May, through sultry June,
    I loved her with a love eternal;
I spoke her praises to the moon,
    I wrote them to *The Sunday Journal:*
My mother laughed; I soon found out
    That ancient ladies have no feeling:
My father frowned; but how should gout
    See any happiness in kneeling? 40

She was the daughter of a Dean,
    Rich, fat, and rather apoplectic;
She had one brother, just thirteen,
    Whose colour was extremely hectic;
Her grandmother for many a year
    Had fed the parish with her bounty;
Her second cousin was a peer,
    And Lord Lieutenant of the County.

But titles, and the three per cents,
    And mortgages, and great relations, 50
And India bonds, and tithes and rents,
    Oh, what are they to love's sensations?
Black eyes, fair forehead, clustering locks—
    Such wealth, such honours, Cupid chooses;
He cares as little for the Stocks,
    As Baron Rothschild[5] for the Muses.

She sketched; the vale, the wood, the beach,
    Grew lovelier from her pencil's shading:
She botanized; I envied each
    Young blossom in her boudoir fading: 60
She warbled Handel;[6] it was grand;
    She made the Catalani[7] jealous:
She touched the organ; I could stand
    For hours and hours to blow the bellows.

She kept an album, too, at home,
    Well filled with all an album's glories;

---

8 'Here lies William Brown, a man to whom some honour is due.'

1 'We should judge of a woman without taking into account her
shoes and head-dress, and, almost as we measure a fish, from
head to tail.'
2 Joseph Chitty, 1776–1841, English jurist and legal writer.

3 John Locke, 1632–1704, the celebrated English philosopher.
4 a pseudonym of Thomas Moore.
5 Nathan Mayer de Rothschild, 1777–1836, London banker.
6 Georg Friedrich Handel, 1685–1759, German musical composer.
7 Angelica Catalani, 1780–1849, an Italian singer.

Paintings of butterflies, and Rome,
  Patterns for trimmings, Persian stories;
Soft songs to Julia's cockatoo,
  Fierce odes to Famine and to Slaughter;   70
And autographs of Prince Leboo,[8]
  And recipes for elder-water.

And she was flattered, worshipped, bored;
  Her steps were watched, her dress was noted,
Her poodle dog was quite adored,
  Her sayings were extremely quoted;
She laughed, and every heart was glad,
  As if the taxes were abolished;
She frowned, and every look was sad,
  As if the Opera were demolished.   80

She smiled on many, just for fun,—
  I knew that there was nothing in it;
I was the first—the only one
  Her heart had thought of for a minute.—
I knew it, for she told me so,
  In phrase which was divinely moulded;
She wrote a charming hand,—and oh!
  How sweetly all her notes were folded!

Our love was like most other loves;—
  A little glow, a little shiver,   90
A rose-bud, and a pair of gloves,
  And 'Fly not yet'—upon the river;
Some jealousy of some one's heir,
  Some hopes of dying broken-hearted;
A miniature, a lock of hair,
  The usual vows,—and then we parted.

We parted; months and years rolled by;
  We met again four summers after:
Our parting was all sob and sigh;
  Our meeting was all mirth and laughter: 100
For in my heart's most secret cell
  There had been many other lodgers;
And she was not the ball-room's belle,
  But only—Mrs. Something Rogers!

                                              1830

From LETTERS FROM TEIGNMOUTH[1]

OUR BALL

Comment! c'est lui? que je le regarde encore!
C'est que vraiment il est bien changé; n'est-ce pas,
mon papa.[2]—*Les Premiers Amours.*

YOU'LL come to our ball;—since we parted
  I've thought of you more than I'll say;
Indeed, I was half broken-hearted
  For a week, when they took you away.
Fond fancy brought back to my slumbers
  Our walks on the Ness and the Den,
And echoed the musical numbers
  Which you used to sing to me then.
I know the romance, since it's over,
  'Twere idle, or worse, to recall;—   10
I know you're a terrible rover;
  But, Clarence, you'll come to our Ball!

It's only a year since, at College,
  You put on your cap and your gown;
But, Clarence, you're grown out of knowledge,
  And changed from the spur to the crown;
The voice that was best when it faltered,
  Is fuller and firmer in tone;
And the smile that should never have altered,—
  Dear Clarence,—it is not your own;   20
Your cravat was badly selected,
  Your coat don't become you at all;
And why is your hair so neglected?
  You must have it curled for our Ball.

I've often been out upon Haldon[3]
  To look for a covey with Pup;
I've often been over to Shaldon,[4]
  To see how your boat is laid up.
In spite of the terrors of Aunty,
  I've ridden the filly you broke;   30
And I've studied your sweet little Dante
  In the shade of your favourite oak:
When I sat in July to Sir Lawrence,
  I sat in your love of a shawl;
And I'll wear what you brought me from Flor-
    ence,
  Perhaps, if you'll come to our Ball.

You'll find us all changed since you vanished;
  We've set up a National School;[5]
And waltzing is utterly banished;
  And Ellen has married a fool;   40
The Major is going to travel;
  Miss Hyacinth threatens a rout;[6]
The walk is laid down with fresh gravel;
  Papa is laid up with the gout;
And Jane has gone on with her easels,
  And Anne has gone off with Sir Paul;
And Fanny is sick with the measles,
  And I'll tell you the rest at the Ball.

---

8 Jean Louis Joseph Lebeau, 1794–1865, a Belgian diplomat who in 1830–31 carried on important negotiations with England.

1 This is one of two 'letters' written from Teignmouth, Devonshire, a seaport and fashionable watering place at the mouth of the river Teign, on the English Channel.
2 'What! is it he? Let me look at him again! He is truly much changed; is he not, papa?'

3 a range of hills in Devonshire.
4 a village on the river Teign across from Teignmouth.
5 a school established by a national society for educating the poor.
6 a large fashionable evening party.

You'll meet all your beauties;—the Lily,
    And the Fairy of Willowbrook Farm,   50
And Lucy, who made me so silly
    At Dawlish, by taking your arm;
Miss Manners, who always abused you,
    For talking so much about Hock;[7]
And her sister, who often amused you,
    By raving of rebels and Rock;[8]
And something which surely would answer,
    An heiress quite fresh from Bengal:—
So, though you were seldom a dancer,
    You'll dance, just for once, at our Ball.   60

But out on the world!—from the flowers
    It shuts out the sunshine of truth;
It blights the green leaves in the bowers,
    It makes an old age of our youth:
And the flow of our feeling, once in it,
    Like a streamlet beginning to freeze,
Though it cannot turn ice in a minute,
    Grows harder by sudden degrees.
Time treads o'er the graves of affection;
    Sweet honey is turned into gall;   70
Perhaps you have no recollection
    That ever you danced at our Ball.

You once could be pleased with our ballads—
    Today you have critical ears;
You once could be charmed with our salads—
    Alas! you've been dining with Peers;
You trifled and flirted with many;
    You've forgotten the when and the how;
There was one you liked better than any—
    Perhaps you've forgotten her now.   80
But of those you remember most newly,
    Of those who delight or enthrall,
None love you a quarter so truly
    As some you will find at our Ball.

They tell me you've many who flatter,
    Because of your wit and your song;
They tell me (and what does it matter?)
    You like to be praised by the throng;
They tell me you're shadowed with laurel,
    They tell me you're loved by a Blue;[9]   90
They tell me you're sadly immoral—
    Dear Clarence, that cannot be true!
But to me you are still what I found you
    Before you grew clever and tall;
And you'll think of the spell that once bound
    you;

And you'll come, WON'T you come? to our
Ball?

                          1829

THE TALENTED MAN

A LETTER FROM A LADY IN LONDON TO A LADY AT LAUSANNE[1]

DEAR Alice! you'll laugh when you know it,—
    Last week, at the Duchess's ball,
I danced with the clever new poet,—
    You've heard of him,—Tully St. Paul.
Miss Jonquil was perfectly frantic;
    I wish you had seen Lady Anne!
It really was very romantic,
    He *is* such a talented man!

He came up from Brazenose College,[2]
    Just caught, as they call it, this spring;   10
And his head, love, is stuffed full of knowledge
    Of every conceivable thing.
Of science and logic he chatters,
    As fine and as fast as he can;
Though I am no judge of such matters,
    I'm sure he's a talented man.

His stories and jests are delightful;—
    Not stories, or jests, dear, for you;
The jests are exceedingly spiteful,
    The stories not always *quite* true.   20
Perhaps to be kind and veracious
    May do pretty well at Lausanne;
But it never would answer,—good gracious!
    Chez nous[3]—in a talented man.

He sneers,—how my Alice would scold him!—
    At the bliss of a sigh or a tear;
He laughed—only think!—when I told him
    How we cried o'er Trevelyan[4] last year;
I vow I was quite in a passion;
    I broke all the sticks of my fan;   30
But sentiment's quite out of fashion,
    It seems, in a talented man.

Lady Bab, who is terribly moral,
    Has told me that Tully is vain,
And apt—which is silly—to quarrel,
    And fond—which is sad—of champagne.
I listened, and doubted, dear Alice,
    For I saw, when my Lady began,

---

7 Hochheimer, a kind of wine.
8 a fictitious name signed to public notices by a leader of the Irish insurgents of 1822.
9 Bluestocking, i. e. a woman affecting an interest in learning and literature.

1 a city in Switzerland.
2 one of the colleges at Oxford University.
3 'with us.'
4 Raleigh Trevelyan, 1781–1865, English writer of slight importance who wrote on various subjects.

It was only the Dowager's malice;—
  She *does* hate a talented man! 40

He's hideous, I own it. But fame, love,
  Is all that these eyes can adore;
He's lame,—but Lord Byron was lame, love,
  And dumpy,—but so is Tom Moore.
Then his voice,—*such* a voice! my sweet creature,
  It's like your Aunt Lucy's toucan;[5]
But oh! what's a tone or a feature,
  When once one's a talented man?

My mother, you know, all the season,
  Has talked of Sir Geoffrey's estate; 50
And truly, to do the fool reason,
  He *has* been less horrid of late.
But today, when we drive in the carriage,
  I'll tell her to lay down her plan;—
If ever I venture on marriage
  It must be a talented man!

P.S.—I have found on reflection,
  One fault in my friend,—*entre nous,*[6]
Without it, he'd just be perfection;—
  Poor fellow, he has not a *sou!* 60
And so, when he comes in September
  To shoot with my uncle, Sir Dan,
I've promised mamma to remember
  He's *only* a talented man!

1831

STANZAS

ON SEEING THE SPEAKER ASLEEP IN HIS CHAIR
DURING ONE OF THE DEBATES OF THE
FIRST REFORMED PARLIAMENT[1]

S<small>LEEP</small>, Mr. Speaker;[2] it's surely fair
If you don't in your bed, that you should in your
  chair,
Longer and longer still they grow,

---

5 a brilliantly-colored tropical bird with a harsh voice.
6 'between us.'

1 This Parliament met in 1833, in the year following the Reform Act. It legislated many reforms including the abolition of slavery, the prohibition of child labor, and the appropriation of funds for public education and for the relief of the poor.
2 Charles Manners Sutton, 1780–1845, a Tory, who was for many years speaker of the House of Commons.

Tory and Radical, Aye and No;
Talking by night, and talking by day;—
Sleep, Mr. Speaker; sleep, sleep while you may!

Sleep, Mr. Speaker; slumber lies
Light and brief on a Speaker's eyes;
Fielden[3] or Finn,[4] in a minute or two,
Some disorderly thing will do; 10
Riot will chase repose away;—
Sleep, Mr. Speaker; sleep, sleep while you may!

Sleep, Mr. Speaker; Cobbett[5] will soon
Move to abolish the sun and moon;
Hume, no doubt, will be taking the sense
Of the House on a saving of thirteen pence;
Grattan[6] will growl, or Baldwin[7] bray;—
Sleep, Mr. Speaker; sleep, sleep while you may!

Sleep, Mr. Speaker; dream of the time
When loyalty was not quite a crime; 20
When Grant[8] was a pupil in Canning's[9] school;
When Palmerston[10] fancied Wood[11] a fool;
Lord, how principles pass away!
Sleep, Mr. Speaker; sleep, sleep while you may!

Sleep, Mr. Speaker; sweet to men
Is the sleep that cometh but now and then;
Sweet to the sorrowful, sweet to the ill,
Sweet to the children that work in a mill;
You have more need of sleep than they;—
Sleep, Mr. Speaker; sleep, sleep while you
  may! 30

1833

---

3 John Fielden, 1784–1849, a radical reformer.
4 an Irish politician.
5 William Cobbett, 1763–1835, writer of political tracts and a member of the House of Commons, who violently attacked all sorts of institutions and measures.
6 Henry Grattan, Jr., 1746–1820, an Irish Member of Parliament noted for his quarrels with regard to legislation.
7 a member of the House of Commons, 1833–5.
8 Charles Grant, 1778–1866, an unpopular politician who entered Canning's ministry in 1827 as president of the Board of Trade.
9 George Canning, 1770–1827, secretary for Foreign Affairs in 1822 and Premier in 1827, celebrated for his foreign policy of non-intervention.
10 John Temple Palmerston, 1784–1865, an English statesman who championed liberal causes.
11 Sir Matthew Wood, 1768–1843, an English political reformer who consistently and strenuously supported the Whig ministries.

1793 · JOHN CLARE · 1864

1793   Born the son of a Northamptonshire farm laborer.

1800–27   At various times herd-boy, gardener, lime burner, militiaman, vagrant, unsuccessful farmer.

1820   Published *Poems Descriptive of Rural Life and Scenery,* which went through three editions; and the next year,

1821   *Village Minstrel and other Poems.*

1827   Published *The Shepherd's Calendar.*

1835   Published *Rural Muse,* containing much of the poet's best work, which went unregarded at the time.

1837   Removed to an insane asylum.

1864   Died in the Northampton asylum.

JOHN CLARE, the 'Northamptonshire peasant poet,' was a sensitive and frail individual who lived out of harmony with his harsh environment and finally escaped from it into madness. His early verse, produced chiefly during respites from hard manual labor in the fields, treats of rustic life and the world of nature. He loved the countryside beyond anything else and never abandoned his first principle of fidelity to nature. His method of composition was to go into the fields with pencil and paper exactly as a landscape artist would do and roughly sketch his subjects there. In this way observation and expression were firmly bound together on the scene in sinewy, physical phrases. Clare happily had a storehouse of homespun local words—such as, 'drowking meadow sweet,' 'chumbling mouse,' 'limping flail'—with which he flavored his verses of country life. His nature poetry is characteristically descriptive of small creatures and the less obtrusive growing things in the fields. It has a pensiveness of tone; often, the delicacy of etchings. Distinct from the nature poetry are the love songs and ballads of the later years written during lucid intervals in a madhouse. Age brought on 'an exaltation of memory and a new tenderness for children.' In the asylum verses, Clare's lyrical faculty gets free. *The Dying Child* with its intimate, indefinable pathos is one of the poet's most perfect utterances.

   Clare is something of a minor discovery for twentieth-century readers. Although he has been known to specialists, much of his best work remained unpublished until 1920 and the bulk of the poems was not issued until 1935. He composed with too easy fluency, and nearly everywhere a childlike awkwardness betrays his lack of training and discipline. Yet Clare has written verses of subtle charm, wholly spontaneous and sincere, and of near lyrical perfection in expression, passion, and music.

THE WOOD-CUTTER'S NIGHT SONG

WELCOME, red and roundy sun,
　Dropping lowly in the west;
Now my hard day's work is done,
　I'm as happy as the best.

Joyful are the thoughts of home,
　Now I'm ready for my chair,
So, till morrow-morning's come,
　Bill[1] and mittens, lie ye there!

Though to leave your pretty song,
　Little birds, it gives me pain,　　　　10
Yet to-morrow is not long,
　Then I'm with you all again.

If I stop, and stand about,
　Well I know how things will be,
Judy will be looking out
　Every now-and-then for me.

So fare-ye-well! and hold your tongues,
　Sing no more until I come;
They're not worthy of your songs
　That never care to drop a crumb.　　　20

All day long I love the oaks,
　But, at nights, yon little cot,
Where I see the chimney smokes,
　Is by far the prettiest spot.

Wife and children all are there,
　To revive with pleasant looks,
Table ready set, and chair,
　Supper hanging on the hooks.

Soon as ever I get in,
　When my faggot[2] down I fling,　　　30
Little prattlers they begin
　Teasing me to talk and sing.

Welcome, red and roundy sun,
　Dropping lowly in the west;
Now my hard day's work is done,
　I'm as happy as the best.

Joyful are the thoughts of home,
　Now I'm ready for my chair,
So, till morrow-morning's come,
　Bill and mittens, lie ye there!　　　40

1821

---

1 a cutting instrument used for pruning branches.
2 bundle of sticks.

SOLITUDE

Now as even's warning bell
Rings the day's departing knell,
Leaving me from labour free,
Solitude, I'll walk with thee:
Whether 'side the woods we rove,
Or sweep beneath the willow grove;
Whether sauntering we proceed
Cross the green, or down the mead;
Whether, sitting down, we look
On the bubbles of the brook;　　　10
Whether, curious, waste an hour,
Pausing o'er each tasty flower;
Or, expounding nature's spells,
From the sand pick out the shells;
Or, while lingering by the streams,
Where more sweet the music seems,
Listen to the soft'ning swells
Of some distant chiming bells
Mellowing sweetly on the breeze,
Rising, falling by degrees,　　　20
Dying now, then wak'd again
In full many a 'witching strain,
Sounding, as the gale flits by,
Flats and sharps of melody.

Sweet it is to wind the rill,
Sweet with thee to climb the hill,
On whose lap the bullock free
Chews his cud most placidly;
Or o'er fallows bare and brown
Beaten sheep-tracks wander down,　　　30
Where the mole unwearied still
Roots up many a crumbling hill,
And the little chumbling mouse
Gnarls the dead weed for her house,
While the plough's unfeeling share
Lays full many a dwelling bare;—
Where the lark with russet breast
'Hind the big clod hides her nest,
And the black snail's founder'd pace
Finds from noon a hiding-place,　　　40
Breaking off the scorching sun
Where the matted twitches run.

Solitude! I love thee well,
Brushing through the wilder'd dell,
Picking from the ramping[1] grass
Nameless blossoms as I pass,
Which the dews of eve bedeck,
Fair as pearls on woman's neck;
Marking shepherds rous'd from sleep
Blundering off to fold their sheep;　　　50
And the swain, with toils distrest,

---

1 entwined with vines.

Hide his tools to seek his rest:
While the cows, with hobbling strides,
Twitching slow their fly-bit hides,
Rub the pasture's creaking gate,
Milking maids and boys to wait.
Or as sunshine leaves the sky,
As the daylight shuts her eye,
Sweet it is to meet the breeze
'Neath the shade of hawthorn trees,   60
By the pasture's wilder'd round,
Where the pismire² hills abound,
Where the blushing fin-weed's flower
Closes up at even's hour:
Leaving then the green behind,
Narrow hoof-plod lanes to wind,
Oak and ash embower'd beneath,
Leading to the lonely heath,
Where the unmolested furze
And the burdock's clinging burs,   70
And the briars, by freedom sown,
Claim the wilder'd spots their own.

There while we the scene survey
Deck'd in nature's wild array,
Swell'd with ling-clad³ hillocks green
Suiting the disorder'd scene,
Haply we may rest us then
In the banish'd herdsman's den;
Where the wattled hulk is fixt,
Propt some double oak betwixt,   80
Where the swain the branches lops,
And o'erhead with rushes tops;
Where, with woodbine's sweet perfume,
And the rose's blushing bloom,
Loveliest ceiling of the bower,
Arching in, peeps many a flower;
While a hill of thyme so sweet,
Or a moss'd stone, forms a seat.
There, as 'tween-light hangs the eve,
I will watch thy bosom heave;   90
Marking then the darksome flows
Night's gloom o'er thy mantle throws;
Fondly gazing on thine eye
As it rolls its extasy,
When thy solemn musings caught
Tell thy soul's absorb'd in thought;
When thy finely folded arm
O'er thy bosom beating warm
Wraps thee melancholy round;
And thy ringlets wild unbound   100
On thy lily shoulders lie,
Like dark streaks in morning's sky.
Peace and silence sit with thee,

---
2 ant.
3 covered with heather.

And peace alone is heaven to me:
While the moonlight's infant hour
Faint 'gins creep to gild the bower,
And the wattled hedge gleams round
Its diamond shadows on the ground.
—O thou soothing Solitude,
From the vain and from the rude,   110
When this silent hour is come,
And I meet thy welcome home,
What balm is thine to troubles deep,
As on thy breast I sink to sleep;
What bliss on even's silence flows,
When thy wish'd opiate brings repose.

And I have found thee wondrous sweet,
Sheltering from the noon-day heat,
As 'neath hazels I have stood
In the gloomy hanging wood,   120
Where the sunbeams, filtering small,
Freckling through the branches fall;
And the flapping leaf the ground
Shadows, flitting round and round:
Where the glimmering streamlets wreathe
Many a crooked root beneath,
Unseen gliding day by day
O'er their solitary way,
Smooth or rough, as onward led
Where the wild-weed dips its head,   130
Murmuring,—dribbling drop by drop
When dead leaves their progress stop,—
Or winding sweet their restless way
While the frothy bubbles play.
And I love thy presence drear
In such wildernesses, where
Ne'er an axe was heard to sound,
Or a tree's fall gulsh'd the ground,
Where (as if that spot could be)
First foot-mark'd the ground by me,   140
All is still, and wild, and gay,
Left as at creation's day.
Pleasant too it is to look
For thy steps in shady nook,
Where, by hedge-side coolly led,
Brooks curl o'er their sandy bed;
On whose tide the clouds reflect,
In whose margin flags are freckt;
Where the waters, winding blue,
Single-arch'd brig flutter through,   150
While the willow-branches grey
Damp the sultry eye of day,
And in whispers mildly sooth
Chafe the mossy keystone smooth;
Where the banks, beneath them spread,
Level in an easy bed;
While the wild-thyme's pinky bells

Circulate reviving smells;
And the breeze, with feather-feet,
Crimping o'er the waters sweet,   160
Trembling fans the sun-tann'd cheek,
And gives the comfort one would seek.
Stretching there in soft repose,
Far from peace and freedom's foes,
In a spot, so wild, so rude,
Dear to me is solitude!
Soothing then to watch the ground,—
Every insect flitting round,
Such as painted summer brings;—
Lady-fly with freckled wings,   170
Watch her up the tall bent climb;
And from knotted flowers of thyme,
Where the woodland banks are deckt,
See the bee his load collect;
Mark him turn the petals by,
Gold dust gathering on his thigh,
As full many a hum he heaves,
While he pats th' intruding leaves,
Lost in many a heedless spring,
Then wearing home on heavy wing.   180

But when sorrows more oppress,
When the world brings more distress,
Wishing to despise as then
Brunts of fate, and scorn of men;
When fate's demons thus intrude,
Then I seek thee, Solitude,
Where the abbey's height appears
Hoary 'neath a weight of years;
Where the mouldering walls are seen
Hung with pellitory⁴ green;   190
Where the steeple's taper stretch
Tires the eye its length to reach,
Dizzy, nauntling⁵ high and proud,
Top-stone losing in a cloud;
Where the cross, to time resign'd,
Creaking harshly in the wind,
Crowning high the rifted dome,
Points the pilgrim's wish'd-for home;
While the look fear turns away,
Shuddering at its dread decay.   200
There let me my peace pursue
'Neath the shades of gloomy yew,
Doleful hung with mourning green,
Suiting well the solemn scene;
There, that I may learn to scan
Mites illustrious, called man,
Turn with thee the nettles by
Where the grave-stone meets the eye,
Soon, full soon to read and see

4 a plant resembling yarrow.
5 rising.

That all below is vanity;   210
And man, to me a galling thing,
Own'd creation's lord and king,
A minute's length, a zephyr's breath,
Sport of fate, and prey of death,
Tyrant to-day, to-morrow gone,
Distinguish'd only by a stone,
That fain would have the eye to know
Pride's better dust is lodg'd below—
While worms like me are mouldering laid,
With nothing set to say 'they're dead'—   220
All the difference, trifling thing,
That notes at last the slave and king.
As wither'd leaves, life's bloom when stopt,
That drop in autumn, so they dropt
As snails, which in their painted shell
So snugly once were known to dwell,
When in the schoolboy's care we view
The pleasing toys of varied hue,
By age or accident are flown,
The shell left empty, tenant gone—   230
So pass we from the world's affairs,
And careless vanish from its cares;
So leave, with silent, long farewell,
Vain life—as left the snail his shell.

All this when there my eyes behold
On every stone and heap of mould,
Solitude, though thou art sweet,
Solemn art thou then to meet;
When with list'ning pause I look
Round the pillar's ruin'd nook,   240
Glooms revealing, dim descried,
Ghosts, companion'd by thy side;
Where in old deformity
Ancient arches sweep on high,
And the aisles, to light unknown,
Create a darkness all their own;
Save the moon, as on we pass,
Splinters through the broken glass,
Or the torn roof, patch'd with cloud,
Or the crack'd wall, bulg'd and bow'd—   250
Glimmering faint along the ground,
Shooting solemn and profound,
Lighting up the silent gloom
Just to read an ancient tomb,
'Neath where, as it gliding creeps
We may see some abbot sleeps;
And as on we mete the aisle,
Daring scarce to breathe the while
Soft as creeping feet can fall,
While the damp green-stained wall   260
Swift the startled ghost flits by,
Mocking murmurs faintly sigh,
Reminding our intruding fear

Such visits are unwelcome here.
Seemly then, from hollow urn,
Gentle steps our steps return;
E'er so soft and e'er so still,
Check our breath of how we will,
List'ning spirits still reply
Step for step, and sigh for sigh,   270
Murmuring o'er one's weary woe,
Such as once 'twas theirs to know,
They whisper to such slaves as me,
A buried tale of misery:
'We once had life, ere life's decline,
Flesh, blood, and bones, the same as thine;
We knew its pains, and shar'd its grief,
Till death, long wish'd-for, brought relief;
We had our hopes, and like to thee,
Hoped morrow's better day to see,   280
But like to thine, our hope the same,
To-morrow's kindness never came:
We had our tyrants, e'en as thou;
Our wants met many a scornful brow;
But death laid low their wealthy powers,
Their harmless ashes mix with ours:
And this vain world, its pride, its form,
That treads on thee as on a worm,
Its mighty heirs—the time shall be
When they as quiet sleep by thee!'   290

Oh, here's thy comfort, Solitude,
When overpowering woes intrude!
Then thy sad, thy solemn dress
Owns the balm my soul to bless;
Here I judge the world aright,
Here see vain man in his true light,
Learn patience, in this trying hour,
To gild Life's brambles with a flower,
Take pattern from the hints thou'st given,
And follow in thy steps to heaven.   300

                                                    1821

THE FIRETAIL'S NEST[1]

'TWEET' pipes the robin as the cat creeps by
Her nestling young that in the elderns lie,
And then the bluecap[2] tootles in its glee,
Picking the flies from orchard apple tree,
And 'pink,' the chaffinch cries its well-known
          strain,
Urging its kind to utter 'pink' again,
While in a quiet mood hedge-sparrows try
An inward stir of shadowed melody.

1 The firetail is the European redstart.
2 the blue titmouse.

Around the rotten tree the firetail mourns
As the old hedger to his toil returns,   10
Chopping the grain to stop the gap close by
The hole where her blue eggs in safety lie.
Of everything that stirs she dreameth wrong
And pipes her 'tweet-tut' fears the whole day
          long.

          c. 1830   1908

BADGER

WHEN midnight comes a host of dogs and men
Go out and track the badger to his den,
And put a sack within the hole, and lie
Till the old grunting badger passes by.
He comes and hears—they let the strongest loose.
The old fox hears the noise and drops the goose.
The poacher shoots and hurries from the cry,
And the old hare half wounded buzzes by.
They get a forkèd stick to bear him down
And clap the dogs and take him to the town,   10
And bait him all the day with many dogs,
And laugh and shout and fright the scampering
          hogs.
He runs along and bites at all he meets:
They shout and hollo down the noisy streets.

He turns about to face the loud uproar
And drives the rebels to their very door.
The frequent stone is hurled where'er they go;
When badgers fight, then every one's a foe.
The dogs are clapt and urged to join the fray;
The badger turns and drives them all away.   20
Though scarcely half as big, demure and small,
He fights with dogs for hours and beats them all.
The heavy mastiff, savage in the fray,
Lies down and licks his feet and turns away.
The bulldog knows his match and waxes cold,
The badger grins and never leaves his hold.
He drives the crowd and follows at their heels
And bites them through—the drunkard swears
          and reels.

The frighted women take the boys away,
The blackguard laughs and hurries on the
          fray.   30
He tries to reach the woods, an awkward race,
But sticks and cudgels quickly stop the chase.
He turns agen and drives the noisy crowd
And beats the many dogs in noises loud.
He drives away and beats them every one,
And then they loose them all and set them on.
He falls as dead and kicked by boys and men,
Then starts and grins and drives the crowd agen;

Till kicked and torn and beaten out he lies
And leaves his hold and cackles, groans, and
   dies.   40

  1835   1920

CROWS IN SPRING

THE Crow will tumble up and down
  At the first sight of spring
And in old trees around the town
  Brush winter from its wing.

No longer flapping far away
  To naked fen they fly,
Chill fare as on a winter's day,
  But field and valley nigh;

Where swains are stirring out to plough
  And woods are just at hand,   10
They seek the upland's sunny brow
  And strut from land to land,

And often flap their sooty wing
  And sturt to neighbouring tree,
And seem to try all ways to sing
  And almost speak in glee.

The ploughman hears and turns his head
  Above to wonder why;
And there a new nest nearly made
  Proclaims the winter by.   20

  c. 1835   1935

SILENT LOVE

THE dew it trembles on the thorn,
Then vanishes—so love is born,
Young love that speaks in silent thought
Till scorned, then withers and is naught.

The pleasure of a single hour,
The blooming of a single flower,
The glitter of the morning dew—
Such is young love when it is new.

The twitter of the wild bird's wing,
The murmur of the bees,   10
Lays of hay-crickets when they sing,
Or other things more frail than these—

Such is young love when silence speaks,
Till weary with the joy it seeks:
Then fancy [other] shapes supplies
Till sick of its own heart it dies.

The dewdrop falls at morning hour
  When none are standing by,
And noiseless fades the broken flower:
  So lovers in their silence die.   20

  after 1842   1935

THE DYING CHILD

HE could not die when trees were green,
  For he loved the time too well.
His little hands, when flowers were seen,
  Were held for the bluebell,
    As he was carried o'er the green.

His eye glanced at the white-nosed bee;
  He knew those children of the Spring:
When he was well and on the lea
  He held one in his hands to sing,
    Which filled his heart with glee.   10

Infants, the children of the Spring!
  How can an infant die
When butterflies are on the wing,
  Green grass, and such a sky?
    How can they die at Spring?

He held his hands for daisies white,
  And then for violets blue,
And took them all to bed at night
  That in the green fields grew
    As childhood's sweet delight.   20

And then he shut his little eyes,
  And flowers would notice not;
Birds' nests and eggs caused no surprise,
  He now no blossoms got:
    They met with plaintive sighs.

When Winter came and blasts did sigh,
  And bare were plain and tree,
As he for ease in bed did lie
  His soul seemed with the free,   30
    He died so quietly.

  after 1842   1873

I AM

I AM: yet what I am none cares or knows,
  My friends forsake me like a memory lost;
I am the self-consumer of my woes,
  They rise and vanish in oblivious host,
Like shades in love and death's oblivion lost;
And yet I am, and live with shadows tost

Into the nothingness of scorn and noise,
  Into the living sea of waking dreams,
Where there is neither sense of life nor joys,
  But the vast shipwreck of my life's esteems; 10
And e'en the dearest—that I loved the best—
Are strange—nay, rather stranger than the rest.

I long for scenes where man has never trod,
  A place where woman never smiled or wept;
There to abide with my Creator, God,
  And sleep as I in childhood sweetly slept:
Untroubling and untroubled where I lie,
The grass below—above the vaulted sky.

       after 1842   1865

1803 · THOMAS LOVELL BEDDOES · 1849

1803   Born, son of an eminent physician.

1817–25   Educated at Charterhouse and Pembroke College, Oxford.

1821–2   Published *The Improvisatore* and *The Bride's Tragedy,* while he was still an undergraduate.

1825–32   Went to Germany to study medicine; obtained his doctorate and settled at Zürich.

1825   Began *Death's Jest-Book,* his most important work, which was repeatedly altered but which remained unpublished until 1850.

1832–49   Continued residence in Germany, broken only by brief visits to England.

1849   Died from self-administered poison.

BEDDOES was a solitary and eccentric genius, whose imagination was obsessed with the phenomenon of death. In his dramas he closely imitated the late Elizabethans, especially in their familiar handling of the terror and gruesomeness of death. Many of his shorter poems also are imitative, showing the influence of seventeenth-century models and of Shelley. In *Death's Jest-Book,* however, Beddoes has written occasional fine blank verse which is 'untrammeled and his own,' and his best dramatic lyrics go far beyond mere imitation of other poets. Moreover, he has experimented successfully in a wide variety of original, intricate patterns. His most characteristic verse abounds in beautiful, somber imagery of intense simplicity. Occasionally in his lyrics there are traces of grotesque humor and Mephistophelian irony; sometimes macabre, gallows music is sounded in a strange minor key. Beddoes possessed a poignant lyrical gift and a passion for perfection. He has left us a half dozen lyrics among the most exquisite in nineteenth-century poetry.

POOR OLD PILGRIM MISERY

SONG FROM THE BRIDE'S TRAGEDY

POOR old pilgrim Misery,
  Beneath the silent moon he sate,
A-listening to the screech owl's cry,
  And the cold wind's goblin prate;
Beside him lay his staff of yew
  With withered willow twined,
His scant grey hair all wet with dew,
  His cheeks with grief ybrined;
    And his cry it was ever, alack!
    Alack, and woe is me!

Anon a wanton imp astray
  His piteous moaning hears,
And from his bosom steals away
  His rosary of tears:
With his plunder fled that urchin elf,
  And hid it in your eyes,
Then tell me back the stolen pelf,
  Give up the lawless prize;
    Or your cry shall be ever, alack!
    Alack, and woe is me!

10

1822

SONGS FROM DEATH'S JEST-BOOK

(Published in 1850)

I

IF THOU WILT EASE THINE HEART

IF thou wilt ease thine heart
Of love and all its smart,
　　　Then sleep, dear, sleep;
And not a sorrow
　Hang any tear on your eyelashes;
　　　Lie still and deep,
　Sad soul, until the sea-wave washes
The rim o' the sun tomorrow,
　　　In eastern sky.

But wilt thou cure thine heart　　　　　10
Of love and all its smart,
　　　Then die, dear, die;
'Tis deeper, sweeter,
　Than on a rose bank to lie dreaming
　　　With folded eye;
　And then alone, amid the beaming
Of love's stars, thou'lt meet her
　　　In eastern sky.

II

OLD ADAM, THE CARRION CROW

OLD Adam, the carrion crow,
　The old crow of Cairo;
He sat in the shower, and let it flow
　Under his tail and over his crest;
　　　And through every feather
　　　Leaked the wet weather;
　And the bough swung under his nest;
　For his beak it was heavy with marrow.
　　　Is that the wind dying? O no;
　　　It's only two devils, that blow　　　10
　　　Through a murderer's bones, to and fro,
　　　　In the ghosts' moonshine.

Ho! Eve, my grey carrion wife,
　When we have supped on kings' marrow,
Where shall we drink and make merry our life?
　Our nest it is queen Cleopatra's skull,
　　　'Tis cloven and cracked,
　　　And battered and hacked,
　But with tears of blue eyes it is full:
　Let us drink then, my raven of Cairo.　　　20
　　　Is that the wind dying? O no;
　　　It's only two devils, that blow
　　　Through a murderer's bones, to and fro,
　　　　In the ghosts' moonshine.

'HOW MANY TIMES DO I LOVE THEE, DEAR?'

SONG FROM TORRISMOND

How many times do I love thee, dear?
　Tell me how many thoughts there be
　　　In the atmosphere
　　　Of a new-fall'n year,
Whose white and sable hours appear
　The latest flake of Eternity;
So many times do I love thee, dear.

How many times do I love again?
　Tell me how many beads there are
　　　In a silver chain　　　　　10
　　　Of evening rain,
Unravelled from the tumbling main,
　And threading the eye of a yellow star:
So many times do I love again.

　　　　　　　　　　　1851

DREAM-PEDLARY

IF there were dreams to sell,
　What would you buy?
Some cost a passing bell;
　Some a light sigh,
That shakes from Life's fresh crown
Only a rose-leaf down.
If there were dreams to sell,
Merry and sad to tell,
And the crier rung the bell,
　What would you buy?　　　　　10

A cottage lone and still,
　With bowers nigh,
Shadowy, my woes to still,
　Until I die.
Such pearl from Life's fresh crown
Fain would I shake me down.
Were dreams to have at will,
This would best heal my ill,
　This would I buy.

But there were dreams to sell　　　20
　Ill didst thou buy;
Life is a dream, they tell,
　Waking, to die.
Dreaming a dream to prize,
Is wishing ghosts to rise;
And if I had the spell
To call the buried well,
　Which one would I?

If there are ghosts to raise,
  What shall I call,   30
Out of hell's murky haze,
  Heaven's blue pall?
Raise my loved long-lost boy,
To lead me to his joy.—
There are no ghosts to raise;
Out of death lead no ways;
  Vain is the call.

Know'st thou not ghosts to sue,
  No love thou hast.
Else lie, as I will do,   40
  And breathe thy last.
So out of Life's fresh crown
Fall like a rose-leaf down.
Thus are the ghosts to woo;
Thus are all dreams made true,
  Ever to last!

                      1851

THE PHANTOM-WOOER

A GHOST, that loved a lady fair,
Ever in the starry air
  Of midnight at her pillow stood;
And, with a sweetness skies above
The luring words of human love,
  Her soul the phantom wooed.
Sweet and sweet is their poisoned note,
The little snakes of silver throat,
In mossy skulls that nest and lie,
Ever singing 'die, oh! die.'   10

Young soul put off your flesh, and come
With me into the quiet tomb,
  Our bed is lovely, dark, and sweet;
The earth will swing us, as she goes,
Beneath our coverlid of snows,
  And the warm leaden sheet.
Dear and dear is their poisoned note,
The little snakes, of silver throat,
In mossy skulls that nest and lie,
Ever singing 'die, oh! die.'   20

                      1851

DIRGE WRITTEN FOR A DRAMA

TODAY is a thought, a fear is tomorrow,
And yesterday is our sin and our sorrow;
And life is a death,
  Where the body's the tomb,
And the pale sweet breath
  Is buried alive in its hideous gloom.
Then waste no tear,

For we are the dead; the living are here,
In the stealing earth, and the heavy bier.
Death lives but an instant, and is but a sigh,   10
And his son is unnamed immortality,
Whose being is thine. Dear ghost, so to die
Is to live,—and life is a worthless lie.—
Then we weep for ourselves, and wish thee good-
    bye.

                      1851

SONG OF THE STYGIAN NAIADES[1]

PROSERPINE[2] may pull her flowers,
  Wet with dew or wet with tears,
  Red with anger, pale with fears,
Is it any fault of ours,
If Pluto be an amorous king,
  And comes home nightly, laden,
Underneath his broad bat-wing,
  With a gentle, mortal maiden?
Is it so? Wind, is it so?
All that you and I do know   10
Is, that we saw fly and fix
'Mongst the reeds and flowers of Styx,
    Yesterday,
Where the Furies made their hay
For a bed of tiger cubs,
A great fly of Beelzebub's,[3]
The bee of hearts, which mortals name
Cupid, Love, and Fie for shame.

Proserpine may weep in rage,
  But, ere I and you have done
  Kissing, bathing in the sun,
What I have in yonder cage,   20
Bird or serpent, wild or tame,
  She shall guess and ask in vain;
  But, if Pluto does't again,
It shall sing out loud his shame.
  What hast caught then? What hast caught?
  Nothing but a poet's thought,
  Which so light did fall and fix
'Mongst the reeds and flowers of Styx,
    Yesterday,
Where the Furies made their hay   30
For a bed of tiger cubs,—
A great fly of Beelzebub's,
The bee of hearts, which mortals name
Cupid, Love, and Fie for shame.

                      1851

---

1 Naiads were nymphs of fresh water. Beddoes is the first to place
them in the Styx, one of the rivers of hell.
2 Proserpine was a mortal princess carried off by Pluto to the
lower world and made his queen.
3 Beelzebub is the prince of demons, Satan's chief lieutenant.

STANZAS FROM THE IVORY GATE

THE mighty thought of an old world
Fans, like a dragon's wing unfurled,
   The surface of my yearnings, deep;
And solemn shadows then awake,
Like the fish-lizard in the lake,
   Troubling a planet's morning sleep.

My waking is a Titan's dream,
Where a strange sun, long set, doth beam
   Through Montezuma's cypress bough:
Through the fern wilderness forlorn   10
Glisten the giant harts' great horn,
   And serpents vast with helmed brow.

The measureless from caverns rise
With steps of earthquake, thunderous cries,
   And graze upon the lofty wood;
The palmy grove, through which doth gleam
Such antediluvian ocean's stream,
   Haunts shadowy my domestic mood.

    *   *   *

1851

THRENODY

No sunny ray, no silver night,
   Here cruelly alight!
    Glare of noontide, star of e'en,
      Otherwhere descend!
    No violet-eyed green,
      With its daisies' yellow end,
The dewy debt receive of any eye!
It is a grave: and *she* doth lie
    'Neath roses' root,
    And the fawn's mossy foot,   10
   Under the skylark's grassy floor,
Whose graceful life held every day,—
As lilies, dew—as dews, and starry ray—
More music, grace delight than they.

When stars are few let light be here,
   Of the softest, through the boughs
    Berry-laden, sad and few;
And the wings of one small bird,
His form unseen, his voice unheard—

    *   *   *

1851

SILENUS IN PROTEUS[1]

OH those were happy days, heaped up with wine-
   skins,
And ivy-wreathed and thyrsus-swinging days,
Swimming like streamy-tressed wanton Bac-
   chantes,
When I was with thee, and sat kingly on thee,
My ass of asses. Then quite full of wine—
Morning, eve—and leaning on a fawn,
Still pretty steady, and on t'other side
Some vinous-lipped nymph of Ariadne,[2]
Her bosom a soft cushion for my right:
Half dreaming and half waking, both in bliss,   10
I sat upon my ass and laughed at Jove.
But thou art dead, my dapple, and I too
Shall ride thee soon about the Elysian meadow,
Almost a skeleton as well as thou.
And why, oh dearest, could'st not keep thy legs
That sacred hair, sacred to sacred me?
Was this thy gratitude for pats and fondlings,
To die like any other mortal ass?
Was it for this, oh son of Semele,[3]
I taught thee then, a little tumbling one,   20
To suck the goatskin oftener than the goat?

1890

---

1 Silenus, companion of Bacchus, was a jovial fat old man who usually rode an ass because he was too drunk to walk. The title of the poem means 'Silenus in an altered condition.' Proteus was a sea god who often changed his shape.
2 princess of Crete who after being abandoned by Theseus was rescued by Bacchus and became the wine-god's mistress.
3 Bacchus.

1796 · HARTLEY COLERIDGE · 1849

1796   Born at Clevedon, eldest son of the poet Samuel Taylor Coleridge.

1805–20   Educated at Ambleside and Merton College, Oxford; was appointed a probationer fellow of Oriel College, but was dismissed on a vague charge of intemperance.

1820–49   Tried writing and teaching school, but with little success; lived for the most part at Grasmere spending his time in studying and in wandering about the countryside.

1849   Died and lies buried in Grasmere churchyard.

HARTLEY COLERIDGE's poetry is, as his biographer Griggs says, like himself—'sincere, wistful, and touched with genius.' It is intimately self-revealing, full of Nature, and possessed of a singular melancholy sweetness and meditative reverence. It soars to no majestic heights. Hartley Coleridge knew his limitations: 'I am one of the small poets,' he said. The sonnet exactly suited his powers, and in this form he has achieved true excellence.

SONG

SHE is not fair to outward view
  As many maidens be,
Her loveliness I never knew
  Until she smil'd on me;
Oh! then I saw her eye was bright,
A well of love, a spring of light.

But now her looks are coy and cold,
  To mine they ne'er reply,
And yet I cease not to behold
  The love-light in her eye: 10
Her very frowns are fairer far
Than smiles of other maidens are.

                1833

LONG TIME A CHILD

LONG time a child, and still a child, when years
Had painted manhood on my cheek, was I,—
For yet I lived like one not born to die;
A thriftless prodigal of smiles and tears,
No hope I needed, and I knew no fears.
But sleep, though sweet, is only sleep, and waking,

I waked to sleep no more, at once o'ertaking
The vanguard of my age, with all arrears
Of duty on my back. Nor child, nor man,
Nor youth, nor sage, I find my head is grey,   10
For I have lost the race I never ran:
A rathe[1] December blights my lagging May;
And still I am a child, tho' I be old,
Time is my debtor for my years untold.

                1833

'MULTUM DILEXIT'[1]

SHE sat and wept beside His feet; the weight
Of sin oppressed her heart; for all the blame,
And the poor malice of the worldly shame,
To her was past, extinct, and out of date,
Only the sin remained,—the leprous state;
She would be melted by the heart of love,
By fires far fiercer than are blown to prove
And purge the silver ore adulterate.
She sat and wept, and with her untressed hair
Still wiped the feet she was so blessed to
  touch;   10

1 early.

1 'Much hath she loved.' See Luke, vii, 37–50.

And He wiped off the soiling of despair
From her sweet soul, because she loved so much.
I am a sinner, full of doubts and fears:
Make me a humble thing of love and tears.

                                        1851

HAST THOU NOT SEEN AN AGED
RIFTED TOWER

HAST thou not seen an aged rifted tower,
Meet habitation for the Ghost of Time,
Where fearful ravage makes decay sublime,
And destitution wears the face of power?

Yet is the fabric deck'd with many a flower
Of fragrance wild, and many-dappled hue,
Gold streak'd with iron-brown, and nodding
     blue,
Making each ruinous chink a fairy bower.
E'en such a thing methinks I fain would be,
Should Heaven appoint me to a lengthen'd
     age;   10
So old in look, that Young and Old may see
The record of my closing pilgrimage:
Yet, to the last, a rugged wrinkled thing
To which young sweetness may delight to cling!

                                        1851

1803 · JAMES CLARENCE MANGAN · 1849

1803   Irish poet, born in Dublin, the son of a grocer.

1818–28   After a rudimentary schooling, drudged for seven years as a copying clerk and for another three years as a clerk in an attorney's office.

1828–33   Through the intercession of friends, found a place in the Irish Ordinance Society and employment in the library of Trinity College.

1833–47   By the irregularity of his habits and an increasing addiction to drink and opium, was forced to depend upon his writing for support; contributed to various Dublin newspapers and magazines and to the *Nation*.

1849   Died.

JAMES CLARENCE MANGAN, who, because of the similarities between his life and Edgar Allan Poe's, has been called 'an Irish Poe,' led a life of wretched poverty and loneliness. Disappointment in love and continued ill-health drove him to the use of opium and alcohol, which despite a heartbreaking struggle to free himself of addiction brought him to an untimely death. He has left between eight hundred and nine hundred poems, the bulk consisting of journalistic hack-work; but Mangan had the touch of genius and for his worthiest efforts holds a high place among Irish poets. He passed off much of his writing as translations, but the truth is that of the languages he chiefly 'translated' he knew only German and only a little of either the Oriental tongues or Gaelic. From these latter languages he worked from the prose renderings accepting suggestions, making adaptations and paraphrases, and elaborating until a new poem emerged dominated by his own creative passion. His versions of the old Irish poems (some of which like O'Hussey's *Ode* are close to the originals) are among his most inspired. In these pieces, Mangan expressed with rare sincerity his own passionate enthusiasm for his country's freedom, and the tragedy of Irish hopes and aspirations. Outside his native tradition, Mangan was widely read in Oriental subjects and often reveals unusual sympathy in his rendering of Oriental themes, as in *The Time of the Barmecides*. As proof of his versatility his extraordinary nonsense verses (witness the inimitable, sarcastic *Woman with Three Cows*) stand in striking contrast to the general tenor of his work.

DARK ROSALEEN

[This poem is a free rendering of a composition written in the sixteenth century by an unknown minstrel of the Tyrconnel chief, Hugh Roe O'Donnell. After the manner of the Celtic bards of personifying their country as a distressed maiden, the minstrel puts upon the lips of his lord as personifying Ireland the love-name of Roisin Dubh, 'Dark-haired little Rose.']

OH! my dark Rosaleen,
    Do not sigh, do not weep!

The priests are on the ocean green,
    They march along the deep.
There's wine from the royal Pope
    Upon the ocean green,
And Spanish ale shall give you hope,[1]
    My dark Rosaleen!
    My own Rosaleen!

1 At the time of the struggle of the northern clans against Queen Elizabeth the Irish were encouraged by promises of help from the Pope and the King of Spain.

1284

Shall glad your heart, shall give you hope,　　10
Shall give you health, and help, and hope,
　　My dark Rosaleen!

Over hills and through dales
　　Have I roamed for your sake;
All yesterday I sailed with sails
　　On river and on lake.
The Erne, at its highest flood,
　　I dashed across unseen,
For there was lightning in my blood,
　　My dark Rosaleen!　　20
　　My own Rosaleen!
Oh! there was lightning in my blood,
Red lightning lightened through my blood,
　　My dark Rosaleen!

All day long, in unrest,
　　To and fro do I move.
The very soul within my breast
　　Is wasted for you, love!
The heart in my bosom faints
　　To think of you, my Queen,　　30
My life of life, my saint of saints,
　　My dark Rosaleen!
　　My own Rosaleen!
To hear your sweet and sad complaints,
My life, my love, my saint of saints,
　　My dark Rosaleen!

Woe and pain, pain and woe,
　　Are my lot, night and noon,
To see your bright face clouded so,
　　Like to the mournful moon.　　40
But yet will I rear your throne
　　Again in golden sheen;
'Tis you shall reign, shall reign alone,
　　My dark Rosaleen!
　　My own Rosaleen!
'Tis you shall have the golden throne,
'Tis you shall reign, and reign alone,
　　My dark Rosaleen!

Over dews, over sands,
　　Will I fly for your weal:　　50
Your holy delicate white hands
　　Shall girdle me with steel.
At home in your emerald bowers,
　　From morning's dawn till e'en,
You'll pray for me, my flower of flowers,
　　My dark Rosaleen!
　　My own Rosaleen!
You'll think of me through daylight's hours,
My virgin flower, my flower of flowers,
　　My dark Rosaleen!　　60

I could scale the blue air,
　　I could plough the high hills,
Oh! I could kneel all night in prayer,
　　To heal your many ills!
And one beamy smile from you
　　Would float like light between
My toils and me, my own, my true,
　　My dark Rosaleen!
　　My own Rosaleen!
Would give me life and soul anew,　　70
A second life, a soul anew,
　　My dark Rosaleen!

Oh! the Erne shall run red
　　With redundance of blood,
The earth shall rock beneath our tread,
　　And flames wrap hill and wood,
And gun-peal and slogan-cry
　　Wake many a glen serene,
Ere you shall fade, ere you shall die,
　　My dark Rosaleen!　　80
　　My own Rosaleen!
The Judgement Hour must first be nigh,
Ere you can fade, ere you can die,
　　My dark Rosaleen!

1846

ST. PATRICK'S HYMN BEFORE TARA

FROM THE IRISH

[The Hill of Tara, located about twenty miles northwest of Dublin, was famous in the early history of Ireland as a royal residence and as the scene of popular assemblies. By the fifth century, during the time of St. Patrick, Tara had become the chief seat of druidism and
idolatry. On the occasion of a great annual festival, surrounded by pagan worshipers, St. Patrick prays to His
God to protect him from the powers of evil and darkness.]

At Tara today, in this awful hour,
　　I call on the Holy Trinity!
Glory to Him who reigneth in power,
The God of the elements, Father, and Son,
And Paraclete Spirit,[1] which Three are the One,
　　The ever-existing Divinity!

At Tara today I call on the Lord,
On Christ, the Omnipotent Word,
Who came to redeem from death and sin
　　　　Our fallen race;　　10
　　　　And I put and I place
The virtue that lieth and liveth in
　　　　His Incarnation lowly,
　　　　His Baptism pure and holy,
His life of toil, and tears, and affliction,

1 Comforting Spirit; Comforter.

His dolorous Death, his Crucifixion,
His Burial, sacred and sad and lone,
　　His Resurrection to life again,
His glorious Ascension to Heaven's high throne,
And, lastly, his future dread　　　　　　20
　　And terrible Coming to judge all men,
　　Both the living and dead.—

At Tara today I put and I place
　　The virtue that dwells in the Seraphim's love,
And the virtue and grace
　　　　That are in the obedience
　　　　And unshaken allegiance
Of all the Archangels and Angels above,
And in the hope of the Resurrection
To everlasting reward and election,　　　30
And in the prayers of the Fathers of old,
And in the truths the Prophets foretold,
And in the Apostles' manifold preachings,
And in the Confessors' faith and teachings,
And in the purity ever dwelling
　　　　Within the immaculate Virgin's breast,
And in the actions bright and excelling
　　Of all good men, and just and the blest.—

At Tara today, in this fateful hour,
I place all Heaven with its power,　　　40
And the sun with its brightness,
And the snow with its whiteness,
And fire with all the strength it hath,
And lightning with its rapid wrath,
And the winds with their swiftness along their
　　path,
And the sea with its deepness,
And the rocks with their steepness,
And the earth with its starkness—
　　　　All these I place,
　　　　By God's almighty help and grace,　　50
Between myself and the Powers of Darkness!

　　At Tara today
　　May God be my stay!
May the strength of God now nerve me!
May the power of God preserve me!
May God the Almighty be near me!
　May God the Almighty espy me!
May God the Almighty hear me!
　May God give me eloquent speech!
May the arm of God protect me!　　　60
May the wisdom of God direct me!
　May God give me power to teach and to
　　preach!

May the shield of God defend me!
May the host of God attend me,
　　And ward me,

　　　　And guard me
Against the wiles of demons and devils,
Against the temptations of vices and evils,
Against the bad passions and wrathful will
　Of the reckless mind and the wicked heart;　70
Against every man who designs me ill,
　Whether leagued with others or plotting apart!

　　　In this hour of hours,
　　　I place all those powers
Between myself and every foe
　　Who threatens my body and soul
　　With danger or dole,
To protect me against the evils that flow
From lying soothsayers' incantations,
From the gloomy laws of the Gentile nations,　80
From heresy's hateful innovations,
From idolatry's rites and invocation;
　　Be those my defenders,
　　My guards against every ban,
And spells of smiths, and Druids, and women;
In fine, against every knowledge that renders
The light Heaven sends us dim in
　　The spirit and soul of man!
　　May Christ, I pray,
　　Protect me today　　　　　　90
　Against poison and fire,
　Against drowning and wounding,
　That so, in His grace abounding,
　　I may earn the preacher's hire!

　　Christ, as a light,
　　Illumine and guide me!
Christ as a shield, o'ershadow and cover me!
Christ be under me! Christ be over me!
　　Christ be beside me
　　On left hand and right!　　　100
Christ be before me, behind me, about me!
Christ this day be within and without me!

Christ, the lowly and meek,
　　Christ, the All-Powerful, be
In the heart of each to whom I speak,
　In the mouth of each who speaks to me!
　　In all who draw near me,
　　Or see me or hear me!

At Tara today, in this awful hour,
　I call on the Holy Trinity!　　　110
Glory to Him who reigneth in power,
The God of the Elements, Father, and Son,
And Paraclete Spirit, which Three are the One,
　　The ever-existing Divinity!

Salvation dwells with the Lord,
With Christ, the Omnipotent Word:

From generation to generation
Grant us, O Lord, thy grace and salvation!

1848

THE WOMAN OF THREE COWS

TRADITIONAL

O Woman of Three Cows, agragh![1] don't let your
    tongue thus rattle!
O don't be saucy, don't be stiff, because you may
    have cattle.
I've seen (and here's my hand to you, I only say
    what's true!)
A many a one with twice your stock not half so
    proud as you.

Good luck to you, don't scorn the poor, and
    don't be their despiser,
For worldly wealth soon melts away, and cheats
    the very miser.
And death soon strips the proudest wreath from
    haughty human brows:
Then don't be stiff, and don't be proud, good
    Woman of Three Cows!

See where Momonia's heroes lie, proud Owen
    More's descendants!
'Tis they that won the glorious name and had the
    grand attendants!   10
If they were forced to bow to fate, as every mortal
    bows,
Can you be proud, can you be stiff, my Woman
    of Three Cows?

The brave sons of the Lord of Clare, they left the
    land to mourning,
Mavrone! for they were banished, with no hope
    of their returning:
Who knows in what abodes of want those youths
    were driven to house?
Yet you can give yourself these airs, O Woman
    of Three Cows!

O think of Donnell of the Ships, the chief whom
    nothing daunted!
See how he fell in distant Spain, unchronicled,
    unchanted!
He sleeps, the great O'Sullivan, whom thunder
    cannot rouse:
Then ask yourself, should you be proud, good
    Woman of Three Cows!   20

O'Ruark, Maguire, those souls of fire whose
    names are shrined in story,

Think how their high achievements once made
    Erin's greatest glory;
Yet now their bones lie mouldering under weeds
    and cypress boughs,
And so, for all your pride, will yours, O Woman
    of Three Cows!

The O'Carrolls, also, famed when fame was only
    for the boldest,
Rest in forgotten sepulchres with Erin's best and
    oldest;
Yet who so great as they of yore in battle and
    carouse?
Just think of that, and hide your head, good
    Woman of Three Cows.

Your neighbour's poor, and you, it seems, are big
    with vain ideas,
Because, inagh,[2] you've got three cows; one
    more, I see, than she has!   30
That tongue of yours wags more, at times, than
    charity allows:
But if you're strong, be merciful, great Woman of
    Three Cows!

AVRAN

*Now there you go: you still, of course, keep up your
    scornful bearing;*
*And I'm too poor to hinder you. But, by the cloak
    I'm wearing,*
*If I had but four cows myself, even though you were
    my spouse,*
*I'd thwack you well to cure your pride, my Woman
    of Three Cows!*

1848

THE TIME OF THE BARMECIDES[1]

FROM THE ARABIC

My eyes are filmed, my beard is grey,
    I am bowed with the weight of years;
I would I were stretched in my bed of clay,
    With my long-lost youth's compeers!
For back to the past, tho' the thought brings woe,
    My memory ever glides—
To the old, old time, long, long ago,
    The time of the Barmecides!
To the old, old time, long, long ago,
    The time of the Barmecides.   10

---

2 forsooth.

---

1 my dear!

1 The Barmecides was a Persian family who acquired power in
the eighth century under the Abbasid Caliphate. Eventually the
grandson fell under the displeasure of his reigning calif and in
803 was put to death with nearly all of the Barmecide family.

Then youth was mine, and a fierce wild will,
  And an iron arm in war,
And a fleet foot high upon Ishkar's hill,
  When the watch-lights glimmered afar;
And as fiery a barb as any I know
  That Kurd[2] or Bedouin[2] rides,
Ere my friends lay low, long, long ago,
  In the time of the Barmecides.
Ere my friends lay low, long, long ago,
  In the time of the Barmecides.   20

One golden goblet illumed my board,
  One silver dish was there;
At hand my tried Karamanian[3] sword
  Lay always bright and bare;
For those were the days when the angry blow
  Supplanted the word that chides,
When hearts could glow, long, long ago,
  In the time of the Barmecides;
When hearts could glow, long, long ago,
  In the time of the Barmecides.   30

Through city and desert my mates and I
  Were free to rove and roam,
Our diapered[4] canopy the deep of the sky,
  Or the roof of the palace dome:
Of ours was that vivid life to and fro
  Which only sloth derides!
Men spent life so, long, long ago,
  In the time of the Barmecides;
Men spent life so, long, long ago,
  In the time of the Barmecides.   40

I see rich Bagdad once again,
  With its turrets of Moorish mould,
And the Caliph's twice five hundred men
  Whose binishes[5] flamed with gold;
I call up many a gorgeous show
  Which the pall of oblivion hides:
All passed like snow, long, long ago,
  With the time of the Barmecides.
All passed like snow, long, long ago,
  With the time of the Barmecides.   50

But mine eye is dim, and my beard is grey,
  And I bend with the weight of years.
May I soon go down to the house of clay
  Where slumber my youth's compeers!
For with them and the past, though the thought
    wakes woe,
  My memory ever abides;

---

2 members of nomadic races inhabiting the Near East.
3 Turkish.
4 ornamented.
5 helmets.

And I mourn for the times gone long ago,
  For the times of the Barmecides!
I mourn for the times gone lone ago,
  For the times of the Barmecides!   60

          1839

THE NAMELESS ONE

ROLL forth, my song, like the rushing river,
  That sweeps along to the mighty sea;
God will inspire me while I deliver
  My soul of thee!

Tell thou the world, when my bones lie whitening
  Amid the last homes of youth and eld,
That there was once one whose veins ran light-
    ning
  No eye beheld.

Tell how his boyhood was one drear night-hour,
  How shone for *him,* through his griefs and
    gloom,   10
No star of all heaven sends to light our
  Path to the tomb.

Roll on, my song, and to after ages
  Tell how, disdaining all earth can give,
He would have taught men, from wisdom's
    pages,
  The way to live.

And tell how trampled, derided, hated,
  And worn by weakness, disease, and wrong,
He fled for shelter to God, who mated
  His soul with song—   20

With song which alway, sublime or vapid,
  Flowed like a rill in the morning beam,
Perchance not deep, but intense and rapid—
  A mountain stream.

Tell how this Nameless, condemned for years
    long
  To herd with demons from hell beneath.
Saw things that made him, with groans and tears,
    long
  For even death.

Go on to tell how, with genius wasted,
  Betrayed in friendship, befooled in love,   30
With spirit shipwrecked, and young hopes
    blasted,
  He still, still strove.

Till, spent with toil, dreeing death for others,
  And some whose hands should have wrought
      for *him*
(If children live not for sires and mothers,)
    His mind grew dim.

And he fell far through that pit abysmal
  The gulf and grave of Maginn and Burns,
And pawned his soul for the devil's dismal
    Stock of returns.   40

But yet redeemed it in days of darkness
  And shakes and signs of the final wrath,
When death, in hideous and ghastly starkness,
    Stood on his path.

And tell how now, amid wreck and sorrow,
  And want, and sickness, and houseless nights,
He bides in calmness the silent morrow,
    That no ray lights.

And lives he still, then? Yes! Old and hoary
  At thirty-nine, from despair and woe,   50
He lives enduring what future story
    Will never know.

Him grant a grave to, ye pitying noble,
  Deep in your bosoms! There let him dwell!
He, too, had tears for all souls in trouble,
    Here and in hell.

                                        1849

1803 · ROBERT STEPHEN HAWKER · 1875

1803   Born in Devonshire, son of a clergyman.
1823–8   Educated at Pembroke College, Oxford.
1834–75   Vicar of Morwenstow in Cornwall.
1864   Published *The Quest of the Sangraal,* a portion of a long unfinished poem.
1869   Published *Cornish Ballads.*
1875   Died.

ROBERT STEPHEN HAWKER, clergyman and antiquarian of the west of England, was a
man of great originality of whom numerous stories are told of his striking sayings
and eccentricities. As a poet he is remembered principally for his *Song of the Western
Men;* but he wrote some other creditable poems portraying life among his parishioners
on the Cornish coast, a community described by Hawker as consisting for the most part
of 'a mixed multitude of smugglers, wreckers, and dissenters of various hues.'

THE SONG OF THE WESTERN MEN

[Sir Jonathan Trelawny, a native Cornishman, was
one of seven bishops imprisoned in London tower for
resisting James II's order in 1688 to read the Declaration
of Indulgences in his church. The refrain of Hawker's
poem dates from the event, but the rest is the poet's own.
On its appearance anonymously in 1826 Sir Walter Scott
and others believed it to be the original ballad.]

A GOOD sword and a trusty hand!
  A merry heart and true!
King James's men shall understand
  What Cornish lads can do.

And have they fix'd the where and when?
  And shall Trelawny die?
Here's twenty thousand Cornish men
  Will know the reason why!

Out spake their captain brave and bold,
  A merry wight was he: 10

'If London Tower were Michael's hold,[1]
  We'll set Trelawny free!

'We'll cross the Tamar,[2] land to land,
  The Severn[2] is no stay,
With "one and all," and hand in hand,
  And who shall bid us nay?

'And when we come to London Wall,
  A pleasant sight to view,
Come forth! come forth, ye cowards all,
  Here's men as good as you!   20

'Trelawny he's in keep and hold,
  Trelawny he may die;
But here's twenty thousand Cornish bold
  Will know the reason why!'
     1825   1826

---

1 St. Michael's Mount, a high pyramidal rock off the coast of
Cornwall.
2 the Tamar and the Severn are English rivers.

BIBLIOGRAPHIES

A selected list of references useful to the student of the English Romantic Movement is provided in the following bibliographies. A General Bibliography covers background studies in the Political, Economic, and Social History of the movement and in Literary History and Criticism. Following the General Bibliography and arranged in alphabetical order are bibliographies for each author represented in this anthology. The author bibliographies include definitive scholarly editions of the complete works wherever they exist, special editions of single works, and volumes of selections of special merit. Most of these editions have biographical and critical accounts. The more extended and usually more important criticism, however, is to be found in the articles and books listed under Biography and Criticism. Brief critical and descriptive comments are provided for each entry whose contents or value is not readily apparent from the title. Except for the texts of the authors, which are arranged with complete works first and individual or selected works following, all titles are arranged in chronological order.

For more extensive bibliographies than those given here the student should consult:
The Cambridge Bibliography of English Literature, ed. F. W. Bateson, vol. III, 1940, with its supplement, 1957.
The English Romantic Poets: A Review of Research, ed. T. M. Raysor, 1950; revised, 1956.
Ernest Bernbaum, *Guide through the Romantic Movement*, rev. ed., 1949.
The English Romantic Poets and Essayists: A Review of Research and Criticism, eds. C. W. and L. H. Houtchens, 1957.
The Year's Work in English Studies, ed. F. S. Boas for The English Association (London), annually since 1919.
Annual Bibliography of English Language and Literature, Modern Humanities Research Association, since 1920.
English Literature: 1660–1800, annually in *PQ* since 1926.
The Romantic Movement: A Selective and Critical Bibliography, annually in *ELH* from March 1937 to 1949; in *PQ* from April 1950 to 1964; taken over by *English Language Notes* Sept. 1965.
Annual bibliographies in *PMLA*, since 1922.

General Bibliography

POLITICAL, ECONOMIC, AND SOCIAL HISTORY

H. D. Traill, ed., *Social England*, 1896–7. Especially vol. v, chs. xix, xx, and vol. vi, ch. xxi.
G. M. Trevelyan, *British History in the Nineteenth Century (1782–1901)*, 1922, rev., 1937.
Élie Halévy, *England in 1815*, 1924, rev., 1949;

and *The Liberal Awakening, 1815–1830*, 1927, rev., 1949.
Elizabeth Manwaring, *Italian Landscape in Eighteenth Century England: A Study Chiefly of the Influence of Claude Lorrain and Salva-*

tor *Rosa on English Taste: 1700–1800,* 1925.

Christopher Hussey, *The Picturesque,* 1927. Includes chapters on the cult of 'the Picturesque' in landscape, travel, garden scenes, and architecture.

Alfred Cobban, *Edmund Burke and the Revolt Against the Eighteenth Century,* 1929.

W. J. Warner, *The Wesleyan Movement in the Industrial Revolution,* 1930.

E. L. Griggs, *Thomas Clarkson: The Friend of Slaves,* 1936.

R. B. Mowat, *The Romantic Age: Europe in the Early Nineteenth Century,* 1937.

J. M. Thompson, ed., *English Witnesses of the French Revolution,* 1938. Selections from the narratives of fifty eyewitnesses of the French Revolution including Mary Wollstonecraft, Thomas Paine, Samuel Rogers, and William Wordsworth.

G. D. H. Cole and Raymond Postgate, *The British Common People: 1746–1938,* 1939, rev., 1947.

M. J. Quinlan, *Victorian Prelude: A History of English Manners, 1700–1830,* 1941.

Arthur Bryant, *The Years of Endurance: 1793–1802,* 1942; *Years of Victory: 1802–1812,* 1944; *The Age of Elegance, 1812–1822,* 1950.

Carola Oman, *Britain Against Napoleon,* 1942.

G. M. Trevelyan, *English Social History,* 1942.

Maldwyn Edwards, *Methodism and England,* 1943.

J. M. Thompson, *The French Revolution,* 1943.

F. E. Mineka, *The Dissidence of Dissent: The Monthly Repository, 1806–1838,* 1944.

Sacheverell Sitwell, *British Architects and Craftsmen: A Survey of Taste, Design, and Style: 1600–1830,* 1945.

R. F. Wearmouth, *Methodism and the Common People,* 1945.

M. R. Adams, *Studies in the Literary Backgrounds of English Radicalism, with Special Reference to the French Revolution,* 1947.

Mary C. Park, *Joseph Priestley and the Problem of Pantisocracy,* 1947.

Crane Brinton, *English Political Thought in the Nineteenth Century,* 1950.

Kenneth MacLean, *Agrarian Age,* 1951.

R. J. White, *Waterloo to Peterloo,* 1957.

LITERARY HISTORY AND CRITICISM

Heinrich Heine, *Die Romantische Schule,* 1867, trans. 1882.

Leslie Stephen, *History of English Thought in the Eighteenth Century,* 2 vols., 1876.

F. H. Hedge, 'Classic and Romantic,' *Atlantic Monthly,* LVII (1886), 309–16.

Walter Pater, *Appreciations,* 1889. Includes Pater's famous essay on style and 'appreciations' on Wordsworth, on Coleridge, and on Lamb.

W. L. Phelps, *The Beginnings of the English Romantic Movement,* 1893.

H. D. Rawnsley, *Literary Associations of the English Lakes,* 2 vols., 1894.

Myra Reynolds, *The Treatment of Nature in English Poetry between Pope and Wordsworth,* 1896.

Edward Dowden, *The French Revolution and English Literature,* 1897.

C. H. Herford, *The Age of Wordsworth,* 1897.

H. A. Beers, *A History of English Romanticism in the Eighteenth Century,* 1899; *A History of English Romanticism in the Nineteenth Century,* 1901.

A. E. Hancock, *The French Revolution and the English Poets,* 1899.

T. S. Omond, *The Romantic Triumph,* 1900.

F. E. Farley, *Scandinavian Influences in the English Romantic Movement,* 1903.

Theodore Watts-Dunton, 'The Renascence of Wonder in Poetry,' *Chambers's Cyclopaedia of English Literature,* III, 1903.

Leslie Stephen, *English Literature and Society in the Eighteenth Century,* 1904.

C. E. Vaughan, *The Romantic Revolt,* 1907.

Martha P. Conant, *The Oriental Tale in England in the Eighteenth Century,* 1908.

Arthur Symons, *The Romantic Movement in English Poetry,* 1909.

Hugh Walker, *The Literature of the Victorian Era,* 1910.

Oliver Elton, *A Survey of English Literature: 1780–1830,* 2 vols., 1912; *A Survey of English Literature: 1730–1780,* 2 vols., 1928.

R. D. Havens, 'Romantic Aspects of the Age of Pope,' *PMLA,* XXVII (1912), 297–324.

P. E. More, *The Drift of Romanticism: Shelburne Essays,* Eighth Series, 1913. A comprehensive survey of degenerate tendencies in modern society.

Allene Gregory, *The French Revolution and the English Novel,* 1915.

G. F. Richardson, *A Neglected Aspect of the English Romantic Revolt,* 1915. Economic, social, and political conditions gave to romantic literature its leading characteristics.

Walter Raleigh, *Romance,* 1916. On the origin and meaning of 'Romance' and its revival in England during the eighteenth and nineteenth centuries.

C. A. Moore, 'The Return to Nature in English Poetry of the Eighteenth Century,' *SP,* XIV (1917), 243–91.

F. E. Pierce, *Currents and Eddies in the English Romantic Generation,* 1918. A study of the major and minor authors arranged according to their environmental groups.

Arthur Quiller-Couch, 'On the Terms "Classical" and "Romantic," ' in *Studies in Literature,* 1918.

Irving Babbitt, *Rousseau and Romanticism,* 1919. A vigorous and brilliant but intensely partisan attack on romanticism.

T. S. Eliot, *The Sacred Wood,* 1920; *The Use of Poetry and the Use of Criticism,* 1933. Essays by one of the most influential of the twentieth-century anti-romantic critics. Romanticism is immature and fails to present the heterogeneity of life. *The Use of Poetry* contains a chapter on Shelley and Keats.

Edith Birkhead, *The Tale of Terror: A Study of the Gothic Romance,* 1921.

Walter Graham, 'The Politics of the Greater Romantic Poets,' *PMLA,* XXXVI (1921), 60–78.

Paul Van Tieghem, *La Poésie de la nuit et des tombeaux en Europe au XVIIIe siècle,* 1921.

P. H. Frye, 'The Terms Classic and Romantic, in *Romance and Tragedy,* 1922.

R. D. Havens, *The Influence of Milton on English Poetry,* 1922.

C. H. Herford, 'Romanticism in the Modern World,' English Assn. *Essays and Studies,* VIII (1922), 109–34. Answers the attacks on romanticism by the modern humanists, in particular Irving Babbitt.

B. H. Lehman, 'The Doctrine of Leadership in the Greater Romantic Poets,' *PMLA,* XXXVII (1922), 639–61.

C. B. Tinker, *Nature's Simple Plan: A Phase of Radical Thought in the Mid-Eighteenth Century,* 1922.

N. I. White, 'The English Romantic Writers as Dramatists,' *Sewanee Review,* XXX (1922), 206–15.

W. P. Ker, 'Romantic Fallacies,' in *The Art of Poetry,* 1923. Critics and historians have made too much of the name romantic.

J. G. Robertson, *Studies in the Genesis of Romantic Theory in the Eighteenth Century,* 1923.

E. D. Snyder, *The Celtic Revival in English Literature: 1760–1800,* 1923.

Olwen W. Campbell, 'Some Suggestions on the Romantic Revival and Its Effects,' in *Shelley and the Unromantics,* 1924. Romanticism is inseparable from a certain kind of faith in man.

S. F. Gingerich, *Essays in the Romantic Poets,* 1924. Includes substantial chapters on Coleridge, Wordsworth, Shelley, and Byron.

T. E. Hulme, 'Romanticism and Classicism,' in *Speculations,* 1924. Romanticism is 'spilt religion.'

Émile Legouis and Louis Cazamian, *A History of English Literature,* (1924), trans. 1926–7, 2 vols., rev. in one volume, 1929, 1947.

Amy L. Reed, *The Background of Gray's Elegy: A Study in the Taste for Melancholy Poetry: 1700–1751,* 1924.

I. A. Richards, *Principles of Literary Criticism,* 1924. Establishes the bases for the new psychology and aesthetics which are hostile to romanticism.

L. P. Smith, *Four Words: Romantic, Originality, Creative, Genius,* 1924; reprinted in *Words and Idioms,* 1925.

Paul Van Tieghem, *Le Préromantisme,* I, 1924; II, 1930; III, 1947.

H. J. C. Grierson, 'Classical and Romantic,' in *The Background of English Literature,* 1925.

Paul Kaufman, 'Defining Romanticism,' *MLN,* XL (1925), 193–204.

W. P. Ker, 'On the Value of the Terms "Classical" and "Romantic" as Applied to Literature,' in *Collected Essays,* 2 vols., 1925.

J. G. Robertson, *The Reconciliation of Classic and Romantic,* 1925.

A. N. Whitehead, 'The Romantic Reaction,' in *Science and the Modern World,* 1925.

Lascelles Abercrombie, *Romanticism,* 1926. Romanticism is 'a recurring disposition, a typical attitude of the human mind in its reaction to experience.'

C. C. Brinton, *The Political Ideas of the English Romanticists,* 1926.

W. R. Inge, *The Platonic Tradition in English Religious Thought,* 1926.

W. R. Inge, 'Romanticism,' in *Lay Thoughts of a Dean,* 1926.

Annie E. Powell, *The Romantic Theory of Poetry: An Examination in the Light of Croce's Aesthetic,* 1926.

F. W. Stokoe, *German Influence in the English Romantic Period, 1788–1818,* 1926.

F. E. Pierce, 'Romanticism and Other Isms,' *JEGP,* XXVI (1927), 451–66. There are four main tendencies in romanticism—popular, exploratory, mystical-ethical, and purely aesthetic.

Eino Railo, *The Haunted Castle: A Study of the Elements of English Romanticism,* 1927.

K. M. Clark, *The Gothic Revival,* 1928. Traces interrelations between architecture and literature.

H. N. Fairchild, *The Noble Savage: A Study in Romantic Naturalism*, 1928.

D. N. Smith, *Shakespeare in the Eighteenth Century*, 1928.

J. W. Draper, *The Funeral Elegy and the Rise of English Romanticism*, 1929.

H. I'A. Fausset, *The Proving of Psyche*, 1929. Pleads for a new romanticism as the salvation of the modern Western world.

Violet A. A. Stockley, *German Literature as Known in England: 1750–1830*, 1929.

Ernest Bernbaum, *Guide through the Romantic Movement*, 1930, rev., 1949.

Allardyce Nicoll, *A History of Early Nineteenth-Century Drama: 1800–1850*, 2 vols., 1930.

Mario Praz, *The Romantic Agony* (1930), trans. 1933. Decadent European romanticism in the nineteenth century as revealed chiefly in sexual aberration.

Ernest Bernbaum, 'The Practical Results of the Humanistic Theories,' *English Journal*, XX (1931), 103–9. Twentieth-century humanism is not likely to prosper in America.

H. N. Fairchild, *The Romantic Quest*, 1931. Classroom lectures on naturalism, medievalism, and transcendentalism as found in the writings of the chief romantic poets. Views romanticism as a tragic failure.

Harry Levin, *The Broken Column: A Study in Romantic Hellenism*, 1931.

René Wellek, *Immanuel Kant in England: 1793–1883*, 1931.

Edmund Wilson, 'Symbolism,' in *Axel's Castle*, 1931. French Symbolism is represented as a second flood tide of romanticism.

Paul Yvon, *Le Gothique et la renaissance gothique en Angleterre: 1750–1880*, 1931.

R. C. Bald, ed., *Literary Friendships in the Age of Wordsworth: An Anthology*, 1932. What the more important authors of the period said to or about one another.

Eleanor M. Sickels, *The Gloomy Egoist: Moods and Themes of Melancholy from Gray to Keats*, 1932.

J. M. S. Tompkins, *The Popular Novel in England, 1770–1800*, 1932.

R. E. Jones, 'Romanticism Reconsidered: Humanism and Romantic Poetry,' *Sewanee Review*, XLI (1933), 396–418.

M. H. Abrams, *The Milk of Paradise: The Effect of Opium Visions on the Works of De Quincey, Crabbe, Francis Thompson, and Coleridge*, 1934. Cf. Elisabeth Schneider, 'The "Dream" of *Kubla Khan*,' *PMLA*, LX (1945), 784–801.

E. A. Baker, *The History of the English Novel*, vols. V, VI, VII, and VIII, 1934–7.

C. H. Dawson, 'The Origins of the Romantic Tradition,' in *Medieval Religion and Other Essays*, 1934.

Marie H. Law, *The English Familiar Essay in the Early Nineteenth Century*, 1934. Cf. M. R. Watson, 'The *Spectator* Tradition and the Development of the Familiar Essay,' *ELH*, XIII (1946), 189–215.

Margaret P. Sherwood, *Undercurrents of Influence in English Romantic Poetry*, 1934. Traces the development of 'the organic idea' of the universe in representative romantic poets.

Lois Whitney, *Primitivism and the Idea of Progress in English Popular Literature of the Eighteenth Century*, 1934.

C. V. Deane, *Aspects of Eighteenth-Century Nature Poetry*, 1935.

S. H. Monk, *The Sublime: A Study of Critical Theories in Eighteenth-Century England*, 1935.

J. W. Beach, *The Concept of Nature in Nineteenth-Century English Poetry*, 1936.

F. R. Leavis, *Revaluation: Tradition and Development in English Poetry*, 1936. Includes chapters on the Augustan tradition, Wordsworth, Shelley, and Keats.

A. O. Lovejoy, *The Great Chain of Being: A Study of the History of an Idea*, 1936.

F. L. Lucas, *The Decline and Fall of the Romantic Ideal*, 1936. Romanticism is 'intoxicated dreaming,' 'a revolt of the unconscious'; it became more and more decadent and died finally of old age in the 1890's.

B. S. Allen, *Tides in English Taste: 1619–1800*, 2 vols., 1937. An illustrated survey of changing tastes in art, decoration, gardens, etc.

Douglas Bush, *Mythology and the Romantic Tradition in English Poetry*, 1937.

Mary M. Colum, *From These Roots: The Ideas That Have Made Modern Literature*, 1937. A fervent vindication of the European romantic adventure.

F. C. Gill, *The Romantic Movement and Methodism: A Study of English Romanticism and the Evangelical Revival*, 1937.

D. G. James, *Scepticism and Poetry*, 1937. Opposing I. A. Richard's literary esthetic, reiterates the doctrine of the imagination as creative.

W. F. Wright, *Sensibility in English Prose Fiction: 1760–1814*, 1937.

Agnes E. Addison, *Romanticism and the Gothic Revival*, 1938. Relates the role of Gothic architecture in the development of romanticism.

Sukumar Dutt, *The Supernatural in English Romantic Poetry: 1780–1830*, 1938.

J. M. Murry, *Heroes of Thought*, 1938. Includes chapters on Godwin, Wordsworth, and Shelley.

J. C. Ransom, *The World's Body*, 1938; also *The New Criticism*, 1941. Disparages the poetry 'written by romantics.' Romanticism denies the real world by idealizing it.

Montague Summers, *The Gothic Quest: A History of the Gothic Novel*, 1938; *A Gothic Bibliography*, 1941.

C. B. Tinker, *Painter and Poet*, 1938. Studies in literary relations to English painting during the period of the romantic revival.

Jacob Bronowski, *The Poet's Defence*, 1939. Includes evaluations of the essays on poetry of Shelley, Wordsworth, and Coleridge.

Cleanth Brooks, *Modern Poetry and the Tradition*, 1939. Gives the body of doctrine of the 'New Criticism' in a 'fully developed and rounded system.' Reprinted 1965, with a retrospective introduction.

H. N. Fairchild, *Religious Trends in English Poetry;* vol. I: *1700–1740: Protestantism and the Cult of Sentiment*, 1939; vol. II: *1740–1780: Religious Sentimentalism in the Age of Johnson*, 1942; vol. III: *1780–1830: Romantic Faith*, 1949.

E. A. Whitney, 'Humanitarianism and Romanticism,' *Huntington Library Quarterly*, II (1939), 159–78.

B. I. Evans, *Tradition and Romanticism: Studies in English Poetry from Chaucer to W. B. Yeats*, 1940. Romanticism has a continuity in English literature and cannot be restricted to a specific school as in France and Germany.

H. N. Fairchild, Elizabeth Nitchie, and others, 'Romanticism: A Symposium,' *PMLA*, LV (1940), 1–60.

T. B. Shepherd, *Methodism and the Literature of the Eighteenth Century*, 1940.

B. H. Stern, *The Rise of Romantic Hellenism in English Literature: 1732–1786*, 1940.

Basil Willey, *The Eighteenth-Century Background: Studies of the Idea of Nature in the Thought of the Period*, 1940.

E. B. Hungerford, *Shores of Darkness*, 1941. A study of the influence of the 'speculative mythologists' of the eighteenth and early nineteenth centuries upon Blake, Keats, Shelley, and Goethe.

G. W. Knight, *The Starlit Dome: Studies in the Poetry of Vision*, 1941. Includes essays on Wordsworth, Coleridge, Shelley, and Keats.

A. O. Lovejoy, 'The Meaning of Romanticism for the Historian of Ideas,' *JHI*, II (1941), 257–78.

David Ash, 'Creative Romanticism,' *College English*, IV (1942), 100–110. Polemic for romanticism in literature and life.

Edmund Blunden, *Romantic Poetry and the Fine Arts*, 1942.

Eva B. Dykes, *The Negro in English Romantic Thought: or, A Study of Sympathy for the Oppressed*, 1942.

Jacques Barzun, *Romanticism and the Modern Ego*, 1943. *Intrinsic* romanticism is just as important and alive today as it ever was.

S. A. Larrabee, *English Bards and Grecian Marbles: The Relationship between Sculpture and Poetry Especially in the Romantic Period*, 1943.

Owen Barfield, *Romanticism Comes of Age*, 1944. Romantic idealism is explained and defended in terms of the theosophical cult of Rudolf Steiner. Two chapters are on Coleridge.

J. W. Beach, *A Romantic View of Poetry*, 1944. The romantic way as recorded by the poets leads to a fuller realization in living than the humanistic way.

E. R. Bentley, 'Romanticism: A Re-Evaluation,' *Antioch Review*, IV (1944), 6–20.

R. H. Fogle, 'Romantic Bards and Metaphysical Reviewers,' *ELH*, XII (1945), 221–50; 'A Recent Attack upon Romanticism,' *College English*, IX (1948), 356–61. Defense of the English romantic poets (in particular, Shelley) against the charges of the 'New Critics.'

W. J. Bate, *From Classic to Romantic: Premises of Taste in Eighteenth-Century England*, 1946.

Marjorie H. Nicolson, *Newton Demands the Muse: Newton's 'Opticks' and the Eighteenth-Century Poets*, 1946. Cf. F. E. L. Priestley, 'Newton and the Romantic Concept of Nature,' *UTQ*, XVII (1948), 323–36.

Cleanth Brooks, *The Well Wrought Urn: Studies in the Structure of Poetry*, 1947. 'New Criticism' of poems selected from the Renaissance to the present, including Gray's *Elegy*, Wordsworth's *Intimations Ode*, and Keats's *Grecian Urn*.

Malcolm Elwin, *The First Romantics*, 1947. A lively narrative presenting Wordsworth, Coleridge, and Southey in their interrelationships.

Bertrand Evans, *Gothic Drama from Walpole to Shelley*, 1947.

Margaret M. Fitzgerald, *First Follow Nature: Primitivism in English Poetry, 1725–1750*, 1947.

Wilma L. Kennedy, *The English Heritage of Coleridge of Bristol, 1798: The Basis in Eighteenth-Century English Thought for His Distinction between Imagination and Fancy,* 1947.

Paul Roubiczek, *The Misinterpretation of Man,* 1947. Traces the perversions of the romantic concept and states the present-day need in Europe for a revival of romantic idealism.

R. S. Crane, 'Cleanth Brooks; or, The Bankruptcy of Critical Monism,' *MP,* XLV (1948), 226–45. Contrasts the narrowness and unsoundness of the 'New Criticism's' theories with the comprehensiveness of Coleridge's philosophy of literature.

D. G. James, *The Romantic Comedy,* 1948. A philosophical inquiry into the nature, methods, and results of the mythical imagination. Chapters on Blake, Coleridge, Shelley, and Keats.

A. O. Lovejoy, *Essays in the History of Ideas,* 1948. Includes chapters on the Gothic Revival and on the discrimination of romanticisms.

A. D. McKillop, *English Literature from Dryden to Burns,* 1948. Includes sections on Romanticism, Sentimentalism, Medieval Revival, and Primitivism.

Paul Van Tieghem, *L'Ère romantique: le romantisme dans la littérature européenne,* 1948.

John Arthos, *The Language of Natural Description in Eighteenth-Century Poetry,* 1949.

C. M. Bowra, *The Romantic Imagination,* 1949.

René Wellek, 'The Concept of "Romanticism" in Literary History,' *Comparative Literature,* I (1949), 1–23, 147–72.

Josephine Miles, *The Primary Language of Poetry in the 1740's and the 1840's,* 1950.

W. H. Auden, *The Enchafèd Flood: Three Critical Essays on the Romantic Spirit,* 1950.

Morse Peckham, 'Towards a Theory of Romanticism,' *PMLA,* LXVI (1951), 5–23.

Herbert Read, *The True Voice of Feeling,* 1953. On organic form in the style of modern English poetry, chiefly of the early nineteenth and early twentieth centuries.

M. H. Abrams, *The Mirror and the Lamp: Romantic Theory and Critical Tradition,* 1954.

René Wellek, *A History of Modern Criticism,* 1955, vol. I: *The Later Eighteenth Century;* vol. II: *The Romantic Age.*

C. P. Brand, *Italy and the English Romantics,* 1957.

C. D. Thorpe and others, eds., *The Major Romantic Poets: A Symposium in Reappraisal,* 1957.

M. H. Abrams, ed., *English Romantic Poets: Modern Essays in Criticism,* 1960.

Karl Kroeber, *Romantic Narrative Art,* 1960.

Harold Bloom, *The Visionary Company,* 1961.

James Benziger, *Images of Eternity: Studies in the Poetry of Religious Vision,* 1962.

R. F. Gleckner and G. E. Enscoe, eds., *Romanticism: Points of View,* 1962. A useful collection of major essays on romanticism.

E. E. Bostetter, *The Romantic Ventriloquists,* 1963.

Northrop Frye, ed., *Romanticism Reconsidered: Selected Papers from the English Institute,* 1963.

F. W. Hilles and Harold Bloom, eds., *From Sensibility to Romanticism: Essays Presented to Frederick A. Pottle,* 1965.

Brian Wilkie, *Romantic Poets and Epic Tradition,* 1965.

AUTHOR BIBLIOGRAPHIES

MARK AKENSIDE   1721–70

EDITIONS

Poetical Works, ed. Alexander Dyce, 1835 (Aldine ed.), 1894.

BIOGRAPHY AND CRITICISM

Edward Dowden, in *English Poets,* 1880.

A. O. Aldridge, 'The Eclecticism of *The Pleasures of Imagination,*' *JHI,* V (1944), 292–314.

C. T. Houpt, *Mark Akenside,* 1944.

A. O. Aldridge, 'Akenside and the Imagination,' *SP,* XLII (1945), 769–92.

Martin Kallich, 'The Association of Ideas and Akenside's *Pleasures of Imagination,*' *MLN,* LXII (1947), 166–73.

WILLIAM BECKFORD   1760–1844

EDITIONS

Vathek, printed with the original Prefaces and Notes by Samuel Henley, the translator of the first French ed., 1900.

Vathek, ed. with an Introduction by R. B. Johnson, 1922.

BIOGRAPHY AND CRITICISM

Lewis Melville, *The Life and Letters of William Beckford* 1910. A pioneer biography.

Sacheverell Sitwell, *Beckford and Beckfordism*, 1930.

J. W. Oliver, *The Life of William Beckford*, 1932. The best-balanced study; emphasizes Beckford as a romantic.

Guy Chapman, *Beckford*, 1937. Presents documentary evidence not included in Oliver; uses the psychological approach.

F. M. Mahmoud, ed., *William Beckford of Fonthill, 1760–1844: Bicentenary Essays*, 1960.

Boyd Alexander, *England's Wealthiest Son: A Study of William Beckford*, 1962.

THOMAS LOVELL BEDDOES   1803–49

EDITIONS

Complete Works, ed. H. W. Donner, 1935; 2nd ed., 1950. The definitive edition.

Thomas Lovell Beddoes: An Anthology, ed. F. L. Lucas, 1932. Contains selections from both the poems and letters, with an introduction.

BIOGRAPHY AND CRITICISM

Edgell Rickword, 'Thomas Lovell Beddoes,' *London Mercury*, IX (1923), 162–74. A useful biographical and critical sketch.

R. H. Snow, *Thomas Lovell Beddoes, Eccentric and Poet*, 1928.

H. W. Donner, ed. *The Browning Box*, 1935. Beddoes' life and works as reflected in letters by his friends and admirers; contains an introduction by the editor.

H. W. Donner, *Thomas Lovell Beddoes: The Making of a Poet*, 1935. Shares with Snow the claim to being the 'standard' life.

Horace Gregory, 'On the Gothic Imagination in Romantic Poetry and the Survival of Thomas Lovell Beddoes,' in *The Shield of Achilles*, 1944.

John Heath-Stubbs, 'The Defeat of Romanticism,' in *The Darkling Plain*, 1950.

Harold Bloom, 'Beddoes, Clare, Darley, and Others,' in *The Visionary Company*, 1961.

ROBERT BLAIR   1699–1746

EDITIONS

The Grave, ed. F. W. Farrar, 1858.

BIOGRAPHY AND CRITICISM

H. G. Graham, *Robert Blair*, 1901.

Carl Müller, *Robert Blair's 'Grave' und die Grabes—und Nachtdichtung*, 1909.

J. W. Draper, in *The Funeral Elegy and the Rise of English Romanticism*, 1929.

WILLIAM BLAKE   1757–1827

EDITIONS

Writings, ed. Geoffrey Keynes, 3 vols., 1925; rev., 1957. The definitive edition, provided with variant readings and notes. One-volume edition with all variant readings (Random House), 1958.

The Poetry and Prose of William Blake, ed. David V. Erdman, 1966. Commentary by Harold Bloom.

Poetical Works, ed. John Sampson (Oxford ed.), 1905, rev., 1934. The shorter poems.

The Prophetic Writings, ed. with an introduction and commentary by D. J. Sloss and J. P. R. Wallis, 2 vols., 1926. Included is a concordance to Blake's symbolism.

Selected Poetry and Prose, ed. Northrop Frye, 1953. A generous selection with a valuable introduction to Blake's leading ideas.

Letters, ed. Geoffrey Keynes, 1956.

BIOGRAPHY AND CRITICISM

Alexander Gilchrist, *Life of William Blake*, 2 vols., 1863, rev., 1880; ed. W. G. Robertson, 1906. This early life has served as an important source book for later biographers.

S. F. Damon, *William Blake: His Philosophy and Symbolism*, 1924, reprinted, 1947. Emphasizes Blake's mysticism and his originality; provides a full commentary.

J. H. Wicksteed, *Blake's Vision of the Book of Job*, rev. ed., 1924.

Darrell Figgis, *The Paintings of William Blake*, illustrated, 1925.

Laurence Binyon, *The Engravings of William Blake*, illustrated, 1926.

Jack Lindsay, *William Blake, Creative Will and the Poetic Image*, 1927.

Max Plowman, *Introduction to the Study of Blake*, 1927. An excellent first book.

Helen C. White, *The Mysticism of Blake*, 1927.

Philippe Soupault, *William Blake*, 1928.

Mona Wilson, *The Life of William Blake*, 1927, new eds., 1932, 1948. The standard biography.

J. H. Wicksteed, *Songs of Innocence and Experience*, 1928. Illustrated.

Denis Saurat, *Blake and Modern Thought*, 1929.

Thomas Wright, *The Life of William Blake*, 2 vols., 1929. A detailed and liberally illustrated biography, prepared by the secretary of the Blake Society.

J. M. Murry, *William Blake*, 1933. One of the best introductions to Blake's thought.

M. O. Percival, *William Blake's Circle of Destiny*, 1937.

Margaret R. Lowery, *Windows of the Morning: A Critical Study of Poetical Sketches*, 1939.

Jacob Bronowski, *A Man without a Mask: William Blake*, 1944. Emphasizes Blake's political and social dissent and his kinship with Marx.

Mark Schorer, *William Blake: The Politics of Vision* 1946. A comprehensive study showing Blake in relation to his times: his social and political thought.

W. P. Witcutt, *Blake: A Psychological Study*, 1946. Uses Jungian psychology as a key to Blake.

Northrop Frye, *Fearful Symmetry: A Study of William Blake*, 1947. Exposition of Blake's mythology with emphasis on the Prophecies.

J. G. Davies, *The Theology of William Blake*, 1948. Good on Swedenborg.

Bernard Blackstone, *English Blake*, 1949. A study of Blake 'concerned chiefly with his position within the tradition of English thought.'

Geoffrey Keynes, *Blake Studies: Notes on His Life and Works*, 1949.

H. M. Margoliouth, *William Blake*, 1951. A good general introduction.

D. V. Erdman, *Blake: Prophet Against Empire*, 1954. An intensive study of English social and political thought during Blake's time and their effect upon him.

Stanley Gardner, *Infinity on the Anvil: A Critical Study of Blake's Poetry*, 1954. A stimulating reading of Blake's symbolism, though marred at times by faulty scholarship.

Joseph Wicksteed, *William Blake's Jerusalem*, 1954.

Hazard Adams, *Blake and Yeats: The Contrary Vision*, 1956.

V. de S. Pinto, ed., *The Divine Vision: Studies in the Poetry and Art of William Blake*, 1957.

R. F. Gleckner, *The Piper and the Bard*, 1959. A perceptive reading of symbolic meaning in the *Songs of Innocence and Experience*.

Peter Fisher, *The Valley of Vision*, 1961.

J. E. Grant, ed., *Discussions of William Blake*, 1961. A useful reprint of the essays of ten modern critics.

G. M. Harper, *The Neoplatonism of William Blake*, 1961.

Hazard Adams, *William Blake: A Reading of the Shorter Poems*, 1963.

Harold Bloom, *Blake's Apocalypse: A Study in Poetic Argument*, 1963.

J. H. Hagstrum, *William Blake, Poet and Painter: An Introduction to the Illuminated Verse*, 1964.

Jacob Bronowski, *William Blake and the Age of Revolution*, 1965.

S. Foster Damon, *A Blake Dictionary: The Ideas and Symbols of William Blake*, 1965.

WILLIAM LISLE BOWLES 1762–1850

EDITIONS

Poetical Works, ed., with a Memoir by George Gilfillan, 2 vols., 1855.

BIOGRAPHY AND CRITICISM

T. E. Casson, in *Eighteenth-Century Literature*, 1909.

Garland Greever, *A Wiltshire Parson and His Friends*, 1926.

ROBERT BURNS 1759–96

EDITIONS

Complete Writings, with an Essay by W. E. Henley, and an Introduction by John Buchan, 10 vols., 1926–7.

Poetry, ed. W. E. Henley and T. F. Henderson (Centenary ed.), 4 vols., 1896–7; in one volume (Cambridge ed.), 1897.

Poems, ed. C. S. Dougall, 1927. The most reliable text.

The Songs of Robert Burns (with their music), ed. J. C. Dick 1903.

Notes on Scottish Song by Robert Burns, ed. J. C. Dick, 1908.

Letters, ed. J. De L. Ferguson, 2 vols., 1931.

BIOGRAPHY AND CRITICISM

Thomas Carlyle, *Robert Burns*, 1828. A famous appreciation by a Victorian and fellow-Scotsman.

W. A. Neilson, *Robert Burns: How To Know Him*, 1917. A good first book.

Hans Hecht, *Robert Burns: Leben und Wirken des schottischen Volksdichters*, 1919, rev. and expanded in the English version, 1936, reprinted, 1950. A thorough account of Burns's life and works.

Catherine Carswell, *The Life of Robert Burns*, 1930. A popular biography.

A. B. Jamieson, *Burns and Religion*, 1931.

J. D. Ross, *A Burns Handbook*, 1931.

F. B. Snyder, *The Life of Robert Burns,* 1932. The standard biography.

F. B. Snyder, *Robert Burns, His Personality, His Reputation, and His Art,* 1936. Toronto University Alexander Lectures.

R. T. Fitzhugh, 'Burns' Highland Mary,' *PMLA,* LII (1937), 829–34.

J. De L. Ferguson, *Pride and Passion: Robert Burns,* 1939. A study of Burns's personality discarding time-sequence for a discussion of the 'relationships of everyday life.'

R. T. Fitzhugh, *Robert Burns: His Associates and Contemporaries,* 1943.

Russell Noyes, 'Wordsworth and Burns,' *PMLA,* LIX (1944), 813–32.

David Daiches, *Robert Burns,* 1950. A biographical and critical sketch, including analyses of the better-known poems.

Thomas Crawford, *Burns: A Study of the Poems and Songs,* 1960. A perceptive and trustworthy reading of the poetry.

GEORGE NOEL GORDON, LORD BYRON
1788–1824

EDITIONS

Poetical Works, ed. E. H. Coleridge, 7 vols., and *Letters and Journals,* ed. R. E. Prothero, 6 vols., 1898–1904. The standard edition.

Poetical Works, ed. E. H. Coleridge, 1905. An excellent one-volume edition.

Don Juan: A Variorum Edition, eds., T. G. Steffan and W. W. Pratt, 4 vols., 1957. Includes a detailed history of the writing of the poem and Byron's method of composition.

Poetic and Dramatic Works, ed. P. E. More (Cambridge ed.), 1905. A valuable introduction by the editor.

Correspondence, ed. John Murray, 2 vols., 1922.

Letters and Diaries, 1798 to 1824, ed. Peter Quennell, 2 vols., 1950. A self-portrait.

Lord Byron in His Letters, ed. V. H. Collins, 1927. An excellent anthology of representative letters with an informative introduction.

BIOGRAPHY AND CRITICISM

Leigh Hunt, *Lord Byron and Some of His Contemporaries,* 3 vols., 1828. A firsthand, though somewhat prejudiced, account.

Thomas Moore, *The Life of Lord Byron, with His Letters and Journals,* 2 vols., 1830. The best of the contemporary accounts.

E. J. Trelawny, *Recollections of the Last Days of Shelley and Byron,* 1858. A vivid firsthand portrayal of the poet, though not always reliable.

Matthew Arnold, in *Essays in Criticism,* Second Series, 1888. Byron is next to Wordsworth among Romantic poets.

Ethel C. Mayne, *Byron,* 2 vols., 1912, rev., 1924. The story of Byron's life told with discrimination and insight.

S. C. Chew, *The Dramas of Lord Byron, A Critical Study,* 1915.

S. C. Chew, *Byron in England, His Fame and After-fame,* 1924. A complete record of Byron's English reputation.

H. G. Nicolson, *Byron: The Last Journey, April, 1823-April, 1824,* 1924; new eds., 1940, 1948.

John Drinkwater, *The Pilgrim of Eternity,* 1925. A substantial biography, but tends to see Byron's faults in a favorable light.

André Maurois, *Byron,* 1929, trans. 1930. A popular, romanticized biography.

W. J. Calvert, *Byron: Romantic Paradox,* 1935. The emphasis is on Byron as poet and thinker.

Peter Quennell, *Byron: The Years of Fame,* 1935; *Byron in Italy,* 1941. Sparkling but not profound biographical studies.

E. M. Marjarum, *Byron as Skeptic and Believer,* 1939.

Elizabeth F. Boyd, *Byron's Don Juan,* 1945. A first-rate scholarly study.

P. G. Trueblood, *The Flowering of Byron's Genius: Studies in Byron's Don Juan,* 1945.

W. A. Borst, *Lord Byron's First Pilgrimage, 1809–1811,* 1948.

Ernest J. Lovell, *Byron: The Record of a Quest. Studies in a Poet's Concept and Treatment of Nature,* 1949.

C. L. Cline, *Byron, Shelley, and Their Pisan Circle,* 1952. A useful supplement to other biographies.

E. J. Lovell, Jr., *His Very Self and Voice,* 1954. A valuable compilation of impressions of Byron by his contemporaries.

Leslie A. Marchand, *Lord Byron,* 3 vols., 1957. The definitive life.

G. M. Ridenour, *The Style of Don Juan,* 1960.

Andrew Rutherford, *Byron,* 1961.

W. H. Marshall *The Structure of Byron's Major Poems,* 1962.

P. L. Thorslev, Jr., *The Byronic Hero: Types and Prototypes,* 1962.

Paul West, ed., *Byron: A Collection of Critical Essays,* 1963.

Leslie A. Marchand, *Byron's Poetry: A Critical Introduction,* 1965.

THOMAS CAMPBELL 1777–1844

EDITIONS

Complete Poetical Works, ed. J. L. Robertson, 1907.

BIOGRAPHY AND CRITICISM

William Beattie, *Life and Letters of Thomas Campbell,* 3 vols., 1850. A scholarly and complete biography.

G. E. B. Saintsbury, 'The English War Songs,' in *Essays in English Literature,* Second Series, 1895.

J. C. Hadden, *Thomas Campbell,* 1899. Shares with Beattie's *Life* the claim to being the standard biography.

W. M. Dixon, 'Thomas Campbell,' in *An Apology for the Arts,* 1944.

S. K. Ratcliffe, 'A Poet of Battle,' *Spectator,* June 16, 1944.

THOMAS CHATTERTON 1752–70

EDITIONS

Poetical Works, ed. with an Essay on the Rowley Poems by W. W. Skeat, 2 vols., 1871.

Complete Poetical Works, ed. with a Life by H. D. Roberts, 2 vols., 1906.

The Rowley Poems, ed. with an Introduction by M. E. Hare, 1911.

BIOGRAPHY AND CRITICISM

Daniel Wilson, *Chatterton: A Biographical Study,* 1869. A very good life.

Esther P. Ellinger, *Thomas Chatterton, the Marvelous Boy,* 1930. An Adler-Freudian interpretation of the poet.

E. H. W. Meyerstein, *A Life of Thomas Chatterton,* 1930. Supplements but does not supersede Wilson

Alun Watkin-Jones, 'Bishop Percy, Thomas Warton and Chatterton's Rowley Poems,' *PMLA,* L (1935), 769–84.

E. H. W. Meyerstein, 'Chatterton: His Significance Today,' *Essays by Divers Hands* (*Transactions of the Royal Society of Literature*), XVI (1937), 61–91.

Frances S. Miller, 'The Historic Sense of Thomas Chatterton,' *ELH,* XI (1944), 117–34.

JOHN CLARE 1793–1864

EDITIONS

Poems, ed. Edmund Blunden and Alan Porter, 1920. Contains an excellent biographical introduction.

Poems, ed. J. W. Tibble, 2 vols., 1935. The standard edition.

Poems of John Clare's Madness, ed. Geoffrey Grigson, 1949.

The Later Poems, ed. Eric Robinson and Geoffrey Summerfield, 1964.

The Prose of John Clare, ed. J. W. and Anne Tibble, 1951.

BIOGRAPHY AND CRITICISM

J. M. Murry, 'The Poetry of John Clare,' in *Countries of the Mind,* 1922; rev., 1931.

J. W. and Anne Tibble, *John Clare, A Life,* 1932; rev., 1956. The standard biography.

Horace Gregory, 'On John Clare, and the Sight of Nature in His Poetry,' in *The Shield of Achilles,* 1944.

John Heath-Stubbs, 'John Clare and the Peasant Tradition,' in *The Darkling Plain,* 1950.

June Wilson, *Green Shadows,* 1951. A new life of Clare.

F. W. Martin, *The Life of John Clare,* ed. Eric Robinson and Geoffrey Summerfield, 1964.

Robert Graves, 'Peasant Poet,' *The Hudson Review,* VIII, no. 1 (Spring 1955), 99–105.

Harold Bloom, 'John Clare: The Wordsworthian Shadow,' in *The Visionary Company,* 1962.

WILLIAM COBBETT 1763–1835

EDITIONS

Selections from Political Works, ed. J. M. and J. P. Cobbett, 4 vols., 1835.

Selections, ed. A. M. D. Hughes, 1923. Contains Hazlitt's essay and other critical estimates, with an introduction and notes.

Opinions of William Cobbett, ed. G. D. H. and Margaret Cole, 1944. Selections from the *Political Register.*

Rural Rides, ed. G. D. H. and Margaret Cole, 3 vols., 1930.

Rural Rides, ed. E. W. Martin, 1959. Illustrated with Gillray's cartoons.

The Progess of a Ploughboy to a Seat in Parliament, ed. William Reitzel, 1933, rev. as *The Autobiography of William Cobbett,* 1947. An autobiography constructed by arranging passages in a connected narrative.

BIOGRAPHY AND CRITICISM

G. D. H. Cole, *The Life of William Cobbett,* 1924. The standard biography.

G. K. Chesterton, *William Cobbett,* 1925. A brilliant study.

Marjorie Bowen, *Peter Porcupine,* 1936. A good popular biography.

H. J. Massingham, *Wisdom of the Fields,* 1945.

W. B. Pemberton, *William Cobbett,* 1949.

J. W. Osborne, *William Cobbett: His Thoughts and His Times,* 1966.

HARTLEY COLERIDGE   1796–1849

EDITIONS

Complete Poetical Works, ed. Ramsay Colles, 1908. The standard edition.

New Poems by Hartley Coleridge, ed. E. L. Griggs, 1942. A selection of the best and most significant poems old and new with a critical preface.

Letters, ed. Grace E. and E. L. Griggs, 1936.

BIOGRAPHY AND CRITICISM

M. J. Pomeroy, *The Poetry of Hartley Coleridge,* 1927.

E. L. Griggs, *Hartley Coleridge, His Life and Work,* 1929. The standard biography.

H. W. Hartman, *Hartley Coleridge: Poet's Son and Poet,* 1931. A scholarly and sympathetic account.

SAMUEL TAYLOR COLERIDGE
1772–1834

EDITIONS

Complete Works, ed. W. G. T. Shedd, 7 vols., 1884. The nearest approach to a complete edition.

Complete Poetical Works, ed. E. H. Coleridge, 2 vols., 1912. Textually the best edition of the poetry. Reprinted, 1957.

Poetical Works, ed. J. D. Campbell, 1909. The preferred one-volume edition.

Christabel, ed. E. H. Coleridge, 1907. Excellent for its critical notes.

Biographia Literaria, ed. John Shawcross, 2 vols., 1908. Contains an excellent introductory essay on Coleridge's literary theory. See also Everyman's edition, ed. George Watson, 1956.

Shakespearean Criticism, ed. T. M. Raysor, 2 vols., 1930; reprinted, 1960.

Miscellaneous Criticism, ed. T. M. Raysor, 1936.

Philosophical Lectures: 1818–1819, ed. Kathleen Coburn, 1949.

Letters, ed. E. H. Coleridge, 2 vols., 1895.

Inquiring Spirit, ed. Kathleen Coburn, 1950. Anthology of Coleridge's speculative prose.

The Notebooks, ed. Kathleen Coburn, vols. I and II (1794–1808), 1957–61.

Collected Letters, ed. E. L. Griggs, vols. I–IV (1785–1819), 1956–59.

BIOGRAPHY AND CRITICISM

Margaret E. Sandford, *Thomas Poole and His Friends,* 2 vols., 1888. A delightfully written book dealing with the relations of the poet and his merchant friend and benefactor.

J. D. Campbell, *Samuel Taylor Coleridge,* 1894. At one time considered the standard life, now superseded by Chambers and Hanson.

Claud Howard, *Coleridge's Idealism,* 1924.

H. I'A. Fausset, *Samuel Taylor Coleridge,* 1926. An impressionistic study of the inner life of Coleridge purporting to show that his poetry is the expression of an 'escape from reality,' the result of an unresolved spiritual conflict.

A. E. Powell (Mrs. E. R. Dodds), *The Romantic Theory of Poetry,* 1926. Interprets Coleridge's early neo-Platonism.

John Charpentier, *Coleridge the Sublime Somnambulist* (1927), trans. 1929. An interesting life with abundant anecdotal material, and containing sound literary appraisals.

J. L. Lowes, *The Road to Xanadu,* 1927, enlarged, 1930. A monumental study 'in the ways of the imagination,' revealing how Coleridge's observation of phenomena and his vast and curious reading became sublimated into poetry.

J. H. Muirhead, *Coleridge as Philosopher,* 1930.

I. A. Richards, *Coleridge on Imagination,* 1934.

Stephen Potter, *Coleridge and S. T. C.,* 1935. A study of Coleridge's dual nature.

Margaret Sherwood, *Coleridge's Imaginative Concept of Imagination,* 1937; reprinted, 1960.

E. K. Chambers, *S. T. Coleridge,* 1938. An admirably compact and scholarly life.

Laurence Hanson, *The Life of S. T. Coleridge: The Early Years,* 1938. A scholarly work on a larger scale than that by Chambers, but covering only the years 1772–1800.

Gordon McKenzie, *Organic Unity in Coleridge,* 1939.

A. H. Nethercott, *The Road to Tryermaine,* 1939. A study of the history, background, and purposes of *Christabel.*

R. W. Armour and R. F. Howes, *Coleridge the Talker: A Series of Contemporary Descriptions and Comments,* 1940. A lengthy critical introduction helps toward an understanding of Coleridge's temperament and literary gift and suggests relations between his talk and his writing.

C. R. Sanders, *Coleridge and the Broad Church Movement,* 1942.

Robert Penn Warren, ed., *The Rime of the Ancient Mariner,* 1946. The most notable symbolist reading of this famous poem.

Basil Willey, *Coleridge on Imagination and Fancy,* 1946.

Malcolm Elwin, *The First Romantics*, 1947. A lively narrative presenting Coleridge, Southey, and Wordsworth in their interrelationships.

E. E. Stoll, 'Symbolism in Coleridge,' *PMLA*, LXIII (1948), 214–23. A defense against the 'New Critics.'

Herbert Read, *Coleridge as Critic*, 1949.

Basil Willey, 'Coleridge,' in *Nineteenth Century Studies*, 1949.

W. J. Bate, 'Coleridge on the Function of Art,' in *Perspectives of Criticism* (ed. Harry Levin), 1950. Incisive discussion of Coleridge's aesthetics.

Humphrey House, *Coleridge*, 1953. Includes perceptive analyses of the major poems.

H. M. Margoliouth, *Wordsworth and Coleridge*, 1953. Compact and readable.

Elisabeth Schneider, *Coleridge, Opium, and 'Kubla Khan*,' 1953.

George Whalley, *Coleridge and Sara Hutchinson and the Asra Poems*, 1955.

J. V. Baker, *The Sacred River: Coleridge's Theory of Imagination*, 1957.

J. B. Beer, *Coleridge the Visionary*, 1959.

J. A. Colmer, *Coleridge: Critic of Society*, 1959.

Marshall Suther, *The Dark Night of Samuel Taylor Coleridge*, 1960.

J. D. Boulger, *Coleridge as Religious Thinker*, 1961.

R. A. Gettman, ed., *The Rime of the Ancient Mariner: A Handbook*, 1961.

Carl Woodring, *Politics in the Poetry of Coleridge*, 1961.

R. H. Fogle, *The Idea of Coleridge's Criticism*, 1962. Includes a good reading of *Christabel*.

M. F. Schulz, *The Poetic Voices of Coleridge*, 1963.

Marshall Suther, *Visions of Xanadu*, 1965. A study of 'Kubla Khan' as a complete, coherent, and symbolic poem.

J. A. Appleyard, *Coleridge's Philosophy of Literature, 1791–1819*, 1965.

WILLIAM COLLINS 1721–59

EDITIONS

Poems, ed. W. C. Bronson, 1898.

Poems, ed. Edmund Blunden, 1929. Contains some material not in Bronson's edition.

BIOGRAPHY AND CRITICISM

H. W. Garrod, *The Poetry of Collins*, 1928.

A. S. P. Woodhouse, 'Collins and the Creative Imagination,' in *Toronto Studies in English*, 1931.

E. G. Ainsworth, *Poor Collins: His Life, His Art, and His Influence*, 1937.

WILLIAM COWPER 1731–1800

EDITIONS

Works, with a Life by Robert Southey, 15 vols., 1836–7.

Poems, ed. H. S. Milford (Oxford), 1906, 3rd ed., 1926.

Correspondence, ed. Thomas Wright, 4 vols., 1904.

Unpublished and Uncollected Letters, ed. Thomas Wright, 1925.

Selected Letters, ed. William Hadley, 1925.

BIOGRAPHY AND CRITICISM

Goldwin Smith, *Cowper*, 1880.

Thomas Wright, *The Life of William Cowper*, 1892, rev. 1921.

H. I'A. Fausset, *William Cowper*, 1928. A psychological study; includes interpretation of the poetry.

Lord David Cecil, *The Stricken Deer*, 1929. The emphasis is upon the man and his madness.

Gilbert Thomas, *William Cowper and the Eighteenth Century*, 1935, rev. 1948. Presents Cowper in relation to his century, stressing the Evangelical background of his writings.

L. C. Hartley, *William Cowper, Humanitarian*, 1938. Discusses Cowper as a figure in the history of liberalism.

A. E. Thein, 'The Religion of John Newton,' *PQ*, XXI (1942), 146–70.

M. J. Quinlan, 'Cowper and the Unpardonable Sin,' *Journal of Religion*, XXIII (1943), 110–16.

Norman Nicholson, *William Cowper*, 1951. A brief, readable life.

M. J. Quinlan, *William Cowper, A Critical Life*, 1952. A well-balanced and sympathetic life.

GEORGE CRABBE 1754–1832

EDITIONS

Poetical Works, with the Letters and Journals and a Life by Crabbe's son, 8 vols., 1834; re-edited by E. M. Forster, 1932.

Poems, ed. A. W. Ward, 3 vols., 1905–7.

Poetical Works, ed. A. J. and R. M. Carlyle (Oxford ed.), 1914.

Poems, selected by Phillip Henderson, 1946. Includes an introduction.

New Poems by George Crabbe, ed. Arthur Pollard, 1960.

BIOGRAPHY AND CRITICISM

G. E. B. Saintsbury, in *Essays in English Literature, 1780–1860*, 1890.

Alfred Ainger, *Crabbe*, 1903.

P. E. More, in *Shelburne Essays*, First Series, 1904.

René Huchon, *George Crabbe and His Times*, trans. 1908.

J. H. Evans, *The Poems of George Crabbe: A Literary and Historical Study*, 1933.

Varley Lang, 'Crabbe and the Eighteenth Century,' *ELH*, v (1938), 305–33.

Vivian Mercier, 'The Poet as Sociologist—George Crabbe,' *Dublin Magazine*, XXII, no. 4 (1947), 19–27.

George Crabbe, *Life of George Crabbe*, by his son, with an introduction by Edmund Blunden, 1947.

Lilian Haddakin, *The Poetry of Crabbe*, 1955.

O. F. Sigworth, *Nature's Sternest Painter: Five Essays on the Poetry of George Crabbe*, 1965.

JOHN WILSON CROKER   1780–1857

EDITIONS

Essays, reprinted from the *Quarterly Review*, 1857.

BIOGRAPHY AND CRITICISM

William Maginn, in *A Gallery of Illustrious Characters*, ed. William Bates, 1873.

M. F. Brightfield, *John Wilson Croker*, 1940.

ALLAN CUNNINGHAM   1784–1842

EDITIONS

Songs and Poems, ed. Paul Cunningham, 1875.

BIOGRAPHY AND CRITICISM

David Hogg, *The Life of Allan Cunningham*, 1875. Includes selections from his poetry.

'Allan Cunningham: A Centenary Tribute,' *TLS*, 31 Oct. 1942, p. 535.

THOMAS DE QUINCEY   1785–1859

EDITIONS

Collected Writings, ed. David Masson, 14 vols., 1889–90. The standard edition.

Confessions, ed. Malcolm Elwin, 1956.

Reminiscences of the English Lake Poets, ed. J. E. Jordan, 1958.

Selected Writings, ed. P. V. D. Stern, 1937.

BIOGRAPHY AND CRITICISM

Lane Cooper, *The Prose Poetry of Thomas De Quincey*, 1902.

C. T. Winchester, in *A Group of English Essayists*, 1910.

J. H. Fowler, 'De Quincey as a Literary Critic,' *English Association Pamphlet*, 1922.

G. E. B. Saintsbury, in *Collected Essays and Papers*, First Series, 1923.

Jeanette A. Marks, *Genius and Disaster*, 1925. Traces the disastrous effects of alcohol and opium upon De Quincey.

M. H. Abrams, *The Milk of Paradise*, 1934. A study of the effect of opium visions on the works of De Quincey and others.

Malcolm Elwin, *De Quincey*, 1935. Great Lives Series.

H. A. Eaton, *Thomas De Quincey*, 1936. A well-documented, scholarly life.

Edward Sackville-West, *A Flame in Sunlight: The Life and Work of Thomas De Quincey*, 1936. Judicious and well-proportioned. Unlike Eaton's biography includes criticism on the literary works.

J. C. Metcalf, *De Quincey: A Portrait*, 1940. Uncovers no new facts, but is a sympathetic 'portrait' freed from academic impedimenta.

S. K. Proctor, *Thomas De Quincey's Theory of Literature*, 1943. A corrective is René Wellek, 'De Quincey's Status in the History of Ideas,' *PQ*, XXIII (1944), 248–72.

J. E. Jordan, *Thomas De Quincey: Literary Critic*, 1952.

J. E. Jordan, *De Quincey to Wordsworth: A Biography of Relationship, with the Letters of Thomas De Quincey to the Wordsworth Family*, 1962.

J. H. Miller, *The Disappearance of God: Five Nineteenth-Century Writers*, 1963.

Françoise Moreux, *Thomas De Quincey, la vie—l'homme—l'œuvre*, 1964.

JOHN DYER   1699–1757

EDITIONS

Poems, ed. with a biographical introduction by Edward Thomas, 1903.

Grongar Hill, ed. R. C. Boys, 1941.

BIOGRAPHY AND CRITICISM

Samuel Johnson, in *Lives of the English Poets*, 1777–80.

Edward Dowden, in *English Poets*, 1880.

WILLIAM GODWIN   1756–1836

EDITIONS

Enquiry Concerning Political Justice, facsimile of the 3rd ed., ed. with critical introduction and notes by F. E. L. Priestley, 3 vols., 1946.

BIOGRAPHY AND CRITICISM

C. K. Paul, *William Godwin: His Friends and Contemporaries*, 2 vols., 1876. Based on source material.

Edward Dowden, 'Theorists of Revolution,' in *The French Revolution and English Literature*, 1897.

Leslie Stephen, 'The Revolutionists,' in *History of English Thought in the Eighteenth Century*, 1902.

Raymond Gourg, *William Godwin: sa vie, ses oeuvres principales*, 1908. Primarily a study of *Political Justice*.

G. M. Harper, 'Rousseau, Godwin, and Wordsworth,' *Atlantic Monthly*, CIX (1912), 639–50.

H. N. Brailsford, *Shelley, Godwin, and their Circle*, 1913. Vigorous study stressing the intellectual and political milieu.

F. K. Brown, *The Life of William Godwin*, 1926. Emphasizes Godwin's business and personal affairs; little discussion of his ideas. Patronizing.

Basil Willey, in *The Eighteenth-Century Background*, 1940.

George Woodcock, *William Godwin: A Biographical Study*, 1946. Possibly the sanest biography; contains an adequate treatment of Godwin's ideas.

D. H. Monro, *Godwin's Moral Philosophy*, 1953.

Rosalie G. Grylls, *William Godwin and His World*, 1954.

OLIVER GOLDSMITH 1730–74

EDITIONS

Collected Works, ed. Arthur Friedman, 5 vols., 1966.

Complete Poetical Works, ed. Austin Dobson, 1906.

Collected Letters, ed. K. C. Balderston, 1928.

BIOGRAPHY AND CRITICISM

John Forster, *Life and Adventures of Oliver Goldsmith*, 2 vols., 1854, final ed., 1877.

Austin Dobson, *Life of Goldsmith*, 1888, rev., 1899.

W. F. Gallaway, Jr., 'The Sentimentalism of Goldsmith,' *PMLA*, XLVIII (1933), 1167–81.

H. J. Bell, Jr., '*The Deserted Village* and Goldsmith's Social Doctrines,' *PMLA*, LIX (1944), 747–72.

R. M. Wardle, *Oliver Goldsmith*, 1957. The only scholarly biography to appear in the twentieth century.

THOMAS GRAY 1716–71

EDITIONS

Works, ed. Edmund Gosse, 4 vols., 1884, rev., 1902–6.

Selected Poetry and Prose, ed. J. E. Crofts, 1926.

Correspondence, ed. Paget Toynbee and Leonard Whibley, 3 vols., 1935.

BIOGRAPHY AND CRITICISM

Edmund Gosse, *Life of Gray*, 1882.

Matthew Arnold, in *Essays in Criticism*, Second Series, 1888.

W. H. Hudson, *Gray and His Poetry*, 1911.

Amy L. Reed, *The Background of Gray's Elegy: A Study in the Taste for Melancholy Poetry, 1700–1751*, 1924.

W. P. Jones, *Thomas Gray, Scholar*, 1937. Emphasis is upon Gray's scholarly interests.

H. W. Starr, *Gray as a Literary Critic*, 1941.

Lord David Cecil, *The Poetry of Thomas Gray*, 1945. Warton Lecture.

H. W. Starr, 'Gray's Craftsmanship,' *JEGP*, XLV (1946), 415–29.

Cleanth Brooks, *The Well Wrought Urn*, 1947. Includes an extended analysis of the 'Elegy.'

Lord David Cecil, *Two Quiet Lives*, 1948. Studies of two shy people—Thomas Gray and Dorothy Osborne.

F. H. Ellis, 'Gray's *Elegy*: The Biographical Problem in Literary Criticism,' *PMLA*, LXVI (1951), 971–1008. One of the best analyses of this world-famous poem.

R. W. Ketton-Cremer, *Thomas Gray*, 1955. The best biography.

Morris Golden, *Thomas Gray*, 1964. The most useful guide to the poetry.

ROBERT STEPHEN HAWKER 1803–75

EDITIONS

Poetical Works, ed. Alfred Wallis, 1899. The best edition; includes an excellent introduction and a full bibliography.

Cornish Ballads and Other Poems, ed. C. E. Byles, 1904. Illustrated.

A Selection of the Cornish Ballads, ed. F. C. Hamlyn, 1928.

BIOGRAPHY AND CRITICISM

C. E. Byles, *Life and Letters of Robert Stephen Hawker*, 1905.

P. E. More, 'The Vicar of Morsenstow,' in *Shelburne Essays*, Fourth Series, 1906.

M. F. Burrows, *Robert Stephen Hawker: A Study of His Thought and Poetry*, 1926.

WILLIAM HAZLITT 1778–1830

EDITIONS

The Complete Works of William Hazlitt, ed. P. P. Howe, 21 vols., 1931. The standard edition.

Selected Essays, ed. Geoffrey Keynes, 1930. The most comprehensive selection.

Shakespeare Criticism, ed. L. B. Bennion, 1947.

Hazlitt on English Literature, ed. Jacob Zeitlin, 1913. Includes a good introduction to Hazlitt as a critic of literature.

Hazlitt Painted by Himself and Presented by Catherine Macdonald Maclean, 1948.

BIOGRAPHY AND CRITICISM

Augustine Birrell, *William Hazlitt* (English Men of Letters Series), 1902. A satisfactory brief life.

P. P. Howe, *Life of William Hazlitt*, 1922; new eds., 1928, 1947.

H. W. Garrod, 'The Place of Hazlitt in English Criticism,' in *The Profession of Poetry*, 1929.

Hesketh Pearson, *The Fool of Love*, 1934. A popular life with the emphasis upon Hazlitt's unhappy love affair with Sarah Walker.

Elisabeth Schneider, *The Aesthetics of William Hazlitt*, 1933; second printing, 1952.

S. C. Wilcox, *Hazlitt in the Workshop*, 1943.

Catherine Maclean, *Born under Saturn: A Biography of Hazlitt*, 1944. A sympathetic portrait, representing Hazlitt as 'a stalwart in the war of liberation.'

W. P. Albrecht, *William Hazlitt and the Malthusian Controversy*, 1950.

René Wellek, chapter in *A History of Modern Criticism: 1750–1950*, 1955. A scholarly account of Hazlitt's literary criticism.

Herschel Baker, *William Hazlitt*, 1962. Replaces Howe's as the standard biography.

THOMAS HOOD 1799–1845

EDITIONS

Complete Works, ed. by his son and daughter, 11 vols., 1882–4.

Complete Poetical Works, ed. W. C. Jerrold, 1911. The best one-volume edition.

Thomas Hood and Charles Lamb, ed. W. C. Jerrold, 1930. A reprint of Hood's 'Literary Reminiscences' with notes by the editor.

Letters, ed. L. A. Marchand, 1945.

BIOGRAPHY AND CRITICISM

W. E. Henley, in *Views and Reviews*, 1890. Stresses the intellectual element in Hood.

W. C. Jerrold, *Thomas Hood: His Life and Times*, 1907. The standard biography.

P. E. More, in *Shelburne Essays*, Seventh Series, 1910. Designates Hood the master of the pun.

W. H. Hudson, 'Tom Hood: the Man, the Wit, and the Poet,' in *A Quiet Corner in a Library*, 1915.

John Heath-Stubbs, 'The Defeat of Romanticism,' in *The Darkling Plain*, 1950.

D. L. Hobman, 'Thomas Hood,' *Contemporary Review*, CLXXXVII (June 1955), 397–401.

Edmund Blunden, 'The Poet Hood,' *A Review of English Literature*, I (January 1960), 26–34.

LEIGH HUNT 1784–1859

EDITIONS

Poetical Works, ed. H. S. Milford, 1923. The definitive edition.

Essays and Poems, ed. R. B. Johnson, 2 vols., 1891. The best selection containing both the prose and poetry.

Essays (Selected), ed. J. B. Priestley (Everyman's Library), 1929.

Autobiography, ed. J. E. Morpurgo, 1949.

Autobiography, ed. S. F. Fogle, 1959. Contains an excellent introduction and helpful notes.

Dramatic Criticism, ed. L. H. and Carolyn W. Houtchens, 1949.

Literary Criticism, ed. L. H. and Carolyn W. Houtchens, 1956. Contains an essay by C. D. Thorpe on 'Leigh Hunt as Man of Letters.'

Political and Occasional Essays, ed. L. H. and Carolyn W. Houtchens, 1962.

BIOGRAPHY AND CRITICISM

G. E. B. Saintsbury, in *Essays in English Literature*, 1890.

R. B. Johnson, *Leigh Hunt*, 1896. A satisfactory brief life.

R. B. Johnson, *Shelley—Leigh Hunt: How a Friendship Made History*, 1928.

Edmund Blunden, *Leigh Hunt and his Circle*, 1930. A scholarly, yet fascinating and humane biography.

Louis Landré, *Leigh Hunt, 1784–1859: Contribution à l'histoire du romantisme anglais*, 2 vols., 1936. A monumental study of first importance. Contains a full bibliography.

G. D. Stout, *The Political History of Leigh Hunt's Examiner*, 1949.

FRANCIS JEFFREY 1773–1850

EDITIONS

Contributions to the Edinburgh Review, 4 vols., 1844. Jeffrey's own selection from his voluminous critical contributions.

Literary Criticism, ed. D. Nichol Smith, 1910. Contains an introduction by the editor and a list of Jeffrey's articles in the *Edinburgh Review*.

BIOGRAPHY AND CRITICISM

H. T. Cockburn, *Life of Lord Jeffrey with a Selection from His Correspondence*, 2 vols., 1856.

Thomas Carlyle, in *Reminiscences*, 1881. Pays tribute to Jeffrey's sincerity.

L. E. Gates, in *Three Studies in Literature*, 1899.

M. Y. Hughes, 'The Humanism of Francis Jeffrey,' *MLR*, XVI (1921), 243–51.

R. C. Bald, 'Francis Jeffrey as a Literary Critic,' *Nineteenth Century*, XCVII (1925), 201–5.

Russell Noyes, *Wordsworth and Jeffrey in Controversy*, 1941.

Robert Daniel, 'Jeffrey and Wordsworth: The Shape of Persecution,' *Sewanee Review*, L (1942), 195–213.

J. R. Derby, 'The Paradox of Francis Jeffrey,' *MLQ*, VII (1946), 489–500.

J. A. Greig, *Francis Jeffrey of the Edinburgh Review*, 1948. Jeffrey's judgment of his age was 'as able and as significant as was that of most of his successors in criticism.'

Byron Guyer, 'Francis Jeffrey's *Essay on Beauty*,' *Huntington Library Quarterly*, XIII (1949), 71–85.

J. A. Greig, *Francis Jeffrey of the Edinburgh Review*, 1949.

Thomas Crawford, *'The Edinburgh Review' and Romantic Poetry* (1802–29), 1955.

John Clive, *Scotch Reviewers: The Edinburgh Review, 1802–1815*, 1957.

JOHN KEATS　1795–1821

EDITIONS

Complete Works, ed. H. B. Forman, 5 vols., 1901, rev. as *Poetical Works and Other Writings*, 8 vols., 1938–9. The standard edition.

Poetical Works, ed. Ernest de Selincourt, one volume, 1905, 5th ed., rev., 1926. Excellent scholarly notes on Keats' style.

Poetical Works, ed. H. W. Garrod, 1956; 2nd ed., 1958. Definitive, well-edited text.

Letters, ed. H. E. Rollins, 2 vols., 1958. The standard edition.

The Keats Circle: Letters and Papers 1816–1878, ed. H. E. Rollins, 2 vols., 1948. *More Letters and Poems of the Keats Circle*, 1955.

Selected Poems and Letters, ed. Douglas Bush, 1959. Excels in authenticity of text and quality of notes.

BIOGRAPHY AND CRITICISM

Sidney Colvin, *John Keats, His Life and Poetry*, 1917, rev., 1925.

Amy Lowell, *John Keats*, 2 vols., 1925.

J. M. Murry, *Keats and Shakespeare*, 1925.

C. D. Thorpe, *The Mind of John Keats*, 1926.

J. M. Murry, *Studies in Keats*, 1930, enlarged, 1939, rev. as *The Mystery of Keats*, 1949, as *Keats*, 1950. Emphasizes the 'uniqueness' of Keats and the prophetic element in his work and life.

M. R. Ridley, *Keats' Craftsmanship: A Study in Poetic Development*, 1933.

Margaret Sherwood, 'Keats' Imaginative Approach to Myth,' in *Undercurrents of Influence in English Romantic Poetry*, 1934.

C. L. Finney, *The Evolution of Keats' Poetry*, 2 vols., 1936. A source book of details on Keats' poetic development.

F. R. Leavis. 'Keats' in *Revaluation*, 1936.

W. J. Bate, *Negative Capability: The Intuitive Approach to Keats*, 1939.

H. W. Garrod, *Keats*, 2nd ed., 1939. A useful study of Keats as a thinker and poet.

L. J. Zillman, *Keats and the Sonnet Tradition*, 1939.

G. H. Ford, *Keats and the Victorians: A Study of His Influence and Rise to Fame, 1821–1895*, 1944.

W. J. Bate, *The Stylistic Development of Keats*, 1945.

J. R. Caldwell, *John Keats' Fancy: The Effect on Keats of the Psychology of His Day*, 1945.

W. W. Beyer, *Keats and Daemon King*, 1947. The theme is the influence of Wieland's *Oberon* on Keats' poetry.

D. G. James, 'Purgatory Blind' in *The Romantic Comedy*, 1948.

R. H. Fogle, *The Imagery of Keats and Shelley: A Comparative Study*, 1949.

J. R. MacGillivray, *Keats: A Bibliography and Reference Guide, with an Essay on Keats's Reputation*, 1949.

Edmund Blunden, *John Keats*, 1950.

Douglas Bush, 'Keats and His Ideas,' in *The Major Romantic Poets*, ed. C. D. Thorpe, 1950.

Dorothy Hewlett, *A Life of John Keats*, 1937, rev., 1950. The story of Keats' life related with sincerity and understanding.

N. F. Ford, *The Prefigurative Imagination of John Keats: A Study of the Beauty-Truth Indentification and Its Implications*, 1951.

E. R. Wasserman, *The Finer Tone: Keats' Major Poems*, 1953.

Robert Gittings, *John Keats: The Living Year*, 1954. A day by day account of the most creative year in Keats' life (21 September 1818 to 21 September 1819).

Lionel Trilling, 'The Poet as Hero: Keats in His Letters,' in *The Opposing Self*, 1955.

Robert Gittings, *The Mask of Keats: A Study of Problems*, 1956.

E. C. Pettet, *On the Poetry of Keats*, 1957.

Kenneth Muir, ed., *John Keats: A Reassessment*, 1958.

Bernice Slote, *Keats and the Dramatic Principle*, 1958.

D. D. Perkins, *The Quest for Permanence: the Symbolism of Wordsworth, Shelley, and Keats*, 1959.

H. T. Lyon, *Keats' Well-Read Urn*, 1958. A useful compilation of interpretations.

W. J. Bate, *John Keats*, 1963. The definitive biography.

Aileen Ward, *John Keats: The Making of a Poet*, 1963. A competent and gracefully written biography.

W. J. Bate, ed., *Keats: A Collection of Critical Essays*, 1964.

W. H. Evert, *Aesthetic and Myth in the Poetry of Keats*, 1965.

Douglas Bush, *John Keats*, 1966. The best short critical biography.

CHARLES LAMB   1775–1834

EDITIONS

The Works of Charles and Mary Lamb, ed. E. V. Lucas, 7 vols., 1903–5. The standard edition.

The Works of Charles Lamb, ed. Thomas Hutchinson, 2 vols., 1924. A recommended inexpensive edition.

The Letters of Charles and Mary Lamb, ed. E. V. Lucas, 3 vols., 1935. The first complete edition of the letters.

Essays and Letters, ed. J. M. French, 1937. A selection with introduction and notes.

The Portable Charles Lamb, ed. J. M. Brown, 1949. Excellent introduction by one of the foremost modern practitioners in the informal essay.

BIOGRAPHY AND CRITICISM

Jules Derocquigny, *Charles Lamb*, 1904.

E. V. Lucas *The Life of Charles Lamb*, 2 vols., 1905, rev., 1921. The standard biography, ample and illuminating.

C. T. Winchester, in *A Group of English Essayists*, 1910.

Walter Pater, in *Appreciations*, 1913. A famous essay.

Edmund Blunden, *Charles Lamb and His Contemporaries*, 1933. An excellent series of sketches given originally as the Clark lectures at Trinity College, Oxford.

Edith C. Johnson, *Lamb Always Elia*, 1935.

E. C. Ross, *The Ordeal of Bridget Elia*, 1940. A life of Mary Lamb revealing her influence upon Charles and emphasizing her own contributions to literature.

W. D. Howe, *Charles Lamb and His Friends*, 1944. A satisfactory first book, but adding nothing new to the scholarship on Lamb.

'The Letters of Charles Lamb,' *TLS*, 15 June 1946, p. 282.

R. L. Hine, *Charles Lamb and His Hertfordshire*, 1949.

George Barnett, *Charles Lamb: The Evolution of Elia*, 1964.

WALTER SAVAGE LANDOR   1775–1864

EDITIONS

Imaginary Conversations, ed. C. G. Crump, 6 vols., 1891; *Longer Prose Works*, 2 vols., 1892–93. More satisfactory for prose than Welby.

Complete Works, ed. T. E. Welby and Stephen Wheeler, 16 vols., 1927–36. Definitive edition. Wheeler is best for the poetry.

Selections, ed. Sidney Colvin, 1882; frequently reprinted. Contains both poetry and prose, with a good brief introduction.

Poetry and Prose, ed. E. K. Chambers, 1946. A selection.

Imaginary Conversations, ed. Ernest de Selincourt, 1915. The most satisfactory selection with an introduction by the editor. The introduction is reprinted in *Wordsworthian and Other Studies*, 1947.

BIOGRAPHY AND CRITICISM

John Forster, *Walter Savage Landor*, 2 vols., 1869; condensed and issued as the first volume of *Works*, 1876.

Sidney Colvin, *Landor* (English Men of Letters Series), 1881. A readable brief life, but with some inaccuracies.

G. E. B. Saintsbury, in *Essays in English Literature*, Second Series, 1895. A judicious appraisal of the man and his literary accomplishment.

William Bradley, *The Early Poems of Landor: A Study of His Development and Debt to Milton*, 1914.

Ernest de Selincourt, 'Classicism and Romanticism in the Poetry of Landor,' *England und die Antike: Vortrage der Bibliothek Warburg, 1930–1931*, 1932.

R. H. Super, 'Landor and the "Satanic School," ' *SP*, XLII (1945), 793–810. Includes interesting materials on Hunt, Byron, Shelley, and others in relation to Landor.

Ernest de Selincourt, 'Landor's Prose,' in *Wordsworthian and Other Studies*, 1947.

R. H. Super, *Walter Savage Landor: A Biography*, 1954. The standard life.

Malcolm Elwin, *Landor: A Replevin*, 1958. Supersedes this author's *Savage Landor*, 1941.

Pierre Vitoux, *L'Œuvre de Walter Savage Landor*, 1964. A discriminating critical study of all of Landor's writings.

JOHN GIBSON LOCKHART 1794–1854

EDITIONS

Memoirs of the Life of Sir Walter Scott, 7 vols., 1837–8. The best abridgment is by Andrew Lang (Everyman's Library), 1906.

Literary Criticism, with an Introduction and Bibliography by M. C. Hildyard, 1931.

BIOGRAPHY AND CRITICISM

William Maginn, in *A Gallery of Illustrious Characters*, ed. William Bates, 1873.

Andrew Lang, *The Life and Letters of John Gibson Lockhart*, 2 vols., 1897. The standard biography.

Augustine Birrell, 'The Biographer of Sir Walter Scott,' in *Et Cetera, a Collection*, 1930.

Donald Carswell, in *Scott and His Circle*, 1930.

Gilbert Macbeth, *John Gibson Lockhart: A Critical Study*, 1935. Contains a bibliography.

Marion Lochhead, *John Gibson Lockhart*, 1954.

JAMES MACPHERSON 1736–96

EDITIONS

Works of Ossian, ed. with an Introduction by William Sharp, 1896.

BIOGRAPHY AND CRITICISM

J. S. Smart, *James Macpherson: An Episode in Literature*, 1905.

Paul Van Tieghem, *Ossian en France*, 1917.

Paul Van Tieghem, in *Le Préromantisme*, 1924.

G. M. Fraser, 'The Truth about Macpherson's Ossian,' *Quarterly Review*, CCXLV (1925), 331–45.

R. T. Clark, Jr., 'Herder, Percy, and the Song of Songs,' *PMLA*, LXI (1946), 1087–1100.

E. D. Snyder, 'James Macpherson,' in *The Celtic Revival in English Literature*, 1923.

JAMES CLARENCE MANGAN 1803–49

EDITIONS

Poems, ed. D. J. O'Donoghue, 1903. The Centenary edition, provided with a preface and notes by the editor, and with a biographical introduction by John Mitchel.

Selected Poems, ed. Louise I. Guiney, 1897. Contains an excellent prefatory essay.

Prose Writings, ed. D. J. O'Donoghue, 1904.

BIOGRAPHY AND CRITICISM

Louise I. Guiney, 'James Clarence Mangan,' *Atlantic Monthly*, LXVIII (1891), 641–59. A discriminating biographical and critical essay.

D. J. O'Donoghue, *The Life and Writings of James Clarence Mangan*, 1897. A fully documented life.

James Joyce, in *St. Stephens*, 1930.

J. D. Sheridan, *James Clarence Mangan*, 1937. A brief readable sketch.

THOMAS MOORE 1779–1852

EDITIONS

Complete Poetical Works, 2 vols., 1930. A reprint of the collection made by the poet himself in 1840–41.

Poetical Works, ed. A. D. Godley, 1910. The best one-volume edition; contains an excellent scholarly introduction.

Selected Poems, ed. C. L. Falkiner, 1903.

Tom Moore's Diary: A Selection, ed. J. B. Priestley, 1925. An introduction provides the biographical background.

BIOGRAPHY AND CRITICISM

A. J. Symington, *Thomas Moore, His Life and Works*, 1880. A good brief biography, with critical appraisals of the poet's works.

G. E. B. Saintsbury, in *Essays in English Literature*, First Series, 1890.

Richard Garnett, in *Essays of an Ex-Librarian*, 1901.

S. L. Gwynn, *Thomas Moore* (English Men of Letters Series), 1924. A recommended brief biography.

W. F. Trench, *Tom Moore*, 1934. Good for critical appraisal of the *Irish Melodies*.

H. M. Jones, *The Harp That Once—A Chronicle of the Life of Thomas Moore*, 1937. The standard biography.

L. A. G. Strong, *The Minstrel Boy: A Portrait of Tom Moore*, 1937. One of the best on the *Irish Melodies*.

THOMAS PAINE 1737–1809

EDITIONS

Complete Writings, ed. P. S. Foner, 2 vols., 1945. The standard edition.

Selections, with a scholarly introduction by

H. H. Clark, 1944. Contains an excellent critical bibliography.

BIOGRAPHY AND CRITICISM

M. D. Conway, *The Life of Thomas Paine*, 2 vols., 1892. Elaborate and admiring, but still the most satisfactory biography.

Leslie Stephen, in *History of English Thought in the Eighteenth Century*, 1902. The standard treatment on Paine's doctrine.

Gamaliel Bradford, in *Damaged Souls*, 1923. Presents Paine as a radical with a 'screw loose.'

F. J. Gould, *Thomas Paine*, 1925. A satisfactory popular life.

Mary A. Best, *Thomas Paine, Prophet and Martyr of Democracy*, 1927. Uncritical and enthusiastic.

H. H. Clark, 'Toward a Reinterpretation of Thomas Paine,' *American Literature*, v (1933), 133–45.

Hesketh Pearson, *Tom Paine, Friend of Mankind*, 1937. Sympathetic, readable; adds nothing new.

Frank Smith, *Thomas Paine, Liberator*, 1938. A popular short biography, emphasizing Paine's contributions to democracy.

Richard Gimbel, *Thomas Paine*, 1956.

A. O. Aldridge, *Man of Reason: The Life of Thomas Paine*, 1959.

THOMAS LOVE PEACOCK   1785–1866

EDITIONS

Works, ed. H. F. B. Brett-Smith and C. E. Jones, 10 vols., 1928. The standard edition, with a biographical introduction and full bibliography and notes.

Poems, ed. R. B. Johnson, 1906. A recommended one-volume edition of the poetry.

Selections, ed. H. F. B. Brett-Smith, 1928. Provided with an excellent scholarly biographical and critical introduction.

The Pleasures of Peacock, ed. B. R. Redman, 1947. Comprises in whole or in part the seven novels of Peacock.

Defence of Poetry and Four Ages of Poetry, ed. J. E. Jordan, 1965. Contains introduction and notes.

BIOGRAPHY AND CRITICISM

Richard Garnett, in *Essays of an Ex-Librarian*, 1901. The best short account of Peacock as man and author.

A. M. Freeman, *Thomas Love Peacock: A Critical Study*, 1911.

C. C. Van Doren, *Life of Thomas Love Peacock*, 1911. The most reliable biography.

Osbert Burdett, 'Peacock the Epicurean,' in *Critical Essays*, 1925. Emphasizes Peacock's wit and humor.

J. B. Priestley, *Thomas Love Peacock* (English Men of Letters Series), 1927. A recommended brief biography.

Jean-Jacques Mayoux, *Un Epicurien anglais: Thomas Love Peacock*, 1932.

Ronald Mason, 'Notes for an Estimate of Peacock,' *Horizon* (London), ix (1944), 238–50.

Olwen W. Campbell, *Thomas Love Peacock*, 1953.

THOMAS PERCY (1729–1811) AND THE BALLAD REVIVAL

EDITIONS

Thomas Percy, ed., *Reliques of Ancient English Poetry*, 3 vols., 1765; ed. H. B. Wheatley, 1876.

Sir Walter Scott, ed., *Minstrelsy of the Scottish Border*, 2 vols., 1802; ed. T. F. Henderson, 1902.

William Motherwell, ed., *Minstrelsy: Ancient and Modern*, 1827.

F. J. Child, ed., *The English and Scottish Popular Ballads*, 5 vols., 1882–98, a monumental and definitive work reissued in a convenient one-volume edition, with an introduction by G. L. Kittredge, 1904.

BIOGRAPHY AND CRITICISM

H. A. Beers, 'Percy and the Ballads,' in *A History of English Romanticism in the Eighteenth Century*, 1898.

S. B. Hustvedt, *Ballad Books and Ballad Men*, 1930. A definitive history of ballad scholarship.

G. H. Gerould, *The Ballad of Tradition*, 1932. An historical analysis of the popular ballad.

Leah A. Dennis, 'Thomas Percy: Antiquarian *vs.* Man of Taste,' *PMLA*, lvii (1942), 140–54.

R. T. Clark, Jr., 'Herder, Percy, and the Song of Songs,' *PMLA*, lxi (1946), 1087–1100.

Evelyn K. Wells, *The Ballad Tree*, 1950. A comprehensive treatment of British and American ballads.

A. B. Friedman, *The Ballad Revival*, 1961. The only book dealing with the folk ballad and literary relationships which is both sound from a scholarly point of view and readable. Provides illuminating comments on the artistic intentions of Blake, Burns, Wordsworth, Coleridge, and Scott.

WINTHROP MACKWORTH PRAED
1802–39

EDITIONS

Poems, 2 vols., 1864. The authorized and standard edition.
The Poetical Works, ed. Kenneth Allott, 1955.
Poems, ed. Ferris Greenslet, 1909. A recommended volume of selections, provided with an introductory essay.

BIOGRAPHY AND CRITICISM

H. G. Hewlett, 'Poets of Society,' *Contemporary Review*, xx (1872), 238–68.
G. E. B. Saintsbury, in *Essays in English Literature*, First Series, 1890.
Derek Hudson, *A Poet in Parliament: A Life of Winthrop Mackworth Praed*, 1939. The first full-length biography.

ANN RADCLIFFE   1764–1823

EDITIONS

The Romance of the Forest, 1791.
The Mysteries of Udolpho, 1794.
The Italian, 1797.

BIOGRAPHY AND CRITICISM

Montague Summers, *A Great Mistress of Romance: Ann Radcliffe*, 1917. Lecture to the Royal Society of Literature.
Clara F. McIntyre, *Ann Radcliffe in Relation to Her Time*, 1920. Includes discussion of her life, her work, and her contribution to the novel.
Edith Birkhead, in *The Tale of Terror*, 1921.
Alida A. S. Wieten, *Mrs. Radcliffe: Her Relation toward Romanticism*, 1926. Includes a discussion of her poetry. Finds her important as a forerunner of romanticism.
Joyce M. S. Tompkins, in *The Popular Novel in England, 1770–1800*, 1932. Contains an appreciation of Mrs. Radcliffe as a Gothic novelist. An appendix lists her sources.

HENRY CRABB ROBINSON   1775–1867

EDITIONS

Diary, Reminiscences and Correspondence, ed. Thomas Sadler, 2 vols., 1872.
Blake, Coleridge, Wordsworth, etc., being Selections from the Remains, ed. Edith J. Morley, 1922.
Correspondence with the Wordsworth Circle, ed. Edith J. Morley, 2 vols., 1927.
Henry Crabb Robinson on Books and Their Writers, ed. Edith J. Morley, 3 vols., 1938.

BIOGRAPHY AND CRITICISM

Edith J. Morley, *The Life and Times of Henry Crabb Robinson*, 1935. The standard biography.
J. M. Baker, *Henry Crabb Robinson of Bury, Jena, The Times, and Russell Square*, 1937.

SIR WALTER SCOTT   1771–1832

EDITIONS

Poems and Ballads, ed. Andrew Lang, 6 vols., 1902. A limited edition with excellent introduction and notes.
Complete Poetical Works, ed. H. E. Scudder (Cambridge ed.), 1900. A recommended one-volume edition.
Minstrelsy of the Scottish Border, ed. T. F. Henderson, 4 vols., 1902.
Journal: 1825–1832, ed. J. G. Tait and W. M. Parker, 3 vols., 1939–47.
The Letters of Sir Walter Scott, ed. H. J. C. Grierson and others, 12 vols., 1932–7.
The Waverley Novels, in many good editions of which The Border Edition, ed. Andrew Lang, 1892–4, has the best introductions.

BIOGRAPHY AND CRITICISM

J. G. Lockhart, *Life of Sir Walter Scott*, in various editions since 1837. The authoritative, and a monumental, biography. A recommended one-volume abridgment by Andrew Lang (Everyman's edition), 1906.
J. C. Shairp, 'The Homeric Spirit in Walter Scott,' in *Aspects of English Poetry*, 1881.
R. L. Stevenson, 'A Gossip on Romance,' in *Memories and Portraits*, 1887. Contains wholehearted praise by a distinguished literary successor.
G. E. B. Saintsbury, *Sir Walter Scott*, 1897. An excellent short biography and appreciation.
Andrew Lang, *Sir Walter Scott and the Border Minstrelsy* (Literary Lives Series), 1902. A scholarly and delightful short biography.
Stephen Gwynn, *Sir Walter Scott*, 1930. One of the best brief accounts.
John Buchan, *Sir Walter Scott*, 1932. One of the best biographies; includes critical estimates of the poetry and prose.
Lord David Cecil, *Sir Walter Scott*, 1933. A reappraisal of his work and worth.
J. T. Hillhouse, *The Waverley Novels and Their Critics*, 1936.
H. J. C. Grierson, *Sir Walter Scott*, 1938. A new life supplementary to and corrective of Lockhart's biography.

Hesketh Pearson, *Walter Scott, His Life and Personality*, 1954.

Donald Davie, *The Heyday of Sir Walter Scott*, 1961.

C. O. Parsons, *Witchcraft and Demonology in Scott's Fiction*, 1964.

PERCY BYSSHE SHELLEY 1792–1822

EDITIONS

Complete Works, ed. H. B. Forman, 8 vols., 1880.

Complete Works, ed. Roger Ingpen and W. E. Peck (Julian ed.), 10 vols., 1926–30. The standard edition: includes letters, poems, and prose.

Complete Poetical Works, ed. Thomas Hutchinson with an introduction by B. P. Kurtz (Oxford ed.), 1933. The best one-volume edition.

Prometheus Unbound: A Variorum Edition, ed. L. J. Zillman, 1959.

Letters of Mary Shelley, ed. F. L. Jones, 2 vols., 1944.

Mary Shelley's Journal, ed. F. L. Jones, 1947.

New Shelley Letters, ed. W. S. Scott, 1949.

Shelley's Lost Letters to Harriet, ed. Leslie Hotson, 1930.

Letters, ed. F. L. Jones, 2 vols., 1964.

Shelley's Prose: or The Trumpet of a Prophecy, ed. D. L. Clark, 1954. Provided with an excellent introduction.

Selected Poems, Essays, and Letters, ed. Ellsworth Barnard, 1944. Contains a well-balanced introductory essay.

BIOGRAPHY AND CRITICISM

Leigh Hunt, *Autobiography*, 1850; ed. J. E. Morpurgo, 1949. Contains significant passages on Shelley.

E. J. Trelawny, *Recollections of the Last Days of Shelley and Byron*, 1858. A vivid firsthand portrayal; tends to be hero-worshiping.

Edward Dowden, *The Life of Shelley*, 2 vols., 1886, rev. in one volume, 1896. Before the appearance of White's biography was considered the standard life.

Matthew Arnold, in *Essays in Criticism*, Second Series, 1888. Contains the celebrated and influential judgment that Shelley is a 'beautiful and ineffectual angel.'

Francis Thompson, *Shelley*, 1909. A famous essay.

Arthur Clutton-Brock, *Shelley the Man and the Poet*, 1910, rev., 1923. Portrays Shelley as a developing personality.

H. N. Brailsford, *Shelley, Godwin, and Their Circle*, 1913; 2nd ed., 1951. A useful book on the Shelley-Godwin relationship.

Roger Ingpen, *Shelley in England*, 2 vols., 1917. A day-by-day account up to 1816.

A. T. Strong, *Three Studies in Shelley*, 1921. Penetrating studies of Shelley's social philosophy.

Olwen W. Campbell, *Shelley and the Unromantics*, 1924.

W. E. Peck, *Shelley, His Life and Work*, 2 vols., 1927. Contains some new material, but is not of primary value.

M. T. Solve, *Shelley: His Theory of Poetry*, 1927. The best book on the subject.

C. H. Grabo, *A Newton among Poets*, 1930. Shows the extensive influence of science on Shelley.

Floyd Stovall, *Desire and Restraint in Shelley*, 1931. A consecutive record of the poet's development.

Bennett Weaver, *Toward the Understanding of Shelley*, 1932. Reveals the important influence of the Bible.

H. L. Hoffman, *An Odyssey of the Soul: Shelley's 'Alastor,'* 1933. For a brief well-balanced reading of *Alastor* see E. K. Gibson, 'Alastor: A Reinterpretation,' *PMLA*, LXII (1947), 1022–45.

B. P. Kurtz, *The Pursuit of Death*, 1933. From a study of Shelley's attitude toward death much may be discovered of his attitude toward life.

Isabel C. Clarke, *Shelley and Byron*, 1934.

C. H. Grabo, *'Prometheus Unbound': An Interpretation*, 1935. Cf. K. N. Cameron, 'The Political Symbolism of *Prometheus Unbound*,' *PMLA*, LVIII (1943), 728–53.

Ellsworth Barnard, *Shelley's Religion*, 1936.

C. H. Grabo, *The Magic Plant: The Growth of Shelley's Mind*, 1936. Stresses the Platonic influence.

O. W. Firkins, *Power and Elusiveness in Shelley*, 1937. Analyzes the thought and art of Shelley's poetry; copiously illustrated.

Rosalie G. Grylls, *Mary Shelley*, 1938. The standard life of Mary Shelley.

N. I. White, *The Unextinguished Hearth: Shelley and His Contemporary Critics*, 1938.

N. I. White, *Shelley*, 2 vols., 1940. The standard biography. A condensation in one volume, entitled *Portrait of Shelley*, was published in 1945.

Edmund Blunden, *Shelley: A Life Story*, 1946. A readable biography, but uncritical and sometimes superficial.

Joseph Barrell, *Shelley and the Thought of His Time: A Study in the History of Ideas,* 1947.

A. M. D. Hughes, *The Nascent Mind of Shelley,* 1947. Stresses the ethical elements of Shelley's thought.

Carlos Baker, *Shelley's Major Poetry: The Fabric of a Vision,* 1948. A balanced and judicious estimate of the major poetry, emphasizing moral and aesthetic beliefs.

R. H. Fogle *The Imagery of Keats and Shelley: A Comparative Study,* 1949.

J. A. Notopoulos, *The Platonism of Shelley,* 1949.

K. N. Cameron, *The Young Shelley: Genesis of a Radical,* 1950. Traces the development of Shelley's radical thinking up to the publication of *Queen Mab.*

Carl H. Grabo, *Shelley's Eccentricities,* 1950.

F. A. Pottle, 'The Case of Shelley,' *PMLA,* LXVII (1952), 589–608. Reviews the decline of Shelley's reputation and examines some of the weaknesses in the 'new' criticism of the poet.

C. E. Pulos, *The Deep Truth: A Study of Shelley's Scepticism,* 1954.

Sylva Norman, *The Flight of the Skylark: The Development of Shelley's Reputation,* 1954.

Bennett Weaver, *Prometheus Unbound,* 1957.

Harold Bloom, *Shelley's Mythmaking,* 1959.

David Perkins, *The Quest for Permanence: The Symbolism of Wordsworth, Shelley, and Keats,* 1959.

E. R. Wasserman, *The Subtler Language,* 1959. Brilliant explications of the major poems.

Milton Wilson, *Shelley's Later Poetry,* 1959.

Desmond King-Hele, *Shelley: The Man and the Poet,* 1960.

Glenn O'Malley, *Shelley and Synesthesia,* 1964.

R. G. Woodman, *The Apocalyptic Vision in the Poetry of Shelley,* 1964.

D. H. Reiman, *Shelley's 'The Triumph of Life,'* 1965.

G. M. Ridenour, *Shelley, A Collection of Critical Essays,* 1965.

E. R. Wasserman, *Shelley's Prometheus Unbound, A Critical Reading,* 1965.

R. A. Duerksen, *Shelleyan Ideas in Victorian Literature,* 1966.

Neville Rogers, ed., *Shelley at Work: A Critical Inquiry,* 2nd ed., 1967.

ROBERT SOUTHEY   1774–1843

EDITIONS

Poetical Works, ed. H. T. Tuckerman, 5 vols., 1884.

Poems, ed. Edward Dowden (Golden Treasury Series), 1895. The best volume of selections; provided with a scholarly introduction.

Poems, ed. M. H. Fitzgerald (Oxford ed.), 1909.

Life of Nelson, ed. E. R. H. Harvey, 1953.

Select Prose, ed. Jacob Zeitlin, 1916. Contains a substantial and well-balanced appraisal of Southey's many-sided activities as a prose writer.

Letters, ed. M. H. Fitzgerald (World's Classics), 1912. A selection.

BIOGRAPHY AND CRITICISM

C. C. Southey, *Life and Correspondence of Robert Southey,* 6 vols., 1849–50. By Southey's son; for many years the standard biography, now superseded by Simmons.

Edward Dowden, *Southey* (English Men of Letters Series), 1880. A brief scholarly life.

William Haller, *The Early Life of Robert Southey,* 1917. The most detailed account of the early period.

William Haller, 'Southey's Later Radicalism,' *PMLA,* XXXVII (1922), 281–92.

Malcolm Elwin, 'Robert Southey,' *Quarterly Review,* CCLXXXI (1943), 187–201.

'Robert Southey, A Problem of Romanticism: Poet Who Lost His Way,' *TLS,* 20 Mar. 1943, p. 142.

'The Industrious Poet: In Southey's Workshop,' *TLS,* 21 Apr. 1945, p. 186.

Jack Simmons, *Southey,* 1945. The standard biography.

Geoffrey Carnall, *Robert Southey and His Age,* 1960.

JAMES THOMSON   1700–1748

EDITIONS

Complete Poetical Works, ed. J. L. Robertson (Oxford ed.), 1908.

The Castle of Indolence and Other Poems, ed. A. D. McKillop, 1961.

BIOGRAPHY AND CRITICISM

Leon Morel, *James Thomson, sa vie et ses oeuvres,* 1895.

G. C. Macaulay, *James Thomson,* 1908.

H. E. Cory, 'Spenser, Thomson and Romanticism,' *PMLA,* XXVI (1911), 51–91.

C. A. Moore, 'Shaftesbury and the Ethical Poets in England, *PMLA,* XXXI (1916), 264–325.

Herbert Drennon, 'Newtonianism in James Thomson's Poetry,' *Englische Studien,* LXX (1936), 358–72.

A. D. McKillop, *The Background of Thomson's Seasons,* 1942.

Douglas Grant, *James Thomson: The Poet of 'The Seasons,'* 1951. A well-informed biography.

Patricia M. Spacks, *The Varied God: A Critical Study of Thomson's 'The Seasons,'* 1959.

HORACE WALPOLE   1717–97

EDITIONS

The Castle of Otranto, 1765, numerously reprinted; ed. Montague Summers, 1924, Oswald Doughty, 1929, and W. S. Lewis, 1964. Doughty's edition contains an attractive memoir and Lewis's a rich introduction.

Letters, ed. Mrs. Paget Toynbee, 16 vols., 1903–5. Supplements to *Letters,* ed. Paget Toynbee, 3 vols., 1918–25.

A Selection of Letters, ed. W. S. Lewis, 2 vols., 1926.

Yale edition of the *Correspondence,* ed. W. S. Lewis, thirty-four volumes published from 1937 to 1966 and when completed may run to over fifty.

BIOGRAPHY AND CRITICISM

Austin Dobson, *Horace Walpole,* 1890, 4th ed. (rev. by Paget Toynbee), 1927. A well-written early life.

Paul Yvon, *La Vie d'un dilettante: Horace Walpole,* 1924. The longest biography.

Dorothy M. Stuart, *Horace Walpole* (English Men of Letters Series), 1927. Good coverage of Walpole's literary career.

Lewis Melville, *Horace Walpole,* 1930. Depicts Walpole as a man of inaction and noteworthy as a letter-writer.

Stephen Gwynn, *The Life of Horace Walpole,* 1932. Chiefly selections from the letters to form a biography.

K. K. Mehrotra, *Horace Walpole and the English Novel: A Study of the Influence of The Castle of Otranto,* 1934.

R. W. Ketton-Cremer, *Horace Walpole,* 1940, rev., 1946. The standard biography.

Isabel W. U. Chase, *Horace Walpole, Gardenist,* 1943.

JOSEPH WARTON   1722–1800

EDITIONS

Poems, in *The Works of the English Poets,* ed. Alexander Chalmers, 1810.

The Three Wartons: A Choice of Their Verse, ed. Eric Partridge, 1927.

An Essay on the Genius and Writings of Pope, 2 vols., 1782.

BIOGRAPHY AND CRITICISM

John Wooll, *Biographical Memoirs of the Reverend Joseph Warton,* 1806.

Edmund Gosse, *Two Pioneers of Romanticism, Joseph and Thomas Warton,* 1915.

Edith J. Morley, 'Joseph Warton: A Comparison of his *Essay* with his Edition of Pope's Works,' Engl. Assn. *Essays and Studies,* IX (1924), 98–114.

Hoyt Trowbridge, 'Joseph Warton on the Imagination,' *MP,* XXXV (1937), 73–87.

THOMAS WARTON   1728–90

EDITIONS

Poetical Works, ed. Richard Mant, 2 vols., 1802.

The Three Wartons, A Choice of Their Verse, ed. Eric Partridge, 1927.

BIOGRAPHY AND CRITICISM

W. P. Ker, *Thomas Warton,* 1912.

Edmund Gosse, *Two Pioneers of Romanticism, Joseph and Thomas Warton,* 1915.

Clarissa Rinaker, *Thomas Warton,* 1916. The standard biography.

René Wellek, in *The Rise of English Literary History,* 1941.

CHARLES WOLFE   1791–1817

EDITIONS

Remains of the Rev. Charles Wolfe, ed. with a Memoir by J. A. Russell, 2 vols., 1825, often reprinted.

The Burial of Sir John Moore, and Other Poems, ed. with a Memoir by C. L. Falkiner, 1909.

MARY WOLLSTONECRAFT 1759–97

EDITIONS

A Vindication of the Rights of Woman, 1792; ed. E. R. Pennell, 1892.

BIOGRAPHY AND CRITICISM

E. R. Pennell, *Mary Wollstonecraft Godwin,* 1885. The first complete life after Godwin's memoirs. Tends to be apologetic.

G. R. Stirling Taylor, *Mary Wollstonecraft: A Study in Economics and Romance,* 1911. A well-balanced study.

H. N. Brailsford, in *Shelley, Godwin, and Their Circle,* 1913. The best brief essay.

Madeline Linford, *Mary Wollstonecraft,* 1925. Adequate and judicious.

H. R. James, *Mary Wollstonecraft: A Sketch,* 1932. Adds no new information.

George Preedy, *This Shining Woman,* 1937. Romanticized biography.

R. M. Wardle, *Mary Wollstonecraft: A Critical Biography,* 1951. The most satisfactory life.

DOROTHY WORDSWORTH   1771–1855

EDITIONS

The Journals of Dorothy Wordsworth, ed. Ernest de Selincourt, 2 vols., 1941. The definitive edition.

The Letters of William and Dorothy Wordsworth, ed. Ernest de Selincourt, 6 vols., 1935–8.

BIOGRAPHY AND CRITICISM

H. W. Garrod, in *Wordsworth: Lectures and Essays,* 2nd ed., 1927.

Catherine M. Maclean, *Dorothy and William Wordsworth,* 1927. A reinterpretation of Wordsworth's poetry in the light of Dorothy's influence upon it.

Catherine M. Maclean, *Dorothy Wordsworth: The Early Years,* 1932. A skillfully wrought portrait.

Ernest de Selincourt, *Dorothy Wordsworth,* 1933. The definitive biography.

WILLIAM WORDSWORTH   1770–1850

EDITIONS

Poetical Works, ed. Ernest de Selincourt and Helen Darbishire, 5 vols., 1940–49. An authoritative and definitive edition. A second edition of vols. I–III was issued by Miss Darbishire in 1952–54.

Poetical Works, ed. Thomas Hutchinson (Oxford ed.), 1911. The standard one-volume edition with Wordsworth's arrangement of the poems.

Complete Poetical Works, ed. A. J. George (Cambridge ed.), one volume, 1904. Poems are arranged in chronological order.

The Prelude, ed. Ernest de Selincourt, Oxford, 1926. The text of 1805 printed opposite the text of 1850, with variant readings, notes, and commentary. Second edition, revised by Helen Darbishire, 1959.

Lyrical Ballads, ed. Thomas Hutchinson, 1907. Valuable introduction and notes.

Lyrical Ballads, ed. R. L. Brett and A. R. Jones, 1963. The text of the 1798 edition with the additional 1800 poems and preface. Provided with an introduction and notes.

The Prose Works, ed. Alexander B. Grosart, 3 vols., 1876. Better than the two-vol. edition by William Knight, 1896.

Letters of William and Dorothy Wordsworth, ed. Ernest de Selincourt, 6 vols., 1935–9.

BIOGRAPHY AND CRITICISM

Matthew Arnold, ed., *Poems of Wordsworth,* 1879. Contains Arnold's famous and influential introductory essay.

Emile Legouis, *La Jeunesse de William Wordsworth, 1770–1798,* 1896, trans. 1897, and reprinted, with new material in 1921 and 1932.

Sir Walter Raleigh, *Wordsworth,* 1903.

A. C. Bradley, *Oxford Lectures on Poetry,* 1909. Wordsworth is the most sublime of our poets since Milton.

G. M. Harper, *William Wordsworth, His Life, Works, and Influence,* 2 vols., 1916; revised and abridged in one volume, 1929.

Arthur Beatty, *William Wordsworth: His Doctrine and Art in Their Historical Relations,* 1922, rev., 1927. Emphasizes Wordsworth's indebtedness to the psychology of David Hartley.

H. W. Garrod, *Wordsworth: Lectures and Essays,* 1923, enlarged, 1927.

C. H. Herford, *Wordsworth,* 1930. A dependable brief biography including a critical appraisal of the poetry.

Srikumar Bannerjee, *Critical Theories and Poetic Practice in the Lyrical Ballads,* 1931.

M. M. Rader, *Presiding Ideas in Wordsworth's Poetry,* 1931. One of the most valuable studies of Wordsworth's idealism.

Edith C. Batho, *The Later Wordsworth,* 1933; reprinted, 1963.

Basil Willey, 'On Wordsworth and the Locke Tradition,' in *The Seventeenth-Century Background,* 1934.

J. W. Beach, *The Concept of Nature in Nineteenth-Century English Poetry,* 1936. See especially chapters II–VI.

R. D. Havens, *The Mind of a Poet: A Study of Wordsworth's Thought with Particular Reference to* The Prelude, 1941.

Russell Noyes, *Wordsworth and Jeffrey in Controversy,* 1941.

Josephine Miles, *Wordsworth and the Vocabulary of Emotion,* 1942.

G. W. Meyer, *Wordsworth's Formative Years,* 1943.

J. C. Smith, *A Study of Wordsworth,* 1944. An

excellent first book on Wordsworth's poetic equipment and ideas.

N. P. Stallknecht, *Strange Seas of Thought: Studies in William Wordsworth's Philosophy of Man and Nature*, 1945; reprinted, 1958.

Francis Christensen, 'Creative Sensibility in Wordsworth,' *JEGP*, XLV (1946), 361–68.

J. V. Logan, *Wordsworthian Criticism*, 1947. A guide with selected critical bibliography. E. F. Henley and D. H. Stam in *Wordsworthian Criticism, 1945–1964*, 1965, continue the work begun by Logan.

Helen Darbishire, *The Poet Wordsworth*, 1950. An enlightened appraisal of Wordsworth's poetic achievement.

G. T. Dunklin, ed., *Wordsworth: Centenary Studies*, 1951. The poet is reappraised in seven separate essays.

Lascelles Abercrombie, *The Art of Wordsworth*, 1952.

Florence Marsh, *Wordsworth's Imagery: A Study in Poetic Vision*, 1952.

H. M. Margoliouth, *Wordsworth and Coleridge, 1795–1834*, 1953.

Abbie Findlay Potts, *Wordsworth's 'Prelude': A Study of Its Literary Form*, 1953.

F. W. Bateson, *Wordsworth: A Re-Interpretation*, 1954; 2nd ed., 1956. Stimulating criticism, marred by unsupportable theorizing of an 'incestuous' relationship between the poet and his sister.

Geoffrey Hartman, *The Unmediated Vision*, 1954.

John Jones, *The Egotistical Sublime: A History of Wordsworth's Imagination*, 1954.

Mary Moorman, *William Wordsworth: A Biography. The Early Years, 1770–1803*, 1957. A second volume, *The Later Years, 1803–1850*, was published in 1965. The standard biography.

F. M. Todd, *Politics and the Poet: A Study of Wordsworth*, 1957.

David Ferry, *The Limits of Mortality: An Essay on Wordsworth's Major Poems*, 1959. A challenging study, which will doubtless provoke disagreement at times. See as a corrective, Alan Grob, 'Wordsworth's Nutting,' *JEGP*, LXI (1962), 826–32.

John F. Danby, *The Simple Wordsworth: Studies in the Poems 1797–1807*, 1960. Useful for the sensitive reading of some of the 'simple' poems, such as, 'The Fountain,' 'The Solitary Reaper,' and 'The White Doe.'

H. W. Piper, *The Active Universe: Pantheism and the Concept of the Imagination in the English Romantic Poets*, 1962.

Colin C. Clarke, *Romantic Paradox: An Essay on the Poetry of Wordsworth*, 1963. Wordsworth's poetry has a far richer texture and is more loaded with ambivalent meanings than has hitherto been recognized.

Jack Davis, ed., *Discussions of William Wordsworth*, 1963. Reprints pages from critical studies of Wordsworth by Coleridge, Arnold, Bradley, Willey, Abrams, Leavis, and others. Paper-bound. An excellent representative selection of the best criticism.

Herbert Lindenberger, *On Wordsworth's Prelude*, 1963.

Geoffrey H. Hartman, *Wordsworth's Poetry 1787–1814*, 1964. An illuminating study containing useful bibliographies of criticism.

David Perkins, *Wordsworth and the Poetry of Sincerity*, 1964. Perceptive and sensitive criticism of a considerable body of Wordsworth's poetry. See also this author's chapter on Wordsworth in *The Quest for Permanence*, 1959.

T. J. Roundtree, *This Mighty Sum of Things: Wordsworth's Theme of Benevolent Necessity*, 1965.

Bennett Weaver, *Wordsworth: Poet of the Unconquerable Mind*, 1965. The psychological approach is used to interpret the inter-relations of sense-experience and imagination in Wordsworth's poetry.

Carl Woodring, *Wordsworth*, 1965. A compact, scholarly introduction to the poetry and prose.

EDWARD YOUNG   1683–1765

EDITIONS

Poetical Works, ed. with a Life by John Mitford, 2 vols., 1834 (Aldine ed.), 1871.

The Complaint, or Night Thoughts has appeared in many editions.

BIOGRAPHY AND CRITICISM

George Eliot, 'Worldliness and Otherworldliness: The Poet Young,' in *Essays*, 1884.

Walter Thomas, *Le Poete Edward Young*, 1901.

H. C. Shelley, *Life and Letters of Edward Young*, 1914.

H. H. Clark, 'The Romanticism of Edward Young,' *Transactions of the Wisconsin Academy*, XXIV (1929), 1–45.

Paul Van Tieghem, 'Le Poésie de la nuit et des tombeaux,' in *Le Préromantisme*, 1930.

C. V. Wicker, *Edward Young and the Fear of Death: A Study in Romantic Melancholy*, 1952.

INDEX TO AUTHORS, TITLES, AND FIRST LINES

Authors' names are set in CAPITALS, *titles are set in italics,* and first lines of poems are set in roman capitals and lower case. When the first line of a poem is used as a title, the entry is by first line only.